This book belongs to:

_____

_____

_____

THE
HOLY BIBLE

WITH APOCRYPHA

THE
HOLY BIBLE

ENGLISH STANDARD VERSION
Containing the Old and New Testaments

ANGLICIZED EDITION
WITH APOCRYPHA

Published in Great Britain in 2021
Society for Promoting Christian Knowledge
36 Causton Street
London SW1P 4ST
www.spck.org.uk

English Standard Version ® with Apocrypha copyright © 2017

The Holy Bible, English Standard Version ® (ESV®)
Copyright © 2001 by Crossway,
a publishing ministry of Good News Publishers.

ESV with Apocrypha copyright © 2017 by Crossway.
ESV Text Edition: 2016

Anglicized ESV copyright © 2002
by Crossway and HarperCollins Publishers, London.

Anglicized ESV Apocrypha copyright © 2009, 2017 by Crossway.
Anglicized ESV Apocrypha copyright © 2017 by Crossway
Used by permission. All rights reserved.

Map illustrations by Maproom.net

British Library Cataloguing-in-Publication Data
A catalogue record for this book is available from the British Library

Holy Bible with Apocrypha, Anglicized ESV Edition ISBN 978–0–281–08534–7; Holy Bible with Apocrypha, Anglicized ESV Deluxe Edition ISBN 978–0–281–08535–4; Holy Bible with Apocrypha, Anglicized ESV Deluxe Leatherette Midnight Blue Edition ISBN 978-0-281-08536-1

1 3 5 7 9 10 8 6 4 2

Typeset by 2K/DENMARK, DK-8270 Højbjerg, Denmark
Printed and bound in Italy by Lego S.P.A.

Produced on paper from sustainable sources

Permissions notice: The text of the ESV with Apocrypha (ESV+A) may be quoted in written, visual, audio, or electronic form up to and inclusive of five hundred (500) verses without express written permission of the publisher, provided that the verses quoted do not amount to more than one-half of any one book of the Bible or its equivalent measured in bytes and provided that the verses quoted do not account for twenty-five percent (25%) or more of the total text of the work in which they are quoted.

Notice of copyright must appear as follows on the title page or copyright page of printed works quoting from the ESV+A, or in a corresponding location when the ESV+A is quoted in other media:

"Scripture quotations are from The ESV® with Apocrypha, copyright © 2009, 2017 by Crossway,

a publishing ministry of Good News Publishers. Used by permission. All rights reserved."

When more than one translation is quoted in printed works or another media, the foregoing notice of copyright should begin as follows:

"Unless otherwise indicated, all Scriptures are from ... [etc.]", or,

"Scripture quotations marked ESV+A are from ... [etc.]."

The "ESV" and "English Standard Version" are registered trademarks of Crossway. Use of either trademark requires the permission of Crossway.

When quotations from the ESV+A texts are used in non-saleable media, such as church bulletins, orders of services, posters, transparencies, or similar media, a complete copyright notice is not required, but the initials (ESV+A) must appear at the end of a quotation.

Publication of any commentary or other biblical reference work produced for commercial sale that uses the ESV+A must include written permission for the use of the ESV+A text.

Permission requests for use of the ESV+A within the UK and EU that exceed the above guidelines must be directed to: SPCK, Attn: Rights and Permissions, 36 Causton Street, London SW1P 4ST, UK.

Other permissions requests must be directed to: rights@crossway.org or Crossway, Attn: Bible Rights, 1300 Crescent Street, Wheaton, IL 60187, USA.

English Standard Version, ESV, and the ESV logo are registered trademarks of Crossway. English Standard Version, ESV, and the ESV logo are registered in the United States of America. ESV and the ESV logo are registered in the European Union. Used by permission.

Supplemental material: The ESV Preface and headings in the Bible text copyright © 2001 by Crossway. The Preface to the ESV Apocrypha copyright © 2017 by Crossway.

The Holy Bible, English Standard Version, with Apocrypha is adapted from the Revised Standard Version of the Bible, with Apocrypha, copyright Division of Christian Education of the National Council of the Churches of Christ in the U.S.A. All rights reserved.

CONTENTS

Preface to the ESV Bible vii
Preface to the Apocrypha xi

THE OLD TESTAMENT

Genesis 1	Ecclesiastes 567
Exodus 45	Song of Solomon 575
Leviticus 81	Isaiah 581
Numbers 108	Jeremiah 645
Deuteronomy 146	Lamentations 705
Joshua 180	Ezekiel 712
Judges 202	Daniel 759
Ruth 224	Hosea 773
1 Samuel 227	Joel 783
2 Samuel 256	Amos 787
1 Kings 281	Obadiah 795
2 Kings 309	Jonah 797
1 Chronicles 336	Micah 799
2 Chronicles 360	Nahum 805
Ezra 391	Habakkuk 808
Nehemiah 400	Zephaniah 811
Esther 412	Haggai 815
Job 419	Zechariah 817
Psalms 452	Malachi 826
Proverbs 539	

THE APOCRYPHA

Tobit 831	Bel and The Dragon 956
Judith 843	1 Maccabees 958
Esther 857	2 Maccabees 986
Wisdom of Solomon 868	1 Esdras 1007
Sirach 888	Prayer of Manasseh 1021
Baruch 943	Psalm 151 1022
Letter of Jeremiah 948	3 Maccabees 1023
Prayer of Azariah 951	2 Esdras 1033
Susanna 954	4 Maccabees 1062

THE NEW TESTAMENT

Matthew 1079	1 Timothy 1266
Mark 1109	2 Timothy 1270
Luke 1128	Titus 1273
John 1160	Philemon 1275
Acts 1183	Hebrews 1276
Romans 1213	James 1286
1 Corinthians 1226	1 Peter 1290
2 Corinthians 1238	2 Peter 1294
Galatians 1246	1 John 1297
Ephesians 1251	2 John 1301
Philippians 1255	3 John 1302
Colossians 1258	Jude 1303
1 Thessalonians 1261	Revelation 1305
2 Thessalonians 1264	

Table of Weights and Measures 1321
Maps 1323

THE BOOKS OF THE BIBLE IN ALPHABETICAL ORDER
WITH APOCRYPHAL BOOKS*

Acts....1183	Lamentations....705
Amos....787	Letter of Jeremiah....948
Baruch....943	Leviticus....81
Bel and The Dragon....956	Luke....1128
1 Chronicles....336	1 Maccabees....958
2 Chronicles....360	2 Maccabees....986
Colossians....1258	3 Maccabees....1023
1 Corinthians....1226	4 Maccabees....1062
2 Corinthians....1238	Malachi....826
Daniel....759	Mark....1109
Deuteronomy....146	Matthew....1079
Ecclesiastes....567	Micah....799
Ephesians....1251	Nahum....805
1 Esdras....1007	Nehemiah....400
2 Esdras....1033	Numbers....108
Esther....412	Obadiah....795
Esther (apocrypha)....857	1 Peter....1290
Exodus....45	2 Peter....1294
Ezekiel....712	Philemon....1275
Ezra....391	Philippians....1255
Galatians....1246	Prayer of Azariah....951
Genesis....1	Prayer of Manasseh....1021
Habakkuk....808	Proverbs....539
Haggai....815	Psalms....452
Hebrews....1276	Psalm 151....1022
Hosea....773	Revelation....1305
Isaiah....581	Romans....1213
James....1286	Ruth....224
Jeremiah....645	1 Samuel....227
Job....419	2 Samuel....256
Joel....783	Sirach....888
John....1160	Song of Solomon....575
1 John....1297	Susanna....954
2 John....1301	1 Thessalonians....1261
3 John....1302	2 Thessalonians....1264
Jonah....797	1 Timothy....1266
Joshua....180	2 Timothy....1270
Jude....1303	Titus....1273
Judges....202	Tobit....831
Judith....863	Wisdom of Solomon....868
1 Kings....281	Zechariah....817
2 Kings....309	Zephaniah....811

* This ESV edition includes the following apocryphal books in the Old Testament that have survived in their entirety only in Greek: Tobit, Judith, 1–2 Maccabees, the Wisdom of Solomon, Sirach, and Baruch.

PREFACE
TO THE ESV BIBLE

THE BIBLE

The Bible is the most valuable treasure there is in all of life. The words of the Bible are "trustworthy and true" (Revelation 21:5). "The word of the Lord remains forever" (1 Peter 1:25). These are "the words of eternal life" (John 6:68). As the translators of the King James Bible wrote, "God's sacred Word . . . is the inestimable treasure that excelleth all the riches of the earth." This assessment of the Bible is the motivating force behind the publication of the English Standard Version.

TRANSLATION LEGACY

The English Standard Version (ESV) stands in the classic mainstream of English Bible translations over the past half-millennium. The fountainhead of that stream was William Tyndale's New Testament of 1526; marking its course were the King James Version of 1611 (KJV), the English Revised Version of 1885 (RV), the American Standard Version of 1901 (ASV), and the Revised Standard Version of 1952 and 1971 (RSV). In that stream, faithfulness to the text and vigorous pursuit of precision were combined with simplicity, beauty, and dignity of expression. Our goal has been to carry forward this legacy for this generation and generations to come.

To this end each word and phrase in the ESV has been carefully weighed against the original Hebrew, Aramaic, and Greek, to ensure the fullest accuracy and clarity and to avoid under-translating or overlooking any nuance of the original text. The words and phrases themselves grow out of the Tyndale–King James legacy, and most recently out of the RSV, with the 1971 RSV text providing the starting point for our work. Archaic language has been brought into line with current usage and significant corrections have been made in the translation of key texts. But throughout, our goal has been to retain the depth of meaning and enduring quality of language that have made their indelible mark on the English-speaking world and have defined the life and doctrine of its church over the last five centuries.

TRANSLATION PHILOSOPHY

The ESV is an "essentially literal" translation that seeks as far as possible to reproduce the precise wording of the original text and the personal style of each Bible writer. As such, its emphasis is on "word-for-word" correspondence, at the same time taking full account of differences in grammar, syntax, and idiom between current literary English and the original languages. Thus it seeks to be transparent to the original text, letting the reader see as directly as possible the structure and exact force of the original.

In contrast to the ESV, some Bible versions have followed a "thought-for-thought" rather than "word-for-word" translation philosophy, emphasizing "dynamic equiva-lence" rather than the "essentially literal" meaning of the original. A "thought-for-thought" translation is of necessity more inclined to reflect the interpretive views of the translator and the influences of contemporary culture.

Every translation is at many points a trade-off between literal precision and read-ability, between "formal equivalence" in expression and "functional equivalence" in communication, and the ESV is no exception. Within this framework we have sought to be "as literal as possible" while maintaining clarity of expression and literary excel-lence. Therefore, to the extent that plain English permits and the meaning in each case allows, we have sought to use the same English word for important recurring words in the original; and, as far as grammar and syntax allow, we have rendered Old Testament passages cited in the New in ways that show their correspondence. Thus in each of these areas, as well as throughout the Bible as a whole, we have sought to capture all the echoes and overtones of meaning that are so abundantly present in the original texts.

As an essentially literal translation, taking into account grammar and syntax, the ESV thus seeks to carry over every possible nuance of meaning in the original words of Scripture into our own language. As such, the ESV is ideally suited for in-depth study of the Bible. Indeed, with its commitment to literary excellence, the ESV is equally well suited for public reading and preaching, for private reading and reflection, for both academic and devotional study, and for Scripture memorization.

TRANSLATION PRINCIPLES AND STYLE

The ESV also carries forward classic translation principles in its literary style. Accordingly it retains theological terminology—words such as grace, faith, justification, sanctification, redemption, regeneration, reconciliation, propitiation—because of their central importance for Christian doctrine and also because the underlying Greek words were already becoming key words and technical terms among Christians in New Testament times.

The ESV lets the stylistic variety of the biblical writers fully express itself—from the exalted prose that opens Genesis, to the flowing narratives of the historical books, to the rich metaphors and dramatic imagery of the poetic books, to the ringing rhetoric in the prophetic books, to the smooth elegance of Luke, to the profound simplicities of John, and the closely reasoned logic of Paul.

In punctuating, paragraphing, dividing long sentences, and rendering connectives, the ESV follows the path that seems to make the ongoing flow of thought clearest in English. The biblical languages regularly connect sentences by frequent repetition of words such as "and," "but," and "for," in a way that goes beyond the conventions of current literary English. Effective translation, however, requires that these links in the original be reproduced so that the flow of the argument will be transparent to the reader. We have therefore normally translated these connectives, though occasionally we have varied the rendering by using alternatives (such as "also," "however," "now," "so," "then," or "thus") when they better express the linkage in specific instances.

In the area of gender language, the goal of the ESV is to render literally what is in the original. For example, "anyone" replaces "any man" where there is no word corre-sponding to "man" in the original languages, and "people" rather than "men" is regularly used where the original languages refer to both men and women. But the words "man" and "men" are retained where a male meaning component is part of the original Greek or Hebrew. Likewise, the word "man" has been retained where the original text intends to convey a clear contrast between "God" on the one hand and "man" on the other hand, with "man" being used in the collective sense of the whole human race (see Luke 2:52). Similarly, the English word "brothers" (translating the Greek word *adelphoi*) is retained as an important familial form of address between fellow-Jews and fellow-Christians in the first century. A recurring note is included to indicate that the term "brothers" (*adelphoi*) was often used in Greek to refer to both men and women, and to indicate the specific instances in the text where this is the case. In addition, the English word "sons" (translating the Greek word *huioi*) is retained in specific instances because the underlying Greek term usually includes a male meaning component and it was used as a legal term in the adoption and inheritance laws of first-century Rome. As used by the apostle Paul, this term refers to the status of all Christians, both men and women, who, having been adopted into God's family, now enjoy all the privileges, obligations, and inheritance rights of God's children.

The inclusive use of the generic "he" has also regularly been retained, because this is consistent with similar usage in the original languages and because an essentially literal translation would be impossible without it.

In each case the objective has been transparency to the original text, allowing the reader to understand the original on its own terms rather than in the terms of our present-day culture.

THE TRANSLATION OF SPECIALIZED TERMS

In the translation of biblical terms referring to God, the ESV takes great care to convey the specific nuances of meaning of the original Hebrew and Greek words. First, concerning terms that refer to God in the Old Testament: God, the Maker of heaven and earth, introduced himself to the people of Israel with a special personal name, the consonants for which are YHWH (see Exodus 3:14–15). Scholars call this the "Tetragrammaton," a Greek term referring to the four

Hebrew letters YHWH. The exact pronunciation of YHWH is uncertain, because the Jewish people considered the personal name of God to be so holy that it should never be spoken aloud. Instead of reading the word YHWH, therefore, they would normally read the Hebrew word *'adonay* ("Lord"), and the ancient translations into Greek, Syriac, and Aramaic also followed this practice. When the vowels of the word *'adonay* are placed with the consonants of YHWH, this results in the familiar word *Jehovah* that was used in some earlier English Bible translations. As is common among English translations today, the ESV usually renders the personal name of God (YHWH) by the word Lord (printed in small capitals). An exception to this is when the Hebrew word *'adonay* appears together with YHWH, in which case the two words are rendered together as "the Lord [in lowercase] God [in small capitals]." In contrast to the personal name for God (YHWH), the more general name for God in Old Testament Hebrew is *'elohim* and its related forms of *'el* or *'eloah*, all of which are normally translated "God" (in lowercase letters). The use of these different ways to translate the Hebrew words for God is especially beneficial to English readers, enabling them to see and understand the different ways that the *personal* name and the *general* name for God are both used to refer to the *One True God* of the Old Testament.

Second, in the New Testament, the Greek word *Christos* has been translated consis-tently as "Christ." Although the term originally meant simply "anointed," among Jews in New Testament times it had specifically come to designate the Messiah, the great Savior that God had promised to raise up. In other New Testament contexts, however, especially among Gentiles, *Christos* ("Christ") was on its way to becoming a proper name. It is important, therefore, to keep the context in mind in understanding the various ways that *Christos* ("Christ") is used in the New Testament. At the same time, in accord with its "essentially literal" translation philosophy, the ESV has retained consistency and concordance in the translation of *Christos* ("Christ") throughout the New Testament.

Third, a particular difficulty is presented when words in biblical Hebrew and Greek refer to ancient practices and institutions that do not correspond directly to those in the modern world. Such is the case in the translation of *'ebed* (Hebrew) and *doulos* (Greek), terms which are often rendered "slave." These terms, however, actually cover a range of relationships that requires a range of renderings—"slave," "bondservant," or "servant"—depending on the context. Further, the word "slave" currently carries asso-ciations with the often brutal and dehumanizing institution of slavery particularly in nineteenth-century America. For this reason, the ESV translation of the words *'ebed* and *doulos* has been undertaken with particular attention to their meaning in each specific context. Thus in Old Testament times, one might enter slavery either voluntarily (e.g., to escape poverty or to pay off a debt) or involuntarily (e.g., by birth, by being captured in battle, or by judicial sentence). Protection for all in servitude in ancient Israel was provided by the Mosaic Law, including specific provisions for release from slavery. In New Testament times, a *doulos* is often best described as a "bondservant"—that is, someone in the Roman Empire officially bound under contract to serve his master for seven years (except for those in Caesar's household in Rome who were contracted for fourteen years). When the contract expired, the person was freed, given his wage that had been saved by the master, and officially declared a freedman. The ESV usage thus seeks to express the most fitting nuance of meaning in each context. Where absolute ownership by a master is envisaged (as in Romans 6), "slave" is used; where a more limited form of servitude is in view, "bondservant" is used (as in 1 Corinthians 7:21–24); where the context indicates a wide range of freedom (as in John 4:51), "servant" is preferred. Footnotes are generally provided to identify the Hebrew or Greek and the range of meaning that these terms may carry in each case. The issues involved in translating the Greek word *doulos* apply also to the Greek word *sundoulos*, translated in the text as "fellow servant."

Fourth, it is sometimes suggested that Bible translations should capitalize pronouns referring to deity. It has seemed best not to capitalize deity pronouns in the ESV, however, for the following reasons: first, there is nothing in the original Hebrew and Greek manuscripts that corresponds to such capitalization; second, the practice of capi-talizing deity pronouns in English Bible translations is a recent innovation, which began only in the mid-twentieth century; and, third, such capitalization is absent from the KJV Bible and the whole stream of Bible translations that the ESV carries forward.

A fifth specialized term, the word "behold," usually has been retained as the most common translation for the Hebrew word *hinneh* and the Greek word *idou*. Both of these words mean something like "Pay careful attention to what follows! This is impor-tant!" Other than the word "behold," there is no single word in English that fits well in most contexts. Although "Look!" and "See!" and "Listen!" would be workable in some contexts, in many others these words lack sufficient weight and dignity. Given the principles of "essentially literal" translation, it is important not to leave *hinneh* and *idou* completely untranslated and so to lose the intended emphasis in the original languages. The older and more formal word "behold" has usually been retained, therefore, as the best available option for conveying the original weight of meaning.

TEXTUAL BASIS AND RESOURCES

The ESV is based on the Masoretic text of the Hebrew Bible as found in *Biblia Hebraica Stuttgartensia* (5th ed., 1997), and on the Greek text in the 2014 editions of the *Greek New Testament* (5th corrected ed.), published by the United Bible Societies (UBS), and *Novum Testamentum Graece* (28th ed., 2012), edited by Nestle and Aland. The currently renewed respect among Old Testament scholars for the Masoretic text is reflected in the ESV's attempt, wherever possible, to translate difficult Hebrew passages as they stand in the Masoretic text rather than resorting to emendations or to finding an alternative reading in the ancient versions. In exceptional, difficult cases, the Dead Sea Scrolls, the Septuagint, the Samaritan Pentateuch, the Syriac Peshitta, the Latin Vulgate, and other sources were consulted to shed possible light on the text, or, if necessary, to support a divergence from the Masoretic text. Similarly, in a few difficult cases in the New Testament, the ESV has followed a Greek text different from the text given preference in the UBS/Nestle-Aland 28th edition. Throughout, the translation team has benefited greatly from the massive textual resources that have become readily available recently, from new insights into biblical laws and culture, and from current advances in Hebrew and Greek lexicography and grammatical understanding.

TEXTUAL FOOTNOTES

The footnotes that are included in most editions of the ESV are therefore an integral part of the ESV translation, informing the reader of textual variations and difficulties and showing how these have been resolved by the ESV translation team. In addition to this, the footnotes indicate significant alternative readings and occasionally provide an explanation for technical terms or for a difficult reading in the text.

PUBLISHING TEAM

The ESV publishing team has included more than a hundred people. The fourteen-member Translation Oversight Committee benefited from the work of more than fifty biblical experts serving as Translation Review Scholars and from the comments of the more than fifty members of the Advisory Council, all of which was carried out under the auspices of the Crossway Board of Directors. This hundred-plus-member team shares a common commitment to the truth of God's Word and to historic Christian orthodoxy and is international in scope, including leaders in many denominations.

TO GOD'S HONOR AND PRAISE

We know that no Bible translation is perfect; but we also know that God uses imperfect and inadequate things to his honor and praise. So to our triune God and to his people we offer what we have done, with our prayers that it may prove useful, with gratitude for much help given, and with ongoing wonder that our God should ever have entrusted to us so momentous a task.

Soli Deo Gloria!—To God alone be the glory!

The Translation Oversight Committee

PREFACE
TO THE APOCRYPHA

HISTORIC STREAM

Translations of the Apocrypha from Greek to English date back to the Geneva Bible (1560), which Cambridge University Press began publishing in 1591. This SPCK edition of the English Standard Version (ESV) with Apocrypha stands in this historic stream. We are pleased to acknowledge further that the bulk of this edition is an adaptation of the ESV with Apocrypha first published by Oxford University Press in 2009. That edition used the Revised Standard Version (RSV) Apocrypha (1971) and the RSV Expanded Apocrypha (1977) as its base. In 2016, a team of Catholic and Protestant scholars from the United Kingdom, Australia, India, and the United States completed a final revision of Tobit, 1–2 Maccabees, Wisdom of Solomon, Sirach, Judith, Baruch, and the Greek additions to Esther and Daniel, thus creating this present edition of the ESV Apocrypha. Like the ESV Bible itself, the ESV Apocrypha has been translated in an essentially literal way that seeks to provide linguistic accuracy and literary excellence.

ORIGINS

The word "Apocrypha" literally means "hidden." It is a general term used to distinguish books that are not universally accepted as Scripture from the 39 books of the Old Testament that all Christian communions consider Scripture. This distinction goes back to the third-century BC, when Hebrew scholars began to translate the Hebrew Scriptures into Greek, the dominant language of that day. This translation, called the Septuagint, eventually contained all the Old Testament books now found in the Catholic, Protestant, and Orthodox editions of the Bible. When quoting from the Old Testament, New Testament writers generally cited the Septuagint. The Septuagint also contained several additional writings that were not deemed to be canonical.

St. Jerome (c. 342–420 AD) translated the Bible from its original languages into Latin, which was the chief written language of the church used in his day and for the next several centuries. Jerome's translation, called the Vulgate, is the most influential version of the Bible in Catholic history. Jerome affirmed as Scripture the 39 books of the Old Testament and the 27 books of the New Testament that Protestants, Catholics, and Orthodox currently share in common. At the same time, Jerome's Vulgate translation included a number of additional "pre-New Testament books," which he designated as "Apocrypha" (i.e. "hidden"), due to their uncertain linguistic and historical origins. Over time, more than one version of the Vulgate circulated, with different books and parts of books included in the Apocrypha.

ACCEPTANCE

Until the sixteenth century, many, if not most, Christians accepted some of the Apocrypha as part of the Bible. In either case, the Apocrypha was generally regarded as worthy of reading for spiritual enrichment. During the sixteenth century, some books of the Apocrypha began to be called "deuterocanonical" (i.e. "second canon" or "secondary canon"), as Protestants and Catholics began to make decisions about the role that these writings should (or should not) have in the canon of Scripture. For example, Martin Luther's first translation of the Bible (1534) included several books of the Apocrypha. Luther identified these as "books which are not considered equal to the Holy Scriptures, but useful and good to read." Luther placed these books between the Old and New Testaments, though many later Lutheran editions omitted them altogether. In 1560, the Geneva Bible (a translation done by English Puritans exiled in Geneva, Switzerland) also printed books of the Apocrypha between the Old and New Testaments. Early editions of the King James Version (1611) did the same. The 1662 Anglican Book of Common Prayer cited Jerome on the deuterocanonical books,

PREFACE TO THE APOCRYPHA

and it described them as good to "read for example of life and instruction of manners," yet not "to establish any doctrine" (see Article VI of the Thirty-nine Articles of Religion). Most Protestant churches eventually decided not to include the Apocrypha in printings of the Bible —mainly because these books do not exist in their entirety in Hebrew or Aramaic, but also for doctrinal reasons. Today, Protestant editions of the Bible rarely include them. By 1592, Roman Catholics had decided to include seven books of the Apocrypha interspersed throughout the Old Testament (Tobit, 1–2 Maccabees, Wisdom of Solomon, Sirach, Judith, and Baruch, along with some additions to Esther and Daniel). These writings remain part of the Catholic canon. Many Anglicans, Lutherans, and other Protestants continue to affirm the spiritual value of reading the Apocrypha.

TEXTS INCLUDED IN THIS EDITION

Beyond the books already mentioned, the ESV Apocrypha includes 3 and 4 Maccabees and Psalm 151, which were included in the Revised Standard Version Expanded Apocrypha (1977). Except for these three additional books, the Apocrypha as translated here are those books and portions of books which appear in the Latin Vulgate. With the exception of 2 Esdras, these books also appear as part of the Greek Septuagint, though they were never included in the Hebrew Canon of Holy Scripture. As noted above, because the Latin Vulgate included books of the Apocrypha, the Apocrypha was often read by the church throughout the medieval period along with the universally accepted canonical books. This present edition also includes the Septuagint books that the Orthodox Christian communion considers Scripture, which include some books besides those in Protestant and Catholic Bibles.

TEXTUAL BASIS OF THIS EDITION

The ESV translators[1] utilized the best standard underlying texts as the basis for their work. In keeping with this striving for accuracy, the ESV Apocrypha used the Göttingen Septuagint as its textual base, with the following exceptions: 4 Maccabees was translated from Rahlfs' Septuagint and 2 Esdras was translated from the 1983 Vulgate published by the German Bible Society. In the special case of Tobit, the translators used the longer Greek text (Sinaiticus) supplemented by the shorter Greek text (Vaticanus) and the Old Latin version at points where the longer text lacks some verses (4:7–18; 13:6b–10a).

We are pleased now to provide this new version of the ESV Apocrypha to all those readers who wish to explore these ancient writings, which provide additional insight into the history and thought of the Jewish people before the time of Jesus Christ and of the major branches of Christianity.

The Apocrypha Translation Team

---

[1] A team of more than twenty scholars, well versed in in the ancient Bible languages of Hebrew, Aramaic, and Greek, reviewed the text of the Apocrypha and the Deuterocanonical books and additions—incorporating in particular the most recent scholarship related to the special cases of Tobit and Esther (with Greek additions).

THE OLD TESTAMENT

GENESIS

THE CREATION OF THE WORLD

1 In the beginning, God created the heavens and the earth. ²The earth was without form and void, and darkness was over the face of the deep. And the Spirit of God was hovering over the face of the waters.

³And God said, "Let there be light", and there was light. ⁴And God saw that the light was good. And God separated the light from the darkness. ⁵God called the light Day, and the darkness he called Night. And there was evening and there was morning, the first day.

⁶And God said, "Let there be an expanse[a] in the midst of the waters, and let it separate the waters from the waters." ⁷And God made[b] the expanse and separated the waters that were under the expanse from the waters that were above the expanse. And it was so. ⁸And God called the expanse Heaven.[c] And there was evening and there was morning, the second day.

⁹And God said, "Let the waters under the heavens be gathered together into one place, and let the dry land appear." And it was so. ¹⁰God called the dry land Earth,[d] and the waters that were gathered together he called Seas. And God saw that it was good.

¹¹And God said, "Let the earth sprout vegetation, plants[e] yielding seed, and fruit trees bearing fruit in which is their seed, each according to its kind, on the earth." And it was so. ¹²The earth brought forth vegetation, plants yielding seed according to their own kinds, and trees bearing fruit in which is their seed, each according to its kind. And God saw that it was good. ¹³And there was evening and there was morning, the third day.

¹⁴And God said, "Let there be lights in the expanse of the heavens to separate the day from the night. And let them be for signs and for seasons,[f] and for days and years, ¹⁵and let them be lights in the expanse of the heavens to give light upon the earth." And it was so. ¹⁶And God made the two great lights—the greater light to rule the day and the lesser light to rule the night—and the stars. ¹⁷And God set them in the expanse of the heavens to give light on the earth, ¹⁸to rule over the day and over the night, and to separate the light from the darkness. And God saw that it was good. ¹⁹And there was evening and there was morning, the fourth day.

²⁰And God said, "Let the waters swarm with swarms of living creatures, and let birds[g] fly above the earth across the expanse of the heavens." ²¹So God created the great sea creatures and every living creature that moves, with which the waters swarm, according to their kinds, and every winged bird according to its kind. And God saw that it was good. ²²And God blessed them, saying, "Be fruitful and multiply and fill the waters in the seas, and let birds multiply on the earth." ²³And there was evening and there was morning, the fifth day.

²⁴And God said, "Let the earth bring forth living creatures according to their kinds—livestock and creeping things and beasts of the earth according to their kinds." And it was so. ²⁵And God made the beasts of the earth according to their kinds and the livestock according to their kinds, and everything that creeps on the ground according to its kind. And God saw that it was good.

²⁶Then God said, "Let us make man[h] in our image, after our likeness. And let them have dominion over the fish of the sea and over the birds of the heavens and over the livestock and over all the earth and over every creeping thing that creeps on the earth."

²⁷ So God created man in his own image,
in the image of God he created him;
male and female he created them.

²⁸And God blessed them. And God said to them, "Be fruitful and multiply and fill the earth and subdue it, and have dominion over the fish of the sea and over the birds of the heavens and over every living thing that moves on the earth." ²⁹And God said, "Behold,

---

[a] Or *a canopy*; also verses 7, 8, 14, 15, 17, 20 [b] Or *fashioned*; also verse 16 [c] Or *Sky*; also verses 9, 14, 15, 17, 20, 26, 28, 30; 2:1 [d] Or *Land*; also verses 11, 12, 22, 24, 25, 26, 28, 30; 2:1 [e] Or *small plants*; also verses 12, 29 [f] Or *appointed times* [g] Or *flying things*; see Leviticus 11:19–20 [h] The Hebrew word for *man (adam)* is the generic term for mankind and becomes the proper name *Adam*

I have given you every plant yielding seed that is on the face of all the earth, and every tree with seed in its fruit. You shall have them for food. ³⁰And to every beast of the earth and to every bird of the heavens and to everything that creeps on the earth, everything that has the breath of life, I have given every green plant for food." And it was so. ³¹And God saw everything that he had made, and behold, it was very good. And there was evening and there was morning, the sixth day.

THE SEVENTH DAY, GOD RESTS

2 Thus the heavens and the earth were finished, and all the host of them. ²And on the seventh day God finished his work that he had done, and he rested on the seventh day from all his work that he had done. ³So God blessed the seventh day and made it holy, because on it God rested from all his work that he had done in creation.

THE CREATION OF MAN AND WOMAN

⁴ These are the generations
 of the heavens and the earth
  when they were created,
 in the day that the LORD God made
  the earth and the heavens.

⁵When no bush of the field^a was yet in the land^b and no small plant of the field had yet sprung up—for the LORD God had not caused it to rain on the land, and there was no man to work the ground, ⁶and a mist^c was going up from the land and was watering the whole face of the ground— ⁷then the LORD God formed the man of dust from the ground and breathed into his nostrils the breath of life, and the man became a living creature. ⁸And the LORD God planted a garden in Eden, in the east, and there he put the man whom he had formed. ⁹And out of the ground the LORD God made to spring up every tree that is pleasant to the sight and good for food. The tree of life was in the midst of the garden, and the tree of the knowledge of good and evil.

¹⁰A river flowed out of Eden to water the garden, and there it divided and became four rivers. ¹¹The name of the first is the Pishon. It is the one that flowed around the whole land of Havilah, where there is gold. ¹²And the gold of that land is good; bdellium and onyx stone are there. ¹³The name of the second river is the Gihon. It is the one that flowed around the whole land of Cush. ¹⁴And the name of the third river is the Tigris, which flows east of Assyria. And the fourth river is the Euphrates.

¹⁵The LORD God took the man and put him in the garden of Eden to work it and keep it. ¹⁶And the LORD God commanded the man, saying, "You may surely eat of every tree of the garden, ¹⁷but of the tree of the knowledge of good and evil you shall not eat, for in the day that you eat^d of it you shall surely die."

¹⁸Then the LORD God said, "It is not good that the man should be alone; I will make him a helper fit for^e him." ¹⁹Now out of the ground the LORD God had formed^f every beast of the field and every bird of the heavens and brought them to the man to see what he would call them. And whatever the man called every living creature, that was its name. ²⁰The man gave names to all livestock and to the birds of the heavens and to every beast of the field. But for Adam^g there was not found a helper fit for him. ²¹So the LORD God caused a deep sleep to fall upon the man, and while he slept took one of his ribs and closed up its place with flesh. ²²And the rib that the LORD God had taken from the man he made^h into a woman and brought her to the man. ²³Then the man said,

"This at last is bone of my bones
 and flesh of my flesh;
she shall be called Woman,
 because she was taken out of Man."^{i}

²⁴Therefore a man shall leave his father and his mother and hold fast to his wife, and they shall become one flesh. ²⁵And the man and his wife were both naked and were not ashamed.

THE FALL

3 Now the serpent was more crafty than any other beast of the field that the LORD God had made.

He said to the woman, "Did God actually say, 'You^j shall not eat of any tree in the garden'?" ²And the woman said to the serpent, "We may eat of the fruit of the trees in the garden, ³but God said, 'You shall not eat of the fruit of the tree that is in the midst of the garden, neither shall you touch it, lest you die.'" ⁴But the serpent said to the woman, "You will not surely die. ⁵For God knows that when you eat of it your eyes will be opened,

---

^{a}Or open country ^{b}Or earth; also verse 6 ^{c}Or spring ^{d}Or when you eat ^{e}Or corresponding to; also verse 20 ^{f}Or And out of the ground the LORD God formed ^{g}Or the man ^{h}Hebrew built ^{i}The Hebrew words for woman (ishshah) and man (ish) sound alike ^{j}In Hebrew you is plural in verses 1–5

and you will be like God, knowing good and evil." ⁶So when the woman saw that the tree was good for food, and that it was a delight to the eyes, and that the tree was to be desired to make one wise,ᵃ she took of its fruit and ate, and she also gave some to her husband who was with her, and he ate. ⁷Then the eyes of both were opened, and they knew that they were naked. And they sewed fig leaves together and made themselves loincloths.

⁸And they heard the sound of the Lord God walking in the garden in the coolᵇ of the day, and the man and his wife hid themselves from the presence of the Lord God among the trees of the garden. ⁹But the Lord God called to the man and said to him, "Where are you?"ᶜ ¹⁰And he said, "I heard the sound of you in the garden, and I was afraid, because I was naked, and I hid myself." ¹¹He said, "Who told you that you were naked? Have you eaten of the tree of which I commanded you not to eat?" ¹²The man said, "The woman whom you gave to be with me, she gave me fruit of the tree, and I ate." ¹³Then the Lord God said to the woman, "What is this that you have done?" The woman said, "The serpent deceived me, and I ate."

¹⁴The Lord God said to the serpent,

"Because you have done this,
 cursed are you above all livestock
 and above all beasts of the field;
on your belly you shall go,
 and dust you shall eat
 all the days of your life.
¹⁵ I will put enmity between
 you and the woman,
 and between your offspringᵈ
 and her offspring;
he shall bruise your head,
 and you shall bruise his heel."

¹⁶To the woman he said,

"I will surely multiply your
 pain in childbearing;
in pain you shall bring
 forth children.
Your desire shall be contrary
 toᵉ your husband,
 but he shall rule over you."

¹⁷And to Adam he said,

"Because you have listened to
 the voice of your wife
 and have eaten of the tree
 of which I commanded you,
 'You shall not eat of it',
cursed is the ground because of you;
 in pain you shall eat of it all
 the days of your life;
¹⁸ thorns and thistles it shall
 bring forth for you;
 and you shall eat the plants
 of the field.
¹⁹ By the sweat of your face
 you shall eat bread,
till you return to the ground,
 for out of it you were taken;
 for you are dust,
 and to dust you shall return."

²⁰The man called his wife's name Eve, because she was the mother of all living.ᶠ ²¹And the Lord God made for Adam and for his wife garments of skins and clothed them.

²²Then the Lord God said, "Behold, the man has become like one of us in knowing good and evil. Now, lest he reach out his hand and take also of the tree of life and eat, and live for ever—" ²³therefore the Lord God sent him out from the garden of Eden to work the ground from which he was taken. ²⁴He drove out the man, and at the east of the garden of Eden he placed the cherubim and a flaming sword that turned every way to guard the way to the tree of life.

CAIN AND ABEL

4 Now Adam knew Eve his wife, and she conceived and bore Cain, saying, "I have producedᵍ a man with the help of the Lord." ²And again, she bore his brother Abel. Now Abel was a keeper of sheep, and Cain a worker of the ground. ³In the course of time Cain brought to the Lord an offering of the fruit of the ground, ⁴and Abel also brought of the firstborn of his flock and of their fat portions. And the Lord had regard for Abel and his offering, ⁵but for Cain and his offering he had no regard. So Cain was very angry, and his face fell. ⁶The Lord said to Cain, "Why are you angry, and why has your face fallen? ⁷If you do well, will you not be accepted?ʰ And if you do not do well, sin is crouching at the door. Its desire is contrary toⁱ you, but you must rule over it."

ᵃOr *to give insight* ᵇHebrew *wind* ᶜIn Hebrew *you* is singular in verses 9 and 11 ᵈHebrew *seed*; so throughout Genesis ᵉOr *shall be towards* (see 4:7) ᶠ*Eve* sounds like the Hebrew for *life-giver* and resembles the word for *living* ᵍ*Cain* sounds like the Hebrew for *produced* ʰHebrew *will there not be a lifting up* [of your face]? ⁱOr *is towards*

⁸Cain spoke to Abel his brother.ᵃ And when they were in the field, Cain rose up against his brother Abel and killed him. ⁹Then the LORD said to Cain, "Where is Abel your brother?" He said, "I do not know; am I my brother's keeper?" ¹⁰And the LORD said, "What have you done? The voice of your brother's blood is crying to me from the ground. ¹¹And now you are cursed from the ground, which has opened its mouth to receive your brother's blood from your hand. ¹²When you work the ground, it shall no longer yield to you its strength. You shall be a fugitive and a wanderer on the earth." ¹³Cain said to the LORD, "My punishment is greater than I can bear.ᵇ ¹⁴Behold, you have driven me today away from the ground, and from your face I shall be hidden. I shall be a fugitive and a wanderer on the earth, and whoever finds me will kill me." ¹⁵Then the LORD said to him, "Not so! If anyone kills Cain, vengeance shall be taken on him sevenfold." And the LORD put a mark on Cain, lest any who found him should attack him. ¹⁶Then Cain went away from the presence of the LORD and settled in the land of Nod,ᶜ east of Eden.

¹⁷Cain knew his wife, and she conceived and bore Enoch. When he built a city, he called the name of the city after the name of his son, Enoch. ¹⁸To Enoch was born Irad, and Irad fathered Mehujael, and Mehujael fathered Methushael, and Methushael fathered Lamech. ¹⁹And Lamech took two wives. The name of one was Adah, and the name of the other Zillah. ²⁰Adah bore Jabal; he was the father of those who dwell in tents and have livestock. ²¹His brother's name was Jubal; he was the father of all those who play the lyre and pipe. ²²Zillah also bore Tubal-cain; he was the forger of all instruments of bronze and iron. The sister of Tubal-cain was Naamah.

²³Lamech said to his wives:

"Adah and Zillah, hear my voice;
  you wives of Lamech, listen
    to what I say:
I have killed a man for wounding me,
  a young man for striking me.
²⁴ If Cain's revenge is sevenfold,
  then Lamech's is seventy-sevenfold."

²⁵And Adam knew his wife again, and she bore a son and called his name Seth, for she said, "God has appointedᵈ for me another offspring instead of Abel, for Cain killed him." ²⁶To Seth also a son was born, and he called his name Enosh. At that time people began to call upon the name of the LORD.

ADAM'S DESCENDANTS TO NOAH

5 This is the book of the generations of Adam. When God created man, he made him in the likeness of God. ²Male and female he created them, and he blessed them and named them Manᵉ when they were created. ³When Adam had lived for 130 years, he fathered a son in his own likeness, after his image, and named him Seth. ⁴The days of Adam after he fathered Seth were 800 years; and he had other sons and daughters. ⁵Thus all the days that Adam lived were 930 years, and he died.

⁶When Seth had lived for 105 years, he fathered Enosh. ⁷Seth lived after he fathered Enosh for 807 years and had other sons and daughters. ⁸Thus all the days of Seth were 912 years, and he died.

⁹When Enosh had lived for 90 years, he fathered Kenan. ¹⁰Enosh lived after he fathered Kenan for 815 years and had other sons and daughters. ¹¹Thus all the days of Enosh were 905 years, and he died.

¹²When Kenan had lived for 70 years, he fathered Mahalalel. ¹³Kenan lived after he fathered Mahalalel for 840 years and had other sons and daughters. ¹⁴Thus all the days of Kenan were 910 years, and he died.

¹⁵When Mahalalel had lived for 65 years, he fathered Jared. ¹⁶Mahalalel lived after he fathered Jared for 830 years and had other sons and daughters. ¹⁷Thus all the days of Mahalalel were 895 years, and he died.

¹⁸When Jared had lived for 162 years, he fathered Enoch. ¹⁹Jared lived after he fathered Enoch for 800 years and had other sons and daughters. ²⁰Thus all the days of Jared were 962 years, and he died.

²¹When Enoch had lived for 65 years, he fathered Methuselah. ²²Enoch walked with Godᶠ after he fathered Methuselah for 300 years and had other sons and daughters. ²³Thus all the days of Enoch were 365 years. ²⁴Enoch walked with God, and he was not,ᵍ for God took him.

²⁵When Methuselah had lived for 187 years, he fathered Lamech. ²⁶Methuselah lived after he fathered Lamech for 782 years and had

---

ᵃHebrew; Samaritan, Septuagint, Syriac, Vulgate add *Let us go out to the field*   ᵇOr *My guilt is too great to bear*   ᶜ*Nod* means *wandering*   ᵈ*Seth* sounds like the Hebrew for *he appointed*   ᵉHebrew *adam*   ᶠSeptuagint *pleased God*; also verse 24   ᵍSeptuagint *was not found*

other sons and daughters. ²⁷Thus all the days of Methuselah were 969 years, and he died.

²⁸When Lamech had lived for 182 years, he fathered a son ²⁹and called his name Noah, saying, "Out of the ground that the LORD has cursed, this one shall bring us relief[a] from our work and from the painful toil of our hands." ³⁰Lamech lived after he fathered Noah for 595 years and had other sons and daughters. ³¹Thus all the days of Lamech were 777 years, and he died.

³²After Noah was 500 years old, Noah fathered Shem, Ham, and Japheth.

INCREASING CORRUPTION ON EARTH

6 When man began to multiply on the face of the land and daughters were born to them, ²the sons of God saw that the daughters of man were attractive. And they took as their wives any they chose. ³Then the LORD said, "My Spirit shall not abide in[b] man for ever, for he is flesh: his days shall be 120 years." ⁴The Nephilim[c] were on the earth in those days, and also afterwards, when the sons of God came in to the daughters of man and they bore children to them. These were the mighty men who were of old, the men of renown.

⁵The LORD saw that the wickedness of man was great in the earth, and that every intention of the thoughts of his heart was only evil continually. ⁶And the LORD regretted that he had made man on the earth, and it grieved him to his heart. ⁷So the LORD said, "I will blot out man whom I have created from the face of the land, man and animals and creeping things and birds of the heavens, for I am sorry that I have made them." ⁸But Noah found favour in the eyes of the LORD.

NOAH AND THE FLOOD

⁹These are the generations of Noah. Noah was a righteous man, blameless in his generation. Noah walked with God. ¹⁰And Noah had three sons, Shem, Ham, and Japheth.

¹¹Now the earth was corrupt in God's sight, and the earth was filled with violence. ¹²And God saw the earth, and behold, it was corrupt, for all flesh had corrupted their way on the earth. ¹³And God said to Noah, "I have determined to make an end of all flesh,[d] for the earth is filled with violence through them. Behold, I will destroy them with the earth. ¹⁴Make yourself an ark of gopher wood.[e] Make rooms in the ark, and cover it inside and out with pitch. ¹⁵This is how you are to make it: the length of the ark 300 cubits,[f] its breadth 50 cubits, and its height 30 cubits. ¹⁶Make a roof[g] for the ark, and finish it to a cubit above, and set the door of the ark in its side. Make it with lower, second, and third decks. ¹⁷For behold, I will bring a flood of waters upon the earth to destroy all flesh in which is the breath of life under heaven. Everything that is on the earth shall die. ¹⁸But I will establish my covenant with you, and you shall come into the ark, you, your sons, your wife, and your sons' wives with you. ¹⁹And of every living thing of all flesh, you shall bring two of every sort into the ark to keep them alive with you. They shall be male and female. ²⁰Of the birds according to their kinds, and of the animals according to their kinds, of every creeping thing of the ground, according to its kind, two of every sort shall come in to you to keep them alive. ²¹Also take with you every sort of food that is eaten, and store it up. It shall serve as food for you and for them." ²²Noah did this; he did all that God commanded him.

7 Then the LORD said to Noah, "Go into the ark, you and all your household, for I have seen that you are righteous before me in this generation. ²Take with you seven pairs of all clean animals,[h] the male and his mate, and a pair of the animals that are not clean, the male and his mate, ³and seven pairs[i] of the birds of the heavens also, male and female, to keep their offspring alive on the face of all the earth. ⁴For in seven days I will send rain on the earth for forty days and forty nights, and every living thing[j] that I have made I will blot out from the face of the ground." ⁵And Noah did all that the LORD had commanded him.

⁶Noah was six hundred years old when the flood of waters came upon the earth. ⁷And Noah and his sons and his wife and his sons' wives with him went into the ark to escape the waters of the flood. ⁸Of clean animals, and of animals that are not clean, and of birds, and of everything that creeps on the ground, ⁹two and two, male and female, went into the ark with Noah, as God had commanded Noah. ¹⁰And after seven days the waters of the flood came upon the earth.

---

[a] *Noah* sounds like the Hebrew for *rest* [b] Or *My Spirit shall not contend with* [c] Or *giants* [d] Hebrew *The end of all flesh has come before me* [e] An unknown kind of tree; transliterated from Hebrew [f] *A cubit* was about 18 inches or 45 centimetres [g] Or *skylight* [h] Or *seven of each kind of clean animal* [i] Or *seven of each kind* [j] Hebrew *all existence*; also verse 23

¹¹In the six hundredth year of Noah's life, in the second month, on the seventeenth day of the month, on that day all the fountains of the great deep burst forth, and the windows of the heavens were opened. ¹²And rain fell upon the earth for forty days and forty nights. ¹³On the very same day Noah and his sons, Shem and Ham and Japheth, and Noah's wife and the three wives of his sons with them entered the ark, ¹⁴they and every beast, according to its kind, and all the livestock according to their kinds, and every creeping thing that creeps on the earth, according to its kind, and every bird, according to its kind, every winged creature. ¹⁵They went into the ark with Noah, two and two of all flesh in which there was the breath of life. ¹⁶And those that entered, male and female of all flesh, went in as God had commanded him. And the LORD shut him in.

¹⁷The flood continued for forty days on the earth. The waters increased and bore up the ark, and it rose high above the earth. ¹⁸The waters prevailed and increased greatly on the earth, and the ark floated on the face of the waters. ¹⁹And the waters prevailed so mightily on the earth that all the high mountains under the whole heaven were covered. ²⁰The waters prevailed above the mountains, covering them fifteen cubits^a deep. ²¹And all flesh died that moved on the earth, birds, livestock, beasts, all swarming creatures that swarm on the earth, and all mankind. ²²Everything on the dry land in whose nostrils was the breath of life died. ²³He blotted out every living thing that was on the face of the ground, man and animals and creeping things and birds of the heavens. They were blotted out from the earth. Only Noah was left, and those who were with him in the ark. ²⁴And the waters prevailed on the earth for 150 days.

THE FLOOD SUBSIDES

8 But God remembered Noah and all the beasts and all the livestock that were with him in the ark. And God made a wind blow over the earth, and the waters subsided. ²The fountains of the deep and the windows of the heavens were closed, the rain from the heavens was restrained, ³and the waters receded from the earth continually. At the end of 150 days the waters had abated, ⁴and in the seventh month, on the seventeenth day of the month, the ark came to rest on the mountains of Ararat. ⁵And the waters continued to abate until the tenth month; in the tenth month, on the first day of the month, the tops of the mountains were seen.

⁶At the end of forty days Noah opened the window of the ark that he had made ⁷and sent forth a raven. It went to and fro until the waters were dried up from the earth. ⁸Then he sent forth a dove from him, to see if the waters had subsided from the face of the ground. ⁹But the dove found no place to set her foot, and she returned to him to the ark, for the waters were still on the face of the whole earth. So he put out his hand and took her and brought her into the ark with him. ¹⁰He waited another seven days, and again he sent forth the dove out of the ark. ¹¹And the dove came back to him in the evening, and behold, in her mouth was a freshly plucked olive leaf. So Noah knew that the waters had subsided from the earth. ¹²Then he waited another seven days and sent forth the dove, and she did not return to him any more.

¹³In the six hundred and first year, in the first month, the first day of the month, the waters were dried from off the earth. And Noah removed the covering of the ark and looked, and behold, the face of the ground was dry. ¹⁴In the second month, on the twenty-seventh day of the month, the earth had dried out. ¹⁵Then God said to Noah, ¹⁶"Go out from the ark, you and your wife, and your sons and your sons' wives with you. ¹⁷Bring out with you every living thing that is with you of all flesh—birds and animals and every creeping thing that creeps on the earth—that they may swarm on the earth, and be fruitful and multiply on the earth." ¹⁸So Noah went out, and his sons and his wife and his sons' wives with him. ¹⁹Every beast, every creeping thing, and every bird, everything that moves on the earth, went out by families from the ark.

GOD'S COVENANT WITH NOAH

²⁰Then Noah built an altar to the LORD and took some of every clean animal and some of every clean bird and offered burnt offerings on the altar. ²¹And when the LORD smelt the pleasing aroma, the LORD said in his heart, "I will never again curse^b the ground because of man, for the intention of man's heart is evil from his youth. Neither will I ever again strike down every living creature as I have done. ²²While the earth remains, seedtime and harvest, cold and heat, summer and winter, day and night, shall not cease."

---

^{a}A *cubit* was about 18 inches or 45 centimetres ^{b}Or *dishonour*

9 And God blessed Noah and his sons and said to them, "Be fruitful and multiply and fill the earth. ²The fear of you and the dread of you shall be upon every beast of the earth and upon every bird of the heavens, upon everything that creeps on the ground and all the fish of the sea. Into your hand they are delivered. ³Every moving thing that lives shall be food for you. And as I gave you the green plants, I give you everything. ⁴But you shall not eat flesh with its life, that is, its blood. ⁵And for your lifeblood I will require a reckoning: from every beast I will require it and from man. From his fellow man I will require a reckoning for the life of man.

⁶ "Whoever sheds the blood of man,
   by man shall his blood be shed,
for God made man in his own image.

⁷And you,[a] be fruitful and multiply, increase greatly on the earth and multiply in it."

⁸Then God said to Noah and to his sons with him, ⁹"Behold, I establish my covenant with you and your offspring after you, ¹⁰and with every living creature that is with you, the birds, the livestock, and every beast of the earth with you, as many as came out of the ark; it is for every beast of the earth. ¹¹I establish my covenant with you, that never again shall all flesh be cut off by the waters of the flood, and never again shall there be a flood to destroy the earth." ¹²And God said, "This is the sign of the covenant that I make between me and you and every living creature that is with you, for all future generations: ¹³I have set my bow in the cloud, and it shall be a sign of the covenant between me and the earth. ¹⁴When I bring clouds over the earth and the bow is seen in the clouds, ¹⁵I will remember my covenant that is between me and you and every living creature of all flesh. And the waters shall never again become a flood to destroy all flesh. ¹⁶When the bow is in the clouds, I will see it and remember the everlasting covenant between God and every living creature of all flesh that is on the earth." ¹⁷God said to Noah, "This is the sign of the covenant that I have established between me and all flesh that is on the earth."

NOAH'S DESCENDANTS

¹⁸The sons of Noah who went forth from the ark were Shem, Ham, and Japheth. (Ham was the father of Canaan.) ¹⁹These three were the sons of Noah, and from these the people of the whole earth were dispersed.[b]

²⁰Noah began to be a man of the soil, and he planted a vineyard.[c] ²¹He drank of the wine and became drunk and lay uncovered in his tent. ²²And Ham, the father of Canaan, saw the nakedness of his father and told his two brothers outside. ²³Then Shem and Japheth took a garment, laid it on both their shoulders, and walked backwards and covered the nakedness of their father. Their faces were turned backwards, and they did not see their father's nakedness. ²⁴When Noah awoke from his wine and knew what his youngest son had done to him, ²⁵he said,

"Cursed be Canaan;
   a servant of servants shall he
     be to his brothers."

²⁶He also said,

"Blessed be the LORD, the God of Shem;
   and let Canaan be his servant.
²⁷ May God enlarge Japheth,[d]
   and let him dwell in the
     tents of Shem,
   and let Canaan be his servant."

²⁸After the flood Noah lived for 350 years. ²⁹All the days of Noah were 950 years, and he died.

NATIONS DESCENDED FROM NOAH

10 These are the generations of the sons of Noah, Shem, Ham, and Japheth. Sons were born to them after the flood.

²The sons of Japheth: Gomer, Magog, Madai, Javan, Tubal, Meshech, and Tiras. ³The sons of Gomer: Ashkenaz, Riphath, and Togarmah. ⁴The sons of Javan: Elishah, Tarshish, Kittim, and Dodanim. ⁵From these the coastland peoples spread in their lands, each with his own language, by their clans, in their nations.

⁶The sons of Ham: Cush, Egypt, Put, and Canaan. ⁷The sons of Cush: Seba, Havilah, Sabtah, Raamah, and Sabteca. The sons of Raamah: Sheba and Dedan. ⁸Cush fathered Nimrod; he was the first on earth to be a mighty man.[e] ⁹He was a mighty hunter before the LORD. Therefore it is said, "Like Nimrod a

---

[a]In Hebrew *you* is plural   [b]Or *from these the whole earth was populated*   [c]Or *Noah, a man of the soil, was the first to plant a vineyard.*   [d]*Japheth* sounds like the Hebrew for *enlarge*   [e]Or *he began to be a mighty man on the earth*

mighty hunter before the LORD." ¹⁰The beginning of his kingdom was Babel, Erech, Accad, and Calneh, in the land of Shinar. ¹¹From that land he went into Assyria and built Nineveh, Rehoboth-Ir, Calah, and ¹²Resen between Nineveh and Calah; that is the great city. ¹³Egypt fathered Ludim, Anamim, Lehabim, Naphtuhim, ¹⁴Pathrusim, Casluhim (from whom^a the Philistines came), and Caphtorim.

¹⁵Canaan fathered Sidon his firstborn and Heth, ¹⁶and the Jebusites, the Amorites, the Girgashites, ¹⁷the Hivites, the Arkites, the Sinites, ¹⁸the Arvadites, the Zemarites, and the Hamathites. Afterwards the clans of the Canaanites dispersed. ¹⁹And the territory of the Canaanites extended from Sidon in the direction of Gerar as far as Gaza, and in the direction of Sodom, Gomorrah, Admah, and Zeboiim, as far as Lasha. ²⁰These are the sons of Ham, by their clans, their languages, their lands, and their nations.

²¹To Shem also, the father of all the children of Eber, the elder brother of Japheth, children were born. ²²The sons of Shem: Elam, Asshur, Arpachshad, Lud, and Aram. ²³The sons of Aram: Uz, Hul, Gether, and Mash. ²⁴Arpachshad fathered Shelah; and Shelah fathered Eber. ²⁵To Eber were born two sons: the name of the one was Peleg,^b for in his days the earth was divided, and his brother's name was Joktan. ²⁶Joktan fathered Almodad, Sheleph, Hazarmaveth, Jerah, ²⁷Hadoram, Uzal, Diklah, ²⁸Obal, Abimael, Sheba, ²⁹Ophir, Havilah, and Jobab; all these were the sons of Joktan. ³⁰The territory in which they lived extended from Mesha in the direction of Sephar to the hill country of the east. ³¹These are the sons of Shem, by their clans, their languages, their lands, and their nations.

³²These are the clans of the sons of Noah, according to their genealogies, in their nations, and from these the nations spread abroad on the earth after the flood.

THE TOWER OF BABEL

11 Now the whole earth had one language and the same words. ²And as people migrated from the east, they found a plain in the land of Shinar and settled there. ³And they said to one another, "Come, let us make bricks, and burn them thoroughly." And they had brick for stone, and bitumen for mortar. ⁴Then they said, "Come, let us build ourselves a city and a tower with its top in the heavens, and let us make a name for ourselves, lest we be dispersed over the face of the whole earth." ⁵And the LORD came down to see the city and the tower, which the children of man had built. ⁶And the LORD said, "Behold, they are one people, and they have all one language, and this is only the beginning of what they will do. And nothing that they propose to do will now be impossible for them. ⁷Come, let us go down and there confuse their language, so that they may not understand one another's speech." ⁸So the LORD dispersed them from there over the face of all the earth, and they left off building the city. ⁹Therefore its name was called Babel, because there the LORD confused^c the language of all the earth. And from there the LORD dispersed them over the face of all the earth.

SHEM'S DESCENDANTS

¹⁰These are the generations of Shem. When Shem was 100 years old, he fathered Arpachshad two years after the flood. ¹¹And Shem lived after he fathered Arpachshad for 500 years and had other sons and daughters.

¹²When Arpachshad had lived for 35 years, he fathered Shelah. ¹³And Arpachshad lived after he fathered Shelah for 403 years and had other sons and daughters.

¹⁴When Shelah had lived for 30 years, he fathered Eber. ¹⁵And Shelah lived after he fathered Eber for 403 years and had other sons and daughters.

¹⁶When Eber had lived for 34 years, he fathered Peleg. ¹⁷And Eber lived after he fathered Peleg for 430 years and had other sons and daughters.

¹⁸When Peleg had lived for 30 years, he fathered Reu. ¹⁹And Peleg lived after he fathered Reu for 209 years and had other sons and daughters.

²⁰When Reu had lived for 32 years, he fathered Serug. ²¹And Reu lived after he fathered Serug for 207 years and had other sons and daughters.

²²When Serug had lived for 30 years, he fathered Nahor. ²³And Serug lived after he fathered Nahor for 200 years and had other sons and daughters.

²⁴When Nahor had lived for 29 years, he fathered Terah. ²⁵And Nahor lived after he fathered Terah for 119 years and had other sons and daughters.

²⁶When Terah had lived for 70 years, he fathered Abram, Nahor, and Haran.

---

^a Or *from where*   ^b *Peleg* means *division*   ^c *Babel* sounds like the Hebrew for *confused*

TERAH'S DESCENDANTS

²⁷Now these are the generations of Terah. Terah fathered Abram, Nahor, and Haran; and Haran fathered Lot. ²⁸Haran died in the presence of his father Terah in the land of his kindred, in Ur of the Chaldeans. ²⁹And Abram and Nahor took wives. The name of Abram's wife was Sarai, and the name of Nahor's wife, Milcah, the daughter of Haran the father of Milcah and Iscah. ³⁰Now Sarai was barren; she had no child.

³¹Terah took Abram his son and Lot the son of Haran, his grandson, and Sarai his daughter-in-law, his son Abram's wife, and they went forth together from Ur of the Chaldeans to go into the land of Canaan, but when they came to Haran, they settled there. ³²The days of Terah were 205 years, and Terah died in Haran.

THE CALL OF ABRAM

12 Now the LORD said^a to Abram, "Go from your country^b and your kindred and your father's house to the land that I will show you. ²And I will make of you a great nation, and I will bless you and make your name great, so that you will be a blessing. ³I will bless those who bless you, and him who dishonours you I will curse, and in you all the families of the earth shall be blessed."^{c}

⁴So Abram went, as the LORD had told him, and Lot went with him. Abram was seventy-five years old when he departed from Haran. ⁵And Abram took Sarai his wife, and Lot his brother's son, and all their possessions that they had gathered, and the people that they had acquired in Haran, and they set out to go to the land of Canaan. When they came to the land of Canaan, ⁶Abram passed through the land to the place at Shechem, to the oak^d of Moreh. At that time the Canaanites were in the land. ⁷Then the LORD appeared to Abram and said, "To your offspring I will give this land." So he built there an altar to the LORD, who had appeared to him. ⁸From there he moved to the hill country on the east of Bethel and pitched his tent, with Bethel on the west and Ai on the east. And there he built an altar to the LORD and called upon the name of the LORD. ⁹And Abram journeyed on, still going towards the Negeb.

ABRAM AND SARAI IN EGYPT

¹⁰Now there was a famine in the land. So Abram went down to Egypt to sojourn there, for the famine was severe in the land. ¹¹When he was about to enter Egypt, he said to Sarai his wife, "I know that you are a woman beautiful in appearance, ¹²and when the Egyptians see you, they will say, 'This is his wife.' Then they will kill me, but they will let you live. ¹³Say you are my sister, that it may go well with me because of you, and that my life may be spared for your sake." ¹⁴When Abram entered Egypt, the Egyptians saw that the woman was very beautiful. ¹⁵And when the princes of Pharaoh saw her, they praised her to Pharaoh. And the woman was taken into Pharaoh's house. ¹⁶And for her sake he dealt well with Abram; and he had sheep, oxen, male donkeys, male servants, female servants, female donkeys, and camels.

¹⁷But the LORD afflicted Pharaoh and his house with great plagues because of Sarai, Abram's wife. ¹⁸So Pharaoh called Abram and said, "What is this you have done to me? Why did you not tell me that she was your wife? ¹⁹Why did you say, 'She is my sister', so that I took her for my wife? Now then, here is your wife; take her, and go." ²⁰And Pharaoh gave men orders concerning him, and they sent him away with his wife and all that he had.

ABRAM AND LOT SEPARATE

13 So Abram went up from Egypt, he and his wife and all that he had, and Lot with him, into the Negeb. ²Now Abram was very rich in livestock, in silver, and in gold. ³And he journeyed on from the Negeb as far as Bethel to the place where his tent had been at the beginning, between Bethel and Ai, ⁴to the place where he had made an altar at the first. And there Abram called upon the name of the LORD. ⁵And Lot, who went with Abram, also had flocks and herds and tents, ⁶so that the land could not support both of them dwelling together; for their possessions were so great that they could not dwell together, ⁷and there was strife between the herdsmen of Abram's livestock and the herdsmen of Lot's livestock. At that time the Canaanites and the Perizzites were dwelling in the land.

⁸Then Abram said to Lot, "Let there be no strife between you and me, and between your herdsmen and my herdsmen, for we are kinsmen.^{e} ⁹Is not the whole land before you? Separate yourself from me. If you take

---

^{a}Or had said ^{b}Or land ^{c}Or by you all the families of the earth shall bless themselves ^{d}Or terebinth ^{e}Hebrew we are men, brothers

the left hand, then I will go to the right, or if you take the right hand, then I will go to the left." ¹⁰And Lot lifted up his eyes and saw that the Jordan Valley was well watered everywhere like the garden of the LORD, like the land of Egypt, in the direction of Zoar. (This was before the LORD destroyed Sodom and Gomorrah.) ¹¹So Lot chose for himself all the Jordan Valley, and Lot journeyed east. Thus they separated from each other. ¹²Abram settled in the land of Canaan, while Lot settled among the cities of the valley and moved his tent as far as Sodom. ¹³Now the men of Sodom were wicked, great sinners against the LORD.

¹⁴The LORD said to Abram, after Lot had separated from him, "Lift up your eyes and look from the place where you are, northwards and southwards and eastwards and westwards, ¹⁵for all the land that you see I will give to you and to your offspring for ever. ¹⁶I will make your offspring as the dust of the earth, so that if one can count the dust of the earth, your offspring also can be counted. ¹⁷Arise, walk through the length and the breadth of the land, for I will give it to you." ¹⁸So Abram moved his tent and came and settled by the oaks[a] of Mamre, which are at Hebron, and there he built an altar to the LORD.

ABRAM RESCUES LOT

14 In the days of Amraphel king of Shinar, Arioch king of Ellasar, Chedorlaomer king of Elam, and Tidal king of Goiim, ²these kings made war with Bera king of Sodom, Birsha king of Gomorrah, Shinab king of Admah, Shemeber king of Zeboiim, and the king of Bela (that is, Zoar). ³And all these joined forces in the Valley of Siddim (that is, the Salt Sea). ⁴Twelve years they had served Chedorlaomer, but in the thirteenth year they rebelled. ⁵In the fourteenth year Chedorlaomer and the kings who were with him came and defeated the Rephaim in Ashteroth-karnaim, the Zuzim in Ham, the Emim in Shaveh-kiriathaim, ⁶and the Horites in their hill country of Seir as far as El-paran on the border of the wilderness. ⁷Then they turned back and came to En-mishpat (that is, Kadesh) and defeated all the country of the Amalekites, and also the Amorites who were dwelling in Hazazon-tamar.

⁸Then the king of Sodom, the king of Gomorrah, the king of Admah, the king of Zeboiim, and the king of Bela (that is, Zoar) went out, and they joined battle in the Valley of Siddim ⁹with Chedorlaomer king of Elam, Tidal king of Goiim, Amraphel king of Shinar, and Arioch king of Ellasar, four kings against five. ¹⁰Now the Valley of Siddim was full of bitumen pits, and as the kings of Sodom and Gomorrah fled, some fell into them, and the rest fled to the hill country. ¹¹So the enemy took all the possessions of Sodom and Gomorrah, and all their provisions, and went their way. ¹²They also took Lot, the son of Abram's brother, who was dwelling in Sodom, and his possessions, and went their way.

¹³Then one who had escaped came and told Abram the Hebrew, who was living by the oaks[b] of Mamre the Amorite, brother of Eshcol and of Aner. These were allies of Abram. ¹⁴When Abram heard that his kinsman had been taken captive, he led forth his trained men, born in his house, 318 of them, and went in pursuit as far as Dan. ¹⁵And he divided his forces against them by night, he and his servants, and defeated them and pursued them to Hobah, north of Damascus. ¹⁶Then he brought back all the possessions, and also brought back his kinsman Lot with his possessions, and the women and the people.

ABRAM BLESSED BY MELCHIZEDEK

¹⁷After his return from the defeat of Chedorlaomer and the kings who were with him, the king of Sodom went out to meet him at the Valley of Shaveh (that is, the King's Valley). ¹⁸And Melchizedek king of Salem brought out bread and wine. (He was priest of God Most High.) ¹⁹And he blessed him and said,

"Blessed be Abram by God Most High,
  Possessor[c] of heaven and earth;
²⁰ and blessed be God Most High,
  who has delivered your enemies
    into your hand!"

And Abram gave him a tenth of everything. ²¹And the king of Sodom said to Abram, "Give me the persons, but take the goods for yourself." ²²But Abram said to the king of Sodom, "I have lifted my hand[d] to the LORD, God Most High, Possessor of heaven and earth, ²³that I would not take a thread or a sandal strap or anything that is yours, lest you should say, 'I have made Abram rich.' ²⁴I will take nothing but what the young men have eaten, and the share of the men who went with me. Let Aner, Eshcol, and Mamre take their share."

---

[a] Or terebinths [b] Or terebinths [c] Or Creator; also verse 22 [d] Or I have taken a solemn oath

GOD'S COVENANT WITH ABRAM

15 After these things the word of the LORD came to Abram in a vision: "Fear not, Abram, I am your shield; your reward shall be very great." ²But Abram said, "O Lord GOD, what will you give me, for I continue[a] childless, and the heir of my house is Eliezer of Damascus?" ³And Abram said, "Behold, you have given me no offspring, and a member of my household will be my heir." ⁴And behold, the word of the LORD came to him: "This man shall not be your heir; your very own son[b] shall be your heir." ⁵And he brought him outside and said, "Look towards heaven, and number the stars, if you are able to number them." Then he said to him, "So shall your offspring be." ⁶And he believed the LORD, and he counted it to him as righteousness.

⁷And he said to him, "I am the LORD who brought you out from Ur of the Chaldeans to give you this land to possess." ⁸But he said, "O Lord GOD, how am I to know that I shall possess it?" ⁹He said to him, "Bring me a heifer three years old, a female goat three years old, a ram three years old, a turtle-dove, and a young pigeon." ¹⁰And he brought him all these, cut them in half, and laid each half over against the other. But he did not cut the birds in half. ¹¹And when birds of prey came down on the carcasses, Abram drove them away.

¹²As the sun was going down, a deep sleep fell on Abram. And behold, dreadful and great darkness fell upon him. ¹³Then the LORD said to Abram, "Know for certain that your offspring will be sojourners in a land that is not theirs and will be servants there, and they will be afflicted for four hundred years. ¹⁴But I will bring judgement on the nation that they serve, and afterwards they shall come out with great possessions. ¹⁵As for you, you shall go to your fathers in peace; you shall be buried in a good old age. ¹⁶And they shall come back here in the fourth generation, for the iniquity of the Amorites is not yet complete."

¹⁷When the sun had gone down and it was dark, behold, a smoking firepot and a flaming torch passed between these pieces. ¹⁸On that day the LORD made a covenant with Abram, saying, "To your offspring I give[c] this land, from the river of Egypt to the great river, the river Euphrates, ¹⁹the land of the Kenites, the Kenizzites, the Kadmonites, ²⁰the Hittites, the Perizzites, the Rephaim, ²¹the Amorites, the Canaanites, the Girgashites and the Jebusites."

SARAI AND HAGAR

16 Now Sarai, Abram's wife, had borne him no children. She had a female Egyptian servant whose name was Hagar. ²And Sarai said to Abram, "Behold now, the LORD has prevented me from bearing children. Go in to my servant; it may be that I shall obtain children[d] by her." And Abram listened to the voice of Sarai. ³So, after Abram had lived ten years in the land of Canaan, Sarai, Abram's wife, took Hagar the Egyptian, her servant, and gave her to Abram her husband as a wife. ⁴And he went in to Hagar, and she conceived. And when she saw that she had conceived, she looked with contempt on her mistress.[e] ⁵And Sarai said to Abram, "May the wrong done to me be on you! I gave my servant to your embrace, and when she saw that she had conceived, she looked on me with contempt. May the LORD judge between you and me!" ⁶But Abram said to Sarai, "Behold, your servant is in your power; do to her as you please." Then Sarai dealt harshly with her, and she fled from her.

⁷The angel of the LORD found her by a spring of water in the wilderness, the spring on the way to Shur. ⁸And he said, "Hagar, servant of Sarai, where have you come from and where are you going?" She said, "I am fleeing from my mistress Sarai." ⁹The angel of the LORD said to her, "Return to your mistress and submit to her." ¹⁰The angel of the LORD also said to her, "I will surely multiply your offspring so that they cannot be numbered for multitude." ¹¹And the angel of the LORD said to her,

"Behold, you are pregnant
    and shall bear a son.
You shall call his name Ishmael,[f]
    because the LORD has listened
        to your affliction.
¹² He shall be a wild donkey of a man,
    his hand against everyone
    and everyone's hand against him,
    and he shall dwell over against
        all his kinsmen."

¹³So she called the name of the LORD who spoke to her, "You are a God of seeing",[g] for she said, "Truly here I have seen him who looks after me."[h] ¹⁴Therefore the well was

---

[a]Or *I shall die* [b]Hebrew *what will come out of your own loins* [c]Or *have given* [d]Hebrew *be built up*, which sounds like the Hebrew for *children* [e]Hebrew *her mistress was dishonourable in her eyes*; similarly in verse 5 [f]*Ishmael* means *God hears* [g]Or *You are a God who sees me* [h]Hebrew *Have I really seen him here who sees me?* or *Would I have looked here for the one who sees me?*

called Beer-lahai-roi;[a] it lies between Kadesh and Bered. ¹⁵And Hagar bore Abram a son, and Abram called the name of his son, whom Hagar bore, Ishmael. ¹⁶Abram was eighty-six years old when Hagar bore Ishmael to Abram.

ABRAHAM AND THE COVENANT OF CIRCUMCISION

17 When Abram was ninety-nine years old the LORD appeared to Abram and said to him, "I am God Almighty;[b] walk before me, and be blameless, ²that I may make my covenant between me and you, and may multiply you greatly." ³Then Abram fell on his face. And God said to him, ⁴"Behold, my covenant is with you, and you shall be the father of a multitude of nations. ⁵No longer shall your name be called Abram,[c] but your name shall be Abraham,[d] for I have made you the father of a multitude of nations. ⁶I will make you exceedingly fruitful, and I will make you into nations, and kings shall come from you. ⁷And I will establish my covenant between me and you and your offspring after you throughout their generations for an everlasting covenant, to be God to you and to your offspring after you. ⁸And I will give to you and to your offspring after you the land of your sojournings, all the land of Canaan, for an everlasting possession, and I will be their God."

⁹And God said to Abraham, "As for you, you shall keep my covenant, you and your offspring after you throughout their generations. ¹⁰This is my covenant, which you shall keep, between me and you and your offspring after you: Every male among you shall be circumcised. ¹¹You shall be circumcised in the flesh of your foreskins, and it shall be a sign of the covenant between me and you. ¹²He who is eight days old among you shall be circumcised. Every male throughout your generations, whether born in your house or bought with your money from any foreigner who is not of your offspring, ¹³both he who is born in your house and he who is bought with your money, shall surely be circumcised. So shall my covenant be in your flesh an everlasting covenant. ¹⁴Any uncircumcised male who is not circumcised in the flesh of his foreskin shall be cut off from his people; he has broken my covenant."

ISAAC'S BIRTH PROMISED

¹⁵And God said to Abraham, "As for Sarai your wife, you shall not call her name Sarai, but Sarah[e] shall be her name. ¹⁶I will bless her, and moreover, I will give[f] you a son by her. I will bless her, and she shall become nations; kings of peoples shall come from her." ¹⁷Then Abraham fell on his face and laughed and said to himself, "Shall a child be born to a man who is a hundred years old? Shall Sarah, who is ninety years old, bear a child?" ¹⁸And Abraham said to God, "Oh that Ishmael might live before you!" ¹⁹God said, "No, but Sarah your wife shall bear you a son, and you shall call his name Isaac.[g] I will establish my covenant with him as an everlasting covenant for his offspring after him. ²⁰As for Ishmael, I have heard you; behold, I have blessed him and will make him fruitful and multiply him greatly. He shall father twelve princes, and I will make him into a great nation. ²¹But I will establish my covenant with Isaac, whom Sarah shall bear to you at this time next year."

²²When he had finished talking with him, God went up from Abraham. ²³Then Abraham took Ishmael his son and all those born in his house or bought with his money, every male among the men of Abraham's house, and he circumcised the flesh of their foreskins that very day, as God had said to him. ²⁴Abraham was ninety-nine years old when he was circumcised in the flesh of his foreskin. ²⁵And Ishmael his son was thirteen years old when he was circumcised in the flesh of his foreskin. ²⁶That very day Abraham and his son Ishmael were circumcised. ²⁷And all the men of his house, those born in the house and those bought with money from a foreigner, were circumcised with him.

18 And the LORD appeared to him by the oaks[h] of Mamre, as he sat at the door of his tent in the heat of the day. ²He lifted up his eyes and looked, and behold, three men were standing in front of him. When he saw them, he ran from the tent door to meet them and bowed himself to the earth ³and said, "O Lord,[i] if I have found favour in your sight, do not pass by your servant. ⁴Let a little water be brought, and wash your feet, and rest yourselves under the tree, ⁵while I bring a morsel of bread, that you may refresh yourselves, and after that you may pass on—since you have come to your servant." So they said, "Do as you have said." ⁶And Abraham went quickly into the tent to

---

[a] Beer-lahai-roi means *the well of the Living One who sees me* [b] Hebrew *El Shaddai* [c] *Abram* means *exalted father* [d] *Abraham* means *father of a multitude* [e] *Sarai* and *Sarah* mean *princess* [f] Hebrew *have given* [g] *Isaac* means *he laughs* [h] Or *terebinths* [i] Or *My lord*

Sarah and said, "Quick! Three seahs[a] of fine flour! Knead it, and make cakes." [7]And Abraham ran to the herd and took a calf, tender and good, and gave it to a young man, who prepared it quickly. [8]Then he took curds and milk and the calf that he had prepared, and set it before them. And he stood by them under the tree while they ate.

[9]They said to him, "Where is Sarah your wife?" And he said, "She is in the tent." [10]The LORD said, "I will surely return to you about this time next year, and Sarah your wife shall have a son." And Sarah was listening at the tent door behind him. [11]Now Abraham and Sarah were old, advanced in years. The way of women had ceased to be with Sarah. [12]So Sarah laughed to herself, saying, "After I am worn out, and my lord is old, shall I have pleasure?" [13]The LORD said to Abraham, "Why did Sarah laugh and say, 'Shall I indeed bear a child, now that I am old?' [14]Is anything too hard[b] for the LORD? At the appointed time I will return to you, about this time next year, and Sarah shall have a son." [15]But Sarah denied it,[c] saying, "I did not laugh", for she was afraid. He said, "No, but you did laugh."

[16]Then the men set out from there, and they looked down towards Sodom. And Abraham went with them to set them on their way. [17]The LORD said, "Shall I hide from Abraham what I am about to do, [18]seeing that Abraham shall surely become a great and mighty nation, and all the nations of the earth shall be blessed in him? [19]For I have chosen[d] him, that he may command his children and his household after him to keep the way of the LORD by doing righteousness and justice, so that the LORD may bring to Abraham what he has promised him." [20]Then the LORD said, "Because the outcry against Sodom and Gomorrah is great and their sin is very grave, [21]I will go down to see whether they have done altogether[e] according to the outcry that has come to me. And if not, I will know."

ABRAHAM INTERCEDES FOR SODOM

[22]So the men turned from there and went towards Sodom, but Abraham still stood before the LORD. [23]Then Abraham drew near and said, "Will you indeed sweep away the righteous with the wicked? [24]Suppose there are fifty righteous within the city. Will you then sweep away the place and not spare it for the fifty righteous who are in it? [25]Far be it from you to do such a thing, to put the righteous to death with the wicked, so that the righteous fare as the wicked! Far be that from you! Shall not the Judge of all the earth do what is just?" [26]And the LORD said, "If I find at Sodom fifty righteous in the city, I will spare the whole place for their sake."

[27]Abraham answered and said, "Behold, I have undertaken to speak to the Lord, I who am but dust and ashes. [28]Suppose five of the fifty righteous are lacking. Will you destroy the whole city for lack of five?" And he said, "I will not destroy it if I find forty-five there." [29]Again he spoke to him and said, "Suppose forty are found there." He answered, "For the sake of forty I will not do it." [30]Then he said, "Oh let not the Lord be angry, and I will speak. Suppose thirty are found there." He answered, "I will not do it, if I find thirty there." [31]He said, "Behold, I have undertaken to speak to the Lord. Suppose twenty are found there." He answered, "For the sake of twenty I will not destroy it." [32]Then he said, "Oh let not the Lord be angry, and I will speak again but this once. Suppose ten are found there." He answered, "For the sake of ten I will not destroy it." [33]And the LORD went his way, when he had finished speaking to Abraham, and Abraham returned to his place.

GOD RESCUES LOT

19 The two angels came to Sodom in the evening, and Lot was sitting in the gate of Sodom. When Lot saw them, he rose to meet them and bowed himself with his face to the earth [2]and said, "My lords, please turn aside to your servant's house and spend the night and wash your feet. Then you may rise up early and go on your way." They said, "No; we will spend the night in the town square." [3]But he pressed them strongly; so they turned aside to him and entered his house. And he made them a feast and baked unleavened bread, and they ate.

[4]But before they lay down, the men of the city, the men of Sodom, both young and old, all the people to the last man, surrounded the house. [5]And they called to Lot, "Where are the men who came to you tonight? Bring them out to us, that we may know them." [6]Lot went out to the men at the entrance, shut the door after him, [7]and said, "I beg you, my brothers, do not act so wickedly. [8]Behold, I

---

[a]A *seah* was about 7 quarts or 7.3 litres [b]Or *wonderful* [c]Or *acted falsely* [d]Hebrew *known* [e]Or *they deserve destruction*; Hebrew *they have made a complete end*

have two daughters who have not known any man. Let me bring them out to you, and do to them as you please. Only do nothing to these men, for they have come under the shelter of my roof." ⁹But they said, "Stand back!" And they said, "This fellow came to sojourn, and he has become the judge! Now we will deal worse with you than with them." Then they pressed hard against the man Lot, and drew near to break the door down. ¹⁰But the men reached out their hands and brought Lot into the house with them and shut the door. ¹¹And they struck with blindness the men who were at the entrance of the house, both small and great, so that they wore themselves out groping for the door.

¹²Then the men said to Lot, "Have you anyone else here? Sons-in-law, sons, daughters, or anyone you have in the city, bring them out of the place. ¹³For we are about to destroy this place, because the outcry against its people has become great before the LORD, and the LORD has sent us to destroy it." ¹⁴So Lot went out and said to his sons-in-law, who were to marry his daughters, "Up! Get out of this place, for the LORD is about to destroy the city." But he seemed to his sons-in-law to be jesting.

¹⁵As morning dawned, the angels urged Lot, saying, "Up! Take your wife and your two daughters who are here, lest you be swept away in the punishment of the city." ¹⁶But he lingered. So the men seized him and his wife and his two daughters by the hand, the LORD being merciful to him, and they brought him out and set him outside the city. ¹⁷And as they brought them out, one said, "Escape for your life. Do not look back or stop anywhere in the valley. Escape to the hills, lest you be swept away." ¹⁸And Lot said to them, "Oh, no, my lords. ¹⁹Behold, your servant has found favour in your sight, and you have shown me great kindness in saving my life. But I cannot escape to the hills, lest the disaster overtake me and I die. ²⁰Behold, this city is near enough to flee to, and it is a little one. Let me escape there—is it not a little one?—and my life will be saved!" ²¹He said to him, "Behold, I grant you this favour also, that I will not overthrow the city of which you have spoken. ²²Escape there quickly, for I can do nothing till you arrive there." Therefore the name of the city was called Zoar.ᵃ

GOD DESTROYS SODOM

²³The sun had risen on the earth when Lot came to Zoar. ²⁴Then the LORD rained on Sodom and Gomorrah sulphur and fire from the LORD out of heaven. ²⁵And he overthrew those cities, and all the valley, and all the inhabitants of the cities, and what grew on the ground. ²⁶But Lot's wife, behind him, looked back, and she became a pillar of salt.

²⁷And Abraham went early in the morning to the place where he had stood before the LORD. ²⁸And he looked down towards Sodom and Gomorrah and towards all the land of the valley, and he looked and, behold, the smoke of the land went up like the smoke of a furnace. ²⁹So it was that, when God destroyed the cities of the valley, God remembered Abraham and sent Lot out of the midst of the overthrow when he overthrew the cities in which Lot had lived.

LOT AND HIS DAUGHTERS

³⁰Now Lot went up out of Zoar and lived in the hills with his two daughters, for he was afraid to live in Zoar. So he lived in a cave with his two daughters. ³¹And the firstborn said to the younger, "Our father is old, and there is not a man on earth to come in to us after the manner of all the earth. ³²Come, let us make our father drink wine, and we will lie with him, that we may preserve offspring from our father." ³³So they made their father drink wine that night. And the firstborn went in and lay with her father. He did not know when she lay down or when she arose.

³⁴The next day, the firstborn said to the younger, "Behold, I lay last night with my father. Let us make him drink wine tonight also. Then you go in and lie with him, that we may preserve offspring from our father." ³⁵So they made their father drink wine that night also. And the younger arose and lay with him, and he did not know when she lay down or when she arose. ³⁶Thus both the daughters of Lot became pregnant by their father. ³⁷The firstborn bore a son and called his name Moab.ᵇ He is the father of the Moabites to this day. ³⁸The younger also bore a son and called his name Ben-ammi.ᶜ He is the father of the Ammonites to this day.

ABRAHAM AND ABIMELECH

20 From there Abraham journeyed towards the territory of the Negeb and lived between Kadesh and Shur; and he sojourned in Gerar. ²And

---

ᵃ*Zoar* means *little* ᵇ*Moab* sounds like the Hebrew for *from father* ᶜ*Ben-ammi* means *son of my people*

Abraham said of Sarah his wife, "She is my sister." And Abimelech king of Gerar sent and took Sarah. ³But God came to Abimelech in a dream by night and said to him, "Behold, you are a dead man because of the woman whom you have taken, for she is a man's wife." ⁴Now Abimelech had not approached her. So he said, "Lord, will you kill an innocent people? ⁵Did he not himself say to me, 'She is my sister'? And she herself said, 'He is my brother.' In the integrity of my heart and the innocence of my hands I have done this." ⁶Then God said to him in the dream, "Yes, I know that you have done this in the integrity of your heart, and it was I who kept you from sinning against me. Therefore I did not let you touch her. ⁷Now then, return the man's wife, for he is a prophet, so that he will pray for you, and you shall live. But if you do not return her, know that you shall surely die, you and all who are yours."

⁸So Abimelech rose early in the morning and called all his servants and told them all these things. And the men were very much afraid. ⁹Then Abimelech called Abraham and said to him, "What have you done to us? And how have I sinned against you, that you have brought on me and my kingdom a great sin? You have done to me things that ought not to be done." ¹⁰And Abimelech said to Abraham, "What did you see, that you did this thing?" ¹¹Abraham said, "I did it because I thought, 'There is no fear of God at all in this place, and they will kill me because of my wife.' ¹²Besides, she is indeed my sister, the daughter of my father though not the daughter of my mother, and she became my wife. ¹³And when God caused me to wander from my father's house, I said to her, 'This is the kindness you must do me: at every place to which we come, say of me, "He is my brother."'"

¹⁴Then Abimelech took sheep and oxen, and male servants and female servants, and gave them to Abraham, and returned Sarah his wife to him. ¹⁵And Abimelech said, "Behold, my land is before you; dwell where it pleases you." ¹⁶To Sarah he said, "Behold, I have given your brother a thousand pieces of silver. It is a sign of your innocence in the eyes of all[a] who are with you, and before everyone you are vindicated." ¹⁷Then Abraham prayed to God, and God healed Abimelech, and also healed his wife and female slaves so that they bore children. ¹⁸For the LORD had closed all the wombs of the house of Abimelech because of Sarah, Abraham's wife.

THE BIRTH OF ISAAC

21 The LORD visited Sarah as he had said, and the LORD did to Sarah as he had promised. ²And Sarah conceived and bore Abraham a son in his old age at the time of which God had spoken to him. ³Abraham called the name of his son who was born to him, whom Sarah bore him, Isaac.[b] ⁴And Abraham circumcised his son Isaac when he was eight days old, as God had commanded him. ⁵Abraham was a hundred years old when his son Isaac was born to him. ⁶And Sarah said, "God has made laughter for me; everyone who hears will laugh over me." ⁷And she said, "Who would have said to Abraham that Sarah would nurse children? Yet I have borne him a son in his old age."

GOD PROTECTS HAGAR AND ISHMAEL

⁸And the child grew and was weaned. And Abraham made a great feast on the day that Isaac was weaned. ⁹But Sarah saw the son of Hagar the Egyptian, whom she had borne to Abraham, laughing.[c] ¹⁰So she said to Abraham, "Cast out this slave woman with her son, for the son of this slave woman shall not be heir with my son Isaac." ¹¹And the thing was very displeasing to Abraham on account of his son. ¹²But God said to Abraham, "Be not displeased because of the boy and because of your slave woman. Whatever Sarah says to you, do as she tells you, for through Isaac shall your offspring be named. ¹³And I will make a nation of the son of the slave woman also, because he is your offspring." ¹⁴So Abraham rose early in the morning and took bread and a skin of water and gave it to Hagar, putting it on her shoulder, along with the child, and sent her away. And she departed and wandered in the wilderness of Beersheba.

¹⁵When the water in the skin was gone, she put the child under one of the bushes. ¹⁶Then she went and sat down opposite him a good way off, about the distance of a bowshot, for she said, "Let me not look on the death of the child." And as she sat opposite him, she lifted up her voice and wept. ¹⁷And God heard the voice of the boy, and the angel of God called to Hagar from heaven and said to her, "What troubles you, Hagar? Fear not, for God has heard the voice of the boy where he is. ¹⁸Up! Lift up the boy, and hold him fast with your hand, for I will make him into a

---

[a]Hebrew *It is a covering of eyes for all* [b]*Isaac* means *he laughs*
[c]Possibly *laughing in mockery*

great nation." ¹⁹Then God opened her eyes, and she saw a well of water. And she went and filled the skin with water and gave the boy a drink. ²⁰And God was with the boy, and he grew up. He lived in the wilderness and became an expert with the bow. ²¹He lived in the wilderness of Paran, and his mother took a wife for him from the land of Egypt.

A TREATY WITH ABIMELECH

²²At that time Abimelech and Phicol the commander of his army said to Abraham, "God is with you in all that you do. ²³Now therefore swear to me here by God that you will not deal falsely with me or with my descendants or with my posterity, but as I have dealt kindly with you, so you will deal with me and with the land where you have sojourned." ²⁴And Abraham said, "I will swear."

²⁵When Abraham reproved Abimelech about a well of water that Abimelech's servants had seized, ²⁶Abimelech said, "I do not know who has done this thing; you did not tell me, and I have not heard of it until today." ²⁷So Abraham took sheep and oxen and gave them to Abimelech, and the two men made a covenant. ²⁸Abraham set seven ewe lambs of the flock apart. ²⁹And Abimelech said to Abraham, "What is the meaning of these seven ewe lambs that you have set apart?" ³⁰He said, "These seven ewe lambs you will take from my hand, that this[a] may be a witness for me that I dug this well." ³¹Therefore that place was called Beersheba,[b] because there both of them swore an oath. ³²So they made a covenant at Beersheba. Then Abimelech and Phicol the commander of his army rose up and returned to the land of the Philistines. ³³Abraham planted a tamarisk tree in Beersheba and called there on the name of the LORD, the Everlasting God. ³⁴And Abraham sojourned many days in the land of the Philistines.

THE SACRIFICE OF ISAAC

22 After these things God tested Abraham and said to him, "Abraham!" And he said, "Here I am." ²He said, "Take your son, your only son Isaac, whom you love, and go to the land of Moriah, and offer him there as a burnt offering on one of the mountains of which I shall tell you." ³So Abraham rose early in the morning, saddled his donkey, and took two of his young men with him, and his son Isaac. And he cut the wood for the burnt offering and arose and went to the place of which God had told him. ⁴On the third day Abraham lifted up his eyes and saw the place from afar. ⁵Then Abraham said to his young men, "Stay here with the donkey; I and the boy[c] will go over there and worship and come again to you." ⁶And Abraham took the wood of the burnt offering and laid it on Isaac his son. And he took in his hand the fire and the knife. So they went both of them together. ⁷And Isaac said to his father Abraham, "My father!" And he said, "Here I am, my son." He said, "Behold, the fire and the wood, but where is the lamb for a burnt offering?" ⁸Abraham said, "God will provide for himself the lamb for a burnt offering, my son." So they went both of them together.

⁹When they came to the place of which God had told him, Abraham built the altar there and laid the wood in order and bound Isaac his son and laid him on the altar, on top of the wood. ¹⁰Then Abraham reached out his hand and took the knife to slaughter his son. ¹¹But the angel of the LORD called to him from heaven and said, "Abraham, Abraham!" And he said, "Here I am." ¹²He said, "Do not lay your hand on the boy or do anything to him, for now I know that you fear God, seeing you have not withheld your son, your only son, from me." ¹³And Abraham lifted up his eyes and looked, and behold, behind him was a ram, caught in a thicket by his horns. And Abraham went and took the ram and offered it up as a burnt offering instead of his son. ¹⁴So Abraham called the name of that place, "The LORD will provide";[d] as it is said to this day, "On the mount of the LORD it shall be provided."[e]

¹⁵And the angel of the LORD called to Abraham a second time from heaven ¹⁶and said, "By myself I have sworn, declares the LORD, because you have done this and have not withheld your son, your only son, ¹⁷I will surely bless you, and I will surely multiply your offspring as the stars of heaven and as the sand that is on the seashore. And your offspring shall possess the gate of his[f] enemies, ¹⁸and in your offspring shall all the nations of the earth be blessed, because you have obeyed my voice." ¹⁹So Abraham returned to his young men, and they arose and went together to Beersheba. And Abraham lived at Beersheba.

---

[a] Or you [b] Beersheba means well of seven or well of the oath [c] Or young man; also verse 12 [d] Or will see [e] Or he will be seen [f] Or their

²⁰Now after these things it was told to Abraham, "Behold, Milcah also has borne children to your brother Nahor: ²¹Uz his firstborn, Buz his brother, Kemuel the father of Aram, ²²Chesed, Hazo, Pildash, Jidlaph, and Bethuel." ²³(Bethuel fathered Rebekah.) These eight Milcah bore to Nahor, Abraham's brother. ²⁴Moreover, his concubine, whose name was Reumah, bore Tebah, Gaham, Tahash, and Maacah.

SARAH'S DEATH AND BURIAL

23 Sarah lived for 127 years; these were the years of the life of Sarah. ²And Sarah died at Kiriath-arba (that is, Hebron) in the land of Canaan, and Abraham went in to mourn for Sarah and to weep for her. ³And Abraham rose up from before his dead and said to the Hittites,ᵃ ⁴"I am a sojourner and foreigner among you; give me property among you for a burying place, that I may bury my dead out of my sight." ⁵The Hittites answered Abraham, ⁶"Hear us, my lord; you are a prince of Godᵇ among us. Bury your dead in the choicest of our tombs. None of us will withhold from you his tomb to hinder you from burying your dead." ⁷Abraham rose and bowed to the Hittites, the people of the land. ⁸And he said to them, "If you are willing that I should bury my dead out of my sight, hear me and entreat for me Ephron the son of Zohar, ⁹that he may give me the cave of Machpelah, which he owns; it is at the end of his field. For the full price let him give it to me in your presence as property for a burying place."

¹⁰Now Ephron was sitting among the Hittites, and Ephron the Hittite answered Abraham in the hearing of the Hittites, of all who went in at the gate of his city, ¹¹"No, my lord, hear me: I give you the field, and I give you the cave that is in it. In the sight of the sons of my people I give it to you. Bury your dead." ¹²Then Abraham bowed down before the people of the land. ¹³And he said to Ephron in the hearing of the people of the land, "But if you will, hear me: I give the price of the field. Accept it from me, that I may bury my dead there." ¹⁴Ephron answered Abraham, ¹⁵"My lord, listen to me: a piece of land worth four hundred shekelsᶜ of silver, what is that between you and me? Bury your dead." ¹⁶Abraham listened to Ephron, and Abraham weighed out for Ephron the silver that he had named in the hearing of the Hittites, four hundred shekels of silver, according to the weights current among the merchants.

¹⁷So the field of Ephron in Machpelah, which was to the east of Mamre, the field with the cave that was in it and all the trees that were in the field, throughout its whole area, was made over ¹⁸to Abraham as a possession in the presence of the Hittites, before all who went in at the gate of his city. ¹⁹After this, Abraham buried Sarah his wife in the cave of the field of Machpelah east of Mamre (that is, Hebron) in the land of Canaan. ²⁰The field and the cave that is in it were made over to Abraham as property for a burying place by the Hittites.

ISAAC AND REBEKAH

24 Now Abraham was old, well advanced in years. And the LORD had blessed Abraham in all things. ²And Abraham said to his servant, the oldest of his household, who had charge of all that he had, "Put your hand under my thigh, ³that I may make you swear by the LORD, the God of heaven and God of the earth, that you will not take a wife for my son from the daughters of the Canaanites, among whom I dwell, ⁴but will go to my country and to my kindred, and take a wife for my son Isaac." ⁵The servant said to him, "Perhaps the woman may not be willing to follow me to this land. Must I then take your son back to the land from which you came?" ⁶Abraham said to him, "See to it that you do not take my son back there. ⁷The LORD, the God of heaven, who took me from my father's house and from the land of my kindred, and who spoke to me and swore to me, 'To your offspring I will give this land', he will send his angel before you, and you shall take a wife for my son from there. ⁸But if the woman is not willing to follow you, then you will be free from this oath of mine; only you must not take my son back there." ⁹So the servant put his hand under the thigh of Abraham his master and swore to him concerning this matter.

¹⁰Then the servant took ten of his master's camels and departed, taking all sorts of choice gifts from his master; and he arose and went to Mesopotamiaᵈ to the city of Nahor. ¹¹And he made the camels kneel down outside the city by the well of water at the time of evening, the time when women go out to draw water. ¹²And he said, "O LORD, God of my master

---

ᵃHebrew *sons of Heth*; also verses 5, 7, 10, 16, 18, 20 ᵇOr *a mighty prince* ᶜA *shekel* was about 2/5 of an ounce or 11 grams ᵈHebrew *Aram-naharaim*

Abraham, please grant me success today and show steadfast love to my master Abraham. ¹³Behold, I am standing by the spring of water, and the daughters of the men of the city are coming out to draw water. ¹⁴Let the young woman to whom I shall say, 'Please let down your jar that I may drink', and who shall say, 'Drink, and I will water your camels'—let her be the one whom you have appointed for your servant Isaac. By this*ᵃ* I shall know that you have shown steadfast love to my master."

¹⁵Before he had finished speaking, behold, Rebekah, who was born to Bethuel the son of Milcah, the wife of Nahor, Abraham's brother, came out with her water jar on her shoulder. ¹⁶The young woman was very attractive in appearance, a maiden*ᵇ* whom no man had known. She went down to the spring and filled her jar and came up. ¹⁷Then the servant ran to meet her and said, "Please give me a little water to drink from your jar." ¹⁸She said, "Drink, my lord." And she quickly let down her jar upon her hand and gave him a drink. ¹⁹When she had finished giving him a drink, she said, "I will draw water for your camels also, until they have finished drinking." ²⁰So she quickly emptied her jar into the trough and ran again to the well to draw water, and she drew for all his camels. ²¹The man gazed at her in silence to learn whether the LORD had prospered his journey or not.

²²When the camels had finished drinking, the man took a gold ring weighing a half shekel,*ᶜ* and two bracelets for her arms weighing ten gold shekels, ²³and said, "Please tell me whose daughter you are. Is there room in your father's house for us to spend the night?" ²⁴She said to him, "I am the daughter of Bethuel the son of Milcah, whom she bore to Nahor." ²⁵She added, "We have plenty of both straw and fodder, and room to spend the night." ²⁶The man bowed his head and worshipped the LORD ²⁷and said, "Blessed be the LORD, the God of my master Abraham, who has not forsaken his steadfast love and his faithfulness towards my master. As for me, the LORD has led me in the way to the house of my master's kinsmen." ²⁸Then the young woman ran and told her mother's household about these things.

²⁹Rebekah had a brother whose name was Laban. Laban ran out towards the man, to the spring. ³⁰As soon as he saw the ring and the bracelets on his sister's arms, and heard the words of Rebekah his sister, "Thus the man spoke to me", he went to the man. And behold, he was standing by the camels at the spring. ³¹He said, "Come in, O blessed of the LORD. Why do you stand outside? For I have prepared the house and a place for the camels." ³²So the man came to the house and unharnessed the camels, and gave straw and fodder to the camels, and there was water to wash his feet and the feet of the men who were with him. ³³Then food was set before him to eat. But he said, "I will not eat until I have said what I have to say." He said, "Speak on."

³⁴So he said, "I am Abraham's servant. ³⁵The LORD has greatly blessed my master, and he has become great. He has given him flocks and herds, silver and gold, male servants and female servants, camels and donkeys. ³⁶And Sarah my master's wife bore a son to my master when she was old, and to him he has given all that he has. ³⁷My master made me swear, saying, 'You shall not take a wife for my son from the daughters of the Canaanites, in whose land I dwell, ³⁸but you shall go to my father's house and to my clan and take a wife for my son.' ³⁹I said to my master, 'Perhaps the woman will not follow me.' ⁴⁰But he said to me, 'The LORD, before whom I have walked, will send his angel with you and prosper your way. You shall take a wife for my son from my clan and from my father's house. ⁴¹Then you will be free from my oath, when you come to my clan. And if they will not give her to you, you will be free from my oath.'

⁴²"I came today to the spring and said, 'O LORD, the God of my master Abraham, if now you are prospering the way that I go, ⁴³behold, I am standing by the spring of water. Let the virgin who comes out to draw water, to whom I shall say, "Please give me a little water from your jar to drink", ⁴⁴and who will say to me, "Drink, and I will draw for your camels also", let her be the woman whom the LORD has appointed for my master's son.'

⁴⁵"Before I had finished speaking in my heart, behold, Rebekah came out with her water jar on her shoulder, and she went down to the spring and drew water. I said to her, 'Please let me drink.' ⁴⁶She quickly let down her jar from her shoulder and said, 'Drink, and I will give your camels drink also.' So I drank, and she gave the camels drink also. ⁴⁷Then I asked her, 'Whose daughter are you?' She said, 'The daughter of Bethuel, Nahor's son, whom Milcah bore to him.' So I put the ring on her nose and the bracelets on her arms. ⁴⁸Then

---

*ᵃ*Or *By her*   *ᵇ*Or *a woman of marriageable age*   *ᶜA shekel* was about 2/5 of an ounce or 11 grams

I bowed my head and worshipped the Lord and blessed the Lord, the God of my master Abraham, who had led me by the right way[a] to take the daughter of my master's kinsman for his son. ⁴⁹Now then, if you are going to show steadfast love and faithfulness to my master, tell me; and if not, tell me, that I may turn to the right hand or to the left."

⁵⁰Then Laban and Bethuel answered and said, "The thing has come from the Lord; we cannot speak to you bad or good. ⁵¹Behold, Rebekah is before you; take her and go, and let her be the wife of your master's son, as the Lord has spoken."

⁵²When Abraham's servant heard their words, he bowed himself to the earth before the Lord. ⁵³And the servant brought out jewellery of silver and of gold, and garments, and gave them to Rebekah. He also gave to her brother and to her mother costly ornaments. ⁵⁴And he and the men who were with him ate and drank, and they spent the night there. When they arose in the morning, he said, "Send me away to my master." ⁵⁵Her brother and her mother said, "Let the young woman remain with us a while, at least ten days; after that she may go." ⁵⁶But he said to them, "Do not delay me, since the Lord has prospered my way. Send me away that I may go to my master." ⁵⁷They said, "Let us call the young woman and ask her." ⁵⁸And they called Rebekah and said to her, "Will you go with this man?" She said, "I will go." ⁵⁹So they sent away Rebekah their sister and her nurse, and Abraham's servant and his men. ⁶⁰And they blessed Rebekah and said to her,

> "Our sister, may you become
> thousands of ten thousands,
> and may your offspring possess
> the gate of those who hate him!"[b]

⁶¹Then Rebekah and her young women arose and rode on the camels and followed the man. Thus the servant took Rebekah and went his way.

⁶²Now Isaac had returned from Beer-lahai-roi and was dwelling in the Negeb. ⁶³And Isaac went out to meditate in the field towards evening. And he lifted up his eyes and saw, and behold, there were camels coming. ⁶⁴And Rebekah lifted up her eyes, and when she saw Isaac, she dismounted from the camel ⁶⁵and said to the servant, "Who is that man, walking in the field to meet us?" The servant said, "It is my master." So she took her veil and covered herself. ⁶⁶And the servant told Isaac all the things that he had done. ⁶⁷Then Isaac brought her into the tent of Sarah his mother and took Rebekah, and she became his wife, and he loved her. So Isaac was comforted after his mother's death.

ABRAHAM'S DEATH AND HIS DESCENDANTS

25 Abraham took another wife, whose name was Keturah. ²She bore him Zimran, Jokshan, Medan, Midian, Ishbak, and Shuah. ³Jokshan fathered Sheba and Dedan. The sons of Dedan were Asshurim, Letushim, and Leummim. ⁴The sons of Midian were Ephah, Epher, Hanoch, Abida, and Eldaah. All these were the children of Keturah. ⁵Abraham gave all he had to Isaac. ⁶But to the sons of his concubines Abraham gave gifts, and while he was still living he sent them away from his son Isaac, eastwards to the east country.

⁷These are the days of the years of Abraham's life, 175 years. ⁸Abraham breathed his last and died in a good old age, an old man and full of years, and was gathered to his people. ⁹Isaac and Ishmael his sons buried him in the cave of Machpelah, in the field of Ephron the son of Zohar the Hittite, east of Mamre, ¹⁰the field that Abraham purchased from the Hittites. There Abraham was buried, with Sarah his wife. ¹¹After the death of Abraham, God blessed Isaac his son. And Isaac settled at Beer-lahai-roi.

¹²These are the generations of Ishmael, Abraham's son, whom Hagar the Egyptian, Sarah's servant, bore to Abraham. ¹³These are the names of the sons of Ishmael, named in the order of their birth: Nebaioth, the firstborn of Ishmael; and Kedar, Adbeel, Mibsam, ¹⁴Mishma, Dumah, Massa, ¹⁵Hadad, Tema, Jetur, Naphish, and Kedemah. ¹⁶These are the sons of Ishmael and these are their names, by their villages and by their encampments, twelve princes according to their tribes. ¹⁷(These are the years of the life of Ishmael: 137 years. He breathed his last and died, and was gathered to his people.) ¹⁸They settled from Havilah to Shur, which is opposite Egypt in the direction of Assyria. He settled[c] over against all his kinsmen.

THE BIRTH OF ESAU AND JACOB

¹⁹These are the generations of Isaac, Abraham's son: Abraham fathered Isaac, ²⁰and

---

[a] Or faithfully [b] Or hate them [c] Hebrew fell

Isaac was forty years old when he took Rebekah, the daughter of Bethuel the Aramean of Paddan-aram, the sister of Laban the Aramean, to be his wife. ²¹And Isaac prayed to the LORD for his wife, because she was barren. And the LORD granted his prayer, and Rebekah his wife conceived. ²²The children struggled together within her, and she said, "If it is thus, why is this happening to me?"[a] So she went to enquire of the LORD. ²³And the LORD said to her,

"Two nations are in your womb,
 and two peoples from within
  you[b] shall be divided;
the one shall be stronger
 than the other,
the older shall serve the younger."

²⁴When her days to give birth were completed, behold, there were twins in her womb. ²⁵The first came out red, all his body like a hairy cloak, so they called his name Esau. ²⁶Afterwards his brother came out with his hand holding Esau's heel, so his name was called Jacob.[c] Isaac was sixty years old when she bore them.

²⁷When the boys grew up, Esau was a skilful hunter, a man of the field, while Jacob was a quiet man, dwelling in tents. ²⁸Isaac loved Esau because he ate of his game, but Rebekah loved Jacob.

ESAU SELLS HIS BIRTHRIGHT

²⁹Once when Jacob was cooking stew, Esau came in from the field, and he was exhausted. ³⁰And Esau said to Jacob, "Let me eat some of that red stew, for I am exhausted!" (Therefore his name was called Edom.[d]) ³¹Jacob said, "Sell me your birthright now." ³²Esau said, "I am about to die; of what use is a birthright to me?" ³³Jacob said, "Swear to me now." So he swore to him and sold his birthright to Jacob. ³⁴Then Jacob gave Esau bread and lentil stew, and he ate and drank and rose and went his way. Thus Esau despised his birthright.

GOD'S PROMISE TO ISAAC

26 Now there was a famine in the land, besides the former famine that was in the days of Abraham. And Isaac went to Gerar to Abimelech king of the Philistines. ²And the LORD appeared to him and said, "Do not go down to Egypt; dwell in the land of which I shall tell you. ³Sojourn in this land, and I will be with you and will bless you, for to you and to your offspring I will give all these lands, and I will establish the oath that I swore to Abraham your father. ⁴I will multiply your offspring as the stars of heaven and will give to your offspring all these lands. And in your offspring all the nations of the earth shall be blessed, ⁵because Abraham obeyed my voice and kept my charge, my commandments, my statutes, and my laws."

ISAAC AND ABIMELECH

⁶So Isaac settled in Gerar. ⁷When the men of the place asked him about his wife, he said, "She is my sister", for he feared to say, "My wife", thinking, "lest the men of the place should kill me because of Rebekah", because she was attractive in appearance. ⁸When he had been there a long time, Abimelech king of the Philistines looked out of a window and saw Isaac laughing with[e] Rebekah his wife. ⁹So Abimelech called Isaac and said, "Behold, she is your wife. How then could you say, 'She is my sister'?" Isaac said to him, "Because I thought, 'Lest I die because of her.'" ¹⁰Abimelech said, "What is this you have done to us? One of the people might easily have lain with your wife, and you would have brought guilt upon us." ¹¹So Abimelech warned all the people, saying, "Whoever touches this man or his wife shall surely be put to death."

¹²And Isaac sowed in that land and reaped in the same year a hundredfold. The LORD blessed him, ¹³and the man became rich, and gained more and more until he became very wealthy. ¹⁴He had possessions of flocks and herds and many servants, so that the Philistines envied him. ¹⁵(Now the Philistines had stopped and filled with earth all the wells that his father's servants had dug in the days of Abraham his father.) ¹⁶And Abimelech said to Isaac, "Go away from us, for you are much mightier than we."

¹⁷So Isaac departed from there and encamped in the Valley of Gerar and settled there. ¹⁸And Isaac dug again the wells of water that had been dug in the days of Abraham his father, which the Philistines had stopped after the death of Abraham. And he gave them the names that his father had given them. ¹⁹But when Isaac's servants dug in the valley and found there a well of spring water, ²⁰the

---

[a] Or why do I live? [b] Or from birth [c] Jacob means He takes by the heel, or He cheats [d] Edom sounds like the Hebrew for red [e] Hebrew may suggest an intimate relationship

herdsmen of Gerar quarrelled with Isaac's herdsmen, saying, "The water is ours." So he called the name of the well Esek,[a] because they contended with him. ²¹Then they dug another well, and they quarrelled over that also, so he called its name Sitnah.[b] ²²And he moved from there and dug another well, and they did not quarrel over it. So he called its name Rehoboth,[c] saying, "For now the LORD has made room for us, and we shall be fruitful in the land."

²³From there he went up to Beersheba. ²⁴And the LORD appeared to him the same night and said, "I am the God of Abraham your father. Fear not, for I am with you and will bless you and multiply your offspring for my servant Abraham's sake." ²⁵So he built an altar there and called upon the name of the LORD and pitched his tent there. And there Isaac's servants dug a well.

²⁶When Abimelech went to him from Gerar with Ahuzzath his adviser and Phicol the commander of his army, ²⁷Isaac said to them, "Why have you come to me, seeing that you hate me and have sent me away from you?" ²⁸They said, "We see plainly that the LORD has been with you. So we said, let there be a sworn pact between us, between you and us, and let us make a covenant with you, ²⁹that you will do us no harm, just as we have not touched you and have done to you nothing but good and have sent you away in peace. You are now the blessed of the LORD." ³⁰So he made them a feast, and they ate and drank. ³¹In the morning they rose early and exchanged oaths. And Isaac sent them on their way, and they departed from him in peace. ³²That same day Isaac's servants came and told him about the well that they had dug and said to him, "We have found water." ³³He called it Shibah;[d] therefore the name of the city is Beersheba to this day.

³⁴When Esau was forty years old, he took Judith the daughter of Beeri the Hittite to be his wife, and Basemath the daughter of Elon the Hittite, ³⁵and they made life bitter[e] for Isaac and Rebekah.

ISAAC BLESSES JACOB

27 When Isaac was old and his eyes were dim so that he could not see, he called Esau his older son and said to him, "My son"; and he answered, "Here I am." ²He said, "Behold, I am old; I do not know the day of my death. ³Now then, take your weapons, your quiver and your bow, and go out to the field and hunt game for me, ⁴and prepare for me delicious food, such as I love, and bring it to me so that I may eat, that my soul may bless you before I die."

⁵Now Rebekah was listening when Isaac spoke to his son Esau. So when Esau went to the field to hunt for game and bring it, ⁶Rebekah said to her son Jacob, "I heard your father speak to your brother Esau, ⁷'Bring me game and prepare for me delicious food, that I may eat it and bless you before the LORD before I die.' ⁸Now therefore, my son, obey my voice as I command you. ⁹Go to the flock and bring me two good young goats, so that I may prepare from them delicious food for your father, such as he loves. ¹⁰And you shall bring it to your father to eat, so that he may bless you before he dies." ¹¹But Jacob said to Rebekah his mother, "Behold, my brother Esau is a hairy man, and I am a smooth man. ¹²Perhaps my father will feel me, and I shall seem to be mocking him and bring a curse upon myself and not a blessing." ¹³His mother said to him, "Let your curse be on me, my son; only obey my voice, and go, bring them to me."

¹⁴So he went and took them and brought them to his mother, and his mother prepared delicious food, such as his father loved. ¹⁵Then Rebekah took the best garments of Esau her older son, which were with her in the house, and put them on Jacob her younger son. ¹⁶And the skins of the young goats she put on his hands and on the smooth part of his neck. ¹⁷And she put the delicious food and the bread, which she had prepared, into the hand of her son Jacob.

¹⁸So he went in to his father and said, "My father." And he said, "Here I am. Who are you, my son?" ¹⁹Jacob said to his father, "I am Esau your firstborn. I have done as you told me; now sit up and eat of my game, that your soul may bless me." ²⁰But Isaac said to his son, "How is it that you have found it so quickly, my son?" He answered, "Because the LORD your God granted me success." ²¹Then Isaac said to Jacob, "Please come near, that I may feel you, my son, to know whether you are really my son Esau or not." ²²So Jacob went near to Isaac his father, who felt him and said, "The voice is Jacob's voice, but the hands are the hands of Esau." ²³And he did not recognize him, because his hands were

---

[a]*Esek* means *contention* [b]*Sitnah* means *enmity* [c]*Rehoboth* means *broad places*, or *room* [d]*Shibah* sounds like the Hebrew for *oath* [e]Hebrew *they were bitterness of spirit*

hairy like his brother Esau's hands. So he blessed him. ²⁴He said, "Are you really my son Esau?" He answered, "I am." ²⁵Then he said, "Bring it near to me, that I may eat of my son's game and bless you." So he brought it near to him, and he ate; and he brought him wine, and he drank.

²⁶Then his father Isaac said to him, "Come near and kiss me, my son." ²⁷So he came near and kissed him. And Isaac smelled the smell of his garments and blessed him and said,

"See, the smell of my son
is as the smell of a field that
the LORD has blessed!
²⁸ May God give you of the dew of heaven
and of the fatness of the earth
and plenty of grain and wine.
²⁹ Let peoples serve you,
and nations bow down to you.
Be lord over your brothers,
and may your mother's sons
bow down to you.
Cursed be everyone who curses you,
and blessed be everyone
who blesses you!"

³⁰As soon as Isaac had finished blessing Jacob, when Jacob had scarcely gone out from the presence of Isaac his father, Esau his brother came in from his hunting. ³¹He also prepared delicious food and brought it to his father. And he said to his father, "Let my father arise and eat of his son's game, that you may bless me." ³²His father Isaac said to him, "Who are you?" He answered, "I am your son, your firstborn, Esau." ³³Then Isaac trembled very violently and said, "Who was it then that hunted game and brought it to me, and I ate it all before you came, and I have blessed him? Yes, and he shall be blessed." ³⁴As soon as Esau heard the words of his father, he cried out with an exceedingly great and bitter cry and said to his father, "Bless me, even me also, O my father!" ³⁵But he said, "Your brother came deceitfully, and he has taken away your blessing." ³⁶Esau said, "Is he not rightly named Jacob?ᵃ For he has cheated me these two times. He took away my birthright, and behold, now he has taken away my blessing." Then he said, "Have you not reserved a blessing for me?" ³⁷Isaac answered and said to Esau, "Behold, I have made him lord over you, and all his brothers I have given to him for servants, and with grain and wine I have sustained him. What then can I do for you, my son?" ³⁸Esau said to his father, "Have you but one blessing, my father? Bless me, even me also, O my father." And Esau lifted up his voice and wept.

³⁹Then Isaac his father answered and said to him:

"Behold, away fromᵇ the fatness of the
earth shall your dwelling be,
and away fromᶜ the dew of
heaven on high.
⁴⁰ By your sword you shall live,
and you shall serve your brother;
but when you grow restless
you shall break his yoke
from your neck."

⁴¹Now Esau hated Jacob because of the blessing with which his father had blessed him, and Esau said to himself, "The days of mourning for my father are approaching; then I will kill my brother Jacob." ⁴²But the words of Esau her older son were told to Rebekah. So she sent and called Jacob her younger son and said to him, "Behold, your brother Esau comforts himself about you by planning to kill you. ⁴³Now therefore, my son, obey my voice. Arise, flee to Laban my brother in Haran ⁴⁴and stay with him a while, until your brother's fury turns away — ⁴⁵until your brother's anger turns away from you, and he forgets what you have done to him. Then I will send and bring you from there. Why should I be bereft of you both in one day?"

⁴⁶Then Rebekah said to Isaac, "I loathe my life because of the Hittite women.ᵈ If Jacob marries one of the Hittite women like these, one of the women of the land, what good will my life be to me?"

JACOB SENT TO LABAN

28 Then Isaac called Jacob and blessed him and directed him, "You must not take a wife from the Canaanite women. ²Arise, go to Paddan-aram to the house of Bethuel your mother's father, and take as your wife from there one of the daughters of Laban your mother's brother. ³God Almightyᵉ bless you and make you fruitful and multiply you, that you may become a company of peoples. ⁴May he give the blessing of Abraham to you and to your offspring with you, that you may take possession of

---

ᵃ*Jacob* means *He takes by the heel*, or *He cheats*   ᵇOr *Behold, of*   ᶜOr *and of*   ᵈHebrew *daughters of Heth*   ᵉHebrew *El Shaddai*

the land of your sojournings that God gave to Abraham!" ⁵Thus Isaac sent Jacob away. And he went to Paddan-aram, to Laban, the son of Bethuel the Aramean, the brother of Rebekah, Jacob's and Esau's mother.

ESAU MARRIES AN ISHMAELITE

⁶Now Esau saw that Isaac had blessed Jacob and sent him away to Paddan-aram to take a wife from there, and that as he blessed him he directed him, "You must not take a wife from the Canaanite women", ⁷and that Jacob had obeyed his father and his mother and gone to Paddan-aram. ⁸So when Esau saw that the Canaanite women did not please Isaac his father, ⁹Esau went to Ishmael and took as his wife, besides the wives he had, Mahalath the daughter of Ishmael, Abraham's son, the sister of Nebaioth.

JACOB'S DREAM

¹⁰Jacob left Beersheba and went towards Haran. ¹¹And he came to a certain place and stayed there that night, because the sun had set. Taking one of the stones of the place, he put it under his head and lay down in that place to sleep. ¹²And he dreamed, and behold, there was a ladder*ᵃ* set up on the earth, and the top of it reached to heaven. And behold, the angels of God were ascending and descending on it! ¹³And behold, the LORD stood above it*ᵇ* and said, "I am the LORD, the God of Abraham your father and the God of Isaac. The land on which you lie I will give to you and to your offspring. ¹⁴Your offspring shall be like the dust of the earth, and you shall spread abroad to the west and to the east and to the north and to the south, and in you and your offspring shall all the families of the earth be blessed. ¹⁵Behold, I am with you and will keep you wherever you go, and will bring you back to this land. For I will not leave you until I have done what I have promised you." ¹⁶Then Jacob awoke from his sleep and said, "Surely the LORD is in this place, and I did not know it." ¹⁷And he was afraid and said, "How awesome is this place! This is none other than the house of God, and this is the gate of heaven."

¹⁸So early in the morning Jacob took the stone that he had put under his head and set it up for a pillar and poured oil on the top of it. ¹⁹He called the name of that place Bethel,*ᶜ* but the name of the city was Luz at the first. ²⁰Then Jacob made a vow, saying, "If God will be with me and will keep me in this way that I go, and will give me bread to eat and clothing to wear, ²¹so that I come again to my father's house in peace, then the LORD shall be my God, ²²and this stone, which I have set up for a pillar, shall be God's house. And of all that you give me I will give a full tenth to you."

JACOB MARRIES LEAH AND RACHEL

29 Then Jacob went on his journey and came to the land of the people of the east. ²As he looked, he saw a well in the field, and behold, three flocks of sheep lying beside it, for out of that well the flocks were watered. The stone on the well's mouth was large, ³and when all the flocks were gathered there, the shepherds would roll the stone from the mouth of the well and water the sheep, and put the stone back in its place over the mouth of the well.

⁴Jacob said to them, "My brothers, where do you come from?" They said, "We are from Haran." ⁵He said to them, "Do you know Laban the son of Nahor?" They said, "We know him." ⁶He said to them, "Is it well with him?" They said, "It is well; and see, Rachel his daughter is coming with the sheep!" ⁷He said, "Behold, it is still high day; it is not time for the livestock to be gathered together. Water the sheep and go, pasture them." ⁸But they said, "We cannot until all the flocks are gathered together and the stone is rolled from the mouth of the well; then we water the sheep."

⁹While he was still speaking with them, Rachel came with her father's sheep, for she was a shepherdess. ¹⁰Now as soon as Jacob saw Rachel the daughter of Laban his mother's brother, and the sheep of Laban his mother's brother, Jacob came near and rolled the stone from the well's mouth and watered the flock of Laban his mother's brother. ¹¹Then Jacob kissed Rachel and wept aloud. ¹²And Jacob told Rachel that he was her father's kinsman, and that he was Rebekah's son, and she ran and told her father.

¹³As soon as Laban heard the news about Jacob, his sister's son, he ran to meet him and embraced him and kissed him and brought him to his house. Jacob told Laban all these things, ¹⁴and Laban said to him, "Surely you are my bone and my flesh!" And he stayed with him for a month.

¹⁵Then Laban said to Jacob, "Because you are my kinsman, should you therefore serve me for nothing? Tell me, what shall your wages

---

ᵃOr a flight of steps ᵇOr beside him ᶜBethel means the house of God

be?" ¹⁶Now Laban had two daughters. The name of the older was Leah, and the name of the younger was Rachel. ¹⁷Leah's eyes were weak,ᵃ but Rachel was beautiful in form and appearance. ¹⁸Jacob loved Rachel. And he said, "I will serve you seven years for your younger daughter Rachel." ¹⁹Laban said, "It is better that I give her to you than that I should give her to any other man; stay with me." ²⁰So Jacob served seven years for Rachel, and they seemed to him but a few days because of the love he had for her.

²¹Then Jacob said to Laban, "Give me my wife that I may go in to her, for my time is completed." ²²So Laban gathered together all the people of the place and made a feast. ²³But in the evening he took his daughter Leah and brought her to Jacob, and he went in to her. ²⁴(Laban gaveᵇ his female servant Zilpah to his daughter Leah to be her servant.) ²⁵And in the morning, behold, it was Leah! And Jacob said to Laban, "What is this you have done to me? Did I not serve with you for Rachel? Why then have you deceived me?" ²⁶Laban said, "It is not so done in our country, to give the younger before the firstborn. ²⁷Complete the week of this one, and we will give you the other also in return for serving me another seven years." ²⁸Jacob did so, and completed her week. Then Laban gave him his daughter Rachel to be his wife. ²⁹(Laban gave his female servant Bilhah to his daughter Rachel to be her servant.) ³⁰So Jacob went in to Rachel also, and he loved Rachel more than Leah, and served Laban for another seven years.

JACOB'S CHILDREN

³¹When the LORD saw that Leah was hated, he opened her womb, but Rachel was barren. ³²And Leah conceived and bore a son, and she called his name Reuben,ᶜ for she said, "Because the LORD has looked upon my affliction; for now my husband will love me." ³³She conceived again and bore a son, and said, "Because the LORD has heard that I am hated, he has given me this son also." And she called his name Simeon.ᵈ ³⁴Again she conceived and bore a son, and said, "Now this time my husband will be attached to me, because I have borne him three sons." Therefore his name was called Levi.ᵉ ³⁵And she conceived again and bore a son, and said, "This time I will praise the LORD." Therefore she called his name Judah.ᶠ Then she ceased bearing.

30 When Rachel saw that she bore Jacob no children, she envied her sister. She said to Jacob, "Give me children, or I shall die!" ²Jacob's anger was kindled against Rachel, and he said, "Am I in the place of God, who has withheld from you the fruit of the womb?" ³Then she said, "Here is my servant Bilhah; go in to her, so that she may give birth on my behalf,ᵍ that even I may have childrenʰ through her." ⁴So she gave him her servant Bilhah as a wife, and Jacob went in to her. ⁵And Bilhah conceived and bore Jacob a son. ⁶Then Rachel said, "God has judged me, and has also heard my voice and given me a son." Therefore she called his name Dan.ⁱ ⁷Rachel's servant Bilhah conceived again and bore Jacob a second son. ⁸Then Rachel said, "With mighty wrestlingsʲ I have wrestled with my sister and have prevailed." So she called his name Naphtali.ᵏ

⁹When Leah saw that she had ceased bearing children, she took her servant Zilpah and gave her to Jacob as a wife. ¹⁰Then Leah's servant Zilpah bore Jacob a son. ¹¹And Leah said, "Good fortune has come!" so she called his name Gad.ˡ ¹²Leah's servant Zilpah bore Jacob a second son. ¹³And Leah said, "Happy am I! For women have called me happy." So she called his name Asher.ᵐ

¹⁴In the days of wheat harvest Reuben went and found mandrakes in the field and brought them to his mother Leah. Then Rachel said to Leah, "Please give me some of your son's mandrakes." ¹⁵But she said to her, "Is it a small matter that you have taken away my husband? Would you take away my son's mandrakes also?" Rachel said, "Then he may lie with you tonight in exchange for your son's mandrakes." ¹⁶When Jacob came from the field in the evening, Leah went out to meet him and said, "You must come in to me, for I have hired you with my son's mandrakes." So he lay with her that night. ¹⁷And God listened to Leah, and she conceived and bore Jacob a fifth son. ¹⁸Leah said, "God has given me my wages because I gave my servant to my husband." So she called his name Issachar.ⁿ

ᵃOr soft ᵇOr had given; also verse 29 ᶜReuben means See, a son ᵈSimeon sounds like the Hebrew for heard ᵉLevi sounds like the Hebrew for attached ᶠJudah sounds like the Hebrew for praise ᵍHebrew on my knees ʰHebrew be built up, which sounds like the Hebrew for children ⁱDan sounds like the Hebrew for judged ʲHebrew With wrestlings of God ᵏNaphtali sounds like the Hebrew for wrestling ˡGad sounds like the Hebrew for good fortune ᵐAsher sounds like the Hebrew for happy ⁿIssachar sounds like the Hebrew for wages, or hire

¹⁹And Leah conceived again, and she bore Jacob a sixth son. ²⁰Then Leah said, "God has endowed me with a good endowment; now my husband will honour me, because I have borne him six sons." So she called his name Zebulun.[a] ²¹Afterwards she bore a daughter and called her name Dinah.

²²Then God remembered Rachel, and God listened to her and opened her womb. ²³She conceived and bore a son and said, "God has taken away my reproach." ²⁴And she called his name Joseph,[b] saying, "May the LORD add to me another son!"

JACOB'S PROSPERITY

²⁵As soon as Rachel had borne Joseph, Jacob said to Laban, "Send me away, that I may go to my own home and country. ²⁶Give me my wives and my children for whom I have served you, that I may go, for you know the service that I have given you." ²⁷But Laban said to him, "If I have found favour in your sight, I have learned by divination that[c] the LORD has blessed me because of you. ²⁸Name your wages, and I will give it." ²⁹Jacob said to him, "You yourself know how I have served you, and how your livestock has fared with me. ³⁰For you had little before I came, and it has increased abundantly, and the LORD has blessed you wherever I turned. But now when shall I provide for my own household also?" ³¹He said, "What shall I give you?" Jacob said, "You shall not give me anything. If you will do this for me, I will again pasture your flock and keep it: ³²let me pass through all your flock today, removing from it every speckled and spotted sheep and every black lamb, and the spotted and speckled among the goats, and they shall be my wages. ³³So my honesty will answer for me later, when you come to look into my wages with you. Every one that is not speckled and spotted among the goats and black among the lambs, if found with me, shall be counted stolen." ³⁴Laban said, "Good! Let it be as you have said." ³⁵But that day Laban removed the male goats that were striped and spotted, and all the female goats that were speckled and spotted, every one that had white on it, and every lamb that was black, and put them in the charge of his sons. ³⁶And he set a distance of three days' journey between himself and Jacob, and Jacob pastured the rest of Laban's flock.

³⁷Then Jacob took fresh sticks of poplar and almond and plane trees, and peeled white streaks in them, exposing the white of the sticks. ³⁸He set the sticks that he had peeled in front of the flocks in the troughs, that is, the watering places, where the flocks came to drink. And since they bred when they came to drink, ³⁹the flocks bred in front of the sticks and so the flocks brought forth striped, speckled, and spotted. ⁴⁰And Jacob separated the lambs and set the faces of the flocks towards the striped and all the black in the flock of Laban. He put his own droves apart and did not put them with Laban's flock. ⁴¹Whenever the stronger of the flock were breeding, Jacob would lay the sticks in the troughs before the eyes of the flock, that they might breed among the sticks, ⁴²but for the feebler of the flock he would not lay them there. So the feebler would be Laban's, and the stronger Jacob's. ⁴³Thus the man increased greatly and had large flocks, female servants and male servants, and camels and donkeys.

JACOB FLEES FROM LABAN

31 Now Jacob heard that the sons of Laban were saying, "Jacob has taken all that was our father's, and from what was our father's he has gained all this wealth." ²And Jacob saw that Laban did not regard him with favour as before. ³Then the LORD said to Jacob, "Return to the land of your fathers and to your kindred, and I will be with you."

⁴So Jacob sent and called Rachel and Leah into the field where his flock was ⁵and said to them, "I see that your father does not regard me with favour as he did before. But the God of my father has been with me. ⁶You know that I have served your father with all my strength, ⁷yet your father has cheated me and changed my wages ten times. But God did not permit him to harm me. ⁸If he said, 'The spotted shall be your wages', then all the flock bore spotted; and if he said, 'The striped shall be your wages', then all the flock bore striped. ⁹Thus God has taken away the livestock of your father and given them to me. ¹⁰In the breeding season of the flock I lifted up my eyes and saw in a dream that the goats that mated with the flock were striped, spotted, and mottled. ¹¹Then the angel of God said to me in the dream, 'Jacob,' and I said, 'Here I am!' ¹²And he said, 'Lift up your eyes and see, all the goats that mate with the flock are

---

[a]*Zebulun* sounds like the Hebrew for *honour* [b]*Joseph* means *May he add*, and sounds like the Hebrew for *taken away* [c]Or *have become rich and*

striped, spotted, and mottled, for I have seen all that Laban is doing to you. **13**I am the God of Bethel, where you anointed a pillar and made a vow to me. Now arise, go out from this land and return to the land of your kindred.'" **14**Then Rachel and Leah answered and said to him, "Is there any portion or inheritance left to us in our father's house? **15**Are we not regarded by him as foreigners? For he has sold us, and he has indeed devoured our money. **16**All the wealth that God has taken away from our father belongs to us and to our children. Now then, whatever God has said to you, do."

17So Jacob arose and set his sons and his wives on camels. **18**He drove away all his livestock, all his property that he had gained, the livestock in his possession that he had acquired in Paddan-aram, to go to the land of Canaan to his father Isaac. **19**Laban had gone to shear his sheep, and Rachel stole her father's household gods. **20**And Jacob tricked*ᵃ* Laban the Aramean, by not telling him that he intended to flee. **21**He fled with all that he had and arose and crossed the Euphrates,*ᵇ* and set his face towards the hill country of Gilead.

22When it was told Laban on the third day that Jacob had fled, **23**he took his kinsmen with him and pursued him for seven days and followed close after him into the hill country of Gilead. **24**But God came to Laban the Aramean in a dream by night and said to him, "Be careful not to say anything to Jacob, either good or bad."

25And Laban overtook Jacob. Now Jacob had pitched his tent in the hill country, and Laban with his kinsmen pitched tents in the hill country of Gilead. **26**And Laban said to Jacob, "What have you done, that you have tricked me and driven away my daughters like captives of the sword? **27**Why did you flee secretly and trick me, and did not tell me, so that I might have sent you away with mirth and songs, with tambourine and lyre? **28**And why did you not permit me to kiss my sons and my daughters farewell? Now you have done foolishly. **29**It is in my power to do you harm. But the God of your*ᶜ* father spoke to me last night, saying, 'Be careful not to say anything to Jacob, either good or bad.' **30**And now you have gone away because you longed greatly for your father's house, but why did you steal my gods?" **31**Jacob answered and said to Laban, "Because I was afraid, for I thought that you would take your daughters from me by force. **32**Anyone with whom you find your gods shall not live. In the presence of our kinsmen point out what I have that is yours, and take it." Now Jacob did not know that Rachel had stolen them.

33So Laban went into Jacob's tent and into Leah's tent and into the tent of the two female servants, but he did not find them. And he went out of Leah's tent and entered Rachel's. **34**Now Rachel had taken the household gods and put them in the camel's saddle and sat on them. Laban felt all about the tent, but did not find them. **35**And she said to her father, "Let not my lord be angry that I cannot rise before you, for the way of women is upon me." So he searched but did not find the household gods.

36Then Jacob became angry and berated Laban. Jacob said to Laban, "What is my offence? What is my sin, that you have hotly pursued me? **37**For you have felt through all my goods; what have you found of all your household goods? Set it here before my kinsmen and your kinsmen, that they may decide between us two. **38**These twenty years I have been with you. Your ewes and your female goats have not miscarried, and I have not eaten the rams of your flocks. **39**What was torn by wild beasts I did not bring to you. I bore the loss of it myself. From my hand you required it, whether stolen by day or stolen by night. **40**There I was: by day the heat consumed me, and the cold by night, and my sleep fled from my eyes. **41**These twenty years I have been in your house. I served you for fourteen years for your two daughters, and six years for your flock, and you have changed my wages ten times. **42**If the God of my father, the God of Abraham and the Fear of Isaac, had not been on my side, surely now you would have sent me away empty-handed. God saw my affliction and the labour of my hands and rebuked you last night."

43Then Laban answered and said to Jacob, "The daughters are my daughters, the children are my children, the flocks are my flocks, and all that you see is mine. But what can I do this day for these my daughters or for their children whom they have borne? **44**Come now, let us make a covenant, you and I. And let it be a witness between you and me." **45**So Jacob took a stone and set it up as a pillar. **46**And Jacob said to his kinsmen, "Gather stones." And they took stones and made a heap, and they ate there by the heap. **47**Laban called it Jegar-sahadutha,*ᵈ* but Jacob called it Galeed.*ᵉ*

---

*ᵃ*Hebrew *stole the heart of*; also verses 26, 27   *ᵇ*Hebrew *the River*
*ᶜ*The Hebrew for *your* is plural here   *ᵈ*Aramaic *the heap of witness*
*ᵉ*Hebrew *the heap of witness*

⁴⁸Laban said, "This heap is a witness between you and me today." Therefore he named it Galeed, ⁴⁹and Mizpah,ᵃ for he said, "The LORD watch between you and me, when we are out of one another's sight. ⁵⁰If you oppress my daughters, or if you take wives besides my daughters, although no one is with us, see, God is witness between you and me."

⁵¹Then Laban said to Jacob, "See this heap and the pillar, which I have set between you and me. ⁵²This heap is a witness, and the pillar is a witness, that I will not pass over this heap to you, and you will not pass over this heap and this pillar to me, to do harm. ⁵³The God of Abraham and the God of Nahor, the God of their father, judge between us." So Jacob swore by the Fear of his father Isaac, ⁵⁴and Jacob offered a sacrifice in the hill country and called his kinsmen to eat bread. They ate bread and spent the night in the hill country.

⁵⁵ᵇ Early in the morning Laban arose and kissed his grandchildren and his daughters and blessed them. Then Laban departed and returned home.

JACOB FEARS ESAU

32 Jacob went on his way, and the angels of God met him. ²And when Jacob saw them he said, "This is God's camp!" So he called the name of that place Mahanaim.ᶜ

³And Jacob sentᵈ messengers before him to Esau his brother in the land of Seir, the country of Edom, ⁴instructing them, "Thus you shall say to my lord Esau: Thus says your servant Jacob, 'I have sojourned with Laban and stayed until now. ⁵I have oxen, donkeys, flocks, male servants, and female servants. I have sent to tell my lord, in order that I may find favour in your sight.'"

⁶And the messengers returned to Jacob, saying, "We came to your brother Esau, and he is coming to meet you, and there are four hundred men with him." ⁷Then Jacob was greatly afraid and distressed. He divided the people who were with him, and the flocks and herds and camels, into two camps, ⁸thinking, "If Esau comes to one camp and attacks it, then the camp that is left will escape."

⁹And Jacob said, "O God of my father Abraham and God of my father Isaac, O LORD who said to me, 'Return to your country and to your kindred, that I may do you good,' ¹⁰I am not worthy of the least of all the deeds of steadfast love and all the faithfulness that you have shown to your servant, for with only my staff I crossed this Jordan, and now I have become two camps. ¹¹Please deliver me from the hand of my brother, from the hand of Esau, for I fear him, that he may come and attack me, the mothers with the children. ¹²But you said, 'I will surely do you good, and make your offspring as the sand of the sea, which cannot be numbered for multitude.'"

¹³So he stayed there that night, and from what he had with him he took a present for his brother Esau, ¹⁴two hundred female goats and twenty male goats, two hundred ewes and twenty rams, ¹⁵thirty milking camels and their calves, forty cows and ten bulls, twenty female donkeys and ten male donkeys. ¹⁶These he handed over to his servants, every drove by itself, and said to his servants, "Pass on ahead of me and put a space between drove and drove." ¹⁷He instructed the first, "When Esau my brother meets you and asks you, 'To whom do you belong? Where are you going? And whose are these ahead of you?' ¹⁸then you shall say, 'They belong to your servant Jacob. They are a present sent to my lord Esau. And moreover, he is behind us.'" ¹⁹He likewise instructed the second and the third and all who followed the droves, "You shall say the same thing to Esau when you find him, ²⁰and you shall say, 'Moreover, your servant Jacob is behind us.'" For he thought, "I may appease himᵉ with the present that goes ahead of me, and afterwards I shall see his face. Perhaps he will accept me."ᶠ ²¹So the present passed on ahead of him, and he himself stayed that night in the camp.

JACOB WRESTLES WITH GOD

²²The same night he arose and took his two wives, his two female servants, and his eleven children,ᵍ and crossed the ford of the Jabbok. ²³He took them and sent them across the stream, and everything else that he had. ²⁴And Jacob was left alone. And a man wrestled with him until the breaking of the day. ²⁵When the man saw that he did not prevail against Jacob, he touched his hip socket, and Jacob's hip was put out of joint as he wrestled with him. ²⁶Then he said, "Let me go, for the day has broken." But Jacob said, "I will not let you go unless you bless me." ²⁷And he said to him, "What is your name?" And he said, "Jacob." ²⁸Then he said, "Your

---

ᵃMizpah means watchpost ᵇCh 32:1 in Hebrew ᶜMahanaim means two camps ᵈOr had sent ᵉHebrew appease his face ᶠHebrew he will lift my face ᵍOr sons

name shall no longer be called Jacob, but Israel,[a] for you have striven with God and with men, and have prevailed." ²⁹Then Jacob asked him, "Please tell me your name." But he said, "Why is it that you ask my name?" And there he blessed him. ³⁰So Jacob called the name of the place Peniel,[b] saying, "For I have seen God face to face, and yet my life has been delivered." ³¹The sun rose upon him as he passed Penuel, limping because of his hip. ³²Therefore to this day the people of Israel do not eat the sinew of the thigh that is on the hip socket, because he touched the socket of Jacob's hip on the sinew of the thigh.

JACOB MEETS ESAU

33 And Jacob lifted up his eyes and looked, and behold, Esau was coming, and four hundred men with him. So he divided the children among Leah and Rachel and the two female servants. ²And he put the servants with their children in front, then Leah with her children, and Rachel and Joseph last of all. ³He himself went on before them, bowing himself to the ground seven times, until he came near to his brother.

⁴But Esau ran to meet him and embraced him and fell on his neck and kissed him, and they wept. ⁵And when Esau lifted up his eyes and saw the women and children, he said, "Who are these with you?" Jacob said, "The children whom God has graciously given your servant." ⁶Then the servants drew near, they and their children, and bowed down. ⁷Leah likewise and her children drew near and bowed down. And last Joseph and Rachel drew near, and they bowed down. ⁸Esau said, "What do you mean by all this company[c] that I met?" Jacob answered, "To find favour in the sight of my lord." ⁹But Esau said, "I have enough, my brother; keep what you have for yourself." ¹⁰Jacob said, "No, please, if I have found favour in your sight, then accept my present from my hand. For I have seen your face, which is like seeing the face of God, and you have accepted me. ¹¹Please accept my blessing that is brought to you, because God has dealt graciously with me, and because I have enough." Thus he urged him, and he took it.

¹²Then Esau said, "Let us journey on our way, and I will go ahead of[d] you." ¹³But Jacob said to him, "My lord knows that the children are frail, and that the nursing flocks and herds are a care to me. If they are driven hard for one day, all the flocks will die. ¹⁴Let my lord pass on ahead of his servant, and I will lead on slowly, at the pace of the livestock that are ahead of me and at the pace of the children, until I come to my lord in Seir."

¹⁵So Esau said, "Let me leave with you some of the people who are with me." But he said, "What need is there? Let me find favour in the sight of my lord." ¹⁶So Esau returned that day on his way to Seir. ¹⁷But Jacob journeyed to Succoth, and built himself a house and made booths for his livestock. Therefore the name of the place is called Succoth.[e]

¹⁸And Jacob came safely[f] to the city of Shechem, which is in the land of Canaan, on his way from Paddan-aram, and he camped before the city. ¹⁹And from the sons of Hamor, Shechem's father, he bought for a hundred pieces of money[g] the piece of land on which he had pitched his tent. ²⁰There he erected an altar and called it El-Elohe-Israel.[h]

THE DEFILING OF DINAH

34 Now Dinah the daughter of Leah, whom she had borne to Jacob, went out to see the women of the land. ²And when Shechem the son of Hamor the Hivite, the prince of the land, saw her, he seized her and lay with her and humiliated her. ³And his soul was drawn to Dinah the daughter of Jacob. He loved the young woman and spoke tenderly to her. ⁴So Shechem spoke to his father Hamor, saying, "Get me this girl for my wife."

⁵Now Jacob heard that he had defiled his daughter Dinah. But his sons were with his livestock in the field, so Jacob held his peace until they came. ⁶And Hamor the father of Shechem went out to Jacob to speak with him. ⁷The sons of Jacob had come in from the field as soon as they heard of it, and the men were indignant and very angry, because he had done an outrageous thing in Israel by lying with Jacob's daughter, for such a thing must not be done.

⁸But Hamor spoke with them, saying, "The soul of my son Shechem longs for your[i] daughter. Please give her to him to be his wife. ⁹Make marriages with us. Give your daughters to us, and take our daughters for yourselves. ¹⁰You shall dwell with us, and the land shall be open to you. Dwell and trade in it, and get property

---

[a]*Israel* means *He strives with God*, or *God strives* [b]*Peniel* means *the face of God* [c]Hebrew *camp* [d]Or *along with* [e]*Succoth* means *booths* [f]Or *peacefully* [g]Hebrew *a hundred qesitah*; a unit of money of unknown value [h]*El-Elohe-Israel* means *God, the God of Israel* [i]The Hebrew for *your* is plural here

in it." ¹¹Shechem also said to her father and to her brothers, "Let me find favour in your eyes, and whatever you say to me I will give. ¹²Ask me for as great a bride-price[a] and gift as you will, and I will give whatever you say to me. Only give me the young woman to be my wife."

¹³The sons of Jacob answered Shechem and his father Hamor deceitfully, because he had defiled their sister Dinah. ¹⁴They said to them, "We cannot do this thing, to give our sister to one who is uncircumcised, for that would be a disgrace to us. ¹⁵Only on this condition will we agree with you — that you will become as we are by every male among you being circumcised. ¹⁶Then we will give our daughters to you, and we will take your daughters to ourselves, and we will dwell with you and become one people. ¹⁷But if you will not listen to us and be circumcised, then we will take our daughter, and we will be gone."

¹⁸Their words pleased Hamor and Hamor's son Shechem. ¹⁹And the young man did not delay to do the thing, because he delighted in Jacob's daughter. Now he was the most honoured of all his father's house. ²⁰So Hamor and his son Shechem came to the gate of their city and spoke to the men of their city, saying, ²¹"These men are at peace with us; let them dwell in the land and trade in it, for behold, the land is large enough for them. Let us take their daughters as wives, and let us give them our daughters. ²²Only on this condition will the men agree to dwell with us to become one people — when every male among us is circumcised as they are circumcised. ²³Will not their livestock, their property and all their beasts be ours? Only let us agree with them, and they will dwell with us." ²⁴And all who went out of the gate of his city listened to Hamor and his son Shechem, and every male was circumcised, all who went out of the gate of his city.

²⁵On the third day, when they were sore, two of the sons of Jacob, Simeon and Levi, Dinah's brothers, took their swords and came against the city while it felt secure and killed all the males. ²⁶They killed Hamor and his son Shechem with the sword and took Dinah out of Shechem's house and went away. ²⁷The sons of Jacob came upon the slain and plundered the city, because they had defiled their sister. ²⁸They took their flocks and their herds, their donkeys, and whatever was in the city and in the field. ²⁹All their wealth, all their little ones and their wives, all that was in the houses, they captured and plundered.

³⁰Then Jacob said to Simeon and Levi, "You have brought trouble on me by making me stink to the inhabitants of the land, the Canaanites and the Perizzites. My numbers are few, and if they gather themselves against me and attack me, I shall be destroyed, both I and my household." ³¹But they said, "Should he treat our sister like a prostitute?"

GOD BLESSES AND RENAMES JACOB

35 God said to Jacob, "Arise, go up to Bethel and dwell there. Make an altar there to the God who appeared to you when you fled from your brother Esau." ²So Jacob said to his household and to all who were with him, "Put away the foreign gods that are among you and purify yourselves and change your garments. ³Then let us arise and go up to Bethel, so that I may make there an altar to the God who answers me in the day of my distress and has been with me wherever I have gone." ⁴So they gave to Jacob all the foreign gods that they had, and the rings that were in their ears. Jacob hid them under the terebinth tree that was near Shechem.

⁵And as they journeyed, a terror from God fell upon the cities that were around them, so that they did not pursue the sons of Jacob. ⁶And Jacob came to Luz (that is, Bethel), which is in the land of Canaan, he and all the people who were with him, ⁷and there he built an altar and called the place El-bethel,[b] because there God had revealed himself to him when he fled from his brother. ⁸And Deborah, Rebekah's nurse, died, and she was buried under an oak below Bethel. So he called its name Allon-bacuth.[c]

⁹God appeared[d] to Jacob again, when he came from Paddan-aram, and blessed him. ¹⁰And God said to him, "Your name is Jacob; no longer shall your name be called Jacob, but Israel shall be your name." So he called his name Israel. ¹¹And God said to him, "I am God Almighty:[e] be fruitful and multiply. A nation and a company of nations shall come from you, and kings shall come from your own body.[f] ¹²The land that I gave to Abraham and Isaac I will give to you, and I will give the land to your offspring after you." ¹³Then God went up from him in the place where he had spoken with him. ¹⁴And Jacob set up a pillar in the place where he had spoken with him, a

---

[a]Or *engagement present* [b]*El-bethel* means *God of Bethel* [c]*Allon-bacuth* means *oak of weeping* [d]Or *had appeared* [e]Hebrew *El Shaddai* [f]Hebrew *from your loins*

pillar of stone. He poured out a drink offering on it and poured oil on it. ¹⁵So Jacob called the name of the place where God had spoken with him Bethel.

THE DEATHS OF RACHEL AND ISAAC

¹⁶Then they journeyed from Bethel. When they were still some distance*ᵃ* from Ephrath, Rachel went into labour, and she had hard labour. ¹⁷And when her labour was at its hardest, the midwife said to her, "Do not fear, for you have another son." ¹⁸And as her soul was departing (for she was dying), she called his name Ben-oni;*ᵇ* but his father called him Benjamin.*ᶜ* ¹⁹So Rachel died, and she was buried on the way to Ephrath (that is, Bethlehem), ²⁰and Jacob set up a pillar over her tomb. It is the pillar of Rachel's tomb, which is there to this day. ²¹Israel journeyed on and pitched his tent beyond the tower of Eder.

²²While Israel lived in that land, Reuben went and lay with Bilhah his father's concubine. And Israel heard of it.

Now the sons of Jacob were twelve. ²³The sons of Leah: Reuben (Jacob's firstborn), Simeon, Levi, Judah, Issachar, and Zebulun. ²⁴The sons of Rachel: Joseph and Benjamin. ²⁵The sons of Bilhah, Rachel's servant: Dan and Naphtali. ²⁶The sons of Zilpah, Leah's servant: Gad and Asher. These were the sons of Jacob who were born to him in Paddan-aram.

²⁷And Jacob came to his father Isaac at Mamre, or Kiriath-arba (that is, Hebron), where Abraham and Isaac had sojourned. ²⁸Now the days of Isaac were 180 years. ²⁹And Isaac breathed his last, and he died and was gathered to his people, old and full of days. And his sons Esau and Jacob buried him.

ESAU'S DESCENDANTS

36 These are the generations of Esau (that is, Edom). ²Esau took his wives from the Canaanites: Adah the daughter of Elon the Hittite, Oholibamah the daughter of Anah the daughter*ᵈ* of Zibeon the Hivite, ³and Basemath, Ishmael's daughter, the sister of Nebaioth. ⁴And Adah bore to Esau, Eliphaz; Basemath bore Reuel; ⁵and Oholibamah bore Jeush, Jalam, and Korah. These are the sons of Esau who were born to him in the land of Canaan.

⁶Then Esau took his wives, his sons, his daughters, and all the members of his household, his livestock, all his beasts, and all his property that he had acquired in the land of Canaan. He went into a land away from his brother Jacob. ⁷For their possessions were too great for them to dwell together. The land of their sojournings could not support them because of their livestock. ⁸So Esau settled in the hill country of Seir. (Esau is Edom.)

⁹These are the generations of Esau the father of the Edomites in the hill country of Seir. ¹⁰These are the names of Esau's sons: Eliphaz the son of Adah the wife of Esau, Reuel the son of Basemath the wife of Esau. ¹¹The sons of Eliphaz were Teman, Omar, Zepho, Gatam, and Kenaz. ¹²(Timna was a concubine of Eliphaz, Esau's son; she bore Amalek to Eliphaz.) These are the sons of Adah, Esau's wife. ¹³These are the sons of Reuel: Nahath, Zerah, Shammah, and Mizzah. These are the sons of Basemath, Esau's wife. ¹⁴These are the sons of Oholibamah the daughter of Anah the daughter of Zibeon, Esau's wife: she bore to Esau Jeush, Jalam, and Korah.

¹⁵These are the chiefs of the sons of Esau. The sons of Eliphaz the firstborn of Esau: the chiefs Teman, Omar, Zepho, Kenaz, ¹⁶Korah, Gatam, and Amalek; these are the chiefs of Eliphaz in the land of Edom; these are the sons of Adah. ¹⁷These are the sons of Reuel, Esau's son: the chiefs Nahath, Zerah, Shammah, and Mizzah; these are the chiefs of Reuel in the land of Edom; these are the sons of Basemath, Esau's wife. ¹⁸These are the sons of Oholibamah, Esau's wife: the chiefs Jeush, Jalam, and Korah; these are the chiefs born of Oholibamah the daughter of Anah, Esau's wife. ¹⁹These are the sons of Esau (that is, Edom), and these are their chiefs.

²⁰These are the sons of Seir the Horite, the inhabitants of the land: Lotan, Shobal, Zibeon, Anah, ²¹Dishon, Ezer, and Dishan; these are the chiefs of the Horites, the sons of Seir in the land of Edom. ²²The sons of Lotan were Hori and Hemam; and Lotan's sister was Timna. ²³These are the sons of Shobal: Alvan, Manahath, Ebal, Shepho, and Onam. ²⁴These are the sons of Zibeon: Aiah and Anah; he is the Anah who found the hot springs in the wilderness, as he pastured the donkeys of Zibeon his father. ²⁵These are the children of Anah: Dishon and Oholibamah the daughter of Anah. ²⁶These are the sons of Dishon: Hemdan, Eshban, Ithran, and Cheran. ²⁷These are the sons of Ezer: Bilhan, Zaavan, and Akan. ²⁸These are

---

ᵃOr about two hours' distance ᵇBen-oni could mean son of my sorrow, or son of my strength ᶜBenjamin means son of the right hand ᵈHebrew; Samaritan, Septuagint, Syriac son; also verse 14

the sons of Dishan: Uz and Aran. ²⁹These are the chiefs of the Horites: the chiefs Lotan, Shobal, Zibeon, Anah, ³⁰Dishon, Ezer, and Dishan; these are the chiefs of the Horites, chief by chief in the land of Seir.

³¹These are the kings who reigned in the land of Edom, before any king reigned over the Israelites. ³²Bela the son of Beor reigned in Edom, the name of his city being Dinhabah. ³³Bela died, and Jobab the son of Zerah of Bozrah reigned in his place. ³⁴Jobab died, and Husham of the land of the Temanites reigned in his place. ³⁵Husham died, and Hadad the son of Bedad, who defeated Midian in the country of Moab, reigned in his place, the name of his city being Avith. ³⁶Hadad died, and Samlah of Masrekah reigned in his place. ³⁷Samlah died, and Shaul of Rehoboth on the Euphrates[a] reigned in his place. ³⁸Shaul died, and Baal-hanan the son of Achbor reigned in his place. ³⁹Baal-hanan the son of Achbor died, and Hadar reigned in his place, the name of his city being Pau; his wife's name was Mehetabel, the daughter of Matred, daughter of Mezahab.

⁴⁰These are the names of the chiefs of Esau, according to their clans and their dwelling places, by their names: the chiefs Timna, Alvah, Jetheth, ⁴¹Oholibamah, Elah, Pinon, ⁴²Kenaz, Teman, Mibzar, ⁴³Magdiel, and Iram; these are the chiefs of Edom (that is, Esau, the father of Edom), according to their dwelling places in the land of their possession.

JOSEPH'S DREAMS

37 Jacob lived in the land of his father's sojournings, in the land of Canaan.

²These are the generations of Jacob.

Joseph, being seventeen years old, was pasturing the flock with his brothers. He was a boy with the sons of Bilhah and Zilpah, his father's wives. And Joseph brought a bad report of them to their father. ³Now Israel loved Joseph more than any other of his sons, because he was the son of his old age. And he made him a robe of many colours.[b] ⁴But when his brothers saw that their father loved him more than all his brothers, they hated him and could not speak peacefully to him.

⁵Now Joseph had a dream, and when he told it to his brothers they hated him even more. ⁶He said to them, "Hear this dream that I have dreamed: ⁷Behold, we were binding sheaves in the field, and behold, my sheaf arose and stood upright. And behold, your sheaves gathered round it and bowed down to my sheaf." ⁸His brothers said to him, "Are you indeed to reign over us? Or are you indeed to rule over us?" So they hated him even more for his dreams and for his words.

⁹Then he dreamed another dream and told it to his brothers and said, "Behold, I have dreamed another dream. Behold, the sun, the moon, and eleven stars were bowing down to me." ¹⁰But when he told it to his father and to his brothers, his father rebuked him and said to him, "What is this dream that you have dreamed? Shall I and your mother and your brothers indeed come to bow ourselves to the ground before you?" ¹¹And his brothers were jealous of him, but his father kept the saying in mind.

JOSEPH SOLD BY HIS BROTHERS

¹²Now his brothers went to pasture their father's flock near Shechem. ¹³And Israel said to Joseph, "Are not your brothers pasturing the flock at Shechem? Come, I will send you to them." And he said to him, "Here I am." ¹⁴So he said to him, "Go now, see if it is well with your brothers and with the flock, and bring me word." So he sent him from the Valley of Hebron, and he came to Shechem. ¹⁵And a man found him wandering in the fields. And the man asked him, "What are you seeking?" ¹⁶"I am seeking my brothers," he said. "Tell me, please, where they are pasturing the flock." ¹⁷And the man said, "They have gone away, for I heard them say, 'Let us go to Dothan.'" So Joseph went after his brothers and found them at Dothan.

¹⁸They saw him from afar, and before he came near to them they conspired against him to kill him. ¹⁹They said to one another, "Here comes this dreamer. ²⁰Come now, let us kill him and throw him into one of the pits.[c] Then we will say that a fierce animal has devoured him, and we will see what will become of his dreams." ²¹But when Reuben heard it, he rescued him out of their hands, saying, "Let us not take his life." ²²And Reuben said to them, "Shed no blood; throw him into this pit here in the wilderness, but do not lay a hand on him"—that he might rescue him out of their hand to restore him to his father. ²³So when Joseph came to his brothers, they

---

[a]Hebrew *the River* [b]See Septuagint, Vulgate; or (with Syriac) *a robe with long sleeves*. The meaning of the Hebrew is uncertain; also verses 23, 32 [c]Or *cisterns*; also verses 22, 24

stripped him of his robe, the robe of many colours that he wore. ²⁴And they took him and threw him into a pit. The pit was empty; there was no water in it.

²⁵Then they sat down to eat. And looking up they saw a caravan of Ishmaelites coming from Gilead, with their camels bearing gum, balm, and myrrh, on their way to carry it down to Egypt. ²⁶Then Judah said to his brothers, "What profit is it if we kill our brother and conceal his blood? ²⁷Come, let us sell him to the Ishmaelites, and let not our hand be upon him, for he is our brother, our own flesh." And his brothers listened to him. ²⁸Then Midianite traders passed by. And they drew Joseph up and lifted him out of the pit, and sold him to the Ishmaelites for twenty shekels^a of silver. They took Joseph to Egypt.

²⁹When Reuben returned to the pit and saw that Joseph was not in the pit, he tore his clothes ³⁰and returned to his brothers and said, "The boy is gone, and I, where shall I go?" ³¹Then they took Joseph's robe and slaughtered a goat and dipped the robe in the blood. ³²And they sent the robe of many colours and brought it to their father and said, "This we have found; please identify whether it is your son's robe or not." ³³And he identified it and said, "It is my son's robe. A fierce animal has devoured him. Joseph is without doubt torn to pieces." ³⁴Then Jacob tore his garments and put sackcloth on his loins and mourned for his son for many days. ³⁵All his sons and all his daughters rose up to comfort him, but he refused to be comforted and said, "No, I shall go down to Sheol to my son, mourning." Thus his father wept for him. ³⁶Meanwhile the Midianites had sold him in Egypt to Potiphar, an officer of Pharaoh, the captain of the guard.

JUDAH AND TAMAR

38 It happened at that time that Judah went down from his brothers and turned aside to a certain Adullamite, whose name was Hirah. ²There Judah saw the daughter of a certain Canaanite whose name was Shua. He took her and went in to her, ³and she conceived and bore a son, and he called his name Er. ⁴She conceived again and bore a son, and she called his name Onan. ⁵Yet again she bore a son, and she called his name Shelah. Judah^b was in Chezib when she bore him.

⁶And Judah took a wife for Er his firstborn, and her name was Tamar. ⁷But Er, Judah's firstborn, was wicked in the sight of the LORD, and the LORD put him to death. ⁸Then Judah said to Onan, "Go in to your brother's wife and perform the duty of a brother-in-law to her, and raise up offspring for your brother." ⁹But Onan knew that the offspring would not be his. So whenever he went in to his brother's wife he would waste the semen on the ground, so as not to give offspring to his brother. ¹⁰And what he did was wicked in the sight of the LORD, and he put him to death also. ¹¹Then Judah said to Tamar his daughter-in-law, "Remain a widow in your father's house, till Shelah my son grows up"—for he feared that he would die, like his brothers. So Tamar went and remained in her father's house.

¹²In the course of time the wife of Judah, Shua's daughter, died. When Judah was comforted, he went up to Timnah to his sheep shearers, he and his friend Hirah the Adullamite. ¹³And when Tamar was told, "Your father-in-law is going up to Timnah to shear his sheep," ¹⁴she took off her widow's garments and covered herself with a veil, wrapping herself up, and sat at the entrance to Enaim, which is on the road to Timnah. For she saw that Shelah was grown up, and she had not been given to him in marriage. ¹⁵When Judah saw her, he thought she was a prostitute, for she had covered her face. ¹⁶He turned to her at the roadside and said, "Come, let me come in to you", for he did not know that she was his daughter-in-law. She said, "What will you give me, that you may come in to me?" ¹⁷He answered, "I will send you a young goat from the flock." And she said, "If you give me a pledge, until you send it—" ¹⁸He said, "What pledge shall I give you?" She replied, "Your signet and your cord and your staff that is in your hand." So he gave them to her and went in to her, and she conceived by him. ¹⁹Then she arose and went away, and taking off her veil she put on the garments of her widowhood.

²⁰When Judah sent the young goat by his friend the Adullamite to take back the pledge from the woman's hand, he did not find her. ²¹And he asked the men of the place, "Where is the cult prostitute^c who was at Enaim at the roadside?" And they said, "No cult prostitute has been here." ²²So he returned to Judah and said, "I have not found her. Also, the men of the place said, 'No cult prostitute has been here.'" ²³And Judah replied, "Let her keep the

---

^{a}A *shekel* was about 2/5 of an ounce or 11 grams ^{b}Hebrew *He*
^{c}Hebrew *sacred woman*; a woman who served a pagan deity by prostitution; also verse 22

Pharaoh was angry with his two officers, the chief cupbearer and the chief baker, ³and he put them in custody in the house of the captain of the guard, in the prison where Joseph was confined. ⁴The captain of the guard appointed Joseph to be with them, and he attended them. They continued for some time in custody.

⁵And one night they both dreamed—the cupbearer and the baker of the king of Egypt, who were confined in the prison—each his own dream, and each dream with its own interpretation. ⁶When Joseph came to them in the morning, he saw that they were troubled. ⁷So he asked Pharaoh's officers who were with him in custody in his master's house, "Why are your faces downcast today?" ⁸They said to him, "We have had dreams, and there is no one to interpret them." And Joseph said to them, "Do not interpretations belong to God? Please tell them to me."

⁹So the chief cupbearer told his dream to Joseph and said to him, "In my dream there was a vine before me, ¹⁰and on the vine there were three branches. As soon as it budded, its blossoms shot forth, and the clusters ripened into grapes. ¹¹Pharaoh's cup was in my hand, and I took the grapes and pressed them into Pharaoh's cup and placed the cup in Pharaoh's hand." ¹²Then Joseph said to him, "This is its interpretation: the three branches are three days. ¹³In three days Pharaoh will lift up your head and restore you to your office, and you shall place Pharaoh's cup in his hand as formerly, when you were his cupbearer. ¹⁴Only remember me, when it is well with you, and please do me the kindness to mention me to Pharaoh, and so get me out of this house. ¹⁵For I was indeed stolen out of the land of the Hebrews, and here also I have done nothing that they should put me into the pit."

¹⁶When the chief baker saw that the interpretation was favourable, he said to Joseph, "I also had a dream: there were three cake baskets on my head, ¹⁷and in the uppermost basket there were all sorts of baked food for Pharaoh, but the birds were eating it out of the basket on my head." ¹⁸And Joseph answered and said, "This is its interpretation: the three baskets are three days. ¹⁹In three days Pharaoh will lift up your head—from you!—and hang you on a tree. And the birds will eat the flesh from you."

²⁰On the third day, which was Pharaoh's birthday, he made a feast for all his servants and lifted up the head of the chief cupbearer and the head of the chief baker among his servants. ²¹He restored the chief cupbearer to his position, and he placed the cup in Pharaoh's hand. ²²But he hanged the chief baker, as Joseph had interpreted to them. ²³Yet the chief cupbearer did not remember Joseph, but forgot him.

JOSEPH INTERPRETS PHARAOH'S DREAMS

41 After two whole years, Pharaoh dreamed that he was standing by the Nile, ²and behold, there came up out of the Nile seven cows, attractive and plump, and they fed in the reed grass. ³And behold, seven other cows, ugly and thin, came up out of the Nile after them, and stood by the other cows on the bank of the Nile. ⁴And the ugly, thin cows ate up the seven attractive, plump cows. And Pharaoh awoke. ⁵And he fell asleep and dreamed a second time. And behold, seven ears of corn, plump and good, were growing on one stalk. ⁶And behold, after them sprouted seven ears, thin and blighted by the east wind. ⁷And the thin ears swallowed up the seven plump, full ears. And Pharaoh awoke, and behold, it was a dream. ⁸So in the morning his spirit was troubled, and he sent and called for all the magicians of Egypt and all its wise men. Pharaoh told them his dreams, but there was none who could interpret them to Pharaoh.

⁹Then the chief cupbearer said to Pharaoh, "I remember my offences today. ¹⁰When Pharaoh was angry with his servants and put me and the chief baker in custody in the house of the captain of the guard, ¹¹we dreamed on the same night, he and I, each having a dream with its own interpretation. ¹²A young Hebrew was there with us, a servant of the captain of the guard. When we told him, he interpreted our dreams to us, giving an interpretation to each man according to his dream. ¹³And as he interpreted to us, so it came about. I was restored to my office, and the baker was hanged."

¹⁴Then Pharaoh sent and called Joseph, and they quickly brought him out of the pit. And when he had shaved himself and changed his clothes, he came in before Pharaoh. ¹⁵And Pharaoh said to Joseph, "I have had a dream, and there is no one who can interpret it. I have heard it said of you that when you hear a dream you can interpret it." ¹⁶Joseph answered Pharaoh, "It is not in me; God will give Pharaoh a favourable answer."[a]

---

[a] Or (compare Samaritan, Septuagint) *Without God it is not possible to give Pharaoh an answer about his welfare*

things as her own, or we shall be laughed at. You see, I sent this young goat, and you did not find her." ²⁴About three months later Judah was told, "Tamar your daughter-in-law has been immoral.ᵃ Moreover, she is pregnant by immorality."ᵇ And Judah said, "Bring her out, and let her be burned." ²⁵As she was being brought out, she sent word to her father-in-law, "By the man to whom these belong, I am pregnant." And she said, "Please identify whose these are, the signet and the cord and the staff." ²⁶Then Judah identified them and said, "She is more righteous than I, since I did not give her to my son Shelah." And he did not know her again.

²⁷When the time of her labour came, there were twins in her womb. ²⁸And when she was in labour, one put out a hand, and the midwife took and tied a scarlet thread on his hand, saying, "This one came out first." ²⁹But as he drew back his hand, behold, his brother came out. And she said, "What a breach you have made for yourself!" Therefore his name was called Perez.ᶜ ³⁰Afterwards his brother came out with the scarlet thread on his hand, and his name was called Zerah.

JOSEPH AND POTIPHAR'S WIFE

39 Now Joseph had been brought down to Egypt, and Potiphar, an officer of Pharaoh, the captain of the guard, an Egyptian, had bought him from the Ishmaelites who had brought him down there. ²The LORD was with Joseph, and he became a successful man, and he was in the house of his Egyptian master. ³His master saw that the LORD was with him and that the LORD caused all that he did to succeed in his hands. ⁴So Joseph found favour in his sight and attended him, and he made him overseer of his house and put him in charge of all that he had. ⁵From the time that he made him overseer in his house and over all that he had, the LORD blessed the Egyptian's house for Joseph's sake; the blessing of the LORD was on all that he had, in house and field. ⁶So he left all that he had in Joseph's charge, and because of him he had no concern about anything but the food he ate.

Now Joseph was handsome in form and appearance. ⁷And after a time his master's wife cast her eyes on Joseph and said, "Lie with me." ⁸But he refused and said to his master's wife, "Behold, because of me my master has no concern about anything in the house, and he has put everything that he has in my charge. ⁹He is not greater in this house than I am, nor has he kept back anything from me except you, because you are his wife. How then can I do this great wickedness and sin against God?" ¹⁰And as she spoke to Joseph day after day, he would not listen to her, to lie beside her or to be with her.

¹¹But one day, when he went into the house to do his work and none of the men of the house was there in the house, ¹²she caught him by his garment, saying, "Lie with me." But he left his garment in her hand and fled and got out of the house. ¹³And as soon as she saw that he had left his garment in her hand and had fled out of the house, ¹⁴she called to the men of her household and said to them, "See, he has brought among us a Hebrew to laugh at us. He came in to me to lie with me, and I cried out with a loud voice. ¹⁵And as soon as he heard that I lifted up my voice and cried out, he left his garment beside me and fled and got out of the house." ¹⁶Then she laid up his garment by her until his master came home, ¹⁷and she told him the same story, saying, "The Hebrew servant, whom you have brought among us, came in to me to laugh at me. ¹⁸But as soon as I lifted up my voice and cried, he left his garment beside me and fled out of the house."

¹⁹As soon as his master heard the words that his wife spoke to him, "This is the way your servant treated me", his anger was kindled. ²⁰And Joseph's master took him and put him into the prison, the place where the king's prisoners were confined, and he was there in prison. ²¹But the LORD was with Joseph and showed him steadfast love and gave him favour in the sight of the keeper of the prison. ²²And the keeper of the prison put Joseph in charge of all the prisoners who were in the prison. Whatever was done there, he was the one who did it. ²³The keeper of the prison paid no attention to anything that was in Joseph's charge, because the LORD was with him. And whatever he did, the LORD made it succeed.

JOSEPH INTERPRETS TWO PRISONERS' DREAMS

40 Some time after this, the cupbearer of the king of Egypt and his baker committed an offence against their lord the king of Egypt. ²And

---

ᵃOr has committed prostitution ᵇOr by prostitution ᶜPerez means a breach

¹⁷Then Pharaoh said to Joseph, "Behold, in my dream I was standing on the banks of the Nile. ¹⁸Seven cows, plump and attractive, came up out of the Nile and fed in the reed grass. ¹⁹Seven other cows came up after them, poor and very ugly and thin, such as I had never seen in all the land of Egypt. ²⁰And the thin, ugly cows ate up the first seven plump cows, ²¹but when they had eaten them no one would have known that they had eaten them, for they were still as ugly as at the beginning. Then I awoke. ²²I also saw in my dream seven ears growing on one stalk, full and good. ²³Seven ears, withered, thin, and blighted by the east wind, sprouted after them, ²⁴and the thin ears swallowed up the seven good ears. And I told it to the magicians, but there was no one who could explain it to me."

²⁵Then Joseph said to Pharaoh, "The dreams of Pharaoh are one; God has revealed to Pharaoh what he is about to do. ²⁶The seven good cows are seven years, and the seven good ears are seven years; the dreams are one. ²⁷The seven lean and ugly cows that came up after them are seven years, and the seven empty ears blighted by the east wind are also seven years of famine. ²⁸It is as I told Pharaoh; God has shown to Pharaoh what he is about to do. ²⁹There will come seven years of great plenty throughout all the land of Egypt, ³⁰but after them there will arise seven years of famine, and all the plenty will be forgotten in the land of Egypt. The famine will consume the land, ³¹and the plenty will be unknown in the land by reason of the famine that will follow, for it will be very severe. ³²And the doubling of Pharaoh's dream means that the thing is fixed by God, and God will shortly bring it about. ³³Now therefore let Pharaoh select a discerning and wise man, and set him over the land of Egypt. ³⁴Let Pharaoh proceed to appoint overseers over the land and take one-fifth of the produce of the land*ᵃ* of Egypt during the seven plentiful years. ³⁵And let them gather all the food of these good years that are coming and store up grain under the authority of Pharaoh for food in the cities, and let them keep it. ³⁶That food shall be a reserve for the land against the seven years of famine that are to occur in the land of Egypt, so that the land may not perish through the famine."

JOSEPH RISES TO POWER

³⁷This proposal pleased Pharaoh and all his servants. ³⁸And Pharaoh said to his servants, "Can we find a man like this, in whom is the Spirit of God?"*ᵇ* ³⁹Then Pharaoh said to Joseph, "Since God has shown you all this, there is none so discerning and wise as you are. ⁴⁰You shall be over my house, and all my people shall order themselves as you command.*ᶜ* Only as regards the throne will I be greater than you." ⁴¹And Pharaoh said to Joseph, "See, I have set you over all the land of Egypt." ⁴²Then Pharaoh took his signet ring from his hand and put it on Joseph's hand, and clothed him in garments of fine linen and put a gold chain about his neck. ⁴³And he made him ride in his second chariot. And they called out before him, "Bow the knee!"*ᵈ* Thus he set him over all the land of Egypt. ⁴⁴Moreover, Pharaoh said to Joseph, "I am Pharaoh, and without your consent no one shall lift up hand or foot in all the land of Egypt." ⁴⁵And Pharaoh called Joseph's name Zaphenath-paneah. And he gave him in marriage Asenath, the daughter of Potiphera priest of On. So Joseph went out over the land of Egypt.

⁴⁶Joseph was thirty years old when he entered the service of Pharaoh king of Egypt. And Joseph went out from the presence of Pharaoh and went through all the land of Egypt. ⁴⁷During the seven plentiful years the earth produced abundantly, ⁴⁸and he gathered up all the food of these seven years, which occurred in the land of Egypt, and put the food in the cities. He put in every city the food from the fields around it. ⁴⁹And Joseph stored up grain in great abundance, like the sand of the sea, until he ceased to measure it, for it could not be measured.

⁵⁰Before the year of famine came, two sons were born to Joseph. Asenath, the daughter of Potiphera priest of On, bore them to him. ⁵¹Joseph called the name of the firstborn Manasseh. "For," he said, "God has made me forget all my hardship and all my father's house."*ᵉ* ⁵²The name of the second he called Ephraim, "For God has made me fruitful in the land of my affliction."*ᶠ*

⁵³The seven years of plenty that occurred in the land of Egypt came to an end, ⁵⁴and the seven years of famine began to come, as Joseph had said. There was famine in all lands, but in all the land of Egypt there was bread. ⁵⁵When all the land of Egypt was

---

ᵃ Or *over the land and organize the land* *ᵇ* Or *of the gods* *ᶜ* Hebrew *and according to your command all my people shall kiss the ground* *ᵈ* *Abrek*, probably an Egyptian word, similar in sound to the Hebrew word meaning *to kneel* *ᵉ* *Manasseh* sounds like the Hebrew for *making to forget* *ᶠ* *Ephraim* sounds like the Hebrew for *making fruitful*

famished, the people cried to Pharaoh for bread. Pharaoh said to all the Egyptians, "Go to Joseph. What he says to you, do."

⁵⁶So when the famine had spread over all the land, Joseph opened all the storehouses[a] and sold to the Egyptians, for the famine was severe in the land of Egypt. ⁵⁷Moreover, all the earth came to Egypt to Joseph to buy grain, because the famine was severe over all the earth.

JOSEPH'S BROTHERS GO TO EGYPT

42 When Jacob learned that there was grain for sale in Egypt, he said to his sons, "Why do you look at one another?" ²And he said, "Behold, I have heard that there is grain for sale in Egypt. Go down and buy grain for us there, that we may live and not die." ³So ten of Joseph's brothers went down to buy grain in Egypt. ⁴But Jacob did not send Benjamin, Joseph's brother, with his brothers, for he feared that harm might happen to him. ⁵Thus the sons of Israel came to buy among the others who came, for the famine was in the land of Canaan.

⁶Now Joseph was governor over the land. He was the one who sold to all the people of the land. And Joseph's brothers came and bowed themselves before him with their faces to the ground. ⁷Joseph saw his brothers and recognized them, but he treated them like strangers and spoke roughly to them. "Where do you come from?" he said. They said, "From the land of Canaan, to buy food." ⁸And Joseph recognized his brothers, but they did not recognize him. ⁹And Joseph remembered the dreams that he had dreamed of them. And he said to them, "You are spies; you have come to see the nakedness of the land." ¹⁰They said to him, "No, my lord, your servants have come to buy food. ¹¹We are all sons of one man. We are honest men. Your servants have never been spies."

¹²He said to them, "No, it is the nakedness of the land that you have come to see." ¹³And they said, "We, your servants, are twelve brothers, the sons of one man in the land of Canaan, and behold, the youngest is this day with our father, and one is no more." ¹⁴But Joseph said to them, "It is as I said to you. You are spies. ¹⁵By this you shall be tested: by the life of Pharaoh, you shall not go from this place unless your youngest brother comes here. ¹⁶Send one of you, and let him bring your brother, while you remain confined, that your words may be tested, whether there is truth in you. Or else, by the life of Pharaoh, surely you are spies." ¹⁷And he put them all together in custody for three days.

¹⁸On the third day Joseph said to them, "Do this and you will live, for I fear God: ¹⁹if you are honest men, let one of your brothers remain confined where you are in custody, and let the rest go and carry grain for the famine of your households, ²⁰and bring your youngest brother to me. So your words will be verified, and you shall not die." And they did so. ²¹Then they said to one another, "In truth we are guilty concerning our brother, in that we saw the distress of his soul, when he begged us and we did not listen. That is why this distress has come upon us." ²²And Reuben answered them, "Did I not tell you not to sin against the boy? But you did not listen. So now there comes a reckoning for his blood." ²³They did not know that Joseph understood them, for there was an interpreter between them. ²⁴Then he turned away from them and wept. And he returned to them and spoke to them. And he took Simeon from them and bound him before their eyes. ²⁵And Joseph gave orders to fill their bags with grain, and to replace every man's money in his sack, and to give them provisions for the journey. This was done for them.

²⁶Then they loaded their donkeys with their grain and departed. ²⁷And as one of them opened his sack to give his donkey fodder at the lodging place, he saw his money in the mouth of his sack. ²⁸He said to his brothers, "My money has been put back; here it is in the mouth of my sack!" At this their hearts failed them, and they turned trembling to one another, saying, "What is this that God has done to us?"

²⁹When they came to Jacob their father in the land of Canaan, they told him all that had happened to them, saying, ³⁰"The man, the lord of the land, spoke roughly to us and took us to be spies of the land. ³¹But we said to him, 'We are honest men; we have never been spies. ³²We are twelve brothers, sons of our father. One is no more, and the youngest is this day with our father in the land of Canaan.' ³³Then the man, the lord of the land, said to us, 'By this I shall know that you are honest men: leave one of your brothers with me, and take grain for the famine of your households, and go your way. ³⁴Bring your youngest brother to me. Then I shall know

---

[a] Hebrew *all that was in them*

that you are not spies but honest men, and I will deliver your brother to you, and you shall trade in the land.'"

³⁵As they emptied their sacks, behold, every man's bundle of money was in his sack. And when they and their father saw their bundles of money, they were afraid. ³⁶And Jacob their father said to them, "You have bereaved me of my children: Joseph is no more, and Simeon is no more, and now you would take Benjamin. All this has come against me." ³⁷Then Reuben said to his father, "Kill my two sons if I do not bring him back to you. Put him in my hands, and I will bring him back to you." ³⁸But he said, "My son shall not go down with you, for his brother is dead, and he is the only one left. If harm should happen to him on the journey that you are to make, you would bring down my grey hairs with sorrow to Sheol."

JOSEPH'S BROTHERS RETURN TO EGYPT

43 Now the famine was severe in the land. ²And when they had eaten the grain that they had brought from Egypt, their father said to them, "Go again, buy us a little food." ³But Judah said to him, "The man solemnly warned us, saying, 'You shall not see my face unless your brother is with you.' ⁴If you will send our brother with us, we will go down and buy you food. ⁵But if you will not send him, we will not go down, for the man said to us, 'You shall not see my face, unless your brother is with you.'" ⁶Israel said, "Why did you treat me so badly as to tell the man that you had another brother?" ⁷They replied, "The man questioned us carefully about ourselves and our kindred, saying, 'Is your father still alive? Do you have another brother?' What we told him was in answer to these questions. Could we in any way know that he would say, 'Bring your brother down'?" ⁸And Judah said to Israel his father, "Send the boy with me, and we will arise and go, that we may live and not die, both we and you and also our little ones. ⁹I will be a pledge of his safety. From my hand you shall require him. If I do not bring him back to you and set him before you, then let me bear the blame for ever. ¹⁰If we had not delayed, we would now have returned twice."

¹¹Then their father Israel said to them, "If it must be so, then do this: take some of the choice fruits of the land in your bags, and carry a present down to the man, a little balm and a little honey, gum, myrrh, pistachio nuts, and almonds. ¹²Take double the money with you. Carry back with you the money that was returned in the mouth of your sacks. Perhaps it was an oversight. ¹³Take also your brother, and arise, go again to the man. ¹⁴May God Almighty*ᵃ* grant you mercy before the man, and may he send back your other brother and Benjamin. And as for me, if I am bereaved of my children, I am bereaved."

¹⁵So the men took this present, and they took double the money with them, and Benjamin. They arose and went down to Egypt and stood before Joseph.

¹⁶When Joseph saw Benjamin with them, he said to the steward of his house, "Bring the men into the house, and slaughter an animal and make ready, for the men are to dine with me at noon." ¹⁷The man did as Joseph told him and brought the men to Joseph's house. ¹⁸And the men were afraid because they were brought to Joseph's house, and they said, "It is because of the money, which was replaced in our sacks the first time, that we are brought in, so that he may assault us and fall upon us to make us servants and seize our donkeys." ¹⁹So they went up to the steward of Joseph's house and spoke with him at the door of the house, ²⁰and said, "Oh, my lord, we came down the first time to buy food. ²¹And when we came to the lodging place we opened our sacks, and there was each man's money in the mouth of his sack, our money in full weight. So we have brought it again with us, ²²and we have brought other money down with us to buy food. We do not know who put our money in our sacks." ²³He replied, "Peace to you, do not be afraid. Your God and the God of your father has put treasure in your sacks for you. I received your money." Then he brought Simeon out to them. ²⁴And when the man had brought the men into Joseph's house and given them water, and they had washed their feet, and when he had given their donkeys fodder, ²⁵they prepared the present for Joseph's coming at noon, for they heard that they should eat bread there.

²⁶When Joseph came home, they brought into the house to him the present that they had with them and bowed down to him to the ground. ²⁷And he enquired about their welfare and said, "Is your father well, the old man of whom you spoke? Is he still alive?" ²⁸They said, "Your servant our father is well; he is still alive." And they bowed their heads and prostrated themselves. ²⁹And he lifted up

---

*ᵃ*Hebrew *El Shaddai*

his eyes and saw his brother Benjamin, his mother's son, and said, "Is this your youngest brother, of whom you spoke to me? God be gracious to you, my son!" 30Then Joseph hurried out, for his compassion grew warm for his brother, and he sought a place to weep. And he entered his chamber and wept there. 31Then he washed his face and came out. And controlling himself he said, "Serve the food." 32They served him by himself, and them by themselves, and the Egyptians who ate with him by themselves, because the Egyptians could not eat with the Hebrews, for that is an abomination to the Egyptians. 33And they sat before him, the firstborn according to his birthright and the youngest according to his youth. And the men looked at one another in amazement. 34Portions were taken to them from Joseph's table, but Benjamin's portion was five times as much as any of theirs. And they drank and were merry[a] with him.

JOSEPH TESTS HIS BROTHERS

44 Then he commanded the steward of his house, "Fill the men's sacks with food, as much as they can carry, and put each man's money in the mouth of his sack, 2and put my cup, the silver cup, in the mouth of the sack of the youngest, with his money for the grain." And he did as Joseph told him.

3As soon as the morning was light, the men were sent away with their donkeys. 4They had gone only a short distance from the city. Now Joseph said to his steward, "Up, follow after the men, and when you overtake them, say to them, 'Why have you repaid evil for good?[b] 5Is it not from this that my lord drinks, and by this that he practises divination? You have done evil in doing this.'"

6When he overtook them, he spoke to them these words. 7They said to him, "Why does my lord speak such words as these? Far be it from your servants to do such a thing! 8Behold, the money that we found in the mouths of our sacks we brought back to you from the land of Canaan. How then could we steal silver or gold from your lord's house? 9Whichever of your servants is found with it shall die, and we also will be my lord's servants." 10He said, "Let it be as you say: he who is found with it shall be my servant, and the rest of you shall be innocent." 11Then each man quickly lowered his sack to the ground, and each man opened his sack. 12And he searched, beginning with the eldest and ending with the youngest. And the cup was found in Benjamin's sack. 13Then they tore their clothes, and every man loaded his donkey, and they returned to the city.

14When Judah and his brothers came to Joseph's house, he was still there. They fell before him to the ground. 15Joseph said to them, "What deed is this that you have done? Do you not know that a man like me can indeed practise divination?" 16And Judah said, "What shall we say to my lord? What shall we speak? Or how can we clear ourselves? God has found out the guilt of your servants; behold, we are my lord's servants, both we and he also in whose hand the cup has been found." 17But he said, "Far be it from me that I should do so! Only the man in whose hand the cup was found shall be my servant. But as for you, go up in peace to your father."

18Then Judah went up to him and said, "Oh, my lord, please let your servant speak a word in my lord's ears, and let not your anger burn against your servant, for you are like Pharaoh himself. 19My lord asked his servants, saying, 'Have you a father, or a brother?' 20And we said to my lord, 'We have a father, an old man, and a young brother, the child of his old age. His brother is dead, and he alone is left of his mother's children, and his father loves him.' 21Then you said to your servants, 'Bring him down to me, that I may set my eyes on him.' 22We said to my lord, 'The boy cannot leave his father, for if he should leave his father, his father would die.' 23Then you said to your servants, 'Unless your youngest brother comes down with you, you shall not see my face again.'

24"When we went back to your servant my father, we told him the words of my lord. 25And when our father said, 'Go again, buy us a little food', 26we said, 'We cannot go down. If our youngest brother goes with us, then we will go down. For we cannot see the man's face unless our youngest brother is with us.' 27Then your servant my father said to us, 'You know that my wife bore me two sons. 28One left me, and I said, "Surely he has been torn to pieces," and I have never seen him since. 29If you take this one also from me, and harm happens to him, you will bring down my grey hairs in evil to Sheol.'

30"Now therefore, as soon as I come to your servant my father, and the boy is not with

---

[a]Hebrew *and became intoxicated* [b]Septuagint (compare Vulgate) adds *Why have you stolen my silver cup?*

us, then, as his life is bound up in the boy's life, ³¹as soon as he sees that the boy is not with us, he will die, and your servants will bring down the grey hairs of your servant our father with sorrow to Sheol. ³²For your servant became a pledge of safety for the boy to my father, saying, 'If I do not bring him back to you, then I shall bear the blame before my father all my life.' ³³Now therefore, please let your servant remain instead of the boy as a servant to my lord, and let the boy go back with his brothers. ³⁴For how can I go back to my father if the boy is not with me? I fear to see the evil that would find my father."

JOSEPH PROVIDES FOR HIS BROTHERS AND FAMILY

45 Then Joseph could not control himself before all those who stood by him. He cried, "Make everyone go out from me." So no one stayed with him when Joseph made himself known to his brothers. ²And he wept aloud, so that the Egyptians heard it, and the household of Pharaoh heard it. ³And Joseph said to his brothers, "I am Joseph! Is my father still alive?" But his brothers could not answer him, for they were dismayed at his presence.

⁴So Joseph said to his brothers, "Come near to me, please." And they came near. And he said, "I am your brother, Joseph, whom you sold into Egypt. ⁵And now do not be distressed or angry with yourselves because you sold me here, for God sent me before you to preserve life. ⁶For the famine has been in the land these two years, and there are yet five years in which there will be neither ploughing nor harvest. ⁷And God sent me before you to preserve for you a remnant on earth, and to keep alive for you many survivors. ⁸So it was not you who sent me here, but God. He has made me a father to Pharaoh, and lord of all his house and ruler over all the land of Egypt. ⁹Hurry and go up to my father and say to him, 'Thus says your son Joseph, God has made me lord of all Egypt. Come down to me; do not tarry. ¹⁰You shall dwell in the land of Goshen, and you shall be near me, you and your children and your children's children, and your flocks, your herds, and all that you have. ¹¹There I will provide for you, for there are yet five years of famine to come, so that you and your household, and all that you have, do not come to poverty.' ¹²And now your eyes see, and the eyes of my brother Benjamin see, that it is my mouth that speaks to you. ¹³You must tell my father of all my honour in Egypt, and of all that you have seen. Hurry and bring my father down here." ¹⁴Then he fell upon his brother Benjamin's neck and wept, and Benjamin wept upon his neck. ¹⁵And he kissed all his brothers and wept upon them. After that his brothers talked with him.

¹⁶When the report was heard in Pharaoh's house, "Joseph's brothers have come", it pleased Pharaoh and his servants. ¹⁷And Pharaoh said to Joseph, "Say to your brothers, 'Do this: load your beasts and go back to the land of Canaan, ¹⁸and take your father and your households, and come to me, and I will give you the best of the land of Egypt, and you shall eat the fat of the land.' ¹⁹And you, Joseph, are commanded to say, 'Do this: take wagons from the land of Egypt for your little ones and for your wives, and bring your father, and come. ²⁰Have no concern for[a] your goods, for the best of all the land of Egypt is yours.'"

²¹The sons of Israel did so: and Joseph gave them wagons, according to the command of Pharaoh, and gave them provisions for the journey. ²²To each and all of them he gave a change of clothes, but to Benjamin he gave three hundred shekels[b] of silver and five changes of clothes. ²³To his father he sent as follows: ten donkeys loaded with the good things of Egypt, and ten female donkeys loaded with grain, bread, and provision for his father on the journey. ²⁴Then he sent his brothers away, and as they departed, he said to them, "Do not quarrel on the way."

²⁵So they went up out of Egypt and came to the land of Canaan to their father Jacob. ²⁶And they told him, "Joseph is still alive, and he is ruler over all the land of Egypt." And his heart became numb, for he did not believe them. ²⁷But when they told him all the words of Joseph, which he had said to them, and when he saw the wagons that Joseph had sent to carry him, the spirit of their father Jacob revived. ²⁸And Israel said, "It is enough; Joseph my son is still alive. I will go and see him before I die."

JOSEPH BRINGS HIS FAMILY TO EGYPT

46 So Israel took his journey with all that he had and came to Beersheba, and offered sacrifices to the God of his father Isaac. ²And God spoke to

---

[a] Hebrew *Let your eye not pity* [b] A *shekel* was about 2/5 of an ounce or 11 grams

Israel in visions of the night and said, "Jacob, Jacob." And he said, "Here I am." ³Then he said, "I am God, the God of your father. Do not be afraid to go down to Egypt, for there I will make you into a great nation. ⁴I myself will go down with you to Egypt, and I will also bring you up again, and Joseph's hand shall close your eyes."

⁵Then Jacob set out from Beersheba. The sons of Israel carried Jacob their father, their little ones, and their wives, in the wagons that Pharaoh had sent to carry him. ⁶They also took their livestock and their goods, which they had gained in the land of Canaan, and came into Egypt, Jacob and all his offspring with him, ⁷his sons, and his sons' sons with him, his daughters, and his sons' daughters. All his offspring he brought with him into Egypt.

⁸Now these are the names of the descendants of Israel, who came into Egypt, Jacob and his sons. Reuben, Jacob's firstborn, ⁹and the sons of Reuben: Hanoch, Pallu, Hezron, and Carmi. ¹⁰The sons of Simeon: Jemuel, Jamin, Ohad, Jachin, Zohar, and Shaul, the son of a Canaanite woman. ¹¹The sons of Levi: Gershon, Kohath, and Merari. ¹²The sons of Judah: Er, Onan, Shelah, Perez, and Zerah (but Er and Onan died in the land of Canaan); and the sons of Perez were Hezron and Hamul. ¹³The sons of Issachar: Tola, Puvah, Yob, and Shimron. ¹⁴The sons of Zebulun: Sered, Elon, and Jahleel. ¹⁵These are the sons of Leah, whom she bore to Jacob in Paddan-aram, together with his daughter Dinah; altogether his sons and his daughters numbered thirty-three.

¹⁶The sons of Gad: Ziphion, Haggi, Shuni, Ezbon, Eri, Arodi, and Areli. ¹⁷The sons of Asher: Imnah, Ishvah, Ishvi, Beriah, with Serah their sister. And the sons of Beriah: Heber and Malchiel. ¹⁸These are the sons of Zilpah, whom Laban gave to Leah his daughter; and these she bore to Jacob—sixteen persons.

¹⁹The sons of Rachel, Jacob's wife: Joseph and Benjamin. ²⁰And to Joseph in the land of Egypt were born Manasseh and Ephraim, whom Asenath, the daughter of Potiphera the priest of On, bore to him. ²¹And the sons of Benjamin: Bela, Becher, Ashbel, Gera, Naaman, Ehi, Rosh, Muppim, Huppim, and Ard. ²²These are the sons of Rachel, who were born to Jacob—fourteen persons in all.

²³The son*ᵃ* of Dan: Hushim. ²⁴The sons of Naphtali: Jahzeel, Guni, Jezer, and Shillem. ²⁵These are the sons of Bilhah, whom Laban gave to Rachel his daughter, and these she bore to Jacob—seven persons in all.

²⁶All the persons belonging to Jacob who came into Egypt, who were his own descendants, not including Jacob's sons' wives, were sixty-six persons in all. ²⁷And the sons of Joseph, who were born to him in Egypt, were two. All the persons of the house of Jacob who came into Egypt were seventy.

JACOB AND JOSEPH REUNITED

²⁸He had sent Judah ahead of him to Joseph to show the way before him in Goshen, and they came into the land of Goshen. ²⁹Then Joseph prepared his chariot and went up to meet Israel his father in Goshen. He presented himself to him and fell on his neck and wept on his neck a good while. ³⁰Israel said to Joseph, "Now let me die, since I have seen your face and know that you are still alive." ³¹Joseph said to his brothers and to his father's household, "I will go up and tell Pharaoh and will say to him, 'My brothers and my father's household, who were in the land of Canaan, have come to me. ³²And the men are shepherds, for they have been keepers of livestock, and they have brought their flocks and their herds and all that they have.' ³³When Pharaoh calls you and says, 'What is your occupation?' ³⁴you shall say, 'Your servants have been keepers of livestock from our youth even until now, both we and our fathers,' in order that you may dwell in the land of Goshen, for every shepherd is an abomination to the Egyptians."

JACOB'S FAMILY SETTLES IN GOSHEN

47 So Joseph went in and told Pharaoh, "My father and my brothers, with their flocks and herds and all that they possess, have come from the land of Canaan. They are now in the land of Goshen." ²And from among his brothers he took five men and presented them to Pharaoh. ³Pharaoh said to his brothers, "What is your occupation?" And they said to Pharaoh, "Your servants are shepherds, as our fathers were." ⁴They said to Pharaoh, "We have come to sojourn in the land, for there is no pasture for your servants' flocks, for the famine is severe in the land of Canaan. And now, please let your servants dwell in the land of Goshen." ⁵Then Pharaoh said to Joseph, "Your father and your brothers have come to you. ⁶The land of Egypt is before you. Settle your father and your brothers in the best of the

---
ᵃHebrew *sons*

land. Let them settle in the land of Goshen, and if you know any able men among them, put them in charge of my livestock." ⁷Then Joseph brought in Jacob his father and stood him before Pharaoh, and Jacob blessed Pharaoh. ⁸And Pharaoh said to Jacob, "How many are the days of the years of your life?" ⁹And Jacob said to Pharaoh, "The days of the years of my sojourning are 130 years. Few and evil have been the days of the years of my life, and they have not attained to the days of the years of the life of my fathers in the days of their sojourning." ¹⁰And Jacob blessed Pharaoh and went out from the presence of Pharaoh. ¹¹Then Joseph settled his father and his brothers and gave them a possession in the land of Egypt, in the best of the land, in the land of Rameses, as Pharaoh had commanded. ¹²And Joseph provided his father, his brothers, and all his father's household with food, according to the number of their dependants.

JOSEPH AND THE FAMINE

¹³Now there was no food in all the land, for the famine was very severe, so that the land of Egypt and the land of Canaan languished by reason of the famine. ¹⁴And Joseph gathered up all the money that was found in the land of Egypt and in the land of Canaan, in exchange for the grain that they bought. And Joseph brought the money into Pharaoh's house. ¹⁵And when the money was all spent in the land of Egypt and in the land of Canaan, all the Egyptians came to Joseph and said, "Give us food. Why should we die before your eyes? For our money is gone." ¹⁶And Joseph answered, "Give your livestock, and I will give you food in exchange for your livestock, if your money is gone." ¹⁷So they brought their livestock to Joseph, and Joseph gave them food in exchange for the horses, the flocks, the herds, and the donkeys. He supplied them with food in exchange for all their livestock that year. ¹⁸And when that year was ended, they came to him the following year and said to him, "We will not hide from my lord that our money is all spent. The herds of livestock are my lord's. There is nothing left in the sight of my lord but our bodies and our land. ¹⁹Why should we die before your eyes, both we and our land? Buy us and our land for food, and we with our land will be servants to Pharaoh. And give us seed that we may live and not die, and that the land may not be desolate."

²⁰So Joseph bought all the land of Egypt for Pharaoh, for all the Egyptians sold their fields, because the famine was severe on them. The land became Pharaoh's. ²¹As for the people, he made servants of them[a] from one end of Egypt to the other. ²²Only the land of the priests he did not buy, for the priests had a fixed allowance from Pharaoh and lived on the allowance that Pharaoh gave them; therefore they did not sell their land.

²³Then Joseph said to the people, "Behold, I have this day bought you and your land for Pharaoh. Now here is seed for you, and you shall sow the land. ²⁴And at the harvests you shall give a fifth to Pharaoh, and four fifths shall be your own, as seed for the field and as food for yourselves and your households, and as food for your little ones." ²⁵And they said, "You have saved our lives; may it please my lord, we will be servants to Pharaoh." ²⁶So Joseph made it a statute concerning the land of Egypt, and it stands to this day, that Pharaoh should have the fifth; the land of the priests alone did not become Pharaoh's.

²⁷Thus Israel settled in the land of Egypt, in the land of Goshen. And they gained possessions in it, and were fruitful and multiplied greatly. ²⁸And Jacob lived in the land of Egypt for seventeen years. So the days of Jacob, the years of his life, were 147 years.

²⁹And when the time drew near that Israel must die, he called his son Joseph and said to him, "If now I have found favour in your sight, put your hand under my thigh and promise to deal kindly and truly with me. Do not bury me in Egypt, ³⁰but let me lie with my fathers. Carry me out of Egypt and bury me in their burying place." He answered, "I will do as you have said." ³¹And he said, "Swear to me"; and he swore to him. Then Israel bowed himself upon the head of his bed.[b]

JACOB BLESSES EPHRAIM AND MANASSEH

48 After this, Joseph was told, "Behold, your father is ill." So he took with him his two sons, Manasseh and Ephraim. ²And it was told to Jacob, "Your son Joseph has come to you." Then Israel summoned his strength and sat up in bed. ³And Jacob said to Joseph, "God Almighty[c] appeared to me at Luz in the land of Canaan and blessed me, ⁴and said to me, 'Behold, I will make you fruitful and multiply

---

[a]Samaritan, Septuagint, Vulgate; Hebrew *he removed them to the cities*
[b]Hebrew; Septuagint *staff* [c]Hebrew *El Shaddai*

you, and I will make of you a company of peoples and will give this land to your offspring after you for an everlasting possession.' ⁵And now your two sons, who were born to you in the land of Egypt before I came to you in Egypt, are mine; Ephraim and Manasseh shall be mine, as Reuben and Simeon are. ⁶And the children that you fathered after them shall be yours. They shall be called by the name of their brothers in their inheritance. ⁷As for me, when I came from Paddan, to my sorrow Rachel died in the land of Canaan on the way, when there was still some distance[a] to go to Ephrath, and I buried her there on the way to Ephrath (that is, Bethlehem)."

⁸When Israel saw Joseph's sons, he said, "Who are these?" ⁹Joseph said to his father, "They are my sons, whom God has given me here." And he said, "Bring them to me, please, that I may bless them." ¹⁰Now the eyes of Israel were dim with age, so that he could not see. So Joseph brought them near him, and he kissed them and embraced them. ¹¹And Israel said to Joseph, "I never expected to see your face; and behold, God has let me see your offspring also." ¹²Then Joseph removed them from his knees, and he bowed himself with his face to the earth. ¹³And Joseph took them both, Ephraim in his right hand towards Israel's left hand, and Manasseh in his left hand towards Israel's right hand, and brought them near him. ¹⁴And Israel stretched out his right hand and laid it on the head of Ephraim, who was the younger, and his left hand on the head of Manasseh, crossing his hands (for Manasseh was the firstborn). ¹⁵And he blessed Joseph and said,

"The God before whom my fathers
   Abraham and Isaac walked,
the God who has been my shepherd
   all my life long to this day,
¹⁶   the angel who has redeemed me
      from all evil, bless the boys;
   and in them let my name be carried
      on, and the name of my
   fathers Abraham and Isaac;
and let them grow into a multitude[b]
   in the midst of the earth."

¹⁷When Joseph saw that his father laid his right hand on the head of Ephraim, it displeased him, and he took his father's hand to move it from Ephraim's head to Manasseh's head. ¹⁸And Joseph said to his father, "Not this way, my father; since this one is the firstborn, put your right hand on his head." ¹⁹But his father refused and said, "I know, my son, I know. He also shall become a people, and he also shall be great. Nevertheless, his younger brother shall be greater than he, and his offspring shall become a multitude[c] of nations." ²⁰So he blessed them that day, saying,

"By you Israel will pronounce
   blessings, saying,
'God make you as Ephraim
   and as Manasseh.'"

Thus he put Ephraim before Manasseh. ²¹Then Israel said to Joseph, "Behold, I am about to die, but God will be with you and will bring you again to the land of your fathers. ²²Moreover, I have given to you rather than to your brothers one mountain slope[d] that I took from the hand of the Amorites with my sword and with my bow."

JACOB BLESSES HIS SONS

49 Then Jacob called his sons and said, "Gather yourselves together, that I may tell you what shall happen to you in days to come.

² "Assemble and listen, O sons of Jacob,
      listen to Israel your father.

³ "Reuben, you are my firstborn,
      my might, and the firstfruits
         of my strength,
      pre-eminent in dignity and
         pre-eminent in power.
⁴ Unstable as water, you shall not
      have pre-eminence,
   because you went up to
      your father's bed;
   then you defiled it—he went
      up to my couch!

⁵ "Simeon and Levi are brothers;
      weapons of violence are
         their swords.
⁶ Let my soul come not into their council;
   O my glory, be not joined
      to their company.
   For in their anger they killed men,
      and in their wilfulness they
         hamstrung oxen.

---

[a] Or *about two hours' distance*   [b] Or *let them be like fish for multitude*
[c] Hebrew *fullness*   [d] Or *one portion of the land*; Hebrew *shekem*, which sounds like the town and district called *Shechem*

7 Cursed be their anger, for it is fierce,
    and their wrath, for it is cruel!
  I will divide them in Jacob
    and scatter them in Israel.

8 "Judah, your brothers shall praise you;
    your hand shall be on the
      neck of your enemies;
    your father's sons shall bow
      down before you.
9 Judah is a lion's cub;
    from the prey, my son, you
      have gone up.
  He stooped down; he crouched as
      a lion
    and as a lioness; who
      dares rouse him?
10 The sceptre shall not depart
      from Judah,
    nor the ruler's staff from
      between his feet,
  until tribute comes to him;[a]
    and to him shall be the
      obedience of the peoples.
11 Binding his foal to the vine
    and his donkey's colt to
      the choice vine,
  he has washed his garments in wine
    and his vesture in the
      blood of grapes.
12 His eyes are darker than wine,
    and his teeth whiter than milk.

13 "Zebulun shall dwell at the
      shore of the sea;
  he shall become a haven for ships,
    and his border shall be at Sidon.

14 "Issachar is a strong donkey,
    crouching between the sheepfolds.[b]
15 He saw that a resting-place was good,
    and that the land was pleasant,
  so he bowed his shoulder to bear,
    and became a servant at
      forced labour.

16 "Dan shall judge his people
    as one of the tribes of Israel.
17 Dan shall be a serpent in the way,
    a viper by the path,
  that bites the horse's heels
    so that his rider falls backwards.
18 I wait for your salvation, O LORD.

19 "Raiders shall raid Gad,[c]
    but he shall raid at their heels.

20 "Asher's food shall be rich,
    and he shall yield royal delicacies.

21 "Naphtali is a doe let loose
    that bears beautiful fawns.[d]

22 "Joseph is a fruitful bough,
    a fruitful bough by a spring;
    his branches run over the wall.[e]
23 The archers bitterly attacked him,
    shot at him, and harassed
      him severely,
24 yet his bow remained unmoved;
    his arms[f] were made agile
  by the hands of the Mighty One of Jacob
    (from there is the Shepherd,[g]
      the Stone of Israel),
25 by the God of your father
    who will help you,
  by the Almighty[h] who will bless you
    with blessings of heaven above,
  blessings of the deep that
    crouches beneath,
  blessings of the breasts
    and of the womb.
26 The blessings of your father
    are mighty beyond the
      blessings of my parents,
  up to the bounties of the
    everlasting hills.[i]
  May they be on the head of Joseph,
    and on the brow of him who was
      set apart from his brothers.

27 "Benjamin is a ravenous wolf,
    in the morning devouring the prey
    and at evening dividing the spoil."

JACOB'S DEATH AND BURIAL

28 All these are the twelve tribes of Israel. This is what their father said to them as he blessed them, blessing each with the blessing suitable to him. 29 Then he commanded them and said to them, "I am to be gathered to my people; bury me with my fathers in the cave that is in the field of Ephron the Hittite, 30 in the cave that is in the field at Machpelah, to the east of Mamre, in the land of Canaan,

---

[a] By a slight revocalization; a slight emendation yields (compare Septuagint, Syriac, Targum) *until he comes to whom it belongs*; Hebrew *until Shiloh comes*, or *until he comes to Shiloh* [b] Or *between its saddlebags* [c] *Gad* sounds like the Hebrew for *raiders* and *raid* [d] Or *he gives beautiful words*, or *that bears fawns of the fold* [e] Or *Joseph is a wild donkey, a wild donkey beside a spring, his wild colts beside the wall* [f] Hebrew *the arms of his hands* [g] Or *by the name of the Shepherd* [h] Hebrew *Shaddai* [i] A slight emendation yields (compare Septuagint) *the blessings of the eternal mountains, the bounties of the everlasting hills*

which Abraham bought with the field from Ephron the Hittite to possess as a burying place. ³¹There they buried Abraham and Sarah his wife. There they buried Isaac and Rebekah his wife, and there I buried Leah— ³²the field and the cave that is in it were bought from the Hittites." ³³When Jacob finished commanding his sons, he drew up his feet into the bed and breathed his last and was gathered to his people.

50 Then Joseph fell on his father's face and wept over him and kissed him. ²And Joseph commanded his servants the physicians to embalm his father. So the physicians embalmed Israel. ³Forty days were required for it, for that is how many are required for embalming. And the Egyptians wept for him for seventy days.

⁴And when the days of weeping for him were past, Joseph spoke to the household of Pharaoh, saying, "If now I have found favour in your eyes, please speak in the ears of Pharaoh, saying, ⁵'My father made me swear, saying, "I am about to die: in my tomb that I hewed out for myself in the land of Canaan, there shall you bury me." Now therefore, let me please go up and bury my father. Then I will return.'" ⁶And Pharaoh answered, "Go up, and bury your father, as he made you swear." ⁷So Joseph went up to bury his father. With him went up all the servants of Pharaoh, the elders of his household, and all the elders of the land of Egypt, ⁸as well as all the household of Joseph, his brothers, and his father's household. Only their children, their flocks, and their herds were left in the land of Goshen. ⁹And there went up with him both chariots and horsemen. It was a very great company. ¹⁰When they came to the threshing floor of Atad, which is beyond the Jordan, they lamented there with a very great and grievous lamentation, and he made a mourning for his father for seven days. ¹¹When the inhabitants of the land, the Canaanites, saw the mourning on the threshing floor of Atad, they said, "This is a grievous mourning by the Egyptians." Therefore the place was named Abel-mizraim;[a] it is beyond the Jordan. ¹²Thus his sons did for him as he had commanded them, ¹³for his sons carried him to the land of Canaan and buried him in the cave of the field at Machpelah, to the east of Mamre, which Abraham bought with the field from Ephron the Hittite to possess as a burying place. ¹⁴After he had buried his father, Joseph returned to Egypt with his brothers and all who had gone up with him to bury his father.

GOD'S GOOD PURPOSES

¹⁵When Joseph's brothers saw that their father was dead, they said, "It may be that Joseph will hate us and pay us back for all the evil that we did to him." ¹⁶So they sent a message to Joseph, saying, "Your father gave this command before he died: ¹⁷'Say to Joseph, "Please forgive the transgression of your brothers and their sin, because they did evil to you."' And now, please forgive the transgression of the servants of the God of your father." Joseph wept when they spoke to him. ¹⁸His brothers also came and fell down before him and said, "Behold, we are your servants." ¹⁹But Joseph said to them, "Do not fear, for am I in the place of God? ²⁰As for you, you meant evil against me, but God meant it for good, to bring it about that many people[b] should be kept alive, as they are today. ²¹So do not fear; I will provide for you and your little ones." Thus he comforted them and spoke kindly to them.

THE DEATH OF JOSEPH

²²So Joseph remained in Egypt, he and his father's house. Joseph lived for 110 years. ²³And Joseph saw Ephraim's children of the third generation. The children also of Machir the son of Manasseh were counted as Joseph's own.[c] ²⁴And Joseph said to his brothers, "I am about to die, but God will visit you and bring you up out of this land to the land that he swore to Abraham, to Isaac, and to Jacob." ²⁵Then Joseph made the sons of Israel swear, saying, "God will surely visit you, and you shall carry up my bones from here." ²⁶So Joseph died, being 110 years old. They embalmed him, and he was put in a coffin in Egypt.

---

[a]*Abel-mizraim* means mourning (or meadow) of Egypt [b]Or a numerous people [c]Hebrew *were born on Joseph's knees*

EXODUS

ISRAEL INCREASES GREATLY IN EGYPT

1 These are the names of the sons of Israel who came to Egypt with Jacob, each with his household: ²Reuben, Simeon, Levi, and Judah, ³Issachar, Zebulun, and Benjamin, ⁴Dan and Naphtali, Gad and Asher. ⁵All the descendants of Jacob were seventy persons; Joseph was already in Egypt. ⁶Then Joseph died, and all his brothers and all that generation. ⁷But the people of Israel were fruitful and increased greatly; they multiplied and grew exceedingly strong, so that the land was filled with them.

PHARAOH OPPRESSES ISRAEL

⁸Now there arose a new king over Egypt, who did not know Joseph. ⁹And he said to his people, "Behold, the people of Israel are too many and too mighty for us. ¹⁰Come, let us deal shrewdly with them, lest they multiply, and, if war breaks out, they join our enemies and fight against us and escape from the land." ¹¹Therefore they set taskmasters over them to afflict them with heavy burdens. They built for Pharaoh store cities, Pithom and Raamses. ¹²But the more they were oppressed, the more they multiplied and the more they spread abroad. And the Egyptians were in dread of the people of Israel. ¹³So they ruthlessly made the people of Israel work as slaves ¹⁴and made their lives bitter with hard service, in mortar and brick, and in all kinds of work in the field. In all their work they ruthlessly made them work as slaves.

¹⁵Then the king of Egypt said to the Hebrew midwives, one of whom was named Shiphrah and the other Puah, ¹⁶"When you serve as midwife to the Hebrew women and see them on the birthstool, if it is a son, you shall kill him, but if it is a daughter, she shall live." ¹⁷But the midwives feared God and did not do as the king of Egypt commanded them, but let the male children live. ¹⁸So the king of Egypt called the midwives and said to them, "Why have you done this, and let the male children live?" ¹⁹The midwives said to Pharaoh, "Because the Hebrew women are not like the Egyptian women, for they are vigorous and give birth before the midwife comes to them." ²⁰So God dealt well with the midwives. And the people multiplied and grew very strong. ²¹And because the midwives feared God, he gave them families. ²²Then Pharaoh commanded all his people, "Every son that is born to the Hebrews[a] you shall cast into the Nile, but you shall let every daughter live."

THE BIRTH OF MOSES

2 Now a man from the house of Levi went and took as his wife a Levite woman. ²The woman conceived and bore a son, and when she saw that he was a fine child, she hid him for three months. ³When she could hide him no longer, she took for him a basket made of bulrushes[b] and daubed it with bitumen and pitch. She put the child in it and placed it among the reeds by the river bank. ⁴And his sister stood at a distance to know what would be done to him. ⁵Now the daughter of Pharaoh came down to bathe at the river, while her young women walked beside the river. She saw the basket among the reeds and sent her servant woman, and she took it. ⁶When she opened it, she saw the child, and behold, the baby was crying. She took pity on him and said, "This is one of the Hebrews' children." ⁷Then his sister said to Pharaoh's daughter, "Shall I go and call you a nurse from the Hebrew women to nurse the child for you?" ⁸And Pharaoh's daughter said to her, "Go." So the girl went and called the child's mother. ⁹And Pharaoh's daughter said to her, "Take this child away and nurse him for me, and I will give you your wages." So the woman took the child and nursed him. ¹⁰When the child grew older, she brought him to Pharaoh's daughter, and he became her son. She named him Moses, "Because," she said, "I drew him out of the water."[c]

MOSES FLEES TO MIDIAN

¹¹One day, when Moses had grown up, he went out to his people and looked on their burdens, and he saw an Egyptian beating a

---

[a] Samaritan, Septuagint, Targum; Hebrew lacks *to the Hebrews*
[b] Hebrew *papyrus reeds* [c] *Moses* sounds like the Hebrew for *draw out*

Hebrew, one of his people.[a] ¹²He looked this way and that, and seeing no one, he struck down the Egyptian and hid him in the sand. ¹³When he went out the next day, behold, two Hebrews were struggling together. And he said to the man in the wrong, "Why do you strike your companion?" ¹⁴He answered, "Who made you a prince and a judge over us? Do you mean to kill me as you killed the Egyptian?" Then Moses was afraid, and thought, "Surely the thing is known." ¹⁵When Pharaoh heard of it, he sought to kill Moses. But Moses fled from Pharaoh and stayed in the land of Midian. And he sat down by a well.

¹⁶Now the priest of Midian had seven daughters, and they came and drew water and filled the troughs to water their father's flock. ¹⁷The shepherds came and drove them away, but Moses stood up and saved them, and watered their flock. ¹⁸When they came home to their father Reuel, he said, "How is it that you have come home so soon today?" ¹⁹They said, "An Egyptian delivered us out of the hand of the shepherds and even drew water for us and watered the flock." ²⁰He said to his daughters, "Then where is he? Why have you left the man? Call him, that he may eat bread." ²¹And Moses was content to dwell with the man, and he gave Moses his daughter Zipporah. ²²She gave birth to a son, and he called his name Gershom, for he said, "I have been a sojourner[b] in a foreign land."

GOD HEARS ISRAEL'S GROANING

²³During those many days the king of Egypt died, and the people of Israel groaned because of their slavery and cried out for help. Their cry for rescue from slavery came up to God. ²⁴And God heard their groaning, and God remembered his covenant with Abraham, with Isaac, and with Jacob. ²⁵God saw the people of Israel—and God knew.

THE BURNING BUSH

3 Now Moses was keeping the flock of his father-in-law, Jethro, the priest of Midian, and he led his flock to the west side of the wilderness and came to Horeb, the mountain of God. ²And the angel of the LORD appeared to him in a flame of fire out of the midst of a bush. He looked, and behold, the bush was burning, yet it was not consumed. ³And Moses said, "I will turn aside to see this great sight, why the bush is not burned." ⁴When the LORD saw that he turned aside to see, God called to him out of the bush, "Moses, Moses!" And he said, "Here I am." ⁵Then he said, "Do not come near; take your sandals off your feet, for the place on which you are standing is holy ground." ⁶And he said, "I am the God of your father, the God of Abraham, the God of Isaac, and the God of Jacob." And Moses hid his face, for he was afraid to look at God.

⁷Then the LORD said, "I have surely seen the affliction of my people who are in Egypt and have heard their cry because of their taskmasters. I know their sufferings, ⁸and I have come down to deliver them out of the hand of the Egyptians and to bring them up out of that land to a good and broad land, a land flowing with milk and honey, to the place of the Canaanites, the Hittites, the Amorites, the Perizzites, the Hivites, and the Jebusites. ⁹And now, behold, the cry of the people of Israel has come to me, and I have also seen the oppression with which the Egyptians oppress them. ¹⁰Come, I will send you to Pharaoh that you may bring my people, the children of Israel, out of Egypt." ¹¹But Moses said to God, "Who am I that I should go to Pharaoh and bring the children of Israel out of Egypt?" ¹²He said, "But I will be with you, and this shall be the sign for you, that I have sent you: when you have brought the people out of Egypt, you shall serve God on this mountain."

¹³Then Moses said to God, "If I come to the people of Israel and say to them, 'The God of your fathers has sent me to you', and they ask me, 'What is his name?' what shall I say to them?" ¹⁴God said to Moses, "I AM WHO I AM."[c] And he said, "Say this to the people of Israel: 'I AM has sent me to you.'" ¹⁵God also said to Moses, "Say this to the people of Israel: 'The LORD,[d] the God of your fathers, the God of Abraham, the God of Isaac, and the God of Jacob, has sent me to you.' This is my name for ever, and thus I am to be remembered throughout all generations. ¹⁶Go and gather the elders of Israel together and say to them, 'The LORD, the God of your fathers, the God of Abraham, of Isaac, and of Jacob, has appeared to me, saying, "I have observed you and what has been done to you in Egypt, ¹⁷and I promise that I will bring you up out of the affliction of Egypt to the land of the Canaanites, the Hittites, the Amorites, the Perizzites, the Hivites, and the Jebusites, a

---

[a] Hebrew *brothers* [b] *Gershom* sounds like the Hebrew for *sojourner* [c] Or *I AM WHAT I AM*, or *I WILL BE WHAT I WILL BE* [d] The word LORD, when spelled with capital letters, stands for the divine name, YHWH, which is here connected with the verb *hayah*, "to be" in verse 14

land flowing with milk and honey."' ¹⁸And they will listen to your voice, and you and the elders of Israel shall go to the king of Egypt and say to him, 'The LORD, the God of the Hebrews, has met with us; and now, please let us go a three days' journey into the wilderness, that we may sacrifice to the LORD our God.' ¹⁹But I know that the king of Egypt will not let you go unless compelled by a mighty hand.[a] ²⁰So I will stretch out my hand and strike Egypt with all the wonders that I will do in it; after that he will let you go. ²¹And I will give this people favour in the sight of the Egyptians; and when you go, you shall not go empty, ²²but each woman shall ask of her neighbour, and any woman who lives in her house, for silver and gold jewellery, and for clothing. You shall put them on your sons and on your daughters. So you shall plunder the Egyptians."

MOSES GIVEN POWERFUL SIGNS

4 Then Moses answered, "But behold, they will not believe me or listen to my voice, for they will say, 'The LORD did not appear to you.'" ²The LORD said to him, "What is that in your hand?" He said, "A staff." ³And he said, "Throw it on the ground." So he threw it on the ground, and it became a serpent, and Moses ran from it. ⁴But the LORD said to Moses, "Put out your hand and catch it by the tail"—so he put out his hand and caught it, and it became a staff in his hand— ⁵"that they may believe that the LORD, the God of their fathers, the God of Abraham, the God of Isaac, and the God of Jacob, has appeared to you." ⁶Again, the LORD said to him, "Put your hand inside your cloak."[b] And he put his hand inside his cloak, and when he took it out, behold, his hand was leprous[c] like snow. ⁷Then God said, "Put your hand back inside your cloak." So he put his hand back inside his cloak, and when he took it out, behold, it was restored like the rest of his flesh. ⁸"If they will not believe you," God said, "or listen to the first sign, they may believe the latter sign. ⁹If they will not believe even these two signs or listen to your voice, you shall take some water from the Nile and pour it on the dry ground, and the water that you shall take from the Nile will become blood on the dry ground."

¹⁰But Moses said to the LORD, "Oh, my Lord, I am not eloquent, either in the past or since you have spoken to your servant, but I am slow of speech and of tongue." ¹¹Then the LORD said to him, "Who has made man's mouth? Who makes him mute, or deaf, or seeing, or blind? Is it not I, the LORD? ¹²Now therefore go, and I will be with your mouth and teach you what you shall speak." ¹³But he said, "Oh, my Lord, please send someone else." ¹⁴Then the anger of the LORD was kindled against Moses and he said, "Is there not Aaron, your brother, the Levite? I know that he can speak well. Behold, he is coming out to meet you, and when he sees you, he will be glad in his heart. ¹⁵You shall speak to him and put the words in his mouth, and I will be with your mouth and with his mouth and will teach you both what to do. ¹⁶He shall speak for you to the people, and he shall be your mouth, and you shall be as God to him. ¹⁷And take in your hand this staff, with which you shall do the signs."

MOSES RETURNS TO EGYPT

¹⁸Moses went back to Jethro his father-in-law and said to him, "Please let me go back to my brothers in Egypt to see whether they are still alive." And Jethro said to Moses, "Go in peace." ¹⁹And the LORD said to Moses in Midian, "Go back to Egypt, for all the men who were seeking your life are dead." ²⁰So Moses took his wife and his sons and put them on a donkey, and went back to the land of Egypt. And Moses took the staff of God in his hand.

²¹And the LORD said to Moses, "When you go back to Egypt, see that you do before Pharaoh all the miracles that I have put in your power. But I will harden his heart, so that he will not let the people go. ²²Then you shall say to Pharaoh, 'Thus says the LORD, Israel is my firstborn son, ²³and I say to you, "Let my son go that he may serve me." If you refuse to let him go, behold, I will kill your firstborn son.'"

²⁴At a lodging place on the way the LORD met him and sought to put him to death. ²⁵Then Zipporah took a flint and cut off her son's foreskin and touched Moses'[d] feet with it and said, "Surely you are a bridegroom of blood to me!" ²⁶So he let him alone. It was then that she said, "A bridegroom of blood", because of the circumcision.

²⁷The LORD said to Aaron, "Go into the wilderness to meet Moses." So he went and met him at the mountain of God and kissed him. ²⁸And Moses told Aaron all the words of the LORD with which he had sent him to speak,

---

[a]Septuagint, Vulgate; Hebrew *go, not by a mighty hand*   [b]Hebrew *into your bosom*; also verse 7   [c]*Leprosy* was a term for several skin diseases; see Leviticus 13   [d]Hebrew *his*

and all the signs that he had commanded him to do. ²⁹Then Moses and Aaron went and gathered together all the elders of the people of Israel. ³⁰Aaron spoke all the words that the Lord had spoken to Moses and did the signs in the sight of the people. ³¹And the people believed; and when they heard that the Lord had visited the people of Israel and that he had seen their affliction, they bowed their heads and worshipped.

MAKING BRICKS WITHOUT STRAW

5 Afterwards Moses and Aaron went and said to Pharaoh, "Thus says the Lord, the God of Israel, 'Let my people go, that they may hold a feast to me in the wilderness.'" ²But Pharaoh said, "Who is the Lord, that I should obey his voice and let Israel go? I do not know the Lord, and moreover, I will not let Israel go." ³Then they said, "The God of the Hebrews has met with us. Please let us go a three days' journey into the wilderness that we may sacrifice to the Lord our God, lest he fall upon us with pestilence or with the sword." ⁴But the king of Egypt said to them, "Moses and Aaron, why do you take the people away from their work? Get back to your burdens." ⁵And Pharaoh said, "Behold, the people of the land are now many,ᵃ and you make them rest from their burdens!" ⁶The same day Pharaoh commanded the taskmasters of the people and their foremen, ⁷"You shall no longer give the people straw to make bricks, as in the past; let them go and gather straw for themselves. ⁸But the number of bricks that they made in the past you shall impose on them, you shall by no means reduce it, for they are idle. Therefore they cry, 'Let us go and offer sacrifice to our God.' ⁹Let heavier work be laid on the men that they may labour at it and pay no regard to lying words."

¹⁰So the taskmasters and the foremen of the people went out and said to the people, "Thus says Pharaoh, 'I will not give you straw. ¹¹Go and get your straw yourselves wherever you can find it, but your work will not be reduced in the least.'" ¹²So the people were scattered throughout all the land of Egypt to gather stubble for straw. ¹³The taskmasters were urgent, saying, "Complete your work, your daily task each day, as when there was straw." ¹⁴And the foremen of the people of Israel, whom Pharaoh's taskmasters had set over them, were beaten and were asked, "Why have you not done all your task of making bricks today and yesterday, as in the past?"

¹⁵Then the foremen of the people of Israel came and cried to Pharaoh, "Why do you treat your servants like this? ¹⁶No straw is given to your servants, yet they say to us, 'Make bricks!' And behold, your servants are beaten; but the fault is in your own people." ¹⁷But he said, "You are idle, you are idle; that is why you say, 'Let us go and sacrifice to the Lord.' ¹⁸Go now and work. No straw will be given you, but you must still deliver the same number of bricks." ¹⁹The foremen of the people of Israel saw that they were in trouble when they said, "You shall by no means reduce your number of bricks, your daily task each day." ²⁰They met Moses and Aaron, who were waiting for them, as they came out from Pharaoh; ²¹and they said to them, "The Lord look on you and judge, because you have made us stink in the sight of Pharaoh and his servants, and have put a sword in their hand to kill us."

²²Then Moses turned to the Lord and said, "O Lord, why have you done evil to this people? Why did you ever send me? ²³For since I came to Pharaoh to speak in your name, he has done evil to this people, and you have not delivered your people at all."

GOD PROMISES DELIVERANCE

6 But the Lord said to Moses, "Now you shall see what I will do to Pharaoh; for with a strong hand he will send them out, and with a strong hand he will drive them out of his land."

²God spoke to Moses and said to him, "I am the Lord. ³I appeared to Abraham, to Isaac, and to Jacob, as God Almighty,ᵇ but by my name the Lord I did not make myself known to them. ⁴I also established my covenant with them to give them the land of Canaan, the land in which they lived as sojourners. ⁵Moreover, I have heard the groaning of the people of Israel whom the Egyptians hold as slaves, and I have remembered my covenant. ⁶Say therefore to the people of Israel, 'I am the Lord, and I will bring you out from under the burdens of the Egyptians, and I will deliver you from slavery to them, and I will redeem you with an outstretched arm and with great acts of judgement. ⁷I will take you to be my people, and I will be your God, and you shall know that I am the Lord your God, who has brought you out from under the burdens of the Egyptians. ⁸I will bring you into the land

---
ᵃSamaritan *they are now more numerous than the people of the land*
ᵇHebrew *El Shaddai*

that I swore to give to Abraham, to Isaac, and to Jacob. I will give it to you for a possession. I am the LORD.'" ⁹Moses spoke thus to the people of Israel, but they did not listen to Moses, because of their broken spirit and harsh slavery.

¹⁰So the LORD said to Moses, ¹¹"Go in, tell Pharaoh king of Egypt to let the people of Israel go out of his land." ¹²But Moses said to the LORD, "Behold, the people of Israel have not listened to me. How then shall Pharaoh listen to me, for I am of uncircumcised lips?" ¹³But the LORD spoke to Moses and Aaron and gave them a charge about the people of Israel and about Pharaoh king of Egypt: to bring the people of Israel out of the land of Egypt.

THE GENEALOGY OF MOSES AND AARON

¹⁴These are the heads of their fathers' houses: the sons of Reuben, the firstborn of Israel: Hanoch, Pallu, Hezron, and Carmi; these are the clans of Reuben. ¹⁵The sons of Simeon: Jemuel, Jamin, Ohad, Jachin, Zohar, and Shaul, the son of a Canaanite woman; these are the clans of Simeon. ¹⁶These are the names of the sons of Levi according to their generations: Gershon, Kohath, and Merari, the years of the life of Levi being 137 years. ¹⁷The sons of Gershon: Libni and Shimei, by their clans. ¹⁸The sons of Kohath: Amram, Izhar, Hebron, and Uzziel, the years of the life of Kohath being 133 years. ¹⁹The sons of Merari: Mahli and Mushi. These are the clans of the Levites according to their generations. ²⁰Amram took as his wife Jochebed his father's sister, and she bore him Aaron and Moses, the years of the life of Amram being 137 years. ²¹The sons of Izhar: Korah, Nepheg, and Zichri. ²²The sons of Uzziel: Mishael, Elzaphan, and Sithri. ²³Aaron took as his wife Elisheba, the daughter of Amminadab and the sister of Nahshon, and she bore him Nadab, Abihu, Eleazar, and Ithamar. ²⁴The sons of Korah: Assir, Elkanah, and Abiasaph; these are the clans of the Korahites. ²⁵Eleazar, Aaron's son, took as his wife one of the daughters of Putiel, and she bore him Phinehas. These are the heads of the fathers' houses of the Levites by their clans.

²⁶These are the Aaron and Moses to whom the LORD said: "Bring out the people of Israel from the land of Egypt by their hosts." ²⁷It was they who spoke to Pharaoh king of Egypt about bringing out the people of Israel from Egypt, this Moses and this Aaron.

²⁸On the day when the LORD spoke to Moses in the land of Egypt, ²⁹the LORD said to Moses, "I am the LORD; tell Pharaoh king of Egypt all that I say to you." ³⁰But Moses said to the LORD, "Behold, I am of uncircumcised lips. How will Pharaoh listen to me?"

MOSES AND AARON BEFORE PHARAOH

7 And the LORD said to Moses, "See, I have made you like God to Pharaoh, and your brother Aaron shall be your prophet. ²You shall speak all that I command you, and your brother Aaron shall tell Pharaoh to let the people of Israel go out of his land. ³But I will harden Pharaoh's heart, and though I multiply my signs and wonders in the land of Egypt, ⁴Pharaoh will not listen to you. Then I will lay my hand on Egypt and bring my hosts, my people the children of Israel, out of the land of Egypt by great acts of judgement. ⁵The Egyptians shall know that I am the LORD, when I stretch out my hand against Egypt and bring out the people of Israel from among them." ⁶Moses and Aaron did so; they did just as the LORD commanded them. ⁷Now Moses was eighty years old, and Aaron eighty-three years old, when they spoke to Pharaoh.

⁸Then the LORD said to Moses and Aaron, ⁹"When Pharaoh says to you, 'Prove yourselves by working a miracle', then you shall say to Aaron, 'Take your staff and cast it down before Pharaoh, that it may become a serpent.'" ¹⁰So Moses and Aaron went to Pharaoh and did just as the LORD commanded. Aaron cast down his staff before Pharaoh and his servants, and it became a serpent. ¹¹Then Pharaoh summoned the wise men and the sorcerers, and they, the magicians of Egypt, also did the same by their secret arts. ¹²For each man cast down his staff, and they became serpents. But Aaron's staff swallowed up their staffs. ¹³Still Pharaoh's heart was hardened, and he would not listen to them, as the LORD had said.

THE FIRST PLAGUE: WATER TURNED TO BLOOD

¹⁴Then the LORD said to Moses, "Pharaoh's heart is hardened; he refuses to let the people go. ¹⁵Go to Pharaoh in the morning, as he is going out to the water. Stand on the bank of the Nile to meet him, and take in your hand the staff that turned into a serpent. ¹⁶And you shall say to him, 'The LORD, the God of the Hebrews, sent me to you, saying, "Let my people go, that they may serve me in the

wilderness.' But so far, you have not obeyed. ¹⁷Thus says the LORD, "By this you shall know that I am the LORD: behold, with the staff that is in my hand I will strike the water that is in the Nile, and it shall turn into blood. ¹⁸The fish in the Nile shall die, and the Nile will stink, and the Egyptians will grow weary of drinking water from the Nile.'" ¹⁹And the LORD said to Moses, "Say to Aaron, 'Take your staff and stretch out your hand over the waters of Egypt, over their rivers, their canals, and their ponds, and all their pools of water, so that they may become blood, and there shall be blood throughout all the land of Egypt, even in vessels of wood and in vessels of stone.'"

²⁰Moses and Aaron did as the LORD commanded. In the sight of Pharaoh and in the sight of his servants he lifted up the staff and struck the water in the Nile, and all the water in the Nile turned into blood. ²¹And the fish in the Nile died, and the Nile stank, so that the Egyptians could not drink water from the Nile. There was blood throughout all the land of Egypt. ²²But the magicians of Egypt did the same by their secret arts. So Pharaoh's heart remained hardened, and he would not listen to them, as the LORD had said. ²³Pharaoh turned and went into his house, and he did not take even this to heart. ²⁴And all the Egyptians dug along the Nile for water to drink, for they could not drink the water of the Nile.

²⁵Seven full days passed after the LORD had struck the Nile.

THE SECOND PLAGUE: FROGS

8 ᵃ Then the LORD said to Moses, "Go in to Pharaoh and say to him, 'Thus says the LORD, "Let my people go, that they may serve me. ²But if you refuse to let them go, behold, I will plague all your country with frogs. ³The Nile shall swarm with frogs that shall come up into your house and into your bedroom and on your bed and into the houses of your servants and your people,ᵇ and into your ovens and your kneading bowls. ⁴The frogs shall come up on you and on your people and on all your servants."'" ⁵ᶜ And the LORD said to Moses, "Say to Aaron, 'Stretch out your hand with your staff over the rivers, over the canals and over the pools, and make frogs come up on the land of Egypt!'" ⁶So Aaron stretched out his hand over the waters of Egypt, and the frogs came up and covered the land of Egypt. ⁷But the magicians did the same by their secret arts and made frogs come up on the land of Egypt.

⁸Then Pharaoh called Moses and Aaron and said, "Plead with the LORD to take away the frogs from me and from my people, and I will let the people go to sacrifice to the LORD." ⁹Moses said to Pharaoh, "Be pleased to command me when I am to plead for you and for your servants and for your people, that the frogs be cut off from you and your houses and be left only in the Nile." ¹⁰And he said, "Tomorrow." Moses said, "Be it as you say, so that you may know that there is no one like the LORD our God. ¹¹The frogs shall go away from you and your houses and your servants and your people. They shall be left only in the Nile." ¹²So Moses and Aaron went out from Pharaoh, and Moses cried to the LORD about the frogs, as he had agreed with Pharaoh.ᵈ ¹³And the LORD did according to the word of Moses. The frogs died out in the houses, the courtyards, and the fields. ¹⁴And they gathered them together in heaps, and the land stank. ¹⁵But when Pharaoh saw that there was a respite, he hardened his heart and would not listen to them, as the LORD had said.

THE THIRD PLAGUE: GNATS

¹⁶Then the LORD said to Moses, "Say to Aaron, 'Stretch out your staff and strike the dust of the earth, so that it may become gnats in all the land of Egypt.'" ¹⁷And they did so. Aaron stretched out his hand with his staff and struck the dust of the earth, and there were gnats on man and beast. All the dust of the earth became gnats in all the land of Egypt. ¹⁸The magicians tried by their secret arts to produce gnats, but they could not. So there were gnats on man and beast. ¹⁹Then the magicians said to Pharaoh, "This is the finger of God." But Pharaoh's heart was hardened, and he would not listen to them, as the LORD had said.

THE FOURTH PLAGUE: FLIES

²⁰Then the LORD said to Moses, "Rise up early in the morning and present yourself to Pharaoh, as he goes out to the water, and say to him, 'Thus says the LORD, "Let my people go, that they may serve me. ²¹Or else, if you will not let my people go, behold, I will send swarms of flies on you and your servants and your people, and into your houses. And the

---
ᵃCh 7:26 in Hebrew ᵇOr *among your people* ᶜCh 8:1 in Hebrew
ᵈOr *which he had brought upon Pharaoh*

houses of the Egyptians shall be filled with swarms of flies, and also the ground on which they stand. ²²But on that day I will set apart the land of Goshen, where my people dwell, so that no swarms of flies shall be there, that you may know that I am the Lord in the midst of the earth.*a* ²³Thus I will put a division*b* between my people and your people. Tomorrow this sign shall happen."'" ²⁴And the Lord did so. There came great swarms of flies into the house of Pharaoh and into his servants' houses. Throughout all the land of Egypt the land was ruined by the swarms of flies.

²⁵Then Pharaoh called Moses and Aaron and said, "Go, sacrifice to your God within the land." ²⁶But Moses said, "It would not be right to do so, for the offerings we shall sacrifice to the Lord our God are an abomination to the Egyptians. If we sacrifice offerings abominable to the Egyptians before their eyes, will they not stone us? ²⁷We must go three days' journey into the wilderness and sacrifice to the Lord our God as he tells us." ²⁸So Pharaoh said, "I will let you go to sacrifice to the Lord your God in the wilderness; only you must not go very far away. Plead for me." ²⁹Then Moses said, "Behold, I am going out from you and I will plead with the Lord that the swarms of flies may depart from Pharaoh, from his servants, and from his people, tomorrow. Only let not Pharaoh cheat again by not letting the people go to sacrifice to the Lord." ³⁰So Moses went out from Pharaoh and prayed to the Lord. ³¹And the Lord did as Moses asked, and removed the swarms of flies from Pharaoh, from his servants, and from his people; not one remained. ³²But Pharaoh hardened his heart this time also, and did not let the people go.

THE FIFTH PLAGUE: EGYPTIAN LIVESTOCK DIE

9 Then the Lord said to Moses, "Go in to Pharaoh and say to him, 'Thus says the Lord, the God of the Hebrews, "Let my people go, that they may serve me. ²For if you refuse to let them go and still hold them, ³behold, the hand of the Lord will fall with a very severe plague upon your livestock that are in the field, the horses, the donkeys, the camels, the herds, and the flocks. ⁴But the Lord will make a distinction between the livestock of Israel and the livestock of Egypt, so that nothing of all that belongs to the people of Israel shall die."'" ⁵And the Lord set a time, saying, "Tomorrow the Lord will do this thing in the land." ⁶And the next day the Lord did this thing. All the livestock of the Egyptians died, but not one of the livestock of the people of Israel died. ⁷And Pharaoh sent, and behold, not one of the livestock of Israel was dead. But the heart of Pharaoh was hardened, and he did not let the people go.

THE SIXTH PLAGUE: BOILS

⁸And the Lord said to Moses and Aaron, "Take handfuls of soot from the kiln, and let Moses throw them in the air in the sight of Pharaoh. ⁹It shall become fine dust over all the land of Egypt, and become boils breaking out in sores on man and beast throughout all the land of Egypt." ¹⁰So they took soot from the kiln and stood before Pharaoh. And Moses threw it in the air, and it became boils breaking out in sores on man and beast. ¹¹And the magicians could not stand before Moses because of the boils, for the boils came upon the magicians and upon all the Egyptians. ¹²But the Lord hardened the heart of Pharaoh, and he did not listen to them, as the Lord had spoken to Moses.

THE SEVENTH PLAGUE: HAIL

¹³Then the Lord said to Moses, "Rise up early in the morning and present yourself before Pharaoh and say to him, 'Thus says the Lord, the God of the Hebrews, "Let my people go, that they may serve me. ¹⁴For this time I will send all my plagues on you yourself,*c* and on your servants and your people, so that you may know that there is none like me in all the earth. ¹⁵For by now I could have put out my hand and struck you and your people with pestilence, and you would have been cut off from the earth. ¹⁶But for this purpose I have raised you up, to show you my power, so that my name may be proclaimed in all the earth. ¹⁷You are still exalting yourself against my people and will not let them go. ¹⁸Behold, about this time tomorrow I will cause very heavy hail to fall, such as never has been in Egypt from the day it was founded until now. ¹⁹Now therefore send, get your livestock and all that you have in the field into safe shelter, for every man and beast that is in the field and is not brought home will die when the hail falls on them."'" ²⁰Then whoever feared the word of the Lord among the servants of Pharaoh hurried his slaves and his livestock into the houses, ²¹but whoever did not pay

---

*a*Or *that I the Lord am in the land*   *b*Septuagint, Vulgate; Hebrew *set redemption*   *c*Hebrew *on your heart*

attention to the word of the LORD left his slaves and his livestock in the field.

²²Then the LORD said to Moses, "Stretch out your hand towards heaven, so that there may be hail in all the land of Egypt, on man and beast and every plant of the field, in the land of Egypt." ²³Then Moses stretched out his staff towards heaven, and the LORD sent thunder and hail, and fire ran down to the earth. And the LORD rained hail upon the land of Egypt. ²⁴There was hail and fire flashing continually in the midst of the hail, very heavy hail, such as had never been in all the land of Egypt since it became a nation. ²⁵The hail struck down everything that was in the field in all the land of Egypt, both man and beast. And the hail struck down every plant of the field and broke every tree of the field. ²⁶Only in the land of Goshen, where the people of Israel were, was there no hail.

²⁷Then Pharaoh sent and called Moses and Aaron and said to them, "This time I have sinned; the LORD is in the right, and I and my people are in the wrong. ²⁸Plead with the LORD, for there has been enough of God's thunder and hail. I will let you go, and you shall stay no longer." ²⁹Moses said to him, "As soon as I have gone out of the city, I will stretch out my hands to the LORD. The thunder will cease, and there will be no more hail, so that you may know that the earth is the LORD's. ³⁰But as for you and your servants, I know that you do not yet fear the LORD God." ³¹(The flax and the barley were struck down, for the barley was in the ear and the flax was in bud. ³²But the wheat and the emmer*a* were not struck down, for they are late in coming up.) ³³So Moses went out of the city from Pharaoh and stretched out his hands to the LORD, and the thunder and the hail ceased, and the rain no longer poured upon the earth. ³⁴But when Pharaoh saw that the rain and the hail and the thunder had ceased, he sinned yet again and hardened his heart, he and his servants. ³⁵So the heart of Pharaoh was hardened, and he did not let the people of Israel go, just as the LORD had spoken through Moses.

THE EIGHTH PLAGUE: LOCUSTS

10 Then the LORD said to Moses, "Go in to Pharaoh, for I have hardened his heart and the heart of his servants, that I may show these signs of mine among them, ²and that you may tell in the hearing of your son and of your grandson how I have dealt harshly with the Egyptians and what signs I have done among them, that you may know that I am the LORD."

³So Moses and Aaron went in to Pharaoh and said to him, "Thus says the LORD, the God of the Hebrews, 'How long will you refuse to humble yourself before me? Let my people go, that they may serve me. ⁴For if you refuse to let my people go, behold, tomorrow I will bring locusts into your country, ⁵and they shall cover the face of the land, so that no one can see the land. And they shall eat what is left to you after the hail, and they shall eat every tree of yours that grows in the field, ⁶and they shall fill your houses and the houses of all your servants and of all the Egyptians, as neither your fathers nor your grandfathers have seen, from the day they came on earth to this day.'" Then he turned and went out from Pharaoh.

⁷Then Pharaoh's servants said to him, "How long shall this man be a snare to us? Let the men go, that they may serve the LORD their God. Do you not yet understand that Egypt is ruined?" ⁸So Moses and Aaron were brought back to Pharaoh. And he said to them, "Go, serve the LORD your God. But which ones are to go?" ⁹Moses said, "We will go with our young and our old. We will go with our sons and daughters and with our flocks and herds, for we must hold a feast to the LORD." ¹⁰But he said to them, "The LORD be with you, if ever I let you and your little ones go! Look, you have some evil purpose in mind.*b* ¹¹No! Go, the men among you, and serve the LORD, for that is what you are asking." And they were driven out from Pharaoh's presence.

¹²Then the LORD said to Moses, "Stretch out your hand over the land of Egypt for the locusts, so that they may come upon the land of Egypt and eat every plant in the land, all that the hail has left." ¹³So Moses stretched out his staff over the land of Egypt, and the LORD brought an east wind upon the land all that day and all that night. When it was morning, the east wind had brought the locusts. ¹⁴The locusts came up over all the land of Egypt and settled on the whole country of Egypt, such a dense swarm of locusts as had never been before, nor ever will be again. ¹⁵They covered the face of the whole land, so that the land was darkened, and they ate all the plants in the land and all the fruit of the trees that the hail had left. Not a green thing remained, neither tree nor plant of the field, through all the land

---

a A type of wheat *b* Hebrew *before your face*

of Egypt. ¹⁶Then Pharaoh hastily called Moses and Aaron and said, "I have sinned against the LORD your God, and against you. ¹⁷Now therefore, forgive my sin, please, only this once, and plead with the LORD your God only to remove this death from me." ¹⁸So he went out from Pharaoh and pleaded with the LORD. ¹⁹And the LORD turned the wind into a very strong west wind, which lifted the locusts and drove them into the Red Sea. Not a single locust was left in all the country of Egypt. ²⁰But the LORD hardened Pharaoh's heart, and he did not let the people of Israel go.

THE NINTH PLAGUE: DARKNESS

²¹Then the LORD said to Moses, "Stretch out your hand towards heaven, that there may be darkness over the land of Egypt, a darkness to be felt." ²²So Moses stretched out his hand towards heaven, and there was pitch darkness in all the land of Egypt for three days. ²³They did not see one another, nor did anyone rise from his place for three days, but all the people of Israel had light where they lived. ²⁴Then Pharaoh called Moses and said, "Go, serve the LORD; your little ones also may go with you; only let your flocks and your herds remain behind." ²⁵But Moses said, "You must also let us have sacrifices and burnt offerings, that we may sacrifice to the LORD our God. ²⁶Our livestock also must go with us; not a hoof shall be left behind, for we must take of them to serve the LORD our God, and we do not know with what we must serve the LORD until we arrive there." ²⁷But the LORD hardened Pharaoh's heart, and he would not let them go. ²⁸Then Pharaoh said to him, "Get away from me; take care never to see my face again, for on the day you see my face you shall die." ²⁹Moses said, "As you say! I will not see your face again."

A FINAL PLAGUE THREATENED

11 The LORD said to Moses, "Yet one plague more I will bring upon Pharaoh and upon Egypt. Afterwards he will let you go from here. When he lets you go, he will drive you away completely. ²Speak now in the hearing of the people, that they ask, every man of his neighbour and every woman of her neighbour, for silver and gold jewellery." ³And the LORD gave the people favour in the sight of the Egyptians. Moreover, the man Moses was very great in the land of Egypt, in the sight of Pharaoh's servants and in the sight of the people.

⁴So Moses said, "Thus says the LORD: 'About midnight I will go out in the midst of Egypt, ⁵and every firstborn in the land of Egypt shall die, from the firstborn of Pharaoh who sits on his throne, even to the firstborn of the slave girl who is behind the handmill, and all the firstborn of the cattle. ⁶There shall be a great cry throughout all the land of Egypt, such as there has never been, nor ever will be again. ⁷But not a dog shall growl against any of the people of Israel, either man or beast, that you may know that the LORD makes a distinction between Egypt and Israel.' ⁸And all these your servants shall come down to me and bow down to me, saying, 'Get out, you and all the people who follow you.' And after that I will go out." And he went out from Pharaoh in hot anger. ⁹Then the LORD said to Moses, "Pharaoh will not listen to you, that my wonders may be multiplied in the land of Egypt."

¹⁰Moses and Aaron did all these wonders before Pharaoh, and the LORD hardened Pharaoh's heart, and he did not let the people of Israel go out of his land.

THE PASSOVER

12 The LORD said to Moses and Aaron in the land of Egypt, ²"This month shall be for you the beginning of months. It shall be the first month of the year for you. ³Tell all the congregation of Israel that on the tenth day of this month every man shall take a lamb according to their fathers' houses, a lamb for a household. ⁴And if the household is too small for a lamb, then he and his nearest neighbour shall take according to the number of persons; according to what each can eat you shall make your count for the lamb. ⁵Your lamb shall be without blemish, a male a year old. You may take it from the sheep or from the goats, ⁶and you shall keep it until the fourteenth day of this month, when the whole assembly of the congregation of Israel shall kill their lambs at twilight.ᵃ

⁷"Then they shall take some of the blood and put it on the two doorposts and the lintel of the houses in which they eat it. ⁸They shall eat the flesh that night, roasted on the fire; with unleavened bread and bitter herbs they shall eat it. ⁹Do not eat any of it raw or boiled in water, but roasted, its head with its legs and its inner parts. ¹⁰And you shall let none of it remain until the morning; anything that

---
ᵃHebrew *between the two evenings*

remains until the morning you shall burn. ¹¹In this manner you shall eat it: with your belt fastened, your sandals on your feet, and your staff in your hand. And you shall eat it in haste. It is the LORD's Passover. ¹²For I will pass through the land of Egypt that night, and I will strike all the firstborn in the land of Egypt, both man and beast; and on all the gods of Egypt I will execute judgements: I am the LORD. ¹³The blood shall be a sign for you, on the houses where you are. And when I see the blood, I will pass over you, and no plague will befall you to destroy you, when I strike the land of Egypt.

¹⁴"This day shall be for you a memorial day, and you shall keep it as a feast to the LORD; throughout your generations, as a statute for ever, you shall keep it as a feast. ¹⁵For seven days you shall eat unleavened bread. On the first day you shall remove leaven out of your houses, for if anyone eats what is leavened, from the first day until the seventh day, that person shall be cut off from Israel. ¹⁶On the first day you shall hold a holy assembly, and on the seventh day a holy assembly. No work shall be done on those days. But what everyone needs to eat, that alone may be prepared by you. ¹⁷And you shall observe the Feast of Unleavened Bread, for on this very day I brought your hosts out of the land of Egypt. Therefore you shall observe this day, throughout your generations, as a statute for ever. ¹⁸In the first month, from the fourteenth day of the month at evening, you shall eat unleavened bread until the twenty-first day of the month at evening. ¹⁹For seven days no leaven is to be found in your houses. If anyone eats what is leavened, that person will be cut off from the congregation of Israel, whether he is a sojourner or a native of the land. ²⁰You shall eat nothing leavened; in all your dwelling places you shall eat unleavened bread."

²¹Then Moses called all the elders of Israel and said to them, "Go and select lambs for yourselves according to your clans, and kill the Passover lamb. ²²Take a bunch of hyssop and dip it in the blood that is in the basin, and touch the lintel and the two doorposts with the blood that is in the basin. None of you shall go out of the door of his house until the morning. ²³For the LORD will pass through to strike the Egyptians, and when he sees the blood on the lintel and on the two doorposts, the LORD will pass over the door and will not allow the destroyer to enter your houses to strike you. ²⁴You shall observe this rite as a statute for you and for your sons for ever. ²⁵And when you come to the land that the LORD will give you, as he has promised, you shall keep this service. ²⁶And when your children say to you, 'What do you mean by this service?' ²⁷you shall say, 'It is the sacrifice of the LORD's Passover, for he passed over the houses of the people of Israel in Egypt, when he struck the Egyptians but spared our houses.'" And the people bowed their heads and worshipped.

²⁸Then the people of Israel went and did so; as the LORD had commanded Moses and Aaron, so they did.

THE TENTH PLAGUE: DEATH OF THE FIRSTBORN

²⁹At midnight the LORD struck down all the firstborn in the land of Egypt, from the firstborn of Pharaoh who sat on his throne to the firstborn of the captive who was in the dungeon, and all the firstborn of the livestock. ³⁰And Pharaoh rose up in the night, he and all his servants and all the Egyptians. And there was a great cry in Egypt, for there was not a house where someone was not dead. ³¹Then he summoned Moses and Aaron by night and said, "Up, go out from among my people, both you and the people of Israel; and go, serve the LORD, as you have said. ³²Take your flocks and your herds, as you have said, and be gone, and bless me also!"

THE EXODUS

³³The Egyptians were urgent with the people to send them out of the land in haste. For they said, "We shall all be dead." ³⁴So the people took their dough before it was leavened, their kneading bowls being bound up in their cloaks on their shoulders. ³⁵The people of Israel had also done as Moses told them, for they had asked the Egyptians for silver and gold jewellery and for clothing. ³⁶And the LORD had given the people favour in the sight of the Egyptians, so that they let them have what they asked. Thus they plundered the Egyptians.

³⁷And the people of Israel journeyed from Rameses to Succoth, about six hundred thousand men on foot, besides women and children. ³⁸A mixed multitude also went up with them, and very much livestock, both flocks and herds. ³⁹And they baked unleavened cakes of the dough that they had brought out of Egypt, for it was not leavened, because they were thrust out of Egypt and

could not wait, nor had they prepared any provisions for themselves. ⁴⁰The time that the people of Israel lived in Egypt was 430 years. ⁴¹At the end of 430 years, on that very day, all the hosts of the LORD went out from the land of Egypt. ⁴²It was a night of watching by the LORD, to bring them out of the land of Egypt; so this same night is a night of watching kept to the LORD by all the people of Israel throughout their generations.

INSTITUTION OF THE PASSOVER

⁴³And the LORD said to Moses and Aaron, "This is the statute of the Passover: no foreigner shall eat of it, ⁴⁴but every slave[a] that is bought for money may eat of it after you have circumcised him. ⁴⁵No foreigner or hired worker may eat of it. ⁴⁶It shall be eaten in one house; you shall not take any of the flesh outside the house, and you shall not break any of its bones. ⁴⁷All the congregation of Israel shall keep it. ⁴⁸If a stranger shall sojourn with you and would keep the Passover to the LORD, let all his males be circumcised. Then he may come near and keep it; he shall be as a native of the land. But no uncircumcised person shall eat of it. ⁴⁹There shall be one law for the native and for the stranger who sojourns among you."

⁵⁰All the people of Israel did just as the LORD commanded Moses and Aaron. ⁵¹And on that very day the LORD brought the people of Israel out of the land of Egypt by their hosts.

CONSECRATION OF THE FIRSTBORN

13 The LORD said to Moses, ²"Consecrate to me all the firstborn. Whatever is the first to open the womb among the people of Israel, both of man and of beast, is mine."

THE FEAST OF UNLEAVENED BREAD

³Then Moses said to the people, "Remember this day in which you came out from Egypt, out of the house of slavery, for by a strong hand the LORD brought you out from this place. No leavened bread shall be eaten. ⁴Today, in the month of Abib, you are going out. ⁵And when the LORD brings you into the land of the Canaanites, the Hittites, the Amorites, the Hivites, and the Jebusites, which he swore to your fathers to give you, a land flowing with milk and honey, you shall keep this service in this month. ⁶For seven days you shall eat unleavened bread, and on the seventh day there shall be a feast to the LORD. ⁷Unleavened bread shall be eaten for seven days; no leavened bread shall be seen with you, and no leaven shall be seen with you in all your territory. ⁸You shall tell your son on that day, 'It is because of what the LORD did for me when I came out of Egypt.' ⁹And it shall be to you as a sign on your hand and as a memorial between your eyes, that the law of the LORD may be in your mouth. For with a strong hand the LORD has brought you out of Egypt. ¹⁰You shall therefore keep this statute at its appointed time from year to year.

¹¹"When the LORD brings you into the land of the Canaanites, as he swore to you and your fathers, and shall give it to you, ¹²you shall set apart to the LORD all that first opens the womb. All the firstborn of your animals that are males shall be the LORD's. ¹³Every firstborn of a donkey you shall redeem with a lamb, or if you will not redeem it you shall break its neck. Every firstborn of man among your sons you shall redeem. ¹⁴And when in time to come your son asks you, 'What does this mean?' you shall say to him, 'By a strong hand the LORD brought us out of Egypt, from the house of slavery. ¹⁵For when Pharaoh stubbornly refused to let us go, the LORD killed all the firstborn in the land of Egypt, both the firstborn of man and the firstborn of animals. Therefore I sacrifice to the LORD all the males that first open the womb, but all the firstborn of my sons I redeem.' ¹⁶It shall be as a mark on your hand or frontlets between your eyes, for by a strong hand the LORD brought us out of Egypt."

PILLARS OF CLOUD AND FIRE

¹⁷When Pharaoh let the people go, God did not lead them by way of the land of the Philistines, although that was near. For God said, "Lest the people change their minds when they see war and return to Egypt." ¹⁸But God led the people round by the way of the wilderness towards the Red Sea. And the people of Israel went up out of the land of Egypt equipped for battle. ¹⁹Moses took the bones of Joseph with him, for Joseph[b] had made the sons of Israel solemnly swear, saying, "God will surely visit you, and you shall carry up my bones with you from here." ²⁰And they moved on from Succoth and encamped at Etham, on the edge of the wilderness. ²¹And the LORD went before them by day in a pillar of cloud to lead them

---

[a] Or *servant*; the Hebrew term *'ebed* designates a range of social and economic roles (see Preface) [b] Samaritan, Septuagint; Hebrew *he*

along the way, and by night in a pillar of fire to give them light, that they might travel by day and by night. ²²The pillar of cloud by day and the pillar of fire by night did not depart from before the people.

CROSSING THE RED SEA

14 Then the LORD said to Moses, ²"Tell the people of Israel to turn back and encamp in front of Pi-hahiroth, between Migdol and the sea, in front of Baal-zephon; you shall encamp facing it, by the sea. ³For Pharaoh will say of the people of Israel, 'They are wandering in the land; the wilderness has shut them in.' ⁴And I will harden Pharaoh's heart, and he will pursue them, and I will get glory over Pharaoh and all his host, and the Egyptians shall know that I am the LORD." And they did so.

⁵When the king of Egypt was told that the people had fled, the mind of Pharaoh and his servants was changed towards the people, and they said, "What is this we have done, that we have let Israel go from serving us?" ⁶So he made ready his chariot and took his army with him, ⁷and took six hundred chosen chariots and all the other chariots of Egypt with officers over all of them. ⁸And the LORD hardened the heart of Pharaoh king of Egypt, and he pursued the people of Israel while the people of Israel were going out defiantly. ⁹The Egyptians pursued them, all Pharaoh's horses and chariots and his horsemen and his army, and overtook them encamped at the sea, by Pi-hahiroth, in front of Baal-zephon.

¹⁰When Pharaoh drew near, the people of Israel lifted up their eyes, and behold, the Egyptians were marching after them, and they feared greatly. And the people of Israel cried out to the LORD. ¹¹They said to Moses, "Is it because there are no graves in Egypt that you have taken us away to die in the wilderness? What have you done to us in bringing us out of Egypt? ¹²Is not this what we said to you in Egypt: 'Leave us alone that we may serve the Egyptians'? For it would have been better for us to serve the Egyptians than to die in the wilderness." ¹³And Moses said to the people, "Fear not, stand firm, and see the salvation of the LORD, which he will work for you today. For the Egyptians whom you see today, you shall never see again. ¹⁴The LORD will fight for you, and you have only to be silent."

¹⁵The LORD said to Moses, "Why do you cry to me? Tell the people of Israel to go forward. ¹⁶Lift up your staff, and stretch out your hand over the sea and divide it, that the people of Israel may go through the sea on dry ground. ¹⁷And I will harden the hearts of the Egyptians so that they shall go in after them, and I will get glory over Pharaoh and all his host, his chariots, and his horsemen. ¹⁸And the Egyptians shall know that I am the LORD, when I have gained glory over Pharaoh, his chariots, and his horsemen."

¹⁹Then the angel of God who was going before the host of Israel moved and went behind them, and the pillar of cloud moved from before them and stood behind them, ²⁰coming between the host of Egypt and the host of Israel. And there was the cloud and the darkness. And it lit up the night[a] without one coming near the other all night.

²¹Then Moses stretched out his hand over the sea, and the LORD drove the sea back by a strong east wind all night and made the sea dry land, and the waters were divided. ²²And the people of Israel went into the midst of the sea on dry ground, the waters being a wall to them on their right hand and on their left. ²³The Egyptians pursued and went in after them into the midst of the sea, all Pharaoh's horses, his chariots, and his horsemen. ²⁴And in the morning watch the LORD in the pillar of fire and of cloud looked down on the Egyptian forces and threw the Egyptian forces into a panic, ²⁵clogging[b] their chariot wheels so that they drove heavily. And the Egyptians said, "Let us flee from before Israel, for the LORD fights for them against the Egyptians."

²⁶Then the LORD said to Moses, "Stretch out your hand over the sea, that the water may come back upon the Egyptians, upon their chariots, and upon their horsemen." ²⁷So Moses stretched out his hand over the sea, and the sea returned to its normal course when the morning appeared. And as the Egyptians fled into it, the LORD threw[c] the Egyptians into the midst of the sea. ²⁸The waters returned and covered the chariots and the horsemen; of all the host of Pharaoh that had followed them into the sea, not one of them remained. ²⁹But the people of Israel walked on dry ground through the sea, the waters being a wall to them on their right hand and on their left.

³⁰Thus the LORD saved Israel that day from the hand of the Egyptians, and Israel saw the Egyptians dead on the seashore. ³¹Israel saw the great power that the LORD used against

---

[a]Septuagint *and the night passed*   [b]Or *binding* (compare Samaritan, Septuagint, Syriac); Hebrew *removing*   [c]Hebrew *shook off*

the Egyptians, so the people feared the Lord, and they believed in the Lord and in his servant Moses.

THE SONG OF MOSES

15 Then Moses and the people of Israel sang this song to the Lord, saying,

"I will sing to the Lord, for he has
    triumphed gloriously;
the horse and his rider[a] he has
    thrown into the sea.
2 The Lord is my strength and my song,
    and he has become my salvation;
this is my God, and I will praise him,
    my father's God, and I will exalt him.
3 The Lord is a man of war;
    the Lord is his name.

4 "Pharaoh's chariots and his host
    he cast into the sea,
and his chosen officers were
    sunk in the Red Sea.
5 The floods covered them;
    they went down into the
    depths like a stone.
6 Your right hand, O Lord,
    glorious in power,
your right hand, O Lord,
    shatters the enemy.
7 In the greatness of your majesty you
    overthrow your adversaries;
you send out your fury; it
    consumes them like stubble.
8 At the blast of your nostrils
    the waters piled up;
the floods stood up in a pile;
    the deeps congealed in the
    heart of the sea.
9 The enemy said, 'I will pursue,
    I will overtake,
I will divide the spoil, my desire
    shall have its fill of them.
I will draw my sword; my hand
    shall destroy them.'
10 You blew with your wind; the
    sea covered them;
they sank like lead in the
    mighty waters.

11 "Who is like you, O Lord,
    among the gods?
Who is like you, majestic
    in holiness,
awesome in glorious deeds,
    doing wonders?
12 You stretched out your right hand;
    the earth swallowed them.

13 "You have led in your steadfast love the
    people whom you have redeemed;
you have guided them by your
    strength to your holy abode.
14 The peoples have heard; they tremble;
    pangs have seized the
    inhabitants of Philistia.
15 Now are the chiefs of Edom dismayed;
    trembling seizes the
    leaders of Moab;
all the inhabitants of Canaan
    have melted away.
16 Terror and dread fall upon them;
    because of the greatness of your
    arm, they are still as a stone,
till your people, O Lord, pass by,
    till the people pass by whom
    you have purchased.
17 You will bring them in and plant
    them on your own mountain,
the place, O Lord, which you
    have made for your abode,
the sanctuary, O Lord, which your
    hands have established.
18 The Lord will reign for ever and ever."

19 For when the horses of Pharaoh with his chariots and his horsemen went into the sea, the Lord brought back the waters of the sea upon them, but the people of Israel walked on dry ground in the midst of the sea. 20 Then Miriam the prophetess, the sister of Aaron, took a tambourine in her hand, and all the women went out after her with tambourines and dancing. 21 And Miriam sang to them:

"Sing to the Lord, for he has
    triumphed gloriously;
the horse and his rider he has
    thrown into the sea."

BITTER WATER MADE SWEET

22 Then Moses made Israel set out from the Red Sea, and they went into the wilderness of Shur. They went three days in the wilderness and found no water. 23 When they came to Marah, they could not drink the water of Marah because it was bitter; therefore it was named Marah.[b] 24 And the people grumbled against Moses, saying, "What shall we drink?" 25 And he cried to the Lord, and the Lord

---

[a] Or *its chariot*; also verse 21   [b] *Marah* means *bitterness*

showed him a log,*a* and he threw it into the water, and the water became sweet.

There the LORD*b* made for them a statute and a rule, and there he tested them, 26saying, "If you will diligently listen to the voice of the LORD your God, and do that which is right in his eyes, and give ear to his commandments and keep all his statutes, I will put none of the diseases on you that I put on the Egyptians, for I am the LORD, your healer."

27Then they came to Elim, where there were twelve springs of water and seventy palm trees, and they encamped there by the water.

BREAD FROM HEAVEN

16 They set out from Elim, and all the congregation of the people of Israel came to the wilderness of Sin, which is between Elim and Sinai, on the fifteenth day of the second month after they had departed from the land of Egypt. 2And the whole congregation of the people of Israel grumbled against Moses and Aaron in the wilderness, 3and the people of Israel said to them, "Would that we had died by the hand of the LORD in the land of Egypt, when we sat by the meat pots and ate bread to the full, for you have brought us out into this wilderness to kill this whole assembly with hunger."

4Then the LORD said to Moses, "Behold, I am about to rain bread from heaven for you, and the people shall go out and gather a day's portion every day, that I may test them, whether they will walk in my law or not. 5On the sixth day, when they prepare what they bring in, it will be twice as much as they gather daily." 6So Moses and Aaron said to all the people of Israel, "At evening you shall know that it was the LORD who brought you out of the land of Egypt, 7and in the morning you shall see the glory of the LORD, because he has heard your grumbling against the LORD. For what are we, that you grumble against us?" 8And Moses said, "When the LORD gives you in the evening meat to eat and in the morning bread to the full, because the LORD has heard your grumbling that you grumble against him—what are we? Your grumbling is not against us but against the LORD."

9Then Moses said to Aaron, "Say to the whole congregation of the people of Israel, 'Come near before the LORD, for he has heard your grumbling.'" 10And as soon as Aaron spoke to the whole congregation of the people of Israel, they looked towards the wilderness, and behold, the glory of the LORD appeared in the cloud. 11And the LORD said to Moses, 12"I have heard the grumbling of the people of Israel. Say to them, 'At twilight you shall eat meat, and in the morning you shall be filled with bread. Then you shall know that I am the LORD your God.'"

13In the evening quail came up and covered the camp, and in the morning dew lay around the camp. 14And when the dew had gone up, there was on the face of the wilderness a fine, flake-like thing, fine as frost on the ground. 15When the people of Israel saw it, they said to one another, "What is it?"*c* For they did not know what it was. And Moses said to them, "It is the bread that the LORD has given you to eat. 16This is what the LORD has commanded: 'Gather of it, each one of you, as much as he can eat. You shall each take an omer,*d* according to the number of the persons that each of you has in his tent.'"
17And the people of Israel did so. They gathered, some more, some less. 18But when they measured it with an omer, whoever gathered much had nothing left over, and whoever gathered little had no lack. Each of them gathered as much as he could eat. 19And Moses said to them, "Let no one leave any of it over till the morning." 20But they did not listen to Moses. Some left part of it till the morning, and it bred worms and stank. And Moses was angry with them. 21Morning by morning they gathered it, each as much as he could eat; but when the sun grew hot, it melted.

22On the sixth day they gathered twice as much bread, two omers each. And when all the leaders of the congregation came and told Moses, 23he said to them, "This is what the LORD has commanded: 'Tomorrow is a day of solemn rest, a holy Sabbath to the LORD; bake what you will bake and boil what you will boil, and all that is left over lay aside to be kept till the morning.'" 24So they laid it aside till the morning, as Moses commanded them, and it did not stink, and there were no worms in it. 25Moses said, "Eat it today, for today is a Sabbath to the LORD; today you will not find it in the field. 26For six days you shall gather it, but on the seventh day, which is a Sabbath, there will be none."

27On the seventh day some of the people went out to gather, but they found none. 28And the LORD said to Moses, "How long will you refuse to keep my commandments and

---

*a*Or tree   *b*Hebrew he   *c*Or "It is manna"; Hebrew man hu
*d*An omer was about 2 quarts or 2 litres

my laws? ²⁹See! The LORD has given you the Sabbath; therefore on the sixth day he gives you bread for two days. Remain each of you in his place; let no one go out of his place on the seventh day." ³⁰So the people rested on the seventh day.

³¹Now the house of Israel called its name manna. It was like coriander seed, white, and the taste of it was like wafers made with honey. ³²Moses said, "This is what the LORD has commanded: 'Let an omer of it be kept throughout your generations, so that they may see the bread with which I fed you in the wilderness, when I brought you out of the land of Egypt.'" ³³And Moses said to Aaron, "Take a jar, and put an omer of manna in it, and place it before the LORD to be kept throughout your generations." ³⁴As the LORD commanded Moses, so Aaron placed it before the testimony to be kept. ³⁵The people of Israel ate the manna for forty years, till they came to a habitable land. They ate the manna till they came to the border of the land of Canaan. ³⁶(An omer is the tenth part of an ephah.)ᵃ

WATER FROM THE ROCK

17 All the congregation of the people of Israel moved on from the wilderness of Sin by stages, according to the commandment of the LORD, and camped at Rephidim, but there was no water for the people to drink. ²Therefore the people quarrelled with Moses and said, "Give us water to drink." And Moses said to them, "Why do you quarrel with me? Why do you test the LORD?" ³But the people thirsted there for water, and the people grumbled against Moses and said, "Why did you bring us up out of Egypt, to kill us and our children and our livestock with thirst?" ⁴So Moses cried to the LORD, "What shall I do with this people? They are almost ready to stone me." ⁵And the LORD said to Moses, "Pass on before the people, taking with you some of the elders of Israel, and take in your hand the staff with which you struck the Nile, and go. ⁶Behold, I will stand before you there on the rock at Horeb, and you shall strike the rock, and water shall come out of it, and the people will drink." And Moses did so, in the sight of the elders of Israel. ⁷And he called the name of the place Massahᵇ and Meribah,ᶜ because of the quarrelling of the people of Israel, and because they tested the LORD by saying, "Is the LORD among us or not?"

ISRAEL DEFEATS AMALEK

⁸Then Amalek came and fought with Israel at Rephidim. ⁹So Moses said to Joshua, "Choose for us men, and go out and fight with Amalek. Tomorrow I will stand on the top of the hill with the staff of God in my hand." ¹⁰So Joshua did as Moses told him, and fought with Amalek, while Moses, Aaron, and Hur went up to the top of the hill. ¹¹Whenever Moses held up his hand, Israel prevailed, and whenever he lowered his hand, Amalek prevailed. ¹²But Moses' hands grew weary, so they took a stone and put it under him, and he sat on it, while Aaron and Hur held up his hands, one on one side, and the other on the other side. So his hands were steady until the going down of the sun. ¹³And Joshua overwhelmed Amalek and his people with the sword.

¹⁴Then the LORD said to Moses, "Write this as a memorial in a book and recite it in the ears of Joshua, that I will utterly blot out the memory of Amalek from under heaven." ¹⁵And Moses built an altar and called the name of it, The LORD Is My Banner, ¹⁶saying, "A hand upon the throneᵈ of the LORD! The LORD will have war with Amalek from generation to generation."

JETHRO'S ADVICE

18 Jethro, the priest of Midian, Moses' father-in-law, heard of all that God had done for Moses and for Israel his people, how the LORD had brought Israel out of Egypt. ²Now Jethro, Moses' father-in-law, had taken Zipporah, Moses' wife, after he had sent her home, ³along with her two sons. The name of one was Gershom (for he said, "I have been a sojournerᵉ in a foreign land"), ⁴and the name of the other, Eliezerᶠ (for he said, "The God of my father was my help, and delivered me from the sword of Pharaoh"). ⁵Jethro, Moses' father-in-law, came with his sons and his wife to Moses in the wilderness where he was encamped at the mountain of God. ⁶And when he sent word to Moses, "I,ᵍ your father-in-law Jethro, am coming to you with your wife and her two sons with her," ⁷Moses went out to meet his father-in-law and bowed down and kissed him. And they asked each other of their welfare and went into the tent. ⁸Then Moses told his father-in-law all

---

ᵃAn *ephah* was about 3/5 of a bushel or 22 litres ᵇ*Massah* means *testing* ᶜ*Meribah* means *quarrelling* ᵈA slight change would yield *upon the banner* ᵉ*Gershom* sounds like the Hebrew for *sojourner* ᶠ*Eliezer* means *My God is help* ᵍHebrew; Samaritan, Septuagint, Syriac *behold*

that the Lord had done to Pharaoh and to the Egyptians for Israel's sake, all the hardship that had come upon them in the way, and how the Lord had delivered them. ⁹And Jethro rejoiced for all the good that the Lord had done to Israel, in that he had delivered them out of the hand of the Egyptians.

¹⁰Jethro said, "Blessed be the Lord, who has delivered you out of the hand of the Egyptians and out of the hand of Pharaoh and has delivered the people from under the hand of the Egyptians. ¹¹Now I know that the Lord is greater than all gods, because in this affair they dealt arrogantly with the people."ᵃ ¹²And Jethro, Moses' father-in-law, brought a burnt offering and sacrifices to God; and Aaron came with all the elders of Israel to eat bread with Moses' father-in-law before God.

¹³The next day Moses sat to judge the people, and the people stood around Moses from morning till evening. ¹⁴When Moses' father-in-law saw all that he was doing for the people, he said, "What is this that you are doing for the people? Why do you sit alone, and all the people stand around you from morning till evening?" ¹⁵And Moses said to his father-in-law, "Because the people come to me to enquire of God; ¹⁶when they have a dispute, they come to me and I decide between one person and another, and I make them know the statutes of God and his laws." ¹⁷Moses' father-in-law said to him, "What you are doing is not good. ¹⁸You and the people with you will certainly wear yourselves out, for the thing is too heavy for you. You are not able to do it alone. ¹⁹Now obey my voice; I will give you advice, and God be with you! You shall represent the people before God and bring their cases to God, ²⁰and you shall warn them about the statutes and the laws, and make them know the way in which they must walk and what they must do. ²¹Moreover, look for able men from all the people, men who fear God, who are trustworthy and hate a bribe, and place such men over the people as chiefs of thousands, of hundreds, of fifties, and of tens. ²²And let them judge the people at all times. Every great matter they shall bring to you, but any small matter they shall decide themselves. So it will be easier for you, and they will bear the burden with you. ²³If you do this, God will direct you, you will be able to endure, and all this people also will go to their place in peace."

²⁴So Moses listened to the voice of his father-in-law and did all that he had said. ²⁵Moses chose able men out of all Israel and made them heads over the people, chiefs of thousands, of hundreds, of fifties, and of tens. ²⁶And they judged the people at all times. Any hard case they brought to Moses, but any small matter they decided themselves. ²⁷Then Moses let his father-in-law depart, and he went away to his own country.

ISRAEL AT MOUNT SINAI

19 On the third new moon after the people of Israel had gone out of the land of Egypt, on that day they came into the wilderness of Sinai. ²They set out from Rephidim and came into the wilderness of Sinai, and they encamped in the wilderness. There Israel encamped before the mountain, ³while Moses went up to God. The Lord called to him out of the mountain, saying, "Thus you shall say to the house of Jacob, and tell the people of Israel: ⁴'You yourselves have seen what I did to the Egyptians, and how I bore you on eagles' wings and brought you to myself. ⁵Now therefore, if you will indeed obey my voice and keep my covenant, you shall be my treasured possession among all peoples, for all the earth is mine; ⁶and you shall be to me a kingdom of priests and a holy nation.' These are the words that you shall speak to the people of Israel."

⁷So Moses came and called the elders of the people and set before them all these words that the Lord had commanded him. ⁸All the people answered together and said, "All that the Lord has spoken we will do." And Moses reported the words of the people to the Lord. ⁹And the Lord said to Moses, "Behold, I am coming to you in a thick cloud, that the people may hear when I speak with you, and may also believe you for ever."

When Moses told the words of the people to the Lord, ¹⁰the Lord said to Moses, "Go to the people and consecrate them today and tomorrow, and let them wash their garments ¹¹and be ready for the third day. For on the third day the Lord will come down on Mount Sinai in the sight of all the people. ¹²And you shall set limits for the people all round, saying, 'Take care not to go up into the mountain or touch the edge of it. Whoever touches the mountain shall be put to death. ¹³No hand shall touch him, but he shall be stoned or shot;ᵇ whether beast or man, he shall not live.' When the trumpet sounds a long blast, they shall come up to the mountain."

ᵃHebrew *with them* ᵇThat is, shot with an arrow

¹⁴So Moses went down from the mountain to the people and consecrated the people; and they washed their garments. ¹⁵And he said to the people, "Be ready for the third day; do not go near a woman."

¹⁶On the morning of the third day there were thunders and lightnings and a thick cloud on the mountain and a very loud trumpet blast, so that all the people in the camp trembled. ¹⁷Then Moses brought the people out of the camp to meet God, and they took their stand at the foot of the mountain. ¹⁸Now Mount Sinai was wrapped in smoke because the LORD had descended on it in fire. The smoke of it went up like the smoke of a kiln, and the whole mountain trembled greatly. ¹⁹And as the sound of the trumpet grew louder and louder, Moses spoke, and God answered him in thunder. ²⁰The LORD came down on Mount Sinai, to the top of the mountain. And the LORD called Moses to the top of the mountain, and Moses went up.

²¹And the LORD said to Moses, "Go down and warn the people, lest they break through to the LORD to look and many of them perish. ²²Also let the priests who come near to the LORD consecrate themselves, lest the LORD break out against them." ²³And Moses said to the LORD, "The people cannot come up to Mount Sinai, for you yourself warned us, saying, 'Set limits round the mountain and consecrate it.'" ²⁴And the LORD said to him, "Go down, and come up bringing Aaron with you. But do not let the priests and the people break through to come up to the LORD, lest he break out against them." ²⁵So Moses went down to the people and told them.

THE TEN COMMANDMENTS

20 And God spoke all these words, saying,

²"I am the LORD your God, who brought you out of the land of Egypt, out of the house of slavery.

³"You shall have no other gods before[a] me.

⁴"You shall not make for yourself a carved image, or any likeness of anything that is in heaven above, or that is in the earth beneath, or that is in the water under the earth. ⁵You shall not bow down to them or serve them, for I the LORD your God am a jealous God, visiting the iniquity of the fathers on the children to the third and the fourth generation of those who hate me, ⁶but showing steadfast love to thousands[b] of those who love me and keep my commandments.

⁷"You shall not take the name of the LORD your God in vain, for the LORD will not hold him guiltless who takes his name in vain.

⁸"Remember the Sabbath day, to keep it holy. ⁹Six days you shall labour, and do all your work, ¹⁰but the seventh day is a Sabbath to the LORD your God. On it you shall not do any work, you, or your son, or your daughter, your male servant, or your female servant, or your livestock, or the sojourner who is within your gates. ¹¹For in six days the LORD made heaven and earth, the sea, and all that is in them, and rested on the seventh day. Therefore the LORD blessed the Sabbath day and made it holy.

¹²"Honour your father and your mother, that your days may be long in the land that the LORD your God is giving you.

¹³"You shall not murder.[c]

¹⁴"You shall not commit adultery.

¹⁵"You shall not steal.

¹⁶"You shall not bear false witness against your neighbour.

¹⁷"You shall not covet your neighbour's house; you shall not covet your neighbour's wife, or his male servant, or his female servant, or his ox, or his donkey, or anything that is your neighbour's."

¹⁸Now when all the people saw the thunder and the flashes of lightning and the sound of the trumpet and the mountain smoking, the people were afraid[d] and trembled, and they stood far off ¹⁹and said to Moses, "You speak to us, and we will listen; but do not let God speak to us, lest we die." ²⁰Moses said to the people, "Do not fear, for God has come to test you, that the fear of him may be before you, that you may not sin." ²¹The people stood far off, while Moses drew near to the thick darkness where God was.

LAWS ABOUT ALTARS

²²And the LORD said to Moses, "Thus you shall say to the people of Israel: 'You have seen for yourselves that I have talked with you from heaven. ²³You shall not make gods of silver to be with me, nor shall you make for yourselves gods of gold. ²⁴An altar of earth you shall make for me and sacrifice on it your burnt offerings and your peace offerings, your sheep and your oxen. In every place where I cause my name to be remembered I

---

[a]Or besides [b]Or to the thousandth generation [c]The Hebrew word also covers causing human death through carelessness or negligence [d]Samaritan, Septuagint, Syriac, Vulgate; Masoretic Text the people saw

will come to you and bless you. ²⁵If you make me an altar of stone, you shall not build it of hewn stones, for if you wield your tool on it you profane it. ²⁶And you shall not go up by steps to my altar, that your nakedness be not exposed on it.'

LAWS ABOUT SLAVES

21 "Now these are the rules that you shall set before them. ²When you buy a Hebrew slave,ᵃ he shall serve for six years, and in the seventh he shall go out free, for nothing. ³If he comes in single, he shall go out single; if he comes in married, then his wife shall go out with him. ⁴If his master gives him a wife and she bears him sons or daughters, the wife and her children shall be her master's, and he shall go out alone. ⁵But if the slave plainly says, 'I love my master, my wife, and my children; I will not go out free', ⁶then his master shall bring him to God, and he shall bring him to the door or the doorpost. And his master shall bore his ear through with an awl, and he shall be his slave for ever.

⁷"When a man sells his daughter as a slave, she shall not go out as the male slaves do. ⁸If she does not please her master, who has designated herᵇ for himself, then he shall let her be redeemed. He shall have no right to sell her to a foreign people, since he has broken faith with her. ⁹If he designates her for his son, he shall deal with her as with a daughter. ¹⁰If he takes another wife to himself, he shall not diminish her food, her clothing, or her marital rights. ¹¹And if he does not do these three things for her, she shall go out for nothing, without payment of money.

¹²"Whoever strikes a man so that he dies shall be put to death. ¹³But if he did not lie in wait for him, but God let him fall into his hand, then I will appoint for you a place to which he may flee. ¹⁴But if a man wilfully attacks another to kill him by cunning, you shall take him from my altar, that he may die.

¹⁵"Whoever strikes his father or his mother shall be put to death.

¹⁶"Whoever steals a man and sells him, and anyone found in possession of him, shall be put to death.

¹⁷"Whoever cursesᶜ his father or his mother shall be put to death.

¹⁸"When men quarrel and one strikes the other with a stone or with his fist and the man does not die but takes to his bed, ¹⁹then if the man rises again and walks outdoors with his staff, he who struck him shall be clear; only he shall pay for the loss of his time, and shall have him thoroughly healed.

²⁰"When a man strikes his slave, male or female, with a rod and the slave dies under his hand, he shall be avenged. ²¹But if the slave survives a day or two, he is not to be avenged, for the slave is his money.

²²"When men strive together and hit a pregnant woman, so that her children come out, but there is no harm, the one who hit her shall surely be fined, as the woman's husband shall impose on him, and he shall pay as the judges determine. ²³But if there is harm,ᵈ then you shall pay life for life, ²⁴eye for eye, tooth for tooth, hand for hand, foot for foot, ²⁵burn for burn, wound for wound, stripe for stripe.

²⁶"When a man strikes the eye of his slave, male or female, and destroys it, he shall let the slave go free because of his eye. ²⁷If he knocks out the tooth of his slave, male or female, he shall let the slave go free because of his tooth.

²⁸"When an ox gores a man or a woman to death, the ox shall be stoned, and its flesh shall not be eaten, but the owner of the ox shall not be liable. ²⁹But if the ox has been accustomed to gore in the past, and its owner has been warned but has not kept it in, and it kills a man or a woman, the ox shall be stoned, and its owner also shall be put to death. ³⁰If a ransom is imposed on him, then he shall give for the redemption of his life whatever is imposed on him. ³¹If it gores a man's son or daughter, he shall be dealt with according to this same rule. ³²If the ox gores a slave, male or female, the owner shall give to their master thirty shekelsᵉ of silver, and the ox shall be stoned.

LAWS ABOUT RESTITUTION

³³"When a man opens a pit, or when a man digs a pit and does not cover it, and an ox or a donkey falls into it, ³⁴the owner of the pit shall make restoration. He shall give money to its owner, and the dead beast shall be his.

³⁵"When one man's ox butts another's, so that it dies, then they shall sell the live ox and share its price, and the dead beast also they shall share. ³⁶Or if it is known that the ox has

---
ᵃOr *servant*; the Hebrew term *'ebed* designates a range of social and economic roles; also verses 5, 6, 7, 20, 21, 26, 27, 32 (see Preface)
ᵇOr so that he has not designated her   ᶜOr *dishonours*; Septuagint *reviles*   ᵈOr so that her children come out and it is clear who was to blame, he shall be fined as the woman's husband shall impose on him, and he alone shall pay. ²³If it is unclear who was to blame . . .
ᵉA *shekel* was about 2/5 of an ounce or 11 grams

been accustomed to gore in the past, and its owner has not kept it in, he shall repay ox for ox, and the dead beast shall be his.

22

[a] "If a man steals an ox or a sheep, and kills it or sells it, he shall repay five oxen for an ox, and four sheep for a sheep. [2b] If a thief is found breaking in and is struck so that he dies, there shall be no bloodguilt for him, [3] but if the sun has risen on him, there shall be bloodguilt for him. He[c] shall surely pay. If he has nothing, then he shall be sold for his theft. [4] If the stolen beast is found alive in his possession, whether it is an ox or a donkey or a sheep, he shall pay double.

[5] "If a man causes a field or vineyard to be grazed over, or lets his beast loose and it feeds in another man's field, he shall make restitution from the best in his own field and in his own vineyard.

[6] "If fire breaks out and catches in thorns so that the stacked corn or the standing corn or the field is consumed, he who started the fire shall make full restitution.

[7] "If a man gives to his neighbour money or goods to keep safe, and it is stolen from the man's house, then, if the thief is found, he shall pay double. [8] If the thief is not found, the owner of the house shall come near to God to show whether or not he has put his hand to his neighbour's property. [9] For every breach of trust, whether it is for an ox, for a donkey, for a sheep, for a cloak, or for any kind of lost thing, of which one says, 'This is it,' the case of both parties shall come before God. The one whom God condemns shall pay double to his neighbour.

[10] "If a man gives to his neighbour a donkey or an ox or a sheep or any beast to keep safe, and it dies or is injured or is driven away, without anyone seeing it, [11] an oath by the LORD shall be between them both to see whether or not he has put his hand to his neighbour's property. The owner shall accept the oath, and he shall not make restitution. [12] But if it is stolen from him, he shall make restitution to its owner. [13] If it is torn by beasts, let him bring it as evidence. He shall not make restitution for what has been torn.

[14] "If a man borrows anything of his neighbour, and it is injured or dies, the owner not being with it, he shall make full restitution. [15] If the owner was with it, he shall not make restitution; if it was hired, it came for its hiring fee.[d]

LAWS ABOUT SOCIAL JUSTICE

[16] "If a man seduces a virgin[e] who is not betrothed and lies with her, he shall give the bride price[f] for her and make her his wife. [17] If her father utterly refuses to give her to him, he shall pay money equal to the bride price for virgins.

[18] "You shall not permit a sorceress to live.

[19] "Whoever lies with an animal shall be put to death.

[20] "Whoever sacrifices to any god, other than the LORD alone, shall be devoted to destruction.[g]

[21] "You shall not wrong a sojourner or oppress him, for you were sojourners in the land of Egypt. [22] You shall not mistreat any widow or fatherless child. [23] If you do mistreat them, and they cry out to me, I will surely hear their cry, [24] and my wrath will burn, and I will kill you with the sword, and your wives shall become widows and your children fatherless.

[25] "If you lend money to any of my people with you who is poor, you shall not be like a money-lender to him, and you shall not exact interest from him. [26] If ever you take your neighbour's cloak in pledge, you shall return it to him before the sun goes down, [27] for that is his only covering, and it is his cloak for his body; in what else shall he sleep? And if he cries to me, I will hear, for I am compassionate.

[28] "You shall not revile God, nor curse a ruler of your people.

[29] "You shall not delay to offer from the fullness of your harvest and from the outflow of your presses. The firstborn of your sons you shall give to me. [30] You shall do the same with your oxen and with your sheep; for seven days it shall be with its mother; on the eighth day you shall give it to me.

[31] "You shall be consecrated to me. Therefore you shall not eat any flesh that is torn by beasts in the field; you shall throw it to the dogs.

23

"You shall not spread a false report. You shall not join hands with a wicked man to be a malicious witness. [2] You shall not fall in with the many to do evil, nor shall you bear witness in a lawsuit, siding with the many, so as to pervert

---
[a] Ch 21:37 in Hebrew [b] Ch 22:1 in Hebrew [c] That is, the thief [d] Or it is reckoned in (Hebrew comes into) its hiring fee [e] Or a girl of marriageable age; also verse 17 [f] Or engagement present; also verse 17 [g] That is, set apart (devoted) as an offering to the Lord (for destruction)

justice, ³nor shall you be partial to a poor man in his lawsuit.

⁴"If you meet your enemy's ox or his donkey going astray, you shall bring it back to him. ⁵If you see the donkey of one who hates you lying down under its burden, you shall refrain from leaving him with it; you shall rescue it with him.

⁶"You shall not pervert the justice due to your poor in his lawsuit. ⁷Keep far from a false charge, and do not kill the innocent and righteous, for I will not acquit the wicked. ⁸And you shall take no bribe, for a bribe blinds the clear-sighted and subverts the cause of those who are in the right.

⁹"You shall not oppress a sojourner. You know the heart of a sojourner, for you were sojourners in the land of Egypt.

LAWS ABOUT THE SABBATH AND FESTIVALS

¹⁰"For six years you shall sow your land and gather in its yield, ¹¹but the seventh year you shall let it rest and lie fallow, that the poor of your people may eat; and what they leave the beasts of the field may eat. You shall do likewise with your vineyard, and with your olive orchard.

¹²"For six days you shall do your work, but on the seventh day you shall rest; that your ox and your donkey may have rest, and the son of your servant woman, and the alien, may be refreshed.

¹³"Pay attention to all that I have said to you, and make no mention of the names of other gods, nor let it be heard on your lips.

¹⁴"Three times in the year you shall keep a feast to me. ¹⁵You shall keep the Feast of Unleavened Bread. As I commanded you, you shall eat unleavened bread for seven days at the appointed time in the month of Abib, for in it you came out of Egypt. None shall appear before me empty-handed. ¹⁶You shall keep the Feast of Harvest, of the firstfruits of your labour, of what you sow in the field. You shall keep the Feast of Ingathering at the end of the year, when you gather in from the field the fruit of your labour. ¹⁷Three times in the year shall all your males appear before the Lord God.

¹⁸"You shall not offer the blood of my sacrifice with anything leavened, or let the fat of my feast remain until the morning.

¹⁹"The best of the firstfruits of your ground you shall bring into the house of the Lord your God.

"You shall not boil a young goat in its mother's milk.

CONQUEST OF CANAAN PROMISED

²⁰"Behold, I send an angel before you to guard you on the way and to bring you to the place that I have prepared. ²¹Pay careful attention to him and obey his voice; do not rebel against him, for he will not pardon your transgression, for my name is in him.

²²"But if you carefully obey his voice and do all that I say, then I will be an enemy to your enemies and an adversary to your adversaries.

²³"When my angel goes before you and brings you to the Amorites and the Hittites and the Perizzites and the Canaanites, the Hivites and the Jebusites, and I blot them out, ²⁴you shall not bow down to their gods nor serve them, nor do as they do, but you shall utterly overthrow them and break their pillars in pieces. ²⁵You shall serve the Lord your God, and he[a] will bless your bread and your water, and I will take sickness away from among you. ²⁶None shall miscarry or be barren in your land; I will fulfil the number of your days. ²⁷I will send my terror before you and will throw into confusion all the people against whom you shall come, and I will make all your enemies turn their backs to you. ²⁸And I will send hornets[b] before you, which shall drive out the Hivites, the Canaanites, and the Hittites from before you. ²⁹I will not drive them out from before you in one year, lest the land become desolate and the wild beasts multiply against you. ³⁰Little by little I will drive them out from before you, until you have increased and possess the land. ³¹And I will set your border from the Red Sea to the Sea of the Philistines, and from the wilderness to the Euphrates,[c] for I will give the inhabitants of the land into your hand, and you shall drive them out before you. ³²You shall make no covenant with them and their gods. ³³They shall not dwell in your land, lest they make you sin against me; for if you serve their gods, it will surely be a snare to you."

THE COVENANT CONFIRMED

24 Then he said to Moses, "Come up to the Lord, you and Aaron, Nadab, and Abihu, and seventy of the elders of Israel, and worship from afar. ²Moses alone shall come near to the Lord, but the others shall not come near, and the people shall not come up with him."

---

[a]Septuagint, Vulgate *I* [b]Or *the hornet* [c]Hebrew *the River*

for its two tenons, and two bases under the next frame for its two tenons; ²⁰and for the second side of the tabernacle, on the north side twenty frames, ²¹and their forty bases of silver, two bases under one frame, and two bases under the next frame. ²²And for the rear of the tabernacle westward you shall make six frames. ²³And you shall make two frames for corners of the tabernacle in the rear; ²⁴they shall be separate beneath, but joined at the top, at the first ring. Thus shall it be with both of them; they shall form the two corners. ²⁵And there shall be eight frames, with their bases of silver, sixteen bases; two bases under one frame, and two bases under another frame.

²⁶"You shall make bars of acacia wood, five for the frames of one side of the tabernacle, ²⁷and five bars for the frames of the other side of the tabernacle, and five bars for the frames of the side of the tabernacle at the rear westward. ²⁸The middle bar, halfway up the frames, shall run from end to end. ²⁹You shall overlay the frames with gold and shall make their rings of gold for holders for the bars, and you shall overlay the bars with gold. ³⁰Then you shall erect the tabernacle according to the plan for it that you were shown on the mountain.

³¹"And you shall make a veil of blue and purple and scarlet yarns and fine twined linen. It shall be made with cherubim skilfully worked into it. ³²And you shall hang it on four pillars of acacia overlaid with gold, with hooks of gold, on four bases of silver. ³³And you shall hang the veil from the clasps, and bring the ark of the testimony in there within the veil. And the veil shall separate for you the Holy Place from the Most Holy. ³⁴You shall put the mercy seat on the ark of the testimony in the Most Holy Place. ³⁵And you shall set the table outside the veil, and the lampstand on the south side of the tabernacle opposite the table, and you shall put the table on the north side.

³⁶"You shall make a screen for the entrance of the tent, of blue and purple and scarlet yarns and fine twined linen, embroidered with needlework. ³⁷And you shall make for the screen five pillars of acacia, and overlay them with gold. Their hooks shall be of gold, and you shall cast five bases of bronze for them.

THE BRONZE ALTAR

27 "You shall make the altar of acacia wood, five cubits^a long and five cubits broad. The altar shall be square, and its height shall be three cubits. ²And you shall make horns for it on its four corners; its horns shall be of one piece with it, and you shall overlay it with bronze. ³You shall make pots for it to receive its ashes, and shovels and basins and forks and firepans. You shall make all its utensils of bronze. ⁴You shall also make for it a grating, a network of bronze, and on the net you shall make four bronze rings at its four corners. ⁵And you shall set it under the ledge of the altar so that the net extends halfway down the altar. ⁶And you shall make poles for the altar, poles of acacia wood, and overlay them with bronze. ⁷And the poles shall be put through the rings, so that the poles are on the two sides of the altar when it is carried. ⁸You shall make it hollow, with boards. As it has been shown you on the mountain, so shall it be made.

THE COURT OF THE TABERNACLE

⁹"You shall make the court of the tabernacle. On the south side the court shall have hangings of fine twined linen a hundred cubits long for one side. ¹⁰Its twenty pillars and their twenty bases shall be of bronze, but the hooks of the pillars and their fillets shall be of silver. ¹¹And likewise for its length on the north side there shall be hangings a hundred cubits long, its pillars twenty and their bases twenty, of bronze, but the hooks of the pillars and their fillets shall be of silver. ¹²And for the breadth of the court on the west side there shall be hangings for fifty cubits, with ten pillars and ten bases. ¹³The breadth of the court on the front to the east shall be fifty cubits. ¹⁴The hangings for one side of the gate shall be fifteen cubits, with their three pillars and three bases. ¹⁵On the other side the hangings shall be fifteen cubits, with their three pillars and three bases. ¹⁶For the gate of the court there shall be a screen twenty cubits long, of blue and purple and scarlet yarns and fine twined linen, embroidered with needlework. It shall have four pillars and with them four bases. ¹⁷All the pillars round the court shall be filleted with silver. Their hooks shall be of silver, and their bases of bronze. ¹⁸The length of the court shall be a hundred cubits, the breadth fifty, and the height five cubits, with hangings of fine twined linen and bases of bronze. ¹⁹All the utensils of the tabernacle for every use, and all its pegs and all the pegs of the court, shall be of bronze.

---
^{a}A *cubit* was about 18 inches or 45 centimetres

OIL FOR THE LAMP

20"You shall command the people of Israel that they bring to you pure beaten olive oil for the light, that a lamp may regularly be set up to burn. 21In the tent of meeting, outside the veil that is before the testimony, Aaron and his sons shall tend it from evening to morning before the LORD. It shall be a statute for ever to be observed throughout their generations by the people of Israel.

THE PRIESTS' GARMENTS

28 "Then bring near to you Aaron your brother, and his sons with him, from among the people of Israel, to serve me as priests—Aaron and Aaron's sons, Nadab and Abihu, Eleazar and Ithamar. 2And you shall make holy garments for Aaron your brother, for glory and for beauty. 3You shall speak to all the skilful, whom I have filled with a spirit of skill, that they make Aaron's garments to consecrate him for my priesthood. 4These are the garments that they shall make: a breastpiece, an ephod, a robe, a coat of chequerwork, a turban, and a sash. They shall make holy garments for Aaron your brother and his sons to serve me as priests. 5They shall receive gold, blue and purple and scarlet yarns, and fine twined linen.

6"And they shall make the ephod of gold, of blue and purple and scarlet yarns, and of fine twined linen, skilfully worked. 7It shall have two shoulder pieces attached to its two edges, so that it may be joined together. 8And the skilfully woven band on it shall be made like it and be of one piece with it, of gold, blue and purple and scarlet yarns, and fine twined linen. 9You shall take two onyx stones, and engrave on them the names of the sons of Israel, 10six of their names on one stone, and the names of the remaining six on the other stone, in the order of their birth. 11As a jeweller engraves signets, so shall you engrave the two stones with the names of the sons of Israel. You shall enclose them in settings of gold filigree. 12And you shall set the two stones on the shoulder pieces of the ephod, as stones of remembrance for the sons of Israel. And Aaron shall bear their names before the LORD on his two shoulders for remembrance. 13You shall make settings of gold filigree, 14and two chains of pure gold, twisted like cords; and you shall attach the corded chains to the settings.

15"You shall make a breastpiece of judgement, in skilled work. In the style of the ephod you shall make it—of gold, blue and purple and scarlet yarns, and fine twined linen shall you make it. 16It shall be square and doubled, a span[a] its length and a span its breadth. 17You shall set in it four rows of stones. A row of sardius,[b] topaz, and carbuncle shall be the first row; 18and the second row an emerald, a sapphire, and a diamond; 19and the third row a jacinth, an agate, and an amethyst; 20and the fourth row a beryl, an onyx, and a jasper. They shall be set in gold filigree. 21There shall be twelve stones with their names according to the names of the sons of Israel. They shall be like signets, each engraved with its name, for the twelve tribes. 22You shall make for the breastpiece twisted chains like cords, of pure gold. 23And you shall make for the breastpiece two rings of gold, and put the two rings on the two edges of the breastpiece. 24And you shall put the two cords of gold in the two rings at the edges of the breastpiece. 25The two ends of the two cords you shall attach to the two settings of filigree, and so attach it in front to the shoulder pieces of the ephod. 26You shall make two rings of gold, and put them at the two ends of the breastpiece, on its inside edge next to the ephod. 27And you shall make two rings of gold, and attach them in front to the lower part of the two shoulder pieces of the ephod, at its seam above the skilfully woven band of the ephod. 28And they shall bind the breastpiece by its rings to the rings of the ephod with a lace of blue, so that it may lie on the skilfully woven band of the ephod, so that the breastpiece shall not come loose from the ephod. 29So Aaron shall bear the names of the sons of Israel in the breastpiece of judgement on his heart, when he goes into the Holy Place, to bring them to regular remembrance before the LORD. 30And in the breastpiece of judgement you shall put the Urim and the Thummim, and they shall be on Aaron's heart, when he goes in before the LORD. Thus Aaron shall bear the judgement of the people of Israel on his heart before the LORD regularly.

31"You shall make the robe of the ephod all of blue. 32It shall have an opening for the head in the middle of it, with a woven binding round the opening, like the opening in a garment,[c] so that it may not tear. 33On its

---

[a] A *span* was about 9 inches or 22 centimetres [b] The identity of some of these stones is uncertain [c] The meaning of the Hebrew word is uncertain; possibly *coat of mail*

hem you shall make pomegranates of blue and purple and scarlet yarns, round its hem, with bells of gold between them, ³⁴a golden bell and a pomegranate, a golden bell and a pomegranate, round the hem of the robe. ³⁵And it shall be on Aaron when he ministers, and its sound shall be heard when he goes into the Holy Place before the LORD, and when he comes out, so that he does not die.

³⁶"You shall make a plate of pure gold and engrave on it, like the engraving of a signet, 'Holy to the LORD.' ³⁷And you shall fasten it on the turban by a cord of blue. It shall be on the front of the turban. ³⁸It shall be on Aaron's forehead, and Aaron shall bear any guilt from the holy things that the people of Israel consecrate as their holy gifts. It shall regularly be on his forehead, that they may be accepted before the LORD.

³⁹"You shall weave the coat in chequerwork of fine linen, and you shall make a turban of fine linen, and you shall make a sash embroidered with needlework.

⁴⁰"For Aaron's sons you shall make coats and sashes and caps. You shall make them for glory and beauty. ⁴¹And you shall put them on Aaron your brother, and on his sons with him, and shall anoint them and ordain them and consecrate them, that they may serve me as priests. ⁴²You shall make for them linen undergarments to cover their naked flesh. They shall reach from the hips to the thighs; ⁴³and they shall be on Aaron and on his sons when they go into the tent of meeting or when they come near the altar to minister in the Holy Place, lest they bear guilt and die. This shall be a statute for ever for him and for his offspring after him.

CONSECRATION OF THE PRIESTS

29 "Now this is what you shall do to them to consecrate them, that they may serve me as priests. Take one bull of the herd and two rams without blemish, ²and unleavened bread, unleavened cakes mixed with oil, and unleavened wafers smeared with oil. You shall make them of fine wheat flour. ³You shall put them in one basket and bring them in the basket, and bring the bull and the two rams. ⁴You shall bring Aaron and his sons to the entrance of the tent of meeting and wash them with water. ⁵Then you shall take the garments, and put on Aaron the coat and the robe of the ephod, and the ephod, and the breastpiece, and gird him with the skilfully woven band of the ephod. ⁶And you shall set the turban on his head and put the holy crown on the turban. ⁷You shall take the anointing oil and pour it on his head and anoint him. ⁸Then you shall bring his sons and put coats on them, ⁹and you shall gird Aaron and his sons with sashes and bind caps on them. And the priesthood shall be theirs by a statute for ever. Thus you shall ordain Aaron and his sons.

¹⁰"Then you shall bring the bull before the tent of meeting. Aaron and his sons shall lay their hands on the head of the bull. ¹¹Then you shall kill the bull before the LORD at the entrance of the tent of meeting, ¹²and shall take part of the blood of the bull and put it on the horns of the altar with your finger, and the rest of[a] the blood you shall pour out at the base of the altar. ¹³And you shall take all the fat that covers the entrails, and the long lobe of the liver, and the two kidneys with the fat that is on them, and burn them on the altar. ¹⁴But the flesh of the bull and its skin and its dung you shall burn with fire outside the camp; it is a sin offering.

¹⁵"Then you shall take one of the rams, and Aaron and his sons shall lay their hands on the head of the ram, ¹⁶and you shall kill the ram and shall take its blood and throw it against the sides of the altar. ¹⁷Then you shall cut the ram into pieces, and wash its entrails and its legs, and put them with its pieces and its head, ¹⁸and burn the whole ram on the altar. It is a burnt offering to the LORD. It is a pleasing aroma, a food offering[b] to the LORD.

¹⁹"You shall take the other ram, and Aaron and his sons shall lay their hands on the head of the ram, ²⁰and you shall kill the ram and take part of its blood and put it on the tip of the right ear of Aaron and on the tips of the right ears of his sons, and on the thumbs of their right hands and on the great toes of their right feet, and throw the rest of the blood against the sides of the altar. ²¹Then you shall take part of the blood that is on the altar, and of the anointing oil, and sprinkle it on Aaron and his garments, and on his sons and his sons' garments with him. He and his garments shall be holy, and his sons and his sons' garments with him.

²²"You shall also take the fat from the ram and the fat tail and the fat that covers the entrails, and the long lobe of the liver and the two kidneys with the fat that is on them, and the right thigh (for it is a ram of ordination),

---

[a]Hebrew *all*   [b]Or *an offering by fire*; also verses 25, 41

²³and one loaf of bread and one cake of bread made with oil, and one wafer out of the basket of unleavened bread that is before the LORD. ²⁴You shall put all these on the palms of Aaron and on the palms of his sons, and wave them for a wave offering before the LORD. ²⁵Then you shall take them from their hands and burn them on the altar on top of the burnt offering, as a pleasing aroma before the LORD. It is a food offering to the LORD.

²⁶"You shall take the breast of the ram of Aaron's ordination and wave it for a wave offering before the LORD, and it shall be your portion. ²⁷And you shall consecrate the breast of the wave offering that is waved and the thigh of the priests' portion that is contributed from the ram of ordination, from what was Aaron's and his sons'. ²⁸It shall be for Aaron and his sons as a perpetual due from the people of Israel, for it is a contribution. It shall be a contribution from the people of Israel from their peace offerings, their contribution to the LORD.

²⁹"The holy garments of Aaron shall be for his sons after him; they shall be anointed in them and ordained in them. ³⁰The son who succeeds him as priest, who comes into the tent of meeting to minister in the Holy Place, shall wear them for seven days.

³¹"You shall take the ram of ordination and boil its flesh in a holy place. ³²And Aaron and his sons shall eat the flesh of the ram and the bread that is in the basket in the entrance of the tent of meeting. ³³They shall eat those things with which atonement was made at their ordination and consecration, but an outsider shall not eat of them, because they are holy. ³⁴And if any of the flesh for the ordination or of the bread remain until the morning, then you shall burn the remainder with fire. It shall not be eaten, because it is holy.

³⁵"Thus you shall do to Aaron and to his sons, according to all that I have commanded you. Over seven days shall you ordain them, ³⁶and every day you shall offer a bull as a sin offering for atonement. Also you shall purify the altar, when you make atonement for it, and shall anoint it to consecrate it. ³⁷For seven days you shall make atonement for the altar and consecrate it, and the altar shall be most holy. Whatever touches the altar shall become holy.

³⁸"Now this is what you shall offer on the altar: two lambs a year old day by day regularly. ³⁹One lamb you shall offer in the morning, and the other lamb you shall offer at twilight. ⁴⁰And with the first lamb a tenth measure^a of fine flour mingled with a quarter of a hin^b of beaten oil, and a quarter of a hin of wine for a drink offering. ⁴¹The other lamb you shall offer at twilight, and shall offer with it a grain offering and its drink offering, as in the morning, for a pleasing aroma, a food offering to the LORD. ⁴²It shall be a regular burnt offering throughout your generations at the entrance of the tent of meeting before the LORD, where I will meet with you, to speak to you there. ⁴³There I will meet with the people of Israel, and it shall be sanctified by my glory. ⁴⁴I will consecrate the tent of meeting and the altar. Aaron also and his sons I will consecrate to serve me as priests. ⁴⁵I will dwell among the people of Israel and will be their God. ⁴⁶And they shall know that I am the LORD their God, who brought them out of the land of Egypt that I might dwell among them. I am the LORD their God.

THE ALTAR OF INCENSE

30 "You shall make an altar on which to burn incense; you shall make it of acacia wood. ²A cubit^c shall be its length, and a cubit its breadth. It shall be square, and two cubits shall be its height. Its horns shall be of one piece with it. ³You shall overlay it with pure gold, its top and round its sides and its horns. And you shall make a moulding of gold round it. ⁴And you shall make two golden rings for it. Under its moulding on two opposite sides of it you shall make them, and they shall be holders for poles with which to carry it. ⁵You shall make the poles of acacia wood and overlay them with gold. ⁶And you shall put it in front of the veil that is above the ark of the testimony, in front of the mercy seat that is above the testimony, where I will meet with you. ⁷And Aaron shall burn fragrant incense on it. Every morning when he dresses the lamps he shall burn it, ⁸and when Aaron sets up the lamps at twilight, he shall burn it, a regular incense offering before the LORD throughout your generations. ⁹You shall not offer unauthorized incense on it, or a burnt offering, or a grain offering, and you shall not pour a drink offering on it. ¹⁰Aaron shall make atonement on its horns once a year. With the blood of the sin offering of atonement he shall make atonement for it once in the

---

^{a}Possibly an ephah (about 3/5 of a bushel or 22 litres) ^{b}A *hin* was about 4 quarts or 3.5 litres ^{c}A *cubit* was about 18 inches or 45 centimetres

THE CENSUS TAX

¹¹The Lord said to Moses, ¹²"When you take the census of the people of Israel, then each shall give a ransom for his life to the Lord when you number them, that there be no plague among them when you number them. ¹³Each one who is numbered in the census shall give this: half a shekel[a] according to the shekel of the sanctuary (the shekel is twenty gerahs),[b] half a shekel as an offering to the Lord. ¹⁴Everyone who is numbered in the census, from twenty years old and upwards, shall give the Lord's offering. ¹⁵The rich shall not give more, and the poor shall not give less, than the half shekel, when you give the Lord's offering to make atonement for your lives. ¹⁶You shall take the atonement money from the people of Israel and shall give it for the service of the tent of meeting, that it may bring the people of Israel to remembrance before the Lord, so as to make atonement for your lives."

THE BRONZE BASIN

¹⁷The Lord said to Moses, ¹⁸"You shall also make a basin of bronze, with its stand of bronze, for washing. You shall put it between the tent of meeting and the altar, and you shall put water in it, ¹⁹with which Aaron and his sons shall wash their hands and their feet. ²⁰When they go into the tent of meeting, or when they come near the altar to minister, to burn a food offering[c] to the Lord, they shall wash with water, so that they may not die. ²¹They shall wash their hands and their feet, so that they may not die. It shall be a statute for ever to them, even to him and to his offspring throughout their generations."

THE ANOINTING OIL AND INCENSE

²²The Lord said to Moses, ²³"Take the finest spices: of liquid myrrh 500 shekels, and of sweet-smelling cinnamon half as much, that is, 250, and 250 of aromatic cane, ²⁴and 500 of cassia, according to the shekel of the sanctuary, and a hin[d] of olive oil. ²⁵And you shall make of these a sacred anointing oil blended as by the perfumer; it shall be a holy anointing oil. ²⁶With it you shall anoint the tent of meeting and the ark of the testimony, ²⁷and the table and all its utensils, and the lampstand and its utensils, and the altar of incense, ²⁸and the altar of burnt offering with all its utensils and the basin and its stand. ²⁹You shall consecrate them, that they may be most holy. Whatever touches them will become holy. ³⁰You shall anoint Aaron and his sons, and consecrate them, that they may serve me as priests. ³¹And you shall say to the people of Israel, 'This shall be my holy anointing oil throughout your generations. ³²It shall not be poured on the body of an ordinary person, and you shall make no other like it in composition. It is holy, and it shall be holy to you. ³³Whoever compounds any like it or whoever puts any of it on an outsider shall be cut off from his people.'"

³⁴The Lord said to Moses, "Take sweet spices, stacte, and onycha, and galbanum, sweet spices with pure frankincense (of each shall there be an equal part), ³⁵and make an incense blended as by the perfumer, seasoned with salt, pure and holy. ³⁶You shall beat some of it very small, and put part of it before the testimony in the tent of meeting where I shall meet with you. It shall be most holy for you. ³⁷And the incense that you shall make according to its composition, you shall not make for yourselves. It shall be for you holy to the Lord. ³⁸Whoever makes any like it to use as perfume shall be cut off from his people."

OHOLIAB AND BEZALEL

31 The Lord said to Moses, ²"See, I have called by name Bezalel the son of Uri, son of Hur, of the tribe of Judah, ³and I have filled him with the Spirit of God, with ability and intelligence, with knowledge and all craftsmanship, ⁴to devise artistic designs, to work in gold, silver, and bronze, ⁵in cutting stones for setting, and in carving wood, to work in every craft. ⁶And behold, I have appointed with him Oholiab, the son of Ahisamach, of the tribe of Dan. And I have given to all able men ability, that they may make all that I have commanded you: ⁷the tent of meeting, and the ark of the testimony, and the mercy seat that is on it, and all the furnishings of the tent, ⁸the table and its utensils, and the pure lampstand with all its utensils, and the altar of incense, ⁹and the altar of burnt offering with all its utensils, and the basin and its stand, ¹⁰and the finely worked garments,[e] the holy garments for Aaron the priest and

---

[a] A *shekel* was about 2/5 of an ounce or 11 grams [b] A *gerah* was about 1/50 of an ounce or 0.6 gram [c] Or *an offering by fire* [d] A *hin* was about 4 quarts or 3.5 litres [e] Or *garments for worship*

the garments of his sons, for their service as priests, ¹¹and the anointing oil and the fragrant incense for the Holy Place. According to all that I have commanded you, they shall do."

THE SABBATH

¹²And the LORD said to Moses, ¹³"You are to speak to the people of Israel and say, 'Above all you shall keep my Sabbaths, for this is a sign between me and you throughout your generations, that you may know that I, the LORD, sanctify you. ¹⁴You shall keep the Sabbath, because it is holy for you. Everyone who profanes it shall be put to death. Whoever does any work on it, that soul shall be cut off from among his people. ¹⁵For six days shall work be done, but the seventh day is a Sabbath of solemn rest, holy to the LORD. Whoever does any work on the Sabbath day shall be put to death. ¹⁶Therefore the people of Israel shall keep the Sabbath, observing the Sabbath throughout their generations, as a covenant for ever. ¹⁷It is a sign for ever between me and the people of Israel that in six days the LORD made heaven and earth, and on the seventh day he rested and was refreshed.'"

¹⁸And he gave to Moses, when he had finished speaking with him on Mount Sinai, the two tablets of the testimony, tablets of stone, written with the finger of God.

THE GOLDEN CALF

32 When the people saw that Moses delayed to come down from the mountain, the people gathered themselves together to Aaron and said to him, "Up, make us gods who shall go before us. As for this Moses, the man who brought us up out of the land of Egypt, we do not know what has become of him." ²So Aaron said to them, "Take off the rings of gold that are in the ears of your wives, your sons, and your daughters, and bring them to me." ³So all the people took off the rings of gold that were in their ears and brought them to Aaron. ⁴And he received the gold from their hand and fashioned it with a graving tool and made a golden*ᵃ* calf. And they said, "These are your gods, O Israel, who brought you up out of the land of Egypt!" ⁵When Aaron saw this, he built an altar before it. And Aaron made a proclamation and said, "Tomorrow shall be a feast to the LORD." ⁶And they rose up early the next day and offered burnt offerings and brought peace offerings. And the people sat down to eat and drink and rose up to play.

⁷And the LORD said to Moses, "Go down, for your people, whom you brought up out of the land of Egypt, have corrupted themselves. ⁸They have turned aside quickly out of the way that I commanded them. They have made for themselves a golden calf and have worshipped it and sacrificed to it and said, 'These are your gods, O Israel, who brought you up out of the land of Egypt!'" ⁹And the LORD said to Moses, "I have seen this people, and behold, it is a stiff-necked people. ¹⁰Now therefore let me alone, that my wrath may burn hot against them and I may consume them, in order that I may make a great nation of you."

¹¹But Moses implored the LORD his God and said, "O LORD, why does your wrath burn hot against your people, whom you have brought out of the land of Egypt with great power and with a mighty hand? ¹²Why should the Egyptians say, 'With evil intent did he bring them out, to kill them in the mountains and to consume them from the face of the earth'? Turn from your burning anger and relent from this disaster against your people. ¹³Remember Abraham, Isaac, and Israel, your servants, to whom you swore by your own self, and said to them, 'I will multiply your offspring as the stars of heaven, and all this land that I have promised I will give to your offspring, and they shall inherit it for ever.'" ¹⁴And the LORD relented from the disaster that he had spoken of bringing on his people.

¹⁵Then Moses turned and went down from the mountain with the two tablets of the testimony in his hand, tablets that were written on both sides; on the front and on the back they were written. ¹⁶The tablets were the work of God, and the writing was the writing of God, engraved on the tablets. ¹⁷When Joshua heard the noise of the people as they shouted, he said to Moses, "There is a noise of war in the camp." ¹⁸But he said, "It is not the sound of shouting for victory, or the sound of the cry of defeat, but the sound of singing that I hear." ¹⁹And as soon as he came near the camp and saw the calf and the dancing, Moses' anger burned hot, and he threw the tablets out of his hands and broke them at the foot of the mountain. ²⁰He took the calf that they had made and burned it with fire and ground it to powder and scattered it on the water and made the people of Israel drink it.

---

*ᵃ*Hebrew *cast-metal*; also verse 8

²¹And Moses said to Aaron, "What did this people do to you that you have brought such a great sin upon them?" ²²And Aaron said, "Let not the anger of my lord burn hot. You know the people, that they are set on evil. ²³For they said to me, 'Make us gods who shall go before us. As for this Moses, the man who brought us up out of the land of Egypt, we do not know what has become of him.' ²⁴So I said to them, 'Let any who have gold take it off.' So they gave it to me, and I threw it into the fire, and out came this calf."

²⁵And when Moses saw that the people had broken loose (for Aaron had let them break loose, to the derision of their enemies), ²⁶then Moses stood in the gate of the camp and said, "Who is on the LORD's side? Come to me." And all the sons of Levi gathered round him. ²⁷And he said to them, "Thus says the LORD God of Israel, 'Put your sword on your side each of you, and go to and fro from gate to gate throughout the camp, and each of you kill his brother and his companion and his neighbour.'" ²⁸And the sons of Levi did according to the word of Moses. And that day about three thousand men of the people fell. ²⁹And Moses said, "Today you have been ordained for the service of the LORD, each one at the cost of his son and of his brother, so that he might bestow a blessing upon you this day."

³⁰The next day Moses said to the people, "You have sinned a great sin. And now I will go up to the LORD; perhaps I can make atonement for your sin." ³¹So Moses returned to the LORD and said, "Alas, this people has sinned a great sin. They have made for themselves gods of gold. ³²But now, if you will forgive their sin—but if not, please blot me out of your book that you have written." ³³But the LORD said to Moses, "Whoever has sinned against me, I will blot out of my book. ³⁴But now go, lead the people to the place about which I have spoken to you; behold, my angel shall go before you. Nevertheless, in the day when I visit, I will visit their sin upon them."

³⁵Then the LORD sent a plague on the people, because they made the calf, the one that Aaron made.

THE COMMAND TO LEAVE SINAI

33 The LORD said to Moses, "Depart; go up from here, you and the people whom you have brought up out of the land of Egypt, to the land of which I swore to Abraham, Isaac, and Jacob, saying, 'To your offspring I will give it.' ²I will send an angel before you, and I will drive out the Canaanites, the Amorites, the Hittites, the Perizzites, the Hivites, and the Jebusites. ³Go up to a land flowing with milk and honey; but I will not go up among you, lest I consume you on the way, for you are a stiff-necked people."

⁴When the people heard this disastrous word, they mourned, and no one put on his ornaments. ⁵For the LORD had said to Moses, "Say to the people of Israel, 'You are a stiff-necked people; if for a single moment I should go up among you, I would consume you. So now take off your ornaments, that I may know what to do with you.'" ⁶Therefore the people of Israel stripped themselves of their ornaments, from Mount Horeb onwards.

THE TENT OF MEETING

⁷Now Moses used to take the tent and pitch it outside the camp, far off from the camp, and he called it the tent of meeting. And everyone who sought the LORD would go out to the tent of meeting, which was outside the camp. ⁸Whenever Moses went out to the tent, all the people would rise up, and each would stand at his tent door, and watch Moses until he had gone into the tent. ⁹When Moses entered the tent, the pillar of cloud would descend and stand at the entrance of the tent, and the LORD*ᵃ* would speak with Moses. ¹⁰And when all the people saw the pillar of cloud standing at the entrance of the tent, all the people would rise up and worship, each at his tent door. ¹¹Thus the LORD used to speak to Moses face to face, as a man speaks to his friend. When Moses turned again into the camp, his assistant Joshua the son of Nun, a young man, would not depart from the tent.

MOSES' INTERCESSION

¹²Moses said to the LORD, "See, you say to me, 'Bring up this people', but you have not let me know whom you will send with me. Yet you have said, 'I know you by name, and you have also found favour in my sight.' ¹³Now therefore, if I have found favour in your sight, please show me now your ways, that I may know you in order to find favour in your sight. Consider too that this nation is your people." ¹⁴And he said, "My presence will go with you, and I will give you rest." ¹⁵And he said to him, "If your presence will not go with me, do not bring us up from here. ¹⁶For how shall it be known that I have found favour

---
*ᵃ*Hebrew *he*

in your sight, I and your people? Is it not in your going with us, so that we are distinct, I and your people, from every other people on the face of the earth?"

¹⁷And the LORD said to Moses, "This very thing that you have spoken I will do, for you have found favour in my sight, and I know you by name." ¹⁸Moses said, "Please show me your glory." ¹⁹And he said, "I will make all my goodness pass before you and will proclaim before you my name 'The LORD'. And I will be gracious to whom I will be gracious, and will show mercy on whom I will show mercy. ²⁰But," he said, "you cannot see my face, for man shall not see me and live." ²¹And the LORD said, "Behold, there is a place by me where you shall stand on the rock, ²²and while my glory passes by I will put you in a cleft of the rock, and I will cover you with my hand until I have passed by. ²³Then I will take away my hand, and you shall see my back, but my face shall not be seen."

MOSES MAKES NEW TABLETS

34 The LORD said to Moses, "Cut for yourself two tablets of stone like the first, and I will write on the tablets the words that were on the first tablets, which you broke. ²Be ready by the morning, and come up in the morning to Mount Sinai, and present yourself there to me on the top of the mountain. ³No one shall come up with you, and let no one be seen throughout all the mountain. Let no flocks or herds graze opposite that mountain." ⁴So Moses cut two tablets of stone like the first. And he rose early in the morning and went up on Mount Sinai, as the LORD had commanded him, and took in his hand two tablets of stone. ⁵The LORD descended in the cloud and stood with him there, and proclaimed the name of the LORD. ⁶The LORD passed before him and proclaimed, "The LORD, the LORD, a God merciful and gracious, slow to anger, and abounding in steadfast love and faithfulness, ⁷keeping steadfast love for thousands,^a forgiving iniquity and transgression and sin, but who will by no means clear the guilty, visiting the iniquity of the fathers on the children and the children's children, to the third and the fourth generation." ⁸And Moses quickly bowed his head towards the earth and worshipped. ⁹And he said, "If now I have found favour in your sight, O Lord, please let the Lord go in the midst of us, for it is a stiff-necked people, and pardon our iniquity and our sin, and take us for your inheritance."

THE COVENANT RENEWED

¹⁰And he said, "Behold, I am making a covenant. Before all your people I will do marvels, such as have not been created in all the earth or in any nation. And all the people among whom you are shall see the work of the LORD, for it is an awesome thing that I will do with you.

¹¹"Observe what I command you this day. Behold, I will drive out before you the Amorites, the Canaanites, the Hittites, the Perizzites, the Hivites, and the Jebusites. ¹²Take care, lest you make a covenant with the inhabitants of the land to which you go, lest it become a snare in your midst. ¹³You shall tear down their altars and break their pillars and cut down their Asherim ¹⁴(for you shall worship no other god, for the LORD, whose name is Jealous, is a jealous God), ¹⁵lest you make a covenant with the inhabitants of the land, and when they whore after their gods and sacrifice to their gods and you are invited, you eat of his sacrifice, ¹⁶and you take of their daughters for your sons, and their daughters whore after their gods and make your sons whore after their gods.

¹⁷"You shall not make for yourself any gods of cast metal.

¹⁸"You shall keep the Feast of Unleavened Bread. For seven days you shall eat unleavened bread, as I commanded you, at the time appointed in the month Abib, for in the month Abib you came out from Egypt. ¹⁹All that open the womb are mine, all your male^b livestock, the firstborn of cow and sheep. ²⁰The firstborn of a donkey you shall redeem with a lamb, or if you will not redeem it you shall break its neck. All the firstborn of your sons you shall redeem. And none shall appear before me empty-handed.

²¹"For six days you shall work, but on the seventh day you shall rest. In ploughing time and in harvest you shall rest. ²²You shall observe the Feast of Weeks, the firstfruits of wheat harvest, and the Feast of Ingathering at the year's end. ²³Three times in the year shall all your males appear before the LORD God, the God of Israel. ²⁴For I will cast out nations before you and enlarge your borders; no one shall covet your land, when you go

---

^aOr *to the thousandth generation*   ^bSeptuagint, Theodotion, Vulgate, Targum; the meaning of the Hebrew is uncertain

up to appear before the Lord your God three times in the year.

²⁵"You shall not offer the blood of my sacrifice with anything leavened, or let the sacrifice of the Feast of the Passover remain until the morning. ²⁶The best of the firstfruits of your ground you shall bring to the house of the Lord your God. You shall not boil a young goat in its mother's milk."

²⁷And the Lord said to Moses, "Write these words, for in accordance with these words I have made a covenant with you and with Israel." ²⁸So he was there with the Lord for forty days and forty nights. He neither ate bread nor drank water. And he wrote on the tablets the words of the covenant, the Ten Commandments.[a]

THE SHINING FACE OF MOSES

²⁹When Moses came down from Mount Sinai, with the two tablets of the testimony in his hand as he came down from the mountain, Moses did not know that the skin of his face shone because he had been talking with God.[b] ³⁰Aaron and all the people of Israel saw Moses, and behold, the skin of his face shone, and they were afraid to come near him. ³¹But Moses called to them, and Aaron and all the leaders of the congregation returned to him, and Moses talked with them. ³²Afterwards all the people of Israel came near, and he commanded them all that the Lord had spoken with him in Mount Sinai. ³³And when Moses had finished speaking with them, he put a veil over his face.

³⁴Whenever Moses went in before the Lord to speak with him, he would remove the veil, until he came out. And when he came out and told the people of Israel what he was commanded, ³⁵the people of Israel would see the face of Moses, that the skin of Moses' face was shining. And Moses would put the veil over his face again, until he went in to speak with him.

SABBATH REGULATIONS

35 Moses assembled all the congregation of the people of Israel and said to them, "These are the things that the Lord has commanded you to do. ²For six days work shall be done, but on the seventh day you shall have a Sabbath of solemn rest, holy to the Lord. Whoever does any work on it shall be put to death. ³You shall kindle no fire in all your dwelling places on the Sabbath day."

CONTRIBUTIONS FOR THE TABERNACLE

⁴Moses said to all the congregation of the people of Israel, "This is the thing that the Lord has commanded. ⁵Take from among you a contribution to the Lord. Whoever is of a generous heart, let him bring the Lord's contribution: gold, silver, and bronze; ⁶blue and purple and scarlet yarns and fine twined linen; goats' hair, ⁷tanned rams' skins, and goatskins;[c] acacia wood, ⁸oil for the light, spices for the anointing oil and for the fragrant incense, ⁹and onyx stones and stones for setting, for the ephod and for the breastpiece.

¹⁰"Let every skilful craftsman among you come and make all that the Lord has commanded: ¹¹the tabernacle, its tent and its covering, its hooks and its frames, its bars, its pillars, and its bases; ¹²the ark with its poles, the mercy seat, and the veil of the screen; ¹³the table with its poles and all its utensils, and the bread of the Presence; ¹⁴the lampstand also for the light, with its utensils and its lamps, and the oil for the light; ¹⁵and the altar of incense, with its poles, and the anointing oil and the fragrant incense, and the screen for the door, at the door of the tabernacle; ¹⁶the altar of burnt offering, with its grating of bronze, its poles, and all its utensils, the basin and its stand; ¹⁷the hangings of the court, its pillars and its bases, and the screen for the gate of the court; ¹⁸the pegs of the tabernacle and the pegs of the court, and their cords; ¹⁹the finely worked garments for ministering[d] in the Holy Place, the holy garments for Aaron the priest, and the garments of his sons, for their service as priests."

²⁰Then all the congregation of the people of Israel departed from the presence of Moses. ²¹And they came, everyone whose heart stirred him, and everyone whose spirit moved him, and brought the Lord's contribution to be used for the tent of meeting, and for all its service, and for the holy garments. ²²So they came, both men and women. All who were of a willing heart brought brooches and earrings and signet rings and armlets, all sorts of gold objects, every man dedicating an offering of gold to the Lord. ²³And everyone who possessed blue or purple or scarlet yarns or fine linen or goats' hair or tanned rams' skins or goatskins brought them. ²⁴Everyone who could

---

[a]Hebrew *the ten words* [b]Hebrew *him* [c]The meaning of the Hebrew word is uncertain; also verse 23; compare 25:5 [d]Or *garments for worship*; see 31:10

make a contribution of silver or bronze brought it as the Lord's contribution. And everyone who possessed acacia wood of any use in the work brought it. 25And every skilful woman spun with her hands, and they all brought what they had spun in blue and purple and scarlet yarns and fine twined linen. 26All the women whose hearts stirred them to use their skill spun the goats' hair. 27And the leaders brought onyx stones and stones to be set, for the ephod and for the breastpiece, 28and spices and oil for the light, and for the anointing oil, and for the fragrant incense. 29All the men and women, the people of Israel, whose heart moved them to bring anything for the work that the Lord had commanded by Moses to be done brought it as a freewill offering to the Lord.

CONSTRUCTION OF THE TABERNACLE

30Then Moses said to the people of Israel, "See, the Lord has called by name Bezalel the son of Uri, son of Hur, of the tribe of Judah; 31and he has filled him with the Spirit of God, with skill, with intelligence, with knowledge, and with all craftsmanship, 32to devise artistic designs, to work in gold and silver and bronze, 33in cutting stones for setting, and in carving wood, for work in every skilled craft. 34And he has inspired him to teach, both him and Oholiab the son of Ahisamach of the tribe of Dan. 35He has filled them with skill to do every sort of work done by an engraver or by a designer or by an embroiderer in blue and purple and scarlet yarns and fine twined linen, or by a weaver—by any sort of workman or skilled designer.

36 "Bezalel and Oholiab and every craftsman in whom the Lord has put skill and intelligence to know how to do any work in the construction of the sanctuary shall work in accordance with all that the Lord has commanded."

2And Moses called Bezalel and Oholiab and every craftsman in whose mind the Lord had put skill, everyone whose heart stirred him up to come to do the work. 3And they received from Moses all the contribution that the people of Israel had brought for doing the work on the sanctuary. They still kept bringing him freewill offerings every morning, 4so that all the craftsmen who were doing every sort of task on the sanctuary came, each from the task that he was doing, 5and said to Moses, "The people bring much more than enough for doing the work that the Lord has commanded us to do." 6So Moses gave command, and word was proclaimed throughout the camp, "Let no man or woman do anything more for the contribution for the sanctuary." So the people were restrained from bringing, 7for the material they had was sufficient to do all the work, and more.

8And all the craftsmen among the workmen made the tabernacle with ten curtains. They were made of fine twined linen and blue and purple and scarlet yarns, with cherubim skilfully worked. 9The length of each curtain was twenty-eight cubits,[a] and the breadth of each curtain four cubits. All the curtains were the same size.

10He[b] coupled five curtains to one another, and the other five curtains he coupled to one another. 11He made loops of blue on the edge of the outermost curtain of the first set. Likewise he made them on the edge of the outermost curtain of the second set. 12He made fifty loops on the one curtain, and he made fifty loops on the edge of the curtain that was in the second set. The loops were opposite one another. 13And he made fifty clasps of gold, and coupled the curtains one to the other with clasps. So the tabernacle was a single whole.

14He also made curtains of goats' hair for a tent over the tabernacle. He made eleven curtains. 15The length of each curtain was thirty cubits, and the breadth of each curtain four cubits. The eleven curtains were the same size. 16He coupled five curtains by themselves, and six curtains by themselves. 17And he made fifty loops on the edge of the outermost curtain of one set, and fifty loops on the edge of the other connecting curtain. 18And he made fifty clasps of bronze to couple the tent together that it might be a single whole. 19And he made for the tent a covering of tanned rams' skins and goatskins.

20Then he made the upright frames for the tabernacle of acacia wood. 21Ten cubits was the length of a frame, and a cubit and a half the breadth of each frame. 22Each frame had two tenons for fitting together. He did this for all the frames of the tabernacle. 23The frames for the tabernacle he made thus: twenty frames for the south side. 24And he made forty bases of silver under the twenty frames, two bases under one frame for its two tenons, and two bases under the next frame for its two tenons. 25For the second side of the tabernacle,

---

[a]A *cubit* was about 18 inches or 45 centimetres [b]Probably Bezalel (compare 35:30; 37:1)

on the north side, he made twenty frames ²⁶and their forty bases of silver, two bases under one frame and two bases under the next frame. ²⁷For the rear of the tabernacle westward he made six frames. ²⁸He made two frames for corners of the tabernacle in the rear. ²⁹And they were separate beneath but joined at the top, at the first ring. He made two of them this way for the two corners. ³⁰There were eight frames with their bases of silver: sixteen bases, under every frame two bases.

³¹He made bars of acacia wood, five for the frames of one side of the tabernacle, ³²and five bars for the frames of the other side of the tabernacle, and five bars for the frames of the tabernacle at the rear westward. ³³And he made the middle bar to run from end to end halfway up the frames. ³⁴And he overlaid the frames with gold, and made their rings of gold for holders for the bars, and overlaid the bars with gold.

³⁵He made the veil of blue and purple and scarlet yarns and fine twined linen; with cherubim skilfully worked into it he made it. ³⁶And for it he made four pillars of acacia and overlaid them with gold. Their hooks were of gold, and he cast for them four bases of silver. ³⁷He also made a screen for the entrance of the tent, of blue and purple and scarlet yarns and fine twined linen, embroidered with needlework, ³⁸and its five pillars with their hooks. He overlaid their capitals, and their fillets were of gold, but their five bases were of bronze.

MAKING THE ARK

37 Bezalel made the ark of acacia wood. Two cubits^a and a half was its length, a cubit and a half its breadth, and a cubit and a half its height. ²And he overlaid it with pure gold inside and outside, and made a moulding of gold round it. ³And he cast for it four rings of gold for its four feet, two rings on its one side and two rings on its other side. ⁴And he made poles of acacia wood and overlaid them with gold ⁵and put the poles into the rings on the sides of the ark to carry the ark. ⁶And he made a mercy seat of pure gold. Two cubits and a half was its length, and a cubit and a half its breadth. ⁷And he made two cherubim of gold. He made them of hammered work on the two ends of the mercy seat, ⁸one cherub on one end, and one cherub on the other end. Of one piece with the mercy seat he made the cherubim on its two ends. ⁹The cherubim spread out their wings above, overshadowing the mercy seat with their wings, with their faces one to another; towards the mercy seat were the faces of the cherubim.

MAKING THE TABLE

¹⁰He also made the table of acacia wood. Two cubits was its length, a cubit its breadth, and a cubit and a half its height. ¹¹And he overlaid it with pure gold, and made a moulding of gold round it. ¹²And he made a rim round it a handbreadth^b wide, and made a moulding of gold round the rim. ¹³He cast for it four rings of gold and fastened the rings to the four corners at its four legs. ¹⁴Close to the frame were the rings, as holders for the poles to carry the table. ¹⁵He made the poles of acacia wood to carry the table, and overlaid them with gold. ¹⁶And he made the vessels of pure gold that were to be on the table, its plates and dishes for incense, and its bowls and flagons with which to pour drink offerings.

MAKING THE LAMPSTAND

¹⁷He also made the lampstand of pure gold. He made the lampstand of hammered work. Its base, its stem, its cups, its calyxes, and its flowers were of one piece with it. ¹⁸And there were six branches going out of its sides, three branches of the lampstand out of one side of it and three branches of the lampstand out of the other side of it; ¹⁹three cups made like almond blossoms, each with calyx and flower, on one branch, and three cups made like almond blossoms, each with calyx and flower, on the other branch — so for the six branches going out of the lampstand. ²⁰And on the lampstand itself were four cups made like almond blossoms, with their calyxes and flowers, ²¹and a calyx of one piece with it under each pair of the six branches going out of it. ²²Their calyxes and their branches were of one piece with it. The whole of it was a single piece of hammered work of pure gold. ²³And he made its seven lamps and its tongs and its trays of pure gold. ²⁴He made it and all its utensils out of a talent^c of pure gold.

MAKING THE ALTAR OF INCENSE

²⁵He made the altar of incense of acacia wood. Its length was a cubit, and its breadth was a cubit. It was square, and two cubits was its height. Its horns were of one piece with it. ²⁶He overlaid it with pure gold, its top and

---
^{a}A *cubit* was about 18 inches or 45 centimetres ^{b}A *handbreadth* was about 3 inches or 7.5 centimetres ^{c}A *talent* was about 75 pounds or 34 kilograms

round its sides and its horns. And he made a moulding of gold round it, ²⁷and made two rings of gold on it under its moulding, on two opposite sides of it, as holders for the poles with which to carry it. ²⁸And he made the poles of acacia wood and overlaid them with gold.

²⁹He made the holy anointing oil also, and the pure fragrant incense, blended as by the perfumer.

MAKING THE ALTAR OF BURNT OFFERING

38 He made the altar of burnt offering of acacia wood. Five cubits*ᵃ* was its length, and five cubits its breadth. It was square, and three cubits was its height. ²He made horns for it on its four corners. Its horns were of one piece with it, and he overlaid it with bronze. ³And he made all the utensils of the altar, the pots, the shovels, the basins, the forks, and the firepans. He made all its utensils of bronze. ⁴And he made for the altar a grating, a network of bronze, under its ledge, extending halfway down. ⁵He cast four rings on the four corners of the bronze grating as holders for the poles. ⁶He made the poles of acacia wood and overlaid them with bronze. ⁷And he put the poles through the rings on the sides of the altar to carry it with them. He made it hollow, with boards.

MAKING THE BRONZE BASIN

⁸He made the basin of bronze and its stand of bronze, from the mirrors of the ministering women who ministered in the entrance of the tent of meeting.

MAKING THE COURT

⁹And he made the court. For the south side the hangings of the court were of fine twined linen, a hundred cubits; ¹⁰their twenty pillars and their twenty bases were of bronze, but the hooks of the pillars and their fillets were of silver. ¹¹And for the north side there were hangings of a hundred cubits; their twenty pillars and their twenty bases were of bronze, but the hooks of the pillars and their fillets were of silver. ¹²And for the west side were hangings of fifty cubits, their ten pillars, and their ten bases; the hooks of the pillars and their fillets were of silver. ¹³And for the front to the east, fifty cubits. ¹⁴The hangings for one side of the gate were fifteen cubits, with their three pillars and three bases. ¹⁵And so for the other side. On both sides of the gate of the court were hangings of fifteen cubits, with their three pillars and their three bases. ¹⁶All the hangings round the court were of fine twined linen. ¹⁷And the bases for the pillars were of bronze, but the hooks of the pillars and their fillets were of silver. The overlaying of their capitals was also of silver, and all the pillars of the court were filleted with silver. ¹⁸And the screen for the gate of the court was embroidered with needlework in blue and purple and scarlet yarns and fine twined linen. It was twenty cubits long and five cubits high in its breadth, corresponding to the hangings of the court. ¹⁹And their pillars were four in number. Their four bases were of bronze, their hooks of silver, and the overlaying of their capitals and their fillets of silver. ²⁰And all the pegs for the tabernacle and for the court all round were of bronze.

MATERIALS FOR THE TABERNACLE

²¹These are the records of the tabernacle, the tabernacle of the testimony, as they were recorded at the commandment of Moses, the responsibility of the Levites under the direction of Ithamar the son of Aaron the priest. ²²Bezalel the son of Uri, son of Hur, of the tribe of Judah, made all that the LORD commanded Moses; ²³and with him was Oholiab the son of Ahisamach, of the tribe of Dan, an engraver and designer and embroiderer in blue and purple and scarlet yarns and fine twined linen. ²⁴All the gold that was used for the work, in all the construction of the sanctuary, the gold from the offering, was twenty-nine talents and 730 shekels,*ᵇ* by the shekel of the sanctuary. ²⁵The silver from those of the congregation who were recorded was a hundred talents and 1,775 shekels, by the shekel of the sanctuary: ²⁶a beka*ᶜ* a head (that is, half a shekel, by the shekel of the sanctuary), for everyone who was listed in the records, from twenty years old and upwards, for 603,550 men. ²⁷The hundred talents of silver were for casting the bases of the sanctuary and the bases of the veil; a hundred bases for the hundred talents, a talent a base. ²⁸And of the 1,775 shekels he made hooks for the pillars and overlaid their capitals and made fillets for them. ²⁹The bronze that was offered was seventy talents and 2,400 shekels; ³⁰with it he made the bases for the entrance of the tent of meeting, the bronze altar and the bronze grating for it and all the utensils of the altar,

---

ᵃA cubit was about 18 inches or 45 centimetres *ᵇA talent* was about 75 pounds or 34 kilograms; a *shekel* was about 2/5 of an ounce or 11 grams   *ᶜA beka* was about 1/5 of an ounce or 5.5 grams

³¹the bases round the court, and the bases of the gate of the court, all the pegs of the tabernacle, and all the pegs round the court.

MAKING THE PRIESTLY GARMENTS

39 From the blue and purple and scarlet yarns they made finely woven garments,[a] for ministering in the Holy Place. They made the holy garments for Aaron, as the LORD had commanded Moses. ²He made the ephod of gold, blue and purple and scarlet yarns, and fine twined linen. ³And they hammered out gold leaf, and he cut it into threads to work into the blue and purple and the scarlet yarns, and into the fine twined linen, in skilled design. ⁴They made for the ephod attaching shoulder pieces, joined to it at its two edges. ⁵And the skilfully woven band on it was of one piece with it and made like it, of gold, blue and purple and scarlet yarns, and fine twined linen, as the LORD had commanded Moses.

⁶They made the onyx stones, enclosed in settings of gold filigree, and engraved like the engravings of a signet, according to the names of the sons of Israel. ⁷And he set them on the shoulder pieces of the ephod to be stones of remembrance for the sons of Israel, as the LORD had commanded Moses.

⁸He made the breastpiece, in skilled work, in the style of the ephod, of gold, blue and purple and scarlet yarns, and fine twined linen. ⁹It was square. They made the breastpiece doubled, a span[b] its length and a span its breadth when doubled. ¹⁰And they set in it four rows of stones. A row of sardius, topaz, and carbuncle was the first row; ¹¹and the second row, an emerald, a sapphire, and a diamond; ¹²and the third row, a jacinth, an agate, and an amethyst; ¹³and the fourth row, a beryl, an onyx, and a jasper. They were enclosed in settings of gold filigree. ¹⁴There were twelve stones with their names according to the names of the sons of Israel. They were like signets, each engraved with its name, for the twelve tribes. ¹⁵And they made on the breastpiece twisted chains like cords, of pure gold. ¹⁶And they made two settings of gold filigree and two gold rings, and put the two rings on the two edges of the breastpiece. ¹⁷And they put the two cords of gold in the two rings at the edges of the breastpiece. ¹⁸They attached the two ends of the two cords to the two settings of filigree. Thus they attached it in front to the shoulder pieces of the ephod. ¹⁹Then they made two rings of gold, and put them at the two ends of the breastpiece, on its inside edge next to the ephod. ²⁰And they made two rings of gold, and attached them in front to the lower part of the two shoulder pieces of the ephod, at its seam above the skilfully woven band of the ephod. ²¹And they bound the breastpiece by its rings to the rings of the ephod with a lace of blue, so that it should lie on the skilfully woven band of the ephod, and that the breastpiece should not come loose from the ephod, as the LORD had commanded Moses.

²²He also made the robe of the ephod woven all of blue, ²³and the opening of the robe in it was like the opening in a garment, with a binding round the opening, so that it might not tear. ²⁴On the hem of the robe they made pomegranates of blue and purple and scarlet yarns and fine twined linen. ²⁵They also made bells of pure gold, and put the bells between the pomegranates all round the hem of the robe, between the pomegranates — ²⁶a bell and a pomegranate, a bell and a pomegranate around the hem of the robe for ministering, as the LORD had commanded Moses.

²⁷They also made the coats, woven of fine linen, for Aaron and his sons, ²⁸and the turban of fine linen, and the caps of fine linen, and the linen undergarments of fine twined linen, ²⁹and the sash of fine twined linen and of blue and purple and scarlet yarns, embroidered with needlework, as the LORD had commanded Moses.

³⁰They made the plate of the holy crown of pure gold, and wrote on it an inscription, like the engraving of a signet, "Holy to the LORD." ³¹And they tied to it a cord of blue to fasten it on the turban above, as the LORD had commanded Moses.

³²Thus all the work of the tabernacle of the tent of meeting was finished, and the people of Israel did according to all that the LORD had commanded Moses; so they did. ³³Then they brought the tabernacle to Moses, the tent and all its utensils, its hooks, its frames, its bars, its pillars, and its bases; ³⁴the covering of tanned rams' skins and goatskins, and the veil of the screen; ³⁵the ark of the testimony with its poles and the mercy seat; ³⁶the table with all its utensils, and the bread of the Presence; ³⁷the lampstand of pure gold and its lamps with the lamps set and all its utensils, and the oil for the light; ³⁸the golden altar, the anointing oil and the fragrant incense, and the screen

---

[a] Or *garments for worship* [b] A *span* was about 9 inches or 22 centimetres

for the entrance of the tent; ³⁹the bronze altar, and its grating of bronze, its poles, and all its utensils; the basin and its stand; ⁴⁰the hangings of the court, its pillars, and its bases, and the screen for the gate of the court, its cords, and its pegs; and all the utensils for the service of the tabernacle, for the tent of meeting; ⁴¹the finely worked garments for ministering in the Holy Place, the holy garments for Aaron the priest, and the garments of his sons for their service as priests. ⁴²According to all that the LORD had commanded Moses, so the people of Israel had done all the work. ⁴³And Moses saw all the work, and behold, they had done it; as the LORD had commanded, so had they done it. Then Moses blessed them.

THE TABERNACLE ERECTED

40 The LORD spoke to Moses, saying, ²"On the first day of the first month you shall erect the tabernacle of the tent of meeting. ³And you shall put in it the ark of the testimony, and you shall screen the ark with the veil. ⁴And you shall bring in the table and arrange it, and you shall bring in the lampstand and set up its lamps. ⁵And you shall put the golden altar for incense before the ark of the testimony, and set up the screen for the door of the tabernacle. ⁶You shall set the altar of burnt offering before the door of the tabernacle of the tent of meeting, ⁷and place the basin between the tent of meeting and the altar, and put water in it. ⁸And you shall set up the court all round, and hang up the screen for the gate of the court.

⁹"Then you shall take the anointing oil and anoint the tabernacle and all that is in it, and consecrate it and all its furniture, so that it may become holy. ¹⁰You shall also anoint the altar of burnt offering and all its utensils, and consecrate the altar, so that the altar may become most holy. ¹¹You shall also anoint the basin and its stand, and consecrate it. ¹²Then you shall bring Aaron and his sons to the entrance of the tent of meeting and shall wash them with water ¹³and put on Aaron the holy garments. And you shall anoint him and consecrate him, that he may serve me as priest. ¹⁴You shall bring his sons also and put coats on them, ¹⁵and anoint them, as you anointed their father, that they may serve me as priests. And their anointing shall admit them to a perpetual priesthood throughout their generations."

¹⁶This Moses did; according to all that the LORD commanded him, so he did. ¹⁷In the first month in the second year, on the first day of the month, the tabernacle was erected. ¹⁸Moses erected the tabernacle. He laid its bases, and set up its frames, and put in its poles, and raised up its pillars. ¹⁹And he spread the tent over the tabernacle and put the covering of the tent over it, as the LORD had commanded Moses. ²⁰He took the testimony and put it into the ark, and put the poles on the ark and set the mercy seat above on the ark. ²¹And he brought the ark into the tabernacle and set up the veil of the screen, and screened the ark of the testimony, as the LORD had commanded Moses. ²²He put the table in the tent of meeting, on the north side of the tabernacle, outside the veil, ²³and arranged the bread on it before the LORD, as the LORD had commanded Moses. ²⁴He put the lampstand in the tent of meeting, opposite the table on the south side of the tabernacle, ²⁵and set up the lamps before the LORD, as the LORD had commanded Moses. ²⁶He put the golden altar in the tent of meeting before the veil, ²⁷and burned fragrant incense on it, as the LORD had commanded Moses. ²⁸He put in place the screen for the door of the tabernacle. ²⁹And he set the altar of burnt offering at the entrance of the tabernacle of the tent of meeting, and offered on it the burnt offering and the grain offering, as the LORD had commanded Moses. ³⁰He set the basin between the tent of meeting and the altar, and put water in it for washing, ³¹with which Moses and Aaron and his sons washed their hands and their feet. ³²When they went into the tent of meeting, and when they approached the altar, they washed, as the LORD commanded Moses. ³³And he erected the court round the tabernacle and the altar, and set up the screen of the gate of the court. So Moses finished the work.

THE GLORY OF THE LORD

³⁴Then the cloud covered the tent of meeting, and the glory of the LORD filled the tabernacle. ³⁵And Moses was not able to enter the tent of meeting because the cloud settled on it, and the glory of the LORD filled the tabernacle. ³⁶Throughout all their journeys, whenever the cloud was taken up from over the tabernacle, the people of Israel would set out. ³⁷But if the cloud was not taken up, then they did not set out till the day that it was taken up. ³⁸For the cloud of the LORD was on the tabernacle by day, and fire was in it by night, in the sight of all the house of Israel throughout all their journeys.

LEVITICUS

LAWS FOR BURNT OFFERINGS

1 The LORD called Moses and spoke to him from the tent of meeting, saying, ²"Speak to the people of Israel and say to them, When any one of you brings an offering to the LORD, you shall bring your offering of livestock from the herd or from the flock.

³"If his offering is a burnt offering from the herd, he shall offer a male without blemish. He shall bring it to the entrance of the tent of meeting, that he may be accepted before the LORD. ⁴He shall lay his hand on the head of the burnt offering, and it shall be accepted for him to make atonement for him. ⁵Then he shall kill the bull before the LORD, and Aaron's sons the priests shall bring the blood and throw the blood against the sides of the altar that is at the entrance of the tent of meeting. ⁶Then he shall flay the burnt offering and cut it into pieces, ⁷and the sons of Aaron the priest shall put fire on the altar and arrange wood on the fire. ⁸And Aaron's sons the priests shall arrange the pieces, the head, and the fat, on the wood that is on the fire on the altar; ⁹but its entrails and its legs he shall wash with water. And the priest shall burn all of it on the altar, as a burnt offering, a food offering*ᵃ* with a pleasing aroma to the LORD.

¹⁰"If his gift for a burnt offering is from the flock, from the sheep or goats, he shall bring a male without blemish, ¹¹and he shall kill it on the north side of the altar before the LORD, and Aaron's sons the priests shall throw its blood against the sides of the altar. ¹²And he shall cut it into pieces, with its head and its fat, and the priest shall arrange them on the wood that is on the fire on the altar, ¹³but the entrails and the legs he shall wash with water. And the priest shall offer all of it and burn it on the altar; it is a burnt offering, a food offering with a pleasing aroma to the LORD.

¹⁴"If his offering to the LORD is a burnt offering of birds, then he shall bring his offering of turtle-doves or pigeons. ¹⁵And the priest shall bring it to the altar and wring off its head and burn it on the altar. Its blood shall be drained out on the side of the altar. ¹⁶He shall remove its crop with its contents*ᵇ* and cast it beside the altar on the east side, in the place for ashes. ¹⁷He shall tear it open by its wings, but shall not sever it completely. And the priest shall burn it on the altar, on the wood that is on the fire. It is a burnt offering, a food offering with a pleasing aroma to the LORD.

LAWS FOR GRAIN OFFERINGS

2 "When anyone brings a grain offering as an offering to the LORD, his offering shall be of fine flour. He shall pour oil on it and put frankincense on it ²and bring it to Aaron's sons the priests. And he shall take from it a handful of the fine flour and oil, with all of its frankincense, and the priest shall burn this as its memorial portion on the altar, a food offering with a pleasing aroma to the LORD. ³But the rest of the grain offering shall be for Aaron and his sons; it is a most holy part of the LORD's food offerings.

⁴"When you bring a grain offering baked in the oven as an offering, it shall be unleavened loaves of fine flour mixed with oil or unleavened wafers smeared with oil. ⁵And if your offering is a grain offering baked on a griddle, it shall be of fine flour unleavened, mixed with oil. ⁶You shall break it in pieces and pour oil on it; it is a grain offering. ⁷And if your offering is a grain offering cooked in a pan, it shall be made of fine flour with oil. ⁸And you shall bring the grain offering that is made of these things to the LORD, and when it is presented to the priest, he shall bring it to the altar. ⁹And the priest shall take from the grain offering its memorial portion and burn this on the altar, a food offering with a pleasing aroma to the LORD. ¹⁰But the rest of the grain offering shall be for Aaron and his sons; it is a most holy part of the LORD's food offerings.

¹¹"No grain offering that you bring to the LORD shall be made with leaven, for you shall burn no leaven nor any honey as a food offering to the LORD. ¹²As an offering of firstfruits you may bring them to the LORD, but they

---

*ᵃ*Or *an offering by fire;* so throughout Leviticus *ᵇ*Or *feathers*

shall not be offered on the altar for a pleasing aroma. ¹³You shall season all your grain offerings with salt. You shall not let the salt of the covenant with your God be missing from your grain offering; with all your offerings you shall offer salt.

¹⁴"If you offer a grain offering of firstfruits to the Lord, you shall offer for the grain offering of your firstfruits fresh ears, roasted with fire, crushed new grain. ¹⁵And you shall put oil on it and lay frankincense on it; it is a grain offering. ¹⁶And the priest shall burn as its memorial portion some of the crushed grain and some of the oil with all of its frankincense; it is a food offering to the Lord.

LAWS FOR PEACE OFFERINGS

3 "If his offering is a sacrifice of peace offering, if he offers an animal from the herd, male or female, he shall offer it without blemish before the Lord. ²And he shall lay his hand on the head of his offering and kill it at the entrance of the tent of meeting, and Aaron's sons the priests shall throw the blood against the sides of the altar. ³And from the sacrifice of the peace offering, as a food offering to the Lord, he shall offer the fat covering the entrails and all the fat that is on the entrails, ⁴and the two kidneys with the fat that is on them at the loins, and the long lobe of the liver that he shall remove with the kidneys. ⁵Then Aaron's sons shall burn it on the altar on top of the burnt offering, which is on the wood on the fire; it is a food offering with a pleasing aroma to the Lord.

⁶"If his offering for a sacrifice of peace offering to the Lord is an animal from the flock, male or female, he shall offer it without blemish. ⁷If he offers a lamb for his offering, then he shall offer it before the Lord, ⁸lay his hand on the head of his offering, and kill it in front of the tent of meeting; and Aaron's sons shall throw its blood against the sides of the altar. ⁹Then from the sacrifice of the peace offering he shall offer as a food offering to the Lord its fat; he shall remove the whole fat tail, cut off close to the backbone, and the fat that covers the entrails and all the fat that is on the entrails ¹⁰and the two kidneys with the fat that is on them at the loins and the long lobe of the liver that he shall remove with the kidneys. ¹¹And the priest shall burn it on the altar as a food offering to the Lord.

¹²"If his offering is a goat, then he shall offer it before the Lord ¹³and lay his hand on its head and kill it in front of the tent of meeting, and the sons of Aaron shall throw its blood against the sides of the altar. ¹⁴Then he shall offer from it, as his offering for a food offering to the Lord, the fat covering the entrails and all the fat that is on the entrails ¹⁵and the two kidneys with the fat that is on them at the loins and the long lobe of the liver that he shall remove with the kidneys. ¹⁶And the priest shall burn them on the altar as a food offering with a pleasing aroma. All fat is the Lord's. ¹⁷It shall be a statute for ever throughout your generations, in all your dwelling places, that you eat neither fat nor blood."

LAWS FOR SIN OFFERINGS

4 And the Lord spoke to Moses, saying, ²"Speak to the people of Israel, saying, If anyone sins unintentionally[a] in any of the Lord's commandments about things not to be done, and does any one of them, ³if it is the anointed priest who sins, thus bringing guilt on the people, then he shall offer for the sin that he has committed a bull from the herd without blemish to the Lord for a sin offering. ⁴He shall bring the bull to the entrance of the tent of meeting before the Lord and lay his hand on the head of the bull and kill the bull before the Lord. ⁵And the anointed priest shall take some of the blood of the bull and bring it into the tent of meeting, ⁶and the priest shall dip his finger in the blood and sprinkle part of the blood seven times before the Lord in front of the veil of the sanctuary. ⁷And the priest shall put some of the blood on the horns of the altar of fragrant incense before the Lord that is in the tent of meeting, and all the rest of the blood of the bull he shall pour out at the base of the altar of burnt offering that is at the entrance of the tent of meeting. ⁸And all the fat of the bull of the sin offering he shall remove from it, the fat that covers the entrails and all the fat that is on the entrails ⁹and the two kidneys with the fat that is on them at the loins and the long lobe of the liver that he shall remove with the kidneys ¹⁰(just as these are taken from the ox of the sacrifice of the peace offerings); and the priest shall burn them on the altar of burnt offering. ¹¹But the skin of the bull and all its flesh, with its head, its legs, its entrails, and its dung— ¹²all the rest of the bull—he shall carry outside the camp to a clean place, to the ash heap, and shall burn it up on a fire of wood. On the ash heap it shall be burned up.

---

[a] Or *by mistake*; so throughout Leviticus

¹³"If the whole congregation of Israel sins unintentionally[a] and the thing is hidden from the eyes of the assembly, and they do any one of the things that by the LORD's commandments ought not to be done, and they realize their guilt,[b] ¹⁴when the sin which they have committed becomes known, the assembly shall offer a bull from the herd for a sin offering and bring it in front of the tent of meeting. ¹⁵And the elders of the congregation shall lay their hands on the head of the bull before the LORD, and the bull shall be killed before the LORD. ¹⁶Then the anointed priest shall bring some of the blood of the bull into the tent of meeting, ¹⁷and the priest shall dip his finger in the blood and sprinkle it seven times before the LORD in front of the veil. ¹⁸And he shall put some of the blood on the horns of the altar that is in the tent of meeting before the LORD, and the rest of the blood he shall pour out at the base of the altar of burnt offering that is at the entrance of the tent of meeting. ¹⁹And all its fat he shall take from it and burn on the altar. ²⁰Thus shall he do with the bull. As he did with the bull of the sin offering, so shall he do with this. And the priest shall make atonement for them, and they shall be forgiven. ²¹And he shall carry the bull outside the camp and burn it up as he burned the first bull; it is the sin offering for the assembly.

²²"When a leader sins, doing unintentionally any one of all the things that by the commandments of the LORD his God ought not to be done, and realizes his guilt, ²³or the sin which he has committed is made known to him, he shall bring as his offering a goat, a male without blemish, ²⁴and shall lay his hand on the head of the goat and kill it in the place where they kill the burnt offering before the LORD; it is a sin offering. ²⁵Then the priest shall take some of the blood of the sin offering with his finger and put it on the horns of the altar of burnt offering and pour out the rest of its blood at the base of the altar of burnt offering. ²⁶And all its fat he shall burn on the altar, like the fat of the sacrifice of peace offerings. So the priest shall make atonement for him for his sin, and he shall be forgiven.

²⁷"If any one of the common people sins unintentionally in doing any one of the things that by the LORD's commandments ought not to be done, and realizes his guilt, ²⁸or the sin which he has committed is made known to him, he shall bring for his offering a goat, a female without blemish, for his sin which he has committed. ²⁹And he shall lay his hand on the head of the sin offering and kill the sin offering in the place of burnt offering. ³⁰And the priest shall take some of its blood with his finger and put it on the horns of the altar of burnt offering and pour out all the rest of its blood at the base of the altar. ³¹And all its fat he shall remove, as the fat is removed from the peace offerings, and the priest shall burn it on the altar for a pleasing aroma to the LORD. And the priest shall make atonement for him, and he shall be forgiven.

³²"If he brings a lamb as his offering for a sin offering, he shall bring a female without blemish ³³and lay his hand on the head of the sin offering and kill it for a sin offering in the place where they kill the burnt offering. ³⁴Then the priest shall take some of the blood of the sin offering with his finger and put it on the horns of the altar of burnt offering and pour out all the rest of its blood at the base of the altar. ³⁵And all its fat he shall remove as the fat of the lamb is removed from the sacrifice of peace offerings, and the priest shall burn it on the altar, on top of the LORD's food offerings. And the priest shall make atonement for him for the sin which he has committed, and he shall be forgiven.

5 "If anyone sins in that he hears a public adjuration to testify, and though he is a witness, whether he has seen or come to know the matter, yet does not speak, he shall bear his iniquity; ²or if anyone touches an unclean thing, whether a carcass of an unclean wild animal or a carcass of unclean livestock or a carcass of unclean swarming things, and it is hidden from him and he has become unclean, and he realizes his guilt; ³or if he touches human uncleanness, of whatever sort the uncleanness may be with which one becomes unclean, and it is hidden from him, when he comes to know it, and realizes his guilt; ⁴or if anyone utters with his lips a rash oath to do evil or to do good, any sort of rash oath that people swear, and it is hidden from him, when he comes to know it, and he realizes his guilt in any of these; ⁵when he realizes his guilt in any of these and confesses the sin he has committed, ⁶he shall bring to the LORD as his compensation[c] for the sin that he has committed, a female from

---

[a] Or *makes a mistake* [b] Or *suffer for their guilt*, or *are guilty*; also verses 22, 27, and chapter 5 [c] Hebrew *his guilt penalty*; so throughout Leviticus

the flock, a lamb or a goat, for a sin offering. And the priest shall make atonement for him for his sin.

⁷"But if he cannot afford a lamb, then he shall bring to the LORD as his compensation for the sin that he has committed two turtle-doves or two pigeons,ᵃ one for a sin offering and the other for a burnt offering. ⁸He shall bring them to the priest, who shall offer first the one for the sin offering. He shall wring its head from its neck but shall not sever it completely, ⁹and he shall sprinkle some of the blood of the sin offering on the side of the altar, while the rest of the blood shall be drained out at the base of the altar; it is a sin offering. ¹⁰Then he shall offer the second for a burnt offering according to the rule. And the priest shall make atonement for him for the sin that he has committed, and he shall be forgiven.

¹¹"But if he cannot afford two turtle-doves or two pigeons, then he shall bring as his offering for the sin that he has committed a tenth of an ephahᵇ of fine flour for a sin offering. He shall put no oil on it and shall put no frankincense on it, for it is a sin offering. ¹²And he shall bring it to the priest, and the priest shall take a handful of it as its memorial portion and burn this on the altar, on the LORD's food offerings; it is a sin offering. ¹³Thus the priest shall make atonement for him for the sin which he has committed in any one of these things, and he shall be forgiven. And the remainderᶜ shall be for the priest, as in the grain offering."

LAWS FOR GUILT OFFERINGS

¹⁴The LORD spoke to Moses, saying, ¹⁵"If anyone commits a breach of faith and sins unintentionally in any of the holy things of the LORD, he shall bring to the LORD as his compensation, a ram without blemish out of the flock, valuedᵈ in silver shekels,ᵉ according to the shekel of the sanctuary, for a guilt offering. ¹⁶He shall also make restitution for what he has done amiss in the holy thing and shall add a fifth to it and give it to the priest. And the priest shall make atonement for him with the ram of the guilt offering, and he shall be forgiven.

¹⁷"If anyone sins, doing any of the things that by the LORD's commandments ought not to be done, though he did not know it, then realizes his guilt, he shall bear his iniquity. ¹⁸He shall bring to the priest a ram without blemish out of the flock, or its equivalent, for a guilt offering, and the priest shall make atonement for him for the mistake that he made unintentionally, and he shall be forgiven. ¹⁹It is a guilt offering; he has indeed incurred guilt beforeᶠ the LORD."

6ᵍ The LORD spoke to Moses, saying, ²"If anyone sins and commits a breach of faith against the LORD by deceiving his neighbour in a matter of deposit or security, or through robbery, or if he has oppressed his neighbour ³or has found something lost and lied about it, swearing falsely—in any of all the things that people do and sin thereby— ⁴if he has sinned and has realized his guilt and will restore what he took by robbery or what he got by oppression or the deposit that was committed to him or the lost thing that he found ⁵or anything about which he has sworn falsely, he shall restore it in full and shall add a fifth to it, and give it to him to whom it belongs on the day he realizes his guilt. ⁶And he shall bring to the priest as his compensation to the LORD a ram without blemish out of the flock, or its equivalent, for a guilt offering. ⁷And the priest shall make atonement for him before the LORD, and he shall be forgiven for any of the things that one may do and thereby become guilty."

THE PRIESTS AND THE OFFERINGS

⁸ʰ The LORD spoke to Moses, saying, ⁹"Command Aaron and his sons, saying, This is the law of the burnt offering. The burnt offering shall be on the hearth on the altar all night until the morning, and the fire of the altar shall be kept burning on it. ¹⁰And the priest shall put on his linen garment and put his linen undergarment on his body, and he shall take up the ashes to which the fire has reduced the burnt offering on the altar and put them beside the altar. ¹¹Then he shall take off his garments and put on other garments and carry the ashes outside the camp to a clean place. ¹²The fire on the altar shall be kept burning on it; it shall not go out. The priest shall burn wood on it every morning, and he shall arrange the burnt offering on it and shall burn on it the fat of the peace offerings. ¹³Fire shall be kept burning on the altar continually; it shall not go out.

¹⁴"And this is the law of the grain offering. The sons of Aaron shall offer it before the

---

ᵃSeptuagint *two young pigeons*; also verse 11   ᵇAn *ephah* was about 3/5 of a bushel or 22 litres   ᶜSeptuagint; Hebrew *it*   ᵈOr *flock, or its equivalent*   ᵉA *shekel* was about 2/5 of an ounce or 11 grams   ᶠOr *he has paid full compensation to*   ᵍCh 5:20 in Hebrew   ʰCh 6:1 in Hebrew

Lord in front of the altar. ¹⁵And one shall take from it a handful of the fine flour of the grain offering and its oil and all the frankincense that is on the grain offering and burn this as its memorial portion on the altar, a pleasing aroma to the Lord. ¹⁶And the rest of it Aaron and his sons shall eat. It shall be eaten unleavened in a holy place. In the court of the tent of meeting they shall eat it. ¹⁷It shall not be baked with leaven. I have given it as their portion of my food offerings. It is a thing most holy, like the sin offering and the guilt offering. ¹⁸Every male among the children of Aaron may eat of it, as decreed for ever throughout your generations, from the Lord's food offerings. Whatever touches them shall become holy."

¹⁹The Lord spoke to Moses, saying, ²⁰"This is the offering that Aaron and his sons shall offer to the Lord on the day when he is anointed: a tenth of an ephah*ᵃ* of fine flour as a regular grain offering, half of it in the morning and half in the evening. ²¹It shall be made with oil on a griddle. You shall bring it well mixed, in baked*ᵇ* pieces like a grain offering, and offer it for a pleasing aroma to the Lord. ²²The priest from among Aaron's sons, who is anointed to succeed him, shall offer it to the Lord as decreed for ever. The whole of it shall be burned. ²³Every grain offering of a priest shall be wholly burned. It shall not be eaten."

²⁴The Lord spoke to Moses, saying, ²⁵"Speak to Aaron and his sons, saying, This is the law of the sin offering. In the place where the burnt offering is killed shall the sin offering be killed before the Lord; it is most holy. ²⁶The priest who offers it for sin shall eat it. In a holy place it shall be eaten, in the court of the tent of meeting. ²⁷Whatever touches its flesh shall be holy, and when any of its blood is splashed on a garment, you shall wash that on which it was splashed in a holy place. ²⁸And the earthenware vessel in which it is boiled shall be broken. But if it is boiled in a bronze vessel, that shall be scoured and rinsed in water. ²⁹Every male among the priests may eat of it; it is most holy. ³⁰But no sin offering shall be eaten from which any blood is brought into the tent of meeting to make atonement in the Holy Place; it shall be burned up with fire.

7 "This is the law of the guilt offering. It is most holy. ²In the place where they kill the burnt offering they shall kill the guilt offering, and its blood shall be thrown against the sides of the altar. ³And all its fat shall be offered, the fat tail, the fat that covers the entrails, ⁴the two kidneys with the fat that is on them at the loins, and the long lobe of the liver that he shall remove with the kidneys. ⁵The priest shall burn them on the altar as a food offering to the Lord; it is a guilt offering. ⁶Every male among the priests may eat of it. It shall be eaten in a holy place. It is most holy. ⁷The guilt offering is just like the sin offering; there is one law for them. The priest who makes atonement with it shall have it. ⁸And the priest who offers any man's burnt offering shall have for himself the skin of the burnt offering that he has offered. ⁹And every grain offering baked in the oven and all that is prepared on a pan or a griddle shall belong to the priest who offers it. ¹⁰And every grain offering, mixed with oil or dry, shall be shared equally among all the sons of Aaron.

¹¹"And this is the law of the sacrifice of peace offerings that one may offer to the Lord. ¹²If he offers it for a thanksgiving, then he shall offer with the thanksgiving sacrifice unleavened loaves mixed with oil, unleavened wafers smeared with oil, and loaves of fine flour well mixed with oil. ¹³With the sacrifice of his peace offerings for thanksgiving he shall bring his offering with loaves of leavened bread. ¹⁴And from it he shall offer one loaf from each offering, as a gift to the Lord. It shall belong to the priest who throws the blood of the peace offerings. ¹⁵And the flesh of the sacrifice of his peace offerings for thanksgiving shall be eaten on the day of his offering. He shall not leave any of it until the morning. ¹⁶But if the sacrifice of his offering is a vow offering or a freewill offering, it shall be eaten on the day that he offers his sacrifice, and on the next day what remains of it shall be eaten. ¹⁷But what remains of the flesh of the sacrifice on the third day shall be burned up with fire. ¹⁸If any of the flesh of the sacrifice of his peace offering is eaten on the third day, he who offers it shall not be accepted, neither shall it be credited to him. It is tainted, and he who eats of it shall bear his iniquity.

¹⁹"Flesh that touches any unclean thing shall not be eaten. It shall be burned up with fire. All who are clean may eat flesh, ²⁰but the person who eats of the flesh of the sacrifice of the Lord's peace offerings while an

---

*ᵃ*An *ephah* was about 3/5 of a bushel or 22 litres *ᵇ*The meaning of the Hebrew is uncertain

uncleanness is on him, that person shall be cut off from his people. ²¹And if anyone touches an unclean thing, whether human uncleanness or an unclean beast or any unclean detestable creature, and then eats some flesh from the sacrifice of the LORD's peace offerings, that person shall be cut off from his people."

²²The LORD spoke to Moses, saying, ²³"Speak to the people of Israel, saying, You shall eat no fat, of ox or sheep or goat. ²⁴The fat of an animal that dies of itself and the fat of one that is torn by beasts may be put to any other use, but on no account shall you eat it. ²⁵For every person who eats of the fat of an animal of which a food offering may be made to the LORD shall be cut off from his people. ²⁶Moreover, you shall eat no blood whatever, whether of fowl or of animal, in any of your dwelling places. ²⁷Whoever eats any blood, that person shall be cut off from his people."

²⁸The LORD spoke to Moses, saying, ²⁹"Speak to the people of Israel, saying, Whoever offers the sacrifice of his peace offerings to the LORD shall bring his offering to the LORD from the sacrifice of his peace offerings. ³⁰His own hands shall bring the LORD's food offerings. He shall bring the fat with the breast, that the breast may be waved as a wave offering before the LORD. ³¹The priest shall burn the fat on the altar, but the breast shall be for Aaron and his sons. ³²And the right thigh you shall give to the priest as a contribution from the sacrifice of your peace offerings. ³³Whoever among the sons of Aaron offers the blood of the peace offerings and the fat shall have the right thigh for a portion. ³⁴For the breast that is waved and the thigh that is contributed I have taken from the people of Israel, out of the sacrifices of their peace offerings, and have given them to Aaron the priest and to his sons, as a perpetual due from the people of Israel. ³⁵This is the portion of Aaron and of his sons from the LORD's food offerings, from the day they were presented to serve as priests of the LORD. ³⁶The LORD commanded this to be given them by the people of Israel, from the day that he anointed them. It is a perpetual due throughout their generations."

³⁷This is the law of the burnt offering, of the grain offering, of the sin offering, of the guilt offering, of the ordination offering, and of the peace offering, ³⁸which the LORD commanded Moses on Mount Sinai, on the day that he commanded the people of Israel to bring their offerings to the LORD, in the wilderness of Sinai.

CONSECRATION OF AARON AND HIS SONS

8 The LORD spoke to Moses, saying, ²"Take Aaron and his sons with him, and the garments and the anointing oil and the bull of the sin offering and the two rams and the basket of unleavened bread. ³And assemble all the congregation at the entrance of the tent of meeting." ⁴And Moses did as the LORD commanded him, and the congregation was assembled at the entrance of the tent of meeting.

⁵And Moses said to the congregation, "This is the thing that the LORD has commanded to be done." ⁶And Moses brought Aaron and his sons and washed them with water. ⁷And he put the coat on him and tied the sash round his waist and clothed him with the robe and put the ephod on him and tied the skilfully woven band of the ephod round him, binding it to him with the band.[a] ⁸And he placed the breastpiece on him, and in the breastpiece he put the Urim and the Thummim. ⁹And he set the turban on his head, and on the turban, in front, he set the golden plate, the holy crown, as the LORD commanded Moses.

¹⁰Then Moses took the anointing oil and anointed the tabernacle and all that was in it, and consecrated them. ¹¹And he sprinkled some of it on the altar seven times, and anointed the altar and all its utensils and the basin and its stand, to consecrate them. ¹²And he poured some of the anointing oil on Aaron's head and anointed him to consecrate him. ¹³And Moses brought Aaron's sons and clothed them with coats and tied sashes round their waists and bound caps on them, as the LORD commanded Moses.

¹⁴Then he brought the bull of the sin offering, and Aaron and his sons laid their hands on the head of the bull of the sin offering. ¹⁵And he[b] killed it, and Moses took the blood, and with his finger put it on the horns of the altar around it and purified the altar and poured out the blood at the base of the altar and consecrated it to make atonement for it. ¹⁶And he took all the fat that was on the entrails and the long lobe of the liver and the two kidneys with their fat, and Moses burned them on the altar. ¹⁷But the bull and its skin and its flesh and its dung he burned

---

[a]Hebrew *with it* [b]Probably Aaron or his representative; possibly Moses; also verses 16–23

up with fire outside the camp, as the LORD commanded Moses. ¹⁸Then he presented the ram of the burnt offering, and Aaron and his sons laid their hands on the head of the ram. ¹⁹And he killed it, and Moses threw the blood against the sides of the altar. ²⁰He cut the ram into pieces, and Moses burned the head and the pieces and the fat. ²¹He washed the entrails and the legs with water, and Moses burned the whole ram on the altar. It was a burnt offering with a pleasing aroma, a food offering for the LORD, as the LORD commanded Moses.

²²Then he presented the other ram, the ram of ordination, and Aaron and his sons laid their hands on the head of the ram. ²³And he killed it, and Moses took some of its blood and put it on the lobe of Aaron's right ear and on the thumb of his right hand and on the big toe of his right foot. ²⁴Then he presented Aaron's sons, and Moses put some of the blood on the lobes of their right ears and on the thumbs of their right hands and on the big toes of their right feet. And Moses threw the blood against the sides of the altar. ²⁵Then he took the fat and the fat tail and all the fat that was on the entrails and the long lobe of the liver and the two kidneys with their fat and the right thigh, ²⁶and out of the basket of unleavened bread that was before the LORD he took one unleavened loaf and one loaf of bread with oil and one wafer and placed them on the pieces of fat and on the right thigh. ²⁷And he put all these in the hands of Aaron and in the hands of his sons and waved them as a wave offering before the LORD. ²⁸Then Moses took them from their hands and burned them on the altar with the burnt offering. This was an ordination offering with a pleasing aroma, a food offering to the LORD. ²⁹And Moses took the breast and waved it for a wave offering before the LORD. It was Moses' portion of the ram of ordination, as the LORD commanded Moses.

³⁰Then Moses took some of the anointing oil and of the blood that was on the altar and sprinkled it on Aaron and his garments, and also on his sons and his sons' garments. So he consecrated Aaron and his garments, and his sons and his sons' garments with him.

³¹And Moses said to Aaron and his sons, "Boil the flesh at the entrance of the tent of meeting, and there eat it and the bread that is in the basket of ordination offerings, as I commanded, saying, 'Aaron and his sons shall eat it.' ³²And what remains of the flesh and the bread you shall burn up with fire. ³³And you shall not go outside the entrance of the tent of meeting for seven days, until the days of your ordination are completed, for it will take seven days to ordain you. ³⁴As has been done today, the LORD has commanded to be done to make atonement for you. ³⁵At the entrance of the tent of meeting you shall remain day and night for seven days, performing what the LORD has charged, so that you do not die, for so I have been commanded." ³⁶And Aaron and his sons did all the things that the LORD commanded by Moses.

THE LORD ACCEPTS AARON'S OFFERING

9 On the eighth day Moses called Aaron and his sons and the elders of Israel, ²and he said to Aaron, "Take for yourself a bull calf for a sin offering and a ram for a burnt offering, both without blemish, and offer them before the LORD. ³And say to the people of Israel, 'Take a male goat for a sin offering, and a calf and a lamb, both a year old without blemish, for a burnt offering, ⁴and an ox and a ram for peace offerings, to sacrifice before the LORD, and a grain offering mixed with oil, for today the LORD will appear to you.'" ⁵And they brought what Moses commanded in front of the tent of meeting, and all the congregation drew near and stood before the LORD. ⁶And Moses said, "This is the thing that the LORD commanded you to do, that the glory of the LORD may appear to you." ⁷Then Moses said to Aaron, "Draw near to the altar and offer your sin offering and your burnt offering and make atonement for yourself and for the people, and bring the offering of the people and make atonement for them, as the LORD has commanded."

⁸So Aaron drew near to the altar and killed the calf of the sin offering, which was for himself. ⁹And the sons of Aaron presented the blood to him, and he dipped his finger in the blood and put it on the horns of the altar and poured out the blood at the base of the altar. ¹⁰But the fat and the kidneys and the long lobe of the liver from the sin offering he burned on the altar, as the LORD commanded Moses. ¹¹The flesh and the skin he burned up with fire outside the camp.

¹²Then he killed the burnt offering, and Aaron's sons handed him the blood, and he threw it against the sides of the altar. ¹³And they handed the burnt offering to him, piece by piece, and the head, and he burned them on the altar. ¹⁴And he washed the entrails

and the legs and burned them with the burnt offering on the altar.

¹⁵Then he presented the people's offering and took the goat of the sin offering that was for the people and killed it and offered it as a sin offering, like the first one. ¹⁶And he presented the burnt offering and offered it according to the rule. ¹⁷And he presented the grain offering, took a handful of it, and burned it on the altar, besides the burnt offering of the morning.

¹⁸Then he killed the ox and the ram, the sacrifice of peace offerings for the people. And Aaron's sons handed him the blood, and he threw it against the sides of the altar. ¹⁹But the fat pieces of the ox and of the ram, the fat tail and that which covers the entrails and the kidneys and the long lobe of the liver— ²⁰they put the fat pieces on the breasts, and he burned the fat pieces on the altar, ²¹but the breasts and the right thigh Aaron waved for a wave offering before the Lord, as Moses commanded.

²²Then Aaron lifted up his hands towards the people and blessed them, and he came down from offering the sin offering and the burnt offering and the peace offerings. ²³And Moses and Aaron went into the tent of meeting, and when they came out they blessed the people, and the glory of the Lord appeared to all the people. ²⁴And fire came out from before the Lord and consumed the burnt offering and the pieces of fat on the altar, and when all the people saw it, they shouted and fell on their faces.

THE DEATH OF NADAB AND ABIHU

10 Now Nadab and Abihu, the sons of Aaron, each took his censer and put fire in it and laid incense on it and offered unauthorized*ᵃ* fire before the Lord, which he had not commanded them. ²And fire came out from before the Lord and consumed them, and they died before the Lord. ³Then Moses said to Aaron, "This is what the Lord has said: 'Among those who are near me I will be sanctified, and before all the people I will be glorified.'" And Aaron held his peace.

⁴And Moses called Mishael and Elzaphan, the sons of Uzziel the uncle of Aaron, and said to them, "Come near; carry your brothers away from the front of the sanctuary and out of the camp." ⁵So they came near and carried them in their coats out of the camp, as Moses had said. ⁶And Moses said to Aaron and to Eleazar and Ithamar his sons, "Do not let the hair of your heads hang loose, and do not tear your clothes, lest you die, and wrath come upon all the congregation; but let your brothers, the whole house of Israel, bewail the burning that the Lord has kindled. ⁷And do not go outside the entrance of the tent of meeting, lest you die, for the anointing oil of the Lord is upon you." And they did according to the word of Moses.

⁸And the Lord spoke to Aaron, saying, ⁹"Drink no wine or strong drink, you or your sons with you, when you go into the tent of meeting, lest you die. It shall be a statute for ever throughout your generations. ¹⁰You are to distinguish between the holy and the common, and between the unclean and the clean, ¹¹and you are to teach the people of Israel all the statutes that the Lord has spoken to them by Moses."

¹²Moses spoke to Aaron and to Eleazar and Ithamar, his surviving sons: "Take the grain offering that is left of the Lord's food offerings, and eat it unleavened beside the altar, for it is most holy. ¹³You shall eat it in a holy place, because it is your due and your sons' due, from the Lord's food offerings, for so I am commanded. ¹⁴But the breast that is waved and the thigh that is contributed you shall eat in a clean place, you and your sons and your daughters with you, for they are given as your due and your sons' due from the sacrifices of the peace offerings of the people of Israel. ¹⁵The thigh that is contributed and the breast that is waved they shall bring with the food offerings of the fat pieces to wave for a wave offering before the Lord, and it shall be yours and your sons' with you as a due for ever, as the Lord has commanded."

¹⁶Now Moses diligently enquired about the goat of the sin offering, and behold, it was burned up! And he was angry with Eleazar and Ithamar, the surviving sons of Aaron, saying, ¹⁷"Why have you not eaten the sin offering in the place of the sanctuary, since it is a thing most holy and has been given to you that you may bear the iniquity of the congregation, to make atonement for them before the Lord? ¹⁸Behold, its blood was not brought into the inner part of the sanctuary. You certainly ought to have eaten it in the sanctuary, as I commanded." ¹⁹And Aaron said to Moses, "Behold, today they have offered their sin offering and their burnt offering before the

---

ᵃ Or *strange*

LORD, and yet such things as these have happened to me! If I had eaten the sin offering today, would the LORD have approved?" ²⁰And when Moses heard that, he approved.

CLEAN AND UNCLEAN ANIMALS

11 And the LORD spoke to Moses and Aaron, saying to them, ²"Speak to the people of Israel, saying, These are the living things that you may eat among all the animals that are on the earth. ³Whatever parts the hoof and is cloven-footed and chews the cud, among the animals, you may eat. ⁴Nevertheless, among those that chew the cud or part the hoof, you shall not eat these: The camel, because it chews the cud but does not part the hoof, is unclean to you. ⁵And the rock badger, because it chews the cud but does not part the hoof, is unclean to you. ⁶And the hare, because it chews the cud but does not part the hoof, is unclean to you. ⁷And the pig, because it parts the hoof and is cloven-footed but does not chew the cud, is unclean to you. ⁸You shall not eat any of their flesh, and you shall not touch their carcasses; they are unclean to you.

⁹"These you may eat, of all that are in the waters. Everything in the waters that has fins and scales, whether in the seas or in the rivers, you may eat. ¹⁰But anything in the seas or the rivers that does not have fins and scales, of the swarming creatures in the waters and of the living creatures that are in the waters, is detestable to you. ¹¹You shall regard them as detestable; you shall not eat any of their flesh, and you shall detest their carcasses. ¹²Everything in the waters that does not have fins and scales is detestable to you.

¹³"And these you shall detest among the birds;[a] they shall not be eaten; they are detestable: the eagle,[b] the bearded vulture, the black vulture, ¹⁴the kite, the falcon of any kind, ¹⁵every raven of any kind, ¹⁶the ostrich, the nighthawk, the seagull, the hawk of any kind, ¹⁷the little owl, the cormorant, the short-eared owl, ¹⁸the barn owl, the tawny owl, the carrion vulture, ¹⁹the stork, the heron of any kind, the hoopoe, and the bat.

²⁰"All winged insects that go on all fours are detestable to you. ²¹Yet among the winged insects that go on all fours you may eat those that have jointed legs above their feet, with which to hop on the ground. ²²Of them you may eat: the locust of any kind, the bald locust of any kind, the cricket of any kind, and the grasshopper of any kind. ²³But all other winged insects that have four feet are detestable to you.

²⁴"And by these you shall become unclean. Whoever touches their carcass shall be unclean until the evening, ²⁵and whoever carries any part of their carcass shall wash his clothes and be unclean until the evening. ²⁶Every animal that parts the hoof but is not cloven-footed or does not chew the cud is unclean to you. Everyone who touches them shall be unclean. ²⁷And all that walk on their paws, among the animals that go on all fours, are unclean to you. Whoever touches their carcass shall be unclean until the evening, ²⁸and he who carries their carcass shall wash his clothes and be unclean until the evening; they are unclean to you.

²⁹"And these are unclean to you among the swarming things that swarm on the ground: the mole rat, the mouse, the great lizard of any kind, ³⁰the gecko, the monitor lizard, the lizard, the sand lizard, and the chameleon. ³¹These are unclean to you among all that swarm. Whoever touches them when they are dead shall be unclean until the evening. ³²And anything on which any of them falls when they are dead shall be unclean, whether it is an article of wood or a garment or a skin or a sack, any article that is used for any purpose. It must be put into water, and it shall be unclean until the evening; then it shall be clean. ³³And if any of them falls into any earthenware vessel, all that is in it shall be unclean, and you shall break it. ³⁴Any food in it that could be eaten, on which water comes, shall be unclean. And all drink that could be drunk from every such vessel shall be unclean. ³⁵And everything on which any part of their carcass falls shall be unclean. Whether oven or stove, it shall be broken in pieces. They are unclean and shall remain unclean for you. ³⁶Nevertheless, a spring or a cistern holding water shall be clean, but whoever touches a carcass in them shall be unclean. ³⁷And if any part of their carcass falls upon any seed that is to be sown, it is clean, ³⁸but if water is put on the seed and any part of their carcass falls on it, it is unclean to you.

³⁹"And if any animal which you may eat dies, whoever touches its carcass shall be unclean until the evening, ⁴⁰and whoever eats of its carcass shall wash his clothes and be unclean until the evening. And whoever

---

[a] Or *things that fly*; compare Genesis 1:20 [b] The identity of many of these birds is uncertain

carries the carcass shall wash his clothes and be unclean until the evening.

⁴¹"Every swarming thing that swarms on the ground is detestable; it shall not be eaten. ⁴²Whatever goes on its belly, and whatever goes on all fours, or whatever has many feet, any swarming thing that swarms on the ground, you shall not eat, for they are detestable. ⁴³You shall not make yourselves detestable with any swarming thing that swarms, and you shall not defile yourselves with them, and become unclean through them. ⁴⁴For I am the LORD your God. Consecrate yourselves therefore, and be holy, for I am holy. You shall not defile yourselves with any swarming thing that crawls on the ground. ⁴⁵For I am the LORD who brought you up out of the land of Egypt to be your God. You shall therefore be holy, for I am holy."

⁴⁶This is the law about beast and bird and every living creature that moves through the waters and every creature that swarms on the ground, ⁴⁷to make a distinction between the unclean and the clean and between the living creature that may be eaten and the living creature that may not be eaten.

PURIFICATION AFTER CHILDBIRTH

12 The LORD spoke to Moses, saying, ²"Speak to the people of Israel, saying, If a woman conceives and bears a male child, then she shall be unclean for seven days. As at the time of her menstruation, she shall be unclean. ³And on the eighth day the flesh of his foreskin shall be circumcised. ⁴Then she shall continue for thirty-three days in the blood of her purifying. She shall not touch anything holy, nor come into the sanctuary, until the days of her purifying are completed. ⁵But if she bears a female child, then she shall be unclean for two weeks, as in her menstruation. And she shall continue in the blood of her purifying for sixty-six days.

⁶"And when the days of her purifying are completed, whether for a son or for a daughter, she shall bring to the priest at the entrance of the tent of meeting a lamb a year old for a burnt offering, and a pigeon or a turtle-dove for a sin offering, ⁷and he shall offer it before the LORD and make atonement for her. Then she shall be clean from the flow of her blood. This is the law for her who bears a child, either male or female. ⁸And if she cannot afford a lamb, then she shall take two turtle-doves or two pigeons,ᵃ one for a burnt offering and the other for a sin offering. And the priest shall make atonement for her, and she shall be clean."

LAWS ABOUT LEPROSY

13 The LORD spoke to Moses and Aaron, saying, ²"When a person has on the skin of his body a swelling or an eruption or a spot, and it turns into a case of leprousᵇ disease on the skin of his body, then he shall be brought to Aaron the priest or to one of his sons the priests, ³and the priest shall examine the diseased area on the skin of his body. And if the hair in the diseased area has turned white and the disease appears to be deeper than the skin of his body, it is a case of leprous disease. When the priest has examined him, he shall pronounce him unclean. ⁴But if the spot is white in the skin of his body and appears no deeper than the skin, and the hair in it has not turned white, the priest shall shut up the diseased person for seven days. ⁵And the priest shall examine him on the seventh day, and if in his eyes the disease is checked and the disease has not spread in the skin, then the priest shall shut him up for another seven days. ⁶And the priest shall examine him again on the seventh day, and if the diseased area has faded and the disease has not spread in the skin, then the priest shall pronounce him clean; it is only an eruption. And he shall wash his clothes and be clean. ⁷But if the eruption spreads in the skin, after he has shown himself to the priest for his cleansing, he shall appear again before the priest. ⁸And the priest shall look, and if the eruption has spread in the skin, then the priest shall pronounce him unclean; it is a leprous disease.

⁹"When a man is afflicted with a leprous disease, he shall be brought to the priest, ¹⁰and the priest shall look. And if there is a white swelling in the skin that has turned the hair white, and there is raw flesh in the swelling, ¹¹it is a chronic leprous disease in the skin of his body, and the priest shall pronounce him unclean. He shall not shut him up, for he is unclean. ¹²And if the leprous disease breaks out in the skin, so that the leprous disease covers all the skin of the diseased person from head to foot, so far as the priest can see, ¹³then the priest shall look, and if the leprous disease has covered

---

ᵃSeptuagint *two young pigeons* ᵇ*Leprosy* was a term for several skin diseases

all his body, he shall pronounce him clean of the disease; it has all turned white, and he is clean. ¹⁴But when raw flesh appears on him, he shall be unclean. ¹⁵And the priest shall examine the raw flesh and pronounce him unclean. Raw flesh is unclean, for it is a leprous disease. ¹⁶But if the raw flesh recovers and turns white again, then he shall come to the priest, ¹⁷and the priest shall examine him, and if the disease has turned white, then the priest shall pronounce the diseased person clean; he is clean.

¹⁸"If there is in the skin of one's body a boil and it heals, ¹⁹and in the place of the boil there comes a white swelling or a reddish-white spot, then it shall be shown to the priest. ²⁰And the priest shall look, and if it appears deeper than the skin and its hair has turned white, then the priest shall pronounce him unclean. It is a case of leprous disease that has broken out in the boil. ²¹But if the priest examines it and there is no white hair in it and it is not deeper than the skin, but has faded, then the priest shall shut him up for seven days. ²²And if it spreads in the skin, then the priest shall pronounce him unclean; it is a disease. ²³But if the spot remains in one place and does not spread, it is the scar of the boil, and the priest shall pronounce him clean.

²⁴"Or, when the body has a burn on its skin and the raw flesh of the burn becomes a spot, reddish-white or white, ²⁵the priest shall examine it, and if the hair in the spot has turned white and it appears deeper than the skin, then it is a leprous disease. It has broken out in the burn, and the priest shall pronounce him unclean; it is a case of leprous disease. ²⁶But if the priest examines it and there is no white hair in the spot and it is no deeper than the skin, but has faded, the priest shall shut him up for seven days, ²⁷and the priest shall examine him on the seventh day. If it is spreading in the skin, then the priest shall pronounce him unclean; it is a case of leprous disease. ²⁸But if the spot remains in one place and does not spread in the skin, but has faded, it is a swelling from the burn, and the priest shall pronounce him clean, for it is the scar of the burn.

²⁹"When a man or woman has a disease on the head or the beard, ³⁰the priest shall examine the disease. And if it appears deeper than the skin, and the hair in it is yellow and thin, then the priest shall pronounce him unclean. It is an itch, a leprous disease of the head or the beard. ³¹And if the priest examines the itching disease and it appears no deeper than the skin and there is no black hair in it, then the priest shall shut up the person with the itching disease for seven days, ³²and on the seventh day the priest shall examine the disease. If the itch has not spread, and there is in it no yellow hair, and the itch appears to be no deeper than the skin, ³³then he shall shave himself, but the itch he shall not shave; and the priest shall shut up the person with the itching disease for another seven days. ³⁴And on the seventh day the priest shall examine the itch, and if the itch has not spread in the skin and it appears to be no deeper than the skin, then the priest shall pronounce him clean. And he shall wash his clothes and be clean. ³⁵But if the itch spreads in the skin after his cleansing, ³⁶then the priest shall examine him, and if the itch has spread in the skin, the priest need not seek for the yellow hair; he is unclean. ³⁷But if in his eyes the itch is unchanged and black hair has grown in it, the itch is healed and he is clean, and the priest shall pronounce him clean.

³⁸"When a man or a woman has spots on the skin of the body, white spots, ³⁹the priest shall look, and if the spots on the skin of the body are of a dull white, it is leucoderma that has broken out in the skin; he is clean.

⁴⁰"If a man's hair falls out from his head, he is bald; he is clean. ⁴¹And if a man's hair falls out from his forehead, he has baldness of the forehead; he is clean. ⁴²But if there is on the bald head or the bald forehead a reddish-white diseased area, it is a leprous disease breaking out on his bald head or his bald forehead. ⁴³Then the priest shall examine him, and if the diseased swelling is reddish-white on his bald head or on his bald forehead, like the appearance of leprous disease in the skin of the body, ⁴⁴he is a leprous man, he is unclean. The priest must pronounce him unclean; his disease is on his head.

⁴⁵"The leprous person who has the disease shall wear torn clothes and let the hair of his head hang loose, and he shall cover his upper lip[a] and cry out, 'Unclean, unclean.' ⁴⁶He shall remain unclean as long as he has the disease. He is unclean. He shall live alone. His dwelling shall be outside the camp.

⁴⁷"When there is a case of leprous disease in a garment, whether a woollen or a linen garment, ⁴⁸in warp or woof of linen or wool, or

---

[a] Or *moustache*

in a skin or in anything made of skin, ⁴⁹if the disease is greenish or reddish in the garment, or in the skin or in the warp or the woof or in any article made of skin, it is a case of leprous disease, and it shall be shown to the priest. ⁵⁰And the priest shall examine the disease and shut up that which has the disease for seven days. ⁵¹Then he shall examine the disease on the seventh day. If the disease has spread in the garment, in the warp or the woof, or in the skin, whatever be the use of the skin, the disease is a persistent leprous disease; it is unclean. ⁵²And he shall burn the garment, or the warp or the woof, the wool or the linen, or any article made of skin that is diseased, for it is a persistent leprous disease. It shall be burned in the fire.

⁵³"And if the priest examines, and if the disease has not spread in the garment, in the warp or the woof or in any article made of skin, ⁵⁴then the priest shall command that they wash the thing in which is the disease, and he shall shut it up for another seven days. ⁵⁵And the priest shall examine the diseased thing after it has been washed. And if the appearance of the diseased area has not changed, though the disease has not spread, it is unclean. You shall burn it in the fire, whether the rot is on the back or on the front.

⁵⁶"But if the priest examines, and if the diseased area has faded after it has been washed, he shall tear it out of the garment or the skin or the warp or the woof. ⁵⁷Then if it appears again in the garment, in the warp or the woof, or in any article made of skin, it is spreading. You shall burn with fire whatever has the disease. ⁵⁸But the garment, or the warp or the woof, or any article made of skin from which the disease departs when you have washed it, shall then be washed a second time, and be clean."

⁵⁹This is the law for a case of leprous disease in a garment of wool or linen, either in the warp or the woof, or in any article made of skin, to determine whether it is clean or unclean.

LAWS FOR CLEANSING LEPERS

14 The LORD spoke to Moses, saying, ²"This shall be the law of the leprous person for the day of his cleansing. He shall be brought to the priest, ³and the priest shall go out of the camp, and the priest shall look. Then, if the case of leprous disease is healed in the leprous person, ⁴the priest shall command them to take for him who is to be cleansed two live*ᵃ* clean birds and cedarwood and scarlet yarn and hyssop. ⁵And the priest shall command them to kill one of the birds in an earthenware vessel over fresh*ᵇ* water. ⁶He shall take the live bird with the cedarwood and the scarlet yarn and the hyssop, and dip them and the live bird in the blood of the bird that was killed over the fresh water. ⁷And he shall sprinkle it seven times on him who is to be cleansed of the leprous disease. Then he shall pronounce him clean and shall let the living bird go into the open field. ⁸And he who is to be cleansed shall wash his clothes and shave off all his hair and bathe himself in water, and he shall be clean. And after that he may come into the camp, but shall live outside his tent for seven days. ⁹And on the seventh day he shall shave off all his hair from his head, his beard, and his eyebrows. He shall shave off all his hair, and then he shall wash his clothes and bathe his body in water, and he shall be clean.

¹⁰"And on the eighth day he shall take two male lambs without blemish, and one ewe lamb a year old without blemish, and a grain offering of three tenths of an ephah*ᶜ* of fine flour mixed with oil, and one log*ᵈ* of oil. ¹¹And the priest who cleanses him shall set the man who is to be cleansed and these things before the LORD, at the entrance of the tent of meeting. ¹²And the priest shall take one of the male lambs and offer it for a guilt offering, along with the log of oil, and wave them for a wave offering before the LORD. ¹³And he shall kill the lamb in the place where they kill the sin offering and the burnt offering, in the place of the sanctuary. For the guilt offering, like the sin offering, belongs to the priest; it is most holy. ¹⁴The priest shall take some of the blood of the guilt offering, and the priest shall put it on the lobe of the right ear of him who is to be cleansed and on the thumb of his right hand and on the big toe of his right foot. ¹⁵Then the priest shall take some of the log of oil and pour it into the palm of his own left hand ¹⁶and dip his right finger in the oil that is in his left hand and sprinkle some oil with his finger seven times before the LORD. ¹⁷And some of the oil that remains in his hand the priest shall put

---

*ᵃ*Or *wild* *ᵇ*Or *running;* Hebrew *living;* also verses 6, 50, 51, 52 *ᶜ*An *ephah* was about 3/5 of a bushel or 22 litres *ᵈ*A *log* was about 1/3 of a quart or 0.3 litre

on the lobe of the right ear of him who is to be cleansed and on the thumb of his right hand and on the big toe of his right foot, on top of the blood of the guilt offering. ¹⁸And the rest of the oil that is in the priest's hand he shall put on the head of him who is to be cleansed. Then the priest shall make atonement for him before the LORD. ¹⁹The priest shall offer the sin offering, to make atonement for him who is to be cleansed from his uncleanness. And afterwards he shall kill the burnt offering. ²⁰And the priest shall offer the burnt offering and the grain offering on the altar. Thus the priest shall make atonement for him, and he shall be clean.

²¹"But if he is poor and cannot afford so much, then he shall take one male lamb for a guilt offering to be waved, to make atonement for him, and a tenth of an ephah of fine flour mixed with oil for a grain offering, and a log of oil; ²²also two turtle-doves or two pigeons, whichever he can afford. One shall be a sin offering and the other a burnt offering. ²³And on the eighth day he shall bring them for his cleansing to the priest, to the entrance of the tent of meeting, before the LORD. ²⁴And the priest shall take the lamb of the guilt offering and the log of oil, and the priest shall wave them for a wave offering before the LORD. ²⁵And he shall kill the lamb of the guilt offering. And the priest shall take some of the blood of the guilt offering and put it on the lobe of the right ear of him who is to be cleansed, and on the thumb of his right hand and on the big toe of his right foot. ²⁶And the priest shall pour some of the oil into the palm of his own left hand, ²⁷and shall sprinkle with his right finger some of the oil that is in his left hand seven times before the LORD. ²⁸And the priest shall put some of the oil that is in his hand on the lobe of the right ear of him who is to be cleansed and on the thumb of his right hand and on the big toe of his right foot, in the place where the blood of the guilt offering was put. ²⁹And the rest of the oil that is in the priest's hand he shall put on the head of him who is to be cleansed, to make atonement for him before the LORD. ³⁰And he shall offer, of the turtle-doves or pigeons, whichever he can afford, ³¹one[a] for a sin offering and the other for a burnt offering, along with a grain offering. And the priest shall make atonement before the LORD for him who is being cleansed. ³²This is the law for him in whom is a case of leprous disease, who cannot afford the offerings for his cleansing."

LAWS FOR CLEANSING HOUSES

³³The LORD spoke to Moses and Aaron, saying, ³⁴"When you come into the land of Canaan, which I give you for a possession, and I put a case of leprous disease in a house in the land of your possession, ³⁵then he who owns the house shall come and tell the priest, 'There seems to me to be some case of disease in my house.' ³⁶Then the priest shall command that they empty the house before the priest goes to examine the disease, lest all that is in the house be declared unclean. And afterwards the priest shall go in to see the house. ³⁷And he shall examine the disease. And if the disease is in the walls of the house with greenish or reddish spots, and if it appears to be deeper than the surface, ³⁸then the priest shall go out of the house to the door of the house and shut up the house for seven days. ³⁹And the priest shall come again on the seventh day, and look. If the disease has spread in the walls of the house, ⁴⁰then the priest shall command that they take out the stones in which is the disease and throw them into an unclean place outside the city. ⁴¹And he shall have the inside of the house scraped all round, and the plaster that they scrape off they shall pour out in an unclean place outside the city. ⁴²Then they shall take other stones and put them in the place of those stones, and he shall take other plaster and plaster the house.

⁴³"If the disease breaks out again in the house, after he has taken out the stones and scraped the house and plastered it, ⁴⁴then the priest shall go and look. And if the disease has spread in the house, it is a persistent leprous disease in the house; it is unclean. ⁴⁵And he shall break down the house, its stones and timber and all the plaster of the house, and he shall carry them out of the city to an unclean place. ⁴⁶Moreover, whoever enters the house while it is shut up shall be unclean until the evening, ⁴⁷and whoever sleeps in the house shall wash his clothes, and whoever eats in the house shall wash his clothes.

⁴⁸"But if the priest comes and looks, and if the disease has not spread in the house after the house was plastered, then the priest shall pronounce the house clean, for the disease is healed. ⁴⁹And for the cleansing of the house he shall take two small birds, with cedarwood and scarlet yarn and hyssop, ⁵⁰and shall kill one of the birds in an earthenware vessel over

---

[a]Septuagint, Syriac; Hebrew *afford, ³¹such as he can afford, one*

fresh water ⁵¹and shall take the cedarwood and the hyssop and the scarlet yarn, along with the live bird, and dip them in the blood of the bird that was killed and in the fresh water and sprinkle the house seven times. ⁵²Thus he shall cleanse the house with the blood of the bird and with the fresh water and with the live bird and with the cedarwood and hyssop and scarlet yarn. ⁵³And he shall let the live bird go out of the city into the open country. So he shall make atonement for the house, and it shall be clean."

⁵⁴This is the law for any case of leprous disease: for an itch, ⁵⁵for leprous disease in a garment or in a house, ⁵⁶and for a swelling or an eruption or a spot, ⁵⁷to show when it is unclean and when it is clean. This is the law for leprous disease.

LAWS ABOUT BODILY DISCHARGES

15 The Lord spoke to Moses and Aaron, saying, ²"Speak to the people of Israel and say to them, When any man has a discharge from his body,ᵃ his discharge is unclean. ³And this is the law of his uncleanness for a discharge: whether his body runs with his discharge, or his body is blocked up by his discharge, it is his uncleanness. ⁴Every bed on which the one with the discharge lies shall be unclean, and everything on which he sits shall be unclean. ⁵And anyone who touches his bed shall wash his clothes and bathe himself in water and be unclean until the evening. ⁶And whoever sits on anything on which the one with the discharge has sat shall wash his clothes and bathe himself in water and be unclean until the evening. ⁷And whoever touches the body of the one with the discharge shall wash his clothes and bathe himself in water and be unclean until the evening. ⁸And if the one with the discharge spits on someone who is clean, then he shall wash his clothes and bathe himself in water and be unclean until the evening. ⁹And any saddle on which the one with the discharge rides shall be unclean. ¹⁰And whoever touches anything that was under him shall be unclean until the evening. And whoever carries such things shall wash his clothes and bathe himself in water and be unclean until the evening. ¹¹Anyone whom the one with the discharge touches without having rinsed his hands in water shall wash his clothes and bathe himself in water and be unclean until the evening. ¹²And an earthenware vessel that the one with the discharge touches shall be broken, and every vessel of wood shall be rinsed in water.

¹³"And when the one with a discharge is cleansed of his discharge, then he shall count for himself seven days for his cleansing, and wash his clothes. And he shall bathe his body in fresh water and shall be clean. ¹⁴And on the eighth day he shall take two turtle-doves or two pigeons and come before the Lord to the entrance of the tent of meeting and give them to the priest. ¹⁵And the priest shall use them, one for a sin offering and the other for a burnt offering. And the priest shall make atonement for him before the Lord for his discharge.

¹⁶"If a man has an emission of semen, he shall bathe his whole body in water and be unclean until the evening. ¹⁷And every garment and every skin on which the semen comes shall be washed with water and be unclean until the evening. ¹⁸If a man lies with a woman and has an emission of semen, both of them shall bathe themselves in water and be unclean until the evening.

¹⁹"When a woman has a discharge, and the discharge in her body is blood, she shall be in her menstrual impurity for seven days, and whoever touches her shall be unclean until the evening. ²⁰And everything on which she lies during her menstrual impurity shall be unclean. Everything also on which she sits shall be unclean. ²¹And whoever touches her bed shall wash his clothes and bathe himself in water and be unclean until the evening. ²²And whoever touches anything on which she sits shall wash his clothes and bathe himself in water and be unclean until the evening. ²³Whether it is the bed or anything on which she sits, when he touches it he shall be unclean until the evening. ²⁴And if any man lies with her and her menstrual impurity comes upon him, he shall be unclean for seven days, and every bed on which he lies shall be unclean.

²⁵"If a woman has a discharge of blood for many days, not at the time of her menstrual impurity, or if she has a discharge beyond the time of her impurity, for all the days of the discharge she shall continue in uncleanness. As in the days of her impurity, she shall be unclean. ²⁶Every bed on which she lies, all the days of her discharge, shall be to her as the bed of her impurity. And everything on which she sits shall be unclean, as in the uncleanness

---

ᵃ Hebrew *flesh*; also verse 3

of her menstrual impurity. ²⁷And whoever touches these things shall be unclean, and shall wash his clothes and bathe himself in water and be unclean until the evening. ²⁸But if she is cleansed of her discharge, she shall count for herself seven days, and after that she shall be clean. ²⁹And on the eighth day she shall take two turtle-doves or two pigeons and bring them to the priest, to the entrance of the tent of meeting. ³⁰And the priest shall use one for a sin offering and the other for a burnt offering. And the priest shall make atonement for her before the LORD for her unclean discharge.

³¹"Thus you shall keep the people of Israel separate from their uncleanness, lest they die in their uncleanness by defiling my tabernacle that is in their midst."

³²This is the law for him who has a discharge and for him who has an emission of semen, becoming unclean thereby; ³³also for her who is unwell with her menstrual impurity, that is, for anyone, male or female, who has a discharge, and for the man who lies with a woman who is unclean.

THE DAY OF ATONEMENT

16 The LORD spoke to Moses after the death of the two sons of Aaron, when they drew near before the LORD and died, ²and the LORD said to Moses, "Tell Aaron your brother not to come at any time into the Holy Place inside the veil, before the mercy seat that is on the ark, so that he may not die. For I will appear in the cloud over the mercy seat. ³But in this way Aaron shall come into the Holy Place: with a bull from the herd for a sin offering and a ram for a burnt offering. ⁴He shall put on the holy linen coat and shall have the linen undergarment on his body, and he shall tie the linen sash round his waist, and wear the linen turban; these are the holy garments. He shall bathe his body in water and then put them on. ⁵And he shall take from the congregation of the people of Israel two male goats for a sin offering, and one ram for a burnt offering.

⁶"Aaron shall offer the bull as a sin offering for himself and shall make atonement for himself and for his house. ⁷Then he shall take the two goats and set them before the LORD at the entrance of the tent of meeting. ⁸And Aaron shall cast lots over the two goats, one lot for the LORD and the other lot for Azazel.ᵃ ⁹And Aaron shall present the goat on which the lot fell for the LORD and use it as a sin offering, ¹⁰but the goat on which the lot fell for Azazel shall be presented alive before the LORD to make atonement over it, that it may be sent away into the wilderness to Azazel.

¹¹"Aaron shall present the bull as a sin offering for himself, and shall make atonement for himself and for his house. He shall kill the bull as a sin offering for himself. ¹²And he shall take a censer full of coals of fire from the altar before the LORD, and two handfuls of sweet incense beaten small, and he shall bring it inside the veil ¹³and put the incense on the fire before the LORD, that the cloud of the incense may cover the mercy seat that is over the testimony, so that he does not die. ¹⁴And he shall take some of the blood of the bull and sprinkle it with his finger on the front of the mercy seat on the east side, and in front of the mercy seat he shall sprinkle some of the blood with his finger seven times.

¹⁵"Then he shall kill the goat of the sin offering that is for the people and bring its blood inside the veil and do with its blood as he did with the blood of the bull, sprinkling it over the mercy seat and in front of the mercy seat. ¹⁶Thus he shall make atonement for the Holy Place, because of the uncleannesses of the people of Israel and because of their transgressions, all their sins. And so he shall do for the tent of meeting, which dwells with them in the midst of their uncleannesses. ¹⁷No one may be in the tent of meeting from the time he enters to make atonement in the Holy Place until he comes out and has made atonement for himself and for his house and for all the assembly of Israel. ¹⁸Then he shall go out to the altar that is before the LORD and make atonement for it, and shall take some of the blood of the bull and some of the blood of the goat, and put it on the horns of the altar all round. ¹⁹And he shall sprinkle some of the blood on it with his finger seven times, and cleanse it and consecrate it from the uncleannesses of the people of Israel.

²⁰"And when he has made an end of atoning for the Holy Place and the tent of meeting and the altar, he shall present the live goat. ²¹And Aaron shall lay both his hands on the head of the live goat, and confess over it all the iniquities of the people of Israel, and all their transgressions, all their sins. And he shall put them on the head of the goat and send it away into the wilderness by the hand

---

ᵃThe meaning of *Azazel* is uncertain; possibly the name of a place or a demon, traditionally a scapegoat; also verses 10, 26

of a man who is in readiness. ²²The goat shall bear all their iniquities on itself to a remote area, and he shall let the goat go free in the wilderness.

²³"Then Aaron shall come into the tent of meeting and shall take off the linen garments that he put on when he went into the Holy Place and shall leave them there. ²⁴And he shall bathe his body in water in a holy place and put on his garments and come out and offer his burnt offering and the burnt offering of the people and make atonement for himself and for the people. ²⁵And the fat of the sin offering he shall burn on the altar. ²⁶And he who lets the goat go to Azazel shall wash his clothes and bathe his body in water, and afterwards he may come into the camp. ²⁷And the bull for the sin offering and the goat for the sin offering, whose blood was brought in to make atonement in the Holy Place, shall be carried outside the camp. Their skin and their flesh and their dung shall be burned up with fire. ²⁸And he who burns them shall wash his clothes and bathe his body in water, and afterwards he may come into the camp.

²⁹"And it shall be a statute to you for ever that in the seventh month, on the tenth day of the month, you shall afflict yourselves[a] and shall do no work, either the native or the stranger who sojourns among you. ³⁰For on this day shall atonement be made for you to cleanse you. You shall be clean before the LORD from all your sins. ³¹It is a Sabbath of solemn rest to you, and you shall afflict yourselves; it is a statute for ever. ³²And the priest who is anointed and consecrated as priest in his father's place shall make atonement, wearing the holy linen garments. ³³He shall make atonement for the holy sanctuary, and he shall make atonement for the tent of meeting and for the altar, and he shall make atonement for the priests and for all the people of the assembly. ³⁴And this shall be a statute for ever for you, that atonement may be made for the people of Israel once in the year because of all their sins." And Aaron[b] did as the LORD commanded Moses.

THE PLACE OF SACRIFICE

17 And the LORD spoke to Moses, saying, ²"Speak to Aaron and his sons and to all the people of Israel and say to them, This is the thing that the LORD has commanded. ³If any one of the house of Israel kills an ox or a lamb or a goat in the camp, or kills it outside the camp, ⁴and does not bring it to the entrance of the tent of meeting to offer it as a gift to the LORD in front of the tabernacle of the LORD, bloodguilt shall be imputed to that man. He has shed blood, and that man shall be cut off from among his people. ⁵This is to the end that the people of Israel may bring their sacrifices that they sacrifice in the open field, that they may bring them to the LORD, to the priest at the entrance of the tent of meeting, and sacrifice them as sacrifices of peace offerings to the LORD. ⁶And the priest shall throw the blood on the altar of the LORD at the entrance of the tent of meeting and burn the fat for a pleasing aroma to the LORD. ⁷So they shall no more sacrifice their sacrifices to goat demons, after whom they whore. This shall be a statute for ever for them throughout their generations.

⁸"And you shall say to them, Any one of the house of Israel, or of the strangers who sojourn among them, who offers a burnt offering or sacrifice ⁹and does not bring it to the entrance of the tent of meeting to offer it to the LORD, that man shall be cut off from his people.

LAWS AGAINST EATING BLOOD

¹⁰"If any one of the house of Israel or of the strangers who sojourn among them eats any blood, I will set my face against that person who eats blood and will cut him off from among his people. ¹¹For the life of the flesh is in the blood, and I have given it for you on the altar to make atonement for your souls, for it is the blood that makes atonement by the life. ¹²Therefore I have said to the people of Israel, No person among you shall eat blood, neither shall any stranger who sojourns among you eat blood.

¹³"Any one also of the people of Israel, or of the strangers who sojourn among them, who takes in hunting any beast or bird that may be eaten shall pour out its blood and cover it with earth. ¹⁴For the life of every creature[c] is its blood: its blood is its life.[d] Therefore I have said to the people of Israel, You shall not eat the blood of any creature, for the life of every creature is its blood. Whoever eats it shall be cut off. ¹⁵And every person who eats what dies of itself or what is torn by beasts, whether he is a native or a sojourner, shall wash his clothes and bathe himself in water and be unclean until the evening; then he

---
[a]Or *shall fast*; also verse 31 [b]Hebrew *he* [c]Hebrew *all flesh*
[d]Hebrew *it is in its life*

shall be clean. ¹⁶But if he does not wash them or bathe his flesh, he shall bear his iniquity."

UNLAWFUL SEXUAL RELATIONS

18 And the LORD spoke to Moses, saying, ²"Speak to the people of Israel and say to them, I am the LORD your God. ³You shall not do as they do in the land of Egypt, where you lived, and you shall not do as they do in the land of Canaan, to which I am bringing you. You shall not walk in their statutes. ⁴You shall follow my rules[a] and keep my statutes and walk in them. I am the LORD your God. ⁵You shall therefore keep my statutes and my rules; if a person does them, he shall live by them: I am the LORD.

⁶"None of you shall approach any one of his close relatives to uncover nakedness. I am the LORD. ⁷You shall not uncover the nakedness of your father, which is the nakedness of your mother; she is your mother, you shall not uncover her nakedness. ⁸You shall not uncover the nakedness of your father's wife; it is your father's nakedness. ⁹You shall not uncover the nakedness of your sister, your father's daughter or your mother's daughter, whether brought up in the family or in another home. ¹⁰You shall not uncover the nakedness of your son's daughter or of your daughter's daughter, for their nakedness is your own nakedness. ¹¹You shall not uncover the nakedness of your father's wife's daughter, brought up in your father's family, since she is your sister. ¹²You shall not uncover the nakedness of your father's sister; she is your father's relative. ¹³You shall not uncover the nakedness of your mother's sister, for she is your mother's relative. ¹⁴You shall not uncover the nakedness of your father's brother, that is, you shall not approach his wife; she is your aunt. ¹⁵You shall not uncover the nakedness of your daughter-in-law; she is your son's wife, you shall not uncover her nakedness. ¹⁶You shall not uncover the nakedness of your brother's wife; it is your brother's nakedness. ¹⁷You shall not uncover the nakedness of a woman and of her daughter, and you shall not take her son's daughter or her daughter's daughter to uncover her nakedness; they are relatives; it is depravity. ¹⁸And you shall not take a woman as a rival wife to her sister, uncovering her nakedness while her sister is still alive.

¹⁹"You shall not approach a woman to uncover her nakedness while she is in her menstrual uncleanness. ²⁰And you shall not lie sexually with your neighbour's wife and so make yourself unclean with her. ²¹You shall not give any of your children to offer them[b] to Molech, and so profane the name of your God: I am the LORD. ²²You shall not lie with a male as with a woman; it is an abomination. ²³And you shall not lie with any animal and so make yourself unclean with it, neither shall any woman give herself to an animal to lie with it: it is perversion.

²⁴"Do not make yourselves unclean by any of these things, for by all these the nations I am driving out before you have become unclean, ²⁵and the land became unclean, so that I punished its iniquity, and the land vomited out its inhabitants. ²⁶But you shall keep my statutes and my rules and do none of these abominations, either the native or the stranger who sojourns among you ²⁷(for the people of the land, who were before you, did all of these abominations, so that the land became unclean), ²⁸lest the land vomit you out when you make it unclean, as it vomited out the nation that was before you. ²⁹For everyone who does any of these abominations, the persons who do them shall be cut off from among their people. ³⁰So keep my charge never to practise any of these abominable customs that were practised before you, and never to make yourselves unclean by them: I am the LORD your God."

THE LORD IS HOLY

19 And the LORD spoke to Moses, saying, ²"Speak to all the congregation of the people of Israel and say to them, You shall be holy, for I the LORD your God am holy. ³Every one of you shall revere his mother and his father, and you shall keep my Sabbaths: I am the LORD your God. ⁴Do not turn to idols or make for yourselves any gods of cast metal: I am the LORD your God.

⁵"When you offer a sacrifice of peace offerings to the LORD, you shall offer it so that you may be accepted. ⁶It shall be eaten the same day you offer it or on the day after, and anything left over until the third day shall be burned up with fire. ⁷If it is eaten at all on the third day, it is tainted; it will not be accepted, ⁸and everyone who eats it shall bear his iniquity, because he has profaned what is holy to the LORD, and that person shall be cut off from his people.

---

[a] Or *my just decrees*; also verse 5 [b] Hebrew *to make them pass through* [*the fire*]

LOVE YOUR NEIGHBOUR AS YOURSELF

⁹"When you reap the harvest of your land, you shall not reap your field right up to its edge, neither shall you gather the gleanings after your harvest. ¹⁰And you shall not strip your vineyard bare, neither shall you gather the fallen grapes of your vineyard. You shall leave them for the poor and for the sojourner: I am the LORD your God.

¹¹"You shall not steal; you shall not deal falsely; you shall not lie to one another. ¹²You shall not swear by my name falsely, and so profane the name of your God: I am the LORD.

¹³"You shall not oppress your neighbour or rob him. The wages of a hired worker shall not remain with you all night until the morning. ¹⁴You shall not curse the deaf or put a stumbling block before the blind, but you shall fear your God: I am the LORD.

¹⁵"You shall do no injustice in court. You shall not be partial to the poor or defer to the great, but in righteousness shall you judge your neighbour. ¹⁶You shall not go around as a slanderer among your people, and you shall not stand up against the life[a] of your neighbour: I am the LORD.

¹⁷"You shall not hate your brother in your heart, but you shall reason frankly with your neighbour, lest you incur sin because of him. ¹⁸You shall not take vengeance or bear a grudge against the sons of your own people, but you shall love your neighbour as yourself: I am the LORD.

YOU SHALL KEEP MY STATUTES

¹⁹"You shall keep my statutes. You shall not let your cattle breed with a different kind. You shall not sow your field with two kinds of seed, nor shall you wear a garment of cloth made of two kinds of material.

²⁰"If a man lies sexually with a woman who is a slave, assigned to another man and not yet ransomed or given her freedom, a distinction shall be made. They shall not be put to death, because she was not free; ²¹but he shall bring his compensation to the LORD, to the entrance of the tent of meeting, a ram for a guilt offering. ²²And the priest shall make atonement for him with the ram of the guilt offering before the LORD for his sin that he has committed, and he shall be forgiven for the sin that he has committed.

²³"When you come into the land and plant any kind of tree for food, then you shall regard its fruit as forbidden.[b] For three years it shall be forbidden to you; it must not be eaten. ²⁴And in the fourth year all its fruit shall be holy, an offering of praise to the LORD. ²⁵But in the fifth year you may eat of its fruit, to increase its yield for you: I am the LORD your God.

²⁶"You shall not eat any flesh with the blood in it. You shall not interpret omens or tell fortunes. ²⁷You shall not round off the hair on your temples or mar the edges of your beard. ²⁸You shall not make any cuts on your body for the dead or tattoo yourselves: I am the LORD.

²⁹"Do not profane your daughter by making her a prostitute, lest the land fall into prostitution and the land become full of depravity. ³⁰You shall keep my Sabbaths and reverence my sanctuary: I am the LORD.

³¹"Do not turn to mediums or necromancers; do not seek them out, and so make yourselves unclean by them: I am the LORD your God.

³²"You shall stand up before the grey head and honour the face of an old man, and you shall fear your God: I am the LORD.

³³"When a stranger sojourns with you in your land, you shall not do him wrong. ³⁴You shall treat the stranger who sojourns with you as the native among you, and you shall love him as yourself, for you were strangers in the land of Egypt: I am the LORD your God.

³⁵"You shall do no wrong in judgement, in measures of length or weight or quantity. ³⁶You shall have just balances, just weights, a just ephah, and a just hin:[c] I am the LORD your God, who brought you out of the land of Egypt. ³⁷And you shall observe all my statutes and all my rules, and do them: I am the LORD."

PUNISHMENT FOR CHILD SACRIFICE

20 The LORD spoke to Moses, saying, ²"Say to the people of Israel, Any one of the people of Israel or of the strangers who sojourn in Israel who gives any of his children to Molech shall surely be put to death. The people of the land shall stone him with stones. ³I myself will set my face against that man and will cut him off from among his people, because he has given one of his children to Molech, to make my sanctuary unclean and to profane my holy name. ⁴And if the people of the land do at all close their eyes to that man when he gives one of his children to Molech, and do not put him to death, ⁵then I will set my face against

---

[a]Hebrew blood [b]Hebrew as its uncircumcision [c]An ephah was about 3/5 of a bushel or 22 litres; a hin was about 4 quarts or 3.5 litres

that man and against his clan and will cut them off from among their people, him and all who follow him in whoring after Molech.

⁶"If a person turns to mediums and necromancers, whoring after them, I will set my face against that person and will cut him off from among his people. ⁷Consecrate yourselves, therefore, and be holy, for I am the LORD your God. ⁸Keep my statutes and do them; I am the LORD who sanctifies you. ⁹For anyone who curses his father or his mother shall surely be put to death; he has cursed his father or his mother; his blood is upon him.

PUNISHMENTS FOR SEXUAL IMMORALITY

¹⁰"If a man commits adultery with the wife of[a] his neighbour, both the adulterer and the adulteress shall surely be put to death. ¹¹If a man lies with his father's wife, he has uncovered his father's nakedness; both of them shall surely be put to death; their blood is upon them. ¹²If a man lies with his daughter-in-law, both of them shall surely be put to death; they have committed perversion; their blood is upon them. ¹³If a man lies with a male as with a woman, both of them have committed an abomination; they shall surely be put to death; their blood is upon them. ¹⁴If a man takes a woman and her mother also, it is depravity; he and they shall be burned with fire, that there may be no depravity among you. ¹⁵If a man lies with an animal, he shall surely be put to death, and you shall kill the animal. ¹⁶If a woman approaches any animal and lies with it, you shall kill the woman and the animal; they shall surely be put to death; their blood is upon them.

¹⁷"If a man takes his sister, a daughter of his father or a daughter of his mother, and sees her nakedness, and she sees his nakedness, it is a disgrace, and they shall be cut off in the sight of the children of their people. He has uncovered his sister's nakedness, and he shall bear his iniquity. ¹⁸If a man lies with a woman during her menstrual period and uncovers her nakedness, he has made naked her fountain, and she has uncovered the fountain of her blood. Both of them shall be cut off from among their people. ¹⁹You shall not uncover the nakedness of your mother's sister or of your father's sister, for that is to make naked one's relative; they shall bear their iniquity. ²⁰If a man lies with his uncle's wife, he has uncovered his uncle's nakedness; they shall bear their sin; they shall die childless. ²¹If a man takes his brother's wife, it is impurity.[b] He has uncovered his brother's nakedness; they shall be childless.

YOU SHALL BE HOLY

²²"You shall therefore keep all my statutes and all my rules and do them, that the land where I am bringing you to live may not vomit you out. ²³And you shall not walk in the customs of the nation that I am driving out before you, for they did all these things, and therefore I detested them. ²⁴But I have said to you, 'You shall inherit their land, and I will give it to you to possess, a land flowing with milk and honey.' I am the LORD your God, who has separated you from the peoples. ²⁵You shall therefore separate the clean beast from the unclean, and the unclean bird from the clean. You shall not make yourselves detestable by beast or by bird or by anything with which the ground crawls, which I have set apart for you to hold unclean. ²⁶You shall be holy to me, for I the LORD am holy and have separated you from the peoples, that you should be mine.

²⁷"A man or a woman who is a medium or a necromancer shall surely be put to death. They shall be stoned with stones; their blood shall be upon them."

HOLINESS AND THE PRIESTS

21 And the LORD said to Moses, "Speak to the priests, the sons of Aaron, and say to them, No one shall make himself unclean for the dead among his people, ²except for his closest relatives, his mother, his father, his son, his daughter, his brother, ³or his virgin sister (who is near to him because she has had no husband; for her he may make himself unclean). ⁴He shall not make himself unclean as a husband among his people and so profane himself. ⁵They shall not make bald patches on their heads, nor shave off the edges of their beards, nor make any cuts on their body. ⁶They shall be holy to their God and not profane the name of their God. For they offer the LORD's food offerings, the bread of their God; therefore they shall be holy. ⁷They shall not marry a prostitute or a woman who has been defiled, neither shall they marry a woman divorced from her husband, for the priest is holy to his God. ⁸You shall sanctify him, for he offers the bread of your God. He shall be holy to you, for I, the LORD, who sanctify you, am holy. ⁹And the

---

[a] Hebrew repeats *if a man commits adultery with the wife of*
[b] Literally *menstrual impurity*

daughter of any priest, if she profanes herself by whoring, profanes her father; she shall be burned with fire.

¹⁰"The priest who is chief among his brothers, on whose head the anointing oil is poured and who has been consecrated to wear the garments, shall not let the hair of his head hang loose nor tear his clothes. ¹¹He shall not go in to any dead bodies nor make himself unclean, even for his father or for his mother. ¹²He shall not go out of the sanctuary, lest he profane the sanctuary of his God, for the consecration of the anointing oil of his God is on him: I am the LORD. ¹³And he shall take a wife in her virginity.[a] ¹⁴A widow, or a divorced woman, or a woman who has been defiled, or a prostitute, these he shall not marry. But he shall take as his wife a virgin[b] of his own people, ¹⁵that he may not profane his offspring among his people, for I am the LORD who sanctifies him."

¹⁶And the LORD spoke to Moses, saying, ¹⁷"Speak to Aaron, saying, None of your offspring throughout their generations who has a blemish may approach to offer the bread of his God. ¹⁸For no one who has a blemish shall draw near, a man blind or lame, or one who has a mutilated face or a limb too long, ¹⁹or a man who has an injured foot or an injured hand, ²⁰or a hunchback or a dwarf or a man with a defect in his sight or an itching disease or scabs or crushed testicles. ²¹No man of the offspring of Aaron the priest who has a blemish shall come near to offer the LORD's food offerings; since he has a blemish, he shall not come near to offer the bread of his God. ²²He may eat the bread of his God, both of the most holy and of the holy things, ²³but he shall not go through the veil or approach the altar, because he has a blemish, that he may not profane my sanctuaries,[c] for I am the LORD who sanctifies them." ²⁴So Moses spoke to Aaron and to his sons and to all the people of Israel.

22 And the LORD spoke to Moses, saying, ²"Speak to Aaron and his sons so that they abstain from the holy things of the people of Israel, which they dedicate to me, so that they do not profane my holy name: I am the LORD. ³Say to them, 'If any one of all your offspring throughout your generations approaches the holy things that the people of Israel dedicate to the LORD, while he has an uncleanness, that person shall be cut off from my presence: I am the LORD. ⁴None of the offspring of Aaron who has a leprous disease or a discharge may eat of the holy things until he is clean. Whoever touches anything that is unclean through contact with the dead or a man who has had an emission of semen, ⁵and whoever touches a swarming thing by which he may be made unclean or a person from whom he may take uncleanness, whatever his uncleanness may be— ⁶the person who touches such a thing shall be unclean until the evening and shall not eat of the holy things unless he has bathed his body in water. ⁷When the sun goes down he shall be clean, and afterwards he may eat of the holy things, because they are his food. ⁸He shall not eat what dies of itself or is torn by beasts, and so make himself unclean by it: I am the LORD.' ⁹They shall therefore keep my charge, lest they bear sin for it and die thereby when they profane it: I am the LORD who sanctifies them.

¹⁰"A lay person shall not eat of a holy thing; no foreign guest of the priest or hired worker shall eat of a holy thing, ¹¹but if a priest buys a slave[d] as his property for money, the slave[e] may eat of it, and anyone born in his house may eat of his food. ¹²If a priest's daughter marries a layman, she shall not eat of the contribution of the holy things. ¹³But if a priest's daughter is widowed or divorced and has no child and returns to her father's house, as in her youth, she may eat of her father's food; yet no lay person shall eat of it. ¹⁴And if anyone eats of a holy thing unintentionally, he shall add the fifth of its value to it and give the holy thing to the priest. ¹⁵They shall not profane the holy things of the people of Israel, which they contribute to the LORD, ¹⁶and so cause them to bear iniquity and guilt, by eating their holy things: for I am the LORD who sanctifies them."

ACCEPTABLE OFFERINGS

¹⁷And the LORD spoke to Moses, saying, ¹⁸"Speak to Aaron and his sons and all the people of Israel and say to them, When any one of the house of Israel or of the sojourners in Israel presents a burnt offering as his offering, for any of their vows or freewill offerings that they offer to the LORD, ¹⁹if it is to be accepted for you it shall be a male without blemish, of the bulls or the sheep or the goats. ²⁰You shall not offer anything that has a blemish, for it will not be acceptable for you.

---

[a] Or *a young wife* [b] Hebrew *young woman* [c] Or *my holy precincts*
[d] Or *servant*; twice in this verse [e] Hebrew *he*

²¹And when anyone offers a sacrifice of peace offerings to the LORD to fulfil a vow or as a freewill offering from the herd or from the flock, to be accepted it must be perfect; there shall be no blemish in it. ²²Animals blind or disabled or mutilated or having a discharge or an itch or scabs you shall not offer to the LORD or give them to the LORD as a food offering on the altar. ²³You may present a bull or a lamb that has a part too long or too short for a freewill offering, but for a vow offering it cannot be accepted. ²⁴Any animal that has its testicles bruised or crushed or torn or cut you shall not offer to the LORD; you shall not do it within your land, ²⁵neither shall you offer as the bread of your God any such animals obtained from a foreigner. Since there is a blemish in them, because of their mutilation, they will not be accepted for you."

²⁶And the LORD spoke to Moses, saying, ²⁷"When an ox or sheep or goat is born, it shall remain for seven days with its mother, and from the eighth day on it shall be acceptable as a food offering to the LORD. ²⁸But you shall not kill an ox or a sheep and her young in one day. ²⁹And when you sacrifice a sacrifice of thanksgiving to the LORD, you shall sacrifice it so that you may be accepted. ³⁰It shall be eaten on the same day; you shall leave none of it until morning: I am the LORD.

³¹"So you shall keep my commandments and do them: I am the LORD. ³²And you shall not profane my holy name, that I may be sanctified among the people of Israel. I am the LORD who sanctifies you, ³³who brought you out of the land of Egypt to be your God: I am the LORD."

FEASTS OF THE LORD

23 The LORD spoke to Moses, saying, ²"Speak to the people of Israel and say to them, These are the appointed feasts of the LORD that you shall proclaim as holy convocations; they are my appointed feasts.

THE SABBATH

³"For six days shall work be done, but on the seventh day is a Sabbath of solemn rest, a holy convocation. You shall do no work. It is a Sabbath to the LORD in all your dwelling places.

THE PASSOVER

⁴"These are the appointed feasts of the LORD, the holy convocations, which you shall proclaim at the time appointed for them. ⁵In the first month, on the fourteenth day of the month at twilight,ᵃ is the LORD's Passover. ⁶And on the fifteenth day of the same month is the Feast of Unleavened Bread to the LORD; for seven days you shall eat unleavened bread. ⁷On the first day you shall have a holy convocation; you shall not do any ordinary work. ⁸But you shall present a food offering to the LORD for seven days. On the seventh day is a holy convocation; you shall not do any ordinary work."

THE FEAST OF FIRSTFRUITS

⁹And the LORD spoke to Moses, saying, ¹⁰"Speak to the people of Israel and say to them, When you come into the land that I give you and reap its harvest, you shall bring the sheaf of the firstfruits of your harvest to the priest, ¹¹and he shall wave the sheaf before the LORD, so that you may be accepted. On the day after the Sabbath the priest shall wave it. ¹²And on the day when you wave the sheaf, you shall offer a male lamb a year old without blemish as a burnt offering to the LORD. ¹³And the grain offering with it shall be two tenths of an ephahᵇ of fine flour mixed with oil, a food offering to the LORD with a pleasing aroma, and the drink offering with it shall be of wine, a quarter of a hin.ᶜ ¹⁴And you shall eat neither bread nor grain parched or fresh until this same day, until you have brought the offering of your God: it is a statute for ever throughout your generations in all your dwellings.

THE FEAST OF WEEKS

¹⁵"You shall count seven full weeks from the day after the Sabbath, from the day that you brought the sheaf of the wave offering. ¹⁶You shall count fifty days to the day after the seventh Sabbath. Then you shall present a grain offering of new grain to the LORD. ¹⁷You shall bring from your dwelling places two loaves of bread to be waved, made of two tenths of an ephah. They shall be of fine flour, and they shall be baked with leaven, as firstfruits to the LORD. ¹⁸And you shall present with the bread seven lambs a year old without blemish, and one bull from the herd and two rams. They shall be a burnt offering to the LORD, with their grain offering and their drink offerings,

---

ᵃHebrew *between the two evenings* ᵇAn *ephah* was about 3/5 of a bushel or 22 litres ᶜA *hin* was about 4 quarts or 3.5 litres

a food offering with a pleasing aroma to the LORD. ¹⁹And you shall offer one male goat for a sin offering, and two male lambs a year old as a sacrifice of peace offerings. ²⁰And the priest shall wave them with the bread of the firstfruits as a wave offering before the LORD, with the two lambs. They shall be holy to the LORD for the priest. ²¹And you shall make a proclamation on the same day. You shall hold a holy convocation. You shall not do any ordinary work. It is a statute for ever in all your dwelling places throughout your generations.

²²"And when you reap the harvest of your land, you shall not reap your field right up to its edge, nor shall you gather the gleanings after your harvest. You shall leave them for the poor and for the sojourner: I am the LORD your God."

THE FEAST OF TRUMPETS

²³And the LORD spoke to Moses, saying, ²⁴"Speak to the people of Israel, saying, In the seventh month, on the first day of the month, you shall observe a day of solemn rest, a memorial proclaimed with blast of trumpets, a holy convocation. ²⁵You shall not do any ordinary work, and you shall present a food offering to the LORD."

THE DAY OF ATONEMENT

²⁶And the LORD spoke to Moses, saying, ²⁷"Now on the tenth day of this seventh month is the Day of Atonement. It shall be for you a time of holy convocation, and you shall afflict yourselves[a] and present a food offering to the LORD. ²⁸And you shall not do any work on that very day, for it is a Day of Atonement, to make atonement for you before the LORD your God. ²⁹For whoever is not afflicted[b] on that very day shall be cut off from his people. ³⁰And whoever does any work on that very day, that person I will destroy from among his people. ³¹You shall not do any work. It is a statute for ever throughout your generations in all your dwelling places. ³²It shall be to you a Sabbath of solemn rest, and you shall afflict yourselves. On the ninth day of the month beginning at evening, from evening to evening shall you keep your Sabbath."

THE FEAST OF BOOTHS

³³And the LORD spoke to Moses, saying, ³⁴"Speak to the people of Israel, saying, On the fifteenth day of this seventh month and for seven days is the Feast of Booths[c] to the LORD. ³⁵On the first day shall be a holy convocation; you shall not do any ordinary work. ³⁶For seven days you shall present food offerings to the LORD. On the eighth day you shall hold a holy convocation and present a food offering to the LORD. It is a solemn assembly; you shall not do any ordinary work.

³⁷"These are the appointed feasts of the LORD, which you shall proclaim as times of holy convocation, for presenting to the LORD food offerings, burnt offerings and grain offerings, sacrifices and drink offerings, each on its proper day, ³⁸besides the LORD's Sabbaths and besides your gifts and besides all your vow offerings and besides all your freewill offerings, which you give to the LORD.

³⁹"On the fifteenth day of the seventh month, when you have gathered in the produce of the land, you shall celebrate the feast of the LORD for seven days. On the first day shall be a solemn rest, and on the eighth day shall be a solemn rest. ⁴⁰And you shall take on the first day the fruit of splendid trees, branches of palm trees and boughs of leafy trees and willows of the brook, and you shall rejoice before the LORD your God for seven days. ⁴¹You shall celebrate it as a feast to the LORD for seven days in the year. It is a statute for ever throughout your generations; you shall celebrate it in the seventh month. ⁴²You shall dwell in booths for seven days. All native Israelites shall dwell in booths, ⁴³that your generations may know that I made the people of Israel dwell in booths when I brought them out of the land of Egypt: I am the LORD your God."

⁴⁴Thus Moses declared to the people of Israel the appointed feasts of the LORD.

THE LAMPS

24 The LORD spoke to Moses, saying, ²"Command the people of Israel to bring you pure oil from beaten olives for the lamp, that a light may be kept burning regularly. ³Outside the veil of the testimony, in the tent of meeting, Aaron shall arrange it from evening to morning before the LORD regularly. It shall be a statute for ever throughout your generations. ⁴He shall arrange the lamps on the lampstand of pure gold[d] before the LORD regularly.

---

[a] Or *shall fast*; also verse 32   [b] Or *is not fasting*   [c] Or *Tabernacles*   [d] Hebrew *the pure lampstand*

BREAD FOR THE TABERNACLE

⁵"You shall take fine flour and bake twelve loaves from it; two tenths of an ephah[a] shall be in each loaf. ⁶And you shall set them in two piles, six in a pile, on the table of pure gold[b] before the LORD. ⁷And you shall put pure frankincense on each pile, that it may go with the bread as a memorial portion as a food offering to the LORD. ⁸Every Sabbath day Aaron shall arrange it before the LORD regularly; it is from the people of Israel as a covenant for ever. ⁹And it shall be for Aaron and his sons, and they shall eat it in a holy place, since it is for him a most holy portion out of the LORD's food offerings, a perpetual due."

PUNISHMENT FOR BLASPHEMY

¹⁰Now an Israelite woman's son, whose father was an Egyptian, went out among the people of Israel. And the Israelite woman's son and a man of Israel fought in the camp, ¹¹and the Israelite woman's son blasphemed the Name, and cursed. Then they brought him to Moses. His mother's name was Shelomith, the daughter of Dibri, of the tribe of Dan. ¹²And they put him in custody, till the will of the LORD should be clear to them.

¹³Then the LORD spoke to Moses, saying, ¹⁴"Bring out of the camp the one who cursed, and let all who heard him lay their hands on his head, and let all the congregation stone him. ¹⁵And speak to the people of Israel, saying, Whoever curses his God shall bear his sin. ¹⁶Whoever blasphemes the name of the LORD shall surely be put to death. All the congregation shall stone him. The sojourner as well as the native, when he blasphemes the Name, shall be put to death.

AN EYE FOR AN EYE

¹⁷"Whoever takes a human life shall surely be put to death. ¹⁸Whoever takes an animal's life shall make it good, life for life. ¹⁹If anyone injures his neighbour, as he has done it shall be done to him, ²⁰fracture for fracture, eye for eye, tooth for tooth; whatever injury he has given a person shall be given to him. ²¹Whoever kills an animal shall make it good, and whoever kills a person shall be put to death. ²²You shall have the same rule for the sojourner and for the native, for I am the LORD your God." ²³So Moses spoke to the people of Israel, and they brought out of the camp the one who had cursed and stoned him with stones. Thus the people of Israel did as the LORD commanded Moses.

THE SABBATH YEAR

25 The LORD spoke to Moses on Mount Sinai, saying, ²"Speak to the people of Israel and say to them, When you come into the land that I give you, the land shall keep a Sabbath to the LORD. ³For six years you shall sow your field, and for six years you shall prune your vineyard and gather in its fruits, ⁴but in the seventh year there shall be a Sabbath of solemn rest for the land, a Sabbath to the LORD. You shall not sow your field or prune your vineyard. ⁵You shall not reap what grows of itself in your harvest, or gather the grapes of your undressed vine. It shall be a year of solemn rest for the land. ⁶The Sabbath of the land[c] shall provide food for you, for yourself and for your male and female slaves[d] and for your hired worker and the sojourner who lives with you, ⁷and for your cattle and for the wild animals that are in your land: all its yield shall be for food.

THE YEAR OF JUBILEE

⁸"You shall count seven weeks[e] of years, seven times seven years, so that the time of the seven weeks of years shall give you forty-nine years. ⁹Then you shall sound the loud trumpet on the tenth day of the seventh month. On the Day of Atonement you shall sound the trumpet throughout all your land. ¹⁰And you shall consecrate the fiftieth year, and proclaim liberty throughout the land to all its inhabitants. It shall be a jubilee for you, when each of you shall return to his property and each of you shall return to his clan. ¹¹That fiftieth year shall be a jubilee for you; in it you shall neither sow nor reap what grows of itself nor gather the grapes from the undressed vines. ¹²For it is a jubilee. It shall be holy to you. You may eat the produce of the field.[f]

¹³"In this year of jubilee each of you shall return to his property. ¹⁴And if you make a sale to your neighbour or buy from your neighbour, you shall not wrong one another. ¹⁵You shall pay your neighbour according to the number of years after the jubilee, and he shall sell to you according to the number of years for crops. ¹⁶If the years are many, you shall increase the price, and if the years are few, you shall reduce the price, for it is the number of the crops that he is selling

---

[a]An *ephah* was about 3/5 of a bushel or 22 litres [b]Hebrew *the pure table* [c]That is, the Sabbath produce of the land [d]Or *servants* [e]Or *Sabbaths* [f]Or *countryside*

to you. ⁷¹You shall not wrong one another, but you shall fear your God, for I am the LORD your God.

¹⁸"Therefore you shall do my statutes and keep my rules and perform them, and then you will dwell in the land securely. ¹⁹The land will yield its fruit, and you will eat your fill and dwell in it securely. ²⁰And if you say, 'What shall we eat in the seventh year, if we may not sow or gather in our crop?' ²¹I will command my blessing on you in the sixth year, so that it will produce a crop sufficient for three years. ²²When you sow in the eighth year, you will be eating some of the old crop; you shall eat the old until the ninth year, when its crop arrives.

REDEMPTION OF PROPERTY

²³"The land shall not be sold in perpetuity, for the land is mine. For you are strangers and sojourners with me. ²⁴And in all the country you possess, you shall allow a redemption of the land.

²⁵"If your brother becomes poor and sells part of his property, then his nearest redeemer shall come and redeem what his brother has sold. ²⁶If a man has no one to redeem it and then himself becomes prosperous and finds sufficient means to redeem it, ²⁷let him calculate the years since he sold it and pay back the balance to the man to whom he sold it, and then return to his property. ²⁸But if he does not have sufficient means to recover it, then what he sold shall remain in the hand of the buyer until the year of jubilee. In the jubilee it shall be released, and he shall return to his property.

²⁹"If a man sells a dwelling house in a walled city, he may redeem it within a year of its sale. For a full year he shall have the right of redemption. ³⁰If it is not redeemed within a full year, then the house in the walled city shall belong in perpetuity to the buyer, throughout his generations; it shall not be released in the jubilee. ³¹But the houses of the villages that have no wall round them shall be classified with the fields of the land. They may be redeemed, and they shall be released in the jubilee. ³²As for the cities of the Levites, the Levites may redeem at any time the houses in the cities they possess. ³³And if one of the Levites exercises his right of redemption, then the house that was sold in a city they possess shall be released in the jubilee. For the houses in the cities of the Levites are their possession among the people of Israel.

³⁴But the fields of pasture land belonging to their cities may not be sold, for that is their possession for ever.

KINDNESS FOR POOR BROTHERS

³⁵"If your brother becomes poor and cannot maintain himself with you, you shall support him as though he were a stranger and a sojourner, and he shall live with you. ³⁶Take no interest from him or profit, but fear your God, that your brother may live beside you. ³⁷You shall not lend him your money at interest, nor give him your food for profit. ³⁸I am the LORD your God, who brought you out of the land of Egypt to give you the land of Canaan, and to be your God.

³⁹"If your brother becomes poor beside you and sells himself to you, you shall not make him serve as a slave: ⁴⁰he shall be with you as a hired worker and as a sojourner. He shall serve with you until the year of the jubilee. ⁴¹Then he shall go out from you, he and his children with him, and go back to his own clan and return to the possession of his fathers. ⁴²For they are my servants,[a] whom I brought out of the land of Egypt; they shall not be sold as slaves. ⁴³You shall not rule over him ruthlessly but shall fear your God. ⁴⁴As for your male and female slaves whom you may have: you may buy male and female slaves from among the nations that are around you. ⁴⁵You may also buy from among the strangers who sojourn with you and their clans that are with you, who have been born in your land, and they may be your property. ⁴⁶You may bequeath them to your sons after you to inherit as a possession for ever. You may make slaves of them, but over your brothers the people of Israel you shall not rule, one over another ruthlessly.

REDEEMING A POOR MAN

⁴⁷"If a stranger or sojourner with you becomes rich, and your brother beside him becomes poor and sells himself to the stranger or sojourner with you or to a member of the stranger's clan, ⁴⁸then after he is sold he may be redeemed. One of his brothers may redeem him, ⁴⁹or his uncle or his cousin may redeem him, or a close relative from his clan may redeem him. Or if he grows rich he may redeem himself. ⁵⁰He shall calculate with his buyer from the year when he sold himself to him until the year of jubilee, and

---

[a] Hebrew *slaves*

the price of his sale shall vary with the number of years. The time he was with his owner shall be rated as the time of a hired worker. ⁵¹If there are still many years left, he shall pay proportionately for his redemption some of his sale price. ⁵²If there remain but a few years until the year of jubilee, he shall calculate and pay for his redemption in proportion to his years of service. ⁵³He shall treat him as a worker hired year by year. He shall not rule ruthlessly over him in your sight. ⁵⁴And if he is not redeemed by these means, then he and his children with him shall be released in the year of jubilee. ⁵⁵For it is to me that the people of Israel are servants.ᵃ They are my servants whom I brought out of the land of Egypt: I am the LORD your God.

BLESSINGS FOR OBEDIENCE

26 "You shall not make idols for yourselves or erect an image or pillar, and you shall not set up a figured stone in your land to bow down to it, for I am the LORD your God. ²You shall keep my Sabbaths and reverence my sanctuary: I am the LORD.

³"If you walk in my statutes and observe my commandments and do them, ⁴then I will give you your rains in their season, and the land shall yield its increase, and the trees of the field shall yield their fruit. ⁵Your threshing shall last to the time of the grape harvest, and the grape harvest shall last to the time for sowing. And you shall eat your bread to the full and dwell in your land securely. ⁶I will give peace in the land, and you shall lie down, and none shall make you afraid. And I will remove harmful beasts from the land, and the sword shall not go through your land. ⁷You shall chase your enemies, and they shall fall before you by the sword. ⁸Five of you shall chase a hundred, and a hundred of you shall chase ten thousand, and your enemies shall fall before you by the sword. ⁹I will turn to you and make you fruitful and multiply you and will confirm my covenant with you. ¹⁰You shall eat old store long kept, and you shall clear out the old to make way for the new. ¹¹I will make my dwellingᵇ among you, and my soul shall not abhor you. ¹²And I will walk among you and will be your God, and you shall be my people. ¹³I am the LORD your God, who brought you out of the land of Egypt, that you should not be their slaves. And I have broken the bars of your yoke and made you walk erect.

PUNISHMENT FOR DISOBEDIENCE

¹⁴"But if you will not listen to me and will not do all these commandments, ¹⁵if you spurn my statutes, and if your soul abhors my rules, so that you will not do all my commandments, but break my covenant, ¹⁶then I will do this to you: I will visit you with panic, with wasting disease and fever that consume the eyes and make the heart ache. And you shall sow your seed in vain, for your enemies shall eat it. ¹⁷I will set my face against you, and you shall be struck down before your enemies. Those who hate you shall rule over you, and you shall flee when none pursues you. ¹⁸And if in spite of this you will not listen to me, then I will discipline you again sevenfold for your sins, ¹⁹and I will break the pride of your power, and I will make your heavens like iron and your earth like bronze. ²⁰And your strength shall be spent in vain, for your land shall not yield its increase, and the trees of the land shall not yield their fruit.

²¹"Then if you walk contrary to me and will not listen to me, I will continue striking you, sevenfold for your sins. ²²And I will let loose the wild beasts against you, which shall bereave you of your children and destroy your livestock and make you few in number, so that your roads shall be deserted.

²³"And if by this discipline you are not turned to me but walk contrary to me, ²⁴then I also will walk contrary to you, and I myself will strike you sevenfold for your sins. ²⁵And I will bring a sword upon you, that shall execute vengeance for the covenant. And if you gather within your cities, I will send pestilence among you, and you shall be delivered into the hand of the enemy. ²⁶When I break your supplyᶜ of bread, ten women shall bake your bread in a single oven and shall dole out your bread again by weight, and you shall eat and not be satisfied.

²⁷"But if in spite of this you will not listen to me, but walk contrary to me, ²⁸then I will walk contrary to you in fury, and I myself will discipline you sevenfold for your sins. ²⁹You shall eat the flesh of your sons, and you shall eat the flesh of your daughters. ³⁰And I will destroy your high places and cut down your incense altars and cast your dead bodies upon the dead bodies of your idols, and my soul will abhor you. ³¹And I will lay your cities waste and will make your sanctuaries desolate, and I will not smell your pleasing

---

ᵃOr *slaves* ᵇHebrew *tabernacle* ᶜHebrew *staff*

aromas. ³²And I myself will devastate the land, so that your enemies who settle in it shall be appalled at it. ³³And I will scatter you among the nations, and I will unsheathe the sword after you, and your land shall be a desolation, and your cities shall be a waste.

³⁴"Then the land shall enjoy*ᵃ* its Sabbaths as long as it lies desolate, while you are in your enemies' land; then the land shall rest, and enjoy its Sabbaths. ³⁵As long as it lies desolate it shall have rest, the rest that it did not have on your Sabbaths when you were dwelling in it. ³⁶And as for those of you who are left, I will send faintness into their hearts in the lands of their enemies. The sound of a driven leaf shall put them to flight, and they shall flee as one flees from the sword, and they shall fall when none pursues. ³⁷They shall stumble over one another, as if to escape a sword, though none pursues. And you shall have no power to stand before your enemies. ³⁸And you shall perish among the nations, and the land of your enemies shall eat you up. ³⁹And those of you who are left shall rot away in your enemies' lands because of their iniquity, and also because of the iniquities of their fathers they shall rot away like them.

⁴⁰"But if they confess their iniquity and the iniquity of their fathers in their treachery that they committed against me, and also in walking contrary to me, ⁴¹so that I walked contrary to them and brought them into the land of their enemies—if then their uncircumcised heart is humbled and they make amends for their iniquity, ⁴²then I will remember my covenant with Jacob, and I will remember my covenant with Isaac and my covenant with Abraham, and I will remember the land. ⁴³But the land shall be abandoned by them and enjoy its Sabbaths while it lies desolate without them, and they shall make amends for their iniquity, because they spurned my rules and their soul abhorred my statutes. ⁴⁴Yet for all that, when they are in the land of their enemies, I will not spurn them, neither will I abhor them so as to destroy them utterly and break my covenant with them, for I am the LORD their God. ⁴⁵But I will for their sake remember the covenant with their forefathers, whom I brought out of the land of Egypt in the sight of the nations, that I might be their God: I am the LORD."

⁴⁶These are the statutes and rules and laws that the LORD made between himself and the people of Israel through Moses on Mount Sinai.

LAWS ABOUT VOWS

27 The LORD spoke to Moses, saying, ²"Speak to the people of Israel and say to them, If anyone makes a special vow to the LORD involving the valuation of persons, ³then the valuation of a male from twenty years old up to sixty years old shall be fifty shekels*ᵇ* of silver, according to the shekel of the sanctuary. ⁴If the person is a female, the valuation shall be thirty shekels. ⁵If the person is from five years old up to twenty years old, the valuation shall be for a male twenty shekels, and for a female ten shekels. ⁶If the person is from a month old up to five years old, the valuation shall be for a male five shekels of silver, and for a female the valuation shall be three shekels of silver. ⁷And if the person is sixty years old or over, then the valuation for a male shall be fifteen shekels, and for a female ten shekels. ⁸And if someone is too poor to pay the valuation, then he shall be made to stand before the priest, and the priest shall value him; the priest shall value him according to what the vower can afford.

⁹"If the vow*ᶜ* is an animal that may be offered as an offering to the LORD, all of it that he gives to the LORD is holy. ¹⁰He shall not exchange it or make a substitute for it, good for bad, or bad for good; and if he does in fact substitute one animal for another, then both it and the substitute shall be holy. ¹¹And if it is any unclean animal that may not be offered as an offering to the LORD, then he shall stand the animal before the priest, ¹²and the priest shall value it as either good or bad; as the priest values it, so it shall be. ¹³But if he wishes to redeem it, he shall add a fifth to the valuation.

¹⁴"When a man dedicates his house as a holy gift to the LORD, the priest shall value it as either good or bad; as the priest values it, so it shall stand. ¹⁵And if the donor wishes to redeem his house, he shall add a fifth to the valuation price, and it shall be his.

¹⁶"If a man dedicates to the LORD part of the land that is his possession, then the valuation shall be in proportion to its seed. A homer*ᵈ* of barley seed shall be valued at fifty shekels of silver. ¹⁷If he dedicates his field from the year of jubilee, the valuation shall stand, ¹⁸but if he dedicates his field after

---

*ᵃ*Or *pay for*; twice in this verse; also verse 43　*ᵇ*A *shekel* was about 2/5 of an ounce or 11 grams　*ᶜ*Hebrew *it*　*ᵈ*A *homer* was about 6 bushels or 220 litres

the jubilee, then the priest shall calculate the price according to the years that remain until the year of jubilee, and a deduction shall be made from the valuation. ¹⁹And if he who dedicates the field wishes to redeem it, then he shall add a fifth to its valuation price, and it shall remain his. ²⁰But if he does not wish to redeem the field, or if he has sold the field to another man, it shall not be redeemed any more. ²¹But the field, when it is released in the jubilee, shall be a holy gift to the LORD, like a field that has been devoted. The priest shall be in possession of it. ²²If he dedicates to the LORD a field that he has bought, which is not a part of his possession, ²³then the priest shall calculate the amount of the valuation for it up to the year of jubilee, and the man shall give the valuation on that day as a holy gift to the LORD. ²⁴In the year of jubilee the field shall return to him from whom it was bought, to whom the land belongs as a possession. ²⁵Every valuation shall be according to the shekel of the sanctuary: twenty gerahs^a shall make a shekel.

²⁶"But a firstborn of animals, which as a firstborn belongs to the LORD, no man may dedicate; whether ox or sheep, it is the LORD's. ²⁷And if it is an unclean animal, then he shall buy it back at the valuation, and add a fifth to it; or, if it is not redeemed, it shall be sold at the valuation.

²⁸"But no devoted thing that a man devotes to the LORD, of anything that he has, whether man or beast, or of his inherited field, shall be sold or redeemed; every devoted thing is most holy to the LORD. ²⁹No one devoted, who is to be devoted for destruction^b from mankind, shall be ransomed; he shall surely be put to death.

³⁰"Every tithe of the land, whether of the seed of the land or of the fruit of the trees, is the LORD's; it is holy to the LORD. ³¹If a man wishes to redeem some of his tithe, he shall add a fifth to it. ³²And every tithe of herds and flocks, every tenth animal of all that pass under the herdsman's staff, shall be holy to the LORD. ³³One shall not differentiate between good or bad, neither shall he make a substitute for it; and if he does substitute for it, then both it and the substitute shall be holy; it shall not be redeemed."

³⁴These are the commandments that the LORD commanded Moses for the people of Israel on Mount Sinai.

---

^{a}A *gerah* was about 1/50 of an ounce or 0.6 gram ^{b}That is, set apart (devoted) as an offering to the Lord (for destruction)

NUMBERS

A CENSUS OF ISRAEL'S WARRIORS

1 The LORD spoke to Moses in the wilderness of Sinai, in the tent of meeting, on the first day of the second month, in the second year after they had come out of the land of Egypt, saying, ²"Take a census of all the congregation of the people of Israel, by clans, by fathers' houses, according to the number of names, every male, head by head. ³From twenty years old and upwards, all in Israel who are able to go to war, you and Aaron shall list them, company by company. ⁴And there shall be with you a man from each tribe, each man being the head of the house of his fathers. ⁵And these are the names of the men who shall assist you. From Reuben, Elizur the son of Shedeur; ⁶from Simeon, Shelumiel the son of Zurishaddai; ⁷from Judah, Nahshon the son of Amminadab; ⁸from Issachar, Nethanel the son of Zuar; ⁹from Zebulun, Eliab the son of Helon; ¹⁰from the sons of Joseph, from Ephraim, Elishama the son of Ammihud, and from Manasseh, Gamaliel the son of Pedahzur; ¹¹from Benjamin, Abidan the son of Gideoni; ¹²from Dan, Ahiezer the son of Ammishaddai; ¹³from Asher, Pagiel the son of Ochran; ¹⁴from Gad, Eliasaph the son of Deuel; ¹⁵from Naphtali, Ahira the son of Enan." ¹⁶These were the ones chosen from the congregation, the chiefs of their ancestral tribes, the heads of the clans of Israel.

¹⁷Moses and Aaron took these men who had been named, ¹⁸and on the first day of the second month, they assembled the whole congregation together, who registered themselves by clans, by fathers' houses, according to the number of names from twenty years old and upwards, head by head, ¹⁹as the LORD commanded Moses. So he listed them in the wilderness of Sinai.

²⁰The people of Reuben, Israel's firstborn, their generations, by their clans, by their fathers' houses, according to the number of names, head by head, every male from twenty years old and upwards, all who were able to go to war: ²¹those listed of the tribe of Reuben were 46,500.

²²Of the people of Simeon, their generations, by their clans, by their fathers' houses, those of them who were listed, according to the number of names, head by head, every male from twenty years old and upwards, all who were able to go to war: ²³those listed of the tribe of Simeon were 59,300.

²⁴Of the people of Gad, their generations, by their clans, by their fathers' houses, according to the number of the names, from twenty years old and upwards, all who were able to go to war: ²⁵those listed of the tribe of Gad were 45,650.

²⁶Of the people of Judah, their generations, by their clans, by their fathers' houses, according to the number of names, from twenty years old and upwards, every man able to go to war: ²⁷those listed of the tribe of Judah were 74,600.

²⁸Of the people of Issachar, their generations, by their clans, by their fathers' houses, according to the number of names, from twenty years old and upwards, every man able to go to war: ²⁹those listed of the tribe of Issachar were 54,400.

³⁰Of the people of Zebulun, their generations, by their clans, by their fathers' houses, according to the number of names, from twenty years old and upwards, every man able to go to war: ³¹those listed of the tribe of Zebulun were 57,400.

³²Of the people of Joseph, namely, of the people of Ephraim, their generations, by their clans, by their fathers' houses, according to the number of names, from twenty years old and upwards, every man able to go to war: ³³those listed of the tribe of Ephraim were 40,500.

³⁴Of the people of Manasseh, their generations, by their clans, by their fathers' houses, according to the number of names, from twenty years old and upwards, every man able to go to war: ³⁵those listed of the tribe of Manasseh were 32,200.

³⁶Of the people of Benjamin, their generations, by their clans, by their fathers' houses, according to the number of names, from twenty years old and upwards, every man

able to go to war: ³⁷those listed of the tribe of Benjamin were 35,400.

³⁸Of the people of Dan, their generations, by their clans, by their fathers' houses, according to the number of names, from twenty years old and upwards, every man able to go to war: ³⁹those listed of the tribe of Dan were 62,700.

⁴⁰Of the people of Asher, their generations, by their clans, by their fathers' houses, according to the number of names, from twenty years old and upwards, every man able to go to war: ⁴¹those listed of the tribe of Asher were 41,500.

⁴²Of the people of Naphtali, their generations, by their clans, by their fathers' houses, according to the number of names, from twenty years old and upwards, every man able to go to war: ⁴³those listed of the tribe of Naphtali were 53,400.

⁴⁴These are those who were listed, whom Moses and Aaron listed with the help of the chiefs of Israel, twelve men, each representing his fathers' house. ⁴⁵So all those listed of the people of Israel, by their fathers' houses, from twenty years old and upwards, every man able to go to war in Israel— ⁴⁶all those listed were 603,550.

LEVITES EXEMPTED

⁴⁷But the Levites were not listed along with them by their ancestral tribe. ⁴⁸For the LORD spoke to Moses, saying, ⁴⁹"Only the tribe of Levi you shall not list, and you shall not take a census of them among the people of Israel. ⁵⁰But appoint the Levites over the tabernacle of the testimony, and over all its furnishings, and over all that belongs to it. They are to carry the tabernacle and all its furnishings, and they shall take care of it and shall camp round the tabernacle. ⁵¹When the tabernacle is to set out, the Levites shall take it down, and when the tabernacle is to be pitched, the Levites shall set it up. And if any outsider comes near, he shall be put to death. ⁵²The people of Israel shall pitch their tents by their companies, each man in his own camp and each man by his own standard. ⁵³But the Levites shall camp round the tabernacle of the testimony, so that there may be no wrath on the congregation of the people of Israel. And the Levites shall keep guard over the tabernacle of the testimony." ⁵⁴Thus did the people of Israel; they did according to all that the LORD commanded Moses.

ARRANGEMENT OF THE CAMP

2 The LORD spoke to Moses and Aaron, saying, ²"The people of Israel shall camp each by his own standard, with the banners of their fathers' houses. They shall camp facing the tent of meeting on every side. ³Those to camp on the east side towards the sunrise shall be of the standard of the camp of Judah by their companies, the chief of the people of Judah being Nahshon the son of Amminadab, ⁴his company as listed being 74,600. ⁵Those to camp next to him shall be the tribe of Issachar, the chief of the people of Issachar being Nethanel the son of Zuar, ⁶his company as listed being 54,400. ⁷Then the tribe of Zebulun, the chief of the people of Zebulun being Eliab the son of Helon, ⁸his company as listed being 57,400. ⁹All those listed of the camp of Judah, by their companies, were 186,400. They shall set out first on the march.

¹⁰"On the south side shall be the standard of the camp of Reuben by their companies, the chief of the people of Reuben being Elizur the son of Shedeur, ¹¹his company as listed being 46,500. ¹²And those to camp next to him shall be the tribe of Simeon, the chief of the people of Simeon being Shelumiel the son of Zurishaddai, ¹³his company as listed being 59,300. ¹⁴Then the tribe of Gad, the chief of the people of Gad being Eliasaph the son of Reuel, ¹⁵his company as listed being 45,650. ¹⁶All those listed of the camp of Reuben, by their companies, were 151,450. They shall set out second.

¹⁷"Then the tent of meeting shall set out, with the camp of the Levites in the midst of the camps; as they camp, so shall they set out, each in position, standard by standard.

¹⁸"On the west side shall be the standard of the camp of Ephraim by their companies, the chief of the people of Ephraim being Elishama the son of Ammihud, ¹⁹his company as listed being 40,500. ²⁰And next to him shall be the tribe of Manasseh, the chief of the people of Manasseh being Gamaliel the son of Pedahzur, ²¹his company as listed being 32,200. ²²Then the tribe of Benjamin, the chief of the people of Benjamin being Abidan the son of Gideoni, ²³his company as listed being 35,400. ²⁴All those listed of the camp of Ephraim, by their companies, were 108,100. They shall set out third on the march.

²⁵"On the north side shall be the standard of the camp of Dan by their companies, the chief of the people of Dan being Ahiezer the son of

Ammishaddai, ²⁶his company as listed being 62,700. ²⁷And those to camp next to him shall be the tribe of Asher, the chief of the people of Asher being Pagiel the son of Ochran, ²⁸his company as listed being 41,500. ²⁹Then the tribe of Naphtali, the chief of the people of Naphtali being Ahira the son of Enan, ³⁰his company as listed being 53,400. ³¹All those listed of the camp of Dan were 157,600. They shall set out last, standard by standard."

³²These are the people of Israel as listed by their fathers' houses. All those listed in the camps by their companies were 603,550. ³³But the Levites were not listed among the people of Israel, as the LORD commanded Moses.

³⁴Thus did the people of Israel. According to all that the LORD commanded Moses, so they camped by their standards, and so they set out, each one in his clan, according to his fathers' house.

THE SONS OF AARON

3 These are the generations of Aaron and Moses at the time when the LORD spoke with Moses on Mount Sinai. ²These are the names of the sons of Aaron: Nadab the firstborn, and Abihu, Eleazar, and Ithamar. ³These are the names of the sons of Aaron, the anointed priests, whom he ordained to serve as priests. ⁴But Nadab and Abihu died before the LORD when they offered unauthorized fire before the LORD in the wilderness of Sinai, and they had no children. So Eleazar and Ithamar served as priests in the lifetime of Aaron their father.

DUTIES OF THE LEVITES

⁵And the LORD spoke to Moses, saying, ⁶"Bring the tribe of Levi near, and set them before Aaron the priest, that they may minister to him. ⁷They shall keep guard over him and over the whole congregation before the tent of meeting, as they minister at the tabernacle. ⁸They shall guard all the furnishings of the tent of meeting, and keep guard over the people of Israel as they minister at the tabernacle. ⁹And you shall give the Levites to Aaron and his sons; they are wholly given to him from among the people of Israel. ¹⁰And you shall appoint Aaron and his sons, and they shall guard their priesthood. But if any outsider comes near, he shall be put to death."

¹¹And the LORD spoke to Moses, saying, ¹²"Behold, I have taken the Levites from among the people of Israel instead of every firstborn who opens the womb among the people of Israel. The Levites shall be mine, ¹³for all the firstborn are mine. On the day that I struck down all the firstborn in the land of Egypt, I consecrated for my own all the firstborn in Israel, both of man and of beast. They shall be mine: I am the LORD."

¹⁴And the LORD spoke to Moses in the wilderness of Sinai, saying, ¹⁵"List the sons of Levi, by fathers' houses and by clans; every male from a month old and upwards you shall list." ¹⁶So Moses listed them according to the word of the LORD, as he was commanded. ¹⁷And these were the sons of Levi by their names: Gershon and Kohath and Merari. ¹⁸And these are the names of the sons of Gershon by their clans: Libni and Shimei. ¹⁹And the sons of Kohath by their clans: Amram, Izhar, Hebron, and Uzziel. ²⁰And the sons of Merari by their clans: Mahli and Mushi. These are the clans of the Levites, by their fathers' houses.

²¹To Gershon belonged the clan of the Libnites and the clan of the Shimeites; these were the clans of the Gershonites. ²²Their listing according to the number of all the males from a month old and upwards was*ᵃ* 7,500. ²³The clans of the Gershonites were to camp behind the tabernacle on the west, ²⁴with Eliasaph, the son of Lael as chief of the fathers' house of the Gershonites. ²⁵And the guard duty of the sons of Gershon in the tent of meeting involved the tabernacle, the tent with its covering, the screen for the entrance of the tent of meeting, ²⁶the hangings of the court, the screen for the door of the court that is round the tabernacle and the altar, and its cords—all the service connected with these.

²⁷To Kohath belonged the clan of the Amramites and the clan of the Izharites and the clan of the Hebronites and the clan of the Uzzielites; these are the clans of the Kohathites. ²⁸According to the number of all the males, from a month old and upwards, there were 8,600, keeping guard over the sanctuary. ²⁹The clans of the sons of Kohath were to camp on the south side of the tabernacle, ³⁰with Elizaphan the son of Uzziel as chief of the fathers' house of the clans of the Kohathites. ³¹And their guard duty involved the ark, the table, the lampstand, the altars, the vessels of the sanctuary with which the priests minister, and the screen; all the service connected with these. ³²And

---

ᵃHebrew *their listing was*

Eleazar the son of Aaron the priest was to be chief over the chiefs of the Levites, and to have oversight of those who kept guard over the sanctuary. ³³To Merari belonged the clan of the Mahlites and the clan of the Mushites: these are the clans of Merari. ³⁴Their listing according to the number of all the males from a month old and upwards was 6,200. ³⁵And the chief of the fathers' house of the clans of Merari was Zuriel the son of Abihail. They were to camp on the north side of the tabernacle. ³⁶And the appointed guard duty of the sons of Merari involved the frames of the tabernacle, the bars, the pillars, the bases, and all their accessories; all the service connected with these; ³⁷also the pillars round the court, with their bases and pegs and cords.

³⁸Those who were to camp before the tabernacle on the east, before the tent of meeting towards the sunrise, were Moses and Aaron and his sons, guarding the sanctuary itself, to protect[a] the people of Israel. And any outsider who came near was to be put to death. ³⁹All those listed among the Levites, whom Moses and Aaron listed at the commandment of the LORD, by clans, all the males from a month old and upwards, were 22,000.

REDEMPTION OF THE FIRSTBORN

⁴⁰And the LORD said to Moses, "List all the firstborn males of the people of Israel, from a month old and upwards, taking the number of their names. ⁴¹And you shall take the Levites for me—I am the LORD—instead of all the firstborn among the people of Israel, and the cattle of the Levites instead of all the firstborn among the cattle of the people of Israel." ⁴²So Moses listed all the firstborn among the people of Israel, as the LORD commanded him. ⁴³And all the firstborn males, according to the number of names, from a month old and upwards as listed were 22,273.

⁴⁴And the LORD spoke to Moses, saying, ⁴⁵"Take the Levites instead of all the firstborn among the people of Israel, and the cattle of the Levites instead of their cattle. The Levites shall be mine: I am the LORD. ⁴⁶And as the redemption price for the 273 of the firstborn of the people of Israel, over and above the number of the male Levites, ⁴⁷you shall take five shekels[b] per head; you shall take them according to the shekel of the sanctuary (the shekel of twenty gerahs[c]), ⁴⁸and give the money to Aaron and his sons as the redemption price for those who are over." ⁴⁹So Moses took the redemption money from those who were over and above those redeemed by the Levites. ⁵⁰From the firstborn of the people of Israel he took the money, 1,365 shekels, by the shekel of the sanctuary. ⁵¹And Moses gave the redemption money to Aaron and his sons, according to the word of the LORD, as the LORD commanded Moses.

DUTIES OF THE KOHATHITES, GERSHONITES, AND MERARITES

4 The LORD spoke to Moses and Aaron, saying, ²"Take a census of the sons of Kohath from among the sons of Levi, by their clans and their fathers' houses, ³from thirty years old up to fifty years old, all who can come on duty, to do the work in the tent of meeting. ⁴This is the service of the sons of Kohath in the tent of meeting: the most holy things. ⁵When the camp is to set out, Aaron and his sons shall go in and take down the veil of the screen and cover the ark of the testimony with it. ⁶Then they shall put on it a covering of goatskin[d] and spread on top of that a cloth all of blue, and shall put in its poles. ⁷And over the table of the bread of the Presence they shall spread a cloth of blue and put on it the plates, the dishes for incense, the bowls, and the flagons for the drink offering; the regular showbread also shall be on it. ⁸Then they shall spread over them a cloth of scarlet and cover the same with a covering of goatskin, and shall put in its poles. ⁹And they shall take a cloth of blue and cover the lampstand for the light, with its lamps, its tongs, its trays, and all the vessels for oil with which it is supplied. ¹⁰And they shall put it with all its utensils in a covering of goatskin and put it on the carrying frame. ¹¹And over the golden altar they shall spread a cloth of blue and cover it with a covering of goatskin, and shall put in its poles. ¹²And they shall take all the vessels of the service that are used in the sanctuary and put them in a cloth of blue and cover them with a covering of goatskin and put them on the carrying frame. ¹³And they shall take away the ashes from the altar and spread a purple cloth over it. ¹⁴And they shall put on it all the utensils of the altar, which are used for the service there, the firepans, the forks, the shovels, and the basins, all the

---

[a] Hebrew *guard* [b] A *shekel* was about 2/5 of an ounce or 11 grams [c] A *gerah* was about 1/50 of an ounce or 0.6 gram [d] The meaning of the Hebrew word is uncertain; compare Exodus 25:5

utensils of the altar; and they shall spread on it a covering of goatskin, and shall put in its poles. **15**And when Aaron and his sons have finished covering the sanctuary and all the furnishings of the sanctuary, as the camp sets out, after that the sons of Kohath shall come to carry these, but they must not touch the holy things, lest they die. These are the things of the tent of meeting that the sons of Kohath are to carry.

16"And Eleazar the son of Aaron the priest shall have charge of the oil for the light, the fragrant incense, the regular grain offering, and the anointing oil, with the oversight of the whole tabernacle and all that is in it, of the sanctuary and its vessels."

17The Lord spoke to Moses and Aaron, saying, **18**"Let not the tribe of the clans of the Kohathites be destroyed from among the Levites, **19**but deal thus with them, that they may live and not die when they come near to the most holy things: Aaron and his sons shall go in and appoint them each to his task and to his burden, **20**but they shall not go in to look on the holy things even for a moment, lest they die."

21The Lord spoke to Moses, saying, **22**"Take a census of the sons of Gershon also, by their fathers' houses and by their clans. **23**From thirty years old up to fifty years old, you shall list them, all who can come to do duty, to do service in the tent of meeting. **24**This is the service of the clans of the Gershonites, in serving and bearing burdens: **25**they shall carry the curtains of the tabernacle and the tent of meeting with its covering and the covering of goatskin that is on top of it and the screen for the entrance of the tent of meeting **26**and the hangings of the court and the screen for the entrance of the gate of the court that is round the tabernacle and the altar, and their cords and all the equipment for their service. And they shall do all that needs to be done with regard to them. **27**All the service of the sons of the Gershonites shall be at the command of Aaron and his sons, in all that they are to carry and in all that they have to do. And you shall assign to their charge all that they are to carry. **28**This is the service of the clans of the sons of the Gershonites in the tent of meeting, and their guard duty is to be under the direction of Ithamar the son of Aaron the priest.

29"As for the sons of Merari, you shall list them by their clans and their fathers' houses. **30**From thirty years old up to fifty years old, you shall list them, everyone who can come on duty, to do the service of the tent of meeting. **31**And this is what they are charged to carry, as the whole of their service in the tent of meeting: the frames of the tabernacle, with its bars, pillars, and bases, **32**and the pillars round the court with their bases, pegs, and cords, with all their equipment and all their accessories. And you shall list by name the objects that they are required to carry. **33**This is the service of the clans of the sons of Merari, the whole of their service in the tent of meeting, under the direction of Ithamar the son of Aaron the priest."

34And Moses and Aaron and the chiefs of the congregation listed the sons of the Kohathites, by their clans and their fathers' houses, **35**from thirty years old up to fifty years old, everyone who could come on duty, for service in the tent of meeting; **36**and those listed by clans were 2,750. **37**This was the list of the clans of the Kohathites, all who served in the tent of meeting, whom Moses and Aaron listed according to the commandment of the Lord by Moses.

38Those listed of the sons of Gershon, by their clans and their fathers' houses, **39**from thirty years old up to fifty years old, everyone who could come on duty for service in the tent of meeting— **40**those listed by their clans and their fathers' houses were 2,630. **41**This was the list of the clans of the sons of Gershon, all who served in the tent of meeting, whom Moses and Aaron listed according to the commandment of the Lord.

42Those listed of the clans of the sons of Merari, by their clans and their fathers' houses, **43**from thirty years old up to fifty years old, everyone who could come on duty, for service in the tent of meeting— **44**those listed by clans were 3,200. **45**This was the list of the clans of the sons of Merari, whom Moses and Aaron listed according to the commandment of the Lord by Moses.

46All those who were listed of the Levites, whom Moses and Aaron and the chiefs of Israel listed, by their clans and their fathers' houses, **47**from thirty years old up to fifty years old, everyone who could come to do the service of ministry and the service of bearing burdens in the tent of meeting, **48**those listed were 8,580. **49**According to the commandment of the Lord through Moses they were listed, each one with his task of serving or carrying. Thus they were listed by him, as the Lord commanded Moses.

UNCLEAN PEOPLE

5 The LORD spoke to Moses, saying, ²"Command the people of Israel that they put out of the camp everyone who is leprous[a] or has a discharge and everyone who is unclean through contact with the dead. ³You shall put out both male and female, putting them outside the camp, that they may not defile their camp, in the midst of which I dwell." ⁴And the people of Israel did so, and put them outside the camp; as the LORD said to Moses, so the people of Israel did.

CONFESSION AND RESTITUTION

⁵And the LORD spoke to Moses, saying, ⁶"Speak to the people of Israel, When a man or woman commits any of the sins that people commit by breaking faith with the LORD, and that person realizes his guilt, ⁷he shall confess his sin that he has committed.[b] And he shall make full restitution for his wrong, adding a fifth to it and giving it to him to whom he did the wrong. ⁸But if the man has no next of kin to whom restitution may be made for the wrong, the restitution for wrong shall go to the LORD for the priest, in addition to the ram of atonement with which atonement is made for him. ⁹And every contribution, all the holy donations of the people of Israel, which they bring to the priest, shall be his. ¹⁰Each one shall keep his holy donations: whatever anyone gives to the priest shall be his."

A TEST FOR ADULTERY

¹¹And the LORD spoke to Moses, saying, ¹²"Speak to the people of Israel, If any man's wife goes astray and breaks faith with him, ¹³if a man lies with her sexually, and it is hidden from the eyes of her husband, and she is undetected though she has defiled herself, and there is no witness against her, since she was not taken in the act, ¹⁴and if the spirit of jealousy comes over him and he is jealous of his wife who has defiled herself, or if the spirit of jealousy comes over him and he is jealous of his wife, though she has not defiled herself, ¹⁵then the man shall bring his wife to the priest and bring the offering required of her, a tenth of an ephah[c] of barley flour. He shall pour no oil on it and put no frankincense on it, for it is a grain offering of jealousy, a grain offering of remembrance, bringing iniquity to remembrance.

¹⁶"And the priest shall bring her near and set her before the LORD. ¹⁷And the priest shall take holy water in an earthenware vessel and take some of the dust that is on the floor of the tabernacle and put it into the water. ¹⁸And the priest shall set the woman before the LORD and unbind the hair of the woman's head and place in her hands the grain offering of remembrance, which is the grain offering of jealousy. And in his hand the priest shall have the water of bitterness that brings the curse. ¹⁹Then the priest shall make her take an oath, saying, 'If no man has lain with you, and if you have not turned aside to uncleanness while you were under your husband's authority, be free from this water of bitterness that brings the curse. ²⁰But if you have gone astray, though you are under your husband's authority, and if you have defiled yourself, and some man other than your husband has lain with you, ²¹then' (let the priest make the woman take the oath of the curse, and say to the woman) 'the LORD make you a curse and an oath among your people, when the LORD makes your thigh fall away and your body swell. ²²May this water that brings the curse pass into your bowels and make your womb swell and your thigh fall away.' And the woman shall say, 'Amen, Amen.'

²³"Then the priest shall write these curses in a book and wash them off into the water of bitterness. ²⁴And he shall make the woman drink the water of bitterness that brings the curse, and the water that brings the curse shall enter into her and cause bitter pain. ²⁵And the priest shall take the grain offering of jealousy out of the woman's hand and shall wave the grain offering before the LORD and bring it to the altar. ²⁶And the priest shall take a handful of the grain offering, as its memorial portion, and burn it on the altar, and afterwards shall make the woman drink the water. ²⁷And when he has made her drink the water, then, if she has defiled herself and has broken faith with her husband, the water that brings the curse shall enter into her and cause bitter pain, and her womb shall swell, and her thigh shall fall away, and the woman shall become a curse among her people. ²⁸But if the woman has not defiled herself and is clean, then she shall be free and shall conceive children.

²⁹"This is the law in cases of jealousy, when a wife, though under her husband's authority, goes astray and defiles herself, ³⁰or when the spirit of jealousy comes over a man and

---

[a] *Leprosy* was a term for several skin diseases; see Leviticus 13
[b] Hebrew *they shall confess their sin that they have committed*
[c] An *ephah* was about 3/5 of a bushel or 22 litres

he is jealous of his wife. Then he shall set the woman before the Lord, and the priest shall carry out for her all this law. ³¹The man shall be free from iniquity, but the woman shall bear her iniquity."

THE NAZIRITE VOW

6 And the Lord spoke to Moses, saying, ²"Speak to the people of Israel and say to them, When either a man or a woman makes a special vow, the vow of a Nazirite,ᵃ to separate himself to the Lord, ³he shall separate himself from wine and strong drink. He shall drink no vinegar made from wine or strong drink and shall not drink any juice of grapes or eat grapes, fresh or dried. ⁴All the days of his separationᵇ he shall eat nothing that is produced by the grapevine, not even the seeds or the skins.

⁵"All the days of his vow of separation, no razor shall touch his head. Until the time is completed for which he separates himself to the Lord, he shall be holy. He shall let the locks of hair of his head grow long.

⁶"All the days that he separates himself to the Lord he shall not go near a dead body. ⁷Not even for his father or for his mother, for brother or sister, if they die, shall he make himself unclean, because his separation to God is on his head. ⁸All the days of his separation he is holy to the Lord.

⁹"And if any man dies very suddenly beside him and he defiles his consecrated head, then he shall shave his head on the day of his cleansing; on the seventh day he shall shave it. ¹⁰On the eighth day he shall bring two turtle-doves or two pigeons to the priest to the entrance of the tent of meeting, ¹¹and the priest shall offer one for a sin offering and the other for a burnt offering, and make atonement for him, because he sinned by reason of the dead body. And he shall consecrate his head that same day ¹²and separate himself to the Lord for the days of his separation and bring a male lamb a year old for a guilt offering. But the previous period shall be void, because his separation was defiled.

¹³"And this is the law for the Nazirite, when the time of his separation has been completed: he shall be brought to the entrance of the tent of meeting, ¹⁴and he shall bring his gift to the Lord, one male lamb a year old without blemish for a burnt offering, and one ewe lamb a year old without blemish as a sin offering, and one ram without blemish as a peace offering, ¹⁵and a basket of unleavened bread, loaves of fine flour mixed with oil, and unleavened wafers smeared with oil, and their grain offering and their drink offerings. ¹⁶And the priest shall bring them before the Lord and offer his sin offering and his burnt offering, ¹⁷and he shall offer the ram as a sacrifice of peace offering to the Lord, with the basket of unleavened bread. The priest shall offer also its grain offering and its drink offering. ¹⁸And the Nazirite shall shave his consecrated head at the entrance of the tent of meeting and shall take the hair from his consecrated head and put it on the fire that is under the sacrifice of the peace offering. ¹⁹And the priest shall take the shoulder of the ram, when it is boiled, and one unleavened loaf out of the basket and one unleavened wafer, and shall put them on the hands of the Nazirite, after he has shaved the hair of his consecration, ²⁰and the priest shall wave them for a wave offering before the Lord. They are a holy portion for the priest, together with the breast that is waved and the thigh that is contributed. And after that the Nazirite may drink wine.

²¹"This is the law of the Nazirite. But if he vows an offering to the Lord above his Nazirite vow, as he can afford, in exact accordance with the vow that he takes, then he shall do in addition to the law of the Nazirite."

AARON'S BLESSING

²²The Lord spoke to Moses, saying, ²³"Speak to Aaron and his sons, saying, Thus you shall bless the people of Israel: you shall say to them,

²⁴   The Lord bless you and keep you;
²⁵   the Lord make his face to shine upon
        you and be gracious to you;
²⁶   the Lord lift up his countenanceᶜ
        upon you and give you peace.

²⁷"So shall they put my name upon the people of Israel, and I will bless them."

OFFERINGS AT THE TABERNACLE'S CONSECRATION

7 On the day when Moses had finished setting up the tabernacle and had anointed and consecrated it with all its furnishings and had anointed and consecrated the altar with all its utensils, ²the chiefs of Israel, heads of their fathers' houses, who were the

---
ᵃ*Nazirite* means *one separated,* or *one consecrated*   ᵇOr *Naziriteship*   ᶜOr *face*

chiefs of the tribes, who were over those who were listed, approached ³and brought their offerings before the LORD, six wagons and twelve oxen, a wagon for every two of the chiefs, and for each one an ox. They brought them before the tabernacle. ⁴Then the LORD said to Moses, ⁵"Accept these from them, that they may be used in the service of the tent of meeting, and give them to the Levites, to each man according to his service." ⁶So Moses took the wagons and the oxen and gave them to the Levites. ⁷Two wagons and four oxen he gave to the sons of Gershon, according to their service. ⁸And four wagons and eight oxen he gave to the sons of Merari, according to their service, under the direction of Ithamar the son of Aaron the priest. ⁹But to the sons of Kohath he gave none, because they were charged with the service of the holy things that had to be carried on the shoulder. ¹⁰And the chiefs offered offerings for the dedication of the altar on the day it was anointed; and the chiefs offered their offering before the altar. ¹¹And the LORD said to Moses, "They shall offer their offerings, one chief each day, for the dedication of the altar."

¹²He who offered his offering on the first day was Nahshon the son of Amminadab, of the tribe of Judah. ¹³And his offering was one silver plate whose weight was 130 shekels,ᵃ one silver basin of 70 shekels, according to the shekel of the sanctuary, both of them full of fine flour mixed with oil for a grain offering; ¹⁴one golden dish of 10 shekels, full of incense; ¹⁵one bull from the herd, one ram, one male lamb a year old, for a burnt offering; ¹⁶one male goat for a sin offering; ¹⁷and for the sacrifice of peace offerings, two oxen, five rams, five male goats, and five male lambs a year old. This was the offering of Nahshon the son of Amminadab.

¹⁸On the second day Nethanel the son of Zuar, the chief of Issachar, made an offering. ¹⁹He offered for his offering one silver plate whose weight was 130 shekels, one silver basin of 70 shekels, according to the shekel of the sanctuary, both of them full of fine flour mixed with oil for a grain offering; ²⁰one golden dish of 10 shekels, full of incense; ²¹one bull from the herd, one ram, one male lamb a year old, for a burnt offering; ²²one male goat for a sin offering; ²³and for the sacrifice of peace offerings, two oxen, five rams, five male goats, and five male lambs a year old. This was the offering of Nethanel the son of Zuar.

²⁴On the third day Eliab the son of Helon, the chief of the people of Zebulun: ²⁵his offering was one silver plate whose weight was 130 shekels, one silver basin of 70 shekels, according to the shekel of the sanctuary, both of them full of fine flour mixed with oil for a grain offering; ²⁶one golden dish of 10 shekels, full of incense; ²⁷one bull from the herd, one ram, one male lamb a year old, for a burnt offering; ²⁸one male goat for a sin offering; ²⁹and for the sacrifice of peace offerings, two oxen, five rams, five male goats, and five male lambs a year old. This was the offering of Eliab the son of Helon.

³⁰On the fourth day Elizur the son of Shedeur, the chief of the people of Reuben: ³¹his offering was one silver plate whose weight was 130 shekels, one silver basin of 70 shekels, according to the shekel of the sanctuary, both of them full of fine flour mixed with oil for a grain offering; ³²one golden dish of 10 shekels, full of incense; ³³one bull from the herd, one ram, one male lamb a year old, for a burnt offering; ³⁴one male goat for a sin offering; ³⁵and for the sacrifice of peace offerings, two oxen, five rams, five male goats, and five male lambs a year old. This was the offering of Elizur the son of Shedeur.

³⁶On the fifth day Shelumiel the son of Zurishaddai, the chief of the people of Simeon: ³⁷his offering was one silver plate whose weight was 130 shekels, one silver basin of 70 shekels, according to the shekel of the sanctuary, both of them full of fine flour mixed with oil for a grain offering; ³⁸one golden dish of 10 shekels, full of incense; ³⁹one bull from the herd, one ram, one male lamb a year old, for a burnt offering; ⁴⁰one male goat for a sin offering; ⁴¹and for the sacrifice of peace offerings, two oxen, five rams, five male goats, and five male lambs a year old. This was the offering of Shelumiel the son of Zurishaddai.

⁴²On the sixth day Eliasaph the son of Deuel, the chief of the people of Gad: ⁴³his offering was one silver plate whose weight was 130 shekels, one silver basin of 70 shekels, according to the shekel of the sanctuary, both of them full of fine flour mixed with oil for a grain offering; ⁴⁴one golden dish of 10 shekels, full of incense; ⁴⁵one bull from the herd, one ram, one male lamb a year old, for a burnt offering; ⁴⁶one male goat for a sin offering; ⁴⁷and for the sacrifice of peace offerings,

---

ᵃ A *shekel* was about 2/5 of an ounce or 11 grams

two oxen, five rams, five male goats, and five male lambs a year old. This was the offering of Eliasaph the son of Deuel.

⁴⁸On the seventh day Elishama the son of Ammihud, the chief of the people of Ephraim: ⁴⁹his offering was one silver plate whose weight was 130 shekels, one silver basin of 70 shekels, according to the shekel of the sanctuary, both of them full of fine flour mixed with oil for a grain offering; ⁵⁰one golden dish of 10 shekels, full of incense; ⁵¹one bull from the herd, one ram, one male lamb a year old, for a burnt offering; ⁵²one male goat for a sin offering; ⁵³and for the sacrifice of peace offerings, two oxen, five rams, five male goats, and five male lambs a year old. This was the offering of Elishama the son of Ammihud.

⁵⁴On the eighth day Gamaliel the son of Pedahzur, the chief of the people of Manasseh: ⁵⁵his offering was one silver plate whose weight was 130 shekels, one silver basin of 70 shekels, according to the shekel of the sanctuary, both of them full of fine flour mixed with oil for a grain offering; ⁵⁶one golden dish of 10 shekels, full of incense; ⁵⁷one bull from the herd, one ram, one male lamb a year old, for a burnt offering; ⁵⁸one male goat for a sin offering; ⁵⁹and for the sacrifice of peace offerings, two oxen, five rams, five male goats, and five male lambs a year old. This was the offering of Gamaliel the son of Pedahzur.

⁶⁰On the ninth day Abidan the son of Gideoni, the chief of the people of Benjamin: ⁶¹his offering was one silver plate whose weight was 130 shekels, one silver basin of 70 shekels, according to the shekel of the sanctuary, both of them full of fine flour mixed with oil for a grain offering; ⁶²one golden dish of 10 shekels, full of incense; ⁶³one bull from the herd, one ram, one male lamb a year old, for a burnt offering; ⁶⁴one male goat for a sin offering; ⁶⁵and for the sacrifice of peace offerings, two oxen, five rams, five male goats, and five male lambs a year old. This was the offering of Abidan the son of Gideoni.

⁶⁶On the tenth day Ahiezer the son of Ammishaddai, the chief of the people of Dan: ⁶⁷his offering was one silver plate whose weight was 130 shekels, one silver basin of 70 shekels, according to the shekel of the sanctuary, both of them full of fine flour mixed with oil for a grain offering; ⁶⁸one golden dish of 10 shekels, full of incense; ⁶⁹one bull from the herd, one ram, one male lamb a year old, for a burnt offering; ⁷⁰one male goat for a sin offering; ⁷¹and for the sacrifice of peace offerings, two oxen, five rams, five male goats, and five male lambs a year old. This was the offering of Ahiezer the son of Ammishaddai.

⁷²On the eleventh day Pagiel the son of Ochran, the chief of the people of Asher: ⁷³his offering was one silver plate whose weight was 130 shekels, one silver basin of 70 shekels, according to the shekel of the sanctuary, both of them full of fine flour mixed with oil for a grain offering; ⁷⁴one golden dish of 10 shekels, full of incense; ⁷⁵one bull from the herd, one ram, one male lamb a year old, for a burnt offering; ⁷⁶one male goat for a sin offering; ⁷⁷and for the sacrifice of peace offerings, two oxen, five rams, five male goats, and five male lambs a year old. This was the offering of Pagiel the son of Ochran.

⁷⁸On the twelfth day Ahira the son of Enan, the chief of the people of Naphtali: ⁷⁹his offering was one silver plate whose weight was 130 shekels, one silver basin of 70 shekels, according to the shekel of the sanctuary, both of them full of fine flour mixed with oil for a grain offering; ⁸⁰one golden dish of 10 shekels, full of incense; ⁸¹one bull from the herd, one ram, one male lamb a year old, for a burnt offering; ⁸²one male goat for a sin offering; ⁸³and for the sacrifice of peace offerings, two oxen, five rams, five male goats, and five male lambs a year old. This was the offering of Ahira the son of Enan.

⁸⁴This was the dedication offering for the altar on the day when it was anointed, from the chiefs of Israel: twelve silver plates, twelve silver basins, twelve golden dishes, ⁸⁵each silver plate weighing 130 shekels and each basin 70, all the silver of the vessels 2,400 shekels according to the shekel of the sanctuary, ⁸⁶the twelve golden dishes, full of incense, weighing 10 shekels apiece according to the shekel of the sanctuary, all the gold of the dishes being 120 shekels; ⁸⁷all the cattle for the burnt offering twelve bulls, twelve rams, twelve male lambs a year old, with their grain offering; and twelve male goats for a sin offering; ⁸⁸and all the cattle for the sacrifice of peace offerings twenty-four bulls, the rams sixty, the male goats sixty, the male lambs a year old sixty. This was the dedication offering for the altar after it was anointed.

⁸⁹And when Moses went into the tent of meeting to speak with the LORD, he heard the voice speaking to him from above the mercy seat that was on the ark of the testimony, from between the two cherubim; and it spoke to him.

THE SEVEN LAMPS

8 Now the LORD spoke to Moses, saying, ²"Speak to Aaron and say to him, When you set up the lamps, the seven lamps shall give light in front of the lampstand." ³And Aaron did so: he set up its lamps in front of the lampstand, as the LORD commanded Moses. ⁴And this was the workmanship of the lampstand, hammered work of gold. From its base to its flowers, it was hammered work; according to the pattern that the LORD had shown Moses, so he made the lampstand.

CLEANSING OF THE LEVITES

⁵And the LORD spoke to Moses, saying, ⁶"Take the Levites from among the people of Israel and cleanse them. ⁷Thus you shall do to them to cleanse them: sprinkle the water of purification upon them, and let them go with a razor over all their body, and wash their clothes and cleanse themselves. ⁸Then let them take a bull from the herd and its grain offering of fine flour mixed with oil, and you shall take another bull from the herd for a sin offering. ⁹And you shall bring the Levites before the tent of meeting and assemble the whole congregation of the people of Israel. ¹⁰When you bring the Levites before the LORD, the people of Israel shall lay their hands on the Levites, ¹¹and Aaron shall offer the Levites before the LORD as a wave offering from the people of Israel, that they may do the service of the LORD. ¹²Then the Levites shall lay their hands on the heads of the bulls, and you shall offer one for a sin offering and the other for a burnt offering to the LORD to make atonement for the Levites. ¹³And you shall set the Levites before Aaron and his sons, and shall offer them as a wave offering to the LORD.

¹⁴"Thus you shall separate the Levites from among the people of Israel, and the Levites shall be mine. ¹⁵And after that the Levites shall go in to serve at the tent of meeting, when you have cleansed them and offered them as a wave offering. ¹⁶For they are wholly given to me from among the people of Israel. Instead of all who open the womb, the firstborn of all the people of Israel, I have taken them for myself. ¹⁷For all the firstborn among the people of Israel are mine, both of man and of beast. On the day that I struck down all the firstborn in the land of Egypt I consecrated them for myself, ¹⁸and I have taken the Levites instead of all the firstborn among the people of Israel. ¹⁹And I have given the Levites as a gift to Aaron and his sons from among the people of Israel, to do the service for the people of Israel at the tent of meeting and to make atonement for the people of Israel, that there may be no plague among the people of Israel when the people of Israel come near the sanctuary."

²⁰Thus did Moses and Aaron and all the congregation of the people of Israel to the Levites. According to all that the LORD commanded Moses concerning the Levites, the people of Israel did to them. ²¹And the Levites purified themselves from sin and washed their clothes, and Aaron offered them as a wave offering before the LORD, and Aaron made atonement for them to cleanse them. ²²And after that the Levites went in to do their service in the tent of meeting before Aaron and his sons; as the LORD had commanded Moses concerning the Levites, so they did to them.

RETIREMENT OF THE LEVITES

²³And the LORD spoke to Moses, saying, ²⁴"This applies to the Levites: from twenty-five years old and upwards they[a] shall come to do duty in the service of the tent of meeting. ²⁵And from the age of fifty years they shall withdraw from the duty of the service and serve no more. ²⁶They minister[b] to their brothers in the tent of meeting by keeping guard, but they shall do no service. Thus shall you do to the Levites in assigning their duties."

THE PASSOVER CELEBRATED

9 And the LORD spoke to Moses in the wilderness of Sinai, in the first month of the second year after they had come out of the land of Egypt, saying, ²"Let the people of Israel keep the Passover at its appointed time. ³On the fourteenth day of this month, at twilight, you shall keep it at its appointed time; according to all its statutes and all its rules you shall keep it." ⁴So Moses told the people of Israel that they should keep the Passover. ⁵And they kept the Passover in the first month, on the fourteenth day of the month, at twilight, in the wilderness of Sinai; according to all that the LORD commanded Moses, so the people of Israel did. ⁶And there were certain men who were unclean through touching a dead body, so that they could not keep the Passover on that day, and they came before Moses and Aaron on that day. ⁷And those

---

[a] Hebrew *he*; also verses 25, 26 [b] Hebrew *He ministers*

men said to him, "We are unclean through touching a dead body. Why are we kept from bringing the LORD's offering at its appointed time among the people of Israel?" ⁸And Moses said to them, "Wait, that I may hear what the LORD will command concerning you."

⁹The LORD spoke to Moses, saying, ¹⁰"Speak to the people of Israel, saying, If any one of you or of your descendants is unclean through touching a dead body, or is on a long journey, he shall still keep the Passover to the LORD. ¹¹In the second month on the fourteenth day at twilight they shall keep it. They shall eat it with unleavened bread and bitter herbs. ¹²They shall leave none of it until the morning, nor break any of its bones; according to all the statute for the Passover they shall keep it. ¹³But if anyone who is clean and is not on a journey fails to keep the Passover, that person shall be cut off from his people because he did not bring the LORD's offering at its appointed time; that man shall bear his sin. ¹⁴And if a stranger sojourns among you and would keep the Passover to the LORD, according to the statute of the Passover and according to its rule, so shall he do. You shall have one statute, both for the sojourner and for the native."

THE CLOUD COVERING THE TABERNACLE

¹⁵On the day that the tabernacle was set up, the cloud covered the tabernacle, the tent of the testimony. And at evening it was over the tabernacle like the appearance of fire until morning. ¹⁶So it was always: the cloud covered it by day[a] and the appearance of fire by night. ¹⁷And whenever the cloud lifted from over the tent, after that the people of Israel set out, and in the place where the cloud settled down, there the people of Israel camped. ¹⁸At the command of the LORD the people of Israel set out, and at the command of the LORD they camped. As long as the cloud rested over the tabernacle, they remained in camp. ¹⁹Even when the cloud continued over the tabernacle for many days, the people of Israel kept the charge of the LORD and did not set out. ²⁰Sometimes the cloud would remain for a few days over the tabernacle, and according to the command of the LORD they remained in camp; then according to the command of the LORD they set out. ²¹And sometimes the cloud remained from evening until morning. And when the cloud lifted in the morning, they set out, or if it continued for a day and a night, when the cloud lifted they set out. ²²Whether it was two days, or a month, or a longer time, that the cloud continued over the tabernacle, abiding there, the people of Israel remained in camp and did not set out, but when it lifted they set out. ²³At the command of the LORD they camped, and at the command of the LORD they set out. They kept the charge of the LORD, at the command of the LORD by Moses.

THE SILVER TRUMPETS

10 The LORD spoke to Moses, saying, ²"Make two silver trumpets. Of hammered work you shall make them, and you shall use them for summoning the congregation and for breaking camp. ³And when both are blown, all the congregation shall gather themselves to you at the entrance of the tent of meeting. ⁴But if they blow only one, then the chiefs, the heads of the tribes of Israel, shall gather themselves to you. ⁵When you blow an alarm, the camps that are on the east side shall set out. ⁶And when you blow an alarm the second time, the camps that are on the south side shall set out. An alarm is to be blown whenever they are to set out. ⁷But when the assembly is to be gathered together, you shall blow a long blast, but you shall not sound an alarm. ⁸And the sons of Aaron, the priests, shall blow the trumpets. The trumpets shall be to you for a perpetual statute throughout your generations. ⁹And when you go to war in your land against the adversary who oppresses you, then you shall sound an alarm with the trumpets, that you may be remembered before the LORD your God, and you shall be saved from your enemies. ¹⁰On the day of your gladness also, and at your appointed feasts and at the beginnings of your months, you shall blow the trumpets over your burnt offerings and over the sacrifices of your peace offerings. They shall be a reminder of you before your God: I am the LORD your God."

ISRAEL LEAVES SINAI

¹¹In the second year, in the second month, on the twentieth day of the month, the cloud lifted from over the tabernacle of the testimony, ¹²and the people of Israel set out by stages from the wilderness of Sinai. And the cloud settled down in the wilderness of Paran. ¹³They set out for the first time at the command of the LORD by Moses. ¹⁴The

---

[a]Septuagint, Syriac, Vulgate; Hebrew lacks *by day*

standard of the camp of the people of Judah set out first by their companies, and over their company was Nahshon the son of Amminadab. ¹⁵And over the company of the tribe of the people of Issachar was Nethanel the son of Zuar. ¹⁶And over the company of the tribe of the people of Zebulun was Eliab the son of Helon.

¹⁷And when the tabernacle was taken down, the sons of Gershon and the sons of Merari, who carried the tabernacle, set out. ¹⁸And the standard of the camp of Reuben set out by their companies, and over their company was Elizur the son of Shedeur. ¹⁹And over the company of the tribe of the people of Simeon was Shelumiel the son of Zurishaddai. ²⁰And over the company of the tribe of the people of Gad was Eliasaph the son of Deuel.

²¹Then the Kohathites set out, carrying the holy things, and the tabernacle was set up before their arrival. ²²And the standard of the camp of the people of Ephraim set out by their companies, and over their company was Elishama the son of Ammihud. ²³And over the company of the tribe of the people of Manasseh was Gamaliel the son of Pedahzur. ²⁴And over the company of the tribe of the people of Benjamin was Abidan the son of Gideoni.

²⁵Then the standard of the camp of the people of Dan, acting as the rearguard of all the camps, set out by their companies, and over their company was Ahiezer the son of Ammishaddai. ²⁶And over the company of the tribe of the people of Asher was Pagiel the son of Ochran. ²⁷And over the company of the tribe of the people of Naphtali was Ahira the son of Enan. ²⁸This was the order of march of the people of Israel by their companies, when they set out.

²⁹And Moses said to Hobab the son of Reuel the Midianite, Moses' father-in-law, "We are setting out for the place of which the Lord said, 'I will give it to you.' Come with us, and we will do good to you, for the Lord has promised good to Israel." ³⁰But he said to him, "I will not go. I will depart to my own land and to my kindred." ³¹And he said, "Please do not leave us, for you know where we should camp in the wilderness, and you will serve as eyes for us. ³²And if you do go with us, whatever good the Lord will do to us, the same will we do to you."

³³So they set out from the mount of the Lord for three days' journey. And the ark of the covenant of the Lord went before them for three days' journey, to seek out a resting-place for them. ³⁴And the cloud of the Lord was over them by day, whenever they set out from the camp.

³⁵And whenever the ark set out, Moses said, "Arise, O Lord, and let your enemies be scattered, and let those who hate you flee before you." ³⁶And when it rested, he said, "Return, O Lord, to the ten thousand thousands of Israel."

THE PEOPLE COMPLAIN

11 And the people complained in the hearing of the Lord about their misfortunes, and when the Lord heard it, his anger was kindled, and the fire of the Lord burned among them and consumed some outlying parts of the camp. ²Then the people cried out to Moses, and Moses prayed to the Lord, and the fire died down. ³So the name of that place was called Taberah,ᵃ because the fire of the Lord burned among them.

⁴Now the rabble that was among them had a strong craving. And the people of Israel also wept again and said, "Oh that we had meat to eat! ⁵We remember the fish we ate in Egypt that cost nothing, the cucumbers, the melons, the leeks, the onions, and the garlic. ⁶But now our strength is dried up, and there is nothing at all but this manna to look at."

⁷Now the manna was like coriander seed, and its appearance like that of bdellium. ⁸The people went about and gathered it and ground it in handmills or beat it in mortars and boiled it in pots and made cakes of it. And the taste of it was like the taste of cakes baked with oil. ⁹When the dew fell upon the camp in the night, the manna fell with it.

¹⁰Moses heard the people weeping throughout their clans, each one at the door of his tent. And the anger of the Lord blazed hotly, and Moses was displeased. ¹¹Moses said to the Lord, "Why have you dealt ill with your servant? And why have I not found favour in your sight, that you lay the burden of all this people on me? ¹²Did I conceive all this people? Did I give them birth, that you should say to me, 'Carry them in your bosom, as a nurse carries a sucking child,' to the land that you swore to give their fathers? ¹³Where am I to get meat to give to all this people? For they weep before me and say, 'Give us meat, that we may eat.' ¹⁴I am not able to carry all this people alone; the burden is too heavy for me. ¹⁵If you will treat me like this, kill me at once,

---

ᵃ*Taberah* means *burning*

if I find favour in your sight, that I may not see my wretchedness."

ELDERS APPOINTED TO AID MOSES

16Then the LORD said to Moses, "Gather for me seventy men of the elders of Israel, whom you know to be the elders of the people and officers over them, and bring them to the tent of meeting, and let them take their stand there with you. 17And I will come down and talk with you there. And I will take some of the Spirit that is on you and put it on them, and they shall bear the burden of the people with you, so that you may not bear it yourself alone. 18And say to the people, 'Consecrate yourselves for tomorrow, and you shall eat meat, for you have wept in the hearing of the LORD, saying, "Who will give us meat to eat? For it was better for us in Egypt." Therefore the LORD will give you meat, and you shall eat. 19You shall not eat for just one day, or two days, or five days, or ten days, or twenty days, 20but for a whole month, until it comes out at your nostrils and becomes loathsome to you, because you have rejected the LORD who is among you and have wept before him, saying, "Why did we come out of Egypt?"'" 21But Moses said, "The people among whom I am number six hundred thousand on foot, and you have said, 'I will give them meat, that they may eat for a whole month!' 22Shall flocks and herds be slaughtered for them, and be enough for them? Or shall all the fish of the sea be gathered together for them, and be enough for them?" 23And the LORD said to Moses, "Is the LORD's hand shortened? Now you shall see whether my word will come true for you or not."

24So Moses went out and told the people the words of the LORD. And he gathered seventy men of the elders of the people and placed them round the tent. 25Then the LORD came down in the cloud and spoke to him, and took some of the Spirit that was on him and put it on the seventy elders. And as soon as the Spirit rested on them, they prophesied. But they did not continue doing it.

26Now two men remained in the camp, one named Eldad, and the other named Medad, and the Spirit rested on them. They were among those registered, but they had not gone out to the tent, and so they prophesied in the camp. 27And a young man ran and told Moses, "Eldad and Medad are prophesying in the camp." 28And Joshua the son of Nun, the assistant of Moses from his youth, said, "My lord Moses, stop them." 29But Moses said to him, "Are you jealous for my sake? Would that all the LORD's people were prophets, that the LORD would put his Spirit on them!" 30And Moses and the elders of Israel returned to the camp.

QUAIL AND A PLAGUE

31Then a wind from the LORD sprang up, and it brought quail from the sea and let them fall beside the camp, about a day's journey on this side and a day's journey on the other side, round the camp, and about two cubits[a] above the ground. 32And the people rose all that day and all night and all the next day, and gathered the quail. Those who gathered least gathered ten homers.[b] And they spread them out for themselves all round the camp. 33While the meat was yet between their teeth, before it was consumed, the anger of the LORD was kindled against the people, and the LORD struck down the people with a very great plague. 34Therefore the name of that place was called Kibroth-hattaavah,[c] because there they buried the people who had the craving. 35From Kibroth-hattaavah the people journeyed to Hazeroth, and they remained at Hazeroth.

MIRIAM AND AARON OPPOSE MOSES

12 Miriam and Aaron spoke against Moses because of the Cushite woman whom he had married, for he had married a Cushite woman. 2And they said, "Has the LORD indeed spoken only through Moses? Has he not spoken through us also?" And the LORD heard it. 3Now the man Moses was very meek, more than all people who were on the face of the earth. 4And suddenly the LORD said to Moses and to Aaron and Miriam, "Come out, you three, to the tent of meeting." And the three of them came out. 5And the LORD came down in a pillar of cloud and stood at the entrance of the tent and called Aaron and Miriam, and they both came forward. 6And he said, "Hear my words: If there is a prophet among you, I the LORD make myself known to him in a vision; I speak with him in a dream. 7Not so with my servant Moses. He is faithful in all my house. 8With him I speak mouth to mouth, clearly, and not in riddles, and he beholds the form of the LORD. Why then were you not afraid to

---
[a]*A cubit* was about 18 inches or 45 centimetres   [b]*A homer* was about 6 bushels or 220 litres   [c]*Kibroth-hattaavah* means *graves of craving*

speak against my servant Moses?" ⁹And the anger of the LORD was kindled against them, and he departed.

¹⁰When the cloud removed from over the tent, behold, Miriam was leprous,[a] like snow. And Aaron turned towards Miriam, and behold, she was leprous. ¹¹And Aaron said to Moses, "Oh, my lord, do not punish us[b] because we have done foolishly and have sinned. ¹²Let her not be as one dead, whose flesh is half eaten away when he comes out of his mother's womb." ¹³And Moses cried to the LORD, "O God, please heal her—please." ¹⁴But the LORD said to Moses, "If her father had but spat in her face, should she not be shamed for seven days? Let her be shut outside the camp for seven days, and after that she may be brought in again." ¹⁵So Miriam was shut outside the camp for seven days, and the people did not set out on the march till Miriam was brought in again. ¹⁶After that the people set out from Hazeroth, and camped in the wilderness of Paran.

SPIES SENT INTO CANAAN

13 The LORD spoke to Moses, saying, ²"Send men to spy out the land of Canaan, which I am giving to the people of Israel. From each tribe of their fathers you shall send a man, every one a chief among them." ³So Moses sent them from the wilderness of Paran, according to the command of the LORD, all of them men who were heads of the people of Israel. ⁴And these were their names: From the tribe of Reuben, Shammua the son of Zaccur; ⁵from the tribe of Simeon, Shaphat the son of Hori; ⁶from the tribe of Judah, Caleb the son of Jephunneh; ⁷from the tribe of Issachar, Igal the son of Joseph; ⁸from the tribe of Ephraim, Hoshea the son of Nun; ⁹from the tribe of Benjamin, Palti the son of Raphu; ¹⁰from the tribe of Zebulun, Gaddiel the son of Sodi; ¹¹from the tribe of Joseph (that is, from the tribe of Manasseh), Gaddi the son of Susi; ¹²from the tribe of Dan, Ammiel the son of Gemalli; ¹³from the tribe of Asher, Sethur the son of Michael; ¹⁴from the tribe of Naphtali, Nahbi the son of Vophsi; ¹⁵from the tribe of Gad, Geuel the son of Machi. ¹⁶These were the names of the men whom Moses sent to spy out the land. And Moses called Hoshea the son of Nun Joshua.

¹⁷Moses sent them to spy out the land of Canaan and said to them, "Go up into the Negeb and go up into the hill country, ¹⁸and see what the land is, and whether the people who dwell in it are strong or weak, whether they are few or many, ¹⁹and whether the land that they dwell in is good or bad, and whether the cities that they dwell in are camps or strongholds, ²⁰and whether the land is rich or poor, and whether there are trees in it or not. Be of good courage and bring some of the fruit of the land." Now the time was the season of the first ripe grapes.

²¹So they went up and spied out the land from the wilderness of Zin to Rehob, near Lebo-hamath. ²²They went up into the Negeb and came to Hebron. Ahiman, Sheshai, and Talmai, the descendants of Anak, were there. (Hebron was built seven years before Zoan in Egypt.) ²³And they came to the Valley of Eshcol and cut down from there a branch with a single cluster of grapes, and they carried it on a pole between two of them; they also brought some pomegranates and figs. ²⁴That place was called the Valley of Eshcol,[c] because of the cluster that the people of Israel cut down from there.

REPORT OF THE SPIES

²⁵At the end of forty days they returned from spying out the land. ²⁶And they came to Moses and Aaron and to all the congregation of the people of Israel in the wilderness of Paran, at Kadesh. They brought back word to them and to all the congregation, and showed them the fruit of the land. ²⁷And they told him, "We came to the land to which you sent us. It flows with milk and honey, and this is its fruit. ²⁸However, the people who dwell in the land are strong, and the cities are fortified and very large. And besides, we saw the descendants of Anak there. ²⁹The Amalekites dwell in the land of the Negeb. The Hittites, the Jebusites, and the Amorites dwell in the hill country. And the Canaanites dwell by the sea, and along the Jordan."

³⁰But Caleb quietened the people before Moses and said, "Let us go up at once and occupy it, for we are well able to overcome it." ³¹Then the men who had gone up with him said, "We are not able to go up against the people, for they are stronger than we are." ³²So they brought to the people of Israel a bad report of the land that they had spied out, saying, "The land, through which we have gone to spy it out, is a land that devours its

---

[a] *Leprosy* was a term for several skin diseases; see Leviticus 13
[b] Hebrew *do not lay sin upon us* [c] *Eshcol* means *cluster*

inhabitants, and all the people that we saw in it are of great height. ³³And there we saw the Nephilim (the sons of Anak, who come from the Nephilim), and we seemed to ourselves like grasshoppers, and so we seemed to them."

THE PEOPLE REBEL

14 Then all the congregation raised a loud cry, and the people wept that night. ²And all the people of Israel grumbled against Moses and Aaron. The whole congregation said to them, "Would that we had died in the land of Egypt! Or would that we had died in this wilderness! ³Why is the LORD bringing us into this land, to fall by the sword? Our wives and our little ones will become a prey. Would it not be better for us to go back to Egypt?" ⁴And they said to one another, "Let us choose a leader and go back to Egypt."

⁵Then Moses and Aaron fell on their faces before all the assembly of the congregation of the people of Israel. ⁶And Joshua the son of Nun and Caleb the son of Jephunneh, who were among those who had spied out the land, tore their clothes ⁷and said to all the congregation of the people of Israel, "The land, which we passed through to spy it out, is an exceedingly good land. ⁸If the LORD delights in us, he will bring us into this land and give it to us, a land that flows with milk and honey. ⁹Only do not rebel against the LORD. And do not fear the people of the land, for they are bread for us. Their protection is removed from them, and the LORD is with us; do not fear them." ¹⁰Then all the congregation said to stone them with stones. But the glory of the LORD appeared at the tent of meeting to all the people of Israel.

¹¹And the LORD said to Moses, "How long will this people despise me? And how long will they not believe in me, in spite of all the signs that I have done among them? ¹²I will strike them with the pestilence and disinherit them, and I will make of you a nation greater and mightier than they."

MOSES INTERCEDES FOR THE PEOPLE

¹³But Moses said to the LORD, "Then the Egyptians will hear of it, for you brought up this people in your might from among them, ¹⁴and they will tell the inhabitants of this land. They have heard that you, O LORD, are in the midst of this people. For you, O LORD, are seen face to face, and your cloud stands over them and you go before them, in a pillar of cloud by day and in a pillar of fire by night. ¹⁵Now if you kill this people as one man, then the nations who have heard your fame will say, ¹⁶'It is because the LORD was not able to bring this people into the land that he swore to give to them that he has killed them in the wilderness.' ¹⁷And now, please let the power of the Lord be great as you have promised, saying, ¹⁸'The LORD is slow to anger and abounding in steadfast love, forgiving iniquity and transgression, but he will by no means clear the guilty, visiting the iniquity of the fathers on the children, to the third and the fourth generation.' ¹⁹Please pardon the iniquity of this people, according to the greatness of your steadfast love, just as you have forgiven this people, from Egypt until now."

GOD PROMISES JUDGEMENT

²⁰Then the LORD said, "I have pardoned, according to your word. ²¹But truly, as I live, and as all the earth shall be filled with the glory of the LORD, ²²none of the men who have seen my glory and my signs that I did in Egypt and in the wilderness, and yet have put me to the test these ten times and have not obeyed my voice, ²³shall see the land that I swore to give to their fathers. And none of those who despised me shall see it. ²⁴But my servant Caleb, because he has a different spirit and has followed me fully, I will bring into the land into which he went, and his descendants shall possess it. ²⁵Now, since the Amalekites and the Canaanites dwell in the valleys, turn tomorrow and set out for the wilderness by the way to the Red Sea."

²⁶And the LORD spoke to Moses and to Aaron, saying, ²⁷"How long shall this wicked congregation grumble against me? I have heard the grumblings of the people of Israel, which they grumble against me. ²⁸Say to them, 'As I live, declares the LORD, what you have said in my hearing I will do to you: ²⁹your dead bodies shall fall in this wilderness, and of all your number, listed in the census from twenty years old and upwards, who have grumbled against me, ³⁰not one shall come into the land where I swore that I would make you dwell, except Caleb the son of Jephunneh and Joshua the son of Nun. ³¹But your little ones, who you said would become a prey, I will bring in, and they shall know the land that you have rejected. ³²But as for you, your dead bodies shall fall in this wilderness. ³³And your children shall be shepherds in the wilderness for forty years and shall suffer for

your faithlessness, until the last of your dead bodies lies in the wilderness. ³⁴According to the number of the days in which you spied out the land, forty days, a year for each day, you shall bear your iniquity for forty years, and you shall know my displeasure.' ³⁵I, the LORD, have spoken. Surely this will I do to all this wicked congregation who are gathered together against me: in this wilderness they shall come to a full end, and there they shall die."

³⁶And the men whom Moses sent to spy out the land, who returned and made all the congregation grumble against him by bringing up a bad report about the land— ³⁷the men who brought up a bad report of the land—died by plague before the LORD. ³⁸Of those men who went to spy out the land, only Joshua the son of Nun and Caleb the son of Jephunneh remained alive.

ISRAEL DEFEATED IN BATTLE

³⁹When Moses told these words to all the people of Israel, the people mourned greatly. ⁴⁰And they rose early in the morning and went up to the heights of the hill country, saying, "Here we are. We will go up to the place that the LORD has promised, for we have sinned." ⁴¹But Moses said, "Why now are you transgressing the command of the LORD, when that will not succeed? ⁴²Do not go up, for the LORD is not among you, lest you be struck down before your enemies. ⁴³For there the Amalekites and the Canaanites are facing you, and you shall fall by the sword. Because you have turned back from following the LORD, the LORD will not be with you." ⁴⁴But they presumed to go up to the heights of the hill country, although neither the ark of the covenant of the LORD nor Moses departed out of the camp. ⁴⁵Then the Amalekites and the Canaanites who lived in that hill country came down and defeated them and pursued them, even to Hormah.

LAWS ABOUT SACRIFICES

15 The LORD spoke to Moses, saying, ²"Speak to the people of Israel and say to them, When you come into the land you are to inhabit, which I am giving you, ³and you offer to the LORD from the herd or from the flock a food offering[a] or a burnt offering or a sacrifice, to fulfil a vow or as a freewill offering or at your appointed feasts, to make a pleasing aroma to the LORD, ⁴then he who brings his offering shall offer to the LORD a grain offering of a tenth of an ephah[b] of fine flour, mixed with a quarter of a hin[c] of oil; ⁵and you shall offer with the burnt offering, or for the sacrifice, a quarter of a hin of wine for the drink offering for each lamb. ⁶Or for a ram, you shall offer for a grain offering two tenths of an ephah of fine flour mixed with a third of a hin of oil. ⁷And for the drink offering you shall offer a third of a hin of wine, a pleasing aroma to the LORD. ⁸And when you offer a bull as a burnt offering or sacrifice, to fulfil a vow or for peace offerings to the LORD, ⁹then one shall offer with the bull a grain offering of three tenths of an ephah of fine flour, mixed with half a hin of oil. ¹⁰And you shall offer for the drink offering half a hin of wine, as a food offering, a pleasing aroma to the LORD.

¹¹"Thus it shall be done for each bull or ram, or for each lamb or young goat. ¹²As many as you offer, so shall you do with each one, as many as there are. ¹³Every native Israelite shall do these things in this way, in offering a food offering, with a pleasing aroma to the LORD. ¹⁴And if a stranger is sojourning with you, or anyone is living permanently among you, and he wishes to offer a food offering, with a pleasing aroma to the LORD, he shall do as you do. ¹⁵For the assembly, there shall be one statute for you and for the stranger who sojourns with you, a statute for ever throughout your generations. You and the sojourner shall be alike before the LORD. ¹⁶One law and one rule shall be for you and for the stranger who sojourns with you."

¹⁷The LORD spoke to Moses, saying, ¹⁸"Speak to the people of Israel and say to them, When you come into the land to which I bring you ¹⁹and when you eat of the bread of the land, you shall present a contribution to the LORD. ²⁰Of the first of your dough you shall present a loaf as a contribution; like a contribution from the threshing floor, so shall you present it. ²¹Some of the first of your dough you shall give to the LORD as a contribution throughout your generations.

LAWS ABOUT UNINTENTIONAL SINS

²²"But if you sin unintentionally,[d] and do not observe all these commandments that the LORD has spoken to Moses, ²³all that the LORD has commanded you by Moses, from

---

[a] Or *an offering by fire*; so throughout Numbers [b] An *ephah* was about 3/5 of a bushel or 22 litres [c] A *hin* was about 4 quarts or 3.5 litres [d] Or *by mistake*; also verses 24, 27, 28, 29

the day that the LORD gave commandment, and onward throughout your generations, ²⁴then if it was done unintentionally without the knowledge of the congregation, all the congregation shall offer one bull from the herd for a burnt offering, a pleasing aroma to the LORD, with its grain offering and its drink offering, according to the rule, and one male goat for a sin offering. ²⁵And the priest shall make atonement for all the congregation of the people of Israel, and they shall be forgiven, because it was a mistake, and they have brought their offering, a food offering to the LORD, and their sin offering before the LORD for their mistake. ²⁶And all the congregation of the people of Israel shall be forgiven, and the stranger who sojourns among them, because the whole population was involved in the mistake.

²⁷"If one person sins unintentionally, he shall offer a female goat a year old for a sin offering. ²⁸And the priest shall make atonement before the LORD for the person who makes a mistake, when he sins unintentionally, to make atonement for him, and he shall be forgiven. ²⁹You shall have one law for him who does anything unintentionally, for him who is native among the people of Israel and for the stranger who sojourns among them. ³⁰But the person who does anything with a high hand, whether he is native or a sojourner, reviles the LORD, and that person shall be cut off from among his people. ³¹Because he has despised the word of the LORD and has broken his commandment, that person shall be utterly cut off; his iniquity shall be on him."

A SABBATH-BREAKER EXECUTED

³²While the people of Israel were in the wilderness, they found a man gathering sticks on the Sabbath day. ³³And those who found him gathering sticks brought him to Moses and Aaron and to all the congregation. ³⁴They put him in custody, because it had not been made clear what should be done to him. ³⁵And the LORD said to Moses, "The man shall be put to death; all the congregation shall stone him with stones outside the camp." ³⁶And all the congregation brought him outside the camp and stoned him to death with stones, as the LORD commanded Moses.

TASSELS ON GARMENTS

³⁷The LORD said to Moses, ³⁸"Speak to the people of Israel, and tell them to make tassels on the corners of their garments throughout their generations, and to put a cord of blue on the tassel of each corner. ³⁹And it shall be a tassel for you to look at and remember all the commandments of the LORD, to do them, not to follow*ᵃ* after your own heart and your own eyes, which you are inclined to whore after. ⁴⁰So you shall remember and do all my commandments, and be holy to your God. ⁴¹I am the LORD your God, who brought you out of the land of Egypt to be your God: I am the LORD your God."

KORAH'S REBELLION

16 Now Korah the son of Izhar, son of Kohath, son of Levi, and Dathan and Abiram the sons of Eliab, and On the son of Peleth, sons of Reuben, took men. ²And they rose up before Moses, with a number of the people of Israel, 250 chiefs of the congregation, chosen from the assembly, well-known men. ³They assembled themselves together against Moses and against Aaron and said to them, "You have gone too far! For all in the congregation are holy, every one of them, and the LORD is among them. Why then do you exalt yourselves above the assembly of the LORD?" ⁴When Moses heard it, he fell on his face, ⁵and he said to Korah and all his company, "In the morning the LORD will show who is his,*ᵇ* and who is holy, and will bring him near to him. The one whom he chooses he will bring near to him. ⁶Do this: take censers, Korah and all his company; ⁷put fire in them and put incense on them before the LORD tomorrow, and the man whom the LORD chooses shall be the holy one. You have gone too far, sons of Levi!" ⁸And Moses said to Korah, "Hear now, you sons of Levi: ⁹is it too small a thing for you that the God of Israel has separated you from the congregation of Israel, to bring you near to himself, to do service in the tabernacle of the LORD and to stand before the congregation to minister to them, ¹⁰and that he has brought you near him, and all your brothers the sons of Levi with you? And would you seek the priesthood also? ¹¹Therefore it is against the LORD that you and all your company have gathered together. What is Aaron that you grumble against him?"

¹²And Moses sent to call Dathan and Abiram the sons of Eliab, and they said, "We will not come up. ¹³Is it a small thing that you have brought us up out of a land flowing with milk

---

*ᵃ*Hebrew *to spy out*   *ᵇ*Septuagint *The LORD knows those who are his*

and honey, to kill us in the wilderness, that you must also make yourself a prince over us? ¹⁴Moreover, you have not brought us into a land flowing with milk and honey, nor given us inheritance of fields and vineyards. Will you put out the eyes of these men? We will not come up." ¹⁵And Moses was very angry and said to the Lord, "Do not respect their offering. I have not taken one donkey from them, and I have not harmed one of them."

¹⁶And Moses said to Korah, "Be present, you and all your company, before the Lord, you and they, and Aaron, tomorrow. ¹⁷And let every one of you take his censer and put incense on it, and every one of you bring before the Lord his censer, 250 censers; you also, and Aaron, each his censer." ¹⁸So every man took his censer and put fire in them and laid incense on them and stood at the entrance of the tent of meeting with Moses and Aaron. ¹⁹Then Korah assembled all the congregation against them at the entrance of the tent of meeting. And the glory of the Lord appeared to all the congregation.

²⁰And the Lord spoke to Moses and to Aaron, saying, ²¹"Separate yourselves from among this congregation, that I may consume them in a moment." ²²And they fell on their faces and said, "O God, the God of the spirits of all flesh, shall one man sin, and will you be angry with all the congregation?" ²³And the Lord spoke to Moses, saying, ²⁴"Say to the congregation, Get away from the dwelling of Korah, Dathan, and Abiram."

²⁵Then Moses rose and went to Dathan and Abiram, and the elders of Israel followed him. ²⁶And he spoke to the congregation, saying, "Depart, please, from the tents of these wicked men, and touch nothing of theirs, lest you be swept away with all their sins." ²⁷So they got away from the dwelling of Korah, Dathan, and Abiram. And Dathan and Abiram came out and stood at the door of their tents, together with their wives, their sons, and their little ones. ²⁸And Moses said, "Hereby you shall know that the Lord has sent me to do all these works, and that it has not been of my own accord. ²⁹If these men die as all men die, or if they are visited by the fate of all mankind, then the Lord has not sent me. ³⁰But if the Lord creates something new, and the ground opens its mouth and swallows them up with all that belongs to them, and they go down alive into Sheol, then you shall know that these men have despised the Lord."

³¹And as soon as he had finished speaking all these words, the ground under them split apart. ³²And the earth opened its mouth and swallowed them up, with their households and all the people who belonged to Korah and all their goods. ³³So they and all that belonged to them went down alive into Sheol, and the earth closed over them, and they perished from the midst of the assembly. ³⁴And all Israel who were around them fled at their cry, for they said, "Lest the earth swallow us up!" ³⁵And fire came out from the Lord and consumed the 250 men offering the incense.

³⁶ᵃ Then the Lord spoke to Moses, saying, ³⁷"Tell Eleazar the son of Aaron the priest to take up the censers out of the blaze. Then scatter the fire far and wide, for they have become holy. ³⁸As for the censers of these men who have sinned at the cost of their lives, let them be made into hammered plates as a covering for the altar, for they offered them before the Lord, and they became holy. Thus they shall be a sign to the people of Israel." ³⁹So Eleazar the priest took the bronze censers, which those who were burned had offered, and they were hammered out as a covering for the altar, ⁴⁰to be a reminder to the people of Israel, so that no outsider, who is not of the descendants of Aaron, should draw near to burn incense before the Lord, lest he become like Korah and his company—as the Lord said to him through Moses.

⁴¹But on the next day all the congregation of the people of Israel grumbled against Moses and against Aaron, saying, "You have killed the people of the Lord." ⁴²And when the congregation had assembled against Moses and against Aaron, they turned towards the tent of meeting. And behold, the cloud covered it, and the glory of the Lord appeared. ⁴³And Moses and Aaron came to the front of the tent of meeting, ⁴⁴and the Lord spoke to Moses, saying, ⁴⁵"Get away from the midst of this congregation, that I may consume them in a moment." And they fell on their faces. ⁴⁶And Moses said to Aaron, "Take your censer, and put fire on it from the altar and lay incense on it and carry it quickly to the congregation and make atonement for them, for wrath has gone out from the Lord; the plague has begun." ⁴⁷So Aaron took it as Moses said and ran into the midst of the assembly. And behold, the plague had already begun among the people. And he put on the incense and made atonement for

---
ᵃ Ch 17:1 in Hebrew

the people. ⁴⁸And he stood between the dead and the living, and the plague was stopped. ⁴⁹Now those who died in the plague were 14,700, besides those who died in the affair of Korah. ⁵⁰And Aaron returned to Moses at the entrance of the tent of meeting, when the plague was stopped.

AARON'S STAFF BUDS

17 ᵃ The LORD spoke to Moses, saying, ²"Speak to the people of Israel, and get from them staffs, one for each fathers' house, from all their chiefs according to their fathers' houses, twelve staffs. Write each man's name on his staff, ³and write Aaron's name on the staff of Levi. For there shall be one staff for the head of each fathers' house. ⁴Then you shall deposit them in the tent of meeting before the testimony, where I meet with you. ⁵And the staff of the man whom I choose shall sprout. Thus I will make to cease from me the grumblings of the people of Israel, which they grumble against you." ⁶Moses spoke to the people of Israel. And all their chiefs gave him staffs, one for each chief, according to their fathers' houses, twelve staffs. And the staff of Aaron was among their staffs. ⁷And Moses deposited the staffs before the LORD in the tent of the testimony.

⁸On the next day Moses went into the tent of the testimony, and behold, the staff of Aaron for the house of Levi had sprouted and put forth buds and produced blossoms, and it bore ripe almonds. ⁹Then Moses brought out all the staffs from before the LORD to all the people of Israel. And they looked, and each man took his staff. ¹⁰And the LORD said to Moses, "Put back the staff of Aaron before the testimony, to be kept as a sign for the rebels, that you may make an end of their grumblings against me, lest they die." ¹¹Thus did Moses; as the LORD commanded him, so he did.

¹²And the people of Israel said to Moses, "Behold, we perish, we are undone, we are all undone. ¹³Everyone who comes near, who comes near to the tabernacle of the LORD, shall die. Are we all to perish?"

DUTIES OF PRIESTS AND LEVITES

18 So the LORD said to Aaron, "You and your sons and your father's house with you shall bear iniquity connected with the sanctuary, and you and your sons with you shall bear iniquity connected with your priesthood. ²And with you bring your brothers also, the tribe of Levi, the tribe of your father, that they may join you and minister to you while you and your sons with you are before the tent of the testimony. ³They shall keep guard over you and over the whole tent, but shall not come near to the vessels of the sanctuary or to the altar lest they, and you, die. ⁴They shall join you and keep guard over the tent of meeting for all the service of the tent, and no outsider shall come near you. ⁵And you shall keep guard over the sanctuary and over the altar, that there may never again be wrath on the people of Israel. ⁶And behold, I have taken your brothers the Levites from among the people of Israel. They are a gift to you, given to the LORD, to do the service of the tent of meeting. ⁷And you and your sons with you shall guard your priesthood for all that concerns the altar and that is within the veil; and you shall serve. I give your priesthood as a gift,ᵇ and any outsider who comes near shall be put to death."

⁸Then the LORD spoke to Aaron, "Behold, I have given you charge of the contributions made to me, all the consecrated things of the people of Israel. I have given them to you as a portion and to your sons as a perpetual due. ⁹This shall be yours of the most holy things, reserved from the fire: every offering of theirs, every grain offering of theirs and every sin offering of theirs and every guilt offering of theirs, which they render to me, shall be most holy to you and to your sons. ¹⁰In a most holy place shall you eat it. Every male may eat it; it is holy to you. ¹¹This also is yours: the contribution of their gift, all the wave offerings of the people of Israel. I have given them to you, and to your sons and daughters with you, as a perpetual due. Everyone who is clean in your house may eat it. ¹²All the best of the oil and all the best of the wine and of the grain, the firstfruits of what they give to the LORD, I give to you. ¹³The first ripe fruits of all that is in their land, which they bring to the LORD, shall be yours. Everyone who is clean in your house may eat it. ¹⁴Every devoted thing in Israel shall be yours. ¹⁵Everything that opens the womb of all flesh, whether man or beast, which they offer to the LORD, shall be yours. Nevertheless, the firstborn of man you shall redeem, and the firstborn of unclean animals you shall redeem. ¹⁶And their redemption price (at a month old you shall redeem them) you shall fix at five

---

ᵃCh 17:16 in Hebrew   ᵇHebrew *service of gift*

shekels*ᵃ* in silver, according to the shekel of the sanctuary, which is twenty gerahs. ¹⁷But the firstborn of a cow, or the firstborn of a sheep, or the firstborn of a goat, you shall not redeem; they are holy. You shall sprinkle their blood on the altar and shall burn their fat as a food offering, with a pleasing aroma to the LORD. ¹⁸But their flesh shall be yours, as the breast that is waved and as the right thigh are yours. ¹⁹All the holy contributions that the people of Israel present to the LORD I give to you, and to your sons and daughters with you, as a perpetual due. It is a covenant of salt for ever before the LORD for you and for your offspring with you." ²⁰And the LORD said to Aaron, "You shall have no inheritance in their land, neither shall you have any portion among them. I am your portion and your inheritance among the people of Israel.

²¹"To the Levites I have given every tithe in Israel for an inheritance, in return for their service that they do, their service in the tent of meeting, ²²so that the people of Israel do not come near the tent of meeting, lest they bear sin and die. ²³But the Levites shall do the service of the tent of meeting, and they shall bear their iniquity. It shall be a perpetual statute throughout your generations, and among the people of Israel they shall have no inheritance. ²⁴For the tithe of the people of Israel, which they present as a contribution to the LORD, I have given to the Levites for an inheritance. Therefore I have said of them that they shall have no inheritance among the people of Israel."

²⁵And the LORD spoke to Moses, saying, ²⁶"Moreover, you shall speak and say to the Levites, 'When you take from the people of Israel the tithe that I have given you from them for your inheritance, then you shall present a contribution from it to the LORD, a tithe of the tithe. ²⁷And your contribution shall be counted to you as though it were the grain of the threshing floor, and as the fullness of the wine press. ²⁸So you shall also present a contribution to the LORD from all your tithes, which you receive from the people of Israel. And from it you shall give the LORD's contribution to Aaron the priest. ²⁹Out of all the gifts to you, you shall present every contribution due to the LORD; from each its best part is to be dedicated.' ³⁰Therefore you shall say to them, 'When you have offered from it the best of it, then the rest shall be counted to the Levites as produce of the threshing floor, and as produce of the wine press. ³¹And you may eat it in any place, you and your households, for it is your reward in return for your service in the tent of meeting. ³²And you shall bear no sin by reason of it, when you have contributed the best of it. But you shall not profane the holy things of the people of Israel, lest you die.'"

LAWS FOR PURIFICATION

19 Now the LORD spoke to Moses and to Aaron, saying, ²"This is the statute of the law that the LORD has commanded: Tell the people of Israel to bring you a red heifer without defect, in which there is no blemish, and on which a yoke has never come. ³And you shall give it to Eleazar the priest, and it shall be taken outside the camp and slaughtered before him. ⁴And Eleazar the priest shall take some of its blood with his finger, and sprinkle some of its blood towards the front of the tent of meeting seven times. ⁵And the heifer shall be burned in his sight. Its skin, its flesh, and its blood, with its dung, shall be burned. ⁶And the priest shall take cedarwood and hyssop and scarlet yarn, and throw them into the fire burning the heifer. ⁷Then the priest shall wash his clothes and bathe his body in water, and afterwards he may come into the camp. But the priest shall be unclean until evening. ⁸The one who burns the heifer shall wash his clothes in water and bathe his body in water and shall be unclean until evening. ⁹And a man who is clean shall gather up the ashes of the heifer and deposit them outside the camp in a clean place. And they shall be kept for the water for impurity for the congregation of the people of Israel; it is a sin offering. ¹⁰And the one who gathers the ashes of the heifer shall wash his clothes and be unclean until evening. And this shall be a perpetual statute for the people of Israel, and for the stranger who sojourns among them.

¹¹"Whoever touches the dead body of any person shall be unclean for seven days. ¹²He shall cleanse himself with the water on the third day and on the seventh day, and so be clean. But if he does not cleanse himself on the third day and on the seventh day, he will not become clean. ¹³Whoever touches a dead person, the body of anyone who has died, and does not cleanse himself, defiles the tabernacle of the LORD, and that person shall be cut off from Israel; because the water

---

ᵃA shekel was about 2/5 of an ounce or 11 grams

for impurity was not thrown on him, he shall be unclean. His uncleanness is still on him. ¹⁴"This is the law when someone dies in a tent: everyone who comes into the tent and everyone who is in the tent shall be unclean for seven days. ¹⁵And every open vessel that has no cover fastened on it is unclean. ¹⁶Whoever in the open field touches someone who was killed with a sword or who died naturally, or touches a human bone or a grave, shall be unclean seven days. ¹⁷For the unclean they shall take some ashes of the burnt sin offering, and fresh[a] water shall be added in a vessel. ¹⁸Then a clean person shall take hyssop and dip it in the water and sprinkle it on the tent and on all the furnishings and on the persons who were there and on whoever touched the bone, or the slain or the dead or the grave. ¹⁹And the clean person shall sprinkle it on the unclean on the third day and on the seventh day. Thus on the seventh day he shall cleanse him, and he shall wash his clothes and bathe himself in water, and at evening he shall be clean.

²⁰"If the man who is unclean does not cleanse himself, that person shall be cut off from the midst of the assembly, since he has defiled the sanctuary of the LORD. Because the water for impurity has not been thrown on him, he is unclean. ²¹And it shall be a statute for ever for them. The one who sprinkles the water for impurity shall wash his clothes, and the one who touches the water for impurity shall be unclean until evening. ²²And whatever the unclean person touches shall be unclean, and anyone who touches it shall be unclean until evening."

THE DEATH OF MIRIAM

20 And the people of Israel, the whole congregation, came into the wilderness of Zin in the first month, and the people stayed in Kadesh. And Miriam died there and was buried there.

THE WATERS OF MERIBAH

²Now there was no water for the congregation. And they assembled themselves together against Moses and against Aaron. ³And the people quarrelled with Moses and said, "Would that we had perished when our brothers perished before the LORD! ⁴Why have you brought the assembly of the LORD into this wilderness, that we should die here, both we and our cattle? ⁵And why have you made us come up out of Egypt to bring us to this evil place? It is no place for grain or figs or vines or pomegranates, and there is no water to drink." ⁶Then Moses and Aaron went from the presence of the assembly to the entrance of the tent of meeting and fell on their faces. And the glory of the LORD appeared to them, ⁷and the LORD spoke to Moses, saying, ⁸"Take the staff, and assemble the congregation, you and Aaron your brother, and tell the rock before their eyes to yield its water. So you shall bring water out of the rock for them and give drink to the congregation and their cattle." ⁹And Moses took the staff from before the LORD, as he commanded him.

MOSES STRIKES THE ROCK

¹⁰Then Moses and Aaron gathered the assembly together before the rock, and he said to them, "Hear now, you rebels: shall we bring water for you out of this rock?" ¹¹And Moses lifted up his hand and struck the rock with his staff twice, and water came out abundantly, and the congregation drank, and their livestock. ¹²And the LORD said to Moses and Aaron, "Because you did not believe in me, to uphold me as holy in the eyes of the people of Israel, therefore you shall not bring this assembly into the land that I have given them." ¹³These are the waters of Meribah,[b] where the people of Israel quarrelled with the LORD, and through them he showed himself holy.

EDOM REFUSES PASSAGE

¹⁴Moses sent messengers from Kadesh to the king of Edom: "Thus says your brother Israel: You know all the hardship that we have met: ¹⁵how our fathers went down to Egypt, and we lived in Egypt for a long time. And the Egyptians dealt harshly with us and our fathers. ¹⁶And when we cried to the LORD, he heard our voice and sent an angel and brought us out of Egypt. And here we are in Kadesh, a city on the edge of your territory. ¹⁷Please let us pass through your land. We will not pass through field or vineyard, or drink water from a well. We will go along the King's Highway. We will not turn aside to the right hand or to the left until we have passed through your territory." ¹⁸But Edom said to him, "You shall not pass through, lest I come out with the sword against you." ¹⁹And the people of Israel said to him, "We will go up by the highway, and if we drink of your

---

[a]Hebrew *living* [b]*Meribah* means *quarrelling*

water, I and my livestock, then I will pay for it. Let me only pass through on foot, nothing more." ²⁰But he said, "You shall not pass through." And Edom came out against them with a large army and with a strong force. ²¹Thus Edom refused to give Israel passage through his territory, so Israel turned away from him.

THE DEATH OF AARON

²²And they journeyed from Kadesh, and the people of Israel, the whole congregation, came to Mount Hor. ²³And the LORD said to Moses and Aaron at Mount Hor, on the border of the land of Edom, ²⁴"Let Aaron be gathered to his people, for he shall not enter the land that I have given to the people of Israel, because you rebelled against my command at the waters of Meribah. ²⁵Take Aaron and Eleazar his son and bring them up to Mount Hor. ²⁶And strip Aaron of his garments and put them on Eleazar his son. And Aaron shall be gathered to his people and shall die there." ²⁷Moses did as the LORD commanded. And they went up Mount Hor in the sight of all the congregation. ²⁸And Moses stripped Aaron of his garments and put them on Eleazar his son. And Aaron died there on the top of the mountain. Then Moses and Eleazar came down from the mountain. ²⁹And when all the congregation saw that Aaron had perished, all the house of Israel wept for Aaron for thirty days.

ARAD DESTROYED

21 When the Canaanite, the king of Arad, who lived in the Negeb, heard that Israel was coming by the way of Atharim, he fought against Israel, and took some of them captive. ²And Israel vowed a vow to the LORD and said, "If you will indeed give this people into my hand, then I will devote their cities to destruction."ᵃ ³And the LORD heeded the voice of Israel and gave over the Canaanites, and they devoted them and their cities to destruction. So the name of the place was called Hormah.ᵇ

THE BRONZE SERPENT

⁴From Mount Hor they set out by the way to the Red Sea, to go round the land of Edom. And the people became impatient on the way. ⁵And the people spoke against God and against Moses, "Why have you brought us up out of Egypt to die in the wilderness? For there is no food and no water, and we loathe this worthless food." ⁶Then the LORD sent fiery serpents among the people, and they bit the people, so that many people of Israel died. ⁷And the people came to Moses and said, "We have sinned, for we have spoken against the LORD and against you. Pray to the LORD, that he take away the serpents from us." So Moses prayed for the people. ⁸And the LORD said to Moses, "Make a fiery serpent and set it on a pole, and everyone who is bitten, when he sees it, shall live." ⁹So Moses made a bronzeᶜ serpent and set it on a pole. And if a serpent bit anyone, he would look at the bronze serpent and live.

THE SONG OF THE WELL

¹⁰And the people of Israel set out and camped in Oboth. ¹¹And they set out from Oboth and camped at Iye-abarim, in the wilderness that is opposite Moab, towards the sunrise. ¹²From there they set out and camped in the Valley of Zered. ¹³From there they set out and camped on the other side of the Arnon, which is in the wilderness that extends from the border of the Amorites, for the Arnon is the border of Moab, between Moab and the Amorites. ¹⁴Therefore it is said in the Book of the Wars of the LORD,

> "Waheb in Suphah, and the
>   valleys of the Arnon,
> ¹⁵ and the slope of the valleys
>   that extends to the seat of Ar,
>   and leans to the border of Moab."

¹⁶And from there they continued to Beer;ᵈ that is the well of which the LORD said to Moses, "Gather the people together, so that I may give them water." ¹⁷Then Israel sang this song:

> "Spring up, O well!—Sing to it!—
> ¹⁸ the well that the princes made,
>   that the nobles of the people dug,
>   with the sceptre and with their staffs."

And from the wilderness they went on to Mattanah, ¹⁹and from Mattanah to Nahaliel, and from Nahaliel to Bamoth, ²⁰and from Bamoth to the valley lying in the region of Moab by the top of Pisgah that looks down on the desert.ᵉ

ᵃThat is, set apart (devote) as an offering to the Lord (for destruction); also verse 3 ᵇ*Hormah* means *destruction* ᶜOr *copper* ᵈ*Beer* means *well* ᵉOr *Jeshimon*

KING SIHON DEFEATED

21 Then Israel sent messengers to Sihon king of the Amorites, saying, **22** "Let me pass through your land. We will not turn aside into field or vineyard. We will not drink the water of a well. We will go by the King's Highway until we have passed through your territory." **23** But Sihon would not allow Israel to pass through his territory. He gathered all his people together and went out against Israel to the wilderness and came to Jahaz and fought against Israel. **24** And Israel defeated him with the edge of the sword and took possession of his land from the Arnon to the Jabbok, as far as to the Ammonites, for the border of the Ammonites was strong. **25** And Israel took all these cities, and Israel settled in all the cities of the Amorites, in Heshbon, and in all its villages. **26** For Heshbon was the city of Sihon the king of the Amorites, who had fought against the former king of Moab and taken all his land out of his hand, as far as the Arnon. **27** Therefore the ballad singers say,

> "Come to Heshbon, let it be built;
>   let the city of Sihon be established.
> **28** For fire came out from Heshbon,
>   flame from the city of Sihon.
> It devoured Ar of Moab,
>   and swallowed*ᵃ* the heights
>   of the Arnon.
> **29** Woe to you, O Moab!
>   You are undone, O people
>   of Chemosh!
> He has made his sons fugitives,
>   and his daughters captives,
>   to an Amorite king, Sihon.
> **30** So we overthrew them;
>   Heshbon, as far as Dibon, perished;
>   and we laid waste as far as Nophah;
>   fire spread as far as Medeba."*ᵇ*

KING OG DEFEATED

31 Thus Israel lived in the land of the Amorites. **32** And Moses sent to spy out Jazer, and they captured its villages and dispossessed the Amorites who were there. **33** Then they turned and went up by the way to Bashan. And Og the king of Bashan came out against them, he and all his people, to battle at Edrei. **34** But the LORD said to Moses, "Do not fear him, for I have given him into your hand, and all his people, and his land. And you shall do to him as you did to Sihon king of the Amorites, who lived at Heshbon." **35** So they defeated him and his sons and all his people, until he had no survivor left. And they possessed his land.

BALAK SUMMONS BALAAM

22 Then the people of Israel set out and camped in the plains of Moab beyond the Jordan at Jericho. **2** And Balak the son of Zippor saw all that Israel had done to the Amorites. **3** And Moab was in great dread of the people, because they were many. Moab was overcome with fear of the people of Israel. **4** And Moab said to the elders of Midian, "This horde will now lick up all that is around us, as the ox licks up the grass of the field." So Balak the son of Zippor, who was king of Moab at that time, **5** sent messengers to Balaam the son of Beor at Pethor, which is near the River*ᶜ* in the land of the people of Amaw,*ᵈ* to call him, saying, "Behold, a people has come out of Egypt. They cover the face of the earth, and they are dwelling opposite me. **6** Come now, curse this people for me, since they are too mighty for me. Perhaps I shall be able to defeat them and drive them from the land, for I know that he whom you bless is blessed, and he whom you curse is cursed."

7 So the elders of Moab and the elders of Midian departed with the fees for divination in their hand. And they came to Balaam and gave him Balak's message. **8** And he said to them, "Lodge here tonight, and I will bring back word to you, as the LORD speaks to me." So the princes of Moab stayed with Balaam. **9** And God came to Balaam and said, "Who are these men with you?" **10** And Balaam said to God, "Balak the son of Zippor, king of Moab, has sent to me, saying, **11** 'Behold, a people has come out of Egypt, and it covers the face of the earth. Now come, curse them for me. Perhaps I shall be able to fight against them and drive them out.'" **12** God said to Balaam, "You shall not go with them. You shall not curse the people, for they are blessed." **13** So Balaam rose in the morning and said to the princes of Balak, "Go to your own land, for the LORD has refused to let me go with you." **14** So the princes of Moab rose and went to Balak and said, "Balaam refuses to come with us."

15 Once again Balak sent princes, more in number and more honourable than these. **16** And they came to Balaam and said to him, "Thus says Balak the son of Zippor: 'Let

---

*ᵃ*Septuagint; Hebrew *the lords of* *ᵇ*Compare Samaritan and Septuagint; Hebrew *and we laid waste as far as Nophah, which is as far as Medeba* *ᶜ*That is, the Euphrates *ᵈ*Or *the people of his kindred*

nothing hinder you from coming to me, ¹⁷for I will surely do you great honour, and whatever you say to me I will do. Come, curse this people for me.'" ¹⁸But Balaam answered and said to the servants of Balak, "Though Balak were to give me his house full of silver and gold, I could not go beyond the command of the Lord my God to do less or more. ¹⁹So you, too, please stay here tonight, that I may know what more the Lord will say to me." ²⁰And God came to Balaam at night and said to him, "If the men have come to call you, rise, go with them; but only do what I tell you." ²¹So Balaam rose in the morning and saddled his donkey and went with the princes of Moab.

BALAAM'S DONKEY AND THE ANGEL

²²But God's anger was kindled because he went, and the angel of the Lord took his stand in the way as his adversary. Now he was riding on the donkey, and his two servants were with him. ²³And the donkey saw the angel of the Lord standing in the road, with a drawn sword in his hand. And the donkey turned aside out of the road and went into the field. And Balaam struck the donkey, to turn her into the road. ²⁴Then the angel of the Lord stood in a narrow path between the vineyards, with a wall on either side. ²⁵And when the donkey saw the angel of the Lord, she pushed against the wall and pressed Balaam's foot against the wall. So he struck her again. ²⁶Then the angel of the Lord went ahead and stood in a narrow place, where there was no way to turn either to the right or to the left. ²⁷When the donkey saw the angel of the Lord, she lay down under Balaam. And Balaam's anger was kindled, and he struck the donkey with his staff. ²⁸Then the Lord opened the mouth of the donkey, and she said to Balaam, "What have I done to you, that you have struck me these three times?" ²⁹And Balaam said to the donkey, "Because you have made a fool of me. I wish I had a sword in my hand, for then I would kill you." ³⁰And the donkey said to Balaam, "Am I not your donkey, on which you have ridden all your life long to this day? Is it my habit to treat you this way?" And he said, "No."

³¹Then the Lord opened the eyes of Balaam, and he saw the angel of the Lord standing in the way, with his drawn sword in his hand. And he bowed down and fell on his face. ³²And the angel of the Lord said to him, "Why have you struck your donkey these three times? Behold, I have come out to oppose you because your way is perverse[a] before me. ³³The donkey saw me and turned aside before me these three times. If she had not turned aside from me, surely just now I would have killed you and let her live." ³⁴Then Balaam said to the angel of the Lord, "I have sinned, for I did not know that you stood in the road against me. Now therefore, if it is evil in your sight, I will turn back." ³⁵And the angel of the Lord said to Balaam, "Go with the men, but speak only the word that I tell you." So Balaam went on with the princes of Balak.

³⁶When Balak heard that Balaam had come, he went out to meet him at the city of Moab, on the border formed by the Arnon, at the extremity of the border. ³⁷And Balak said to Balaam, "Did I not send to you to call you? Why did you not come to me? Am I not able to honour you?" ³⁸Balaam said to Balak, "Behold, I have come to you! Have I now any power of my own to speak anything? The word that God puts in my mouth, that must I speak." ³⁹Then Balaam went with Balak, and they came to Kiriath-huzoth. ⁴⁰And Balak sacrificed oxen and sheep, and sent for Balaam and for the princes who were with him.

⁴¹And in the morning Balak took Balaam and brought him up to Bamoth-baal, and from there he saw a fraction of the people.

BALAAM'S FIRST ORACLE

23 And Balaam said to Balak, "Build for me here seven altars, and prepare for me here seven bulls and seven rams." ²Balak did as Balaam had said. And Balak and Balaam offered on each altar a bull and a ram. ³And Balaam said to Balak, "Stand beside your burnt offering, and I will go. Perhaps the Lord will come to meet me, and whatever he shows me I will tell you." And he went to a bare height, ⁴and God met Balaam. And Balaam said to him, "I have arranged the seven altars and I have offered on each altar a bull and a ram." ⁵And the Lord put a word in Balaam's mouth and said, "Return to Balak, and thus you shall speak." ⁶And he returned to him, and behold, he and all the princes of Moab were standing beside his burnt offering. ⁷And Balaam took up his discourse and said,

"From Aram Balak has brought me,
the king of Moab from the
eastern mountains:

---

[a] Or reckless

'Come, curse Jacob for me,
 and come, denounce Israel!'
8 How can I curse whom God
  has not cursed?
 How can I denounce whom the
  LORD has not denounced?
9 For from the top of the crags I see him,
  from the hills I behold him;
 behold, a people dwelling alone,
  and not counting itself
   among the nations!
10 Who can count the dust of Jacob
   or number the fourth part[a] of Israel?
  Let me die the death of the upright,
   and let my end be like his!"

11And Balak said to Balaam, "What have you done to me? I took you to curse my enemies, and behold, you have done nothing but bless them." 12And he answered and said, "Must I not take care to speak what the LORD puts in my mouth?"

BALAAM'S SECOND ORACLE

13And Balak said to him, "Please come with me to another place, from which you may see them. You shall see only a fraction of them and shall not see them all. Then curse them for me from there." 14And he took him to the field of Zophim, to the top of Pisgah, and built seven altars and offered a bull and a ram on each altar. 15Balaam said to Balak, "Stand here beside your burnt offering, while I meet the LORD over there." 16And the LORD met Balaam and put a word in his mouth and said, "Return to Balak, and thus shall you speak." 17And he came to him, and behold, he was standing beside his burnt offering, and the princes of Moab with him. And Balak said to him, "What has the LORD spoken?" 18And Balaam took up his discourse and said,

 "Rise, Balak, and hear;
  give ear to me, O son of Zippor:
19 God is not man, that he should lie,
   or a son of man, that he should
    change his mind.
  Has he said, and will he not do it?
   Or has he spoken, and will
    he not fulfil it?
20 Behold, I received a command to bless:
   he has blessed, and I
    cannot revoke it.
21 He has not beheld misfortune in Jacob,
   nor has he seen trouble in Israel.

 The LORD their God is with them,
  and the shout of a king is
   among them.
22 God brings them out of Egypt
   and is for them like the
    horns of the wild ox.
23 For there is no enchantment
    against Jacob,
   no divination against Israel;
  now it shall be said of Jacob and Israel,
   'What has God wrought!'
24 Behold, a people! As a lioness it rises up
   and as a lion it lifts itself;
  it does not lie down until it
   has devoured the prey
  and drunk the blood of the slain."

25And Balak said to Balaam, "Do not curse them at all, and do not bless them at all." 26But Balaam answered Balak, "Did I not tell you, 'All that the LORD says, that I must do'?" 27And Balak said to Balaam, "Come now, I will take you to another place. Perhaps it will please God that you may curse them for me from there." 28So Balak took Balaam to the top of Peor, which overlooks the desert.[b] 29And Balaam said to Balak, "Build for me here seven altars and prepare for me here seven bulls and seven rams." 30And Balak did as Balaam had said, and offered a bull and a ram on each altar.

BALAAM'S THIRD ORACLE

24 When Balaam saw that it pleased the LORD to bless Israel, he did not go, as at other times, to look for omens, but set his face towards the wilderness. 2And Balaam lifted up his eyes and saw Israel camping tribe by tribe. And the Spirit of God came upon him, 3and he took up his discourse and said,

 "The oracle of Balaam the son of Beor,
   the oracle of the man whose
    eye is opened,[c]
4 the oracle of him who hears
    the words of God,
   who sees the vision of the Almighty,
    falling down with his
     eyes uncovered:
5 How lovely are your tents, O Jacob,
    your encampments, O Israel!
6 Like palm groves[d] that stretch afar,
    like gardens beside a river,

---

[a] Or *dust clouds* [b] Or *Jeshimon* [c] Or *closed, or perfect*; also verse 15
[d] Or *valleys*

like aloes that the LORD has planted,
　　like cedar trees beside the waters.
⁷ Water shall flow from his buckets,
　　and his seed shall be in
　　　　many waters;
　his king shall be higher than Agag,
　　and his kingdom shall be exalted.
⁸ God brings him out of Egypt
　　and is for him like the horns
　　　　of the wild ox;
　he shall eat up the nations,
　　his adversaries,
　and shall break their bones in pieces
　　and pierce them through
　　　　with his arrows.
⁹ He crouched, he lay down like a lion
　　and like a lioness; who will
　　　　rouse him up?
　Blessed are those who bless you,
　　and cursed are those who curse you."

¹⁰And Balak's anger was kindled against Balaam, and he struck his hands together. And Balak said to Balaam, "I called you to curse my enemies, and behold, you have blessed them these three times. ¹¹Therefore now flee to your own place. I said, 'I will certainly honour you', but the LORD has held you back from honour." ¹²And Balaam said to Balak, "Did I not tell your messengers whom you sent to me, ¹³'If Balak should give me his house full of silver and gold, I would not be able to go beyond the word of the LORD, to do either good or bad of my own will. What the LORD speaks, that will I speak'? ¹⁴And now, behold, I am going to my people. Come, I will let you know what this people will do to your people in the latter days."

BALAAM'S FINAL ORACLE

¹⁵And he took up his discourse and said,

"The oracle of Balaam the son of Beor,
　　the oracle of the man whose
　　　　eye is opened,
¹⁶ the oracle of him who hears
　　　　the words of God,
　　and knows the knowledge
　　　　of the Most High,
　who sees the vision of the Almighty,
　　falling down with his
　　　　eyes uncovered:
¹⁷ I see him, but not now;
　　I behold him, but not near:
　a star shall come out of Jacob,
　　and a sceptre shall rise out of Israel;

　it shall crush the forehead^a of Moab
　　and break down all the
　　　　sons of Sheth.
¹⁸ Edom shall be dispossessed;
　　Seir also, his enemies, shall
　　　　be dispossessed.
　Israel is doing valiantly.
¹⁹ And one from Jacob shall
　　　　exercise dominion
　　and destroy the survivors of cities!"

²⁰Then he looked on Amalek and took up his discourse and said,

"Amalek was the first among
　　the nations,
　but its end is utter destruction."

²¹And he looked on the Kenite, and took up his discourse and said,

"Enduring is your dwelling place,
　　and your nest is set in the rock.
²² Nevertheless, Kain shall be burned
　　when Asshur takes you
　　　　away captive."

²³And he took up his discourse and said,

"Alas, who shall live when
　　God does this?
²⁴ But ships shall come from Kittim
　　and shall afflict Asshur and Eber;
　　and he too shall come to
　　　　utter destruction."

²⁵Then Balaam rose and went back to his place. And Balak also went his way.

BAAL WORSHIP AT PEOR

25 While Israel lived in Shittim, the people began to whore with the daughters of Moab. ²These invited the people to the sacrifices of their gods, and the people ate and bowed down to their gods. ³So Israel yoked himself to Baal of Peor. And the anger of the LORD was kindled against Israel. ⁴And the LORD said to Moses, "Take all the chiefs of the people and hang^b them in the sun before the LORD, that the fierce anger of the LORD may turn away from Israel." ⁵And Moses said to the judges of Israel, "Each of you kill those of his men who have yoked themselves to Baal of Peor."

---

^{a}Hebrew *corners* [of the head]　^{b}Or *impale*

⁶And behold, one of the people of Israel came and brought a Midianite woman to his family, in the sight of Moses and in the sight of the whole congregation of the people of Israel, while they were weeping in the entrance of the tent of meeting. ⁷When Phinehas the son of Eleazar, son of Aaron the priest, saw it, he rose and left the congregation and took a spear in his hand ⁸and went after the man of Israel into the chamber and pierced both of them, the man of Israel and the woman through her belly. Thus the plague on the people of Israel was stopped. ⁹Nevertheless, those who died by the plague were twenty-four thousand.

THE ZEAL OF PHINEHAS

¹⁰And the LORD said to Moses, ¹¹"Phinehas the son of Eleazar, son of Aaron the priest, has turned back my wrath from the people of Israel, in that he was jealous with my jealousy among them, so that I did not consume the people of Israel in my jealousy. ¹²Therefore say, 'Behold, I give to him my covenant of peace, ¹³and it shall be to him and to his descendants after him the covenant of a perpetual priesthood, because he was jealous for his God and made atonement for the people of Israel.'"

¹⁴The name of the slain man of Israel, who was killed with the Midianite woman, was Zimri the son of Salu, chief of a father's house belonging to the Simeonites. ¹⁵And the name of the Midianite woman who was killed was Cozbi the daughter of Zur, who was the tribal head of a father's house in Midian.

¹⁶And the LORD spoke to Moses, saying, ¹⁷"Harass the Midianites and strike them down, ¹⁸for they have harassed you with their wiles, with which they beguiled you in the matter of Peor, and in the matter of Cozbi, the daughter of the chief of Midian, their sister, who was killed on the day of the plague on account of Peor."

CENSUS OF THE NEW GENERATION

26 After the plague, the LORD said to Moses and to Eleazar the son of Aaron, the priest, ²"Take a census of all the congregation of the people of Israel, from twenty years old and upwards, by their fathers' houses, all in Israel who are able to go to war." ³And Moses and Eleazar the priest spoke with them in the plains of Moab by the Jordan at Jericho, saying, ⁴"Take a census of the people,ᵃ from twenty years old and upwards", as the LORD commanded Moses. The people of Israel who came out of the land of Egypt were:

⁵Reuben, the firstborn of Israel; the sons of Reuben: of Hanoch, the clan of the Hanochites; of Pallu, the clan of the Palluites; ⁶of Hezron, the clan of the Hezronites; of Carmi, the clan of the Carmites. ⁷These are the clans of the Reubenites, and those listed were 43,730. ⁸And the sons of Pallu: Eliab. ⁹The sons of Eliab: Nemuel, Dathan, and Abiram. These are the Dathan and Abiram, chosen from the congregation, who contended against Moses and Aaron in the company of Korah, when they contended against the LORD ¹⁰and the earth opened its mouth and swallowed them up together with Korah, when that company died, when the fire devoured 250 men, and they became a warning. ¹¹But the sons of Korah did not die.

¹²The sons of Simeon according to their clans: of Nemuel, the clan of the Nemuelites; of Jamin, the clan of the Jaminites; of Jachin, the clan of the Jachinites; ¹³of Zerah, the clan of the Zerahites; of Shaul, the clan of the Shaulites. ¹⁴These are the clans of the Simeonites, 22,200.

¹⁵The sons of Gad according to their clans: of Zephon, the clan of the Zephonites; of Haggi, the clan of the Haggites; of Shuni, the clan of the Shunites; ¹⁶of Ozni, the clan of the Oznites; of Eri, the clan of the Erites; ¹⁷of Arod, the clan of the Arodites; of Areli, the clan of the Arelites. ¹⁸These are the clans of the sons of Gad as they were listed, 40,500.

¹⁹The sons of Judah were Er and Onan; and Er and Onan died in the land of Canaan. ²⁰And the sons of Judah according to their clans were: of Shelah, the clan of the Shelanites; of Perez, the clan of the Perezites; of Zerah, the clan of the Zerahites. ²¹And the sons of Perez were: of Hezron, the clan of the Hezronites; of Hamul, the clan of the Hamulites. ²²These are the clans of Judah as they were listed, 76,500.

²³The sons of Issachar according to their clans: of Tola, the clan of the Tolaites; of Puvah, the clan of the Punites; ²⁴of Jashub, the clan of the Jashubites; of Shimron, the clan of the Shimronites. ²⁵These are the clans of Issachar as they were listed, 64,300.

²⁶The sons of Zebulun, according to their clans: of Sered, the clan of the Seredites; of Elon, the clan of the Elonites; of Jahleel, the

---

ᵃ*Take a census of the people* is implied (compare verse 2)

clan of the Jahleelites. ²⁷These are the clans of the Zebulunites as they were listed, 60,500.

²⁸The sons of Joseph according to their clans: Manasseh and Ephraim. ²⁹The sons of Manasseh: of Machir, the clan of the Machirites; and Machir was the father of Gilead; of Gilead, the clan of the Gileadites. ³⁰These are the sons of Gilead: of Iezer, the clan of the Iezerites; of Helek, the clan of the Helekites; ³¹and of Asriel, the clan of the Asrielites; and of Shechem, the clan of the Shechemites; ³²and of Shemida, the clan of the Shemidaites; and of Hepher, the clan of the Hepherites. ³³Now Zelophehad the son of Hepher had no sons, but daughters. And the names of the daughters of Zelophehad were Mahlah, Noah, Hoglah, Milcah, and Tirzah. ³⁴These are the clans of Manasseh, and those listed were 52,700.

³⁵These are the sons of Ephraim according to their clans: of Shuthelah, the clan of the Shuthelahites; of Becher, the clan of the Becherites; of Tahan, the clan of the Tahanites. ³⁶And these are the sons of Shuthelah: of Eran, the clan of the Eranites. ³⁷These are the clans of the sons of Ephraim as they were listed, 32,500. These are the sons of Joseph according to their clans.

³⁸The sons of Benjamin according to their clans: of Bela, the clan of the Belaites; of Ashbel, the clan of the Ashbelites; of Ahiram, the clan of the Ahiramites; ³⁹of Shephupham, the clan of the Shuphamites; of Hupham, the clan of the Huphamites. ⁴⁰And the sons of Bela were Ard and Naaman: of Ard, the clan of the Ardites; of Naaman, the clan of the Naamites. ⁴¹These are the sons of Benjamin according to their clans, and those listed were 45,600.

⁴²These are the sons of Dan according to their clans: of Shuham, the clan of the Shuhamites. These are the clans of Dan according to their clans. ⁴³All the clans of the Shuhamites, as they were listed, were 64,400.

⁴⁴The sons of Asher according to their clans: of Imnah, the clan of the Imnites; of Ishvi, the clan of the Ishvites; of Beriah, the clan of the Beriites. ⁴⁵Of the sons of Beriah: of Heber, the clan of the Heberites; of Malchiel, the clan of the Malchielites. ⁴⁶And the name of the daughter of Asher was Serah. ⁴⁷These are the clans of the sons of Asher as they were listed, 53,400.

⁴⁸The sons of Naphtali according to their clans: of Jahzeel, the clan of the Jahzeelites; of Guni, the clan of the Gunites; ⁴⁹of Jezer, the clan of the Jezerites; of Shillem, the clan of the Shillemites. ⁵⁰These are the clans of Naphtali according to their clans, and those listed were 45,400.

⁵¹This was the list of the people of Israel, 601,730.

⁵²The LORD spoke to Moses, saying, ⁵³"Among these the land shall be divided for inheritance according to the number of names. ⁵⁴To a large tribe you shall give a large inheritance, and to a small tribe you shall give a small inheritance; every tribe shall be given its inheritance in proportion to its list. ⁵⁵But the land shall be divided by lot. According to the names of the tribes of their fathers they shall inherit. ⁵⁶Their inheritance shall be divided according to lot between the larger and the smaller."

⁵⁷This was the list of the Levites according to their clans: of Gershon, the clan of the Gershonites; of Kohath, the clan of the Kohathites; of Merari, the clan of the Merarites. ⁵⁸These are the clans of Levi: the clan of the Libnites, the clan of the Hebronites, the clan of the Mahlites, the clan of the Mushites, the clan of the Korahites. And Kohath was the father of Amram. ⁵⁹The name of Amram's wife was Jochebed the daughter of Levi, who was born to Levi in Egypt. And she bore to Amram Aaron and Moses and Miriam their sister. ⁶⁰And to Aaron were born Nadab, Abihu, Eleazar, and Ithamar. ⁶¹But Nadab and Abihu died when they offered unauthorized fire before the LORD. ⁶²And those listed were 23,000, every male from a month old and upwards. For they were not listed among the people of Israel, because there was no inheritance given to them among the people of Israel.

⁶³These were those listed by Moses and Eleazar the priest, who listed the people of Israel in the plains of Moab by the Jordan at Jericho. ⁶⁴But among these there was not one of those listed by Moses and Aaron the priest, who had listed the people of Israel in the wilderness of Sinai. ⁶⁵For the LORD had said of them, "They shall die in the wilderness." Not one of them was left, except Caleb the son of Jephunneh and Joshua the son of Nun.

THE DAUGHTERS OF ZELOPHEHAD

27 Then drew near the daughters of Zelophehad the son of Hepher, son of Gilead, son of Machir, son of Manasseh, from the clans of Manasseh the son of Joseph. The names of his daughters were: Mahlah, Noah, Hoglah, Milcah, and

Tirzah. ²And they stood before Moses and before Eleazar the priest and before the chiefs and all the congregation, at the entrance of the tent of meeting, saying, ³"Our father died in the wilderness. He was not among the company of those who gathered themselves together against the LORD in the company of Korah, but died for his own sin. And he had no sons. ⁴Why should the name of our father be taken away from his clan because he had no son? Give to us a possession among our father's brothers."

⁵Moses brought their case before the LORD. ⁶And the LORD said to Moses, ⁷"The daughters of Zelophehad are right. You shall give them possession of an inheritance among their father's brothers and transfer the inheritance of their father to them. ⁸And you shall speak to the people of Israel, saying, 'If a man dies and has no son, then you shall transfer his inheritance to his daughter. ⁹And if he has no daughter, then you shall give his inheritance to his brothers. ¹⁰And if he has no brothers, then you shall give his inheritance to his father's brothers. ¹¹And if his father has no brothers, then you shall give his inheritance to the nearest kinsman of his clan, and he shall possess it. And it shall be for the people of Israel a statute and rule, as the LORD commanded Moses.'"

JOSHUA TO SUCCEED MOSES

¹²The LORD said to Moses, "Go up into this mountain of Abarim and see the land that I have given to the people of Israel. ¹³When you have seen it, you also shall be gathered to your people, as your brother Aaron was, ¹⁴because you rebelled against my word in the wilderness of Zin when the congregation quarrelled, failing to uphold me as holy at the waters before their eyes." (These are the waters of Meribah of Kadesh in the wilderness of Zin.) ¹⁵Moses spoke to the LORD, saying, ¹⁶"Let the LORD, the God of the spirits of all flesh, appoint a man over the congregation ¹⁷who shall go out before them and come in before them, who shall lead them out and bring them in, that the congregation of the LORD may not be as sheep that have no shepherd." ¹⁸So the LORD said to Moses, "Take Joshua the son of Nun, a man in whom is the Spirit, and lay your hand on him. ¹⁹Make him stand before Eleazar the priest and all the congregation, and you shall commission him in their sight. ²⁰You shall invest him with some of your authority, that all the congregation of the people of Israel may obey. ²¹And he shall stand before Eleazar the priest, who shall enquire for him by the judgement of the Urim before the LORD. At his word they shall go out, and at his word they shall come in, both he and all the people of Israel with him, the whole congregation." ²²And Moses did as the LORD commanded him. He took Joshua and made him stand before Eleazar the priest and the whole congregation, ²³and he laid his hands on him and commissioned him as the LORD directed through Moses.

DAILY OFFERINGS

28 The LORD spoke to Moses, saying, ²"Command the people of Israel and say to them, 'My offering, my food for my food offerings, my pleasing aroma, you shall be careful to offer to me at its appointed time.' ³And you shall say to them, This is the food offering that you shall offer to the LORD: two male lambs a year old without blemish, day by day, as a regular offering. ⁴One lamb you shall offer in the morning, and the other lamb you shall offer at twilight; ⁵also a tenth of an ephah^a of fine flour for a grain offering, mixed with a quarter of a hin^b of beaten oil. ⁶It is a regular burnt offering, which was ordained at Mount Sinai for a pleasing aroma, a food offering to the LORD. ⁷Its drink offering shall be a quarter of a hin for each lamb. In the Holy Place you shall pour out a drink offering of strong drink to the LORD. ⁸The other lamb you shall offer at twilight. Like the grain offering of the morning, and like its drink offering, you shall offer it as a food offering, with a pleasing aroma to the LORD.

SABBATH OFFERINGS

⁹"On the Sabbath day, two male lambs a year old without blemish, and two tenths of an ephah of fine flour for a grain offering, mixed with oil, and its drink offering: ¹⁰this is the burnt offering of every Sabbath, besides the regular burnt offering and its drink offering.

MONTHLY OFFERINGS

¹¹"At the beginnings of your months, you shall offer a burnt offering to the LORD: two bulls from the herd, one ram, seven male lambs a year old without blemish; ¹²also three tenths of an ephah of fine flour for a grain

---

^{a}An *ephah* was about 3/5 of a bushel or 22 litres ^{b}A *hin* was about 4 quarts or 3.5 litres

offering, mixed with oil, for each bull, and two tenths of fine flour for a grain offering, mixed with oil, for the one ram; ¹³and a tenth of fine flour mixed with oil as a grain offering for every lamb; for a burnt offering with a pleasing aroma, a food offering to the LORD. ¹⁴Their drink offerings shall be half a hin of wine for a bull, a third of a hin for a ram, and a quarter of a hin for a lamb. This is the burnt offering of each month throughout the months of the year. ¹⁵Also one male goat for a sin offering to the LORD; it shall be offered besides the regular burnt offering and its drink offering.

PASSOVER OFFERINGS

¹⁶"On the fourteenth day of the first month is the LORD's Passover, ¹⁷and on the fifteenth day of this month is a feast. For seven days shall unleavened bread be eaten. ¹⁸On the first day there shall be a holy convocation. You shall not do any ordinary work, ¹⁹but shall offer a food offering, a burnt offering to the LORD: two bulls from the herd, one ram, and seven male lambs a year old; see that they are without blemish; ²⁰also their grain offering of fine flour mixed with oil; three tenths of an ephah shall you offer for a bull, and two tenths for a ram; ²¹a tenth shall you offer for each of the seven lambs; ²²also one male goat for a sin offering, to make atonement for you. ²³You shall offer these besides the burnt offering of the morning, which is for a regular burnt offering. ²⁴In the same way you shall offer daily, for seven days, the food of a food offering, with a pleasing aroma to the LORD. It shall be offered besides the regular burnt offering and its drink offering. ²⁵And on the seventh day you shall have a holy convocation. You shall not do any ordinary work.

OFFERINGS FOR THE FEAST OF WEEKS

²⁶"On the day of the firstfruits, when you offer a grain offering of new grain to the LORD at your Feast of Weeks, you shall have a holy convocation. You shall not do any ordinary work, ²⁷but shall offer a burnt offering, with a pleasing aroma to the LORD: two bulls from the herd, one ram, seven male lambs a year old; ²⁸also their grain offering of fine flour mixed with oil, three tenths of an ephah for each bull, two tenths for one ram, ²⁹a tenth for each of the seven lambs; ³⁰with one male goat, to make atonement for you. ³¹Besides the regular burnt offering and its grain offering, you shall offer them and their drink offering. See that they are without blemish.

OFFERINGS FOR THE FEAST OF TRUMPETS

29 "On the first day of the seventh month you shall have a holy convocation. You shall not do any ordinary work. It is a day for you to blow the trumpets, ²and you shall offer a burnt offering, for a pleasing aroma to the LORD: one bull from the herd, one ram, seven male lambs a year old without blemish; ³also their grain offering of fine flour mixed with oil, three tenths of an ephah*ᵃ* for the bull, two tenths for the ram, ⁴and one tenth for each of the seven lambs; ⁵with one male goat for a sin offering, to make atonement for you; ⁶besides the burnt offering of the new moon, and its grain offering, and the regular burnt offering and its grain offering, and their drink offering, according to the rule for them, for a pleasing aroma, a food offering to the LORD.

OFFERINGS FOR THE DAY OF ATONEMENT

⁷"On the tenth day of this seventh month you shall have a holy convocation and afflict yourselves.*ᵇ* You shall do no work, ⁸but you shall offer a burnt offering to the LORD, a pleasing aroma: one bull from the herd, one ram, seven male lambs a year old: see that they are without blemish. ⁹And their grain offering shall be of fine flour mixed with oil, three tenths of an ephah for the bull, two tenths for the one ram, ¹⁰a tenth for each of the seven lambs: ¹¹also one male goat for a sin offering, besides the sin offering of atonement, and the regular burnt offering and its grain offering, and their drink offerings.

OFFERINGS FOR THE FEAST OF BOOTHS

¹²"On the fifteenth day of the seventh month you shall have a holy convocation. You shall not do any ordinary work, and you shall keep a feast to the LORD for seven days. ¹³And you shall offer a burnt offering, a food offering, with a pleasing aroma to the LORD, thirteen bulls from the herd, two rams, fourteen male lambs a year old; they shall be without blemish; ¹⁴and their grain offering of fine flour mixed with oil, three tenths of an ephah for each of the thirteen bulls, two tenths for each of the two rams, ¹⁵and a tenth for each of the fourteen lambs; ¹⁶also one male goat for a sin offering, besides the regular burnt offering, its grain offering and its drink offering.

ᵃAn ephah was about 3/5 of a bushel or 22 litres ᵇOr and fast

17"On the second day twelve bulls from the herd, two rams, fourteen male lambs a year old without blemish, 18with the grain offering and the drink offerings for the bulls, for the rams, and for the lambs, in the prescribed quantities; 19also one male goat for a sin offering, besides the regular burnt offering and its grain offering, and their drink offerings.

20"On the third day eleven bulls, two rams, fourteen male lambs a year old without blemish, 21with the grain offering and the drink offerings for the bulls, for the rams, and for the lambs, in the prescribed quantities; 22also one male goat for a sin offering, besides the regular burnt offering and its grain offering and its drink offering.

23"On the fourth day ten bulls, two rams, fourteen male lambs a year old without blemish, 24with the grain offering and the drink offerings for the bulls, for the rams, and for the lambs, in the prescribed quantities; 25also one male goat for a sin offering, besides the regular burnt offering, its grain offering and its drink offering.

26"On the fifth day nine bulls, two rams, fourteen male lambs a year old without blemish, 27with the grain offering and the drink offerings for the bulls, for the rams, and for the lambs, in the prescribed quantities; 28also one male goat for a sin offering; besides the regular burnt offering and its grain offering and its drink offering.

29"On the sixth day eight bulls, two rams, fourteen male lambs a year old without blemish, 30with the grain offering and the drink offerings for the bulls, for the rams, and for the lambs, in the prescribed quantities; 31also one male goat for a sin offering; besides the regular burnt offering, its grain offering, and its drink offerings.

32"On the seventh day seven bulls, two rams, fourteen male lambs a year old without blemish, 33with the grain offering and the drink offerings for the bulls, for the rams, and for the lambs, in the prescribed quantities; 34also one male goat for a sin offering; besides the regular burnt offering, its grain offering, and its drink offering.

35"On the eighth day you shall have a solemn assembly. You shall not do any ordinary work, 36but you shall offer a burnt offering, a food offering, with a pleasing aroma to the LORD: one bull, one ram, seven male lambs a year old without blemish, 37and the grain offering and the drink offerings for the bull, for the ram, and for the lambs, in the prescribed quantities; 38also one male goat for a sin offering; besides the regular burnt offering and its grain offering and its drink offering.

39"These you shall offer to the LORD at your appointed feasts, in addition to your vow offerings and your freewill offerings, for your burnt offerings, and for your grain offerings, and for your drink offerings, and for your peace offerings."

40a So Moses told the people of Israel everything just as the LORD had commanded Moses.

MEN AND VOWS

30 Moses spoke to the heads of the tribes of the people of Israel, saying, "This is what the LORD has commanded. 2If a man vows a vow to the LORD, or swears an oath to bind himself by a pledge, he shall not break his word. He shall do according to all that proceeds out of his mouth.

WOMEN AND VOWS

3"If a woman vows a vow to the LORD and binds herself by a pledge, while within her father's house in her youth, 4and her father hears of her vow and of her pledge by which she has bound herself and says nothing to her, then all her vows shall stand, and every pledge by which she has bound herself shall stand. 5But if her father opposes her on the day that he hears of it, no vow of hers, no pledge by which she has bound herself shall stand. And the LORD will forgive her, because her father opposed her.

6"If she marries a husband, while under her vows or any thoughtless utterance of her lips by which she has bound herself, 7and her husband hears of it and says nothing to her on the day that he hears, then her vows shall stand, and her pledges by which she has bound herself shall stand. 8But if, on the day that her husband comes to hear of it, he opposes her, then he makes void her vow that was on her, and the thoughtless utterance of her lips by which she bound herself. And the LORD will forgive her. 9(But any vow of a widow or of a divorced woman, anything by which she has bound herself, shall stand against her.) 10And if she vowed in her husband's house or bound herself by a pledge with an oath, 11and her husband

---
a Ch 30:1 in Hebrew

heard of it and said nothing to her and did not oppose her, then all her vows shall stand, and every pledge by which she bound herself shall stand. ¹²But if her husband makes them null and void on the day that he hears them, then whatever proceeds out of her lips concerning her vows or concerning her pledge of herself shall not stand. Her husband has made them void, and the LORD will forgive her. ¹³Any vow and any binding oath to afflict herself,*a* her husband may establish,*b* or her husband may make void. ¹⁴But if her husband says nothing to her from day to day, then he establishes all her vows or all her pledges that are upon her. He has established them, because he said nothing to her on the day that he heard of them. ¹⁵But if he makes them null and void after he has heard of them, then he shall bear her iniquity."

¹⁶These are the statutes that the LORD commanded Moses about a man and his wife and about a father and his daughter while she is in her youth within her father's house.

VENGEANCE ON MIDIAN

31 The LORD spoke to Moses, saying, ²"Avenge the people of Israel on the Midianites. Afterwards you shall be gathered to your people." ³So Moses spoke to the people, saying, "Arm men from among you for the war, that they may go against Midian to execute the LORD's vengeance on Midian. ⁴You shall send a thousand from each of the tribes of Israel to the war." ⁵So there were provided, out of the thousands of Israel, a thousand from each tribe, twelve thousand armed for war. ⁶And Moses sent them to the war, a thousand from each tribe, together with Phinehas the son of Eleazar the priest, with the vessels of the sanctuary and the trumpets for the alarm in his hand. ⁷They warred against Midian, as the LORD commanded Moses, and killed every male. ⁸They killed the kings of Midian with the rest of their slain, Evi, Rekem, Zur, Hur, and Reba, the five kings of Midian. And they also killed Balaam the son of Beor with the sword. ⁹And the people of Israel took captive the women of Midian and their little ones, and they took as plunder all their cattle, their flocks, and all their goods. ¹⁰All their cities in the places where they lived, and all their encampments, they burned with fire, ¹¹and took all the spoil and all the plunder, both of man and of beast. ¹²Then they brought the captives and the plunder and the spoil to Moses, and to Eleazar the priest, and to the congregation of the people of Israel, at the camp on the plains of Moab by the Jordan at Jericho.

¹³Moses and Eleazar the priest and all the chiefs of the congregation went to meet them outside the camp. ¹⁴And Moses was angry with the officers of the army, the commanders of thousands and the commanders of hundreds, who had come from service in the war. ¹⁵Moses said to them, "Have you let all the women live? ¹⁶Behold, these, on Balaam's advice, caused the people of Israel to act treacherously against the LORD in the incident of Peor, and so the plague came among the congregation of the LORD. ¹⁷Now therefore, kill every male among the little ones, and kill every woman who has known man by lying with him. ¹⁸But all the young girls who have not known man by lying with him keep alive for yourselves. ¹⁹Encamp outside the camp for seven days. Whoever of you has killed any person and whoever has touched any slain, purify yourselves and your captives on the third day and on the seventh day. ²⁰You shall purify every garment, every article of skin, all work of goats' hair, and every article of wood."

²¹Then Eleazar the priest said to the men in the army who had gone to battle: "This is the statute of the law that the LORD has commanded Moses: ²²only the gold, the silver, the bronze, the iron, the tin, and the lead, ²³everything that can stand the fire, you shall pass through the fire, and it shall be clean. Nevertheless, it shall also be purified with the water for impurity. And whatever cannot stand the fire, you shall pass through the water. ²⁴You must wash your clothes on the seventh day, and you shall be clean. And afterwards you may come into the camp."

²⁵The LORD said to Moses, ²⁶"Take the count of the plunder that was taken, both of man and of beast, you and Eleazar the priest and the heads of the fathers' houses of the congregation, ²⁷and divide the plunder into two parts between the warriors who went out to battle and all the congregation. ²⁸And levy for the LORD a tribute from the men of war who went out to battle, one out of five hundred, of the people and of the oxen and of the donkeys and of the flocks. ²⁹Take it from their half and give it to Eleazar the priest as a contribution to the LORD. ³⁰And from

---

a Or *to fast* *b* Or *may allow to stand*

the people of Israel's half you shall take one drawn out of every fifty, of the people, of the oxen, of the donkeys, and of the flocks, of all the cattle, and give them to the Levites who keep guard over the tabernacle of the LORD." ³¹And Moses and Eleazar the priest did as the LORD commanded Moses.

³²Now the plunder remaining of the spoil that the army took was 675,000 sheep, ³³72,000 cattle, ³⁴61,000 donkeys, ³⁵and 32,000 persons in all, women who had not known man by lying with him. ³⁶And the half, the portion of those who had gone out in the army, numbered 337,500 sheep, ³⁷and the LORD's tribute of sheep was 675. ³⁸The cattle were 36,000, of which the LORD's tribute was 72. ³⁹The donkeys were 30,500, of which the LORD's tribute was 61. ⁴⁰The persons were 16,000, of which the LORD's tribute was 32 persons. ⁴¹And Moses gave the tribute, which was the contribution for the LORD, to Eleazar the priest, as the LORD commanded Moses.

⁴²From the people of Israel's half, which Moses separated from that of the men who had served in the army— ⁴³now the congregation's half was 337,500 sheep, ⁴⁴36,000 cattle, ⁴⁵and 30,500 donkeys, ⁴⁶and 16,000 persons— ⁴⁷from the people of Israel's half Moses took one of every 50, both of persons and of beasts, and gave them to the Levites who kept guard over the tabernacle of the LORD, as the LORD commanded Moses.

⁴⁸Then the officers who were over the thousands of the army, the commanders of thousands and the commanders of hundreds, came near to Moses ⁴⁹and said to Moses, "Your servants have counted the men of war who are under our command, and there is not a man missing from us. ⁵⁰And we have brought the LORD's offering, what each man found, articles of gold, armlets and bracelets, signet rings, earrings, and beads, to make atonement for ourselves before the LORD." ⁵¹And Moses and Eleazar the priest received from them the gold, all crafted articles. ⁵²And all the gold of the contribution that they presented to the LORD, from the commanders of thousands and the commanders of hundreds, was 16,750 shekels.ᵃ ⁵³(The men in the army had each taken plunder for himself.) ⁵⁴And Moses and Eleazar the priest received the gold from the commanders of thousands and of hundreds, and brought it into the tent of meeting, as a memorial for the people of Israel before the LORD.

REUBEN AND GAD SETTLE IN GILEAD

32 Now the people of Reuben and the people of Gad had a very great number of livestock. And they saw the land of Jazer and the land of Gilead, and behold, the place was a place for livestock. ²So the people of Gad and the people of Reuben came and said to Moses and to Eleazar the priest and to the chiefs of the congregation, ³"Ataroth, Dibon, Jazer, Nimrah, Heshbon, Elealeh, Sebam, Nebo, and Beon, ⁴the land that the LORD struck down before the congregation of Israel, is a land for livestock, and your servants have livestock." ⁵And they said, "If we have found favour in your sight, let this land be given to your servants for a possession. Do not take us across the Jordan."

⁶But Moses said to the people of Gad and to the people of Reuben, "Shall your brothers go to the war while you sit here? ⁷Why will you discourage the heart of the people of Israel from going over into the land that the LORD has given them? ⁸Your fathers did this, when I sent them from Kadesh-barnea to see the land. ⁹For when they went up to the Valley of Eshcol and saw the land, they discouraged the heart of the people of Israel from going into the land that the LORD had given them. ¹⁰And the LORD's anger was kindled on that day, and he swore, saying, ¹¹'Surely none of the men who came up out of Egypt, from twenty years old and upwards, shall see the land that I swore to give to Abraham, to Isaac, and to Jacob, because they have not wholly followed me, ¹²none except Caleb the son of Jephunneh the Kenizzite and Joshua the son of Nun, for they have wholly followed the LORD.' ¹³And the LORD's anger was kindled against Israel, and he made them wander in the wilderness forty years, until all the generation that had done evil in the sight of the LORD was gone. ¹⁴And behold, you have risen in your fathers' place, a brood of sinful men, to increase still more the fierce anger of the LORD against Israel! ¹⁵For if you turn away from following him, he will again abandon them in the wilderness, and you will destroy all this people."

¹⁶Then they came near to him and said, "We will build sheepfolds here for our livestock, and cities for our little ones, ¹⁷but we will take up arms, ready to go before the people of Israel, until we have brought them to their place. And our little ones shall live in the

---

ᵃA *shekel* was about 2/5 of an ounce or 11 grams

fortified cities because of the inhabitants of the land. ¹⁸We will not return to our homes until each of the people of Israel has gained his inheritance. ¹⁹For we will not inherit with them on the other side of the Jordan and beyond, because our inheritance has come to us on this side of the Jordan to the east." ²⁰So Moses said to them, "If you will do this, if you will take up arms to go before the LORD for the war, ²¹and every armed man of you will pass over the Jordan before the LORD, until he has driven out his enemies from before him ²²and the land is subdued before the LORD; then after that you shall return and be free of obligation to the LORD and to Israel, and this land shall be your possession before the LORD. ²³But if you will not do so, behold, you have sinned against the LORD, and be sure your sin will find you out. ²⁴Build cities for your little ones and folds for your sheep, and do what you have promised." ²⁵And the people of Gad and the people of Reuben said to Moses, "Your servants will do as my lord commands. ²⁶Our little ones, our wives, our livestock, and all our cattle shall remain there in the cities of Gilead, ²⁷but your servants will pass over, every man who is armed for war, before the LORD to battle, as my lord orders."

²⁸So Moses gave command concerning them to Eleazar the priest and to Joshua the son of Nun and to the heads of the fathers' houses of the tribes of the people of Israel. ²⁹And Moses said to them, "If the people of Gad and the people of Reuben, every man who is armed to battle before the LORD, will pass with you over the Jordan and the land shall be subdued before you, then you shall give them the land of Gilead for a possession. ³⁰However, if they will not pass over with you armed, they shall have possessions among you in the land of Canaan." ³¹And the people of Gad and the people of Reuben answered, "What the LORD has said to your servants, we will do. ³²We will pass over armed before the LORD into the land of Canaan, and the possession of our inheritance shall remain with us beyond the Jordan."

³³And Moses gave to them, to the people of Gad and to the people of Reuben and to the half-tribe of Manasseh the son of Joseph, the kingdom of Sihon king of the Amorites and the kingdom of Og king of Bashan, the land and its cities with their territories, the cities of the land throughout the country. ³⁴And the people of Gad built Dibon, Ataroth, Aroer, ³⁵Atroth-shophan, Jazer, Jogbehah, ³⁶Beth-nimrah and Beth-haran, fortified cities, and folds for sheep. ³⁷And the people of Reuben built Heshbon, Elealeh, Kiriathaim, ³⁸Nebo, and Baal-meon (their names were changed), and Sibmah. And they gave other names to the cities that they built. ³⁹And the sons of Machir the son of Manasseh went to Gilead and captured it, and dispossessed the Amorites who were in it. ⁴⁰And Moses gave Gilead to Machir the son of Manasseh, and he settled in it. ⁴¹And Jair the son of Manasseh went and captured their villages, and called them Havvoth-jair.[a] ⁴²And Nobah went and captured Kenath and its villages, and called it Nobah, after his own name.

RECOUNTING ISRAEL'S JOURNEY

33 These are the stages of the people of Israel, when they went out of the land of Egypt by their companies under the leadership of Moses and Aaron. ²Moses wrote down their starting places, stage by stage, by command of the LORD, and these are their stages according to their starting places. ³They set out from Rameses in the first month, on the fifteenth day of the first month. On the day after the Passover, the people of Israel went out triumphantly in the sight of all the Egyptians, ⁴while the Egyptians were burying all their firstborn, whom the LORD had struck down among them. On their gods also the LORD executed judgements.

⁵So the people of Israel set out from Rameses and camped at Succoth. ⁶And they set out from Succoth and camped at Etham, which is on the edge of the wilderness. ⁷And they set out from Etham and turned back to Pi-hahiroth, which is east of Baal-zephon, and they camped before Migdol. ⁸And they set out from before Hahiroth[b] and passed through the midst of the sea into the wilderness, and they went a three days' journey in the wilderness of Etham and camped at Marah. ⁹And they set out from Marah and came to Elim; at Elim there were twelve springs of water and seventy palm trees, and they camped there. ¹⁰And they set out from Elim and camped by the Red Sea. ¹¹And they set out from the Red Sea and camped in the wilderness of Sin. ¹²And they set out from the wilderness of Sin and camped at Dophkah. ¹³And they set out from Dophkah

---

[a]*Havvoth-jair* means *the villages of Jair* [b]Some manuscripts and versions *Pi-hahiroth*

and camped at Alush. ¹⁴And they set out from Alush and camped at Rephidim, where there was no water for the people to drink. ¹⁵And they set out from Rephidim and camped in the wilderness of Sinai. ¹⁶And they set out from the wilderness of Sinai and camped at Kibroth-hattaavah. ¹⁷And they set out from Kibroth-hattaavah and camped at Hazeroth. ¹⁸And they set out from Hazeroth and camped at Rithmah. ¹⁹And they set out from Rithmah and camped at Rimmon-perez. ²⁰And they set out from Rimmon-perez and camped at Libnah. ²¹And they set out from Libnah and camped at Rissah. ²²And they set out from Rissah and camped at Kehelathah. ²³And they set out from Kehelathah and camped at Mount Shepher. ²⁴And they set out from Mount Shepher and camped at Haradah. ²⁵And they set out from Haradah and camped at Makheloth. ²⁶And they set out from Makheloth and camped at Tahath. ²⁷And they set out from Tahath and camped at Terah. ²⁸And they set out from Terah and camped at Mithkah. ²⁹And they set out from Mithkah and camped at Hashmonah. ³⁰And they set out from Hashmonah and camped at Moseroth. ³¹And they set out from Moseroth and camped at Bene-jaakan. ³²And they set out from Bene-jaakan and camped at Hor-haggidgad. ³³And they set out from Hor-haggidgad and camped at Jotbathah. ³⁴And they set out from Jotbathah and camped at Abronah. ³⁵And they set out from Abronah and camped at Ezion-geber. ³⁶And they set out from Ezion-geber and camped in the wilderness of Zin (that is, Kadesh). ³⁷And they set out from Kadesh and camped at Mount Hor, on the edge of the land of Edom.

³⁸And Aaron the priest went up Mount Hor at the command of the LORD and died there, in the fortieth year after the people of Israel had come out of the land of Egypt, on the first day of the fifth month. ³⁹And Aaron was 123 years old when he died on Mount Hor.

⁴⁰And the Canaanite, the king of Arad, who lived in the Negeb in the land of Canaan, heard of the coming of the people of Israel.

⁴¹And they set out from Mount Hor and camped at Zalmonah. ⁴²And they set out from Zalmonah and camped at Punon. ⁴³And they set out from Punon and camped at Oboth. ⁴⁴And they set out from Oboth and camped at Iye-abarim, in the territory of Moab. ⁴⁵And they set out from Iyim and camped at Dibon-gad. ⁴⁶And they set out from Dibon-gad and camped at Almon-diblathaim. ⁴⁷And they set out from Almon-diblathaim and camped in the mountains of Abarim, before Nebo. ⁴⁸And they set out from the mountains of Abarim and camped in the plains of Moab by the Jordan at Jericho; ⁴⁹they camped by the Jordan from Beth-jeshimoth as far as Abel-shittim in the plains of Moab.

DRIVE OUT THE INHABITANTS

⁵⁰And the LORD spoke to Moses in the plains of Moab by the Jordan at Jericho, saying, ⁵¹"Speak to the people of Israel and say to them, When you pass over the Jordan into the land of Canaan, ⁵²then you shall drive out all the inhabitants of the land from before you and destroy all their figured stones and destroy all their metal images and demolish all their high places. ⁵³And you shall take possession of the land and settle in it, for I have given the land to you to possess it. ⁵⁴You shall inherit the land by lot according to your clans. To a large tribe you shall give a large inheritance, and to a small tribe you shall give a small inheritance. Wherever the lot falls for anyone, that shall be his. According to the tribes of your fathers you shall inherit. ⁵⁵But if you do not drive out the inhabitants of the land from before you, then those of them whom you let remain shall be as barbs in your eyes and thorns in your sides, and they shall trouble you in the land where you dwell. ⁵⁶And I will do to you as I thought to do to them."

BOUNDARIES OF THE LAND

34 The LORD spoke to Moses, saying, ²"Command the people of Israel, and say to them, When you enter the land of Canaan (this is the land that shall fall to you for an inheritance, the land of Canaan as defined by its borders), ³your south side shall be from the wilderness of Zin alongside Edom, and your southern border shall run from the end of the Salt Sea on the east. ⁴And your border shall turn south of the ascent of Akrabbim, and cross to Zin, and its limit shall be south of Kadesh-barnea. Then it shall go on to Hazar-addar, and pass along to Azmon. ⁵And the border shall turn from Azmon to the Brook of Egypt, and its limit shall be at the sea.

⁶"For the western border, you shall have the Great Sea and its[a] coast. This shall be your western border.

---

[a] Syriac; Hebrew lacks *its*

⁷"This shall be your northern border: from the Great Sea you shall draw a line to Mount Hor. ⁸From Mount Hor you shall draw a line to Lebo-hamath, and the limit of the border shall be at Zedad. ⁹Then the border shall extend to Ziphron, and its limit shall be at Hazar-enan. This shall be your northern border.

¹⁰"You shall draw a line for your eastern border from Hazar-enan to Shepham. ¹¹And the border shall go down from Shepham to Riblah on the east side of Ain. And the border shall go down and reach to the shoulder of the Sea of Chinnereth on the east. ¹²And the border shall go down to the Jordan, and its limit shall be at the Salt Sea. This shall be your land as defined by its borders all round."

¹³Moses commanded the people of Israel, saying, "This is the land that you shall inherit by lot, which the LORD has commanded to give to the nine tribes and to the half-tribe. ¹⁴For the tribe of the people of Reuben by fathers' houses and the tribe of the people of Gad by their fathers' houses have received their inheritance, and also the half-tribe of Manasseh. ¹⁵The two tribes and the half-tribe have received their inheritance beyond the Jordan east of Jericho, towards the sunrise."

LIST OF TRIBAL CHIEFS

¹⁶The LORD spoke to Moses, saying, ¹⁷"These are the names of the men who shall divide the land to you for inheritance: Eleazar the priest and Joshua the son of Nun. ¹⁸You shall take one chief from every tribe to divide the land for inheritance. ¹⁹These are the names of the men: Of the tribe of Judah, Caleb the son of Jephunneh. ²⁰Of the tribe of the people of Simeon, Shemuel the son of Ammihud. ²¹Of the tribe of Benjamin, Elidad the son of Chislon. ²²Of the tribe of the people of Dan a chief, Bukki the son of Jogli. ²³Of the people of Joseph: of the tribe of the people of Manasseh a chief, Hanniel the son of Ephod. ²⁴And of the tribe of the people of Ephraim a chief, Kemuel the son of Shiphtan. ²⁵Of the tribe of the people of Zebulun a chief, Elizaphan the son of Parnach. ²⁶Of the tribe of the people of Issachar a chief, Paltiel the son of Azzan. ²⁷And of the tribe of the people of Asher a chief, Ahihud the son of Shelomi. ²⁸Of the tribe of the people of Naphtali a chief, Pedahel the son of Ammihud." ²⁹These are the men whom the LORD commanded to divide the inheritance for the people of Israel in the land of Canaan.

CITIES FOR THE LEVITES

35 The LORD spoke to Moses in the plains of Moab by the Jordan at Jericho, saying, ²"Command the people of Israel to give to the Levites some of the inheritance of their possession as cities for them to dwell in. And you shall give to the Levites pasture lands round the cities. ³The cities shall be theirs to dwell in, and their pasture lands shall be for their cattle and for their livestock and for all their beasts. ⁴The pasture lands of the cities, which you shall give to the Levites, shall reach from the wall of the city outwards a thousand cubits*ᵃ* all round. ⁵And you shall measure, outside the city, on the east side two thousand cubits, and on the south side two thousand cubits, and on the west side two thousand cubits, and on the north side two thousand cubits, the city being in the middle. This shall belong to them as pasture land for their cities.

⁶"The cities that you give to the Levites shall be the six cities of refuge, where you shall permit the manslayer to flee, and in addition to them you shall give forty-two cities. ⁷All the cities that you give to the Levites shall be forty-eight, with their pasture lands. ⁸And as for the cities that you shall give from the possession of the people of Israel, from the larger tribes you shall take many, and from the smaller tribes you shall take few; each, in proportion to the inheritance that it inherits, shall give of its cities to the Levites."

CITIES OF REFUGE

⁹And the LORD spoke to Moses, saying, ¹⁰"Speak to the people of Israel and say to them, When you cross the Jordan into the land of Canaan, ¹¹then you shall select cities to be cities of refuge for you, that the manslayer who kills any person without intent may flee there. ¹²The cities shall be for you a refuge from the avenger, that the manslayer may not die until he stands before the congregation for judgement. ¹³And the cities that you give shall be your six cities of refuge. ¹⁴You shall give three cities beyond the Jordan, and three cities in the land of Canaan, to be cities of refuge. ¹⁵These six cities shall be for refuge for the people of Israel, and for the stranger and for the sojourner among them, that anyone who kills any person without intent may flee there.

ᵃA cubit was about 18 inches or 45 centimetres

16"But if he struck him down with an iron object, so that he died, he is a murderer. The murderer shall be put to death. 17And if he struck him down with a stone tool that could cause death, and he died, he is a murderer. The murderer shall be put to death. 18Or if he struck him down with a wooden tool that could cause death, and he died, he is a murderer. The murderer shall be put to death. 19The avenger of blood shall himself put the murderer to death; when he meets him, he shall put him to death. 20And if he pushed him out of hatred or hurled something at him, lying in wait, so that he died, 21or in enmity struck him down with his hand, so that he died, then he who struck the blow shall be put to death. He is a murderer. The avenger of blood shall put the murderer to death when he meets him.

22"But if he pushed him suddenly without enmity, or hurled anything on him without lying in wait 23or used a stone that could cause death, and without seeing him dropped it on him, so that he died, though he was not his enemy and did not seek his harm, 24then the congregation shall judge between the manslayer and the avenger of blood, in accordance with these rules. 25And the congregation shall rescue the manslayer from the hand of the avenger of blood, and the congregation shall restore him to his city of refuge to which he had fled, and he shall live in it until the death of the high priest who was anointed with the holy oil. 26But if the manslayer shall at any time go beyond the boundaries of his city of refuge to which he fled, 27and the avenger of blood finds him outside the boundaries of his city of refuge, and the avenger of blood kills the manslayer, he shall not be guilty of blood. 28For he must remain in his city of refuge until the death of the high priest, but after the death of the high priest the manslayer may return to the land of his possession. 29And these things shall be for a statute and rule for you throughout your generations in all your dwelling places.

30"If anyone kills a person, the murderer shall be put to death on the evidence of witnesses. But no person shall be put to death on the testimony of one witness. 31Moreover, you shall accept no ransom for the life of a murderer, who is guilty of death, but he shall be put to death. 32And you shall accept no ransom for him who has fled to his city of refuge, that he may return to dwell in the land before the death of the high priest. 33You shall not pollute the land in which you live, for blood pollutes the land, and no atonement can be made for the land for the blood that is shed in it, except by the blood of the one who shed it. 34You shall not defile the land in which you live, in the midst of which I dwell, for I the LORD dwell in the midst of the people of Israel."

MARRIAGE OF FEMALE HEIRS

36 The heads of the fathers' houses of the clan of the people of Gilead the son of Machir, son of Manasseh, from the clans of the people of Joseph, came near and spoke before Moses and before the chiefs, the heads of the fathers' houses of the people of Israel. 2They said, "The LORD commanded my lord to give the land for inheritance by lot to the people of Israel, and my lord was commanded by the LORD to give the inheritance of Zelophehad our brother to his daughters. 3But if they are married to any of the sons of the other tribes of the people of Israel, then their inheritance will be taken from the inheritance of our fathers and added to the inheritance of the tribe into which they marry. So it will be taken away from the lot of our inheritance. 4And when the jubilee of the people of Israel comes, then their inheritance will be added to the inheritance of the tribe into which they marry, and their inheritance will be taken from the inheritance of the tribe of our fathers."

5And Moses commanded the people of Israel according to the word of the LORD, saying, "The tribe of the people of Joseph is right. 6This is what the LORD commands concerning the daughters of Zelophehad: 'Let them marry whom they think best, only they shall marry within the clan of the tribe of their father. 7The inheritance of the people of Israel shall not be transferred from one tribe to another, for every one of the people of Israel shall hold on to the inheritance of the tribe of his fathers. 8And every daughter who possesses an inheritance in any tribe of the people of Israel shall be wife to one of the clan of the tribe of her father, so that every one of the people of Israel may possess the inheritance of his fathers. 9So no inheritance shall be transferred from one tribe to another, for each of the tribes of the people of Israel shall hold on to its own inheritance.'"

¹⁰The daughters of Zelophehad did as the LORD commanded Moses, ¹¹for Mahlah, Tirzah, Hoglah, Milcah, and Noah, the daughters of Zelophehad, were married to sons of their father's brothers. ¹²They were married into the clans of the people of Manasseh the son of Joseph, and their inheritance remained in the tribe of their father's clan.

¹³These are the commandments and the rules that the LORD commanded through Moses to the people of Israel in the plains of Moab by the Jordan at Jericho.

DEUTERONOMY

THE COMMAND TO LEAVE HOREB

1 These are the words that Moses spoke to all Israel beyond the Jordan in the wilderness, in the Arabah opposite Suph, between Paran and Tophel, Laban, Hazeroth, and Dizahab. ²It is eleven days' journey from Horeb by the way of Mount Seir to Kadesh-barnea. ³In the fortieth year, on the first day of the eleventh month, Moses spoke to the people of Israel according to all that the Lord had given him in commandment to them, ⁴after he had defeated Sihon the king of the Amorites, who lived in Heshbon, and Og the king of Bashan, who lived in Ashtaroth and in Edrei. ⁵Beyond the Jordan, in the land of Moab, Moses undertook to explain this law, saying, ⁶"The Lord our God said to us in Horeb, 'You have stayed long enough at this mountain. ⁷Turn and take your journey, and go to the hill country of the Amorites and to all their neighbours in the Arabah, in the hill country and in the lowland and in the Negeb and by the sea coast, the land of the Canaanites, and Lebanon, as far as the great river, the river Euphrates. ⁸See, I have set the land before you. Go in and take possession of the land that the Lord swore to your fathers, to Abraham, to Isaac, and to Jacob, to give to them and to their offspring after them.'

LEADERS APPOINTED

⁹"At that time I said to you, 'I am not able to bear you by myself. ¹⁰The Lord your God has multiplied you, and behold, you are today as numerous as the stars of heaven. ¹¹May the Lord, the God of your fathers, make you a thousand times as many as you are and bless you, as he has promised you! ¹²How can I bear by myself the weight and burden of you and your strife? ¹³Choose for your tribes wise, understanding, and experienced men, and I will appoint them as your heads.' ¹⁴And you answered me, 'The thing that you have spoken is good for us to do.' ¹⁵So I took the heads of your tribes, wise and experienced men, and set them as heads over you, commanders of thousands, commanders of hundreds, commanders of fifties, commanders of tens, and officers, throughout your tribes. ¹⁶And I charged your judges at that time, 'Hear the cases between your brothers, and judge righteously between a man and his brother or the alien who is with him. ¹⁷You shall not be partial in judgement. You shall hear the small and the great alike. You shall not be intimidated by anyone, for the judgement is God's. And the case that is too hard for you, you shall bring to me, and I will hear it.' ¹⁸And I commanded you at that time all the things that you should do.

ISRAEL'S REFUSAL TO ENTER THE LAND

¹⁹"Then we set out from Horeb and went through all that great and terrifying wilderness that you saw, on the way to the hill country of the Amorites, as the Lord our God commanded us. And we came to Kadesh-barnea. ²⁰And I said to you, 'You have come to the hill country of the Amorites, which the Lord our God is giving us. ²¹See, the Lord your God has set the land before you. Go up, take possession, as the Lord, the God of your fathers, has told you. Do not fear or be dismayed.' ²²Then all of you came near me and said, 'Let us send men before us, that they may explore the land for us and bring us word again of the way by which we must go up and the cities into which we shall come.' ²³The thing seemed good to me, and I took twelve men from you, one man from each tribe. ²⁴And they turned and went up into the hill country, and came to the Valley of Eshcol and spied it out. ²⁵And they took in their hands some of the fruit of the land and brought it down to us, and brought us word again and said, 'It is a good land that the Lord our God is giving us.'

²⁶"Yet you would not go up, but rebelled against the command of the Lord your God. ²⁷And you murmured in your tents and said, 'Because the Lord hated us he has brought us out of the land of Egypt, to give us into the hand of the Amorites, to destroy us. ²⁸Where are we going up? Our brothers have made our hearts melt, saying, "The people are greater and taller than we. The cities are great and

fortified up to heaven. And besides, we have seen the sons of the Anakim there.'" ²⁹Then I said to you, 'Do not be in dread or afraid of them. ³⁰The Lord your God who goes before you will himself fight for you, just as he did for you in Egypt before your eyes, ³¹and in the wilderness, where you have seen how the Lord your God carried you, as a man carries his son, all the way that you went until you came to this place.' ³²Yet in spite of this word you did not believe the Lord your God, ³³who went before you in the way to seek you out a place to pitch your tents, in fire by night and in the cloud by day, to show you by what way you should go.

THE PENALTY FOR ISRAEL'S REBELLION

³⁴"And the Lord heard your words and was angered, and he swore, ³⁵'Not one of these men of this evil generation shall see the good land that I swore to give to your fathers, ³⁶except Caleb the son of Jephunneh. He shall see it, and to him and to his children I will give the land on which he has trodden, because he has wholly followed the Lord!' ³⁷Even with me the Lord was angry on your account and said, 'You also shall not go in there. ³⁸Joshua the son of Nun, who stands before you, he shall enter. Encourage him, for he shall cause Israel to inherit it. ³⁹And as for your little ones, who you said would become a prey, and your children, who today have no knowledge of good or evil, they shall go in there. And to them I will give it, and they shall possess it. ⁴⁰But as for you, turn, and journey into the wilderness in the direction of the Red Sea.'

⁴¹"Then you answered me, 'We have sinned against the Lord. We ourselves will go up and fight, just as the Lord our God commanded us.' And every one of you fastened on his weapons of war and thought it easy to go up into the hill country. ⁴²And the Lord said to me, 'Say to them, Do not go up or fight, for I am not in your midst, lest you be defeated before your enemies.' ⁴³So I spoke to you, and you would not listen; but you rebelled against the command of the Lord and presumptuously went up into the hill country. ⁴⁴Then the Amorites who lived in that hill country came out against you and chased you as bees do and beat you down in Seir as far as Hormah. ⁴⁵And you returned and wept before the Lord, but the Lord did not listen to your voice or give ear to you. ⁴⁶So you remained at Kadesh for many days, the days that you remained there.

THE WILDERNESS YEARS

2 "Then we turned and journeyed into the wilderness in the direction of the Red Sea, as the Lord told me. And for many days we travelled round Mount Seir. ²Then the Lord said to me, ³'You have been travelling around this mountain country long enough. Turn northwards ⁴and command the people, "You are about to pass through the territory of your brothers, the people of Esau, who live in Seir; and they will be afraid of you. So be very careful. ⁵Do not contend with them, for I will not give you any of their land, no, not so much as for the sole of the foot to tread on, because I have given Mount Seir to Esau as a possession. ⁶You shall purchase food from them with money, that you may eat, and you shall also buy water from them with money, that you may drink. ⁷For the Lord your God has blessed you in all the work of your hands. He knows your going through this great wilderness. These forty years the Lord your God has been with you. You have lacked nothing."' ⁸So we went on, away from our brothers, the people of Esau, who live in Seir, away from the Arabah road from Elath and Ezion-geber.

"And we turned and went in the direction of the wilderness of Moab. ⁹And the Lord said to me, 'Do not harass Moab or contend with them in battle, for I will not give you any of their land for a possession, because I have given Ar to the people of Lot for a possession.' ¹⁰(The Emim formerly lived there, a people great and many, and tall as the Anakim. ¹¹Like the Anakim they are also counted as Rephaim, but the Moabites call them Emim. ¹²The Horites also lived in Seir formerly, but the people of Esau dispossessed them and destroyed them from before them and settled in their place, as Israel did to the land of their possession, which the Lord gave to them.) ¹³'Now rise up and go over the brook Zered.' So we went over the brook Zered. ¹⁴And the time from our leaving Kadesh-barnea until we crossed the brook Zered was thirty-eight years, until the entire generation, that is, the men of war, had perished from the camp, as the Lord had sworn to them. ¹⁵For indeed the hand of the Lord was against them, to destroy them from the camp, until they had perished.

¹⁶"So as soon as all the men of war had perished and were dead from among the people, ¹⁷the Lord said to me, ¹⁸'Today you are to cross the border of Moab at Ar. ¹⁹And when you approach the territory of the people of

Ammon, do not harass them or contend with them, for I will not give you any of the land of the people of Ammon as a possession, because I have given it to the sons of Lot for a possession.' ²⁰(It is also counted as a land of Rephaim. Rephaim formerly lived there—but the Ammonites call them Zamzummim— ²¹a people great and many, and tall as the Anakim; but the LORD destroyed them before the Ammonites,ᵃ and they dispossessed them and settled in their place, ²²as he did for the people of Esau, who live in Seir, when he destroyed the Horites before them and they dispossessed them and settled in their place even to this day. ²³As for the Avvim, who lived in villages as far as Gaza, the Caphtorim, who came from Caphtor, destroyed them and settled in their place.) ²⁴'Rise up, set out on your journey and go over the Valley of the Arnon. Behold, I have given into your hand Sihon the Amorite, king of Heshbon, and his land. Begin to take possession, and contend with him in battle. ²⁵This day I will begin to put the dread and fear of you on the peoples who are under the whole heaven, who shall hear the report of you and shall tremble and be in anguish because of you.'

THE DEFEAT OF KING SIHON

²⁶"So I sent messengers from the wilderness of Kedemoth to Sihon the king of Heshbon, with words of peace, saying, ²⁷'Let me pass through your land. I will go only by the road; I will turn aside neither to the right nor to the left. ²⁸You shall sell me food for money, that I may eat, and give me water for money, that I may drink. Only let me pass through on foot, ²⁹as the sons of Esau who live in Seir and the Moabites who live in Ar did for me, until I go over the Jordan into the land that the LORD our God is giving to us.' ³⁰But Sihon the king of Heshbon would not let us pass by him, for the LORD your God hardened his spirit and made his heart obstinate, that he might give him into your hand, as he is this day. ³¹And the LORD said to me, 'Behold, I have begun to give Sihon and his land over to you. Begin to take possession, that you may occupy his land.' ³²Then Sihon came out against us, he and all his people, to battle at Jahaz. ³³And the LORD our God gave him over to us, and we defeated him and his sons and all his people. ³⁴And we captured all his cities at that time and devoted to destructionᵇ every city, men, women, and children. We left no survivors. ³⁵Only the livestock we took as spoil for ourselves, with the plunder of the cities that we captured. ³⁶From Aroer, which is on the edge of the Valley of the Arnon, and from the city that is in the valley, as far as Gilead, there was not a city too high for us. The LORD our God gave all into our hands. ³⁷Only to the land of the sons of Ammon you did not draw near, that is, to all the banks of the river Jabbok and the cities of the hill country, whatever the LORD our God had forbidden us.

THE DEFEAT OF KING OG

3 "Then we turned and went up the way to Bashan. And Og the king of Bashan came out against us, he and all his people, to battle at Edrei. ²But the LORD said to me, 'Do not fear him, for I have given him and all his people and his land into your hand. And you shall do to him as you did to Sihon the king of the Amorites, who lived at Heshbon.' ³So the LORD our God gave into our hand Og also, the king of Bashan, and all his people, and we struck him down until he had no survivor left. ⁴And we took all his cities at that time—there was not a city that we did not take from them—sixty cities, the whole region of Argob, the kingdom of Og in Bashan. ⁵All these were cities fortified with high walls, gates, and bars, besides very many unwalled villages. ⁶And we devoted them to destruction,ᶜ as we did to Sihon the king of Heshbon, devoting to destruction every city, men, women, and children. ⁷But all the livestock and the spoil of the cities we took as our plunder. ⁸So we took the land at that time out of the hand of the two kings of the Amorites who were beyond the Jordan, from the Valley of the Arnon to Mount Hermon ⁹(the Sidonians call Hermon Sirion, while the Amorites call it Senir), ¹⁰all the cities of the tableland and all Gilead and all Bashan, as far as Salecah and Edrei, cities of the kingdom of Og in Bashan. ¹¹(For only Og the king of Bashan was left of the remnant of the Rephaim. Behold, his bed was a bed of iron. Is it not in Rabbah of the Ammonites? Nine cubitsᵈ was its length, and four cubits its breadth, according to the common cubit.ᵉ)

¹²"When we took possession of this land at that time, I gave to the Reubenites and the Gadites the territory beginning at Aroer, which is on the edge of the Valley of the Arnon, and

---

ᵃHebrew *them*   ᵇThat is, set apart (devoted) as an offering to the Lord (for destruction)   ᶜThat is, set apart (devoted) as an offering to the Lord (for destruction); twice in this verse   ᵈA *cubit* was about 18 inches or 45 centimetres   ᵉHebrew *cubit of a man*

half the hill country of Gilead with its cities. ¹³The rest of Gilead, and all Bashan, the kingdom of Og, that is, all the region of Argob, I gave to the half-tribe of Manasseh. (All that portion of Bashan is called the land of Rephaim. ¹⁴Jair the Manassite took all the region of Argob, that is, Bashan, as far as the border of the Geshurites and the Maacathites, and called the villages after his own name, Havvoth-jair, as it is to this day.) ¹⁵To Machir I gave Gilead, ¹⁶and to the Reubenites and the Gadites I gave the territory from Gilead as far as the Valley of the Arnon, with the middle of the valley as a border, as far over as the river Jabbok, the border of the Ammonites; ¹⁷the Arabah also, with the Jordan as the border, from Chinnereth as far as the Sea of the Arabah, the Salt Sea, under the slopes of Pisgah on the east.

¹⁸"And I commanded you at that time, saying, 'The LORD your God has given you this land to possess. All your men of valour shall cross over armed before your brothers, the people of Israel. ¹⁹Only your wives, your little ones, and your livestock (I know that you have much livestock) shall remain in the cities that I have given you, ²⁰until the LORD gives rest to your brothers, as to you, and they also occupy the land that the LORD your God gives them beyond the Jordan. Then each of you may return to his possession which I have given you.' ²¹And I commanded Joshua at that time, 'Your eyes have seen all that the LORD your God has done to these two kings. So will the LORD do to all the kingdoms into which you are crossing. ²²You shall not fear them, for it is the LORD your God who fights for you.'

MOSES FORBIDDEN TO ENTER THE LAND

²³"And I pleaded with the LORD at that time, saying, ²⁴'O Lord GOD, you have only begun to show your servant your greatness and your mighty hand. For what god is there in heaven or on earth who can do such works and mighty acts as yours? ²⁵Please let me go over and see the good land beyond the Jordan, that good hill country and Lebanon.' ²⁶But the LORD was angry with me because of you and would not listen to me. And the LORD said to me, 'Enough from you; do not speak to me of this matter again. ²⁷Go up to the top of Pisgah and lift up your eyes westwards and northwards and southwards and eastwards, and look at it with your eyes, for you shall not go over this Jordan. ²⁸But charge Joshua, and encourage and strengthen him, for he shall go over at the head of this people, and he shall put them in possession of the land that you shall see.' ²⁹So we remained in the valley opposite Beth-peor.

MOSES COMMANDS OBEDIENCE

4 "And now, O Israel, listen to the statutes and the rules[a] that I am teaching you, and do them, that you may live, and go in and take possession of the land that the LORD, the God of your fathers, is giving you. ²You shall not add to the word that I command you, nor take from it, that you may keep the commandments of the LORD your God that I command you. ³Your eyes have seen what the LORD did at Baal-peor, for the LORD your God destroyed from among you all the men who followed the Baal of Peor. ⁴But you who held fast to the LORD your God are all alive today. ⁵See, I have taught you statutes and rules, as the LORD my God commanded me, that you should do them in the land that you are entering to take possession of it. ⁶Keep them and do them, for that will be your wisdom and your understanding in the sight of the peoples, who, when they hear all these statutes, will say, 'Surely this great nation is a wise and understanding people.' ⁷For what great nation is there that has a god so near to it as the LORD our God is to us, whenever we call upon him? ⁸And what great nation is there, that has statutes and rules so righteous as all this law that I set before you today?

⁹"Only take care, and keep your soul diligently, lest you forget the things that your eyes have seen, and lest they depart from your heart all the days of your life. Make them known to your children and your children's children— ¹⁰how on the day that you stood before the LORD your God at Horeb, the LORD said to me, 'Gather the people to me, that I may let them hear my words, so that they may learn to fear me all the days that they live on the earth, and that they may teach their children so.' ¹¹And you came near and stood at the foot of the mountain, while the mountain burned with fire to the heart of heaven, wrapped in darkness, cloud, and gloom. ¹²Then the LORD spoke to you out of the midst of the fire. You heard the sound of words, but saw no form; there was only a voice. ¹³And he declared to you his covenant, which he commanded you to perform, that is, the Ten Commandments,[b] and he wrote them on two tablets of stone. ¹⁴And the LORD

---

[a] Or *just decrees*; also verses 5, 8, 14, 45 [b] Hebrew *the ten words*

commanded me at that time to teach you statutes and rules, that you might do them in the land that you are going over to possess.

IDOLATRY FORBIDDEN

¹⁵"Therefore watch yourselves very carefully. Since you saw no form on the day that the LORD spoke to you at Horeb out of the midst of the fire, ¹⁶beware lest you act corruptly by making a carved image for yourselves, in the form of any figure, the likeness of male or female, ¹⁷the likeness of any animal that is on the earth, the likeness of any winged bird that flies in the air, ¹⁸the likeness of anything that creeps on the ground, the likeness of any fish that is in the water under the earth. ¹⁹And beware lest you raise your eyes to heaven, and when you see the sun and the moon and the stars, all the host of heaven, you be drawn away and bow down to them and serve them, things that the LORD your God has allotted to all the peoples under the whole heaven. ²⁰But the LORD has taken you and brought you out of the iron furnace, out of Egypt, to be a people of his own inheritance, as you are this day. ²¹Furthermore, the LORD was angry with me because of you, and he swore that I should not cross the Jordan, and that I should not enter the good land that the LORD your God is giving you for an inheritance. ²²For I must die in this land; I must not go over the Jordan. But you shall go over and take possession of that good land. ²³Take care, lest you forget the covenant of the LORD your God, which he made with you, and make a carved image, the form of anything that the LORD your God has forbidden you. ²⁴For the LORD your God is a consuming fire, a jealous God.

²⁵"When you father children and children's children, and have grown old in the land, if you act corruptly by making a carved image in the form of anything, and by doing what is evil in the sight of the LORD your God, so as to provoke him to anger, ²⁶I call heaven and earth to witness against you today, that you will soon utterly perish from the land that you are going over the Jordan to possess. You will not live long in it, but will be utterly destroyed. ²⁷And the LORD will scatter you among the peoples, and you will be left few in number among the nations where the LORD will drive you. ²⁸And there you will serve gods of wood and stone, the work of human hands, that neither see, nor hear, nor eat, nor smell. ²⁹But from there you will seek the LORD your God and you will find him, if you search after him with all your heart and with all your soul. ³⁰When you are in tribulation, and all these things come upon you in the latter days, you will return to the LORD your God and obey his voice. ³¹For the LORD your God is a merciful God. He will not leave you or destroy you or forget the covenant with your fathers that he swore to them.

THE LORD ALONE IS GOD

³²"For ask now of the days that are past, which were before you, since the day that God created man on the earth, and ask from one end of heaven to the other, whether such a great thing as this has ever happened or was ever heard of. ³³Did any people ever hear the voice of a god speaking out of the midst of the fire, as you have heard, and still live? ³⁴Or has any god ever attempted to go and take a nation for himself from the midst of another nation, by trials, by signs, by wonders, and by war, by a mighty hand and an outstretched arm, and by great deeds of terror, all of which the LORD your God did for you in Egypt before your eyes? ³⁵To you it was shown, that you might know that the LORD is God; there is no other besides him. ³⁶Out of heaven he let you hear his voice, that he might discipline you. And on earth he let you see his great fire, and you heard his words out of the midst of the fire. ³⁷And because he loved your fathers and chose their offspring after them[a] and brought you out of Egypt with his own presence, by his great power, ³⁸driving out before you nations greater and mightier than you, to bring you in, to give you their land for an inheritance, as it is this day, ³⁹know therefore today, and lay it to your heart, that the LORD is God in heaven above and on the earth beneath; there is no other. ⁴⁰Therefore you shall keep his statutes and his commandments, which I command you today, that it may go well with you and with your children after you, and that you may prolong your days in the land that the LORD your God is giving you for all time."

CITIES OF REFUGE

⁴¹Then Moses set apart three cities in the east beyond the Jordan, ⁴²that the manslayer might flee there, anyone who kills his neighbour unintentionally, without being at

---

[a] Hebrew *his offspring after him*

enmity with him in time past; he may flee to one of these cities and save his life: ⁴³Bezer in the wilderness on the tableland for the Reubenites, Ramoth in Gilead for the Gadites, and Golan in Bashan for the Manassites.

INTRODUCTION TO THE LAW

⁴⁴This is the law that Moses set before the people of Israel. ⁴⁵These are the testimonies, the statutes, and the rules, which Moses spoke to the people of Israel when they came out of Egypt, ⁴⁶beyond the Jordan in the valley opposite Beth-peor, in the land of Sihon the king of the Amorites, who lived at Heshbon, whom Moses and the people of Israel defeated when they came out of Egypt. ⁴⁷And they took possession of his land and the land of Og, the king of Bashan, the two kings of the Amorites, who lived to the east beyond the Jordan; ⁴⁸from Aroer, which is on the edge of the Valley of the Arnon, as far as Mount Sirion^a (that is, Hermon), ⁴⁹together with all the Arabah on the east side of the Jordan as far as the Sea of the Arabah, under the slopes of Pisgah.

THE TEN COMMANDMENTS

5 And Moses summoned all Israel and said to them, "Hear, O Israel, the statutes and the rules that I speak in your hearing today, and you shall learn them and be careful to do them. ²The LORD our God made a covenant with us in Horeb. ³Not with our fathers did the LORD make this covenant, but with us, who are all of us here alive today. ⁴The LORD spoke with you face to face at the mountain, out of the midst of the fire, ⁵while I stood between the LORD and you at that time, to declare to you the word of the LORD. For you were afraid because of the fire, and you did not go up into the mountain. He said:

⁶" 'I am the LORD your God, who brought you out of the land of Egypt, out of the house of slavery.

⁷" 'You shall have no other gods before^b me.

⁸" 'You shall not make for yourself a carved image, or any likeness of anything that is in heaven above, or that is on the earth beneath, or that is in the water under the earth. ⁹You shall not bow down to them or serve them; for I the LORD your God am a jealous God, visiting the iniquity of the fathers on the children to the third and fourth generation of those who hate me, ¹⁰but showing steadfast love to thousands^c of those who love me and keep my commandments.

¹¹" 'You shall not take the name of the LORD your God in vain, for the LORD will not hold him guiltless who takes his name in vain.

¹²" 'Observe the Sabbath day, to keep it holy, as the LORD your God commanded you. ¹³For six days you shall labour and do all your work, ¹⁴but the seventh day is a Sabbath to the LORD your God. On it you shall not do any work, you or your son or your daughter or your male servant or your female servant, or your ox or your donkey or any of your livestock, or the sojourner who is within your gates, that your male servant and your female servant may rest as well as you. ¹⁵You shall remember that you were a slave^d in the land of Egypt, and the LORD your God brought you out from there with a mighty hand and an outstretched arm. Therefore the LORD your God commanded you to keep the Sabbath day.

¹⁶" 'Honour your father and your mother, as the LORD your God commanded you, that your days may be long, and that it may go well with you in the land that the LORD your God is giving you.

¹⁷" 'You shall not murder.^{e}

¹⁸" 'And you shall not commit adultery.

¹⁹" 'And you shall not steal.

²⁰" 'And you shall not bear false witness against your neighbour.

²¹" 'And you shall not covet your neighbour's wife. And you shall not desire your neighbour's house, his field, or his male servant, or his female servant, his ox, or his donkey, or anything that is your neighbour's.'

²²"These words the LORD spoke to all your assembly at the mountain out of the midst of the fire, the cloud, and the thick darkness, with a loud voice; and he added no more. And he wrote them on two tablets of stone and gave them to me. ²³And as soon as you heard the voice out of the midst of the darkness, while the mountain was burning with fire, you came near to me, all the heads of your tribes, and your elders. ²⁴And you said, 'Behold, the LORD our God has shown us his glory and greatness, and we have heard his voice out of the midst of the fire. This day we have seen God speak with man, and man still live. ²⁵Now therefore why should we die? For this great fire will consume us. If we hear the voice of the LORD our God any more, we shall die. ²⁶For who is there of all

---

^{a}Syriac; Hebrew *Sion* ^{b}Or *besides* ^{c}Or *to the thousandth generation* ^{d}Or *servant* ^{e}The Hebrew word also covers causing human death through carelessness or negligence

flesh, that has heard the voice of the living God speaking out of the midst of fire as we have, and has still lived? ²⁷Go near and hear all that the LORD our God will say, and speak to us all that the LORD our God will speak to you, and we will hear and do it.'

²⁸And the LORD heard your words, when you spoke to me. And the LORD said to me, 'I have heard the words of this people, which they have spoken to you. They are right in all that they have spoken. ²⁹Oh that they had such a heart as this always, to fear me and to keep all my commandments, that it might go well with them and with their descendants[a] for ever! ³⁰Go and say to them, "Return to your tents." ³¹But you, stand here by me, and I will tell you the whole commandment and the statutes and the rules that you shall teach them, that they may do them in the land that I am giving them to possess.' ³²You shall be careful therefore to do as the LORD your God has commanded you. You shall not turn aside to the right hand or to the left. ³³You shall walk in all the way that the LORD your God has commanded you, that you may live, and that it may go well with you, and that you may live long in the land that you shall possess.

THE GREATEST COMMANDMENT

6 "Now this is the commandment—the statutes and the rules[b]—that the LORD your God commanded me to teach you, that you may do them in the land to which you are going over, to possess it, ²that you may fear the LORD your God, you and your son and your son's son, by keeping all his statutes and his commandments, which I command you, all the days of your life, and that your days may be long. ³Hear therefore, O Israel, and be careful to do them, that it may go well with you, and that you may multiply greatly, as the LORD, the God of your fathers, has promised you, in a land flowing with milk and honey.

⁴"Hear, O Israel: The LORD our God, the LORD is one.[c] ⁵You shall love the LORD your God with all your heart and with all your soul and with all your might. ⁶And these words that I command you today shall be on your heart. ⁷You shall teach them diligently to your children, and shall talk of them when you sit in your house, and when you walk by the way, and when you lie down, and when you rise. ⁸You shall bind them as a sign on your hand, and they shall be as frontlets between your eyes. ⁹You shall write them on the doorposts of your house and on your gates.

¹⁰"And when the LORD your God brings you into the land that he swore to your fathers, to Abraham, to Isaac, and to Jacob, to give you—with great and good cities that you did not build, ¹¹and houses full of all good things that you did not fill, and cisterns that you did not dig, and vineyards and olive trees that you did not plant—and when you eat and are full, ¹²then take care lest you forget the LORD, who brought you out of the land of Egypt, out of the house of slavery. ¹³It is the LORD your God you shall fear. Him you shall serve and by his name you shall swear. ¹⁴You shall not go after other gods, the gods of the peoples who are around you—¹⁵for the LORD your God in your midst is a jealous God—lest the anger of the LORD your God be kindled against you, and he destroy you from off the face of the earth.

¹⁶"You shall not put the LORD your God to the test, as you tested him at Massah. ¹⁷You shall diligently keep the commandments of the LORD your God, and his testimonies and his statutes, which he has commanded you. ¹⁸And you shall do what is right and good in the sight of the LORD, that it may go well with you, and that you may go in and take possession of the good land that the LORD swore to give to your fathers ¹⁹by thrusting out all your enemies from before you, as the LORD has promised.

²⁰"When your son asks you in time to come, 'What is the meaning of the testimonies and the statutes and the rules that the LORD our God has commanded you?' ²¹then you shall say to your son, 'We were Pharaoh's slaves in Egypt. And the LORD brought us out of Egypt with a mighty hand. ²²And the LORD showed signs and wonders, great and grievous, against Egypt and against Pharaoh and all his household, before our eyes. ²³And he brought us out from there, that he might bring us in and give us the land that he swore to give to our fathers. ²⁴And the LORD commanded us to do all these statutes, to fear the LORD our God, for our good always, that he might preserve us alive, as we are this day. ²⁵And it will be righteousness for us, if we are careful to do all this commandment before the LORD our God, as he has commanded us.'

---

[a] Or sons [b] Or just decrees; also verse 20 [c] Or The LORD our God is one LORD; or The LORD is our God, the LORD is one; or The LORD is our God, the LORD alone

A CHOSEN PEOPLE

7 "When the Lord your God brings you into the land that you are entering to take possession of it, and clears away many nations before you, the Hittites, the Girgashites, the Amorites, the Canaanites, the Perizzites, the Hivites, and the Jebusites, seven nations more numerous and mightier than you, ²and when the Lord your God gives them over to you, and you defeat them, then you must devote them to complete destruction.*a* You shall make no covenant with them and show no mercy to them. ³You shall not intermarry with them, giving your daughters to their sons or taking their daughters for your sons, ⁴for they would turn away your sons from following me, to serve other gods. Then the anger of the Lord would be kindled against you, and he would destroy you quickly. ⁵But thus shall you deal with them: you shall break down their altars and dash in pieces their pillars and chop down their Asherim and burn their carved images with fire.

⁶"For you are a people holy to the Lord your God. The Lord your God has chosen you to be a people for his treasured possession, out of all the peoples who are on the face of the earth. ⁷It was not because you were more in number than any other people that the Lord set his love on you and chose you, for you were the fewest of all peoples, ⁸but it is because the Lord loves you and is keeping the oath that he swore to your fathers, that the Lord has brought you out with a mighty hand and redeemed you from the house of slavery, from the hand of Pharaoh king of Egypt. ⁹Know therefore that the Lord your God is God, the faithful God who keeps covenant and steadfast love with those who love him and keep his commandments, to a thousand generations, ¹⁰and repays to their face those who hate him, by destroying them. He will not be slack with one who hates him. He will repay him to his face. ¹¹You shall therefore be careful to do the commandment and the statutes and the rules that I command you today.

¹²"And because you listen to these rules and keep and do them, the Lord your God will keep with you the covenant and the steadfast love that he swore to your fathers. ¹³He will love you, bless you, and multiply you. He will also bless the fruit of your womb and the fruit of your ground, your grain and your wine and your oil, the increase of your herds and the young of your flock, in the land that he swore to your fathers to give you. ¹⁴You shall be blessed above all peoples. There shall not be male or female barren among you or among your livestock. ¹⁵And the Lord will take away from you all sickness, and none of the evil diseases of Egypt, which you knew, will he inflict on you, but he will lay them on all who hate you. ¹⁶And you shall consume all the peoples that the Lord your God will give over to you. Your eye shall not pity them, neither shall you serve their gods, for that would be a snare to you.

¹⁷"If you say in your heart, 'These nations are greater than I. How can I dispossess them?' ¹⁸you shall not be afraid of them but you shall remember what the Lord your God did to Pharaoh and to all Egypt, ¹⁹the great trials that your eyes saw, the signs, the wonders, the mighty hand, and the outstretched arm, by which the Lord your God brought you out. So will the Lord your God do to all the peoples of whom you are afraid. ²⁰Moreover, the Lord your God will send hornets among them, until those who are left and hide themselves from you are destroyed. ²¹You shall not be in dread of them, for the Lord your God is in your midst, a great and awesome God. ²²The Lord your God will clear away these nations before you little by little. You may not make an end of them at once,*b* lest the wild beasts grow too numerous for you. ²³But the Lord your God will give them over to you and throw them into great confusion, until they are destroyed. ²⁴And he will give their kings into your hand, and you shall make their name perish from under heaven. No one shall be able to stand against you until you have destroyed them. ²⁵The carved images of their gods you shall burn with fire. You shall not covet the silver or the gold that is on them or take it for yourselves, lest you be ensnared by it, for it is an abomination to the Lord your God. ²⁶And you shall not bring an abominable thing into your house and become devoted to destruction*c* like it. You shall utterly detest and abhor it, for it is devoted to destruction.

REMEMBER THE LORD YOUR GOD

8 "The whole commandment that I command you today you shall be careful to do, that you may live and multiply, and go in and possess the land that the Lord

---

a That is, set apart (devote) as an offering to the Lord (for destruction)
b Or *quickly* *c* That is, set apart (devoted) as an offering to the Lord (for destruction); twice in this verse

swore to give to your fathers. ²And you shall remember the whole way that the LORD your God has led you these forty years in the wilderness, that he might humble you, testing you to know what was in your heart, whether you would keep his commandments or not. ³And he humbled you and let you hunger and fed you with manna, which you did not know, nor did your fathers know, that he might make you know that man does not live by bread alone, but man lives by every word[a] that comes from the mouth of the LORD. ⁴Your clothing did not wear out on you and your foot did not swell these forty years. ⁵Know then in your heart that, as a man disciplines his son, the LORD your God disciplines you. ⁶So you shall keep the commandments of the LORD your God by walking in his ways and by fearing him. ⁷For the LORD your God is bringing you into a good land, a land of brooks of water, of fountains and springs, flowing out in the valleys and hills, ⁸a land of wheat and barley, of vines and fig trees and pomegranates, a land of olive trees and honey, ⁹a land in which you will eat bread without scarcity, in which you will lack nothing, a land whose stones are iron, and out of whose hills you can dig copper. ¹⁰And you shall eat and be full, and you shall bless the LORD your God for the good land he has given you.

¹¹"Take care lest you forget the LORD your God by not keeping his commandments and his rules and his statutes, which I command you today, ¹²lest, when you have eaten and are full and have built good houses and live in them, ¹³and when your herds and flocks multiply and your silver and gold is multiplied and all that you have is multiplied, ¹⁴then your heart be lifted up, and you forget the LORD your God, who brought you out of the land of Egypt, out of the house of slavery, ¹⁵who led you through the great and terrifying wilderness, with its fiery serpents and scorpions and thirsty ground where there was no water, who brought you water out of the flinty rock, ¹⁶who fed you in the wilderness with manna that your fathers did not know, that he might humble you and test you, to do you good in the end. ¹⁷Beware lest you say in your heart, 'My power and the might of my hand have gained me this wealth.' ¹⁸You shall remember the LORD your God, for it is he who gives you power to get wealth, that he may confirm his covenant that he swore to your fathers, as it is this day. ¹⁹And if you forget the LORD your God and go after other gods and serve them and worship them, I solemnly warn you today that you shall surely perish. ²⁰Like the nations that the LORD makes to perish before you, so shall you perish, because you would not obey the voice of the LORD your God.

NOT BECAUSE OF RIGHTEOUSNESS

9 "Hear, O Israel: you are to cross over the Jordan today, to go in to dispossess nations greater and mightier than you, cities great and fortified up to heaven, ²a people great and tall, the sons of the Anakim, whom you know, and of whom you have heard it said, 'Who can stand before the sons of Anak?' ³Know therefore today that he who goes over before you as a consuming fire is the LORD your God. He will destroy them and subdue them before you. So you shall drive them out and make them perish quickly, as the LORD has promised you.

⁴"Do not say in your heart, after the LORD your God has thrust them out before you, 'It is because of my righteousness that the LORD has brought me in to possess this land,' whereas it is because of the wickedness of these nations that the LORD is driving them out before you. ⁵Not because of your righteousness or the uprightness of your heart are you going in to possess their land, but because of the wickedness of these nations the LORD your God is driving them out from before you, and that he may confirm the word that the LORD swore to your fathers, to Abraham, to Isaac, and to Jacob.

⁶"Know, therefore, that the LORD your God is not giving you this good land to possess because of your righteousness, for you are a stubborn people. ⁷Remember and do not forget how you provoked the LORD your God to wrath in the wilderness. From the day you came out of the land of Egypt until you came to this place, you have been rebellious against the LORD. ⁸Even at Horeb you provoked the LORD to wrath, and the LORD was so angry with you that he was ready to destroy you. ⁹When I went up the mountain to receive the tablets of stone, the tablets of the covenant that the LORD made with you, I remained on the mountain for forty days and forty nights. I neither ate bread nor drank water. ¹⁰And the LORD gave me the two tablets of stone written with the finger of God, and on them were all the words that the LORD had spoken with

---

[a] Hebrew *by all*

you on the mountain out of the midst of the fire on the day of the assembly. ¹¹And at the end of forty days and forty nights the LORD gave me the two tablets of stone, the tablets of the covenant. ¹²Then the LORD said to me, 'Arise, go down quickly from here, for your people whom you have brought from Egypt have acted corruptly. They have turned aside quickly out of the way that I commanded them; they have made themselves a metal image.'

THE GOLDEN CALF

¹³"Furthermore, the LORD said to me, 'I have seen this people, and behold, it is a stubborn people. ¹⁴Let me alone, that I may destroy them and blot out their name from under heaven. And I will make of you a nation mightier and greater than they.' ¹⁵So I turned and came down from the mountain, and the mountain was burning with fire. And the two tablets of the covenant were in my two hands. ¹⁶And I looked, and behold, you had sinned against the LORD your God. You had made yourselves a golden*ᵃ* calf. You had turned aside quickly from the way that the LORD had commanded you. ¹⁷So I took hold of the two tablets and threw them out of my two hands and broke them before your eyes. ¹⁸Then I lay prostrate before the LORD as before, for forty days and forty nights. I neither ate bread nor drank water, because of all the sin that you had committed, in doing what was evil in the sight of the LORD to provoke him to anger. ¹⁹For I was afraid of the anger and hot displeasure that the LORD bore against you, so that he was ready to destroy you. But the LORD listened to me that time also. ²⁰And the LORD was so angry with Aaron that he was ready to destroy him. And I prayed for Aaron also at the same time. ²¹Then I took the sinful thing, the calf that you had made, and burned it with fire and crushed it, grinding it very small, until it was as fine as dust. And I threw the dust of it into the brook that ran down from the mountain.

²²"At Taberah also, and at Massah and at Kibroth-hattaavah you provoked the LORD to wrath. ²³And when the LORD sent you from Kadesh-barnea, saying, 'Go up and take possession of the land that I have given you', then you rebelled against the commandment of the LORD your God and did not believe him or obey his voice. ²⁴You have been rebellious against the LORD from the day that I knew you.

²⁵"So I lay prostrate before the LORD for these forty days and forty nights, because the LORD had said he would destroy you. ²⁶And I prayed to the LORD, 'O Lord GOD, do not destroy your people and your heritage, whom you have redeemed through your greatness, whom you have brought out of Egypt with a mighty hand. ²⁷Remember your servants, Abraham, Isaac, and Jacob. Do not regard the stubbornness of this people, or their wickedness or their sin, ²⁸lest the land from which you brought us say, "Because the LORD was not able to bring them into the land that he promised them, and because he hated them, he has brought them out to put them to death in the wilderness." ²⁹For they are your people and your heritage, whom you brought out by your great power and by your outstretched arm.'

NEW TABLETS OF STONE

10 "At that time the LORD said to me, 'Cut for yourself two tablets of stone like the first, and come up to me on the mountain and make an ark of wood. ²And I will write on the tablets the words that were on the first tablets that you broke, and you shall put them in the ark.' ³So I made an ark of acacia wood, and cut two tablets of stone like the first, and went up the mountain with the two tablets in my hand. ⁴And he wrote on the tablets, in the same writing as before, the Ten Commandments*ᵇ* that the LORD had spoken to you on the mountain out of the midst of the fire on the day of the assembly. And the LORD gave them to me. ⁵Then I turned and came down from the mountain and put the tablets in the ark that I had made. And there they are, as the LORD commanded me."

⁶(The people of Israel journeyed from Beeroth Bene-jaakan*ᶜ* to Moserah. There Aaron died, and there he was buried. And his son Eleazar ministered as priest in his place. ⁷From there they journeyed to Gudgodah, and from Gudgodah to Jotbathah, a land with brooks of water. ⁸At that time the LORD set apart the tribe of Levi to carry the ark of the covenant of the LORD to stand before the LORD to minister to him and to bless in his name, to this day. ⁹Therefore Levi has no portion or inheritance with his brothers. The LORD is his inheritance, as the LORD your God said to him.)

---

*ᵃ*Hebrew *cast-metal* *ᵇ*Hebrew *the ten words* *ᶜ*Or *the wells of the Bene-jaakan*

¹⁰"I myself stayed on the mountain, as at the first time, for forty days and forty nights, and the LORD listened to me that time also. The LORD was unwilling to destroy you. ¹¹And the LORD said to me, 'Arise, go on your journey at the head of the people, so that they may go in and possess the land, which I swore to their fathers to give them.'

CIRCUMCISE YOUR HEART

¹²"And now, Israel, what does the LORD your God require of you, but to fear the LORD your God, to walk in all his ways, to love him, to serve the LORD your God with all your heart and with all your soul, ¹³and to keep the commandments and statutes of the LORD, which I am commanding you today for your good? ¹⁴Behold, to the LORD your God belong heaven and the heaven of heavens, the earth with all that is in it. ¹⁵Yet the LORD set his heart in love on your fathers and chose their offspring after them, you above all peoples, as you are this day. ¹⁶Circumcise therefore the foreskin of your heart, and be no longer stubborn. ¹⁷For the LORD your God is God of gods and Lord of lords, the great, the mighty, and the awesome God, who is not partial and takes no bribe. ¹⁸He executes justice for the fatherless and the widow, and loves the sojourner, giving him food and clothing. ¹⁹Love the sojourner, therefore, for you were sojourners in the land of Egypt. ²⁰You shall fear the LORD your God. You shall serve him and hold fast to him, and by his name you shall swear. ²¹He is your praise. He is your God, who has done for you these great and terrifying things that your eyes have seen. ²²Your fathers went down to Egypt seventy persons, and now the LORD your God has made you as numerous as the stars of heaven.

LOVE AND SERVE THE LORD

11 "You shall therefore love the LORD your God and keep his charge, his statutes, his rules, and his commandments always. ²And consider today (since I am not speaking to your children who have not known or seen it), consider the discipline*ᵃ* of the LORD your God, his greatness, his mighty hand and his outstretched arm, ³his signs and his deeds that he did in Egypt to Pharaoh the king of Egypt and to all his land, ⁴and what he did to the army of Egypt, to their horses and to their chariots, how he made the water of the Red Sea flow over them as they pursued after you, and how the LORD has destroyed them to this day, ⁵and what he did to you in the wilderness, until you came to this place, ⁶and what he did to Dathan and Abiram the sons of Eliab, son of Reuben, how the earth opened its mouth and swallowed them up, with their households, their tents, and every living thing that followed them, in the midst of all Israel. ⁷For your eyes have seen all the great work of the LORD that he did.

⁸"You shall therefore keep the whole commandment that I command you today, that you may be strong, and go in and take possession of the land that you are going over to possess, ⁹and that you may live long in the land that the LORD swore to your fathers to give to them and to their offspring, a land flowing with milk and honey. ¹⁰For the land that you are entering to take possession of it is not like the land of Egypt, from which you have come, where you sowed your seed and irrigated it,*ᵇ* like a garden of vegetables. ¹¹But the land that you are going over to possess is a land of hills and valleys, which drinks water by the rain from heaven, ¹²a land that the LORD your God cares for. The eyes of the LORD your God are always upon it, from the beginning of the year to the end of the year.

¹³"And if you will indeed obey my commandments that I command you today, to love the LORD your God, and to serve him with all your heart and with all your soul, ¹⁴he*ᶜ* will give the rain for your land in its season, the early rain and the later rain, that you may gather in your grain and your wine and your oil. ¹⁵And he will give grass in your fields for your livestock, and you shall eat and be full. ¹⁶Take care lest your heart be deceived, and you turn aside and serve other gods and worship them; ¹⁷then the anger of the LORD will be kindled against you, and he will shut up the heavens, so that there will be no rain, and the land will yield no fruit, and you will perish quickly off the good land that the LORD is giving you.

¹⁸"You shall therefore lay up these words of mine in your heart and in your soul, and you shall bind them as a sign on your hand, and they shall be as frontlets between your eyes. ¹⁹You shall teach them to your children, talking of them when you are sitting in your house, and when you are walking by the way, and when you lie down, and when you rise. ²⁰You shall write them on the doorposts of

---

*ᵃ*Or *instruction* *ᵇ*Hebrew *watered it with your feet* *ᶜ*Samaritan, Septuagint, Vulgate; Hebrew *I*; also verse 15

your house and on your gates, ²¹that your days and the days of your children may be multiplied in the land that the LORD swore to your fathers to give them, as long as the heavens are above the earth. ²²For if you will be careful to do all this commandment that I command you to do, loving the LORD your God, walking in all his ways, and holding fast to him, ²³then the LORD will drive out all these nations before you, and you will dispossess nations greater and mightier than you. ²⁴Every place on which the sole of your foot treads shall be yours. Your territory shall be from the wilderness to*ᵃ* the Lebanon and from the River, the river Euphrates, to the western sea. ²⁵No one shall be able to stand against you. The LORD your God will lay the fear of you and the dread of you on all the land that you shall tread, as he promised you.

²⁶"See, I am setting before you today a blessing and a curse: ²⁷the blessing, if you obey the commandments of the LORD your God, which I command you today, ²⁸and the curse, if you do not obey the commandments of the LORD your God, but turn aside from the way that I am commanding you today, to go after other gods that you have not known. ²⁹And when the LORD your God brings you into the land that you are entering to take possession of it, you shall set the blessing on Mount Gerizim and the curse on Mount Ebal. ³⁰Are they not beyond the Jordan, west of the road, towards the going down of the sun, in the land of the Canaanites who live in the Arabah, opposite Gilgal, beside the oak*ᵇ* of Moreh? ³¹For you are to cross over the Jordan to go in to take possession of the land that the LORD your God is giving you. And when you possess it and live in it, ³²you shall be careful to do all the statutes and the rules that I am setting before you today.

THE LORD'S CHOSEN PLACE OF WORSHIP

12 "These are the statutes and rules that you shall be careful to do in the land that the LORD, the God of your fathers, has given you to possess, all the days that you live on the earth. ²You shall surely destroy all the places where the nations whom you shall dispossess served their gods, on the high mountains and on the hills and under every green tree. ³You shall tear down their altars and dash in pieces their pillars and burn their Asherim with fire. You shall chop down the carved images of their gods and destroy their name out of that place. ⁴You shall not worship the LORD your God in that way. ⁵But you shall seek the place that the LORD your God will choose out of all your tribes to put his name and make his habitation*ᶜ* there. There you shall go, ⁶and there you shall bring your burnt offerings and your sacrifices, your tithes and the contribution that you present, your vow offerings, your freewill offerings, and the firstborn of your herd and of your flock. ⁷And there you shall eat before the LORD your God, and you shall rejoice, you and your households, in all that you undertake, in which the LORD your God has blessed you.

⁸"You shall not do according to all that we are doing here today, everyone doing whatever is right in his own eyes, ⁹for you have not as yet come to the rest and to the inheritance that the LORD your God is giving you. ¹⁰But when you go over the Jordan and live in the land that the LORD your God is giving you to inherit, and when he gives you rest from all your enemies around, so that you live in safety, ¹¹then to the place that the LORD your God will choose, to make his name dwell there, there you shall bring all that I command you: your burnt offerings and your sacrifices, your tithes and the contribution that you present, and all your finest vow offerings that you vow to the LORD. ¹²And you shall rejoice before the LORD your God, you and your sons and your daughters, your male servants and your female servants, and the Levite who is within your towns, since he has no portion or inheritance with you. ¹³Take care that you do not offer your burnt offerings at any place that you see, ¹⁴but at the place that the LORD will choose in one of your tribes, there you shall offer your burnt offerings, and there you shall do all that I am commanding you.

¹⁵"However, you may slaughter and eat meat within any of your towns, as much as you desire, according to the blessing of the LORD your God that he has given you. The unclean and the clean may eat of it, as of the gazelle and as of the deer. ¹⁶Only you shall not eat the blood; you shall pour it out on the earth like water. ¹⁷You may not eat within your towns the tithe of your grain or of your wine or of your oil, or the firstborn of your herd or of your flock, or any of your vow offerings that you vow, or your freewill offerings or the contribution that you present,

---
*ᵃ*Hebrew *and* *ᵇ*Septuagint, Syriac; see Genesis 12:6. Hebrew *oaks*, or *terebinths* *ᶜ*Or *name as its habitation*

18but you shall eat them before the Lord your God in the place that the Lord your God will choose, you and your son and your daughter, your male servant and your female servant, and the Levite who is within your towns. And you shall rejoice before the Lord your God in all that you undertake. 19Take care that you do not neglect the Levite as long as you live in your land.

20"When the Lord your God enlarges your territory, as he has promised you, and you say, 'I will eat meat', because you crave meat, you may eat meat whenever you desire. 21If the place that the Lord your God will choose to put his name there is too far from you, then you may kill any of your herd or your flock, which the Lord has given you, as I have commanded you, and you may eat within your towns whenever you desire. 22Just as the gazelle or the deer is eaten, so you may eat of it. The unclean and the clean alike may eat of it. 23Only be sure that you do not eat the blood, for the blood is the life, and you shall not eat the life with the flesh. 24You shall not eat it; you shall pour it out on the earth like water. 25You shall not eat it, that all may go well with you and with your children after you, when you do what is right in the sight of the Lord. 26But the holy things that are due from you, and your vow offerings, you shall take, and you shall go to the place that the Lord will choose, 27and offer your burnt offerings, the flesh and the blood, on the altar of the Lord your God. The blood of your sacrifices shall be poured out on the altar of the Lord your God, but the flesh you may eat. 28Be careful to obey all these words that I command you, that it may go well with you and with your children after you for ever, when you do what is good and right in the sight of the Lord your God.

WARNING AGAINST IDOLATRY

29"When the Lord your God cuts off before you the nations whom you go in to dispossess, and you dispossess them and dwell in their land, 30take care that you are not ensnared to follow them, after they have been destroyed before you, and that you do not enquire about their gods, saying, 'How did these nations serve their gods?—that I also may do the same.' 31You shall not worship the Lord your God in that way, for every abominable thing that the Lord hates they have done for their gods, for they even burn their sons and their daughters in the fire to their gods.

32a "Everything that I command you, you shall be careful to do. You shall not add to it or take from it.

13 "If a prophet or a dreamer of dreams arises among you and gives you a sign or a wonder, 2and the sign or wonder that he tells you comes to pass, and if he says, 'Let us go after other gods', which you have not known, 'and let us serve them', 3you shall not listen to the words of that prophet or that dreamer of dreams. For the Lord your God is testing you, to know whether you love the Lord your God with all your heart and with all your soul. 4You shall walk after the Lord your God and fear him and keep his commandments and obey his voice, and you shall serve him and hold fast to him. 5But that prophet or that dreamer of dreams shall be put to death, because he has taught rebellion against the Lord your God, who brought you out of the land of Egypt and redeemed you out of the house of slavery, to make you leave the way in which the Lord your God commanded you to walk. So you shall purge the evil[b] from your midst.

6"If your brother, the son of your mother, or your son or your daughter or the wife you embrace[c] or your friend who is as your own soul entices you secretly, saying, 'Let us go and serve other gods', which neither you nor your fathers have known, 7some of the gods of the peoples who are around you, whether near you or far off from you, from one end of the earth to the other, 8you shall not yield to him or listen to him, nor shall your eye pity him, nor shall you spare him, nor shall you conceal him. 9But you shall kill him. Your hand shall be first against him to put him to death, and afterwards the hand of all the people. 10You shall stone him to death with stones, because he sought to draw you away from the Lord your God, who brought you out of the land of Egypt, out of the house of slavery. 11And all Israel shall hear and fear and never again do any such wickedness as this among you.

12"If you hear in one of your cities, which the Lord your God is giving you to dwell there, 13that certain worthless fellows have gone out among you and have drawn away the inhabitants of their city, saying, 'Let us go and serve other gods', which you have not known, 14then you shall enquire and make search and ask diligently. And behold, if it is

---

[a]Ch 13:1 in Hebrew   [b]Or evil person   [c]Hebrew the wife of your bosom

true and certain that such an abomination has been done among you, ¹⁵you shall surely put the inhabitants of that city to the sword, devoting it to destruction,ᵃ all who are in it and its cattle, with the edge of the sword. ¹⁶You shall gather all its spoil into the midst of its open square and burn the city and all its spoil with fire, as a whole burnt offering to the LORD your God. It shall be a heap for ever. It shall not be built again. ¹⁷None of the devoted things shall stick to your hand, that the LORD may turn from the fierceness of his anger and show you mercy and have compassion on you and multiply you, as he swore to your fathers, ¹⁸if you obey the voice of the LORD your God, keeping all his commandments that I am commanding you today, and doing what is right in the sight of the LORD your God.

CLEAN AND UNCLEAN FOOD

14 "You are the sons of the LORD your God. You shall not cut yourselves or make any baldness on your foreheads for the dead. ²For you are a people holy to the LORD your God, and the LORD has chosen you to be a people for his treasured possession, out of all the peoples who are on the face of the earth.

³"You shall not eat any abomination. ⁴These are the animals you may eat: the ox, the sheep, the goat, ⁵the deer, the gazelle, the roebuck, the wild goat, the ibex,ᵇ the antelope, and the mountain sheep. ⁶Every animal that parts the hoof and has the hoof cloven in two and chews the cud, among the animals, you may eat. ⁷Yet of those that chew the cud or have the hoof cloven you shall not eat these: the camel, the hare, and the rock badger, because they chew the cud but do not part the hoof, are unclean for you. ⁸And the pig, because it parts the hoof but does not chew the cud, is unclean for you. Their flesh you shall not eat, and their carcasses you shall not touch.

⁹"Of all that are in the waters you may eat these: whatever has fins and scales you may eat. ¹⁰And whatever does not have fins and scales you shall not eat; it is unclean for you.

¹¹"You may eat all clean birds. ¹²But these are the ones that you shall not eat: the eagle,ᶜ the bearded vulture, the black vulture, ¹³the kite, the falcon of any kind; ¹⁴every raven of any kind; ¹⁵the ostrich, the nighthawk, the seagull, the hawk of any kind; ¹⁶the little owl and the short-eared owl, the barn owl ¹⁷and the tawny owl, the carrion vulture and the cormorant, ¹⁸the stork, the heron of any kind; the hoopoe and the bat. ¹⁹And all winged insects are unclean for you; they shall not be eaten. ²⁰All clean winged things you may eat.

²¹"You shall not eat anything that has died naturally. You may give it to the sojourner who is within your towns, that he may eat it, or you may sell it to a foreigner. For you are a people holy to the LORD your God.

"You shall not boil a young goat in its mother's milk.

TITHES

²²"You shall tithe all the yield of your seed that comes from the field year by year. ²³And before the LORD your God, in the place that he will choose, to make his name dwell there, you shall eat the tithe of your grain, of your wine, and of your oil, and the firstborn of your herd and flock, that you may learn to fear the LORD your God always. ²⁴And if the way is too long for you, so that you are not able to carry the tithe, when the LORD your God blesses you, because the place is too far from you, which the LORD your God chooses, to set his name there, ²⁵then you shall turn it into money and bind up the money in your hand and go to the place that the LORD your God chooses ²⁶and spend the money for whatever you desire—oxen or sheep or wine or strong drink, whatever your appetite craves. And you shall eat there before the LORD your God and rejoice, you and your household. ²⁷And you shall not neglect the Levite who is within your towns, for he has no portion or inheritance with you.

²⁸"At the end of every three years you shall bring out all the tithe of your produce in the same year and lay it up within your towns. ²⁹And the Levite, because he has no portion or inheritance with you, and the sojourner, the fatherless, and the widow, who are within your towns, shall come and eat and be filled, that the LORD your God may bless you in all the work of your hands that you do.

THE SABBATICAL YEAR

15 "At the end of every seven years you shall grant a release. ²And this is the manner of the release: every creditor shall release what he has lent to his neighbour. He shall not exact it of his neighbour,

---

ᵃThat is, setting apart (devoting) as an offering to the Lord (for destruction) ᵇOr *addax* ᶜThe identity of many of these birds is uncertain

his brother, because the LORD's release has been proclaimed. ³Of a foreigner you may exact it, but whatever of yours is with your brother your hand shall release. ⁴But there will be no poor among you; for the LORD will bless you in the land that the LORD your God is giving you for an inheritance to possess— ⁵if only you will strictly obey the voice of the LORD your God, being careful to do all this commandment that I command you today. ⁶For the LORD your God will bless you, as he promised you, and you shall lend to many nations, but you shall not borrow, and you shall rule over many nations, but they shall not rule over you.

⁷"If among you, one of your brothers should become poor, in any of your towns within your land that the LORD your God is giving you, you shall not harden your heart or shut your hand against your poor brother, ⁸but you shall open your hand to him and lend him sufficient for his need, whatever it may be. ⁹Take care lest there be an unworthy thought in your heart and you say, 'The seventh year, the year of release is near', and your eye look grudgingly[a] on your poor brother, and you give him nothing, and he cry to the LORD against you, and you be guilty of sin. ¹⁰You shall give to him freely, and your heart shall not be grudging when you give to him, because for this the LORD your God will bless you in all your work and in all that you undertake. ¹¹For there will never cease to be poor in the land. Therefore I command you, 'You shall open wide your hand to your brother, to the needy and to the poor, in your land.'

¹²"If your brother, a Hebrew man or a Hebrew woman, is sold[b] to you, he shall serve you for six years, and in the seventh year you shall let him go free from you. ¹³And when you let him go free from you, you shall not let him go empty-handed. ¹⁴You shall furnish him liberally out of your flock, out of your threshing floor, and out of your wine press. As the LORD your God has blessed you, you shall give to him. ¹⁵You shall remember that you were a slave in the land of Egypt, and the LORD your God redeemed you; therefore I command you this today. ¹⁶But if he says to you, 'I will not go out from you,' because he loves you and your household, since he is well off with you, ¹⁷then you shall take an awl, and put it through his ear into the door, and he shall be your slave[c] for ever. And to your female slave[d] you shall do the same. ¹⁸It shall not seem hard to you when you let him go free from you, for at half the cost of a hired worker he has served you for six years. So the LORD your God will bless you in all that you do.

¹⁹"All the firstborn males that are born of your herd and flock you shall dedicate to the LORD your God. You shall do no work with the firstborn of your herd, nor shear the firstborn of your flock. ²⁰You shall eat it, you and your household, before the LORD your God year by year at the place that the LORD will choose. ²¹But if it has any blemish, if it is lame or blind or has any serious blemish whatever, you shall not sacrifice it to the LORD your God. ²²You shall eat it within your towns. The unclean and the clean alike may eat it, as though it were a gazelle or a deer. ²³Only you shall not eat its blood; you shall pour it out on the ground like water.

PASSOVER

16 "Observe the month of Abib and keep the Passover to the LORD your God, for in the month of Abib the LORD your God brought you out of Egypt by night. ²And you shall offer the Passover sacrifice to the LORD your God, from the flock or the herd, at the place that the LORD will choose, to make his name dwell there. ³You shall eat no leavened bread with it. For seven days you shall eat it with unleavened bread, the bread of affliction—for you came out of the land of Egypt in haste—that all the days of your life you may remember the day when you came out of the land of Egypt. ⁴No leaven shall be seen with you in all your territory for seven days, nor shall any of the flesh that you sacrifice on the evening of the first day remain all night until morning. ⁵You may not offer the Passover sacrifice within any of your towns that the LORD your God is giving you, ⁶but at the place that the LORD your God will choose, to make his name dwell in it, there you shall offer the Passover sacrifice, in the evening at sunset, at the time you came out of Egypt. ⁷And you shall cook it and eat it at the place that the LORD your God will choose. And in the morning you shall turn and go to your tents. ⁸For six days you shall eat unleavened bread, and on the seventh day there shall be a solemn assembly to the LORD your God. You shall do no work on it.

---

[a] Or *be evil*; also verse 10 [b] Or *sells himself* [c] Or *servant*; the Hebrew term *'ebed* designates a range of social and economic roles (see Preface) [d] Or *servant*

THE FEAST OF WEEKS

⁹"You shall count seven weeks. Begin to count the seven weeks from the time the sickle is first put to the standing corn. ¹⁰Then you shall keep the Feast of Weeks to the LORD your God with the tribute of a freewill offering from your hand, which you shall give as the LORD your God blesses you. ¹¹And you shall rejoice before the LORD your God, you and your son and your daughter, your male servant and your female servant, the Levite who is within your towns, the sojourner, the fatherless, and the widow who are among you, at the place that the LORD your God will choose, to make his name dwell there. ¹²You shall remember that you were a slave in Egypt; and you shall be careful to observe these statutes.

THE FEAST OF BOOTHS

¹³"You shall keep the Feast of Booths for seven days, when you have gathered in the produce from your threshing floor and your wine press. ¹⁴You shall rejoice in your feast, you and your son and your daughter, your male servant and your female servant, the Levite, the sojourner, the fatherless, and the widow who are within your towns. ¹⁵For seven days you shall keep the feast to the LORD your God at the place that the LORD will choose, because the LORD your God will bless you in all your produce and in all the work of your hands, so that you will be altogether joyful.

¹⁶"Three times a year all your males shall appear before the LORD your God at the place that he will choose: at the Feast of Unleavened Bread, at the Feast of Weeks, and at the Feast of Booths. They shall not appear before the LORD empty-handed. ¹⁷Every man shall give as he is able, according to the blessing of the LORD your God that he has given you.

JUSTICE

¹⁸"You shall appoint judges and officers in all your towns that the LORD your God is giving you, according to your tribes, and they shall judge the people with righteous judgement. ¹⁹You shall not pervert justice. You shall not show partiality, and you shall not accept a bribe, for a bribe blinds the eyes of the wise and subverts the cause of the righteous. ²⁰Justice, and only justice, you shall follow, that you may live and inherit the land that the LORD your God is giving you.

FORBIDDEN FORMS OF WORSHIP

²¹"You shall not plant any tree as an Asherah beside the altar of the LORD your God that you shall make. ²²And you shall not set up a pillar, which the LORD your God hates.

17 "You shall not sacrifice to the LORD your God an ox or a sheep in which is a blemish, any defect whatever, for that is an abomination to the LORD your God.

²"If there is found among you, within any of your towns that the LORD your God is giving you, a man or woman who does what is evil in the sight of the LORD your God, in transgressing his covenant, ³and has gone and served other gods and worshipped them, or the sun or the moon or any of the host of heaven, which I have forbidden, ⁴and it is told you and you hear of it, then you shall enquire diligently, and if it is true and certain that such an abomination has been done in Israel, ⁵then you shall bring out to your gates that man or woman who has done this evil thing, and you shall stone that man or woman to death with stones. ⁶On the evidence of two witnesses or of three witnesses the one who is to die shall be put to death; a person shall not be put to death on the evidence of one witness. ⁷The hand of the witnesses shall be first against him to put him to death, and afterwards the hand of all the people. So you shall purge[a] the evil[b] from your midst.

LEGAL DECISIONS BY PRIESTS AND JUDGES

⁸"If any case arises requiring decision between one kind of homicide and another, one kind of legal right and another, or one kind of assault and another, any case within your towns that is too difficult for you, then you shall arise and go up to the place that the LORD your God will choose. ⁹And you shall come to the Levitical priests and to the judge who is in office in those days, and you shall consult them, and they shall declare to you the decision. ¹⁰Then you shall do according to what they declare to you from that place that the LORD will choose. And you shall be careful to do according to all that they direct you. ¹¹According to the instructions that they give you, and according to the decision which they pronounce to you, you shall do. You shall not turn aside from the verdict that they declare to you, either to the right hand or to the left. ¹²The man who acts presumptuously by not obeying the priest who

---

[a]Septuagint *drive out*; also verse 12 [b]Or *evil person*; also verse 12

stands to minister there before the LORD your God, or the judge, that man shall die. So you shall purge the evil from Israel. ¹³And all the people shall hear and fear and not act presumptuously again.

LAWS CONCERNING ISRAEL'S KINGS

¹⁴"When you come to the land that the LORD your God is giving you, and you possess it and dwell in it and then say, 'I will set a king over me, like all the nations that are around me', ¹⁵you may indeed set a king over you whom the LORD your God will choose. One from among your brothers you shall set as king over you. You may not put a foreigner over you, who is not your brother. ¹⁶Only he must not acquire many horses for himself or cause the people to return to Egypt in order to acquire many horses, since the LORD has said to you, 'You shall never return that way again.' ¹⁷And he shall not acquire many wives for himself, lest his heart turn away, nor shall he acquire for himself excessive silver and gold. ¹⁸"And when he sits on the throne of his kingdom, he shall write for himself in a book a copy of this law, approved by[a] the Levitical priests. ¹⁹And it shall be with him, and he shall read in it all the days of his life, that he may learn to fear the LORD his God by keeping all the words of this law and these statutes, and doing them, ²⁰that his heart may not be lifted up above his brothers, and that he may not turn aside from the commandment, either to the right hand or to the left, so that he may continue long in his kingdom, he and his children, in Israel.

PROVISION FOR PRIESTS AND LEVITES

18 "The Levitical priests, all the tribe of Levi, shall have no portion or inheritance with Israel. They shall eat the LORD's food offerings[b] as their[c] inheritance. ²They shall have no inheritance among their brothers; the LORD is their inheritance, as he promised them. ³And this shall be the priests' due from the people, from those offering a sacrifice, whether an ox or a sheep: they shall give to the priest the shoulder and the two cheeks and the stomach. ⁴The firstfruits of your grain, of your wine and of your oil, and the first fleece of your sheep, you shall give him. ⁵For the LORD your God has chosen him out of all your tribes to stand and minister in the name of the LORD, him and his sons for all time.

⁶"And if a Levite comes from any of your towns out of all Israel, where he lives—and he may come when he desires[d]—to the place that the LORD will choose, ⁷and ministers in the name of the LORD his God, like all his fellow Levites who stand to minister there before the LORD, ⁸then he may have equal portions to eat, besides what he receives from the sale of his patrimony.[e]

ABOMINABLE PRACTICES

⁹"When you come into the land that the LORD your God is giving you, you shall not learn to follow the abominable practices of those nations. ¹⁰There shall not be found among you anyone who burns his son or his daughter as an offering,[f] anyone who practises divination or tells fortunes or interprets omens, or a sorcerer ¹¹or a charmer or a medium or a necromancer or one who enquires of the dead, ¹²for whoever does these things is an abomination to the LORD. And because of these abominations the LORD your God is driving them out before you. ¹³You shall be blameless before the LORD your God, ¹⁴for these nations, which you are about to dispossess, listen to fortune-tellers and to diviners. But as for you, the LORD your God has not allowed you to do this.

A NEW PROPHET LIKE MOSES

¹⁵"The LORD your God will raise up for you a prophet like me from among you, from your brothers—it is to him you shall listen— ¹⁶just as you desired of the LORD your God at Horeb on the day of the assembly, when you said, 'Let me not hear again the voice of the LORD my God or see this great fire any more, lest I die.' ¹⁷And the LORD said to me, 'They are right in what they have spoken. ¹⁸I will raise up for them a prophet like you from among their brothers. And I will put my words in his mouth, and he shall speak to them all that I command him. ¹⁹And whoever will not listen to my words that he shall speak in my name, I myself will require it of him. ²⁰But the prophet who presumes to speak a word in my name that I have not commanded him to speak, or[g] who speaks in the name of other gods, that same prophet shall die.' ²¹And if you say in your heart, 'How may we know the word that the LORD has

---

[a] Hebrew *from before* [b] Or *the offerings by fire to the LORD* [c] Hebrew *his* [d] Or *lives—if he comes enthusiastically* [e] The meaning of the Hebrew is uncertain [f] Hebrew *makes his son or his daughter pass through the fire* [g] Or *and*

not spoken?'— ²²when a prophet speaks in the name of the LORD, if the word does not come to pass or come true, that is a word that the LORD has not spoken; the prophet has spoken it presumptuously. You need not be afraid of him.

LAWS CONCERNING CITIES OF REFUGE

19 "When the LORD your God cuts off the nations whose land the LORD your God is giving you, and you dispossess them and dwell in their cities and in their houses, ²you shall set apart three cities for yourselves in the land that the LORD your God is giving you to possess. ³You shall measure the distances^a and divide into three parts the area of the land that the LORD your God gives you as a possession, so that any manslayer can flee to them.

⁴"This is the provision for the manslayer, who by fleeing there may save his life. If anyone kills his neighbour unintentionally without having hated him in the past— ⁵as when someone goes into the forest with his neighbour to cut wood, and his hand swings the axe to cut down a tree, and the head slips from the handle and strikes his neighbour so that he dies—he may flee to one of these cities and live, ⁶lest the avenger of blood in hot anger pursue the manslayer and overtake him, because the way is long, and strike him fatally, though the man did not deserve to die, since he had not hated his neighbour in the past. ⁷Therefore I command you, You shall set apart three cities. ⁸And if the LORD your God enlarges your territory, as he has sworn to your fathers, and gives you all the land that he promised to give to your fathers— ⁹provided you are careful to keep all this commandment, which I command you today, by loving the LORD your God and by walking ever in his ways—then you shall add three other cities to these three, ¹⁰lest innocent blood be shed in your land that the LORD your God is giving you for an inheritance, and so the guilt of bloodshed be upon you.

¹¹"But if anyone hates his neighbour and lies in wait for him and attacks him and strikes him fatally so that he dies, and he flees into one of these cities, ¹²then the elders of his city shall send and take him from there, and hand him over to the avenger of blood, so that he may die. ¹³Your eye shall not pity him, but you shall purge the guilt of innocent blood^b from Israel, so that it may be well with you.

PROPERTY BOUNDARIES

¹⁴"You shall not move your neighbour's landmark, which the men of old have set, in the inheritance that you will hold in the land that the LORD your God is giving you to possess.

LAWS CONCERNING WITNESSES

¹⁵"A single witness shall not suffice against a person for any crime or for any wrong in connection with any offence that he has committed. Only on the evidence of two witnesses or of three witnesses shall a charge be established. ¹⁶If a malicious witness arises to accuse a person of wrongdoing, ¹⁷then both parties to the dispute shall appear before the LORD, before the priests and the judges who are in office in those days. ¹⁸The judges shall enquire diligently, and if the witness is a false witness and has accused his brother falsely, ¹⁹then you shall do to him as he had meant to do to his brother. So you shall purge the evil^c from your midst. ²⁰And the rest shall hear and fear, and shall never again commit any such evil among you. ²¹Your eye shall not pity. It shall be life for life, eye for eye, tooth for tooth, hand for hand, foot for foot.

LAWS CONCERNING WARFARE

20 "When you go out to war against your enemies, and see horses and chariots and an army larger than your own, you shall not be afraid of them, for the LORD your God is with you, who brought you up out of the land of Egypt. ²And when you draw near to the battle, the priest shall come forward and speak to the people ³and shall say to them, 'Hear, O Israel, today you are drawing near for battle against your enemies: let not your heart faint. Do not fear or panic or be in dread of them, ⁴for the LORD your God is he who goes with you to fight for you against your enemies, to give you the victory.' ⁵Then the officers shall speak to the people, saying, 'Is there any man who has built a new house and has not dedicated it? Let him go back to his house, lest he die in the battle and another man dedicate it. ⁶And is there any man who has planted a vineyard and has not enjoyed its fruit? Let him go back to his house, lest he die in the battle and another man enjoy its fruit. ⁷And is there any man who has betrothed a wife and has not taken her? Let him go back to his

---

^{a}Hebrew road ^{b}Or the blood of the innocent ^{c}Or evil person

house, lest he die in the battle and another man take her.' ⁸And the officers shall speak further to the people, and say, 'Is there any man who is fearful and faint-hearted? Let him go back to his house, lest he make the heart of his fellows melt like his own.' ⁹And when the officers have finished speaking to the people, then commanders shall be appointed at the head of the people.

¹⁰"When you draw near to a city to fight against it, offer terms of peace to it. ¹¹And if it responds to you peaceably and it opens to you, then all the people who are found in it shall do forced labour for you and shall serve you. ¹²But if it makes no peace with you, but makes war against you, then you shall besiege it. ¹³And when the LORD your God gives it into your hand, you shall put all its males to the sword, ¹⁴but the women and the little ones, the livestock, and everything else in the city, all its spoil, you shall take as plunder for yourselves. And you shall enjoy the spoil of your enemies, which the LORD your God has given you. ¹⁵Thus you shall do to all the cities that are very far from you, which are not cities of the nations here. ¹⁶But in the cities of these peoples that the LORD your God is giving you for an inheritance, you shall save alive nothing that breathes, ¹⁷but you shall devote them to complete destruction,ᵃ the Hittites and the Amorites, the Canaanites and the Perizzites, the Hivites and the Jebusites, as the LORD your God has commanded, ¹⁸that they may not teach you to do according to all their abominable practices that they have done for their gods, and so you sin against the LORD your God.

¹⁹"When you besiege a city for a long time, making war against it in order to take it, you shall not destroy its trees by wielding an axe against them. You may eat from them, but you shall not cut them down. Are the trees in the field human, that they should be besieged by you? ²⁰Only the trees that you know are not trees for food you may destroy and cut down, that you may build siege works against the city that makes war with you, until it falls.

ATONEMENT FOR UNSOLVED MURDERS

21 "If in the land that the LORD your God is giving you to possess someone is found slain, lying in the open country, and it is not known who killed him, ²then your elders and your judges shall come out, and they shall measure the distance to the surrounding cities. ³And the elders of the city that is nearest to the slain man shall take a heifer that has never been worked and that has not pulled in a yoke. ⁴And the elders of that city shall bring the heifer down to a valley with running water, which is neither ploughed nor sown, and shall break the heifer's neck there in the valley. ⁵Then the priests, the sons of Levi, shall come forward, for the LORD your God has chosen them to minister to him and to bless in the name of the LORD, and by their word every dispute and every assault shall be settled. ⁶And all the elders of that city nearest to the slain man shall wash their hands over the heifer whose neck was broken in the valley, ⁷and they shall testify, 'Our hands did not shed this blood, nor did our eyes see it shed. ⁸Accept atonement, O LORD, for your people Israel, whom you have redeemed, and do not set the guilt of innocent blood in the midst of your people Israel, so that their bloodguilt may be atoned for.' ⁹So you shall purge the guilt of innocent blood from your midst, when you do what is right in the sight of the LORD.

MARRYING FEMALE CAPTIVES

¹⁰"When you go out to war against your enemies, and the LORD your God gives them into your hand and you take them captive, ¹¹and you see among the captives a beautiful woman, and you desire to take her to be your wife, ¹²and you bring her home to your house, she shall shave her head and pare her nails. ¹³And she shall take off the clothes in which she was captured and shall remain in your house and lament her father and her mother for a full month. After that you may go in to her and be her husband, and she shall be your wife. ¹⁴But if you no longer delight in her, you shall let her go where she wants. But you shall not sell her for money, nor shall you treat her as a slave, since you have humiliated her.

INHERITANCE RIGHTS OF THE FIRSTBORN

¹⁵"If a man has two wives, one loved and the other unloved, and both the loved and the unloved have borne him children, and if the firstborn son belongs to the unloved,ᵇ ¹⁶then on the day when he assigns his possessions as an inheritance to his sons, he may not treat the son of the loved as the firstborn in preference to the son of the unloved, who is

---

ᵃThat is, set apart (devote) as an offering to the Lord (for destruction)
ᵇOr *hated*; also verses 16, 17

the firstborn, ¹⁷but he shall acknowledge the firstborn, the son of the unloved, by giving him a double portion of all that he has, for he is the firstfruits of his strength. The right of the firstborn is his.

A REBELLIOUS SON

¹⁸"If a man has a stubborn and rebellious son who will not obey the voice of his father or the voice of his mother, and, though they discipline him, will not listen to them, ¹⁹then his father and his mother shall take hold of him and bring him out to the elders of his city at the gate of the place where he lives, ²⁰and they shall say to the elders of his city, 'This our son is stubborn and rebellious; he will not obey our voice; he is a glutton and a drunkard.' ²¹Then all the men of the city shall stone him to death with stones. So you shall purge the evil from your midst, and all Israel shall hear, and fear.

A MAN HANGED ON A TREE IS CURSED

²²"And if a man has committed a crime punishable by death and he is put to death, and you hang him on a tree, ²³his body shall not remain all night on the tree, but you shall bury him the same day, for a hanged man is cursed by God. You shall not defile your land that the LORD your God is giving you for an inheritance.

VARIOUS LAWS

22 "You shall not see your brother's ox or his sheep going astray and ignore them. You shall take them back to your brother. ²And if he does not live near you and you do not know who he is, you shall bring it home to your house, and it shall stay with you until your brother seeks it. Then you shall restore it to him. ³And you shall do the same with his donkey or with his garment, or with any lost thing of your brother's, which he loses and you find; you may not ignore it. ⁴You shall not see your brother's donkey or his ox fallen down by the way and ignore them. You shall help him to lift them up again.

⁵"A woman shall not wear a man's garment, nor shall a man put on a woman's cloak, for whoever does these things is an abomination to the LORD your God.

⁶"If you come across a bird's nest in any tree or on the ground, with young ones or eggs and the mother sitting on the young or on the eggs, you shall not take the mother with the young. ⁷You shall let the mother go, but the young you may take for yourself, that it may go well with you, and that you may live long.

⁸"When you build a new house, you shall make a parapet for your roof, that you may not bring the guilt of blood upon your house, if anyone should fall from it.

⁹"You shall not sow your vineyard with two kinds of seed, lest the whole yield be forfeited,ᵃ the crop that you have sown and the yield of the vineyard. ¹⁰You shall not plough with an ox and a donkey together. ¹¹You shall not wear cloth of wool and linen mixed together.

¹²"You shall make yourself tassels on the four corners of the garment with which you cover yourself.

LAWS CONCERNING SEXUAL IMMORALITY

¹³"If any man takes a wife and goes in to her and then hates her ¹⁴and accuses her of misconduct and brings a bad name upon her, saying, 'I took this woman, and when I came near her, I did not find in her evidence of virginity,' ¹⁵then the father of the young woman and her mother shall take and bring out the evidence of her virginity to the elders of the city in the gate. ¹⁶And the father of the young woman shall say to the elders, 'I gave my daughter to this man to marry, and he hates her; ¹⁷and behold, he has accused her of misconduct, saying, "I did not find in your daughter evidence of virginity." And yet this is the evidence of my daughter's virginity.' And they shall spread the cloak before the elders of the city. ¹⁸Then the elders of that city shall take the man and whipᵇ him, ¹⁹and they shall fine him a hundred shekelsᶜ of silver and give them to the father of the young woman, because he has brought a bad name upon a virginᵈ of Israel. And she shall be his wife. He may not divorce her all his days. ²⁰But if the thing is true, that evidence of virginity was not found in the young woman, ²¹then they shall bring out the young woman to the door of her father's house, and the men of her city shall stone her to death with stones, because she has done an outrageous thing in Israel by whoring in her father's house. So you shall purge the evil from your midst.

²²"If a man is found lying with the wife of another man, both of them shall die, the man who lay with the woman, and the woman. So you shall purge the evil from Israel.

ᵃHebrew *become holy* ᵇOr *discipline* ᶜA *shekel* was about 2/5 of an ounce or 11 grams ᵈOr *girl of marriageable age*

²³"If there is a betrothed virgin, and a man meets her in the city and lies with her, ²⁴then you shall bring them both out to the gate of that city, and you shall stone them to death with stones, the young woman because she did not cry for help though she was in the city, and the man because he violated his neighbour's wife. So you shall purge the evil from your midst.

²⁵"But if in the open country a man meets a young woman who is betrothed, and the man seizes her and lies with her, then only the man who lay with her shall die. ²⁶But you shall do nothing to the young woman; she has committed no offence punishable by death. For this case is like that of a man attacking and murdering his neighbour, ²⁷because he met her in the open country, and though the betrothed young woman cried for help there was no one to rescue her.

²⁸"If a man meets a virgin who is not betrothed, and seizes her and lies with her, and they are found, ²⁹then the man who lay with her shall give to the father of the young woman fifty shekels of silver, and she shall be his wife, because he has violated her. He may not divorce her all his days.

³⁰ᵃ"A man shall not take his father's wife, so that he does not uncover his father's nakedness.ᵇ

THOSE EXCLUDED FROM THE ASSEMBLY

23 "No one whose testicles are crushed or whose male organ is cut off shall enter the assembly of the LORD.

²"No one born of a forbidden union may enter the assembly of the LORD. Even to the tenth generation, none of his descendants may enter the assembly of the LORD.

³"No Ammonite or Moabite may enter the assembly of the LORD. Even to the tenth generation, none of them may enter the assembly of the LORD for ever, ⁴because they did not meet you with bread and with water on the way, when you came out of Egypt, and because they hired against you Balaam the son of Beor from Pethor of Mesopotamia, to curse you. ⁵But the LORD your God would not listen to Balaam; instead the LORD your God turned the curse into a blessing for you, because the LORD your God loved you. ⁶You shall not seek their peace or their prosperity all your days for ever.

⁷"You shall not abhor an Edomite, for he is your brother. You shall not abhor an Egyptian, because you were a sojourner in his land. ⁸Children born to them in the third generation may enter the assembly of the LORD.

UNCLEANNESS IN THE CAMP

⁹"When you are encamped against your enemies, then you shall keep yourself from every evil thing.

¹⁰"If any man among you becomes unclean because of a nocturnal emission, then he shall go outside the camp. He shall not come inside the camp, ¹¹but when evening comes, he shall bathe himself in water, and as the sun sets, he may come inside the camp.

¹²"You shall have a place outside the camp, and you shall go out to it. ¹³And you shall have a trowel with your tools, and when you sit down outside, you shall dig a hole with it and turn back and cover up your excrement. ¹⁴Because the LORD your God walks in the midst of your camp, to deliver you and to give up your enemies before you, therefore your camp must be holy, so that he may not see anything indecent among you and turn away from you.

MISCELLANEOUS LAWS

¹⁵"You shall not give up to his master a slaveᶜ who has escaped from his master to you. ¹⁶He shall dwell with you, in your midst, in the place that he shall choose within one of your towns, wherever it suits him. You shall not wrong him.

¹⁷"None of the daughters of Israel shall be a cult prostitute, and none of the sons of Israel shall be a cult prostitute. ¹⁸You shall not bring the fee of a prostitute or the wages of a dogᵈ into the house of the LORD your God in payment for any vow, for both of these are an abomination to the LORD your God.

¹⁹"You shall not charge interest on loans to your brother, interest on money, interest on food, interest on anything that is lent for interest. ²⁰You may charge a foreigner interest, but you may not charge your brother interest, that the LORD your God may bless you in all that you undertake in the land that you are entering to take possession of it.

²¹"If you make a vow to the LORD your God, you shall not delay fulfilling it, for the LORD your God will surely require it of you, and you will be guilty of sin. ²²But if you refrain from vowing, you will not be guilty

---

ᵃCh 23:1 in Hebrew ᵇHebrew *uncover his father's skirt* ᶜOr *servant*; the Hebrew term *'ebed* designates a range of social and economic roles (see Preface) ᵈOr *male prostitute*

of sin. ²³You shall be careful to do what has passed your lips, for you have voluntarily vowed to the LORD your God what you have promised with your mouth.

²⁴"If you go into your neighbour's vineyard, you may eat your fill of grapes, as many as you wish, but you shall not put any in your bag. ²⁵If you go into your neighbour's standing corn, you may pluck the ears with your hand, but you shall not put a sickle to your neighbour's standing corn.

LAWS CONCERNING DIVORCE

24 "When a man takes a wife and marries her, if then she finds no favour in his eyes because he has found some indecency in her, and he writes her a certificate of divorce and puts it in her hand and sends her out of his house, and she departs out of his house, ²and if she goes and becomes another man's wife, ³and the latter man hates her and writes her a certificate of divorce and puts it in her hand and sends her out of his house, or if the latter man dies, who took her to be his wife, ⁴then her former husband, who sent her away, may not take her again to be his wife, after she has been defiled, for that is an abomination before the LORD. And you shall not bring sin upon the land that the LORD your God is giving you for an inheritance.

MISCELLANEOUS LAWS

⁵"When a man is newly married, he shall not go out with the army or be liable for any other public duty. He shall be free at home for one year to be happy with his wife*ᵃ* whom he has taken.

⁶"No one shall take a mill or an upper millstone in pledge, for that would be taking a life in pledge.

⁷"If a man is found stealing one of his brothers of the people of Israel, and if he treats him as a slave or sells him, then that thief shall die. So you shall purge the evil from your midst.

⁸"Take care, in a case of leprous*ᵇ* disease, to be very careful to do according to all that the Levitical priests shall direct you. As I commanded them, so you shall be careful to do. ⁹Remember what the LORD your God did to Miriam on the way as you came out of Egypt.

¹⁰"When you make your neighbour a loan of any sort, you shall not go into his house to collect his pledge. ¹¹You shall stand outside, and the man to whom you make the loan shall bring the pledge out to you. ¹²And if he is a poor man, you shall not sleep in his pledge. ¹³You shall restore to him the pledge as the sun sets, that he may sleep in his cloak and bless you. And it shall be righteousness for you before the LORD your God.

¹⁴"You shall not oppress a hired worker who is poor and needy, whether he is one of your brothers or one of the sojourners who are in your land within your towns. ¹⁵You shall give him his wages on the same day, before the sun sets (for he is poor and counts on it), lest he cry against you to the LORD, and you be guilty of sin.

¹⁶"Fathers shall not be put to death because of their children, nor shall children be put to death because of their fathers. Each one shall be put to death for his own sin.

¹⁷"You shall not pervert the justice due to the sojourner or to the fatherless, or take a widow's garment in pledge, ¹⁸but you shall remember that you were a slave in Egypt and the LORD your God redeemed you from there; therefore I command you to do this.

¹⁹"When you reap your harvest in your field and forget a sheaf in the field, you shall not go back to get it. It shall be for the sojourner, the fatherless, and the widow, that the LORD your God may bless you in all the work of your hands. ²⁰When you beat your olive trees, you shall not go over them again. It shall be for the sojourner, the fatherless, and the widow. ²¹When you gather the grapes of your vineyard, you shall not strip it afterwards. It shall be for the sojourner, the fatherless, and the widow. ²²You shall remember that you were a slave in the land of Egypt; therefore I command you to do this.

25 "If there is a dispute between men and they come into court and the judges decide between them, acquitting the innocent and condemning the guilty, ²then if the guilty man deserves to be beaten, the judge shall cause him to lie down and be beaten in his presence with a number of stripes in proportion to his offence. ³Forty stripes may be given him, but not more, lest, if one should go on to beat him with more stripes than these, your brother be degraded in your sight.

⁴"You shall not muzzle an ox when it is treading out the grain.

ᵃOr to make happy his wife *ᵇLeprosy* was a term for several skin diseases; see Leviticus 13

LAWS CONCERNING LEVIRATE MARRIAGE

5 "If brothers dwell together, and one of them dies and has no son, the wife of the dead man shall not be married outside the family to a stranger. Her husband's brother shall go in to her and take her as his wife and perform the duty of a husband's brother to her. 6 And the first son whom she bears shall succeed to the name of his dead brother, that his name may not be blotted out of Israel. 7 And if the man does not wish to take his brother's wife, then his brother's wife shall go up to the gate to the elders and say, 'My husband's brother refuses to perpetuate his brother's name in Israel; he will not perform the duty of a husband's brother to me.' 8 Then the elders of his city shall call him and speak to him, and if he persists, saying, 'I do not wish to take her', 9 then his brother's wife shall go up to him in the presence of the elders and pull his sandal off his foot and spit in his face. And she shall answer and say, 'So shall it be done to the man who does not build up his brother's house.' 10 And the name of his house[a] shall be called in Israel, 'The house of him who had his sandal pulled off.'

MISCELLANEOUS LAWS

11 "When men fight with one another and the wife of the one draws near to rescue her husband from the hand of him who is beating him and puts out her hand and seizes him by the private parts, 12 then you shall cut off her hand. Your eye shall have no pity.

13 "You shall not have in your bag two kinds of weights, a large and a small. 14 You shall not have in your house two kinds of measures, a large and a small. 15 A full and fair[b] weight you shall have, a full and fair measure you shall have, that your days may be long in the land that the LORD your God is giving you. 16 For all who do such things, all who act dishonestly, are an abomination to the LORD your God.

17 "Remember what Amalek did to you on the way as you came out of Egypt, 18 how he attacked you on the way when you were faint and weary, and cut off your tail, those who were lagging behind you, and he did not fear God. 19 Therefore when the LORD your God has given you rest from all your enemies around you, in the land that the LORD your God is giving you for an inheritance to possess, you shall blot out the memory of Amalek from under heaven; you shall not forget.

OFFERINGS OF FIRSTFRUITS AND TITHES

26 "When you come into the land that the LORD your God is giving you for an inheritance and have taken possession of it and live in it, 2 you shall take some of the first of all the fruit of the ground, which you harvest from your land that the LORD your God is giving you, and you shall put it in a basket, and you shall go to the place that the LORD your God will choose, to make his name to dwell there. 3 And you shall go to the priest who is in office at that time and say to him, 'I declare today to the LORD your God that I have come into the land that the LORD swore to our fathers to give us.' 4 Then the priest shall take the basket from your hand and set it down before the altar of the LORD your God.

5 "And you shall make response before the LORD your God, 'A wandering Aramean was my father. And he went down into Egypt and sojourned there, few in number, and there he became a nation, great, mighty, and populous. 6 And the Egyptians treated us harshly and humiliated us and laid on us hard labour. 7 Then we cried to the LORD, the God of our fathers, and the LORD heard our voice and saw our affliction, our toil, and our oppression. 8 And the LORD brought us out of Egypt with a mighty hand and an outstretched arm, with great deeds of terror,[c] with signs and wonders. 9 And he brought us into this place and gave us this land, a land flowing with milk and honey. 10 And behold, now I bring the first of the fruit of the ground, which you, O LORD, have given me.' And you shall set it down before the LORD your God and worship before the LORD your God. 11 And you shall rejoice in all the good that the LORD your God has given to you and to your house, you, and the Levite, and the sojourner who is among you.

12 "When you have finished paying all the tithe of your produce in the third year, which is the year of tithing, giving it to the Levite, the sojourner, the fatherless, and the widow, so that they may eat within your towns and be filled, 13 then you shall say before the LORD your God, 'I have removed the sacred portion out of my house, and moreover, I have given it to the Levite, the sojourner, the fatherless, and the widow, according to all your commandment that you have commanded me. I

---

[a]Hebrew *its name*   [b]Or *just*, or *righteous*; twice in this verse
[c]Hebrew *with great terror*

have not transgressed any of your commandments, nor have I forgotten them. ¹⁴I have not eaten of the tithe while I was mourning, or removed any of it while I was unclean, or offered any of it to the dead. I have obeyed the voice of the LORD my God. I have done according to all that you have commanded me. ¹⁵Look down from your holy habitation, from heaven, and bless your people Israel and the ground that you have given us, as you swore to our fathers, a land flowing with milk and honey.'

¹⁶"This day the LORD your God commands you to do these statutes and rules. You shall therefore be careful to do them with all your heart and with all your soul. ¹⁷You have declared today that the LORD is your God, and that you will walk in his ways, and keep his statutes and his commandments and his rules, and will obey his voice. ¹⁸And the LORD has declared today that you are a people for his treasured possession, as he has promised you, and that you are to keep all his commandments, ¹⁹and that he will set you in praise and in fame and in honour high above all nations that he has made, and that you shall be a people holy to the LORD your God, as he promised."

THE ALTAR ON MOUNT EBAL

27 Now Moses and the elders of Israel commanded the people, saying, "Keep the whole commandment that I command you today. ²And on the day you cross over the Jordan to the land that the LORD your God is giving you, you shall set up large stones and plaster them with plaster. ³And you shall write on them all the words of this law, when you cross over to enter the land that the LORD your God is giving you, a land flowing with milk and honey, as the LORD, the God of your fathers, has promised you. ⁴And when you have crossed over the Jordan, you shall set up these stones, concerning which I command you today, on Mount Ebal, and you shall plaster them with plaster. ⁵And there you shall build an altar to the LORD your God, an altar of stones. You shall wield no iron tool on them; ⁶you shall build an altar to the LORD your God of uncut*a* stones. And you shall offer burnt offerings on it to the LORD your God, ⁷and you shall sacrifice peace offerings and shall eat there, and you shall rejoice before the LORD your God. ⁸And you shall write on the stones all the words of this law very plainly."

CURSES FROM MOUNT EBAL

⁹Then Moses and the Levitical priests said to all Israel, "Keep silence and hear, O Israel: this day you have become the people of the LORD your God. ¹⁰You shall therefore obey the voice of the LORD your God, keeping his commandments and his statutes, which I command you today."

¹¹That day Moses charged the people, saying, ¹²"When you have crossed over the Jordan, these shall stand on Mount Gerizim to bless the people: Simeon, Levi, Judah, Issachar, Joseph, and Benjamin. ¹³And these shall stand on Mount Ebal for the curse: Reuben, Gad, Asher, Zebulun, Dan, and Naphtali. ¹⁴And the Levites shall declare to all the men of Israel in a loud voice:

¹⁵" 'Cursed be the man who makes a carved or cast-metal image, an abomination to the LORD, a thing made by the hands of a craftsman, and sets it up in secret.' And all the people shall answer and say, 'Amen.'

¹⁶" 'Cursed be anyone who dishonours his father or his mother.' And all the people shall say, 'Amen.'

¹⁷" 'Cursed be anyone who moves his neighbour's landmark.' And all the people shall say, 'Amen.'

¹⁸" 'Cursed be anyone who misleads a blind man on the road.' And all the people shall say, 'Amen.'

¹⁹" 'Cursed be anyone who perverts the justice due to the sojourner, the fatherless, and the widow.' And all the people shall say, 'Amen.'

²⁰" 'Cursed be anyone who lies with his father's wife, because he has uncovered his father's nakedness.'*b* And all the people shall say, 'Amen.'

²¹" 'Cursed be anyone who lies with any kind of animal.' And all the people shall say, 'Amen.'

²²" 'Cursed be anyone who lies with his sister, whether the daughter of his father or the daughter of his mother.' And all the people shall say, 'Amen.'

²³" 'Cursed be anyone who lies with his mother-in-law.' And all the people shall say, 'Amen.'

²⁴" 'Cursed be anyone who strikes down his neighbour in secret.' And all the people shall say, 'Amen.'

²⁵" 'Cursed be anyone who takes a bribe to shed innocent blood.' And all the people shall say, 'Amen.'

---

a Hebrew *whole*   *b* Hebrew *uncovered his father's skirt*

26"'Cursed be anyone who does not confirm the words of this law by doing them.' And all the people shall say, 'Amen.'

BLESSINGS FOR OBEDIENCE

28 "And if you faithfully obey the voice of the LORD your God, being careful to do all his commandments that I command you today, the LORD your God will set you high above all the nations of the earth. ²And all these blessings shall come upon you and overtake you, if you obey the voice of the LORD your God. ³Blessed shall you be in the city, and blessed shall you be in the field. ⁴Blessed shall be the fruit of your womb and the fruit of your ground and the fruit of your cattle, the increase of your herds and the young of your flock. ⁵Blessed shall be your basket and your kneading bowl. ⁶Blessed shall you be when you come in, and blessed shall you be when you go out.

⁷"The LORD will cause your enemies who rise against you to be defeated before you. They shall come out against you one way and flee before you seven ways. ⁸The LORD will command the blessing on you in your barns and in all that you undertake. And he will bless you in the land that the LORD your God is giving you. ⁹The LORD will establish you as a people holy to himself, as he has sworn to you, if you keep the commandments of the LORD your God and walk in his ways. ¹⁰And all the peoples of the earth shall see that you are called by the name of the LORD, and they shall be afraid of you. ¹¹And the LORD will make you abound in prosperity, in the fruit of your womb and in the fruit of your livestock and in the fruit of your ground, within the land that the LORD swore to your fathers to give you. ¹²The LORD will open to you his good treasury, the heavens, to give the rain to your land in its season and to bless all the work of your hands. And you shall lend to many nations, but you shall not borrow. ¹³And the LORD will make you the head and not the tail, and you shall only go up and not down, if you obey the commandments of the LORD your God, which I command you today, being careful to do them, ¹⁴and if you do not turn aside from any of the words that I command you today, to the right hand or to the left, to go after other gods to serve them.

CURSES FOR DISOBEDIENCE

¹⁵"But if you will not obey the voice of the LORD your God or be careful to do all his commandments and his statutes that I command you today, then all these curses shall come upon you and overtake you. ¹⁶Cursed shall you be in the city, and cursed shall you be in the field. ¹⁷Cursed shall be your basket and your kneading bowl. ¹⁸Cursed shall be the fruit of your womb and the fruit of your ground, the increase of your herds and the young of your flock. ¹⁹Cursed shall you be when you come in, and cursed shall you be when you go out.

²⁰"The LORD will send on you curses, confusion, and frustration in all that you undertake to do, until you are destroyed and perish quickly on account of the evil of your deeds, because you have forsaken me. ²¹The LORD will make the pestilence stick to you until he has consumed you off the land that you are entering to take possession of it. ²²The LORD will strike you with wasting disease and with fever, inflammation and fiery heat, and with drought*a* and with blight and with mildew. They shall pursue you until you perish. ²³And the heavens over your head shall be bronze, and the earth under you shall be iron. ²⁴The LORD will make the rain of your land powder. From heaven dust shall come down on you until you are destroyed.

²⁵"The LORD will cause you to be defeated before your enemies. You shall go out one way against them and flee seven ways before them. And you shall be a horror to all the kingdoms of the earth. ²⁶And your dead body shall be food for all birds of the air and for the beasts of the earth, and there shall be no one to frighten them away. ²⁷The LORD will strike you with the boils of Egypt, and with tumours and scabs and itch, of which you cannot be healed. ²⁸The LORD will strike you with madness and blindness and confusion of mind, ²⁹and you shall grope at noonday, as the blind grope in darkness, and you shall not prosper in your ways.*b* And you shall be only oppressed and robbed continually, and there shall be no one to help you. ³⁰You shall betroth a wife, but another man shall ravish her. You shall build a house, but you shall not dwell in it. You shall plant a vineyard, but you shall not enjoy its fruit. ³¹Your ox shall be slaughtered before your eyes, but you shall not eat any of it. Your donkey shall be seized before your face, but shall not be restored to you. Your sheep shall be given to your enemies, but there shall be no one to help you.

---

a Or sword *b* Or shall not succeed in finding your ways

³²Your sons and your daughters shall be given to another people, while your eyes look on and fail with longing for them all day long, but you shall be helpless. ³³A nation that you have not known shall eat up the fruit of your ground and of all your labours, and you shall be only oppressed and crushed continually, ³⁴so that you are driven mad by the sights that your eyes see. ³⁵The LORD will strike you on the knees and on the legs with grievous boils of which you cannot be healed, from the sole of your foot to the crown of your head.

³⁶"The LORD will bring you and your king whom you set over you to a nation that neither you nor your fathers have known. And there you shall serve other gods of wood and stone. ³⁷And you shall become a horror, a proverb, and a byword among all the peoples where the LORD will lead you away. ³⁸You shall carry much seed into the field and shall gather in little, for the locust shall consume it. ³⁹You shall plant vineyards and dress them, but you shall neither drink of the wine nor gather the grapes, for the worm shall eat them. ⁴⁰You shall have olive trees throughout all your territory, but you shall not anoint yourself with the oil, for your olives shall drop off. ⁴¹You shall father sons and daughters, but they shall not be yours, for they shall go into captivity. ⁴²The cricket*ᵃ* shall possess all your trees and the fruit of your ground. ⁴³The sojourner who is among you shall rise higher and higher above you, and you shall come down lower and lower. ⁴⁴He shall lend to you, and you shall not lend to him. He shall be the head, and you shall be the tail.

⁴⁵"All these curses shall come upon you and pursue you and overtake you till you are destroyed, because you did not obey the voice of the LORD your God, to keep his commandments and his statutes that he commanded you. ⁴⁶They shall be a sign and a wonder against you and your offspring for ever. ⁴⁷Because you did not serve the LORD your God with joyfulness and gladness of heart, because of the abundance of all things, ⁴⁸therefore you shall serve your enemies whom the LORD will send against you, in hunger and thirst, in nakedness, and lacking everything. And he will put a yoke of iron on your neck until he has destroyed you. ⁴⁹The LORD will bring a nation against you from far away, from the end of the earth, swooping down like the eagle, a nation whose language you do not understand, ⁵⁰a hard-faced nation who shall not respect the old or show mercy to the young. ⁵¹It shall eat the offspring of your cattle and the fruit of your ground, until you are destroyed; it also shall not leave you grain, wine, or oil, the increase of your herds or the young of your flock, until they have caused you to perish.

⁵²"They shall besiege you in all your towns, until your high and fortified walls, in which you trusted, come down throughout all your land. And they shall besiege you in all your towns throughout all your land, which the LORD your God has given you. ⁵³And you shall eat the fruit of your womb, the flesh of your sons and daughters, whom the LORD your God has given you, in the siege and in the distress with which your enemies shall distress you. ⁵⁴The man who is the most tender and refined among you will begrudge food to his brother, to the wife he embraces,*ᵇ* and to the last of the children whom he has left, ⁵⁵so that he will not give to any of them any of the flesh of his children whom he is eating, because he has nothing else left, in the siege and in the distress with which your enemy shall distress you in all your towns. ⁵⁶The most tender and refined woman among you, who would not venture to set the sole of her foot on the ground because she is so delicate and tender, will begrudge to the husband she embraces,*ᶜ* to her son and to her daughter, ⁵⁷her afterbirth that comes out from between her feet and her children whom she bears, because lacking everything she will eat them secretly, in the siege and in the distress with which your enemy shall distress you in your towns.

⁵⁸"If you are not careful to do all the words of this law that are written in this book, that you may fear this glorious and awesome name, the LORD your God, ⁵⁹then the LORD will bring on you and your offspring extraordinary afflictions, afflictions severe and lasting, and sicknesses grievous and lasting. ⁶⁰And he will bring upon you again all the diseases of Egypt, of which you were afraid, and they shall cling to you. ⁶¹Every sickness also and every affliction that is not recorded in the book of this law, the LORD will bring upon you, until you are destroyed. ⁶²Whereas you were as numerous as the stars of heaven, you shall be left few in number, because you did not obey the voice of the LORD your God. ⁶³And as the LORD took delight in doing you

---

ᵃIdentity uncertain ᵇHebrew *the wife of his bosom* ᶜHebrew *the husband of her bosom*

good and multiplying you, so the Lord will take delight in bringing ruin upon you and destroying you. And you shall be plucked off the land that you are entering to take possession of it.

⁶⁴"And the Lord will scatter you among all peoples, from one end of the earth to the other, and there you shall serve other gods of wood and stone, which neither you nor your fathers have known. ⁶⁵And among these nations you shall find no respite, and there shall be no resting-place for the sole of your foot, but the Lord will give you there a trembling heart and failing eyes and a languishing soul. ⁶⁶Your life shall hang in doubt before you. Night and day you shall be in dread and have no assurance of your life. ⁶⁷In the morning you shall say, 'If only it were evening!' and at evening you shall say, 'If only it were morning!' because of the dread that your heart shall feel, and the sights that your eyes shall see. ⁶⁸And the Lord will bring you back in ships to Egypt, a journey that I promised that you should never make again; and there you shall offer yourselves for sale to your enemies as male and female slaves, but there will be no buyer."

THE COVENANT RENEWED IN MOAB

29 ᵃ These are the words of the covenant that the Lord commanded Moses to make with the people of Israel in the land of Moab, besides the covenant that he had made with them at Horeb.

²ᵇ And Moses summoned all Israel and said to them: "You have seen all that the Lord did before your eyes in the land of Egypt, to Pharaoh and to all his servants and to all his land, ³the great trials that your eyes saw, the signs, and those great wonders. ⁴But to this day the Lord has not given you a heart to understand or eyes to see or ears to hear. ⁵I have led you for forty years in the wilderness. Your clothes have not worn out on you, and your sandals have not worn off your feet. ⁶You have not eaten bread, and you have not drunk wine or strong drink, that you may know that I am the Lord your God. ⁷And when you came to this place, Sihon the king of Heshbon and Og the king of Bashan came out against us to battle, but we defeated them. ⁸We took their land and gave it for an inheritance to the Reubenites, the Gadites, and the half-tribe of the Manassites. ⁹Therefore keep the words of this covenant and do them, that you may prosperᶜ in all that you do.

¹⁰"You are standing today, all of you, before the Lord your God: the heads of your tribes,ᵈ your elders, and your officers, all the men of Israel, ¹¹your little ones, your wives, and the sojourner who is in your camp, from the one who chops your wood to the one who draws your water, ¹²so that you may enter into the sworn covenant of the Lord your God, which the Lord your God is making with you today, ¹³that he may establish you today as his people, and that he may be your God, as he promised you, and as he swore to your fathers, to Abraham, to Isaac, and to Jacob. ¹⁴It is not with you alone that I am making this sworn covenant, ¹⁵but with whoever is standing here with us today before the Lord our God, and with whoever is not here with us today.

¹⁶"You know how we lived in the land of Egypt, and how we came through the midst of the nations through which you passed. ¹⁷And you have seen their detestable things, their idols of wood and stone, of silver and gold, which were among them. ¹⁸Beware lest there be among you a man or woman or clan or tribe whose heart is turning away today from the Lord our God to go and serve the gods of those nations. Beware lest there be among you a root bearing poisonous and bitter fruit, ¹⁹one who, when he hears the words of this sworn covenant, blesses himself in his heart, saying, 'I shall be safe, though I walk in the stubbornness of my heart.' This will lead to the sweeping away of moist and dry alike. ²⁰The Lord will not be willing to forgive him, but rather the anger of the Lord and his jealousy will smoke against that man, and the curses written in this book will settle upon him, and the Lord will blot out his name from under heaven. ²¹And the Lord will single him out from all the tribes of Israel for calamity, in accordance with all the curses of the covenant written in this Book of the Law. ²²And the next generation, your children who rise up after you, and the foreigner who comes from a far land, will say, when they see the afflictions of that land and the sicknesses with which the Lord has made it sick— ²³the whole land burned out with brimstone and salt, nothing sown and nothing growing, where no plant can sprout, an overthrow like that of Sodom and Gomorrah, Admah, and Zeboiim, which the Lord overthrew in his anger and wrath— ²⁴all the nations will say, 'Why has the Lord

---

ᵃCh 28:69 in Hebrew   ᵇCh 29:1 in Hebrew   ᶜOr *deal wisely*
ᵈSeptuagint, Syriac; Hebrew *your heads, your tribes*

done thus to this land? What caused the heat of this great anger?' ²⁵Then people will say, 'It is because they abandoned the covenant of the Lord, the God of their fathers, which he made with them when he brought them out of the land of Egypt, ²⁶and went and served other gods and worshipped them, gods whom they had not known and whom he had not allotted to them. ²⁷Therefore the anger of the Lord was kindled against this land, bringing upon it all the curses written in this book, ²⁸and the Lord uprooted them from their land in anger and fury and great wrath, and cast them into another land, as they are this day.'

²⁹"The secret things belong to the Lord our God, but the things that are revealed belong to us and to our children for ever, that we may do all the words of this law.

REPENTANCE AND FORGIVENESS

30 "And when all these things come upon you, the blessing and the curse, which I have set before you, and you call them to mind among all the nations where the Lord your God has driven you, ²and return to the Lord your God, you and your children, and obey his voice in all that I command you today, with all your heart and with all your soul, ³then the Lord your God will restore your fortunes and have mercy on you, and he will gather you again from all the peoples where the Lord your God has scattered you. ⁴If your outcasts are in the uttermost parts of heaven, from there the Lord your God will gather you, and from there he will take you. ⁵And the Lord your God will bring you into the land that your fathers possessed, that you may possess it. And he will make you more prosperous and numerous than your fathers. ⁶And the Lord your God will circumcise your heart and the heart of your offspring, so that you will love the Lord your God with all your heart and with all your soul, that you may live. ⁷And the Lord your God will put all these curses on your foes and enemies who persecuted you. ⁸And you shall again obey the voice of the Lord and keep all his commandments that I command you today. ⁹The Lord your God will make you abundantly prosperous in all the work of your hand, in the fruit of your womb and in the fruit of your cattle and in the fruit of your ground. For the Lord will again take delight in prospering you, as he took delight in your fathers, ¹⁰when you obey the voice of the Lord your God, to keep his commandments and his statutes that are written in this Book of the Law, when you turn to the Lord your God with all your heart and with all your soul.

THE CHOICE OF LIFE AND DEATH

¹¹"For this commandment that I command you today is not too hard for you, neither is it far off. ¹²It is not in heaven, that you should say, 'Who will ascend to heaven for us and bring it to us, that we may hear it and do it?' ¹³Neither is it beyond the sea, that you should say, 'Who will go over the sea for us and bring it to us, that we may hear it and do it?' ¹⁴But the word is very near you. It is in your mouth and in your heart, so that you can do it.

¹⁵"See, I have set before you today life and good, death and evil. ¹⁶If you obey the commandments of the Lord your God^a that I command you today, by loving the Lord your God, by walking in his ways, and by keeping his commandments and his statutes and his rules,^{b} then you shall live and multiply, and the Lord your God will bless you in the land that you are entering to take possession of it. ¹⁷But if your heart turns away, and you will not hear, but are drawn away to worship other gods and serve them, ¹⁸I declare to you today, that you shall surely perish. You shall not live long in the land that you are going over the Jordan to enter and possess. ¹⁹I call heaven and earth to witness against you today, that I have set before you life and death, blessing and curse. Therefore choose life, that you and your offspring may live, ²⁰loving the Lord your God, obeying his voice and holding fast to him, for he is your life and length of days, that you may dwell in the land that the Lord swore to your fathers, to Abraham, to Isaac, and to Jacob, to give them."

JOSHUA TO SUCCEED MOSES

31 So Moses continued to speak these words to all Israel. ²And he said to them, "I am 120 years old today. I am no longer able to go out and come in. The Lord has said to me, 'You shall not go over this Jordan.' ³The Lord your God himself will go over before you. He will destroy these nations before you, so that you shall dispossess them, and Joshua will go over at your head, as the Lord has spoken. ⁴And the Lord will do to them as he did to Sihon

---

^{a}Septuagint; Hebrew lacks *If you obey the commandments of the Lord your God* ^{b}Or *his just decrees*

and Og, the kings of the Amorites, and to their land, when he destroyed them. ⁵And the LORD will give them over to you, and you shall do to them according to the whole commandment that I have commanded you. ⁶Be strong and courageous. Do not fear or be in dread of them, for it is the LORD your God who goes with you. He will not leave you or forsake you."

⁷Then Moses summoned Joshua and said to him in the sight of all Israel, "Be strong and courageous, for you shall go with this people into the land that the LORD has sworn to their fathers to give them, and you shall put them in possession of it. ⁸It is the LORD who goes before you. He will be with you; he will not leave you or forsake you. Do not fear or be dismayed."

THE READING OF THE LAW

⁹Then Moses wrote this law and gave it to the priests, the sons of Levi, who carried the ark of the covenant of the LORD, and to all the elders of Israel. ¹⁰And Moses commanded them, "At the end of every seven years, at the set time in the year of release, at the Feast of Booths, ¹¹when all Israel comes to appear before the LORD your God at the place that he will choose, you shall read this law before all Israel in their hearing. ¹²Assemble the people, men, women, and little ones, and the sojourner within your towns, that they may hear and learn to fear the LORD your God, and be careful to do all the words of this law, ¹³and that their children, who have not known it, may hear and learn to fear the LORD your God, as long as you live in the land that you are going over the Jordan to possess."

JOSHUA COMMISSIONED TO LEAD ISRAEL

¹⁴And the LORD said to Moses, "Behold, the days approach when you must die. Call Joshua and present yourselves in the tent of meeting, that I may commission him." And Moses and Joshua went and presented themselves in the tent of meeting. ¹⁵And the LORD appeared in the tent in a pillar of cloud. And the pillar of cloud stood over the entrance of the tent.

¹⁶And the LORD said to Moses, "Behold, you are about to lie down with your fathers. Then this people will rise and whore after the foreign gods among them in the land that they are entering, and they will forsake me and break my covenant that I have made with them. ¹⁷Then my anger will be kindled against them in that day, and I will forsake them and hide my face from them, and they will be devoured. And many evils and troubles will come upon them, so that they will say in that day, 'Have not these evils come upon us because our God is not among us?' ¹⁸And I will surely hide my face in that day because of all the evil that they have done, because they have turned to other gods.

¹⁹"Now therefore write this song and teach it to the people of Israel. Put it in their mouths, that this song may be a witness for me against the people of Israel. ²⁰For when I have brought them into the land flowing with milk and honey, which I swore to give to their fathers, and they have eaten and are full and grown fat, they will turn to other gods and serve them, and despise me and break my covenant. ²¹And when many evils and troubles have come upon them, this song shall confront them as a witness (for it will live unforgotten in the mouths of their offspring). For I know what they are inclined to do even today, before I have brought them into the land that I swore to give." ²²So Moses wrote this song the same day and taught it to the people of Israel.

²³And the LORD*ᵃ* commissioned Joshua the son of Nun and said, "Be strong and courageous, for you shall bring the people of Israel into the land that I swore to give them. I will be with you."

²⁴When Moses had finished writing the words of this law in a book to the very end, ²⁵Moses commanded the Levites who carried the ark of the covenant of the LORD, ²⁶"Take this Book of the Law and put it by the side of the ark of the covenant of the LORD your God, that it may be there for a witness against you. ²⁷For I know how rebellious and stubborn you are. Behold, even today while I am yet alive with you, you have been rebellious against the LORD. How much more after my death! ²⁸Assemble to me all the elders of your tribes and your officers, that I may speak these words in their ears and call heaven and earth to witness against them. ²⁹For I know that after my death you will surely act corruptly and turn aside from the way that I have commanded you. And in the days to come evil will befall you, because you will do what is evil in the sight of the LORD, provoking him to anger through the work of your hands."

---

*ᵃ*Hebrew *he*

THE SONG OF MOSES

30 Then Moses spoke the words of this song until they were finished, in the ears of all the assembly of Israel:

32

"Give ear, O heavens, and I will speak,
 and let the earth hear the words of my mouth.
2 May my teaching drop as the rain,
 my speech distil as the dew,
 like gentle rain upon the tender grass,
 and like showers upon the herb.
3 For I will proclaim the name of the LORD;
 ascribe greatness to our God!

4 "The Rock, his work is perfect,
 for all his ways are justice.
 A God of faithfulness and without iniquity,
 just and upright is he.
5 They have dealt corruptly with him;
 they are no longer his children because they are blemished;
 they are a crooked and twisted generation.
6 Do you thus repay the LORD,
 you foolish and senseless people?
 Is not he your father, who created you,
 who made you and established you?
7 Remember the days of old;
 consider the years of many generations;
 ask your father, and he will show you,
 your elders, and they will tell you.
8 When the Most High gave to the nations their inheritance,
 when he divided mankind,
 he fixed the borders[a] of the peoples
 according to the number of the sons of God.[b]
9 But the LORD's portion is his people,
 Jacob his allotted heritage.

10 "He found him in a desert land,
 and in the howling waste of the wilderness;
 he encircled him, he cared for him,
 he kept him as the apple of his eye.
11 Like an eagle that stirs up its nest,
 that flutters over its young,
 spreading out its wings, catching them,
 bearing them on its pinions,
12 the LORD alone guided him,
 no foreign god was with him.
13 He made him ride on the high places of the land,
 and he ate the produce of the field,
 and he suckled him with honey out of the rock,
 and oil out of the flinty rock.
14 Curds from the herd, and milk from the flock,
 with fat[c] of lambs,
 rams of Bashan and goats,
 with the very finest[d] of the wheat—
 and you drank foaming wine made from the blood of the grape.

15 "But Jeshurun grew fat, and kicked;
 you grew fat, stout, and sleek;
 then he forsook God who made him
 and scoffed at the Rock of his salvation.
16 They stirred him to jealousy with strange gods;
 with abominations they provoked him to anger.
17 They sacrificed to demons that were no gods,
 to gods they had never known,
 to new gods that had come recently,
 whom your fathers had never dreaded.
18 You were unmindful of the Rock that bore[e] you,
 and you forgot the God who gave you birth.

19 "The LORD saw it and spurned them,
 because of the provocation of his sons and his daughters.
20 And he said, 'I will hide my face from them;
 I will see what their end will be,
 for they are a perverse generation,
 children in whom is no faithfulness.
21 They have made me jealous with what is no god;
 they have provoked me to anger with their idols.
 So I will make them jealous with those who are no people;
 I will provoke them to anger with a foolish nation.
22 For a fire is kindled by my anger,
 and it burns to the depths of Sheol,

---

[a] Or *territories* [b] Compare Dead Sea Scroll, Septuagint; Masoretic Text *sons of Israel* [c] That is, with the best [d] Hebrew *with the kidney fat* [e] Or *fathered*

devours the earth and its increase,
and sets on fire the foundations
of the mountains.

23 "'And I will heap disasters upon them;
I will expend my arrows on them;
24 they shall be wasted with hunger,
and devoured by plague
and poisonous pestilence;
I will send the teeth of beasts
against them,
with the venom of things that
crawl in the dust.
25 Outdoors the sword shall bereave,
and indoors terror,
for young man and woman alike,
the nursing child with the
man of grey hairs.
26 I would have said, "I will cut
them to pieces;
I will wipe them from
human memory,"
27 had I not feared provocation
by the enemy,
lest their adversaries should
misunderstand,
lest they should say, "Our
hand is triumphant,
it was not the LORD who did
all this."'

28 "For they are a nation void of counsel,
and there is no understanding
in them.
29 If they were wise, they would
understand this;
they would discern their
latter end!
30 How could one have chased
a thousand,
and two have put ten
thousand to flight,
unless their Rock had sold them,
and the LORD had given them up?
31 For their rock is not as our Rock;
our enemies are by themselves.
32 For their vine comes from
the vine of Sodom
and from the fields of Gomorrah;
their grapes are grapes of poison;
their clusters are bitter;
33 their wine is the poison of serpents
and the cruel venom of asps.

34 "'Is not this laid up in store with me,
sealed up in my treasuries?
35 Vengeance is mine, and recompense,*a*
for the time when their
foot shall slip;
for the day of their calamity is at hand,
and their doom comes swiftly.'
36 For the LORD will vindicate*b* his people
and have compassion on
his servants,
when he sees that their power is gone
and there is none remaining,
bond or free.
37 Then he will say, 'Where are their gods,
the rock in which they took refuge,
38 who ate the fat of their sacrifices
and drank the wine of their
drink offering?
Let them rise up and help you;
let them be your protection!

39 "'See now that I, even I, am he,
and there is no god beside me;
I kill and I make alive;
I wound and I heal;
and there is none that can
deliver out of my hand.
40 For I lift up my hand to heaven
and swear, As I live for ever,
41 if I sharpen my flashing sword*c*
and my hand takes hold
on judgement,
I will take vengeance on
my adversaries
and will repay those who hate me.
42 I will make my arrows
drunk with blood,
and my sword shall devour flesh —
with the blood of the slain
and the captives,
from the long-haired heads
of the enemy.'

43 "Rejoice with him, O heavens;*d*
bow down to him, all gods,*e*
for he avenges the blood
of his children*f*
and takes vengeance on
his adversaries.
He repays those who hate him*g*
and cleanses*h* his people's land."*i*

---

*a*Septuagint *and I will repay* *b*Septuagint *judge* *c*Hebrew *the lightning of my sword* *d*Dead Sea Scroll, Septuagint; Masoretic Text *Rejoice his people, O nations* *e*Masoretic Text lacks *bow down to him, all gods* *f*Dead Sea Scroll, Septuagint; Masoretic Text *servants* *g*Dead Sea Scroll, Septuagint; Masoretic Text lacks *He repays those who hate him* *h*Or *atones for* *i*Septuagint, Vulgate; Hebrew *his land his people*

⁴⁴Moses came and recited all the words of this song in the hearing of the people, he and Joshua[a] the son of Nun. ⁴⁵And when Moses had finished speaking all these words to all Israel, ⁴⁶he said to them, "Take to heart all the words by which I am warning you today, that you may command them to your children, that they may be careful to do all the words of this law. ⁴⁷For it is no empty word for you, but your very life, and by this word you shall live long in the land that you are going over the Jordan to possess."

MOSES' DEATH FORETOLD

⁴⁸That very day the LORD spoke to Moses, ⁴⁹"Go up this mountain of the Abarim, Mount Nebo, which is in the land of Moab, opposite Jericho, and view the land of Canaan, which I am giving to the people of Israel for a possession. ⁵⁰And die on the mountain which you go up, and be gathered to your people, as Aaron your brother died in Mount Hor and was gathered to his people, ⁵¹because you broke faith with me in the midst of the people of Israel at the waters of Meribah-kadesh, in the wilderness of Zin, and because you did not treat me as holy in the midst of the people of Israel. ⁵²For you shall see the land before you, but you shall not go there, into the land that I am giving to the people of Israel."

MOSES' FINAL BLESSING ON ISRAEL

33 This is the blessing with which Moses the man of God blessed the people of Israel before his death. ²He said,

"The LORD came from Sinai
  and dawned from Seir upon us;[b]
he shone forth from Mount Paran;
he came from the ten thousands
  of holy ones,
  with flaming fire[c] at his right hand.
³ Yes, he loved his people,[d]
  all his holy ones were in his[e] hand;
so they followed[f] in your steps,
  receiving direction from you,
⁴ when Moses commanded us a law,
  as a possession for the
    assembly of Jacob.
⁵ Thus the LORD[g] became
    king in Jeshurun,
  when the heads of the people
    were gathered,
  all the tribes of Israel together.

⁶ "Let Reuben live, and not die,
  but let his men be few."

⁷And this he said of Judah:

"Hear, O LORD, the voice of Judah,
  and bring him in to his people.
With your hands contend[h] for him,
  and be a help against his adversaries."

⁸And of Levi he said,

"Give to Levi[i] your Thummim,
  and your Urim to your godly one,
whom you tested at Massah,
  with whom you quarrelled at
    the waters of Meribah;
⁹ who said of his father and mother,
    'I regard them not';
  he disowned his brothers
    and ignored his children.
  For they observed your word
    and kept your covenant.
¹⁰ They shall teach Jacob your rules
    and Israel your law;
  they shall put incense before you
    and whole burnt offerings
      on your altar.
¹¹ Bless, O LORD, his substance,
    and accept the work of his hands;
  crush the loins of his adversaries,
    of those who hate him, that
      they rise not again."

¹²Of Benjamin he said,

"The beloved of the LORD
    dwells in safety.
The High God[j] surrounds
    him all day long,
  and dwells between his shoulders."

¹³And of Joseph he said,

"Blessed by the LORD be his land,
  with the choicest gifts of
    heaven above,[k]
  and of the deep that
    crouches beneath,

---

[a]Septuagint, Syriac, Vulgate; Hebrew *Hoshea* [b]Septuagint, Syriac, Vulgate; Hebrew *them* [c]The meaning of the Hebrew word is uncertain [d]Septuagint; Hebrew *peoples* [e]Hebrew *your* [f]The meaning of the Hebrew word is uncertain [g]Hebrew *Thus he* [h]Probable reading; Hebrew *With his hands he contended* [i]Dead Sea Scroll, Septuagint; Masoretic Text lacks *Give to Levi* [j]Septuagint; Hebrew *dwells in safety by him. He* [k]Two Hebrew manuscripts and Targum; Hebrew *with the dew*

14   with the choicest fruits of
>   the sun
>   and the rich yield of the months,
15   with the finest produce of the
>   ancient mountains
>   and the abundance of the
>   everlasting hills,
16   with the best gifts of the earth
>   and its fullness
>   and the favour of him who
>   dwells in the bush.
>   May these rest on the head
>   of Joseph,
>   on the pate of him who is prince
>   among his brothers.
17   A firstborn bull[a]—he has majesty,
>   and his horns are the horns
>   of a wild ox;
>   with them he shall gore the peoples,
>   all of them, to the ends of the earth;
>   they are the ten thousands
>   of Ephraim,
>   and they are the thousands
>   of Manasseh."

18 And of Zebulun he said,

> "Rejoice, Zebulun, in your going out,
>   and Issachar, in your tents.
19   They shall call peoples to
>   their mountain;
>   there they offer right sacrifices;
>   for they draw from the
>   abundance of the seas
>   and the hidden treasures
>   of the sand."

20 And of Gad he said,

> "Blessed be he who enlarges Gad!
>   Gad crouches like a lion;
>   he tears off arm and scalp.
21   He chose the best of the
>   land for himself,
>   for there a commander's
>   portion was reserved;
>   and he came with the heads
>   of the people,
>   with Israel he executed the
>   justice of the LORD,
>   and his judgements for Israel."

22 And of Dan he said,

> "Dan is a lion's cub
>   that leaps from Bashan."

23 And of Naphtali he said,

> "O Naphtali, sated with favour,
>   and full of the blessing of the LORD,
>   possess the lake[b] and the south."

24 And of Asher he said,

> "Most blessed of sons be Asher;
>   let him be the favourite
>   of his brothers,
>   and let him dip his foot in oil.
25   Your bars shall be iron and bronze,
>   and as your days, so shall
>   your strength be.

26   "There is none like God, O Jeshurun,
>   who rides through the
>   heavens to your help,
>   through the skies in his majesty.
27   The eternal God is your dwelling place,[c]
>   and underneath are the
>   everlasting arms.[d]
>   And he thrust out the
>   enemy before you
>   and said, 'Destroy.'
28   So Israel lived in safety,
>   Jacob lived alone,[e]
>   in a land of grain and wine,
>   whose heavens drop down dew.
29   Happy are you, O Israel!
>   Who is like you,
>   a people saved by the LORD,
>   the shield of your help,
>   and the sword of your triumph!
>   Your enemies shall come
>   fawning to you,
>   and you shall tread upon
>   their backs."

THE DEATH OF MOSES

34 Then Moses went up from the plains of Moab to Mount Nebo, to the top of Pisgah, which is opposite Jericho. And the LORD showed him all the land, Gilead as far as Dan, ²all Naphtali, the land of Ephraim and Manasseh, all the land of Judah as far as the western sea, ³the Negeb, and the Plain, that is, the Valley of Jericho the city of palm trees, as far as Zoar. ⁴And the LORD said to him, "This is the land of which I swore to Abraham, to Isaac, and to Jacob, 'I

---

[a] Dead Sea Scroll, Septuagint, Samaritan; Masoretic Text *His firstborn bull*   [b] Or *west*   [c] Or *a dwelling place*   [d] Revocalization of verse 27 yields *He subdues the ancient gods, and shatters the forces of old*
[e] Hebrew *the abode of Jacob was alone*

will give it to your offspring.' I have let you see it with your eyes, but you shall not go over there." ⁵So Moses the servant of the LORD died there in the land of Moab, according to the word of the LORD, ⁶and he buried him in the valley in the land of Moab opposite Beth-peor; but no one knows the place of his burial to this day. ⁷Moses was 120 years old when he died. His eye was undimmed, and his vigour unabated. ⁸And the people of Israel wept for Moses in the plains of Moab for thirty days. Then the days of weeping and mourning for Moses were ended.

⁹And Joshua the son of Nun was full of the spirit of wisdom, for Moses had laid his hands on him. So the people of Israel obeyed him and did as the LORD had commanded Moses. ¹⁰And there has not arisen a prophet since in Israel like Moses, whom the LORD knew face to face, ¹¹none like him for all the signs and the wonders that the LORD sent him to do in the land of Egypt, to Pharaoh and to all his servants and to all his land, ¹²and for all the mighty power and all the great deeds of terror that Moses did in the sight of all Israel.

JOSHUA

GOD COMMISSIONS JOSHUA

1 After the death of Moses the servant of the Lord, the Lord said to Joshua the son of Nun, Moses' assistant, ²"Moses my servant is dead. Now therefore arise, go over this Jordan, you and all this people, into the land that I am giving to them, to the people of Israel. ³Every place that the sole of your foot will tread upon I have given to you, just as I promised to Moses. ⁴From the wilderness and this Lebanon as far as the great river, the river Euphrates, all the land of the Hittites to the Great Sea towards the going down of the sun shall be your territory. ⁵No man shall be able to stand before you all the days of your life. Just as I was with Moses, so I will be with you. I will not leave you or forsake you. ⁶Be strong and courageous, for you shall cause this people to inherit the land that I swore to their fathers to give them. ⁷Only be strong and very courageous, being careful to do according to all the law that Moses my servant commanded you. Do not turn from it to the right hand or to the left, that you may have good success[a] wherever you go. ⁸This Book of the Law shall not depart from your mouth, but you shall meditate on it day and night, so that you may be careful to do according to all that is written in it. For then you will make your way prosperous, and then you will have good success. ⁹Have I not commanded you? Be strong and courageous. Do not be frightened, and do not be dismayed, for the Lord your God is with you wherever you go."

JOSHUA ASSUMES COMMAND

¹⁰And Joshua commanded the officers of the people, ¹¹"Pass through the midst of the camp and command the people, 'Prepare your provisions, for within three days you are to pass over this Jordan to go in to take possession of the land that the Lord your God is giving you to possess.'"

¹²And to the Reubenites, the Gadites, and the half-tribe of Manasseh Joshua said, ¹³"Remember the word that Moses the servant of the Lord commanded you, saying, 'The Lord your God is providing you a place of rest and will give you this land.' ¹⁴Your wives, your little ones, and your livestock shall remain in the land that Moses gave you beyond the Jordan, but all the men of valour among you shall pass over armed before your brothers and shall help them, ¹⁵until the Lord gives rest to your brothers as he has to you, and they also take possession of the land that the Lord your God is giving them. Then you shall return to the land of your possession and shall possess it, the land that Moses the servant of the Lord gave you beyond the Jordan towards the sunrise."

¹⁶And they answered Joshua, "All that you have commanded us we will do, and wherever you send us we will go. ¹⁷Just as we obeyed Moses in all things, so we will obey you. Only may the Lord your God be with you, as he was with Moses! ¹⁸Whoever rebels against your commandment and disobeys your words, whatever you command him, shall be put to death. Only be strong and courageous."

RAHAB HIDES THE SPIES

2 And Joshua the son of Nun sent[b] two men secretly from Shittim as spies, saying, "Go, view the land, especially Jericho." And they went and came into the house of a prostitute whose name was Rahab and lodged there. ²And it was told to the king of Jericho, "Behold, men of Israel have come here tonight to search out the land." ³Then the king of Jericho sent to Rahab, saying, "Bring out the men who have come to you, who entered your house, for they have come to search out all the land." ⁴But the woman had taken the two men and hidden them. And she said, "True, the men came to me, but I did not know where they were from. ⁵And when the gate was about to be closed at dark, the men went out. I do not know where the men went. Pursue them quickly, for you will overtake them." ⁶But she had brought them up to the roof and hid them with the stalks of flax that she had laid in order on the roof. ⁷So the men pursued after them on the way to the

---

[a] Or may act wisely [b] Or had sent

Jordan as far as the fords. And the gate was shut as soon as the pursuers had gone out.

⁸Before the men[a] lay down, she came up to them on the roof ⁹and said to the men, "I know that the LORD has given you the land, and that the fear of you has fallen upon us, and that all the inhabitants of the land melt away before you. ¹⁰For we have heard how the LORD dried up the water of the Red Sea before you when you came out of Egypt, and what you did to the two kings of the Amorites who were beyond the Jordan, to Sihon and Og, whom you devoted to destruction.[b] ¹¹And as soon as we heard it, our hearts melted, and there was no spirit left in any man because of you, for the LORD your God, he is God in the heavens above and on the earth beneath. ¹²Now then, please swear to me by the LORD that, as I have dealt kindly with you, you also will deal kindly with my father's house, and give me a sure sign ¹³that you will save alive my father and mother, my brothers and sisters, and all who belong to them, and deliver our lives from death." ¹⁴And the men said to her, "Our life for yours even to death! If you do not tell this business of ours, then when the LORD gives us the land we will deal kindly and faithfully with you."

¹⁵Then she let them down by a rope through the window, for her house was built into the city wall, so that she lived in the wall. ¹⁶And she said[c] to them, "Go into the hills, or the pursuers will encounter you, and hide there three days until the pursuers have returned. Then afterwards you may go your way." ¹⁷The men said to her, "We will be guiltless with respect to this oath of yours that you have made us swear. ¹⁸Behold, when we come into the land, you shall tie this scarlet cord in the window through which you let us down, and you shall gather into your house your father and mother, your brothers, and all your father's household. ¹⁹Then if anyone goes out of the doors of your house into the street, his blood shall be on his own head, and we shall be guiltless. But if a hand is laid on anyone who is with you in the house, his blood shall be on our head. ²⁰But if you tell this business of ours, then we shall be guiltless with respect to your oath that you have made us swear." ²¹And she said, "According to your words, so be it." Then she sent them away, and they departed. And she tied the scarlet cord in the window.

²²They departed and went into the hills and remained there three days until the pursuers returned, and the pursuers searched all along the way and found nothing. ²³Then the two men returned. They came down from the hills and passed over and came to Joshua the son of Nun, and they told him all that had happened to them. ²⁴And they said to Joshua, "Truly the LORD has given all the land into our hands. And also, all the inhabitants of the land melt away because of us."

ISRAEL CROSSES THE JORDAN

3 Then Joshua rose early in the morning and they set out from Shittim. And they came to the Jordan, he and all the people of Israel, and lodged there before they passed over. ²At the end of three days the officers went through the camp ³and commanded the people, "As soon as you see the ark of the covenant of the LORD your God being carried by the Levitical priests, then you shall set out from your place and follow it. ⁴Yet there shall be a distance between you and it, about 2,000 cubits[d] in length. Do not come near it, in order that you may know the way you shall go, for you have not passed this way before." ⁵Then Joshua said to the people, "Consecrate yourselves, for tomorrow the LORD will do wonders among you." ⁶And Joshua said to the priests, "Take up the ark of the covenant and pass on before the people." So they took up the ark of the covenant and went before the people.

⁷The LORD said to Joshua, "Today I will begin to exalt you in the sight of all Israel, that they may know that, as I was with Moses, so I will be with you. ⁸And as for you, command the priests who bear the ark of the covenant, 'When you come to the brink of the waters of the Jordan, you shall stand still in the Jordan.'" ⁹And Joshua said to the people of Israel, "Come here and listen to the words of the LORD your God." ¹⁰And Joshua said, "Here is how you shall know that the living God is among you and that he will without fail drive out from before you the Canaanites, the Hittites, the Hivites, the Perizzites, the Girgashites, the Amorites, and the Jebusites. ¹¹Behold, the ark of the covenant of the Lord of all the earth[e] is passing over before you into the Jordan. ¹²Now therefore take twelve men from the tribes of Israel, from each tribe a man. ¹³And when the soles of the feet of the priests bearing the ark of the LORD, the Lord of all the earth, shall rest in the waters of

---

[a]Hebrew *they* [b]That is, set apart (devoted) as an offering to the Lord (for destruction) [c]Or *had said* [d]A *cubit* was about 18 inches or 45 centimetres [e]Hebrew *the ark of the covenant, the Lord of all the earth*

the Jordan, the waters of the Jordan shall be cut off from flowing, and the waters coming down from above shall stand in one heap." **14**So when the people set out from their tents to pass over the Jordan with the priests bearing the ark of the covenant before the people, **15**and as soon as those bearing the ark had come as far as the Jordan, and the feet of the priests bearing the ark were dipped in the brink of the water (now the Jordan overflows all its banks throughout the time of harvest), **16**the waters coming down from above stood and rose up in a heap very far away, at Adam, the city that is beside Zarethan, and those flowing down towards the Sea of the Arabah, the Salt Sea, were completely cut off. And the people passed over opposite Jericho. **17**Now the priests bearing the ark of the covenant of the LORD stood firmly on dry ground in the midst of the Jordan, and all Israel was passing over on dry ground until all the nation finished passing over the Jordan.

TWELVE MEMORIAL STONES FROM THE JORDAN

4 When all the nation had finished passing over the Jordan, the LORD said to Joshua, **2**"Take twelve men from the people, from each tribe a man, **3**and command them, saying, 'Take twelve stones from here out of the midst of the Jordan, from the very place where the priests' feet stood firmly, and bring them over with you and lay them down in the place where you lodge tonight.'" **4**Then Joshua called the twelve men from the people of Israel, whom he had appointed, a man from each tribe. **5**And Joshua said to them, "Pass on before the ark of the LORD your God into the midst of the Jordan, and take up each of you a stone upon his shoulder, according to the number of the tribes of the people of Israel, **6**that this may be a sign among you. When your children ask in time to come, 'What do those stones mean to you?' **7**then you shall tell them that the waters of the Jordan were cut off before the ark of the covenant of the LORD. When it passed over the Jordan, the waters of the Jordan were cut off. So these stones shall be to the people of Israel a memorial for ever."

8And the people of Israel did just as Joshua commanded and took up twelve stones out of the midst of the Jordan, according to the number of the tribes of the people of Israel, just as the LORD told Joshua. And they carried them over with them to the place where they lodged and laid them down[a] there. **9**And Joshua set up[b] twelve stones in the midst of the Jordan, in the place where the feet of the priests bearing the ark of the covenant had stood; and they are there to this day. **10**For the priests bearing the ark stood in the midst of the Jordan until everything was finished that the LORD commanded Joshua to tell the people, according to all that Moses had commanded Joshua.

The people passed over in haste. **11**And when all the people had finished passing over, the ark of the LORD and the priests passed over before the people. **12**The sons of Reuben and the sons of Gad and the half-tribe of Manasseh passed over armed before the people of Israel, as Moses had told them. **13**About 40,000 ready for war passed over before the LORD for battle, to the plains of Jericho. **14**On that day the LORD exalted Joshua in the sight of all Israel, and they stood in awe of him just as they had stood in awe of Moses, all the days of his life.

15And the LORD said to Joshua, **16**"Command the priests bearing the ark of the testimony to come up out of the Jordan." **17**So Joshua commanded the priests, "Come up out of the Jordan." **18**And when the priests bearing the ark of the covenant of the LORD came up from the midst of the Jordan, and the soles of the priests' feet were lifted up on dry ground, the waters of the Jordan returned to their place and overflowed all its banks, as before.

19The people came up out of the Jordan on the tenth day of the first month, and they encamped at Gilgal on the east border of Jericho. **20**And those twelve stones, which they took out of the Jordan, Joshua set up at Gilgal. **21**And he said to the people of Israel, "When your children ask their fathers in times to come, 'What do these stones mean?' **22**then you shall let your children know, 'Israel passed over this Jordan on dry ground.' **23**For the LORD your God dried up the waters of the Jordan for you until you passed over, as the LORD your God did to the Red Sea, which he dried up for us until we passed over, **24**so that all the peoples of the earth may know that the hand of the LORD is mighty, that you may fear the LORD your God for ever."[c]

THE NEW GENERATION CIRCUMCISED

5 As soon as all the kings of the Amorites who were beyond the Jordan to the west, and all the kings of the Canaanites who were by the sea, heard that the LORD had dried

---

[a]Or *to rest* [b]Or *Joshua had set up* [c]Or *all the days*

up the waters of the Jordan for the people of Israel until they had crossed over, their hearts melted and there was no longer any spirit in them because of the people of Israel.

²At that time the LORD said to Joshua, "Make flint knives and circumcise the sons of Israel a second time." ³So Joshua made flint knives and circumcised the sons of Israel at Gibeath-haaraloth.*ᵃ* ⁴And this is the reason why Joshua circumcised them: all the males of the people who came out of Egypt, all the men of war, had died in the wilderness on the way after they had come out of Egypt. ⁵Though all the people who came out had been circumcised, yet all the people who were born on the way in the wilderness after they had come out of Egypt had not been circumcised. ⁶For the people of Israel walked forty years in the wilderness, until all the nation, the men of war who came out of Egypt, perished, because they did not obey the voice of the LORD; the LORD swore to them that he would not let them see the land that the LORD had sworn to their fathers to give to us, a land flowing with milk and honey. ⁷So it was their children, whom he raised up in their place, that Joshua circumcised. For they were uncircumcised, because they had not been circumcised on the way.

⁸When the circumcising of the whole nation was finished, they remained in their places in the camp until they were healed. ⁹And the LORD said to Joshua, "Today I have rolled away the reproach of Egypt from you." And so the name of that place is called Gilgal*ᵇ* to this day.

FIRST PASSOVER IN CANAAN

¹⁰While the people of Israel were encamped at Gilgal, they kept the Passover on the fourteenth day of the month in the evening on the plains of Jericho. ¹¹And the day after the Passover, on that very day, they ate of the produce of the land, unleavened cakes and parched grain. ¹²And the manna ceased the day after they ate of the produce of the land. And there was no longer manna for the people of Israel, but they ate of the fruit of the land of Canaan that year.

THE COMMANDER OF THE LORD'S ARMY

¹³When Joshua was by Jericho, he lifted up his eyes and looked, and behold, a man was standing before him with his drawn sword in his hand. And Joshua went to him and said to him, "Are you for us, or for our adversaries?" ¹⁴And he said, "No; but I am the commander of the army of the LORD. Now I have come." And Joshua fell on his face to the earth and worshipped*ᶜ* and said to him, "What does my lord say to his servant?" ¹⁵And the commander of the LORD's army said to Joshua, "Take off your sandals from your feet, for the place where you are standing is holy." And Joshua did so.

THE FALL OF JERICHO

6 Now Jericho was shut up inside and outside because of the people of Israel. None went out, and none came in. ²And the LORD said to Joshua, "See, I have given Jericho into your hand, with its king and mighty men of valour. ³You shall march round the city, all the men of war going round the city once. Thus shall you do for six days. ⁴Seven priests shall bear seven trumpets of rams' horns before the ark. On the seventh day you shall march round the city seven times, and the priests shall blow the trumpets. ⁵And when they make a long blast with the ram's horn, when you hear the sound of the trumpet, then all the people shall shout with a great shout, and the wall of the city will fall down flat,*ᵈ* and the people shall go up, everyone straight before him." ⁶So Joshua the son of Nun called the priests and said to them, "Take up the ark of the covenant and let seven priests bear seven trumpets of rams' horns before the ark of the LORD." ⁷And he said to the people, "Go forward. March round the city and let the armed men pass on before the ark of the LORD."

⁸And just as Joshua had commanded the people, the seven priests bearing the seven trumpets of rams' horns before the LORD went forward, blowing the trumpets, with the ark of the covenant of the LORD following them. ⁹The armed men were walking before the priests who were blowing the trumpets, and the rearguard was walking after the ark, while the trumpets blew continually. ¹⁰But Joshua commanded the people, "You shall not shout or make your voice heard, neither shall any word go out of your mouth, until the day I tell you to shout. Then you shall shout." ¹¹So he caused the ark of the LORD to circle the city, going round it once. And they came into the camp and spent the night in the camp.

ᵃGibeath-haaraloth means *the hill of the foreskins* *ᵇGilgal* sounds like the Hebrew for *to roll* *ᶜOr and paid homage* *ᵈ*Hebrew *under itself*; also verse 20

¹²Then Joshua rose early in the morning, and the priests took up the ark of the LORD. ¹³And the seven priests bearing the seven trumpets of rams' horns before the ark of the LORD walked on, and they blew the trumpets continually. And the armed men were walking before them, and the rearguard was walking after the ark of the LORD, while the trumpets blew continually. ¹⁴And the second day they marched round the city once, and returned into the camp. So they did for six days.

¹⁵On the seventh day they rose early, at the dawn of day, and marched around the city in the same manner seven times. It was only on that day that they marched around the city seven times. ¹⁶And at the seventh time, when the priests had blown the trumpets, Joshua said to the people, "Shout, for the LORD has given you the city. ¹⁷And the city and all that is within it shall be devoted to the LORD for destruction.ᵃ Only Rahab the prostitute and all who are with her in her house shall live, because she hid the messengers whom we sent. ¹⁸But you, keep yourselves from the things devoted to destruction, lest when you have devoted them you take any of the devoted things and make the camp of Israel a thing for destruction and bring trouble upon it. ¹⁹But all silver and gold, and every vessel of bronze and iron, are holy to the LORD; they shall go into the treasury of the LORD." ²⁰So the people shouted, and the trumpets were blown. As soon as the people heard the sound of the trumpet, the people shouted a great shout, and the wall fell down flat, so that the people went up into the city, every man straight before him, and they captured the city. ²¹Then they devoted all in the city to destruction, both men and women, young and old, oxen, sheep, and donkeys, with the edge of the sword.

²²But to the two men who had spied out the land, Joshua said, "Go into the prostitute's house and bring out from there the woman and all who belong to her, as you swore to her." ²³So the young men who had been spies went in and brought out Rahab and her father and mother and brothers and all who belonged to her. And they brought all her relatives and put them outside the camp of Israel. ²⁴And they burned the city with fire, and everything in it. Only the silver and gold, and the vessels of bronze and of iron, they put into the treasury of the house of the LORD. ²⁵But Rahab the prostitute and her father's household and all who belonged to her, Joshua saved alive. And she has lived in Israel to this day, because she hid the messengers whom Joshua sent to spy out Jericho.

²⁶Joshua laid an oath on them at that time, saying, "Cursed before the LORD be the man who rises up and rebuilds this city, Jericho.

> "At the cost of his firstborn shall he
>   lay its foundation,
> and at the cost of his youngest son
>   shall he set up its gates."

²⁷So the LORD was with Joshua, and his fame was in all the land.

ISRAEL DEFEATED AT AI

7 But the people of Israel broke faith in regard to the devoted things, for Achan the son of Carmi, son of Zabdi, son of Zerah, of the tribe of Judah, took some of the devoted things. And the anger of the LORD burned against the people of Israel.

²Joshua sent men from Jericho to Ai, which is near Beth-aven, east of Bethel, and said to them, "Go up and spy out the land." And the men went up and spied out Ai. ³And they returned to Joshua and said to him, "Do not make all the people go up, but let about two or three thousand men go up and attack Ai. Do not make the whole people toil up there, for they are few." ⁴So about three thousand men went up there from the people. And they fled before the men of Ai, ⁵and the men of Ai killed about thirty-six of their men and chased them before the gate as far as Shebarim and struck them at the descent. And the hearts of the people melted and became as water.

⁶Then Joshua tore his clothes and fell to the earth on his face before the ark of the LORD until the evening, he and the elders of Israel. And they put dust on their heads. ⁷And Joshua said, "Alas, O Lord GOD, why have you brought this people over the Jordan at all, to give us into the hands of the Amorites, to destroy us? Would that we had been content to dwell beyond the Jordan! ⁸O Lord, what can I say, when Israel has turned their backs before their enemies! ⁹For the Canaanites and all the inhabitants of the land will hear of it and will surround us and cut off our name from the earth. And what will you do for your great name?"

ᵃThat is, set apart (devoted) as an offering to the Lord (for destruction); also verses 18, 21

THE SIN OF ACHAN

¹⁰The Lord said to Joshua, "Get up! Why have you fallen on your face? ¹¹Israel has sinned; they have transgressed my covenant that I commanded them; they have taken some of the devoted things; they have stolen and lied and put them among their own belongings. ¹²Therefore the people of Israel cannot stand before their enemies. They turn their backs to their enemies, because they have become devoted for destruction.[a] I will be with you no more, unless you destroy the devoted things from among you. ¹³Get up! Consecrate the people and say, 'Consecrate yourselves for tomorrow; for thus says the Lord, God of Israel, "There are devoted things in your midst, O Israel. You cannot stand before your enemies until you take away the devoted things from among you." ¹⁴In the morning therefore you shall be brought near by your tribes. And the tribe that the Lord takes by lot shall come near by clans. And the clan that the Lord takes shall come near by households. And the household that the Lord takes shall come near man by man. ¹⁵And he who is taken with the devoted things shall be burned with fire, he and all that he has, because he has transgressed the covenant of the Lord, and because he has done an outrageous thing in Israel.'"

¹⁶So Joshua rose early in the morning and brought Israel near tribe by tribe, and the tribe of Judah was taken. ¹⁷And he brought near the clans of Judah, and the clan of the Zerahites was taken. And he brought near the clan of the Zerahites man by man, and Zabdi was taken. ¹⁸And he brought near his household man by man, and Achan the son of Carmi, son of Zabdi, son of Zerah, of the tribe of Judah, was taken. ¹⁹Then Joshua said to Achan, "My son, give glory to the Lord God of Israel and give praise[b] to him. And tell me now what you have done; do not hide it from me." ²⁰And Achan answered Joshua, "Truly I have sinned against the Lord God of Israel, and this is what I did: ²¹when I saw among the spoil a beautiful cloak from Shinar, and 200 shekels of silver, and a bar of gold weighing 50 shekels,[c] then I coveted them and took them. And see, they are hidden in the earth inside my tent, with the silver underneath."

²²So Joshua sent messengers, and they ran to the tent; and behold, it was hidden in his tent with the silver underneath. ²³And they took them out of the tent and brought them to Joshua and to all the people of Israel. And they laid them down before the Lord. ²⁴And Joshua and all Israel with him took Achan the son of Zerah, and the silver and the cloak and the bar of gold, and his sons and daughters and his oxen and donkeys and sheep and his tent and all that he had. And they brought them up to the Valley of Achor. ²⁵And Joshua said, "Why did you bring trouble on us? The Lord brings trouble on you today." And all Israel stoned him with stones. They burned them with fire and stoned them with stones. ²⁶And they raised over him a great heap of stones that remains to this day. Then the Lord turned from his burning anger. Therefore, to this day the name of that place is called the Valley of Achor.[d]

THE FALL OF AI

8 And the Lord said to Joshua, "Do not fear and do not be dismayed. Take all the fighting men with you, and arise, go up to Ai. See, I have given into your hand the king of Ai, and his people, his city, and his land. ²And you shall do to Ai and its king as you did to Jericho and its king. Only its spoil and its livestock you shall take as plunder for yourselves. Lay an ambush against the city, behind it."

³So Joshua and all the fighting men arose to go up to Ai. And Joshua chose 30,000 mighty men of valour and sent them out by night. ⁴And he commanded them, "Behold, you shall lie in ambush against the city, behind it. Do not go very far from the city, but all of you remain ready. ⁵And I and all the people who are with me will approach the city. And when they come out against us just as before, we shall flee before them. ⁶And they will come out after us, until we have drawn them away from the city. For they will say, 'They are fleeing from us, just as before.' So we will flee before them. ⁷Then you shall rise up from the ambush and seize the city, for the Lord your God will give it into your hand. ⁸And as soon as you have taken the city, you shall set the city on fire. You shall do according to the word of the Lord. See, I have commanded you." ⁹So Joshua sent them out. And they went to the place of ambush and lay between Bethel and Ai, to the west of Ai, but Joshua spent that night among the people.

---

[a]That is, set apart (devoted) as an offering to the Lord (for destruction) [b]Or *and make confession* [c]A *shekel* was about 2/5 of an ounce or 11 grams [d]*Achor* means *trouble*

¹⁰Joshua arose early in the morning and mustered the people and went up, he and the elders of Israel, before the people to Ai. ¹¹And all the fighting men who were with him went up and drew near before the city and encamped on the north side of Ai, with a ravine between them and Ai. ¹²He took about 5,000 men and set them in ambush between Bethel and Ai, to the west of the city. ¹³So they stationed the forces, the main encampment that was north of the city and its rearguard west of the city. But Joshua spent that night in the valley. ¹⁴And as soon as the king of Ai saw this, he and all his people, the men of the city, hurried and went out early to the appointed place[a] towards the Arabah to meet Israel in battle. But he did not know that there was an ambush against him behind the city. ¹⁵And Joshua and all Israel pretended to be beaten before them and fled in the direction of the wilderness. ¹⁶So all the people who were in the city were called together to pursue them, and as they pursued Joshua they were drawn away from the city. ¹⁷Not a man was left in Ai or Bethel who did not go out after Israel. They left the city open and pursued Israel.

¹⁸Then the LORD said to Joshua, "Stretch out the javelin that is in your hand towards Ai, for I will give it into your hand." And Joshua stretched out the javelin that was in his hand towards the city. ¹⁹And the men in the ambush rose quickly out of their place, and as soon as he had stretched out his hand, they ran and entered the city and captured it. And they hurried to set the city on fire. ²⁰So when the men of Ai looked back, behold, the smoke of the city went up to heaven, and they had no power to flee this way or that, for the people who fled to the wilderness turned back against the pursuers. ²¹And when Joshua and all Israel saw that the ambush had captured the city, and that the smoke of the city went up, then they turned back and struck down the men of Ai. ²²And the others came out from the city against them, so they were in the midst of Israel, some on this side, and some on that side. And Israel struck them down, until there was left none that survived or escaped. ²³But the king of Ai they took alive, and brought him near to Joshua.

²⁴When Israel had finished killing all the inhabitants of Ai in the open wilderness where they pursued them, and all of them to the very last had fallen by the edge of the sword, all Israel returned to Ai and struck it down with the edge of the sword. ²⁵And all who fell that day, both men and women, were 12,000, all the people of Ai. ²⁶But Joshua did not draw back his hand with which he stretched out the javelin until he had devoted all the inhabitants of Ai to destruction.[b] ²⁷Only the livestock and the spoil of that city Israel took as their plunder, according to the word of the LORD that he had commanded Joshua. ²⁸So Joshua burned Ai and made it for ever a heap of ruins, as it is to this day. ²⁹And he hanged the king of Ai on a tree until evening. And at sunset Joshua commanded, and they took his body down from the tree and threw it at the entrance of the gate of the city and raised over it a great heap of stones, which stands there to this day.

JOSHUA RENEWS THE COVENANT

³⁰At that time Joshua built an altar to the LORD, the God of Israel, on Mount Ebal, ³¹just as Moses the servant of the LORD had commanded the people of Israel, as it is written in the Book of the Law of Moses, "an altar of uncut stones, upon which no man has wielded an iron tool." And they offered on it burnt offerings to the LORD and sacrificed peace offerings. ³²And there, in the presence of the people of Israel, he wrote on the stones a copy of the law of Moses, which he had written. ³³And all Israel, sojourner as well as native born, with their elders and officers and their judges, stood on opposite sides of the ark before the Levitical priests who carried the ark of the covenant of the LORD, half of them in front of Mount Gerizim and half of them in front of Mount Ebal, just as Moses the servant of the LORD had commanded at the first, to bless the people of Israel. ³⁴And afterwards he read all the words of the law, the blessing and the curse, according to all that is written in the Book of the Law. ³⁵There was not a word of all that Moses commanded that Joshua did not read before all the assembly of Israel, and the women, and the little ones, and the sojourners who lived[c] among them.

THE GIBEONITE DECEPTION

9 As soon as all the kings who were beyond the Jordan in the hill country and in the lowland all along the coast of the Great Sea towards Lebanon, the Hittites, the Amorites, the Canaanites, the Perizzites, the Hivites, and the Jebusites, heard of this,

---

[a]Hebrew *appointed time* [b]That is, set apart (devoted) as an offering to the Lord (for destruction) [c]Or *travelled*

²they gathered together as one to fight against Joshua and Israel.

³But when the inhabitants of Gibeon heard what Joshua had done to Jericho and to Ai, ⁴they on their part acted with cunning and went and made ready provisions and took worn-out sacks for their donkeys, and wineskins, worn-out and torn and mended, ⁵with worn-out, patched sandals on their feet, and worn-out clothes. And all their provisions were dry and crumbly. ⁶And they went to Joshua in the camp at Gilgal and said to him and to the men of Israel, "We have come from a distant country, so now make a covenant with us." ⁷But the men of Israel said to the Hivites, "Perhaps you live among us; then how can we make a covenant with you?" ⁸They said to Joshua, "We are your servants." And Joshua said to them, "Who are you? And where do you come from?" ⁹They said to him, "From a very distant country your servants have come, because of the name of the LORD your God. For we have heard a report of him, and all that he did in Egypt, ¹⁰and all that he did to the two kings of the Amorites who were beyond the Jordan, to Sihon the king of Heshbon, and to Og king of Bashan, who lived in Ashtaroth. ¹¹So our elders and all the inhabitants of our country said to us, 'Take provisions in your hand for the journey and go to meet them and say to them, "We are your servants. Come now, make a covenant with us."' ¹²Here is our bread. It was still warm when we took it from our houses as our food for the journey on the day we set out to come to you, but now, behold, it is dry and crumbly. ¹³These wineskins were new when we filled them, and behold, they have burst. And these garments and sandals of ours are worn out from the very long journey." ¹⁴So the men took some of their provisions, but did not ask counsel from the LORD. ¹⁵And Joshua made peace with them and made a covenant with them, to let them live, and the leaders of the congregation swore to them.

¹⁶At the end of three days after they had made a covenant with them, they heard that they were their neighbours and that they lived among them. ¹⁷And the people of Israel set out and reached their cities on the third day. Now their cities were Gibeon, Chephirah, Beeroth, and Kiriath-jearim. ¹⁸But the people of Israel did not attack them, because the leaders of the congregation had sworn to them by the LORD, the God of Israel. Then all the congregation murmured against the leaders. ¹⁹But all the leaders said to all the congregation, "We have sworn to them by the LORD, the God of Israel, and now we may not touch them. ²⁰This we will do to them: let them live, lest wrath be upon us, because of the oath that we swore to them." ²¹And the leaders said to them, "Let them live." So they became cutters of wood and drawers of water for all the congregation, just as the leaders had said of them.

²²Joshua summoned them, and he said to them, "Why did you deceive us, saying, 'We are very far from you', when you dwell among us? ²³Now therefore you are cursed, and some of you shall never be anything but servants, cutters of wood and drawers of water for the house of my God." ²⁴They answered Joshua, "Because it was told to your servants for a certainty that the LORD your God had commanded his servant Moses to give you all the land and to destroy all the inhabitants of the land from before you—so we feared greatly for our lives because of you and did this thing. ²⁵And now, behold, we are in your hand. Whatever seems good and right in your sight to do to us, do it." ²⁶So he did this to them and delivered them out of the hand of the people of Israel, and they did not kill them. ²⁷But Joshua made them that day cutters of wood and drawers of water for the congregation and for the altar of the LORD, to this day, in the place that he should choose.

THE SUN STANDS STILL

10 As soon as Adoni-zedek, king of Jerusalem, heard how Joshua had captured Ai and had devoted it to destruction,ᵃ doing to Ai and its king as he had done to Jericho and its king, and how the inhabitants of Gibeon had made peace with Israel and were among them, ²heᵇ feared greatly, because Gibeon was a great city, like one of the royal cities, and because it was greater than Ai, and all its men were warriors. ³So Adoni-zedek king of Jerusalem sent to Hoham king of Hebron, to Piram king of Jarmuth, to Japhia king of Lachish, and to Debir king of Eglon, saying, ⁴"Come up to me and help me, and let us strike Gibeon. For it has made peace with Joshua and with the people of Israel." ⁵Then the five kings of the Amorites, the king of Jerusalem, the

---

ᵃThat is, set apart (devoted) as an offering to the Lord (for destruction); also verses 28, 35, 37, 39, 40   ᵇOne Hebrew manuscript, Vulgate (compare Syriac); most Hebrew manuscripts *they*

king of Hebron, the king of Jarmuth, the king of Lachish, and the king of Eglon, gathered their forces and went up with all their armies and encamped against Gibeon and made war against it.

⁶And the men of Gibeon sent to Joshua at the camp in Gilgal, saying, "Do not relax your hand from your servants. Come up to us quickly and save us and help us, for all the kings of the Amorites who dwell in the hill country are gathered against us." ⁷So Joshua went up from Gilgal, he and all the people of war with him, and all the mighty men of valour. ⁸And the LORD said to Joshua, "Do not fear them, for I have given them into your hands. Not a man of them shall stand before you." ⁹So Joshua came upon them suddenly, having marched up all night from Gilgal. ¹⁰And the LORD threw them into a panic before Israel, whoᵃ struck them with a great blow at Gibeon and chased them by the way of the ascent of Beth-horon and struck them as far as Azekah and Makkedah. ¹¹And as they fled before Israel, while they were going down the ascent of Beth-horon, the LORD threw down large stones from heaven on them as far as Azekah, and they died. There were more who died because of the hailstones than the sons of Israel killed with the sword.

¹²At that time Joshua spoke to the LORD in the day when the LORD gave the Amorites over to the sons of Israel, and he said in the sight of Israel,

> "Sun, stand still at Gibeon,
>   and moon, in the Valley of Aijalon."
> ¹³ And the sun stood still, and
>   the moon stopped,
>   until the nation took vengeance
>   on their enemies.

Is this not written in the Book of Jashar? The sun stopped in the midst of heaven and did not hurry to set for about a whole day. ¹⁴There has been no day like it before or since, when the LORD heeded the voice of a man, for the LORD fought for Israel.

¹⁵So Joshua returned, and all Israel with him, to the camp at Gilgal.

FIVE AMORITE KINGS EXECUTED

¹⁶These five kings fled and hid themselves in the cave at Makkedah. ¹⁷And it was told to Joshua, "The five kings have been found, hidden in the cave at Makkedah." ¹⁸And Joshua said, "Roll large stones against the mouth of the cave and set men by it to guard them, ¹⁹but do not stay there yourselves. Pursue your enemies; attack their rearguard. Do not let them enter their cities, for the LORD your God has given them into your hand." ²⁰When Joshua and the sons of Israel had finished striking them with a great blow until they were wiped out, and when the remnant that remained of them had entered into the fortified cities, ²¹then all the people returned safe to Joshua in the camp at Makkedah. Not a man moved his tongue against any of the people of Israel.

²²Then Joshua said, "Open the mouth of the cave and bring those five kings out to me from the cave." ²³And they did so, and brought those five kings out to him from the cave, the king of Jerusalem, the king of Hebron, the king of Jarmuth, the king of Lachish, and the king of Eglon. ²⁴And when they brought those kings out to Joshua, Joshua summoned all the men of Israel and said to the chiefs of the men of war who had gone with him, "Come near; put your feet on the necks of these kings." Then they came near and put their feet on their necks. ²⁵And Joshua said to them, "Do not be afraid or dismayed; be strong and courageous. For thus the LORD will do to all your enemies against whom you fight." ²⁶And afterwards Joshua struck them and put them to death, and he hanged them on five trees. And they hung on the trees until evening. ²⁷But at the time of the going down of the sun, Joshua commanded, and they took them down from the trees and threw them into the cave where they had hidden themselves, and they set large stones against the mouth of the cave, which remain to this very day.

²⁸As for Makkedah, Joshua captured it on that day and struck it, and its king, with the edge of the sword. He devoted to destruction every person in it; he left none remaining. And he did to the king of Makkedah just as he had done to the king of Jericho.

CONQUEST OF SOUTHERN CANAAN

²⁹Then Joshua and all Israel with him passed on from Makkedah to Libnah and fought against Libnah. ³⁰And the LORD gave it also and its king into the hand of Israel. And he struck it with the edge of the sword, and every person in it; he left none remaining in it. And he did to its king as he had done to the king of Jericho.

ᵃ Or *and he*

³¹Then Joshua and all Israel with him passed on from Libnah to Lachish and laid siege to it and fought against it. ³²And the Lord gave Lachish into the hand of Israel, and he captured it on the second day and struck it with the edge of the sword, and every person in it, as he had done to Libnah.

³³Then Horam king of Gezer came up to help Lachish. And Joshua struck him and his people, until he left none remaining.

³⁴Then Joshua and all Israel with him passed on from Lachish to Eglon. And they laid siege to it and fought against it. ³⁵And they captured it on that day, and struck it with the edge of the sword. And he devoted every person in it to destruction that day, as he had done to Lachish.

³⁶Then Joshua and all Israel with him went up from Eglon to Hebron. And they fought against it ³⁷and captured it and struck it with the edge of the sword, and its king and its towns, and every person in it. He left none remaining, as he had done to Eglon, and devoted it to destruction and every person in it.

³⁸Then Joshua and all Israel with him turned back to Debir and fought against it ³⁹and he captured it with its king and all its towns. And they struck them with the edge of the sword and devoted to destruction every person in it; he left none remaining. Just as he had done to Hebron and to Libnah and its king, so he did to Debir and to its king.

⁴⁰So Joshua struck the whole land, the hill country and the Negeb and the lowland and the slopes, and all their kings. He left none remaining, but devoted to destruction all that breathed, just as the Lord God of Israel commanded. ⁴¹And Joshua struck them from Kadesh-barnea as far as Gaza, and all the country of Goshen, as far as Gibeon. ⁴²And Joshua captured all these kings and their land at one time, because the Lord God of Israel fought for Israel. ⁴³Then Joshua returned, and all Israel with him, to the camp at Gilgal.

CONQUESTS IN NORTHERN CANAAN

11 When Jabin, king of Hazor, heard of this, he sent to Jobab king of Madon, and to the king of Shimron, and to the king of Achshaph, ²and to the kings who were in the northern hill country, and in the Arabah south of Chinneroth, and in the lowland, and in Naphoth-dor on the west, ³to the Canaanites in the east and the west, the Amorites, the Hittites, the Perizzites, and the Jebusites in the hill country, and the Hivites under Hermon in the land of Mizpah. ⁴And they came out with all their troops, a great horde, in number like the sand that is on the seashore, with very many horses and chariots. ⁵And all these kings joined their forces and came and encamped together at the waters of Merom to fight against Israel.

⁶And the Lord said to Joshua, "Do not be afraid of them, for tomorrow at this time I will give over all of them, slain, to Israel. You shall hamstring their horses and burn their chariots with fire." ⁷So Joshua and all his warriors came suddenly against them by the waters of Merom and fell upon them. ⁸And the Lord gave them into the hand of Israel, who struck them and chased them as far as Great Sidon and Misrephoth-maim, and eastwards as far as the Valley of Mizpeh. And they struck them until he left none remaining. ⁹And Joshua did to them just as the Lord said to him: he hamstrung their horses and burned their chariots with fire.

¹⁰And Joshua turned back at that time and captured Hazor and struck its king with the sword, for Hazor formerly was the head of all those kingdoms. ¹¹And they struck with the sword all who were in it, devoting them to destruction;ᵃ there was none left that breathed. And he burned Hazor with fire. ¹²And all the cities of those kings, and all their kings, Joshua captured, and struck them with the edge of the sword, devoting them to destruction, just as Moses the servant of the Lord had commanded. ¹³But none of the cities that stood on mounds did Israel burn, except Hazor alone; that Joshua burned. ¹⁴And all the spoil of these cities and the livestock, the people of Israel took for their plunder. But every person they struck with the edge of the sword until they had destroyed them, and they did not leave any who breathed. ¹⁵Just as the Lord had commanded Moses his servant, so Moses commanded Joshua, and so Joshua did. He left nothing undone of all that the Lord had commanded Moses.

¹⁶So Joshua took all that land, the hill country and all the Negeb and all the land of Goshen and the lowland and the Arabah and the hill country of Israel and its lowland ¹⁷from Mount Halak, which rises towards Seir, as far as Baal-gad in the Valley of Lebanon below Mount Hermon. And he captured all

---

ᵃThat is, setting apart (devoting) as an offering to the Lord (for destruction); also verses 12, 20, 21

their kings and struck them and put them to death. ¹⁸Joshua made war for a long time with all those kings. ¹⁹There was not a city that made peace with the people of Israel except the Hivites, the inhabitants of Gibeon. They took them all in battle. ²⁰For it was the LORD's doing to harden their hearts that they should come against Israel in battle, in order that they should be devoted to destruction and should receive no mercy but be destroyed, just as the LORD commanded Moses.

²¹And Joshua came at that time and cut off the Anakim from the hill country, from Hebron, from Debir, from Anab, and from all the hill country of Judah, and from all the hill country of Israel. Joshua devoted them to destruction with their cities. ²²There was none of the Anakim left in the land of the people of Israel. Only in Gaza, in Gath, and in Ashdod did some remain. ²³So Joshua took the whole land, according to all that the LORD had spoken to Moses. And Joshua gave it for an inheritance to Israel according to their tribal allotments. And the land had rest from war.

KINGS DEFEATED BY MOSES

12 Now these are the kings of the land whom the people of Israel defeated and took possession of their land beyond the Jordan towards the sunrise, from the Valley of the Arnon to Mount Hermon, with all the Arabah eastwards: ²Sihon king of the Amorites who lived at Heshbon and ruled from Aroer, which is on the edge of the Valley of the Arnon, and from the middle of the valley as far as the river Jabbok, the boundary of the Ammonites, that is, half of Gilead, ³and the Arabah to the Sea of Chinneroth eastwards, and in the direction of Beth-jeshimoth, to the Sea of the Arabah, the Salt Sea, southwards to the foot of the slopes of Pisgah; ⁴and Og[a] king of Bashan, one of the remnant of the Rephaim, who lived at Ashtaroth and at Edrei ⁵and ruled over Mount Hermon and Salecah and all Bashan to the boundary of the Geshurites and the Maacathites, and over half of Gilead to the boundary of Sihon king of Heshbon. ⁶Moses, the servant of the LORD, and the people of Israel defeated them. And Moses the servant of the LORD gave their land for a possession to the Reubenites and the Gadites and the half-tribe of Manasseh.

KINGS DEFEATED BY JOSHUA

⁷And these are the kings of the land whom Joshua and the people of Israel defeated on the west side of the Jordan, from Baal-gad in the Valley of Lebanon to Mount Halak, that rises towards Seir (and Joshua gave their land to the tribes of Israel as a possession according to their allotments, ⁸in the hill country, in the lowland, in the Arabah, in the slopes, in the wilderness, and in the Negeb, the land of the Hittites, the Amorites, the Canaanites, the Perizzites, the Hivites, and the Jebusites): ⁹the king of Jericho, one; the king of Ai, which is beside Bethel, one; ¹⁰the king of Jerusalem, one; the king of Hebron, one; ¹¹the king of Jarmuth, one; the king of Lachish, one; ¹²the king of Eglon, one; the king of Gezer, one; ¹³the king of Debir, one; the king of Geder, one; ¹⁴the king of Hormah, one; the king of Arad, one; ¹⁵the king of Libnah, one; the king of Adullam, one; ¹⁶the king of Makkedah, one; the king of Bethel, one; ¹⁷the king of Tappuah, one; the king of Hepher, one; ¹⁸the king of Aphek, one; the king of Lasharon, one; ¹⁹the king of Madon, one; the king of Hazor, one; ²⁰the king of Shimron-meron, one; the king of Achshaph, one; ²¹the king of Taanach, one; the king of Megiddo, one; ²²the king of Kedesh, one; the king of Jokneam in Carmel, one; ²³the king of Dor in Naphath-dor, one; the king of Goiim in Galilee,[b] one; ²⁴the king of Tirzah, one: in all, thirty-one kings.

LAND STILL TO BE CONQUERED

13 Now Joshua was old and advanced in years, and the LORD said to him, "You are old and advanced in years, and there remains yet very much land to possess. ²This is the land that yet remains: all the regions of the Philistines, and all those of the Geshurites ³(from the Shihor, which is east of Egypt, northwards to the boundary of Ekron, it is counted as Canaanite; there are five rulers of the Philistines, those of Gaza, Ashdod, Ashkelon, Gath, and Ekron), and those of the Avvim, ⁴in the south, all the land of the Canaanites, and Mearah that belongs to the Sidonians, to Aphek, to the boundary of the Amorites, ⁵and the land of the Gebalites, and all Lebanon, towards the sunrise, from Baal-gad below Mount Hermon to Lebo-hamath, ⁶all the inhabitants of the hill country from Lebanon to Misrephoth-maim, even all the Sidonians. I myself will drive them out from before the people of Israel. Only allot the land to Israel for an inheritance, as I have

---

[a]Septuagint; Hebrew *the boundary of Og* [b]Septuagint; Hebrew *Gilgal*

commanded you. ⁷Now therefore divide this land for an inheritance to the nine tribes and half the tribe of Manasseh."

THE INHERITANCE EAST OF THE JORDAN

⁸With the other half of the tribe of Manasseh[a] the Reubenites and the Gadites received their inheritance, which Moses gave them, beyond the Jordan eastwards, as Moses the servant of the LORD gave them: ⁹from Aroer, which is on the edge of the Valley of the Arnon, and the city that is in the middle of the valley, and all the tableland of Medeba as far as Dibon; ¹⁰and all the cities of Sihon king of the Amorites, who reigned in Heshbon, as far as the boundary of the Ammonites; ¹¹and Gilead, and the region of the Geshurites and Maacathites, and all Mount Hermon, and all Bashan to Salecah; ¹²all the kingdom of Og in Bashan, who reigned in Ashtaroth and in Edrei (he alone was left of the remnant of the Rephaim); these Moses had struck and driven out. ¹³Yet the people of Israel did not drive out the Geshurites or the Maacathites, but Geshur and Maacath dwell in the midst of Israel to this day.

¹⁴To the tribe of Levi alone Moses gave no inheritance. The offerings by fire to the LORD God of Israel are their inheritance, as he said to him.

¹⁵And Moses gave an inheritance to the tribe of the people of Reuben according to their clans. ¹⁶So their territory was from Aroer, which is on the edge of the Valley of the Arnon, and the city that is in the middle of the valley, and all the tableland by Medeba; ¹⁷with Heshbon, and all its cities that are in the tableland; Dibon, and Bamoth-baal, and Beth-baal-meon, ¹⁸and Jahaz, and Kedemoth, and Mephaath, ¹⁹and Kiriathaim, and Sibmah, and Zereth-shahar on the hill of the valley, ²⁰and Beth-peor, and the slopes of Pisgah, and Beth-jeshimoth, ²¹that is, all the cities of the tableland, and all the kingdom of Sihon king of the Amorites, who reigned in Heshbon, whom Moses defeated with the leaders of Midian, Evi and Rekem and Zur and Hur and Reba, the princes of Sihon, who lived in the land. ²²Balaam also, the son of Beor, the one who practised divination, was killed with the sword by the people of Israel among the rest of their slain. ²³And the border of the people of Reuben was the Jordan as a boundary. This was the inheritance of the people of Reuben, according to their clans with their cities and villages.

²⁴Moses gave an inheritance also to the tribe of Gad, to the people of Gad, according to their clans. ²⁵Their territory was Jazer, and all the cities of Gilead, and half the land of the Ammonites, to Aroer, which is east of Rabbah, ²⁶and from Heshbon to Ramath-mizpeh and Betonim, and from Mahanaim to the territory of Debir,[b] ²⁷and in the valley Beth-haram, Beth-nimrah, Succoth, and Zaphon, the rest of the kingdom of Sihon king of Heshbon, having the Jordan as a boundary, to the lower end of the Sea of Chinnereth, eastwards beyond the Jordan. ²⁸This is the inheritance of the people of Gad according to their clans, with their cities and villages.

²⁹And Moses gave an inheritance to the half-tribe of Manasseh. It was allotted to the half-tribe of the people of Manasseh according to their clans. ³⁰Their region extended from Mahanaim, through all Bashan, the whole kingdom of Og king of Bashan, and all the towns of Jair, which are in Bashan, sixty cities, ³¹and half Gilead, and Ashtaroth, and Edrei, the cities of the kingdom of Og in Bashan. These were allotted to the people of Machir the son of Manasseh for the half of the people of Machir according to their clans.

³²These are the inheritances that Moses distributed in the plains of Moab, beyond the Jordan east of Jericho. ³³But to the tribe of Levi Moses gave no inheritance; the LORD God of Israel is their inheritance, just as he said to them.

THE INHERITANCE WEST OF THE JORDAN

14 These are the inheritances that the people of Israel received in the land of Canaan, which Eleazar the priest and Joshua the son of Nun and the heads of the fathers' houses of the tribes of the people of Israel gave them to inherit. ²Their inheritance was by lot, just as the LORD had commanded by the hand of Moses for the nine and a half tribes. ³For Moses had given an inheritance to the two and a half tribes beyond the Jordan, but to the Levites he gave no inheritance among them. ⁴For the people of Joseph were two tribes, Manasseh and Ephraim. And no portion was given to the Levites in the land, but only cities to dwell in, with their pasture lands for their livestock and their substance. ⁵The people of Israel did as the LORD commanded Moses; they allotted the land.

---

[a]Hebrew *With it* [b]Septuagint, Syriac, Vulgate; Hebrew *Lidebir*

JOSHUA 14–15

CALEB'S REQUEST AND INHERITANCE

⁶Then the people of Judah came to Joshua at Gilgal. And Caleb the son of Jephunneh the Kenizzite said to him, "You know what the LORD said to Moses the man of God in Kadesh-barnea concerning you and me. ⁷I was forty years old when Moses the servant of the LORD sent me from Kadesh-barnea to spy out the land, and I brought him word again as it was in my heart. ⁸But my brothers who went up with me made the heart of the people melt; yet I wholly followed the LORD my God. ⁹And Moses swore on that day, saying, 'Surely the land on which your foot has trodden shall be an inheritance for you and your children for ever, because you have wholly followed the LORD my God.' ¹⁰And now, behold, the LORD has kept me alive, just as he said, these forty-five years since the time that the LORD spoke this word to Moses, while Israel walked in the wilderness. And now, behold, I am this day eighty-five years old. ¹¹I am still as strong today as I was in the day that Moses sent me; my strength now is as my strength was then, for war and for going and coming. ¹²So now give me this hill country of which the LORD spoke on that day, for you heard on that day how the Anakim were there, with great fortified cities. It may be that the LORD will be with me, and I shall drive them out just as the LORD said."

¹³Then Joshua blessed him, and he gave Hebron to Caleb the son of Jephunneh for an inheritance. ¹⁴Therefore Hebron became the inheritance of Caleb the son of Jephunneh the Kenizzite to this day, because he wholly followed the LORD, the God of Israel. ¹⁵Now the name of Hebron formerly was Kiriath-arba.ᵃ (Arbaᵇ was the greatest man among the Anakim.) And the land had rest from war.

THE ALLOTMENT FOR JUDAH

15 The allotment for the tribe of the people of Judah according to their clans reached southwards to the boundary of Edom, to the wilderness of Zin at the farthest south. ²And their southern boundary ran from the end of the Salt Sea, from the bay that faces southwards. ³It goes out southwards of the ascent of Akrabbim, passes along to Zin, and goes up south of Kadesh-barnea, along by Hezron, up to Addar, turns round to Karka, ⁴passes along to Azmon, goes out by the Brook of Egypt, and comes to its end at the sea. This shall be your southern boundary. ⁵And the eastern boundary is the Salt Sea, to the mouth of the Jordan. And the boundary on the north side runs from the bay of the sea at the mouth of the Jordan. ⁶And the boundary goes up to Beth-hoglah and passes along north of Beth-arabah. And the boundary goes up to the stone of Bohan the son of Reuben. ⁷And the boundary goes up to Debir from the Valley of Achor, and so northwards, turning towards Gilgal, which is opposite the ascent of Adummim, which is on the south side of the valley. And the boundary passes along to the waters of En-shemesh and ends at En-rogel. ⁸Then the boundary goes up by the Valley of the Son of Hinnom at the southern shoulder of the Jebusite (that is, Jerusalem). And the boundary goes up to the top of the mountain that lies over against the Valley of Hinnom, on the west, at the northern end of the Valley of Rephaim. ⁹Then the boundary extends from the top of the mountain to the spring of the waters of Nephtoah, and from there to the cities of Mount Ephron. Then the boundary bends round to Baalah (that is, Kiriath-jearim). ¹⁰And the boundary circles west of Baalah to Mount Seir, passes along to the northern shoulder of Mount Jearim (that is, Chesalon), and goes down to Beth-shemesh and passes along by Timnah. ¹¹The boundary goes out to the shoulder of the hill north of Ekron, then the boundary bends round to Shikkeron and passes along to Mount Baalah and goes out to Jabneel. Then the boundary comes to an end at the sea. ¹²And the west boundary was the Great Sea with its coastline. This is the boundary round the people of Judah according to their clans.

¹³According to the commandment of the LORD to Joshua, he gave to Caleb the son of Jephunneh a portion among the people of Judah, Kiriath-arba, that is, Hebron (Arba was the father of Anak). ¹⁴And Caleb drove out from there the three sons of Anak, Sheshai and Ahiman and Talmai, the descendants of Anak. ¹⁵And he went up from there against the inhabitants of Debir. Now the name of Debir formerly was Kiriath-sepher. ¹⁶And Caleb said, "Whoever strikes Kiriath-sepher and captures it, to him will I give Achsah my daughter as wife." ¹⁷And Othniel the son of Kenaz, the brother of Caleb, captured it. And he gave him Achsah his daughter as wife. ¹⁸When she came to him, she urged him to ask her father for a field. And she got off her donkey, and Caleb said to her, "What

---

ᵃ*Kiriath-arba* means *the city of Arba* ᵇHebrew *He*

do you want?" ¹⁹She said to him, "Give me a blessing. Since you have given me the land of the Negeb, give me also springs of water." And he gave her the upper springs and the lower springs.

²⁰This is the inheritance of the tribe of the people of Judah according to their clans. ²¹The cities belonging to the tribe of the people of Judah in the extreme south, towards the boundary of Edom, were Kabzeel, Eder, Jagur, ²²Kinah, Dimonah, Adadah, ²³Kedesh, Hazor, Ithnan, ²⁴Ziph, Telem, Bealoth, ²⁵Hazor-hadattah, Kerioth-hezron (that is, Hazor), ²⁶Amam, Shema, Moladah, ²⁷Hazar-gaddah, Heshmon, Beth-pelet, ²⁸Hazar-shual, Beer-sheba, Biziothiah, ²⁹Baalah, Iim, Ezem, ³⁰Eltolad, Chesil, Hormah, ³¹Ziklag, Madmannah, Sansannah, ³²Lebaoth, Shilhim, Ain, and Rimmon: in all, twenty-nine cities with their villages.

³³And in the lowland, Eshtaol, Zorah, Ashnah, ³⁴Zanoah, En-gannim, Tappuah, Enam, ³⁵Jarmuth, Adullam, Socoh, Azekah, ³⁶Shaaraim, Adithaim, Gederah, Gederothaim: fourteen cities with their villages.

³⁷Zenan, Hadashah, Migdal-gad, ³⁸Dilean, Mizpeh, Joktheel, ³⁹Lachish, Bozkath, Eglon, ⁴⁰Cabbon, Lahmam, Chitlish, ⁴¹Gederoth, Beth-dagon, Naamah, and Makkedah: sixteen cities with their villages.

⁴²Libnah, Ether, Ashan, ⁴³Iphtah, Ashnah, Nezib, ⁴⁴Keilah, Achzib, and Mareshah: nine cities with their villages.

⁴⁵Ekron, with its towns and its villages; ⁴⁶from Ekron to the sea, all that were by the side of Ashdod, with their villages.

⁴⁷Ashdod, its towns and its villages; Gaza, its towns and its villages; to the Brook of Egypt, and the Great Sea with its coastline.

⁴⁸And in the hill country, Shamir, Jattir, Socoh, ⁴⁹Dannah, Kiriath-sannah (that is, Debir), ⁵⁰Anab, Eshtemoh, Anim, ⁵¹Goshen, Holon, and Giloh: eleven cities with their villages.

⁵²Arab, Dumah, Eshan, ⁵³Janim, Beth-tappuah, Aphekah, ⁵⁴Humtah, Kiriath-arba (that is, Hebron), and Zior: nine cities with their villages.

⁵⁵Maon, Carmel, Ziph, Juttah, ⁵⁶Jezreel, Jokdeam, Zanoah, ⁵⁷Kain, Gibeah, and Timnah: ten cities with their villages.

⁵⁸Halhul, Beth-zur, Gedor, ⁵⁹Maarath, Beth-anoth, and Eltekon: six cities with their villages.

⁶⁰Kiriath-baal (that is, Kiriath-jearim), and Rabbah: two cities with their villages.

⁶¹In the wilderness, Beth-arabah, Middin, Secacah, ⁶²Nibshan, the City of Salt, and Engedi: six cities with their villages.

⁶³But the Jebusites, the inhabitants of Jerusalem, the people of Judah could not drive out, so the Jebusites dwell with the people of Judah at Jerusalem to this day.

THE ALLOTMENT FOR EPHRAIM AND MANASSEH

16 The allotment of the people of Joseph went from the Jordan by Jericho, east of the waters of Jericho, into the wilderness, going up from Jericho into the hill country to Bethel. ²Then going from Bethel to Luz, it passes along to Ataroth, the territory of the Archites. ³Then it goes down westwards to the territory of the Japhletites, as far as the territory of Lower Beth-horon, then to Gezer, and it ends at the sea.

⁴The people of Joseph, Manasseh and Ephraim, received their inheritance.

⁵The territory of the people of Ephraim by their clans was as follows: the boundary of their inheritance on the east was Ataroth-addar as far as Upper Beth-horon, ⁶and the boundary goes from there to the sea. On the north is Michmethath. Then on the east the boundary turns round towards Taanath-shiloh and passes along beyond it on the east to Janoah, ⁷then it goes down from Janoah to Ataroth and to Naarah, and touches Jericho, ending at the Jordan. ⁸From Tappuah the boundary goes westwards to the brook Kanah and ends at the sea. Such is the inheritance of the tribe of the people of Ephraim by their clans, ⁹together with the towns that were set apart for the people of Ephraim within the inheritance of the Manassites, all those towns with their villages. ¹⁰However, they did not drive out the Canaanites who lived in Gezer, so the Canaanites have lived in the midst of Ephraim to this day but have been made to do forced labour.

17 Then allotment was made to the people of Manasseh, for he was the firstborn of Joseph. To Machir the firstborn of Manasseh, the father of Gilead, were allotted Gilead and Bashan, because he was a man of war. ²And allotments were made to the rest of the people of Manasseh by their clans, Abiezer, Helek, Asriel, Shechem, Hepher, and Shemida. These were the male descendants of Manasseh the son of Joseph, by their clans.

³Now Zelophehad the son of Hepher, son of Gilead, son of Machir, son of Manasseh, had no sons, but only daughters, and these are the names of his daughters: Mahlah, Noah, Hoglah, Milcah, and Tirzah. ⁴They approached Eleazar the priest and Joshua the son of Nun and the leaders and said, "The LORD commanded Moses to give us an inheritance along with our brothers." So according to the mouth of the LORD he gave them an inheritance among the brothers of their father. ⁵Thus there fell to Manasseh ten portions, besides the land of Gilead and Bashan, which is on the other side of the Jordan, ⁶because the daughters of Manasseh received an inheritance along with his sons. The land of Gilead was allotted to the rest of the people of Manasseh.

⁷The territory of Manasseh reached from Asher to Michmethath, which is east of Shechem. Then the boundary goes along southwards to the inhabitants of En-tappuah. ⁸The land of Tappuah belonged to Manasseh, but the town of Tappuah on the boundary of Manasseh belonged to the people of Ephraim. ⁹Then the boundary went down to the brook Kanah. These cities, to the south of the brook, among the cities of Manasseh, belong to Ephraim. Then the boundary of Manasseh goes on the north side of the brook and ends at the sea, ¹⁰the land to the south being Ephraim's and that to the north being Manasseh's, with the sea forming its boundary. On the north Asher is reached, and on the east Issachar. ¹¹Also in Issachar and in Asher Manasseh had Beth-shean and its villages, and Ibleam and its villages, and the inhabitants of Dor and its villages, and the inhabitants of En-dor and its villages, and the inhabitants of Taanach and its villages, and the inhabitants of Megiddo and its villages; the third is Naphath.ᵃ ¹²Yet the people of Manasseh could not take possession of those cities, but the Canaanites persisted in dwelling in that land. ¹³Now when the people of Israel grew strong, they put the Canaanites to forced labour, but did not utterly drive them out.

¹⁴Then the people of Joseph spoke to Joshua, saying, "Why have you given me but one lot and one portion as an inheritance, although I am a numerous people, since all along the LORD has blessed me?" ¹⁵And Joshua said to them, "If you are a numerous people, go up by yourselves to the forest, and there clear ground for yourselves in the land of the Perizzites and the Rephaim, since the hill country of Ephraim is too narrow for you." ¹⁶The people of Joseph said, "The hill country is not enough for us. Yet all the Canaanites who dwell in the plain have chariots of iron, both those in Beth-shean and its villages and those in the Valley of Jezreel." ¹⁷Then Joshua said to the house of Joseph, to Ephraim and Manasseh, "You are a numerous people and have great power. You shall not have one allotment only, ¹⁸but the hill country shall be yours, for though it is a forest, you shall clear it and possess it to its farthest borders. For you shall drive out the Canaanites, though they have chariots of iron, and though they are strong."

ALLOTMENT OF THE REMAINING LAND

18 Then the whole congregation of the people of Israel assembled at Shiloh and set up the tent of meeting there. The land lay subdued before them.

²There remained among the people of Israel seven tribes whose inheritance had not yet been apportioned. ³So Joshua said to the people of Israel, "How long will you put off going in to take possession of the land, which the LORD, the God of your fathers, has given you? ⁴Provide three men from each tribe, and I will send them out that they may set out and go up and down the land. They shall write a description of it with a view to their inheritances, and then come to me. ⁵They shall divide it into seven portions. Judah shall continue in his territory on the south, and the house of Joseph shall continue in their territory on the north. ⁶And you shall describe the land in seven divisions and bring the description here to me. And I will cast lots for you here before the LORD our God. ⁷The Levites have no portion among you, for the priesthood of the LORD is their heritage. And Gad and Reuben and half the tribe of Manasseh have received their inheritance beyond the Jordan eastwards, which Moses the servant of the LORD gave them."

⁸So the men arose and went, and Joshua charged those who went to write the description of the land, saying, "Go up and down in the land and write a description and return to me. And I will cast lots for you here before the LORD in Shiloh." ⁹So the men went and passed up and down in the land and wrote in a book a description of it by towns in seven divisions. Then they came to Joshua to the

---

ᵃThe meaning of the Hebrew is uncertain

camp at Shiloh, ¹⁰and Joshua cast lots for them in Shiloh before the LORD. And there Joshua apportioned the land to the people of Israel, to each his portion.

THE INHERITANCE FOR BENJAMIN

¹¹The lot of the tribe of the people of Benjamin according to its clans came up, and the territory allotted to it fell between the people of Judah and the people of Joseph. ¹²On the north side their boundary began at the Jordan. Then the boundary goes up to the shoulder north of Jericho, then up through the hill country westwards, and it ends at the wilderness of Beth-aven. ¹³From there the boundary passes along southwards in the direction of Luz, to the shoulder of Luz (that is, Bethel), then the boundary goes down to Ataroth-addar, on the mountain that lies south of Lower Beth-horon. ¹⁴Then the boundary goes in another direction, turning on the western side southwards from the mountain that lies to the south, opposite Beth-horon, and it ends at Kiriath-baal (that is, Kiriath-jearim), a city belonging to the people of Judah. This forms the western side. ¹⁵And the southern side begins at the outskirts of Kiriath-jearim. And the boundary goes from there to Ephron,^{a} to the spring of the waters of Nephtoah. ¹⁶Then the boundary goes down to the border of the mountain that overlooks the Valley of the Son of Hinnom, which is at the north end of the Valley of Rephaim. And it then goes down the Valley of Hinnom, south of the shoulder of the Jebusites, and downwards to En-rogel. ¹⁷Then it bends in a northerly direction going on to En-shemesh, and from there goes to Geliloth, which is opposite the ascent of Adummim. Then it goes down to the stone of Bohan the son of Reuben, ¹⁸and passing on to the north of the shoulder of Beth-arabah^b it goes down to the Arabah. ¹⁹Then the boundary passes on to the north of the shoulder of Beth-hoglah. And the boundary ends at the northern bay of the Salt Sea, at the south end of the Jordan: this is the southern border. ²⁰The Jordan forms its boundary on the eastern side. This is the inheritance of the people of Benjamin, according to their clans, boundary by boundary all round.

²¹Now the cities of the tribe of the people of Benjamin according to their clans were Jericho, Beth-hoglah, Emek-keziz, ²²Beth-arabah, Zemaraim, Bethel, ²³Avvim, Parah, Ophrah, ²⁴Chephar-ammoni, Ophni, Geba—twelve cities with their villages: ²⁵Gibeon, Ramah, Beeroth, ²⁶Mizpeh, Chephirah, Mozah, ²⁷Rekem, Irpeel, Taralah, ²⁸Zela, Haeleph, Jebus^c (that is, Jerusalem), Gibeah^d and Kiriath-jearim^e—fourteen cities with their villages. This is the inheritance of the people of Benjamin according to its clans.

THE INHERITANCE FOR SIMEON

19 The second lot came out for Simeon, for the tribe of the people of Simeon, according to their clans, and their inheritance was in the midst of the inheritance of the people of Judah. ²And they had for their inheritance Beersheba, Sheba, Moladah, ³Hazar-shual, Balah, Ezem, ⁴Eltolad, Bethul, Hormah, ⁵Ziklag, Beth-marcaboth, Hazar-susah, ⁶Beth-lebaoth, and Sharuhen—thirteen cities with their villages; ⁷Ain, Rimmon, Ether, and Ashan—four cities with their villages, ⁸together with all the villages round these cities as far as Baalath-beer, Ramah of the Negeb. This was the inheritance of the tribe of the people of Simeon according to their clans. ⁹The inheritance of the people of Simeon formed part of the territory of the people of Judah. Because the portion of the people of Judah was too large for them, the people of Simeon obtained an inheritance in the midst of their inheritance.

THE INHERITANCE FOR ZEBULUN

¹⁰The third lot came up for the people of Zebulun, according to their clans. And the territory of their inheritance reached as far as Sarid. ¹¹Then their boundary goes up westwards and on to Mareal and touches Dabbesheth, then the brook that is east of Jokneam. ¹²From Sarid it goes in the other direction eastwards towards the sunrise to the boundary of Chisloth-tabor. From there it goes to Daberath, then up to Japhia. ¹³From there it passes along on the east towards the sunrise to Gath-hepher, to Eth-kazin, and going on to Rimmon it bends towards Neah, ¹⁴then on the north the boundary turns about to Hannathon, and it ends at the Valley of Iphtahel; ¹⁵and Kattath, Nahalal, Shimron, Idalah, and Bethlehem—twelve cities with their villages. ¹⁶This is the inheritance of the people of Zebulun, according to their clans—these cities with their villages.

---

^{a}See 15:9; Hebrew *westward* ^{b}Septuagint; Hebrew *to the shoulder over against the Arabah* ^{c}Septuagint, Syriac, Vulgate; Hebrew *the Jebusite* ^{d}Hebrew *Gibeath* ^{e}Septuagint; Hebrew *Kiriath*

THE INHERITANCE FOR ISSACHAR

¹⁷The fourth lot came out for Issachar, for the people of Issachar, according to their clans. ¹⁸Their territory included Jezreel, Chesulloth, Shunem, ¹⁹Hapharaim, Shion, Anaharath, ²⁰Rabbith, Kishion, Ebez, ²¹Remeth, En-gannim, En-haddah, Beth-pazzez. ²²The boundary also touches Tabor, Shahazumah, and Beth-shemesh, and its boundary ends at the Jordan—sixteen cities with their villages. ²³This is the inheritance of the tribe of the people of Issachar, according to their clans—the cities with their villages.

THE INHERITANCE FOR ASHER

²⁴The fifth lot came out for the tribe of the people of Asher according to their clans. ²⁵Their territory included Helkath, Hali, Beten, Achshaph, ²⁶Allammelech, Amad, and Mishal. On the west it touches Carmel and Shihor-libnath, ²⁷then it turns eastwards, it goes to Beth-dagon, and touches Zebulun and the Valley of Iphtahel northwards to Beth-emek and Neiel. Then it continues in the north to Cabul, ²⁸Ebron, Rehob, Hammon, Kanah, as far as Sidon the Great. ²⁹Then the boundary turns to Ramah, reaching to the fortified city of Tyre. Then the boundary turns to Hosah, and it ends at the sea; Mahalab,[a] Achzib, ³⁰Ummah, Aphek and Rehob—twenty-two cities with their villages. ³¹This is the inheritance of the tribe of the people of Asher according to their clans—these cities with their villages.

THE INHERITANCE FOR NAPHTALI

³²The sixth lot came out for the people of Naphtali, for the people of Naphtali, according to their clans. ³³And their boundary ran from Heleph, from the oak in Zaanannim, and Adami-nekeb, and Jabneel, as far as Lakkum, and it ended at the Jordan. ³⁴Then the boundary turns westwards to Aznoth-tabor and goes from there to Hukkok, touching Zebulun at the south and Asher on the west and Judah on the east at the Jordan. ³⁵The fortified cities are Ziddim, Zer, Hammath, Rakkath, Chinnereth, ³⁶Adamah, Ramah, Hazor, ³⁷Kedesh, Edrei, En-hazor, ³⁸Yiron, Migdal-el, Horem, Beth-anath, and Beth-shemesh—nineteen cities with their villages. ³⁹This is the inheritance of the tribe of the people of Naphtali according to their clans—the cities with their villages.

THE INHERITANCE FOR DAN

⁴⁰The seventh lot came out for the tribe of the people of Dan, according to their clans. ⁴¹And the territory of its inheritance included Zorah, Eshtaol, Ir-shemesh, ⁴²Shaalabbin, Aijalon, Ithlah, ⁴³Elon, Timnah, Ekron, ⁴⁴Eltekeh, Gibbethon, Baalath, ⁴⁵Jehud, Bene-berak, Gath-rimmon, ⁴⁶and Me-jarkon and Rakkon with the territory over against Joppa. ⁴⁷When the territory of the people of Dan was lost to them, the people of Dan went up and fought against Leshem, and after capturing it and striking it with the sword they took possession of it and settled in it, calling Leshem, Dan, after the name of Dan their ancestor. ⁴⁸This is the inheritance of the tribe of the people of Dan, according to their clans—these cities with their villages.

THE INHERITANCE FOR JOSHUA

⁴⁹When they had finished distributing the several territories of the land as inheritances, the people of Israel gave an inheritance among them to Joshua the son of Nun. ⁵⁰By command of the LORD they gave him the city that he asked, Timnath-serah in the hill country of Ephraim. And he rebuilt the city and settled in it.

⁵¹These are the inheritances that Eleazar the priest and Joshua the son of Nun and the heads of the fathers' houses of the tribes of the people of Israel distributed by lot at Shiloh before the LORD, at the entrance of the tent of meeting. So they finished dividing the land.

THE CITIES OF REFUGE

20 Then the LORD said to Joshua, ²"Say to the people of Israel, 'Appoint the cities of refuge, of which I spoke to you through Moses, ³that the manslayer who strikes any person without intent or unknowingly may flee there. They shall be for you a refuge from the avenger of blood. ⁴He shall flee to one of these cities and shall stand at the entrance of the gate of the city and explain his case to the elders of that city. Then they shall take him into the city and give him a place, and he shall remain with them. ⁵And if the avenger of blood pursues him, they shall not give up the manslayer into his hand, because he struck his neighbour unknowingly, and did not hate him in the past. ⁶And he shall remain in that city until he has stood before the congregation for judgement, until the death of him who is high priest at the time. Then the manslayer may

---

[a] Compare Septuagint; Hebrew *Mehebel*

return to his own town and his own home, to the town from which he fled.'"

⁷So they set apart Kedesh in Galilee in the hill country of Naphtali, and Shechem in the hill country of Ephraim, and Kiriath-arba (that is, Hebron) in the hill country of Judah. ⁸And beyond the Jordan east of Jericho, they appointed Bezer in the wilderness on the tableland, from the tribe of Reuben, and Ramoth in Gilead, from the tribe of Gad, and Golan in Bashan, from the tribe of Manasseh. ⁹These were the cities designated for all the people of Israel and for the stranger sojourning among them, that anyone who killed a person without intent could flee there, so that he might not die by the hand of the avenger of blood, till he stood before the congregation.

CITIES AND PASTURE LANDS ALLOTTED TO LEVI

21 Then the heads of the fathers' houses of the Levites came to Eleazar the priest and to Joshua the son of Nun and to the heads of the fathers' houses of the tribes of the people of Israel. ²And they said to them at Shiloh in the land of Canaan, "The LORD commanded through Moses that we be given cities to dwell in, along with their pasture lands for our livestock." ³So by command of the LORD the people of Israel gave to the Levites the following cities and pasture lands out of their inheritance.

⁴The lot came out for the clans of the Kohathites. So those Levites who were descendants of Aaron the priest received by lot from the tribes of Judah, Simeon, and Benjamin, thirteen cities.

⁵And the rest of the Kohathites received by lot from the clans of the tribe of Ephraim, from the tribe of Dan and the half-tribe of Manasseh, ten cities.

⁶The Gershonites received by lot from the clans of the tribe of Issachar, from the tribe of Asher, from the tribe of Naphtali, and from the half-tribe of Manasseh in Bashan, thirteen cities.

⁷The Merarites according to their clans received from the tribe of Reuben, the tribe of Gad, and the tribe of Zebulun, twelve cities.

⁸These cities and their pasture lands the people of Israel gave by lot to the Levites, as the LORD had commanded through Moses.

⁹Out of the tribe of the people of Judah and the tribe of the people of Simeon they gave the following cities mentioned by name, ¹⁰which went to the descendants of Aaron, one of the clans of the Kohathites who belonged to the people of Levi; since the lot fell to them first. ¹¹They gave them Kiriath-arba (Arba being the father of Anak), that is Hebron, in the hill country of Judah, along with the pasture lands round it. ¹²But the fields of the city and its villages had been given to Caleb the son of Jephunneh as his possession.

¹³And to the descendants of Aaron the priest they gave Hebron, the city of refuge for the manslayer, with its pasture lands, Libnah with its pasture lands, ¹⁴Jattir with its pasture lands, Eshtemoa with its pasture lands, ¹⁵Holon with its pasture lands, Debir with its pasture lands, ¹⁶Ain with its pasture lands, Juttah with its pasture lands, Beth-shemesh with its pasture lands — nine cities out of these two tribes; ¹⁷then out of the tribe of Benjamin, Gibeon with its pasture lands, Geba with its pasture lands, ¹⁸Anathoth with its pasture lands, and Almon with its pasture lands — four cities. ¹⁹The cities of the descendants of Aaron, the priests, were in all thirteen cities with their pasture lands.

²⁰As to the rest of the Kohathites belonging to the Kohathite clans of the Levites, the cities allotted to them were out of the tribe of Ephraim. ²¹To them were given Shechem, the city of refuge for the manslayer, with its pasture lands in the hill country of Ephraim, Gezer with its pasture lands, ²²Kibzaim with its pasture lands, Beth-horon with its pasture lands — four cities; ²³and out of the tribe of Dan, Elteke with its pasture lands, Gibbethon with its pasture lands, ²⁴Aijalon with its pasture lands, Gath-rimmon with its pasture lands — four cities; ²⁵and out of the half-tribe of Manasseh, Taanach with its pasture lands, and Gath-rimmon with its pasture lands — two cities. ²⁶The cities of the clans of the rest of the Kohathites were ten in all with their pasture lands.

²⁷And to the Gershonites, one of the clans of the Levites, were given out of the half-tribe of Manasseh, Golan in Bashan with its pasture lands, the city of refuge for the manslayer, and Beeshterah with its pasture lands — two cities; ²⁸and out of the tribe of Issachar, Kishion with its pasture lands, Daberath with its pasture lands, ²⁹Jarmuth with its pasture lands, En-gannim with its pasture lands — four cities; ³⁰and out of the tribe of Asher, Mishal with its pasture lands, Abdon with its pasture lands, ³¹Helkath with its pasture lands, and Rehob with its pasture

lands—four cities; ³²and out of the tribe of Naphtali, Kedesh in Galilee with its pasture lands, the city of refuge for the manslayer, Hammoth-dor with its pasture lands, and Kartan with its pasture lands—three cities. ³³The cities of the several clans of the Gershonites were in all thirteen cities with their pasture lands.

³⁴And to the rest of the Levites, the Merarite clans, were given out of the tribe of Zebulun, Jokneam with its pasture lands, Kartah with its pasture lands, ³⁵Dimnah with its pasture lands, Nahalal with its pasture lands—four cities; ³⁶and out of the tribe of Reuben, Bezer with its pasture lands, Jahaz with its pasture lands, ³⁷Kedemoth with its pasture lands, and Mephaath with its pasture lands—four cities; ³⁸and out of the tribe of Gad, Ramoth in Gilead with its pasture lands, the city of refuge for the manslayer, Mahanaim with its pasture lands, ³⁹Heshbon with its pasture lands, Jazer with its pasture lands—four cities in all. ⁴⁰As for the cities of the several Merarite clans, that is, the remainder of the clans of the Levites, those allotted to them were in all twelve cities.

⁴¹The cities of the Levites in the midst of the possession of the people of Israel were in all forty-eight cities with their pasture lands. ⁴²These cities each had its pasture lands round it. So it was with all these cities.

⁴³Thus the LORD gave to Israel all the land that he swore to give to their fathers. And they took possession of it, and they settled there. ⁴⁴And the LORD gave them rest on every side just as he had sworn to their fathers. Not one of all their enemies had withstood them, for the LORD had given all their enemies into their hands. ⁴⁵Not one word of all the good promises that the LORD had made to the house of Israel had failed; all came to pass.

THE EASTERN TRIBES RETURN HOME

22 At that time Joshua summoned the Reubenites and the Gadites and the half-tribe of Manasseh, ²and said to them, "You have kept all that Moses the servant of the LORD commanded you and have obeyed my voice in all that I have commanded you. ³You have not forsaken your brothers these many days, down to this day, but have been careful to keep the charge of the LORD your God. ⁴And now the LORD your God has given rest to your brothers, as he promised them. Therefore turn and go to your tents in the land where your possession lies, which Moses the servant of the LORD gave you on the other side of the Jordan. ⁵Only be very careful to observe the commandment and the law that Moses the servant of the LORD commanded you, to love the LORD your God, and to walk in all his ways and to keep his commandments and to cling to him and to serve him with all your heart and with all your soul." ⁶So Joshua blessed them and sent them away, and they went to their tents.

⁷Now to one half of the tribe of Manasseh Moses had given a possession in Bashan, but to the other half Joshua had given a possession beside their brothers in the land west of the Jordan. And when Joshua sent them away to their homes and blessed them, ⁸he said to them, "Go back to your tents with much wealth and with very much livestock, with silver, gold, bronze, and iron, and with much clothing. Divide the spoil of your enemies with your brothers." ⁹So the people of Reuben and the people of Gad and the half-tribe of Manasseh returned home, parting from the people of Israel at Shiloh, which is in the land of Canaan, to go to the land of Gilead, their own land of which they had possessed themselves by command of the LORD through Moses.

THE EASTERN TRIBES' ALTAR OF WITNESS

¹⁰And when they came to the region of the Jordan that is in the land of Canaan, the people of Reuben and the people of Gad and the half-tribe of Manasseh built there an altar by the Jordan, an altar of imposing size. ¹¹And the people of Israel heard it said, "Behold, the people of Reuben and the people of Gad and the half-tribe of Manasseh have built the altar at the frontier of the land of Canaan, in the region about the Jordan, on the side that belongs to the people of Israel." ¹²And when the people of Israel heard of it, the whole assembly of the people of Israel gathered at Shiloh to make war against them.

¹³Then the people of Israel sent to the people of Reuben and the people of Gad and the half-tribe of Manasseh, in the land of Gilead, Phinehas the son of Eleazar the priest, ¹⁴and with him ten chiefs, one from each of the tribal families of Israel, every one of them the head of a family among the clans of Israel. ¹⁵And they came to the people of Reuben, the people of Gad, and the half-tribe of Manasseh, in the land of Gilead, and they said to them, ¹⁶"Thus says the whole congregation of the

LORD, 'What is this breach of faith that you have committed against the God of Israel in turning away this day from following the LORD by building yourselves an altar this day in rebellion against the LORD? ¹⁷Have we not had enough of the sin at Peor from which even yet we have not cleansed ourselves, and for which there came a plague upon the congregation of the LORD, ¹⁸that you too must turn away this day from following the LORD? And if you too rebel against the LORD today then tomorrow he will be angry with the whole congregation of Israel. ¹⁹But now, if the land of your possession is unclean, pass over into the LORD's land where the LORD's tabernacle stands, and take for yourselves a possession among us. Only do not rebel against the LORD or make us as rebels by building for yourselves an altar other than the altar of the LORD our God. ²⁰Did not Achan the son of Zerah break faith in the matter of the devoted things, and wrath fell upon all the congregation of Israel? And he did not perish alone for his iniquity.'"

²¹Then the people of Reuben, the people of Gad, and the half-tribe of Manasseh said in answer to the heads of the families of Israel, ²²"The Mighty One, God, the LORD! The Mighty One, God, the LORD! He knows; and let Israel itself know! If it was in rebellion or in breach of faith against the LORD, do not spare us today ²³for building an altar to turn away from following the LORD. Or if we did so to offer burnt offerings or grain offerings or peace offerings on it, may the LORD himself take vengeance. ²⁴No, but we did it from fear that in time to come your children might say to our children, 'What have you to do with the LORD, the God of Israel? ²⁵For the LORD has made the Jordan a boundary between us and you, you people of Reuben and people of Gad. You have no portion in the LORD.' So your children might make our children cease to worship the LORD. ²⁶Therefore we said, 'Let us now build an altar, not for burnt offering, nor for sacrifice, ²⁷but to be a witness between us and you, and between our generations after us, that we do perform the service of the LORD in his presence with our burnt offerings and sacrifices and peace offerings, so your children will not say to our children in time to come, "You have no portion in the LORD."' ²⁸And we thought, 'If this should be said to us or to our descendants in time to come, we should say, "Behold, the copy of the altar of the LORD, which our fathers made, not for burnt offerings, nor for sacrifice, but to be a witness between us and you."' ²⁹Far be it from us that we should rebel against the LORD and turn away this day from following the LORD by building an altar for burnt offering, grain offering, or sacrifice, other than the altar of the LORD our God that stands before his tabernacle!"

³⁰When Phinehas the priest and the chiefs of the congregation, the heads of the families of Israel who were with him, heard the words that the people of Reuben and the people of Gad and the people of Manasseh spoke, it was good in their eyes. ³¹And Phinehas the son of Eleazar the priest said to the people of Reuben and the people of Gad and the people of Manasseh, "Today we know that the LORD is in our midst, because you have not committed this breach of faith against the LORD. Now you have delivered the people of Israel from the hand of the LORD."

³²Then Phinehas the son of Eleazar the priest, and the chiefs, returned from the people of Reuben and the people of Gad in the land of Gilead to the land of Canaan, to the people of Israel, and brought back word to them. ³³And the report was good in the eyes of the people of Israel. And the people of Israel blessed God and spoke no more of making war against them to destroy the land where the people of Reuben and the people of Gad were settled. ³⁴The people of Reuben and the people of Gad called the altar Witness, "For," they said, "it is a witness between us that the LORD is God."

JOSHUA'S CHARGE TO ISRAEL'S LEADERS

23 A long time afterwards, when the LORD had given rest to Israel from all their surrounding enemies, and Joshua was old and well advanced in years, ²Joshua summoned all Israel, its elders and heads, its judges and officers, and said to them, "I am now old and well advanced in years. ³And you have seen all that the LORD your God has done to all these nations for your sake, for it is the LORD your God who has fought for you. ⁴Behold, I have allotted to you as an inheritance for your tribes those nations that remain, along with all the nations that I have already cut off, from the Jordan to the Great Sea in the west. ⁵The LORD your God will push them back before you and drive them out of your sight. And you shall possess their land, just as the LORD your God promised you. ⁶Therefore, be very strong to keep

and to do all that is written in the Book of the Law of Moses, turning aside from it neither to the right hand nor to the left, ⁷that you may not mix with these nations remaining among you or make mention of the names of their gods or swear by them or serve them or bow down to them, ⁸but you shall cling to the LORD your God just as you have done to this day. ⁹For the LORD has driven out before you great and strong nations. And as for you, no man has been able to stand before you to this day. ¹⁰One man of you puts to flight a thousand, since it is the LORD your God who fights for you, just as he promised you. ¹¹Be very careful, therefore, to love the LORD your God. ¹²For if you turn back and cling to the remnant of these nations remaining among you and make marriages with them, so that you associate with them and they with you, ¹³know for certain that the LORD your God will no longer drive out these nations before you, but they shall be a snare and a trap for you, a whip on your sides and thorns in your eyes, until you perish from off this good ground that the LORD your God has given you.

¹⁴"And now I am about to go the way of all the earth, and you know in your hearts and souls, all of you, that not one word has failed of all the good things*ᵃ* that the LORD your God promised concerning you. All have come to pass for you; not one of them has failed. ¹⁵But just as all the good things that the LORD your God promised concerning you have been fulfilled for you, so the LORD will bring upon you all the evil things, until he has destroyed you from off this good land that the LORD your God has given you, ¹⁶if you transgress the covenant of the LORD your God, which he commanded you, and go and serve other gods and bow down to them. Then the anger of the LORD will be kindled against you, and you shall perish quickly from off the good land that he has given to you."

THE COVENANT RENEWAL AT SHECHEM

24 Joshua gathered all the tribes of Israel to Shechem and summoned the elders, the heads, the judges, and the officers of Israel. And they presented themselves before God. ²And Joshua said to all the people, "Thus says the LORD, the God of Israel, 'Long ago, your fathers lived beyond the Euphrates,*ᵇ* Terah, the father of Abraham and of Nahor; and they served other gods. ³Then I took your father Abraham from beyond the River*ᶜ* and led him through all the land of Canaan, and made his offspring many. I gave him Isaac. ⁴And to Isaac I gave Jacob and Esau. And I gave Esau the hill country of Seir to possess, but Jacob and his children went down to Egypt. ⁵And I sent Moses and Aaron, and I plagued Egypt with what I did in the midst of it, and afterwards I brought you out.

⁶"'Then I brought your fathers out of Egypt, and you came to the sea. And the Egyptians pursued your fathers with chariots and horsemen to the Red Sea. ⁷And when they cried to the LORD, he put darkness between you and the Egyptians and made the sea come upon them and cover them; and your eyes saw what I did in Egypt. And you lived in the wilderness a long time. ⁸Then I brought you to the land of the Amorites, who lived on the other side of the Jordan. They fought with you, and I gave them into your hand, and you took possession of their land, and I destroyed them before you. ⁹Then Balak the son of Zippor, king of Moab, arose and fought against Israel. And he sent and invited Balaam the son of Beor to curse you, ¹⁰but I would not listen to Balaam. Indeed, he blessed you. So I delivered you out of his hand. ¹¹And you went over the Jordan and came to Jericho, and the leaders of Jericho fought against you, and also the Amorites, the Perizzites, the Canaanites, the Hittites, the Girgashites, the Hivites, and the Jebusites. And I gave them into your hand. ¹²And I sent the hornet before you, which drove them out before you, the two kings of the Amorites; it was not by your sword or by your bow. ¹³I gave you a land on which you had not laboured and cities that you had not built, and you dwell in them. You eat the fruit of vineyards and olive orchards that you did not plant.'

CHOOSE WHOM YOU WILL SERVE

¹⁴"Now therefore fear the LORD and serve him in sincerity and in faithfulness. Put away the gods that your fathers served beyond the River and in Egypt, and serve the LORD. ¹⁵And if it is evil in your eyes to serve the LORD, choose this day whom you will serve, whether the gods your fathers served in the region beyond the River, or the gods of the Amorites in whose land you dwell. But as for me and my house, we will serve the LORD."

¹⁶Then the people answered, "Far be it from us that we should forsake the LORD to serve

---

*ᵃ*Or *words*; also twice in verse 15 *ᵇ*Hebrew *the River* *ᶜ*That is, the Euphrates; also verses 14, 15

other gods, ¹⁷for it is the LORD our God who brought us and our fathers up from the land of Egypt, out of the house of slavery, and who did those great signs in our sight and preserved us in all the way that we went, and among all the peoples through whom we passed. ¹⁸And the LORD drove out before us all the peoples, the Amorites who lived in the land. Therefore we also will serve the LORD, for he is our God."

¹⁹But Joshua said to the people, "You are not able to serve the LORD, for he is a holy God. He is a jealous God; he will not forgive your transgressions or your sins. ²⁰If you forsake the LORD and serve foreign gods, then he will turn and do you harm and consume you, after having done you good." ²¹And the people said to Joshua, "No, but we will serve the LORD." ²²Then Joshua said to the people, "You are witnesses against yourselves that you have chosen the LORD, to serve him." And they said, "We are witnesses." ²³He said, "Then put away the foreign gods that are among you, and incline your heart to the LORD, the God of Israel." ²⁴And the people said to Joshua, "The LORD our God we will serve, and his voice we will obey." ²⁵So Joshua made a covenant with the people that day, and put in place statutes and rules for them at Shechem. ²⁶And Joshua wrote these words in the Book of the Law of God. And he took a large stone and set it up there under the terebinth that was by the sanctuary of the LORD. ²⁷And Joshua said to all the people, "Behold, this stone shall be a witness against us, for it has heard all the words of the LORD that he spoke to us. Therefore it shall be a witness against you, lest you deal falsely with your God." ²⁸So Joshua sent the people away, every man to his inheritance.

JOSHUA'S DEATH AND BURIAL

²⁹After these things Joshua the son of Nun, the servant of the LORD, died, being 110 years old. ³⁰And they buried him in his own inheritance at Timnath-serah, which is in the hill country of Ephraim, north of the mountain of Gaash.

³¹Israel served the LORD all the days of Joshua, and all the days of the elders who outlived Joshua and had known all the work that the LORD did for Israel.

³²As for the bones of Joseph, which the people of Israel brought up from Egypt, they buried them at Shechem, in the piece of land that Jacob bought from the sons of Hamor the father of Shechem for a hundred pieces of money.¹ It became an inheritance of the descendants of Joseph.

³³And Eleazar the son of Aaron died, and they buried him at Gibeah, the town of Phinehas his son, which had been given him in the hill country of Ephraim.

---

¹Hebrew *for a hundred qesitah*; a unit of money of unknown value

JUDGES

THE CONTINUING CONQUEST OF CANAAN

1 After the death of Joshua, the people of Israel enquired of the LORD, "Who shall go up first for us against the Canaanites, to fight against them?" ²The LORD said, "Judah shall go up; behold, I have given the land into his hand." ³And Judah said to Simeon his brother, "Come up with me into the territory allotted to me, that we may fight against the Canaanites. And I likewise will go with you into the territory allotted to you." So Simeon went with him. ⁴Then Judah went up and the LORD gave the Canaanites and the Perizzites into their hand, and they defeated 10,000 of them at Bezek. ⁵They found Adoni-bezek at Bezek and fought against him and defeated the Canaanites and the Perizzites. ⁶Adoni-bezek fled, but they pursued him and caught him and cut off his thumbs and his big toes. ⁷And Adoni-bezek said, "Seventy kings with their thumbs and their big toes cut off used to pick up scraps under my table. As I have done, so God has repaid me." And they brought him to Jerusalem, and he died there.

⁸And the men of Judah fought against Jerusalem and captured it and struck it with the edge of the sword and set the city on fire. ⁹And afterwards the men of Judah went down to fight against the Canaanites who lived in the hill country, in the Negeb, and in the lowland. ¹⁰And Judah went against the Canaanites who lived in Hebron (now the name of Hebron was formerly Kiriath-arba), and they defeated Sheshai and Ahiman and Talmai.

¹¹From there they went against the inhabitants of Debir. The name of Debir was formerly Kiriath-sepher. ¹²And Caleb said, "He who attacks Kiriath-sepher and captures it, I will give him Achsah my daughter for a wife." ¹³And Othniel the son of Kenaz, Caleb's younger brother, captured it. And he gave him Achsah his daughter for a wife. ¹⁴When she came to him, she urged him to ask her father for a field. And she dismounted from her donkey, and Caleb said to her, "What do you want?" ¹⁵She said to him, "Give me a blessing. Since you have set me in the land of the Negeb, give me also springs of water." And Caleb gave her the upper springs and the lower springs.

¹⁶And the descendants of the Kenite, Moses' father-in-law, went up with the people of Judah from the city of palms into the wilderness of Judah, which lies in the Negeb near Arad, and they went and settled with the people. ¹⁷And Judah went with Simeon his brother, and they defeated the Canaanites who inhabited Zephath and devoted it to destruction. So the name of the city was called Hormah.ᵃ ¹⁸Judah also captured Gaza with its territory, and Ashkelon with its territory, and Ekron with its territory. ¹⁹And the LORD was with Judah, and he took possession of the hill country, but he could not drive out the inhabitants of the plain because they had chariots of iron. ²⁰And Hebron was given to Caleb, as Moses had said. And he drove out from it the three sons of Anak. ²¹But the people of Benjamin did not drive out the Jebusites who lived in Jerusalem, so the Jebusites have lived with the people of Benjamin in Jerusalem to this day.

²²The house of Joseph also went up against Bethel, and the LORD was with them. ²³And the house of Joseph scouted out Bethel. (Now the name of the city was formerly Luz.) ²⁴And the spies saw a man coming out of the city, and they said to him, "Please show us the way into the city, and we will deal kindly with you." ²⁵And he showed them the way into the city. And they struck the city with the edge of the sword, but they let the man and all his family go. ²⁶And the man went to the land of the Hittites and built a city and called its name Luz. That is its name to this day.

FAILURE TO COMPLETE THE CONQUEST

²⁷Manasseh did not drive out the inhabitants of Beth-shean and its villages, or Taanach and its villages, or the inhabitants of Dor and its villages, or the inhabitants of Ibleam and its villages, or the inhabitants of Megiddo and its villages, for the Canaanites persisted in dwelling in that land. ²⁸When Israel grew

---

ᵃ*Hormah means utter destruction*

strong, they put the Canaanites to forced labour, but did not drive them out completely. ²⁹And Ephraim did not drive out the Canaanites who lived in Gezer, so the Canaanites lived in Gezer among them.

³⁰Zebulun did not drive out the inhabitants of Kitron, or the inhabitants of Nahalol, so the Canaanites lived among them, but became subject to forced labour.

³¹Asher did not drive out the inhabitants of Acco, or the inhabitants of Sidon or of Ahlab or of Achzib or of Helbah or of Aphik or of Rehob, ³²so the Asherites lived among the Canaanites, the inhabitants of the land, for they did not drive them out.

³³Naphtali did not drive out the inhabitants of Beth-shemesh, or the inhabitants of Beth-anath, so they lived among the Canaanites, the inhabitants of the land. Nevertheless, the inhabitants of Beth-shemesh and of Beth-anath became subject to forced labour for them.

³⁴The Amorites pressed the people of Dan back into the hill country, for they did not allow them to come down to the plain. ³⁵The Amorites persisted in dwelling in Mount Heres, in Aijalon, and in Shaalbim, but the hand of the house of Joseph rested heavily on them, and they became subject to forced labour. ³⁶And the border of the Amorites ran from the ascent of Akrabbim, from Sela and upwards.

ISRAEL'S DISOBEDIENCE

2 Now the angel of the LORD went up from Gilgal to Bochim. And he said, "I brought you up from Egypt and brought you into the land that I swore to give to your fathers. I said, 'I will never break my covenant with you, ²and you shall make no covenant with the inhabitants of this land; you shall break down their altars.' But you have not obeyed my voice. What is this you have done? ³So now I say, I will not drive them out before you, but they shall become thorns in your sides, and their gods shall be a snare to you." ⁴As soon as the angel of the LORD spoke these words to all the people of Israel, the people lifted up their voices and wept. ⁵And they called the name of that place Bochim.ᵃ And they sacrificed there to the LORD.

THE DEATH OF JOSHUA

⁶When Joshua dismissed the people, the people of Israel went each to his inheritance to take possession of the land. ⁷And the people served the LORD all the days of Joshua, and all the days of the elders who outlived Joshua, who had seen all the great work that the LORD had done for Israel. ⁸And Joshua the son of Nun, the servant of the LORD, died at the age of 110 years. ⁹And they buried him within the boundaries of his inheritance in Timnath-heres, in the hill country of Ephraim, north of the mountain of Gaash. ¹⁰And all that generation also were gathered to their fathers. And there arose another generation after them who did not know the LORD or the work that he had done for Israel.

ISRAEL'S UNFAITHFULNESS

¹¹And the people of Israel did what was evil in the sight of the LORD and served the Baals. ¹²And they abandoned the LORD, the God of their fathers, who had brought them out of the land of Egypt. They went after other gods, from among the gods of the peoples who were around them, and bowed down to them. And they provoked the LORD to anger. ¹³They abandoned the LORD and served the Baals and the Ashtaroth. ¹⁴So the anger of the LORD was kindled against Israel, and he gave them over to plunderers, who plundered them. And he sold them into the hand of their surrounding enemies, so that they could no longer withstand their enemies. ¹⁵Whenever they marched out, the hand of the LORD was against them for harm, as the LORD had warned, and as the LORD had sworn to them. And they were in terrible distress.

THE LORD RAISES UP JUDGES

¹⁶Then the LORD raised up judges, who saved them out of the hand of those who plundered them. ¹⁷Yet they did not listen to their judges, for they whored after other gods and bowed down to them. They soon turned aside from the way in which their fathers had walked, who had obeyed the commandments of the LORD, and they did not do so. ¹⁸Whenever the LORD raised up judges for them, the LORD was with the judge, and he saved them from the hand of their enemies all the days of the judge. For the LORD was moved to pity by their groaning because of those who afflicted and oppressed them. ¹⁹But whenever the judge died, they turned back and were more corrupt than their fathers, going after other gods, serving

---

ᵃ*Bochim* means *weepers*

them and bowing down to them. They did not drop any of their practices or their stubborn ways. ²⁰So the anger of the LORD was kindled against Israel, and he said, "Because this people have transgressed my covenant that I commanded their fathers and have not obeyed my voice, ²¹I will no longer drive out before them any of the nations that Joshua left when he died, ²²in order to test Israel by them, whether they will take care to walk in the way of the LORD as their fathers did, or not." ²³So the LORD left those nations, not driving them out quickly, and he did not give them into the hand of Joshua.

3 Now these are the nations that the LORD left, to test Israel by them, that is, all in Israel who had not experienced all the wars in Canaan. ²It was only in order that the generations of the people of Israel might know war, to teach war to those who had not known it before. ³These are the nations: the five lords of the Philistines and all the Canaanites and the Sidonians and the Hivites who lived on Mount Lebanon, from Mount Baal-hermon as far as Lebo-hamath. ⁴They were for the testing of Israel, to know whether Israel would obey the commandments of the LORD, which he commanded their fathers by the hand of Moses. ⁵So the people of Israel lived among the Canaanites, the Hittites, the Amorites, the Perizzites, the Hivites, and the Jebusites. ⁶And their daughters they took to themselves for wives, and their own daughters they gave to their sons, and they served their gods.

OTHNIEL

⁷And the people of Israel did what was evil in the sight of the LORD. They forgot the LORD their God and served the Baals and the Asheroth. ⁸Therefore the anger of the LORD was kindled against Israel, and he sold them into the hand of Cushan-rishathaim king of Mesopotamia. And the people of Israel served Cushan-rishathaim eight years. ⁹But when the people of Israel cried out to the LORD, the LORD raised up a deliverer for the people of Israel, who saved them, Othniel the son of Kenaz, Caleb's younger brother. ¹⁰The Spirit of the LORD was upon him, and he judged Israel. He went out to war, and the LORD gave Cushan-rishathaim king of Mesopotamia into his hand. And his hand prevailed over Cushan-rishathaim. ¹¹So the land had rest for forty years. Then Othniel the son of Kenaz died.

EHUD

¹²And the people of Israel again did what was evil in the sight of the LORD, and the LORD strengthened Eglon the king of Moab against Israel, because they had done what was evil in the sight of the LORD. ¹³He gathered to himself the Ammonites and the Amalekites, and went and defeated Israel. And they took possession of the city of palms. ¹⁴And the people of Israel served Eglon the king of Moab for eighteen years.

¹⁵Then the people of Israel cried out to the LORD, and the LORD raised up for them a deliverer, Ehud, the son of Gera, the Benjaminite, a left-handed man. The people of Israel sent tribute by him to Eglon the king of Moab. ¹⁶And Ehud made for himself a sword with two edges, a cubit[a] in length, and he bound it on his right thigh under his clothes. ¹⁷And he presented the tribute to Eglon king of Moab. Now Eglon was a very fat man. ¹⁸And when Ehud had finished presenting the tribute, he sent away the people who carried the tribute. ¹⁹But he himself turned back at the idols near Gilgal and said, "I have a secret message for you, O king." And he commanded, "Silence." And all his attendants went out from his presence. ²⁰And Ehud came to him as he was sitting alone in his cool roof chamber. And Ehud said, "I have a message from God for you." And he arose from his seat. ²¹And Ehud reached with his left hand, took the sword from his right thigh, and thrust it into his belly. ²²And the hilt also went in after the blade, and the fat closed over the blade, for he did not pull the sword out of his belly; and the excrement came out. ²³Then Ehud went out into the porch[b] and closed the doors of the roof chamber behind him and locked them.

²⁴When he had gone, the servants came, and when they saw that the doors of the roof chamber were locked, they thought, "Surely he is relieving himself in the closet of the cool chamber." ²⁵And they waited till they were embarrassed. But when he still did not open the doors of the roof chamber, they took the key and opened them, and there lay their lord dead on the floor.

²⁶Ehud escaped while they delayed, and he passed beyond the idols and escaped to Seirah. ²⁷When he arrived, he sounded the trumpet in the hill country of Ephraim. Then the people of Israel went down with

---

[a] A *cubit* was about 18 inches or 45 centimetres [b] The meaning of the Hebrew word is uncertain

him from the hill country, and he was their leader. ²⁸And he said to them, "Follow after me, for the LORD has given your enemies the Moabites into your hand." So they went down after him and seized the fords of the Jordan against the Moabites and did not allow anyone to pass over. ²⁹And they killed at that time about 10,000 of the Moabites, all strong, able-bodied men; not a man escaped. ³⁰So Moab was subdued that day under the hand of Israel. And the land had rest for eighty years.

SHAMGAR

³¹After him was Shamgar the son of Anath, who killed 600 of the Philistines with an ox goad, and he also saved Israel.

DEBORAH AND BARAK

4 And the people of Israel again did what was evil in the sight of the LORD after Ehud died. ²And the LORD sold them into the hand of Jabin king of Canaan, who reigned in Hazor. The commander of his army was Sisera, who lived in Harosheth-hagoyim. ³Then the people of Israel cried out to the LORD for help, for he had 900 chariots of iron and he oppressed the people of Israel cruelly for twenty years.

⁴Now Deborah, a prophetess, the wife of Lappidoth, was judging Israel at that time. ⁵She used to sit under the palm of Deborah between Ramah and Bethel in the hill country of Ephraim, and the people of Israel came up to her for judgement. ⁶She sent and summoned Barak the son of Abinoam from Kedesh-naphtali and said to him, "Has not the LORD, the God of Israel, commanded you, 'Go, gather your men at Mount Tabor, taking 10,000 from the people of Naphtali and the people of Zebulun. ⁷And I will draw out Sisera, the general of Jabin's army, to meet you by the river Kishon with his chariots and his troops, and I will give him into your hand'?" ⁸Barak said to her, "If you will go with me, I will go, but if you will not go with me, I will not go." ⁹And she said, "I will surely go with you. Nevertheless, the road on which you are going will not lead to your glory, for the LORD will sell Sisera into the hand of a woman." Then Deborah arose and went with Barak to Kedesh. ¹⁰And Barak called out Zebulun and Naphtali to Kedesh. And 10,000 men went up at his heels, and Deborah went up with him.

¹¹Now Heber the Kenite had separated from the Kenites, the descendants of Hobab the father-in-law of Moses, and had pitched his tent as far away as the oak in Zaanannim, which is near Kedesh.

¹²When Sisera was told that Barak the son of Abinoam had gone up to Mount Tabor, ¹³Sisera called out all his chariots, 900 chariots of iron, and all the men who were with him, from Harosheth-hagoyim to the river Kishon. ¹⁴And Deborah said to Barak, "Up! For this is the day in which the LORD has given Sisera into your hand. Does not the LORD go out before you?" So Barak went down from Mount Tabor with 10,000 men following him. ¹⁵And the LORD routed Sisera and all his chariots and all his army before Barak by the edge of the sword. And Sisera got down from his chariot and fled away on foot. ¹⁶And Barak pursued the chariots and the army to Harosheth-hagoyim, and all the army of Sisera fell by the edge of the sword; not a man was left.

¹⁷But Sisera fled away on foot to the tent of Jael, the wife of Heber the Kenite, for there was peace between Jabin the king of Hazor and the house of Heber the Kenite. ¹⁸And Jael came out to meet Sisera and said to him, "Turn aside, my lord; turn aside to me; do not be afraid." So he turned aside to her into the tent, and she covered him with a rug. ¹⁹And he said to her, "Please give me a little water to drink, for I am thirsty." So she opened a skin of milk and gave him a drink and covered him. ²⁰And he said to her, "Stand at the opening of the tent, and if any man comes and asks you, 'Is anyone here?' say, 'No.'" ²¹But Jael the wife of Heber took a tent peg, and took a hammer in her hand. Then she went softly to him and drove the peg into his temple until it went down into the ground while he was lying fast asleep from weariness. So he died. ²²And behold, as Barak was pursuing Sisera, Jael went out to meet him and said to him, "Come, and I will show you the man whom you are seeking." So he went in to her tent, and there lay Sisera dead, with the tent peg in his temple.

²³So on that day God subdued Jabin the king of Canaan before the people of Israel. ²⁴And the hand of the people of Israel pressed harder and harder against Jabin the king of Canaan, until they destroyed Jabin king of Canaan.

THE SONG OF DEBORAH AND BARAK

5 Then sang Deborah and Barak the son of Abinoam on that day:

²"That the leaders took the lead
  in Israel,

that the people offered
themselves willingly,
bless the LORD!

3 "Hear, O kings; give ear, O princes;
to the LORD I will sing;
I will make melody to the
LORD, the God of Israel.

4 "LORD, when you went out from Seir,
when you marched from
the region of Edom,
the earth trembled
and the heavens dropped,
yes, the clouds dropped water.
5 The mountains quaked
before the LORD,
even Sinai before the LORD,[a]
the God of Israel.

6 "In the days of Shamgar, son of Anath,
in the days of Jael, the highways
were abandoned,
and travellers kept to the byways.
7 The villagers ceased in Israel;
they ceased to be until I arose;
I, Deborah, arose as a
mother in Israel.
8 When new gods were chosen,
then war was in the gates.
Was shield or spear to be seen
among forty thousand in Israel?
9 My heart goes out to the
commanders of Israel
who offered themselves willingly
among the people.
Bless the LORD.

10 "Tell of it, you who ride on
white donkeys,
you who sit on rich carpets[b]
and you who walk by the way.
11 To the sound of musicians[c] at
the watering places,
there they repeat the righteous
triumphs of the LORD,
the righteous triumphs of his
villagers in Israel.

"Then down to the gates marched
the people of the LORD.

12 "Awake, awake, Deborah!
Awake, awake, break out in a song!
Arise, Barak, lead away your captives,
O son of Abinoam.

13 Then down marched the
remnant of the noble;
the people of the LORD marched
down for me against the mighty.
14 From Ephraim their root they
marched down into the valley,[d]
following you, Benjamin,
with your kinsmen;
from Machir marched down
the commanders,
and from Zebulun those who
bear the lieutenant's[e] staff;
15 the princes of Issachar came
with Deborah,
and Issachar faithful to Barak;
into the valley they rushed
at his heels.
Among the clans of Reuben
there were great searchings of heart.
16 Why did you sit still among
the sheepfolds,
to hear the whistling for the flocks?
Among the clans of Reuben
there were great searchings of heart.
17 Gilead stayed beyond the Jordan;
and Dan, why did he stay
with the ships?
Asher sat still at the coast of the sea,
staying by his landings.
18 Zebulun is a people who risked
their lives to the death;
Naphtali, too, on the heights
of the field.

19 "The kings came, they fought;
then fought the kings of Canaan,
at Taanach, by the waters of Megiddo;
they got no spoils of silver.
20 From heaven the stars fought,
from their courses they
fought against Sisera.
21 The torrent Kishon swept them away,
the ancient torrent, the
torrent Kishon.
March on, my soul, with might!
22 "Then loud beat the horses' hoofs
with the galloping, galloping
of his steeds.
23 "Curse Meroz, says the angel of the LORD,
curse its inhabitants thoroughly,

---
[a] Or *before the LORD, the One of Sinai, before the LORD* [b] The meaning of the Hebrew word is uncertain; it may connote *saddle blankets* [c] Or *archers*; the meaning of the Hebrew word is uncertain [d] Septuagint; Hebrew *in Amalek* [e] Hebrew *commander's*

because they did not come to
to the help of the LORD,
to the help of the LORD
against the mighty.

24 "Most blessed of women be Jael,
the wife of Heber the Kenite,
of tent-dwelling women
most blessed.
25 He asked for water and she
gave him milk;
she brought him curds in
a noble's bowl.
26 She sent her hand to the tent peg
and her right hand to the
workmen's mallet;
she struck Sisera;
she crushed his head;
she shattered and pierced
his temple.
27 Between her feet
he sank, he fell, he lay still;
between her feet
he sank, he fell;
where he sank,
there he fell—dead.

28 "Out of the window she peered,
the mother of Sisera wailed
through the lattice:
'Why is his chariot so long in coming?
Why tarry the hoofbeats
of his chariots?'
29 Her wisest princesses answer,
indeed, she answers herself,
30 'Have they not found and
divided the spoil?—
A womb or two for every man;
spoil of dyed materials for Sisera,
spoil of dyed materials embroidered,
two pieces of dyed work
embroidered for the
neck as spoil?'

31 "So may all your enemies
perish, O LORD!
But your friends be like the sun
as he rises in his might."

And the land had rest for forty years.

MIDIAN OPPRESSES ISRAEL

6 The people of Israel did what was evil in the sight of the LORD, and the LORD gave them into the hand of Midian for seven years. ²And the hand of Midian overpowered Israel, and because of Midian the people of Israel made for themselves the dens that are in the mountains and the caves and the strongholds. ³For whenever the Israelites planted crops, the Midianites and the Amalekites and the people of the East would come up against them. ⁴They would encamp against them and devour the produce of the land, as far as Gaza, and leave no sustenance in Israel and no sheep or ox or donkey. ⁵For they would come up with their livestock and their tents; they would come like locusts in number—both they and their camels could not be counted—so that they laid waste the land as they came in. ⁶And Israel was brought very low because of Midian. And the people of Israel cried out for help to the LORD.

⁷When the people of Israel cried out to the LORD on account of the Midianites, ⁸the LORD sent a prophet to the people of Israel. And he said to them, "Thus says the LORD, the God of Israel: I led you up from Egypt and brought you out of the house of slavery. ⁹And I delivered you from the hand of the Egyptians and from the hand of all who oppressed you, and drove them out before you and gave you their land. ¹⁰And I said to you, 'I am the LORD your God; you shall not fear the gods of the Amorites in whose land you dwell.' But you have not obeyed my voice."

THE CALL OF GIDEON

¹¹Now the angel of the LORD came and sat under the terebinth at Ophrah, which belonged to Joash the Abiezrite, while his son Gideon was beating out wheat in the wine press to hide it from the Midianites. ¹²And the angel of the LORD appeared to him and said to him, "The LORD is with you, O mighty man of valour." ¹³And Gideon said to him, "Please, my lord, if the LORD is with us, why then has all this happened to us? And where are all his wonderful deeds that our fathers recounted to us, saying, 'Did not the LORD bring us up from Egypt?' But now the LORD has forsaken us and given us into the hand of Midian." ¹⁴And the LORD[a] turned to him and said, "Go in this might of yours and save Israel from the hand of Midian; do not I send you?" ¹⁵And he said to him, "Please, Lord, how can I save Israel? Behold, my clan is the weakest in Manasseh, and I am the least in my father's house." ¹⁶And the LORD said to him, "But I will be with you, and you shall

---

[a]Septuagint *the angel of the* LORD; also verse 16

strike the Midianites as one man." ¹⁷And he said to him, "If now I have found favour in your eyes, then show me a sign that it is you who speak with me. ¹⁸Please do not depart from here until I come to you and bring out my present and set it before you." And he said, "I will stay till you return."

¹⁹So Gideon went into his house and prepared a young goat and unleavened cakes from an ephah[a] of flour. The meat he put in a basket, and the broth he put in a pot, and brought them to him under the terebinth and presented them. ²⁰And the angel of God said to him, "Take the meat and the unleavened cakes, and put them on this rock, and pour the broth over them." And he did so. ²¹Then the angel of the LORD reached out the tip of the staff that was in his hand and touched the meat and the unleavened cakes. And fire sprang up from the rock and consumed the meat and the unleavened cakes. And the angel of the LORD vanished from his sight. ²²Then Gideon perceived that he was the angel of the LORD. And Gideon said, "Alas, O Lord GOD! For now I have seen the angel of the LORD face to face." ²³But the LORD said to him, "Peace be to you. Do not fear; you shall not die." ²⁴Then Gideon built an altar there to the LORD and called it, The LORD Is Peace. To this day it still stands at Ophrah, which belongs to the Abiezrites.

²⁵That night the LORD said to him, "Take your father's bull, and the second bull seven years old, and pull down the altar of Baal that your father has, and cut down the Asherah that is beside it ²⁶and build an altar to the LORD your God on the top of the stronghold here, with stones laid in due order. Then take the second bull and offer it as a burnt offering with the wood of the Asherah that you shall cut down." ²⁷So Gideon took ten men of his servants and did as the LORD had told him. But because he was too afraid of his family and the men of the town to do it by day, he did it by night.

GIDEON DESTROYS THE ALTAR OF BAAL

²⁸When the men of the town rose early in the morning, behold, the altar of Baal was broken down, and the Asherah beside it was cut down, and the second bull was offered on the altar that had been built. ²⁹And they said to one another, "Who has done this thing?" And after they had searched and enquired, they said, "Gideon the son of Joash has done this thing." ³⁰Then the men of the town said to Joash, "Bring out your son, that he may die, for he has broken down the altar of Baal and cut down the Asherah beside it." ³¹But Joash said to all who stood against him, "Will you contend for Baal? Or will you save him? Whoever contends for him shall be put to death by morning. If he is a god, let him contend for himself, because his altar has been broken down." ³²Therefore on that day Gideon[b] was called Jerubbaal, that is to say, "Let Baal contend against him," because he broke down his altar.

³³Now all the Midianites and the Amalekites and the people of the East came together, and they crossed the Jordan and encamped in the Valley of Jezreel. ³⁴But the Spirit of the LORD clothed Gideon, and he sounded the trumpet, and the Abiezrites were called out to follow him. ³⁵And he sent messengers throughout all Manasseh, and they too were called out to follow him. And he sent messengers to Asher, Zebulun, and Naphtali, and they went up to meet them.

THE SIGN OF THE FLEECE

³⁶Then Gideon said to God, "If you will save Israel by my hand, as you have said, ³⁷behold, I am laying a fleece of wool on the threshing floor. If there is dew on the fleece alone, and it is dry on all the ground, then I shall know that you will save Israel by my hand, as you have said." ³⁸And it was so. When he rose early next morning and squeezed the fleece, he wrung enough dew from the fleece to fill a bowl with water. ³⁹Then Gideon said to God, "Let not your anger burn against me; let me speak just once more. Please let me test just once more with the fleece. Please let it be dry on the fleece only, and on all the ground let there be dew." ⁴⁰And God did so that night; and it was dry on the fleece only, and on all the ground there was dew.

GIDEON'S THREE HUNDRED MEN

7 Then Jerubbaal (that is, Gideon) and all the people who were with him rose early and encamped beside the spring of Harod. And the camp of Midian was north of them, by the hill of Moreh, in the valley.

²The LORD said to Gideon, "The people with you are too many for me to give the Midianites into their hand, lest Israel boast over me, saying, 'My own hand has saved me.' ³Now therefore proclaim in the ears of the people,

---

[a] An *ephah* was about 3/5 of a bushel or 22 litres   [b] Hebrew *he*

saying, 'Whoever is fearful and trembling, let him return home and hurry away from Mount Gilead.'" Then 22,000 of the people returned, and 10,000 remained.

⁴And the LORD said to Gideon, "The people are still too many. Take them down to the water, and I will test them for you there, and any one of whom I say to you, 'This one shall go with you', shall go with you, and any one of whom I say to you, 'This one shall not go with you', shall not go." ⁵So he brought the people down to the water. And the LORD said to Gideon, "Every one who laps the water with his tongue, as a dog laps, you shall set by himself. Likewise, every one who kneels down to drink." ⁶And the number of those who lapped, putting their hands to their mouths, was 300 men, but all the rest of the people knelt down to drink water. ⁷And the LORD said to Gideon, "With the 300 men who lapped I will save you and give the Midianites into your hand, and let all the others go every man to his home." ⁸So the people took provisions in their hands, and their trumpets. And he sent all the rest of Israel every man to his tent, but retained the 300 men. And the camp of Midian was below him in the valley.

⁹That same night the LORD said to him, "Arise, go down against the camp, for I have given it into your hand. ¹⁰But if you are afraid to go down, go down to the camp with Purah your servant. ¹¹And you shall hear what they say, and afterwards your hands shall be strengthened to go down against the camp." Then he went down with Purah his servant to the outposts of the armed men who were in the camp. ¹²And the Midianites and the Amalekites and all the people of the East lay along the valley like locusts in abundance, and their camels were without number, as the sand that is on the seashore in abundance. ¹³When Gideon came, behold, a man was telling a dream to his comrade. And he said, "Behold, I dreamed a dream, and behold, a cake of barley bread tumbled into the camp of Midian and came to the tent and struck it so that it fell and turned it upside down, so that the tent lay flat." ¹⁴And his comrade answered, "This is no other than the sword of Gideon the son of Joash, a man of Israel; God has given into his hand Midian and all the camp."

¹⁵As soon as Gideon heard the telling of the dream and its interpretation, he worshipped. And he returned to the camp of Israel and said, "Arise, for the LORD has given the host of Midian into your hand." ¹⁶And he divided the 300 men into three companies and put trumpets into the hands of all of them and empty jars, with torches inside the jars. ¹⁷And he said to them, "Look at me, and do likewise. When I come to the outskirts of the camp, do as I do. ¹⁸When I blow the trumpet, I and all who are with me, then blow the trumpets also on every side of all the camp and shout, 'For the LORD and for Gideon.'"

GIDEON DEFEATS MIDIAN

¹⁹So Gideon and the hundred men who were with him came to the outskirts of the camp at the beginning of the middle watch, when they had just set the watch. And they blew the trumpets and smashed the jars that were in their hands. ²⁰Then the three companies blew the trumpets and broke the jars. They held in their left hands the torches, and in their right hands the trumpets to blow. And they cried out, "A sword for the LORD and for Gideon!" ²¹Every man stood in his place around the camp, and all the army ran. They cried out and fled. ²²When they blew the 300 trumpets, the LORD set every man's sword against his comrade and against all the army. And the army fled as far as Beth-shittah towards Zererah,ᵃ as far as the border of Abel-meholah, by Tabbath. ²³And the men of Israel were called out from Naphtali and from Asher and from all Manasseh, and they pursued after Midian.

²⁴Gideon sent messengers throughout all the hill country of Ephraim, saying, "Come down against the Midianites and capture the waters against them, as far as Beth-barah, and also the Jordan." So all the men of Ephraim were called out, and they captured the waters as far as Beth-barah, and also the Jordan. ²⁵And they captured the two princes of Midian, Oreb and Zeeb. They killed Oreb at the rock of Oreb, and Zeeb they killed at the wine press of Zeeb. Then they pursued Midian, and they brought the heads of Oreb and Zeeb to Gideon across the Jordan.

GIDEON DEFEATS ZEBAH AND ZALMUNNA

8 Then the men of Ephraim said to him, "What is this that you have done to us, not to call us when you went to fight against Midian?" And they accused him fiercely. ²And he said to them, "What have I done now in comparison with you? Is not the gleaning of the grapes of Ephraim better

---
ᵃSome Hebrew manuscripts *Zeredah*

than the grape harvest of Abiezer? ³God has given into your hands the princes of Midian, Oreb and Zeeb. What have I been able to do in comparison with you?" Then their anger¹ against him subsided when he said this.

⁴And Gideon came to the Jordan and crossed over, he and the 300 men who were with him, exhausted yet pursuing. ⁵So he said to the men of Succoth, "Please give loaves of bread to the people who follow me, for they are exhausted, and I am pursuing after Zebah and Zalmunna, the kings of Midian." ⁶And the officials of Succoth said, "Are the hands of Zebah and Zalmunna already in your hand, that we should give bread to your army?" ⁷So Gideon said, "Well then, when the LORD has given Zebah and Zalmunna into my hand, I will flail your flesh with the thorns of the wilderness and with briers." ⁸And from there he went up to Penuel, and spoke to them in the same way, and the men of Penuel answered him as the men of Succoth had answered. ⁹And he said to the men of Penuel, "When I come again in peace, I will break down this tower."

¹⁰Now Zebah and Zalmunna were in Karkor with their army, about 15,000 men, all who were left of all the army of the people of the East, for there had fallen 120,000 men who drew the sword. ¹¹And Gideon went up by the way of the tent dwellers east of Nobah and Jogbehah and attacked the army, for the army felt secure. ¹²And Zebah and Zalmunna fled, and he pursued them and captured the two kings of Midian, Zebah and Zalmunna, and he threw all the army into a panic.

¹³Then Gideon the son of Joash returned from the battle by the ascent of Heres. ¹⁴And he captured a young man of Succoth and questioned him. And he wrote down for him the officials and elders of Succoth, seventy-seven men. ¹⁵And he came to the men of Succoth and said, "Behold Zebah and Zalmunna, about whom you taunted me, saying, 'Are the hands of Zebah and Zalmunna already in your hand, that we should give bread to your men who are exhausted?'" ¹⁶And he took the elders of the city, and he took thorns of the wilderness and briers and with them taught the men of Succoth a lesson. ¹⁷And he broke down the tower of Penuel and killed the men of the city.

¹⁸Then he said to Zebah and Zalmunna, "Where are the men whom you killed at Tabor?" They answered, "As you are, so were they. Every one of them resembled the son of a king." ¹⁹And he said, "They were my brothers, the sons of my mother. As the LORD lives, if you had saved them alive, I would not kill you." ²⁰So he said to Jether his firstborn, "Rise and kill them!" But the young man did not draw his sword, for he was afraid, because he was still a young man. ²¹Then Zebah and Zalmunna said, "Rise yourself and fall upon us, for as the man is, so is his strength." And Gideon arose and killed Zebah and Zalmunna, and he took the crescent ornaments that were on the necks of their camels.

GIDEON'S EPHOD

²²Then the men of Israel said to Gideon, "Rule over us, you and your son and your grandson also, for you have saved us from the hand of Midian." ²³Gideon said to them, "I will not rule over you, and my son will not rule over you; the LORD will rule over you." ²⁴And Gideon said to them, "Let me make a request of you: every one of you give me the earrings from his spoil." (For they had golden earrings, because they were Ishmaelites.) ²⁵And they answered, "We will willingly give them." And they spread a cloak, and every man threw in it the earrings of his spoil. ²⁶And the weight of the golden earrings that he requested was 1,700 shekels¹ of gold, besides the crescent ornaments and the pendants and the purple garments worn by the kings of Midian, and besides the collars that were round the necks of their camels. ²⁷And Gideon made an ephod of it and put it in his city, in Ophrah. And all Israel whored after it there, and it became a snare to Gideon and to his family. ²⁸So Midian was subdued before the people of Israel, and they raised their heads no more. And the land had rest for forty years in the days of Gideon.

THE DEATH OF GIDEON

²⁹Jerubbaal the son of Joash went and lived in his own house. ³⁰Now Gideon had seventy sons, his own offspring,¹ for he had many wives. ³¹And his concubine who was in Shechem also bore him a son, and he called his name Abimelech. ³²And Gideon the son of Joash died in a good old age and was buried in the tomb of Joash his father, at Ophrah of the Abiezrites.

³³As soon as Gideon died, the people of Israel turned again and whored after the Baals

---

¹Hebrew *their spirit*   ¹A *shekel* was about 2/5 of an ounce or 11 grams
¹Hebrew *who came from his own loins*

and made Baal-berith their god. ³⁴And the people of Israel did not remember the LORD their God, who had delivered them from the hand of all their enemies on every side, ³⁵and they did not show steadfast love to the family of Jerubbaal (that is, Gideon) in return for all the good that he had done to Israel.

ABIMELECH'S CONSPIRACY

9 Now Abimelech the son of Jerubbaal went to Shechem to his mother's relatives and said to them and to the whole clan of his mother's family, ²"Say in the ears of all the leaders of Shechem, 'Which is better for you, that all seventy of the sons of Jerubbaal rule over you, or that one rule over you?' Remember also that I am your bone and your flesh."

³And his mother's relatives spoke all these words on his behalf in the ears of all the leaders of Shechem, and their hearts inclined to follow Abimelech, for they said, "He is our brother." ⁴And they gave him seventy pieces of silver out of the house of Baal-berith with which Abimelech hired worthless and reckless fellows, who followed him. ⁵And he went to his father's house at Ophrah and killed his brothers the sons of Jerubbaal, seventy men, on one stone. But Jotham the youngest son of Jerubbaal was left, for he hid himself. ⁶And all the leaders of Shechem came together, and all Beth-millo, and they went and made Abimelech king, by the oak of the pillar at Shechem.

⁷When it was told to Jotham, he went and stood on top of Mount Gerizim and cried aloud and said to them, "Listen to me, you leaders of Shechem, that God may listen to you. ⁸The trees once went out to anoint a king over them, and they said to the olive tree, 'Reign over us.' ⁹But the olive tree said to them, 'Shall I leave my abundance, by which gods and men are honoured, and go to hold sway over the trees?' ¹⁰And the trees said to the fig tree, 'You come and reign over us.' ¹¹But the fig tree said to them, 'Shall I leave my sweetness and my good fruit and go to hold sway over the trees?' ¹²And the trees said to the vine, 'You come and reign over us.' ¹³But the vine said to them, 'Shall I leave my wine that cheers God and men and go to hold sway over the trees?' ¹⁴Then all the trees said to the bramble, 'You come and reign over us.' ¹⁵And the bramble said to the trees, 'If in good faith you are anointing me king over you, then come and take refuge in my shade, but if not, let fire come out of the bramble and devour the cedars of Lebanon.'

¹⁶"Now therefore, if you acted in good faith and integrity when you made Abimelech king, and if you have dealt well with Jerubbaal and his house and have done to him as his deeds deserved— ¹⁷for my father fought for you and risked his life and delivered you from the hand of Midian, ¹⁸and you have risen up against my father's house this day and have killed his sons, seventy men on one stone, and have made Abimelech, the son of his female servant, king over the leaders of Shechem, because he is your relative— ¹⁹if you then have acted in good faith and integrity with Jerubbaal and with his house this day, then rejoice in Abimelech, and let him also rejoice in you. ²⁰But if not, let fire come out from Abimelech and devour the leaders of Shechem and Beth-millo; and let fire come out from the leaders of Shechem and from Beth-millo and devour Abimelech." ²¹And Jotham ran away and fled and went to Beer and lived there, because of Abimelech his brother.

THE DOWNFALL OF ABIMELECH

²²Abimelech ruled over Israel for three years. ²³And God sent an evil spirit between Abimelech and the leaders of Shechem, and the leaders of Shechem dealt treacherously with Abimelech, ²⁴that the violence done to the seventy sons of Jerubbaal might come, and their blood be laid on Abimelech their brother, who killed them, and on the men of Shechem, who strengthened his hands to kill his brothers. ²⁵And the leaders of Shechem put men in ambush against him on the mountaintops, and they robbed all who passed by them along that way. And it was told to Abimelech.

²⁶And Gaal the son of Ebed moved into Shechem with his relatives, and the leaders of Shechem put their confidence in him. ²⁷And they went out into the field and gathered the grapes from their vineyards and trod them and held a festival; and they went into the house of their god and ate and drank and reviled Abimelech. ²⁸And Gaal the son of Ebed said, "Who is Abimelech, and who are we of Shechem, that we should serve him? Is he not the son of Jerubbaal, and is not Zebul his officer? Serve the men of Hamor the father of Shechem; but why should we serve him? ²⁹Would that this people were under my hand! Then I would remove Abimelech.

I would say*ᵃ* to Abimelech, 'Increase your army, and come out.'" ³⁰When Zebul the ruler of the city heard the words of Gaal the son of Ebed, his anger was kindled. ³¹And he sent messengers to Abimelech secretly,*ᵇ* saying, "Behold, Gaal the son of Ebed and his relatives have come to Shechem, and they are stirring up*ᶜ* the city against you. ³²Now therefore, go by night, you and the people who are with you, and set an ambush in the field. ³³Then in the morning, as soon as the sun is up, rise early and rush upon the city. And when he and the people who are with him come out against you, you may do to them as your hand finds to do." ³⁴So Abimelech and all the men who were with him rose up by night and set an ambush against Shechem in four companies. ³⁵And Gaal the son of Ebed went out and stood in the entrance of the gate of the city, and Abimelech and the people who were with him rose from the ambush. ³⁶And when Gaal saw the people, he said to Zebul, "Look, people are coming down from the mountaintops!" And Zebul said to him, "You mistake*ᵈ* the shadow of the mountains for men." ³⁷Gaal spoke again and said, "Look, people are coming down from the centre of the land, and one company is coming from the direction of the Diviners' Oak." ³⁸Then Zebul said to him, "Where is your mouth now, you who said, 'Who is Abimelech, that we should serve him?' Are not these the people whom you despised? Go out now and fight with them." ³⁹And Gaal went out at the head of the leaders of Shechem and fought with Abimelech. ⁴⁰And Abimelech chased him, and he fled before him. And many fell wounded, up to the entrance of the gate. ⁴¹And Abimelech lived at Arumah, and Zebul drove out Gaal and his relatives, so that they could not dwell at Shechem.

⁴²On the following day, the people went out into the field, and Abimelech was told. ⁴³He took his people and divided them into three companies and set an ambush in the fields. And he looked and saw the people coming out of the city. So he rose against them and killed them. ⁴⁴Abimelech and the company that was with him rushed forward and stood at the entrance of the gate of the city, while the two companies rushed upon all who were in the field and killed them. ⁴⁵And Abimelech fought against the city all that day. He captured the city and killed the people who were in it, and he razed the city and sowed it with salt.

⁴⁶When all the leaders of the Tower of Shechem heard of it, they entered the stronghold of the house of El-berith. ⁴⁷Abimelech was told that all the leaders of the Tower of Shechem were gathered together. ⁴⁸And Abimelech went up to Mount Zalmon, he and all the people who were with him. And Abimelech took an axe in his hand and cut down a bundle of brushwood and took it up and laid it on his shoulder. And he said to the men who were with him, "What you have seen me do, hurry and do as I have done." ⁴⁹So every one of the people cut down his bundle and following Abimelech put it against the stronghold, and they set the stronghold on fire over them, so that all the people of the Tower of Shechem also died, about 1,000 men and women.

⁵⁰Then Abimelech went to Thebez and encamped against Thebez and captured it. ⁵¹But there was a strong tower within the city, and all the men and women and all the leaders of the city fled to it and shut themselves in, and they went up to the roof of the tower. ⁵²And Abimelech came to the tower and fought against it and drew near to the door of the tower to burn it with fire. ⁵³And a certain woman threw an upper millstone on Abimelech's head and crushed his skull. ⁵⁴Then he called quickly to the young man his armour bearer and said to him, "Draw your sword and kill me, lest they say of me, 'A woman killed him.'" And his young man thrust him through, and he died. ⁵⁵And when the men of Israel saw that Abimelech was dead, everyone departed to his home. ⁵⁶Thus God returned the evil of Abimelech, which he committed against his father in killing his seventy brothers. ⁵⁷And God also made all the evil of the men of Shechem return on their heads, and upon them came the curse of Jotham the son of Jerubbaal.

TOLA AND JAIR

10 After Abimelech there arose to save Israel Tola the son of Puah, son of Dodo, a man of Issachar, and he lived at Shamir in the hill country of Ephraim. ²And he judged Israel for twenty-three years. Then he died and was buried at Shamir.

³After him arose Jair the Gileadite, who judged Israel for twenty-two years. ⁴And he had thirty sons who rode on thirty donkeys, and they had thirty cities, called Havvoth-jair

---

*ᵃ*Septuagint; Hebrew *and he said*   *ᵇ*Or *at Tormah*   *ᶜ*Hebrew *besieging, or closing up*   *ᵈ*Hebrew *You see*

to this day, which are in the land of Gilead. ⁵And Jair died and was buried in Kamon.

FURTHER DISOBEDIENCE AND OPPRESSION

⁶The people of Israel again did what was evil in the sight of the LORD and served the Baals and the Ashtaroth, the gods of Syria, the gods of Sidon, the gods of Moab, the gods of the Ammonites, and the gods of the Philistines. And they forsook the LORD and did not serve him. ⁷So the anger of the LORD was kindled against Israel, and he sold them into the hand of the Philistines and into the hand of the Ammonites, ⁸and they crushed and oppressed the people of Israel that year. For eighteen years they oppressed all the people of Israel who were beyond the Jordan in the land of the Amorites, which is in Gilead. ⁹And the Ammonites crossed the Jordan to fight also against Judah and against Benjamin and against the house of Ephraim, so that Israel was severely distressed.

¹⁰And the people of Israel cried out to the LORD, saying, "We have sinned against you, because we have forsaken our God and have served the Baals." ¹¹And the LORD said to the people of Israel, "Did I not save you from the Egyptians and from the Amorites, from the Ammonites and from the Philistines? ¹²The Sidonians also, and the Amalekites and the Maonites oppressed you, and you cried out to me, and I saved you out of their hand. ¹³Yet you have forsaken me and served other gods; therefore I will save you no more. ¹⁴Go and cry out to the gods whom you have chosen; let them save you in the time of your distress." ¹⁵And the people of Israel said to the LORD, "We have sinned; do to us whatever seems good to you. Only please deliver us this day." ¹⁶So they put away the foreign gods from among them and served the LORD, and he became impatient over the misery of Israel.

¹⁷Then the Ammonites were called to arms, and they encamped in Gilead. And the people of Israel came together, and they encamped at Mizpah. ¹⁸And the people, the leaders of Gilead, said one to another, "Who is the man who will begin to fight against the Ammonites? He shall be head over all the inhabitants of Gilead."

JEPHTHAH DELIVERS ISRAEL

11 Now Jephthah the Gileadite was a mighty warrior, but he was the son of a prostitute. Gilead was the father of Jephthah. ²And Gilead's wife also bore him sons. And when his wife's sons grew up, they drove Jephthah out and said to him, "You shall not have an inheritance in our father's house, for you are the son of another woman." ³Then Jephthah fled from his brothers and lived in the land of Tob, and worthless fellows collected around Jephthah and went out with him.

⁴After a time the Ammonites made war against Israel. ⁵And when the Ammonites made war against Israel, the elders of Gilead went to bring Jephthah from the land of Tob. ⁶And they said to Jephthah, "Come and be our leader, that we may fight against the Ammonites." ⁷But Jephthah said to the elders of Gilead, "Did you not hate me and drive me out of my father's house? Why have you come to me now when you are in distress?" ⁸And the elders of Gilead said to Jephthah, "That is why we have turned to you now, that you may go with us and fight against the Ammonites and be our head over all the inhabitants of Gilead." ⁹Jephthah said to the elders of Gilead, "If you bring me home again to fight against the Ammonites, and the LORD gives them over to me, I will be your head." ¹⁰And the elders of Gilead said to Jephthah, "The LORD will be witness between us, if we do not do as you say." ¹¹So Jephthah went with the elders of Gilead, and the people made him head and leader over them. And Jephthah spoke all his words before the LORD at Mizpah.

¹²Then Jephthah sent messengers to the king of the Ammonites and said, "What do you have against me, that you have come to me to fight against my land?" ¹³And the king of the Ammonites answered the messengers of Jephthah, "Because Israel on coming up from Egypt took away my land, from the Arnon to the Jabbok and to the Jordan; now therefore restore it peaceably." ¹⁴Jephthah again sent messengers to the king of the Ammonites ¹⁵and said to him, "Thus says Jephthah: Israel did not take away the land of Moab or the land of the Ammonites, ¹⁶but when they came up from Egypt, Israel went through the wilderness to the Red Sea and came to Kadesh. ¹⁷Israel then sent messengers to the king of Edom, saying, 'Please let us pass through your land', but the king of Edom would not listen. And they sent also to the king of Moab, but he would not consent. So Israel remained at Kadesh.

¹⁸"Then they journeyed through the wilderness and went round the land of Edom and the land of Moab and arrived on the east

side of the land of Moab and camped on the other side of the Arnon. But they did not enter the territory of Moab, for the Arnon was the boundary of Moab. ¹⁹Israel then sent messengers to Sihon king of the Amorites, king of Heshbon, and Israel said to him, 'Please let us pass through your land to our country,' ²⁰but Sihon did not trust Israel to pass through his territory, so Sihon gathered all his people together and encamped at Jahaz and fought with Israel. ²¹And the LORD, the God of Israel, gave Sihon and all his people into the hand of Israel, and they defeated them. So Israel took possession of all the land of the Amorites, who inhabited that country. ²²And they took possession of all the territory of the Amorites from the Arnon to the Jabbok and from the wilderness to the Jordan. ²³So then the LORD, the God of Israel, dispossessed the Amorites from before his people Israel; and are you to take possession of them? ²⁴Will you not possess what Chemosh your god gives you to possess? And all that the LORD our God has dispossessed before us, we will possess. ²⁵Now are you any better than Balak the son of Zippor, king of Moab? Did he ever contend against Israel, or did he ever go to war with them? ²⁶While Israel lived in Heshbon and its villages, and in Aroer and its villages, and in all the cities that are on the banks of the Arnon, 300 years, why did you not deliver them within that time? ²⁷I therefore have not sinned against you, and you do me wrong by making war on me. The LORD, the Judge, decide this day between the people of Israel and the people of Ammon." ²⁸But the king of the Ammonites did not listen to the words of Jephthah that he sent to him.

JEPHTHAH'S TRAGIC VOW

²⁹Then the Spirit of the LORD was upon Jephthah, and he passed through Gilead and Manasseh and passed on to Mizpah of Gilead, and from Mizpah of Gilead he passed on to the Ammonites. ³⁰And Jephthah made a vow to the LORD and said, "If you will give the Ammonites into my hand, ³¹then whatever*ᵃ* comes out from the doors of my house to meet me when I return in peace from the Ammonites shall be the LORD's, and I will offer it*ᵇ* up for a burnt offering." ³²So Jephthah crossed over to the Ammonites to fight against them, and the LORD gave them into his hand. ³³And he struck them from Aroer to the neighbourhood of Minnith, twenty cities, and as far as Abel-keramim, with a great blow. So the Ammonites were subdued before the people of Israel.

³⁴Then Jephthah came to his home at Mizpah. And behold, his daughter came out to meet him with tambourines and with dances. She was his only child; besides her he had neither son nor daughter. ³⁵And as soon as he saw her, he tore his clothes and said, "Alas, my daughter! You have brought me very low, and you have become the cause of great trouble to me. For I have opened my mouth to the LORD, and I cannot take back my vow." ³⁶And she said to him, "My father, you have opened your mouth to the LORD; do to me according to what has gone out of your mouth, now that the LORD has avenged you of your enemies, on the Ammonites." ³⁷So she said to her father, "Let this thing be done for me: leave me alone for two months, that I may go up and down on the mountains and weep for my virginity, I and my companions." ³⁸So he said, "Go." Then he sent her away for two months, and she departed, she and her companions, and wept for her virginity on the mountains. ³⁹And at the end of two months, she returned to her father, who did with her according to his vow that he had made. She had never known a man, and it became a custom in Israel ⁴⁰that the daughters of Israel went year by year to lament the daughter of Jephthah the Gileadite for four days in the year.

JEPHTHAH'S CONFLICT WITH EPHRAIM

12 The men of Ephraim were called to arms, and they crossed to Zaphon and said to Jephthah, "Why did you cross over to fight against the Ammonites and did not call us to go with you? We will burn your house over you with fire." ²And Jephthah said to them, "I and my people had a great dispute with the Ammonites, and when I called you, you did not save me from their hand. ³And when I saw that you would not save me, I took my life in my hand and crossed over against the Ammonites, and the LORD gave them into my hand. Why then have you come up to me this day to fight against me?" ⁴Then Jephthah gathered all the men of Gilead and fought with Ephraim. And the men of Gilead struck Ephraim, because they said, "You are fugitives of Ephraim, you Gileadites, in the midst of Ephraim and Manasseh." ⁵And the Gileadites captured the fords of the Jordan against the Ephraimites. And when any of the

---

ᵃ Or whoever   ᵇ Or him

fugitives of Ephraim said, "Let me go over", the men of Gilead said to him, "Are you an Ephraimite?" When he said, "No", ⁶they said to him, "Then say Shibboleth", and he said, "Sibboleth", for he could not pronounce it right. Then they seized him and slaughtered him at the fords of the Jordan. At that time 42,000 of the Ephraimites fell.

⁷Jephthah judged Israel for six years. Then Jephthah the Gileadite died and was buried in his city in Gilead.*ᵃ*

IBZAN, ELON, AND ABDON

⁸After him Ibzan of Bethlehem judged Israel. ⁹He had thirty sons, and thirty daughters he gave in marriage outside his clan, and thirty daughters he brought in from outside for his sons. And he judged Israel for seven years. ¹⁰Then Ibzan died and was buried at Bethlehem.

¹¹After him Elon the Zebulunite judged Israel, and he judged Israel for ten years. ¹²Then Elon the Zebulunite died and was buried at Aijalon in the land of Zebulun.

¹³After him Abdon the son of Hillel the Pirathonite judged Israel. ¹⁴He had forty sons and thirty grandsons, who rode on seventy donkeys, and he judged Israel for eight years. ¹⁵Then Abdon the son of Hillel the Pirathonite died and was buried at Pirathon in the land of Ephraim, in the hill country of the Amalekites.

THE BIRTH OF SAMSON

13 And the people of Israel again did what was evil in the sight of the LORD, so the LORD gave them into the hand of the Philistines for forty years.

²There was a certain man of Zorah, of the tribe of the Danites, whose name was Manoah. And his wife was barren and had no children. ³And the angel of the LORD appeared to the woman and said to her, "Behold, you are barren and have not borne children, but you shall conceive and bear a son. ⁴Therefore be careful and drink no wine or strong drink, and eat nothing unclean, ⁵for behold, you shall conceive and bear a son. No razor shall come upon his head, for the child shall be a Nazirite to God from the womb, and he shall begin to save Israel from the hand of the Philistines." ⁶Then the woman came and told her husband, "A man of God came to me, and his appearance was like the appearance of the angel of God, very awesome. I did not ask him where he was from, and he did not tell me his name, ⁷but he said to me, 'Behold, you shall conceive and bear a son. So then drink no wine or strong drink, and eat nothing unclean, for the child shall be a Nazirite to God from the womb to the day of his death.'"

⁸Then Manoah prayed to the LORD and said, "O Lord, please let the man of God whom you sent come again to us and teach us what we are to do with the child who will be born." ⁹And God listened to the voice of Manoah, and the angel of God came again to the woman as she sat in the field. But Manoah her husband was not with her. ¹⁰So the woman ran quickly and told her husband, "Behold, the man who came to me the other day has appeared to me." ¹¹And Manoah arose and went after his wife and came to the man and said to him, "Are you the man who spoke to this woman?" And he said, "I am." ¹²And Manoah said, "Now when your words come true, what is to be the child's manner of life, and what is his mission?" ¹³And the angel of the LORD said to Manoah, "Of all that I said to the woman let her be careful. ¹⁴She may not eat of anything that comes from the vine, neither let her drink wine or strong drink, or eat any unclean thing. All that I commanded her let her observe."

¹⁵Manoah said to the angel of the LORD, "Please let us detain you and prepare a young goat for you." ¹⁶And the angel of the LORD said to Manoah, "If you detain me, I will not eat of your food. But if you prepare a burnt offering, then offer it to the LORD." (For Manoah did not know that he was the angel of the LORD.) ¹⁷And Manoah said to the angel of the LORD, "What is your name, so that, when your words come true, we may honour you?" ¹⁸And the angel of the LORD said to him, "Why do you ask my name, seeing it is wonderful?" ¹⁹So Manoah took the young goat with the grain offering, and offered it on the rock to the LORD, to the one who works*ᵇ* wonders, and Manoah and his wife were watching. ²⁰And when the flame went up towards heaven from the altar, the angel of the LORD went up in the flame of the altar. Now Manoah and his wife were watching, and they fell on their faces to the ground.

²¹The angel of the LORD appeared no more to Manoah and to his wife. Then Manoah knew that he was the angel of the LORD. ²²And Manoah said to his wife, "We shall surely die, for we have seen God." ²³But his wife said to him, "If the LORD had meant to kill us, he

---

*ᵃ*Septuagint; Hebrew *in the cities of Gilead* *ᵇ*Septuagint, Vulgate; Hebrew LORD, *and working*

would not have accepted a burnt offering and a grain offering at our hands, or shown us all these things, or now announced to us such things as these." ²⁴And the woman bore a son and called his name Samson. And the young man grew, and the Lord blessed him. ²⁵And the Spirit of the Lord began to stir him in Mahaneh-dan, between Zorah and Eshtaol.

SAMSON'S MARRIAGE

14 Samson went down to Timnah, and at Timnah he saw one of the daughters of the Philistines. ²Then he came up and told his father and mother, "I saw one of the daughters of the Philistines at Timnah. Now get her for me as my wife." ³But his father and mother said to him, "Is there not a woman among the daughters of your relatives, or among all our people, that you must go to take a wife from the uncircumcised Philistines?" But Samson said to his father, "Get her for me, for she is right in my eyes."

⁴His father and mother did not know that it was from the Lord, for he was seeking an opportunity against the Philistines. At that time the Philistines ruled over Israel.

⁵Then Samson went down with his father and mother to Timnah, and they came to the vineyards of Timnah. And behold, a young lion came towards him roaring. ⁶Then the Spirit of the Lord rushed upon him, and although he had nothing in his hand, he tore the lion in pieces as one tears a young goat. But he did not tell his father or his mother what he had done. ⁷Then he went down and talked with the woman, and she was right in Samson's eyes.

⁸After some days he returned to take her. And he turned aside to see the carcass of the lion, and behold, there was a swarm of bees in the body of the lion, and honey. ⁹He scraped it out into his hands and went on, eating as he went. And he came to his father and mother and gave some to them, and they ate. But he did not tell them that he had scraped the honey from the carcass of the lion.

¹⁰His father went down to the woman, and Samson prepared a feast there, for so the young men used to do. ¹¹As soon as the people saw him, they brought thirty companions to be with him. ¹²And Samson said to them, "Let me now put a riddle to you. If you can tell me what it is, within the seven days of the feast, and find it out, then I will give you thirty linen garments and thirty changes of clothes, ¹³but if you cannot tell me what it is,

then you shall give me thirty linen garments and thirty changes of clothes." And they said to him, "Put your riddle, that we may hear it." ¹⁴And he said to them,

> "Out of the eater came something to eat.
> Out of the strong came
>   something sweet."

And in three days they could not solve the riddle.

¹⁵On the fourth*ᵃ* day they said to Samson's wife, "Entice your husband to tell us what the riddle is, lest we burn you and your father's house with fire. Have you invited us here to impoverish us?" ¹⁶And Samson's wife wept over him and said, "You only hate me; you do not love me. You have put a riddle to my people, and you have not told me what it is." And he said to her, "Behold, I have not told my father nor my mother, and shall I tell you?" ¹⁷She wept before him for the seven days that their feast lasted, and on the seventh day he told her, because she pressed him hard. Then she told the riddle to her people. ¹⁸And the men of the city said to him on the seventh day before the sun went down,

> "What is sweeter than honey?
> What is stronger than a lion?"

And he said to them,

> "If you had not ploughed
>   with my heifer,
> you would not have found
>   out my riddle."

¹⁹And the Spirit of the Lord rushed upon him, and he went down to Ashkelon and struck down thirty men of the town and took their spoil and gave the garments to those who had explained the riddle. In hot anger he went back to his father's house. ²⁰And Samson's wife was given to his companion, who had been his best man.

SAMSON DEFEATS THE PHILISTINES

15 After some days, at the time of wheat harvest, Samson went to visit his wife with a young goat. And he said, "I will go in to my wife in the chamber." But her father would not allow him to go in. ²And her father said, "I really thought that you

---
*ᵃ*Septuagint, Syriac; Hebrew *seventh*

utterly hated her, so I gave her to your companion. Is not her younger sister more beautiful than she? Please take her instead." ³And Samson said to them, "This time I shall be innocent in regard to the Philistines, when I do them harm." ⁴So Samson went and caught 300 foxes and took torches. And he turned them tail to tail and put a torch between each pair of tails. ⁵And when he had set fire to the torches, he let the foxes go into the standing corn of the Philistines and set fire to the stacked corn and the standing corn, as well as the olive orchards. ⁶Then the Philistines said, "Who has done this?" And they said, "Samson, the son-in-law of the Timnite, because he has taken his wife and given her to his companion." And the Philistines came up and burned her and her father with fire. ⁷And Samson said to them, "If this is what you do, I swear I will be avenged on you, and after that I will quit." ⁸And he struck them hip and thigh with a great blow, and he went down and stayed in the cleft of the rock of Etam.

⁹Then the Philistines came up and encamped in Judah and made a raid on Lehi. ¹⁰And the men of Judah said, "Why have you come up against us?" They said, "We have come up to bind Samson, to do to him as he did to us." ¹¹Then 3,000 men of Judah went down to the cleft of the rock of Etam, and said to Samson, "Do you not know that the Philistines are rulers over us? What then is this that you have done to us?" And he said to them, "As they did to me, so have I done to them." ¹²And they said to him, "We have come down to bind you, that we may give you into the hands of the Philistines." And Samson said to them, "Swear to me that you will not attack me yourselves." ¹³They said to him, "No; we will only bind you and give you into their hands. We will surely not kill you." So they bound him with two new ropes and brought him up from the rock.

¹⁴When he came to Lehi, the Philistines came shouting to meet him. Then the Spirit of the LORD rushed upon him, and the ropes that were on his arms became as flax that has caught fire, and his bonds melted off his hands. ¹⁵And he found a fresh jawbone of a donkey, and put out his hand and took it, and with it he struck 1,000 men. ¹⁶And Samson said,

> "With the jawbone of a donkey,
>   heaps upon heaps,
> with the jawbone of a donkey
>   have I struck down a thousand men."

¹⁷As soon as he had finished speaking, he threw away the jawbone out of his hand. And that place was called Ramath-lehi.ᵃ

¹⁸And he was very thirsty, and he called upon the LORD and said, "You have granted this great salvation by the hand of your servant, and shall I now die of thirst and fall into the hands of the uncircumcised?" ¹⁹And God split open the hollow place that is at Lehi, and water came out from it. And when he drank, his spirit returned, and he revived. Therefore the name of it was called En-hakkore;ᵇ it is at Lehi to this day. ²⁰And he judged Israel in the days of the Philistines for twenty years.

SAMSON AND DELILAH

16 Samson went to Gaza, and there he saw a prostitute, and he went in to her. ²The Gazites were told, "Samson has come here." And they surrounded the place and set an ambush for him all night at the gate of the city. They kept quiet all night, saying, "Let us wait till the light of the morning; then we will kill him." ³But Samson lay till midnight, and at midnight he arose and took hold of the doors of the gate of the city and the two posts, and pulled them up, bar and all, and put them on his shoulders and carried them to the top of the hill that is in front of Hebron.

⁴After this he loved a woman in the Valley of Sorek, whose name was Delilah. ⁵And the lords of the Philistines came up to her and said to her, "Seduce him, and see where his great strength lies, and by what means we may overpower him, that we may bind him to humble him. And we will each give you 1,100 pieces of silver." ⁶So Delilah said to Samson, "Please tell me where your great strength lies, and how you might be bound, that one could subdue you."

⁷Samson said to her, "If they bind me with seven fresh bowstrings that have not been dried, then I shall become weak and be like any other man." ⁸Then the lords of the Philistines brought up to her seven fresh bowstrings that had not been dried, and she bound him with them. ⁹Now she had men lying in ambush in an inner chamber. And she said to him, "The Philistines are upon you, Samson!" But he snapped the bowstrings, as a thread of flax snaps when it touches the fire. So the secret of his strength was not known.

ᵃ*Ramath-lehi* means *the hill of the jawbone* ᵇ*En-hakkore* means *the spring of him who called*

[10] Then Delilah said to Samson, "Behold, you have mocked me and told me lies. Please tell me how you might be bound." [11] And he said to her, "If they bind me with new ropes that have not been used, then I shall become weak and be like any other man." [12] So Delilah took new ropes and bound him with them and said to him, "The Philistines are upon you, Samson!" And the men lying in ambush were in an inner chamber. But he snapped the ropes off his arms like a thread.

[13] Then Delilah said to Samson, "Until now you have mocked me and told me lies. Tell me how you might be bound." And he said to her, "If you weave the seven locks of my head with the web and fasten it tight with the pin, then I shall become weak and be like any other man." [14] So while he slept, Delilah took the seven locks of his head and wove them into the web.[a] And she made them tight with the pin and said to him, "The Philistines are upon you, Samson!" But he awoke from his sleep and pulled away the pin, the loom, and the web.

[15] And she said to him, "How can you say, 'I love you', when your heart is not with me? You have mocked me these three times, and you have not told me where your great strength lies." [16] And when she pressed him hard with her words day after day, and urged him, his soul was vexed to death. [17] And he told her all his heart, and said to her, "A razor has never come upon my head, for I have been a Nazirite to God from my mother's womb. If my head is shaved, then my strength will leave me, and I shall become weak and be like any other man."

[18] When Delilah saw that he had told her all his heart, she sent and called the lords of the Philistines, saying, "Come up again, for he has told me all his heart." Then the lords of the Philistines came up to her and brought the money in their hands. [19] She made him sleep on her knees. And she called a man and had him shave off the seven locks of his head. Then she began to torment him, and his strength left him. [20] And she said, "The Philistines are upon you, Samson!" And he awoke from his sleep and said, "I will go out as at other times and shake myself free." But he did not know that the Lord had left him. [21] And the Philistines seized him and gouged out his eyes and brought him down to Gaza and bound him with bronze shackles. And he ground at the mill in the prison. [22] But the hair of his head began to grow again after it had been shaved.

THE DEATH OF SAMSON

[23] Now the lords of the Philistines gathered to offer a great sacrifice to Dagon their god and to rejoice, and they said, "Our god has given Samson our enemy into our hand." [24] And when the people saw him, they praised their god. For they said, "Our god has given our enemy into our hand, the ravager of our country, who has killed many of us."[b] [25] And when their hearts were merry, they said, "Call Samson, that he may entertain us." So they called Samson out of the prison, and he entertained them. They made him stand between the pillars. [26] And Samson said to the young man who held him by the hand, "Let me feel the pillars on which the house rests, that I may lean against them." [27] Now the house was full of men and women. All the lords of the Philistines were there, and on the roof there were about 3,000 men and women, who looked on while Samson entertained.

[28] Then Samson called to the Lord and said, "O Lord God, please remember me and please strengthen me only this once, O God, that I may be avenged on the Philistines for my two eyes." [29] And Samson grasped the two middle pillars on which the house rested, and he leaned his weight against them, his right hand on the one and his left hand on the other. [30] And Samson said, "Let me die with the Philistines." Then he bowed with all his strength, and the house fell upon the lords and upon all the people who were in it. So the dead whom he killed at his death were more than those whom he had killed during his life. [31] Then his brothers and all his family came down and took him and brought him up and buried him between Zorah and Eshtaol in the tomb of Manoah his father. He had judged Israel for twenty years.

MICAH AND THE LEVITE

17 There was a man of the hill country of Ephraim, whose name was Micah. [2] And he said to his mother, "The 1,100 pieces of silver that were taken from you, about which you uttered a curse, and also spoke it in my ears, behold, the silver is with me; I took it." And his mother said, "Blessed be my son by the Lord." [3] And he restored the 1,100 pieces of silver to his mother. And his mother said, "I dedicate the silver to the Lord from my hand for my son,

---
[a] Compare Septuagint; Hebrew lacks *and fasten it tight . . . into the web*
[b] Or *who has multiplied our slain*

to make a carved image and a metal image. Now therefore I will restore it to you." ⁴So when he restored the money to his mother, his mother took 200 pieces of silver and gave it to the silversmith, who made it into a carved image and a metal image. And it was in the house of Micah. ⁵And the man Micah had a shrine, and he made an ephod and household gods, and ordained[a] one of his sons, who became his priest. ⁶In those days there was no king in Israel. Everyone did what was right in his own eyes.

⁷Now there was a young man of Bethlehem in Judah, of the family of Judah, who was a Levite, and he sojourned there. ⁸And the man departed from the town of Bethlehem in Judah to sojourn where he could find a place. And as he journeyed, he came to the hill country of Ephraim to the house of Micah. ⁹And Micah said to him, "Where do you come from?" And he said to him, "I am a Levite of Bethlehem in Judah, and I am going to sojourn where I may find a place." ¹⁰And Micah said to him, "Stay with me, and be to me a father and a priest, and I will give you ten pieces of silver a year and a suit of clothes and your living." And the Levite went in. ¹¹And the Levite was content to dwell with the man, and the young man became to him like one of his sons. ¹²And Micah ordained the Levite, and the young man became his priest, and was in the house of Micah. ¹³Then Micah said, "Now I know that the LORD will prosper me, because I have a Levite as priest."

DANITES TAKE THE LEVITE AND THE IDOL

18 In those days there was no king in Israel. And in those days the tribe of the people of Dan was seeking for itself an inheritance to dwell in, for until then no inheritance among the tribes of Israel had fallen to them. ²So the people of Dan sent five able men from the whole number of their tribe, from Zorah and from Eshtaol, to spy out the land and to explore it. And they said to them, "Go and explore the land." And they came to the hill country of Ephraim, to the house of Micah, and lodged there. ³When they were by the house of Micah, they recognized the voice of the young Levite. And they turned aside and said to him, "Who brought you here? What are you doing in this place? What is your business here?" ⁴And he said to them, "This is how Micah dealt with me: he has hired me, and I have become his priest." ⁵And they said to him, "Enquire of God, please, that we may know whether the journey on which we are setting out will succeed." ⁶And the priest said to them, "Go in peace. The journey on which you go is under the eye of the LORD."

⁷Then the five men departed and came to Laish and saw the people who were there, how they lived in security, after the manner of the Sidonians, quiet and unsuspecting, lacking[b] nothing that is in the earth and possessing wealth, and how they were far from the Sidonians and had no dealings with anyone. ⁸And when they came to their brothers at Zorah and Eshtaol, their brothers said to them, "What do you report?" ⁹They said, "Arise, and let us go up against them, for we have seen the land, and behold, it is very good. And will you do nothing? Do not be slow to go, to enter in and possess the land. ¹⁰As soon as you go, you will come to an unsuspecting people. The land is spacious, for God has given it into your hands, a place where there is no lack of anything that is in the earth."

¹¹So 600 men of the tribe of Dan, armed with weapons of war, set out from Zorah and Eshtaol, ¹²and went up and encamped at Kiriath-jearim in Judah. On this account that place is called Mahaneh-dan[c] to this day; behold, it is west of Kiriath-jearim. ¹³And they passed on from there to the hill country of Ephraim, and came to the house of Micah.

¹⁴Then the five men who had gone to scout out the country of Laish said to their brothers, "Do you know that in these houses there are an ephod, household gods, a carved image, and a metal image? Now therefore consider what you will do." ¹⁵And they turned aside there and came to the house of the young Levite, at the home of Micah, and asked him about his welfare. ¹⁶Now the 600 men of the Danites, armed with their weapons of war, stood by the entrance of the gate. ¹⁷And the five men who had gone to scout out the land went up and entered and took the carved image, the ephod, the household gods, and the metal image, while the priest stood by the entrance of the gate with the 600 men armed with weapons of war. ¹⁸And when these went into Micah's house and took the carved image, the ephod, the household gods, and the metal image, the priest said to them, "What are you doing?" ¹⁹And they said to him,

---

[a]Hebrew *filled the hand of*; also verse 12 [b]Compare 18:10; the meaning of the Hebrew word is uncertain [c]*Mahaneh-dan* means *camp of Dan*

"Keep quiet; put your hand on your mouth and come with us and be to us a father and a priest. Is it better for you to be priest to the house of one man, or to be priest to a tribe and clan in Israel?" ²⁰And the priest's heart was glad. He took the ephod and the household gods and the carved image and went along with the people.

²¹So they turned and departed, putting the little ones and the livestock and the goods in front of them. ²²When they had gone a distance from the home of Micah, the men who were in the houses near Micah's house were called out, and they overtook the people of Dan. ²³And they shouted to the people of Dan, who turned round and said to Micah, "What is the matter with you, that you come with such a company?" ²⁴And he said, "You take my gods that I made and the priest, and go away, and what have I left? How then do you ask me, 'What is the matter with you?'" ²⁵And the people of Dan said to him, "Do not let your voice be heard among us, lest angry fellows fall upon you, and you lose your life with the lives of your household." ²⁶Then the people of Dan went their way. And when Micah saw that they were too strong for him, he turned and went back to his home.

²⁷But the people of Dan took what Micah had made, and the priest who belonged to him, and they came to Laish, to a people quiet and unsuspecting, and struck them with the edge of the sword and burned the city with fire. ²⁸And there was no deliverer because it was far from Sidon, and they had no dealings with anyone. It was in the valley that belongs to Beth-rehob. Then they rebuilt the city and lived in it. ²⁹And they named the city Dan, after the name of Dan their ancestor, who was born to Israel; but the name of the city was Laish at the first. ³⁰And the people of Dan set up the carved image for themselves, and Jonathan the son of Gershom, son of Moses,[a] and his sons were priests to the tribe of the Danites until the day of the captivity of the land. ³¹So they set up Micah's carved image that he made, as long as the house of God was at Shiloh.

A LEVITE AND HIS CONCUBINE

19 In those days, when there was no king in Israel, a certain Levite was sojourning in the remote parts of the hill country of Ephraim, who took to himself a concubine from Bethlehem in Judah. ²And his concubine was unfaithful to[b] him, and she went away from him to her father's house at Bethlehem in Judah, and was there for some four months. ³Then her husband arose and went after her, to speak kindly to her and bring her back. He had with him his servant and a couple of donkeys. And she brought him into her father's house. And when the girl's father saw him, he came with joy to meet him. ⁴And his father-in-law, the girl's father, made him stay, and he remained with him three days. So they ate and drank and spent the night there. ⁵And on the fourth day they arose early in the morning, and he prepared to go, but the girl's father said to his son-in-law, "Strengthen your heart with a morsel of bread, and after that you may go." ⁶So the two of them sat and ate and drank together. And the girl's father said to the man, "Be pleased to spend the night, and let your heart be merry." ⁷And when the man rose up to go, his father-in-law pressed him, till he spent the night there again. ⁸And on the fifth day he arose early in the morning to depart. And the girl's father said, "Strengthen your heart and wait until the day declines." So they ate, both of them. ⁹And when the man and his concubine and his servant rose up to depart, his father-in-law, the girl's father, said to him, "Behold, now the day has waned towards evening. Please, spend the night. Behold, the day draws to its close. Lodge here and let your heart be merry, and tomorrow you shall arise early in the morning for your journey, and go home."

¹⁰But the man would not spend the night. He rose up and departed and arrived opposite Jebus (that is, Jerusalem). He had with him a couple of saddled donkeys, and his concubine was with him. ¹¹When they were near Jebus, the day was nearly over, and the servant said to his master, "Come now, let us turn aside to this city of the Jebusites and spend the night in it." ¹²And his master said to him, "We will not turn aside into the city of foreigners, who do not belong to the people of Israel, but we will pass on to Gibeah." ¹³And he said to his young man, "Come and let us draw near to one of these places and spend the night at Gibeah or at Ramah." ¹⁴So they passed on and went their way. And the sun went down on them near Gibeah, which belongs to Benjamin, ¹⁵and they turned aside there, to go in and spend the night at Gibeah. And he went in and sat down in the open square of the

---

[a] Or *Manasseh* [b] Septuagint, Old Latin *became angry with*

city, for no one took them into his house to spend the night. ¹⁶And behold, an old man was coming from his work in the field at evening. The man was from the hill country of Ephraim, and he was sojourning in Gibeah. The men of the place were Benjaminites. ¹⁷And he lifted up his eyes and saw the traveller in the open square of the city. And the old man said, "Where are you going? And where do you come from?" ¹⁸And he said to him, "We are passing from Bethlehem in Judah to the remote parts of the hill country of Ephraim, from which I come. I went to Bethlehem in Judah, and I am going to the house of the Lord,ᵃ but no one has taken me into his house. ¹⁹We have straw and feed for our donkeys, with bread and wine for me and your female servant and the young man with your servants. There is no lack of anything." ²⁰And the old man said, "Peace be to you; I will care for all your wants. Only, do not spend the night in the square." ²¹So he brought him into his house and gave the donkeys feed. And they washed their feet, and ate and drank.

GIBEAH'S CRIME

²²As they were making their hearts merry, behold, the men of the city, worthless fellows, surrounded the house, beating on the door. And they said to the old man, the master of the house, "Bring out the man who came into your house, that we may know him." ²³And the man, the master of the house, went out to them and said to them, "No, my brothers, do not act so wickedly; since this man has come into my house, do not do this vile thing. ²⁴Behold, here are my virgin daughter and his concubine. Let me bring them out now. Violate them and do with them what seems good to you, but against this man do not do this outrageous thing." ²⁵But the men would not listen to him. So the man seized his concubine and made her go out to them. And they knew her and abused her all night until the morning. And as the dawn began to break, they let her go. ²⁶And as morning appeared, the woman came and fell down at the door of the man's house where her master was, until it was light.

²⁷And her master rose up in the morning, and when he opened the doors of the house and went out to go on his way, behold, there was his concubine lying at the door of the house, with her hands on the threshold. ²⁸He said to her, "Get up, let us be going." But there was no answer. Then he put her on the donkey, and the man rose up and went away to his home. ²⁹And when he entered his house, he took a knife, and taking hold of his concubine he divided her, limb by limb, into twelve pieces, and sent her throughout all the territory of Israel. ³⁰And all who saw it said, "Such a thing has never happened or been seen from the day that the people of Israel came up out of the land of Egypt until this day; consider it, take counsel, and speak."

ISRAEL'S WAR WITH THE TRIBE OF BENJAMIN

20 Then all the people of Israel came out, from Dan to Beersheba, including the land of Gilead, and the congregation assembled as one man to the Lord at Mizpah. ²And the chiefs of all the people, of all the tribes of Israel, presented themselves in the assembly of the people of God, 400,000 men on foot that drew the sword. ³(Now the people of Benjamin heard that the people of Israel had gone up to Mizpah.) And the people of Israel said, "Tell us, how did this evil happen?" ⁴And the Levite, the husband of the woman who was murdered, answered and said, "I came to Gibeah that belongs to Benjamin, I and my concubine, to spend the night. ⁵And the leaders of Gibeah rose against me and surrounded the house against me by night. They meant to kill me, and they violated my concubine, and she is dead. ⁶So I took hold of my concubine and cut her in pieces and sent her throughout all the country of the inheritance of Israel, for they have committed abomination and outrage in Israel. ⁷Behold, you people of Israel, all of you, give your advice and counsel here."

⁸And all the people arose as one man, saying, "None of us will go to his tent, and none of us will return to his house. ⁹But now this is what we will do to Gibeah: we will go up against it by lot, ¹⁰and we will take ten men of a hundred throughout all the tribes of Israel, and a hundred of a thousand, and a thousand of ten thousand, to bring provisions for the people, that when they come they may repay Gibeah of Benjamin for all the outrage that they have committed in Israel." ¹¹So all the men of Israel gathered against the city, united as one man.

¹²And the tribes of Israel sent men through all the tribe of Benjamin, saying, "What evil

---
ᵃSeptuagint *my home*; compare verse 29

is this that has taken place among you? [13]Now therefore give up the men, the worthless fellows in Gibeah, that we may put them to death and purge evil from Israel." But the Benjaminites would not listen to the voice of their brothers, the people of Israel. [14]Then the people of Benjamin came together out of the cities to Gibeah to go out to battle against the people of Israel. [15]And the people of Benjamin mustered out of their cities on that day 26,000 men who drew the sword, besides the inhabitants of Gibeah, who mustered 700 chosen men. [16]Among all these were 700 chosen men who were left-handed; every one could sling a stone at a hair and not miss. [17]And the men of Israel, apart from Benjamin, mustered 400,000 men who drew the sword; all these were men of war.

[18]The people of Israel arose and went up to Bethel and enquired of God, "Who shall go up first for us to fight against the people of Benjamin?" And the LORD said, "Judah shall go up first."

[19]Then the people of Israel rose in the morning and encamped against Gibeah. [20]And the men of Israel went out to fight against Benjamin, and the men of Israel drew up the battle line against them at Gibeah. [21]The people of Benjamin came out of Gibeah and destroyed on that day 22,000 men of the Israelites. [22]But the people, the men of Israel, took courage, and again formed the battle line in the same place where they had formed it on the first day. [23]And the people of Israel went up and wept before the LORD until the evening. And they enquired of the LORD, "Shall we again draw near to fight against our brothers, the people of Benjamin?" And the LORD said, "Go up against them."

[24]So the people of Israel came near against the people of Benjamin the second day. [25]And Benjamin went against them out of Gibeah on the second day, and destroyed 18,000 men of the people of Israel. All these were men who drew the sword. [26]Then all the people of Israel, the whole army, went up and came to Bethel and wept. They sat there before the LORD and fasted that day until evening, and offered burnt offerings and peace offerings before the LORD. [27]And the people of Israel enquired of the LORD (for the ark of the covenant of God was there in those days, [28]and Phinehas the son of Eleazar, son of Aaron, ministered before it in those days), saying, "Shall we go out once more to battle against our brothers, the people of Benjamin, or shall we cease?" And the LORD said, "Go up, for tomorrow I will give them into your hand."

[29]So Israel set men in ambush around Gibeah. [30]And the people of Israel went up against the people of Benjamin on the third day and set themselves in array against Gibeah, as at other times. [31]And the people of Benjamin went out against the people and were drawn away from the city. And as at other times they began to strike and kill some of the people in the highways, one of which goes up to Bethel and the other to Gibeah, and in the open country, about thirty men of Israel. [32]And the people of Benjamin said, "They are routed before us, as at the first." But the people of Israel said, "Let us flee and draw them away from the city to the highways." [33]And all the men of Israel rose up out of their place and set themselves in array at Baal-tamar, and the men of Israel who were in ambush rushed out of their place from Maareh-geba.[a] [34]And there came against Gibeah 10,000 chosen men out of all Israel, and the battle was hard, but the Benjaminites did not know that disaster was close upon them. [35]And the LORD defeated Benjamin before Israel, and the people of Israel destroyed 25,100 men of Benjamin that day. All these were men who drew the sword. [36]So the people of Benjamin saw that they were defeated.

The men of Israel gave ground to Benjamin, because they trusted the men in ambush whom they had set against Gibeah. [37]Then the men in ambush hurried and rushed against Gibeah; the men in ambush moved out and struck all the city with the edge of the sword. [38]Now the appointed signal between the men of Israel and the men in the main ambush was that when they made a great cloud of smoke rise up out of the city [39]the men of Israel should turn in battle. Now Benjamin had begun to strike and kill about thirty men of Israel. They said, "Surely they are defeated before us, as in the first battle." [40]But when the signal began to rise out of the city in a column of smoke, the Benjaminites looked behind them, and behold, the whole of the city went up in smoke to heaven. [41]Then the men of Israel turned, and the men of Benjamin were dismayed, for they saw that disaster was close upon them. [42]Therefore they turned their backs before the men of Israel in the direction of the wilderness, but the battle overtook them. And those who came

---

[a]Some Septuagint manuscripts *place west of Geba*

out of the cities were destroying them in their midst. ⁴³Surrounding the Benjaminites, they pursued them and trod them down from Nohah[a] as far as opposite Gibeah on the east. ⁴⁴Eighteen thousand men of Benjamin fell, all of them men of valour. ⁴⁵And they turned and fled towards the wilderness to the rock of Rimmon. Five thousand men of them were cut down in the highways. And they were pursued hard to Gidom, and 2,000 men of them were struck down. ⁴⁶So all who fell that day of Benjamin were 25,000 men who drew the sword, all of them men of valour. ⁴⁷But 600 men turned and fled towards the wilderness to the rock of Rimmon and remained at the rock of Rimmon four months. ⁴⁸And the men of Israel turned back against the people of Benjamin and struck them with the edge of the sword, the city, men and beasts and all that they found. And all the towns that they found they set on fire.

WIVES PROVIDED FOR THE TRIBE OF BENJAMIN

21 Now the men of Israel had sworn at Mizpah, "No one of us shall give his daughter in marriage to Benjamin." ²And the people came to Bethel and sat there till evening before God, and they lifted up their voices and wept bitterly. ³And they said, "O LORD, the God of Israel, why has this happened in Israel, that today there should be one tribe lacking in Israel?" ⁴And the next day the people rose early and built there an altar and offered burnt offerings and peace offerings. ⁵And the people of Israel said, "Which of all the tribes of Israel did not come up in the assembly to the LORD?" For they had taken a great oath concerning him who did not come up to the LORD to Mizpah, saying, "He shall surely be put to death." ⁶And the people of Israel had compassion for Benjamin their brother and said, "One tribe is cut off from Israel this day. ⁷What shall we do for wives for those who are left, since we have sworn by the LORD that we will not give them any of our daughters for wives?"

⁸And they said, "What one is there of the tribes of Israel that did not come up to the LORD to Mizpah?" And behold, no one had come to the camp from Jabesh-gilead, to the assembly. ⁹For when the people were mustered, behold, not one of the inhabitants of Jabesh-gilead was there. ¹⁰So the congregation sent 12,000 of their bravest men there and commanded them, "Go and strike the inhabitants of Jabesh-gilead with the edge of the sword; also the women and the little ones. ¹¹This is what you shall do: every male and every woman that has lain with a male you shall devote to destruction." ¹²And they found among the inhabitants of Jabesh-gilead 400 young virgins who had not known a man by lying with him, and they brought them to the camp at Shiloh, which is in the land of Canaan.

¹³Then the whole congregation sent word to the people of Benjamin who were at the rock of Rimmon and proclaimed peace to them. ¹⁴And Benjamin returned at that time. And they gave them the women whom they had saved alive of the women of Jabesh-gilead, but they were not enough for them. ¹⁵And the people had compassion on Benjamin because the LORD had made a breach in the tribes of Israel.

¹⁶Then the elders of the congregation said, "What shall we do for wives for those who are left, since the women are destroyed out of Benjamin?" ¹⁷And they said, "There must be an inheritance for the survivors of Benjamin, that a tribe may not be blotted out from Israel. ¹⁸Yet we cannot give them wives from our daughters." For the people of Israel had sworn, "Cursed be he who gives a wife to Benjamin." ¹⁹So they said, "Behold, there is the yearly feast of the LORD at Shiloh, which is north of Bethel, on the east of the highway that goes up from Bethel to Shechem, and south of Lebonah." ²⁰And they commanded the people of Benjamin, saying, "Go and lie in ambush in the vineyards ²¹and watch. If the daughters of Shiloh come out to dance in the dances, then come out of the vineyards and snatch each man his wife from the daughters of Shiloh, and go to the land of Benjamin. ²²And when their fathers or their brothers come to complain to us, we will say to them, 'Grant them graciously to us, because we did not take for each man of them his wife in battle, neither did you give them to them, else you would now be guilty.'" ²³And the people of Benjamin did so and took their wives, according to their number, from the dancers whom they carried off. Then they went and returned to their inheritance and rebuilt the towns and lived in them. ²⁴And the people of Israel departed from there at that time, every man to his tribe and family, and they went out from there every man to his inheritance.

²⁵In those days there was no king in Israel. Everyone did what was right in his own eyes.

---

[a]Septuagint; Hebrew [at their] *resting place*

RUTH

NAOMI WIDOWED

1 In the days when the judges ruled there was a famine in the land, and a man of Bethlehem in Judah went to sojourn in the country of Moab, he and his wife and his two sons. ²The name of the man was Elimelech and the name of his wife Naomi, and the names of his two sons were Mahlon and Chilion. They were Ephrathites from Bethlehem in Judah. They went into the country of Moab and remained there. ³But Elimelech, the husband of Naomi, died, and she was left with her two sons. ⁴These took Moabite wives; the name of one was Orpah and the name of the other Ruth. They lived there about ten years, ⁵and both Mahlon and Chilion died, so that the woman was left without her two sons and her husband.

RUTH'S LOYALTY TO NAOMI

⁶Then she arose with her daughters-in-law to return from the country of Moab, for she had heard in the fields of Moab that the LORD had visited his people and given them food. ⁷So she set out from the place where she was with her two daughters-in-law, and they went on the way to return to the land of Judah. ⁸But Naomi said to her two daughters-in-law, "Go, return each of you to her mother's house. May the LORD deal kindly with you, as you have dealt with the dead and with me. ⁹The LORD grant that you may find rest, each of you in the house of her husband!" Then she kissed them, and they lifted up their voices and wept. ¹⁰And they said to her, "No, we will return with you to your people." ¹¹But Naomi said, "Turn back, my daughters; why will you go with me? Have I yet sons in my womb that they may become your husbands? ¹²Turn back, my daughters; go your way, for I am too old to have a husband. If I should say I have hope, even if I should have a husband this night and should bear sons, ¹³would you therefore wait till they were grown? Would you therefore refrain from marrying? No, my daughters, for it is exceedingly bitter to me for your sake that the hand of the LORD has gone out against me." ¹⁴Then they lifted up their voices and wept again. And Orpah kissed her mother-in-law, but Ruth clung to her.

¹⁵And she said, "See, your sister-in-law has gone back to her people and to her gods; return after your sister-in-law." ¹⁶But Ruth said, "Do not urge me to leave you or to return from following you. For where you go I will go, and where you lodge I will lodge. Your people shall be my people, and your God my God. ¹⁷Where you die I will die, and there will I be buried. May the LORD do so to me and more also if anything but death parts me from you." ¹⁸And when Naomi saw that she was determined to go with her, she said no more.

NAOMI AND RUTH RETURN

¹⁹So the two of them went on until they came to Bethlehem. And when they came to Bethlehem, the whole town was stirred because of them. And the women said, "Is this Naomi?" ²⁰She said to them, "Do not call me Naomi;*ᵃ* call me Mara,*ᵇ* for the Almighty has dealt very bitterly with me. ²¹I went away full, and the LORD has brought me back empty. Why call me Naomi, when the LORD has testified against me and the Almighty has brought calamity upon me?"

²²So Naomi returned, and Ruth the Moabite her daughter-in-law with her, who returned from the country of Moab. And they came to Bethlehem at the beginning of barley harvest.

RUTH MEETS BOAZ

2 Now Naomi had a relative of her husband's, a worthy man of the clan of Elimelech, whose name was Boaz. ²And Ruth the Moabite said to Naomi, "Let me go to the field and glean among the ears of grain after him in whose sight I shall find favour." And she said to her, "Go, my daughter." ³So she set out and went and gleaned in the field after the reapers, and she happened to come to the part of the field belonging to Boaz, who was of the clan of Elimelech. ⁴And behold, Boaz came from Bethlehem. And he

---

ᵃNaomi means *pleasant* *ᵇMara* means *bitter*

said to the reapers, "The LORD be with you!" And they answered, "The LORD bless you." ⁵Then Boaz said to his young man who was in charge of the reapers, "Whose young woman is this?" ⁶And the servant who was in charge of the reapers answered, "She is the young Moabite woman, who came back with Naomi from the country of Moab. ⁷She said, 'Please let me glean and gather among the sheaves after the reapers.' So she came, and she has continued from early morning until now, except for a short rest."ᵃ

⁸Then Boaz said to Ruth, "Now, listen, my daughter, do not go to glean in another field or leave this one, but keep close to my young women. ⁹Let your eyes be on the field that they are reaping, and go after them. Have I not charged the young men not to touch you? And when you are thirsty, go to the vessels and drink what the young men have drawn." ¹⁰Then she fell on her face, bowing to the ground, and said to him, "Why have I found favour in your eyes, that you should take notice of me, since I am a foreigner?" ¹¹But Boaz answered her, "All that you have done for your mother-in-law since the death of your husband has been fully told to me, and how you left your father and mother and your native land and came to a people that you did not know before. ¹²The LORD repay you for what you have done, and a full reward be given you by the LORD, the God of Israel, under whose wings you have come to take refuge!" ¹³Then she said, "I have found favour in your eyes, my lord, for you have comforted me and spoken kindly to your servant, though I am not one of your servants."

¹⁴And at mealtime Boaz said to her, "Come here and eat some bread and dip your morsel in the wine." So she sat beside the reapers, and he passed to her roasted grain. And she ate until she was satisfied, and she had some left over. ¹⁵When she rose to glean, Boaz instructed his young men, saying, "Let her glean even among the sheaves, and do not reproach her. ¹⁶And also pull out some from the bundles for her and leave it for her to glean, and do not rebuke her."

¹⁷So she gleaned in the field until evening. Then she beat out what she had gleaned, and it was about an ephahᵇ of barley. ¹⁸And she took it up and went into the city. Her mother-in-law saw what she had gleaned. She also brought out and gave her what food she had left over after being satisfied. ¹⁹And her mother-in-law said to her, "Where did you glean today? And where have you worked? Blessed be the man who took notice of you." So she told her mother-in-law with whom she had worked and said, "The man's name with whom I worked today is Boaz." ²⁰And Naomi said to her daughter-in-law, "May he be blessed by the LORD, whose kindness has not forsaken the living or the dead!" Naomi also said to her, "The man is a close relative of ours, one of our redeemers." ²¹And Ruth the Moabite said, "Besides, he said to me, 'You shall keep close by my young men until they have finished all my harvest.'" ²²And Naomi said to Ruth, her daughter-in-law, "It is good, my daughter, that you go out with his young women, lest in another field you be assaulted." ²³So she kept close to the young women of Boaz, gleaning until the end of the barley and wheat harvests. And she lived with her mother-in-law.

RUTH AND BOAZ AT THE THRESHING FLOOR

3 Then Naomi her mother-in-law said to her, "My daughter, should I not seek rest for you, that it may be well with you? ²Is not Boaz our relative, with whose young women you were? See, he is winnowing barley tonight at the threshing floor. ³Wash therefore and anoint yourself, and put on your cloak and go down to the threshing floor, but do not make yourself known to the man until he has finished eating and drinking. ⁴But when he lies down, observe the place where he lies. Then go and uncover his feet and lie down, and he will tell you what to do." ⁵And she replied, "All that you say I will do."

⁶So she went down to the threshing floor and did just as her mother-in-law had commanded her. ⁷And when Boaz had eaten and drunk, and his heart was merry, he went to lie down at the end of the heap of grain. Then she came softly and uncovered his feet and lay down. ⁸At midnight the man was startled and turned over, and behold, a woman lay at his feet! ⁹He said, "Who are you?" And she answered, "I am Ruth, your servant. Spread your wingsᶜ over your servant, for you are a redeemer." ¹⁰And he said, "May you be blessed by the LORD, my daughter. You have made this last kindness greater than the first in that you have not gone after young men, whether poor

---
ᵃCompare Septuagint, Vulgate; the meaning of the Hebrew phrase is uncertain ᵇAn *ephah* was about 3/5 of a bushel or 22 litres
ᶜCompare 2:12; the word for *wings* can also mean *corners of a garment*

or rich. ⁱⁱAnd now, my daughter, do not fear. I will do for you all that you ask, for all my fellow townsmen know that you are a worthy woman. ¹²And now it is true that I am a redeemer. Yet there is a redeemer nearer than I. ¹³Remain tonight, and in the morning, if he will redeem you, good; let him do it. But if he is not willing to redeem you, then, as the LORD lives, I will redeem you. Lie down until the morning."

¹⁴So she lay at his feet until the morning, but arose before one could recognize another. And he said, "Let it not be known that the woman came to the threshing floor." ¹⁵And he said, "Bring the garment you are wearing and hold it out." So she held it, and he measured out six measures of barley and put it on her. Then she went into the city. ¹⁶And when she came to her mother-in-law, she said, "How did you fare, my daughter?" Then she told her all that the man had done for her, ¹⁷saying, "These six measures of barley he gave to me, for he said to me, 'You must not go back empty-handed to your mother-in-law.'" ¹⁸She replied, "Wait, my daughter, until you learn how the matter turns out, for the man will not rest but will settle the matter today."

BOAZ REDEEMS RUTH

4 Now Boaz had gone up to the gate and sat down there. And behold, the redeemer, of whom Boaz had spoken, came by. So Boaz said, "Turn aside, friend; sit down here." And he turned aside and sat down. ²And he took ten men of the elders of the city and said, "Sit down here." So they sat down. ³Then he said to the redeemer, "Naomi, who has come back from the country of Moab, is selling the parcel of land that belonged to our relative Elimelech. ⁴So I thought I would tell you of it and say, 'Buy it in the presence of those sitting here and in the presence of the elders of my people.' If you will redeem it, redeem it. But if you*ᵃ* will not, tell me, that I may know, for there is no one besides you to redeem it, and I come after you." And he said, "I will redeem it." ⁵Then Boaz said, "The day you buy the field from the hand of Naomi, you also acquire Ruth*ᵇ* the Moabite, the widow of the dead, in order to perpetuate the name of the dead in his inheritance." ⁶Then the redeemer said, "I cannot redeem it for myself, lest I impair my own inheritance. Take my right of redemption yourself, for I cannot redeem it."

⁷Now this was the custom in former times in Israel concerning redeeming and exchanging: to confirm a transaction, one drew off his sandal and gave it to the other, and this was the manner of attesting in Israel. ⁸So when the redeemer said to Boaz, "Buy it for yourself," he drew off his sandal. ⁹Then Boaz said to the elders and all the people, "You are witnesses this day that I have bought from the hand of Naomi all that belonged to Elimelech and all that belonged to Chilion and to Mahlon. ¹⁰Also Ruth the Moabite, the widow of Mahlon, I have bought to be my wife, to perpetuate the name of the dead in his inheritance, that the name of the dead may not be cut off from among his brothers and from the gate of his native place. You are witnesses this day." ¹¹Then all the people who were at the gate and the elders said, "We are witnesses. May the LORD make the woman, who is coming into your house, like Rachel and Leah, who together built up the house of Israel. May you act worthily in Ephrathah and be renowned in Bethlehem, ¹²and may your house be like the house of Perez, whom Tamar bore to Judah, because of the offspring that the LORD will give you by this young woman."

RUTH AND BOAZ MARRY

¹³So Boaz took Ruth, and she became his wife. And he went in to her, and the LORD gave her conception, and she bore a son. ¹⁴Then the women said to Naomi, "Blessed be the LORD, who has not left you this day without a redeemer, and may his name be renowned in Israel! ¹⁵He shall be to you a restorer of life and a nourisher of your old age, for your daughter-in-law who loves you, who is more to you than seven sons, has given birth to him." ¹⁶Then Naomi took the child and laid him on her lap and became his nurse. ¹⁷And the women of the neighbourhood gave him a name, saying, "A son has been born to Naomi." They named him Obed. He was the father of Jesse, the father of David.

THE GENEALOGY OF DAVID

¹⁸Now these are the generations of Perez: Perez fathered Hezron, ¹⁹Hezron fathered Ram, Ram fathered Amminadab, ²⁰Amminadab fathered Nahshon, Nahshon fathered Salmon, ²¹Salmon fathered Boaz, Boaz fathered Obed, ²²Obed fathered Jesse, and Jesse fathered David.

---

*ᵃ*Hebrew *he* *ᵇ*Masoretic Text *you also buy it from Ruth*

1 SAMUEL

THE BIRTH OF SAMUEL

1 There was a certain man of Ramathaim-zophim of the hill country of Ephraim whose name was Elkanah the son of Jeroham, son of Elihu, son of Tohu, son of Zuph, an Ephrathite. ²He had two wives. The name of one was Hannah, and the name of the other, Peninnah. And Peninnah had children, but Hannah had no children.

³Now this man used to go up year by year from his city to worship and to sacrifice to the LORD of hosts at Shiloh, where the two sons of Eli, Hophni and Phinehas, were priests of the LORD. ⁴On the day when Elkanah sacrificed, he would give portions to Peninnah his wife and to all her sons and daughters. ⁵But to Hannah he gave a double portion, because he loved her, though the LORD had closed her womb.*ᵃ* ⁶And her rival used to provoke her grievously to irritate her, because the LORD had closed her womb. ⁷So it went on year by year. As often as she went up to the house of the LORD, she used to provoke her. Therefore Hannah wept and would not eat. ⁸And Elkanah, her husband, said to her, "Hannah, why do you weep? And why do you not eat? And why is your heart sad? Am I not more to you than ten sons?"

⁹After they had eaten and drunk in Shiloh, Hannah rose. Now Eli the priest was sitting on the seat beside the doorpost of the temple of the LORD. ¹⁰She was deeply distressed and prayed to the LORD and wept bitterly. ¹¹And she vowed a vow and said, "O LORD of hosts, if you will indeed look on the affliction of your servant and remember me and not forget your servant, but will give to your servant a son, then I will give him to the LORD all the days of his life, and no razor shall touch his head."

¹²As she continued praying before the LORD, Eli observed her mouth. ¹³Hannah was speaking in her heart; only her lips moved, and her voice was not heard. Therefore Eli took her to be a drunken woman. ¹⁴And Eli said to her, "How long will you go on being drunk? Put your wine away from you." ¹⁵But Hannah answered, "No, my lord, I am a woman troubled in spirit. I have drunk neither wine nor strong drink, but I have been pouring out my soul before the LORD. ¹⁶Do not regard your servant as a worthless woman, for all along I have been speaking out of my great anxiety and vexation." ¹⁷Then Eli answered, "Go in peace, and the God of Israel grant your petition that you have made to him." ¹⁸And she said, "Let your servant find favour in your eyes." Then the woman went on her way and ate, and her face was no longer sad.

¹⁹They rose early in the morning and worshipped before the LORD; then they went back to their house at Ramah. And Elkanah knew Hannah his wife, and the LORD remembered her. ²⁰And in due time Hannah conceived and bore a son, and she called his name Samuel, for she said, "I have asked for him from the LORD."*ᵇ*

SAMUEL GIVEN TO THE LORD

²¹The man Elkanah and all his house went up to offer to the LORD the yearly sacrifice and to pay his vow. ²²But Hannah did not go up, for she said to her husband, "As soon as the child is weaned, I will bring him, so that he may appear in the presence of the LORD and dwell there for ever." ²³Elkanah her husband said to her, "Do what seems best to you; wait until you have weaned him; only, may the LORD establish his word." So the woman remained and nursed her son until she weaned him. ²⁴And when she had weaned him, she took him up with her, along with a three-year-old bull,*ᶜ* an ephah*ᵈ* of flour, and a skin of wine, and she brought him to the house of the LORD at Shiloh. And the child was young. ²⁵Then they slaughtered the bull, and they brought the child to Eli. ²⁶And she said, "Oh, my lord! As you live, my lord, I am the woman who was standing here in your presence, praying to the LORD. ²⁷For this child I prayed, and the LORD has granted me my

---

*ᵃ*Syriac; the meaning of the Hebrew is uncertain. Septuagint *And, although he loved Hannah, he would give Hannah only one portion, because the LORD had closed her womb* *ᵇSamuel* sounds like the Hebrew for *heard of God* *ᶜ*Dead Sea Scroll, Septuagint, Syriac; Masoretic Text *three bulls* *ᵈ*An *ephah* was about 3/5 of a bushel or 22 litres

petition that I made to him. ²⁸Therefore I have lent him to the LORD. As long as he lives, he is lent to the LORD."

And he worshipped the LORD there.

HANNAH'S PRAYER

2 And Hannah prayed and said,

"My heart exults in the LORD;
   my horn is exalted in the LORD.
My mouth derides my enemies,
   because I rejoice in your salvation.

² "There is none holy like the LORD:
   for there is none besides you;
   there is no rock like our God.
³ Talk no more so very proudly,
   let not arrogance come
      from your mouth;
for the LORD is a God of knowledge,
   and by him actions are weighed.
⁴ The bows of the mighty are broken,
   but the feeble bind on strength.
⁵ Those who were full have hired
      themselves out for bread,
   but those who were hungry
      have ceased to hunger.
The barren has borne seven,
   but she who has many
      children is forlorn.
⁶ The LORD kills and brings to life;
   he brings down to Sheol
      and raises up.
⁷ The LORD makes poor and makes rich;
   he brings low and he exalts.
⁸ He raises up the poor from the dust;
   he lifts the needy from the ash heap
to make them sit with princes
   and inherit a seat of honour.
For the pillars of the earth
   are the LORD's,
   and on them he has set the world.

⁹ "He will guard the feet of
      his faithful ones,
   but the wicked shall be cut
      off in darkness,
for not by might shall a man prevail.
¹⁰ The adversaries of the LORD shall
      be broken to pieces;
   against them he will
      thunder in heaven.
The LORD will judge the
   ends of the earth;
he will give strength to his king
   and exalt the horn of his anointed."

¹¹Then Elkanah went home to Ramah. And the boy[a] was ministering to the LORD in the presence of Eli the priest.

ELI'S WORTHLESS SONS

¹²Now the sons of Eli were worthless men. They did not know the LORD. ¹³The custom of the priests with the people was that when any man offered sacrifice, the priest's servant would come, while the meat was boiling, with a three-pronged fork in his hand, ¹⁴and he would thrust it into the pan or kettle or cauldron or pot. All that the fork brought up the priest would take for himself. This is what they did at Shiloh to all the Israelites who came there. ¹⁵Moreover, before the fat was burned, the priest's servant would come and say to the man who was sacrificing, "Give meat for the priest to roast, for he will not accept boiled meat from you but only raw." ¹⁶And if the man said to him, "Let them burn the fat first, and then take as much as you wish," he would say, "No, you must give it now, and if not, I will take it by force." ¹⁷Thus the sin of the young men was very great in the sight of the LORD, for the men treated the offering of the LORD with contempt.

¹⁸Samuel was ministering before the LORD, a boy clothed with a linen ephod. ¹⁹And his mother used to make for him a little robe and take it to him each year when she went up with her husband to offer the yearly sacrifice. ²⁰Then Eli would bless Elkanah and his wife, and say, "May the LORD give you children by this woman for the petition she asked of the LORD." So then they would return to their home.

²¹Indeed the LORD visited Hannah, and she conceived and bore three sons and two daughters. And the boy Samuel grew in the presence of the LORD.

ELI REBUKES HIS SONS

²²Now Eli was very old, and he kept hearing all that his sons were doing to all Israel, and how they lay with the women who were serving at the entrance to the tent of meeting. ²³And he said to them, "Why do you do such things? For I hear of your evil dealings from all these people. ²⁴No, my sons; it is not a good report that I hear the people of the LORD spreading abroad. ²⁵If

---

[a]Hebrew *na'ar* can be rendered *boy* (2:11, 18, 21, 26; 3:1, 8), *servant* (2:13, 15), or *young man* (2:17), depending on the context

someone sins against a man, God will mediate for him, but if someone sins against the LORD, who can intercede for him?" But they would not listen to the voice of their father, for it was the will of the LORD to put them to death. ²⁶Now the boy Samuel continued to grow both in stature and in favour with the LORD and also with man.

THE LORD REJECTS ELI'S HOUSEHOLD

²⁷And there came a man of God to Eli and said to him, "Thus says the LORD, 'Did I indeed reveal myself to the house of your father when they were in Egypt subject to the house of Pharaoh? ²⁸Did I choose him out of all the tribes of Israel to be my priest, to go up to my altar, to burn incense, to wear an ephod before me? I gave to the house of your father all my offerings by fire from the people of Israel. ²⁹Why then do you scorn[a] my sacrifices and my offerings that I commanded for my dwelling, and honour your sons above me by fattening yourselves on the choicest parts of every offering of my people Israel?' ³⁰Therefore the LORD, the God of Israel, declares: 'I promised that your house and the house of your father should go in and out before me for ever,' but now the LORD declares: 'Far be it from me, for those who honour me I will honour, and those who despise me shall be lightly esteemed. ³¹Behold, the days are coming when I will cut off your strength and the strength of your father's house, so that there will not be an old man in your house. ³²Then in distress you will look with envious eye on all the prosperity that shall be bestowed on Israel, and there shall not be an old man in your house for ever. ³³The only one of you whom I shall not cut off from my altar shall be spared to weep his[b] eyes out to grieve his heart, and all the descendants[c] of your house shall die by the sword of men.[d] ³⁴And this that shall come upon your two sons, Hophni and Phinehas, shall be the sign to you: both of them shall die on the same day. ³⁵And I will raise up for myself a faithful priest, who shall do according to what is in my heart and in my mind. And I will build him a sure house, and he shall go in and out before my anointed for ever. ³⁶And everyone who is left in your house shall come to implore him for a piece of silver or a loaf of bread and shall say, "Please put me in one of the priests' places, that I may eat a morsel of bread."'"

THE LORD CALLS SAMUEL

3 Now the boy Samuel was ministering to the LORD in the presence of Eli. And the word of the LORD was rare in those days; there was no frequent vision.

²At that time Eli, whose eyesight had begun to grow dim so that he could not see, was lying down in his own place. ³The lamp of God had not yet gone out, and Samuel was lying down in the temple of the LORD, where the ark of God was. ⁴Then the LORD called Samuel, and he said, "Here I am!" ⁵and ran to Eli and said, "Here I am, for you called me." But he said, "I did not call; lie down again." So he went and lay down. ⁶And the LORD called again, "Samuel!" and Samuel arose and went to Eli and said, "Here I am, for you called me." But he said, "I did not call, my son; lie down again." ⁷Now Samuel did not yet know the LORD, and the word of the LORD had not yet been revealed to him. ⁸And the LORD called Samuel again the third time. And he arose and went to Eli and said, "Here I am, for you called me." Then Eli perceived that the LORD was calling the boy. ⁹Therefore Eli said to Samuel, "Go, lie down, and if he calls you, you shall say, 'Speak, LORD, for your servant hears.'" So Samuel went and lay down in his place.

¹⁰And the LORD came and stood, calling as at other times, "Samuel! Samuel!" And Samuel said, "Speak, for your servant hears." ¹¹Then the LORD said to Samuel, "Behold, I am about to do a thing in Israel at which the two ears of everyone who hears it will tingle. ¹²On that day I will fulfil against Eli all that I have spoken concerning his house, from beginning to end. ¹³And I declare to him that I am about to punish his house for ever, for the iniquity that he knew, because his sons were blaspheming God,[e] and he did not restrain them. ¹⁴Therefore I swear to the house of Eli that the iniquity of Eli's house shall not be atoned for by sacrifice or offering for ever."

¹⁵Samuel lay until morning; then he opened the doors of the house of the LORD. And Samuel was afraid to tell the vision to Eli. ¹⁶But Eli called Samuel and said, "Samuel, my son." And he said, "Here I am." ¹⁷And Eli said, "What was it that he told you? Do not hide it from me. May God do so to you and more also if you hide anything from me of all that he told

---

[a]Hebrew *kick at* [b]Septuagint; Hebrew *your*; twice in this verse
[c]Hebrew *increase* [d]Septuagint; Hebrew *die as men* [e]Or *blaspheming for themselves*

you." ¹⁸So Samuel told him everything and hid nothing from him. And he said, "It is the LORD. Let him do what seems good to him."

¹⁹And Samuel grew, and the LORD was with him and let none of his words fall to the ground. ²⁰And all Israel from Dan to Beersheba knew that Samuel was established as a prophet of the LORD. ²¹And the LORD appeared again at Shiloh, for the LORD revealed himself to Samuel at Shiloh by the word of the LORD.

THE PHILISTINES CAPTURE THE ARK

4 And the word of Samuel came to all Israel.

Now Israel went out to battle against the Philistines. They encamped at Ebenezer, and the Philistines encamped at Aphek. ²The Philistines drew up in line against Israel, and when the battle spread, Israel was defeated before the Philistines, who killed about four thousand men on the field of battle. ³And when the people came to the camp, the elders of Israel said, "Why has the LORD defeated us today before the Philistines? Let us bring the ark of the covenant of the LORD here from Shiloh, that it^a may come among us and save us from the power of our enemies." ⁴So the people sent to Shiloh and brought from there the ark of the covenant of the LORD of hosts, who is enthroned on the cherubim. And the two sons of Eli, Hophni and Phinehas, were there with the ark of the covenant of God.

⁵As soon as the ark of the covenant of the LORD came into the camp, all Israel gave a mighty shout, so that the earth resounded. ⁶And when the Philistines heard the noise of the shouting, they said, "What does this great shouting in the camp of the Hebrews mean?" And when they learned that the ark of the LORD had come to the camp, ⁷the Philistines were afraid, for they said, "A god has come into the camp." And they said, "Woe to us! For nothing like this has happened before. ⁸Woe to us! Who can deliver us from the power of these mighty gods? These are the gods who struck the Egyptians with every sort of plague in the wilderness. ⁹Take courage, and be men, O Philistines, lest you become slaves to the Hebrews as they have been to you; be men and fight."

¹⁰So the Philistines fought, and Israel was defeated, and they fled, every man to his home. And there was a very great slaughter, for thirty thousand foot soldiers of Israel fell. ¹¹And the ark of God was captured, and the two sons of Eli, Hophni and Phinehas, died.

THE DEATH OF ELI

¹²A man of Benjamin ran from the battle line and came to Shiloh the same day, with his clothes torn and with dirt on his head. ¹³When he arrived, Eli was sitting on his seat by the road watching, for his heart trembled for the ark of God. And when the man came into the city and told the news, all the city cried out. ¹⁴When Eli heard the sound of the outcry, he said, "What is this uproar?" Then the man hurried and came and told Eli. ¹⁵Now Eli was ninety-eight years old and his eyes were set so that he could not see. ¹⁶And the man said to Eli, "I am he who has come from the battle; I fled from the battle today." And he said, "How did it go, my son?" ¹⁷He who brought the news answered and said, "Israel has fled before the Philistines, and there has also been a great defeat among the people. Your two sons also, Hophni and Phinehas, are dead, and the ark of God has been captured." ¹⁸As soon as he mentioned the ark of God, Eli fell over backwards from his seat by the side of the gate, and his neck was broken and he died, for the man was old and heavy. He had judged Israel for forty years.

¹⁹Now his daughter-in-law, the wife of Phinehas, was pregnant, about to give birth. And when she heard the news that the ark of God was captured, and that her father-in-law and her husband were dead, she bowed and gave birth, for her pains came upon her. ²⁰And about the time of her death the women attending her said to her, "Do not be afraid, for you have borne a son." But she did not answer or pay attention. ²¹And she named the child Ichabod, saying, "The glory has departed^b from Israel!" because the ark of God had been captured and because of her father-in-law and her husband. ²²And she said, "The glory has departed from Israel, for the ark of God has been captured."

THE PHILISTINES AND THE ARK

5 When the Philistines captured the ark of God, they brought it from Ebenezer to Ashdod. ²Then the Philistines took the ark of God and brought it into the house of Dagon and set it up beside Dagon. ³And when the people of Ashdod rose early the next day, behold, Dagon had fallen face down on the ground before the ark of the LORD. So they took Dagon and put him back in his place. ⁴But when they rose early on the next

---

^{a}Or he ^{b}Or gone into exile; also verse 22

morning, behold, Dagon had fallen face down on the ground before the ark of the LORD, and the head of Dagon and both his hands were lying cut off on the threshold. Only the trunk of Dagon was left to him. ⁵This is why the priests of Dagon and all who enter the house of Dagon do not tread on the threshold of Dagon in Ashdod to this day.

⁶The hand of the LORD was heavy against the people of Ashdod, and he terrified and afflicted them with tumours, both in Ashdod and its territory. ⁷And when the men of Ashdod saw how things were, they said, "The ark of the God of Israel must not remain with us, for his hand is hard against us and against Dagon our god." ⁸So they sent and gathered together all the lords of the Philistines and said, "What shall we do with the ark of the God of Israel?" They answered, "Let the ark of the God of Israel be brought round to Gath." So they brought the ark of the God of Israel there. ⁹But after they had brought it round, the hand of the LORD was against the city, causing a very great panic, and he afflicted the men of the city, both young and old, so that tumours broke out on them. ¹⁰So they sent the ark of God to Ekron. But as soon as the ark of God came to Ekron, the people of Ekron cried out, "They have brought round to us the ark of the God of Israel to kill us and our people." ¹¹They sent therefore and gathered together all the lords of the Philistines and said, "Send away the ark of the God of Israel, and let it return to its own place, that it may not kill us and our people." For there was a deathly panic throughout the whole city. The hand of God was very heavy there. ¹²The men who did not die were struck with tumours, and the cry of the city went up to heaven.

THE ARK RETURNED TO ISRAEL

6 The ark of the LORD was in the country of the Philistines for seven months. ²And the Philistines called for the priests and the diviners and said, "What shall we do with the ark of the LORD? Tell us with what we shall send it to its place." ³They said, "If you send away the ark of the God of Israel, do not send it empty, but by all means return him a guilt offering. Then you will be healed, and it will be known to you why his hand does not turn away from you." ⁴And they said, "What is the guilt offering that we shall return to him?" They answered, "Five golden tumours and five golden mice, according to the number of the lords of the Philistines, for the same plague was on all of you and on your lords. ⁵So you must make images of your tumours and images of your mice that ravage the land, and give glory to the God of Israel. Perhaps he will lighten his hand from off you and your gods and your land. ⁶Why should you harden your hearts as the Egyptians and Pharaoh hardened their hearts? After he had dealt severely with them, did they not send the people away, and they departed? ⁷Now then, take and prepare a new cart and two milk cows on which there has never come a yoke, and yoke the cows to the cart, but take their calves home, away from them. ⁸And take the ark of the LORD and place it on the cart and put in a box at its side the figures of gold, which you are returning to him as a guilt offering. Then send it off and let it go its way ⁹and watch. If it goes up on the way to its own land, to Beth-shemesh, then it is he who has done us this great harm, but if not, then we shall know that it is not his hand that struck us; it happened to us by coincidence."

¹⁰The men did so, and took two milk cows and yoked them to the cart and shut up their calves at home. ¹¹And they put the ark of the LORD on the cart and the box with the golden mice and the images of their tumours. ¹²And the cows went straight in the direction of Beth-shemesh along one highway, lowing as they went. They turned neither to the right nor to the left, and the lords of the Philistines went after them as far as the border of Beth-shemesh. ¹³Now the people of Beth-shemesh were reaping their wheat harvest in the valley. And when they lifted up their eyes and saw the ark, they rejoiced to see it. ¹⁴The cart came into the field of Joshua of Beth-shemesh and stopped there. A great stone was there. And they split up the wood of the cart and offered the cows as a burnt offering to the LORD. ¹⁵And the Levites took down the ark of the LORD and the box that was beside it, in which were the golden figures, and set them upon the great stone. And the men of Beth-shemesh offered burnt offerings and sacrificed sacrifices on that day to the LORD. ¹⁶And when the five lords of the Philistines saw it, they returned that day to Ekron.

¹⁷These are the golden tumours that the Philistines returned as a guilt offering to the LORD: one for Ashdod, one for Gaza, one for Ashkelon, one for Gath, one for Ekron, ¹⁸and the golden mice, according to the number of all the cities of the Philistines belonging to the five lords, both fortified cities and

unwalled villages. The great stone beside which they set down the ark of the Lord is a witness to this day in the field of Joshua of Beth-shemesh. ¹⁹And he struck some of the men of Beth-shemesh, because they looked upon the ark of the Lord. He struck seventy men of them,ᵃ and the people mourned because the Lord had struck the people with a great blow. ²⁰Then the men of Beth-shemesh said, "Who is able to stand before the Lord, this holy God? And to whom shall he go up away from us?" ²¹So they sent messengers to the inhabitants of Kiriath-jearim, saying, "The Philistines have returned the ark of the Lord. Come down and take it up to you."

7 And the men of Kiriath-jearim came and took up the ark of the Lord and brought it to the house of Abinadab on the hill. And they consecrated his son Eleazar to have charge of the ark of the Lord. ²From the day that the ark was lodged at Kiriath-jearim, a long time passed, some twenty years, and all the house of Israel lamented after the Lord.

SAMUEL JUDGES ISRAEL

³And Samuel said to all the house of Israel, "If you are returning to the Lord with all your heart, then put away the foreign gods and the Ashtaroth from among you and direct your heart to the Lord and serve him only, and he will deliver you out of the hand of the Philistines." ⁴So the people of Israel put away the Baals and the Ashtaroth, and they served the Lord only.

⁵Then Samuel said, "Gather all Israel at Mizpah, and I will pray to the Lord for you." ⁶So they gathered at Mizpah and drew water and poured it out before the Lord and fasted on that day and said there, "We have sinned against the Lord." And Samuel judged the people of Israel at Mizpah. ⁷Now when the Philistines heard that the people of Israel had gathered at Mizpah, the lords of the Philistines went up against Israel. And when the people of Israel heard of it, they were afraid of the Philistines. ⁸And the people of Israel said to Samuel, "Do not cease to cry out to the Lord our God for us, that he may save us from the hand of the Philistines." ⁹So Samuel took a sucking lamb and offered it as a whole burnt offering to the Lord. And Samuel cried out to the Lord for Israel, and the Lord answered him. ¹⁰As Samuel was offering up the burnt offering, the Philistines drew near to attack Israel. But the Lord thundered with a mighty sound that day against the Philistines and threw them into confusion, and they were defeated before Israel. ¹¹And the men of Israel went out from Mizpah and pursued the Philistines and struck them, as far as below Beth-car.

¹²Then Samuel took a stone and set it up between Mizpah and Shenᵇ and called its name Ebenezer;ᶜ for he said, "Till now the Lord has helped us." ¹³So the Philistines were subdued and did not again enter the territory of Israel. And the hand of the Lord was against the Philistines all the days of Samuel. ¹⁴The cities that the Philistines had taken from Israel were restored to Israel, from Ekron to Gath, and Israel delivered their territory from the hand of the Philistines. There was peace also between Israel and the Amorites.

¹⁵Samuel judged Israel all the days of his life. ¹⁶And he went on a circuit year by year to Bethel, Gilgal, and Mizpah. And he judged Israel in all these places. ¹⁷Then he would return to Ramah, for his home was there, and there also he judged Israel. And he built there an altar to the Lord.

ISRAEL DEMANDS A KING

8 When Samuel became old, he made his sons judges over Israel. ²The name of his firstborn son was Joel, and the name of his second, Abijah; they were judges in Beersheba. ³Yet his sons did not walk in his ways but turned aside after gain. They took bribes and perverted justice.

⁴Then all the elders of Israel gathered together and came to Samuel at Ramah ⁵and said to him, "Behold, you are old and your sons do not walk in your ways. Now appoint for us a king to judge us like all the nations." ⁶But the thing displeased Samuel when they said, "Give us a king to judge us." And Samuel prayed to the Lord. ⁷And the Lord said to Samuel, "Obey the voice of the people in all that they say to you, for they have not rejected you, but they have rejected me from being king over them. ⁸According to all the deeds that they have done, from the day I brought them up out of Egypt even to this day, forsaking me and serving other gods, so they are also doing to you. ⁹Now then, obey their voice; only you shall solemnly warn them and show them the ways of the king who shall reign over them."

ᵃMost Hebrew manuscripts *struck of the people seventy men, fifty thousand men* ᵇHebrew; Septuagint, Syriac *Jeshanah* ᶜ*Ebenezer* means *stone of help*

SAMUEL'S WARNING AGAINST KINGS

¹⁰So Samuel told all the words of the LORD to the people who were asking for a king from him. ¹¹He said, "These will be the ways of the king who will reign over you: he will take your sons and appoint them to his chariots and to be his horsemen and to run before his chariots. ¹²And he will appoint for himself commanders of thousands and commanders of fifties, and some to plough his ground and to reap his harvest, and to make his implements of war and the equipment of his chariots. ¹³He will take your daughters to be perfumers and cooks and bakers. ¹⁴He will take the best of your fields and vineyards and olive orchards and give them to his servants. ¹⁵He will take the tenth of your grain and of your vineyards and give it to his officers and to his servants. ¹⁶He will take your male servants and female servants and the best of your young men[a] and your donkeys, and put them to his work. ¹⁷He will take the tenth of your flocks, and you shall be his slaves. ¹⁸And in that day you will cry out because of your king, whom you have chosen for yourselves, but the LORD will not answer you in that day."

THE LORD GRANTS ISRAEL'S REQUEST

¹⁹But the people refused to obey the voice of Samuel. And they said, "No! But there shall be a king over us, ²⁰that we also may be like all the nations, and that our king may judge us and go out before us and fight our battles." ²¹And when Samuel had heard all the words of the people, he repeated them in the ears of the LORD. ²²And the LORD said to Samuel, "Obey their voice and make them a king." Samuel then said to the men of Israel, "Go every man to his city."

SAUL CHOSEN TO BE KING

9 There was a man of Benjamin whose name was Kish, the son of Abiel, son of Zeror, son of Becorath, son of Aphiah, a Benjaminite, a man of wealth. ²And he had a son whose name was Saul, a handsome young man. There was not a man among the people of Israel more handsome than he. From his shoulders upwards he was taller than any of the people.

³Now the donkeys of Kish, Saul's father, were lost. So Kish said to Saul his son, "Take one of the young men with you, and arise, go and look for the donkeys." ⁴And he passed through the hill country of Ephraim and passed through the land of Shalishah, but they did not find them. And they passed through the land of Shaalim, but they were not there. Then they passed through the land of Benjamin, but did not find them.

⁵When they came to the land of Zuph, Saul said to his servant[b] who was with him, "Come, let us go back, lest my father cease to care about the donkeys and become anxious about us." ⁶But he said to him, "Behold, there is a man of God in this city, and he is a man who is held in honour; all that he says comes true. So now let us go there. Perhaps he can tell us the way we should go." ⁷Then Saul said to his servant, "But if we go, what can we bring the man? For the bread in our sacks is gone, and there is no present to bring to the man of God. What do we have?" ⁸The servant answered Saul again, "Here, I have with me a quarter of a shekel[c] of silver, and I will give it to the man of God to tell us our way." ⁹(Formerly in Israel, when a man went to enquire of God, he said, "Come, let us go to the seer", for today's "prophet" was formerly called a seer.) ¹⁰And Saul said to his servant, "Well said; come, let us go." So they went to the city where the man of God was.

¹¹As they went up the hill to the city, they met young women coming out to draw water and said to them, "Is the seer here?" ¹²They answered, "He is; behold, he is just ahead of you. Hurry. He has come just now to the city, because the people have a sacrifice today on the high place. ¹³As soon as you enter the city you will find him, before he goes up to the high place to eat. For the people will not eat till he comes, since he must bless the sacrifice; afterwards those who are invited will eat. Now go up, for you will meet him immediately." ¹⁴So they went up to the city. As they were entering the city, they saw Samuel coming out towards them on his way up to the high place.

¹⁵Now the day before Saul came, the LORD had revealed to Samuel: ¹⁶"Tomorrow about this time I will send to you a man from the land of Benjamin, and you shall anoint him to be prince[d] over my people Israel. He shall save my people from the hand of the Philistines. For I have seen[e] my people, because their cry has come to me." ¹⁷When Samuel saw Saul, the LORD told him, "Here is the man of whom I spoke to you! He it is who shall

---

[a]Septuagint *cattle* [b]Hebrew *young man*; also verses 7, 8, 10, 27 [c]A *shekel* was about 2/5 of an ounce or 11 grams [d]Or *leader* [e]Septuagint adds *the affliction of*

restrain my people." ⁱ⁸Then Saul approached Samuel in the gate and said, "Tell me where is the house of the seer?" ¹⁹Samuel answered Saul, "I am the seer. Go up before me to the high place, for today you shall eat with me, and in the morning I will let you go and will tell you all that is on your mind. ²⁰As for your donkeys that were lost three days ago, do not set your mind on them, for they have been found. And for whom is all that is desirable in Israel? Is it not for you and for all your father's house?" ²¹Saul answered, "Am I not a Benjaminite, from the least of the tribes of Israel? And is not my clan the humblest of all the clans of the tribe of Benjamin? Why then have you spoken to me in this way?"

²²Then Samuel took Saul and his young man and brought them into the hall and gave them a place at the head of those who had been invited, who were about thirty persons. ²³And Samuel said to the cook, "Bring the portion I gave you, of which I said to you, 'Put it aside.'" ²⁴So the cook took up the leg and what was on it and set them before Saul. And Samuel said, "See, what was kept is set before you. Eat, because it was kept for you until the hour appointed, that you might eat with the guests."ᵃ

So Saul ate with Samuel that day. ²⁵And when they came down from the high place into the city, a bed was spread for Saul on the roof, and he lay down to sleep.ᵇ ²⁶Then at the break of dawnᶜ Samuel called to Saul on the roof, "Get up, that I may send you on your way." So Saul arose, and both he and Samuel went out into the street.

²⁷As they were going down to the outskirts of the city, Samuel said to Saul, "Tell the servant to pass on before us, and when he has passed on, stop here yourself for a while, that I may make known to you the word of God."

SAUL ANOINTED KING

10 Then Samuel took a flask of oil and poured it on his head and kissed him and said, "Has not the LORD anointed you to be princeᵈ over his people Israel? And you shall reign over the people of the LORD and you will save them from the hand of their surrounding enemies. And this shall be the sign to you that the LORD has anointed you to be princeᵉ over his heritage. ²When you depart from me today, you will meet two men by Rachel's tomb in the territory of Benjamin at Zelzah, and they will say to you, 'The donkeys that you went to seek are found, and now your father has ceased to care about the donkeys and is anxious about you, saying, "What shall I do about my son?"' ³Then you shall go on from there farther and come to the oak of Tabor. Three men going up to God at Bethel will meet you there, one carrying three young goats, another carrying three loaves of bread, and another carrying a skin of wine. ⁴And they will greet you and give you two loaves of bread, which you shall accept from their hand. ⁵After that you shall come to Gibeath-elohim,ᶠ where there is a garrison of the Philistines. And there, as soon as you come to the city, you will meet a group of prophets coming down from the high place with harp, tambourine, flute, and lyre before them, prophesying. ⁶Then the Spirit of the LORD will rush upon you, and you will prophesy with them and be turned into another man. ⁷Now when these signs meet you, do what your hand finds to do, for God is with you. ⁸Then go down before me to Gilgal. And behold, I am coming down to you to offer burnt offerings and to sacrifice peace offerings. Seven days you shall wait, until I come to you and show you what you shall do."

⁹When he turned his back to leave Samuel, God gave him another heart. And all these signs came to pass that day. ¹⁰When they came to Gibeah,ᵍ behold, a group of prophets met him, and the Spirit of God rushed upon him, and he prophesied among them. ¹¹And when all who knew him previously saw how he prophesied with the prophets, the people said to one another, "What has come over the son of Kish? Is Saul also among the prophets?" ¹²And a man of the place answered, "And who is their father?" Therefore it became a proverb, "Is Saul also among the prophets?" ¹³When he had finished prophesying, he came to the high place.

¹⁴Saul's uncle said to him and to his servant, "Where did you go?" And he said, "To seek the donkeys. And when we saw they were not to be found, we went to Samuel." ¹⁵And Saul's uncle said, "Please tell me what Samuel said to you." ¹⁶And Saul said to his uncle, "He told us plainly that the donkeys had been found." But about the matter of the kingdom, of which Samuel had spoken, he did not tell him anything.

ᵃHebrew *appointed, saying, 'I have invited the people'* ᵇSeptuagint; Hebrew *city, he spoke with Saul on the roof* ᶜSeptuagint; Hebrew *And they arose early, and at the break of dawn* ᵈOr *leader* ᵉSeptuagint; Hebrew lacks *over his people Israel? And you shall. . . . to be prince* ᶠ*Gibeath-elohim* means *the hill of God* ᵍ*Gibeah* means *the hill*

SAUL PROCLAIMED KING

17Now Samuel called the people together to the LORD at Mizpah. **18**And he said to the people of Israel, "Thus says the LORD, the God of Israel, 'I brought up Israel out of Egypt, and I delivered you from the hand of the Egyptians and from the hand of all the kingdoms that were oppressing you.' **19**But today you have rejected your God, who saves you from all your calamities and your distresses, and you have said to him, 'Set a king over us.' Now therefore present yourselves before the LORD by your tribes and by your thousands."

20Then Samuel brought all the tribes of Israel near, and the tribe of Benjamin was taken by lot. **21**He brought the tribe of Benjamin near by its clans, and the clan of the Matrites was taken by lot;[a] and Saul the son of Kish was taken by lot. But when they sought him, he could not be found. **22**So they enquired again of the LORD, "Is there a man still to come?" and the LORD said, "Behold, he has hidden himself among the baggage." **23**Then they ran and took him from there. And when he stood among the people, he was taller than any of the people from his shoulders upwards. **24**And Samuel said to all the people, "Do you see him whom the LORD has chosen? There is none like him among all the people." And all the people shouted, "Long live the king!"

25Then Samuel told the people the rights and duties of the kingship, and he wrote them in a book and laid it up before the LORD. Then Samuel sent all the people away, each one to his home. **26**Saul also went to his home at Gibeah, and with him went men of valour whose hearts God had touched. **27**But some worthless fellows said, "How can this man save us?" And they despised him and brought him no present. But he held his peace.

SAUL DEFEATS THE AMMONITES

11 Then Nahash the Ammonite went up and besieged Jabesh-gilead, and all the men of Jabesh said to Nahash, "Make a treaty with us, and we will serve you." **2**But Nahash the Ammonite said to them, "On this condition I will make a treaty with you, that I gouge out all your right eyes, and thus bring disgrace on all Israel." **3**The elders of Jabesh said to him, "Give us seven days' respite that we may send messengers through all the territory of Israel. Then, if there is no one to save us, we will give ourselves up to you." **4**When the messengers came to Gibeah of Saul, they reported the matter in the ears of the people, and all the people wept aloud.

5Now, behold, Saul was coming from the field behind the oxen. And Saul said, "What is wrong with the people, that they are weeping?" So they told him the news of the men of Jabesh. **6**And the Spirit of God rushed upon Saul when he heard these words, and his anger was greatly kindled. **7**He took a yoke of oxen and cut them in pieces and sent them throughout all the territory of Israel by the hand of the messengers, saying, "Whoever does not come out after Saul and Samuel, so shall it be done to his oxen!" Then the dread of the LORD fell upon the people, and they came out as one man. **8**When he mustered them at Bezek, the people of Israel were three hundred thousand, and the men of Judah thirty thousand. **9**And they said to the messengers who had come, "Thus shall you say to the men of Jabesh-gilead: 'Tomorrow, by the time the sun is hot, you shall have salvation.'" When the messengers came and told the men of Jabesh, they were glad. **10**Therefore the men of Jabesh said, "Tomorrow we will give ourselves up to you, and you may do to us whatever seems good to you." **11**And the next day Saul put the people in three companies. And they came into the midst of the camp in the morning watch and struck down the Ammonites until the heat of the day. And those who survived were scattered, so that no two of them were left together.

THE KINGDOM IS RENEWED

12Then the people said to Samuel, "Who is it that said, 'Shall Saul reign over us?' Bring the men, that we may put them to death." **13**But Saul said, "Not a man shall be put to death this day, for today the LORD has worked salvation in Israel." **14**Then Samuel said to the people, "Come, let us go to Gilgal and there renew the kingdom." **15**So all the people went to Gilgal, and there they made Saul king before the LORD in Gilgal. There they sacrificed peace offerings before the LORD, and there Saul and all the men of Israel rejoiced greatly.

SAMUEL'S FAREWELL ADDRESS

12 And Samuel said to all Israel, "Behold, I have obeyed your voice in all that you have said to me and have made a king over you. **2**And now, behold,

---

[a]Septuagint adds *finally he brought the family of the Matrites near, man by man*

the king walks before you, and I am old and grey; and behold, my sons are with you. I have walked before you from my youth until this day. ³Here I am; testify against me before the LORD and before his anointed. Whose ox have I taken? Or whose donkey have I taken? Or whom have I defrauded? Whom have I oppressed? Or from whose hand have I taken a bribe to blind my eyes with it? Testify against me¹ and I will restore it to you." ⁴They said, "You have not defrauded us or oppressed us or taken anything from any man's hand." ⁵And he said to them, "The LORD is witness against you, and his anointed is witness this day, that you have not found anything in my hand." And they said, "He is witness."

⁶And Samuel said to the people, "The LORD is witness,¹ who appointed Moses and Aaron and brought your fathers up out of the land of Egypt. ⁷Now therefore stand still that I may plead with you before the LORD concerning all the righteous deeds of the LORD that he performed for you and for your fathers. ⁸When Jacob went into Egypt, and the Egyptians oppressed them,¹ then your fathers cried out to the LORD and the LORD sent Moses and Aaron, who brought your fathers out of Egypt and made them dwell in this place. ⁹But they forgot the LORD their God. And he sold them into the hand of Sisera, commander of the army of Hazor,¹ and into the hand of the Philistines, and into the hand of the king of Moab. And they fought against them. ¹⁰And they cried out to the LORD and said, 'We have sinned, because we have forsaken the LORD and have served the Baals and the Ashtaroth. But now deliver us out of the hand of our enemies, that we may serve you.' ¹¹And the LORD sent Jerubbaal and Barak¹ and Jephthah and Samuel and delivered you out of the hand of your enemies on every side, and you lived in safety. ¹²And when you saw that Nahash the king of the Ammonites came against you, you said to me, 'No, but a king shall reign over us', when the LORD your God was your king. ¹³And now behold the king whom you have chosen, for whom you have asked; behold, the LORD has set a king over you. ¹⁴If you will fear the LORD and serve him and obey his voice and not rebel against the commandment of the LORD, and if both you and the king who reigns over you will follow the LORD your God, it will be well. ¹⁵But if you will not obey the voice of the LORD, but rebel against the commandment of the LORD, then the hand of the LORD will be against you and your king.¹ ¹⁶Now therefore stand still and see this great thing that the LORD will do before your eyes. ¹⁷Is it not wheat harvest today? I will call upon the LORD, that he may send thunder and rain. And you shall know and see that your wickedness is great, which you have done in the sight of the LORD, in asking for yourselves a king." ¹⁸So Samuel called upon the LORD, and the LORD sent thunder and rain that day, and all the people greatly feared the LORD and Samuel.

¹⁹And all the people said to Samuel, "Pray for your servants to the LORD your God, that we may not die, for we have added to all our sins this evil, to ask for ourselves a king." ²⁰And Samuel said to the people, "Do not be afraid; you have done all this evil. Yet do not turn aside from following the LORD, but serve the LORD with all your heart. ²¹And do not turn aside after empty things that cannot profit or deliver, for they are empty. ²²For the LORD will not forsake his people, for his great name's sake, because it has pleased the LORD to make you a people for himself. ²³Moreover, as for me, far be it from me that I should sin against the LORD by ceasing to pray for you, and I will instruct you in the good and the right way. ²⁴Only fear the LORD and serve him faithfully with all your heart. For consider what great things he has done for you. ²⁵But if you still do wickedly, you shall be swept away, both you and your king."

SAUL FIGHTS THE PHILISTINES

13 Saul lived for one year and then became king, and when he had reigned for two years over Israel,¹ ²Saul chose three thousand men of Israel. Two thousand were with Saul in Michmash and the hill country of Bethel, and a thousand were with Jonathan in Gibeah of Benjamin. The rest of the people he sent home, every man to his tent. ³Jonathan defeated the garrison of the Philistines that was at Geba, and the Philistines heard of it. And Saul blew the trumpet throughout all the land, saying, "Let the Hebrews hear." ⁴And all Israel heard it said that Saul had defeated the garrison of the Philistines, and also that Israel had

---

¹Septuagint; Hebrew lacks *Testify against me* ¹Septuagint; Hebrew lacks *is witness* ¹Septuagint; Hebrew lacks *and the Egyptians oppressed them* ¹Septuagint *the army of Jabin king of Hazor* ¹Septuagint, Syriac; Hebrew *Bedan* ¹Septuagint; Hebrew *fathers* ¹Hebrew *Saul was one year old when he became king, and he reigned for two years over Israel*; some Greek manuscripts give Saul's age when he began to reign as thirty years

become a stench to the Philistines. And the people were called out to join Saul at Gilgal.

⁵And the Philistines mustered to fight with Israel, thirty thousand chariots and six thousand horsemen and troops like the sand on the seashore in multitude. They came up and encamped in Michmash, to the east of Beth-aven. ⁶When the men of Israel saw that they were in trouble (for the people were hard pressed), the people hid themselves in caves and in holes and in rocks and in tombs and in cisterns, ⁷and some Hebrews crossed the fords of the Jordan to the land of Gad and Gilead. Saul was still at Gilgal, and all the people followed him trembling.

SAUL'S UNLAWFUL SACRIFICE

⁸He waited for seven days, the time appointed by Samuel. But Samuel did not come to Gilgal, and the people were scattering from him. ⁹So Saul said, "Bring the burnt offering here to me, and the peace offerings." And he offered the burnt offering. ¹⁰As soon as he had finished offering the burnt offering, behold, Samuel came. And Saul went out to meet him and greet him. ¹¹Samuel said, "What have you done?" And Saul said, "When I saw that the people were scattering from me, and that you did not come within the days appointed, and that the Philistines had mustered at Michmash, ¹²I said, 'Now the Philistines will come down against me at Gilgal, and I have not sought the favour of the Lord.' So I forced myself, and offered the burnt offering." ¹³And Samuel said to Saul, "You have done foolishly. You have not kept the command of the Lord your God, with which he commanded you. For then the Lord would have established your kingdom over Israel for ever. ¹⁴But now your kingdom shall not continue. The Lord has sought out a man after his own heart, and the Lord has commanded him to be prince*ᵃ* over his people, because you have not kept what the Lord commanded you." ¹⁵And Samuel arose and went up from Gilgal. The rest of the people went up after Saul to meet the army; they went up from Gilgal*ᵇ* to Gibeah of Benjamin.

And Saul numbered the people who were present with him, about six hundred men. ¹⁶And Saul and Jonathan his son and the people who were present with them stayed in Geba of Benjamin, but the Philistines encamped in Michmash. ¹⁷And raiders came out of the camp of the Philistines in three companies. One company turned towards Ophrah, to the land of Shual; ¹⁸another company turned towards Beth-horon; and another company turned towards the border that looks down on the Valley of Zeboim towards the wilderness.

¹⁹Now there was no blacksmith to be found throughout all the land of Israel, for the Philistines said, "Lest the Hebrews make themselves swords or spears." ²⁰But every one of the Israelites went down to the Philistines to sharpen his ploughshare, his mattock, his axe, or his sickle,*ᶜ* ²¹and the charge was two-thirds of a shekel*ᵈ* for the ploughshares and for the mattocks, and a third of a shekel*ᵉ* for sharpening the axes and for setting the goads.*ᶠ* ²²So on the day of the battle there was neither sword nor spear found in the hand of any of the people with Saul and Jonathan, but Saul and Jonathan his son had them. ²³And the garrison of the Philistines went out to the pass of Michmash.

JONATHAN DEFEATS THE PHILISTINES

14 One day Jonathan the son of Saul said to the young man who carried his armour, "Come, let us go over to the Philistine garrison on the other side." But he did not tell his father. ²Saul was staying in the outskirts of Gibeah in the pomegranate cave*ᵍ* at Migron. The people who were with him were about six hundred men, ³including Ahijah the son of Ahitub, Ichabod's brother, son of Phinehas, son of Eli, the priest of the Lord in Shiloh, wearing an ephod. And the people did not know that Jonathan had gone. ⁴Within the passes, by which Jonathan sought to go over to the Philistine garrison, there was a rocky crag on the one side and a rocky crag on the other side. The name of one was Bozez, and the name of the other Seneh. ⁵The one crag rose on the north in front of Michmash, and the other on the south in front of Geba.

⁶Jonathan said to the young man who carried his armour, "Come, let us go over to the garrison of these uncircumcised. It may be that the Lord will work for us, for nothing can hinder the Lord from saving by many or by few." ⁷And his armour bearer said to him, "Do all that is in your heart. Do as you wish.*ʰ* Behold, I am with you heart and soul." ⁸Then Jonathan said, "Behold, we will cross

---

*ᵃ*Or leader   *ᵇ*Septuagint; Hebrew lacks *The rest of the people . . . from Gilgal*   *ᶜ*Septuagint; Hebrew *ploughshare*   *ᵈ*Hebrew *was a pim*   *ᵉ*A *shekel* was about 2/5 of an ounce or 11 grams   *ᶠ*The meaning of the Hebrew verse is uncertain   *ᵍ*Or *under the pomegranate* [tree]   *ʰ*Septuagint *Do all that your mind inclines to*

over to the men, and we will show ourselves to them. ⁹If they say to us, 'Wait until we come to you', then we will stand still in our place, and we will not go up to them. ¹⁰But if they say, 'Come up to us', then we will go up, for the LORD has given them into our hand. And this shall be the sign to us." ¹¹So both of them showed themselves to the garrison of the Philistines. And the Philistines said, "Look, Hebrews are coming out of the holes where they have hidden themselves." ¹²And the men of the garrison hailed Jonathan and his armour bearer and said, "Come up to us, and we will show you something." And Jonathan said to his armour bearer, "Come up after me, for the LORD has given them into the hand of Israel." ¹³Then Jonathan climbed up on his hands and feet, and his armour bearer after him. And they fell before Jonathan, and his armour bearer killed them after him. ¹⁴And that first strike, which Jonathan and his armour bearer made, killed about twenty men within as it were half a furrow's length in an acre*ᵃ* of land. ¹⁵And there was a panic in the camp, in the field, and among all the people. The garrison and even the raiders trembled, the earth quaked, and it became a very great panic.*ᵇ*

¹⁶And the watchmen of Saul in Gibeah of Benjamin looked, and behold, the multitude was dispersing here and there.*ᶜ* ¹⁷Then Saul said to the people who were with him, "Count and see who has gone from us." And when they had counted, behold, Jonathan and his armour bearer were not there. ¹⁸So Saul said to Ahijah, "Bring the ark of God here." For the ark of God went at that time with the people*ᵈ* of Israel. ¹⁹Now while Saul was talking to the priest, the tumult in the camp of the Philistines increased more and more. So Saul said to the priest, "Withdraw your hand." ²⁰Then Saul and all the people who were with him rallied and went into the battle. And behold, every Philistine's sword was against his fellow, and there was very great confusion. ²¹Now the Hebrews who had been with the Philistines before that time and who had gone up with them into the camp, even they also turned to be with the Israelites who were with Saul and Jonathan. ²²Likewise, when all the men of Israel who had hidden themselves in the hill country of Ephraim heard that the Philistines were fleeing, they too followed hard after them in the battle. ²³So the LORD saved Israel that day. And the battle passed beyond Beth-aven.

SAUL'S RASH VOW

²⁴And the men of Israel had been hard pressed that day, so Saul had laid an oath on the people, saying, "Cursed be the man who eats food until it is evening and I am avenged on my enemies." So none of the people had tasted food. ²⁵Now when all the people*ᵉ* came to the forest, behold, there was honey on the ground. ²⁶And when the people entered the forest, behold, the honey was dropping, but no one put his hand to his mouth, for the people feared the oath. ²⁷But Jonathan had not heard his father charge the people with the oath, so he put out the tip of the staff that was in his hand and dipped it in the honeycomb and put his hand to his mouth, and his eyes became bright. ²⁸Then one of the people said, "Your father strictly charged the people with an oath, saying, 'Cursed be the man who eats food this day.'" And the people were faint. ²⁹Then Jonathan said, "My father has troubled the land. See how my eyes have become bright because I tasted a little of this honey. ³⁰How much better if the people had eaten freely today of the spoil of their enemies that they found. For now the defeat among the Philistines has not been great."

³¹They struck down the Philistines that day from Michmash to Aijalon. And the people were very faint. ³²The people pounced on the spoil and took sheep and oxen and calves and slaughtered them on the ground. And the people ate them with the blood. ³³Then they told Saul, "Behold, the people are sinning against the LORD by eating with the blood." And he said, "You have dealt treacherously; roll a great stone to me here."*ᶠ* ³⁴And Saul said, "Disperse yourselves among the people and say to them, 'Let every man bring his ox or his sheep and slaughter them here and eat, and do not sin against the LORD by eating with the blood.'" So every one of the people brought his ox with him that night and they slaughtered them there. ³⁵And Saul built an altar to the LORD; it was the first altar that he built to the LORD.

³⁶Then Saul said, "Let us go down after the Philistines by night and plunder them until the morning light; let us not leave a man of them." And they said, "Do whatever seems good to you." But the priest said, "Let us draw near to God here." ³⁷And Saul enquired of

---

*ᵃ*Hebrew *a yoke* *ᵇ*Or *became a panic from God* *ᶜ*Septuagint; Hebrew *they went here and there* *ᵈ*Hebrew; Septuagint *"Bring the ephod." For at that time he wore the ephod before the people* *ᵉ*Hebrew *land* *ᶠ*Septuagint; Hebrew *this day*

God, "Shall I go down after the Philistines? Will you give them into the hand of Israel?" But he did not answer him that day. ³⁸And Saul said, "Come here, all you leaders of the people, and know and see how this sin has arisen today. ³⁹For as the LORD lives who saves Israel, though it be in Jonathan my son, he shall surely die." But there was not a man among all the people who answered him. ⁴⁰Then he said to all Israel, "You shall be on one side, and I and Jonathan my son will be on the other side." And the people said to Saul, "Do what seems good to you." ⁴¹Therefore Saul said, "O LORD God of Israel, why have you not answered your servant this day? If this guilt is in me or in Jonathan my son, O LORD, God of Israel, give Urim. But if this guilt is in your people Israel, give Thummim."ᵃ And Jonathan and Saul were taken, but the people escaped. ⁴²Then Saul said, "Cast the lot between me and my son Jonathan." And Jonathan was taken.

⁴³Then Saul said to Jonathan, "Tell me what you have done." And Jonathan told him, "I tasted a little honey with the tip of the staff that was in my hand. Here I am; I will die." ⁴⁴And Saul said, "God do so to me and more also; you shall surely die, Jonathan." ⁴⁵Then the people said to Saul, "Shall Jonathan die, who has worked this great salvation in Israel? Far from it! As the LORD lives, there shall not one hair of his head fall to the ground, for he has worked with God this day." So the people ransomed Jonathan, so that he did not die. ⁴⁶Then Saul went up from pursuing the Philistines, and the Philistines went to their own place.

SAUL FIGHTS ISRAEL'S ENEMIES

⁴⁷When Saul had taken the kingship over Israel, he fought against all his enemies on every side, against Moab, against the Ammonites, against Edom, against the kings of Zobah, and against the Philistines. Wherever he turned he routed them. ⁴⁸And he did valiantly and struck the Amalekites and delivered Israel out of the hands of those who plundered them.

⁴⁹Now the sons of Saul were Jonathan, Ishvi, and Malchi-shua. And the names of his two daughters were these: the name of the firstborn was Merab, and the name of the younger Michal. ⁵⁰And the name of Saul's wife was Ahinoam the daughter of Ahimaaz. And the name of the commander of his army was Abner the son of Ner, Saul's uncle. ⁵¹Kish was the father of Saul, and Ner the father of Abner was the son of Abiel.

⁵²There was hard fighting against the Philistines all the days of Saul. And when Saul saw any strong man, or any valiant man, he attached him to himself.

THE LORD REJECTS SAUL

15 And Samuel said to Saul, "The LORD sent me to anoint you king over his people Israel; now therefore listen to the words of the LORD. ²Thus says the LORD of hosts, 'I have noted what Amalek did to Israel in opposing them on the way when they came up out of Egypt. ³Now go and strike Amalek and devote to destructionᵇ all that they have. Do not spare them, but kill both man and woman, child and infant, ox and sheep, camel and donkey.'"

⁴So Saul summoned the people and numbered them in Telaim, two hundred thousand men on foot, and ten thousand men of Judah. ⁵And Saul came to the city of Amalek and lay in wait in the valley. ⁶Then Saul said to the Kenites, "Go, depart; go down from among the Amalekites, lest I destroy you with them. For you showed kindness to all the people of Israel when they came up out of Egypt." So the Kenites departed from among the Amalekites. ⁷And Saul defeated the Amalekites from Havilah as far as Shur, which is east of Egypt. ⁸And he took Agag the king of the Amalekites alive and devoted to destruction all the people with the edge of the sword. ⁹But Saul and the people spared Agag and the best of the sheep and of the oxen and of the fattened calvesᶜ and the lambs, and all that was good, and would not utterly destroy them. All that was despised and worthless they devoted to destruction.

¹⁰The word of the LORD came to Samuel: ¹¹"I regretᵈ that I have made Saul king, for he has turned back from following me and has not performed my commandments." And Samuel was angry, and he cried to the LORD all night. ¹²And Samuel rose early to meet Saul in the morning. And it was told to Samuel, "Saul came to Carmel, and behold, he set up a monument for himself and turned and passed on and went down to Gilgal." ¹³And Samuel came to Saul, and Saul said to him, "Blessed be you to the LORD. I have performed the

---

ᵃVulgate and Septuagint; Hebrew *Therefore Saul said to the LORD, the God of Israel, "Give Thummim."* ᵇThat is, set apart (devote) as an offering to the Lord (for destruction); also verses 8, 9, 15, 18, 20, 21 ᶜThe meaning of the Hebrew term is uncertain ᵈSee also verses 29, 35

commandment of the LORD." ¹⁴And Samuel said, "What then is this bleating of the sheep in my ears and the lowing of the oxen that I hear?" ¹⁵Saul said, "They have brought them from the Amalekites, for the people spared the best of the sheep and of the oxen to sacrifice to the LORD your God, and the rest we have devoted to destruction." ¹⁶Then Samuel said to Saul, "Stop! I will tell you what the LORD said to me this night." And he said to him, "Speak."

¹⁷And Samuel said, "Though you are little in your own eyes, are you not the head of the tribes of Israel? The LORD anointed you king over Israel. ¹⁸And the LORD sent you on a mission and said, 'Go, devote to destruction the sinners, the Amalekites, and fight against them until they are consumed.' ¹⁹Why then did you not obey the voice of the LORD? Why did you pounce on the spoil and do what was evil in the sight of the LORD?" ²⁰And Saul said to Samuel, "I have obeyed the voice of the LORD. I have gone on the mission on which the LORD sent me. I have brought Agag the king of Amalek, and I have devoted the Amalekites to destruction. ²¹But the people took of the spoil, sheep and oxen, the best of the things devoted to destruction, to sacrifice to the LORD your God in Gilgal." ²²And Samuel said,

> "Has the LORD as great delight in
>   burnt offerings and sacrifices,
>   as in obeying the voice of the LORD?
> Behold, to obey is better than sacrifice,
>   and to listen than the fat of rams.
> ²³ For rebellion is as the sin of divination,
>   and presumption is as
>   iniquity and idolatry.
> Because you have rejected the
>   word of the LORD,
>   he has also rejected you
>   from being king."

²⁴Saul said to Samuel, "I have sinned, for I have transgressed the commandment of the LORD and your words, because I feared the people and obeyed their voice. ²⁵Now therefore, please pardon my sin and return with me that I may bow before the LORD." ²⁶And Samuel said to Saul, "I will not return with you. For you have rejected the word of the LORD, and the LORD has rejected you from being king over Israel." ²⁷As Samuel turned to go away, Saul seized the skirt of his robe, and it tore. ²⁸And Samuel said to him, "The LORD has torn the kingdom of Israel from you this day and has given it to a neighbour of yours, who is better than you. ²⁹And also the Glory of Israel will not lie or have regret, for he is not a man, that he should have regret." ³⁰Then he said, "I have sinned; yet honour me now before the elders of my people and before Israel, and return with me, that I may bow before the LORD your God." ³¹So Samuel turned back after Saul, and Saul bowed before the LORD.

³²Then Samuel said, "Bring here to me Agag the king of the Amalekites." And Agag came to him cheerfully.ᵃ Agag said, "Surely the bitterness of death is past." ³³And Samuel said, "As your sword has made women childless, so shall your mother be childless among women." And Samuel hacked Agag to pieces before the LORD in Gilgal.

³⁴Then Samuel went to Ramah, and Saul went up to his house in Gibeah of Saul. ³⁵And Samuel did not see Saul again until the day of his death, but Samuel grieved over Saul. And the LORD regretted that he had made Saul king over Israel.

DAVID ANOINTED KING

16 The LORD said to Samuel, "How long will you grieve over Saul, since I have rejected him from being king over Israel? Fill your horn with oil, and go. I will send you to Jesse the Bethlehemite, for I have provided for myself a king among his sons." ²And Samuel said, "How can I go? If Saul hears it, he will kill me." And the LORD said, "Take a heifer with you and say, 'I have come to sacrifice to the LORD.' ³And invite Jesse to the sacrifice, and I will show you what you shall do. And you shall anoint for me him whom I declare to you." ⁴Samuel did what the LORD commanded and came to Bethlehem. The elders of the city came to meet him trembling and said, "Do you come peaceably?" ⁵And he said, "Peaceably; I have come to sacrifice to the LORD. Consecrate yourselves, and come with me to the sacrifice." And he consecrated Jesse and his sons and invited them to the sacrifice.

⁶When they came, he looked on Eliab and thought, "Surely the LORD's anointed is before him." ⁷But the LORD said to Samuel, "Do not look on his appearance or on the height of his stature, because I have rejected him. For the LORD sees not as man

---

ᵃOr *haltingly* (compare Septuagint); the Hebrew is uncertain

sees: man looks on the outward appearance, but the LORD looks on the heart." ⁸Then Jesse called Abinadab and made him pass before Samuel. And he said, "Neither has the LORD chosen this one." ⁹Then Jesse made Shammah pass by. And he said, "Neither has the LORD chosen this one." ¹⁰And Jesse made seven of his sons pass before Samuel. And Samuel said to Jesse, "The LORD has not chosen these." ¹¹Then Samuel said to Jesse, "Are all your sons here?" And he said, "There remains yet the youngest,ᵃ but behold, he is keeping the sheep." And Samuel said to Jesse, "Send and get him, for we will not sit down till he comes here." ¹²And he sent and brought him in. Now he was ruddy and had beautiful eyes and was handsome. And the LORD said, "Arise, anoint him, for this is he." ¹³Then Samuel took the horn of oil and anointed him in the midst of his brothers. And the Spirit of the LORD rushed upon David from that day forward. And Samuel rose up and went to Ramah.

DAVID IN SAUL'S SERVICE

¹⁴Now the Spirit of the LORD departed from Saul, and a harmful spirit from the LORD tormented him. ¹⁵And Saul's servants said to him, "Behold now, a harmful spirit from God is tormenting you. ¹⁶Let our lord now command your servants who are before you to seek out a man who is skilful in playing the lyre, and when the harmful spirit from God is upon you, he will play it, and you will be well." ¹⁷So Saul said to his servants, "Provide for me a man who can play well and bring him to me." ¹⁸One of the young men answered, "Behold, I have seen a son of Jesse the Bethlehemite, who is skilful in playing, a man of valour, a man of war, prudent in speech, and a man of good presence, and the LORD is with him." ¹⁹Therefore Saul sent messengers to Jesse and said, "Send me David your son, who is with the sheep." ²⁰And Jesse took a donkey laden with bread and a skin of wine and a young goat and sent them by David his son to Saul. ²¹And David came to Saul and entered his service. And Saul loved him greatly, and he became his armour bearer. ²²And Saul sent to Jesse, saying, "Let David remain in my service, for he has found favour in my sight." ²³And whenever the harmful spirit from God was upon Saul, David took the lyre and played it with his hand. So Saul was refreshed and was well, and the harmful spirit departed from him.

DAVID AND GOLIATH

17 Now the Philistines gathered their armies for battle. And they were gathered at Socoh, which belongs to Judah, and encamped between Socoh and Azekah, in Ephes-dammim. ²And Saul and the men of Israel were gathered, and encamped in the Valley of Elah, and drew up in line of battle against the Philistines. ³And the Philistines stood on the mountain on one side, and Israel stood on the mountain on the other side, with a valley between them. ⁴And there came out from the camp of the Philistines a champion named Goliath of Gath, whose height was sixᵇ cubitsᶜ and a span. ⁵He had a helmet of bronze on his head, and he was armed with a coat of mail, and the weight of the coat was five thousand shekelsᵈ of bronze. ⁶And he had bronze armour on his legs, and a javelin of bronze slung between his shoulders. ⁷The shaft of his spear was like a weaver's beam, and his spear's head weighed six hundred shekels of iron. And his shield bearer went before him. ⁸He stood and shouted to the ranks of Israel, "Why have you come out to draw up for battle? Am I not a Philistine, and are you not servants of Saul? Choose a man for yourselves, and let him come down to me. ⁹If he is able to fight with me and kill me, then we will be your servants. But if I prevail against him and kill him, then you shall be our servants and serve us." ¹⁰And the Philistine said, "I defy the ranks of Israel this day. Give me a man, that we may fight together." ¹¹When Saul and all Israel heard these words of the Philistine, they were dismayed and greatly afraid.

¹²Now David was the son of an Ephrathite of Bethlehem in Judah, named Jesse, who had eight sons. In the days of Saul the man was already old and advanced in years.ᵉ ¹³The three oldest sons of Jesse had followed Saul to the battle. And the names of his three sons who went to the battle were Eliab the firstborn, and next to him Abinadab, and the third Shammah. ¹⁴David was the youngest. The three eldest followed Saul, ¹⁵but David went back and forth from Saul to feed his father's sheep at Bethlehem. ¹⁶For forty days the Philistine came forward and took his stand, morning and evening.

ᵃOr *smallest* ᵇHebrew; Septuagint, Dead Sea Scroll and Josephus *four* ᶜA *cubit* was about 18 inches or 45 centimetres ᵈA *shekel* was about 2/5 of an ounce or 11 grams ᵉSeptuagint, Syriac; Hebrew *advanced among men*

1 SAMUEL 17

¹⁷And Jesse said to David his son, "Take for your brothers an ephah[a] of this parched grain, and these ten loaves, and carry them quickly to the camp to your brothers. ¹⁸Also take these ten cheeses to the commander of their thousand. See if your brothers are well, and bring some token from them."

¹⁹Now Saul and they and all the men of Israel were in the Valley of Elah, fighting with the Philistines. ²⁰And David rose early in the morning and left the sheep with a keeper and took the provisions and went, as Jesse had commanded him. And he came to the encampment as the host was going out to the battle line, shouting the war cry. ²¹And Israel and the Philistines drew up for battle, army against army. ²²And David left the things in charge of the keeper of the baggage and ran to the ranks and went and greeted his brothers. ²³As he talked with them, behold, the champion, the Philistine of Gath, Goliath by name, came up out of the ranks of the Philistines and spoke the same words as before. And David heard him.

²⁴All the men of Israel, when they saw the man, fled from him and were much afraid. ²⁵And the men of Israel said, "Have you seen this man who has come up? Surely he has come up to defy Israel. And the king will enrich the man who kills him with great riches and will give him his daughter and make his father's house free in Israel." ²⁶And David said to the men who stood by him, "What shall be done for the man who kills this Philistine and takes away the reproach from Israel? For who is this uncircumcised Philistine, that he should defy the armies of the living God?" ²⁷And the people answered him in the same way, "So shall it be done to the man who kills him."

²⁸Now Eliab his oldest brother heard when he spoke to the men. And Eliab's anger was kindled against David, and he said, "Why have you come down? And with whom have you left those few sheep in the wilderness? I know your presumption and the evil of your heart, for you have come down to see the battle." ²⁹And David said, "What have I done now? Was it not but a word?" ³⁰And he turned away from him towards another, and spoke in the same way, and the people answered him again as before.

³¹When the words that David spoke were heard, they repeated them before Saul, and he sent for him. ³²And David said to Saul, "Let no man's heart fail because of him. Your servant will go and fight with this Philistine." ³³And Saul said to David, "You are not able to go against this Philistine to fight with him, for you are but a youth, and he has been a man of war from his youth." ³⁴But David said to Saul, "Your servant used to keep sheep for his father. And when there came a lion, or a bear, and took a lamb from the flock, ³⁵I went after him and struck him and delivered it out of his mouth. And if he arose against me, I caught him by his beard and struck him and killed him. ³⁶Your servant has struck down both lions and bears, and this uncircumcised Philistine shall be like one of them, for he has defied the armies of the living God." ³⁷And David said, "The LORD who delivered me from the paw of the lion and from the paw of the bear will deliver me from the hand of this Philistine." And Saul said to David, "Go, and the LORD be with you!"

³⁸Then Saul clothed David with his armour. He put a helmet of bronze on his head and clothed him with a coat of mail, ³⁹and David strapped his sword over his armour. And he tried in vain to go, for he had not tested them. Then David said to Saul, "I cannot go with these, for I have not tested them." So David put them off. ⁴⁰Then he took his staff in his hand and chose five smooth stones from the brook and put them in his shepherd's pouch. His sling was in his hand, and he approached the Philistine.

⁴¹And the Philistine moved forward and came near to David, with his shield bearer in front of him. ⁴²And when the Philistine looked and saw David, he disdained him, for he was but a youth, ruddy and handsome in appearance. ⁴³And the Philistine said to David, "Am I a dog, that you come to me with sticks?" And the Philistine cursed David by his gods. ⁴⁴The Philistine said to David, "Come to me, and I will give your flesh to the birds of the air and to the beasts of the field." ⁴⁵Then David said to the Philistine, "You come to me with a sword and with a spear and with a javelin, but I come to you in the name of the LORD of hosts, the God of the armies of Israel, whom you have defied. ⁴⁶This day the LORD will deliver you into my hand, and I will strike you down and cut off your head. And I will give the dead bodies of the host of the Philistines this day to the birds of the air and to the wild beasts of the earth, that all the earth may know that there is a God in Israel,

---

[a] An *ephah* was about 3/5 of a bushel or 22 litres

⁴⁷and that all this assembly may know that the LORD saves not with sword and spear. For the battle is the LORD's, and he will give you into our hand."

⁴⁸When the Philistine arose and came and drew near to meet David, David ran quickly towards the battle line to meet the Philistine. ⁴⁹And David put his hand in his bag and took out a stone and slung it and struck the Philistine on his forehead. The stone sank into his forehead, and he fell on his face to the ground. ⁵⁰So David prevailed over the Philistine with a sling and with a stone, and struck the Philistine and killed him. There was no sword in the hand of David. ⁵¹Then David ran and stood over the Philistine and took his sword and drew it out of its sheath and killed him and cut off his head with it. When the Philistines saw that their champion was dead, they fled. ⁵²And the men of Israel and Judah rose with a shout and pursued the Philistines as far as Gath[a] and the gates of Ekron, so that the wounded Philistines fell on the way from Shaaraim as far as Gath and Ekron. ⁵³And the people of Israel came back from chasing the Philistines, and they plundered their camp. ⁵⁴And David took the head of the Philistine and brought it to Jerusalem, but he put his armour in his tent.

⁵⁵As soon as Saul saw David go out against the Philistine, he said to Abner, the commander of the army, "Abner, whose son is this youth?" And Abner said, "As your soul lives, O king, I do not know." ⁵⁶And the king said, "Enquire whose son the boy is." ⁵⁷And as soon as David returned from the striking down of the Philistine, Abner took him, and brought him before Saul with the head of the Philistine in his hand. ⁵⁸And Saul said to him, "Whose son are you, young man?" And David answered, "I am the son of your servant Jesse the Bethlehemite."

DAVID AND JONATHAN'S FRIENDSHIP

18 As soon as he had finished speaking to Saul, the soul of Jonathan was knit to the soul of David, and Jonathan loved him as his own soul. ²And Saul took him that day and would not let him return to his father's house. ³Then Jonathan made a covenant with David, because he loved him as his own soul. ⁴And Jonathan stripped himself of the robe that was on him and gave it to David, and his armour, and even his sword and his bow and his belt. ⁵And David went out and was successful wherever Saul sent him, so that Saul set him over the men of war. And this was good in the sight of all the people and also in the sight of Saul's servants.

SAUL'S JEALOUSY OF DAVID

⁶As they were coming home, when David returned from striking down the Philistine, the women came out of all the cities of Israel, singing and dancing, to meet King Saul, with tambourines, with songs of joy, and with musical instruments.[b] ⁷And the women sang to one another as they celebrated,

"Saul has struck down his thousands,
    and David his ten thousands."

⁸And Saul was very angry, and this saying displeased him. He said, "They have ascribed to David ten thousands, and to me they have ascribed thousands, and what more can he have but the kingdom?" ⁹And Saul kept an eye on David from that day on.

¹⁰The next day a harmful spirit from God rushed upon Saul, and he raved within his house while David was playing the lyre, as he did day by day. Saul had his spear in his hand. ¹¹And Saul hurled the spear, for he thought, "I will pin David to the wall." But David evaded him twice.

¹²Saul was afraid of David because the LORD was with him but had departed from Saul. ¹³So Saul removed him from his presence and made him a commander of a thousand. And he went out and came in before the people. ¹⁴And David had success in all his undertakings, for the LORD was with him. ¹⁵And when Saul saw that he had great success, he stood in fearful awe of him. ¹⁶But all Israel and Judah loved David, for he went out and came in before them.

DAVID MARRIES MICHAL

¹⁷Then Saul said to David, "Here is my elder daughter Merab. I will give her to you for a wife. Only be valiant for me and fight the LORD's battles." For Saul thought, "Let not my hand be against him, but let the hand of the Philistines be against him." ¹⁸And David said to Saul, "Who am I, and who are my relatives, my father's clan in Israel, that I should be son-in-law to the king?" ¹⁹But at the time when Merab, Saul's daughter, should have been given to David, she was given to Adriel the Meholathite for a wife.

---

[a]Septuagint; Hebrew *Gai*   [b]Or *triangles*, or *three-stringed instruments*

20Now Saul's daughter Michal loved David. And they told Saul, and the thing pleased him. **21**Saul thought, "Let me give her to him, that she may be a snare for him and that the hand of the Philistines may be against him." Therefore Saul said to David a second time,[a] "You shall now be my son-in-law." **22**And Saul commanded his servants, "Speak to David in private and say, 'Behold, the king has delight in you, and all his servants love you. Now then become the king's son-in-law.'" **23**And Saul's servants spoke those words in the ears of David. And David said, "Does it seem to you a little thing to become the king's son-in-law, since I am a poor man and have no reputation?" **24**And the servants of Saul told him, "Thus and so did David speak." **25**Then Saul said, "Thus shall you say to David, 'The king desires no bride price except a hundred foreskins of the Philistines, that he may be avenged of the king's enemies.'" Now Saul thought to make David fall by the hand of the Philistines. **26**And when his servants told David these words, it pleased David well to be the king's son-in-law. Before the time had expired, **27**David arose and went, along with his men, and killed two hundred of the Philistines. And David brought their foreskins, which were given in full number to the king, that he might become the king's son-in-law. And Saul gave him his daughter Michal for a wife. **28**But when Saul saw and knew that the LORD was with David, and that Michal, Saul's daughter, loved him, **29**Saul was even more afraid of David. So Saul was David's enemy continually.

30Then the commanders of the Philistines came out to battle, and as often as they came out David had more success than all the servants of Saul, so that his name was highly esteemed.

SAUL TRIES TO KILL DAVID

19 And Saul spoke to Jonathan his son and to all his servants, that they should kill David. But Jonathan, Saul's son, delighted much in David. **2**And Jonathan told David, "Saul my father seeks to kill you. Therefore be on your guard in the morning. Stay in a secret place and hide yourself. **3**And I will go out and stand beside my father in the field where you are, and I will speak to my father about you. And if I learn anything I will tell you." **4**And Jonathan spoke well of David to Saul his father and said to him, "Let not the king sin against his servant David, because he has not sinned against you, and because his deeds have brought good to you. **5**For he took his life in his hand and he struck down the Philistine, and the LORD worked a great salvation for all Israel. You saw it, and rejoiced. Why then will you sin against innocent blood by killing David without cause?" **6**And Saul listened to the voice of Jonathan. Saul swore, "As the LORD lives, he shall not be put to death." **7**And Jonathan called David, and Jonathan reported to him all these things. And Jonathan brought David to Saul, and he was in his presence as before.

8And there was war again. And David went out and fought with the Philistines and struck them with a great blow, so that they fled before him. **9**Then a harmful spirit from the LORD came upon Saul, as he sat in his house with his spear in his hand. And David was playing the lyre. **10**And Saul sought to pin David to the wall with the spear, but he eluded Saul, so that he struck the spear into the wall. And David fled and escaped that night.

11Saul sent messengers to David's house to watch him, that he might kill him in the morning. But Michal, David's wife, told him, "If you do not escape with your life tonight, tomorrow you will be killed." **12**So Michal let David down through the window, and he fled away and escaped. **13**Michal took an image[b] and laid it on the bed and put a pillow of goats' hair at its head and covered it with the clothes. **14**And when Saul sent messengers to take David, she said, "He is sick." **15**Then Saul sent the messengers to see David, saying, "Bring him up to me in the bed, that I may kill him." **16**And when the messengers came in, behold, the image was in the bed, with the pillow of goats' hair at its head. **17**Saul said to Michal, "Why have you deceived me thus and let my enemy go, so that he has escaped?" And Michal answered Saul, "He said to me, 'Let me go. Why should I kill you?'"

18Now David fled and escaped, and he came to Samuel at Ramah and told him all that Saul had done to him. And he and Samuel went and lived at Naioth. **19**And it was told Saul, "Behold, David is at Naioth in Ramah." **20**Then Saul sent messengers to take David, and when they saw the company of the prophets prophesying, and Samuel standing as head over them, the Spirit of God came upon the messengers of Saul, and they also prophesied. **21**When it was told Saul, he sent other messengers, and they

---

[a] Hebrew *by two*   [b] Or *a household god*

Bethlehem. ²⁹He said, 'Let me go, for our clan holds a sacrifice in the city, and my brother has commanded me to be there. So now, if I have found favour in your eyes, let me get away and see my brothers.' For this reason he has not come to the king's table."

³⁰Then Saul's anger was kindled against Jonathan, and he said to him, "You son of a perverse, rebellious woman, do I not know that you have chosen the son of Jesse to your own shame, and to the shame of your mother's nakedness? ³¹For as long as the son of Jesse lives on the earth, neither you nor your kingdom shall be established. Therefore send and bring him to me, for he shall surely die." ³²Then Jonathan answered Saul his father, "Why should he be put to death? What has he done?" ³³But Saul hurled his spear at him to strike him. So Jonathan knew that his father was determined to put David to death. ³⁴And Jonathan rose from the table in fierce anger and ate no food the second day of the month, for he was grieved for David, because his father had disgraced him.

³⁵In the morning Jonathan went out into the field to the appointment with David, and with him a little boy. ³⁶And he said to his boy, "Run and find the arrows that I shoot." As the boy ran, he shot an arrow beyond him. ³⁷And when the boy came to the place of the arrow that Jonathan had shot, Jonathan called after the boy and said, "Is not the arrow beyond you?" ³⁸And Jonathan called after the boy, "Hurry! Be quick! Do not stay!" So Jonathan's boy gathered up the arrows and came to his master. ³⁹But the boy knew nothing. Only Jonathan and David knew the matter. ⁴⁰And Jonathan gave his weapons to his boy and said to him, "Go and carry them to the city." ⁴¹And as soon as the boy had gone, David rose from beside the stone heap*ᵃ* and fell on his face to the ground and bowed three times. And they kissed one another and wept with one another, David weeping the most. ⁴²Then Jonathan said to David, "Go in peace, because we have sworn both of us in the name of the LORD, saying, 'The LORD shall be between me and you, and between my offspring and your offspring, for ever.'" And he rose and departed, and Jonathan went into the city.*ᵇ*

DAVID AND THE HOLY BREAD

21ᶜ Then David came to Nob, to Ahimelech the priest. And Ahimelech came to meet David, trembling, and said to him, "Why are you alone, and no one with you?" ²And David said to Ahimelech the priest, "The king has charged me with a matter and said to me, 'Let no one know anything of the matter about which I send you, and with which I have charged you.' I have made an appointment with the young men for such and such a place. ³Now then, what do you have at hand? Give me five loaves of bread, or whatever is here." ⁴And the priest answered David, "I have no common bread at hand, but there is holy bread—if the young men have kept themselves from women." ⁵And David answered the priest, "Truly women have been kept from us as always when I go on an expedition. The vessels of the young men are holy even when it is an ordinary journey. How much more today will their vessels be holy?" ⁶So the priest gave him the holy bread, for there was no bread there but the bread of the Presence, which is removed from before the LORD, to be replaced by hot bread on the day it is taken away.

⁷Now a certain man of the servants of Saul was there that day, detained before the LORD. His name was Doeg the Edomite, the chief of Saul's herdsmen.

⁸Then David said to Ahimelech, "Then have you not here a spear or a sword at hand? For I have brought neither my sword nor my weapons with me, because the king's business required haste." ⁹And the priest said, "The sword of Goliath the Philistine, whom you struck down in the Valley of Elah, behold, it is here wrapped in a cloth behind the ephod. If you will take that, take it, for there is none but that here." And David said, "There is none like that; give it to me."

DAVID FLEES TO GATH

¹⁰And David rose and fled that day from Saul and went to Achish the king of Gath. ¹¹And the servants of Achish said to him, "Is not this David the king of the land? Did they not sing to one another of him in dances,

'Saul has struck down his thousands,
and David his ten thousands'?"

¹²And David took these words to heart and was much afraid of Achish the king of Gath. ¹³So he changed his behaviour before them and pretended to be insane in their hands and made marks on the doors of the gate

---

ᵃSeptuagint; Hebrew *from beside the south* ᵇThis sentence is 21:1 in Hebrew ᶜCh 21:2 in Hebrew

also prophesied. And Saul sent messengers again the third time, and they also prophesied. ²²Then he himself went to Ramah and came to the great well that is in Secu. And he asked, "Where are Samuel and David?" And one said, "Behold, they are at Naioth in Ramah." ²³And he went there to Naioth in Ramah. And the Spirit of God came upon him also, and as he went he prophesied until he came to Naioth in Ramah. ²⁴And he too stripped off his clothes, and he too prophesied before Samuel and lay naked all that day and all that night. Thus it is said, "Is Saul also among the prophets?"

JONATHAN WARNS DAVID

20 Then David fled from Naioth in Ramah and came and said before Jonathan, "What have I done? What is my guilt? And what is my sin before your father, that he seeks my life?" ²And he said to him, "Far from it! You shall not die. Behold, my father does nothing either great or small without disclosing it to me. And why should my father hide this from me? It is not so." ³But David vowed again, saying, "Your father knows well that I have found favour in your eyes, and he thinks, 'Do not let Jonathan know this, lest he be grieved.' But truly, as the LORD lives and as your soul lives, there is but a step between me and death." ⁴Then Jonathan said to David, "Whatever you say, I will do for you." ⁵David said to Jonathan, "Behold, tomorrow is the new moon, and I should not fail to sit at table with the king. But let me go, that I may hide myself in the field till the third day at evening. ⁶If your father misses me at all, then say, 'David earnestly asked leave of me to run to Bethlehem his city, for there is a yearly sacrifice there for all the clan.' ⁷If he says, 'Good!' it will be well with your servant, but if he is angry, then know that harm is determined by him. ⁸Therefore deal kindly with your servant, for you have brought your servant into a covenant of the LORD with you. But if there is guilt in me, kill me yourself, for why should you bring me to your father?" ⁹And Jonathan said, "Far be it from you! If I knew that it was determined by my father that harm should come to you, would I not tell you?" ¹⁰Then David said to Jonathan, "Who will tell me if your father answers you roughly?" ¹¹And Jonathan said to David, "Come, let us go out into the field." So they both went out into the field.

¹²And Jonathan said to David, "The LORD, the God of Israel, be witness!ᵃ When I have sounded out my father, about this time tomorrow, or the third day, behold, if he is well disposed towards David, shall I not then send and disclose it to you? ¹³But should it please my father to do you harm, the LORD do so to Jonathan and more also if I do not disclose it to you and send you away, that you may go in safety. May the LORD be with you, as he has been with my father. ¹⁴If I am still alive, show me the steadfast love of the LORD, that I may not die; ¹⁵and do not cut offᵇ your steadfast love from my house for ever, when the LORD cuts off every one of the enemies of David from the face of the earth." ¹⁶And Jonathan made a covenant with the house of David, saying, "Mayᶜ the LORD take vengeance on David's enemies." ¹⁷And Jonathan made David swear again by his love for him, for he loved him as he loved his own soul.

¹⁸Then Jonathan said to him, "Tomorrow is the new moon, and you will be missed, because your seat will be empty. ¹⁹On the third day go down quickly to the place where you hid yourself when the matter was in hand, and remain beside the stone heap.ᵈ ²⁰And I will shoot three arrows to the side of it, as though I shot at a mark. ²¹And behold, I will send the boy, saying, 'Go, find the arrows.' If I say to the boy, 'Look, the arrows are on this side of you, take them,' then you are to come, for, as the LORD lives, it is safe for you and there is no danger. ²²But if I say to the youth, 'Look, the arrows are beyond you', then go, for the LORD has sent you away. ²³And as for the matter of which you and I have spoken, behold, the LORD is between you and me for ever."

²⁴So David hid himself in the field. And when the new moon came, the king sat down to eat food. ²⁵The king sat on his seat, as at other times, on the seat by the wall. Jonathan sat opposite,ᵉ and Abner sat by Saul's side, but David's place was empty.

²⁶Yet Saul did not say anything that day, for he thought, "Something has happened to him. He is not clean; surely he is not clean." ²⁷But on the second day, the day after the new moon, David's place was empty. And Saul said to Jonathan his son, "Why has not the son of Jesse come to the meal, either yesterday or today?" ²⁸Jonathan answered Saul, "David earnestly asked leave of me to go to

---

ᵃHebrew lacks *be witness* ᵇOr *but if I die, do not cut off* ᶜSeptuagint *earth*, ¹⁶*let not the name of Jonathan be cut off from the house of David. And may* ᵈSeptuagint; Hebrew *the stone Ezel* ᵉCompare Septuagint; Hebrew *stood up*

and let his spittle run down his beard. ¹⁴Then Achish said to his servants, "Behold, you see the man is mad. Why then have you brought him to me? ¹⁵Do I lack madmen, that you have brought this fellow to behave as a madman in my presence? Shall this fellow come into my house?"

DAVID AT THE CAVE OF ADULLAM

22 David departed from there and escaped to the cave of Adullam. And when his brothers and all his father's house heard it, they went down there to him. ²And everyone who was in distress, and everyone who was in debt, and everyone who was bitter in soul,ᵃ gathered to him. And he became commander over them. And there were with him about four hundred men.

³And David went from there to Mizpeh of Moab. And he said to the king of Moab, "Please let my father and my mother stayᵇ with you, till I know what God will do for me." ⁴And he left them with the king of Moab, and they stayed with him all the time that David was in the stronghold. ⁵Then the prophet Gad said to David, "Do not remain in the stronghold; depart, and go into the land of Judah." So David departed and went into the forest of Hereth.

SAUL KILLS THE PRIESTS AT NOB

⁶Now Saul heard that David was discovered, and the men who were with him. Saul was sitting at Gibeah under the tamarisk tree on the height with his spear in his hand, and all his servants were standing about him. ⁷And Saul said to his servants who stood about him, "Hear now, people of Benjamin; will the son of Jesse give every one of you fields and vineyards, will he make you all commanders of thousands and commanders of hundreds, ⁸that all of you have conspired against me? No one discloses to me when my son makes a covenant with the son of Jesse. None of you is sorry for me or discloses to me that my son has stirred up my servant against me, to lie in wait, as at this day." ⁹Then answered Doeg the Edomite, who stood by the servants of Saul, "I saw the son of Jesse coming to Nob, to Ahimelech the son of Ahitub, ¹⁰and he enquired of the LORD for him and gave him provisions and gave him the sword of Goliath the Philistine."

¹¹Then the king sent to summon Ahimelech the priest, the son of Ahitub, and all his father's house, the priests who were at Nob, and all of them came to the king. ¹²And Saul said, "Hear now, son of Ahitub." And he answered, "Here I am, my lord." ¹³And Saul said to him, "Why have you conspired against me, you and the son of Jesse, in that you have given him bread and a sword and have enquired of God for him, so that he has risen against me, to lie in wait, as at this day?" ¹⁴Then Ahimelech answered the king, "And who among all your servants is so faithful as David, who is the king's son-in-law, and captain overᶜ your bodyguard, and honoured in your house? ¹⁵Is today the first time that I have enquired of God for him? No! Let not the king impute anything to his servant or to all the house of my father, for your servant has known nothing of all this, much or little." ¹⁶And the king said, "You shall surely die, Ahimelech, you and all your father's house." ¹⁷And the king said to the guard who stood about him, "Turn and kill the priests of the LORD, because their hand also is with David, and they knew that he fled and did not disclose it to me." But the servants of the king would not put out their hand to strike the priests of the LORD. ¹⁸Then the king said to Doeg, "You turn and strike the priests." And Doeg the Edomite turned and struck down the priests, and he killed on that day eighty-five persons who wore the linen ephod. ¹⁹And Nob, the city of the priests, he put to the sword; both man and woman, child and infant, ox, donkey and sheep, he put to the sword.

²⁰But one of the sons of Ahimelech the son of Ahitub, named Abiathar, escaped and fled after David. ²¹And Abiathar told David that Saul had killed the priests of the LORD. ²²And David said to Abiathar, "I knew on that day, when Doeg the Edomite was there, that he would surely tell Saul. I have occasioned the death of all the persons of your father's house. ²³Stay with me; do not be afraid, for he who seeks my life seeks your life. With me you shall be in safekeeping."

DAVID SAVES THE CITY OF KEILAH

23 Now they told David, "Behold, the Philistines are fighting against Keilah and are robbing the threshing floors." ²Therefore David enquired of the LORD, "Shall I go and attack these Philistines?" And the LORD said to David, "Go and

---

ᵃOr *discontented* ᵇSyriac, Vulgate; Hebrew *go out* ᶜSeptuagint, Targum; Hebrew *and has turned aside to*

attack the Philistines and save Keilah." ³But David's men said to him, "Behold, we are afraid here in Judah; how much more then if we go to Keilah against the armies of the Philistines?" ⁴Then David enquired of the LORD again. And the LORD answered him, "Arise, go down to Keilah, for I will give the Philistines into your hand." ⁵And David and his men went to Keilah and fought with the Philistines and brought away their livestock and struck them with a great blow. So David saved the inhabitants of Keilah.

⁶When Abiathar the son of Ahimelech had fled to David to Keilah, he had come down with an ephod in his hand. ⁷Now it was told Saul that David had come to Keilah. And Saul said, "God has given him into my hand, for he has shut himself in by entering a town that has gates and bars." ⁸And Saul summoned all the people to war, to go down to Keilah, to besiege David and his men. ⁹David knew that Saul was plotting harm against him. And he said to Abiathar the priest, "Bring the ephod here." ¹⁰Then David said, "O LORD, the God of Israel, your servant has surely heard that Saul seeks to come to Keilah, to destroy the city on my account. ¹¹Will the men of Keilah surrender me into his hand? Will Saul come down, as your servant has heard? O LORD, the God of Israel, please tell your servant." And the LORD said, "He will come down." ¹²Then David said, "Will the men of Keilah surrender me and my men into the hand of Saul?" And the LORD said, "They will surrender you." ¹³Then David and his men, who were about six hundred, arose and departed from Keilah, and they went wherever they could go. When Saul was told that David had escaped from Keilah, he gave up the expedition. ¹⁴And David remained in the strongholds in the wilderness, in the hill country of the wilderness of Ziph. And Saul sought him every day, but God did not give him into his hand.

SAUL PURSUES DAVID

¹⁵David saw that Saul had come out to seek his life. David was in the wilderness of Ziph at Horesh. ¹⁶And Jonathan, Saul's son, rose and went to David at Horesh, and strengthened his hand in God. ¹⁷And he said to him, "Do not fear, for the hand of Saul my father shall not find you. You shall be king over Israel, and I shall be next to you. Saul my father also knows this." ¹⁸And the two of them made a covenant before the LORD. David remained at Horesh, and Jonathan went home.

¹⁹Then the Ziphites went up to Saul at Gibeah, saying, "Is not David hiding among us in the strongholds at Horesh, on the hill of Hachilah, which is south of Jeshimon? ²⁰Now come down, O king, according to all your heart's desire to come down, and our part shall be to surrender him into the king's hand." ²¹And Saul said, "May you be blessed by the LORD, for you have had compassion on me. ²²Go, make yet more sure. Know and see the place where his foot is, and who has seen him there, for it is told me that he is very cunning. ²³See therefore and take note of all the lurking places where he hides, and come back to me with sure information. Then I will go with you. And if he is in the land, I will search him out among all the thousands of Judah." ²⁴And they arose and went to Ziph ahead of Saul.

Now David and his men were in the wilderness of Maon, in the Arabah to the south of Jeshimon. ²⁵And Saul and his men went to seek him. And David was told, so he went down to the rock and lived in the wilderness of Maon. And when Saul heard that, he pursued after David in the wilderness of Maon. ²⁶Saul went on one side of the mountain, and David and his men on the other side of the mountain. And David was hurrying to get away from Saul. As Saul and his men were closing in on David and his men to capture them, ²⁷a messenger came to Saul, saying, "Hurry and come, for the Philistines have made a raid against the land." ²⁸So Saul returned from pursuing after David and went against the Philistines. Therefore that place was called the Rock of Escape.[a] ²⁹[b] And David went up from there and lived in the strongholds of Engedi.

DAVID SPARES SAUL'S LIFE

24[c] When Saul returned from following the Philistines, he was told, "Behold, David is in the wilderness of Engedi." ²Then Saul took three thousand chosen men out of all Israel and went to seek David and his men in front of the Wildgoats' Rocks. ³And he came to the sheepfolds by the way, where there was a cave, and Saul went in to relieve himself.[d] Now David and his men were sitting in the innermost parts of the cave. ⁴And the men of David said to him, "Here is the day of which the LORD

---
[a] Or Rock of Divisions [b] Ch 24:1 in Hebrew [c] Ch 24:2 in Hebrew
[d] Hebrew *cover his feet*

said to you, 'Behold, I will give your enemy into your hand, and you shall do to him as it shall seem good to you.'" Then David arose and stealthily cut off a corner of Saul's robe. ⁵And afterwards David's heart struck him, because he had cut off a corner of Saul's robe. ⁶He said to his men, "The LORD forbid that I should do this thing to my lord, the LORD's anointed, to put out my hand against him, seeing he is the LORD's anointed." ⁷So David persuaded his men with these words and did not permit them to attack Saul. And Saul rose up and left the cave and went on his way.

⁸Afterwards David also arose and went out of the cave, and called after Saul, "My lord the king!" And when Saul looked behind him, David bowed with his face to the earth and paid homage. ⁹And David said to Saul, "Why do you listen to the words of men who say, 'Behold, David seeks your harm'? ¹⁰Behold, this day your eyes have seen how the LORD gave you today into my hand in the cave. And some told me to kill you, but I spared you.ᵃ I said, 'I will not put out my hand against my lord, for he is the LORD's anointed.' ¹¹See, my father, see the corner of your robe in my hand. For by the fact that I cut off the corner of your robe and did not kill you, you may know and see that there is no wrong or treason in my hands. I have not sinned against you, though you hunt my life to take it. ¹²May the LORD judge between me and you, may the LORD avenge me against you, but my hand shall not be against you. ¹³As the proverb of the ancients says, 'Out of the wicked comes wickedness.' But my hand shall not be against you. ¹⁴After whom has the king of Israel come out? After whom do you pursue? After a dead dog! After a flea! ¹⁵May the LORD therefore be judge and give sentence between me and you, and see to it and plead my cause and deliver me from your hand."

¹⁶As soon as David had finished speaking these words to Saul, Saul said, "Is this your voice, my son David?" And Saul lifted up his voice and wept. ¹⁷He said to David, "You are more righteous than I, for you have repaid me good, whereas I have repaid you evil. ¹⁸And you have declared this day how you have dealt well with me, in that you did not kill me when the LORD put me into your hands. ¹⁹For if a man finds his enemy, will he let him go away safe? So may the LORD reward you with good for what you have done to me this day. ²⁰And now, behold, I know that you shall surely be king, and that the kingdom of Israel shall be established in your hand. ²¹Swear to me therefore by the LORD that you will not cut off my offspring after me, and that you will not destroy my name out of my father's house." ²²And David swore this to Saul. Then Saul went home, but David and his men went up to the stronghold.

THE DEATH OF SAMUEL

25 Now Samuel died. And all Israel assembled and mourned for him, and they buried him in his house at Ramah.

DAVID AND ABIGAIL

Then David rose and went down to the wilderness of Paran. ²And there was a man in Maon whose business was in Carmel. The man was very rich; he had three thousand sheep and a thousand goats. He was shearing his sheep in Carmel. ³Now the name of the man was Nabal, and the name of his wife was Abigail. The woman was discerning and beautiful, but the man was harsh and badly behaved; he was a Calebite. ⁴David heard in the wilderness that Nabal was shearing his sheep. ⁵So David sent ten young men. And David said to the young men, "Go up to Carmel, and go to Nabal and greet him in my name. ⁶And thus you shall greet him: 'Peace be to you, and peace be to your house, and peace be to all that you have. ⁷I hear that you have shearers. Now your shepherds have been with us, and we did them no harm, and they missed nothing all the time they were in Carmel. ⁸Ask your young men, and they will tell you. Therefore let my young men find favour in your eyes, for we come on a feast day. Please give whatever you have at hand to your servants and to your son David.'"

⁹When David's young men came, they said all this to Nabal in the name of David, and then they waited. ¹⁰And Nabal answered David's servants, "Who is David? Who is the son of Jesse? There are many servants these days who are breaking away from their masters. ¹¹Shall I take my bread and my water and my meat that I have killed for my shearers and give it to men who come from I do not know where?" ¹²So David's young men turned away and came back and told him all this. ¹³And David said to his men, "Every man strap on his sword!" And every man of them strapped on his sword. David also strapped on his

---
ᵃSeptuagint, Syriac, Targum; Hebrew *it* [my eye] *spared you*

sword. And about four hundred men went up after David, while two hundred remained with the baggage.

¹⁴But one of the young men told Abigail, Nabal's wife, "Behold, David sent messengers out of the wilderness to greet our master, and he railed at them. ¹⁵Yet the men were very good to us, and we suffered no harm, and we did not miss anything when we were in the fields, as long as we went with them. ¹⁶They were a wall to us both by night and by day, all the while we were with them keeping the sheep. ¹⁷Now therefore know this and consider what you should do, for harm is determined against our master and against all his house, and he is such a worthless man that one cannot speak to him."

¹⁸Then Abigail made haste and took two hundred loaves and two skins of wine and five sheep already prepared and five seahs*ᵃ* of parched grain and a hundred clusters of raisins and two hundred cakes of figs, and laid them on donkeys. ¹⁹And she said to her young men, "Go on before me; behold, I come after you." But she did not tell her husband Nabal. ²⁰And as she rode on the donkey and came down under cover of the mountain, behold, David and his men came down towards her, and she met them. ²¹Now David had said, "Surely in vain have I guarded all that this fellow has in the wilderness, so that nothing was missed of all that belonged to him, and he has returned me evil for good. ²²God do so to the enemies of David*ᵇ* and more also, if by morning I leave so much as one male of all who belong to him."

²³When Abigail saw David, she hurried and got down from the donkey and fell before David on her face and bowed to the ground. ²⁴She fell at his feet and said, "On me alone, my lord, be the guilt. Please let your servant speak in your ears, and hear the words of your servant. ²⁵Let not my lord regard this worthless fellow, Nabal, for as his name is, so is he. Nabal*ᶜ* is his name, and folly is with him. But I your servant did not see the young men of my lord, whom you sent. ²⁶Now then, my lord, as the LORD lives, and as your soul lives, because the LORD has restrained you from bloodguilt and from saving with your own hand, now then let your enemies and those who seek to do evil to my lord be as Nabal. ²⁷And now let this present that your servant has brought to my lord be given to the young men who follow my lord. ²⁸Please forgive the trespass of your servant. For the LORD will certainly make my lord a sure house, because my lord is fighting the battles of the LORD, and evil shall not be found in you so long as you live. ²⁹If men rise up to pursue you and to seek your life, the life of my lord shall be bound in the bundle of the living in the care of the LORD your God. And the lives of your enemies he shall sling out as from the hollow of a sling. ³⁰And when the LORD has done to my lord according to all the good that he has spoken concerning you and has appointed you prince*ᵈ* over Israel, ³¹my lord shall have no cause of grief or pangs of conscience for having shed blood without cause or for my lord working salvation himself. And when the LORD has dealt well with my lord, then remember your servant."

³²And David said to Abigail, "Blessed be the LORD, the God of Israel, who sent you this day to meet me! ³³Blessed be your discretion, and blessed be you, who have kept me this day from bloodguilt and from working salvation with my own hand! ³⁴For as surely as the LORD, the God of Israel, lives, who has restrained me from hurting you, unless you had hurried and come to meet me, truly by morning there had not been left to Nabal so much as one male." ³⁵Then David received from her hand what she had brought him. And he said to her, "Go up in peace to your house. See, I have obeyed your voice, and I have granted your petition."

³⁶And Abigail came to Nabal, and behold, he was holding a feast in his house, like the feast of a king. And Nabal's heart was merry within him, for he was very drunk. So she told him nothing at all until the morning light. ³⁷In the morning, when the wine had gone out of Nabal, his wife told him these things, and his heart died within him, and he became as a stone. ³⁸And about ten days later the LORD struck Nabal, and he died.

³⁹When David heard that Nabal was dead, he said, "Blessed be the LORD who has avenged the insult I received at the hand of Nabal, and has kept back his servant from wrongdoing. The LORD has returned the evil of Nabal on his own head." Then David sent and spoke to Abigail, to take her as his wife. ⁴⁰When the servants of David came to Abigail at Carmel, they said to her, "David has sent us to you to take you to him as his wife." ⁴¹And she rose and bowed with her face to the ground and

---

ᵃA seah was about 7 quarts or 7.3 litres ᵇSeptuagint to David ᶜNabal means fool ᵈOr leader

said, "Behold, your handmaid is a servant to wash the feet of the servants of my lord." ⁴²And Abigail hurried and rose and mounted a donkey, and her five young women attended her. She followed the messengers of David and became his wife.

⁴³David also took Ahinoam of Jezreel, and both of them became his wives. ⁴⁴Saul had given Michal his daughter, David's wife, to Palti the son of Laish, who was of Gallim.

DAVID SPARES SAUL AGAIN

26 Then the Ziphites came to Saul at Gibeah, saying, "Is not David hiding himself on the hill of Hachilah, which is on the east of Jeshimon?" ²So Saul arose and went down to the wilderness of Ziph with three thousand chosen men of Israel to seek David in the wilderness of Ziph. ³And Saul encamped on the hill of Hachilah, which is beside the road on the east of Jeshimon. But David remained in the wilderness. When he saw that Saul came after him into the wilderness, ⁴David sent out spies and learned that Saul had indeed come. ⁵Then David rose and came to the place where Saul had encamped. And David saw the place where Saul lay, with Abner the son of Ner, the commander of his army. Saul was lying within the encampment, while the army was encamped round him.

⁶Then David said to Ahimelech the Hittite, and to Joab's brother Abishai the son of Zeruiah, "Who will go down with me into the camp to Saul?" And Abishai said, "I will go down with you." ⁷So David and Abishai went to the army by night. And there lay Saul sleeping within the encampment, with his spear stuck in the ground at his head, and Abner and the army lay round him. ⁸Then Abishai said to David, "God has given your enemy into your hand this day. Now please let me pin him to the earth with one stroke of the spear, and I will not strike him twice." ⁹But David said to Abishai, "Do not destroy him, for who can put out his hand against the LORD's anointed and be guiltless?" ¹⁰And David said, "As the LORD lives, the LORD will strike him, or his day will come to die, or he will go down into battle and perish. ¹¹The LORD forbid that I should put out my hand against the LORD's anointed. But take now the spear that is at his head and the jar of water, and let us go." ¹²So David took the spear and the jar of water from Saul's head, and they went away. No man saw it or knew it, nor did any awake, for they were all asleep, because a deep sleep from the LORD had fallen upon them.

¹³Then David went over to the other side and stood far off on the top of the hill, with a great space between them. ¹⁴And David called to the army, and to Abner the son of Ner, saying, "Will you not answer, Abner?" Then Abner answered, "Who are you who calls to the king?" ¹⁵And David said to Abner, "Are you not a man? Who is like you in Israel? Why then have you not kept watch over your lord the king? For one of the people came in to destroy the king your lord. ¹⁶This thing that you have done is not good. As the LORD lives, you deserve to die, because you have not kept watch over your lord, the LORD's anointed. And now see where the king's spear is and the jar of water that was at his head."

¹⁷Saul recognized David's voice and said, "Is this your voice, my son David?" And David said, "It is my voice, my lord, O king." ¹⁸And he said, "Why does my lord pursue after his servant? For what have I done? What evil is on my hands? ¹⁹Now therefore let my lord the king hear the words of his servant. If it is the LORD who has stirred you up against me, may he accept an offering, but if it is men, may they be cursed before the LORD, for they have driven me out this day that I should have no share in the heritage of the LORD, saying, 'Go, serve other gods.' ²⁰Now therefore, let not my blood fall to the earth away from the presence of the LORD, for the king of Israel has come out to seek a single flea like one who hunts a partridge in the mountains."

²¹Then Saul said, "I have sinned. Return, my son David, for I will no more do you harm, because my life was precious in your eyes this day. Behold, I have acted foolishly, and have made a great mistake." ²²And David answered and said, "Here is the spear, O king! Let one of the young men come over and take it. ²³The LORD rewards every man for his righteousness and his faithfulness, for the LORD gave you into my hand today, and I would not put out my hand against the LORD's anointed. ²⁴Behold, as your life was precious this day in my sight, so may my life be precious in the sight of the LORD, and may he deliver me out of all tribulation." ²⁵Then Saul said to David, "Blessed be you, my son David! You will do many things and will succeed in them." So David went his way, and Saul returned to his place.

DAVID FLEES TO THE PHILISTINES

27 Then David said in his heart, "Now I shall perish one day by the hand of Saul. There is nothing better for me than that I should escape to the land of the Philistines. Then Saul will despair of seeking me any longer within the borders of Israel, and I shall escape out of his hand." ²So David arose and went over, he and the six hundred men who were with him, to Achish the son of Maoch, king of Gath. ³And David lived with Achish at Gath, he and his men, every man with his household, and David with his two wives, Ahinoam of Jezreel, and Abigail of Carmel, Nabal's widow. ⁴And when it was told Saul that David had fled to Gath, he no longer sought him.

⁵Then David said to Achish, "If I have found favour in your eyes, let a place be given to me in one of the country towns, that I may dwell there. For why should your servant dwell in the royal city with you?" ⁶So that day Achish gave him Ziklag. Therefore Ziklag has belonged to the kings of Judah to this day. ⁷And the number of the days that David lived in the country of the Philistines was a year and four months.

⁸Now David and his men went up and made raids against the Geshurites, the Girzites, and the Amalekites, for these were the inhabitants of the land from of old, as far as Shur, to the land of Egypt. ⁹And David would strike the land and would leave neither man nor woman alive, but would take away the sheep, the oxen, the donkeys, the camels, and the garments, and come back to Achish. ¹⁰When Achish asked, "Where have you made a raid today?" David would say, "Against the Negeb of Judah", or, "Against the Negeb of the Jerahmeelites", or, "Against the Negeb of the Kenites." ¹¹And David would leave neither man nor woman alive to bring news to Gath, thinking, "lest they should tell about us and say, 'So David has done.'" Such was his custom all the while he lived in the country of the Philistines. ¹²And Achish trusted David, thinking, "He has made himself an utter stench to his people Israel; therefore he shall always be my servant."

SAUL AND THE MEDIUM OF EN-DOR

28 In those days the Philistines gathered their forces for war, to fight against Israel. And Achish said to David, "Understand that you and your men are to go out with me in the army." ²David said to Achish, "Very well, you shall know what your servant can do." And Achish said to David, "Very well, I will make you my bodyguard for life."

³Now Samuel had died, and all Israel had mourned for him and buried him in Ramah, his own city. And Saul had put the mediums and the necromancers out of the land. ⁴The Philistines assembled and came and encamped at Shunem. And Saul gathered all Israel, and they encamped at Gilboa. ⁵When Saul saw the army of the Philistines, he was afraid, and his heart trembled greatly. ⁶And when Saul enquired of the LORD, the LORD did not answer him, either by dreams, or by Urim, or by prophets. ⁷Then Saul said to his servants, "Seek out for me a woman who is a medium, that I may go to her and enquire of her." And his servants said to him, "Behold, there is a medium at En-dor."

⁸So Saul disguised himself and put on other garments and went, he and two men with him. And they came to the woman by night. And he said, "Divine for me by a spirit and bring up for me whomever I shall name to you." ⁹The woman said to him, "Surely you know what Saul has done, how he has cut off the mediums and the necromancers from the land. Why then are you laying a trap for my life to bring about my death?" ¹⁰But Saul swore to her by the LORD, "As the LORD lives, no punishment shall come upon you for this thing." ¹¹Then the woman said, "Whom shall I bring up for you?" He said, "Bring up Samuel for me." ¹²When the woman saw Samuel, she cried out with a loud voice. And the woman said to Saul, "Why have you deceived me? You are Saul." ¹³The king said to her, "Do not be afraid. What do you see?" And the woman said to Saul, "I see a god coming up out of the earth." ¹⁴He said to her, "What is his appearance?" And she said, "An old man is coming up, and he is wrapped in a robe." And Saul knew that it was Samuel, and he bowed with his face to the ground and paid homage.

¹⁵Then Samuel said to Saul, "Why have you disturbed me by bringing me up?" Saul answered, "I am in great distress, for the Philistines are warring against me, and God has turned away from me and answers me no more, either by prophets or by dreams. Therefore I have summoned you to tell me what I shall do." ¹⁶And Samuel said, "Why then do you ask me, since the LORD has turned from you and become your enemy? ¹⁷The LORD has done to you as he spoke by me, for the LORD

has torn the kingdom out of your hand and given it to your neighbour, David. ¹⁸Because you did not obey the voice of the LORD and did not carry out his fierce wrath against Amalek, therefore the LORD has done this thing to you this day. ¹⁹Moreover, the LORD will give Israel also with you into the hand of the Philistines, and tomorrow you and your sons shall be with me. The LORD will give the army of Israel also into the hand of the Philistines."

²⁰Then Saul fell at once full length on the ground, filled with fear because of the words of Samuel. And there was no strength in him, for he had eaten nothing all day and all night. ²¹And the woman came to Saul, and when she saw that he was terrified, she said to him, "Behold, your servant has obeyed you. I have taken my life in my hand and have listened to what you have said to me. ²²Now therefore, you also obey your servant. Let me set a morsel of bread before you; and eat, that you may have strength when you go on your way." ²³He refused and said, "I will not eat." But his servants, together with the woman, urged him, and he listened to their words. So he arose from the earth and sat on the bed. ²⁴Now the woman had a fattened calf in the house, and she quickly killed it, and she took flour and kneaded it and baked unleavened bread from it, ²⁵and she put it before Saul and his servants, and they ate. Then they rose and went away that night.

THE PHILISTINES REJECT DAVID

29 Now the Philistines had gathered all their forces at Aphek. And the Israelites were encamped by the spring that is in Jezreel. ²As the lords of the Philistines were passing on by hundreds and by thousands, and David and his men were passing on in the rear with Achish, ³the commanders of the Philistines said, "What are these Hebrews doing here?" And Achish said to the commanders of the Philistines, "Is this not David, the servant of Saul, king of Israel, who has been with me now for days and years, and since he deserted to me I have found no fault in him to this day." ⁴But the commanders of the Philistines were angry with him. And the commanders of the Philistines said to him, "Send the man back, that he may return to the place to which you have assigned him. He shall not go down with us to battle, lest in the battle he become an adversary to us. For how could this fellow reconcile himself to his lord? Would it not be with the heads of the men here? ⁵Is not this David, of whom they sing to one another in dances,

> 'Saul has struck down his thousands,
> and David his ten thousands'?"

⁶Then Achish called David and said to him, "As the LORD lives, you have been honest, and to me it seems right that you should march out and in with me in the campaign. For I have found nothing wrong in you from the day of your coming to me to this day. Nevertheless, the lords do not approve of you. ⁷So go back now; and go peaceably, that you may not displease the lords of the Philistines." ⁸And David said to Achish, "But what have I done? What have you found in your servant from the day I entered your service until now, that I may not go and fight against the enemies of my lord the king?" ⁹And Achish answered David and said, "I know that you are as blameless in my sight as an angel of God. Nevertheless, the commanders of the Philistines have said, 'He shall not go up with us to the battle.' ¹⁰Now then rise early in the morning with the servants of your lord who came with you, and start early in the morning, and depart as soon as you have light." ¹¹So David set out with his men early in the morning to return to the land of the Philistines. But the Philistines went up to Jezreel.

DAVID'S WIVES ARE CAPTURED

30 Now when David and his men came to Ziklag on the third day, the Amalekites had made a raid against the Negeb and against Ziklag. They had overcome Ziklag and burned it with fire ²and taken captive the women and all[a] who were in it, both small and great. They killed no one, but carried them off and went their way. ³And when David and his men came to the city, they found it burned with fire, and their wives and sons and daughters taken captive. ⁴Then David and the people who were with him raised their voices and wept until they had no more strength to weep. ⁵David's two wives also had been taken captive, Ahinoam of Jezreel and Abigail the widow of Nabal of Carmel. ⁶And David was greatly distressed, for the people spoke of stoning him, because all the people were bitter in soul,[b] each for his sons and daughters. But David strengthened himself in the LORD his God.

---

[a]Septuagint; Hebrew lacks *and all* [b]Compare 22:2

⁷And David said to Abiathar the priest, the son of Ahimelech, "Bring me the ephod." So Abiathar brought the ephod to David. ⁸And David enquired of the LORD, "Shall I pursue after this band? Shall I overtake them?" He answered him, "Pursue, for you shall surely overtake and shall surely rescue." ⁹So David set out, and the six hundred men who were with him, and they came to the brook Besor, where those who were left behind stayed. ¹⁰But David pursued, he and four hundred men. Two hundred stayed behind, who were too exhausted to cross the brook Besor.

¹¹They found an Egyptian in the open country and brought him to David. And they gave him bread and he ate. They gave him water to drink, ¹²and they gave him a piece of a cake of figs and two clusters of raisins. And when he had eaten, his spirit revived, for he had not eaten bread or drunk water for three days and three nights. ¹³And David said to him, "To whom do you belong? And where are you from?" He said, "I am a young man of Egypt, servant to an Amalekite, and my master left me behind because I fell sick three days ago. ¹⁴We had made a raid against the Negeb of the Cherethites and against that which belongs to Judah and against the Negeb of Caleb, and we burned Ziklag with fire." ¹⁵And David said to him, "Will you take me down to this band?" And he said, "Swear to me by God that you will not kill me or deliver me into the hands of my master, and I will take you down to this band."

DAVID DEFEATS THE AMALEKITES

¹⁶And when he had taken him down, behold, they were spread abroad over all the land, eating and drinking and dancing, because of all the great spoil they had taken from the land of the Philistines and from the land of Judah. ¹⁷And David struck them down from twilight until the evening of the next day, and not a man of them escaped, except four hundred young men, who mounted camels and fled. ¹⁸David recovered all that the Amalekites had taken, and David rescued his two wives. ¹⁹Nothing was missing, whether small or great, sons or daughters, spoil or anything that had been taken. David brought back everything. ²⁰David also captured all the flocks and herds, and the people drove the livestock before him,ᵃ and said, "This is David's spoil."

²¹Then David came to the two hundred men who had been too exhausted to follow David, and who had been left at the brook Besor. And they went out to meet David and to meet the people who were with him. And when David came near to the people he greeted them. ²²Then all the wicked and worthless fellows among the men who had gone with David said, "Because they did not go with us, we will not give them any of the spoil that we have recovered, except that each man may lead away his wife and children, and depart." ²³But David said, "You shall not do so, my brothers, with what the LORD has given us. He has preserved us and given into our hand the band that came against us. ²⁴Who would listen to you in this matter? For as his share is who goes down into the battle, so shall his share be who stays by the baggage. They shall share alike." ²⁵And he made it a statute and a rule for Israel from that day forward to this day.

²⁶When David came to Ziklag, he sent part of the spoil to his friends, the elders of Judah, saying, "Here is a present for you from the spoil of the enemies of the LORD." ²⁷It was for those in Bethel, in Ramoth of the Negeb, in Jattir, ²⁸in Aroer, in Siphmoth, in Eshtemoa, ²⁹in Racal, in the cities of the Jerahmeelites, in the cities of the Kenites, ³⁰in Hormah, in Bor-ashan, in Athach, ³¹in Hebron, for all the places where David and his men had roamed.

THE DEATH OF SAUL

31 Now the Philistines were fighting against Israel, and the men of Israel fled before the Philistines and fell slain on Mount Gilboa. ²And the Philistines overtook Saul and his sons, and the Philistines struck down Jonathan and Abinadab and Malchi-shua, the sons of Saul. ³The battle pressed hard against Saul, and the archers found him, and he was badly wounded by the archers. ⁴Then Saul said to his armour bearer, "Draw your sword, and thrust me through with it, lest these uncircumcised come and thrust me through, and mistreat me." But his armour bearer would not, for he feared greatly. Therefore Saul took his own sword and fell upon it. ⁵And when his armour bearer saw that Saul was dead, he also fell upon his sword and died with him. ⁶Thus Saul died, and his three sons, and his armour bearer, and all his men, on the same day together. ⁷And when the men of Israel who were on the other side of the valley and those beyond

---

ᵃThe meaning of the Hebrew clause is uncertain

the Jordan saw that the men of Israel had fled and that Saul and his sons were dead, they abandoned their cities and fled. And the Philistines came and lived in them.

⁸The next day, when the Philistines came to strip the slain, they found Saul and his three sons fallen on Mount Gilboa. ⁹So they cut off his head and stripped off his armour and sent messengers throughout the land of the Philistines, to carry the good news to the house of their idols and to the people. ¹⁰They put his armour in the temple of Ashtaroth, and they fastened his body to the wall of Beth-shan. ¹¹But when the inhabitants of Jabesh-gilead heard what the Philistines had done to Saul, ¹²all the valiant men arose and went all night and took the body of Saul and the bodies of his sons from the wall of Beth-shan, and they came to Jabesh and burned them there. ¹³And they took their bones and buried them under the tamarisk tree in Jabesh and fasted for seven days.

2 SAMUEL

DAVID HEARS OF SAUL'S DEATH

1 After the death of Saul, when David had returned from striking down the Amalekites, David remained two days in Ziklag. ²And on the third day, behold, a man came from Saul's camp, with his clothes torn and dirt on his head. And when he came to David, he fell to the ground and paid homage. ³David said to him, "Where do you come from?" And he said to him, "I have escaped from the camp of Israel." ⁴And David said to him, "How did it go? Tell me." And he answered, "The people fled from the battle, and also many of the people have fallen and are dead, and Saul and his son Jonathan are also dead." ⁵Then David said to the young man who told him, "How do you know that Saul and his son Jonathan are dead?" ⁶And the young man who told him said, "By chance I happened to be on Mount Gilboa, and there was Saul leaning on his spear, and behold, the chariots and the horsemen were close upon him. ⁷And when he looked behind him, he saw me, and called to me. And I answered, 'Here I am.' ⁸And he said to me, 'Who are you?' I answered him, 'I am an Amalekite.' ⁹And he said to me, 'Stand beside me and kill me, for anguish has seized me, and yet my life still lingers.' ¹⁰So I stood beside him and killed him, because I was sure that he could not live after he had fallen. And I took the crown that was on his head and the armlet that was on his arm, and I have brought them here to my lord."

¹¹Then David took hold of his clothes and tore them, and so did all the men who were with him. ¹²And they mourned and wept and fasted until evening for Saul and for Jonathan his son and for the people of the LORD and for the house of Israel, because they had fallen by the sword. ¹³And David said to the young man who told him, "Where do you come from?" And he answered, "I am the son of a sojourner, an Amalekite." ¹⁴David said to him, "How is it you were not afraid to put out your hand to destroy the LORD's anointed?" ¹⁵Then David called one of the young men and said, "Go, execute him." And he struck him down so that he died. ¹⁶And David said to him, "Your blood be on your head, for your own mouth has testified against you, saying, 'I have killed the LORD's anointed.'"

DAVID'S LAMENT FOR SAUL AND JONATHAN

¹⁷And David lamented with this lamentation over Saul and Jonathan his son, ¹⁸and he said it*ᵃ* should be taught to the people of Judah; behold, it is written in the Book of Jashar.*ᵇ* He said:

¹⁹ "Your glory, O Israel, is slain
    on your high places!
  How the mighty have fallen!
²⁰ Tell it not in Gath,
    publish it not in the streets
      of Ashkelon,
  lest the daughters of the
    Philistines rejoice,
  lest the daughters of the
    uncircumcised exult.

²¹ "You mountains of Gilboa,
    let there be no dew or rain upon you,
    nor fields of offerings!*ᶜ*
  For there the shield of the
    mighty was defiled,
  the shield of Saul, not
    anointed with oil.

²² "From the blood of the slain,
    from the fat of the mighty,
  the bow of Jonathan turned not back,
    and the sword of Saul
      returned not empty.

²³ "Saul and Jonathan, beloved and lovely!
    In life and in death they
      were not divided;
  they were swifter than eagles;
    they were stronger than lions.

²⁴ "You daughters of Israel,
    weep over Saul,

---

*ᵃ*Septuagint; Hebrew *the Bow*, which may be the name of the lament's tune   *ᵇ*Or *of the upright*   *ᶜ*Septuagint *firstfruits*

> who clothed you luxuriously
> in scarlet,
> who put ornaments of gold
> on your apparel.
>
> 25 "How the mighty have fallen
> in the midst of the battle!
>
> "Jonathan lies slain on your
> high places.
> 26 I am distressed for you, my
> brother Jonathan;
> very pleasant have you been to me;
> your love to me was extraordinary,
> surpassing the love of women.
>
> 27 "How the mighty have fallen,
> and the weapons of war perished!"

DAVID ANOINTED KING OF JUDAH

2 After this David enquired of the LORD, "Shall I go up into any of the cities of Judah?" And the LORD said to him, "Go up." David said, "To which shall I go up?" And he said, "To Hebron." ²So David went up there, and his two wives also, Ahinoam of Jezreel and Abigail the widow of Nabal of Carmel. ³And David brought up his men who were with him, everyone with his household, and they lived in the towns of Hebron. ⁴And the men of Judah came, and there they anointed David king over the house of Judah.

When they told David, "It was the men of Jabesh-gilead who buried Saul", ⁵David sent messengers to the men of Jabesh-gilead and said to them, "May you be blessed by the LORD, because you showed this loyalty to Saul your lord and buried him. ⁶Now may the LORD show steadfast love and faithfulness to you. And I will do good to you because you have done this thing. ⁷Now therefore let your hands be strong, and be valiant, for Saul your lord is dead, and the house of Judah has anointed me king over them."

ISH-BOSHETH MADE KING OF ISRAEL

⁸But Abner the son of Ner, commander of Saul's army, took Ish-bosheth the son of Saul and brought him over to Mahanaim, ⁹and he made him king over Gilead and the Ashurites and Jezreel and Ephraim and Benjamin and all Israel. ¹⁰Ish-bosheth, Saul's son, was forty years old when he began to reign over Israel, and he reigned for two years. But the house of Judah followed David. ¹¹And the time that David was king in Hebron over the house of Judah was seven years and six months.

THE BATTLE OF GIBEON

¹²Abner the son of Ner, and the servants of Ish-bosheth the son of Saul, went out from Mahanaim to Gibeon. ¹³And Joab the son of Zeruiah and the servants of David went out and met them at the pool of Gibeon. And they sat down, one on one side of the pool, and the other on the other side of the pool. ¹⁴And Abner said to Joab, "Let the young men arise and compete before us." And Joab said, "Let them arise." ¹⁵Then they arose and passed over by number, twelve for Benjamin and Ish-bosheth the son of Saul, and twelve of the servants of David. ¹⁶And each caught his opponent by the head and thrust his sword in his opponent's side, so they fell down together. Therefore that place was called Helkath-hazzurim,ᵃ which is at Gibeon. ¹⁷And the battle was very fierce that day. And Abner and the men of Israel were beaten before the servants of David.

¹⁸And the three sons of Zeruiah were there, Joab, Abishai, and Asahel. Now Asahel was as swift of foot as a wild gazelle. ¹⁹And Asahel pursued Abner, and as he went, he turned neither to the right hand nor to the left from following Abner. ²⁰Then Abner looked behind him and said, "Is it you, Asahel?" And he answered, "It is I." ²¹Abner said to him, "Turn aside to your right hand or to your left, and seize one of the young men and take his spoil." But Asahel would not turn aside from following him. ²²And Abner said again to Asahel, "Turn aside from following me. Why should I strike you to the ground? How then could I lift up my face to your brother Joab?" ²³But he refused to turn aside. Therefore Abner struck him in the stomach with the butt of his spear, so that the spear came out at his back. And he fell there and died where he was. And all who came to the place where Asahel had fallen and died, stood still.

²⁴But Joab and Abishai pursued Abner. And as the sun was going down they came to the hill of Ammah, which lies before Giah on the way to the wilderness of Gibeon. ²⁵And the people of Benjamin gathered themselves together behind Abner and became one group and took their stand on the top of a hill. ²⁶Then Abner called to Joab, "Shall the sword devour for ever? Do you not know that the end will

---

ᵃ*Helkath-hazzurim* means *the field of sword-edges*

be bitter? How long will it be before you tell your people to turn from the pursuit of their brothers?" ²⁷And Joab said, "As God lives, if you had not spoken, surely the men would not have given up the pursuit of their brothers until the morning." ²⁸So Joab blew the trumpet, and all the men stopped and pursued Israel no more, nor did they fight any more.

²⁹And Abner and his men went all that night through the Arabah. They crossed the Jordan, and marching the whole morning, they came to Mahanaim. ³⁰Joab returned from the pursuit of Abner. And when he had gathered all the people together, there were missing from David's servants nineteen men besides Asahel. ³¹But the servants of David had struck down of Benjamin 360 of Abner's men. ³²And they took up Asahel and buried him in the tomb of his father, which was at Bethlehem. And Joab and his men marched all night, and the day broke upon them at Hebron.

ABNER JOINS DAVID

3 There was a long war between the house of Saul and the house of David. And David grew stronger and stronger, while the house of Saul became weaker and weaker.

²And sons were born to David at Hebron: his firstborn was Amnon, of Ahinoam of Jezreel; ³and his second, Chileab, of Abigail the widow of Nabal of Carmel; and the third, Absalom the son of Maacah the daughter of Talmai king of Geshur; ⁴and the fourth, Adonijah the son of Haggith; and the fifth, Shephatiah the son of Abital; ⁵and the sixth, Ithream, of Eglah, David's wife. These were born to David in Hebron.

⁶While there was war between the house of Saul and the house of David, Abner was making himself strong in the house of Saul. ⁷Now Saul had a concubine whose name was Rizpah, the daughter of Aiah. And Ish-bosheth said to Abner, "Why have you gone in to my father's concubine?" ⁸Then Abner was very angry over the words of Ish-bosheth and said, "Am I a dog's head of Judah? To this day I keep showing steadfast love to the house of Saul your father, to his brothers, and to his friends, and have not given you into the hand of David. And yet you charge me today with a fault concerning a woman. ⁹God do so to Abner and more also, if I do not accomplish for David what the LORD has sworn to him, ¹⁰to transfer the kingdom from the house of Saul and set up the throne of David over Israel and over Judah, from Dan to Beersheba." ¹¹And Ish-bosheth could not answer Abner another word, because he feared him.

¹²And Abner sent messengers to David on his behalf,ᵃ saying, "To whom does the land belong? Make your covenant with me, and behold, my hand shall be with you to bring over all Israel to you." ¹³And he said, "Good; I will make a covenant with you. But one thing I require of you; that is, you shall not see my face unless you first bring Michal, Saul's daughter, when you come to see my face." ¹⁴Then David sent messengers to Ish-bosheth, Saul's son, saying, "Give me my wife Michal, for whom I paid the bridal price of a hundred foreskins of the Philistines." ¹⁵And Ish-bosheth sent and took her from her husband Paltiel the son of Laish. ¹⁶But her husband went with her, weeping after her all the way to Bahurim. Then Abner said to him, "Go, return." And he returned.

¹⁷And Abner conferred with the elders of Israel, saying, "For some time past you have been seeking David as king over you. ¹⁸Now then bring it about, for the LORD has promised David, saying, 'By the hand of my servant David I will save my people Israel from the hand of the Philistines, and from the hand of all their enemies.'" ¹⁹Abner also spoke to Benjamin. And then Abner went to tell David at Hebron all that Israel and the whole house of Benjamin thought good to do.

²⁰When Abner came with twenty men to David at Hebron, David made a feast for Abner and the men who were with him. ²¹And Abner said to David, "I will arise and go and will gather all Israel to my lord the king, that they may make a covenant with you, and that you may reign over all that your heart desires." So David sent Abner away, and he went in peace.

²²Just then the servants of David arrived with Joab from a raid, bringing much spoil with them. But Abner was not with David at Hebron, for he had sent him away, and he had gone in peace. ²³When Joab and all the army that was with him came, it was told Joab, "Abner the son of Ner came to the king, and he has let him go, and he has gone in peace." ²⁴Then Joab went to the king and said, "What have you done? Behold, Abner came to you. Why is it that you have sent him away, so that he is gone? ²⁵You know that Abner the son of Ner came to deceive you and to know your going out and your coming in, and to know all that you are doing."

ᵃ Or *where he was*; Septuagint *at Hebron*

JOAB MURDERS ABNER

26When Joab came out from David's presence, he sent messengers after Abner, and they brought him back from the cistern of Sirah. But David did not know about it. 27And when Abner returned to Hebron, Joab took him aside into the midst of the gate to speak with him privately, and there he struck him in the stomach, so that he died, for the blood of Asahel his brother. 28Afterwards, when David heard of it, he said, "I and my kingdom are for ever guiltless before the LORD for the blood of Abner the son of Ner. 29May it fall upon the head of Joab and upon all his father's house, and may the house of Joab never be without one who has a discharge or who is leprous or who holds a spindle or who falls by the sword or who lacks bread!" 30So Joab and Abishai his brother killed Abner, because he had put their brother Asahel to death in the battle at Gibeon.

DAVID MOURNS ABNER

31Then David said to Joab and to all the people who were with him, "Tear your clothes and put on sackcloth and mourn before Abner." And King David followed the bier. 32They buried Abner at Hebron. And the king lifted up his voice and wept at the grave of Abner, and all the people wept. 33And the king lamented for Abner, saying,

> "Should Abner die as a fool dies?
> 34 Your hands were not bound;
>   your feet were not fettered;
> as one falls before the wicked
>   you have fallen."

And all the people wept again over him. 35Then all the people came to persuade David to eat bread while it was yet day. But David swore, saying, "God do so to me and more also, if I taste bread or anything else till the sun goes down!" 36And all the people took notice of it, and it pleased them, as everything that the king did pleased all the people. 37So all the people and all Israel understood that day that it had not been the king's will to put to death Abner the son of Ner. 38And the king said to his servants, "Do you not know that a prince and a great man has fallen this day in Israel? 39And I was gentle today, though anointed king. These men, the sons of Zeruiah, are more severe than I. The LORD repay the evildoer according to his wickedness!"

ISH-BOSHETH MURDERED

4 When Ish-bosheth, Saul's son, heard that Abner had died at Hebron, his courage failed, and all Israel was dismayed. 2Now Saul's son had two men who were captains of raiding bands; the name of one was Baanah, and the name of the other Rechab, sons of Rimmon a man of Benjamin from Beeroth (for Beeroth also is counted part of Benjamin; 3the Beerothites fled to Gittaim and have been sojourners there to this day).

4Jonathan, the son of Saul, had a son who was crippled in his feet. He was five years old when the news about Saul and Jonathan came from Jezreel, and his nurse took him up and fled, and as she fled in her haste, he fell and became lame. And his name was Mephibosheth.

5Now the sons of Rimmon the Beerothite, Rechab and Baanah, set out, and about the heat of the day they came to the house of Ish-bosheth as he was taking his noonday rest. 6And they came into the midst of the house as if to get wheat, and they stabbed him in the stomach. Then Rechab and Baanah his brother escaped.*a* 7When they came into the house, as he lay on his bed in his bedroom, they struck him and put him to death and beheaded him. They took his head and went by the way of the Arabah all night, 8and brought the head of Ish-bosheth to David at Hebron. And they said to the king, "Here is the head of Ish-bosheth, the son of Saul, your enemy, who sought your life. The LORD has avenged my lord the king this day on Saul and on his offspring." 9But David answered Rechab and Baanah his brother, the sons of Rimmon the Beerothite, "As the LORD lives, who has redeemed my life out of every adversity, 10when one told me, 'Behold, Saul is dead', and thought he was bringing good news, I seized him and killed him at Ziklag, which was the reward I gave him for his news. 11How much more, when wicked men have killed a righteous man in his own house on his bed, shall I not now require his blood at your hand and destroy you from the earth?" 12And David commanded his young men, and they killed them and cut off their hands and feet and hanged them beside the pool at Hebron. But they took the head of Ish-bosheth and buried it in the tomb of Abner at Hebron.

---

a Septuagint *And behold, the doorkeeper of the house had been cleaning wheat, but she grew drowsy and slept. So Rechab and Baanah his brother slipped in*

DAVID ANOINTED KING OF ISRAEL

5 Then all the tribes of Israel came to David at Hebron and said, "Behold, we are your bone and flesh. ²In times past, when Saul was king over us, it was you who led out and brought in Israel. And the LORD said to you, 'You shall be shepherd of my people Israel, and you shall be prince[a] over Israel.'" ³So all the elders of Israel came to the king at Hebron, and King David made a covenant with them at Hebron before the LORD, and they anointed David king over Israel. ⁴David was thirty years old when he began to reign, and he reigned for forty years. ⁵At Hebron he reigned over Judah for seven years and six months, and at Jerusalem he reigned over all Israel and Judah for thirty-three years.[b]

⁶And the king and his men went to Jerusalem against the Jebusites, the inhabitants of the land, who said to David, "You will not come in here, but the blind and the lame will ward you off"—thinking, "David cannot come in here." ⁷Nevertheless, David took the stronghold of Zion, that is, the city of David. ⁸And David said on that day, "Whoever would strike the Jebusites, let him get up the water shaft to attack 'the lame and the blind,' who are hated by David's soul." Therefore it is said, "The blind and the lame shall not come into the house." ⁹And David lived in the stronghold and called it the city of David. And David built the city all round from the Millo inwards. ¹⁰And David became greater and greater, for the LORD, the God of hosts, was with him.

¹¹And Hiram king of Tyre sent messengers to David, and cedar trees, also carpenters and masons who built David a house. ¹²And David knew that the LORD had established him king over Israel, and that he had exalted his kingdom for the sake of his people Israel.

¹³And David took more concubines and wives from Jerusalem, after he came from Hebron, and more sons and daughters were born to David. ¹⁴And these are the names of those who were born to him in Jerusalem: Shammua, Shobab, Nathan, Solomon, ¹⁵Ibhar, Elishua, Nepheg, Japhia, ¹⁶Elishama, Eliada, and Eliphelet.

DAVID DEFEATS THE PHILISTINES

¹⁷When the Philistines heard that David had been anointed king over Israel, all the Philistines went up to search for David. But David heard of it and went down to the stronghold. ¹⁸Now the Philistines had come and spread out in the Valley of Rephaim. ¹⁹And David enquired of the LORD, "Shall I go up against the Philistines? Will you give them into my hand?" And the LORD said to David, "Go up, for I will certainly give the Philistines into your hand." ²⁰And David came to Baal-perazim, and David defeated them there. And he said, "The LORD has broken through my enemies before me like a breaking flood." Therefore the name of that place is called Baal-perazim.[c] ²¹And the Philistines left their idols there, and David and his men carried them away.

²²And the Philistines came up yet again and spread out in the Valley of Rephaim. ²³And when David enquired of the LORD, he said, "You shall not go up; go round to their rear, and come against them opposite the balsam trees. ²⁴And when you hear the sound of marching in the tops of the balsam trees, then rouse yourself, for then the LORD has gone out before you to strike down the army of the Philistines." ²⁵And David did as the LORD commanded him, and struck down the Philistines from Geba to Gezer.

THE ARK BROUGHT TO JERUSALEM

6 David again gathered all the chosen men of Israel, thirty thousand. ²And David arose and went with all the people who were with him from Baale-judah to bring up from there the ark of God, which is called by the name of the LORD of hosts who sits enthroned on the cherubim. ³And they carried the ark of God on a new cart and brought it out of the house of Abinadab, which was on the hill. And Uzzah and Ahio,[d] the sons of Abinadab, were driving the new cart, ⁴with the ark of God,[e] and Ahio went before the ark.

UZZAH AND THE ARK

⁵And David and all the house of Israel were celebrating before the LORD, with songs[f] and lyres and harps and tambourines and castanets and cymbals. ⁶And when they came to the threshing floor of Nacon, Uzzah put out his hand to the ark of God and took hold of it, for the oxen stumbled. ⁷And the anger of the LORD was kindled against Uzzah, and God struck him down there because of his error, and he died there beside the ark of God.

---

[a] Or *leader* [b] Dead Sea Scroll lacks verses 4–5 [c] *Baal-perazim* means *Lord of breaking through* [d] Or *and his brother*; also verse 4
[e] Compare Septuagint; Hebrew *the new cart,* ⁴*and brought it out of the house of Abinadab, which was on the hill, with the ark of God*
[f] Septuagint, 1 Chronicles 13:8; Hebrew *fir trees*

⁸And David was angry because the LORD had broken out against Uzzah. And that place is called Perez-uzzah[a] to this day. ⁹And David was afraid of the LORD that day, and he said, "How can the ark of the LORD come to me?" ¹⁰So David was not willing to take the ark of the LORD into the city of David. But David took it aside to the house of Obed-edom the Gittite. ¹¹And the ark of the LORD remained in the house of Obed-edom the Gittite for three months, and the LORD blessed Obed-edom and all his household.

¹²And it was told King David, "The LORD has blessed the household of Obed-edom and all that belongs to him, because of the ark of God." So David went and brought up the ark of God from the house of Obed-edom to the city of David with rejoicing. ¹³And when those who bore the ark of the LORD had gone six steps, he sacrificed an ox and a fattened animal. ¹⁴And David danced before the LORD with all his might. And David was wearing a linen ephod. ¹⁵So David and all the house of Israel brought up the ark of the LORD with shouting and with the sound of the horn.

DAVID AND MICHAL

¹⁶As the ark of the LORD came into the city of David, Michal the daughter of Saul looked out of the window and saw King David leaping and dancing before the LORD, and she despised him in her heart. ¹⁷And they brought in the ark of the LORD and set it in its place, inside the tent that David had pitched for it. And David offered burnt offerings and peace offerings before the LORD. ¹⁸And when David had finished offering the burnt offerings and the peace offerings, he blessed the people in the name of the LORD of hosts ¹⁹and distributed among all the people, the whole multitude of Israel, both men and women, a cake of bread, a portion of meat,[b] and a cake of raisins to each one. Then all the people departed, each to his house.

²⁰And David returned to bless his household. But Michal the daughter of Saul came out to meet David and said, "How the king of Israel honoured himself today, uncovering himself today before the eyes of his servants' female servants, as one of the vulgar fellows shamelessly uncovers himself!" ²¹And David said to Michal, "It was before the LORD, who chose me above your father and above all his house, to appoint me as prince[c] over Israel, the people of the LORD — and I will celebrate before the LORD. ²²I will make myself yet more contemptible than this, and I will be abased in your[d] eyes. But by the female servants of whom you have spoken, by them I shall be held in honour." ²³And Michal the daughter of Saul had no child to the day of her death.

THE LORD'S COVENANT WITH DAVID

7 Now when the king lived in his house and the LORD had given him rest from all his surrounding enemies, ²the king said to Nathan the prophet, "See now, I dwell in a house of cedar, but the ark of God dwells in a tent." ³And Nathan said to the king, "Go, do all that is in your heart, for the LORD is with you."

⁴But that same night the word of the LORD came to Nathan, ⁵"Go and tell my servant David, 'Thus says the LORD: Would you build me a house to dwell in? ⁶I have not lived in a house since the day I brought up the people of Israel from Egypt to this day, but I have been moving about in a tent for my dwelling. ⁷In all places where I have moved with all the people of Israel, did I speak a word with any of the judges[e] of Israel, whom I commanded to shepherd my people Israel, saying, "Why have you not built me a house of cedar?"' ⁸Now, therefore, thus you shall say to my servant David, 'Thus says the LORD of hosts, I took you from the pasture, from following the sheep, that you should be prince[f] over my people Israel. ⁹And I have been with you wherever you went and have cut off all your enemies from before you. And I will make for you a great name, like the name of the great ones of the earth. ¹⁰And I will appoint a place for my people Israel and will plant them, so that they may dwell in their own place and be disturbed no more. And violent men shall afflict them no more, as formerly, ¹¹from the time that I appointed judges over my people Israel. And I will give you rest from all your enemies. Moreover, the LORD declares to you that the LORD will make you a house. ¹²When your days are fulfilled and you lie down with your fathers, I will raise up your offspring after you, who shall come from your body, and I will establish his kingdom. ¹³He shall build a house for my name, and I will establish the throne of his kingdom for ever. ¹⁴I will be to him a father, and he shall be to me a son. When he commits

---

[a]Perez-uzzah means *the breaking out against Uzzah* [b]Vulgate; the meaning of the Hebrew term is uncertain [c]Or *leader* [d]Septuagint; Hebrew *my* [e]Compare 1 Chronicles 17:6; Hebrew *tribes* [f]Or *leader*

iniquity, I will discipline him with the rod of men, with the stripes of the sons of men, ¹⁵but my steadfast love will not depart from him, as I took it from Saul, whom I put away from before you. ¹⁶And your house and your kingdom shall be made sure for ever before me.ᵃ Your throne shall be established for ever.'" ¹⁷In accordance with all these words, and in accordance with all this vision, Nathan spoke to David.

DAVID'S PRAYER OF GRATITUDE

¹⁸Then King David went in and sat before the LORD and said, "Who am I, O Lord GOD, and what is my house, that you have brought me thus far? ¹⁹And yet this was a small thing in your eyes, O Lord GOD. You have spoken also of your servant's house for a great while to come, and this is instruction for mankind, O Lord GOD! ²⁰And what more can David say to you? For you know your servant, O Lord GOD! ²¹Because of your promise, and according to your own heart, you have brought about all this greatness, to make your servant know it. ²²Therefore you are great, O LORD God. For there is none like you, and there is no God besides you, according to all that we have heard with our ears. ²³And who is like your people Israel, the one nation on earth whom God went to redeem to be his people, making himself a name and doing for themᵇ great and awesome things by driving out before your people,ᶜ whom you redeemed for yourself from Egypt, a nation and its gods? ²⁴And you established for yourself your people Israel to be your people for ever. And you, O LORD, became their God. ²⁵And now, O LORD God, confirm for ever the word that you have spoken concerning your servant and concerning his house, and do as you have spoken. ²⁶And your name will be magnified for ever, saying, 'The LORD of hosts is God over Israel', and the house of your servant David will be established before you. ²⁷For you, O LORD of hosts, the God of Israel, have made this revelation to your servant, saying, 'I will build you a house.' Therefore your servant has found courage to pray this prayer to you. ²⁸And now, O Lord GOD, you are God, and your words are true, and you have promised this good thing to your servant. ²⁹Now therefore may it please you to bless the house of your servant, so that it may continue for ever before you. For you, O Lord GOD, have spoken, and with your blessing shall the house of your servant be blessed for ever."

DAVID'S VICTORIES

8 After this David defeated the Philistines and subdued them, and David took Metheg-ammah out of the hand of the Philistines.

²And he defeated Moab and he measured them with a line, making them lie down on the ground. Two lines he measured to be put to death, and one full line to be spared. And the Moabites became servants to David and brought tribute.

³David also defeated Hadadezer the son of Rehob, king of Zobah, as he went to restore his power at the river Euphrates. ⁴And David took from him 1,700 horsemen, and 20,000 foot soldiers. And David hamstrung all the chariot horses but left enough for 100 chariots. ⁵And when the Syrians of Damascus came to help Hadadezer king of Zobah, David struck down 22,000 men of the Syrians. ⁶Then David put garrisons in Aram of Damascus, and the Syrians became servants to David and brought tribute. And the LORD gave victory to David wherever he went. ⁷And David took the shields of gold that were carried by the servants of Hadadezer and brought them to Jerusalem. ⁸And from Betah and from Berothai, cities of Hadadezer, King David took very much bronze.

⁹When Toi king of Hamath heard that David had defeated the whole army of Hadadezer, ¹⁰Toi sent his son Joram to King David, to ask about his health and to bless him because he had fought against Hadadezer and defeated him, for Hadadezer had often been at war with Toi. And Joram brought with him articles of silver, of gold, and of bronze. ¹¹These also King David dedicated to the LORD, together with the silver and gold that he dedicated from all the nations he subdued, ¹²from Edom, Moab, the Ammonites, the Philistines, Amalek, and from the spoil of Hadadezer the son of Rehob, king of Zobah.

¹³And David made a name for himself when he returned from striking down 18,000 Edomites in the Valley of Salt. ¹⁴Then he put garrisons in Edom; throughout all Edom he put garrisons, and all the Edomites became David's servants. And the LORD gave victory to David wherever he went.

DAVID'S OFFICIALS

¹⁵So David reigned over all Israel. And David administered justice and equity to all his

---

ᵃSeptuagint; Hebrew *you* ᵇWith a few Targums, Vulgate, Syriac; Hebrew *you* ᶜSeptuagint (compare 1 Chronicles 17:21); Hebrew *awesome things for your land, before your people*

people. ¹⁶Joab the son of Zeruiah was over the army, and Jehoshaphat the son of Ahilud was recorder, ¹⁷and Zadok the son of Ahitub and Ahimelech the son of Abiathar were priests, and Seraiah was secretary, ¹⁸and Benaiah the son of Jehoiada was over[a] the Cherethites and the Pelethites, and David's sons were priests.

DAVID'S KINDNESS TO MEPHIBOSHETH

9 And David said, "Is there still anyone left of the house of Saul, that I may show him kindness for Jonathan's sake?" ²Now there was a servant of the house of Saul whose name was Ziba, and they called him to David. And the king said to him, "Are you Ziba?" And he said, "I am your servant." ³And the king said, "Is there not still someone of the house of Saul, that I may show the kindness of God to him?" Ziba said to the king, "There is still a son of Jonathan; he is crippled in his feet." ⁴The king said to him, "Where is he?" And Ziba said to the king, "He is in the house of Machir the son of Ammiel, at Lo-debar." ⁵Then King David sent and brought him from the house of Machir the son of Ammiel, at Lo-debar. ⁶And Mephibosheth the son of Jonathan, son of Saul, came to David and fell on his face and paid homage. And David said, "Mephibosheth!" And he answered, "Behold, I am your servant." ⁷And David said to him, "Do not fear, for I will show you kindness for the sake of your father Jonathan, and I will restore to you all the land of Saul your father, and you shall eat at my table always." ⁸And he paid homage and said, "What is your servant, that you should show regard for a dead dog such as I?"

⁹Then the king called Ziba, Saul's servant, and said to him, "All that belonged to Saul and to all his house I have given to your master's grandson. ¹⁰And you and your sons and your servants shall till the land for him and shall bring in the produce, that your master's grandson may have bread to eat. But Mephibosheth your master's grandson shall always eat at my table." Now Ziba had fifteen sons and twenty servants. ¹¹Then Ziba said to the king, "According to all that my lord the king commands his servant, so will your servant do." So Mephibosheth ate at David's[b] table, like one of the king's sons. ¹²And Mephibosheth had a young son, whose name was Mica. And all who lived in Ziba's house became Mephibosheth's servants. ¹³So Mephibosheth lived in Jerusalem, for he ate always at the king's table. Now he was lame in both his feet.

DAVID DEFEATS AMMON AND SYRIA

10 After this the king of the Ammonites died, and Hanun his son reigned in his place. ²And David said, "I will deal loyally[c] with Hanun the son of Nahash, as his father dealt loyally with me." So David sent his servants to console him concerning his father. And David's servants came into the land of the Ammonites. ³But the princes of the Ammonites said to Hanun their lord, "Do you think, because David has sent comforters to you, that he is honouring your father? Has not David sent his servants to you to search the city and to spy it out and to overthrow it?" ⁴So Hanun took David's servants and shaved off half the beard of each and cut off their garments in the middle, at their hips, and sent them away. ⁵When it was told David, he sent to meet them, for the men were greatly ashamed. And the king said, "Remain at Jericho until your beards have grown and then return."

⁶When the Ammonites saw that they had become a stench to David, the Ammonites sent and hired the Syrians of Beth-rehob, and the Syrians of Zobah, 20,000 foot soldiers, and the king of Maacah with 1,000 men, and the men of Tob, 12,000 men. ⁷And when David heard of it, he sent Joab and all the host of the mighty men. ⁸And the Ammonites came out and drew up in battle array at the entrance of the gate, and the Syrians of Zobah and of Rehob and the men of Tob and Maacah were by themselves in the open country.

⁹When Joab saw that the battle was set against him both in front and in the rear, he chose some of the best men of Israel and arrayed them against the Syrians. ¹⁰The rest of his men he put in the charge of Abishai his brother, and he arrayed them against the Ammonites. ¹¹And he said, "If the Syrians are too strong for me, then you shall help me, but if the Ammonites are too strong for you, then I will come and help you. ¹²Be of good courage, and let us be courageous for our people, and for the cities of our God, and may the LORD do what seems good to him." ¹³So Joab and the people who were with him drew near to battle against the Syrians, and they fled before him. ¹⁴And when the Ammonites saw that the Syrians fled, they likewise fled before Abishai and entered the city. Then Joab returned from fighting against the Ammonites and came to Jerusalem.

---

[a]Compare 20:23, 1 Chronicles 18:17, Syriac, Targum, Vulgate; Hebrew lacks *was over* [b]Septuagint; Hebrew *my* [c]Or *kindly*; twice in this verse

¹⁵But when the Syrians saw that they had been defeated by Israel, they gathered themselves together. ¹⁶And Hadadezer sent and brought out the Syrians who were beyond the Euphrates.[a] They came to Helam, with Shobach the commander of the army of Hadadezer at their head. ¹⁷And when it was told David, he gathered all Israel together and crossed the Jordan and came to Helam. The Syrians arrayed themselves against David and fought with him. ¹⁸And the Syrians fled before Israel, and David killed of the Syrians the men of 700 chariots, and 40,000 horsemen, and wounded Shobach the commander of their army, so that he died there. ¹⁹And when all the kings who were servants of Hadadezer saw that they had been defeated by Israel, they made peace with Israel and became subject to them. So the Syrians were afraid to save the Ammonites any more.

DAVID AND BATHSHEBA

11 In the spring of the year, the time when kings go out to battle, David sent Joab, and his servants with him, and all Israel. And they ravaged the Ammonites and besieged Rabbah. But David remained at Jerusalem.

²It happened, late one afternoon, when David arose from his couch and was walking on the roof of the king's house, that he saw from the roof a woman bathing; and the woman was very beautiful. ³And David sent and enquired about the woman. And one said, "Is not this Bathsheba, the daughter of Eliam, the wife of Uriah the Hittite?" ⁴So David sent messengers and took her, and she came to him, and he lay with her. (Now she had been purifying herself from her uncleanness.) Then she returned to her house. ⁵And the woman conceived, and she sent and told David, "I am pregnant."

⁶So David sent word to Joab, "Send me Uriah the Hittite." And Joab sent Uriah to David. ⁷When Uriah came to him, David asked how Joab was doing and how the people were doing and how the war was going. ⁸Then David said to Uriah, "Go down to your house and wash your feet." And Uriah went out of the king's house, and there followed him a present from the king. ⁹But Uriah slept at the door of the king's house with all the servants of his lord, and did not go down to his house. ¹⁰When they told David, "Uriah did not go down to his house", David said to Uriah, "Have you not come from a journey? Why did you not go down to your house?" ¹¹Uriah said to David, "The ark and Israel and Judah dwell in booths, and my lord Joab and the servants of my lord are camping in the open field. Shall I then go to my house, to eat and to drink and to lie with my wife? As you live, and as your soul lives, I will not do this thing." ¹²Then David said to Uriah, "Remain here today also, and tomorrow I will send you back." So Uriah remained in Jerusalem that day and the next. ¹³And David invited him, and he ate in his presence and drank, so that he made him drunk. And in the evening he went out to lie on his couch with the servants of his lord, but he did not go down to his house.

¹⁴In the morning David wrote a letter to Joab and sent it by the hand of Uriah. ¹⁵In the letter he wrote, "Set Uriah in the forefront of the hardest fighting, and then draw back from him, that he may be struck down, and die." ¹⁶And as Joab was besieging the city, he assigned Uriah to the place where he knew there were valiant men. ¹⁷And the men of the city came out and fought with Joab, and some of the servants of David among the people fell. Uriah the Hittite also died. ¹⁸Then Joab sent and told David all the news about the fighting. ¹⁹And he instructed the messenger, "When you have finished telling all the news about the fighting to the king, ²⁰then, if the king's anger rises, and if he says to you, 'Why did you go so near the city to fight? Did you not know that they would shoot from the wall? ²¹Who killed Abimelech the son of Jerubbesheth? Did not a woman cast an upper millstone on him from the wall, so that he died at Thebez? Why did you go so near the wall?' then you shall say, 'Your servant Uriah the Hittite is dead also.'"

²²So the messenger went and came and told David all that Joab had sent him to tell. ²³The messenger said to David, "The men gained an advantage over us and came out against us in the field, but we drove them back to the entrance of the gate. ²⁴Then the archers shot at your servants from the wall. Some of the king's servants are dead, and your servant Uriah the Hittite is dead also." ²⁵David said to the messenger, "Thus shall you say to Joab, 'Do not let this matter displease you, for the sword devours now one and now another. Strengthen your attack against the city and overthrow it.' And encourage him."

---

[a] Hebrew *the River*

²⁶When the wife of Uriah heard that Uriah her husband was dead, she lamented over her husband. ²⁷And when the mourning was over, David sent and brought her to his house, and she became his wife and bore him a son. But the thing that David had done displeased the LORD.

NATHAN REBUKES DAVID

12 And the LORD sent Nathan to David. He came to him and said to him, "There were two men in a certain city, one rich and the other poor. ²The rich man had very many flocks and herds, ³but the poor man had nothing but one little ewe lamb, which he had bought. And he brought it up, and it grew up with him and with his children. It used to eat of his morsel and drink from his cup and lie in his arms,ᵃ and it was like a daughter to him. ⁴Now there came a traveller to the rich man, and he was unwilling to take one of his own flock or herd to prepare for the guest who had come to him, but he took the poor man's lamb and prepared it for the man who had come to him." ⁵Then David's anger was greatly kindled against the man, and he said to Nathan, "As the LORD lives, the man who has done this deserves to die, ⁶and he shall restore the lamb fourfold, because he did this thing, and because he had no pity."

⁷Nathan said to David, "You are the man! Thus says the LORD, the God of Israel, 'I anointed you king over Israel, and I delivered you out of the hand of Saul. ⁸And I gave you your master's house and your master's wives into your arms and gave you the house of Israel and of Judah. And if this were too little, I would add to you as much more. ⁹Why have you despised the word of the LORD, to do what is evil in his sight? You have struck down Uriah the Hittite with the sword and have taken his wife to be your wife and have killed him with the sword of the Ammonites. ¹⁰Now therefore the sword shall never depart from your house, because you have despised me and have taken the wife of Uriah the Hittite to be your wife.' ¹¹Thus says the LORD, 'Behold, I will raise up evil against you out of your own house. And I will take your wives before your eyes and give them to your neighbour, and he shall lie with your wives in the sight of this sun. ¹²For you did it secretly, but I will do this thing before all Israel and before the sun.'"

¹³David said to Nathan, "I have sinned against the LORD." And Nathan said to David, "The LORD also has put away your sin; you shall not die. ¹⁴Nevertheless, because by this deed you have utterly scorned the LORD,ᵇ the child who is born to you shall die." ¹⁵Then Nathan went to his house.

DAVID'S CHILD DIES

And the LORD afflicted the child that Uriah's wife bore to David, and he became sick. ¹⁶David therefore sought God on behalf of the child. And David fasted and went in and lay all night on the ground. ¹⁷And the elders of his house stood beside him, to raise him from the ground, but he would not, nor did he eat food with them. ¹⁸On the seventh day the child died. And the servants of David were afraid to tell him that the child was dead, for they said, "Behold, while the child was yet alive, we spoke to him, and he did not listen to us. How then can we say to him the child is dead? He may do himself some harm." ¹⁹But when David saw that his servants were whispering together, David understood that the child was dead. And David said to his servants, "Is the child dead?" They said, "He is dead." ²⁰Then David arose from the earth and washed and anointed himself and changed his clothes. And he went into the house of the LORD and worshipped. He then went to his own house. And when he asked, they set food before him, and he ate. ²¹Then his servants said to him, "What is this thing that you have done? You fasted and wept for the child while he was alive; but when the child died, you arose and ate food." ²²He said, "While the child was still alive, I fasted and wept, for I said, 'Who knows whether the LORD will be gracious to me, that the child may live?' ²³But now he is dead. Why should I fast? Can I bring him back again? I shall go to him, but he will not return to me."

SOLOMON'S BIRTH

²⁴Then David comforted his wife, Bathsheba, and went in to her and lay with her, and she bore a son, and he called his name Solomon. And the LORD loved him ²⁵and sent a message by Nathan the prophet. So he called his name Jedidiah,ᶜ because of the LORD.

RABBAH IS CAPTURED

²⁶Now Joab fought against Rabbah of the Ammonites and took the royal city. ²⁷And Joab sent messengers to David and said, "I have

---

ᵃHebrew *bosom*; also verse 8 ᵇMasoretic Text *the enemies of the LORD*; Dead Sea Scroll *the word of the LORD* ᶜ*Jedidiah* means *beloved of the LORD*

fought against Rabbah; moreover, I have taken the city of waters. ²⁸Now then gather the rest of the people together and encamp against the city and take it, lest I take the city and it be called by my name." ²⁹So David gathered all the people together and went to Rabbah and fought against it and took it. ³⁰And he took the crown of their king from his head. The weight of it was a talent[a] of gold, and in it was a precious stone, and it was placed on David's head. And he brought out the spoil of the city, a very great amount. ³¹And he brought out the people who were in it and set them to labour with saws and iron picks and iron axes and made them toil at[b] the brick kilns. And thus he did to all the cities of the Ammonites. Then David and all the people returned to Jerusalem.

AMNON AND TAMAR

13 Now Absalom, David's son, had a beautiful sister, whose name was Tamar. And after a time Amnon, David's son, loved her. ²And Amnon was so tormented that he made himself ill because of his sister Tamar, for she was a virgin, and it seemed impossible to Amnon to do anything to her. ³But Amnon had a friend, whose name was Jonadab, the son of Shimeah, David's brother. And Jonadab was a very crafty man. ⁴And he said to him, "O son of the king, why are you so haggard morning after morning? Will you not tell me?" Amnon said to him, "I love Tamar, my brother Absalom's sister." ⁵Jonadab said to him, "Lie down on your bed and pretend to be ill. And when your father comes to see you, say to him, 'Let my sister Tamar come and give me bread to eat, and prepare the food in my sight, that I may see it and eat it from her hand.'" ⁶So Amnon lay down and pretended to be ill. And when the king came to see him, Amnon said to the king, "Please let my sister Tamar come and make a couple of cakes in my sight, that I may eat from her hand."

⁷Then David sent home to Tamar, saying, "Go to your brother Amnon's house and prepare food for him." ⁸So Tamar went to her brother Amnon's house, where he was lying down. And she took dough and kneaded it and made cakes in his sight and baked the cakes. ⁹And she took the pan and emptied it out before him, but he refused to eat. And Amnon said, "Send out everyone from me." So everyone went out from him. ¹⁰Then Amnon said to Tamar, "Bring the food into the chamber, that I may eat from your hand." And Tamar took the cakes she had made and brought them into the chamber to Amnon her brother. ¹¹But when she brought them near him to eat, he took hold of her and said to her, "Come, lie with me, my sister." ¹²She answered him, "No, my brother, do not violate[c] me, for such a thing is not done in Israel; do not do this outrageous thing. ¹³As for me, where could I carry my shame? And as for you, you would be as one of the outrageous fools in Israel. Now therefore, please speak to the king, for he will not withhold me from you." ¹⁴But he would not listen to her, and being stronger than she, he violated her and lay with her.

¹⁵Then Amnon hated her with very great hatred, so that the hatred with which he hated her was greater than the love with which he had loved her. And Amnon said to her, "Get up! Go!" ¹⁶But she said to him, "No, my brother, for this wrong in sending me away is greater than the other that you did to me."[d] But he would not listen to her. ¹⁷He called the young man who served him and said, "Put this woman out of my presence and bolt the door after her." ¹⁸Now she was wearing a long robe with sleeves,[e] for thus were the virgin daughters of the king dressed. So his servant put her out and bolted the door after her. ¹⁹And Tamar put ashes on her head and tore the long robe that she wore. And she laid her hand on her head and went away, crying aloud as she went.

²⁰And her brother Absalom said to her, "Has Amnon your brother been with you? Now hold your peace, my sister. He is your brother; do not take this to heart." So Tamar lived, a desolate woman, in her brother Absalom's house. ²¹When King David heard of all these things, he was very angry.[f] ²²But Absalom spoke to Amnon neither good nor bad, for Absalom hated Amnon, because he had violated his sister Tamar.

ABSALOM MURDERS AMNON

²³After two full years Absalom had sheepshearers at Baal-hazor, which is near Ephraim, and Absalom invited all the king's sons. ²⁴And Absalom came to the king and

---

[a] A *talent* was about 75 pounds or 34 kilograms [b] Hebrew *pass through* [c] Or *humiliate*; also verses 14, 22, 32 [d] Compare Septuagint, Vulgate; the meaning of the Hebrew is uncertain [e] Or *a robe of many colours* (compare Genesis 37:3); compare *long robe*, verse 19 [f] Dead Sea Scroll, Septuagint add *But he would not punish his son Amnon, because he loved him, since he was his firstborn*

said, "Behold, your servant has sheep shearers. Please let the king and his servants go with your servant." ²⁵But the king said to Absalom, "No, my son, let us not all go, lest we be burdensome to you." He pressed him, but he would not go but gave him his blessing. ²⁶Then Absalom said, "If not, please let my brother Amnon go with us." And the king said to him, "Why should he go with you?" ²⁷But Absalom pressed him until he let Amnon and all the king's sons go with him. ²⁸Then Absalom commanded his servants, "Mark when Amnon's heart is merry with wine, and when I say to you, 'Strike Amnon', then kill him. Do not fear; have I not commanded you? Be courageous and be valiant." ²⁹So the servants of Absalom did to Amnon as Absalom had commanded. Then all the king's sons arose, and each mounted his mule and fled.

³⁰While they were on the way, news came to David, "Absalom has struck down all the king's sons, and not one of them is left." ³¹Then the king arose and tore his garments and lay on the earth. And all his servants who were standing by tore their garments. ³²But Jonadab the son of Shimeah, David's brother, said, "Let not my lord suppose that they have killed all the young men, the king's sons, for Amnon alone is dead. For by the command of Absalom this has been determined from the day he violated his sister Tamar. ³³Now therefore let not my lord the king so take it to heart as to suppose that all the king's sons are dead, for Amnon alone is dead."

ABSALOM FLEES TO GESHUR

³⁴But Absalom fled. And the young man who kept the watch lifted up his eyes and looked, and behold, many people were coming from the road behind him*ᵃ* by the side of the mountain. ³⁵And Jonadab said to the king, "Behold, the king's sons have come; as your servant said, so it has come about." ³⁶And as soon as he had finished speaking, behold, the king's sons came and lifted up their voice and wept. And the king also and all his servants wept very bitterly.

³⁷But Absalom fled and went to Talmai the son of Ammihud, king of Geshur. And David mourned for his son day after day. ³⁸So Absalom fled and went to Geshur, and was there for three years. ³⁹And the spirit of the king*ᵇ* longed to go out*ᶜ* to Absalom, because he was comforted about Amnon, since he was dead.

ABSALOM RETURNS TO JERUSALEM

14 Now Joab the son of Zeruiah knew that the king's heart went out to Absalom. ²And Joab sent to Tekoa and brought from there a wise woman and said to her, "Pretend to be a mourner and put on mourning garments. Do not anoint yourself with oil, but behave like a woman who has been mourning many days for the dead. ³Go to the king and speak thus to him." So Joab put the words in her mouth.

⁴When the woman of Tekoa came to the king, she fell on her face to the ground and paid homage and said, "Save me, O king." ⁵And the king said to her, "What is your trouble?" She answered, "Alas, I am a widow; my husband is dead. ⁶And your servant had two sons, and they quarrelled with one another in the field. There was no one to separate them, and one struck the other and killed him. ⁷And now the whole clan has risen against your servant, and they say, 'Give up the man who struck his brother, that we may put him to death for the life of his brother whom he killed.' And so they would destroy the heir also. Thus they would quench my coal that is left and leave to my husband neither name nor remnant on the face of the earth."

⁸Then the king said to the woman, "Go to your house, and I will give orders concerning you." ⁹And the woman of Tekoa said to the king, "On me be the guilt, my lord the king, and on my father's house; let the king and his throne be guiltless." ¹⁰The king said, "If anyone says anything to you, bring him to me, and he shall never touch you again." ¹¹Then she said, "Please let the king invoke the LORD your God, that the avenger of blood kill no more, and my son be not destroyed." He said, "As the LORD lives, not one hair of your son shall fall to the ground."

¹²Then the woman said, "Please let your servant speak a word to my lord the king." He said, "Speak." ¹³And the woman said, "Why then have you planned such a thing against the people of God? For in giving this decision the king convicts himself, inasmuch as the king does not bring his banished one home again. ¹⁴We must all die; we are like water spilled on the ground, which cannot be gathered up again. But God will not take away life, and he devises means so that the banished one will not remain an outcast. ¹⁵Now I have

---

*ᵃ*Septuagint *the Horonaim Road* *ᵇ*Dead Sea Scroll, Septuagint; Hebrew *David* *ᶜ*Compare Vulgate *ceased to go out*

come to say this to my lord the king because the people have made me afraid, and your servant thought, 'I will speak to the king; it may be that the king will perform the request of his servant. ¹⁶For the king will hear and deliver his servant from the hand of the man who would destroy me and my son together from the heritage of God.' ¹⁷And your servant thought, 'The word of my lord the king will set me at rest', for my lord the king is like the angel of God to discern good and evil. The LORD your God be with you!"

¹⁸Then the king answered the woman, "Do not hide from me anything I ask you." And the woman said, "Let my lord the king speak." ¹⁹The king said, "Is the hand of Joab with you in all this?" The woman answered and said, "As surely as you live, my lord the king, one cannot turn to the right hand or to the left from anything that my lord the king has said. It was your servant Joab who commanded me; it was he who put all these words in the mouth of your servant. ²⁰In order to change the course of things your servant Joab did this. But my lord has wisdom like the wisdom of the angel of God to know all things that are on the earth."

²¹Then the king said to Joab, "Behold now, I grant this; go, bring back the young man Absalom." ²²And Joab fell on his face to the ground and paid homage and blessed the king. And Joab said, "Today your servant knows that I have found favour in your sight, my lord the king, in that the king has granted the request of his servant." ²³So Joab arose and went to Geshur and brought Absalom to Jerusalem. ²⁴And the king said, "Let him dwell apart in his own house; he is not to come into my presence." So Absalom lived apart in his own house and did not come into the king's presence.

²⁵Now in all Israel there was no one so much to be praised for his handsome appearance as Absalom. From the sole of his foot to the crown of his head there was no blemish in him. ²⁶And when he cut the hair of his head (for at the end of every year he used to cut it; when it was heavy on him, he cut it), he weighed the hair of his head, two hundred shekels[a] by the king's weight. ²⁷There were born to Absalom three sons, and one daughter whose name was Tamar. She was a beautiful woman.

²⁸So Absalom lived for two full years in Jerusalem, without coming into the king's presence. ²⁹Then Absalom sent for Joab, to send him to the king, but Joab would not come to him. And he sent a second time, but Joab would not come. ³⁰Then he said to his servants, "See, Joab's field is next to mine, and he has barley there; go and set it on fire." So Absalom's servants set the field on fire.[b] ³¹Then Joab arose and went to Absalom at his house and said to him, "Why have your servants set my field on fire?" ³²Absalom answered Joab, "Behold, I sent word to you, 'Come here, that I may send you to the king, to ask, "Why have I come from Geshur? It would be better for me to be there still." Now therefore let me go into the presence of the king, and if there is guilt in me, let him put me to death.'" ³³Then Joab went to the king and told him, and he summoned Absalom. So he came to the king and bowed himself with his face to the ground before the king, and the king kissed Absalom.

ABSALOM'S CONSPIRACY

15 After this Absalom got himself a chariot and horses, and fifty men to run before him. ²And Absalom used to rise early and stand beside the way of the gate. And when any man had a dispute to come before the king for judgement, Absalom would call to him and say, "From what city are you?" And when he said, "Your servant is of such and such a tribe in Israel", ³Absalom would say to him, "See, your claims are good and right, but there is no man designated by the king to hear you." ⁴Then Absalom would say, "Oh that I were judge in the land! Then every man with a dispute or cause might come to me, and I would give him justice." ⁵And whenever a man came near to pay homage to him, he would put out his hand and take hold of him and kiss him. ⁶Thus Absalom did to all of Israel who came to the king for judgement. So Absalom stole the hearts of the men of Israel.

⁷And at the end of four[c] years Absalom said to the king, "Please let me go and pay my vow, which I have vowed to the LORD, in Hebron. ⁸For your servant vowed a vow while I lived at Geshur in Aram, saying, 'If the LORD will indeed bring me back to Jerusalem, then I will offer worship to[d] the LORD.'" ⁹The king said to him, "Go in peace." So he arose and went to Hebron. ¹⁰But Absalom sent secret

---

[a] A *shekel* was about 2/5 of an ounce or 11 grams   [b] Septuagint, Dead Sea Scroll add *So Joab's servants came to him with their clothes torn, and they said to him, "The servants of Absalom have set your field on fire."*
[c] Septuagint, Syriac; Hebrew *forty*   [d] Or *will serve*

messengers throughout all the tribes of Israel, saying, "As soon as you hear the sound of the trumpet, then say, 'Absalom is king at Hebron!'" ¹¹With Absalom went two hundred men from Jerusalem who were invited guests, and they went in their innocence and knew nothing. ¹²And while Absalom was offering the sacrifices, he sent for[a] Ahithophel the Gilonite, David's counsellor, from his city Giloh. And the conspiracy grew strong, and the people with Absalom kept increasing.

DAVID FLEES JERUSALEM

¹³And a messenger came to David, saying, "The hearts of the men of Israel have gone after Absalom." ¹⁴Then David said to all his servants who were with him at Jerusalem, "Arise, and let us flee, or else there will be no escape for us from Absalom. Go quickly, lest he overtake us quickly and bring down ruin on us and strike the city with the edge of the sword." ¹⁵And the king's servants said to the king, "Behold, your servants are ready to do whatever my lord the king decides." ¹⁶So the king went out, and all his household after him. And the king left ten concubines to keep the house. ¹⁷And the king went out, and all the people after him. And they halted at the last house.

¹⁸And all his servants passed by him, and all the Cherethites, and all the Pelethites, and all the six hundred Gittites who had followed him from Gath, passed on before the king. ¹⁹Then the king said to Ittai the Gittite, "Why do you also go with us? Go back and stay with the king, for you are a foreigner and also an exile from your home. ²⁰You came only yesterday, and shall I today make you wander about with us, since I go I know not where? Go back and take your brothers with you, and may the LORD show[b] steadfast love and faithfulness to you." ²¹But Ittai answered the king, "As the LORD lives, and as my lord the king lives, wherever my lord the king shall be, whether for death or for life, there also will your servant be." ²²And David said to Ittai, "Go then, pass on." So Ittai the Gittite passed on with all his men and all the little ones who were with him. ²³And all the land wept aloud as all the people passed by, and the king crossed the brook Kidron, and all the people passed on towards the wilderness.

²⁴And Abiathar came up, and behold, Zadok came also with all the Levites, bearing the ark of the covenant of God. And they set down the ark of God until the people had all passed out of the city. ²⁵Then the king said to Zadok, "Carry the ark of God back into the city. If I find favour in the eyes of the LORD, he will bring me back and let me see both it and his dwelling place. ²⁶But if he says, 'I have no pleasure in you', behold, here I am, let him do to me what seems good to him." ²⁷The king also said to Zadok the priest, "Are you not a seer? Go back[c] to the city in peace, with your two sons, Ahimaaz your son, and Jonathan the son of Abiathar. ²⁸See, I will wait at the fords of the wilderness until word comes from you to inform me." ²⁹So Zadok and Abiathar carried the ark of God back to Jerusalem, and they remained there.

³⁰But David went up the ascent of the Mount of Olives, weeping as he went, barefoot and with his head covered. And all the people who were with him covered their heads, and they went up, weeping as they went. ³¹And it was told David, "Ahithophel is among the conspirators with Absalom." And David said, "O LORD, please turn the counsel of Ahithophel into foolishness."

³²While David was coming to the summit, where God was worshipped, behold, Hushai the Archite came to meet him with his coat torn and dirt on his head. ³³David said to him, "If you go on with me, you will be a burden to me. ³⁴But if you return to the city and say to Absalom, 'I will be your servant, O king; as I have been your father's servant in time past, so now I will be your servant', then you will defeat for me the counsel of Ahithophel. ³⁵Are not Zadok and Abiathar the priests with you there? So whatever you hear from the king's house, tell it to Zadok and Abiathar the priests. ³⁶Behold, their two sons are with them there, Ahimaaz, Zadok's son, and Jonathan, Abiathar's son, and by them you shall send to me everything you hear." ³⁷So Hushai, David's friend, came into the city, just as Absalom was entering Jerusalem.

DAVID AND ZIBA

16 When David had passed a little beyond the summit, Ziba the servant of Mephibosheth met him, with a couple of donkeys saddled, bearing two hundred loaves of bread, a hundred bunches of raisins, a hundred of summer fruits, and a skin of wine. ²And the king said to Ziba, "Why have you brought these?" Ziba answered, "The

---

[a]Or *sent* [b]Septuagint; Hebrew lacks *may the LORD show*
[c]Septuagint *The king also said to Zadok the priest, "Look, go back*

donkeys are for the king's household to ride on, the bread and summer fruit for the young men to eat, and the wine for those who faint in the wilderness to drink." ³And the king said, "And where is your master's son?" Ziba said to the king, "Behold, he remains in Jerusalem, for he said, 'Today the house of Israel will give me back the kingdom of my father.'" ⁴Then the king said to Ziba, "Behold, all that belonged to Mephibosheth is now yours." And Ziba said, "I pay homage; let me ever find favour in your sight, my lord the king."

SHIMEI CURSES DAVID

⁵When King David came to Bahurim, there came out a man of the family of the house of Saul, whose name was Shimei, the son of Gera, and as he came he cursed continually. ⁶And he threw stones at David and at all the servants of King David, and all the people and all the mighty men were on his right hand and on his left. ⁷And Shimei said as he cursed, "Get out, get out, you man of blood, you worthless man! ⁸The LORD has avenged on you all the blood of the house of Saul, in whose place you have reigned, and the LORD has given the kingdom into the hand of your son Absalom. See, your evil is on you, for you are a man of blood."

⁹Then Abishai the son of Zeruiah said to the king, "Why should this dead dog curse my lord the king? Let me go over and take off his head." ¹⁰But the king said, "What have I to do with you, you sons of Zeruiah? If he is cursing because the LORD has said to him, 'Curse David', who then shall say, 'Why have you done so?'" ¹¹And David said to Abishai and to all his servants, "Behold, my own son seeks my life; how much more now may this Benjaminite! Leave him alone, and let him curse, for the LORD has told him to. ¹²It may be that the LORD will look on the wrong done to me,[a] and that the LORD will repay me with good for his cursing today." ¹³So David and his men went on the road, while Shimei went along on the hillside opposite him and cursed as he went and threw stones at him and flung dust. ¹⁴And the king, and all the people who were with him, arrived weary at the Jordan.[b] And there he refreshed himself.

ABSALOM ENTERS JERUSALEM

¹⁵Now Absalom and all the people, the men of Israel, came to Jerusalem, and Ahithophel with him. ¹⁶And when Hushai the Archite, David's friend, came to Absalom, Hushai said to Absalom, "Long live the king! Long live the king!" ¹⁷And Absalom said to Hushai, "Is this your loyalty to your friend? Why did you not go with your friend?" ¹⁸And Hushai said to Absalom, "No, for whom the LORD and this people and all the men of Israel have chosen, his I will be, and with him I will remain. ¹⁹And again, whom should I serve? Should it not be his son? As I have served your father, so I will serve you."

²⁰Then Absalom said to Ahithophel, "Give your counsel. What shall we do?" ²¹Ahithophel said to Absalom, "Go in to your father's concubines, whom he has left to keep the house, and all Israel will hear that you have made yourself a stench to your father, and the hands of all who are with you will be strengthened." ²²So they pitched a tent for Absalom on the roof. And Absalom went in to his father's concubines in the sight of all Israel. ²³Now in those days the counsel that Ahithophel gave was as if one consulted the word of God; so was all the counsel of Ahithophel esteemed, both by David and by Absalom.

HUSHAI SAVES DAVID

17 Moreover, Ahithophel said to Absalom, "Let me choose twelve thousand men, and I will arise and pursue David tonight. ²I will come upon him while he is weary and discouraged and throw him into a panic, and all the people who are with him will flee. I will strike down only the king, ³and I will bring all the people back to you as a bride comes home to her husband. You seek the life of only one man,[c] and all the people will be at peace." ⁴And the advice seemed right in the eyes of Absalom and all the elders of Israel.

⁵Then Absalom said, "Call Hushai the Archite also, and let us hear what he has to say." ⁶And when Hushai came to Absalom, Absalom said to him, "Thus has Ahithophel spoken; shall we do as he says? If not, you speak." ⁷Then Hushai said to Absalom, "This time the counsel that Ahithophel has given is not good." ⁸Hushai said, "You know that your father and his men are mighty men, and that they are enraged,[d] like a bear robbed of her cubs in the field. Besides, your father is experienced in war; he will not spend the night with the people. ⁹Behold, even now he has hidden himself in one of the pits or

---

[a]Septuagint, Vulgate *will look upon my affliction* [b]Septuagint; Hebrew lacks *at the Jordan* [c]Septuagint; Hebrew *back to you. Like the return of the whole is the man whom you seek* [d]Hebrew *bitter of soul*

in some other place. And as soon as some of the people fall[a] at the first attack, whoever hears it will say, 'There has been a slaughter among the people who follow Absalom.' ¹⁰Then even the valiant man, whose heart is like the heart of a lion, will utterly melt with fear, for all Israel knows that your father is a mighty man, and that those who are with him are valiant men. ¹¹But my counsel is that all Israel be gathered to you, from Dan to Beersheba, as the sand by the sea for multitude, and that you go to battle in person. ¹²So we shall come upon him in some place where he is to be found, and we shall light upon him as the dew falls on the ground, and of him and all the men with him not one will be left. ¹³If he withdraws into a city, then all Israel will bring ropes to that city, and we shall drag it into the valley, until not even a pebble is to be found there." ¹⁴And Absalom and all the men of Israel said, "The counsel of Hushai the Archite is better than the counsel of Ahithophel." For the LORD had ordained[b] to defeat the good counsel of Ahithophel, so that the LORD might bring harm upon Absalom.

¹⁵Then Hushai said to Zadok and Abiathar the priests, "Thus and so did Ahithophel counsel Absalom and the elders of Israel, and thus and so have I counselled. ¹⁶Now therefore send quickly and tell David, 'Do not stay tonight at the fords of the wilderness, but by all means pass over, lest the king and all the people who are with him be swallowed up.'" ¹⁷Now Jonathan and Ahimaaz were waiting at En-rogel. A female servant was to go and tell them, and they were to go and tell King David, for they were not to be seen entering the city. ¹⁸But a young man saw them and told Absalom. So both of them went away quickly and came to the house of a man at Bahurim, who had a well in his courtyard. And they went down into it. ¹⁹And the woman took and spread a covering over the well's mouth and scattered grain on it, and nothing was known of it. ²⁰When Absalom's servants came to the woman at the house, they said, "Where are Ahimaaz and Jonathan?" And the woman said to them, "They have gone over the brook[c] of water." And when they had sought and could not find them, they returned to Jerusalem.

²¹After they had gone, the men came up out of the well, and went and told King David. They said to David, "Arise, and go quickly over the water, for thus and so has Ahithophel counselled against you." ²²Then David arose, and all the people who were with him, and they crossed the Jordan. By daybreak not one was left who had not crossed the Jordan.

²³When Ahithophel saw that his counsel was not followed, he saddled his donkey and went off home to his own city. He set his house in order and hanged himself, and he died and was buried in the tomb of his father.

²⁴Then David came to Mahanaim. And Absalom crossed the Jordan with all the men of Israel. ²⁵Now Absalom had set Amasa over the army instead of Joab. Amasa was the son of a man named Ithra the Ishmaelite,[d] who had married Abigal the daughter of Nahash, sister of Zeruiah, Joab's mother. ²⁶And Israel and Absalom encamped in the land of Gilead.

²⁷When David came to Mahanaim, Shobi the son of Nahash from Rabbah of the Ammonites, and Machir the son of Ammiel from Lo-debar, and Barzillai the Gileadite from Rogelim, ²⁸brought beds, basins, and earthen vessels, wheat, barley, flour, parched grain, beans and lentils,[e] ²⁹honey and curds and sheep and cheese from the herd, for David and the people with him to eat, for they said, "The people are hungry and weary and thirsty in the wilderness."

ABSALOM KILLED

18 Then David mustered the men who were with him and set over them commanders of thousands and commanders of hundreds. ²And David sent out the army, one third under the command of Joab, one third under the command of Abishai the son of Zeruiah, Joab's brother, and one third under the command of Ittai the Gittite. And the king said to the men, "I myself will also go out with you." ³But the men said, "You shall not go out. For if we flee, they will not care about us. If half of us die, they will not care about us. But you are worth ten thousand of us. Therefore it is better that you send us help from the city." ⁴The king said to them, "Whatever seems best to you I will do." So the king stood at the side of the gate, while all the army marched out by hundreds and by thousands. ⁵And the king ordered Joab and Abishai and Ittai, "Deal gently for my sake with the young man Absalom." And all the people heard when the king gave orders to all the commanders about Absalom.

---

[a] Or *And as he falls on them* [b] Hebrew *commanded* [c] The meaning of the Hebrew word is uncertain [d] Compare 1 Chronicles 2:17; Hebrew *Israelite* [e] Hebrew adds *and parched grain*

⁶So the army went out into the field against Israel, and the battle was fought in the forest of Ephraim. ⁷And the men of Israel were defeated there by the servants of David, and the loss there was great on that day, twenty thousand men. ⁸The battle spread over the face of all the country, and the forest devoured more people that day than the sword.

⁹And Absalom happened to meet the servants of David. Absalom was riding on his mule, and the mule went under the thick branches of a great oak,[a] and his head caught fast in the oak, and he was suspended between heaven and earth, while the mule that was under him went on. ¹⁰And a certain man saw it and told Joab, "Behold, I saw Absalom hanging in an oak." ¹¹Joab said to the man who told him, "What, you saw him! Why then did you not strike him there to the ground? I would have been glad to give you ten pieces of silver and a belt." ¹²But the man said to Joab, "Even if I felt in my hand the weight of a thousand pieces of silver, I would not reach out my hand against the king's son, for in our hearing the king commanded you and Abishai and Ittai, 'For my sake protect the young man Absalom.' ¹³On the other hand, if I had dealt treacherously against his life[b] (and there is nothing hidden from the king), then you yourself would have stood aloof." ¹⁴Joab said, "I will not waste time like this with you." And he took three javelins in his hand and thrust them into the heart of Absalom while he was still alive in the oak. ¹⁵And ten young men, Joab's armour bearers, surrounded Absalom and struck him and killed him.

¹⁶Then Joab blew the trumpet, and the troops came back from pursuing Israel, for Joab restrained them. ¹⁷And they took Absalom and threw him into a great pit in the forest and raised over him a very great heap of stones. And all Israel fled every one to his own home. ¹⁸Now Absalom in his lifetime had taken and set up for himself the pillar that is in the King's Valley, for he said, "I have no son to keep my name in remembrance." He called the pillar after his own name, and it is called Absalom's monument[c] to this day.

DAVID HEARS OF ABSALOM'S DEATH

¹⁹Then Ahimaaz the son of Zadok said, "Let me run and carry news to the king that the LORD has delivered him from the hand of his enemies." ²⁰And Joab said to him, "You are not to carry news today. You may carry news another day, but today you shall carry no news, because the king's son is dead." ²¹Then Joab said to the Cushite, "Go, tell the king what you have seen." The Cushite bowed before Joab, and ran. ²²Then Ahimaaz the son of Zadok said again to Joab, "Come what may, let me also run after the Cushite." And Joab said, "Why will you run, my son, seeing that you will have no reward for the news?" ²³"Come what may," he said, "I will run." So he said to him, "Run." Then Ahimaaz ran by the way of the plain, and outran the Cushite.

²⁴Now David was sitting between the two gates, and the watchman went up to the roof of the gate by the wall, and when he lifted up his eyes and looked, he saw a man running alone. ²⁵The watchman called out and told the king. And the king said, "If he is alone, there is news in his mouth." And he drew nearer and nearer. ²⁶The watchman saw another man running. And the watchman called to the gate and said, "See, another man running alone!" The king said, "He also brings news." ²⁷The watchman said, "I think the running of the first is like the running of Ahimaaz the son of Zadok." And the king said, "He is a good man and comes with good news."

²⁸Then Ahimaaz cried out to the king, "All is well." And he bowed before the king with his face to the earth and said, "Blessed be the LORD your God, who has delivered up the men who raised their hand against my lord the king." ²⁹And the king said, "Is it well with the young man Absalom?" Ahimaaz answered, "When Joab sent the king's servant, your servant, I saw a great commotion, but I do not know what it was." ³⁰And the king said, "Turn aside and stand here." So he turned aside and stood still.

DAVID'S GRIEF

³¹And behold, the Cushite came, and the Cushite said, "Good news for my lord the king! For the LORD has delivered you this day from the hand of all who rose up against you." ³²The king said to the Cushite, "Is it well with the young man Absalom?" And the Cushite answered, "May the enemies of my lord the king and all who rise up against you for evil be like that young man." ³³[d] And the king was deeply moved and went up to the chamber over the gate and wept. And as he went, he said, "O my son Absalom, my son, my son Absalom! Would that I had died instead of you, O Absalom, my son, my son!"

---

[a]Or *terebinth*; also verses 10, 14   [b]Or *at the risk of my life*
[c]Or *Absalom's hand*   [d]Ch 19:1 in Hebrew

JOAB REBUKES DAVID

19 It was told Joab, "Behold, the king is weeping and mourning for Absalom." ²So the victory that day was turned into mourning for all the people, for the people heard that day, "The king is grieving for his son." ³And the people stole into the city that day as people steal in who are ashamed when they flee in battle. ⁴The king covered his face, and the king cried with a loud voice, "O my son Absalom, O Absalom, my son, my son!" ⁵Then Joab came into the house to the king and said, "You have today covered with shame the faces of all your servants, who have this day saved your life and the lives of your sons and your daughters and the lives of your wives and your concubines, ⁶because you love those who hate you and hate those who love you. For you have made it clear today that commanders and servants are nothing to you, for today I know that if Absalom were alive and all of us were dead today, then you would be pleased. ⁷Now therefore arise, go out and speak kindly to your servants, for I swear by the LORD, if you do not go, not a man will stay with you this night, and this will be worse for you than all the evil that has come upon you from your youth until now." ⁸Then the king arose and took his seat in the gate. And the people were all told, "Behold, the king is sitting in the gate." And all the people came before the king.

DAVID RETURNS TO JERUSALEM

Now Israel had fled every man to his own home. ⁹And all the people were arguing throughout all the tribes of Israel, saying, "The king delivered us from the hand of our enemies and saved us from the hand of the Philistines, and now he has fled out of the land from Absalom. ¹⁰But Absalom, whom we anointed over us, is dead in battle. Now therefore why do you say nothing about bringing the king back?"

¹¹And King David sent this message to Zadok and Abiathar the priests: "Say to the elders of Judah, 'Why should you be the last to bring the king back to his house, when the word of all Israel has come to the king?ᵃ ¹²You are my brothers; you are my bone and my flesh. Why then should you be the last to bring back the king?' ¹³And say to Amasa, 'Are you not my bone and my flesh? God do so to me and more also, if you are not commander of my army from now on in place of Joab.'" ¹⁴And he swayed the heart of all the men of Judah as one man, so that they sent word to the king, "Return, both you and all your servants." ¹⁵So the king came back to the Jordan, and Judah came to Gilgal to meet the king and to bring the king over the Jordan.

DAVID PARDONS HIS ENEMIES

¹⁶And Shimei the son of Gera, the Benjaminite, from Bahurim, hurried to come down with the men of Judah to meet King David. ¹⁷And with him were a thousand men from Benjamin. And Ziba the servant of the house of Saul, with his fifteen sons and his twenty servants, rushed down to the Jordan before the king, ¹⁸and they crossed the ford to bring over the king's household and to do his pleasure. And Shimei the son of Gera fell down before the king, as he was about to cross the Jordan, ¹⁹and said to the king, "Let not my lord hold me guilty or remember how your servant did wrong on the day my lord the king left Jerusalem. Do not let the king take it to heart. ²⁰For your servant knows that I have sinned. Therefore, behold, I have come this day, the first of all the house of Joseph to come down to meet my lord the king." ²¹Abishai the son of Zeruiah answered, "Shall not Shimei be put to death for this, because he cursed the LORD's anointed?" ²²But David said, "What have I to do with you, you sons of Zeruiah, that you should this day be as an adversary to me? Shall anyone be put to death in Israel this day? For do I not know that I am this day king over Israel?" ²³And the king said to Shimei, "You shall not die." And the king gave him his oath.

²⁴And Mephibosheth the son of Saul came down to meet the king. He had neither taken care of his feet nor trimmed his beard nor washed his clothes, from the day the king departed until the day he came back in safety. ²⁵And when he came to Jerusalem to meet the king, the king said to him, "Why did you not go with me, Mephibosheth?" ²⁶He answered, "My lord, O king, my servant deceived me, for your servant said to him, 'I will saddle a donkey for myself,ᵇ that I may ride on it and go with the king.' For your servant is lame. ²⁷He has slandered your servant to my lord the king. But my lord the king is like the angel of God; do therefore what seems good to you. ²⁸For all my father's house were but men doomed to death before my lord the king,

---

ᵃSeptuagint; Hebrew *to the king, to his house* ᵇSeptuagint, Syriac, Vulgate *Saddle a donkey for me*

but you set your servant among those who eat at your table. What further right have I, then, to cry to the king?" ²⁹And the king said to him, "Why speak any more of your affairs? I have decided: you and Ziba shall divide the land." ³⁰And Mephibosheth said to the king, "Oh, let him take it all, since my lord the king has come safely home."

³¹Now Barzillai the Gileadite had come down from Rogelim, and he went on with the king to the Jordan, to escort him over the Jordan. ³²Barzillai was a very aged man, eighty years old. He had provided the king with food while he stayed at Mahanaim, for he was a very wealthy man. ³³And the king said to Barzillai, "Come over with me, and I will provide for you with me in Jerusalem." ³⁴But Barzillai said to the king, "How many years have I still to live, that I should go up with the king to Jerusalem? ³⁵I am this day eighty years old. Can I discern what is pleasant and what is not? Can your servant taste what he eats or what he drinks? Can I still listen to the voice of singing men and singing women? Why then should your servant be an added burden to my lord the king? ³⁶Your servant will go a little way over the Jordan with the king. Why should the king repay me with such a reward? ³⁷Please let your servant return, that I may die in my own city near the grave of my father and my mother. But here is your servant Chimham. Let him go over with my lord the king, and do for him whatever seems good to you." ³⁸And the king answered, "Chimham shall go over with me, and I will do for him whatever seems good to you, and all that you desire of me I will do for you." ³⁹Then all the people went over the Jordan, and the king went over. And the king kissed Barzillai and blessed him, and he returned to his own home. ⁴⁰The king went on to Gilgal, and Chimham went on with him. All the people of Judah, and also half the people of Israel, brought the king on his way.

⁴¹Then all the men of Israel came to the king and said to the king, "Why have our brothers the men of Judah stolen you away and brought the king and his household over the Jordan, and all David's men with him?" ⁴²All the men of Judah answered the men of Israel, "Because the king is our close relative. Why then are you angry over this matter? Have we eaten at all at the king's expense? Or has he given us any gift?" ⁴³And the men of Israel answered the men of Judah, "We have ten shares in the king, and in David also we have more than you. Why then did you despise us? Were we not the first to speak of bringing back our king?" But the words of the men of Judah were fiercer than the words of the men of Israel.

THE REBELLION OF SHEBA

20 Now there happened to be there a worthless man, whose name was Sheba, the son of Bichri, a Benjaminite. And he blew the trumpet and said,

"We have no portion in David,
  and we have no inheritance
    in the son of Jesse;
  every man to his tents, O Israel!"

²So all the men of Israel withdrew from David and followed Sheba the son of Bichri. But the men of Judah followed their king steadfastly from the Jordan to Jerusalem.

³And David came to his house at Jerusalem. And the king took the ten concubines whom he had left to care for the house and put them in a house under guard and provided for them, but did not go in to them. So they were shut up until the day of their death, living as if in widowhood.

⁴Then the king said to Amasa, "Call the men of Judah together to me within three days, and be here yourself." ⁵So Amasa went to summon Judah, but he delayed beyond the set time that had been appointed him. ⁶And David said to Abishai, "Now Sheba the son of Bichri will do us more harm than Absalom. Take your lord's servants and pursue him, lest he get himself to fortified cities and escape from us."[a] ⁷And there went out after him Joab's men and the Cherethites and the Pelethites, and all the mighty men. They went out from Jerusalem to pursue Sheba the son of Bichri. ⁸When they were at the great stone that is in Gibeon, Amasa came to meet them. Now Joab was wearing a soldier's garment, and over it was a belt with a sword in its sheath fastened on his thigh, and as he went forward it fell out. ⁹And Joab said to Amasa, "Is it well with you, my brother?" And Joab took Amasa by the beard with his right hand to kiss him. ¹⁰But Amasa did not observe the sword that was in Joab's hand. So Joab struck him with it in the stomach and spilled his entrails to the ground without striking a second blow, and he died.

---

[a] Hebrew *and snatch away our eyes*

Then Joab and Abishai his brother pursued Sheba the son of Bichri. ¹¹And one of Joab's young men took his stand by Amasa and said, "Whoever favours Joab, and whoever is for David, let him follow Joab." ¹²And Amasa lay wallowing in his blood in the highway. And anyone who came by, seeing him, stopped. And when the man saw that all the people stopped, he carried Amasa out of the highway into the field and threw a garment over him. ¹³When he was taken out of the highway, all the people went on after Joab to pursue Sheba the son of Bichri.

¹⁴And Sheba passed through all the tribes of Israel to Abel of Beth-maacah,ᵃ and all the Bichritesᵇ assembled and followed him in. ¹⁵And all the men who were with Joab came and besieged him in Abel of Beth-maacah. They cast up a mound against the city, and it stood against the rampart, and they were battering the wall to throw it down. ¹⁶Then a wise woman called from the city, "Listen! Listen! Tell Joab, 'Come here, that I may speak to you.' " ¹⁷And he came near her, and the woman said, "Are you Joab?" He answered, "I am." Then she said to him, "Listen to the words of your servant." And he answered, "I am listening." ¹⁸Then she said, "They used to say in former times, 'Let them but ask counsel at Abel', and so they settled a matter. ¹⁹I am one of those who are peaceable and faithful in Israel. You seek to destroy a city that is a mother in Israel. Why will you swallow up the heritage of the LORD?" ²⁰Joab answered, "Far be it from me, far be it, that I should swallow up or destroy! ²¹That is not true. But a man of the hill country of Ephraim, called Sheba the son of Bichri, has lifted up his hand against King David. Give up him alone, and I will withdraw from the city." And the woman said to Joab, "Behold, his head shall be thrown to you over the wall." ²²Then the woman went to all the people in her wisdom. And they cut off the head of Sheba the son of Bichri and threw it out to Joab. So he blew the trumpet, and they dispersed from the city, every man to his home. And Joab returned to Jerusalem to the king.

²³Now Joab was in command of all the army of Israel; and Benaiah the son of Jehoiada was in command of the Cherethites and the Pelethites; ²⁴and Adoram was in charge of the forced labour; and Jehoshaphat the son of Ahilud was the recorder; ²⁵and Sheva was secretary; and Zadok and Abiathar were priests; ²⁶and Ira the Jairite was also David's priest.

DAVID AVENGES THE GIBEONITES

21 Now there was a famine in the days of David for three years, year after year. And David sought the face of the LORD. And the LORD said, "There is bloodguilt on Saul and on his house, because he put the Gibeonites to death." ²So the king called the Gibeonites and spoke to them. Now the Gibeonites were not of the people of Israel but of the remnant of the Amorites. Although the people of Israel had sworn to spare them, Saul had sought to strike them down in his zeal for the people of Israel and Judah. ³And David said to the Gibeonites, "What shall I do for you? And how shall I make atonement, that you may bless the heritage of the LORD?" ⁴The Gibeonites said to him, "It is not a matter of silver or gold between us and Saul or his house; neither is it for us to put any man to death in Israel." And he said, "What do you say that I shall do for you?" ⁵They said to the king, "The man who consumed us and planned to destroy us, so that we should have no place in all the territory of Israel, ⁶let seven of his sons be given to us, so that we may hang them before the LORD at Gibeah of Saul, the chosen of the LORD." And the king said, "I will give them."

⁷But the king spared Mephibosheth, the son of Saul's son Jonathan, because of the oath of the LORD that was between them, between David and Jonathan the son of Saul. ⁸The king took the two sons of Rizpah the daughter of Aiah, whom she bore to Saul, Armoni and Mephibosheth; and the five sons of Merabᶜ the daughter of Saul, whom she bore to Adriel the son of Barzillai the Meholathite; ⁹and he gave them into the hands of the Gibeonites, and they hanged them on the mountain before the LORD, and the seven of them perished together. They were put to death in the first days of harvest, at the beginning of barley harvest.

¹⁰Then Rizpah the daughter of Aiah took sackcloth and spread it for herself on the rock, from the beginning of harvest until rain fell upon them from the heavens. And she did not allow the birds of the air to come upon them by day, or the beasts of the field by night. ¹¹When David was told what Rizpah the daughter of Aiah, the concubine of Saul, had done, ¹²David went and took the bones of

---

ᵃCompare 20:15; Hebrew *and Beth-maacah* ᵇHebrew *Berites*
ᶜTwo Hebrew manuscripts, Septuagint; most Hebrew manuscripts *Michal*

Saul and the bones of his son Jonathan from the men of Jabesh-gilead, who had stolen them from the public square of Beth-shan, where the Philistines had hanged them, on the day the Philistines killed Saul on Gilboa. ¹³And he brought up from there the bones of Saul and the bones of his son Jonathan; and they gathered the bones of those who were hanged. ¹⁴And they buried the bones of Saul and his son Jonathan in the land of Benjamin in Zela, in the tomb of Kish his father. And they did all that the king commanded. And after that God responded to the plea for the land.

WAR WITH THE PHILISTINES

¹⁵There was war again between the Philistines and Israel, and David went down together with his servants, and they fought against the Philistines. And David grew weary. ¹⁶And Ishbi-benob, one of the descendants of the giants, whose spear weighed three hundred shekels[a] of bronze, and who was armed with a new sword, thought to kill David. ¹⁷But Abishai the son of Zeruiah came to his aid and attacked the Philistine and killed him. Then David's men swore to him, "You shall no longer go out with us to battle, lest you quench the lamp of Israel."

¹⁸After this there was again war with the Philistines at Gob. Then Sibbecai the Hushathite struck down Saph, who was one of the descendants of the giants. ¹⁹And there was again war with the Philistines at Gob, and Elhanan the son of Jaare-oregim, the Bethlehemite, struck down Goliath the Gittite, the shaft of whose spear was like a weaver's beam.[b] ²⁰And there was again war at Gath, where there was a man of great stature, who had six fingers on each hand, and six toes on each foot, twenty-four in number, and he also was descended from the giants. ²¹And when he taunted Israel, Jonathan the son of Shimei, David's brother, struck him down. ²²These four were descended from the giants in Gath, and they fell by the hand of David and by the hand of his servants.

DAVID'S SONG OF DELIVERANCE

22 And David spoke to the LORD the words of this song on the day when the LORD delivered him from the hand of all his enemies, and from the hand of Saul. ²He said,

"The LORD is my rock and my
 fortress and my deliverer,
³ my[c] God, my rock, in whom
 I take refuge,
my shield, and the horn
 of my salvation,
my stronghold and my refuge,
 my saviour; you save me
 from violence.
⁴ I call upon the LORD, who is
 worthy to be praised,
and I am saved from my enemies.

⁵ "For the waves of death
 encompassed me,
the torrents of destruction
 assailed me;[d]
⁶ the cords of Sheol entangled me;
 the snares of death confronted me.

⁷ "In my distress I called upon the LORD;
 to my God I called.
From his temple he heard my voice,
 and my cry came to his ears.

⁸ "Then the earth reeled and rocked;
 the foundations of the
 heavens trembled
and quaked, because he was angry.
⁹ Smoke went up from his nostrils,[e]
 and devouring fire from his mouth;
 glowing coals flamed
 forth from him.
¹⁰ He bowed the heavens and came down;
 thick darkness was under his feet.
¹¹ He rode on a cherub and flew;
 he was seen on the wings
 of the wind.
¹² He made darkness around
 him his canopy,
 thick clouds, a gathering of water.
¹³ Out of the brightness before him
 coals of fire flamed forth.
¹⁴ The LORD thundered from heaven,
 and the Most High uttered his voice.
¹⁵ And he sent out arrows and
 scattered them;
 lightning, and routed them.
¹⁶ Then the channels of the sea
 were seen;
the foundations of the world
 were laid bare,

---

[a] A *shekel* was about 2/5 of an ounce or 11 grams
[b] Contrast 1 Chronicles 20:5, which may preserve the original reading
[c] Septuagint (compare Psalm 18:2); Hebrew lacks *my*
[d] Or *terrified me*
[e] Or *in his wrath*

at the rebuke of the LORD,
   at the blast of the breath
      of his nostrils.
17 "He sent from on high, he took me;
   he drew me out of many waters.
18 He rescued me from my strong enemy,
   from those who hated me,
      for they were too mighty for me.
19 They confronted me in the
      day of my calamity,
   but the LORD was my support.
20 He brought me out into a broad place;
   he rescued me, because he
      delighted in me.

21 "The LORD dealt with me according
      to my righteousness;
   according to the cleanness of my
      hands he rewarded me.
22 For I have kept the ways of the LORD
   and have not wickedly
      departed from my God.
23 For all his rules were before me,
   and from his statutes I did
      not turn aside.
24 I was blameless before him,
   and I kept myself from guilt.
25 And the LORD has rewarded me
   according to my righteousness,
      according to my cleanness
         in his sight.

26 "With the merciful you show
      yourself merciful;
   with the blameless man you
      show yourself blameless;
27 with the purified you deal purely,
   and with the crooked you make
      yourself seem tortuous.
28 You save a humble people,
   but your eyes are on the haughty
      to bring them down.
29 For you are my lamp, O LORD,
   and my God lightens my darkness.
30 For by you I can run against a troop,
   and by my God I can leap over a wall.
31 This God—his way is perfect;
   the word of the LORD proves true;
   he is a shield for all those who
      take refuge in him.

32 "For who is God, but the LORD?
   And who is a rock, except our God?
33 This God is my strong refuge
   and has made my[a] way blameless.[b]

34 He made my feet like the feet of a deer
   and set me secure on the heights.
35 He trains my hands for war,
   so that my arms can bend
      a bow of bronze.
36 You have given me the shield
      of your salvation,
   and your gentleness made me great.
37 You gave a wide place for my
      steps under me,
   and my feet[c] did not slip;
38 I pursued my enemies and
      destroyed them,
   and did not turn back until
      they were consumed.
39 I consumed them; I thrust them
      through, so that they did not rise;
   they fell under my feet.
40 For you equipped me with
      strength for the battle;
   you made those who rise against
      me sink under me.
41 You made my enemies turn
      their backs to me,[d]
   those who hated me, and I
      destroyed them.
42 They looked, but there was
      none to save;
   they cried to the LORD, but he
      did not answer them.
43 I beat them fine as the dust of the earth;
   I crushed them and stamped them
      down like the mire of the streets.

44 "You delivered me from strife
      with my people;[e]
   you kept me as the head
      of the nations;
   people whom I had not
      known served me.
45 Foreigners came cringing to me;
   as soon as they heard of me,
      they obeyed me.
46 Foreigners lost heart
   and came trembling[f] out of
      their fortresses.

47 "The LORD lives, and blessed
      be my rock,
   and exalted be my God, the
      rock of my salvation,

---

[a] Or his; also verse 34 [b] Compare Psalm 18:32; Hebrew he has blamelessly set my way free, or he has made my way spring up blamelessly [c] Hebrew ankles [d] Or You gave me my enemies' necks [e] Septuagint with the peoples [f] Compare Psalm 18:45; Hebrew equipped themselves

48 the God who gave me vengeance
    and brought down peoples
        under me,
49 who brought me out from my enemies;
    you exalted me above those
        who rose against me;
    you delivered me from
        men of violence.

50 "For this I will praise you, O LORD,
        among the nations,
    and sing praises to your name.
51 Great salvation he brings[a] to his king,
    and shows steadfast love
        to his anointed,
    to David and his offspring for ever."

THE LAST WORDS OF DAVID

23 Now these are the last words of David:

The oracle of David, the son of Jesse,
    the oracle of the man who
        was raised on high,
    the anointed of the God of Jacob,
    the sweet psalmist of Israel:[b]

2 "The Spirit of the LORD speaks by me;
    his word is on my tongue.
3 The God of Israel has spoken;
    the Rock of Israel has said to me:
When one rules justly over men,
    ruling in the fear of God,
4 he dawns on them like the
        morning light,
    like the sun shining forth on
        a cloudless morning,
    like rain[c] that makes grass to
        sprout from the earth.

5 "For does not my house
        stand so with God?
    For he has made with me an
        everlasting covenant,
    ordered in all things and secure.
    For will he not cause to prosper
    all my help and my desire?
6 But worthless men[d] are all like
        thorns that are thrown away,
    for they cannot be taken
        with the hand;
7 but the man who touches them
    arms himself with iron and
        the shaft of a spear,
    and they are utterly consumed
        with fire."[e]

DAVID'S MIGHTY MEN

8These are the names of the mighty men whom David had: Josheb-basshebeth a Tahchemonite; he was chief of the three.[f] He wielded his spear[g] against eight hundred whom he killed at one time.

9And next to him among the three mighty men was Eleazar the son of Dodo, son of Ahohi. He was with David when they defied the Philistines who were gathered there for battle, and the men of Israel withdrew. 10He rose and struck down the Philistines until his hand was weary, and his hand clung to the sword. And the LORD brought about a great victory that day, and the men returned after him only to strip the slain.

11And next to him was Shammah, the son of Agee the Hararite. The Philistines gathered together at Lehi,[h] where there was a plot of ground full of lentils, and the men fled from the Philistines. 12But he took his stand in the midst of the plot and defended it and struck down the Philistines, and the LORD worked a great victory.

13And three of the thirty chief men went down and came about harvest time to David at the cave of Adullam, when a band of Philistines was encamped in the Valley of Rephaim. 14David was then in the stronghold, and the garrison of the Philistines was then at Bethlehem. 15And David said longingly, "Oh, that someone would give me water to drink from the well of Bethlehem that is by the gate!" 16Then the three mighty men broke through the camp of the Philistines and drew water out of the well of Bethlehem that was by the gate and carried and brought it to David. But he would not drink of it. He poured it out to the LORD 17and said, "Far be it from me, O LORD, that I should do this. Shall I drink the blood of the men who went at the risk of their lives?" Therefore he would not drink it. These things the three mighty men did.

18Now Abishai, the brother of Joab, the son of Zeruiah, was chief of the thirty.[i] And he wielded his spear against three hundred men[j] and killed them and won a name beside the three. 19He was the most renowned of the thirty[k] and became their commander, but he did not attain to the three.

---

[a]Or *He is a tower of salvation* [b]Or *the favourite of the songs of Israel* [c]Hebrew *from rain* [d]Hebrew *worthlessness* [e]Hebrew *consumed with fire in the sitting* [f]Or *of the captains* [g]Compare 1 Chronicles 11:11; the meaning of the Hebrew expression is uncertain [h]Or *gathered together as a camp* [i]Two Hebrew manuscripts, Syriac; most Hebrew manuscripts *three* [j]Or *slain ones* [k]Compare 1 Chronicles 11:21; Hebrew *Was he the most renowned of the three?*

²⁰And Benaiah the son of Jehoiada was a valiant man[a] of Kabzeel, a doer of great deeds. He struck down two ariels[b] of Moab. He also went down and struck down a lion in a pit on a day when snow had fallen. ²¹And he struck down an Egyptian, a handsome man. The Egyptian had a spear in his hand, but Benaiah went down to him with a staff and snatched the spear out of the Egyptian's hand and killed him with his own spear. ²²These things did Benaiah the son of Jehoiada, and won a name beside the three mighty men. ²³He was renowned among the thirty, but he did not attain to the three. And David set him over his bodyguard.

²⁴Asahel the brother of Joab was one of the thirty; Elhanan the son of Dodo of Bethlehem, ²⁵Shammah of Harod, Elika of Harod, ²⁶Helez the Paltite, Ira the son of Ikkesh of Tekoa, ²⁷Abiezer of Anathoth, Mebunnai the Hushathite, ²⁸Zalmon the Ahohite, Maharai of Netophah, ²⁹Heleb the son of Baanah of Netophah, Ittai the son of Ribai of Gibeah of the people of Benjamin, ³⁰Benaiah of Pirathon, Hiddai of the brooks of Gaash, ³¹Abi-albon the Arbathite, Azmaveth of Bahurim, ³²Eliahba the Shaalbonite, the sons of Jashen, Jonathan, ³³Shammah the Hararite, Ahiam the son of Sharar the Hararite, ³⁴Eliphelet the son of Ahasbai of Maacah, Eliam the son of Ahithophel the Gilonite, ³⁵Hezro[c] of Carmel, Paarai the Arbite, ³⁶Igal the son of Nathan of Zobah, Bani the Gadite, ³⁷Zelek the Ammonite, Naharai of Beeroth, the armour bearer of Joab the son of Zeruiah, ³⁸Ira the Ithrite, Gareb the Ithrite, ³⁹Uriah the Hittite: thirty-seven in all.

DAVID'S CENSUS

24 Again the anger of the LORD was kindled against Israel, and he incited David against them, saying, "Go, number Israel and Judah." ²So the king said to Joab, the commander of the army,[d] who was with him, "Go through all the tribes of Israel, from Dan to Beersheba, and number the people, that I may know the number of the people." ³But Joab said to the king, "May the LORD your God add to the people a hundred times as many as they are, while the eyes of my lord the king still see it, but why does my lord the king delight in this thing?" ⁴But the king's word prevailed against Joab and the commanders of the army. So Joab and the commanders of the army went out from the presence of the king to number the people of Israel. ⁵They crossed the Jordan and began from Aroer,[e] and from the city that is in the middle of the valley, towards Gad and on to Jazer. ⁶Then they came to Gilead, and to Kadesh in the land of the Hittites;[f] and they came to Dan, and from Dan[g] they went round to Sidon, ⁷and came to the fortress of Tyre and to all the cities of the Hivites and Canaanites; and they went out to the Negeb of Judah at Beersheba. ⁸So when they had gone through all the land, they came to Jerusalem at the end of nine months and twenty days. ⁹And Joab gave the sum of the numbering of the people to the king: in Israel there were 800,000 valiant men who drew the sword, and the men of Judah were 500,000.

THE LORD'S JUDGEMENT OF DAVID'S SIN

¹⁰But David's heart struck him after he had numbered the people. And David said to the LORD, "I have sinned greatly in what I have done. But now, O LORD, please take away the iniquity of your servant, for I have done very foolishly." ¹¹And when David arose in the morning, the word of the LORD came to the prophet Gad, David's seer, saying, ¹²"Go and say to David, 'Thus says the LORD, Three things I offer[h] you. Choose one of them, that I may do it to you.'" ¹³So Gad came to David and told him, and said to him, "Shall three[i] years of famine come to you in your land? Or will you flee three months before your foes while they pursue you? Or shall there be three days' pestilence in your land? Now consider, and decide what answer I shall return to him who sent me." ¹⁴Then David said to Gad, "I am in great distress. Let us fall into the hand of the LORD, for his mercy is great; but let me not fall into the hand of man."

¹⁵So the LORD sent a pestilence on Israel from the morning until the appointed time. And there died of the people from Dan to Beersheba 70,000 men. ¹⁶And when the angel stretched out his hand towards Jerusalem to destroy it, the LORD relented from the calamity and said to the angel who was working destruction among the people, "It is enough; now stay your hand." And the angel of the LORD was by the threshing floor of Araunah the Jebusite. ¹⁷Then David spoke to the LORD when he saw the angel who was striking the

---

[a] Or *the son of Ishhai* [b] The meaning of the word *ariel* is unknown [c] Or *Hezrai* [d] Septuagint *to Joab and the commanders of the army* [e] Septuagint; Hebrew *encamped in Aroer* [f] Septuagint; Hebrew *to the land of Tahtim-hodshi* [g] Septuagint; Hebrew *they came to Dan-jaan and* [h] Or *hold over* [i] Compare 1 Chronicles 21:12, Septuagint; Hebrew *seven*

people, and said, "Behold, I have sinned, and I have done wickedly. But these sheep, what have they done? Please let your hand be against me and against my father's house."

DAVID BUILDS AN ALTAR

¹⁸And Gad came that day to David and said to him, "Go up, raise an altar to the LORD on the threshing floor of Araunah the Jebusite." ¹⁹So David went up at Gad's word, as the LORD commanded. ²⁰And when Araunah looked down, he saw the king and his servants coming on towards him. And Araunah went out and paid homage to the king with his face to the ground. ²¹And Araunah said, "Why has my lord the king come to his servant?" David said, "To buy the threshing floor from you, in order to build an altar to the LORD, that the plague may be averted from the people." ²²Then Araunah said to David, "Let my lord the king take and offer up what seems good to him. Here are the oxen for the burnt offering and the threshing sledges and the yokes of the oxen for the wood. ²³All this, O king, Araunah gives to the king." And Araunah said to the king, "May the LORD your God accept you." ²⁴But the king said to Araunah, "No, but I will buy it from you for a price. I will not offer burnt offerings to the LORD my God that cost me nothing." So David bought the threshing floor and the oxen for fifty shekels[a] of silver. ²⁵And David built there an altar to the LORD and offered burnt offerings and peace offerings. So the LORD responded to the plea for the land, and the plague was averted from Israel.

---

[a] A *shekel* was about 2/5 of an ounce or 11 grams

1 KINGS

DAVID IN HIS OLD AGE

1 Now King David was old and advanced in years. And although they covered him with clothes, he could not get warm. ²Therefore his servants said to him, "Let a young woman be sought for my lord the king, and let her wait on the king and be in his service. Let her lie in your arms,ᵃ that my lord the king may be warm." ³So they sought for a beautiful young woman throughout all the territory of Israel, and found Abishag the Shunammite, and brought her to the king. ⁴The young woman was very beautiful, and she was of service to the king and attended to him, but the king knew her not.

ADONIJAH SETS HIMSELF UP AS KING

⁵Now Adonijah the son of Haggith exalted himself, saying, "I will be king." And he prepared for himself chariots and horsemen, and fifty men to run before him. ⁶His father had never at any time displeased him by asking, "Why have you done thus and so?" He was also a very handsome man, and he was born next after Absalom. ⁷He conferred with Joab the son of Zeruiah and with Abiathar the priest. And they followed Adonijah and helped him. ⁸But Zadok the priest and Benaiah the son of Jehoiada and Nathan the prophet and Shimei and Rei and David's mighty men were not with Adonijah.

⁹Adonijah sacrificed sheep, oxen, and fattened cattle by the Serpent's Stone, which is beside En-rogel, and he invited all his brothers, the king's sons, and all the royal officials of Judah, ¹⁰but he did not invite Nathan the prophet or Benaiah or the mighty men or Solomon his brother.

NATHAN AND BATHSHEBA BEFORE DAVID

¹¹Then Nathan said to Bathsheba the mother of Solomon, "Have you not heard that Adonijah the son of Haggith has become king and David our lord does not know it? ¹²Now therefore come, let me give you advice, that you may save your own life and the life of your son Solomon. ¹³Go in at once to King David, and say to him, 'Did you not, my lord the king, swear to your servant, saying, "Solomon your son shall reign after me, and he shall sit on my throne"? Why then is Adonijah king?' ¹⁴Then while you are still speaking with the king, I also will come in after you and confirmᵇ your words."

¹⁵So Bathsheba went to the king in his chamber (now the king was very old, and Abishag the Shunammite was attending to the king). ¹⁶Bathsheba bowed and paid homage to the king, and the king said, "What do you desire?" ¹⁷She said to him, "My lord, you swore to your servant by the LORD your God, saying, 'Solomon your son shall reign after me, and he shall sit on my throne.' ¹⁸And now, behold, Adonijah is king, although you, my lord the king, do not know it. ¹⁹He has sacrificed oxen, fattened cattle, and sheep in abundance, and has invited all the sons of the king, Abiathar the priest, and Joab the commander of the army, but Solomon your servant he has not invited. ²⁰And now, my lord the king, the eyes of all Israel are on you, to tell them who shall sit on the throne of my lord the king after him. ²¹Otherwise it will come to pass, when my lord the king sleeps with his fathers, that I and my son Solomon will be counted offenders."

²²While she was still speaking with the king, Nathan the prophet came in. ²³And they told the king, "Here is Nathan the prophet." And when he came in before the king, he bowed before the king, with his face to the ground. ²⁴And Nathan said, "My lord the king, have you said, 'Adonijah shall reign after me, and he shall sit on my throne'? ²⁵For he has gone down this day and has sacrificed oxen, fattened cattle, and sheep in abundance, and has invited all the king's sons, the commandersᶜ of the army, and Abiathar the priest. And behold, they are eating and drinking before him, and saying, 'Long live King Adonijah!' ²⁶But me, your servant, and Zadok the priest, and Benaiah the son of Jehoiada, and your servant Solomon he has not invited. ²⁷Has

---

ᵃOr *in your bosom* ᵇOr *expand on* ᶜHebrew; Septuagint *Joab the commander* this thing been brought about by my lord the king and you have not told your servants who should sit on the throne of my lord the king after him?"

SOLOMON ANOINTED KING

28Then King David answered, "Call Bathsheba to me." So she came into the king's presence and stood before the king. **29**And the king swore, saying, "As the LORD lives, who has redeemed my soul out of every adversity, **30**as I swore to you by the LORD, the God of Israel, saying, 'Solomon your son shall reign after me, and he shall sit on my throne in my place', even so will I do this day." **31**Then Bathsheba bowed with her face to the ground and paid homage to the king and said, "May my lord King David live for ever!"

32King David said, "Call to me Zadok the priest, Nathan the prophet, and Benaiah the son of Jehoiada." So they came before the king. **33**And the king said to them, "Take with you the servants of your lord and have Solomon my son ride on my own mule, and bring him down to Gihon. **34**And let Zadok the priest and Nathan the prophet there anoint him king over Israel. Then blow the trumpet and say, 'Long live King Solomon!' **35**You shall then come up after him, and he shall come and sit on my throne, for he shall be king in my place. And I have appointed him to be ruler over Israel and over Judah." **36**And Benaiah the son of Jehoiada answered the king, "Amen! May the LORD, the God of my lord the king, say so. **37**As the LORD has been with my lord the king, even so may he be with Solomon, and make his throne greater than the throne of my lord King David."

38So Zadok the priest, Nathan the prophet, and Benaiah the son of Jehoiada, and the Cherethites and the Pelethites went down and made Solomon ride on King David's mule and brought him to Gihon. **39**There Zadok the priest took the horn of oil from the tent and anointed Solomon. Then they blew the trumpet, and all the people said, "Long live King Solomon!" **40**And all the people went up after him, playing on pipes, and rejoicing with great joy, so that the earth was split by their noise.

41Adonijah and all the guests who were with him heard it as they finished feasting. And when Joab heard the sound of the trumpet, he said, "What does this uproar in the city mean?" **42**While he was still speaking, behold, Jonathan the son of Abiathar the priest came. And Adonijah said, "Come in, for you are a worthy man and bring good news." **43**Jonathan answered Adonijah, "No, for our lord King David has made Solomon king, **44**and the king has sent with him Zadok the priest, Nathan the prophet, and Benaiah the son of Jehoiada, and the Cherethites and the Pelethites. And they made him ride on the king's mule. **45**And Zadok the priest and Nathan the prophet have anointed him king at Gihon, and they have gone up from there rejoicing, so that the city is in an uproar. This is the noise that you have heard. **46**Solomon sits on the royal throne. **47**Moreover, the king's servants came to congratulate our lord King David, saying, 'May your God make the name of Solomon more famous than yours, and make his throne greater than your throne.' And the king bowed himself on the bed. **48**And the king also said, 'Blessed be the LORD, the God of Israel, who has granted someone*a* to sit on my throne this day, my own eyes seeing it.'"

49Then all the guests of Adonijah trembled and rose, and each went his own way. **50**And Adonijah feared Solomon. So he arose and went and took hold of the horns of the altar. **51**Then it was told Solomon, "Behold, Adonijah fears King Solomon, for behold, he has laid hold of the horns of the altar, saying, 'Let King Solomon swear to me first that he will not put his servant to death with the sword.'" **52**And Solomon said, "If he will show himself a worthy man, not one of his hairs shall fall to the earth, but if wickedness is found in him, he shall die." **53**So King Solomon sent, and they brought him down from the altar. And he came and paid homage to King Solomon, and Solomon said to him, "Go to your house."

DAVID'S INSTRUCTIONS TO SOLOMON

2 When David's time to die drew near, he commanded Solomon his son, saying, **2**"I am about to go the way of all the earth. Be strong, and show yourself a man, **3**and keep the charge of the LORD your God, walking in his ways and keeping his statutes, his commandments, his rules, and his testimonies, as it is written in the Law of Moses, that you may prosper in all that you do and wherever you turn, **4**that the LORD may establish his word that he spoke concerning me, saying, 'If your sons pay close

---
a Septuagint *one of my offspring*

attention to their way, to walk before me in faithfulness with all their heart and with all their soul, you shall not lack[a] a man on the throne of Israel.'

⁵"Moreover, you also know what Joab the son of Zeruiah did to me, how he dealt with the two commanders of the armies of Israel, Abner the son of Ner, and Amasa the son of Jether, whom he killed, avenging[b] in time of peace for blood that had been shed in war, and putting the blood of war[c] on the belt round his[d] waist and on the sandals on his feet. ⁶Act therefore according to your wisdom, but do not let his grey head go down to Sheol in peace. ⁷But deal loyally with the sons of Barzillai the Gileadite, and let them be among those who eat at your table, for with such loyalty[e] they met me when I fled from Absalom your brother. ⁸And there is also with you Shimei the son of Gera, the Benjaminite from Bahurim, who cursed me with a grievous curse on the day when I went to Mahanaim. But when he came down to meet me at the Jordan, I swore to him by the LORD, saying, 'I will not put you to death with the sword.' ⁹Now therefore do not hold him guiltless, for you are a wise man. You will know what you ought to do to him, and you shall bring his grey head down with blood to Sheol."

THE DEATH OF DAVID

¹⁰Then David slept with his fathers and was buried in the city of David. ¹¹And the time that David reigned over Israel was forty years. He reigned for seven years in Hebron and for thirty-three years in Jerusalem. ¹²So Solomon sat on the throne of David his father, and his kingdom was firmly established.

SOLOMON'S REIGN ESTABLISHED

¹³Then Adonijah the son of Haggith came to Bathsheba the mother of Solomon. And she said, "Do you come peacefully?" He said, "Peacefully." ¹⁴Then he said, "I have something to say to you." She said, "Speak." ¹⁵He said, "You know that the kingdom was mine, and that all Israel fully expected me to reign. However, the kingdom has turned about and become my brother's, for it was his from the LORD. ¹⁶And now I have one request to make of you; do not refuse me." She said to him, "Speak." ¹⁷And he said, "Please ask King Solomon—he will not refuse you—to give me Abishag the Shunammite as my wife." ¹⁸Bathsheba said, "Very well; I will speak for you to the king."

¹⁹So Bathsheba went to King Solomon to speak to him on behalf of Adonijah. And the king rose to meet her and bowed down to her. Then he sat on his throne and had a seat brought for the king's mother, and she sat on his right. ²⁰Then she said, "I have one small request to make of you; do not refuse me." And the king said to her, "Make your request, my mother, for I will not refuse you." ²¹She said, "Let Abishag the Shunammite be given to Adonijah your brother as his wife." ²²King Solomon answered his mother, "And why do you ask Abishag the Shunammite for Adonijah? Ask for him the kingdom also, for he is my older brother, and on his side are Abiathar[f] the priest and Joab the son of Zeruiah." ²³Then King Solomon swore by the LORD, saying, "God do so to me and more also if this word does not cost Adonijah his life! ²⁴Now therefore as the LORD lives, who has established me and placed me on the throne of David my father, and who has made me a house, as he promised, Adonijah shall be put to death today." ²⁵So King Solomon sent Benaiah the son of Jehoiada, and he struck him down, and he died.

²⁶And to Abiathar the priest the king said, "Go to Anathoth, to your estate, for you deserve death. But I will not at this time put you to death, because you carried the ark of the Lord GOD before David my father, and because you shared in all my father's affliction." ²⁷So Solomon expelled Abiathar from being priest to the LORD, thus fulfilling the word of the LORD that he had spoken concerning the house of Eli in Shiloh.

²⁸When the news came to Joab—for Joab had supported Adonijah although he had not supported Absalom—Joab fled to the tent of the LORD and caught hold of the horns of the altar. ²⁹And when it was told King Solomon, "Joab has fled to the tent of the LORD, and behold, he is beside the altar," Solomon sent Benaiah the son of Jehoiada, saying, "Go, strike him down." ³⁰So Benaiah came to the tent of the LORD and said to him, "The king commands, 'Come out.'" But he said, "No, I will die here." Then Benaiah brought the king word again, saying, "Thus said Joab, and thus he answered me." ³¹The king replied to him, "Do as he has said, strike him down and bury him, and thus take away from me and from

---

[a] Hebrew *there shall not be cut off for you* [b] Septuagint; Hebrew *placing* [c] Septuagint *innocent blood* [d] Septuagint *my*; twice in this verse [e] Or *steadfast love* [f] Septuagint, Syriac, Vulgate; Hebrew *and for him and for Abiathar*

my father's house the guilt for the blood that Joab shed without cause. ³²The LORD will bring back his bloody deeds on his own head, because, without the knowledge of my father David, he attacked and killed with the sword two men more righteous and better than himself, Abner the son of Ner, commander of the army of Israel, and Amasa the son of Jether, commander of the army of Judah. ³³So shall their blood come back on the head of Joab and on the head of his descendants for ever. But for David and for his descendants and for his house and for his throne there shall be peace from the LORD for evermore." ³⁴Then Benaiah the son of Jehoiada went up and struck him down and put him to death. And he was buried in his own house in the wilderness. ³⁵The king put Benaiah the son of Jehoiada over the army in place of Joab, and the king put Zadok the priest in the place of Abiathar.

³⁶Then the king sent and summoned Shimei and said to him, "Build yourself a house in Jerusalem and dwell there, and do not go out from there to any place whatever. ³⁷For on the day you go out and cross the brook Kidron, know for certain that you shall die. Your blood shall be on your own head." ³⁸And Shimei said to the king, "What you say is good; as my lord the king has said, so will your servant do." So Shimei lived in Jerusalem for many days.

³⁹But it happened at the end of three years that two of Shimei's servants ran away to Achish, son of Maacah, king of Gath. And when it was told Shimei, "Behold, your servants are in Gath", ⁴⁰Shimei arose and saddled a donkey and went to Gath to Achish to seek his servants. Shimei went and brought his servants from Gath. ⁴¹And when Solomon was told that Shimei had gone from Jerusalem to Gath and returned, ⁴²the king sent and summoned Shimei and said to him, "Did I not make you swear by the LORD and solemnly warn you, saying, 'Know for certain that on the day you go out and go to any place whatever, you shall die'? And you said to me, 'What you say is good; I will obey.' ⁴³Why then have you not kept your oath to the LORD and the commandment with which I commanded you?" ⁴⁴The king also said to Shimei, "You know in your own heart all the harm that you did to David my father. So the LORD will bring back your harm on your own head. ⁴⁵But King Solomon shall be blessed, and the throne of David shall be established before the LORD for ever." ⁴⁶Then the king commanded Benaiah the son of Jehoiada, and he went out and struck him down, and he died.

So the kingdom was established in the hand of Solomon.

SOLOMON'S PRAYER FOR WISDOM

3 Solomon made a marriage alliance with Pharaoh king of Egypt. He took Pharaoh's daughter and brought her into the city of David until he had finished building his own house and the house of the LORD and the wall round Jerusalem. ²The people were sacrificing at the high places, however, because no house had yet been built for the name of the LORD.

³Solomon loved the LORD, walking in the statutes of David his father, only he sacrificed and made offerings at the high places. ⁴And the king went to Gibeon to sacrifice there, for that was the great high place. Solomon used to offer a thousand burnt offerings on that altar. ⁵At Gibeon the LORD appeared to Solomon in a dream by night, and God said, "Ask what I shall give you." ⁶And Solomon said, "You have shown great and steadfast love to your servant David my father, because he walked before you in faithfulness, in righteousness, and in uprightness of heart towards you. And you have kept for him this great and steadfast love and have given him a son to sit on his throne this day. ⁷And now, O LORD my God, you have made your servant king in place of David my father, although I am but a little child. I do not know how to go out or come in. ⁸And your servant is in the midst of your people whom you have chosen, a great people, too many to be numbered or counted for multitude. ⁹Give your servant therefore an understanding mind to govern your people, that I may discern between good and evil, for who is able to govern this your great people?"

¹⁰It pleased the Lord that Solomon had asked this. ¹¹And God said to him, "Because you have asked this, and have not asked for yourself long life or riches or the life of your enemies, but have asked for yourself understanding to discern what is right, ¹²behold, I now do according to your word. Behold, I give you a wise and discerning mind, so that none like you has been before you and none like you shall arise after you. ¹³I give you also what you have not asked, both riches and honour, so that no other king shall compare with you, all your days. ¹⁴And if you will walk in my ways, keeping my statutes and my

commandments, as your father David walked, then I will lengthen your days."

¹⁵And Solomon awoke, and behold, it was a dream. Then he came to Jerusalem and stood before the ark of the covenant of the Lord, and offered up burnt offerings and peace offerings, and made a feast for all his servants.

SOLOMON'S WISDOM

¹⁶Then two prostitutes came to the king and stood before him. ¹⁷The one woman said, "Oh, my lord, this woman and I live in the same house, and I gave birth to a child while she was in the house. ¹⁸Then on the third day after I gave birth, this woman also gave birth. And we were alone. There was no one else with us in the house; only we two were in the house. ¹⁹And this woman's son died in the night, because she lay on him. ²⁰And she arose at midnight and took my son from beside me, while your servant slept, and laid him at her breast, and laid her dead son at my breast. ²¹When I rose in the morning to nurse my child, behold, he was dead. But when I looked at him closely in the morning, behold, he was not the child that I had borne." ²²But the other woman said, "No, the living child is mine, and the dead child is yours." The first said, "No, the dead child is yours, and the living child is mine." Thus they spoke before the king.

²³Then the king said, "One says, 'This is my son that is alive, and your son is dead'; and the other says, 'No; but your son is dead, and my son is the living one.'" ²⁴And the king said, "Bring me a sword." So a sword was brought before the king. ²⁵And the king said, "Divide the living child in two, and give half to one and half to the other." ²⁶Then the woman whose son was alive said to the king, because her heart yearned for her son, "Oh, my lord, give her the living child, and by no means put him to death." But the other said, "He shall be neither mine nor yours; divide him." ²⁷Then the king answered and said, "Give the living child to the first woman, and by no means put him to death; she is his mother." ²⁸And all Israel heard of the judgement that the king had rendered, and they stood in awe of the king, because they perceived that the wisdom of God was in him to do justice.

SOLOMON'S OFFICIALS

4 King Solomon was king over all Israel, ²and these were his high officials: Azariah the son of Zadok was the priest; ³Elihoreph and Ahijah the sons of Shisha were secretaries; Jehoshaphat the son of Ahilud was recorder; ⁴Benaiah the son of Jehoiada was in command of the army; Zadok and Abiathar were priests; ⁵Azariah the son of Nathan was over the officers; Zabud the son of Nathan was priest and king's friend; ⁶Ahishar was in charge of the palace; and Adoniram the son of Abda was in charge of the forced labour.

⁷Solomon had twelve officers over all Israel, who provided food for the king and his household. Each man had to make provision for one month in the year. ⁸These were their names: Ben-hur, in the hill country of Ephraim; ⁹Ben-deker, in Makaz, Shaalbim, Beth-shemesh, and Elonbeth-hanan; ¹⁰Ben-hesed, in Arubboth (to him belonged Socoh and all the land of Hepher); ¹¹Ben-abinadab, in all Naphath-dor (he had Taphath the daughter of Solomon as his wife); ¹²Baana the son of Ahilud, in Taanach, Megiddo, and all Beth-shean that is beside Zarethan below Jezreel, and from Beth-shean to Abel-meholah, as far as the other side of Jokmeam; ¹³Ben-geber, in Ramoth-gilead (he had the villages of Jair the son of Manasseh, which are in Gilead, and he had the region of Argob, which is in Bashan, sixty great cities with walls and bronze bars); ¹⁴Ahinadab the son of Iddo, in Mahanaim; ¹⁵Ahimaaz, in Naphtali (he had taken Basemath the daughter of Solomon as his wife); ¹⁶Baana the son of Hushai, in Asher and Bealoth; ¹⁷Jehoshaphat the son of Paruah, in Issachar; ¹⁸Shimei the son of Ela, in Benjamin; ¹⁹Geber the son of Uri, in the land of Gilead, the country of Sihon king of the Amorites and of Og king of Bashan. And there was one governor who was over the land.

SOLOMON'S WEALTH AND WISDOM

²⁰Judah and Israel were as many as the sand by the sea. They ate and drank and were happy. ²¹ᵃ Solomon ruled over all the kingdoms from the Euphratesᵇ to the land of the Philistines and to the border of Egypt. They brought tribute and served Solomon all the days of his life.

²²Solomon's provision for one day was thirty corsᶜ of fine flour and sixty cors of meal, ²³ten fat oxen, and twenty pasture-fed cattle, a hundred sheep, besides deer, gazelles, roebucks, and fattened fowl. ²⁴For he had dominion over all the region west of the Euphratesᵈ

ᵃCh 5:1 in Hebrew ᵇHebrew *the River* ᶜA *cor* was about 6 bushels or 220 litres ᵈHebrew *the River*; twice in this verse

from Tiphsah to Gaza, over all the kings west of the Euphrates. And he had peace on all sides around him. 25And Judah and Israel lived in safety, from Dan even to Beersheba, every man under his vine and under his fig tree, all the days of Solomon. 26Solomon also had 40,000[a] stalls of horses for his chariots, and 12,000 horsemen. 27And those officers supplied provisions for King Solomon, and for all who came to King Solomon's table, each one in his month. They let nothing be lacking. 28Barley also and straw for the horses and swift steeds they brought to the place where it was required, each according to his duty.

29And God gave Solomon wisdom and understanding beyond measure, and breadth of mind like the sand on the seashore, 30so that Solomon's wisdom surpassed the wisdom of all the people of the east and all the wisdom of Egypt. 31For he was wiser than all other men, wiser than Ethan the Ezrahite, and Heman, Calcol, and Darda, the sons of Mahol, and his fame was in all the surrounding nations. 32He also spoke 3,000 proverbs, and his songs were 1,005. 33He spoke of trees, from the cedar that is in Lebanon to the hyssop that grows out of the wall. He spoke also of beasts, and of birds, and of reptiles, and of fish. 34And people of all nations came to hear the wisdom of Solomon, and from all the kings of the earth, who had heard of his wisdom.

PREPARATIONS FOR BUILDING THE TEMPLE

5 [b] Now Hiram king of Tyre sent his servants to Solomon when he heard that they had anointed him king in place of his father, for Hiram always loved David. 2And Solomon sent word to Hiram, 3"You know that David my father could not build a house for the name of the LORD his God because of the warfare with which his enemies surrounded him, until the LORD put them under the soles of his feet. 4But now the LORD my God has given me rest on every side. There is neither adversary nor misfortune. 5And so I intend to build a house for the name of the LORD my God, as the LORD said to David my father, 'Your son, whom I will set on your throne in your place, shall build the house for my name.' 6Now therefore command that cedars of Lebanon be cut for me. And my servants will join your servants, and I will pay you for your servants such wages as you set, for you know that there is no one among us who knows how to cut timber like the Sidonians."

7As soon as Hiram heard the words of Solomon, he rejoiced greatly and said, "Blessed be the LORD this day, who has given to David a wise son to be over this great people." 8And Hiram sent to Solomon, saying, "I have heard the message that you have sent to me. I am ready to do all you desire in the matter of cedar and cypress timber. 9My servants shall bring it down to the sea from Lebanon, and I will make it into rafts to go by sea to the place you direct. And I will have them broken up there, and you shall receive it. And you shall meet my wishes by providing food for my household." 10So Hiram supplied Solomon with all the timber of cedar and cypress that he desired, 11while Solomon gave Hiram 20,000 cors[c] of wheat as food for his household, and 20,000[d] cors of pressed oil. Solomon gave this to Hiram year by year. 12And the LORD gave Solomon wisdom, as he promised him. And there was peace between Hiram and Solomon, and the two of them made a treaty.

13King Solomon drafted forced labour out of all Israel, and the draft numbered 30,000 men. 14And he sent them to Lebanon, 10,000 a month in shifts. They would be a month in Lebanon and two months at home. Adoniram was in charge of the draft. 15Solomon also had 70,000 burden-bearers and 80,000 stonecutters in the hill country, 16besides Solomon's 3,300 chief officers who were over the work, who had charge of the people who carried on the work. 17At the king's command they quarried out great, costly stones in order to lay the foundation of the house with dressed stones. 18So Solomon's builders and Hiram's builders and the men of Gebal did the cutting and prepared the timber and the stone to build the house.

SOLOMON BUILDS THE TEMPLE

6 In the four hundred and eightieth year after the people of Israel came out of the land of Egypt, in the fourth year of Solomon's reign over Israel, in the month of Ziv, which is the second month, he began to build the house of the LORD. 2The house that King Solomon built for the LORD was sixty cubits[e] long, twenty cubits wide, and thirty cubits high. 3The vestibule in front of the nave of the house was twenty cubits long, equal to the width of the house, and ten cubits deep

---

[a]Hebrew; one Hebrew manuscript (see 2 Chronicles 9:25 and Septuagint of 1 Kings 10:26) 4,000 [b]Ch 5:15 in Hebrew [c]A *cor* was about 6 bushels or 220 litres [d]Septuagint; Hebrew *twenty*
[e]A *cubit* was about 18 inches or 45 centimetres

in front of the house. ⁴And he made for the house windows with recessed frames.ᵃ ⁵He also built a structureᵇ against the wall of the house, running round the walls of the house, both the nave and the inner sanctuary. And he made side chambers all round. ⁶The lowest storeyᶜ was five cubits broad, the middle one was six cubits broad, and the third was seven cubits broad. For round the outside of the house he made offsets on the wall in order that the supporting beams should not be inserted into the walls of the house.

⁷When the house was built, it was with stone prepared at the quarry, so that neither hammer nor axe nor any tool of iron was heard in the house while it was being built.

⁸The entrance for the lowestᵈ storey was on the south side of the house, and one went up by stairs to the middle storey, and from the middle storey to the third. ⁹So he built the house and finished it, and he made the ceiling of the house of beams and planks of cedar. ¹⁰He built the structure against the whole house, five cubits high, and it was joined to the house with timbers of cedar.

¹¹Now the word of the LORD came to Solomon, ¹²"Concerning this house that you are building, if you will walk in my statutes and obey my rules and keep all my commandments and walk in them, then I will establish my word with you, which I spoke to David your father. ¹³And I will dwell among the children of Israel and will not forsake my people Israel."

¹⁴So Solomon built the house and finished it. ¹⁵He lined the walls of the house on the inside with boards of cedar. From the floor of the house to the walls of the ceiling, he covered them on the inside with wood, and he covered the floor of the house with boards of cypress. ¹⁶He built twenty cubits of the rear of the house with boards of cedar from the floor to the walls, and he built this within as an inner sanctuary, as the Most Holy Place. ¹⁷The house, that is, the nave in front of the inner sanctuary, was forty cubits long. ¹⁸The cedar within the house was carved in the form of gourds and open flowers. All was cedar; no stone was seen. ¹⁹The inner sanctuary he prepared in the innermost part of the house, to set there the ark of the covenant of the LORD. ²⁰The inner sanctuaryᵉ was twenty cubits long, twenty cubits wide, and twenty cubits high, and he overlaid it with pure gold. He also overlaidᶠ an altar of cedar. ²¹And Solomon overlaid the inside of the house with pure gold, and he drew chains of gold across, in front of the inner sanctuary, and overlaid it with gold. ²²And he overlaid the whole house with gold, until all the house was finished. Also the whole altar that belonged to the inner sanctuary he overlaid with gold.

²³In the inner sanctuary he made two cherubim of olive wood, each ten cubits high. ²⁴Five cubits was the length of one wing of the cherub, and five cubits the length of the other wing of the cherub; it was ten cubits from the tip of one wing to the tip of the other. ²⁵The other cherub also measured ten cubits; both cherubim had the same measure and the same form. ²⁶The height of one cherub was ten cubits, and so was that of the other cherub. ²⁷He put the cherubim in the innermost part of the house. And the wings of the cherubim were spread out so that a wing of one touched one wall, and a wing of the other cherub touched the other wall; their other wings touched each other in the middle of the house. ²⁸And he overlaid the cherubim with gold.

²⁹Round all the walls of the house he carved engraved figures of cherubim and palm trees and open flowers, in the inner and outer rooms. ³⁰The floor of the house he overlaid with gold in the inner and outer rooms.

³¹For the entrance to the inner sanctuary he made doors of olive wood; the lintel and the doorposts were five-sided.ᵍ ³²He covered the two doors of olive wood with carvings of cherubim, palm trees, and open flowers. He overlaid them with gold and spread gold on the cherubim and on the palm trees.

³³So also he made for the entrance to the nave doorposts of olive wood, in the form of a square, ³⁴and two doors of cypress wood. The two leaves of one door were folding, and the two leaves of the other door were folding. ³⁵On them he carved cherubim and palm trees and open flowers, and he overlaid them with gold evenly applied on the carved work. ³⁶He built the inner court with three courses of cut stone and one course of cedar beams.

³⁷In the fourth year the foundation of the house of the LORD was laid, in the month of Ziv. ³⁸And in the eleventh year, in the month of Bul, which is the eighth month, the house was finished in all its parts, and according to all its specifications. He was seven years in building it.

ᵃOr *blocked lattice windows*   ᵇOr *platform*; also verse 10   ᶜSeptuagint; Hebrew *structure*, or *platform*   ᵈSeptuagint, Targum; Hebrew *middle*
ᵉVulgate; Hebrew *And before the inner sanctuary*   ᶠSeptuagint *made*
ᵍThe meaning of the Hebrew phrase is uncertain

SOLOMON BUILDS HIS PALACE

7 Solomon was building his own house for thirteen years, and he finished his entire house. ²He built the House of the Forest of Lebanon. Its length was a hundred cubits[a] and its breadth fifty cubits and its height thirty cubits, and it was built on four[b] rows of cedar pillars, with cedar beams on the pillars. ³And it was covered with cedar above the chambers that were on the forty-five pillars, fifteen in each row. ⁴There were window frames in three rows, and window opposite window in three tiers. ⁵All the doorways and windows[c] had square frames, and window was opposite window in three tiers.

⁶And he made the Hall of Pillars; its length was fifty cubits, and its breadth thirty cubits. There was a porch in front with pillars, and a canopy in front of them.

⁷And he made the Hall of the Throne where he was to pronounce judgement, even the Hall of Judgement. It was finished with cedar from floor to rafters.[d]

⁸His own house where he was to dwell, in the other court back of the hall, was of like workmanship. Solomon also made a house like this hall for Pharaoh's daughter whom he had taken in marriage.

⁹All these were made of costly stones, cut according to measure, sawn with saws, back and front, even from the foundation to the coping, and from the outside to the great court. ¹⁰The foundation was of costly stones, huge stones, stones of eight and ten cubits. ¹¹And above were costly stones, cut according to measurement, and cedar. ¹²The great court had three courses of cut stone all round, and a course of cedar beams; so had the inner court of the house of the LORD and the vestibule of the house.

THE TEMPLE FURNISHINGS

¹³And King Solomon sent and brought Hiram from Tyre. ¹⁴He was the son of a widow of the tribe of Naphtali, and his father was a man of Tyre, a worker in bronze. And he was full of wisdom, understanding, and skill for making any work in bronze. He came to King Solomon and did all his work.

¹⁵He cast two pillars of bronze. Eighteen cubits was the height of one pillar, and a line of twelve cubits measured its circumference. It was hollow, and its thickness was four fingers. The second pillar was the same.[e] ¹⁶He also made two capitals of cast bronze to set on the tops of the pillars. The height of one capital was five cubits, and the height of the other capital was five cubits. ¹⁷There were lattices of chequerwork with wreaths of chainwork for the capitals on the tops of the pillars, a lattice[f] for one capital and a lattice for the other capital. ¹⁸Likewise he made pomegranates[g] in two rows round the one latticework to cover the capital that was on the top of the pillar, and he did the same with the other capital. ¹⁹Now the capitals that were on the tops of the pillars in the vestibule were of lily-work, four cubits. ²⁰The capitals were on the two pillars and also above the rounded projection which was beside the latticework. There were two hundred pomegranates in two rows all round, and so with the other capital. ²¹He set up the pillars at the vestibule of the temple. He set up the pillar on the south and called its name Jachin, and he set up the pillar on the north and called its name Boaz. ²²And on the tops of the pillars was lily-work. Thus the work of the pillars was finished.

²³Then he made the sea of cast metal. It was round, ten cubits from brim to brim, and five cubits high, and a line of thirty cubits measured its circumference. ²⁴Under its brim were gourds, for ten cubits, compassing the sea all round. The gourds were in two rows, cast with it when it was cast. ²⁵It stood on twelve oxen, three facing north, three facing west, three facing south, and three facing east. The sea was set on them, and all their rear parts were inward. ²⁶Its thickness was a handbreadth,[h] and its brim was made like the brim of a cup, like the flower of a lily. It held two thousand baths.[i]

²⁷He also made the ten stands of bronze. Each stand was four cubits long, four cubits wide, and three cubits high. ²⁸This was the construction of the stands: they had panels, and the panels were set in the frames, ²⁹and on the panels that were set in the frames were lions, oxen, and cherubim. On the frames, both above and below the lions and oxen, there were wreaths of bevelled work. ³⁰Moreover, each stand had four bronze wheels and axles of bronze, and at the four corners were supports for a basin. The supports were cast with wreaths at the side of each. ³¹Its opening

---

[a] A *cubit* was about 18 inches or 45 centimetres [b] Septuagint *three* [c] Septuagint; Hebrew *posts* [d] Syriac, Vulgate; Hebrew *floor* [e] Targum, Syriac (compare Septuagint and Jeremiah 52:21); Hebrew *and a line of twelve cubits measured the circumference of the second pillar* [f] Septuagint; Hebrew *seven*; twice in this verse [g] Two manuscripts (compare Septuagint); Hebrew *pillars* [h] A *handbreadth* was about 3 inches or 7.5 centimetres [i] A *bath* was about 6 gallons or 22 litres

was within a crown that projected upwards one cubit. Its opening was round, as a pedestal is made, a cubit and a half deep. At its opening there were carvings, and its panels were square, not round. ³²And the four wheels were underneath the panels. The axles of the wheels were of one piece with the stands, and the height of a wheel was a cubit and a half. ³³The wheels were made like a chariot wheel; their axles, their rims, their spokes, and their hubs were all cast. ³⁴There were four supports at the four corners of each stand. The supports were of one piece with the stands. ³⁵And on the top of the stand there was a round band half a cubit high; and on the top of the stand its stays and its panels were of one piece with it. ³⁶And on the surfaces of its stays and on its panels, he carved cherubim, lions, and palm trees, according to the space of each, with wreaths all round. ³⁷After this manner he made the ten stands. All of them were cast alike, of the same measure and the same form.

³⁸And he made ten basins of bronze. Each basin held forty baths, each basin measured four cubits, and there was a basin for each of the ten stands. ³⁹And he set the stands, five on the south side of the house, and five on the north side of the house. And he set the sea at the southeast corner of the house.

⁴⁰Hiram also made the pots, the shovels, and the basins. So Hiram finished all the work that he did for King Solomon on the house of the LORD: ⁴¹the two pillars, the two bowls of the capitals that were on the tops of the pillars, and the two latticeworks to cover the two bowls of the capitals that were on the tops of the pillars; ⁴²and the four hundred pomegranates for the two latticeworks, two rows of pomegranates for each latticework, to cover the two bowls of the capitals that were on the pillars; ⁴³the ten stands, and the ten basins on the stands; ⁴⁴and the one sea, and the twelve oxen underneath the sea.

⁴⁵Now the pots, the shovels, and the basins, all these vessels in the house of the LORD, which Hiram made for King Solomon, were of burnished bronze. ⁴⁶In the plain of the Jordan the king cast them, in the clay ground between Succoth and Zarethan. ⁴⁷And Solomon left all the vessels unweighed, because there were so many of them; the weight of the bronze was not ascertained.

⁴⁸So Solomon made all the vessels that were in the house of the LORD: the golden altar, the golden table for the bread of the Presence, ⁴⁹the lampstands of pure gold, five on the south side and five on the north, before the inner sanctuary; the flowers, the lamps, and the tongs, of gold; ⁵⁰the cups, snuffers, basins, dishes for incense, and firepans, of pure gold; and the sockets of gold, for the doors of the innermost part of the house, the Most Holy Place, and for the doors of the nave of the temple.

⁵¹Thus all the work that King Solomon did on the house of the LORD was finished. And Solomon brought in the things that David his father had dedicated, the silver, the gold, and the vessels, and stored them in the treasuries of the house of the LORD.

THE ARK BROUGHT INTO THE TEMPLE

8 Then Solomon assembled the elders of Israel and all the heads of the tribes, the leaders of the fathers' houses of the people of Israel, before King Solomon in Jerusalem, to bring up the ark of the covenant of the LORD out of the city of David, which is Zion. ²And all the men of Israel assembled to King Solomon at the feast in the month Ethanim, which is the seventh month. ³And all the elders of Israel came, and the priests took up the ark. ⁴And they brought up the ark of the LORD, the tent of meeting, and all the holy vessels that were in the tent; the priests and the Levites brought them up. ⁵And King Solomon and all the congregation of Israel, who had assembled before him, were with him before the ark, sacrificing so many sheep and oxen that they could not be counted or numbered. ⁶Then the priests brought the ark of the covenant of the LORD to its place in the inner sanctuary of the house, in the Most Holy Place, underneath the wings of the cherubim. ⁷For the cherubim spread out their wings over the place of the ark, so that the cherubim overshadowed the ark and its poles. ⁸And the poles were so long that the ends of the poles were seen from the Holy Place before the inner sanctuary; but they could not be seen from outside. And they are there to this day. ⁹There was nothing in the ark except the two tablets of stone that Moses put there at Horeb, where the LORD made a covenant with the people of Israel, when they came out of the land of Egypt. ¹⁰And when the priests came out of the Holy Place, a cloud filled the house of the LORD, ¹¹so that the priests could not stand to minister because of the cloud, for the glory of the LORD filled the house of the LORD.

SOLOMON BLESSES THE LORD

12 Then Solomon said, "The LORD[a] has said that he would dwell in thick darkness. **13** I have indeed built you an exalted house, a place for you to dwell in for ever." **14** Then the king turned round and blessed all the assembly of Israel, while all the assembly of Israel stood. **15** And he said, "Blessed be the LORD, the God of Israel, who with his hand has fulfilled what he promised with his mouth to David my father, saying, **16** 'Since the day that I brought my people Israel out of Egypt, I chose no city out of all the tribes of Israel in which to build a house, that my name might be there. But I chose David to be over my people Israel.' **17** Now it was in the heart of David my father to build a house for the name of the LORD, the God of Israel. **18** But the LORD said to David my father, 'Whereas it was in your heart to build a house for my name, you did well that it was in your heart. **19** Nevertheless, you shall not build the house, but your son who shall be born to you shall build the house for my name.' **20** Now the LORD has fulfilled his promise that he made. For I have risen in the place of David my father, and sit on the throne of Israel, as the LORD promised, and I have built the house for the name of the LORD, the God of Israel. **21** And there I have provided a place for the ark, in which is the covenant of the LORD that he made with our fathers, when he brought them out of the land of Egypt."

SOLOMON'S PRAYER OF DEDICATION

22 Then Solomon stood before the altar of the LORD in the presence of all the assembly of Israel and spread out his hands towards heaven, **23** and said, "O LORD, God of Israel, there is no God like you, in heaven above or on earth beneath, keeping covenant and showing steadfast love to your servants who walk before you with all their heart; **24** you have kept with your servant David my father what you declared to him. You spoke with your mouth, and with your hand have fulfilled it this day. **25** Now therefore, O LORD, God of Israel, keep for your servant David my father what you have promised him, saying, 'You shall not lack a man to sit before me on the throne of Israel, if only your sons pay close attention to their way, to walk before me as you have walked before me.' **26** Now therefore, O God of Israel, let your word be confirmed, which you have spoken to your servant David my father.

27 "But will God indeed dwell on the earth? Behold, heaven and the highest heaven cannot contain you; how much less this house that I have built! **28** Yet have regard to the prayer of your servant and to his plea, O LORD my God, listening to the cry and to the prayer that your servant prays before you this day, **29** that your eyes may be open night and day towards this house, the place of which you have said, 'My name shall be there', that you may listen to the prayer that your servant offers towards this place. **30** And listen to the plea of your servant and of your people Israel, when they pray towards this place. And listen in heaven your dwelling place, and when you hear, forgive.

31 "If a man sins against his neighbour and is made to take an oath and comes and swears his oath before your altar in this house, **32** then hear in heaven and act and judge your servants, condemning the guilty by bringing his conduct on his own head, and vindicating the righteous by rewarding him according to his righteousness.

33 "When your people Israel are defeated before the enemy because they have sinned against you, and if they turn again to you and acknowledge your name and pray and plead with you in this house, **34** then hear in heaven and forgive the sin of your people Israel and bring them again to the land that you gave to their fathers.

35 "When heaven is shut up and there is no rain because they have sinned against you, if they pray towards this place and acknowledge your name and turn from their sin, when you afflict them, **36** then hear in heaven and forgive the sin of your servants, your people Israel, when you teach them the good way in which they should walk, and grant rain upon your land, which you have given to your people as an inheritance.

37 "If there is famine in the land, if there is pestilence or blight or mildew or locust or caterpillar, if their enemy besieges them in the land at their gates,[b] whatever plague, whatever sickness there is, **38** whatever prayer, whatever plea is made by any man or by all your people Israel, each knowing the affliction of his own heart and stretching out his hands towards this house, **39** then hear in heaven your dwelling place and forgive and act and render to each whose heart you know,

---
[a] Septuagint *The LORD has set the sun in the heavens, but* [b] Septuagint, Syriac *in any of their cities*

according to all his ways (for you, you only, know the hearts of all the children of mankind), ⁴⁰that they may fear you all the days that they live in the land that you gave to our fathers.

⁴¹"Likewise, when a foreigner, who is not of your people Israel, comes from a far country for your name's sake ⁴²(for they shall hear of your great name and your mighty hand, and of your outstretched arm), when he comes and prays towards this house, ⁴³hear in heaven your dwelling place and do according to all for which the foreigner calls to you, in order that all the peoples of the earth may know your name and fear you, as do your people Israel, and that they may know that this house that I have built is called by your name.

⁴⁴"If your people go out to battle against their enemy, by whatever way you shall send them, and they pray to the LORD towards the city that you have chosen and the house that I have built for your name, ⁴⁵then hear in heaven their prayer and their plea, and maintain their cause.

⁴⁶"If they sin against you—for there is no one who does not sin—and you are angry with them and give them to an enemy, so that they are carried away captive to the land of the enemy, far off or near, ⁴⁷yet if they turn their heart in the land to which they have been carried captive, and repent and plead with you in the land of their captors, saying, 'We have sinned and have acted perversely and wickedly', ⁴⁸if they repent with all their heart and with all their soul in the land of their enemies, who carried them captive, and pray to you towards their land, which you gave to their fathers, the city that you have chosen, and the house that I have built for your name, ⁴⁹then hear in heaven your dwelling place their prayer and their plea, and maintain their cause ⁵⁰and forgive your people who have sinned against you, and all their transgressions that they have committed against you, and grant them compassion in the sight of those who carried them captive, that they may have compassion on them ⁵¹(for they are your people, and your heritage, which you brought out of Egypt, from the midst of the iron furnace). ⁵²Let your eyes be open to the plea of your servant and to the plea of your people Israel, giving ear to them whenever they call to you. ⁵³For you separated them from among all the peoples of the earth to be your heritage, as you declared through Moses your servant, when you brought our fathers out of Egypt, O Lord GOD."

SOLOMON'S BENEDICTION

⁵⁴Now as Solomon finished offering all this prayer and plea to the LORD, he arose from before the altar of the LORD, where he had knelt with hands outstretched towards heaven. ⁵⁵And he stood and blessed all the assembly of Israel with a loud voice, saying, ⁵⁶"Blessed be the LORD who has given rest to his people Israel, according to all that he promised. Not one word has failed of all his good promise, which he spoke by Moses his servant. ⁵⁷The LORD our God be with us, as he was with our fathers. May he not leave us or forsake us, ⁵⁸that he may incline our hearts to him, to walk in all his ways and to keep his commandments, his statutes, and his rules, which he commanded our fathers. ⁵⁹Let these words of mine, with which I have pleaded before the LORD, be near to the LORD our God day and night, and may he maintain the cause of his servant and the cause of his people Israel, as each day requires, ⁶⁰that all the peoples of the earth may know that the LORD is God; there is no other. ⁶¹Let your heart therefore be wholly true to the LORD our God, walking in his statutes and keeping his commandments, as at this day."

SOLOMON'S SACRIFICES

⁶²Then the king, and all Israel with him, offered sacrifice before the LORD. ⁶³Solomon offered as peace offerings to the LORD 22,000 oxen and 120,000 sheep. So the king and all the people of Israel dedicated the house of the LORD. ⁶⁴The same day the king consecrated the middle of the court that was before the house of the LORD, for there he offered the burnt offering and the grain offering and the fat pieces of the peace offerings, because the bronze altar that was before the LORD was too small to receive the burnt offering and the grain offering and the fat pieces of the peace offerings.

⁶⁵So Solomon held the feast at that time, and all Israel with him, a great assembly, from Lebo-hamath to the Brook of Egypt, before the LORD our God, seven days.[a] ⁶⁶On the eighth day he sent the people away, and they blessed the king and went to their homes joyful and glad of heart for all the goodness that the LORD had shown to David his servant and to Israel his people.

---

[a] Septuagint; Hebrew *seven days and seven days, fourteen days*

THE LORD APPEARS TO SOLOMON

9 As soon as Solomon had finished building the house of the LORD and the king's house and all that Solomon desired to build, ²the LORD appeared to Solomon a second time, as he had appeared to him at Gibeon. ³And the LORD said to him, "I have heard your prayer and your plea, which you have made before me. I have consecrated this house that you have built, by putting my name there for ever. My eyes and my heart will be there for all time. ⁴And as for you, if you will walk before me, as David your father walked, with integrity of heart and uprightness, doing according to all that I have commanded you, and keeping my statutes and my rules, ⁵then I will establish your royal throne over Israel for ever, as I promised David your father, saying, 'You shall not lack a man on the throne of Israel.' ⁶But if you turn aside from following me, you or your children, and do not keep my commandments and my statutes that I have set before you, but go and serve other gods and worship them, ⁷then I will cut off Israel from the land that I have given them, and the house that I have consecrated for my name I will cast out of my sight, and Israel will become a proverb and a byword among all peoples. ⁸And this house will become a heap of ruins.ᵃ Everyone passing by it will be astonished and will hiss, and they will say, 'Why has the LORD done thus to this land and to this house?' ⁹Then they will say, 'Because they abandoned the LORD their God who brought their fathers out of the land of Egypt and laid hold on other gods and worshipped them and served them. Therefore the LORD has brought all this disaster on them.'"

SOLOMON'S OTHER ACTS

¹⁰At the end of twenty years, in which Solomon had built the two houses, the house of the LORD and the king's house, ¹¹and Hiram king of Tyre had supplied Solomon with cedar and cypress timber and gold, as much as he desired, King Solomon gave to Hiram twenty cities in the land of Galilee. ¹²But when Hiram came from Tyre to see the cities that Solomon had given him, they did not please him. ¹³Therefore he said, "What kind of cities are these that you have given me, my brother?" So they are called the land of Cabul to this day. ¹⁴Hiram had sent to the king 120 talentsᵇ of gold.

¹⁵And this is the account of the forced labour that King Solomon drafted to build the house of the LORD and his own house and the Millo and the wall of Jerusalem and Hazor and Megiddo and Gezer ¹⁶(Pharaoh king of Egypt had gone up and captured Gezer and burned it with fire, and had killed the Canaanites who lived in the city, and had given it as dowry to his daughter, Solomon's wife; ¹⁷so Solomon rebuilt Gezer) and Lower Beth-horon ¹⁸and Baalath and Tamar in the wilderness, in the land of Judah,ᶜ ¹⁹and all the store cities that Solomon had, and the cities for his chariots, and the cities for his horsemen, and whatever Solomon desired to build in Jerusalem, in Lebanon, and in all the land of his dominion. ²⁰All the people who were left of the Amorites, the Hittites, the Perizzites, the Hivites, and the Jebusites, who were not of the people of Israel — ²¹their descendants who were left after them in the land, whom the people of Israel were unable to devote to destructionᵈ — these Solomon drafted to be slaves, and so they are to this day. ²²But of the people of Israel Solomon made no slaves. They were the soldiers, they were his officials, his commanders, his captains, his chariot commanders and his horsemen.

²³These were the chief officers who were over Solomon's work: 550 who had charge of the people who carried on the work.

²⁴But Pharaoh's daughter went up from the city of David to her own house that Solomon had built for her. Then he built the Millo.

²⁵Three times a year Solomon used to offer up burnt offerings and peace offerings on the altar that he built to the LORD, making offerings with itᵉ before the LORD. So he finished the house.

²⁶King Solomon built a fleet of ships at Ezion-geber, which is near Eloth on the shore of the Red Sea, in the land of Edom. ²⁷And Hiram sent with the fleet his servants, seamen who were familiar with the sea, together with the servants of Solomon. ²⁸And they went to Ophir and brought from there gold, 420 talents, and they brought it to King Solomon.

THE QUEEN OF SHEBA

10 Now when the queen of Sheba heard of the fame of Solomon concerning the name of the LORD, she came to test him with hard questions. ²She came to Jerusalem with a very great retinue,

---

ᵃSyriac, Old Latin; Hebrew *will become high* ᵇA *talent* was about 75 pounds or 34 kilograms ᶜHebrew lacks *of Judah* ᵈThat is, set apart (devote) as an offering to the Lord (for destruction) ᵉSeptuagint lacks *with it*

with camels bearing spices and very much gold and precious stones. And when she came to Solomon, she told him all that was on her mind. ³And Solomon answered all her questions; there was nothing hidden from the king that he could not explain to her. ⁴And when the queen of Sheba had seen all the wisdom of Solomon, the house that he had built, ⁵the food of his table, the seating of his officials, and the attendance of his servants, their clothing, his cupbearers, and his burnt offerings that he offered at the house of the LORD, there was no more breath in her.

⁶And she said to the king, "The report was true that I heard in my own land of your words and of your wisdom, ⁷but I did not believe the reports until I came and my own eyes had seen it. And behold, the half was not told me. Your wisdom and prosperity surpass the report that I heard. ⁸Happy are your men! Happy are your servants, who continually stand before you and hear your wisdom! ⁹Blessed be the LORD your God, who has delighted in you and set you on the throne of Israel! Because the LORD loved Israel for ever, he has made you king, that you may execute justice and righteousness." ¹⁰Then she gave the king 120 talents[a] of gold, and a very great quantity of spices and precious stones. Never again came such an abundance of spices as these that the queen of Sheba gave to King Solomon.

¹¹Moreover, the fleet of Hiram, which brought gold from Ophir, brought from Ophir a very great amount of almug wood and precious stones. ¹²And the king made of the almug wood supports for the house of the LORD and for the king's house, also lyres and harps for the singers. No such almug wood has come or been seen to this day.

¹³And King Solomon gave to the queen of Sheba all that she desired, whatever she asked besides what was given her by the bounty of King Solomon. So she turned and went back to her own land with her servants.

SOLOMON'S GREAT WEALTH

¹⁴Now the weight of gold that came to Solomon in one year was 666 talents of gold, ¹⁵besides that which came from the explorers and from the business of the merchants, and from all the kings of the west and from the governors of the land. ¹⁶King Solomon made 200 large shields of beaten gold; 600 shekels[b] of gold went into each shield. ¹⁷And he made 300 shields of beaten gold; three minas[c] of gold went into each shield. And the king put them in the House of the Forest of Lebanon. ¹⁸The king also made a great ivory throne and overlaid it with the finest gold. ¹⁹The throne had six steps, and the throne had a round top,[d] and on each side of the seat were armrests and two lions standing beside the armrests, ²⁰while twelve lions stood there, one on each end of a step on the six steps. The like of it was never made in any kingdom. ²¹All King Solomon's drinking vessels were of gold, and all the vessels of the House of the Forest of Lebanon were of pure gold. None were of silver; silver was not considered as anything in the days of Solomon. ²²For the king had a fleet of ships of Tarshish at sea with the fleet of Hiram. Once every three years the fleet of ships of Tarshish used to come bringing gold, silver, ivory, apes, and peacocks.[e]

²³Thus King Solomon excelled all the kings of the earth in riches and in wisdom. ²⁴And the whole earth sought the presence of Solomon to hear his wisdom, which God had put into his mind. ²⁵Every one of them brought his present, articles of silver and gold, garments, myrrh,[f] spices, horses, and mules, so much year by year.

²⁶And Solomon gathered together chariots and horsemen. He had 1,400 chariots and 12,000 horsemen, whom he stationed in the chariot cities and with the king in Jerusalem. ²⁷And the king made silver as common in Jerusalem as stone, and he made cedar as plentiful as the sycamore of the Shephelah. ²⁸And Solomon's import of horses was from Egypt and Kue, and the king's traders received them from Kue at a price. ²⁹A chariot could be imported from Egypt for 600 shekels of silver and a horse for 150, and so through the king's traders they were exported to all the kings of the Hittites and the kings of Syria.

SOLOMON TURNS FROM THE LORD

11 Now King Solomon loved many foreign women, along with the daughter of Pharaoh: Moabite, Ammonite, Edomite, Sidonian, and Hittite women, ²from the nations concerning which the LORD had said to the people of Israel, "You shall not enter into marriage with them, neither shall they with you, for surely they will turn away your heart after their gods." Solomon clung

---

[a]A *talent* was about 75 pounds or 34 kilograms [b]A *shekel* was about 2/5 of an ounce or 11 grams [c]A *mina* was about 1 1/4 pounds or 0.6 kilogram [d]Or *and at the back of the throne was a calf's head* [e]Or *baboons* [f]Or *armour*

to these in love. ³He had 700 wives, who were princesses, and 300 concubines. And his wives turned away his heart. ⁴For when Solomon was old his wives turned away his heart after other gods, and his heart was not wholly true to the LORD his God, as was the heart of David his father. ⁵For Solomon went after Ashtoreth the goddess of the Sidonians, and after Milcom the abomination of the Ammonites. ⁶So Solomon did what was evil in the sight of the LORD and did not wholly follow the LORD, as David his father had done. ⁷Then Solomon built a high place for Chemosh the abomination of Moab, and for Molech the abomination of the Ammonites, on the mountain east of Jerusalem. ⁸And so he did for all his foreign wives, who made offerings and sacrificed to their gods.

THE LORD RAISES ADVERSARIES

⁹And the LORD was angry with Solomon, because his heart had turned away from the LORD, the God of Israel, who had appeared to him twice ¹⁰and had commanded him concerning this thing, that he should not go after other gods. But he did not keep what the LORD commanded. ¹¹Therefore the LORD said to Solomon, "Since this has been your practice and you have not kept my covenant and my statutes that I have commanded you, I will surely tear the kingdom from you and will give it to your servant. ¹²Yet for the sake of David your father I will not do it in your days, but I will tear it out of the hand of your son. ¹³However, I will not tear away all the kingdom, but I will give one tribe to your son, for the sake of David my servant and for the sake of Jerusalem, which I have chosen."

¹⁴And the LORD raised up an adversary against Solomon, Hadad the Edomite. He was of the royal house in Edom. ¹⁵For when David was in Edom, and Joab the commander of the army went up to bury the slain, he struck down every male in Edom ¹⁶(for Joab and all Israel remained there for six months, until he had cut off every male in Edom). ¹⁷But Hadad fled to Egypt, together with certain Edomites of his father's servants, Hadad still being a little child. ¹⁸They set out from Midian and came to Paran and took men with them from Paran and came to Egypt, to Pharaoh king of Egypt, who gave him a house and assigned him an allowance of food and gave him land. ¹⁹And Hadad found great favour in the sight of Pharaoh, so that he gave him in marriage the sister of his own wife, the sister of Tahpenes the queen. ²⁰And the sister of Tahpenes bore him Genubath his son, whom Tahpenes weaned in Pharaoh's house. And Genubath was in Pharaoh's house among the sons of Pharaoh. ²¹But when Hadad heard in Egypt that David slept with his fathers and that Joab the commander of the army was dead, Hadad said to Pharaoh, "Let me depart, that I may go to my own country." ²²But Pharaoh said to him, "What have you lacked with me that you are now seeking to go to your own country?" And he said to him, "Only let me depart."

²³God also raised up as an adversary to him, Rezon the son of Eliada, who had fled from his master Hadadezer king of Zobah. ²⁴And he gathered men about him and became leader of a marauding band, after the killing by David. And they went to Damascus and lived there and made him king in Damascus. ²⁵He was an adversary of Israel all the days of Solomon, doing harm as Hadad did. And he loathed Israel and reigned over Syria.

²⁶Jeroboam the son of Nebat, an Ephraimite of Zeredah, a servant of Solomon, whose mother's name was Zeruah, a widow, also lifted up his hand against the king. ²⁷And this was the reason why he lifted up his hand against the king. Solomon built the Millo, and closed up the breach of the city of David his father. ²⁸The man Jeroboam was very able, and when Solomon saw that the young man was industrious he gave him charge over all the forced labour of the house of Joseph. ²⁹And at that time, when Jeroboam went out of Jerusalem, the prophet Ahijah the Shilonite found him on the road. Now Ahijah had dressed himself in a new garment, and the two of them were alone in the open country. ³⁰Then Ahijah laid hold of the new garment that was on him, and tore it into twelve pieces. ³¹And he said to Jeroboam, "Take for yourself ten pieces, for thus says the LORD, the God of Israel, 'Behold, I am about to tear the kingdom from the hand of Solomon and will give you ten tribes ³²(but he shall have one tribe, for the sake of my servant David and for the sake of Jerusalem, the city that I have chosen out of all the tribes of Israel), ³³because they have[a] forsaken me and worshipped Ashtoreth the goddess of the Sidonians, Chemosh the god of Moab, and Milcom the god of the Ammonites, and they have not walked in my ways, doing what is right in my sight and keeping

---

[a]Septuagint, Syriac, Vulgate *he has*; twice in this verse

my statutes and my rules, as David his father did. ³⁴Nevertheless, I will not take the whole kingdom out of his hand, but I will make him ruler all the days of his life, for the sake of David my servant whom I chose, who kept my commandments and my statutes. ³⁵But I will take the kingdom out of his son's hand and will give it to you, ten tribes. ³⁶Yet to his son I will give one tribe, that David my servant may always have a lamp before me in Jerusalem, the city where I have chosen to put my name. ³⁷And I will take you, and you shall reign over all that your soul desires, and you shall be king over Israel. ³⁸And if you will listen to all that I command you, and will walk in my ways, and do what is right in my eyes by keeping my statutes and my commandments, as David my servant did, I will be with you and will build you a sure house, as I built for David, and I will give Israel to you. ³⁹And I will afflict the offspring of David because of this, but not for ever.'" ⁴⁰Solomon sought therefore to kill Jeroboam. But Jeroboam arose and fled into Egypt, to Shishak king of Egypt, and was in Egypt until the death of Solomon.

⁴¹Now the rest of the acts of Solomon, and all that he did, and his wisdom, are they not written in the Book of the Acts of Solomon? ⁴²And the time that Solomon reigned in Jerusalem over all Israel was forty years. ⁴³And Solomon slept with his fathers and was buried in the city of David his father. And Rehoboam his son reigned in his place.

REHOBOAM'S FOLLY

12 Rehoboam went to Shechem, for all Israel had come to Shechem to make him king. ²And as soon as Jeroboam the son of Nebat heard of it (for he was still in Egypt, where he had fled from King Solomon), then Jeroboam returned from*ᵃ* Egypt. ³And they sent and called him, and Jeroboam and all the assembly of Israel came and said to Rehoboam, ⁴"Your father made our yoke heavy. Now therefore lighten the hard service of your father and his heavy yoke on us, and we will serve you." ⁵He said to them, "Go away for three days, then come again to me." So the people went away.

⁶Then King Rehoboam took counsel with the old men, who had stood before Solomon his father while he was yet alive, saying, "How do you advise me to answer this people?" ⁷And they said to him, "If you will be a servant to this people today and serve them, and speak good words to them when you answer them, then they will be your servants for ever." ⁸But he abandoned the counsel that the old men gave him and took counsel with the young men who had grown up with him and stood before him. ⁹And he said to them, "What do you advise that we answer this people who have said to me, 'Lighten the yoke that your father put on us'?" ¹⁰And the young men who had grown up with him said to him, "Thus shall you speak to this people who said to you, 'Your father made our yoke heavy, but you lighten it for us', thus shall you say to them, 'My little finger is thicker than my father's thighs. ¹¹And now, whereas my father laid on you a heavy yoke, I will add to your yoke. My father disciplined you with whips, but I will discipline you with scorpions.'"

¹²So Jeroboam and all the people came to Rehoboam on the third day, as the king said, "Come to me again on the third day." ¹³And the king answered the people harshly, and forsaking the counsel that the old men had given him, ¹⁴he spoke to them according to the counsel of the young men, saying, "My father made your yoke heavy, but I will add to your yoke. My father disciplined you with whips, but I will discipline you with scorpions." ¹⁵So the king did not listen to the people, for it was a turn of affairs brought about by the LORD that he might fulfil his word, which the LORD spoke by Ahijah the Shilonite to Jeroboam the son of Nebat.

THE KINGDOM DIVIDED

¹⁶And when all Israel saw that the king did not listen to them, the people answered the king, "What portion do we have in David? We have no inheritance in the son of Jesse. To your tents, O Israel! Look now to your own house, David." So Israel went to their tents. ¹⁷But Rehoboam reigned over the people of Israel who lived in the cities of Judah. ¹⁸Then King Rehoboam sent Adoram, who was taskmaster over the forced labour, and all Israel stoned him to death with stones. And King Rehoboam hurried to mount his chariot to flee to Jerusalem. ¹⁹So Israel has been in rebellion against the house of David to this day. ²⁰And when all Israel heard that Jeroboam had returned, they sent and called him to the assembly and made him king over all Israel. There was none that followed the house of David but the tribe of Judah only.

---

*ᵃ*Septuagint, Vulgate (compare 2 Chronicles 10:2); Hebrew *lived in*

21When Rehoboam came to Jerusalem, he assembled all the house of Judah and the tribe of Benjamin, 180,000 chosen warriors, to fight against the house of Israel, to restore the kingdom to Rehoboam the son of Solomon. 22But the word of God came to Shemaiah the man of God: 23"Say to Rehoboam the son of Solomon, king of Judah, and to all the house of Judah and Benjamin, and to the rest of the people, 24'Thus says the LORD, You shall not go up or fight against your relatives the people of Israel. Every man return to his home, for this thing is from me.'" So they listened to the word of the LORD and went home again, according to the word of the LORD.

JEROBOAM'S GOLDEN CALVES

25Then Jeroboam built Shechem in the hill country of Ephraim and lived there. And he went out from there and built Penuel. 26And Jeroboam said in his heart, "Now the kingdom will turn back to the house of David. 27If this people go up to offer sacrifices in the temple of the LORD at Jerusalem, then the heart of this people will turn again to their lord, to Rehoboam king of Judah, and they will kill me and return to Rehoboam king of Judah." 28So the king took counsel and made two calves of gold. And he said to the people, "You have gone up to Jerusalem long enough. Behold your gods, O Israel, who brought you up out of the land of Egypt." 29And he set one in Bethel, and the other he put in Dan. 30Then this thing became a sin, for the people went as far as Dan to be before one.[a] 31He also made temples on high places and appointed priests from among all the people, who were not of the Levites. 32And Jeroboam appointed a feast on the fifteenth day of the eighth month like the feast that was in Judah, and he offered sacrifices on the altar. So he did in Bethel, sacrificing to the calves that he made. And he placed in Bethel the priests of the high places that he had made. 33He went up to the altar that he had made in Bethel on the fifteenth day in the eighth month, in the month that he had devised from his own heart. And he instituted a feast for the people of Israel and went up to the altar to make offerings.

A MAN OF GOD CONFRONTS JEROBOAM

13 And behold, a man of God came out of Judah by the word of the LORD to Bethel. Jeroboam was standing by the altar to make offerings. 2And the man cried against the altar by the word of the LORD and said, "O altar, altar, thus says the LORD: 'Behold, a son shall be born to the house of David, Josiah by name, and he shall sacrifice on you the priests of the high places who make offerings on you, and human bones shall be burned on you.'" 3And he gave a sign the same day, saying, "This is the sign that the LORD has spoken: 'Behold, the altar shall be torn down, and the ashes that are on it shall be poured out.'" 4And when the king heard the saying of the man of God, which he cried against the altar at Bethel, Jeroboam stretched out his hand from the altar, saying, "Seize him." And his hand, which he stretched out against him, dried up, so that he could not draw it back to himself. 5The altar also was torn down, and the ashes poured out from the altar, according to the sign that the man of God had given by the word of the LORD. 6And the king said to the man of God, "Entreat now the favour of the LORD your God, and pray for me, that my hand may be restored to me." And the man of God entreated the LORD, and the king's hand was restored to him and became as it was before. 7And the king said to the man of God, "Come home with me, and refresh yourself, and I will give you a reward." 8And the man of God said to the king, "If you give me half your house, I will not go in with you. And I will not eat bread or drink water in this place, 9for so was it commanded me by the word of the LORD, saying, 'You shall neither eat bread nor drink water nor return by the way that you came.'" 10So he went another way and did not return by the way that he came to Bethel.

THE PROPHET'S DISOBEDIENCE

11Now an old prophet lived in Bethel. And his sons[b] came and told him all that the man of God had done that day in Bethel. They also told to their father the words that he had spoken to the king. 12And their father said to them, "Which way did he go?" And his sons showed him the way that the man of God who came from Judah had gone. 13And he said to his sons, "Saddle the donkey for me." So they saddled the donkey for him and he mounted it. 14And he went after the man of God and found him sitting under an oak. And he said to him, "Are you the man of God who came from Judah?" And he said, "I am." 15Then he said to him, "Come home with

---
[a]Septuagint *went to the one at Bethel and to the other as far as Dan*
[b]Septuagint, Syriac, Vulgate; Hebrew *son*

me and eat bread." ¹⁶And he said, "I may not return with you, or go in with you, neither will I eat bread nor drink water with you in this place, ¹⁷for it was said to me by the word of the LORD, 'You shall neither eat bread nor drink water there, nor return by the way that you came.'" ¹⁸And he said to him, "I also am a prophet as you are, and an angel spoke to me by the word of the LORD, saying, 'Bring him back with you into your house that he may eat bread and drink water.'" But he lied to him. ¹⁹So he went back with him and ate bread in his house and drank water.

²⁰And as they sat at the table, the word of the LORD came to the prophet who had brought him back. ²¹And he cried to the man of God who came from Judah, "Thus says the LORD, 'Because you have disobeyed the word of the LORD and have not kept the command that the LORD your God commanded you, ²²but have come back and have eaten bread and drunk water in the place of which he said to you, "Eat no bread and drink no water", your body shall not come to the tomb of your fathers.'" ²³And after he had eaten bread and drunk, he saddled the donkey for the prophet whom he had brought back. ²⁴And as he went away a lion met him on the road and killed him. And his body was thrown in the road, and the donkey stood beside it; the lion also stood beside the body. ²⁵And behold, men passed by and saw the body thrown in the road and the lion standing by the body. And they came and told it in the city where the old prophet lived.

²⁶And when the prophet who had brought him back from the way heard of it, he said, "It is the man of God who disobeyed the word of the LORD, therefore the LORD has given him to the lion, which has torn him and killed him, according to the word that the LORD spoke to him." ²⁷And he said to his sons, "Saddle the donkey for me." And they saddled it. ²⁸And he went and found his body thrown in the road, and the donkey and the lion standing beside the body. The lion had not eaten the body or torn the donkey. ²⁹And the prophet took up the body of the man of God and laid it on the donkey and brought it back to the city*ᵃ* to mourn and to bury him. ³⁰And he laid the body in his own grave. And they mourned over him, saying, "Alas, my brother!" ³¹And after he had buried him, he said to his sons, "When I die, bury me in the grave in which the man of God is buried; lay my bones beside his bones. ³²For the saying that he called out by the word of the LORD against the altar in Bethel and against all the houses of the high places that are in the cities of Samaria shall surely come to pass."

³³After this thing Jeroboam did not turn from his evil way, but made priests for the high places again from among all the people. Any who would, he ordained to be priests of the high places. ³⁴And this thing became sin to the house of Jeroboam, so as to cut it off and to destroy it from the face of the earth.

PROPHECY AGAINST JEROBOAM

14 At that time Abijah the son of Jeroboam fell sick. ²And Jeroboam said to his wife, "Arise, and disguise yourself, that it not be known that you are the wife of Jeroboam, and go to Shiloh. Behold, Ahijah the prophet is there, who said of me that I should be king over this people. ³Take with you ten loaves, some cakes, and a jar of honey, and go to him. He will tell you what shall happen to the child."

⁴Jeroboam's wife did so. She arose and went to Shiloh and came to the house of Ahijah. Now Ahijah could not see, for his eyes were dim because of his age. ⁵And the LORD said to Ahijah, "Behold, the wife of Jeroboam is coming to enquire of you concerning her son, for he is sick. Thus and thus shall you say to her."

When she came, she pretended to be another woman. ⁶But when Ahijah heard the sound of her feet, as she came in at the door, he said, "Come in, wife of Jeroboam. Why do you pretend to be another? For I am charged with unbearable news for you. ⁷Go, tell Jeroboam, 'Thus says the LORD, the God of Israel: "Because I exalted you from among the people and made you leader over my people Israel ⁸and tore the kingdom away from the house of David and gave it to you, and yet you have not been like my servant David, who kept my commandments and followed me with all his heart, doing only that which was right in my eyes, ⁹but you have done evil above all who were before you and have gone and made for yourself other gods and metal images, provoking me to anger, and have cast me behind your back, ¹⁰therefore behold, I will bring harm upon the house of Jeroboam and will cut off from Jeroboam every male, both bond and free in Israel, and will burn up the house of Jeroboam, as a man burns up dung until it is all gone. ¹¹Anyone belonging

---

*ᵃ*Septuagint; Hebrew *he came to the city of the old prophet*

to Jeroboam who dies in the city the dogs shall eat, and anyone who dies in the open country the birds of the heavens shall eat, for the LORD has spoken it."' ¹²Arise therefore, go to your house. When your feet enter the city, the child shall die. ¹³And all Israel shall mourn for him and bury him, for he only of Jeroboam shall come to the grave, because in him there is found something pleasing to the LORD, the God of Israel, in the house of Jeroboam. ¹⁴Moreover, the LORD will raise up for himself a king over Israel who shall cut off the house of Jeroboam today. And henceforth, ¹⁵the LORD will strike Israel as a reed is shaken in the water, and root up Israel out of this good land that he gave to their fathers and scatter them beyond the Euphrates,ᵃ because they have made their Asherim, provoking the LORD to anger. ¹⁶And he will give Israel up because of the sins of Jeroboam, which he sinned and made Israel to sin."

¹⁷Then Jeroboam's wife arose and departed and came to Tirzah. And as she came to the threshold of the house, the child died. ¹⁸And all Israel buried him and mourned for him, according to the word of the LORD, which he spoke by his servant Ahijah the prophet.

THE DEATH OF JEROBOAM

¹⁹Now the rest of the acts of Jeroboam, how he warred and how he reigned, behold, they are written in the Book of the Chronicles of the Kings of Israel. ²⁰And the time that Jeroboam reigned was twenty-two years. And he slept with his fathers, and Nadab his son reigned in his place.

REHOBOAM REIGNS IN JUDAH

²¹Now Rehoboam the son of Solomon reigned in Judah. Rehoboam was forty-one years old when he began to reign, and he reigned for seventeen years in Jerusalem, the city that the LORD had chosen out of all the tribes of Israel, to put his name there. His mother's name was Naamah the Ammonite. ²²And Judah did what was evil in the sight of the LORD, and they provoked him to jealousy with their sins that they committed, more than all that their fathers had done. ²³For they also built for themselves high places and pillars and Asherim on every high hill and under every green tree, ²⁴and there were also male cult prostitutes in the land. They did according to all the abominations of the nations that the LORD drove out before the people of Israel.

²⁵In the fifth year of King Rehoboam, Shishak king of Egypt came up against Jerusalem. ²⁶He took away the treasures of the house of the LORD and the treasures of the king's house. He took away everything. He also took away all the shields of gold that Solomon had made, ²⁷and King Rehoboam made in their place shields of bronze, and committed them to the hands of the officers of the guard, who kept the door of the king's house. ²⁸And as often as the king went into the house of the LORD, the guard carried them and brought them back to the guardroom.

²⁹Now the rest of the acts of Rehoboam and all that he did, are they not written in the Book of the Chronicles of the Kings of Judah? ³⁰And there was war between Rehoboam and Jeroboam continually. ³¹And Rehoboam slept with his fathers and was buried with his fathers in the city of David. His mother's name was Naamah the Ammonite. And Abijam his son reigned in his place.

ABIJAM REIGNS IN JUDAH

15 Now in the eighteenth year of King Jeroboam the son of Nebat, Abijam began to reign over Judah. ²He reigned for three years in Jerusalem. His mother's name was Maacah the daughter of Abishalom. ³And he walked in all the sins that his father did before him, and his heart was not wholly true to the LORD his God, as the heart of David his father. ⁴Nevertheless, for David's sake the LORD his God gave him a lamp in Jerusalem, setting up his son after him, and establishing Jerusalem, ⁵because David did what was right in the eyes of the LORD and did not turn aside from anything that he commanded him all the days of his life, except in the matter of Uriah the Hittite. ⁶Now there was war between Rehoboam and Jeroboam all the days of his life. ⁷The rest of the acts of Abijam and all that he did, are they not written in the Book of the Chronicles of the Kings of Judah? And there was war between Abijam and Jeroboam. ⁸And Abijam slept with his fathers, and they buried him in the city of David. And Asa his son reigned in his place.

ASA REIGNS IN JUDAH

⁹In the twentieth year of Jeroboam king of Israel, Asa began to reign over Judah, ¹⁰and he reigned for forty-one years in Jerusalem.

ᵃ Hebrew *the River*

His mother's name was Maacah the daughter of Abishalom. ¹¹And Asa did what was right in the eyes of the LORD, as David his father had done. ¹²He put away the male cult prostitutes out of the land and removed all the idols that his fathers had made. ¹³He also removed Maacah his mother from being queen mother because she had made an abominable image for Asherah. And Asa cut down her image and burned it at the brook Kidron. ¹⁴But the high places were not taken away. Nevertheless, the heart of Asa was wholly true to the LORD all his days. ¹⁵And he brought into the house of the LORD the sacred gifts of his father and his own sacred gifts, silver, and gold, and vessels.

¹⁶And there was war between Asa and Baasha king of Israel all their days. ¹⁷Baasha king of Israel went up against Judah and built Ramah, that he might permit no one to go out or come in to Asa king of Judah. ¹⁸Then Asa took all the silver and the gold that were left in the treasures of the house of the LORD and the treasures of the king's house and gave them into the hands of his servants. And King Asa sent them to Ben-hadad the son of Tabrimmon, the son of Hezion, king of Syria, who lived in Damascus, saying, ¹⁹"Let there be a covenant[a] between me and you, as there was between my father and your father. Behold, I am sending to you a present of silver and gold. Go, break your covenant with Baasha king of Israel, that he may withdraw from me." ²⁰And Ben-hadad listened to King Asa and sent the commanders of his armies against the cities of Israel and conquered Ijon, Dan, Abel-beth-maacah, and all Chinneroth, with all the land of Naphtali. ²¹And when Baasha heard of it, he stopped building Ramah, and he lived in Tirzah. ²²Then King Asa made a proclamation to all Judah, none was exempt, and they carried away the stones of Ramah and its timber, with which Baasha had been building, and with them King Asa built Geba of Benjamin and Mizpah. ²³Now the rest of all the acts of Asa, all his might, and all that he did, and the cities that he built, are they not written in the Book of the Chronicles of the Kings of Judah? But in his old age he was diseased in his feet. ²⁴And Asa slept with his fathers and was buried with his fathers in the city of David his father, and Jehoshaphat his son reigned in his place.

NADAB REIGNS IN ISRAEL

²⁵Nadab the son of Jeroboam began to reign over Israel in the second year of Asa king of Judah, and he reigned over Israel for two years. ²⁶He did what was evil in the sight of the LORD and walked in the way of his father, and in his sin which he made Israel to sin.

²⁷Baasha the son of Ahijah, of the house of Issachar, conspired against him. And Baasha struck him down at Gibbethon, which belonged to the Philistines, for Nadab and all Israel were laying siege to Gibbethon. ²⁸So Baasha killed him in the third year of Asa king of Judah and reigned in his place. ²⁹And as soon as he was king, he killed all the house of Jeroboam. He left to the house of Jeroboam not one that breathed, until he had destroyed it, according to the word of the LORD that he spoke by his servant Ahijah the Shilonite. ³⁰It was for the sins of Jeroboam that he sinned and that he made Israel to sin, and because of the anger to which he provoked the LORD, the God of Israel.

³¹Now the rest of the acts of Nadab and all that he did, are they not written in the Book of the Chronicles of the Kings of Israel? ³²And there was war between Asa and Baasha king of Israel all their days.

BAASHA REIGNS IN ISRAEL

³³In the third year of Asa king of Judah, Baasha the son of Ahijah began to reign over all Israel at Tirzah, and he reigned for twenty-four years. ³⁴He did what was evil in the sight of the LORD and walked in the way of Jeroboam and in his sin which he made Israel to sin.

16 And the word of the LORD came to Jehu the son of Hanani against Baasha, saying, ²"Since I exalted you out of the dust and made you leader over my people Israel, and you have walked in the way of Jeroboam and have made my people Israel to sin, provoking me to anger with their sins, ³behold, I will utterly sweep away Baasha and his house, and I will make your house like the house of Jeroboam the son of Nebat. ⁴Anyone belonging to Baasha who dies in the city the dogs shall eat, and anyone of his who dies in the field the birds of the heavens shall eat."

⁵Now the rest of the acts of Baasha and what he did, and his might, are they not written in the Book of the Chronicles of the Kings of Israel? ⁶And Baasha slept with his fathers and was buried at Tirzah, and Elah

---

[a] Or *treaty*; twice in this verse

his son reigned in his place. ⁷Moreover, the word of the LORD came by the prophet Jehu the son of Hanani against Baasha and his house, both because of all the evil that he did in the sight of the LORD, provoking him to anger with the work of his hands, in being like the house of Jeroboam, and also because he destroyed it.

ELAH REIGNS IN ISRAEL

⁸In the twenty-sixth year of Asa king of Judah, Elah the son of Baasha began to reign over Israel in Tirzah, and he reigned for two years. ⁹But his servant Zimri, commander of half his chariots, conspired against him. When he was at Tirzah, drinking himself drunk in the house of Arza, who was over the household in Tirzah, ¹⁰Zimri came in and struck him down and killed him, in the twenty-seventh year of Asa king of Judah, and reigned in his place.

¹¹When he began to reign, as soon as he had seated himself on his throne, he struck down all the house of Baasha. He did not leave him a single male of his relatives or his friends. ¹²Thus Zimri destroyed all the house of Baasha, according to the word of the LORD, which he spoke against Baasha by Jehu the prophet, ¹³for all the sins of Baasha and the sins of Elah his son, that they sinned and that they made Israel to sin, provoking the LORD God of Israel to anger with their idols. ¹⁴Now the rest of the acts of Elah and all that he did, are they not written in the Book of the Chronicles of the Kings of Israel?

ZIMRI REIGNS IN ISRAEL

¹⁵In the twenty-seventh year of Asa king of Judah, Zimri reigned for seven days in Tirzah. Now the troops were encamped against Gibbethon, which belonged to the Philistines, ¹⁶and the troops who were encamped heard it said, "Zimri has conspired, and he has killed the king." Therefore all Israel made Omri, the commander of the army, king over Israel that day in the camp. ¹⁷So Omri went up from Gibbethon, and all Israel with him, and they besieged Tirzah. ¹⁸And when Zimri saw that the city was taken, he went into the citadel of the king's house and burned the king's house over him with fire and died, ¹⁹because of his sins that he committed, doing evil in the sight of the LORD, walking in the way of Jeroboam, and for his sin that he committed, making Israel to sin. ²⁰Now the rest of the acts of Zimri, and the conspiracy that he made, are they not written in the Book of the Chronicles of the Kings of Israel?

OMRI REIGNS IN ISRAEL

²¹Then the people of Israel were divided into two parts. Half of the people followed Tibni the son of Ginath, to make him king, and half followed Omri. ²²But the people who followed Omri overcame the people who followed Tibni the son of Ginath. So Tibni died, and Omri became king. ²³In the thirty-first year of Asa king of Judah, Omri began to reign over Israel, and he reigned for twelve years; for six years he reigned in Tirzah. ²⁴He bought the hill of Samaria from Shemer for two talents[a] of silver, and he fortified the hill and called the name of the city that he built Samaria, after the name of Shemer, the owner of the hill.

²⁵Omri did what was evil in the sight of the LORD, and did more evil than all who were before him. ²⁶For he walked in all the way of Jeroboam the son of Nebat, and in the sins that he made Israel to sin, provoking the LORD, the God of Israel, to anger by their idols. ²⁷Now the rest of the acts of Omri that he did, and the might that he showed, are they not written in the Book of the Chronicles of the Kings of Israel? ²⁸And Omri slept with his fathers and was buried in Samaria, and Ahab his son reigned in his place.

AHAB REIGNS IN ISRAEL

²⁹In the thirty-eighth year of Asa king of Judah, Ahab the son of Omri began to reign over Israel, and Ahab the son of Omri reigned over Israel in Samaria for twenty-two years. ³⁰And Ahab the son of Omri did evil in the sight of the LORD, more than all who were before him. ³¹And as if it had been a light thing for him to walk in the sins of Jeroboam the son of Nebat, he took for his wife Jezebel the daughter of Ethbaal king of the Sidonians, and went and served Baal and worshipped him. ³²He erected an altar for Baal in the house of Baal, which he built in Samaria. ³³And Ahab made an Asherah. Ahab did more to provoke the LORD, the God of Israel, to anger than all the kings of Israel who were before him. ³⁴In his days Hiel of Bethel built Jericho. He laid its foundation at the cost of Abiram his firstborn, and set up its gates at the cost of his youngest son Segub, according to the word of the LORD, which he spoke by Joshua the son of Nun.

---

[a] A *talent* was about 75 pounds or 34 kilograms

ELIJAH PREDICTS A DROUGHT

17 Now Elijah the Tishbite, of Tishbe[a] in Gilead, said to Ahab, "As the LORD, the God of Israel, lives, before whom I stand, there shall be neither dew nor rain these years, except by my word." ²And the word of the LORD came to him: ³"Depart from here and turn eastwards and hide yourself by the brook Cherith, which is east of the Jordan. ⁴You shall drink from the brook, and I have commanded the ravens to feed you there." ⁵So he went and did according to the word of the LORD. He went and lived by the brook Cherith that is east of the Jordan. ⁶And the ravens brought him bread and meat in the morning, and bread and meat in the evening, and he drank from the brook. ⁷And after a while the brook dried up, because there was no rain in the land.

THE WIDOW OF ZAREPHATH

⁸Then the word of the LORD came to him, ⁹"Arise, go to Zarephath, which belongs to Sidon, and dwell there. Behold, I have commanded a widow there to feed you." ¹⁰So he arose and went to Zarephath. And when he came to the gate of the city, behold, a widow was there gathering sticks. And he called to her and said, "Bring me a little water in a vessel, that I may drink." ¹¹And as she was going to bring it, he called to her and said, "Bring me a morsel of bread in your hand." ¹²And she said, "As the LORD your God lives, I have nothing baked, only a handful of flour in a jar and a little oil in a jug. And now I am gathering a couple of sticks that I may go in and prepare it for myself and my son, that we may eat it and die." ¹³And Elijah said to her, "Do not fear; go and do as you have said. But first make me a little cake of it and bring it to me, and afterwards make something for yourself and your son. ¹⁴For thus says the LORD, the God of Israel, 'The jar of flour shall not be spent, and the jug of oil shall not be empty, until the day that the LORD sends rain upon the earth.'" ¹⁵And she went and did as Elijah said. And she and he and her household ate for many days. ¹⁶The jar of flour was not spent, neither did the jug of oil become empty, according to the word of the LORD that he spoke by Elijah.

ELIJAH RAISES THE WIDOW'S SON

¹⁷After this the son of the woman, the mistress of the house, became ill. And his illness was so severe that there was no breath left in him. ¹⁸And she said to Elijah, "What have you against me, O man of God? You have come to me to bring my sin to remembrance and to cause the death of my son!" ¹⁹And he said to her, "Give me your son." And he took him from her arms and carried him up into the upper chamber where he lodged, and laid him on his own bed. ²⁰And he cried to the LORD, "O LORD my God, have you brought calamity even upon the widow with whom I sojourn, by killing her son?" ²¹Then he stretched himself upon the child three times and cried to the LORD, "O LORD my God, let this child's life[b] come into him again." ²²And the LORD listened to the voice of Elijah. And the life of the child came into him again, and he revived. ²³And Elijah took the child and brought him down from the upper chamber into the house and delivered him to his mother. And Elijah said, "See, your son lives." ²⁴And the woman said to Elijah, "Now I know that you are a man of God, and that the word of the LORD in your mouth is truth."

ELIJAH CONFRONTS AHAB

18 After many days the word of the LORD came to Elijah, in the third year, saying, "Go, show yourself to Ahab, and I will send rain upon the earth." ²So Elijah went to show himself to Ahab. Now the famine was severe in Samaria. ³And Ahab called Obadiah, who was over the household. (Now Obadiah feared the LORD greatly, ⁴and when Jezebel cut off the prophets of the LORD, Obadiah took a hundred prophets and hid them by fifties in a cave and fed them with bread and water.) ⁵And Ahab said to Obadiah, "Go through the land to all the springs of water and to all the valleys. Perhaps we may find grass and save the horses and mules alive, and not lose some of the animals." ⁶So they divided the land between them to pass through it. Ahab went in one direction by himself, and Obadiah went in another direction by himself.

⁷And as Obadiah was on the way, behold, Elijah met him. And Obadiah recognized him and fell on his face and said, "Is it you, my lord Elijah?" ⁸And he answered him, "It is I. Go, tell your lord, 'Behold, Elijah is here.'" ⁹And he said, "How have I sinned, that you would give your servant into the hand of Ahab, to kill me? ¹⁰As the LORD your God lives, there is no nation or kingdom where my lord has

---

[a]Septuagint; Hebrew *of the settlers* [b]Or *soul*; also verse 22

not sent to seek you. And when they would say, 'He is not here', he would take an oath of the kingdom or nation, that they had not found you. ¹¹And now you say, 'Go, tell your lord, "Behold, Elijah is here."' ¹²And as soon as I have gone from you, the Spirit of the LORD will carry you I know not where. And so, when I come and tell Ahab and he cannot find you, he will kill me, although I your servant have feared the LORD from my youth. ¹³Has it not been told my lord what I did when Jezebel killed the prophets of the LORD, how I hid a hundred men of the LORD's prophets by fifties in a cave and fed them with bread and water? ¹⁴And now you say, 'Go, tell your lord, "Behold, Elijah is here"'; and he will kill me." ¹⁵And Elijah said, "As the LORD of hosts lives, before whom I stand, I will surely show myself to him today." ¹⁶So Obadiah went to meet Ahab, and told him. And Ahab went to meet Elijah.

¹⁷When Ahab saw Elijah, Ahab said to him, "Is it you, you troubler of Israel?" ¹⁸And he answered, "I have not troubled Israel, but you have, and your father's house, because you have abandoned the commandments of the LORD and followed the Baals. ¹⁹Now therefore send and gather all Israel to me at Mount Carmel, and the 450 prophets of Baal and the 400 prophets of Asherah, who eat at Jezebel's table."

THE PRIESTS OF BAAL DEFEATED

²⁰So Ahab sent to all the people of Israel and gathered the prophets together at Mount Carmel. ²¹And Elijah came near to all the people and said, "How long will you go limping between two different opinions? If the LORD is God, follow him; but if Baal, then follow him." And the people did not answer him a word. ²²Then Elijah said to the people, "I, even I only, am left a prophet of the LORD, but Baal's prophets are 450 men. ²³Let two bulls be given to us, and let them choose one bull for themselves and cut it in pieces and lay it on the wood, but put no fire to it. And I will prepare the other bull and lay it on the wood and put no fire to it. ²⁴And you call upon the name of your god, and I will call upon the name of the LORD, and the God who answers by fire, he is God." And all the people answered, "It is well spoken." ²⁵Then Elijah said to the prophets of Baal, "Choose for yourselves one bull and prepare it first, for you are many, and call upon the name of your god, but put no fire to it." ²⁶And they took the bull that was given them, and they prepared it and called upon the name of Baal from morning until noon, saying, "O Baal, answer us!" But there was no voice, and no one answered. And they limped round the altar that they had made. ²⁷And at noon Elijah mocked them, saying, "Cry aloud, for he is a god. Either he is musing, or he is relieving himself, or he is on a journey, or perhaps he is asleep and must be awakened." ²⁸And they cried aloud and cut themselves after their custom with swords and lances, until the blood gushed out upon them. ²⁹And as midday passed, they raved on until the time of the offering of the oblation, but there was no voice. No one answered; no one paid attention.

³⁰Then Elijah said to all the people, "Come near to me." And all the people came near to him. And he repaired the altar of the LORD that had been thrown down. ³¹Elijah took twelve stones, according to the number of the tribes of the sons of Jacob, to whom the word of the LORD came, saying, "Israel shall be your name", ³²and with the stones he built an altar in the name of the LORD. And he made a trench about the altar, as great as would contain two seahs[a] of seed. ³³And he put the wood in order and cut the bull in pieces and laid it on the wood. And he said, "Fill four jars with water and pour it on the burnt offering and on the wood." ³⁴And he said, "Do it a second time." And they did it a second time. And he said, "Do it a third time." And they did it a third time. ³⁵And the water ran round the altar and filled the trench also with water.

³⁶And at the time of the offering of the oblation, Elijah the prophet came near and said, "O LORD, God of Abraham, Isaac, and Israel, let it be known this day that you are God in Israel, and that I am your servant, and that I have done all these things at your word. ³⁷Answer me, O LORD, answer me, that this people may know that you, O LORD, are God, and that you have turned their hearts back." ³⁸Then the fire of the LORD fell and consumed the burnt offering and the wood and the stones and the dust, and licked up the water that was in the trench. ³⁹And when all the people saw it, they fell on their faces and said, "The LORD, he is God; the LORD, he is God." ⁴⁰And Elijah said to them, "Seize the prophets of Baal; let not one of them escape." And they seized them. And Elijah brought them down to the brook Kishon and slaughtered them there.

---

[a] *A seah* was about 7 quarts or 7.3 litres

THE LORD SENDS RAIN

⁴¹And Elijah said to Ahab, "Go up, eat and drink, for there is a sound of the rushing of rain." ⁴²So Ahab went up to eat and to drink. And Elijah went up to the top of Mount Carmel. And he bowed himself down on the earth and put his face between his knees. ⁴³And he said to his servant, "Go up now, look towards the sea." And he went up and looked and said, "There is nothing." And he said, "Go again," seven times. ⁴⁴And at the seventh time he said, "Behold, a little cloud like a man's hand is rising from the sea." And he said, "Go up, say to Ahab, 'Prepare your chariot and go down, lest the rain stop you.'" ⁴⁵And in a little while the heavens grew black with clouds and wind, and there was a great rain. And Ahab rode and went to Jezreel. ⁴⁶And the hand of the LORD was on Elijah, and he gathered up his garment and ran before Ahab to the entrance of Jezreel.

ELIJAH FLEES JEZEBEL

19 Ahab told Jezebel all that Elijah had done, and how he had killed all the prophets with the sword. ²Then Jezebel sent a messenger to Elijah, saying, "So may the gods do to me and more also, if I do not make your life as the life of one of them by this time tomorrow." ³Then he was afraid, and he arose and ran for his life and came to Beersheba, which belongs to Judah, and left his servant there.

⁴But he himself went a day's journey into the wilderness and came and sat down under a broom tree. And he asked that he might die, saying, "It is enough; now, O LORD, take away my life, for I am no better than my fathers." ⁵And he lay down and slept under a broom tree. And behold, an angel touched him and said to him, "Arise and eat." ⁶And he looked, and behold, there was at his head a cake baked on hot stones and a jar of water. And he ate and drank and lay down again. ⁷And the angel of the LORD came again a second time and touched him and said, "Arise and eat, for the journey is too great for you." ⁸And he arose and ate and drank, and went in the strength of that food forty days and forty nights to Horeb, the mount of God.

THE LORD SPEAKS TO ELIJAH

⁹There he came to a cave and lodged in it. And behold, the word of the LORD came to him, and he said to him, "What are you doing here, Elijah?" ¹⁰He said, "I have been very jealous for the LORD, the God of hosts. For the people of Israel have forsaken your covenant, thrown down your altars, and killed your prophets with the sword, and I, even I only, am left, and they seek my life, to take it away." ¹¹And he said, "Go out and stand on the mount before the LORD." And behold, the LORD passed by, and a great and strong wind tore the mountains and broke in pieces the rocks before the LORD, but the LORD was not in the wind. And after the wind an earthquake, but the LORD was not in the earthquake. ¹²And after the earthquake a fire, but the LORD was not in the fire. And after the fire the sound of a low whisper.ᵃ ¹³And when Elijah heard it, he wrapped his face in his cloak and went out and stood at the entrance of the cave. And behold, there came a voice to him and said, "What are you doing here, Elijah?" ¹⁴He said, "I have been very jealous for the LORD, the God of hosts. For the people of Israel have forsaken your covenant, thrown down your altars, and killed your prophets with the sword, and I, even I only, am left, and they seek my life, to take it away." ¹⁵And the LORD said to him, "Go, return on your way to the wilderness of Damascus. And when you arrive, you shall anoint Hazael to be king over Syria. ¹⁶And Jehu the son of Nimshi you shall anoint to be king over Israel, and Elisha the son of Shaphat of Abel-meholah you shall anoint to be prophet in your place. ¹⁷And the one who escapes from the sword of Hazael shall Jehu put to death, and the one who escapes from the sword of Jehu shall Elisha put to death. ¹⁸Yet I will leave seven thousand in Israel, all the knees that have not bowed to Baal, and every mouth that has not kissed him."

THE CALL OF ELISHA

¹⁹So he departed from there and found Elisha the son of Shaphat, who was ploughing with twelve yoke of oxen in front of him, and he was with the twelfth. Elijah passed by him and cast his cloak upon him. ²⁰And he left the oxen and ran after Elijah and said, "Let me kiss my father and my mother, and then I will follow you." And he said to him, "Go back again, for what have I done to you?" ²¹And he returned from following him and took the yoke of oxen and sacrificed them and boiled their flesh with the yokes of the oxen and gave it to the people, and they ate. Then he arose and went after Elijah and assisted him.

ᵃ Or a sound, a thin silence

AHAB'S WARS WITH SYRIA

20 Ben-hadad the king of Syria gathered all his army together. Thirty-two kings were with him, and horses and chariots. And he went up and closed in on Samaria and fought against it. ²And he sent messengers into the city to Ahab king of Israel and said to him, "Thus says Ben-hadad: ³'Your silver and your gold are mine; your best wives and children also are mine.'" ⁴And the king of Israel answered, "As you say, my lord, O king, I am yours, and all that I have." ⁵The messengers came again and said, "Thus says Ben-hadad: 'I sent to you, saying, "Deliver to me your silver and your gold, your wives and your children." ⁶Nevertheless I will send my servants to you tomorrow about this time, and they shall search your house and the houses of your servants and lay hands on whatever pleases you and take it away.'"

⁷Then the king of Israel called all the elders of the land and said, "Mark, now, and see how this man is seeking trouble, for he sent to me for my wives and my children, and for my silver and my gold, and I did not refuse him." ⁸And all the elders and all the people said to him, "Do not listen or consent." ⁹So he said to the messengers of Ben-hadad, "Tell my lord the king, 'All that you first demanded of your servant I will do, but this thing I cannot do.'" And the messengers departed and brought him word again. ¹⁰Ben-hadad sent to him and said, "The gods do so to me and more also, if the dust of Samaria shall suffice for handfuls for all the people who follow me." ¹¹And the king of Israel answered, "Tell him, 'Let not him who straps on his armour boast himself as he who takes it off.'" ¹²When Ben-hadad heard this message as he was drinking with the kings in the booths, he said to his men, "Take your positions." And they took their positions against the city.

AHAB DEFEATS BEN-HADAD

¹³And behold, a prophet came near to Ahab king of Israel and said, "Thus says the LORD, Have you seen all this great multitude? Behold, I will give it into your hand this day, and you shall know that I am the LORD." ¹⁴And Ahab said, "By whom?" He said, "Thus says the LORD, By the servants of the governors of the districts." Then he said, "Who shall begin the battle?" He answered, "You." ¹⁵Then he mustered the servants of the governors of the districts, and they were 232. And after them he mustered all the people of Israel, seven thousand.

¹⁶And they went out at noon, while Ben-hadad was drinking himself drunk in the booths, he and the thirty-two kings who helped him. ¹⁷The servants of the governors of the districts went out first. And Ben-hadad sent out scouts, and they reported to him, "Men are coming out from Samaria." ¹⁸He said, "If they have come out for peace, take them alive. Or if they have come out for war, take them alive."

¹⁹So these went out of the city, the servants of the governors of the districts and the army that followed them. ²⁰And each struck down his man. The Syrians fled, and Israel pursued them, but Ben-hadad king of Syria escaped on a horse with horsemen. ²¹And the king of Israel went out and struck the horses and chariots, and struck the Syrians with a great blow.

²²Then the prophet came near to the king of Israel and said to him, "Come, strengthen yourself, and consider well what you have to do, for in the spring the king of Syria will come up against you."

²³And the servants of the king of Syria said to him, "Their gods are gods of the hills, and so they were stronger than we. But let us fight against them in the plain, and surely we shall be stronger than they. ²⁴And do this: remove the kings, each from his post, and put commanders in their places, ²⁵and muster an army like the army that you have lost, horse for horse, and chariot for chariot. Then we will fight against them in the plain, and surely we shall be stronger than they." And he listened to their voice and did so.

AHAB DEFEATS BEN-HADAD AGAIN

²⁶In the spring, Ben-hadad mustered the Syrians and went up to Aphek to fight against Israel. ²⁷And the people of Israel were mustered and were provisioned and went against them. The people of Israel encamped before them like two little flocks of goats, but the Syrians filled the country. ²⁸And a man of God came near and said to the king of Israel, "Thus says the LORD, 'Because the Syrians have said, "The LORD is a god of the hills but he is not a god of the valleys", therefore I will give all this great multitude into your hand, and you shall know that I am the LORD.'" ²⁹And they encamped opposite one another seven days. Then on the seventh day the battle was joined. And the people of Israel struck down of the

two worthless men came in and sat opposite him. And the worthless men brought a charge against Naboth in the presence of the people, saying, "Naboth cursed God and the king." So they took him outside the city and stoned him to death with stones. ¹⁴Then they sent to Jezebel, saying, "Naboth has been stoned; he is dead."

¹⁵As soon as Jezebel heard that Naboth had been stoned and was dead, Jezebel said to Ahab, "Arise, take possession of the vineyard of Naboth the Jezreelite, which he refused to give you for money, for Naboth is not alive, but dead." ¹⁶And as soon as Ahab heard that Naboth was dead, Ahab arose to go down to the vineyard of Naboth the Jezreelite, to take possession of it.

THE LORD CONDEMNS AHAB

¹⁷Then the word of the LORD came to Elijah the Tishbite, saying, ¹⁸"Arise, go down to meet Ahab king of Israel, who is in Samaria; behold, he is in the vineyard of Naboth, where he has gone to take possession. ¹⁹And you shall say to him, 'Thus says the LORD, "Have you killed and also taken possession?"' And you shall say to him, 'Thus says the LORD: "In the place where dogs licked up the blood of Naboth shall dogs lick your own blood."'"

²⁰Ahab said to Elijah, "Have you found me, O my enemy?" He answered, "I have found you, because you have sold yourself to do what is evil in the sight of the LORD. ²¹Behold, I will bring disaster upon you. I will utterly burn you up, and will cut off from Ahab every male, bond or free, in Israel. ²²And I will make your house like the house of Jeroboam the son of Nebat, and like the house of Baasha the son of Ahijah, for the anger to which you have provoked me, and because you have made Israel to sin. ²³And of Jezebel the LORD also said, 'The dogs shall eat Jezebel within the walls of Jezreel.' ²⁴Anyone belonging to Ahab who dies in the city the dogs shall eat, and anyone of his who dies in the open country the birds of the heavens shall eat."

AHAB'S REPENTANCE

²⁵(There was none who sold himself to do what was evil in the sight of the LORD like Ahab, whom Jezebel his wife incited. ²⁶He acted very abominably in going after idols, as the Amorites had done, whom the LORD cast out before the people of Israel.)

²⁷And when Ahab heard those words, he tore his clothes and put sackcloth on his flesh and fasted and lay in sackcloth and went about dejectedly. ²⁸And the word of the LORD came to Elijah the Tishbite, saying, ²⁹"Have you seen how Ahab has humbled himself before me? Because he has humbled himself before me, I will not bring the disaster in his days; but in his son's days I will bring the disaster upon his house."

AHAB AND THE FALSE PROPHETS

22 For three years Syria and Israel continued without war. ²But in the third year Jehoshaphat the king of Judah came down to the king of Israel. ³And the king of Israel said to his servants, "Do you know that Ramoth-gilead belongs to us, and we keep quiet and do not take it out of the hand of the king of Syria?" ⁴And he said to Jehoshaphat, "Will you go with me to battle at Ramoth-gilead?" And Jehoshaphat said to the king of Israel, "I am as you are, my people as your people, my horses as your horses."

⁵And Jehoshaphat said to the king of Israel, "Enquire first for the word of the LORD." ⁶Then the king of Israel gathered the prophets together, about four hundred men, and said to them, "Shall I go to battle against Ramoth-gilead, or shall I refrain?" And they said, "Go up, for the Lord will give it into the hand of the king." ⁷But Jehoshaphat said, "Is there not here another prophet of the LORD of whom we may enquire?" ⁸And the king of Israel said to Jehoshaphat, "There is yet one man by whom we may enquire of the LORD, Micaiah the son of Imlah, but I hate him, for he never prophesies good concerning me, but evil." And Jehoshaphat said, "Let not the king say so." ⁹Then the king of Israel summoned an officer and said, "Bring quickly Micaiah the son of Imlah." ¹⁰Now the king of Israel and Jehoshaphat the king of Judah were sitting on their thrones, arrayed in their robes, at the threshing floor at the entrance of the gate of Samaria, and all the prophets were prophesying before them. ¹¹And Zedekiah the son of Chenaanah made for himself horns of iron and said, "Thus says the LORD, 'With these you shall push the Syrians until they are destroyed.'" ¹²And all the prophets prophesied so and said, "Go up to Ramoth-gilead and triumph; the LORD will give it into the hand of the king."

Syrians 100,000 foot soldiers in one day. ³⁰And the rest fled into the city of Aphek, and the wall fell upon 27,000 men who were left.

Ben-hadad also fled and entered an inner chamber in the city. ³¹And his servants said to him, "Behold now, we have heard that the kings of the house of Israel are merciful kings. Let us put sackcloth round our waists and ropes on our heads and go out to the king of Israel. Perhaps he will spare your life." ³²So they tied sackcloth round their waists and put ropes on their heads and went to the king of Israel and said, "Your servant Ben-hadad says, 'Please, let me live.'" And he said, "Does he still live? He is my brother." ³³Now the men were watching for a sign, and they quickly took it up from him and said, "Yes, your brother Ben-hadad." Then he said, "Go and bring him." Then Ben-hadad came out to him, and he caused him to come up into the chariot. ³⁴And Ben-hadad said to him, "The cities that my father took from your father I will restore, and you may establish bazaars for yourself in Damascus, as my father did in Samaria." And Ahab said, "I will let you go on these terms." So he made a covenant with him and let him go.

A PROPHET CONDEMNS BEN-HADAD'S RELEASE

³⁵And a certain man of the sons of the prophets said to his fellow at the command of the LORD, "Strike me, please." But the man refused to strike him. ³⁶Then he said to him, "Because you have not obeyed the voice of the LORD, behold, as soon as you have gone from me, a lion shall strike you down." And as soon as he had departed from him, a lion met him and struck him down. ³⁷Then he found another man and said, "Strike me, please." And the man struck him—struck him and wounded him. ³⁸So the prophet departed and waited for the king by the way, disguising himself with a bandage over his eyes. ³⁹And as the king passed, he cried to the king and said, "Your servant went out into the midst of the battle, and behold, a soldier turned and brought a man to me and said, 'Guard this man; if by any means he is missing, your life shall be for his life, or else you shall pay a talent*ᵃ* of silver.' ⁴⁰And as your servant was busy here and there, he was gone." The king of Israel said to him, "So shall your judgement be; you yourself have decided it." ⁴¹Then he hurried to take the bandage away from his eyes, and the king of Israel recognized him as one of the prophets. ⁴²And he said to him, "Thus says the LORD, 'Because you have let go out of your hand the man whom I had devoted to destruction,*ᵇ* therefore your life shall be for his life, and your people for his people.'" ⁴³And the king of Israel went to his house vexed and sullen and came to Samaria.

NABOTH'S VINEYARD

21 Now Naboth the Jezreelite had a vineyard in Jezreel, beside the palace of Ahab king of Samaria. ²And after this Ahab said to Naboth, "Give me your vineyard, that I may have it for a vegetable garden, because it is near my house, and I will give you a better vineyard for it; or, if it seems good to you, I will give you its value in money." ³But Naboth said to Ahab, "The LORD forbid that I should give you the inheritance of my fathers." ⁴And Ahab went into his house vexed and sullen because of what Naboth the Jezreelite had said to him, for he had said, "I will not give you the inheritance of my fathers." And he lay down on his bed and turned away his face and would eat no food.

⁵But Jezebel his wife came to him and said to him, "Why is your spirit so vexed that you eat no food?" ⁶And he said to her, "Because I spoke to Naboth the Jezreelite and said to him, 'Give me your vineyard for money, or else, if it please you, I will give you another vineyard for it.' And he answered, 'I will not give you my vineyard.'" ⁷And Jezebel his wife said to him, "Do you now govern Israel? Arise and eat bread and let your heart be cheerful; I will give you the vineyard of Naboth the Jezreelite."

⁸So she wrote letters in Ahab's name and sealed them with his seal, and she sent the letters to the elders and the leaders who lived with Naboth in his city. ⁹And she wrote in the letters, "Proclaim a fast, and set Naboth at the head of the people. ¹⁰And set two worthless men opposite him, and let them bring a charge against him, saying, 'You have cursed*ᶜ* God and the king.' Then take him out and stone him to death." ¹¹And the men of his city, the elders and the leaders who lived in his city, did as Jezebel had sent word to them. As it was written in the letters that she had sent to them, ¹²they proclaimed a fast and set Naboth at the head of the people. ¹³And the

---

ᵃA talent was about 75 pounds or 34 kilograms   *ᵇ*That is, set apart (devoted) as an offering to the Lord (for destruction)   *ᶜ*Hebrew *blessed*; also verse 13

MICAIAH PROPHESIES AGAINST AHAB

¹³And the messenger who went to summon Micaiah said to him, "Behold, the words of the prophets with one accord are favourable to the king. Let your word be like the word of one of them, and speak favourably." ¹⁴But Micaiah said, "As the LORD lives, what the LORD says to me, that I will speak." ¹⁵And when he had come to the king, the king said to him, "Micaiah, shall we go to Ramoth-gilead to battle, or shall we refrain?" And he answered him, "Go up and triumph; the LORD will give it into the hand of the king." ¹⁶But the king said to him, "How many times shall I make you swear that you speak to me nothing but the truth in the name of the LORD?" ¹⁷And he said, "I saw all Israel scattered on the mountains, as sheep that have no shepherd. And the LORD said, 'These have no master; let each return to his home in peace.'" ¹⁸And the king of Israel said to Jehoshaphat, "Did I not tell you that he would not prophesy good concerning me, but evil?" ¹⁹And Micaiah said, "Therefore hear the word of the LORD: I saw the LORD sitting on his throne, and all the host of heaven standing beside him on his right hand and on his left; ²⁰and the LORD said, 'Who will entice Ahab, that he may go up and fall at Ramoth-gilead?' And one said one thing, and another said another. ²¹Then a spirit came forward and stood before the LORD, saying, 'I will entice him.' ²²And the LORD said to him, 'By what means?' And he said, 'I will go out, and will be a lying spirit in the mouth of all his prophets.' And he said, 'You are to entice him, and you shall succeed; go out and do so.' ²³Now therefore behold, the LORD has put a lying spirit in the mouth of all these your prophets; the LORD has declared disaster for you."

²⁴Then Zedekiah the son of Chenaanah came near and struck Micaiah on the cheek and said, "How did the Spirit of the LORD go from me to speak to you?" ²⁵And Micaiah said, "Behold, you shall see on that day when you go into an inner chamber to hide yourself." ²⁶And the king of Israel said, "Seize Micaiah, and take him back to Amon the governor of the city and to Joash the king's son, ²⁷and say, 'Thus says the king, "Put this fellow in prison and feed him meagre rations of bread and water, until I come in peace."'" ²⁸And Micaiah said, "If you return in peace, the LORD has not spoken by me." And he said, "Hear, all you peoples!"

AHAB KILLED IN BATTLE

²⁹So the king of Israel and Jehoshaphat the king of Judah went up to Ramoth-gilead. ³⁰And the king of Israel said to Jehoshaphat, "I will disguise myself and go into battle, but you wear your robes." And the king of Israel disguised himself and went into battle. ³¹Now the king of Syria had commanded the thirty-two captains of his chariots, "Fight with neither small nor great, but only with the king of Israel." ³²And when the captains of the chariots saw Jehoshaphat, they said, "It is surely the king of Israel." So they turned to fight against him. And Jehoshaphat cried out. ³³And when the captains of the chariots saw that it was not the king of Israel, they turned back from pursuing him. ³⁴But a certain man drew his bow at random[a] and struck the king of Israel between the scale armour and the breastplate. Therefore he said to the driver of his chariot, "Turn round and carry me out of the battle, for I am wounded." ³⁵And the battle continued that day, and the king was propped up in his chariot facing the Syrians, until at evening he died. And the blood of the wound flowed into the bottom of the chariot. ³⁶And about sunset a cry went through the army, "Every man to his city, and every man to his country!"

³⁷So the king died, and was brought to Samaria. And they buried the king in Samaria. ³⁸And they washed the chariot by the pool of Samaria, and the dogs licked up his blood, and the prostitutes washed themselves in it, according to the word of the LORD that he had spoken. ³⁹Now the rest of the acts of Ahab and all that he did, and the ivory house that he built and all the cities that he built, are they not written in the Book of the Chronicles of the Kings of Israel? ⁴⁰So Ahab slept with his fathers, and Ahaziah his son reigned in his place.

JEHOSHAPHAT REIGNS IN JUDAH

⁴¹Jehoshaphat the son of Asa began to reign over Judah in the fourth year of Ahab king of Israel. ⁴²Jehoshaphat was thirty-five years old when he began to reign, and he reigned for twenty-five years in Jerusalem. His mother's name was Azubah the daughter of Shilhi. ⁴³He walked in all the way of Asa his father. He did not turn aside from it, doing what was right in the sight of the LORD. Yet the high places were not taken away, and the people still

---

[a] Hebrew *in his innocence*

sacrificed and made offerings on the high places. ⁴⁴Jehoshaphat also made peace with the king of Israel.

⁴⁵Now the rest of the acts of Jehoshaphat, and his might that he showed, and how he warred, are they not written in the Book of the Chronicles of the Kings of Judah? ⁴⁶And from the land he exterminated the remnant of the male cult prostitutes who remained in the days of his father Asa.

⁴⁷There was no king in Edom; a deputy was king. ⁴⁸Jehoshaphat made ships of Tarshish to go to Ophir for gold, but they did not go, for the ships were wrecked at Ezion-geber. ⁴⁹Then Ahaziah the son of Ahab said to Jehoshaphat, "Let my servants go with your servants in the ships," but Jehoshaphat was not willing. ⁵⁰And Jehoshaphat slept with his fathers and was buried with his fathers in the city of David his father, and Jehoram his son reigned in his place.

AHAZIAH REIGNS IN ISRAEL

⁵¹Ahaziah the son of Ahab began to reign over Israel in Samaria in the seventeenth year of Jehoshaphat king of Judah, and he reigned for two years over Israel. ⁵²He did what was evil in the sight of the LORD and walked in the way of his father and in the way of his mother and in the way of Jeroboam the son of Nebat, who made Israel to sin. ⁵³He served Baal and worshipped him and provoked the LORD, the God of Israel, to anger in every way that his father had done.

2 KINGS

ELIJAH DENOUNCES AHAZIAH

1 After the death of Ahab, Moab rebelled against Israel.
²Now Ahaziah fell through the lattice in his upper chamber in Samaria, and lay sick; so he sent messengers, telling them, "Go, enquire of Baal-zebub, the god of Ekron, whether I shall recover from this sickness." ³But the angel of the LORD said to Elijah the Tishbite, "Arise, go up to meet the messengers of the king of Samaria, and say to them, 'Is it because there is no God in Israel that you are going to enquire of Baal-zebub, the god of Ekron? ⁴Now therefore thus says the LORD, You shall not come down from the bed to which you have gone up, but you shall surely die.'" So Elijah went.
⁵The messengers returned to the king, and he said to them, "Why have you returned?" ⁶And they said to him, "There came a man to meet us, and said to us, 'Go back to the king who sent you, and say to him, Thus says the LORD, Is it because there is no God in Israel that you are sending to enquire of Baal-zebub, the god of Ekron? Therefore you shall not come down from the bed to which you have gone up, but you shall surely die.'" ⁷He said to them, "What kind of man was he who came to meet you and told you these things?" ⁸They answered him, "He wore a garment of hair, with a belt of leather about his waist." And he said, "It is Elijah the Tishbite."
⁹Then the king sent to him a captain of fifty men with his fifty. He went up to Elijah, who was sitting on the top of a hill, and said to him, "O man of God, the king says, 'Come down.'" ¹⁰But Elijah answered the captain of fifty, "If I am a man of God, let fire come down from heaven and consume you and your fifty." Then fire came down from heaven and consumed him and his fifty.
¹¹Again the king sent to him another captain of fifty men with his fifty. And he answered and said to him, "O man of God, this is the king's order, 'Come down quickly!'" ¹²But Elijah answered them, "If I am a man of God, let fire come down from heaven and consume you and your fifty." Then the fire of God came down from heaven and consumed him and his fifty.
¹³Again the king sent the captain of a third fifty with his fifty. And the third captain of fifty went up and came and fell on his knees before Elijah and entreated him, "O man of God, please let my life, and the life of these fifty servants of yours, be precious in your sight. ¹⁴Behold, fire came down from heaven and consumed the two former captains of fifty men with their fifties, but now let my life be precious in your sight." ¹⁵Then the angel of the LORD said to Elijah, "Go down with him; do not be afraid of him." So he arose and went down with him to the king ¹⁶and said to him, "Thus says the LORD, 'Because you have sent messengers to enquire of Baal-zebub, the god of Ekron—is it because there is no God in Israel to enquire of his word?—therefore you shall not come down from the bed to which you have gone up, but you shall surely die.'"
¹⁷So he died according to the word of the LORD that Elijah had spoken. Jehoram became king in his place in the second year of Jehoram the son of Jehoshaphat, king of Judah, because Ahaziah had no son. ¹⁸Now the rest of the acts of Ahaziah that he did, are they not written in the Book of the Chronicles of the Kings of Israel?

ELIJAH TAKEN TO HEAVEN

2 Now when the LORD was about to take Elijah up to heaven by a whirlwind, Elijah and Elisha were on their way from Gilgal. ²And Elijah said to Elisha, "Please stay here, for the LORD has sent me as far as Bethel." But Elisha said, "As the LORD lives, and as you yourself live, I will not leave you." So they went down to Bethel. ³And the sons of the prophets who were in Bethel came out to Elisha and said to him, "Do you know that today the LORD will take away your master from over you?" And he said, "Yes, I know it; keep quiet."
⁴Elijah said to him, "Elisha, please stay here, for the LORD has sent me to Jericho." But he said, "As the LORD lives, and as you yourself live, I will not leave you." So they came to

Jericho. ⁵The sons of the prophets who were at Jericho drew near to Elisha and said to him, "Do you know that today the LORD will take away your master from over you?" And he answered, "Yes, I know it; keep quiet."

⁶Then Elijah said to him, "Please stay here, for the LORD has sent me to the Jordan." But he said, "As the LORD lives, and as you yourself live, I will not leave you." So the two of them went on. ⁷Fifty men of the sons of the prophets also went and stood at some distance from them, as they both were standing by the Jordan. ⁸Then Elijah took his cloak and rolled it up and struck the water, and the water was parted to one side and to the other, till the two of them could go over on dry ground.

⁹When they had crossed, Elijah said to Elisha, "Ask what I shall do for you, before I am taken from you." And Elisha said, "Please let there be a double portion of your spirit on me." ¹⁰And he said, "You have asked a hard thing; yet, if you see me as I am being taken from you, it shall be so for you, but if you do not see me, it shall not be so." ¹¹And as they still went on and talked, behold, chariots of fire and horses of fire separated the two of them. And Elijah went up by a whirlwind into heaven. ¹²And Elisha saw it and he cried, "My father, my father! The chariots of Israel and its horsemen!" And he saw him no more.

Then he took hold of his own clothes and tore them in two pieces. ¹³And he took up the cloak of Elijah that had fallen from him and went back and stood on the bank of the Jordan. ¹⁴Then he took the cloak of Elijah that had fallen from him and struck the water, saying, "Where is the LORD, the God of Elijah?" And when he had struck the water, the water was parted to the one side and to the other, and Elisha went over.

ELISHA SUCCEEDS ELIJAH

¹⁵Now when the sons of the prophets who were at Jericho saw him opposite them, they said, "The spirit of Elijah rests on Elisha." And they came to meet him and bowed to the ground before him. ¹⁶And they said to him, "Behold now, there are with your servants fifty strong men. Please let them go and seek your master. It may be that the Spirit of the LORD has caught him up and cast him upon some mountain or into some valley." And he said, "You shall not send." ¹⁷But when they urged him till he was ashamed, he said, "Send." They sent therefore fifty men. And for three days they sought him but did not find him. ¹⁸And they came back to him while he was staying at Jericho, and he said to them, "Did I not say to you, 'Do not go'?"

¹⁹Now the men of the city said to Elisha, "Behold, the situation of this city is pleasant, as my lord sees, but the water is bad, and the land is unfruitful." ²⁰He said, "Bring me a new bowl, and put salt in it." So they brought it to him. ²¹Then he went to the spring of water and threw salt in it and said, "Thus says the LORD, I have healed this water; from now on neither death nor miscarriage shall come from it." ²²So the water has been healed to this day, according to the word that Elisha spoke.

²³He went up from there to Bethel, and while he was going up on the way, some small boys came out of the city and jeered at him, saying, "Go up, you baldhead! Go up, you baldhead!" ²⁴And he turned round, and when he saw them, he cursed them in the name of the LORD. And two she-bears came out of the woods and tore forty-two of the boys. ²⁵From there he went on to Mount Carmel, and from there he returned to Samaria.

MOAB REBELS AGAINST ISRAEL

3 In the eighteenth year of Jehoshaphat king of Judah, Jehoram the son of Ahab became king over Israel in Samaria, and he reigned for twelve years. ²He did what was evil in the sight of the LORD, though not like his father and mother, for he put away the pillar of Baal that his father had made. ³Nevertheless, he clung to the sin of Jeroboam the son of Nebat, which he made Israel to sin; he did not depart from it.

⁴Now Mesha king of Moab was a sheep breeder, and he had to deliver to the king of Israel 100,000 lambs and the wool of 100,000 rams. ⁵But when Ahab died, the king of Moab rebelled against the king of Israel. ⁶So King Jehoram marched out of Samaria at that time and mustered all Israel. ⁷And he went and sent word to Jehoshaphat king of Judah: "The king of Moab has rebelled against me. Will you go with me to battle against Moab?" And he said, "I will go. I am as you are, my people as your people, my horses as your horses." ⁸Then he said, "By which way shall we march?" Jehoram answered, "By the way of the wilderness of Edom."

⁹So the king of Israel went with the king of Judah and the king of Edom. And when they had made a circuitous march of seven days, there was no water for the army or for the animals that followed them. ¹⁰Then the

king of Israel said, "Alas! The LORD has called these three kings to give them into the hand of Moab." ¹¹And Jehoshaphat said, "Is there no prophet of the LORD here, through whom we may enquire of the LORD?" Then one of the king of Israel's servants answered, "Elisha the son of Shaphat is here, who poured water on the hands of Elijah." ¹²And Jehoshaphat said, "The word of the LORD is with him." So the king of Israel and Jehoshaphat and the king of Edom went down to him.

¹³And Elisha said to the king of Israel, "What have I to do with you? Go to the prophets of your father and to the prophets of your mother." But the king of Israel said to him, "No; it is the LORD who has called these three kings to give them into the hand of Moab." ¹⁴And Elisha said, "As the LORD of hosts lives, before whom I stand, were it not that I have regard for Jehoshaphat the king of Judah, I would neither look at you nor see you. ¹⁵But now bring me a musician." And when the musician played, the hand of the LORD came upon him. ¹⁶And he said, "Thus says the LORD, 'I will make this dry streambed full of pools.' ¹⁷For thus says the LORD, 'You shall not see wind or rain, but that streambed shall be filled with water, so that you shall drink, you, your livestock, and your animals.' ¹⁸This is a light thing in the sight of the LORD. He will also give the Moabites into your hand, ¹⁹and you shall attack every fortified city and every choice city, and shall fell every good tree and stop up all springs of water and ruin every good piece of land with stones." ²⁰The next morning, about the time of offering the sacrifice, behold, water came from the direction of Edom, till the country was filled with water.

²¹When all the Moabites heard that the kings had come up to fight against them, all who were able to put on armour, from the youngest to the oldest, were called out and were drawn up at the border. ²²And when they rose early in the morning and the sun shone on the water, the Moabites saw the water opposite them as red as blood. ²³And they said, "This is blood; the kings have surely fought together and struck one another down. Now then, Moab, to the spoil!" ²⁴But when they came to the camp of Israel, the Israelites rose and struck the Moabites, till they fled before them. And they went forward, striking the Moabites as they went.*ᵃ* ²⁵And they overthrew the cities, and on every good piece of land every man threw a stone until it was covered. They stopped every spring of water and felled all the good trees, till only its stones were left in Kir-hareseth, and the slingers surrounded and attacked it. ²⁶When the king of Moab saw that the battle was going against him, he took with him 700 swordsmen to break through, opposite the king of Edom, but they could not. ²⁷Then he took his oldest son who was to reign in his place and offered him for a burnt offering on the wall. And there came great wrath against Israel. And they withdrew from him and returned to their own land.

ELISHA AND THE WIDOW'S OIL

4 Now the wife of one of the sons of the prophets cried to Elisha, "Your servant my husband is dead, and you know that your servant feared the LORD, but the creditor has come to take my two children to be his slaves." ²And Elisha said to her, "What shall I do for you? Tell me; what have you in the house?" And she said, "Your servant has nothing in the house except a jar of oil." ³Then he said, "Go outside, borrow vessels from all your neighbours, empty vessels and not too few. ⁴Then go in and shut the door behind yourself and your sons and pour into all these vessels. And when one is full, set it aside." ⁵So she went from him and shut the door behind herself and her sons. And as she poured they brought the vessels to her. ⁶When the vessels were full, she said to her son, "Bring me another vessel." And he said to her, "There is not another." Then the oil stopped flowing. ⁷She came and told the man of God, and he said, "Go, sell the oil and pay your debts, and you and your sons can live on the rest."

ELISHA AND THE SHUNAMMITE WOMAN

⁸One day Elisha went on to Shunem, where a wealthy woman lived, who urged him to eat some food. So whenever he passed that way, he would turn in there to eat food. ⁹And she said to her husband, "Behold now, I know that this is a holy man of God who is continually passing our way. ¹⁰Let us make a small room on the roof with walls and put there for him a bed, a table, a chair, and a lamp, so that whenever he comes to us, he can go in there."

¹¹One day he came there, and he turned into the chamber and rested there. ¹²And he said to Gehazi his servant, "Call this Shunammite." When he had called her, she stood before him. ¹³And he said to him, "Say now

---
*ᵃ*Septuagint; the meaning of the Hebrew is uncertain

to her, 'See, you have taken all this trouble for us; what is to be done for you? Would you have a word spoken on your behalf to the king or to the commander of the army?'" She answered, "I dwell among my own people." **¹⁴**And he said, "What then is to be done for her?" Gehazi answered, "Well, she has no son, and her husband is old." **¹⁵**He said, "Call her." And when he had called her, she stood in the doorway. **¹⁶**And he said, "At this season, about this time next year, you shall embrace a son." And she said, "No, my lord, O man of God; do not lie to your servant." **¹⁷**But the woman conceived, and she bore a son about that time the following spring, as Elisha had said to her.

ELISHA RAISES THE SHUNAMMITE'S SON

¹⁸When the child had grown, he went out one day to his father among the reapers. **¹⁹**And he said to his father, "Oh, my head, my head!" The father said to his servant, "Carry him to his mother." **²⁰**And when he had lifted him and brought him to his mother, the child sat on her lap till noon, and then he died. **²¹**And she went up and laid him on the bed of the man of God and shut the door behind him and went out. **²²**Then she called to her husband and said, "Send me one of the servants and one of the donkeys, that I may quickly go to the man of God and come back again." **²³**And he said, "Why will you go to him today? It is neither new moon nor Sabbath." She said, "All is well." **²⁴**Then she saddled the donkey, and she said to her servant, "Urge the animal on; do not slacken the pace for me unless I tell you." **²⁵**So she set out and came to the man of God at Mount Carmel.

When the man of God saw her coming, he said to Gehazi his servant, "Look, there is the Shunammite. **²⁶**Run at once to meet her and say to her, 'Is all well with you? Is all well with your husband? Is all well with the child?'" And she answered, "All is well." **²⁷**And when she came to the mountain to the man of God, she caught hold of his feet. And Gehazi came to push her away. But the man of God said, "Leave her alone, for she is in bitter distress, and the LORD has hidden it from me and has not told me." **²⁸**Then she said, "Did I ask my lord for a son? Did I not say, 'Do not deceive me?'" **²⁹**He said to Gehazi, "Tie up your garment and take my staff in your hand and go. If you meet anyone, do not greet him, and if anyone greets you, do not reply. And lay my staff on the face of the child." **³⁰**Then the mother of the child said, "As the LORD lives and as you yourself live, I will not leave you." So he arose and followed her. **³¹**Gehazi went on ahead and laid the staff on the face of the child, but there was no sound or sign of life. Therefore he returned to meet him and told him, "The child has not awakened."

³²When Elisha came into the house, he saw the child lying dead on his bed. **³³**So he went in and shut the door behind the two of them and prayed to the LORD. **³⁴**Then he went up and lay on the child, putting his mouth on his mouth, his eyes on his eyes, and his hands on his hands. And as he stretched himself upon him, the flesh of the child became warm. **³⁵**Then he got up again and walked once back and forth in the house, and went up and stretched himself upon him. The child sneezed seven times, and the child opened his eyes. **³⁶**Then he summoned Gehazi and said, "Call this Shunammite." So he called her. And when she came to him, he said, "Pick up your son." **³⁷**She came and fell at his feet, bowing to the ground. Then she picked up her son and went out.

ELISHA PURIFIES THE DEADLY STEW

³⁸And Elisha came again to Gilgal when there was a famine in the land. And as the sons of the prophets were sitting before him, he said to his servant, "Set on the large pot, and boil stew for the sons of the prophets." **³⁹**One of them went out into the field to gather herbs, and found a wild vine and gathered from it his lap full of wild gourds, and came and cut them up into the pot of stew, not knowing what they were. **⁴⁰**And they poured out some for the men to eat. But while they were eating of the stew, they cried out, "O man of God, there is death in the pot!" And they could not eat it. **⁴¹**He said, "Then bring flour." And he threw it into the pot and said, "Pour some out for the men, that they may eat." And there was no harm in the pot.

⁴²A man came from Baal-shalishah, bringing the man of God bread of the firstfruits, twenty loaves of barley and fresh ears of grain in his sack. And Elisha said, "Give to the men, that they may eat." **⁴³**But his servant said, "How can I set this before a hundred men?" So he repeated, "Give them to the men, that they may eat, for thus says the LORD, 'They shall eat and have some left.'" **⁴⁴**So he set it before them. And they ate and had some left, according to the word of the LORD.

NAAMAN HEALED OF LEPROSY

5 Naaman, commander of the army of the king of Syria, was a great man with his master and in high favour, because by him the Lord had given victory to Syria. He was a mighty man of valour, but he was a leper.[a] ²Now the Syrians on one of their raids had carried off a little girl from the land of Israel, and she worked in the service of Naaman's wife. ³She said to her mistress, "Would that my lord were with the prophet who is in Samaria! He would cure him of his leprosy." ⁴So Naaman went in and told his lord, "Thus and so spoke the girl from the land of Israel." ⁵And the king of Syria said, "Go now, and I will send a letter to the king of Israel."

So he went, taking with him ten talents of silver, six thousand shekels[b] of gold, and ten changes of clothing. ⁶And he brought the letter to the king of Israel, which read, "When this letter reaches you, know that I have sent to you Naaman my servant, that you may cure him of his leprosy." ⁷And when the king of Israel read the letter, he tore his clothes and said, "Am I God, to kill and to make alive, that this man sends word to me to cure a man of his leprosy? Only consider, and see how he is seeking a quarrel with me."

⁸But when Elisha the man of God heard that the king of Israel had torn his clothes, he sent to the king, saying, "Why have you torn your clothes? Let him come now to me, that he may know that there is a prophet in Israel." ⁹So Naaman came with his horses and chariots and stood at the door of Elisha's house. ¹⁰And Elisha sent a messenger to him, saying, "Go and wash in the Jordan seven times, and your flesh shall be restored, and you shall be clean." ¹¹But Naaman was angry and went away, saying, "Behold, I thought that he would surely come out to me and stand and call upon the name of the Lord his God, and wave his hand over the place and cure the leper. ¹²Are not Abana[c] and Pharpar, the rivers of Damascus, better than all the waters of Israel? Could I not wash in them and be clean?" So he turned and went away in a rage. ¹³But his servants came near and said to him, "My father, it is a great word the prophet has spoken to you; will you not do it? Has he actually said to you, 'Wash, and be clean'?" ¹⁴So he went down and dipped himself seven times in the Jordan, according to the word of the man of God, and his flesh was restored like the flesh of a little child, and he was clean.

GEHAZI'S GREED AND PUNISHMENT

¹⁵Then he returned to the man of God, he and all his company, and he came and stood before him. And he said, "Behold, I know that there is no God in all the earth but in Israel; so accept now a present from your servant." ¹⁶But he said, "As the Lord lives, before whom I stand, I will receive none." And he urged him to take it, but he refused. ¹⁷Then Naaman said, "If not, please let there be given to your servant two mule-loads of earth, for from now on your servant will not offer burnt offering or sacrifice to any god but the Lord. ¹⁸In this matter may the Lord pardon your servant: when my master goes into the house of Rimmon to worship there, leaning on my arm, and I bow myself in the house of Rimmon, when I bow myself in the house of Rimmon, the Lord pardon your servant in this matter." ¹⁹He said to him, "Go in peace."

But when Naaman had gone from him a short distance, ²⁰Gehazi, the servant of Elisha the man of God, said, "See, my master has spared this Naaman the Syrian, in not accepting from his hand what he brought. As the Lord lives, I will run after him and get something from him." ²¹So Gehazi followed Naaman. And when Naaman saw someone running after him, he got down from the chariot to meet him and said, "Is all well?" ²²And he said, "All is well. My master has sent me to say, 'There have just now come to me from the hill country of Ephraim two young men of the sons of the prophets. Please give them a talent of silver and two changes of clothing.'" ²³And Naaman said, "Be pleased to accept two talents." And he urged him and tied up two talents of silver in two bags, with two changes of clothing, and laid them on two of his servants. And they carried them before Gehazi. ²⁴And when he came to the hill, he took them from their hand and put them in the house, and he sent the men away, and they departed. ²⁵He went in and stood before his master, and Elisha said to him, "Where have you been, Gehazi?" And he said, "Your servant went nowhere." ²⁶But he said to him, "Did not my heart go when the man turned from his chariot to meet you? Was it a time to accept money and garments, olive orchards and vineyards, sheep and oxen, male servants and female servants? ²⁷Therefore the

---

[a] *Leprosy* was a term for several skin diseases; see Leviticus 13
[b] A *talent* was about 75 pounds or 34 kilograms; a *shekel* was about 2/5 of an ounce or 11 grams   [c] Or *Amana*

leprosy of Naaman shall cling to you and to your descendants for ever." So he went out from his presence a leper, like snow.

THE AXE HEAD RECOVERED

6 Now the sons of the prophets said to Elisha, "See, the place where we dwell under your charge is too small for us. ²Let us go to the Jordan and each of us get there a log, and let us make a place for us to dwell there." And he answered, "Go." ³Then one of them said, "Be pleased to go with your servants." And he answered, "I will go." ⁴So he went with them. And when they came to the Jordan, they cut down trees. ⁵But as one was felling a log, his axe head fell into the water, and he cried out, "Alas, my master! It was borrowed." ⁶Then the man of God said, "Where did it fall?" When he showed him the place, he cut off a stick and threw it in there and made the iron float. ⁷And he said, "Take it up." So he reached out his hand and took it.

HORSES AND CHARIOTS OF FIRE

⁸Once when the king of Syria was warring against Israel, he took counsel with his servants, saying, "At such and such a place shall be my camp." ⁹But the man of God sent word to the king of Israel, "Beware that you do not pass this place, for the Syrians are going down there." ¹⁰And the king of Israel sent to the place about which the man of God told him. Thus he used to warn him, so that he saved himself there more than once or twice.

¹¹And the mind of the king of Syria was greatly troubled because of this thing, and he called his servants and said to them, "Will you not show me who of us is for the king of Israel?" ¹²And one of his servants said, "None, my lord, O king; but Elisha, the prophet who is in Israel, tells the king of Israel the words that you speak in your bedroom." ¹³And he said, "Go and see where he is, that I may send and seize him." It was told him, "Behold, he is in Dothan." ¹⁴So he sent there horses and chariots and a great army, and they came by night and surrounded the city.

¹⁵When the servant of the man of God rose early in the morning and went out, behold, an army with horses and chariots was all round the city. And the servant said, "Alas, my master! What shall we do?" ¹⁶He said, "Do not be afraid, for those who are with us are more than those who are with them." ¹⁷Then Elisha prayed and said, "O LORD, please open his eyes that he may see." So the LORD opened the eyes of the young man, and he saw, and behold, the mountain was full of horses and chariots of fire all round Elisha. ¹⁸And when the Syrians came down against him, Elisha prayed to the LORD and said, "Please strike this people with blindness." So he struck them with blindness in accordance with the prayer of Elisha. ¹⁹And Elisha said to them, "This is not the way, and this is not the city. Follow me, and I will bring you to the man whom you seek." And he led them to Samaria.

²⁰As soon as they entered Samaria, Elisha said, "O LORD, open the eyes of these men, that they may see." So the LORD opened their eyes and they saw, and behold, they were in the midst of Samaria. ²¹As soon as the king of Israel saw them, he said to Elisha, "My father, shall I strike them down? Shall I strike them down?" ²²He answered, "You shall not strike them down. Would you strike down those whom you have taken captive with your sword and with your bow? Set bread and water before them, that they may eat and drink and go to their master." ²³So he prepared for them a great feast, and when they had eaten and drunk, he sent them away, and they went to their master. And the Syrians did not come again on raids into the land of Israel.

BEN-HADAD'S SIEGE OF SAMARIA

²⁴Afterwards Ben-hadad king of Syria mustered his entire army and went up and besieged Samaria. ²⁵And there was a great famine in Samaria, as they besieged it, until a donkey's head was sold for eighty shekels of silver, and the fourth part of a kab[a] of dove's dung for five shekels of silver. ²⁶Now as the king of Israel was passing by on the wall, a woman cried out to him, saying, "Help, my lord, O king!" ²⁷And he said, "If the LORD will not help you, how shall I help you? From the threshing floor, or from the wine press?" ²⁸And the king asked her, "What is your trouble?" She answered, "This woman said to me, 'Give your son, that we may eat him today, and we will eat my son tomorrow.' ²⁹So we boiled my son and ate him. And on the next day I said to her, 'Give your son, that we may eat him.' But she has hidden her son." ³⁰When the king heard the words of the woman, he tore his clothes—now he was passing by on the wall—and the people looked, and behold, he had sackcloth beneath on his body—³¹and he

---

[a] A *shekel* was about 2/5 of an ounce or 11 grams; a *kab* was about 1 quart or 1 litre

said, "May God do so to me and more also, if the head of Elisha the son of Shaphat remains on his shoulders today."

³²Elisha was sitting in his house, and the elders were sitting with him. Now the king had dispatched a man from his presence, but before the messenger arrived Elisha said to the elders, "Do you see how this murderer has sent to take off my head? Look, when the messenger comes, shut the door and hold the door fast against him. Is not the sound of his master's feet behind him?" ³³And while he was still speaking with them, the messenger came down to him and said, "This trouble is from the LORD! Why should I wait for the LORD any longer?"

ELISHA PROMISES FOOD

7 But Elisha said, "Hear the word of the LORD: thus says the LORD, Tomorrow about this time a seah¹ of fine flour shall be sold for a shekel,¹ and two seahs of barley for a shekel, at the gate of Samaria." ²Then the captain on whose hand the king leaned said to the man of God, "If the LORD himself should make windows in heaven, could this thing be?" But he said, "You shall see it with your own eyes, but you shall not eat of it."

THE SYRIANS FLEE

³Now there were four men who were lepers¹ at the entrance to the gate. And they said to one another, "Why are we sitting here until we die? ⁴If we say, 'Let us enter the city', the famine is in the city, and we shall die there. And if we sit here, we die also. So now come, let us go over to the camp of the Syrians. If they spare our lives we shall live, and if they kill us we shall but die." ⁵So they arose at twilight to go to the camp of the Syrians. But when they came to the edge of the camp of the Syrians, behold, there was no one there. ⁶For the Lord had made the army of the Syrians hear the sound of chariots and of horses, the sound of a great army, so that they said to one another, "Behold, the king of Israel has hired against us the kings of the Hittites and the kings of Egypt to come against us." ⁷So they fled away in the twilight and abandoned their tents, their horses, and their donkeys, leaving the camp as it was, and fled for their lives. ⁸And when these lepers came to the edge of the camp, they went into a tent and ate and drank, and they carried off silver and gold and clothing and went and hid them. Then they came back and entered another tent and carried off things from it and went and hid them.

⁹Then they said to one another, "We are not doing right. This day is a day of good news. If we are silent and wait until the morning light, punishment will overtake us. Now therefore come; let us go and tell the king's household." ¹⁰So they came and called to the gatekeepers of the city and told them, "We came to the camp of the Syrians, and behold, there was no one to be seen or heard there, nothing but the horses tied and the donkeys tied and the tents as they were." ¹¹Then the gatekeepers called out, and it was told within the king's household. ¹²And the king rose in the night and said to his servants, "I will tell you what the Syrians have done to us. They know that we are hungry. Therefore they have gone out of the camp to hide themselves in the open country, thinking, 'When they come out of the city, we shall take them alive and get into the city.'" ¹³And one of his servants said, "Let some men take five of the remaining horses, seeing that those who are left here will fare like the whole multitude of Israel who have already perished. Let us send and see." ¹⁴So they took two horsemen, and the king sent them after the army of the Syrians, saying, "Go and see." ¹⁵So they went after them as far as the Jordan, and behold, all the way was littered with garments and equipment that the Syrians had thrown away in their haste. And the messengers returned and told the king.

¹⁶Then the people went out and plundered the camp of the Syrians. So a seah of fine flour was sold for a shekel, and two seahs of barley for a shekel, according to the word of the LORD. ¹⁷Now the king had appointed the captain on whose hand he leaned to have charge of the gate. And the people trampled him in the gate, so that he died, as the man of God had said when the king came down to him. ¹⁸For when the man of God had said to the king, "Two seahs of barley shall be sold for a shekel, and a seah of fine flour for a shekel, about this time tomorrow in the gate of Samaria," ¹⁹the captain had answered the man of God, "If the LORD himself should make windows in heaven, could such a thing be?" And he had said, "You shall see it with your own eyes, but you shall not eat of it." ²⁰And so it happened to him, for the people trampled him in the gate and he died.

---

¹A *seah* was about 7 quarts or 7.3 litres ¹A *shekel* was about 2/5 of an ounce or 11 grams ¹*Leprosy* was a term for several skin diseases; see Leviticus 13

THE SHUNAMMITE'S LAND RESTORED

8 Now Elisha had said to the woman whose son he had restored to life, "Arise, and depart with your household, and sojourn wherever you can, for the LORD has called for a famine, and it will come upon the land for seven years." ²So the woman arose and did according to the word of the man of God. She went with her household and sojourned in the land of the Philistines for seven years. ³And at the end of the seven years, when the woman returned from the land of the Philistines, she went to appeal to the king for her house and her land. ⁴Now the king was talking with Gehazi the servant of the man of God, saying, "Tell me all the great things that Elisha has done." ⁵And while he was telling the king how Elisha had restored the dead to life, behold, the woman whose son he had restored to life appealed to the king for her house and her land. And Gehazi said, "My lord, O king, here is the woman, and here is her son whom Elisha restored to life." ⁶And when the king asked the woman, she told him. So the king appointed an official for her, saying, "Restore all that was hers, together with all the produce of the fields from the day that she left the land until now."

HAZAEL MURDERS BEN-HADAD

⁷Now Elisha came to Damascus. Ben-hadad the king of Syria was sick. And when it was told him, "The man of God has come here," ⁸the king said to Hazael, "Take a present with you and go to meet the man of God, and enquire of the LORD through him, saying, 'Shall I recover from this sickness?'" ⁹So Hazael went to meet him, and took a present with him, all kinds of goods of Damascus, forty camels' loads. When he came and stood before him, he said, "Your son Ben-hadad king of Syria has sent me to you, saying, 'Shall I recover from this sickness?'" ¹⁰And Elisha said to him, "Go, say to him, 'You shall certainly recover', but^a the LORD has shown me that he shall certainly die." ¹¹And he fixed his gaze and stared at him, until he was embarrassed. And the man of God wept. ¹²And Hazael said, "Why does my lord weep?" He answered, "Because I know the evil that you will do to the people of Israel. You will set on fire their fortresses, and you will kill their young men with the sword and dash in pieces their little ones and rip open their pregnant women." ¹³And Hazael said, "What is your servant, who is but a dog, that he should do this great thing?" Elisha answered, "The LORD has shown me that you are to be king over Syria." ¹⁴Then he departed from Elisha and came to his master, who said to him, "What did Elisha say to you?" And he answered, "He told me that you would certainly recover." ¹⁵But the next day he took the bed cloth^b and dipped it in water and spread it over his face, till he died. And Hazael became king in his place.

JEHORAM REIGNS IN JUDAH

¹⁶In the fifth year of Joram the son of Ahab, king of Israel, when Jehoshaphat was king of Judah,^{c} Jehoram the son of Jehoshaphat, king of Judah, began to reign. ¹⁷He was thirty-two years old when he became king, and he reigned for eight years in Jerusalem. ¹⁸And he walked in the way of the kings of Israel, as the house of Ahab had done, for the daughter of Ahab was his wife. And he did what was evil in the sight of the LORD. ¹⁹Yet the LORD was not willing to destroy Judah, for the sake of David his servant, since he promised to give a lamp to him and to his sons for ever.

²⁰In his days Edom revolted from the rule of Judah and set up a king of their own. ²¹Then Joram^d passed over to Zair with all his chariots and rose by night, and he and his chariot commanders struck the Edomites who had surrounded him, but his army fled home. ²²So Edom revolted from the rule of Judah to this day. Then Libnah revolted at the same time. ²³Now the rest of the acts of Joram, and all that he did, are they not written in the Book of the Chronicles of the Kings of Judah? ²⁴So Joram slept with his fathers and was buried with his fathers in the city of David, and Ahaziah his son reigned in his place.

AHAZIAH REIGNS IN JUDAH

²⁵In the twelfth year of Joram the son of Ahab, king of Israel, Ahaziah the son of Jehoram, king of Judah, began to reign. ²⁶Ahaziah was twenty-two years old when he began to reign, and he reigned for one year in Jerusalem. His mother's name was Athaliah; she was a granddaughter of Omri king of Israel. ²⁷He also walked in the way of the house of Ahab and did what was evil in the sight of the LORD, as the house of Ahab had done, for he was son-in-law to the house of Ahab.

---

^{a}Some manuscripts say, 'You shall certainly not recover,' for
^{b}The meaning of the Hebrew is uncertain ^{c}Septuagint, Syriac lack *when Jehoshaphat was king of Judah* ^{d}*Joram* is an alternate spelling of *Jehoram* (the son of Jehoshaphat) as in verse 16; also verses 23, 24

²⁸He went with Joram the son of Ahab to make war against Hazael king of Syria at Ramoth-gilead, and the Syrians wounded Joram. ²⁹And King Joram returned to be healed in Jezreel of the wounds that the Syrians had given him at Ramah, when he fought against Hazael king of Syria. And Ahaziah the son of Jehoram king of Judah went down to see Joram the son of Ahab in Jezreel, because he was sick.

JEHU ANOINTED KING OF ISRAEL

9 Then Elisha the prophet called one of the sons of the prophets and said to him, "Tie up your garments, and take this flask of oil in your hand, and go to Ramoth-gilead. ²And when you arrive, look there for Jehu the son of Jehoshaphat, son of Nimshi. And go in and get him to rise from among his fellows, and lead him to an inner chamber. ³Then take the flask of oil and pour it on his head and say, 'Thus says the LORD, I anoint you king over Israel.' Then open the door and flee; do not linger."

⁴So the young man, the servant of the prophet, went to Ramoth-gilead. ⁵And when he came, behold, the commanders of the army were in council. And he said, "I have a word for you, O commander." And Jehu said, "To which of us all?" And he said, "To you, O commander." ⁶So he arose and went into the house. And the young man poured the oil on his head, saying to him, "Thus says the LORD, the God of Israel, I anoint you king over the people of the LORD, over Israel. ⁷And you shall strike down the house of Ahab your master, so that I may avenge on Jezebel the blood of my servants the prophets, and the blood of all the servants of the LORD. ⁸For the whole house of Ahab shall perish, and I will cut off from Ahab every male, bond or free, in Israel. ⁹And I will make the house of Ahab like the house of Jeroboam the son of Nebat, and like the house of Baasha the son of Ahijah. ¹⁰And the dogs shall eat Jezebel in the territory of Jezreel, and none shall bury her." Then he opened the door and fled.

¹¹When Jehu came out to the servants of his master, they said to him, "Is all well? Why did this mad fellow come to you?" And he said to them, "You know the fellow and his talk." ¹²And they said, "That is not true; tell us now." And he said, "Thus and so he spoke to me, saying, 'Thus says the LORD, I anoint you king over Israel.'" ¹³Then in haste every man of them took his garment and put it under him on the bare*ᵃ* steps, and they blew the trumpet and proclaimed, "Jehu is king."

JEHU ASSASSINATES JORAM AND AHAZIAH

¹⁴Thus Jehu the son of Jehoshaphat the son of Nimshi conspired against Joram. (Now Joram with all Israel had been on guard at Ramoth-gilead against Hazael king of Syria, ¹⁵but King Joram had returned to be healed in Jezreel of the wounds that the Syrians had given him, when he fought with Hazael king of Syria.) So Jehu said, "If this is your decision, then let no one slip out of the city to go and tell the news in Jezreel." ¹⁶Then Jehu mounted his chariot and went to Jezreel, for Joram lay there. And Ahaziah king of Judah had come down to visit Joram.

¹⁷Now the watchman was standing on the tower in Jezreel, and he saw the company of Jehu as he came and said, "I see a company." And Joram said, "Take a horseman and send to meet them, and let him say, 'Is it peace?'" ¹⁸So a man on horseback went to meet him and said, "Thus says the king, 'Is it peace?'" And Jehu said, "What do you have to do with peace? Turn round and ride behind me." And the watchman reported, saying, "The messenger reached them, but he is not coming back." ¹⁹Then he sent out a second horseman, who came to them and said, "Thus the king has said, 'Is it peace?'" And Jehu answered, "What do you have to do with peace? Turn round and ride behind me." ²⁰Again the watchman reported, "He reached them, but he is not coming back. And the driving is like the driving of Jehu the son of Nimshi, for he drives furiously."

²¹Joram said, "Make ready." And they made ready his chariot. Then Joram king of Israel and Ahaziah king of Judah set out, each in his chariot, and went to meet Jehu, and met him at the property of Naboth the Jezreelite. ²²And when Joram saw Jehu, he said, "Is it peace, Jehu?" He answered, "What peace can there be, so long as the whorings and the sorceries of your mother Jezebel are so many?" ²³Then Joram reined about and fled, saying to Ahaziah, "Treachery, O Ahaziah!" ²⁴And Jehu drew his bow with his full strength, and shot Joram between the shoulders, so that the arrow pierced his heart, and he sank in his chariot. ²⁵Jehu said to Bidkar his assistant, "Take him up and throw him on the plot of ground belonging to Naboth the Jezreelite. For

---

ᵃ The meaning of the Hebrew word is uncertain

remember, when you and I rode side by side behind Ahab his father, how the LORD made this pronouncement against him: ²⁶'As surely as I saw yesterday the blood of Naboth and the blood of his sons—declares the LORD—I will repay you on this plot of ground.' Now therefore take him up and throw him on the plot of ground, in accordance with the word of the LORD."

²⁷When Ahaziah the king of Judah saw this, he fled in the direction of Beth-haggan. And Jehu pursued him and said, "Shoot him also." And they shot him*ᵃ* in the chariot at the ascent of Gur, which is by Ibleam. And he fled to Megiddo and died there. ²⁸His servants carried him in a chariot to Jerusalem, and buried him in his tomb with his fathers in the city of David.

²⁹In the eleventh year of Joram the son of Ahab, Ahaziah began to reign over Judah.

JEHU EXECUTES JEZEBEL

³⁰When Jehu came to Jezreel, Jezebel heard of it. And she painted her eyes and adorned her head and looked out of the window. ³¹And as Jehu entered the gate, she said, "Is it peace, you Zimri, murderer of your master?" ³²And he lifted up his face to the window and said, "Who is on my side? Who?" Two or three eunuchs looked out at him. ³³He said, "Throw her down." So they threw her down. And some of her blood spattered on the wall and on the horses, and they trampled on her. ³⁴Then he went in and ate and drank. And he said, "See now to this cursed woman and bury her, for she is a king's daughter." ³⁵But when they went to bury her, they found no more of her than the skull and the feet and the palms of her hands. ³⁶When they came back and told him, he said, "This is the word of the LORD, which he spoke by his servant Elijah the Tishbite: 'In the territory of Jezreel the dogs shall eat the flesh of Jezebel, ³⁷and the corpse of Jezebel shall be as dung on the face of the field in the territory of Jezreel, so that no one can say, This is Jezebel.'"

JEHU SLAUGHTERS AHAB'S DESCENDANTS

10 Now Ahab had seventy sons in Samaria. So Jehu wrote letters and sent them to Samaria, to the rulers of the city,*ᵇ* to the elders, and to the guardians of the sons*ᶜ* of Ahab, saying, ²"Now then, as soon as this letter comes to you, seeing your master's sons are with you, and there are with you chariots and horses, fortified cities also, and weapons, ³select the best and fittest of your master's sons and set him on his father's throne and fight for your master's house." ⁴But they were exceedingly afraid and said, "Behold, the two kings could not stand before him. How then can we stand?" ⁵So he who was over the palace, and he who was over the city, together with the elders and the guardians, sent to Jehu, saying, "We are your servants, and we will do all that you tell us. We will not make anyone king. Do whatever is good in your eyes." ⁶Then he wrote to them a second letter, saying, "If you are on my side, and if you are ready to obey me, take the heads of your master's sons and come to me at Jezreel tomorrow at this time." Now the king's sons, seventy persons, were with the great men of the city, who were bringing them up. ⁷And as soon as the letter came to them, they took the king's sons and slaughtered them, seventy persons, and put their heads in baskets and sent them to him at Jezreel. ⁸When the messenger came and told him, "They have brought the heads of the king's sons," he said, "Lay them in two heaps at the entrance of the gate until the morning." ⁹Then in the morning, when he went out, he stood and said to all the people, "You are innocent. It was I who conspired against my master and killed him, but who struck down all these? ¹⁰Know then that there shall fall to the earth nothing of the word of the LORD, which the LORD spoke concerning the house of Ahab, for the LORD has done what he said by his servant Elijah." ¹¹So Jehu struck down all who remained of the house of Ahab in Jezreel, all his great men and his close friends and his priests, until he left him none remaining.

¹²Then he set out and went to Samaria. On the way, when he was at Beth-eked of the Shepherds, ¹³Jehu met the relatives of Ahaziah king of Judah, and he said, "Who are you?" And they answered, "We are the relatives of Ahaziah, and we came down to visit the royal princes and the sons of the queen mother." ¹⁴He said, "Take them alive." And they took them alive and slaughtered them at the pit of Beth-eked, forty-two persons, and he spared none of them.

¹⁵And when he departed from there, he met Jehonadab the son of Rechab coming to meet him. And he greeted him and said to him, "Is your heart true to my heart as mine is to

---

*ᵃ*Syriac, Vulgate (compare Septuagint); Hebrew lacks *and they shot him* *ᵇ*Septuagint, Vulgate; Hebrew *rulers of Jezreel* *ᶜ*Hebrew lacks *of the sons*

yours?" And Jehonadab answered, "It is." Jehu said,[a] "If it is, give me your hand." So he gave him his hand. And Jehu took him up with him into the chariot. ¹⁶And he said, "Come with me, and see my zeal for the LORD." So he[b] had him ride in his chariot. ¹⁷And when he came to Samaria, he struck down all who remained to Ahab in Samaria, till he had wiped them out, according to the word of the LORD that he spoke to Elijah.

JEHU STRIKES DOWN THE PROPHETS OF BAAL

¹⁸Then Jehu assembled all the people and said to them, "Ahab served Baal a little, but Jehu will serve him much. ¹⁹Now therefore call to me all the prophets of Baal, all his worshippers and all his priests. Let none be missing, for I have a great sacrifice to offer to Baal. Whoever is missing shall not live." But Jehu did it with cunning in order to destroy the worshippers of Baal. ²⁰And Jehu ordered, "Sanctify a solemn assembly for Baal." So they proclaimed it. ²¹And Jehu sent throughout all Israel, and all the worshippers of Baal came, so that there was not a man left who did not come. And they entered the house of Baal, and the house of Baal was filled from one end to the other. ²²He said to him who was in charge of the wardrobe, "Bring out the vestments for all the worshippers of Baal." So he brought out the vestments for them. ²³Then Jehu went into the house of Baal with Jehonadab the son of Rechab, and he said to the worshippers of Baal, "Search, and see that there is no servant of the LORD here among you, but only the worshippers of Baal." ²⁴Then they[c] went in to offer sacrifices and burnt offerings.

Now Jehu had stationed eighty men outside and said, "The man who allows any of those whom I give into your hands to escape shall forfeit his life." ²⁵So as soon as he had made an end of offering the burnt offering, Jehu said to the guard and to the officers, "Go in and strike them down; let not a man escape." So when they put them to the sword, the guard and the officers cast them out and went into the inner room of the house of Baal, ²⁶and they brought out the pillar that was in the house of Baal and burned it. ²⁷And they demolished the pillar of Baal, and demolished the house of Baal, and made it a latrine to this day.

JEHU REIGNS IN ISRAEL

²⁸Thus Jehu wiped out Baal from Israel. ²⁹But Jehu did not turn aside from the sins of Jeroboam the son of Nebat, which he made Israel to sin—that is, the golden calves that were in Bethel and in Dan. ³⁰And the LORD said to Jehu, "Because you have done well in carrying out what is right in my eyes, and have done to the house of Ahab according to all that was in my heart, your sons of the fourth generation shall sit on the throne of Israel." ³¹But Jehu was not careful to walk in the law of the LORD, the God of Israel, with all his heart. He did not turn from the sins of Jeroboam, which he made Israel to sin.

³²In those days the LORD began to cut off parts of Israel. Hazael defeated them throughout the territory of Israel: ³³from the Jordan eastwards, all the land of Gilead, the Gadites, and the Reubenites, and the Manassites, from Aroer, which is by the Valley of the Arnon, that is, Gilead and Bashan. ³⁴Now the rest of the acts of Jehu and all that he did, and all his might, are they not written in the Book of the Chronicles of the Kings of Israel? ³⁵So Jehu slept with his fathers, and they buried him in Samaria. And Jehoahaz his son reigned in his place. ³⁶The time that Jehu reigned over Israel in Samaria was twenty-eight years.

ATHALIAH REIGNS IN JUDAH

11 Now when Athaliah the mother of Ahaziah saw that her son was dead, she arose and destroyed all the royal family. ²But Jehosheba, the daughter of King Joram, sister of Ahaziah, took Joash the son of Ahaziah and stole him away from among the king's sons who were being put to death, and she put[d] him and his nurse in a bedroom. Thus they[e] hid him from Athaliah, so that he was not put to death. ³And he remained with her for six years, hidden in the house of the LORD, while Athaliah reigned over the land.

JOASH ANOINTED KING IN JUDAH

⁴But in the seventh year Jehoiada sent and brought the captains of the Carites and of the guards, and had them come to him in the house of the LORD. And he made a covenant with them and put them under oath in the house of the LORD, and he showed them the king's son. ⁵And he commanded them, "This is the thing that you shall do: one third of you, those who come off duty on the Sabbath and guard the king's house ⁶(another third being

---

[a]Septuagint; Hebrew lacks *Jehu said* [b]Septuagint, Syriac, Targum; Hebrew *they* [c]Septuagint *he* (compare verse 25)
[d]Compare 2 Chronicles 22:11; Hebrew lacks *and she put*
[e]Septuagint, Syriac, Vulgate (compare 2 Chronicles 22:11) *she*

at the gate Sur and a third at the gate behind the guards) shall guard the palace.ᵃ ⁷And the two divisions of you, which come on duty in force on the Sabbath and guard the house of the LORD on behalf of the king, ⁸shall surround the king, each with his weapons in his hand. And whoever approaches the ranks is to be put to death. Be with the king when he goes out and when he comes in."

⁹The captains did according to all that Jehoiada the priest commanded, and they each brought his men who were to go off duty on the Sabbath, with those who were to come on duty on the Sabbath, and came to Jehoiada the priest. ¹⁰And the priest gave to the captains the spears and shields that had been King David's, which were in the house of the LORD. ¹¹And the guards stood, every man with his weapons in his hand, from the south side of the house to the north side of the house, round the altar and the house on behalf of the king. ¹²Then he brought out the king's son and put the crown on him and gave him the testimony. And they proclaimed him king and anointed him, and they clapped their hands and said, "Long live the king!"

¹³When Athaliah heard the noise of the guard and of the people, she went into the house of the LORD to the people. ¹⁴And when she looked, there was the king standing by the pillar, according to the custom, and the captains and the trumpeters beside the king, and all the people of the land rejoicing and blowing trumpets. And Athaliah tore her clothes and cried, "Treason! Treason!" ¹⁵Then Jehoiada the priest commanded the captains who were set over the army, "Bring her out between the ranks, and put to death with the sword anyone who follows her." For the priest said, "Let her not be put to death in the house of the LORD." ¹⁶So they laid hands on her; and she went through the horses' entrance to the king's house, and there she was put to death.

¹⁷And Jehoiada made a covenant between the LORD and the king and people, that they should be the LORD's people, and also between the king and the people. ¹⁸Then all the people of the land went to the house of Baal and tore it down; his altars and his images they broke in pieces, and they killed Mattan the priest of Baal before the altars. And the priest posted watchmen over the house of the LORD. ¹⁹And he took the captains, the Carites, the guards, and all the people of the land, and they brought the king down from the house of the LORD, marching through the gate of the guards to the king's house. And he took his seat on the throne of the kings. ²⁰So all the people of the land rejoiced, and the city was quiet after Athaliah had been put to death with the sword at the king's house.

JEHOASH REIGNS IN JUDAH

²¹ᵇ Jehoashᶜ was seven years old when he began to reign.

12 In the seventh year of Jehu, Jehoashᵈ began to reign, and he reigned for forty years in Jerusalem. His mother's name was Zibiah of Beersheba. ²And Jehoash did what was right in the eyes of the LORD all his days, because Jehoiada the priest instructed him. ³Nevertheless, the high places were not taken away; the people continued to sacrifice and make offerings on the high places.

JEHOASH REPAIRS THE TEMPLE

⁴Jehoash said to the priests, "All the money of the holy things that is brought into the house of the LORD, the money for which each man is assessed—the money from the assessment of persons—and the money that a man's heart prompts him to bring into the house of the LORD, ⁵let the priests take, each from his donor, and let them repair the house wherever any need of repairs is discovered." ⁶But by the twenty-third year of King Jehoash, the priests had made no repairs on the house. ⁷Therefore King Jehoash summoned Jehoiada the priest and the other priests and said to them, "Why are you not repairing the house? Now therefore take no more money from your donors, but hand it over for the repair of the house." ⁸So the priests agreed that they should take no more money from the people, and that they should not repair the house.

⁹Then Jehoiada the priest took a chest and bored a hole in the lid of it and set it beside the altar on the right side as one entered the house of the LORD. And the priests who guarded the threshold put in it all the money that was brought into the house of the LORD. ¹⁰And whenever they saw that there was much money in the chest, the king's secretary and the high priest came up and they bagged and counted the money that was found in the house of the LORD. ¹¹Then they would give the

---

ᵃThe meaning of the Hebrew word is uncertain   ᵇCh 12:1 in Hebrew   ᶜJehoash is an alternate spelling of Joash (son of Ahaziah) as in verse 2   ᵈJehoash is an alternate spelling of Joash (son of Ahaziah) as in 11:2; also verses 2, 4, 6, 7, 18

money that was weighed out into the hands of the workmen who had the oversight of the house of the LORD. And they paid it out to the carpenters and the builders who worked on the house of the LORD, ¹²and to the masons and the stonecutters, as well as to buy timber and quarried stone for making repairs on the house of the LORD, and for any outlay for the repairs of the house. ¹³But there were not made for the house of the LORD basins of silver, snuffers, bowls, trumpets, or any vessels of gold, or of silver, from the money that was brought into the house of the LORD, ¹⁴for that was given to the workmen who were repairing the house of the LORD with it. ¹⁵And they did not ask for an accounting from the men into whose hand they delivered the money to pay out to the workmen, for they dealt honestly. ¹⁶The money from the guilt offerings and the money from the sin offerings was not brought into the house of the LORD; it belonged to the priests.

¹⁷At that time Hazael king of Syria went up and fought against Gath and took it. But when Hazael set his face to go up against Jerusalem, ¹⁸Jehoash king of Judah took all the sacred gifts that Jehoshaphat and Jehoram and Ahaziah his fathers, the kings of Judah, had dedicated, and his own sacred gifts, and all the gold that was found in the treasuries of the house of the LORD and of the king's house, and sent these to Hazael king of Syria. Then Hazael went away from Jerusalem.

THE DEATH OF JOASH

¹⁹Now the rest of the acts of Joash and all that he did, are they not written in the Book of the Chronicles of the Kings of Judah? ²⁰His servants arose and made a conspiracy and struck down Joash in the house of Millo, on the way that goes down to Silla. ²¹It was Jozacar the son of Shimeath and Jehozabad the son of Shomer, his servants, who struck him down, so that he died. And they buried him with his fathers in the city of David, and Amaziah his son reigned in his place.

JEHOAHAZ REIGNS IN ISRAEL

13 In the twenty-third year of Joash the son of Ahaziah, king of Judah, Jehoahaz the son of Jehu began to reign over Israel in Samaria, and he reigned for seventeen years. ²He did what was evil in the sight of the LORD and followed the sins of Jeroboam the son of Nebat, which he made Israel to sin; he did not depart from them. ³And the anger of the LORD was kindled against Israel, and he gave them continually into the hand of Hazael king of Syria and into the hand of Ben-hadad the son of Hazael. ⁴Then Jehoahaz sought the favour of the LORD, and the LORD listened to him, for he saw the oppression of Israel, how the king of Syria oppressed them. ⁵(Therefore the LORD gave Israel a saviour, so that they escaped from the hand of the Syrians, and the people of Israel lived in their homes as formerly. ⁶Nevertheless, they did not depart from the sins of the house of Jeroboam, which he made Israel to sin, but walked[a] in them; and the Asherah also remained in Samaria.) ⁷For there was not left to Jehoahaz an army of more than fifty horsemen and ten chariots and ten thousand footmen, for the king of Syria had destroyed them and made them like the dust at threshing. ⁸Now the rest of the acts of Jehoahaz and all that he did, and his might, are they not written in the Book of the Chronicles of the Kings of Israel? ⁹So Jehoahaz slept with his fathers, and they buried him in Samaria, and Joash his son reigned in his place.

JEHOASH REIGNS IN ISRAEL

¹⁰In the thirty-seventh year of Joash king of Judah, Jehoash[b] the son of Jehoahaz began to reign over Israel in Samaria, and he reigned for sixteen years. ¹¹He also did what was evil in the sight of the LORD. He did not depart from all the sins of Jeroboam the son of Nebat, which he made Israel to sin, but he walked in them. ¹²Now the rest of the acts of Joash and all that he did, and the might with which he fought against Amaziah king of Judah, are they not written in the Book of the Chronicles of the Kings of Israel? ¹³So Joash slept with his fathers, and Jeroboam sat on his throne. And Joash was buried in Samaria with the kings of Israel.

THE DEATH OF ELISHA

¹⁴Now when Elisha had fallen sick with the illness of which he was to die, Joash king of Israel went down to him and wept before him, crying, "My father, my father! The chariots of Israel and its horsemen!" ¹⁵And Elisha said to him, "Take a bow and arrows." So he took a bow and arrows. ¹⁶Then he said to the

---

[a]Septuagint, Syriac, Targum, Vulgate; Hebrew *he walked* [b]*Jehoash* is an alternate spelling of *Joash* (son of Jehoahaz) as in verses 9, 12–14; also verse 25

king of Israel, "Draw the bow," and he drew it. And Elisha laid his hands on the king's hands. ¹⁷And he said, "Open the window eastwards", and he opened it. Then Elisha said, "Shoot", and he shot. And he said, "The LORD's arrow of victory, the arrow of victory over Syria! For you shall fight the Syrians in Aphek until you have made an end of them." ¹⁸And he said, "Take the arrows", and he took them. And he said to the king of Israel, "Strike the ground with them." And he struck three times and stopped. ¹⁹Then the man of God was angry with him and said, "You should have struck five or six times; then you would have struck down Syria until you had made an end of it, but now you will strike down Syria only three times."

²⁰So Elisha died, and they buried him. Now bands of Moabites used to invade the land in the spring of the year. ²¹And as a man was being buried, behold, a marauding band was seen and the man was thrown into the grave of Elisha, and as soon as the man touched the bones of Elisha, he revived and stood on his feet.

²²Now Hazael king of Syria oppressed Israel all the days of Jehoahaz. ²³But the LORD was gracious to them and had compassion on them, and he turned towards them, because of his covenant with Abraham, Isaac, and Jacob, and would not destroy them, nor has he cast them from his presence until now.

²⁴When Hazael king of Syria died, Ben-hadad his son became king in his place. ²⁵Then Jehoash the son of Jehoahaz took again from Ben-hadad the son of Hazael the cities that he had taken from Jehoahaz his father in war. Three times Joash defeated him and recovered the cities of Israel.

AMAZIAH REIGNS IN JUDAH

14 In the second year of Joash the son of Joahaz, king of Israel, Amaziah the son of Joash, king of Judah, began to reign. ²He was twenty-five years old when he began to reign, and he reigned for twenty-nine years in Jerusalem. His mother's name was Jehoaddin of Jerusalem. ³And he did what was right in the eyes of the LORD, yet not like David his father. He did in all things as Joash his father had done. ⁴But the high places were not removed; the people still sacrificed and made offerings on the high places. ⁵And as soon as the royal power was firmly in his hand, he struck down his servants who had struck down the king his father. ⁶But he did not put to death the children of the murderers, according to what is written in the Book of the Law of Moses, where the LORD commanded, "Fathers shall not be put to death because of their children, nor shall children be put to death because of their fathers. But each one shall die for his own sin."

⁷He struck down ten thousand Edomites in the Valley of Salt and took Sela by storm, and called it Joktheel, which is its name to this day.

⁸Then Amaziah sent messengers to Jehoash[a] the son of Jehoahaz, son of Jehu, king of Israel, saying, "Come, let us look one another in the face." ⁹And Jehoash king of Israel sent word to Amaziah king of Judah, "A thistle on Lebanon sent to a cedar on Lebanon, saying, 'Give your daughter to my son for a wife', and a wild beast of Lebanon passed by and trampled down the thistle. ¹⁰You have indeed struck down Edom, and your heart has lifted you up. Be content with your glory, and stay at home, for why should you provoke trouble so that you fall, you and Judah with you?"

¹¹But Amaziah would not listen. So Jehoash king of Israel went up, and he and Amaziah king of Judah faced one another in battle at Beth-shemesh, which belongs to Judah. ¹²And Judah was defeated by Israel, and every man fled to his home. ¹³And Jehoash king of Israel captured Amaziah king of Judah, the son of Jehoash, son of Ahaziah, at Beth-shemesh, and came to Jerusalem and broke down the wall of Jerusalem for four hundred cubits,[b] from the Ephraim Gate to the Corner Gate. ¹⁴And he seized all the gold and silver, and all the vessels that were found in the house of the LORD and in the treasuries of the king's house, also hostages, and he returned to Samaria.

¹⁵Now the rest of the acts of Jehoash that he did, and his might, and how he fought with Amaziah king of Judah, are they not written in the Book of the Chronicles of the Kings of Israel? ¹⁶And Jehoash slept with his fathers and was buried in Samaria with the kings of Israel, and Jeroboam his son reigned in his place.

¹⁷Amaziah the son of Joash, king of Judah, lived for fifteen years after the death of Jehoash son of Jehoahaz, king of Israel. ¹⁸Now the rest of the deeds of Amaziah, are they not written in the Book of the Chronicles of

---

[a] *Jehoash* is an alternate spelling of *Joash* (son of Jehoahaz) as in 13:9, 12–14; also verses 9, 11–16   [b] A *cubit* was about 18 inches or 45 centimetres

the Kings of Judah? ¹⁹And they made a conspiracy against him in Jerusalem, and he fled to Lachish. But they sent after him to Lachish and put him to death there. ²⁰And they brought him on horses; and he was buried in Jerusalem with his fathers in the city of David. ²¹And all the people of Judah took Azariah, who was sixteen years old, and made him king instead of his father Amaziah. ²²He built Elath and restored it to Judah, after the king slept with his fathers.

JEROBOAM II REIGNS IN ISRAEL

²³In the fifteenth year of Amaziah the son of Joash, king of Judah, Jeroboam the son of Joash, king of Israel, began to reign in Samaria, and he reigned for forty-one years. ²⁴And he did what was evil in the sight of the LORD. He did not depart from all the sins of Jeroboam the son of Nebat, which he made Israel to sin. ²⁵He restored the border of Israel from Lebo-hamath as far as the Sea of the Arabah, according to the word of the LORD, the God of Israel, which he spoke by his servant Jonah the son of Amittai, the prophet, who was from Gath-hepher. ²⁶For the LORD saw that the affliction of Israel was very bitter, for there was none left, bond or free, and there was none to help Israel. ²⁷But the LORD had not said that he would blot out the name of Israel from under heaven, so he saved them by the hand of Jeroboam the son of Joash.

²⁸Now the rest of the acts of Jeroboam and all that he did, and his might, how he fought, and how he restored Damascus and Hamath to Judah in Israel, are they not written in the Book of the Chronicles of the Kings of Israel? ²⁹And Jeroboam slept with his fathers, the kings of Israel, and Zechariah his son reigned in his place.

AZARIAH REIGNS IN JUDAH

15 In the twenty-seventh year of Jeroboam king of Israel, Azariah the son of Amaziah, king of Judah, began to reign. ²He was sixteen years old when he began to reign, and he reigned for fifty-two years in Jerusalem. His mother's name was Jecoliah of Jerusalem. ³And he did what was right in the eyes of the LORD, according to all that his father Amaziah had done. ⁴Nevertheless, the high places were not taken away. The people still sacrificed and made offerings on the high places. ⁵And the LORD touched the king, so that he was a leper*ᵃ* to the day of his death, and he lived in a separate house.*ᵇ* And Jotham the king's son was over the household, governing the people of the land. ⁶Now the rest of the acts of Azariah, and all that he did, are they not written in the Book of the Chronicles of the Kings of Judah? ⁷And Azariah slept with his fathers, and they buried him with his fathers in the city of David, and Jotham his son reigned in his place.

ZECHARIAH REIGNS IN ISRAEL

⁸In the thirty-eighth year of Azariah king of Judah, Zechariah the son of Jeroboam reigned over Israel in Samaria for six months. ⁹And he did what was evil in the sight of the LORD, as his fathers had done. He did not depart from the sins of Jeroboam the son of Nebat, which he made Israel to sin. ¹⁰Shallum the son of Jabesh conspired against him and struck him down at Ibleam and put him to death and reigned in his place. ¹¹Now the rest of the deeds of Zechariah, behold, they are written in the Book of the Chronicles of the Kings of Israel. ¹²(This was the promise of the LORD that he gave to Jehu, "Your sons shall sit on the throne of Israel to the fourth generation." And so it came to pass.)

SHALLUM REIGNS IN ISRAEL

¹³Shallum the son of Jabesh began to reign in the thirty-ninth year of Uzziah*ᶜ* king of Judah, and he reigned for one month in Samaria. ¹⁴Then Menahem the son of Gadi came up from Tirzah and came to Samaria, and he struck down Shallum the son of Jabesh in Samaria and put him to death and reigned in his place. ¹⁵Now the rest of the deeds of Shallum, and the conspiracy that he made, behold, they are written in the Book of the Chronicles of the Kings of Israel. ¹⁶At that time Menahem sacked Tiphsah and all who were in it and its territory from Tirzah on, because they did not open it to him. Therefore he sacked it, and he ripped open all the women in it who were pregnant.

MENAHEM REIGNS IN ISRAEL

¹⁷In the thirty-ninth year of Azariah king of Judah, Menahem the son of Gadi began to reign over Israel, and he reigned for ten years in Samaria. ¹⁸And he did what was evil in the sight of the LORD. He did not depart all his days from all the sins of Jeroboam the son of

---

ᵃLeprosy was a term for several skin diseases; see Leviticus 13 *ᵇ*The meaning of the Hebrew word is uncertain *ᶜ*Another name for *Azariah*

Nebat, which he made Israel to sin. ¹⁹Pul[a] the king of Assyria came against the land, and Menahem gave Pul a thousand talents[b] of silver, that he might help him to confirm his hold on the royal power. ²⁰Menahem exacted the money from Israel, that is, from all the wealthy men, fifty shekels[c] of silver from every man, to give to the king of Assyria. So the king of Assyria turned back and did not stay there in the land. ²¹Now the rest of the deeds of Menahem and all that he did, are they not written in the Book of the Chronicles of the Kings of Israel? ²²And Menahem slept with his fathers, and Pekahiah his son reigned in his place.

PEKAHIAH REIGNS IN ISRAEL

²³In the fiftieth year of Azariah king of Judah, Pekahiah the son of Menahem began to reign over Israel in Samaria, and he reigned for two years. ²⁴And he did what was evil in the sight of the LORD. He did not turn away from the sins of Jeroboam the son of Nebat, which he made Israel to sin. ²⁵And Pekah the son of Remaliah, his captain, conspired against him with fifty men of the people of Gilead, and struck him down in Samaria, in the citadel of the king's house with Argob and Arieh; he put him to death and reigned in his place. ²⁶Now the rest of the deeds of Pekahiah and all that he did, behold, they are written in the Book of the Chronicles of the Kings of Israel.

PEKAH REIGNS IN ISRAEL

²⁷In the fifty-second year of Azariah king of Judah, Pekah the son of Remaliah began to reign over Israel in Samaria, and he reigned for twenty years. ²⁸And he did what was evil in the sight of the LORD. He did not depart from the sins of Jeroboam the son of Nebat, which he made Israel to sin.

²⁹In the days of Pekah king of Israel, Tiglath-pileser king of Assyria came and captured Ijon, Abel-beth-maacah, Janoah, Kedesh, Hazor, Gilead, and Galilee, all the land of Naphtali, and he carried the people captive to Assyria. ³⁰Then Hoshea the son of Elah made a conspiracy against Pekah the son of Remaliah and struck him down and put him to death and reigned in his place, in the twentieth year of Jotham the son of Uzziah. ³¹Now the rest of the acts of Pekah and all that he did, behold, they are written in the Book of the Chronicles of the Kings of Israel.

JOTHAM REIGNS IN JUDAH

³²In the second year of Pekah the son of Remaliah, king of Israel, Jotham the son of Uzziah, king of Judah, began to reign. ³³He was twenty-five years old when he began to reign, and he reigned for sixteen years in Jerusalem. His mother's name was Jerusha the daughter of Zadok. ³⁴And he did what was right in the eyes of the LORD, according to all that his father Uzziah had done. ³⁵Nevertheless, the high places were not removed. The people still sacrificed and made offerings on the high places. He built the upper gate of the house of the LORD. ³⁶Now the rest of the acts of Jotham and all that he did, are they not written in the Book of the Chronicles of the Kings of Judah? ³⁷In those days the LORD began to send Rezin the king of Syria and Pekah the son of Remaliah against Judah. ³⁸Jotham slept with his fathers and was buried with his fathers in the city of David his father, and Ahaz his son reigned in his place.

AHAZ REIGNS IN JUDAH

16 In the seventeenth year of Pekah the son of Remaliah, Ahaz the son of Jotham, king of Judah, began to reign. ²Ahaz was twenty years old when he began to reign, and he reigned for sixteen years in Jerusalem. And he did not do what was right in the eyes of the LORD his God, as his father David had done, ³but he walked in the way of the kings of Israel. He even burned his son as an offering,[d] according to the despicable practices of the nations whom the LORD drove out before the people of Israel. ⁴And he sacrificed and made offerings on the high places and on the hills and under every green tree.

⁵Then Rezin king of Syria and Pekah the son of Remaliah, king of Israel, came up to wage war on Jerusalem, and they besieged Ahaz but could not conquer him. ⁶At that time Rezin the king of Syria recovered Elath for Syria and drove the men of Judah from Elath, and the Edomites came to Elath, where they dwell to this day. ⁷So Ahaz sent messengers to Tiglath-pileser king of Assyria, saying, "I am your servant and your son. Come up and rescue me from the hand of the king of Syria and from the hand of the king of Israel, who are attacking me." ⁸Ahaz also took the silver and gold that was found in the house of the

---

[a]Another name for *Tiglath-pileser III* (compare verse 29) [b]A *talent* was about 75 pounds or 34 kilograms [c]A *shekel* was about 2/5 of an ounce or 11 grams [d]Or *made his son pass through the fire*

LORD and in the treasures of the king's house and sent a present to the king of Assyria. ⁹And the king of Assyria listened to him. The king of Assyria marched up against Damascus and took it, carrying its people captive to Kir, and he killed Rezin.

¹⁰When King Ahaz went to Damascus to meet Tiglath-pileser king of Assyria, he saw the altar that was at Damascus. And King Ahaz sent to Uriah the priest a model of the altar, and its pattern, exact in all its details. ¹¹And Uriah the priest built the altar; in accordance with all that King Ahaz had sent from Damascus, so Uriah the priest made it, before King Ahaz arrived from Damascus. ¹²And when the king came from Damascus, the king viewed the altar. Then the king drew near to the altar and went up on it ¹³and burned his burnt offering and his grain offering and poured his drink offering and threw the blood of his peace offerings on the altar. ¹⁴And the bronze altar that was before the LORD he removed from the front of the house, from the place between his altar and the house of the LORD, and put it on the north side of his altar. ¹⁵And King Ahaz commanded Uriah the priest, saying, "On the great altar burn the morning burnt offering and the evening grain offering and the king's burnt offering and his grain offering, with the burnt offering of all the people of the land, and their grain offering and their drink offering. And throw on it all the blood of the burnt offering and all the blood of the sacrifice, but the bronze altar shall be for me to enquire by." ¹⁶Uriah the priest did all this, as King Ahaz commanded.

¹⁷And King Ahaz cut off the frames of the stands and removed the basin from them, and he took down the sea*ᵃ* from off the bronze oxen that were under it and put it on a stone pedestal. ¹⁸And the covered way for the Sabbath that had been built inside the house and the outer entrance for the king he caused to go round the house of the LORD, because of the king of Assyria. ¹⁹Now the rest of the acts of Ahaz that he did, are they not written in the Book of the Chronicles of the Kings of Judah? ²⁰And Ahaz slept with his fathers and was buried with his fathers in the city of David, and Hezekiah his son reigned in his place.

HOSHEA REIGNS IN ISRAEL

17 In the twelfth year of Ahaz king of Judah, Hoshea the son of Elah began to reign in Samaria over Israel, and he reigned for nine years. ²And he did what was evil in the sight of the LORD, yet not as the kings of Israel who were before him. ³Against him came up Shalmaneser king of Assyria. And Hoshea became his vassal and paid him tribute. ⁴But the king of Assyria found treachery in Hoshea, for he had sent messengers to So, king of Egypt, and offered no tribute to the king of Assyria, as he had done year by year. Therefore the king of Assyria shut him up and bound him in prison. ⁵Then the king of Assyria invaded all the land and came to Samaria, and for three years he besieged it.

THE FALL OF ISRAEL

⁶In the ninth year of Hoshea, the king of Assyria captured Samaria, and he carried the Israelites away to Assyria and placed them in Halah, and on the Habor, the river of Gozan, and in the cities of the Medes.

EXILE BECAUSE OF IDOLATRY

⁷And this occurred because the people of Israel had sinned against the LORD their God, who had brought them up out of the land of Egypt from under the hand of Pharaoh king of Egypt, and had feared other gods ⁸and walked in the customs of the nations whom the LORD drove out before the people of Israel, and in the customs that the kings of Israel had practised. ⁹And the people of Israel did secretly against the LORD their God things that were not right. They built for themselves high places in all their towns, from watchtower to fortified city. ¹⁰They set up for themselves pillars and Asherim on every high hill and under every green tree, ¹¹and there they made offerings on all the high places, as the nations did whom the LORD carried away before them. And they did wicked things, provoking the LORD to anger, ¹²and they served idols, of which the LORD had said to them, "You shall not do this." ¹³Yet the LORD warned Israel and Judah by every prophet and every seer, saying, "Turn from your evil ways and keep my commandments and my statutes, in accordance with all the Law that I commanded your fathers, and that I sent to you by my servants the prophets."

¹⁴But they would not listen, but were stubborn, as their fathers had been, who did not believe in the LORD their God. ¹⁵They despised his statutes and his covenant that he made with their fathers and the warnings that he gave them. They went after false idols and

---

*ᵃ*Compare 1 Kings 7:23

became false, and they followed the nations that were around them, concerning whom the LORD had commanded them that they should not do like them. ¹⁶And they abandoned all the commandments of the LORD their God, and made for themselves metal images of two calves; and they made an Asherah and worshipped all the host of heaven and served Baal. ¹⁷And they burned their sons and their daughters as offerings[a] and used divination and omens and sold themselves to do evil in the sight of the LORD, provoking him to anger. ¹⁸Therefore the LORD was very angry with Israel and removed them out of his sight. None was left but the tribe of Judah only.

¹⁹Judah also did not keep the commandments of the LORD their God, but walked in the customs that Israel had introduced. ²⁰And the LORD rejected all the descendants of Israel and afflicted them and gave them into the hand of plunderers, until he had cast them out of his sight.

²¹When he had torn Israel from the house of David, they made Jeroboam the son of Nebat king. And Jeroboam drove Israel from following the LORD and made them commit great sin. ²²The people of Israel walked in all the sins that Jeroboam did. They did not depart from them, ²³until the LORD removed Israel out of his sight, as he had spoken by all his servants the prophets. So Israel was exiled from their own land to Assyria until this day.

ASSYRIA RESETTLES SAMARIA

²⁴And the king of Assyria brought people from Babylon, Cuthah, Avva, Hamath, and Sepharvaim, and placed them in the cities of Samaria instead of the people of Israel. And they took possession of Samaria and lived in its cities. ²⁵And at the beginning of their dwelling there, they did not fear the LORD. Therefore the LORD sent lions among them, which killed some of them. ²⁶So the king of Assyria was told, "The nations that you have carried away and placed in the cities of Samaria do not know the law of the god of the land. Therefore he has sent lions among them, and behold, they are killing them, because they do not know the law of the god of the land." ²⁷Then the king of Assyria commanded, "Send there one of the priests whom you carried away from there, and let him[b] go and dwell there and teach them the law of the god of the land." ²⁸So one of the priests whom they had carried away from Samaria came and lived in Bethel and taught them how they should fear the LORD.

²⁹But every nation still made gods of its own and put them in the shrines of the high places that the Samaritans had made, every nation in the cities in which they lived. ³⁰The men of Babylon made Succoth-benoth, the men of Cuth made Nergal, the men of Hamath made Ashima, ³¹and the Avvites made Nibhaz and Tartak; and the Sepharvites burned their children in the fire to Adrammelech and Anammelech, the gods of Sepharvaim. ³²They also feared the LORD and appointed from among themselves all sorts of people as priests of the high places, who sacrificed for them in the shrines of the high places. ³³So they feared the LORD but also served their own gods, after the manner of the nations from among whom they had been carried away.

³⁴To this day they do according to the former manner. They do not fear the LORD, and they do not follow the statutes or the rules or the law or the commandment that the LORD commanded the children of Jacob, whom he named Israel. ³⁵The LORD made a covenant with them and commanded them, "You shall not fear other gods or bow yourselves to them or serve them or sacrifice to them, ³⁶but you shall fear the LORD, who brought you out of the land of Egypt with great power and with an outstretched arm. You shall bow yourselves to him, and to him you shall sacrifice. ³⁷And the statutes and the rules and the law and the commandment that he wrote for you, you shall always be careful to do. You shall not fear other gods, ³⁸and you shall not forget the covenant that I have made with you. You shall not fear other gods, ³⁹but you shall fear the LORD your God, and he will deliver you out of the hand of all your enemies." ⁴⁰However, they would not listen, but they did according to their former manner.

⁴¹So these nations feared the LORD and also served their carved images. Their children did likewise, and their children's children—as their fathers did, so they do to this day.

HEZEKIAH REIGNS IN JUDAH

18 In the third year of Hoshea son of Elah, king of Israel, Hezekiah the son of Ahaz, king of Judah, began to reign. ²He was twenty-five years old when he began to reign, and he reigned for

---

[a] Or made their sons and their daughters pass through the fire
[b] Syriac, Vulgate; Hebrew *them*

twenty-nine years in Jerusalem. His mother's name was Abi the daughter of Zechariah. ³And he did what was right in the eyes of the LORD, according to all that David his father had done. ⁴He removed the high places and broke the pillars and cut down the Asherah. And he broke in pieces the bronze serpent that Moses had made, for until those days the people of Israel had made offerings to it (it was called Nehushtan).[a] ⁵He trusted in the LORD, the God of Israel, so that there was none like him among all the kings of Judah after him, nor among those who were before him. ⁶For he held fast to the LORD. He did not depart from following him, but kept the commandments that the LORD commanded Moses. ⁷And the LORD was with him; wherever he went out, he prospered. He rebelled against the king of Assyria and would not serve him. ⁸He struck down the Philistines as far as Gaza and its territory, from watchtower to fortified city.

⁹In the fourth year of King Hezekiah, which was the seventh year of Hoshea son of Elah, king of Israel, Shalmaneser king of Assyria came up against Samaria and besieged it, ¹⁰and at the end of three years he took it. In the sixth year of Hezekiah, which was the ninth year of Hoshea king of Israel, Samaria was taken. ¹¹The king of Assyria carried the Israelites away to Assyria and put them in Halah, and on the Habor, the river of Gozan, and in the cities of the Medes, ¹²because they did not obey the voice of the LORD their God but transgressed his covenant, even all that Moses the servant of the LORD commanded. They neither listened nor obeyed.

SENNACHERIB ATTACKS JUDAH

¹³In the fourteenth year of King Hezekiah, Sennacherib king of Assyria came up against all the fortified cities of Judah and took them. ¹⁴And Hezekiah king of Judah sent to the king of Assyria at Lachish, saying, "I have done wrong; withdraw from me. Whatever you impose on me I will bear." And the king of Assyria required of Hezekiah king of Judah three hundred talents[b] of silver and thirty talents of gold. ¹⁵And Hezekiah gave him all the silver that was found in the house of the LORD and in the treasuries of the king's house. ¹⁶At that time Hezekiah stripped the gold from the doors of the temple of the LORD and from the doorposts that Hezekiah king of Judah had overlaid and gave it to the king of Assyria. ¹⁷And the king of Assyria sent the Tartan, the Rab-saris, and the Rabshakeh with a great army from Lachish to King Hezekiah at Jerusalem. And they went up and came to Jerusalem. When they arrived, they came and stood by the conduit of the upper pool, which is on the highway to the Washer's Field. ¹⁸And when they called for the king, there came out to them Eliakim the son of Hilkiah, who was over the household, and Shebnah the secretary, and Joah the son of Asaph, the recorder.

¹⁹And the Rabshakeh said to them, "Say to Hezekiah, 'Thus says the great king, the king of Assyria: On what do you rest this trust of yours? ²⁰Do you think that mere words are strategy and power for war? In whom do you now trust, that you have rebelled against me? ²¹Behold, you are trusting now in Egypt, that broken reed of a staff, which will pierce the hand of any man who leans on it. Such is Pharaoh king of Egypt to all who trust in him. ²²But if you say to me, "We trust in the LORD our God", is it not he whose high places and altars Hezekiah has removed, saying to Judah and to Jerusalem, "You shall worship before this altar in Jerusalem"? ²³Come now, make a wager with my master the king of Assyria: I will give you two thousand horses, if you are able on your part to set riders on them. ²⁴How then can you repulse a single captain among the least of my master's servants, when you trust in Egypt for chariots and for horsemen? ²⁵Moreover, is it without the LORD that I have come up against this place to destroy it? The LORD said to me, "Go up against this land and destroy it."'"

²⁶Then Eliakim the son of Hilkiah, and Shebnah, and Joah, said to the Rabshakeh, "Please speak to your servants in Aramaic, for we understand it. Do not speak to us in the language of Judah within the hearing of the people who are on the wall." ²⁷But the Rabshakeh said to them, "Has my master sent me to speak these words to your master and to you, and not to the men sitting on the wall, who are doomed with you to eat their own dung and to drink their own urine?"

²⁸Then the Rabshakeh stood and called out in a loud voice in the language of Judah: "Hear the word of the great king, the king of Assyria! ²⁹Thus says the king: 'Do not let Hezekiah deceive you, for he will not be able to deliver you out of my[c] hand. ³⁰Do not let Hezekiah make you trust in the LORD by saying,

---

[a] *Nehushtan* sounds like the Hebrew for both *bronze* and *serpent* [b] A *talent* was about 75 pounds or 34 kilograms [c] Hebrew *his*

The LORD will surely deliver us, and this city will not be given into the hand of the king of Assyria.' ³¹Do not listen to Hezekiah, for thus says the king of Assyria: 'Make your peace with me[a] and come out to me. Then each one of you will eat of his own vine, and each one of his own fig tree, and each one of you will drink the water of his own cistern, ³²until I come and take you away to a land like your own land, a land of grain and wine, a land of bread and vineyards, a land of olive trees and honey, that you may live, and not die. And do not listen to Hezekiah when he misleads you by saying, "The LORD will deliver us." ³³Has any of the gods of the nations ever delivered his land out of the hand of the king of Assyria? ³⁴Where are the gods of Hamath and Arpad? Where are the gods of Sepharvaim, Hena, and Ivvah? Have they delivered Samaria out of my hand? ³⁵Who among all the gods of the lands have delivered their lands out of my hand, that the LORD should deliver Jerusalem out of my hand?'"

³⁶But the people were silent and answered him not a word, for the king's command was, "Do not answer him." ³⁷Then Eliakim the son of Hilkiah, who was over the household, and Shebna the secretary, and Joah the son of Asaph, the recorder, came to Hezekiah with their clothes torn and told him the words of the Rabshakeh.

ISAIAH REASSURES HEZEKIAH

19 As soon as King Hezekiah heard it, he tore his clothes and covered himself with sackcloth and went into the house of the LORD. ²And he sent Eliakim, who was over the household, and Shebna the secretary, and the senior priests, covered with sackcloth, to the prophet Isaiah the son of Amoz. ³They said to him, "Thus says Hezekiah, This day is a day of distress, of rebuke, and of disgrace; children have come to the point of birth, and there is no strength to bring them forth. ⁴It may be that the LORD your God heard all the words of the Rabshakeh, whom his master the king of Assyria has sent to mock the living God, and will rebuke the words that the LORD your God has heard; therefore lift up your prayer for the remnant that is left." ⁵When the servants of King Hezekiah came to Isaiah, ⁶Isaiah said to them, "Say to your master, 'Thus says the LORD: Do not be afraid because of the words that you have heard, with which the servants of the king of Assyria have reviled me. ⁷Behold, I will put a spirit in him, so that he shall hear a rumour and return to his own land, and I will make him fall by the sword in his own land.'"

SENNACHERIB DEFIES THE LORD

⁸The Rabshakeh returned, and found the king of Assyria fighting against Libnah, for he heard that the king had left Lachish. ⁹Now the king heard concerning Tirhakah king of Cush, "Behold, he has set out to fight against you." So he sent messengers again to Hezekiah, saying, ¹⁰"Thus shall you speak to Hezekiah king of Judah: 'Do not let your God in whom you trust deceive you by promising that Jerusalem will not be given into the hand of the king of Assyria. ¹¹Behold, you have heard what the kings of Assyria have done to all lands, devoting them to destruction. And shall you be delivered? ¹²Have the gods of the nations delivered them, the nations that my fathers destroyed, Gozan, Haran, Rezeph, and the people of Eden who were in Telassar? ¹³Where is the king of Hamath, the king of Arpad, the king of the city of Sepharvaim, the king of Hena, or the king of Ivvah?'"

HEZEKIAH'S PRAYER

¹⁴Hezekiah received the letter from the hand of the messengers and read it; and Hezekiah went up to the house of the LORD and spread it before the LORD. ¹⁵And Hezekiah prayed before the LORD and said: "O LORD, the God of Israel, enthroned above the cherubim, you are the God, you alone, of all the kingdoms of the earth; you have made heaven and earth. ¹⁶Incline your ear, O LORD, and hear; open your eyes, O LORD, and see; and hear the words of Sennacherib, which he has sent to mock the living God. ¹⁷Truly, O LORD, the kings of Assyria have laid waste the nations and their lands ¹⁸and have cast their gods into the fire, for they were not gods, but the work of men's hands, wood and stone. Therefore they were destroyed. ¹⁹So now, O LORD our God, save us, please, from his hand, that all the kingdoms of the earth may know that you, O LORD, are God alone."

ISAIAH PROPHESIES SENNACHERIB'S FALL

²⁰Then Isaiah the son of Amoz sent to Hezekiah, saying, "Thus says the LORD, the God of Israel: Your prayer to me about Sennacherib king of Assyria I have heard. ²¹This is the word that the LORD has spoken concerning him:

---

[a] Hebrew *Make a blessing with me*

"She despises you, she scorns you—
   the virgin daughter of Zion;
she wags her head behind you—
   the daughter of Jerusalem.

22 "Whom have you mocked and reviled?
   Against whom have you
      raised your voice
and lifted your eyes to the heights?
   Against the Holy One of Israel!
23 By your messengers you have
   mocked the Lord,
   and you have said, 'With
      my many chariots
I have gone up the heights
   of the mountains,
to the far recesses of Lebanon;
I felled its tallest cedars,
   its choicest cypresses;
I entered its farthest lodging place,
   its most fruitful forest.
24 I dug wells
   and drank foreign waters,
and I dried up with the sole of my foot
   all the streams of Egypt.'

25 "Have you not heard
   that I determined it long ago?
   I planned from days of old
      what now I bring to pass,
that you should turn fortified cities
   into heaps of ruins,
26 while their inhabitants,
   shorn of strength,
   are dismayed and confounded,
and have become like plants of the field
   and like tender grass,
like grass on the housetops,
   blighted before it is grown.

27 "But I know your sitting down
   and your going out and coming in,
   and your raging against me.
28 Because you have raged against me
   and your complacency has
      come into my ears,
I will put my hook in your nose
   and my bit in your mouth,
and I will turn you back on the way
   by which you came.

29 "And this shall be the sign for you: this year eat what grows of itself, and in the second year what springs of the same. Then in the third year sow and reap and plant vineyards, and eat their fruit. 30 And the surviving remnant of the house of Judah shall again take root downwards and bear fruit upwards. 31 For out of Jerusalem shall go a remnant, and out of Mount Zion a band of survivors. The zeal of the Lord will do this.

32 "Therefore thus says the Lord concerning the king of Assyria: He shall not come into this city or shoot an arrow there, or come before it with a shield or cast up a siege mound against it. 33 By the way that he came, by the same he shall return, and he shall not come into this city, declares the Lord. 34 For I will defend this city to save it, for my own sake and for the sake of my servant David."

35 And that night the angel of the Lord went out and struck down 185,000 in the camp of the Assyrians. And when people arose early in the morning, behold, these were all dead bodies. 36 Then Sennacherib king of Assyria departed and went home and lived at Nineveh. 37 And as he was worshipping in the house of Nisroch his god, Adrammelech and Sharezer, his sons, struck him down with the sword and escaped into the land of Ararat. And Esarhaddon his son reigned in his place.

HEZEKIAH'S ILLNESS AND RECOVERY

20 In those days Hezekiah became sick and was at the point of death. And Isaiah the prophet the son of Amoz came to him and said to him, "Thus says the Lord, 'Set your house in order, for you shall die; you shall not recover.'" 2 Then Hezekiah turned his face to the wall and prayed to the Lord, saying, 3 "Now, O Lord, please remember how I have walked before you in faithfulness and with a whole heart, and have done what is good in your sight." And Hezekiah wept bitterly. 4 And before Isaiah had gone out of the middle court, the word of the Lord came to him: 5 "Turn back, and say to Hezekiah the leader of my people, Thus says the Lord, the God of David your father: I have heard your prayer; I have seen your tears. Behold, I will heal you. On the third day you shall go up to the house of the Lord, 6 and I will add fifteen years to your life. I will deliver you and this city out of the hand of the king of Assyria, and I will defend this city for my own sake and for my servant David's sake." 7 And Isaiah said, "Bring a cake of figs. And let them take and lay it on the boil, that he may recover."

8 And Hezekiah said to Isaiah, "What shall be the sign that the Lord will heal me, and that I shall go up to the house of the Lord on the third day?" 9 And Isaiah said, "This shall be

the sign to you from the LORD, that the LORD will do the thing that he has promised: shall the shadow go forward ten steps, or go back ten steps?" 10And Hezekiah answered, "It is an easy thing for the shadow to lengthen ten steps. Rather let the shadow go back ten steps." 11And Isaiah the prophet called to the LORD, and he brought the shadow back ten steps, by which it had gone down on the steps of Ahaz.

HEZEKIAH AND THE BABYLONIAN ENVOYS

12At that time Merodach-baladan the son of Baladan, king of Babylon, sent envoys with letters and a present to Hezekiah, for he heard that Hezekiah had been sick. 13And Hezekiah welcomed them, and he showed them all his treasure house, the silver, the gold, the spices, the precious oil, his armoury, all that was found in his storehouses. There was nothing in his house or in all his realm that Hezekiah did not show them. 14Then Isaiah the prophet came to King Hezekiah, and said to him, "What did these men say? And from where did they come to you?" And Hezekiah said, "They have come from a far country, from Babylon." 15He said, "What have they seen in your house?" And Hezekiah answered, "They have seen all that is in my house; there is nothing in my storehouses that I did not show them."

16Then Isaiah said to Hezekiah, "Hear the word of the LORD: 17Behold, the days are coming, when all that is in your house, and that which your fathers have stored up till this day, shall be carried to Babylon. Nothing shall be left, says the LORD. 18And some of your own sons, who will come from you, whom you will father, shall be taken away, and they shall be eunuchs in the palace of the king of Babylon." 19Then Hezekiah said to Isaiah, "The word of the LORD that you have spoken is good." For he thought, "Why not, if there will be peace and security in my days?"

20The rest of the deeds of Hezekiah and all his might and how he made the pool and the conduit and brought water into the city, are they not written in the Book of the Chronicles of the Kings of Judah? 21And Hezekiah slept with his fathers, and Manasseh his son reigned in his place.

MANASSEH REIGNS IN JUDAH

21 Manasseh was twelve years old when he began to reign, and he reigned for fifty-five years in Jerusalem. His mother's name was Hephzibah. 2And he did what was evil in the sight of the LORD, according to the despicable practices of the nations whom the LORD drove out before the people of Israel. 3For he rebuilt the high places that Hezekiah his father had destroyed, and he erected altars for Baal and made an Asherah, as Ahab king of Israel had done, and worshipped all the host of heaven and served them. 4And he built altars in the house of the LORD, of which the LORD had said, "In Jerusalem will I put my name." 5And he built altars for all the host of heaven in the two courts of the house of the LORD. 6And he burned his son as an offering[a] and used fortune-telling and omens and dealt with mediums and with necromancers. He did much evil in the sight of the LORD, provoking him to anger. 7And the carved image of Asherah that he had made he set in the house of which the LORD said to David and to Solomon his son, "In this house, and in Jerusalem, which I have chosen out of all the tribes of Israel, I will put my name for ever. 8And I will not cause the feet of Israel to wander any more out of the land that I gave to their fathers, if only they will be careful to do according to all that I have commanded them, and according to all the Law that my servant Moses commanded them." 9But they did not listen, and Manasseh led them astray to do more evil than the nations had done whom the LORD destroyed before the people of Israel.

MANASSEH'S IDOLATRY DENOUNCED

10And the LORD said by his servants the prophets, 11"Because Manasseh king of Judah has committed these abominations and has done things more evil than all that the Amorites did, who were before him, and has made Judah also to sin with his idols, 12therefore thus says the LORD, the God of Israel: Behold, I am bringing upon Jerusalem and Judah such disaster[b] that the ears of everyone who hears of it will tingle. 13And I will stretch over Jerusalem the measuring line of Samaria, and the plumb line of the house of Ahab, and I will wipe Jerusalem as one wipes a dish, wiping it and turning it upside down. 14And I will forsake the remnant of my heritage and give them into the hand of their enemies, and they shall become a prey and a spoil to all their enemies, 15because they have done what is evil in my sight and have provoked me to anger, since the day their fathers came out of Egypt, even to this day."

---

[a]Hebrew *made his son pass through the fire* [b]Or *evil*

[16] Moreover, Manasseh shed very much innocent blood, till he had filled Jerusalem from one end to another, besides the sin that he made Judah to sin so that they did what was evil in the sight of the LORD.

[17] Now the rest of the acts of Manasseh and all that he did, and the sin that he committed, are they not written in the Book of the Chronicles of the Kings of Judah? [18] And Manasseh slept with his fathers and was buried in the garden of his house, in the garden of Uzza, and Amon his son reigned in his place.

AMON REIGNS IN JUDAH

[19] Amon was twenty-two years old when he began to reign, and he reigned for two years in Jerusalem. His mother's name was Meshullemeth the daughter of Haruz of Jotbah. [20] And he did what was evil in the sight of the LORD, as Manasseh his father had done. [21] He walked in all the way in which his father walked and served the idols that his father served and worshipped them. [22] He abandoned the LORD, the God of his fathers, and did not walk in the way of the LORD. [23] And the servants of Amon conspired against him and put the king to death in his house. [24] But the people of the land struck down all those who had conspired against King Amon, and the people of the land made Josiah his son king in his place. [25] Now the rest of the acts of Amon that he did, are they not written in the Book of the Chronicles of the Kings of Judah? [26] And he was buried in his tomb in the garden of Uzza, and Josiah his son reigned in his place.

JOSIAH REIGNS IN JUDAH

22 [1] Josiah was eight years old when he began to reign, and he reigned for thirty-one years in Jerusalem. His mother's name was Jedidah the daughter of Adaiah of Bozkath. [2] And he did what was right in the eyes of the LORD and walked in all the way of David his father, and he did not turn aside to the right or to the left.

JOSIAH REPAIRS THE TEMPLE

[3] In the eighteenth year of King Josiah, the king sent Shaphan the son of Azaliah, son of Meshullam, the secretary, to the house of the LORD, saying, [4] "Go up to Hilkiah the high priest, that he may count the money that has been brought into the house of the LORD, which the keepers of the threshold have collected from the people. [5] And let it be given into the hand of the workmen who have the oversight of the house of the LORD, and let them give it to the workmen who are at the house of the LORD, repairing the house [6] (that is, to the carpenters, and to the builders, and to the masons), and let them use it for buying timber and quarried stone to repair the house. [7] But no accounting shall be asked from them for the money that is delivered into their hand, for they deal honestly."

HILKIAH FINDS THE BOOK OF THE LAW

[8] And Hilkiah the high priest said to Shaphan the secretary, "I have found the Book of the Law in the house of the LORD." And Hilkiah gave the book to Shaphan, and he read it. [9] And Shaphan the secretary came to the king, and reported to the king, "Your servants have emptied out the money that was found in the house and have delivered it into the hand of the workmen who have the oversight of the house of the LORD." [10] Then Shaphan the secretary told the king, "Hilkiah the priest has given me a book." And Shaphan read it before the king.

[11] When the king heard the words of the Book of the Law, he tore his clothes. [12] And the king commanded Hilkiah the priest, and Ahikam the son of Shaphan, and Achbor the son of Micaiah, and Shaphan the secretary, and Asaiah the king's servant, saying, [13] "Go, enquire of the LORD for me, and for the people, and for all Judah, concerning the words of this book that has been found. For great is the wrath of the LORD that is kindled against us, because our fathers have not obeyed the words of this book, to do according to all that is written concerning us."

[14] So Hilkiah the priest, and Ahikam, and Achbor, and Shaphan, and Asaiah went to Huldah the prophetess, the wife of Shallum the son of Tikvah, son of Harhas, keeper of the wardrobe (now she lived in Jerusalem in the Second Quarter), and they talked with her. [15] And she said to them, "Thus says the LORD, the God of Israel: 'Tell the man who sent you to me, [16] Thus says the LORD, Behold, I will bring disaster upon this place and upon its inhabitants, all the words of the book that the king of Judah has read. [17] Because they have forsaken me and have made offerings to other gods, that they might provoke me to anger with all the work of their hands, therefore my wrath will be kindled against this place, and it will not be quenched. [18] But to the king of Judah, who sent you to enquire

of the LORD, thus shall you say to him, Thus says the LORD, the God of Israel: Regarding the words that you have heard, ¹⁹because your heart was penitent, and you humbled yourself before the LORD, when you heard how I spoke against this place and against its inhabitants, that they should become a desolation and a curse, and you have torn your clothes and wept before me, I also have heard you, declares the LORD. ²⁰Therefore, behold, I will gather you to your fathers, and you shall be gathered to your grave in peace, and your eyes shall not see all the disaster that I will bring upon this place.'" And they brought back word to the king.

JOSIAH'S REFORMS

23 Then the king sent, and all the elders of Judah and Jerusalem were gathered to him. ²And the king went up to the house of the LORD, and with him all the men of Judah and all the inhabitants of Jerusalem and the priests and the prophets, all the people, both small and great. And he read in their hearing all the words of the Book of the Covenant that had been found in the house of the LORD. ³And the king stood by the pillar and made a covenant before the LORD, to walk after the LORD and to keep his commandments and his testimonies and his statutes with all his heart and all his soul, to perform the words of this covenant that were written in this book. And all the people joined in the covenant.

⁴And the king commanded Hilkiah the high priest and the priests of the second order and the keepers of the threshold to bring out of the temple of the LORD all the vessels made for Baal, for Asherah, and for all the host of heaven. He burned them outside Jerusalem in the fields of the Kidron and carried their ashes to Bethel. ⁵And he deposed the priests whom the kings of Judah had ordained to make offerings in the high places at the cities of Judah and round Jerusalem; those also who burned incense to Baal, to the sun and the moon and the constellations and all the host of the heavens. ⁶And he brought out the Asherah from the house of the LORD, outside Jerusalem, to the brook Kidron, and burned it at the brook Kidron and beat it to dust and cast the dust of it upon the graves of the common people. ⁷And he broke down the houses of the male cult prostitutes who were in the house of the LORD, where the women wove hangings for the Asherah. ⁸And he brought all the priests out of the cities of Judah, and defiled the high places where the priests had made offerings, from Geba to Beersheba. And he broke down the high places of the gates that were at the entrance of the gate of Joshua the governor of the city, which were on one's left at the gate of the city. ⁹However, the priests of the high places did not come up to the altar of the LORD in Jerusalem, but they ate unleavened bread among their brothers. ¹⁰And he defiled Topheth, which is in the Valley of the Son of Hinnom, that no one might burn his son or his daughter as an offering to Molech.ᵃ ¹¹And he removed the horses that the kings of Judah had dedicated to the sun, at the entrance to the house of the LORD, by the chamber of Nathan-melech the chamberlain, which was in the precincts.ᵇ And he burned the chariots of the sun with fire. ¹²And the altars on the roof of the upper chamber of Ahaz, which the kings of Judah had made, and the altars that Manasseh had made in the two courts of the house of the LORD, he pulled down and broke in piecesᶜ and cast the dust of them into the brook Kidron. ¹³And the king defiled the high places that were east of Jerusalem, to the south of the mount of corruption, which Solomon the king of Israel had built for Ashtoreth the abomination of the Sidonians, and for Chemosh the abomination of Moab, and for Milcom the abomination of the Ammonites. ¹⁴And he broke in pieces the pillars and cut down the Asherim and filled their places with the bones of men.

¹⁵Moreover, the altar at Bethel, the high place erected by Jeroboam the son of Nebat, who made Israel to sin, that altar with the high place he pulled down and burned,ᵈ reducing it to dust. He also burned the Asherah. ¹⁶And as Josiah turned, he saw the tombs there on the mount. And he sent and took the bones out of the tombs and burned them on the altar and defiled it, according to the word of the LORD that the man of God proclaimed, who had predicted these things. ¹⁷Then he said, "What is that monument that I see?" And the men of the city told him, "It is the tomb of the man of God who came from Judah and predictedᵉ these things that you have done against the altar at Bethel." ¹⁸And he said, "Let him be; let no man move his bones." So they left his bones alone, with the bones of the prophet who came

---

ᵃHebrew *might cause his son or daughter to pass through the fire for Molech* ᵇThe meaning of the Hebrew word is uncertain ᶜHebrew *pieces from there* ᵈSeptuagint *broke in pieces its stones* ᵉHebrew *called*

out of Samaria. ¹⁹And Josiah removed all the shrines also of the high places that were in the cities of Samaria, which kings of Israel had made, provoking the LORD to anger. He did to them according to all that he had done at Bethel. ²⁰And he sacrificed all the priests of the high places who were there, on the altars, and burned human bones on them. Then he returned to Jerusalem.

JOSIAH RESTORES THE PASSOVER

²¹And the king commanded all the people, "Keep the Passover to the LORD your God, as it is written in this Book of the Covenant." ²²For no such Passover had been kept since the days of the judges who judged Israel, or during all the days of the kings of Israel or of the kings of Judah. ²³But in the eighteenth year of King Josiah this Passover was kept to the LORD in Jerusalem.

²⁴Moreover, Josiah put away the mediums and the necromancers and the household gods and the idols and all the abominations that were seen in the land of Judah and in Jerusalem, that he might establish the words of the law that were written in the book that Hilkiah the priest found in the house of the LORD. ²⁵Before him there was no king like him, who turned to the LORD with all his heart and with all his soul and with all his might, according to all the Law of Moses, nor did any like him arise after him.

²⁶Still the LORD did not turn from the burning of his great wrath, by which his anger was kindled against Judah, because of all the provocations with which Manasseh had provoked him. ²⁷And the LORD said, "I will remove Judah also out of my sight, as I have removed Israel, and I will cast off this city that I have chosen, Jerusalem, and the house of which I said, My name shall be there."

JOSIAH'S DEATH IN BATTLE

²⁸Now the rest of the acts of Josiah and all that he did, are they not written in the Book of the Chronicles of the Kings of Judah? ²⁹In his days Pharaoh Neco king of Egypt went up to the king of Assyria to the river Euphrates. King Josiah went to meet him, and Pharaoh Neco killed him at Megiddo, as soon as he saw him. ³⁰And his servants carried him dead in a chariot from Megiddo and brought him to Jerusalem and buried him in his own tomb. And the people of the land took Jehoahaz the son of Josiah, and anointed him, and made him king in his father's place.

JEHOAHAZ'S REIGN AND CAPTIVITY

³¹Jehoahaz was twenty-three years old when he began to reign, and he reigned for three months in Jerusalem. His mother's name was Hamutal the daughter of Jeremiah of Libnah. ³²And he did what was evil in the sight of the LORD, according to all that his fathers had done. ³³And Pharaoh Neco put him in bonds at Riblah in the land of Hamath, that he might not reign in Jerusalem, and laid on the land a tribute of a hundred talents[a] of silver and a talent of gold. ³⁴And Pharaoh Neco made Eliakim the son of Josiah king in the place of Josiah his father, and changed his name to Jehoiakim. But he took Jehoahaz away, and he came to Egypt and died there. ³⁵And Jehoiakim gave the silver and the gold to Pharaoh, but he taxed the land to give the money according to the command of Pharaoh. He exacted the silver and the gold of the people of the land, from everyone according to his assessment, to give it to Pharaoh Neco.

JEHOIAKIM REIGNS IN JUDAH

³⁶Jehoiakim was twenty-five years old when he began to reign, and he reigned for eleven years in Jerusalem. His mother's name was Zebidah the daughter of Pedaiah of Rumah. ³⁷And he did what was evil in the sight of the LORD, according to all that his fathers had done.

24 In his days, Nebuchadnezzar king of Babylon came up, and Jehoiakim became his servant for three years. Then he turned and rebelled against him. ²And the LORD sent against him bands of the Chaldeans and bands of the Syrians and bands of the Moabites and bands of the Ammonites, and sent them against Judah to destroy it, according to the word of the LORD that he spoke by his servants the prophets. ³Surely this came upon Judah at the command of the LORD, to remove them out of his sight, for the sins of Manasseh, according to all that he had done, ⁴and also for the innocent blood that he had shed. For he filled Jerusalem with innocent blood, and the LORD would not pardon. ⁵Now the rest of the deeds of Jehoiakim and all that he did, are they not written in the Book of the Chronicles of the Kings of Judah? ⁶So Jehoiakim slept with his fathers, and Jehoiachin his son reigned in his place. ⁷And the king of Egypt did not come again out of his land, for the king of Babylon had taken

---

[a] A *talent* was about 75 pounds or 34 kilograms

all that belonged to the king of Egypt from the Brook of Egypt to the river Euphrates.

JEHOIACHIN REIGNS IN JUDAH

⁸Jehoiachin was eighteen years old when he became king, and he reigned for three months in Jerusalem. His mother's name was Nehushta the daughter of Elnathan of Jerusalem. ⁹And he did what was evil in the sight of the LORD, according to all that his father had done.

JERUSALEM CAPTURED

¹⁰At that time the servants of Nebuchadnezzar king of Babylon came up to Jerusalem, and the city was besieged. ¹¹And Nebuchadnezzar king of Babylon came to the city while his servants were besieging it, ¹²and Jehoiachin the king of Judah gave himself up to the king of Babylon, himself and his mother and his servants and his officials and his palace officials. The king of Babylon took him prisoner in the eighth year of his reign ¹³and carried off all the treasures of the house of the LORD and the treasures of the king's house, and cut in pieces all the vessels of gold in the temple of the LORD, which Solomon king of Israel had made, as the LORD had foretold. ¹⁴He carried away all Jerusalem and all the officials and all the mighty men of valour, 10,000 captives, and all the craftsmen and the smiths. None remained, except the poorest people of the land. ¹⁵And he carried away Jehoiachin to Babylon. The king's mother, the king's wives, his officials, and the chief men of the land he took into captivity from Jerusalem to Babylon. ¹⁶And the king of Babylon brought captive to Babylon all the men of valour, 7,000, and the craftsmen and the metal workers, 1,000, all of them strong and fit for war. ¹⁷And the king of Babylon made Mattaniah, Jehoiachin's uncle, king in his place, and changed his name to Zedekiah.

ZEDEKIAH REIGNS IN JUDAH

¹⁸Zedekiah was twenty-one years old when he became king, and he reigned for eleven years in Jerusalem. His mother's name was Hamutal the daughter of Jeremiah of Libnah. ¹⁹And he did what was evil in the sight of the LORD, according to all that Jehoiakim had done. ²⁰For because of the anger of the LORD it came to the point in Jerusalem and Judah that he cast them out from his presence.

And Zedekiah rebelled against the king of Babylon.

FALL AND CAPTIVITY OF JUDAH

25 And in the ninth year of his reign, in the tenth month, on the tenth day of the month, Nebuchadnezzar king of Babylon came with all his army against Jerusalem and laid siege to it. And they built siege works all round it. ²So the city was besieged till the eleventh year of King Zedekiah. ³On the ninth day of the fourth month the famine was so severe in the city that there was no food for the people of the land. ⁴Then a breach was made in the city, and all the men of war fled by night by the way of the gate between the two walls, by the king's garden, and the Chaldeans were round the city. And they went in the direction of the Arabah. ⁵But the army of the Chaldeans pursued the king and overtook him in the plains of Jericho, and all his army was scattered from him. ⁶Then they captured the king and brought him up to the king of Babylon at Riblah, and they passed sentence on him. ⁷They slaughtered the sons of Zedekiah before his eyes, and put out the eyes of Zedekiah and bound him in chains and took him to Babylon.

⁸In the fifth month, on the seventh day of the month—that was the nineteenth year of King Nebuchadnezzar, king of Babylon— Nebuzaradan, the captain of the bodyguard, a servant of the king of Babylon, came to Jerusalem. ⁹And he burned the house of the LORD and the king's house and all the houses of Jerusalem; every great house he burned down. ¹⁰And all the army of the Chaldeans, who were with the captain of the guard, broke down the walls round Jerusalem. ¹¹And the rest of the people who were left in the city and the deserters who had deserted to the king of Babylon, together with the rest of the multitude, Nebuzaradan the captain of the guard carried into exile. ¹²But the captain of the guard left some of the poorest of the land to be vine dressers and ploughmen.

¹³And the pillars of bronze that were in the house of the LORD, and the stands and the bronze sea that were in the house of the LORD, the Chaldeans broke in pieces and carried the bronze to Babylon. ¹⁴And they took away the pots and the shovels and the snuffers and the dishes for incense and all the vessels of bronze used in the temple service, ¹⁵the firepans also and the bowls. What was of gold the captain of the guard took away as gold, and what was of silver, as silver. ¹⁶As for the two pillars, the one sea, and the stands that

Solomon had made for the house of the LORD, the bronze of all these vessels was beyond weight. ¹⁷The height of one pillar was eighteen cubits,ᵃ and on it was a capital of bronze. The height of the capital was three cubits. A latticework and pomegranates, all of bronze, were all round the capital. And the second pillar had the same, with the latticework.

¹⁸And the captain of the guard took Seraiah the chief priest and Zephaniah the second priest and the three keepers of the threshold; ¹⁹and from the city he took an officer who had been in command of the men of war, and five men of the king's council who were found in the city; and the secretary of the commander of the army, who mustered the people of the land; and sixty men of the people of the land, who were found in the city. ²⁰And Nebuzaradan the captain of the guard took them and brought them to the king of Babylon at Riblah. ²¹And the king of Babylon struck them down and put them to death at Riblah in the land of Hamath. So Judah was taken into exile out of its land.

GEDALIAH MADE GOVERNOR OF JUDAH

²²And over the people who remained in the land of Judah, whom Nebuchadnezzar king of Babylon had left, he appointed Gedaliah the son of Ahikam, son of Shaphan, governor. ²³Now when all the captains and their men heard that the king of Babylon had appointed Gedaliah governor, they came with their men to Gedaliah at Mizpah, namely, Ishmael the son of Nethaniah, and Johanan the son of Kareah, and Seraiah the son of Tanhumeth the Netophathite, and Jaazaniah the son of the Maacathite. ²⁴And Gedaliah swore to them and their men, saying, "Do not be afraid because of the Chaldean officials. Live in the land and serve the king of Babylon, and it shall be well with you." ²⁵But in the seventh month, Ishmael the son of Nethaniah, son of Elishama, of the royal family, came with ten men and struck down Gedaliah and put him to death along with the Jews and the Chaldeans who were with him at Mizpah. ²⁶Then all the people, both small and great, and the captains of the forces arose and went to Egypt, for they were afraid of the Chaldeans.

JEHOIACHIN RELEASED FROM PRISON

²⁷And in the thirty-seventh year of the exile of Jehoiachin king of Judah, in the twelfth month, on the twenty-seventh day of the month, Evil-merodach king of Babylon, in the year that he began to reign, graciously freedᵇ Jehoiachin king of Judah from prison. ²⁸And he spoke kindly to him and gave him a seat above the seats of the kings who were with him in Babylon. ²⁹So Jehoiachin put off his prison garments. And every day of his life he dined regularly at the king's table, ³⁰and for his allowance, a regular allowance was given him by the king, according to his daily needs, as long as he lived.

ᵃA *cubit* was about 18 inches or 45 centimetres   ᵇHebrew *reign, lifted up the head of*

1 CHRONICLES

FROM ADAM TO ABRAHAM

1 [a] Adam, Seth, Enosh; ²Kenan, Mahalalel, Jared; ³Enoch, Methuselah, Lamech; ⁴Noah, Shem, Ham, and Japheth.

⁵The sons of Japheth: Gomer, Magog, Madai, Javan, Tubal, Meshech, and Tiras. ⁶The sons of Gomer: Ashkenaz, Riphath,[b] and Togarmah. ⁷The sons of Javan: Elishah, Tarshish, Kittim, and Rodanim.

⁸The sons of Ham: Cush, Egypt, Put, and Canaan. ⁹The sons of Cush: Seba, Havilah, Sabta, Raamah, and Sabteca. The sons of Raamah: Sheba and Dedan. ¹⁰Cush fathered Nimrod. He was the first on earth to be a mighty man.[c]

¹¹Egypt fathered Ludim, Anamim, Lehabim, Naphtuhim, ¹²Pathrusim, Casluhim (from whom the Philistines came), and Caphtorim.

¹³Canaan fathered Sidon his firstborn and Heth, ¹⁴and the Jebusites, the Amorites, the Girgashites, ¹⁵the Hivites, the Arkites, the Sinites, ¹⁶the Arvadites, the Zemarites, and the Hamathites.

¹⁷The sons of Shem: Elam, Asshur, Arpachshad, Lud, and Aram. And the sons of Aram:[d] Uz, Hul, Gether, and Meshech. ¹⁸Arpachshad fathered Shelah, and Shelah fathered Eber. ¹⁹To Eber were born two sons: the name of one was Peleg[e] (for in his days the earth was divided), and his brother's name was Joktan. ²⁰Joktan fathered Almodad, Sheleph, Hazarmaveth, Jerah, ²¹Hadoram, Uzal, Diklah, ²²Obal,[f] Abimael, Sheba, ²³Ophir, Havilah, and Jobab; all these were the sons of Joktan.

²⁴Shem, Arpachshad, Shelah; ²⁵Eber, Peleg, Reu; ²⁶Serug, Nahor, Terah; ²⁷Abram, that is, Abraham.

FROM ABRAHAM TO JACOB

²⁸The sons of Abraham: Isaac and Ishmael. ²⁹These are their genealogies: the firstborn of Ishmael, Nebaioth, and Kedar, Adbeel, Mibsam, ³⁰Mishma, Dumah, Massa, Hadad, Tema, ³¹Jetur, Naphish, and Kedemah. These are the sons of Ishmael. ³²The sons of Keturah, Abraham's concubine: she bore Zimran, Jokshan, Medan, Midian, Ishbak, and Shuah. The sons of Jokshan: Sheba and Dedan. ³³The sons of Midian: Ephah, Epher, Hanoch, Abida, and Eldaah. All these were the descendants of Keturah.

³⁴Abraham fathered Isaac. The sons of Isaac: Esau and Israel. ³⁵The sons of Esau: Eliphaz, Reuel, Jeush, Jalam, and Korah. ³⁶The sons of Eliphaz: Teman, Omar, Zepho, Gatam, Kenaz, and of Timna,[g] Amalek. ³⁷The sons of Reuel: Nahath, Zerah, Shammah, and Mizzah.

³⁸The sons of Seir: Lotan, Shobal, Zibeon, Anah, Dishon, Ezer, and Dishan. ³⁹The sons of Lotan: Hori and Hemam;[h] and Lotan's sister was Timna. ⁴⁰The sons of Shobal: Alvan,[i] Manahath, Ebal, Shepho,[j] and Onam. The sons of Zibeon: Aiah and Anah. ⁴¹The son[k] of Anah: Dishon. The sons of Dishon: Hemdan,[l] Eshban, Ithran, and Cheran. ⁴²The sons of Ezer: Bilhan, Zaavan, and Akan.[m] The sons of Dishan: Uz and Aran.

⁴³These are the kings who reigned in the land of Edom before any king reigned over the people of Israel: Bela the son of Beor, the name of his city being Dinhabah. ⁴⁴Bela died, and Jobab the son of Zerah of Bozrah reigned in his place. ⁴⁵Jobab died, and Husham of the land of the Temanites reigned in his place. ⁴⁶Husham died, and Hadad the son of Bedad, who defeated Midian in the country of Moab, reigned in his place, the name of his city being Avith. ⁴⁷Hadad died, and Samlah of Masrekah reigned in his place. ⁴⁸Samlah died, and Shaul of Rehoboth on the Euphrates[n] reigned in his place. ⁴⁹Shaul died, and Baal-hanan, the son of Achbor, reigned in his place. ⁵⁰Baal-hanan died, and Hadad reigned in his place, the name of his city being Pai; and his wife's name was Mehetabel, the daughter of Matred, the daughter of Mezahab. ⁵¹And Hadad died.

---

[a]Many names in these genealogies are spelled differently in other biblical books [b]Septuagint; Hebrew *Diphath* [c]Or *He began to be a mighty man on the earth* [d]Septuagint; Hebrew lacks *And the sons of Aram* [e]*Peleg* means *division* [f]Septuagint, Syriac (compare Genesis 10:28); Hebrew *Ebal* [g]Septuagint (compare Genesis 36:12); Hebrew lacks *and of* [h]Septuagint (compare Genesis 36:22); Hebrew *Homam* [i]Septuagint (compare Genesis 36:23); Hebrew *Alian* [j]Septuagint (compare Genesis 36:23); Hebrew *Shephi* [k]Hebrew *sons* [l]Septuagint (compare Genesis 36:26); Hebrew *Hamran* [m]Septuagint (compare Genesis 36:27); Hebrew *Jaakan* [n]Hebrew *the River*

The chiefs of Edom were: chiefs Timna, Alvah, Jetheth, ⁵²Oholibamah, Elah, Pinon, ⁵³Kenaz, Teman, Mibzar, ⁵⁴Magdiel, and Iram; these are the chiefs of Edom.

A GENEALOGY OF DAVID

2 These are the sons of Israel: Reuben, Simeon, Levi, Judah, Issachar, Zebulun, ²Dan, Joseph, Benjamin, Naphtali, Gad, and Asher. ³The sons of Judah: Er, Onan and Shelah; these three Bath-shua the Canaanite bore to him. Now Er, Judah's firstborn, was evil in the sight of the Lord, and he put him to death. ⁴His daughter-in-law Tamar also bore him Perez and Zerah. Judah had five sons in all.

⁵The sons of Perez: Hezron and Hamul. ⁶The sons of Zerah: Zimri, Ethan, Heman, Calcol, and Dara, five in all. ⁷The son[a] of Carmi: Achan, the troubler of Israel, who broke faith in the matter of the devoted thing; ⁸and Ethan's son was Azariah.

⁹The sons of Hezron that were born to him: Jerahmeel, Ram, and Chelubai. ¹⁰Ram fathered Amminadab, and Amminadab fathered Nahshon, prince of the sons of Judah. ¹¹Nahshon fathered Salmon,[b] Salmon fathered Boaz, ¹²Boaz fathered Obed, Obed fathered Jesse. ¹³Jesse fathered Eliab his firstborn, Abinadab the second, Shimea the third, ¹⁴Nethanel the fourth, Raddai the fifth, ¹⁵Ozem the sixth, David the seventh. ¹⁶And their sisters were Zeruiah and Abigail. The sons of Zeruiah: Abishai, Joab, and Asahel, three. ¹⁷Abigail bore Amasa, and the father of Amasa was Jether the Ishmaelite.

¹⁸Caleb the son of Hezron fathered children by his wife Azubah, and by Jerioth; and these were her sons: Jesher, Shobab, and Ardon. ¹⁹When Azubah died, Caleb married Ephrath, who bore him Hur. ²⁰Hur fathered Uri, and Uri fathered Bezalel.

²¹Afterwards Hezron went in to the daughter of Machir the father of Gilead, whom he married when he was sixty years old, and she bore him Segub. ²²And Segub fathered Jair, who had twenty-three cities in the land of Gilead. ²³But Geshur and Aram took from them Havvoth-jair, Kenath, and its villages, sixty towns. All these were descendants of Machir, the father of Gilead. ²⁴After the death of Hezron, Caleb went in to Ephrathah,[c] the wife of Hezron his father, and she bore him Ashhur, the father of Tekoa.

²⁵The sons of Jerahmeel, the firstborn of Hezron: Ram, his firstborn, Bunah, Oren, Ozem, and Ahijah. ²⁶Jerahmeel also had another wife, whose name was Atarah; she was the mother of Onam. ²⁷The sons of Ram, the firstborn of Jerahmeel: Maaz, Jamin, and Eker. ²⁸The sons of Onam: Shammai and Jada. The sons of Shammai: Nadab and Abishur. ²⁹The name of Abishur's wife was Abihail, and she bore him Ahban and Molid. ³⁰The sons of Nadab: Seled and Appaim; and Seled died childless. ³¹The son[d] of Appaim: Ishi. The son of Ishi: Sheshan. The son of Sheshan: Ahlai. ³²The sons of Jada, Shammai's brother: Jether and Jonathan; and Jether died childless. ³³The sons of Jonathan: Peleth and Zaza. These were the descendants of Jerahmeel. ³⁴Now Sheshan had no sons, only daughters, but Sheshan had an Egyptian slave whose name was Jarha. ³⁵So Sheshan gave his daughter in marriage to Jarha his slave, and she bore him Attai. ³⁶Attai fathered Nathan, and Nathan fathered Zabad. ³⁷Zabad fathered Ephlal, and Ephlal fathered Obed. ³⁸Obed fathered Jehu, and Jehu fathered Azariah. ³⁹Azariah fathered Helez, and Helez fathered Eleasah. ⁴⁰Eleasah fathered Sismai, and Sismai fathered Shallum. ⁴¹Shallum fathered Jekamiah, and Jekamiah fathered Elishama.

⁴²The sons of Caleb the brother of Jerahmeel: Mareshah[e] his firstborn, who fathered Ziph. The son[f] of Mareshah: Hebron.[g] ⁴³The sons of Hebron: Korah, Tappuah, Rekem and Shema. ⁴⁴Shema fathered Raham, the father of Jorkeam; and Rekem fathered Shammai. ⁴⁵The son of Shammai: Maon; and Maon fathered Beth-zur. ⁴⁶Ephah also, Caleb's concubine, bore Haran, Moza, and Gazez; and Haran fathered Gazez. ⁴⁷The sons of Jahdai: Regem, Jotham, Geshan, Pelet, Ephah, and Shaaph. ⁴⁸Maacah, Caleb's concubine, bore Sheber and Tirhanah. ⁴⁹She also bore Shaaph the father of Madmannah, Sheva the father of Machbenah and the father of Gibea; and the daughter of Caleb was Achsah. ⁵⁰These were the descendants of Caleb.

The sons[h] of Hur the firstborn of Ephrathah: Shobal the father of Kiriath-jearim, ⁵¹Salma, the father of Bethlehem, and Hareph the father of Beth-gader. ⁵²Shobal the father of Kiriath-jearim had other sons: Haroeh, half of the Menuhoth. ⁵³And the clans of Kiriath-jearim: the Ithrites, the Puthites, the Shumathites, and the Mishraites; from

---

[a]Hebrew sons [b]Septuagint (compare Ruth 4:21); Hebrew Salma
[c]Septuagint, Vulgate; Hebrew in Caleb Ephrathah [d]Hebrew sons;
three times in this verse [e]Septuagint; Hebrew Mesha [f]Hebrew sons
[g]Hebrew the father of Hebron [h]Septuagint, Vulgate; Hebrew son

these came the Zorathites and the Eshtaolites. **54**The sons of Salma: Bethlehem, the Netophathites, Atroth-beth-joab and half of the Manahathites, the Zorites. **55**The clans also of the scribes who lived at Jabez: the Tirathites, the Shimeathites and the Sucathites. These are the Kenites who came from Hammath, the father of the house of Rechab.

DESCENDANTS OF DAVID

3 These are the sons of David who were born to him in Hebron: the firstborn, Amnon, by Ahinoam the Jezreelite; the second, Daniel, by Abigail the Carmelite, **2**the third, Absalom, whose mother was Maacah, the daughter of Talmai, king of Geshur; the fourth, Adonijah, whose mother was Haggith; **3**the fifth, Shephatiah, by Abital; the sixth, Ithream, by his wife Eglah; **4**six were born to him in Hebron, where he reigned for seven years and six months. And he reigned for thirty-three years in Jerusalem. **5**These were born to him in Jerusalem: Shimea, Shobab, Nathan and Solomon, four by Bath-shua, the daughter of Ammiel; **6**then Ibhar, Elishama, Eliphelet, **7**Nogah, Nepheg, Japhia, **8**Elishama, Eliada, and Eliphelet, nine. **9**All these were David's sons, besides the sons of the concubines, and Tamar was their sister.

10The son of Solomon was Rehoboam, Abijah his son, Asa his son, Jehoshaphat his son, **11**Joram his son, Ahaziah his son, Joash his son, **12**Amaziah his son, Azariah his son, Jotham his son, **13**Ahaz his son, Hezekiah his son, Manasseh his son, **14**Amon his son, Josiah his son. **15**The sons of Josiah: Johanan the firstborn, the second Jehoiakim, the third Zedekiah, the fourth Shallum. **16**The descendants of Jehoiakim: Jeconiah his son, Zedekiah his son; **17**and the sons of Jeconiah, the captive: Shealtiel his son, **18**Malchiram, Pedaiah, Shenazzar, Jekamiah, Hoshama and Nedabiah; **19**and the sons of Pedaiah: Zerubbabel and Shimei; and the sons of Zerubbabel: Meshullam and Hananiah, and Shelomith was their sister; **20**and Hashubah, Ohel, Berechiah, Hasadiah, and Jushab-hesed, five. **21**The sons of Hananiah: Pelatiah and Jeshaiah, his son[a] Rephaiah, his son Arnan, his son Obadiah, his son Shecaniah. **22**The son[b] of Shecaniah: Shemaiah. And the sons of Shemaiah: Hattush, Igal, Bariah, Neariah, and Shaphat, six. **23**The sons of Neariah: Elioenai, Hizkiah, and Azrikam, three. **24**The sons of Elioenai: Hodaviah, Eliashib, Pelaiah, Akkub, Johanan, Delaiah, and Anani, seven.

DESCENDANTS OF JUDAH

4 The sons of Judah: Perez, Hezron, Carmi, Hur, and Shobal. **2**Reaiah the son of Shobal fathered Jahath, and Jahath fathered Ahumai and Lahad. These were the clans of the Zorathites. **3**These were the sons[c] of Etam: Jezreel, Ishma, and Idbash; and the name of their sister was Hazzelelponi, **4**and Penuel fathered Gedor, and Ezer fathered Hushah. These were the sons of Hur, the firstborn of Ephrathah, the father of Bethlehem. **5**Ashhur, the father of Tekoa, had two wives, Helah and Naarah; **6**Naarah bore him Ahuzzam, Hepher, Temeni, and Haahashtari. These were the sons of Naarah. **7**The sons of Helah: Zereth, Izhar, and Ethnan. **8**Koz fathered Anub, Zobebah, and the clans of Aharhel, the son of Harum. **9**Jabez was more honourable than his brothers; and his mother called his name Jabez, saying, "Because I bore him in pain."[d] **10**Jabez called upon the God of Israel, saying, "Oh that you would bless me and enlarge my border, and that your hand might be with me, and that you would keep me from harm[e] so that it might not bring me pain!" And God granted what he asked. **11**Chelub, the brother of Shuhah, fathered Mehir, who fathered Eshton. **12**Eshton fathered Beth-rapha, Paseah, and Tehinnah, the father of Ir-nahash. These are the men of Recah. **13**The sons of Kenaz: Othniel and Seraiah; and the sons of Othniel: Hathath and Meonothai.[f] **14**Meonothai fathered Ophrah; and Seraiah fathered Joab, the father of Ge-harashim,[g] so-called because they were craftsmen. **15**The sons of Caleb the son of Jephunneh: Iru, Elah, and Naam; and the son[h] of Elah: Kenaz. **16**The sons of Jehallelel: Ziph, Ziphah, Tiria, and Asarel. **17**The sons of Ezrah: Jether, Mered, Epher, and Jalon. These are the sons of Bithiah, the daughter of Pharaoh, whom Mered married;[i] and she conceived and bore[j] Miriam, Shammai, and Ishbah, the father of Eshtemoa. **18**And his Judahite wife bore Jered the father of Gedor, Heber the father of Soco, and Jekuthiel the father of Zanoah. **19**The sons of the wife of Hodiah, the sister of Naham, were the fathers of Keilah the Garmite and Eshtemoa the Maacathite. **20**The sons of Shimon:

---

[a]Septuagint (compare Syriac, Vulgate); Hebrew *sons of*; four times in this verse [b]Hebrew *sons* [c]Septuagint (compare Vulgate); Hebrew *father* [d]*Jabez* sounds like the Hebrew for *pain* [e]Or *evil* [f]Septuagint, Vulgate; Hebrew lacks *Meonothai* [g]*Ge-harashim* means *valley of craftsmen* [h]Hebrew *sons* [i]The clause *These are ... married* is transposed from verse 18 [j]Hebrew lacks *and bore*

Amnon, Rinnah, Ben-hanan, and Tilon. The sons of Ishi: Zoheth and Ben-zoheth. ²¹The sons of Shelah the son of Judah: Er the father of Lecah, Laadah the father of Mareshah, and the clans of the house of linen workers at Beth-ashbea; ²²and Jokim, and the men of Cozeba, and Joash, and Saraph, who ruled in Moab and returned to Lehem[a] (now the records[b] are ancient). ²³These were the potters who were inhabitants of Netaim and Gederah. They lived there in the king's service.

DESCENDANTS OF SIMEON

²⁴The sons of Simeon: Nemuel, Jamin, Jarib, Zerah, Shaul; ²⁵Shallum was his son, Mibsam his son, Mishma his son. ²⁶The sons of Mishma: Hammuel his son, Zaccur his son, Shimei his son. ²⁷Shimei had sixteen sons and six daughters; but his brothers did not have many children, nor did all their clan multiply like the men of Judah. ²⁸They lived in Beer-sheba, Moladah, Hazar-shual, ²⁹Bilhah, Ezem, Tolad, ³⁰Bethuel, Hormah, Ziklag, ³¹Beth-marcaboth, Hazar-susim, Beth-biri, and Shaaraim. These were their cities until David reigned. ³²And their villages were Etam, Ain, Rimmon, Tochen, and Ashan, five cities, ³³along with all their villages that were round these cities as far as Baal. These were their settlements, and they kept a genealogical record.

³⁴Meshobab, Jamlech, Joshah the son of Amaziah, ³⁵Joel, Jehu the son of Joshibiah, son of Seraiah, son of Asiel, ³⁶Elioenai, Jaakobah, Jeshohaiah, Asaiah, Adiel, Jesimiel, Benaiah, ³⁷Ziza the son of Shiphi, son of Allon, son of Jedaiah, son of Shimri, son of Shemaiah — ³⁸these mentioned by name were princes in their clans, and their fathers' houses increased greatly. ³⁹They journeyed to the entrance of Gedor, to the east side of the valley, to seek pasture for their flocks, ⁴⁰where they found rich, good pasture, and the land was very broad, quiet, and peaceful, for the former inhabitants there belonged to Ham. ⁴¹These, registered by name, came in the days of Hezekiah, king of Judah, and destroyed their tents and the Meunites who were found there, and marked them for destruction to this day, and settled in their place, because there was pasture there for their flocks. ⁴²And some of them, five hundred men of the Simeonites, went to Mount Seir, having as their leaders Pelatiah, Neariah, Rephaiah, and Uzziel, the sons of Ishi. ⁴³And they defeated the remnant of the Amalekites who had escaped, and they have lived there to this day.

DESCENDANTS OF REUBEN

5 The sons of Reuben the firstborn of Israel (for he was the firstborn, but because he defiled his father's bed, his birthright was given to the sons of Joseph the son of Israel, so that he could not be enrolled as the oldest son; ²though Judah became strong among his brothers and a chief came from him, yet the birthright belonged to Joseph), ³the sons of Reuben, the firstborn of Israel: Hanoch, Pallu, Hezron, and Carmi. ⁴The sons of Joel: Shemaiah his son, Gog his son, Shimei his son, ⁵Micah his son, Reaiah his son, Baal his son, ⁶Beerah his son, whom Tiglath-pileser[c] king of Assyria carried away into exile; he was a chief of the Reubenites. ⁷And his kinsmen by their clans, when the genealogy of their generations was recorded: the chief, Jeiel, and Zechariah, ⁸and Bela the son of Azaz, son of Shema, son of Joel, who lived in Aroer, as far as Nebo and Baal-meon. ⁹He also lived to the east as far as the entrance of the desert this side of the Euphrates, because their livestock had multiplied in the land of Gilead. ¹⁰And in the days of Saul they waged war against the Hagrites, who fell into their hand. And they lived in their tents throughout all the region east of Gilead.

DESCENDANTS OF GAD

¹¹The sons of Gad lived over against them in the land of Bashan as far as Salecah: ¹²Joel the chief, Shapham the second, Janai, and Shaphat in Bashan. ¹³And their kinsmen according to their fathers' houses: Michael, Meshullam, Sheba, Jorai, Jacan, Zia and Eber, seven. ¹⁴These were the sons of Abihail the son of Huri, son of Jaroah, son of Gilead, son of Michael, son of Jeshishai, son of Jahdo, son of Buz. ¹⁵Ahi the son of Abdiel, son of Guni, was chief in their fathers' houses, ¹⁶and they lived in Gilead, in Bashan and in its towns, and in all the pasture lands of Sharon to their limits. ¹⁷All of these were recorded in genealogies in the days of Jotham king of Judah, and in the days of Jeroboam king of Israel.

¹⁸The Reubenites, the Gadites, and the half-tribe of Manasseh had valiant men who carried shield and sword, and drew the bow, expert in war, 44,760, able to go to war. ¹⁹They waged war against the Hagrites, Jetur, Naphish, and Nodab. ²⁰And when they prevailed[d] over them,

---
[a]Vulgate (compare Septuagint); Hebrew *and Jashubi-lahem*
[b]Or *matters* [c]Hebrew *Tilgath-pilneser*; also verse 26 [d]Or *they were helped to prevail*

the Hagrites and all who were with them were given into their hands, for they cried out to God in the battle, and he granted their urgent plea because they trusted in him. ²¹They carried off their livestock: 50,000 of their camels, 250,000 sheep, 2,000 donkeys, and 100,000 men alive. ²²For many fell, because the war was of God. And they lived in their place until the exile.

THE HALF-TRIBE OF MANASSEH

²³The members of the half-tribe of Manasseh lived in the land. They were very numerous from Bashan to Baal-hermon, Senir, and Mount Hermon. ²⁴These were the heads of their fathers' houses: Epher,[a] Ishi, Eliel, Azriel, Jeremiah, Hodaviah, and Jahdiel, mighty warriors, famous men, heads of their fathers' houses. ²⁵But they broke faith with the God of their fathers, and whored after the gods of the peoples of the land, whom God had destroyed before them. ²⁶So the God of Israel stirred up the spirit of Pul king of Assyria, the spirit of Tiglath-pileser king of Assyria, and he took them into exile, namely, the Reubenites, the Gadites, and the half-tribe of Manasseh, and brought them to Halah, Habor, Hara, and the river Gozan, to this day.

DESCENDANTS OF LEVI

6[b] The sons of Levi: Gershon, Kohath, and Merari. ²The sons of Kohath: Amram, Izhar, Hebron, and Uzziel. ³The children of Amram: Aaron, Moses, and Miriam. The sons of Aaron: Nadab, Abihu, Eleazar, and Ithamar. ⁴Eleazar fathered Phinehas, Phinehas fathered Abishua, ⁵Abishua fathered Bukki, Bukki fathered Uzzi, ⁶Uzzi fathered Zerahiah, Zerahiah fathered Meraioth, ⁷Meraioth fathered Amariah, Amariah fathered Ahitub, ⁸Ahitub fathered Zadok, Zadok fathered Ahimaaz, ⁹Ahimaaz fathered Azariah, Azariah fathered Johanan, ¹⁰and Johanan fathered Azariah (it was he who served as priest in the house that Solomon built in Jerusalem). ¹¹Azariah fathered Amariah, Amariah fathered Ahitub, ¹²Ahitub fathered Zadok, Zadok fathered Shallum, ¹³Shallum fathered Hilkiah, Hilkiah fathered Azariah, ¹⁴Azariah fathered Seraiah, Seraiah fathered Jehozadak; ¹⁵and Jehozadak went into exile when the LORD sent Judah and Jerusalem into exile by the hand of Nebuchadnezzar.

¹⁶[c] The sons of Levi: Gershom, Kohath, and Merari. ¹⁷And these are the names of the sons of Gershom: Libni and Shimei. ¹⁸The sons of Kohath: Amram, Izhar, Hebron and Uzziel. ¹⁹The sons of Merari: Mahli and Mushi. These are the clans of the Levites according to their fathers. ²⁰Of Gershom: Libni his son, Jahath his son, Zimmah his son, ²¹Joah his son, Iddo his son, Zerah his son, Jeatherai his son. ²²The sons of Kohath: Amminadab his son, Korah his son, Assir his son, ²³Elkanah his son, Ebiasaph his son, Assir his son, ²⁴Tahath his son, Uriel his son, Uzziah his son, and Shaul his son. ²⁵The sons of Elkanah: Amasai and Ahimoth, ²⁶Elkanah his son, Zophai his son, Nahath his son, ²⁷Eliab his son, Jeroham his son, Elkanah his son. ²⁸The sons of Samuel: Joel[d] his firstborn, the second Abijah.[e] ²⁹The sons of Merari: Mahli, Libni his son, Shimei his son, Uzzah his son, ³⁰Shimea his son, Haggiah his son, and Asaiah his son.

³¹These are the men whom David put in charge of the service of song in the house of the LORD after the ark rested there. ³²They ministered with song before the tabernacle of the tent of meeting until Solomon built the house of the LORD in Jerusalem, and they performed their service according to their order. ³³These are the men who served and their sons. Of the sons of the Kohathites: Heman the singer the son of Joel, son of Samuel, ³⁴son of Elkanah, son of Jeroham, son of Eliel, son of Toah, ³⁵son of Zuph, son of Elkanah, son of Mahath, son of Amasai, ³⁶son of Elkanah, son of Joel, son of Azariah, son of Zephaniah, ³⁷son of Tahath, son of Assir, son of Ebiasaph, son of Korah, ³⁸son of Izhar, son of Kohath, son of Levi, son of Israel; ³⁹and his brother Asaph, who stood on his right hand, namely, Asaph the son of Berechiah, son of Shimea, ⁴⁰son of Michael, son of Baaseiah, son of Malchijah, ⁴¹son of Ethni, son of Zerah, son of Adaiah, ⁴²son of Ethan, son of Zimmah, son of Shimei, ⁴³son of Jahath, son of Gershom, son of Levi. ⁴⁴On the left hand were their brothers, the sons of Merari: Ethan the son of Kishi, son of Abdi, son of Malluch, ⁴⁵son of Hashabiah, son of Amaziah, son of Hilkiah, ⁴⁶son of Amzi, son of Bani, son of Shemer, ⁴⁷son of Mahli, son of Mushi, son of Merari, son of Levi. ⁴⁸And their brothers the Levites were appointed for all the service of the tabernacle of the house of God.

⁴⁹But Aaron and his sons made offerings on the altar of burnt offering and on the altar

---
[a]Septuagint, Vulgate; Hebrew *and Epher* [b]Ch 5:27 in Hebrew [c]Ch 6:1 in Hebrew [d]Septuagint, Syriac (compare verse 33 and 1 Samuel 8:2); Hebrew lacks *Joel* [e]Hebrew *and Abijah*

of incense for all the work of the Most Holy Place, and to make atonement for Israel, according to all that Moses the servant of God had commanded. ⁵⁰These are the sons of Aaron: Eleazar his son, Phinehas his son, Abishua his son, ⁵¹Bukki his son, Uzzi his son, Zerahiah his son, ⁵²Meraioth his son, Amariah his son, Ahitub his son, ⁵³Zadok his son, Ahimaaz his son.

⁵⁴These are their dwelling places according to their settlements within their borders: to the sons of Aaron of the clans of Kohathites, for theirs was the first lot, ⁵⁵to them they gave Hebron in the land of Judah and its surrounding pasture lands, ⁵⁶but the fields of the city and its villages they gave to Caleb the son of Jephunneh. ⁵⁷To the sons of Aaron they gave the cities of refuge: Hebron, Libnah with its pasture lands, Jattir, Eshtemoa with its pasture lands, ⁵⁸Hilen with its pasture lands, Debir with its pasture lands, ⁵⁹Ashan with its pasture lands, and Beth-shemesh with its pasture lands; ⁶⁰and from the tribe of Benjamin, Gibeon,ᵃ Geba with its pasture lands, Alemeth with its pasture lands, and Anathoth with its pasture lands. All their cities throughout their clans were thirteen.

⁶¹To the rest of the Kohathites were given by lot out of the clan of the tribe, out of the half-tribe, the half of Manasseh, ten cities. ⁶²To the Gershomites according to their clans were allotted thirteen cities out of the tribes of Issachar, Asher, Naphtali and Manasseh in Bashan. ⁶³To the Merarites according to their clans were allotted twelve cities out of the tribes of Reuben, Gad, and Zebulun. ⁶⁴So the people of Israel gave the Levites the cities with their pasture lands. ⁶⁵They gave by lot out of the tribes of Judah, Simeon, and Benjamin these cities that are mentioned by name.

⁶⁶And some of the clans of the sons of Kohath had cities of their territory out of the tribe of Ephraim. ⁶⁷They were given the cities of refuge: Shechem with its pasture lands in the hill country of Ephraim, Gezer with its pasture lands, ⁶⁸Jokmeam with its pasture lands, Beth-horon with its pasture lands, ⁶⁹Aijalon with its pasture lands, Gath-rimmon with its pasture lands, ⁷⁰and out of the half-tribe of Manasseh, Aner with its pasture lands, and Bileam with its pasture lands, for the rest of the clans of the Kohathites.

⁷¹To the Gershomites were given out of the clan of the half-tribe of Manasseh: Golan in Bashan with its pasture lands and Ashtaroth with its pasture lands; ⁷²and out of the tribe of Issachar: Kedesh with its pasture lands, Daberath with its pasture lands, ⁷³Ramoth with its pasture lands, and Anem with its pasture lands; ⁷⁴out of the tribe of Asher: Mashal with its pasture lands, Abdon with its pasture lands, ⁷⁵Hukok with its pasture lands, and Rehob with its pasture lands; ⁷⁶and out of the tribe of Naphtali: Kedesh in Galilee with its pasture lands, Hammon with its pasture lands, and Kiriathaim with its pasture lands. ⁷⁷To the rest of the Merarites were allotted out of the tribe of Zebulun: Rimmono with its pasture lands, Tabor with its pasture lands, ⁷⁸and beyond the Jordan at Jericho, on the east side of the Jordan, out of the tribe of Reuben: Bezer in the wilderness with its pasture lands, Jahzah with its pasture lands, ⁷⁹Kedemoth with its pasture lands, and Mephaath with its pasture lands; ⁸⁰and out of the tribe of Gad: Ramoth in Gilead with its pasture lands, Mahanaim with its pasture lands, ⁸¹Heshbon with its pasture lands, and Jazer with its pasture lands.

DESCENDANTS OF ISSACHAR

7 The sonsᵇ of Issachar: Tola, Puah, Jashub, and Shimron, four. ²The sons of Tola: Uzzi, Rephaiah, Jeriel, Jahmai, Ibsam, and Shemuel, heads of their fathers' houses, namely of Tola, mighty warriors of their generations, their number in the days of David being 22,600. ³The sonᶜ of Uzzi: Izrahiah. And the sons of Izrahiah: Michael, Obadiah, Joel, and Isshiah, all five of them were chief men. ⁴And along with them, by their generations, according to their fathers' houses, were units of the army for war, 36,000, for they had many wives and sons. ⁵Their kinsmen belonging to all the clans of Issachar were in all 87,000 mighty warriors, enrolled by genealogy.

DESCENDANTS OF BENJAMIN

⁶The sons of Benjamin: Bela, Becher, and Jediael, three. ⁷The sons of Bela: Ezbon, Uzzi, Uzziel, Jerimoth, and Iri, five, heads of fathers' houses, mighty warriors. And their enrolment by genealogies was 22,034. ⁸The sons of Becher: Zemirah, Joash, Eliezer, Elioenai, Omri, Jeremoth, Abijah, Anathoth, and Alemeth. All these were the sons of Becher. ⁹And their enrolment by genealogies, according to their generations, as heads of their

---

ᵃSeptuagint, Syriac (compare Joshua 21:17); Hebrew lacks *Gibeon*
ᵇSyriac (compare Vulgate); Hebrew *And to the sons* ᶜHebrew *sons*; also verses 10, 12, 17

fathers' houses, mighty warriors, was 20,200. ¹⁰The son of Jediael: Bilhan. And the sons of Bilhan: Jeush, Benjamin, Ehud, Chenaanah, Zethan, Tarshish, and Ahishahar. ¹¹All these were the sons of Jediael according to the heads of their fathers' houses, mighty warriors, 17,200, able to go to war. ¹²And Shuppim and Huppim were the sons of Ir, Hushim the son of Aher.

DESCENDANTS OF NAPHTALI

¹³The sons of Naphtali: Jahziel, Guni, Jezer and Shallum, the descendants of Bilhah.

DESCENDANTS OF MANASSEH

¹⁴The sons of Manasseh: Asriel, whom his Aramean concubine bore; she bore Machir the father of Gilead. ¹⁵And Machir took a wife for Huppim and for Shuppim. The name of his sister was Maacah. And the name of the second was Zelophehad, and Zelophehad had daughters. ¹⁶And Maacah the wife of Machir bore a son, and she called his name Peresh; and the name of his brother was Sheresh; and his sons were Ulam and Rakem. ¹⁷The son of Ulam: Bedan. These were the sons of Gilead the son of Machir, son of Manasseh. ¹⁸And his sister Hammolecheth bore Ishhod, Abiezer, and Mahlah. ¹⁹The sons of Shemida were Ahian, Shechem, Likhi, and Aniam.

DESCENDANTS OF EPHRAIM

²⁰The sons of Ephraim: Shuthelah, and Bered his son, Tahath his son, Eleadah his son, Tahath his son, ²¹Zabad his son, Shuthelah his son, and Ezer and Elead, whom the men of Gath who were born in the land killed, because they came down to raid their livestock. ²²And Ephraim their father mourned many days, and his brothers came to comfort him. ²³And Ephraim went in to his wife, and she conceived and bore a son. And he called his name Beriah, because disaster had befallen his house.ᵃ ²⁴His daughter was Sheerah, who built both Lower and Upper Beth-horon, and Uzzen-sheerah. ²⁵Rephah was his son, Resheph his son, Telah his son, Tahan his son, ²⁶Ladan his son, Ammihud his son, Elishama his son, ²⁷Nunᵇ his son, Joshua his son. ²⁸Their possessions and settlements were Bethel and its towns, and to the east Naaran, and to the west Gezer and its towns, Shechem and its towns, and Ayyah and its towns; ²⁹also in possession of the Manassites, Beth-shean and its towns, Taanach and its towns, Megiddo and its towns, Dor and its towns. In these lived the sons of Joseph the son of Israel.

DESCENDANTS OF ASHER

³⁰The sons of Asher: Imnah, Ishvah, Ishvi, Beriah, and their sister Serah. ³¹The sons of Beriah: Heber, and Malchiel, who fathered Birzaith. ³²Heber fathered Japhlet, Shomer, Hotham, and their sister Shua. ³³The sons of Japhlet: Pasach, Bimhal, and Ashvath. These are the sons of Japhlet. ³⁴The sons of Shemer his brother: Rohgah, Jehubbah, and Aram. ³⁵The sons of Helem his brother: Zophah, Imna, Shelesh, and Amal. ³⁶The sons of Zophah: Suah, Harnepher, Shual, Beri, Imrah. ³⁷Bezer, Hod, Shamma, Shilshah, Ithran, and Beera. ³⁸The sons of Jether: Jephunneh, Pispa, and Ara. ³⁹The sons of Ulla: Arah, Hanniel, and Rizia. ⁴⁰All of these were men of Asher, heads of fathers' houses, approved, mighty warriors, chiefs of the princes. Their number enrolled by genealogies, for service in war, was 26,000 men.

A GENEALOGY OF SAUL

8 Benjamin fathered Bela his firstborn, Ashbel the second, Aharah the third, ²Nohah the fourth, and Rapha the fifth. ³And Bela had sons: Addar, Gera, Abihud, ⁴Abishua, Naaman, Ahoah, ⁵Gera, Shephuphan, and Huram. ⁶These are the sons of Ehud (they were heads of fathers' houses of the inhabitants of Geba, and they were carried into exile to Manahath): ⁷Naaman,ᶜ Ahijah, and Gera, that is, Heglam, who fatheredᵈ Uzza and Ahihud. ⁸And Shaharaim fathered sons in the country of Moab after he had sent away Hushim and Baara his wives. ⁹He fathered sons by Hodesh his wife: Jobab, Zibia, Mesha, Malcam, ¹⁰Jeuz, Sachia, and Mirmah. These were his sons, heads of fathers' houses. ¹¹He also fathered sons by Hushim: Abitub and Elpaal. ¹²The sons of Elpaal: Eber, Misham, and Shemed, who built Ono and Lod with its towns, ¹³and Beriah and Shema (they were heads of fathers' houses of the inhabitants of Aijalon, who caused the inhabitants of Gath to flee); ¹⁴and Ahio, Shashak, and Jeremoth. ¹⁵Zebadiah, Arad, Eder, ¹⁶Michael, Ishpah, and Joha were sons of Beriah. ¹⁷Zebadiah, Meshullam, Hizki, Heber, ¹⁸Ishmerai, Izliah, and Jobab were the sons of Elpaal. ¹⁹Jakim, Zichri, Zabdi, ²⁰Elienai, Zillethai,

---

ᵃ*Beriah* sounds like the Hebrew for *disaster* ᵇHebrew *Non*
ᶜHebrew *and Naaman* ᵈOr *Gera; he carried them into exile and fathered*

Eliel, ²¹Adaiah, Beraiah, and Shimrath were the sons of Shimei. ²²Ishpan, Eber, Eliel, ²³Abdon, Zichri, Hanan, ²⁴Hananiah, Elam, Anthothijah, ²⁵Iphdeiah, and Penuel were the sons of Shashak. ²⁶Shamsherai, Shehariah, Athaliah, ²⁷Jaareshiah, Elijah, and Zichri were the sons of Jeroham. ²⁸These were the heads of fathers' houses, according to their generations, chief men. These lived in Jerusalem.

²⁹Jeiel[a] the father of Gibeon lived in Gibeon, and the name of his wife was Maacah. ³⁰His firstborn son: Abdon, then Zur, Kish, Baal, Nadab, ³¹Gedor, Ahio, Zecher, ³²and Mikloth (he fathered Shimeah). Now these also lived opposite their kinsmen in Jerusalem, with their kinsmen. ³³Ner was the father of Kish, Kish of Saul, Saul of Jonathan, Malchi-shua, Abinadab and Eshbaal; ³⁴and the son of Jonathan was Merib-baal; and Merib-baal was the father of Micah. ³⁵The sons of Micah: Pithon, Melech, Tarea, and Ahaz. ³⁶Ahaz fathered Jehoaddah, and Jehoaddah fathered Alemeth, Azmaveth, and Zimri. Zimri fathered Moza. ³⁷Moza fathered Binea; Raphah was his son, Eleasah his son, Azel his son. ³⁸Azel had six sons, and these are their names: Azrikam, Bocheru, Ishmael, Sheariah, Obadiah, and Hanan. All these were the sons of Azel. ³⁹The sons of Eshek his brother: Ulam his firstborn, Jeush the second, and Eliphelet the third. ⁴⁰The sons of Ulam were men who were mighty warriors, bowmen, having many sons and grandsons, 150. All these were Benjaminites.

A GENEALOGY OF THE RETURNED EXILES

9 So all Israel was recorded in genealogies, and these are written in the Book of the Kings of Israel. And Judah was taken into exile in Babylon because of their breach of faith. ²Now the first to dwell again in their possessions in their cities were Israel, the priests, the Levites, and the temple servants. ³And some of the people of Judah, Benjamin, Ephraim, and Manasseh lived in Jerusalem: ⁴Uthai the son of Ammihud, son of Omri, son of Imri, son of Bani, from the sons of Perez the son of Judah. ⁵And of the Shilonites: Asaiah the firstborn, and his sons. ⁶Of the sons of Zerah: Jeuel and their kinsmen, 690. ⁷Of the Benjaminites: Sallu the son of Meshullam, son of Hodaviah, son of Hassenuah, ⁸Ibneiah the son of Jeroham, Elah the son of Uzzi, son of Michri, and Meshullam the son of Shephatiah, son of Reuel, son of Ibnijah; ⁹and their kinsmen according to their generations, 956. All these were heads of fathers' houses according to their fathers' houses.

¹⁰Of the priests: Jedaiah, Jehoiarib, Jachin, ¹¹and Azariah the son of Hilkiah, son of Meshullam, son of Zadok, son of Meraioth, son of Ahitub, the chief officer of the house of God; ¹²and Adaiah the son of Jeroham, son of Pashhur, son of Malchijah, and Maasai the son of Adiel, son of Jahzerah, son of Meshullam, son of Meshillemith, son of Immer; ¹³besides their kinsmen, heads of their fathers' houses, 1,760, mighty men for the work of the service of the house of God.

¹⁴Of the Levites: Shemaiah the son of Hasshub, son of Azrikam, son of Hashabiah, of the sons of Merari; ¹⁵and Bakbakkar, Heresh, Galal and Mattaniah the son of Mica, son of Zichri, son of Asaph; ¹⁶and Obadiah the son of Shemaiah, son of Galal, son of Jeduthun, and Berechiah the son of Asa, son of Elkanah, who lived in the villages of the Netophathites.

¹⁷The gatekeepers were Shallum, Akkub, Talmon, Ahiman, and their kinsmen (Shallum was the chief); ¹⁸until then they were in the king's gate on the east side as the gatekeepers of the camps of the Levites. ¹⁹Shallum the son of Kore, son of Ebiasaph, son of Korah, and his kinsmen of his fathers' house, the Korahites, were in charge of the work of the service, keepers of the thresholds of the tent, as their fathers had been in charge of the camp of the LORD, keepers of the entrance. ²⁰And Phinehas the son of Eleazar was the chief officer over them in time past; the LORD was with him. ²¹Zechariah the son of Meshelemiah was gatekeeper at the entrance of the tent of meeting. ²²All these, who were chosen as gatekeepers at the thresholds, were 212. They were enrolled by genealogies in their villages. David and Samuel the seer established them in their office of trust. ²³So they and their sons were in charge of the gates of the house of the LORD, that is, the house of the tent, as guards. ²⁴The gatekeepers were on the four sides, east, west, north, and south. ²⁵And their kinsmen who were in their villages were bound to come in every seven days, in turn, to be with these, ²⁶for the four chief gatekeepers, who were Levites, were entrusted to be over the chambers and the treasures of the house of God. ²⁷And they lodged round the house of God, for on them lay the duty of watching, and they had charge of opening it every morning.

---

[a] Compare 9:35; Hebrew lacks *Jeiel*

28 Some of them had charge of the utensils of service, for they were required to count them when they were brought in and taken out. 29 Others of them were appointed over the furniture and over all the holy utensils, also over the fine flour, the wine, the oil, the incense, and the spices. 30 Others, of the sons of the priests, prepared the mixing of the spices, 31 and Mattithiah, one of the Levites, the firstborn of Shallum the Korahite, was entrusted with making the flat cakes. 32 Also some of their kinsmen of the Kohathites had charge of the showbread, to prepare it every Sabbath.

33 Now these, the singers, the heads of fathers' houses of the Levites, were in the chambers of the temple free from other service, for they were on duty day and night. 34 These were heads of fathers' houses of the Levites, according to their generations, leaders. These lived in Jerusalem.

SAUL'S GENEALOGY REPEATED

35 In Gibeon lived the father of Gibeon, Jeiel, and the name of his wife was Maacah, 36 and his firstborn son Abdon, then Zur, Kish, Baal, Ner, Nadab, 37 Gedor, Ahio, Zechariah, and Mikloth; 38 and Mikloth was the father of Shimeam; and these also lived opposite their kinsmen in Jerusalem, with their kinsmen. 39 Ner fathered Kish, Kish fathered Saul, Saul fathered Jonathan, Malchi-shua, Abinadab, and Eshbaal. 40 And the son of Jonathan was Merib-baal, and Merib-baal fathered Micah. 41 The sons of Micah: Pithon, Melech, Tahrea, and Ahaz.[a] 42 And Ahaz fathered Jarah, and Jarah fathered Alemeth, Azmaveth, and Zimri. And Zimri fathered Moza. 43 Moza fathered Binea, and Rephaiah was his son, Eleasah his son, Azel his son. 44 Azel had six sons and these are their names: Azrikam, Bocheru, Ishmael, Sheariah, Obadiah, and Hanan; these were the sons of Azel.

THE DEATH OF SAUL AND HIS SONS

10 Now the Philistines fought against Israel, and the men of Israel fled before the Philistines and fell slain on Mount Gilboa. 2 And the Philistines overtook Saul and his sons, and the Philistines struck down Jonathan and Abinadab and Malchi-shua, the sons of Saul. 3 The battle pressed hard against Saul, and the archers found him, and he was wounded by the archers. 4 Then Saul said to his armour bearer, "Draw your sword and thrust me through with it, lest these uncircumcised come and mistreat me." But his armour bearer would not, for he feared greatly. Therefore Saul took his own sword and fell upon it. 5 And when his armour bearer saw that Saul was dead, he also fell upon his sword and died. 6 Thus Saul died; he and his three sons and all his house died together. 7 And when all the men of Israel who were in the valley saw that the army[b] had fled and that Saul and his sons were dead, they abandoned their cities and fled, and the Philistines came and lived in them.

8 The next day, when the Philistines came to strip the slain, they found Saul and his sons fallen on Mount Gilboa. 9 And they stripped him and took his head and his armour, and sent messengers throughout the land of the Philistines to carry the good news to their idols and to the people. 10 And they put his armour in the temple of their gods and fastened his head in the temple of Dagon. 11 But when all Jabesh-gilead heard all that the Philistines had done to Saul, 12 all the valiant men arose and took away the body of Saul and the bodies of his sons, and brought them to Jabesh. And they buried their bones under the oak in Jabesh and fasted for seven days.

13 So Saul died for his breach of faith. He broke faith with the LORD in that he did not keep the command of the LORD, and also consulted a medium, seeking guidance. 14 He did not seek guidance from the LORD. Therefore the LORD put him to death and turned the kingdom over to David the son of Jesse.

DAVID ANOINTED KING

11 Then all Israel gathered together to David at Hebron and said, "Behold, we are your bone and flesh. 2 In times past, even when Saul was king, it was you who led out and brought in Israel. And the LORD your God said to you, 'You shall be shepherd of my people Israel, and you shall be prince over my people Israel.'" 3 So all the elders of Israel came to the king at Hebron, and David made a covenant with them at Hebron before the LORD. And they anointed David king over Israel, according to the word of the LORD by Samuel.

DAVID TAKES JERUSALEM

4 And David and all Israel went to Jerusalem, that is, Jebus, where the Jebusites were, the inhabitants of the land. 5 The inhabitants of Jebus said to David, "You will not come in here." Nevertheless, David took the

---
[a] Compare 8:35; Hebrew lacks *and Ahaz* [b] Hebrew *they*

stronghold of Zion, that is, the city of David. ⁶David said, "Whoever strikes the Jebusites first shall be chief and commander." And Joab the son of Zeruiah went up first, so he became chief. ⁷And David lived in the stronghold; therefore it was called the city of David. ⁸And he built the city all round from the Millo in complete circuit, and Joab repaired the rest of the city. ⁹And David became greater and greater, for the LORD of hosts was with him.

DAVID'S MIGHTY MEN

¹⁰Now these are the chiefs of David's mighty men, who gave him strong support in his kingdom, together with all Israel, to make him king, according to the word of the LORD concerning Israel. ¹¹This is an account of David's mighty men: Jashobeam, a Hachmonite, was chief of the three.ᵃ He wielded his spear against 300 whom he killed at one time.

¹²And next to him among the three mighty men was Eleazar the son of Dodo, the Ahohite. ¹³He was with David at Pas-dammim when the Philistines were gathered there for battle. There was a plot of ground full of barley, and the men fled from the Philistines. ¹⁴But he took hisᵇ stand in the midst of the plot and defended it and killed the Philistines. And the LORD saved them by a great victory.

¹⁵Three of the thirty chief men went down to the rock to David at the cave of Adullam, when the army of Philistines was encamped in the Valley of Rephaim. ¹⁶David was then in the stronghold, and the garrison of the Philistines was then at Bethlehem. ¹⁷And David said longingly, "Oh that someone would give me water to drink from the well of Bethlehem that is by the gate!" ¹⁸Then the three mighty men broke through the camp of the Philistines and drew water out of the well of Bethlehem that was by the gate and took it and brought it to David. But David would not drink it. He poured it out to the LORD ¹⁹and said, "Far be it from me before my God that I should do this. Shall I drink the lifeblood of these men? For at the risk of their lives they brought it." Therefore he would not drink it. These things did the three mighty men.

²⁰Now Abishai, the brother of Joab, was chief of the thirty.ᶜ And he wielded his spear against 300 men and killed them and won a name beside the three. ²¹He was the most renownedᵈ of the thirtyᵉ and became their commander, but he did not attain to the three.

²²And Benaiah the son of Jehoiada was a valiant manᶠ of Kabzeel, a doer of great deeds. He struck down two heroes of Moab. He also went down and struck down a lion in a pit on a day when snow had fallen. ²³And he struck down an Egyptian, a man of great stature, five cubitsᵍ tall. The Egyptian had in his hand a spear like a weaver's beam, but Benaiah went down to him with a staff and snatched the spear out of the Egyptian's hand and killed him with his own spear. ²⁴These things did Benaiah the son of Jehoiada and won a name beside the three mighty men. ²⁵He was renowned among the thirty, but he did not attain to the three. And David set him over his bodyguard.

²⁶The mighty men were Asahel the brother of Joab, Elhanan the son of Dodo of Bethlehem, ²⁷Shammoth of Harod,ʰ Helez the Pelonite, ²⁸Ira the son of Ikkesh of Tekoa, Abiezer of Anathoth, ²⁹Sibbecai the Hushathite, Ilai the Ahohite, ³⁰Maharai of Netophah, Heled the son of Baanah of Netophah, ³¹Ithai the son of Ribai of Gibeah of the people of Benjamin, Benaiah of Pirathon, ³²Hurai of the brooks of Gaash, Abiel the Arbathite, ³³Azmaveth of Baharum, Eliahba the Shaalbonite, ³⁴Hashemⁱ the Gizonite, Jonathan the son of Shagee the Hararite, ³⁵Ahiam the son of Sachar the Hararite, Eliphal the son of Ur, ³⁶Hepher the Mecherathite, Ahijah the Pelonite, ³⁷Hezro of Carmel, Naarai the son of Ezbai, ³⁸Joel the brother of Nathan, Mibhar the son of Hagri, ³⁹Zelek the Ammonite, Naharai of Beeroth, the armour bearer of Joab the son of Zeruiah, ⁴⁰Ira the Ithrite, Gareb the Ithrite, ⁴¹Uriah the Hittite, Zabad the son of Ahlai, ⁴²Adina the son of Shiza the Reubenite, a leader of the Reubenites, and thirty with him, ⁴³Hanan the son of Maacah, and Joshaphat the Mithnite, ⁴⁴Uzzia the Ashterathite, Shama and Jeiel the sons of Hotham the Aroerite, ⁴⁵Jediael the son of Shimri, and Joha his brother, the Tizite, ⁴⁶Eliel the Mahavite, and Jeribai, and Joshaviah, the sons of Elnaam, and Ithmah the Moabite, ⁴⁷Eliel, and Obed, and Jaasiel the Mezobaite.

THE MIGHTY MEN JOIN DAVID

12 Now these are the men who came to David at Ziklag, while he could not move about freely because of Saul the son of Kish. And they were among the mighty men who helped him in war. ²They

---

ᵃCompare 2 Samuel 23:8; Hebrew *thirty*, or *captains* ᵇCompare 2 Samuel 23:12; Hebrew *they... their* ᶜSyriac; Hebrew *three* ᵈCompare 2 Samuel 23:19; Hebrew *more renowned among the two* ᵉSyriac; Hebrew *three* ᶠSyriac; Hebrew *the son of a valiant man* ᵍA *cubit* was about 18 inches or 45 centimetres ʰCompare 2 Samuel 23:25; Hebrew *the Harorite* ⁱCompare Septuagint and 2 Samuel 23:32; Hebrew *the sons of Hashem*

1 CHRONICLES 12

were bowmen and could shoot arrows and sling stones with either the right or the left hand; they were Benjaminites, Saul's kinsmen. ³The chief was Ahiezer, then Joash, both sons of Shemaah of Gibeah; also Jeziel and Pelet, the sons of Azmaveth; Beracah, Jehu of Anathoth, ⁴Ishmaiah of Gibeon, a mighty man among the thirty and a leader over the thirty; Jeremiah,[a] Jahaziel, Johanan, Jozabad of Gederah, ⁵Eluzai,[b] Jerimoth, Bealiah, Shemariah, Shephatiah the Haruphite; ⁶Elkanah, Isshiah, Azarel, Joezer, and Jashobeam, the Korahites; ⁷And Joelah and Zebadiah, the sons of Jeroham of Gedor.

⁸From the Gadites there went over to David at the stronghold in the wilderness mighty and experienced warriors, expert with shield and spear, whose faces were like the faces of lions and who were swift as gazelles upon the mountains: ⁹Ezer the chief, Obadiah second, Eliab third, ¹⁰Mishmannah fourth, Jeremiah fifth, ¹¹Attai sixth, Eliel seventh, ¹²Johanan eighth, Elzabad ninth, ¹³Jeremiah tenth, Machbannai eleventh. ¹⁴These Gadites were officers of the army; the least was a match for a hundred men and the greatest for a thousand. ¹⁵These are the men who crossed the Jordan in the first month, when it was overflowing all its banks, and put to flight all those in the valleys, to the east and to the west.

¹⁶And some of the men of Benjamin and Judah came to the stronghold to David. ¹⁷David went out to meet them and said to them, "If you have come to me in friendship to help me, my heart will be joined to you; but if to betray me to my adversaries, although there is no wrong in my hands, then may the God of our fathers see and rebuke you." ¹⁸Then the Spirit clothed Amasai, chief of the thirty, and he said,

"We are yours, O David,
    and with you, O son of Jesse!
Peace, peace to you,
    and peace to your helpers!
For your God helps you."

Then David received them and made them officers of his troops.

¹⁹Some of the men of Manasseh deserted to David when he came with the Philistines for the battle against Saul. (Yet he did not help them, for the rulers of the Philistines took counsel and sent him away, saying, "At peril to our heads he will desert to his master Saul.") ²⁰As he went to Ziklag, these men of Manasseh deserted to him: Adnah, Jozabad, Jediael, Michael, Jozabad, Elihu, and Zillethai, chiefs of thousands in Manasseh. ²¹They helped David against the band of raiders, for they were all mighty men of valour and were commanders in the army. ²²For from day to day men came to David to help him, until there was a great army, like an army of God.

²³These are the numbers of the divisions of the armed troops who came to David in Hebron to turn the kingdom of Saul over to him, according to the word of the LORD. ²⁴The men of Judah bearing shield and spear were 6,800 armed troops. ²⁵Of the Simeonites, mighty men of valour for war, 7,100. ²⁶Of the Levites 4,600. ²⁷The prince Jehoiada, of the house of Aaron, and with him 3,700. ²⁸Zadok, a young man mighty in valour, and twenty-two commanders from his own fathers' house. ²⁹Of the Benjaminites, the kinsmen of Saul, 3,000, of whom the majority had to that point kept their allegiance to the house of Saul. ³⁰Of the Ephraimites 20,800, mighty men of valour, famous men in their fathers' houses. ³¹Of the half-tribe of Manasseh 18,000, who were expressly named to come and make David king. ³²Of Issachar, men who had understanding of the times, to know what Israel ought to do, 200 chiefs, and all their kinsmen under their command. ³³Of Zebulun 50,000 seasoned troops, equipped for battle with all the weapons of war, to help David[c] with singleness of purpose. ³⁴Of Naphtali 1,000 commanders with whom were 37,000 men armed with shield and spear. ³⁵Of the Danites 28,600 men equipped for battle. ³⁶Of Asher 40,000 seasoned troops ready for battle. ³⁷Of the Reubenites and Gadites and the half-tribe of Manasseh from beyond the Jordan, 120,000 men armed with all the weapons of war.

³⁸All these, men of war, arrayed in battle order, came to Hebron with a whole heart to make David king over all Israel. Likewise, all the rest of Israel were of a single mind to make David king. ³⁹And they were there with David for three days, eating and drinking, for their brothers had made preparation for them. ⁴⁰And also their relatives, from as far as Issachar and Zebulun and Naphtali, came bringing food on donkeys and on camels and on mules and on oxen, abundant provisions of flour, cakes of figs, clusters of raisins, and wine and oil, oxen and sheep, for there was joy in Israel.

---

[a] Hebrew verse 5   [b] Hebrew verse 6   [c] Septuagint; Hebrew lacks *David*

THE ARK BROUGHT FROM KIRIATH-JEARIM

13 David consulted with the commanders of thousands and of hundreds, with every leader. ²And David said to all the assembly of Israel, "If it seems good to you and from the Lord our God, let us send abroad to our brothers who remain in all the lands of Israel, as well as to the priests and Levites in the cities that have pasture lands, that they may be gathered to us. ³Then let us bring again the ark of our God to us, for we did not seek it*a* in the days of Saul." ⁴All the assembly agreed to do so, for the thing was right in the eyes of all the people.

UZZAH AND THE ARK

⁵So David assembled all Israel from the Nile*b* of Egypt to Lebo-hamath, to bring the ark of God from Kiriath-jearim. ⁶And David and all Israel went up to Baalah, that is, to Kiriath-jearim that belongs to Judah, to bring up from there the ark of God, which is called by the name of the Lord who sits enthroned above the cherubim. ⁷And they carried the ark of God on a new cart, from the house of Abinadab, and Uzzah and Ahio*c* were driving the cart. ⁸And David and all Israel were celebrating before God with all their might, with song and lyres and harps and tambourines and cymbals and trumpets.

⁹And when they came to the threshing floor of Chidon, Uzzah put out his hand to take hold of the ark, for the oxen stumbled. ¹⁰And the anger of the Lord was kindled against Uzzah, and he struck him down because he put out his hand to the ark, and he died there before God. ¹¹And David was angry because the Lord had broken out against Uzzah. And that place is called Perez-uzza*d* to this day. ¹²And David was afraid of God that day, and he said, "How can I bring the ark of God home to me?" ¹³So David did not take the ark home into the city of David, but took it aside to the house of Obed-edom the Gittite. ¹⁴And the ark of God remained with the household of Obed-edom in his house for three months. And the Lord blessed the household of Obed-edom and all that he had.

DAVID'S WIVES AND CHILDREN

14 And Hiram king of Tyre sent messengers to David, and cedar trees, also masons and carpenters to build a house for him. ²And David knew that the Lord had established him as king over Israel, and that his kingdom was highly exalted for the sake of his people Israel.

³And David took more wives in Jerusalem, and David fathered more sons and daughters. ⁴These are the names of the children born to him in Jerusalem: Shammua, Shobab, Nathan, Solomon, ⁵Ibhar, Elishua, Elpelet, ⁶Nogah, Nepheg, Japhia, ⁷Elishama, Beeliada and Eliphelet.

PHILISTINES DEFEATED

⁸When the Philistines heard that David had been anointed king over all Israel, all the Philistines went up to search for David. But David heard of it and went out against them. ⁹Now the Philistines had come and made a raid in the Valley of Rephaim. ¹⁰And David enquired of God, "Shall I go up against the Philistines? Will you give them into my hand?" And the Lord said to him, "Go up, and I will give them into your hand." ¹¹And he went up to Baal-perazim, and David struck them down there. And David said, "God has broken through*e* my enemies by my hand, like a bursting flood." Therefore the name of that place is called Baal-perazim. ¹²And they left their gods there, and David gave command, and they were burned.

¹³And the Philistines yet again made a raid in the valley. ¹⁴And when David again enquired of God, God said to him, "You shall not go up after them; go round and come against them opposite the balsam trees. ¹⁵And when you hear the sound of marching in the tops of the balsam trees, then go out to battle, for God has gone out before you to strike down the army of the Philistines." ¹⁶And David did as God commanded him, and they struck down the Philistine army from Gibeon to Gezer. ¹⁷And the fame of David went out into all lands, and the Lord brought the fear of him upon all nations.

THE ARK BROUGHT TO JERUSALEM

15 David*f* built houses for himself in the city of David. And he prepared a place for the ark of God and pitched a tent for it. ²Then David said that no one but the Levites may carry the ark of God, for the Lord had chosen them to carry the ark of the Lord and to minister to him for ever. ³And David assembled all Israel at Jerusalem to bring up

---

a Or *him* *b* Hebrew *Shihor* *c* Or *and his brother* *d* *Perez-uzza* means *the breaking out against Uzzah* *e* *Baal-perazim* means *Lord of breaking through* *f* Hebrew *He*

the ark of the LORD to its place, which he had prepared for it. ⁴And David gathered together the sons of Aaron and the Levites: ⁵of the sons of Kohath, Uriel the chief, with 120 of his brothers; ⁶of the sons of Merari, Asaiah the chief, with 220 of his brothers; ⁷of the sons of Gershom, Joel the chief, with 130 of his brothers; ⁸of the sons of Elizaphan, Shemaiah the chief, with 200 of his brothers; ⁹of the sons of Hebron, Eliel the chief, with 80 of his brothers; ¹⁰of the sons of Uzziel, Amminadab the chief, with 112 of his brothers. ¹¹Then David summoned the priests Zadok and Abiathar, and the Levites Uriel, Asaiah, Joel, Shemaiah, Eliel, and Amminadab, ¹²and said to them, "You are the heads of the fathers' houses of the Levites. Consecrate yourselves, you and your brothers, so that you may bring up the ark of the LORD, the God of Israel, to the place that I have prepared for it. ¹³Because you did not carry it the first time, the LORD our God broke out against us, because we did not seek him according to the rule." ¹⁴So the priests and the Levites consecrated themselves to bring up the ark of the LORD, the God of Israel. ¹⁵And the Levites carried the ark of God on their shoulders with the poles, as Moses had commanded according to the word of the LORD.

¹⁶David also commanded the chiefs of the Levites to appoint their brothers as the singers who should play loudly on musical instruments, on harps and lyres and cymbals, to raise sounds of joy. ¹⁷So the Levites appointed Heman the son of Joel; and of his brothers Asaph the son of Berechiah; and of the sons of Merari, their brothers, Ethan the son of Kushaiah; ¹⁸and with them their brothers of the second order, Zechariah, Jaaziel, Shemiramoth, Jehiel, Unni, Eliab, Benaiah, Maaseiah, Mattithiah, Eliphelehu, and Mikneiah, and the gatekeepers Obed-edom and Jeiel. ¹⁹The singers, Heman, Asaph, and Ethan, were to sound bronze cymbals; ²⁰Zechariah, Aziel, Shemiramoth, Jehiel, Unni, Eliab, Maaseiah, and Benaiah were to play harps according to Alamoth; ²¹but Mattithiah, Eliphelehu, Mikneiah, Obed-edom, Jeiel, and Azaziah were to lead with lyres according to the Sheminith. ²²Chenaniah, leader of the Levites in music, should direct the music, for he understood it. ²³Berechiah and Elkanah were to be gatekeepers for the ark. ²⁴Shebaniah, Joshaphat, Nethanel, Amasai, Zechariah, Benaiah, and Eliezer, the priests, should blow the trumpets before the ark of God. Obed-edom and Jehiah were to be gatekeepers for the ark.

²⁵So David and the elders of Israel and the commanders of thousands went to bring up the ark of the covenant of the LORD from the house of Obed-edom with rejoicing. ²⁶And because God helped the Levites who were carrying the ark of the covenant of the LORD, they sacrificed seven bulls and seven rams. ²⁷David was clothed with a robe of fine linen, as also were all the Levites who were carrying the ark, and the singers and Chenaniah the leader of the music of the singers. And David wore a linen ephod. ²⁸So all Israel brought up the ark of the covenant of the LORD with shouting, to the sound of the horn, trumpets, and cymbals, and made loud music on harps and lyres.

²⁹And as the ark of the covenant of the LORD came to the city of David, Michal the daughter of Saul looked out of the window and saw King David dancing and celebrating, and she despised him in her heart.

THE ARK PLACED IN A TENT

16 And they brought in the ark of God and set it inside the tent that David had pitched for it, and they offered burnt offerings and peace offerings before God. ²And when David had finished offering the burnt offerings and the peace offerings, he blessed the people in the name of the LORD ³and distributed to all Israel, both men and women, to each a loaf of bread, a portion of meat,ᵃ and a cake of raisins.

⁴Then he appointed some of the Levites as ministers before the ark of the LORD, to invoke, to thank, and to praise the LORD, the God of Israel. ⁵Asaph was the chief, and second to him were Zechariah, Jeiel, Shemiramoth, Jehiel, Mattithiah, Eliab, Benaiah, Obed-edom, and Jeiel, who were to play harps and lyres; Asaph was to sound the cymbals, ⁶and Benaiah and Jahaziel the priests were to blow trumpets regularly before the ark of the covenant of God. ⁷Then on that day David first appointed that thanksgiving be sung to the LORD by Asaph and his brothers.

DAVID'S SONG OF THANKS

⁸ Oh give thanks to the LORD;
    call upon his name;
    make known his deeds
        among the peoples!
⁹ Sing to him, sing praises to him;
    tell of all his wondrous works!

ᵃCompare Septuagint, Syriac, Vulgate; the meaning of the Hebrew is uncertain

10   Glory in his holy name;
      let the hearts of those who
         seek the LORD rejoice!
11   Seek the LORD and his strength;
      seek his presence continually!
12   Remember the wondrous
        works that he has done,
      his miracles and the
        judgements he uttered,
13   O offspring of Israel his servant,
      children of Jacob, his chosen ones!

14   He is the LORD our God;
      his judgements are in all the earth.
15   Remember his covenant for ever,
      the word that he commanded, for
        a thousand generations,
16   the covenant that he made
      with Abraham,
      his sworn promise to Isaac,
17   which he confirmed to
        Jacob as a statute,
      to Israel as an everlasting covenant,
18   saying, "To you I will give
      the land of Canaan,
      as your portion for an inheritance."

19   When you were few in number,
      of little account, and sojourners in it,
20   wandering from nation to nation,
      from one kingdom to
        another people,
21   he allowed no one to oppress them;
      he rebuked kings on their account,
22   saying, "Touch not my anointed ones,
      do my prophets no harm!"

23   Sing to the LORD, all the earth!
      Tell of his salvation from day to day.
24   Declare his glory among the nations,
      his marvellous works among
        all the peoples!
25   For great is the LORD, and
        greatly to be praised,
      and he is to be feared above all gods.
26   For all the gods of the peoples
      are worthless idols,
      but the LORD made the heavens.
27   Splendour and majesty are
        before him;
      strength and joy are in his place.

28   Ascribe to the LORD, O families
        of the peoples,
      ascribe to the LORD glory
        and strength!
29   Ascribe to the LORD the glory
        due his name;
      bring an offering and
        come before him!
      Worship the LORD in the
        splendour of holiness;[a]
30   tremble before him, all the earth;
      yes, the world is established; it
        shall never be moved.
31   Let the heavens be glad, and
      let the earth rejoice,
      and let them say among the
        nations, "The LORD reigns!"
32   Let the sea roar, and all that fills it;
      let the field exult, and
        everything in it!
33   Then shall the trees of the
        forest sing for joy
      before the LORD, for he comes
        to judge the earth.
34   Oh give thanks to the LORD,
        for he is good;
      for his steadfast love
        endures for ever!

35 Say also:

"Save us, O God of our salvation,
   and gather and deliver us from
      among the nations,
that we may give thanks to
   your holy name
and glory in your praise.
36   Blessed be the LORD, the God of Israel,
      from everlasting to everlasting!"

Then all the people said, "Amen!" and praised the LORD.

WORSHIP BEFORE THE ARK

37 So David left Asaph and his brothers there before the ark of the covenant of the LORD to minister regularly before the ark as each day required, 38 and also Obed-edom and his[b] sixty-eight brothers, while Obed-edom, the son of Jeduthun, and Hosah were to be gatekeepers. 39 And he left Zadok the priest and his brothers the priests before the tabernacle of the LORD in the high place that was at Gibeon 40 to offer burnt offerings to the LORD on the altar of burnt offering regularly morning and evening, to do all that is written in the Law of the LORD that he commanded Israel. 41 With them were Heman and Jeduthun and

---

[a] Or in holy attire   [b] Hebrew their

the rest of those chosen and expressly named to give thanks to the LORD, for his steadfast love endures for ever. ⁴²Heman and Jeduthun had trumpets and cymbals for the music and instruments for sacred song. The sons of Jeduthun were appointed to the gate.

⁴³Then all the people departed each to his house, and David went home to bless his household.

THE LORD'S COVENANT WITH DAVID

17 Now when David lived in his house, David said to Nathan the prophet, "Behold, I dwell in a house of cedar, but the ark of the covenant of the LORD is under a tent." ²And Nathan said to David, "Do all that is in your heart, for God is with you."

³But that same night the word of the LORD came to Nathan, ⁴"Go and tell my servant David, 'Thus says the LORD: It is not you who will build me a house to dwell in. ⁵For I have not lived in a house since the day I brought up Israel to this day, but I have gone from tent to tent and from dwelling to dwelling. ⁶In all places where I have moved with all Israel, did I speak a word with any of the judges of Israel, whom I commanded to shepherd my people, saying, "Why have you not built me a house of cedar?"' ⁷Now, therefore, thus shall you say to my servant David, 'Thus says the LORD of hosts, I took you from the pasture, from following the sheep, to be prince over my people Israel, ⁸and I have been with you wherever you have gone and have cut off all your enemies from before you. And I will make for you a name, like the name of the great ones of the earth. ⁹And I will appoint a place for my people Israel and will plant them, that they may dwell in their own place and be disturbed no more. And violent men shall waste them no more, as formerly, ¹⁰from the time that I appointed judges over my people Israel. And I will subdue all your enemies. Moreover, I declare to you that the LORD will build you a house. ¹¹When your days are fulfilled to walk with your fathers, I will raise up your offspring after you, one of your own sons, and I will establish his kingdom. ¹²He shall build a house for me, and I will establish his throne for ever. ¹³I will be to him a father, and he shall be to me a son. I will not take my steadfast love from him, as I took it from him who was before you, ¹⁴but I will confirm him in my house and in my kingdom for ever, and his throne shall be established for ever.'" ¹⁵In accordance with all these words, and in accordance with all this vision, Nathan spoke to David.

DAVID'S PRAYER

¹⁶Then King David went in and sat before the LORD and said, "Who am I, O LORD God, and what is my house, that you have brought me thus far? ¹⁷And this was a small thing in your eyes, O God. You have also spoken of your servant's house for a great while to come, and have shown me future generations,[a] O LORD God! ¹⁸And what more can David say to you for honouring your servant? For you know your servant. ¹⁹For your servant's sake, O LORD, and according to your own heart, you have done all this greatness, in making known all these great things. ²⁰There is none like you, O LORD, and there is no God besides you, according to all that we have heard with our ears. ²¹And who is like your people Israel, the one[b] nation on earth whom God went to redeem to be his people, making for yourself a name for great and awesome things, in driving out nations before your people whom you redeemed from Egypt? ²²And you made your people Israel to be your people for ever, and you, O LORD, became their God. ²³And now, O LORD, let the word that you have spoken concerning your servant and concerning his house be established for ever, and do as you have spoken, ²⁴and your name will be established and magnified for ever, saying, 'The LORD of hosts, the God of Israel, is Israel's God', and the house of your servant David will be established before you. ²⁵For you, my God, have revealed to your servant that you will build a house for him. Therefore your servant has found courage to pray before you. ²⁶And now, O LORD, you are God, and you have promised this good thing to your servant. ²⁷Now you have been pleased to bless the house of your servant, that it may continue for ever before you, for it is you, O LORD, who have blessed, and it is blessed for ever."

DAVID DEFEATS HIS ENEMIES

18 After this David defeated the Philistines and subdued them, and he took Gath and its villages out of the hand of the Philistines.

²And he defeated Moab, and the Moabites became servants to David and brought tribute.

---

[a] Or and you look upon me as a man of high rank
[b] Septuagint, Vulgate other

³David also defeated Hadadezer king of Zobah-Hamath, as he went to set up his monument[a] at the river Euphrates. ⁴And David took from him 1,000 chariots, 7,000 horsemen, and 20,000 foot soldiers. And David hamstrung all the chariot horses, but left enough for 100 chariots. ⁵And when the Syrians of Damascus came to help Hadadezer king of Zobah, David struck down 22,000 men of the Syrians. ⁶Then David put garrisons[b] in Syria of Damascus, and the Syrians became servants to David and brought tribute. And the LORD gave victory to David[c] wherever he went. ⁷And David took the shields of gold that were carried by the servants of Hadadezer and brought them to Jerusalem. ⁸And from Tibhath and from Cun, cities of Hadadezer, David took a large amount of bronze. With it Solomon made the bronze sea and the pillars and the vessels of bronze.

⁹When Tou king of Hamath heard that David had defeated the whole army of Hadadezer, king of Zobah, ¹⁰he sent his son Hadoram to King David, to ask about his health and to bless him because he had fought against Hadadezer and defeated him; for Hadadezer had often been at war with Tou. And he sent all sorts of articles of gold, of silver, and of bronze. ¹¹These also King David dedicated to the LORD, together with the silver and gold that he had carried off from all the nations, from Edom, Moab, the Ammonites, the Philistines, and Amalek.

¹²And Abishai, the son of Zeruiah, killed 18,000 Edomites in the Valley of Salt. ¹³Then he put garrisons in Edom, and all the Edomites became David's servants. And the LORD gave victory to David wherever he went.

DAVID'S ADMINISTRATION

¹⁴So David reigned over all Israel, and he administered justice and equity to all his people. ¹⁵And Joab the son of Zeruiah was over the army; and Jehoshaphat the son of Ahilud was recorder; ¹⁶and Zadok the son of Ahitub and Ahimelech the son of Abiathar were priests; and Shavsha was secretary; ¹⁷and Benaiah the son of Jehoiada was over the Cherethites and the Pelethites; and David's sons were the chief officials in the service of the king.

THE AMMONITES DISGRACE DAVID'S MEN

19 Now after this Nahash the king of the Ammonites died, and his son reigned in his place. ²And David said, "I will deal kindly with Hanun the son of Nahash, for his father dealt kindly with me." So David sent messengers to console him concerning his father. And David's servants came to the land of the Ammonites to Hanun to console him. ³But the princes of the Ammonites said to Hanun, "Do you think, because David has sent comforters to you, that he is honouring your father? Have not his servants come to you to search and to overthrow and to spy out the land?" ⁴So Hanun took David's servants and shaved them and cut off their garments in the middle, at their hips, and sent them away; ⁵and they departed. When David was told concerning the men, he sent messengers to meet them, for the men were greatly ashamed. And the king said, "Remain at Jericho until your beards have grown and then return."

⁶When the Ammonites saw that they had become a stench to David, Hanun and the Ammonites sent 1,000 talents[d] of silver to hire chariots and horsemen from Mesopotamia, from Aram-maacah, and from Zobah. ⁷They hired 32,000 chariots and the king of Maacah with his army, who came and encamped before Medeba. And the Ammonites were mustered from their cities and came to battle. ⁸When David heard of it, he sent Joab and all the army of the mighty men. ⁹And the Ammonites came out and drew up in battle array at the entrance of the city, and the kings who had come were by themselves in the open country.

AMMONITES AND SYRIANS DEFEATED

¹⁰When Joab saw that the battle was set against him both in front and in the rear, he chose some of the best men of Israel and arrayed them against the Syrians. ¹¹The rest of his men he put in the charge of Abishai his brother, and they were arrayed against the Ammonites. ¹²And he said, "If the Syrians are too strong for me, then you shall help me, but if the Ammonites are too strong for you, then I will help you. ¹³Be strong, and let us use our strength for our people and for the cities of our God, and may the LORD do what seems good to him." ¹⁴So Joab and the people who were with him drew near before the Syrians for battle, and they fled before him. ¹⁵And when the Ammonites saw that the Syrians fled, they likewise fled before Abishai, Joab's brother, and entered the city. Then Joab came to Jerusalem.

---

[a]Hebrew *hand* [b]Septuagint, Vulgate, 2 Samuel 8:6 (compare Syriac); Hebrew lacks *garrisons* [c]Hebrew *the LORD saved David*; also verse 13 [d]A *talent* was about 75 pounds or 34 kilograms

¹⁶But when the Syrians saw that they had been defeated by Israel, they sent messengers and brought out the Syrians who were beyond the Euphrates,ᵃ with Shophach the commander of the army of Hadadezer at their head. ¹⁷And when it was told to David, he gathered all Israel together and crossed the Jordan and came to them and drew up his forces against them. And when David set the battle in array against the Syrians, they fought with him. ¹⁸And the Syrians fled before Israel, and David killed of the Syrians the men of 7,000 chariots and 40,000 foot soldiers, and put to death also Shophach the commander of their army. ¹⁹And when the servants of Hadadezer saw that they had been defeated by Israel, they made peace with David and became subject to him. So the Syrians were not willing to save the Ammonites any more.

THE CAPTURE OF RABBAH

20 In the spring of the year, the time when kings go out to battle, Joab led out the army and ravaged the country of the Ammonites and came and besieged Rabbah. But David remained at Jerusalem. And Joab struck down Rabbah and overthrew it. ²And David took the crown of their king from his head. He found that it weighed a talentᵇ of gold, and in it was a precious stone. And it was placed on David's head. And he brought out the spoil of the city, a very great amount. ³And he brought out the people who were in it and set them to labourᶜ with saws and iron picks and axes.ᵈ And thus David did to all the cities of the Ammonites. Then David and all the people returned to Jerusalem.

PHILISTINE GIANTS KILLED

⁴And after this there arose war with the Philistines at Gezer. Then Sibbecai the Hushathite struck down Sippai, who was one of the descendants of the giants, and the Philistines were subdued. ⁵And there was again war with the Philistines, and Elhanan the son of Jair struck down Lahmi the brother of Goliath the Gittite, the shaft of whose spear was like a weaver's beam. ⁶And there was again war at Gath, where there was a man of great stature, who had six fingers on each hand and six toes on each foot, twenty-four in number, and he also was descended from the giants. ⁷And when he taunted Israel, Jonathan the son of Shimea, David's brother, struck him down. ⁸These were descended from the giants in Gath, and they fell by the hand of David and by the hand of his servants.

DAVID'S CENSUS BRINGS PESTILENCE

21 Then Satan stood against Israel and incited David to number Israel. ²So David said to Joab and the commanders of the army, "Go, number Israel, from Beersheba to Dan, and bring me a report, that I may know their number." ³But Joab said, "May the LORD add to his people a hundred times as many as they are! Are they not, my lord the king, all of them my lord's servants? Why then should my lord require this? Why should it be a cause of guilt for Israel?" ⁴But the king's word prevailed against Joab. So Joab departed and went throughout all Israel and came back to Jerusalem. ⁵And Joab gave the sum of the numbering of the people to David. In all Israel there were 1,100,000 men who drew the sword, and in Judah 470,000 who drew the sword. ⁶But he did not include Levi and Benjamin in the numbering, for the king's command was abhorrent to Joab.

⁷But God was displeased with this thing, and he struck Israel. ⁸And David said to God, "I have sinned greatly in that I have done this thing. But now, please take away the iniquity of your servant, for I have acted very foolishly." ⁹And the LORD spoke to Gad, David's seer, saying, ¹⁰"Go and say to David, 'Thus says the LORD, Three things I offer you; choose one of them, that I may do it to you.'" ¹¹So Gad came to David and said to him, "Thus says the LORD, 'Choose what you will: ¹²either three years of famine, or three months of devastation by your foes while the sword of your enemies overtakes you, or else three days of the sword of the LORD, pestilence on the land, with the angel of the LORD destroying throughout all the territory of Israel.' Now decide what answer I shall return to him who sent me." ¹³Then David said to Gad, "I am in great distress. Let me fall into the hand of the LORD, for his mercy is very great, but do not let me fall into the hand of man."

¹⁴So the LORD sent a pestilence on Israel, and 70,000 men of Israel fell. ¹⁵And God sent the angel to Jerusalem to destroy it, but as he was about to destroy it, the LORD saw, and he relented from the calamity. And he said to the angel who was working destruction,

---

ᵃHebrew *the River* ᵇA *talent* was about 75 pounds or 34 kilograms ᶜCompare 2 Samuel 12:31; Hebrew *he sawed* ᵈCompare 2 Samuel 12:31; Hebrew *saws*

"It is enough; now stay your hand." And the angel of the LORD was standing by the threshing floor of Ornan the Jebusite. ¹⁶And David lifted his eyes and saw the angel of the LORD standing between earth and heaven, and in his hand a drawn sword stretched out over Jerusalem. Then David and the elders, clothed in sackcloth, fell upon their faces. ¹⁷And David said to God, "Was it not I who gave command to number the people? It is I who have sinned and done great evil. But these sheep, what have they done? Please let your hand, O LORD my God, be against me and against my father's house. But do not let the plague be on your people."

DAVID BUILDS AN ALTAR

¹⁸Now the angel of the LORD had commanded Gad to say to David that David should go up and raise an altar to the LORD on the threshing floor of Ornan the Jebusite. ¹⁹So David went up at Gad's word, which he had spoken in the name of the LORD. ²⁰Now Ornan was threshing wheat. He turned and saw the angel, and his four sons who were with him hid themselves. ²¹As David came to Ornan, Ornan looked and saw David and went out from the threshing floor and paid homage to David with his face to the ground. ²²And David said to Ornan, "Give me the site of the threshing floor that I may build on it an altar to the LORD—give it to me at its full price—that the plague may be averted from the people." ²³Then Ornan said to David, "Take it, and let my lord the king do what seems good to him. See, I give the oxen for burnt offerings and the threshing sledges for the wood and the wheat for a grain offering; I give it all." ²⁴But King David said to Ornan, "No, but I will buy them for the full price. I will not take for the LORD what is yours, nor offer burnt offerings that cost me nothing." ²⁵So David paid Ornan 600 shekels*ᵃ* of gold by weight for the site. ²⁶And David built there an altar to the LORD and presented burnt offerings and peace offerings and called on the LORD, and the LORD*ᵇ* answered him with fire from heaven upon the altar of burnt offering. ²⁷Then the LORD commanded the angel, and he put his sword back into its sheath.

²⁸At that time, when David saw that the LORD had answered him at the threshing floor of Ornan the Jebusite, he sacrificed there. ²⁹For the tabernacle of the LORD, which Moses had made in the wilderness, and the altar of burnt offering were at that time in the high place at Gibeon, ³⁰but David could not go before it to enquire of God, for he was afraid of the sword of the angel of the LORD.

22 Then David said, "Here shall be the house of the LORD God and here the altar of burnt offering for Israel."

DAVID PREPARES FOR TEMPLE BUILDING

²David commanded to gather together the resident aliens who were in the land of Israel, and he set stonecutters to prepare dressed stones for building the house of God. ³David also provided great quantities of iron for nails for the doors of the gates and for clamps, as well as bronze in quantities beyond weighing, ⁴and cedar timbers without number, for the Sidonians and Tyrians brought great quantities of cedar to David. ⁵For David said, "Solomon my son is young and inexperienced, and the house that is to be built for the LORD must be exceedingly magnificent, of fame and glory throughout all lands. I will therefore make preparation for it." So David provided materials in great quantity before his death.

SOLOMON CHARGED TO BUILD THE TEMPLE

⁶Then he called for Solomon his son and charged him to build a house for the LORD, the God of Israel. ⁷David said to Solomon, "My son, I had it in my heart to build a house to the name of the LORD my God. ⁸But the word of the LORD came to me, saying, 'You have shed much blood and have waged great wars. You shall not build a house to my name, because you have shed so much blood before me on the earth. ⁹Behold, a son shall be born to you who shall be a man of rest. I will give him rest from all his surrounding enemies. For his name shall be Solomon, and I will give peace and quiet to Israel in his days. ¹⁰He shall build a house for my name. He shall be my son, and I will be his father, and I will establish his royal throne in Israel for ever.'

¹¹"Now, my son, the LORD be with you, so that you may succeed in building the house of the LORD your God, as he has spoken concerning you. ¹²Only, may the LORD grant you discretion and understanding, that when he gives you charge over Israel you may keep the law of the LORD your God. ¹³Then you will prosper if you are careful to observe the statutes and the rules that the LORD commanded

---

ᵃA shekel was about 2/5 of an ounce or 11 grams   *ᵇ*Hebrew *he*

Moses for Israel. Be strong and courageous. Fear not; do not be dismayed. **14**With great pains I have provided for the house of the LORD 100,000 talents*a* of gold, a million talents of silver, and bronze and iron beyond weighing, for there is so much of it; timber and stone, too, I have provided. To these you must add. **15**You have an abundance of workmen: stonecutters, masons, carpenters, and all kinds of craftsmen without number, skilled in working **16**gold, silver, bronze, and iron. Arise and work! The LORD be with you!"

17David also commanded all the leaders of Israel to help Solomon his son, saying, **18**"Is not the LORD your God with you? And has he not given you peace*b* on every side? For he has delivered the inhabitants of the land into my hand, and the land is subdued before the LORD and his people. **19**Now set your mind and heart to seek the LORD your God. Arise and build the sanctuary of the LORD God, so that the ark of the covenant of the LORD and the holy vessels of God may be brought into a house built for the name of the LORD."

DAVID ORGANIZES THE LEVITES

23 When David was old and full of days, he made Solomon his son king over Israel. **2**David*c* assembled all the leaders of Israel and the priests and the Levites. **3**The Levites, thirty years old and upwards, were numbered, and the total was 38,000 men. **4**"Twenty-four thousand of these," David said,*d* "shall have charge of the work in the house of the LORD, 6,000 shall be officers and judges, **5**4,000 gatekeepers, and 4,000 shall offer praises to the LORD with the instruments that I have made for praise." **6**And David organized them into divisions corresponding to the sons of Levi: Gershon, Kohath, and Merari.

7The sons of Gershon*e* were Ladan and Shimei. **8**The sons of Ladan: Jehiel the chief, and Zetham, and Joel, three. **9**The sons of Shimei: Shelomoth, Haziel, and Haran, three. These were the heads of the fathers' houses of Ladan. **10**And the sons of Shimei: Jahath, Zina, and Jeush and Beriah. These four were the sons of Shimei. **11**Jahath was the chief, and Zizah the second; but Jeush and Beriah did not have many sons, therefore they became counted as a single father's house.

12The sons of Kohath: Amram, Izhar, Hebron, and Uzziel, four. **13**The sons of Amram: Aaron and Moses. Aaron was set apart to dedicate the most holy things, that he and his sons for ever should make offerings before the LORD and minister to him and pronounce blessings in his name for ever. **14**But the sons of Moses the man of God were named among the tribe of Levi. **15**The sons of Moses: Gershom and Eliezer. **16**The sons of Gershom: Shebuel the chief. **17**The sons of Eliezer: Rehabiah the chief. Eliezer had no other sons, but the sons of Rehabiah were very many. **18**The sons of Izhar: Shelomith the chief. **19**The sons of Hebron: Jeriah the chief, Amariah the second, Jahaziel the third, and Jekameam the fourth. **20**The sons of Uzziel: Micah the chief and Isshiah the second.

21The sons of Merari: Mahli and Mushi. The sons of Mahli: Eleazar and Kish. **22**Eleazar died having no sons, but only daughters; their kinsmen, the sons of Kish, married them. **23**The sons of Mushi: Mahli, Eder, and Jeremoth, three.

24These were the sons of Levi by their fathers' houses, the heads of fathers' houses as they were listed according to the number of the names of the individuals from twenty years old and upwards who were to do the work for the service of the house of the LORD. **25**For David said, "The LORD, the God of Israel, has given rest to his people, and he dwells in Jerusalem for ever. **26**And so the Levites no longer need to carry the tabernacle or any of the things for its service." **27**For by the last words of David the sons of Levi were numbered from twenty years old and upwards. **28**For their duty was to assist the sons of Aaron for the service of the house of the LORD, having the care of the courts and the chambers, the cleansing of all that is holy, and any work for the service of the house of God. **29**Their duty was also to assist with the showbread, the flour for the grain offering, the wafers of unleavened bread, the baked offering, the offering mixed with oil, and all measures of quantity or size. **30**And they were to stand every morning, thanking and praising the LORD, and likewise at evening, **31**and whenever burnt offerings were offered to the LORD on Sabbaths, new moons, and feast days, according to the number required of them, regularly before the LORD. **32**Thus they were to keep charge of the tent of meeting and the sanctuary, and to attend the sons of Aaron, their brothers, for the service of the house of the LORD.

---

*a*A *talent* was about 75 pounds or 34 kilograms *b*Or *rest* (see 22:9) *c*Hebrew *He* *d*Hebrew lacks *David said* *e*Vulgate (compare Septuagint, Syriac); Hebrew *to the Gershonite*

DAVID ORGANIZES THE PRIESTS

24 The divisions of the sons of Aaron were these. The sons of Aaron: Nadab, Abihu, Eleazar, and Ithamar. ²But Nadab and Abihu died before their father and had no children, so Eleazar and Ithamar became the priests. ³With the help of Zadok of the sons of Eleazar, and Ahimelech of the sons of Ithamar, David organized them according to the appointed duties in their service. ⁴Since more chief men were found among the sons of Eleazar than among the sons of Ithamar, they organized them under sixteen heads of fathers' houses of the sons of Eleazar, and eight of the sons of Ithamar. ⁵They divided them by lot, all alike, for there were sacred officers and officers of God among both the sons of Eleazar and the sons of Ithamar. ⁶And the scribe Shemaiah, the son of Nethanel, a Levite, recorded them in the presence of the king and the princes and Zadok the priest and Ahimelech the son of Abiathar and the heads of the fathers' houses of the priests and of the Levites, one father's house being chosen for Eleazar and one chosen for Ithamar.

⁷The first lot fell to Jehoiarib, the second to Jedaiah, ⁸the third to Harim, the fourth to Seorim, ⁹the fifth to Malchijah, the sixth to Mijamin, ¹⁰the seventh to Hakkoz, the eighth to Abijah, ¹¹the ninth to Jeshua, the tenth to Shecaniah, ¹²the eleventh to Eliashib, the twelfth to Jakim, ¹³the thirteenth to Huppah, the fourteenth to Jeshebeab, ¹⁴the fifteenth to Bilgah, the sixteenth to Immer, ¹⁵the seventeenth to Hezir, the eighteenth to Happizzez, ¹⁶the nineteenth to Pethahiah, the twentieth to Jehezkel, ¹⁷the twenty-first to Jachin, the twenty-second to Gamul, ¹⁸the twenty-third to Delaiah, the twenty-fourth to Maaziah. ¹⁹These had as their appointed duty in their service to come into the house of the LORD according to the procedure established for them by Aaron their father, as the LORD God of Israel had commanded him.

²⁰And of the rest of the sons of Levi: of the sons of Amram, Shubael; of the sons of Shubael, Jehdeiah. ²¹Of Rehabiah: of the sons of Rehabiah, Isshiah the chief. ²²Of the Izharites, Shelomoth; of the sons of Shelomoth, Jahath. ²³The sons of Hebron:[a] Jeriah the chief,[b] Amariah the second, Jahaziel the third, Jekameam the fourth. ²⁴The sons of Uzziel, Micah; of the sons of Micah, Shamir. ²⁵The brother of Micah, Isshiah; of the sons of Isshiah, Zechariah. ²⁶The sons of Merari: Mahli and Mushi. The sons of Jaaziah: Beno.[c] ²⁷The sons of Merari: of Jaaziah, Beno, Shoham, Zaccur, and Ibri. ²⁸Of Mahli: Eleazar, who had no sons. ²⁹Of Kish, the sons of Kish: Jerahmeel. ³⁰The sons of Mushi: Mahli, Eder, and Jerimoth. These were the sons of the Levites according to their fathers' houses. ³¹These also, the head of each father's house and his younger brother alike, cast lots, just as their brothers the sons of Aaron, in the presence of King David, Zadok, Ahimelech, and the heads of fathers' houses of the priests and of the Levites.

DAVID ORGANIZES THE MUSICIANS

25 David and the chiefs of the service also set apart for the service the sons of Asaph, and of Heman, and of Jeduthun, who prophesied with lyres, with harps, and with cymbals. The list of those who did the work and of their duties was: ²Of the sons of Asaph: Zaccur, Joseph, Nethaniah, and Asharelah, sons of Asaph, under the direction of Asaph, who prophesied under the direction of the king. ³Of Jeduthun, the sons of Jeduthun: Gedaliah, Zeri, Jeshaiah, Shimei,[d] Hashabiah, and Mattithiah, six, under the direction of their father Jeduthun, who prophesied with the lyre in thanksgiving and praise to the LORD. ⁴Of Heman, the sons of Heman: Bukkiah, Mattaniah, Uzziel, Shebuel and Jerimoth, Hananiah, Hanani, Eliathah, Giddalti and Romamti-ezer, Joshbekashah, Mallothi, Hothir, Mahazioth. ⁵All these were the sons of Heman the king's seer, according to the promise of God to exalt him, for God had given Heman fourteen sons and three daughters. ⁶They were all under the direction of their father in the music in the house of the LORD with cymbals, harps, and lyres for the service of the house of God. Asaph, Jeduthun, and Heman were under the order of the king. ⁷The number of them along with their brothers, who were trained in singing to the LORD, all who were skilful, was 288. ⁸And they cast lots for their duties, small and great, teacher and pupil alike.

⁹The first lot fell for Asaph to Joseph; the second to Gedaliah, to him and his brothers and his sons, twelve; ¹⁰the third to Zaccur, his sons and his brothers, twelve; ¹¹the fourth to Izri, his sons and his brothers, twelve; ¹²the fifth to Nethaniah, his sons and his brothers,

---

[a]Compare 23:19; Hebrew lacks *Hebron* [b]Compare 23:19; Hebrew lacks *the chief* [c]*Or his son*; also verse 27 [d]One Hebrew manuscript, Septuagint; most Hebrew manuscripts lack *Shimei*

twelve; ¹³the sixth to Bukkiah, his sons and his brothers, twelve; ¹⁴the seventh to Jesharelah, his sons and his brothers, twelve; ¹⁵the eighth to Jeshaiah, his sons and his brothers, twelve; ¹⁶the ninth to Mattaniah, his sons and his brothers, twelve; ¹⁷the tenth to Shimei, his sons and his brothers, twelve; ¹⁸the eleventh to Azarel, his sons and his brothers, twelve; ¹⁹the twelfth to Hashabiah, his sons and his brothers, twelve; ²⁰to the thirteenth, Shubael, his sons and his brothers, twelve; ²¹to the fourteenth, Mattithiah, his sons and his brothers, twelve; ²²to the fifteenth, to Jeremoth, his sons and his brothers, twelve; ²³to the sixteenth, to Hananiah, his sons and his brothers, twelve; ²⁴to the seventeenth, to Joshbekashah, his sons and his brothers, twelve; ²⁵to the eighteenth, to Hanani, his sons and his brothers, twelve; ²⁶to the nineteenth, to Mallothi, his sons and his brothers, twelve; ²⁷to the twentieth, to Eliathah, his sons and his brothers, twelve; ²⁸to the twenty-first, to Hothir, his sons and his brothers, twelve; ²⁹to the twenty-second, to Giddalti, his sons and his brothers, twelve; ³⁰to the twenty-third, to Mahazioth, his sons and his brothers, twelve; ³¹to the twenty-fourth, to Romamti-ezer, his sons and his brothers, twelve.

DIVISIONS OF THE GATEKEEPERS

26 As for the divisions of the gatekeepers: of the Korahites, Meshelemiah the son of Kore, of the sons of Asaph. ²And Meshelemiah had sons: Zechariah the firstborn, Jediael the second, Zebadiah the third, Jathniel the fourth, ³Elam the fifth, Jehohanan the sixth, Eliehoenai the seventh. ⁴And Obed-edom had sons: Shemaiah the firstborn, Jehozabad the second, Joah the third, Sachar the fourth, Nethanel the fifth, ⁵Ammiel the sixth, Issachar the seventh, Peullethai the eighth, for God blessed him. ⁶Also to his son Shemaiah were sons born who were rulers in their fathers' houses, for they were men of great ability. ⁷The sons of Shemaiah: Othni, Rephael, Obed and Elzabad, whose brothers were able men, Elihu and Semachiah. ⁸All these were of the sons of Obed-edom with their sons and brothers, able men qualified for the service; sixty-two of Obed-edom. ⁹And Meshelemiah had sons and brothers, able men, eighteen. ¹⁰And Hosah, of the sons of Merari, had sons: Shimri the chief (for though he was not the firstborn, his father made him chief), ¹¹Hilkiah the second, Tebaliah the third, Zechariah the fourth: all the sons and brothers of Hosah were thirteen.

¹²These divisions of the gatekeepers, corresponding to their chief men, had duties, just as their brothers did, ministering in the house of the LORD. ¹³And they cast lots by fathers' houses, small and great alike, for their gates. ¹⁴The lot for the east fell to Shelemiah. They cast lots also for his son Zechariah, a shrewd counsellor, and his lot came out for the north. ¹⁵Obed-edom's came out for the south, and to his sons was allotted the gatehouse. ¹⁶For Shuppim and Hosah it came out for the west, at the gate of Shallecheth on the road that goes up. Watch corresponded to watch. ¹⁷On the east there were six each day,ᵃ on the north four each day, on the south four each day, as well as two and two at the gatehouse. ¹⁸And for the colonnadeᵇ on the west there were four at the road and two at the colonnade. ¹⁹These were the divisions of the gatekeepers among the Korahites and the sons of Merari.

TREASURERS AND OTHER OFFICIALS

²⁰And of the Levites, Ahijah had charge of the treasuries of the house of God and the treasuries of the dedicated gifts. ²¹The sons of Ladan, the sons of the Gershonites belonging to Ladan, the heads of the fathers' houses belonging to Ladan the Gershonite: Jehieli.ᶜ ²²The sons of Jehieli, Zetham, and Joel his brother, were in charge of the treasuries of the house of the LORD. ²³Of the Amramites, the Izharites, the Hebronites, and the Uzzielites— ²⁴and Shebuel the son of Gershom, son of Moses, was chief officer in charge of the treasuries. ²⁵His brothers: from Eliezer were his son Rehabiah, and his son Jeshaiah, and his son Joram, and his son Zichri, and his son Shelomoth. ²⁶This Shelomoth and his brothers were in charge of all the treasuries of the dedicated gifts that David the king and the heads of the fathers' houses and the officers of the thousands and the hundreds and the commanders of the army had dedicated. ²⁷From spoil won in battles they dedicated gifts for the maintenance of the house of the LORD. ²⁸Also all that Samuel the seer and Saul the son of Kish and Abner the son of Ner and Joab the son of Zeruiah had dedicated—all dedicated gifts were in the care of Shelomothᵈ and his brothers.

ᵃSeptuagint; Hebrew *six Levites* ᵇOr *court*; Hebrew *parbar* (meaning unknown); twice in this verse ᶜThe Hebrew of verse 21 is uncertain ᵈHebrew *Shelomith*

²⁹Of the Izharites, Chenaniah and his sons were appointed to external duties for Israel, as officers and judges. ³⁰Of the Hebronites, Hashabiah and his brothers, 1,700 men of ability, had the oversight of Israel westwards of the Jordan for all the work of the LORD and for the service of the king. ³¹Of the Hebronites, Jerijah was chief of the Hebronites of whatever genealogy or fathers' houses. (In the fortieth year of David's reign search was made and men of great ability among them were found at Jazer in Gilead.) ³²King David appointed him and his brothers, 2,700 men of ability, heads of fathers' houses, to have the oversight of the Reubenites, the Gadites and the half-tribe of the Manassites for everything pertaining to God and for the affairs of the king.

MILITARY DIVISIONS

27 This is the number of the people of Israel, the heads of fathers' houses, the commanders of thousands and hundreds, and their officers who served the king in all matters concerning the divisions that came and went, month after month throughout the year, each division numbering 24,000: ²Jashobeam the son of Zabdiel was in charge of the first division in the first month; in his division were 24,000. ³He was a descendant of Perez and was chief of all the commanders. He served for the first month. ⁴Dodai the Ahohite[a] was in charge of the division of the second month; in his division were 24,000. ⁵The third commander, for the third month, was Benaiah, the son of Jehoiada the chief priest; in his division were 24,000. ⁶This is the Benaiah who was a mighty man of the thirty and in command of the thirty; Ammizabad his son was in charge of his division.[b] ⁷Asahel the brother of Joab was fourth, for the fourth month, and his son Zebadiah after him; in his division were 24,000. ⁸The fifth commander, for the fifth month, was Shamhuth the Izrahite; in his division were 24,000. ⁹Sixth, for the sixth month, was Ira, the son of Ikkesh the Tekoite; in his division were 24,000. ¹⁰Seventh, for the seventh month, was Helez the Pelonite, of the sons of Ephraim; in his division were 24,000. ¹¹Eighth, for the eighth month, was Sibbecai the Hushathite, of the Zerahites; in his division were 24,000. ¹²Ninth, for the ninth month, was Abiezer of Anathoth, a Benjaminite; in his division were 24,000. ¹³Tenth, for the tenth month, was Maharai of Netophah, of the Zerahites; in his division were 24,000. ¹⁴Eleventh, for the eleventh month, was Benaiah of Pirathon, of the sons of Ephraim; in his division were 24,000. ¹⁵Twelfth, for the twelfth month, was Heldai the Netophathite, of Othniel; in his division were 24,000.

LEADERS OF TRIBES

¹⁶Over the tribes of Israel, for the Reubenites, Eliezer the son of Zichri was chief officer; for the Simeonites, Shephatiah the son of Maacah; ¹⁷for Levi, Hashabiah the son of Kemuel; for Aaron, Zadok; ¹⁸for Judah, Elihu, one of David's brothers; for Issachar, Omri the son of Michael; ¹⁹for Zebulun, Ishmaiah the son of Obadiah; for Naphtali, Jeremoth the son of Azriel; ²⁰for the Ephraimites, Hoshea the son of Azaziah; for the half-tribe of Manasseh, Joel the son of Pedaiah; ²¹for the half-tribe of Manasseh in Gilead, Iddo the son of Zechariah; for Benjamin, Jaasiel the son of Abner; ²²for Dan, Azarel the son of Jeroham. These were the leaders of the tribes of Israel. ²³David did not count those below twenty years of age, for the LORD had promised to make Israel as many as the stars of heaven. ²⁴Joab the son of Zeruiah began to count, but did not finish. Yet wrath came upon Israel for this, and the number was not entered in the chronicles of King David.

²⁵Over the king's treasuries was Azmaveth the son of Adiel; and over the treasuries in the country, in the cities, in the villages, and in the towers, was Jonathan the son of Uzziah; ²⁶and over those who did the work of the field for tilling the soil was Ezri the son of Chelub; ²⁷and over the vineyards was Shimei the Ramathite; and over the produce of the vineyards for the wine cellars was Zabdi the Shiphmite. ²⁸Over the olive and sycamore trees in the Shephelah was Baal-hanan the Gederite; and over the stores of oil was Joash. ²⁹Over the herds that pastured in Sharon was Shitrai the Sharonite; over the herds in the valleys was Shaphat the son of Adlai. ³⁰Over the camels was Obil the Ishmaelite; and over the donkeys was Jehdeiah the Meronothite. Over the flocks was Jaziz the Hagrite. ³¹All these were stewards of King David's property.

³²Jonathan, David's uncle, was a counsellor, being a man of understanding and a scribe. He and Jehiel the son of Hachmoni attended the king's sons. ³³Ahithophel was the king's counsellor, and Hushai the Archite was the

---
[a]Septuagint; Hebrew *Ahohite and his division and Mikloth the chief officer* [b]Septuagint, Vulgate; Hebrew *was his division*

king's friend. ³⁴Ahithophel was succeeded by Jehoiada the son of Benaiah, and Abiathar. Joab was commander of the king's army.

DAVID'S CHARGE TO ISRAEL

28 David assembled at Jerusalem all the officials of Israel, the officials of the tribes, the officers of the divisions that served the king, the commanders of thousands, the commanders of hundreds, the stewards of all the property and livestock of the king and his sons, together with the palace officials, the mighty men and all the seasoned warriors. ²Then King David rose to his feet and said: "Hear me, my brothers and my people. I had it in my heart to build a house of rest for the ark of the covenant of the LORD and for the footstool of our God, and I made preparations for building. ³But God said to me, 'You may not build a house for my name, for you are a man of war and have shed blood.' ⁴Yet the LORD God of Israel chose me from all my father's house to be king over Israel for ever. For he chose Judah as leader, and in the house of Judah my father's house, and among my father's sons he took pleasure in me to make me king over all Israel. ⁵And of all my sons (for the LORD has given me many sons) he has chosen Solomon my son to sit on the throne of the kingdom of the LORD over Israel. ⁶He said to me, 'It is Solomon your son who shall build my house and my courts, for I have chosen him to be my son, and I will be his father. ⁷I will establish his kingdom for ever if he continues strong in keeping my commandments and my rules, as he is today.' ⁸Now therefore in the sight of all Israel, the assembly of the LORD, and in the hearing of our God, observe and seek out all the commandments of the LORD your God, that you may possess this good land and leave it for an inheritance to your children after you for ever.

DAVID'S CHARGE TO SOLOMON

⁹"And you, Solomon my son, know the God of your father and serve him with a whole heart and with a willing mind, for the LORD searches all hearts and understands every plan and thought. If you seek him, he will be found by you, but if you forsake him, he will cast you off for ever. ¹⁰Be careful now, for the LORD has chosen you to build a house for the sanctuary; be strong and do it."

¹¹Then David gave Solomon his son the plan of the vestibule of the temple,ᵃ and of its houses, its treasuries, its upper rooms, and its inner chambers, and of the room for the mercy seat; ¹²and the plan of all that he had in mind for the courts of the house of the LORD, all the surrounding chambers, the treasuries of the house of God, and the treasuries for dedicated gifts; ¹³for the divisions of the priests and of the Levites, and all the work of the service in the house of the LORD; for all the vessels for the service in the house of the LORD, ¹⁴the weight of gold for all golden vessels for each service, the weight of silver vessels for each service, ¹⁵the weight of the golden lampstands and their lamps, the weight of gold for each lampstand and its lamps, the weight of silver for a lampstand and its lamps, according to the use of each lampstand in the service, ¹⁶the weight of gold for each table for the showbread, the silver for the silver tables, ¹⁷and pure gold for the forks, the basins and the cups; for the golden bowls and the weight of each; for the silver bowls and the weight of each; ¹⁸for the altar of incense made of refined gold, and its weight; also his plan for the golden chariot of the cherubim that spread their wings and covered the ark of the covenant of the LORD. ¹⁹"All this he made clear to me in writing from the hand of the LORD, all the work to be done according to the plan."

²⁰Then David said to Solomon his son, "Be strong and courageous and do it. Do not be afraid and do not be dismayed, for the LORD God, even my God, is with you. He will not leave you or forsake you, until all the work for the service of the house of the LORD is finished. ²¹And behold the divisions of the priests and the Levites for all the service of the house of God; and with you in all the work will be every willing man who has skill for any kind of service; also the officers and all the people will be wholly at your command."

OFFERINGS FOR THE TEMPLE

29 And David the king said to all the assembly, "Solomon my son, whom alone God has chosen, is young and inexperienced, and the work is great, for the palace will not be for man but for the LORD God. ²So I have provided for the house of my God, so far as I was able, the gold for the things of gold, the silver for the things of silver, and the bronze for the things of bronze, the iron for the things of iron, and wood for the things of wood, besides great quantities of onyx and stones for setting,

---

ᵃHebrew lacks *of the temple*

antimony, coloured stones, all sorts of precious stones and marble. ³Moreover, in addition to all that I have provided for the holy house, I have a treasure of my own of gold and silver, and because of my devotion to the house of my God I give it to the house of my God: ⁴3,000 talents[a] of gold, of the gold of Ophir, and 7,000 talents of refined silver, for overlaying the walls of the house,[b] ⁵and for all the work to be done by craftsmen, gold for the things of gold and silver for the things of silver. Who then will offer willingly, consecrating himself[c] today to the LORD?"

⁶Then the leaders of fathers' houses made their freewill offerings, as did also the leaders of the tribes, the commanders of thousands and of hundreds, and the officers over the king's work. ⁷They gave for the service of the house of God 5,000 talents and 10,000 darics[d] of gold, 10,000 talents of silver, 18,000 talents of bronze and 100,000 talents of iron. ⁸And whoever had precious stones gave them to the treasury of the house of the LORD, in the care of Jehiel the Gershonite. ⁹Then the people rejoiced because they had given willingly, for with a whole heart they had offered freely to the LORD. David the king also rejoiced greatly.

DAVID PRAYS IN THE ASSEMBLY

¹⁰Therefore David blessed the LORD in the presence of all the assembly. And David said: "Blessed are you, O LORD, the God of Israel our father, for ever and ever. ¹¹Yours, O LORD, is the greatness and the power and the glory and the victory and the majesty, for all that is in the heavens and in the earth is yours. Yours is the kingdom, O LORD, and you are exalted as head above all. ¹²Both riches and honour come from you, and you rule over all. In your hand are power and might, and in your hand it is to make great and to give strength to all. ¹³And now we thank you, our God, and praise your glorious name.

¹⁴"But who am I, and what is my people, that we should be able thus to offer willingly? For all things come from you, and of your own have we given you. ¹⁵For we are strangers before you and sojourners, as all our fathers were. Our days on the earth are like a shadow, and there is no abiding.[e] ¹⁶O LORD our God, all this abundance that we have provided for building you a house for your holy name comes from your hand and is all your own. ¹⁷I know, my God, that you test the heart and have pleasure in uprightness. In the uprightness of my heart I have freely offered all these things, and now I have seen your people, who are present here, offering freely and joyously to you. ¹⁸O LORD, the God of Abraham, Isaac, and Israel, our fathers, keep for ever such purposes and thoughts in the hearts of your people, and direct their hearts towards you. ¹⁹Grant to Solomon my son a whole heart that he may keep your commandments, your testimonies, and your statutes, performing all, and that he may build the palace for which I have made provision."

²⁰Then David said to all the assembly, "Bless the LORD your God." And all the assembly blessed the LORD, the God of their fathers, and bowed their heads and paid homage to the LORD and to the king. ²¹And they offered sacrifices to the LORD, and on the next day offered burnt offerings to the LORD, 1,000 bulls, 1,000 rams, and 1,000 lambs, with their drink offerings, and sacrifices in abundance for all Israel. ²²And they ate and drank before the LORD on that day with great gladness.

SOLOMON ANOINTED KING

And they made Solomon the son of David king the second time, and they anointed him as prince for the LORD, and Zadok as priest.

²³Then Solomon sat on the throne of the LORD as king in place of David his father. And he prospered, and all Israel obeyed him. ²⁴All the leaders and the mighty men, and also all the sons of King David, pledged their allegiance to King Solomon. ²⁵And the LORD made Solomon very great in the sight of all Israel and bestowed on him such royal majesty as had not been on any king before him in Israel.

THE DEATH OF DAVID

²⁶Thus David the son of Jesse reigned over all Israel. ²⁷The time that he reigned over Israel was forty years. He reigned for seven years in Hebron and thirty-three years in Jerusalem. ²⁸Then he died at a good age, full of days, riches, and honour. And Solomon his son reigned in his place. ²⁹Now the acts of King David, from first to last, are written in the Chronicles of Samuel the seer, and in the Chronicles of Nathan the prophet, and in the Chronicles of Gad the seer, ³⁰with accounts of all his rule and his might and of the circumstances that came upon him and upon Israel and upon all the kingdoms of the countries.

---

[a] A *talent* was about 75 pounds or 34 kilograms [b] Septuagint; Hebrew *houses* [c] Or *ordaining himself*; Hebrew *filling his hand*
[d] A *daric* was a coin weighing about 1/4 of an ounce or 8.5 grams
[e] Septuagint, Vulgate; Hebrew *hope*, or *prospect*

2 CHRONICLES

SOLOMON WORSHIPS AT GIBEON

1 Solomon the son of David established himself in his kingdom, and the LORD his God was with him and made him exceedingly great. ²Solomon spoke to all Israel, to the commanders of thousands and of hundreds, to the judges, and to all the leaders in all Israel, the heads of fathers' houses. ³And Solomon, and all the assembly with him, went to the high place that was at Gibeon, for the tent of meeting of God, which Moses the servant of the LORD had made in the wilderness, was there. ⁴(But David had brought up the ark of God from Kiriath-jearim to the place that David had prepared for it, for he had pitched a tent for it in Jerusalem.) ⁵Moreover, the bronze altar that Bezalel the son of Uri, son of Hur, had made, was there before the tabernacle of the LORD. And Solomon and the assembly sought it[a] out. ⁶And Solomon went up there to the bronze altar before the LORD, which was at the tent of meeting, and offered a thousand burnt offerings on it.

SOLOMON PRAYS FOR WISDOM

⁷In that night God appeared to Solomon, and said to him, "Ask what I shall give you." ⁸And Solomon said to God, "You have shown great and steadfast love to David my father, and have made me king in his place. ⁹O LORD God, let your word to David my father be now fulfilled, for you have made me king over a people as numerous as the dust of the earth. ¹⁰Give me now wisdom and knowledge to go out and come in before this people, for who can govern this people of yours, which is so great?" ¹¹God answered Solomon, "Because this was in your heart, and you have not asked for possessions, wealth, honour, or the life of those who hate you, and have not even asked for long life, but have asked for wisdom and knowledge for yourself that you may govern my people over whom I have made you king, ¹²wisdom and knowledge are granted to you. I will also give you riches, possessions, and honour, such as none of the kings had who were before you, and none after you shall have the like." ¹³So Solomon came from[b] the high place at Gibeon, from before the tent of meeting, to Jerusalem. And he reigned over Israel.

SOLOMON GIVEN WEALTH

¹⁴Solomon gathered together chariots and horsemen. He had 1,400 chariots and 12,000 horsemen, whom he stationed in the chariot cities and with the king in Jerusalem. ¹⁵And the king made silver and gold as common in Jerusalem as stone, and he made cedar as plentiful as the sycamore of the Shephelah. ¹⁶And Solomon's import of horses was from Egypt and Kue, and the king's traders would buy them from Kue for a price. ¹⁷They imported a chariot from Egypt for 600 shekels[c] of silver, and a horse for 150. Likewise through them these were exported to all the kings of the Hittites and the kings of Syria.

PREPARING TO BUILD THE TEMPLE

2[d] Now Solomon purposed to build a temple for the name of the LORD, and a royal palace for himself. ²[e] And Solomon assigned 70,000 men to bear burdens and 80,000 to quarry in the hill country, and 3,600 to oversee them. ³And Solomon sent word to Hiram the king of Tyre: "As you dealt with David my father and sent him cedar to build himself a house to dwell in, so deal with me. ⁴Behold, I am about to build a house for the name of the LORD my God and dedicate it to him for the burning of incense of sweet spices before him, and for the regular arrangement of the showbread, and for burnt offerings morning and evening, on the Sabbaths and the new moons and the appointed feasts of the LORD our God, as ordained for ever for Israel. ⁵The house that I am to build will be great, for our God is greater than all gods. ⁶But who is able to build him a house, since heaven, even highest heaven, cannot contain him? Who am I to build a house for him, except as a place to make offerings before

---

[a] Or *him* [b] Septuagint, Vulgate; Hebrew *to* [c] A *shekel* was about 2/5 of an ounce or 11 grams [d] Ch 1:18 in Hebrew [e] Ch 2:1 in Hebrew

him? ⁷So now send me a man skilled to work in gold, silver, bronze, and iron, and in purple, crimson, and blue fabrics, trained also in engraving, to be with the skilled workers who are with me in Judah and Jerusalem, whom David my father provided. ⁸Send me also cedar, cypress, and algum timber from Lebanon, for I know that your servants know how to cut timber in Lebanon. And my servants will be with your servants, ⁹to prepare timber for me in abundance, for the house I am to build will be great and wonderful. ¹⁰I will give for your servants, the woodsmen who cut timber, 20,000 cors[a] of crushed wheat, 20,000 cors of barley, 20,000 baths[b] of wine, and 20,000 baths of oil."

¹¹Then Hiram the king of Tyre answered in a letter that he sent to Solomon, "Because the LORD loves his people, he has made you king over them." ¹²Hiram also said, "Blessed be the LORD God of Israel, who made heaven and earth, who has given King David a wise son, who has discretion and understanding, who will build a temple for the LORD and a royal palace for himself.

¹³"Now I have sent a skilled man, who has understanding, Huram-abi, ¹⁴the son of a woman of the daughters of Dan, and his father was a man of Tyre. He is trained to work in gold, silver, bronze, iron, stone, and wood, and in purple, blue, and crimson fabrics and fine linen, and to do all sorts of engraving and execute any design that may be assigned him, with your craftsmen, the craftsmen of my lord, David your father. ¹⁵Now therefore the wheat and barley, oil and wine, of which my lord has spoken, let him send to his servants. ¹⁶And we will cut whatever timber you need from Lebanon and bring it to you in rafts by sea to Joppa, so that you may take it up to Jerusalem."

¹⁷Then Solomon counted all the resident aliens who were in the land of Israel, after the census of them that David his father had taken, and there were found to be 153,600. ¹⁸Seventy thousand of them he assigned to bear burdens, 80,000 to quarry in the hill country, and 3,600 as overseers to make the people work.

SOLOMON BUILDS THE TEMPLE

3 Then Solomon began to build the house of the LORD in Jerusalem on Mount Moriah, where the LORD[c] had appeared to David his father, at the place that David had appointed, on the threshing floor of Ornan the Jebusite. ²He began to build in the second month of the fourth year of his reign. ³These are Solomon's measurements[d] for building the house of God: the length, in cubits[e] of the old standard, was sixty cubits, and the breadth twenty cubits. ⁴The vestibule in front of the nave of the house was twenty cubits long, equal to the width of the house,[f] and its height was 120 cubits. He overlaid it on the inside with pure gold. ⁵The nave he lined with cypress and covered it with fine gold and made palms and chains on it. ⁶He adorned the house with settings of precious stones. The gold was gold of Parvaim. ⁷So he lined the house with gold — its beams, its thresholds, its walls, and its doors — and he carved cherubim on the walls.

⁸And he made the Most Holy Place. Its length, corresponding to the breadth of the house, was twenty cubits, and its breadth was twenty cubits. He overlaid it with 600 talents[g] of fine gold. ⁹The weight of gold for the nails was fifty shekels.[h] And he overlaid the upper chambers with gold.

¹⁰In the Most Holy Place he made two cherubim of wood[i] and overlaid[j] them with gold. ¹¹The wings of the cherubim together extended twenty cubits: one wing of one, of five cubits, touched the wall of the house, and its other wing, of five cubits, touched the wing of the other cherub; ¹²and of this cherub, one wing, of five cubits, touched the wall of the house, and the other wing, also of five cubits, was joined to the wing of the first cherub. ¹³The wings of these cherubim extended twenty cubits. The cherubim[k] stood on their feet, facing the nave. ¹⁴And he made the veil of blue and purple and crimson fabrics and fine linen, and he worked cherubim on it.

¹⁵In front of the house he made two pillars thirty-five cubits high, with a capital of five cubits on the top of each. ¹⁶He made chains like a necklace[l] and put them on the tops of the pillars, and he made a hundred pomegranates and put them on the chains. ¹⁷He set up the pillars in front of the temple, one on the south, the other on the north; the one on the south he called Jachin, and the one on the north Boaz.

---

[a] A *cor* was about 6 bushels or 220 litres [b] A *bath* was about 6 gallons or 22 litres [c] Septuagint; Hebrew lacks *the LORD* [d] Syriac; Hebrew *foundations* [e] A *cubit* was about 18 inches or 45 centimetres [f] Compare 1 Kings 6:3; the meaning of the Hebrew is uncertain [g] A *talent* was about 75 pounds or 34 kilograms [h] A *shekel* was about 2/5 of an ounce or 11 grams [i] Septuagint; the meaning of the Hebrew is uncertain [j] Hebrew *they overlaid* [k] Hebrew *they* [l] Hebrew *chains in the inner sanctuary*

THE TEMPLE'S FURNISHINGS

4 He made an altar of bronze, twenty cubits[a] long and twenty cubits wide and ten cubits high. ²Then he made the sea of cast metal. It was round, ten cubits from brim to brim, and five cubits high, and a line of thirty cubits measured its circumference. ³Under it were figures of gourds,[b] for ten cubits, compassing the sea all round. The gourds were in two rows, cast with it when it was cast. ⁴It stood on twelve oxen, three facing north, three facing west, three facing south, and three facing east. The sea was set on them, and all their rear parts were inward. ⁵Its thickness was a handbreadth.[c] And its brim was made like the brim of a cup, like the flower of a lily. It held 3,000 baths.[d] ⁶He also made ten basins in which to wash, and set five on the south side, and five on the north side. In these they were to rinse off what was used for the burnt offering, and the sea was for the priests to wash in.

⁷And he made ten golden lampstands as prescribed, and set them in the temple, five on the south side and five on the north. ⁸He also made ten tables and placed them in the temple, five on the south side and five on the north. And he made a hundred basins of gold. ⁹He made the court of the priests and the great court and doors for the court and overlaid their doors with bronze. ¹⁰And he set the sea at the southeast corner of the house.

¹¹Hiram also made the pots, the shovels, and the basins. So Hiram finished the work that he did for King Solomon on the house of God: ¹²the two pillars, the bowls, and the two capitals on the top of the pillars; and the two latticeworks to cover the two bowls of the capitals that were on the top of the pillars; ¹³and the 400 pomegranates for the two latticeworks, two rows of pomegranates for each latticework, to cover the two bowls of the capitals that were on the pillars. ¹⁴He made the stands also, and the basins on the stands, ¹⁵and the one sea, and the twelve oxen underneath it. ¹⁶The pots, the shovels, the forks, and all the equipment for these Huram-abi made of burnished bronze for King Solomon for the house of the Lord. ¹⁷In the plain of the Jordan the king cast them, in the clay ground between Succoth and Zeredah.[e] ¹⁸Solomon made all these things in great quantities, for the weight of the bronze was not sought.

¹⁹So Solomon made all the vessels that were in the house of God: the golden altar, the tables for the bread of the Presence, ²⁰the lampstands and their lamps of pure gold to burn before the inner sanctuary, as prescribed; ²¹the flowers, the lamps, and the tongs, of purest gold; ²²the snuffers, basins, dishes for incense, and firepans, of pure gold, and the sockets[f] of the temple, for the inner doors to the Most Holy Place and for the doors of the nave of the temple were of gold.

5 Thus all the work that Solomon did for the house of the Lord was finished. And Solomon brought in the things that David his father had dedicated, and stored the silver, the gold, and all the vessels in the treasuries of the house of God.

THE ARK BROUGHT TO THE TEMPLE

²Then Solomon assembled the elders of Israel and all the heads of the tribes, the leaders of the fathers' houses of the people of Israel, in Jerusalem, to bring up the ark of the covenant of the Lord out of the city of David, which is Zion. ³And all the men of Israel assembled before the king at the feast that is in the seventh month. ⁴And all the elders of Israel came, and the Levites took up the ark. ⁵And they brought up the ark, the tent of meeting, and all the holy vessels that were in the tent; the Levitical priests brought them up. ⁶And King Solomon and all the congregation of Israel, who had assembled before him, were before the ark, sacrificing so many sheep and oxen that they could not be counted or numbered. ⁷Then the priests brought the ark of the covenant of the Lord to its place, in the inner sanctuary of the house, in the Most Holy Place, underneath the wings of the cherubim. ⁸The cherubim spread out their wings over the place of the ark, so that the cherubim made a covering above the ark and its poles. ⁹And the poles were so long that the ends of the poles were seen from the Holy Place before the inner sanctuary, but they could not be seen from outside. And they are[g] there to this day. ¹⁰There was nothing in the ark except the two tablets that Moses put there at Horeb, where the Lord made a covenant with the people of Israel, when they came out of Egypt. ¹¹And when the priests came out of the Holy Place (for all the priests who were present had

---

[a] A *cubit* was about 18 inches or 45 centimetres   [b] Compare 1 Kings 7:24; Hebrew *oxen*; twice in this verse   [c] A *handbreadth* was about 3 inches or 7.5 centimetres   [d] A *bath* was about 6 gallons or 22 litres   [e] Spelled *Zarethan* in 1 Kings 7:46   [f] Compare 1 Kings 7:50; Hebrew *the entrance of the house*   [g] Hebrew *it is*

consecrated themselves, without regard to their divisions, ¹²and all the Levitical singers, Asaph, Heman, and Jeduthun, their sons and kinsmen, arrayed in fine linen, with cymbals, harps, and lyres, stood east of the altar with 120 priests who were trumpeters; ¹³and it was the duty of the trumpeters and singers to make themselves heard in unison in praise and thanksgiving to the LORD), and when the song was raised, with trumpets and cymbals and other musical instruments, in praise to the LORD,

"For he is good,
for his steadfast love
endures for ever,"

the house, the house of the LORD, was filled with a cloud, ¹⁴so that the priests could not stand to minister because of the cloud, for the glory of the LORD filled the house of God.

SOLOMON BLESSES THE PEOPLE

6 Then Solomon said, "The LORD has said that he would dwell in thick darkness. ²But I have built you an exalted house, a place for you to dwell in for ever." ³Then the king turned round and blessed all the assembly of Israel, while all the assembly of Israel stood. ⁴And he said, "Blessed be the LORD, the God of Israel, who with his hand has fulfilled what he promised with his mouth to David my father, saying, ⁵'Since the day that I brought my people out of the land of Egypt, I chose no city out of all the tribes of Israel in which to build a house, that my name might be there, and I chose no man as prince over my people Israel; ⁶but I have chosen Jerusalem that my name may be there, and I have chosen David to be over my people Israel.' ⁷Now it was in the heart of David my father to build a house for the name of the LORD, the God of Israel. ⁸But the LORD said to David my father, 'Whereas it was in your heart to build a house for my name, you did well that it was in your heart. ⁹Nevertheless, it is not you who shall build the house, but your son who shall be born to you shall build the house for my name.' ¹⁰Now the LORD has fulfilled his promise that he made. For I have risen in the place of David my father and sit on the throne of Israel, as the LORD promised, and I have built the house for the name of the LORD, the God of Israel. ¹¹And there I have set the ark, in which is the covenant of the LORD that he made with the people of Israel."

SOLOMON'S PRAYER OF DEDICATION

¹²Then Solomon stood before the altar of the LORD in the presence of all the assembly of Israel and spread out his hands. ¹³Solomon had made a bronze platform five cubits^a long, five cubits wide, and three cubits high, and had set it in the court, and he stood on it. Then he knelt on his knees in the presence of all the assembly of Israel, and spread out his hands towards heaven, ¹⁴and said, "O LORD, God of Israel, there is no God like you, in heaven or on earth, keeping covenant and showing steadfast love to your servants who walk before you with all their heart, ¹⁵who have kept with your servant David my father what you declared to him. You spoke with your mouth, and with your hand have fulfilled it this day. ¹⁶Now therefore, O LORD, God of Israel, keep for your servant David my father what you have promised him, saying, 'You shall not lack a man to sit before me on the throne of Israel, if only your sons pay close attention to their way, to walk in my law as you have walked before me.' ¹⁷Now therefore, O LORD, God of Israel, let your word be confirmed, which you have spoken to your servant David.

¹⁸"But will God indeed dwell with man on the earth? Behold, heaven and the highest heaven cannot contain you, how much less this house that I have built! ¹⁹Yet have regard to the prayer of your servant and to his plea, O LORD my God, listening to the cry and to the prayer that your servant prays before you, ²⁰that your eyes may be open day and night towards this house, the place where you have promised to set your name, that you may listen to the prayer that your servant offers towards this place. ²¹And listen to the pleas of your servant and of your people Israel, when they pray towards this place. And listen from heaven your dwelling place, and when you hear, forgive.

²²"If a man sins against his neighbour and is made to take an oath and comes and swears his oath before your altar in this house, ²³then hear from heaven and act and judge your servants, repaying the guilty by bringing his conduct on his own head, and vindicating the righteous by rewarding him according to his righteousness.

²⁴"If your people Israel are defeated before the enemy because they have sinned against you, and they turn again and acknowledge

---

^{a}A *cubit* was about 18 inches or 45 centimetres

your name and pray and plead with you in this house, ²⁵then hear from heaven and forgive the sin of your people Israel and bring them again to the land, which you gave to them and to their fathers.

²⁶"When heaven is shut up and there is no rain because they have sinned against you, if they pray towards this place and acknowledge your name and turn from their sin, when you afflict[a] them, ²⁷then hear in heaven and forgive the sin of your servants, your people Israel, when you teach them the good way[b] in which they should walk, and grant rain upon your land, which you have given to your people as an inheritance.

²⁸"If there is famine in the land, if there is pestilence or blight or mildew or locust or caterpillar, if their enemies besiege them in the land at their gates, whatever plague, whatever sickness there is, ²⁹whatever prayer, whatever plea is made by any man or by all your people Israel, each knowing his own affliction and his own sorrow and stretching out his hands towards this house, ³⁰then hear from heaven your dwelling place and forgive and render to each whose heart you know, according to all his ways, for you, you only, know the hearts of the children of mankind, ³¹that they may fear you and walk in your ways all the days that they live in the land that you gave to our fathers.

³²"Likewise, when a foreigner, who is not of your people Israel, comes from a far country for the sake of your great name and your mighty hand and your outstretched arm, when he comes and prays towards this house, ³³hear from heaven your dwelling place and do according to all for which the foreigner calls to you, in order that all the peoples of the earth may know your name and fear you, as do your people Israel, and that they may know that this house that I have built is called by your name.

³⁴"If your people go out to battle against their enemies, by whatever way you shall send them, and they pray to you towards this city that you have chosen and the house that I have built for your name, ³⁵then hear from heaven their prayer and their plea, and maintain their cause.

³⁶"If they sin against you—for there is no one who does not sin—and you are angry with them and give them to an enemy, so that they are carried away captive to a land far or near, ³⁷yet if they turn their heart in the land to which they have been carried captive, and repent and plead with you in the land of their captivity, saying, 'We have sinned and have acted perversely and wickedly', ³⁸if they repent with all their heart and with all their soul in the land of their captivity to which they were carried captive, and pray towards their land, which you gave to their fathers, the city that you have chosen and the house that I have built for your name, ³⁹then hear from heaven your dwelling place their prayer and their pleas, and maintain their cause and forgive your people who have sinned against you. ⁴⁰Now, O my God, let your eyes be open and your ears attentive to the prayer of this place.

⁴¹ "And now arise, O LORD God, and
go to your resting-place,
you and the ark of your might.
Let your priests, O LORD God, be
clothed with salvation,
and let your saints rejoice
in your goodness.
⁴² O LORD God, do not turn away the
face of your anointed one!
Remember your steadfast love
for David your servant."

FIRE FROM HEAVEN

7 As soon as Solomon finished his prayer, fire came down from heaven and consumed the burnt offering and the sacrifices, and the glory of the LORD filled the temple. ²And the priests could not enter the house of the LORD, because the glory of the LORD filled the LORD's house. ³When all the people of Israel saw the fire come down and the glory of the LORD on the temple, they bowed down with their faces to the ground on the pavement and worshipped and gave thanks to the LORD, saying, "For he is good, for his steadfast love endures for ever."

THE DEDICATION OF THE TEMPLE

⁴Then the king and all the people offered sacrifice before the LORD. ⁵King Solomon offered as a sacrifice 22,000 oxen and 120,000 sheep. So the king and all the people dedicated the house of God. ⁶The priests stood at their posts; the Levites also, with the instruments for music to the LORD that King David had made for giving thanks to the LORD—for his steadfast love endures for

---

[a]Septuagint, Vulgate; Hebrew *answer* [b]Septuagint, Syriac, Vulgate (compare 1 Kings 8:36); Hebrew *towards the good way*

ever—whenever David offered praises by their ministry;[a] opposite them the priests sounded trumpets, and all Israel stood.

⁷And Solomon consecrated the middle of the court that was before the house of the LORD, for there he offered the burnt offering and the fat of the peace offerings, because the bronze altar Solomon had made could not hold the burnt offering and the grain offering and the fat.

⁸At that time Solomon held the feast for seven days, and all Israel with him, a very great assembly, from Lebo-hamath to the Brook of Egypt. ⁹And on the eighth day they held a solemn assembly, for they had kept the dedication of the altar seven days and the feast seven days. ¹⁰On the twenty-third day of the seventh month he sent the people away to their homes, joyful and glad of heart for the prosperity[b] that the LORD had granted to David and to Solomon and to Israel his people.

IF MY PEOPLE PRAY

¹¹Thus Solomon finished the house of the LORD and the king's house. All that Solomon had planned to do in the house of the LORD and in his own house he successfully accomplished. ¹²Then the LORD appeared to Solomon in the night and said to him: "I have heard your prayer and have chosen this place for myself as a house of sacrifice. ¹³When I shut up the heavens so that there is no rain, or command the locust to devour the land, or send pestilence among my people, ¹⁴if my people who are called by my name humble themselves, and pray and seek my face and turn from their wicked ways, then I will hear from heaven and will forgive their sin and heal their land. ¹⁵Now my eyes will be open and my ears attentive to the prayer that is made in this place. ¹⁶For now I have chosen and consecrated this house that my name may be there for ever. My eyes and my heart will be there for all time. ¹⁷And as for you, if you will walk before me as David your father walked, doing according to all that I have commanded you and keeping my statutes and my rules, ¹⁸then I will establish your royal throne, as I covenanted with David your father, saying, 'You shall not lack a man to rule Israel.'

¹⁹"But if you[c] turn aside and forsake my statutes and my commandments that I have set before you, and go and serve other gods and worship them, ²⁰then I will pluck you[d] up from my land that I have given you, and this house that I have consecrated for my name, I will cast out of my sight, and I will make it a proverb and a byword among all peoples. ²¹And at this house, which was exalted, everyone passing by will be astonished and say, 'Why has the LORD done thus to this land and to this house?' ²²Then they will say, 'Because they abandoned the LORD, the God of their fathers who brought them out of the land of Egypt, and laid hold on other gods and worshipped them and served them. Therefore he has brought all this disaster on them.'"

SOLOMON'S ACCOMPLISHMENTS

8 At the end of twenty years, in which Solomon had built the house of the LORD and his own house, ²Solomon rebuilt the cities that Hiram had given to him, and settled the people of Israel in them.

³And Solomon went to Hamath-zobah and took it. ⁴He built Tadmor in the wilderness and all the store cities that he built in Hamath. ⁵He also built Upper Beth-horon and Lower Beth-horon, fortified cities with walls, gates, and bars, ⁶and Baalath, and all the store cities that Solomon had and all the cities for his chariots and the cities for his horsemen, and whatever Solomon desired to build in Jerusalem, in Lebanon, and in all the land of his dominion. ⁷All the people who were left of the Hittites, the Amorites, the Perizzites, the Hivites, and the Jebusites, who were not of Israel, ⁸from their descendants who were left after them in the land, whom the people of Israel had not destroyed—these Solomon drafted as forced labour, and so they are to this day. ⁹But of the people of Israel Solomon made no slaves for his work; they were soldiers, and his officers, the commanders of his chariots, and his horsemen. ¹⁰And these were the chief officers of King Solomon, 250, who exercised authority over the people.

¹¹Solomon brought Pharaoh's daughter up from the city of David to the house that he had built for her, for he said, "My wife shall not live in the house of David king of Israel, for the places to which the ark of the LORD has come are holy."

¹²Then Solomon offered up burnt offerings to the LORD on the altar of the LORD that he had built before the vestibule, ¹³as the duty of each day required, offering according to the commandment of Moses for the Sabbaths, the new moons, and the three annual feasts—the Feast

---

[a]Hebrew *by their hand* [b]Or *good* [c]The Hebrew for *you* is plural here [d]Hebrew *them*; twice in this verse

of Unleavened Bread, the Feast of Weeks, and the Feast of Booths. **14**According to the ruling of David his father, he appointed the divisions of the priests for their service, and the Levites for their offices of praise and ministry before the priests as the duty of each day required, and the gatekeepers in their divisions at each gate, for so David the man of God had commanded. **15**And they did not turn aside from what the king had commanded the priests and Levites concerning any matter and concerning the treasuries.

16Thus was accomplished all the work of Solomon from[a] the day the foundation of the house of the LORD was laid until it was finished. So the house of the LORD was completed.

17Then Solomon went to Ezion-geber and Eloth on the shore of the sea, in the land of Edom. **18**And Hiram sent to him by the hand of his servants ships and servants familiar with the sea, and they went to Ophir together with the servants of Solomon and brought from there 450 talents[b] of gold and brought it to King Solomon.

THE QUEEN OF SHEBA

9 Now when the queen of Sheba heard of the fame of Solomon, she came to Jerusalem to test him with hard questions, having a very great retinue and camels bearing spices and very much gold and precious stones. And when she came to Solomon, she told him all that was on her mind. **2**And Solomon answered all her questions. There was nothing hidden from Solomon that he could not explain to her. **3**And when the queen of Sheba had seen the wisdom of Solomon, the house that he had built, **4**the food of his table, the seating of his officials, and the attendance of his servants, and their clothing, his cupbearers, and their clothing, and his burnt offerings that he offered at the house of the LORD, there was no more breath in her.

5And she said to the king, "The report was true that I heard in my own land of your words and of your wisdom, **6**but I did not believe the[c] reports until I came and my own eyes had seen it. And behold, half the greatness of your wisdom was not told me; you surpass the report that I heard. **7**Happy are your wives![d] Happy are these your servants, who continually stand before you and hear your wisdom! **8**Blessed be the LORD your God, who has delighted in you and set you on his throne as king for the LORD your God! Because your God loved Israel and would establish them for ever, he has made you king over them, that you may execute justice and righteousness." **9**Then she gave the king 120 talents[e] of gold, and a very great quantity of spices, and precious stones. There were no spices such as those that the queen of Sheba gave to King Solomon.

10Moreover, the servants of Hiram and the servants of Solomon, who brought gold from Ophir, brought algum wood and precious stones. **11**And the king made from the algum wood supports for the house of the LORD and for the king's house, lyres also and harps for the singers. There never was seen the like of them before in the land of Judah.

12And King Solomon gave to the queen of Sheba all that she desired, whatever she asked besides what she had brought to the king. So she turned and went back to her own land with her servants.

SOLOMON'S WEALTH

13Now the weight of gold that came to Solomon in one year was 666 talents of gold, **14**besides that which the explorers and merchants brought. And all the kings of Arabia and the governors of the land brought gold and silver to Solomon. **15**King Solomon made 200 large shields of beaten gold; 600 shekels[f] of beaten gold went into each shield. **16**And he made 300 shields of beaten gold; 300 shekels of gold went into each shield; and the king put them in the House of the Forest of Lebanon. **17**The king also made a great ivory throne and overlaid it with pure gold. **18**The throne had six steps and a footstool of gold, which were attached to the throne, and on each side of the seat were armrests and two lions standing beside the armrests, **19**while twelve lions stood there, one on each end of a step on the six steps. Nothing like it was ever made for any kingdom. **20**All King Solomon's drinking vessels were of gold, and all the vessels of the House of the Forest of Lebanon were of pure gold. Silver was not considered as anything in the days of Solomon. **21**For the king's ships went to Tarshish with the servants of Hiram. Once every three years the ships of Tarshish used to come bringing gold, silver, ivory, apes, and peacocks.[g]

---

[a]Septuagint, Syriac, Vulgate; Hebrew *to* [b]*A talent* was about 75 pounds or 34 kilograms [c]Hebrew *their* [d]Septuagint (compare 1 Kings 10:8); Hebrew *men* [e]*A talent* was about 75 pounds or 34 kilograms [f]*A shekel* was about 2/5 of an ounce or 11 grams [g]Or *baboons*

²²Thus King Solomon excelled all the kings of the earth in riches and in wisdom. ²³And all the kings of the earth sought the presence of Solomon to hear his wisdom, which God had put into his mind. ²⁴Every one of them brought his present, articles of silver and of gold, garments, myrrh,[a] spices, horses, and mules, so much year by year. ²⁵And Solomon had 4,000 stalls for horses and chariots, and 12,000 horsemen, whom he stationed in the chariot cities and with the king in Jerusalem. ²⁶And he ruled over all the kings from the Euphrates[b] to the land of the Philistines and to the border of Egypt. ²⁷And the king made silver as common in Jerusalem as stone, and he made cedar as plentiful as the sycamore of the Shephelah. ²⁸And horses were imported for Solomon from Egypt and from all lands.

SOLOMON'S DEATH

²⁹Now the rest of the acts of Solomon, from first to last, are they not written in the history of Nathan the prophet, and in the prophecy of Ahijah the Shilonite, and in the visions of Iddo the seer concerning Jeroboam the son of Nebat? ³⁰Solomon reigned in Jerusalem over all Israel for forty years. ³¹And Solomon slept with his fathers and was buried in the city of David his father, and Rehoboam his son reigned in his place.

THE REVOLT AGAINST REHOBOAM

10 Rehoboam went to Shechem, for all Israel had come to Shechem to make him king. ²And as soon as Jeroboam the son of Nebat heard of it (for he was in Egypt, where he had fled from King Solomon), then Jeroboam returned from Egypt. ³And they sent and called him. And Jeroboam and all Israel came and said to Rehoboam, ⁴"Your father made our yoke heavy. Now therefore lighten the hard service of your father and his heavy yoke on us, and we will serve you." ⁵He said to them, "Come to me again in three days." So the people went away.

⁶Then King Rehoboam took counsel with the old men,[c] who had stood before Solomon his father while he was yet alive, saying, "How do you advise me to answer this people?" ⁷And they said to him, "If you will be good to this people and please them and speak good words to them, then they will be your servants for ever." ⁸But he abandoned the counsel that the old men gave him, and took counsel with the young men who had grown up with him and stood before him. ⁹And he said to them, "What do you advise that we answer this people who have said to me, 'Lighten the yoke that your father put on us'?" ¹⁰And the young men who had grown up with him said to him, "Thus shall you speak to the people who said to you, 'Your father made our yoke heavy, but you lighten it for us'; thus shall you say to them, 'My little finger is thicker than my father's thighs. ¹¹And now, whereas my father laid on you a heavy yoke, I will add to your yoke. My father disciplined you with whips, but I will discipline you with scorpions.'"

¹²So Jeroboam and all the people came to Rehoboam on the third day, as the king said, "Come to me again on the third day." ¹³And the king answered them harshly; and forsaking the counsel of the old men, ¹⁴King Rehoboam spoke to them according to the counsel of the young men, saying, "My father made your yoke heavy, but I will add to it. My father disciplined you with whips, but I will discipline you with scorpions." ¹⁵So the king did not listen to the people, for it was a turn of affairs brought about by God that the LORD might fulfil his word, which he spoke by Ahijah the Shilonite to Jeroboam the son of Nebat.

¹⁶And when all Israel saw that the king did not listen to them, the people answered the king, "What portion have we in David? We have no inheritance in the son of Jesse. Each of you to your tents, O Israel! Look now to your own house, David." So all Israel went to their tents. ¹⁷But Rehoboam reigned over the people of Israel who lived in the cities of Judah. ¹⁸Then King Rehoboam sent Hadoram,[d] who was taskmaster over the forced labour, and the people of Israel stoned him to death with stones. And King Rehoboam quickly mounted his chariot to flee to Jerusalem. ¹⁹So Israel has been in rebellion against the house of David to this day.

REHOBOAM SECURES HIS KINGDOM

11 When Rehoboam came to Jerusalem, he assembled the house of Judah and Benjamin, 180,000 chosen warriors, to fight against Israel, to restore the kingdom to Rehoboam. ²But the word of the LORD came to Shemaiah the man of God: ³"Say to Rehoboam the son of Solomon, king of Judah, and to all Israel in Judah and Benjamin, ⁴"Thus

---

[a] Or *armour* [b] Hebrew *the River* [c] Or *the elders*; also verses 8, 13
[d] Spelled *Adoram* in 1 Kings 12:18

says the LORD, You shall not go up or fight against your relatives. Return every man to his home, for this thing is from me.'" So they listened to the word of the LORD and returned and did not go against Jeroboam.

⁵Rehoboam lived in Jerusalem, and he built cities for defence in Judah. ⁶He built Bethlehem, Etam, Tekoa, ⁷Beth-zur, Soco, Adullam, ⁸Gath, Mareshah, Ziph, ⁹Adoraim, Lachish, Azekah, ¹⁰Zorah, Aijalon, and Hebron, fortified cities that are in Judah and in Benjamin. ¹¹He made the fortresses strong, and put commanders in them, and stores of food, oil, and wine. ¹²And he put shields and spears in all the cities and made them very strong. So he held Judah and Benjamin.

PRIESTS AND LEVITES COME TO JERUSALEM

¹³And the priests and the Levites who were in all Israel presented themselves to him from all places where they lived. ¹⁴For the Levites left their common lands and their holdings and came to Judah and Jerusalem, because Jeroboam and his sons cast them out from serving as priests of the LORD, ¹⁵and he appointed his own priests for the high places and for the goat idols and for the calves that he had made. ¹⁶And those who had set their hearts to seek the LORD God of Israel came after them from all the tribes of Israel to Jerusalem to sacrifice to the LORD, the God of their fathers. ¹⁷They strengthened the kingdom of Judah, and for three years they made Rehoboam the son of Solomon secure, for they walked for three years in the way of David and Solomon.

REHOBOAM'S FAMILY

¹⁸Rehoboam took as wife Mahalath the daughter of Jerimoth the son of David, and of Abihail the daughter of Eliab the son of Jesse, ¹⁹and she bore him sons, Jeush, Shemariah, and Zaham. ²⁰After her he took Maacah the daughter of Absalom, who bore him Abijah, Attai, Ziza, and Shelomith. ²¹Rehoboam loved Maacah the daughter of Absalom above all his wives and concubines (he took eighteen wives and sixty concubines, and fathered twenty-eight sons and sixty daughters). ²²And Rehoboam appointed Abijah the son of Maacah as chief prince among his brothers, for he intended to make him king. ²³And he dealt wisely and distributed some of his sons through all the districts of Judah and Benjamin, in all the fortified cities, and he gave them abundant provisions and procured wives for them.ᵃ

EGYPT PLUNDERS JERUSALEM

12 When the rule of Rehoboam was established and he was strong, he abandoned the law of the LORD, and all Israel with him. ²In the fifth year of King Rehoboam, because they had been unfaithful to the LORD, Shishak king of Egypt came up against Jerusalem ³with 1,200 chariots and 60,000 horsemen. And the people were without number who came with him from Egypt—Libyans, Sukkiim, and Ethiopians. ⁴And he took the fortified cities of Judah and came as far as Jerusalem. ⁵Then Shemaiah the prophet came to Rehoboam and to the princes of Judah, who had gathered at Jerusalem because of Shishak, and said to them, "Thus says the LORD, 'You abandoned me, so I have abandoned you to the hand of Shishak.'" ⁶Then the princes of Israel and the king humbled themselves and said, "The LORD is righteous." ⁷When the LORD saw that they humbled themselves, the word of the LORD came to Shemaiah: "They have humbled themselves. I will not destroy them, but I will grant them some deliverance, and my wrath shall not be poured out on Jerusalem by the hand of Shishak. ⁸Nevertheless, they shall be servants to him, that they may know my service and the service of the kingdoms of the countries."

⁹So Shishak king of Egypt came up against Jerusalem. He took away the treasures of the house of the LORD and the treasures of the king's house. He took away everything. He also took away the shields of gold that Solomon had made, ¹⁰and King Rehoboam made in their place shields of bronze and committed them to the hands of the officers of the guard, who kept the door of the king's house. ¹¹And as often as the king went into the house of the LORD, the guard came and carried them and brought them back to the guardroom. ¹²And when he humbled himself the wrath of the LORD turned from him, so as not to make a complete destruction. Moreover, conditions were goodᵇ in Judah.

¹³So King Rehoboam grew strong in Jerusalem and reigned. Rehoboam was forty-one years old when he began to reign, and he reigned for seventeen years in Jerusalem, the city that the LORD had chosen out of all the tribes of Israel to put his name there. His mother's name was Naamah the Ammonite.

ᵃHebrew *and sought a multitude of wives* ᵇHebrew *good things were found*

¹⁴And he did evil, for he did not set his heart to seek the LORD.

¹⁵Now the acts of Rehoboam, from first to last, are they not written in the chronicles of Shemaiah the prophet and of Iddo the seer?ᵃ There were continual wars between Rehoboam and Jeroboam. ¹⁶And Rehoboam slept with his fathers and was buried in the city of David, and Abijahᵇ his son reigned in his place.

ABIJAH REIGNS IN JUDAH

13 In the eighteenth year of King Jeroboam, Abijah began to reign over Judah. ²He reigned for three years in Jerusalem. His mother's name was Micaiahᶜ the daughter of Uriel of Gibeah.

Now there was war between Abijah and Jeroboam. ³Abijah went out to battle, having an army of valiant men of war, 400,000 chosen men. And Jeroboam drew up his line of battle against him with 800,000 chosen mighty warriors. ⁴Then Abijah stood up on Mount Zemaraim that is in the hill country of Ephraim and said, "Hear me, O Jeroboam and all Israel! ⁵Ought you not to know that the LORD God of Israel gave the kingship over Israel for ever to David and his sons by a covenant of salt? ⁶Yet Jeroboam the son of Nebat, a servant of Solomon the son of David, rose up and rebelled against his lord, ⁷and certain worthless scoundrelsᵈ gathered about him and defied Rehoboam the son of Solomon, when Rehoboam was young and irresoluteᵉ and could not withstand them.

⁸"And now you think to withstand the kingdom of the LORD in the hand of the sons of David, because you are a great multitude and have with you the golden calves that Jeroboam made you for gods. ⁹Have you not driven out the priests of the LORD, the sons of Aaron, and the Levites, and made priests for yourselves like the peoples of other lands? Whoever comes for ordinationᶠ with a young bull or seven rams becomes a priest of what are not gods. ¹⁰But as for us, the LORD is our God, and we have not forsaken him. We have priests ministering to the LORD who are sons of Aaron, and Levites for their service. ¹¹They offer to the LORD every morning and every evening burnt offerings and incense of sweet spices, set out the showbread on the table of pure gold, and care for the golden lampstand that its lamps may burn every evening. For we keep the charge of the LORD our God, but you have forsaken him. ¹²Behold, God is with us at our head, and his priests with their battle trumpets to sound the call to battle against you. O sons of Israel, do not fight against the LORD, the God of your fathers, for you cannot succeed."

¹³Jeroboam had sent an ambush round to come upon them from behind. Thus his troopsᵍ were in front of Judah, and the ambush was behind them. ¹⁴And when Judah looked, behold, the battle was in front of and behind them. And they cried to the LORD, and the priests blew the trumpets. ¹⁵Then the men of Judah raised the battle shout. And when the men of Judah shouted, God defeated Jeroboam and all Israel before Abijah and Judah. ¹⁶The men of Israel fled before Judah, and God gave them into their hand. ¹⁷Abijah and his people struck them with great force, so there fell slain of Israel 500,000 chosen men. ¹⁸Thus the men of Israel were subdued at that time, and the men of Judah prevailed, because they relied on the LORD, the God of their fathers. ¹⁹And Abijah pursued Jeroboam and took cities from him, Bethel with its villages and Jeshanah with its villages and Ephronʰ with its villages. ²⁰Jeroboam did not recover his power in the days of Abijah. And the LORD struck him down, and he died. ²¹But Abijah grew mighty. And he took fourteen wives and had twenty-two sons and sixteen daughters. ²²The rest of the acts of Abijah, his ways and his sayings, are written in the story of the prophet Iddo.

ASA REIGNS IN JUDAH

14 ⁱ Abijah slept with his fathers, and they buried him in the city of David. And Asa his son reigned in his place. In his days the land had rest for ten years. ²ʲ And Asa did what was good and right in the eyes of the LORD his God. ³He took away the foreign altars and the high places and broke down the pillars and cut down the Asherim ⁴and commanded Judah to seek the LORD, the God of their fathers, and to keep the law and the commandment. ⁵He also took out of all the cities of Judah the high places and the incense altars. And the kingdom had rest under him. ⁶He built fortified cities in Judah, for the land had rest. He had no war in those years, for the LORD gave him peace. ⁷And he said to Judah, "Let us build

---

ᵃAfter *seer*, Hebrew adds *according to genealogy* ᵇSpelled *Abijam* in 1 Kings 14:31 ᶜSpelled *Maacah* in 1 Kings 15:2 ᵈHebrew *worthless men, sons of Belial* ᵉHebrew *soft of heart* ᶠHebrew *to fill his hand* ᵍHebrew *they* ʰOr *Ephrain* ⁱCh 13:23 in Hebrew ʲCh 14:1 in Hebrew

these cities and surround them with walls and towers, gates and bars. The land is still ours, because we have sought the LORD our God. We have sought him, and he has given us peace on every side." So they built and prospered. ⁸And Asa had an army of 300,000 from Judah, armed with large shields and spears, and 280,000 men from Benjamin that carried shields and drew bows. All these were mighty men of valour.

⁹Zerah the Ethiopian came out against them with an army of a million men and 300 chariots, and came as far as Mareshah. ¹⁰And Asa went out to meet him, and they drew up their lines of battle in the Valley of Zephathah at Mareshah. ¹¹And Asa cried to the LORD his God, "O LORD, there is none like you to help, between the mighty and the weak. Help us, O LORD our God, for we rely on you, and in your name we have come against this multitude. O LORD, you are our God; let not man prevail against you." ¹²So the LORD defeated the Ethiopians before Asa and before Judah, and the Ethiopians fled. ¹³Asa and the people who were with him pursued them as far as Gerar, and the Ethiopians fell until none remained alive, for they were broken before the LORD and his army. The men of Judah*a* carried away very much spoil. ¹⁴And they attacked all the cities around Gerar, for the fear of the LORD was upon them. They plundered all the cities, for there was much plunder in them. ¹⁵And they struck down the tents of those who had livestock and carried away sheep in abundance and camels. Then they returned to Jerusalem.

ASA'S RELIGIOUS REFORMS

15 The Spirit of God came*b* upon Azariah the son of Oded, ²and he went out to meet Asa and said to him, "Hear me, Asa, and all Judah and Benjamin: The LORD is with you while you are with him. If you seek him, he will be found by you, but if you forsake him, he will forsake you. ³For a long time Israel was without the true God, and without a teaching priest and without law, ⁴but when in their distress they turned to the LORD, the God of Israel, and sought him, he was found by them. ⁵In those times there was no peace to him who went out or to him who came in, for great disturbances afflicted all the inhabitants of the lands. ⁶They were broken in pieces. Nation was crushed by nation and city by city, for God troubled them with every sort of distress. ⁷But you, take courage! Do not let your hands be weak, for your work shall be rewarded."

⁸As soon as Asa heard these words, the prophecy of Azariah the son of Oded, he took courage and put away the detestable idols from all the land of Judah and Benjamin and from the cities that he had taken in the hill country of Ephraim, and he repaired the altar of the LORD that was in front of the vestibule of the house of the LORD.*c* ⁹And he gathered all Judah and Benjamin, and those from Ephraim, Manasseh, and Simeon who were residing with them, for great numbers had deserted to him from Israel when they saw that the LORD his God was with him. ¹⁰They were gathered at Jerusalem in the third month of the fifteenth year of the reign of Asa. ¹¹They sacrificed to the LORD on that day from the spoil that they had brought 700 oxen and 7,000 sheep. ¹²And they entered into a covenant to seek the LORD, the God of their fathers, with all their heart and with all their soul, ¹³but that whoever would not seek the LORD, the God of Israel, should be put to death, whether young or old, man or woman. ¹⁴They swore an oath to the LORD with a loud voice and with shouting and with trumpets and with horns. ¹⁵And all Judah rejoiced over the oath, for they had sworn with all their heart and had sought him with their whole desire, and he was found by them, and the LORD gave them rest all round.

¹⁶Even Maacah, his mother, King Asa removed from being queen mother because she had made a detestable image for Asherah. Asa cut down her image, crushed it, and burned it at the brook Kidron. ¹⁷But the high places were not taken out of Israel. Nevertheless, the heart of Asa was wholly true all his days. ¹⁸And he brought into the house of God the sacred gifts of his father and his own sacred gifts, silver, and gold, and vessels. ¹⁹And there was no more war until the thirty-fifth year of the reign of Asa.

ASA'S LAST YEARS

16 In the thirty-sixth year of the reign of Asa, Baasha king of Israel went up against Judah and built Ramah, that he might permit no one to go out or come in to Asa king of Judah. ²Then Asa took silver and gold from the treasures of the house of the LORD and the king's house and sent them to Ben-hadad king of Syria, who lived

---
a Hebrew *They* *b* Or *was* *c* Hebrew *the vestibule of the* LORD

in Damascus, saying, ³"There is a covenant^a between me and you, as there was between my father and your father. Behold, I am sending to you silver and gold. Go, break your covenant with Baasha king of Israel, that he may withdraw from me." ⁴And Ben-hadad listened to King Asa and sent the commanders of his armies against the cities of Israel, and they conquered Ijon, Dan, Abel-maim, and all the store cities of Naphtali. ⁵And when Baasha heard of it, he stopped building Ramah and let his work cease. ⁶Then King Asa took all Judah, and they carried away the stones of Ramah and its timber, with which Baasha had been building, and with them he built Geba and Mizpah.

⁷At that time Hanani the seer came to Asa king of Judah and said to him, "Because you relied on the king of Syria, and did not rely on the LORD your God, the army of the king of Syria has escaped you. ⁸Were not the Ethiopians and the Libyans a huge army with very many chariots and horsemen? Yet because you relied on the LORD, he gave them into your hand. ⁹For the eyes of the LORD run to and fro throughout the whole earth, to give strong support to those whose heart is blameless^b towards him. You have done foolishly in this, for from now on you will have wars." ¹⁰Then Asa was angry with the seer and put him in the stocks in prison, for he was in a rage with him because of this. And Asa inflicted cruelties upon some of the people at the same time.

¹¹The acts of Asa, from first to last, are written in the Book of the Kings of Judah and Israel. ¹²In the thirty-ninth year of his reign Asa was diseased in his feet, and his disease became severe. Yet even in his disease he did not seek the LORD, but sought help from physicians. ¹³And Asa slept with his fathers, dying in the forty-first year of his reign. ¹⁴They buried him in the tomb that he had cut for himself in the city of David. They laid him on a bier that had been filled with various kinds of spices prepared by the perfumer's art, and they made a very great fire in his honour.

JEHOSHAPHAT REIGNS IN JUDAH

17 Jehoshaphat his son reigned in his place and strengthened himself against Israel. ²He placed forces in all the fortified cities of Judah and set garrisons in the land of Judah, and in the cities of Ephraim that Asa his father had captured. ³The LORD was with Jehoshaphat, because he walked in the earlier ways of his father David. He did not seek the Baals, ⁴but sought the God of his father and walked in his commandments, and not according to the practices of Israel. ⁵Therefore the LORD established the kingdom in his hand. And all Judah brought tribute to Jehoshaphat, and he had great riches and honour. ⁶His heart was courageous in the ways of the LORD. And furthermore, he took the high places and the Asherim out of Judah.

⁷In the third year of his reign he sent his officials, Ben-hail, Obadiah, Zechariah, Nethanel, and Micaiah, to teach in the cities of Judah; ⁸and with them the Levites, Shemaiah, Nethaniah, Zebadiah, Asahel, Shemiramoth, Jehonathan, Adonijah, Tobijah, and Tobadonijah; and with these Levites, the priests Elishama and Jehoram. ⁹And they taught in Judah, having the Book of the Law of the LORD with them. They went about through all the cities of Judah and taught among the people.

¹⁰And the fear of the LORD fell upon all the kingdoms of the lands that were round Judah, and they made no war against Jehoshaphat. ¹¹Some of the Philistines brought Jehoshaphat presents and silver for tribute, and the Arabians also brought him 7,700 rams and 7,700 goats. ¹²And Jehoshaphat grew steadily greater. He built in Judah fortresses and store cities, ¹³and he had large supplies in the cities of Judah. He had soldiers, mighty men of valour, in Jerusalem. ¹⁴This was the muster of them by fathers' houses: Of Judah, the commanders of thousands: Adnah the commander, with 300,000 mighty men of valour; ¹⁵and next to him Jehohanan the commander, with 280,000; ¹⁶and next to him Amasiah the son of Zichri, a volunteer for the service of the LORD, with 200,000 mighty men of valour. ¹⁷Of Benjamin: Eliada, a mighty man of valour, with 200,000 men armed with bow and shield; ¹⁸and next to him Jehozabad with 180,000 armed for war. ¹⁹These were in the service of the king, besides those whom the king had placed in the fortified cities throughout all Judah.

JEHOSHAPHAT ALLIES WITH AHAB

18 Now Jehoshaphat had great riches and honour, and he made a marriage alliance with Ahab. ²After some years he went down to Ahab in Samaria. And Ahab killed an abundance of sheep and

---

^{a}Or *treaty*; twice in this verse ^{b}Or *whole*

oxen for him and for the people who were with him, and induced him to go up against Ramoth-gilead. ³Ahab king of Israel said to Jehoshaphat king of Judah, "Will you go with me to Ramoth-gilead?" He answered him, "I am as you are, my people as your people. We will be with you in the war."

⁴And Jehoshaphat said to the king of Israel, "Enquire first for the word of the LORD." ⁵Then the king of Israel gathered the prophets together, four hundred men, and said to them, "Shall we go to battle against Ramoth-gilead, or shall I refrain?" And they said, "Go up, for God will give it into the hand of the king." ⁶But Jehoshaphat said, "Is there not here another prophet of the LORD of whom we may enquire?" ⁷And the king of Israel said to Jehoshaphat, "There is yet one man by whom we may enquire of the LORD, Micaiah the son of Imlah; but I hate him, for he never prophesies good concerning me, but always evil." And Jehoshaphat said, "Let not the king say so." ⁸Then the king of Israel summoned an officer and said, "Bring quickly Micaiah the son of Imlah." ⁹Now the king of Israel and Jehoshaphat the king of Judah were sitting on their thrones, arrayed in their robes. And they were sitting at the threshing floor at the entrance of the gate of Samaria, and all the prophets were prophesying before them. ¹⁰And Zedekiah the son of Chenaanah made for himself horns of iron and said, "Thus says the LORD, 'With these you shall push the Syrians until they are destroyed.'" ¹¹And all the prophets prophesied so and said, "Go up to Ramoth-gilead and triumph. The LORD will give it into the hand of the king."

¹²And the messenger who went to summon Micaiah said to him, "Behold, the words of the prophets with one accord are favourable to the king. Let your word be like the word of one of them, and speak favourably." ¹³But Micaiah said, "As the LORD lives, what my God says, that I will speak." ¹⁴And when he had come to the king, the king said to him, "Micaiah, shall we go to Ramoth-gilead to battle, or shall I refrain?" And he answered, "Go up and triumph; they will be given into your hand." ¹⁵But the king said to him, "How many times shall I make you swear that you speak to me nothing but the truth in the name of the LORD?" ¹⁶And he said, "I saw all Israel scattered on the mountains, as sheep that have no shepherd. And the LORD said, 'These have no master; let each return to his home in peace.'" ¹⁷And the king of Israel said to Jehoshaphat, "Did I not tell you that he would not prophesy good concerning me, but evil?" ¹⁸And Micaiah said, "Therefore hear the word of the LORD: I saw the LORD sitting on his throne, and all the host of heaven standing on his right hand and on his left. ¹⁹And the LORD said, 'Who will entice Ahab the king of Israel, that he may go up and fall at Ramoth-gilead?' And one said one thing, and another said another. ²⁰Then a spirit came forward and stood before the LORD, saying, 'I will entice him.' And the LORD said to him, 'By what means?' ²¹And he said, 'I will go out, and will be a lying spirit in the mouth of all his prophets.' And he said, 'You are to entice him, and you shall succeed; go out and do so.' ²²Now therefore behold, the LORD has put a lying spirit in the mouth of these your prophets. The LORD has declared disaster concerning you."

²³Then Zedekiah the son of Chenaanah came near and struck Micaiah on the cheek and said, "Which way did the Spirit of the LORD go from me to speak to you?" ²⁴And Micaiah said, "Behold, you shall see on that day when you go into an inner chamber to hide yourself." ²⁵And the king of Israel said, "Seize Micaiah and take him back to Amon the governor of the city and to Joash the king's son, ²⁶and say, 'Thus says the king, Put this fellow in prison and feed him with meagre rations of bread and water until I return in peace.'" ²⁷And Micaiah said, "If you return in peace, the LORD has not spoken by me." And he said, "Hear, all you peoples!"

THE DEFEAT AND DEATH OF AHAB

²⁸So the king of Israel and Jehoshaphat the king of Judah went up to Ramoth-gilead. ²⁹And the king of Israel said to Jehoshaphat, "I will disguise myself and go into battle, but you wear your robes." And the king of Israel disguised himself, and they went into battle. ³⁰Now the king of Syria had commanded the captains of his chariots, "Fight with neither small nor great, but only with the king of Israel." ³¹As soon as the captains of the chariots saw Jehoshaphat, they said, "It is the king of Israel." So they turned to fight against him. And Jehoshaphat cried out, and the LORD helped him; God drew them away from him. ³²For as soon as the captains of the chariots saw that it was not the king of Israel, they turned back from pursuing him. ³³But a certain man drew his bow at random[a] and

---
[a] Hebrew *in his innocence*

struck the king of Israel between the scale armour and the breastplate. Therefore he said to the driver of his chariot, "Turn round and carry me out of the battle, for I am wounded." ³⁴And the battle continued that day, and the king of Israel was propped up in his chariot facing the Syrians until evening. Then at sunset he died.

JEHOSHAPHAT'S REFORMS

19 Jehoshaphat the king of Judah returned in safety to his house in Jerusalem. ²But Jehu the son of Hanani the seer went out to meet him and said to King Jehoshaphat, "Should you help the wicked and love those who hate the LORD? Because of this, wrath has gone out against you from the LORD. ³Nevertheless, some good is found in you, for you destroyed the Asheroth out of the land, and have set your heart to seek God."

⁴Jehoshaphat lived at Jerusalem. And he went out again among the people, from Beersheba to the hill country of Ephraim, and brought them back to the LORD, the God of their fathers. ⁵He appointed judges in the land in all the fortified cities of Judah, city by city, ⁶and said to the judges, "Consider what you do, for you judge not for man but for the LORD. He is with you in giving judgement. ⁷Now then, let the fear of the LORD be upon you. Be careful what you do, for there is no injustice with the LORD our God, or partiality or taking bribes."

⁸Moreover, in Jerusalem Jehoshaphat appointed certain Levites and priests and heads of families of Israel, to give judgement for the LORD and to decide disputed cases. They had their seat at Jerusalem. ⁹And he charged them: "Thus you shall do in the fear of the LORD, in faithfulness, and with your whole heart: ¹⁰whenever a case comes to you from your brothers who live in their cities, concerning bloodshed, law or commandment, statutes or rules, then you shall warn them, that they may not incur guilt before the LORD and wrath may not come upon you and your brothers. Thus you shall do, and you will not incur guilt. ¹¹And behold, Amariah the chief priest is over you in all matters of the LORD; and Zebadiah the son of Ishmael, the governor of the house of Judah, in all the king's matters, and the Levites will serve you as officers. Deal courageously, and may the LORD be with the upright!"ᵃ

JEHOSHAPHAT'S PRAYER

20 After this the Moabites and Ammonites, and with them some of the Meunites,ᵇ came against Jehoshaphat for battle. ²Some men came and told Jehoshaphat, "A great multitude is coming against you from Edom,ᶜ from beyond the sea; and, behold, they are in Hazazon-tamar" (that is, Engedi). ³Then Jehoshaphat was afraid and set his face to seek the LORD, and proclaimed a fast throughout all Judah. ⁴And Judah assembled to seek help from the LORD; from all the cities of Judah they came to seek the LORD.

⁵And Jehoshaphat stood in the assembly of Judah and Jerusalem, in the house of the LORD, before the new court, ⁶and said, "O LORD, God of our fathers, are you not God in heaven? You rule over all the kingdoms of the nations. In your hand are power and might, so that none is able to withstand you. ⁷Did you not, our God, drive out the inhabitants of this land before your people Israel, and give it for ever to the descendants of Abraham your friend? ⁸And they have lived in it and have built for you in it a sanctuary for your name, saying, ⁹'If disaster comes upon us, the sword, judgement,ᵈ or pestilence, or famine, we will stand before this house and before you—for your name is in this house—and cry out to you in our affliction, and you will hear and save.' ¹⁰And now behold, the men of Ammon and Moab and Mount Seir, whom you would not let Israel invade when they came from the land of Egypt, and whom they avoided and did not destroy—¹¹behold, they reward us by coming to drive us out of your possession, which you have given us to inherit. ¹²O our God, will you not execute judgement on them? For we are powerless against this great horde that is coming against us. We do not know what to do, but our eyes are on you."

¹³Meanwhile all Judah stood before the LORD, with their little ones, their wives, and their children. ¹⁴And the Spirit of the LORD cameᵉ upon Jahaziel the son of Zechariah, son of Benaiah, son of Jeiel, son of Mattaniah, a Levite of the sons of Asaph, in the midst of the assembly. ¹⁵And he said, "Listen, all Judah and inhabitants of Jerusalem and King Jehoshaphat: Thus says the LORD to you, 'Do not be afraid and do not be dismayed at this great

---
ᵃHebrew *the good* ᵇCompare 26:7; Hebrew *Ammonites*
ᶜOne Hebrew manuscript; most Hebrew manuscripts *Aram* (Syria)
ᵈOr *the sword of judgement* ᵉOr *was*

horde, for the battle is not yours but God's. ¹⁶Tomorrow go down against them. Behold, they will come up by the ascent of Ziz. You will find them at the end of the valley, east of the wilderness of Jeruel. ¹⁷You will not need to fight in this battle. Stand firm, hold your position, and see the salvation of the LORD on your behalf, O Judah and Jerusalem.' Do not be afraid and do not be dismayed. Tomorrow go out against them, and the LORD will be with you."

¹⁸Then Jehoshaphat bowed his head with his face to the ground, and all Judah and the inhabitants of Jerusalem fell down before the LORD, worshipping the LORD. ¹⁹And the Levites, of the Kohathites and the Korahites, stood up to praise the LORD, the God of Israel, with a very loud voice.

²⁰And they rose early in the morning and went out into the wilderness of Tekoa. And when they went out, Jehoshaphat stood and said, "Hear me, Judah and inhabitants of Jerusalem! Believe in the LORD your God, and you will be established; believe his prophets, and you will succeed." ²¹And when he had taken counsel with the people, he appointed those who were to sing to the LORD and praise him in holy attire, as they went before the army, and say,

> "Give thanks to the LORD,
>   for his steadfast love
>   endures for ever."

²²And when they began to sing and praise, the LORD set an ambush against the men of Ammon, Moab, and Mount Seir, who had come against Judah, so that they were routed. ²³For the men of Ammon and Moab rose against the inhabitants of Mount Seir, devoting them to destruction, and when they had made an end of the inhabitants of Seir, they all helped to destroy one another.

THE LORD DELIVERS JUDAH

²⁴When Judah came to the watchtower of the wilderness, they looked towards the horde, and behold, there[a] were dead bodies lying on the ground; none had escaped. ²⁵When Jehoshaphat and his people came to take their spoil, they found among them, in great numbers, goods, clothing, and precious things, which they took for themselves until they could carry no more. They were three days in taking the spoil, it was so much. ²⁶On the fourth day they assembled in the Valley of Beracah,[b] for there they blessed the LORD. Therefore the name of that place has been called the Valley of Beracah to this day. ²⁷Then they returned, every man of Judah and Jerusalem, and Jehoshaphat at their head, returning to Jerusalem with joy, for the LORD had made them rejoice over their enemies. ²⁸They came to Jerusalem with harps and lyres and trumpets, to the house of the LORD. ²⁹And the fear of God came on all the kingdoms of the countries when they heard that the LORD had fought against the enemies of Israel. ³⁰So the realm of Jehoshaphat was quiet, for his God gave him rest all round.

³¹Thus Jehoshaphat reigned over Judah. He was thirty-five years old when he began to reign, and he reigned for twenty-five years in Jerusalem. His mother's name was Azubah the daughter of Shilhi. ³²He walked in the way of Asa his father and did not turn aside from it, doing what was right in the sight of the LORD. ³³The high places, however, were not taken away; the people had not yet set their hearts upon the God of their fathers.

³⁴Now the rest of the acts of Jehoshaphat, from first to last, are written in the chronicles of Jehu the son of Hanani, which are recorded in the Book of the Kings of Israel.

THE END OF JEHOSHAPHAT'S REIGN

³⁵After this Jehoshaphat king of Judah joined with Ahaziah king of Israel, who acted wickedly. ³⁶He joined him in building ships to go to Tarshish, and they built the ships in Ezion-geber. ³⁷Then Eliezer the son of Dodavahu of Mareshah prophesied against Jehoshaphat, saying, "Because you have joined with Ahaziah, the LORD will destroy what you have made." And the ships were wrecked and were not able to go to Tarshish.

JEHORAM REIGNS IN JUDAH

21 Jehoshaphat slept with his fathers and was buried with his fathers in the city of David, and Jehoram his son reigned in his place. ²He had brothers, the sons of Jehoshaphat: Azariah, Jehiel, Zechariah, Azariah, Michael, and Shephatiah; all these were the sons of Jehoshaphat king of Israel.[c] ³Their father gave them great gifts of silver, gold, and valuable possessions, together with fortified cities in Judah, but he gave the kingdom to Jehoram, because he was the firstborn. ⁴When Jehoram had

---
[a] Hebrew *they*   [b] *Beracah* means *blessing*   [c] That is, Judah

ascended the throne of his father and was established, he killed all his brothers with the sword, and also some of the princes of Israel. ⁵Jehoram was thirty-two years old when he became king, and he reigned for eight years in Jerusalem. ⁶And he walked in the way of the kings of Israel, as the house of Ahab had done, for the daughter of Ahab was his wife. And he did what was evil in the sight of the Lord. ⁷Yet the Lord was not willing to destroy the house of David, because of the covenant that he had made with David, and since he had promised to give a lamp to him and to his sons for ever.

⁸In his days Edom revolted from the rule of Judah and set up a king of their own. ⁹Then Jehoram passed over with his commanders and all his chariots, and he rose by night and struck the Edomites who had surrounded him and his chariot commanders. ¹⁰So Edom revolted from the rule of Judah to this day. At that time Libnah also revolted from his rule, because he had forsaken the Lord, the God of his fathers.

¹¹Moreover, he made high places in the hill country of Judah and led the inhabitants of Jerusalem into whoredom and made Judah go astray. ¹²And a letter came to him from Elijah the prophet, saying, "Thus says the Lord, the God of David your father, 'Because you have not walked in the ways of Jehoshaphat your father, or in the ways of Asa king of Judah, ¹³but have walked in the way of the kings of Israel and have enticed Judah and the inhabitants of Jerusalem into whoredom, as the house of Ahab led Israel into whoredom, and also you have killed your brothers, of your father's house, who were better than you, ¹⁴behold, the Lord will bring a great plague on your people, your children, your wives, and all your possessions, ¹⁵and you yourself will have a severe sickness with a disease of your bowels, until your bowels come out because of the disease, day by day.'"

¹⁶And the Lord stirred up against Jehoram the anger*ᵃ* of the Philistines and of the Arabians who are near the Ethiopians. ¹⁷And they came up against Judah and invaded it and carried away all the possessions they found that belonged to the king's house, and also his sons and his wives, so that no son was left to him except Jehoahaz, his youngest son.

¹⁸And after all this the Lord struck him in his bowels with an incurable disease. ¹⁹In the course of time, at the end of two years, his bowels came out because of the disease, and he died in great agony. His people made no fire in his honour, like the fires made for his fathers. ²⁰He was thirty-two years old when he began to reign, and he reigned for eight years in Jerusalem. And he departed with no one's regret. They buried him in the city of David, but not in the tombs of the kings.

AHAZIAH REIGNS IN JUDAH

22 And the inhabitants of Jerusalem made Ahaziah, his youngest son, king in his place, for the band of men that came with the Arabians to the camp had killed all the older sons. So Ahaziah the son of Jehoram king of Judah reigned. ²Ahaziah was twenty-two*ᵇ* years old when he began to reign, and he reigned for one year in Jerusalem. His mother's name was Athaliah, the granddaughter of Omri. ³He also walked in the ways of the house of Ahab, for his mother was his counsellor in doing wickedly. ⁴He did what was evil in the sight of the Lord, as the house of Ahab had done. For after the death of his father they were his counsellors, to his undoing. ⁵He even followed their counsel and went with Jehoram the son of Ahab king of Israel to make war against Hazael king of Syria at Ramoth-gilead. And the Syrians wounded Joram, ⁶and he returned to be healed in Jezreel of the wounds that he had received at Ramah, when he fought against Hazael king of Syria. And Ahaziah the son of Jehoram king of Judah went down to see Joram the son of Ahab in Jezreel, because he was wounded.

⁷But it was ordained by*ᶜ* God that the downfall of Ahaziah should come about through his going to visit Joram. For when he came there, he went out with Jehoram to meet Jehu the son of Nimshi, whom the Lord had anointed to destroy the house of Ahab. ⁸And when Jehu was executing judgement on the house of Ahab, he met the princes of Judah and the sons of Ahaziah's brothers, who attended Ahaziah, and he killed them. ⁹He searched for Ahaziah, and he was captured while hiding in Samaria, and he was brought to Jehu and put to death. They buried him, for they said, "He is the grandson of Jehoshaphat, who sought the Lord with all his heart." And the house of Ahaziah had no one able to rule the kingdom.

---

*ᵃ*Hebrew *spirit* *ᵇ*See 2 Kings 8:26; Hebrew *forty-two*; Septuagint *twenty* *ᶜ*Hebrew *was from*

ATHALIAH REIGNS IN JUDAH

10 Now when Athaliah the mother of Ahaziah saw that her son was dead, she arose and destroyed all the royal family of the house of Judah. **11** But Jehoshabeath,[a] the daughter of the king, took Joash the son of Ahaziah and stole him away from among the king's sons who were about to be put to death, and she put him and his nurse in a bedroom. Thus Jehoshabeath, the daughter of King Jehoram and wife of Jehoiada the priest, because she was a sister of Ahaziah, hid him[b] from Athaliah, so that she did not put him to death. **12** And he remained with them for six years, hidden in the house of God, while Athaliah reigned over the land.

JOASH MADE KING

23 But in the seventh year Jehoiada took courage and entered into a covenant with the commanders of hundreds, Azariah the son of Jeroham, Ishmael the son of Jehohanan, Azariah the son of Obed, Maaseiah the son of Adaiah, and Elishaphat the son of Zichri. **2** And they went about through Judah and gathered the Levites from all the cities of Judah, and the heads of fathers' houses of Israel, and they came to Jerusalem. **3** And all the assembly made a covenant with the king in the house of God. And Jehoiada[c] said to them, "Behold, the king's son! Let him reign, as the LORD spoke concerning the sons of David. **4** This is the thing that you shall do: of you priests and Levites who come off duty on the Sabbath, one third shall be gatekeepers, **5** and one third shall be at the king's house and one third at the Gate of the Foundation. And all the people shall be in the courts of the house of the LORD. **6** Let no one enter the house of the LORD except the priests and ministering Levites. They may enter, for they are holy, but all the people shall keep the charge of the LORD. **7** The Levites shall surround the king, each with his weapons in his hand. And whoever enters the house shall be put to death. Be with the king when he comes in and when he goes out."

8 The Levites and all Judah did according to all that Jehoiada the priest commanded, and they each brought his men, who were to go off duty on the Sabbath, with those who were to come on duty on the Sabbath, for Jehoiada the priest did not dismiss the divisions. **9** And Jehoiada the priest gave to the captains the spears and the large and small shields that had been King David's, which were in the house of God. **10** And he set all the people as a guard for the king, every man with his weapon in his hand, from the south side of the house to the north side of the house, round the altar and the house. **11** Then they brought out the king's son and put the crown on him and gave him the testimony. And they proclaimed him king, and Jehoiada and his sons anointed him, and they said, "Long live the king."

ATHALIAH EXECUTED

12 When Athaliah heard the noise of the people running and praising the king, she went into the house of the LORD to the people. **13** And when she looked, there was the king standing by his pillar at the entrance, and the captains and the trumpeters beside the king, and all the people of the land rejoicing and blowing trumpets, and the singers with their musical instruments leading in the celebration. And Athaliah tore her clothes and cried, "Treason! Treason!" **14** Then Jehoiada the priest brought out the captains who were set over the army, saying to them, "Bring her out between the ranks, and anyone who follows her is to be put to death with the sword." For the priest said, "Do not put her to death in the house of the LORD." **15** So they laid hands on her,[d] and she went into the entrance of the horse gate of the king's house, and they put her to death there.

JEHOIADA'S REFORMS

16 And Jehoiada made a covenant between himself and all the people and the king that they should be the LORD's people. **17** Then all the people went to the house of Baal and tore it down; his altars and his images they broke in pieces, and they killed Mattan the priest of Baal before the altars. **18** And Jehoiada posted watchmen for the house of the LORD under the direction of the Levitical priests and the Levites whom David had organized to be in charge of the house of the LORD, to offer burnt offerings to the LORD, as it is written in the Law of Moses, with rejoicing and with singing, according to the order of David. **19** He stationed the gatekeepers at the gates of the house of the LORD so that no one should enter who was in any way unclean. **20** And he took the captains, the nobles, the governors of the

---

[a] Spelled *Jehosheba* in 2 Kings 11:2   [b] That is, Joash   [c] Hebrew *he*
[d] Or *they made a passage for her*

people, and all the people of the land, and they brought the king down from the house of the Lord, marching through the upper gate to the king's house. And they set the king on the royal throne. ²¹So all the people of the land rejoiced, and the city was quiet after Athaliah had been put to death with the sword.

JOASH REPAIRS THE TEMPLE

24 Joash[a] was seven years old when he began to reign, and he reigned for forty years in Jerusalem. His mother's name was Zibiah of Beersheba. ²And Joash did what was right in the eyes of the Lord all the days of Jehoiada the priest. ³Jehoiada got for him two wives, and he had sons and daughters.

⁴After this Joash decided to restore the house of the Lord. ⁵And he gathered the priests and the Levites and said to them, "Go out to the cities of Judah and gather from all Israel money to repair the house of your God from year to year, and see that you act quickly." But the Levites did not act quickly. ⁶So the king summoned Jehoiada the chief and said to him, "Why have you not required the Levites to bring in from Judah and Jerusalem the tax levied by Moses, the servant of the Lord, and the congregation of Israel for the tent of testimony?" ⁷For the sons of Athaliah, that wicked woman, had broken into the house of God, and had also used all the dedicated things of the house of the Lord for the Baals.

⁸So the king commanded, and they made a chest and set it outside the gate of the house of the Lord. ⁹And proclamation was made throughout Judah and Jerusalem to bring in for the Lord the tax that Moses the servant of God laid on Israel in the wilderness. ¹⁰And all the princes and all the people rejoiced and brought their tax and dropped it into the chest until they had finished.[b] ¹¹And whenever the chest was brought to the king's officers by the Levites, when they saw that there was much money in it, the king's secretary and the officer of the chief priest would come and empty the chest and take it and return it to its place. Thus they did day after day, and collected money in abundance. ¹²And the king and Jehoiada gave it to those who had charge of the work of the house of the Lord, and they hired masons and carpenters to restore the house of the Lord, and also workers in iron and bronze to repair the house of the Lord. ¹³So those who were engaged in the work laboured, and the repairing went forward in their hands, and they restored the house of God to its proper condition and strengthened it. ¹⁴And when they had finished, they brought the rest of the money before the king and Jehoiada, and with it were made utensils for the house of the Lord, both for the service and for the burnt offerings, and dishes for incense and vessels of gold and silver. And they offered burnt offerings in the house of the Lord regularly all the days of Jehoiada.

¹⁵But Jehoiada grew old and full of days, and died. He was 130 years old at his death. ¹⁶And they buried him in the city of David among the kings, because he had done good in Israel, and towards God and his house.

¹⁷Now after the death of Jehoiada the princes of Judah came and paid homage to the king. Then the king listened to them. ¹⁸And they abandoned the house of the Lord, the God of their fathers, and served the Asherim and the idols. And wrath came upon Judah and Jerusalem for this guilt of theirs. ¹⁹Yet he sent prophets among them to bring them back to the Lord. These testified against them, but they would not pay attention.

JOASH'S TREACHERY

²⁰Then the Spirit of God clothed Zechariah the son of Jehoiada the priest, and he stood above the people, and said to them, "Thus says God, 'Why do you break the commandments of the Lord, so that you cannot prosper? Because you have forsaken the Lord, he has forsaken you.'" ²¹But they conspired against him, and by command of the king they stoned him with stones in the court of the house of the Lord. ²²Thus Joash the king did not remember the kindness that Jehoiada, Zechariah's father, had shown him, but killed his son. And when he was dying, he said, "May the Lord see and avenge!"[c]

JOASH ASSASSINATED

²³At the end of the year the army of the Syrians came up against Joash. They came to Judah and Jerusalem and destroyed all the princes of the people from among the people and sent all their spoil to the king of Damascus. ²⁴Though the army of the Syrians had come with few men, the Lord delivered into their hand a very great army, because Judah[d] had forsaken the Lord, the God of

---

[a] Spelled *Jehoash* in 2 Kings 12:1 [b] Or *until it was full* [c] Or *and require it*
[d] Hebrew *they*

their fathers. Thus they executed judgement on Joash.

²⁵When they had departed from him, leaving him severely wounded, his servants conspired against him because of the blood of the son[a] of Jehoiada the priest, and killed him on his bed. So he died, and they buried him in the city of David, but they did not bury him in the tombs of the kings. ²⁶Those who conspired against him were Zabad the son of Shimeath the Ammonite, and Jehozabad the son of Shimrith the Moabite. ²⁷Accounts of his sons and of the many oracles against him and of the rebuilding[b] of the house of God are written in the Story[c] of the Book of the Kings. And Amaziah his son reigned in his place.

AMAZIAH REIGNS IN JUDAH

25 Amaziah was twenty-five years old when he began to reign, and he reigned for twenty-nine years in Jerusalem. His mother's name was Jehoaddan of Jerusalem. ²And he did what was right in the eyes of the LORD, yet not with a whole heart. ³And as soon as the royal power was firmly his, he killed his servants who had struck down the king his father. ⁴But he did not put their children to death, according to what is written in the Law, in the Book of Moses, where the LORD commanded, "Fathers shall not die because of their children, nor children die because of their fathers, but each one shall die for his own sin."

AMAZIAH'S VICTORIES

⁵Then Amaziah assembled the men of Judah and set them by fathers' houses under commanders of thousands and of hundreds for all Judah and Benjamin. He mustered those twenty years old and upwards, and found that they were 300,000 choice men, fit for war, able to handle spear and shield. ⁶He hired also 100,000 mighty men of valour from Israel for 100 talents[d] of silver. ⁷But a man of God came to him and said, "O king, do not let the army of Israel go with you, for the LORD is not with Israel, with all these Ephraimites. ⁸But go, act, be strong for the battle. Why should you suppose that God will cast you down before the enemy? For God has power to help or to cast down." ⁹And Amaziah said to the man of God, "But what shall we do about the hundred talents that I have given to the army of Israel?" The man of God answered, "The LORD is able to give you much more than this." ¹⁰Then Amaziah discharged the army that had come to him from Ephraim to go home again. And they became very angry with Judah and returned home in fierce anger. ¹¹But Amaziah took courage and led out his people and went to the Valley of Salt and struck down 10,000 men of Seir. ¹²The men of Judah captured another 10,000 alive and took them to the top of a rock and threw them down from the top of the rock, and they were all dashed to pieces. ¹³But the men of the army whom Amaziah sent back, not letting them go with him to battle, raided the cities of Judah, from Samaria to Beth-horon, and struck down 3,000 people in them and took much spoil.

AMAZIAH'S IDOLATRY

¹⁴After Amaziah came from striking down the Edomites, he brought the gods of the men of Seir and set them up as his gods and worshipped them, making offerings to them. ¹⁵Therefore the LORD was angry with Amaziah and sent to him a prophet, who said to him, "Why have you sought the gods of a people who did not deliver their own people from your hand?" ¹⁶But as he was speaking, the king said to him, "Have we made you a royal counsellor? Stop! Why should you be struck down?" So the prophet stopped, but said, "I know that God has determined to destroy you, because you have done this and have not listened to my counsel."

ISRAEL DEFEATS AMAZIAH

¹⁷Then Amaziah king of Judah took counsel and sent to Joash the son of Jehoahaz, son of Jehu, king of Israel, saying, "Come, let us look one another in the face." ¹⁸And Joash the king of Israel sent word to Amaziah king of Judah, "A thistle on Lebanon sent to a cedar on Lebanon, saying, 'Give your daughter to my son for a wife', and a wild beast of Lebanon passed by and trampled down the thistle. ¹⁹You say, 'See, I[e] have struck down Edom', and your heart has lifted you up in boastfulness. But now stay at home. Why should you provoke trouble so that you fall, you and Judah with you?"

²⁰But Amaziah would not listen, for it was of God, in order that he might give them into the hand of their enemies, because they had sought the gods of Edom. ²¹So Joash king of

---

[a]Septuagint, Vulgate; Hebrew sons [b]Hebrew founding
[c]Or Exposition [d]A talent was about 75 pounds or 34 kilograms
[e]Hebrew you

Israel went up, and he and Amaziah king of Judah faced one another in battle at Beth-shemesh, which belongs to Judah. ²²And Judah was defeated by Israel, and every man fled to his home. ²³And Joash king of Israel captured Amaziah king of Judah, the son of Joash, son of Ahaziah, at Beth-shemesh, and brought him to Jerusalem and broke down the wall of Jerusalem for 400 cubits,*ᵃ* from the Ephraim Gate to the Corner Gate. ²⁴And he seized all the gold and silver, and all the vessels that were found in the house of God, in the care of Obed-edom. He seized also the treasuries of the king's house, also hostages, and he returned to Samaria.

²⁵Amaziah the son of Joash, king of Judah, lived fifteen years after the death of Joash the son of Jehoahaz, king of Israel. ²⁶Now the rest of the deeds of Amaziah, from first to last, are they not written in the Book of the Kings of Judah and Israel? ²⁷From the time when he turned away from the Lord they made a conspiracy against him in Jerusalem, and he fled to Lachish. But they sent after him to Lachish and put him to death there. ²⁸And they brought him upon horses, and he was buried with his fathers in the city of David.*ᵇ*

UZZIAH REIGNS IN JUDAH

26 And all the people of Judah took Uzziah, who was sixteen years old, and made him king instead of his father Amaziah. ²He built Eloth and restored it to Judah, after the king slept with his fathers. ³Uzziah was sixteen years old when he began to reign, and he reigned for fifty-two years in Jerusalem. His mother's name was Jecoliah of Jerusalem. ⁴And he did what was right in the eyes of the Lord, according to all that his father Amaziah had done. ⁵He set himself to seek God in the days of Zechariah, who instructed him in the fear of God, and as long as he sought the Lord, God made him prosper.

⁶He went out and made war against the Philistines and broke through the wall of Gath and the wall of Jabneh and the wall of Ashdod, and he built cities in the territory of Ashdod and elsewhere among the Philistines. ⁷God helped him against the Philistines and against the Arabians who lived in Gurbaal and against the Meunites. ⁸The Ammonites paid tribute to Uzziah, and his fame spread even to the border of Egypt, for he became very strong. ⁹Moreover, Uzziah built towers in Jerusalem at the Corner Gate and at the Valley Gate and at the Angle, and fortified them. ¹⁰And he built towers in the wilderness and cut out many cisterns, for he had large herds, both in the Shephelah and in the plain, and he had farmers and vine dressers in the hills and in the fertile lands, for he loved the soil. ¹¹Moreover, Uzziah had an army of soldiers, fit for war, in divisions according to the numbers in the muster made by Jeiel the secretary and Maaseiah the officer, under the direction of Hananiah, one of the king's commanders. ¹²The whole number of the heads of fathers' houses of mighty men of valour was 2,600. ¹³Under their command was an army of 307,500, who could make war with mighty power, to help the king against the enemy. ¹⁴And Uzziah prepared for all the army shields, spears, helmets, coats of mail, bows, and stones for slinging. ¹⁵In Jerusalem he made machines, invented by skilful men, to be on the towers and the corners, to shoot arrows and great stones. And his fame spread far, for he was marvellously helped, till he was strong.

UZZIAH'S PRIDE AND PUNISHMENT

¹⁶But when he was strong, he grew proud, to his destruction. For he was unfaithful to the Lord his God and entered the temple of the Lord to burn incense on the altar of incense. ¹⁷But Azariah the priest went in after him, with eighty priests of the Lord who were men of valour, ¹⁸and they withstood King Uzziah and said to him, "It is not for you, Uzziah, to burn incense to the Lord, but for the priests, the sons of Aaron, who are consecrated to burn incense. Go out of the sanctuary, for you have done wrong, and it will bring you no honour from the Lord God." ¹⁹Then Uzziah was angry. Now he had a censer in his hand to burn incense, and when he became angry with the priests, leprosy*ᶜ* broke out on his forehead in the presence of the priests in the house of the Lord, by the altar of incense. ²⁰And Azariah the chief priest and all the priests looked at him, and behold, he was leprous in his forehead! And they rushed him out quickly, and he himself hurried to go out, because the Lord had struck him. ²¹And King Uzziah was a leper to the day of his death, and being a leper lived in a separate house, for he was excluded from the house of the Lord. And Jotham his son

---

ᵃA cubit was about 18 inches or 45 centimetres   ᵇHebrew of Judah
ᶜLeprosy was a term for several skin diseases; see Leviticus 13

was over the king's household, governing the people of the land.

²²Now the rest of the acts of Uzziah, from first to last, Isaiah the prophet the son of Amoz wrote. ²³And Uzziah slept with his fathers, and they buried him with his fathers in the burial field that belonged to the kings, for they said, "He is a leper." And Jotham his son reigned in his place.

JOTHAM REIGNS IN JUDAH

27 Jotham was twenty-five years old when he began to reign, and he reigned for sixteen years in Jerusalem. His mother's name was Jerushah the daughter of Zadok. ²And he did what was right in the eyes of the LORD according to all that his father Uzziah had done, except he did not enter the temple of the LORD. But the people still followed corrupt practices. ³He built the upper gate of the house of the LORD and did much building on the wall of Ophel. ⁴Moreover, he built cities in the hill country of Judah, and forts and towers on the wooded hills. ⁵He fought with the king of the Ammonites and prevailed against them. And the Ammonites gave him that year 100 talents^a of silver, and 10,000 cors^b of wheat and 10,000 of barley. The Ammonites paid him the same amount in the second and the third years. ⁶So Jotham became mighty, because he ordered his ways before the LORD his God. ⁷Now the rest of the acts of Jotham, and all his wars and his ways, behold, they are written in the Book of the Kings of Israel and Judah. ⁸He was twenty-five years old when he began to reign, and he reigned for sixteen years in Jerusalem. ⁹And Jotham slept with his fathers, and they buried him in the city of David, and Ahaz his son reigned in his place.

AHAZ REIGNS IN JUDAH

28 Ahaz was twenty years old when he began to reign, and he reigned for sixteen years in Jerusalem. And he did not do what was right in the eyes of the LORD, as his father David had done, ²but he walked in the ways of the kings of Israel. He even made metal images for the Baals, ³and he made offerings in the Valley of the Son of Hinnom and burned his sons as an offering,^{c} according to the abominations of the nations whom the LORD drove out before the people of Israel. ⁴And he sacrificed and made offerings on the high places and on the hills and under every green tree.

JUDAH DEFEATED

⁵Therefore the LORD his God gave him into the hand of the king of Syria, who defeated him and took captive a great number of his people and brought them to Damascus. He was also given into the hand of the king of Israel, who struck him with great force. ⁶For Pekah the son of Remaliah killed 120,000 from Judah in one day, all of them men of valour, because they had forsaken the LORD, the God of their fathers. ⁷And Zichri, a mighty man of Ephraim, killed Maaseiah the king's son and Azrikam the commander of the palace and Elkanah the next in authority to the king.

⁸The men of Israel took captive 200,000 of their relatives, women, sons, and daughters. They also took much spoil from them and brought the spoil to Samaria. ⁹But a prophet of the LORD was there, whose name was Oded, and he went out to meet the army that came to Samaria and said to them, "Behold, because the LORD, the God of your fathers, was angry with Judah, he gave them into your hand, but you have killed them in a rage that has reached up to heaven. ¹⁰And now you intend to subjugate the people of Judah and Jerusalem, male and female, as your slaves. Have you not sins of your own against the LORD your God? ¹¹Now hear me, and send back the captives from your relatives whom you have taken, for the fierce wrath of the LORD is upon you."

¹²Certain chiefs also of the men of Ephraim, Azariah the son of Johanan, Berechiah the son of Meshillemoth, Jehizkiah the son of Shallum, and Amasa the son of Hadlai, stood up against those who were coming from the war ¹³and said to them, "You shall not bring the captives in here, for you propose to bring upon us guilt against the LORD in addition to our present sins and guilt. For our guilt is already great, and there is fierce wrath against Israel." ¹⁴So the armed men left the captives and the spoil before the princes and all the assembly. ¹⁵And the men who have been mentioned by name rose and took the captives, and with the spoil they clothed all who were naked among them. They clothed them, gave them sandals, provided them with food and drink, and anointed them, and carrying all the feeble among them on donkeys, they brought them to their kinsfolk at Jericho, the city of palm trees. Then they returned to Samaria.

---

^{a}A *talent* was about 75 pounds or 34 kilograms ^{b}A *cor* was about 6 bushels or 220 litres ^{c}Hebrew *made his sons pass through the fire*

¹⁶At that time King Ahaz sent to the king[a] of Assyria for help. ¹⁷For the Edomites had again invaded and defeated Judah and carried away captives. ¹⁸And the Philistines had made raids on the cities in the Shephelah and the Negeb of Judah, and had taken Beth-shemesh, Aijalon, Gederoth, Soco with its villages, Timnah with its villages, and Gimzo with its villages. And they settled there. ¹⁹For the LORD humbled Judah because of Ahaz king of Israel, for he had made Judah act sinfully[b] and had been very unfaithful to the LORD. ²⁰So Tiglath-pileser[c] king of Assyria came against him and afflicted him instead of strengthening him. ²¹For Ahaz took a portion from the house of the LORD and the house of the king and of the princes, and gave tribute to the king of Assyria, but it did not help him.

AHAZ'S IDOLATRY

²²In the time of his distress he became yet more faithless to the LORD—this same King Ahaz. ²³For he sacrificed to the gods of Damascus, which had defeated him and said, "Because the gods of the kings of Syria helped them, I will sacrifice to them that they may help me." But they were the ruin of him and of all Israel. ²⁴And Ahaz gathered together the vessels of the house of God and cut in pieces the vessels of the house of God, and he shut up the doors of the house of the LORD, and he made himself altars in every corner of Jerusalem. ²⁵In every city of Judah he made high places to make offerings to other gods, provoking to anger the LORD, the God of his fathers. ²⁶Now the rest of his acts and all his ways, from first to last, behold, they are written in the Book of the Kings of Judah and Israel. ²⁷And Ahaz slept with his fathers, and they buried him in the city, in Jerusalem, for they did not bring him into the tombs of the kings of Israel. And Hezekiah his son reigned in his place.

HEZEKIAH REIGNS IN JUDAH

29 Hezekiah began to reign when he was twenty-five years old, and he reigned for twenty-nine years in Jerusalem. His mother's name was Abijah[d] the daughter of Zechariah. ²And he did what was right in the eyes of the LORD, according to all that David his father had done.

HEZEKIAH CLEANSES THE TEMPLE

³In the first year of his reign, in the first month, he opened the doors of the house of the LORD and repaired them. ⁴He brought in the priests and the Levites and assembled them in the square on the east ⁵and said to them, "Hear me, Levites! Now consecrate yourselves, and consecrate the house of the LORD, the God of your fathers, and carry out the filth[e] from the Holy Place. ⁶For our fathers have been unfaithful and have done what was evil in the sight of the LORD our God. They have forsaken him and have turned away their faces from the habitation of the LORD and turned their backs. ⁷They also shut the doors of the vestibule and put out the lamps and have not burned incense or offered burnt offerings in the Holy Place to the God of Israel. ⁸Therefore the wrath of the LORD came on Judah and Jerusalem, and he has made them an object of horror, of astonishment, and of hissing, as you see with your own eyes. ⁹For behold, our fathers have fallen by the sword, and our sons and our daughters and our wives are in captivity for this. ¹⁰Now it is in my heart to make a covenant with the LORD, the God of Israel, in order that his fierce anger may turn away from us. ¹¹My sons, do not now be negligent, for the LORD has chosen you to stand in his presence, to minister to him and to be his ministers and make offerings to him."

¹²Then the Levites arose, Mahath the son of Amasai, and Joel the son of Azariah, of the sons of the Kohathites; and of the sons of Merari, Kish the son of Abdi, and Azariah the son of Jehallelel; and of the Gershonites, Joah the son of Zimmah, and Eden the son of Joah; ¹³and of the sons of Elizaphan, Shimri and Jeuel; and of the sons of Asaph, Zechariah and Mattaniah; ¹⁴and of the sons of Heman, Jehuel and Shimei; and of the sons of Jeduthun, Shemaiah and Uzziel. ¹⁵They gathered their brothers and consecrated themselves and went in as the king had commanded, by the words of the LORD, to cleanse the house of the LORD. ¹⁶The priests went into the inner part of the house of the LORD to cleanse it, and they brought out all the uncleanness that they found in the temple of the LORD into the court of the house of the LORD. And the Levites took it and carried it out to the brook Kidron. ¹⁷They began to consecrate on the first day of the first month, and on the eighth day of the month they came to the vestibule of the LORD. Then for eight days they consecrated

---

[a]Septuagint, Syriac, Vulgate (compare 2 Kings 16:7); Hebrew *kings*
[b]Or *wildly* [c]Hebrew *Tilgath-pilneser* [d]Spelled *Abi* in 2 Kings 18:2
[e]Hebrew *impurity*

the house of the LORD, and on the sixteenth day of the first month they finished. [18]Then they went in to Hezekiah the king and said, "We have cleansed all the house of the LORD, the altar of burnt offering and all its utensils, and the table for the showbread and all its utensils. [19]All the utensils that King Ahaz discarded in his reign when he was faithless, we have made ready and consecrated, and behold, they are before the altar of the LORD."

HEZEKIAH RESTORES TEMPLE WORSHIP

[20]Then Hezekiah the king rose early and gathered the officials of the city and went up to the house of the LORD. [21]And they brought seven bulls, seven rams, seven lambs, and seven male goats for a sin offering for the kingdom and for the sanctuary and for Judah. And he commanded the priests, the sons of Aaron, to offer them on the altar of the LORD. [22]So they slaughtered the bulls, and the priests received the blood and threw it against the altar. And they slaughtered the rams, and their blood was thrown against the altar. And they slaughtered the lambs, and their blood was thrown against the altar. [23]Then the goats for the sin offering were brought to the king and the assembly, and they laid their hands on them, [24]and the priests slaughtered them and made a sin offering with their blood on the altar, to make atonement for all Israel. For the king commanded that the burnt offering and the sin offering should be made for all Israel.

[25]And he stationed the Levites in the house of the LORD with cymbals, harps, and lyres, according to the commandment of David and of Gad the king's seer and of Nathan the prophet, for the commandment was from the LORD through his prophets. [26]The Levites stood with the instruments of David, and the priests with the trumpets. [27]Then Hezekiah commanded that the burnt offering be offered on the altar. And when the burnt offering began, the song to the LORD began also, and the trumpets, accompanied by the instruments of David king of Israel. [28]The whole assembly worshipped, and the singers sang, and the trumpeters sounded. All this continued until the burnt offering was finished. [29]When the offering was finished, the king and all who were present with him bowed themselves and worshipped. [30]And Hezekiah the king and the officials commanded the Levites to sing praises to the LORD with the words of David and of Asaph the seer. And they sang praises with gladness, and they bowed down and worshipped.

[31]Then Hezekiah said, "You have now consecrated yourselves to[a] the LORD. Come near; bring sacrifices and thank offerings to the house of the LORD." And the assembly brought sacrifices and thank offerings, and all who were of a willing heart brought burnt offerings. [32]The number of the burnt offerings that the assembly brought was 70 bulls, 100 rams, and 200 lambs; all these were for a burnt offering to the LORD. [33]And the consecrated offerings were 600 bulls and 3,000 sheep. [34]But the priests were too few and could not flay all the burnt offerings, so until other priests had consecrated themselves, their brothers the Levites helped them, until the work was finished—for the Levites were more upright in heart than the priests in consecrating themselves. [35]Besides the great number of burnt offerings, there was the fat of the peace offerings, and there were the drink offerings for the burnt offerings. Thus the service of the house of the LORD was restored. [36]And Hezekiah and all the people rejoiced because God had provided for the people, for the thing came about suddenly.

PASSOVER CELEBRATED

30 Hezekiah sent to all Israel and Judah, and wrote letters also to Ephraim and Manasseh, that they should come to the house of the LORD at Jerusalem to keep the Passover to the LORD, the God of Israel. [2]For the king and his princes and all the assembly in Jerusalem had taken counsel to keep the Passover in the second month— [3]for they could not keep it at that time because the priests had not consecrated themselves in sufficient number, nor had the people assembled in Jerusalem— [4]and the plan seemed right to the king and all the assembly. [5]So they decreed to make a proclamation throughout all Israel, from Beersheba to Dan, that the people should come and keep the Passover to the LORD, the God of Israel, at Jerusalem, for they had not kept it as often as prescribed. [6]So couriers went throughout all Israel and Judah with letters from the king and his princes, as the king had commanded, saying, "O people of Israel, return to the LORD, the God of Abraham, Isaac, and Israel, that he may turn again to the remnant of you who have escaped from the hand of the kings of

---

[a] Hebrew *filled your hand for*

Assyria. ⁷Do not be like your fathers and your brothers, who were faithless to the LORD God of their fathers, so that he made them a desolation, as you see. ⁸Do not now be stiff-necked as your fathers were, but yield yourselves to the LORD and come to his sanctuary, which he has consecrated for ever, and serve the LORD your God, that his fierce anger may turn away from you. ⁹For if you return to the LORD, your brothers and your children will find compassion with their captors and return to this land. For the LORD your God is gracious and merciful and will not turn away his face from you, if you return to him."

¹⁰So the couriers went from city to city through the country of Ephraim and Manasseh, and as far as Zebulun, but they laughed them to scorn and mocked them. ¹¹However, some men of Asher, of Manasseh, and of Zebulun humbled themselves and came to Jerusalem. ¹²The hand of God was also on Judah to give them one heart to do what the king and the princes commanded by the word of the LORD.

¹³And many people came together in Jerusalem to keep the Feast of Unleavened Bread in the second month, a very great assembly. ¹⁴They set to work and removed the altars that were in Jerusalem, and all the altars for burning incense they took away and threw into the brook Kidron. ¹⁵And they slaughtered the Passover lamb on the fourteenth day of the second month. And the priests and the Levites were ashamed, so that they consecrated themselves and brought burnt offerings into the house of the LORD. ¹⁶They took their accustomed posts according to the Law of Moses the man of God. The priests threw the blood that they received from the hand of the Levites. ¹⁷For there were many in the assembly who had not consecrated themselves. Therefore the Levites had to slaughter the Passover lamb for everyone who was not clean, to consecrate it to the LORD. ¹⁸For a majority of the people, many of them from Ephraim, Manasseh, Issachar, and Zebulun, had not cleansed themselves, yet they ate the Passover otherwise than as prescribed. For Hezekiah had prayed for them, saying, "May the good LORD pardon everyone ¹⁹who sets his heart to seek God, the LORD, the God of his fathers, even though not according to the sanctuary's rules of cleanness."ᵃ ²⁰And the LORD heard Hezekiah and healed the people. ²¹And the people of Israel who were present at Jerusalem kept the Feast of Unleavened Bread seven days with great gladness, and the Levites and the priests praised the LORD day by day, singing with all their mightᵇ to the LORD. ²²And Hezekiah spoke encouragingly to all the Levites who showed good skill in the service of the LORD. So they ate the food of the festival for seven days, sacrificing peace offerings and giving thanks to the LORD, the God of their fathers.

²³Then the whole assembly agreed together to keep the feast for another seven days. So they kept it for another seven days with gladness. ²⁴For Hezekiah king of Judah gave the assembly 1,000 bulls and 7,000 sheep for offerings, and the princes gave the assembly 1,000 bulls and 10,000 sheep. And the priests consecrated themselves in great numbers. ²⁵The whole assembly of Judah, and the priests and the Levites, and the whole assembly that came out of Israel, and the sojourners who came out of the land of Israel, and the sojourners who lived in Judah, rejoiced. ²⁶So there was great joy in Jerusalem, for since the time of Solomon the son of David king of Israel there had been nothing like this in Jerusalem. ²⁷Then the priests and the Levites arose and blessed the people, and their voice was heard, and their prayer came to his holy habitation in heaven.

HEZEKIAH ORGANIZES THE PRIESTS

31 Now when all this was finished, all Israel who were present went out to the cities of Judah and broke in pieces the pillars and cut down the Asherim and broke down the high places and the altars throughout all Judah and Benjamin, and in Ephraim and Manasseh, until they had destroyed them all. Then all the people of Israel returned to their cities, every man to his possession.

²And Hezekiah appointed the divisions of the priests and of the Levites, division by division, each according to his service, the priests and the Levites, for burnt offerings and peace offerings, to minister in the gates of the camp of the LORD and to give thanks and praise. ³The contribution of the king from his own possessions was for the burnt offerings: the burnt offerings of morning and evening, and the burnt offerings for the Sabbaths, the new moons, and the appointed feasts, as it is written in the Law of the LORD.

ᵃ Hebrew *not according to the cleanness of holiness*
ᵇ Compare 1 Chronicles 13:8; Hebrew *with instruments of might*

⁴And he commanded the people who lived in Jerusalem to give the portion due to the priests and the Levites, that they might give themselves to the Law of the Lord. ⁵As soon as the command was spread abroad, the people of Israel gave in abundance the firstfruits of grain, wine, oil, honey, and of all the produce of the field. And they brought in abundantly the tithe of everything. ⁶And the people of Israel and Judah who lived in the cities of Judah also brought in the tithe of cattle and sheep, and the tithe of the dedicated things that had been dedicated to the Lord their God, and laid them in heaps. ⁷In the third month they began to pile up the heaps, and finished them in the seventh month. ⁸When Hezekiah and the princes came and saw the heaps, they blessed the Lord and his people Israel. ⁹And Hezekiah questioned the priests and the Levites about the heaps. ¹⁰Azariah the chief priest, who was of the house of Zadok, answered him, "Since they began to bring the contributions into the house of the Lord, we have eaten and had enough and have plenty left, for the Lord has blessed his people, so that we have this large amount left."

¹¹Then Hezekiah commanded them to prepare chambers in the house of the Lord, and they prepared them. ¹²And they faithfully brought in the contributions, the tithes, and the dedicated things. The chief officer in charge of them was Conaniah the Levite, with Shimei his brother as second, ¹³while Jehiel, Azaziah, Nahath, Asahel, Jerimoth, Jozabad, Eliel, Ismachiah, Mahath, and Benaiah were overseers assisting Conaniah and Shimei his brother, by the appointment of Hezekiah the king and Azariah the chief officer of the house of God. ¹⁴And Kore the son of Imnah the Levite, keeper of the east gate, was over the freewill offerings to God, to apportion the contribution reserved for the Lord and the most holy offerings. ¹⁵Eden, Miniamin, Jeshua, Shemaiah, Amariah, and Shecaniah were faithfully assisting him in the cities of the priests, to distribute the portions to their brothers, old and young alike, by divisions, ¹⁶except those enrolled by genealogy, males from three years old and upwards—all who entered the house of the Lord as the duty of each day required—for their service according to their offices, by their divisions. ¹⁷The enrolment of the priests was according to their fathers' houses; that of the Levites from twenty years old and upwards was according to their offices, by their divisions. ¹⁸They were enrolled with all their little children, their wives, their sons, and their daughters, the whole assembly, for they were faithful in keeping themselves holy. ¹⁹And for the sons of Aaron, the priests, who were in the fields of common land belonging to their cities, there were men in the several cities who were designated by name to distribute portions to every male among the priests and to everyone among the Levites who was enrolled.

²⁰Thus Hezekiah did throughout all Judah, and he did what was good and right and faithful before the Lord his God. ²¹And every work that he undertook in the service of the house of God and in accordance with the law and the commandments, seeking his God, he did with all his heart, and prospered.

SENNACHERIB INVADES JUDAH

32 After these things and these acts of faithfulness, Sennacherib king of Assyria came and invaded Judah and encamped against the fortified cities, thinking to win them for himself. ²And when Hezekiah saw that Sennacherib had come and intended to fight against Jerusalem, ³he planned with his officers and his mighty men to stop the water of the springs that were outside the city; and they helped him. ⁴A great many people were gathered, and they stopped all the springs and the brook that flowed through the land, saying, "Why should the kings of Assyria come and find much water?" ⁵He set to work resolutely and built up all the wall that was broken down and raised towers upon it,ᵃ and outside it he built another wall, and he strengthened the Millo in the city of David. He also made weapons and shields in abundance. ⁶And he set combat commanders over the people and gathered them together to him in the square at the gate of the city and spoke encouragingly to them, saying, ⁷"Be strong and courageous. Do not be afraid or dismayed before the king of Assyria and all the horde that is with him, for there are more with us than with him. ⁸With him is an arm of flesh, but with us is the Lord our God, to help us and to fight our battles." And the people took confidence from the words of Hezekiah king of Judah.

SENNACHERIB BLASPHEMES

⁹After this, Sennacherib king of Assyria, who was besieging Lachish with all his forces,

---
ᵃVulgate; Hebrew *and raised upon the towers*

sent his servants to Jerusalem to Hezekiah king of Judah and to all the people of Judah who were in Jerusalem, saying, ¹⁰"Thus says Sennacherib king of Assyria, 'On what are you trusting, that you endure the siege in Jerusalem? ¹¹Is not Hezekiah misleading you, that he may give you over to die by famine and by thirst, when he tells you, "The LORD our God will deliver us from the hand of the king of Assyria"? ¹²Has not this same Hezekiah taken away his high places and his altars and commanded Judah and Jerusalem, "Before one altar you shall worship, and on it you shall burn your sacrifices"? ¹³Do you not know what I and my fathers have done to all the peoples of other lands? Were the gods of the nations of those lands at all able to deliver their lands out of my hand? ¹⁴Who among all the gods of those nations that my fathers devoted to destruction was able to deliver his people from my hand, that your God should be able to deliver you from my hand? ¹⁵Now, therefore, do not let Hezekiah deceive you or mislead you in this fashion, and do not believe him, for no god of any nation or kingdom has been able to deliver his people from my hand or from the hand of my fathers. How much less will your God deliver you out of my hand!'"

¹⁶And his servants said still more against the LORD God and against his servant Hezekiah. ¹⁷And he wrote letters to cast contempt on the LORD, the God of Israel, and to speak against him, saying, "Like the gods of the nations of the lands who have not delivered their people from my hands, so the God of Hezekiah will not deliver his people from my hand." ¹⁸And they shouted it with a loud voice in the language of Judah to the people of Jerusalem who were on the wall, to frighten and terrify them, in order that they might take the city. ¹⁹And they spoke of the God of Jerusalem as they spoke of the gods of the peoples of the earth, which are the work of men's hands.

THE LORD DELIVERS JERUSALEM

²⁰Then Hezekiah the king and Isaiah the prophet, the son of Amoz, prayed because of this and cried to heaven. ²¹And the LORD sent an angel, who cut off all the mighty warriors and commanders and officers in the camp of the king of Assyria. So he returned with shame of face to his own land. And when he came into the house of his god, some of his own sons struck him down there with the sword. ²²So the LORD saved Hezekiah and the inhabitants of Jerusalem from the hand of Sennacherib king of Assyria and from the hand of all his enemies, and he provided for them on every side. ²³And many brought gifts to the LORD to Jerusalem and precious things to Hezekiah king of Judah, so that he was exalted in the sight of all nations from that time onward.

HEZEKIAH'S PRIDE AND ACHIEVEMENTS

²⁴In those days Hezekiah became sick and was at the point of death, and he prayed to the LORD, and he answered him and gave him a sign. ²⁵But Hezekiah did not make return according to the benefit done to him, for his heart was proud. Therefore wrath came upon him and Judah and Jerusalem. ²⁶But Hezekiah humbled himself for the pride of his heart, both he and the inhabitants of Jerusalem, so that the wrath of the LORD did not come upon them in the days of Hezekiah.

²⁷And Hezekiah had very great riches and honour, and he made for himself treasuries for silver, for gold, for precious stones, for spices, for shields, and for all kinds of costly vessels; ²⁸storehouses also for the yield of grain, wine, and oil; and stalls for all kinds of cattle, and sheepfolds. ²⁹He likewise provided cities for himself, and flocks and herds in abundance, for God had given him very great possessions. ³⁰This same Hezekiah closed the upper outlet of the waters of Gihon and directed them down to the west side of the city of David. And Hezekiah prospered in all his works. ³¹And so in the matter of the envoys of the princes of Babylon, who had been sent to him to enquire about the sign that had been done in the land, God left him to himself, in order to test him and to know all that was in his heart.

³²Now the rest of the acts of Hezekiah and his good deeds, behold, they are written in the vision of Isaiah the prophet, the son of Amoz, in the Book of the Kings of Judah and Israel. ³³And Hezekiah slept with his fathers, and they buried him in the upper part of the tombs of the sons of David, and all Judah and the inhabitants of Jerusalem did him honour at his death. And Manasseh his son reigned in his place.

MANASSEH REIGNS IN JUDAH

33 Manasseh was twelve years old when he began to reign, and he reigned for fifty-five years in Jerusalem. ²And he did what was evil in the sight of the LORD, according to the abominations of the nations whom the LORD drove out before the people of Israel. ³For he rebuilt the high places that his father Hezekiah had broken down, and he erected altars to the Baals, and made Asheroth, and worshipped all the host of heaven and served them. ⁴And he built altars in the house of the LORD, of which the LORD had said, "In Jerusalem shall my name be for ever." ⁵And he built altars for all the host of heaven in the two courts of the house of the LORD. ⁶And he burned his sons as an offering in the Valley of the Son of Hinnom, and used fortune-telling and omens and sorcery, and dealt with mediums and with necromancers. He did much evil in the sight of the LORD, provoking him to anger. ⁷And the carved image of the idol that he had made he set in the house of God, of which God said to David and to Solomon his son, "In this house, and in Jerusalem, which I have chosen out of all the tribes of Israel, I will put my name for ever, ⁸and I will no more remove the foot of Israel from the land that I appointed for your fathers, if only they will be careful to do all that I have commanded them, all the law, the statutes, and the rules given through Moses." ⁹Manasseh led Judah and the inhabitants of Jerusalem astray, to do more evil than the nations whom the LORD destroyed before the people of Israel.

MANASSEH'S REPENTANCE

¹⁰The LORD spoke to Manasseh and to his people, but they paid no attention. ¹¹Therefore the LORD brought upon them the commanders of the army of the king of Assyria, who captured Manasseh with hooks and bound him with chains of bronze and brought him to Babylon. ¹²And when he was in distress, he entreated the favour of the LORD his God and humbled himself greatly before the God of his fathers. ¹³He prayed to him, and God was moved by his entreaty and heard his plea and brought him again to Jerusalem into his kingdom. Then Manasseh knew that the LORD was God.

¹⁴Afterwards he built an outer wall for the city of David west of Gihon, in the valley, and for the entrance into the Fish Gate, and carried it round Ophel, and raised it to a very great height. He also put commanders of the army in all the fortified cities in Judah. ¹⁵And he took away the foreign gods and the idol from the house of the LORD, and all the altars that he had built on the mountain of the house of the LORD and in Jerusalem, and he threw them outside the city. ¹⁶He also restored the altar of the LORD and offered on it sacrifices of peace offerings and of thanksgiving, and he commanded Judah to serve the LORD, the God of Israel. ¹⁷Nevertheless, the people still sacrificed at the high places, but only to the LORD their God.

¹⁸Now the rest of the acts of Manasseh, and his prayer to his God, and the words of the seers who spoke to him in the name of the LORD, the God of Israel, behold, they are in the Chronicles of the Kings of Israel. ¹⁹And his prayer, and how God was moved by his entreaty, and all his sin and his faithlessness, and the sites on which he built high places and set up the Asherim and the images, before he humbled himself, behold, they are written in the Chronicles of the Seers.[a] ²⁰So Manasseh slept with his fathers, and they buried him in his house, and Amon his son reigned in his place.

AMON'S REIGN AND DEATH

²¹Amon was twenty-two years old when he began to reign, and he reigned for two years in Jerusalem. ²²And he did what was evil in the sight of the LORD, as Manasseh his father had done. Amon sacrificed to all the images that Manasseh his father had made, and served them. ²³And he did not humble himself before the LORD, as Manasseh his father had humbled himself, but this Amon incurred guilt more and more. ²⁴And his servants conspired against him and put him to death in his house. ²⁵But the people of the land struck down all those who had conspired against King Amon. And the people of the land made Josiah his son king in his place.

JOSIAH REIGNS IN JUDAH

34 Josiah was eight years old when he began to reign, and he reigned for thirty-one years in Jerusalem. ²And he did what was right in the eyes of the LORD, and walked in the ways of David his father; and he did not turn aside to the right hand or to the left. ³For in the eighth year of his reign, while he was yet a boy, he began to seek the God of David his father, and in the twelfth year he began to purge Judah and Jerusalem of the high places, the Asherim, and the carved and the metal images. ⁴And

---

[a] One Hebrew manuscript, Septuagint; most Hebrew manuscripts of *Hozai*

they chopped down the altars of the Baals in his presence, and he cut down the incense altars that stood above them. And he broke in pieces the Asherim and the carved and the metal images, and he made dust of them and scattered it over the graves of those who had sacrificed to them. ⁵He also burned the bones of the priests on their altars and cleansed Judah and Jerusalem. ⁶And in the cities of Manasseh, Ephraim, and Simeon, and as far as Naphtali, in their ruins*ᵃ* all round, ⁷he broke down the altars and beat the Asherim and the images into powder and cut down all the incense altars throughout all the land of Israel. Then he returned to Jerusalem.

THE BOOK OF THE LAW FOUND

⁸Now in the eighteenth year of his reign, when he had cleansed the land and the house, he sent Shaphan the son of Azaliah, and Maaseiah the governor of the city, and Joah the son of Joahaz, the recorder, to repair the house of the LORD his God. ⁹They came to Hilkiah the high priest and gave him the money that had been brought into the house of God, which the Levites, the keepers of the threshold, had collected from Manasseh and Ephraim and from all the remnant of Israel and from all Judah and Benjamin and from the inhabitants of Jerusalem. ¹⁰And they gave it to the workmen who were working in the house of the LORD. And the workmen who were working in the house of the LORD gave it for repairing and restoring the house. ¹¹They gave it to the carpenters and the builders to buy quarried stone, and timber for binders and beams for the buildings that the kings of Judah had let go to ruin. ¹²And the men did the work faithfully. Over them were set Jahath and Obadiah the Levites, of the sons of Merari, and Zechariah and Meshullam, of the sons of the Kohathites, to have oversight. The Levites, all who were skilful with instruments of music, ¹³were over the burden-bearers and directed all who did work in every kind of service, and some of the Levites were scribes and officials and gatekeepers.

¹⁴While they were bringing out the money that had been brought into the house of the LORD, Hilkiah the priest found the Book of the Law of the LORD given through*ᵇ* Moses. ¹⁵Then Hilkiah answered and said to Shaphan the secretary, "I have found the Book of the Law in the house of the LORD." And Hilkiah gave the book to Shaphan. ¹⁶Shaphan brought the book to the king, and further reported to the king, "All that was committed to your servants they are doing. ¹⁷They have emptied out the money that was found in the house of the LORD and have given it into the hand of the overseers and the workmen." ¹⁸Then Shaphan the secretary told the king, "Hilkiah the priest has given me a book." And Shaphan read from it before the king.

¹⁹And when the king heard the words of the Law, he tore his clothes. ²⁰And the king commanded Hilkiah, Ahikam the son of Shaphan, Abdon the son of Micah, Shaphan the secretary, and Asaiah the king's servant, saying, ²¹"Go, enquire of the LORD for me and for those who are left in Israel and in Judah, concerning the words of the book that has been found. For great is the wrath of the LORD that is poured out on us, because our fathers have not kept the word of the LORD, to do according to all that is written in this book."

HULDAH PROPHESIES DISASTER

²²So Hilkiah and those whom the king had sent*ᶜ* went to Huldah the prophetess, the wife of Shallum the son of Tokhath, son of Hasrah, keeper of the wardrobe (now she lived in Jerusalem in the Second Quarter) and spoke to her to that effect. ²³And she said to them, "Thus says the LORD, the God of Israel: 'Tell the man who sent you to me, ²⁴Thus says the LORD, Behold, I will bring disaster upon this place and upon its inhabitants, all the curses that are written in the book that was read before the king of Judah. ²⁵Because they have forsaken me and have made offerings to other gods, that they might provoke me to anger with all the works of their hands, therefore my wrath will be poured out on this place and will not be quenched. ²⁶But to the king of Judah, who sent you to enquire of the LORD, thus shall you say to him, Thus says the LORD, the God of Israel: Regarding the words that you have heard, ²⁷because your heart was tender and you humbled yourself before God when you heard his words against this place and its inhabitants, and you have humbled yourself before me and have torn your clothes and wept before me, I also have heard you, declares the LORD. ²⁸Behold, I will gather you to your fathers, and you shall be gathered to your grave in peace, and your eyes shall not see all the disaster that I will bring

---

*ᵃ*The meaning of the Hebrew is uncertain *ᵇ*Hebrew *by the hand of* *ᶜ*Syriac, Vulgate; Hebrew lacks *had sent*

upon this place and its inhabitants.'" And they brought back word to the king. ²⁹Then the king sent and gathered together all the elders of Judah and Jerusalem. ³⁰And the king went up to the house of the Lord, with all the men of Judah and the inhabitants of Jerusalem and the priests and the Levites, all the people both great and small. And he read in their hearing all the words of the Book of the Covenant that had been found in the house of the Lord. ³¹And the king stood in his place and made a covenant before the Lord, to walk after the Lord and to keep his commandments and his testimonies and his statutes, with all his heart and all his soul, to perform the words of the covenant that were written in this book. ³²Then he made all who were present in Jerusalem and in Benjamin join in it. And the inhabitants of Jerusalem did according to the covenant of God, the God of their fathers. ³³And Josiah took away all the abominations from all the territory that belonged to the people of Israel and made all who were present in Israel serve the Lord their God. All his days they did not turn away from following the Lord, the God of their fathers.

JOSIAH KEEPS THE PASSOVER

35 Josiah kept a Passover to the Lord in Jerusalem. And they slaughtered the Passover lamb on the fourteenth day of the first month. ²He appointed the priests to their offices and encouraged them in the service of the house of the Lord. ³And he said to the Levites who taught all Israel and who were holy to the Lord, "Put the holy ark in the house that Solomon the son of David, king of Israel, built. You need not carry it on your shoulders. Now serve the Lord your God and his people Israel. ⁴Prepare yourselves according to your fathers' houses by your divisions, as prescribed in the writing of David king of Israel and the document of Solomon his son. ⁵And stand in the Holy Place according to the groupings of the fathers' houses of your brothers the lay people, and according to the division of the Levites by fathers' household. ⁶And slaughter the Passover lamb, and consecrate yourselves, and prepare for your brothers, to do according to the word of the Lord by[a] Moses."

⁷Then Josiah contributed to the lay people, as Passover offerings for all who were present, lambs and young goats from the flock to the number of 30,000, and 3,000 bulls; these were from the king's possessions. ⁸And his officials contributed willingly to the people, to the priests, and to the Levites. Hilkiah, Zechariah, and Jehiel, the chief officers of the house of God, gave to the priests for the Passover offerings 2,600 Passover lambs and 300 bulls. ⁹Conaniah also, and Shemaiah and Nethanel his brothers, and Hashabiah and Jeiel and Jozabad, the chiefs of the Levites, gave to the Levites for the Passover offerings 5,000 lambs and young goats and 500 bulls.

¹⁰When the service had been prepared for, the priests stood in their place, and the Levites in their divisions according to the king's command. ¹¹And they slaughtered the Passover lamb, and the priests threw the blood that they received from them while the Levites flayed the sacrifices. ¹²And they set aside the burnt offerings that they might distribute them according to the groupings of the fathers' houses of the lay people, to offer to the Lord, as it is written in the Book of Moses. And so they did with the bulls. ¹³And they roasted the Passover lamb with fire according to the rule; and they boiled the holy offerings in pots, in cauldrons, and in pans, and carried them quickly to all the lay people. ¹⁴And afterwards they prepared for themselves and for the priests, because the priests, the sons of Aaron, were offering the burnt offerings and the fat parts until night; so the Levites prepared for themselves and for the priests, the sons of Aaron. ¹⁵The singers, the sons of Asaph, were in their place according to the command of David, and Asaph, and Heman, and Jeduthun the king's seer; and the gatekeepers were at each gate. They did not need to depart from their service, for their brothers the Levites prepared for them.

¹⁶So all the service of the Lord was prepared that day, to keep the Passover and to offer burnt offerings on the altar of the Lord, according to the command of King Josiah. ¹⁷And the people of Israel who were present kept the Passover at that time, and the Feast of Unleavened Bread seven days. ¹⁸No Passover like it had been kept in Israel since the days of Samuel the prophet. None of the kings of Israel had kept such a Passover as was kept by Josiah, and the priests and the Levites, and all Judah and Israel who were present, and the inhabitants of Jerusalem. ¹⁹In the

---
[a] Hebrew *by the hand of*

eighteenth year of the reign of Josiah this Passover was kept.

JOSIAH KILLED IN BATTLE

²⁰After all this, when Josiah had prepared the temple, Neco king of Egypt went up to fight at Carchemish on the Euphrates, and Josiah went out to meet him. ²¹But he sent envoys to him, saying, "What have we to do with each other, king of Judah? I am not coming against you this day, but against the house with which I am at war. And God has commanded me to hurry. Cease opposing God, who is with me, lest he destroy you." ²²Nevertheless, Josiah did not turn away from him, but disguised himself in order to fight with him. He did not listen to the words of Neco from the mouth of God, but came to fight in the plain of Megiddo. ²³And the archers shot King Josiah. And the king said to his servants, "Take me away, for I am badly wounded." ²⁴So his servants took him out of the chariot and carried him in his second chariot and brought him to Jerusalem. And he died and was buried in the tombs of his fathers. All Judah and Jerusalem mourned for Josiah. ²⁵Jeremiah also uttered a lament for Josiah; and all the singing men and singing women have spoken of Josiah in their laments to this day. They made these a rule in Israel; behold, they are written in the Laments. ²⁶Now the rest of the acts of Josiah, and his good deeds according to what is written in the Law of the LORD, ²⁷and his acts, first and last, behold, they are written in the Book of the Kings of Israel and Judah.

JUDAH'S DECLINE

36 The people of the land took Jehoahaz the son of Josiah and made him king in his father's place in Jerusalem. ²Jehoahaz was twenty-three years old when he began to reign, and he reigned for three months in Jerusalem. ³Then the king of Egypt deposed him in Jerusalem and laid on the land a tribute of a hundred talents of silver and a talent^a of gold. ⁴And the king of Egypt made Eliakim his brother king over Judah and Jerusalem, and changed his name to Jehoiakim. But Neco took Jehoahaz his brother and carried him to Egypt.

⁵Jehoiakim was twenty-five years old when he began to reign, and he reigned for eleven years in Jerusalem. He did what was evil in the sight of the LORD his God. ⁶Against him came up Nebuchadnezzar king of Babylon and bound him in chains to take him to Babylon. ⁷Nebuchadnezzar also carried part of the vessels of the house of the LORD to Babylon and put them in his palace in Babylon. ⁸Now the rest of the acts of Jehoiakim, and the abominations that he did, and what was found against him, behold, they are written in the Book of the Kings of Israel and Judah. And Jehoiachin his son reigned in his place.

⁹Jehoiachin was eighteen^b years old when he became king, and he reigned for three months and ten days in Jerusalem. He did what was evil in the sight of the LORD. ¹⁰In the spring of the year King Nebuchadnezzar sent and brought him to Babylon, with the precious vessels of the house of the LORD, and made his brother Zedekiah king over Judah and Jerusalem.

¹¹Zedekiah was twenty-one years old when he began to reign, and he reigned for eleven years in Jerusalem. ¹²He did what was evil in the sight of the LORD his God. He did not humble himself before Jeremiah the prophet, who spoke from the mouth of the LORD. ¹³He also rebelled against King Nebuchadnezzar, who had made him swear by God. He stiffened his neck and hardened his heart against turning to the LORD, the God of Israel. ¹⁴All the officers of the priests and the people likewise were exceedingly unfaithful, following all the abominations of the nations. And they polluted the house of the LORD that he had made holy in Jerusalem.

¹⁵The LORD, the God of their fathers, sent persistently to them by his messengers, because he had compassion on his people and on his dwelling place. ¹⁶But they kept mocking the messengers of God, despising his words and scoffing at his prophets, until the wrath of the LORD rose against his people, until there was no remedy.

JERUSALEM CAPTURED AND BURNED

¹⁷Therefore he brought up against them the king of the Chaldeans, who killed their young men with the sword in the house of their sanctuary and had no compassion on young man or virgin, old man or aged. He gave them all into his hand. ¹⁸And all the vessels of the house of God, great and small, and the treasures of the house of the LORD, and the treasures of the king and of

---

^{a}A *talent* was about 75 pounds or 34 kilograms ^{b}Septuagint (compare 2 Kings 24:8); most Hebrew manuscripts *eight*

his princes, all these he brought to Babylon. ¹⁹And they burned the house of God and broke down the wall of Jerusalem and burned all its palaces with fire and destroyed all its precious vessels. ²⁰He took into exile in Babylon those who had escaped from the sword, and they became servants to him and to his sons until the establishment of the kingdom of Persia, ²¹to fulfil the word of the LORD by the mouth of Jeremiah, until the land had enjoyed its Sabbaths. All the days that it lay desolate it kept Sabbath, to fulfil seventy years.

THE PROCLAMATION OF CYRUS

²²Now in the first year of Cyrus king of Persia, that the word of the LORD by the mouth of Jeremiah might be fulfilled, the LORD stirred up the spirit of Cyrus king of Persia, so that he made a proclamation throughout all his kingdom and also put it in writing: ²³"Thus says Cyrus king of Persia, 'The LORD, the God of heaven, has given me all the kingdoms of the earth, and he has charged me to build him a house at Jerusalem, which is in Judah. Whoever is among you of all his people, may the LORD his God be with him. Let him go up.'"

EZRA

THE PROCLAMATION OF CYRUS

1 In the first year of Cyrus king of Persia, that the word of the LORD by the mouth of Jeremiah might be fulfilled, the LORD stirred up the spirit of Cyrus king of Persia, so that he made a proclamation throughout all his kingdom and also put it in writing:

²"Thus says Cyrus king of Persia: The LORD, the God of heaven, has given me all the kingdoms of the earth, and he has charged me to build him a house at Jerusalem, which is in Judah. ³Whoever is among you of all his people, may his God be with him, and let him go up to Jerusalem, which is in Judah, and rebuild the house of the LORD, the God of Israel—he is the God who is in Jerusalem. ⁴And let each survivor, in whatever place he sojourns, be assisted by the men of his place with silver and gold, with goods and with beasts, besides freewill offerings for the house of God that is in Jerusalem."

⁵Then rose up the heads of the fathers' houses of Judah and Benjamin, and the priests and the Levites, everyone whose spirit God had stirred to go up to rebuild the house of the LORD that is in Jerusalem. ⁶And all who were about them aided them with vessels of silver, with gold, with goods, with beasts, and with costly wares, besides all that was freely offered. ⁷Cyrus the king also brought out the vessels of the house of the LORD that Nebuchadnezzar had carried away from Jerusalem and placed in the house of his gods. ⁸Cyrus king of Persia brought these out in the charge of Mithredath the treasurer, who counted them out to Sheshbazzar the prince of Judah. ⁹And this was the number of them: 30 basins of gold, 1,000 basins of silver, 29 censers, ¹⁰30 bowls of gold, 410 bowls of silver, and 1,000 other vessels; ¹¹all the vessels of gold and of silver were 5,400. All these did Sheshbazzar bring up, when the exiles were brought up from Babylonia to Jerusalem.

THE EXILES RETURN

2 Now these were the people of the province who came up out of the captivity of those exiles whom Nebuchadnezzar the king of Babylon had carried captive to Babylonia. They returned to Jerusalem and Judah, each to his own town. ²They came with Zerubbabel, Jeshua, Nehemiah, Seraiah, Reelaiah, Mordecai, Bilshan, Mispar, Bigvai, Rehum, and Baanah.

The number of the men of the people of Israel: ³the sons of Parosh, 2,172. ⁴The sons of Shephatiah, 372. ⁵The sons of Arah, 775. ⁶The sons of Pahath-moab, namely the sons of Jeshua and Joab, 2,812. ⁷The sons of Elam, 1,254. ⁸The sons of Zattu, 945. ⁹The sons of Zaccai, 760. ¹⁰The sons of Bani, 642. ¹¹The sons of Bebai, 623. ¹²The sons of Azgad, 1,222. ¹³The sons of Adonikam, 666. ¹⁴The sons of Bigvai, 2,056. ¹⁵The sons of Adin, 454. ¹⁶The sons of Ater, namely of Hezekiah, 98. ¹⁷The sons of Bezai, 323. ¹⁸The sons of Jorah, 112. ¹⁹The sons of Hashum, 223. ²⁰The sons of Gibbar, 95. ²¹The sons of Bethlehem, 123. ²²The men of Netophah, 56. ²³The men of Anathoth, 128. ²⁴The sons of Azmaveth, 42. ²⁵The sons of Kiriath-arim, Chephirah, and Beeroth, 743. ²⁶The sons of Ramah and Geba, 621. ²⁷The men of Michmas, 122. ²⁸The men of Bethel and Ai, 223. ²⁹The sons of Nebo, 52. ³⁰The sons of Magbish, 156. ³¹The sons of the other Elam, 1,254. ³²The sons of Harim, 320. ³³The sons of Lod, Hadid, and Ono, 725. ³⁴The sons of Jericho, 345. ³⁵The sons of Senaah, 3,630.

³⁶The priests: the sons of Jedaiah, of the house of Jeshua, 973. ³⁷The sons of Immer, 1,052. ³⁸The sons of Pashhur, 1,247. ³⁹The sons of Harim, 1,017.

⁴⁰The Levites: the sons of Jeshua and Kadmiel, of the sons of Hodaviah, 74. ⁴¹The singers: the sons of Asaph, 128. ⁴²The sons of the gatekeepers: the sons of Shallum, the sons of Ater, the sons of Talmon, the sons of Akkub, the sons of Hatita, and the sons of Shobai, in all 139.

⁴³The temple servants: the sons of Ziha, the sons of Hasupha, the sons of Tabbaoth, ⁴⁴the sons of Keros, the sons of Siaha, the sons of Padon, ⁴⁵the sons of Lebanah, the sons of Hagabah, the sons of Akkub, ⁴⁶the sons of Hagab, the sons of Shamlai, the sons of Hanan, ⁴⁷the sons of Giddel, the sons of Gahar, the sons of Reaiah, ⁴⁸the sons of Rezin, the sons of Nekoda, the sons of Gazzam, ⁴⁹the

sons of Uzza, the sons of Paseah, the sons of Besai, ⁵⁰the sons of Asnah, the sons of Meunim, the sons of Nephisim, ⁵¹the sons of Bakbuk, the sons of Hakupha, the sons of Harhur, ⁵²the sons of Bazluth, the sons of Mehida, the sons of Harsha, ⁵³the sons of Barkos, the sons of Sisera, the sons of Temah, ⁵⁴the sons of Neziah, and the sons of Hatipha.

⁵⁵The sons of Solomon's servants: the sons of Sotai, the sons of Hassophereth, the sons of Peruda, ⁵⁶the sons of Jaalah, the sons of Darkon, the sons of Giddel, ⁵⁷the sons of Shephatiah, the sons of Hattil, the sons of Pochereth-hazzebaim, and the sons of Ami.

⁵⁸All the temple servants and the sons of Solomon's servants were 392.

⁵⁹The following were those who came up from Tel-melah, Tel-harsha, Cherub, Addan, and Immer, though they could not prove their fathers' houses or their descent, whether they belonged to Israel: ⁶⁰the sons of Delaiah, the sons of Tobiah, and the sons of Nekoda, 652. ⁶¹Also, of the sons of the priests: the sons of Habaiah, the sons of Hakkoz, and the sons of Barzillai (who had taken a wife from the daughters of Barzillai the Gileadite, and was called by their name). ⁶²These sought their registration among those enrolled in the genealogies, but they were not found there, and so they were excluded from the priesthood as unclean. ⁶³The governor told them that they were not to partake of the most holy food, until there should be a priest to consult Urim and Thummim.

⁶⁴The whole assembly together was 42,360, ⁶⁵besides their male and female servants, of whom there were 7,337, and they had 200 male and female singers. ⁶⁶Their horses were 736, their mules were 245, ⁶⁷their camels were 435, and their donkeys were 6,720.

⁶⁸Some of the heads of families, when they came to the house of the Lord that is in Jerusalem, made freewill offerings for the house of God, to erect it on its site. ⁶⁹According to their ability they gave to the treasury of the work 61,000 darics*a* of gold, 5,000 minas*b* of silver, and 100 priests' garments.

⁷⁰Now the priests, the Levites, some of the people, the singers, the gatekeepers, and the temple servants lived in their towns, and all the rest of Israel*c* in their towns.

REBUILDING THE ALTAR

3 When the seventh month came, and the children of Israel were in the towns, the people gathered as one man to Jerusalem. ²Then arose Jeshua the son of Jozadak, with his fellow priests, and Zerubbabel the son of Shealtiel with his kinsmen, and they built the altar of the God of Israel, to offer burnt offerings on it, as it is written in the Law of Moses the man of God. ³They set the altar in its place, for fear was on them because of the peoples of the lands, and they offered burnt offerings on it to the Lord, burnt offerings morning and evening. ⁴And they kept the Feast of Booths, as it is written, and offered the daily burnt offerings by number according to the rule, as each day required, ⁵and after that the regular burnt offerings, the offerings at the new moon and at all the appointed feasts of the Lord, and the offerings of everyone who made a freewill offering to the Lord. ⁶From the first day of the seventh month they began to offer burnt offerings to the Lord. But the foundation of the temple of the Lord was not yet laid. ⁷So they gave money to the masons and the carpenters, and food, drink, and oil to the Sidonians and the Tyrians to bring cedar trees from Lebanon to the sea, to Joppa, according to the grant that they had from Cyrus king of Persia.

REBUILDING THE TEMPLE

⁸Now in the second year after their coming to the house of God at Jerusalem, in the second month, Zerubbabel the son of Shealtiel and Jeshua the son of Jozadak made a beginning, together with the rest of their kinsmen, the priests and the Levites and all who had come to Jerusalem from the captivity. They appointed the Levites, from twenty years old and upwards, to supervise the work of the house of the Lord. ⁹And Jeshua with his sons and his brothers, and Kadmiel and his sons, the sons of Judah, together supervised the workmen in the house of God, along with the sons of Henadad and the Levites, their sons and brothers.

¹⁰And when the builders laid the foundation of the temple of the Lord, the priests in their vestments came forward with trumpets, and the Levites, the sons of Asaph, with cymbals, to praise the Lord, according to the directions of David king of Israel. ¹¹And they sang responsively, praising and giving thanks to the Lord,

"For he is good,
    for his steadfast love endures
        for ever towards Israel."

---

a A *daric* was a coin weighing about 1/4 of an ounce or 8.5 grams
b A *mina* was about 1 1/4 pounds or 0.6 kilogram   *c* Hebrew *all Israel*

And all the people shouted with a great shout when they praised the LORD, because the foundation of the house of the LORD was laid. ¹²But many of the priests and Levites and heads of fathers' houses, old men who had seen the first house, wept with a loud voice when they saw the foundation of this house being laid, though many shouted aloud for joy, ¹³so that the people could not distinguish the sound of the joyful shout from the sound of the people's weeping, for the people shouted with a great shout, and the sound was heard far away.

ADVERSARIES OPPOSE THE REBUILDING

4 Now when the adversaries of Judah and Benjamin heard that the returned exiles were building a temple to the LORD, the God of Israel, ²they approached Zerubbabel and the heads of fathers' houses and said to them, "Let us build with you, for we worship your God as you do, and we have been sacrificing to him ever since the days of Esarhaddon king of Assyria who brought us here." ³But Zerubbabel, Jeshua, and the rest of the heads of fathers' houses in Israel said to them, "You have nothing to do with us in building a house to our God; but we alone will build to the LORD, the God of Israel, as King Cyrus the king of Persia has commanded us."

⁴Then the people of the land discouraged the people of Judah and made them afraid to build ⁵and bribed counsellors against them to frustrate their purpose, all the days of Cyrus king of Persia, even until the reign of Darius king of Persia.

⁶And in the reign of Ahasuerus, in the beginning of his reign, they wrote an accusation against the inhabitants of Judah and Jerusalem.

THE LETTER TO KING ARTAXERXES

⁷In the days of Artaxerxes, Bishlam and Mithredath and Tabeel and the rest of their associates wrote to Artaxerxes king of Persia. The letter was written in Aramaic and translated.[a] ⁸Rehum the commander and Shimshai the scribe wrote a letter against Jerusalem to Artaxerxes the king as follows: ⁹Rehum the commander, Shimshai the scribe, and the rest of their associates, the judges, the governors, the officials, the Persians, the men of Erech, the Babylonians, the men of Susa, that is, the Elamites, ¹⁰and the rest of the nations whom the great and noble Osnappar deported and settled in the cities of Samaria and in the rest of the province Beyond the River. ¹¹(This is a copy of the letter that they sent.) "To Artaxerxes the king: Your servants, the men of the province Beyond the River, send greeting. And now ¹²be it known to the king that the Jews who came up from you to us have gone to Jerusalem. They are rebuilding that rebellious and wicked city. They are finishing the walls and repairing the foundations. ¹³Now be it known to the king that if this city is rebuilt and the walls finished, they will not pay tribute, custom, or toll, and the royal revenue will be impaired. ¹⁴Now because we eat the salt of the palace[b] and it is not fitting for us to witness the king's dishonour, therefore we send and inform the king, ¹⁵in order that search may be made in the book of the records of your fathers. You will find in the book of the records and learn that this city is a rebellious city, hurtful to kings and provinces, and that sedition was stirred up in it from of old. That was why this city was laid waste. ¹⁶We make known to the king that if this city is rebuilt and its walls finished, you will then have no possession in the province Beyond the River."

THE KING ORDERS THE WORK TO CEASE

¹⁷The king sent an answer: "To Rehum the commander and Shimshai the scribe and the rest of their associates who live in Samaria and in the rest of the province Beyond the River, greeting. And now ¹⁸the letter that you sent to us has been plainly read before me. ¹⁹And I made a decree, and search has been made, and it has been found that this city from of old has risen against kings, and that rebellion and sedition have been made in it. ²⁰And mighty kings have been over Jerusalem, who ruled over the whole province Beyond the River, to whom tribute, custom, and toll were paid. ²¹Therefore make a decree that these men be made to cease, and that this city be not rebuilt, until a decree is made by me. ²²And take care not to be slack in this matter. Why should damage grow to the hurt of the king?"

²³Then, when the copy of King Artaxerxes' letter was read before Rehum and Shimshai the scribe and their associates, they went in haste to the Jews at Jerusalem and by force and power made them cease. ²⁴Then the

---

[a] Hebrew *written in Aramaic and translated in Aramaic*, indicating that 4:8–6:18 is in Aramaic; another interpretation is *The letter was written in the Aramaic script and set forth in the Aramaic language*
[b] Aramaic *because the salt of the palace is our salt*

REBUILDING BEGINS ANEW

5 Now the prophets, Haggai and Zechariah the son of Iddo, prophesied to the Jews who were in Judah and Jerusalem, in the name of the God of Israel who was over them. ²Then Zerubbabel the son of Shealtiel and Jeshua the son of Jozadak arose and began to rebuild the house of God that is in Jerusalem, and the prophets of God were with them, supporting them.

³At the same time Tattenai the governor of the province Beyond the River and Shethar-bozenai and their associates came to them and spoke to them thus: "Who gave you a decree to build this house and to finish this structure?" ⁴They also asked them this:[a] "What are the names of the men who are building this building?" ⁵But the eye of their God was on the elders of the Jews, and they did not stop them until the report should reach Darius and then an answer be returned by letter concerning it.

TATTENAI'S LETTER TO KING DARIUS

⁶This is a copy of the letter that Tattenai the governor of the province Beyond the River and Shethar-bozenai and his associates, the governors who were in the province Beyond the River, sent to Darius the king. ⁷They sent him a report, in which was written as follows: "To Darius the king, all peace. ⁸Be it known to the king that we went to the province of Judah, to the house of the great God. It is being built with huge stones, and timber is laid in the walls. This work goes on diligently and prospers in their hands. ⁹Then we asked those elders and spoke to them thus: 'Who gave you a decree to build this house and to finish this structure?' ¹⁰We also asked them their names, for your information, that we might write down the names of their leaders.[b] ¹¹And this was their reply to us: 'We are the servants of the God of heaven and earth, and we are rebuilding the house that was built many years ago, which a great king of Israel built and finished. ¹²But because our fathers had angered the God of heaven, he gave them into the hand of Nebuchadnezzar king of Babylon, the Chaldean, who destroyed this house and carried away the people to Babylonia. ¹³However, in the first year of Cyrus king of Babylon, Cyrus the king made a decree that this house of God should be rebuilt. ¹⁴And the gold and silver vessels of the house of God, which Nebuchadnezzar had taken out of the temple that was in Jerusalem and brought into the temple of Babylon, these Cyrus the king took out of the temple of Babylon, and they were delivered to one whose name was Sheshbazzar, whom he had made governor; ¹⁵and he said to him, "Take these vessels, go and put them in the temple that is in Jerusalem, and let the house of God be rebuilt on its site." ¹⁶Then this Sheshbazzar came and laid the foundations of the house of God that is in Jerusalem, and from that time until now it has been in building, and it is not yet finished.' ¹⁷Therefore, if it seems good to the king, let search be made in the royal archives there in Babylon, to see whether a decree was issued by Cyrus the king for the rebuilding of this house of God in Jerusalem. And let the king send us his pleasure in this matter."

THE DECREE OF DARIUS

6 Then Darius the king made a decree, and search was made in Babylonia, in the house of the archives where the documents were stored. ²And in Ecbatana, the citadel that is in the province of Media, a scroll was found on which this was written: "A record. ³In the first year of Cyrus the king, Cyrus the king issued a decree: Concerning the house of God at Jerusalem, let the house be rebuilt, the place where sacrifices were offered, and let its foundations be retained. Its height shall be sixty cubits[c] and its breadth sixty cubits, ⁴with three layers of great stones and one layer of timber. Let the cost be paid from the royal treasury. ⁵And also let the gold and silver vessels of the house of God, which Nebuchadnezzar took out of the temple that is in Jerusalem and brought to Babylon, be restored and brought back to the temple that is in Jerusalem, each to its place. You shall put them in the house of God."

⁶"Now therefore, Tattenai, governor of the province Beyond the River, Shethar-bozenai, and your[d] associates the governors who are in the province Beyond the River, keep away. ⁷Leave the work on this house of God alone. Let the governor of the Jews and the elders of the Jews rebuild this house of God on its site. ⁸Moreover, I make a decree regarding what

---

[a]Septuagint, Syriac; Aramaic *Then we said to them,* [b]Aramaic *of the men at their heads* [c]A *cubit* was about 18 inches or 45 centimetres [d]Aramaic *their*

you shall do for these elders of the Jews for the rebuilding of this house of God. The cost is to be paid to these men in full and without delay from the royal revenue, the tribute of the province from Beyond the River. ⁹And whatever is needed—bulls, rams, or sheep for burnt offerings to the God of heaven, wheat, salt, wine, or oil, as the priests at Jerusalem require—let that be given to them day by day without fail, ¹⁰that they may offer pleasing sacrifices to the God of heaven and pray for the life of the king and his sons. ¹¹Also I make a decree that if anyone alters this edict, a beam shall be pulled out of his house, and he shall be impaled on it, and his house shall be made a dunghill. ¹²May the God who has caused his name to dwell there overthrow any king or people who shall put out a hand to alter this, or to destroy this house of God that is in Jerusalem. I Darius make a decree; let it be done with all diligence."

THE TEMPLE FINISHED AND DEDICATED

¹³Then, according to the word sent by Darius the king, Tattenai, the governor of the province Beyond the River, Shethar-bozenai, and their associates did with all diligence what Darius the king had ordered. ¹⁴And the elders of the Jews built and prospered through the prophesying of Haggai the prophet and Zechariah the son of Iddo. They finished their building by decree of the God of Israel and by decree of Cyrus and Darius and Artaxerxes king of Persia; ¹⁵and this house was finished on the third day of the month of Adar, in the sixth year of the reign of Darius the king.

¹⁶And the people of Israel, the priests and the Levites, and the rest of the returned exiles, celebrated the dedication of this house of God with joy. ¹⁷They offered at the dedication of this house of God 100 bulls, 200 rams, 400 lambs, and as a sin offering for all Israel 12 male goats, according to the number of the tribes of Israel. ¹⁸And they set the priests in their divisions and the Levites in their divisions, for the service of God at Jerusalem, as it is written in the Book of Moses.

PASSOVER CELEBRATED

¹⁹On the fourteenth day of the first month, the returned exiles kept the Passover. ²⁰For the priests and the Levites had purified themselves together; all of them were clean. So they slaughtered the Passover lamb for all the returned exiles, for their fellow priests, and for themselves. ²¹It was eaten by the people of Israel who had returned from exile, and also by every one who had joined them and separated himself from the uncleanness of the peoples of the land to worship the LORD, the God of Israel. ²²And they kept the Feast of Unleavened Bread for seven days with joy, for the LORD had made them joyful and had turned the heart of the king of Assyria to them, so that he aided them in the work of the house of God, the God of Israel.

EZRA SENT TO TEACH THE PEOPLE

7 Now after this, in the reign of Artaxerxes king of Persia, Ezra the son of Seraiah, son of Azariah, son of Hilkiah, ²son of Shallum, son of Zadok, son of Ahitub, ³son of Amariah, son of Azariah, son of Meraioth, ⁴son of Zerahiah, son of Uzzi, son of Bukki, ⁵son of Abishua, son of Phinehas, son of Eleazar, son of Aaron the chief priest— ⁶this Ezra went up from Babylonia. He was a scribe skilled in the Law of Moses that the LORD, the God of Israel, had given, and the king granted him all that he asked, for the hand of the LORD his God was on him.

⁷And there went up also to Jerusalem, in the seventh year of Artaxerxes the king, some of the people of Israel, and some of the priests and Levites, the singers and gatekeepers, and the temple servants. ⁸And Ezra[a] came to Jerusalem in the fifth month, which was in the seventh year of the king. ⁹For on the first day of the first month he began to go up from Babylonia, and on the first day of the fifth month he came to Jerusalem, for the good hand of his God was on him. ¹⁰For Ezra had set his heart to study the Law of the LORD, and to do it and to teach his statutes and rules in Israel.

¹¹This is a copy of the letter that King Artaxerxes gave to Ezra the priest, the scribe, a man learned in matters of the commandments of the LORD and his statutes for Israel: ¹²"Artaxerxes, king of kings, to Ezra the priest, the scribe of the Law of the God of heaven. Peace.[b] And now ¹³I make a decree that anyone of the people of Israel or their priests or Levites in my kingdom, who freely offers to go to Jerusalem, may go with you. ¹⁴For you are sent by the king and his seven counsellors to make enquiries about Judah and Jerusalem according to the Law of your God, which is in your hand, ¹⁵and also to carry the silver and gold that the king and his counsellors have freely

---

[a] Aramaic *he* [b] Aramaic *Perfect* (probably a greeting)

offered to the God of Israel, whose dwelling is in Jerusalem, ¹⁶with all the silver and gold that you shall find in the whole province of Babylonia, and with the freewill offerings of the people and the priests, vowed willingly for the house of their God that is in Jerusalem. ¹⁷With this money, then, you shall with all diligence buy bulls, rams, and lambs, with their grain offerings and their drink offerings, and you shall offer them on the altar of the house of your God that is in Jerusalem. ¹⁸Whatever seems good to you and your brothers to do with the rest of the silver and gold, you may do, according to the will of your God. ¹⁹The vessels that have been given to you for the service of the house of your God, you shall deliver before the God of Jerusalem. ²⁰And whatever else is required for the house of your God, which it falls to you to provide, you may provide it out of the king's treasury.

²¹"And I, Artaxerxes the king, make a decree to all the treasurers in the province Beyond the River: Whatever Ezra the priest, the scribe of the Law of the God of heaven, requires of you, let it be done with all diligence, ²²up to 100 talents[a] of silver, 100 cors[b] of wheat, 100 baths[c] of wine, 100 baths of oil, and salt without prescribing how much. ²³Whatever is decreed by the God of heaven, let it be done in full for the house of the God of heaven, lest his wrath be against the realm of the king and his sons. ²⁴We also notify you that it shall not be lawful to impose tribute, custom, or toll on anyone of the priests, the Levites, the singers, the doorkeepers, the temple servants, or other servants of this house of God.

²⁵"And you, Ezra, according to the wisdom of your God that is in your hand, appoint magistrates and judges who may judge all the people in the province Beyond the River, all such as know the laws of your God. And those who do not know them, you shall teach. ²⁶Whoever will not obey the law of your God and the law of the king, let judgement be strictly executed on him, whether for death or for banishment or for confiscation of his goods or for imprisonment."

²⁷Blessed be the LORD, the God of our fathers, who put such a thing as this into the heart of the king, to beautify the house of the LORD that is in Jerusalem, ²⁸and who extended to me his steadfast love before the king and his counsellors, and before all the king's mighty officers. I took courage, for the hand of the LORD my God was on me, and I gathered leading men from Israel to go up with me.

GENEALOGY OF THOSE WHO RETURNED WITH EZRA

8 These are the heads of their fathers' houses, and this is the genealogy of those who went up with me from Babylonia, in the reign of Artaxerxes the king: ²Of the sons of Phinehas, Gershom. Of the sons of Ithamar, Daniel. Of the sons of David, Hattush. ³Of the sons of Shecaniah, who was of the sons of Parosh, Zechariah, with whom were registered 150 men. ⁴Of the sons of Pahath-moab, Eliehoenai the son of Zerahiah, and with him 200 men. ⁵Of the sons of Zattu,[d] Shecaniah the son of Jahaziel, and with him 300 men. ⁶Of the sons of Adin, Ebed the son of Jonathan, and with him 50 men. ⁷Of the sons of Elam, Jeshaiah the son of Athaliah, and with him 70 men. ⁸Of the sons of Shephatiah, Zebadiah the son of Michael, and with him 80 men. ⁹Of the sons of Joab, Obadiah the son of Jehiel, and with him 218 men. ¹⁰Of the sons of Bani,[e] Shelomith the son of Josiphiah, and with him 160 men. ¹¹Of the sons of Bebai, Zechariah, the son of Bebai, and with him 28 men. ¹²Of the sons of Azgad, Johanan the son of Hakkatan, and with him 110 men. ¹³Of the sons of Adonikam, those who came later, their names being Eliphelet, Jeuel, and Shemaiah, and with them 60 men. ¹⁴Of the sons of Bigvai, Uthai and Zaccur, and with them 70 men.

EZRA SENDS FOR LEVITES

¹⁵I gathered them to the river that runs to Ahava, and there we camped three days. As I reviewed the people and the priests, I found there none of the sons of Levi. ¹⁶Then I sent for Eliezer, Ariel, Shemaiah, Elnathan, Jarib, Elnathan, Nathan, Zechariah, and Meshullam, leading men, and for Joiarib and Elnathan, who were men of insight, ¹⁷and sent them to Iddo, the leading man at the place Casiphia, telling them what to say to Iddo and his brothers and[f] the temple servants at the place Casiphia, namely, to send us ministers for the house of our God. ¹⁸And by the good hand of our God on us, they brought us a man of discretion, of the sons of Mahli the son of Levi, son of Israel, namely Sherebiah with his sons and kinsmen, 18; ¹⁹also Hashabiah, and with him Jeshaiah of the sons of Merari, with his kinsmen and their

---

[a] A *talent* was about 75 pounds or 34 kilograms   [b] A *cor* was about 6 bushels or 220 litres   [c] A *bath* was about 6 gallons or 22 litres
[d] Septuagint; Hebrew lacks *of Zattu*   [e] Septuagint; Hebrew lacks *Bani*
[f] Hebrew lacks *and*

sons, 20; ²⁰besides 220 of the temple servants, whom David and his officials had set apart to attend the Levites. These were all mentioned by name.

FASTING AND PRAYER FOR PROTECTION

²¹Then I proclaimed a fast there, at the river Ahava, that we might humble ourselves before our God, to seek from him a safe journey for ourselves, our children, and all our goods. ²²For I was ashamed to ask the king for a band of soldiers and horsemen to protect us against the enemy on our way, since we had told the king, "The hand of our God is for good on all who seek him, and the power of his wrath is against all who forsake him." ²³So we fasted and implored our God for this, and he listened to our entreaty.

PRIESTS TO GUARD OFFERINGS

²⁴Then I set apart twelve of the leading priests: Sherebiah, Hashabiah, and ten of their kinsmen with them. ²⁵And I weighed out to them the silver and the gold and the vessels, the offering for the house of our God that the king and his counsellors and his lords and all Israel there present had offered. ²⁶I weighed out into their hand 650 talents^a of silver, and silver vessels worth 200 talents,^{b} and 100 talents of gold, ²⁷20 bowls of gold worth 1,000 darics,^{c} and two vessels of fine bright bronze as precious as gold. ²⁸And I said to them, "You are holy to the LORD, and the vessels are holy, and the silver and the gold are a freewill offering to the LORD, the God of your fathers. ²⁹Guard them and keep them until you weigh them before the chief priests and the Levites and the heads of fathers' houses in Israel at Jerusalem, within the chambers of the house of the LORD." ³⁰So the priests and the Levites took over the weight of the silver and the gold and the vessels, to bring them to Jerusalem, to the house of our God.

³¹Then we departed from the river Ahava on the twelfth day of the first month, to go to Jerusalem. The hand of our God was on us, and he delivered us from the hand of the enemy and from ambushes by the way. ³²We came to Jerusalem, and there we remained three days. ³³On the fourth day, within the house of our God, the silver and the gold and the vessels were weighed into the hands of Meremoth the priest, son of Uriah, and with him was Eleazar the son of Phinehas, and with them were the Levites, Jozabad the son of Jeshua and Noadiah the son of Binnui. ³⁴The total was counted and weighed, and the weight of everything was recorded.

³⁵At that time those who had come from captivity, the returned exiles, offered burnt offerings to the God of Israel, twelve bulls for all Israel, ninety-six rams, seventy-seven lambs, and as a sin offering twelve male goats. All this was a burnt offering to the LORD. ³⁶They also delivered the king's commissions to the king's satraps^d and to the governors of the province Beyond the River, and they aided the people and the house of God.

EZRA PRAYS ABOUT INTERMARRIAGE

9 After these things had been done, the officials approached me and said, "The people of Israel and the priests and the Levites have not separated themselves from the peoples of the lands with their abominations, from the Canaanites, the Hittites, the Perizzites, the Jebusites, the Ammonites, the Moabites, the Egyptians, and the Amorites. ²For they have taken some of their daughters to be wives for themselves and for their sons, so that the holy race^e has mixed itself with the peoples of the lands. And in this faithlessness the hand of the officials and chief men has been foremost." ³As soon as I heard this, I tore my garment and my cloak and pulled hair from my head and beard and sat appalled. ⁴Then all who trembled at the words of the God of Israel, because of the faithlessness of the returned exiles, gathered round me while I sat appalled until the evening sacrifice. ⁵And at the evening sacrifice I rose from my fasting, with my garment and my cloak torn, and fell upon my knees and spread out my hands to the LORD my God, ⁶saying:

"O my God, I am ashamed and blush to lift my face to you, my God, for our iniquities have risen higher than our heads, and our guilt has mounted up to the heavens. ⁷From the days of our fathers to this day we have been in great guilt. And for our iniquities we, our kings, and our priests have been given into the hand of the kings of the lands, to the sword, to captivity, to plundering, and to utter shame, as it is today. ⁸But now for a brief moment favour has been shown by the LORD our God, to leave us a remnant and to give us a secure hold^f within his holy place,

---

^{a}A *talent* was about 75 pounds or 34 kilograms ^{b}Revocalization; the number is missing in the Masoretic Text ^{c}A *daric* was a coin weighing about 1/4 of an ounce or 8.5 grams ^{d}A *satrap* was a Persian official ^{e}Hebrew *offspring* ^{f}Hebrew *nail*, or *tent-peg*

that our God may brighten our eyes and grant us a little reviving in our slavery. ⁹For we are slaves. Yet our God has not forsaken us in our slavery, but has extended to us his steadfast love before the kings of Persia, to grant us some reviving to set up the house of our God, to repair its ruins, and to give us protection[a] in Judea and Jerusalem.

¹⁰"And now, O our God, what shall we say after this? For we have forsaken your commandments, ¹¹which you commanded by your servants the prophets, saying, 'The land that you are entering, to take possession of it, is a land impure with the impurity of the peoples of the lands, with their abominations that have filled it from end to end with their uncleanness. ¹²Therefore do not give your daughters to their sons, neither take their daughters for your sons, and never seek their peace or prosperity, that you may be strong and eat the good of the land and leave it for an inheritance to your children for ever.' ¹³And after all that has come upon us for our evil deeds and for our great guilt, seeing that you, our God, have punished us less than our iniquities deserved and have given us such a remnant as this, ¹⁴shall we break your commandments again and intermarry with the peoples who practise these abominations? Would you not be angry with us until you consumed us, so that there should be no remnant, nor any to escape? ¹⁵O Lord, the God of Israel, you are just, for we are left a remnant that has escaped, as it is today. Behold, we are before you in our guilt, for none can stand before you because of this."

THE PEOPLE CONFESS THEIR SIN

10 While Ezra prayed and made confession, weeping and casting himself down before the house of God, a very great assembly of men, women, and children, gathered to him out of Israel, for the people wept bitterly. ²And Shecaniah the son of Jehiel, of the sons of Elam, addressed Ezra: "We have broken faith with our God and have married foreign women from the peoples of the land, but even now there is hope for Israel in spite of this. ³Therefore let us make a covenant with our God to put away all these wives and their children, according to the counsel of my lord[b] and of those who tremble at the commandment of our God, and let it be done according to the Law. ⁴Arise, for it is your task, and we are with you; be strong and do it." ⁵Then Ezra arose and made the leading priests and Levites and all Israel swear that they would do as had been said. So they took the oath.

⁶Then Ezra withdrew from before the house of God and went to the chamber of Jehohanan the son of Eliashib, where he spent the night,[c] neither eating bread nor drinking water, for he was mourning over the faithlessness of the exiles. ⁷And a proclamation was made throughout Judah and Jerusalem to all the returned exiles that they should assemble at Jerusalem, ⁸and that if anyone did not come within three days, by order of the officials and the elders all his property should be forfeited, and he himself banned from the congregation of the exiles.

⁹Then all the men of Judah and Benjamin assembled at Jerusalem within the three days. It was the ninth month, on the twentieth day of the month. And all the people sat in the open square before the house of God, trembling because of this matter and because of the heavy rain. ¹⁰And Ezra the priest stood up and said to them, "You have broken faith and married foreign women, and so increased the guilt of Israel. ¹¹Now then make confession to the Lord, the God of your fathers and do his will. Separate yourselves from the peoples of the land and from the foreign wives." ¹²Then all the assembly answered with a loud voice, "It is so; we must do as you have said. ¹³But the people are many, and it is a time of heavy rain; we cannot stand in the open. Nor is this a task for one day or for two, for we have greatly transgressed in this matter. ¹⁴Let our officials stand for the whole assembly. Let all in our cities who have taken foreign wives come at appointed times, and with them the elders and judges of every city, until the fierce wrath of our God over this matter is turned away from us." ¹⁵Only Jonathan the son of Asahel and Jahzeiah the son of Tikvah opposed this, and Meshullam and Shabbethai the Levite supported them.

¹⁶Then the returned exiles did so. Ezra the priest selected men,[d] heads of fathers' houses, according to their fathers' houses, each of them designated by name. On the first day of the tenth month they sat down to examine the matter; ¹⁷and by the first day of the first month they had come to the end of all the men who had married foreign women.

---

[a]Hebrew *a wall* [b]Or *of the Lord* [c]Probable reading; Hebrew *where he went* [d]Syriac; Hebrew *And there were selected Ezra . . .*

THOSE GUILTY OF INTERMARRIAGE

¹⁸Now there were found some of the sons of the priests who had married foreign women: Maaseiah, Eliezer, Jarib, and Gedaliah, some of the sons of Jeshua the son of Jozadak and his brothers. ¹⁹They pledged themselves to put away their wives, and their guilt offering was a ram of the flock for their guilt.ᵃ ²⁰Of the sons of Immer: Hanani and Zebadiah. ²¹Of the sons of Harim: Maaseiah, Elijah, Shemaiah, Jehiel, and Uzziah. ²²Of the sons of Pashhur: Elioenai, Maaseiah, Ishmael, Nethanel, Jozabad, and Elasah.

²³Of the Levites: Jozabad, Shimei, Kelaiah (that is, Kelita), Pethahiah, Judah, and Eliezer. ²⁴Of the singers: Eliashib. Of the gatekeepers: Shallum, Telem, and Uri.

²⁵And of Israel: of the sons of Parosh: Ramiah, Izziah, Malchijah, Mijamin, Eleazar, Hashabiah,ᵇ and Benaiah. ²⁶Of the sons of Elam: Mattaniah, Zechariah, Jehiel, Abdi, Jeremoth, and Elijah. ²⁷Of the sons of Zattu: Elioenai, Eliashib, Mattaniah, Jeremoth, Zabad, and Aziza. ²⁸Of the sons of Bebai were Jehohanan, Hananiah, Zabbai, and Athlai. ²⁹Of the sons of Bani were Meshullam, Malluch, Adaiah, Jashub, Sheal, and Jeremoth. ³⁰Of the sons of Pahath-moab: Adna, Chelal, Benaiah, Maaseiah, Mattaniah, Bezalel, Binnui, and Manasseh. ³¹Of the sons of Harim: Eliezer, Isshijah, Malchijah, Shemaiah, Shimeon, ³²Benjamin, Malluch, and Shemariah. ³³Of the sons of Hashum: Mattenai, Mattattah, Zabad, Eliphelet, Jeremai, Manasseh, and Shimei. ³⁴Of the sons of Bani: Maadai, Amram, Uel, ³⁵Benaiah, Bedeiah, Cheluhi, ³⁶Vaniah, Meremoth, Eliashib, ³⁷Mattaniah, Mattenai, Jaasu. ³⁸Of the sons of Binnui:ᶜ Shimei, ³⁹Shelemiah, Nathan, Adaiah, ⁴⁰Machnadebai, Shashai, Sharai, ⁴¹Azarel, Shelemiah, Shemariah, ⁴²Shallum, Amariah, and Joseph. ⁴³Of the sons of Nebo: Jeiel, Mattithiah, Zabad, Zebina, Jaddai, Joel, and Benaiah. ⁴⁴All these had married foreign women, and some of the women had even borne children.ᵈ

ᵃOr *as their reparation* ᵇSeptuagint; Hebrew *Malchijah* ᶜSeptuagint; Hebrew *Bani, Binnui* ᵈOr *and they put them away with their children*

NEHEMIAH

REPORT FROM JERUSALEM

1 The words of Nehemiah the son of Hacaliah.

Now it happened in the month of Chislev, in the twentieth year, as I was in Susa the citadel, ²that Hanani, one of my brothers, came with certain men from Judah. And I asked them concerning the Jews who escaped, who had survived the exile, and concerning Jerusalem. ³And they said to me, "The remnant there in the province who had survived the exile is in great trouble and shame. The wall of Jerusalem is broken down, and its gates are destroyed by fire."

NEHEMIAH'S PRAYER

⁴As soon as I heard these words I sat down and wept and mourned for days, and I continued fasting and praying before the God of heaven. ⁵And I said, "O LORD God of heaven, the great and awesome God who keeps covenant and steadfast love with those who love him and keep his commandments, ⁶let your ear be attentive and your eyes open, to hear the prayer of your servant that I now pray before you day and night for the people of Israel your servants, confessing the sins of the people of Israel, which we have sinned against you. Even I and my father's house have sinned. ⁷We have acted very corruptly against you and have not kept the commandments, the statutes, and the rules that you commanded your servant Moses. ⁸Remember the word that you commanded your servant Moses, saying, 'If you are unfaithful, I will scatter you among the peoples, ⁹but if you return to me and keep my commandments and do them, though your outcasts are in the uttermost parts of heaven, from there I will gather them and bring them to the place that I have chosen, to make my name dwell there.' ¹⁰They are your servants and your people, whom you have redeemed by your great power and by your strong hand. ¹¹O Lord, let your ear be attentive to the prayer of your servant, and to the prayer of your servants who delight to fear your name, and give success to your servant today, and grant him mercy in the sight of this man."

Now I was cupbearer to the king.

NEHEMIAH SENT TO JUDAH

2 In the month of Nisan, in the twentieth year of King Artaxerxes, when wine was before him, I took up the wine and gave it to the king. Now I had not been sad in his presence. ²And the king said to me, "Why is your face sad, seeing you are not sick? This is nothing but sadness of the heart." Then I was very much afraid. ³I said to the king, "Let the king live for ever! Why should not my face be sad, when the city, the place of my fathers' graves, lies in ruins, and its gates have been destroyed by fire?" ⁴Then the king said to me, "What are you requesting?" So I prayed to the God of heaven. ⁵And I said to the king, "If it pleases the king, and if your servant has found favour in your sight, that you send me to Judah, to the city of my fathers' graves, that I may rebuild it." ⁶And the king said to me (the queen sitting beside him), "How long will you be gone, and when will you return?" So it pleased the king to send me when I had given him a time. ⁷And I said to the king, "If it pleases the king, let letters be given to me for the governors of the province Beyond the River, that they may let me pass through until I come to Judah, ⁸and a letter to Asaph, the keeper of the king's forest, that he may give me timber to make beams for the gates of the fortress of the temple, and for the wall of the city, and for the house that I shall occupy." And the king granted me what I asked, for the good hand of my God was upon me.

NEHEMIAH INSPECTS JERUSALEM'S WALLS

⁹Then I came to the governors of the province Beyond the River and gave them the king's letters. Now the king had sent with me officers of the army and horsemen. ¹⁰But when Sanballat the Horonite and Tobiah the Ammonite servant heard this, it displeased them greatly that someone had come to seek the welfare of the people of Israel.

¹¹So I went to Jerusalem and was there for three days. ¹²Then I arose in the night, I and a few men with me. And I told no one what my God had put into my heart to do for Jerusalem. There was no animal with me but the one on which I rode. ¹³I went out by night by the Valley Gate to the Dragon Spring and to the Dung Gate, and I inspected the walls of Jerusalem that were broken down and its gates that had been destroyed by fire. ¹⁴Then I went on to the Fountain Gate and to the King's Pool, but there was no room for the animal that was under me to pass. ¹⁵Then I went up in the night by the valley and inspected the wall, and I turned back and entered by the Valley Gate, and so returned. ¹⁶And the officials did not know where I had gone or what I was doing, and I had not yet told the Jews, the priests, the nobles, the officials, and the rest who were to do the work.

¹⁷Then I said to them, "You see the trouble we are in, how Jerusalem lies in ruins with its gates burned. Come, let us build the wall of Jerusalem, that we may no longer suffer derision." ¹⁸And I told them of the hand of my God that had been upon me for good, and also of the words that the king had spoken to me. And they said, "Let us rise up and build." So they strengthened their hands for the good work. ¹⁹But when Sanballat the Horonite and Tobiah the Ammonite servant and Geshem the Arab heard of it, they jeered at us and despised us and said, "What is this thing that you are doing? Are you rebelling against the king?" ²⁰Then I replied to them, "The God of heaven will make us prosper, and we his servants will arise and build, but you have no portion or right or claim^a in Jerusalem."

REBUILDING THE WALL

3 Then Eliashib the high priest rose up with his brothers the priests, and they built the Sheep Gate. They consecrated it and set up its doors. They consecrated it as far as the Tower of the Hundred, as far as the Tower of Hananel. ²And next to him the men of Jericho built. And next to them^b Zaccur the son of Imri built.

³The sons of Hassenaah built the Fish Gate. They laid its beams and set up its doors, its bolts, and its bars. ⁴And next to them Meremoth the son of Uriah, son of Hakkoz repaired. And next to them Meshullam the son of Berechiah, son of Meshezabel repaired. And next to them Zadok the son of Baana repaired. ⁵And next to them the Tekoites repaired, but their nobles would not stoop to serve their Lord.^{c}

⁶Joiada the son of Paseah and Meshullam the son of Besodeiah repaired the Gate of Yeshanah.^{d} They laid its beams and set up its doors, its bolts, and its bars. ⁷And next to them repaired Melatiah the Gibeonite and Jadon the Meronothite, the men of Gibeon and of Mizpah, the seat of the governor of the province Beyond the River. ⁸Next to them Uzziel the son of Harhaiah, goldsmiths, repaired. Next to him Hananiah, one of the perfumers, repaired, and they restored Jerusalem as far as the Broad Wall. ⁹Next to them Rephaiah the son of Hur, ruler of half the district of^e Jerusalem, repaired. ¹⁰Next to them Jedaiah the son of Harumaph repaired opposite his house. And next to him Hattush the son of Hashabneiah repaired. ¹¹Malchijah the son of Harim and Hasshub the son of Pahath-moab repaired another section and the Tower of the Ovens. ¹²Next to him Shallum the son of Hallohesh, ruler of half the district of Jerusalem, repaired, he and his daughters.

¹³Hanun and the inhabitants of Zanoah repaired the Valley Gate. They rebuilt it and set up its doors, its bolts, and its bars, and repaired a thousand cubits^f of the wall, as far as the Dung Gate.

¹⁴Malchijah the son of Rechab, ruler of the district of Beth-haccherem, repaired the Dung Gate. He rebuilt it and set up its doors, its bolts, and its bars.

¹⁵And Shallum the son of Col-hozeh, ruler of the district of Mizpah, repaired the Fountain Gate. He rebuilt it and covered it and set up its doors, its bolts, and its bars. And he built the wall of the Pool of Shelah of the king's garden, as far as the steps that go down from the city of David. ¹⁶After him Nehemiah the son of Azbuk, ruler of half the district of Beth-zur, repaired to a point opposite the tombs of David, as far as the artificial pool, and as far as the house of the mighty men. ¹⁷After him the Levites repaired: Rehum the son of Bani. Next to him Hashabiah, ruler of half the district of Keilah, repaired for his district. ¹⁸After him their brothers repaired: Bavvai the son of Henadad, ruler of half the district of Keilah. ¹⁹Next to him Ezer the son of Jeshua, ruler of Mizpah, repaired another section opposite the ascent to the armoury

---

^{a}Or memorial ^{b}Hebrew him ^{c}Or lords ^{d}Or of the old city
^{e}Or foreman of half the portion assigned to; also verses 12, 14, 15, 16, 17, 18 ^{f}A cubit was about 18 inches or 45 centimetres

at the buttress.[a] [20]After him Baruch the son of Zabbai repaired[b] another section from the buttress to the door of the house of Eliashib the high priest. [21]After him Meremoth the son of Uriah, son of Hakkoz repaired another section from the door of the house of Eliashib to the end of the house of Eliashib. [22]After him the priests, the men of the surrounding area, repaired. [23]After them Benjamin and Hasshub repaired opposite their house. After them Azariah the son of Maaseiah, son of Ananiah repaired beside his own house. [24]After him Binnui the son of Henadad repaired another section, from the house of Azariah to the buttress and to the corner. [25]Palal the son of Uzai repaired opposite the buttress and the tower projecting from the upper house of the king at the court of the guard. After him Pedaiah the son of Parosh [26]and the temple servants living on Ophel repaired to a point opposite the Water Gate on the east and the projecting tower. [27]After him the Tekoites repaired another section opposite the great projecting tower as far as the wall of Ophel.

[28]Above the Horse Gate the priests repaired, each one opposite his own house. [29]After them Zadok the son of Immer repaired opposite his own house. After him Shemaiah the son of Shecaniah, the keeper of the East Gate, repaired. [30]After him Hananiah the son of Shelemiah and Hanun the sixth son of Zalaph repaired another section. After him Meshullam the son of Berechiah repaired opposite his chamber. [31]After him Malchijah, one of the goldsmiths, repaired as far as the house of the temple servants and of the merchants, opposite the Muster Gate,[c] and to the upper chamber of the corner. [32]And between the upper chamber of the corner and the Sheep Gate the goldsmiths and the merchants repaired.

OPPOSITION TO THE WORK

4 [d] Now when Sanballat heard that we were building the wall, he was angry and greatly enraged, and he jeered at the Jews. [2]And he said in the presence of his brothers and of the army of Samaria, "What are these feeble Jews doing? Will they restore it for themselves?[e] Will they sacrifice? Will they finish in a day? Will they revive the stones out of the heaps of rubbish, and burned ones at that?" [3]Tobiah the Ammonite was beside him, and he said, "Yes, what they are building—if a fox goes up on it he will break down their stone wall!" [4]Hear, O our God, for we are despised. Turn back their taunt on their own heads and give them up to be plundered in a land where they are captives. [5]Do not cover their guilt, and let not their sin be blotted out from your sight, for they have provoked you to anger in the presence of the builders.

[6]So we built the wall. And all the wall was joined together to half its height, for the people had a mind to work.

[7][f] But when Sanballat and Tobiah and the Arabs and the Ammonites and the Ashdodites heard that the repairing of the walls of Jerusalem was going forward and that the breaches were beginning to be closed, they were very angry. [8]And they all plotted together to come and fight against Jerusalem and to cause confusion in it. [9]And we prayed to our God and set a guard as a protection against them day and night.

[10]In Judah it was said,[g] "The strength of those who bear the burdens is failing. There is too much rubble. By ourselves we will not be able to rebuild the wall." [11]And our enemies said, "They will not know or see till we come among them and kill them and stop the work." [12]At that time the Jews who lived near them came from all directions and said to us ten times, "You must return to us."[h] [13]So in the lowest parts of the space behind the wall, in open places, I stationed the people by their clans, with their swords, their spears, and their bows. [14]And I looked and arose and said to the nobles and to the officials and to the rest of the people, "Do not be afraid of them. Remember the Lord, who is great and awesome, and fight for your brothers, your sons, your daughters, your wives, and your homes."

THE WORK RESUMES

[15]When our enemies heard that it was known to us and that God had frustrated their plan, we all returned to the wall, each to his work. [16]From that day on, half of my servants worked on construction, and half held the spears, shields, bows, and coats of mail. And the leaders stood behind the whole house of Judah, [17]who were building on the wall. Those who carried burdens were loaded in such a way that each laboured on the work with one hand and held his weapon with the other. [18]And each of the builders had his sword strapped at his side while he

---

[a]Or *corner*; also verses 20, 24, 25 [b]Some manuscripts *vigorously repaired* [c]Or *Hammiphkad Gate* [d]Ch 3:33 in Hebrew [e]Or *Will they commit themselves to God?* [f]Ch 4:1 in Hebrew [g]Hebrew *Judah said* [h]The meaning of the Hebrew is uncertain

built. The man who sounded the trumpet was beside me. ¹⁹And I said to the nobles and to the officials and to the rest of the people, "The work is great and widely spread, and we are separated on the wall, far from one another. ²⁰In the place where you hear the sound of the trumpet, rally to us there. Our God will fight for us."

²¹So we laboured at the work, and half of them held the spears from the break of dawn until the stars came out. ²²I also said to the people at that time, "Let every man and his servant pass the night within Jerusalem, that they may be a guard for us by night and may labour by day." ²³So neither I nor my brothers nor my servants nor the men of the guard who followed me, none of us took off our clothes; each kept his weapon at his right hand.[a]

NEHEMIAH STOPS OPPRESSION OF THE POOR

5 Now there arose a great outcry of the people and of their wives against their Jewish brothers. ²For there were those who said, "With our sons and our daughters, we are many. So let us get grain, that we may eat and keep alive." ³There were also those who said, "We are mortgaging our fields, our vineyards, and our houses to get grain because of the famine." ⁴And there were those who said, "We have borrowed money for the king's tax on our fields and our vineyards. ⁵Now our flesh is as the flesh of our brothers, our children are as their children. Yet we are forcing our sons and our daughters to be slaves, and some of our daughters have already been enslaved, but it is not in our power to help it, for other men have our fields and our vineyards."

⁶I was very angry when I heard their outcry and these words. ⁷I took counsel with myself, and I brought charges against the nobles and the officials. I said to them, "You are exacting interest, each from his brother." And I held a great assembly against them ⁸and said to them, "We, as far as we are able, have bought back our Jewish brothers who have been sold to the nations, but you even sell your brothers that they may be sold to us!" They were silent and could not find a word to say. ⁹So I said, "The thing that you are doing is not good. Ought you not to walk in the fear of our God to prevent the taunts of the nations our enemies? ¹⁰Moreover, I and my brothers and my servants are lending them money and grain. Let us abandon this exacting of interest. ¹¹Return to them this very day their fields, their vineyards, their olive orchards, and their houses, and the percentage of money, grain, wine, and oil that you have been exacting from them." ¹²Then they said, "We will restore these and require nothing from them. We will do as you say." And I called the priests and made them swear to do as they had promised. ¹³I also shook out the fold[b] of my garment and said, "So may God shake out every man from his house and from his labour who does not keep this promise. So may he be shaken out and emptied." And all the assembly said "Amen" and praised the LORD. And the people did as they had promised.

NEHEMIAH'S GENEROSITY

¹⁴Moreover, from the time that I was appointed to be their governor in the land of Judah, from the twentieth year to the thirty-second year of Artaxerxes the king, twelve years, neither I nor my brothers ate the food allowance of the governor. ¹⁵The former governors who were before me laid heavy burdens on the people and took from them for their daily ration[c] forty shekels[d] of silver. Even their servants lorded it over the people. But I did not do so, because of the fear of God. ¹⁶I also persevered in the work on this wall, and we acquired no land, and all my servants were gathered there for the work. ¹⁷Moreover, there were at my table 150 men, Jews and officials, besides those who came to us from the nations that were around us. ¹⁸Now what was prepared at my expense[e] for each day was one ox and six choice sheep and birds, and every ten days all kinds of wine in abundance. Yet for all this I did not demand the food allowance of the governor, because the service was too heavy on this people. ¹⁹Remember for my good, O my God, all that I have done for this people.

CONSPIRACY AGAINST NEHEMIAH

6 Now when Sanballat and Tobiah and Geshem the Arab and the rest of our enemies heard that I had built the wall and that there was no breach left in it (although up to that time I had not set up the doors in the gates), ²Sanballat and Geshem sent to me, saying, "Come and let us meet

---

[a]Or *his weapon when drinking* [b]Hebrew *bosom* [c]Compare Vulgate; Hebrew *took from them for food and wine after* [d]A *shekel* was about 2/5 of an ounce or 11 grams [e]Or *prepared for me*

together at Hakkephirim in the plain of Ono." But they intended to do me harm. ³And I sent messengers to them, saying, "I am doing a great work and I cannot come down. Why should the work stop while I leave it and come down to you?" ⁴And they sent to me four times in this way, and I answered them in the same manner. ⁵In the same way Sanballat for the fifth time sent his servant to me with an open letter in his hand. ⁶In it was written, "It is reported among the nations, and Geshem[a] also says it, that you and the Jews intend to rebel; that is why you are building the wall. And according to these reports you wish to become their king. ⁷And you have also set up prophets to proclaim concerning you in Jerusalem, 'There is a king in Judah.' And now the king will hear of these reports. So now come and let us take counsel together." ⁸Then I sent to him, saying, "No such things as you say have been done, for you are inventing them out of your own mind." ⁹For they all wanted to frighten us, thinking, "Their hands will drop from the work, and it will not be done." But now, O God,[b] strengthen my hands.

¹⁰Now when I went into the house of Shemaiah the son of Delaiah, son of Mehetabel, who was confined to his home, he said, "Let us meet together in the house of God, within the temple. Let us close the doors of the temple, for they are coming to kill you. They are coming to kill you by night." ¹¹But I said, "Should such a man as I run away? And what man such as I could go into the temple and live?[c] I will not go in." ¹²And I understood and saw that God had not sent him, but he had pronounced the prophecy against me because Tobiah and Sanballat had hired him. ¹³For this purpose he was hired, that I should be afraid and act in this way and sin, and so they could give me a bad name in order to taunt me. ¹⁴Remember Tobiah and Sanballat, O my God, according to these things that they did, and also the prophetess Noadiah and the rest of the prophets who wanted to make me afraid.

THE WALL IS FINISHED

¹⁵So the wall was finished on the twenty-fifth day of the month Elul, in fifty-two days. ¹⁶And when all our enemies heard of it, all the nations around us were afraid and fell greatly in their own esteem, for they perceived that this work had been accomplished with the help of our God. ¹⁷Moreover, in those days the nobles of Judah sent many letters to Tobiah, and Tobiah's letters came to them. ¹⁸For many in Judah were bound by oath to him, because he was the son-in-law of Shecaniah the son of Arah: and his son Jehohanan had taken the daughter of Meshullam the son of Berechiah as his wife. ¹⁹Also they spoke of his good deeds in my presence and reported my words to him. And Tobiah sent letters to make me afraid.

7 Now when the wall had been built and I had set up the doors, and the gatekeepers, the singers, and the Levites had been appointed, ²I gave my brother Hanani and Hananiah the governor of the castle charge over Jerusalem, for he was a more faithful and God-fearing man than many. ³And I said to them, "Let not the gates of Jerusalem be opened until the sun is hot. And while they are still standing guard, let them shut and bar the doors. Appoint guards from among the inhabitants of Jerusalem, some at their guard posts and some in front of their own homes." ⁴The city was wide and large, but the people within it were few, and no houses had been rebuilt.

LISTS OF RETURNED EXILES

⁵Then my God put it into my heart to assemble the nobles and the officials and the people to be enrolled by genealogy. And I found the book of the genealogy of those who came up at the first, and I found written in it:

⁶These were the people of the province who came up out of the captivity of those exiles whom Nebuchadnezzar the king of Babylon had carried into exile. They returned to Jerusalem and Judah, each to his town. ⁷They came with Zerubbabel, Jeshua, Nehemiah, Azariah, Raamiah, Nahamani, Mordecai, Bilshan, Mispereth, Bigvai, Nehum, Baanah.

The number of the men of the people of Israel: ⁸the sons of Parosh, 2,172. ⁹The sons of Shephatiah, 372. ¹⁰The sons of Arah, 652. ¹¹The sons of Pahath-moab, namely the sons of Jeshua and Joab, 2,818. ¹²The sons of Elam, 1,254. ¹³The sons of Zattu, 845. ¹⁴The sons of Zaccai, 760. ¹⁵The sons of Binnui, 648. ¹⁶The sons of Bebai, 628. ¹⁷The sons of Azgad, 2,322. ¹⁸The sons of Adonikam, 667. ¹⁹The sons of Bigvai, 2,067. ²⁰The sons of Adin, 655. ²¹The sons of Ater, namely of Hezekiah, 98. ²²The sons of Hashum, 328. ²³The sons of Bezai, 324. ²⁴The sons of Hariph, 112. ²⁵The sons of Gibeon, 95. ²⁶The men of Bethlehem and Netophah, 188. ²⁷The men of Anathoth, 128. ²⁸The men of Beth-azmaveth, 42. ²⁹The men

---

[a]Hebrew *Gashmu* [b]Hebrew lacks *O God* [c]Or *would go into the temple to save his life*

of Kiriath-jearim, Chephirah, and Beeroth, 743. ³⁰The men of Ramah and Geba, 621. ³¹The men of Michmas, 122. ³²The men of Bethel and Ai, 123. ³³The men of the other Nebo, 52. ³⁴The sons of the other Elam, 1,254. ³⁵The sons of Harim, 320. ³⁶The sons of Jericho, 345. ³⁷The sons of Lod, Hadid, and Ono, 721. ³⁸The sons of Senaah, 3,930.

³⁹The priests: the sons of Jedaiah, namely the house of Jeshua, 973. ⁴⁰The sons of Immer, 1,052. ⁴¹The sons of Pashhur, 1,247. ⁴²The sons of Harim, 1,017.

⁴³The Levites: the sons of Jeshua, namely of Kadmiel of the sons of Hodevah, 74. ⁴⁴The singers: the sons of Asaph, 148. ⁴⁵The gatekeepers: the sons of Shallum, the sons of Ater, the sons of Talmon, the sons of Akkub, the sons of Hatita, the sons of Shobai, 138.

⁴⁶The temple servants: the sons of Ziha, the sons of Hasupha, the sons of Tabbaoth, ⁴⁷the sons of Keros, the sons of Sia, the sons of Padon, ⁴⁸the sons of Lebana, the sons of Hagaba, the sons of Shalmai, ⁴⁹the sons of Hanan, the sons of Giddel, the sons of Gahar, ⁵⁰the sons of Reaiah, the sons of Rezin, the sons of Nekoda, ⁵¹the sons of Gazzam, the sons of Uzza, the sons of Paseah, ⁵²the sons of Besai, the sons of Meunim, the sons of Nephushesim, ⁵³the sons of Bakbuk, the sons of Hakupha, the sons of Harhur, ⁵⁴the sons of Bazlith, the sons of Mehida, the sons of Harsha, ⁵⁵the sons of Barkos, the sons of Sisera, the sons of Temah, ⁵⁶the sons of Neziah, the sons of Hatipha.

⁵⁷The sons of Solomon's servants: the sons of Sotai, the sons of Sophereth, the sons of Perida, ⁵⁸the sons of Jaala, the sons of Darkon, the sons of Giddel, ⁵⁹the sons of Shephatiah, the sons of Hattil, the sons of Pochereth-hazzebaim, the sons of Amon.

⁶⁰All the temple servants and the sons of Solomon's servants were 392.

⁶¹The following were those who came up from Tel-melah, Tel-harsha, Cherub, Addon, and Immer, but they could not prove their fathers' houses nor their descent, whether they belonged to Israel: ⁶²the sons of Delaiah, the sons of Tobiah, the sons of Nekoda, 642. ⁶³Also, of the priests: the sons of Hobaiah, the sons of Hakkoz, the sons of Barzillai (who had taken a wife of the daughters of Barzillai the Gileadite and was called by their name). ⁶⁴These sought their registration among those enrolled in the genealogies, but it was not found there, so they were excluded from the priesthood as unclean. ⁶⁵The governor told them that they were not to partake of the most holy food until a priest with Urim and Thummim should arise.

TOTALS OF PEOPLE AND GIFTS

⁶⁶The whole assembly together was 42,360, ⁶⁷besides their male and female servants, of whom there were 7,337. And they had 245 singers, male and female. ⁶⁸Their horses were 736, their mules 245,ᵃ ⁶⁹their camels 435, and their donkeys 6,720.

⁷⁰Now some of the heads of fathers' houses gave to the work. The governor gave to the treasury 1,000 darics^b of gold, 50 basins, 30 priests' garments and 500 minas^c of silver.^{d} ⁷¹And some of the heads of fathers' houses gave into the treasury of the work 20,000 darics of gold and 2,200 minas of silver. ⁷²And what the rest of the people gave was 20,000 darics of gold, 2,000 minas of silver, and 67 priests' garments.

⁷³So the priests, the Levites, the gatekeepers, the singers, some of the people, the temple servants, and all Israel, lived in their towns.

And when the seventh month had come, the people of Israel were in their towns.

EZRA READS THE LAW

8 And all the people gathered as one man into the square before the Water Gate. And they told Ezra the scribe to bring the Book of the Law of Moses that the LORD had commanded Israel. ²So Ezra the priest brought the Law before the assembly, both men and women and all who could understand what they heard, on the first day of the seventh month. ³And he read from it facing the square before the Water Gate from early morning until midday, in the presence of the men and the women and those who could understand. And the ears of all the people were attentive to the Book of the Law. ⁴And Ezra the scribe stood on a wooden platform that they had made for the purpose. And beside him stood Mattithiah, Shema, Anaiah, Uriah, Hilkiah, and Maaseiah on his right hand, and Pedaiah, Mishael, Malchijah, Hashum, Hashbaddanah, Zechariah, and Meshullam on his left hand. ⁵And Ezra opened the book in the sight of all the people, for he was above all the people, and as he opened it all the people stood. ⁶And Ezra blessed the LORD, the great God, and all the

---

^{a}Compare Ezra 2:66 and the margins of some Hebrew manuscripts; Hebrew lacks *Their horses . . . 245* ^{b}A *daric* was a coin weighing about 1/4 of an ounce or 8.5 grams ^{c}A *mina* was about 1 1/4 pounds or 0.6 kilogram ^{d}Probable reading; Hebrew lacks *minas of silver*

people answered, "Amen, Amen," lifting up their hands. And they bowed their heads and worshipped the LORD with their faces to the ground. ⁷Also Jeshua, Bani, Sherebiah, Jamin, Akkub, Shabbethai, Hodiah, Maaseiah, Kelita, Azariah, Jozabad, Hanan, Pelaiah, the Levites,ᵃ helped the people to understand the Law, while the people remained in their places. ⁸They read from the book, from the Law of God, clearly,ᵇ and they gave the meaning, so that the people understood the reading.

THIS DAY IS HOLY

⁹And Nehemiah, who was the governor, and Ezra the priest and scribe, and the Levites who taught the people said to all the people, "This day is holy to the LORD your God; do not mourn or weep." For all the people wept as they heard the words of the Law. ¹⁰Then he said to them, "Go on your way. Eat the fat and drink sweet wine and send portions to anyone who has nothing ready, for this day is holy to our Lord. And do not be grieved, for the joy of the LORD is your strength." ¹¹So the Levites calmed all the people, saying, "Be quiet, for this day is holy; do not be grieved." ¹²And all the people went on their way to eat and drink and to send portions and to make great rejoicing, because they had understood the words that were declared to them.

FEAST OF BOOTHS CELEBRATED

¹³On the second day the heads of fathers' houses of all the people, with the priests and the Levites, came together to Ezra the scribe in order to study the words of the Law. ¹⁴And they found it written in the Law that the LORD had commanded by Moses that the people of Israel should dwell in boothsᶜ during the feast of the seventh month, ¹⁵and that they should proclaim it and publish it in all their towns and in Jerusalem, "Go out to the hills and bring branches of olive, wild olive, myrtle, palm, and other leafy trees to make booths, as it is written." ¹⁶So the people went out and brought them and made booths for themselves, each on his roof, and in their courts and in the courts of the house of God, and in the square at the Water Gate and in the square at the Gate of Ephraim. ¹⁷And all the assembly of those who had returned from the captivity made booths and lived in the booths, for from the days of Jeshua the son of Nun to that day the people of Israel had not done so. And there was very great rejoicing. ¹⁸And day by day, from the first day to the last day, he read from the Book of the Law of God. They kept the feast seven days, and on the eighth day there was a solemn assembly, according to the rule.

THE PEOPLE OF ISRAEL CONFESS THEIR SIN

9 Now on the twenty-fourth day of this month the people of Israel were assembled with fasting and in sackcloth, and with earth on their heads. ²And the Israelitesᵈ separated themselves from all foreigners and stood and confessed their sins and the iniquities of their fathers. ³And they stood up in their place and read from the Book of the Law of the LORD their God for a quarter of the day; for another quarter of it they made confession and worshipped the LORD their God. ⁴On the stairs of the Levites stood Jeshua, Bani, Kadmiel, Shebaniah, Bunni, Sherebiah, Bani, and Chenani; and they cried with a loud voice to the LORD their God. ⁵Then the Levites, Jeshua, Kadmiel, Bani, Hashabneiah, Sherebiah, Hodiah, Shebaniah, and Pethahiah, said, "Stand up and bless the LORD your God from everlasting to everlasting. Blessed be your glorious name, which is exalted above all blessing and praise.

⁶ᵉ "You are the LORD, you alone. You have made heaven, the heaven of heavens, with all their host, the earth and all that is on it, the seas and all that is in them; and you preserve all of them; and the host of heaven worships you. ⁷You are the LORD, the God who chose Abram and brought him out of Ur of the Chaldeans and gave him the name Abraham. ⁸You found his heart faithful before you, and made with him the covenant to give to his offspring the land of the Canaanite, the Hittite, the Amorite, the Perizzite, the Jebusite, and the Girgashite. And you have kept your promise, for you are righteous.

⁹"And you saw the affliction of our fathers in Egypt and heard their cry at the Red Sea, ¹⁰and performed signs and wonders against Pharaoh and all his servants and all the people of his land, for you knew that they acted arrogantly against our fathers. And you made a name for yourself, as it is to this day. ¹¹And you divided the sea before them, so that they went through the midst of the sea on dry land, and you cast their pursuers into the depths, as a stone into mighty waters. ¹²By a pillar of cloud you led them in the day, and by a pillar of fire in the

---

ᵃVulgate; Hebrew *and the Levites* ᵇOr *with interpretation*, or *paragraph by paragraph* ᶜOr *temporary shelters* ᵈHebrew *the offspring of Israel* ᵉSeptuagint adds *And Ezra said*

night to light for them the way in which they should go. ¹³You came down on Mount Sinai and spoke with them from heaven and gave them right rules and true laws, good statutes and commandments, ¹⁴and you made known to them your holy Sabbath and commanded them commandments and statutes and a law by Moses your servant. ¹⁵You gave them bread from heaven for their hunger and brought water for them out of the rock for their thirst, and you told them to go in to possess the land that you had sworn to give them.

¹⁶"But they and our fathers acted presumptuously and stiffened their neck and did not obey your commandments. ¹⁷They refused to obey and were not mindful of the wonders that you performed among them, but they stiffened their neck and appointed a leader to return to their slavery in Egypt.ᵃ But you are a God ready to forgive, gracious and merciful, slow to anger and abounding in steadfast love, and did not forsake them. ¹⁸Even when they had made for themselves a goldenᵇ calf and said, 'This is your God who brought you up out of Egypt', and had committed great blasphemies, ¹⁹you in your great mercies did not forsake them in the wilderness. The pillar of cloud to lead them in the way did not depart from them by day, nor the pillar of fire by night to light for them the way by which they should go. ²⁰You gave your good Spirit to instruct them and did not withhold your manna from their mouth and gave them water for their thirst. ²¹For forty years you sustained them in the wilderness, and they lacked nothing. Their clothes did not wear out and their feet did not swell.

²²"And you gave them kingdoms and peoples and allotted to them every corner. So they took possession of the land of Sihon king of Heshbon and the land of Og king of Bashan. ²³You multiplied their children as the stars of heaven, and you brought them into the land that you had told their fathers to enter and possess. ²⁴So the descendants went in and possessed the land, and you subdued before them the inhabitants of the land, the Canaanites, and gave them into their hand, with their kings and the peoples of the land, that they might do with them as they would. ²⁵And they captured fortified cities and a rich land, and took possession of houses full of all good things, cisterns already hewn, vineyards, olive orchards and fruit trees in abundance. So they ate and were filled and became fat and delighted themselves in your great goodness.

²⁶"Nevertheless, they were disobedient and rebelled against you and cast your law behind their back and killed your prophets, who had warned them in order to turn them back to you, and they committed great blasphemies. ²⁷Therefore you gave them into the hand of their enemies, who made them suffer. And in the time of their suffering they cried out to you and you heard them from heaven, and according to your great mercies you gave them saviours who saved them from the hand of their enemies. ²⁸But after they had rest they did evil again before you, and you abandoned them to the hand of their enemies, so that they had dominion over them. Yet when they turned and cried to you, you heard from heaven, and many times you delivered them according to your mercies. ²⁹And you warned them in order to turn them back to your law. Yet they acted presumptuously and did not obey your commandments, but sinned against your rules, which if a person does them, he shall live by them, and they turned a stubborn shoulder and stiffened their neck and would not obey. ³⁰For many years you bore with them and warned them by your Spirit through your prophets. Yet they would not give ear. Therefore you gave them into the hand of the peoples of the lands. ³¹Nevertheless, in your great mercies you did not make an end of them or forsake them, for you are a gracious and merciful God.

³²"Now, therefore, our God, the great, the mighty, and the awesome God, who keeps covenant and steadfast love, let not all the hardship seem little to you that has come upon us, upon our kings, our princes, our priests, our prophets, our fathers, and all your people, since the time of the kings of Assyria until this day. ³³Yet you have been righteous in all that has come upon us, for you have dealt faithfully and we have acted wickedly. ³⁴Our kings, our princes, our priests, and our fathers have not kept your law or paid attention to your commandments and your warnings that you gave them. ³⁵Even in their own kingdom, and amid your great goodness that you gave them, and in the large and rich land that you set before them, they did not serve you or turn from their wicked works. ³⁶Behold, we are slaves this day; in the land that you gave to our fathers to enjoy its fruit and its good gifts, behold, we are slaves. ³⁷And

---

ᵃSome Hebrew manuscripts; many Hebrew manuscripts *and in their rebellion appointed a leader to return to their slavery* ᵇHebrew *metal*

its rich yield goes to the kings whom you have set over us because of our sins. They rule over our bodies and over our livestock as they please, and we are in great distress. ³⁸ᵃ"Because of all this we make a firm covenant in writing; on the sealed document are the names ofᵇ our princes, our Levites, and our priests.

THE PEOPLE WHO SEALED THE COVENANT

10 ᶜ"On the seals are the names ofᵈ Nehemiah the governor, the son of Hacaliah, Zedekiah, ²Seraiah, Azariah, Jeremiah, ³Pashhur, Amariah, Malchijah, ⁴Hattush, Shebaniah, Malluch, ⁵Harim, Meremoth, Obadiah, ⁶Daniel, Ginnethon, Baruch, ⁷Meshullam, Abijah, Mijamin, ⁸Maaziah, Bilgai, Shemaiah; these are the priests. ⁹And the Levites: Jeshua the son of Azaniah, Binnui of the sons of Henadad, Kadmiel; ¹⁰and their brothers, Shebaniah, Hodiah, Kelita, Pelaiah, Hanan, ¹¹Mica, Rehob, Hashabiah, ¹²Zaccur, Sherebiah, Shebaniah, ¹³Hodiah, Bani, Beninu. ¹⁴The chiefs of the people: Parosh, Pahath-moab, Elam, Zattu, Bani, ¹⁵Bunni, Azgad, Bebai, ¹⁶Adonijah, Bigvai, Adin, ¹⁷Ater, Hezekiah, Azzur, ¹⁸Hodiah, Hashum, Bezai, ¹⁹Hariph, Anathoth, Nebai, ²⁰Magpiash, Meshullam, Hezir, ²¹Meshezabel, Zadok, Jaddua, ²²Pelatiah, Hanan, Anaiah, ²³Hoshea, Hananiah, Hasshub, ²⁴Hallohesh, Pilha, Shobek, ²⁵Rehum, Hashabnah, Maaseiah, ²⁶Ahiah, Hanan, Anan, ²⁷Malluch, Harim, Baanah.

THE OBLIGATIONS OF THE COVENANT

²⁸"The rest of the people, the priests, the Levites, the gatekeepers, the singers, the temple servants, and all who have separated themselves from the peoples of the lands to the Law of God, their wives, their sons, their daughters, all who have knowledge and understanding, ²⁹join with their brothers, their nobles, and enter into a curse and an oath to walk in God's Law that was given by Moses the servant of God, and to observe and do all the commandments of the LORD our Lord and his rules and his statutes. ³⁰We will not give our daughters to the peoples of the land or take their daughters for our sons. ³¹And if the peoples of the land bring in goods or any grain on the Sabbath day to sell, we will not buy from them on the Sabbath or on a holy day. And we will forego the crops of the seventh year and the exaction of every debt.

³²"We also take on ourselves the obligation to give yearly a third part of a shekelᵉ for the service of the house of our God: ³³for the showbread, the regular grain offering, the regular burnt offering, the Sabbaths, the new moons, the appointed feasts, the holy things, and the sin offerings to make atonement for Israel, and for all the work of the house of our God. ³⁴We, the priests, the Levites, and the people, have likewise cast lots for the wood offering, to bring it into the house of our God, according to our fathers' houses, at times appointed, year by year, to burn on the altar of the LORD our God, as it is written in the Law. ³⁵We bind ourselves to bring the firstfruits of our ground and the firstfruits of all fruit of every tree, year by year, to the house of the LORD; ³⁶also to bring to the house of our God, to the priests who minister in the house of our God, the firstborn of our sons and of our cattle, as it is written in the Law, and the firstborn of our herds and of our flocks; ³⁷and to bring the first of our dough, and our contributions, the fruit of every tree, the wine and the oil, to the priests, to the chambers of the house of our God; and to bring to the Levites the tithes from our ground, for it is the Levites who collect the tithes in all our towns where we labour. ³⁸And the priest, the son of Aaron, shall be with the Levites when the Levites receive the tithes. And the Levites shall bring up the tithe of the tithes to the house of our God, to the chambers of the storehouse. ³⁹For the people of Israel and the sons of Levi shall bring the contribution of grain, wine, and oil to the chambers, where the vessels of the sanctuary are, as well as the priests who minister, and the gatekeepers and the singers. We will not neglect the house of our God."

THE LEADERS IN JERUSALEM

11 Now the leaders of the people lived in Jerusalem. And the rest of the people cast lots to bring one out of ten to live in Jerusalem the holy city, while nine out of tenᶠ remained in the other towns. ²And the people blessed all the men who willingly offered to live in Jerusalem.

³These are the chiefs of the province who lived in Jerusalem; but in the towns of Judah everyone lived on his property in their towns: Israel, the priests, the Levites, the temple

---

ᵃCh 10:1 in Hebrew ᵇHebrew lacks *the names of* ᶜCh 10:2 in Hebrew ᵈHebrew lacks *the names of* ᵉA *shekel* was about 2/5 of an ounce or 11 grams ᶠHebrew *nine hands*

servants, and the descendants of Solomon's servants. ⁴And in Jerusalem lived certain of the sons of Judah and of the sons of Benjamin. Of the sons of Judah: Athaiah the son of Uzziah, son of Zechariah, son of Amariah, son of Shephatiah, son of Mahalalel, of the sons of Perez; ⁵and Maaseiah the son of Baruch, son of Col-hozeh, son of Hazaiah, son of Adaiah, son of Joiarib, son of Zechariah, son of the Shilonite. ⁶All the sons of Perez who lived in Jerusalem were 468 valiant men.

⁷And these are the sons of Benjamin: Sallu the son of Meshullam, son of Joed, son of Pedaiah, son of Kolaiah, son of Maaseiah, son of Ithiel, son of Jeshaiah, ⁸and his brothers, men of valour, 928.ᵃ ⁹Joel the son of Zichri was their overseer; and Judah the son of Hassenuah was second over the city.

¹⁰Of the priests: Jedaiah the son of Joiarib, Jachin, ¹¹Seraiah the son of Hilkiah, son of Meshullam, son of Zadok, son of Meraioth, son of Ahitub, ruler of the house of God, ¹²and their brothers who did the work of the house, 822; and Adaiah the son of Jeroham, son of Pelaliah, son of Amzi, son of Zechariah, son of Pashhur, son of Malchijah, ¹³and his brothers, heads of fathers' houses, 242; and Amashsai, the son of Azarel, son of Ahzai, son of Meshillemoth, son of Immer, ¹⁴and their brothers, mighty men of valour, 128; their overseer was Zabdiel the son of Haggedolim.

¹⁵And of the Levites: Shemaiah the son of Hasshub, son of Azrikam, son of Hashabiah, son of Bunni; ¹⁶and Shabbethai and Jozabad, of the chiefs of the Levites, who were over the outside work of the house of God; ¹⁷and Mattaniah the son of Mica, son of Zabdi, son of Asaph, who was the leader of the praise,ᵇ who gave thanks, and Bakbukiah, the second among his brothers; and Abda the son of Shammua, son of Galal, son of Jeduthun. ¹⁸All the Levites in the holy city were 284.

¹⁹The gatekeepers, Akkub, Talmon and their brothers, who kept watch at the gates, were 172. ²⁰And the rest of Israel, and of the priests and the Levites, were in all the towns of Judah, every one in his inheritance. ²¹But the temple servants lived on Ophel; and Ziha and Gishpa were over the temple servants.

²²The overseer of the Levites in Jerusalem was Uzzi the son of Bani, son of Hashabiah, son of Mattaniah, son of Mica, of the sons of Asaph, the singers, over the work of the house of God. ²³For there was a command from the king concerning them, and a fixed provision for the singers, as every day required. ²⁴And Pethahiah the son of Meshezabel, of the sons of Zerah the son of Judah, was at the king's sideᶜ in all matters concerning the people.

VILLAGES OUTSIDE JERUSALEM

²⁵And as for the villages, with their fields, some of the people of Judah lived in Kiriath-arba and its villages, and in Dibon and its villages, and in Jekabzeel and its villages, ²⁶and in Jeshua and in Moladah and Beth-pelet, ²⁷in Hazar-shual, in Beersheba and its villages, ²⁸in Ziklag, in Meconah and its villages, ²⁹in En-rimmon, in Zorah, in Jarmuth, ³⁰Zanoah, Adullam, and their villages, Lachish and its fields, and Azekah and its villages. So they encamped from Beersheba to the Valley of Hinnom. ³¹The people of Benjamin also lived from Geba onward, at Michmash, Aija, Bethel and its villages, ³²Anathoth, Nob, Ananiah, ³³Hazor, Ramah, Gittaim, ³⁴Hadid, Zeboim, Neballat, ³⁵Lod, and Ono, the valley of craftsmen. ³⁶And certain divisions of the Levites in Judah were assigned to Benjamin.

PRIESTS AND LEVITES

12 These are the priests and the Levites who came up with Zerubbabel the son of Shealtiel, and Jeshua: Seraiah, Jeremiah, Ezra, ²Amariah, Malluch, Hattush, ³Shecaniah, Rehum, Meremoth, ⁴Iddo, Ginnethoi, Abijah, ⁵Mijamin, Maadiah, Bilgah, ⁶Shemaiah, Joiarib, Jedaiah, ⁷Sallu, Amok, Hilkiah, Jedaiah. These were the chiefs of the priests and of their brothers in the days of Jeshua.

⁸And the Levites: Jeshua, Binnui, Kadmiel, Sherebiah, Judah, and Mattaniah, who with his brothers was in charge of the songs of thanksgiving. ⁹And Bakbukiah and Unni and their brothers stood opposite them in the service. ¹⁰And Jeshua was the father of Joiakim, Joiakim the father of Eliashib, Eliashib the father of Joiada, ¹¹Joiada the father of Jonathan, and Jonathan the father of Jaddua.

¹²And in the days of Joiakim were priests, heads of fathers' houses: of Seraiah, Meraiah; of Jeremiah, Hananiah; ¹³of Ezra, Meshullam; of Amariah, Jehohanan; ¹⁴of Malluchi, Jonathan; of Shebaniah, Joseph; ¹⁵of Harim, Adna; of Meraioth, Helkai; ¹⁶of Iddo, Zechariah; of Ginnethon, Meshullam; ¹⁷of Abijah, Zichri; of Miniamin, of Moadiah, Piltai; ¹⁸of Bilgah, Shammua; of Shemaiah, Jehonathan; ¹⁹of

---

ᵃCompare Septuagint; Hebrew *Jeshaiah, and after him Gabbai, Sallai, 928* ᵇCompare Septuagint, Vulgate; Hebrew *beginning* ᶜHebrew *hand*

Joiarib, Mattenai; of Jedaiah, Uzzi; ²⁰of Sallai, Kallai; of Amok, Eber; ²¹of Hilkiah, Hashabiah; of Jedaiah, Nethanel.

²²In the days of Eliashib, Joiada, Johanan, and Jaddua, the Levites were recorded as heads of fathers' houses; so too were the priests in the reign of Darius the Persian. ²³As for the sons of Levi, their heads of fathers' houses were written in the Book of the Chronicles until the days of Johanan the son of Eliashib. ²⁴And the chiefs of the Levites: Hashabiah, Sherebiah, and Jeshua the son of Kadmiel, with their brothers who stood opposite them, to praise and to give thanks, according to the commandment of David the man of God, watch by watch. ²⁵Mattaniah, Bakbukiah, Obadiah, Meshullam, Talmon, and Akkub were gatekeepers standing guard at the storehouses of the gates. ²⁶These were in the days of Joiakim the son of Jeshua son of Jozadak, and in the days of Nehemiah the governor and of Ezra, the priest and scribe.

DEDICATION OF THE WALL

²⁷And at the dedication of the wall of Jerusalem they sought the Levites in all their places, to bring them to Jerusalem to celebrate the dedication with gladness, with thanksgivings and with singing, with cymbals, harps, and lyres. ²⁸And the sons of the singers gathered together from the district surrounding Jerusalem and from the villages of the Netophathites; ²⁹also from Beth-gilgal and from the region of Geba and Azmaveth, for the singers had built for themselves villages round Jerusalem. ³⁰And the priests and the Levites purified themselves, and they purified the people and the gates and the wall.

³¹Then I brought the leaders of Judah up onto the wall and appointed two great choirs that gave thanks. One went to the south on the wall to the Dung Gate. ³²And after them went Hoshaiah and half of the leaders of Judah, ³³and Azariah, Ezra, Meshullam, ³⁴Judah, Benjamin, Shemaiah, and Jeremiah, ³⁵and certain of the priests' sons with trumpets: Zechariah the son of Jonathan, son of Shemaiah, son of Mattaniah, son of Micaiah, son of Zaccur, son of Asaph; ³⁶and his relatives, Shemaiah, Azarel, Milalai, Gilalai, Maai, Nethanel, Judah, and Hanani, with the musical instruments of David the man of God. And Ezra the scribe went before them. ³⁷At the Fountain Gate they went up straight before them by the stairs of the city of David, at the ascent of the wall, above the house of David, to the Water Gate on the east.

³⁸The other choir of those who gave thanks went to the north, and I followed them with half of the people, on the wall, above the Tower of the Ovens, to the Broad Wall, ³⁹and above the Gate of Ephraim, and by the Gate of Yeshanah,ᵃ and by the Fish Gate and the Tower of Hananel and the Tower of the Hundred, to the Sheep Gate; and they came to a halt at the Gate of the Guard. ⁴⁰So both choirs of those who gave thanks stood in the house of God, and I and half of the officials with me; ⁴¹and the priests Eliakim, Maaseiah, Miniamin, Micaiah, Elioenai, Zechariah, and Hananiah, with trumpets; ⁴²and Maaseiah, Shemaiah, Eleazar, Uzzi, Jehohanan, Malchijah, Elam, and Ezer. And the singers sang with Jezrahiah as their leader. ⁴³And they offered great sacrifices that day and rejoiced, for God had made them rejoice with great joy; the women and children also rejoiced. And the joy of Jerusalem was heard far away.

SERVICE AT THE TEMPLE

⁴⁴On that day men were appointed over the storerooms, the contributions, the firstfruits, and the tithes, to gather into them the portions required by the Law for the priests and for the Levites according to the fields of the towns, for Judah rejoiced over the priests and the Levites who ministered. ⁴⁵And they performed the service of their God and the service of purification, as did the singers and the gatekeepers, according to the command of David and his son Solomon. ⁴⁶For long ago in the days of David and Asaph there were directors of the singers, and there were songsᵇ of praise and thanksgiving to God. ⁴⁷And all Israel in the days of Zerubbabel and in the days of Nehemiah gave the daily portions for the singers and the gatekeepers; and they set apart that which was for the Levites; and the Levites set apart that which was for the sons of Aaron.

NEHEMIAH'S FINAL REFORMS

13 On that day they read from the Book of Moses in the hearing of the people. And in it was found written that no Ammonite or Moabite should ever enter the assembly of God, ²for they did not meet the people of Israel with bread and water, but hired Balaam against them to curse them—yet our God turned the curse into a blessing. ³As soon as the people heard the law, they separated from Israel all those of foreign descent.

ᵃOr of the old city ᵇOr leaders

⁴Now before this, Eliashib the priest, who was appointed over the chambers of the house of our God, and who was related to Tobiah, ⁵prepared for Tobiah a large chamber where they had previously put the grain offering, the frankincense, the vessels, and the tithes of grain, wine, and oil, which were given by commandment to the Levites, singers, and gatekeepers, and the contributions for the priests. ⁶While this was taking place, I was not in Jerusalem, for in the thirty-second year of Artaxerxes king of Babylon I went to the king. And after some time I asked leave of the king ⁷and came to Jerusalem, and I then discovered the evil that Eliashib had done for Tobiah, preparing for him a chamber in the courts of the house of God. ⁸And I was very angry, and I threw all the household furniture of Tobiah out of the chamber. ⁹Then I gave orders, and they cleansed the chambers, and I brought back there the vessels of the house of God, with the grain offering and the frankincense.

¹⁰I also found out that the portions of the Levites had not been given to them, so that the Levites and the singers, who did the work, had fled each to his field. ¹¹So I confronted the officials and said, "Why is the house of God forsaken?" And I gathered them together and set them in their stations. ¹²Then all Judah brought the tithe of the grain, wine, and oil into the storehouses. ¹³And I appointed as treasurers over the storehouses Shelemiah the priest, Zadok the scribe, and Pedaiah of the Levites, and as their assistant Hanan the son of Zaccur, son of Mattaniah, for they were considered reliable, and their duty was to distribute to their brothers. ¹⁴Remember me, O my God, concerning this, and do not wipe out my good deeds which I have done for the house of my God and for his service.

¹⁵In those days I saw in Judah people treading wine presses on the Sabbath, and bringing in heaps of grain and loading them on donkeys, and also wine, grapes, figs, and all kinds of loads, which they brought into Jerusalem on the Sabbath day. And I warned them on the day when they sold food. ¹⁶Tyrians also, who lived in the city, brought in fish and all kinds of goods and sold them on the Sabbath to the people of Judah, in Jerusalem itself! ¹⁷Then I confronted the nobles of Judah and said to them, "What is this evil thing that you are doing, profaning the Sabbath day? ¹⁸Did not your fathers act in this way, and did not our God bring all this disaster[a] on us and on this city? Now you are bringing more wrath on Israel by profaning the Sabbath."

¹⁹As soon as it began to grow dark at the gates of Jerusalem before the Sabbath, I commanded that the doors should be shut and gave orders that they should not be opened until after the Sabbath. And I stationed some of my servants at the gates, that no load might be brought in on the Sabbath day. ²⁰Then the merchants and sellers of all kinds of wares lodged outside Jerusalem once or twice. ²¹But I warned them and said to them, "Why do you lodge outside the wall? If you do so again, I will lay hands on you." From that time on they did not come on the Sabbath. ²²Then I commanded the Levites that they should purify themselves and come and guard the gates, to keep the Sabbath day holy. Remember this also in my favour, O my God, and spare me according to the greatness of your steadfast love.

²³In those days also I saw the Jews who had married women of Ashdod, Ammon, and Moab. ²⁴And half of their children spoke the language of Ashdod, and they could not speak the language of Judah, but only the language of each people. ²⁵And I confronted them and cursed them and beat some of them and pulled out their hair. And I made them swear in the name of God, saying, "You shall not give your daughters to their sons, or take their daughters for your sons or for yourselves. ²⁶Did not Solomon king of Israel sin on account of such women? Among the many nations there was no king like him, and he was beloved by his God, and God made him king over all Israel. Nevertheless, foreign women made even him to sin. ²⁷Shall we then listen to you and do all this great evil and act treacherously against our God by marrying foreign women?"

²⁸And one of the sons of Jehoiada, the son of Eliashib the high priest, was the son-in-law of Sanballat the Horonite. Therefore I chased him from me. ²⁹Remember them, O my God, because they have desecrated the priesthood and the covenant of the priesthood and the Levites.

³⁰Thus I cleansed them from everything foreign, and I established the duties of the priests and Levites, each in his work; ³¹and I provided for the wood offering at appointed times, and for the firstfruits.

Remember me, O my God, for good.

---

[a] The Hebrew word can mean *evil*, *harm*, or *disaster*, depending on the context

ESTHER

THE KING'S BANQUETS

1 Now in the days of Ahasuerus, the Ahasuerus who reigned from India to Ethiopia over 127 provinces, ²in those days when King Ahasuerus sat on his royal throne in Susa, the citadel, ³in the third year of his reign he gave a feast for all his officials and servants. The army of Persia and Media and the nobles and governors of the provinces were before him, ⁴while he showed the riches of his royal glory and the splendour and pomp of his greatness for many days, 180 days. ⁵And when these days were completed, the king gave for all the people present in Susa the citadel, both great and small, a feast lasting for seven days in the court of the garden of the king's palace. ⁶There were white cotton curtains and violet hangings fastened with cords of fine linen and purple to silver rods[a] and marble pillars, and also couches of gold and silver on a mosaic pavement of porphyry, marble, mother-of-pearl, and precious stones. ⁷Drinks were served in golden vessels, vessels of different kinds, and the royal wine was lavished according to the bounty of the king. ⁸And drinking was according to this edict: "There is no compulsion." For the king had given orders to all the staff of his palace to do as each man desired. ⁹Queen Vashti also gave a feast for the women in the palace that belonged to King Ahasuerus.

QUEEN VASHTI'S REFUSAL

¹⁰On the seventh day, when the heart of the king was merry with wine, he commanded Mehuman, Biztha, Harbona, Bigtha and Abagtha, Zethar and Carkas, the seven eunuchs who served in the presence of King Ahasuerus, ¹¹to bring Queen Vashti before the king with her royal crown,[b] in order to show the peoples and the princes her beauty, for she was lovely to look at. ¹²But Queen Vashti refused to come at the king's command delivered by the eunuchs. At this the king became enraged, and his anger burned within him.

¹³Then the king said to the wise men who knew the times (for this was the king's procedure towards all who were versed in law and judgement, ¹⁴the men next to him being Carshena, Shethar, Admatha, Tarshish, Meres, Marsena, and Memucan, the seven princes of Persia and Media, who saw the king's face, and sat first in the kingdom): ¹⁵"According to the law, what is to be done to Queen Vashti, because she has not performed the command of King Ahasuerus delivered by the eunuchs?" ¹⁶Then Memucan said in the presence of the king and the officials, "Not only against the king has Queen Vashti done wrong, but also against all the officials and all the peoples who are in all the provinces of King Ahasuerus. ¹⁷For the queen's behaviour will be made known to all women, causing them to look at their husbands with contempt,[c] since they will say, 'King Ahasuerus commanded Queen Vashti to be brought before him, and she did not come.' ¹⁸This very day the noble women of Persia and Media who have heard of the queen's behaviour will say the same to all the king's officials, and there will be contempt and wrath in plenty. ¹⁹If it please the king, let a royal order go out from him, and let it be written among the laws of the Persians and the Medes so that it may not be repealed, that Vashti is never again to come before King Ahasuerus. And let the king give her royal position to another who is better than she. ²⁰So when the decree made by the king is proclaimed throughout all his kingdom, for it is vast, all women will give honour to their husbands, high and low alike." ²¹This advice pleased the king and the princes, and the king did as Memucan proposed. ²²He sent letters to all the royal provinces, to every province in its own script and to every people in its own language, that every man be master in his own household and speak according to the language of his people.

---

[a] Or *rings* [b] Or *headdress* [c] Hebrew *to disdain their husbands in their eyes*

ESTHER CHOSEN QUEEN

2 After these things, when the anger of King Ahasuerus had abated, he remembered Vashti and what she had done and what had been decreed against her. ²Then the king's young men who attended him said, "Let beautiful young virgins be sought out for the king. ³And let the king appoint officers in all the provinces of his kingdom to gather all the beautiful young virgins to the harem in Susa the citadel, under custody of Hegai, the king's eunuch, who is in charge of the women. Let their cosmetics be given to them. ⁴And let the young woman who pleases the king[a] be queen instead of Vashti." This pleased the king, and he did so.

⁵Now there was a Jew in Susa the citadel whose name was Mordecai, the son of Jair, son of Shimei, son of Kish, a Benjaminite, ⁶who had been carried away from Jerusalem among the captives carried away with Jeconiah king of Judah, whom Nebuchadnezzar king of Babylon had carried away. ⁷He was bringing up Hadassah, that is Esther, the daughter of his uncle, for she had neither father nor mother. The young woman had a beautiful figure and was lovely to look at, and when her father and her mother died, Mordecai took her as his own daughter. ⁸So when the king's order and his edict were proclaimed, and when many young women were gathered in Susa the citadel in the custody of Hegai, Esther also was taken into the king's palace and put in the custody of Hegai, who had charge of the women. ⁹And the young woman pleased him and won his favour. And he quickly provided her with her cosmetics and her portion of food, and with seven chosen young women from the king's palace, and advanced her and her young women to the best place in the harem. ¹⁰Esther had not made known her people or kindred, for Mordecai had commanded her not to make it known. ¹¹And every day Mordecai walked in front of the court of the harem to learn how Esther was and what was happening to her.

¹²Now when the turn came for each young woman to go in to King Ahasuerus, after being twelve months under the regulations for the women, since this was the regular period of their beautifying, six months with oil of myrrh and six months with spices and ointments for women— ¹³when the young woman went in to the king in this way, she was given whatever she desired to take with her from the harem to the king's palace. ¹⁴In the evening she would go in, and in the morning she would return to the second harem in custody of Shaashgaz, the king's eunuch, who was in charge of the concubines. She would not go in to the king again, unless the king delighted in her and she was summoned by name.

¹⁵When the turn came for Esther the daughter of Abihail the uncle of Mordecai, who had taken her as his own daughter, to go in to the king, she asked for nothing except what Hegai the king's eunuch, who had charge of the women, advised. Now Esther was winning favour in the eyes of all who saw her. ¹⁶And when Esther was taken to King Ahasuerus, into his royal palace, in the tenth month, which is the month of Tebeth, in the seventh year of his reign, ¹⁷the king loved Esther more than all the women, and she won grace and favour in his sight more than all the virgins, so he set the royal crown[b] on her head and made her queen instead of Vashti. ¹⁸Then the king gave a great feast for all his officials and servants; it was Esther's feast. He also granted a remission of taxes to the provinces and gave gifts with royal generosity.

MORDECAI DISCOVERS A PLOT

¹⁹Now when the virgins were gathered together the second time, Mordecai was sitting at the king's gate. ²⁰Esther had not made known her kindred or her people, as Mordecai had commanded her, for Esther obeyed Mordecai just as when she was brought up by him. ²¹In those days, as Mordecai was sitting at the king's gate, Bigthan and Teresh, two of the king's eunuchs, who guarded the threshold, became angry and sought to lay hands on King Ahasuerus. ²²And this came to the knowledge of Mordecai, and he told it to Queen Esther, and Esther told the king in the name of Mordecai. ²³When the affair was investigated and found to be so, the men were both hanged on the gallows.[c] And it was recorded in the book of the chronicles in the presence of the king.

HAMAN PLOTS AGAINST THE JEWS

3 After these things King Ahasuerus promoted Haman the Agagite, the son of Hammedatha, and advanced him and set his throne above all the officials who

---

[a]Hebrew *who is good in the eyes of the king* [b]Or *headdress*
[c]Or *wooden beam* or *stake*; Hebrew *tree* or *wood*. This Persian execution practice involved affixing or impaling a person on a stake or pole (compare Ezra 6:11)

were with him. ²And all the king's servants who were at the king's gate bowed down and paid homage to Haman, for the king had so commanded concerning him. But Mordecai did not bow down or pay homage. ³Then the king's servants who were at the king's gate said to Mordecai, "Why do you transgress the king's command?" ⁴And when they spoke to him day after day and he would not listen to them, they told Haman, in order to see whether Mordecai's words would stand, for he had told them that he was a Jew. ⁵And when Haman saw that Mordecai did not bow down or pay homage to him, Haman was filled with fury. ⁶But he disdained*ᵃ* to lay hands on Mordecai alone. So, as they had made known to him the people of Mordecai, Haman sought to destroy*ᵇ* all the Jews, the people of Mordecai, throughout the whole kingdom of Ahasuerus.

⁷In the first month, which is the month of Nisan, in the twelfth year of King Ahasuerus, they cast Pur (that is, they cast lots) before Haman day after day; and they cast it month after month till the twelfth month, which is the month of Adar. ⁸Then Haman said to King Ahasuerus, "There is a certain people scattered abroad and dispersed among the peoples in all the provinces of your kingdom. Their laws are different from those of every other people, and they do not keep the king's laws, so that it is not to the king's profit to tolerate them. ⁹If it please the king, let it be decreed that they be destroyed, and I will pay 10,000 talents*ᶜ* of silver into the hands of those who have charge of the king's business, that they may put it into the king's treasuries." ¹⁰So the king took his signet ring from his hand and gave it to Haman the Agagite, the son of Hammedatha, the enemy of the Jews. ¹¹And the king said to Haman, "The money is given to you, the people also, to do with them as it seems good to you."

¹²Then the king's scribes were summoned on the thirteenth day of the first month, and an edict, according to all that Haman commanded, was written to the king's satraps and to the governors over all the provinces and to the officials of all the peoples, to every province in its own script and every people in its own language. It was written in the name of King Ahasuerus and sealed with the king's signet ring. ¹³Letters were sent by couriers to all the king's provinces with instruction to destroy, to kill, and to annihilate all Jews, young and old, women and children, in one day, the thirteenth day of the twelfth month, which is the month of Adar, and to plunder their goods.

¹⁴A copy of the document was to be issued as a decree in every province by proclamation to all the peoples to be ready for that day. ¹⁵The couriers went out hurriedly by order of the king, and the decree was issued in Susa the citadel. And the king and Haman sat down to drink, but the city of Susa was thrown into confusion.

ESTHER AGREES TO HELP THE JEWS

4 When Mordecai learned all that had been done, Mordecai tore his clothes and put on sackcloth and ashes, and went out into the midst of the city, and he cried out with a loud and bitter cry. ²He went up to the entrance of the king's gate, for no one was allowed to enter the king's gate clothed in sackcloth. ³And in every province, wherever the king's command and his decree reached, there was great mourning among the Jews, with fasting and weeping and lamenting, and many of them lay in sackcloth and ashes.

⁴When Esther's young women and her eunuchs came and told her, the queen was deeply distressed. She sent garments to clothe Mordecai, so that he might take off his sackcloth, but he would not accept them. ⁵Then Esther called for Hathach, one of the king's eunuchs, who had been appointed to attend her, and ordered him to go to Mordecai to learn what this was and why it was. ⁶Hathach went out to Mordecai in the open square of the city in front of the king's gate, ⁷and Mordecai told him all that had happened to him, and the exact sum of money that Haman had promised to pay into the king's treasuries for the destruction of the Jews. ⁸Mordecai also gave him a copy of the written decree issued in Susa for their destruction,*ᵈ* that he might show it to Esther and explain it to her and command her to go to the king to beg his favour and plead with him*ᵉ* on behalf of her people.

⁹And Hathach went and told Esther what Mordecai had said. ¹⁰Then Esther spoke to Hathach and commanded him to go to Mordecai and say, ¹¹"All the king's servants and the people of the king's provinces know that

---

*ᵃ*Hebrew *disdained in his eyes*   *ᵇ*Or *annihilate*   *ᶜA talent* was about 75 pounds or 34 kilograms   *ᵈ*Or *annihilation*   *ᵉ*Hebrew *and seek from before his face*

if any man or woman goes to the king inside the inner court without being called, there is but one law—to be put to death, except the one to whom the king holds out the golden sceptre so that he may live. But as for me, I have not been called to come in to the king these thirty days."

¹²And they told Mordecai what Esther had said. ¹³Then Mordecai told them to reply to Esther, "Do not think to yourself that in the king's palace you will escape any more than all the other Jews. ¹⁴For if you keep silent at this time, relief and deliverance will rise for the Jews from another place, but you and your father's house will perish. And who knows whether you have not come to the kingdom for such a time as this?" ¹⁵Then Esther told them to reply to Mordecai, ¹⁶"Go, gather all the Jews to be found in Susa, and hold a fast on my behalf, and do not eat or drink for three days, night or day. I and my young women will also fast as you do. Then I will go to the king, though it is against the law, and if I perish, I perish."[a] ¹⁷Mordecai then went away and did everything as Esther had ordered him.

ESTHER PREPARES A BANQUET

5 On the third day Esther put on her royal robes and stood in the inner court of the king's palace, in front of the king's quarters, while the king was sitting on his royal throne inside the throne room opposite the entrance to the palace. ²And when the king saw Queen Esther standing in the court, she won favour in his sight, and he held out to Esther the golden sceptre that was in his hand. Then Esther approached and touched the tip of the sceptre.

³And the king said to her, "What is it, Queen Esther? What is your request? It shall be given you, even to the half of my kingdom." ⁴And Esther said, "If it please the king,[b] let the king and Haman come today to a feast that I have prepared for the king." ⁵Then the king said, "Bring Haman quickly, so that we may do as Esther has asked." So the king and Haman came to the feast that Esther had prepared. ⁶And as they were drinking wine after the feast, the king said to Esther, "What is your wish? It shall be granted you. And what is your request? Even to the half of my kingdom, it shall be fulfilled."[c] ⁷Then Esther answered, "My wish and my request is: ⁸If I have found favour in the sight of the king, and if it please the king[d] to grant my wish and fulfil my request, let the king and Haman come to the feast that I will prepare for them, and tomorrow I will do as the king has said."

HAMAN PLANS TO HANG MORDECAI

⁹And Haman went out that day joyful and glad of heart. But when Haman saw Mordecai in the king's gate, that he neither rose nor trembled before him, he was filled with wrath against Mordecai. ¹⁰Nevertheless, Haman restrained himself and went home, and he sent and brought his friends and his wife Zeresh. ¹¹And Haman recounted to them the splendour of his riches, the number of his sons, all the promotions with which the king had honoured him, and how he had advanced him above the officials and the servants of the king. ¹²Then Haman said, "Even Queen Esther let no one but me come with the king to the feast she prepared. And tomorrow also I am invited by her together with the king. ¹³Yet all this is worth nothing to me, so long as I see Mordecai the Jew sitting at the king's gate." ¹⁴Then his wife Zeresh and all his friends said to him, "Let a gallows[e] fifty cubits[f] high be made, and in the morning tell the king to have Mordecai hanged upon it. Then go joyfully with the king to the feast." This idea pleased Haman, and he had the gallows made.

THE KING HONOURS MORDECAI

6 On that night the king could not sleep. And he gave orders to bring the book of memorable deeds, the chronicles, and they were read before the king. ²And it was found written how Mordecai had told about Bigthana[g] and Teresh, two of the king's eunuchs, who guarded the threshold, and who had sought to lay hands on King Ahasuerus. ³And the king said, "What honour or distinction has been bestowed on Mordecai for this?" The king's young men who attended him said, "Nothing has been done for him." ⁴And the king said, "Who is in the court?" Now Haman had just entered the outer court of the king's palace to speak to the king about having Mordecai hanged on the gallows[h] that he had prepared for him. ⁵And the king's young men told him, "Haman is there, standing in the court." And the king

---
[a]Hebrew *if I am destroyed, then I will be destroyed* [b]Hebrew *If it is good to the king* [c]Or *done* [d]Hebrew *if it is good to the king* [e]Or *wooden beam*; twice in this verse (see note on 2:23) [f]A *cubit* was about 18 inches or 45 centimetres [g]*Bigthana* is an alternate spelling of *Bigthan* (see 2:21) [h]Or *wooden beam* (see note on 2:23)

said, "Let him come in." ⁶So Haman came in, and the king said to him, "What should be done to the man whom the king delights to honour?" And Haman said to himself, "Whom would the king delight to honour more than me?" ⁷And Haman said to the king, "For the man whom the king delights to honour, ⁸let royal robes be brought, which the king has worn, and the horse that the king has ridden, and on whose head a royal crown*ᵃ* is set. ⁹And let the robes and the horse be handed over to one of the king's most noble officials. Let them dress the man whom the king delights to honour, and let them lead him on the horse through the square of the city, proclaiming before him: 'Thus shall it be done to the man whom the king delights to honour.'" ¹⁰Then the king said to Haman, "Hurry; take the robes and the horse, as you have said, and do so to Mordecai the Jew, who sits at the king's gate. Leave out nothing that you have mentioned." ¹¹So Haman took the robes and the horse, and he dressed Mordecai and led him through the square of the city, proclaiming before him, "Thus shall it be done to the man whom the king delights to honour."

¹²Then Mordecai returned to the king's gate. But Haman hurried to his house, mourning and with his head covered. ¹³And Haman told his wife Zeresh and all his friends everything that had happened to him. Then his wise men and his wife Zeresh said to him, "If Mordecai, before whom you have begun to fall, is of the Jewish people, you will not overcome him but will surely fall before him."

ESTHER REVEALS HAMAN'S PLOT

¹⁴While they were yet talking with him, the king's eunuchs arrived and hurried to bring Haman to the feast that Esther had prepared.

7 So the king and Haman went in to feast with Queen Esther. ²And on the second day, as they were drinking wine after the feast, the king again said to Esther, "What is your wish, Queen Esther? It shall be granted you. And what is your request? Even to the half of my kingdom, it shall be fulfilled." ³Then Queen Esther answered, "If I have found favour in your sight, O king, and if it please the king, let my life be granted me for my wish, and my people for my request. ⁴For we have been sold, I and my people, to be destroyed, to be killed, and to be annihilated. If we had been sold merely as slaves, men and women, I would have been silent, for our affliction is not to be compared with the loss to the king." ⁵Then King Ahasuerus said to Queen Esther, "Who is he, and where is he, who has dared*ᵇ* to do this?" ⁶And Esther said, "A foe and enemy! This wicked Haman!" Then Haman was terrified before the king and the queen.

HAMAN IS HANGED

⁷And the king arose in his wrath from the wine-drinking and went into the palace garden, but Haman stayed to beg for his life from Queen Esther, for he saw that harm was determined against him by the king. ⁸And the king returned from the palace garden to the place where they were drinking wine, as Haman was falling on the couch where Esther was. And the king said, "Will he even assault the queen in my presence, in my own house?" As the word left the mouth of the king, they covered Haman's face. ⁹Then Harbona, one of the eunuchs in attendance on the king, said, "Moreover, the gallows*ᶜ* that Haman has prepared for Mordecai, whose word saved the king, is standing at Haman's house, fifty cubits*ᵈ* high." And the king said, "Hang him on that." ¹⁰So they hanged Haman on the gallows that he had prepared for Mordecai. Then the wrath of the king abated.

ESTHER SAVES THE JEWS

8 On that day King Ahasuerus gave to Queen Esther the house of Haman, the enemy of the Jews. And Mordecai came before the king, for Esther had told what he was to her. ²And the king took off his signet ring, which he had taken from Haman, and gave it to Mordecai. And Esther set Mordecai over the house of Haman.

³Then Esther spoke again to the king. She fell at his feet and wept and pleaded with him to avert the evil plan of Haman the Agagite and the plot that he had devised against the Jews. ⁴When the king held out the golden sceptre to Esther, Esther rose and stood before the king. ⁵And she said, "If it please the king, and if I have found favour in his sight, and if the thing seems right before the king, and I am pleasing in his eyes, let an order be written to revoke the letters devised by Haman the Agagite, the son

---

*ᵃ*Or *headdress* *ᵇ*Hebrew *whose heart has filled him* *ᶜ*Or *wooden beam*; also verse 10 (see note on 2:23) *ᵈ*A *cubit* was about 18 inches or 45 centimetres

of Hammedatha, which he wrote to destroy the Jews who are in all the provinces of the king. ⁶For how can I bear to see the calamity that is coming to my people? Or how can I bear to see the destruction of my kindred?" ⁷Then King Ahasuerus said to Queen Esther and to Mordecai the Jew, "Behold, I have given Esther the house of Haman, and they have hanged him on the gallows,ᵃ because he intended to lay hands on the Jews. ⁸But you may write as you please with regard to the Jews, in the name of the king, and seal it with the king's ring, for an edict written in the name of the king and sealed with the king's ring cannot be revoked."

⁹The king's scribes were summoned at that time, in the third month, which is the month of Sivan, on the twenty-third day. And an edict was written, according to all that Mordecai commanded concerning the Jews, to the satraps and the governors and the officials of the provinces from India to Ethiopia, 127 provinces, to each province in its own script and to each people in its own language, and also to the Jews in their script and their language. ¹⁰And he wrote in the name of King Ahasuerus and sealed it with the king's signet ring. Then he sent the letters by mounted couriers riding on swift horses that were used in the king's service, bred from the royal stud, ¹¹saying that the king allowed the Jews who were in every city to gather and defend their lives, to destroy, to kill, and to annihilate any armed force of any people or province that might attack them, children and women included, and to plunder their goods, ¹²on one day throughout all the provinces of King Ahasuerus, on the thirteenth day of the twelfth month, which is the month of Adar.

¹³A copy of what was written was to be issued as a decree in every province, being publicly displayed to all peoples, and the Jews were to be ready on that day to take vengeance on their enemies. ¹⁴So the couriers, mounted on their swift horses that were used in the king's service, rode out hurriedly, urged by the king's command. And the decree was issued in Susa the citadel.

¹⁵Then Mordecai went out from the presence of the king in royal robes of blue and white, with a great golden crownᵇ and a robe of fine linen and purple, and the city of Susa shouted and rejoiced. ¹⁶The Jews had light and gladness and joy and honour. ¹⁷And in every province and in every city, wherever the king's command and his edict reached, there was gladness and joy among the Jews, a feast and a holiday. And many from the peoples of the country declared themselves Jews, for fear of the Jews had fallen on them.

THE JEWS DESTROY THEIR ENEMIES

9 Now in the twelfth month, which is the month of Adar, on the thirteenth day of the same, when the king's command and edict were about to be carried out, on the very day when the enemies of the Jews hoped to gain the mastery over them, the reverse occurred: the Jews gained mastery over those who hated them. ²The Jews gathered in their cities throughout all the provinces of King Ahasuerus to lay hands on those who sought their harm. And no one could stand against them, for the fear of them had fallen on all peoples. ³All the officials of the provinces and the satraps and the governors and the royal agents also helped the Jews, for the fear of Mordecai had fallen on them. ⁴For Mordecai was great in the king's house, and his fame spread throughout all the provinces, for the man Mordecai grew more and more powerful. ⁵The Jews struck all their enemies with the sword, killing and destroying them, and did as they pleased to those who hated them. ⁶In Susa the citadel itself the Jews killed and destroyed 500 men, ⁷and also killed Parshandatha and Dalphon and Aspatha ⁸and Poratha and Adalia and Aridatha ⁹and Parmashta and Arisai and Aridai and Vaizatha, ¹⁰the ten sons of Haman the son of Hammedatha, the enemy of the Jews, but they laid no hand on the plunder.

¹¹That very day the number of those killed in Susa the citadel was reported to the king. ¹²And the king said to Queen Esther, "In Susa the citadel the Jews have killed and destroyed 500 men and also the ten sons of Haman. What then have they done in the rest of the king's provinces! Now what is your wish? It shall be granted you. And what further is your request? It shall be fulfilled." ¹³And Esther said, "If it please the king, let the Jews who are in Susa be allowed tomorrow also to do according to this day's edict. And let the ten sons of Haman be hanged on the gallows."ᶜ ¹⁴So the king commanded this to be done. A decree was issued in Susa, and the ten sons of Haman were hanged. ¹⁵The Jews who were

---

ᵃOr *wooden beam* (see note on 2:23) ᵇOr *headdress* ᶜOr *wooden beam*; also verse 25 (see note on 2:23)

in Susa gathered also on the fourteenth day of the month of Adar and they killed 300 men in Susa, but they laid no hands on the plunder. [16]Now the rest of the Jews who were in the king's provinces also gathered to defend their lives, and got relief from their enemies and killed 75,000 of those who hated them, but they laid no hands on the plunder. [17]This was on the thirteenth day of the month of Adar, and on the fourteenth day they rested and made that a day of feasting and gladness. [18]But the Jews who were in Susa gathered on the thirteenth day and on the fourteenth, and rested on the fifteenth day, making that a day of feasting and gladness. [19]Therefore the Jews of the villages, who live in the rural towns, hold the fourteenth day of the month of Adar as a day for gladness and feasting, as a holiday, and as a day on which they send gifts of food to one another.

THE FEAST OF PURIM INAUGURATED

[20]And Mordecai recorded these things and sent letters to all the Jews who were in all the provinces of King Ahasuerus, both near and far, [21]obliging them to keep the fourteenth day of the month Adar and also the fifteenth day of the same, year by year, [22]as the days on which the Jews got relief from their enemies, and as the month that had been turned for them from sorrow into gladness and from mourning into a holiday; that they should make them days of feasting and gladness, days for sending gifts of food to one another and gifts to the poor.

[23]So the Jews accepted what they had started to do, and what Mordecai had written to them. [24]For Haman the Agagite, the son of Hammedatha, the enemy of all the Jews, had plotted against the Jews to destroy them, and had cast Pur (that is, cast lots), to crush and to destroy them. [25]But when it came before the king, he gave orders in writing that his evil plan which he had devised against the Jews should return on his own head, and that he and his sons should be hanged on the gallows. [26]Therefore they called these days Purim, after the term Pur. Therefore, because of all that was written in this letter, and of what they had faced in this matter, and of what had happened to them, [27]the Jews firmly bound themselves and their offspring and all who joined them, that without fail they would keep these two days according to what was written and at the time appointed every year, [28]that these days should be remembered and kept throughout every generation, in every clan, province, and city, and that these days of Purim should never fall into disuse among the Jews, nor should the commemoration of these days cease among their descendants.

[29]Then Queen Esther, the daughter of Abihail, and Mordecai the Jew gave full written authority, confirming this second letter about Purim. [30]Letters were sent to all the Jews, to the 127 provinces of the kingdom of Ahasuerus, in words of peace and truth, [31]that these days of Purim should be observed at their appointed seasons, as Mordecai the Jew and Queen Esther bound them, and as they had bound themselves and their offspring, with regard to their fasts and their lamenting. [32]The command of Esther confirmed these practices of Purim, and it was recorded in writing.

THE GREATNESS OF MORDECAI

10 King Ahasuerus imposed tax on the land and on the coastlands of the sea. [2]And all the acts of his power and might, and the full account of the high honour of Mordecai, to which the king advanced him, are they not written in the Book of the Chronicles of the kings of Media and Persia? [3]For Mordecai the Jew was second in rank to King Ahasuerus, and he was great among the Jews and popular with the multitude of his brothers, for he sought the welfare of his people and spoke peace to all his people.

JOB

JOB'S CHARACTER AND WEALTH

1 There was a man in the land of Uz whose name was Job, and that man was blameless and upright, one who feared God and turned away from evil. ²There were born to him seven sons and three daughters. ³He possessed 7,000 sheep, 3,000 camels, 500 yoke of oxen, and 500 female donkeys, and very many servants, so that this man was the greatest of all the people of the east. ⁴His sons used to go and hold a feast in the house of each one on his day, and they would send and invite their three sisters to eat and drink with them. ⁵And when the days of the feast had run their course, Job would send and consecrate them, and he would rise early in the morning and offer burnt offerings according to the number of them all. For Job said, "It may be that my children have sinned, and cursed[a] God in their hearts." Thus Job did continually.

SATAN ALLOWED TO TEST JOB

⁶Now there was a day when the sons of God came to present themselves before the Lord, and Satan[b] also came among them. ⁷The Lord said to Satan, "From where have you come?" Satan answered the Lord and said, "From going to and fro on the earth, and from walking up and down on it." ⁸And the Lord said to Satan, "Have you considered my servant Job, that there is none like him on the earth, a blameless and upright man, who fears God and turns away from evil?" ⁹Then Satan answered the Lord and said, "Does Job fear God for no reason? ¹⁰Have you not put a hedge around him and his house and all that he has, on every side? You have blessed the work of his hands, and his possessions have increased in the land. ¹¹But stretch out your hand and touch all that he has, and he will curse you to your face." ¹²And the Lord said to Satan, "Behold, all that he has is in your hand. Only against him do not stretch out your hand." So Satan went out from the presence of the Lord.

SATAN TAKES JOB'S PROPERTY AND CHILDREN

¹³Now there was a day when his sons and daughters were eating and drinking wine in their oldest brother's house, ¹⁴and there came a messenger to Job and said, "The oxen were ploughing and the donkeys feeding beside them, ¹⁵and the Sabeans fell upon them and took them and struck down the servants[c] with the edge of the sword, and I alone have escaped to tell you." ¹⁶While he was yet speaking, there came another and said, "The fire of God fell from heaven and burned up the sheep and the servants and consumed them, and I alone have escaped to tell you." ¹⁷While he was yet speaking, there came another and said, "The Chaldeans formed three groups and made a raid on the camels and took them and struck down the servants with the edge of the sword, and I alone have escaped to tell you." ¹⁸While he was yet speaking, there came another and said, "Your sons and daughters were eating and drinking wine in their oldest brother's house, ¹⁹and behold, a great wind came across the wilderness and struck the four corners of the house, and it fell upon the young people, and they are dead, and I alone have escaped to tell you."

²⁰Then Job arose and tore his robe and shaved his head and fell on the ground and worshipped. ²¹And he said, "Naked I came from my mother's womb, and naked shall I return. The Lord gave, and the Lord has taken away; blessed be the name of the Lord."

²²In all this Job did not sin or charge God with wrong.

SATAN ATTACKS JOB'S HEALTH

2 Again there was a day when the sons of God came to present themselves before the Lord, and Satan also came among them to present himself before the Lord. ²And the Lord said to Satan, "From where have you come?" Satan answered the Lord and said, "From going to and fro on the earth, and from walking up and down on it." ³And the Lord said to Satan, "Have you considered my servant Job, that there is none like him

---

[a] The Hebrew word *bless* is used euphemistically for *curse* in 1:5, 11; 2:5, 9
[b] Hebrew *the Accuser* or *the Adversary*; so throughout chapters 1–2
[c] Hebrew *the young men*; also verses 16, 17

on the earth, a blameless and upright man, who fears God and turns away from evil? He still holds fast his integrity, although you incited me against him to destroy him without reason." ⁴Then Satan answered the LORD and said, "Skin for skin! All that a man has he will give for his life. ⁵But stretch out your hand and touch his bone and his flesh, and he will curse you to your face." ⁶And the LORD said to Satan, "Behold, he is in your hand; only spare his life."

⁷So Satan went out from the presence of the LORD and struck Job with loathsome sores from the sole of his foot to the crown of his head. ⁸And he took a piece of broken pottery with which to scrape himself while he sat in the ashes.

⁹Then his wife said to him, "Do you still hold fast your integrity? Curse God and die." ¹⁰But he said to her, "You speak as one of the foolish women would speak. Shall we receive good from God, and shall we not receive evil?"ᵃ In all this Job did not sin with his lips.

JOB'S THREE FRIENDS

¹¹Now when Job's three friends heard of all this evil that had come upon him, they came each from his own place, Eliphaz the Temanite, Bildad the Shuhite, and Zophar the Naamathite. They made an appointment together to come to show him sympathy and comfort him. ¹²And when they saw him from a distance, they did not recognize him. And they raised their voices and wept, and they tore their robes and sprinkled dust on their heads towards heaven. ¹³And they sat with him on the ground seven days and seven nights, and no one spoke a word to him, for they saw that his suffering was very great.

JOB LAMENTS HIS BIRTH

3 After this Job opened his mouth and cursed the day of his birth. ²And Job said:

³ "Let the day perish on which I was born,
 and the night that said,
 'A man is conceived.'
⁴ Let that day be darkness!
 May God above not seek it,
 nor light shine upon it.
⁵ Let gloom and deep darkness claim it.
 Let clouds dwell upon it;
 let the blackness of the day terrify it.
⁶ That night—let thick darkness seize it!
 Let it not rejoice among the
 days of the year;
 let it not come into the number
 of the months.
⁷ Behold, let that night be barren;
 let no joyful cry enter it.
⁸ Let those curse it who curse the day,
 who are ready to rouse up Leviathan.
⁹ Let the stars of its dawn be dark;
 let it hope for light, but have none,
 nor see the eyelids of the morning,
¹⁰ because it did not shut the doors
 of my mother's womb,
 nor hide trouble from my eyes.

¹¹ "Why did I not die at birth,
 come out from the womb
 and expire?
¹² Why did the knees receive me?
 Or why the breasts, that
 I should nurse?
¹³ For then I would have lain
 down and been quiet;
 I would have slept; then I
 would have been at rest,
¹⁴ with kings and counsellors of the earth
 who rebuilt ruins for themselves,
¹⁵ or with princes who had gold,
 who filled their houses with silver.
¹⁶ Or why was I not as a hidden
 stillborn child,
 as infants who never see the light?
¹⁷ There the wicked cease
 from troubling,
 and there the weary are at rest.
¹⁸ There the prisoners are at
 ease together;
 they hear not the voice of
 the taskmaster.
¹⁹ The small and the great are there,
 and the slave is free from his master.

²⁰ "Why is light given to him
 who is in misery,
 and life to the bitter in soul,
²¹ who long for death, but it comes not,
 and dig for it more than for
 hidden treasures,
²² who rejoice exceedingly
 and are glad when they
 find the grave?
²³ Why is light given to a man
 whose way is hidden,
 whom God has hedged in?
²⁴ For my sighing comes instead
 ofᵇ my bread,

ᵃOr *disaster*; also verse 11 ᵇOr *like*; Hebrew *before*

and my groanings are poured
  out like water.
25 For the thing that I fear comes upon me,
  and what I dread befalls me.
26 I am not at ease, nor am I quiet;
  I have no rest, but trouble comes."

ELIPHAZ SPEAKS: THE INNOCENT PROSPER

4 Then Eliphaz the Temanite answered and said:

2 " If one ventures a word with you,
  will you be impatient?
  Yet who can keep from speaking?
3 Behold, you have instructed many,
  and you have strengthened
    the weak hands.
4 Your words have upheld him
    who was stumbling,
  and you have made firm
    the feeble knees.
5 But now it has come to you,
    and you are impatient;
  it touches you, and you
    are dismayed.
6 Is not your fear of God^a
    your confidence,
  and the integrity of your
    ways your hope?

7 " Remember: who that was
    innocent ever perished?
  Or where were the upright cut off?
8 As I have seen, those who
    plough iniquity
  and sow trouble reap the same.
9 By the breath of God they perish,
  and by the blast of his anger
    they are consumed.
10 The roar of the lion, the voice
    of the fierce lion,
  the teeth of the young
    lions are broken.
11 The strong lion perishes
    for lack of prey,
  and the cubs of the lioness
    are scattered.

12 " Now a word was brought
    to me stealthily;
  my ear received the whisper of it.
13 Amid thoughts from visions
    of the night,
  when deep sleep falls on men,
14 dread came upon me, and trembling,
  which made all my bones shake.
15 A spirit glided past my face;
  the hair of my flesh stood up.
16 It stood still,
    but I could not discern
      its appearance.
  A form was before my eyes;
    there was silence, then I
      heard a voice:
17 'Can mortal man be in the
    right before^b God?
  Can a man be pure before his Maker?
18 Even in his servants he puts no trust,
  and his angels he charges
    with error;
19 how much more those who
    dwell in houses of clay,
  whose foundation is in the dust,
  who are crushed like^c the moth.
20 Between morning and evening
    they are beaten to pieces;
  they perish for ever without
    anyone regarding it.
21 Is not their tent-cord plucked
    up within them,
  do they not die, and that
    without wisdom?'

5 "Call now; is there anyone who will answer you?
  To which of the holy ones
    will you turn?
2 Surely vexation kills the fool,
  and jealousy slays the simple.
3 I have seen the fool taking root,
  but suddenly I cursed his dwelling.
4 His children are far from safety;
  they are crushed in the gate,
  and there is no one to deliver them.
5 The hungry eat his harvest,
  and he takes it even out of thorns,^{d}
  and the thirsty pant^e after
    his^f wealth.
6 For affliction does not come
    from the dust,
  nor does trouble sprout
    from the ground,
7 but man is born to trouble
  as the sparks fly upwards.

8 "As for me, I would seek God,
  and to God would I commit
    my cause,

---

^{a}Hebrew lacks *of God* ^{b}Or *more than*; twice in this verse ^{c}Or *before* ^{d}The meaning of the Hebrew is uncertain ^{e}Aquila, Symmachus, Syriac, Vulgate; Hebrew could be read as *and the snare pants* ^{f}Hebrew *their*

9   who does great things and
      unsearchable,
    marvellous things without
      number:
10 he gives rain on the earth
    and sends waters on the fields;
11 he sets on high those who are lowly,
    and those who mourn are
      lifted to safety.
12 He frustrates the devices of the crafty,
    so that their hands achieve
      no success.
13 He catches the wise in their
      own craftiness,
    and the schemes of the wily are
      brought to a quick end.
14 They meet with darkness
      in the daytime
    and grope at noonday as
      in the night.
15 But he saves the needy from the
      sword of their mouth
    and from the hand of the mighty.
16 So the poor have hope,
    and injustice shuts her mouth.

17 "Behold, blessed is the one
      whom God reproves;
    therefore despise not the
      discipline of the Almighty.
18 For he wounds, but he binds up;
    he shatters, but his hands heal.
19 He will deliver you from six troubles;
    in seven no evil[a] shall touch you.
20 In famine he will redeem
      you from death,
    and in war from the power
      of the sword.
21 You shall be hidden from the
      lash of the tongue,
    and shall not fear destruction
      when it comes.
22 At destruction and famine
      you shall laugh,
    and shall not fear the beasts
      of the earth.
23 For you shall be in league with
      the stones of the field,
    and the beasts of the field shall
      be at peace with you.
24 You shall know that your
      tent is at peace,
    and you shall inspect your
      fold and miss nothing.
25 You shall know also that your
      offspring shall be many,
    and your descendants as the
      grass of the earth.
26 You shall come to your grave
      in ripe old age,
    like a sheaf gathered up
      in its season.
27 Behold, this we have searched
      out; it is true.
    Hear, and know it for your good."[b]

JOB REPLIES: MY COMPLAINT IS JUST

6 Then Job answered and said:

2 "Oh that my vexation were
      weighed,
    and all my calamity laid
      in the balances!
3   For then it would be heavier
      than the sand of the sea;
    therefore my words have been rash.
4   For the arrows of the
      Almighty are in me;
    my spirit drinks their poison;
    the terrors of God are
      arrayed against me.
5   Does the wild donkey bray
      when he has grass,
    or the ox low over his fodder?
6   Can that which is tasteless be
      eaten without salt,
    or is there any taste in the
      juice of the mallow?[c]
7   My appetite refuses to touch them;
    they are as food that is
      loathsome to me.[d]

8   "Oh that I might have my request,
    and that God would fulfil my hope,
9   that it would please God to crush me,
    that he would let loose his
      hand and cut me off!
10 This would be my comfort;
    I would even exult[e] in
      pain unsparing,
    for I have not denied the
      words of the Holy One.
11 What is my strength, that
      I should wait?
    And what is my end, that I
      should be patient?
12 Is my strength the strength of
      stones, or is my flesh bronze?

---

[a] Or *disaster*   [b] Hebrew *for yourself*   [c] The meaning of the Hebrew word is uncertain   [d] The meaning of the Hebrew is uncertain   [e] The meaning of the Hebrew word is uncertain

13 Have I any help in me,
    when resource is driven from me?

14 "He who withholds[1] kindness
    from a friend
    forsakes the fear of the Almighty.
15 My brothers are treacherous
    as a torrent-bed,
    as torrential streams that pass away,
16 which are dark with ice,
    and where the snow hides itself.
17 When they melt, they disappear;
    when it is hot, they vanish
        from their place.
18 The caravans turn aside
    from their course;
    they go up into the waste
        and perish.
19 The caravans of Tema look,
    the travellers of Sheba hope.
20 They are ashamed because
    they were confident;
    they come there and are
        disappointed.
21 For you have now become nothing;
    you see my calamity and are afraid.
22 Have I said, 'Make me a gift'?
    Or, 'From your wealth offer
        a bribe for me'?
23 Or, 'Deliver me from the
        adversary's hand'?
    Or, 'Redeem me from the
        hand of the ruthless'?

24 "Teach me, and I will be silent;
    make me understand how
        I have gone astray.
25 How forceful are upright words!
    But what does reproof
        from you reprove?
26 Do you think that you can
        reprove words,
    when the speech of a despairing
        man is wind?
27 You would even cast lots
        over the fatherless,
    and bargain over your friend.

28 "But now, be pleased to look at me,
    for I will not lie to your face.
29 Please turn; let no injustice be done.
    Turn now; my vindication
        is at stake.
30 Is there any injustice on my tongue?
    Cannot my palate discern the
        cause of calamity?

JOB CONTINUES: MY LIFE HAS NO HOPE

7 "Has not man a hard service on earth,
    and are not his days like the
        days of a hired hand?
2 Like a slave who longs for the shadow,
    and like a hired hand who
        looks for his wages,
3 so I am allotted months of emptiness,
    and nights of misery are
        apportioned to me.
4 When I lie down I say, 'When
        shall I arise?'
    But the night is long,
    and I am full of tossing till the dawn.
5 My flesh is clothed with
        worms and dirt;
    my skin hardens, then
        breaks out afresh.
6 My days are swifter than a
        weaver's shuttle
    and come to their end without hope.

7 "Remember that my life is a breath;
    my eye will never again see good.
8 The eye of him who sees me will
        behold me no more;
    while your eyes are on me,
        I shall be gone.
9 As the cloud fades and vanishes,
    so he who goes down to Sheol
        does not come up;
10 he returns no more to his house,
    nor does his place know
        him any more.

11 "Therefore I will not restrain
        my mouth;
    I will speak in the anguish
        of my spirit;
    I will complain in the
        bitterness of my soul.
12 Am I the sea, or a sea monster,
    that you set a guard over me?
13 When I say, 'My bed will comfort me,
    my couch will ease my complaint',
14 then you scare me with dreams
    and terrify me with visions,
15 so that I would choose strangling
    and death rather than my bones.
16 I loathe my life; I would
        not live for ever.
    Leave me alone, for my
        days are a breath.

---

[1]Syriac, Vulgate (compare Targum); the meaning of the Hebrew word is uncertain

17 What is man, that you make
so much of him,
and that you set your heart on him,
18 visit him every morning
and test him every moment?
19 How long will you not look
away from me,
nor leave me alone till I
swallow my spittle?
20 If I sin, what do I do to you, you
watcher of mankind?
Why have you made me your mark?
Why have I become a burden to you?
21 Why do you not pardon my
transgression
and take away my iniquity?
For now I shall lie in the earth;
you will seek me, but I shall not be."

BILDAD SPEAKS: JOB SHOULD REPENT

8 Then Bildad the Shuhite answered and said:

2 "How long will you say these things,
and the words of your mouth
be a great wind?
3 Does God pervert justice?
Or does the Almighty
pervert the right?
4 If your children have sinned
against him,
he has delivered them into the
hand of their transgression.
5 If you will seek God
and plead with the Almighty
for mercy,
6 if you are pure and upright,
surely then he will rouse
himself for you
and restore your rightful habitation.
7 And though your beginning
was small,
your latter days will be very great.

8 "For enquire, please, of bygone ages,
and consider what the fathers
have searched out.
9 For we are but of yesterday
and know nothing,
for our days on earth are a shadow.
10 Will they not teach you and tell you
and utter words out of their
understanding?

11 "Can papyrus grow where
there is no marsh?
Can reeds flourish where
there is no water?
12 While yet in flower and not cut down,
they wither before any other plant.
13 Such are the paths of all
who forget God;
the hope of the godless shall perish.
14 His confidence is severed,
and his trust is a spider's web.[a]
15 He leans against his house,
but it does not stand;
he lays hold of it, but it
does not endure.
16 He is a lush plant before the sun,
and his shoots spread
over his garden.
17 His roots entwine the stone heap;
he looks upon a house of stones.
18 If he is destroyed from his place,
then it will deny him, saying,
'I have never seen you.'
19 Behold, this is the joy of his way,
and out of the soil others will spring.

20 "Behold, God will not reject
a blameless man,
nor take the hand of evildoers.
21 He will yet fill your mouth
with laughter,
and your lips with shouting.
22 Those who hate you will be
clothed with shame,
and the tent of the wicked
will be no more."

JOB REPLIES: THERE IS NO ARBITER

9 Then Job answered and said:

2 "Truly I know that it is so:
But how can a man be in the
right before God?
3 If one wished to contend with him,
one could not answer him once
in a thousand times.
4 He is wise in heart and
mighty in strength
—who has hardened himself
against him, and succeeded?—
5 he who removes mountains,
and they know it not,
when he overturns them
in his anger,
6 who shakes the earth out of its place,
and its pillars tremble;

---
[a] Hebrew *house*

7 who commands the sun,
   and it does not rise;
   who seals up the stars;
8 who alone stretched out the heavens
   and trampled the waves of
      the sea;
9 who made the Bear and Orion,
   the Pleiades and the chambers
      of the south;
10 who does great things beyond
      searching out,
   and marvellous things
      beyond number.
11 Behold, he passes by me,
   and I see him not;
   he moves on, but I do not
      perceive him.
12 Behold, he snatches away; who
      can turn him back?
   Who will say to him, 'What
      are you doing?'

13 "God will not turn back his anger;
   beneath him bowed the
      helpers of Rahab.
14 How then can I answer him,
   choosing my words with him?
15 Though I am in the right, I
      cannot answer him;
   I must appeal for mercy
      to my accuser.*a*
16 If I summoned him and he
      answered me,
   I would not believe that he was
      listening to my voice.
17 For he crushes me with a tempest
   and multiplies my wounds
      without cause;
18 he will not let me get my breath,
   but fills me with bitterness.
19 If it is a contest of strength,
   behold, he is mighty!
   If it is a matter of justice, who
      can summon him?*b*
20 Though I am in the right, my own
      mouth would condemn me;
   though I am blameless, he
      would prove me perverse.
21 I am blameless; I regard not myself;
   I loathe my life.
22 It is all one; therefore I say,
   'He destroys both the blameless
      and the wicked.'
23 When disaster brings sudden death,
   he mocks at the calamity*c*
      of the innocent.

24 The earth is given into the
      hand of the wicked;
   he covers the faces of its judges—
   if it is not he, who then is it?

25 "My days are swifter than a runner;
   they flee away; they see no good.
26 They go by like skiffs of reed,
   like an eagle swooping on the prey.
27 If I say, 'I will forget my complaint,
   I will put off my sad face, and
      be of good cheer',
28 I become afraid of all my suffering,
   for I know you will not
      hold me innocent.
29 I shall be condemned;
   why then do I labour in vain?
30 If I wash myself with snow
   and cleanse my hands with lye,
31 yet you will plunge me into a pit,
   and my own clothes will abhor me.
32 For he is not a man, as I am, that
      I might answer him,
   that we should come to
      trial together.
33 There is no*d* arbiter between us,
   who might lay his hand on
      us both.
34 Let him take his rod away from me,
   and let not dread of him terrify me.
35 Then I would speak without
      fear of him,
   for I am not so in myself.

JOB CONTINUES: A PLEA TO GOD

10 "I loathe my life;
   I will give free utterance to my
      complaint;
   I will speak in the bitterness
      of my soul.
2 I will say to God, Do not condemn me;
   let me know why you
      contend against me.
3 Does it seem good to you to oppress,
   to despise the work of your hands
   and favour the designs
      of the wicked?
4 Have you eyes of flesh?
   Do you see as man sees?
5 Are your days as the days of man,
   or your years as a man's years,
6 that you seek out my iniquity
   and search for my sin,

---

*a*Or *to my judge* *b*Or *who can grant me a hearing?* *c*The meaning of the Hebrew word is uncertain *d*Or *Would that there were an*

⁷ although you know that I am not guilty,
  and there is none to deliver
    out of your hand?
⁸ Your hands fashioned and made me,
  and now you have destroyed
    me altogether.
⁹ Remember that you have
    made me like clay;
  and will you return me to the dust?
¹⁰ Did you not pour me out like milk
  and curdle me like cheese?
¹¹ You clothed me with skin and flesh,
  and knit me together with
    bones and sinews.
¹² You have granted me life
    and steadfast love,
  and your care has preserved my spirit.
¹³ Yet these things you hid in your heart;
  I know that this was your purpose.
¹⁴ If I sin, you watch me
  and do not acquit me of my iniquity.
¹⁵ If I am guilty, woe to me!
  If I am in the right, I cannot
    lift up my head,
  for I am filled with disgrace
    and look on my affliction.
¹⁶ And were my head lifted up,ᵃ you
    would hunt me like a lion
  and again work wonders against me.
¹⁷ You renew your witnesses against me
  and increase your vexation
    towards me;
  you bring fresh troops against me.

¹⁸ "Why did you bring me out
    from the womb?
  Would that I had died before
    any eye had seen me
¹⁹ and were as though I had not been,
  carried from the womb to the grave.
²⁰ Are not my days few?
  Then cease, and leave me alone,
    that I may find a little cheer
²¹ before I go—and I shall not return—
    to the land of darkness
      and deep shadow,
²² the land of gloom like thick darkness,
    like deep shadow without any order,
  where light is as thick darkness."

ZOPHAR SPEAKS: YOU DESERVE WORSE

11 Then Zophar the Naamathite
    answered and said:

² "Should a multitude of words go
    unanswered,
  and a man full of talk be
    judged right?
³ Should your babble silence men,
  and when you mock, shall
    no one shame you?
⁴ For you say, 'My doctrine is pure,
  and I am clean in God'sᵇ eyes.'
⁵ But oh, that God would speak
  and open his lips to you,
⁶ and that he would tell you the
    secrets of wisdom!
  For he is manifold in
    understanding.ᶜ
  Know then that God exacts of you
    less than your guilt deserves.

⁷ "Can you find out the deep
    things of God?
  Can you find out the limit
    of the Almighty?
⁸ It is higher than heavenᵈ—
    what can you do?
  Deeper than Sheol—what
    can you know?
⁹ Its measure is longer than the earth
  and broader than the sea.
¹⁰ If he passes through and imprisons
  and summons the court, who
    can turn him back?
¹¹ For he knows worthless men;
  when he sees iniquity, will
    he not consider it?
¹² But a stupid man will get
    understanding
  when a wild donkey's colt
    is born a man!

¹³ "If you prepare your heart,
  you will stretch out your
    hands towards him.
¹⁴ If iniquity is in your hand,
    put it far away,
  and let not injustice dwell
    in your tents.
¹⁵ Surely then you will lift up your
    face without blemish;
  you will be secure and will
    not fear.
¹⁶ You will forget your misery;
  you will remember it as waters
    that have passed away.
¹⁷ And your life will be brighter
    than the noonday;

ᵃHebrew lacks *my head* ᵇHebrew *your* ᶜThe meaning of the Hebrew is uncertain ᵈHebrew *The heights of heaven*

its darkness will be like
  the morning.
18 And you will feel secure,
  because there is hope;
  you will look around and take
  your rest in security.
19 You will lie down, and none
  will make you afraid;
  many will court your favour.
20 But the eyes of the wicked will fail;
  all way of escape will be lost to them,
  and their hope is to breathe
  their last."

JOB REPLIES: THE LORD HAS DONE THIS

12

Then Job answered and said:

2 "No doubt you are the people,
  and wisdom will die with you.
3 But I have understanding
  as well as you;
  I am not inferior to you.
  Who does not know such
  things as these?
4 I am a laughing-stock to my friends;
  I, who called to God and
  he answered me,
  a just and blameless man,
  am a laughing-stock.
5 In the thought of one who is at ease
  there is contempt for misfortune;
  it is ready for those whose feet slip.
6 The tents of robbers are at peace,
  and those who provoke
  God are secure,
  who bring their god in their hand.[a]

7 "But ask the beasts, and they
  will teach you;
  the birds of the heavens, and
  they will tell you;
8 or the bushes of the earth, and
  they will teach you;[b]
  and the fish of the sea will
  declare to you.
9 Who among all these does not know
  that the hand of the LORD
  has done this?
10 In his hand is the life of
  every living thing
  and the breath of all mankind.
11 Does not the ear test words
  as the palate tastes food?
12 Wisdom is with the aged,
  and understanding in length
  of days.

13 "With God[c] are wisdom and might;
  he has counsel and understanding.
14 If he tears down, none can rebuild;
  if he shuts a man in, none can open.
15 If he withholds the waters, they dry up;
  if he sends them out, they
  overwhelm the land.
16 With him are strength and
  sound wisdom;
  the deceived and the
  deceiver are his.
17 He leads counsellors away stripped,
  and judges he makes fools.
18 He looses the bonds of kings
  and binds a waistcloth on their hips.
19 He leads priests away stripped
  and overthrows the mighty.
20 He deprives of speech those
  who are trusted
  and takes away the discernment
  of the elders.
21 He pours contempt on princes
  and loosens the belt of the strong.
22 He uncovers the deeps out of darkness
  and brings deep darkness to light.
23 He makes nations great, and
  he destroys them;
  he enlarges nations, and
  leads them away.
24 He takes away understanding from the
  chiefs of the people of the earth
  and makes them wander in
  a trackless waste.
25 They grope in the dark without light,
  and he makes them stagger
  like a drunken man.

JOB CONTINUES: STILL I WILL HOPE IN GOD

13

"Behold, my eye has seen all this,
  my ear has heard and
  understood it.
2 What you know, I also know;
  I am not inferior to you.
3 But I would speak to the Almighty,
  and I desire to argue my
  case with God.
4 As for you, you whitewash with lies;
  worthless physicians are you all.
5 Oh that you would keep silent,
  and it would be your wisdom!
6 Hear now my argument
  and listen to the pleadings
  of my lips.

---

[a] The meaning of the Hebrew is uncertain [b] Or *or speak to the earth, and it will teach you* [c] Hebrew *him*

7 Will you speak falsely for God
    and speak deceitfully for him?
8 Will you show partiality towards him?
    Will you plead the case for God?
9 Will it be well with you when
        he searches you out?
    Or can you deceive him, as
        one deceives a man?
10 He will surely rebuke you
    if in secret you show partiality.
11 Will not his majesty terrify you,
    and the dread of him fall upon you?
12 Your maxims are proverbs of ashes;
    your defences are defences of clay.

13 "Let me have silence, and I will speak,
    and let come on me what may.
14 Why should I take my flesh in my teeth
    and put my life in my hand?
15 Though he slay me, I will hope in him;^{a}
    yet I will argue my ways to his face.
16 This will be my salvation,
    that the godless shall not
        come before him.
17 Keep listening to my words,
    and let my declaration
        be in your ears.
18 Behold, I have prepared my case;
    I know that I shall be in the right.
19 Who is there who will
        contend with me?
    For then I would be silent and die.
20 Only grant me two things,
    then I will not hide myself
        from your face:
21 withdraw your hand far from me,
    and let not dread of you terrify me.
22 Then call, and I will answer;
    or let me speak, and you reply to me.
23 How many are my iniquities
        and my sins?
    Make me know my transgression
        and my sin.
24 Why do you hide your face
    and count me as your enemy?
25 Will you frighten a driven leaf
    and pursue dry chaff?
26 For you write bitter things against me
    and make me inherit the
        iniquities of my youth.
27 You put my feet in the stocks
    and watch all my paths;
    you set a limit for^b the
        soles of my feet.
28 Man^c wastes away like a rotten thing,
    like a garment that is moth-eaten.

JOB CONTINUES: DEATH COMES SOON TO ALL

14 "Man who is born of a woman
    is few of days and full of trouble.
2 He comes out like a flower
        and withers;
    he flees like a shadow and
        continues not.
3 And do you open your eyes
        on such a one
    and bring me into judgement
        with you?
4 Who can bring a clean thing
        out of an unclean?
    There is not one.
5 Since his days are determined,
    and the number of his
        months is with you,
    and you have appointed his
        limits that he cannot pass,
6 look away from him and
        leave him alone,^{d}
    that he may enjoy, like a
        hired hand, his day.

7 "For there is hope for a tree,
    if it be cut down, that it
        will sprout again,
    and that its shoots will not cease.
8 Though its root grow old in the earth,
    and its stump die in the soil,
9 yet at the scent of water it will bud
    and put out branches like
        a young plant.
10 But a man dies and is laid low;
    man breathes his last,
        and where is he?
11 As waters fail from a lake
    and a river wastes away and dries up,
12 so a man lies down and rises
        not again;
    till the heavens are no more
        he will not awake
    or be roused out of his sleep.
13 Oh that you would hide me in Sheol,
    that you would conceal me
        until your wrath be past,
    that you would appoint me a set
        time, and remember me!
14 If a man dies, shall he live again?
    All the days of my service
        I would wait,
    till my renewal^e should come.

---
^{a} Or *Behold, he will slay me; I have no hope* ^{b} Or *you marked* ^{c} Hebrew *He*
^{d} Probable reading; Hebrew *look away from him, that he may cease*
^{e} Or *relief*

15 You would call, and I would
    answer you;
  you would long for the work
    of your hands.
16 For then you would number
    my steps;
  you would not keep watch
    over my sin;
17 my transgression would be
    sealed up in a bag,
  and you would cover over
    my iniquity.

18 "But the mountain falls and
    crumbles away,
  and the rock is removed
    from its place;
19 the waters wear away the stones;
  the torrents wash away the
    soil of the earth;
  so you destroy the hope of man.
20 You prevail for ever against
    him, and he passes;
  you change his countenance,
    and send him away.
21 His sons come to honour, and
    he does not know it;
  they are brought low, and
    he perceives it not.
22 He feels only the pain of his own body,
  and he mourns only for himself."

ELIPHAZ ACCUSES: JOB DOES NOT FEAR GOD

15

Then Eliphaz the Temanite answered and said:

2 "Should a wise man answer with
    windy knowledge,
  and fill his belly with the east wind?
3 Should he argue in unprofitable talk,
  or in words with which he
    can do no good?
4 But you are doing away with
    the fear of God[a]
  and hindering meditation
    before God.
5 For your iniquity teaches your mouth,
  and you choose the tongue
    of the crafty.
6 Your own mouth condemns
    you, and not I;
  your own lips testify against you.

7 "Are you the first man who was born?
  Or were you brought forth
    before the hills?
8 Have you listened in the
    council of God?
  And do you limit wisdom
    to yourself?
9 What do you know that
    we do not know?
  What do you understand that
    is not clear to us?
10 Both the grey-haired and the
    aged are among us,
  older than your father.
11 Are the comforts of God
    too small for you,
  or the word that deals
    gently with you?
12 Why does your heart carry you away,
  and why do your eyes flash,
13 that you turn your spirit against God
  and bring such words out
    of your mouth?
14 What is man, that he can be pure?
  Or he who is born of a woman,
    that he can be righteous?
15 Behold, God[b] puts no trust
    in his holy ones,
  and the heavens are not
    pure in his sight;
16 how much less one who is
    abominable and corrupt,
  a man who drinks injustice
    like water!

17 "I will show you; hear me,
  and what I have seen I will declare
18 (what wise men have told,
    without hiding it from
      their fathers,
19 to whom alone the land was given,
  and no stranger passed
    among them).
20 The wicked man writhes in
    pain all his days,
  through all the years that are
    laid up for the ruthless.
21 Dreadful sounds are in his ears;
  in prosperity the destroyer
    will come upon him.
22 He does not believe that he will
    return out of darkness,
  and he is marked for the sword.
23 He wanders abroad for bread,
    saying, 'Where is it?'
  He knows that a day of darkness
    is ready at his hand;

---

[a]Hebrew lacks of God [b]Hebrew he

24 distress and anguish terrify him;
  they prevail against him, like
    a king ready for battle.
25 Because he has stretched out
    his hand against God
  and defies the Almighty,
26 running stubbornly against him
  with a thickly bossed shield;
27 because he has covered his
    face with his fat
  and gathered fat upon his waist
28 and has lived in desolate cities,
  in houses that none should inhabit,
  which were ready to become
    heaps of ruins;
29 he will not be rich, and his
    wealth will not endure,
  nor will his possessions
    spread over the earth;^{a}
30 he will not depart from darkness;
  the flame will dry up his shoots,
  and by the breath of his
    mouth he will depart.
31 Let him not trust in emptiness,
    deceiving himself,
  for emptiness will be his payment.
32 It will be paid in full before his time,
  and his branch will not be green.
33 He will shake off his unripe
    grape like the vine,
  and cast off his blossom
    like the olive tree.
34 For the company of the
    godless is barren,
  and fire consumes the
    tents of bribery.
35 They conceive trouble and
    give birth to evil,
  and their womb prepares deceit."

JOB REPLIES: MISERABLE COMFORTERS ARE YOU

16 Then Job answered and said:

2 "I have heard many such things;
  miserable comforters are you all.
3 Shall windy words have an end?
  Or what provokes you
    that you answer?
4 I also could speak as you do,
    if you were in my place;
  I could join words together
    against you
  and shake my head at you.
5 I could strengthen you
    with my mouth,
  and the solace of my lips would
    assuage your pain.
6 "If I speak, my pain is not assuaged,
  and if I forbear, how much
    of it leaves me?
7 Surely now God has worn me out;
  he has^b made desolate all
    my company.
8 And he has shrivelled me up,
  which is a witness against me,
  and my leanness has risen
    up against me;
  it testifies to my face.
9 He has torn me in his wrath
    and hated me;
  he has gnashed his teeth at me;
  my adversary sharpens his
    eyes against me.
10 Men have gaped at me with
    their mouth;
  they have struck me insolently
    on the cheek;
  they mass themselves
    together against me.
11 God gives me up to the ungodly
  and casts me into the hands
    of the wicked.
12 I was at ease, and he broke me apart;
  he seized me by the neck and
    dashed me to pieces;
  he set me up as his target;
13 his archers surround me.
  He slashes open my kidneys
    and does not spare;
  he pours out my gall on the ground.
14 He breaks me with breach
    upon breach;
  he runs upon me like a warrior.
15 I have sewed sackcloth upon my skin
  and have laid my strength
    in the dust.
16 My face is red with weeping,
  and on my eyelids is deep
    darkness,
17 although there is no violence
    in my hands,
  and my prayer is pure.
18 "O earth, cover not my blood,
  and let my cry find no resting-place.
19 Even now, behold, my
    witness is in heaven,

---
^{a}Or *nor will his produce bend down to the earth* ^{b}Hebrew *you have*; also verse 8

and he who testifies for
me is on high.
20 My friends scorn me;
my eye pours out tears to God,
21 that he would argue the case
of a man with God,
as^a a son of man does with
his neighbour.
22 For when a few years have come
I shall go the way from which
I shall not return.

JOB CONTINUES: WHERE THEN IS MY HOPE?

17 "My spirit is broken; my days
are extinct;
the graveyard is ready for me.
2 Surely there are mockers about me,
and my eye dwells on their
provocation.

3 "Lay down a pledge for me with you;
who is there who will put
up security for me?
4 Since you have closed their
hearts to understanding,
therefore you will not let
them triumph.
5 He who informs against his friends
to get a share of their property—
the eyes of his children will fail.

6 "He has made me a byword
of the peoples,
and I am one before whom
men spit.
7 My eye has grown dim from vexation,
and all my members are
like a shadow.
8 The upright are appalled at this,
and the innocent stirs himself
up against the godless.
9 Yet the righteous holds to his way,
and he who has clean hands grows
stronger and stronger.
10 But you, come on again, all of you,
and I shall not find a wise
man among you.
11 My days are past; my plans
are broken off,
the desires of my heart.
12 They make night into day:
'The light,' they say, 'is near
to the darkness.'^{b}
13 If I hope for Sheol as my house,
if I make my bed in darkness,
14 if I say to the pit, 'You are my father',

and to the worm, 'My mother',
or 'My sister',
15 where then is my hope?
Who will see my hope?
16 Will it go down to the bars of Sheol?
Shall we descend together
into the dust?"^{c}

BILDAD SPEAKS: GOD PUNISHES THE WICKED

18 Then Bildad the Shuhite answered
and said:
2 "How long will you hunt for words?
Consider, and then we will speak.
3 Why are we counted as cattle?
Why are we stupid in your sight?
4 You who tear yourself in your anger,
shall the earth be forsaken for you,
or the rock be removed
out of its place?

5 "Indeed, the light of the
wicked is put out,
and the flame of his fire
does not shine.
6 The light is dark in his tent,
and his lamp above him is put out.
7 His strong steps are shortened,
and his own schemes
throw him down.
8 For he is cast into a net by his
own feet,
and he walks on its mesh.
9 A trap seizes him by the heel;
a snare lays hold of him.
10 A rope is hidden for him in the ground,
a trap for him in the path.
11 Terrors frighten him on every side,
and chase him at his heels.
12 His strength is famished,
and calamity is ready for
his stumbling.
13 It consumes the parts of his skin;
the firstborn of death
consumes his limbs.
14 He is torn from the tent in
which he trusted
and is brought to the king of terrors.
15 In his tent dwells that which
is none of his;
sulphur is scattered over
his habitation.

---

^{a}Hebrew and ^{b}The meaning of the Hebrew is uncertain
^{c}Or *Will they go down to the bars of Sheol? Is rest to be found together in the dust?*

16 His roots dry up beneath,
 and his branches wither above.
17 His memory perishes from the earth,
 and he has no name in the street.
18 He is thrust from light into darkness,
 and driven out of the world.
19 He has no posterity or progeny
 among his people,
 and no survivor where
 he used to live.
20 They of the west are appalled
 at his day,
 and horror seizes them of the east.
21 Surely such are the dwellings
 of the unrighteous,
 such is the place of him who
 knows not God."

JOB REPLIES: MY REDEEMER LIVES

19
Then Job answered and said:

2 "How long will you torment me
 and break me in pieces
 with words?
3 These ten times you have cast
 reproach upon me;
 are you not ashamed to wrong me?
4 And even if it be true that I have erred,
 my error remains with myself.
5 If indeed you magnify
 yourselves against me
 and make my disgrace an
 argument against me,
6 know then that God has put
 me in the wrong
 and closed his net about me.
7 Behold, I cry out, 'Violence!'
 but I am not answered;
 I call for help, but there is
 no justice.
8 He has walled up my way, so
 that I cannot pass,
 and he has set darkness
 upon my paths.
9 He has stripped from me my glory
 and taken the crown from my head.
10 He breaks me down on every
 side, and I am gone,
 and my hope has he pulled
 up like a tree.
11 He has kindled his wrath against me
 and counts me as his adversary.
12 His troops come on together;
 they have cast up their siege
 ramp[a] against me
 and encamp round my tent.

13 "He has put my brothers far from me,
 and those who knew me are
 wholly estranged from me.
14 My relatives have failed me,
 my close friends have forgotten me.
15 The guests in my house and
 my maidservants count
 me as a stranger;
 I have become a foreigner
 in their eyes.
16 I call to my servant, but he
 gives me no answer;
 I must plead with him with
 my mouth for mercy.
17 My breath is strange to my wife,
 and I am a stench to the children
 of my own mother.
18 Even young children despise me;
 when I rise they talk against me.
19 All my intimate friends abhor me,
 and those whom I loved have
 turned against me.
20 My bones stick to my skin
 and to my flesh,
 and I have escaped by the
 skin of my teeth.
21 Have mercy on me, have mercy
 on me, O you my friends,
 for the hand of God has
 touched me!
22 Why do you, like God, pursue me?
 Why are you not satisfied
 with my flesh?

23 "Oh that my words were written!
 Oh that they were inscribed
 in a book!
24 Oh that with an iron pen and lead
 they were engraved in the
 rock for ever!
25 For I know that my Redeemer lives,
 and at the last he will stand
 upon the earth.[b]
26 And after my skin has been
 thus destroyed,
 yet in[c] my flesh I shall see God,
27 whom I shall see for myself,
 and my eyes shall behold,
 and not another.
 My heart faints within me!
28 If you say, 'How we will pursue him!'
 and, 'The root of the matter
 is found in him',[d]

---

[a]Hebrew *their way* [b]Hebrew *dust* [c]Or *without* [d]Many Hebrew manuscripts *in me*

29 be afraid of the sword,
   for wrath brings the punishment
      of the sword,
   that you may know there
      is a judgement."

ZOPHAR SPEAKS: THE WICKED WILL SUFFER

20 Then Zophar the Naamathite answered and said:

2 "Therefore my thoughts answer me,
   because of my haste within me.
3 I hear censure that insults me,
   and out of my understanding
      a spirit answers me.
4 Do you not know this from of old,
   since man was placed on earth,
5 that the exulting of the wicked is short,
   and the joy of the godless
      but for a moment?
6 Though his height mount
      up to the heavens,
   and his head reach to the clouds,
7 he will perish for ever like
      his own dung;
   those who have seen him will
      say, 'Where is he?'
8 He will fly away like a dream
      and not be found;
   he will be chased away like a
      vision of the night.
9 The eye that saw him will
      see him no more,
   nor will his place any more
      behold him.
10 His children will seek the
      favour of the poor,
   and his hands will give
      back his wealth.
11 His bones are full of his
      youthful vigour,
   but it will lie down with
      him in the dust.

12 "Though evil is sweet in his mouth,
   though he hides it under his tongue,
13 though he is loath to let it go
   and holds it in his mouth,
14 yet his food is turned in his stomach;
   it is the venom of cobras
      within him.
15 He swallows down riches and
      vomits them up again;
   God casts them out of his belly.
16 He will suck the poison of cobras;
   the tongue of a viper will kill him.
17 He will not look upon the rivers,
   the streams flowing with
      honey and curds.
18 He will give back the fruit of
      his toil
   and will not swallow it down;
   from the profit of his trading
      he will get no enjoyment.
19 For he has crushed and
      abandoned the poor;
   he has seized a house that
      he did not build.

20 "Because he knew no contentment
      in his belly,
   he will not let anything in which
      he delights escape him.
21 There was nothing left after
      he had eaten;
   therefore his prosperity
      will not endure.
22 In the fullness of his sufficiency
      he will be in distress;
   the hand of everyone in misery
      will come against him.
23 To fill his belly to the full,
   God^a will send his burning
      anger against him
   and rain it upon him into
      his body.
24 He will flee from an iron weapon;
   a bronze arrow will strike
      him through.
25 It is drawn forth and comes
      out of his body;
   the glittering point comes
      out of his gallbladder;
   terrors come upon him.
26 Utter darkness is laid up
      for his treasures;
   a fire not fanned will devour him;
   what is left in his tent will
      be consumed.
27 The heavens will reveal his iniquity,
   and the earth will rise up
      against him.
28 The possessions of his house
      will be carried away,
   dragged off in the day of
      God's^b wrath.
29 This is the wicked man's
      portion from God,
   the heritage decreed for
      him by God."

---

^{a}Hebrew *he* ^{b}Hebrew *his*

JOB REPLIES: THE WICKED DO PROSPER

21 Then Job answered and said:

2 "Keep listening to my words,
  and let this be your comfort.
3 Bear with me, and I will speak,
  and after I have spoken, mock on.
4 As for me, is my complaint
    against man?
  Why should I not be impatient?
5 Look at me and be appalled,
  and lay your hand over your mouth.
6 When I remember, I am dismayed,
  and shuddering seizes my flesh.
7 Why do the wicked live,
  reach old age, and grow
    mighty in power?
8 Their offspring are established
    in their presence,
  and their descendants
    before their eyes.
9 Their houses are safe from fear,
  and no rod of God is upon them.
10 Their bull breeds without fail;
  their cow calves and does
    not miscarry.
11 They send out their little
    boys like a flock,
  and their children dance.
12 They sing to the tambourine
    and the lyre
  and rejoice to the sound of the pipe.
13 They spend their days in prosperity,
  and in peace they go down to Sheol.
14 They say to God, 'Depart from us!
  We do not desire the knowledge
    of your ways.
15 What is the Almighty, that we
    should serve him?
  And what profit do we get
    if we pray to him?'
16 Behold, is not their prosperity
    in their hand?
  The counsel of the wicked
    is far from me.

17 "How often is it that the lamp of
    the wicked is put out?
  That their calamity comes
    upon them?
  That God[a] distributes pains
    in his anger?
18 That they are like straw
    before the wind,
  and like chaff that the storm
    carries away?

19 You say, 'God stores up their
    iniquity for their children.'
  Let him pay it out to them,
    that they may know it.
20 Let their own eyes see their
    destruction,
  and let them drink of the
    wrath of the Almighty.
21 For what do they care for their
    houses after them,
  when the number of their
    months is cut off?
22 Will any teach God knowledge,
  seeing that he judges those
    who are on high?
23 One dies in his full vigour,
  being wholly at ease and secure,
24 his pails[b] full of milk
  and the marrow of his bones
    moist.
25 Another dies in bitterness of soul,
  never having tasted of
    prosperity.
26 They lie down alike in the dust,
  and the worms cover them.

27 "Behold, I know your thoughts
  and your schemes to wrong me.
28 For you say, 'Where is the
    house of the prince?
  Where is the tent in which
    the wicked lived?'
29 Have you not asked those
    who travel the roads,
  and do you not accept
    their testimony
30 that the evil man is spared in
    the day of calamity,
  that he is rescued in the
    day of wrath?
31 Who declares his way to his face,
  and who repays him for
    what he has done?
32 When he is carried to the grave,
  watch is kept over his tomb.
33 The clods of the valley are
    sweet to him;
  all mankind follows after him,
  and those who go before him
    are innumerable.
34 How then will you comfort me
    with empty nothings?
  There is nothing left of your
    answers but falsehood."

---
[a] Hebrew *he* [b] The meaning of the Hebrew word is uncertain

ELIPHAZ SPEAKS: JOB'S WICKEDNESS IS GREAT

22 Then Eliphaz the Temanite answered and said:

2 "Can a man be profitable to God?
    Surely he who is wise is
        profitable to himself.
3 Is it any pleasure to the Almighty
    if you are in the right,
    or is it gain to him if you make
        your ways blameless?
4 Is it for your fear of him that
        he reproves you
    and enters into judgement
        with you?
5 Is not your evil abundant?
    There is no end to your iniquities.
6 For you have exacted pledges of
        your brothers for nothing
    and stripped the naked of
        their clothing.
7 You have given no water to
        the weary to drink,
    and you have withheld bread
        from the hungry.
8 The man with power
        possessed the land,
    and the favoured man lived in it.
9 You have sent widows away empty,
    and the arms of the fatherless
        were crushed.
10 Therefore snares are all round you,
    and sudden terror overwhelms you,
11 or darkness, so that you cannot see,
    and a flood of water covers you.

12 "Is not God high in the heavens?
    See the highest stars, how
        lofty they are!
13 But you say, 'What does God know?
    Can he judge through the
        deep darkness?
14 Thick clouds veil him, so
        that he does not see,
    and he walks on the vault of heaven.'
15 Will you keep to the old way
        that wicked men have trod?
16 They were snatched away
        before their time;
    their foundation was washed away.[a]
17 They said to God, 'Depart from us',
    and 'What can the Almighty
        do to us?'[b]
18 Yet he filled their houses
        with good things—
    but the counsel of the wicked
        is far from me.
19 The righteous see it and are glad;
    the innocent one mocks at them,
20 saying, 'Surely our adversaries
        are cut off,
    and what they left the fire
        has consumed.'

21 "Agree with God, and be at peace;
    thereby good will come to you.
22 Receive instruction from his mouth,
    and lay up his words in your heart.
23 If you return to the Almighty
        you will be built up;
    if you remove injustice far
        from your tents,
24 if you lay gold in the dust,
    and gold of Ophir among the
        stones of the torrent-bed,
25 then the Almighty will be your gold
    and your precious silver.
26 For then you will delight
        yourself in the Almighty
    and lift up your face to God.
27 You will make your prayer to
        him, and he will hear you,
    and you will pay your vows.
28 You will decide on a matter, and it
        will be established for you,
    and light will shine on your ways.
29 For when they are humbled you
        say, 'It is because of pride';[c]
    but he saves the lowly.
30 He delivers even the one who
        is not innocent,
    who will be delivered through the
        cleanness of your hands."

JOB REPLIES: WHERE IS GOD?

23 Then Job answered and said:

2 "Today also my complaint
        is bitter;[d]
    my hand is heavy on account
        of my groaning.
3 Oh, that I knew where I
        might find him,
    that I might come even to his seat!
4 I would lay my case before him
    and fill my mouth with arguments.
5 I would know what he
        would answer me

---
[a]Or their foundation was poured out as a stream (or river)
[b]Hebrew them [c]Or you say, 'It is exaltation' [d]Or defiant

and understand what he
  would say to me.
6 Would he contend with me in the
    greatness of his power?
  No; he would pay attention to me.
7 There an upright man could
    argue with him,
  and I would be acquitted for
    ever by my judge.

8 "Behold, I go forwards, but
    he is not there,
  and backwards, but I do
    not perceive him;
9 on the left hand when he is working,
    I do not behold him;
  he turns to the right hand,
    but I do not see him.
10 But he knows the way that I take;
    when he has tried me, I shall
    come out as gold.
11 My foot has held fast to his steps;
    I have kept his way and have
    not turned aside.
12 I have not departed from the
    commandment of his lips;
  I have treasured the words
    of his mouth more than
    my portion of food.
13 But he is unchangeable,^{a} and
    who can turn him back?
  What he desires, that he does.
14 For he will complete what
    he appoints for me,
  and many such things
    are in his mind.
15 Therefore I am terrified at his presence;
    when I consider, I am in
    dread of him.
16 God has made my heart faint;
    the Almighty has terrified me;
17 yet I am not silenced because
    of the darkness,
  nor because thick darkness
    covers my face.

24

"Why are not times of
  judgement kept by the Almighty,
  and why do those who know
    him never see his days?
2 Some move landmarks;
    they seize flocks and pasture them.
3 They drive away the donkey
    of the fatherless;
  they take the widow's ox
    for a pledge.

4 They thrust the poor off the road;
    the poor of the earth all
    hide themselves.
5 Behold, like wild donkeys in the desert
    the poor^b go out to their
    toil, seeking game;
  the wasteland yields food
    for their children.
6 They gather their^c fodder in the field,
    and they glean the vineyard
    of the wicked man.
7 They lie all night naked,
    without clothing,
  and have no covering in the cold.
8 They are wet with the rain
    of the mountains
  and cling to the rock for
    lack of shelter.
9 (There are those who snatch the
    fatherless child from the breast,
  and they take a pledge
    against the poor.)
10 They go about naked,
    without clothing;
  hungry, they carry the sheaves;
11 among the olive rows of the
    wicked^d they make oil;
  they tread the wine presses,
    but suffer thirst.
12 From out of the city the dying^e groan,
    and the soul of the wounded
    cries for help;
  yet God charges no one with wrong.

13 "There are those who rebel
    against the light,
  who are not acquainted
    with its ways,
  and do not stay in its paths.
14 The murderer rises before it is light,
    that he may kill the poor and needy,
    and in the night he is like a thief.
15 The eye of the adulterer also
    waits for the twilight,
  saying, 'No eye will see me';
    and he veils his face.
16 In the dark they dig through houses;
    by day they shut themselves up;
    they do not know the light.
17 For deep darkness is morning
    to all of them;
  for they are friends with the
    terrors of deep darkness.

---

^{a}Or one ^{b}Hebrew they ^{c}Hebrew his ^{d}Hebrew their olive rows ^{e}Or the men

18 "You say, 'Swift are they on the
         face of the waters;
       their portion is cursed in the land;
       no treader turns towards
         their vineyards.
19 Drought and heat snatch away
         the snow waters;
       so does Sheol those who
         have sinned.
20 The womb forgets them;
       the worm finds them sweet;
       they are no longer remembered,
       so wickedness is broken like a tree.'
21 "They wrong the barren,
         childless woman,
       and do no good to the widow.
22 Yet God[a] prolongs the life of the
         mighty by his power;
       they rise up when they despair of life.
23 He gives them security, and
         they are supported,
       and his eyes are upon their ways.
24 They are exalted a little while,
         and then are gone;
       they are brought low and
         gathered up like all others;
       they are cut off like the ears of corn.
25 If it is not so, who will prove me a liar
       and show that there is nothing
         in what I say?"

BILDAD SPEAKS: MAN CANNOT BE RIGHTEOUS

25 Then Bildad the Shuhite answered and said:

2 "Dominion and fear are with God;[b]
       he makes peace in his high heaven.
3 Is there any number to his armies?
       Upon whom does his light not arise?
4 How then can man be in the
         right before God?
       How can he who is born of
         woman be pure?
5 Behold, even the moon is not bright,
       and the stars are not pure in his eyes;
6 how much less man, who is a maggot,
       and the son of man, who is a worm!"

JOB REPLIES: GOD'S MAJESTY IS UNSEARCHABLE

26 Then Job answered and said:

2 "How you have helped him
       who has no power!
     How you have saved the arm
       that has no strength!
3 How you have counselled him
       who has no wisdom,
     and plentifully declared
       sound knowledge!
4 With whose help have you
       uttered words,
     and whose breath has come
       out from you?
5 The dead tremble
       under the waters and their
         inhabitants.
6 Sheol is naked before God,[c]
       and Abaddon has no covering.
7 He stretches out the north over the void
       and hangs the earth on nothing.
8 He binds up the waters in
         his thick clouds,
       and the cloud is not split
         open under them.
9 He covers the face of the full moon[d]
       and spreads over it his cloud.
10 He has inscribed a circle on
         the face of the waters
       at the boundary between
         light and darkness.
11 The pillars of heaven tremble
       and are astounded at his rebuke.
12 By his power he stilled the sea;
       by his understanding he
         shattered Rahab.
13 By his wind the heavens
         were made fair;
       his hand pierced the fleeing serpent.
14 Behold, these are but the
         outskirts of his ways,
       and how small a whisper
         do we hear of him!
       But the thunder of his power
         who can understand?"

JOB CONTINUES: I WILL MAINTAIN MY INTEGRITY

27 And Job again took up his discourse, and said:

2 "As God lives, who has taken
       away my right,
     and the Almighty, who has
       made my soul bitter,
3 as long as my breath is in me,
       and the spirit of God is
         in my nostrils,

---
[a]Hebrew he [b]Hebrew him [c]Hebrew him [d]Or his throne

⁴ my lips will not speak falsehood,
  and my tongue will not utter deceit.
⁵ Far be it from me to say
    that you are right;
  till I die I will not put away
    my integrity from me.
⁶ I hold fast my righteousness
    and will not let it go;
  my heart does not reproach
    me for any of my days.

⁷ "Let my enemy be as the wicked,
  and let him who rises up against
    me be as the unrighteous.
⁸ For what is the hope of the godless
    when God cuts him off,
  when God takes away his life?
⁹ Will God hear his cry
    when distress comes upon him?
¹⁰ Will he take delight in the Almighty?
   Will he call upon God at all times?
¹¹ I will teach you concerning
     the hand of God;
   what is with the Almighty
     I will not conceal.
¹² Behold, all of you have seen
     it yourselves;
   why then have you become
     altogether vain?

¹³ "This is the portion of a wicked
     man with God,
   and the heritage that oppressors
     receive from the Almighty:
¹⁴ If his children are multiplied,
     it is for the sword,
   and his descendants have
     not enough bread.
¹⁵ Those who survive him the
     pestilence buries,
   and his widows do not weep.
¹⁶ Though he heap up silver like dust,
     and pile up clothing like clay,
¹⁷ he may pile it up, but the
     righteous will wear it,
   and the innocent will
     divide the silver.
¹⁸ He builds his house like a moth's,
     like a booth that a watchman makes.
¹⁹ He goes to bed rich, but will
     do so no more;
   he opens his eyes, and his
     wealth is gone.
²⁰ Terrors overtake him like a flood;
     in the night a whirlwind
     carries him off.

²¹ The east wind lifts him up
     and he is gone;
   it sweeps him out of his place.
²² It^a hurls at him without pity;
   he flees from its^b power in
     headlong flight.
²³ It claps its hands at him
   and hisses at him from its place.

JOB CONTINUES: WHERE IS WISDOM?

28 "Surely there is a mine for silver,
     and a place for gold that
       they refine.
² Iron is taken out of the earth,
   and copper is smelted from the ore.
³ Man puts an end to darkness
   and searches out to the farthest limit
     the ore in gloom and deep darkness.
⁴ He opens shafts in a valley away
     from where anyone lives;
   they are forgotten by travellers;
   they hang in the air, far away from
     mankind; they swing to and fro.
⁵ As for the earth, out of it comes bread,
   but underneath it is turned
     up as by fire.
⁶ Its stones are the place of sapphires,^{c}
   and it has dust of gold.

⁷ "That path no bird of prey knows,
   and the falcon's eye has not seen it.
⁸ The proud beasts have not trodden it;
   the lion has not passed over it.

⁹ "Man puts his hand to the flinty rock
     and overturns mountains
       by the roots.
¹⁰ He cuts out channels in the rocks,
     and his eye sees every
       precious thing.
¹¹ He dams up the streams so that
     they do not trickle,
   and the thing that is hidden
     he brings out to light.

¹² "But where shall wisdom be found?
   And where is the place of
     understanding?
¹³ Man does not know its worth,
   and it is not found in the
     land of the living.
¹⁴ The deep says, 'It is not in me',
   and the sea says, 'It is not with me.'

---

^{a}Or *He* (that is, God); also verse 23 ^{b}Or *his*; also verse 23 ^{c}Or *lapis lazuli*; also verse 16

15 It cannot be bought for gold,
      and silver cannot be weighed
         as its price.
16 It cannot be valued in the
      gold of Ophir,
         in precious onyx or sapphire.
17 Gold and glass cannot equal it,
      nor can it be exchanged for
         jewels of fine gold.
18 No mention shall be made of
      coral or of crystal;
         the price of wisdom is above pearls.
19 The topaz of Ethiopia cannot equal it,
      nor can it be valued in pure gold.

20 "From where, then, does wisdom come?
      And where is the place of
         understanding?
21 It is hidden from the eyes of all living
      and concealed from the
         birds of the air.
22 Abaddon and Death say,
      'We have heard a rumour of
         it with our ears.'

23 "God understands the way to it,
      and he knows its place.
24 For he looks to the ends of the earth
      and sees everything under
         the heavens.
25 When he gave to the wind its weight
      and apportioned the waters
         by measure,
26 when he made a decree for the rain
      and a way for the lightning
         of the thunder,
27 then he saw it and declared it;
      he established it, and
         searched it out.
28 And he said to man,
      'Behold, the fear of the Lord,
         that is wisdom,
      and to turn away from evil
         is understanding.'"

JOB'S SUMMARY DEFENCE

29 And Job again took up his discourse, and said:

2 "Oh, that I were as in the months
      of old,
      as in the days when God
         watched over me,
3 when his lamp shone upon my head,
      and by his light I walked
         through darkness,
4 as I was in my prime,[a]
      when the friendship of God
         was upon my tent,
5 when the Almighty was yet with me,
      when my children were
         all round me,
6 when my steps were washed
      with butter,
      and the rock poured out for
         me streams of oil!
7 When I went out to the gate of the city,
      when I prepared my seat
         in the square,
8 the young men saw me and withdrew,
      and the aged rose and stood;
9 the princes refrained from talking
      and laid their hand on their mouth;
10 the voice of the nobles was hushed,
      and their tongue stuck to the
         roof of their mouth.
11 When the ear heard, it
      called me blessed,
      and when the eye saw, it approved,
12 because I delivered the poor
      who cried for help,
      and the fatherless who had
         none to help him.
13 The blessing of him who was about
      to perish came upon me,
      and I caused the widow's
         heart to sing for joy.
14 I put on righteousness, and
      it clothed me;
      my justice was like a robe
         and a turban.
15 I was eyes to the blind
      and feet to the lame.
16 I was a father to the needy,
      and I searched out the cause of
         him whom I did not know.
17 I broke the fangs of the unrighteous
      and made him drop his prey
         from his teeth.
18 Then I thought, 'I shall die in my nest,
      and I shall multiply my
         days as the sand,
19 my roots spread out to the waters,
      with the dew all night on
         my branches,
20 my glory fresh with me,
      and my bow ever new in my hand.'

21 "Men listened to me and waited
      and kept silence for my counsel.

---
[a]Hebrew *my autumn days*

22 After I spoke they did not speak again,
   and my word dropped upon them.
23 They waited for me as for the rain,
   and they opened their mouths
     as for the spring rain.
24 I smiled on them when they
     had no confidence,
   and the light of my face they
     did not cast down.
25 I chose their way and sat as chief,
   and I lived like a king
     among his troops,
   like one who comforts mourners.

30

"But now they laugh at me,
   men who are younger than I,
   whose fathers I would have
     disdained
   to set with the dogs of my flock.
2 What could I gain from the
     strength of their hands,
   men whose vigour is gone?
3 Through want and hard hunger
     they gnaw the dry ground by night
     in waste and desolation;
4 they pick saltwort and the
     leaves of bushes,
   and the roots of the broom
     tree for their food.[a]
5 They are driven out from
     human company;
   they shout after them as after a thief.
6 In the gullies of the torrents
     they must dwell,
   in holes of the earth and of the rocks.
7 Among the bushes they bray;
   under the nettles they
     huddle together.
8 A senseless, a nameless brood,
   they have been whipped
     out of the land.

9 "And now I have become their song;
   I am a byword to them.
10 They abhor me; they keep
     aloof from me;
   they do not hesitate to spit
     at the sight of me.
11 Because God has loosed my
     cord and humbled me,
   they have cast off restraint[b]
     in my presence.
12 On my right hand the rabble rise;
   they push away my feet;
   they cast up against me their
     ways of destruction.
13 They break up my path;
   they promote my calamity;
   they need no one to help them.
14 As through a wide breach they come;
   amid the crash they roll on.
15 Terrors are turned upon me;
   my honour is pursued
     as by the wind,
   and my prosperity has passed
     away like a cloud.

16 "And now my soul is poured
     out within me;
   days of affliction have
     taken hold of me.
17 The night racks my bones,
   and the pain that gnaws
     me takes no rest.
18 With great force my garment
     is disfigured;
   it binds me about like the
     collar of my tunic.
19 God[c] has cast me into the mire,
   and I have become like
     dust and ashes.
20 I cry to you for help and you
     do not answer me;
   I stand, and you only look at me.
21 You have turned cruel to me;
   with the might of your hand
     you persecute me.
22 You lift me up on the wind; you
     make me ride on it,
   and you toss me about in the
     roar of the storm.
23 For I know that you will
     bring me to death
   and to the house appointed
     for all living.

24 "Yet does not one in a heap of
     ruins stretch out his hand,
   and in his disaster cry for help?[d]
25 Did not I weep for him whose
     day was hard?
   Was not my soul grieved
     for the needy?
26 But when I hoped for good, evil came,
   and when I waited for light,
     darkness came.
27 My inward parts are in turmoil
     and never still;
   days of affliction come to meet me.

[a]Or *warmth* [b]Hebrew *the bridle* [c]Hebrew *He* [d]The meaning of the Hebrew is uncertain

28 I go about darkened, but
        not by the sun;
    I stand up in the assembly
        and cry for help.
29 I am a brother of jackals
        and a companion of ostriches.
30 My skin turns black and falls from me,
        and my bones burn with heat.
31 My lyre is turned to mourning,
        and my pipe to the voice of
            those who weep.

JOB'S FINAL APPEAL

31 "I have made a covenant with
        my eyes;
    how then could I gaze at a virgin?
2 What would be my portion
        from God above
    and my heritage from the
        Almighty on high?
3 Is not calamity for the unrighteous,
        and disaster for the workers
            of iniquity?
4 Does not he see my ways
        and number all my steps?

5 "If I have walked with falsehood
        and my foot has hastened to deceit;
6 (Let me be weighed in a just balance,
        and let God know my integrity!)
7 if my step has turned aside
        from the way
    and my heart has gone after
        my eyes,
    and if any spot has stuck
        to my hands,
8 then let me sow, and another eat,
    and let what grows for me[a]
        be rooted out.

9 "If my heart has been enticed
        towards a woman,
    and I have lain in wait at my
        neighbour's door,
10 then let my wife grind for another,
        and let others bow down on her.
11 For that would be a heinous crime;
        that would be an iniquity to be
            punished by the judges;
12 for that would be a fire that
        consumes as far as Abaddon,
    and it would burn to the
        root all my increase.

13 "If I have rejected the cause of my
        manservant or my maidservant,
    when they brought a
        complaint against me,
14 what then shall I do when
        God rises up?
    When he makes enquiry, what
        shall I answer him?
15 Did not he who made me in
        the womb make him?
    And did not one fashion
        us in the womb?

16 "If I have withheld anything
        that the poor desired,
    or have caused the eyes of
        the widow to fail,
17 or have eaten my morsel alone,
        and the fatherless has not eaten of it
18 (for from my youth the fatherless[b]
        grew up with me as with a father,
    and from my mother's womb
        I guided the widow[c]),
19 if I have seen anyone perish
        for lack of clothing,
    or the needy without covering,
20 if his body has not blessed me,[d]
    and if he was not warmed with
        the fleece of my sheep,
21 if I have raised my hand
        against the fatherless,
    because I saw my help in the gate,
22 then let my shoulder blade fall
        from my shoulder,
    and let my arm be broken
        from its socket.
23 For I was in terror of
        calamity from God,
    and I could not have faced
        his majesty.

24 "If I have made gold my trust
        or called fine gold my confidence,
25 if I have rejoiced because my
        wealth was abundant
    or because my hand had
        found much,
26 if I have looked at the sun[e]
        when it shone,
    or the moon moving in splendour,
27 and my heart has been
        secretly enticed,
    and my mouth has kissed my hand,
28 this also would be an iniquity to
        be punished by the judges,

---

[a]Or *let my descendants* [b]Hebrew *he* [c]Hebrew *her* [d]Hebrew *if his loins have not blessed me* [e]Hebrew *the light*

      for I would have been false
         to God above.
29 "If I have rejoiced at the ruin of
         him who hated me,
      or exulted when evil overtook him
30 (I have not let my mouth sin
         by asking for his life with a curse),
31 if the men of my tent have not said,
      'Who is there that has not been
         filled with his meat?'
32 (the sojourner has not
         lodged in the street;
      I have opened my doors
         to the traveller),
33 if I have concealed my
         transgressions as others do[a]
      by hiding my iniquity in my heart,
34 because I stood in great fear
         of the multitude,
      and the contempt of families
         terrified me,
      so that I kept silence, and did
         not go out of doors —
35 Oh, that I had one to hear me!
      (Here is my signature! Let the
         Almighty answer me!)
      Oh, that I had the indictment
         written by my adversary!
36 Surely I would carry it on my shoulder;
      I would bind it on me as a crown;
37 I would give him an account
         of all my steps;
      like a prince I would approach him.

38 "If my land has cried out against me
      and its furrows have wept together,
39 if I have eaten its yield
         without payment
      and made its owners
         breathe their last,
40 let thorns grow instead of wheat,
      and foul weeds instead of barley."

The words of Job are ended.

ELIHU REBUKES JOB'S THREE FRIENDS

32 So these three men ceased to answer Job, because he was righteous in his own eyes. ²Then Elihu the son of Barachel the Buzite, of the family of Ram, burned with anger. He burned with anger at Job because he justified himself rather than God. ³He burned with anger also at Job's three friends because they had found no answer, although they had declared Job to be in the wrong. ⁴Now Elihu had waited to speak to Job because they were older than he. ⁵And when Elihu saw that there was no answer in the mouth of these three men, he burned with anger.

⁶And Elihu the son of Barachel the Buzite answered and said:

  "I am young in years,
      and you are aged;
  therefore I was timid and afraid
      to declare my opinion to you.
7 I said, 'Let days speak,
      and many years teach wisdom.'
8 But it is the spirit in man,
      the breath of the Almighty, that
         makes him understand.
9 It is not the old[b] who are wise,
      nor the aged who understand
         what is right.
10 Therefore I say, 'Listen to me;
      let me also declare my opinion.'

11 "Behold, I waited for your words,
      I listened for your wise sayings,
      while you searched out what to say.
12 I gave you my attention,
      and, behold, there was none
         among you who refuted Job
      or who answered his words.
13 Beware lest you say, 'We have
         found wisdom;
      God may vanquish him, not a man.'
14 He has not directed his
         words against me,
      and I will not answer him
         with your speeches.

15 "They are dismayed; they
         answer no more;
      they have not a word to say.
16 And shall I wait, because
         they do not speak,
      because they stand there,
         and answer no more?
17 I also will answer with my share;
      I also will declare my opinion.
18 For I am full of words;
      the spirit within me constrains me.
19 Behold, my belly is like wine
         that has no vent;
      like new wineskins ready to burst.
20 I must speak, that I may find relief;
      I must open my lips and answer.

---

[a] Or *as Adam did*   [b] Hebrew *many* [in years]

21 I will not show partiality to any man
    or use flattery towards any person.
22 For I do not know how to flatter,
    else my Maker would soon
        take me away.

ELIHU REBUKES JOB

33 "But now, hear my speech, O Job,
    and listen to all my words.
2 Behold, I open my mouth;
    the tongue in my mouth speaks.
3 My words declare the uprightness
        of my heart,
    and what my lips know they
        speak sincerely.
4 The Spirit of God has made me,
    and the breath of the Almighty
        gives me life.
5 Answer me, if you can;
    set your words in order before
        me; take your stand.
6 Behold, I am towards God as you are;
    I too was pinched off from
        a piece of clay.
7 Behold, no fear of me need terrify you;
    my pressure will not be
        heavy upon you.

8 "Surely you have spoken in my ears,
    and I have heard the sound
        of your words.
9 You say, 'I am pure, without
        transgression;
    I am clean, and there is no
        iniquity in me.
10 Behold, he finds occasions against me,
    he counts me as his enemy,
11 he puts my feet in the stocks
    and watches all my paths.'

12 "Behold, in this you are not
        right. I will answer you,
    for God is greater than man.
13 Why do you contend against him,
    saying, 'He will answer none
        of man's[a] words'?[b]
14 For God speaks in one way,
    and in two, though man
        does not perceive it.
15 In a dream, in a vision of the night,
    when deep sleep falls on men,
    while they slumber on their beds,
16 then he opens the ears of men
    and terrifies[c] them with warnings,
17 that he may turn man aside
        from his deed

and conceal pride from a man;
18 he keeps back his soul from the pit,
    his life from perishing by the sword.

19 "Man is also rebuked with
        pain on his bed
    and with continual strife
        in his bones,
20 so that his life loathes bread,
    and his appetite the choicest food.
21 His flesh is so wasted away
        that it cannot be seen,
    and his bones that were
        not seen stick out.
22 His soul draws near the pit,
    and his life to those who
        bring death.
23 If there be for him an angel,
    a mediator, one of the thousand,
        to declare to man what is
            right for him,
24 and he is merciful to him, and says,
    'Deliver him from going
        down into the pit;
    I have found a ransom;
25 let his flesh become fresh with youth;
    let him return to the days of
        his youthful vigour';
26 then man[d] prays to God, and
        he accepts him;
    he sees his face with a shout of joy,
    and he restores to man his
        righteousness.
27 He sings before men and says:
    'I sinned and perverted what was right,
        and it was not repaid to me.
28 He has redeemed my soul from
        going down into the pit,
    and my life shall look
        upon the light.'

29 "Behold, God does all these things,
    twice, three times, with a man,
30 to bring back his soul from the pit,
    that he may be lighted with
        the light of life.
31 Pay attention, O Job, listen to me;
    be silent, and I will speak.
32 If you have any words, answer me;
    speak, for I desire to justify you.
33 If not, listen to me;
    be silent, and I will teach
        you wisdom."

---

[a] Hebrew *his* [b] Or *He will not answer for any of his own words*
[c] Or *seals* [d] Hebrew *he*

JOB 34

ELIHU ASSERTS GOD'S JUSTICE

34 Then Elihu answered and said:

2 "Hear my words, you wise men,
  and give ear to me, you who know;
3 for the ear tests words
  as the palate tastes food.
4 Let us choose what is right;
  let us know among ourselves
  what is good.
5 For Job has said, 'I am in the right,
  and God has taken away my right;
6 in spite of my right I am counted a liar;
  my wound is incurable, though I
  am without transgression.'
7 What man is like Job,
  who drinks up scoffing like water,
8 who travels in company
  with evildoers
  and walks with wicked men?
9 For he has said, 'It profits
  a man nothing
  that he should take delight in God.'

10 "Therefore, hear me, you men
  of understanding:
  far be it from God that he
  should do wickedness,
  and from the Almighty that
  he should do wrong.
11 For according to the work of a
  man he will repay him,
  and according to his ways he
  will make it befall him.
12 Of a truth, God will not do wickedly,
  and the Almighty will not
  pervert justice.
13 Who gave him charge over the earth,
  and who laid on him[a] the
  whole world?
14 If he should set his heart to it
  and gather to himself his
  spirit and his breath,
15 all flesh would perish together,
  and man would return to dust.

16 "If you have understanding, hear this;
  listen to what I say.
17 Shall one who hates justice govern?
  Will you condemn him who is
  righteous and mighty,
18 who says to a king, 'Worthless one',
  and to nobles, 'Wicked man',
19 who shows no partiality to princes,
  nor regards the rich more
  than the poor,
  for they are all the work
  of his hands?
20 In a moment they die;
  at midnight the people are
  shaken and pass away,
  and the mighty are taken away
  by no human hand.

21 "For his eyes are on the ways of a man,
  and he sees all his steps.
22 There is no gloom or deep darkness
  where evildoers may hide
  themselves.
23 For God[b] has no need to
  consider a man further,
  that he should go before
  God in judgement.
24 He shatters the mighty
  without investigation
  and sets others in their place.
25 Thus, knowing their works,
  he overturns them in the night,
  and they are crushed.
26 He strikes them for their
  wickedness
  in a place for all to see,
27 because they turned aside
  from following him
  and had no regard for
  any of his ways,
28 so that they caused the cry of
  the poor to come to him,
  and he heard the cry of
  the afflicted —
29 When he is quiet, who can condemn?
  When he hides his face, who
  can behold him,
  whether it be a nation or a man? —
30 that a godless man should not reign,
  that he should not ensnare
  the people.

31 "For has anyone said to God,
  'I have borne punishment; I will
  not offend any more;
32 teach me what I do not see;
  if I have done iniquity, I
  will do it no more'?
33 Will he then make repayment
  to suit you,
  because you reject it?
  For you must choose, and not I;
  therefore declare what you know.[c]

---

[a] Hebrew lacks *on him* [b] Hebrew *he* [c] The meaning of the Hebrew in verses 29–33 is uncertain

34 Men of understanding will say to me,
   and the wise man who
      hears me will say:
35 'Job speaks without knowledge;
   his words are without insight.'
36 Would that Job were tried to the end,
   because he answers like
      wicked men.
37 For he adds rebellion to his sin;
   he claps his hands among us
   and multiplies his words
      against God."

ELIHU CONDEMNS JOB

35

And Elihu answered and said:

2 "Do you think this to be just?
   Do you say, 'It is my right
      before God',
3 that you ask, 'What advantage
      have I?
   How am I better off than
      if I had sinned?'
4 I will answer you
   and your friends with you.
5 Look at the heavens, and see;
   and behold the clouds, which
      are higher than you.
6 If you have sinned, what do you
      accomplish against him?
   And if your transgressions
      are multiplied, what
      do you do to him?
7 If you are righteous, what
      do you give to him?
   Or what does he receive
      from your hand?
8 Your wickedness concerns a
      man like yourself,
   and your righteousness
      a son of man.

9 "Because of the multitude of
      oppressions people cry out;
   they call for help because of
      the arm of the mighty.ᵃ
10 But none says, 'Where is
      God my Maker,
   who gives songs in the night,
11 who teaches us more than the
      beasts of the earth
   and makes us wiser than the
      birds of the heavens?'
12 There they cry out, but he
      does not answer,
   because of the pride of evil men.
13 Surely God does not hear
      an empty cry,
   nor does the Almighty regard it.
14 How much less when you say
      that you do not see him,
   that the case is before him, and
      you are waiting for him!
15 And now, because his anger
      does not punish,
   and he does not take much
      note of transgression,ᵇ
16 Job opens his mouth in empty talk;
   he multiplies words without
      knowledge."

ELIHU EXTOLS GOD'S GREATNESS

36

And Elihu continued, and said:

2 "Bear with me a little, and I will
      show you,
   for I have yet something to
      say on God's behalf.
3 I will get my knowledge from afar
   and ascribe righteousness
      to my Maker.
4 For truly my words are not false;
   one who is perfect in
      knowledge is with you.

5 "Behold, God is mighty, and
      does not despise any;
   he is mighty in strength of
      understanding.
6 He does not keep the wicked alive,
   but gives the afflicted their right.
7 He does not withdraw his eyes
      from the righteous,
   but with kings on the throne
      he sets them for ever, and
      they are exalted.
8 And if they are bound in chains
   and caught in the cords
      of affliction,
9 then he declares to them their work
   and their transgressions, that they
      are behaving arrogantly.
10 He opens their ears to instruction
   and commands that they
      return from iniquity.
11 If they listen and serve him,
   they complete their days
      in prosperity,
   and their years in pleasantness.

ᵃOr *the many* ᵇTheodotion, Symmachus (compare Vulgate); the meaning of the Hebrew word is uncertain

12 But if they do not listen, they
perish by the sword
and die without knowledge.

13 "The godless in heart cherish anger;
they do not cry for help when
he binds them.
14 They die in youth,
and their life ends among
the cult prostitutes.
15 He delivers the afflicted by
their affliction
and opens their ear by adversity.
16 He also allured you out of distress
into a broad place where there
was no cramping,
and what was set on your table
was full of fatness.

17 "But you are full of the judgement
on the wicked;
judgement and justice seize you.
18 Beware lest wrath entice
you into scoffing,
and let not the greatness of the
ransom turn you aside.
19 Will your cry for help avail to
keep you from distress,
or all the force of your strength?
20 Do not long for the night,
when peoples vanish in
their place.
21 Take care; do not turn to iniquity,
for this you have chosen
rather than affliction.
22 Behold, God is exalted in his power;
who is a teacher like him?
23 Who has prescribed for him his way,
or who can say, 'You have
done wrong'?

24 "Remember to extol his work,
of which men have sung.
25 All mankind has looked on it;
man beholds it from afar.
26 Behold, God is great, and
we know him not;
the number of his years
is unsearchable.
27 For he draws up the drops of water;
they distil his mist in rain,
28 which the skies pour down
and drop on mankind abundantly.
29 Can anyone understand the
spreading of the clouds,
the thunderings of his pavilion?
30 Behold, he scatters his
lightning about him
and covers the roots of the sea.
31 For by these he judges peoples;
he gives food in abundance.
32 He covers his hands with
the lightning
and commands it to strike the mark.
33 Its crashing declares his presence;[a]
the cattle also declare that he rises.

ELIHU PROCLAIMS GOD'S MAJESTY

37 "At this also my heart trembles
and leaps out of its place.
² Keep listening to the thunder
of his voice
and the rumbling that comes
from his mouth.
3 Under the whole heaven he lets it go,
and his lightning to the
corners of the earth.
4 After it his voice roars;
he thunders with his majestic voice,
and he does not restrain
the lightnings[b] when
his voice is heard.
5 God thunders wondrously
with his voice;
he does great things that we
cannot comprehend.
6 For to the snow he says,
'Fall on the earth',
likewise to the downpour, his
mighty downpour.
7 He seals up the hand of every man,
that all men whom he made
may know it.
8 Then the beasts go into their lairs,
and remain in their dens.
9 From its chamber comes
the whirlwind,
and cold from the scattering winds.
10 By the breath of God ice is given,
and the broad waters are frozen fast.
11 He loads the thick cloud
with moisture;
the clouds scatter his lightning.
12 They turn round and round
by his guidance,
to accomplish all that he
commands them
on the face of the habitable world.
13 Whether for correction or for his land
or for love, he causes it to happen.

---
[a]Hebrew *declares concerning him*   [b]Hebrew *them*

14 "Hear this, O Job;
   stop and consider the wondrous
      works of God.
15 Do you know how God lays his
      command upon them
   and causes the lightning of
      his cloud to shine?
16 Do you know the balancings*a*
      of the clouds,
   the wondrous works of him who
      is perfect in knowledge,
17 you whose garments are hot
   when the earth is still because
      of the south wind?
18 Can you, like him, spread out
      the skies,
   hard as a cast-metal mirror?
19 Teach us what we shall say to him;
   we cannot draw up our case
      because of darkness.
20 Shall it be told him that I would speak?
   Did a man ever wish that he
      would be swallowed up?

21 "And now no one looks on the light
      when it is bright in the skies,
   when the wind has passed
      and cleared them.
22 Out of the north comes
      golden splendour;
   God is clothed with
      awesome majesty.
23 The Almighty—we cannot find him;
      he is great in power;
   justice and abundant righteousness
      he will not violate.
24 Therefore men fear him;
   he does not regard any who are
      wise in their own conceit."*b*

THE LORD ANSWERS JOB

38

Then the LORD answered Job out
   of the whirlwind and said:

2 "Who is this that darkens counsel by
      words without knowledge?
3 Dress for action*c* like a man;
   I will question you, and you
      make it known to me.

4 "Where were you when I laid the
      foundation of the earth?
   Tell me, if you have understanding.
5 Who determined its measurements—
      surely you know!
   Or who stretched the line upon it?
6 On what were its bases sunk,
      or who laid its cornerstone,
7 when the morning stars sang
      together
   and all the sons of God
      shouted for joy?

8 "Or who shut in the sea with doors
      when it burst out from the womb,
9 when I made clouds its garment
   and thick darkness its
      swaddling band,
10 and prescribed limits for it
   and set bars and doors,
11 and said, 'Thus far shall you
      come, and no farther,
   and here shall your proud
      waves be stayed'?

12 "Have you commanded the morning
      since your days began,
   and caused the dawn to
      know its place,
13 that it might take hold of the
      skirts of the earth,
   and the wicked be shaken out of it?
14 It is changed like clay under the seal,
   and its features stand out
      like a garment.
15 From the wicked their
      light is withheld,
   and their uplifted arm is broken.

16 "Have you entered into the
      springs of the sea,
   or walked in the recesses
      of the deep?
17 Have the gates of death been
      revealed to you,
   or have you seen the gates
      of deep darkness?
18 Have you comprehended the
      expanse of the earth?
   Declare, if you know all this.

19 "Where is the way to the
      dwelling of light,
   and where is the place of darkness,
20 that you may take it to its territory
   and that you may discern the
      paths to its home?
21 You know, for you were born then,
   and the number of your days
      is great!

---

*a*Or *hoverings* *b*Hebrew *in heart* *c*Hebrew *Gird up your loins*

22 "Have you entered the
        storehouses of the snow,
    or have you seen the
        storehouses of the hail,
23 which I have reserved for
        the time of trouble,
    for the day of battle and war?
24 What is the way to the place where
        the light is distributed,
    or where the east wind is
        scattered upon the earth?

25 "Who has cleft a channel for
        the torrents of rain
    and a way for the thunderbolt,
26 to bring rain on a land
        where no man is,
    on the desert in which
        there is no man,
27 to satisfy the waste and desolate land,
    and to make the ground
        sprout with grass?

28 "Has the rain a father,
    or who has begotten the
        drops of dew?
29 From whose womb did the
        ice come forth,
    and who has given birth to
        the frost of heaven?
30 The waters become hard like stone,
    and the face of the deep is frozen.

31 "Can you bind the chains of the Pleiades
    or loose the cords of Orion?
32 Can you lead forth the Mazzaroth^a
        in their season,
    or can you guide the Bear
        with its children?
33 Do you know the ordinances
        of the heavens?
    Can you establish their
        rule on the earth?

34 "Can you lift up your voice
        to the clouds,
    that a flood of waters may cover you?
35 Can you send forth lightnings,
        that they may go
    and say to you, 'Here we are'?
36 Who has put wisdom in
        the inward parts^b
    or given understanding
        to the mind?^{c}
37 Who can number the clouds
        by wisdom?
    Or who can tilt the waterskins
        of the heavens,
38 when the dust runs into a mass
    and the clods stick fast together?

39 "Can you hunt the prey for the lion,
    or satisfy the appetite of
        the young lions,
40 when they crouch in their dens
    or lie in wait in their thicket?
41 Who provides for the raven its prey,
    when its young ones cry
        to God for help,
    and wander about for lack of food?

39

"Do you know when the
        mountain goats give birth?
    Do you observe the calving of
        the does?
2 Can you number the months
        that they fulfil,
    and do you know the time
        when they give birth,
3 when they crouch, bring
        forth their offspring,
    and are delivered of their young?
4 Their young ones become strong;
        they grow up in the open;
    they go out and do not
        return to them.

5 "Who has let the wild donkey go free?
    Who has loosed the bonds
        of the swift donkey,
6 to whom I have given the arid
        plain for his home
    and the salt land for his
        dwelling place?
7 He scorns the tumult of the city;
    he hears not the shouts of the driver.
8 He ranges the mountains
        as his pasture,
    and he searches after every
        green thing.

9 "Is the wild ox willing to serve you?
    Will he spend the night
        at your manger?
10 Can you bind him in the
        furrow with ropes,
    or will he harrow the
        valleys after you?
11 Will you depend on him because
        his strength is great,

---

^{a}Probably the name of a constellation ^{b}Or *in the ibis* ^{c}Or *cock*

and will you leave to him
  your labour?
12 Do you have faith in him that he
  will return your grain
  and gather it to your threshing floor?

13 "The wings of the ostrich wave proudly,
  but are they the pinions and
    plumage of love?[a]
14 For she leaves her eggs to the earth
  and lets them be warmed
    on the ground,
15 forgetting that a foot may crush them
  and that the wild beast may
    trample them.
16 She deals cruelly with her young,
  as if they were not hers;
  though her labour be in vain,
    yet she has no fear,
17 because God has made her
    forget wisdom
  and given her no share in
    understanding.
18 When she rouses herself to flee,[b]
  she laughs at the horse and
    his rider.

19 "Do you give the horse his might?
  Do you clothe his neck with a mane?
20 Do you make him leap like the locust?
  His majestic snorting is terrifying.
21 He paws[c] in the valley and
    exults in his strength;
  he goes out to meet the weapons.
22 He laughs at fear and is not dismayed;
  he does not turn back
    from the sword.
23 Upon him rattle the quiver,
  the flashing spear, and the javelin.
24 With fierceness and rage he
    swallows the ground;
  he cannot stand still at the
    sound of the trumpet.
25 When the trumpet sounds,
  he says 'Aha!'
  He smells the battle from afar,
  the thunder of the captains,
    and the shouting.

26 "Is it by your understanding
    that the hawk soars
  and spreads his wings
    towards the south?
27 Is it at your command that
    the eagle mounts up
  and makes his nest on high?

28 On the rock he dwells and
    makes his home,
  on the rocky crag and stronghold.
29 From there he spies out the prey;
  his eyes behold it from far away.
30 His young ones suck up blood,
  and where the slain are, there is he."

40

And the LORD said to Job:

2 "Shall a fault-finder contend
    with the Almighty?
  He who argues with God,
    let him answer it."

JOB PROMISES SILENCE

3 Then Job answered the LORD and said:

4 "Behold, I am of small account;
    what shall I answer you?
  I lay my hand on my mouth.
5 I have spoken once, and I
    will not answer;
  twice, but I will proceed no further."

THE LORD CHALLENGES JOB

6 Then the LORD answered Job out of the whirlwind and said:

7 "Dress for action[d] like a man;
  I will question you, and you
    make it known to me.
8 Will you even put me in the wrong?
  Will you condemn me that you
    may be in the right?
9 Have you an arm like God,
  and can you thunder with
    a voice like his?

10 "Adorn yourself with majesty
    and dignity;
  clothe yourself with glory
    and splendour.
11 Pour out the overflowings of your anger,
  and look on everyone who is
    proud and abase him.
12 Look on everyone who is proud
    and bring him low
  and tread down the wicked
    where they stand.
13 Hide them all in the dust together;
  bind their faces in the world below.[e]

---

[a]The meaning of the Hebrew is uncertain [b]The meaning of the Hebrew is uncertain [c]Hebrew *They paw* [d]Hebrew *Gird up your loins* [e]Hebrew *in the hidden place*

14 Then will I also acknowledge to you
 that your own right hand
  can save you.

15 "Behold, Behemoth,ᵃ
 which I made as I made you;
  he eats grass like an ox.
16 Behold, his strength in his loins,
 and his power in the muscles
  of his belly.
17 He makes his tail stiff like a cedar;
 the sinews of his thighs
  are knit together.
18 His bones are tubes of bronze,
 his limbs like bars of iron.
19 "He is the first of the worksᵇ of God;
 let him who made him bring
  near his sword!
20 For the mountains yield food for him
 where all the wild beasts play.
21 Under the lotus plants he lies,
 in the shelter of the reeds
  and in the marsh.
22 For his shade the lotus trees cover him;
 the willows of the brook
  surround him.
23 Behold, if the river is turbulent
 he is not frightened;
 he is confident though Jordan
  rushes against his mouth.
24 Can one take him by his eyes,ᶜ
 or pierce his nose with a snare?

41 ᵈ "Can you draw out Leviathanᵉ with a fish-hook or press down his tongue with a cord?

2 Can you put a rope in his nose
 or pierce his jaw with a hook?
3 Will he make many pleas to you?
 Will he speak to you soft words?
4 Will he make a covenant with you
 to take him for your servant
  for ever?
5 Will you play with him as with a bird,
 or will you put him on a
  leash for your girls?
6 Will traders bargain over him?
 Will they divide him up
  among the merchants?
7 Can you fill his skin with harpoons
 or his head with fishing spears?
8 Lay your hands on him;
 remember the battle—you
  will not do it again!

9ᶠ Behold, the hope of a man is false;
 he is laid low even at the
  sight of him.
10 No one is so fierce that he
  dares to stir him up.
 Who then is he who can
  stand before me?
11 Who has first given to me, that
  I should repay him?
 Whatever is under the whole
  heaven is mine.

12 "I will not keep silence
  concerning his limbs,
 or his mighty strength, or
  his goodly frame.
13 Who can strip off his outer garment?
 Who would come near
  him with a bridle?
14 Who can open the doors of his face?
 Around his teeth is terror.
15 His back is made ofᵍ rows of shields,
 shut up closely as with a seal.
16 One is so near to another
 that no air can come between
  them.
17 They are joined one to another;
 they clasp each other and
  cannot be separated.
18 His sneezings flash forth light,
 and his eyes are like the
  eyelids of the dawn.
19 Out of his mouth go flaming torches;
 sparks of fire leap forth.
20 Out of his nostrils comes forth
  smoke,
 as from a boiling pot and
  burning rushes.
21 His breath kindles coals,
 and a flame comes forth
  from his mouth.
22 In his neck abides strength,
 and terror dances before him.
23 The folds of his flesh stick together,
 firmly cast on him and immovable.
24 His heart is hard as a stone,
 hard as the lower millstone.
25 When he raises himself up,
  the mightyʰ are afraid;
 at the crashing they are
  beside themselves.
26 Though the sword reaches
  him, it does not avail,

ᵃA large animal, exact identity unknown ᵇHebrew *ways* ᶜOr *in his sight* ᵈCh 40:25 in Hebrew ᵉA large sea animal, exact identity unknown ᶠCh 41:1 in Hebrew ᵍOr *His pride is in his* ʰOr *gods*

      nor the spear, the dart, or
         the javelin.
27 He counts iron as straw,
      and bronze as rotten wood.
28 The arrow cannot make him flee;
      for him, sling stones are
         turned to stubble.
29 Clubs are counted as stubble;
      he laughs at the rattle of javelins.
30 His underparts are like
         sharp potsherds;
      he spreads himself like a threshing
         sledge on the mire.
31 He makes the deep boil like a pot;
      he makes the sea like a
         pot of ointment.
32 Behind him he leaves a shining
         wake;
      one would think the deep
         to be white-haired.
33 On earth there is not his like,
      a creature without fear.
34 He sees everything that is high;
      he is king over all the sons
         of pride."

JOB'S CONFESSION AND REPENTANCE

42 Then Job answered the LORD and said:

2 "I know that you can do all things,
      and that no purpose of yours
         can be thwarted.
3 'Who is this that hides counsel
         without knowledge?'
    Therefore I have uttered what
      I did not understand,
    things too wonderful for me,
      which I did not know.
4 'Hear, and I will speak;
      I will question you, and you
         make it known to me.'
5 I had heard of you by the
         hearing of the ear,
    but now my eye sees you;
6 therefore I despise myself,
      and repent[a] in dust and ashes."

THE LORD REBUKES JOB'S FRIENDS

7 After the LORD had spoken these words to Job, the LORD said to Eliphaz the Temanite: "My anger burns against you and against your two friends, for you have not spoken of me what is right, as my servant Job has. 8 Now therefore take seven bulls and seven rams and go to my servant Job and offer up a burnt offering for yourselves. And my servant Job shall pray for you, for I will accept his prayer not to deal with you according to your folly. For you have not spoken of me what is right, as my servant Job has." 9 So Eliphaz the Temanite and Bildad the Shuhite and Zophar the Naamathite went and did what the LORD had told them, and the LORD accepted Job's prayer.

THE LORD RESTORES JOB'S FORTUNES

10 And the LORD restored the fortunes of Job, when he had prayed for his friends. And the LORD gave Job twice as much as he had before. 11 Then came to him all his brothers and sisters and all who had known him before, and ate bread with him in his house. And they showed him sympathy and comforted him for all the evil[b] that the LORD had brought upon him. And each of them gave him a piece of money[c] and a ring of gold.

12 And the LORD blessed the latter days of Job more than his beginning. And he had 14,000 sheep, 6,000 camels, 1,000 yoke of oxen, and 1,000 female donkeys. 13 He had also seven sons and three daughters. 14 And he called the name of the first daughter Jemimah, and the name of the second Keziah, and the name of the third Keren-happuch. 15 And in all the land there were no women so beautiful as Job's daughters. And their father gave them an inheritance among their brothers. 16 And after this Job lived for 140 years, and saw his sons, and his sons' sons, four generations. 17 And Job died, an old man, and full of days.

---

[a] Or *and am comforted* [b] Or *disaster* [c] Hebrew *a qesitah*; a unit of money of unknown value

THE PSALMS

BOOK ONE

THE WAY OF THE RIGHTEOUS AND THE WICKED

1
1 Blessed is the man[a]
  who walks not in the counsel of
    the wicked,
nor stands in the way of sinners,
  nor sits in the seat of scoffers;
2 but his delight is in the
    law[b] of the LORD,
  and on his law he meditates
    day and night.

3 He is like a tree
    planted by streams of water
  that yields its fruit in its season,
    and its leaf does not wither.
  In all that he does, he prospers.
4 The wicked are not so,
    but are like chaff that the
      wind drives away.

5 Therefore the wicked will not
    stand in the judgement,
  nor sinners in the congregation
    of the righteous;
6 for the LORD knows the way
    of the righteous,
  but the way of the wicked
    will perish.

THE REIGN OF THE LORD'S ANOINTED

2
Why do the nations rage[c]
  and the peoples plot in vain?
2 The kings of the earth set
    themselves,
  and the rulers take counsel together,
    against the LORD and against
      his Anointed, saying,
3 "Let us burst their bonds apart
    and cast away their cords from us."

4 He who sits in the heavens laughs;
    the Lord holds them in derision.
5 Then he will speak to them
    in his wrath,
  and terrify them in his fury, saying,

6 "As for me, I have set my King
    on Zion, my holy hill."

7 I will tell of the decree:
  The LORD said to me, "You are
      my Son;
    today I have begotten you.
8 Ask of me, and I will make the
      nations your heritage,
    and the ends of the earth
      your possession.
9 You shall break[d] them with
      a rod of iron
    and dash them in pieces like
      a potter's vessel."

10 Now therefore, O kings, be wise;
    be warned, O rulers of the earth.
11 Serve the LORD with fear,
    and rejoice with trembling.
12 Kiss the Son,
    lest he be angry, and you
      perish in the way,
    for his wrath is quickly kindled.
  Blessed are all who take refuge in him.

SAVE ME, O MY GOD

3
*A Psalm of David, when he fled
from Absalom his son.*

1 O LORD, how many are my foes!
    Many are rising against me;
2 many are saying of my soul,
    "There is no salvation for him in
      God."   *Selah*[e]

3 But you, O LORD, are a shield about me,
    my glory, and the lifter of my head.
4 I cried aloud to the LORD,
    and he answered me from his holy
      hill.   *Selah*

---

[a]The singular Hebrew word for *man* (*ish*) is used here to portray a representative example of a godly person; see Preface [b]Or *instruction* [c]Or *nations noisily assemble* [d]Revocalization yields (compare Septuagint) *You shall rule* [e]The meaning of the Hebrew word *Selah*, used frequently in the Psalms, is uncertain. It may be a musical or liturgical direction

5 I lay down and slept;
  I woke again, for the LORD
    sustained me.
6 I will not be afraid of many
    thousands of people
  who have set themselves
    against me all round.

7 Arise, O LORD!
    Save me, O my God!
  For you strike all my enemies
    on the cheek;
  you break the teeth of the wicked.

8 Salvation belongs to the LORD;
  your blessing be on your
    people!   Selah

ANSWER ME WHEN I CALL

4 *To the choirmaster: with stringed instruments. A Psalm of David.*

1 Answer me when I call, O God
    of my righteousness!
  You have given me relief when
    I was in distress.
  Be gracious to me and
    hear my prayer!

2 O men,[a] how long shall my honour
    be turned into shame?
  How long will you love vain words
    and seek after lies?   Selah
3 But know that the LORD has set
    apart the godly for himself;
  the LORD hears when I call
    to him.

4 Be angry,[b] and do not sin;
  ponder in your own hearts on your
    beds, and be silent.   Selah
5 Offer right sacrifices,
  and put your trust in the LORD.

6 There are many who say, "Who
    will show us some good?
  Lift up the light of your face
    upon us, O LORD!"
7 You have put more joy in my heart
    than they have when their
      grain and wine abound.

8 In peace I will both lie down
    and sleep;
  for you alone, O LORD, make
    me dwell in safety.

LEAD ME IN YOUR RIGHTEOUSNESS

5 *To the choirmaster: for the flutes. A Psalm of David.*

1 Give ear to my words, O LORD;
    consider my groaning.
2 Give attention to the sound of my cry,
    my King and my God,
    for to you do I pray.
3 O LORD, in the morning you
    hear my voice;
  in the morning I prepare a
    sacrifice for you[c] and watch.

4 For you are not a God who
    delights in wickedness;
  evil may not dwell with you.
5 The boastful shall not stand
    before your eyes;
  you hate all evildoers.
6 You destroy those who speak lies;
  the LORD abhors the bloodthirsty
    and deceitful man.

7 But I, through the abundance
    of your steadfast love,
  will enter your house.
  I will bow down towards
    your holy temple
    in the fear of you.
8 Lead me, O LORD, in your
    righteousness
  because of my enemies;
  make your way straight before me.

9 For there is no truth in their mouth;
  their inmost self is destruction;
  their throat is an open grave;
  they flatter with their tongue.
10 Make them bear their guilt, O God;
  let them fall by their own counsels;
  because of the abundance of their
    transgressions cast them out,
  for they have rebelled against you.

11 But let all who take refuge
    in you rejoice;
  let them ever sing for joy,
  and spread your protection over them,
    that those who love your name
      may exult in you.
12 For you bless the righteous, O LORD;
  you cover him with favour
    as with a shield.

---

[a] Or *O men of rank*   [b] Or *Be agitated*   [c] Or *I direct my prayer to you*

O LORD, DELIVER MY LIFE

6 *To the choirmaster: with stringed instruments; according to The Sheminith.[a] A Psalm of David.*

1 O LORD, rebuke me not in your anger,
    nor discipline me in your wrath.
2 Be gracious to me, O LORD,
    for I am languishing;
  heal me, O LORD, for my
    bones are troubled.
3 My soul also is greatly troubled.
    But you, O LORD—how long?

4 Turn, O LORD, deliver my life;
    save me for the sake of your
      steadfast love.
5 For in death there is no
    remembrance of you;
  in Sheol who will give you praise?

6 I am weary with my moaning;
    every night I flood my
      bed with tears;
  I drench my couch with my weeping.
7 My eye wastes away because of grief;
    it grows weak because of all my foes.

8 Depart from me, all you
    workers of evil,
  for the LORD has heard the
    sound of my weeping.
9 The LORD has heard my plea;
    the LORD accepts my prayer.
10 All my enemies shall be ashamed
    and greatly troubled;
  they shall turn back and be put
    to shame in a moment.

IN YOU DO I TAKE REFUGE

7 *A Shiggaion[b] of David, which he sang to the LORD concerning the words of Cush, a Benjaminite.*

1 O LORD my God, in you do I take refuge;
    save me from all my pursuers
      and deliver me,
2 lest like a lion they tear my soul apart,
    rending it in pieces, with
      none to deliver.

3 O LORD my God, if I have done this,
    if there is wrong in my hands,
4 if I have repaid my friend[c] with evil
    or plundered my enemy
      without cause,
5 let the enemy pursue my
    soul and overtake it,
  and let him trample my
    life to the ground
  and lay my glory in the dust. Selah

6 Arise, O LORD, in your anger;
    lift yourself up against the
      fury of my enemies;
  awake for me; you have
    appointed a judgement.
7 Let the assembly of the peoples
    be gathered about you;
  over it return on high.

8 The LORD judges the peoples;
    judge me, O LORD, according
      to my righteousness
  and according to the integrity
    that is in me.
9 Oh, let the evil of the wicked
    come to an end,
  and may you establish
    the righteous—
  you who test the minds and hearts,[d]
    O righteous God!
10 My shield is with God,
    who saves the upright in heart.
11 God is a righteous judge,
    and a God who feels
      indignation every day.

12 If a man[e] does not repent, God[f]
    will whet his sword;
  he has bent and readied his bow;
13 he has prepared for him his
      deadly weapons,
  making his arrows fiery shafts.
14 Behold, the wicked man conceives evil
    and is pregnant with mischief
    and gives birth to lies.
15 He makes a pit, digging it out,
    and falls into the hole that
      he has made.
16 His mischief returns upon
    his own head,
  and on his own skull his
    violence descends.

17 I will give to the LORD the thanks
    due to his righteousness,

---

[a]Probably a musical or liturgical term [b]Probably a musical or liturgical term [c]Hebrew *the one at peace with me* [d]Hebrew *the hearts and kidneys* [e]Hebrew *he* [f]Hebrew *he*

and I will sing praise to the name
    of the LORD, the Most High.

HOW MAJESTIC IS YOUR NAME

8 *To the choirmaster: according to
The Gittith.[a] A Psalm of David.*

1 O LORD, our Lord,
    how majestic is your name
        in all the earth!
  You have set your glory
    above the heavens.
2 Out of the mouth of babies
        and infants,
    you have established strength
        because of your foes,
    to still the enemy and the avenger.

3 When I look at your heavens,
        the work of your fingers,
    the moon and the stars, which
        you have set in place,
4 what is man that you are
        mindful of him,
    and the son of man that
        you care for him?

5 Yet you have made him a little lower
        than the heavenly beings[b]
    and crowned him with
        glory and honour.
6 You have given him dominion over
        the works of your hands;
    you have put all things under his feet,
7 all sheep and oxen,
        and also the beasts of the field,
8 the birds of the heavens, and
        the fish of the sea,
    whatever passes along the
        paths of the seas.

9 O LORD, our Lord,
    how majestic is your name
        in all the earth!

I WILL RECOUNT YOUR WONDERFUL DEEDS

9[c] *To the choirmaster: according to
Muth-labben.[d] A Psalm of David.*

1 I will give thanks to the LORD
        with my whole heart;
    I will recount all of your
        wonderful deeds.
2 I will be glad and exult in you;
    I will sing praise to your
        name, O Most High.
3 When my enemies turn back,
    they stumble and perish
        before[e] your presence.
4 For you have maintained
        my just cause;
    you have sat on the throne, giving
        righteous judgement.

5 You have rebuked the nations; you
        have made the wicked perish;
    you have blotted out their
        name for ever and ever.
6 The enemy came to an end
        in everlasting ruins;
    their cities you rooted out;
    the very memory of them
        has perished.

7 But the LORD sits enthroned for ever;
    he has established his
        throne for justice,
8 and he judges the world with
        righteousness;
    he judges the peoples with
        uprightness.
9 The LORD is a stronghold
        for the oppressed,
    a stronghold in times of trouble.
10 And those who know your name
        put their trust in you,
    for you, O LORD, have not forsaken
        those who seek you.

11 Sing praises to the LORD, who
        sits enthroned in Zion!
    Tell among the peoples his deeds!
12 For he who avenges blood is
        mindful of them;
    he does not forget the cry
        of the afflicted.

13 Be gracious to me, O LORD!
    See my affliction from
        those who hate me,
    O you who lift me up from
        the gates of death,
14 that I may recount all your praises,
    that in the gates of the
        daughter of Zion
    I may rejoice in your salvation.

---

[a]Probably a musical or liturgical term [b]Or *than God*; Septuagint *than the angels* [c]Psalms 9 and 10 together follow an acrostic pattern, each stanza beginning with the successive letters of the Hebrew alphabet. In the Septuagint they form one psalm [d]Probably a musical or liturgical term [e]Or *because of*

15 The nations have sunk in the
        pit that they made;
     in the net that they hid, their
        own foot has been caught.
16 The LORD has made himself known;
     he has executed judgement;
   the wicked are snared in
        the work of their
        own hands.   Higgaion.[a] Selah

17 The wicked shall return to Sheol,
     all the nations that forget God.

18 For the needy shall not
        always be forgotten,
   and the hope of the poor shall
        not perish for ever.

19 Arise, O LORD! Let not man prevail;
     let the nations be judged before you!
20 Put them in fear, O LORD!
     Let the nations know that they are
        but men!   Selah

WHY DO YOU HIDE YOURSELF?

10 Why, O LORD, do you stand
        far away?
     Why do you hide yourself
        in times of trouble?

2 In arrogance the wicked hotly
        pursue the poor;
     let them be caught in the schemes
        that they have devised.
3 For the wicked boasts of the
        desires of his soul,
     and the one greedy for gain curses[b]
        and renounces the LORD.
4 In the pride of his face[c] the wicked
        does not seek him;[d]
     all his thoughts are, "There is no God."
5 His ways prosper at all times;
     your judgements are on high,
        out of his sight;
     as for all his foes, he puffs at them.
6 He says in his heart, "I shall
        not be moved;
     throughout all generations I
        shall not meet adversity."
7 His mouth is filled with cursing
        and deceit and oppression;
     under his tongue are mischief
        and iniquity.
8 He sits in ambush in the villages;
     in hiding places he murders
        the innocent.
   His eyes stealthily watch
        for the helpless;
9 he lurks in ambush like a
        lion in his thicket;
   he lurks that he may seize the poor;
     he seizes the poor when he
        draws him into his net.
10 The helpless are crushed, sink down,
     and fall by his might.
11 He says in his heart, "God
        has forgotten,
     he has hidden his face, he
        will never see it."

12 Arise, O LORD; O God, lift up your hand;
     forget not the afflicted.
13 Why does the wicked renounce God
   and say in his heart, "You will
        not call to account"?
14 But you do see, for you note
        mischief and vexation,
   that you may take it into your hands;
   to you the helpless commits himself;
     you have been the helper
        of the fatherless.
15 Break the arm of the wicked
        and evildoer;
     call his wickedness to account
        till you find none.

16 The LORD is king for ever and ever;
     the nations perish from his land.
17 O LORD, you hear the desire
        of the afflicted;
     you will strengthen their heart;
        you will incline your ear
18 to do justice to the fatherless
        and the oppressed,
   so that man who is of the earth
        may strike terror no more.

THE LORD IS IN HIS HOLY TEMPLE

11 *To the choirmaster. Of David.*

¹In the LORD I take refuge;
   how can you say to my soul,
     "Flee like a bird to your mountain,
2 for behold, the wicked bend the bow;
     they have fitted their arrow
        to the string
     to shoot in the dark at the
        upright in heart;

---

[a]Probably a musical or liturgical term   [b]Or *and he blesses the one greedy for gain*   [c]Or *of his anger*   [d]Or *the wicked says, "He will not call to account"*

³ if the foundations are destroyed,
what can the righteous do?"ᵃ

⁴ The Lord is in his holy temple;
the Lord's throne is in heaven;
his eyes see, his eyelids test
the children of man.
⁵ The Lord tests the righteous,
but his soul hates the wicked and
the one who loves violence.
⁶ Let him rain coals on the wicked;
fire and sulphur and a
scorching wind shall be
the portion of their cup.
⁷ For the Lord is righteous;
he loves righteous deeds;
the upright shall behold his face.

THE FAITHFUL HAVE VANISHED

12 *To the choirmaster: according to The Sheminith.ᵇ A Psalm of David.*

¹ Save, O Lord, for the godly one
is gone;
for the faithful have vanished from
among the children of man.
² Everyone utters lies to his neighbour;
with flattering lips and a double
heart they speak.

³ May the Lord cut off all
flattering lips,
the tongue that makes
great boasts,
⁴ those who say, "With our
tongue we will prevail,
our lips are with us; who is
master over us?"

⁵ "Because the poor are plundered,
because the needy groan,
I will now arise," says the Lord;
"I will place him in the safety
for which he longs."
⁶ The words of the Lord are
pure words,
like silver refined in a furnace
on the ground,
purified seven times.

⁷ You, O Lord, will keep them;
you will guard usᶜ from this
generation for ever.
⁸ On every side the wicked prowl,
as vileness is exalted among
the children of man.

HOW LONG, O LORD?

13 *To the choirmaster. A Psalm of David.*

¹ How long, O Lord? Will
you forget me for ever?
How long will you hide
your face from me?
² How long must I take
counsel in my soul
and have sorrow in my
heart all the day?
How long shall my enemy
be exalted over me?

³ Consider and answer me,
O Lord my God;
light up my eyes, lest I sleep
the sleep of death,
⁴ lest my enemy say, "I have
prevailed over him",
lest my foes rejoice because
I am shaken.

⁵ But I have trusted in your steadfast love;
my heart shall rejoice in
your salvation.
⁶ I will sing to the Lord,
because he has dealt
bountifully with me.

THE FOOL SAYS, THERE IS NO GOD

14 *To the choirmaster. Of David.*

¹ The fool says in his heart,
"There is no God."
They are corrupt, they do
abominable deeds;
there is none who does good.

² The Lord looks down from heaven
on the children of man,
to see if there are any who
understand,ᵈ
who seek after God.

³ They have all turned aside; together
they have become corrupt;
there is none who does good,
not even one.

⁴ Have they no knowledge,
all the evildoers

ᵃOr *for the foundations will be destroyed; what has the righteous done?*
ᵇProbably a musical or liturgical term   ᶜOr *guard him*
ᵈOr *that act wisely*

who eat up my people as
  they eat bread
  and do not call upon the Lord?

5 There they are in great terror,
  for God is with the generation
  of the righteous.
6 You would shame the plans of the poor,
  but[a] the Lord is his refuge.

7 Oh, that salvation for Israel
    would come out of Zion!
  When the Lord restores the
    fortunes of his people,
  let Jacob rejoice, let Israel be glad.

WHO SHALL DWELL ON YOUR HOLY HILL?

15 A Psalm of David.

¹O Lord, who shall
    sojourn in your tent?
  Who shall dwell on your holy hill?

2 He who walks blamelessly
    and does what is right
    and speaks truth in his heart;
3 who does not slander with his tongue
    and does no evil to his neighbour,
    nor takes up a reproach
    against his friend;
4 in whose eyes a vile person is despised,
    but who honours those
      who fear the Lord;
  who swears to his own hurt
    and does not change;
5 who does not put out his
    money at interest
  and does not take a bribe
    against the innocent.
  He who does these things
    shall never be moved.

YOU WILL NOT ABANDON MY SOUL

16 A Miktam[b] of David.

¹Preserve me, O God, for
    in you I take refuge.
2 I say to the Lord, "You are my Lord;
    I have no good apart from you."

3 As for the saints in the land, they
    are the excellent ones,
    in whom is all my delight.[c]

4 The sorrows of those who run after[d]
    another god shall multiply;
  their drink offerings of blood
    I will not pour out
  or take their names on my lips.

5 The Lord is my chosen
    portion and my cup;
    you hold my lot.
6 The lines have fallen for me
    in pleasant places;
  indeed, I have a beautiful inheritance.

7 I bless the Lord who gives me counsel;
    in the night also my heart
      instructs me.[e]
8 I have set the Lord always before me;
  because he is at my right hand,
    I shall not be shaken.

9 Therefore my heart is glad, and
    my whole being[f] rejoices;
    my flesh also dwells secure.
10 For you will not abandon
    my soul to Sheol,
  or let your holy one see corruption.[g]

11 You make known to me the path of life;
    in your presence there is
      fullness of joy;
    at your right hand are pleasures
      for evermore.

IN THE SHADOW OF YOUR WINGS

17 A Prayer of David.

¹Hear a just cause, O Lord;
    attend to my cry!
  Give ear to my prayer from
    lips free of deceit!
2 From your presence let my
    vindication come!
  Let your eyes behold the right!

3 You have tried my heart, you
    have visited me by night,
  you have tested me, and you
    will find nothing;
  I have purposed that my mouth
    will not transgress.
4 With regard to the works of man,
    by the word of your lips
  I have avoided the ways
    of the violent.

---

[a]Or for [b]Probably a musical or liturgical term [c]Or To the saints in the land, the excellent in whom is all my delight, I say: [d]Or who acquire [e]Hebrew my kidneys instruct me [f]Hebrew my glory [g]Or see the pit

⁵ My steps have held fast to your paths;
   my feet have not slipped.
⁶ I call upon you, for you will
      answer me, O God;
   incline your ear to me;
      hear my words.
⁷ Wondrously show*ᵃ* your steadfast love,
   O Saviour of those who seek refuge
      from their adversaries at
         your right hand.

⁸ Keep me as the apple of your eye;
   hide me in the shadow of your wings,
⁹ from the wicked who do me violence,
   my deadly enemies who
      surround me.

¹⁰ They close their hearts to pity;
    with their mouths they
       speak arrogantly.
¹¹ They have now surrounded our steps;
    they set their eyes to cast
       us to the ground.
¹² He is like a lion eager to tear,
    as a young lion lurking in ambush.

¹³ Arise, O Lord! Confront
       him, subdue him!
    Deliver my soul from the
       wicked by your sword,
¹⁴ from men by your hand, O Lord,
    from men of the world whose
       portion is in this life.*ᵇ*
    You fill their womb with treasure;*ᶜ*
       they are satisfied with children,
    and they leave their abundance
       to their infants.

¹⁵ As for me, I shall behold your
       face in righteousness;
    when I awake, I shall be satisfied
       with your likeness.

THE LORD IS MY ROCK AND MY FORTRESS

18 *To the choirmaster. A Psalm of David, the servant of the Lord, who addressed the words of this song to the Lord on the day when the Lord delivered him from the hand of all his enemies, and from the hand of Saul. He said:*

¹ I love you, O Lord, my strength.
² The Lord is my rock and my
      fortress and my deliverer,
   my God, my rock, in whom
      I take refuge,
   my shield, and the horn of my
      salvation, my stronghold.
³ I call upon the Lord, who is
      worthy to be praised,
   and I am saved from my enemies.

⁴ The cords of death encompassed me;
   the torrents of destruction
      assailed me;*ᵈ*
⁵ the cords of Sheol entangled me;
   the snares of death confronted me.

⁶ In my distress I called upon the Lord;
      to my God I cried for help.
   From his temple he heard my voice,
      and my cry to him reached his ears.

⁷ Then the earth reeled and rocked;
    the foundations also of the
       mountains trembled
    and quaked, because he was angry.
⁸ Smoke went up from his nostrils,*ᵉ*
    and devouring fire from his mouth;
    glowing coals flamed
       forth from him.
⁹ He bowed the heavens
       and came down;
    thick darkness was under his feet.
¹⁰ He rode on a cherub and flew;
    he came swiftly on the
       wings of the wind.
¹¹ He made darkness his covering,
    his canopy around him,
    thick clouds dark with water.
¹² Out of the brightness before him
    hailstones and coals of fire
       broke through his clouds.

¹³ The Lord also thundered
       in the heavens,
    and the Most High uttered
       his voice,
    hailstones and coals of fire.
¹⁴ And he sent out his arrows
       and scattered them;
    he flashed forth lightnings
       and routed them.
¹⁵ Then the channels of the
       sea were seen,
    and the foundations of the
       world were laid bare

---
*ᵃ*Or *Distinguish me by*   *ᵇ*Or *from men whose portion in life is of the world*
*ᶜ*Or *As for your treasured ones, you fill their womb*   *ᵈ*Or *terrified me*
*ᵉ*Or *in his wrath*

at your rebuke, O Lord,
    at the blast of the breath
        of your nostrils.

16 He sent from on high, he took me;
    he drew me out of many waters.
17 He rescued me from my strong enemy
    and from those who hated me,
        for they were too mighty for me.
18 They confronted me in the
        day of my calamity,
    but the Lord was my support.
19 He brought me out into a broad place;
    he rescued me, because he
        delighted in me.

20 The Lord dealt with me according
        to my righteousness;
    according to the cleanness of my
        hands he rewarded me.
21 For I have kept the ways of the Lord,
    and have not wickedly
        departed from my God.
22 For all his rules[a] were before me,
    and his statutes I did not
        put away from me.
23 I was blameless before him,
    and I kept myself from my guilt.
24 So the Lord has rewarded me
        according to my righteousness,
    according to the cleanness of
        my hands in his sight.

25 With the merciful you show
        yourself merciful;
    with the blameless man you
        show yourself blameless;
26 with the purified you show
        yourself pure;
    and with the crooked you make
        yourself seem tortuous.
27 For you save a humble people,
    but the haughty eyes you
        bring down.
28 For it is you who light my lamp;
    the Lord my God lightens
        my darkness.
29 For by you I can run against a troop,
    and by my God I can leap over a wall.
30 This God—his way is perfect;[b]
    the word of the Lord proves true;
    he is a shield for all those who
        take refuge in him.

31 For who is God, but the Lord?
    And who is a rock, except our God?—
32 the God who equipped me
        with strength
    and made my way blameless.
33 He made my feet like the feet of a deer
    and set me secure on the heights.
34 He trains my hands for war,
    so that my arms can bend
        a bow of bronze.
35 You have given me the shield
        of your salvation,
    and your right hand supported me,
    and your gentleness made me great.
36 You gave a wide place for my
        steps under me,
    and my feet did not slip.
37 I pursued my enemies and
        overtook them,
    and did not turn back till
        they were consumed.
38 I thrust them through, so that
    they were not able to rise;
    they fell under my feet.
39 For you equipped me with
        strength for the battle;
    you made those who rise against
        me sink under me.
40 You made my enemies turn
        their backs to me,[c]
    and those who hated me I
        destroyed.
41 They cried for help, but there
        was none to save;
    they cried to the Lord, but he
        did not answer them.
42 I beat them fine as dust
        before the wind;
    I cast them out like the
        mire of the streets.

43 You delivered me from strife
        with the people;
    you made me the head
        of the nations;
    people whom I had not
        known served me.
44 As soon as they heard of me
        they obeyed me;
    foreigners came cringing to me.
45 Foreigners lost heart
    and came trembling out of
        their fortresses.

46 The Lord lives, and blessed
        be my rock,

---

[a] Or just decrees   [b] Or blameless   [c] Or You gave me my enemies' necks

and exalted be the God of
  my salvation—
47 the God who gave me vengeance
  and subdued peoples under me,
48 who rescued me from my enemies;
  yes, you exalted me above those
    who rose against me;
  you delivered me from the
    man of violence.

49 For this I will praise you, O Lord,
    among the nations,
  and sing to your name.
50 Great salvation he brings to his king,
  and shows steadfast love
    to his anointed,
  to David and his offspring for ever.

THE LAW OF THE LORD IS PERFECT

19

To the choirmaster. A Psalm of David.

1 The heavens declare
    the glory of God,
  and the sky above[a] proclaims
    his handiwork.
2 Day to day pours out speech,
  and night to night reveals
    knowledge.
3 There is no speech, nor
    are there words,
  whose voice is not heard.
4 Their voice[b] goes out through
    all the earth,
  and their words to the end
    of the world.
  In them he has set a tent for the sun,
5   which comes out like
    a bridegroom leaving
      his chamber,
  and, like a strong man, runs
    its course with joy.
6 Its rising is from the end
    of the heavens,
  and its circuit to the end of them,
  and there is nothing hidden
    from its heat.

7 The law of the Lord is perfect,[c]
    reviving the soul;
  the testimony of the Lord is sure,
    making wise the simple;
8 the precepts of the Lord are right,
    rejoicing the heart;
  the commandment of the
    Lord is pure,
    enlightening the eyes;

9 the fear of the Lord is clean,
    enduring for ever;
  the rules[d] of the Lord are true,
    and righteous altogether.
10 More to be desired are they than gold,
    even much fine gold;
  sweeter also than honey
    and drippings of the honeycomb.
11 Moreover, by them is your
    servant warned;
  in keeping them there is
    great reward.

12 Who can discern his errors?
    Declare me innocent from
      hidden faults.
13 Keep back your servant also from
    presumptuous sins;
  let them not have dominion
    over me!
  Then I shall be blameless,
    and innocent of great transgression.

14 Let the words of my mouth and
    the meditation of my heart
  be acceptable in your sight,
  O Lord, my rock and my redeemer.

TRUST IN THE NAME OF THE LORD OUR GOD

20

*To the choirmaster.
A Psalm of David.*

1 May the Lord answer you in
    the day of trouble!
  May the name of the God of
    Jacob protect you!
2 May he send you help from
    the sanctuary
  and give you support from Zion!
3 May he remember all your offerings
  and regard with favour your burnt
    sacrifices!   *Selah*

4 May he grant you your heart's desire
  and fulfil all your plans!
5 May we shout for joy over
    your salvation,
  and in the name of our God
    set up our banners!
  May the Lord fulfil all your petitions!

6 Now I know that the Lord
    saves his anointed;

---

[a]Hebrew *the expanse*; compare Genesis 1:6–8   [b]Or *Their measuring line*   [c]Or *blameless*   [d]Or *just decrees*

he will answer him from
   his holy heaven
with the saving might of
   his right hand.
7 Some trust in chariots and
      some in horses,
   but we trust in the name of
      the Lord our God.
8 They collapse and fall,
   but we rise and stand upright.

9 O Lord, save the king!
   May he answer us when we call.

THE KING REJOICES IN THE LORD'S STRENGTH

21

To the choirmaster. A Psalm of David.

¹ O Lord, in your strength
   the king rejoices,
and in your salvation how
   greatly he exults!
² You have given him his heart's desire
   and have not withheld the request of
      his lips.   *Selah*
³ For you meet him with rich blessings;
   you set a crown of fine gold
      upon his head.
⁴ He asked life of you; you gave it to him,
   length of days for ever and ever.
⁵ His glory is great through
      your salvation;
   splendour and majesty you
      bestow on him.
⁶ For you make him most
      blessed for ever;[a]
   you make him glad with the
      joy of your presence.
⁷ For the king trusts in the Lord,
   and through the steadfast
      love of the Most High he
      shall not be moved.

⁸ Your hand will find out all
      your enemies;
   your right hand will find out
      those who hate you.
⁹ You will make them as a blazing oven
      when you appear.
   The Lord will swallow them
      up in his wrath,
   and fire will consume them.
¹⁰ You will destroy their descendants
      from the earth,
   and their offspring from among
      the children of man.

¹¹ Though they plan evil against you,
      though they devise mischief,
      they will not succeed.
¹² For you will put them to flight;
      you will aim at their faces
         with your bows.

¹³ Be exalted, O Lord, in your strength!
      We will sing and praise your power.

WHY HAVE YOU FORSAKEN ME?

22

To the choirmaster: according to The Doe of the Dawn. A Psalm of David.

¹ My God, my God, why have
      you forsaken me?
   Why are you so far from saving me,
      from the words of my groaning?
² O my God, I cry by day, but
      you do not answer,
   and by night, but I find no rest.

³ Yet you are holy,
      enthroned on the praises[b] of Israel.
⁴ In you our fathers trusted;
      they trusted, and you delivered them.
⁵ To you they cried and were rescued;
      in you they trusted and were
         not put to shame.

⁶ But I am a worm and not a man,
      scorned by mankind and
         despised by the people.
⁷ All who see me mock me;
      they make mouths at me;
      they wag their heads;
⁸ "He trusts in the Lord; let
      him deliver him;
   let him rescue him, for he
      delights in him!"

⁹ Yet you are he who took me
      from the womb;
   you made me trust you at my
      mother's breasts.
¹⁰ On you was I cast from my birth,
      and from my mother's womb
         you have been my God.
¹¹ Be not far from me,
      for trouble is near,
      and there is none to help.

¹² Many bulls encompass me;
      strong bulls of Bashan surround me;

---

[a] Or *make him a source of blessing for ever*   [b] Or *dwelling in the praises*

13 they open wide their mouths at me,
     like a ravening and roaring lion.

14 I am poured out like water,
     and all my bones are out of joint;
   my heart is like wax;
     it is melted within my breast;
15 my strength is dried up like a potsherd,
     and my tongue sticks to my jaws;
   you lay me in the dust of death.

16 For dogs encompass me;
     a company of evildoers
       encircles me;
   they have pierced my
       hands and feet[a]—
17 I can count all my bones—
   they stare and gloat over me;
18 they divide my garments
       among them,
   and for my clothing they cast lots.

19 But you, O Lord, do not be far off!
   O you my help, come
       quickly to my aid!
20 Deliver my soul from the sword,
     my precious life from the
       power of the dog!
21 Save me from the mouth of the lion!
   You have rescued[b] me from the
       horns of the wild oxen!

22 I will tell of your name to
       my brothers;
   in the midst of the congregation
       I will praise you:
23 You who fear the Lord, praise him!
   All you offspring of Jacob,
       glorify him,
     and stand in awe of him, all
       you offspring of Israel!
24 For he has not despised or abhorred
     the affliction of the afflicted,
   and he has not hidden his
       face from him,
     but has heard, when he cried
       to him.

25 From you comes my praise in
       the great congregation;
   my vows I will perform before
       those who fear him.
26 The afflicted[c] shall eat and be satisfied;
     those who seek him shall
       praise the Lord!
   May your hearts live for ever!

27 All the ends of the earth
       shall remember
     and turn to the Lord,
   and all the families of the nations
     shall worship before you.
28 For kingship belongs to the Lord,
     and he rules over the nations.

29 All the prosperous of the earth
     eat and worship;
   before him shall bow all who
       go down to the dust,
     even the one who could not
       keep himself alive.
30 Posterity shall serve him;
     it shall be told of the Lord to
       the coming generation;
31 they shall come and proclaim
     his righteousness to a
       people yet unborn,
   that he has done it.

THE LORD IS MY SHEPHERD

23

A Psalm of David.

1 The Lord is my shepherd;
     I shall not want.
2   He makes me lie down in
       green pastures.
   He leads me beside still waters.[d]
3   He restores my soul.
   He leads me in paths of righteousness[e]
       for his name's sake.

4   Even though I walk through the
       valley of the shadow of death,[f]
   I will fear no evil,
   for you are with me;
     your rod and your staff,
       they comfort me.

5   You prepare a table before me
       in the presence of my enemies;
   you anoint my head with oil;
     my cup overflows.
6   Surely[g] goodness and mercy[h]
       shall follow me
     all the days of my life,
   and I shall dwell[i] in the
       house of the Lord
     for ever.[j]

---

[a]Some Hebrew manuscripts, Septuagint, Vulgate, Syriac; most Hebrew manuscripts *like a lion* [they are at] *my hands and feet* [b]Hebrew *answered* [c]Or *The meek* [d]Hebrew *beside waters of rest* [e]Or *in right paths* [f]Or *the valley of deep darkness* [g]Or *Only* [h]Or *steadfast love* [i]Or *shall return to dwell* [j]Hebrew *for length of days*

THE KING OF GLORY

24 A Psalm of David.

1 The earth is the LORD's and
   the fullness thereof,[a]
the world and those who
   dwell therein,
2 for he has founded it upon the seas
   and established it upon the rivers.

3 Who shall ascend the hill of the LORD?
   And who shall stand in his holy place?
4 He who has clean hands
      and a pure heart,
   who does not lift up his soul
      to what is false
   and does not swear deceitfully.
5 He will receive blessing from the LORD
   and righteousness from the
      God of his salvation.
6 Such is the generation of
      those who seek him,
   who seek the face of the God
      of Jacob.[b]   Selah

7 Lift up your heads, O gates!
   And be lifted up, O ancient doors,
   that the King of glory may come in.
8 Who is this King of glory?
   The LORD, strong and mighty,
   the LORD, mighty in battle!
9 Lift up your heads, O gates!
   And lift them up, O ancient doors,
   that the King of glory may come in.
10 Who is this King of glory?
   The LORD of hosts,
   he is the King of glory!   Selah

TEACH ME YOUR PATHS

25[c] Of David.

1 To you, O LORD,
   I lift up my soul.
2 O my God, in you I trust;
   let me not be put to shame;
   let not my enemies exult over me.
3 Indeed, none who wait for you
      shall be put to shame;
   they shall be ashamed who are
      wantonly treacherous.

4 Make me to know your ways, O LORD;
   teach me your paths.
5 Lead me in your truth and teach me,
   for you are the God of my salvation;
   for you I wait all the day long.

6 Remember your mercy, O LORD,
   and your steadfast love,
   for they have been from of old.
7 Remember not the sins of my
      youth or my transgressions;
   according to your steadfast
      love remember me,
   for the sake of your
      goodness, O LORD!

8 Good and upright is the LORD;
   therefore he instructs
      sinners in the way.
9 He leads the humble in what is right,
   and teaches the humble his way.
10 All the paths of the LORD are steadfast
      love and faithfulness,
   for those who keep his covenant
      and his testimonies.

11 For your name's sake, O LORD,
   pardon my guilt, for it is great.
12 Who is the man who fears the LORD?
   Him will he instruct in the way
      that he should choose.
13 His soul shall abide in well-being,
   and his offspring shall
      inherit the land.
14 The friendship[d] of the LORD is
      for those who fear him,
   and he makes known to
      them his covenant.
15 My eyes are ever towards the LORD,
   for he will pluck my feet
      out of the net.

16 Turn to me and be gracious to me,
   for I am lonely and afflicted.
17 The troubles of my heart are enlarged;
   bring me out of my distresses.
18 Consider my affliction and my trouble,
   and forgive all my sins.

19 Consider how many are my foes,
   and with what violent hatred
      they hate me.
20 Oh, guard my soul, and deliver me!
   Let me not be put to shame,
      for I take refuge in you.
21 May integrity and uprightness
      preserve me,
   for I wait for you.

---

[a]Or *and all that fills it* [b]Septuagint, Syriac, and two Hebrew manuscripts; Masoretic Text *who seek your face, Jacob* [c]This psalm is an acrostic poem, each verse beginning with the successive letters of the Hebrew alphabet [d]Or *The secret counsel*

22 Redeem Israel, O God,
out of all his troubles.

I WILL BLESS THE LORD

26 Of David.

1 Vindicate me, O LORD,
for I have walked in my integrity,
and I have trusted in the LORD
without wavering.
2 Prove me, O LORD, and try me;
test my heart and my mind.^a
3 For your steadfast love is
before my eyes,
and I walk in your faithfulness.

4 I do not sit with men of falsehood,
nor do I consort with hypocrites.
5 I hate the assembly of evildoers,
and I will not sit with the wicked.

6 I wash my hands in innocence
and go round your altar, O LORD,
7 proclaiming thanksgiving aloud,
and telling all your wondrous deeds.

8 O LORD, I love the habitation
of your house
and the place where your
glory dwells.
9 Do not sweep my soul away
with sinners,
nor my life with bloodthirsty men,
10 in whose hands are evil devices,
and whose right hands
are full of bribes.

11 But as for me, I shall walk
in my integrity;
redeem me, and be gracious to me.
12 My foot stands on level ground;
in the great assembly I will
bless the LORD.

THE LORD IS MY LIGHT AND MY SALVATION

27 Of David.

1 The LORD is my light and
my salvation;
whom shall I fear?
The LORD is the stronghold^b
of my life;
of whom shall I be afraid?

2 When evildoers assail me
to eat up my flesh,
my adversaries and foes,
it is they who stumble and fall.
3 Though an army encamp against me,
my heart shall not fear;
though war arise against me,
yet^c I will be confident.

4 One thing have I asked of the LORD,
that will I seek after:
that I may dwell in the
house of the LORD
all the days of my life,
to gaze upon the beauty of the LORD
and to enquire^d in his temple.
5 For he will hide me in his shelter
in the day of trouble;
he will conceal me under the
cover of his tent;
he will lift me high upon a rock.

6 And now my head shall be lifted up
above my enemies all round me,
and I will offer in his tent
sacrifices with shouts of joy;
I will sing and make melody
to the LORD.

7 Hear, O LORD, when I cry aloud;
be gracious to me and answer me!
8 You have said, "Seek^e my face."
My heart says to you,
"Your face, LORD, do I seek."^f
9 Hide not your face from me.
Turn not your servant away
in anger,
O you who have been my help.
Cast me not off; forsake me not,
O God of my salvation!
10 For my father and my mother
have forsaken me,
but the LORD will take me in.

11 Teach me your way, O LORD,
and lead me on a level path
because of my enemies.
12 Give me not up to the will
of my adversaries;
for false witnesses have
risen against me,
and they breathe out violence.

---

^aHebrew *test my kidneys and my heart* ^bOr *refuge* ^cOr *in this* ^dOr *meditate* ^eThe command (*seek*) is addressed to more than one person ^fThe meaning of the Hebrew verse is uncertain

THE LORD IS MY STRENGTH AND MY SHIELD

28 Of David.

1 To you, O LORD, I call;
   my rock, be not deaf to me,
lest, if you be silent to me,
   I become like those who go
      down to the pit.
2 Hear the voice of my pleas for mercy,
   when I cry to you for help,
when I lift up my hands
   towards your most holy sanctuary.[b]
3 Do not drag me off with the wicked,
   with the workers of evil,
who speak peace with
      their neighbours
   while evil is in their hearts.
4 Give to them according to
      their work
   and according to the evil
      of their deeds;
give to them according to the
      work of their hands;
   render them their due reward.
5 Because they do not regard
      the works of the LORD
   or the work of his hands,
he will tear them down and
   build them up no more.

6 Blessed be the LORD!
   For he has heard the voice of
      my pleas for mercy.
7 The LORD is my strength
      and my shield;
   in him my heart trusts,
      and I am helped;
my heart exults,
   and with my song I give
      thanks to him.
8 The LORD is the strength of
      his people;[c]
   he is the saving refuge of
      his anointed.
9 Oh, save your people and
      bless your heritage!
   Be their shepherd and carry
      them for ever.

ASCRIBE TO THE LORD GLORY

29 A Psalm of David.

1 Ascribe to the LORD,
      O heavenly beings,[d]
   ascribe to the LORD glory
      and strength.
2 Ascribe to the LORD the glory
      due his name;
   worship the LORD in the
      splendour of holiness.[e]

3 The voice of the LORD is
      over the waters;
   the God of glory thunders,
      the LORD, over many waters.
4 The voice of the LORD is powerful;
   the voice of the LORD is
      full of majesty.

5 The voice of the LORD
      breaks the cedars;
   the LORD breaks the cedars
      of Lebanon.
6 He makes Lebanon to skip like a calf,
   and Sirion like a young wild ox.

7 The voice of the LORD flashes
      forth flames of fire.
8 The voice of the LORD shakes
      the wilderness;
   the LORD shakes the
      wilderness of Kadesh.

9 The voice of the LORD makes
      the deer give birth[f]
   and strips the forests bare,
   and in his temple all cry, "Glory!"

10 The LORD sits enthroned
      over the flood;
   the LORD sits enthroned
      as king for ever.
11 May the LORD give strength
      to his people!
   May the LORD bless[g] his
      people with peace!

---

[a]Other Hebrew manuscripts *Oh! Had I not believed that I would look*   [b]Hebrew *your innermost sanctuary*   [c]Some Hebrew manuscripts, Septuagint, Syriac; most Hebrew manuscripts *is their strength*   [d]Hebrew *sons of God*, or *sons of might*   [e]Or *in holy attire*   [f]Revocalization yields *makes the oaks to shake*   [g]Or *The LORD will give . . . The LORD will bless*

JOY COMES WITH THE MORNING

30 A Psalm of David. A song at the dedication of the temple.

1 I will extol you, O Lord, for
 you have drawn me up
 and have not let my foes
 rejoice over me.
2 O Lord my God, I cried to you for help,
 and you have healed me.
3 O Lord, you have brought up
 my soul from Sheol;
 you restored me to life from among
 those who go down to the pit.[a]

4 Sing praises to the Lord,
 O you his saints,
 and give thanks to his holy name.[b]
5 For his anger is but for a moment,
 and his favour is for a lifetime.[c]
 Weeping may tarry for the night,
 but joy comes with the morning.

6 As for me, I said in my prosperity,
 "I shall never be moved."
7 By your favour, O Lord,
 you made my mountain
 stand strong;
 you hid your face;
 I was dismayed.

8 To you, O Lord, I cry,
 and to the Lord I plead for mercy:
9 "What profit is there in my death,[d]
 if I go down to the pit?[e]
 Will the dust praise you?
 Will it tell of your faithfulness?
10 Hear, O Lord, and be merciful to me!
 O Lord, be my helper!"

11 You have turned for me my
 mourning into dancing;
 you have loosed my sackcloth
 and clothed me with gladness,
12 that my glory may sing your
 praise and not be silent.
 O Lord my God, I will give
 thanks to you for ever!

INTO YOUR HAND I COMMIT MY SPIRIT

31 To the choirmaster. A Psalm of David.

1 In you, O Lord, do I take refuge;
 let me never be put to shame;
 in your righteousness deliver me!
2 Incline your ear to me;
 rescue me speedily!
 Be a rock of refuge for me,
 a strong fortress to save me!
3 For you are my rock and my fortress;
 and for your name's sake you
 lead me and guide me;
4 you take me out of the net they
 have hidden for me,
 for you are my refuge.
5 Into your hand I commit my spirit;
 you have redeemed me, O
 Lord, faithful God.

6 I hate[f] those who pay regard
 to worthless idols,
 but I trust in the Lord.
7 I will rejoice and be glad in
 your steadfast love,
 because you have seen my
 affliction;
 you have known the distress
 of my soul,
8 and you have not delivered me
 into the hand of the enemy;
 you have set my feet in a
 broad place.

9 Be gracious to me, O Lord,
 for I am in distress;
 my eye is wasted from grief;
 my soul and my body also.
10 For my life is spent with sorrow,
 and my years with sighing;
 my strength fails because
 of my iniquity,
 and my bones waste away.

11 Because of all my adversaries I
 have become a reproach,
 especially to my neighbours,
 and an object of dread to my
 acquaintances;
 those who see me in the
 street flee from me.
12 I have been forgotten like
 one who is dead;
 I have become like a broken vessel.
13 For I hear the whispering of many—
 terror on every side!—
 as they scheme together against me,
 as they plot to take my life.

---

[a] Or to life, that I should not go down to the pit [b] Hebrew to the memorial of his holiness (see Exodus 3:15) [c] Or and in his favour is life [d] Hebrew in my blood [e] Or to corruption [f] Masoretic Text; one Hebrew manuscript, Septuagint, Syriac, Jerome You hate

14 But I trust in you, O LORD;
   I say, "You are my God."
15 My times are in your hand;
   rescue me from the hand of
      my enemies and from
      my persecutors!
16 Make your face shine on your servant;
   save me in your steadfast love!
17 O LORD, let me not be put to shame,
   for I call upon you;
   let the wicked be put to shame;
   let them go silently to Sheol.
18 Let the lying lips be mute,
   which speak insolently
      against the righteous
   in pride and contempt.

19 Oh, how abundant is your goodness,
   which you have stored up for
      those who fear you
   and worked for those who
      take refuge in you,
   in the sight of the children
      of mankind!
20 In the cover of your presence
   you hide them
      from the plots of men;
   you store them in your shelter
      from the strife of tongues.

21 Blessed be the LORD,
   for he has wondrously shown
      his steadfast love to me
   when I was in a besieged city.
22 I had said in my alarm,[a]
   "I am cut off from your sight."
   But you heard the voice of
      my pleas for mercy
   when I cried to you for help.

23 Love the LORD, all you his saints!
   The LORD preserves the faithful
   but abundantly repays the
      one who acts in pride.
24 Be strong, and let your heart
      take courage,
   all you who wait for the LORD!

BLESSED ARE THE FORGIVEN

32
A Maskil[b] of David.

¹Blessed is the one whose
   transgression is forgiven,
   whose sin is covered.
² Blessed is the man against whom
   the LORD counts no iniquity,
   and in whose spirit there
      is no deceit.

³ For when I kept silent, my
      bones wasted away
   through my groaning all day long.
⁴ For day and night your hand
      was heavy upon me;
   my strength was dried up[c] as by the
      heat of summer.   *Selah*

⁵ I acknowledged my sin to you,
   and I did not cover my iniquity;
   I said, "I will confess my
      transgressions to the LORD",
   and you forgave the iniquity of my
      sin.   *Selah*

⁶ Therefore let everyone who is godly
   offer prayer to you at a time
      when you may be found;
   surely in the rush of great waters,
      they shall not reach him.
⁷ You are a hiding place for me;
   you preserve me from trouble;
   you surround me with shouts of
      deliverance.   *Selah*

⁸ I will instruct you and teach you
      in the way you should go;
   I will counsel you with my
      eye upon you.
⁹ Be not like a horse or a mule,
      without understanding,
   which must be curbed with
      bit and bridle,
   or it will not stay near you.

¹⁰ Many are the sorrows of the wicked,
    but steadfast love surrounds the
       one who trusts in the LORD.
¹¹ Be glad in the LORD, and
    rejoice, O righteous,
    and shout for joy, all you
       upright in heart!

THE STEADFAST LOVE OF THE LORD

33
Shout for joy in the LORD,
   O you righteous!
   Praise befits the upright.
² Give thanks to the LORD with the lyre;
   make melody to him with the
      harp of ten strings!

---

[a] Or *in my haste*   [b] Probably a musical or liturgical term   [c] Hebrew *my vitality was changed*

3 Sing to him a new song;
  play skilfully on the strings,
    with loud shouts.

4 For the word of the LORD is upright,
    and all his work is done
      in faithfulness.
5 He loves righteousness and justice;
    the earth is full of the steadfast
      love of the LORD.

6 By the word of the LORD the
    heavens were made,
    and by the breath of his
      mouth all their host.
7 He gathers the waters of
    the sea as a heap;
    he puts the deeps in storehouses.

8 Let all the earth fear the LORD;
    let all the inhabitants of the
      world stand in awe of him!
9 For he spoke, and it came to be;
    he commanded, and it stood firm.

10 The LORD brings the counsel of
    the nations to nothing;
    he frustrates the plans
      of the peoples.
11 The counsel of the LORD
    stands for ever,
    the plans of his heart to
      all generations.
12 Blessed is the nation whose
    God is the LORD,
    the people whom he has
      chosen as his heritage!

13 The LORD looks down from heaven;
    he sees all the children of man;
14 from where he sits enthroned
    he looks out
      on all the inhabitants of the earth,
15 he who fashions the hearts of
    them all
    and observes all their deeds.
16 The king is not saved by his great army;
    a warrior is not delivered by
      his great strength.
17 The war horse is a false
    hope for salvation,
    and by its great might it
      cannot rescue.

18 Behold, the eye of the LORD is
    on those who fear him,
      on those who hope in his
        steadfast love,
19 that he may deliver their
    soul from death
    and keep them alive in famine.

20 Our soul waits for the LORD;
    he is our help and our shield.
21 For our heart is glad in him,
    because we trust in his holy name.
22 Let your steadfast love, O
    LORD, be upon us,
    even as we hope in you.

TASTE AND SEE THAT THE LORD IS GOOD

34

[a] Of David, when he changed his behaviour before Abimelech, so that he drove him out, and he went away.

1 I will bless the LORD at all times;
    his praise shall continually
      be in my mouth.
2 My soul makes its boast in the LORD;
    let the humble hear and be glad.
3 Oh, magnify the LORD with me,
    and let us exalt his name together!

4 I sought the LORD, and he
    answered me
    and delivered me from all my fears.
5 Those who look to him are radiant,
    and their faces shall never
      be ashamed.
6 This poor man cried, and the
    LORD heard him
    and saved him out of all his troubles.
7 The angel of the LORD encamps
    round those who fear him,
      and delivers them.

8 Oh, taste and see that the LORD is good!
    Blessed is the man who
      takes refuge in him!
9 Oh, fear the LORD, you his saints,
    for those who fear him have no lack!
10 The young lions suffer
    want and hunger;
    but those who seek the LORD
      lack no good thing.

11 Come, O children, listen to me;
    I will teach you the fear of the LORD.

---

[a]This psalm is an acrostic poem, each verse beginning with the successive letters of the Hebrew alphabet

12 What man is there who desires life
   and loves many days, that
      he may see good?
13 Keep your tongue from evil
   and your lips from speaking deceit.
14 Turn away from evil and do good;
   seek peace and pursue it.

15 The eyes of the LORD are
      towards the righteous
   and his ears towards their cry.
16 The face of the LORD is against
      those who do evil,
   to cut off the memory of
      them from the earth.
17 When the righteous cry for
      help, the LORD hears
   and delivers them out of
      all their troubles.
18 The LORD is near to the broken-hearted
   and saves the crushed in spirit.

19 Many are the afflictions of
      the righteous,
   but the LORD delivers him
      out of them all.
20 He keeps all his bones;
   not one of them is broken.
21 Affliction will slay the wicked,
   and those who hate the righteous
      will be condemned.
22 The LORD redeems the life
      of his servants;
   none of those who take refuge in
      him will be condemned.

GREAT IS THE LORD

35

Of David.

1 Contend, O LORD, with those
      who contend with me;
   fight against those who
      fight against me!
2 Take hold of shield and buckler
   and rise for my help!
3 Draw the spear and javelin*a*
      against my pursuers!
   Say to my soul,
      "I am your salvation!"

4 Let them be put to shame
      and dishonour
   who seek after my life!
   Let them be turned back
      and disappointed
   who devise evil against me!

5 Let them be like chaff before the wind,
   with the angel of the LORD
      driving them away!
6 Let their way be dark and slippery,
   with the angel of the LORD
      pursuing them!

7 For without cause they hid
      their net for me;
   without cause they dug a
      pit for my life.*b*
8 Let destruction come upon him
      when he does not know it!
   And let the net that he hid ensnare him;
   let him fall into it—to his
      destruction!

9 Then my soul will rejoice in the LORD,
   exulting in his salvation.
10 All my bones shall say,
   "O LORD, who is like you,
delivering the poor
   from him who is too strong for him,
   the poor and needy from
      him who robs him?"

11 Malicious*c* witnesses rise up;
   they ask me of things that
      I do not know.
12 They repay me evil for good;
   my soul is bereft.*d*
13 But I, when they were sick—
   I wore sackcloth;
   I afflicted myself with fasting;
   I prayed with head bowed*e* on my chest.
14   I went about as though I grieved
      for my friend or my brother;
   as one who laments his mother,
   I bowed down in mourning.

15 But at my stumbling they
      rejoiced and gathered;
   they gathered together against me;
   wretches whom I did not know
      tore at me without ceasing;
16 like profane mockers at a feast,*f*
   they gnash at me with their teeth.

17 How long, O Lord, will you look on?
   Rescue me from their destruction,
   my precious life from the lions!

---

a Or *and close the way* *b* The word *pit* is transposed from the preceding line; Hebrew *For without cause they hid the pit of their net for me; without cause they dug a pit for my life* *c* Or *Violent* *d* Hebrew *it is bereavement to my soul* *e* Or *my prayer shall turn back* *f* The meaning of the Hebrew phrase is uncertain

¹⁸ I will thank you in the great congregation;
 in the mighty throng I will praise you.

¹⁹ Let not those rejoice over me
 who are wrongfully my foes,
and let not those wink the eye
 who hate me without cause.
²⁰ For they do not speak peace,
 but against those who are quiet in the land
 they devise words of deceit.
²¹ They open wide their mouths against me;
 they say, "Aha, Aha!
 Our eyes have seen it!"

²² You have seen, O LORD; be not silent!
 O Lord, be not far from me!
²³ Awake and rouse yourself for my vindication,
 for my cause, my God and my Lord!
²⁴ Vindicate me, O LORD, my God,
 according to your righteousness,
 and let them not rejoice over me!
²⁵ Let them not say in their hearts,
 "Aha, our heart's desire!"
Let them not say, "We have swallowed him up."

²⁶ Let them be put to shame and disappointed altogether
 who rejoice at my calamity!
Let them be clothed with shame and dishonour
 who magnify themselves against me!

²⁷ Let those who delight in my righteousness
 shout for joy and be glad
 and say evermore,
"Great is the LORD,
 who delights in the welfare of his servant!"
²⁸ Then my tongue shall tell of your righteousness
 and of your praise all the day long.

HOW PRECIOUS IS YOUR STEADFAST LOVE

36 *To the choirmaster. Of David, the servant of the LORD.*

¹ Transgression speaks to the wicked
 deep in his heart;[a]
 there is no fear of God before his eyes.
² For he flatters himself in his own eyes
 that his iniquity cannot be found out and hated.
³ The words of his mouth are trouble and deceit;
 he has ceased to act wisely and do good.
⁴ He plots trouble while on his bed;
 he sets himself in a way that is not good;
 he does not reject evil.

⁵ Your steadfast love, O LORD, extends to the heavens,
 your faithfulness to the clouds.
⁶ Your righteousness is like the mountains of God;
 your judgements are like the great deep;
 man and beast you save, O LORD.

⁷ How precious is your steadfast love, O God!
 The children of mankind take refuge
 in the shadow of your wings.
⁸ They feast on the abundance of your house,
 and you give them drink from the river of your delights.
⁹ For with you is the fountain of life;
 in your light do we see light.

¹⁰ Oh, continue your steadfast love to those who know you,
 and your righteousness to the upright of heart!
¹¹ Let not the foot of arrogance come upon me,
 nor the hand of the wicked drive me away.
¹² There the evildoers lie fallen;
 they are thrust down, unable to rise.

HE WILL NOT FORSAKE HIS SAINTS

37[b] *Of David.*

¹ Fret not yourself because of evildoers;
 be not envious of wrongdoers!

---

[a] Some Hebrew manuscripts, Syriac, Jerome (compare Septuagint); most Hebrew manuscripts *in my heart*   [b] This psalm is an acrostic poem, each stanza beginning with the successive letters of the Hebrew alphabet

2 For they will soon fade like the grass
   and wither like the green herb.
3 Trust in the LORD, and do good;
   dwell in the land and befriend
     faithfulness.ᵃ
4 Delight yourself in the LORD,
   and he will give you the
     desires of your heart.
5 Commit your way to the LORD;
   trust in him, and he will act.
6 He will bring forth your
     righteousness as the light,
   and your justice as the noonday.
7 Be still before the LORD and
     wait patiently for him;
   fret not yourself over the one
     who prospers in his way,
   over the man who carries
     out evil devices!
8 Refrain from anger, and forsake wrath!
   Fret not yourself; it tends
     only to evil.
9 For the evildoers shall be cut off,
   but those who wait for the LORD
     shall inherit the land.
10 In just a little while, the wicked
     will be no more;
   though you look carefully at his
     place, he will not be there.
11 But the meek shall inherit the land
   and delight themselves in
     abundant peace.
12 The wicked plots against the
     righteous
   and gnashes his teeth at him,
13 but the Lord laughs at the wicked,
   for he sees that his day is coming.
14 The wicked draw the sword
     and bend their bows
   to bring down the poor and needy,
   to slay those whose way is upright;
15 their sword shall enter
     their own heart,
   and their bows shall be broken.
16 Better is the little that the
     righteous has
   than the abundance of
     many wicked.

17 For the arms of the wicked
     shall be broken,
   but the LORD upholds the righteous.
18 The LORD knows the days
     of the blameless,
   and their heritage will
     remain for ever;
19 they are not put to shame in evil times;
   in the days of famine they
     have abundance.
20 But the wicked will perish;
   the enemies of the LORD are like
     the glory of the pastures;
   they vanish—like smoke
     they vanish away.
21 The wicked borrows but
     does not pay back,
   but the righteous is
     generous and gives;
22 for those blessed by the LORDᵇ
     shall inherit the land,
   but those cursed by him
     shall be cut off.
23 The steps of a man are
     established by the LORD,
   when he delights in his way;
24 though he fall, he shall not
     be cast headlong,
   for the LORD upholds his hand.
25 I have been young, and now am old,
   yet I have not seen the
     righteous forsaken
   or his children begging for bread.
26 He is ever lending generously,
   and his children become a blessing.
27 Turn away from evil and do good;
   so shall you dwell for ever.
28 For the LORD loves justice;
   he will not forsake his saints.
   They are preserved for ever,
     but the children of the wicked
       shall be cut off.
29 The righteous shall inherit the land
   and dwell upon it for ever.
30 The mouth of the righteous
     utters wisdom,
   and his tongue speaks justice.

ᵃ Or *and feed on faithfulness*, or *and find safe pasture*   ᵇ Hebrew *by him*

31 The law of his God is in his heart;
    his steps do not slip.
32 The wicked watches for the righteous
    and seeks to put him to death.
33 The LORD will not abandon
    him to his power
  or let him be condemned when
    he is brought to trial.

34 Wait for the LORD and keep his way,
  and he will exalt you to
    inherit the land;
  you will look on when the
    wicked are cut off.

35 I have seen a wicked, ruthless man,
  spreading himself like a
    green laurel tree.[a]
36 But he passed away,[b] and
    behold, he was no more;
  though I sought him, he
    could not be found.

37 Mark the blameless and
    behold the upright,
  for there is a future for the
    man of peace.
38 But transgressors shall be
    altogether destroyed;
  the future of the wicked
    shall be cut off.

39 The salvation of the righteous
    is from the LORD;
  he is their stronghold in the time
    of trouble.
40 The LORD helps them and
    delivers them;
  he delivers them from the
    wicked and saves them,
  because they take refuge in him.

DO NOT FORSAKE ME, O LORD

38
A Psalm of David, for the memorial offering.

1 O LORD, rebuke me not in your anger,
    nor discipline me in your wrath!
2 For your arrows have sunk into me,
    and your hand has come down on me.

3 There is no soundness in my flesh
    because of your indignation;
  there is no health in my bones
    because of my sin.
4 For my iniquities have gone
    over my head;
  like a heavy burden, they are
    too heavy for me.

5 My wounds stink and fester
    because of my foolishness,
6 I am utterly bowed down
    and prostrate;
  all the day I go about mourning.
7 For my sides are filled with burning,
    and there is no soundness
      in my flesh.
8 I am feeble and crushed;
  I groan because of the
    tumult of my heart.

9 O Lord, all my longing is before you;
    my sighing is not hidden from you.
10 My heart throbs; my strength fails me,
    and the light of my eyes—it
      also has gone from me.
11 My friends and companions stand
    aloof from my plague,
  and my nearest kin stand far off.

12 Those who seek my life
    lay their snares;
  those who seek my hurt
    speak of ruin
  and meditate treachery all day long.

13 But I am like a deaf man; I do not hear,
    like a mute man who does
      not open his mouth.
14 I have become like a man
    who does not hear,
  and in whose mouth are
    no rebukes.

15 But for you, O LORD, do I wait;
    it is you, O Lord my God,
      who will answer.
16 For I said, "Only let them not
    rejoice over me,
  who boast against me when
    my foot slips!"

17 For I am ready to fall,
    and my pain is ever before me.
18 I confess my iniquity;
    I am sorry for my sin.
19 But my foes are vigorous,
    they are mighty,

---
[a]The identity of this tree is uncertain [b]Or *But one passed by*

and many are those who
    hate me wrongfully.
20 Those who render me evil for good
    accuse me because I follow
        after good.

21 Do not forsake me, O Lord!
    O my God, be not far from me!
22 Make haste to help me,
    O Lord, my salvation!

WHAT IS THE MEASURE OF MY DAYS?

39 *To the choirmaster:
to Jeduthun. A Psalm of David.*

1 I said, "I will guard my ways,
    that I may not sin with my tongue;
  I will guard my mouth with a muzzle,
    so long as the wicked are
        in my presence."
2 I was mute and silent;
    I held my peace to no avail,
  and my distress grew worse.
3 My heart became hot within me.
    As I mused, the fire burned;
  then I spoke with my tongue:

4 "O Lord, make me know my end
    and what is the measure of my days;
    let me know how fleeting I am!
5 Behold, you have made my days
        a few handbreadths,
    and my lifetime is as
        nothing before you.
  Surely all mankind stands as a
        mere breath!   *Selah*
6 Surely a man goes about as a shadow!
    Surely for nothing[a] they are in turmoil;
  man heaps up wealth and does
        not know who will gather!

7 "And now, O Lord, for what do I wait?
    My hope is in you.
8 Deliver me from all my transgressions.
    Do not make me the scorn of the fool!
9 I am mute; I do not open my mouth,
    for it is you who have done it.
10 Remove your stroke from me;
    I am spent by the hostility
        of your hand.
11 When you discipline a man
        with rebukes for sin,
    you consume like a moth
        what is dear to him;
  surely all mankind is a
        mere breath!   *Selah*

12 "Hear my prayer, O Lord,
    and give ear to my cry;
    hold not your peace at my tears!
  For I am a sojourner with you,
    a guest, like all my fathers.
13 Look away from me, that I
        may smile again,
    before I depart and am no more!"

MY HELP AND MY DELIVERER

40 *To the choirmaster.
A Psalm of David.*

1 I waited patiently for the Lord;
    he inclined to me and heard my cry.
2 He drew me up from the pit
        of destruction,
    out of the miry bog,
  and set my feet upon a rock,
    making my steps secure.
3 He put a new song in my mouth,
    a song of praise to our God.
  Many will see and fear,
    and put their trust in the Lord.

4 Blessed is the man who makes
        the Lord his trust,
  who does not turn to the proud,
    to those who go astray after a lie!
5 You have multiplied, O Lord my God,
    your wondrous deeds and your
        thoughts towards us;
    none can compare with you!
  I will proclaim and tell of them,
    yet they are more than can be told.

6 In sacrifice and offering you
        have not delighted,
    but you have given me an
        open ear.[b]
  Burnt offering and sin offering
    you have not required.
7 Then I said, "Behold, I have come;
    in the scroll of the book it
        is written of me:
8 I delight to do your will, O my God;
    your law is within my heart."

9 I have told the glad news
        of deliverance[c]
    in the great congregation;
  behold, I have not restrained my lips,
    as you know, O Lord.

---
[a]Hebrew *Surely as a breath*   [b]Hebrew *ears you have dug for me*
[c]Hebrew *righteousness*; also verse 10

10 I have not hidden your deliverance
      within my heart;
   I have spoken of your faithfulness
      and your salvation;
   I have not concealed your steadfast
      love and your faithfulness
      from the great congregation.
11 As for you, O Lord, you
      will not restrain
      your mercy from me;
   your steadfast love and your
      faithfulness will
      ever preserve me!
12 For evils have encompassed me
      beyond number;
   my iniquities have overtaken me,
      and I cannot see;
   they are more than the
      hairs of my head;
   my heart fails me.

13 Be pleased, O Lord, to deliver me!
      O Lord, make haste to help me!
14 Let those be put to shame and
      disappointed altogether
      who seek to snatch away my life;
   let those be turned back and
      brought to dishonour
      who delight in my hurt!
15 Let those be appalled because
      of their shame
   who say to me, "Aha, Aha!"

16 But may all who seek you
      rejoice and be glad in you;
   may those who love your salvation
      say continually, "Great is
      the Lord!"
17 As for me, I am poor and needy,
      but the Lord takes thought for me.
   You are my help and my deliverer;
      do not delay, O my God!

O LORD, BE GRACIOUS TO ME

41

To the choirmaster. A Psalm of David.

¹ Blessed is the one who
      considers the poor!*a*
   In the day of trouble the
      Lord delivers him;
² the Lord protects him and
      keeps him alive;
   he is called blessed in the land;
      you do not give him up to the
      will of his enemies.

³ The Lord sustains him on his sickbed;
      in his illness you restore
      him to full health.*b*
⁴ As for me, I said, "O Lord,
      be gracious to me;
   heal me,*c* for I have sinned
      against you!"
⁵ My enemies say of me in malice,
      "When will he die, and his
      name perish?"
⁶ And when one comes to see me,
      he utters empty words,
      while his heart gathers iniquity;
      when he goes out, he tells it abroad.
⁷ All who hate me whisper
      together about me;
      they imagine the worst for me.*d*
⁸ They say, "A deadly thing is
      poured out*e* on him;
   he will not rise again from
      where he lies."
⁹ Even my close friend in
      whom I trusted,
   who ate my bread, has lifted
      his heel against me.
¹⁰ But you, O Lord, be gracious to me,
      and raise me up, that I
      may repay them!

¹¹ By this I know that you delight in me:
      my enemy will not shout in
      triumph over me.
¹² But you have upheld me
      because of my integrity,
      and set me in your presence for ever.

¹³ Blessed be the Lord, the God of Israel,
      from everlasting to everlasting!
      Amen and Amen.

BOOK TWO

WHY ARE YOU CAST DOWN, O MY SOUL?

42

*To the choirmaster. A Maskil*f*
of the Sons of Korah.*

¹ As a deer pants for flowing streams,
      so pants my soul for you, O God.
² My soul thirsts for God,
      for the living God.

---

a Or *weak* *b* Hebrew *you turn all his bed* *c* Hebrew *my soul* *d* Or *they devise evil against me* *e* Or *has fastened* *f* Probably a musical or liturgical term

When shall I come and
 appear before God?ᵃ
3 My tears have been my food
 day and night,
while they say to me all the day long,
 "Where is your God?"
4 These things I remember,
 as I pour out my soul:
how I would go with the throng
 and lead them in procession
  to the house of God
with glad shouts and songs of praise,
 a multitude keeping festival.

5 Why are you cast down, O my soul,
 and why are you in turmoil
  within me?
Hope in God; for I shall
 again praise him,
 my salvationᵇ ⁶and my God.

My soul is cast down within me;
 therefore I remember you
from the land of Jordan and of Hermon,
 from Mount Mizar.
7 Deep calls to deep
 at the roar of your waterfalls;
all your breakers and your waves
 have gone over me.
8 By day the LORD commands
 his steadfast love,
 and at night his song is with me,
 a prayer to the God of my life.
9 I say to God, my rock:
 "Why have you forgotten me?
Why do I go mourning
 because of the oppression
  of the enemy?"
10 As with a deadly wound in my bones,
 my adversaries taunt me,
while they say to me all the day long,
 "Where is your God?"

11 Why are you cast down, O my soul,
 and why are you in turmoil
  within me?
Hope in God; for I shall
 again praise him,
 my salvation and my God.

SEND OUT YOUR LIGHT AND YOUR TRUTH

43
Vindicate me, O God,
 and defend my cause
 against an ungodly people,
from the deceitful and unjust man
 deliver me!

2 For you are the God in whom
 I take refuge;
why have you rejected me?
Why do I go about mourning
 because of the oppression
  of the enemy?

3 Send out your light and your truth;
 let them lead me;
let them bring me to your holy hill
 and to your dwelling!
4 Then I will go to the altar of God,
 to God my exceeding joy,
and I will praise you with the lyre,
 O God, my God.

5 Why are you cast down, O my soul,
 and why are you in turmoil
  within me?
Hope in God; for I shall
 again praise him,
 my salvation and my God.

COME TO OUR HELP

44
To the choirmaster. A Maskilᶜ of the Sons of Korah.

1 O God, we have heard with our ears,
 our fathers have told us,
what deeds you performed in their days,
 in the days of old:
2 you with your own hand drove
 out the nations,
 but them you planted;
you afflicted the peoples,
 but them you set free;
3 for not by their own sword did
 they win the land,
 nor did their own arm save them,
but your right hand and your arm,
 and the light of your face,
 for you delighted in them.

4 You are my King, O God;
 ordain salvation for Jacob!
5 Through you we push down our foes;
 through your name we tread down
  those who rise up against us.
6 For not in my bow do I trust,
 nor can my sword save me.
7 But you have saved us from our foes
 and have put to shame
  those who hate us.

ᵃRevocalization yields *and see the face of God* ᵇHebrew *the salvation of my face*; also verse 11 and 43:5 ᶜProbably a musical or liturgical term

8 In God we have boasted continually,
and we will give thanks to your
name for ever. *Selah*

9 But you have rejected us
and disgraced us
and have not gone out
with our armies.
10 You have made us turn
back from the foe,
and those who hate us
have taken spoil.
11 You have made us like sheep
for slaughter
and have scattered us
among the nations.
12 You have sold your people for a trifle,
demanding no high price
for them.
13 You have made us the taunt
of our neighbours,
the derision and scorn of
those around us.
14 You have made us a byword
among the nations,
a laughing-stock[a] among
the peoples.
15 All day long my disgrace is before me,
and shame has covered my face
16 at the sound of the taunter
and reviler,
at the sight of the enemy
and the avenger.

17 All this has come upon us,
though we have not forgotten you,
and we have not been false
to your covenant.
18 Our heart has not turned back,
nor have our steps departed
from your way;
19 yet you have broken us in
the place of jackals
and covered us with the
shadow of death.
20 If we had forgotten the
name of our God
or spread out our hands
to a foreign god,
21 would not God discover this?
For he knows the secrets
of the heart.
22 Yet for your sake we are killed
all the day long;
we are regarded as sheep
to be slaughtered.

23 Awake! Why are you sleeping, O Lord?
Rouse yourself! Do not
reject us for ever!
24 Why do you hide your face?
Why do you forget our affliction
and oppression?
25 For our soul is bowed down to
the dust;
our belly clings to the ground.
26 Rise up; come to our help!
Redeem us for the sake of
your steadfast love!

YOUR THRONE, O GOD, IS FOR EVER

45

To the choirmaster: according to Lilies. A Maskil[b] of the Sons of Korah; a love song.

1 My heart overflows with a
pleasing theme;
I address my verses to the king;
my tongue is like the pen
of a ready scribe.

2 You are the most handsome
of the sons of men;
grace is poured upon your lips;
therefore God has blessed
you for ever.
3 Gird your sword on your
thigh, O mighty one,
in your splendour and majesty!

4 In your majesty ride out victoriously
for the cause of truth and meekness
and righteousness;
let your right hand teach you
awesome deeds!
5 Your arrows are sharp
in the heart of the king's enemies;
the peoples fall under you.

6 Your throne, O God, is for
ever and ever.
The sceptre of your kingdom is
a sceptre of uprightness;
7 you have loved righteousness
and hated wickedness.
Therefore God, your God,
has anointed you
with the oil of gladness beyond
your companions;
8 your robes are all fragrant with
myrrh and aloes and cassia.

---

[a]Hebrew *a shaking of the head* [b]Probably a musical or liturgical term

From ivory palaces stringed
     instruments make you glad;
9 daughters of kings are among
     your ladies of honour;
  at your right hand stands the
     queen in gold of Ophir.

10 Hear, O daughter, and consider,
     and incline your ear:
  forget your people and your
     father's house,
11 and the king will desire your beauty.
  Since he is your lord, bow to him.
12 The people[a] of Tyre will seek
     your favour with gifts,
   the richest of the people.[b]

13 All glorious is the princess in
     her chamber, with robes
     interwoven with gold.
14 In many-coloured robes she
     is led to the king,
   with her virgin companions
     following behind her.
15 With joy and gladness they
     are led along
   as they enter the palace of the king.

16 In place of your fathers
     shall be your sons;
   you will make them princes
     in all the earth.
17 I will cause your name to be
     remembered in all generations;
   therefore nations will praise
     you for ever and ever.

GOD IS OUR FORTRESS

46

To the choirmaster. Of the Sons of Korah. According to Alamoth.[c] A Song.

1 God is our refuge and strength,
     a very present[d] help in trouble.
2 Therefore we will not fear though
     the earth gives way,
   though the mountains be moved
     into the heart of the sea,
3 though its waters roar and foam,
   though the mountains tremble at
     its swelling. *Selah*

4 There is a river whose streams
     make glad the city of God,
   the holy habitation of
     the Most High.

5 God is in the midst of her; she
     shall not be moved;
   God will help her when
     morning dawns.
6 The nations rage, the kingdoms totter;
   he utters his voice, the earth melts.
7 The LORD of hosts is with us;
   the God of Jacob is our fortress. *Selah*

8 Come, behold the works of the LORD,
   how he has brought desolations
     on the earth.
9 He makes wars cease to the
     end of the earth;
   he breaks the bow and
     shatters the spear;
   he burns the chariots with fire.
10 "Be still, and know that I am God.
   I will be exalted among the nations,
   I will be exalted in the earth!"
11 The LORD of hosts is with us;
   the God of Jacob is our fortress. *Selah*

GOD IS KING OVER ALL THE EARTH

47

To the choirmaster. A Psalm of the Sons of Korah.

1 Clap your hands, all peoples!
   Shout to God with loud songs of joy!
2 For the LORD, the Most High,
     is to be feared,
   a great king over all the earth.
3 He subdued peoples under us,
   and nations under our feet.
4 He chose our heritage for us,
   the pride of Jacob whom
     he loves. *Selah*

5 God has gone up with a shout,
   the LORD with the sound
     of a trumpet.
6 Sing praises to God, sing praises!
   Sing praises to our King,
     sing praises!
7 For God is the King of all the earth;
   sing praises with a psalm![e]

8 God reigns over the nations;
   God sits on his holy throne.
9 The princes of the peoples gather
   as the people of the God
     of Abraham.

---

[a]Hebrew *daughter* [b]Or *The daughter of Tyre is here with gifts, the richest of people seek your favour* [c]Probably a musical or liturgical term [d]Or *well proved* [e]Hebrew *maskil*

For the shields of the earth
    belong to God;
he is highly exalted!

ZION, THE CITY OF OUR GOD

48 *A Song. A Psalm of the Sons of Korah.*

1 Great is the LORD and greatly
        to be praised
    in the city of our God!
His holy mountain, ²beautiful
        in elevation,
    is the joy of all the earth,
Mount Zion, in the far north,
    the city of the great King.
3 Within her citadels God
        has made himself known
    as a fortress.

4 For behold, the kings assembled;
    they came on together.
5 As soon as they saw it, they
        were astounded;
    they were in panic; they
        took to flight.
6 Trembling took hold of them there,
    anguish as of a woman in labour.
7 By the east wind you shattered
    the ships of Tarshish.
8 As we have heard, so have we seen
    in the city of the LORD of hosts,
in the city of our God,
    which God will establish
        for ever.   *Selah*

9 We have thought on your
        steadfast love, O God,
    in the midst of your temple.
10 As your name, O God,
    so your praise reaches to the
        ends of the earth.
Your right hand is filled with
        righteousness.
11 Let Mount Zion be glad!
Let the daughters of Judah rejoice
    because of your judgements!

12 Walk about Zion, go round her,
    number her towers,
13 consider well her ramparts,
    go through her citadels,
that you may tell the next generation
14   that this is God,
    our God for ever and ever.
He will guide us for ever.[a]

WHY SHOULD I FEAR IN TIMES OF TROUBLE?

49 *To the choirmaster. A Psalm of the Sons of Korah.*

1 Hear this, all peoples!
    Give ear, all inhabitants of
        the world,
2 both low and high,
    rich and poor together!
3 My mouth shall speak wisdom;
    the meditation of my heart
        shall be understanding.
4 I will incline my ear to a proverb;
    I will solve my riddle to the
        music of the lyre.

5 Why should I fear in times of trouble,
    when the iniquity of those who
        cheat me surrounds me,
6 those who trust in their wealth
    and boast of the abundance
        of their riches?
7 Truly no man can ransom another,
    or give to God the price of his life,
8 for the ransom of their life is costly
    and can never suffice,
9 that he should live on for ever
    and never see the pit.

10 For he sees that even the wise die;
    the fool and the stupid
        alike must perish
    and leave their wealth to others.
11 Their graves are their homes for ever,[b]
    their dwelling places to
        all generations,
    though they called lands by
        their own names.
12 Man in his pomp will not remain;
    he is like the beasts that perish.

13 This is the path of those who
        have foolish confidence;
    yet after them people approve of
        their boasts.[c]   *Selah*
14 Like sheep they are appointed
        for Sheol;
    death shall be their shepherd,
and the upright shall rule over
        them in the morning.
    Their form shall be consumed in
        Sheol, with no place to dwell.

---

[a]Septuagint; another reading is (compare Jerome, Syriac) *He will guide us beyond death*   [b]Septuagint, Syriac, Targum; Hebrew *Their inward thought was that their homes were for ever*   [c]Or *and of those after them who approve of their boasts*

15 But God will ransom my soul
    from the power of Sheol,
    for he will receive me. *Selah*

16 Be not afraid when a man
    becomes rich,
    when the glory of his
    house increases.
17 For when he dies he will
    carry nothing away;
    his glory will not go down after him.
18 For though, while he lives, he
    counts himself blessed
    —and though you get praise when
    you do well for yourself—
19 his soul will go to the generation
    of his fathers,
    who will never again see light.
20 Man in his pomp yet without
    understanding is like the
    beasts that perish.

GOD HIMSELF IS JUDGE

50

A Psalm of Asaph.

1 The Mighty One,
    God the LORD,
speaks and summons the earth
    from the rising of the sun
    to its setting.
2 Out of Zion, the perfection of beauty,
    God shines forth.

3 Our God comes; he does
    not keep silence;[a]
    before him is a devouring fire,
    around him a mighty tempest.
4 He calls to the heavens above
    and to the earth, that he may
    judge his people:
5 "Gather to me my faithful ones,
    who made a covenant with
    me by sacrifice!"
6 The heavens declare his righteousness,
    for God himself is judge! *Selah*

7 "Hear, O my people, and I will speak;
    O Israel, I will testify against you.
    I am God, your God.
8 Not for your sacrifices do I rebuke you;
    your burnt offerings are
    continually before me.
9 I will not accept a bull from your house
    or goats from your folds.
10 For every beast of the forest is mine,
    the cattle on a thousand hills.
11 I know all the birds of the hills,
    and all that moves in the field
    is mine.

12 "If I were hungry, I would not tell you,
    for the world and its
    fullness are mine.
13 Do I eat the flesh of bulls
    or drink the blood of goats?
14 Offer to God a sacrifice of thanksgiving,[b]
    and perform your vows to
    the Most High,
15 and call upon me in the day of trouble;
    I will deliver you, and you
    shall glorify me."

16 But to the wicked God says:
    "What right have you to
    recite my statutes
    or take my covenant on your lips?
17 For you hate discipline,
    and you cast my words behind you.
18 If you see a thief, you are
    pleased with him,
    and you keep company
    with adulterers.

19 "You give your mouth free rein for evil,
    and your tongue frames deceit.
20 You sit and speak against your brother;
    you slander your own mother's son.
21 These things you have done,
    and I have been silent;
    you thought that I[c] was
    one like yourself.
But now I rebuke you and lay
    the charge before you.

22 "Mark this, then, you who forget God,
    lest I tear you apart, and there
    be none to deliver!
23 The one who offers thanksgiving
    as his sacrifice glorifies me;
    to one who orders his way rightly
    I will show the salvation of God!"

CREATE IN ME A CLEAN HEART, O GOD

51

To the choirmaster. A Psalm of David, when Nathan the prophet went to him, after he had gone in to Bathsheba.

1 Have mercy on me,[d] O God,
    according to your steadfast love;

---

[a] Or *May our God come, and not keep silence* [b] Or *Make thanksgiving your sacrifice to God* [c] Or *that the I AM* [d] Or *Be gracious to me*

according to your abundant mercy
   blot out my transgressions.
2 Wash me thoroughly from
      my iniquity,
   and cleanse me from my sin!

3 For I know my transgressions,
   and my sin is ever before me.
4 Against you, you only, have I sinned
      and done what is evil in your sight,
   so that you may be justified
      in your words
   and blameless in your judgement.
5 Behold, I was brought forth
      in iniquity,
   and in sin did my mother
      conceive me.
6 Behold, you delight in truth
      in the inward being,
   and you teach me wisdom
      in the secret heart.

7 Purge me with hyssop, and
      I shall be clean;
   wash me, and I shall be
      whiter than snow.
8 Let me hear joy and gladness;
   let the bones that you have
      broken rejoice.
9 Hide your face from my sins,
   and blot out all my iniquities.
10 Create in me a clean heart, O God,
   and renew a right^a spirit within me.
11 Cast me not away from your presence,
   and take not your Holy
      Spirit from me.
12 Restore to me the joy of your salvation,
   and uphold me with a willing spirit.

13 Then I will teach transgressors
      your ways,
   and sinners will return to you.
14 Deliver me from bloodguiltiness,
      O God,
   O God of my salvation,
   and my tongue will sing aloud
      of your righteousness.
15 O Lord, open my lips,
   and my mouth will declare
      your praise.
16 For you will not delight in
      sacrifice, or I would give it;
   you will not be pleased with
      a burnt offering.
17 The sacrifices of God are
      a broken spirit;
   a broken and contrite heart, O
      God, you will not despise.

18 Do good to Zion in your good pleasure;
   build up the walls of Jerusalem;
19 then will you delight in
      right sacrifices,
   in burnt offerings and whole
      burnt offerings;
   then bulls will be offered
      on your altar.

THE STEADFAST LOVE OF GOD ENDURES

52 To the choirmaster. A Maskil^b of David, when Doeg, the Edomite, came and told Saul, "David has come to the house of Ahimelech."

1 Why do you boast of evil,
      O mighty man?
   The steadfast love of God
      endures all the day.
2 Your tongue plots destruction,
      like a sharp razor, you
      worker of deceit.
3 You love evil more than good,
   and lying more than speaking what
      is right.   Selah
4 You love all words that devour,
      O deceitful tongue.

5 But God will break you down for ever;
   he will snatch and tear you
      from your tent;
   he will uproot you from the land of
      the living.   Selah
6 The righteous shall see and fear,
   and shall laugh at him, saying,
7 "See the man who would not make
      God his refuge,
   but trusted in the abundance
      of his riches
   and sought refuge in his
      own destruction!"^{c}

8 But I am like a green olive tree
      in the house of God.
   I trust in the steadfast love of God
      for ever and ever.
9 I will thank you for ever,
      because you have done it.
   I will wait for your name, for it is good,
      in the presence of the godly.

---

^{a}Or *steadfast* ^{b}Probably a musical or liturgical term ^{c}Or *in his work of destruction*

THERE IS NONE WHO DOES GOOD

53
To the choirmaster: according to Mahalath. A Maskil[a] of David.

1 The fool says in his heart,
    "There is no God."
  They are corrupt, doing
      abominable iniquity;
    there is none who does good.

2 God looks down from heaven
      on the children of man
  to see if there are any who understand,[b]
    who seek after God.

3 They have all fallen away;
    together they have become corrupt;
  there is none who does good,
    not even one.

4 Have those who work evil no knowledge,
    who eat up my people as they eat bread,
    and do not call upon God?

5 There they are, in great terror,
    where there is no terror!
  For God scatters the bones of him
      who encamps against you;
    you put them to shame, for
      God has rejected them.

6 Oh, that salvation for Israel
      would come out of Zion!
  When God restores the
      fortunes of his people,
    let Jacob rejoice, let Israel be glad.

THE LORD UPHOLDS MY LIFE

54
To the choirmaster: with stringed instruments. A Maskil[c] of David, when the Ziphites went and told Saul, "Is not David hiding among us?"

1 O God, save me by your name,
    and vindicate me by your might.
2 O God, hear my prayer;
    give ear to the words of my mouth.

3 For strangers[d] have risen against me;
    ruthless men seek my life;
  they do not set God before
      themselves.   *Selah*

4 Behold, God is my helper;
    the Lord is the upholder of my life.

5 He will return the evil to my enemies;
    in your faithfulness put
      an end to them.

6 With a freewill offering I will
      sacrifice to you;
    I will give thanks to your name,
      O LORD, for it is good.
7 For he has delivered me
      from every trouble,
    and my eye has looked in
      triumph on my enemies.

CAST YOUR BURDEN ON THE LORD

55
To the choirmaster: with stringed instruments. A Maskil[e] of David.

1 Give ear to my prayer, O God,
    and hide not yourself from
      my plea for mercy!
2 Attend to me, and answer me;
    I am restless in my complaint
      and I moan,
3 because of the noise of the enemy,
    because of the oppression
      of the wicked.
  For they drop trouble upon me,
    and in anger they bear a
      grudge against me.

4 My heart is in anguish within me;
    the terrors of death have
      fallen upon me.
5 Fear and trembling come upon me,
    and horror overwhelms me.
6 And I say, "Oh, that I had
      wings like a dove!
    I would fly away and be at rest;
7 yes, I would wander far away;
    I would lodge in the
      wilderness;   *Selah*
8 I would hurry to find a shelter
    from the raging wind and tempest."

9 Destroy, O Lord, divide their tongues;
    for I see violence and strife in the city.
10 Day and night they go round it
      on its walls,
    and iniquity and trouble are within it;
11   ruin is in its midst;
    oppression and fraud
      do not depart from its market-place.

---

[a] Probably musical or liturgical terms [b] Or *who act wisely* [c] Probably a musical or liturgical term [d] Some Hebrew manuscripts and Targum *insolent men* (compare Psalm 86:14) [e] Probably a musical or liturgical term

12 For it is not an enemy who taunts me—
    then I could bear it;
  it is not an adversary who deals
      insolently with me—
    then I could hide from him.
13 But it is you, a man, my equal,
    my companion, my familiar friend.
14 We used to take sweet counsel together;
    within God's house we
      walked in the throng.
15 Let death steal over them;
    let them go down to Sheol alive;
  for evil is in their dwelling
    place and in their heart.

16 But I call to God,
    and the LORD will save me.
17 Evening and morning and at noon
    I utter my complaint and moan,
    and he hears my voice.
18 He redeems my soul in safety
    from the battle that I wage,
    for many are arrayed against me.
19 God will give ear and humble them,
    he who is enthroned from
      of old,   Selah
  because they do not change
    and do not fear God.

20 My companion[a] stretched out his
    hand against his friends;
    he violated his covenant.
21 His speech was smooth as butter,
    yet war was in his heart;
  his words were softer than oil,
    yet they were drawn swords.

22 Cast your burden on the LORD,
    and he will sustain you;
  he will never permit
    the righteous to be moved.

23 But you, O God, will cast them down
    into the pit of destruction;
  men of blood and treachery
    shall not live out half their days.
  But I will trust in you.

IN GOD I TRUST

56

To the choirmaster: according to The Dove on Far-off Terebinths. A Miktam[b] of David, when the Philistines seized him in Gath.

1 Be gracious to me, O God, for
    man tramples on me;
  all day long an attacker
    oppresses me;
2 my enemies trample on
    me all day long,
  for many attack me proudly.
3 When I am afraid,
    I put my trust in you.
4 In God, whose word I praise,
    in God I trust; I shall not be afraid.
    What can flesh do to me?

5 All day long they injure my cause;[c]
    all their thoughts are
      against me for evil.
6 They stir up strife, they lurk;
    they watch my steps,
    as they have waited for my life.
7 For their crime will they escape?
    In wrath cast down the
      peoples, O God!

8 You have kept count of my tossings;[d]
    put my tears in your bottle.
    Are they not in your book?
9 Then my enemies will turn back
    in the day when I call.
    This I know, that[e] God is for me.
10 In God, whose word I praise,
    in the LORD, whose word I praise,
11 in God I trust; I shall not be afraid.
    What can man do to me?

12 I must perform my vows to you, O God;
    I will render thank offerings to you.
13 For you have delivered my
      soul from death,
    yes, my feet from falling,
  that I may walk before God
    in the light of life.

LET YOUR GLORY BE OVER ALL THE EARTH

57

To the choirmaster: according to Do Not Destroy. A Miktam[f] of David, when he fled from Saul, in the cave.

1 Be merciful to me, O God,
    be merciful to me,
    for in you my soul takes refuge;
  in the shadow of your wings
    I will take refuge,
  till the storms of destruction
    pass by.

---

[a]Hebrew He [b]Probably a musical or liturgical term [c]Or they twist my words [d]Or wanderings [e]Or because [f]Probably a musical or liturgical term

2 I cry out to God Most High,
   to God who fulfils his
      purpose for me.
3 He will send from heaven and save me;
   he will put to shame him who
      tramples on me. *Selah*
  God will send out his steadfast
      love and his faithfulness!

4 My soul is in the midst of lions;
   I lie down amid fiery beasts—
  the children of man, whose teeth
      are spears and arrows,
   whose tongues are sharp swords.

5 Be exalted, O God, above the heavens!
   Let your glory be over all the earth!

6 They set a net for my steps;
      my soul was bowed down.
   They dug a pit in my way,
      but they have fallen into it
         themselves. *Selah*
7 My heart is steadfast, O God,
      my heart is steadfast!
   I will sing and make melody!
8 Awake, my glory!*a*
   Awake, O harp and lyre!
      I will awake the dawn!
9 I will give thanks to you, O Lord,
      among the peoples;
   I will sing praises to you
      among the nations.
10 For your steadfast love is
      great to the heavens,
   your faithfulness to the clouds.

11 Be exalted, O God, above the heavens!
   Let your glory be over all the earth!

GOD WHO JUDGES THE EARTH

58 *To the choirmaster: according to Do Not Destroy. A Miktam*[b] *of David.*

1 Do you indeed decree what
      is right, you gods?[c]
   Do you judge the children
      of man uprightly?
2 No, in your hearts you devise wrongs;
      your hands deal out
         violence on earth.

3 The wicked are estranged
      from the womb;
   they go astray from birth,
      speaking lies.

4 They have venom like the
      venom of a serpent,
   like the deaf adder that stops its ear,
5 so that it does not hear the
      voice of charmers
   or of the cunning enchanter.

6 O God, break the teeth in their mouths;
   tear out the fangs of the
      young lions, O LORD!
7 Let them vanish like water
      that runs away;
   when he aims his arrows,
      let them be blunted.
8 Let them be like the snail that
      dissolves into slime,
   like the stillborn child who
      never sees the sun.
9 Sooner than your pots can feel
      the heat of thorns,
   whether green or ablaze, may
      he sweep them away![d]

10 The righteous will rejoice when
      he sees the vengeance;
   he will bathe his feet in the
      blood of the wicked.
11 Mankind will say, "Surely there is
      a reward for the righteous;
   surely there is a God who
      judges on earth."

DELIVER ME FROM MY ENEMIES

59 *To the choirmaster: according to Do Not Destroy. A Miktam*[e] *of David, when Saul sent men to watch his house in order to kill him.*

1 Deliver me from my enemies,
      O my God;
   protect me from those who
      rise up against me;
2 deliver me from those who work evil,
   and save me from bloodthirsty men.

3 For behold, they lie in wait for my life;
   fierce men stir up strife against me.
   For no transgression or sin
      of mine, O LORD,
4 for no fault of mine, they
      run and make ready.
   Awake, come to meet me, and see!

---

[a] Or *my whole being* [b] Probably a musical or liturgical term [c] Or *you mighty lords* (by revocalization; Hebrew *in silence*) [d] The meaning of the Hebrew verse is uncertain [e] Probably a musical or liturgical term

5 You, LORD God of hosts,
      are God of Israel.
   Rouse yourself to punish
      all the nations;
   spare none of those who
        treacherously plot evil.   Selah

6 Each evening they come back,
      howling like dogs
      and prowling about the city.
7 There they are, bellowing
      with their mouths
   with swords in their lips—
   for "Who," they think,[a]
      "will hear us?"

8 But you, O LORD, laugh at them;
      you hold all the nations in derision.
9 O my Strength, I will watch for you,
      for you, O God, are my fortress.
10 My God in his steadfast
      love[b] will meet me;
   God will let me look in triumph
      on my enemies.

11 Kill them not, lest my people forget;
      make them totter[c] by your power
      and bring them down,
      O Lord, our shield!
12 For the sin of their mouths,
      the words of their lips,
      let them be trapped in their pride.
   For the cursing and lies that they utter,
13   consume them in wrath;
   consume them till they are no more,
   that they may know that God
      rules over Jacob
   to the ends of the earth.   Selah

14 Each evening they come back,
      howling like dogs
      and prowling about the city.
15 They wander about for food
      and growl if they do not get their fill.

16 But I will sing of your strength;
      I will sing aloud of your steadfast
        love in the morning.
   For you have been to me a fortress
      and a refuge in the day
      of my distress.
17 O my Strength, I will sing
      praises to you,
   for you, O God, are my fortress,
      the God who shows me
        steadfast love.

HE WILL TREAD DOWN OUR FOES

60

To the choirmaster: according to Shushan Eduth. A Miktam[d] of David; for instruction; when he strove with Aram-naharaim and with Aram-zobah, and when Joab on his return struck down twelve thousand of Edom in the Valley of Salt.

1 O God, you have rejected us,
      broken our defences;
   you have been angry; oh, restore us.
2 You have made the land to quake;
      you have torn it open;
   repair its breaches, for it totters.
3 You have made your people
      see hard things;
   you have given us wine to drink
      that made us stagger.

4 You have set up a banner for
      those who fear you,
   that they may flee to it from
      the bow.[e]   Selah
5 That your beloved ones
      may be delivered,
   give salvation by your right
      hand and answer us!

6 God has spoken in his holiness:[f]
      "With exultation I will
        divide up Shechem
   and portion out the Vale of Succoth.
7 Gilead is mine; Manasseh is mine;
      Ephraim is my helmet;
      Judah is my sceptre.
8 Moab is my washbasin;
      upon Edom I cast my shoe;
   over Philistia I shout in triumph."[g]

9 Who will bring me to the
      fortified city?
   Who will lead me to Edom?
10 Have you not rejected us, O God?
   You do not go forth, O God,
      with our armies.
11 Oh, grant us help against the foe,
      for vain is the salvation of man!
12 With God we shall do valiantly;
      it is he who will tread down
      our foes.

---

[a]Hebrew lacks *they think*   [b]Or *The God who shows me steadfast love*   [c]Or *wander*   [d]Probably musical or liturgical terms   [e]Or *that it may be displayed because of truth*   [f]Or *sanctuary*   [g]Revocalization (compare Psalm 108:10); Masoretic Text *over me, O Philistia, shout in triumph*

LEAD ME TO THE ROCK

61 *To the choirmaster: with stringed instruments. Of David.*

1 Hear my cry, O God,
 listen to my prayer;
2 from the end of the earth I call to you
 when my heart is faint.
 Lead me to the rock
 that is higher than I,
3 for you have been my refuge,
 a strong tower against the enemy.

4 Let me dwell in your tent for ever!
 Let me take refuge under the shelter
 of your wings! *Selah*
5 For you, O God, have heard my vows;
 you have given me the heritage of
 those who fear your name.

6 Prolong the life of the king;
 may his years endure to
 all generations!
7 May he be enthroned for
 ever before God;
 appoint steadfast love and
 faithfulness to watch over him!

8 So will I ever sing praises
 to your name,
 as I perform my vows day after day.

MY SOUL WAITS FOR GOD ALONE

62 *To the choirmaster: according to Jeduthun. A Psalm of David.*

1 For God alone my soul waits in silence;
 from him comes my salvation.
2 He alone is my rock and my salvation,
 my fortress; I shall not be
 greatly shaken.

3 How long will all of you attack a man
 to batter him,
 like a leaning wall, a tottering fence?
4 They only plan to thrust him down
 from his high position.
 They take pleasure in falsehood.
 They bless with their mouths,
 but inwardly they curse. *Selah*

5 For God alone, O my soul,
 wait in silence,
 for my hope is from him.
6 He only is my rock and my salvation,
 my fortress; I shall not be shaken.
7 On God rests my salvation
 and my glory;
 my mighty rock, my refuge is God.

8 Trust in him at all times, O people;
 pour out your heart before him;
 God is a refuge for us. *Selah*

9 Those of low estate are but a breath;
 those of high estate are a delusion;
 in the balances they go up;
 they are together lighter
 than a breath.
10 Put no trust in extortion;
 set no vain hopes on robbery;
 if riches increase, set not
 your heart on them.

11 Once God has spoken;
 twice have I heard this:
 that power belongs to God,
12 and that to you, O Lord,
 belongs steadfast love.
 For you will render to a man
 according to his work.

MY SOUL THIRSTS FOR YOU

63 *A Psalm of David, when he was in the wilderness of Judah.*

1 O God, you are my God;
 earnestly I seek you;
 my soul thirsts for you;
 my flesh faints for you,
 as in a dry and weary land
 where there is no water.
2 So I have looked upon you
 in the sanctuary,
 beholding your power and glory.
3 Because your steadfast love
 is better than life,
 my lips will praise you.
4 So I will bless you as long as I live;
 in your name I will lift up
 my hands.

5 My soul will be satisfied as
 with fat and rich food,
 and my mouth will praise
 you with joyful lips,
6 when I remember you upon my bed,
 and meditate on you in the
 watches of the night;
7 for you have been my help,
 and in the shadow of your
 wings I will sing for joy.

8 My soul clings to you;
    your right hand upholds me.

9 But those who seek to destroy
       my life
    shall go down into the
       depths of the earth;
10 they shall be given over to the
       power of the sword;
    they shall be a portion for jackals.
11 But the king shall rejoice in God;
    all who swear by him shall exult,
    for the mouths of liars
       will be stopped.

HIDE ME FROM THE WICKED

64

To the choirmaster. A Psalm of David.

1 Hear my voice, O God, in
       my complaint;
    preserve my life from dread
       of the enemy.
2 Hide me from the secret
       plots of the wicked,
    from the throng of evildoers,
3 who whet their tongues like swords,
    who aim bitter words like arrows,
4 shooting from ambush at
       the blameless,
    shooting at him suddenly
       and without fear.
5 They hold fast to their evil purpose;
    they talk of laying snares secretly,
    thinking, "Who can see them?"
6 They search out injustice,
    saying, "We have accomplished
       a diligent search."
    For the inward mind and heart
       of a man are deep.

7 But God shoots his arrow at them;
    they are wounded suddenly.
8 They are brought to ruin, with their
       own tongues turned against them;
    all who see them will wag
       their heads.
9 Then all mankind fears;
    they tell what God has brought
       about
    and ponder what he has done.

10 Let the righteous one rejoice
       in the LORD
    and take refuge in him!
    Let all the upright in heart exult!

O GOD OF OUR SALVATION

65

To the choirmaster. A Psalm of David. A Song.

1 Praise is due to you,[a] O God, in Zion,
    and to you shall vows be performed.
2 O you who hear prayer,
    to you shall all flesh come.
3 When iniquities prevail against me,
    you atone for our transgressions.
4 Blessed is the one you choose
       and bring near,
    to dwell in your courts!
    We shall be satisfied with the
       goodness of your house,
    the holiness of your temple!

5 By awesome deeds you answer
       us with righteousness,
    O God of our salvation,
    the hope of all the ends of the earth
       and of the farthest seas;
6 the one who by his strength
       established the mountains,
    being girded with might;
7 who stills the roaring of the seas,
    the roaring of their waves,
    the tumult of the peoples,
8 so that those who dwell at the ends of
       the earth are in awe at your signs.
    You make the going out of the morning
       and the evening to shout for joy.

9 You visit the earth and water it;[b]
    you greatly enrich it;
    the river of God is full of water;
    you provide their corn,
    for so you have prepared it.
10 You water its furrows abundantly,
    settling its ridges,
    softening it with showers,
    and blessing its growth.
11 You crown the year with your bounty;
    your wagon tracks overflow
       with abundance.
12 The pastures of the wilderness
       overflow,
    the hills gird themselves with joy,
13 the meadows clothe themselves
       with flocks,
    the valleys deck themselves
       with corn,
    they shout and sing together
       for joy.

---

[a]Or *Praise waits for you in silence* [b]Or *and make it overflow*

HOW AWESOME ARE YOUR DEEDS

66 *To the choirmaster. A Song. A Psalm.*

1 Shout for joy to God, all the earth;
2 sing the glory of his name;
 give to him glorious praise!
3 Say to God, "How awesome
  are your deeds!
 So great is your power that your
  enemies come cringing to you.
4 All the earth worships you
  and sings praises to you;
 they sing praises to your
  name." *Selah*

5 Come and see what God has done:
 he is awesome in his deeds towards
  the children of man.
6 He turned the sea into dry land;
 they passed through the
  river on foot.
 There did we rejoice in him,
7 who rules by his might for ever,
 whose eyes keep watch on
  the nations—
 let not the rebellious exalt
  themselves. *Selah*

8 Bless our God, O peoples;
 let the sound of his praise be heard,
9 who has kept our soul among the living
 and has not let our feet slip.
10 For you, O God, have tested us;
 you have tried us as silver is tried.
11 You brought us into the net;
 you laid a crushing burden
  on our backs;
12 you let men ride over our heads;
 we went through fire and
  through water;
 yet you have brought us out to
  a place of abundance.

13 I will come into your house
  with burnt offerings;
 I will perform my vows to you,
14 that which my lips uttered
 and my mouth promised
  when I was in trouble.
15 I will offer to you burnt offerings
  of fattened animals,
 with the smoke of the
  sacrifice of rams;
 I will make an offering of bulls
  and goats. *Selah*

16 Come and hear, all you who fear God,
 and I will tell what he has
  done for my soul.
17 I cried to him with my mouth,
 and high praise was on[a] my tongue.[b]
18 If I had cherished iniquity in my heart,
 the Lord would not have listened.
19 But truly God has listened;
 he has attended to the voice
  of my prayer.

20 Blessed be God,
 because he has not rejected
  my prayer
 or removed his steadfast
  love from me!

MAKE YOUR FACE SHINE UPON US

67 *To the choirmaster: with stringed instruments. A Psalm. A Song.*

1 May God be gracious to us and bless us
 and make his face to shine
  upon us, *Selah*
2 that your way may be known on earth,
 your saving power among
  all nations.
3 Let the peoples praise you, O God;
 let all the peoples praise you!

4 Let the nations be glad and sing for joy,
 for you judge the peoples
  with equity
 and guide the nations upon
  earth. *Selah*
5 Let the peoples praise you, O God;
 let all the peoples praise you!

6 The earth has yielded its increase;
 God, our God, shall bless us.
7 God shall bless us;
 let all the ends of the earth fear him!

GOD SHALL SCATTER HIS ENEMIES

68 *To the choirmaster. A Psalm of David. A Song.*

1 God shall arise, his enemies
  shall be scattered;
 and those who hate him shall
  flee before him!
2 As smoke is driven away, so you
  shall drive them away;
 as wax melts before fire,

---

[a]Hebrew *under* [b]Or *and he was exalted with my tongue*

so the wicked shall perish
　　before God!
3 But the righteous shall be glad;
　　they shall exult before God;
　　they shall be jubilant with joy!

4 Sing to God, sing praises to his name;
　　lift up a song to him who rides
　　　through the deserts;
　his name is the LORD;
　　exult before him!
5 Father of the fatherless and
　　　protector of widows
　is God in his holy habitation.
6 God settles the solitary in a home;
　　he leads out the prisoners
　　　to prosperity,
　but the rebellious dwell in
　　　a parched land.

7 O God, when you went out
　　before your people,
　when you marched through
　　　the wilderness,　　　　Selah
8 the earth quaked, the heavens
　　poured down rain,
　before God, the One of Sinai,
　before God,[a] the God of Israel.
9 Rain in abundance, O God,
　　you shed abroad;
　you restored your inheritance
　　as it languished;
10 your flock[b] found a dwelling in it;
　in your goodness, O God, you
　　provided for the needy.

11 The Lord gives the word;
　　the women who announce the
　　　news are a great host:
12 "The kings of the armies—
　　they flee, they flee!"
　The women at home divide the spoil—
13 　though you men lie among
　　　the sheepfolds—
　the wings of a dove covered with silver,
　　its pinions with shimmering gold.
14 When the Almighty scatters
　　kings there,
　let snow fall on Zalmon.

15 O mountain of God, mountain
　　of Bashan;
　O many-peaked[c] mountain,
　　mountain of Bashan!
16 Why do you look with hatred, O
　　many-peaked mountain,
　at the mount that God desired
　　for his abode,
　yes, where the LORD will
　　dwell for ever?
17 The chariots of God are twice
　　ten thousand,
　　thousands upon thousands;
　the Lord is among them; Sinai
　　is now in the sanctuary.
18 You ascended on high,
　　leading a host of captives
　　　in your train
　and receiving gifts among men,
　even among the rebellious, that the
　　LORD God may dwell there.

19 Blessed be the Lord,
　　who daily bears us up;
　God is our salvation.　　　　Selah
20 Our God is a God of salvation,
　　and to GOD, the Lord, belong
　　　deliverances from death.
21 But God will strike the heads
　　of his enemies,
　　the hairy crown of him who
　　　walks in his guilty ways.
22 The Lord said,
　　"I will bring them back from
　　　Bashan,
　I will bring them back from
　　the depths of the sea,
23 that you may strike your
　　feet in their blood,
　that the tongues of your dogs may
　　have their portion from the foe."

24 Your procession is[d] seen, O God,
　　the procession of my God, my
　　　King, into the sanctuary—
25 the singers in front, the
　　musicians last,
　between them virgins playing
　　tambourines:
26 "Bless God in the great congregation,
　　the LORD, O you[e] who are of
　　Israel's fountain!"
27 There is Benjamin, the least
　　of them, in the lead,
　the princes of Judah in their
　　　throng,
　the princes of Zebulun, the
　　princes of Naphtali.

---

[a]Or *before God, even Sinai before God*　　[b]Or *your congregation*
[c]Or *hunch-backed*; also verse 16　　[d]Or *has been*　　[e]The Hebrew for *you* is plural here

28 Summon your power, O God,[a]
   the power, O God, by which
      you have worked for us.
29 Because of your temple at Jerusalem
   kings shall bear gifts to you.
30 Rebuke the beasts that dwell
      among the reeds,
   the herd of bulls with the
      calves of the peoples.
   Trample underfoot those who
      lust after tribute;
   scatter the peoples who
      delight in war.[b]
31 Nobles shall come from Egypt;
   Cush shall hasten to stretch
      out her hands to God.

32 O kingdoms of the earth,
      sing to God;
   sing praises to the Lord,   Selah
33 to him who rides in the heavens,
      the ancient heavens;
   behold, he sends out his voice,
      his mighty voice.
34 Ascribe power to God,
   whose majesty is over Israel,
   and whose power is in the skies.
35 Awesome is God from his[c] sanctuary;
   the God of Israel—he is the
      one who gives power and
      strength to his people.
   Blessed be God!

SAVE ME, O GOD

69

To the choirmaster: according to Lilies. Of David.

1 Save me, O God!
   For the waters have come
      up to my neck.[d]
2 I sink in deep mire,
      where there is no foothold;
   I have come into deep waters,
      and the flood sweeps over me.
3 I am weary with my crying out;
      my throat is parched.
   My eyes grow dim
      with waiting for my God.

4 More in number than the
      hairs of my head
   are those who hate me
      without cause;
   mighty are those who
      would destroy me,
   those who attack me with lies.
   What I did not steal
      must I now restore?
5 O God, you know my folly;
   the wrongs I have done are
      not hidden from you.

6 Let not those who hope in you be
      put to shame through me,
   O Lord GOD of hosts;
   let not those who seek you be brought
      to dishonour through me,
   O God of Israel.
7 For it is for your sake that I
      have borne reproach,
   that dishonour has covered
      my face.
8 I have become a stranger
      to my brothers,
   an alien to my mother's sons.

9 For zeal for your house has
      consumed me,
   and the reproaches of those who
      reproach you have fallen on me.
10 When I wept and humbled[e]
      my soul with fasting,
   it became my reproach.
11 When I made sackcloth my clothing,
   I became a byword to them.
12 I am the talk of those who
      sit in the gate,
   and the drunkards make
      songs about me.

13 But as for me, my prayer is
      to you, O LORD.
   At an acceptable time, O God,
   in the abundance of your
      steadfast love answer me in
      your saving faithfulness.
14 Deliver me
   from sinking in the mire;
   let me be delivered from my enemies
      and from the deep waters.
15 Let not the flood sweep over me,
   or the deep swallow me up,
   or the pit close its mouth over me.

16 Answer me, O LORD, for your
      steadfast love is good;
   according to your abundant
      mercy, turn to me.

---

[a] By revocalization (compare Septuagint); Hebrew *Your God has summoned your power*   [b] The meaning of the Hebrew verse is uncertain   [c] Septuagint; Hebrew *your*   [d] Or *waters threaten my life*   [e] Hebrew lacks *and humbled*

17 Hide not your face from your servant,
for I am in distress; make
haste to answer me.
18 Draw near to my soul, redeem me;
ransom me because of
my enemies!

19 You know my reproach,
and my shame and my dishonour;
my foes are all known to you.
20 Reproaches have broken my heart,
so that I am in despair.
I looked for pity, but there was none,
and for comforters, but
I found none.
21 They gave me poison for food,
and for my thirst they gave me
sour wine to drink.

22 Let their own table before
them become a snare;
and when they are at peace,
let it become a trap.[a]
23 Let their eyes be darkened, so
that they cannot see,
and make their loins tremble
continually.
24 Pour out your indignation upon them,
and let your burning anger
overtake them.
25 May their camp be a desolation;
let no one dwell in their tents.
26 For they persecute him whom
you have struck down,
and they recount the pain of
those you have wounded.
27 Add to them punishment
upon punishment;
may they have no acquittal
from you.[b]
28 Let them be blotted out of the
book of the living;
let them not be enrolled
among the righteous.

29 But I am afflicted and in pain;
let your salvation, O God,
set me on high!

30 I will praise the name of
God with a song;
I will magnify him with
thanksgiving.
31 This will please the LORD
more than an ox
or a bull with horns and hoofs.

32 When the humble see it
they will be glad;
you who seek God, let your
hearts revive.
33 For the LORD hears the needy
and does not despise his own
people who are prisoners.

34 Let heaven and earth praise him,
the seas and everything that
moves in them.
35 For God will save Zion
and build up the cities of Judah,
and people shall dwell there
and possess it;
36 the offspring of his servants
shall inherit it,
and those who love his name
shall dwell in it.

O LORD, DO NOT DELAY

70

*To the choirmaster. Of David,
for the memorial offering.*

1 Make haste, O God, to deliver me!
O LORD, make haste to help me!
2 Let them be put to shame
and confusion
who seek my life!
Let them be turned back and
brought to dishonour
who delight in my hurt!
3 Let them turn back because
of their shame
who say, "Aha, Aha!"

4 May all who seek you
rejoice and be glad in you!
May those who love your salvation
say evermore, "God is great!"
5 But I am poor and needy;
hasten to me, O God!
You are my help and my deliverer;
O LORD, do not delay!

FORSAKE ME NOT WHEN MY STRENGTH IS SPENT

71

In you, O LORD, do I take refuge;
let me never be put to shame!
2 In your righteousness deliver
me and rescue me;
incline your ear to me, and save me!

---

[a]Hebrew; a slight revocalization yields (compare Septuagint, Syriac, Jerome) *a snare, and retribution and a trap* [b]Hebrew *may they not come into your righteousness*

3 Be to me a rock of refuge,
    to which I may continually come;
you have given the command
    to save me,
for you are my rock and my fortress.

4 Rescue me, O my God, from the
    hand of the wicked,
from the grasp of the unjust
    and cruel man.
5 For you, O Lord, are my hope,
    my trust, O LORD, from my youth.
6 Upon you I have leaned from
    before my birth;
you are he who took me from
    my mother's womb.
My praise is continually of you.

7 I have been as a portent to many,
    but you are my strong refuge.
8 My mouth is filled with your praise,
    and with your glory all the day.
9 Do not cast me off in the
    time of old age;
forsake me not when my
    strength is spent.
10 For my enemies speak concerning me;
    those who watch for my life
    consult together
11 and say, "God has forsaken him;
    pursue and seize him,
for there is none to deliver him."

12 O God, be not far from me;
    O my God, make haste to help me!
13 May my accusers be put to
    shame and consumed;
with scorn and disgrace may
    they be covered
who seek my hurt.
14 But I will hope continually
    and will praise you yet
    more and more.
15 My mouth will tell of your
    righteous acts,
of your deeds of salvation all
    the day,
for their number is past
    my knowledge.
16 With the mighty deeds of the
    Lord GOD I will come;
I will remind them of your
    righteousness, yours alone.

17 O God, from my youth you
    have taught me,
and I still proclaim your
    wondrous deeds.
18 So even to old age and grey hairs,
    O God, do not forsake me,
until I proclaim your might to
    another generation,
your power to all those to come.
19 Your righteousness, O God,
    reaches the high heavens.
You who have done great things,
    O God, who is like you?
20 You who have made me see many
    troubles and calamities
    will revive me again;
from the depths of the earth
    you will bring me up again.
21 You will increase my greatness
    and comfort me again.

22 I will also praise you with the harp
    for your faithfulness, O my God;
I will sing praises to you with the lyre,
    O Holy One of Israel.
23 My lips will shout for joy,
    when I sing praises to you;
my soul also, which you
    have redeemed.
24 And my tongue will talk of your
    righteous help all the day long,
for they have been put to shame
    and disappointed
who sought to do me hurt.

GIVE THE KING YOUR JUSTICE

72 *Of Solomon.*

1 Give the king your justice,
    O God,
and your righteousness
    to the royal son!
2 May he judge your people
    with righteousness,
    and your poor with justice!
3 Let the mountains bear
    prosperity for the people,
and the hills, in righteousness!
4 May he defend the cause of the
    poor of the people,
give deliverance to the
    children of the needy,
and crush the oppressor!

5 May they fear you[a] while
    the sun endures,

---
[a] Septuagint *He shall endure*

and as long as the moon,
throughout all generations!
6 May he be like rain that falls
on the mown grass,
like showers that water the earth!
7 In his days may the righteous flourish,
and peace abound, till the
moon be no more!

8 May he have dominion from sea to sea,
and from the River[a] to the
ends of the earth!
9 May desert tribes bow
down before him,
and his enemies lick the dust!
10 May the kings of Tarshish and
of the coastlands
render him tribute;
may the kings of Sheba and Seba
bring gifts!
11 May all kings fall down before him,
all nations serve him!

12 For he delivers the needy when he calls,
the poor and him who has no helper.
13 He has pity on the weak and the needy,
and saves the lives of the needy.
14 From oppression and violence
he redeems their life,
and precious is their blood
in his sight.

15 Long may he live;
may gold of Sheba be given to him!
May prayer be made for
him continually,
and blessings invoked for
him all the day!
16 May there be abundance of
corn in the land;
on the tops of the mountains
may it wave;
may its fruit be like Lebanon;
and may people blossom in the cities
like the grass of the field!
17 May his name endure for ever,
his fame continue as long as the sun!
May people be blessed in him,
all nations call him blessed!

18 Blessed be the LORD, the God of Israel,
who alone does wondrous things.
19 Blessed be his glorious name for ever;
may the whole earth be
filled with his glory!
Amen and Amen!

20 The prayers of David, the son
of Jesse, are ended.

BOOK THREE

GOD IS MY STRENGTH AND PORTION FOR EVER

73

A Psalm of Asaph.

1 Truly God is good to Israel,
to those who are pure in heart.
2 But as for me, my feet had
almost stumbled,
my steps had nearly slipped.
3 For I was envious of the arrogant
when I saw the prosperity
of the wicked.

4 For they have no pangs until death;
their bodies are fat and sleek.
5 They are not in trouble as others are;
they are not stricken like the
rest of mankind.
6 Therefore pride is their necklace;
violence covers them as a garment.
7 Their eyes swell out through fatness;
their hearts overflow with follies.
8 They scoff and speak with malice;
loftily they threaten oppression.
9 They set their mouths against
the heavens,
and their tongue struts
through the earth.
10 Therefore his people turn
back to them,
and find no fault in them.[b]
11 And they say, "How can God know?
Is there knowledge in the
Most High?"
12 Behold, these are the wicked;
always at ease, they
increase in riches.
13 All in vain have I kept my heart clean
and washed my hands in innocence.
14 For all the day long I have been stricken
and rebuked every morning.
15 If I had said, "I will speak thus",
I would have betrayed the
generation of your children.
16 But when I thought how to
understand this,
it seemed to me a wearisome task,

---

[a]That is, the Euphrates [b]Probable reading; Hebrew *the waters of a full cup are drained by them*

17 until I went into the sanctuary of God;
   then I discerned their end.
18 Truly you set them in slippery places;
   you make them fall to ruin.
19 How they are destroyed in a moment,
   swept away utterly by terrors!
20 Like a dream when one awakes,
   O Lord, when you rouse yourself,
     you despise them as phantoms.
21 When my soul was embittered,
   when I was pricked in heart,
22 I was brutish and ignorant;
   I was like a beast towards you.

23 Nevertheless, I am continually
     with you;
   you hold my right hand.
24 You guide me with your counsel,
   and afterwards you will
     receive me to glory.
25 Whom have I in heaven but you?
   And there is nothing on earth
     that I desire besides you.
26 My flesh and my heart may fail,
   but God is the strength^a of my heart
     and my portion for ever.

27 For behold, those who are far
     from you shall perish;
   you put an end to everyone who
     is unfaithful to you.
28 But for me it is good to be near God;
   I have made the Lord GOD my refuge,
   that I may tell of all your works.

ARISE, O GOD, DEFEND YOUR CAUSE

74
A Maskil^b of Asaph.

1 O God, why do you cast us off
     for ever?
   Why does your anger smoke against
     the sheep of your pasture?
2 Remember your congregation, which
     you have purchased of old,
   which you have redeemed to be
     the tribe of your heritage!
   Remember Mount Zion,
     where you have dwelt.
3 Direct your steps to the perpetual ruins;
   the enemy has destroyed
     everything in the sanctuary!

4 Your foes have roared in the midst
     of your meeting place;
   they set up their own signs for signs.
5 They were like those who swing axes
     in a forest of trees.^{c}
6 And all its carved wood
   they broke down with hatchets
     and hammers.
7 They set your sanctuary on fire;
   they profaned the dwelling
     place of your name,
   bringing it down to the ground.
8 They said to themselves, "We will
     utterly subdue them";
   they burned all the meeting
     places of God in the land.

9 We do not see our signs;
   there is no longer any prophet,
   and there is none among us
     who knows how long.
10 How long, O God, is the foe to scoff?
   Is the enemy to revile your
     name for ever?
11 Why do you hold back your
     hand, your right hand?
   Take it from the fold of your
     garment^d and destroy them!

12 Yet God my King is from of old,
   working salvation in the
     midst of the earth.
13 You divided the sea by your might;
   you broke the heads of the sea
     monsters^e on the waters.
14 You crushed the heads of Leviathan;
   you gave him as food for the
     creatures of the wilderness.
15 You split open springs and brooks;
   you dried up ever-flowing streams.
16 Yours is the day, yours also the night;
   you have established the heavenly
     lights and the sun.
17 You have fixed all the
     boundaries of the earth;
   you have made summer and winter.

18 Remember this, O LORD, how
     the enemy scoffs,
   and a foolish people reviles
     your name.
19 Do not deliver the soul of your
     dove to the wild beasts;
   do not forget the life of
     your poor for ever.

---

^{a}Hebrew *rock* ^{b}Probably a musical or liturgical term ^{c}The meaning of the Hebrew is uncertain ^{d}Hebrew *from your bosom* ^{e}Or *the great sea creatures*

⁲⁰ Have regard for the covenant,
    for the dark places of the land are full
        of the habitations of violence.
²¹ Let not the downtrodden
        turn back in shame;
    let the poor and needy
        praise your name.

²² Arise, O God, defend your cause;
    remember how the foolish
        scoff at you all the day!
²³ Do not forget the clamour of your foes,
    the uproar of those who rise against
        you, which goes up continually!

GOD WILL JUDGE WITH EQUITY

75

To the choirmaster: according to Do Not Destroy. A Psalm of Asaph. A Song.

¹ We give thanks to you, O God;
    we give thanks, for your
        name is near.
  We[a] recount your wondrous deeds.

² "At the set time that I appoint
    I will judge with equity.
³ When the earth totters, and
        all its inhabitants,
    it is I who keep steady
        its pillars.   Selah
⁴ I say to the boastful, 'Do not boast',
    and to the wicked, 'Do not
        lift up your horn;
⁵ do not lift up your horn on high,
    or speak with haughty neck.'"

⁶ For not from the east or from the west
    and not from the wilderness
        comes lifting up,
⁷ but it is God who executes judgement,
    putting down one and
        lifting up another.
⁸ For in the hand of the Lord
        there is a cup
    with foaming wine, well mixed,
    and he pours out from it,
    and all the wicked of the earth
        shall drain it down to the dregs.

⁹ But I will declare it for ever;
    I will sing praises to the God of Jacob.
¹⁰ All the horns of the wicked
        I will cut off,
    but the horns of the righteous
        shall be lifted up.

WHO CAN STAND BEFORE YOU?

76

To the choirmaster: with stringed instruments. A Psalm of Asaph. A Song.

¹ In Judah God is known;
    his name is great in Israel.
² His abode has been
        established in Salem,
    his dwelling place in Zion.
³ There he broke the flashing arrows,
    the shield, the sword, and the
        weapons of war.   Selah

⁴ Glorious are you, more majestic
    than the mountains full of prey.
⁵ The stout-hearted were
        stripped of their spoil;
    they sank into sleep;
  all the men of war
    were unable to use their hands.
⁶ At your rebuke, O God of Jacob,
    both rider and horse lay stunned.

⁷ But you, you are to be feared!
    Who can stand before you
        when once your anger is roused?
⁸ From the heavens you
        uttered judgement;
    the earth feared and was still,
⁹ when God arose to establish
        judgement,
    to save all the humble of
        the earth.   Selah

¹⁰ Surely the wrath of man
        shall praise you;
    the remnant[b] of wrath you
        will put on like a belt.
¹¹ Make your vows to the Lord your
        God and perform them;
    let all round him bring gifts
        to him who is to be feared,
¹² who cuts off the spirit of princes,
    who is to be feared by the
        kings of the earth.

IN THE DAY OF TROUBLE I SEEK THE LORD

77

To the choirmaster: according to Jeduthun. A Psalm of Asaph.

¹ I cry aloud to God,
    aloud to God, and he will
        hear me.

---
[a]Hebrew *They* [b]Or *extremity*

2 In the day of my trouble I seek the Lord;
   in the night my hand is stretched
      out without wearying;
   my soul refuses to be comforted.
3 When I remember God, I moan;
   when I meditate, my spirit faints. *Selah*

4 You hold my eyelids open;
   I am so troubled that I cannot speak.
5 I consider the days of old,
   the years long ago.
6 I said,[a] "Let me remember my
      song in the night;
   let me meditate in my heart."
   Then my spirit made a
      diligent search:
7 "Will the Lord spurn for ever,
   and never again be favourable?
8 Has his steadfast love for ever ceased?
   Are his promises at an
      end for all time?
9 Has God forgotten to be gracious?
   Has he in anger shut up his
      compassion?" *Selah*

10 Then I said, "I will appeal to this,
      to the years of the right hand
      of the Most High."[b]

11 I will remember the deeds of the LORD;
   yes, I will remember your
      wonders of old.
12 I will ponder all your work,
   and meditate on your mighty deeds.
13 Your way, O God, is holy.
   What god is great like our God?
14 You are the God who works wonders;
   you have made known your
      might among the peoples.
15 You with your arm redeemed
      your people,
   the children of Jacob and Joseph. *Selah*

16 When the waters saw you, O God,
      when the waters saw you,
         they were afraid;
      indeed, the deep trembled.
17 The clouds poured out water;
   the skies gave forth thunder;
   your arrows flashed on every side.
18 The crash of your thunder was
      in the whirlwind;
   your lightnings lighted
      up the world;
   the earth trembled and shook.
19 Your way was through the sea,
   your path through the great waters;
   yet your footprints were unseen.[c]
20 You led your people like a flock
   by the hand of Moses and Aaron.

TELL THE COMING GENERATION

78 A Maskil[d] of Asaph.

¹Give ear, O my people,
      to my teaching;
   incline your ears to the
      words of my mouth!
2 I will open my mouth in a parable;
   I will utter dark sayings from of old,
3 things that we have heard and known,
   that our fathers have told us.
4 We will not hide them from
      their children,
   but tell to the coming generation
   the glorious deeds of the
      LORD, and his might,
   and the wonders that he has done.

5 He established a testimony in Jacob
   and appointed a law in Israel,
   which he commanded our fathers
      to teach to their children,
6 that the next generation
      might know them,
   the children yet unborn,
   and arise and tell them to
      their children,
7 so that they should set
      their hope in God
   and not forget the works of God,
   but keep his commandments;
8 and that they should not be
      like their fathers,
   a stubborn and rebellious
      generation,
   a generation whose heart
      was not steadfast,
   whose spirit was not faithful to God.

9 The Ephraimites, armed with[e]
      the bow,
   turned back on the day of battle.
10 They did not keep God's covenant,
   but refused to walk
      according to his law.

---

[a] Hebrew lacks *I said* [b] Or *This is my grief: that the right hand of the Most High has changed* [c] Hebrew unknown [d] Probably a musical or liturgical term [e] Hebrew *armed and shooting*

45 He sent among them swarms of
  flies, which devoured them,
 and frogs, which destroyed them.
46 He gave their crops to the
  destroying locust
 and the fruit of their labour
  to the locust.
47 He destroyed their vines with hail
  and their sycamores with frost.
48 He gave over their cattle to the hail
  and their flocks to thunderbolts.
49 He let loose on them his
  burning anger,
 wrath, indignation, and distress,
  a company of destroying angels.
50 He made a path for his anger;
 he did not spare them from death,
  but gave their lives over
   to the plague.
51 He struck down every
  firstborn in Egypt,
 the firstfruits of their strength
  in the tents of Ham.
52 Then he led out his people like sheep
 and guided them in the
  wilderness like a flock.
53 He led them in safety, so that
  they were not afraid,
 but the sea overwhelmed
  their enemies.
54 And he brought them to his
  holy land,
 to the mountain which his
  right hand had won.
55 He drove out nations before them;
 he apportioned them for
  a possession
 and settled the tribes of
  Israel in their tents.

56 Yet they tested and rebelled
  against the Most High God
 and did not keep his testimonies,
57 but turned away and acted
  treacherously like their fathers;
 they twisted like a deceitful bow.
58 For they provoked him to anger
  with their high places;
 they moved him to jealousy
  with their idols.
59 When God heard, he was full
  of wrath,
 and he utterly rejected Israel.
60 He forsook his dwelling at Shiloh,
  the tent where he dwelt
   among mankind,
61 and delivered his power to captivity,
 his glory to the hand of the foe.
62 He gave his people over to the sword
 and vented his wrath on
  his heritage.
63 Fire devoured their young men,
 and their young women had
  no marriage song.
64 Their priests fell by the sword,
 and their widows made
  no lamentation.
65 Then the Lord awoke as from sleep,
 like a strong man shouting
  because of wine.
66 And he put his adversaries to rout;
 he put them to everlasting shame.

67 He rejected the tent of Joseph;
 he did not choose the
  tribe of Ephraim,
68 but he chose the tribe of Judah,
 Mount Zion, which he loves.
69 He built his sanctuary like
  the high heavens,
 like the earth, which he has
  founded for ever.
70 He chose David his servant
 and took him from the sheepfolds;
71 from following the nursing
  ewes he brought him
 to shepherd Jacob his people,
 Israel his inheritance.
72 With upright heart he
  shepherded them
 and guided them with his
  skilful hand.

HOW LONG, O LORD?

79

A Psalm of Asaph.

¹ O God, the nations have come
  into your inheritance;
 they have defiled your holy
  temple;
 they have laid Jerusalem in ruins.
² They have given the bodies
  of your servants
 to the birds of the heavens for food,
 the flesh of your faithful to
  the beasts of the earth.
³ They have poured out their
  blood like water
 all round Jerusalem,
 and there was no one to bury them.
⁴ We have become a taunt to
  our neighbours,

11 They forgot his works
 and the wonders that he
  had shown them.
12 In the sight of their fathers he
  performed wonders
 in the land of Egypt, in the
  fields of Zoan.
13 He divided the sea and let
  them pass through it,
 and made the waters
  stand like a heap.
14 In the daytime he led them
  with a cloud,
 and all the night with a fiery light.
15 He split rocks in the wilderness
 and gave them drink abundantly
  as from the deep.
16 He made streams come out of
  the rock
 and caused waters to flow
  down like rivers.

17 Yet they sinned still more against him,
 rebelling against the Most
  High in the desert.
18 They tested God in their heart
 by demanding the food they craved.
19 They spoke against God, saying,
 "Can God spread a table in
  the wilderness?
20 He struck the rock so that
  water gushed out
 and streams overflowed.
 Can he also give bread
  or provide meat for his people?"

21 Therefore, when the LORD heard,
  he was full of wrath;
 a fire was kindled against Jacob;
  his anger rose against Israel,
22 because they did not believe in God
  and did not trust his saving power.
23 Yet he commanded the skies above
  and opened the doors of heaven,
24 and he rained down on
  them manna to eat
 and gave them the grain of heaven.
25 Man ate of the bread of the angels;
  he sent them food in abundance.
26 He caused the east wind to
  blow in the heavens,
 and by his power he led out
  the south wind;
27 he rained meat on them like dust,
  winged birds like the
  sand of the seas;

28 he let them fall in the midst
  of their camp,
 all round their dwellings.
29 And they ate and were well filled,
  for he gave them what they craved.
30 But before they had satisfied
  their craving,
 while the food was still
  in their mouths,
31 the anger of God rose against them,
  and he killed the strongest of them
  and laid low the young men of Israel.

32 In spite of all this, they still sinned;
  despite his wonders, they
  did not believe.
33 So he made their days vanish
  like^a a breath,^{b}
  and their years in terror.
34 When he killed them, they sought him;
  they repented and sought
  God earnestly.
35 They remembered that God
  was their rock,
  the Most High God their redeemer.
36 But they flattered him with
  their mouths;
  they lied to him with their tongues.
37 Their heart was not steadfast
  towards him;
  they were not faithful to
  his covenant.
38 Yet he, being compassionate,
  atoned for their iniquity
  and did not destroy them;
 he restrained his anger often
  and did not stir up all his wrath.
39 He remembered that they
  were but flesh,
  a wind that passes and
  comes not again.
40 How often they rebelled against
  him in the wilderness
  and grieved him in the desert!
41 They tested God again and again
  and provoked the Holy One of Israel.
42 They did not remember his power^c
  or the day when he redeemed
  them from the foe,
43 when he performed his signs in Egypt
  and his marvels in the fields of Zoan.
44 He turned their rivers to blood,
  so that they could not drink
  of their streams.

---

^{a}Hebrew *in* ^{b}Or *vapour* ^{c}Hebrew *hand*

mocked and derided by
those around us.

5 How long, O LORD? Will you
be angry for ever?
Will your jealousy burn like fire?
6 Pour out your anger on the nations
that do not know you,
and on the kingdoms
that do not call upon your name!
7 For they have devoured Jacob
and laid waste his habitation.

8 Do not remember against us
our former iniquities;[a]
let your compassion come
speedily to meet us,
for we are brought very low.
9 Help us, O God of our salvation,
for the glory of your name;
deliver us, and atone for our sins,
for your name's sake!
10 Why should the nations say,
"Where is their God?"
Let the avenging of the outpoured
blood of your servants
be known among the nations
before our eyes!

11 Let the groans of the prisoners
come before you;
according to your great power,
preserve those doomed to die!
12 Return sevenfold into the lap
of our neighbours
the taunts with which they have
taunted you, O Lord!
13 But we your people, the sheep
of your pasture,
will give thanks to you for ever;
from generation to generation we
will recount your praise.

RESTORE US, O GOD

80

*To the choirmaster: according
to Lilies. A Testimony.
Of Asaph, a Psalm.*

1 Give ear, O Shepherd of Israel,
you who lead Joseph like a flock.
You who are enthroned upon the
cherubim, shine forth.
2 Before Ephraim and Benjamin
and Manasseh,
stir up your might
and come to save us!

3 Restore us,[b] O God;
let your face shine, that
we may be saved!

4 O LORD God of hosts,
how long will you be angry with
your people's prayers?
5 You have fed them with
the bread of tears
and given them tears to drink
in full measure.
6 You make us an object of contention
for our neighbours,
and our enemies laugh
among themselves.

7 Restore us, O God of hosts;
let your face shine, that
we may be saved!

8 You brought a vine out of Egypt;
you drove out the nations
and planted it.
9 You cleared the ground for it;
it took deep root and filled the land.
10 The mountains were covered
with its shade,
the mighty cedars with its branches.
11 It sent out its branches to the sea
and its shoots to the River.[c]
12 Why then have you broken
down its walls,
so that all who pass along the
way pluck its fruit?
13 The boar from the forest ravages it,
and all that move in the
field feed on it.

14 Turn again, O God of hosts!
Look down from heaven, and see;
have regard for this vine,
15 the stock that your right
hand planted,
and for the son whom you made
strong for yourself.
16 They have burned it with fire;
they have cut it down;
may they perish at the
rebuke of your face!
17 But let your hand be on the man
of your right hand,
the son of man whom you have
made strong for yourself!

---

[a]Or *the iniquities of former generations* [b]Or *Turn us again*; also verses 7, 19 [c]That is, the Euphrates

18 Then we shall not turn back from you;
   give us life, and we will call
       upon your name!

19 Restore us, O LORD God of hosts!
   Let your face shine, that
       we may be saved!

OH, THAT MY PEOPLE WOULD LISTEN TO ME

81

To the choirmaster: according to The Gittith.^{a} Of Asaph.

1 Sing aloud to God our strength;
   shout for joy to the God of Jacob!
2 Raise a song; sound the tambourine,
   the sweet lyre with the harp.
3 Blow the trumpet at the new moon,
   at the full moon, on our feast day.
4 For it is a statute for Israel,
   a rule^b of the God of Jacob.
5 He made it a decree in Joseph
   when he went out over^c
       the land of Egypt.
   I hear a language I had not known:
6 "I relieved your^d shoulder of the burden;
   your hands were freed
       from the basket.
7 In distress you called, and
       I delivered you;
   I answered you in the secret
       place of thunder;
   I tested you at the waters of
       Meribah.   Selah
8 Hear, O my people, while
       I admonish you!
   O Israel, if you would but listen to me!
9 There shall be no strange
       god among you;
   you shall not bow down
       to a foreign god.
10 I am the LORD your God,
    who brought you up out of
        the land of Egypt.
    Open your mouth wide,
        and I will fill it.

11 "But my people did not listen to my voice;
    Israel would not submit to me.
12 So I gave them over to their
        stubborn hearts,
    to follow their own counsels.
13 Oh, that my people would listen to me,
    that Israel would walk in my ways!
14 I would soon subdue their enemies
    and turn my hand against their foes.

15 Those who hate the LORD would
        cringe towards him,
    and their fate would last for ever.
16 But he would feed you^e with
        the finest of the wheat,
    and with honey from the rock
        I would satisfy you."

RESCUE THE WEAK AND NEEDY

82

A Psalm of Asaph.

1 God has taken his place in
       the divine council;
   in the midst of the gods he
       holds judgement:
2 "How long will you judge unjustly
   and show partiality to the
       wicked?   Selah
3 Give justice to the weak and
       the fatherless;
   maintain the right of the afflicted
       and the destitute.
4 Rescue the weak and the needy;
   deliver them from the hand
       of the wicked."

5 They have neither knowledge
       nor understanding,
   they walk about in darkness;
   all the foundations of the
       earth are shaken.

6 I said, "You are gods,
   sons of the Most High, all of you;
7 nevertheless, like men you shall die,
   and fall like any prince."^{f}

8 Arise, O God, judge the earth;
   for you shall inherit all the nations!

O GOD, DO NOT KEEP SILENCE

83

A Song. A Psalm of Asaph.

1 O God, do not keep silence;
   do not hold your peace or
       be still, O God!
2 For behold, your enemies
       make an uproar;
   those who hate you have
       raised their heads.
3 They lay crafty plans against
       your people;

---

^{a}Probably a musical or liturgical term ^{b}Or *just decree* ^{c}Or *against* ^{d}Hebrew *his*; also next line ^{e}That is, Israel; Hebrew *him* ^{f}Or *fall as one man, O princes*

they consult together against
  your treasured ones.
4 They say, "Come, let us wipe
   them out as a nation;
  let the name of Israel be
   remembered no more!"
5 For they conspire with one accord;
  against you they make a covenant—
6 the tents of Edom and the Ishmaelites,
   Moab and the Hagrites,
7 Gebal and Ammon and Amalek,
  Philistia with the inhabitants of Tyre;
8 Asshur also has joined them;
   they are the strong arm of the
    children of Lot.   Selah

9 Do to them as you did to Midian,
  as to Sisera and Jabin at
   the river Kishon,
10 who were destroyed at En-dor,
   who became dung for the ground.
11 Make their nobles like Oreb and Zeeb,
   all their princes like Zebah
    and Zalmunna,
12 who said, "Let us take possession
   for ourselves
    of the pastures of God."

13 O my God, make them like
    whirling dust,[a]
   like chaff before the wind.
14 As fire consumes the forest,
   as the flame sets the
    mountains ablaze,
15 so may you pursue them
   with your tempest
   and terrify them with
    your hurricane!
16 Fill their faces with shame,
   that they may seek your
    name, O LORD.
17 Let them be put to shame and
    dismayed for ever;
   let them perish in disgrace,
18 that they may know that you alone,
    whose name is the LORD,
   are the Most High over all the earth.

MY SOUL LONGS FOR THE COURTS OF THE LORD

84

To the choirmaster: according to The Gittith.[b] A Psalm of the Sons of Korah.

1 How lovely is your dwelling place,
   O LORD of hosts!
2 My soul longs, yes, faints
   for the courts of the LORD;
  my heart and flesh sing for joy
   to the living God.

3 Even the sparrow finds a home,
   and the swallow a nest for herself,
   where she may lay her young,
  at your altars, O LORD of hosts,
   my King and my God.
4 Blessed are those who dwell
   in your house,
   ever singing your praise!   Selah

5 Blessed are those whose
    strength is in you,
   in whose heart are the
    highways to Zion.[c]
6 As they go through the Valley of Baca
   they make it a place of springs;
   the early rain also covers
    it with pools.
7 They go from strength to strength;
   each one appears before God in Zion.

8 O LORD God of hosts, hear my prayer;
   give ear, O God of Jacob!   Selah
9 Behold our shield, O God;
   look on the face of your anointed!

10 For a day in your courts is better
    than a thousand elsewhere.
   I would rather be a doorkeeper
    in the house of my God
   than dwell in the tents
    of wickedness.
11 For the LORD God is a sun and shield;
   the LORD bestows favour
    and honour.
  No good thing does he withhold
   from those who walk uprightly.
12 O LORD of hosts,
   blessed is the one who trusts in you!

REVIVE US AGAIN

85

To the choirmaster. A Psalm of the Sons of Korah.

1 LORD, you were favourable to your land;
   you restored the fortunes of Jacob.
2 You forgave the iniquity
    of your people;
   you covered all their sin.   Selah

---

[a]Or *like a tumbleweed* [b]Probably a musical or liturgical term
[c]Hebrew lacks *to Zion*

3 You withdrew all your wrath;
　　you turned from your hot anger.

4 Restore us again, O God of
　　our salvation,
　and put away your indignation
　　towards us!
5 Will you be angry with us for ever?
　Will you prolong your anger
　　to all generations?
6 Will you not revive us again,
　　that your people may rejoice in you?
7 Show us your steadfast love, O LORD,
　　and grant us your salvation.

8 Let me hear what God the
　　LORD will speak,
　for he will speak peace to his
　　people, to his saints;
　　but let them not turn back to folly.
9 Surely his salvation is near to
　　those who fear him,
　　that glory may dwell in our land.
10 Steadfast love and faithfulness meet;
　　righteousness and peace
　　　kiss each other.
11 Faithfulness springs up
　　from the ground,
　and righteousness looks
　　down from the sky.
12 Yes, the LORD will give what is good,
　　and our land will yield its increase.
13 Righteousness will go before him
　　and make his footsteps a way.

GREAT IS YOUR STEADFAST LOVE

86
A Prayer of David.

1 Incline your ear, O LORD,
　　and answer me,
　for I am poor and needy.
2 Preserve my life, for I am godly;
　save your servant, who trusts
　　in you—you are my God.
3 Be gracious to me, O Lord,
　　for to you do I cry all the day.
4 Gladden the soul of your servant,
　　for to you, O Lord, do I
　　　lift up my soul.
5 For you, O Lord, are good
　　and forgiving,
　abounding in steadfast love to
　　all who call upon you.
6 Give ear, O LORD, to my prayer;
　　listen to my plea for grace.
7 In the day of my trouble I call
　　upon you,
　　for you answer me.

8 There is none like you among
　　the gods, O Lord,
　　nor are there any works like yours.
9 All the nations you have
　　made shall come
　　and worship before you, O Lord,
　　and shall glorify your name.
10 For you are great and do
　　wondrous things;
　　you alone are God.
11 Teach me your way, O LORD,
　　that I may walk in your truth;
　　unite my heart to fear your name.
12 I give thanks to you, O Lord my
　　God, with my whole heart,
　　and I will glorify your name
　　　for ever.
13 For great is your steadfast
　　love towards me;
　　you have delivered my soul
　　　from the depths of Sheol.

14 O God, insolent men have
　　risen up against me;
　a band of ruthless men seeks
　　my life,
　　and they do not set you before them.
15 But you, O Lord, are a God
　　merciful and gracious,
　　slow to anger and abounding in
　　　steadfast love and faithfulness.
16 Turn to me and be gracious to me;
　　give your strength to your servant,
　　and save the son of your
　　　maidservant.
17 Show me a sign of your favour,
　　that those who hate me may
　　　see and be put to shame
　because you, LORD, have helped
　　me and comforted me.

GLORIOUS THINGS OF YOU ARE SPOKEN

87
*A Psalm of the Sons of Korah.
A Song.*

1 On the holy mount stands
　　the city he founded;
2 the LORD loves the gates of Zion
　　more than all the dwelling
　　　places of Jacob.
3 Glorious things of you are spoken,
　　O city of God. *Selah*

⁴ Among those who know me I
    mention Rahab and Babylon;
  behold, Philistia and Tyre,
      with Cush*ᵃ*—
    "This one was born there", they say.
⁵ And of Zion it shall be said,
    "This one and that one were
      born in her";
  for the Most High himself
    will establish her.
⁶ The LORD records as he
    registers the peoples,
  "This one was born there."   *Selah*

⁷ Singers and dancers alike say,
    "All my springs are in you."

I CRY OUT DAY AND NIGHT BEFORE YOU

88 A Song. A Psalm of the Sons of Korah. To the choirmaster: according to Mahalath Leannoth. A Maskil*ᵇ* of Heman the Ezrahite.

¹ O LORD, God of my salvation,
    I cry out day and night before you.
² Let my prayer come before you;
    incline your ear to my cry!

³ For my soul is full of troubles,
    and my life draws near to Sheol.
⁴ I am counted among those who
    go down to the pit;
  I am a man who has no strength,
⁵ like one set loose among the dead,
    like the slain that lie in the grave,
  like those whom you
    remember no more,
  for they are cut off from your hand.
⁶ You have put me in the
    depths of the pit,
  in the regions dark and deep.
⁷ Your wrath lies heavy upon me,
    and you overwhelm me with all
      your waves.   *Selah*

⁸ You have caused my companions
    to shun me;
  you have made me a horror*ᶜ*
    to them.
  I am shut in so that I cannot escape;
⁹ my eye grows dim through sorrow.
  Every day I call upon you, O LORD;
    I spread out my hands to you.
¹⁰ Do you work wonders for the dead?
    Do the departed rise up to
      praise you?   *Selah*

¹¹ Is your steadfast love declared
      in the grave,
    or your faithfulness in Abaddon?
¹² Are your wonders known
      in the darkness,
    or your righteousness in the
      land of forgetfulness?

¹³ But I, O LORD, cry to you;
    in the morning my prayer
      comes before you.
¹⁴ O LORD, why do you cast my soul away?
    Why do you hide your face from me?
¹⁵ Afflicted and close to death
      from my youth up,
    I suffer your terrors; I am helpless.*ᵈ*
¹⁶ Your wrath has swept over me;
    your dreadful assaults destroy me.
¹⁷ They surround me like a
      flood all day long;
    they close in on me together.
¹⁸ You have caused my beloved and
      my friend to shun me;
    my companions have
      become darkness.*ᵉ*

I WILL SING OF THE STEADFAST LOVE OF THE LORD

89 A Maskil*ᶠ* of Ethan the Ezrahite.

¹ I will sing of the steadfast love
    of the LORD, for ever;
  with my mouth I will make
    known your faithfulness
      to all generations.
² For I said, "Steadfast love will
    be built up for ever;
  in the heavens you will establish
    your faithfulness."
³ You have said, "I have made a
    covenant with my chosen one;
  I have sworn to David my servant:
⁴ 'I will establish your offspring for ever,
    and build your throne for all
      generations.'"   *Selah*

⁵ Let the heavens praise your
    wonders, O LORD,
  your faithfulness in the assembly
    of the holy ones!
⁶ For who in the skies can be
    compared to the LORD?

---

*ᵃ*Probably *Nubia*   *ᵇ*Probably musical or liturgical terms   *ᶜ*Or *an abomination*   *ᵈ*The meaning of the Hebrew word is uncertain   *ᵉ*Or *darkness has become my only companion*   *ᶠ*Probably a musical or liturgical term

Who among the heavenly
    beings[a] is like the LORD,
7 a God greatly to be feared in the
    council of the holy ones,
  and awesome above all who
    are around him?
8 O LORD God of hosts,
    who is mighty as you are, O LORD,
  with your faithfulness
    all round you?
9 You rule the raging of the sea;
    when its waves rise, you still them.
10 You crushed Rahab like a carcass;
    you scattered your enemies
    with your mighty arm.
11 The heavens are yours; the
    earth also is yours;
  the world and all that is in it,
    you have founded them.
12 The north and the south, you
    have created them;
  Tabor and Hermon joyously
    praise your name.
13 You have a mighty arm;
    strong is your hand, high
    your right hand.
14 Righteousness and justice are the
    foundation of your throne;
  steadfast love and faithfulness
    go before you.
15 Blessed are the people who
    know the festal shout,
  who walk, O LORD, in the
    light of your face,
16 who exult in your name all the day
    and in your righteousness
    are exalted.
17 For you are the glory of their strength;
    by your favour our horn is exalted.
18 For our shield belongs to the LORD,
    our king to the Holy One of Israel.

19 Of old you spoke in a vision to
    your godly one,[b] and said:
  "I have granted help to one
    who is mighty;
  I have exalted one chosen
    from the people.
20 I have found David, my servant;
    with my holy oil I have
    anointed him,
21 so that my hand shall be
    established with him;
  my arm also shall strengthen him.
22 The enemy shall not outwit him;
    the wicked shall not humble him.
23 I will crush his foes before him
    and strike down those
    who hate him.
24 My faithfulness and my steadfast
    love shall be with him,
  and in my name shall his
    horn be exalted.
25 I will set his hand on the sea
    and his right hand on the rivers.
26 He shall cry to me, 'You are my Father,
    my God, and the Rock of
    my salvation.'
27 And I will make him the firstborn,
    the highest of the kings of the earth.
28 My steadfast love I will keep
    for him for ever,
  and my covenant will stand
    firm[c] for him.
29 I will establish his offspring for ever
    and his throne as the days
    of the heavens.
30 If his children forsake my law
    and do not walk according
    to my rules,[d]
31 if they violate my statutes
    and do not keep my
    commandments,
32 then I will punish their
    transgression with the rod
  and their iniquity with stripes,
33 but I will not remove from
    him my steadfast love
  or be false to my faithfulness.
34 I will not violate my covenant
    or alter the word that went
    forth from my lips.
35 Once for all I have sworn
    by my holiness;
  I will not lie to David.
36 His offspring shall endure for ever,
    his throne as long as the
    sun before me.
37 Like the moon it shall be
    established for ever,
  a faithful witness in the skies." *Selah*

38 But now you have cast off and rejected;
    you are full of wrath against
    your anointed.
39 You have renounced the covenant
    with your servant;
  you have defiled his crown
    in the dust.

---

[a]Hebrew *the sons of God*, or *the sons of might* [b]Some Hebrew manuscripts *godly ones* [c]Or *will remain faithful* [d]Or *my just decrees*

40 You have breached all his walls;
        you have laid his strongholds
            in ruins.
41 All who pass by plunder him;
        he has become the scorn
            of his neighbours.
42 You have exalted the right
        hand of his foes;
    you have made all his
        enemies rejoice.
43 You have also turned back the
        edge of his sword,
    and you have not made him
        stand in battle.
44 You have made his splendour to cease
        and cast his throne to the ground.
45 You have cut short the days
        of his youth;
    you have covered him with
        shame.   Selah

46 How long, O Lord? Will you
        hide yourself for ever?
    How long will your wrath
        burn like fire?
47 Remember how short my time is!
    For what vanity you have created
        all the children of man!
48 What man can live and
        never see death?
    Who can deliver his soul from the
        power of Sheol?   Selah

49 Lord, where is your steadfast love of old,
        which by your faithfulness
            you swore to David?
50 Remember, O Lord, how your
        servants are mocked,
    and how I bear in my heart the
        insults[a] of all the many nations,
51 with which your enemies
        mock, O Lord,
    with which they mock the
        footsteps of your anointed.

52 Blessed be the Lord for ever!
        Amen and Amen.

BOOK FOUR
FROM EVERLASTING TO EVERLASTING

90
A Prayer of Moses, the man of God.

1 Lord, you have been
        our dwelling place[b]
    in all generations.

2 Before the mountains were
        brought forth,
    or ever you had formed the
        earth and the world,
    from everlasting to everlasting
        you are God.

3 You return man to dust
    and say, "Return, O
        children of man!"[c]
4 For a thousand years in your sight
    are but as yesterday when it is past,
        or as a watch in the night.

5 You sweep them away as with a
        flood; they are like a dream,
    like grass that is renewed
        in the morning:
6 in the morning it flourishes
        and is renewed;
    in the evening it fades and withers.

7 For we are brought to an
        end by your anger;
    by your wrath we are dismayed.
8 You have set our iniquities before you,
        our secret sins in the light
            of your presence.

9 For all our days pass away
        under your wrath;
    we bring our years to an
        end like a sigh.
10 The years of our life are seventy,
        or even by reason of strength
            eighty;
    yet their span[d] is but toil and trouble;
        they are soon gone, and we fly away.
11 Who considers the power
        of your anger,
    and your wrath according
        to the fear of you?

12 So teach us to number our days
    that we may get a heart of wisdom.
13 Return, O Lord! How long?
        Have pity on your servants!
14 Satisfy us in the morning with
        your steadfast love,
    that we may rejoice and be
        glad all our days.
15 Make us glad for as many days
        as you have afflicted us,

---
[a]Hebrew lacks *the insults* [b]Some Hebrew manuscripts (compare Septuagint) *our refuge* [c]Or *of Adam* [d]Or *pride*

and for as many years as
   we have seen evil.
16 Let your work be shown to
      your servants,
   and your glorious power
      to their children.
17 Let the favour[a] of the Lord
      our God be upon us,
   and establish the work of
      our hands upon us;
   yes, establish the work of our hands!

MY REFUGE AND MY FORTRESS

91 He who dwells in the shelter of
      the Most High
   will abide in the shadow of
      the Almighty.
2 I will say[b] to the LORD, "My
      refuge and my fortress,
   my God, in whom I trust."

3 For he will deliver you from
      the snare of the fowler
   and from the deadly pestilence.
4 He will cover you with his pinions,
   and under his wings you
      will find refuge;
   his faithfulness is a shield
      and buckler.
5 You will not fear the terror of
      the night,
   nor the arrow that flies by day,
6 nor the pestilence that
      stalks in darkness,
   nor the destruction that
      wastes at noonday.

7 A thousand may fall at your side,
   ten thousand at your right hand,
   but it will not come near you.
8 You will only look with your eyes
   and see the recompense
      of the wicked.

9 Because you have made the LORD
      your dwelling place—
   the Most High, who is my refuge[c]—
10 no evil shall be allowed to befall you,
   no plague come near your tent.

11 For he will command his
      angels concerning you
   to guard you in all your ways.
12 On their hands they will bear you up,
   lest you strike your foot
      against a stone.

13 You will tread on the lion
      and the adder;
   the young lion and the serpent
      you will trample underfoot.

14 "Because he holds fast to me in
      love, I will deliver him;
   I will protect him, because
      he knows my name.
15 When he calls to me, I will answer him;
   I will be with him in trouble;
   I will rescue him and honour him.
16 With long life I will satisfy him
   and show him my salvation."

HOW GREAT ARE YOUR WORKS

92 *A Psalm. A Song for the Sabbath.*

¹It is good to give thanks to
      the LORD,
   to sing praises to your
      name, O Most High;
2 to declare your steadfast love
      in the morning,
   and your faithfulness by night,
3 to the music of the lute and the harp,
   to the melody of the lyre.
4 For you, O LORD, have made
      me glad by your work;
   at the works of your hands
      I sing for joy.

5 How great are your works, O LORD!
   Your thoughts are very deep!
6 The stupid man cannot know;
   the fool cannot understand this:
7 that though the wicked
      sprout like grass
   and all evildoers flourish,
   they are doomed to
      destruction for ever;
8 but you, O LORD, are on high for ever.
9 For behold, your enemies, O LORD,
   for behold, your enemies
      shall perish;
   all evildoers shall be scattered.

10 But you have exalted my horn
      like that of the wild ox;
   you have poured over me[d] fresh oil.
11 My eyes have seen the downfall
      of my enemies;

---
[a]Or *beauty* [b]Septuagint *He will say* [c]Or *For you, O LORD, are my refuge! You have made the Most High your dwelling place*
[d]Compare Syriac; the meaning of the Hebrew is uncertain

> my ears have heard the doom
> > of my evil assailants.
>
> 12 The righteous flourish like
> > the palm tree
> > and grow like a cedar in Lebanon.
> 13 They are planted in the
> > house of the Lord;
> > they flourish in the courts
> > > of our God.
> 14 They still bear fruit in old age;
> > they are ever full of sap and green,
> 15 to declare that the Lord is upright;
> > he is my rock, and there is no
> > > unrighteousness in him.

THE LORD REIGNS

93

> The Lord reigns; he is robed
> > in majesty;
> > the Lord is robed; he has put on
> > > strength as his belt.
> > Yes, the world is established; it
> > > shall never be moved.
> 2 Your throne is established from
> > of old;
> > you are from everlasting.
>
> 3 The floods have lifted up, O Lord,
> > the floods have lifted up their voice;
> > the floods lift up their roaring.
> 4 Mightier than the thunders
> > of many waters,
> > mightier than the waves of the sea,
> > the Lord on high is mighty!
>
> 5 Your decrees are very trustworthy;
> > holiness befits your house,
> > O Lord, for evermore.

THE LORD WILL NOT FORSAKE HIS PEOPLE

94

> O Lord, God of vengeance,
> > O God of vengeance,
> > > shine forth!
> 2 Rise up, O judge of the earth;
> > repay to the proud what
> > > they deserve!
> 3 O Lord, how long shall the wicked,
> > how long shall the wicked exult?
> 4 They pour out their arrogant words;
> > all the evildoers boast.
> 5 They crush your people, O Lord,
> > and afflict your heritage.
> 6 They kill the widow and the sojourner,
> > and murder the fatherless;
> 7 and they say, "The Lord does not see;
> > the God of Jacob does not perceive."

> 8 Understand, O dullest of the people!
> > Fools, when will you be wise?
> 9 He who planted the ear,
> > does he not hear?
> > He who formed the eye,
> > > does he not see?
> 10 He who disciplines the nations,
> > does he not rebuke?
> > He who teaches man knowledge—
> 11 the Lord—knows the
> > thoughts of man,
> > that they are but a breath.[a]
>
> 12 Blessed is the man whom you
> > discipline, O Lord,
> > and whom you teach out of your law,
> 13 to give him rest from days of trouble,
> > until a pit is dug for the wicked.
> 14 For the Lord will not
> > forsake his people;
> > he will not abandon his heritage;
> 15 for justice will return to the righteous,
> > and all the upright in heart
> > > will follow it.
>
> 16 Who rises up for me against
> > the wicked?
> > Who stands up for me
> > > against evildoers?
> 17 If the Lord had not been my help,
> > my soul would soon have lived
> > > in the land of silence.
> 18 When I thought, "My foot slips",
> > your steadfast love, O
> > > Lord, held me up.
> 19 When the cares of my heart are many,
> > your consolations cheer my soul.
> 20 Can wicked rulers be allied with you,
> > those who frame[b] injustice
> > > by statute?
> 21 They band together against the
> > life of the righteous
> > and condemn the innocent
> > > to death.[c]
> 22 But the Lord has become
> > my stronghold,
> > and my God the rock of my refuge.
> 23 He will bring back on them
> > their iniquity
> > and wipe them out for
> > > their wickedness;
> > the Lord our God will
> > > wipe them out.

---

[a] Septuagint *they are futile* [b] Or *fashion* [c] Hebrew *condemn innocent blood*

LET US SING SONGS OF PRAISE

95 Oh come, let us sing to the LORD;
let us make a joyful noise to the
rock of our salvation!
2 Let us come into his presence
with thanksgiving;
let us make a joyful noise to
him with songs of praise!
3 For the LORD is a great God,
and a great King above all gods.
4 In his hand are the depths of the earth;
the heights of the mountains
are his also.
5 The sea is his, for he made it,
and his hands formed the dry land.

6 Oh come, let us worship
and bow down;
let us kneel before the
LORD, our Maker!
7 For he is our God,
and we are the people of his pasture,
and the sheep of his hand.
Today, if you hear his voice,
8 do not harden your hearts,
as at Meribah,
as on the day at Massah in
the wilderness,
9 when your fathers put me to the test
and put me to the proof, though
they had seen my work.
10 For forty years I loathed that generation
and said, "They are a people who
go astray in their heart,
and they have not known my ways."
11 Therefore I swore in my wrath,
"They shall not enter my rest."

WORSHIP IN THE SPLENDOUR OF HOLINESS

96 Oh sing to the LORD a new song;
sing to the LORD, all the earth!
2 Sing to the LORD,
bless his name;
tell of his salvation from day to day.
3 Declare his glory among the nations,
his marvellous works among
all the peoples!
4 For great is the LORD, and
greatly to be praised;
he is to be feared above all gods.
5 For all the gods of the peoples
are worthless idols,
but the LORD made the heavens.
6 Splendour and majesty are before him;
strength and beauty are
in his sanctuary.

7 Ascribe to the LORD, O families
of the peoples,
ascribe to the LORD glory
and strength!
8 Ascribe to the LORD the glory
due his name;
bring an offering, and come
into his courts!
9 Worship the LORD in the
splendour of holiness;[a]
tremble before him, all the earth!

10 Say among the nations,
"The LORD reigns!
Yes, the world is established;
it shall never be moved;
he will judge the peoples
with equity."

11 Let the heavens be glad, and
let the earth rejoice;
let the sea roar, and all that fills it;
12 let the field exult, and
everything in it!
Then shall all the trees of the
forest sing for joy
13 before the LORD, for he comes,
for he comes to judge the earth.
He will judge the world in
righteousness,
and the peoples in his faithfulness.

THE LORD REIGNS

97 The LORD reigns, let the earth
rejoice;
let the many coastlands be glad!
2 Clouds and thick darkness
are all round him;
righteousness and justice are the
foundation of his throne.
3 Fire goes before him
and burns up his adversaries
all round.
4 His lightnings light up the world;
the earth sees and trembles.
5 The mountains melt like wax
before the LORD,
before the Lord of all the earth.
6 The heavens proclaim his
righteousness,
and all the peoples see his glory.
7 All worshippers of images
are put to shame,

---
[a] Or in holy attire

who make their boast in
    worthless idols;
worship him, all you gods!

8 Zion hears and is glad,
    and the daughters of Judah rejoice,
    because of your judgements,
        O Lord.
9 For you, O Lord, are most high
    over all the earth;
you are exalted far above all gods.

10 O you who love the Lord, hate evil!
He preserves the lives of his saints;
    he delivers them from the
        hand of the wicked.
11 Light is sown[a] for the righteous,
    and joy for the upright in heart.
12 Rejoice in the Lord, O you righteous,
    and give thanks to his holy name!

MAKE A JOYFUL NOISE TO THE LORD

98

A Psalm.

¹ Oh sing to the Lord
    a new song,
for he has done marvellous things!
His right hand and his holy arm
    have worked salvation for him.
2 The Lord has made known
    his salvation;
he has revealed his righteousness
    in the sight of the nations.
3 He has remembered his steadfast
        love and faithfulness
    to the house of Israel.
All the ends of the earth have seen
    the salvation of our God.

4 Make a joyful noise to the
        Lord, all the earth;
    break forth into joyous song
        and sing praises!
5 Sing praises to the Lord with the lyre,
    with the lyre and the
        sound of melody!
6 With trumpets and the
        sound of the horn
    make a joyful noise before
        the King, the Lord!

7 Let the sea roar, and all that fills it;
    the world and those who
        dwell in it!
8 Let the rivers clap their hands;
    let the hills sing for joy together

9 before the Lord, for he comes
    to judge the earth.
He will judge the world with
    righteousness,
and the peoples with equity.

THE LORD OUR GOD IS HOLY

99

The Lord reigns; let the
    peoples tremble!
He sits enthroned upon
    the cherubim; let the
        earth quake!
2 The Lord is great in Zion;
    he is exalted over all the peoples.
3 Let them praise your great
    and awesome name!
    Holy is he!
4 The King in his might loves justice.[b]
    You have established equity;
you have executed justice
    and righteousness in Jacob.
5 Exalt the Lord our God;
    worship at his footstool!
    Holy is he!

6 Moses and Aaron were
        among his priests,
    Samuel also was among those
        who called upon his name.
They called to the Lord, and
    he answered them.
7 In the pillar of the cloud he
        spoke to them;
    they kept his testimonies
    and the statute that he gave them.

8 O Lord our God, you answered them;
    you were a forgiving God to them,
    but an avenger of their
        wrongdoings.
9 Exalt the Lord our God,
    and worship at his holy
        mountain;
for the Lord our God is holy!

HIS STEADFAST LOVE ENDURES FOR EVER

100

A Psalm for giving thanks.

¹ Make a joyful noise to the
    Lord, all the earth!
2 Serve the Lord with gladness!
    Come into his presence
        with singing!

---

[a]Most Hebrew manuscripts; one Hebrew manuscript, Septuagint, Syriac, Jerome *Light dawns*   [b]Or *The might of the King loves justice*

³ Know that the LORD, he is God!
  It is he who made us, and we
      are his;ᵃ
  we are his people, and the
      sheep of his pasture.

⁴ Enter his gates with thanksgiving,
      and his courts with praise!
  Give thanks to him; bless his name!

⁵ For the LORD is good;
      his steadfast love endures for ever,
  and his faithfulness to
      all generations.

I WILL WALK WITH INTEGRITY

101   A Psalm of David.

¹ I will sing of steadfast love
      and justice;
  to you, O LORD, I will make music.
² I will ponder the way that is
      blameless.
  Oh when will you come to me?
  I will walk with integrity of heart
      within my house;
³ I will not set before my eyes
      anything that is worthless.
  I hate the work of those who fall away;
      it shall not cling to me.
⁴ A perverse heart shall be far from me;
      I will know nothing of evil.

⁵ Whoever slanders his
      neighbour secretly
      I will destroy.
  Whoever has a haughty look
      and an arrogant heart
      I will not endure.

⁶ I will look with favour on the
      faithful in the land,
      that they may dwell with me;
  he who walks in the way
      that is blameless
      shall minister to me.

⁷ No one who practises deceit
      shall dwell in my house;
  no one who utters lies
      shall continue before my eyes.

⁸ Morning by morning I will destroy
      all the wicked in the land,
  cutting off all the evildoers
      from the city of the LORD.

DO NOT HIDE YOUR FACE FROM ME

102   A Prayer of one afflicted, when he is faint and pours out his complaint before the LORD.

¹ Hear my prayer, O LORD;
      let my cry come to you!
² Do not hide your face from me
      in the day of my distress!
  Incline your ear to me;
      answer me speedily in the
          day when I call!

³ For my days pass away like smoke,
      and my bones burn like a furnace.
⁴ My heart is struck down like
      grass and has withered;
      I forget to eat my bread.
⁵ Because of my loud groaning
      my bones cling to my flesh.
⁶ I am like a desert owl of
      the wilderness,
  like an owlᵇ of the waste places;
⁷ I lie awake;
  I am like a lonely sparrow
      on the housetop.
⁸ All the day my enemies taunt me;
      those who deride me use my
          name for a curse.
⁹ For I eat ashes like bread
      and mingle tears with my drink,
¹⁰ because of your indignation
      and anger;
  for you have taken me up and
      thrown me down.
¹¹ My days are like an evening shadow;
      I wither away like grass.

¹² But you, O LORD, are
      enthroned for ever;
  you are remembered throughout
      all generations.
¹³ You will arise and have pity on Zion;
      it is the time to favour her;
      the appointed time has come.
¹⁴ For your servants hold her stones dear
      and have pity on her dust.
¹⁵ Nations will fear the name of
      the LORD,
  and all the kings of the earth
      will fear your glory.
¹⁶ For the LORD builds up Zion;
      he appears in his glory;

ᵃOr *und not we ourselves*   ᵇThe precise identity of these birds is uncertain

17 he regards the prayer of the destitute
     and does not despise their prayer.
18 Let this be recorded for a
     generation to come,
   so that a people yet to be created
     may praise the LORD:
19 that he looked down from
     his holy height;
   from heaven the LORD
     looked at the earth,
20 to hear the groans of the prisoners,
     to set free those who were
     doomed to die,
21 that they may declare in Zion
     the name of the LORD,
   and in Jerusalem his praise,
22 when peoples gather together,
     and kingdoms, to worship the LORD.

23 He has broken my strength
     in midcourse;
   he has shortened my days.
24 "O my God," I say, "take me not away
     in the midst of my days—
   you whose years endure
     throughout all generations!"

25 Of old you laid the foundation
     of the earth,
   and the heavens are the
     work of your hands.
26 They will perish, but you will remain;
     they will all wear out like a garment.
   You will change them like a robe,
     and they will pass away,
27 but you are the same, and your
     years have no end.
28 The children of your servants
     shall dwell secure;
   their offspring shall be
     established before you.

BLESS THE LORD, O MY SOUL

103 *Of David.*

¹ Bless the LORD, O my soul,
   and all that is within me,
   bless his holy name!
2 Bless the LORD, O my soul,
   and forget not all his benefits,
3 who forgives all your iniquity,
   who heals all your diseases,
4 who redeems your life from the pit,
   who crowns you with steadfast
     love and mercy,
5 who satisfies you with good
   so that your youth is renewed
     like the eagle's.

6 The LORD works righteousness
   and justice for all who
     are oppressed.
7 He made known his ways to Moses,
   his acts to the people of Israel.
8 The LORD is merciful and gracious,
   slow to anger and abounding
     in steadfast love.
9 He will not always chide,
   nor will he keep his anger
     for ever.
10 He does not deal with us
    according to our sins,
   nor repay us according to
     our iniquities.
11 For as high as the heavens
     are above the earth,
   so great is his steadfast love
     towards those who fear him;
12 as far as the east is from the west,
   so far does he remove our
     transgressions from us.
13 As a father shows compassion
     to his children,
   so the LORD shows compassion
     to those who fear him.
14 For he knows our frame;*a*
   he remembers that we are dust.

15 As for man, his days are like grass;
   he flourishes like a flower
     of the field;
16 for the wind passes over
     it, and it is gone,
   and its place knows it no more.
17 But the steadfast love of the LORD is
     from everlasting to everlasting
     on those who fear him,
   and his righteousness to
     children's children,
18 to those who keep his covenant
   and remember to do his
     commandments.
19 The LORD has established his
     throne in the heavens,
   and his kingdom rules over all.

20 Bless the LORD, O you his angels,
   you mighty ones who do his word,
   obeying the voice of his word!

---

a Or *knows how we are formed*

21 Bless the LORD, all his hosts,
    his ministers, who do his will!
22 Bless the LORD, all his works,
    in all places of his dominion.
    Bless the LORD, O my soul!

O LORD MY GOD, YOU ARE VERY GREAT

104

Bless the LORD, O my soul!
    O LORD my God, you are
        very great!
You are clothed with splendour
    and majesty,
2   covering yourself with light
        as with a garment,
    stretching out the heavens
        like a tent.
3 He lays the beams of his
        chambers on the waters;
    he makes the clouds his chariot;
        he rides on the wings of the wind;
4   he makes his messengers winds,
        his ministers a flaming fire.

5 He set the earth on its foundations,
    so that it should never
        be moved.
6 You covered it with the deep
        as with a garment;
    the waters stood above
        the mountains.
7 At your rebuke they fled;
    at the sound of your thunder
        they took to flight.
8 The mountains rose, the
        valleys sank down
    to the place that you
        appointed for them.
9 You set a boundary that
        they may not pass,
    so that they might not again
        cover the earth.

10 You make springs gush forth
        in the valleys;
    they flow between the hills;
11 they give drink to every
        beast of the field;
    the wild donkeys quench
        their thirst.
12 Beside them the birds of the
        heavens dwell;
    they sing among the branches.
13 From your lofty abode you
        water the mountains;
    the earth is satisfied with the
        fruit of your work.

14 You cause the grass to grow
        for the livestock
    and plants for man to cultivate,
    that he may bring forth food
        from the earth
15 and wine to gladden the
        heart of man,
    oil to make his face shine
    and bread to strengthen man's heart.
16 The trees of the LORD are
        watered abundantly,
    the cedars of Lebanon
        that he planted.
17 In them the birds build their nests;
    the stork has her home
        in the fir trees.
18 The high mountains are for
        the wild goats;
    the rocks are a refuge for
        the rock badgers.

19 He made the moon to mark
        the seasons;[a]
    the sun knows its time for setting.
20 You make darkness, and it is night,
    when all the beasts of the
        forest creep about.
21 The young lions roar for their prey,
    seeking their food from God.
22 When the sun rises, they steal away
    and lie down in their dens.
23 Man goes out to his work
    and to his labour until the evening.

24 O LORD, how manifold are your works!
    In wisdom have you made them all;
    the earth is full of your creatures.
25 Here is the sea, great and wide,
    which teems with creatures
        innumerable,
    living things both small and great.
26 There go the ships,
    and Leviathan, which you
        formed to play in it.[b]

27 These all look to you,
    to give them their food
        in due season.
28 When you give it to them,
        they gather it up;
    when you open your hand, they
        are filled with good things.

---

[a] Or *the appointed times* (compare Genesis 1:14)   [b] Or *you formed to play with*

29 When you hide your face,
   they are dismayed;
   when you take away their
      breath, they die
   and return to their dust.
30 When you send forth your Spirit,*a*
   they are created,
   and you renew the face of the ground.
31 May the glory of the LORD
      endure for ever;
   may the LORD rejoice in his works,
32 who looks on the earth and it trembles,
   who touches the mountains
      and they smoke!
33 I will sing to the LORD as long as I live;
   I will sing praise to my God
      while I have being.
34 May my meditation be pleasing to him,
   for I rejoice in the LORD.
35 Let sinners be consumed
      from the earth,
   and let the wicked be no more!
   Bless the LORD, O my soul!
   Praise the LORD!

TELL OF ALL HIS WONDROUS WORKS

105

Oh give thanks to the LORD;
   call upon his name;
   make known his deeds
      among the peoples!
2 Sing to him, sing praises to him;
   tell of all his wondrous works!
3 Glory in his holy name;
   let the hearts of those who
      seek the LORD rejoice!
4 Seek the LORD and his strength;
   seek his presence continually!
5 Remember the wondrous
      works that he has done,
   his miracles, and the
      judgements he uttered,
6 O offspring of Abraham, his servant,
   children of Jacob, his chosen ones!

7 He is the LORD our God;
   his judgements are in all the earth.
8 He remembers his covenant for ever,
   the word that he commanded, for
      a thousand generations,
9 the covenant that he made
      with Abraham,
   his sworn promise to Isaac,
10 which he confirmed to Jacob
      as a statute,
   to Israel as an everlasting covenant,

11 saying, "To you I will give
      the land of Canaan
   as your portion for an inheritance."
12 When they were few in number,
   of little account, and
      sojourners in it,
13 wandering from nation to nation,
   from one kingdom to
      another people,
14 he allowed no one to oppress them;
   he rebuked kings on their account,
15 saying, "Touch not my anointed ones,
   do my prophets no harm!"
16 When he summoned a
      famine on the land
   and broke all supply*b* of bread,
17 he had sent a man ahead of them,
   Joseph, who was sold as a slave.
18 His feet were hurt with fetters;
   his neck was put in a collar of iron;
19 until what he had said came to pass,
   the word of the LORD tested him.
20 The king sent and released him;
   the ruler of the peoples set him free;
21 he made him lord of his house
   and ruler of all his possessions,
22 to bind*c* his princes at his pleasure
   and to teach his elders wisdom.
23 Then Israel came to Egypt;
   Jacob sojourned in the land of Ham.
24 And the LORD made his
      people very fruitful
   and made them stronger
      than their foes.
25 He turned their hearts to
      hate his people,
   to deal craftily with his servants.
26 He sent Moses, his servant,
   and Aaron, whom he had chosen.
27 They performed his signs among them
   and miracles in the land of Ham.
28 He sent darkness, and made
      the land dark;
   they did not rebel*d* against
      his words.
29 He turned their waters into blood
   and caused their fish to die.
30 Their land swarmed with frogs,
   even in the chambers of their kings.

---

*a*Or breath *b*Hebrew *staff* *c*Septuagint, Syriac, Jerome *instruct*
*d*Septuagint, Syriac omit *not*

31 He spoke, and there came
    swarms of flies,
    and gnats throughout their country.
32 He gave them hail for rain,
    and fiery lightning bolts
        through their land.
33 He struck down their vines
        and fig trees,
    and shattered the trees of
        their country.
34 He spoke, and the locusts came,
    young locusts without number,
35 which devoured all the
        vegetation in their land
    and ate up the fruit of their ground.
36 He struck down all the
        firstborn in their land,
    the firstfruits of all their strength.

37 Then he brought out Israel
        with silver and gold,
    and there was none among his
        tribes who stumbled.
38 Egypt was glad when they departed,
    for dread of them had fallen upon it.
39 He spread a cloud for a covering,
    and fire to give light by night.
40 They asked, and he brought quail,
    and gave them bread from
        heaven in abundance.
41 He opened the rock, and
        water gushed out;
    it flowed through the
        desert like a river.
42 For he remembered his holy promise,
    and Abraham, his servant.

43 So he brought his people out with joy,
    his chosen ones with singing.
44 And he gave them the lands
        of the nations,
    and they took possession of the
        fruit of the peoples' toil,
45 that they might keep his statutes
    and observe his laws.
    Praise the LORD!

GIVE THANKS TO THE LORD, FOR HE IS GOOD

106
Praise the LORD!
Oh give thanks to the LORD,
    for he is good,
for his steadfast love endures
    for ever!
2 Who can utter the mighty
        deeds of the LORD,
    or declare all his praise?
3 Blessed are they who observe justice,
    who do righteousness at all times!

4 Remember me, O LORD, when you
        show favour to your people;
    help me when you save them,[a]
5 that I may look upon the prosperity
        of your chosen ones,
    that I may rejoice in the
        gladness of your nation,
    that I may glory with your
        inheritance.

6 Both we and our fathers have sinned;
    we have committed iniquity; we
        have done wickedness.
7 Our fathers, when they were in Egypt,
        did not consider your
        wondrous works;
    they did not remember the abundance
        of your steadfast love,
    but rebelled by the sea,
        at the Red Sea.
8 Yet he saved them for his name's sake,
    that he might make known
        his mighty power.
9 He rebuked the Red Sea,
        and it became dry,
    and he led them through the
        deep as through a desert.
10 So he saved them from the
        hand of the foe
    and redeemed them from the
        power of the enemy.
11 And the waters covered
        their adversaries;
    not one of them was left.
12 Then they believed his words;
    they sang his praise.

13 But they soon forgot his works;
    they did not wait for his counsel.
14 But they had a wanton craving
        in the wilderness,
    and put God to the test in the desert;
15 he gave them what they asked,
    but sent a wasting disease
        among them.

16 When men in the camp were
        jealous of Moses
    and Aaron, the holy one of the LORD,

---
[a] Or *Remember me, O LORD, with the favour you show to your people; help me with your salvation*

17 the earth opened and
      swallowed up Dathan,
    and covered the company
      of Abiram.
18 Fire also broke out in their company;
    the flame burned up the wicked.

19 They made a calf in Horeb
    and worshipped a metal image.
20 They exchanged the glory of God^a
    for the image of an ox that eats grass.
21 They forgot God, their Saviour,
    who had done great things in Egypt,
22 wondrous works in the land of Ham,
    and awesome deeds by the Red Sea.
23 Therefore he said he would
      destroy them—
    had not Moses, his chosen one,
    stood in the breach before him,
    to turn away his wrath from
      destroying them.

24 Then they despised the pleasant land,
    having no faith in his promise.
25 They murmured in their tents,
    and did not obey the voice
      of the LORD.
26 Therefore he raised his hand
      and swore to them
    that he would make them fall
      in the wilderness,
27 and would make their offspring
      fall among the nations,
    scattering them among the lands.

28 Then they yoked themselves
      to the Baal of Peor,
    and ate sacrifices offered
      to the dead;
29 they provoked the LORD to
      anger with their deeds,
    and a plague broke out among them.
30 Then Phinehas stood up
      and intervened,
    and the plague was stayed.
31 And that was counted to him
      as righteousness
    from generation to
      generation for ever.

32 They angered him at the
      waters of Meribah,
    and it went ill with Moses
      on their account,
33 for they made his spirit bitter,^b
    and he spoke rashly with his lips.

34 They did not destroy the peoples,
    as the LORD commanded them,
35 but they mixed with the nations
    and learned to do as they did.
36 They served their idols,
    which became a snare to them.
37 They sacrificed their sons
    and their daughters to the demons;
38 they poured out innocent blood,
    the blood of their sons
      and daughters,
    whom they sacrificed to the
      idols of Canaan,
    and the land was polluted
      with blood.
39 Thus they became unclean
      by their acts,
    and played the whore in their deeds.

40 Then the anger of the LORD was
      kindled against his people,
    and he abhorred his heritage;
41 he gave them into the hand
      of the nations,
    so that those who hated them
      ruled over them.
42 Their enemies oppressed them,
    and they were brought into
      subjection under their power.
43 Many times he delivered them,
    but they were rebellious
      in their purposes
    and were brought low through
      their iniquity.

44 Nevertheless, he looked
      upon their distress,
    when he heard their cry.
45 For their sake he remembered
      his covenant,
    and relented according to the
      abundance of his steadfast love.
46 He caused them to be pitied
    by all those who held them captive.

47 Save us, O LORD our God,
    and gather us from among
      the nations,
    that we may give thanks to
      your holy name
    and glory in your praise.

48 Blessed be the LORD, the God of Israel,
    from everlasting to everlasting!

---
^aHebrew *exchanged their glory* ^bOr *they rebelled against God's Spirit*

And let all the people say, "Amen!"
Praise the LORD!

BOOK FIVE

LET THE REDEEMED OF THE LORD SAY SO

107

Oh give thanks to the LORD,
for he is good,
for his steadfast love
endures for ever!
2 Let the redeemed of the LORD say so,
whom he has redeemed
from trouble[a]
3 and gathered in from the lands,
from the east and from the west,
from the north and from the south.

4 Some wandered in desert wastes,
finding no way to a city to dwell in;
5 hungry and thirsty,
their soul fainted within them.
6 Then they cried to the LORD
in their trouble,
and he delivered them from
their distress.
7 He led them by a straight way
till they reached a city to dwell in.
8 Let them thank the LORD for
his steadfast love,
for his wondrous works to
the children of man!
9 For he satisfies the longing soul,
and the hungry soul he fills
with good things.

10 Some sat in darkness and in
the shadow of death,
prisoners in affliction and in irons,
11 for they had rebelled against
the words of God,
and spurned the counsel
of the Most High.
12 So he bowed their hearts down
with hard labour;
they fell down, with none to help.
13 Then they cried to the LORD
in their trouble,
and he delivered them from
their distress.
14 He brought them out of darkness
and the shadow of death,
and burst their bonds apart.
15 Let them thank the LORD for
his steadfast love,
for his wondrous works to
the children of man!

16 For he shatters the doors of bronze
and cuts in two the bars of iron.

17 Some were fools through
their sinful ways,
and because of their iniquities
suffered affliction;
18 they loathed any kind of food,
and they drew near to the
gates of death.
19 Then they cried to the LORD
in their trouble,
and he delivered them from
their distress.
20 He sent out his word and healed them,
and delivered them from
their destruction.
21 Let them thank the LORD for
his steadfast love,
for his wondrous works to
the children of man!
22 And let them offer sacrifices
of thanksgiving,
and tell of his deeds in songs of joy!

23 Some went down to the sea in ships,
doing business on the great waters;
24 they saw the deeds of the LORD,
his wondrous works in the deep.
25 For he commanded and raised
the stormy wind,
which lifted up the waves of
the sea.
26 They mounted up to heaven; they
went down to the depths;
their courage melted away
in their evil plight;
27 they reeled and staggered
like drunken men
and were at their wits' end.[b]
28 Then they cried to the LORD
in their trouble,
and he delivered them from
their distress.
29 He made the storm be still,
and the waves of the sea
were hushed.
30 Then they were glad that the
waters[c] were quiet,
and he brought them to
their desired haven.
31 Let them thank the LORD for
his steadfast love,

---

[a] Or from the hand of the foe [b] Hebrew and all their wisdom was swallowed up [c] Hebrew they

5 The Lord is at your right hand;
 he will shatter kings on the
  day of his wrath.
6 He will execute judgement
  among the nations,
 filling them with corpses;
 he will shatter chiefs[a]
  over the wide earth.
7 He will drink from the
  brook by the way;
 therefore he will lift up his head.

GREAT ARE THE LORD'S WORKS

111
[b] Praise the LORD!
 I will give thanks to the LORD
  with my whole heart,
 in the company of the upright,
  in the congregation.
2 Great are the works of the LORD,
 studied by all who delight in them.
3 Full of splendour and
  majesty is his work,
 and his righteousness
  endures for ever.
4 He has caused his wondrous
  works to be remembered;
 the LORD is gracious and merciful.
5 He provides food for those
  who fear him;
 he remembers his covenant for ever.
6 He has shown his people the
  power of his works,
 in giving them the inheritance
  of the nations.
7 The works of his hands are
  faithful and just;
 all his precepts are trustworthy;
8 they are established for ever and ever,
 to be performed with faithfulness
  and uprightness.
9 He sent redemption to his people;
 he has commanded his
  covenant for ever.
 Holy and awesome is his name!
10 The fear of the LORD is the
  beginning of wisdom;
 all those who practise it have
  a good understanding.
 His praise endures for ever!

THE RIGHTEOUS WILL NEVER BE MOVED

112
[c] Praise the LORD!
 Blessed is the man who fears
  the LORD,
 who greatly delights in his
  commandments!
2 His offspring will be mighty
  in the land;
 the generation of the upright
  will be blessed.
3 Wealth and riches are in his house,
 and his righteousness
  endures for ever.
4 Light dawns in the darkness
  for the upright;
 he is gracious, merciful,
  and righteous.
5 It is well with the man who deals
  generously and lends;
 who conducts his affairs
  with justice.
6 For the righteous will never be moved;
 he will be remembered for ever.
7 He is not afraid of bad news;
 his heart is firm, trusting
  in the LORD.
8 His heart is steady;[d] he will
  not be afraid,
 until he looks in triumph
  on his adversaries.
9 He has distributed freely; he
  has given to the poor;
 his righteousness endures for ever;
 his horn is exalted in honour.
10 The wicked man sees it and is angry;
 he gnashes his teeth and
  melts away;
 the desire of the wicked will perish!

WHO IS LIKE THE LORD OUR GOD?

113
Praise the LORD!
 Praise, O servants of the LORD,
 praise the name of the LORD!

2 Blessed be the name of the LORD
 from this time forth and
  for evermore!
3 From the rising of the sun
  to its setting,
 the name of the LORD is
  to be praised!

4 The LORD is high above all nations,
 and his glory above the heavens!
5 Who is like the LORD our God,
 who is seated on high,
6 who looks far down
 on the heavens and the earth?

---

[a]Or *the head* [b]This psalm is an acrostic poem, each line beginning with the successive letters of the Hebrew alphabet [c]This psalm is an acrostic poem, each line beginning with the successive letters of the Hebrew alphabet [d]Or *established* (compare 111:8)

7 He raises the poor from the dust
  and lifts the needy from
    the ash heap,
8 to make them sit with princes,
  with the princes of his people.
9 He gives the barren woman a home,
  making her the joyous
    mother of children.
  Praise the LORD!

TREMBLE AT THE PRESENCE OF THE LORD

114
When Israel went out
    from Egypt,
  the house of Jacob from
    a people of strange
      language,
2 Judah became his sanctuary,
  Israel his dominion.

3 The sea looked and fled;
    Jordan turned back.
4 The mountains skipped like rams,
    the hills like lambs.

5 What ails you, O sea, that you flee?
    O Jordan, that you turn back?
6 O mountains, that you skip like rams?
    O hills, like lambs?

7 Tremble, O earth, at the
      presence of the Lord,
    at the presence of the God of Jacob,
8 who turns the rock into a pool of water,
    the flint into a spring of water.

TO YOUR NAME GIVE GLORY

115
Not to us, O LORD, not to us, but
    to your name give glory,
  for the sake of your steadfast
    love and your faithfulness!

2 Why should the nations say,
    "Where is their God?"
3 Our God is in the heavens;
    he does all that he pleases.

4 Their idols are silver and gold,
    the work of human hands.
5 They have mouths, but do not speak;
    eyes, but do not see.
6 They have ears, but do not hear;
    noses, but do not smell.
7 They have hands, but do not feel;
    feet, but do not walk;
  and they do not make a sound
    in their throat.
8 Those who make them
    become like them;
  so do all who trust in them.

9 O Israel,[a] trust in the LORD!
    He is their help and their shield.
10 O house of Aaron, trust in the LORD!
    He is their help and their shield.
11 You who fear the LORD,
    trust in the LORD!
  He is their help and their shield.

12 The LORD has remembered
      us; he will bless us;
    he will bless the house of Israel;
    he will bless the house of Aaron;
13 he will bless those who fear the LORD,
    both the small and the great.

14 May the LORD give you increase,
    you and your children!
15 May you be blessed by the LORD,
    who made heaven and earth!

16 The heavens are the LORD's heavens,
    but the earth he has given to
      the children of man.
17 The dead do not praise the LORD,
    nor do any who go down into silence.
18 But we will bless the LORD
    from this time forth and
      for evermore.
  Praise the LORD!

I LOVE THE LORD

116
I love the LORD, because he
    has heard
  my voice and my pleas
    for mercy.
2 Because he inclined his ear to me,
    therefore I will call on him
      as long as I live.
3 The snares of death encompassed me;
    the pangs of Sheol laid hold on me;
    I suffered distress and anguish.
4 Then I called on the name of the LORD:
    "O LORD, I pray, deliver my soul!"

5 Gracious is the LORD, and righteous;
    our God is merciful.
6 The LORD preserves the simple;
    when I was brought low,
      he saved me.

---
[a] Masoretic Text; many Hebrew manuscripts, Septuagint, Syriac *O house of Israel*

7 Return, O my soul, to your rest;
  for the LORD has dealt
    bountifully with you.
8 For you have delivered my
    soul from death,
  my eyes from tears,
  my feet from stumbling;
9 I will walk before the LORD
    in the land of the living.
10 I believed, even when[a] I spoke:
    "I am greatly afflicted";
11 I said in my alarm,
    "All mankind are liars."
12 What shall I render to the LORD
    for all his benefits to me?
13 I will lift up the cup of salvation
    and call on the name of the LORD,
14 I will pay my vows to the LORD
    in the presence of all his people.
15 Precious in the sight of the LORD
    is the death of his saints.
16 O LORD, I am your servant;
    I am your servant, the son of
      your maidservant.
  You have loosed my bonds.
17 I will offer to you the sacrifice
    of thanksgiving
  and call on the name of the LORD.
18 I will pay my vows to the LORD
    in the presence of all his people,
19 in the courts of the house of the LORD,
    in your midst, O Jerusalem.
  Praise the LORD!

THE LORD'S FAITHFULNESS ENDURES FOR EVER

117

Praise the LORD, all nations!
Extol him, all peoples!
2 For great is his steadfast love
    towards us,
  and the faithfulness of the LORD
    endures for ever.
Praise the LORD!

HIS STEADFAST LOVE ENDURES FOR EVER

118

Oh give thanks to the LORD,
    for he is good;
  for his steadfast love endures
    for ever!

2 Let Israel say,
    "His steadfast love endures for ever."
3 Let the house of Aaron say,
    "His steadfast love endures for ever."
4 Let those who fear the LORD say,
    "His steadfast love endures for ever."

5 Out of my distress I called on the LORD;
    the LORD answered me
      and set me free.
6 The LORD is on my side; I will not fear.
    What can man do to me?
7 The LORD is on my side as my helper;
    I shall look in triumph on
      those who hate me.

8 It is better to take refuge in the LORD
    than to trust in man.
9 It is better to take refuge in the LORD
    than to trust in princes.

10 All nations surrounded me;
    in the name of the LORD
      I cut them off!
11 They surrounded me, surrounded
      me on every side;
    in the name of the LORD
      I cut them off!
12 They surrounded me like bees;
    they went out like a fire
      among thorns;
    in the name of the LORD
      I cut them off!
13 I was pushed hard,[b] so that I was falling,
    but the LORD helped me.

14 The LORD is my strength and my song;
    he has become my salvation.
15 Glad songs of salvation
    are in the tents of the righteous:
  "The right hand of the LORD
      does valiantly,
16 the right hand of the LORD exalts,
    the right hand of the LORD
      does valiantly!"

17 I shall not die, but I shall live,
    and recount the deeds of the LORD.
18 The LORD has disciplined me severely,
    but he has not given me
      over to death.

19 Open to me the gates of righteousness,
    that I may enter through them
    and give thanks to the LORD.

---

[a] Or *believed, indeed*; Septuagint *believed, therefore* [b] Hebrew *You (that is, the enemy) pushed me hard*

20 This is the gate of the Lord;
　　 the righteous shall enter through it.
21 I thank you that you have answered me
　　 and have become my salvation.
22 The stone that the builders rejected
　　 has become the cornerstone.[a]
23 This is the Lord's doing;
　　 it is marvellous in our eyes.
24 This is the day that the Lord has made;
　　 let us rejoice and be glad in it.

25 Save us, we pray, O Lord!
　　 O Lord, we pray, give us success!

26 Blessed is he who comes in
　　　 the name of the Lord!
　　 We bless you from the
　　　 house of the Lord.
27 The Lord is God,
　　 and he has made his light
　　　 to shine upon us.
　　 Bind the festal sacrifice with cords,
　　　 up to the horns of the altar!

28 You are my God, and I will
　　　 give thanks to you;
　　 you are my God; I will extol you.
29 Oh give thanks to the Lord,
　　　 for he is good;
　　 for his steadfast love
　　　 endures for ever!

YOUR WORD IS A LAMP TO MY FEET

Aleph

119
[b] Blessed are those whose way
　　 is blameless,
　　 who walk in the law of
　　　 the Lord!
2 Blessed are those who keep
　　 his testimonies,
　　 who seek him with their
　　　 whole heart,
3 who also do no wrong,
　　 but walk in his ways!
4 You have commanded your precepts
　　 to be kept diligently.
5 Oh that my ways may be steadfast
　　 in keeping your statutes!
6 Then I shall not be put to shame,
　　 having my eyes fixed on all
　　　 your commandments.
7 I will praise you with an upright heart,
　　 when I learn your righteous rules.[c]
8 I will keep your statutes;
　　 do not utterly forsake me!

Beth

9 How can a young man keep
　　 his way pure?
　　 By guarding it according
　　　 to your word.
10 With my whole heart I seek you;
　　 let me not wander from your
　　　 commandments!
11 I have stored up your word in my heart,
　　 that I might not sin against you.
12 Blessed are you, O Lord;
　　 teach me your statutes!
13 With my lips I declare
　　 all the rules[d] of your mouth.
14 In the way of your testimonies I delight
　　 as much as in all riches.
15 I will meditate on your precepts
　　 and fix my eyes on your ways.
16 I will delight in your statutes;
　　 I will not forget your word.

Gimel

17 Deal bountifully with your servant,
　　 that I may live and keep your word.
18 Open my eyes, that I may behold
　　 wondrous things out of your law.
19 I am a sojourner on the earth;
　　 hide not your commandments
　　　 from me!
20 My soul is consumed with longing
　　 for your rules[e] at all times.
21 You rebuke the insolent, accursed ones,
　　 who wander from your
　　　 commandments.
22 Take away from me scorn
　　 and contempt,
　　 for I have kept your testimonies.
23 Even though princes sit
　　　 plotting against me,
　　 your servant will meditate
　　　 on your statutes.
24 Your testimonies are my delight;
　　 they are my counsellors.

Daleth

25 My soul clings to the dust;
　　 give me life according to your word!
26 When I told of my ways,
　　　 you answered me;
　　 teach me your statutes!

---

[a] Hebrew *the head of the corner*　[b] This psalm is an acrostic poem of twenty-two stanzas, following the letters of the Hebrew alphabet; within a stanza, each verse begins with the same Hebrew letter　[c] Or *your just and righteous decrees*; also verses 62, 106, 160, 164　[d] Or *all the just decrees*　[e] Or *your just decrees*; also verses 30, 39, 43, 52, 75, 102, 108, 137, 156, 175

27 Make me understand the way
   of your precepts,
   and I will meditate on your
   wondrous works.
28 My soul melts away for sorrow;
   strengthen me according
   to your word!
29 Put false ways far from me
   and graciously teach me your law!
30 I have chosen the way of
   faithfulness;
   I set your rules before me.
31 I cling to your testimonies, O Lord;
   let me not be put to shame!
32 I will run in the way of your
   commandments
   when you enlarge my heart!*a*

He

33 Teach me, O Lord, the way
   of your statutes;
   and I will keep it to the end.*b*
34 Give me understanding, that
   I may keep your law
   and observe it with my whole heart.
35 Lead me in the path of your
   commandments,
   for I delight in it.
36 Incline my heart to your testimonies,
   and not to selfish gain!
37 Turn my eyes from looking
   at worthless things;
   and give me life in your ways.
38 Confirm to your servant your
   promise,
   that you may be feared.
39 Turn away the reproach that I dread,
   for your rules are good.
40 Behold, I long for your precepts;
   in your righteousness give me life!

Waw

41 Let your steadfast love come
   to me, O Lord,
   your salvation according
   to your promise;
42 then shall I have an answer for
   him who taunts me,
   for I trust in your word.
43 And take not the word of truth
   utterly out of my mouth,
   for my hope is in your rules.
44 I will keep your law continually,
   for ever and ever,
45 and I shall walk in a wide place,
   for I have sought your precepts.
46 I will also speak of your
   testimonies before kings
   and shall not be put to shame,
47 for I find my delight in your
   commandments,
   which I love.
48 I will lift up my hands towards your
   commandments, which I love,
   and I will meditate on your statutes.

Zayin

49 Remember your word to your servant,
   in which you have made me hope.
50 This is my comfort in my affliction,
   that your promise gives me life.
51 The insolent utterly deride me,
   but I do not turn away from your law.
52 When I think of your rules from of old,
   I take comfort, O Lord.
53 Hot indignation seizes me
   because of the wicked,
   who forsake your law.
54 Your statutes have been my songs
   in the house of my sojourning.
55 I remember your name in
   the night, O Lord,
   and keep your law.
56 This blessing has fallen to me,
   that I have kept your precepts.

Heth

57 The Lord is my portion;
   I promise to keep your words.
58 I entreat your favour with all my heart;
   be gracious to me according
   to your promise.
59 When I think on my ways,
   I turn my feet to your testimonies;
60 I hasten and do not delay
   to keep your commandments.
61 Though the cords of the
   wicked ensnare me,
   I do not forget your law.
62 At midnight I rise to praise you,
   because of your righteous rules.
63 I am a companion of all who fear you,
   of those who keep your precepts.
64 The earth, O Lord, is full of
   your steadfast love;
   teach me your statutes!

Teth

65 You have dealt well with your servant,
   O Lord, according to your word.

---

a Or *for you set my heart free* *b* Or *keep it as my reward*

66 Teach me good judgement
    and knowledge,
  for I believe in your
    commandments.
67 Before I was afflicted I went astray,
  but now I keep your word.
68 You are good and do good;
  teach me your statutes.
69 The insolent smear me with lies,
  but with my whole heart I
    keep your precepts;
70 their heart is unfeeling like fat,
  but I delight in your law.
71 It is good for me that I was afflicted,
  that I might learn your statutes.
72 The law of your mouth is better to me
  than thousands of gold
    and silver pieces.

Yodh

73 Your hands have made and
    fashioned me;
  give me understanding that I may
    learn your commandments.
74 Those who fear you shall
    see me and rejoice,
  because I have hoped in your word.
75 I know, O Lord, that your
    rules are righteous,
  and that in faithfulness you
    have afflicted me.
76 Let your steadfast love comfort me
  according to your promise
    to your servant.
77 Let your mercy come to me,
    that I may live;
  for your law is my delight.
78 Let the insolent be put to shame,
  because they have wronged
    me with falsehood;
  as for me, I will meditate
    on your precepts.
79 Let those who fear you turn to me,
  that they may know your
    testimonies.
80 May my heart be blameless
    in your statutes,
  that I may not be put to shame!

Kaph

81 My soul longs for your salvation;
  I hope in your word.
82 My eyes long for your promise;
  I ask, "When will you comfort me?"
83 For I have become like a
    wineskin in the smoke,
  yet I have not forgotten
    your statutes.
84 How long must your servant endure?[a]
  When will you judge those
    who persecute me?
85 The insolent have dug pitfalls for me;
  they do not live according
    to your law.
86 All your commandments are sure;
  they persecute me with
    falsehood; help me!
87 They have almost made an
    end of me on earth,
  but I have not forsaken
    your precepts.
88 In your steadfast love give me life,
  that I may keep the testimonies
    of your mouth.

Lamedh

89 For ever, O Lord, your word
  is firmly fixed in the heavens.
90 Your faithfulness endures
    to all generations;
  you have established the earth,
    and it stands fast.
91 By your appointment they
    stand this day,
  for all things are your servants.
92 If your law had not been my delight,
  I would have perished in
    my affliction.
93 I will never forget your precepts,
  for by them you have given me life.
94 I am yours; save me,
  for I have sought your precepts.
95 The wicked lie in wait to destroy me,
  but I consider your testimonies.
96 I have seen a limit to all perfection,
  but your commandment is
    exceedingly broad.

Mem

97 Oh how I love your law!
  It is my meditation all the day.
98 Your commandment makes me
    wiser than my enemies,
  for it is ever with me.
99 I have more understanding
    than all my teachers,
  for your testimonies are
    my meditation.
100 I understand more than the aged,[b]
  for I keep your precepts.

---

[a] Hebrew *How many are the days of your servant?* [b] Or *the elders*

101 I hold back my feet from every evil way,
    in order to keep your word.
102 I do not turn aside from your rules,
    for you have taught me.
103 How sweet are your words to my taste,
    sweeter than honey to my mouth!
104 Through your precepts I get understanding;
    therefore I hate every false way.

Nun

105 Your word is a lamp to my feet
    and a light to my path.
106 I have sworn an oath and confirmed it,
    to keep your righteous rules.
107 I am severely afflicted;
    give me life, O Lord, according to your word!
108 Accept my freewill offerings of praise, O Lord,
    and teach me your rules.
109 I hold my life in my hand continually,
    but I do not forget your law.
110 The wicked have laid a snare for me,
    but I do not stray from your precepts.
111 Your testimonies are my heritage for ever,
    for they are the joy of my heart.
112 I incline my heart to perform your statutes
    for ever, to the end.[a]

Samekh

113 I hate the double-minded,
    but I love your law.
114 You are my hiding place and my shield;
    I hope in your word.
115 Depart from me, you evildoers,
    that I may keep the commandments of my God.
116 Uphold me according to your promise, that I may live,
    and let me not be put to shame in my hope!
117 Hold me up, that I may be safe
    and have regard for your statutes continually!
118 You spurn all who go astray from your statutes,
    for their cunning is in vain.
119 All the wicked of the earth you discard like dross,
    therefore I love your testimonies.
120 My flesh trembles for fear of you,
    and I am afraid of your judgements.

Ayin

121 I have done what is just and right;
    do not leave me to my oppressors.
122 Give your servant a pledge of good;
    let not the insolent oppress me.
123 My eyes long for your salvation
    and for the fulfilment of your righteous promise.
124 Deal with your servant according to your steadfast love,
    and teach me your statutes.
125 I am your servant; give me understanding,
    that I may know your testimonies!
126 It is time for the Lord to act,
    for your law has been broken.
127 Therefore I love your commandments
    above gold, above fine gold.
128 Therefore I consider all your precepts to be right;
    I hate every false way.

Pe

129 Your testimonies are wonderful;
    therefore my soul keeps them.
130 The unfolding of your words gives light;
    it imparts understanding to the simple.
131 I open my mouth and pant,
    because I long for your commandments.
132 Turn to me and be gracious to me,
    as is your way with those who love your name.
133 Keep steady my steps according to your promise,
    and let no iniquity get dominion over me.
134 Redeem me from man's oppression,
    that I may keep your precepts.
135 Make your face shine upon your servant,
    and teach me your statutes.
136 My eyes shed streams of tears,
    because people do not keep your law.

Tsadhe

137 Righteous are you, O Lord,
    and right are your rules.
138 You have appointed your testimonies in righteousness
    and in all faithfulness.

---

[a] Or statutes; the reward is eternal

139 My zeal consumes me,
  because my foes forget your words.
140 Your promise is well tried,
  and your servant loves it.
141 I am small and despised,
  yet I do not forget your precepts.
142 Your righteousness is
    righteous for ever,
  and your law is true.
143 Trouble and anguish have
    found me out,
  but your commandments
    are my delight.
144 Your testimonies are
    righteous for ever;
  give me understanding
    that I may live.

QOPH

145 With my whole heart I cry;
    answer me, O LORD!
  I will keep your statutes.
146 I call to you; save me,
  that I may observe your
    testimonies.
147 I rise before dawn and cry for help;
  I hope in your words.
148 My eyes are awake before the
    watches of the night,
  that I may meditate on
    your promise.
149 Hear my voice according to
    your steadfast love;
  O LORD, according to your
    justice give me life.
150 They draw near who persecute
    me with evil purpose;
  they are far from your law.
151 But you are near, O LORD,
  and all your commandments
    are true.
152 Long have I known from
    your testimonies
  that you have founded them
    for ever.

RESH

153 Look on my affliction and deliver me,
  for I do not forget your law.
154 Plead my cause and redeem me;
  give me life according to
    your promise!
155 Salvation is far from the wicked,
  for they do not seek your statutes.
156 Great is your mercy, O LORD;
  give me life according to your rules.
157 Many are my persecutors
    and my adversaries,
  but I do not swerve from
    your testimonies.
158 I look at the faithless with disgust,
  because they do not keep
    your commands.
159 Consider how I love your precepts!
  Give me life according to
    your steadfast love.
160 The sum of your word is truth,
  and every one of your righteous
    rules endures for ever.

SIN AND SHIN

161 Princes persecute me without cause,
  but my heart stands in awe
    of your words.
162 I rejoice at your word
  like one who finds great spoil.
163 I hate and abhor falsehood,
  but I love your law.
164 Seven times a day I praise you
  for your righteous rules.
165 Great peace have those who
    love your law;
  nothing can make them stumble.
166 I hope for your salvation, O LORD,
  and I do your commandments.
167 My soul keeps your testimonies;
  I love them exceedingly.
168 I keep your precepts and
    testimonies,
  for all my ways are before you.

TAW

169 Let my cry come before you, O LORD;
  give me understanding
    according to your word!
170 Let my plea come before you;
  deliver me according to your word.
171 My lips will pour forth praise,
  for you teach me your statutes.
172 My tongue will sing of your word,
  for all your commandments
    are right.
173 Let your hand be ready to help me,
  for I have chosen your precepts.
174 I long for your salvation, O LORD,
  and your law is my delight.
175 Let my soul live and praise you,
  and let your rules help me.
176 I have gone astray like a lost
    sheep; seek your servant,
  for I do not forget your
    commandments.

DELIVER ME, O LORD

120 *A Song of Ascents.*

¹ In my distress I called to
    the LORD,
  and he answered me.
² Deliver me, O LORD,
    from lying lips,
    from a deceitful tongue.

³ What shall be given to you,
    and what more shall be done to you,
    you deceitful tongue?
⁴ A warrior's sharp arrows,
    with glowing coals of the broom tree!

⁵ Woe to me, that I sojourn in Meshech,
    that I dwell among the
      tents of Kedar!
⁶ Too long have I had my dwelling
    among those who hate peace.
⁷ I am for peace,
    but when I speak, they are for war!

MY HELP COMES FROM THE LORD

121 *A Song of Ascents.*

¹ I lift up my eyes to the hills.
    From where does my help come?
² My help comes from the LORD,
    who made heaven and earth.

³ He will not let your foot be moved;
    he who keeps you will not slumber.
⁴ Behold, he who keeps Israel
    will neither slumber nor sleep.

⁵ The LORD is your keeper;
    the LORD is your shade on
      your right hand.
⁶ The sun shall not strike you by day,
    nor the moon by night.

⁷ The LORD will keep you from all evil;
    he will keep your life.
⁸ The LORD will keep
    your going out and your coming in
    from this time forth and
      for evermore.

LET US GO TO THE HOUSE OF THE LORD

122 *A Song of Ascents. Of David.*

¹ I was glad when they
    said to me,
  "Let us go to the house of the LORD!"
² Our feet have been standing
    within your gates, O Jerusalem!

³ Jerusalem—built as a city
    that is bound firmly together,
⁴ to which the tribes go up,
    the tribes of the LORD,
  as was decreed for*ᵃ* Israel,
    to give thanks to the name
      of the LORD.
⁵ There thrones for judgement were set,
    the thrones of the house of David.

⁶ Pray for the peace of Jerusalem!
    "May they be secure who love you!
⁷ Peace be within your walls
    and security within your towers!"
⁸ For my brothers and companions'
      sake
    I will say, "Peace be within you!"
⁹ For the sake of the house of
    the LORD our God,
  I will seek your good.

OUR EYES LOOK TO THE LORD OUR GOD

123 *A Song of Ascents.*

¹ To you I lift up my eyes,
    O you who are enthroned
      in the heavens!
² Behold, as the eyes of servants
    look to the hand of their master,
  as the eyes of a maidservant
    to the hand of her mistress,
  so our eyes look to the LORD our God,
    till he has mercy upon us.

³ Have mercy upon us, O LORD,
    have mercy upon us,
  for we have had more than
      enough of contempt.
⁴ Our soul has had more than enough
    of the scorn of those who are at ease,
    of the contempt of the proud.

OUR HELP IS IN THE NAME OF THE LORD

124 *A Song of Ascents. Of David.*

¹ If it had not been the LORD
    who was on our side—
  let Israel now say—
² if it had not been the LORD
    who was on our side
  when people rose up against us,

ᵃ Or as a testimony for

3   then they would have
       swallowed us up alive,
     when their anger was
       kindled against us;
4   then the flood would have
       swept us away,
     the torrent would have gone over us;
5   then over us would have gone
       the raging waters.

6   Blessed be the LORD,
     who has not given us
       as prey to their teeth!
7   We have escaped like a bird
       from the snare of the fowlers;
     the snare is broken,
       and we have escaped!
8   Our help is in the name of the LORD,
     who made heaven and earth.

THE LORD SURROUNDS HIS PEOPLE

125
A Song of Ascents.

1   Those who trust in the LORD
       are like Mount Zion,
     which cannot be moved,
       but abides for ever.
2   As the mountains surround Jerusalem,
     so the LORD surrounds his people,
       from this time forth and
         for evermore.
3   For the sceptre of wickedness
       shall not rest
     on the land allotted to the righteous,
     lest the righteous stretch out
       their hands to do wrong.
4   Do good, O LORD, to those
       who are good,
     and to those who are upright
       in their hearts!
5   But those who turn aside to
       their crooked ways
     the LORD will lead away
       with evildoers!
     Peace be upon Israel!

RESTORE OUR FORTUNES, O LORD

126
A Song of Ascents.

1   When the LORD restored
       the fortunes of Zion,
     we were like those who dream.
2   Then our mouth was filled
       with laughter,
     and our tongue with shouts of joy;

    then they said among the nations,
     "The LORD has done great
       things for them."
3   The LORD has done great things
       for us;
     we are glad.

4   Restore our fortunes, O LORD,
       like streams in the Negeb!
5   Those who sow in tears
       shall reap with shouts of joy!
6   He who goes out weeping,
       bearing the seed for sowing,
     shall come home with shouts of joy,
       bringing his sheaves with him.

UNLESS THE LORD BUILDS THE HOUSE

127
A Song of Ascents. Of Solomon.

1   Unless the LORD builds
       the house,
     those who build it labour in vain.
     Unless the LORD watches over the city,
       the watchman stays awake in vain.
2   It is in vain that you rise up early
       and go late to rest,
     eating the bread of anxious toil;
       for he gives to his beloved sleep.

3   Behold, children are a heritage
       from the LORD,
     the fruit of the womb a reward.
4   Like arrows in the hand of a warrior
       are the children[a] of one's youth.
5   Blessed is the man
       who fills his quiver with them!
     He shall not be put to shame
       when he speaks with his
         enemies in the gate.[b]

BLESSED IS EVERYONE WHO FEARS THE LORD

128
A Song of Ascents.

1   Blessed is everyone who
       fears the LORD,
     who walks in his ways!
2   You shall eat the fruit of the
       labour of your hands;
     you shall be blessed, and it
       shall be well with you.

3   Your wife will be like a fruitful vine
       within your house;

---

[a] Or sons   [b] Or They shall not be put to shame when they speak with their enemies in the gate

your children will be like olive shoots
round your table.
4 Behold, thus shall the man be blessed
who fears the LORD.

5 The LORD bless you from Zion!
May you see the prosperity
of Jerusalem
all the days of your life!
6 May you see your children's children!
Peace be upon Israel!

THEY HAVE AFFLICTED ME FROM MY YOUTH

129

A Song of Ascents.

1 "Greatly^a have they afflicted
me from my youth"—
let Israel now say—
2 "Greatly have they afflicted
me from my youth,
yet they have not prevailed
against me.
3 The ploughers ploughed
upon my back;
they made long their furrows."
4 The LORD is righteous;
he has cut the cords of the wicked.
5 May all who hate Zion
be put to shame and turned
backwards!
6 Let them be like the grass
on the housetops,
which withers before it grows up,
7 with which the reaper does
not fill his hand
nor the binder of sheaves his arms,
8 nor do those who pass by say,
"The blessing of the LORD
be upon you!
We bless you in the name
of the LORD!"

MY SOUL WAITS FOR THE LORD

130

A Song of Ascents.

1 Out of the depths I cry
to you, O LORD!
2 O Lord, hear my voice!
Let your ears be attentive
to the voice of my pleas for mercy!

3 If you, O LORD, should mark
iniquities,
O Lord, who could stand?
4 But with you there is forgiveness,
that you may be feared.

5 I wait for the LORD, my soul waits,
and in his word I hope;
6 my soul waits for the Lord
more than watchmen for
the morning,
more than watchmen for
the morning.

7 O Israel, hope in the LORD!
For with the LORD there
is steadfast love,
and with him is plentiful
redemption.
8 And he will redeem Israel
from all his iniquities.

I HAVE CALMED AND QUIETENED MY SOUL

131

A Song of Ascents. Of David.

1 O LORD, my heart is not
lifted up;
my eyes are not raised too high;
I do not occupy myself with things
too great and too marvellous
for me.
2 But I have calmed and
quietened my soul,
like a weaned child with its mother;
like a weaned child is my
soul within me.

3 O Israel, hope in the LORD
from this time forth and
for evermore.

THE LORD HAS CHOSEN ZION

132

A Song of Ascents.

1 Remember, O LORD,
in David's favour,
all the hardships he endured,
2 how he swore to the LORD
and vowed to the Mighty
One of Jacob,
3 "I will not enter my house
or get into my bed,
4 I will not give sleep to my eyes
or slumber to my eyelids,
5 until I find a place for the LORD,
a dwelling place for the
Mighty One of Jacob."

6 Behold, we heard of it in Ephrathah;
we found it in the fields of Jaar.

---

^{a}Or *Often*; also verse 2

7 "Let us go to his dwelling place;
    let us worship at his footstool!"

8 Arise, O LORD, and go to
      your resting-place,
    you and the ark of your might.

9 Let your priests be clothed
      with righteousness,
    and let your saints shout for joy.

10 For the sake of your servant David,
     do not turn away the face of
       your anointed one.

11 The LORD swore to David a sure oath
     from which he will not turn back:
   "One of the sons of your body[a]
     I will set on your throne.

12 If your sons keep my covenant
     and my testimonies that I
       shall teach them,
   their sons also for ever
     shall sit on your throne."

13 For the LORD has chosen Zion;
     he has desired it for his
       dwelling place:

14 "This is my resting-place for ever;
     here I will dwell, for I have desired it.

15 I will abundantly bless her provisions;
     I will satisfy her poor with bread.

16 Her priests I will clothe with salvation,
     and her saints will shout for joy.

17 There I will make a horn to
       sprout for David;
     I have prepared a lamp for
       my anointed.

18 His enemies I will clothe with shame,
     but on him his crown will shine."

WHEN BROTHERS DWELL IN UNITY

133
A Song of Ascents. Of David.

1 Behold, how good and
     pleasant it is
   when brothers dwell in unity![b]

2 It is like the precious oil on the head,
     running down on the beard,
   on the beard of Aaron,
     running down on the collar
       of his robes!

3 It is like the dew of Hermon,
     which falls on the
       mountains of Zion!
   For there the LORD has
     commanded the blessing,
       life for evermore.

COME, BLESS THE LORD

134
A Song of Ascents.

1 Come, bless the LORD, all
       you servants of the
         LORD,
     who stand by night in the
       house of the LORD!

2 Lift up your hands to the holy place
     and bless the LORD!

3 May the LORD bless you from Zion,
     he who made heaven and earth!

YOUR NAME, O LORD, ENDURES FOR EVER

135

1 Praise the LORD!
   Praise the name of the LORD,
     give praise, O servants of
       the LORD,
2 who stand in the house of the LORD,
     in the courts of the house of
       our God!
3 Praise the LORD, for the LORD is good;
     sing to his name, for it is pleasant![c]
4 For the LORD has chosen
       Jacob for himself,
     Israel as his own possession.

5 For I know that the LORD is great,
     and that our Lord is above all gods.
6 Whatever the LORD pleases, he does,
     in heaven and on earth,
     in the seas and all deeps.
7 He it is who makes the clouds rise
     at the end of the earth,
   who makes lightnings for the rain
     and brings forth the wind
       from his storehouses.

8 He it was who struck down
     the firstborn of Egypt,
   both of man and of beast;
9 who in your midst, O Egypt,
     sent signs and wonders
   against Pharaoh and all his
     servants;
10 who struck down many nations
     and killed mighty kings,
11 Sihon, king of the Amorites,
     and Og, king of Bashan,
   and all the kingdoms of Canaan,
12 and gave their land as a heritage,
     a heritage to his people Israel.

---

[a] Hebrew *of your fruit of the womb* [b] Or *dwell together* [c] Or *for he is beautiful*

13 Your name, O Lord, endures for ever,
   your renown,[a] O Lord,
      throughout all ages.
14 For the Lord will vindicate his people
   and have compassion on
      his servants.

15 The idols of the nations are
      silver and gold,
   the work of human hands.
16 They have mouths, but do not speak;
   they have eyes, but do not see;
17 they have ears, but do not hear,
   nor is there any breath in
      their mouths.
18 Those who make them
      become like them,
   so do all who trust in them.

19 O house of Israel, bless the Lord!
   O house of Aaron, bless the Lord!
20 O house of Levi, bless the Lord!
   You who fear the Lord,
      bless the Lord!
21 Blessed be the Lord from Zion,
   he who dwells in Jerusalem!
      Praise the Lord!

HIS STEADFAST LOVE ENDURES FOR EVER

136 Give thanks to the Lord,
      for he is good,
   for his steadfast love
      endures for ever.
2 Give thanks to the God of gods,
   for his steadfast love endures for ever.
3 Give thanks to the Lord of lords,
   for his steadfast love
      endures for ever;

4 to him who alone does great wonders,
   for his steadfast love
      endures for ever;
5 to him who by understanding
      made the heavens,
   for his steadfast love
      endures for ever;
6 to him who spread out the
      earth above the waters,
   for his steadfast love
      endures for ever;
7 to him who made the great lights,
   for his steadfast love
      endures for ever;
8 the sun to rule over the day,
   for his steadfast love
      endures for ever;
9 the moon and stars to rule
      over the night,
   for his steadfast love
      endures for ever;

10 to him who struck down the
      firstborn of Egypt,
   for his steadfast love
      endures for ever;
11 and brought Israel out from
      among them,
   for his steadfast love
      endures for ever;
12 with a strong hand and an
      outstretched arm,
   for his steadfast love
      endures for ever;
13 to him who divided the Red Sea in two,
   for his steadfast love
      endures for ever;
14 and made Israel pass through
      the midst of it,
   for his steadfast love
      endures for ever;
15 but overthrew[b] Pharaoh and
      his host in the Red Sea,
   for his steadfast love
      endures for ever;
16 to him who led his people
      through the wilderness,
   for his steadfast love
      endures for ever;

17 to him who struck down great kings,
   for his steadfast love
      endures for ever;
18 and killed mighty kings,
   for his steadfast love
      endures for ever;
19 Sihon, king of the Amorites,
   for his steadfast love
      endures for ever;
20 and Og, king of Bashan,
   for his steadfast love
      endures for ever;
21 and gave their land as a heritage,
   for his steadfast love
      endures for ever;
22 a heritage to Israel his servant,
   for his steadfast love
      endures for ever.

23 It is he who remembered us
      in our low estate,

---

[a] Or remembrance   [b] Hebrew shook off

for his steadfast love
   endures for ever;
24 and rescued us from our foes,
   for his steadfast love
   endures for ever;
25 he who gives food to all flesh,
   for his steadfast love endures for ever.

26 Give thanks to the God of heaven,
   for his steadfast love endures for ever.

HOW SHALL WE SING THE LORD'S SONG?

137

By the waters of Babylon,
   there we sat down and wept,
   when we remembered Zion.
2 On the willows[1] there
   we hung up our lyres.
3 For there our captors
   required of us songs,
   and our tormentors, mirth, saying,
   "Sing us one of the songs of Zion!"

4 How shall we sing the LORD's song
   in a foreign land?
5 If I forget you, O Jerusalem,
   let my right hand forget its skill!
6 Let my tongue stick to the
   roof of my mouth,
   if I do not remember you,
   if I do not set Jerusalem
   above my highest joy!

7 Remember, O LORD, against
   the Edomites
   the day of Jerusalem,
   how they said, "Lay it bare, lay it bare,
   down to its foundations!"
8 O daughter of Babylon, doomed
   to be destroyed,
   blessed shall he be who
   repays you
   with what you have done to us!
9 Blessed shall he be who takes
   your little ones
   and dashes them against the rock!

GIVE THANKS TO THE LORD

138

Of David.

1 I give you thanks, O LORD,
   with my whole heart;
   before the gods I sing your praise;
2 I bow down towards your holy temple
   and give thanks to your name
   for your steadfast love
   and your faithfulness,
   for you have exalted above all things
   your name and your word.[1]
3 On the day I called, you answered me;
   my strength of soul you increased.[1]

4 All the kings of the earth shall
   give you thanks, O LORD,
   for they have heard the words
   of your mouth,
5 and they shall sing of the
   ways of the LORD,
   for great is the glory of the LORD.
6 For though the LORD is high,
   he regards the lowly,
   but the haughty he knows from afar.

7 Though I walk in the midst of trouble,
   you preserve my life;
   you stretch out your hand against
   the wrath of my enemies,
   and your right hand delivers me.
8 The LORD will fulfil his
   purpose for me;
   your steadfast love, O LORD,
   endures for ever.
   Do not forsake the work
   of your hands.

SEARCH ME, O GOD, AND KNOW MY HEART

139

To the choirmaster.
A Psalm of David.

1 O LORD, you have searched
   me and known me!
2 You know when I sit down
   and when I rise up;
   you discern my thoughts from afar.
3 You search out my path and
   my lying down
   and are acquainted with all my ways.
4 Even before a word is on my tongue,
   behold, O LORD, you know
   it altogether.
5 You hem me in, behind and before,
   and lay your hand upon me.
6 Such knowledge is too
   wonderful for me;
   it is high; I cannot attain it.

7 Where shall I go from your Spirit?
   Or where shall I flee from
   your presence?

---

[1] Or poplars   [1] Or you have exalted your word above all your name
[1] Hebrew *you made me bold in my soul with strength*

5 I remember the days of old;
   I meditate on all that you have done;
   I ponder the work of your hands.
6 I stretch out my hands to you;
   my soul thirsts for you like a
      parched land. *Selah*

7 Answer me quickly, O Lord!
   My spirit fails!
   Hide not your face from me,
   lest I be like those who go
      down to the pit.
8 Let me hear in the morning of
      your steadfast love,
   for in you I trust.
   Make me know the way I should go,
   for to you I lift up my soul.

9 Deliver me from my enemies,
      O Lord!
   I have fled to you for refuge.[a]
10 Teach me to do your will,
    for you are my God!
   Let your good Spirit lead me
      on level ground!

11 For your name's sake, O Lord,
      preserve my life!
   In your righteousness bring
      my soul out of trouble!
12 And in your steadfast love you
      will cut off my enemies,
   and you will destroy all the
      adversaries of my soul,
   for I am your servant.

MY ROCK AND MY FORTRESS

144 *Of David.*

¹ Blessed be the Lord,
      my rock,
   who trains my hands for war,
      and my fingers for battle;
² he is my steadfast love
      and my fortress,
   my stronghold and my deliverer,
   my shield and he in whom
      I take refuge,
   who subdues peoples[b] under me.

³ O Lord, what is man that
      you regard him,
   or the son of man that you
      think of him?
⁴ Man is like a breath;
   his days are like a passing shadow.

5 Bow your heavens, O Lord,
      and come down!
   Touch the mountains so
      that they smoke!
6 Flash forth the lightning
      and scatter them;
   send out your arrows and rout them!
7 Stretch out your hand from on high;
      rescue me and deliver me
         from the many waters,
      from the hand of foreigners,
8 whose mouths speak lies
   and whose right hand is a right
      hand of falsehood.

9 I will sing a new song to you, O God;
      upon a ten-stringed harp
      I will play to you,
10 who gives victory to kings,
      who rescues David his servant
         from the cruel sword.
11 Rescue me and deliver me
      from the hand of foreigners,
   whose mouths speak lies
   and whose right hand is a right
      hand of falsehood.

12 May our sons in their youth
      be like plants full grown,
   our daughters like corner pillars
      cut for the structure of a palace;
13 may our granaries be full,
      providing all kinds of produce;
   may our sheep bring forth thousands
      and ten thousands in our fields;
14 may our cattle be heavy with young,
      suffering no mishap or
         failure in bearing;[c]
   may there be no cry of distress
      in our streets!
15 Blessed are the people to whom
      such blessings fall!
   Blessed are the people whose
      God is the Lord!

GREAT IS THE LORD

145[d] *A Song of Praise. Of David.*

¹ I will extol you, my God
      and King,

---

[a] One Hebrew manuscript, Septuagint; most Hebrew manuscripts *To you I have covered* [b] Many Hebrew manuscripts, Dead Sea Scroll, Jerome, Syriac, Aquila; most Hebrew manuscripts *subdues my people* [c] Hebrew *with no breaking in or going out* [d] This psalm is an acrostic poem, each verse beginning with the successive letters of the Hebrew alphabet

and bless your name for
    ever and ever.
2 Every day I will bless you
   and praise your name for
    ever and ever.
3 Great is the LORD, and greatly
    to be praised,
   and his greatness is unsearchable.

4 One generation shall commend
    your works to another,
   and shall declare your mighty acts.
5 On the glorious splendour
    of your majesty,
   and on your wondrous works,
    I will meditate.
6 They shall speak of the might
    of your awesome deeds,
   and I will declare your greatness.
7 They shall pour forth the fame of
    your abundant goodness
   and shall sing aloud of your
    righteousness.

8 The LORD is gracious and merciful,
   slow to anger and abounding
    in steadfast love.
9 The LORD is good to all,
   and his mercy is over all
    that he has made.

10 All your works shall give
    thanks to you, O LORD,
   and all your saints shall bless you!
11 They shall speak of the glory
    of your kingdom
   and tell of your power,
12 to make known to the children of
    man your[a] mighty deeds,
   and the glorious splendour
    of your kingdom.
13 Your kingdom is an everlasting
    kingdom,
   and your dominion endures
    throughout all generations.

   [The LORD is faithful in all
    his words
   and kind in all his works.][b]
14 The LORD upholds all who
    are falling
   and raises up all who are
    bowed down.
15 The eyes of all look to you,
   and you give them their
    food in due season.

16 You open your hand;
   you satisfy the desire of
    every living thing.
17 The LORD is righteous in all his ways
   and kind in all his works.
18 The LORD is near to all
    who call on him,
   to all who call on him in truth.
19 He fulfils the desire of those
    who fear him;
   he also hears their cry
    and saves them.
20 The LORD preserves all who love him,
   but all the wicked he will destroy.

21 My mouth will speak the
    praise of the LORD,
   and let all flesh bless his holy
    name for ever and ever.

PUT NOT YOUR TRUST IN PRINCES

146 Praise the LORD!
    Praise the LORD, O my soul!
2 I will praise the LORD
    as long as I live;
I will sing praises to my God
    while I have my being.

3 Put not your trust in princes,
   in a son of man, in whom
    there is no salvation.
4 When his breath departs, he
    returns to the earth;
   on that very day his plans perish.

5 Blessed is he whose help is
    the God of Jacob,
   whose hope is in the LORD his God,
6 who made heaven and earth,
   the sea, and all that is in them,
who keeps faith for ever;
7 who executes justice for
    the oppressed,
   who gives food to the hungry.

The LORD sets the prisoners free;
8 the LORD opens the eyes of the blind.
The LORD lifts up those who
    are bowed down;
   the LORD loves the righteous.
9 The LORD watches over the sojourners;
   he upholds the widow and
    the fatherless,

---

[a] Hebrew *his*; also next line   [b] These two lines are supplied by one Hebrew manuscript, Septuagint, Syriac (compare Dead Sea Scroll)

but the way of the wicked
    he brings to ruin.

10 The Lord will reign for ever,
    your God, O Zion, to all generations.
Praise the Lord!

HE HEALS THE BROKEN-HEARTED

147 Praise the Lord!
    For it is good to sing praises
        to our God;
for it is pleasant,[a] and a song
    of praise is fitting.
2 The Lord builds up Jerusalem;
    he gathers the outcasts of Israel.
3 He heals the broken-hearted
    and binds up their wounds.
4 He determines the number
    of the stars;
    he gives to all of them their names.
5 Great is our Lord, and
        abundant in power;
    his understanding is
        beyond measure.
6 The Lord lifts up the humble;[b]
    he casts the wicked to the ground.

7 Sing to the Lord with thanksgiving;
    make melody to our God on
        the lyre!
8 He covers the heavens with clouds;
    he prepares rain for the earth;
    he makes grass grow on the hills.
9 He gives to the beasts their food,
    and to the young ravens that cry.
10 His delight is not in the
        strength of the horse,
    nor his pleasure in the legs of a man,
11 but the Lord takes pleasure in
        those who fear him,
    in those who hope in his
        steadfast love.

12 Praise the Lord, O Jerusalem!
    Praise your God, O Zion!
13 For he strengthens the bars
        of your gates;
    he blesses your children within you.
14 He makes peace in your borders;
    he fills you with the finest
        of the wheat.
15 He sends out his command
        to the earth;
    his word runs swiftly.
16 He gives snow like wool;
    he scatters frost like ashes.
17 He hurls down his crystals
        of ice like crumbs;
    who can stand before his cold?
18 He sends out his word,
        and melts them;
    he makes his wind blow and
        the waters flow.
19 He declares his word to Jacob,
    his statutes and rules[c] to Israel.
20 He has not dealt thus with
        any other nation;
    they do not know his rules.[d]
Praise the Lord!

PRAISE THE NAME OF THE LORD

148 Praise the Lord!
    Praise the Lord from
        the heavens;
    praise him in the heights!
2 Praise him, all his angels;
    praise him, all his hosts!

3 Praise him, sun and moon,
    praise him, all you shining stars!
4 Praise him, you highest heavens,
    and you waters above the heavens!

5 Let them praise the name of the Lord!
    For he commanded and
        they were created.
6 And he established them
        for ever and ever;
    he gave a decree, and it shall
        not pass away.[e]

7 Praise the Lord from the earth,
    you great sea creatures and
        all deeps,
8 fire and hail, snow and mist,
    stormy wind fulfilling his word!

9 Mountains and all hills,
    fruit trees and all cedars!
10 Beasts and all livestock,
    creeping things and flying birds!

11 Kings of the earth and all peoples,
    princes and all rulers of the earth!
12 Young men and maidens together,
    old men and children!

13 Let them praise the name of the Lord,
    for his name alone is exalted;

---

[a] Or *for he is beautiful*   [b] Or *afflicted*   [c] Or *and just decrees*
[d] Or *his just decrees*   [e] Or *it shall not be transgressed*

his majesty is above earth
and heaven.
14 He has raised up a horn for
his people,
praise for all his saints,
for the people of Israel who
are near to him.
Praise the LORD!

SING TO THE LORD A NEW SONG

149 Praise the LORD!
Sing to the LORD a new song,
his praise in the assembly
of the godly!
2 Let Israel be glad in his Maker;
let the children of Zion
rejoice in their King!
3 Let them praise his name
with dancing,
making melody to him with
tambourine and lyre!
4 For the LORD takes pleasure
in his people;
he adorns the humble
with salvation.
5 Let the godly exult in glory;
let them sing for joy on their beds.
6 Let the high praises of God
be in their throats
and two-edged swords
in their hands,

7 to execute vengeance on the nations
and punishments on the peoples,
8 to bind their kings with chains
and their nobles with fetters of iron,
9 to execute on them the
judgement written!
This is honour for all his godly ones.
Praise the LORD!

LET EVERYTHING PRAISE THE LORD

150 Praise the LORD!
Praise God in his sanctuary;
praise him in his mighty
heavens!^a
2 Praise him for his mighty deeds;
praise him according to his
excellent greatness!
3 Praise him with trumpet sound;
praise him with lute and harp!
4 Praise him with tambourine
and dance;
praise him with strings and pipe!
5 Praise him with sounding cymbals;
praise him with loud
clashing cymbals!
6 Let everything that has breath
praise the LORD!
Praise the LORD!

---

^aHebrew *expanse* (compare Genesis 1:6–8)

PROVERBS

THE BEGINNING OF KNOWLEDGE

1 The proverbs of Solomon, son of David, king of Israel:

2 To know wisdom and instruction,
   to understand words of insight,
3 to receive instruction in wise dealing,
   in righteousness, justice, and equity;
4 to give prudence to the simple,
   knowledge and discretion to the youth—
5 Let the wise hear and increase in learning,
   and the one who understands obtain guidance,
6 to understand a proverb and a saying,
   the words of the wise and their riddles.

7 The fear of the LORD is the beginning of knowledge;
   fools despise wisdom and instruction.

THE ENTICEMENT OF SINNERS

8 Hear, my son, your father's instruction,
   and forsake not your mother's teaching,
9 for they are a graceful garland for your head
   and pendants for your neck.
10 My son, if sinners entice you,
    do not consent.
11 If they say, "Come with us, let us lie in wait for blood;
    let us ambush the innocent without reason;
12 like Sheol let us swallow them alive,
    and whole, like those who go down to the pit;
13 we shall find all precious goods,
    we shall fill our houses with plunder;
14 throw in your lot among us;
    we will all have one purse"—
15 my son, do not walk in the way with them;
    hold back your foot from their paths,
16 for their feet run to evil,
    and they make haste to shed blood.
17 For in vain is a net spread
    in the sight of any bird,
18 but these men lie in wait for their own blood;
    they set an ambush for their own lives.
19 Such are the ways of everyone who is greedy for unjust gain;
    it takes away the life of its possessors.

THE CALL OF WISDOM

20 Wisdom cries aloud in the street,
    in the markets she raises her voice;
21 at the head of the noisy streets she cries out;
    at the entrance of the city gates she speaks:
22 "How long, O simple ones, will you love being simple?
    How long will scoffers delight in their scoffing
    and fools hate knowledge?
23 If you turn at my reproof,[1]
    behold, I will pour out my spirit to you;
    I will make my words known to you.
24 Because I have called and you refused to listen,
    have stretched out my hand and no one has heeded,
25 because you have ignored all my counsel
    and would have none of my reproof,
26 I also will laugh at your calamity;
    I will mock when terror strikes you,
27 when terror strikes you like a storm
    and your calamity comes like a whirlwind,
    when distress and anguish come upon you.

---

[1] Or *Will you turn away at my reproof?*

28 Then they will call upon me,
    but I will not answer;
  they will seek me diligently
    but will not find me.
29 Because they hated knowledge
    and did not choose the
      fear of the Lord,
30 would have none of my counsel
    and despised all my reproof,
31 therefore they shall eat the
      fruit of their way,
    and have their fill of their
      own devices.
32 For the simple are killed by
      their turning away,
    and the complacency of
      fools destroys them;
33 but whoever listens to me
      will dwell secure
    and will be at ease, without
      dread of disaster."

THE VALUE OF WISDOM

2 My son, if you receive my words
    and treasure up my
      commandments with you,
2 making your ear attentive to wisdom
    and inclining your heart
      to understanding;
3 yes, if you call out for insight
    and raise your voice for
      understanding,
4 if you seek it like silver
    and search for it as for
      hidden treasures,
5 then you will understand
      the fear of the Lord
    and find the knowledge of God.
6 For the Lord gives wisdom;
    from his mouth come knowledge
      and understanding;
7 he stores up sound wisdom
      for the upright;
    he is a shield to those who
      walk in integrity,
8 guarding the paths of justice
    and watching over the
      way of his saints.
9 Then you will understand
      righteousness and justice
    and equity, every good path;
10 for wisdom will come into your heart,
    and knowledge will be
      pleasant to your soul;
11 discretion will watch over you,
    understanding will guard you,

12 delivering you from the way of evil,
    from men of perverted speech,
13 who forsake the paths of uprightness
    to walk in the ways of darkness,
14 who rejoice in doing evil
    and delight in the
      perverseness of evil,
15 men whose paths are crooked,
    and who are devious in their ways.

16 So you will be delivered from
      the forbidden[a] woman,
    from the adulteress[b] with
      her smooth words,
17 who forsakes the companion
      of her youth
    and forgets the covenant of her God;
18 for her house sinks down to death,
    and her paths to the departed;[c]
19 none who go to her come back,
    nor do they regain the paths of life.

20 So you will walk in the way of
      the good
    and keep to the paths of
      the righteous.
21 For the upright will inhabit the land,
    and those with integrity
      will remain in it,
22 but the wicked will be cut
      off from the land,
    and the treacherous will
      be rooted out of it.

TRUST IN THE LORD WITH ALL YOUR HEART

3 My son, do not forget my teaching,
    but let your heart keep my
      commandments,
2 for length of days and years of life
    and peace they will add to you.
3 Let not steadfast love and
      faithfulness forsake you;
    bind them round your neck;
    write them on the tablet
      of your heart.
4 So you will find favour and
      good success[d]
    in the sight of God and man.

5 Trust in the Lord with all your heart,
    and do not lean on your own
      understanding.

---
[a]Hebrew *strange* [b]Hebrew *foreign woman* [c]Hebrew *to the Rephaim*
[d]Or *repute*

6 In all your ways acknowledge him,
  and he will make straight
    your paths.
7 Be not wise in your own eyes;
  fear the LORD, and turn
    away from evil.
8 It will be healing to your flesh[a]
  and refreshment[b] to your bones.

9 Honour the LORD with your wealth
  and with the firstfruits of
    all your produce;
10 then your barns will be
    filled with plenty,
  and your vats will be
    bursting with wine.

11 My son, do not despise the
    LORD's discipline
  or be weary of his reproof,
12 for the LORD reproves him
    whom he loves,
  as a father the son in whom
    he delights.

BLESSED IS THE ONE WHO FINDS WISDOM

13 Blessed is the one who finds wisdom,
  and the one who gets
    understanding,
14 for the gain from her is better
    than gain from silver
  and her profit better than gold.
15 She is more precious than jewels,
  and nothing you desire can
    compare with her.
16 Long life is in her right hand;
  in her left hand are riches
    and honour.
17 Her ways are ways of pleasantness,
  and all her paths are peace.
18 She is a tree of life to those
    who lay hold of her;
  those who hold her fast are
    called blessed.

19 The LORD by wisdom
    founded the earth;
  by understanding he
    established the heavens;
20 by his knowledge the deeps
    broke open,
  and the clouds drop down the dew.

21 My son, do not lose sight of these—
  keep sound wisdom and
    discretion,
22 and they will be life for your soul
  and adornment for your neck.
23 Then you will walk on your
    way securely,
  and your foot will not stumble.
24 If you lie down, you will not be afraid;
  when you lie down, your
    sleep will be sweet.
25 Do not be afraid of sudden terror
  or of the ruin[c] of the wicked,
    when it comes,
26 for the LORD will be your confidence
  and will keep your foot
    from being caught.
27 Do not withhold good from
    those to whom it is due,[d]
  when it is in your power to do it.

28 Do not say to your neighbour,
    "Go, and come again,
    tomorrow I will give it"—when
    you have it with you.
29 Do not plan evil against
    your neighbour,
  who dwells trustingly beside you.
30 Do not contend with a man
    for no reason,
  when he has done you no harm.
31 Do not envy a man of violence
  and do not choose any of his ways,
32 for the devious person is an
    abomination to the LORD,
  but the upright are in his
    confidence.
33 The LORD's curse is on the
    house of the wicked,
  but he blesses the dwelling
    of the righteous.
34 Towards the scorners he is scornful,
  but to the humble he gives favour.[e]
35 The wise will inherit honour,
  but fools get[f] disgrace.

A FATHER'S WISE INSTRUCTION

4 Hear, O sons, a father's instruction,
    and be attentive, that you
    may gain[g] insight,
2 for I give you good precepts;
  do not forsake my teaching.
3 When I was a son with my father,
  tender, the only one in the
    sight of my mother,

---

[a]Hebrew *navel* [b]Or *medicine* [c]Hebrew *storm* [d]Hebrew *Do not withhold good from its owners* [e]Or *grace* [f]The meaning of the Hebrew word is uncertain [g]Hebrew *know*

4   he taught me and said to me,
"Let your heart hold fast my words;
    keep my commandments, and live.
5   Get wisdom; get insight;
    do not forget, and do not turn away
      from the words of my mouth.
6   Do not forsake her, and she
    will keep you;
    love her, and she will guard you.
7   The beginning of wisdom is
    this: Get wisdom,
    and whatever you get, get insight.
8   Prize her highly, and she will exalt you;
    she will honour you if you
      embrace her.
9   She will place on your head
    a graceful garland;
    she will bestow on you a
      beautiful crown."

10   Hear, my son, and accept my words,
     that the years of your life
       may be many.
11   I have taught you the way of wisdom;
     I have led you in the paths
       of uprightness.
12   When you walk, your step will
     not be hampered,
     and if you run, you will not
       stumble.
13   Keep hold of instruction; do not let go;
     guard her, for she is your life.
14   Do not enter the path of the wicked,
     and do not walk in the
       way of the evil.
15   Avoid it; do not go on it;
     turn away from it and pass on.
16   For they cannot sleep unless
     they have done wrong;
     they are robbed of sleep unless they
       have made someone stumble.
17   For they eat the bread of wickedness
     and drink the wine of violence.
18   But the path of the righteous is
     like the light of dawn,
     which shines brighter and
       brighter until full day.
19   The way of the wicked is like
     deep darkness;
     they do not know over what
       they stumble.

20   My son, be attentive to my words;
     incline your ear to my sayings.
21   Let them not escape from your sight;
     keep them within your heart.
22   For they are life to those
     who find them,
     and healing to all their[a] flesh.
23   Keep your heart with all vigilance,
     for from it flow the springs of life.
24   Put away from you crooked speech,
     and put devious talk far from you.
25   Let your eyes look directly forwards,
     and your gaze be straight before you.
26   Ponder[b] the path of your feet;
     then all your ways will be sure.
27   Do not swerve to the right or to the left;
     turn your foot away from evil.

WARNING AGAINST ADULTERY

5 My son, be attentive to my wisdom;
    incline your ear to my
      understanding,
2   that you may keep discretion,
    and your lips may guard knowledge.
3   For the lips of a forbidden[c]
    woman drip honey,
    and her speech[d] is smoother
      than oil,
4   but in the end she is bitter
    as wormwood,
    sharp as a two-edged sword.
5   Her feet go down to death;
    her steps follow the path to[e] Sheol;
6   she does not ponder the path of life;
    her ways wander, and she
      does not know it.

7   And now, O sons, listen to me,
    and do not depart from the
      words of my mouth.
8   Keep your way far from her,
    and do not go near the
      door of her house,
9   lest you give your honour to others
    and your years to the merciless,
10   lest strangers take their fill
     of your strength,
     and your labours go to the
       house of a foreigner,
11   and at the end of your life you groan,
     when your flesh and body
       are consumed,
12   and you say, "How I hated discipline,
     and my heart despised reproof!
13   I did not listen to the voice
     of my teachers
     or incline my ear to my instructors.

---

[a] Hebrew *his* [b] Or *Make level* [c] Hebrew *strange*; also verse 20
[d] Hebrew *palate* [e] Hebrew *lay hold of*

¹⁴ I am at the brink of utter ruin
   in the assembled congregation."

¹⁵ Drink water from your own cistern,
   flowing water from your own well.
¹⁶ Should your springs be
      scattered abroad,
   streams of water in the streets?
¹⁷ Let them be for yourself alone,
   and not for strangers with you.
¹⁸ Let your fountain be blessed,
   and rejoice in the wife of your youth,
¹⁹   a lovely deer, a graceful doe.
   Let her breasts fill you at all
      times with delight;
   be intoxicated[a] always in her love.
²⁰ Why should you be intoxicated, my
      son, with a forbidden woman
   and embrace the bosom of
      an adulteress?[b]
²¹ For a man's ways are before
      the eyes of the LORD,
   and he ponders[c] all his paths.
²² The iniquities of the wicked
      ensnare him,
   and he is held fast in the
      cords of his sin.
²³ He dies for lack of discipline,
   and because of his great
      folly he is led astray.

PRACTICAL WARNINGS

6 My son, if you have put up security
      for your neighbour,
   have given your pledge
      for a stranger,
² if you are snared in the words
      of your mouth,
   caught in the words of your mouth,
³ then do this, my son, and
      save yourself,
   for you have come into the
      hand of your neighbour:
   go, hasten,[d] and plead urgently
      with your neighbour.
⁴ Give your eyes no sleep
   and your eyelids no slumber;
⁵ save yourself like a gazelle from
      the hand of the hunter,[e]
   like a bird from the hand
      of the fowler.

⁶ Go to the ant, O sluggard;
   consider her ways, and be wise.
⁷ Without having any chief,
      officer, or ruler,
⁸ she prepares her bread in summer
   and gathers her food in harvest.
⁹ How long will you lie there,
      O sluggard?
   When will you arise from
      your sleep?
¹⁰ A little sleep, a little slumber,
   a little folding of the hands to rest,
¹¹ and poverty will come upon
      you like a robber,
   and want like an armed man.

¹² A worthless person, a wicked man,
   goes about with crooked speech,
¹³ winks with his eyes, signals[f]
      with his feet,
   points with his finger,
¹⁴ with perverted heart devises evil,
   continually sowing discord;
¹⁵ therefore calamity will come
      upon him suddenly;
   in a moment he will be broken
      beyond healing.

¹⁶ There are six things that
      the LORD hates,
   seven that are an
      abomination to him:
¹⁷ haughty eyes, a lying tongue,
   and hands that shed innocent blood,
¹⁸ a heart that devises wicked plans,
   feet that make haste to run to evil,
¹⁹ a false witness who breathes out lies,
   and one who sows discord
      among brothers.

WARNINGS AGAINST ADULTERY

²⁰ My son, keep your father's
      commandment,
   and forsake not your
      mother's teaching.
²¹ Bind them on your heart always;
   tie them round your neck.
²² When you walk, they[g] will lead you;
   when you lie down, they
      will watch over you;
   and when you awake, they
      will talk with you.
²³ For the commandment is a lamp
   and the teaching a light,
   and the reproofs of discipline
      are the way of life,

---

[a]Hebrew *be led astray*; also verse 20. [b]Hebrew *a foreign woman*
[c]Or *makes level* [d]Or *humble yourself* [e]Hebrew *lacks of the hunter*
[f]Hebrew *scrapes* [g]Hebrew *it*; three times in this verse

24 to preserve you from the evil woman,[a]
   from the smooth tongue
      of the adulteress.[b]
25 Do not desire her beauty in your heart,
   and do not let her capture you
      with her eyelashes;
26 for the price of a prostitute is
      only a loaf of bread,[c]
   but a married woman[d] hunts
      down a precious life.
27 Can a man carry fire next to his chest
   and his clothes not be burned?
28 Or can one walk on hot coals
   and his feet not be scorched?
29 So is he who goes in to his
      neighbour's wife;
   none who touches her will
      go unpunished.
30 People do not despise a
      thief if he steals
   to satisfy his appetite when
      he is hungry,
31 but if he is caught, he will
      pay sevenfold;
   he will give all the goods
      of his house.
32 He who commits adultery lacks
      sense;
   he who does it destroys himself.
33 He will get wounds and dishonour,
   and his disgrace will not
      be wiped away.
34 For jealousy makes a man furious,
   and he will not spare when
      he takes revenge.
35 He will accept no compensation;
   he will refuse though you
      multiply gifts.

WARNING AGAINST THE ADULTERESS

7 My son, keep my words
   and treasure up my
      commandments with you;
2 keep my commandments and live;
   keep my teaching as the
      apple of your eye;
3 bind them on your fingers;
   write them on the tablet
      of your heart.
4 Say to wisdom, "You are my sister",
   and call insight your
      intimate friend,
5 to keep you from the
      forbidden[e] woman,
   from the adulteress[f] with
      her smooth words.

6 For at the window of my house
   I have looked out through my lattice,
7 and I have seen among the simple,
   I have perceived among the youths,
      a young man lacking sense,
8 passing along the street
      near her corner,
   taking the road to her house
9 in the twilight, in the evening,
   at the time of night and darkness.
10 And behold, the woman meets him,
      dressed as a prostitute,
         wily of heart.[g]
11 She is loud and wayward;
   her feet do not stay at home;
12 now in the street, now in the market,
   and at every corner she lies in wait.
13 She seizes him and kisses him,
   and with bold face she says to him,
14 "I had to offer sacrifices,[h]
   and today I have paid my vows;
15 so now I have come out to meet you,
   to seek you eagerly, and I
      have found you.
16 I have spread my couch
      with coverings,
   coloured linens from
      Egyptian linen;
17 I have perfumed my bed with myrrh,
   aloes, and cinnamon.
18 Come, let us take our fill of
      love till morning;
   let us delight ourselves with love.
19 For my husband is not at home;
   he has gone on a long journey;
20 he took a bag of money with him;
   at full moon he will come home."
21 With much seductive speech
      she persuades him;
   with her smooth talk she
      compels him.
22 All at once he follows her,
   as an ox goes to the slaughter,
   or as a stag is caught fast[i]
23 till an arrow pierces its liver;
   as a bird rushes into a snare;
   he does not know that it will
      cost him his life.

---

[a]Revocalization (compare Septuagint) yields *from the wife of a neighbour* [b]Hebrew *the foreign woman* [c]Or (compare Septuagint, Syriac, Vulgate) *for a prostitute leaves a man with nothing but a loaf of bread* [d]Hebrew *a man's wife* [e]Hebrew *strange* [f]Hebrew *the foreign woman* [g]Hebrew *guarded in heart* [h]Hebrew *peace offerings* [i]Probable reading (compare Septuagint, Vulgate, Syriac); Hebrew *as a chain to discipline a fool*

24 And now, O sons, listen to me,
and be attentive to the
words of my mouth.
25 Let not your heart turn
aside to her ways;
do not stray into her paths,
26 for many a victim has she laid low,
and all her slain are a mighty throng.
27 Her house is the way to Sheol,
going down to the chambers
of death.

THE BLESSINGS OF WISDOM

8 Does not wisdom call?
Does not understanding raise
her voice?
2 On the heights beside the way,
at the crossroads she
takes her stand;
3 beside the gates in front of the town,
at the entrance of the portals
she cries aloud:
4 "To you, O men, I call,
and my cry is to the children of man.
5 O simple ones, learn prudence;
O fools, learn sense.
6 Hear, for I will speak noble things,
and from my lips will come
what is right,
7 for my mouth will utter truth;
wickedness is an abomination
to my lips.
8 All the words of my mouth
are righteous;
there is nothing twisted or
crooked in them.
9 They are all straight to him
who understands,
and right to those who
find knowledge.
10 Take my instruction instead of silver,
and knowledge rather
than choice gold,
11 for wisdom is better than jewels,
and all that you may desire
cannot compare with her.

12 "I, wisdom, dwell with prudence,
and I find knowledge and discretion.
13 The fear of the LORD is hatred of evil.
Pride and arrogance and the way of evil
and perverted speech I hate.
14 I have counsel and sound wisdom;
I have insight; I have strength.
15 By me kings reign,
and rulers decree what is just;
16 by me princes rule,
and nobles, all who govern justly.[a]
17 I love those who love me,
and those who seek me
diligently find me.
18 Riches and honour are with me,
enduring wealth and
righteousness.
19 My fruit is better than gold,
even fine gold,
and my yield than choice silver.
20 I walk in the way of righteousness,
in the paths of justice,
21 granting an inheritance to
those who love me,
and filling their treasuries.

22 "The LORD possessed[b] me at the
beginning of his work,[c]
the first of his acts of old.
23 Ages ago I was set up,
at the first, before the
beginning of the earth.
24 When there were no depths
I was brought forth,
when there were no springs
abounding with water.
25 Before the mountains had
been shaped,
before the hills, I was brought forth,
26 before he had made the earth
with its fields,
or the first of the dust of the world.
27 When he established the
heavens, I was there;
when he drew a circle on
the face of the deep,
28 when he made firm the skies above,
when he established[d] the
fountains of the deep,
29 when he assigned to the sea its limit,
so that the waters might not
transgress his command,
when he marked out the
foundations of the earth,
30 then I was beside him, like
a master workman,
and I was daily his[e] delight,
rejoicing before him always,
31 rejoicing in his inhabited world
and delighting in the
children of man.

---
[a]Most Hebrew manuscripts; many Hebrew manuscripts, Septuagint *govern the earth* [b]Or *fathered*; Septuagint *created* [c]Hebrew *way* [d]The meaning of the Hebrew is uncertain [e]Or *daily filled with*

32 "And now, O sons, listen to me:
    blessed are those who keep my ways.
33 Hear instruction and be wise,
    and do not neglect it.
34 Blessed is the one who listens to me,
    watching daily at my gates,
    waiting beside my doors.
35 For whoever finds me finds life
    and obtains favour from the LORD,
36 but he who fails to find me
    injures himself;
    all who hate me love death."

THE WAY OF WISDOM

9

Wisdom has built her house;
    she has hewn her seven pillars.
² She has slaughtered her beasts;
    she has mixed her wine;
    she has also set her table.
³ She has sent out her young women to call
    from the highest places in the town,
⁴ "Whoever is simple, let him turn in here!"
    To him who lacks sense she says,
⁵ "Come, eat of my bread
    and drink of the wine I have mixed.
⁶ Leave your simple ways,^{a} and live,
    and walk in the way of insight."

⁷ Whoever corrects a scoffer
    gets himself abuse,
    and he who reproves a wicked man incurs injury.
⁸ Do not reprove a scoffer, or
    he will hate you;
    reprove a wise man, and
    he will love you.
⁹ Give instruction^b to a wise man,
    and he will be still wiser;
    teach a righteous man, and he
    will increase in learning.
¹⁰ The fear of the LORD is the
    beginning of wisdom,
    and the knowledge of the
    Holy One is insight.
¹¹ For by me your days will be multiplied,
    and years will be added to your life.
¹² If you are wise, you are
    wise for yourself;
    if you scoff, you alone will bear it.

THE WAY OF FOLLY

¹³ The woman Folly is loud;
    she is seductive^c and
    knows nothing.

¹⁴ She sits at the door of her house;
    she takes a seat on the highest
    places of the town,
¹⁵ calling to those who pass by,
    who are going straight on their way,
¹⁶ "Whoever is simple, let him
    turn in here!"
    And to him who lacks
    sense she says,
¹⁷ "Stolen water is sweet,
    and bread eaten in secret
    is pleasant."
¹⁸ But he does not know that
    the dead^d are there,
    that her guests are in the
    depths of Sheol.

THE PROVERBS OF SOLOMON

10

The proverbs of Solomon.

A wise son makes a glad father,
    but a foolish son is a sorrow to
    his mother.
² Treasures gained by wickedness
    do not profit,
    but righteousness delivers
    from death.
³ The LORD does not let the
    righteous go hungry,
    but he thwarts the craving
    of the wicked.
⁴ A slack hand causes poverty,
    but the hand of the diligent
    makes rich.
⁵ He who gathers in summer
    is a prudent son,
    but he who sleeps in harvest is
    a son who brings shame.
⁶ Blessings are on the head
    of the righteous,
    but the mouth of the wicked
    conceals violence.^{e}
⁷ The memory of the righteous
    is a blessing,
    but the name of the wicked will rot.
⁸ The wise of heart will receive
    commandments,
    but a babbling fool will come to ruin.
⁹ Whoever walks in integrity
    walks securely,
    but he who makes his ways
    crooked will be found out.

---

^{a}Or *Leave the company of the simple* ^{b}Hebrew *lacks instruction* ^{c}Or *full of simpleness* ^{d}Hebrew *Rephaim* ^{e}Or *but violence covers the mouth of the wicked*; also verse 11

10 Whoever winks the eye causes trouble,
   and a babbling fool will come to ruin.
11 The mouth of the righteous
       is a fountain of life,
   but the mouth of the wicked
       conceals violence.
12 Hatred stirs up strife,
   but love covers all offences.
13 On the lips of him who has
       understanding, wisdom is found,
   but a rod is for the back of
       him who lacks sense.
14 The wise lay up knowledge,
   but the mouth of a fool
       brings ruin near.
15 A rich man's wealth is his strong city;
   the poverty of the poor is their ruin.
16 The wage of the righteous leads to life,
   the gain of the wicked to sin.
17 Whoever heeds instruction
       is on the path to life,
   but he who rejects reproof
       leads others astray.
18 The one who conceals hatred
       has lying lips,
   and whoever utters slander is a fool.
19 When words are many,
       transgression is not lacking,
   but whoever restrains his
       lips is prudent.
20 The tongue of the righteous
       is choice silver;
   the heart of the wicked is
       of little worth.
21 The lips of the righteous feed many,
   but fools die for lack of sense.
22 The blessing of the LORD makes rich,
   and he adds no sorrow with it.[a]
23 Doing wrong is like a joke to a fool,
   but wisdom is pleasure to a
       man of understanding.
24 What the wicked dreads will
       come upon him,
   but the desire of the righteous
       will be granted.
25 When the tempest passes, the
       wicked is no more,
   but the righteous is
       established for ever.
26 Like vinegar to the teeth and
       smoke to the eyes,
   so is the sluggard to those
       who send him.
27 The fear of the LORD prolongs life,
   but the years of the wicked
       will be short.
28 The hope of the righteous brings joy,
   but the expectation of the
       wicked will perish.
29 The way of the LORD is a stronghold
       to the blameless,
   but destruction to evildoers.
30 The righteous will never be removed,
   but the wicked will not
       dwell in the land.
31 The mouth of the righteous
       brings forth wisdom,
   but the perverse tongue
       will be cut off.
32 The lips of the righteous know
       what is acceptable,
   but the mouth of the wicked,
       what is perverse.

11 A false balance is an abomination to the LORD,
   but a just weight is his delight.
2 When pride comes, then
       comes disgrace,
   but with the humble is wisdom.
3 The integrity of the upright
       guides them,
   but the crookedness of the
       treacherous destroys them.
4 Riches do not profit in the
       day of wrath,
   but righteousness delivers
       from death.
5 The righteousness of the blameless
       keeps his way straight,
   but the wicked falls by his
       own wickedness.
6 The righteousness of the
       upright delivers them,
   but the treacherous are taken
       captive by their lust.
7 When the wicked dies, his
       hope will perish,
   and the expectation of
       wealth[b] perishes too.
8 The righteous is delivered
       from trouble,
   and the wicked walks into it instead.
9 With his mouth the godless man
       would destroy his neighbour,
   but by knowledge the righteous
       are delivered.
10 When it goes well with the
       righteous, the city rejoices,
   and when the wicked perish there
       are shouts of gladness.

---

[a]Or and toil adds nothing to it   [b]Or of his strength, or of iniquity

11 By the blessing of the upright
a city is exalted,
but by the mouth of the wicked
it is overthrown.
12 Whoever belittles his
neighbour lacks sense,
but a man of understanding
remains silent.
13 Whoever goes about slandering
reveals secrets,
but he who is trustworthy in spirit
keeps a thing covered.
14 Where there is no guidance,
a people falls,
but in an abundance of
counsellors there is safety.
15 Whoever puts up security for a
stranger will surely suffer harm,
but he who hates striking hands
in pledge is secure.
16 A gracious woman gets honour,
and violent men get riches.
17 A man who is kind benefits himself,
but a cruel man hurts himself.
18 The wicked earns deceptive wages,
but one who sows righteousness
gets a sure reward.
19 Whoever is steadfast in
righteousness will live,
but he who pursues evil will die.
20 Those of crooked heart are an
abomination to the LORD,
but those of blameless ways
are his delight.
21 Be assured, an evil person will
not go unpunished,
but the offspring of the righteous
will be delivered.
22 Like a gold ring in a pig's snout
is a beautiful woman
without discretion.
23 The desire of the righteous
ends only in good,
the expectation of the
wicked in wrath.
24 One gives freely, yet grows all the richer;
another withholds what he should
give, and only suffers want.
25 Whoever brings blessing
will be enriched,
and one who waters will
himself be watered.
26 The people curse him who
holds back grain,
but a blessing is on the head
of him who sells it.
27 Whoever diligently seeks
good seeks favour,^{a}
but evil comes to him who
searches for it.
28 Whoever trusts in his riches will fall,
but the righteous will flourish
like a green leaf.
29 Whoever troubles his own household
will inherit the wind,
and the fool will be servant
to the wise of heart.
30 The fruit of the righteous
is a tree of life,
and whoever captures souls is wise.
31 If the righteous is repaid on earth,
how much more the wicked
and the sinner!

12

Whoever loves discipline loves
knowledge,
but he who hates reproof
is stupid.
2 A good man obtains favour
from the LORD,
but a man of evil devices
he condemns.
3 No one is established by wickedness,
but the root of the righteous
will never be moved.
4 An excellent wife is the crown
of her husband,
but she who brings shame is like
rottenness in his bones.
5 The thoughts of the righteous are just;
the counsels of the wicked
are deceitful.
6 The words of the wicked lie
in wait for blood,
but the mouth of the upright
delivers them.
7 The wicked are overthrown
and are no more,
but the house of the
righteous will stand.
8 A man is commended according
to his good sense,
but one of twisted mind is despised.
9 Better to be lowly and have a servant
than to play the great man
and lack bread.
10 Whoever is righteous has regard
for the life of his beast,
but the mercy of the wicked is cruel.
11 Whoever works his land will
have plenty of bread,

---

^{a}Or *acceptance*

but he who follows worthless
      pursuits lacks sense.
12 Whoever is wicked covets the
      spoil of evildoers,
   but the root of the righteous
      bears fruit.
13 An evil man is ensnared by the
      transgression of his lips,[a]
   but the righteous escapes
      from trouble.
14 From the fruit of his mouth a man
      is satisfied with good,
   and the work of a man's hand
      comes back to him.
15 The way of a fool is right
      in his own eyes,
   but a wise man listens to advice.
16 The vexation of a fool is
      known at once,
   but the prudent ignores an insult.
17 Whoever speaks[b] the truth
      gives honest evidence,
   but a false witness utters deceit.
18 There is one whose rash words
      are like sword thrusts,
   but the tongue of the wise
      brings healing.
19 Truthful lips endure for ever,
   but a lying tongue is but
      for a moment.
20 Deceit is in the heart of those
      who devise evil,
   but those who plan peace
      have joy.
21 No ill befalls the righteous,
   but the wicked are filled
      with trouble.
22 Lying lips are an abomination
      to the LORD,
   but those who act faithfully
      are his delight.
23 A prudent man conceals knowledge,
   but the heart of fools
      proclaims folly.
24 The hand of the diligent will rule,
   while the slothful will be
      put to forced labour.
25 Anxiety in a man's heart
      weighs him down,
   but a good word makes him glad.
26 One who is righteous is a guide
      to his neighbour,[c]
   but the way of the wicked
      leads them astray.
27 Whoever is slothful will not
      roast his game,
   but the diligent man will get
      precious wealth.[d]
28 In the path of righteousness is life,
   and in its pathway there is no death.

13

A wise son hears his father's
      instruction,
   but a scoffer does not listen
      to rebuke.
2 From the fruit of his mouth a
      man eats what is good,
   but the desire of the treacherous
      is for violence.
3 Whoever guards his mouth
      preserves his life;
   he who opens wide his lips
      comes to ruin.
4 The soul of the sluggard craves
      and gets nothing,
   while the soul of the diligent
      is richly supplied.
5 The righteous hates falsehood,
   but the wicked brings shame[e]
      and disgrace.
6 Righteousness guards him
      whose way is blameless,
   but sin overthrows the wicked.
7 One pretends to be rich,[f]
      yet has nothing;
   another pretends to be poor,[g]
      yet has great wealth.
8 The ransom of a man's life
      is his wealth,
   but a poor man hears no threat.
9 The light of the righteous rejoices,
   but the lamp of the wicked
      will be put out.
10 By insolence comes nothing but strife,
   but with those who take
      advice is wisdom.
11 Wealth gained hastily[h] will dwindle,
   but whoever gathers little by
      little will increase it.
12 Hope deferred makes the heart sick,
   but a desire fulfilled is a tree of life.
13 Whoever despises the word[i] brings
      destruction on himself,
   but he who reveres the
      commandment[j] will
      be rewarded.
14 The teaching of the wise is
      a fountain of life,

---

[a] Or *In the transgression of the lips, there is an evil snare*
[b] Hebrew *breathes out* [c] Or *The righteous chooses his friends carefully*
[d] Or *but diligence is precious wealth* [e] Or *stench* [f] Or *One makes himself rich* [g] Or *another makes himself poor* [h] Or *by fraud*
[i] Or *a word* [j] Or *a commandment*

that one may turn away from
    the snares of death.
15 Good sense wins favour,
    but the way of the treacherous
        is their ruin.*a*
16 Every prudent man acts
        with knowledge,
    but a fool flaunts his folly.
17 A wicked messenger falls into
        trouble,
    but a faithful envoy brings healing.
18 Poverty and disgrace come to him
        who ignores instruction,
    but whoever heeds reproof
        is honoured.
19 A desire fulfilled is sweet to the soul,
    but to turn away from evil is an
        abomination to fools.
20 Whoever walks with the
        wise becomes wise,
    but the companion of fools
        will suffer harm.
21 Disaster*b* pursues sinners,
    but the righteous are
        rewarded with good.
22 A good man leaves an inheritance
        to his children's children,
    but the sinner's wealth is laid
        up for the righteous.
23 The fallow ground of the poor
        would yield much food,
    but it is swept away
        through injustice.
24 Whoever spares the rod hates his son,
    but he who loves him is diligent
        to discipline him.*c*
25 The righteous has enough to
        satisfy his appetite,
    but the belly of the wicked
        suffers want.

14

The wisest of women builds
    her house,
but folly with her own hands
    tears it down.
2 Whoever walks in uprightness
    fears the Lord,
    but he who is devious in his
        ways despises him.
3 By the mouth of a fool comes
        a rod for his back,*d*
    but the lips of the wise will
        preserve them.
4 Where there are no oxen, the
        manger is clean,
    but abundant crops come by
        the strength of the ox.
5 A faithful witness does not lie,
    but a false witness breathes out lies.
6 A scoffer seeks wisdom in vain,
    but knowledge is easy for a
        man of understanding.
7 Leave the presence of a fool,
    for there you do not meet
        words of knowledge.
8 The wisdom of the prudent
        is to discern his way,
    but the folly of fools is deceiving.
9 Fools mock at the guilt offering,
    but the upright enjoy acceptance.*e*
10 The heart knows its own bitterness,
    and no stranger shares its joy.
11 The house of the wicked
        will be destroyed,
    but the tent of the upright
        will flourish.
12 There is a way that seems right to a man,
    but its end is the way to death.*f*
13 Even in laughter the heart may ache,
    and the end of joy may be grief.
14 The backslider in heart will be filled
        with the fruit of his ways,
    and a good man will be filled
        with the fruit of his ways.
15 The simple believes everything,
    but the prudent gives
        thought to his steps.
16 One who is wise is cautious*g* and
        turns away from evil,
    but a fool is reckless and careless.
17 A man of quick temper acts foolishly,
    and a man of evil devices is hated.
18 The simple inherit folly,
    but the prudent are crowned
        with knowledge.
19 The evil bow down before the good,
    the wicked at the gates of
        the righteous.
20 The poor is disliked even
        by his neighbour,
    but the rich has many friends.
21 Whoever despises his
        neighbour is a sinner,
    but blessed is he who is
        generous to the poor.
22 Do they not go astray who devise evil?
    Those who devise good meet*h*
        steadfast love and faithfulness.

---

*a*Probable reading (compare Septuagint, Syriac, Vulgate); Hebrew *is rugged*, or *is an enduring rut* *b*Or *Evil* *c*Or *who loves him disciplines him early* *d*Or *In the mouth of a fool is a rod of pride* *e*Hebrew *but among the upright is acceptance* *f*Hebrew *ways of death* *g*Or *fears* [the Lord] *h*Or *show*

23 In all toil there is profit,
     but mere talk tends only to poverty.
24 The crown of the wise is their wealth,
     but the folly of fools brings folly.
25 A truthful witness saves lives,
     but one who breathes out
       lies is deceitful.
26 In the fear of the Lord one has
       strong confidence,
     and his children will have a refuge.
27 The fear of the Lord is a
       fountain of life,
     that one may turn away from
       the snares of death.
28 In a multitude of people is
       the glory of a king,
     but without people a
       prince is ruined.
29 Whoever is slow to anger has
       great understanding,
     but he who has a hasty
       temper exalts folly.
30 A tranquil[a] heart gives life to the flesh,
     but envy[b] makes the bones rot.
31 Whoever oppresses a poor
       man insults his Maker,
     but he who is generous to the
       needy honours him.
32 The wicked is overthrown
       through his evildoing,
     but the righteous finds
       refuge in his death.
33 Wisdom rests in the heart of a
       man of understanding,
     but it makes itself known even
       in the midst of fools.[c]
34 Righteousness exalts a nation,
     but sin is a reproach to any people.
35 A servant who deals wisely
       has the king's favour,
     but his wrath falls on one
       who acts shamefully.

15

A soft answer turns away wrath,
   but a harsh word stirs up anger.
2 The tongue of the wise
     commends knowledge,
   but the mouths of fools
     pour out folly.
3 The eyes of the Lord are in every place,
   keeping watch on the evil
     and the good.
4 A gentle[d] tongue is a tree of life,
   but perverseness in it
     breaks the spirit.
5 A fool despises his father's
     instruction,
   but whoever heeds reproof
     is prudent.
6 In the house of the righteous
     there is much treasure,
   but trouble befalls the income
     of the wicked.
7 The lips of the wise spread knowledge;
   not so the hearts of fools.[e]
8 The sacrifice of the wicked is an
     abomination to the Lord,
   but the prayer of the upright
     is acceptable to him.
9 The way of the wicked is an
     abomination to the Lord,
   but he loves him who pursues
     righteousness.
10 There is severe discipline for him
     who forsakes the way;
   whoever hates reproof will die.
11 Sheol and Abaddon lie open
     before the Lord;
   how much more the hearts of
     the children of man!
12 A scoffer does not like to be reproved;
   he will not go to the wise.
13 A glad heart makes a cheerful face,
   but by sorrow of heart the
     spirit is crushed.
14 The heart of him who has
     understanding seeks knowledge,
   but the mouths of fools feed
     on folly.
15 All the days of the afflicted are evil,
   but the cheerful of heart has
     a continual feast.
16 Better is a little with the
     fear of the Lord
   than great treasure and
     trouble with it.
17 Better is a dinner of herbs where
     love is
   than a fattened ox and hatred with it.
18 A hot-tempered man stirs up strife,
   but he who is slow to anger
     quiets contention.
19 The way of a sluggard is like
     a hedge of thorns,
   but the path of the upright
     is a level highway.
20 A wise son makes a glad father,
   but a foolish man despises
     his mother.

---

[a] Or healing [b] Or jealousy [c] Or Wisdom rests quietly in the heart of a man of understanding, but makes itself known in the midst of fools [d] Or healing [e] Or the hearts of fools are not steadfast

21 Folly is a joy to him who lacks sense,
   but a man of understanding
     walks straight ahead.
22 Without counsel plans fail,
   but with many advisers
     they succeed.
23 To make an apt answer is
     a joy to a man,
   and a word in season, how good it is!
24 The path of life leads upwards
     for the prudent,
   that he may turn away from
     Sheol beneath.
25 The LORD tears down the
     house of the proud
   but maintains the widow's
     boundaries.
26 The thoughts of the wicked are an
     abomination to the LORD,
   but gracious words are pure.
27 Whoever is greedy for unjust gain
     troubles his own household,
   but he who hates bribes will live.
28 The heart of the righteous
     ponders how to answer,
   but the mouth of the wicked
     pours out evil things.
29 The LORD is far from the wicked,
   but he hears the prayer of
     the righteous.
30 The light of the eyes rejoices the heart,
   and good news refreshes*a* the bones.
31 The ear that listens to life-
     giving reproof
   will dwell among the wise.
32 Whoever ignores instruction
     despises himself,
   but he who listens to reproof
     gains intelligence.
33 The fear of the LORD is
     instruction in wisdom,
   and humility comes before honour.

16

The plans of the heart belong
     to man,
   but the answer of the tongue is
     from the LORD.
2 All the ways of a man are pure
     in his own eyes,
   but the LORD weighs the spirit.*b*
3 Commit your work to the LORD,
   and your plans will be established.
4 The LORD has made everything
     for its purpose,
   even the wicked for the
     day of trouble.

5 Everyone who is arrogant in heart is
     an abomination to the LORD;
   be assured, he will not go
     unpunished.
6 By steadfast love and faithfulness
     iniquity is atoned for,
   and by the fear of the LORD one
     turns away from evil.
7 When a man's ways please the LORD,
   he makes even his enemies to
     be at peace with him.
8 Better is a little with righteousness
   than great revenues with injustice.
9 The heart of man plans his way,
   but the LORD establishes his steps.
10 An oracle is on the lips of a king;
    his mouth does not sin
      in judgement.
11 A just balance and scales
      are the LORD's;
    all the weights in the bag
      are his work.
12 It is an abomination to kings to do evil,
    for the throne is established
      by righteousness.
13 Righteous lips are the delight of a king,
    and he loves him who speaks
      what is right.
14 A king's wrath is a messenger of death,
    and a wise man will appease it.
15 In the light of a king's face there is life,
    and his favour is like the clouds
      that bring the spring rain.
16 How much better to get
      wisdom than gold!
    To get understanding is to be
      chosen rather than silver.
17 The highway of the upright
      turns aside from evil;
    whoever guards his way
      preserves his life.
18 Pride goes before destruction,
    and a haughty spirit before a fall.
19 It is better to be of a lowly
      spirit with the poor
    than to divide the spoil
      with the proud.
20 Whoever gives thought to the
      word*c* will discover good,
    and blessed is he who
      trusts in the LORD.
21 The wise of heart is called discerning,
    and sweetness of speech
      increases persuasiveness.

---
*a*Hebrew *makes fat* *b*Or *spirits* *c*Or *to a matter*

6 Many seek the favour of a
 generous man,^a
 and everyone is a friend to a
 man who gives gifts.
7 All a poor man's brothers hate him;
 how much more do his friends
 go far from him!
 He pursues them with words,
 but does not have them.^b
8 Whoever gets sense loves
 his own soul;
 he who keeps understanding
 will discover good.
9 A false witness will not
 go unpunished,
 and he who breathes out
 lies will perish.
10 It is not fitting for a fool
 to live in luxury,
 much less for a slave to
 rule over princes.
11 Good sense makes one slow to anger,
 and it is his glory to overlook
 an offence.
12 A king's wrath is like the
 growling of a lion,
 but his favour is like dew
 on the grass.
13 A foolish son is ruin to his father,
 and a wife's quarrelling is a
 continual dripping of rain.
14 House and wealth are inherited
 from fathers,
 but a prudent wife is from the LORD.
15 Slothfulness casts into a deep sleep,
 and an idle person will
 suffer hunger.
16 Whoever keeps the commandment
 keeps his life;
 he who despises his ways will die.
17 Whoever is generous to the
 poor lends to the LORD,
 and he will repay him for his deed.
18 Discipline your son, for there is hope;
 do not set your heart on
 putting him to death.
19 A man of great wrath will
 pay the penalty,
 for if you deliver him, you will
 only have to do it again.
20 Listen to advice and accept
 instruction,
 that you may gain wisdom
 in the future.
21 Many are the plans in the
 mind of a man,
 but it is the purpose of the
 LORD that will stand.
22 What is desired in a man
 is steadfast love,
 and a poor man is better than a liar.
23 The fear of the LORD leads to life,
 and whoever has it rests satisfied;
 he will not be visited by harm.
24 The sluggard buries his
 hand in the dish
 and will not even bring it
 back to his mouth.
25 Strike a scoffer, and the simple
 will learn prudence;
 reprove a man of understanding,
 and he will gain knowledge.
26 He who does violence to his father
 and chases away his mother
 is a son who brings shame
 and reproach.
27 Cease to hear instruction, my son,
 and you will stray from the
 words of knowledge.
28 A worthless witness mocks at justice,
 and the mouth of the wicked
 devours iniquity.
29 Condemnation is ready for scoffers,
 and beating for the backs of fools.

20

Wine is a mocker, strong
 drink a brawler,
 and whoever is led astray by it
 is not wise.^c
2 The terror of a king is like the
 growling of a lion;
 whoever provokes him to
 anger forfeits his life.
3 It is an honour for a man to
 keep aloof from strife,
 but every fool will be quarrelling.
4 The sluggard does not plough
 in the autumn;
 he will seek at harvest and
 have nothing.
5 The purpose in a man's heart
 is like deep water,
 but a man of understanding
 will draw it out.
6 Many a man proclaims his
 own steadfast love,
 but a faithful man who can find?
7 The righteous who walks
 in his integrity—
 blessed are his children after him!

---

^aOr *of a noble* ^bThe meaning of the Hebrew sentence is uncertain
^cOr *will not become wise*

8 A king who sits on the throne
   of judgement
   winnows all evil with his eyes.
9 Who can say, "I have made
   my heart pure;
   I am clean from my sin"?
10 Unequal[a] weights and
   unequal measures
   are both alike an abomination
   to the LORD.
11 Even a child makes himself
   known by his acts,
   by whether his conduct is
   pure and upright.[b]
12 The hearing ear and the seeing eye,
   the LORD has made them both.
13 Love not sleep, lest you
   come to poverty;
   open your eyes, and you will
   have plenty of bread.
14 "Bad, bad," says the buyer,
   but when he goes away,
   then he boasts.
15 There is gold and abundance
   of costly stones,
   but the lips of knowledge
   are a precious jewel.
16 Take a man's garment when he has
   put up security for a stranger,
   and hold it in pledge when he puts
   up security for foreigners.[c]
17 Bread gained by deceit is
   sweet to a man,
   but afterwards his mouth
   will be full of gravel.
18 Plans are established by counsel;
   by wise guidance wage war.
19 Whoever goes about slandering
   reveals secrets;
   therefore do not associate
   with a simple babbler.[d]
20 If one curses his father or his mother,
   his lamp will be put out in
   utter darkness.
21 An inheritance gained hastily
   in the beginning
   will not be blessed in the end.
22 Do not say, "I will repay evil";
   wait for the LORD, and he
   will deliver you.
23 Unequal weights are an
   abomination to the LORD,
   and false scales are not good.
24 A man's steps are from the LORD;
   how then can man
   understand his way?
25 It is a snare to say rashly, "It is holy",
   and to reflect only after
   making vows.
26 A wise king winnows the wicked
   and drives the wheel over them.
27 The spirit[e] of man is the
   lamp of the LORD,
   searching all his innermost parts.
28 Steadfast love and faithfulness
   preserve the king,
   and by steadfast love his
   throne is upheld.
29 The glory of young men is
   their strength,
   but the splendour of old men
   is their grey hair.
30 Blows that wound cleanse away evil;
   strokes make clean the
   innermost parts.

21

The king's heart is a stream of
   water in the hand of
   the LORD;
he turns it wherever he will.
2 Every way of a man is right
   in his own eyes,
   but the LORD weighs the heart.
3 To do righteousness and justice
   is more acceptable to the
   LORD than sacrifice.
4 Haughty eyes and a proud heart,
   the lamp[f] of the wicked, are sin.
5 The plans of the diligent lead
   surely to abundance,
   but everyone who is hasty
   comes only to poverty.
6 The getting of treasures by
   a lying tongue
   is a fleeting vapour and a
   snare of death.[g]
7 The violence of the wicked
   will sweep them away,
   because they refuse to
   do what is just.
8 The way of the guilty is crooked,
   but the conduct of the
   pure is upright.
9 It is better to live in a corner
   of the housetop
   than in a house shared with
   a quarrelsome wife.

---

[a]Or *Two kinds of*; also verse 23 [b]Or *Even a child can dissemble in his actions, though his conduct seems pure and upright* [c]Or *for an adulteress* (compare 27:13) [d]Hebrew *with one who is simple in his lips* [e]Hebrew *breath* [f]Or *the ploughing* [g]Some Hebrew manuscripts, Septuagint, Latin; most Hebrew manuscripts *vapour for those who seek death*

10 The soul of the wicked desires evil;
   his neighbour finds no
     mercy in his eyes.
11 When a scoffer is punished, the
     simple becomes wise;
   when a wise man is instructed,
     he gains knowledge.
12 The Righteous One observes the
     house of the wicked;
   he throws the wicked down to ruin.
13 Whoever closes his ear to
     the cry of the poor
   will himself call out and
     not be answered.
14 A gift in secret averts anger,
   and a concealed bribe,[a] strong wrath.
15 When justice is done, it is a
     joy to the righteous
   but terror to evildoers.
16 One who wanders from the
     way of good sense
   will rest in the assembly of the dead.
17 Whoever loves pleasure will
     be a poor man;
   he who loves wine and oil
     will not be rich.
18 The wicked is a ransom for
     the righteous,
   and the traitor for the upright.
19 It is better to live in a desert land
     than with a quarrelsome
     and fretful woman.
20 Precious treasure and oil are in
     a wise man's dwelling,
   but a foolish man devours it.
21 Whoever pursues righteousness
     and kindness
   will find life, righteousness,
     and honour.
22 A wise man scales the city
     of the mighty
   and brings down the stronghold
     in which they trust.
23 Whoever keeps his mouth
     and his tongue
   keeps himself out of trouble.
24 "Scoffer" is the name of the
     arrogant, haughty man
   who acts with arrogant pride.
25 The desire of the sluggard kills him,
     for his hands refuse to labour.
26 All day long he craves and craves,
     but the righteous gives and
     does not hold back.
27 The sacrifice of the wicked
     is an abomination;
   how much more when he brings
     it with evil intent.
28 A false witness will perish,
   but the word of a man who
     hears will endure.
29 A wicked man puts on a bold face,
   but the upright gives thought
     to[b] his ways.
30 No wisdom, no understanding,
     no counsel
   can avail against the Lord.
31 The horse is made ready for
     the day of battle,
   but the victory belongs to the Lord.

22

A good name is to be chosen
   rather than great riches,
   and favour is better than silver
     or gold.
2 The rich and the poor meet together;
   the Lord is the Maker of them all.
3 The prudent sees danger
     and hides himself,
   but the simple go on and
     suffer for it.
4 The reward for humility and
     fear of the Lord
   is riches and honour and life.[c]
5 Thorns and snares are in the
     way of the crooked;
   whoever guards his soul will
     keep far from them.
6 Train up a child in the way
     he should go;
   even when he is old he will
     not depart from it.
7 The rich rules over the poor,
   and the borrower is the
     slave of the lender.
8 Whoever sows injustice
     will reap calamity,
   and the rod of his fury will fail.
9 Whoever has a bountiful[d]
     eye will be blessed,
   for he shares his bread
     with the poor.
10 Drive out a scoffer, and
     strife will go out,
   and quarrelling and abuse
     will cease.
11 He who loves purity of heart,
   and whose speech is gracious, will
     have the king as his friend.

---

[a]Hebrew *a bribe in the bosom* [b]Or *establishes* [c]Or *The reward for humility is the fear of the Lord, riches and honour and life* [d]Hebrew *good*

PROVERBS 22–23

12 The eyes of the Lord keep watch over knowledge,
     but he overthrows the words of the traitor.
13 The sluggard says, "There is a lion outside!
     I shall be killed in the streets!"
14 The mouth of forbidden[a] women is a deep pit;
     he with whom the Lord is angry will fall into it.
15 Folly is bound up in the heart of a child,
     but the rod of discipline drives it far from him.
16 Whoever oppresses the poor to increase his own wealth,
     or gives to the rich, will only come to poverty.

WORDS OF THE WISE

17 Incline your ear, and hear the words of the wise,
     and apply your heart to my knowledge,
18 for it will be pleasant if you keep them within you,
     if all of them are ready on your lips.
19 That your trust may be in the Lord,
     I have made them known to you today, even to you.
20 Have I not written for you thirty sayings
     of counsel and knowledge,
21 to make you know what is right and true,
     that you may give a true answer to those who sent you?

22 Do not rob the poor, because he is poor,
     or crush the afflicted at the gate,
23 for the Lord will plead their cause
     and rob of life those who rob them.
24 Make no friendship with a man given to anger,
     nor go with a wrathful man,
25 lest you learn his ways
     and entangle yourself in a snare.
26 Be not one of those who give pledges,
     who put up security for debts.
27 If you have nothing with which to pay,
     why should your bed be taken from under you?
28 Do not move the ancient landmark
     that your fathers have set.
29 Do you see a man skilful in his work?
     He will stand before kings;
     he will not stand before obscure men.

23

When you sit down to eat with a ruler,
     observe carefully what[b] is before you,
2 and put a knife to your throat
     if you are given to appetite.
3 Do not desire his delicacies,
     for they are deceptive food.
4 Do not toil to acquire wealth;
     be discerning enough to desist.
5 When your eyes light on it, it is gone,
     for suddenly it sprouts wings,
     flying like an eagle towards heaven.
6 Do not eat the bread of a man who is stingy;[c]
     do not desire his delicacies,
7 for he is like one who is inwardly calculating.[d]
     "Eat and drink!" he says to you,
     but his heart is not with you.
8 You will vomit up the morsels that you have eaten,
     and waste your pleasant words.
9 Do not speak in the hearing of a fool,
     for he will despise the good sense of your words.
10 Do not move an ancient landmark
     or enter the fields of the fatherless,
11 for their Redeemer is strong;
     he will plead their cause against you.
12 Apply your heart to instruction
     and your ear to words of knowledge.
13 Do not withhold discipline from a child;
     if you strike him with a rod, he will not die.
14 If you strike him with the rod,
     you will save his soul from Sheol.
15 My son, if your heart is wise,
     my heart too will be glad.
16 My inmost being[e] will exult
     when your lips speak what is right.
17 Let not your heart envy sinners,
     but continue in the fear of the Lord all the day.
18 Surely there is a future,
     and your hope will not be cut off.

---

[a]Hebrew *strange* [b]Or *who* [c]Hebrew *whose eye is evil* [d]Or *for as he calculates in his soul, so is he* [e]Hebrew *My kidneys*

19 Hear, my son, and be wise,
   and direct your heart in the way.
20 Be not among drunkards[a]
   or among gluttonous eaters of meat,
21 for the drunkard and the glutton
   will come to poverty,
   and slumber will clothe
   them with rags.

22 Listen to your father who gave you life,
   and do not despise your mother
   when she is old.
23 Buy truth, and do not sell it;
   buy wisdom, instruction,
   and understanding.
24 The father of the righteous
   will greatly rejoice;
   he who fathers a wise son
   will be glad in him.
25 Let your father and mother be glad;
   let her who bore you rejoice.

26 My son, give me your heart,
   and let your eyes observe[b] my ways.
27 For a prostitute is a deep pit;
   an adulteress[c] is a narrow well.
28 She lies in wait like a robber
   and increases the traitors
   among mankind.

29 Who has woe? Who has sorrow?
   Who has strife? Who has
   complaining?
   Who has wounds without cause?
   Who has redness of eyes?
30 Those who tarry long over wine;
   those who go to try mixed wine.
31 Do not look at wine when it is red,
   when it sparkles in the cup
   and goes down smoothly.
32 In the end it bites like a serpent
   and stings like an adder.
33 Your eyes will see strange things,
   and your heart utter perverse things.
34 You will be like one who lies down
   in the midst of the sea,
   like one who lies on the top of a mast.[d]
35 "They struck me," you will say,[e]
   "but I was not hurt;
   they beat me, but I did not feel it.
   When shall I awake?
   I must have another drink."

24

Be not envious of evil men,
   nor desire to be with them,
2 for their hearts devise violence,
   and their lips talk of trouble.

3 By wisdom a house is built,
   and by understanding it
   is established;
4 by knowledge the rooms are filled
   with all precious and
   pleasant riches.
5 A wise man is full of strength,
   and a man of knowledge
   enhances his might,
6 for by wise guidance you
   can wage your war,
   and in abundance of counsellors
   there is victory.
7 Wisdom is too high for a fool;
   in the gate he does not
   open his mouth.

8 Whoever plans to do evil
   will be called a schemer.
9 The devising[f] of folly is sin,
   and the scoffer is an abomination
   to mankind.

10 If you faint in the day of adversity,
   your strength is small.
11 Rescue those who are being
   taken away to death;
   hold back those who are
   stumbling to the slaughter.
12 If you say, "Behold, we did
   not know this",
   does not he who weighs the
   heart perceive it?
   Does not he who keeps watch
   over your soul know it,
   and will he not repay man
   according to his work?

13 My son, eat honey, for it is good,
   and the drippings of the honeycomb
   are sweet to your taste.
14 Know that wisdom is such to your soul;
   if you find it, there will be a future,
   and your hope will not be cut off.

15 Lie not in wait as a wicked man against
   the dwelling of the righteous;
   do no violence to his home;
16 for the righteous falls seven
   times and rises again,
   but the wicked stumble in
   times of calamity.

---

[a]Hebrew *those who drink too much wine* [b]Or *delight in* [c]Hebrew *a foreign woman* [d]Or *of the rigging* [e]Hebrew lacks *you will say* [f]Or *scheming*

¹⁷ Do not rejoice when your enemy falls,
    and let not your heart be glad
        when he stumbles,
¹⁸ lest the LORD see it and be displeased,
    and turn away his anger from him.

¹⁹ Fret not yourself because of evildoers,
    and be not envious of the wicked,
²⁰ for the evil man has no future;
    the lamp of the wicked
        will be put out.

²¹ My son, fear the LORD and the king,
    and do not join with those
        who do otherwise,
²² for disaster will arise
        suddenly from them,
    and who knows the ruin that will
        come from them both?

MORE SAYINGS OF THE WISE

²³These also are sayings of the wise.

Partiality in judging is not good.
²⁴ Whoever says to the wicked,
        "You are in the right",
    will be cursed by peoples,
        abhorred by nations,
²⁵ but those who rebuke the wicked
        will have delight,
    and a good blessing will
        come upon them.
²⁶ Whoever gives an honest answer
        kisses the lips.

²⁷ Prepare your work outside;
    get everything ready for
        yourself in the field,
    and after that build your house.

²⁸ Be not a witness against your
        neighbour without cause,
    and do not deceive with your lips.
²⁹ Do not say, "I will do to him
        as he has done to me;
    I will pay the man back for
        what he has done."

³⁰ I passed by the field of a sluggard,
    by the vineyard of a man
        lacking sense,
³¹ and behold, it was all overgrown
        with thorns;
    the ground was covered with
        nettles,
    and its stone wall was broken down.

³² Then I saw and considered it;
    I looked and received instruction.
³³ A little sleep, a little slumber,
    a little folding of the hands to rest,
³⁴ and poverty will come upon
        you like a robber,
    and want like an armed man.

MORE PROVERBS OF SOLOMON

25 These also are proverbs of Solomon which the men of Hezekiah king of Judah copied.

² It is the glory of God to conceal things,
    but the glory of kings is to
        search things out.
³ As the heavens for height, and
        the earth for depth,
    so the heart of kings is unsearchable.
⁴ Take away the dross from the silver,
    and the smith has material
        for a vessel;
⁵ take away the wicked from the
        presence of the king,
    and his throne will be established
        in righteousness.
⁶ Do not put yourself forward
        in the king's presence
    or stand in the place of the great,
⁷ for it is better to be told,
        "Come up here",
    than to be put lower in the
        presence of a noble.

What your eyes have seen
⁸ do not hastily bring into court,[a]
    for[b] what will you do in the end,
        when your neighbour puts
            you to shame?
⁹ Argue your case with your
        neighbour himself,
    and do not reveal another's secret,
¹⁰ lest he who hears you bring
        shame upon you,
    and your ill repute have no end.

¹¹ A word fitly spoken
    is like apples of gold in a
        setting of silver.
¹² Like a gold ring or an ornament of gold
    is a wise reprover to a listening ear.
¹³ Like the cold of snow in the
        time of harvest

---

[a]Or *presence of a noble, as your eyes have seen.* ⁸*Do not go hastily out to court*   [b]Hebrew *or else*

is a faithful messenger to
  those who send him;
he refreshes the soul of his masters.
14 Like clouds and wind without rain
  is a man who boasts of a gift
  he does not give.

15 With patience a ruler may
    be persuaded,
  and a soft tongue will break a bone.
16 If you have found honey, eat
    only enough for you,
  lest you have your fill of
    it and vomit it.
17 Let your foot be seldom in your
    neighbour's house,
  lest he have his fill of you
    and hate you.
18 A man who bears false witness
    against his neighbour
  is like a war club, or a sword,
    or a sharp arrow.
19 Trusting in a treacherous man
    in time of trouble
  is like a bad tooth or a foot
    that slips.
20 Whoever sings songs to a heavy heart
  is like one who takes off a
    garment on a cold day,
  and like vinegar on soda.
21 If your enemy is hungry, give
    him bread to eat,
  and if he is thirsty, give him
    water to drink,
22 for you will heap burning
    coals on his head,
  and the LORD will reward you.
23 The north wind brings forth rain,
  and a backbiting tongue,
    angry looks.
24 It is better to live in a corner
    of the housetop
  than in a house shared with
    a quarrelsome wife.
25 Like cold water to a thirsty soul,
  so is good news from a far country.
26 Like a muddied spring or a
    polluted fountain
  is a righteous man who gives
    way before the wicked.
27 It is not good to eat much honey,
  nor is it glorious to seek
    one's own glory.[a]
28 A man without self-control
  is like a city broken into and
    left without walls.

26

Like snow in summer or rain
    in harvest,
  so honour is not fitting for a fool.
2 Like a sparrow in its flitting, like
    a swallow in its flying,
  a curse that is causeless
    does not alight.
3 A whip for the horse, a bridle
    for the donkey,
  and a rod for the back of fools.
4 Answer not a fool according
    to his folly,
  lest you be like him yourself.
5 Answer a fool according to his folly,
  lest he be wise in his own eyes.
6 Whoever sends a message by
    the hand of a fool
  cuts off his own feet and
    drinks violence.
7 Like a lame man's legs, which
    hang useless,
  is a proverb in the mouth of fools.
8 Like one who binds the
    stone in the sling
  is one who gives honour to a fool.
9 Like a thorn that goes up into
    the hand of a drunkard
  is a proverb in the mouth of fools.
10 Like an archer who wounds everyone
  is one who hires a passing
    fool or drunkard.[b]
11 Like a dog that returns to his vomit
  is a fool who repeats his folly.
12 Do you see a man who is wise
    in his own eyes?
  There is more hope for a
    fool than for him.
13 The sluggard says, "There is
    a lion in the road!
  There is a lion in the streets!"
14 As a door turns on its hinges,
  so does a sluggard on his bed.
15 The sluggard buries his
    hand in the dish;
  it wears him out to bring it
    back to his mouth.
16 The sluggard is wiser in his own eyes
  than seven men who can
    answer sensibly.
17 Whoever meddles in a
    quarrel not his own
  is like one who takes a passing
    dog by the ears.

---

[a]The meaning of the Hebrew line is uncertain [b]Or *hires a fool or passers-by*

18 Like a madman who throws
    firebrands, arrows, and death
19 is the man who deceives his neighbour
    and says, "I am only joking!"
20 For lack of wood the fire goes out,
    and where there is no whisperer,
        quarrelling ceases.
21 As charcoal to hot embers
    and wood to fire,
        so is a quarrelsome man
        for kindling strife.
22 The words of a whisperer are
    like delicious morsels;
        they go down into the inner
        parts of the body.
23 Like the glaze^a covering an
    earthen vessel
        are fervent lips with an evil heart.
24 Whoever hates disguises
    himself with his lips
        and harbours deceit in his heart;
25 when he speaks graciously,
    believe him not,
        for there are seven abominations
        in his heart;
26 though his hatred be covered
    with deception,
        his wickedness will be exposed
        in the assembly.
27 Whoever digs a pit will fall into it,
    and a stone will come back on
        him who starts it rolling.
28 A lying tongue hates its victims,
    and a flattering mouth works ruin.

27

Do not boast about tomorrow,
    for you do not know what a day
        may bring.
2 Let another praise you, and
    not your own mouth;
        a stranger, and not your own lips.
3 A stone is heavy, and sand is weighty,
    but a fool's provocation is
        heavier than both.
4 Wrath is cruel, anger is overwhelming,
    but who can stand before jealousy?
5 Better is open rebuke
    than hidden love.
6 Faithful are the wounds of a friend;
    profuse are the kisses of an enemy.
7 One who is full loathes honey,
    but to one who is hungry
        everything bitter is sweet.
8 Like a bird that strays from its nest
    is a man who strays from his home.
9 Oil and perfume make the
    heart glad,
        and the sweetness of a friend comes
        from his earnest counsel.^{b}
10 Do not forsake your friend and
    your father's friend,
        and do not go to your
        brother's house in the
        day of your calamity.
    Better is a neighbour who is near
        than a brother who is far away.
11 Be wise, my son, and make
    my heart glad,
        that I may answer him who
        reproaches me.
12 The prudent sees danger
    and hides himself,
        but the simple go on and
        suffer for it.
13 Take a man's garment when he has
    put up security for a stranger,
        and hold it in pledge when he puts
        up security for an adulteress.^{c}
14 Whoever blesses his neighbour
    with a loud voice,
        rising early in the morning,
        will be counted as cursing.
15 A continual dripping on a rainy day
    and a quarrelsome wife are alike;
16 to restrain her is to restrain the wind
    or to grasp^d oil in one's right hand.
17 Iron sharpens iron,
    and one man sharpens another.^{e}
18 Whoever tends a fig tree
    will eat its fruit,
        and he who guards his master
        will be honoured.
19 As in water face reflects face,
    so the heart of man reflects the man.
20 Sheol and Abaddon are never satisfied,
    and never satisfied are
        the eyes of man.
21 The crucible is for silver, and
    the furnace is for gold,
        and a man is tested by his praise.
22 Crush a fool in a mortar with a pestle
    along with crushed grain,
        yet his folly will not
        depart from him.

23 Know well the condition
    of your flocks,
        and give attention to your herds,

---

^{a}By revocalization; Hebrew *silver of dross* ^{b}Or *and so does the sweetness of a friend that comes from his earnest counsel* ^{c}Hebrew *a foreign woman*; a slight emendation yields (compare Vulgate; see also 20:16) *foreigners* ^{d}Hebrew *to meet with* ^{e}Hebrew *sharpens the face of another*

24 for riches do not last for ever;
   and does a crown endure
      to all generations?
25 When the grass is gone and the
      new growth appears
   and the vegetation of the
      mountains is gathered,
26 the lambs will provide your clothing,
   and the goats the price of a field.
27 There will be enough goats'
      milk for your food,
   for the food of your household
   and maintenance for your girls.

28

1 The wicked flee when no one
      pursues,
   but the righteous are bold as
      a lion.
2 When a land transgresses,
      it has many rulers,
   but with a man of understanding
      and knowledge,
      its stability will long continue.
3 A poor man who oppresses the poor
   is a beating rain that leaves no food.
4 Those who forsake the law
      praise the wicked,
   but those who keep the law
      strive against them.
5 Evil men do not understand justice,
   but those who seek the LORD
      understand it completely.
6 Better is a poor man who
      walks in his integrity
   than a rich man who is
      crooked in his ways.
7 The one who keeps the law is a
      son with understanding,
   but a companion of gluttons
      shames his father.
8 Whoever multiplies his wealth
      by interest and profit[a]
   gathers it for him who is
      generous to the poor.
9 If one turns away his ear from
      hearing the law,
   even his prayer is an abomination.
10 Whoever misleads the upright
      into an evil way
   will fall into his own pit,
   but the blameless will have a
      goodly inheritance.
11 A rich man is wise in his own eyes,
   but a poor man who has
      understanding will find him out.
12 When the righteous triumph,
      there is great glory,
   but when the wicked rise,
      people hide themselves.
13 Whoever conceals his transgressions
      will not prosper,
   but he who confesses and forsakes
      them will obtain mercy.
14 Blessed is the one who fears
      the LORD[b] always,
   but whoever hardens his heart
      will fall into calamity.
15 Like a roaring lion or a charging bear
   is a wicked ruler over a poor people.
16 A ruler who lacks understanding
      is a cruel oppressor,
   but he who hates unjust gain
      will prolong his days.
17 If one is burdened with the
      blood of another,
   he will be a fugitive until death;[c]
      let no one help him.
18 Whoever walks in integrity
      will be delivered,
   but he who is crooked in his
      ways will suddenly fall.
19 Whoever works his land will
      have plenty of bread,
   but he who follows worthless
      pursuits will have
      plenty of poverty.
20 A faithful man will abound
      with blessings,
   but whoever hastens to be rich
      will not go unpunished.
21 To show partiality is not good,
   but for a piece of bread a
      man will do wrong.
22 A stingy man[d] hastens after wealth
   and does not know that poverty
      will come upon him.
23 Whoever rebukes a man will
      afterwards find more favour
   than he who flatters with his tongue.
24 Whoever robs his father or his mother
   and says, "That is no transgression",
   is a companion to a man
      who destroys.
25 A greedy man stirs up strife,
   but the one who trusts in the
      LORD will be enriched.
26 Whoever trusts in his own
      mind is a fool,
   but he who walks in wisdom
      will be delivered.

---

[a]That is, profit that comes from charging interest to the poor [b]Hebrew lacks the LORD [c]Hebrew until the pit [d]Hebrew A man whose eye is evil

²⁷ Whoever gives to the poor
       will not want,
   but he who hides his eyes
       will get many a curse.
²⁸ When the wicked rise, people
       hide themselves,
   but when they perish, the
       righteous increase.

29

He who is often reproved,
       yet stiffens his neck,
   will suddenly be broken beyond
       healing.
² When the righteous increase,
       the people rejoice,
   but when the wicked rule,
       the people groan.
³ He who loves wisdom makes
       his father glad,
   but a companion of prostitutes
       squanders his wealth.
⁴ By justice a king builds up the land,
   but he who exacts gifts[1]
       tears it down.
⁵ A man who flatters his neighbour
   spreads a net for his feet.
⁶ An evil man is ensnared in
       his transgression,
   but a righteous man sings
       and rejoices.
⁷ A righteous man knows the
       rights of the poor;
   a wicked man does not understand
       such knowledge.
⁸ Scoffers set a city aflame,
   but the wise turn away wrath.
⁹ If a wise man has an argument
       with a fool,
   the fool only rages and laughs,
       and there is no quiet.
¹⁰ Bloodthirsty men hate one
       who is blameless
   and seek the life of the upright.[1]
¹¹ A fool gives full vent to his spirit,
   but a wise man quietly holds it back.
¹² If a ruler listens to falsehood,
   all his officials will be wicked.
¹³ The poor man and the oppressor
       meet together;
   the LORD gives light to
       the eyes of both.
¹⁴ If a king faithfully judges the poor,
   his throne will be established
       for ever.
¹⁵ The rod and reproof give wisdom,
   but a child left to himself brings
       shame to his mother.
¹⁶ When the wicked increase,
       transgression increases,
   but the righteous will look
       upon their downfall.
¹⁷ Discipline your son, and he
       will give you rest;
   he will give delight to your heart.
¹⁸ Where there is no prophetic vision
       the people cast off restraint,[1]
   but blessed is he who keeps
       the law.
¹⁹ By mere words a servant is
       not disciplined,
   for though he understands,
       he will not respond.
²⁰ Do you see a man who is
       hasty in his words?
   There is more hope for a
       fool than for him.
²¹ Whoever pampers his servant
       from childhood
   will in the end find him his heir.[1]
²² A man of wrath stirs up strife,
   and one given to anger causes
       much transgression.
²³ One's pride will bring him low,
   but he who is lowly in spirit
       will obtain honour.
²⁴ The partner of a thief hates
       his own life;
   he hears the curse, but
       discloses nothing.
²⁵ The fear of man lays a snare,
   but whoever trusts in the
       LORD is safe.
²⁶ Many seek the face of a ruler,
   but it is from the LORD that
       a man gets justice.
²⁷ An unjust man is an abomination
       to the righteous,
   but one whose way is straight is an
       abomination to the wicked.

THE WORDS OF AGUR

30

The words of Agur son of Jakeh.
The oracle.[1]

The man declares, I am weary, O God;
   I am weary, O God, and worn out.[1]
² Surely I am too stupid to be a man.
   I have not the understanding
       of a man.

---

[1] Or *who taxes heavily* [1] Or *but the upright seek his soul* [1] Or *the people are discouraged* [1] The meaning of the Hebrew word rendered *his heir* is uncertain [1] Or *Jakeh, the man of Massa* [1] Revocalization; Hebrew *The man declares to Ithiel, to Ithiel and Ucal*

3 I have not learned wisdom,
    nor have I knowledge of
      the Holy One.
4 Who has ascended to heaven
      and come down?
  Who has gathered the
      wind in his fists?
  Who has wrapped up the
      waters in a garment?
  Who has established all the
      ends of the earth?
  What is his name, and what
      is his son's name?
  Surely you know!

5 Every word of God proves true;
    he is a shield to those who
      take refuge in him.
6 Do not add to his words,
    lest he rebuke you and you
      be found a liar.

7 Two things I ask of you;
    deny them not to me before I die:
8 Remove far from me
      falsehood and lying;
    give me neither poverty nor riches;
      feed me with the food that
        is needful for me,
9 lest I be full and deny you
      and say, "Who is the LORD?"
    or lest I be poor and steal
      and profane the name of my God.

10 Do not slander a servant to his
        master,
      lest he curse you, and you
        be held guilty.

11 There are those[a] who curse
        their fathers
      and do not bless their mothers.
12 There are those who are clean
        in their own eyes
      but are not washed of their filth.
13 There are those—how lofty
        are their eyes,
      how high their eyelids lift!
14 There are those whose
        teeth are swords,
      whose fangs are knives,
    to devour the poor from off the earth,
      the needy from among mankind.

15 The leech has two daughters:
      Give and Give.[b]
  Three things are never satisfied;
      four never say, "Enough":
16 Sheol, the barren womb,
      the land never satisfied with water,
    and the fire that never
        says, "Enough."

17 The eye that mocks a father
      and scorns to obey a mother
    will be picked out by the
        ravens of the valley
      and eaten by the vultures.

18 Three things are too wonderful for me;
      four I do not understand:
19 the way of an eagle in the sky,
      the way of a serpent on a rock,
    the way of a ship on the high seas,
      and the way of a man with a virgin.

20 This is the way of an adulteress:
      she eats and wipes her mouth
      and says, "I have done no wrong."

21 Under three things the earth trembles;
      under four it cannot bear up:
22 a slave when he becomes king,
      and a fool when he is
        filled with food;
23 an unloved woman when
        she gets a husband,
      and a maidservant when she
        displaces her mistress.

24 Four things on earth are small,
      but they are exceedingly wise:
25 the ants are a people not strong,
      yet they provide their food
        in the summer;
26 the rock badgers are a
        people not mighty,
      yet they make their homes
        in the cliffs;
27 the locusts have no king,
      yet all of them march in rank;
28 the lizard you can take in your hands,
      yet it is in kings' palaces.

29 Three things are stately in their tread;
      four are stately in their stride:
30 the lion, which is mightiest
        among beasts
      and does not turn back before any;

---

[a]Hebrew *There is a generation*; also verses 12, 13, 14 [b]Or *"Give, give,"* they cry

³¹ the strutting cock,ᵃ the he-goat,
  and a king whose army is with him.ᵇ

³² If you have been foolish,
    exalting yourself,
  or if you have been devising evil,
    put your hand on your mouth.
³³ For pressing milk produces curds,
    pressing the nose produces blood,
    and pressing anger produces strife.

THE WORDS OF KING LEMUEL

31 The words of King Lemuel. An oracle
  that his mother taught him:
² What are you doing, my son?ᶜ What
    are you doing, son of my womb?
  What are you doing, son of
    my vows?
³ Do not give your strength to women,
    your ways to those who
    destroy kings.
⁴ It is not for kings, O Lemuel,
    it is not for kings to drink wine,
    or for rulers to take strong drink,
⁵ lest they drink and forget what
    has been decreed
    and pervert the rights of
    all the afflicted.
⁶ Give strong drink to the one
    who is perishing,
    and wine to those in bitter distress;ᵈ
⁷ let them drink and forget their poverty
    and remember their
    misery no more.
⁸ Open your mouth for the mute,
    for the rights of all who
    are destitute.ᵉ
⁹ Open your mouth, judge righteously,
    defend the rights of the
    poor and needy.

THE WOMAN WHO FEARS THE LORD

¹⁰ᶠ An excellent wife who can find?
  She is far more precious
    than jewels.
¹¹ The heart of her husband trusts in her,
    and he will have no lack of gain.
¹² She does him good, and not harm,
    all the days of her life.
¹³ She seeks wool and flax,
    and works with willing hands.
¹⁴ She is like the ships of the merchant;
    she brings her food from afar.
¹⁵ She rises while it is yet night
    and provides food for her household
    and portions for her maidens.
¹⁶ She considers a field and buys it;
    with the fruit of her hands
    she plants a vineyard.
¹⁷ She dresses herselfᵍ with strength
    and makes her arms strong.
¹⁸ She perceives that her
    merchandise is profitable.
  Her lamp does not go out at night.
¹⁹ She puts her hands to the distaff,
    and her hands hold the spindle.
²⁰ She opens her hand to the poor
    and reaches out her hands
    to the needy.
²¹ She is not afraid of snow for
    her household,
  for all her household are
    clothed in scarlet.ʰ
²² She makes bed coverings for herself;
    her clothing is fine linen and purple.
²³ Her husband is known in the gates
    when he sits among the
    elders of the land.
²⁴ She makes linen garments
    and sells them;
  she delivers sashes to the merchant.
²⁵ Strength and dignity are her clothing,
    and she laughs at the time to come.
²⁶ She opens her mouth with wisdom,
    and the teaching of kindness
    is on her tongue.
²⁷ She looks well to the ways
    of her household
  and does not eat the bread
    of idleness.
²⁸ Her children rise up and
    call her blessed;
  her husband also, and he praises her:
²⁹ "Many women have done excellently,
    but you surpass them all."
³⁰ Charm is deceitful, and beauty is vain,
    but a woman who fears the
    LORD is to be praised.
³¹ Give her of the fruit of her hands,
    and let her works praise
    her in the gates.

ᵃOr *the magpie*, or *the greyhound*; Hebrew *girt-of-loins* ᵇOr *against whom there is no rising up* ᶜHebrew *What, my son?* ᵈHebrew *those bitter in soul* ᵉHebrew *are sons of passing away* ᶠVerses 10–31 are an acrostic poem, each verse beginning with the successive letters of the Hebrew alphabet ᵍHebrew *She girds her loins* ʰOr *in double thickness*

ECCLESIASTES

ALL IS VANITY

1 The words of the Preacher,[a] the son of David, king in Jerusalem.

² Vanity[b] of vanities, says the Preacher,
  vanity of vanities! All is vanity.
³ What does man gain by all the toil
  at which he toils under the sun?
⁴ A generation goes, and a
   generation comes,
  but the earth remains for ever.
⁵ The sun rises, and the sun goes down,
  and hastens[c] to the place
   where it rises.
⁶ The wind blows to the south
  and goes round to the north;
round and round goes the wind,
  and on its circuits the wind returns.
⁷ All streams run to the sea,
  but the sea is not full;
to the place where the streams flow,
  there they flow again.
⁸ All things are full of weariness;
  a man cannot utter it;
the eye is not satisfied with seeing,
  nor the ear filled with hearing.
⁹ What has been is what will be,
  and what has been done is
   what will be done,
  and there is nothing new
   under the sun.
¹⁰ Is there a thing of which it is said,
   "See, this is new"?
  It has been already
   in the ages before us.
¹¹ There is no remembrance
   of former things,[d]
  nor will there be any remembrance
   of later things[e] yet to be
  among those who come after.

THE VANITY OF WISDOM

¹²I the Preacher have been king over Israel in Jerusalem. ¹³And I applied my heart[f] to seek and to search out by wisdom all that is done under heaven. It is an unhappy business that God has given to the children of man to be busy with. ¹⁴I have seen everything that is done under the sun, and behold, all is vanity[g] and a striving after wind.[h]

¹⁵   What is crooked cannot be
      made straight,
     and what is lacking cannot
      be counted.

¹⁶I said in my heart, "I have acquired great wisdom, surpassing all who were over Jerusalem before me, and my heart has had great experience of wisdom and knowledge." ¹⁷And I applied my heart to know wisdom and to know madness and folly. I perceived that this also is but a striving after wind.

¹⁸   For in much wisdom is much vexation,
     and he who increases knowledge
      increases sorrow.

THE VANITY OF SELF-INDULGENCE

2 I said in my heart, "Come now, I will test you with pleasure; enjoy yourself." But behold, this also was vanity.[i] ²I said of laughter, "It is mad", and of pleasure, "What use is it?" ³I searched with my heart how to cheer my body with wine—my heart still guiding me with wisdom—and how to lay hold on folly, till I might see what was good for the children of man to do under heaven during the few days of their life. ⁴I made great works. I built houses and planted vineyards for myself. ⁵I made myself gardens and parks, and planted in them all kinds of fruit trees. ⁶I made myself pools from which to water the forest of growing trees. ⁷I bought male and female slaves, and had slaves who were born

---

[a]Or *Convener*, or *Collector*; Hebrew *Qoheleth* (so throughout Ecclesiastes)   [b]The Hebrew term *hebel*, translated *vanity* or *vain*, refers concretely to a "mist", "vapour", or "mere breath", and metaphorically to something that is fleeting or elusive (with different nuances depending on the context). It appears five times in this verse and in 29 other verses in Ecclesiastes   [c]Or *and returns panting*   [d]Or *former people*   [e]Or *later people*   [f]The Hebrew term denotes the centre of one's inner life, including mind, will, and emotions   [g]The Hebrew term *hebel* can refer to a "vapour" or "mere breath" (see note on 1:2)   [h]Or *a feeding on wind*; compare Hosea 12:1 (also in Ecclesiastes 1:17; 2:11, 17, 26; 4:4, 6, 16; 6:9)   [i]The Hebrew term *hebel* can refer to a "vapour" or "mere breath"; also verses 11, 15, 17, 19, 21, 23, 26 (see note on 1:2)

in my house. I had also great possessions of herds and flocks, more than any who had been before me in Jerusalem. ⁸I also gathered for myself silver and gold and the treasure of kings and provinces. I got singers, both men and women, and many concubines,ᵃ the delight of the sons of man.

⁹So I became great and surpassed all who were before me in Jerusalem. Also my wisdom remained with me. ¹⁰And whatever my eyes desired I did not keep from them. I kept my heart from no pleasure, for my heart found pleasure in all my toil, and this was my reward for all my toil. ¹¹Then I considered all that my hands had done and the toil I had expended in doing it, and behold, all was vanity and a striving after wind, and there was nothing to be gained under the sun.

THE VANITY OF LIVING WISELY

¹²So I turned to consider wisdom and madness and folly. For what can the man do who comes after the king? Only what has already been done. ¹³Then I saw that there is more gain in wisdom than in folly, as there is more gain in light than in darkness. ¹⁴The wise person has his eyes in his head, but the fool walks in darkness. And yet I perceived that the same event happens to all of them. ¹⁵Then I said in my heart, "What happens to the fool will happen to me also. Why then have I been so very wise?" And I said in my heart that this also is vanity. ¹⁶For of the wise as of the fool there is no enduring remembrance, seeing that in the days to come all will have been long forgotten. How the wise dies just like the fool! ¹⁷So I hated life, because what is done under the sun was grievous to me, for all is vanity and a striving after wind.

THE VANITY OF TOIL

¹⁸I hated all my toil in which I toil under the sun, seeing that I must leave it to the man who will come after me, ¹⁹and who knows whether he will be wise or a fool? Yet he will be master of all for which I toiled and used my wisdom under the sun. This also is vanity. ²⁰So I turned about and gave my heart up to despair over all the toil of my labours under the sun, ²¹because sometimes a person who has toiled with wisdom and knowledge and skill must leave everything to be enjoyed by someone who did not toil for it. This also is vanity and a great evil. ²²What has a man from all the toil and striving of heart with which he toils beneath the sun? ²³For all his days are full of sorrow, and his work is a vexation. Even in the night his heart does not rest. This also is vanity.

²⁴There is nothing better for a person than that he should eat and drink and find enjoyment*ᵇ* in his toil. This also, I saw, is from the hand of God, ²⁵for apart from him*ᶜ* who can eat or who can have enjoyment? ²⁶For to the one who pleases him God has given wisdom and knowledge and joy, but to the sinner he has given the business of gathering and collecting, only to give to one who pleases God. This also is vanity and a striving after wind.

A TIME FOR EVERYTHING

3 For everything there is a season, and a time for every matter under heaven:

² a time to be born, and a time to die;
   a time to plant, and a time to pluck up what is planted;
³ a time to kill, and a time to heal;
   a time to break down, and a time to build up;
⁴ a time to weep, and a time to laugh;
   a time to mourn, and a time to dance;
⁵ a time to cast away stones, and a time to gather stones together;
   a time to embrace, and a time to refrain from embracing;
⁶ a time to seek, and a time to lose;
   a time to keep, and a time to cast away;
⁷ a time to tear, and a time to sew;
   a time to keep silence, and a time to speak;
⁸ a time to love, and a time to hate;
   a time for war, and a time for peace.

THE GOD-GIVEN TASK

⁹What gain has the worker from his toil? ¹⁰I have seen the business that God has given to the children of man to be busy with. ¹¹He has made everything beautiful in its time. Also, he has put eternity into man's heart, yet so that he cannot find out what God has done from the beginning to the end. ¹²I perceived that there is nothing better for them than to be joyful and to do good as long as they live; ¹³also that everyone should eat and drink and take pleasure in all his toil—this is God's gift to man.

ᵃThe meaning of the Hebrew word is uncertain   ᵇOr and make his soul see good   ᶜSome Hebrew manuscripts, Septuagint, Syriac; most Hebrew manuscripts apart from me

¹⁴I perceived that whatever God does endures for ever; nothing can be added to it, nor anything taken from it. God has done it, so that people fear before him. ¹⁵That which is, already has been; that which is to be, already has been; and God seeks what has been driven away.ᵃ

FROM DUST TO DUST

¹⁶Moreover, I saw under the sun that in the place of justice, even there was wickedness, and in the place of righteousness, even there was wickedness. ¹⁷I said in my heart, God will judge the righteous and the wicked, for there is a time for every matter and for every work. ¹⁸I said in my heart with regard to the children of man that God is testing them that they may see that they themselves are but beasts. ¹⁹For what happens to the children of man and what happens to the beasts is the same; as one dies, so dies the other. They all have the same breath, and man has no advantage over the beasts, for all is vanity.ᵇ ²⁰All go to one place. All are from the dust, and to dust all return. ²¹Who knows whether the spirit of man goes upwards and the spirit of the beast goes down into the earth? ²²So I saw that there is nothing better than that a man should rejoice in his work, for that is his lot. Who can bring him to see what will be after him?

EVIL UNDER THE SUN

4 Again I saw all the oppressions that are done under the sun. And behold, the tears of the oppressed, and they had no one to comfort them! On the side of their oppressors there was power, and there was no one to comfort them. ²And I thought the dead who are already dead more fortunate than the living who are still alive. ³But better than both is he who has not yet been and has not seen the evil deeds that are done under the sun.

⁴Then I saw that all toil and all skill in work come from a man's envy of his neighbour. This also is vanityᶜ and a striving after wind.

⁵The fool folds his hands and eats his own flesh.

⁶Better is a handful of quietness than two hands full of toil and a striving after wind.

⁷Again, I saw vanity under the sun: ⁸one person who has no other, either son or brother, yet there is no end to all his toil, and his eyes are never satisfied with riches, so that he never asks, "For whom am I toiling and depriving myself of pleasure?" This also is vanity and an unhappy business.

⁹Two are better than one, because they have a good reward for their toil. ¹⁰For if they fall, one will lift up his fellow. But woe to him who is alone when he falls and has not another to lift him up! ¹¹Again, if two lie together, they keep warm, but how can one keep warm alone? ¹²And though a man might prevail against one who is alone, two will withstand him—a threefold cord is not quickly broken.

¹³Better was a poor and wise youth than an old and foolish king who no longer knew how to take advice. ¹⁴For he went from prison to the throne, though in his own kingdom he had been born poor. ¹⁵I saw all the living who move about under the sun, along with thatᵈ youth who was to stand in the king'sᵉ place. ¹⁶There was no end of all the people, all of whom he led. Yet those who come later will not rejoice in him. Surely this also is vanity and a striving after wind.

FEAR GOD

5 ᶠ Guard your steps when you go to the house of God. To draw near to listen is better than to offer the sacrifice of fools, for they do not know that they are doing evil. ²ᵍ Be not rash with your mouth, nor let your heart be hasty to utter a word before God, for God is in heaven and you are on earth. Therefore let your words be few. ³For a dream comes with much busyness, and a fool's voice with many words.

⁴When you vow a vow to God, do not delay paying it, for he has no pleasure in fools. Pay what you vow. ⁵It is better that you should not vow than that you should vow and not pay. ⁶Let not your mouth lead youʰ into sin, and do not say before the messengerⁱ that it was a mistake. Why should God be angry at your voice and destroy the work of your hands? ⁷For when dreams increase and words grow many, there is vanity;ʲ butᵏ God is the one you must fear.

THE VANITY OF WEALTH AND HONOUR

⁸If you see in a province the oppression of the poor and the violation of justice and righteousness, do not be amazed at the

---

ᵃHebrew *what has been pursued* ᵇThe Hebrew term *hebel* can refer to a "vapour" or "mere breath" (see note on 1:2) ᶜThe Hebrew term *hebel* can refer to a "vapour" or "mere breath"; also verses 7, 8, 16 (see note on 1:2) ᵈHebrew *the second* ᵉHebrew *his* ᶠCh 4:17 in Hebrew ᵍCh 5:1 in Hebrew ʰHebrew *your flesh* ⁱOr *angel* ʲThe Hebrew term *hebel* can refer to a "vapour" or "mere breath"; also verse 10 (see note on 1:2) ᵏOr *For when dreams and vanities increase, words also grow many; but*

matter, for the high official is watched by a higher, and there are yet higher ones over them. ⁹But this is gain for a land in every way: a king committed to cultivated fields.ᵃ

¹⁰He who loves money will not be satisfied with money, nor he who loves wealth with his income; this also is vanity. ¹¹When goods increase, they increase who eat them, and what advantage has their owner but to see them with his eyes? ¹²Sweet is the sleep of a labourer, whether he eats little or much, but the full stomach of the rich will not let him sleep.

¹³There is a grievous evil that I have seen under the sun: riches were kept by their owner to his hurt, ¹⁴and those riches were lost in a bad venture. And he is father of a son, but he has nothing in his hand. ¹⁵As he came from his mother's womb he shall go again, naked as he came, and shall take nothing for his toil that he may carry away in his hand. ¹⁶This also is a grievous evil: just as he came, so shall he go, and what gain is there to him who toils for the wind? ¹⁷Moreover, all his days he eats in darkness in much vexation and sickness and anger.

¹⁸Behold, what I have seen to be good and fitting is to eat and drink and find enjoymentᵇ in all the toil with which one toils under the sun the few days of his life that God has given him, for this is his lot. ¹⁹Everyone also to whom God has given wealth and possessions and power to enjoy them, and to accept his lot and rejoice in his toil—this is the gift of God. ²⁰For he will not much remember the days of his life because God keeps him occupied with joy in his heart.

6 There is an evil that I have seen under the sun, and it lies heavy on mankind: ²a man to whom God gives wealth, possessions, and honour, so that he lacks nothing of all that he desires, yet God does not give him power to enjoy them, but a stranger enjoys them. This is vanity;ᶜ it is a grievous evil. ³If a man fathers a hundred children and lives many years, so that the days of his years are many, but his soul is not satisfied with life's good things, and he also has no burial, I say that a stillborn child is better off than he. ⁴For it comes in vanity and goes in darkness, and in darkness its name is covered. ⁵Moreover, it has not seen the sun or known anything, yet it finds rest rather than he. ⁶Even though he should live a thousand years twice over, yet enjoyᵈ no good—do not all go to the one place?

⁷All the toil of man is for his mouth, yet his appetite is not satisfied.ᵉ ⁸For what advantage has the wise man over the fool? And what does the poor man have who knows how to conduct himself before the living? ⁹Better is the sight of the eyes than the wandering of the appetite: this also is vanity and a striving after wind.

¹⁰Whatever has come to be has already been named, and it is known what man is, and that he is not able to dispute with one stronger than he. ¹¹The more words, the more vanity, and what is the advantage to man? ¹²For who knows what is good for man while he lives the few days of his vainᶠ life, which he passes like a shadow? For who can tell man what will be after him under the sun?

THE CONTRAST OF WISDOM AND FOLLY

7 A good name is better than precious
   ointment,
   and the day of death than the day
   of birth.
² It is better to go to the house
   of mourning
   than to go to the house of feasting,
   for this is the end of all mankind,
   and the living will lay it to heart.
³ Sorrow is better than laughter,
   for by sadness of face the
   heart is made glad.
⁴ The heart of the wise is in the
   house of mourning,
   but the heart of fools is in
   the house of mirth.
⁵ It is better for a man to hear
   the rebuke of the wise
   than to hear the song of fools.
⁶ For as the crackling of thorns
   under a pot,
   so is the laughter of the fools;
   this also is vanity.ᵍ
⁷ Surely oppression drives the
   wise into madness,
   and a bribe corrupts the heart.
⁸ Better is the end of a thing
   than its beginning,
   and the patient in spirit is better
   than the proud in spirit.

ᵃThe meaning of the Hebrew verse is uncertain ᵇOr *and see good* ᶜThe Hebrew term *hebel* can refer to a "vapour" or "mere breath"; also verses 4, 9, 11 (see note on 1:2) ᵈOr *see* ᵉHebrew *filled* ᶠThe Hebrew term *hebel* can refer to a "vapour" or "mere breath" (see note on 1:2) ᵍThe Hebrew term *hebel* can refer to a "vapour" or "mere breath" (see note on 1:2)

9 Be not quick in your spirit
    to become angry,
  for anger lodges in the heart[a]
    of fools.
10 Say not, "Why were the former
    days better than these?"
  For it is not from wisdom
    that you ask this.
11 Wisdom is good with an inheritance,
    an advantage to those
    who see the sun.
12 For the protection of wisdom is like
    the protection of money,
  and the advantage of knowledge
    is that wisdom preserves
    the life of him who has it.
13 Consider the work of God:
    who can make straight what
    he has made crooked?

[14]In the day of prosperity be joyful, and in the day of adversity consider: God has made the one as well as the other, so that man may not find out anything that will be after him. [15]In my vain[b] life I have seen everything. There is a righteous man who perishes in his righteousness, and there is a wicked man who prolongs his life in his evildoing. [16]Be not overly righteous, and do not make yourself too wise. Why should you destroy yourself? [17]Be not overly wicked, neither be a fool. Why should you die before your time? [18]It is good that you should take hold of this, and from that withhold not your hand, for the one who fears God shall come out from both of them.

[19]Wisdom gives strength to the wise man more than ten rulers who are in a city.

[20]Surely there is not a righteous man on earth who does good and never sins.

[21]Do not take to heart all the things that people say, lest you hear your servant cursing you. [22]Your heart knows that many times you yourself have cursed others.

[23]All this I have tested by wisdom. I said, "I will be wise", but it was far from me. [24]That which has been is far off, and deep, very deep; who can find it out?

[25]I turned my heart to know and to search out and to seek wisdom and the scheme of things, and to know the wickedness of folly and the foolishness that is madness. [26]And I find something more bitter than death: the woman whose heart is snares and nets, and whose hands are fetters. He who pleases God escapes her, but the sinner is taken by her. [27]Behold, this is what I found, says the Preacher, while adding one thing to another to find the scheme of things— [28]which my soul has sought repeatedly, but I have not found. One man among a thousand I found, but a woman among all these I have not found. [29]See, this alone I found, that God made man upright, but they have sought out many schemes.

KEEP THE KING'S COMMAND

8 Who is like the wise?
  And who knows the interpretation
    of a thing?
  A man's wisdom makes his face shine,
    and the hardness of his face
    is changed.

[2]I say:[c] Keep the king's command, because of God's oath to him.[d] [3]Be not hasty to go from his presence. Do not take your stand in an evil cause, for he does whatever he pleases. [4]For the word of the king is supreme, and who may say to him, "What are you doing?" [5]Whoever keeps a command will know no evil thing, and the wise heart will know the proper time and the just way.[e] [6]For there is a time and a way for everything, although man's trouble[f] lies heavy on him. [7]For he does not know what is to be, for who can tell him how it will be? [8]No man has power to retain the spirit, or power over the day of death. There is no discharge from war, nor will wickedness deliver those who are given to it. [9]All this I observed while applying my heart to all that is done under the sun, when man had power over man to his hurt.

THOSE WHO FEAR GOD WILL DO WELL

[10]Then I saw the wicked buried. They used to go in and out of the holy place and were praised[g] in the city where they had done such things. This also is vanity.[h] [11]Because the sentence against an evil deed is not executed speedily, the heart of the children of man is fully set to do evil. [12]Though a sinner does evil a hundred times and prolongs his life, yet I know that it will be well with those who fear God, because they fear before him. [13]But it will not be well with the wicked, neither will

---

[a]Hebrew *in the bosom* [b]The Hebrew term *hebel* can refer to a "vapour" or "mere breath" (see note on 1:2) [c]Hebrew lacks *say* [d]Or *because of your oath to God* [e]Or *and judgement* [f]Or *evil* [g]Some Hebrew manuscripts, Septuagint, Vulgate; most Hebrew manuscripts *forgotten* [h]The Hebrew term *hebel* can refer to a "vapour" or "mere breath"; also twice in verse 14 (see note on 1:2)

he prolong his days like a shadow, because he does not fear before God.

MAN CANNOT KNOW GOD'S WAYS

14 There is a vanity that takes place on earth, that there are righteous people to whom it happens according to the deeds of the wicked, and there are wicked people to whom it happens according to the deeds of the righteous. I said that this also is vanity. **15** And I commend joy, for man has nothing better under the sun but to eat and drink and be joyful, for this will go with him in his toil through the days of his life that God has given him under the sun.

16 When I applied my heart to know wisdom, and to see the business that is done on earth, how neither day nor night do one's eyes see sleep, **17** then I saw all the work of God, that man cannot find out the work that is done under the sun. However much man may toil in seeking, he will not find it out. Even though a wise man claims to know, he cannot find it out.

DEATH COMES TO ALL

9 But all this I laid to heart, examining it all, how the righteous and the wise and their deeds are in the hand of God. Whether it is love or hate, man does not know; both are before him. **2** It is the same for all, since the same event happens to the righteous and the wicked, to the good and the evil,^{a} to the clean and the unclean, to him who sacrifices and him who does not sacrifice. As the good one is, so is the sinner, and he who swears is as he who shuns an oath. **3** This is an evil in all that is done under the sun, that the same event happens to all. Also, the hearts of the children of man are full of evil, and madness is in their hearts while they live, and after that they go to the dead. **4** But he who is joined with all the living has hope, for a living dog is better than a dead lion. **5** For the living know that they will die, but the dead know nothing, and they have no more reward, for the memory of them is forgotten. **6** Their love and their hate and their envy have already perished, and for ever they have no more share in all that is done under the sun.

ENJOY LIFE WITH THE ONE YOU LOVE

7 Go, eat your bread with joy, and drink your wine with a merry heart, for God has already approved what you do.

8 Let your garments be always white. Let not oil be lacking on your head.

9 Enjoy life with the wife whom you love, all the days of your vain^b life that he has given you under the sun, because that is your portion in life and in your toil at which you toil under the sun. **10** Whatever your hand finds to do, do it with your might,^{c} for there is no work or thought or knowledge or wisdom in Sheol, to which you are going.

WISDOM BETTER THAN FOLLY

11 Again I saw that under the sun the race is not to the swift, nor the battle to the strong, nor bread to the wise, nor riches to the intelligent, nor favour to those with knowledge, but time and chance happen to them all. **12** For man does not know his time. Like fish that are taken in an evil net, and like birds that are caught in a snare, so the children of man are snared at an evil time, when it suddenly falls upon them.

13 I have also seen this example of wisdom under the sun, and it seemed great to me. **14** There was a little city with few men in it, and a great king came against it and besieged it, building great siege works against it. **15** But there was found in it a poor, wise man, and he by his wisdom delivered the city. Yet no one remembered that poor man. **16** But I say that wisdom is better than might, though the poor man's wisdom is despised and his words are not heard.

17 The words of the wise heard in quiet are better than the shouting of a ruler among fools. **18** Wisdom is better than weapons of war, but one sinner destroys much good.

10 Dead flies make the perfumer's
 ointment give off a stench;
 so a little folly outweighs
 wisdom and honour.
2 A wise man's heart inclines
 him to the right,
 but a fool's heart to the left.
3 Even when the fool walks on
 the road, he lacks sense,
 and he says to everyone
 that he is a fool.
4 If the anger of the ruler rises against
 you, do not leave your place,
 for calmness^d will lay great
 offences to rest.

---

^{a}Septuagint, Syriac, Vulgate; Hebrew lacks *and the evil* ^{b}The Hebrew term *hebel* can refer to a "vapour" or "mere breath" (see note on 1:2) ^{c}Or *finds to do with your might, do it* ^{d}Hebrew *healing*

⁵There is an evil that I have seen under the sun, as it were an error proceeding from the ruler: ⁶folly is set in many high places, and the rich sit in a low place. ⁷I have seen slaves on horses, and princes walking on the ground like slaves.

⁸ He who digs a pit will fall into it,
    and a serpent will bite him who
        breaks through a wall.
⁹ He who quarries stones
    is hurt by them,
  and he who splits logs is
    endangered by them.
¹⁰ If the iron is blunt, and one does
    not sharpen the edge,
  he must use more strength,
    but wisdom helps one to succeed.ᵃ
¹¹ If the serpent bites before
    it is charmed,
  there is no advantage to the charmer.

¹² The words of a wise man's
    mouth win him favour,ᵇ
  but the lips of a fool consume him.
¹³ The beginning of the words of
    his mouth is foolishness,
  and the end of his talk is
    evil madness.
¹⁴ A fool multiplies words,
    though no man knows what is to be,
  and who can tell him what
    will be after him?
¹⁵ The toil of a fool wearies him,
    for he does not know the
        way to the city.

¹⁶ Woe to you, O land, when
    your king is a child,
  and your princes feast in
    the morning!
¹⁷ Happy are you, O land, when your
    king is the son of the nobility,
  and your princes feast at
    the proper time,
  for strength, and not for
    drunkenness!
¹⁸ Through sloth the roof sinks in,
    and through indolence
        the house leaks.
¹⁹ Bread is made for laughter,
    and wine gladdens life,
  and money answers everything.
²⁰ Even in your thoughts, do
    not curse the king,
  nor in your bedroom curse the rich,
    for a bird of the air will
        carry your voice,
  or some winged creature
    tell the matter.

CAST YOUR BREAD UPON THE WATERS

11 Cast your bread upon the waters,
    for you will find it after many days.
²Give a portion to seven,
    or even to eight,
  for you know not what disaster
    may happen on earth.
³ If the clouds are full of rain,
    they empty themselves on the earth,
  and if a tree falls to the south
    or to the north,
  in the place where the tree
    falls, there it will lie.
⁴ He who observes the wind
    will not sow,
  and he who regards the
    clouds will not reap.

⁵As you do not know the way the spirit comes to the bones in the wombᶜ of a woman with child, so you do not know the work of God who makes everything.

⁶In the morning sow your seed, and at evening withhold not your hand, for you do not know which will prosper, this or that, or whether both alike will be good.

⁷Light is sweet, and it is pleasant for the eyes to see the sun.

⁸So if a person lives many years, let him rejoice in them all; but let him remember that the days of darkness will be many. All that comes is vanity.ᵈ

⁹Rejoice, O young man, in your youth, and let your heart cheer you in the days of your youth. Walk in the ways of your heart and the sight of your eyes. But know that for all these things God will bring you into judgement.

¹⁰Remove vexation from your heart, and put away painᵉ from your body, for youth and the dawn of life are vanity.

REMEMBER YOUR CREATOR IN YOUR YOUTH

12 Remember also your Creator in the days of your youth, before the evil days come and the years draw near of which you will say, "I have no pleasure

---

ᵃOr *wisdom is an advantage for success*   ᵇOr *are gracious*   ᶜSome Hebrew manuscripts, Targum; most Hebrew manuscripts *As you do not know the way of the wind, or how the bones grow in the womb*   ᵈThe Hebrew term *hebel* can refer to a "vapour" or "mere breath"; also verse 10 (see note on 1:2)   ᵉOr *evil*

in them"; ²before the sun and the light and the moon and the stars are darkened and the clouds return after the rain, ³in the day when the keepers of the house tremble, and the strong men are bent, and the grinders cease because they are few, and those who look through the windows are dimmed, ⁴and the doors on the street are shut—when the sound of the grinding is low, and one rises up at the sound of a bird, and all the daughters of song are brought low— ⁵they are afraid also of what is high, and terrors are in the way; the almond tree blossoms, the grasshopper drags itself along,ᵃ and desire fails, because man is going to his eternal home, and the mourners go about the streets— ⁶before the silver cord is snapped, or the golden bowl is broken, or the pitcher is shattered at the fountain, or the wheel broken at the cistern, ⁷and the dust returns to the earth as it was, and the spirit returns to God who gave it. ⁸Vanityᵇ of vanities, says the Preacher; all is vanity.

FEAR GOD AND KEEP HIS COMMANDMENTS

⁹Besides being wise, the Preacher also taught the people knowledge, weighing and studying and arranging many proverbs with great care. ¹⁰The Preacher sought to find words of delight, and uprightly he wrote words of truth.

¹¹The words of the wise are like goads, and like nails firmly fixed are the collected sayings; they are given by one Shepherd. ¹²My son, beware of anything beyond these. Of making many books there is no end, and much study is a weariness of the flesh.

¹³The end of the matter; all has been heard. Fear God and keep his commandments, for this is the whole duty of man.ᶜ ¹⁴For God will bring every deed into judgement, withᵈ every secret thing, whether good or evil.

ᵃOr *is a burden* ᵇThe Hebrew term *hebel* can refer to a "vapour" or "mere breath" (three times in this verse); see note on 1:2 ᶜOr *the duty of all mankind* ᵈOr *into the judgement on*

THE SONG OF SOLOMON

1 The Song of Songs, which is Solomon's.

THE BRIDE CONFESSES HER LOVE

She[a]

2 Let him kiss me with the
    kisses of his mouth!
For your love is better than wine;
3   your anointing oils are fragrant;
your name is oil poured out;
    therefore virgins love you.
4 Draw me after you; let us run.
    The king has brought me
      into his chambers.

Others

We will exult and rejoice in you;
  we will extol your love
    more than wine;
  rightly do they love you.

She

5 I am very dark, but lovely,
  O daughters of Jerusalem,
  like the tents of Kedar,
  like the curtains of Solomon.
6 Do not gaze at me because I am dark,
  because the sun has looked upon me.
  My mother's sons were angry with me;
    they made me keeper of
      the vineyards,
  but my own vineyard I have not kept!
7 Tell me, you whom my soul loves,
  where you pasture your flock,
  where you make it lie down at noon;
for why should I be like one
    who veils herself
  beside the flocks of your
      companions?

SOLOMON AND HIS BRIDE DELIGHT IN EACH OTHER

He

8 If you do not know,
  O most beautiful among women,
follow in the tracks of the flock,
  and pasture your young goats
  beside the shepherds' tents.

9 I compare you, my love,
  to a mare among Pharaoh's chariots.
10 Your cheeks are lovely
    with ornaments,
  your neck with strings of jewels.

Others

11 We will make for you[b]
    ornaments of gold,
  studded with silver.

She

12 While the king was on his couch,
  my nard gave forth its fragrance.
13 My beloved is to me a sachet
    of myrrh
  that lies between my breasts.
14 My beloved is to me a cluster
    of henna blossoms
  in the vineyards of Engedi.

He

15 Behold, you are beautiful, my love;
  behold, you are beautiful;
  your eyes are doves.

She

16 Behold, you are beautiful, my
    beloved, truly delightful.
Our couch is green;
17   the beams of our house are cedar;
  our rafters are pine.

2 I am a rose[c] of Sharon,
  a lily of the valleys.

---

[a]The translators have added speaker identifications based on the gender and number of the Hebrew words   [b]The Hebrew for *you* is feminine singular   [c]Probably a bulb, such as a crocus, asphodel, or narcissus

He

2 As a lily among brambles,
    so is my love among the
        young women.

She

3 As an apple tree among the
        trees of the forest,
    so is my beloved among
        the young men.
    With great delight I sat in his shadow,
        and his fruit was sweet to my taste.
4 He brought me to the
        banqueting house,[a]
    and his banner over me was love.
5 Sustain me with raisins;
        refresh me with apples,
    for I am sick with love.
6 His left hand is under my head,
        and his right hand embraces me!
7 I adjure you,[b] O daughters
        of Jerusalem,
    by the gazelles or the does
        of the field,
    that you not stir up or awaken love
        until it pleases.

THE BRIDE ADORES HER BELOVED

8 The voice of my beloved!
        Behold, he comes,
    leaping over the mountains,
        bounding over the hills.
9 My beloved is like a gazelle
        or a young stag.
    Behold, there he stands
        behind our wall,
    gazing through the windows,
        looking through the lattice.
10 My beloved speaks and says to me:
    "Arise, my love, my beautiful one,
        and come away,
11 for behold, the winter is past;
        the rain is over and gone.
12 The flowers appear on the earth,
        the time of singing[c] has come,
    and the voice of the turtle-dove
        is heard in our land.
13 The fig tree ripens its figs,
        and the vines are in blossom;
        they give forth fragrance.
    Arise, my love, my beautiful one,
        and come away.
14 O my dove, in the clefts of the rock,
        in the crannies of the cliff,
    let me see your face,
        let me hear your voice,
    for your voice is sweet,
        and your face is lovely.
15 Catch the foxes[d] for us,
        the little foxes
    that spoil the vineyards,
        for our vineyards are in blossom."

16 My beloved is mine, and I am his;
        he grazes[e] among the lilies.
17 Until the day breathes
        and the shadows flee,
    turn, my beloved, be like a gazelle
        or a young stag on cleft
            mountains.[f]

THE BRIDE'S DREAM

3 On my bed by night
    I sought him whom my soul loves;
    I sought him, but found him not.
2 I will rise now and go about the city,
        in the streets and in the squares;
    I will seek him whom my soul loves.
    I sought him, but found him not.
3 The watchmen found me
        as they went about in the city.
    "Have you seen him whom
        my soul loves?"
4 Scarcely had I passed them
        when I found him whom
            my soul loves.
    I held him, and would not let him go
        until I had brought him into
            my mother's house,
    and into the chamber of her
        who conceived me.
5 I adjure you, O daughters of Jerusalem,
        by the gazelles or the does
            of the field,
    that you not stir up or awaken love
        until it pleases.

SOLOMON ARRIVES FOR THE WEDDING

6 What is that coming up from
        the wilderness
    like columns of smoke,
    perfumed with myrrh and
        frankincense,
    with all the fragrant powders
        of a merchant?
7 Behold, it is the litter[g] of Solomon!
    Around it are sixty mighty men,
        some of the mighty men of Israel,

---

[a] Hebrew *the house of wine*   [b] That is, I put you on oath; so throughout the Song   [c] Or *pruning*   [d] Or *jackals*   [e] Or *he pastures his flock*   [f] Or *mountains of Bether*   [g] That is, the couch on which servants carry a king

8 all of them wearing swords
and expert in war,
each with his sword at his thigh,
against terror by night.
9 King Solomon made himself
a carriage*a*
from the wood of Lebanon.
10 He made its posts of silver,
its back of gold, its seat of purple;
its interior was inlaid with love
by the daughters of Jerusalem.
11 Go out, O daughters of Zion,
and look upon King Solomon,
with the crown with which his
mother crowned him
on the day of his wedding,
on the day of the gladness
of his heart.

SOLOMON ADMIRES HIS BRIDE'S BEAUTY

HE

4 Behold, you are beautiful, my love,
behold, you are beautiful!
Your eyes are doves
behind your veil.
Your hair is like a flock of goats
leaping down the slopes of Gilead.
2 Your teeth are like a flock
of shorn ewes
that have come up from
the washing,
all of which bear twins,
and not one among them
has lost its young.
3 Your lips are like a scarlet thread,
and your mouth is lovely.
Your cheeks are like halves
of a pomegranate
behind your veil.
4 Your neck is like the tower of David,
built in rows of stone;*b*
on it hang a thousand shields,
all of them shields of warriors.
5 Your two breasts are like two fawns,
twins of a gazelle,
that graze among the lilies.
6 Until the day breathes
and the shadows flee,
I will go away to the
mountain of myrrh
and the hill of frankincense.
7 You are altogether beautiful, my love;
there is no flaw in you.
8 Come with me from
Lebanon, my bride;
come with me from Lebanon.
Depart*c* from the peak of Amana,
from the peak of Senir and Hermon,
from the dens of lions,
from the mountains of leopards.
9 You have captivated my heart,
my sister, my bride;
you have captivated my heart with
one glance of your eyes,
with one jewel of your necklace.
10 How beautiful is your love,
my sister, my bride!
How much better is your
love than wine,
and the fragrance of your
oils than any spice!
11 Your lips drip nectar, my bride;
honey and milk are under
your tongue;
the fragrance of your garments is
like the fragrance of Lebanon.
12 A garden locked is my sister,
my bride,
a spring locked, a fountain sealed.
13 Your shoots are an orchard
of pomegranates
with all choicest fruits,
henna with nard,
14 nard and saffron, calamus
and cinnamon,
with all trees of frankincense,
myrrh and aloes,
with all choice spices—
15 a garden fountain, a well
of living water,
and flowing streams from Lebanon.

16 Awake, O north wind,
and come, O south wind!
Blow upon my garden,
let its spices flow.

TOGETHER IN THE GARDEN OF LOVE

SHE

Let my beloved come to his garden,
and eat its choicest fruits.

HE

5 I came to my garden, my sister,
my bride,
I gathered my myrrh with my spice,
I ate my honeycomb with my honey,
I drank my wine with my milk.

---
*a*Or *sedan chair* *b*The meaning of the Hebrew word is uncertain
*c*Or *Look*

OTHERS

Eat, friends, drink,
  and be drunk with love!

THE BRIDE SEARCHES FOR HER BELOVED

SHE

2 I slept, but my heart was awake.
  A sound! My beloved is knocking.
  "Open to me, my sister, my love,
    my dove, my perfect one,
  for my head is wet with dew,
    my locks with the drops
      of the night."
3 I had put off my garment;
    how could I put it on?
  I had bathed my feet;
    how could I soil them?
4 My beloved put his hand to the latch,
    and my heart was thrilled within me.
5 I arose to open to my beloved,
    and my hands dripped with myrrh,
  my fingers with liquid myrrh,
    on the handles of the bolt.
6 I opened to my beloved,
    but my beloved had
      turned and gone.
  My soul failed me when he spoke.
  I sought him, but found him not;
    I called him, but he gave no answer.
7 The watchmen found me
    as they went about in the city;
  they beat me, they bruised me,
    they took away my veil,
  those watchmen of the walls.
8 I adjure you, O daughters of Jerusalem,
    if you find my beloved,
  that you tell him
    I am sick with love.

OTHERS

9 What is your beloved more
    than another beloved,
  O most beautiful among women?
  What is your beloved more
    than another beloved,
  that you thus adjure us?

THE BRIDE PRAISES HER BELOVED

SHE

10 My beloved is radiant and ruddy,
    distinguished among ten thousand.
11 His head is the finest gold;
    his locks are wavy,
      black as a raven.
12 His eyes are like doves
    beside streams of water,
  bathed in milk,
    sitting beside a full pool.[a]
13 His cheeks are like beds of spices,
    mounds of sweet-smelling herbs.
  His lips are lilies,
    dripping liquid myrrh.
14 His arms are rods of gold,
    set with jewels.
  His body is polished ivory,[b]
    bedecked with sapphires.[c]
15 His legs are alabaster columns,
    set on bases of gold.
  His appearance is like Lebanon,
    choice as the cedars.
16 His mouth[d] is most sweet,
    and he is altogether desirable.
  This is my beloved and
    this is my friend,
  O daughters of Jerusalem.

OTHERS

6 Where has your beloved gone,
  O most beautiful among women?
  Where has your beloved turned,
    that we may seek him with you?

TOGETHER IN THE GARDEN OF LOVE

SHE

2 My beloved has gone down
    to his garden
  to the beds of spices,
    to graze[e] in the gardens
    and to gather lilies.
3 I am my beloved's and my
    beloved is mine;
  he grazes among the lilies.

SOLOMON AND HIS BRIDE DELIGHT IN EACH OTHER

HE

4 You are beautiful as Tirzah, my love,
    lovely as Jerusalem,
  awesome as an army with banners.
5 Turn away your eyes from me,
    for they overwhelm me—
  Your hair is like a flock of goats
    leaping down the slopes of Gilead.
6 Your teeth are like a flock of ewes
    that have come up from the washing;
  all of them bear twins;
    not one among them has
      lost its young.

---

[a] The meaning of the Hebrew is uncertain [b] The meaning of the Hebrew word is uncertain [c] Hebrew *lapis lazuli* [d] Hebrew *palate*
[e] Or *to pasture his flock*; also verse 3

7 Your cheeks are like halves
of a pomegranate
behind your veil.
8 There are sixty queens and
eighty concubines,
and virgins without number.
9 My dove, my perfect one,
is the only one,
the only one of her mother,
pure to her who bore her.
The young women saw her and
called her blessed;
the queens and concubines also,
and they praised her.

10 "Who is this who looks down
like the dawn,
beautiful as the moon,
bright as the sun,
awesome as an army with banners?"

SHE

11 I went down to the nut orchard
to look at the blossoms of
the valley,
to see whether the vines had budded,
whether the pomegranates
were in bloom.
12 Before I was aware, my desire set me
among the chariots of my
kinsman, a prince.[a]

OTHERS

13[b] Return, return, O Shulammite,
return, return, that we may
look upon you.

HE

Why should you look upon
the Shulammite,
as upon a dance before two armies?[c]

7 How beautiful are your feet in
sandals,
O noble daughter!
Your rounded thighs are like jewels,
the work of a master hand.
2 Your navel is a rounded bowl
that never lacks mixed wine.
Your belly is a heap of wheat,
encircled with lilies.
3 Your two breasts are like two fawns,
twins of a gazelle.
4 Your neck is like an ivory tower.
Your eyes are pools in Heshbon,
by the gate of Bath-rabbim.
Your nose is like a tower of Lebanon,
which looks towards Damascus.
5 Your head crowns you like Carmel,
and your flowing locks
are like purple;
a king is held captive in the tresses.

6 How beautiful and pleasant you are,
O loved one, with all your delights![d]
7 Your stature is like a palm tree,
and your breasts are like
its clusters.
8 I say I will climb the palm tree
and lay hold of its fruit.
Oh may your breasts be like
clusters of the vine,
and the scent of your breath
like apples,
9 and your mouth[e] like the best wine.

SHE

It goes down smoothly for my beloved,
gliding over lips and teeth.[f]

10 I am my beloved's,
and his desire is for me.

THE BRIDE GIVES HER LOVE

11 Come, my beloved,
let us go out into the fields
and lodge in the villages;[g]
12 let us go out early to the vineyards
and see whether the vines
have budded,
whether the grape blossoms
have opened
and the pomegranates are
in bloom.
There I will give you my love.
13 The mandrakes give forth fragrance,
and beside our doors are
all choice fruits,
new as well as old,
which I have laid up for
you, O my beloved.

LONGING FOR HER BELOVED

8 Oh that you were like a brother to me
who nursed at my mother's breasts!
If I found you outside, I would
kiss you,
and none would despise me.

---

[a]Or chariots of Ammi-Nadib [b]Ch 7:1 in Hebrew [c]Or dance of Mahanaim [d]Or among delights [e]Hebrew palate [f]Septuagint, Syriac, Vulgate; Hebrew causing the lips of sleepers to speak, or gliding over the lips of those who sleep [g]Or among the henna plants

SONG OF SOLOMON 8

2 I would lead you and bring you
    into the house of my mother—
    she who used to teach me.
  I would give you spiced wine to drink,
    the juice of my pomegranate.
3 His left hand is under my head,
    and his right hand embraces me!
4 I adjure you, O daughters of Jerusalem,
    that you not stir up or awaken love
    until it pleases.

5 Who is that coming up from
    the wilderness,
    leaning on her beloved?

Under the apple tree I awakened you.
There your mother was in
    labour with you;
  there she who bore you was in labour.

6 Set me as a seal upon your heart,
    as a seal upon your arm,
  for love is strong as death,
    jealousy[a] is fierce as the grave.[b]
  Its flashes are flashes of fire,
    the very flame of the LORD.
7 Many waters cannot quench love,
    neither can floods drown it.
  If a man offered for love
    all the wealth of his house,
  he[c] would be utterly despised.

FINAL ADVICE

OTHERS
8 We have a little sister,
    and she has no breasts.
  What shall we do for our sister
    on the day when she is spoken for?

9 If she is a wall,
    we will build on her a
    battlement of silver,
  but if she is a door,
    we will enclose her with
    boards of cedar.

SHE
10 I was a wall,
    and my breasts were like towers;
  then I was in his eyes
    as one who finds[d] peace.

11 Solomon had a vineyard
    at Baal-hamon;
  he let out the vineyard to keepers;
    each one was to bring for its fruit
    a thousand pieces of silver.
12 My vineyard, my very own,
    is before me;
  you, O Solomon, may have
    the thousand,
  and the keepers of the fruit
    two hundred.

HE
13 O you who dwell in the gardens,
    with companions listening
    for your voice;
    let me hear it.

SHE
14 Make haste, my beloved,
    and be like a gazelle
  or a young stag
    on the mountains of spices.

---

[a]Or ardour [b]Hebrew as Sheol [c]Or it [d]Or brings out

ISAIAH

1 The vision of Isaiah the son of Amoz, which he saw concerning Judah and Jerusalem in the days of Uzziah, Jotham, Ahaz, and Hezekiah, kings of Judah.

THE WICKEDNESS OF JUDAH

2 Hear, O heavens, and give ear,
 O earth;
 for the LORD has spoken:
 "Children[a] have I reared
 and brought up,
 but they have rebelled against me.
3 The ox knows its owner,
 and the donkey its master's crib,
 but Israel does not know,
 my people do not understand."

4 Ah, sinful nation,
 a people laden with iniquity,
 offspring of evildoers,
 children who deal corruptly!
 They have forsaken the LORD,
 they have despised the
 Holy One of Israel,
 they are utterly estranged.

5 Why will you still be struck down?
 Why will you continue to rebel?
 The whole head is sick,
 and the whole heart faint.
6 From the sole of the foot
 even to the head,
 there is no soundness in it,
 but bruises and sores
 and raw wounds;
 they are not pressed out or bound up
 or softened with oil.

7 Your country lies desolate;
 your cities are burned with fire;
 in your very presence
 foreigners devour your land;
 it is desolate, as overthrown
 by foreigners.
8 And the daughter of Zion is left
 like a booth in a vineyard,
 like a lodge in a cucumber field,
 like a besieged city.

9 If the LORD of hosts
 had not left us a few survivors,
 we should have been like Sodom,
 and become like Gomorrah.

10 Hear the word of the LORD,
 you rulers of Sodom!
 Give ear to the teaching[b] of our God,
 you people of Gomorrah!
11 "What to me is the multitude
 of your sacrifices?
 says the LORD;
 I have had enough of burnt
 offerings of rams
 and the fat of well-fed beasts;
 I do not delight in the blood of bulls,
 or of lambs, or of goats.

12 "When you come to appear before me,
 who has required of you
 this trampling of my courts?
13 Bring no more vain offerings;
 incense is an abomination to me.
 New moon and Sabbath and the
 calling of convocations—
 I cannot endure iniquity and
 solemn assembly.
14 Your new moons and your
 appointed feasts
 my soul hates;
 they have become a burden to me;
 I am weary of bearing them.
15 When you spread out your hands,
 I will hide my eyes from you;
 even though you make many prayers,
 I will not listen;
 your hands are full of blood.
16 Wash yourselves; make
 yourselves clean;
 remove the evil of your deeds
 from before my eyes;
 cease to do evil,
17 learn to do good;
 seek justice,
 correct oppression;

---

[a] Or Sons; also verse 4   [b] Or law

bring justice to the fatherless,
   plead the widow's cause.

18 "Come now, let us reason[a]
      together, says the Lord:
   though your sins are like scarlet,
      they shall be as white as snow;
   though they are red like crimson,
      they shall become like wool.
19 If you are willing and obedient,
      you shall eat the good of the land;
20 but if you refuse and rebel,
      you shall be eaten by the sword;
   for the mouth of the Lord
      has spoken."

THE UNFAITHFUL CITY

21 How the faithful city
      has become a whore,[b]
      she who was full of justice!
   Righteousness lodged in her,
      but now murderers.
22 Your silver has become dross,
      your best wine mixed with water.
23 Your princes are rebels
      and companions of thieves.
   Everyone loves a bribe
      and runs after gifts.
   They do not bring justice
      to the fatherless,
   and the widow's cause does
      not come to them.

24 Therefore the Lord declares,
      the Lord of hosts,
      the Mighty One of Israel:
   "Ah, I will get relief from
      my enemies
      and avenge myself on my foes.
25 I will turn my hand against you
      and will smelt away your
         dross as with lye
      and remove all your alloy.
26 And I will restore your judges
      as at the first,
      and your counsellors as
         at the beginning.
   Afterwards you shall be called
      the city of righteousness,
      the faithful city."

27 Zion shall be redeemed by justice,
      and those in her who repent,
         by righteousness.
28 But rebels and sinners shall
      be broken together,
   and those who forsake the Lord
      shall be consumed.
29 For they[c] shall be ashamed of the oaks
      that you desired;
   and you shall blush for the gardens
      that you have chosen.
30 For you shall be like an oak
      whose leaf withers,
   and like a garden without water.
31 And the strong shall become tinder,
      and his work a spark,
   and both of them shall burn together,
      with none to quench them.

THE MOUNTAIN OF THE LORD

2 The word that Isaiah the son of Amoz saw concerning Judah and Jerusalem.

2 It shall come to pass in the latter days
      that the mountain of the
         house of the Lord
   shall be established as the
      highest of the mountains,
      and shall be lifted up above the hills;
   and all the nations shall flow to it,
3   and many peoples shall
         come, and say:
   "Come, let us go up to the
      mountain of the Lord,
      to the house of the God of Jacob,
   that he may teach us his ways
      and that we may walk in his paths."
   For out of Zion shall go forth the law,[d]
      and the word of the Lord
         from Jerusalem.
4 He shall judge between the nations,
      and shall decide disputes
         for many peoples;
   and they shall beat their swords
      into ploughshares,
      and their spears into pruning-hooks;
   nation shall not lift up sword
      against nation,
   neither shall they learn
      war any more.

5 O house of Jacob,
      come, let us walk
      in the light of the Lord.

THE DAY OF THE LORD

6 For you have rejected your people,
      the house of Jacob,

---

[a] Or dispute [b] Or become unchaste [c] Some Hebrew manuscripts *you* [d] Or *teaching*

because they are full of
things from the east
and of fortune-tellers like
the Philistines,
and they strike hands with the
children of foreigners.
7 Their land is filled with
silver and gold,
and there is no end to
their treasures;
their land is filled with horses,
and there is no end to their
chariots.
8 Their land is filled with idols;
they bow down to the work
of their hands,
to what their own fingers
have made.
9 So man is humbled,
and each one is brought low —
do not forgive them!
10 Enter into the rock
and hide in the dust
from before the terror of the LORD,
and from the splendour
of his majesty.
11 The haughty looks of man
shall be brought low,
and the lofty pride of men
shall be humbled,
and the LORD alone will be
exalted in that day.

12 For the LORD of hosts has a day
against all that is proud and lofty,
against all that is lifted up — and
it shall be brought low;
13 against all the cedars of Lebanon,
lofty and lifted up;
and against all the oaks of Bashan;
14 against all the lofty mountains,
and against all the uplifted hills;
15 against every high tower,
and against every fortified wall;
16 against all the ships of Tarshish,
and against all the beautiful craft.
17 And the haughtiness of man
shall be humbled,
and the lofty pride of men
shall be brought low,
and the LORD alone will be
exalted in that day.
18 And the idols shall utterly pass away.
19 And people shall enter the
caves of the rocks
and the holes of the ground,[a]
from before the terror of the LORD,
and from the splendour
of his majesty,
when he rises to terrify the earth.
20 In that day mankind will cast away
their idols of silver and
their idols of gold,
which they made for
themselves to worship,
to the moles and to the bats,
21 to enter the caverns of the rocks
and the clefts of the cliffs,
from before the terror of the LORD,
and from the splendour
of his majesty,
when he rises to terrify the earth.
22 Stop regarding man
in whose nostrils is breath,
for of what account is he?

JUDGEMENT ON JUDAH AND JERUSALEM

3 For behold, the Lord GOD of hosts
is taking away from Jerusalem and
from Judah
support and supply,[b]
all support of bread,
and all support of water;
2 the mighty man and the soldier,
the judge and the prophet,
the diviner and the elder,
3 the captain of fifty
and the man of rank,
the counsellor and the skilful magician
and the expert in charms.
4 And I will make boys their princes,
and infants[c] shall rule over them.
5 And the people will oppress
one another,
every one his fellow
and every one his neighbour;
the youth will be insolent to the elder,
and the despised to the honourable.

6 For a man will take hold of his brother
in the house of his father, saying:
"You have a cloak;
you shall be our leader,
and this heap of ruins
shall be under your rule";
7 in that day he will speak out, saying:
"I will not be a healer;[d]
in my house there is neither
bread nor cloak;

---

[a]Hebrew *dust* [b]Hebrew *staff* [c]Or *caprice* [d]Hebrew *binder of wounds*

you shall not make me
    leader of the people."
8 For Jerusalem has stumbled,
    and Judah has fallen,
because their speech and their
        deeds are against the Lord,
    defying his glorious presence.^a

9 For the look on their faces bears
        witness against them;
    they proclaim their sin like Sodom;
    they do not hide it.
Woe to them!
    For they have brought evil
        on themselves.
10 Tell the righteous that it shall
        be well with them,
    for they shall eat the fruit
        of their deeds.
11 Woe to the wicked! It shall
        be ill with him,
    for what his hands have dealt
        out shall be done to him.
12 My people—infants are
        their oppressors,
    and women rule over them.
O my people, your guides mislead you
    and they have swallowed up^b
        the course of your paths.

13 The Lord has taken his
        place to contend;
    he stands to judge peoples.
14 The Lord will enter into judgement
        with the elders and princes
            of his people:
    "It is you who have devoured^c
        the vineyard,
    the spoil of the poor is in
        your houses.
15 What do you mean by
        crushing my people,
    by grinding the face of the poor?"
            declares the Lord God of hosts.

16 The Lord said:
    Because the daughters of
        Zion are haughty
    and walk with outstretched necks,
        glancing wantonly with their eyes,
    mincing along as they go,
        tinkling with their feet,
17 therefore the Lord will strike with a scab
        the heads of the daughters of Zion,
    and the Lord will lay bare
        their secret parts.

¹⁸In that day the Lord will take away the finery of the anklets, the headbands, and the crescents; ¹⁹the pendants, the bracelets, and the scarves; ²⁰the headdresses, the armlets, the sashes, the perfume boxes, and the amulets; ²¹the signet rings and nose rings; ²²the festal robes, the mantles, the cloaks, and the handbags; ²³the mirrors, the linen garments, the turbans, and the veils.

24 Instead of perfume there
        will be rottenness;
    and instead of a belt, a rope;
    and instead of well-set hair, baldness;
    and instead of a rich robe, a
        skirt of sackcloth;
    and branding instead of beauty.
25 Your men shall fall by the sword
        and your mighty men in battle.
26 And her gates shall lament and mourn;
        empty, she shall sit on the ground.

4 And seven women shall take hold of one man in that day, saying, "We will eat our own bread and wear our own clothes, only let us be called by your name; take away our reproach."

THE BRANCH OF THE LORD GLORIFIED

²In that day the branch of the Lord shall be beautiful and glorious, and the fruit of the land shall be the pride and honour of the survivors of Israel. ³And he who is left in Zion and remains in Jerusalem will be called holy, everyone who has been recorded for life in Jerusalem, ⁴when the Lord shall have washed away the filth of the daughters of Zion and cleansed the bloodstains of Jerusalem from its midst by a spirit of judgement and by a spirit of burning.^d ⁵Then the Lord will create over the whole site of Mount Zion and over her assemblies a cloud by day, and smoke and the shining of a flaming fire by night; for over all the glory there will be a canopy. ⁶There will be a booth for shade by day from the heat, and for a refuge and a shelter from the storm and rain.

THE VINEYARD OF THE LORD DESTROYED

5 Let me sing for my beloved
        my love song concerning his vineyard:
    My beloved had a vineyard
        on a very fertile hill.

---

^aHebrew *the eyes of his glory* ^bOr *they have confused* ^cOr *grazed over*; compare Exodus 22:5 ^dOr *purging*

2 He dug it and cleared it of stones,
    and planted it with choice vines;
  he built a watchtower in
    the midst of it,
  and hewed out a wine vat in it;
  and he looked for it to yield grapes,
    but it yielded wild grapes.

3 And now, O inhabitants of Jerusalem
    and men of Judah,
  judge between me and my vineyard.
4 What more was there to do
    for my vineyard,
    that I have not done in it?
  When I looked for it to yield grapes,
    why did it yield wild grapes?

5 And now I will tell you
    what I will do to my vineyard.
  I will remove its hedge,
    and it shall be devoured;[a]
  I will break down its wall,
    and it shall be trampled down.
6 I will make it a waste;
    it shall not be pruned or hoed,
    and briers and thorns shall grow up;
  I will also command the clouds
    that they rain no rain upon it.

7 For the vineyard of the LORD of hosts
    is the house of Israel,
  and the men of Judah
    are his pleasant planting;
  and he looked for justice,
    but behold, bloodshed;[b]
  for righteousness,
    but behold, an outcry![c]

WOE TO THE WICKED

8 Woe to those who join house to house,
    who add field to field,
  until there is no more room,
    and you are made to dwell alone
    in the midst of the land.
9 The LORD of hosts has sworn
    in my hearing:
  "Surely many houses shall be desolate,
    large and beautiful houses,
    without inhabitant.
10 For ten acres[d] of vineyard shall
    yield but one bath,
  and a homer of seed shall
    yield but an ephah."[e]

11 Woe to those who rise early
    in the morning,
    that they may run after strong drink,
  who tarry late into the evening
    as wine inflames them!
12 They have lyre and harp,
    tambourine and flute and
    wine at their feasts,
  but they do not regard the
    deeds of the LORD,
  or see the work of his hands.

13 Therefore my people go into exile
    for lack of knowledge;[f]
  their honoured men go hungry,[g]
  and their multitude is
    parched with thirst.
14 Therefore Sheol has enlarged
    its appetite
  and opened its mouth
    beyond measure,
  and the nobility of Jerusalem[h] and
    her multitude will go down,
  her revellers and he who
    exults in her.
15 Man is humbled, and each
    one is brought low,
  and the eyes of the haughty[i]
    are brought low.
16 But the LORD of hosts is
    exalted[j] in justice,
  and the Holy God shows himself
    holy in righteousness.
17 Then shall the lambs graze
    as in their pasture,
  and nomads shall eat among
    the ruins of the rich.

18 Woe to those who draw iniquity
    with cords of falsehood,
  who draw sin as with cart ropes,
19 who say: "Let him be quick,
    let him speed his work
    that we may see it;
  let the counsel of the Holy One
    of Israel draw near,
  and let it come, that we
    may know it!"
20 Woe to those who call evil good
    and good evil,
  who put darkness for light
    and light for darkness,

---

[a]Or *grazed over*; compare Exodus 22:5   [b]The Hebrew words for *justice* and *bloodshed* sound alike   [c]The Hebrew words for *righteous* and *outcry* sound alike   [d]Hebrew *ten yoke*, the area ten yoke of oxen can plough in a day   [e]A *bath* was about 6 gallons or 22 litres; a *homer* was about 6 bushels or 220 litres; an *ephah* was about 3/5 of a bushel or 22 litres   [f]Or *without their knowledge*   [g]*or die of hunger*   [h]Hebrew *her nobility*   [i]Hebrew *high*   [j]Hebrew *high*

who put bitter for sweet
and sweet for bitter!
21 Woe to those who are wise
in their own eyes,
and shrewd in their own sight!
22 Woe to those who are heroes
at drinking wine,
and valiant men in mixing
strong drink,
23 who acquit the guilty for a bribe,
and deprive the innocent
of his right!

24 Therefore, as the tongue of fire
devours the stubble,
and as dry grass sinks down
in the flame,
so their root will be as rottenness,
and their blossom go up like dust;
for they have rejected the law
of the LORD of hosts,
and have despised the word of
the Holy One of Israel.
25 Therefore the anger of the LORD was
kindled against his people,
and he stretched out his hand
against them and struck them,
and the mountains quaked;
and their corpses were as refuse
in the midst of the streets.
For all this his anger has
not turned away,
and his hand is stretched out still.

26 He will raise a signal for
nations far away,
and whistle for them from
the ends of the earth;
and behold, quickly, speedily
they come!
27 None is weary, none stumbles,
none slumbers or sleeps,
not a waistband is loose,
not a sandal strap broken;
28 their arrows are sharp,
all their bows bent,
their horses' hoofs seem like flint,
and their wheels like
the whirlwind.
29 Their roaring is like a lion,
like young lions they roar;
they growl and seize their prey;
they carry it off, and none
can rescue.
30 They will growl over it on that day,
like the growling of the sea.

And if one looks to the land,
behold, darkness and distress;
and the light is darkened by its clouds.

ISAIAH'S VISION OF THE LORD

6 In the year that King Uzziah died I saw the Lord sitting upon a throne, high and lifted up; and the train[a] of his robe filled the temple. ²Above him stood the seraphim. Each had six wings: with two he covered his face, and with two he covered his feet, and with two he flew. ³And one called to another and said:

"Holy, holy, holy is the LORD of hosts;
the whole earth is full of his glory!"[b]

⁴And the foundations of the thresholds shook at the voice of him who called, and the house was filled with smoke. ⁵And I said: "Woe is me! For I am lost; for I am a man of unclean lips, and I dwell in the midst of a people of unclean lips; for my eyes have seen the King, the LORD of hosts!"

⁶Then one of the seraphim flew to me, having in his hand a burning coal that he had taken with tongs from the altar. ⁷And he touched my mouth and said: "Behold, this has touched your lips; your guilt is taken away, and your sin atoned for."

ISAIAH'S COMMISSION FROM THE LORD

⁸And I heard the voice of the Lord saying, "Whom shall I send, and who will go for us?" Then I said, "Here I am! Send me." ⁹And he said, "Go, and say to this people:

"'Keep on hearing,[c] but do
not understand;
keep on seeing,[d] but do not perceive.'
10 Make the heart of this people dull,[e]
and their ears heavy,
and blind their eyes;
lest they see with their eyes,
and hear with their ears,
and understand with their hearts,
and turn and be healed."
11 Then I said, "How long, O Lord?"
And he said:
"Until cities lie waste
without inhabitant,
and houses without people,
and the land is a desolate waste,

---

[a] Or hem [b] Or may his glory fill the whole earth [c] Or Hear indeed
[d] Or see indeed [e] Hebrew fat

12 and the Lord removes people far away,
    and the forsaken places are many
        in the midst of the land.
13 And though a tenth remain in it,
    it will be burned[a] again,
    like a terebinth or an oak,
    whose stump remains
        when it is felled."
The holy seed[b] is its stump.

ISAIAH SENT TO KING AHAZ

7 In the days of Ahaz the son of Jotham, son of Uzziah, king of Judah, Rezin the king of Syria and Pekah the son of Remaliah the king of Israel came up to Jerusalem to wage war against it, but could not yet mount an attack against it. ²When the house of David was told, "Syria is in league with[c] Ephraim," the heart of Ahaz[d] and the heart of his people shook as the trees of the forest shake before the wind.

³And the Lord said to Isaiah, "Go out to meet Ahaz, you and Shear-jashub[e] your son, at the end of the conduit of the upper pool on the highway to the Washer's Field. ⁴And say to him, 'Be careful, be quiet, do not fear, and do not let your heart be faint because of these two smouldering stumps of firebrands, at the fierce anger of Rezin and Syria and the son of Remaliah. ⁵Because Syria, with Ephraim and the son of Remaliah, has devised evil against you, saying, ⁶"Let us go up against Judah and terrify it, and let us conquer it[f] for ourselves, and set up the son of Tabeel as king in the midst of it," ⁷thus says the Lord God:

"'It shall not stand,
    and it shall not come to pass.
8   For the head of Syria is Damascus,
        and the head of Damascus is Rezin.
    And within sixty-five years
        Ephraim will be shattered
            from being a people.
9   And the head of Ephraim is Samaria,
        and the head of Samaria is
            the son of Remaliah.
    If you[g] are not firm in faith,
        you will not be firm at all.'"

THE SIGN OF IMMANUEL

¹⁰Again the Lord spoke to Ahaz: ¹¹"Ask a sign of the Lord your[h] God; let it be deep as Sheol or high as heaven." ¹²But Ahaz said, "I will not ask, and I will not put the Lord to the test." ¹³And he[i] said, "Hear then, O house of David! Is it too little for you to weary men, that you weary my God also? ¹⁴Therefore the Lord himself will give you a sign. Behold, the virgin shall conceive and bear a son, and shall call his name Immanuel.[j] ¹⁵He shall eat curds and honey when he knows how to refuse the evil and choose the good. ¹⁶For before the boy knows how to refuse the evil and choose the good, the land whose two kings you dread will be deserted. ¹⁷The Lord will bring upon you and upon your people and upon your father's house such days as have not come since the day that Ephraim departed from Judah—the king of Assyria!"

¹⁸In that day the Lord will whistle for the fly that is at the end of the streams of Egypt, and for the bee that is in the land of Assyria. ¹⁹And they will all come and settle in the steep ravines, and in the clefts of the rocks, and on all the thorn bushes, and on all the pastures.[k]

²⁰In that day the Lord will shave with a razor that is hired beyond the River[l]—with the king of Assyria—the head and the hair of the feet, and it will sweep away the beard also.

²¹In that day a man will keep alive a young cow and two sheep, ²²and because of the abundance of milk that they give, he will eat curds, for everyone who is left in the land will eat curds and honey.

²³In that day every place where there used to be a thousand vines, worth a thousand shekels[m] of silver, will become briers and thorns. ²⁴With bow and arrows a man will come there, for all the land will be briers and thorns. ²⁵And as for all the hills that used to be hoed with a hoe, you will not come there for fear of briers and thorns, but they will become a place where cattle are let loose and where sheep tread.

THE COMING ASSYRIAN INVASION

8 Then the Lord said to me, "Take a large tablet and write on it in common characters,[n] 'Belonging to Maher-shalal-hash-baz.'[o] ²And I will get reliable witnesses, Uriah the priest and Zechariah the son of Jeberechiah, to attest for me."

³And I went to the prophetess, and she conceived and bore a son. Then the Lord

---

[a] Or purged [b] Or offspring [c] Hebrew Syria has rested upon [d] Hebrew his heart [e] Shear-jashub means A remnant shall return [f] Hebrew let us split it open [g] The Hebrew for you is plural in verses 9, 13, 14 [h] The Hebrew for you and your is singular in verses 11, 16, 17 [i] That is, Isaiah [j] Immanuel means God is with us [k] Or watering holes, or brambles [l] That is, the Euphrates [m] A shekel was about 2/5 of an ounce or 11 grams [n] Hebrew with a man's stylus [o] Maher-shalal-hash-baz means The spoil speeds, the prey hastens

said to me, "Call his name Maher-shalal-hash-baz; ⁴for before the boy knows how to cry 'My father' or 'My mother', the wealth of Damascus and the spoil of Samaria will be carried away before the king of Assyria."

⁵The LORD spoke to me again: ⁶"Because this people has refused the waters of Shiloah that flow gently, and rejoice over Rezin and the son of Remaliah, ⁷therefore, behold, the Lord is bringing up against them the waters of the River,ᵃ mighty and many, the king of Assyria and all his glory. And it will rise over all its channels and go over all its banks, ⁸and it will sweep on into Judah, it will overflow and pass on, reaching even to the neck, and its outspread wings will fill the breadth of your land, O Immanuel."

⁹ Be broken,ᵇ you peoples,
   and be shattered;ᶜ
  give ear, all you far countries;
  strap on your armour and be shattered;
  strap on your armour and
   be shattered.
¹⁰ Take counsel together, but it
   will come to nothing;
  speak a word, but it will not stand,
   for God is with us.ᵈ

FEAR GOD, WAIT FOR THE LORD

¹¹For the LORD spoke thus to me with his strong hand upon me, and warned me not to walk in the way of this people, saying: ¹²"Do not call conspiracy all that this people calls conspiracy, and do not fear what they fear, nor be in dread. ¹³But the LORD of hosts, him you shall honour as holy. Let him be your fear, and let him be your dread. ¹⁴And he will become a sanctuary and a stone of offence and a rock of stumbling to both houses of Israel, a trap and a snare to the inhabitants of Jerusalem. ¹⁵And many shall stumble on it. They shall fall and be broken; they shall be snared and taken."

¹⁶Bind up the testimony; seal the teachingᵉ among my disciples. ¹⁷I will wait for the LORD, who is hiding his face from the house of Jacob, and I will hope in him. ¹⁸Behold, I and the children whom the LORD has given me are signs and portents in Israel from the LORD of hosts, who dwells on Mount Zion. ¹⁹And when they say to you, "Enquire of the mediums and the necromancers who chirp and mutter," should not a people enquire of their God? Should they enquire of the dead on behalf of the living? ²⁰To the teaching and to the testimony! If they will not speak according to this word, it is because they have no dawn. ²¹They will pass through the land,ᶠ greatly distressed and hungry. And when they are hungry, they will be enraged and will speak contemptuously againstᵍ their king and their God, and turn their faces upwards. ²²And they will look to the earth, but behold, distress and darkness, the gloom of anguish. And they will be thrust into thick darkness.

FOR TO US A CHILD IS BORN

9ʰ But there will be no gloom for her who was in anguish. In the former time he brought into contempt the land of Zebulun and the land of Naphtali, but in the latter time he has made glorious the way of the sea, the land beyond the Jordan, Galilee of the nations.ⁱ

²ʲ The people who walked in darkness
   have seen a great light;
  those who dwelt in a land
   of deep darkness,
   on them has light shone.
³ You have multiplied the nation;
   you have increased its joy;
  they rejoice before you
   as with joy at the harvest,
  as they are glad when they
   divide the spoil.
⁴ For the yoke of his burden,
   and the staff for his shoulder,
   the rod of his oppressor,
  you have broken as on the
   day of Midian.
⁵ For every boot of the tramping
   warrior in battle tumult
  and every garment rolled in blood
   will be burned as fuel for the fire.
⁶ For to us a child is born,
   to us a son is given;
  and the government shall be
   uponᵏ his shoulder,
  and his name shall be calledˡ
  Wonderful Counsellor, Mighty God,
   Everlasting Father, Prince of Peace.
⁷ Of the increase of his government
   and of peace
   there will be no end,
  on the throne of David and
   over his kingdom,
  to establish it and to uphold it

ᵃThat is, the Euphrates ᵇOr Be evil ᶜOr dismayed ᵈThe Hebrew for God is with us is Immanuel ᵉOr law; also verse 20 ᶠHebrew it ᵍOr speak contemptuously by ʰCh 8:23 in Hebrew ⁱOr of the Gentiles ʲCh 9:1 in Hebrew ᵏOr is upon ˡOr is called

with justice and with righteousness
from this time forth and
for evermore.
The zeal of the Lord of
hosts will do this.

JUDGEMENT ON ARROGANCE AND OPPRESSION

8 The Lord has sent a word against Jacob,
and it will fall on Israel;
9 and all the people will know,
Ephraim and the inhabitants
of Samaria,
who say in pride and in
arrogance of heart:
10 "The bricks have fallen,
but we will build with
dressed stones;
the sycamores have been cut down,
but we will put cedars in their place."
11 But the Lord raises the adversaries
of Rezin against him,
and stirs up his enemies.
12 The Syrians on the east and the
Philistines on the west
devour Israel with open mouth.
For all this his anger has
not turned away,
and his hand is stretched out still.

13 The people did not turn to him
who struck them,
nor enquire of the Lord of hosts.
14 So the Lord cut off from
Israel head and tail,
palm branch and reed in one day—
15 the elder and honoured
man is the head,
and the prophet who teaches
lies is the tail;
16 for those who guide this people have
been leading them astray,
and those who are guided by
them are swallowed up.
17 Therefore the Lord does not rejoice
over their young men,
and has no compassion on their
fatherless and widows;
for everyone is godless and an evildoer,
and every mouth speaks folly.*a*
For all this his anger has
not turned away,
and his hand is stretched out still.

18 For wickedness burns like a fire;
it consumes briers and thorns;
it kindles the thickets of the forest,
and they roll upwards in a
column of smoke.
19 Through the wrath of the Lord
of hosts
the land is scorched,
and the people are like fuel for the fire;
no one spares another.
20 They slice meat on the right,
but are still hungry,
and they devour on the left,
but are not satisfied;
each devours the flesh of his own arm,
21 Manasseh devours Ephraim, and
Ephraim devours Manasseh;
together they are against Judah.
For all this his anger has
not turned away,
and his hand is stretched out still.

10 Woe to those who decree
iniquitous decrees,
and the writers who keep writing
oppression,
2 to turn aside the needy from justice
and to rob the poor of my
people of their right,
that widows may be their spoil,
and that they may make the
fatherless their prey!
3 What will you do on the day
of punishment,
in the ruin that will come from afar?
To whom will you flee for help,
and where will you leave
your wealth?
4 Nothing remains but to crouch
among the prisoners
or fall among the slain.
For all this his anger has
not turned away,
and his hand is stretched out still.

JUDGEMENT ON ARROGANT ASSYRIA

5 Woe to Assyria, the rod of my anger;
the staff in their hands is my fury!
6 Against a godless nation I send him,
and against the people of my
wrath I command him,
to take spoil and seize plunder,
and to tread them down like
the mire of the streets.
7 But he does not so intend,
and his heart does not so think;

---

a Or *speaks disgraceful things*

but it is in his heart to destroy,
and to cut off nations not a few;
⁸ for he says:
"Are not my commanders all kings?
⁹ Is not Calno like Carchemish?
Is not Hamath like Arpad?
Is not Samaria like Damascus?
¹⁰ As my hand has reached to the
kingdoms of the idols,
whose carved images were
greater than those of
Jerusalem and Samaria,
¹¹ shall I not do to Jerusalem and her idols
as I have done to Samaria
and her images?"

¹²When the Lord has finished all his work on Mount Zion and on Jerusalem, he[a] will punish the speech[b] of the arrogant heart of the king of Assyria and the boastful look in his eyes. ¹³For he says:

"By the strength of my hand
I have done it,
and by my wisdom, for I have
understanding;
I remove the boundaries of peoples,
and plunder their treasures;
like a bull I bring down those
who sit on thrones.
¹⁴ My hand has found like a nest
the wealth of the peoples;
and as one gathers eggs that
have been forsaken,
so I have gathered all the earth;
and there was none that moved a wing
or opened the mouth or chirped."

¹⁵ Shall the axe boast over him
who hews with it,
or the saw magnify itself against
him who wields it?
As if a rod should wield
him who lifts it,
or as if a staff should lift him
who is not wood!
¹⁶ Therefore the Lord GOD of hosts
will send wasting sickness
among his stout warriors,
and under his glory a burning
will be kindled,
like the burning of fire.
¹⁷ The light of Israel will become a fire,
and his Holy One a flame,
and it will burn and devour
his thorns and briers in one day.
¹⁸ The glory of his forest and
of his fruitful land
the LORD will destroy, both
soul and body,
and it will be as when a sick
man wastes away.
¹⁹ The remnant of the trees of his
forest will be so few
that a child can write them down.

THE REMNANT OF ISRAEL WILL RETURN

²⁰In that day the remnant of Israel and the survivors of the house of Jacob will no more lean on him who struck them, but will lean on the LORD, the Holy One of Israel, in truth. ²¹A remnant will return, the remnant of Jacob, to the mighty God. ²²For though your people Israel be as the sand of the sea, only a remnant of them will return. Destruction is decreed, overflowing with righteousness. ²³For the Lord GOD of hosts will make a full end, as decreed, in the midst of all the earth.

²⁴Therefore thus says the Lord GOD of hosts: "O my people, who dwell in Zion, be not afraid of the Assyrians when they strike with the rod and lift up their staff against you as the Egyptians did. ²⁵For in a very little while my fury will come to an end, and my anger will be directed to their destruction. ²⁶And the LORD of hosts will wield against them a whip, as when he struck Midian at the rock of Oreb. And his staff will be over the sea, and he will lift it as he did in Egypt. ²⁷And in that day his burden will depart from your shoulder, and his yoke from your neck; and the yoke will be broken because of the fat."[c]

²⁸ He has come to Aiath;
he has passed through Migron;
at Michmash he stores his baggage;
²⁹ they have crossed over the pass;
at Geba they lodge for the night;
Ramah trembles;
Gibeah of Saul has fled.
³⁰ Cry aloud, O daughter of Gallim!
Give attention, O Laishah!
O poor Anathoth!
³¹ Madmenah is in flight;
the inhabitants of Gebim
flee for safety.
³² This very day he will halt at Nob;
he will shake his fist
at the mount of the daughter of Zion,
the hill of Jerusalem.

[a]Hebrew *I* [b]Hebrew *fruit* [c]The meaning of the Hebrew is uncertain

the greenery is no more.
7 Therefore the abundance
    they have gained
    and what they have laid up
they carry away
    over the Brook of the Willows.
8 For a cry has gone
    around the land of Moab;
her wailing reaches to Eglaim;
    her wailing reaches to Beer-elim.
9 For the waters of Dibon[a]
    are full of blood;
for I will bring upon Dibon
    even more,
a lion for those of Moab who escape,
    for the remnant of the land.

16

Send the lamb to the ruler of the land,
    from Sela, by way of the desert,
to the mount of the
    daughter of Zion.
2 Like fleeing birds,
    like a scattered nest,
so are the daughters of Moab
    at the fords of the Arnon.

3 "Give counsel;
    grant justice;
make your shade like night
    at the height of noon;
shelter the outcasts;
    do not reveal the fugitive;
4 let the outcasts of Moab
    sojourn among you;
be a shelter to them[b]
    from the destroyer.
When the oppressor is no more,
    and destruction has ceased,
and he who tramples underfoot
    has vanished from the land,
5 then a throne will be established
    in steadfast love,
    and on it will sit in faithfulness
    in the tent of David
one who judges and seeks justice
    and is swift to do righteousness."

6 We have heard of the pride of Moab—
    how proud he is!—
of his arrogance, his pride,
    and his insolence;
    in his idle boasting he is not right.
7 Therefore let Moab wail for Moab,
    let everyone wail.
Mourn, utterly stricken,
    for the raisin cakes of Kir-hareseth.
8 For the fields of Heshbon languish,
    and the vine of Sibmah;
the lords of the nations
    have struck down its branches,
which reached to Jazer
    and strayed to the desert;
its shoots spread abroad
    and passed over the sea.
9 Therefore I weep with the
    weeping of Jazer
    for the vine of Sibmah;
I drench you with my tears,
    O Heshbon and Elealeh;
for over your summer fruit
    and your harvest
    the shout has ceased.
10 And joy and gladness are taken
    away from the fruitful field,
and in the vineyards no songs are sung,
    no cheers are raised;
no treader treads out wine
    in the presses;
I have put an end to the shouting.
11 Therefore my inner parts moan
    like a lyre for Moab,
    and my inmost self for Kir-hareseth.

12 And when Moab presents himself, when he wearies himself on the high place, when he comes to his sanctuary to pray, he will not prevail.

13 This is the word that the LORD spoke concerning Moab in the past. 14 But now the LORD has spoken, saying, "In three years, like the years of a hired worker, the glory of Moab will be brought into contempt, in spite of all his great multitude, and those who remain will be very few and feeble."

AN ORACLE CONCERNING DAMASCUS

17

An oracle concerning Damascus.

Behold, Damascus will cease to be
    a city
and will become a heap of ruins.
2 The cities of Aroer are deserted;
    they will be for flocks,
which will lie down, and none
    will make them afraid.
3 The fortress will disappear
    from Ephraim,
and the kingdom from Damascus;

---

[a]Dead Sea Scroll, Vulgate (compare Syriac); Masoretic Text *Dimon*; twice in this verse [b]Some Hebrew manuscripts, Septuagint, Syriac; Masoretic Text *let my outcasts sojourn among you; as for Moab, be a shelter to them*

and the remnant of Syria will be
like the glory of the
children of Israel,
declares the LORD of hosts.

4 And in that day the glory of Jacob
will be brought low,
and the fat of his flesh
will grow lean.
5 And it shall be as when the reaper
gathers standing corn
and his arm harvests the ears,
and as when one gleans
the ears of corn
in the Valley of Rephaim.
6 Gleanings will be left in it,
as when an olive tree is beaten —
two or three berries
in the top of the highest bough,
four or five
on the branches of a fruit tree,
declares the LORD God of Israel.

⁷In that day man will look to his Maker, and his eyes will look on the Holy One of Israel. ⁸He will not look to the altars, the work of his hands, and he will not look on what his own fingers have made, either the Asherim or the altars of incense. ⁹In that day their strong cities will be like the deserted places of the wooded heights and the hilltops, which they deserted because of the children of Israel, and there will be desolation.

10 For you have forgotten the
God of your salvation
and have not remembered the
Rock of your refuge;
therefore, though you plant
pleasant plants
and sow the vine-branch
of a stranger,
11 though you make them grow[a] on
the day that you plant them,
and make them blossom in the
morning that you sow,
yet the harvest will flee away[b]
in a day of grief and incurable pain.

12 Ah, the thunder of many peoples;
they thunder like the
thundering of the sea!
Ah, the roar of nations;
they roar like the roaring
of mighty waters!
13 The nations roar like the
roaring of many waters,
but he will rebuke them, and
they will flee far away,
chased like chaff on the mountains
before the wind
and whirling dust before the storm.
14 At evening time, behold, terror!
Before morning, they are no more!
This is the portion of those
who loot us,
and the lot of those who plunder us.

AN ORACLE CONCERNING CUSH

18 Ah, land of whirring wings
that is beyond the rivers of Cush,[c]
²which sends ambassadors by
the sea,
in vessels of papyrus on the waters!
Go, you swift messengers,
to a nation tall and smooth,
to a people feared near and far,
a nation mighty and conquering,
whose land the rivers divide.
3 All you inhabitants of the world,
you who dwell on the earth,
when a signal is raised on the
mountains, look!
When a trumpet is blown, hear!
4 For thus the LORD said to me:
"I will quietly look from my dwelling
like clear heat in sunshine,
like a cloud of dew in the
heat of harvest."
5 For before the harvest, when
the blossom is over,
and the flower becomes a
ripening grape,
he cuts off the shoots with
pruning-hooks,
and the spreading branches he
lops off and clears away.
6 They shall all of them be left
to the birds of prey of the mountains
and to the beasts of the earth.
And the birds of prey will
summer on them,
and all the beasts of the earth
will winter on them.

⁷At that time tribute will be brought to the LORD of hosts

---
[a] Or though you carefully fence them [b] Or will be a heap
[c] Probably Nubia

from a people tall and smooth,
   from a people feared near and far,
a nation mighty and conquering,
   whose land the rivers divide,

to Mount Zion, the place of the name of the Lord of hosts.

AN ORACLE CONCERNING EGYPT

19 An oracle concerning Egypt.

Behold, the Lord is riding on a
      swift cloud
   and comes to Egypt;
and the idols of Egypt will
      tremble at his presence,
   and the heart of the Egyptians
      will melt within them.
² And I will stir up Egyptians
      against Egyptians,
   and they will fight, each
      against another
   and each against his neighbour,
   city against city, kingdom
      against kingdom;
³ and the spirit of the Egyptians within
      them will be emptied out,
   and I will confound[a] their counsel;
   and they will enquire of the
      idols and the sorcerers,
   and the mediums and the
      necromancers;
⁴ and I will give over the Egyptians
      into the hand of a hard master,
   and a fierce king will rule over them,
      declares the Lord God of hosts.

⁵ And the waters of the sea
      will be dried up,
   and the river will be dry
      and parched,
⁶ and its canals will become foul,
   and the branches of Egypt's Nile
      will diminish and dry up,
   reeds and rushes will rot away.
⁷ There will be bare places by the Nile,
      on the brink of the Nile,
   and all that is sown by the
      Nile will be parched,
   will be driven away, and
      will be no more.
⁸ The fishermen will mourn and
      lament,
   all who cast a hook in the Nile;
   and they will languish
      who spread nets on the water.
⁹ The workers in combed flax
      will be in despair,
   and the weavers of white cotton.
¹⁰ Those who are the pillars of the
      land will be crushed,
   and all who work for pay
      will be grieved.

¹¹ The princes of Zoan are utterly foolish;
      the wisest counsellors of Pharaoh
         give stupid counsel.
   How can you say to Pharaoh,
      "I am a son of the wise,
         a son of ancient kings"?
¹² Where then are your wise men?
      Let them tell you
   that they might know what
      the Lord of hosts has
         purposed against Egypt.
¹³ The princes of Zoan have
         become fools,
   and the princes of Memphis
         are deluded;
   those who are the cornerstones
         of her tribes
   have made Egypt stagger.
¹⁴ The Lord has mingled within
      her a spirit of confusion,
   and they will make Egypt
      stagger in all its deeds,
   as a drunken man staggers
      in his vomit.
¹⁵ And there will be nothing for Egypt
   that head or tail, palm branch
      or reed, may do.

EGYPT, ASSYRIA, ISRAEL BLESSED

¹⁶In that day the Egyptians will be like women, and tremble with fear before the hand that the Lord of hosts shakes over them. ¹⁷And the land of Judah will become a terror to the Egyptians. Everyone to whom it is mentioned will fear because of the purpose that the Lord of hosts has purposed against them.

¹⁸In that day there will be five cities in the land of Egypt that speak the language of Canaan and swear allegiance to the Lord of hosts. One of these will be called the City of Destruction.[b]

¹⁹In that day there will be an altar to the Lord in the midst of the land of Egypt, and a pillar to the Lord at its border. ²⁰It will be

---

[a] Or *I will swallow up* [b] Dead Sea Scroll and some other manuscripts *City of the Sun*

a sign and a witness to the LORD of hosts in the land of Egypt. When they cry to the LORD because of oppressors, he will send them a saviour and defender, and deliver them. ²¹And the LORD will make himself known to the Egyptians, and the Egyptians will know the LORD in that day and worship with sacrifice and offering, and they will make vows to the LORD and perform them. ²²And the LORD will strike Egypt, striking and healing, and they will return to the LORD, and he will listen to their pleas for mercy and heal them.

²³In that day there will be a highway from Egypt to Assyria, and Assyria will come into Egypt, and Egypt into Assyria, and the Egyptians will worship with the Assyrians.

²⁴In that day Israel will be the third with Egypt and Assyria, a blessing in the midst of the earth, ²⁵whom the LORD of hosts has blessed, saying, "Blessed be Egypt my people, and Assyria the work of my hands, and Israel my inheritance."

A SIGN AGAINST EGYPT AND CUSH

20 In the year that the commander-in-chief, who was sent by Sargon the king of Assyria, came to Ashdod and fought against it and captured it — ²at that time the LORD spoke by Isaiah the son of Amoz, saying, "Go, and loose the sackcloth from your waist and take off your sandals from your feet", and he did so, walking naked and barefoot.

³Then the LORD said, "As my servant Isaiah has walked naked and barefoot for three years as a sign and a portent against Egypt and Cush,ᵃ ⁴so shall the king of Assyria lead away the Egyptian captives and the Cushite exiles, both the young and the old, naked and barefoot, with buttocks uncovered, the nakedness of Egypt. ⁵Then they shall be dismayed and ashamed because of Cush their hope and of Egypt their boast. ⁶And the inhabitants of this coastland will say in that day, 'Behold, this is what has happened to those in whom we hoped and to whom we fled for help to be delivered from the king of Assyria! And we, how shall we escape?'"

FALLEN, FALLEN IS BABYLON

21 The oracle concerning the wilderness of the sea.

As whirlwinds in the Negeb sweep on,
   it comes from the wilderness,
   from a terrible land.

² A stern vision is told to me;
   the traitor betrays,
   and the destroyer destroys.
Go up, O Elam;
   lay siege, O Media;
all the sighing she has caused
   I bring to an end.
³ Therefore my loins are filled
   with anguish;
pangs have seized me,
   like the pangs of a woman in labour;
I am bowed down so that I cannot hear;
   I am dismayed so that I cannot see.
⁴ My heart staggers; horror
   has appalled me;
the twilight I longed for
   has been turned for me
   into trembling.
⁵ They prepare the table,
   they spread the rugs,ᵇ
   they eat, they drink.
Arise, O princes;
   oil the shield!

⁶ For thus the Lord said to me:
"Go, set a watchman;
   let him announce what he sees.
⁷ When he sees riders,
   horsemen in pairs,
   riders on donkeys, riders on camels,
let him listen diligently,
   very diligently."
⁸ Then he who saw cried out:ᶜ
"Upon a watchtower I stand, O Lord,
   continually by day,
and at my post I am stationed
   whole nights.
⁹ And behold, here come riders,
   horsemen in pairs!"
And he answered,
   "Fallen, fallen is Babylon;
and all the carved images of her gods
   he has shattered to the ground."
¹⁰ O my threshed and winnowed one,
   what I have heard from the
   LORD of hosts,
   the God of Israel, I announce to you.

¹¹The oracle concerning Dumah.

One is calling to me from Seir,
   "Watchman, what time of the night?
   Watchman, what time of the night?"

ᵃProbably Nubia ᵇOr *they set the watchman* ᶜDead Sea Scroll, Syriac; Masoretic Text *Then a lion cried out*, or *Then he cried out like a lion*

¹² The watchman says:
"Morning comes, and also the night.
If you will enquire, enquire;
come back again."

¹³The oracle concerning Arabia.

In the thickets in Arabia you will lodge,
O caravans of Dedanites.
¹⁴ To the thirsty bring water;
meet the fugitive with bread,
O inhabitants of the land of Tema.
¹⁵ For they have fled from the swords,
from the drawn sword,
from the bent bow,
and from the press of battle.

¹⁶For thus the Lord said to me, "Within a year, according to the years of a hired worker, all the glory of Kedar will come to an end. ¹⁷And the remainder of the archers of the mighty men of the sons of Kedar will be few, for the LORD, the God of Israel, has spoken."

AN ORACLE CONCERNING JERUSALEM

22 The oracle concerning the valley of vision.

What do you mean that you
have gone up,
all of you, to the housetops,
² you who are full of shoutings,
tumultuous city, exultant town?
Your slain are not slain with the sword
or dead in battle.
³ All your leaders have fled together;
without the bow they were captured.
All of you who were found
were captured,
though they had fled far away.
⁴ Therefore I said:
"Look away from me;
let me weep bitter tears;
do not labour to comfort me
concerning the destruction of the
daughter of my people."

⁵ For the Lord GOD of hosts has a day
of tumult and trampling
and confusion
in the valley of vision,
a battering down of walls
and a shouting to the mountains.
⁶ And Elam bore the quiver
with chariots and horsemen,
and Kir uncovered the shield.
⁷ Your choicest valleys were
full of chariots,
and the horsemen took their
stand at the gates.
⁸ He has taken away the
covering of Judah.

In that day you looked to the weapons of the House of the Forest, ⁹and you saw that the breaches of the city of David were many. You collected the waters of the lower pool, ¹⁰and you counted the houses of Jerusalem, and you broke down the houses to fortify the wall. ¹¹You made a reservoir between the two walls for the water of the old pool. But you did not look to him who did it, or see him who planned it long ago.

¹² In that day the Lord GOD of hosts
called for weeping and mourning,
for baldness and wearing sackcloth;
¹³ and behold, joy and gladness,
killing oxen and slaughtering sheep,
eating flesh and drinking wine.
"Let us eat and drink,
for tomorrow we die."
¹⁴ The LORD of hosts has revealed
himself in my ears:
"Surely this iniquity will not be
atoned for you until you die,"
says the Lord GOD of hosts.

¹⁵Thus says the Lord GOD of hosts, "Come, go to this steward, to Shebna, who is over the household, and say to him: ¹⁶What have you to do here, and whom have you here, that you have cut out here a tomb for yourself, you who cut out a tomb on the height and carve a dwelling for yourself in the rock? ¹⁷Behold, the LORD will hurl you away violently, O you strong man. He will seize firm hold on you ¹⁸and whirl you round and round, and throw you like a ball into a wide land. There you shall die, and there shall be your glorious chariots, you shame of your master's house. ¹⁹I will thrust you from your office, and you will be pulled down from your station. ²⁰In that day I will call my servant Eliakim the son of Hilkiah, ²¹and I will clothe him with your robe, and will bind your sash on him, and will commit your authority to his hand. And he shall be a father to the inhabitants of Jerusalem and to the house of Judah. ²²And I will place on his shoulder the key of the house of David. He shall open, and none shall shut; and

he shall shut, and none shall open. ²³And I will fasten him like a peg in a secure place, and he will become a throne of honour to his father's house. ²⁴And they will hang on him the whole honour of his father's house, the offspring and issue, every small vessel, from the cups to all the flagons. ²⁵In that day, declares the LORD of hosts, the peg that was fastened in a secure place will give way, and it will be cut down and fall, and the load that was on it will be cut off, for the LORD has spoken."

AN ORACLE CONCERNING TYRE AND SIDON

23 The oracle concerning Tyre.

Wail, O ships of Tarshish,
    for Tyre is laid waste, without
        house or harbour!
From the land of Cyprus*ᵃ*
    it is revealed to them.
² Be still, O inhabitants of the coast;
    the merchants of Sidon, who cross
        the sea, have filled you.
³ And on many waters
    your revenue was the grain of Shihor,
        the harvest of the Nile;
    you were the merchant
        of the nations.
⁴ Be ashamed, O Sidon, for
    the sea has spoken,
    the stronghold of the sea, saying:
"I have neither laboured
    nor given birth,
I have neither reared young men
    nor brought up young women."
⁵ When the report comes to Egypt,
    they will be in anguish*ᵇ* over
        the report about Tyre.
⁶ Cross over to Tarshish;
    wail, O inhabitants of the coast!
⁷ Is this your exultant city
    whose origin is from days of old,
    whose feet carried her
        to settle far away?
⁸ Who has purposed this
    against Tyre, the bestower
        of crowns,
    whose merchants were princes,
    whose traders were the
        honoured of the earth?
⁹ The LORD of hosts has purposed it,
    to defile the pompous
        pride of all glory,*ᶜ*
    to dishonour all the honoured
        of the earth.
¹⁰ Cross over your land like the Nile,
    O daughter of Tarshish;
    there is no restraint any more.
¹¹ He has stretched out his
        hand over the sea;
    he has shaken the kingdoms;
the LORD has given command
    concerning Canaan
    to destroy its strongholds.
¹² And he said:
"You will no more exult,
    O oppressed virgin
        daughter of Sidon;
arise, cross over to Cyprus,
    even there you will have no rest."

¹³Behold the land of the Chaldeans! This is the people that was not;*ᵈ* Assyria destined it for wild beasts. They erected their siege towers, they stripped her palaces bare, they made her a ruin.

¹⁴ Wail, O ships of Tarshish,
    for your stronghold is laid waste.

¹⁵In that day Tyre will be forgotten for seventy years, like the days*ᵉ* of one king. At the end of seventy years, it will happen to Tyre as in the song of the prostitute:

¹⁶ "Take a harp;
    go about the city,
    O forgotten prostitute!
Make sweet melody;
    sing many songs,
    that you may be remembered."

¹⁷At the end of seventy years, the LORD will visit Tyre, and she will return to her wages and will prostitute herself with all the kingdoms of the world on the face of the earth. ¹⁸Her merchandise and her wages will be holy to the LORD. It will not be stored or hoarded, but her merchandise will supply abundant food and fine clothing for those who dwell before the LORD.

JUDGEMENT ON THE WHOLE EARTH

24 Behold, the LORD will empty
    the earth*ᶠ* and make it desolate,
    and he will twist its surface and
        scatter its inhabitants.

---

*ᵃ*Hebrew *Kittim*; also verse 12   *ᵇ*Hebrew *they will have labour pains*   *ᶜ*The Hebrew words for *glory* and *hosts* sound alike   *ᵈ*Or *that has become nothing*   *ᵉ*Or *lifetime*   *ᶠ*Or *land*; also throughout this chapter

2 And it shall be, as with the
    people, so with the priest;
  as with the slave, so with his master;
  as with the maid, so with
    her mistress;
  as with the buyer, so with the seller;
  as with the lender, so with
    the borrower;
  as with the creditor, so
    with the debtor.
3 The earth shall be utterly empty
    and utterly plundered;
  for the LORD has spoken this word.

4 The earth mourns and withers;
    the world languishes and withers;
    the highest people of the
      earth languish.
5 The earth lies defiled
    under its inhabitants;
  for they have transgressed the laws,
    violated the statutes,
    broken the everlasting covenant.
6 Therefore a curse devours the earth,
    and its inhabitants suffer
      for their guilt;
  therefore the inhabitants of
    the earth are scorched,
    and few men are left.
7 The wine mourns,
    the vine languishes,
    all the merry-hearted sigh.
8 The mirth of the tambourines
      is stilled,
    the noise of the jubilant has ceased,
    the mirth of the lyre is stilled.
9 No more do they drink wine
      with singing;
    strong drink is bitter to
      those who drink it.
10 The wasted city is broken down;
    every house is shut up so
      that none can enter.
11 There is an outcry in the streets
      for lack of wine;
    all joy has grown dark;
    the gladness of the earth
      is banished.
12 Desolation is left in the city;
    the gates are battered into ruins.
13 For thus it shall be in the
      midst of the earth
    among the nations,
  as when an olive tree is beaten,
    as at the gleaning when the
      grape harvest is done.

14 They lift up their voices,
    they sing for joy;
  over the majesty of the LORD
    they shout from the west.[1]
15 Therefore in the east[1] give
    glory to the LORD;
  in the coastlands of the sea, give
    glory to the name of the
      LORD, the God of Israel.
16 From the ends of the earth we
    hear songs of praise,
    of glory to the Righteous One.
  But I say, "I waste away,
    I waste away. Woe is me!
  For the traitors have betrayed,
    with betrayal the traitors
      have betrayed."

17 Terror and the pit and the snare[1]
    are upon you, O inhabitant
      of the earth!
18 He who flees at the sound of
      the terror
    shall fall into the pit,
  and he who climbs out of the pit
    shall be caught in the snare.
  For the windows of heaven are
      opened,
    and the foundations of the
      earth tremble.
19 The earth is utterly broken,
    the earth is split apart,
    the earth is violently shaken.
20 The earth staggers like a
      drunken man;
    it sways like a hut;
  its transgression lies heavy upon it,
    and it falls, and will not rise again.

21 On that day the LORD will punish
    the host of heaven, in heaven,
    and the kings of the earth,
      on the earth.
22 They will be gathered together
    as prisoners in a pit;
  they will be shut up in a prison,
    and after many days they
      will be punished.
23 Then the moon will be confounded
    and the sun ashamed,
  for the LORD of hosts reigns
    on Mount Zion and in Jerusalem,
    and his glory will be before his elders.

---

[1]Hebrew *from the sea*   [1]Hebrew *in the realm of light*, or *with the fires*
[1]The Hebrew words for *terror, pit,* and *snare* sound alike

GOD WILL SWALLOW UP DEATH FOR EVER

25 O Lord, you are my God;
    I will exalt you; I will praise
        your name,
for you have done wonderful things,
    plans formed of old,
        faithful and sure.
2 For you have made the city a heap,
    the fortified city a ruin;
the foreigners' palace is a city
        no more;
    it will never be rebuilt.
3 Therefore strong peoples
        will glorify you;
    cities of ruthless nations
        will fear you.
4 For you have been a stronghold
        to the poor,
    a stronghold to the needy
        in his distress,
    a shelter from the storm and
        a shade from the heat;
for the breath of the ruthless is
        like a storm against a wall,
5   like heat in a dry place.
You subdue the noise of the foreigners;
    as heat by the shade of a cloud,
    so the song of the ruthless
        is put down.

6 On this mountain the Lord of hosts
        will make for all peoples
    a feast of rich food, a feast
        of well-aged wine,
    of rich food full of marrow, of
        aged wine well refined.
7 And he will swallow up on
        this mountain
    the covering that is cast
        over all peoples,
    the veil that is spread
        over all nations.
8 He will swallow up death for ever;
and the Lord God will wipe away
        tears from all faces,
    and the reproach of his people he
        will take away from all the earth,
    for the Lord has spoken.
9 It will be said on that day,
    "Behold, this is our God; we
        have waited for him, that
        he might save us.
    This is the Lord; we have
        waited for him;
    let us be glad and rejoice
        in his salvation."

10 For the hand of the Lord will
        rest on this mountain,
    and Moab shall be trampled
        down in his place,
    as straw is trampled down
        in a dunghill.[a]
11 And he will spread out his
        hands in the midst of it
    as a swimmer spreads his
        hands out to swim,
    but the Lord will lay low his
        pompous pride together
        with the skill[b] of his hands.
12 And the high fortifications of his
        walls he will bring down,
    lay low, and cast to the
        ground, to the dust.

YOU KEEP HIM IN PERFECT PEACE

26 In that day this song will be sung
    in the land of Judah:

"We have a strong city;
    he sets up salvation
        as walls and bulwarks.
2 Open the gates,
    that the righteous nation that
        keeps faith may enter in.
3 You keep him in perfect peace
    whose mind is stayed on you,
    because he trusts in you.
4 Trust in the Lord for ever,
    for the Lord God is an
        everlasting rock.
5 For he has humbled
    the inhabitants of the height,
    the lofty city.
He lays it low, lays it low to the ground,
    casts it to the dust.
6 The foot tramples it,
    the feet of the poor,
    the steps of the needy."

7 The path of the righteous is level;
    you make level the way of
        the righteous.
8 In the path of your judgements,
    O Lord, we wait for you;
your name and remembrance
    are the desire of our soul.
9 My soul yearns for you in the night;
    my spirit within me
        earnestly seeks you.

---

[a] The Hebrew words for *dunghill* and for the Moabite town *Madmen* (Jeremiah 48:2) sound alike   [b] Or *in spite of the skill*

For when your judgements
    are in the earth,
  the inhabitants of the world
    learn righteousness.
10 If favour is shown to the wicked,
    he does not learn righteousness;
  in the land of uprightness
    he deals corruptly
  and does not see the majesty
    of the LORD.
11 O LORD, your hand is lifted up,
    but they do not see it.
  Let them see your zeal for your
    people, and be ashamed.
  Let the fire for your adversaries
    consume them.
12 O LORD, you will ordain peace for us,
    for you have indeed done
    for us all our works.
13 O LORD our God,
    other lords besides you
    have ruled over us,
  but your name alone we bring
    to remembrance.
14 They are dead, they will not live;
    they are shades, they will not arise;
  to that end you have visited
    them with destruction
  and wiped out all remembrance
    of them.
15 But you have increased the
    nation, O LORD,
    you have increased the nation;
    you are glorified;
  you have enlarged all the
    borders of the land.
16 O LORD, in distress they sought you;
    they poured out a whispered prayer
    when your discipline
    was upon them.
17 Like a pregnant woman
    who writhes and cries
    out in her pangs
  when she is near to giving birth,
  so were we because of you, O LORD;
18   we were pregnant, we writhed,
    but we have given birth to wind.
  We have accomplished no
    deliverance in the earth,
  and the inhabitants of the
    world have not fallen.
19 Your dead shall live; their
    bodies shall rise.
  You who dwell in the dust,
    awake and sing for joy!
  For your dew is a dew of light,
    and the earth will give
    birth to the dead.
20 Come, my people, enter
    your chambers,
    and shut your doors behind you;
  hide yourselves for a little while
    until the fury has passed by.
21 For behold, the LORD is coming
    out from his place
  to punish the inhabitants of the
    earth for their iniquity,
  and the earth will disclose
    the blood shed on it,
  and will no more cover its slain.

THE REDEMPTION OF ISRAEL

27 In that day the LORD with his hard and great and strong sword will punish Leviathan the fleeing serpent, Leviathan the twisting serpent, and he will slay the dragon that is in the sea.

2   In that day,
  "A pleasant vineyard,[a] sing of it!
3   I, the LORD, am its keeper;
    every moment I water it.
  Lest anyone punish it,
    I keep it night and day;
4   I have no wrath.
  Would that I had thorns and
    briers to battle!
  I would march against them,
    I would burn them up together.
5   Or let them lay hold of my protection,
    let them make peace with me,
    let them make peace with me."

6   In days to come[b] Jacob shall take root,
    Israel shall blossom and
    put forth shoots
  and fill the whole world with fruit.

7   Has he struck them as he struck
    those who struck them?
  Or have they been slain as their
    slayers were slain?
8   Measure by measure,[c] by exile
    you contended with them;
  he removed them with his
    fierce breath[d] in the day
    of the east wind.

---

[a] Many Hebrew manuscripts *A vineyard of wine*   [b] Hebrew *In those to come*   [c] Or *By driving her away*; the meaning of the Hebrew word is uncertain   [d] Or *wind*

⁹ Therefore by this the guilt of
      Jacob will be atoned for,
   and this will be the full fruit of
      the removal of his sin:ᵃ
 when he makes all the
      stones of the altars
   like chalk-stones crushed
      to pieces,
   no Asherim or incense altars
      will remain standing.
¹⁰ For the fortified city is solitary,
      a habitation deserted and forsaken,
      like the wilderness;
   there the calf grazes;
      there it lies down and strips
      its branches.
¹¹ When its boughs are dry,
      they are broken;
   women come and make
      a fire of them.
   For this is a people without
      discernment;
   therefore he who made them will
      not have compassion on them;
   he who formed them will
      show them no favour.

¹²In that day from the river Euphratesᵇ to the Brook of Egypt the LORD will thresh out the grain, and you will be gleaned one by one, O people of Israel. ¹³And in that day a great trumpet will be blown, and those who were lost in the land of Assyria and those who were driven out to the land of Egypt will come and worship the LORD on the holy mountain at Jerusalem.

JUDGEMENT ON EPHRAIM AND JERUSALEM

28 Ah, the proud crown of the
      drunkards of Ephraim,
   and the fading flower of its
      glorious beauty,
   which is on the head of the
      rich valley of those
      overcome with wine!
² Behold, the Lord has one who
      is mighty and strong;
   like a storm of hail, a
      destroying tempest,
   like a storm of mighty,
      overflowing waters,
   he casts down to the earth
      with his hand.
³ The proud crown of the
      drunkards of Ephraim
   will be trodden underfoot;
⁴ and the fading flower of its
      glorious beauty,
   which is on the head of
      the rich valley,
   will be like a first-ripe figᶜ
      before the summer:
   when someone sees it,
      he swallows it
   as soon as it is in his hand.
⁵ In that day the LORD of hosts
      will be a crown of glory,ᵈ
   and a diadem of beauty, to the
      remnant of his people,
⁶ and a spirit of justice to him
      who sits in judgement,
   and strength to those who turn
      back the battle at the gate.

⁷ These also reel with wine
      and stagger with strong drink;
   the priest and the prophet reel
      with strong drink,
   they are swallowed byᵉ wine,
      they stagger with strong drink,
   they reel in vision,
      they stumble in giving
      judgement.
⁸ For all tables are full of filthy vomit,
      with no space left.

⁹ "To whom will he teach knowledge,
      and to whom will he explain
      the message?
   Those who are weaned from
      the milk,
      those taken from the breast?
¹⁰ For it is precept upon precept,
      precept upon precept,
   line upon line, line upon line,
      here a little, there a little."

¹¹ For by people of strange lips
      and with a foreign tongue
   the LORD will speak to this people,
¹² to whom he has said,
   "This is rest;
      give rest to the weary;
   and this is repose";
      yet they would not hear.
¹³ And the word of the LORD
      will be to them

ᵃSeptuagint *and this is the blessing when I take away his sin*   ᵇHebrew *from the River*   ᶜOr *fruit*   ᵈThe Hebrew words for *glory* and *hosts* sound alike   ᵉOr *confused by*

precept upon precept, precept
  upon precept,
 line upon line, line upon line,
 here a little, there a little,
that they may go, and fall backwards,
 and be broken, and snared,
  and taken.

A CORNERSTONE IN ZION

14 Therefore hear the word of the
   LORD, you scoffers,
  who rule this people in Jerusalem!
15 Because you have said, "We have
   made a covenant with death,
  and with Sheol we have
   an agreement,
  when the overwhelming
   whip passes through
  it will not come to us,
  for we have made lies our refuge,
  and in falsehood we have
   taken shelter";
16 therefore thus says the Lord GOD,
 "Behold, I am the one who has laid[a]
   as a foundation in Zion,
  a stone, a tested stone,
 a precious cornerstone, of
   a sure foundation:
  'Whoever believes will
   not be in haste.'
17 And I will make justice the line,
   and righteousness the plumb line;
  and hail will sweep away
   the refuge of lies,
  and waters will overwhelm
   the shelter."
18 Then your covenant with death
   will be annulled,
  and your agreement with
   Sheol will not stand;
  when the overwhelming
   scourge passes through,
  you will be beaten down by it.
19 As often as it passes through
   it will take you;
  for morning by morning it
   will pass through,
  by day and by night;
  and it will be sheer terror to
   understand the message.
20 For the bed is too short to
   stretch oneself on,
  and the covering too narrow
   to wrap oneself in.
21 For the LORD will rise up as
   on Mount Perazim;
  as in the Valley of Gibeon
   he will be roused;
  to do his deed—strange is his deed!
  and to work his work—
   alien is his work!
22 Now therefore do not scoff,
   lest your bonds be made strong;
  for I have heard a decree of destruction
   from the Lord GOD of hosts
   against the whole land.

23 Give ear, and hear my voice;
   give attention, and hear my speech.
24 Does he who ploughs for sowing
   plough continually?
  Does he continually open and
   harrow his ground?
25 When he has levelled its surface,
   does he not scatter dill, sow cumin,
  and put in wheat in rows
   and barley in its proper place,
   and emmer[b] as the border?
26 For he is rightly instructed;
   his God teaches him.

27 Dill is not threshed with a
   threshing sledge,
  nor is a cart wheel rolled
   over cumin,
  but dill is beaten out with a stick,
   and cumin with a rod.
28 Does one crush grain for bread?
  No, he does not thresh it for ever;[c]
  when he drives his cart wheel over it
   with his horses, he does not crush it.
29 This also comes from the
   LORD of hosts;
  he is wonderful in counsel
   and excellent in wisdom.

THE SIEGE OF JERUSALEM

29 Ah, Ariel, Ariel,
   the city where David encamped!
  Add year to year;
   let the feasts run their round.
2 Yet I will distress Ariel,
   and there shall be moaning
   and lamentation,
  and she shall be to me like an Ariel.[d]
3 And I will encamp against
   you all round,
  and will besiege you with towers

---

[a]Dead Sea Scroll *I am laying* [b]A type of wheat [c]Or *Grain is crushed for bread; he will surely thresh it, but not for ever* [d]*Ariel* could mean *lion of God*, or *hero* (2 Samuel 23:20), or *altar hearth* (Ezekiel 43:15–16)

and I will raise siege works
against you.
4 And you will be brought low; from
the earth you shall speak,
and from the dust your speech
will be bowed down;
your voice shall come from the
ground like the voice of a ghost,
and from the dust your
speech shall whisper.

5 But the multitude of your foreign
foes shall be like small dust,
and the multitude of the ruthless
like passing chaff.
And in an instant, suddenly,
6 you will be visited by the
Lord of hosts
with thunder and with earthquake
and great noise,
with whirlwind and tempest, and
the flame of a devouring fire.
7 And the multitude of all the nations
that fight against Ariel,
all that fight against her and her
stronghold and distress her,
shall be like a dream, a
vision of the night.
8 As when a hungry man dreams,
and behold, he is eating,
and awakes with his hunger
not satisfied,
or as when a thirsty man dreams,
and behold, he is drinking,
and awakes faint, with his
thirst not quenched,
so shall the multitude of
all the nations be
that fight against Mount Zion.

9 Astonish yourselves*a* and
be astonished;
blind yourselves and be blind!
Be drunk,*b* but not with wine;
stagger,*c* but not with strong drink!
10 For the Lord has poured out upon you
a spirit of deep sleep,
and has closed your eyes
(the prophets),
and covered your heads (the seers).

11 And the vision of all this has become to you like the words of a book that is sealed. When men give it to one who can read, saying, "Read this," he says, "I cannot, for it is sealed." 12 And when they give the book to one who cannot read, saying, "Read this," he says, "I cannot read."

13 And the Lord said:
"Because this people draw near
with their mouth
and honour me with their lips,
while their hearts are far from me,
and their fear of me is a
commandment taught by men,
14 therefore, behold, I will again
do wonderful things with
this people,
with wonder upon wonder;
and the wisdom of their wise
men shall perish,
and the discernment of
their discerning men
shall be hidden."

15 Ah, you who hide deep from
the Lord your counsel,
whose deeds are in the dark,
and who say, "Who sees us?
Who knows us?"
16 You turn things upside down!
Shall the potter be regarded as
the clay,
that the thing made should
say of its maker,
"He did not make me";
or the thing formed say of
him who formed it,
"He has no understanding"?

17 Is it not yet a very little while
until Lebanon shall be turned
into a fruitful field,
and the fruitful field shall be
regarded as a forest?
18 In that day the deaf shall hear
the words of a book,
and out of their gloom and darkness
the eyes of the blind shall see.
19 The meek shall obtain fresh
joy in the Lord,
and the poor among mankind shall
exult in the Holy One of Israel.
20 For the ruthless shall come to nothing
and the scoffer cease,
and all who watch to do evil
shall be cut off,
21 who by a word make a man
out to be an offender,

---

a Or *Linger awhile* *b* Or *They are drunk* *c* Or *they stagger*

and lay a snare for him who
    reproves in the gate,
and with an empty plea turn aside
    him who is in the right.

²²Therefore thus says the LORD, who redeemed Abraham, concerning the house of Jacob:

"Jacob shall no more be ashamed,
    no more shall his face grow pale.
²³ For when he sees his children,
    the work of my hands, in his midst,
    they will sanctify my name;
they will sanctify the Holy One
    of Jacob
and will stand in awe of
    the God of Israel.
²⁴ And those who go astray in spirit
    will come to understanding,
and those who murmur will
    accept instruction."

DO NOT GO DOWN TO EGYPT

30 "Ah, stubborn children,"
    declares the LORD,
"who carry out a plan,
    but not mine,
and who make an alliance,ᵃ
    but not of my Spirit,
that they may add sin to sin;
² who set out to go down to Egypt,
    without asking for my direction,
to take refuge in the protection
    of Pharaoh
and to seek shelter in the
    shadow of Egypt!
³ Therefore shall the protection of
    Pharaoh turn to your shame,
and the shelter in the shadow of
    Egypt to your humiliation.
⁴ For though his officials are at Zoan
    and his envoys reach Hanes,
⁵ everyone comes to shame
    through a people that
    cannot profit them,
that brings neither help nor profit,
    but shame and disgrace."

⁶An oracle on the beasts of the Negeb.

Through a land of trouble and anguish,
    from where come the lioness
    and the lion,
    the adder and the flying
    fiery serpent,
they carry their riches on the
    backs of donkeys,
and their treasures on the
    humps of camels,
to a people that cannot profit them.
⁷ Egypt's help is worthless and empty;
    therefore I have called her
    "Rahab who sits still."

A REBELLIOUS PEOPLE

⁸ And now, go, write it before
    them on a tablet
and inscribe it in a book,
that it may be for the time to come
    as a witness for ever.ᵇ
⁹ For they are a rebellious people,
    lying children,
children unwilling to hear
    the instruction of the LORD;
¹⁰ who say to the seers, "Do not see",
    and to the prophets, "Do not
    prophesy to us what is right;
speak to us smooth things,
    prophesy illusions,
¹¹ leave the way, turn aside from the path,
    let us hear no more about the
    Holy One of Israel."
¹² Therefore thus says the
    Holy One of Israel,
"Because you despise this word
    and trust in oppression
    and perverseness
    and rely on them,
¹³ therefore this iniquity shall be to you
    like a breach in a high wall, bulging
    out and about to collapse,
    whose breaking comes
    suddenly, in an instant;
¹⁴ and its breaking is like that
    of a potter's vessel
    that is smashed so ruthlessly
that among its fragments
    not a shard is found
with which to take fire
    from the hearth,
or to dip up water out of the cistern."

¹⁵ For thus said the Lord GOD,
    the Holy One of Israel,
"In returningᶜ and rest you shall be saved;
    in quietness and in trust shall
    be your strength."

ᵃHebrew *who weave a web*   ᵇSome Hebrew manuscripts, Syriac, Targum, Vulgate, and Greek versions; Masoretic Text *for ever and ever*   ᶜOr *repentance*

But you were unwilling,
¹⁶and you said,
"No! We will flee upon horses";
    therefore you shall flee away;
and, "We will ride upon swift steeds";
    therefore your pursuers
        shall be swift.
¹⁷ A thousand shall flee at
        the threat of one;
    at the threat of five you shall flee,
till you are left
    like a flagstaff on the top
        of a mountain,
    like a signal on a hill.

THE LORD WILL BE GRACIOUS

¹⁸   Therefore the LORD waits to
        be gracious to you,
    and therefore he exalts himself
        to show mercy to you.
    For the LORD is a God of justice;
        blessed are all those who
            wait for him.

¹⁹For a people shall dwell in Zion, in Jerusalem; you shall weep no more. He will surely be gracious to you at the sound of your cry. As soon as he hears it, he answers you. ²⁰And though the Lord give you the bread of adversity and the water of affliction, yet your Teacher will not hide himself any more, but your eyes shall see your Teacher. ²¹And your ears shall hear a word behind you, saying, "This is the way, walk in it", when you turn to the right or when you turn to the left. ²²Then you will defile your carved idols overlaid with silver and your gold-plated metal images. You will scatter them as unclean things. You will say to them, "Be gone!"

²³And he will give rain for the seed with which you sow the ground, and bread, the produce of the ground, which will be rich and plenteous. In that day your livestock will graze in large pastures, ²⁴and the oxen and the donkeys that work the ground will eat seasoned fodder, which has been winnowed with shovel and fork. ²⁵And on every lofty mountain and every high hill there will be brooks running with water, in the day of the great slaughter, when the towers fall. ²⁶Moreover, the light of the moon will be as the light of the sun, and the light of the sun will be sevenfold, as the light of seven days, in the day when the LORD binds up the brokenness of his people, and heals the wounds inflicted by his blow.

²⁷   Behold, the name of the LORD
        comes from afar,
    burning with his anger, and
        in thick rising smoke;[a]
    his lips are full of fury,
        and his tongue is like a
            devouring fire;
²⁸   his breath is like an
        overflowing stream
    that reaches up to the neck;
    to sift the nations with the
        sieve of destruction,
    and to place on the jaws of
        the peoples a bridle
            that leads astray.

²⁹You shall have a song as in the night when a holy feast is kept, and gladness of heart, as when one sets out to the sound of the flute to go to the mountain of the LORD, to the Rock of Israel. ³⁰And the LORD will cause his majestic voice to be heard and the descending blow of his arm to be seen, in furious anger and a flame of devouring fire, with a cloudburst and storm and hailstones. ³¹The Assyrians will be terror-stricken at the voice of the LORD, when he strikes with his rod. ³²And every stroke of the appointed staff that the LORD lays on them will be to the sound of tambourines and lyres. Battling with brandished arm, he will fight with them. ³³For a burning place[b] has long been prepared; indeed, for the king it is made ready, its pyre made deep and wide, with fire and wood in abundance; the breath of the LORD, like a stream of sulphur, kindles it.

WOE TO THOSE WHO GO DOWN TO EGYPT

31   Woe[c] to those who go down to
            Egypt for help
        and rely on horses,
    who trust in chariots because
            they are many
        and in horsemen because
            they are very strong,
    but do not look to the Holy
            One of Israel
        or consult the LORD!
²   And yet he is wise and brings disaster;
        he does not call back his words,
    but will arise against the
            house of the evildoers
        and against the helpers of those
            who work iniquity.

---

[a]Hebrew *in weight of uplifted clouds*   [b]Or *For Topheth*   [c]Or *Ah,*

³ The Egyptians are man, and not God,
   and their horses are flesh,
      and not spirit.
   When the LORD stretches out his hand,
      the helper will stumble, and he
         who is helped will fall,
      and they will all perish together.

⁴ For thus the LORD said to me,
   "As a lion or a young lion
      growls over his prey,
   and when a band of shepherds
      is called out against him
   he is not terrified by their shouting
      or daunted at their noise,
   so the LORD of hosts will come down
      to fight[a] on Mount Zion
         and on its hill.
⁵ Like birds hovering, so the
      LORD of hosts
   will protect Jerusalem;
   he will protect and deliver it;
   he will spare and rescue it."

⁶Turn to him from whom people[b] have deeply revolted, O children of Israel. ⁷For in that day everyone shall cast away his idols of silver and his idols of gold, which your hands have sinfully made for you.

⁸ "And the Assyrian shall fall by
      a sword, not of man;
   and a sword, not of man,
      shall devour him;
   and he shall flee from the sword,
      and his young men shall be
         put to forced labour.
⁹ His rock shall pass away in terror,
   and his officers desert the
      standard in panic,"
declares the LORD, whose
      fire is in Zion,
   and whose furnace is in Jerusalem.

A KING WILL REIGN IN RIGHTEOUSNESS

32 Behold, a king will reign in
      righteousness,
   and princes will rule in justice.
² Each will be like a hiding
      place from the wind,
   a shelter from the storm,
   like streams of water in a dry place,
   like the shade of a great rock
      in a weary land.
³ Then the eyes of those who
      see will not be closed,
   and the ears of those who hear
      will give attention.
⁴ The heart of the hasty will
      understand and know,
   and the tongue of the stammerers
      will hasten to speak distinctly.
⁵ The fool will no more be called noble,
      nor the scoundrel said to
         be honourable.
⁶ For the fool speaks folly,
      and his heart is busy with iniquity,
   to practise ungodliness,
      to utter error concerning the LORD,
   to leave the craving of the
      hungry unsatisfied,
   and to deprive the thirsty of drink.
⁷ As for the scoundrel—his
      devices are evil;
   he plans wicked schemes
   to ruin the poor with lying words,
      even when the plea of the
         needy is right.
⁸ But he who is noble plans
      noble things,
   and on noble things he stands.

COMPLACENT WOMEN WARNED OF DISASTER

⁹ Rise up, you women who are
      at ease, hear my voice;
   you complacent daughters,
      give ear to my speech.
¹⁰ In little more than a year
      you will shudder, you
         complacent women;
   for the grape harvest fails,
      the fruit harvest will not come.
¹¹ Tremble, you women who are at ease,
      shudder, you complacent ones;
   strip, and make yourselves bare,
      and tie sackcloth round your waist.
¹² Beat your breasts for the
      pleasant fields,
      for the fruitful vine,
¹³ for the soil of my people
      growing up in thorns and briers,
   yes, for all the joyous houses
      in the exultant city.
¹⁴ For the palace is forsaken,
      the populous city deserted;
   the hill and the watchtower
      will become dens for ever,
   a joy of wild donkeys,
      a pasture of flocks;

---
[a]The Hebrew words for *hosts* and *to fight* sound alike [b]Hebrew *they*

15 until the Spirit is poured upon
     us from on high,
   and the wilderness becomes
     a fruitful field,
   and the fruitful field is
     deemed a forest.
16 Then justice will dwell in
     the wilderness,
   and righteousness abide in
     the fruitful field.
17 And the effect of righteousness
     will be peace,
   and the result of righteousness,
     quietness and trust[a] for ever.
18 My people will abide in a
     peaceful habitation,
   in secure dwellings, and in
     quiet resting-places.
19 And it will hail when the
     forest falls down,
   and the city will be utterly laid low.
20 Happy are you who sow
     beside all waters,
   who let the feet of the ox and
     the donkey range free.

O LORD, BE GRACIOUS TO US

33 Ah, you destroyer,
     who yourself have not been
       destroyed,
   you traitor,
     whom none has betrayed!
   When you have ceased to destroy,
     you will be destroyed;
   and when you have finished betraying,
     they will betray you.

2 O LORD, be gracious to us;
     we wait for you.
   Be our arm every morning,
     our salvation in the time of trouble.
3 At the tumultuous noise peoples flee;
     when you lift yourself up,
     nations are scattered,
4 and your spoil is gathered as
     the caterpillar gathers;
   as locusts leap, it is leapt upon.

5 The LORD is exalted, for he
     dwells on high;
   he will fill Zion with justice
     and righteousness,
6 and he will be the stability
     of your times,
   abundance of salvation,
     wisdom, and knowledge;
   the fear of the LORD is
     Zion's[b] treasure.

7 Behold, their heroes cry in the streets;
     the envoys of peace weep bitterly.
8 The highways lie waste;
     the traveller ceases.
   Covenants are broken;
     cities[c] are despised;
   there is no regard for man.
9 The land mourns and languishes;
     Lebanon is confounded
     and withers away;
   Sharon is like a desert,
     and Bashan and Carmel
     shake off their leaves.

10 "Now I will arise," says the LORD,
     "now I will lift myself up;
     now I will be exalted.
11 You conceive chaff; you give
     birth to stubble;
   your breath is a fire that
     will consume you.
12 And the peoples will be as
     if burned to lime,
   like thorns cut down, that are
     burned in the fire."

13 Hear, you who are far off,
     what I have done;
   and you who are near,
     acknowledge my might.
14 The sinners in Zion are afraid;
     trembling has seized the godless:
   "Who among us can dwell with
     the consuming fire?
   Who among us can dwell with
     everlasting burnings?"
15 He who walks righteously
     and speaks uprightly,
   who despises the gain of
     oppressions,
   who shakes his hands, lest
     they hold a bribe,
   who stops his ears from
     hearing of bloodshed
   and shuts his eyes from
     looking on evil,
16 he will dwell on the heights;
   his place of defence will be
     the fortresses of rocks;
   his bread will be given him;
     his water will be sure.

---

[a] Or *security* [b] Hebrew *his* [c] Masoretic Text; Dead Sea Scroll *witnesses*

¹⁷ Your eyes will behold the
  king in his beauty;
  they will see a land that
  stretches afar.
¹⁸ Your heart will muse on the terror:
  "Where is he who counted, where is
  he who weighed the tribute?
  Where is he who counted
  the towers?"
¹⁹ You will see no more the
  insolent people,
  the people of an obscure speech
   that you cannot comprehend,
   stammering in a tongue that
   you cannot understand.
²⁰ Behold Zion, the city of our
  appointed feasts!
  Your eyes will see Jerusalem,
   an untroubled habitation,
   an immovable tent,
  whose stakes will never be
   plucked up,
   nor will any of its cords be broken.
²¹ But there the Lord in majesty
  will be for us
  a place of broad rivers and streams,
  where no galley with oars can go,
   nor majestic ship can pass.
²² For the Lord is our judge; the
  Lord is our lawgiver;
  the Lord is our king; he will save us.

²³ Your cords hang loose;
  they cannot hold the mast
   firm in its place
   or keep the sail spread out.
  Then prey and spoil in abundance
   will be divided;
   even the lame will take the prey.
²⁴ And no inhabitant will say, "I am sick";
  the people who dwell there will
   be forgiven their iniquity.

JUDGEMENT ON THE NATIONS

34 Draw near, O nations, to hear,
  and give attention, O peoples!
  Let the earth hear, and all that
   fills it;
   the world, and all that comes
   from it.
² For the Lord is enraged against
  all the nations,
  and furious against all their host;
  he has devoted them to
   destruction,[a] has given
   them over for slaughter.
³ Their slain shall be cast out,
  and the stench of their
   corpses shall rise;
  the mountains shall flow
   with their blood.
⁴ All the host of heaven shall rot away,
  and the skies roll up like a scroll.
  All their host shall fall,
   as leaves fall from the vine,
   like leaves falling from the fig tree.

⁵ For my sword has drunk its
  fill in the heavens;
  behold, it descends for
   judgement upon Edom,
   upon the people I have devoted
   to destruction.
⁶ The Lord has a sword; it is
  sated with blood;
  it is gorged with fat,
  with the blood of lambs and goats,
  with the fat of the kidneys of rams.
  For the Lord has a sacrifice in Bozrah,
   a great slaughter in the
   land of Edom.
⁷ Wild oxen shall fall with them,
  and young steers with the
   mighty bulls.
  Their land shall drink its fill of blood,
   and their soil shall be
   gorged with fat.

⁸ For the Lord has a day of vengeance,
  a year of recompense for
   the cause of Zion.
⁹ And the streams of Edom[b] shall
  be turned into pitch,
  and her soil into sulphur;
  her land shall become burning pitch.
¹⁰ Night and day it shall not be quenched;
  its smoke shall go up for ever.
  From generation to generation
   it shall lie waste;
   none shall pass through it
   for ever and ever.
¹¹ But the hawk and the porcupine[c]
  shall possess it,
  the owl and the raven
   shall dwell in it.
  He shall stretch the line of
   confusion[d] over it,
   and the plumb line of emptiness.

---

[a]That is, set apart (devoted) as an offering to the Lord (for destruction); also verse 5   [b]Hebrew *her streams*   [c]The identity of the animals rendered *hawk* and *porcupine* is uncertain   [d]Hebrew *formlessness*

12 Its nobles—there is no one there
  to call it a kingdom,
 and all its princes shall be nothing.
13 Thorns shall grow over
  its strongholds,
 nettles and thistles in its fortresses.
 It shall be the haunt of jackals,
  an abode for ostriches.[a]
14 And wild animals shall
  meet with hyenas;
 the wild goat shall cry to his fellow;
 indeed, there the night bird[b] settles
  and finds for herself a resting-place.
15 There the owl nests and lays
  and hatches and gathers her
  young in her shadow;
 indeed, there the hawks are gathered,
  each one with her mate.
16 Seek and read from the
  book of the LORD:
 Not one of these shall be missing;
  none shall be without her mate.
 For the mouth of the LORD
  has commanded,
  and his Spirit has gathered them.
17 He has cast the lot for them;
  his hand has portioned it out
   to them with the line;
 they shall possess it for ever;
  from generation to generation
   they shall dwell in it.

THE RANSOMED SHALL RETURN

35 The wilderness and the dry land
   shall be glad;
  the desert shall rejoice and
   blossom like the crocus;
2 it shall blossom abundantly
  and rejoice with joy and singing.
 The glory of Lebanon shall
  be given to it,
  the majesty of Carmel and Sharon.
 They shall see the glory of the LORD,
  the majesty of our God.

3 Strengthen the weak hands,
  and make firm the feeble knees.
4 Say to those who have an
   anxious heart,
  "Be strong; fear not!
 Behold, your God
  will come with vengeance,
  with the recompense of God.
 He will come and save you."

5 Then the eyes of the blind
  shall be opened,
  and the ears of the deaf unstopped;
6 then shall the lame man leap like a deer,
  and the tongue of the
   mute sing for joy.
 For waters break forth in
   the wilderness,
  and streams in the desert;
7 the burning sand shall become a pool,
  and the thirsty ground
   springs of water;
 in the haunt of jackals, where
   they lie down,
  the grass shall become
   reeds and rushes.

8 And a highway shall be there,
  and it shall be called the
   Way of Holiness;
 the unclean shall not pass over it.
 It shall belong to those who
   walk on the way;
  even if they are fools, they
   shall not go astray.[c]
9 No lion shall be there,
  nor shall any ravenous beast
   come up on it;
 they shall not be found there,
  but the redeemed shall walk there.
10 And the ransomed of the
   LORD shall return
  and come to Zion with singing;
 everlasting joy shall be
   upon their heads;
  they shall obtain gladness and joy,
  and sorrow and sighing
   shall flee away.

SENNACHERIB INVADES JUDAH

36 In the fourteenth year of King Hezekiah, Sennacherib king of Assyria came up against all the fortified cities of Judah and took them. ²And the king of Assyria sent the Rabshakeh[d] from Lachish to King Hezekiah at Jerusalem, with a great army. And he stood by the conduit of the upper pool on the highway to the Washer's Field. ³And there came out to him Eliakim the son of Hilkiah, who was over the household, and Shebna the secretary, and Joah the son of Asaph, the recorder.

---

[a] Or *owls* [b] Identity uncertain [c] Or *if they are fools, they shall not wander in it* [d] *Rabshakeh* is the title of a high-ranking Assyrian military officer

⁴And the Rabshakeh said to them, "Say to Hezekiah, 'Thus says the great king, the king of Assyria: On what do you rest this trust of yours? ⁵Do you think that mere words are strategy and power for war? In whom do you now trust, that you have rebelled against me? ⁶Behold, you are trusting in Egypt, that broken reed of a staff, which will pierce the hand of any man who leans on it. Such is Pharaoh king of Egypt to all who trust in him. ⁷But if you say to me, "We trust in the LORD our God", is it not he whose high places and altars Hezekiah has removed, saying to Judah and to Jerusalem, "You shall worship before this altar"? ⁸Come now, make a wager with my master the king of Assyria: I will give you two thousand horses, if you are able on your part to set riders on them. ⁹How then can you repulse a single captain among the least of my master's servants, when you trust in Egypt for chariots and for horsemen? ¹⁰Moreover, is it without the LORD that I have come up against this land to destroy it? The LORD said to me, "Go up against this land and destroy it."'"

¹¹Then Eliakim, Shebna, and Joah said to the Rabshakeh, "Please speak to your servants in Aramaic, for we understand it. Do not speak to us in the language of Judah within the hearing of the people who are on the wall." ¹²But the Rabshakeh said, "Has my master sent me to speak these words to your master and to you, and not to the men sitting on the wall, who are doomed with you to eat their own dung and drink their own urine?"

¹³Then the Rabshakeh stood and called out in a loud voice in the language of Judah: "Hear the words of the great king, the king of Assyria! ¹⁴Thus says the king: 'Do not let Hezekiah deceive you, for he will not be able to deliver you. ¹⁵Do not let Hezekiah make you trust in the LORD by saying, "The LORD will surely deliver us. This city will not be given into the hand of the king of Assyria." ¹⁶Do not listen to Hezekiah. For thus says the king of Assyria: Make your peace with me[a] and come out to me. Then each one of you will eat of his own vine, and each one of his own fig tree, and each one of you will drink the water of his own cistern, ¹⁷until I come and take you away to a land like your own land, a land of grain and wine, a land of bread and vineyards. ¹⁸Beware lest Hezekiah mislead you by saying, "The LORD will deliver us." Has any of the gods of the nations delivered his land out of the hand of the king of Assyria? ¹⁹Where are the gods of Hamath and Arpad? Where are the gods of Sepharvaim? Have they delivered Samaria out of my hand? ²⁰Who among all the gods of these lands have delivered their lands out of my hand, that the LORD should deliver Jerusalem out of my hand?'"

²¹But they were silent and answered him not a word, for the king's command was, "Do not answer him." ²²Then Eliakim the son of Hilkiah, who was over the household, and Shebna the secretary, and Joah the son of Asaph, the recorder, came to Hezekiah with their clothes torn, and told him the words of the Rabshakeh.

HEZEKIAH SEEKS ISAIAH'S HELP

37 As soon as King Hezekiah heard it, he tore his clothes and covered himself with sackcloth and went into the house of the LORD. ²And he sent Eliakim, who was over the household, and Shebna the secretary, and the senior priests, covered with sackcloth, to the prophet Isaiah the son of Amoz. ³They said to him, "Thus says Hezekiah, 'This day is a day of distress, of rebuke, and of disgrace; children have come to the point of birth, and there is no strength to bring them forth. ⁴It may be that the LORD your God will hear the words of the Rabshakeh, whom his master the king of Assyria has sent to mock the living God, and will rebuke the words that the LORD your God has heard; therefore lift up your prayer for the remnant that is left.'"

⁵When the servants of King Hezekiah came to Isaiah, ⁶Isaiah said to them, "Say to your master, 'Thus says the LORD: Do not be afraid because of the words that you have heard, with which the young men of the king of Assyria have reviled me. ⁷Behold, I will put a spirit in him, so that he shall hear a rumour and return to his own land, and I will make him fall by the sword in his own land.'"

⁸The Rabshakeh returned, and found the king of Assyria fighting against Libnah, for he had heard that the king had left Lachish. ⁹Now the king heard concerning Tirhakah king of Cush,[b] "He has set out to fight against you." And when he heard it, he sent messengers to Hezekiah, saying, ¹⁰"Thus shall you speak to Hezekiah king of Judah: 'Do not let your God in whom you trust deceive you by promising that Jerusalem will not be

---

[a] Hebrew *Make a blessing with me* [b] Probably *Nubia*

given into the hand of the king of Assyria. ¹¹Behold, you have heard what the kings of Assyria have done to all lands, devoting them to destruction. And shall you be delivered? ¹²Have the gods of the nations delivered them, the nations that my fathers destroyed, Gozan, Haran, Rezeph, and the people of Eden who were in Telassar? ¹³Where is the king of Hamath, the king of Arpad, the king of the city of Sepharvaim, the king of Hena, or the king of Ivvah?'"

HEZEKIAH'S PRAYER FOR DELIVERANCE

¹⁴Hezekiah received the letter from the hand of the messengers, and read it; and Hezekiah went up to the house of the LORD, and spread it before the LORD. ¹⁵And Hezekiah prayed to the LORD: ¹⁶"O LORD of hosts, God of Israel, enthroned above the cherubim, you are the God, you alone, of all the kingdoms of the earth; you have made heaven and earth. ¹⁷Incline your ear, O LORD, and hear; open your eyes, O LORD, and see; and hear all the words of Sennacherib, which he has sent to mock the living God. ¹⁸Truly, O LORD, the kings of Assyria have laid waste all the nations and their lands, ¹⁹and have cast their gods into the fire. For they were no gods, but the work of men's hands, wood and stone. Therefore they were destroyed. ²⁰So now, O LORD our God, save us from his hand, that all the kingdoms of the earth may know that you alone are the LORD."

SENNACHERIB'S FALL

²¹Then Isaiah the son of Amoz sent to Hezekiah, saying, "Thus says the LORD, the God of Israel: Because you have prayed to me concerning Sennacherib king of Assyria, ²²this is the word that the LORD has spoken concerning him:

"'She despises you, she scorns you —
　the virgin daughter of Zion;
she wags her head behind you —
　the daughter of Jerusalem.

²³ "'Whom have you mocked and reviled?
　Against whom have you
　　raised your voice
and lifted your eyes to the heights?
　Against the Holy One of Israel!
²⁴ By your servants you have
　　mocked the Lord,
and you have said, With
　my many chariots
I have gone up the heights
　of the mountains,
to the far recesses of Lebanon,
to cut down its tallest cedars,
　its choicest cypresses,
to come to its remotest height,
　its most fruitful forest.
²⁵ I dug wells
　and drank waters,
to dry up with the sole of my foot
　all the streams of Egypt.

²⁶ "'Have you not heard
　that I determined it long ago?
I planned from days of old
　what now I bring to pass,
that you should make fortified cities
　crash into heaps of ruins,
²⁷ while their inhabitants,
　shorn of strength,
are dismayed and confounded,
and have become like
　plants of the field
and like tender grass,
like grass on the housetops,
　blighted[a] before it is grown.

²⁸ "'I know your sitting down
　and your going out and coming in,
　and your raging against me.
²⁹ Because you have raged against me
　and your complacency has
　　come to my ears,
I will put my hook in your nose
　and my bit in your mouth,
and I will turn you back on the way
　by which you came.'

³⁰"And this shall be the sign for you: this year you shall eat what grows of itself, and in the second year what springs from that. Then in the third year sow and reap, and plant vineyards, and eat their fruit. ³¹And the surviving remnant of the house of Judah shall again take root downwards and bear fruit upwards. ³²For out of Jerusalem shall go a remnant, and out of Mount Zion a band of survivors. The zeal of the LORD of hosts will do this.

³³"Therefore thus says the LORD concerning the king of Assyria: He shall not come into this city or shoot an arrow there or come before it with a shield or cast up a siege

---

[a] Some Hebrew manuscripts and 2 Kings 19:26; most Hebrew manuscripts *a field*

mound against it. ³⁴By the way that he came, by the same he shall return, and he shall not come into this city, declares the LORD. ³⁵For I will defend this city to save it, for my own sake and for the sake of my servant David."

³⁶And the angel of the LORD went out and struck down 185,000 in the camp of the Assyrians. And when people arose early in the morning, behold, these were all dead bodies. ³⁷Then Sennacherib king of Assyria departed and returned home and lived at Nineveh. ³⁸And as he was worshipping in the house of Nisroch his god, Adrammelech and Sharezer, his sons, struck him down with the sword. And after they escaped into the land of Ararat, Esarhaddon his son reigned in his place.

HEZEKIAH'S SICKNESS AND RECOVERY

38 In those days Hezekiah became sick and was at the point of death. And Isaiah the prophet the son of Amoz came to him, and said to him, "Thus says the LORD: Set your house in order, for you shall die, you shall not recover."ᵃ ²Then Hezekiah turned his face to the wall and prayed to the LORD, ³and said, "Please, O LORD, remember how I have walked before you in faithfulness and with a whole heart, and have done what is good in your sight." And Hezekiah wept bitterly.

⁴Then the word of the LORD came to Isaiah: ⁵"Go and say to Hezekiah, Thus says the LORD, the God of David your father: I have heard your prayer; I have seen your tears. Behold, I will add fifteen years to your life.ᵇ ⁶I will deliver you and this city out of the hand of the king of Assyria, and will defend this city.

⁷"This shall be the sign to you from the LORD, that the LORD will do this thing that he has promised: ⁸Behold, I will make the shadow cast by the declining sun on the dial of Ahaz turn back ten steps." So the sun turned back on the dial the ten steps by which it had declined.ᶜ

⁹A writing of Hezekiah king of Judah, after he had been sick and had recovered from his sickness:

¹⁰   I said, In the middleᵈ of my days
        I must depart;
    I am consigned to the gates of Sheol
        for the rest of my years.
¹¹   I said, I shall not see the LORD,
        the LORD in the land of the living;
    I shall look on man no more
        among the inhabitants of the world.
¹²   My dwelling is plucked up and
        removed from me
    like a shepherd's tent;
    like a weaver I have rolled up my life;
        he cuts me off from the loom;
    from day to night you bring
        me to an end;
¹³   I calmed myselfᵉ until morning;
    like a lion he breaks all my bones;
    from day to night you bring
        me to an end.

¹⁴   Like a swallow or a crane I chirp;
        I moan like a dove.
    My eyes are weary with
        looking upwards.
    O Lord, I am oppressed; be
        my pledge of safety!
¹⁵   What shall I say? For he has
        spoken to me,
    and he himself has done it.
    I walk slowly all my years
        because of the bitterness of my soul.

¹⁶   O Lord, by these things men live,
    and in all these is the life of
        my spirit.
    Oh restore me to health
        and make me live!
¹⁷   Behold, it was for my welfare
        that I had great bitterness;
    but in love you have delivered my life
        from the pit of destruction,
    for you have cast all my sins
        behind your back.
¹⁸   For Sheol does not thank you;
        death does not praise you;
    those who go down to the
        pit do not hope
    for your faithfulness.
¹⁹   The living, the living, he thanks you,
        as I do this day;
    the father makes known to the children
        your faithfulness.

²⁰   The LORD will save me,
        and we will play my music on
        stringed instruments
    all the days of our lives,
        at the house of the LORD.

ᵃOr *live*; also verses 9, 21   ᵇHebrew *to your days*   ᶜThe meaning of the Hebrew verse is uncertain   ᵈOr *In the quiet*   ᵉOr (with Targum) *I cried for help*

²¹Now Isaiah had said, "Let them take a cake of figs and apply it to the boil, that he may recover." ²²Hezekiah also had said, "What is the sign that I shall go up to the house of the LORD?"

ENVOYS FROM BABYLON

39

At that time Merodach-baladan the son of Baladan, king of Babylon, sent envoys with letters and a present to Hezekiah, for he heard that he had been sick and had recovered. ²And Hezekiah welcomed them gladly. And he showed them his treasure house, the silver, the gold, the spices, the precious oil, his whole armoury, all that was found in his storehouses. There was nothing in his house or in all his realm that Hezekiah did not show them. ³Then Isaiah the prophet came to King Hezekiah, and said to him, "What did these men say? And from where did they come to you?" Hezekiah said, "They have come to me from a far country, from Babylon." ⁴He said, "What have they seen in your house?" Hezekiah answered, "They have seen all that is in my house. There is nothing in my storehouses that I did not show them."

⁵Then Isaiah said to Hezekiah, "Hear the word of the LORD of hosts: ⁶Behold, the days are coming, when all that is in your house, and that which your fathers have stored up till this day, shall be carried to Babylon. Nothing shall be left, says the LORD. ⁷And some of your own sons, who will come from you, whom you will father, shall be taken away, and they shall be eunuchs in the palace of the king of Babylon." ⁸Then Hezekiah said to Isaiah, "The word of the LORD that you have spoken is good." For he thought, "There will be peace and security in my days."

COMFORT FOR GOD'S PEOPLE

40

Comfort, comfort my people,
 says your God.
²Speak tenderly to Jerusalem,
 and cry to her
that her warfare^a is ended,
 that her iniquity is pardoned,
 that she has received from
  the LORD's hand
 double for all her sins.

³ A voice cries.^{b}
"In the wilderness prepare
 the way of the LORD;
 make straight in the desert a
  highway for our God.
⁴ Every valley shall be lifted up,
 and every mountain and
  hill be made low;
 the uneven ground shall become level,
  and the rough places a plain.
⁵ And the glory of the LORD
  shall be revealed,
 and all flesh shall see it together,
  for the mouth of the LORD
   has spoken."

THE WORD OF GOD STANDS FOR EVER

⁶ A voice says, "Cry!"
 And I said,^{c} "What shall I cry?"
All flesh is grass,
 and all its beauty^d is like the
  flower of the field.
⁷ The grass withers, the flower fades
  when the breath of the
   LORD blows on it;
 surely the people are grass.
⁸ The grass withers, the flower fades,
  but the word of our God
   will stand for ever.

THE GREATNESS OF GOD

⁹ Go on up to a high mountain,
 O Zion, herald of good news;^{e}
lift up your voice with strength,
 O Jerusalem, herald of good news;^{f}
 lift it up, fear not;
say to the cities of Judah,
 "Behold your God!"
¹⁰ Behold, the Lord GOD comes
  with might,
 and his arm rules for him;
behold, his reward is with him,
 and his recompense before him.
¹¹ He will tend his flock like a shepherd;
 he will gather the lambs in his arms;
he will carry them in his bosom,
 and gently lead those that
  are with young.

¹² Who has measured the waters
  in the hollow of his hand
 and marked off the heavens
  with a span,
 enclosed the dust of the
  earth in a measure

---

^{a} Or hardship ^{b} Or A voice of one crying ^{c} Revocalization based on Dead Sea Scroll, Septuagint, Vulgate; Masoretic Text And someone says ^{d} Or all its constancy ^{e} Or O herald of good news to Zion ^{f} Or O herald of good news to Jerusalem

and weighed the mountains
  in scales
  and the hills in a balance?
13 Who has measured[a] the
  Spirit of the Lord,
  or what man shows him his counsel?
14 Whom did he consult,
  and who made him understand?
  Who taught him the path of justice,
  and taught him knowledge,
  and showed him the way
  of understanding?
15 Behold, the nations are like a
  drop from a bucket,
  and are accounted as the
  dust on the scales;
  behold, he takes up the
  coastlands like fine dust.
16 Lebanon would not suffice for fuel,
  nor are its beasts enough
  for a burnt offering.
17 All the nations are as nothing
  before him,
  they are accounted by him as less
  than nothing and emptiness.

18 To whom then will you liken God,
  or what likeness compare with him?
19 An idol! A craftsman casts it,
  and a goldsmith overlays it with gold
  and casts for it silver chains.
20 He who is too impoverished
  for an offering
  chooses wood[b] that will not rot;
  he seeks out a skilful craftsman
  to set up an idol that will not move.

21 Do you not know? Do you not hear?
  Has it not been told you
  from the beginning?
  Have you not understood from the
  foundations of the earth?
22 It is he who sits above the
  circle of the earth,
  and its inhabitants are like
  grasshoppers;
  who stretches out the heavens
  like a curtain,
  and spreads them like a
  tent to dwell in;
23 who brings princes to nothing,
  and makes the rulers of the
  earth as emptiness.

24 Scarcely are they planted,
  scarcely sown,
  scarcely has their stem taken
  root in the earth,
  when he blows on them,
  and they wither,
  and the tempest carries them
  off like stubble.

25 To whom then will you compare me,
  that I should be like him?
  says the Holy One.
26 Lift up your eyes on high and see:
  who created these?
  He who brings out their
  host by number,
  calling them all by name;
  by the greatness of his might
  and because he is strong in power,
  not one is missing.

27 Why do you say, O Jacob,
  and speak, O Israel,
  "My way is hidden from the Lord,
  and my right is disregarded
  by my God"?
28 Have you not known? Have
  you not heard?
  The Lord is the everlasting God,
  the Creator of the ends of the earth.
  He does not faint or grow weary;
  his understanding is unsearchable.
29 He gives power to the faint,
  and to him who has no might
  he increases strength.
30 Even youths shall faint and be weary,
  and young men shall fall exhausted;
31 but they who wait for the Lord
  shall renew their strength;
  they shall mount up with
  wings like eagles;
  they shall run and not be weary;
  they shall walk and not faint.

FEAR NOT, FOR I AM WITH YOU

41 Listen to me in silence,
  O coastlands;
  let the peoples renew their
  strength;
  let them approach, then let them speak;
  let us together draw near for
  judgement.

2 Who stirred up one from the east
  whom victory meets at every step?[c]

---

[a]Or has directed [b]Or He chooses valuable wood [c]Or whom righteousness calls to follow?

He gives up nations before him,
  so that he tramples kings underfoot;
 he makes them like dust
    with his sword,
  like driven stubble with his bow.
3 He pursues them and passes on safely,
  by paths his feet have not trod.
4 Who has performed and done this,
    calling the generations from
    the beginning?
  I, the LORD, the first,
    and with the last; I am he.

5 The coastlands have seen
    and are afraid;
  the ends of the earth tremble;
    they have drawn near and come.
6 Everyone helps his neighbour
    and says to his brother, "Be strong!"
7 The craftsman strengthens
    the goldsmith,
  and he who smooths with
    the hammer him who
    strikes the anvil,
  saying of the soldering, "It is good";
  and they strengthen it with nails
    so that it cannot be moved.

8 But you, Israel, my servant,
  Jacob, whom I have chosen,
    the offspring of Abraham, my friend;
9 you whom I took from the
    ends of the earth,
  and called from its farthest corners,
  saying to you, "You are my servant,
    I have chosen you and not
    cast you off";
10 fear not, for I am with you;
  be not dismayed, for I am your God;
  I will strengthen you, I will help you,
    I will uphold you with my
    righteous right hand.

11 Behold, all who are incensed
    against you
  shall be put to shame and
    confounded;
  those who strive against you
    shall be as nothing and shall perish.
12 You shall seek those who
    contend with you,
  but you shall not find them;
  those who war against you
    shall be as nothing at all.
13 For I, the LORD your God,
  hold your right hand;
  it is I who say to you, "Fear not,
    I am the one who helps you."

14 Fear not, you worm Jacob,
    you men of Israel!
  I am the one who helps you,
    declares the LORD;
  your Redeemer is the Holy
    One of Israel.
15 Behold, I make of you a
    threshing sledge,
  new, sharp, and having teeth;
  you shall thresh the mountains
    and crush them,
    and you shall make the
    hills like chaff;
16 you shall winnow them, and the
    wind shall carry them away,
    and the tempest shall scatter them.
  And you shall rejoice in the LORD;
    in the Holy One of Israel
    you shall glory.

17 When the poor and needy seek water,
    and there is none,
    and their tongue is parched
    with thirst,
  I the LORD will answer them;
    I the God of Israel will not
    forsake them.
18 I will open rivers on the bare heights,
    and fountains in the midst
    of the valleys.
  I will make the wilderness
    a pool of water,
    and the dry land springs of water.
19 I will put in the wilderness the cedar,
    the acacia, the myrtle, and the olive.
  I will set in the desert the cypress,
    the plane and the pine together,
20 that they may see and know,
    may consider and understand
    together,
  that the hand of the LORD
    has done this,
    the Holy One of Israel has created it.

THE FUTILITY OF IDOLS

21 Set forth your case, says the LORD;
    bring your proofs, says
    the King of Jacob.
22 Let them bring them, and tell us
    what is to happen.
  Tell us the former things,
    what they are,
    that we may consider them,

that we may know their outcome;
   or declare to us the things to come.
23 Tell us what is to come hereafter,
   that we may know that you are gods;
do good, or do harm,
   that we may be dismayed
     and terrified.*ᵃ*
24 Behold, you are nothing,
   and your work is less than nothing;
an abomination is he who
   chooses you.

25 I stirred up one from the north,
   and he has come,
from the rising of the sun, and he
   shall call upon my name;
he shall trample on rulers as on mortar,
   as the potter treads clay.
26 Who declared it from the beginning,
   that we might know,
and beforehand, that we might
   say, "He is right"?
There was none who declared it,
   none who proclaimed,
   none who heard your words.
27 I was the first to say*ᵇ* to Zion,
   "Behold, here they are!"
and I give to Jerusalem a
   herald of good news.
28 But when I look, there is no one;
   among these there is no counsellor
who, when I ask, gives an answer.
29 Behold, they are all a delusion;
   their works are nothing;
   their metal images are empty wind.

THE LORD'S CHOSEN SERVANT

42

Behold my servant, whom
   I uphold,
my chosen, in whom my soul
   delights;
I have put my Spirit upon him;
   he will bring forth justice
     to the nations.
2 He will not cry aloud or
   lift up his voice,
or make it heard in the street;
3 a bruised reed he will not break,
   and a faintly burning wick
     he will not quench;
   he will faithfully bring forth justice.
4 He will not grow faint or
   be discouraged*ᶜ*
     till he has established
        justice in the earth;
   and the coastlands wait for his law.

5 Thus says God, the LORD,
   who created the heavens and
     stretched them out,
who spread out the earth and
   what comes from it,
who gives breath to the people on it
   and spirit to those who walk in it:
6 "I am the LORD; I have called
   you*ᵈ* in righteousness;
I will take you by the hand
   and keep you;
I will give you as a covenant
   for the people,
   a light for the nations,
7 to open the eyes that are blind,
to bring out the prisoners
   from the dungeon,
from the prison those who
   sit in darkness.
8 I am the LORD; that is my name;
   my glory I give to no other,
   nor my praise to carved idols.
9 Behold, the former things
   have come to pass,
and new things I now declare;
before they spring forth
   I tell you of them."

SING TO THE LORD A NEW SONG

10 Sing to the LORD a new song,
   his praise from the end of the earth,
you who go down to the sea,
   and all that fills it,
   the coastlands and their
     inhabitants.
11 Let the desert and its cities
   lift up their voice,
   the villages that Kedar inhabits;
let the habitants of Sela sing for joy,
   let them shout from the top
     of the mountains.
12 Let them give glory to the LORD,
   and declare his praise in
     the coastlands.
13 The LORD goes out like a mighty man,
   like a man of war he stirs up his zeal;
he cries out, he shouts aloud,
   he shows himself mighty
     against his foes.

14 For a long time I have held my peace;
   I have kept still and
     restrained myself;

---

*ᵃ*Or *that we may both be dismayed and see*   *ᵇ*Or *Formerly I said*
*ᶜ*Or *bruised*   *ᵈ*The Hebrew for *you* is singular; four times in this verse

now I will cry out like a
    woman in labour;
  I will gasp and pant.
15 I will lay waste mountains and hills,
    and dry up all their vegetation;
  I will turn the rivers into islands,*a*
    and dry up the pools.
16 And I will lead the blind
    in a way that they do not know,
  in paths that they have not known
    I will guide them.
  I will turn the darkness before
    them into light,
    the rough places into level ground.
  These are the things I do,
    and I do not forsake them.
17 They are turned back and
    utterly put to shame,
  who trust in carved idols,
  who say to metal images,
    "You are our gods."

ISRAEL'S FAILURE TO HEAR AND SEE

18 Hear, you deaf,
  and look, you blind, that
    you may see!
19 Who is blind but my servant,
    or deaf as my messenger
      whom I send?
  Who is blind as my dedicated one,*b*
    or blind as the servant of the LORD?
20 He sees many things, but does
    not observe them;
  his ears are open, but he
    does not hear.
21 The LORD was pleased, for his
    righteousness' sake,
  to magnify his law and
    make it glorious.
22 But this is a people plundered
    and looted;
  they are all of them trapped
    in holes
  and hidden in prisons;
  they have become plunder
    with none to rescue,
  spoil with none to say, "Restore!"
23 Who among you will give ear to this,
  will attend and listen for
    the time to come?
24 Who gave up Jacob to the looter,
    and Israel to the plunderers?
  Was it not the LORD, against
    whom we have sinned,
  in whose ways they would not walk,
    and whose law they would not obey?

25 So he poured on him the
    heat of his anger
    and the might of battle;
  it set him on fire all round, but
    he did not understand;
  it burned him up, but he did
    not take it to heart.

ISRAEL'S ONLY SAVIOUR

43

But now thus says the LORD,
  he who created you, O Jacob,
  he who formed you, O Israel:
"Fear not, for I have redeemed you;
  I have called you by name,
    you are mine.
2 When you pass through the
    waters, I will be with you;
  and through the rivers, they
    shall not overwhelm you;
  when you walk through fire you
    shall not be burned,
  and the flame shall not
    consume you.
3 For I am the LORD your God,
    the Holy One of Israel, your Saviour.
  I give Egypt as your ransom,
    Cush and Seba in exchange for you.
4 Because you are precious in my eyes,
    and honoured, and I love you,
  I give men in return for you,
    peoples in exchange for your life.
5 Fear not, for I am with you;
  I will bring your offspring
    from the east,
  and from the west I will gather you.
6 I will say to the north, Give up,
    and to the south, Do not withhold;
  bring my sons from afar
    and my daughters from the
      end of the earth,
7 everyone who is called by my name,
    whom I created for my glory,
    whom I formed and made."

8 Bring out the people who are
    blind, yet have eyes,
  who are deaf, yet have ears!
9 All the nations gather together,
    and the peoples assemble.
  Who among them can declare this,
    and show us the former things?
  Let them bring their witnesses
    to prove them right,
  and let them hear and say, It is true.

---
a Or *into coastlands*   *b* Or *as the one at peace with me*

10 "You are my witnesses,"
    declares the LORD,
   "and my servant whom I have chosen,
  that you may know and believe me
    and understand that I am he.
  Before me no god was formed,
    nor shall there be any after me.
11 I, I am the LORD,
    and besides me there is no saviour.
12 I declared and saved and proclaimed,
    when there was no strange
       god among you;
   and you are my witnesses," declares
       the LORD, "and I am God.
13 Also henceforth I am he;
    there is none who can deliver
       from my hand;
   I work, and who can turn it back?"

14 Thus says the LORD,
    your Redeemer, the Holy
       One of Israel:
   "For your sake I send to Babylon
    and bring them all down as fugitives,
    even the Chaldeans, in the ships
       in which they rejoice.
15 I am the LORD, your Holy One,
    the Creator of Israel, your King."

16 Thus says the LORD,
    who makes a way in the sea,
    a path in the mighty waters,
17 who brings forth chariot and horse,
    army and warrior;
   they lie down, they cannot rise,
    they are extinguished,
       quenched like a wick:
18 "Remember not the former things,
    nor consider the things of old.
19 Behold, I am doing a new thing;
    now it springs forth, do you
       not perceive it?
   I will make a way in the wilderness
    and rivers in the desert.
20 The wild beasts will honour me,
    the jackals and the ostriches,
   for I give water in the wilderness,
    rivers in the desert,
   to give drink to my chosen people,
21   the people whom I formed
       for myself
    that they might declare my praise.

22 "Yet you did not call upon me, O Jacob;
    but you have been weary
       of me, O Israel!
23 You have not brought me your
       sheep for burnt offerings,
    or honoured me with
       your sacrifices.
   I have not burdened you
       with offerings,
    or wearied you with frankincense.
24 You have not bought me sweet
       cane with money,
    or satisfied me with the fat
       of your sacrifices.
   But you have burdened me
       with your sins;
    you have wearied me with
       your iniquities.

25 "I, I am he
    who blots out your transgressions
       for my own sake,
    and I will not remember your sins.
26 Put me in remembrance; let
       us argue together;
    set forth your case, that you
       may be proved right.
27 Your first father sinned,
    and your mediators transgressed
       against me.
28 Therefore I will profane the
       princes of the sanctuary,
    and deliver Jacob to utter
       destruction
    and Israel to reviling.

ISRAEL THE LORD'S CHOSEN

44 "But now hear, O Jacob
       my servant,
    Israel whom I have chosen!
2 Thus says the LORD who made you,
    who formed you from the
       womb and will help you:
   Fear not, O Jacob my servant,
    Jeshurun whom I have chosen.
3 For I will pour water on
       the thirsty land,
    and streams on the dry ground;
   I will pour my Spirit upon
       your offspring,
    and my blessing on your
       descendants.
4 They shall spring up among the grass
    like willows by flowing streams.
5 This one will say, 'I am the LORD's',
    another will call on the name
       of Jacob,
   and another will write on his hand,
       'The LORD's',

and name himself by the name
of Israel."

BESIDES ME THERE IS NO GOD

6 Thus says the LORD, the King of Israel
and his Redeemer, the
LORD of hosts:
"I am the first and I am the last;
besides me there is no god.
7 Who is like me? Let him proclaim it.[a]
Let him declare and set it before me,
since I appointed an ancient people.
Let them declare what is to come,
and what will happen.
8 Fear not, nor be afraid;
have I not told you from of
old and declared it?
And you are my witnesses!
Is there a God besides me?
There is no Rock; I know not any."

THE FOLLY OF IDOLATRY

[9] All who fashion idols are nothing, and the things they delight in do not profit. Their witnesses neither see nor know, that they may be put to shame. [10] Who fashions a god or casts an idol that is profitable for nothing? [11] Behold, all his companions shall be put to shame, and the craftsmen are only human. Let them all assemble, let them stand forth. They shall be terrified; they shall be put to shame together.

[12] The ironsmith takes a cutting tool and works it over the coals. He fashions it with hammers and works it with his strong arm. He becomes hungry, and his strength fails; he drinks no water and is faint. [13] The carpenter stretches a line; he marks it out with a pencil.[b] He shapes it with planes and marks it with a compass. He shapes it into the figure of a man, with the beauty of a man, to dwell in a house. [14] He cuts down cedars, or he chooses a cypress tree or an oak and lets it grow strong among the trees of the forest. He plants a cedar and the rain nourishes it. [15] Then it becomes fuel for a man. He takes a part of it and warms himself; he kindles a fire and bakes bread. Also he makes a god and worships it; he makes it an idol and falls down before it. [16] Half of it he burns in the fire. Over the half he eats meat; he roasts it and is satisfied. Also he warms himself and says, "Aha, I am warm, I have seen the fire!" [17] And the rest of it he makes into a god, his idol, and falls down to it and worships it. He prays to it and says, "Deliver me, for you are my god!"

[18] They know not, nor do they discern, for he has shut their eyes, so that they cannot see, and their hearts, so that they cannot understand. [19] No one considers, nor is there knowledge or discernment to say, "Half of it I burned in the fire; I also baked bread on its coals; I roasted meat and have eaten. And shall I make the rest of it an abomination? Shall I fall down before a block of wood?" [20] He feeds on ashes; a deluded heart has led him astray, and he cannot deliver himself or say, "Is there not a lie in my right hand?"

THE LORD REDEEMS ISRAEL

21 Remember these things, O Jacob,
and Israel, for you are my servant;
I formed you; you are my servant;
O Israel, you will not be
forgotten by me.
22 I have blotted out your
transgressions like a cloud
and your sins like mist;
return to me, for I have
redeemed you.

23 Sing, O heavens, for the
LORD has done it;
shout, O depths of the earth;
break forth into singing, O mountains,
O forest, and every tree in it!
For the LORD has redeemed Jacob,
and will be glorified[c] in Israel.

24 Thus says the LORD, your Redeemer,
who formed you from the womb:
"I am the LORD, who made all things,
who alone stretched out
the heavens,
who spread out the earth by myself,
25 who frustrates the signs of liars
and makes fools of diviners,
who turns wise men back
and makes their knowledge foolish,
26 who confirms the word of his servant
and fulfils the counsel of
his messengers,
who says of Jerusalem, 'She
shall be inhabited',
and of the cities of Judah,
'They shall be built,
and I will raise up their ruins';
27 who says to the deep, 'Be dry;
I will dry up your rivers';

---

[a] Or *Who like me can proclaim it?* [b] Hebrew *stylus* [c] Or *will display his beauty*

²⁸ who says of Cyrus, 'He is my shepherd,
and he shall fulfil all my purpose';
saying of Jerusalem, 'She shall be built',
and of the temple, 'Your
foundation shall be laid.'"

CYRUS, GOD'S INSTRUMENT

45 Thus says the LORD to his
anointed, to Cyrus,
whose right hand I have grasped,
to subdue nations before him
and to loose the belts of kings,
to open doors before him
that gates may not be closed:
² "I will go before you
and level the exalted places,ᵃ
I will break in pieces the doors of bronze
and cut through the bars of iron,
³ I will give you the treasures of darkness
and the hoards in secret places,
that you may know that it is I, the LORD,
the God of Israel, who call
you by your name.
⁴ For the sake of my servant Jacob,
and Israel my chosen,
I call you by your name,
I name you, though you
do not know me.
⁵ I am the LORD, and there is no other,
besides me there is no God;
I equip you, though you
do not know me,
⁶ that people may know, from
the rising of the sun
and from the west, that there
is none besides me;
I am the LORD, and there is
no other.
⁷ I form light and create darkness;
I make well-being and
create calamity;
I am the LORD, who does
all these things.

⁸ "Shower, O heavens, from above,
and let the clouds rain down
righteousness;
let the earth open, that salvation and
righteousness may bear fruit;
let the earth cause them
both to sprout;
I the LORD have created it.

⁹ "Woe to him who strives with
him who formed him,
a pot among earthen pots!
Does the clay say to him who forms
it, 'What are you making?'
or 'Your work has no handles'?
¹⁰ Woe to him who says to a father,
'What are you begetting?'
or to a woman, 'With what
are you in labour?'"

¹¹ Thus says the LORD,
the Holy One of Israel, and the
one who formed him:
"Ask me of things to come;
will you command me concerning
my children and the
work of my hands?ᵇ
¹² I made the earth
and created man on it;
it was my hands that stretched
out the heavens,
and I commanded all their host.
¹³ I have stirred him up in righteousness,
and I will make all his ways level;
he shall build my city
and set my exiles free,
not for price or reward,"
says the LORD of hosts.

THE LORD, THE ONLY SAVIOUR

¹⁴ Thus says the LORD:
"The wealth of Egypt and the
merchandise of Cush,
and the Sabeans, men of stature,
shall come over to you and be yours;
they shall follow you;
they shall come over in chains
and bow down to you.
They will plead with you, saying:
'Surely God is in you, and
there is no other,
no god besides him.'"

¹⁵ Truly, you are a God who hides himself,
O God of Israel, the Saviour.
¹⁶ All of them are put to shame
and confounded;
the makers of idols go in
confusion together.
¹⁷ But Israel is saved by the LORD
with everlasting salvation;
you shall not be put to shame
or confounded
to all eternity.

ᵃMasoretic Text; Dead Sea Scroll, Septuagint *level the mountains*
ᵇA slight emendation yields *will you question me about my children, or command me concerning the work of my hands?*

18 For thus says the LORD,
 who created the heavens
  (he is God!),
 who formed the earth and made it
  (he established it;
 he did not create it empty,
  he formed it to be inhabited!):
 "I am the LORD, and there is no other.
19 I did not speak in secret,
  in a land of darkness;
 I did not say to the offspring of Jacob,
  'Seek me in vain.'[a]
 I the LORD speak the truth;
  I declare what is right.

20 "Assemble yourselves and come;
  draw near together,
  you survivors of the nations!
 They have no knowledge
  who carry about their wooden idols,
 and keep on praying to a god
  that cannot save.
21 Declare and present your case;
  let them take counsel together!
 Who told this long ago?
  Who declared it of old?
 Was it not I, the LORD?
  And there is no other god
   besides me,
 a righteous God and a Saviour;
  there is none besides me.

22 "Turn to me and be saved,
  all the ends of the earth!
 For I am God, and there is no other.
23 By myself I have sworn;
  from my mouth has gone
   out in righteousness
  a word that shall not return:
 'To me every knee shall bow,
  every tongue shall swear allegiance.'[b]

24 "Only in the LORD, it shall be said of me,
  are righteousness and strength;
 to him shall come and be ashamed
  all who were incensed against him.
25 In the LORD all the offspring of Israel
  shall be justified and shall glory."

THE IDOLS OF BABYLON AND THE ONE TRUE GOD

46

Bel bows down; Nebo stoops;
 their idols are on beasts and
  livestock;
these things you carry are borne
 as burdens on weary beasts.

2 They stoop; they bow down together;
  they cannot save the burden,
  but themselves go into captivity.

3 "Listen to me, O house of Jacob,
  all the remnant of the house of Israel,
 who have been borne by me
  from before your birth,
  carried from the womb;
4 even to your old age I am he,
  and to grey hairs I will carry you.
 I have made, and I will bear;
  I will carry and will save.

5 "To whom will you liken me
  and make me equal,
 and compare me, that we
  may be alike?
6 Those who lavish gold from the purse,
  and weigh out silver in the scales,
 hire a goldsmith, and he
  makes it into a god;
 then they fall down and worship!
7 They lift it to their shoulders,
  they carry it,
 they set it in its place, and
  it stands there;
  it cannot move from its place.
 If one cries to it, it does not answer
  or save him from his trouble.

8 "Remember this and stand firm,
  recall it to mind, you transgressors,
9 remember the former things of old;
 for I am God, and there is no other;
  I am God, and there is none like me,
10 declaring the end from the beginning
  and from ancient times
   things not yet done,
 saying, 'My counsel shall stand,
  and I will accomplish all
   my purpose',
11 calling a bird of prey from the east,
  the man of my counsel
   from a far country.
 I have spoken, and I will
  bring it to pass;
 I have purposed, and I will do it.

12 "Listen to me, you stubborn of heart,
  you who are far from righteousness:
13 I bring near my righteousness;
  it is not far off,
 and my salvation will not delay;

---
[a]Hebrew *in emptiness* [b]Septuagint *every tongue shall confess to God*

> he split the rock and the
> water gushed out.

²² "There is no peace," says the Lord,
> "for the wicked."

THE SERVANT OF THE LORD

49

> Listen to me, O coastlands,
> and give attention, you peoples
> from afar.
> The Lord called me from the womb,
> from the body of my mother
> he named my name.
² He made my mouth like a sharp sword;
> in the shadow of his hand he hid me;
> he made me a polished arrow;
> in his quiver he hid me away.
³ And he said to me, "You
> are my servant,
> Israel, in whom I will be glorified."ᵃ
⁴ But I said, "I have laboured in vain;
> I have spent my strength for
> nothing and vanity;
> yet surely my right is with the Lord,
> and my recompense with my God."

⁵ And now the Lord says,
> he who formed me from the
> womb to be his servant,
> to bring Jacob back to him;
> and that Israel might be
> gathered to him —
> for I am honoured in the
> eyes of the Lord,
> and my God has become
> my strength —
⁶ he says:
> "It is too light a thing that you
> should be my servant
> to raise up the tribes of Jacob
> and to bring back the
> preserved of Israel;
> I will make you as a light
> for the nations,
> that my salvation may reach
> to the end of the earth."

⁷ Thus says the Lord,
> the Redeemer of Israel and
> his Holy One,
> to one deeply despised,
> abhorred by the nation,
> the servant of rulers:
> "Kings shall see and arise;
> princes, and they shall
> prostrate themselves;
> because of the Lord, who is faithful,
> the Holy One of Israel, who
> has chosen you."

THE RESTORATION OF ISRAEL

⁸ Thus says the Lord:
> "In a time of favour I have
> answered you;
> in a day of salvation I have
> helped you;
> I will keep you and give you
> as a covenant to the people,
> to establish the land,
> to apportion the desolate heritages,
⁹ saying to the prisoners, 'Come out',
> to those who are in
> darkness, 'Appear.'
> They shall feed along the ways;
> on all bare heights shall
> be their pasture;
¹⁰ they shall not hunger or thirst,
> neither scorching wind nor
> sun shall strike them,
> for he who has pity on them
> will lead them,
> and by springs of water
> will guide them.
¹¹ And I will make all my
> mountains a road,
> and my highways shall be raised up.
¹² Behold, these shall come from afar,
> and behold, these from the
> north and from the west,ᵇ
> and these from the land of Syene."ᶜ

¹³ Sing for joy, O heavens, and
> exult, O earth;
> break forth, O mountains,
> into singing!
> For the Lord has comforted his
> people
> and will have compassion
> on his afflicted.

¹⁴ But Zion said, "The Lord
> has forsaken me;
> my Lord has forgotten me."
¹⁵ "Can a woman forget her nursing child,
> that she should have no compassion
> on the son of her womb?
> Even these may forget,
> yet I will not forget you.

ᵃOr *I will display my beauty*   ᵇHebrew *from the sea*   ᶜDead Sea Scroll; Masoretic Text *Sinim*

16 Behold, I have engraved you on
    the palms of my hands;
  your walls are continually
    before me.
17 Your builders make haste;[a]
  your destroyers and those who laid
    you waste go out from you.
18 Lift up your eyes all round and see;
    they all gather, they come to you.
  As I live, declares the Lord,
  you shall put them all on
    as an ornament;
  you shall bind them on
    as a bride does.
19 "Surely your waste and your
    desolate places
  and your devastated land—
  surely now you will be too narrow
    for your inhabitants,
  and those who swallowed you
    up will be far away.
20 The children of your bereavement
    will yet say in your ears:
  'The place is too narrow for me;
    make room for me to dwell in.'
21 Then you will say in your heart:
  'Who has borne me these?
  I was bereaved and barren,
    exiled and put away,
  but who has brought up these?
  Behold, I was left alone;
    from where have these come?'"
22 Thus says the Lord God:
  "Behold, I will lift up my hand
    to the nations,
    and raise my signal to the peoples;
  and they shall bring your
    sons in their arms,[b]
  and your daughters shall be
    carried on their shoulders.
23 Kings shall be your foster fathers,
    and their queens your
      nursing mothers.
  With their faces to the ground they
    shall bow down to you,
    and lick the dust of your feet.
  Then you will know that
    I am the Lord;
  those who wait for me shall
    not be put to shame."
24 Can the prey be taken from the mighty,
  or the captives of a tyrant[c]
    be rescued?
25 For thus says the Lord:
  "Even the captives of the
    mighty shall be taken,
  and the prey of the tyrant be rescued,
  for I will contend with those
    who contend with you,
  and I will save your children.
26 I will make your oppressors
    eat their own flesh,
  and they shall be drunk with their
    own blood as with wine.
  Then all flesh shall know
    that I am the Lord your Saviour,
    and your Redeemer, the
      Mighty One of Jacob."

ISRAEL'S SIN AND THE SERVANT'S OBEDIENCE

50 Thus says the Lord:
  "Where is your mother's
    certificate of divorce,
  with which I sent her away?
  Or which of my creditors is it
    to whom I have sold you?
  Behold, for your iniquities
    you were sold,
  and for your transgressions your
    mother was sent away.
2 Why, when I came, was there no man;
  why, when I called, was there
    no one to answer?
  Is my hand shortened, that
    it cannot redeem?
  Or have I no power to deliver?
  Behold, by my rebuke I dry up the sea,
    I make the rivers a desert;
  their fish stink for lack of water
    and die of thirst.
3 I clothe the heavens with blackness
    and make sackcloth their covering."

4 The Lord God has given me
    the tongue of those who are taught,
  that I may know how to
    sustain with a word
    him who is weary.
  Morning by morning he awakens;
    he awakens my ear
  to hear as those who are taught.
5 The Lord God has opened my ear,
    and I was not rebellious;
  I turned not backwards.

---

[a]Dead Sea Scroll; Masoretic Text *Your children make haste* [b]Hebrew *in their bosom* [c]Dead Sea Scroll, Syriac, Vulgate (see also verse 25); Masoretic Text *of a righteous man*

⁶ I gave my back to those who strike,
  and my cheeks to those who
    pull out the beard;
 I hid not my face
  from disgrace and spitting.

⁷ But the Lord G<small>OD</small> helps me;
  therefore I have not been disgraced;
 therefore I have set my face like a flint,
  and I know that I shall not
    be put to shame.
⁸ He who vindicates me is near.
 Who will contend with me?
  Let us stand up together.
 Who is my adversary?
  Let him come near to me.
⁹ Behold, the Lord G<small>OD</small> helps me;
  who will declare me guilty?
 Behold, all of them will wear
    out like a garment;
  the moth will eat them up.

¹⁰ Who among you fears the L<small>ORD</small>
   and obeys the voice of his servant?
 Let him who walks in darkness
   and has no light
 trust in the name of the L<small>ORD</small>
   and rely on his God.
¹¹ Behold, all you who kindle a fire,
   who equip yourselves with
     burning torches!
 Walk by the light of your fire,
   and by the torches that
     you have kindled!
 This you have from my hand:
   you shall lie down in torment.

THE LORD'S COMFORT FOR ZION

51

"Listen to me, you who pursue
   righteousness,
   you who seek the L<small>ORD</small>:
 look to the rock from which
     you were hewn,
   and to the quarry from
     which you were dug.
² Look to Abraham your father
   and to Sarah who bore you;
 for he was but one when I called him,
   that I might bless him and
     multiply him.
³ For the L<small>ORD</small> comforts Zion;
   he comforts all her waste places
 and makes her wilderness like Eden,
   her desert like the garden of the L<small>ORD</small>;
 joy and gladness will be found in her,
   thanksgiving and the voice of song.

⁴ "Give attention to me, my people,
   and give ear to me, my nation;
 for a law*ᵃ* will go out from me,
   and I will set my justice for a
     light to the peoples.
⁵ My righteousness draws near,
   my salvation has gone out,
   and my arms will judge the peoples;
 the coastlands hope for me,
   and for my arm they wait.
⁶ Lift up your eyes to the heavens,
   and look at the earth beneath;
 for the heavens vanish like smoke,
   the earth will wear out
     like a garment,
   and they who dwell in it will
     die in like manner;*ᵇ*
 but my salvation will be for ever,
   and my righteousness will
     never be dismayed.

⁷ "Listen to me, you who know
     righteousness,
   the people in whose heart is my law;
 fear not the reproach of man,
   nor be dismayed at their revilings.
⁸ For the moth will eat them
     up like a garment,
   and the worm will eat them like wool,
 but my righteousness will be for ever,
   and my salvation to all generations."

⁹ Awake, awake, put on strength,
     O arm of the L<small>ORD</small>;
 awake, as in days of old,
     the generations of long ago.
 Was it not you who cut Rahab in pieces,
     who pierced the dragon?
¹⁰ Was it not you who dried up the sea,
     the waters of the great deep,
 who made the depths of the sea a way
     for the redeemed to pass over?
¹¹ And the ransomed of the
     L<small>ORD</small> shall return
   and come to Zion with singing;
 everlasting joy shall be
     upon their heads;
 they shall obtain gladness and joy,
   and sorrow and sighing
     shall flee away.

¹² "I, I am he who comforts you;
   who are you that you are afraid
     of man who dies,

ᵃ Or *for teaching*; also verse 7 *ᵇ* Or *will die like gnats*

of the son of man who is
        made like grass,
¹³ and have forgotten the
        Lord, your Maker,
    who stretched out the heavens
    and laid the foundations
        of the earth,
    and you fear continually all the day
        because of the wrath of
            the oppressor,
    when he sets himself to destroy?
    And where is the wrath of
            the oppressor?
¹⁴ He who is bowed down shall
        speedily be released;
    he shall not die and go
        down to the pit,
    neither shall his bread be lacking.
¹⁵ I am the Lord your God,
    who stirs up the sea so that
        its waves roar—
    the Lord of hosts is his name.
¹⁶ And I have put my words
        in your mouth
    and covered you in the
        shadow of my hand,
    establishing[a] the heavens
        and laying the foundations
            of the earth,
    and saying to Zion, 'You
        are my people.'"

¹⁷ Wake yourself, wake yourself,
        stand up, O Jerusalem,
    you who have drunk from the
        hand of the Lord
    the cup of his wrath,
    who have drunk to the dregs
        the bowl, the cup of staggering.
¹⁸ There is none to guide her
        among all the sons she has borne;
    there is none to take her by the hand
        among all the sons she
            has brought up.
¹⁹ These two things have
        happened to you—
    who will console you?—
    devastation and destruction,
        famine and sword;
    who will comfort you?[b]
²⁰ Your sons have fainted;
    they lie at the head of every street
        like an antelope in a net;
    they are full of the wrath of
            the Lord,
        the rebuke of your God.

²¹ Therefore hear this, you
        who are afflicted,
    who are drunk, but not with wine:
²² Thus says your Lord, the Lord,
        your God who pleads the
            cause of his people:
    "Behold, I have taken from your
        hand the cup of staggering;
    the bowl of my wrath you
        shall drink no more;
²³ and I will put it into the hand
        of your tormentors,
    who have said to you,
        'Bow down, that we may pass over';
    and you have made your back
        like the ground
    and like the street for them
        to pass over."

THE LORD'S COMING SALVATION

52 Awake, awake,
        put on your strength, O Zion;
    put on your beautiful garments,
        O Jerusalem, the holy city;
    for there shall no more come into you
        the uncircumcised and the unclean.
² Shake yourself from the dust
        and arise;
    be seated, O Jerusalem;
    loose the bonds from your neck,
        O captive daughter of Zion.

³ For thus says the Lord: "You were sold for nothing, and you shall be redeemed without money." ⁴ For thus says the Lord God: "My people went down at the first into Egypt to sojourn there, and the Assyrian oppressed them for nothing.[c] ⁵ Now therefore what have I here," declares the Lord, "seeing that my people are taken away for nothing? Their rulers wail," declares the Lord, "and continually all the day my name is despised. ⁶ Therefore my people shall know my name. Therefore in that day they shall know that it is I who speak; here I am."

⁷ How beautiful upon the mountains
        are the feet of him who
            brings good news,
    who publishes peace, who brings
        good news of happiness,
    who publishes salvation,
        who says to Zion, "Your God reigns."

---

[a] Or *planting* [b] Dead Sea Scroll, Septuagint, Syriac, Vulgate; Masoretic Text *how shall I comfort you* [c] Or *the Assyrian has oppressed them of late*

8 The voice of your watchmen—
    they lift up their voice;
   together they sing for joy;
   for eye to eye they see
    the return of the LORD to Zion.
9 Break forth together into singing,
    you waste places of Jerusalem,
   for the LORD has comforted his people;
    he has redeemed Jerusalem.
10 The LORD has bared his holy arm
    before the eyes of all the nations,
   and all the ends of the earth shall see
    the salvation of our God.

11 Depart, depart, go out from there;
    touch no unclean thing;
   go out from the midst of her;
    purify yourselves,
   you who bear the vessels
    of the LORD.
12 For you shall not go out in haste,
    and you shall not go in flight,
   for the LORD will go before you,
    and the God of Israel will
    be your rearguard.

HE WAS PIERCED FOR OUR TRANSGRESSIONS

13 Behold, my servant shall act wisely;*a*
    he shall be high and lifted up,
    and shall be exalted.
14 As many were astonished at you—
    his appearance was so marred,
     beyond human semblance,
    and his form beyond that of the
     children of mankind—
15 so shall he sprinkle*b* many nations.
   Kings shall shut their mouths
    because of him,
   for that which has not been
    told them they see,
   and that which they have not
    heard they understand.

53

Who has believed what he has
    heard from us?*c*
   And to whom has the arm of
    the LORD been revealed?
2 For he grew up before him
    like a young plant,
   and like a root out of dry ground;
   he had no form or majesty that
    we should look at him,
   and no beauty that we
    should desire him.
3 He was despised and rejected*d* by men,
    a man of sorrows*e* and
    acquainted with*f* grief;*g*
   and as one from whom men
    hide their faces*h*
   he was despised, and we
    esteemed him not.

4 Surely he has borne our griefs
    and carried our sorrows;
   yet we esteemed him stricken,
    smitten by God, and afflicted.
5 But he was pierced for our
    transgressions;
   he was crushed for our iniquities;
   upon him was the chastisement
    that brought us peace,
   and with his wounds we are healed.
6 All we like sheep have gone astray;
   we have turned—every one—
    to his own way;
   and the LORD has laid on him
    the iniquity of us all.

7 He was oppressed, and he
    was afflicted,
   yet he opened not his mouth;
   like a lamb that is led to the slaughter,
   and like a sheep that before
    its shearers is silent,
   so he opened not his mouth.
8 By oppression and judgement
    he was taken away;
   and as for his generation,
    who considered
   that he was cut off out of the
    land of the living,
   stricken for the transgression
    of my people?
9 And they made his grave
    with the wicked
   and with a rich man in his death,
   although he had done no violence,
   and there was no deceit
    in his mouth.

10 Yet it was the will of the
    LORD to crush him;
   he has put him to grief;*i*
   when his soul makes*j* an
    offering for guilt,
   he shall see his offspring; he
    shall prolong his days;
   the will of the LORD shall
    prosper in his hand.

---

*a*Or shall prosper *b*Or startle *c*Or Who has believed what we have heard? *d*Or forsaken *e*Or pains; also verse 4 *f*Or and knowing *g*Or sickness; also verse 4 *h*Or as one who hides his face from us *i*Or he has made him sick *j*Or when you make his soul

11 Out of the anguish of his soul he
    shall see[a] and be satisfied;
  by his knowledge shall the
    righteous one, my servant,
    make many to be accounted
    righteous,
  and he shall bear their iniquities.
12 Therefore I will divide him a
    portion with the many,[b]
  and he shall divide the spoil
    with the strong,[c]
  because he poured out his
    soul to death
  and was numbered with
    the transgressors;
  yet he bore the sin of many,
  and makes intercession for
    the transgressors.

THE ETERNAL COVENANT OF PEACE

54

"Sing, O barren one, who did
    not bear;
  break forth into singing and
    cry aloud,
  you who have not been in labour!
For the children of the desolate
    one will be more
  than the children of her who is
    married," says the LORD.
2 "Enlarge the place of your tent,
  and let the curtains of your
    habitations be stretched out;
  do not hold back; lengthen your cords
    and strengthen your stakes.
3 For you will spread abroad to
    the right and to the left,
  and your offspring will
    possess the nations
  and will people the desolate cities.
4 "Fear not, for you will not be ashamed;
    be not confounded, for you
    will not be disgraced;
  for you will forget the shame
    of your youth,
  and the reproach of your widowhood
    you will remember no more.
5 For your Maker is your husband,
    the LORD of hosts is his name;
  and the Holy One of Israel
    is your Redeemer,
  the God of the whole earth
    he is called.
6 For the LORD has called you
    like a wife deserted and
    grieved in spirit,
  like a wife of youth when
    she is cast off,
  says your God.
7 For a brief moment I deserted you,
  but with great compassion
    I will gather you.
8 In overflowing anger for a moment
    I hid my face from you,
  but with everlasting love I will
    have compassion on you,"
  says the LORD, your Redeemer.

9 "This is like the days of Noah[d] to me:
  as I swore that the waters of Noah
    should no more go over the earth,
  so I have sworn that I will not
    be angry with you,
    and will not rebuke you.
10 For the mountains may depart
    and the hills be removed,
  but my steadfast love shall
    not depart from you,
  and my covenant of peace
    shall not be removed,"
  says the LORD, who has
    compassion on you.

11 "O afflicted one, storm-tossed
    and not comforted,
  behold, I will set your stones
    in antimony,
  and lay your foundations
    with sapphires.[e]
12 I will make your pinnacles of agate,[f]
  your gates of carbuncles,[g]
  and all your wall of precious stones.
13 All your children shall be
    taught by the LORD,
  and great shall be the peace
    of your children.
14 In righteousness you shall
    be established;
  you shall be far from oppression,
    for you shall not fear;
  and from terror, for it shall
    not come near you.
15 If anyone stirs up strife,
    it is not from me;
  whoever stirs up strife with you
    shall fall because of you.
16 Behold, I have created the smith
  who blows the fire of coals

---

[a]Masoretic Text; Dead Sea Scroll *he shall see light* [b]Or *with the great* [c]Or *with the numerous* [d]Some manuscripts *For this is as the waters of Noah* [e]Or *lapis lazuli* [f]Or *jasper, or ruby* [g]Or *crystal*

and produces a weapon
    for its purpose.
I have also created the
    ravager to destroy;
¹⁷ no weapon that is fashioned
    against you shall succeed,
and you shall refute every
    tongue that rises against
    you in judgement.
This is the heritage of the
    servants of the Lord
and their vindication*ᵃ* from
    me, declares the Lord."

THE COMPASSION OF THE LORD

55 "Come, everyone who thirsts,
    come to the waters;
and he who has no money,
    come, buy and eat!
Come, buy wine and milk
    without money and without price.
² Why do you spend your money
    for that which is not bread,
and your labour for that which
    does not satisfy?
Listen diligently to me, and
    eat what is good,
and delight yourselves in rich food.
³ Incline your ear, and come to me;
    hear, that your soul may live;
and I will make with you an
    everlasting covenant,
my steadfast, sure love for David.
⁴ Behold, I made him a witness
    to the peoples,
a leader and commander
    for the peoples.
⁵ Behold, you shall call a nation
    that you do not know,
and a nation that did not know
    you shall run to you,
because of the Lord your God, and
    of the Holy One of Israel,
    for he has glorified you.

⁶ "Seek the Lord while he may be found;
    call upon him while he is near;
⁷ let the wicked forsake his way,
    and the unrighteous man
        his thoughts;
let him return to the Lord, that he
    may have compassion on him,
and to our God, for he will
    abundantly pardon.
⁸ For my thoughts are not
    your thoughts,
neither are your ways my ways,
    declares the Lord.
⁹ For as the heavens are higher
    than the earth,
so are my ways higher
    than your ways
and my thoughts than
    your thoughts.

¹⁰ "For as the rain and the snow
    come down from heaven
and do not return there but
    water the earth,
making it bring forth and sprout,
    giving seed to the sower and
        bread to the eater,
¹¹ so shall my word be that goes
    out from my mouth;
it shall not return to me empty,
but it shall accomplish that
    which I purpose,
and shall succeed in the thing
    for which I sent it.

¹² "For you shall go out in joy
    and be led forth in peace;
the mountains and the hills
    before you
shall break forth into singing,
    and all the trees of the field
        shall clap their hands.
¹³ Instead of the thorn shall
    come up the cypress;
instead of the brier shall
    come up the myrtle;
and it shall make a name for the Lord,
    an everlasting sign that
        shall not be cut off."

SALVATION FOR FOREIGNERS

56 Thus says the Lord:
    "Keep justice, and do
        righteousness,
for soon my salvation will come,
    and my righteousness be revealed.
² Blessed is the man who does this,
    and the son of man who holds it fast,
who keeps the Sabbath,
    not profaning it,
and keeps his hand from
    doing any evil."

³ Let not the foreigner who has joined
    himself to the Lord say,

ᵃOr righteousness

"The LORD will surely separate
    me from his people";
and let not the eunuch say,
    "Behold, I am a dry tree."
4 For thus says the LORD:
"To the eunuchs who keep my Sabbaths,
    who choose the things
        that please me
    and hold fast my covenant,
5 I will give in my house and
        within my walls
    a monument and a name
    better than sons and daughters;
I will give them an everlasting name
    that shall not be cut off.

6 "And the foreigners who join
        themselves to the LORD,
    to minister to him, to love
        the name of the LORD,
    and to be his servants,
everyone who keeps the Sabbath
    and does not profane it,
    and holds fast my covenant—
7 these I will bring to my holy mountain,
    and make them joyful in my
        house of prayer;
their burnt offerings and
    their sacrifices
    will be accepted on my altar;
for my house shall be called
    a house of prayer
    for all peoples."
8 The Lord GOD,
    who gathers the outcasts
    of Israel, declares,
"I will gather yet others to him
    besides those already gathered."

ISRAEL'S IRRESPONSIBLE LEADERS

9 All you beasts of the field,
    come to devour—
    all you beasts in the forest.
10 His watchmen are blind;
    they are all without knowledge;
they are all silent dogs;
    they cannot bark,
dreaming, lying down,
    loving to slumber.
11 The dogs have a mighty appetite;
    they never have enough.
But they are shepherds who
    have no understanding;
they have all turned to
    their own way,
each to his own gain, one and all.

12 "Come," they say, "let me get wine;
    let us fill ourselves with
        strong drink;
and tomorrow will be like this day,
    great beyond measure."

ISRAEL'S FUTILE IDOLATRY

57 The righteous man perishes,
    and no one lays it to heart;
devout men are taken away,
    while no one understands.
For the righteous man is taken
    away from calamity;
2   he enters into peace;
they rest in their beds
    who walk in their uprightness.
3 But you, draw near,
    sons of the sorceress,
    offspring of the adulterer and
        the loose woman.
4 Whom are you mocking?
    Against whom do you open
        your mouth wide
    and stick out your tongue?
Are you not children of transgression,
    the offspring of deceit,
5 you who burn with lust
        among the oaks,[a]
    under every green tree,
who slaughter your children
    in the valleys,
    under the clefts of the rocks?
6 Among the smooth stones of the
        valley is your portion;
    they, they, are your lot;
to them you have poured out
    a drink offering,
    you have brought a grain offering.
Shall I relent for these things?
7 On a high and lofty mountain
    you have set your bed,
and there you went up to
    offer sacrifice.
8 Behind the door and the doorpost
    you have set up your memorial;
for, deserting me, you have
    uncovered your bed,
you have gone up to it,
    you have made it wide;
and you have made a covenant
    for yourself with them,
you have loved their bed,
    you have looked on nakedness.[b]

---

[a] Or *among the terebinths*   [b] Or *on a monument* (see 56:5); Hebrew *on a hand*

9   You journeyed to the king with oil
     and multiplied your perfumes;
  you sent your envoys far off,
     and sent down even to Sheol.
10 You were wearied with the
     length of your way,
  but you did not say, "It is hopeless";
  you found new life for your strength,
     and so you were not faint.[a]

11 Whom did you dread and fear,
     so that you lied,
  and did not remember me,
     did not lay it to heart?
  Have I not held my peace,
     even for a long time,
  and you do not fear me?
12 I will declare your righteousness
     and your deeds,
  but they will not profit you.
13 When you cry out, let your collection
     of idols deliver you!
  The wind will carry them all off,
     a breath will take them away.
  But he who takes refuge in me
     shall possess the land
     and shall inherit my holy mountain.

COMFORT FOR THE CONTRITE

14 And it shall be said,
  "Build up, build up, prepare the way,
     remove every obstruction
     from my people's way."
15 For thus says the One who is
     high and lifted up,
  who inhabits eternity, whose
     name is Holy:
  "I dwell in the high and holy place,
     and also with him who is of a
     contrite and lowly spirit,
  to revive the spirit of the lowly,
     and to revive the heart
     of the contrite.
16 For I will not contend for ever,
     nor will I always be angry;
  for the spirit would grow
     faint before me,
     and the breath of life that I made.
17 Because of the iniquity of his
     unjust gain I was angry,
  I struck him; I hid my face
     and was angry,
  but he went on backsliding in
     the way of his own heart.
18 I have seen his ways, but
     I will heal him;
  I will lead him and restore comfort
     to him and his mourners,
19 creating the fruit of the lips.
  Peace, peace, to the far and to
     the near," says the LORD,
  "and I will heal him.
20 But the wicked are like the tossing sea;
     for it cannot be quiet,
     and its waters toss up mire and dirt.
21 There is no peace," says my
     God, "for the wicked."

TRUE AND FALSE FASTING

58 "Cry aloud; do not hold back;
     lift up your voice like a trumpet;
     declare to my people their
     transgression,
  to the house of Jacob their sins.
2   Yet they seek me daily
     and delight to know my ways,
  as if they were a nation that
     did righteousness
     and did not forsake the
     judgement of their God;
  they ask of me righteous judgements;
     they delight to draw near to God.
3   'Why have we fasted, and you see it not?
     Why have we humbled
     ourselves, and you take
     no knowledge of it?'
  Behold, in the day of your fast you
     seek your own pleasure,[b]
     and oppress all your workers.
4   Behold, you fast only to
     quarrel and to fight
     and to hit with a wicked fist.
  Fasting like yours this day
     will not make your voice to
     be heard on high.
5   Is such the fast that I choose,
     a day for a person to
     humble himself?
  Is it to bow down his head like a reed,
     and to spread sackcloth and
     ashes under him?
  Will you call this a fast,
     and a day acceptable to the LORD?

6   "Is not this the fast that I choose:
     to loose the bonds of wickedness,
     to undo the straps of the yoke,
     to let the oppressed[c] go free,
     and to break every yoke?

---

[a] Hebrew *and so you were not sick*   [b] Or *pursue your own business*   [c] Or *bruised*

7 Is it not to share your bread
      with the hungry
   and bring the homeless poor
      into your house;
   when you see the naked, to cover him,
   and not to hide yourself from
      your own flesh?
8 Then shall your light break
      forth like the dawn,
   and your healing shall
      spring up speedily;
   your righteousness shall
      go before you;
   the glory of the LORD shall
      be your rearguard.
9 Then you shall call, and the
      LORD will answer;
   you shall cry, and he will
      say, 'Here I am.'
   If you take away the yoke
      from your midst,
   the pointing of the finger, and
      speaking wickedness,
10 if you pour yourself out for the hungry
   and satisfy the desire of the
      afflicted,
   then shall your light rise
      in the darkness
   and your gloom be as the noonday.
11 And the LORD will guide
      you continually
   and satisfy your desire in
      scorched places
   and make your bones strong;
   and you shall be like a watered garden,
      like a spring of water,
   whose waters do not fail.
12 And your ancient ruins
      shall be rebuilt;
   you shall raise up the foundations
      of many generations;
   you shall be called the repairer
      of the breach,
   the restorer of streets to dwell in.
13 "If you turn back your foot
      from the Sabbath,
   from doing your pleasure¹
      on my holy day,
   and call the Sabbath a delight
   and the holy day of the
      LORD honourable;
   if you honour it, not going
      your own ways,
   or seeking your own pleasure,¹
      or talking idly;¹

14 then you shall take delight in the LORD,
   and I will make you ride on the
      heights of the earth;¹
   I will feed you with the heritage
      of Jacob your father,
   for the mouth of the LORD
      has spoken."

EVIL AND OPPRESSION

59 Behold, the LORD's hand
         is not shortened, that
            it cannot save,
      or his ear dull, that it cannot hear;
2 but your iniquities have
         made a separation
      between you and your God,
   and your sins have hidden
         his face from you
      so that he does not hear.
3 For your hands are defiled with blood
      and your fingers with iniquity;
   your lips have spoken lies;
      your tongue mutters wickedness.
4 No one enters suit justly;
      no one goes to law honestly;
   they rely on empty pleas,
      they speak lies,
   they conceive mischief and
      give birth to iniquity.
5 They hatch adders' eggs;
      they weave the spider's web;
   he who eats their eggs dies,
      and from one that is crushed
         a viper is hatched.
6 Their webs will not serve as clothing;
      men will not cover themselves
         with what they make.
   Their works are works of iniquity,
      and deeds of violence are
         in their hands.
7 Their feet run to evil,
      and they are swift to shed
         innocent blood;
   their thoughts are thoughts
         of iniquity;
      desolation and destruction
         are in their highways.
8 The way of peace they do not know,
      and there is no justice in their
         paths;
   they have made their roads crooked;
      no one who treads on them
         knows peace.

---

¹Or *business* ¹Or *pursuing your own business* ¹Hebrew *or speaking a word* ¹Or *of the land*

9 Therefore justice is far from us,
   and righteousness does
      not overtake us;
   we hope for light, and
      behold, darkness,
   and for brightness, but we
      walk in gloom.
10 We grope for the wall like the blind;
   we grope like those who
      have no eyes;
   we stumble at noon as in the twilight,
      among those in full vigour
   we are like dead men.
11 We all growl like bears;
   we moan and moan like doves;
   we hope for justice, but there is none;
      for salvation, but it is far from us.
12 For our transgressions are
      multiplied before you,
   and our sins testify against us;
   for our transgressions are with us,
      and we know our iniquities:
13 transgressing, and denying the Lord,
   and turning back from
      following our God,
   speaking oppression and revolt,
      conceiving and uttering from
         the heart lying words.

JUDGEMENT AND REDEMPTION

14 Justice is turned back,
      and righteousness stands far away;
   for truth has stumbled in
      the public squares,
      and uprightness cannot enter.
15 Truth is lacking,
      and he who departs from evil
         makes himself a prey.

   The Lord saw it, and it
      displeased him[a]
      that there was no justice.
16 He saw that there was no man,
      and wondered that there was
         no one to intercede;
   then his own arm brought
      him salvation,
      and his righteousness upheld him.
17 He put on righteousness
      as a breastplate,
   and a helmet of salvation
      on his head;
   he put on garments of
      vengeance for clothing,
   and wrapped himself in
      zeal as a cloak.

18 According to their deeds,
      so will he repay,
   wrath to his adversaries,
      repayment to his enemies;
   to the coastlands he will
      render repayment.
19 So they shall fear the name of
      the Lord from the west,
   and his glory from the
      rising of the sun;
   for he will come like a rushing stream,[b]
      which the wind of the Lord drives.

20 "And a Redeemer will come to Zion,
      to those in Jacob who turn
         from transgression,"
      declares the Lord.

21 "And as for me, this is my covenant with them," says the Lord: "My Spirit that is upon you, and my words that I have put in your mouth, shall not depart out of your mouth, or out of the mouth of your offspring, or out of the mouth of your children's offspring," says the Lord, "from this time forth and for evermore."

THE FUTURE GLORY OF ISRAEL

60

Arise, shine, for your light
   has come,
and the glory of the Lord has
   risen upon you.
2 For behold, darkness shall
      cover the earth,
   and thick darkness the peoples;
   but the Lord will arise upon you,
      and his glory will be seen upon you.
3 And nations shall come to your light,
      and kings to the brightness
         of your rising.

4 Lift up your eyes all round, and see;
      they all gather together,
         they come to you;
   your sons shall come from afar,
      and your daughters shall be
         carried on the hip.
5 Then you shall see and be radiant;
      your heart shall thrill and exult,[c]
   because the abundance of the
      sea shall be turned to you,
      the wealth of the nations
         shall come to you.

---

[a]Hebrew *and it was evil in his eyes* [b]Hebrew *a narrow river* [c]Hebrew *your heart shall tremble and grow wide*

⁶ A multitude of camels shall cover you,
   the young camels of Midian
      and Ephah;
   all those from Sheba shall come.
   They shall bring gold and
      frankincense,
   and shall bring good news, the
      praises of the LORD.
⁷ All the flocks of Kedar shall
      be gathered to you;
   the rams of Nebaioth shall
      minister to you;
   they shall come up with
      acceptance on my altar,
   and I will beautify my
      beautiful house.

⁸ Who are these that fly like a cloud,
      and like doves to their windows?
⁹ For the coastlands shall hope for me,
      the ships of Tarshish first,
   to bring your children from afar,
      their silver and gold with them,
   for the name of the LORD your God,
      and for the Holy One of Israel,
      because he has made you beautiful.

¹⁰ Foreigners shall build up your walls,
      and their kings shall minister to you;
   for in my wrath I struck you,
      but in my favour I have had
         mercy on you.
¹¹ Your gates shall be open continually;
      day and night they shall not be shut,
   that people may bring to you the
      wealth of the nations,
      with their kings led in procession.
¹² For the nation and kingdom
      that will not serve you shall perish;
   those nations shall be
      utterly laid waste.
¹³ The glory of Lebanon shall come to you,
      the cypress, the plane, and the pine,
   to beautify the place of my sanctuary,
      and I will make the place of
         my feet glorious.
¹⁴ The sons of those who afflicted you
      shall come bending low to you,
   and all who despised you
      shall bow down at your feet;
   they shall call you the City of the LORD,
      the Zion of the Holy One of Israel.

¹⁵ Whereas you have been
      forsaken and hated,
      with no one passing through,
   I will make you majestic for ever,
      a joy from age to age.
¹⁶ You shall suck the milk of nations;
      you shall nurse at the
         breast of kings;
   and you shall know that I, the
      LORD, am your Saviour
   and your Redeemer, the
      Mighty One of Jacob.

¹⁷ Instead of bronze I will bring gold,
      and instead of iron I will bring silver;
   instead of wood, bronze,
      instead of stones, iron.
   I will make your overseers peace
      and your taskmasters
         righteousness.
¹⁸ Violence shall no more be
      heard in your land,
   devastation or destruction
      within your borders;
   you shall call your walls Salvation,
      and your gates Praise.

¹⁹ The sun shall be no more
      your light by day,
   nor for brightness shall the moon
      give you light;ᵃ
   but the LORD will be your
      everlasting light,
      and your God will be your glory.ᵇ
²⁰ Your sun shall no more go down,
      nor your moon withdraw itself;
   for the LORD will be your
      everlasting light,
      and your days of mourning
         shall be ended.
²¹ Your people shall all be righteous;
      they shall possess the land for ever,
   the branch of my planting, the
      work of my hands,
      that I might be glorified.ᶜ
²² The least one shall become a clan,
      and the smallest one a
         mighty nation;
   I am the LORD;
      in its time I will hasten it.

THE YEAR OF THE LORD'S FAVOUR

61 The Spirit of the Lord GOD is
      upon me,
   because the LORD has
      anointed me

ᵃMasoretic Text; Dead Sea Scroll, Septuagint, Targum add *by night*
ᵇOr *your beauty*   ᶜOr *that I might display my beauty*

18 But be glad and rejoice for ever
    in that which I create;
  for behold, I create Jerusalem
    to be a joy,
  and her people to be a gladness.
19 I will rejoice in Jerusalem
    and be glad in my people;
  no more shall be heard in it
    the sound of weeping
  and the cry of distress.
20 No more shall there be in it
    an infant who lives but a few days,
  or an old man who does not
    fill out his days,
  for the young man shall die a
    hundred years old,
  and the sinner a hundred years
    old shall be accursed.
21 They shall build houses
    and inhabit them;
  they shall plant vineyards
    and eat their fruit.
22 They shall not build and
    another inhabit;
  they shall not plant and
    another eat;
  for like the days of a tree shall
    the days of my people be,
  and my chosen shall long enjoy[a]
    the work of their hands.
23 They shall not labour in vain
    or bear children for calamity,[b]
  for they shall be the offspring of
    the blessed of the LORD,
  and their descendants with them.
24 Before they call I will answer;
    while they are yet speaking
    I will hear.
25 The wolf and the lamb shall
    graze together;
  the lion shall eat straw like the ox,
    and dust shall be the serpent's food.
  They shall not hurt or destroy
    in all my holy mountain,"
               says the LORD.

THE HUMBLE AND CONTRITE IN SPIRIT

66 Thus says the LORD:
  "Heaven is my throne,
    and the earth is my footstool;
  what is the house that you
    would build for me,
  and what is the place of my rest?
2 All these things my hand has made,
    and so all these things came to be,
               declares the LORD.
  But this is the one to whom I will look:
    he who is humble and
    contrite in spirit
    and trembles at my word.

3 "He who slaughters an ox is like
    one who kills a man;
  he who sacrifices a lamb, like one
    who breaks a dog's neck;
  he who presents a grain offering,
    like one who offers pig's blood;
  he who makes a memorial
    offering of frankincense, like
    one who blesses an idol.
  These have chosen their own ways,
    and their soul delights in
    their abominations;
4 I also will choose harsh
    treatment for them
  and bring their fears upon them,
  because when I called, no
    one answered,
  when I spoke, they did not listen;
  but they did what was evil in my eyes
    and chose that in which I
    did not delight."

5 Hear the word of the LORD,
    you who tremble at his word:
  "Your brothers who hate you
    and cast you out for my name's sake
  have said, 'Let the LORD be glorified,
    that we may see your joy';
  but it is they who shall be
    put to shame.

6 "The sound of an uproar from the city!
    A sound from the temple!
  The sound of the LORD,
    rendering recompense
    to his enemies!

REJOICE WITH JERUSALEM

7 "Before she was in labour
    she gave birth;
  before her pain came upon her
    she delivered a son.
8 Who has heard such a thing?
    Who has seen such things?
  Shall a land be born in one day?
    Shall a nation be brought
    forth in one moment?
  For as soon as Zion was in labour
    she brought forth her children.

---

[a]Hebrew *shall wear out* [b]Or *for sudden terror*

9 Shall I bring to the point of birth
    and not cause to bring forth?"
  says the LORD;
"shall I, who cause to bring
    forth, shut the womb?"
  says your God.

10 "Rejoice with Jerusalem, and
    be glad for her,
  all you who love her;
  rejoice with her in joy,
  all you who mourn over her;
11 that you may nurse and be satisfied
    from her consoling breast;
  that you may drink deeply with delight
    from her glorious abundance."[a]

12 For thus says the LORD:
"Behold, I will extend peace
    to her like a river,
  and the glory of the nations like
    an overflowing stream;
and you shall nurse, you shall
    be carried upon her hip,
  and bounced upon her knees.
13 As one whom his mother comforts,
    so I will comfort you;
  you shall be comforted in Jerusalem.
14 You shall see, and your
    heart shall rejoice;
  your bones shall flourish
    like the grass;
and the hand of the LORD shall
    be known to his servants,
  and he shall show his indignation
    against his enemies.

FINAL JUDGEMENT AND GLORY OF THE LORD

15 "For behold, the LORD will come in fire,
    and his chariots like the whirlwind,
  to render his anger in fury,
    and his rebuke with flames of fire.
16 For by fire will the LORD enter
    into judgement,
  and by his sword, with all flesh;
  and those slain by the LORD
    shall be many.

17 "Those who sanctify and purify themselves to go into the gardens, following one in the midst, eating pig's flesh and the abomination and mice, shall come to an end together, declares the LORD.

18 "For I know[b] their works and their thoughts, and the time is coming[c] to gather all nations and tongues. And they shall come and shall see my glory, 19 and I will set a sign among them. And from them I will send survivors to the nations, to Tarshish, Pul, and Lud, who draw the bow, to Tubal and Javan, to the coastlands far away, that have not heard my fame or seen my glory. And they shall declare my glory among the nations. 20 And they shall bring all your brothers from all the nations as an offering to the LORD, on horses and in chariots and in litters and on mules and on dromedaries, to my holy mountain Jerusalem, says the LORD, just as the Israelites bring their grain offering in a clean vessel to the house of the LORD. 21 And some of them also I will take for priests and for Levites, says the LORD.

22 "For as the new heavens and
    the new earth
  that I make
shall remain before me, says
    the LORD,
  so shall your offspring and
    your name remain.
23 From new moon to new moon,
    and from Sabbath to Sabbath,
  all flesh shall come to
    worship before me,
  declares the LORD.

24 "And they shall go out and look on the dead bodies of the men who have rebelled against me. For their worm shall not die, their fire shall not be quenched, and they shall be an abhorrence to all flesh."

---

[a]Or breast   [b]Septuagint, Syriac; Hebrew lacks know   [c]Hebrew and it is coming

JEREMIAH

1 The words of Jeremiah, the son of Hilkiah, one of the priests who were in Anathoth in the land of Benjamin, ²to whom the word of the Lord came in the days of Josiah the son of Amon, king of Judah, in the thirteenth year of his reign. ³It came also in the days of Jehoiakim the son of Josiah, king of Judah, and until the end of the eleventh year of Zedekiah, the son of Josiah, king of Judah, until the captivity of Jerusalem in the fifth month.

THE CALL OF JEREMIAH

⁴Now the word of the Lord came to me, saying,

⁵ " Before I formed you in the
womb I knew you,
and before you were born I
consecrated you;
I appointed you a prophet
to the nations."

⁶Then I said, "Ah, Lord God! Behold, I do not know how to speak, for I am only a youth." ⁷But the Lord said to me,

" Do not say, 'I am only a youth';
for to all to whom I send
you, you shall go,
and whatever I command
you, you shall speak.
⁸ Do not be afraid of them,
for I am with you to deliver you,
declares the Lord."

⁹Then the Lord put out his hand and touched my mouth. And the Lord said to me,

" Behold, I have put my words
in your mouth.
¹⁰ See, I have set you this day over
nations and over kingdoms,
to pluck up and to break down,
to destroy and to overthrow,
to build and to plant."

¹¹And the word of the Lord came to me, saying, "Jeremiah, what do you see?" And I said, "I see an almond^a branch." ¹²Then the Lord said to me, "You have seen well, for I am watching over my word to perform it."

¹³The word of the Lord came to me a second time, saying, "What do you see?" And I said, "I see a boiling pot, facing away from the north." ¹⁴Then the Lord said to me, "Out of the north disaster^b shall be let loose upon all the inhabitants of the land. ¹⁵For behold, I am calling all the tribes of the kingdoms of the north, declares the Lord, and they shall come, and every one shall set his throne at the entrance of the gates of Jerusalem, against all its walls all round and against all the cities of Judah. ¹⁶And I will declare my judgements against them, for all their evil in forsaking me. They have made offerings to other gods and worshipped the works of their own hands. ¹⁷But you, dress yourself for work;^c arise, and say to them everything that I command you. Do not be dismayed by them, lest I dismay you before them. ¹⁸And I, behold, I make you this day a fortified city, an iron pillar, and bronze walls, against the whole land, against the kings of Judah, its officials, its priests, and the people of the land. ¹⁹They will fight against you, but they shall not prevail against you, for I am with you, declares the Lord, to deliver you."

ISRAEL FORSAKES THE LORD

2 The word of the Lord came to me, saying, ²"Go and proclaim in the hearing of Jerusalem, Thus says the Lord,

"I remember the devotion of your youth,
your love as a bride,
how you followed me in
the wilderness,
in a land not sown.
³ Israel was holy to the Lord,
the firstfruits of his harvest.
All who ate of it incurred guilt;
disaster came upon them,
declares the Lord."

---

^a*Almond* sounds like the Hebrew for *watching* (compare verse 12)
^bThe Hebrew word can mean *evil, harm,* or *disaster*, depending on the context; so throughout Jeremiah   ^cHebrew *gird up your loins*

⁴Hear the word of the LORD, O house of Jacob, and all the clans of the house of Israel. ⁵Thus says the LORD:

"What wrong did your
 fathers find in me
that they went far from me,
and went after worthlessness,
 and became worthless?
⁶ They did not say, 'Where is the LORD
 who brought us up from
  the land of Egypt,
who led us in the wilderness,
in a land of deserts and pits,
in a land of drought and
 deep darkness,
in a land that none passes through,
 where no man dwells?'
⁷ And I brought you into a plentiful land
 to enjoy its fruits and its
  good things.
But when you came in, you
 defiled my land
and made my heritage an
 abomination.
⁸ The priests did not say,
 'Where is the LORD?'
Those who handle the law
 did not know me;
the shepherds*ᵃ* transgressed
 against me;
the prophets prophesied by Baal
and went after things that
 do not profit.

⁹ "Therefore I still contend with you,
  declares the LORD,
and with your children's
 children I will contend.
¹⁰ For cross to the coasts of
  Cyprus and see,
or send to Kedar and
 examine with care;
see if there has been such a thing.
¹¹ Has a nation changed its gods,
 even though they are no gods?
But my people have changed
 their glory
 for that which does not profit.
¹² Be appalled, O heavens, at this;
 be shocked, be utterly desolate,
  declares the LORD,
¹³ for my people have committed
  two evils:
they have forsaken me,
 the fountain of living waters,
and hewed out cisterns
 for themselves,
broken cisterns that can
 hold no water.

¹⁴ "Is Israel a slave? Is he a
  homeborn servant?
Why then has he become a prey?
¹⁵ The lions have roared against him;
 they have roared loudly.
They have made his land a waste;
 his cities are in ruins,
  without inhabitant.
¹⁶ Moreover, the men of Memphis
  and Tahpanhes
have shaved*ᵇ* the crown
 of your head.
¹⁷ Have you not brought this
  upon yourself
by forsaking the LORD your God,
 when he led you in the way?
¹⁸ And now what do you gain
 by going to Egypt
 to drink the waters of the Nile?
Or what do you gain by
 going to Assyria
 to drink the waters of the
  Euphrates?*ᶜ*
¹⁹ Your evil will chastise you,
 and your apostasy will reprove you.
Know and see that it is evil and bitter
 for you to forsake the
  LORD your God;
the fear of me is not in you,
 declares the Lord GOD of hosts.

²⁰ "For long ago I broke your yoke
 and burst your bonds;
but you said, 'I will not serve.'
Yes, on every high hill
 and under every green tree
 you bowed down like a whore.
²¹ Yet I planted you a choice vine,
 wholly of pure seed.
How then have you turned
 degenerate
 and become a wild vine?
²² Though you wash yourself with lye
 and use much soap,
 the stain of your guilt is
  still before me,
  declares the Lord GOD.
²³ How can you say, 'I am not unclean,
 I have not gone after the Baals'?

---
*ᵃ*Or *rulers*   *ᵇ*Hebrew *grazed*   *ᶜ*Hebrew *the River*

Look at your way in the valley;
　know what you have done—
a restless young camel running
　here and there,
24　a wild donkey used to
　　the wilderness,
in her heat sniffing the wind!
　Who can restrain her lust?
None who seek her need
　weary themselves;
in her month they will find her.
25　Keep your feet from going unshod
　and your throat from thirst.
But you said, 'It is hopeless,
　for I have loved foreigners,
　and after them I will go.'

26　"As a thief is shamed when caught,
　so the house of Israel
　　shall be shamed:
they, their kings, their officials,
　their priests, and their prophets,
27　who say to a tree, 'You are my father',
　and to a stone, 'You gave me birth.'
For they have turned their back to me,
　and not their face.
But in the time of their
　　trouble they say,
　'Arise and save us!'
28　But where are your gods
　that you made for yourself?
Let them arise, if they can save you,
　in your time of trouble;
for as many as your cities
　are your gods, O Judah.

29　"Why do you contend with me?
　You have all transgressed
　　against me,
　　　　　　declares the LORD.
30　In vain have I struck your children;
　they took no correction;
your own sword devoured
　your prophets
like a ravening lion.
31　And you, O generation, behold
　the word of the LORD.
Have I been a wilderness to Israel,
　or a land of thick darkness?
Why then do my people
　say, 'We are free,
we will come no more to you'?
32　Can a virgin forget her ornaments,
　or a bride her attire?
Yet my people have forgotten me
　days without number.

33　"How well you direct your course
　　to seek love!
So that even to wicked women
　you have taught your ways.
34　Also on your skirts is found
　the lifeblood of the guiltless poor;
you did not find them breaking in.
　Yet in spite of all these things
35　you say, 'I am innocent;
　surely his anger has
　　turned from me.'
Behold, I will bring you to judgement
　for saying, 'I have not sinned.'
36　How much you go about,
　changing your way!
You shall be put to shame by Egypt
　as you were put to shame by Assyria.
37　From it too you will come away
　with your hands on your head,
for the LORD has rejected those
　in whom you trust,
and you will not prosper by them.

3 "If[c] a man divorces his wife
　and she goes from him
　and becomes another man's wife,
will he return to her?
Would not that land be
　greatly polluted?
You have played the whore
　with many lovers;
and would you return to me?
　　　　　　declares the LORD.
2　Lift up your eyes to the bare
　　heights, and see!
Where have you not been ravished?
By the waysides you have
　sat awaiting lovers
like an Arab in the wilderness.
You have polluted the land
　with your vile whoredom.
3　Therefore the showers have
　　been withheld,
　and the spring rain has not come;
yet you have the forehead of a whore;
　you refuse to be ashamed.
4　Have you not just now called to me,
　'My father, you are the friend
　　of my youth—
5　will he be angry for ever,
　will he be indignant to the end?'
Behold, you have spoken,
　but you have done all the
　　evil that you could."

---
[c] Septuagint, Syriac; Hebrew *Saying*, "If

FAITHLESS ISRAEL CALLED TO REPENTANCE

⁶The Lord said to me in the days of King Josiah: "Have you seen what she did, that faithless one, Israel, how she went up on every high hill and under every green tree, and there played the whore? ⁷And I thought, 'After she has done all this she will return to me', but she did not return, and her treacherous sister Judah saw it. ⁸She saw that for all the adulteries of that faithless one, Israel, I had sent her away with a decree of divorce. Yet her treacherous sister Judah did not fear, but she too went and played the whore. ⁹Because she took her whoredom lightly, she polluted the land, committing adultery with stone and tree. ¹⁰Yet for all this her treacherous sister Judah did not return to me with her whole heart, but in pretence, declares the Lord."

¹¹And the Lord said to me, "Faithless Israel has shown herself more righteous than treacherous Judah. ¹²Go, and proclaim these words towards the north, and say,

"'Return, faithless Israel,
  declares the Lord.
I will not look on you in anger,
 for I am merciful,
  declares the Lord;
I will not be angry for ever.
¹³ Only acknowledge your guilt,
 that you rebelled against
  the Lord your God
and scattered your favours among
 foreigners under every green tree,
and that you have not
 obeyed my voice,
  declares the Lord.
¹⁴ Return, O faithless children,
  declares the Lord;
for I am your master;
I will take you, one from a city
 and two from a family,
 and I will bring you to Zion.

¹⁵"'And I will give you shepherds after my own heart, who will feed you with knowledge and understanding. ¹⁶And when you have multiplied and been fruitful in the land, in those days, declares the Lord, they shall no more say, "The ark of the covenant of the Lord." It shall not come to mind or be remembered or missed; it shall not be made again. ¹⁷At that time Jerusalem shall be called the throne of the Lord, and all nations shall gather to it, to the presence of the Lord in Jerusalem, and they shall no more stubbornly follow their own evil heart. ¹⁸In those days the house of Judah shall join the house of Israel, and together they shall come from the land of the north to the land that I gave your fathers for a heritage.

¹⁹ "'I said,
 How I would set you
  among my sons,
 and give you a pleasant land,
  a heritage most beautiful
   of all nations.
And I thought you would
 call me, My Father,
 and would not turn from
  following me.
²⁰ Surely, as a treacherous wife
 leaves her husband,
so have you been treacherous
 to me, O house of Israel,
  declares the Lord.'"

²¹ A voice on the bare heights is heard,
 the weeping and pleading
  of Israel's sons
because they have perverted their way;
 they have forgotten the
  Lord their God.
²² "Return, O faithless sons;
 I will heal your faithlessness."
"Behold, we come to you,
 for you are the Lord our God.
²³ Truly the hills are a delusion,
 the orgies*ᵃ* on the mountains.
Truly in the Lord our God
 is the salvation of Israel.

²⁴"But from our youth the shameful thing has devoured all for which our fathers laboured, their flocks and their herds, their sons and their daughters. ²⁵Let us lie down in our shame, and let our dishonour cover us. For we have sinned against the Lord our God, we and our fathers, from our youth even to this day, and we have not obeyed the voice of the Lord our God."

4 "If you return, O Israel,
  declares the Lord,
to me you should return.
If you remove your detestable
 things from my presence,
 and do not waver,

ᵃHebrew *commotion*

² and if you swear, 'As the LORD lives,'
in truth, in justice, and in
righteousness,
then nations shall bless
themselves in him,
and in him shall they glory."

³For thus says the LORD to the men of Judah and Jerusalem:

"Break up your fallow ground,
and sow not among thorns.
⁴ Circumcise yourselves to the LORD;
remove the foreskin of your hearts,
O men of Judah and inhabitants
of Jerusalem;
lest my wrath go forth like fire,
and burn with none to quench it,
because of the evil of your deeds."

DISASTER FROM THE NORTH

⁵Declare in Judah, and proclaim in Jerusalem, and say,

"Blow the trumpet through the land;
cry aloud and say,
'Assemble, and let us go
into the fortified cities!'
⁶ Raise a standard towards Zion,
flee for safety, stay not,
for I bring disaster from the north,
and great destruction.
⁷ A lion has gone up from his thicket,
a destroyer of nations has set out;
he has gone out from his place
to make your land a waste;
your cities will be ruins
without inhabitant.
⁸ For this put on sackcloth,
lament and wail,
for the fierce anger of the LORD
has not turned back from us."

⁹"In that day, declares the LORD, courage shall fail both king and officials. The priests shall be appalled and the prophets astounded." ¹⁰Then I said, "Ah, Lord GOD, surely you have utterly deceived this people and Jerusalem, saying, 'It shall be well with you', whereas the sword has reached their very life."

¹¹At that time it will be said to this people and to Jerusalem, "A hot wind from the bare heights in the desert towards the daughter of my people, not to winnow or cleanse, ¹²a wind too full for this comes for me. Now it is I who speak in judgement upon them."

¹³ Behold, he comes up like clouds;
his chariots like the whirlwind;
his horses are swifter than eagles—
woe to us, for we are ruined!
¹⁴ O Jerusalem, wash your
heart from evil,
that you may be saved.
How long shall your wicked thoughts
lodge within you?
¹⁵ For a voice declares from Dan
and proclaims trouble from
Mount Ephraim.
¹⁶ Warn the nations that he is coming;
announce to Jerusalem,
"Besiegers come from a distant land;
they shout against the
cities of Judah.
¹⁷ Like keepers of a field are they
against her all round,
because she has rebelled
against me,
declares the LORD.
¹⁸ Your ways and your deeds
have brought this upon you.
This is your doom, and it is bitter;
it has reached your very heart."

ANGUISH OVER JUDAH'S DESOLATION

¹⁹ My anguish, my anguish!
I writhe in pain!
Oh the walls of my heart!
My heart is beating wildly;
I cannot keep silent,
for I hear the sound of the trumpet,
the alarm of war.
²⁰ Crash follows hard on crash;
the whole land is laid waste.
Suddenly my tents are laid waste,
my curtains in a moment.
²¹ How long must I see the standard
and hear the sound of the trumpet?

²² "For my people are foolish;
they know me not;
they are stupid children;
they have no understanding.
They are 'wise'—in doing evil!
But how to do good they know not."

²³ I looked on the earth, and behold, it
was without form and void;
and to the heavens, and
they had no light.
²⁴ I looked on the mountains, and
behold, they were quaking,
and all the hills moved to and fro.

²⁵ I looked, and behold, there was
    no man,
  and all the birds of the air had fled.
²⁶ I looked, and behold, the fruitful
    land was a desert,
  and all its cities were laid in ruins
    before the Lord, before
      his fierce anger.

²⁷For thus says the Lord, "The whole land shall be a desolation; yet I will not make a full end.

²⁸ "For this the earth shall mourn,
    and the heavens above be dark;
  for I have spoken; I have purposed;
    I have not relented, nor
      will I turn back."
²⁹ At the noise of horseman and archer
    every city takes to flight;
  they enter thickets; they
    climb among rocks;
  all the cities are forsaken,
    and no man dwells in them.
³⁰ And you, O desolate one,
  what do you mean that you
    dress in scarlet,
  that you adorn yourself with
    ornaments of gold,
  that you enlarge your
    eyes with paint?
  In vain you beautify yourself.
    Your lovers despise you;
    they seek your life.
³¹ For I heard a cry as of a
    woman in labour,
  anguish as of one giving birth
    to her first child,
  the cry of the daughter of Zion
    gasping for breath,
    stretching out her hands,
  "Woe is me! I am fainting
    before murderers."

JERUSALEM REFUSED TO REPENT

5 Run to and fro through the streets
    of Jerusalem,
  look and take note!
  Search her squares to see
    if you can find a man,
  one who does justice
    and seeks truth,
  that I may pardon her.
² Though they say, "As the Lord lives",
    yet they swear falsely.

³ O Lord, do not your eyes look for truth?
    You have struck them down,
      but they felt no anguish;
    you have consumed them,
      but they refused to take correction.
    They have made their faces
      harder than rock;
    they have refused to repent.

⁴ Then I said, "These are only the poor;
    they have no sense;
  for they do not know the
    way of the Lord,
    the justice of their God.
⁵ I will go to the great
    and will speak to them,
  for they know the way of the Lord,
    the justice of their God."
  But they all alike had broken the yoke;
    they had burst the bonds.

⁶ Therefore a lion from the forest
    shall strike them down;
  a wolf from the desert shall
    devastate them.
  A leopard is watching their cities;
    everyone who goes out of them
      shall be torn in pieces,
  because their transgressions are many,
    their apostasies are great.

⁷ "How can I pardon you?
    Your children have forsaken me
    and have sworn by those
      who are no gods.
  When I fed them to the full,
    they committed adultery
    and trooped to the houses of whores.
⁸ They were well-fed, lusty stallions,
    each neighing for his
      neighbour's wife.
⁹ Shall I not punish them
    for these things?
            declares the Lord;
  and shall I not avenge myself
    on a nation such as this?

¹⁰ "Go up through her vine
    rows and destroy,
    but make not a full end;
  strip away her branches,
    for they are not the Lord's.
¹¹ For the house of Israel and
    the house of Judah
  have been utterly treacherous to me,
            declares the Lord.

12 They have spoken falsely of the LORD
and have said, 'He will do nothing;
no disaster will come upon us,
nor shall we see sword or famine.
13 The prophets will become wind;
the word is not in them.
Thus shall it be done to them!'"

THE LORD PROCLAIMS JUDGEMENT

14 Therefore thus says the LORD,
the God of hosts:
"Because you have spoken this word,
behold, I am making my words
in your mouth a fire,
and this people wood, and the
fire shall consume them.
15 Behold, I am bringing against you
a nation from afar, O house of Israel,
declares the LORD.
It is an enduring nation;
it is an ancient nation,
a nation whose language
you do not know,
nor can you understand
what they say.
16 Their quiver is like an open tomb;
they are all mighty warriors.
17 They shall eat up your harvest
and your food;
they shall eat up your sons
and your daughters;
they shall eat up your flocks
and your herds;
they shall eat up your vines
and your fig trees;
your fortified cities in which you trust
they shall beat down with
the sword."

18"But even in those days, declares the LORD, I will not make a full end of you. 19And when your people say, 'Why has the LORD our God done all these things to us?' you shall say to them, 'As you have forsaken me and served foreign gods in your land, so you shall serve foreigners in a land that is not yours.'"

20 Declare this in the house of Jacob;
proclaim it in Judah:
21 "Hear this, O foolish and
senseless people,
who have eyes, but see not,
who have ears, but hear not.
22 Do you not fear me? declares the LORD.
Do you not tremble before me?
I placed the sand as the
boundary for the sea,
a perpetual barrier that
it cannot pass;
though the waves toss, they
cannot prevail;
though they roar, they
cannot pass over it.
23 But this people has a stubborn
and rebellious heart;
they have turned aside
and gone away.
24 They do not say in their hearts,
'Let us fear the LORD our God,
who gives the rain in its season,
the autumn rain and the
spring rain,
and keeps for us
the weeks appointed for
the harvest.'
25 Your iniquities have turned
these away,
and your sins have kept
good from you.
26 For wicked men are found
among my people;
they lurk like fowlers lying in wait.[a]
They set a trap;
they catch men.
27 Like a cage full of birds,
their houses are full of deceit;
therefore they have become
great and rich;
28 they have grown fat and sleek.
They know no bounds in deeds of evil;
they judge not with justice
the cause of the fatherless,
to make it prosper,
and they do not defend the
rights of the needy.
29 Shall I not punish them
for these things?
declares the LORD,
and shall I not avenge myself
on a nation such as this?"

30 An appalling and horrible thing
has happened in the land:
31 the prophets prophesy falsely,
and the priests rule at
their direction;
my people love to have it so,
but what will you do when
the end comes?

---

[a]The meaning of the Hebrew is uncertain

JEREMIAH 6

IMPENDING DISASTER FOR JERUSALEM

6 Flee for safety, O people of Benjamin,
  from the midst of Jerusalem!
 Blow the trumpet in Tekoa,
  and raise a signal on Beth-
   haccherem,
 for disaster looms out of the north,
  and great destruction.
2 The lovely and delicately
   bred I will destroy,
  the daughter of Zion.[a]
3 Shepherds with their flocks
   shall come against her;
  they shall pitch their
   tents round her;
  they shall pasture, each in his place.
4 "Prepare war against her;
  arise, and let us attack at noon!
 Woe to us, for the day declines,
  for the shadows of evening
   lengthen!
5 Arise, and let us attack by night
  and destroy her palaces!"

6 For thus says the LORD of hosts:
 "Cut down her trees;
  cast up a siege mound
   against Jerusalem.
 This is the city that must be punished;
  there is nothing but
   oppression within her.
7 As a well keeps its water fresh,
  so she keeps fresh her evil;
 violence and destruction are
   heard within her;
  sickness and wounds are
   ever before me.
8 Be warned, O Jerusalem,
  lest I turn from you in disgust,
 lest I make you a desolation,
  an uninhabited land."

9 Thus says the LORD of hosts:
 "They shall glean thoroughly as a vine
   the remnant of Israel;
  like a grape gatherer pass
   your hand again
   over its branches."
10 To whom shall I speak and
    give warning,
   that they may hear?
  Behold, their ears are uncircumcised,
   they cannot listen;
  behold, the word of the LORD is
   to them an object of scorn;
   they take no pleasure in it.

11 Therefore I am full of the
    wrath of the LORD;
   I am weary of holding it in.
  "Pour it out upon the children
    in the street,
   and upon the gatherings of
    young men, also;
  both husband and wife shall be taken,
   the elderly and the very aged.
12 Their houses shall be turned
    over to others,
   their fields and wives together,
  for I will stretch out my hand
   against the inhabitants of the land,"
         declares the LORD.
13 "For from the least to the
    greatest of them,
   everyone is greedy for unjust gain;
  and from prophet to priest,
   everyone deals falsely.
14 They have healed the wound
    of my people lightly,
   saying, 'Peace, peace',
   when there is no peace.
15 Were they ashamed when they
    committed abomination?
   No, they were not at all ashamed;
    they did not know how to blush.
  Therefore they shall fall
    among those who fall;
   at the time that I punish them,
    they shall be overthrown,"
         says the LORD.

16 Thus says the LORD:
 "Stand by the roads, and look,
   and ask for the ancient paths,
  where the good way is; and walk in it,
   and find rest for your souls.
  But they said, 'We will not walk in it.'
17 I set watchmen over you, saying,
   'Pay attention to the sound
     of the trumpet!'
  But they said, 'We will not pay attention.'
18 Therefore hear, O nations,
   and know, O congregation, what
    will happen to them.
19 Hear, O earth; behold, I am bringing
    disaster upon this people,
   the fruit of their devices,
  because they have not paid
    attention to my words;
   and as for my law, they
    have rejected it.

---

[a] Or *I have likened the daughter of Zion to the loveliest pasture*

20 What use to me is frankincense
    that comes from Sheba,
    or sweet cane from a distant land?
  Your burnt offerings are
    not acceptable,
    nor your sacrifices pleasing to me.
21 Therefore thus says the LORD:
  'Behold, I will lay before this people
    stumbling blocks against which
      they shall stumble;
    fathers and sons together,
    neighbour and friend
      shall perish.'"

22 Thus says the LORD:
  "Behold, a people is coming
    from the north country,
    a great nation is stirring from the
      farthest parts of the earth.
23 They lay hold on bow and javelin;
    they are cruel and have no mercy;
    the sound of them is like
      the roaring sea;
  they ride on horses,
    set in array as a man for battle,
    against you, O daughter of Zion!"
24 We have heard the report of it;
    our hands fall helpless;
  anguish has taken hold of us,
    pain as of a woman in labour.
25 Go not out into the field,
    nor walk on the road,
  for the enemy has a sword;
    terror is on every side.
26 O daughter of my people,
    put on sackcloth,
    and roll in ashes;
  make mourning as for an only son,
    most bitter lamentation,
  for suddenly the destroyer
    will come upon us.

27 "I have made you a tester of metals
    among my people,
    that you may know and
      test their ways.
28 They are all stubbornly rebellious,
    going about with slanders;
  they are bronze and iron;
    all of them act corruptly.
29 The bellows blow fiercely;
    the lead is consumed by the fire;
  in vain the refining goes on,
    for the wicked are not removed.
30 Rejected silver they are called,
    for the LORD has rejected them."

EVIL IN THE LAND

7 The word that came to Jeremiah from the LORD: ²"Stand in the gate of the LORD's house, and proclaim there this word, and say, Hear the word of the LORD, all you men of Judah who enter these gates to worship the LORD. ³Thus says the LORD of hosts, the God of Israel: Amend your ways and your deeds, and I will let you dwell in this place. ⁴Do not trust in these deceptive words: 'This is the temple of the LORD, the temple of the LORD, the temple of the LORD.'

⁵"For if you truly amend your ways and your deeds, if you truly execute justice one with another, ⁶if you do not oppress the sojourner, the fatherless, or the widow, or shed innocent blood in this place, and if you do not go after other gods to your own harm, ⁷then I will let you dwell in this place, in the land that I gave of old to your fathers for ever.

⁸"Behold, you trust in deceptive words to no avail. ⁹Will you steal, murder, commit adultery, swear falsely, make offerings to Baal, and go after other gods that you have not known, ¹⁰and then come and stand before me in this house, which is called by my name, and say, 'We are delivered!'—only to go on doing all these abominations? ¹¹Has this house, which is called by my name, become a den of robbers in your eyes? Behold, I myself have seen it, declares the LORD. ¹²Go now to my place that was in Shiloh, where I made my name dwell at first, and see what I did to it because of the evil of my people Israel. ¹³And now, because you have done all these things, declares the LORD, and when I spoke to you persistently you did not listen, and when I called you, you did not answer, ¹⁴therefore I will do to the house that is called by my name, and in which you trust, and to the place that I gave to you and to your fathers, as I did to Shiloh. ¹⁵And I will cast you out of my sight, as I cast out all your kinsmen, all the offspring of Ephraim.

¹⁶"As for you, do not pray for this people, or lift up a cry or prayer for them, and do not intercede with me, for I will not hear you. ¹⁷Do you not see what they are doing in the cities of Judah and in the streets of Jerusalem? ¹⁸The children gather wood, the fathers kindle fire, and the women knead dough, to make cakes for the queen of heaven. And they pour out drink offerings to other gods, to provoke me to anger. ¹⁹Is it I whom they provoke? declares the LORD. Is it not themselves, to their own shame? ²⁰Therefore thus

says the Lord God: Behold, my anger and my wrath will be poured out on this place, upon man and beast, upon the trees of the field and the fruit of the ground; it will burn and not be quenched."

²¹Thus says the Lord of hosts, the God of Israel: "Add your burnt offerings to your sacrifices, and eat the flesh. ²²For in the day that I brought them out of the land of Egypt, I did not speak to your fathers or command them concerning burnt offerings and sacrifices. ²³But this command I gave them: 'Obey my voice, and I will be your God, and you shall be my people. And walk in all the way that I command you, that it may be well with you.' ²⁴But they did not obey or incline their ear, but walked in their own counsels and the stubbornness of their evil hearts, and went backwards and not forwards. ²⁵From the day that your fathers came out of the land of Egypt to this day, I have persistently sent all my servants the prophets to them, day after day. ²⁶Yet they did not listen to me or incline their ear, but stiffened their neck. They did worse than their fathers.

²⁷"So you shall speak all these words to them, but they will not listen to you. You shall call to them, but they will not answer you. ²⁸And you shall say to them, 'This is the nation that did not obey the voice of the Lord their God, and did not accept discipline; truth has perished; it is cut off from their lips.'

²⁹ "'Cut off your hair and cast it away;
　　raise a lamentation on
　　　　the bare heights,
for the Lord has rejected and forsaken
　　the generation of his wrath.'

THE VALLEY OF SLAUGHTER

³⁰"For the sons of Judah have done evil in my sight, declares the Lord. They have set their detestable things in the house that is called by my name, to defile it. ³¹And they have built the high places of Topheth, which is in the Valley of the Son of Hinnom, to burn their sons and their daughters in the fire, which I did not command, nor did it come into my mind. ³²Therefore, behold, the days are coming, declares the Lord, when it will no more be called Topheth, or the Valley of the Son of Hinnom, but the Valley of Slaughter; for they will bury in Topheth, because there is no room elsewhere. ³³And the dead bodies of this people will be food for the birds of the air, and for the beasts of the earth, and none will frighten them away. ³⁴And I will silence in the cities of Judah and in the streets of Jerusalem the voice of mirth and the voice of gladness, the voice of the bridegroom and the voice of the bride, for the land shall become a waste.

8

"At that time, declares the Lord, the bones of the kings of Judah, the bones of its officials, the bones of the priests, the bones of the prophets, and the bones of the inhabitants of Jerusalem shall be brought out of their tombs. ²And they shall be spread before the sun and the moon and all the host of heaven, which they have loved and served, which they have gone after, and which they have sought and worshipped. And they shall not be gathered or buried. They shall be as dung on the surface of the ground. ³Death shall be preferred to life by all the remnant that remains of this evil family in all the places where I have driven them, declares the Lord of hosts.

SIN AND TREACHERY

⁴ "You shall say to them, Thus
　　says the Lord:
When men fall, do they not rise again?
　　If one turns away, does
　　　　he not return?
⁵ Why then has this people turned away
　　in perpetual backsliding?
They hold fast to deceit;
　　they refuse to return.
⁶ I have paid attention and listened,
　　but they have not spoken rightly;
no man relents of his evil,
　　saying, 'What have I done?'
Everyone turns to his own course,
　　like a horse plunging
　　　　headlong into battle.
⁷ Even the stork in the heavens
　　knows her times,
and the turtle-dove, swallow,
　　and crane*ᵃ*
keep the time of their coming,
but my people know not
　　the rules*ᵇ* of the Lord.

⁸ "How can you say, 'We are wise,
　　and the law of the Lord is with us'?
But behold, the lying pen of the scribes
　　has made it into a lie.
⁹ The wise men shall be put to shame;
　　they shall be dismayed and taken;

ᵃThe meaning of the Hebrew word is uncertain　　*ᵇOr just decrees*

behold, they have rejected the
        word of the LORD,
    so what wisdom is in them?
10 Therefore I will give their
        wives to others
    and their fields to conquerors,
    because from the least to the greatest
        everyone is greedy for unjust gain;
    from prophet to priest,
        everyone deals falsely.
11 They have healed the wound
        of my people lightly,
    saying, 'Peace, peace',
        when there is no peace.
12 Were they ashamed when they
        committed abomination?
    No, they were not at all ashamed;
        they did not know how to blush.
    Therefore they shall fall
        among the fallen;
    when I punish them, they
        shall be overthrown,
                    says the LORD.
13 When I would gather them,
        declares the LORD,
    there are no grapes on the vine,
        nor figs on the fig tree;
    even the leaves are withered,
        and what I gave them has passed
            away from them."[a]

14 Why do we sit still?
    Gather together; let us go into
        the fortified cities
    and perish there,
    for the LORD our God has
        doomed us to perish
    and has given us poisoned
        water to drink,
    because we have sinned
        against the LORD.
15 We looked for peace, but
        no good came;
    for a time of healing, but
        behold, terror.
16 "The snorting of their horses
        is heard from Dan;
    at the sound of the neighing
        of their stallions
    the whole land quakes.
    They come and devour the land
        and all that fills it,
    the city and those who dwell in it.
17 For behold, I am sending
        among you serpents,
    adders that cannot be charmed,
        and they shall bite you,"
                    declares the LORD.

JEREMIAH GRIEVES FOR HIS PEOPLE

18 My joy is gone; grief is upon me;[b]
        my heart is sick within me.
19 Behold, the cry of the daughter
        of my people
    from the length and breadth
        of the land:
    "Is the LORD not in Zion?
        Is her King not in her?"
    "Why have they provoked me to anger
        with their carved images
        and with their foreign idols?"
20 "The harvest is past, the
        summer is ended,
        and we are not saved."
21 For the wound of the daughter of my
        people is my heart wounded;
    I mourn, and dismay has
        taken hold on me.

22 Is there no balm in Gilead?
        Is there no physician there?
    Why then has the health of the
        daughter of my people
    not been restored?

9 [c] Oh that my head were waters,
        and my eyes a fountain of tears,
    that I might weep day and night
        for the slain of the daughter
            of my people!
2[d] Oh that I had in the desert
        a travellers' lodging place,
    that I might leave my people
        and go away from them!
    For they are all adulterers,
        a company of treacherous men.
3   They bend their tongue like a bow;
        falsehood and not truth has
            grown strong[e] in the land;
    for they proceed from evil to evil,
        and they do not know me,
                    declares the LORD.

4   Let everyone beware of his neighbour,
        and put no trust in any brother,
    for every brother is a deceiver,
        and every neighbour goes
            about as a slanderer.

---

[a]The meaning of the Hebrew is uncertain [b]Compare Septuagint; the meaning of the Hebrew is uncertain [c]Ch 8:23 in Hebrew [d]Ch 9:1 in Hebrew [e]Septuagint; Hebrew *and not for truth they have grown strong*

⁵ Everyone deceives his neighbour,
  and no one speaks the truth;
 they have taught their tongue
   to speak lies;
  they weary themselves
   committing iniquity.
⁶ Heaping oppression upon oppression,
  and deceit upon deceit,
 they refuse to know me,
  declares the LORD.

⁷ Therefore thus says the LORD of hosts:
"Behold, I will refine them
  and test them,
 for what else can I do, because
   of my people?
⁸ Their tongue is a deadly arrow;
 it speaks deceitfully;
with his mouth each speaks
  peace to his neighbour,
 but in his heart he plans an
  ambush for him.
⁹ Shall I not punish them for these
  things? declares the LORD,
 and shall I not avenge myself
  on a nation such as this?

¹⁰ "I will take up weeping and wailing
  for the mountains,
 and a lamentation for the
   pastures of the wilderness,
because they are laid waste so that
  no one passes through,
 and the lowing of cattle is not heard;
both the birds of the air and the beasts
  have fled and are gone.
¹¹ I will make Jerusalem a heap of ruins,
  a lair of jackals,
 and I will make the cities of
   Judah a desolation,
  without inhabitant."

¹²Who is the man so wise that he can understand this? To whom has the mouth of the LORD spoken, that he may declare it? Why is the land ruined and laid waste like a wilderness, so that no one passes through? ¹³And the LORD says: "Because they have forsaken my law that I set before them, and have not obeyed my voice or walked in accord with it, ¹⁴but have stubbornly followed their own hearts and have gone after the Baals, as their fathers taught them. ¹⁵Therefore thus says the LORD of hosts, the God of Israel: Behold, I will feed this people with bitter food, and give them poisonous water to drink. ¹⁶I will scatter them among the nations whom neither they nor their fathers have known, and I will send the sword after them, until I have consumed them."

¹⁷ Thus says the LORD of hosts:
"Consider, and call for the
  mourning women to come;
 send for the skilful women to come;
¹⁸ let them make haste and raise
  a wailing over us,
 that our eyes may run
  down with tears
 and our eyelids flow with water.
¹⁹ For a sound of wailing is
  heard from Zion:
'How we are ruined!
 We are utterly shamed,
because we have left the land,
 because they have cast down
  our dwellings.'"

²⁰ Hear, O women, the word of the LORD,
  and let your ear receive the
   word of his mouth;
 teach to your daughters a lament,
  and each to her neighbour a dirge.
²¹ For death has come up into
  our windows;
 it has entered our palaces,
cutting off the children
  from the streets
 and the young men from
  the squares.
²² Speak: "Thus declares the LORD,
'The dead bodies of men shall fall
 like dung upon the open field,
 like sheaves after the reaper,
 and none shall gather them.'"

²³Thus says the LORD: "Let not the wise man boast in his wisdom, let not the mighty man boast in his might, let not the rich man boast in his riches, ²⁴but let him who boasts boast in this, that he understands and knows me, that I am the LORD who practises steadfast love, justice, and righteousness in the earth. For in these things I delight, declares the LORD.

²⁵"Behold, the days are coming, declares the LORD, when I will punish all those who are circumcised merely in the flesh — ²⁶Egypt, Judah, Edom, the sons of Ammon, Moab, and all who dwell in the desert who cut the corners of their hair, for all these nations are uncircumcised, and all the house of Israel are uncircumcised in heart."

IDOLS AND THE LIVING GOD

10 Hear the word that the Lord speaks to you, O house of Israel. ²Thus says the Lord:

"Learn not the way of the nations,
  nor be dismayed at the signs
    of the heavens
  because the nations are
    dismayed at them,
³ for the customs of the
    peoples are vanity.ᵃ
  A tree from the forest is cut down
    and worked with an axe by the
      hands of a craftsman.
⁴ They decorate it with silver and gold;
    they fasten it with hammer and nails
      so that it cannot move.
⁵ Their idolsᵇ are like scarecrows
    in a cucumber field,
  and they cannot speak;
    they have to be carried,
      for they cannot walk.
  Do not be afraid of them,
    for they cannot do evil,
      neither is it in them to do good."

⁶ There is none like you, O Lord;
    you are great, and your name
      is great in might.
⁷ Who would not fear you, O
    King of the nations?
  For this is your due;
    for among all the wise ones
      of the nations
    and in all their kingdoms
      there is none like you.
⁸ They are both stupid and foolish;
    the instruction of idols is but wood!
⁹ Beaten silver is brought from Tarshish,
    and gold from Uphaz.
  They are the work of the craftsman and
    of the hands of the goldsmith;
      their clothing is violet and purple;
      they are all the work of skilled men.
¹⁰ But the Lord is the true God;
    he is the living God and the
      everlasting King.
  At his wrath the earth quakes,
    and the nations cannot endure
      his indignation.

¹¹Thus shall you say to them: "The gods who did not make the heavens and the earth shall perish from the earth and from under the heavens."ᶜ

¹² It is he who made the earth
    by his power,
  who established the world
    by his wisdom,
  and by his understanding
    stretched out the heavens.
¹³ When he utters his voice, there is a
    tumult of waters in the heavens,
  and he makes the mist rise from
    the ends of the earth.
  He makes lightning for the rain,
    and he brings forth the wind
      from his storehouses.
¹⁴ Every man is stupid and
    without knowledge;
  every goldsmith is put to
    shame by his idols,
  for his images are false,
    and there is no breath in them.
¹⁵ They are worthless, a work of delusion;
    at the time of their punishment
      they shall perish.
¹⁶ Not like these is he who is
    the portion of Jacob,
  for he is the one who
    formed all things,
  and Israel is the tribe of
    his inheritance;
  the Lord of hosts is his name.

¹⁷ Gather up your bundle
    from the ground,
  O you who dwell under siege!
¹⁸ For thus says the Lord:
  "Behold, I am slinging out the
    inhabitants of the land
      at this time,
  and I will bring distress on them,
    that they may feel it."

¹⁹ Woe is me because of my hurt!
    My wound is grievous.
  But I said, "Truly this is an affliction,
    and I must bear it."
²⁰ My tent is destroyed,
    and all my cords are broken;
  my children have gone from me,
    and they are not;
  there is no one to spread my tent again
    and to set up my curtains.
²¹ For the shepherds are stupid
    and do not enquire of the Lord;
  therefore they have not prospered,
    and all their flock is scattered.

ᵃOr *vapour*, or *mist*   ᵇHebrew *They*   ᶜThis verse is in Aramaic

22 A voice, a rumour! Behold, it comes!—
 a great commotion out of
  the north country
 to make the cities of Judah
  a desolation,
  a lair of jackals.

23 I know, O Lord, that the way of
  man is not in himself,
 that it is not in man who walks
  to direct his steps.

24 Correct me, O Lord, but in justice;
 not in your anger, lest you
  bring me to nothing.

25 Pour out your wrath on the
  nations that know you not,
 and on the peoples that call
  not on your name,
 for they have devoured Jacob;
 they have devoured him and
  consumed him,
 and have laid waste his habitation.

THE BROKEN COVENANT

11 The word that came to Jeremiah from the Lord: ²"Hear the words of this covenant, and speak to the men of Judah and the inhabitants of Jerusalem. ³You shall say to them, Thus says the Lord, the God of Israel: Cursed be the man who does not hear the words of this covenant ⁴that I commanded your fathers when I brought them out of the land of Egypt, from the iron furnace, saying, Listen to my voice, and do all that I command you. So shall you be my people, and I will be your God, ⁵that I may confirm the oath that I swore to your fathers, to give them a land flowing with milk and honey, as at this day." Then I answered, "So be it, Lord."

⁶And the Lord said to me, "Proclaim all these words in the cities of Judah and in the streets of Jerusalem: Hear the words of this covenant and do them. ⁷For I solemnly warned your fathers when I brought them up out of the land of Egypt, warning them persistently, even to this day, saying, Obey my voice. ⁸Yet they did not obey or incline their ear, but everyone walked in the stubbornness of his evil heart. Therefore I brought upon them all the words of this covenant, which I commanded them to do, but they did not."

⁹Again the Lord said to me, "A conspiracy exists among the men of Judah and the inhabitants of Jerusalem. ¹⁰They have turned back to the iniquities of their forefathers, who refused to hear my words. They have gone after other gods to serve them. The house of Israel and the house of Judah have broken my covenant that I made with their fathers. ¹¹Therefore, thus says the Lord, Behold, I am bringing disaster upon them that they cannot escape. Though they cry to me, I will not listen to them. ¹²Then the cities of Judah and the inhabitants of Jerusalem will go and cry to the gods to whom they make offerings, but they cannot save them in the time of their trouble. ¹³For your gods have become as many as your cities, O Judah, and as many as the streets of Jerusalem are the altars you have set up to shame, altars to make offerings to Baal.

¹⁴"Therefore do not pray for this people, or lift up a cry or prayer on their behalf, for I will not listen when they call to me in the time of their trouble. ¹⁵What right has my beloved in my house, when she has done many vile deeds? Can even sacrificial flesh avert your doom? Can you then exult? ¹⁶The Lord once called you 'a green olive tree, beautiful with good fruit.' But with the roar of a great tempest he will set fire to it, and its branches will be consumed. ¹⁷The Lord of hosts, who planted you, has decreed disaster against you, because of the evil that the house of Israel and the house of Judah have done, provoking me to anger by making offerings to Baal."

18 The Lord made it known
  to me and I knew;
 then you showed me their deeds.
19 But I was like a gentle lamb
  led to the slaughter.
 I did not know it was against me
  they devised schemes, saying,
 "Let us destroy the tree with its fruit,
 let us cut him off from the
  land of the living,
 that his name be remembered
  no more."
20 But, O Lord of hosts, who
  judges righteously,
 who tests the heart and the mind,
 let me see your vengeance upon them,
 for to you have I committed
  my cause.

²¹Therefore thus says the Lord concerning the men of Anathoth, who seek your life,

and say, "Do not prophesy in the name of the Lord, or you will die by our hand"— ²²therefore thus says the Lord of hosts: "Behold, I will punish them. The young men shall die by the sword, their sons and their daughters shall die by famine, ²³and none of them shall be left. For I will bring disaster upon the men of Anathoth, the year of their punishment."

JEREMIAH'S COMPLAINT

12 Righteous are you, O Lord,
    when I complain to you;
    yet I would plead my case
        before you.
Why does the way of the
        wicked prosper?
Why do all who are
        treacherous thrive?
² You plant them, and they take root;
    they grow and produce fruit;
you are near in their mouth
    and far from their heart.
³ But you, O Lord, know me;
    you see me, and test my
        heart towards you.
Pull them out like sheep
        for the slaughter,
    and set them apart for the
        day of slaughter.
⁴ How long will the land mourn
    and the grass of every field wither?
For the evil of those who dwell in it
    the beasts and the birds
        are swept away,
    because they said, "He will
        not see our latter end."

THE LORD ANSWERS JEREMIAH

⁵ "If you have raced with men on foot,
    and they have wearied you,
    how will you compete with horses?
And if in a safe land you
        are so trusting,
    what will you do in the
        thicket of the Jordan?
⁶ For even your brothers and the
        house of your father,
    even they have dealt
        treacherously with you;
    they are in full cry after you;
    do not believe them,
        though they speak friendly
            words to you."

⁷ "I have forsaken my house;
    I have abandoned my heritage;
I have given the beloved of my soul
    into the hands of her enemies.
⁸ My heritage has become to me
    like a lion in the forest;
she has lifted up her voice against me;
    therefore I hate her.
⁹ Is my heritage to me like a hyena's
        lair?
    Are the birds of prey against
        her all round?
Go, assemble all the wild beasts;
    bring them to devour.
¹⁰ Many shepherds have destroyed
        my vineyard;
    they have trampled down
        my portion;
they have made my pleasant portion
    a desolate wilderness.
¹¹ They have made it a desolation;
    desolate, it mourns to me.
The whole land is made desolate,
    but no man lays it to heart.
¹² Upon all the bare heights in the desert
        destroyers have come,
for the sword of the Lord devours
    from one end of the land
        to the other;
no flesh has peace.
¹³ They have sown wheat and
        have reaped thorns;
    they have tired themselves
        out but profit nothing.
They shall be ashamed of
        their*ᵃ* harvests
    because of the fierce anger
        of the Lord."

¹⁴Thus says the Lord concerning all my evil neighbours who touch the heritage that I have given my people Israel to inherit: "Behold, I will pluck them up from their land, and I will pluck up the house of Judah from among them. ¹⁵And after I have plucked them up, I will again have compassion on them, and I will bring them again each to his heritage and each to his land. ¹⁶And it shall come to pass, if they will diligently learn the ways of my people, to swear by my name, 'As the Lord lives', even as they taught my people to swear by Baal, then they shall be built up in the midst of my people. ¹⁷But if any nation will not listen, then I will utterly pluck it up and destroy it, declares the Lord."

ᵃHebrew *your*

JEREMIAH 13

THE RUINED LOINCLOTH

13 Thus says the LORD to me, "Go and buy a linen loincloth and put it round your waist, and do not dip it in water." ²So I bought a loincloth according to the word of the LORD, and put it round my waist. ³And the word of the LORD came to me a second time, ⁴"Take the loincloth that you have bought, which is round your waist, and arise, go to the Euphrates and hide it there in a cleft of the rock." ⁵So I went and hid it by the Euphrates, as the LORD commanded me. ⁶And after many days the LORD said to me, "Arise, go to the Euphrates, and take from there the loincloth that I commanded you to hide there." ⁷Then I went to the Euphrates, and dug, and I took the loincloth from the place where I had hidden it. And behold, the loincloth was spoiled; it was good for nothing.

⁸Then the word of the LORD came to me: ⁹"Thus says the LORD: Even so will I spoil the pride of Judah and the great pride of Jerusalem. ¹⁰This evil people, who refuse to hear my words, who stubbornly follow their own heart and have gone after other gods to serve them and worship them, shall be like this loincloth, which is good for nothing. ¹¹For as the loincloth clings to the waist of a man, so I made the whole house of Israel and the whole house of Judah cling to me, declares the LORD, that they might be for me a people, a name, a praise, and a glory, but they would not listen.

THE JARS FILLED WITH WINE

¹²"You shall speak to them this word: 'Thus says the LORD, the God of Israel, "Every jar shall be filled with wine."' And they will say to you, 'Do we not indeed know that every jar will be filled with wine?' ¹³Then you shall say to them, 'Thus says the LORD: Behold, I will fill with drunkenness all the inhabitants of this land: the kings who sit on David's throne, the priests, the prophets, and all the inhabitants of Jerusalem. ¹⁴And I will dash them one against another, fathers and sons together, declares the LORD. I will not pity or spare or have compassion, that I should not destroy them.'"

EXILE THREATENED

¹⁵ Hear and give ear; be not proud,
 for the LORD has spoken.
¹⁶ Give glory to the LORD your God
 before he brings darkness,
 before your feet stumble
 on the twilight mountains,
 and while you look for light
 he turns it into gloom
 and makes it deep darkness.
¹⁷ But if you will not listen,
 my soul will weep in secret
 for your pride;
 my eyes will weep bitterly and
 run down with tears,
 because the LORD's flock has
 been taken captive.

¹⁸ Say to the king and the queen mother:
 "Take a lowly seat,
 for your beautiful crown
 has come down from your head."
¹⁹ The cities of the Negeb are shut up,
 with none to open them;
 all Judah is taken into exile,
 wholly taken into exile.

²⁰ "Lift up your eyes and see
 those who come from the north.
 Where is the flock that was
 given you,
 your beautiful flock?
²¹ What will you say when they
 set as head over you
 those whom you yourself have
 taught to be friends to you?
 Will not pangs take hold of you
 like those of a woman in labour?
²² And if you say in your heart,
 'Why have these things
 come upon me?'
 it is for the greatness of your
 iniquity
 that your skirts are lifted up
 and you suffer violence.
²³ Can the Ethiopian change his skin
 or the leopard his spots?
 Then also you can do good
 who are accustomed to do evil.
²⁴ I will scatter you*a* like chaff
 driven by the wind from the desert.
²⁵ This is your lot,
 the portion I have measured out
 to you, declares the LORD,
 because you have forgotten me
 and trusted in lies.
²⁶ I myself will lift up your
 skirts over your face,
 and your shame will be seen.

---

a Hebrew *them*

27 I have seen your abominations,
  your adulteries and neighings,
    your lewd whorings,
  on the hills in the field.
  Woe to you, O Jerusalem!
    How long will it be before
      you are made clean?"

FAMINE, SWORD, AND PESTILENCE

14 The word of the LORD that came to Jeremiah concerning the drought:

2 "Judah mourns,
    and her gates languish;
  her people lament on the ground,
    and the cry of Jerusalem goes up.
3 Her nobles send their
    servants for water;
  they come to the cisterns;
  they find no water;
    they return with their vessels
      empty;
  they are ashamed and confounded
    and cover their heads.
4 Because of the ground that
    is dismayed,
  since there is no rain on the land,
  the farmers are ashamed;
    they cover their heads.
5 Even the doe in the field forsakes
    her newborn fawn
  because there is no grass.
6 The wild donkeys stand on
    the bare heights;
  they pant for air like jackals;
  their eyes fail
    because there is no vegetation.

7 "Though our iniquities
    testify against us,
  act, O LORD, for your name's sake;
  for our backslidings are many;
    we have sinned against you.
8 O you hope of Israel,
    its saviour in time of trouble,
  why should you be like a
    stranger in the land,
  like a traveller who turns aside
    to tarry for a night?
9 Why should you be like a
    man confused,
  like a mighty warrior who
    cannot save?
  Yet you, O LORD, are in the midst of us,
    and we are called by your name;
    do not leave us."

10 Thus says the LORD concerning
    this people:
  "They have loved to wander thus;
    they have not restrained their feet;
  therefore the LORD does
    not accept them;
  now he will remember their iniquity
    and punish their sins."

11 The LORD said to me: "Do not pray for the welfare of this people. 12 Though they fast, I will not hear their cry, and though they offer burnt offering and grain offering, I will not accept them. But I will consume them by the sword, by famine, and by pestilence."

LYING PROPHETS

13 Then I said: "Ah, Lord GOD, behold, the prophets say to them, 'You shall not see the sword, nor shall you have famine, but I will give you assured peace in this place.'" 14 And the LORD said to me: "The prophets are prophesying lies in my name. I did not send them, nor did I command them or speak to them. They are prophesying to you a lying vision, worthless divination, and the deceit of their own minds. 15 Therefore thus says the LORD concerning the prophets who prophesy in my name although I did not send them, and who say, 'Sword and famine shall not come upon this land': By sword and famine those prophets shall be consumed. 16 And the people to whom they prophesy shall be cast out in the streets of Jerusalem, victims of famine and sword, with none to bury them—them, their wives, their sons, and their daughters. For I will pour out their evil upon them.

17 "You shall say to them this word:
  'Let my eyes run down with
    tears night and day,
    and let them not cease,
  for the virgin daughter of my people
    is shattered with a great wound,
    with a very grievous blow.
18 If I go out into the field,
    behold, those pierced by the sword!
  And if I enter the city,
    behold, the diseases of famine!
  For both prophet and priest ply
    their trade through the land
    and have no knowledge.'"

19 Have you utterly rejected Judah?
    Does your soul loathe Zion?

Why have you struck us down
    so that there is no healing for us?
We looked for peace, but
    no good came;
for a time of healing, but
    behold, terror.
20 We acknowledge our
    wickedness, O Lord,
    and the iniquity of our fathers,
for we have sinned against you.
21 Do not spurn us, for your name's sake;
    do not dishonour your
    glorious throne;
remember and do not break
    your covenant with us.
22 Are there any among the false gods of
    the nations that can bring rain?
Or can the heavens give showers?
Are you not he, O Lord our God?
We set our hope on you,
    for you do all these things.

THE LORD WILL NOT RELENT

15 Then the Lord said to me, "Though Moses and Samuel stood before me, yet my heart would not turn towards this people. Send them out of my sight, and let them go! ²And when they ask you, 'Where shall we go?' you shall say to them, 'Thus says the Lord:

"'Those who are for pestilence,
    to pestilence,
and those who are for the
    sword, to the sword;
those who are for famine, to famine,
    and those who are for
    captivity, to captivity.'

³I will appoint over them four kinds of destroyers, declares the Lord: the sword to kill, the dogs to tear, and the birds of the air and the beasts of the earth to devour and destroy. ⁴And I will make them a horror to all the kingdoms of the earth because of what Manasseh the son of Hezekiah, king of Judah, did in Jerusalem.

5 "Who will have pity on you,
    O Jerusalem,
or who will grieve for you?
Who will turn aside
    to ask about your welfare?
6 You have rejected me,
    declares the Lord;
you keep going backwards,
so I have stretched out my hand
    against you and destroyed you—
I am weary of relenting.
7 I have winnowed them with
    a winnowing fork
    in the gates of the land;
I have bereaved them; I have
    destroyed my people;
they did not turn from their ways.
8 I have made their widows
    more in number
    than the sand of the seas;
I have brought against the
    mothers of young men
    a destroyer at noonday;
I have made anguish and terror
    fall upon them suddenly.
9 She who bore seven has grown feeble;
    she has fainted away;
her sun went down while
    it was yet day;
    she has been shamed and disgraced.
And the rest of them I will
    give to the sword
before their enemies,
        declares the Lord."

JEREMIAH'S COMPLAINT

¹⁰Woe is me, my mother, that you bore me, a man of strife and contention to the whole land! I have not lent, nor have I borrowed, yet all of them curse me. ¹¹The Lord said, "Have I not[a] set you free for their good? Have I not pleaded for you before the enemy in the time of trouble and in the time of distress? ¹²Can one break iron, iron from the north, and bronze?

¹³"Your wealth and your treasures I will give as spoil, without price, for all your sins, throughout all your territory. ¹⁴I will make you serve your enemies in a land that you do not know, for in my anger a fire is kindled that shall burn for ever."

15 O Lord, you know;
    remember me and visit me,
    and take vengeance for me
        on my persecutors.
In your forbearance take me not away;
    know that for your sake I
    bear reproach.
16 Your words were found, and I ate them,
    and your words became to me a joy
    and the delight of my heart,

---

[a] The meaning of the Hebrew is uncertain

for I am called by your name,
　　O Lord, God of hosts.
17　I did not sit in the company
　　　　of revellers,
　　nor did I rejoice;
　　I sat alone, because your
　　　　hand was upon me,
　　for you had filled me with
　　　　indignation.
18　Why is my pain unceasing,
　　my wound incurable,
　　refusing to be healed?
　　Will you be to me like a
　　　　deceitful brook,
　　like waters that fail?

19　Therefore thus says the Lord:
　　"If you return, I will restore you,
　　　　and you shall stand before me.
　　If you utter what is precious, and
　　　　not what is worthless,
　　you shall be as my mouth.
　　They shall turn to you,
　　　　but you shall not turn to them.
20　And I will make you to this people
　　　　a fortified wall of bronze;
　　they will fight against you,
　　　　but they shall not prevail over you,
　　for I am with you
　　　　to save you and deliver you,
　　　　　　declares the Lord.
21　I will deliver you out of the
　　　　hand of the wicked,
　　and redeem you from the
　　　　grasp of the ruthless."

FAMINE, SWORD, AND DEATH

16 The word of the Lord came to me: ²"You shall not take a wife, nor shall you have sons or daughters in this place. ³For thus says the Lord concerning the sons and daughters who are born in this place, and concerning the mothers who bore them and the fathers who fathered them in this land: ⁴They shall die of deadly diseases. They shall not be lamented, nor shall they be buried. They shall be as dung on the surface of the ground. They shall perish by the sword and by famine, and their dead bodies shall be food for the birds of the air and for the beasts of the earth.

⁵"For thus says the Lord: Do not enter the house of mourning, or go to lament or grieve for them, for I have taken away my peace from this people, my steadfast love and mercy, declares the Lord. ⁶Both great and small shall die in this land. They shall not be buried, and no one shall lament for them or cut himself or make himself bald for them. ⁷No one shall break bread for the mourner, to comfort him for the dead, nor shall anyone give him the cup of consolation to drink for his father or his mother. ⁸You shall not go into the house of feasting to sit with them, to eat and drink. ⁹For thus says the Lord of hosts, the God of Israel: Behold, I will silence in this place, before your eyes and in your days, the voice of mirth and the voice of gladness, the voice of the bridegroom and the voice of the bride.

¹⁰"And when you tell this people all these words, and they say to you, 'Why has the Lord pronounced all this great evil against us? What is our iniquity? What is the sin that we have committed against the Lord our God?' ¹¹then you shall say to them: 'Because your fathers have forsaken me, declares the Lord, and have gone after other gods and have served and worshipped them, and have forsaken me and have not kept my law, ¹²and because you have done worse than your fathers, for behold, every one of you follows his stubborn, evil will, refusing to listen to me. ¹³Therefore I will hurl you out of this land into a land that neither you nor your fathers have known, and there you shall serve other gods day and night, for I will show you no favour.'

THE LORD WILL RESTORE ISRAEL

¹⁴"Therefore, behold, the days are coming, declares the Lord, when it shall no longer be said, 'As the Lord lives who brought up the people of Israel out of the land of Egypt', ¹⁵but 'As the Lord lives who brought up the people of Israel out of the north country and out of all the countries where he had driven them.' For I will bring them back to their own land that I gave to their fathers.

¹⁶"Behold, I am sending for many fishers, declares the Lord, and they shall catch them. And afterwards I will send for many hunters, and they shall hunt them from every mountain and every hill, and out of the clefts of the rocks. ¹⁷For my eyes are on all their ways. They are not hidden from me, nor is their iniquity concealed from my eyes. ¹⁸But first I will doubly repay their iniquity and their sin, because they have polluted my land with the carcasses of their detestable idols, and have filled my inheritance with their abominations."

¹⁹ O Lord, my strength and
my stronghold,
my refuge in the day of trouble,
to you shall the nations come
from the ends of the earth and say:
"Our fathers have inherited
nothing but lies,
worthless things in which
there is no profit.
²⁰ Can man make for himself gods?
Such are not gods!"

²¹"Therefore, behold, I will make them know, this once I will make them know my power and my might, and they shall know that my name is the Lord."

THE SIN OF JUDAH

17 "The sin of Judah is written with a pen of iron; with a point of diamond it is engraved on the tablet of their heart, and on the horns of their altars, ²while their children remember their altars and their Asherim, beside every green tree and on the high hills, ³on the mountains in the open country. Your wealth and all your treasures I will give for spoil as the price of your high places for sin throughout all your territory. ⁴You shall loosen your hand from your heritage that I gave to you, and I will make you serve your enemies in a land that you do not know, for in my anger a fire is kindled that shall burn for ever."

⁵ Thus says the Lord:
"Cursed is the man who trusts in man
and makes flesh his strength,^{a}
whose heart turns away
from the Lord.
⁶ He is like a shrub in the desert,
and shall not see any good come.
He shall dwell in the parched
places of the wilderness,
in an uninhabited salt land.
⁷ "Blessed is the man who
trusts in the Lord,
whose trust is the Lord.
⁸ He is like a tree planted by water,
that sends out its roots
by the stream,
and does not fear when heat comes,
for its leaves remain green,
and is not anxious in the
year of drought,
for it does not cease to bear fruit."

⁹ The heart is deceitful above all things,
and desperately sick;
who can understand it?
¹⁰ "I the Lord search the heart
and test the mind,^{b}
to give every man according to his ways,
according to the fruit of his deeds."
¹¹ Like the partridge that gathers a
brood that she did not hatch,
so is he who gets riches
but not by justice;
in the midst of his days they
will leave him,
and at his end he will be a fool.

¹² A glorious throne set on high
from the beginning
is the place of our sanctuary.
¹³ O Lord, the hope of Israel,
all who forsake you shall
be put to shame;
those who turn away from you^c
shall be written in the earth,
for they have forsaken the Lord,
the fountain of living water.

JEREMIAH PRAYS FOR DELIVERANCE

¹⁴ Heal me, O Lord, and I shall be healed;
save me, and I shall be saved,
for you are my praise.
¹⁵ Behold, they say to me,
"Where is the word of the Lord?
Let it come!"
¹⁶ I have not run away from
being your shepherd,
nor have I desired the day of sickness.
You know what came out of my lips;
it was before your face.
¹⁷ Be not a terror to me;
you are my refuge in the
day of disaster.
¹⁸ Let those be put to shame
who persecute me,
but let me not be put to shame;
let them be dismayed,
but let me not be dismayed;
bring upon them the day of disaster;
destroy them with double
destruction!

KEEP THE SABBATH HOLY

¹⁹Thus said the Lord to me: "Go and stand in the People's Gate, by which the kings of

---

^{a}Hebrew *arm* ^{b}Hebrew *kidneys* ^{c}Hebrew *me*

Judah enter and by which they go out, and in all the gates of Jerusalem, ²⁰and say: 'Hear the word of the LORD, you kings of Judah, and all Judah, and all the inhabitants of Jerusalem, who enter by these gates. ²¹Thus says the LORD: Take care for the sake of your lives, and do not bear a burden on the Sabbath day or bring it in by the gates of Jerusalem. ²²And do not carry a burden out of your houses on the Sabbath or do any work, but keep the Sabbath day holy, as I commanded your fathers. ²³Yet they did not listen or incline their ear, but stiffened their neck, that they might not hear and receive instruction.

²⁴"'But if you listen to me, declares the LORD, and bring in no burden by the gates of this city on the Sabbath day, but keep the Sabbath day holy and do no work on it, ²⁵then there shall enter by the gates of this city kings and princes who sit on the throne of David, riding in chariots and on horses, they and their officials, the men of Judah and the inhabitants of Jerusalem. And this city shall be inhabited for ever. ²⁶And people shall come from the cities of Judah and the places round Jerusalem, from the land of Benjamin, from the Shephelah, from the hill country, and from the Negeb, bringing burnt offerings and sacrifices, grain offerings and frankincense, and bringing thank offerings to the house of the LORD. ²⁷But if you do not listen to me, to keep the Sabbath day holy, and not to bear a burden and enter by the gates of Jerusalem on the Sabbath day, then I will kindle a fire in its gates, and it shall devour the palaces of Jerusalem and shall not be quenched.'"

THE POTTER AND THE CLAY

18 The word that came to Jeremiah from the LORD: ²"Arise, and go down to the potter's house, and there I will let you hear*ᵃ* my words." ³So I went down to the potter's house, and there he was working at his wheel. ⁴And the vessel he was making of clay was spoiled in the potter's hand, and he reworked it into another vessel, as it seemed good to the potter to do.

⁵Then the word of the LORD came to me: ⁶"O house of Israel, can I not do with you as this potter has done? declares the LORD. Behold, like the clay in the potter's hand, so are you in my hand, O house of Israel. ⁷If at any time I declare concerning a nation or a kingdom, that I will pluck up and break down and destroy it, ⁸and if that nation, concerning which I have spoken, turns from its evil, I will relent of the disaster that I intended to do to it. ⁹And if at any time I declare concerning a nation or a kingdom that I will build and plant it, ¹⁰and if it does evil in my sight, not listening to my voice, then I will relent of the good that I had intended to do to it. ¹¹Now, therefore, say to the men of Judah and the inhabitants of Jerusalem: 'Thus says the LORD, Behold, I am shaping disaster against you and devising a plan against you. Return, every one from his evil way, and amend your ways and your deeds.'

¹²"But they say, 'That is in vain! We will follow our own plans, and will every one act according to the stubbornness of his evil heart.'

13 "Therefore thus says the LORD:
Ask among the nations,
    Who has heard the like of this?
The virgin Israel
    has done a very horrible thing.
14 Does the snow of Lebanon leave
    the crags of Sirion?*ᵇ*
Do the mountain waters run dry,*ᶜ*
    the cold flowing streams?
15 But my people have forgotten me;
    they make offerings to false gods;
they made them stumble in their ways,
    in the ancient roads,
and to walk into side roads,
    not the highway,
16 making their land a horror,
    a thing to be hissed at for ever.
Everyone who passes by it is horrified
    and shakes his head.
17 Like the east wind I will scatter them
    before the enemy.
I will show them my back, not my face,
    in the day of their calamity."

¹⁸Then they said, "Come, let us make plots against Jeremiah, for the law shall not perish from the priest, nor counsel from the wise, nor the word from the prophet. Come, let us strike him with the tongue, and let us not pay attention to any of his words."

19 Hear me, O LORD,
    and listen to the voice of
        my adversaries.
20 Should good be repaid with evil?
    Yet they have dug a pit for my life.

ᵃOr will cause you to hear *ᵇHebrew of the field* *ᶜHebrew Are foreign waters plucked up*

Remember how I stood before you
    to speak good for them,
    to turn away your wrath from them.
21 Therefore deliver up their
      children to famine;
    give them over to the power
      of the sword;
    let their wives become childless
      and widowed.
    May their men meet death
      by pestilence,
    their youths be struck down
      by the sword in battle.
22 May a cry be heard from their houses,
    when you bring the plunderer
      suddenly upon them!
    For they have dug a pit to take me
      and laid snares for my feet.
23 Yet you, O LORD, know
      all their plotting to kill me.
    Forgive not their iniquity,
      nor blot out their sin
        from your sight.
    Let them be overthrown before you;
      deal with them in the time
        of your anger.

THE BROKEN FLASK

19 Thus says the LORD, "Go, buy a potter's earthenware flask, and take some of the elders of the people and some of the elders of the priests, ²and go out to the Valley of the Son of Hinnom at the entry of the Potsherd Gate, and proclaim there the words that I tell you. ³You shall say, 'Hear the word of the LORD, O kings of Judah and inhabitants of Jerusalem. Thus says the LORD of hosts, the God of Israel: Behold, I am bringing such disaster upon this place that the ears of everyone who hears of it will tingle. ⁴Because the people have forsaken me and have profaned this place by making offerings in it to other gods whom neither they nor their fathers nor the kings of Judah have known; and because they have filled this place with the blood of innocents, ⁵and have built the high places of Baal to burn their sons in the fire as burnt offerings to Baal, which I did not command or decree, nor did it come into my mind — ⁶therefore, behold, days are coming, declares the LORD, when this place shall no more be called Topheth, or the Valley of the Son of Hinnom, but the Valley of Slaughter. ⁷And in this place I will make void the plans of Judah and Jerusalem, and will cause their people to fall by the sword before their enemies, and by the hand of those who seek their life. I will give their dead bodies for food to the birds of the air and to the beasts of the earth. ⁸And I will make this city a horror, a thing to be hissed at. Everyone who passes by it will be horrified and will hiss because of all its wounds. ⁹And I will make them eat the flesh of their sons and their daughters, and everyone shall eat the flesh of his neighbour in the siege and in the distress, with which their enemies and those who seek their life afflict them.'

¹⁰"Then you shall break the flask in the sight of the men who go with you, ¹¹and shall say to them, 'Thus says the LORD of hosts: So will I break this people and this city, as one breaks a potter's vessel, so that it can never be mended. Men shall bury in Topheth because there will be no other place to bury. ¹²Thus will I do to this place, declares the LORD, and to its inhabitants, making this city like Topheth. ¹³The houses of Jerusalem and the houses of the kings of Judah — all the houses on whose roofs offerings have been offered to all the host of heaven, and drink offerings have been poured out to other gods — shall be defiled like the place of Topheth.'"

¹⁴Then Jeremiah came from Topheth, where the LORD had sent him to prophesy, and he stood in the court of the LORD's house and said to all the people: ¹⁵"Thus says the LORD of hosts, the God of Israel, behold, I am bringing upon this city and upon all its towns all the disaster that I have pronounced against it, because they have stiffened their neck, refusing to hear my words."

JEREMIAH PERSECUTED BY PASHHUR

20 Now Pashhur the priest, the son of Immer, who was chief officer in the house of the LORD, heard Jeremiah prophesying these things. ²Then Pashhur beat Jeremiah the prophet, and put him in the stocks that were in the upper Benjamin Gate of the house of the LORD. ³The next day, when Pashhur released Jeremiah from the stocks, Jeremiah said to him, "The LORD does not call your name Pashhur, but Terror on Every Side. ⁴For thus says the LORD: Behold, I will make you a terror to yourself and to all your friends. They shall fall by the sword of their enemies while you look on. And I will give all Judah into the hand of the king of Babylon. He shall carry them captive to Babylon, and shall strike them down with the sword. ⁵Moreover, I will give all the wealth of the city, all its gains, all its prized belongings, and all the treasures of the kings of Judah into the hand of their enemies, who shall plunder them and seize them and carry them to Babylon. ⁶And you, Pashhur, and all who dwell in your house, shall go into captivity. To Babylon you shall go, and there you shall die, and there you shall be buried, you and all your friends, to whom you have prophesied falsely."

⁷ O LORD, you have deceived me,
 and I was deceived;
 you are stronger than I,
 and you have prevailed.
 I have become a laughing-
  stock all the day;
  everyone mocks me.
⁸ For whenever I speak, I cry out,
 I shout, "Violence and destruction!"
 For the word of the LORD
  has become for me
  a reproach and derision all day long.
⁹ If I say, "I will not mention him,
  or speak any more in his name",
 there is in my heart as it
  were a burning fire
  shut up in my bones,
 and I am weary with holding it in,
  and I cannot.
¹⁰ For I hear many whispering.
  Terror is on every side!
 "Denounce him! Let us denounce him!"
  say all my close friends,
  watching for my fall.
 "Perhaps he will be deceived;
  then we can overcome him
  and take our revenge on him."
¹¹ But the LORD is with me as
  a dread warrior;
 therefore my persecutors
  will stumble;
  they will not overcome me.
 They will be greatly shamed,
  for they will not succeed.
 Their eternal dishonour
  will never be forgotten.
¹² O LORD of hosts, who tests
  the righteous,
  who sees the heart and the mind,ᵃ
 let me see your vengeance upon them,
  for to you have I committed
  my cause.

¹³ Sing to the LORD;
  praise the LORD!
 For he has delivered the
  life of the needy
  from the hand of evildoers.

¹⁴ Cursed be the day
  on which I was born!
 The day when my mother bore me,
  let it not be blessed!
¹⁵ Cursed be the man who brought
  the news to my father,
 "A son is born to you",
  making him very glad.
¹⁶ Let that man be like the cities
  that the LORD overthrew
  without pity;
 let him hear a cry in the morning
  and an alarm at noon,
¹⁷ because he did not kill me
  in the womb;
 so my mother would have
  been my grave,
 and her womb for ever great.
¹⁸ Why did I come out from the womb
  to see toil and sorrow,
 and spend my days in shame?

JERUSALEM WILL FALL TO NEBUCHADNEZZAR

21 This is the word that came to Jeremiah from the LORD, when King Zedekiah sent to him Pashhur the son of Malchiah and Zephaniah the priest, the son of Maaseiah, saying, ²"Enquire of the LORD for us, for Nebuchadnezzarᵇ king of Babylon is making war against us. Perhaps the LORD will deal with us according to all his wonderful deeds and will make him withdraw from us."

³Then Jeremiah said to them: "Thus you shall say to Zedekiah, ⁴"Thus says the LORD, the God of Israel: Behold, I will turn back the weapons of war that are in your hands and with which you are fighting against the king of Babylon and against the Chaldeans who are besieging you outside the walls. And I will bring them together into the midst of this city. ⁵I myself will fight against you with outstretched hand and strong arm, in anger and in fury and in great wrath. ⁶And I will strike down the inhabitants of this city, both man and beast. They shall die of a great pestilence. ⁷Afterwards, declares the LORD, I will give Zedekiah king of Judah and

---

ᵃHebrew *kidneys* ᵇHebrew *Nebuchadrezzar*, an alternate spelling of *Nebuchadnezzar* (king of Babylon) occurring frequently from Jeremiah 21–52; this latter spelling is used throughout Jeremiah for consistency

his servants and the people in this city who survive the pestilence, sword, and famine into the hand of Nebuchadnezzar king of Babylon and into the hand of their enemies, into the hand of those who seek their lives. He shall strike them down with the edge of the sword. He shall not pity them or spare them or have compassion.'

8"And to this people you shall say: 'Thus says the LORD: Behold, I set before you the way of life and the way of death. 9He who stays in this city shall die by the sword, by famine, and by pestilence, but he who goes out and surrenders to the Chaldeans who are besieging you shall live and shall have his life as a prize of war. 10For I have set my face against this city for harm and not for good, declares the LORD: it shall be given into the hand of the king of Babylon, and he shall burn it with fire.'

MESSAGE TO THE HOUSE OF DAVID

11"And to the house of the king of Judah say, 'Hear the word of the LORD, 12O house of David! Thus says the LORD:

"'Execute justice in the morning,
    and deliver from the hand
      of the oppressor
    him who has been robbed,
lest my wrath go forth like fire,
    and burn with none to quench it,
    because of your evil deeds.'"

13 "Behold, I am against you, O
      inhabitant of the valley,
    O rock of the plain,
              declares the LORD;
you who say, 'Who shall come
    down against us,
or who shall enter our habitations?'
14 I will punish you according to
      the fruit of your deeds,
              declares the LORD;
I will kindle a fire in her forest,
    and it shall devour all that
      is round her."

22 Thus says the LORD: "Go down to the house of the king of Judah and speak there this word, 2and say, 'Hear the word of the LORD, O king of Judah, who sits on the throne of David, you, and your servants, and your people who enter these gates. 3Thus says the LORD: Do justice and righteousness, and deliver from the hand of the oppressor him who has been robbed. And do no wrong or violence to the resident alien, the fatherless, and the widow, nor shed innocent blood in this place. 4For if you will indeed obey this word, then there shall enter the gates of this house kings who sit on the throne of David, riding in chariots and on horses, they and their servants and their people. 5But if you will not obey these words, I swear by myself, declares the LORD, that this house shall become a desolation. 6For thus says the LORD concerning the house of the king of Judah:

"'You are like Gilead to me,
    like the summit of Lebanon,
yet surely I will make you a desert,
    an uninhabited city.[a]
7 I will prepare destroyers against you,
    each with his weapons,
and they shall cut down your
      choicest cedars
    and cast them into the fire.

8"'And many nations will pass by this city, and every man will say to his neighbour, "Why has the LORD dealt thus with this great city?" 9And they will answer, "Because they have forsaken the covenant of the LORD their God and worshipped other gods and served them."'

10 Weep not for him who is dead,
    nor grieve for him,
but weep bitterly for him
    who goes away,
for he shall return no more
    to see his native land.

MESSAGE TO THE SONS OF JOSIAH

11For thus says the LORD concerning Shallum the son of Josiah, king of Judah, who reigned instead of Josiah his father, and who went away from this place: "He shall return here no more, 12but in the place where they have carried him captive, there shall he die, and he shall never see this land again."

13 "Woe to him who builds his house
      by unrighteousness,
    and his upper rooms by injustice,
who makes his neighbour
      serve him for nothing
    and does not give him his wages,

---
[a] Hebrew *cities*

14 who says, 'I will build myself
       a great house
    with spacious upper rooms',
  who cuts out windows for it,
       panelling it with cedar
    and painting it with vermilion.
15 Do you think you are a king
       because you compete in cedar?
    Did not your father eat and drink
       and do justice and righteousness?
    Then it was well with him.
16 He judged the cause of the
       poor and needy;
    then it was well.
    Is not this to know me?
       declares the LORD.
17 But you have eyes and heart
       only for your dishonest gain,
    for shedding innocent blood,
       and for practising oppression
    and violence."

¹⁸Therefore thus says the LORD concerning Jehoiakim the son of Josiah, king of Judah:

  "They shall not lament for him, saying,
       'Ah, my brother!' or 'Ah, sister!'
    They shall not lament for him, saying,
       'Ah, lord!' or 'Ah, his majesty!'
19 With the burial of a donkey
       he shall be buried,
    dragged and dumped beyond
       the gates of Jerusalem."

20 "Go up to Lebanon, and cry out,
       and lift up your voice in Bashan;
    cry out from Abarim,
       for all your lovers are destroyed.
21 I spoke to you in your prosperity,
       but you said, 'I will not listen.'
    This has been your way
       from your youth,
    that you have not obeyed my voice.
22 The wind shall shepherd all
       your shepherds,
    and your lovers shall go
       into captivity;
    then you will be ashamed
       and confounded
    because of all your evil.
23 O inhabitant of Lebanon,
       nested among the cedars,
    how you will be pitied when
       pangs come upon you,
    pain as of a woman in labour!"

²⁴"As I live, declares the LORD, though Coniah the son of Jehoiakim, king of Judah, were the signet ring on my right hand, yet I would tear you off ²⁵and give you into the hand of those who seek your life, into the hand of those of whom you are afraid, even into the hand of Nebuchadnezzar king of Babylon and into the hand of the Chaldeans. ²⁶I will hurl you and the mother who bore you into another country, where you were not born, and there you shall die. ²⁷But to the land to which they will long to return, there they shall not return."

28 Is this man Coniah a despised,
       broken pot,
    a vessel no one cares for?
    Why are he and his children
       hurled and cast
    into a land that they do not know?
29 O land, land, land,
    hear the word of the LORD!
30 Thus says the LORD:
    "Write this man down as childless,
       a man who shall not succeed
    in his days,
    for none of his offspring shall succeed
       in sitting on the throne of David
    and ruling again in Judah."

THE RIGHTEOUS BRANCH

23 "Woe to the shepherds who destroy and scatter the sheep of my pasture!" declares the LORD. ²Therefore thus says the LORD, the God of Israel, concerning the shepherds who care for my people: "You have scattered my flock and have driven them away, and you have not attended to them. Behold, I will attend to you for your evil deeds, declares the LORD. ³Then I will gather the remnant of my flock out of all the countries where I have driven them, and I will bring them back to their fold, and they shall be fruitful and multiply. ⁴I will set shepherds over them who will care for them, and they shall fear no more, nor be dismayed, neither shall any be missing, declares the LORD.

⁵"Behold, the days are coming, declares the LORD, when I will raise up for David a righteous Branch, and he shall reign as king and deal wisely, and shall execute justice and righteousness in the land. ⁶In his days Judah will be saved, and Israel will dwell securely. And this is the name by which he will be called: 'The LORD is our righteousness.'

7"Therefore, behold, the days are coming, declares the LORD, when they shall no longer say, 'As the LORD lives who brought up the people of Israel out of the land of Egypt', 8but 'As the LORD lives who brought up and led the offspring of the house of Israel out of the north country and out of all the countries where he*a* had driven them.' Then they shall dwell in their own land."

LYING PROPHETS

9Concerning the prophets:

My heart is broken within me;
    all my bones shake;
I am like a drunken man,
    like a man overcome by wine,
because of the LORD
    and because of his holy words.
10 For the land is full of adulterers;
    because of the curse the
        land mourns,
    and the pastures of the
        wilderness are dried up.
Their course is evil,
    and their might is not right.
11 "Both prophet and priest are ungodly;
    even in my house I have
        found their evil,
            declares the LORD.
12 Therefore their way shall be to them
    like slippery paths in the darkness,
    into which they shall be
        driven and fall,
for I will bring disaster upon them
    in the year of their punishment,
            declares the LORD.
13 In the prophets of Samaria
    I saw an unsavoury thing:
they prophesied by Baal
    and led my people Israel astray.
14 But in the prophets of Jerusalem
    I have seen a horrible thing:
they commit adultery and walk in lies;
    they strengthen the hands
        of evildoers,
so that no one turns from his evil;
all of them have become
        like Sodom to me,
    and its inhabitants like Gomorrah."
15 Therefore thus says the LORD of
        hosts concerning the prophets:
"Behold, I will feed them
    with bitter food
and give them poisoned
    water to drink,
for from the prophets of Jerusalem
    ungodliness has gone out
        into all the land."

16Thus says the LORD of hosts: "Do not listen to the words of the prophets who prophesy to you, filling you with vain hopes. They speak visions of their own minds, not from the mouth of the LORD. 17They say continually to those who despise the word of the LORD, 'It shall be well with you'; and to everyone who stubbornly follows his own heart, they say, 'No disaster shall come upon you.'"

18   For who among them has stood
        in the council of the LORD
    to see and to hear his word,
        or who has paid attention to
            his word and listened?
19   Behold, the storm of the LORD!
        Wrath has gone forth,
    a whirling tempest;
        it will burst upon the head
            of the wicked.
20   The anger of the LORD will
        not turn back
    until he has executed and
        accomplished
    the intents of his heart.
In the latter days you will
    understand it clearly.

21   "I did not send the prophets,
        yet they ran;
    I did not speak to them,
        yet they prophesied.
22   But if they had stood in my council,
        then they would have proclaimed
            my words to my people,
    and they would have turned
        them from their evil way,
    and from the evil of their deeds.

23"Am I a God at hand, declares the LORD, and not a God far away? 24Can a man hide himself in secret places so that I cannot see him? declares the LORD. Do I not fill heaven and earth? declares the LORD. 25I have heard what the prophets have said who prophesy lies in my name, saying, 'I have dreamed, I have dreamed!' 26How long shall there be lies in the heart of the prophets who prophesy lies, and who prophesy the deceit of their own heart, 27who think to make my people

---
*a*Septuagint; Hebrew *I*

forget my name by their dreams that they tell one another, even as their fathers forgot my name for Baal? ²⁸Let the prophet who has a dream tell the dream, but let him who has my word speak my word faithfully. What has straw in common with wheat? declares the LORD. ²⁹Is not my word like fire, declares the LORD, and like a hammer that breaks the rock in pieces? ³⁰Therefore, behold, I am against the prophets, declares the LORD, who steal my words from one another. ³¹Behold, I am against the prophets, declares the LORD, who use their tongues and declare, 'declares the LORD.' ³²Behold, I am against those who prophesy lying dreams, declares the LORD, and who tell them and lead my people astray by their lies and their recklessness, when I did not send them or charge them. So they do not profit this people at all, declares the LORD.

³³"When one of this people, or a prophet or a priest asks you, 'What is the burden of the LORD?' you shall say to them, 'You are the burden,ᵃ and I will cast you off, declares the LORD.' ³⁴And as for the prophet, priest, or one of the people who says, 'The burden of the LORD', I will punish that man and his household. ³⁵Thus shall you say, every one to his neighbour and every one to his brother, 'What has the LORD answered?' or 'What has the LORD spoken?' ³⁶But 'the burden of the LORD' you shall mention no more, for the burden is every man's own word, and you pervert the words of the living God, the LORD of hosts, our God. ³⁷Thus you shall say to the prophet, 'What has the LORD answered you?' or 'What has the LORD spoken?' ³⁸But if you say, 'The burden of the LORD', thus says the LORD, 'Because you have said these words, "The burden of the LORD", when I sent to you, saying, "You shall not say, 'The burden of the LORD',"' ³⁹therefore, behold, I will surely lift you upᵇ and cast you away from my presence, you and the city that I gave to you and your fathers. ⁴⁰And I will bring upon you everlasting reproach and perpetual shame, which shall not be forgotten.'"

THE GOOD FIGS AND THE BAD FIGS

24 After Nebuchadnezzar king of Babylon had taken into exile from Jerusalem Jeconiah the son of Jehoiakim, king of Judah, together with the officials of Judah, the craftsmen, and the metal workers, and had brought them to Babylon, the LORD showed me this vision: behold, two baskets of figs placed before the temple of the LORD. ²One basket had very good figs, like first-ripe figs, but the other basket had very bad figs, so bad that they could not be eaten. ³And the LORD said to me, "What do you see, Jeremiah?" I said, "Figs, the good figs very good, and the bad figs very bad, so bad that they cannot be eaten."

⁴Then the word of the LORD came to me: ⁵"Thus says the LORD, the God of Israel: Like these good figs, so I will regard as good the exiles from Judah, whom I have sent away from this place to the land of the Chaldeans. ⁶I will set my eyes on them for good, and I will bring them back to this land. I will build them up, and not tear them down; I will plant them, and not pluck them up. ⁷I will give them a heart to know that I am the LORD, and they shall be my people and I will be their God, for they shall return to me with their whole heart.

⁸"But thus says the LORD: Like the bad figs that are so bad they cannot be eaten, so will I treat Zedekiah the king of Judah, his officials, the remnant of Jerusalem who remain in this land, and those who dwell in the land of Egypt. ⁹I will make them a horrorᶜ to all the kingdoms of the earth, to be a reproach, a byword, a taunt, and a curse in all the places where I shall drive them. ¹⁰And I will send sword, famine, and pestilence upon them, until they shall be utterly destroyed from the land that I gave to them and their fathers."

SEVENTY YEARS OF CAPTIVITY

25 The word that came to Jeremiah concerning all the people of Judah, in the fourth year of Jehoiakim the son of Josiah, king of Judah (that was the first year of Nebuchadnezzar king of Babylon), ²which Jeremiah the prophet spoke to all the people of Judah and all the inhabitants of Jerusalem: ³"For twenty-three years, from the thirteenth year of Josiah the son of Amon, king of Judah, to this day, the word of the LORD has come to me, and I have spoken persistently to you, but you have not listened. ⁴You have neither listened nor inclined your ears to hear, although the LORD persistently sent to you all his servants the prophets, ⁵saying, 'Turn now, every one of you, from his evil way and evil deeds, and dwell upon the land that the LORD has given to you and your

---

ᵃSeptuagint, Vulgate; Hebrew *What burden?* ᵇOr *surely forget you*
ᶜCompare Septuagint; Hebrew *horror for evil*

fathers from of old and for ever. ⁶Do not go after other gods to serve and worship them, or provoke me to anger with the work of your hands. Then I will do you no harm.' ⁷Yet you have not listened to me, declares the LORD, that you might provoke me to anger with the work of your hands to your own harm.

⁸"Therefore thus says the LORD of hosts: Because you have not obeyed my words, ⁹behold, I will send for all the tribes of the north, declares the LORD, and for Nebuchadnezzar the king of Babylon, my servant, and I will bring them against this land and its inhabitants, and against all these surrounding nations. I will devote them to destruction, and make them a horror, a hissing, and an everlasting desolation. ¹⁰Moreover, I will banish from them the voice of mirth and the voice of gladness, the voice of the bridegroom and the voice of the bride, the grinding of the millstones and the light of the lamp. ¹¹This whole land shall become a ruin and a waste, and these nations shall serve the king of Babylon seventy years. ¹²Then after seventy years are completed, I will punish the king of Babylon and that nation, the land of the Chaldeans, for their iniquity, declares the LORD, making the land an everlasting waste. ¹³I will bring upon that land all the words that I have uttered against it, everything written in this book, which Jeremiah prophesied against all the nations. ¹⁴For many nations and great kings shall make slaves even of them, and I will recompense them according to their deeds and the work of their hands."

THE CUP OF THE LORD'S WRATH

¹⁵Thus the LORD, the God of Israel, said to me: "Take from my hand this cup of the wine of wrath, and make all the nations to whom I send you drink it. ¹⁶They shall drink and stagger and be crazed because of the sword that I am sending among them."

¹⁷So I took the cup from the LORD's hand, and made all the nations to whom the LORD sent me drink it: ¹⁸Jerusalem and the cities of Judah, its kings and officials, to make them a desolation and a waste, a hissing and a curse, as at this day; ¹⁹Pharaoh king of Egypt, his servants, his officials, all his people, ²⁰and all the mixed tribes among them; all the kings of the land of Uz and all the kings of the land of the Philistines (Ashkelon, Gaza, Ekron, and the remnant of Ashdod); ²¹Edom, Moab, and the sons of Ammon; ²²all the kings of Tyre, all the kings of Sidon, and the kings of the coastland across the sea; ²³Dedan, Tema, Buz, and all who cut the corners of their hair; ²⁴all the kings of Arabia and all the kings of the mixed tribes who dwell in the desert; ²⁵all the kings of Zimri, all the kings of Elam, and all the kings of Media; ²⁶all the kings of the north, far and near, one after another, and all the kingdoms of the world that are on the face of the earth. And after them the king of Babylon[a] shall drink.

²⁷"Then you shall say to them, 'Thus says the LORD of hosts, the God of Israel: Drink, be drunk and vomit, fall and rise no more, because of the sword that I am sending among you.'

²⁸"And if they refuse to accept the cup from your hand to drink, then you shall say to them, 'Thus says the LORD of hosts: You must drink! ²⁹For behold, I begin to work disaster at the city that is called by my name, and shall you go unpunished? You shall not go unpunished, for I am summoning a sword against all the inhabitants of the earth, declares the LORD of hosts.'

³⁰"You, therefore, shall prophesy against them all these words, and say to them:

"'The LORD will roar from on high,
    and from his holy habitation
        utter his voice;
he will roar mightily against his fold,
    and shout, like those who
        tread grapes,
    against all the inhabitants
        of the earth.
³¹   The clamour will resound to
        the ends of the earth,
    for the LORD has an indictment
        against the nations;
he is entering into judgement
    with all flesh,
and the wicked he will
    put to the sword,
        declares the LORD.'

³² "Thus says the LORD of hosts:
Behold, disaster is going forth
    from nation to nation,
and a great tempest is stirring
    from the farthest parts of the earth!

³³"And those pierced by the LORD on that day shall extend from one end of the earth to the other. They shall not be lamented, or

---

[a] Hebrew *Sheshach*, a code name for Babylon

34 "Wail, you shepherds, and cry out,
 and roll in ashes, you
  lords of the flock,
 for the days of your slaughter and
  dispersion have come,
 and you shall fall like a
  choice vessel.
35 No refuge will remain for
  the shepherds,
 nor escape for the lords of the flock.
36 A voice — the cry of the shepherds,
 and the wail of the lords of the flock!
 For the LORD is laying waste
  their pasture,
37 and the peaceful folds
  are devastated
 because of the fierce anger
  of the LORD.
38 Like a lion he has left his lair,
 for their land has become a waste
 because of the sword of the oppressor,
 and because of his fierce anger."

JEREMIAH THREATENED WITH DEATH

26 In the beginning of the reign of Jehoiakim the son of Josiah, king of Judah, this word came from the LORD: ²"Thus says the LORD: Stand in the court of the LORD's house, and speak to all the cities of Judah that come to worship in the house of the LORD all the words that I command you to speak to them; do not hold back a word. ³It may be they will listen, and every one turn from his evil way, that I may relent of the disaster that I intend to do to them because of their evil deeds. ⁴You shall say to them, 'Thus says the LORD: If you will not listen to me, to walk in my law that I have set before you, ⁵and to listen to the words of my servants the prophets whom I send to you urgently, though you have not listened, ⁶then I will make this house like Shiloh, and I will make this city a curse for all the nations of the earth.'"

⁷The priests and the prophets and all the people heard Jeremiah speaking these words in the house of the LORD. ⁸And when Jeremiah had finished speaking all that the LORD had commanded him to speak to all the people, then the priests and the prophets and all the people laid hold of him, saying, "You shall die! ⁹Why have you prophesied in the name of the LORD, saying, 'This house shall be like Shiloh, and this city shall be desolate, without inhabitant'?" And all the people gathered around Jeremiah in the house of the LORD.

¹⁰When the officials of Judah heard these things, they came up from the king's house to the house of the LORD and took their seat in the entry of the New Gate of the house of the LORD. ¹¹Then the priests and the prophets said to the officials and to all the people, "This man deserves the sentence of death, because he has prophesied against this city, as you have heard with your own ears."

¹²Then Jeremiah spoke to all the officials and all the people, saying, "The LORD sent me to prophesy against this house and this city all the words you have heard. ¹³Now therefore mend your ways and your deeds, and obey the voice of the LORD your God, and the LORD will relent of the disaster that he has pronounced against you. ¹⁴But as for me, behold, I am in your hands. Do with me as seems good and right to you. ¹⁵Only know for certain that if you put me to death, you will bring innocent blood upon yourselves and upon this city and its inhabitants, for in truth the LORD sent me to you to speak all these words in your ears."

JEREMIAH SPARED FROM DEATH

¹⁶Then the officials and all the people said to the priests and the prophets, "This man does not deserve the sentence of death, for he has spoken to us in the name of the LORD our God." ¹⁷And certain of the elders of the land arose and spoke to all the assembled people, saying, ¹⁸"Micah of Moresheth prophesied in the days of Hezekiah king of Judah, and said to all the people of Judah: 'Thus says the LORD of hosts,

"'Zion shall be ploughed as a field;
 Jerusalem shall become
  a heap of ruins,
 and the mountain of the house
  a wooded height.'

¹⁹Did Hezekiah king of Judah and all Judah put him to death? Did he not fear the LORD and entreat the favour of the LORD, and did not the LORD relent of the disaster that he had pronounced against them? But we are about to bring great disaster upon ourselves."

²⁰There was another man who prophesied in the name of the LORD, Uriah the son of

Shemaiah from Kiriath-jearim. He prophesied against this city and against this land in words like those of Jeremiah. ²¹And when King Jehoiakim, with all his warriors and all the officials, heard his words, the king sought to put him to death. But when Uriah heard of it, he was afraid and fled and escaped to Egypt. ²²Then King Jehoiakim sent to Egypt certain men, Elnathan the son of Achbor and others with him, ²³and they took Uriah from Egypt and brought him to King Jehoiakim, who struck him down with the sword and dumped his dead body into the burial place of the common people.

²⁴But the hand of Ahikam the son of Shaphan was with Jeremiah so that he was not given over to the people to be put to death.

THE YOKE OF NEBUCHADNEZZAR

27 In the beginning of the reign of Zedekiah*ᵃ* the son of Josiah, king of Judah, this word came to Jeremiah from the LORD. ²Thus the LORD said to me: "Make yourself straps and yoke-bars, and put them on your neck. ³Send word*ᵇ* to the king of Edom, the king of Moab, the king of the sons of Ammon, the king of Tyre, and the king of Sidon by the hand of the envoys who have come to Jerusalem to Zedekiah king of Judah. ⁴Give them this charge for their masters: 'Thus says the LORD of hosts, the God of Israel: This is what you shall say to your masters: ⁵"It is I who by my great power and my outstretched arm have made the earth, with the men and animals that are on the earth, and I give it to whomever it seems right to me. ⁶Now I have given all these lands into the hand of Nebuchadnezzar, the king of Babylon, my servant, and I have given him also the beasts of the field to serve him. ⁷All the nations shall serve him and his son and his grandson, until the time of his own land comes. Then many nations and great kings shall make him their slave.

⁸"'"But if any nation or kingdom will not serve this Nebuchadnezzar king of Babylon, and put its neck under the yoke of the king of Babylon, I will punish that nation with the sword, with famine, and with pestilence, declares the LORD, until I have consumed it by his hand. ⁹So do not listen to your prophets, your diviners, your dreamers, your fortune-tellers, or your sorcerers, who are saying to you, 'You shall not serve the king of Babylon.' ¹⁰For it is a lie that they are prophesying to you, with the result that you will be removed far from your land, and I will drive you out, and you will perish. ¹¹But any nation that will bring its neck under the yoke of the king of Babylon and serve him, I will leave on its own land, to work it and dwell there, declares the LORD."'"

¹²To Zedekiah king of Judah I spoke in like manner: "Bring your necks under the yoke of the king of Babylon, and serve him and his people and live. ¹³Why will you and your people die by the sword, by famine, and by pestilence, as the LORD has spoken concerning any nation that will not serve the king of Babylon? ¹⁴Do not listen to the words of the prophets who are saying to you, 'You shall not serve the king of Babylon', for it is a lie that they are prophesying to you. ¹⁵I have not sent them, declares the LORD, but they are prophesying falsely in my name, with the result that I will drive you out and you will perish, you and the prophets who are prophesying to you."

¹⁶Then I spoke to the priests and to all this people, saying, "Thus says the LORD: Do not listen to the words of your prophets who are prophesying to you, saying, 'Behold, the vessels of the LORD's house will now shortly be brought back from Babylon', for it is a lie that they are prophesying to you. ¹⁷Do not listen to them; serve the king of Babylon and live. Why should this city become a desolation? ¹⁸If they are prophets, and if the word of the LORD is with them, then let them intercede with the LORD of hosts, that the vessels that are left in the house of the LORD, in the house of the king of Judah, and in Jerusalem may not go to Babylon. ¹⁹For thus says the LORD of hosts concerning the pillars, the sea, the stands, and the rest of the vessels that are left in this city, ²⁰which Nebuchadnezzar king of Babylon did not take away, when he took into exile from Jerusalem to Babylon Jeconiah the son of Jehoiakim, king of Judah, and all the nobles of Judah and Jerusalem — ²¹thus says the LORD of hosts, the God of Israel, concerning the vessels that are left in the house of the LORD, in the house of the king of Judah, and in Jerusalem: ²²They shall be carried to Babylon and remain there until the day when I visit them, declares the LORD. Then I will bring them back and restore them to this place."

---

*ᵃ*Or *Jehoiakim* *ᵇ*Hebrew *Send them*

HANANIAH THE FALSE PROPHET

28 In that same year, at the beginning of the reign of Zedekiah king of Judah, in the fifth month of the fourth year, Hananiah the son of Azzur, the prophet from Gibeon, spoke to me in the house of the LORD, in the presence of the priests and all the people, saying, ²"Thus says the LORD of hosts, the God of Israel: I have broken the yoke of the king of Babylon. ³Within two years I will bring back to this place all the vessels of the LORD's house, which Nebuchadnezzar king of Babylon took away from this place and carried to Babylon. ⁴I will also bring back to this place Jeconiah the son of Jehoiakim, king of Judah, and all the exiles from Judah who went to Babylon, declares the LORD, for I will break the yoke of the king of Babylon."

⁵Then the prophet Jeremiah spoke to Hananiah the prophet in the presence of the priests and all the people who were standing in the house of the LORD, ⁶and the prophet Jeremiah said, "Amen! May the LORD do so; may the LORD make the words that you have prophesied come true, and bring back to this place from Babylon the vessels of the house of the LORD, and all the exiles. ⁷Yet hear now this word that I speak in your hearing and in the hearing of all the people. ⁸The prophets who preceded you and me from ancient times prophesied war, famine, and pestilence against many countries and great kingdoms. ⁹As for the prophet who prophesies peace, when the word of that prophet comes to pass, then it will be known that the LORD has truly sent the prophet."

¹⁰Then the prophet Hananiah took the yoke-bars from the neck of Jeremiah the prophet and broke them. ¹¹And Hananiah spoke in the presence of all the people, saying, "Thus says the LORD: Even so will I break the yoke of Nebuchadnezzar king of Babylon from the neck of all the nations within two years." But Jeremiah the prophet went his way.

¹²Sometime after the prophet Hananiah had broken the yoke-bars from off the neck of Jeremiah the prophet, the word of the LORD came to Jeremiah: ¹³"Go, tell Hananiah, 'Thus says the LORD: You have broken wooden bars, but you have made in their place bars of iron. ¹⁴For thus says the LORD of hosts, the God of Israel: I have put upon the neck of all these nations an iron yoke to serve Nebuchadnezzar king of Babylon, and they shall serve him, for I have given to him even the beasts of the field.'" ¹⁵And Jeremiah the prophet said to the prophet Hananiah, "Listen, Hananiah, the LORD has not sent you, and you have made this people trust in a lie. ¹⁶Therefore thus says the LORD: 'Behold, I will remove you from the face of the earth. This year you shall die, because you have uttered rebellion against the LORD.'"

¹⁷In that same year, in the seventh month, the prophet Hananiah died.

JEREMIAH'S LETTER TO THE EXILES

29 These are the words of the letter that Jeremiah the prophet sent from Jerusalem to the surviving elders of the exiles, and to the priests, the prophets, and all the people, whom Nebuchadnezzar had taken into exile from Jerusalem to Babylon. ²This was after King Jeconiah and the queen mother, the eunuchs, the officials of Judah and Jerusalem, the craftsmen, and the metal workers had departed from Jerusalem. ³The letter was sent by the hand of Elasah the son of Shaphan and Gemariah the son of Hilkiah, whom Zedekiah king of Judah sent to Babylon to Nebuchadnezzar king of Babylon. It said: ⁴"Thus says the LORD of hosts, the God of Israel, to all the exiles whom I have sent into exile from Jerusalem to Babylon: ⁵Build houses and live in them; plant gardens and eat their produce. ⁶Take wives and have sons and daughters; take wives for your sons, and give your daughters in marriage, that they may bear sons and daughters; multiply there, and do not decrease. ⁷But seek the welfare of the city where I have sent you into exile, and pray to the LORD on its behalf, for in its welfare you will find your welfare. ⁸For thus says the LORD of hosts, the God of Israel: Do not let your prophets and your diviners who are among you deceive you, and do not listen to the dreams that they dream,ᵃ ⁹for it is a lie that they are prophesying to you in my name; I did not send them, declares the LORD.

¹⁰"For thus says the LORD: When seventy years are completed for Babylon, I will visit you, and I will fulfil to you my promise and bring you back to this place. ¹¹For I know the plans I have for you, declares the LORD, plans for welfareᵇ and not for evil, to give

---

ᵃHebrew *your dreams, which you cause to dream* ᵇOr *peace*

you a future and a hope. ¹²Then you will call upon me and come and pray to me, and I will hear you. ¹³You will seek me and find me, when you seek me with all your heart. ¹⁴I will be found by you, declares the LORD, and I will restore your fortunes and gather you from all the nations and all the places where I have driven you, declares the LORD, and I will bring you back to the place from which I sent you into exile.

¹⁵"Because you have said, 'The LORD has raised up prophets for us in Babylon', ¹⁶thus says the LORD concerning the king who sits on the throne of David, and concerning all the people who dwell in this city, your kinsmen who did not go out with you into exile: ¹⁷Thus says the LORD of hosts, behold, I am sending on them sword, famine, and pestilence, and I will make them like vile figs that are so rotten they cannot be eaten. ¹⁸I will pursue them with sword, famine, and pestilence, and will make them a horror to all the kingdoms of the earth, to be a curse, a terror, a hissing, and a reproach among all the nations where I have driven them, ¹⁹because they did not pay attention to my words, declares the LORD, that I persistently sent to you by my servants the prophets, but you would not listen, declares the LORD.' ²⁰Hear the word of the LORD, all you exiles whom I sent away from Jerusalem to Babylon: ²¹"Thus says the LORD of hosts, the God of Israel, concerning Ahab the son of Kolaiah and Zedekiah the son of Maaseiah, who are prophesying a lie to you in my name: Behold, I will deliver them into the hand of Nebuchadnezzar king of Babylon, and he shall strike them down before your eyes. ²²Because of them this curse shall be used by all the exiles from Judah in Babylon: "The LORD make you like Zedekiah and Ahab, whom the king of Babylon roasted in the fire", ²³because they have done an outrageous thing in Israel, they have committed adultery with their neighbours' wives, and they have spoken in my name lying words that I did not command them. I am the one who knows, and I am witness, declares the LORD.'"

SHEMAIAH'S FALSE PROPHECY

²⁴To Shemaiah of Nehelam you shall say: ²⁵"Thus says the LORD of hosts, the God of Israel: You have sent letters in your name to all the people who are in Jerusalem, and to Zephaniah the son of Maaseiah the priest, and to all the priests, saying, ²⁶'The LORD has made you priest instead of Jehoiada the priest, to have charge in the house of the LORD over every madman who prophesies, to put him in the stocks and neck irons. ²⁷Now why have you not rebuked Jeremiah of Anathoth who is prophesying to you? ²⁸For he has sent to us in Babylon, saying, "Your exile will be long; build houses and live in them, and plant gardens and eat their produce."'"

²⁹Zephaniah the priest read this letter in the hearing of Jeremiah the prophet. ³⁰Then the word of the LORD came to Jeremiah: ³¹"Send to all the exiles, saying, 'Thus says the LORD concerning Shemaiah of Nehelam: Because Shemaiah had prophesied to you when I did not send him, and has made you trust in a lie, ³²therefore thus says the LORD: Behold, I will punish Shemaiah of Nehelam and his descendants. He shall not have anyone living among this people, and he shall not see the good that I will do to my people, declares the LORD, for he has spoken rebellion against the LORD.'"

RESTORATION FOR ISRAEL AND JUDAH

30 The word that came to Jeremiah from the LORD: ²"Thus says the LORD, the God of Israel: Write in a book all the words that I have spoken to you. ³For behold, days are coming, declares the LORD, when I will restore the fortunes of my people, Israel and Judah, says the LORD, and I will bring them back to the land that I gave to their fathers, and they shall take possession of it."

⁴These are the words that the LORD spoke concerning Israel and Judah:

⁵ "Thus says the LORD:
We have heard a cry of panic,
   of terror, and no peace.
⁶ Ask now, and see,
   can a man bear a child?
Why then do I see every man
   with his hands on his stomach
      like a woman in labour?
Why has every face turned pale?
⁷ Alas! That day is so great
   there is none like it;
it is a time of distress for Jacob;
   yet he shall be saved out of it.

⁸"And it shall come to pass in that day, declares the LORD of hosts, that I will break his yoke from off your neck, and I will burst

your bonds, and foreigners shall no more make a servant of him.[a] ⁹But they shall serve the LORD their God and David their king, whom I will raise up for them.

10 "Then fear not, O Jacob my servant,
         declares the LORD,
   nor be dismayed, O Israel;
   for behold, I will save you
         from far away,
      and your offspring from the
         land of their captivity.
   Jacob shall return and have
         quiet and ease,
      and none shall make him afraid.
11 For I am with you to save you,
                     declares the LORD;
   I will make a full end of all the nations
      among whom I scattered you,
   but of you I will not make a full end.
   I will discipline you in just measure,
      and I will by no means leave
         you unpunished.

12 "For thus says the LORD:
   Your hurt is incurable,
      and your wound is grievous.
13 There is none to uphold your cause,
      no medicine for your wound,
         no healing for you.
14 All your lovers have forgotten you;
      they care nothing for you;
   for I have dealt you the
         blow of an enemy,
      the punishment of a merciless foe,
   because your guilt is great,
      because your sins are flagrant.
15 Why do you cry out over your hurt?
      Your pain is incurable.
   Because your guilt is great,
      because your sins are flagrant,
   I have done these things to you.
16 Therefore all who devour you
         shall be devoured,
      and all your foes, every one of
         them, shall go into captivity;
   those who plunder you shall
         be plundered,
      and all who prey on you I
         will make a prey.
17 For I will restore health to you,
      and your wounds I will heal,
                     declares the LORD,
   because they have called
         you an outcast:
   'It is Zion, for whom no one cares!'

18 "Thus says the LORD:
   Behold, I will restore the fortunes
         of the tents of Jacob
      and have compassion on
         his dwellings;
   the city shall be rebuilt on its mound,
      and the palace shall stand
         where it used to be.
19 Out of them shall come songs
         of thanksgiving,
      and the voices of those
         who celebrate.
   I will multiply them, and they
         shall not be few;
   I will make them honoured, and
         they shall not be small.
20 Their children shall be as
         they were of old,
      and their congregation shall be
         established before me,
   and I will punish all who
         oppress them.
21 Their prince shall be one
         of themselves;
      their ruler shall come out
         from their midst;
   I will make him draw near, and
         he shall approach me,
   for who would dare of himself
         to approach me?
                     declares the LORD.
22 And you shall be my people,
      and I will be your God."

23 Behold the storm of the LORD!
      Wrath has gone forth,
   a whirling tempest;
      it will burst upon the head
         of the wicked.
24 The fierce anger of the LORD
         will not turn back
   until he has executed and
         accomplished
      the intentions of his mind.
   In the latter days you will
         understand this.

THE LORD WILL TURN MOURNING TO JOY

31 "At that time, declares the LORD, I will be the God of all the clans of Israel, and they shall be my people."

² Thus says the LORD:
"The people who survived the sword

---
[a] Or *serve him*

found grace in the wilderness;
  when Israel sought for rest,
³ the LORD appeared to him*ᵃ*
    from far away.
I have loved you with an
    everlasting love;
  therefore I have continued my
    faithfulness to you.
⁴ Again I will build you, and
    you shall be built,
  O virgin Israel!
Again you shall adorn yourself
    with tambourines
  and shall go forth in the dance
    of the merrymakers.
⁵ Again you shall plant vineyards
    on the mountains of Samaria;
  the planters shall plant
    and shall enjoy the fruit.
⁶ For there shall be a day when
    watchmen will call
  in the hill country of Ephraim:
'Arise, and let us go up to Zion,
    to the LORD our God.'"

⁷ For thus says the LORD:
"Sing aloud with gladness for Jacob,
    and raise shouts for the
      chief of the nations;
  proclaim, give praise, and say,
'O LORD, save your people,
    the remnant of Israel.'
⁸ Behold, I will bring them from
    the north country
  and gather them from the
    farthest parts of the earth,
among them the blind and the lame,
  the pregnant woman and she
    who is in labour, together;
a great company, they
  shall return here.
⁹ With weeping they shall come,
    and with pleas for mercy I
      will lead them back,
I will make them walk by
    brooks of water,
  in a straight path in which
    they shall not stumble,
for I am a father to Israel,
    and Ephraim is my firstborn.

¹⁰ "Hear the word of the LORD, O nations,
    and declare it in the
      coastlands far away;
  say, 'He who scattered Israel
    will gather him,
and will keep him as a shepherd
    keeps his flock.'
¹¹ For the LORD has ransomed Jacob
    and has redeemed him from
      hands too strong for him.
¹² They shall come and sing aloud
    on the height of Zion,
  and they shall be radiant over
    the goodness of the LORD,
over the grain, the wine, and the oil,
    and over the young of the
      flock and the herd;
their life shall be like a
    watered garden,
  and they shall languish no more.
¹³ Then shall the young women
    rejoice in the dance,
  and the young men and the
    old shall be merry.
I will turn their mourning into joy;
    I will comfort them, and give
      them gladness for sorrow.
¹⁴ I will feast the soul of the priests
    with abundance,
  and my people shall be satisfied
    with my goodness,
      declares the LORD."

¹⁵ Thus says the LORD:
"A voice is heard in Ramah,
    lamentation and bitter weeping.
Rachel is weeping for her children;
    she refuses to be comforted
      for her children,
  because they are no more."

¹⁶ Thus says the LORD:
"Keep your voice from weeping,
    and your eyes from tears,
for there is a reward for your work,
      declares the LORD,
  and they shall come back from
    the land of the enemy.
¹⁷ There is hope for your future,
      declares the LORD,
  and your children shall come
    back to their own country.
¹⁸ I have heard Ephraim grieving,
'You have disciplined me, and
    I was disciplined,
  like an untrained calf;
bring me back that I may be
    restored,
  for you are the LORD my God.

---
*ᵃ*Septuagint; Hebrew *me*

¹⁹ For after I had turned away, I relented,
and after I was instructed,
I struck my thigh;
I was ashamed, and I was confounded,
because I bore the disgrace
of my youth.'
²⁰ Is Ephraim my dear son?
Is he my darling child?
For as often as I speak against him,
I do remember him still.
Therefore my heart[a] yearns for him;
I will surely have mercy on him,
declares the Lord.

²¹ "Set up road markers for yourself;
make yourself guideposts;
consider well the highway,
the road by which you went.
Return, O virgin Israel,
return to these your cities.
²² How long will you waver,
O faithless daughter?
For the Lord has created a new
thing on the earth:
a woman encircles a man."

²³Thus says the Lord of hosts, the God of Israel: "Once more they shall use these words in the land of Judah and in its cities, when I restore their fortunes:

"'The Lord bless you, O habitation
of righteousness,
O holy hill!'

²⁴And Judah and all its cities shall dwell there together, and the farmers and those who wander with their flocks. ²⁵For I will satisfy the weary soul, and every languishing soul I will replenish."

²⁶At this I awoke and looked, and my sleep was pleasant to me.

²⁷"Behold, the days are coming, declares the Lord, when I will sow the house of Israel and the house of Judah with the seed of man and the seed of beast. ²⁸And it shall come to pass that as I have watched over them to pluck up and break down, to overthrow, destroy, and bring harm, so I will watch over them to build and to plant, declares the Lord. ²⁹In those days they shall no longer say:

"'The fathers have eaten sour grapes,
and the children's teeth
are set on edge.'

³⁰But everyone shall die for his own iniquity. Each man who eats sour grapes, his teeth shall be set on edge.

THE NEW COVENANT

³¹"Behold, the days are coming, declares the Lord, when I will make a new covenant with the house of Israel and the house of Judah, ³²not like the covenant that I made with their fathers on the day when I took them by the hand to bring them out of the land of Egypt, my covenant that they broke, though I was their husband, declares the Lord. ³³For this is the covenant that I will make with the house of Israel after those days, declares the Lord: I will put my law within them, and I will write it on their hearts. And I will be their God, and they shall be my people. ³⁴And no longer shall each one teach his neighbour and each his brother, saying, 'Know the Lord', for they shall all know me, from the least of them to the greatest, declares the Lord. For I will forgive their iniquity, and I will remember their sin no more."

³⁵ Thus says the Lord,
who gives the sun for light by day
and the fixed order of the moon and
the stars for light by night,
who stirs up the sea so that
its waves roar—
the Lord of hosts is his name:
³⁶ "If this fixed order departs
from before me, declares the Lord,
then shall the offspring of Israel cease
from being a nation before
me for ever."

³⁷ Thus says the Lord:
"If the heavens above can be measured,
and the foundations of the earth
below can be explored,
then I will cast off all the
offspring of Israel
for all that they have done,
declares the Lord."

³⁸"Behold, the days are coming, declares the Lord, when the city shall be rebuilt for the Lord from the Tower of Hananel to the Corner Gate. ³⁹And the measuring line shall go out farther, straight to the hill Gareb, and shall then turn to Goah. ⁴⁰The whole valley

---
[a] Hebrew *bowels*

of the dead bodies and the ashes, and all the fields as far as the brook Kidron, to the corner of the Horse Gate towards the east, shall be sacred to the LORD. It shall not be plucked up or overthrown any more for ever."

JEREMIAH BUYS A FIELD DURING THE SIEGE

32 The word that came to Jeremiah from the LORD in the tenth year of Zedekiah king of Judah, which was the eighteenth year of Nebuchadnezzar. ²At that time the army of the king of Babylon was besieging Jerusalem, and Jeremiah the prophet was shut up in the court of the guard that was in the palace of the king of Judah. ³For Zedekiah king of Judah had imprisoned him, saying, "Why do you prophesy and say, 'Thus says the LORD: Behold, I am giving this city into the hand of the king of Babylon, and he shall capture it; ⁴Zedekiah king of Judah shall not escape out of the hand of the Chaldeans, but shall surely be given into the hand of the king of Babylon, and shall speak with him face to face and see him eye to eye. ⁵And he shall take Zedekiah to Babylon, and there he shall remain until I visit him, declares the LORD. Though you fight against the Chaldeans, you shall not succeed'?"

⁶Jeremiah said, "The word of the LORD came to me: ⁷Behold, Hanamel the son of Shallum your uncle will come to you and say, 'Buy my field that is at Anathoth, for the right of redemption by purchase is yours.' ⁸Then Hanamel my cousin came to me in the court of the guard, in accordance with the word of the LORD, and said to me, 'Buy my field that is at Anathoth in the land of Benjamin, for the right of possession and redemption is yours; buy it for yourself.' Then I knew that this was the word of the LORD.

⁹"And I bought the field at Anathoth from Hanamel my cousin, and weighed out the money to him, seventeen shekels of silver. ¹⁰I signed the deed, sealed it, got witnesses, and weighed the money on scales. ¹¹Then I took the sealed deed of purchase, containing the terms and conditions and the open copy. ¹²And I gave the deed of purchase to Baruch the son of Neriah son of Mahseiah, in the presence of Hanamel my cousin, in the presence of the witnesses who signed the deed of purchase, and in the presence of all the Judeans who were sitting in the court of the guard. ¹³I charged Baruch in their presence, saying, ¹⁴'Thus says the LORD of hosts, the God of Israel: Take these deeds, both this sealed deed of purchase and this open deed, and put them in an earthenware vessel, that they may last for a long time. ¹⁵For thus says the LORD of hosts, the God of Israel: Houses and fields and vineyards shall again be bought in this land.'

JEREMIAH PRAYS FOR UNDERSTANDING

¹⁶"After I had given the deed of purchase to Baruch the son of Neriah, I prayed to the LORD, saying: ¹⁷'Ah, Lord GOD! It is you who have made the heavens and the earth by your great power and by your outstretched arm! Nothing is too hard for you. ¹⁸You show steadfast love to thousands, but you repay the guilt of fathers to their children after them, O great and mighty God, whose name is the LORD of hosts, ¹⁹great in counsel and mighty in deed, whose eyes are open to all the ways of the children of man, rewarding each one according to his ways and according to the fruit of his deeds. ²⁰You have shown signs and wonders in the land of Egypt, and to this day in Israel and among all mankind, and have made a name for yourself, as at this day. ²¹You brought your people Israel out of the land of Egypt with signs and wonders, with a strong hand and outstretched arm, and with great terror. ²²And you gave them this land, which you swore to their fathers to give them, a land flowing with milk and honey. ²³And they entered and took possession of it. But they did not obey your voice or walk in your law. They did nothing of all you commanded them to do. Therefore you have made all this disaster come upon them. ²⁴Behold, the siege mounds have come up to the city to take it, and because of sword and famine and pestilence the city is given into the hands of the Chaldeans who are fighting against it. What you spoke has come to pass, and behold, you see it. ²⁵Yet you, O Lord GOD, have said to me, "Buy the field for money and get witnesses"—though the city is given into the hands of the Chaldeans.'"

²⁶The word of the LORD came to Jeremiah: ²⁷"Behold, I am the LORD, the God of all flesh. Is anything too hard for me? ²⁸Therefore, thus says the LORD: Behold, I am giving this city into the hands of the Chaldeans and into the hand of Nebuchadnezzar king of Babylon, and he shall capture it. ²⁹The Chaldeans who are fighting against this city shall come

and set this city on fire and burn it, with the houses on whose roofs offerings have been made to Baal and drink offerings have been poured out to other gods, to provoke me to anger. ³⁰For the children of Israel and the children of Judah have done nothing but evil in my sight from their youth. The children of Israel have done nothing but provoke me to anger by the work of their hands, declares the Lord. ³¹This city has aroused my anger and wrath, from the day it was built to this day, so that I will remove it from my sight ³²because of all the evil of the children of Israel and the children of Judah that they did to provoke me to anger—their kings and their officials, their priests and their prophets, the men of Judah and the inhabitants of Jerusalem. ³³They have turned to me their back and not their face. And though I have taught them persistently, they have not listened to receive instruction. ³⁴They set up their abominations in the house that is called by my name, to defile it. ³⁵They built the high places of Baal in the Valley of the Son of Hinnom, to offer up their sons and daughters to Molech, though I did not command them, nor did it enter into my mind, that they should do this abomination, to cause Judah to sin.

THEY SHALL BE MY PEOPLE; I WILL BE THEIR GOD

³⁶"Now therefore thus says the Lord, the God of Israel, concerning this city of which you say, 'It is given into the hand of the king of Babylon by sword, by famine, and by pestilence': ³⁷Behold, I will gather them from all the countries to which I drove them in my anger and my wrath and in great indignation. I will bring them back to this place, and I will make them dwell in safety. ³⁸And they shall be my people, and I will be their God. ³⁹I will give them one heart and one way, that they may fear me for ever, for their own good and the good of their children after them. ⁴⁰I will make with them an everlasting covenant, that I will not turn away from doing good to them. And I will put the fear of me in their hearts, that they may not turn from me. ⁴¹I will rejoice in doing them good, and I will plant them in this land in faithfulness, with all my heart and all my soul.

⁴²"For thus says the Lord: Just as I have brought all this great disaster upon this people, so I will bring upon them all the good that I promise them. ⁴³Fields shall be bought in this land of which you are saying, 'It is a desolation, without man or beast; it is given into the hand of the Chaldeans.' ⁴⁴Fields shall be bought for money, and deeds shall be signed and sealed and witnessed, in the land of Benjamin, in the places about Jerusalem, and in the cities of Judah, in the cities of the hill country, in the cities of the Shephelah, and in the cities of the Negeb; for I will restore their fortunes, declares the Lord."

THE LORD PROMISES PEACE

33 The word of the Lord came to Jeremiah a second time, while he was still shut up in the court of the guard: ²"Thus says the Lord who made the earth,ᵃ the Lord who formed it to establish it—the Lord is his name: ³Call to me and I will answer you, and will tell you great and hidden things that you have not known. ⁴For thus says the Lord, the God of Israel, concerning the houses of this city and the houses of the kings of Judah that were torn down to make a defence against the siege mounds and against the sword: ⁵They are coming in to fight against the Chaldeans and to fill themᵇ with the dead bodies of men whom I shall strike down in my anger and my wrath, for I have hidden my face from this city because of all their evil. ⁶Behold, I will bring to it health and healing, and I will heal them and reveal to them abundance of prosperity and security. ⁷I will restore the fortunes of Judah and the fortunes of Israel, and rebuild them as they were at first. ⁸I will cleanse them from all the guilt of their sin against me, and I will forgive all the guilt of their sin and rebellion against me. ⁹And this cityᶜ shall be to me a name of joy, a praise and a glory before all the nations of the earth who shall hear of all the good that I do for them. They shall fear and tremble because of all the good and all the prosperity I provide for it.

¹⁰"Thus says the Lord: In this place of which you say, 'It is a waste without man or beast', in the cities of Judah and the streets of Jerusalem that are desolate, without man or inhabitant or beast, there shall be heard again ¹¹the voice of mirth and the voice of gladness, the voice of the bridegroom and the voice of the bride, the voices of those who sing, as they bring thank offerings to the house of the Lord:

ᵃSeptuagint; Hebrew *it* ᵇThat is, the torn-down houses
ᶜHebrew *And it*

" 'Give thanks to the LORD of hosts,
for the LORD is good,
for his steadfast love
endures for ever!'

For I will restore the fortunes of the land as at first, says the LORD.

¹²"Thus says the LORD of hosts: In this place that is waste, without man or beast, and in all of its cities, there shall again be habitations of shepherds resting their flocks. ¹³In the cities of the hill country, in the cities of the Shephelah, and in the cities of the Negeb, in the land of Benjamin, the places about Jerusalem, and in the cities of Judah, flocks shall again pass under the hands of the one who counts them, says the LORD.

THE LORD'S ETERNAL COVENANT WITH DAVID

¹⁴"Behold, the days are coming, declares the LORD, when I will fulfil the promise I made to the house of Israel and the house of Judah. ¹⁵In those days and at that time I will cause a righteous Branch to spring up for David, and he shall execute justice and righteousness in the land. ¹⁶In those days Judah will be saved, and Jerusalem will dwell securely. And this is the name by which it will be called: 'The LORD is our righteousness.'

¹⁷"For thus says the LORD: David shall never lack a man to sit on the throne of the house of Israel, ¹⁸and the Levitical priests shall never lack a man in my presence to offer burnt offerings, to burn grain offerings, and to make sacrifices for ever."

¹⁹The word of the LORD came to Jeremiah: ²⁰"Thus says the LORD: If you can break my covenant with the day and my covenant with the night, so that day and night will not come at their appointed time, ²¹then also my covenant with David my servant may be broken, so that he shall not have a son to reign on his throne, and my covenant with the Levitical priests my ministers. ²²As the host of heaven cannot be numbered and the sands of the sea cannot be measured, so I will multiply the offspring of David my servant, and the Levitical priests who minister to me."

²³The word of the LORD came to Jeremiah: ²⁴"Have you not observed that these people are saying, 'The LORD has rejected the two clans that he chose'? Thus they have despised my people so that they are no longer a nation in their sight. ²⁵Thus says the LORD: If I have not established my covenant with day and night and the fixed order of heaven and earth, ²⁶then I will reject the offspring of Jacob and David my servant and will not choose one of his offspring to rule over the offspring of Abraham, Isaac, and Jacob. For I will restore their fortunes and will have mercy on them."

ZEDEKIAH TO DIE IN BABYLON

34 The word that came to Jeremiah from the LORD, when Nebuchadnezzar king of Babylon and all his army and all the kingdoms of the earth under his dominion and all the peoples were fighting against Jerusalem and all of its cities: ²"Thus says the LORD, the God of Israel: Go and speak to Zedekiah king of Judah and say to him, 'Thus says the LORD: Behold, I am giving this city into the hand of the king of Babylon, and he shall burn it with fire. ³You shall not escape from his hand but shall surely be captured and delivered into his hand. You shall see the king of Babylon eye to eye and speak with him face to face. And you shall go to Babylon.' ⁴Yet hear the word of the LORD, O Zedekiah king of Judah! Thus says the LORD concerning you: 'You shall not die by the sword. ⁵You shall die in peace. And as spices were burned for your fathers, the former kings who were before you, so people shall burn spices for you and lament for you, saying, "Alas, lord!" ' For I have spoken the word, declares the LORD."

⁶Then Jeremiah the prophet spoke all these words to Zedekiah king of Judah, in Jerusalem, ⁷when the army of the king of Babylon was fighting against Jerusalem and against all the cities of Judah that were left, Lachish and Azekah, for these were the only fortified cities of Judah that remained.

⁸The word that came to Jeremiah from the LORD, after King Zedekiah had made a covenant with all the people in Jerusalem to make a proclamation of liberty to them, ⁹that everyone should set free his Hebrew slaves, male and female, so that no one should enslave a Jew, his brother. ¹⁰And they obeyed, all the officials and all the people who had entered into the covenant that everyone would set free his slave, male or female, so that they would not be enslaved again. They obeyed and set them free. ¹¹But afterwards they turned round and took back the male and female slaves they had set free, and brought them into subjection as slaves. ¹²The word of the LORD came to Jeremiah from the LORD: ¹³"Thus says the LORD, the God of Israel: I

myself made a covenant with your fathers when I brought them out of the land of Egypt, out of the house of slavery, saying, ¹⁴'At the end of seven years each of you must set free the fellow Hebrew who has been sold to you and has served you six years; you must set him free from your service.' But your fathers did not listen to me or incline their ears to me. ¹⁵You recently repented and did what was right in my eyes by proclaiming liberty, each to his neighbour, and you made a covenant before me in the house that is called by my name, ¹⁶but then you turned round and profaned my name when each of you took back his male and female slaves, whom you had set free according to their desire, and you brought them into subjection to be your slaves.

¹⁷"Therefore, thus says the LORD: You have not obeyed me by proclaiming liberty, every one to his brother and to his neighbour; behold, I proclaim to you liberty to the sword, to pestilence, and to famine, declares the LORD. I will make you a horror to all the kingdoms of the earth. ¹⁸And the men who transgressed my covenant and did not keep the terms of the covenant that they made before me, I will make them like*ᵃ* the calf that they cut in two and passed between its parts — ¹⁹the officials of Judah, the officials of Jerusalem, the eunuchs, the priests, and all the people of the land who passed between the parts of the calf. ²⁰And I will give them into the hand of their enemies and into the hand of those who seek their lives. Their dead bodies shall be food for the birds of the air and the beasts of the earth. ²¹And Zedekiah king of Judah and his officials I will give into the hand of their enemies and into the hand of those who seek their lives, into the hand of the army of the king of Babylon which has withdrawn from you. ²²Behold, I will command, declares the LORD, and will bring them back to this city. And they will fight against it and take it and burn it with fire. I will make the cities of Judah a desolation without inhabitant."

THE OBEDIENCE OF THE RECHABITES

35 The word that came to Jeremiah from the LORD in the days of Jehoiakim the son of Josiah, king of Judah: ²"Go to the house of the Rechabites and speak with them and bring them to the house of the LORD, into one of the chambers; then offer them wine to drink." ³So I took Jaazaniah the son of Jeremiah, son of Habazziniah and his brothers and all his sons and the whole house of the Rechabites. ⁴I brought them to the house of the LORD into the chamber of the sons of Hanan the son of Igdaliah, the man of God, which was near the chamber of the officials, above the chamber of Maaseiah the son of Shallum, keeper of the threshold. ⁵Then I set before the Rechabites pitchers full of wine, and cups, and I said to them, "Drink wine." ⁶But they answered, "We will drink no wine, for Jonadab the son of Rechab, our father, commanded us, 'You shall not drink wine, neither you nor your sons for ever. ⁷You shall not build a house; you shall not sow seed; you shall not plant or have a vineyard; but you shall live in tents all your days, that you may live many days in the land where you sojourn.' ⁸We have obeyed the voice of Jonadab the son of Rechab, our father, in all that he commanded us, to drink no wine all our days, ourselves, our wives, our sons, or our daughters, ⁹and not to build houses to dwell in. We have no vineyard or field or seed, ¹⁰but we have lived in tents and have obeyed and done all that Jonadab our father commanded us. ¹¹But when Nebuchadnezzar king of Babylon came up against the land, we said, 'Come, and let us go to Jerusalem for fear of the army of the Chaldeans and the army of the Syrians.' So we are living in Jerusalem."

¹²Then the word of the LORD came to Jeremiah: ¹³"Thus says the LORD of hosts, the God of Israel: Go and say to the people of Judah and the inhabitants of Jerusalem, Will you not receive instruction and listen to my words? declares the LORD. ¹⁴The command that Jonadab the son of Rechab gave to his sons, to drink no wine, has been kept, and they drink none to this day, for they have obeyed their father's command. I have spoken to you persistently, but you have not listened to me. ¹⁵I have sent to you all my servants the prophets, sending them persistently, saying, 'Turn now every one of you from his evil way, and amend your deeds, and do not go after other gods to serve them, and then you shall dwell in the land that I gave to you and your fathers.' But you did not incline your ear or listen to me. ¹⁶The sons of Jonadab the son of Rechab have kept the command that their father gave them, but this people has not obeyed me. ¹⁷Therefore,

---

ᵃHebrew lacks *them like*

thus says the Lord, the God of hosts, the God of Israel: Behold, I am bringing upon Judah and all the inhabitants of Jerusalem all the disaster that I have pronounced against them, because I have spoken to them and they have not listened, I have called to them and they have not answered."

¹⁸But to the house of the Rechabites Jeremiah said, "Thus says the Lord of hosts, the God of Israel: Because you have obeyed the command of Jonadab your father and kept all his precepts and done all that he commanded you, ¹⁹therefore thus says the Lord of hosts, the God of Israel: Jonadab the son of Rechab shall never lack a man to stand before me."

JEHOIAKIM BURNS JEREMIAH'S SCROLL

36 In the fourth year of Jehoiakim the son of Josiah, king of Judah, this word came to Jeremiah from the Lord: ²"Take a scroll and write on it all the words that I have spoken to you against Israel and Judah and all the nations, from the day I spoke to you, from the days of Josiah until today. ³It may be that the house of Judah will hear all the disaster that I intend to do to them, so that every one may turn from his evil way, and that I may forgive their iniquity and their sin."

⁴Then Jeremiah called Baruch the son of Neriah, and Baruch wrote on a scroll at the dictation of Jeremiah all the words of the Lord that he had spoken to him. ⁵And Jeremiah ordered Baruch, saying, "I am banned from going to the house of the Lord, ⁶so you are to go, and on a day of fasting in the hearing of all the people in the Lord's house you shall read the words of the Lord from the scroll that you have written at my dictation. You shall read them also in the hearing of all the men of Judah who come out of their cities. ⁷It may be that their plea for mercy will come before the Lord, and that every one will turn from his evil way, for great is the anger and wrath that the Lord has pronounced against this people." ⁸And Baruch the son of Neriah did all that Jeremiah the prophet ordered him about reading from the scroll the words of the Lord in the Lord's house.

⁹In the fifth year of Jehoiakim the son of Josiah, king of Judah, in the ninth month, all the people in Jerusalem and all the people who came from the cities of Judah to Jerusalem proclaimed a fast before the Lord. ¹⁰Then, in the hearing of all the people, Baruch read the words of Jeremiah from the scroll, in the house of the Lord, in the chamber of Gemariah the son of Shaphan the secretary, which was in the upper court, at the entry of the New Gate of the Lord's house.

¹¹When Micaiah the son of Gemariah, son of Shaphan, heard all the words of the Lord from the scroll, ¹²he went down to the king's house, into the secretary's chamber, and all the officials were sitting there: Elishama the secretary, Delaiah the son of Shemaiah, Elnathan the son of Achbor, Gemariah the son of Shaphan, Zedekiah the son of Hananiah, and all the officials. ¹³And Micaiah told them all the words that he had heard, when Baruch read the scroll in the hearing of the people. ¹⁴Then all the officials sent Jehudi the son of Nethaniah, son of Shelemiah, son of Cushi, to say to Baruch, "Take in your hand the scroll that you read in the hearing of the people, and come." So Baruch the son of Neriah took the scroll in his hand and came to them. ¹⁵And they said to him, "Sit down and read it." So Baruch read it to them. ¹⁶When they heard all the words, they turned one to another in fear. And they said to Baruch, "We must report all these words to the king." ¹⁷Then they asked Baruch, "Tell us, please, how did you write all these words? Was it at his dictation?" ¹⁸Baruch answered them, "He dictated all these words to me, while I wrote them with ink on the scroll." ¹⁹Then the officials said to Baruch, "Go and hide, you and Jeremiah, and let no one know where you are."

²⁰So they went into the court to the king, having put the scroll in the chamber of Elishama the secretary, and they reported all the words to the king. ²¹Then the king sent Jehudi to get the scroll, and he took it from the chamber of Elishama the secretary. And Jehudi read it to the king and all the officials who stood beside the king. ²²It was the ninth month, and the king was sitting in the winter house, and there was a fire burning in the firepot before him. ²³As Jehudi read three or four columns, the king would cut them off with a knife and throw them into the fire in the firepot, until the entire scroll was consumed in the fire that was in the firepot. ²⁴Yet neither the king nor any of his servants who heard all these words was afraid, nor did they tear their garments. ²⁵Even when Elnathan and Delaiah and Gemariah urged the king not to burn the scroll, he would not listen to them. ²⁶And the king commanded

Jerahmeel the king's son and Seraiah the son of Azriel and Shelemiah the son of Abdeel to seize Baruch the secretary and Jeremiah the prophet, but the LORD hid them.

²⁷Now after the king had burned the scroll with the words that Baruch wrote at Jeremiah's dictation, the word of the LORD came to Jeremiah: ²⁸"Take another scroll and write on it all the former words that were in the first scroll, which Jehoiakim the king of Judah has burned. ²⁹And concerning Jehoiakim king of Judah you shall say, 'Thus says the LORD, You have burned this scroll, saying, "Why have you written in it that the king of Babylon will certainly come and destroy this land, and will cut off from it man and beast?" ³⁰Therefore thus says the LORD concerning Jehoiakim king of Judah: He shall have none to sit on the throne of David, and his dead body shall be cast out to the heat by day and the frost by night. ³¹And I will punish him and his offspring and his servants for their iniquity. I will bring upon them and upon the inhabitants of Jerusalem and upon the people of Judah all the disaster that I have pronounced against them, but they would not hear.'"

³²Then Jeremiah took another scroll and gave it to Baruch the scribe, the son of Neriah, who wrote on it at the dictation of Jeremiah all the words of the scroll that Jehoiakim king of Judah had burned in the fire. And many similar words were added to them.

JEREMIAH WARNS ZEDEKIAH

37 Zedekiah the son of Josiah, whom Nebuchadnezzar king of Babylon made king in the land of Judah, reigned instead of Coniah the son of Jehoiakim. ²But neither he nor his servants nor the people of the land listened to the words of the LORD that he spoke through Jeremiah the prophet.

³King Zedekiah sent Jehucal the son of Shelemiah, and Zephaniah the priest, the son of Maaseiah, to Jeremiah the prophet, saying, "Please pray for us to the LORD our God." ⁴Now Jeremiah was still going in and out among the people, for he had not yet been put in prison. ⁵The army of Pharaoh had come out of Egypt. And when the Chaldeans who were besieging Jerusalem heard news about them, they withdrew from Jerusalem.

⁶Then the word of the LORD came to Jeremiah the prophet: ⁷"Thus says the LORD, God of Israel: Thus shall you say to the king of Judah who sent you to me to enquire of me, 'Behold, Pharaoh's army that came to help you is about to return to Egypt, to its own land. ⁸And the Chaldeans shall come back and fight against this city. They shall capture it and burn it with fire. ⁹Thus says the LORD, Do not deceive yourselves, saying, "The Chaldeans will surely go away from us", for they will not go away. ¹⁰For even if you should defeat the whole army of Chaldeans who are fighting against you, and there remained of them only wounded men, every man in his tent, they would rise up and burn this city with fire.'"

JEREMIAH IMPRISONED

¹¹Now when the Chaldean army had withdrawn from Jerusalem at the approach of Pharaoh's army, ¹²Jeremiah set out from Jerusalem to go to the land of Benjamin to receive his portion there among the people. ¹³When he was at the Benjamin Gate, a sentry there named Irijah the son of Shelemiah, son of Hananiah, seized Jeremiah the prophet, saying, "You are deserting to the Chaldeans." ¹⁴And Jeremiah said, "It is a lie; I am not deserting to the Chaldeans." But Irijah would not listen to him, and seized Jeremiah and brought him to the officials. ¹⁵And the officials were enraged at Jeremiah, and they beat him and imprisoned him in the house of Jonathan the secretary, for it had been made a prison.

¹⁶When Jeremiah had come to the dungeon cells and remained there many days, ¹⁷King Zedekiah sent for him and received him. The king questioned him secretly in his house and said, "Is there any word from the LORD?" Jeremiah said, "There is." Then he said, "You shall be delivered into the hand of the king of Babylon." ¹⁸Jeremiah also said to King Zedekiah, "What wrong have I done to you or your servants or this people, that you have put me in prison? ¹⁹Where are your prophets who prophesied to you, saying, 'The king of Babylon will not come against you and against this land'? ²⁰Now hear, please, O my lord the king: let my humble plea come before you and do not send me back to the house of Jonathan the secretary, lest I die there." ²¹So King Zedekiah gave orders, and they committed Jeremiah to the court of the guard. And a loaf of bread was given him daily from the bakers' street, until all the bread of the city was gone. So Jeremiah remained in the court of the guard.

JEREMIAH 38

JEREMIAH CAST INTO THE CISTERN

38 Now Shephatiah the son of Mattan, Gedaliah the son of Pashhur, Jucal the son of Shelemiah, and Pashhur the son of Malchiah heard the words that Jeremiah was saying to all the people: **2**"Thus says the LORD: He who stays in this city shall die by the sword, by famine, and by pestilence, but he who goes out to the Chaldeans shall live. He shall have his life as a prize of war, and live. **3**Thus says the LORD: This city shall surely be given into the hand of the army of the king of Babylon and be taken." **4**Then the officials said to the king, "Let this man be put to death, for he is weakening the hands of the soldiers who are left in this city, and the hands of all the people, by speaking such words to them. For this man is not seeking the welfare of this people, but their harm." **5**King Zedekiah said, "Behold, he is in your hands, for the king can do nothing against you." **6**So they took Jeremiah and cast him into the cistern of Malchiah, the king's son, which was in the court of the guard, letting Jeremiah down by ropes. And there was no water in the cistern, but only mud, and Jeremiah sank in the mud.

JEREMIAH RESCUED FROM THE CISTERN

7When Ebed-melech the Ethiopian, a eunuch who was in the king's house, heard that they had put Jeremiah into the cistern—the king was sitting in the Benjamin Gate— **8**Ebed-melech went from the king's house and said to the king, **9**"My lord the king, these men have done evil in all that they did to Jeremiah the prophet by casting him into the cistern, and he will die there of hunger, for there is no bread left in the city." **10**Then the king commanded Ebed-melech the Ethiopian, "Take thirty men with you from here, and lift Jeremiah the prophet out of the cistern before he dies." **11**So Ebed-melech took the men with him and went to the house of the king, to a wardrobe in the storehouse, and took from there old rags and worn-out clothes, which he let down to Jeremiah in the cistern by ropes. **12**Then Ebed-melech the Ethiopian said to Jeremiah, "Put the rags and clothes between your armpits and the ropes." Jeremiah did so. **13**Then they drew Jeremiah up with ropes and lifted him out of the cistern. And Jeremiah remained in the court of the guard.

JEREMIAH WARNS ZEDEKIAH AGAIN

14King Zedekiah sent for Jeremiah the prophet and received him at the third entrance of the temple of the LORD. The king said to Jeremiah, "I will ask you a question; hide nothing from me." **15**Jeremiah said to Zedekiah, "If I tell you, will you not surely put me to death? And if I give you counsel, you will not listen to me." **16**Then King Zedekiah swore secretly to Jeremiah, "As the LORD lives, who made our souls, I will not put you to death or deliver you into the hand of these men who seek your life."

17Then Jeremiah said to Zedekiah, "Thus says the LORD, the God of hosts, the God of Israel: If you will surrender to the officials of the king of Babylon, then your life shall be spared, and this city shall not be burned with fire, and you and your house shall live. **18**But if you do not surrender to the officials of the king of Babylon, then this city shall be given into the hand of the Chaldeans, and they shall burn it with fire, and you shall not escape from their hand." **19**King Zedekiah said to Jeremiah, "I am afraid of the Judeans who have deserted to the Chaldeans, lest I be handed over to them and they deal cruelly with me." **20**Jeremiah said, "You shall not be given to them. Obey now the voice of the LORD in what I say to you, and it shall be well with you, and your life shall be spared. **21**But if you refuse to surrender, this is the vision which the LORD has shown to me: **22**Behold, all the women left in the house of the king of Judah were being led out to the officials of the king of Babylon and were saying,

" 'Your trusted friends have deceived you
    and prevailed against you;
now that your feet are
    sunk in the mud,
    they turn away from you.'

23All your wives and your sons shall be led out to the Chaldeans, and you yourself shall not escape from their hand, but shall be seized by the king of Babylon, and this city shall be burned with fire."

24Then Zedekiah said to Jeremiah, "Let no one know of these words, and you shall not die. **25**If the officials hear that I have spoken with you and come to you and say to you, 'Tell us what you said to the king and what the king said to you; hide nothing from us and we will not put you to death', **26**then you shall say to them, 'I made a humble plea to the king that he would not send me back to the house of Jonathan to die there.'" ²⁷Then all the officials came to Jeremiah and asked him, and he answered them as the king had instructed him. So they stopped speaking with him, for the conversation had not been overheard. ²⁸And Jeremiah remained in the court of the guard until the day that Jerusalem was taken.

THE FALL OF JERUSALEM

39 In the ninth year of Zedekiah king of Judah, in the tenth month, Nebuchadnezzar king of Babylon and all his army came against Jerusalem and besieged it. ²In the eleventh year of Zedekiah, in the fourth month, on the ninth day of the month, a breach was made in the city. ³Then all the officials of the king of Babylon came and sat in the middle gate: Nergal-sar-ezer of Samgar, Nebu-sar-sekim the Rab-saris, Nergal-sar-ezer the Rab-mag, with all the rest of the officers of the king of Babylon. ⁴When Zedekiah king of Judah and all the soldiers saw them, they fled, going out of the city at night by way of the king's garden through the gate between the two walls; and they went towards the Arabah. ⁵But the army of the Chaldeans pursued them and overtook Zedekiah in the plains of Jericho. And when they had taken him, they brought him up to Nebuchadnezzar king of Babylon, at Riblah, in the land of Hamath; and he passed sentence on him. ⁶The king of Babylon slaughtered the sons of Zedekiah at Riblah before his eyes, and the king of Babylon slaughtered all the nobles of Judah. ⁷He put out the eyes of Zedekiah and bound him in chains to take him to Babylon. ⁸The Chaldeans burned the king's house and the house of the people, and broke down the walls of Jerusalem. ⁹Then Nebuzaradan, the captain of the guard, carried into exile to Babylon the rest of the people who were left in the city, those who had deserted to him, and the people who remained. ¹⁰Nebuzaradan, the captain of the guard, left in the land of Judah some of the poor people who owned nothing, and gave them vineyards and fields at the same time.

THE LORD DELIVERS JEREMIAH

¹¹Nebuchadnezzar king of Babylon gave command concerning Jeremiah through Nebuzaradan, the captain of the guard, saying, ¹²"Take him, look after him well, and do him no harm, but deal with him as he tells you." ¹³So Nebuzaradan the captain of the guard, Nebushazban the Rab-saris, Nergal-sar-ezer the Rab-mag, and all the chief officers of the king of Babylon ¹⁴sent and took Jeremiah from the court of the guard. They entrusted him to Gedaliah the son of Ahikam, son of Shaphan, that he should take him home. So he lived among the people.

¹⁵The word of the LORD came to Jeremiah while he was shut up in the court of the guard: ¹⁶"Go, and say to Ebed-melech the Ethiopian, 'Thus says the LORD of hosts, the God of Israel: Behold, I will fulfil my words against this city for harm and not for good, and they shall be accomplished before you on that day. ¹⁷But I will deliver you on that day, declares the LORD, and you shall not be given into the hand of the men of whom you are afraid. ¹⁸For I will surely save you, and you shall not fall by the sword, but you shall have your life as a prize of war, because you have put your trust in me, declares the LORD.'"

JEREMIAH REMAINS IN JUDAH

40 The word that came to Jeremiah from the LORD after Nebuzaradan the captain of the guard had let him go from Ramah, when he took him bound in chains along with all the captives of Jerusalem and Judah who were being exiled to Babylon. ²The captain of the guard took Jeremiah and said to him, "The LORD your God pronounced this disaster against this place. ³The LORD has brought it about, and has done as he said. Because you sinned against the LORD and did not obey his voice, this thing has come upon you. ⁴Now, behold, I release you today from the chains on your hands. If it seems good to you to come with me to Babylon, come, and I will look after you well, but if it seems wrong to you to come with me to Babylon, do not come. See, the whole land is before you; go wherever you think it good and right to go. ⁵If you remain,ᵃ then return to Gedaliah the son of Ahikam, son of Shaphan, whom the king of Babylon appointed governor of the cities of Judah, and dwell with him among the people. Or go wherever you think it right to go." So the captain of the guard gave him an allowance of food and a present, and let him go. ⁶Then Jeremiah went to Gedaliah the son of Ahikam, at Mizpah, and lived with him among the people who were left in the land.

ᵃSyriac; the meaning of the Hebrew phrase is uncertain

⁷When all the captains of the forces in the open country and their men heard that the king of Babylon had appointed Gedaliah the son of Ahikam governor in the land and had committed to him men, women, and children, those of the poorest of the land who had not been taken into exile to Babylon, ⁸they went to Gedaliah at Mizpah—Ishmael the son of Nethaniah, Johanan the son of Kareah, Seraiah the son of Tanhumeth, the sons of Ephai the Netophathite, Jezaniah the son of the Maacathite, they and their men. ⁹Gedaliah the son of Ahikam, son of Shaphan, swore to them and their men, saying, "Do not be afraid to serve the Chaldeans. Dwell in the land and serve the king of Babylon, and it shall be well with you. ¹⁰As for me, I will dwell at Mizpah, to represent you before the Chaldeans who will come to us. But as for you, gather wine and summer fruits and oil, and store them in your vessels, and dwell in your cities that you have taken." ¹¹Likewise, when all the Judeans who were in Moab and among the Ammonites and in Edom and in other lands heard that the king of Babylon had left a remnant in Judah and had appointed Gedaliah the son of Ahikam, son of Shaphan, as governor over them, ¹²then all the Judeans returned from all the places to which they had been driven and came to the land of Judah, to Gedaliah at Mizpah. And they gathered wine and summer fruits in great abundance.

¹³Now Johanan the son of Kareah and all the leaders of the forces in the open country came to Gedaliah at Mizpah ¹⁴and said to him, "Do you know that Baalis the king of the Ammonites has sent Ishmael the son of Nethaniah to take your life?" But Gedaliah the son of Ahikam would not believe them. ¹⁵Then Johanan the son of Kareah spoke secretly to Gedaliah at Mizpah, "Please let me go and strike down Ishmael the son of Nethaniah, and no one will know it. Why should he take your life, so that all the Judeans who are gathered about you would be scattered, and the remnant of Judah would perish?" ¹⁶But Gedaliah the son of Ahikam said to Johanan the son of Kareah, "You shall not do this thing, for you are speaking falsely of Ishmael."

GEDALIAH MURDERED

41 In the seventh month, Ishmael the son of Nethaniah, son of Elishama, of the royal family, one of the chief officers of the king, came with ten men to Gedaliah the son of Ahikam, at Mizpah. As they ate bread together there at Mizpah, ²Ishmael the son of Nethaniah and the ten men with him rose up and struck down Gedaliah the son of Ahikam, son of Shaphan, with the sword, and killed him, whom the king of Babylon had appointed governor in the land. ³Ishmael also struck down all the Judeans who were with Gedaliah at Mizpah, and the Chaldean soldiers who happened to be there.

⁴On the day after the murder of Gedaliah, before anyone knew of it, ⁵eighty men arrived from Shechem and Shiloh and Samaria, with their beards shaved and their clothes torn, and their bodies gashed, bringing grain offerings and incense to present at the temple of the LORD. ⁶And Ishmael the son of Nethaniah came out from Mizpah to meet them, weeping as he came. As he met them, he said to them, "Come in to Gedaliah the son of Ahikam." ⁷When they came into the city, Ishmael the son of Nethaniah and the men with him slaughtered them and cast them into a cistern. ⁸But there were ten men among them who said to Ishmael, "Do not put us to death, for we have stores of wheat, barley, oil, and honey hidden in the fields." So he refrained and did not put them to death with their companions.

⁹Now the cistern into which Ishmael had thrown all the bodies of the men whom he had struck down along with*ᵃ* Gedaliah was the large cistern that King Asa had made for defence against Baasha king of Israel; Ishmael the son of Nethaniah filled it with the slain. ¹⁰Then Ishmael took captive all the rest of the people who were in Mizpah, the king's daughters and all the people who were left at Mizpah, whom Nebuzaradan, the captain of the guard, had committed to Gedaliah the son of Ahikam. Ishmael the son of Nethaniah took them captive and set out to cross over to the Ammonites.

¹¹But when Johanan the son of Kareah and all the leaders of the forces with him heard of all the evil that Ishmael the son of Nethaniah had done, ¹²they took all their men and went to fight against Ishmael the son of Nethaniah. They came upon him at the great pool that is in Gibeon. ¹³And when all the people who were with Ishmael saw Johanan the son of Kareah and all the leaders of the forces with him, they rejoiced. ¹⁴So all the people whom Ishmael had carried

---
*ᵃ*Hebrew *by the hand of*

away captive from Mizpah turned round and came back, and went to Johanan the son of Kareah. ¹⁵But Ishmael the son of Nethaniah escaped from Johanan with eight men, and went to the Ammonites. ¹⁶Then Johanan the son of Kareah and all the leaders of the forces with him took from Mizpah all the rest of the people whom he had recovered from Ishmael the son of Nethaniah, after he had struck down Gedaliah the son of Ahikam— soldiers, women, children, and eunuchs, whom Johanan brought back from Gibeon. ¹⁷And they went and stayed at Geruth Chimham near Bethlehem, intending to go to Egypt ¹⁸because of the Chaldeans. For they were afraid of them, because Ishmael the son of Nethaniah had struck down Gedaliah the son of Ahikam, whom the king of Babylon had made governor over the land.

WARNING AGAINST GOING TO EGYPT

42 Then all the commanders of the forces, and Johanan the son of Kareah and Jezaniah the son of Hoshaiah, and all the people from the least to the greatest, came near ²and said to Jeremiah the prophet, "Let our plea for mercy come before you, and pray to the LORD your God for us, for all this remnant—because we are left with but a few, as your eyes see us— ³that the LORD your God may show us the way we should go, and the thing that we should do." ⁴Jeremiah the prophet said to them, "I have heard you. Behold, I will pray to the LORD your God according to your request, and whatever the LORD answers you I will tell you. I will keep nothing back from you." ⁵Then they said to Jeremiah, "May the LORD be a true and faithful witness against us if we do not act according to all the word with which the LORD your God sends you to us. ⁶Whether it is good or bad, we will obey the voice of the LORD our God to whom we are sending you, that it may be well with us when we obey the voice of the LORD our God."

⁷At the end of ten days the word of the LORD came to Jeremiah. ⁸Then he summoned Johanan the son of Kareah and all the commanders of the forces who were with him, and all the people from the least to the greatest, ⁹and said to them, "Thus says the LORD, the God of Israel, to whom you sent me to present your plea for mercy before him: ¹⁰If you will remain in this land, then I will build you up and not pull you down; I will plant you, and not pluck you up; for I relent of the disaster that I did to you. ¹¹Do not fear the king of Babylon, of whom you are afraid. Do not fear him, declares the LORD, for I am with you, to save you and to deliver you from his hand. ¹²I will grant you mercy, that he may have mercy on you and let you remain in your own land. ¹³But if you say, 'We will not remain in this land', disobeying the voice of the LORD your God ¹⁴and saying, 'No, we will go to the land of Egypt, where we shall not see war or hear the sound of the trumpet or be hungry for bread, and we will dwell there', ¹⁵then hear the word of the LORD, O remnant of Judah. Thus says the LORD of hosts, the God of Israel: If you set your faces to enter Egypt and go to live there, ¹⁶then the sword that you fear shall overtake you there in the land of Egypt, and the famine of which you are afraid shall follow close after you to Egypt, and there you shall die. ¹⁷All the men who set their faces to go to Egypt to live there shall die by the sword, by famine, and by pestilence. They shall have no remnant or survivor from the disaster that I will bring upon them.

¹⁸"For thus says the LORD of hosts, the God of Israel: As my anger and my wrath were poured out on the inhabitants of Jerusalem, so my wrath will be poured out on you when you go to Egypt. You shall become an execration, a horror, a curse, and a taunt. You shall see this place no more. ¹⁹The LORD has said to you, O remnant of Judah, 'Do not go to Egypt.' Know for a certainty that I have warned you this day ²⁰that you have gone astray at the cost of your lives. For you sent me to the LORD your God, saying, 'Pray for us to the LORD our God, and whatever the LORD our God says, declare to us and we will do it.' ²¹And I have this day declared it to you, but you have not obeyed the voice of the LORD your God in anything that he sent me to tell you. ²²Now therefore know for a certainty that you shall die by the sword, by famine, and by pestilence in the place where you desire to go to live."

JEREMIAH TAKEN TO EGYPT

43 When Jeremiah finished speaking to all the people all these words of the LORD their God, with which the LORD their God had sent him to them, ²Azariah the son of Hoshaiah and Johanan the son of Kareah and all the insolent men said to Jeremiah, "You are telling a lie. The LORD our God did not send you to say, 'Do

not go to Egypt to live there', ³but Baruch the son of Neriah has set you against us, to deliver us into the hand of the Chaldeans, that they may kill us or take us into exile in Babylon." ⁴So Johanan the son of Kareah and all the commanders of the forces and all the people did not obey the voice of the LORD, to remain in the land of Judah. ⁵But Johanan the son of Kareah and all the commanders of the forces took all the remnant of Judah who had returned to live in the land of Judah from all the nations to which they had been driven — ⁶the men, the women, the children, the princesses, and every person whom Nebuzaradan the captain of the guard had left with Gedaliah the son of Ahikam, son of Shaphan; also Jeremiah the prophet and Baruch the son of Neriah. ⁷And they came into the land of Egypt, for they did not obey the voice of the LORD. And they arrived at Tahpanhes.

⁸Then the word of the LORD came to Jeremiah in Tahpanhes: ⁹"Take in your hands large stones and hide them in the mortar in the pavement that is at the entrance to Pharaoh's palace in Tahpanhes, in the sight of the men of Judah, ¹⁰and say to them, 'Thus says the LORD of hosts, the God of Israel: Behold, I will send and take Nebuchadnezzar the king of Babylon, my servant, and I will set his throne above these stones that I have hidden, and he will spread his royal canopy over them. ¹¹He shall come and strike the land of Egypt, giving over to the pestilence those who are doomed to the pestilence, to captivity those who are doomed to captivity, and to the sword those who are doomed to the sword. ¹²I shall kindle a fire in the temples of the gods of Egypt, and he shall burn them and carry them away captive. And he shall clean the land of Egypt as a shepherd cleans his cloak of vermin, and he shall go away from there in peace. ¹³He shall break the obelisks of Heliopolis, which is in the land of Egypt, and the temples of the gods of Egypt he shall burn with fire.'"

JUDGEMENT FOR IDOLATRY

44 The word that came to Jeremiah concerning all the Judeans who lived in the land of Egypt, at Migdol, at Tahpanhes, at Memphis, and in the land of Pathros, ²"Thus says the LORD of hosts, the God of Israel: You have seen all the disaster that I brought upon Jerusalem and upon all the cities of Judah. Behold, this day they are a desolation, and no one dwells in them, ³because of the evil that they committed, provoking me to anger, in that they went to make offerings and serve other gods that they knew not, neither they, nor you, nor your fathers. ⁴Yet I persistently sent to you all my servants the prophets, saying, 'Oh, do not do this abomination that I hate!' ⁵But they did not listen or incline their ear, to turn from their evil and make no offerings to other gods. ⁶Therefore my wrath and my anger were poured out and kindled in the cities of Judah and in the streets of Jerusalem, and they became a waste and a desolation, as at this day. ⁷And now thus says the LORD God of hosts, the God of Israel: Why do you commit this great evil against yourselves, to cut off from you man and woman, infant and child, from the midst of Judah, leaving you no remnant? ⁸Why do you provoke me to anger with the works of your hands, making offerings to other gods in the land of Egypt where you have come to live, so that you may be cut off and become a curse and a taunt among all the nations of the earth? ⁹Have you forgotten the evil of your fathers, the evil of the kings of Judah, the evil of their*a* wives, your own evil, and the evil of your wives, which they committed in the land of Judah and in the streets of Jerusalem? ¹⁰They have not humbled themselves even to this day, nor have they feared, nor walked in my law and my statutes that I set before you and before your fathers.

¹¹"Therefore thus says the LORD of hosts, the God of Israel: Behold, I will set my face against you for harm, to cut off all Judah. ¹²I will take the remnant of Judah who have set their faces to come to the land of Egypt to live, and they shall all be consumed. In the land of Egypt they shall fall; by the sword and by famine they shall be consumed. From the least to the greatest, they shall die by the sword and by famine, and they shall become an oath, a horror, a curse, and a taunt. ¹³I will punish those who dwell in the land of Egypt, as I have punished Jerusalem, with the sword, with famine, and with pestilence, ¹⁴so that none of the remnant of Judah who have come to live in the land of Egypt shall escape or survive or return to the land of Judah, to which they desire to return to dwell there. For they shall not return, except some fugitives."

---
a Hebrew *his*

¹⁵Then all the men who knew that their wives had made offerings to other gods, and all the women who stood by, a great assembly, all the people who lived in Pathros in the land of Egypt, answered Jeremiah: ¹⁶"As for the word that you have spoken to us in the name of the Lord, we will not listen to you. ¹⁷But we will do everything that we have vowed, make offerings to the queen of heaven and pour out drink offerings to her, as we did, both we and our fathers, our kings and our officials, in the cities of Judah and in the streets of Jerusalem. For then we had plenty of food, and prospered, and saw no disaster. ¹⁸But since we left off making offerings to the queen of heaven and pouring out drink offerings to her, we have lacked everything and have been consumed by the sword and by famine." ¹⁹And the women said,ᵃ "When we made offerings to the queen of heaven and poured out drink offerings to her, was it without our husbands' approval that we made cakes for her bearing her image and poured out drink offerings to her?"

²⁰Then Jeremiah said to all the people, men and women, all the people who had given him this answer: ²¹"As for the offerings that you offered in the cities of Judah and in the streets of Jerusalem, you and your fathers, your kings and your officials, and the people of the land, did not the Lord remember them? Did it not come into his mind? ²²The Lord could no longer bear your evil deeds and the abominations that you committed. Therefore your land has become a desolation and a waste and a curse, without inhabitant, as it is this day. ²³It is because you made offerings and because you sinned against the Lord and did not obey the voice of the Lord or walk in his law and in his statutes and in his testimonies that this disaster has happened to you, as at this day."

²⁴Jeremiah said to all the people and all the women, "Hear the word of the Lord, all you of Judah who are in the land of Egypt. ²⁵Thus says the Lord of hosts, the God of Israel: You and your wives have declared with your mouths, and have fulfilled it with your hands, saying, 'We will surely perform our vows that we have made, to make offerings to the queen of heaven and to pour out drink offerings to her.' Then confirm your vows and perform your vows! ²⁶Therefore hear the word of the Lord, all you of Judah who dwell in the land of Egypt: Behold, I have sworn by my great name, says the Lord, that my name shall no more be invoked by the mouth of any man of Judah in all the land of Egypt, saying, 'As the Lord God lives.' ²⁷Behold, I am watching over them for disaster and not for good. All the men of Judah who are in the land of Egypt shall be consumed by the sword and by famine, until there is an end of them. ²⁸And those who escape the sword shall return from the land of Egypt to the land of Judah, few in number; and all the remnant of Judah, who came to the land of Egypt to live, shall know whose word will stand, mine or theirs. ²⁹This shall be the sign to you, declares the Lord, that I will punish you in this place, in order that you may know that my words will surely stand against you for harm: ³⁰Thus says the Lord, Behold, I will give Pharaoh Hophra king of Egypt into the hand of his enemies and into the hand of those who seek his life, as I gave Zedekiah king of Judah into the hand of Nebuchadnezzar king of Babylon, who was his enemy and sought his life."

MESSAGE TO BARUCH

45 The word that Jeremiah the prophet spoke to Baruch the son of Neriah, when he wrote these words in a book at the dictation of Jeremiah, in the fourth year of Jehoiakim the son of Josiah, king of Judah: ²"Thus says the Lord, the God of Israel, to you, O Baruch: ³You said, 'Woe is me! For the Lord has added sorrow to my pain. I am weary with my groaning, and I find no rest.' ⁴Thus shall you say to him, Thus says the Lord: Behold, what I have built I am breaking down, and what I have planted I am plucking up—that is, the whole land. ⁵And do you seek great things for yourself? Seek them not, for behold, I am bringing disaster upon all flesh, declares the Lord. But I will give you your life as a prize of war in all places to which you may go."

JUDGEMENT ON EGYPT

46 The word of the Lord that came to Jeremiah the prophet concerning the nations.

²About Egypt. Concerning the army of Pharaoh Neco, king of Egypt, which was by the river Euphrates at Carchemish and which Nebuchadnezzar king of Babylon defeated in the fourth year of Jehoiakim the son of Josiah, king of Judah:

ᵃCompare Syriac; Hebrew lacks *And the women said*

JEREMIAH 46

3 "Prepare buckler and shield,
  and advance for battle!
4 Harness the horses;
  mount, O horsemen!
  Take your stations with your helmets,
  polish your spears,
  put on your armour!
5 Why have I seen it?
  They are dismayed
  and have turned backwards.
  Their warriors are beaten down
  and have fled in haste;
  they look not back—
  terror on every side!
        declares the LORD.

6 "The swift cannot flee away,
  nor the warrior escape;
  in the north by the river Euphrates
  they have stumbled and fallen.

7 "Who is this, rising like the Nile,
  like rivers whose waters surge?
8 Egypt rises like the Nile,
  like rivers whose waters surge.
  He said, 'I will rise, I will
    cover the earth,
  I will destroy cities and
    their inhabitants.'
9 Advance, O horses,
  and rage, O chariots!
  Let the warriors go out:
  men of Cush and Put who
    handle the shield,
  men of Lud, skilled in
    handling the bow.
10 That day is the day of the
    Lord GOD of hosts,
   a day of vengeance,
   to avenge himself on his foes.
   The sword shall devour and be sated
   and drink its fill of their blood.
   For the Lord GOD of hosts
     holds a sacrifice
   in the north country by the
     river Euphrates.
11 Go up to Gilead, and take balm,
   O virgin daughter of Egypt!
   In vain you have used
     many medicines;
   there is no healing for you.
12 The nations have heard of your shame,
   and the earth is full of your cry;
   for warrior has stumbled
     against warrior;
   they have both fallen together."

13 The word that the LORD spoke to Jeremiah the prophet about the coming of Nebuchadnezzar king of Babylon to strike the land of Egypt:

14 "Declare in Egypt, and
     proclaim in Migdol;
   proclaim in Memphis
     and Tahpanhes;
   say, 'Stand ready and be prepared,
     for the sword shall devour
       around you.'
15 Why are your mighty ones face down?
   They do not stand[1]
   because the LORD thrust them down.
16 He made many stumble, and they fell,
   and they said one to another,
   'Arise, and let us go back to
     our own people
   and to the land of our birth,
   because of the sword of
     the oppressor.'
17 Call the name of Pharaoh,
     king of Egypt,
   'Noisy one who lets the hour go by.'

18 "As I live, declares the King,
     whose name is the LORD of hosts,
   like Tabor among the mountains
     and like Carmel by the sea,
   shall one come.
19 Prepare yourselves baggage for exile,
     O inhabitants of Egypt!
   For Memphis shall become a waste,
     a ruin, without inhabitant.

20 "A beautiful heifer is Egypt,
     but a biting fly from the north
       has come upon her.
21 Even her hired soldiers in her midst
     are like fattened calves;
   yes, they have turned and fled together;
     they did not stand,
   for the day of their calamity
     has come upon them,
   the time of their punishment.

22 "She makes a sound like a
     serpent gliding away;
   for her enemies march in force
   and come against her with axes
     like those who fell trees.
23 They shall cut down her forest,
        declares the LORD,

---
[1] Hebrew *He does not stand*

though it is impenetrable,
because they are more
numerous than locusts;
they are without number.
²⁴ The daughter of Egypt shall
be put to shame;
she shall be delivered into the hand
of a people from the north."

²⁵The LORD of hosts, the God of Israel, said: "Behold, I am bringing punishment upon Amon of Thebes, and Pharaoh and Egypt and her gods and her kings, upon Pharaoh and those who trust in him. ²⁶I will deliver them into the hand of those who seek their life, into the hand of Nebuchadnezzar king of Babylon and his officers. Afterwards Egypt shall be inhabited as in the days of old, declares the LORD.

²⁷ "But fear not, O Jacob my servant,
nor be dismayed, O Israel,
for behold, I will save you
from far away,
and your offspring from the
land of their captivity.
Jacob shall return and have
quiet and ease,
and none shall make him afraid.
²⁸ Fear not, O Jacob my servant,
declares the LORD,
for I am with you.
I will make a full end of all the nations
to which I have driven you,
but of you I will not make a full end.
I will discipline you in just measure,
and I will by no means leave
you unpunished."

JUDGEMENT ON THE PHILISTINES

47 The word of the LORD that came to Jeremiah the prophet concerning the Philistines, before Pharaoh struck down Gaza.

² "Thus says the LORD:
Behold, waters are rising
out of the north,
and shall become an
overflowing torrent;
they shall overflow the land
and all that fills it,
the city and those who dwell in it.
Men shall cry out,
and every inhabitant of the
land shall wail.
³ At the noise of the stamping of
the hoofs of his stallions,
at the rushing of his chariots, at
the rumbling of their wheels,
the fathers look not back
to their children,
so feeble are their hands,
⁴ because of the day that is
coming to destroy
all the Philistines,
to cut off from Tyre and Sidon
every helper that remains.
For the LORD is destroying
the Philistines,
the remnant of the coastland
of Caphtor.
⁵ Baldness has come upon Gaza;
Ashkelon has perished.
O remnant of their valley,
how long will you gash yourselves?
⁶ Ah, sword of the LORD!
How long till you are quiet?
Put yourself into your scabbard;
rest and be still!
⁷ How can it^a be quiet
when the LORD has given it
a charge?
Against Ashkelon and against
the seashore
he has appointed it."

JUDGEMENT ON MOAB

48 Concerning Moab.
Thus says the LORD of hosts,
the God of Israel:

"Woe to Nebo, for it is laid waste!
Kiriathaim is put to shame,
it is taken;
the fortress is put to shame
and broken down;
² the renown of Moab is no more.
In Heshbon they planned
disaster against her:
'Come, let us cut her off from
being a nation!'
You also, O Madmen, shall be
brought to silence;
the sword shall pursue you.

³ "A voice! A cry from Horonaim,
'Desolation and great destruction!'
⁴ Moab is destroyed;
her little ones have made a cry.

---

^{a}Septuagint, Vulgate; Hebrew *you*

⁵ For at the ascent of Luhith
they go up weeping;ᵃ
for at the descent of Horonaim
they have heard the distressed
cryᵇ of destruction.
⁶ Flee! Save yourselves!
You will be like a juniper
in the desert!
⁷ For, because you trusted in your
works and your treasures,
you also shall be taken;
and Chemosh shall go into exile
with his priests and his officials.
⁸ The destroyer shall come
upon every city,
and no city shall escape;
the valley shall perish,
and the plain shall be destroyed,
as the LORD has spoken.
⁹ "Give wings to Moab,
for she would fly away;
her cities shall become a desolation,
with no inhabitant in them.

¹⁰"Cursed is he who does the work of the LORD with slackness, and cursed is he who keeps back his sword from bloodshed.

¹¹ "Moab has been at ease from
his youth
and has settled on his dregs;
he has not been emptied from
vessel to vessel,
nor has he gone into exile;
so his taste remains in him,
and his scent is not changed.

¹²"Therefore, behold, the days are coming, declares the LORD, when I shall send to him pourers who will pour him, and empty his vessels and break hisᶜ jars in pieces. ¹³Then Moab shall be ashamed of Chemosh, as the house of Israel was ashamed of Bethel, their confidence.

¹⁴ "How do you say, 'We are heroes
and mighty men of war'?
¹⁵ The destroyer of Moab and his
cities has come up,
and the choicest of his young men
have gone down to slaughter,
declares the King, whose name
is the LORD of hosts.
¹⁶ The calamity of Moab is near at hand,
and his affliction hastens swiftly.
¹⁷ Grieve for him, all you who
are round him,
and all who know his name;
say, 'How the mighty sceptre is broken,
the glorious staff.'
¹⁸ "Come down from your glory,
and sit on the parched ground,
O inhabitant of Dibon!
For the destroyer of Moab has
come up against you;
he has destroyed your strongholds.
¹⁹ Stand by the way and watch,
O inhabitant of Aroer!
Ask him who flees and her
who escapes;
say, 'What has happened?'
²⁰ Moab is put to shame, for it is broken;
wail and cry!
Tell it beside the Arnon,
that Moab is laid waste.

²¹"Judgement has come upon the tableland, upon Holon, and Jahzah, and Mephaath, ²²and Dibon, and Nebo, and Beth-diblathaim, ²³and Kiriathaim, and Beth-gamul, and Beth-meon, ²⁴and Kerioth, and Bozrah, and all the cities of the land of Moab, far and near. ²⁵The horn of Moab is cut off, and his arm is broken, declares the LORD.

²⁶"Make him drunk, because he magnified himself against the LORD, so that Moab shall wallow in his vomit, and he too shall be held in derision. ²⁷Was not Israel a derision to you? Was he found among thieves, that whenever you spoke of him you wagged your head?

²⁸ "Leave the cities, and dwell in the rock,
O inhabitants of Moab!
Be like the dove that nests
in the sides of the mouth of a gorge.
²⁹ We have heard of the pride of Moab—
he is very proud—
of his loftiness, his pride,
and his arrogance,
and the haughtiness of his heart.
³⁰ I know his insolence,
declares the LORD;
his boasts are false,
his deeds are false.
³¹ Therefore I wail for Moab;
I cry out for all Moab;
for the men of Kir-hareseth I mourn.

ᵃHebrew *weeping goes up with weeping* ᵇSeptuagint (compare Isaiah 15:5) *heard the cry* ᶜSeptuagint, Aquila; Hebrew *their*

⁣³² More than for Jazer I weep for you,
    O vine of Sibmah!
Your branches passed over the sea,
    reached to the Sea of Jazer;
on your summer fruits and your grapes
    the destroyer has fallen.
³³ Gladness and joy have been taken away
    from the fruitful land of Moab;
I have made the wine cease
    from the wine presses;
no one treads them with
    shouts of joy;
the shouting is not the shout of joy.

³⁴ "From the outcry at Heshbon even to Elealeh, as far as Jahaz they utter their voice, from Zoar to Horonaim and Eglath-shelishiyah. For the waters of Nimrim also have become desolate. ³⁵And I will bring to an end in Moab, declares the LORD, him who offers sacrifice in the high place and makes offerings to his god. ³⁶Therefore my heart moans for Moab like a flute, and my heart moans like a flute for the men of Kir-hareseth. Therefore the riches they gained have perished.

³⁷"For every head is shaved and every beard cut off. On all the hands are gashes, and round the waist is sackcloth. ³⁸On all the housetops of Moab and in the squares there is nothing but lamentation, for I have broken Moab like a vessel for which no one cares, declares the LORD. ³⁹How it is broken! How they wail! How Moab has turned his back in shame! So Moab has become a derision and a horror to all that are round him."

⁴⁰ For thus says the LORD:
"Behold, one shall fly swiftly
    like an eagle
and spread his wings against Moab;
⁴¹ the cities shall be taken
    and the strongholds seized.
The heart of the warriors of
    Moab shall be in that day
like the heart of a woman
    in her birth pains;
⁴² Moab shall be destroyed and
    be no longer a people,
because he magnified himself
    against the LORD.
⁴³ Terror, pit, and snare
    are before you, O inhabitant
        of Moab!
                    declares the LORD.
⁴⁴ He who flees from the terror
    shall fall into the pit,
and he who climbs out of the pit
    shall be caught in the snare.
For I will bring these things
    upon Moab,
the year of their punishment,
            declares the LORD.
⁴⁵ "In the shadow of Heshbon
    fugitives stop without strength,
for fire came out from Heshbon,
    flame from the house of Sihon;
it has destroyed the forehead of Moab,
    the crown of the sons of tumult.
⁴⁶ Woe to you, O Moab!
    The people of Chemosh are undone,
for your sons have been taken captive,
    and your daughters into captivity.
⁴⁷ Yet I will restore the fortunes of Moab
    in the latter days, declares the LORD."
Thus far is the judgement on Moab.

JUDGEMENT ON AMMON

49 Concerning the Ammonites.
    Thus says the LORD:

"Has Israel no sons?
    Has he no heir?
Why then has Milcom[a]
    dispossessed Gad,
and his people settled in its cities?
² Therefore, behold, the days are coming,
    declares the LORD,
when I will cause the battle
    cry to be heard
against Rabbah of the Ammonites;
    it shall become a desolate mound,
    and its villages shall be
        burned with fire;
then Israel shall dispossess those
    who dispossessed him,
        says the LORD.

³ "Wail, O Heshbon, for Ai is laid waste!
    Cry out, O daughters of Rabbah!
Put on sackcloth,
    lament, and run to and fro
        among the hedges!
For Milcom shall go into exile,
    with his priests and his officials.
⁴ Why do you boast of your valleys,[b]
    O faithless daughter,
who trusted in her treasures, saying,
    'Who will come against me?'

---

[a]Or *their king*; also verse 3 [b]Hebrew *boast of your valleys, your valley flows*

5 Behold, I will bring terror upon you,
    declares the Lord GOD of hosts,
    from all who are round you,
and you shall be driven out, every
    man straight before him,
    with none to gather the fugitives.

6 "But afterwards I will restore the fortunes of the Ammonites, declares the LORD."

JUDGEMENT ON EDOM

7 Concerning Edom.
Thus says the LORD of hosts:

"Is wisdom no more in Teman?
    Has counsel perished from
        the prudent?
    Has their wisdom vanished?
8 Flee, turn back, dwell in the depths,
    O inhabitants of Dedan!
For I will bring the calamity
    of Esau upon him,
    the time when I punish him.
9 If grape gatherers came to you,
    would they not leave gleanings?
If thieves came by night,
    would they not destroy only
        enough for themselves?
10 But I have stripped Esau bare;
    I have uncovered his hiding places,
    and he is not able to conceal himself.
His children are destroyed,
    and his brothers,
    and his neighbours; and
        he is no more.
11 Leave your fatherless children;
    I will keep them alive;
    and let your widows trust in me."

12 For thus says the LORD: "If those who did not deserve to drink the cup must drink it, will you go unpunished? You shall not go unpunished, but you must drink. 13 For I have sworn by myself, declares the LORD, that Bozrah shall become a horror, a taunt, a waste, and a curse, and all her cities shall be perpetual wastes."

14 I have heard a message from the LORD,
    and an envoy has been sent
        among the nations:
"Gather yourselves together
    and come against her,
    and rise up for battle!
15 For behold, I will make you small
        among the nations,
        despised among mankind.
16 The horror you inspire has
        deceived you,
    and the pride of your heart,
    you who live in the clefts of the rock,*a*
    who hold the height of the hill.
Though you make your nest
        as high as the eagle's,
    I will bring you down from there,
        declares the LORD.

17 "Edom shall become a horror. Everyone who passes by it will be horrified and will hiss because of all its disasters. 18 As when Sodom and Gomorrah and their neighbouring cities were overthrown, says the LORD, no man shall dwell there, no man shall sojourn in her. 19 Behold, like a lion coming up from the jungle of the Jordan against a perennial pasture, I will suddenly make him*b* run away from her. And I will appoint over her whomever I choose. For who is like me? Who will summon me? What shepherd can stand before me? 20 Therefore hear the plan that the LORD has made against Edom and the purposes that he has formed against the inhabitants of Teman: Even the little ones of the flock shall be dragged away. Surely their fold shall be appalled at their fate. 21 At the sound of their fall the earth shall tremble; the sound of their cry shall be heard at the Red Sea. 22 Behold, one shall mount up and fly swiftly like an eagle and spread his wings against Bozrah, and the heart of the warriors of Edom shall be in that day like the heart of a woman in her birth pains."

JUDGEMENT ON DAMASCUS

23 Concerning Damascus:

"Hamath and Arpad are confounded,
    for they have heard bad news;
    they melt in fear,
    they are troubled like the sea
        that cannot be quiet.
24 Damascus has become feeble,
    she turned to flee,
    and panic seized her;
anguish and sorrows have
        taken hold of her,
    as of a woman in labour.
25 How is the famous city not forsaken,
    the city of my joy?
26 Therefore her young men shall
        fall in her squares,

---

a Or *of Sela* *b* Septuagint, Syriac *them*

and all her soldiers shall be
destroyed in that day,
declares the Lord of hosts.
²⁷ And I will kindle a fire in the
wall of Damascus,
and it shall devour the strongholds
of Ben-hadad."

JUDGEMENT ON KEDAR AND HAZOR

²⁸Concerning Kedar and the kingdoms of Hazor that Nebuchadnezzar king of Babylon struck down.

Thus says the Lord:
"Rise up, advance against Kedar!
Destroy the people of the east!
²⁹ Their tents and their flocks
shall be taken,
their curtains and all their goods;
their camels shall be led
away from them,
and men shall cry to them:
'Terror on every side!'
³⁰ Flee, wander far away, dwell
in the depths,
O inhabitants of Hazor!
declares the Lord.
For Nebuchadnezzar king of Babylon
has made a plan against you
and formed a purpose against you.
³¹ "Rise up, advance against
a nation at ease,
that dwells securely,
declares the Lord,
that has no gates or bars,
that dwells alone.
³² Their camels shall become plunder,
their herds of livestock a spoil.
I will scatter to every wind
those who cut the corners
of their hair,
and I will bring their calamity
from every side of them,
declares the Lord.
³³ Hazor shall become a haunt
of jackals,
an everlasting waste;
no man shall dwell there;
no man shall sojourn in her."

JUDGEMENT ON ELAM

³⁴The word of the Lord that came to Jeremiah the prophet concerning Elam, in the beginning of the reign of Zedekiah king of Judah.

³⁵Thus says the Lord of hosts: "Behold, I will break the bow of Elam, the mainstay of their might. ³⁶And I will bring upon Elam the four winds from the four quarters of heaven. And I will scatter them to all those winds, and there shall be no nation to which those driven out of Elam shall not come. ³⁷I will terrify Elam before their enemies and before those who seek their life. I will bring disaster upon them, my fierce anger, declares the Lord. I will send the sword after them, until I have consumed them, ³⁸and I will set my throne in Elam and destroy their king and officials, declares the Lord.

³⁹"But in the latter days I will restore the fortunes of Elam, declares the Lord."

JUDGEMENT ON BABYLON

50 The word that the Lord spoke concerning Babylon, concerning the land of the Chaldeans, by Jeremiah the prophet:

² "Declare among the nations
and proclaim,
set up a banner and proclaim,
conceal it not, and say:
'Babylon is taken,
Bel is put to shame,
Merodach is dismayed.
Her images are put to shame,
her idols are dismayed.'

³"For out of the north a nation has come up against her, which shall make her land a desolation, and none shall dwell in it; both man and beast shall flee away.

⁴"In those days and in that time, declares the Lord, the people of Israel and the people of Judah shall come together, weeping as they come, and they shall seek the Lord their God. ⁵They shall ask the way to Zion, with faces turned towards it, saying, 'Come, let us join ourselves to the Lord in an everlasting covenant that will never be forgotten.'

⁶"My people have been lost sheep. Their shepherds have led them astray, turning them away on the mountains. From mountain to hill they have gone. They have forgotten their fold. ⁷All who found them have devoured them, and their enemies have said, 'We are not guilty, for they have sinned against the Lord, their habitation of righteousness, the Lord, the hope of their fathers.'

⁸"Flee from the midst of Babylon, and go out of the land of the Chaldeans, and be as

male goats before the flock. ⁹For behold, I am stirring up and bringing against Babylon a gathering of great nations, from the north country. And they shall array themselves against her. From there she shall be taken. Their arrows are like a skilled warrior who does not return empty-handed. ¹⁰Chaldea shall be plundered; all who plunder her shall be sated, declares the LORD.

11 "Though you rejoice, though you exult,
    O plunderers of my heritage,
  though you frolic like a heifer
    in the pasture,
    and neigh like stallions,
12 your mother shall be utterly shamed,
    and she who bore you shall
      be disgraced.
  Behold, she shall be the last
    of the nations,
    a wilderness, a dry land, and a desert.
13 Because of the wrath of the LORD
    she shall not be inhabited
  but shall be an utter desolation;
  everyone who passes by Babylon
    shall be appalled,
    and hiss because of all her wounds.
14 Set yourselves in array against
      Babylon all round,
    all you who bend the bow;
  shoot at her, spare no arrows,
    for she has sinned against the LORD.
15 Raise a shout against her all round;
    she has surrendered;
  her bulwarks have fallen;
    her walls are thrown down.
  For this is the vengeance of the LORD:
    take vengeance on her;
    do to her as she has done.
16 Cut off from Babylon the sower,
    and the one who handles the
      sickle in time of harvest;
  because of the sword of the oppressor,
    every one shall turn to
      his own people,
    and every one shall flee
      to his own land.

¹⁷"Israel is a hunted sheep driven away by lions. First the king of Assyria devoured him, and now at last Nebuchadnezzar king of Babylon has gnawed his bones. ¹⁸Therefore, thus says the LORD of hosts, the God of Israel: Behold, I am bringing punishment on the king of Babylon and his land, as I punished the king of Assyria. ¹⁹I will restore Israel to his pasture, and he shall feed on Carmel and in Bashan, and his desire shall be satisfied on the hills of Ephraim and in Gilead. ²⁰In those days and in that time, declares the LORD, iniquity shall be sought in Israel, and there shall be none, and sin in Judah, and none shall be found, for I will pardon those whom I leave as a remnant.

21 "Go up against the land of Merathaim,ᵃ
      and against the inhabitants
        of Pekod.ᵇ
    Kill, and devote them to destruction,ᶜ
            declares the LORD,
      and do all that I have
        commanded you.
22 The noise of battle is in the land,
      and great destruction!
23 How the hammer of the whole earth
      is cut down and broken!
    How Babylon has become
      a horror among the nations!
24 I set a snare for you and you
      were taken, O Babylon,
      and you did not know it;
    you were found and caught,
      because you opposed the LORD.
25 The LORD has opened his armoury
      and brought out the weapons
        of his wrath,
    for the Lord GOD of hosts
      has a work to do
      in the land of the Chaldeans.
26 Come against her from every quarter;
      open her granaries;
    pile her up like heaps of grain, and
      devote her to destruction;
      let nothing be left of her.
27 Kill all her bulls;
      let them go down to the slaughter.
    Woe to them, for their day has come,
      the time of their punishment.

²⁸"A voice! They flee and escape from the land of Babylon, to declare in Zion the vengeance of the LORD our God, vengeance for his temple.

²⁹"Summon archers against Babylon, all those who bend the bow. Encamp round her; let no one escape. Repay her according to her deeds; do to her according to all that she has done. For she has proudly defied the LORD, the Holy One of Israel. ³⁰Therefore her

---
ᵃ*Merathaim* means *double rebellion* ᵇ*Pekod* means *punishment*
ᶜThat is, set apart (devote) as an offering to the Lord (for destruction)

young men shall fall in her squares, and all her soldiers shall be destroyed on that day, declares the LORD.

31 "Behold, I am against you, O proud one,
    declares the Lord GOD of hosts,
for your day has come,
    the time when I will punish you.
32 The proud one shall stumble and fall,
    with none to raise him up,
and I will kindle a fire in his cities,
    and it will devour all that
        is round him.

33 "Thus says the LORD of hosts: The people of Israel are oppressed, and the people of Judah with them. All who took them captive have held them fast; they refuse to let them go. 34 Their Redeemer is strong; the LORD of hosts is his name. He will surely plead their cause, that he may give rest to the earth, but unrest to the inhabitants of Babylon.

35 "A sword against the Chaldeans,
    declares the LORD,
and against the inhabitants
    of Babylon,
and against her officials
    and her wise men!
36 A sword against the diviners,
    that they may become fools!
A sword against her warriors,
    that they may be destroyed!
37 A sword against her horses and
    against her chariots,
and against all the foreign
    troops in her midst,
    that they may become women!
A sword against all her treasures,
    that they may be plundered!
38 A drought against her waters,
    that they may be dried up!
For it is a land of images,
    and they are mad over idols.

39 "Therefore wild beasts shall dwell with hyenas in Babylon,[a] and ostriches shall dwell in her. She shall never again have people, nor be inhabited for all generations. 40 As when God overthrew Sodom and Gomorrah and their neighbouring cities, declares the LORD, so no man shall dwell there, and no son of man shall sojourn in her.

41 "Behold, a people comes from the north;
    a mighty nation and many kings
    are stirring from the farthest
        parts of the earth.
42 They lay hold of bow and spear;
    they are cruel and have no mercy.
The sound of them is like the
    roaring of the sea;
they ride on horses,
arrayed as a man for battle
    against you, O daughter of Babylon!

43 "The king of Babylon heard
    the report of them,
    and his hands fell helpless;
anguish seized him,
    pain as of a woman in labour.

44 "Behold, like a lion coming up from the thicket of the Jordan against a perennial pasture, I will suddenly make them run away from her, and I will appoint over her whomever I choose. For who is like me? Who will summon me? What shepherd can stand before me? 45 Therefore hear the plan that the LORD has made against Babylon, and the purposes that he has formed against the land of the Chaldeans: Surely the little ones of their flock shall be dragged away; surely their fold shall be appalled at their fate. 46 At the sound of the capture of Babylon the earth shall tremble, and her cry shall be heard among the nations."

THE UTTER DESTRUCTION OF BABYLON

51 Thus says the LORD:
"Behold, I will stir up the spirit
    of a destroyer
against Babylon,
against the inhabitants
    of Leb-kamai,[b]
2 and I will send to Babylon winnowers,
    and they shall winnow her,
and they shall empty her land,
    when they come against
        her from every side
    on the day of trouble.
3 Let not the archer bend his bow,
    and let him not stand up
        in his armour.
Spare not her young men;
    devote to destruction[c] all her army.
4 They shall fall down slain in the
    land of the Chaldeans,
    and wounded in her streets.

---

[a] Hebrew lacks *in Babylon* [b] A code name for Chaldea [c] That is, set apart (devote) as an offering to the Lord (for destruction)

⁵ For Israel and Judah have
    not been forsaken
by their God, the Lord of hosts,
but the land of the Chaldeans*ᵃ*
    is full of guilt
against the Holy One of Israel.

⁶ "Flee from the midst of Babylon;
    let every one save his life!
Be not cut off in her punishment,
    for this is the time of the
        Lord's vengeance,
the repayment he is rendering her.
⁷ Babylon was a golden cup in
    the Lord's hand,
making all the earth drunken;
the nations drank of her wine;
    therefore the nations went mad.
⁸ Suddenly Babylon has fallen
    and been broken;
        wail for her!
Take balm for her pain;
    perhaps she may be healed.
⁹ We would have healed Babylon,
    but she was not healed.
Forsake her, and let us go
    each to his own country,
for her judgement has
    reached up to heaven
    and has been lifted up
        even to the skies.
¹⁰ The Lord has brought about
    our vindication;
come, let us declare in Zion
    the work of the Lord our God.

¹¹ "Sharpen the arrows!
    Take up the shields!

The Lord has stirred up the spirit of the kings of the Medes, because his purpose concerning Babylon is to destroy it, for that is the vengeance of the Lord, the vengeance for his temple.

¹² "Set up a standard against the
    walls of Babylon;
    make the watch strong;
set up watchmen;
    prepare the ambushes;
for the Lord has both
    planned and done
what he spoke concerning the
    inhabitants of Babylon.
¹³ O you who dwell by many waters,
    rich in treasures,
your end has come;
    the thread of your life is cut.
¹⁴ The Lord of hosts has
    sworn by himself:
Surely I will fill you with men,
    as many as locusts,
    and they shall raise the shout
        of victory over you.

¹⁵ "It is he who made the earth
    by his power,
who established the world
    by his wisdom,
and by his understanding
    stretched out the heavens.
¹⁶ When he utters his voice there is a
    tumult of waters in the heavens,
and he makes the mist rise from
    the ends of the earth.
He makes lightning for the rain,
    and he brings forth the wind
        from his storehouses.
¹⁷ Every man is stupid and
    without knowledge;
every goldsmith is put to
    shame by his idols,
for his images are false,
    and there is no breath in them.
¹⁸ They are worthless, a work of
    delusion;
at the time of their punishment
    they shall perish.
¹⁹ Not like these is he who is
    the portion of Jacob,
for he is the one who
    formed all things,
and Israel is the tribe of
    his inheritance;
    the Lord of hosts is his name.

²⁰ "You are my hammer and
    weapon of war:
with you I break nations in pieces;
    with you I destroy kingdoms;
²¹ with you I break in pieces the
    horse and his rider;
with you I break in pieces the
    chariot and the charioteer;
²² with you I break in pieces
    man and woman;
with you I break in pieces the
    old man and the youth;
with you I break in pieces the young
    man and the young woman;

ᵃ Hebrew *their land*

²³ with you I break in pieces the
 shepherd and his flock;
 with you I break in pieces the
 farmer and his team;
 with you I break in pieces
 governors and commanders.

²⁴ "I will repay Babylon and all the inhabitants of Chaldea before your very eyes for all the evil that they have done in Zion, declares the LORD.

²⁵ "Behold, I am against you, O
 destroying mountain,
 declares the LORD,
 which destroys the whole earth;
 I will stretch out my hand against you,
 and roll you down from the crags,
 and make you a burnt mountain.
²⁶ No stone shall be taken from
 you for a corner
 and no stone for a foundation,
 but you shall be a perpetual waste,
 declares the LORD.

²⁷ "Set up a standard on the earth;
 blow the trumpet among
 the nations;
 prepare the nations for
 war against her;
 summon against her the kingdoms,
 Ararat, Minni, and Ashkenaz;
 appoint a marshal against her;
 bring up horses like
 bristling locusts.
²⁸ Prepare the nations for
 war against her,
 the kings of the Medes, with their
 governors and deputies,
 and every land under
 their dominion.
²⁹ The land trembles and writhes in pain,
 for the LORD's purposes
 against Babylon stand,
 to make the land of Babylon
 a desolation,
 without inhabitant.
³⁰ The warriors of Babylon have
 ceased fighting;
 they remain in their strongholds;
 their strength has failed;
 they have become women;
 her dwellings are on fire;
 her bars are broken.
³¹ One runner runs to meet another,
 and one messenger to meet another,
 to tell the king of Babylon
 that his city is taken on every side;
³² the fords have been seized,
 the marshes are burned with fire,
 and the soldiers are in panic.
³³ For thus says the LORD of hosts,
 the God of Israel:
 The daughter of Babylon is
 like a threshing floor
 at the time when it is trodden;
 yet a little while
 and the time of her harvest will come."

³⁴ "Nebuchadnezzar the king of
 Babylon has devoured me;
 he has crushed me;
 he has made me an empty vessel;
 he has swallowed me like a monster;
 he has filled his stomach
 with my delicacies;
 he has rinsed me out.^a
³⁵ The violence done to me and to my
 kinsmen be upon Babylon,"
 let the inhabitant of Zion say.
 "My blood be upon the
 inhabitants of Chaldea,"
 let Jerusalem say.
³⁶ Therefore thus says the LORD:
 "Behold, I will plead your cause
 and take vengeance for you.
 I will dry up her sea
 and make her fountain dry,
³⁷ and Babylon shall become
 a heap of ruins,
 the haunt of jackals,
 a horror and a hissing,
 without inhabitant.

³⁸ "They shall roar together like lions;
 they shall growl like lions' cubs.
³⁹ While they are inflamed I will
 prepare them a feast
 and make them drunk, that
 they may become merry,
 then sleep a perpetual sleep
 and not wake, declares the LORD.
⁴⁰ I will bring them down like
 lambs to the slaughter,
 like rams and male goats.

⁴¹ "How Babylon^b is taken,
 the praise of the whole earth seized!
 How Babylon has become
 a horror among the nations!

---

^aOr he has expelled me   ^bHebrew Sheshach, a code name for Babylon

42 The sea has come up on Babylon;
	she is covered with its
		tumultuous waves.
43 Her cities have become a horror,
	a land of drought and a desert,
	a land in which no one dwells,
	and through which no son
		of man passes.
44 And I will punish Bel in Babylon,
	and take out of his mouth what
		he has swallowed.
   The nations shall no longer
		flow to him;
	the wall of Babylon has fallen.

45 "Go out of the midst of her, my people!
	Let every one save his life
	from the fierce anger of the LORD!
46 Let not your heart faint,
	and be not fearful
	at the report heard in the land,
   when a report comes in one year
	and afterwards a report
		in another year,
   and violence is in the land,
	and ruler is against ruler.

47 "Therefore, behold, the days
		are coming
	when I will punish the
		images of Babylon;
   her whole land shall be put to shame,
	and all her slain shall fall
		in the midst of her.
48 Then the heavens and the earth,
	and all that is in them,
   shall sing for joy over Babylon,
	for the destroyers shall come
		against them out of the north,
			declares the LORD.
49 Babylon must fall for the
		slain of Israel,
	just as for Babylon have fallen
		the slain of all the earth.

50 "You who have escaped from the sword,
		go, do not stand still!
	Remember the LORD from far away,
	and let Jerusalem come
		into your mind:
51 'We are put to shame, for we
		have heard reproach;
	dishonour has covered our face,
	for foreigners have come
		into the holy places of the
			LORD's house.'

52 "Therefore, behold, the days are
		coming, declares the LORD,
	when I will execute judgement
		upon her images,
	and through all her land
		the wounded shall groan.
53 Though Babylon should
		mount up to heaven,
	and though she should fortify
		her strong height,
   yet destroyers would come
		from me against her,
			declares the LORD.

54 "A voice! A cry from Babylon!
	The noise of great destruction from
		the land of the Chaldeans!
55 For the LORD is laying Babylon waste
	and stilling her mighty voice.
   Their waves roar like many waters;
	the noise of their voice is raised,
56 for a destroyer has come upon her,
		upon Babylon;
	her warriors are taken;
		their bows are broken in pieces,
   for the LORD is a God of recompense;
		he will surely repay.
57 I will make drunk her officials
		and her wise men,
	her governors, her commanders,
		and her warriors;
   they shall sleep a perpetual
		sleep and not wake,
	declares the King, whose name
		is the LORD of hosts.

58 "Thus says the LORD of hosts:
   The broad wall of Babylon
		shall be levelled to the ground,
	and her high gates
		shall be burned with fire.
   The peoples labour for nothing,
	and the nations weary
		themselves only for fire."

59 The word that Jeremiah the prophet commanded Seraiah the son of Neriah, son of Mahseiah, when he went with Zedekiah king of Judah to Babylon, in the fourth year of his reign. Seraiah was the quartermaster. 60 Jeremiah wrote in a book all the disaster that should come upon Babylon, all these words that are written concerning Babylon. 61 And Jeremiah said to Seraiah: "When you come to Babylon, see that you read all these words, 62 and say, 'O LORD, you have said concerning

this place that you will cut it off, so that nothing shall dwell in it, neither man nor beast, and it shall be desolate for ever.' ⁶³When you finish reading this book, tie a stone to it and cast it into the midst of the Euphrates, ⁶⁴and say, 'Thus shall Babylon sink, to rise no more, because of the disaster that I am bringing upon her, and they shall become exhausted.'"

Thus far are the words of Jeremiah.

THE FALL OF JERUSALEM RECOUNTED

52 Zedekiah was twenty-one years old when he became king, and he reigned eleven years in Jerusalem. His mother's name was Hamutal the daughter of Jeremiah of Libnah. ²And he did what was evil in the sight of the LORD, according to all that Jehoiakim had done. ³For because of the anger of the LORD it came to the point in Jerusalem and Judah that he cast them out from his presence.

And Zedekiah rebelled against the king of Babylon. ⁴And in the ninth year of his reign, in the tenth month, on the tenth day of the month, Nebuchadnezzar king of Babylon came with all his army against Jerusalem, and laid siege to it. And they built siege works all round it. ⁵So the city was besieged till the eleventh year of King Zedekiah. ⁶On the ninth day of the fourth month the famine was so severe in the city that there was no food for the people of the land. ⁷Then a breach was made in the city, and all the men of war fled and went out from the city by night by the way of a gate between the two walls, by the king's garden, and the Chaldeans were round the city. And they went in the direction of the Arabah. ⁸But the army of the Chaldeans pursued the king and overtook Zedekiah in the plains of Jericho, and all his army was scattered from him. ⁹Then they captured the king and brought him up to the king of Babylon at Riblah in the land of Hamath, and he passed sentence on him. ¹⁰The king of Babylon slaughtered the sons of Zedekiah before his eyes, and also slaughtered all the officials of Judah at Riblah. ¹¹He put out the eyes of Zedekiah, and bound him in chains, and the king of Babylon took him to Babylon, and put him in prison till the day of his death.

THE TEMPLE BURNED

¹²In the fifth month, on the tenth day of the month—that was the nineteenth year of King Nebuchadnezzar, king of Babylon—Nebuzaradan the captain of the bodyguard, who served the king of Babylon, entered Jerusalem. ¹³And he burned the house of the LORD, and the king's house and all the houses of Jerusalem; every great house he burned down. ¹⁴And all the army of the Chaldeans, who were with the captain of the guard, broke down all the walls round Jerusalem. ¹⁵And Nebuzaradan the captain of the guard carried away captive some of the poorest of the people and the rest of the people who were left in the city and the deserters who had deserted to the king of Babylon, together with the rest of the artisans. ¹⁶But Nebuzaradan the captain of the guard left some of the poorest of the land to be vine dressers and ploughmen.

¹⁷And the pillars of bronze that were in the house of the LORD, and the stands and the bronze sea that were in the house of the LORD, the Chaldeans broke in pieces, and carried all the bronze to Babylon. ¹⁸And they took away the pots and the shovels and the snuffers and the basins and the dishes for incense and all the vessels of bronze used in the temple service; ¹⁹also the small bowls and the firepans and the basins and the pots and the lampstands and the dishes for incense and the bowls for drink offerings. What was of gold the captain of the guard took away as gold, and what was of silver, as silver. ²⁰As for the two pillars, the one sea, the twelve bronze bulls that were under the sea,[a] and the stands, which Solomon the king had made for the house of the LORD, the bronze of all these things was beyond weight. ²¹As for the pillars, the height of one pillar was eighteen cubits,[b] its circumference was twelve cubits, and its thickness was four fingers, and it was hollow. ²²On it was a capital of bronze. The height of the capital was five cubits. A network and pomegranates, all of bronze, were round the capital. And the second pillar had the same, with pomegranates. ²³There were ninety-six pomegranates on the sides; all the pomegranates were a hundred upon the network all round.

THE PEOPLE EXILED TO BABYLON

²⁴And the captain of the guard took Seraiah the chief priest, and Zephaniah the second priest and the three keepers of the threshold; ²⁵and from the city he took an officer who had been in command of the men of war, and seven men of the king's council, who were found in the city; and the secretary of the

---

[a]Hebrew lacks *the sea* [b]A *cubit* was about 18 inches or 45 centimetres

JEREMIAH 52

commander of the army, who mustered the people of the land; and sixty men of the people of the land, who were found in the midst of the city. ²⁶And Nebuzaradan the captain of the guard took them and brought them to the king of Babylon at Riblah. ²⁷And the king of Babylon struck them down and put them to death at Riblah in the land of Hamath. So Judah was taken into exile out of its land.

²⁸This is the number of the people whom Nebuchadnezzar carried away captive: in the seventh year, 3,023 Judeans; ²⁹in the eighteenth year of Nebuchadnezzar he carried away captive from Jerusalem 832 persons; ³⁰in the twenty-third year of Nebuchadnezzar, Nebuzaradan the captain of the guard carried away captive of the Judeans 745 persons; all the persons were 4,600.

JEHOIACHIN RELEASED FROM PRISON

³¹And in the thirty-seventh year of the exile of Jehoiachin king of Judah, in the twelfth month, on the twenty-fifth day of the month, Evil-merodach king of Babylon, in the year that he began to reign, graciously freed[a] Jehoiachin king of Judah and brought him out of prison. ³²And he spoke kindly to him and gave him a seat above the seats of the kings who were with him in Babylon. ³³So Jehoiachin put off his prison garments. And every day of his life he dined regularly at the king's table, ³⁴and for his allowance, a regular allowance was given him by the king, according to his daily needs, until the day of his death, as long as he lived.

---

[a] Hebrew *reign, lifted up the head of*

LAMENTATIONS

HOW LONELY SITS THE CITY

1 How lonely sits the city
  that was full of people!
 How like a widow has she become,
  she who was great among
      the nations!
 She who was a princess
  among the provinces
   has become a slave.

2 She weeps bitterly in the night,
  with tears on her cheeks;
 among all her lovers
  she has none to comfort her;
 all her friends have dealt
  treacherously with her;
  they have become her enemies.

3 Judah has gone into exile
   because of affliction[a]
   and hard servitude;
 she dwells now among the
     nations,
  but finds no resting-place;
 her pursuers have all overtaken her
  in the midst of her distress.[b]

4 The roads to Zion mourn,
  for none come to the festival;
 all her gates are desolate;
  her priests groan;
 her virgins have been afflicted,[c]
  and she herself suffers bitterly.

5 Her foes have become the head;
  her enemies prosper,
 because the LORD has afflicted her
  for the multitude of her
      transgressions;
 her children have gone away,
  captives before the foe.

6 From the daughter of Zion
  all her majesty has departed.
 Her princes have become like deer
  that find no pasture;
 they fled without strength
  before the pursuer.

7 Jerusalem remembers
  in the days of her affliction
   and wandering
 all the precious things
  that were hers from days of old.
 When her people fell into
   the hand of the foe,
  and there was none to help her,
 her foes gloated over her;
  they mocked at her downfall.

8 Jerusalem sinned grievously;
  therefore she became filthy;
 all who honoured her despise her,
  for they have seen her nakedness;
 she herself groans
  and turns her face away.

9 Her uncleanness was in her skirts;
  she took no thought of her future;[d]
 therefore her fall is terrible;
  she has no comforter.
 "O LORD, behold my affliction,
  for the enemy has triumphed!"

10 The enemy has stretched out his hands
   over all her precious things;
  for she has seen the nations
   enter her sanctuary,
  those whom you forbade
   to enter your congregation.

11 All her people groan
    as they search for bread;
   they trade their treasures for food
    to revive their strength.
  "Look, O LORD, and see,
    for I am despised."

12 "Is it nothing to you, all you who pass by?
    Look and see
   if there is any sorrow like my sorrow,
    which was brought upon me,
   which the LORD inflicted
    on the day of his fierce anger.

---

[a]Or *under affliction* [b]Or *in the narrow passes* [c]Septuagint, Old Latin *dragged away* [d]Or *end*

13 "From on high he sent fire;
    into my bones[a] he made it descend;
he spread a net for my feet;
    he turned me back;
he has left me stunned,
    faint all the day long.

14 "My transgressions were
        bound[b] into a yoke;
    by his hand they were
        fastened together;
they were set upon my neck;
    he caused my strength to fail;
the Lord gave me into the hands
    of those whom I cannot withstand.

15 "The Lord rejected
    all my mighty men in my midst;
he summoned an assembly against me
    to crush my young men;
the Lord has trodden as in a wine press
    the virgin daughter of Judah.

16 "For these things I weep;
    my eyes flow with tears;
for a comforter is far from me,
    one to revive my spirit;
my children are desolate,
    for the enemy has prevailed."

17 Zion stretches out her hands,
    but there is none to comfort her;
the LORD has commanded against Jacob
    that his neighbours should
        be his foes;
Jerusalem has become
    a filthy thing among them.

18 "The LORD is in the right,
    for I have rebelled against his word;
but hear, all you peoples,
    and see my suffering;
my young women and my young men
    have gone into captivity.

19 "I called to my lovers,
    but they deceived me;
my priests and elders
    perished in the city,
while they sought food
    to revive their strength.

20 "Look, O LORD, for I am in distress;
    my stomach churns;
my heart is wrung within me,
    because I have been very rebellious.
In the street the sword bereaves;
    in the house it is like death.

21 "They heard[c] my groaning,
    yet there is no one to comfort me.
All my enemies have heard
    of my trouble;
they are glad that you have done it.
You have brought[d] the day
    you announced;
now let them be as I am.

22 "Let all their evildoing come before you,
    and deal with them
as you have dealt with me
    because of all my transgressions;
for my groans are many,
    and my heart is faint."

THE LORD HAS DESTROYED WITHOUT PITY

2 How the Lord in his anger
    has set the daughter of Zion under
        a cloud!
He has cast down from heaven to earth
    the splendour of Israel;
he has not remembered his footstool
    in the day of his anger.

2 The Lord has swallowed up
        without mercy
    all the habitations of Jacob;
in his wrath he has broken down
    the strongholds of the
        daughter of Judah;
he has brought down to the
    ground in dishonour
    the kingdom and its rulers.

3 He has cut down in fierce anger
    all the might of Israel;
he has withdrawn from them
    his right hand
    in the face of the enemy;
he has burned like a flaming
    fire in Jacob,
    consuming all round.

4 He has bent his bow like an enemy,
    with his right hand set like a foe;
and he has killed all who were
    delightful in our eyes
    in the tent of the daughter of Zion;
he has poured out his fury like fire.

---

[a]Septuagint; Hebrew *bones and*   [b]The meaning of the Hebrew is uncertain   [c]Septuagint, Syriac *Hear*   [d]Syriac *Bring*

5 The Lord has become like an enemy;
    he has swallowed up Israel;
  he has swallowed up all its palaces;
    he has laid in ruins its strongholds,
  and he has multiplied in the
      daughter of Judah
    mourning and lamentation.

6 He has laid waste his booth
      like a garden,
    laid in ruins his meeting place;
  the LORD has made Zion forget
      festival and Sabbath,
  and in his fierce indignation has
    spurned king and priest.

7 The Lord has scorned his altar,
    disowned his sanctuary;
  he has delivered into the
      hand of the enemy
    the walls of her palaces;
  they raised a clamour in the
      house of the LORD
    as on the day of festival.

8 The LORD determined to lay in ruins
    the wall of the daughter of Zion;
  he stretched out the measuring line;
    he did not restrain his hand
      from destroying;
  he caused rampart and wall to lament;
    they languished together.

9 Her gates have sunk into the ground;
    he has ruined and broken her bars;
  her king and princes are
      among the nations;
    the law is no more,
  and her prophets find
    no vision from the LORD.

10 The elders of the daughter of Zion
      sit on the ground in silence;
    they have thrown dust on their heads
      and put on sackcloth;
    the young women of Jerusalem
      have bowed their heads
        to the ground.

11 My eyes are spent with weeping;
      my stomach churns;
    my bile is poured out to the ground
      because of the destruction of the
        daughter of my people,
    because infants and babies faint
      in the streets of the city.

12 They cry to their mothers,
      "Where is bread and wine?"
    as they faint like a wounded man
      in the streets of the city,
    as their life is poured out
      on their mothers' bosom.

13 What can I say for you, to
      what compare you,
    O daughter of Jerusalem?
  What can I liken to you, that
      I may comfort you,
    O virgin daughter of Zion?
  For your ruin is vast as the sea;
    who can heal you?

14 Your prophets have seen for you
      false and deceptive visions;
    they have not exposed your iniquity
      to restore your fortunes,
    but have seen for you oracles
      that are false and misleading.

15 All who pass along the way
      clap their hands at you;
    they hiss and wag their heads
      at the daughter of Jerusalem:
    "Is this the city that was called
      the perfection of beauty,
      the joy of all the earth?"

16 All your enemies
      rail against you;
    they hiss, they gnash their teeth,
      they cry: "We have swallowed her!
    Ah, this is the day we longed for;
      now we have it; we see it!"

17 The LORD has done what he purposed;
      he has carried out his word,
    which he commanded long ago;
      he has thrown down without pity;
    he has made the enemy
        rejoice over you
      and exalted the might of your foes.

18 Their heart cried to the Lord.
    O wall of the daughter of Zion,
  let tears stream down like a torrent
      day and night!
  Give yourself no rest,
    your eyes no respite!

19 "Arise, cry out in the night,
    at the beginning of the
      night watches!

    Pour out your heart like water
        before the presence of the Lord!
    Lift your hands to him
        for the lives of your children,
    who faint for hunger
        at the head of every street."

20 Look, O Lord, and see!
        With whom have you dealt thus?
    Should women eat the fruit
            of their womb,
        the children of their tender care?
    Should priest and prophet be killed
        in the sanctuary of the Lord?

21 In the dust of the streets
        lie the young and the old;
    my young women and my young men
        have fallen by the sword;
    you have killed them in the
            day of your anger,
        slaughtering without pity.

22 You summoned as if to a festival day
        my terrors on every side,
    and on the day of the anger of
            the Lord
        no one escaped or survived;
    those whom I held and raised
        my enemy destroyed.

GREAT IS YOUR FAITHFULNESS

3 I am the man who has seen affliction
        under the rod of his wrath;
²he has driven and brought me
        into darkness without any light;
³ surely against me he turns his hand
        again and again the whole
            day long.

⁴ He has made my flesh and
        my skin waste away;
    he has broken my bones;
⁵ he has besieged and enveloped me
        with bitterness and tribulation;
⁶ he has made me dwell in darkness
        like the dead of long ago.

⁷ He has walled me about so
            that I cannot escape;
    he has made my chains heavy;
⁸ though I call and cry for help,
        he shuts out my prayer;
⁹ he has blocked my ways with
            blocks of stones;
    he has made my paths crooked.

10 He is a bear lying in wait for me,
        a lion in hiding;
11 he turned aside my steps and
            tore me to pieces;
        he has made me desolate;
12 he bent his bow and set me
        as a target for his arrow.

13 He drove into my kidneys
        the arrows of his quiver;
14 I have become the laughing-
            stock of all peoples,
        the object of their taunts
            all day long.
15 He has filled me with bitterness;
        he has sated me with wormwood.

16 He has made my teeth grind on gravel,
        and made me cower in ashes;
17 my soul is bereft of peace;
        I have forgotten what
            happiness*ᵃ* is;
18 so I say, "My endurance has perished;
        so has my hope from the Lord."

19 Remember my affliction and
            my wanderings,
        the wormwood and the gall!
20 My soul continually remembers it
        and is bowed down within me.
21 But this I call to mind,
        and therefore I have hope:

22 The steadfast love of the
            Lord never ceases;*ᵇ*
        his mercies never come to an end;
23 they are new every morning;
        great is your faithfulness.
24 "The Lord is my portion," says my soul,
        "therefore I will hope in him."

25 The Lord is good to those
            who wait for him,
        to the soul who seeks him.
26 It is good that one should wait quietly
        for the salvation of the Lord.
27 It is good for a man that he bear
        the yoke in his youth.

28 Let him sit alone in silence
        when it is laid on him;
29 let him put his mouth in the dust—
        there may yet be hope;

---

*ᵃ*Hebrew *good* *ᵇ*Syriac, Targum; Hebrew *Because of the steadfast love of the* Lord, *we are not cut off*

30 let him give his cheek to the
     one who strikes,
   and let him be filled with insults.

31 For the Lord will not
     cast off for ever,
32 but, though he cause grief, he
     will have compassion
   according to the abundance
     of his steadfast love;
33 for he does not afflict from his heart
     or grieve the children of men.

34 To crush underfoot
     all the prisoners of the earth,
35 to deny a man justice
     in the presence of the Most High,
36 to subvert a man in his lawsuit,
     the Lord does not approve.

37 Who has spoken and it came to pass,
     unless the Lord has commanded it?
38 Is it not from the mouth
     of the Most High
   that good and bad come?
39 Why should a living man complain,
     a man, about the punishment
     of his sins?

40 Let us test and examine our ways,
     and return to the LORD!
41 Let us lift up our hearts and hands
     to God in heaven:
42 "We have transgressed and rebelled,
     and you have not forgiven.

43 "You have wrapped yourself with
     anger and pursued us,
     killing without pity;
44 you have wrapped yourself with a cloud
     so that no prayer can pass through.
45 You have made us filth and rubbish
     among the peoples.

46 "All our enemies
     open their mouths against us;
47 panic and pitfall have come upon us,
     devastation and destruction;
48 my eyes flow with rivers of tears
     because of the destruction of the
     daughter of my people.

49 "My eyes will flow without ceasing,
     without respite,
50 until the LORD from heaven
     looks down and sees;
51 my eyes cause me grief
     at the fate of all the daughters
     of my city.

52 "I have been hunted like a bird
     by those who were my enemies
     without cause;
53 they flung me alive into the pit
     and cast stones on me;
54 water closed over my head;
     I said, 'I am lost.'

55 "I called on your name, O LORD,
     from the depths of the pit;
56 you heard my plea, 'Do not close
     your ear to my cry for help!'
57 You came near when I called on you;
     you said, 'Do not fear!'

58 "You have taken up my cause, O Lord;
     you have redeemed my life.
59 You have seen the wrong
     done to me, O LORD;
     judge my cause.
60 You have seen all their vengeance,
     all their plots against me.

61 "You have heard their taunts, O LORD,
     all their plots against me.
62 The lips and thoughts of my assailants
     are against me all the day long.
63 Behold their sitting and their rising;
     I am the object of their taunts.

64 "You will repay them,[a] O LORD,
     according to the work of
     their hands.
65 You will give them[b] dullness of heart;
     your curse will be[c] on them.
66 You will pursue them[d] in anger
     and destroy them
     from under your heavens, O LORD."[e]

THE HOLY STONES LIE SCATTERED

4 How the gold has grown dim,
    how the pure gold is changed!
    The holy stones lie scattered
    at the head of every street.

2 The precious sons of Zion,
     worth their weight in fine gold,
   how they are regarded as earthen pots,
     the work of a potter's hands!

---

[a]Or *Repay them* [b]Or *Give them* [c]Or *place your curse* [d]Or *Pursue them*
[e]Syriac (compare Septuagint, Vulgate); Hebrew *the heavens of the LORD*

3   Even jackals offer the breast;
       they nurse their young;
    but the daughter of my people
          has become cruel,
       like the ostriches in the wilderness.

4   The tongue of the nursing infant sticks
       to the roof of its mouth for thirst;
    the children beg for food,
       but no one gives to them.

5   Those who once feasted on delicacies
       perish in the streets;
    those who were brought up in purple
       embrace ash heaps.

6   For the chastisement[a] of the daughter
          of my people has been greater
       than the punishment[b] of Sodom,
    which was overthrown in a moment,
       and no hands were wrung for her.[c]

7   Her princes were purer than snow,
       whiter than milk;
    their bodies were more
          ruddy than coral,
       the beauty of their form[d]
          was like sapphire.[e]

8   Now their face is blacker than soot;
       they are not recognized in the streets;
    their skin has shrivelled
          on their bones;
       it has become as dry as wood.

9   Happier were the victims of the sword
       than the victims of hunger,
    who wasted away, pierced
       by lack of the fruits of the field.

10 The hands of compassionate women
       have boiled their own children;
    they became their food
       during the destruction of the
          daughter of my people.

11 The LORD gave full vent to his wrath;
       he poured out his hot anger,
    and he kindled a fire in Zion
       that consumed its foundations.

12 The kings of the earth did not believe,
       nor any of the inhabitants
          of the world,
    that foe or enemy could enter
       the gates of Jerusalem.

13 This was for the sins of her prophets
       and the iniquities of her priests,
    who shed in the midst of her
       the blood of the righteous.

14 They wandered, blind,
       through the streets;
    they were so defiled with blood
    that no one was able to touch
       their garments.

15 "Away! Unclean!" people cried at them.
       "Away! Away! Do not touch!"
    So they became fugitives
       and wanderers;
       people said among the nations,
    "They shall stay with us no longer."

16 The LORD himself[f] has scattered
          them;
       he will regard them no more;
    no honour was shown to the priests,
       no favour to the elders.

17 Our eyes failed, ever watching
       vainly for help;
    in our watching we watched
       for a nation which could not save.

18 They dogged our steps
       so that we could not walk
          in our streets;
    our end drew near; our days
       were numbered,
       for our end had come.

19 Our pursuers were swifter
       than the eagles in the heavens;
    they chased us on the mountains;
       they lay in wait for us in
          the wilderness.

20 The breath of our nostrils,
       the LORD's anointed,
    was captured in their pits,
    of whom we said, "Under his shadow
       we shall live among the nations."

21 Rejoice and be glad, O
          daughter of Edom,
       you who dwell in the land of Uz;
    but to you also the cup shall pass;

---

[a]Or *iniquity* [b]Or *sin* [c]The meaning of the Hebrew is uncertain [d]The meaning of the Hebrew is uncertain [e]Hebrew *lapis lazuli* [f]Hebrew *The face of the LORD*

you shall become drunk and
   strip yourself bare.

22 The punishment of your
   iniquity, O daughter of
   Zion, is accomplished;
   he will keep you in exile no longer;[a]
   but your iniquity, O daughter of
   Edom, he will punish;
   he will uncover your sins.

RESTORE US TO YOURSELF, O LORD

5 Remember, O LORD, what has
   befallen us;
   look, and see our disgrace!
2 Our inheritance has been turned
   over to strangers,
   our homes to foreigners.
3 We have become orphans, fatherless;
   our mothers are like widows.
4 We must pay for the water we drink;
   the wood we get must be bought.
5 Our pursuers are at our necks;
   we are weary; we are given no rest.
6 We have given the hand to
   Egypt, and to Assyria,
   to get bread enough.
7 Our fathers sinned, and are no more;
   and we bear their iniquities.
8 Slaves rule over us;
   there is none to deliver us
   from their hand.
9 We get our bread at the
   peril of our lives,
   because of the sword in
   the wilderness.
10 Our skin is hot as an oven
   with the burning heat of famine.
11 Women are raped in Zion,
   young women in the towns of Judah.
12 Princes are hung up by their hands;
   no respect is shown to the elders.
13 Young men are compelled
   to grind at the mill,
   and boys stagger under
   loads of wood.
14 The old men have left the city gate,
   the young men their music.
15 The joy of our hearts has ceased;
   our dancing has been turned
   to mourning.
16 The crown has fallen from our head;
   woe to us, for we have sinned!
17 For this our heart has become sick,
   for these things our eyes
   have grown dim,
18 for Mount Zion which lies desolate;
   jackals prowl over it.
19 But you, O LORD, reign for ever;
   your throne endures to
   all generations.
20 Why do you forget us for ever,
   why do you forsake us for
   so many days?
21 Restore us to yourself, O LORD,
   that we may be restored!
   Renew our days as of old —
22 unless you have utterly rejected us,
   and you remain exceedingly
   angry with us.

---

[a] Or he will not exile you again

EZEKIEL

EZEKIEL IN BABYLON

1 In the thirtieth year, in the fourth month, on the fifth day of the month, as I was among the exiles by the Chebar canal, the heavens were opened, and I saw visions of God.[a] ²On the fifth day of the month (it was the fifth year of the exile of King Jehoiachin), ³the word of the Lord came to Ezekiel the priest, the son of Buzi, in the land of the Chaldeans by the Chebar canal, and the hand of the Lord was upon him there.

THE GLORY OF THE LORD

⁴As I looked, behold, a stormy wind came out of the north, and a great cloud, with brightness round it, and fire flashing forth continually, and in the midst of the fire, as it were gleaming metal.[b] ⁵And from the midst of it came the likeness of four living creatures. And this was their appearance: they had a human likeness, ⁶but each had four faces, and each of them had four wings. ⁷Their legs were straight, and the soles of their feet were like the sole of a calf's foot. And they sparkled like burnished bronze. ⁸Under their wings on their four sides they had human hands. And the four had their faces and their wings thus: ⁹their wings touched one another. Each one of them went straight forward, without turning as they went. ¹⁰As for the likeness of their faces, each had a human face. The four had the face of a lion on the right side, the four had the face of an ox on the left side, and the four had the face of an eagle. ¹¹Such were their faces. And their wings were spread out above. Each creature had two wings, each of which touched the wing of another, while two covered their bodies. ¹²And each went straight forward. Wherever the spirit[c] would go, they went, without turning as they went. ¹³As for the likeness of the living creatures, their appearance was like burning coals of fire, like the appearance of torches moving to and fro among the living creatures. And the fire was bright, and out of the fire went forth lightning. ¹⁴And the living creatures darted to and fro, like the appearance of a flash of lightning.

¹⁵Now as I looked at the living creatures, I saw a wheel on the earth beside the living creatures, one for each of the four of them.[d] ¹⁶As for the appearance of the wheels and their construction: their appearance was like the gleaming of beryl. And the four had the same likeness, their appearance and construction being as it were a wheel within a wheel. ¹⁷When they went, they went in any of their four directions[e] without turning as they went. ¹⁸And their rims were tall and awesome, and the rims of all four were full of eyes all round. ¹⁹And when the living creatures went, the wheels went beside them; and when the living creatures rose from the earth, the wheels rose. ²⁰Wherever the spirit wanted to go, they went, and the wheels rose along with them, for the spirit of the living creatures[f] was in the wheels. ²¹When those went, these went; and when those stood, these stood; and when those rose from the earth, the wheels rose along with them, for the spirit of the living creatures was in the wheels.

²²Over the heads of the living creatures there was the likeness of an expanse, shining like awe-inspiring crystal, spread out above their heads. ²³And under the expanse their wings were stretched out straight, one towards another. And each creature had two wings covering its body. ²⁴And when they went, I heard the sound of their wings like the sound of many waters, like the sound of the Almighty, a sound of tumult like the sound of an army. When they stood still, they let down their wings. ²⁵And there came a voice from above the expanse over their heads. When they stood still, they let down their wings.

²⁶And above the expanse over their heads there was the likeness of a throne, in appearance like sapphire;[g] and seated above the likeness of a throne was a likeness with a human appearance. ²⁷And upwards from

---

[a] Or *from God* [b] Or *amber*; also verse 27 [c] Or *Spirit*; also twice in verse 20 and once in verse 21 [d] Hebrew *of their faces* [e] Hebrew *on their four sides* [f] Or *the spirit of life*; also verse 21 [g] Or *lapis lazuli*

what had the appearance of his waist I saw as it were gleaming metal, like the appearance of fire enclosed all round. And downwards from what had the appearance of his waist I saw as it were the appearance of fire, and there was brightness round him.[a] ²⁸Like the appearance of the bow that is in the cloud on the day of rain, so was the appearance of the brightness all round.

Such was the appearance of the likeness of the glory of the Lord. And when I saw it, I fell on my face, and I heard the voice of one speaking.

EZEKIEL'S CALL

2 And he said to me, "Son of man,[b] stand on your feet, and I will speak with you." ²And as he spoke to me, the Spirit entered into me and set me on my feet, and I heard him speaking to me. ³And he said to me, "Son of man, I send you to the people of Israel, to nations of rebels, who have rebelled against me. They and their fathers have transgressed against me to this very day. ⁴The descendants also are impudent and stubborn: I send you to them, and you shall say to them, 'Thus says the Lord God.' ⁵And whether they hear or refuse to hear (for they are a rebellious house) they will know that a prophet has been among them. ⁶And you, son of man, be not afraid of them, nor be afraid of their words, though briers and thorns are with you and you sit on scorpions.[c] Be not afraid of their words, nor be dismayed at their looks, for they are a rebellious house. ⁷And you shall speak my words to them, whether they hear or refuse to hear, for they are a rebellious house.

⁸"But you, son of man, hear what I say to you. Be not rebellious like that rebellious house; open your mouth and eat what I give you." ⁹And when I looked, behold, a hand was stretched out to me, and behold, a scroll of a book was in it. ¹⁰And he spread it before me. And it had writing on the front and on the back, and there were written on it words of lamentation and mourning and woe.

3 And he said to me, "Son of man, eat whatever you find here. Eat this scroll, and go, speak to the house of Israel." ²So I opened my mouth, and he gave me this scroll to eat. ³And he said to me, "Son of man, feed your belly with this scroll that I give you and fill your stomach with it." Then I ate it, and it was in my mouth as sweet as honey.

⁴And he said to me, "Son of man, go to the house of Israel and speak with my words to them. ⁵For you are not sent to a people of foreign speech and a hard language, but to the house of Israel— ⁶not to many peoples of foreign speech and a hard language, whose words you cannot understand. Surely, if I sent you to such, they would listen to you. ⁷But the house of Israel will not be willing to listen to you, for they are not willing to listen to me: because all the house of Israel have a hard forehead and a stubborn heart. ⁸Behold, I have made your face as hard as their faces, and your forehead as hard as their foreheads. ⁹Like emery harder than flint have I made your forehead. Fear them not, nor be dismayed at their looks, for they are a rebellious house." ¹⁰Moreover, he said to me, "Son of man, all my words that I shall speak to you receive in your heart, and hear with your ears. ¹¹And go to the exiles, to your people, and speak to them and say to them, 'Thus says the Lord God', whether they hear or refuse to hear."

¹²Then the Spirit[d] lifted me up, and I heard behind me the voice[e] of a great earthquake: "Blessed be the glory of the Lord from its place!" ¹³It was the sound of the wings of the living creatures as they touched one another, and the sound of the wheels beside them, and the sound of a great earthquake. ¹⁴The Spirit lifted me up and took me away, and I went in bitterness in the heat of my spirit, the hand of the Lord being strong upon me. ¹⁵And I came to the exiles at Tel-abib, who were dwelling by the Chebar canal, and I sat where they were dwelling.[f] And I sat there overwhelmed among them seven days.

A WATCHMAN FOR ISRAEL

¹⁶And at the end of seven days, the word of the Lord came to me: ¹⁷"Son of man, I have made you a watchman for the house of Israel. Whenever you hear a word from my mouth, you shall give them warning from me. ¹⁸If I say to the wicked, 'You shall surely die', and you give him no warning, nor speak to warn the wicked from his wicked way, in order to save his life, that wicked person shall die for[g] his iniquity, but his blood I will require at your hand. ¹⁹But if you warn the wicked, and he does not turn from his wickedness, or

---

[a]Or it [b]Or Son of Adam; so throughout Ezekiel [c]Or on scorpion plants [d]Or the wind; also verse 14 [e]Or sound [f]Or Chebar, and to where they dwelt [g]Or in; also verses 19, 20

from his wicked way, he shall die for his iniquity, but you will have delivered your soul. ²⁰Again, if a righteous person turns from his righteousness and commits injustice, and I lay a stumbling block before him, he shall die. Because you have not warned him, he shall die for his sin, and his righteous deeds that he has done shall not be remembered, but his blood I will require at your hand. ²¹But if you warn the righteous person not to sin, and he does not sin, he shall surely live, because he took warning, and you will have delivered your soul."

²²And the hand of the Lord was upon me there. And he said to me, "Arise, go out into the valley,*ᵃ* and there I will speak with you." ²³So I arose and went out into the valley, and behold, the glory of the Lord stood there, like the glory that I had seen by the Chebar canal, and I fell on my face. ²⁴But the Spirit entered into me and set me on my feet, and he spoke with me and said to me, "Go, shut yourself within your house. ²⁵And you, O son of man, behold, cords will be placed upon you, and you shall be bound with them, so that you cannot go out among the people. ²⁶And I will make your tongue cling to the roof of your mouth, so that you shall be mute and unable to reprove them, for they are a rebellious house. ²⁷But when I speak with you, I will open your mouth, and you shall say to them, 'Thus says the Lord God.' He who will hear, let him hear; and he who will refuse to hear, let him refuse, for they are a rebellious house.

THE SIEGE OF JERUSALEM SYMBOLIZED

4 "And you, son of man, take a brick and lay it before you, and engrave on it a city, even Jerusalem. ²And put siege works against it, and build a siege wall against it, and cast up a mound against it. Set camps also against it, and plant battering rams against it all round. ³And you, take an iron griddle, and place it as an iron wall between you and the city; and set your face towards it, and let it be in a state of siege, and press the siege against it. This is a sign for the house of Israel.

⁴"Then lie on your left side, and place the punishment*ᵇ* of the house of Israel upon it. For the number of the days that you lie on it, you shall bear their punishment. ⁵For I assign to you a number of days, 390 days, equal to the number of the years of their punishment. So long shall you bear the punishment of the house of Israel. ⁶And when you have completed these, you shall lie down a second time, but on your right side, and bear the punishment of the house of Judah. Forty days I assign you, a day for each year. ⁷And you shall set your face towards the siege of Jerusalem, with your arm bared, and you shall prophesy against the city. ⁸And behold, I will place cords upon you, so that you cannot turn from one side to the other, till you have completed the days of your siege.

⁹"And you, take wheat and barley, beans and lentils, millet and emmer,*ᶜ* and put them into a single vessel and make your bread from them. During the number of days that you lie on your side, 390 days, you shall eat it. ¹⁰And your food that you eat shall be by weight, twenty shekels*ᵈ* a day; from day to day*ᵉ* you shall eat it. ¹¹And water you shall drink by measure, the sixth part of a hin;*ᶠ* from day to day you shall drink. ¹²And you shall eat it as a barley cake, baking it in their sight on human dung." ¹³And the Lord said, "Thus shall the people of Israel eat their bread unclean, among the nations where I will drive them." ¹⁴Then I said, "Ah, Lord God! Behold, I have never defiled myself.*ᵍ* From my youth up till now I have never eaten what died of itself or was torn by beasts, nor has tainted meat come into my mouth." ¹⁵Then he said to me, "See, I assign to you cow's dung instead of human dung, on which you may prepare your bread." ¹⁶Moreover, he said to me, "Son of man, behold, I will break the supply*ʰ* of bread in Jerusalem. They shall eat bread by weight and with anxiety, and they shall drink water by measure and in dismay. ¹⁷I will do this that they may lack bread and water, and look at one another in dismay, and rot away because of their punishment.

JERUSALEM WILL BE DESTROYED

5 "And you, O son of man, take a sharp sword. Use it as a barber's razor and pass it over your head and your beard. Then take balances for weighing and divide the hair. ²A third part you shall burn in the fire in the midst of the city, when the days of the siege are completed. And a third part you shall take and strike with the sword all round the city. And a third part you shall scatter to

---

*ᵃ*Or *plain*; also verse 23   *ᵇ*Or *iniquity*; also verses 5, 6, 17
*ᶜ*A type of wheat   *ᵈ*A *shekel* was about 2/5 of an ounce or 11 grams
*ᵉ*Or *at a set time daily*; also verse 11   *ᶠ*A *hin* was about 4 quarts or 3.5 litres   *ᵍ*Hebrew *my soul* (or *throat*) *has never been made unclean*
*ʰ*Hebrew *staff*

the wind, and I will unsheathe the sword after them. ³And you shall take from these a small number and bind them in the skirts of your robe. ⁴And of these again you shall take some and cast them into the midst of the fire and burn them in the fire. From there a fire will come out into all the house of Israel.

⁵"Thus says the Lord GOD: This is Jerusalem. I have set her in the centre of the nations, with countries all around her. ⁶And she has rebelled against my rules by doing wickedness more than the nations, and against my statutes more than the countries all around her; for they have rejected my rules and have not walked in my statutes. ⁷Therefore thus says the Lord GOD: Because you are more turbulent than the nations that are all around you, and have not walked in my statutes or obeyed my rules, and have not*ᵃ* even acted according to the rules of the nations that are all around you, ⁸therefore thus says the Lord GOD: Behold, I, even I, am against you. And I will execute judgements*ᵇ* in your midst in the sight of the nations. ⁹And because of all your abominations I will do with you what I have never yet done, and the like of which I will never do again. ¹⁰Therefore fathers shall eat their sons in your midst, and sons shall eat their fathers. And I will execute judgements on you, and any of you who survive I will scatter to all the winds. ¹¹Therefore, as I live, declares the Lord GOD, surely, because you have defiled my sanctuary with all your detestable things and with all your abominations, therefore I will withdraw.*ᶜ* My eye will not spare, and I will have no pity. ¹²A third part of you shall die of pestilence and be consumed with famine in your midst; a third part shall fall by the sword all round you; and a third part I will scatter to all the winds and will unsheathe the sword after them.

¹³"Thus shall my anger spend itself, and I will vent my fury upon them and satisfy myself. And they shall know that I am the LORD—that I have spoken in my jealousy—when I spend my fury upon them. ¹⁴Moreover, I will make you a desolation and an object of reproach among the nations all around you and in the sight of all who pass by. ¹⁵You shall be*ᵈ* a reproach and a taunt, a warning and a horror, to the nations all around you, when I execute judgements on you in anger and fury, and with furious rebukes—I am the LORD; I have spoken— ¹⁶when I send against you*ᵉ* the deadly arrows of famine, arrows for destruction, which I will send to destroy you, and when I bring more and more famine upon you and break your supply*ᶠ* of bread. ¹⁷I will send famine and wild beasts against you, and they will rob you of your children. Pestilence and blood shall pass through you, and I will bring the sword upon you. I am the LORD; I have spoken."

JUDGEMENT AGAINST IDOLATRY

6 The word of the LORD came to me: ²"Son of man, set your face towards the mountains of Israel, and prophesy against them, ³and say, You mountains of Israel, hear the word of the Lord GOD! Thus says the Lord GOD to the mountains and the hills, to the ravines and the valleys: Behold, I, even I, will bring a sword upon you, and I will destroy your high places. ⁴Your altars shall become desolate, and your incense altars shall be broken, and I will cast down your slain before your idols. ⁵And I will lay the dead bodies of the people of Israel before their idols, and I will scatter your bones around your altars. ⁶Wherever you dwell, the cities shall be waste and the high places ruined, so that your altars will be waste and ruined,*ᵍ* your idols broken and destroyed, your incense altars cut down, and your works wiped out. ⁷And the slain shall fall in your midst, and you shall know that I am the LORD.

⁸"Yet I will leave some of you alive. When you have among the nations some who escape the sword, and when you are scattered through the countries, ⁹then those of you who escape will remember me among the nations where they are carried captive, how I have been broken over their whoring heart that has departed from me and over their eyes that go whoring after their idols. And they will be loathsome in their own sight for the evils that they have committed, for all their abominations. ¹⁰And they shall know that I am the LORD. I have not said in vain that I would do this evil to them."

¹¹Thus says the Lord GOD: "Clap your hands and stamp your foot and say, Alas, because of all the evil abominations of the house of Israel, for they shall fall by the sword, by famine, and by pestilence. ¹²He who is far off shall die of pestilence, and he who is near

---

*ᵃ*Some Hebrew manuscripts and Syriac lack *not* *ᵇ*The same Hebrew expression can mean *obey rules*, or *execute judgements*, depending on the context *ᶜ*Some Hebrew manuscripts *I will cut you down* *ᵈ*Dead Sea Scroll, Septuagint, Syriac, Vulgate, Targum; Masoretic Text *And it shall be* *ᵉ*Hebrew *them* *ᶠ*Hebrew *staff* *ᵍ*Or *and punished*

shall fall by the sword, and he who is left and is preserved shall die of famine. Thus I will spend my fury upon them. **13**And you shall know that I am the Lord, when their slain lie among their idols around their altars, on every high hill, on all the mountaintops, under every green tree, and under every leafy oak, wherever they offered pleasing aroma to all their idols. **14**And I will stretch out my hand against them and make the land desolate and waste, in all their dwelling places, from the wilderness to Riblah.*a* Then they will know that I am the Lord."

THE DAY OF THE WRATH OF THE LORD

7 The word of the Lord came to me: **2**"And you, O son of man, thus says the Lord God to the land of Israel: An end! The end has come upon the four corners of the land.*b* **3**Now the end is upon you, and I will send my anger upon you; I will judge you according to your ways, and I will punish you for all your abominations. **4**And my eye will not spare you, nor will I have pity, but I will punish you for your ways, while your abominations are in your midst. Then you will know that I am the Lord.

5"Thus says the Lord God: Disaster after disaster!*c* Behold, it comes. **6**An end has come; the end has come; it has awakened against you. Behold, it comes. **7**Your doom*d* has come to you, O inhabitant of the land. The time has come; the day is near, a day of tumult, and not of joyful shouting on the mountains. **8**Now I will soon pour out my wrath upon you, and spend my anger against you, and judge you according to your ways, and I will punish you for all your abominations. **9**And my eye will not spare, nor will I have pity. I will punish you according to your ways, while your abominations are in your midst. Then you will know that I am the Lord, who strikes.

10"Behold, the day! Behold, it comes! Your doom has come; the rod has blossomed; pride has budded. **11**Violence has grown up into a rod of wickedness. None of them shall remain, nor their abundance, nor their wealth; neither shall there be pre-eminence among them.*e* **12**The time has come; the day has arrived. Let not the buyer rejoice, nor the seller mourn, for wrath is upon all their multitude.*f* **13**For the seller shall not return to what he has sold, while they live. For the vision concerns all their multitude; it shall not turn back; and because of his iniquity, none can maintain his life.*g*

14"They have blown the trumpet and made everything ready, but none goes to battle, for my wrath is upon all their multitude. **15**The sword is without; pestilence and famine are within. He who is in the field dies by the sword, and him who is in the city famine and pestilence devour. **16**And if any survivors escape, they will be on the mountains, like doves of the valleys, all of them moaning, each one over his iniquity. **17**All hands are feeble, and all knees turn to water. **18**They put on sackcloth, and horror covers them. Shame is on all faces, and baldness on all their heads. **19**They cast their silver into the streets, and their gold is like an unclean thing. Their silver and gold are not able to deliver them in the day of the wrath of the Lord. They cannot satisfy their hunger or fill their stomachs with it. For it was the stumbling block of their iniquity. **20**His beautiful ornament they used for pride, and they made their abominable images and their detestable things of it. Therefore I make it an unclean thing to them. **21**And I will give it into the hands of foreigners for prey, and to the wicked of the earth for spoil, and they shall profane it. **22**I will turn my face from them, and they shall profane my treasured*h* place. Robbers shall enter and profane it.

23"Forge a chain!*i* For the land is full of bloody crimes and the city is full of violence. **24**I will bring the worst of the nations to take possession of their houses. I will put an end to the pride of the strong, and their holy places*j* shall be profaned. **25**When anguish comes, they will seek peace, but there shall be none. **26**Disaster comes upon disaster; rumour follows rumour. They seek a vision from the prophet, while the law*k* perishes from the priest and counsel from the elders. **27**The king mourns, the prince is wrapped in despair, and the hands of the people of the land are paralysed by terror. According to their way I will do to them, and according to their judgements I will judge them, and they shall know that I am the Lord."

---

*a*Some Hebrew manuscripts; most Hebrew manuscripts *Diblah*
*b*Or *earth*   *c*Some Hebrew manuscripts (compare Syriac, Targum); most Hebrew manuscripts *Disaster! A unique disaster!*   *d*The meaning of the Hebrew word is uncertain; also verse 10   *e*The meaning of this last Hebrew sentence is uncertain   *f*Or *abundance*; also verses 13, 14
*g*The meaning of this last Hebrew sentence is uncertain   *h*Or *secret*
*i*Probably refers to an instrument of captivity   *j*By revocalization (compare Septuagint); Hebrew *and those who sanctify them*
*k*Or *instruction*

ABOMINATIONS IN THE TEMPLE

8 In the sixth year, in the sixth month, on the fifth day of the month, as I sat in my house, with the elders of Judah sitting before me, the hand of the Lord God fell upon me there. ²Then I looked, and behold, a form that had the appearance of a man.[a] Below what appeared to be his waist was fire, and above his waist was something like the appearance of brightness, like gleaming metal.[b] ³He put out the form of a hand and took me by a lock of my head, and the Spirit lifted me up between earth and heaven and brought me in visions of God to Jerusalem, to the entrance of the gateway of the inner court that faces north, where was the seat of the image of jealousy, which provokes to jealousy. ⁴And behold, the glory of the God of Israel was there, like the vision that I saw in the valley.

⁵Then he said to me, "Son of man, lift up your eyes now towards the north." So I lifted up my eyes towards the north, and behold, north of the altar gate, in the entrance, was this image of jealousy. ⁶And he said to me, "Son of man, do you see what they are doing, the great abominations that the house of Israel are committing here, to drive me far from my sanctuary? But you will see still greater abominations."

⁷And he brought me to the entrance of the court, and when I looked, behold, there was a hole in the wall. ⁸Then he said to me, "Son of man, dig in the wall." So I dug in the wall, and behold, there was an entrance. ⁹And he said to me, "Go in, and see the vile abominations that they are committing here." ¹⁰So I went in and saw. And there, engraved on the wall all round, was every form of creeping things and loathsome beasts, and all the idols of the house of Israel. ¹¹And before them stood seventy men of the elders of the house of Israel, with Jaazaniah the son of Shaphan standing among them. Each had his censer in his hand, and the smoke of the cloud of incense went up. ¹²Then he said to me, "Son of man, have you seen what the elders of the house of Israel are doing in the dark, each in his room of pictures? For they say, 'The Lord does not see us, the Lord has forsaken the land.'" ¹³He said also to me, "You will see still greater abominations that they commit."

¹⁴Then he brought me to the entrance of the north gate of the house of the Lord, and behold, there sat women weeping for Tammuz. ¹⁵Then he said to me, "Have you seen this, O son of man? You will see still greater abominations than these."

¹⁶And he brought me into the inner court of the house of the Lord. And behold, at the entrance of the temple of the Lord, between the porch and the altar, were about twenty-five men, with their backs to the temple of the Lord, and their faces towards the east, worshipping the sun towards the east. ¹⁷Then he said to me, "Have you seen this, O son of man? Is it too light a thing for the house of Judah to commit the abominations that they commit here, that they should fill the land with violence and provoke me still further to anger? Behold, they put the branch to their[c] nose. ¹⁸Therefore I will act in wrath. My eye will not spare, nor will I have pity. And though they cry in my ears with a loud voice, I will not hear them."

IDOLATERS KILLED

9 Then he cried in my ears with a loud voice, saying, "Bring near the executioners of the city, each with his destroying weapon in his hand." ²And behold, six men came from the direction of the upper gate, which faces north, each with his weapon for slaughter in his hand, and with them was a man clothed in linen, with a writing case at his waist. And they went in and stood beside the bronze altar.

³Now the glory of the God of Israel had gone up from the cherub on which it rested to the threshold of the house. And he called to the man clothed in linen, who had the writing case at his waist. ⁴And the Lord said to him, "Pass through the city, through Jerusalem, and put a mark on the foreheads of the men who sigh and groan over all the abominations that are committed in it." ⁵And to the others he said in my hearing, "Pass through the city after him, and strike. Your eye shall not spare, and you shall show no pity. ⁶Kill old men outright, young men and maidens, little children and women, but touch no one on whom is the mark. And begin at my sanctuary." So they began with the elders who were before the house. ⁷Then he said to them, "Defile the house, and fill the courts with the slain. Go out." So they went out and struck in the city. ⁸And while they were striking, and I was left alone, I fell upon my face, and cried, "Ah, Lord God! Will you destroy

---

[a] By revocalization (compare Septuagint); Hebrew *of fire* [b] Or *amber* [c] Or *my*

all the remnant of Israel in the outpouring of your wrath on Jerusalem?"

⁹Then he said to me, "The guilt of the house of Israel and Judah is exceedingly great. The land is full of blood, and the city full of injustice. For they say, 'The LORD has forsaken the land, and the LORD does not see.' ¹⁰As for me, my eye will not spare, nor will I have pity; I will bring their deeds upon their heads."

¹¹And behold, the man clothed in linen, with the writing case at his waist, brought back word, saying, "I have done as you commanded me."

THE GLORY OF THE LORD LEAVES THE TEMPLE

10 Then I looked, and behold, on the expanse that was over the heads of the cherubim there appeared above them something like a sapphire,ᵃ in appearance like a throne. ²And he said to the man clothed in linen, "Go in among the whirling wheels underneath the cherubim. Fill your hands with burning coals from between the cherubim, and scatter them over the city."

And he went in before my eyes. ³Now the cherubim were standing on the south side of the house, when the man went in, and a cloud filled the inner court. ⁴And the glory of the LORD went up from the cherub to the threshold of the house, and the house was filled with the cloud, and the court was filled with the brightness of the glory of the LORD. ⁵And the sound of the wings of the cherubim was heard as far as the outer court, like the voice of God Almighty when he speaks.

⁶And when he commanded the man clothed in linen, "Take fire from between the whirling wheels, from between the cherubim", he went in and stood beside a wheel. ⁷And a cherub stretched out his hand from between the cherubim to the fire that was between the cherubim, and took some of it and put it into the hands of the man clothed in linen, who took it and went out. ⁸The cherubim appeared to have the form of a human hand under their wings.

⁹And I looked, and behold, there were four wheels beside the cherubim, one beside each cherub, and the appearance of the wheels was like sparkling beryl. ¹⁰And as for their appearance, the four had the same likeness, as if a wheel were within a wheel. ¹¹When they went, they went in any of their four directionsᵇ without turning as they went,

but in whatever direction the front wheelᶜ faced, the others followed without turning as they went. ¹²And their whole body, their rims, and their spokes, their wings,ᵈ and the wheels were full of eyes all round—the wheels that the four of them had. ¹³As for the wheels, they were called in my hearing "the whirling wheels". ¹⁴And every one had four faces: the first face was the face of the cherub, and the second face was a human face, and the third the face of a lion, and the fourth the face of an eagle.

¹⁵And the cherubim mounted up. These were the living creatures that I saw by the Chebar canal. ¹⁶And when the cherubim went, the wheels went beside them. And when the cherubim lifted up their wings to mount up from the earth, the wheels did not turn from beside them. ¹⁷When they stood still, these stood still, and when they mounted up, these mounted up with them, for the spirit of the living creaturesᵉ was in them.

¹⁸Then the glory of the LORD went out from the threshold of the house, and stood over the cherubim. ¹⁹And the cherubim lifted up their wings and mounted up from the earth before my eyes as they went out, with the wheels beside them. And they stood at the entrance of the east gate of the house of the LORD, and the glory of the God of Israel was over them.

²⁰These were the living creatures that I saw underneath the God of Israel by the Chebar canal; and I knew that they were cherubim. ²¹Each had four faces, and each four wings, and underneath their wings the likeness of human hands. ²²And as for the likeness of their faces, they were the same faces whose appearance I had seen by the Chebar canal. Each one of them went straight forward.

JUDGEMENT ON WICKED COUNSELLORS

11 The Spirit lifted me up and brought me to the east gate of the house of the LORD, which faces east. And behold, at the entrance of the gateway there were twenty-five men. And I saw among them Jaazaniah the son of Azzur, and Pelatiah the son of Benaiah, princes of the people. ²And he said to me, "Son of man, these are the men who devise iniquity and who give wicked counsel in this city; ³who say, 'The

---

ᵃOr lapis lazuli ᵇHebrew to their four sides ᶜHebrew the head
ᵈOr their whole body, their backs, their hands, and their wings
ᵉOr spirit of life

time is not near*a* to build houses. This city is the cauldron, and we are the meat.' ⁴Therefore prophesy against them; prophesy, O son of man."

⁵And the Spirit of the LORD fell upon me, and he said to me, "Say, Thus says the LORD: So you think, O house of Israel. For I know the things that come into your mind. ⁶You have multiplied your slain in this city and have filled its streets with the slain. ⁷Therefore thus says the Lord GOD: Your slain whom you have laid in the midst of it, they are the meat, and this city is the cauldron, but you shall be brought out of the midst of it. ⁸You have feared the sword, and I will bring the sword upon you, declares the Lord GOD. ⁹And I will bring you out of the midst of it, and give you into the hands of foreigners, and execute judgements upon you. ¹⁰You shall fall by the sword. I will judge you at the border of Israel, and you shall know that I am the LORD. ¹¹This city shall not be your cauldron, nor shall you be the meat in the midst of it. I will judge you at the border of Israel, ¹²and you shall know that I am the LORD. For you have not walked in my statutes, nor obeyed my rules, but have acted according to the rules of the nations that are around you."

¹³And it came to pass, while I was prophesying, that Pelatiah the son of Benaiah died. Then I fell down on my face and cried out with a loud voice and said, "Ah, Lord GOD! Will you make a full end of the remnant of Israel?"

ISRAEL'S NEW HEART AND SPIRIT

¹⁴And the word of the LORD came to me: ¹⁵"Son of man, your brothers, even your brothers, your kinsmen,*b* the whole house of Israel, all of them, are those of whom the inhabitants of Jerusalem have said, 'Go far from the LORD; to us this land is given for a possession.' ¹⁶Therefore say, 'Thus says the Lord GOD: Though I removed them far off among the nations, and though I scattered them among the countries, yet I have been a sanctuary to them for a while*c* in the countries where they have gone.' ¹⁷Therefore say, 'Thus says the Lord GOD: I will gather you from the peoples and assemble you out of the countries where you have been scattered, and I will give you the land of Israel.' ¹⁸And when they come there, they will remove from it all its detestable things and all its abominations. ¹⁹And I will give them one heart, and a new spirit I will put within them. I will remove the heart of stone from their flesh and give them a heart of flesh, ²⁰that they may walk in my statutes and keep my rules and obey them. And they shall be my people, and I will be their God. ²¹But as for those whose heart goes after their detestable things and their abominations, I will*d* bring their deeds upon their own heads, declares the Lord GOD."

²²Then the cherubim lifted up their wings, with the wheels beside them, and the glory of the God of Israel was over them. ²³And the glory of the LORD went up from the midst of the city and stood on the mountain that is on the east side of the city. ²⁴And the Spirit lifted me up and brought me in the vision by the Spirit of God into Chaldea, to the exiles. Then the vision that I had seen went up from me. ²⁵And I told the exiles all the things that the LORD had shown me.

JUDAH'S CAPTIVITY SYMBOLIZED

12 The word of the LORD came to me: ²"Son of man, you dwell in the midst of a rebellious house, who have eyes to see, but see not, who have ears to hear, but hear not, for they are a rebellious house. ³As for you, son of man, prepare for yourself an exile's baggage, and go into exile by day in their sight. You shall go like an exile from your place to another place in their sight. Perhaps they will understand, though*e* they are a rebellious house. ⁴You shall bring out your baggage by day in their sight, as baggage for exile, and you shall go out yourself at evening in their sight, as those do who must go into exile. ⁵In their sight dig through the wall, and bring your baggage out through it. ⁶In their sight you shall lift the baggage upon your shoulder and carry it out at dusk. You shall cover your face that you may not see the land, for I have made you a sign for the house of Israel."

⁷And I did as I was commanded. I brought out my baggage by day, as baggage for exile, and in the evening I dug through the wall with my own hands. I brought out my baggage at dusk, carrying it on my shoulder in their sight.

⁸In the morning the word of the LORD came to me: ⁹"Son of man, has not the house of Israel, the rebellious house, said to you,

---

*a*Or *Is not the time near...?* *b*Hebrew *the men of your redemption*
*c*Or *in small measure* *d*Hebrew *To the heart of their detestable things and their abominations their heart goes; I will* *e*Or *will see that*

'What are you doing?' ¹⁰Say to them, 'Thus says the Lord GOD: This oracle concerns*ᵃ* the prince in Jerusalem and all the house of Israel who are in it.'*ᵇ* ¹¹Say, 'I am a sign for you: as I have done, so shall it be done to them. They shall go into exile, into captivity.' ¹²And the prince who is among them shall lift his baggage upon his shoulder at dusk, and shall go out. They shall dig through the wall to bring him out through it. He shall cover his face, that he may not see the land with his eyes. ¹³And I will spread my net over him, and he shall be taken in my snare. And I will bring him to Babylon, the land of the Chaldeans, yet he shall not see it, and he shall die there. ¹⁴And I will scatter towards every wind all who are round him, his helpers and all his troops, and I will unsheathe the sword after them. ¹⁵And they shall know that I am the LORD, when I disperse them among the nations and scatter them among the countries. ¹⁶But I will let a few of them escape from the sword, from famine and pestilence, that they may declare all their abominations among the nations where they go, and may know that I am the LORD.'

¹⁷And the word of the LORD came to me: ¹⁸"Son of man, eat your bread with quaking, and drink water with trembling and with anxiety. ¹⁹And say to the people of the land, Thus says the Lord GOD concerning the inhabitants of Jerusalem in the land of Israel: They shall eat their bread with anxiety, and drink water in dismay. In this way her land will be stripped of all it contains, on account of the violence of all those who dwell in it. ²⁰And the inhabited cities shall be laid waste, and the land shall become a desolation; and you shall know that I am the LORD."

²¹And the word of the LORD came to me: ²²"Son of man, what is this proverb that you*ᶜ* have about the land of Israel, saying, 'The days grow long, and every vision comes to nothing'? ²³Tell them therefore, 'Thus says the Lord GOD: I will put an end to this proverb, and they shall no more use it as a proverb in Israel.' But say to them, The days are near, and the fulfilment*ᵈ* of every vision. ²⁴For there shall be no more any false vision or flattering divination within the house of Israel. ²⁵For I am the LORD; I will speak the word that I will speak, and it will be performed. It will no longer be delayed, but in your days, O rebellious house, I will speak the word and perform it, declares the Lord GOD."

²⁶And the word of the LORD came to me: ²⁷"Son of man, behold, they of the house of Israel say, 'The vision that he sees is for many days from now, and he prophesies of times far off.' ²⁸Therefore say to them, Thus says the Lord GOD: None of my words will be delayed any longer, but the word that I speak will be performed, declares the Lord GOD."

FALSE PROPHETS CONDEMNED

13 The word of the LORD came to me: ²"Son of man, prophesy against the prophets of Israel, who are prophesying, and say to those who prophesy from their own hearts: 'Hear the word of the LORD!' ³Thus says the Lord GOD, Woe to the foolish prophets who follow their own spirit, and have seen nothing! ⁴Your prophets have been like jackals among ruins, O Israel. ⁵You have not gone up into the breaches, or built up a wall for the house of Israel, that it might stand in battle in the day of the LORD. ⁶They have seen false visions and lying divinations. They say, 'Declares the LORD', when the LORD has not sent them, and yet they expect him to fulfil their word. ⁷Have you not seen a false vision and uttered a lying divination, whenever you have said, 'Declares the LORD', although I have not spoken?"

⁸Therefore thus says the Lord GOD: "Because you have uttered falsehood and seen lying visions, therefore behold, I am against you, declares the Lord GOD. ⁹My hand will be against the prophets who see false visions and who give lying divinations. They shall not be in the council of my people, nor be enrolled in the register of the house of Israel, nor shall they enter the land of Israel. And you shall know that I am the Lord GOD. ¹⁰Precisely because they have misled my people, saying, 'Peace', when there is no peace, and because, when the people build a wall, these prophets smear it with whitewash,*ᵉ* ¹¹say to those who smear it with whitewash that it shall fall! There will be a deluge of rain, and you, O great hailstones, will fall, and a stormy wind break out. ¹²And when the wall falls, will it not be said to you, 'Where is the coating with which you smeared it?' ¹³Therefore thus says the Lord GOD: I will make a stormy wind break out in my wrath, and there shall be a deluge of rain in my anger, and great hailstones in wrath to

---

*ᵃ*Or *This burden is* *ᵇ*Hebrew *in the midst of them* *ᶜ*The Hebrew for *you* is plural *ᵈ*Hebrew *word* *ᵉ*Or *plaster*; also verses 11, 14, 15

make a full end. ¹⁴And I will break down the wall that you have smeared with whitewash, and bring it down to the ground, so that its foundation will be laid bare. When it falls, you shall perish in the midst of it, and you shall know that I am the LORD. ¹⁵Thus will I spend my wrath upon the wall and upon those who have smeared it with whitewash, and I will say to you, The wall is no more, nor those who smeared it, ¹⁶the prophets of Israel who prophesied concerning Jerusalem and saw visions of peace for her, when there was no peace, declares the Lord GOD.

¹⁷"And you, son of man, set your face against the daughters of your people, who prophesy out of their own hearts. Prophesy against them ¹⁸and say, Thus says the Lord GOD: Woe to the women who sew magic bands upon all wrists, and make veils for the heads of persons of every stature, in the hunt for souls! Will you hunt down souls belonging to my people and keep your own souls alive? ¹⁹You have profaned me among my people for handfuls of barley and for pieces of bread, putting to death souls who should not die and keeping alive souls who should not live, by your lying to my people, who listen to lies.

²⁰"Therefore thus says the Lord GOD: Behold, I am against your magic bands with which you hunt the souls like birds, and I will tear them from your arms, and I will let the souls whom you hunt go free, the souls like birds. ²¹Your veils also I will tear off and deliver my people out of your hand, and they shall be no more in your hand as prey, and you shall know that I am the LORD. ²²Because you have disheartened the righteous falsely, although I have not grieved him, and you have encouraged the wicked, that he should not turn from his evil way to save his life, ²³therefore you shall no more see false visions nor practise divination. I will deliver my people out of your hand. And you shall know that I am the LORD."

IDOLATROUS ELDERS CONDEMNED

14 Then certain of the elders of Israel came to me and sat before me. ²And the word of the LORD came to me: ³"Son of man, these men have taken their idols into their hearts, and set the stumbling block of their iniquity before their faces. Should I indeed let myself be consulted by them? ⁴Therefore speak to them and say to them, Thus says the Lord GOD: Any one of the house of Israel who takes his idols into his heart and sets the stumbling block of his iniquity before his face, and yet comes to the prophet, I the LORD will answer him as he comes with the multitude of his idols, ⁵that I may lay hold of the hearts of the house of Israel, who are all estranged from me through their idols.

⁶"Therefore say to the house of Israel, Thus says the Lord GOD: Repent and turn away from your idols, and turn away your faces from all your abominations. ⁷For any one of the house of Israel, or of the strangers who sojourn in Israel, who separates himself from me, taking his idols into his heart and putting the stumbling block of his iniquity before his face, and yet comes to a prophet to consult me through him, I the LORD will answer him myself. ⁸And I will set my face against that man; I will make him a sign and a byword and cut him off from the midst of my people, and you shall know that I am the LORD. ⁹And if the prophet is deceived and speaks a word, I, the LORD, have deceived that prophet, and I will stretch out my hand against him and will destroy him from the midst of my people Israel. ¹⁰And they shall bear their punishment^a—the punishment of the prophet and the punishment of the enquirer shall be alike— ¹¹that the house of Israel may no more go astray from me, nor defile themselves any more with all their transgressions, but that they may be my people and I may be their God, declares the Lord GOD."

JERUSALEM WILL NOT BE SPARED

¹²And the word of the LORD came to me: ¹³"Son of man, when a land sins against me by acting faithlessly, and I stretch out my hand against it and break its supply^b of bread and send famine upon it, and cut off from it man and beast, ¹⁴even if these three men, Noah, Daniel, and Job, were in it, they would deliver but their own lives by their righteousness, declares the Lord GOD.

¹⁵"If I cause wild beasts to pass through the land, and they ravage it, and it be made desolate, so that no one may pass through because of the beasts, ¹⁶even if these three men were in it, as I live, declares the Lord GOD, they would deliver neither sons nor daughters. They alone would be delivered, but the land would be desolate.

---

^{a}Or *iniquity*; three times in this verse ^{b}Hebrew *staff*

17"Or if I bring a sword upon that land and say, Let a sword pass through the land, and I cut off from it man and beast, 18though these three men were in it, as I live, declares the Lord GOD, they would deliver neither sons nor daughters, but they alone would be delivered.

19"Or if I send a pestilence into that land and pour out my wrath upon it with blood, to cut off from it man and beast, 20even if Noah, Daniel, and Job were in it, as I live, declares the Lord GOD, they would deliver neither son nor daughter. They would deliver but their own lives by their righteousness.

21"For thus says the Lord GOD: How much more when I send upon Jerusalem my four disastrous acts of judgement, sword, famine, wild beasts, and pestilence, to cut off from it man and beast! 22But behold, some survivors will be left in it, sons and daughters who will be brought out; behold, when they come out to you, and you see their ways and their deeds, you will be consoled for the disaster that I have brought upon Jerusalem, for all that I have brought upon it. 23They will console you, when you see their ways and their deeds, and you shall know that I have not done without cause all that I have done in it, declares the Lord GOD."

JERUSALEM, A USELESS VINE

15 And the word of the LORD came to me: 2"Son of man, how does the wood of the vine surpass any wood, the vine branch that is among the trees of the forest? 3Is wood taken from it to make anything? Do people take a peg from it to hang any vessel on it? 4Behold, it is given to the fire for fuel. When the fire has consumed both ends of it, and the middle of it is charred, is it useful for anything? 5Behold, when it was whole, it was used for nothing. How much less, when the fire has consumed it and it is charred, can it ever be used for anything! 6Therefore thus says the Lord GOD: Like the wood of the vine among the trees of the forest, which I have given to the fire for fuel, so have I given up the inhabitants of Jerusalem. 7And I will set my face against them. Though they escape from the fire, the fire shall yet consume them, and you will know that I am the LORD, when I set my face against them. 8And I will make the land desolate, because they have acted faithlessly, declares the Lord GOD."

THE LORD'S FAITHLESS BRIDE

16 Again the word of the LORD came to me: 2"Son of man, make known to Jerusalem her abominations, 3and say, Thus says the Lord GOD to Jerusalem: Your origin and your birth are of the land of the Canaanites; your father was an Amorite and your mother a Hittite. 4And as for your birth, on the day you were born your cord was not cut, nor were you washed with water to cleanse you, nor rubbed with salt, nor wrapped in swaddling cloths. 5No eye pitied you, to do any of these things to you out of compassion for you, but you were cast out on the open field, for you were abhorred, on the day that you were born.

6"And when I passed by you and saw you wallowing in your blood, I said to you in your blood, 'Live!' I said to you in your blood, 'Live!' 7I made you flourish like a plant of the field. And you grew up and became tall and arrived at full adornment. Your breasts were formed, and your hair had grown; yet you were naked and bare.

8"When I passed by you again and saw you, behold, you were at the age for love, and I spread the corner of my garment over you and covered your nakedness; I made my vow to you and entered into a covenant with you, declares the Lord GOD, and you became mine. 9Then I bathed you with water and washed off your blood from you and anointed you with oil. 10I clothed you also with embroidered cloth and shod you with fine leather. I wrapped you in fine linen and covered you with silk.[a] 11And I adorned you with ornaments and put bracelets on your wrists and a chain on your neck. 12And I put a ring on your nose and earrings in your ears and a beautiful crown on your head. 13Thus you were adorned with gold and silver, and your clothing was of fine linen and silk and embroidered cloth. You ate fine flour and honey and oil. You grew exceedingly beautiful and advanced to royalty. 14And your renown went forth among the nations because of your beauty, for it was perfect through the splendour that I had bestowed on you, declares the Lord GOD.

15"But you trusted in your beauty and played the whore[b] because of your renown and lavished your whorings[c] on any passer-by; your beauty[d] became his. 16You took

---
[a] Or with rich fabric   [b] Or were unfaithful; also verses 16, 17, 26, 28
[c] Or unfaithfulness; also verses 20, 22, 25, 26, 29, 33, 34, 36   [d] Hebrew it

some of your garments and made for yourself colourful shrines, and on them played the whore. The like has never been, nor ever shall be.*ᵃ* ¹⁷You also took your beautiful jewels of my gold and of my silver, which I had given you, and made for yourself images of men, and with them played the whore. ¹⁸And you took your embroidered garments to cover them, and set my oil and my incense before them. ¹⁹Also my bread that I gave you—I fed you with fine flour and oil and honey—you set before them for a pleasing aroma; and so it was, declares the Lord GOD. ²⁰And you took your sons and your daughters, whom you had borne to me, and these you sacrificed to them to be devoured. Were your whorings so small a matter ²¹that you slaughtered my children and delivered them up as an offering by fire to them? ²²And in all your abominations and your whorings you did not remember the days of your youth, when you were naked and bare, wallowing in your blood.

²³"And after all your wickedness (woe, woe to you! declares the Lord GOD), ²⁴you built yourself a vaulted chamber and made yourself a lofty place in every square. ²⁵At the head of every street you built your lofty place and made your beauty an abomination, offering yourself*ᵇ* to any passer-by and multiplying your whoring. ²⁶You also played the whore with the Egyptians, your lustful neighbours, multiplying your whoring, to provoke me to anger. ²⁷Behold, therefore, I stretched out my hand against you and diminished your allotted portion and delivered you to the greed of your enemies, the daughters of the Philistines, who were ashamed of your lewd behaviour. ²⁸You played the whore also with the Assyrians, because you were not satisfied; yes, you played the whore with them, and still you were not satisfied. ²⁹You multiplied your whoring also with the trading land of Chaldea, and even with this you were not satisfied.

³⁰"How sick is your heart,*ᶜ* declares the Lord GOD, because you did all these things, the deeds of a brazen prostitute, ³¹building your vaulted chamber at the head of every street, and making your lofty place in every square. Yet you were not like a prostitute, because you scorned payment. ³²Adulterous wife, who receives strangers instead of her husband! ³³Men give gifts to all prostitutes, but you gave your gifts to all your lovers, bribing them to come to you from every side with your whorings. ³⁴So you were different from other women in your whorings. No one solicited you to play the whore, and you gave payment, while no payment was given to you; therefore you were different.

³⁵"Therefore, O prostitute, hear the word of the LORD: ³⁶Thus says the Lord GOD, Because your lust was poured out and your nakedness uncovered in your whorings with your lovers, and with all your abominable idols, and because of the blood of your children that you gave to them, ³⁷therefore, behold, I will gather all your lovers with whom you took pleasure, all those you loved and all those you hated. I will gather them against you from every side and will uncover your nakedness to them, that they may see all your nakedness. ³⁸And I will judge you as women who commit adultery and shed blood are judged, and bring upon you the blood of wrath and jealousy. ³⁹And I will give you into their hands, and they shall throw down your vaulted chamber and break down your lofty places. They shall strip you of your clothes and take your beautiful jewels and leave you naked and bare. ⁴⁰They shall bring up a crowd against you, and they shall stone you and cut you to pieces with their swords. ⁴¹And they shall burn your houses and execute judgements upon you in the sight of many women. I will make you stop playing the whore, and you shall also give payment no more. ⁴²So will I satisfy my wrath on you, and my jealousy shall depart from you. I will be calm and will no more be angry. ⁴³Because you have not remembered the days of your youth, but have enraged me with all these things, therefore, behold, I have returned your deeds upon your head, declares the Lord GOD. Have you not committed lewdness in addition to all your abominations?

⁴⁴"Behold, everyone who uses proverbs will use this proverb about you: 'Like mother, like daughter.' ⁴⁵You are the daughter of your mother, who loathed her husband and her children; and you are the sister of your sisters, who loathed their husbands and their children. Your mother was a Hittite and your father an Amorite. ⁴⁶And your elder sister is Samaria, who lived with her daughters to the north of you; and your younger sister, who lived to the south of you, is Sodom with her daughters. ⁴⁷Not only did you walk in their

---

*ᵃ*The meaning of this Hebrew sentence is uncertain *ᵇ*Hebrew *spreading your legs* *ᶜ*Revocalization yields *How I am filled with anger against you*

ways and do according to their abominations; within a very little time you were more corrupt than they in all your ways. **48**As I live, declares the Lord God, your sister Sodom and her daughters have not done as you and your daughters have done. **49**Behold, this was the guilt of your sister Sodom: she and her daughters had pride, excess of food, and prosperous ease, but did not aid the poor and needy. **50**They were haughty and did an abomination before me. So I removed them, when I saw it. **51**Samaria has not committed half your sins. You have committed more abominations than they, and have made your sisters appear righteous by all the abominations that you have committed. **52**Bear your disgrace, you also, for you have intervened on behalf of your sisters. Because of your sins in which you acted more abominably than they, they are more in the right than you. So be ashamed, you also, and bear your disgrace, for you have made your sisters appear righteous.

53"I will restore their fortunes, both the fortunes of Sodom and her daughters, and the fortunes of Samaria and her daughters, and I will restore your own fortunes in their midst, **54**that you may bear your disgrace and be ashamed of all that you have done, becoming a consolation to them. **55**As for your sisters, Sodom and her daughters shall return to their former state, and Samaria and her daughters shall return to their former state, and you and your daughters shall return to your former state. **56**Was not your sister Sodom a byword in your mouth in the day of your pride, **57**before your wickedness was uncovered? Now you have become an object of reproach for the daughters of Syria*a* and all those around her, and for the daughters of the Philistines, those all around who despise you. **58**You bear the penalty of your lewdness and your abominations, declares the Lord.

THE LORD'S EVERLASTING COVENANT

59"For thus says the Lord God: I will deal with you as you have done, you who have despised the oath in breaking the covenant, **60**yet I will remember my covenant with you in the days of your youth, and I will establish for you an everlasting covenant. **61**Then you will remember your ways and be ashamed when you take your sisters, both your elder and your younger, and I give them to you as daughters, but not on account of*b* the covenant with you. **62**I will establish my covenant with you, and you shall know that I am the Lord, **63**that you may remember and be confounded, and never open your mouth again because of your shame, when I atone for you for all that you have done, declares the Lord God."

PARABLE OF TWO EAGLES AND A VINE

17 The word of the Lord came to me: **2**"Son of man, propound a riddle, and speak a parable to the house of Israel; **3**say, Thus says the Lord God: A great eagle with great wings and long pinions, rich in plumage of many colours, came to Lebanon and took the top of the cedar. **4**He broke off the topmost of its young twigs and carried it to a land of trade and set it in a city of merchants. **5**Then he took from the seed of the land and planted it in fertile soil.*c* He placed it beside abundant waters. He set it like a willow twig, **6**and it sprouted and became a low spreading vine, and its branches turned towards him, and its roots remained where it stood. So it became a vine and produced branches and put out boughs.

7"And there was another great eagle with great wings and much plumage, and behold, this vine bent its roots towards him and shot forth its branches towards him from the bed where it was planted, that he might water it. **8**It had been planted on good soil by abundant waters, that it might produce branches and bear fruit and become a noble vine.

9"Say, Thus says the Lord God: Will it thrive? Will he not pull up its roots and cut off its fruit, so that it withers, so that all its fresh sprouting leaves wither? It will not take a strong arm or many people to pull it from its roots. **10**Behold, it is planted; will it thrive? Will it not utterly wither when the east wind strikes it—wither away on the bed where it sprouted?"

11Then the word of the Lord came to me: **12**"Say now to the rebellious house, Do you not know what these things mean? Tell them, behold, the king of Babylon came to Jerusalem, and took her king and her princes and brought them to him to Babylon. **13**And he took one of the royal offspring*d* and made a covenant with him, putting him under oath (the chief men of the land he had taken away), **14**that the kingdom might be humble and not lift itself up, and keep his covenant

---
*a*Some manuscripts (compare Syriac) *of Edom* *b*Or *not apart from* *c*Hebrew *in a field of seed* *d*Hebrew *seed*

that it might stand. ¹⁵But he rebelled against him by sending his ambassadors to Egypt, that they might give him horses and a large army. Will he thrive? Can one escape who does such things? Can he break the covenant and yet escape?

¹⁶"As I live, declares the Lord GOD, surely in the place where the king dwells who made him king, whose oath he despised, and whose covenant with him he broke, in Babylon he shall die. ¹⁷Pharaoh with his mighty army and great company will not help him in war, when mounds are cast up and siege walls built to cut off many lives. ¹⁸He despised the oath in breaking the covenant, and behold, he gave his hand and did all these things; he shall not escape. ¹⁹Therefore thus says the Lord GOD: As I live, surely it is my oath that he despised, and my covenant that he broke. I will return it upon his head. ²⁰I will spread my net over him, and he shall be taken in my snare, and I will bring him to Babylon and enter into judgement with him there for the treachery he has committed against me. ²¹And all the pick^a of his troops shall fall by the sword, and the survivors shall be scattered to every wind, and you shall know that I am the LORD; I have spoken."

²²Thus says the Lord GOD: "I myself will take a sprig from the lofty top of the cedar and will set it out. I will break off from the topmost of its young twigs a tender one, and I myself will plant it on a high and lofty mountain. ²³On the mountain height of Israel will I plant it, that it may bear branches and produce fruit and become a noble cedar. And under it will dwell every kind of bird; in the shade of its branches birds of every sort will nest. ²⁴And all the trees of the field shall know that I am the LORD; I bring low the high tree, and make high the low tree, dry up the green tree, and make the dry tree flourish. I am the LORD; I have spoken, and I will do it."

THE SOUL WHO SINS SHALL DIE

18 The word of the LORD came to me: ²"What do you^b mean by repeating this proverb concerning the land of Israel, 'The fathers have eaten sour grapes, and the children's teeth are set on edge'? ³As I live, declares the Lord GOD, this proverb shall no more be used by you in Israel. ⁴Behold, all souls are mine; the soul of the father as well as the soul of the son is mine: the soul who sins shall die.

⁵"If a man is righteous and does what is just and right — ⁶if he does not eat upon the mountains or lift up his eyes to the idols of the house of Israel, does not defile his neighbour's wife or approach a woman in her time of menstrual impurity, ⁷does not oppress anyone, but restores to the debtor his pledge, commits no robbery, gives his bread to the hungry and covers the naked with a garment, ⁸does not lend at interest or take any profit,^{c} withholds his hand from injustice, executes true justice between man and man, ⁹walks in my statutes, and keeps my rules by acting faithfully — he is righteous; he shall surely live, declares the Lord GOD.

¹⁰"If he fathers a son who is violent, a shedder of blood, who does any of these things ¹¹(though he himself did none of these things), who even eats upon the mountains, defiles his neighbour's wife, ¹²oppresses the poor and needy, commits robbery, does not restore the pledge, lifts up his eyes to the idols, commits abomination, ¹³lends at interest, and takes profit; shall he then live? He shall not live. He has done all these abominations; he shall surely die; his blood shall be upon himself.

¹⁴"Now suppose this man fathers a son who sees all the sins that his father has done; he sees, and does not do likewise: ¹⁵he does not eat upon the mountains or lift up his eyes to the idols of the house of Israel, does not defile his neighbour's wife, ¹⁶does not oppress anyone, exacts no pledge, commits no robbery, but gives his bread to the hungry and covers the naked with a garment, ¹⁷withholds his hand from iniquity,^{d} takes no interest or profit obeys my rules, and walks in my statutes; he shall not die for his father's iniquity; he shall surely live. ¹⁸As for his father, because he practised extortion, robbed his brother, and did what is not good among his people, behold, he shall die for his iniquity.

¹⁹"Yet you say, 'Why should not the son suffer for the iniquity of the father?' When the son has done what is just and right, and has been careful to observe all my statutes, he shall surely live. ²⁰The soul who sins shall die. The son shall not suffer for the iniquity of the father, nor the father suffer for the iniquity of the son. The righteousness of

---

^{a}Some Hebrew manuscripts, Syriac, Targum; most Hebrew manuscripts *all the fugitives* ^{b}The Hebrew for *you* is plural ^{c}That is, profit that comes from charging interest to the poor; also verses 13, 17 (compare Leviticus 25:36) ^{d}Septuagint; Hebrew *from the poor*

the righteous shall be upon himself, and the wickedness of the wicked shall be upon himself.

²¹"But if a wicked person turns away from all his sins that he has committed and keeps all my statutes and does what is just and right, he shall surely live; he shall not die. ²²None of the transgressions that he has committed shall be remembered against him; for the righteousness that he has done he shall live. ²³Have I any pleasure in the death of the wicked, declares the Lord GOD, and not rather that he should turn from his way and live? ²⁴But when a righteous person turns away from his righteousness and does injustice and does the same abominations that the wicked person does, shall he live? None of the righteous deeds that he has done shall be remembered; for the treachery of which he is guilty and the sin he has committed, for them he shall die.

²⁵"Yet you say, 'The way of the Lord is not just.' Hear now, O house of Israel: Is my way not just? Is it not your ways that are not just? ²⁶When a righteous person turns away from his righteousness and does injustice, he shall die for it; for the injustice that he has done he shall die. ²⁷Again, when a wicked person turns away from the wickedness he has committed and does what is just and right, he shall save his life. ²⁸Because he considered and turned away from all the transgressions that he had committed, he shall surely live; he shall not die. ²⁹Yet the house of Israel says, 'The way of the Lord is not just.' O house of Israel, are my ways not just? Is it not your ways that are not just?

³⁰"Therefore I will judge you, O house of Israel, every one according to his ways, declares the Lord GOD. Repent and turn from all your transgressions, lest iniquity be your ruin.ᵃ ³¹Cast away from you all the transgressions that you have committed, and make yourselves a new heart and a new spirit! Why will you die, O house of Israel? ³²For I have no pleasure in the death of anyone, declares the Lord GOD; so turn, and live."

A LAMENT FOR THE PRINCES OF ISRAEL

19 And you, take up a lamentation for the princes of Israel, ²and say:

What was your mother? A lioness!
  Among lions she crouched;
in the midst of young lions
  she reared her cubs.

3   And she brought up one of her cubs;
      he became a young lion,
    and he learned to catch prey;
      he devoured men.
4   The nations heard about him;
      he was caught in their pit,
    and they brought him with hooks
      to the land of Egypt.
5   When she saw that she waited in vain,
      that her hope was lost,
    she took another of her cubs
      and made him a young lion.
6   He prowled among the lions;
      he became a young lion,
    and he learned to catch prey;
      he devoured men,
7   and seizedᵇ their widows.
    He laid waste their cities,
    and the land was appalled
      and all who were in it
    at the sound of his roaring.
8   Then the nations set against him
      from provinces on every side;
    they spread their net over him;
      he was taken in their pit.
9   With hooks they put him in a cageᶜ
      and brought him to the
        king of Babylon;
    they brought him into custody,
    that his voice should no more
      be heard
    on the mountains of Israel.

10 Your mother was like a vine
      in a vineyardᵈ
    planted by the water,
    fruitful and full of branches
      by reason of abundant water.
11 Its strong stems became
      rulers' sceptres;
    it towered aloft
      among the thick boughs;ᵉ
    it was seen in its height
      with the mass of its branches.
12 But the vine was plucked up in fury,
      cast down to the ground;
    the east wind dried up its fruit;
      they were stripped off and withered.
    As for its strong stem,
      fire consumed it.
13 Now it is planted in the wilderness,
      in a dry and thirsty land.

ᵃOr *lest iniquity be your stumbling block* ᵇHebrew *knew* ᶜOr *in a wooden collar* ᵈSome Hebrew manuscripts; most Hebrew manuscripts *in your blood* ᵉOr *the clouds*

¹⁴ And fire has gone out from
　　the stem of its shoots,
　has consumed its fruit,
so that there remains in it
　no strong stem,
　no sceptre for ruling.

This is a lamentation and has become a lamentation.

ISRAEL'S CONTINUING REBELLION

20 In the seventh year, in the fifth month, on the tenth day of the month, certain of the elders of Israel came to enquire of the LORD, and sat before me. ²And the word of the LORD came to me: ³"Son of man, speak to the elders of Israel, and say to them, Thus says the Lord GOD, Is it to enquire of me that you come? As I live, declares the Lord GOD, I will not be enquired of by you. ⁴Will you judge them, son of man, will you judge them? Let them know the abominations of their fathers, ⁵and say to them, Thus says the Lord GOD: On the day when I chose Israel, I swore*a* to the offspring of the house of Jacob, making myself known to them in the land of Egypt; I swore to them, saying, I am the LORD your God. ⁶On that day I swore to them that I would bring them out of the land of Egypt into a land that I had searched out for them, a land flowing with milk and honey, the most glorious of all lands. ⁷And I said to them, 'Cast away the detestable things your eyes feast on, every one of you, and do not defile yourselves with the idols of Egypt; I am the LORD your God.' ⁸But they rebelled against me and were not willing to listen to me. None of them cast away the detestable things their eyes feasted on, nor did they forsake the idols of Egypt.

"Then I said I would pour out my wrath upon them and spend my anger against them in the midst of the land of Egypt. ⁹But I acted for the sake of my name, that it should not be profaned in the sight of the nations among whom they lived, in whose sight I made myself known to them in bringing them out of the land of Egypt. ¹⁰So I led them out of the land of Egypt and brought them into the wilderness. ¹¹I gave them my statutes and made known to them my rules, by which, if a person does them, he shall live. ¹²Moreover, I gave them my Sabbaths, as a sign between me and them, that they might know that I am the LORD who sanctifies them. ¹³But the house of Israel rebelled against me in the wilderness. They did not walk in my statutes but rejected my rules, by which, if a person does them, he shall live; and my Sabbaths they greatly profaned.

"Then I said I would pour out my wrath upon them in the wilderness, to make a full end of them. ¹⁴But I acted for the sake of my name, that it should not be profaned in the sight of the nations in whose sight I had brought them out. ¹⁵Moreover, I swore to them in the wilderness that I would not bring them into the land that I had given them, a land flowing with milk and honey, the most glorious of all lands, ¹⁶because they rejected my rules and did not walk in my statutes, and profaned my Sabbaths; for their heart went after their idols. ¹⁷Nevertheless, my eye spared them, and I did not destroy them or make a full end of them in the wilderness.

¹⁸"And I said to their children in the wilderness, 'Do not walk in the statutes of your fathers, nor keep their rules, nor defile yourselves with their idols. ¹⁹I am the LORD your God; walk in my statutes, and be careful to obey my rules, ²⁰and keep my Sabbaths holy that they may be a sign between me and you, that you may know that I am the LORD your God.' ²¹But the children rebelled against me. They did not walk in my statutes and were not careful to obey my rules, by which, if a person does them, he shall live; they profaned my Sabbaths.

"Then I said I would pour out my wrath upon them and spend my anger against them in the wilderness. ²²But I withheld my hand and acted for the sake of my name, that it should not be profaned in the sight of the nations, in whose sight I had brought them out. ²³Moreover, I swore to them in the wilderness that I would scatter them among the nations and disperse them through the countries, ²⁴because they had not obeyed my rules, but had rejected my statutes and profaned my Sabbaths, and their eyes were set on their fathers' idols. ²⁵Moreover, I gave them statutes that were not good and rules by which they could not have life, ²⁶and I defiled them through their very gifts in their offering up all their firstborn, that I might devastate them. I did it that they might know that I am the LORD.

²⁷"Therefore, son of man, speak to the house of Israel and say to them, Thus says the Lord GOD: In this also your fathers

---

a Hebrew *I lifted my hand*; twice in this verse; also verses 6, 15, 23, 28, 42 blasphemed me, by dealing treacherously with me. ²⁸For when I had brought them into the land that I swore to give them, then wherever they saw any high hill or any leafy tree, there they offered their sacrifices and there they presented the provocation of their offering; there they sent up their pleasing aromas, and there they poured out their drink offerings. ²⁹(I said to them, 'What is the high place to which you go?' So its name is called Bamah*ᵃ* to this day.)

³⁰"Therefore say to the house of Israel, Thus says the Lord God: Will you defile yourselves after the manner of your fathers and go whoring after their detestable things? ³¹When you present your gifts and offer up your children in fire,*ᵇ* you defile yourselves with all your idols to this day. And shall I be enquired of by you, O house of Israel? As I live, declares the Lord God, I will not be enquired of by you.

³²"What is in your mind shall never happen — the thought, 'Let us be like the nations, like the tribes of the countries, and worship wood and stone.'

THE LORD WILL RESTORE ISRAEL

³³"As I live, declares the Lord God, surely with a mighty hand and an outstretched arm and with wrath poured out I will be king over you. ³⁴I will bring you out from the peoples and gather you out of the countries where you are scattered, with a mighty hand and an outstretched arm, and with wrath poured out. ³⁵And I will bring you into the wilderness of the peoples, and there I will enter into judgement with you face to face. ³⁶As I entered into judgement with your fathers in the wilderness of the land of Egypt, so I will enter into judgement with you, declares the Lord God. ³⁷I will make you pass under the rod, and I will bring you into the bond of the covenant. ³⁸I will purge out the rebels from among you, and those who transgress against me. I will bring them out of the land where they sojourn, but they shall not enter the land of Israel. Then you will know that I am the Lord.

³⁹"As for you, O house of Israel, thus says the Lord God: Go serve every one of you his idols, now and hereafter, if you will not listen to me; but my holy name you shall no more profane with your gifts and your idols.

⁴⁰"For on my holy mountain, the mountain height of Israel, declares the Lord God, there all the house of Israel, all of them, shall serve me in the land. There I will accept them, and there I will require your contributions and the choicest of your gifts, with all your sacred offerings. ⁴¹As a pleasing aroma I will accept you, when I bring you out from the peoples and gather you out of the countries where you have been scattered. And I will manifest my holiness among you in the sight of the nations. ⁴²And you shall know that I am the Lord, when I bring you into the land of Israel, the country that I swore to give to your fathers. ⁴³And there you shall remember your ways and all your deeds with which you have defiled yourselves, and you shall loathe yourselves for all the evils that you have committed. ⁴⁴And you shall know that I am the Lord, when I deal with you for my name's sake, not according to your evil ways, nor according to your corrupt deeds, O house of Israel, declares the Lord God."

⁴⁵*ᶜ* And the word of the Lord came to me: ⁴⁶"Son of man, set your face towards the southland;*ᵈ* preach against the south, and prophesy against the forest land in the Negeb. ⁴⁷Say to the forest of the Negeb, Hear the word of the Lord: Thus says the Lord God, Behold, I will kindle a fire in you, and it shall devour every green tree in you and every dry tree. The blazing flame shall not be quenched, and all faces from south to north shall be scorched by it. ⁴⁸All flesh shall see that I the Lord have kindled it; it shall not be quenched." ⁴⁹Then I said, "Ah, Lord God! They are saying of me, 'Is he not a maker of parables?'"

THE LORD HAS DRAWN HIS SWORD

21*ᵉ* The word of the Lord came to me: ²"Son of man, set your face towards Jerusalem and preach against the sanctuaries.*ᶠ* Prophesy against the land of Israel ³and say to the land of Israel, Thus says the Lord: Behold, I am against you and will draw my sword from its sheath and will cut off from you both righteous and wicked. ⁴Because I will cut off from you both righteous and wicked, therefore my sword shall be drawn from its sheath against all flesh from south to north. ⁵And all flesh shall know that I am the Lord. I have drawn my sword from its sheath; it shall not be sheathed again.

⁶"As for you, son of man, groan; with breaking heart and bitter grief, groan before their

---

ᵃBamah means high place ᵇHebrew and make your children pass through the fire ᶜCh 21:1 in Hebrew ᵈOr towards Teman ᵉCh 21:6 in Hebrew ᶠSome Hebrew manuscripts, compare Septuagint, Syriac against their sanctuary

eyes. ⁷And when they say to you, 'Why do you groan?' you shall say, 'Because of the news that is coming. Every heart will melt, and all hands will be feeble; every spirit will faint, and all knees will be weak as water. Behold, it is coming, and it will be fulfilled,'" declares the Lord GOD.

⁸And the word of the LORD came to me: ⁹"Son of man, prophesy and say, Thus says the Lord, say:

> "A sword, a sword is sharpened
>   and also polished,
> ¹⁰ sharpened for slaughter,
>   polished to flash like lightning!

(Or shall we rejoice? You have despised the rod, my son, with everything of wood.)ᵃ ¹¹So the sword is given to be polished, that it may be grasped in the hand. It is sharpened and polished to be given into the hand of the slayer. ¹²Cry out and wail, son of man, for it is against my people. It is against all the princes of Israel. They are delivered over to the sword with my people. Strike therefore upon your thigh. ¹³For it will not be a testing—what could it do if you despise the rod?"ᵇ declares the Lord GOD.

¹⁴"As for you, son of man, prophesy. Clap your hands and let the sword come down twice, yes, three times,ᶜ the sword for those to be slain. It is the sword for the great slaughter, which surrounds them, ¹⁵that their hearts may melt, and many stumble.ᵈ At all their gates I have given the glittering sword. Ah, it is made like lightning; it is taken upᵉ for slaughter. ¹⁶Cut sharply to the right; set yourself to the left, wherever your face is directed. ¹⁷I also will clap my hands, and I will satisfy my fury; I the LORD have spoken."

¹⁸The word of the LORD came to me again: ¹⁹"As for you, son of man, mark two ways for the sword of the king of Babylon to come. Both of them shall come from the same land. And make a signpost; make it at the head of the way to a city. ²⁰Mark a way for the sword to come to Rabbah of the Ammonites and to Judah, into Jerusalem the fortified. ²¹For the king of Babylon stands at the parting of the way, at the head of the two ways, to use divination. He shakes the arrows; he consults the teraphim;ᶠ he looks at the liver. ²²Into his right hand comes the divination for Jerusalem, to set battering rams, to open the mouth with murder, to lift up the voice with shouting, to set battering rams against the gates, to cast up mounds, to build siege towers. ²³But to them it will seem like a false divination. They have sworn solemn oaths, but he brings their guilt to remembrance, that they may be taken.

²⁴"Therefore thus says the Lord GOD: Because you have made your guilt to be remembered, in that your transgressions are uncovered, so that in all your deeds your sins appear—because you have come to remembrance, you shall be taken in hand. ²⁵And you, O profaneᵍ wicked one, prince of Israel, whose day has come, the time of your final punishment, ²⁶thus says the Lord GOD: Remove the turban and take off the crown. Things shall not remain as they are. Exalt that which is low, and bring low that which is exalted. ²⁷A ruin, ruin, ruin I will make it. This also shall not be, until he comes, the one to whom judgement belongs, and I will give it to him.

²⁸"And you, son of man, prophesy, and say, Thus says the Lord GOD concerning the Ammonites and concerning their reproach; say, A sword, a sword is drawn for the slaughter. It is polished to consume and to flash like lightning—²⁹while they see for you false visions, while they divine lies for you—to place you on the necks of the profane wicked, whose day has come, the time of their final punishment. ³⁰Return it to its sheath. In the place where you were created, in the land of your origin, I will judge you. ³¹And I will pour out my indignation upon you; I will blow upon you with the fire of my wrath and I will deliver you into the hands of brutish men, skilful to destroy. ³²You shall be fuel for the fire. Your blood shall be in the midst of the land. You shall be no more remembered, for I the LORD have spoken."

ISRAEL'S SHEDDING OF BLOOD

22 And the word of the LORD came to me, saying, ²"And you, son of man, will you judge, will you judge the bloody city? Then declare to her all her abominations. ³You shall say, Thus says the Lord GOD: A city that sheds blood in her midst, so that her time may come, and that makes idols to defile herself! ⁴You have become guilty by

---
ᵃProbable reading; Hebrew *The rod of my son despises everything of wood* ᵇOr *For it is a testing; and what if even the rod despises? It shall not be!* ᶜHebrew *its third* ᶜHebrew *many stumbling blocks* ᵉThe meaning of the Hebrew word rendered *taken up* is uncertain ᶠOr *household idols* ᵍOr *slain*; also verse 29

the blood that you have shed, and defiled by the idols that you have made, and you have brought your days near, the appointed time of[a] your years has come. Therefore I have made you a reproach to the nations, and a mockery to all the countries. 5Those who are near and those who are far from you will mock you; your name is defiled; you are full of tumult.

6"Behold, the princes of Israel in you, every one according to his power, have been bent on shedding blood. 7Father and mother are treated with contempt in you; the sojourner suffers extortion in your midst; the fatherless and the widow are wronged in you. 8You have despised my holy things and profaned my Sabbaths. 9There are men in you who slander to shed blood, and people in you who eat on the mountains; they commit lewdness in your midst. 10In you men uncover their fathers' nakedness; in you they violate women who are unclean in their menstrual impurity. 11One commits abomination with his neighbour's wife; another lewdly defiles his daughter-in-law; another in you violates his sister, his father's daughter. 12In you they take bribes to shed blood; you take interest and profit[b] and make gain of your neighbours by extortion; but me you have forgotten, declares the Lord GOD.

13"Behold, I strike my hand at the dishonest gain that you have made, and at the blood that has been in your midst. 14Can your courage endure, or can your hands be strong, in the days that I shall deal with you? I the LORD have spoken, and I will do it. 15I will scatter you among the nations and disperse you through the countries, and I will consume your uncleanness out of you. 16And you shall be profaned by your own doing in the sight of the nations, and you shall know that I am the LORD."

17And the word of the LORD came to me: 18"Son of man, the house of Israel has become dross to me; all of them are bronze and tin and iron and lead in the furnace; they are dross of silver. 19Therefore thus says the Lord GOD: Because you have all become dross, therefore, behold, I will gather you into the midst of Jerusalem. 20As one gathers silver and bronze and iron and lead and tin into a furnace, to blow the fire on it in order to melt it, so I will gather you in my anger and in my wrath, and I will put you in and melt you. 21I will gather you and blow on you with the fire of my wrath, and you shall be melted in the midst of it. 22As silver is melted in a furnace, so you shall be melted in the midst of it, and you shall know that I am the LORD; I have poured out my wrath upon you."

23And the word of the LORD came to me: 24"Son of man, say to her, You are a land that is not cleansed or rained upon in the day of indignation. 25The conspiracy of her prophets in her midst is like a roaring lion tearing the prey; they have devoured human lives; they have taken treasure and precious things; they have made many widows in her midst. 26Her priests have done violence to my law and have profaned my holy things. They have made no distinction between the holy and the common, neither have they taught the difference between the unclean and the clean, and they have disregarded my Sabbaths, so that I am profaned among them. 27Her princes in her midst are like wolves tearing the prey, shedding blood, destroying lives to get dishonest gain. 28And her prophets have smeared whitewash for them, seeing false visions and divining lies for them, saying, 'Thus says the Lord GOD', when the LORD has not spoken. 29The people of the land have practised extortion and committed robbery. They have oppressed the poor and needy, and have extorted from the sojourner without justice. 30And I sought for a man among them who should build up the wall and stand in the breach before me for the land, that I should not destroy it, but I found none. 31Therefore I have poured out my indignation upon them. I have consumed them with the fire of my wrath. I have returned their way upon their heads, declares the Lord GOD."

OHOLAH AND OHOLIBAH

23 The word of the LORD came to me: 2"Son of man, there were two women, the daughters of one mother. 3They played the whore in Egypt; they played the whore in their youth; there their breasts were pressed and their virgin bosoms[c] handled. 4Oholah was the name of the elder and Oholibah the name of her sister. They became mine, and they bore sons and daughters. As for their names, Oholah is Samaria, and Oholibah is Jerusalem.

---

[a]Some Hebrew manuscripts, Septuagint, Syriac, Vulgate, Targum; most Hebrew manuscripts *until*   [b]That is, profit that comes from charging interest to the poor (compare Leviticus 25:36)   [c]Hebrew *nipples*; also verses 8, 21

⁵"Oholah played the whore while she was mine, and she lusted after her lovers the Assyrians, warriors ⁶clothed in purple, governors and commanders, all of them desirable young men, horsemen riding on horses. ⁷She bestowed her whoring upon them, the choicest men of Assyria all of them, and she defiled herself with all the idols of everyone after whom she lusted. ⁸She did not give up her whoring that she had begun in Egypt; for in her youth men had lain with her and handled her virgin bosom and poured out their whoring lust upon her. ⁹Therefore I delivered her into the hands of her lovers, into the hands of the Assyrians, after whom she lusted. ¹⁰These uncovered her nakedness; they seized her sons and her daughters; and as for her, they killed her with the sword; and she became a byword among women, when judgement had been executed on her.

¹¹"Her sister Oholibah saw this, and she became more corrupt than her sister[a] in her lust and in her whoring, which was worse than that of her sister. ¹²She lusted after the Assyrians, governors and commanders, warriors clothed in full armour, horsemen riding on horses, all of them desirable young men. ¹³And I saw that she was defiled; they both took the same way. ¹⁴But she carried her whoring further. She saw men portrayed on the wall, the images of the Chaldeans portrayed in vermilion, ¹⁵wearing belts on their waists, with flowing turbans on their heads, all of them having the appearance of officers, a likeness of Babylonians whose native land was Chaldea. ¹⁶When she saw them, she lusted after them and sent messengers to them in Chaldea. ¹⁷And the Babylonians came to her into the bed of love, and they defiled her with their whoring lust. And after she was defiled by them, she turned from them in disgust. ¹⁸When she carried on her whoring so openly and flaunted her nakedness, I turned in disgust from her, as I had turned in disgust from her sister. ¹⁹Yet she increased her whoring, remembering the days of her youth, when she played the whore in the land of Egypt ²⁰and lusted after her lovers there, whose members were like those of donkeys, and whose issue was like that of horses. ²¹Thus you longed for the lewdness of your youth, when the Egyptians handled your bosom and pressed[b] your young breasts."

²²Therefore, O Oholibah, thus says the Lord GOD: "Behold, I will stir up against you your lovers from whom you turned in disgust, and I will bring them against you from every side: ²³the Babylonians and all the Chaldeans, Pekod and Shoa and Koa, and all the Assyrians with them, desirable young men, governors and commanders all of them, officers and men of renown, all of them riding on horses. ²⁴And they shall come against you from the north[c] with chariots and wagons and a host of peoples. They shall set themselves against you on every side with buckler, shield, and helmet; and I will commit the judgement to them, and they shall judge you according to their judgements. ²⁵And I will direct my jealousy against you, that they may deal with you in fury. They shall cut off your nose and your ears, and your survivors shall fall by the sword. They shall seize your sons and your daughters, and your survivors shall be devoured by fire. ²⁶They shall also strip you of your clothes and take away your beautiful jewels. ²⁷Thus I will put an end to your lewdness and your whoring begun in the land of Egypt, so that you shall not lift up your eyes to them or remember Egypt any more.

²⁸"For thus says the Lord GOD: Behold, I will deliver you into the hands of those whom you hate, into the hands of those from whom you turned in disgust, ²⁹and they shall deal with you in hatred and take away all the fruit of your labour and leave you naked and bare, and the nakedness of your whoring shall be uncovered. Your lewdness and your whoring ³⁰have brought this upon you, because you played the whore with the nations and defiled yourself with their idols. ³¹You have gone the way of your sister; therefore I will give her cup into your hand. ³²Thus says the Lord GOD:

> "You shall drink your sister's cup
>   that is deep and large;
> you shall be laughed at and
>   held in derision,
>   for it contains much;
> ³³ you will be filled with
>   drunkenness and sorrow.
> A cup of horror and desolation,
>   the cup of your sister Samaria;
> ³⁴ you shall drink it and drain it out,
>   and gnaw its shards,
>   and tear your breasts;

---

[a] Hebrew *than she* [b] Vulgate, Syriac: Hebrew *bosom for the sake of* [c] Septuagint; the meaning of the Hebrew word is unknown

for I have spoken, declares the Lord God. ³⁵Therefore thus says the Lord God: Because you have forgotten me and cast me behind your back, you yourself must bear the consequences of your lewdness and whoring."

³⁶The Lord said to me: "Son of man, will you judge Oholah and Oholibah? Declare to them their abominations. ³⁷For they have committed adultery, and blood is on their hands. With their idols they have committed adultery, and they have even offered up*a* to them for food the children whom they had borne to me. ³⁸Moreover, this they have done to me: they have defiled my sanctuary on the same day and profaned my Sabbaths. ³⁹For when they had slaughtered their children in sacrifice to their idols, on the same day they came into my sanctuary to profane it. And behold, this is what they did in my house. ⁴⁰They even sent for men to come from far, to whom a messenger was sent; and behold, they came. For them you bathed yourself, painted your eyes, and adorned yourself with ornaments. ⁴¹You sat on a stately couch, with a table spread before it on which you had placed my incense and my oil. ⁴²The sound of a carefree multitude was with her; and with men of the common sort, drunkards*b* were brought from the wilderness; and they put bracelets on the hands of the women, and beautiful crowns on their heads.

⁴³"Then I said of her who was worn out by adultery, 'Now they will continue to use her for a whore, even her!'*c* ⁴⁴For they have gone in to her, as men go in to a prostitute. Thus they went in to Oholah and to Oholibah, lewd women! ⁴⁵But righteous men shall pass judgement on them with the sentence of adulteresses, and with the sentence of women who shed blood, because they are adulteresses, and blood is on their hands."

⁴⁶For thus says the Lord God: "Bring up a vast host against them, and make them an object of terror and a plunder. ⁴⁷And the host shall stone them and cut them down with their swords. They shall kill their sons and their daughters, and burn up their houses. ⁴⁸Thus will I put an end to lewdness in the land, that all women may take warning and not commit lewdness as you have done. ⁴⁹And they shall return your lewdness upon you, and you shall bear the penalty for your sinful idolatry, and you shall know that I am the Lord God."

THE SIEGE OF JERUSALEM

24 In the ninth year, in the tenth month, on the tenth day of the month, the word of the Lord came to me: ²"Son of man, write down the name of this day, this very day. The king of Babylon has laid siege to Jerusalem this very day. ³And utter a parable to the rebellious house and say to them, Thus says the Lord God:

"Set on the pot, set it on;
  pour in water also;
⁴ put in it the pieces of meat,
  all the good pieces, the thigh
    and the shoulder;
  fill it with choice bones.
⁵ Take the choicest one of the flock;
  pile the logs*d* under it;
  boil it well;
  seethe also its bones in it.

⁶"Therefore thus says the Lord God: Woe to the bloody city, to the pot whose corrosion is in it, and whose corrosion has not gone out of it! Take out of it piece after piece, without making any choice.*e* ⁷For the blood she has shed is in her midst; she put it on the bare rock; she did not pour it out on the ground to cover it with dust. ⁸To rouse my wrath, to take vengeance, I have set on the bare rock the blood she has shed, that it may not be covered. ⁹Therefore thus says the Lord God: Woe to the bloody city! I also will make the pile great. ¹⁰Heap on the logs, kindle the fire, boil the meat well, mix in the spices,*f* and let the bones be burned up. ¹¹Then set it empty upon the coals, that it may become hot, and its copper may burn, that its uncleanness may be melted in it, its corrosion consumed. ¹²She has wearied herself with toil;*g* its abundant corrosion does not go out of it. Into the fire with its corrosion! ¹³On account of your unclean lewdness, because I would have cleansed you and you were not cleansed from your uncleanness, you shall not be cleansed any more till I have satisfied my fury upon you. ¹⁴I am the Lord. I have spoken; it shall come to pass; I will do it. I will not go back; I will not spare; I will not relent; according to your ways and your deeds you will be judged, declares the Lord God."

---

*a*Or *have even made pass through the fire* *b*Or *Sabeans*
*c*The meaning of the Hebrew verse is uncertain *d*Compare verse 10; Hebrew *the bones* *e*Hebrew *no lot has fallen upon it* *f*Or *empty out the broth* *g*The meaning of the Hebrew is uncertain

EZEKIEL'S WIFE DIES

¹⁵The word of the Lord came to me: ¹⁶"Son of man, behold, I am about to take the delight of your eyes away from you at a stroke; yet you shall not mourn or weep, nor shall your tears run down. ¹⁷Sigh, but not aloud; make no mourning for the dead. Bind on your turban, and put your shoes on your feet; do not cover your lips, nor eat the bread of men." ¹⁸So I spoke to the people in the morning, and at evening my wife died. And on the next morning I did as I was commanded.

¹⁹And the people said to me, "Will you not tell us what these things mean for us, that you are acting thus?" ²⁰Then I said to them, "The word of the Lord came to me: ²¹'Say to the house of Israel, Thus says the Lord God: Behold, I will profane my sanctuary, the pride of your power, the delight of your eyes, and the yearning of your soul, and your sons and your daughters whom you left behind shall fall by the sword. ²²And you shall do as I have done; you shall not cover your lips, nor eat the bread of men. ²³Your turbans shall be on your heads and your shoes on your feet; you shall not mourn or weep, but you shall rot away in your iniquities and groan to one another. ²⁴Thus shall Ezekiel be to you a sign; according to all that he has done you shall do. When this comes, then you will know that I am the Lord God.'

²⁵"As for you, son of man, surely on the day when I take from them their stronghold, their joy and glory, the delight of their eyes and their soul's desire, and also their sons and daughters, ²⁶on that day a fugitive will come to you to report to you the news. ²⁷On that day your mouth will be opened to the fugitive, and you shall speak and be no longer mute. So you will be a sign to them, and they will know that I am the Lord."

PROPHECY AGAINST AMMON

25 The word of the Lord came to me: ²"Son of man, set your face towards the Ammonites and prophesy against them. ³Say to the Ammonites, Hear the word of the Lord God: Thus says the Lord God, Because you said, 'Aha!' over my sanctuary when it was profaned, and over the land of Israel when it was made desolate, and over the house of Judah when they went into exile, ⁴therefore behold, I am handing you over to the people of the East for a possession, and they shall set their encampments among you and make their dwellings in your midst. They shall eat your fruit, and they shall drink your milk. ⁵I will make Rabbah a pasture for camels and Ammon*a* a fold for flocks. Then you will know that I am the Lord. ⁶For thus says the Lord God: Because you have clapped your hands and stamped your feet and rejoiced with all the malice within your soul against the land of Israel, ⁷therefore, behold, I have stretched out my hand against you, and will hand you over as plunder to the nations. And I will cut you off from the peoples and will make you perish out of the countries; I will destroy you. Then you will know that I am the Lord.

PROPHECY AGAINST MOAB AND SEIR

⁸"Thus says the Lord God: Because Moab and Seir*b* said, 'Behold, the house of Judah is like all the other nations', ⁹therefore I will lay open the flank of Moab from the cities, from its cities on its frontier, the glory of the country, Beth-jeshimoth, Baal-meon, and Kiriathaim. ¹⁰I will give it along with the Ammonites to the people of the East as a possession, that the Ammonites may be remembered no more among the nations, ¹¹and I will execute judgements upon Moab. Then they will know that I am the Lord.

PROPHECY AGAINST EDOM

¹²"Thus says the Lord God: Because Edom acted revengefully against the house of Judah and has grievously offended in taking vengeance on them, ¹³therefore thus says the Lord God, I will stretch out my hand against Edom and cut off from it man and beast. And I will make it desolate; from Teman even to Dedan they shall fall by the sword. ¹⁴And I will lay my vengeance upon Edom by the hand of my people Israel, and they shall do in Edom according to my anger and according to my wrath, and they shall know my vengeance, declares the Lord God.

PROPHECY AGAINST PHILISTIA

¹⁵"Thus says the Lord God: Because the Philistines acted revengefully and took vengeance with malice of soul to destroy in never-ending enmity, ¹⁶therefore thus says the Lord God, Behold, I will stretch out my hand against the Philistines, and I will cut off the Cherethites and destroy the rest of the sea coast. ¹⁷I will execute great vengeance on them with wrathful rebukes. Then they will

---

a Hebrew *and the Ammonites*   *b* Septuagint lacks *and Seir* know that I am the Lord, when I lay my vengeance upon them."

PROPHECY AGAINST TYRE

26 In the eleventh year, on the first day of the month, the word of the Lord came to me: ²"Son of man, because Tyre said concerning Jerusalem, 'Aha, the gate of the peoples is broken; it has swung open to me. I shall be replenished, now that she is laid waste', ³therefore thus says the Lord God: Behold, I am against you, O Tyre, and will bring up many nations against you, as the sea brings up its waves. ⁴They shall destroy the walls of Tyre and break down her towers, and I will scrape her soil from her and make her a bare rock. ⁵She shall be in the midst of the sea a place for the spreading of nets, for I have spoken, declares the Lord God. And she shall become plunder for the nations, ⁶and her daughters on the mainland shall be killed by the sword. Then they will know that I am the Lord.

⁷"For thus says the Lord God: Behold, I will bring against Tyre from the north Nebuchadnezzar[a] king of Babylon, king of kings, with horses and chariots, and with horsemen and a host of many soldiers. ⁸He will kill with the sword your daughters on the mainland. He will set up a siege wall against you and throw up a mound against you, and raise a roof of shields against you. ⁹He will direct the shock of his battering rams against your walls, and with his axes he will break down your towers. ¹⁰His horses will be so many that their dust will cover you. Your walls will shake at the noise of the horsemen and wagons and chariots, when he enters your gates as men enter a city that has been breached. ¹¹With the hoofs of his horses he will trample all your streets. He will kill your people with the sword, and your mighty pillars will fall to the ground. ¹²They will plunder your riches and loot your merchandise. They will break down your walls and destroy your pleasant houses. Your stones and timber and soil they will cast into the midst of the waters. ¹³And I will stop the music of your songs, and the sound of your lyres shall be heard no more. ¹⁴I will make you a bare rock. You shall be a place for the spreading of nets. You shall never be rebuilt, for I am the Lord; I have spoken, declares the Lord God.

¹⁵"Thus says the Lord God to Tyre: Will not the coastlands shake at the sound of your fall, when the wounded groan, when slaughter is made in your midst? ¹⁶Then all the princes of the sea will step down from their thrones and remove their robes and strip off their embroidered garments. They will clothe themselves with trembling; they will sit on the ground and tremble every moment and be appalled at you. ¹⁷And they will raise a lamentation over you and say to you,

"'How you have perished,
 you who were inhabited
  from the seas,
O city renowned,
 who was mighty on the sea;
she and her inhabitants
 imposed their terror
  on all her inhabitants!
¹⁸ Now the coastlands tremble
 on the day of your fall,
and the coastlands that are on the sea
 are dismayed at your passing.'

¹⁹"For thus says the Lord God: When I make you a city laid waste, like the cities that are not inhabited, when I bring up the deep over you, and the great waters cover you, ²⁰then I will make you go down with those who go down to the pit, to the people of old, and I will make you to dwell in the world below, among ruins from of old, with those who go down to the pit, so that you will not be inhabited; but I will set beauty in the land of the living. ²¹I will bring you to a dreadful end, and you shall be no more. Though you be sought for, you will never be found again, declares the Lord God."

A LAMENT FOR TYRE

27 The word of the Lord came to me: ²"Now you, son of man, raise a lamentation over Tyre, ³and say to Tyre, who dwells at the entrances to the sea, merchant of the peoples to many coastlands, thus says the Lord God:

"O Tyre, you have said,
 'I am perfect in beauty.'
⁴ Your borders are in the
  heart of the seas;
 your builders made perfect
  your beauty.
⁵ They made all your planks
 of fir trees from Senir;

---

[a] Hebrew *Nebuchadrezzar*; so throughout Ezekiel

they took a cedar from Lebanon
    to make a mast for you.
6 Of oaks of Bashan
    they made your oars;
they made your deck of pines
    from the coasts of Cyprus,
    inlaid with ivory.
7 Of fine embroidered linen from Egypt
    was your sail,
    serving as your banner;
blue and purple from the
    coasts of Elishah
    was your awning.
8 The inhabitants of Sidon and Arvad
    were your rowers;
your skilled men, O Tyre, were in you;
    they were your pilots.
9 The elders of Gebal and her
    skilled men were in you,
    caulking your seams;
all the ships of the sea with their
    mariners were in you
    to barter for your wares.

10 "Persia and Lud and Put were in your army as your men of war. They hung the shield and helmet in you; they gave you splendour. 11 Men of Arvad and Helech were on your walls all round, and men of Gamad were in your towers. They hung their shields on your walls all round; they made perfect your beauty.
12 "Tarshish did business with you because of your great wealth of every kind; silver, iron, tin, and lead they exchanged for your wares. 13 Javan, Tubal, and Meshech traded with you; they exchanged human beings and vessels of bronze for your merchandise. 14 From Beth-togarmah they exchanged horses, war horses, and mules for your wares. 15 The men of Dedan[a] traded with you. Many coastlands were your own special markets; they brought you in payment ivory tusks and ebony. 16 Syria did business with you because of your abundant goods; they exchanged for your wares emeralds, purple, embroidered work, fine linen, coral, and ruby. 17 Judah and the land of Israel traded with you; they exchanged for your merchandise wheat of Minnith, meal,[b] honey, oil, and balm. 18 Damascus did business with you for your abundant goods, because of your great wealth of every kind; wine of Helbon and wool of Sahar 19 and casks of wine[c] from Uzal they exchanged for your wares; wrought iron, cassia, and calamus were bartered for your merchandise. 20 Dedan traded with you in saddlecloths for riding. 21 Arabia and all the princes of Kedar were your favoured dealers in lambs, rams, and goats; in these they did business with you. 22 The traders of Sheba and Raamah traded with you; they exchanged for your wares the best of all kinds of spices and all precious stones and gold. 23 Haran, Canneh, Eden, traders of Sheba, Asshur, and Chilmad traded with you. 24 In your market these traded with you in choice garments, in clothes of blue and embroidered work, and in carpets of coloured material, bound with cords and made secure. 25 The ships of Tarshish travelled for you with your merchandise. So you were filled and heavily laden in the heart of the seas.

26   "Your rowers have brought you out
    into the high seas.
The east wind has wrecked you
    in the heart of the seas.
27 Your riches, your wares,
    your merchandise,
your mariners and your pilots,
your caulkers, your dealers
    in merchandise,
and all your men of war
    who are in you,
with all your crew
    that is in your midst,
sink into the heart of the seas
    on the day of your fall.
28 At the sound of the cry of your pilots
    the countryside shakes,
29 and down from their ships
    come all who handle the oar.
The mariners and all the
    pilots of the sea
stand on the land
30 and shout aloud over you
    and cry out bitterly.
They cast dust on their heads
    and wallow in ashes;
31 they make themselves bald for you
    and put sackcloth on their waist,
and they weep over you in
    bitterness of soul,
    with bitter mourning.
32 In their wailing they raise a
    lamentation for you
    and lament over you:

---

[a] Hebrew; Septuagint *Rhodes*   [b] The meaning of the Hebrew word is unknown   [c] Probable reading; Hebrew *wool of Sahar* [19] *and Dan and Javan*

'Who is like Tyre,
  like one destroyed in the
    midst of the sea?
33 When your wares came from
    the seas,
  you satisfied many peoples;
  with your abundant wealth
    and merchandise
  you enriched the kings of the earth.
34 Now you are wrecked by the seas,
    in the depths of the waters;
  your merchandise and all your
    crew in your midst
  have sunk with you.
35 All the inhabitants of the coastlands
    are appalled at you,
  and the hair of their kings
    bristles with horror;
    their faces are convulsed.
36 The merchants among the
    peoples hiss at you;
  you have come to a dreadful end
    and shall be no more for ever.'"

PROPHECY AGAINST THE PRINCE OF TYRE

28 The word of the Lord came to me: ²"Son of man, say to the prince of Tyre, Thus says the Lord God:

"Because your heart is proud,
  and you have said, 'I am a god,
  I sit in the seat of the gods,
    in the heart of the seas',
  yet you are but a man, and no god,
    though you make your heart
      like the heart of a god —
3 you are indeed wiser than Daniel;
    no secret is hidden from you;
4 by your wisdom and your
      understanding
  you have made wealth for yourself,
  and have gathered gold and silver
    into your treasuries;
5 by your great wisdom in your trade
    you have increased your wealth,
  and your heart has become
    proud in your wealth —
6 therefore thus says the Lord God:
  Because you make your heart
    like the heart of a god,
7 therefore, behold, I will bring
    foreigners upon you,
    the most ruthless of the nations;
  and they shall draw their swords
    against the beauty of your wisdom
    and defile your splendour.
8 They shall thrust you down
    into the pit,
  and you shall die the
    death of the slain
    in the heart of the seas.
9 Will you still say, 'I am a god',
    in the presence of those
      who kill you,
  though you are but a man, and no god,
    in the hands of those who slay you?
10 You shall die the death of
      the uncircumcised
    by the hand of foreigners;
  for I have spoken, declares
    the Lord God."

A LAMENT OVER THE KING OF TYRE

¹¹Moreover, the word of the Lord came to me: ¹²"Son of man, raise a lamentation over the king of Tyre, and say to him, Thus says the Lord God:

"You were the signet of perfection,ᵃ
  full of wisdom and perfect in beauty.
13 You were in Eden, the garden of God;
  every precious stone was
    your covering,
  sardius, topaz, and diamond,
    beryl, onyx, and jasper,
    sapphire,ᵇ emerald, and carbuncle;
  and crafted in gold were
    your settings
    and your engravings.ᶜ
  On the day that you were created
    they were prepared.
14 You were an anointed guardian cherub.
    I placed you;ᵈ you were on the
      holy mountain of God;
    in the midst of the stones
      of fire you walked.
15 You were blameless in your ways
    from the day you were created,
    till unrighteousness was
      found in you.
16 In the abundance of your trade
    you were filled with violence in
      your midst, and you sinned;
  so I cast you as a profane thing
    from the mountain of God,
    and I destroyed you,ᵉ O
      guardian cherub,
    from the midst of the stones of fire.

ᵃThe meaning of the Hebrew phrase is uncertain ᵇOr *lapis lazuli*
ᶜThe meaning of the Hebrew phrase is uncertain ᵈThe meaning of the Hebrew phrase is uncertain ᵉOr *banished you*

17 Your heart was proud because
    of your beauty;
  you corrupted your wisdom for
    the sake of your splendour.
  I cast you to the ground;
  I exposed you before kings,
    to feast their eyes on you.
18 By the multitude of your iniquities,
    in the unrighteousness of your trade
  you profaned your sanctuaries;
  so I brought fire out from your midst;
    it consumed you,
  and I turned you to ashes on the earth
    in the sight of all who saw you.
19 All who know you among the peoples
    are appalled at you;
  you have come to a dreadful end
    and shall be no more for ever."

PROPHECY AGAINST SIDON

²⁰The word of the LORD came to me: ²¹"Son of man, set your face towards Sidon, and prophesy against her ²²and say, Thus says the Lord GOD:

  "Behold, I am against you, O Sidon,
    and I will manifest my glory
      in your midst.
  And they shall know that
    I am the LORD
  when I execute judgements in her
    and manifest my holiness in her;
23 for I will send pestilence into her,
    and blood into her streets;
  and the slain shall fall in her midst,
    by the sword that is against
      her on every side.
  Then they will know that
    I am the LORD.

²⁴"And for the house of Israel there shall be no more a brier to prick or a thorn to hurt them among all their neighbours who have treated them with contempt. Then they will know that I am the Lord GOD.

ISRAEL GATHERED IN SECURITY

²⁵"Thus says the Lord GOD: When I gather the house of Israel from the peoples among whom they are scattered, and manifest my holiness in them in the sight of the nations, then they shall dwell in their own land that I gave to my servant Jacob. ²⁶And they shall dwell securely in it, and they shall build houses and plant vineyards. They shall dwell securely, when I execute judgements upon all their neighbours who have treated them with contempt. Then they will know that I am the LORD their God."

PROPHECY AGAINST EGYPT

29 In the tenth year, in the tenth month, on the twelfth day of the month, the word of the LORD came to me: ²"Son of man, set your face against Pharaoh king of Egypt, and prophesy against him and against all Egypt; ³speak, and say, Thus says the Lord GOD:

  "Behold, I am against you,
    Pharaoh king of Egypt,
  the great dragon that lies
    in the midst of his streams,
  that says, 'My Nile is my own;
    I made it for myself.'
4 I will put hooks in your jaws,
    and make the fish of your streams
      stick to your scales;
  and I will draw you up out of the
    midst of your streams,
  with all the fish of your streams
    that stick to your scales.
5 And I will cast you out into
    the wilderness,
  you and all the fish of your streams;
  you shall fall on the open field,
    and not be brought together
      or gathered.
  To the beasts of the earth and to
    the birds of the heavens
  I give you as food.

⁶Then all the inhabitants of Egypt shall know that I am the LORD.

"Because you[a] have been a staff of reed to the house of Israel, ⁷when they grasped you with the hand, you broke and tore all their shoulders; and when they leaned on you, you broke and made all their loins to shake.[b] ⁸Therefore thus says the Lord GOD: Behold, I will bring a sword upon you, and will cut off from you man and beast, ⁹and the land of Egypt shall be a desolation and a waste. Then they will know that I am the LORD.

"Because you[c] said, 'The Nile is mine, and I made it', ¹⁰therefore, behold, I am against you and against your streams, and I will make the land of Egypt an utter waste and desolation, from Migdol to Syene, as far as the border of

---

[a]Hebrew *they* [b]Syriac (compare Psalm 69:23); Hebrew *to stand* [c]Hebrew *he*

Cush. ¹¹No foot of man shall pass through it, and no foot of beast shall pass through it; it shall be uninhabited forty years. ¹²And I will make the land of Egypt a desolation in the midst of desolated countries, and her cities shall be a desolation forty years among cities that are laid waste. I will scatter the Egyptians among the nations, and disperse them through the countries.

¹³"For thus says the Lord God: At the end of forty years I will gather the Egyptians from the peoples among whom they were scattered, ¹⁴and I will restore the fortunes of Egypt and bring them back to the land of Pathros, the land of their origin, and there they shall be a lowly kingdom. ¹⁵It shall be the most lowly of the kingdoms, and never again exalt itself above the nations. And I will make them so small that they will never again rule over the nations. ¹⁶And it shall never again be the reliance of the house of Israel, recalling their iniquity, when they turn to them for aid. Then they will know that I am the Lord God."

¹⁷In the twenty-seventh year, in the first month, on the first day of the month, the word of the Lord came to me: ¹⁸"Son of man, Nebuchadnezzar king of Babylon made his army labour hard against Tyre. Every head was made bald, and every shoulder was rubbed bare, yet neither he nor his army got anything from Tyre to pay for the labour that he had performed against her. ¹⁹Therefore thus says the Lord God: Behold, I will give the land of Egypt to Nebuchadnezzar king of Babylon; and he shall carry off its wealth*a* and despoil it and plunder it; and it shall be the wages for his army. ²⁰I have given him the land of Egypt as his payment for which he laboured, because they worked for me, declares the Lord God.

²¹"On that day I will cause a horn to spring up for the house of Israel, and I will open your lips among them. Then they will know that I am the Lord."

A LAMENT FOR EGYPT

30 The word of the Lord came to me: ²"Son of man, prophesy, and say, Thus says the Lord God:

"Wail, 'Alas for the day!'
³   For the day is near,
     the day of the Lord is near;
it will be a day of clouds,
     a time of doom for*b* the nations.
⁴   A sword shall come upon Egypt,
     and anguish shall be in Cush,
when the slain fall in Egypt,
     and her wealth*c* is carried away,
     and her foundations are torn down.

⁵Cush, and Put, and Lud, and all Arabia, and Libya,*d* and the people of the land that is in league,*e* shall fall with them by the sword.

⁶   "Thus says the Lord:
Those who support Egypt shall fall,
     and her proud might shall
       come down;
from Migdol to Syene
     they shall fall within her
       by the sword,
declares the Lord God.
⁷   And they shall be desolated in the
     midst of desolated countries,
and their cities shall be in the midst
     of cities that are laid waste.
⁸   Then they will know that
     I am the Lord,
when I have set fire to Egypt,
     and all her helpers are broken.

⁹"On that day messengers shall go out from me in ships to terrify the unsuspecting people of Cush, and anguish shall come upon them on the day of Egypt's doom;*f* for, behold, it comes!
¹⁰"Thus says the Lord God:

"I will put an end to the wealth
     of Egypt,
by the hand of Nebuchadnezzar
     king of Babylon.
¹¹   He and his people with him, the
     most ruthless of nations,
shall be brought in to
     destroy the land,
and they shall draw their
     swords against Egypt
and fill the land with the slain.
¹²   And I will dry up the Nile
and will sell the land into the
     hand of evildoers;
I will bring desolation upon the
     land and everything in it,
     by the hand of foreigners;
I am the Lord; I have spoken.

---

*a*Or *multitude*   *b*Hebrew lacks *doom for*   *c*Or *multitude*; also verse 10   *d*With Septuagint; Hebrew *Cub*   *e*Hebrew *and the sons of the land of the covenant*   *f*Hebrew *the day of Egypt*

¹³"Thus says the Lord GOD:

"I will destroy the idols
  and put an end to the images
   in Memphis;
 there shall no longer be a prince
  from the land of Egypt;
 so I will put fear in the land of Egypt.
¹⁴ I will make Pathros a desolation
  and will set fire to Zoan
  and will execute judgements
   on Thebes.
¹⁵ And I will pour out my wrath
   on Pelusium,
  the stronghold of Egypt,
  and cut off the multitude*a* of Thebes.
¹⁶ And I will set fire to Egypt;
  Pelusium shall be in great agony;
  Thebes shall be breached,
  and Memphis shall face
   enemies*b* by day.
¹⁷ The young men of On and of Pi-beseth
   shall fall by the sword,
  and the women*c* shall go
   into captivity.
¹⁸ At Tehaphnehes the day shall be dark,
  when I break there the yoke
   bars of Egypt,
  and her proud might shall
   come to an end in her;
  she shall be covered by a cloud,
  and her daughters shall
   go into captivity.
¹⁹ Thus I will execute judgements
   on Egypt.
  Then they will know that
   I am the LORD."

EGYPT SHALL FALL TO BABYLON

²⁰In the eleventh year, in the first month, on the seventh day of the month, the word of the LORD came to me: ²¹"Son of man, I have broken the arm of Pharaoh king of Egypt, and behold, it has not been bound up, to heal it by binding it with a bandage, so that it may become strong to wield the sword. ²²Therefore thus says the Lord GOD: Behold, I am against Pharaoh king of Egypt and will break his arms, both the strong arm and the one that was broken, and I will make the sword fall from his hand. ²³I will scatter the Egyptians among the nations and disperse them through the countries. ²⁴And I will strengthen the arms of the king of Babylon and put my sword in his hand, but I will break the arms of Pharaoh, and he will groan before him like a man mortally wounded. ²⁵I will strengthen the arms of the king of Babylon, but the arms of Pharaoh shall fall. Then they shall know that I am the LORD, when I put my sword into the hand of the king of Babylon and he stretches it out against the land of Egypt. ²⁶And I will scatter the Egyptians among the nations and disperse them throughout the countries. Then they will know that I am the LORD."

PHARAOH TO BE SLAIN

31 In the eleventh year, in the third month, on the first day of the month, the word of the LORD came to me: ²"Son of man, say to Pharaoh king of Egypt and to his multitude:

"Whom are you like in your greatness?
³ Behold, Assyria was a
   cedar in Lebanon,
  with beautiful branches
   and forest shade,
  and of towering height,
   its top among the clouds.*d*
⁴ The waters nourished it;
  the deep made it grow tall,
  making its rivers flow
   around the place of its planting,
  sending forth its streams
   to all the trees of the field.
⁵ So it towered high
   above all the trees of the field;
  its boughs grew large
   and its branches long
   from abundant water in its shoots.
⁶ All the birds of the heavens
   made their nests in its boughs;
  under its branches all the
   beasts of the field
  gave birth to their young,
  and under its shadow
   lived all great nations.
⁷ It was beautiful in its greatness,
   in the length of its branches;
  for its roots went down
   to abundant waters.
⁸ The cedars in the garden of
   God could not rival it,
  nor the fir trees equal its boughs;
  neither were the plane trees
   like its branches;
  no tree in the garden of God
   was its equal in beauty.

---

*a*Or *wealth* *b*Or *distress* *c*Or *the cities*; Hebrew *they* *d*Or *its top went through the thick boughs*

⁹ I made it beautiful
    in the mass of its branches,
    and all the trees of Eden envied it,
    that were in the garden of God.

¹⁰"Therefore thus says the Lord GOD: Because it[a] towered high and set its top among the clouds,[b] and its heart was proud of its height, ¹¹I will give it into the hand of a mighty one of the nations. He shall surely deal with it as its wickedness deserves. I have cast it out. ¹²Foreigners, the most ruthless of nations, have cut it down and left it. On the mountains and in all the valleys its branches have fallen, and its boughs have been broken in all the ravines of the land, and all the peoples of the earth have gone away from its shadow and left it. ¹³On its fallen trunk dwell all the birds of the heavens, and on its branches are all the beasts of the field. ¹⁴All this is in order that no trees by the waters may grow to towering height or set their tops among the clouds,[c] and that no trees that drink water may reach up to them in height. For they are all given over to death, to the world below, among the children of man,[d] with those who go down to the pit.

¹⁵"Thus says the Lord GOD: On the day the cedar[e] went down to Sheol I caused mourning; I closed the deep over it, and restrained its rivers, and many waters were stopped. I clothed Lebanon in gloom for it, and all the trees of the field fainted because of it. ¹⁶I made the nations quake at the sound of its fall, when I cast it down to Sheol with those who go down to the pit. And all the trees of Eden, the choice and best of Lebanon, all that drink water, were comforted in the world below. ¹⁷They also went down to Sheol with it, to those who are slain by the sword; yes, those who were its arm, who lived under its shadow among the nations.

¹⁸"Whom are you thus like in glory and in greatness among the trees of Eden? You shall be brought down with the trees of Eden to the world below. You shall lie among the uncircumcised, with those who are slain by the sword.

"This is Pharaoh and all his multitude, declares the Lord GOD."

A LAMENT OVER PHARAOH AND EGYPT

32 In the twelfth year, in the twelfth month, on the first day of the month, the word of the LORD came to me: ²"Son of man, raise a lamentation over Pharaoh king of Egypt and say to him:

"You consider yourself a lion
    of the nations,
but you are like a dragon in the seas;
    you burst forth in your rivers,
trouble the waters with your feet,
    and foul their rivers.

³ Thus says the Lord GOD:
    I will throw my net over you
        with a host of many peoples,
    and they will haul you up
        in my dragnet.
⁴ And I will cast you on the ground;
    on the open field I will fling you,
    and will cause all the birds of the
        heavens to settle on you,
    and I will gorge the beasts of the
        whole earth with you.
⁵ I will strew your flesh upon
        the mountains
    and fill the valleys with your carcass.[f]
⁶ I will drench the land even
        to the mountains
        with your flowing blood,
    and the ravines will be full of you.
⁷ When I blot you out, I will
        cover the heavens
        and make their stars dark;
    I will cover the sun with a cloud,
    and the moon shall not give its light.
⁸ All the bright lights of heaven
        will I make dark over you,
    and put darkness on your land,
            declares the Lord GOD.

⁹"I will trouble the hearts of many peoples, when I bring your destruction among the nations, into the countries that you have not known. ¹⁰I will make many peoples appalled at you, and the hair of their kings shall bristle with horror because of you, when I brandish my sword before them. They shall tremble every moment, every one for his own life, on the day of your downfall.

¹¹"For thus says the Lord GOD: The sword of the king of Babylon shall come upon you. ¹²I will cause your multitude to fall by the swords of mighty ones, all of them most ruthless of nations.

"They shall bring to ruin the
        pride of Egypt,
    and all its multitude[g] shall perish.

---
[a]Syriac, Vulgate; Hebrew *you*   [b]Or *its top through the thick boughs*   [c]Or *their tops through the thick boughs*   [d]Or *of Adam*   [e]Hebrew *it*   [f]Hebrew *your height*   [g]Or *wealth*

13 I will destroy all its beasts
    from beside many waters;
  and no foot of man shall trouble
    them any more,
  nor shall the hoofs of beasts
    trouble them.
14 Then I will make their waters clear,
  and cause their rivers to run like oil,
    declares the Lord GOD.
15 When I make the land of
    Egypt desolate,
  and when the land is desolate
    of all that fills it,
  when I strike down all who dwell in it,
  then they will know that
    I am the LORD.

¹⁶This is a lamentation that shall be chanted; the daughters of the nations shall chant it; over Egypt, and over all her multitude, shall they chant it, declares the Lord GOD."

¹⁷In the twelfth year, in the twelfth month,[a] on the fifteenth day of the month, the word of the LORD came to me: ¹⁸"Son of man, wail over the multitude of Egypt, and send them down, her and the daughters of majestic nations, to the world below, to those who have gone down to the pit:

19 'Whom do you surpass in beauty?
    Go down and be laid to rest with
      the uncircumcised.'

²⁰They shall fall amid those who are slain by the sword. Egypt[b] is delivered to the sword; drag her away, and all her multitudes. ²¹The mighty chiefs shall speak of them, with their helpers, out of the midst of Sheol: 'They have come down, they lie still, the uncircumcised, slain by the sword.' ²²"Assyria is there, and all her company, its graves all round it, all of them slain, fallen by the sword, ²³whose graves are set in the uttermost parts of the pit; and her company is all round her grave, all of them slain, fallen by the sword, who spread terror in the land of the living. ²⁴"Elam is there, and all her multitude round her grave; all of them slain, fallen by the sword, who went down uncircumcised into the world below, who spread their terror in the land of the living; and they bear their shame with those who go down to the pit. ²⁵They have made her a bed among the slain with all her multitude, her graves all round it, all of them uncircumcised, slain by the sword; for terror of them was spread in the land of the living, and they bear their shame with those who go down to the pit; they are placed among the slain. ²⁶"Meshech-Tubal is there, and all her multitude, her graves all round it, all of them uncircumcised, slain by the sword; for they spread their terror in the land of the living. ²⁷And they do not lie with the mighty, the fallen from among the uncircumcised, who went down to Sheol with their weapons of war, whose swords were laid under their heads, and whose iniquities are upon their bones; for the terror of the mighty men was in the land of the living. ²⁸But as for you, you shall be broken and lie among the uncircumcised, with those who are slain by the sword.

²⁹"Edom is there, her kings and all her princes, who for all their might are laid with those who are killed by the sword; they lie with the uncircumcised, with those who go down to the pit.

³⁰"The princes of the north are there, all of them, and all the Sidonians, who have gone down in shame with the slain, for all the terror that they caused by their might; they lie uncircumcised with those who are slain by the sword, and bear their shame with those who go down to the pit.

³¹"When Pharaoh sees them, he will be comforted for all his multitude, Pharaoh and all his army, slain by the sword, declares the Lord GOD. ³²For I spread terror in the land of the living; and he shall be laid to rest among the uncircumcised, with those who are slain by the sword, Pharaoh and all his multitude, declares the Lord GOD."

EZEKIEL IS ISRAEL'S WATCHMAN

33 The word of the LORD came to me: ²"Son of man, speak to your people and say to them, If I bring the sword upon a land, and the people of the land take a man from among them, and make him their watchman, ³and if he sees the sword coming upon the land and blows the trumpet and warns the people, ⁴then if anyone who hears the sound of the trumpet does not take warning, and the sword comes and takes him away, his blood shall be upon his own head. ⁵He heard the sound of the trumpet and did not take warning; his blood shall be upon himself. But if he had taken warning, he would have saved his life.

---

[a] Hebrew lacks *in the twelfth month*   [b] Hebrew *She*

6But if the watchman sees the sword coming and does not blow the trumpet, so that the people are not warned, and the sword comes and takes any one of them, that person is taken away in his iniquity, but his blood I will require at the watchman's hand.

7"So you, son of man, I have made a watchman for the house of Israel. Whenever you hear a word from my mouth, you shall give them warning from me. **8**If I say to the wicked, O wicked one, you shall surely die, and you do not speak to warn the wicked to turn from his way, that wicked person shall die in his iniquity, but his blood I will require at your hand. **9**But if you warn the wicked to turn from his way, and he does not turn from his way, that person shall die in his iniquity, but you will have delivered your soul.

WHY WILL YOU DIE, ISRAEL?

10"And you, son of man, say to the house of Israel, Thus have you said: 'Surely our transgressions and our sins are upon us, and we rot away because of them. How then can we live?' **11**Say to them, As I live, declares the Lord GOD, I have no pleasure in the death of the wicked, but that the wicked turn from his way and live; turn back, turn back from your evil ways, for why will you die, O house of Israel?

12"And you, son of man, say to your people, The righteousness of the righteous shall not deliver him when he transgresses, and as for the wickedness of the wicked, he shall not fall by it when he turns from his wickedness, and the righteous shall not be able to live by his righteousness*a* when he sins. **13**Though I say to the righteous that he shall surely live, yet if he trusts in his righteousness and does injustice, none of his righteous deeds shall be remembered, but in his injustice that he has done he shall die. **14**Again, though I say to the wicked, 'You shall surely die', yet if he turns from his sin and does what is just and right, **15**if the wicked restores the pledge, gives back what he has taken by robbery, and walks in the statutes of life, not doing injustice, he shall surely live; he shall not die. **16**None of the sins that he has committed shall be remembered against him. He has done what is just and right; he shall surely live.

17"Yet your people say, 'The way of the Lord is not just', when it is their own way that is not just. **18**When the righteous turns from his righteousness and does injustice, he shall die for it. **19**And when the wicked turns from his wickedness and does what is just and right, he shall live by this. **20**Yet you say, 'The way of the Lord is not just.' O house of Israel, I will judge each of you according to his ways.'

JERUSALEM STRUCK DOWN

21In the twelfth year of our exile, in the tenth month, on the fifth day of the month, a fugitive from Jerusalem came to me and said, "The city has been struck down." **22**Now the hand of the LORD had been upon me the evening before the fugitive came; and he had opened my mouth by the time the man came to me in the morning, so my mouth was opened, and I was no longer mute.

23The word of the LORD came to me: **24**"Son of man, the inhabitants of these waste places in the land of Israel keep saying, 'Abraham was only one man, yet he got possession of the land; but we are many; the land is surely given us to possess.' **25**Therefore say to them, Thus says the Lord GOD: You eat flesh with the blood and lift up your eyes to your idols and shed blood; shall you then possess the land? **26**You rely on the sword, you commit abominations, and each of you defiles his neighbour's wife; shall you then possess the land? **27**Say this to them, Thus says the Lord GOD: As I live, surely those who are in the waste places shall fall by the sword, and whoever is in the open field I will give to the beasts to be devoured, and those who are in strongholds and in caves shall die by pestilence. **28**And I will make the land a desolation and a waste, and her proud might shall come to an end, and the mountains of Israel shall be so desolate that none will pass through. **29**Then they will know that I am the LORD, when I have made the land a desolation and a waste because of all their abominations that they have committed.

30"As for you, son of man, your people who talk together about you by the walls and at the doors of the houses, say to one another, each to his brother, 'Come, and hear what the word is that comes from the LORD.' **31**And they come to you as people come, and they sit before you as my people, and they hear what you say but they will not do it; for with lustful talk in their mouths they act; their heart is set on their gain. **32**And behold, you are to them like one who sings lustful songs with a beautiful voice and plays*b* well on an instrument, for they hear what you say, but

---

*a*Hebrew *by it* *b*Hebrew *like the singing of lustful songs with a beautiful voice and one who plays*

they will not do it. ³³When this comes—and come it will!—then they will know that a prophet has been among them."

PROPHECY AGAINST THE SHEPHERDS OF ISRAEL

34 The word of the LORD came to me: ²"Son of man, prophesy against the shepherds of Israel; prophesy, and say to them, even to the shepherds, Thus says the Lord GOD: Ah, shepherds of Israel who have been feeding yourselves! Should not shepherds feed the sheep? ³You eat the fat, you clothe yourselves with the wool, you slaughter the fat ones, but you do not feed the sheep. ⁴The weak you have not strengthened, the sick you have not healed, the injured you have not bound up, the strayed you have not brought back, the lost you have not sought, and with force and harshness you have ruled them. ⁵So they were scattered, because there was no shepherd, and they became food for all the wild beasts. My sheep were scattered; ⁶they wandered over all the mountains and on every high hill. My sheep were scattered over all the face of the earth, with none to search or seek for them.

⁷"Therefore, you shepherds, hear the word of the LORD: ⁸As I live, declares the Lord GOD, surely because my sheep have become a prey, and my sheep have become food for all the wild beasts, since there was no shepherd, and because my shepherds have not searched for my sheep, but the shepherds have fed themselves, and have not fed my sheep, ⁹therefore, you shepherds, hear the word of the LORD: ¹⁰Thus says the Lord GOD, Behold, I am against the shepherds, and I will require my sheep at their hand and put a stop to their feeding the sheep. No longer shall the shepherds feed themselves. I will rescue my sheep from their mouths, that they may not be food for them.

THE LORD GOD WILL SEEK THEM OUT

¹¹"For thus says the Lord GOD: Behold, I, I myself will search for my sheep and will seek them out. ¹²As a shepherd seeks out his flock when he is among his sheep that have been scattered, so will I seek out my sheep, and I will rescue them from all places where they have been scattered on a day of clouds and thick darkness. ¹³And I will bring them out from the peoples and gather them from the countries, and will bring them into their own land. And I will feed them on the mountains of Israel, by the ravines, and in all the inhabited places of the country. ¹⁴I will feed them with good pasture, and on the mountain heights of Israel shall be their grazing land. There they shall lie down in good grazing land, and on rich pasture they shall feed on the mountains of Israel. ¹⁵I myself will be the shepherd of my sheep, and I myself will make them lie down, declares the Lord GOD. ¹⁶I will seek the lost, and I will bring back the strayed, and I will bind up the injured, and I will strengthen the weak, and the fat and the strong I will destroy.ᵃ I will feed them in justice.

¹⁷"As for you, my flock, thus says the Lord GOD: Behold, I judge between sheep and sheep, between rams and male goats. ¹⁸Is it not enough for you to feed on the good pasture, that you must tread down with your feet the rest of your pasture; and to drink of clear water, that you must muddy the rest of the water with your feet? ¹⁹And must my sheep eat what you have trodden with your feet, and drink what you have muddied with your feet?

²⁰"Therefore, thus says the Lord GOD to them: Behold, I, I myself will judge between the fat sheep and the lean sheep. ²¹Because you push with side and shoulder, and thrust at all the weak with your horns, till you have scattered them abroad, ²²I will rescueᵇ my flock; they shall no longer be a prey. And I will judge between sheep and sheep. ²³And I will set up over them one shepherd, my servant David, and he shall feed them: he shall feed them and be their shepherd. ²⁴And I, the LORD, will be their God, and my servant David shall be prince among them. I am the LORD; I have spoken.

THE LORD'S COVENANT OF PEACE

²⁵"I will make with them a covenant of peace and banish wild beasts from the land, so that they may dwell securely in the wilderness and sleep in the woods. ²⁶And I will make them and the places all round my hill a blessing, and I will send down the showers in their season; they shall be showers of blessing. ²⁷And the trees of the field shall yield their fruit, and the earth shall yield its increase, and they shall be secure in their land. And they shall know that I am the LORD, when I break the bars of their yoke, and deliver them from the hand of those

---

ᵃSeptuagint, Syriac, Vulgate *I will watch over* ᵇOr *save*

who enslaved them. ²⁸They shall no more be a prey to the nations, nor shall the beasts of the land devour them. They shall dwell securely, and none shall make them afraid. ²⁹And I will provide for them renowned plantations so that they shall no more be consumed with hunger in the land, and no longer suffer the reproach of the nations. ³⁰And they shall know that I am the LORD their God with them, and that they, the house of Israel, are my people, declares the Lord GOD. ³¹And you are my sheep, human sheep of my pasture, and I am your God, declares the Lord GOD."

PROPHECY AGAINST MOUNT SEIR

35 The word of the LORD came to me: ²"Son of man, set your face against Mount Seir, and prophesy against it, ³and say to it, Thus says the Lord GOD: Behold, I am against you, Mount Seir, and I will stretch out my hand against you, and I will make you a desolation and a waste. ⁴I will lay your cities waste, and you shall become a desolation, and you shall know that I am the LORD. ⁵Because you cherished perpetual enmity and gave over the people of Israel to the power of the sword at the time of their calamity, at the time of their final punishment, ⁶therefore, as I live, declares the Lord GOD, I will prepare you for blood, and blood shall pursue you; because you did not hate bloodshed, therefore blood shall pursue you. ⁷I will make Mount Seir a waste and a desolation, and I will cut off from it all who come and go. ⁸And I will fill its mountains with the slain. On your hills and in your valleys and in all your ravines those slain with the sword shall fall. ⁹I will make you a perpetual desolation, and your cities shall not be inhabited. Then you will know that I am the LORD.

¹⁰"Because you said, 'These two nations and these two countries shall be mine, and we will take possession of them'—although the LORD was there— ¹¹therefore, as I live, declares the Lord GOD, I will deal with you according to the anger and envy that you showed because of your hatred against them. And I will make myself known among them, when I judge you. ¹²And you shall know that I am the LORD.

"I have heard all the revilings that you uttered against the mountains of Israel, saying, 'They are laid desolate; they are given us to devour.' ¹³And you magnified yourselves against me with your mouth, and multiplied your words against me; I heard it. ¹⁴Thus says the Lord GOD: While the whole earth rejoices, I will make you desolate. ¹⁵As you rejoiced over the inheritance of the house of Israel, because it was desolate, so I will deal with you; you shall be desolate, Mount Seir, and all Edom, all of it. Then they will know that I am the LORD.

PROPHECY TO THE MOUNTAINS OF ISRAEL

36 "And you, son of man, prophesy to the mountains of Israel, and say, O mountains of Israel, hear the word of the LORD. ²Thus says the Lord GOD: Because the enemy said of you, 'Aha!' and, 'The ancient heights have become our possession', ³therefore prophesy, and say, Thus says the Lord GOD: Precisely because they made you desolate and crushed you from all sides, so that you became the possession of the rest of the nations, and you became the talk and evil gossip of the people, ⁴therefore, O mountains of Israel, hear the word of the Lord GOD: Thus says the Lord GOD to the mountains and the hills, the ravines and the valleys, the desolate wastes and the deserted cities, which have become a prey and derision to the rest of the nations all around, ⁵therefore thus says the Lord GOD: Surely I have spoken in my hot jealousy against the rest of the nations and against all Edom, who gave my land to themselves as a possession with wholehearted joy and utter contempt, that they might make its pasture lands a prey. ⁶Therefore prophesy concerning the land of Israel, and say to the mountains and hills, to the ravines and valleys, Thus says the Lord GOD: Behold, I have spoken in my jealous wrath, because you have suffered the reproach of the nations. ⁷Therefore thus says the Lord GOD: I swear that the nations that are all around you shall themselves suffer reproach.

⁸"But you, O mountains of Israel, shall shoot forth your branches and yield your fruit to my people Israel, for they will soon come home. ⁹For behold, I am for you, and I will turn to you, and you shall be tilled and sown. ¹⁰And I will multiply people on you, the whole house of Israel, all of it. The cities shall be inhabited and the waste places rebuilt. ¹¹And I will multiply on you man and beast, and they shall multiply and be fruitful. And I will cause you to be inhabited as in your former times, and will do more good to you than ever before. Then you will know that I

am the Lord. ¹²I will let people walk on you, even my people Israel. And they shall possess you, and you shall be their inheritance, and you shall no longer bereave them of children. ¹³Thus says the Lord God: Because they say to you, 'You devour people, and you bereave your nation of children', ¹⁴therefore you shall no longer devour people and no longer bereave your nation of children, declares the Lord God. ¹⁵And I will not let you hear any more the reproach of the nations, and you shall no longer bear the disgrace of the peoples and no longer cause your nation to stumble, declares the Lord God."

THE LORD'S CONCERN FOR HIS HOLY NAME

¹⁶The word of the Lord came to me: ¹⁷"Son of man, when the house of Israel lived in their own land, they defiled it by their ways and their deeds. Their ways before me were like the uncleanness of a woman in her menstrual impurity. ¹⁸So I poured out my wrath upon them for the blood that they had shed in the land, for the idols with which they had defiled it. ¹⁹I scattered them among the nations, and they were dispersed through the countries. In accordance with their ways and their deeds I judged them. ²⁰But when they came to the nations, wherever they came, they profaned my holy name, in that people said of them, 'These are the people of the Lord, and yet they had to go out of his land.' ²¹But I had concern for my holy name, which the house of Israel had profaned among the nations to which they came.

I WILL PUT MY SPIRIT WITHIN YOU

²²"Therefore say to the house of Israel, Thus says the Lord God: It is not for your sake, O house of Israel, that I am about to act, but for the sake of my holy name, which you have profaned among the nations to which you came. ²³And I will vindicate the holiness of my great name, which has been profaned among the nations, and which you have profaned among them. And the nations will know that I am the Lord, declares the Lord God, when through you I vindicate my holiness before their eyes. ²⁴I will take you from the nations and gather you from all the countries and bring you into your own land. ²⁵I will sprinkle clean water on you, and you shall be clean from all your uncleannesses, and from all your idols I will cleanse you. ²⁶And I will give you a new heart, and a new spirit I will put within you. And I will remove the heart of stone from your flesh and give you a heart of flesh. ²⁷And I will put my Spirit within you, and cause you to walk in my statutes and be careful to obey my rules.ᵃ ²⁸You shall dwell in the land that I gave to your fathers, and you shall be my people, and I will be your God. ²⁹And I will deliver you from all your uncleannesses. And I will summon the grain and make it abundant and lay no famine upon you. ³⁰I will make the fruit of the tree and the increase of the field abundant, that you may never again suffer the disgrace of famine among the nations. ³¹Then you will remember your evil ways, and your deeds that were not good, and you will loathe yourselves for your iniquities and your abominations. ³²It is not for your sake that I will act, declares the Lord God; let that be known to you. Be ashamed and confounded for your ways, O house of Israel.

³³"Thus says the Lord God: On the day that I cleanse you from all your iniquities, I will cause the cities to be inhabited, and the waste places shall be rebuilt. ³⁴And the land that was desolate shall be tilled, instead of being the desolation that it was in the sight of all who passed by. ³⁵And they will say, 'This land that was desolate has become like the garden of Eden, and the waste and desolate and ruined cities are now fortified and inhabited.' ³⁶Then the nations that are left all around you shall know that I am the Lord; I have rebuilt the ruined places and replanted that which was desolate. I am the Lord; I have spoken, and I will do it.

³⁷"Thus says the Lord God: This also I will let the house of Israel ask me to do for them: to increase their people like a flock. ³⁸Like the flock for sacrifices,ᵇ like the flock at Jerusalem during her appointed feasts, so shall the waste cities be filled with flocks of people. Then they will know that I am the Lord."

THE VALLEY OF DRY BONES

37 The hand of the Lord was upon me, and he brought me out in the Spirit of the Lord and set me down in the middle of the valley;ᶜ it was full of bones. ²And he led me around among them, and behold, there were very many on the surface of the valley, and behold, they were very dry. ³And he said to me, "Son of man, can these bones live?" And I answered, "O Lord

---

ᵃOr *my just decrees* ᵇHebrew *flock of holy things* ᶜOr *plain*; also verse 2

God, you know." ⁴Then he said to me, "Prophesy over these bones, and say to them, O dry bones, hear the word of the Lord. ⁵Thus says the Lord God to these bones: Behold, I will cause breath*ᵃ* to enter you, and you shall live. ⁶And I will lay sinews upon you, and will cause flesh to come upon you, and cover you with skin, and put breath in you, and you shall live, and you shall know that I am the Lord."

⁷So I prophesied as I was commanded. And as I prophesied, there was a sound, and behold, a rattling,*ᵇ* and the bones came together, bone to its bone. ⁸And I looked, and behold, there were sinews on them, and flesh had come upon them, and skin had covered them. But there was no breath in them. ⁹Then he said to me, "Prophesy to the breath; prophesy, son of man, and say to the breath, Thus says the Lord God: Come from the four winds, O breath, and breathe on these slain, that they may live." ¹⁰So I prophesied as he commanded me, and the breath came into them, and they lived and stood on their feet, an exceedingly great army.

¹¹Then he said to me, "Son of man, these bones are the whole house of Israel. Behold, they say, 'Our bones are dried up, and our hope is lost; we are indeed cut off.' ¹²Therefore prophesy, and say to them, Thus says the Lord God: Behold, I will open your graves and raise you from your graves, O my people. And I will bring you into the land of Israel. ¹³And you shall know that I am the Lord, when I open your graves, and raise you from your graves, O my people. ¹⁴And I will put my Spirit within you, and you shall live, and I will place you in your own land. Then you shall know that I am the Lord; I have spoken, and I will do it, declares the Lord."

I WILL BE THEIR GOD; THEY SHALL BE MY PEOPLE

¹⁵The word of the Lord came to me: ¹⁶"Son of man, take a stick*ᶜ* and write on it, 'For Judah, and the people of Israel associated with him'; then take another stick and write on it, 'For Joseph (the stick of Ephraim) and all the house of Israel associated with him.' ¹⁷And join them one to another into one stick, that they may become one in your hand. ¹⁸And when your people say to you, 'Will you not tell us what you mean by these?' ¹⁹say to them, Thus says the Lord God: Behold, I am about to take the stick of Joseph (that is in the hand of Ephraim) and the tribes of Israel associated with him. And I will join with it the stick of Judah,*ᵈ* and make them one stick, that they may be one in my hand. ²⁰When the sticks on which you write are in your hand before their eyes, ²¹then say to them, Thus says the Lord God: Behold, I will take the people of Israel from the nations among which they have gone, and will gather them from all around, and bring them to their own land. ²²And I will make them one nation in the land, on the mountains of Israel. And one king shall be king over them all, and they shall be no longer two nations, and no longer divided into two kingdoms. ²³They shall not defile themselves any more with their idols and their detestable things, or with any of their transgressions. But I will save them from all the backsliding*ᵉ* in which they have sinned, and will cleanse them; and they shall be my people, and I will be their God.

²⁴"My servant David shall be king over them, and they shall all have one shepherd. They shall walk in my rules and be careful to obey my statutes. ²⁵They shall dwell in the land that I gave to my servant Jacob, where your fathers lived. They and their children and their children's children shall dwell there for ever, and David my servant shall be their prince for ever. ²⁶I will make a covenant of peace with them. It shall be an everlasting covenant with them. And I will set them in their land*ᶠ* and multiply them, and will set my sanctuary in their midst for evermore. ²⁷My dwelling place shall be with them, and I will be their God, and they shall be my people. ²⁸Then the nations will know that I am the Lord who sanctifies Israel, when my sanctuary is in their midst for evermore."

PROPHECY AGAINST GOG

38 The word of the Lord came to me: ²"Son of man, set your face towards Gog, of the land of Magog, the chief prince of Meshech*ᵍ* and Tubal, and prophesy against him ³and say, Thus says the Lord God: Behold, I am against you, O Gog, chief prince of Meshech*ʰ* and Tubal. ⁴And I will turn you about and put hooks into your jaws, and I will bring you out, and all your army, horses and horsemen, all of them clothed in full armour, a great host,

---

*ᵃ*Or *spirit*; also verses 6, 9, 10 *ᵇ*Or *an earthquake* (compare 3:12, 13) *ᶜ*Or *one piece of wood*; also verses 17, 19, 20 *ᵈ*Hebrew *And I will place them on it, the stick of Judah* *ᵉ*Many Hebrew manuscripts; other Hebrew manuscripts *dwellings* *ᶠ*Hebrew lacks *in their land* *ᵍ*Or *Magog, the prince of Rosh, Meshech* *ʰ*Or *Gog, prince of Rosh, Meshech*

all of them with buckler and shield, wielding swords. ⁵Persia, Cush, and Put are with them, all of them with shield and helmet; ⁶Gomer and all his hordes; Beth-togarmah from the uttermost parts of the north with all his hordes — many peoples are with you.

⁷"Be ready and keep ready, you and all your hosts that are assembled about you, and be a guard for them. ⁸After many days you will be mustered. In the latter years you will go against the land that is restored from war, the land whose people were gathered from many peoples upon the mountains of Israel, which had been a continual waste. Its people were brought out from the peoples and now dwell securely, all of them. ⁹You will advance, coming on like a storm. You will be like a cloud covering the land, you and all your hordes, and many peoples with you.

¹⁰"Thus says the Lord GOD: On that day, thoughts will come into your mind, and you will devise an evil scheme ¹¹and say, 'I will go up against the land of unwalled villages. I will fall upon the quiet people who dwell securely, all of them dwelling without walls, and having no bars or gates', ¹²to seize spoil and carry off plunder, to turn your hand against the waste places that are now inhabited, and the people who were gathered from the nations, who have acquired livestock and goods, who dwell at the centre of the earth. ¹³Sheba and Dedan and the merchants of Tarshish and all its leaders*ᵃ* will say to you, 'Have you come to seize spoil? Have you assembled your hosts to carry off plunder, to carry away silver and gold, to take away livestock and goods, to seize great spoil?'

¹⁴"Therefore, son of man, prophesy, and say to Gog, Thus says the Lord GOD: On that day when my people Israel are dwelling securely, will you not know it? ¹⁵You will come from your place out of the uttermost parts of the north, you and many peoples with you, all of them riding on horses, a great host, a mighty army. ¹⁶You will come up against my people Israel, like a cloud covering the land. In the latter days I will bring you against my land, that the nations may know me, when through you, O Gog, I vindicate my holiness before their eyes.

¹⁷"Thus says the Lord GOD: Are you he of whom I spoke in former days by my servants the prophets of Israel, who in those days prophesied for years that I would bring you against them? ¹⁸But on that day, the day that Gog shall come against the land of Israel, declares the Lord GOD, my wrath will be roused in my anger. ¹⁹For in my jealousy and in my blazing wrath I declare, On that day there shall be a great earthquake in the land of Israel. ²⁰The fish of the sea and the birds of the heavens and the beasts of the field and all creeping things that creep on the ground, and all the people who are on the face of the earth, shall quake at my presence. And the mountains shall be thrown down, and the cliffs shall fall, and every wall shall tumble to the ground. ²¹I will summon a sword against Gog*ᵇ* on all my mountains, declares the Lord GOD. Every man's sword will be against his brother. ²²With pestilence and bloodshed I will enter into judgement with him, and I will rain upon him and his hordes and the many peoples who are with him torrential rains and hailstones, fire and sulphur. ²³So I will show my greatness and my holiness and make myself known in the eyes of many nations. Then they will know that I am the LORD.

39

"And you, son of man, prophesy against Gog and say, Thus says the Lord GOD: Behold, I am against you, O Gog, chief prince of Meshech*ᶜ* and Tubal. ²And I will turn you about and drive you forwards,*ᵈ* and bring you up from the uttermost parts of the north, and lead you against the mountains of Israel. ³Then I will strike your bow from your left hand, and will make your arrows drop out of your right hand. ⁴You shall fall on the mountains of Israel, you and all your hordes and the peoples who are with you. I will give you to birds of prey of every sort and to the beasts of the field to be devoured. ⁵You shall fall in the open field, for I have spoken, declares the Lord GOD. ⁶I will send fire on Magog and on those who dwell securely in the coastlands, and they shall know that I am the LORD.

⁷"And my holy name I will make known in the midst of my people Israel, and I will not let my holy name be profaned any more. And the nations shall know that I am the LORD, the Holy One in Israel. ⁸Behold, it is coming and it will be brought about, declares the Lord GOD. That is the day of which I have spoken.

⁹"Then those who dwell in the cities of Israel will go out and make fires of the weapons and burn them, shields and bucklers, bow and arrows, clubs*ᵉ* and spears; and they will make fires of them for seven years, ¹⁰so

---

*ᵃ*Hebrew *young lions* *ᵇ*Hebrew *against him* *ᶜ*Or *Gog, prince of Rosh, Meshech* *ᵈ*Or *and drag you along* *ᵉ*Or *javelins*

that they will not need to take wood out of the field or cut down any out of the forests, for they will make their fires of the weapons. They will seize the spoil of those who despoiled them, and plunder those who plundered them, declares the Lord GOD.

¹¹"On that day I will give to Gog a place for burial in Israel, the Valley of the Travellers, east of the sea. It will block the travellers, for there Gog and all his multitude will be buried. It will be called the Valley of Hamon-gog.^{a} ¹²For seven months the house of Israel will be burying them, in order to cleanse the land. ¹³All the people of the land will bury them, and it will bring them renown on the day that I show my glory, declares the Lord GOD. ¹⁴They will set apart men to travel through the land regularly and bury those travellers remaining on the face of the land, so as to cleanse it. At^b the end of seven months they will make their search. ¹⁵And when these travel through the land and anyone sees a human bone, then he shall set up a sign by it, till the buriers have buried it in the Valley of Hamon-gog. ¹⁶(Hamonah^c is also the name of the city.) Thus shall they cleanse the land.

¹⁷"As for you, son of man, thus says the Lord GOD: Speak to the birds of every sort and to all beasts of the field: 'Assemble and come, gather from all round to the sacrificial feast that I am preparing for you, a great sacrificial feast on the mountains of Israel, and you shall eat flesh and drink blood. ¹⁸You shall eat the flesh of the mighty, and drink the blood of the princes of the earth—of rams, of lambs, and of he-goats, of bulls, all of them fat beasts of Bashan. ¹⁹And you shall eat fat till you are filled, and drink blood till you are drunk, at the sacrificial feast that I am preparing for you. ²⁰And you shall be filled at my table with horses and charioteers, with mighty men and all kinds of warriors,' declares the Lord GOD.

²¹"And I will set my glory among the nations, and all the nations shall see my judgement that I have executed, and my hand that I have laid on them. ²²The house of Israel shall know that I am the LORD their God, from that day forward. ²³And the nations shall know that the house of Israel went into captivity for their iniquity, because they dealt so treacherously with me that I hid my face from them and gave them into the hand of their adversaries, and they all fell by the sword. ²⁴I dealt with them according to their uncleanness and their transgressions, and hid my face from them.

THE LORD WILL RESTORE ISRAEL

²⁵"Therefore thus says the Lord GOD: Now I will restore the fortunes of Jacob and have mercy on the whole house of Israel, and I will be jealous for my holy name. ²⁶They shall forget their shame and all the treachery they have practised against me, when they dwell securely in their land with none to make them afraid, ²⁷when I have brought them back from the peoples and gathered them from their enemies' lands, and through them have vindicated my holiness in the sight of many nations. ²⁸Then they shall know that I am the LORD their God, because I sent them into exile among the nations and then assembled them into their own land. I will leave none of them remaining among the nations any more. ²⁹And I will not hide my face any more from them, when I pour out my Spirit upon the house of Israel, declares the Lord GOD."

VISION OF THE NEW TEMPLE

40 In the twenty-fifth year of our exile, at the beginning of the year, on the tenth day of the month, in the fourteenth year after the city was struck down, on that very day, the hand of the LORD was upon me, and he brought me to the city.^{d} ²In visions of God he brought me to the land of Israel, and set me down on a very high mountain, on which was a structure like a city to the south. ³When he brought me there, behold, there was a man whose appearance was like bronze, with a linen cord and a measuring reed in his hand. And he was standing in the gateway. ⁴And the man said to me, "Son of man, look with your eyes, and hear with your ears, and set your heart upon all that I shall show you, for you were brought here in order that I might show it to you. Declare all that you see to the house of Israel."

THE EAST GATE TO THE OUTER COURT

⁵And behold, there was a wall all round the outside of the temple area, and the length of the measuring reed in the man's hand was six long cubits, each being a cubit and a handbreadth^e in length. So he measured the thickness of the wall, one reed; and the height, one reed. ⁶Then he went into the gateway facing east, going up its steps, and measured the

---

^{a}Hamon-gog means the multitude of Gog ^{b}Or Until ^{c}Hamonah means multitude ^{d}Hebrew brought me there ^{e}A cubit was about 18 inches or 45 centimetres; a handbreadth was about 3 inches or 7.5 centimetres

threshold of the gate, one reed deep.[a] ⁷And the side rooms, one reed long and one reed broad; and the space between the side rooms, five cubits; and the threshold of the gate by the vestibule of the gate at the inner end, one reed. ⁸Then he measured the vestibule of the gateway, on the inside, one reed. ⁹Then he measured the vestibule of the gateway, eight cubits; and its jambs, two cubits; and the vestibule of the gate was at the inner end. ¹⁰And there were three side rooms on either side of the east gate. The three were of the same size, and the jambs on either side were of the same size. ¹¹Then he measured the width of the opening of the gateway, ten cubits; and the length of the gateway, thirteen cubits. ¹²There was a barrier before the side rooms, one cubit on either side. And the side rooms were six cubits on either side. ¹³Then he measured the gate from the ceiling of one side room to the ceiling of the other, a breadth of twenty-five cubits; the openings faced each other. ¹⁴He measured also the vestibule, sixty cubits. And round the vestibule of the gateway was the court.[b] ¹⁵From the front of the gate at the entrance to the front of the inner vestibule of the gate was fifty cubits. ¹⁶And the gateway had windows all round, narrowing inwards towards the side rooms and towards their jambs, and likewise the vestibule had windows all round inside, and on the jambs were palm trees.

THE OUTER COURT

¹⁷Then he brought me into the outer court. And behold, there were chambers and a pavement, all round the court. Thirty chambers faced the pavement. ¹⁸And the pavement ran along the side of the gates, corresponding to the length of the gates. This was the lower pavement. ¹⁹Then he measured the distance from the inner front of the lower gate to the outer front of the inner court,[c] a hundred cubits on the east side and on the north side.[d]

THE NORTH GATE

²⁰As for the gate that faced towards the north, belonging to the outer court, he measured its length and its breadth. ²¹Its side rooms, three on either side, and its jambs and its vestibule were of the same size as those of the first gate. Its length was fifty cubits, and its breadth twenty-five cubits. ²²And its windows, its vestibule, and its palm trees were of the same size as those of the gate that faced towards the east. And by seven steps people would go up to it, and find its vestibule before them. ²³And opposite the gate on the north, as on the east, was a gate to the inner court. And he measured from gate to gate, a hundred cubits.

THE SOUTH GATE

²⁴And he led me towards the south, and behold, there was a gate on the south. And he measured its jambs and its vestibule; they had the same size as the others. ²⁵Both it and its vestibule had windows all round, like the windows of the others. Its length was fifty cubits, and its breadth twenty-five cubits. ²⁶And there were seven steps leading up to it, and its vestibule was before them, and it had palm trees on its jambs, one on either side. ²⁷And there was a gate on the south of the inner court. And he measured from gate to gate towards the south, a hundred cubits.

THE INNER COURT

²⁸Then he brought me to the inner court through the south gate, and he measured the south gate. It was of the same size as the others. ²⁹Its side rooms, its jambs, and its vestibule were of the same size as the others, and both it and its vestibule had windows all round. Its length was fifty cubits, and its breadth twenty-five cubits. ³⁰And there were vestibules all round, twenty-five cubits long and five cubits broad. ³¹Its vestibule faced the outer court, and palm trees were on its jambs, and its stairway had eight steps.

³²Then he brought me to the inner court on the east side, and he measured the gate. It was of the same size as the others. ³³Its side rooms, its jambs, and its vestibule were of the same size as the others, and both it and its vestibule had windows all round. Its length was fifty cubits, and its breadth twenty-five cubits. ³⁴Its vestibule faced the outer court, and it had palm trees on its jambs, on either side, and its stairway had eight steps.

³⁵Then he brought me to the north gate, and he measured it. It had the same size as the others. ³⁶Its side rooms, its jambs, and its vestibule were of the same size as the others,[e] and it had windows all round. Its length was fifty cubits, and its breadth twenty-five cubits. ³⁷Its vestibule[f] faced the outer court, and it

---

[a]Hebrew *deep, and one threshold, one reed deep* [b]Text uncertain; Hebrew *And he made the jambs sixty cubits, and to the jamb of the court was the gateway all around* [c]Hebrew *distance from before the low gate before the inner court to the outside* [d]Or *cubits. So far the eastern gate; now to the northern gate* [e]One manuscript (compare verses 29 and 33); most manuscripts lack *were of the same size as the others* [f]Septuagint, Vulgate (compare verses 26, 31, 34); Hebrew *jambs*

had palm trees on its jambs, on either side, and its stairway had eight steps.

38 There was a chamber with its door in the vestibule of the gate,*a* where the burnt offering was to be washed. **39** And in the vestibule of the gate were two tables on either side, on which the burnt offering and the sin offering and the guilt offering were to be slaughtered. **40** And off to the side, on the outside as one goes up to the entrance of the north gate, were two tables; and off to the other side of the vestibule of the gate were two tables. **41** Four tables were on either side of the gate, eight tables, on which to slaughter. **42** And there were four tables of hewn stone for the burnt offering, a cubit and a half long, and a cubit and a half broad, and one cubit high, on which the instruments were to be laid with which the burnt offerings and the sacrifices were slaughtered. **43** And hooks,*b* a handbreadth long, were fastened all round within. And on the tables the flesh of the offering was to be laid.

CHAMBERS FOR THE PRIESTS

44 On the outside of the inner gateway there were two chambers*c* in the inner court, one*d* at the side of the north gate facing south, the other at the side of the south*e* gate facing north. **45** And he said to me, "This chamber that faces south is for the priests who have charge of the temple, **46** and the chamber that faces north is for the priests who have charge of the altar. These are the sons of Zadok, who alone*f* among the sons of Levi may come near to the Lord to minister to him." **47** And he measured the court, a hundred cubits long and a hundred cubits broad, a square. And the altar was in front of the temple.

THE VESTIBULE OF THE TEMPLE

48 Then he brought me to the vestibule of the temple and measured the jambs of the vestibule, five cubits on either side. And the breadth of the gate was fourteen cubits, and the side walls of the gate*g* were three cubits on either side. **49** The length of the vestibule was twenty cubits, and the breadth twelve*h* cubits, and people would go up to it by ten steps.*i* And there were pillars beside the jambs, one on either side.

THE INNER TEMPLE

41 Then he brought me to the nave and measured the jambs. On each side six cubits*j* was the breadth of the jambs.*k* **2** And the breadth of the entrance was ten cubits, and the side walls of the entrance were five cubits on either side. And he measured the length of the nave,*l* forty cubits, and its breadth, twenty cubits. **3** Then he went into the inner room and measured the jambs of the entrance, two cubits; and the entrance, six cubits; and the side walls on either side*m* of the entrance, seven cubits. **4** And he measured the length of the room, twenty cubits, and its breadth, twenty cubits, across the nave. And he said to me, "This is the Most Holy Place."

5 Then he measured the wall of the temple, six cubits thick, and the breadth of the side chambers, four cubits, all round the temple. **6** And the side chambers were in three storeys, one over another, thirty in each storey. There were offsets*n* all round the wall of the temple to serve as supports for the side chambers, so that they should not be supported by the wall of the temple. **7** And it became broader as it wound upwards to the side chambers, because the temple was enclosed upwards all round the temple. Thus the temple had a broad area upwards, and so one went up from the lowest storey to the top storey through the middle storey. **8** I saw also that the temple had a raised platform all round; the foundations of the side chambers measured a full reed of six long cubits. **9** The thickness of the outer wall of the side chambers was five cubits. The free space between the side chambers of the temple and the **10** other chambers was a breadth of twenty cubits all round the temple on every side. **11** And the doors of the side chambers opened on the free space, one door towards the north, and another door towards the south. And the breadth of the free space was five cubits all round.

12 The building that was facing the separate yard on the west side was seventy cubits broad, and the wall of the building was five cubits thick all round, and its length ninety cubits.

13 Then he measured the temple, a hundred cubits long; and the yard and the building with its walls, a hundred cubits long; **14** also the breadth of the east front of the temple and the yard, a hundred cubits.

---

*a*Hebrew *at the jambs, the gates* *b*Or *shelves* *c*Septuagint; Hebrew *were chambers for singers* *d*Hebrew lacks *one* *e*Septuagint; Hebrew *east* *f*Hebrew lacks *alone* *g*Septuagint; Hebrew lacks *was fourteen cubits, and the side walls of the gate* *h*Septuagint; Hebrew *eleven* *i*Septuagint; Hebrew *and by steps that would go up to it* *j*A cubit was about 18 inches or 45 centimetres *k*Compare Septuagint; Hebrew *tent* *l*Hebrew *its length* *m*Septuagint; Hebrew *and the breadth* *n*Septuagint, compare 1 Kings 6:6; the meaning of the Hebrew word is uncertain

¹⁵Then he measured the length of the building facing the yard that was at the back and its galleries*ᵃ* on either side, a hundred cubits.

The inside of the nave and the vestibules of the court, ¹⁶the thresholds and the narrow windows and the galleries all round the three of them, opposite the threshold, were panelled with wood all round, from the floor up to the windows (now the windows were covered), ¹⁷to the space above the door, even to the inner room, and on the outside. And on all the walls all round, inside and outside, was a measured pattern.*ᵇ* ¹⁸It was carved of cherubim and palm trees, a palm tree between cherub and cherub. Every cherub had two faces: ¹⁹a human face towards the palm tree on one side, and the face of a young lion towards the palm tree on the other side. They were carved on the whole temple all round. ²⁰From the floor to above the door, cherubim and palm trees were carved; similarly the wall of the nave.

²¹The doorposts of the nave were squared, and in front of the Holy Place was something resembling ²²an altar of wood, three cubits high, two cubits long, and two cubits broad.*ᶜ* Its corners, its base,*ᵈ* and its walls were of wood. He said to me, "This is the table that is before the LORD." ²³The nave and the Holy Place had each a double door. ²⁴The double doors had two leaves apiece, two swinging leaves for each door. ²⁵And on the doors of the nave were carved cherubim and palm trees, such as were carved on the walls. And there was a canopy*ᵉ* of wood in front of the vestibule outside. ²⁶And there were narrow windows and palm trees on either side, on the side walls of the vestibule, the side chambers of the temple, and the canopies.

THE TEMPLE'S CHAMBERS

42 Then he led me out into the outer court, towards the north, and he brought me to the chambers that were opposite the separate yard and opposite the building on the north. ²The length of the building whose door faced north was a hundred cubits,*ᶠ* and the breadth fifty cubits. ³Facing the twenty cubits that belonged to the inner court, and facing the pavement that belonged to the outer court, was gallery*ᵍ* against gallery in three storeys. ⁴And before the chambers was a passage inwards, ten cubits wide and a hundred cubits long,*ʰ* and their doors were on the north. ⁵Now the upper chambers were narrower, for the galleries took more away from them than from the lower and middle chambers of the building. ⁶For they were in three storeys, and they had no pillars like the pillars of the courts. Thus the upper chambers were set back from the ground more than the lower and the middle ones. ⁷And there was a wall outside parallel to the chambers, towards the outer court, opposite the chambers, fifty cubits long. ⁸For the chambers on the outer court were fifty cubits long, while those opposite the nave*ⁱ* were a hundred cubits long. ⁹Below these chambers was an entrance on the east side, as one enters them from the outer court.

¹⁰In the thickness of the wall of the court, on the south*ʲ* also, opposite the yard and opposite the building there were chambers ¹¹with a passage in front of them. They were similar to the chambers on the north, of the same length and breadth, with the same exits*ᵏ* and arrangements and doors, ¹²as were the entrances of the chambers on the south. There was an entrance at the beginning of the passage, the passage before the corresponding wall on the east as one enters them.*ˡ*

¹³Then he said to me, "The north chambers and the south chambers opposite the yard are the holy chambers, where the priests who approach the LORD shall eat the most holy offerings. There they shall put the most holy offerings — the grain offering, the sin offering, and the guilt offering — for the place is holy. ¹⁴When the priests enter the Holy Place, they shall not go out of it into the outer court without laying there the garments in which they minister, for these are holy. They shall put on other garments before they go near to that which is for the people."

¹⁵Now when he had finished measuring the interior of the temple area, he led me out by the gate that faced east, and measured the temple area all round. ¹⁶He measured the east side with the measuring reed, 500 cubits by the measuring reed all round. ¹⁷He measured the north side, 500 cubits by the measuring reed all round. ¹⁸He measured the south side, 500 cubits by the measuring reed. ¹⁹Then he turned to the west side and measured, 500 cubits by the measuring reed. ²⁰He measured

---

*ᵃ*The meaning of the Hebrew term is unknown; also verse 16
*ᵇ*Hebrew *were measurements* *ᶜ*Septuagint; Hebrew lacks *two cubits broad* *ᵈ*Septuagint; Hebrew *length* *ᵉ*The meaning of the Hebrew word is unknown; also verse 26 *ᶠ*A *cubit* was about 18 inches or 45 centimetres *ᵍ*The meaning of the Hebrew word is unknown; also verse 5 *ʰ*Septuagint, Syriac; Hebrew *and a way of one cubit* *ⁱ*Or *temple* *ʲ*Septuagint; Hebrew *east* *ᵏ*Hebrew *and all their exits* *ˡ*The meaning of the Hebrew verse is uncertain

it on the four sides. It had a wall round it, 500 cubits long and 500 cubits broad, to make a separation between the holy and the common.

THE GLORY OF THE LORD FILLS THE TEMPLE

43 Then he led me to the gate, the gate facing east. ²And behold, the glory of the God of Israel was coming from the east. And the sound of his coming was like the sound of many waters, and the earth shone with his glory. ³And the vision I saw was just like the vision that I had seen when he*ᵃ* came to destroy the city, and just like the vision that I had seen by the Chebar canal. And I fell on my face. ⁴As the glory of the LORD entered the temple by the gate facing east, ⁵the Spirit lifted me up and brought me into the inner court; and behold, the glory of the LORD filled the temple.

⁶While the man was standing beside me, I heard one speaking to me out of the temple, ⁷and he said to me, "Son of man, this is the place of my throne and the place of the soles of my feet, where I will dwell in the midst of the people of Israel for ever. And the house of Israel shall no more defile my holy name, neither they, nor their kings, by their whoring and by the dead bodies*ᵇ* of their kings at their high places,*ᶜ* ⁸by setting their threshold by my threshold and their doorposts beside my doorposts, with only a wall between me and them. They have defiled my holy name by their abominations that they have committed, so I have consumed them in my anger. ⁹Now let them put away their whoring and the dead bodies of their kings far from me, and I will dwell in their midst for ever.

¹⁰"As for you, son of man, describe to the house of Israel the temple, that they may be ashamed of their iniquities; and they shall measure the plan. ¹¹And if they are ashamed of all that they have done, make known to them the design of the temple, its arrangement, its exits and its entrances, that is, its whole design; and make known to them as well all its statutes and its whole design and all its laws, and write it down in their sight, so that they may observe all its laws and all its statutes and carry them out. ¹²This is the law of the temple: the whole territory on the top of the mountain all round shall be most holy. Behold, this is the law of the temple.

THE ALTAR

¹³"These are the measurements of the altar by cubits (the cubit being a cubit and a handbreadth):*ᵈ* its base shall be one cubit high*ᵉ* and one cubit broad, with a rim of one span*ᶠ* round its edge. And this shall be the height of the altar: ¹⁴from the base on the ground to the lower ledge, two cubits, with a breadth of one cubit; and from the smaller ledge to the larger ledge, four cubits, with a breadth of one cubit; ¹⁵and the altar hearth, four cubits; and from the altar hearth projecting upwards, four horns. ¹⁶The altar hearth shall be square, twelve cubits long by twelve broad. ¹⁷The ledge also shall be square, fourteen cubits long by fourteen broad, with a rim round it half a cubit broad, and its base one cubit all round. The steps of the altar shall face east."

¹⁸And he said to me, "Son of man, thus says the Lord GOD: These are the ordinances for the altar: On the day when it is erected for offering burnt offerings upon it and for throwing blood against it, ¹⁹you shall give to the Levitical priests of the family of Zadok, who draw near to me to minister to me, declares the Lord GOD, a bull from the herd for a sin offering. ²⁰And you shall take some of its blood and put it on the four horns of the altar and on the four corners of the ledge and upon the rim all round. Thus you shall purify the altar and make atonement for it. ²¹You shall also take the bull of the sin offering, and it shall be burned in the appointed place belonging to the temple, outside the sacred area. ²²And on the second day you shall offer a male goat without blemish for a sin offering; and the altar shall be purified, as it was purified with the bull. ²³When you have finished purifying it, you shall offer a bull from the herd without blemish and a ram from the flock without blemish. ²⁴You shall present them before the LORD, and the priests shall sprinkle salt on them and offer them up as a burnt offering to the LORD. ²⁵For seven days you shall provide daily a male goat for a sin offering; also, a bull from the herd and a ram from the flock, without blemish, shall be provided. ²⁶Seven days shall they make atonement for the altar and cleanse it, and so consecrate it.*ᵍ* ²⁷And when they have completed these days, then from the eighth day onward the priests shall offer on the altar your burnt offerings and your peace offerings, and I will accept you, declares the Lord GOD."

---

*ᵃ*Some Hebrew manuscripts and Vulgate; most Hebrew manuscripts *when I*   *ᵇOr the monuments*; also verse 9   *ᶜOr at their deaths*   *ᵈA cubit* was about 18 inches or 45 centimetres; a *handbreadth* was about 3 inches or 7.5 centimetres   *ᵉOr its gutter shall be one cubit deep*   *ᶠA span* was about 9 inches or 22 centimetres   *ᵍ*Hebrew *fill its hand*

THE GATE FOR THE PRINCE

44 Then he brought me back to the outer gate of the sanctuary, which faces east. And it was shut. ²And the LORD said to me, "This gate shall remain shut; it shall not be opened, and no one shall enter by it, for the LORD, the God of Israel, has entered by it. Therefore it shall remain shut. ³Only the prince may sit in it to eat bread before the LORD. He shall enter by way of the vestibule of the gate, and shall go out by the same way."

⁴Then he brought me by way of the north gate to the front of the temple, and I looked, and behold, the glory of the LORD filled the temple of the LORD. And I fell on my face. ⁵And the LORD said to me, "Son of man, mark well, see with your eyes, and hear with your ears all that I shall tell you concerning all the statutes of the temple of the LORD and all its laws. And mark well the entrance to the temple and all the exits from the sanctuary. ⁶And say to the rebellious house,ᵃ to the house of Israel, Thus says the Lord GOD: O house of Israel, enough of all your abominations, ⁷in admitting foreigners, uncircumcised in heart and flesh, to be in my sanctuary, profaning my temple, when you offer to me my food, the fat and the blood. Youᵇ have broken my covenant, in addition to all your abominations. ⁸And you have not kept charge of my holy things, but you have set others to keep my charge for you in my sanctuary.

⁹"Thus says the Lord GOD: No foreigner, uncircumcised in heart and flesh, of all the foreigners who are among the people of Israel, shall enter my sanctuary. ¹⁰But the Levites who went far from me, going astray from me after their idols when Israel went astray, shall bear their punishment.ᶜ ¹¹They shall be ministers in my sanctuary, having oversight at the gates of the temple and ministering in the temple. They shall slaughter the burnt offering and the sacrifice for the people, and they shall stand before the people, to minister to them. ¹²Because they ministered to them before their idols and became a stumbling block of iniquity to the house of Israel, therefore I have sworn concerning them, declares the Lord GOD, and they shall bear their punishment. ¹³They shall not come near to me, to serve me as priest, nor come near any of my holy things and the things that are most holy, but they shall bear their shame and the abominations that they have committed. ¹⁴Yet I will appoint them to keep charge of the temple, to do all its service and all that is to be done in it.

RULES FOR LEVITICAL PRIESTS

¹⁵"But the Levitical priests, the sons of Zadok, who kept the charge of my sanctuary when the people of Israel went astray from me, shall come near to me to minister to me. And they shall stand before me to offer me the fat and the blood, declares the Lord GOD. ¹⁶They shall enter my sanctuary, and they shall approach my table, to minister to me, and they shall keep my charge. ¹⁷When they enter the gates of the inner court, they shall wear linen garments. They shall have nothing of wool on them, while they minister at the gates of the inner court, and within. ¹⁸They shall have linen turbans on their heads, and linen undergarments round their waists. They shall not bind themselves with anything that causes sweat. ¹⁹And when they go out into the outer court to the people, they shall put off the garments in which they have been ministering and lay them in the holy chambers. And they shall put on other garments, lest they transmit holiness to the people with their garments. ²⁰They shall not shave their heads or let their locks grow long; they shall surely trim the hair of their heads. ²¹No priest shall drink wine when he enters the inner court. ²²They shall not marry a widow or a divorced woman, but only virgins of the offspring of the house of Israel, or a widow who is the widow of a priest. ²³They shall teach my people the difference between the holy and the common, and show them how to distinguish between the unclean and the clean. ²⁴In a dispute, they shall act as judges, and they shall judge it according to my judgements. They shall keep my laws and my statutes in all my appointed feasts, and they shall keep my Sabbaths holy. ²⁵They shall not defile themselves by going near to a dead person. However, for father or mother, for son or daughter, for brother or unmarried sister they may defile themselves. ²⁶After heᵈ has become clean, they shall count seven days for him. ²⁷And on the day that he goes into the Holy Place, into the inner court, to minister in the Holy Place, he shall offer his sin offering, declares the Lord GOD.

²⁸"This shall be their inheritance: I am their inheritance: and you shall give them no possession in Israel; I am their possession.

ᵃSeptuagint; Hebrew lacks *house*   ᵇSeptuagint, Syriac, Vulgate; Hebrew *They*   ᶜOr *iniquity*; also verse 12   ᵈThat is, a priest

29They shall eat the grain offering, the sin offering, and the guilt offering, and every devoted thing in Israel shall be theirs. 30And the first of all the firstfruits of all kinds, and every offering of all kinds from all your offerings, shall belong to the priests. You shall also give to the priests the first of your dough, that a blessing may rest on your house. 31The priests shall not eat of anything, whether bird or beast, that has died of itself or is torn by wild animals.

THE HOLY DISTRICT

45 "When you allot the land as an inheritance, you shall set apart for the Lord a portion of the land as a holy district, 25,000 cubits[a] long and 20,000[b] cubits broad. It shall be holy throughout its whole extent. 2Of this a square plot of 500 by 500 cubits shall be for the sanctuary, with fifty cubits for an open space round it. 3And from this measured district you shall measure off a section 25,000 cubits long and 10,000 broad, in which shall be the sanctuary, the Most Holy Place. 4It shall be the holy portion of the land. It shall be for the priests, who minister in the sanctuary and approach the Lord to minister to him, and it shall be a place for their houses and a holy place for the sanctuary. 5Another section, 25,000 cubits long and 10,000 cubits broad, shall be for the Levites who minister at the temple, as their possession for cities to live in.[c]

6"Alongside the portion set apart as the holy district you shall assign for the property of the city an area 5,000 cubits broad and 25,000 cubits long. It shall belong to the whole house of Israel.

THE PORTION FOR THE PRINCE

7"And to the prince shall belong the land on both sides of the holy district and the property of the city, alongside the holy district and the property of the city, on the west and on the east, corresponding in length to one of the tribal portions, and extending from the western to the eastern boundary 8of the land. It is to be his property in Israel. And my princes shall no more oppress my people, but they shall let the house of Israel have the land according to their tribes.

9"Thus says the Lord God: Enough, O princes of Israel! Put away violence and oppression, and execute justice and righteousness. Cease your evictions of my people, declares the Lord God.

10"You shall have just balances, a just ephah, and a just bath.[d] 11The ephah and the bath shall be of the same measure, the bath containing one tenth of a homer,[e] and the ephah one tenth of a homer; the homer shall be the standard measure. 12The shekel shall be twenty gerahs;[f] twenty shekels plus twenty-five shekels plus fifteen shekels shall be your mina.[g]

13"This is the offering that you shall make: one sixth of an ephah from each homer of wheat, and one sixth of an ephah from each homer of barley, 14and as the fixed portion of oil, measured in baths, one tenth of a bath from each cor[h] (the cor, like the homer, contains ten baths).[i] 15And one sheep from every flock of two hundred, from the watering places of Israel for grain offering, burnt offering, and peace offerings, to make atonement for them, declares the Lord God. 16All the people of the land shall be obliged to give this offering to the prince in Israel. 17It shall be the prince's duty to furnish the burnt offerings, grain offerings, and drink offerings, at the feasts, the new moons, and the Sabbaths, all the appointed feasts of the house of Israel: he shall provide the sin offerings, grain offerings, burnt offerings, and peace offerings, to make atonement on behalf of the house of Israel.

18"Thus says the Lord God: In the first month, on the first day of the month, you shall take a bull from the herd without blemish, and purify the sanctuary. 19The priest shall take some of the blood of the sin offering and put it on the doorposts of the temple, the four corners of the ledge of the altar, and the posts of the gate of the inner court. 20You shall do the same on the seventh day of the month for anyone who has sinned through error or ignorance; so you shall make atonement for the temple.

21"In the first month, on the fourteenth day of the month, you shall celebrate the Feast of the Passover, and for seven days unleavened bread shall be eaten. 22On that day the prince shall provide for himself and all the people of the land a young bull for a sin offering. 23And on the seven days of the

---

[a]A *cubit* was about 18 inches or 45 centimetres [b]Septuagint; Hebrew *10,000* [c]Septuagint; Hebrew *as their possession, twenty chambers* [d]An *ephah* was about 3/5 of a bushel or 22 litres; a *bath* was about 6 gallons or 22 litres [e]A *homer* was about 6 bushels or 220 litres [f]A *shekel* was about 2/5 of an ounce or 11 grams; a *gerah* was about 1/50 of an ounce or 0.6 gram [g]A *mina* was about 1 1/4 pounds or 0.6 kilogram [h]A *cor* was about 6 bushels or 220 litres [i]See Vulgate; Hebrew *(ten baths are a homer, for ten baths are a homer)*

festival he shall provide as a burnt offering to the LORD seven young bulls and seven rams without blemish, on each of the seven days; and a male goat daily for a sin offering. ²⁴And he shall provide as a grain offering an ephah for each bull, an ephah for each ram, and a hin*ᵃ* of oil to each ephah. ²⁵In the seventh month, on the fifteenth day of the month and for the seven days of the feast, he shall make the same provision for sin offerings, burnt offerings, and grain offerings, and for the oil.

THE PRINCE AND THE FEASTS

46 "Thus says the Lord GOD: The gate of the inner court that faces east shall be shut on the six working days, but on the Sabbath day it shall be opened, and on the day of the new moon it shall be opened. ²The prince shall enter by the vestibule of the gate from outside, and shall take his stand by the post of the gate. The priests shall offer his burnt offering and his peace offerings, and he shall worship at the threshold of the gate. Then he shall go out, but the gate shall not be shut until evening. ³The people of the land shall bow down at the entrance of that gate before the LORD on the Sabbaths and on the new moons. ⁴The burnt offering that the prince offers to the LORD on the Sabbath day shall be six lambs without blemish and a ram without blemish. ⁵And the grain offering with the ram shall be an ephah,*ᵇ* and the grain offering with the lambs shall be as much as he is able, together with a hin*ᶜ* of oil to each ephah. ⁶On the day of the new moon he shall offer a bull from the herd without blemish, and six lambs and a ram, which shall be without blemish. ⁷As a grain offering he shall provide an ephah with the bull and an ephah with the ram, and with the lambs as much as he is able, together with a hin of oil to each ephah. ⁸When the prince enters, he shall enter by the vestibule of the gate, and he shall go out by the same way.

⁹"When the people of the land come before the LORD at the appointed feasts, he who enters by the north gate to worship shall go out by the south gate, and he who enters by the south gate shall go out by the north gate: no one shall return by way of the gate by which he entered, but each shall go out straight ahead. ¹⁰When they enter, the prince shall enter with them, and when they go out, he shall go out.

¹¹"At the feasts and the appointed festivals, the grain offering with a young bull shall be an ephah, and with a ram an ephah, and with the lambs as much as one is able to give, together with a hin of oil to an ephah. ¹²When the prince provides a freewill offering, either a burnt offering or peace offerings as a freewill offering to the LORD, the gate facing east shall be opened for him. And he shall offer his burnt offering or his peace offerings as he does on the Sabbath day. Then he shall go out, and after he has gone out the gate shall be shut.

¹³"You shall provide a lamb a year old without blemish for a burnt offering to the LORD daily; morning by morning you shall provide it. ¹⁴And you shall provide a grain offering with it morning by morning, one sixth of an ephah, and one third of a hin of oil to moisten the flour, as a grain offering to the LORD. This is a perpetual statute. ¹⁵Thus the lamb and the meal offering and the oil shall be provided, morning by morning, for a regular burnt offering.

¹⁶"Thus says the Lord GOD: If the prince makes a gift to any of his sons as his inheritance, it shall belong to his sons. It is their property by inheritance. ¹⁷But if he makes a gift out of his inheritance to one of his servants, it shall be his to the year of liberty. Then it shall revert to the prince; surely it is his inheritance—it shall belong to his sons. ¹⁸The prince shall not take any of the inheritance of the people, thrusting them out of their property. He shall give his sons their inheritance out of his own property, so that none of my people shall be scattered from his property."

BOILING PLACES FOR OFFERINGS

¹⁹Then he brought me through the entrance, which was at the side of the gate, to the north row of the holy chambers for the priests, and behold, a place was there at the extreme western end of them. ²⁰And he said to me, "This is the place where the priests shall boil the guilt offering and the sin offering, and where they shall bake the grain offering, in order not to bring them out into the outer court and so transmit holiness to the people."

²¹Then he brought me out to the outer court and led me round to the four corners of the

---

ᵃA hin was about 4 quarts or 3.5 litres *ᵇAn ephah* was about 3/5 of a bushel or 22 litres *ᶜA hin* was about 4 quarts or 3.5 litres

court. And behold, in each corner of the court there was another court— ²²in the four corners of the court were small[a] courts, forty cubits[b] long and thirty broad; the four were of the same size. ²³On the inside, round each of the four courts was a row of masonry, with hearths made at the bottom of the rows all round. ²⁴Then he said to me, "These are the kitchens where those who minister at the temple shall boil the sacrifices of the people."

WATER FLOWING FROM THE TEMPLE

47 Then he brought me back to the door of the temple, and behold, water was issuing from below the threshold of the temple towards the east (for the temple faced east). The water was flowing down from below the south end of the threshold of the temple, south of the altar. ²Then he brought me out by way of the north gate and led me round on the outside to the outer gate that faces towards the east; and behold, the water was trickling out on the south side.

³Going on eastwards with a measuring line in his hand, the man measured a thousand cubits,[c] and then led me through the water, and it was ankle-deep. ⁴Again he measured a thousand, and led me through the water, and it was knee-deep. Again he measured a thousand, and led me through the water, and it was waist-deep. ⁵Again he measured a thousand, and it was a river that I could not pass through, for the water had risen. It was deep enough to swim in, a river that could not be passed through. ⁶And he said to me, "Son of man, have you seen this?"

Then he led me back to the bank of the river. ⁷As I went back, I saw on the bank of the river very many trees on one side and on the other. ⁸And he said to me, "This water flows towards the eastern region and goes down into the Arabah, and enters the sea;[d] when the water flows into the sea, the water will become fresh.[e] ⁹And wherever the river goes,[f] every living creature that swarms will live, and there will be very many fish. For this water goes there, that the waters of the sea[g] may become fresh; so everything will live where the river goes. ¹⁰Fishermen will stand beside the sea. From Engedi to Eneglaim it will be a place for the spreading of nets. Its fish will be of very many kinds, like the fish of the Great Sea.[h] ¹¹But its swamps and marshes will not become fresh; they are to be left for salt. ¹²And on the banks, on both sides of the river, there will grow all kinds of trees for food. Their leaves will not wither, nor their fruit fail, but they will bear fresh fruit every month, because the water for them flows from the sanctuary. Their fruit will be for food, and their leaves for healing."

DIVISION OF THE LAND

¹³Thus says the Lord God: "This is the boundary[i] by which you shall divide the land for inheritance among the twelve tribes of Israel. Joseph shall have two portions. ¹⁴And you shall divide equally what I swore to give to your fathers. This land shall fall to you as your inheritance.

¹⁵"This shall be the boundary of the land: On the north side, from the Great Sea by way of Hethlon to Lebo-hamath, and on to Zedad,[j] ¹⁶Berothah, Sibraim (which lies on the border between Damascus and Hamath), as far as Hazer-hatticon, which is on the border of Hauran. ¹⁷So the boundary shall run from the sea to Hazar-enan, which is on the northern border of Damascus, with the border of Hamath to the north.[k] This shall be the north side.[l]

¹⁸"On the east side, the boundary shall run between Hauran and Damascus; along the Jordan between Gilead and the land of Israel; to the eastern sea and as far as Tamar.[m] This shall be the east side.

¹⁹"On the south side, it shall run from Tamar as far as the waters of Meribah-kadesh, from there along the Brook of Egypt[n] to the Great Sea. This shall be the south side.

²⁰"On the west side, the Great Sea shall be the boundary to a point opposite Lebo-hamath. This shall be the west side.

²¹"So you shall divide this land among you according to the tribes of Israel. ²²You shall allot it as an inheritance for yourselves and for the sojourners who reside among you and have had children among you. They shall be to you as native-born children of Israel. With you they shall be allotted an inheritance among the tribes of Israel. ²³In whatever tribe the sojourner resides, there you shall assign him his inheritance, declares the Lord God.

[a]Septuagint, Syriac, Vulgate; the meaning of the Hebrew word is uncertain [b]A *cubit* was about 18 inches or 45 centimetres [c]A *cubit* was about 18 inches or 45 centimetres [d]That is, the Dead Sea [e]Hebrew *will be healed*; also verses 9, 11 [f]Septuagint, Syriac, Vulgate, Targum; Hebrew *the two rivers go* [g]Hebrew lacks *the waters of the sea* [h]That is, the Mediterranean Sea; also verses 15, 19, 20 [i]Probable reading; Hebrew *The valley of the boundary* [j]Septuagint; Hebrew *the entrance of Zedad, Hamath* [k]The meaning of the Hebrew is uncertain [l]Probable reading; Hebrew *and as for the north side* [m]Compare Syriac; Hebrew *to the eastern sea you shall measure* [n]Hebrew lacks *of Egypt*

48 "These are the names of the tribes: Beginning at the northern extreme, beside the way of Hethlon to Lebo-hamath, as far as Hazar-enan (which is on the northern border of Damascus over against Hamath), and extending[a] from the east side to the west,[b] Dan, one portion. ²Adjoining the territory of Dan, from the east side to the west, Asher, one portion. ³Adjoining the territory of Asher, from the east side to the west, Naphtali, one portion. ⁴Adjoining the territory of Naphtali, from the east side to the west, Manasseh, one portion. ⁵Adjoining the territory of Manasseh, from the east side to the west, Ephraim, one portion. ⁶Adjoining the territory of Ephraim, from the east side to the west, Reuben, one portion. ⁷Adjoining the territory of Reuben, from the east side to the west, Judah, one portion.

⁸"Adjoining the territory of Judah, from the east side to the west, shall be the portion which you shall set apart, 25,000 cubits[c] in breadth, and in length equal to one of the tribal portions, from the east side to the west, with the sanctuary in the midst of it. ⁹The portion that you shall set apart for the LORD shall be 25,000 cubits in length, and 20,000[d] in breadth. ¹⁰These shall be the allotments of the holy portion: the priests shall have an allotment measuring 25,000 cubits on the northern side, 10,000 cubits in breadth on the western side, 10,000 in breadth on the eastern side, and 25,000 in length on the southern side, with the sanctuary of the LORD in the midst of it. ¹¹This shall be for the consecrated priests, the sons of Zadok, who kept my charge, who did not go astray when the people of Israel went astray, as the Levites did. ¹²And it shall belong to them as a special portion from the holy portion of the land, a most holy place, adjoining the territory of the Levites. ¹³And alongside the territory of the priests, the Levites shall have an allotment 25,000 cubits in length and 10,000 in breadth. The whole length shall be 25,000 cubits and the breadth 20,000.[e] ¹⁴They shall not sell or exchange any of it. They shall not alienate this choice portion of the land, for it is holy to the LORD.

¹⁵"The remainder, 5,000 cubits in breadth and 25,000 in length, shall be for common use for the city, for dwellings and for open country. In the midst of it shall be the city, ¹⁶and these shall be its measurements: the north side 4,500 cubits, the south side 4,500, the east side 4,500, and the west side 4,500. ¹⁷And the city shall have open land: on the north 250 cubits, on the south 250, on the east 250, and on the west 250. ¹⁸The remainder of the length alongside the holy portion shall be 10,000 cubits to the east, and 10,000 to the west, and it shall be alongside the holy portion. Its produce shall be food for the workers of the city. ¹⁹And the workers of the city, from all the tribes of Israel, shall till it. ²⁰The whole portion that you shall set apart shall be 25,000 cubits square, that is, the holy portion together with the property of the city.

²¹"What remains on both sides of the holy portion and of the property of the city shall belong to the prince. Extending from the 25,000 cubits of the holy portion to the east border, and westwards from the 25,000 cubits to the west border, parallel to the tribal portions, it shall belong to the prince. The holy portion with the sanctuary of the temple shall be in its midst. ²²It shall be separate from the property of the Levites and the property of the city, which are in the midst of that which belongs to the prince. The portion of the prince shall lie between the territory of Judah and the territory of Benjamin.

²³"As for the rest of the tribes: from the east side to the west, Benjamin, one portion. ²⁴Adjoining the territory of Benjamin, from the east side to the west, Simeon, one portion. ²⁵Adjoining the territory of Simeon, from the east side to the west, Issachar, one portion. ²⁶Adjoining the territory of Issachar, from the east side to the west, Zebulun, one portion. ²⁷Adjoining the territory of Zebulun, from the east side to the west, Gad, one portion. ²⁸And adjoining the territory of Gad to the south, the boundary shall run from Tamar to the waters of Meribah-kadesh, from there along the Brook of Egypt[f] to the Great Sea.[g] ²⁹This is the land that you shall allot as an inheritance among the tribes of Israel, and these are their portions, declares the Lord GOD.

THE GATES OF THE CITY

³⁰"These shall be the exits of the city: On the north side, which is to be 4,500 cubits by measure, ³¹three gates, the gate of Reuben, the gate of Judah, and the gate of Levi,

---

[a] Probable reading; Hebrew *and they shall be his* [b] Septuagint (compare verses 2–8); Hebrew *the east side the west* [c] A *cubit* was about 18 inches or 45 centimetres [d] Compare 45:1; Hebrew *10,000* [e] Septuagint; Hebrew *10,000* [f] Hebrew lacks *of Egypt* [g] That is, the Mediterranean Sea

the gates of the city being named after the tribes of Israel. ³²On the east side, which is to be 4,500 cubits, three gates, the gate of Joseph, the gate of Benjamin, and the gate of Dan. ³³On the south side, which is to be 4,500 cubits by measure, three gates, the gate of Simeon, the gate of Issachar, and the gate of Zebulun. ³⁴On the west side, which is to be 4,500 cubits, three gates,[a] the gate of Gad, the gate of Asher, and the gate of Naphtali. ³⁵The circumference of the city shall be 18,000 cubits. And the name of the city from that time on shall be, The LORD Is There."

---

[a] One Hebrew manuscript, Syriac (compare Septuagint); most Hebrew manuscripts *their gates three*

DANIEL

DANIEL TAKEN TO BABYLON

1 In the third year of the reign of Jehoiakim king of Judah, Nebuchadnezzar king of Babylon came to Jerusalem and besieged it. ²And the Lord gave Jehoiakim king of Judah into his hand, with some of the vessels of the house of God. And he brought them to the land of Shinar, to the house of his god, and placed the vessels in the treasury of his god. ³Then the king commanded Ashpenaz, his chief eunuch, to bring some of the people of Israel, both of the royal family[a] and of the nobility, ⁴youths without blemish, of good appearance and skilful in all wisdom, endowed with knowledge, understanding learning, and competent to stand in the king's palace, and to teach them the literature and language of the Chaldeans. ⁵The king assigned them a daily portion of the food that the king ate, and of the wine that he drank. They were to be educated for three years, and at the end of that time they were to stand before the king. ⁶Among these were Daniel, Hananiah, Mishael, and Azariah of the tribe of Judah. ⁷And the chief of the eunuchs gave them names: Daniel he called Belteshazzar, Hananiah he called Shadrach, Mishael he called Meshach, and Azariah he called Abednego.

DANIEL'S FAITHFULNESS

⁸But Daniel resolved that he would not defile himself[b] with the king's food, or with the wine that he drank. Therefore he asked the chief of the eunuchs to allow him not to defile himself. ⁹And God gave Daniel favour and compassion in the sight of the chief of the eunuchs, ¹⁰and the chief of the eunuchs said to Daniel, "I fear my lord the king, who assigned your food and your drink; for why should he see that you were in worse condition than the youths who are of your own age? So you would endanger my head with the king." ¹¹Then Daniel said to the steward whom the chief of the eunuchs had assigned over Daniel, Hananiah, Mishael, and Azariah, ¹²"Test your servants for ten days; let us be given vegetables to eat and water to drink. ¹³Then let our appearance and the appearance of the youths who eat the king's food be observed by you, and deal with your servants according to what you see." ¹⁴So he listened to them in this matter, and tested them for ten days. ¹⁵At the end of ten days it was seen that they were better in appearance and fatter in flesh than all the youths who ate the king's food. ¹⁶So the steward took away their food and the wine they were to drink, and gave them vegetables.

¹⁷As for these four youths, God gave them learning and skill in all literature and wisdom, and Daniel had understanding in all visions and dreams. ¹⁸At the end of the time, when the king had commanded that they should be brought in, the chief of the eunuchs brought them in before Nebuchadnezzar. ¹⁹And the king spoke with them, and among all of them none was found like Daniel, Hananiah, Mishael, and Azariah. Therefore they stood before the king. ²⁰And in every matter of wisdom and understanding about which the king enquired of them, he found them ten times better than all the magicians and enchanters that were in all his kingdom. ²¹And Daniel was there until the first year of King Cyrus.

NEBUCHADNEZZAR'S DREAM

2 In the second year of the reign of Nebuchadnezzar, Nebuchadnezzar had dreams; his spirit was troubled, and his sleep left him. ²Then the king commanded that the magicians, the enchanters, the sorcerers, and the Chaldeans be summoned to tell the king his dreams. So they came in and stood before the king. ³And the king said to them, "I had a dream, and my spirit is troubled to know the dream." ⁴Then the Chaldeans said to the king in Aramaic,[c] "O king, live for ever! Tell your servants the dream, and we will show the interpretation." ⁵The king answered and said to the Chaldeans, "The word from me is firm: if you do not make known to me

---

[a] Hebrew *of the seed of the kingdom* [b] Daniel believed eating these foods would make him unclean [c] The text from this point to the end of chapter 7 is in Aramaic

the dream and its interpretation, you shall be torn limb from limb, and your houses shall be laid in ruins. ⁶But if you show the dream and its interpretation, you shall receive from me gifts and rewards and great honour. Therefore show me the dream and its interpretation." ⁷They answered a second time and said, "Let the king tell his servants the dream, and we will show its interpretation." ⁸The king answered and said, "I know with certainty that you are trying to gain time, because you see that the word from me is firm— ⁹if you do not make the dream known to me, there is but one sentence for you. You have agreed to speak lying and corrupt words before me till the times change. Therefore tell me the dream, and I shall know that you can show me its interpretation." ¹⁰The Chaldeans answered the king and said, "There is not a man on earth who can meet the king's demand, for no great and powerful king has asked such a thing of any magician or enchanter or Chaldean. ¹¹The thing that the king asks is difficult, and no one can show it to the king except the gods, whose dwelling is not with flesh."

¹²Because of this the king was angry and very furious, and commanded that all the wise men of Babylon be destroyed. ¹³So the decree went out, and the wise men were about to be killed; and they sought Daniel and his companions, to kill them. ¹⁴Then Daniel replied with prudence and discretion to Arioch, the captain of the king's guard, who had gone out to kill the wise men of Babylon. ¹⁵He declared[a] to Arioch, the king's captain, "Why is the decree of the king so urgent?" Then Arioch made the matter known to Daniel. ¹⁶And Daniel went in and requested the king to appoint him a time, that he might show the interpretation to the king.

GOD REVEALS NEBUCHADNEZZAR'S DREAM

¹⁷Then Daniel went to his house and made the matter known to Hananiah, Mishael, and Azariah, his companions, ¹⁸and told them to seek mercy from the God of heaven concerning this mystery, so that Daniel and his companions might not be destroyed with the rest of the wise men of Babylon. ¹⁹Then the mystery was revealed to Daniel in a vision of the night. Then Daniel blessed the God of heaven. ²⁰Daniel answered and said:

> "Blessed be the name of God
>   for ever and ever,
>   to whom belong wisdom and might.

²¹ He changes times and seasons;
   he removes kings and sets up kings;
  he gives wisdom to the wise
    and knowledge to those who
      have understanding;
²² he reveals deep and hidden things;
   he knows what is in the darkness,
   and the light dwells with him.
²³ To you, O God of my fathers,
   I give thanks and praise,
  for you have given me
    wisdom and might,
  and have now made known to
    me what we asked of you,
  for you have made known to
    us the king's matter."

²⁴Therefore Daniel went in to Arioch, whom the king had appointed to destroy the wise men of Babylon. He went and said thus to him: "Do not destroy the wise men of Babylon; bring me in before the king, and I will show the king the interpretation." ²⁵Then Arioch brought in Daniel before the king in haste and said thus to him: "I have found among the exiles from Judah a man who will make known to the king the interpretation." ²⁶The king declared to Daniel, whose name was Belteshazzar, "Are you able to make known to me the dream that I have seen and its interpretation?" ²⁷Daniel answered the king and said, "No wise men, enchanters, magicians, or astrologers can show to the king the mystery that the king has asked, ²⁸but there is a God in heaven who reveals mysteries, and he has made known to King Nebuchadnezzar what will be in the latter days. Your dream and the visions of your head as you lay in bed are these: ²⁹To you, O king, as you lay in bed came thoughts of what would be after this, and he who reveals mysteries made known to you what is to be. ³⁰But as for me, this mystery has been revealed to me, not because of any wisdom that I have more than all the living, but in order that the interpretation may be made known to the king, and that you may know the thoughts of your mind.

DANIEL INTERPRETS THE DREAM

³¹"You saw, O king, and behold, a great image. This image, mighty and of exceeding brightness, stood before you, and its appearance was frightening. ³²The head of

---
[a] Aramaic *answered and said*; also verse 26

this image was of fine gold, its chest and arms of silver, its middle and thighs of bronze, ³³its legs of iron, its feet partly of iron and partly of clay. ³⁴As you looked, a stone was cut out by no human hand, and it struck the image on its feet of iron and clay, and broke them in pieces. ³⁵Then the iron, the clay, the bronze, the silver, and the gold, all together were broken in pieces, and became like the chaff of the summer threshing floors; and the wind carried them away, so that not a trace of them could be found. But the stone that struck the image became a great mountain and filled the whole earth.

³⁶"This was the dream. Now we will tell the king its interpretation. ³⁷You, O king, the king of kings, to whom the God of heaven has given the kingdom, the power, and the might, and the glory, ³⁸and into whose hand he has given, wherever they dwell, the children of man, the beasts of the field, and the birds of the heavens, making you rule over them all—you are the head of gold. ³⁹Another kingdom inferior to you shall arise after you, and yet a third kingdom of bronze, which shall rule over all the earth. ⁴⁰And there shall be a fourth kingdom, strong as iron, because iron breaks to pieces and shatters all things. And like iron that crushes, it shall break and crush all these. ⁴¹And as you saw the feet and toes, partly of potter's clay and partly of iron, it shall be a divided kingdom, but some of the firmness of iron shall be in it, just as you saw iron mixed with the soft clay. ⁴²And as the toes of the feet were partly iron and partly clay, so the kingdom shall be partly strong and partly brittle. ⁴³As you saw the iron mixed with soft clay, so they will mix with one another in marriage,ᵃ but they will not hold together, just as iron does not mix with clay. ⁴⁴And in the days of those kings the God of heaven will set up a kingdom that shall never be destroyed, nor shall the kingdom be left to another people. It shall break in pieces all these kingdoms and bring them to an end, and it shall stand for ever, ⁴⁵just as you saw that a stone was cut from a mountain by no human hand, and that it broke in pieces the iron, the bronze, the clay, the silver, and the gold. A great God has made known to the king what shall be after this. The dream is certain, and its interpretation sure."

DANIEL IS PROMOTED

⁴⁶Then King Nebuchadnezzar fell upon his face and paid homage to Daniel, and commanded that an offering and incense be offered up to him. ⁴⁷The king answered and said to Daniel, "Truly, your God is God of gods and Lord of kings, and a revealer of mysteries, for you have been able to reveal this mystery." ⁴⁸Then the king gave Daniel high honours and many great gifts, and made him ruler over the whole province of Babylon and chief prefect over all the wise men of Babylon. ⁴⁹Daniel made a request of the king, and he appointed Shadrach, Meshach, and Abednego over the affairs of the province of Babylon. But Daniel remained at the king's court.

NEBUCHADNEZZAR'S GOLDEN IMAGE

3 King Nebuchadnezzar made an image of gold, whose height was sixty cubitsᵇ and its breadth six cubits. He set it up on the plain of Dura, in the province of Babylon. ²Then King Nebuchadnezzar sent to gather the satraps, the prefects, and the governors, the counsellors, the treasurers, the justices, the magistrates, and all the officials of the provinces to come to the dedication of the image that King Nebuchadnezzar had set up. ³Then the satraps, the prefects, and the governors, the counsellors, the treasurers, the justices, the magistrates, and all the officials of the provinces gathered for the dedication of the image that King Nebuchadnezzar had set up. And they stood before the image that Nebuchadnezzar had set up. ⁴And the herald proclaimed aloud, "You are commanded, O peoples, nations, and languages, ⁵that when you hear the sound of the horn, pipe, lyre, trigon, harp, bagpipe, and every kind of music, you are to fall down and worship the golden image that King Nebuchadnezzar has set up. ⁶And whoever does not fall down and worship shall immediately be cast into a burning fiery furnace." ⁷Therefore, as soon as all the peoples heard the sound of the horn, pipe, lyre, trigon, harp, bagpipe, and every kind of music, all the peoples, nations, and languages fell down and worshipped the golden image that King Nebuchadnezzar had set up.

THE FIERY FURNACE

⁸Therefore at that time certain Chaldeans came forward and maliciously accused the Jews. ⁹They declaredᶜ to King Nebuchadnezzar, "O king, live for ever! ¹⁰You, O king, have made a decree, that every man who hears the

---

ᵃAramaic *by the seed of men* ᵇA *cubit* was about 18 inches or 45 centimetres ᶜAramaic *answered and said*; also verses 24, 26

sound of the horn, pipe, lyre, trigon, harp, bagpipe, and every kind of music, shall fall down and worship the golden image. ¹¹And whoever does not fall down and worship shall be cast into a burning fiery furnace. ¹²There are certain Jews whom you have appointed over the affairs of the province of Babylon: Shadrach, Meshach, and Abednego. These men, O king, pay no attention to you; they do not serve your gods or worship the golden image that you have set up."

¹³Then Nebuchadnezzar in furious rage commanded that Shadrach, Meshach, and Abednego be brought. So they brought these men before the king. ¹⁴Nebuchadnezzar answered and said to them, "Is it true, O Shadrach, Meshach, and Abednego, that you do not serve my gods or worship the golden image that I have set up? ¹⁵Now if you are ready when you hear the sound of the horn, pipe, lyre, trigon, harp, bagpipe, and every kind of music, to fall down and worship the image that I have made, well and good.ᵃ But if you do not worship, you shall immediately be cast into a burning fiery furnace. And who is the god who will deliver you out of my hands?"

¹⁶Shadrach, Meshach, and Abednego answered and said to the king, "O Nebuchadnezzar, we have no need to answer you in this matter. ¹⁷If this be so, our God whom we serve is able to deliver us from the burning fiery furnace, and he will deliver us out of your hand, O king.ᵇ ¹⁸But if not, be it known to you, O king, that we will not serve your gods or worship the golden image that you have set up."

¹⁹Then Nebuchadnezzar was filled with fury, and the expression of his face was changed against Shadrach, Meshach, and Abednego. He ordered the furnace heated seven times more than it was usually heated. ²⁰And he ordered some of the mighty men of his army to bind Shadrach, Meshach, and Abednego, and to cast them into the burning fiery furnace. ²¹Then these men were bound in their cloaks, their tunics,ᶜ their hats, and their other garments, and they were thrown into the burning fiery furnace. ²²Because the king's order was urgent and the furnace overheated, the flame of the fire killed those men who took up Shadrach, Meshach, and Abednego. ²³And these three men, Shadrach, Meshach, and Abednego, fell bound into the burning fiery furnace.

GOD DELIVERS HIS SERVANTS

²⁴Then King Nebuchadnezzar was astonished and rose up in haste. He declared to his counsellors, "Did we not cast three men bound into the fire?" They answered and said to the king, "True, O king."²⁵He answered and said, "But I see four men unbound, walking in the midst of the fire, and they are not hurt; and the appearance of the fourth is like a son of the gods."

²⁶Then Nebuchadnezzar came near to the door of the burning fiery furnace; he declared, "Shadrach, Meshach, and Abednego, servants of the Most High God, come out, and come here!" Then Shadrach, Meshach, and Abednego came out from the fire.²⁷And the satraps, the prefects, the governors, and the king's counsellors gathered together and saw that the fire had not had any power over the bodies of those men. The hair of their heads was not singed, their cloaks were not harmed, and no smell of fire had come upon them.²⁸Nebuchadnezzar answered and said, "Blessed be the God of Shadrach, Meshach, and Abednego, who has sent his angel and delivered his servants, who trusted in him, and set asideᵃ the king's command, and yielded up their bodies rather than serve and worship any god except their own God.²⁹Therefore I make a decree: Any people, nation, or language that speaks anything against the God of Shadrach, Meshach, and Abednego shall be torn limb from limb, and their houses laid in ruins, for there is no other god who is able to rescue in this way."³⁰Then the king promoted Shadrach, Meshach, and Abednego in the province of Babylon.

NEBUCHADNEZZAR PRAISES GOD

4 ᵈ King Nebuchadnezzar to all peoples, nations, and languages, that dwell in all the earth: Peace be multiplied to you! ²It has seemed good to me to show the signs and wonders that the Most High God has done for me.

³ How great are his signs,
 how mighty his wonders!
His kingdom is an everlasting kingdom,
 and his dominion endures from
  generation to generation.

NEBUCHADNEZZAR'S SECOND DREAM

⁴ᵉ I, Nebuchadnezzar, was at ease in my house and prospering in my palace. ⁵I saw a dream that made me afraid. As I lay in bed the

---

ᵃAramaic lacks *well and good*   ᵇOr *If our God whom we serve is able to deliver us, he will deliver us from the burning fiery furnace and out of your hand, O king*   ᶜThe meaning of the Aramaic words rendered *cloaks* and *tunics* is uncertain; also verse 27   ᵈCh 3:31 in Aramaic   ᵉCh 4:1 in Aramaic

fancies and the visions of my head alarmed me. ⁶So I made a decree that all the wise men of Babylon should be brought before me, that they might make known to me the interpretation of the dream. ⁷Then the magicians, the enchanters, the Chaldeans, and the astrologers came in, and I told them the dream, but they could not make known to me its interpretation. ⁸At last Daniel came in before me—he who was named Belteshazzar after the name of my god, and in whom is the spirit of the holy gods*ᵃ*—and I told him the dream, saying, ⁹"O Belteshazzar, chief of the magicians, because I know that the spirit of the holy gods is in you and that no mystery is too difficult for you, tell me the visions of my dream that I saw and their interpretation. ¹⁰The visions of my head as I lay in bed were these: I saw, and behold, a tree in the midst of the earth, and its height was great. ¹¹The tree grew and became strong, and its top reached to heaven, and it was visible to the end of the whole earth. ¹²Its leaves were beautiful and its fruit abundant, and in it was food for all. The beasts of the field found shade under it, and the birds of the heavens lived in its branches, and all flesh was fed from it.

¹³"I saw in the visions of my head as I lay in bed, and behold, a watcher, a holy one, came down from heaven. ¹⁴He proclaimed aloud and said thus: 'Chop down the tree and lop off its branches, strip off its leaves and scatter its fruit. Let the beasts flee from under it and the birds from its branches. ¹⁵But leave the stump of its roots in the earth, bound with a band of iron and bronze, amid the tender grass of the field. Let him be wet with the dew of heaven. Let his portion be with the beasts in the grass of the earth. ¹⁶Let his mind be changed from a man's, and let a beast's mind be given to him; and let seven periods of time pass over him. ¹⁷The sentence is by the decree of the watchers, the decision by the word of the holy ones, to the end that the living may know that the Most High rules the kingdom of men and gives it to whom he will and sets over it the lowliest of men.' ¹⁸This dream I, King Nebuchadnezzar, saw. And you, O Belteshazzar, tell me the interpretation, because all the wise men of my kingdom are not able to make known to me the interpretation, but you are able, for the spirit of the holy gods is in you."

DANIEL INTERPRETS THE SECOND DREAM

¹⁹Then Daniel, whose name was Belteshazzar, was dismayed for a while, and his thoughts alarmed him. The king answered and said, "Belteshazzar, let not the dream or the interpretation alarm you." Belteshazzar answered and said, "My lord, may the dream be for those who hate you and its interpretation for your enemies! ²⁰The tree you saw, which grew and became strong, so that its top reached to heaven, and it was visible to the end of the whole earth, ²¹whose leaves were beautiful and its fruit abundant, and in which was food for all, under which beasts of the field found shade, and in whose branches the birds of the heavens lived — ²²it is you, O king, who have grown and become strong. Your greatness has grown and reaches to heaven, and your dominion to the ends of the earth. ²³And because the king saw a watcher, a holy one, coming down from heaven and saying, 'Chop down the tree and destroy it, but leave the stump of its roots in the earth, bound with a band of iron and bronze, in the tender grass of the field, and let him be wet with the dew of heaven, and let his portion be with the beasts of the field, till seven periods of time pass over him', ²⁴this is the interpretation, O king: It is a decree of the Most High, which has come upon my lord the king, ²⁵that you shall be driven from among men, and your dwelling shall be with the beasts of the field. You shall be made to eat grass like an ox, and you shall be wet with the dew of heaven, and seven periods of time shall pass over you, till you know that the Most High rules the kingdom of men and gives it to whom he will. ²⁶And as it was commanded to leave the stump of the roots of the tree, your kingdom shall be confirmed for you from the time that you know that Heaven rules. ²⁷Therefore, O king, let my counsel be acceptable to you: break off your sins by practicing righteousness, and your iniquities by showing mercy to the oppressed, that there may perhaps be a lengthening of your prosperity."

NEBUCHADNEZZAR'S HUMILIATION

²⁸All this came upon King Nebuchadnezzar. ²⁹At the end of twelve months he was walking on the roof of the royal palace of Babylon, ³⁰and the king answered and said, "Is not this great Babylon, which I have built by my mighty power as a royal residence and for the glory of my majesty?" ³¹While the words were still in the king's mouth, there fell a voice

---

ᵃOr *Spirit of the holy God*; also verses 9, 18

from heaven, "O King Nebuchadnezzar, to you it is spoken: The kingdom has departed from you, ³²and you shall be driven from among men, and your dwelling shall be with the beasts of the field. And you shall be made to eat grass like an ox, and seven periods of time shall pass over you, until you know that the Most High rules the kingdom of men and gives it to whom he will." ³³Immediately the word was fulfilled against Nebuchadnezzar. He was driven from among men and ate grass like an ox, and his body was wet with the dew of heaven till his hair grew as long as eagles' feathers, and his nails were like birds' claws.

NEBUCHADNEZZAR RESTORED

³⁴At the end of the days I, Nebuchadnezzar, lifted my eyes to heaven, and my reason returned to me, and I blessed the Most High, and praised and honoured him who lives for ever,

> for his dominion is an
> everlasting dominion,
> and his kingdom endures from
> generation to generation;
> ³⁵ all the inhabitants of the earth
> are accounted as nothing,
> and he does according to his will
> among the host of heaven
> and among the inhabitants
> of the earth;
> and none can stay his hand
> or say to him, "What have
> you done?"

³⁶At the same time my reason returned to me, and for the glory of my kingdom, my majesty and splendour returned to me. My counsellors and my lords sought me, and I was established in my kingdom, and still more greatness was added to me. ³⁷Now I, Nebuchadnezzar, praise and extol and honour the King of heaven, for all his works are right and his ways are just; and those who walk in pride he is able to humble.

THE HANDWRITING ON THE WALL

5 King Belshazzar made a great feast for a thousand of his lords and drank wine in front of the thousand.

²Belshazzar, when he tasted the wine, commanded that the vessels of gold and of silver that Nebuchadnezzar his father[a] had taken out of the temple in Jerusalem be brought, that the king and his lords, his wives, and his concubines might drink from them. ³Then they brought in the golden vessels that had been taken out of the temple, the house of God in Jerusalem, and the king and his lords, his wives, and his concubines drank from them. ⁴They drank wine and praised the gods of gold and silver, bronze, iron, wood, and stone.

⁵Immediately the fingers of a human hand appeared and wrote on the plaster of the wall of the king's palace, opposite the lampstand. And the king saw the hand as it wrote. ⁶Then the king's colour changed, and his thoughts alarmed him; his limbs gave way, and his knees knocked together. ⁷The king called loudly to bring in the enchanters, the Chaldeans, and the astrologers. The king declared[b] to the wise men of Babylon, "Whoever reads this writing, and shows me its interpretation, shall be clothed with purple and have a chain of gold round his neck and shall be the third ruler in the kingdom." ⁸Then all the king's wise men came in, but they could not read the writing or make known to the king the interpretation. ⁹Then King Belshazzar was greatly alarmed, and his colour changed, and his lords were perplexed.

¹⁰The queen,[c] because of the words of the king and his lords, came into the banqueting hall, and the queen declared, "O king, live for ever! Let not your thoughts alarm you or your colour change. ¹¹There is a man in your kingdom in whom is the spirit of the holy gods.[d] In the days of your father, light and understanding and wisdom like the wisdom of the gods were found in him, and King Nebuchadnezzar, your father— your father the king—made him chief of the magicians, enchanters, Chaldeans, and astrologers, ¹²because an excellent spirit, knowledge, and understanding to interpret dreams, explain riddles, and solve problems were found in this Daniel, whom the king named Belteshazzar. Now let Daniel be called, and he will show the interpretation."

DANIEL INTERPRETS THE HANDWRITING

¹³Then Daniel was brought in before the king. The king answered and said to Daniel, "You are that Daniel, one of the exiles of Judah, whom the king my father brought from Judah. ¹⁴I have heard of you that the spirit of the gods[e] is in you, and that light

---

[a]Or *predecessor*; also verses 11, 13, 29 [b]Aramaic *answered and said*; also verse 10 [c]Or *queen mother*; twice in this verse [d]Or *Spirit of the holy God* [e]Or *Spirit of God*

and understanding and excellent wisdom are found in you. ¹⁵Now the wise men, the enchanters, have been brought in before me to read this writing and make known to me its interpretation, but they could not show the interpretation of the matter. ¹⁶But I have heard that you can give interpretations and solve problems. Now if you can read the writing and make known to me its interpretation, you shall be clothed with purple and have a chain of gold round your neck and shall be the third ruler in the kingdom."

¹⁷Then Daniel answered and said before the king, "Let your gifts be for yourself, and give your rewards to another. Nevertheless, I will read the writing to the king and make known to him the interpretation. ¹⁸O king, the Most High God gave Nebuchadnezzar your father kingship and greatness and glory and majesty. ¹⁹And because of the greatness that he gave him, all peoples, nations, and languages trembled and feared before him. Whom he would, he killed, and whom he would, he kept alive; whom he would, he raised up, and whom he would, he humbled. ²⁰But when his heart was lifted up and his spirit was hardened so that he dealt proudly, he was brought down from his kingly throne, and his glory was taken from him. ²¹He was driven from among the children of mankind, and his mind was made like that of a beast, and his dwelling was with the wild donkeys. He was fed grass like an ox, and his body was wet with the dew of heaven, until he knew that the Most High God rules the kingdom of mankind and sets over it whom he will. ²²And you his son,ᵃ Belshazzar, have not humbled your heart, though you knew all this, ²³but you have lifted up yourself against the Lord of heaven. And the vessels of his house have been brought in before you, and you and your lords, your wives, and your concubines have drunk wine from them. And you have praised the gods of silver and gold, of bronze, iron, wood, and stone, which do not see or hear or know, but the God in whose hand is your breath, and whose are all your ways, you have not honoured.

²⁴"Then from his presence the hand was sent, and this writing was inscribed. ²⁵And this is the writing that was inscribed: MENE, MENE, TEKEL, and PARSIN. ²⁶This is the interpretation of the matter: MENE, God has numberedᵇ the days of your kingdom and brought it to an end; ²⁷TEKEL, you have been weighedᶜ in the balances and found wanting; ²⁸PERES, your kingdom is divided and given to the Medes and Persians."ᵈ

²⁹Then Belshazzar gave the command, and Daniel was clothed with purple, a chain of gold was put round his neck, and a proclamation was made about him, that he should be the third ruler in the kingdom.

³⁰That very night Belshazzar the Chaldean king was killed. ³¹ᵉ And Darius the Mede received the kingdom, being about sixty-two years old.

DANIEL AND THE LIONS' DEN

6 It pleased Darius to set over the kingdom 120 satraps, to be throughout the whole kingdom; ²and over them three high officials, of whom Daniel was one, to whom these satraps should give account, so that the king might suffer no loss. ³Then this Daniel became distinguished above all the other high officials and satraps, because an excellent spirit was in him. And the king planned to set him over the whole kingdom. ⁴Then the high officials and the satraps sought to find a ground for complaint against Daniel with regard to the kingdom, but they could find no ground for complaint or any fault, because he was faithful, and no error or fault was found in him. ⁵Then these men said, "We shall not find any ground for complaint against this Daniel unless we find it in connection with the law of his God."

⁶Then these high officials and satraps came by agreementᶠ to the king and said to him, "O King Darius, live for ever! ⁷All the high officials of the kingdom, the prefects and the satraps, the counsellors and the governors are agreed that the king should establish an ordinance and enforce an injunction, that whoever makes petition to any god or man for thirty days, except to you, O king, shall be cast into the den of lions. ⁸Now, O king, establish the injunction and sign the document, so that it cannot be changed, according to the law of the Medes and the Persians, which cannot be revoked." ⁹Therefore King Darius signed the document and injunction.

¹⁰When Daniel knew that the document had been signed, he went to his house where he had windows in his upper chamber open towards Jerusalem. He got down on his knees

---

ᵃOr successor ᵇMENE sounds like the Aramaic for numbered ᶜTEKEL sounds like the Aramaic for weighed ᵈPERES (the singular of Parsin) sounds like the Aramaic for divided and for Persia ᵉCh 6:1 in Aramaic ᶠOr came thronging; also verses 11, 15

three times a day and prayed and gave thanks before his God, as he had done previously. **11**Then these men came by agreement and found Daniel making petition and plea before his God. **12**Then they came near and said before the king, concerning the injunction, "O king! Did you not sign an injunction, that anyone who makes petition to any god or man within thirty days except to you, O king, shall be cast into the den of lions?" The king answered and said, "The thing stands fast, according to the law of the Medes and Persians, which cannot be revoked." **13**Then they answered and said before the king, "Daniel, who is one of the exiles from Judah, pays no attention to you, O king, or the injunction you have signed, but makes his petition three times a day."

14Then the king, when he heard these words, was much distressed and set his mind to deliver Daniel. And he laboured till the sun went down to rescue him. **15**Then these men came by agreement to the king and said to the king, "Know, O king, that it is a law of the Medes and Persians that no injunction or ordinance that the king establishes can be changed."

16Then the king commanded, and Daniel was brought and cast into the den of lions. The king declared*a* to Daniel, "May your God, whom you serve continually, deliver you!" **17**And a stone was brought and laid on the mouth of the den, and the king sealed it with his own signet and with the signet of his lords, that nothing might be changed concerning Daniel. **18**Then the king went to his palace and spent the night fasting; no diversions were brought to him, and sleep fled from him.

19Then, at break of day, the king arose and went in haste to the den of lions. **20**As he came near to the den where Daniel was, he cried out in a tone of anguish. The king declared to Daniel, "O Daniel, servant of the living God, has your God, whom you serve continually, been able to deliver you from the lions?" **21**Then Daniel said to the king, "O king, live for ever! **22**My God sent his angel and shut the lions' mouths, and they have not harmed me, because I was found blameless before him; and also before you, O king, I have done no harm." **23**Then the king was exceedingly glad, and commanded that Daniel be taken up out of the den. So Daniel was taken up out of the den, and no kind of harm was found on him, because he had trusted in his God. **24**And the king commanded, and those men who had maliciously accused Daniel were brought and cast into the den of lions—they, their children, and their wives. And before they reached the bottom of the den, the lions overpowered them and broke all their bones in pieces.

25Then King Darius wrote to all the peoples, nations, and languages that dwell in all the earth: "Peace be multiplied to you. **26**I make a decree, that in all my royal dominion people are to tremble and fear before the God of Daniel,

for he is the living God,
    enduring for ever;
his kingdom shall never be destroyed,
    and his dominion shall
        be to the end.
27 He delivers and rescues;
    he works signs and wonders
        in heaven and on earth,
he who has saved Daniel
    from the power of the lions."

28So this Daniel prospered during the reign of Darius and the reign of Cyrus the Persian.

DANIEL'S VISION OF THE FOUR BEASTS

7 In the first year of Belshazzar king of Babylon, Daniel saw a dream and visions of his head as he lay in his bed. Then he wrote down the dream and told the sum of the matter. **2**Daniel declared,*b* "I saw in my vision by night, and behold, the four winds of heaven were stirring up the great sea. **3**And four great beasts came up out of the sea, different from one another. **4**The first was like a lion and had eagles' wings. Then as I looked its wings were plucked off, and it was lifted up from the ground and made to stand on two feet like a man, and the mind of a man was given to it. **5**And behold, another beast, a second one, like a bear. It was raised up on one side. It had three ribs in its mouth between its teeth; and it was told, 'Arise, devour much flesh.' **6**After this I looked, and behold, another, like a leopard, with four wings of a bird on its back. And the beast had four heads, and dominion was given to it. **7**After this I saw in the night visions, and behold, a fourth beast, terrifying and dreadful and exceedingly strong. It had great iron teeth; it devoured and broke in pieces and stamped what was left with its

---

*a*Aramaic *answered and said*; also verse 20   *b*Aramaic *answered and said*

feet. It was different from all the beasts that were before it, and it had ten horns. ⁸I considered the horns, and behold, there came up among them another horn, a little one, before which three of the first horns were plucked up by the roots. And behold, in this horn were eyes like the eyes of a man, and a mouth speaking great things.

THE ANCIENT OF DAYS REIGNS

⁹"As I looked,

> thrones were placed,
>   and the Ancient of Days took his seat;
> his clothing was white as snow,
>   and the hair of his head
>   like pure wool;
> his throne was fiery flames;
>   its wheels were burning fire.
> ¹⁰ A stream of fire issued
>   and came out from before him;
>   a thousand thousands served him,
>   and ten thousand times ten
>   thousand stood before him;
>   the court sat in judgement,
>   and the books were opened.

¹¹"I looked then because of the sound of the great words that the horn was speaking. And as I looked, the beast was killed, and its body destroyed and given over to be burned with fire. ¹²As for the rest of the beasts, their dominion was taken away, but their lives were prolonged for a season and a time.

THE SON OF MAN IS GIVEN DOMINION

¹³"I saw in the night visions,

> and behold, with the clouds of heaven
>   there came one like a son of man,
> and he came to the Ancient of Days
>   and was presented before him.
> ¹⁴ And to him was given dominion
>   and glory and a kingdom,
>   that all peoples, nations,
>   and languages
>   should serve him;
>   his dominion is an everlasting
>   dominion,
>   which shall not pass away,
>   and his kingdom one
>   that shall not be destroyed.

DANIEL'S VISION INTERPRETED

¹⁵"As for me, Daniel, my spirit within me[a] was anxious, and the visions of my head alarmed me. ¹⁶I approached one of those who stood there and asked him the truth concerning all this. So he told me and made known to me the interpretation of the things. ¹⁷'These four great beasts are four kings who shall arise out of the earth. ¹⁸But the saints of the Most High shall receive the kingdom and possess the kingdom for ever, for ever and ever.'

¹⁹"Then I desired to know the truth about the fourth beast, which was different from all the rest, exceedingly terrifying, with its teeth of iron and claws of bronze, and which devoured and broke in pieces and stamped what was left with its feet, ²⁰and about the ten horns that were on its head, and the other horn that came up and before which three of them fell, the horn that had eyes and a mouth that spoke great things, and that seemed greater than its companions. ²¹As I looked, this horn made war with the saints and prevailed over them, ²²until the Ancient of Days came, and judgement was given for the saints of the Most High, and the time came when the saints possessed the kingdom.

²³"Thus he said: 'As for the fourth beast,

> there shall be a fourth
>   kingdom on earth,
>   which shall be different from
>   all the kingdoms,
>   and it shall devour the whole earth,
>   and trample it down, and
>   break it to pieces.
> ²⁴ As for the ten horns,
>   out of this kingdom ten
>   kings shall arise,
>   and another shall arise after them;
>   he shall be different from
>   the former ones,
>   and shall put down three kings.
> ²⁵ He shall speak words against
>   the Most High,
>   and shall wear out the saints
>   of the Most High,
>   and shall think to change the
>   times and the law;
>   and they shall be given into his hand
>   for a time, times, and half a time.
> ²⁶ But the court shall sit in judgement,
>   and his dominion shall
>   be taken away,
>   to be consumed and
>   destroyed to the end.

---

[a] Aramaic *within its sheath*

²⁷ And the kingdom and the dominion
and the greatness of the kingdoms
under the whole heaven
shall be given to the people of the
saints of the Most High;
his kingdom shall be an
everlasting kingdom,
and all dominions shall
serve and obey him.'ᵃ

²⁸"Here is the end of the matter. As for me, Daniel, my thoughts greatly alarmed me, and my colour changed, but I kept the matter in my heart."

DANIEL'S VISION OF THE RAM AND THE GOAT

8 In the third year of the reign of King Belshazzar a vision appeared to me, Daniel, after that which appeared to me at the first. ²And I saw in the vision; and when I saw, I was in Susa the citadel, which is in the province of Elam. And I saw in the vision, and I was at the Ulai canal. ³I raised my eyes and saw, and behold, a ram standing on the bank of the canal. It had two horns, and both horns were high, but one was higher than the other, and the higher one came up last. ⁴I saw the ram charging westwards and northwards and southwards. No beast could stand before him, and there was no one who could rescue from his power. He did as he pleased and became great.

⁵As I was considering, behold, a male goat came from the west across the face of the whole earth, without touching the ground. And the goat had a conspicuous horn between his eyes. ⁶He came to the ram with the two horns, which I had seen standing on the bank of the canal, and he ran at him in his powerful wrath. ⁷I saw him come close to the ram, and he was enraged against him and struck the ram and broke his two horns. And the ram had no power to stand before him, but he cast him down to the ground and trampled on him. And there was no one who could rescue the ram from his power. ⁸Then the goat became exceedingly great, but when he was strong, the great horn was broken, and instead of it there came up four conspicuous horns towards the four winds of heaven.

⁹Out of one of them came a little horn, which grew exceedingly great towards the south, towards the east, and towards the glorious land. ¹⁰It grew great, even to the host of heaven. And some of the host and someᵇ of the stars it threw down to the ground and trampled on them. ¹¹It became great, even as great as the Prince of the host. And the regular burnt offering was taken away from him, and the place of his sanctuary was overthrown. ¹²And a host will be given over to it together with the regular burnt offering because of transgression,ᶜ and it will throw truth to the ground, and it will act and prosper. ¹³Then I heard a holy one speaking, and another holy one said to the one who spoke, "For how long is the vision concerning the regular burnt offering, the transgression that makes desolate, and the giving over of the sanctuary and host to be trampled underfoot?" ¹⁴And he said to me,ᵈ "For 2,300 evenings and mornings. Then the sanctuary shall be restored to its rightful state."

THE INTERPRETATION OF THE VISION

¹⁵When I, Daniel, had seen the vision, I sought to understand it. And behold, there stood before me one having the appearance of a man. ¹⁶And I heard a man's voice between the banks of the Ulai, and it called, "Gabriel, make this man understand the vision." ¹⁷So he came near where I stood. And when he came, I was frightened and fell on my face. But he said to me, "Understand, O son of man, that the vision is for the time of the end."

¹⁸And when he had spoken to me, I fell into a deep sleep with my face to the ground. But he touched me and made me stand up. ¹⁹He said, "Behold, I will make known to you what shall be at the latter end of the indignation, for it refers to the appointed time of the end. ²⁰As for the ram that you saw with the two horns, these are the kings of Media and Persia. ²¹And the goatᵉ is the king of Greece. And the great horn between his eyes is the first king. ²²As for the horn that was broken, in place of which four others arose, four kingdoms shall arise from hisᶠ nation, but not with his power. ²³And at the latter end of their kingdom, when the transgressors have reached their limit, a king of bold countenance, one who understands riddles, shall arise. ²⁴His power shall be great—but not by his own power; and he shall cause fearful destruction and shall succeed in what he does, and destroy mighty men and the people who are the saints. ²⁵By his cunning he shall make deceit prosper under his hand, and in his own mind he shall become great. Without

---

ᵃOr their kingdom shall be an everlasting kingdom, and all dominions shall serve and obey them ᵇOr host, that is, some ᶜOr in an act of rebellion ᵈHebrew; Septuagint, Theodotion, Vulgate to him ᵉOr the shaggy goat ᶠTheodotion, Septuagint, Vulgate; Hebrew a

warning he shall destroy many. And he shall even rise up against the Prince of princes, and he shall be broken — but by no human hand. ²⁶The vision of the evenings and the mornings that has been told is true, but seal up the vision, for it refers to many days from now."

²⁷And I, Daniel, was overcome and lay sick for some days. Then I rose and went about the king's business, but I was appalled by the vision and did not understand it.

DANIEL'S PRAYER FOR HIS PEOPLE

9 In the first year of Darius the son of Ahasuerus, by descent a Mede, who was made king over the realm of the Chaldeans — ²in the first year of his reign, I, Daniel, perceived in the books the number of years that, according to the word of the LORD to Jeremiah the prophet, must pass before the end of the desolations of Jerusalem, namely, seventy years.

³Then I turned my face to the Lord God, seeking him by prayer and pleas for mercy with fasting and sackcloth and ashes. ⁴I prayed to the LORD my God and made confession, saying, "O Lord, the great and awesome God, who keeps covenant and steadfast love with those who love him and keep his commandments, ⁵we have sinned and done wrong and acted wickedly and rebelled, turning aside from your commandments and rules. ⁶We have not listened to your servants the prophets, who spoke in your name to our kings, our princes, and our fathers, and to all the people of the land. ⁷To you, O Lord, belongs righteousness, but to us open shame, as at this day, to the men of Judah, to the inhabitants of Jerusalem, and to all Israel, those who are near and those who are far away, in all the lands to which you have driven them, because of the treachery that they have committed against you. ⁸To us, O LORD, belongs open shame, to our kings, to our princes, and to our fathers, because we have sinned against you. ⁹To the Lord our God belong mercy and forgiveness, for we have rebelled against him ¹⁰and have not obeyed the voice of the LORD our God by walking in his laws, which he set before us by his servants the prophets. ¹¹All Israel has transgressed your law and turned aside, refusing to obey your voice. And the curse and oath that are written in the Law of Moses the servant of God have been poured out upon us, because we have sinned against him. ¹²He has confirmed his words, which he spoke against us and against our rulers who ruled us,ᵃ by bringing upon us a great calamity. For under the whole heaven there has not been done anything like what has been done against Jerusalem. ¹³As it is written in the Law of Moses, all this calamity has come upon us; yet we have not entreated the favour of the LORD our God, turning from our iniquities and gaining insight by your truth. ¹⁴Therefore the LORD has kept ready the calamity and has brought it upon us, for the LORD our God is righteous in all the works that he has done, and we have not obeyed his voice. ¹⁵And now, O Lord our God, who brought your people out of the land of Egypt with a mighty hand, and have made a name for yourself, as at this day, we have sinned, we have done wickedly.

¹⁶"O Lord, according to all your righteous acts, let your anger and your wrath turn away from your city Jerusalem, your holy hill, because for our sins, and for the iniquities of our fathers, Jerusalem and your people have become a byword among all who are around us. ¹⁷Now therefore, O our God, listen to the prayer of your servant and to his pleas for mercy, and for your own sake, O Lord,ᵇ make your face to shine upon your sanctuary, which is desolate. ¹⁸O my God, incline your ear and hear. Open your eyes and see our desolations, and the city that is called by your name. For we do not present our pleas before you because of our righteousness, but because of your great mercy. ¹⁹O Lord, hear; O Lord, forgive. O Lord, pay attention and act. Delay not, for your own sake, O my God, because your city and your people are called by your name."

GABRIEL BRINGS AN ANSWER

²⁰While I was speaking and praying, confessing my sin and the sin of my people Israel, and presenting my plea before the LORD my God for the holy hill of my God, ²¹while I was speaking in prayer, the man Gabriel, whom I had seen in the vision at the first, came to me in swift flight at the time of the evening sacrifice. ²²He made me understand, speaking with me and saying, "O Daniel, I have now come out to give you insight and understanding. ²³At the beginning of your pleas for mercy a word went out, and I have come to tell it to you, for you are greatly loved. Therefore consider the word and understand the vision.

ᵃOr *our judges who judged us*   ᵇHebrew *for the Lord's sake*

THE SEVENTY WEEKS

²⁴"Seventy weeks[a] are decreed about your people and your holy city, to finish the transgression, to put an end to sin, and to atone for iniquity, to bring in everlasting righteousness, to seal both vision and prophet, and to anoint a most holy place.[b] ²⁵Know therefore and understand that from the going out of the word to restore and build Jerusalem to the coming of an anointed one, a prince, there shall be seven weeks. Then for sixty-two weeks it shall be built again[c] with squares and moat, but in a troubled time. ²⁶And after the sixty-two weeks, an anointed one shall be cut off and shall have nothing. And the people of the prince who is to come shall destroy the city and the sanctuary. Its[d] end shall come with a flood, and to the end there shall be war. Desolations are decreed. ²⁷And he shall make a strong covenant with many for one week,[e] and for half of the week he shall put an end to sacrifice and offering. And on the wing of abominations shall come one who makes desolate, until the decreed end is poured out on the desolator."

DANIEL'S TERRIFYING VISION OF A MAN

10 In the third year of Cyrus king of Persia a word was revealed to Daniel, who was named Belteshazzar. And the word was true, and it was a great conflict.[f] And he understood the word and had understanding of the vision.

²In those days I, Daniel, was mourning for three weeks. ³I ate no delicacies, no meat or wine entered my mouth, nor did I anoint myself at all, for the full three weeks. ⁴On the twenty-fourth day of the first month, as I was standing on the bank of the great river (that is, the Tigris) ⁵I lifted up my eyes and looked, and behold, a man clothed in linen, with a belt of fine gold from Uphaz round his waist. ⁶His body was like beryl, his face like the appearance of lightning, his eyes like flaming torches, his arms and legs like the gleam of burnished bronze, and the sound of his words like the sound of a multitude. ⁷And I, Daniel, alone saw the vision, for the men who were with me did not see the vision, but a great trembling fell upon them, and they fled to hide themselves. ⁸So I was left alone and saw this great vision, and no strength was left in me. My radiant appearance was fearfully changed,[g] and I retained no strength. ⁹Then I heard the sound of his words, and as I heard the sound of his words, I fell on my face in deep sleep with my face to the ground.

¹⁰And behold, a hand touched me and set me trembling on my hands and knees. ¹¹And he said to me, "O Daniel, man greatly loved, understand the words that I speak to you, and stand upright, for now I have been sent to you." And when he had spoken this word to me, I stood up trembling. ¹²Then he said to me, "Fear not, Daniel, for from the first day that you set your heart to understand and humbled yourself before your God, your words have been heard, and I have come because of your words. ¹³The prince of the kingdom of Persia withstood me twenty-one days, but Michael, one of the chief princes, came to help me, for I was left there with the kings of Persia, ¹⁴and came to make you understand what is to happen to your people in the latter days. For the vision is for days yet to come."

¹⁵When he had spoken to me according to these words, I turned my face towards the ground and was mute. ¹⁶And behold, one in the likeness of the children of man touched my lips. Then I opened my mouth and spoke. I said to him who stood before me, "O my lord, by reason of the vision pains have come upon me, and I retain no strength. ¹⁷How can my lord's servant talk with my lord? For now no strength remains in me, and no breath is left in me." ¹⁸Again one having the appearance of a man touched me and strengthened me. ¹⁹And he said, "O man greatly loved, fear not, peace be with you; be strong and of good courage." And as he spoke to me, I was strengthened and said, "Let my lord speak, for you have strengthened me." ²⁰Then he said, "Do you know why I have come to you? But now I will return to fight against the prince of Persia; and when I go out, behold, the prince of Greece will come. ²¹But I will tell you what is inscribed in the book of truth: there is none who contends by my side against these except Michael, your prince.

THE KINGS OF THE SOUTH AND THE NORTH

11 "And as for me, in the first year of Darius the Mede, I stood up to confirm and strengthen him.

²"And now I will show you the truth. Behold, three more kings shall arise in Persia, and a fourth shall be far richer than all of them.

---

[a]Or sevens; also twice in verse 25 and once in verse 26 [b]Or thing, or one [c]Or there shall be seven weeks and sixty-two weeks. It shall be built again [d]Or His [e]Or seven; twice in this verse [f]Or and it was about a great conflict [g]Hebrew My splendour was changed to ruin

And when he has become strong through his riches, he shall stir up all against the kingdom of Greece. ³Then a mighty king shall arise, who shall rule with great dominion and do as he wills. ⁴And as soon as he has arisen, his kingdom shall be broken and divided towards the four winds of heaven, but not to his posterity, nor according to the authority with which he ruled, for his kingdom shall be plucked up and go to others besides these.

⁵"Then the king of the south shall be strong, but one of his princes shall be stronger than he and shall rule, and his authority shall be a great authority. ⁶After some years they shall make an alliance, and the daughter of the king of the south shall come to the king of the north to make an agreement. But she shall not retain the strength of her arm, and he and his arm shall not endure, but she shall be given up, and her attendants, he who fathered her, and he who supported[a] her in those times. ⁷"And from a branch from her roots one shall arise in his place. He shall come against the army and enter the fortress of the king of the north, and he shall deal with them and shall prevail. ⁸He shall also carry off to Egypt their gods with their metal images and their precious vessels of silver and gold, and for some years he shall refrain from attacking the king of the north. ⁹Then the latter shall come into the realm of the king of the south but shall return to his own land.

¹⁰"His sons shall wage war and assemble a multitude of great forces, which shall keep coming and overflow and pass through, and again shall carry the war as far as his fortress. ¹¹Then the king of the south, moved with rage, shall come out and fight against the king of the north. And he shall raise a great multitude, but it shall be given into his hand. ¹²And when the multitude is taken away, his heart shall be exalted, and he shall cast down tens of thousands, but he shall not prevail. ¹³For the king of the north shall again raise a multitude, greater than the first. And after some years[b] he shall come on with a great army and abundant supplies.

¹⁴"In those times many shall rise against the king of the south, and the violent among your own people shall lift themselves up in order to fulfil the vision, but they shall fail. ¹⁵Then the king of the north shall come and throw up siege works and take a well-fortified city. And the forces of the south shall not stand, or even his best troops, for there shall be no strength to stand. ¹⁶But he who comes against him shall do as he wills, and none shall stand before him. And he shall stand in the glorious land, with destruction in his hand. ¹⁷He shall set his face to come with the strength of his whole kingdom, and he shall bring terms of an agreement and perform them. He shall give him the daughter of women to destroy the kingdom,[c] but it shall not stand or be to his advantage. ¹⁸Afterwards he shall turn his face to the coastlands and shall capture many of them, but a commander shall put an end to his insolence. Indeed,[d] he shall turn his insolence back upon him. ¹⁹Then he shall turn his face back towards the fortresses of his own land, but he shall stumble and fall, and shall not be found.

²⁰"Then shall arise in his place one who shall send an exactor of tribute for the glory of the kingdom. But within a few days he shall be broken, neither in anger nor in battle. ²¹In his place shall arise a contemptible person to whom royal majesty has not been given. He shall come in without warning and obtain the kingdom by flatteries. ²²Armies shall be utterly swept away before him and broken, even the prince of the covenant. ²³And from the time that an alliance is made with him he shall act deceitfully, and he shall become strong with a small people. ²⁴Without warning he shall come into the richest parts[e] of the province, and he shall do what neither his fathers nor his fathers' fathers have done, scattering among them plunder, spoil, and goods. He shall devise plans against strongholds, but only for a time. ²⁵And he shall stir up his power and his heart against the king of the south with a great army. And the king of the south shall wage war with an exceedingly great and mighty army, but he shall not stand, for plots shall be devised against him. ²⁶Even those who eat his food shall break him. His army shall be swept away, and many shall fall down slain. ²⁷And as for the two kings, their hearts shall be bent on doing evil. They shall speak lies at the same table, but to no avail, for the end is yet to be at the time appointed. ²⁸And he shall return to his land with great wealth, but his heart shall be set against the holy covenant. And he shall work his will and return to his own land.

²⁹"At the time appointed he shall return and come into the south, but it shall not be this time as it was before. ³⁰For ships of Kittim shall come against him, and he shall be afraid and withdraw, and shall turn back and be enraged

---

[a]Or obtained [b]Hebrew *at the end of the times* [c]Hebrew *her*, or *it*
[d]The meaning of the Hebrew is uncertain [e]Or *among the richest men*

and take action against the holy covenant. He shall turn back and pay attention to those who forsake the holy covenant. ³¹Forces from him shall appear and profane the temple and fortress, and shall take away the regular burnt offering. And they shall set up the abomination that makes desolate. ³²He shall seduce with flattery those who violate the covenant, but the people who know their God shall stand firm and take action. ³³And the wise among the people shall make many understand, though for some days they shall stumble by sword and flame, by captivity and plunder. ³⁴When they stumble, they shall receive a little help. And many shall join themselves to them with flattery, ³⁵and some of the wise shall stumble, so that they may be refined, purified, and made white, until the time of the end, for it still awaits the appointed time.

³⁶"And the king shall do as he wills. He shall exalt himself and magnify himself above every god, and shall speak astonishing things against the God of gods. He shall prosper till the indignation is accomplished; for what is decreed shall be done. ³⁷He shall pay no attention to the gods of his fathers, or to the one beloved by women. He shall not pay attention to any other god, for he shall magnify himself above all. ³⁸He shall honour the god of fortresses instead of these. A god whom his fathers did not know he shall honour with gold and silver, with precious stones and costly gifts. ³⁹He shall deal with the strongest fortresses with the help of a foreign god. Those who acknowledge him he shall load with honour. He shall make them rulers over many and shall divide the land for a price.ᵃ

⁴⁰"At the time of the end, the king of the south shall attackᵇ him, but the king of the north shall rush upon him like a whirlwind, with chariots and horsemen, and with many ships. And he shall come into countries and shall overflow and pass through. ⁴¹He shall come into the glorious land. And tens of thousands shall fall, but these shall be delivered out of his hand: Edom and Moab and the main part of the Ammonites. ⁴²He shall stretch out his hand against the countries, and the land of Egypt shall not escape. ⁴³He shall become ruler of the treasures of gold and of silver, and all the precious things of Egypt, and the Libyans and the Cushites shall follow in his train. ⁴⁴But news from the east and the north shall alarm him, and he shall go out with great fury to destroy and devote many to destruction. ⁴⁵And he shall pitch his palatial tents between the sea and the glorious holy mountain. Yet he shall come to his end, with none to help him.

THE TIME OF THE END

12 "At that time shall arise Michael, the great prince who has charge of your people. And there shall be a time of trouble, such as never has been since there was a nation till that time. But at that time your people shall be delivered, everyone whose name shall be found written in the book. ²And many of those who sleep in the dust of the earth shall awake, some to everlasting life, and some to shame and everlasting contempt. ³And those who are wise shall shine like the brightness of the sky above;ᶜ and those who turn many to righteousness, like the stars for ever and ever. ⁴But you, Daniel, shut up the words and seal the book, until the time of the end. Many shall run to and fro, and knowledge shall increase."

⁵Then I, Daniel, looked, and behold, two others stood, one on this bank of the stream and one on that bank of the stream. ⁶And someone said to the man clothed in linen, who was above the waters of the stream,ᵈ "How long shall it be till the end of these wonders?" ⁷And I heard the man clothed in linen, who was above the waters of the stream; he raised his right hand and his left hand towards heaven and swore by him who lives for ever that it would be for a time, times, and half a time, and that when the shattering of the power of the holy people comes to an end all these things would be finished. ⁸I heard, but I did not understand. Then I said, "O my lord, what shall be the outcome of these things?" ⁹He said, "Go your way, Daniel, for the words are shut up and sealed until the time of the end. ¹⁰Many shall purify themselves and make themselves white and be refined, but the wicked shall act wickedly. And none of the wicked shall understand, but those who are wise shall understand. ¹¹And from the time that the regular burnt offering is taken away and the abomination that makes desolate is set up, there shall be 1,290 days. ¹²Blessed is he who waits and arrives at the 1,335 days. ¹³But go your way till the end. And you shall rest and shall stand in your allotted place at the end of the days."

ᵃOr *land as payment* ᵇHebrew *thrust at* ᶜHebrew *the expanse*; compare Genesis 1:6–8 ᵈOr *who was upstream*; also verse 7

HOSEA

1 The word of the LORD that came to Hosea, the son of Beeri, in the days of Uzziah, Jotham, Ahaz, and Hezekiah, kings of Judah, and in the days of Jeroboam the son of Joash, king of Israel.

HOSEA'S WIFE AND CHILDREN

²When the LORD first spoke through Hosea, the LORD said to Hosea, "Go, take to yourself a wife of whoredom and have children of whoredom, for the land commits great whoredom by forsaking the LORD." ³So he went and took Gomer, the daughter of Diblaim, and she conceived and bore him a son.

⁴And the LORD said to him, "Call his name Jezreel, for in just a little while I will punish the house of Jehu for the blood of Jezreel, and I will put an end to the kingdom of the house of Israel. ⁵And on that day I will break the bow of Israel in the Valley of Jezreel."

⁶She conceived again and bore a daughter. And the LORD said to him, "Call her name No Mercy,ᵃ for I will no more have mercy on the house of Israel, to forgive them at all. ⁷But I will have mercy on the house of Judah, and I will save them by the LORD their God. I will not save them by bow or by sword or by war or by horses or by horsemen."

⁸When she had weaned No Mercy, she conceived and bore a son. ⁹And the LORD said, "Call his name Not My People,ᵇ for you are not my people, and I am not your God."ᶜ

¹⁰ᵈ Yet the number of the children of Israel shall be like the sand of the sea, which cannot be measured or numbered. And in the place where it was said to them, "You are not my people", it shall be said to them, "Childrenᵉ of the living God." ¹¹And the children of Judah and the children of Israel shall be gathered together, and they shall appoint for themselves one head. And they shall go up from the land, for great shall be the day of Jezreel.

ISRAEL'S UNFAITHFULNESS PUNISHED

2 Say to your brothers, "You are my people",ᵍ and to your sisters, "You have received mercy."ʰ

² "Plead with your mother, plead—
 for she is not my wife,
 and I am not her husband—
that she put away her whoring
 from her face,
 and her adultery from
 between her breasts;
³ lest I strip her naked
 and make her as in the day
 she was born,
and make her like a wilderness,
 and make her like a parched land,
 and kill her with thirst.
⁴ Upon her children also I will
 have no mercy,
 because they are children
 of whoredom.
⁵ For their mother has played the whore;
 she who conceived them has
 acted shamefully.
For she said, 'I will go after my lovers,
 who give me my bread and my water,
 my wool and my flax, my
 oil and my drink.'
⁶ Therefore I will hedge up herⁱ
 way with thorns,
 and I will build a wall against her,
 so that she cannot find her paths.
⁷ She shall pursue her lovers
 but not overtake them,
and she shall seek them
 but shall not find them.
Then she shall say,
 'I will go and return to my
 first husband,
 for it was better for me
 then than now.'
⁸ And she did not know
 that it was I who gave her
 the grain, the wine, and the oil,
 and who lavished on her
 silver and gold,
 which they used for Baal.

ᵃHebrew Lo-ruhama, which means she has not received mercy ᵇHebrew Lo-ammi, which means not my people ᶜHebrew I am not yours ᵈCh 2:1 in Hebrew ᵉOr Sons ᶠCh 2:3 in Hebrew ᵍHebrew ammi, which means my people ʰHebrew ruhama, which means she has received mercy ⁱHebrew your

⁹ Therefore I will take back
   my grain in its time,
   and my wine in its season,
 and I will take away my
   wool and my flax,
   which were to cover her nakedness.
¹⁰ Now I will uncover her lewdness
   in the sight of her lovers,
   and no one shall rescue her
   out of my hand.
¹¹ And I will put an end to all her mirth,
   her feasts, her new moons,
   her Sabbaths,
   and all her appointed feasts.
¹² And I will lay waste her vines
   and her fig trees,
   of which she said,
 'These are my wages,
   which my lovers have given me.'
 I will make them a forest,
   and the beasts of the field
   shall devour them.
¹³ And I will punish her for the
   feast days of the Baals
   when she burned offerings to them
 and adorned herself with her
   ring and jewellery,
   and went after her lovers
   and forgot me, declares the LORD.

THE LORD'S MERCY ON ISRAEL

¹⁴ "Therefore, behold, I will allure her,
   and bring her into the wilderness,
   and speak tenderly to her.
¹⁵ And there I will give her her vineyards
   and make the Valley of Achor*ᵃ*
   a door of hope.
 And there she shall answer as
   in the days of her youth,
   as at the time when she came
   out of the land of Egypt.

¹⁶"And in that day, declares the LORD, you will call me 'My Husband', and no longer will you call me 'My Baal.' ¹⁷For I will remove the names of the Baals from her mouth, and they shall be remembered by name no more. ¹⁸And I will make for them a covenant on that day with the beasts of the field, the birds of the heavens, and the creeping things of the ground. And I will abolish*ᵇ* the bow, the sword, and war from the land, and I will make you lie down in safety. ¹⁹And I will betroth you to me for ever. I will betroth you to me in righteousness and in justice, in steadfast love and in mercy. ²⁰I will betroth you to me in faithfulness. And you shall know the LORD.

²¹ "And in that day I will answer,
   declares the LORD,
 I will answer the heavens,
   and they shall answer the earth,
²² and the earth shall answer the
   grain, the wine, and the oil,
   and they shall answer Jezreel,*ᶜ*
²³ and I will sow her for
   myself in the land.
 And I will have mercy on No Mercy,*ᵈ*
   and I will say to Not My People,*ᵉ*
   'You are my people';
   and he shall say, 'You are my God.'"

HOSEA REDEEMS HIS WIFE

3 And the LORD said to me, "Go again, love a woman who is loved by another man and is an adulteress, even as the LORD loves the children of Israel, though they turn to other gods and love cakes of raisins." ²So I bought her for fifteen shekels of silver and a homer and a lethech*ᶠ* of barley. ³And I said to her, "You must dwell as mine for many days. You shall not play the whore, or belong to another man; so will I also be to you." ⁴For the children of Israel shall dwell many days without king or prince, without sacrifice or pillar, without ephod or household gods. ⁵Afterwards the children of Israel shall return and seek the LORD their God, and David their king, and they shall come in fear to the LORD and to his goodness in the latter days.

THE LORD ACCUSES ISRAEL

4 Hear the word of the LORD,
   O children of Israel,
   for the LORD has a controversy
   with the inhabitants of the land.
 There is no faithfulness or
   steadfast love,
   and no knowledge of God
   in the land;
² there is swearing, lying,
   murder, stealing, and
   committing adultery;
   they break all bounds, and
   bloodshed follows bloodshed.
³ Therefore the land mourns,
   and all who dwell in it languish,

ᵃAchor means *trouble*; compare Joshua 7:26 *ᵇ*Hebrew *break* *ᶜJezreel* means *God will sow* *ᵈ*Hebrew *Lo-ruhama* *ᵉ*Hebrew *Lo-ammi*
*ᶠ*A *shekel* was about 2/5 of an ounce or 11 grams; a *homer* was about 6 bushels or 220 litres; a *lethech* was about 3 bushels or 110 litres

and also the beasts of the field
and the birds of the heavens,
and even the fish of the sea
are taken away.

4 Yet let no one contend,
and let none accuse,
for with you is my contention,
O priest.[a]
5 You shall stumble by day;
the prophet also shall stumble
with you by night;
and I will destroy your mother.
6 My people are destroyed for
lack of knowledge;
because you have rejected
knowledge,
I reject you from being a priest to me.
And since you have forgotten
the law of your God,
I also will forget your children.

7 The more they increased,
the more they sinned against me;
I will change their glory into shame.
8 They feed on the sin[b] of my people;
they are greedy for their iniquity.
9 And it shall be like people, like priest;
I will punish them for their ways
and repay them for their deeds.
10 They shall eat, but not be satisfied;
they shall play the whore,
but not multiply,
because they have forsaken the LORD
to cherish 11whoredom,
wine, and new wine,
which take away the understanding.
12 My people enquire of a piece of wood,
and their walking staff
gives them oracles.
For a spirit of whoredom has
led them astray,
and they have left their God
to play the whore.
13 They sacrifice on the tops
of the mountains
and burn offerings on the hills,
under oak, poplar, and terebinth,
because their shade is good.
Therefore your daughters
play the whore,
and your brides commit adultery.
14 I will not punish your daughters
when they play the whore,
nor your brides when they
commit adultery;
for the men themselves go
aside with prostitutes
and sacrifice with cult prostitutes,
and a people without understanding
shall come to ruin.

15 Though you play the whore, O Israel,
let not Judah become guilty.
Enter not into Gilgal,
nor go up to Beth-aven,
and swear not, "As the LORD lives."
16 Like a stubborn heifer,
Israel is stubborn;
can the LORD now feed them
like a lamb in a broad pasture?

17 Ephraim is joined to idols;
leave him alone.
18 When their drink is gone, they give
themselves to whoring;
their rulers[c] dearly love shame.
19 A wind has wrapped them[d]
in its wings,
and they shall be ashamed
because of their sacrifices.

PUNISHMENT COMING FOR ISRAEL AND JUDAH

5 Hear this, O priests!
Pay attention, O house of Israel!
Give ear, O house of the king!
For the judgement is for you;
for you have been a snare at Mizpah
and a net spread upon Tabor.
2 And the revolters have gone
deep into slaughter,
but I will discipline all of them.

3 I know Ephraim,
and Israel is not hidden from me;
for now, O Ephraim, you have
played the whore;
Israel is defiled.
4 Their deeds do not permit them
to return to their God.
For the spirit of whoredom
is within them,
and they know not the LORD.

5 The pride of Israel testifies to his face;[e]
Israel and Ephraim shall stumble
in his guilt;
Judah also shall stumble with them.

---

[a] Or for your people are like those who contend with the priest [b] Or sin offering [c] Hebrew shields [d] Hebrew her [e] Or in his presence

6 With their flocks and herds
     they shall go
  to seek the LORD,
  but they will not find him;
     he has withdrawn from them.
7 They have dealt faithlessly
     with the LORD;
  for they have borne alien children.
     Now the new moon shall devour
        them with their fields.

8 Blow the horn in Gibeah,
     the trumpet in Ramah.
  Sound the alarm at Beth-aven;
     we follow you,[a] O Benjamin!
9 Ephraim shall become a desolation
     in the day of punishment;
  among the tribes of Israel
     I make known what is sure.
10 The princes of Judah have become
     like those who move the landmark;
  upon them I will pour out
     my wrath like water.
11 Ephraim is oppressed, crushed
     in judgement,
  because he was determined
     to go after filth.[b]
12 But I am like a moth to Ephraim,
     and like dry rot to the
        house of Judah.
13 When Ephraim saw his sickness,
     and Judah his wound,
  then Ephraim went to Assyria,
     and sent to the great king.[c]
  But he is not able to cure you
     or heal your wound.
14 For I will be like a lion to Ephraim,
     and like a young lion to the
        house of Judah.
  I, even I, will tear and go away;
     I will carry off, and no one
        shall rescue.

15 I will return again to my place,
     until they acknowledge their
        guilt and seek my face,
     and in their distress
        earnestly seek me.

ISRAEL AND JUDAH ARE UNREPENTANT

6 "Come, let us return to the LORD;
     for he has torn us, that he may
        heal us;
  he has struck us down, and
     he will bind us up.
2 After two days he will revive us;
     on the third day he will raise us up,
        that we may live before him.
3 Let us know; let us press on
     to know the LORD;
  his going out is sure as the dawn;
     he will come to us as the showers,
     as the spring rains that
        water the earth."

4 What shall I do with you, O Ephraim?
     What shall I do with you, O Judah?
  Your love is like a morning cloud,
     like the dew that goes early away.
5 Therefore I have hewn them
     by the prophets;
  I have slain them by the
     words of my mouth,
  and my judgement goes
     forth as the light.
6 For I desire steadfast love[d]
     and not sacrifice,
  the knowledge of God rather
     than burnt offerings.

7 But like Adam they transgressed
     the covenant;
  there they dealt faithlessly
     with me.
8 Gilead is a city of evildoers,
     tracked with blood.
9 As robbers lie in wait for a man,
     so the priests band together;
  they murder on the way to Shechem;
     they commit villainy.
10 In the house of Israel I have
     seen a horrible thing;
  Ephraim's whoredom is there;
     Israel is defiled.

11 For you also, O Judah, a
     harvest is appointed.

  When I restore the fortunes of
     my people,
7 when I would heal Israel,
  the iniquity of Ephraim is revealed,
  and the evil deeds of Samaria,
  for they deal falsely;
     the thief breaks in,
     and the bandits raid outside.
2 But they do not consider
     that I remember all their evil.

---
[a] Or *after you* [b] Or *to follow human precepts* [c] Or *to King Jareb*
[d] Septuagint *mercy*

Now their deeds surround them;
  they are before my face.
3 By their evil they make the king glad,
  and the princes by their treachery.
4 They are all adulterers;
  they are like a heated oven
  whose baker ceases to stir the fire,
  from the kneading of the dough
  until it is leavened.
5 On the day of our king, the princes
  became sick with the heat of wine;
  he stretched out his hand
  with mockers.
6 For with hearts like an oven they
  approach their intrigue;
  all night their anger smoulders;
  in the morning it blazes
  like a flaming fire.
7 All of them are hot as an oven,
  and they devour their rulers.
  All their kings have fallen,
  and none of them calls upon me.

8 Ephraim mixes himself
  with the peoples;
  Ephraim is a cake not turned.
9 Strangers devour his strength,
  and he knows it not;
  grey hairs are sprinkled upon him,
  and he knows it not.
10 The pride of Israel testifies to his face;[a]
  yet they do not return to the
  LORD their God,
  nor seek him, for all this.

11 Ephraim is like a dove,
  silly and without sense,
  calling to Egypt, going to Assyria.
12 As they go, I will spread
  over them my net;
  I will bring them down like
  birds of the heavens;
  I will discipline them according
  to the report made to
  their congregation.
13 Woe to them, for they have
  strayed from me!
  Destruction to them, for they
  have rebelled against me!
  I would redeem them,
  but they speak lies against me.
14 They do not cry to me from the heart,
  but they wail upon their beds;
  for grain and wine they gash themselves;
  they rebel against me.
15 Although I trained and
  strengthened their arms,
  yet they devise evil against me.
16 They return, but not upward;[b]
  they are like a treacherous bow;
  their princes shall fall by the sword
  because of the insolence
  of their tongue.
  This shall be their derision
  in the land of Egypt.

ISRAEL WILL REAP THE WHIRLWIND

8 Set the trumpet to your lips!
  One like a vulture is over the house
  of the LORD,
  because they have transgressed
  my covenant
  and rebelled against my law.
2 To me they cry,
  "My God, we —Israel— know you."
3 Israel has spurned the good;
  the enemy shall pursue him.

4 They made kings, but not through me.
  They set up princes, but I knew it not.
  With their silver and gold
  they made idols
  for their own destruction.
5 I have[c] spurned your calf, O Samaria.
  My anger burns against them.
  How long will they be incapable
  of innocence?
6 For it is from Israel;
  a craftsman made it;
  it is not God.
  The calf of Samaria
  shall be broken to pieces.[d]

7 For they sow the wind,
  and they shall reap the whirlwind.
  The standing corn has no heads;
  it shall yield no flour;
  if it were to yield,
  strangers would devour it.
8 Israel is swallowed up;
  already they are among the nations
  as a useless vessel.
9 For they have gone up to Assyria,
  a wild donkey wandering alone;
  Ephraim has hired lovers.
10 Though they hire allies
  among the nations,
  I will soon gather them up.

---

[a] Or *in his presence* [b] Or *to the Most High* [c] Hebrew *He has*
[d] Or *shall go up in flames*

And the king and princes
  shall soon writhe
  because of the tribute.
¹¹ Because Ephraim has multiplied
  altars for sinning,
  they have become to him
  altars for sinning.
¹² Were I to write for him my laws
  by the ten thousands,
  they would be regarded as
  a strange thing.
¹³ As for my sacrificial offerings,
  they sacrifice meat and eat it,
  but the LORD does not accept them.
Now he will remember their iniquity
  and punish their sins;
  they shall return to Egypt.
¹⁴ For Israel has forgotten his Maker
  and built palaces,
and Judah has multiplied
  fortified cities;
  so I will send a fire upon his cities,
  and it shall devour her strongholds.

THE LORD WILL PUNISH ISRAEL

9 Rejoice not, O Israel!
  Exult not like the peoples;
  for you have played the whore,
    forsaking your God.
  You have loved a prostitute's wages
  on all threshing floors.
² Threshing floor and wine vat
  shall not feed them,
  and the new wine shall fail them.
³ They shall not remain in the
    land of the LORD,
  but Ephraim shall return to Egypt,
  and they shall eat unclean
    food in Assyria.

⁴ They shall not pour drink offerings
    of wine to the LORD,
  and their sacrifices shall
    not please him.
It shall be like mourners' bread to them;
  all who eat of it shall be defiled;
for their bread shall be for
    their hunger only;
  it shall not come to the
    house of the LORD.

⁵ What will you do on the day of
    the appointed festival,
  and on the day of the feast
    of the LORD?

⁶ For behold, they are going away
    from destruction;
  but Egypt shall gather them;
  Memphis shall bury them.
Nettles shall possess their
    precious things of silver;
  thorns shall be in their tents.

⁷ The days of punishment have come;
  the days of recompense have come;
  Israel shall know it.
The prophet is a fool;
  the man of the spirit is mad,
because of your great iniquity
  and great hatred.
⁸ The prophet is the watchman of
    Ephraim with my God;
  yet a fowler's snare is on all his ways,
  and hatred in the house of his God.
⁹ They have deeply corrupted
    themselves
  as in the days of Gibeah:
he will remember their iniquity;
  he will punish their sins.

¹⁰ Like grapes in the wilderness,
    I found Israel.
Like the first fruit on the fig tree
    in its first season,
    I saw your fathers.
But they came to Baal-peor
  and consecrated themselves
    to the thing of shame,
  and became detestable like
    the thing they loved.
¹¹ Ephraim's glory shall fly
    away like a bird—
  no birth, no pregnancy,
    no conception!
¹² Even if they bring up children,
  I will bereave them till none is left.
Woe to them
  when I depart from them!
¹³ Ephraim, as I have seen, was like a
    young palm^a planted in a meadow;
  but Ephraim must lead his
    children out to slaughter.^b
¹⁴ Give them, O LORD—
    what will you give?
Give them a miscarrying womb
    and dry breasts.

¹⁵ Every evil of theirs is in Gilgal;
  there I began to hate them.

---

^aOr *like Tyre* ^bHebrew *to him who slaughters*

Because of the wickedness
    of their deeds
I will drive them out of my house.
I will love them no more;
    all their princes are rebels.
16 Ephraim is stricken;
    their root is dried up;
    they shall bear no fruit.
Even though they give birth,
    I will put their beloved
        children to death.
17 My God will reject them
    because they have not
        listened to him;
    they shall be wanderers
        among the nations.

10 Israel is a luxuriant vine
    that yields its fruit.
The more his fruit increased,
    the more altars he built;
as his country improved,
    he improved his pillars.
2 Their heart is false;
    now they must bear their guilt.
The LORD^a will break down their altars
    and destroy their pillars.

3 For now they will say:
    "We have no king,
for we do not fear the LORD;
    and a king—what could
        he do for us?"
4 They utter mere words;
    with empty^b oaths they
        make covenants;
so judgement springs up like
    poisonous weeds
in the furrows of the field.
5 The inhabitants of Samaria tremble
    for the calf^c of Beth-aven.
Its people mourn for it, and so do
    its idolatrous priests—
those who rejoiced over it
    and over its glory—
for it has departed^d from them.
6 The thing itself shall be
        carried to Assyria
    as tribute to the great king.^{e}
Ephraim shall be put to shame,
    and Israel shall be ashamed
        of his idol.^{f}

7 Samaria's king shall perish
    like a twig on the face of the waters.
8 The high places of Aven,
    the sin of Israel,
    shall be destroyed.
Thorn and thistle shall grow up
    on their altars,
and they shall say to the
    mountains, "Cover us,"
and to the hills, "Fall on us."

9 From the days of Gibeah, you
        have sinned, O Israel;
    there they have continued.
Shall not the war against the unjust^g
    overtake them in Gibeah?
10 When I please, I will discipline them,
    and nations shall be gathered
        against them
    when they are bound up for
        their double iniquity.
11 Ephraim was a trained calf
    that loved to thresh,
    and I spared her fair neck;
but I will put Ephraim to the yoke;
    Judah must plough;
    Jacob must harrow for himself.
12 Sow for yourselves righteousness;
    reap steadfast love;
    break up your fallow ground,
for it is the time to seek the LORD,
    that he may come and rain
        righteousness upon you.

13 You have ploughed iniquity;
    you have reaped injustice;
    you have eaten the fruit of lies.
Because you have trusted
    in your own way
and in the multitude of
    your warriors,
14 therefore the tumult of war shall
    arise among your people,
and all your fortresses shall
    be destroyed,
as Shalman destroyed Beth-
    arbel on the day of battle;
    mothers were dashed in pieces
        with their children.
15 Thus it shall be done to you, O Bethel,
    because of your great evil.
At dawn the king of Israel
    shall be utterly cut off.

---

^{a}Hebrew *He* ^{b}Or *vain* (see Exodus 20:7) ^{c}Or *calves* ^{d}Or *has gone into exile* ^{e}Or *to King Jareb* ^{f}Or *counsel* ^{g}Hebrew *the children of injustice*

THE LORD'S LOVE FOR ISRAEL

11 When Israel was a child,
   I loved him,
   and out of Egypt I called my son.
² The more they were called,
   the more they went away;
   they kept sacrificing to the Baals
   and burning offerings to idols.

³ Yet it was I who taught
   Ephraim to walk;
   I took them up by their arms,
   but they did not know that
   I healed them.
⁴ I led them with cords of kindness,ᵃ
   with the bands of love,
   and I became to them as one who
   eases the yoke on their jaws,
   and I bent down to them
   and fed them.

⁵ They shall notᵇ return to
   the land of Egypt,
   but Assyria shall be their king,
   because they have refused
   to return to me.
⁶ The sword shall rage against
   their cities,
   consume the bars of their gates,
   and devour them because of
   their own counsels.
⁷ My people are bent on turning
   away from me,
   and though they call out
   to the Most High,
   he shall not raise them up at all.

⁸ How can I give you up, O Ephraim?
   How can I hand you over,
   O Israel?
   How can I make you like Admah?
   How can I treat you like Zeboiim?
   My heart recoils within me;
   my compassion grows
   warm and tender.
⁹ I will not execute my burning anger;
   I will not again destroy Ephraim;
   for I am God and not a man,
   the Holy One in your midst,
   and I will not come in wrath.ᶜ

¹⁰ They shall go after the LORD;
   he will roar like a lion;
   when he roars,
   his children shall come
   trembling from the west;
¹¹ they shall come trembling
   like birds from Egypt,
   and like doves from the
   land of Assyria,
   and I will return them to their
   homes, declares the LORD.

¹²ᵈ Ephraim has surrounded me with lies,
   and the house of Israel with deceit,
   but Judah still walks with God
   and is faithful to the Holy One.

12 Ephraim feeds on the wind
   and pursues the east wind
   all day long;
   they multiply falsehood and violence;
   they make a covenant with Assyria,
   and oil is carried to Egypt.

THE LORD'S INDICTMENT OF ISRAEL AND JUDAH

² The LORD has an indictment
   against Judah
   and will punish Jacob
   according to his ways;
   he will repay him according
   to his deeds.
³ In the womb he took his
   brother by the heel,
   and in his manhood he
   strove with God.
⁴ He strove with the angel and prevailed;
   he wept and sought his favour.
   He met Godᵉ at Bethel,
   and there God spoke with us—
⁵ the LORD, the God of hosts,
   the LORD is his memorial name:
⁶ "So you, by the help of your God, return,
   hold fast to love and justice,
   and wait continually for your God."

⁷ A merchant, in whose hands
   are false balances,
   he loves to oppress.
⁸ Ephraim has said, "Ah, but I am rich;
   I have found wealth for myself;
   in all my labours they cannot find
   in me iniquity or sin."
⁹ I am the LORD your God
   from the land of Egypt;
   I will again make you dwell in tents,
   as in the days of the appointed feast.

¹⁰ I spoke to the prophets;
   it was I who multiplied visions,

ᵃOr *humaneness*; Hebrew *man*   ᵇOr *surely*   ᶜOr *into the city*
ᵈCh 12:1 in Hebrew   ᵉHebrew *him*

and through the prophets
    gave parables.
11 If there is iniquity in Gilead,
    they shall surely come to nothing:
in Gilgal they sacrifice bulls;
    their altars also are like stone heaps
        on the furrows of the field.
12 Jacob fled to the land of Aram;
    there Israel served for a wife,
    and for a wife he guarded sheep.
13 By a prophet the LORD brought
    Israel up from Egypt,
and by a prophet he was guarded.
14 Ephraim has given bitter provocation;
    so his Lord will leave his
        bloodguilt on him
    and will repay him for his
        disgraceful deeds.

THE LORD'S RELENTLESS JUDGEMENT ON ISRAEL

13

When Ephraim spoke,
    there was trembling;
he was exalted in Israel,
    but he incurred guilt through
        Baal and died.
2 And now they sin more and more,
    and make for themselves
        metal images,
idols skilfully made of their silver,
    all of them the work of craftsmen.
It is said of them,
    "Those who offer human
        sacrifice kiss calves!"
3 Therefore they shall be like
    the morning mist
or like the dew that goes early away,
    like the chaff that swirls from
        the threshing floor
or like smoke from a window.

4 But I am the LORD your God
    from the land of Egypt;
you know no God but me,
    and besides me there is no saviour.
5 It was I who knew you in
    the wilderness,
    in the land of drought;
6 but when they had grazed,[a]
    they became full,
they were filled, and their
    heart was lifted up;
therefore they forgot me.
7 So I am to them like a lion;
    like a leopard I will lurk
        beside the way.
8 I will fall upon them like a bear
    robbed of her cubs;
I will tear open their breast,
    and there I will devour
        them like a lion,
as a wild beast would rip
    them open.

9 He destroys[b] you, O Israel,
    for you are against me,
    against your helper.
10 Where now is your king, to save
    you in all your cities?
Where are all your rulers —
    those of whom you said,
    "Give me a king and princes"?
11 I gave you a king in my anger,
    and I took him away in my wrath.

12 The iniquity of Ephraim is bound up;
    his sin is kept in store.
13 The pangs of childbirth come for him,
    but he is an unwise son,
for at the right time he does
    not present himself
    at the opening of the womb.

14 I shall ransom them from
    the power of Sheol;
I shall redeem them from Death.[c]
O Death, where are your plagues?
O Sheol, where is your sting?
    Compassion is hidden
        from my eyes.

15 Though he may flourish
    among his brothers,
the east wind, the wind of
    the LORD, shall come,
rising from the wilderness,
and his fountain shall dry up;
    his spring shall be parched;
it shall strip his treasury
    of every precious thing.
16[d] Samaria shall bear her guilt,
    because she has rebelled
        against her God;
they shall fall by the sword;
    their little ones shall be
        dashed in pieces,
    and their pregnant women
        ripped open.

---

[a]Hebrew *according to their pasture*   [b]Or *I will destroy*   [c]Or *Shall I ransom them from the power of Sheol? Shall I redeem them from Death?*   [d]Ch 14:1 in Hebrew

HOSEA 14

A PLEA TO RETURN TO THE LORD

14 Return, O Israel, to the LORD
your God,
for you have stumbled because
of your iniquity.
² Take with you words
and return to the LORD;
say to him,
"Take away all iniquity;
accept what is good,
and we will pay with bulls
the vows[a] of our lips.
³ Assyria shall not save us;
we will not ride on horses;
and we will say no more, 'Our God',
to the work of our hands.
In you the orphan finds mercy."

⁴ I will heal their apostasy;
I will love them freely,
for my anger has turned from them.
⁵ I will be like the dew to Israel;
he shall blossom like the lily;
he shall take root like the
trees of Lebanon;
⁶ his shoots shall spread out;
his beauty shall be like the olive,
and his fragrance like Lebanon.
⁷ They shall return and dwell
beneath my[b] shadow;
they shall flourish like the corn;
they shall blossom like the vine;
their fame shall be like the
wine of Lebanon.

⁸ O Ephraim, what have I to
do with idols?
It is I who answer and look after you.[c]
I am like an evergreen cypress;
from me comes your fruit.

⁹ Whoever is wise, let him
understand these things;
whoever is discerning, let
him know them;
for the ways of the LORD are right,
and the upright walk in them,
but transgressors stumble in them.

---

[a]Septuagint, Syriac *pay the fruit* [b]Hebrew *his* [c]Hebrew *him*

JOEL

1 ¹ The word of the Lord that came to Joel, the son of Pethuel:

AN INVASION OF LOCUSTS

² Hear this, you elders;
  give ear, all inhabitants of
    the land!
Has such a thing happened
    in your days,
  or in the days of your fathers?
³ Tell your children of it,
  and let your children tell
    their children,
  and their children to
    another generation.

⁴ What the cutting locust left,
  the swarming locust has eaten.
What the swarming locust left,
  the hopping locust has eaten,
and what the hopping locust left,
  the destroying locust has eaten.

⁵ Awake, you drunkards, and weep,
  and wail, all you drinkers of wine,
because of the sweet wine,
  for it is cut off from your mouth.
⁶ For a nation has come up
    against my land,
  powerful and beyond number;
its teeth are lions' teeth,
  and it has the fangs of a lioness.
⁷ It has laid waste my vine
  and splintered my fig tree;
it has stripped off their bark
    and thrown it down;
  their branches are made white.

⁸ Lament like a virgin[a]
    wearing sackcloth
  for the bridegroom of her youth.
⁹ The grain offering and the drink
    offering are cut off
  from the house of the Lord.
The priests mourn,
  the ministers of the Lord.
¹⁰ The fields are destroyed,
  the ground mourns,
because the grain is destroyed,
  the wine dries up,
  the oil languishes.

¹¹ Be ashamed,[b] O tillers of the soil;
  wail, O vine dressers,
for the wheat and the barley,
  because the harvest of the
    field has perished.
¹² The vine dries up;
  the fig tree languishes.
Pomegranate, palm, and apple,
  all the trees of the field are dried up,
and gladness dries up
  from the children of man.

A CALL TO REPENTANCE

¹³ Put on sackcloth and lament, O priests;
  wail, O ministers of the altar.
Go in, pass the night in sackcloth,
  O ministers of my God!
Because grain offering and
    drink offering
  are withheld from the
    house of your God.

¹⁴ Consecrate a fast;
  call a solemn assembly.
Gather the elders
  and all the inhabitants of the land
to the house of the Lord your God,
  and cry out to the Lord.

¹⁵ Alas for the day!
For the day of the Lord is near,
  and as destruction from the
    Almighty[c] it comes.
¹⁶ Is not the food cut off
    before our eyes,
  joy and gladness
    from the house of our God?

¹⁷ The seed shrivels under the clods;[d]
  the storehouses are desolate;

---

[a] Or *young woman* [b] The Hebrew words for *dry up* and *be ashamed* in verses 10–12, 17 sound alike [c] *Destruction* sounds like the Hebrew for *Almighty* [d] The meaning of the Hebrew line is uncertain

the granaries are torn down
   because the grain has dried up.
¹⁸ How the beasts groan!
   The herds of cattle are perplexed
because there is no pasture for them;
   even the flocks of sheep suffer.ᵃ

¹⁹ To you, O Lord, I call.
   For fire has devoured
      the pastures of the wilderness,
   and flame has burned
      all the trees of the field.
²⁰ Even the beasts of the field pant for you
   because the water brooks
      are dried up,
   and fire has devoured
      the pastures of the wilderness.

THE DAY OF THE LORD

2 Blow a trumpet in Zion;
   sound an alarm on my holy
      mountain!
Let all the inhabitants of
   the land tremble,
for the day of the Lord is
   coming; it is near,
² a day of darkness and gloom,
   a day of clouds and thick darkness!
Like blackness there is spread
   upon the mountains
a great and powerful people;
   their like has never been before,
nor will be again after them
   through the years of all generations.

³ Fire devours before them,
   and behind them a flame burns.
The land is like the garden of
   Eden before them,
but behind them a desolate
   wilderness,
   and nothing escapes them.

⁴ Their appearance is like the
      appearance of horses,
   and like war horses they run.
⁵ As with the rumbling of chariots,
   they leap on the tops of
      the mountains,
like the crackling of a flame of fire
   devouring the stubble,
like a powerful army
   drawn up for battle.

⁶ Before them peoples are in anguish;
   all faces grow pale.

⁷ Like warriors they charge;
   like soldiers they scale the wall.
They march each on his way;
   they do not swerve from their paths.
⁸ They do not jostle one another;
   each marches in his path;
they burst through the weapons
   and are not halted.
⁹ They leap upon the city,
   they run upon the walls,
they climb up into the houses,
   they enter through the
      windows like a thief.

¹⁰ The earth quakes before them;
   the heavens tremble.
The sun and the moon are darkened,
   and the stars withdraw
      their shining.
¹¹ The Lord utters his voice
   before his army,
for his camp is exceedingly great;
   he who executes his word
      is powerful.
For the day of the Lord is great
   and very awesome;
   who can endure it?

RETURN TO THE LORD

¹² "Yet even now," declares the Lord,
   "return to me with all your heart,
with fasting, with weeping,
   and with mourning;
¹³ and rend your hearts and
      not your garments."
Return to the Lord your God,
   for he is gracious and merciful,
slow to anger, and abounding
   in steadfast love;
   and he relents over disaster.
¹⁴ Who knows whether he will
      not turn and relent,
   and leave a blessing behind him,
a grain offering and a drink offering
   for the Lord your God?

¹⁵ Blow the trumpet in Zion;
   consecrate a fast;
call a solemn assembly;
¹⁶   gather the people.
Consecrate the congregation;
   assemble the elders;
gather the children,
   even nursing infants.

ᵃ Or are made desolate

Let the bridegroom leave his room,
  and the bride her chamber.

17 Between the vestibule and the altar
  let the priests, the ministers
    of the Lord, weep
  and say, "Spare your people, O Lord,
    and make not your heritage
      a reproach,
    a byword among the nations.[a]
  Why should they say among the peoples,
    'Where is their God?'"

THE LORD HAD PITY

18 Then the Lord became
    jealous for his land
  and had pity on his people.
19 The Lord answered and
    said to his people,
  "Behold, I am sending to you
    grain, wine, and oil,
    and you will be satisfied;
  and I will no more make you
    a reproach among the nations.

20 "I will remove the northerner
    far from you,
  and drive him into a parched
    and desolate land,
  his vanguard[b] into the eastern sea,
    and his rearguard[c] into
      the western sea;
  the stench and foul smell
    of him will rise,
  for he has done great things.

21 "Fear not, O land;
    be glad and rejoice,
  for the Lord has done great things!
22 Fear not, you beasts of the field,
    for the pastures of the
      wilderness are green;
  the tree bears its fruit;
    the fig tree and vine give
      their full yield.

23 "Be glad, O children of Zion,
    and rejoice in the Lord your God,
  for he has given the early rain
    for your vindication;
  he has poured down for you
    abundant rain,
  the early and the latter rain, as before.

24 "The threshing floors shall
    be full of grain;
  the vats shall overflow
    with wine and oil.
25 I will restore[d] to you the years
    that the swarming locust has eaten,
  the hopper, the destroyer,
    and the cutter,
  my great army, which I
    sent among you.

26 "You shall eat in plenty and be satisfied,
    and praise the name of the
      Lord your God,
  who has dealt wondrously with you.
  And my people shall never
    again be put to shame.
27 You shall know that I am in
    the midst of Israel,
  and that I am the Lord your God
    and there is none else.
  And my people shall never
    again be put to shame.

THE LORD WILL POUR OUT HIS SPIRIT

28[e] "And it shall come to pass afterwards,
    that I will pour out my
      Spirit on all flesh;
  your sons and your daughters
    shall prophesy,
  your old men shall dream dreams,
    and your young men shall
      see visions.
29 Even on the male and female servants
    in those days I will pour out my Spirit.

30 "And I will show wonders in the heavens and on the earth, blood and fire and columns of smoke. 31 The sun shall be turned to darkness, and the moon to blood, before the great and awesome day of the Lord comes. 32 And it shall come to pass that everyone who calls on the name of the Lord shall be saved. For in Mount Zion and in Jerusalem there shall be those who escape, as the Lord has said, and among the survivors shall be those whom the Lord calls.

THE LORD JUDGES THE NATIONS

3[f] "For behold, in those days and at that time, when I restore the fortunes of Judah and Jerusalem, 2 I will gather all the nations and bring them down to the Valley of Jehoshaphat. And I will enter into judgement with them there, on behalf of my

---

[a] Or reproach, that the nations should rule over them [b] Hebrew face [c] Hebrew his end [d] Or pay back [e] Ch 3:1 in Hebrew [f] Ch 4:1 in Hebrew

people and my heritage Israel, because they have scattered them among the nations and have divided up my land, ³and have cast lots for my people, and have traded a boy for a prostitute, and have sold a girl for wine and have drunk it.

⁴"What are you to me, O Tyre and Sidon, and all the regions of Philistia? Are you paying me back for something? If you are paying me back, I will return your payment on your own head swiftly and speedily. ⁵For you have taken my silver and my gold, and have carried my rich treasures into your temples.ᵃ ⁶You have sold the people of Judah and Jerusalem to the Greeks in order to remove them far from their own border. ⁷Behold, I will stir them up from the place to which you have sold them, and I will return your payment on your own head. ⁸I will sell your sons and your daughters into the hand of the people of Judah, and they will sell them to the Sabeans, to a nation far away, for the LORD has spoken."

⁹ Proclaim this among the nations:
  Consecrate for war;ᵇ
   stir up the mighty men.
  Let all the men of war draw near;
   let them come up.
¹⁰ Beat your ploughshares into swords,
   and your pruning-hooks into spears;
   let the weak say, "I am a warrior."
¹¹ Hasten and come,
   all you surrounding nations,
   and gather yourselves there.
  Bring down your warriors, O LORD.
¹² Let the nations stir themselves up
   and come up to the Valley
    of Jehoshaphat;
  for there I will sit to judge
   all the surrounding nations.
¹³ Put in the sickle,
   for the harvest is ripe.
  Go in, tread,
   for the wine press is full.
  The vats overflow,
   for their evil is great.

¹⁴ Multitudes, multitudes,
   in the valley of decision!
  For the day of the LORD is near
   in the valley of decision.
¹⁵ The sun and the moon are darkened,
   and the stars withdraw
    their shining.

¹⁶ The LORD roars from Zion,
   and utters his voice from
    Jerusalem,
   and the heavens and the
    earth quake.
  But the LORD is a refuge to his people,
   a stronghold to the people of Israel.

THE GLORIOUS FUTURE OF JUDAH

¹⁷ "So you shall know that I am
   the LORD your God,
  who dwells in Zion, my
    holy mountain.
  And Jerusalem shall be holy,
   and strangers shall never
    again pass through it.

¹⁸ "And in that day
  the mountains shall drip sweet wine,
   and the hills shall flow with milk,
  and all the stream beds of Judah
   shall flow with water;
  and a fountain shall come forth
   from the house of the LORD
  and water the Valley of Shittim.

¹⁹ "Egypt shall become a desolation
   and Edom a desolate wilderness,
  for the violence done to the
    people of Judah,
   because they have shed innocent
    blood in their land.
²⁰ But Judah shall be inhabited for ever,
   and Jerusalem to all generations.
²¹ I will avenge their blood,
   blood I have not avenged,ᶜ
  for the LORD dwells in Zion."

ᵃOr palaces ᵇOr Consecrate a war ᶜOr I will acquit their bloodguilt that I have not acquitted

AMOS

1 The words of Amos, who was among the shepherds[a] of Tekoa, which he saw concerning Israel in the days of Uzziah king of Judah and in the days of Jeroboam the son of Joash, king of Israel, two years[b] before the earthquake.

JUDGEMENT ON ISRAEL'S NEIGHBOURS

²And he said:

"The LORD roars from Zion
 and utters his voice from Jerusalem;
the pastures of the shepherds mourn,
 and the top of Carmel withers."

³Thus says the LORD:

"For three transgressions of Damascus,
 and for four, I will not revoke
  the punishment,[c]
because they have threshed Gilead
 with threshing sledges of iron.
⁴ So I will send a fire upon the
  house of Hazael,
 and it shall devour the
  strongholds of Ben-hadad.
⁵ I will break the gate-bar of Damascus,
 and cut off the inhabitants
  from the Valley of Aven,[d]
 and him who holds the sceptre
  from Beth-eden;
 and the people of Syria shall
  go into exile to Kir,"
   says the LORD.

⁶Thus says the LORD:

"For three transgressions of Gaza,
 and for four, I will not revoke
  the punishment,
because they carried into
 exile a whole people
 to deliver them up to Edom.
⁷ So I will send a fire upon
  the wall of Gaza,
 and it shall devour her strongholds.
⁸ I will cut off the inhabitants
  from Ashdod,
 and him who holds the sceptre
  from Ashkelon;
 I will turn my hand against Ekron,
 and the remnant of the
  Philistines shall perish,"
   says the Lord GOD.

⁹Thus says the LORD:

"For three transgressions of Tyre,
 and for four, I will not revoke
  the punishment,
because they delivered up a
 whole people to Edom,
 and did not remember the
  covenant of brotherhood.
¹⁰ So I will send a fire upon the wall of Tyre,
 and it shall devour her strongholds."

¹¹Thus says the LORD:

"For three transgressions of Edom,
 and for four, I will not revoke
  the punishment,
because he pursued his brother
 with the sword
 and cast off all pity,
 and his anger tore perpetually,
 and he kept his wrath for ever.
¹² So I will send a fire upon Teman,
 and it shall devour the
  strongholds of Bozrah."

¹³Thus says the LORD:

"For three transgressions of
  the Ammonites,
 and for four, I will not revoke
  the punishment,
because they have ripped open
 pregnant women in Gilead,
 that they might enlarge their border.
¹⁴ So I will kindle a fire in the
  wall of Rabbah,
 and it shall devour her strongholds,

---

[a] Or sheep breeders [b] Or during two years [c] Hebrew *I will not turn it back*; also verses 6, 9, 11, 13 [d] Or On

with shouting on the day of battle,
with a tempest in the day
of the whirlwind;
¹⁵ and their king shall go into exile,
he and his princes^a together,"
says the Lord.

2 Thus says the Lord:
"For three transgressions of Moab,
and for four, I will not revoke
the punishment,^b
because he burned to lime
the bones of the king of Edom.
² So I will send a fire upon Moab,
and it shall devour the
strongholds of Kerioth,
and Moab shall die amid uproar,
amid shouting and the sound
of the trumpet;
³ I will cut off the ruler from its midst,
and will kill all its princes^c
with him,"
says the Lord.

JUDGEMENT ON JUDAH

⁴Thus says the Lord:

"For three transgressions of Judah,
and for four, I will not revoke
the punishment,
because they have rejected
the law of the Lord,
and have not kept his statutes,
but their lies have led them astray,
those after which their
fathers walked.
⁵ So I will send a fire upon Judah,
and it shall devour the
strongholds of Jerusalem."

JUDGEMENT ON ISRAEL

⁶Thus says the Lord:

"For three transgressions of Israel,
and for four, I will not revoke
the punishment,
because they sell the
righteous for silver,
and the needy for a pair of sandals—
⁷ those who trample the head of the
poor into the dust of the earth
and turn aside the way of the afflicted;
a man and his father go in
to the same girl,
so that my holy name is profaned;
⁸ they lay themselves down
beside every altar
on garments taken in pledge,
and in the house of their God they drink
the wine of those who
have been fined.

⁹ "Yet it was I who destroyed the
Amorite before them,
whose height was like the
height of the cedars
and who was as strong as the oaks;
I destroyed his fruit above
and his roots beneath.
¹⁰ Also it was I who brought you up
out of the land of Egypt
and led you for forty years
in the wilderness,
to possess the land of the Amorite.
¹¹ And I raised up some of your
sons for prophets,
and some of your young
men for Nazirites.
Is it not indeed so, O
people of Israel?"
declares the Lord.

¹² "But you made the Nazirites drink wine,
and commanded the prophets,
saying, 'You shall not prophesy.'
¹³ "Behold, I will press you
down in your place,
as a cart full of sheaves presses down.
¹⁴ Flight shall perish from the swift,
and the strong shall not
retain his strength,
nor shall the mighty save his life;
¹⁵ he who handles the bow shall not stand,
and he who is swift of foot
shall not save himself,
nor shall he who rides the
horse save his life;
¹⁶ and he who is stout of heart
among the mighty
shall flee away naked in that day,"
declares the Lord.

ISRAEL'S GUILT AND PUNISHMENT

3 Hear this word that the Lord has
spoken against you, O people of Israel,
against the whole family that I brought
up out of the land of Egypt:

---

^aOr officials ^bHebrew *I will not turn it back*; also verses 4, 6
^cOr officials

2 "You only have I known
    of all the families of the earth;
therefore I will punish you
    for all your iniquities.

3 "Do two walk together,
    unless they have agreed to meet?
4 Does a lion roar in the forest,
    when he has no prey?
Does a young lion cry out from
        his den,
    if he has taken nothing?
5 Does a bird fall in a snare on the earth,
    when there is no trap for it?
Does a snare spring up
        from the ground,
    when it has taken nothing?
6 Is a trumpet blown in a city,
    and the people are not afraid?
Does disaster come to a city,
    unless the Lord has done it?

7 "For the Lord God does nothing
    without revealing his secret
        to his servants the prophets.
8 The lion has roared;
    who will not fear?
The Lord God has spoken;
    who can but prophesy?"

9 Proclaim to the strongholds
        in Ashdod
    and to the strongholds in
        the land of Egypt,
and say, "Assemble yourselves on
        the mountains of Samaria,
    and see the great tumults within her,
        and the oppressed in her midst."
10 "They do not know how to do
        right," declares the Lord,
    "those who store up violence and
        robbery in their strongholds."

11 Therefore thus says the Lord God:

"An adversary shall surround the land
    and bring down^a your
        defences from you,
    and your strongholds shall
        be plundered."

12 Thus says the Lord: "As the shepherd rescues from the mouth of the lion two legs, or a piece of an ear, so shall the people of Israel who dwell in Samaria be rescued, with the corner of a couch and part^b of a bed.

13 "Hear, and testify against the
        house of Jacob,"
    declares the Lord God,
        the God of hosts,
14 "that on the day I punish Israel
        for his transgressions,
    I will punish the altars of Bethel,
    and the horns of the altar
        shall be cut off
    and fall to the ground.
15 I will strike the winter house along
        with the summer house,
    and the houses of ivory shall perish,
    and the great houses^c shall
        come to an end,"
            declares the Lord.

4 "Hear this word, you cows of Bashan,
    who are on the mountain of Samaria,
    who oppress the poor, who crush
        the needy,
    who say to your husbands,
        'Bring, that we may drink!'
2 The Lord God has sworn
        by his holiness
    that, behold, the days are
        coming upon you,
    when they shall take you
        away with hooks,
    even the last of you with fish-hooks.
3 And you shall go out through
        the breaches,
    each one straight ahead;
    and you shall be cast out
        into Harmon,"
            declares the Lord.

4 "Come to Bethel, and transgress;
    to Gilgal, and multiply
        transgression;
    bring your sacrifices every morning,
    your tithes every three days;
5 offer a sacrifice of thanksgiving
        of that which is leavened,
    and proclaim freewill offerings,
        publish them;
    for so you love to do, O people
        of Israel!"
            declares the Lord God.

ISRAEL HAS NOT RETURNED TO THE LORD

6 "I gave you cleanness of teeth
        in all your cities,

---

^{a}Hebrew *An adversary, one who surrounds the land—he shall bring down* ^{b}The meaning of the Hebrew word is uncertain ^{c}Or *and many houses*

and lack of bread in all your places,
yet you did not return to me,"
declares the LORD.

7 "I also withheld the rain from you
when there were yet three
months to the harvest;
I would send rain on one city,
and send no rain on another city;
one field would have rain,
and the field on which it did
not rain would wither;
8 so two or three cities would
wander to another city
to drink water, and would
not be satisfied;
yet you did not return to me,"
declares the LORD.

9 "I struck you with blight and mildew;
your many gardens and
your vineyards,
your fig trees and your olive
trees the locust devoured;
yet you did not return to me,"
declares the LORD.

10 "I sent among you a pestilence
after the manner of Egypt;
I killed your young men
with the sword,
and carried away your horses,[a]
and I made the stench of your camp
go up into your nostrils;
yet you did not return to me,"
declares the LORD.

11 "I overthrew some of you,
as when God overthrew
Sodom and Gomorrah,
and you were as a brand[b] plucked
out of the burning;
yet you did not return to me,"
declares the LORD.

12 "Therefore thus I will do
to you, O Israel;
because I will do this to you,
prepare to meet your God,
O Israel!"

13 For behold, he who forms the
mountains and creates the wind,
and declares to man what
is his thought,
who makes the morning darkness,

and treads on the heights
of the earth—
the LORD, the God of hosts,
is his name!

SEEK THE LORD AND LIVE

5 Hear this word that I take up over you
in lamentation, O house of Israel:

2 "Fallen, no more to rise,
is the virgin Israel;
forsaken on her land,
with none to raise her up."

3 For thus says the Lord GOD:

"The city that went out a thousand
shall have a hundred left,
and that which went out a hundred
shall have ten left
to the house of Israel."

4 For thus says the LORD to the house of Israel:

"Seek me and live;
5   but do not seek Bethel,
and do not enter into Gilgal
or cross over to Beersheba;
for Gilgal shall surely go into exile,
and Bethel shall come to nothing."

6   Seek the LORD and live,
lest he break out like fire in
the house of Joseph,
and it devour, with none to
quench it for Bethel,
7   O you who turn justice to wormwood[c]
and cast down righteousness
to the earth!

8   He who made the Pleiades
and Orion,
and turns deep darkness
into the morning
and darkens the day into night,
who calls for the waters of the sea
and pours them out on the
surface of the earth,
the LORD is his name;
9   who makes destruction flash
forth against the strong,
so that destruction comes
upon the fortress.

---

[a] Hebrew *along with the captivity of your horses*   [b] That is, a burning stick   [c] Or *to bitter fruit*

10 They hate him who reproves
      in the gate,
    and they abhor him who
      speaks the truth.
11 Therefore because you
      trample on[a] the poor
    and you exact taxes of
      grain from him,
    you have built houses of hewn stone,
      but you shall not dwell in them;
    you have planted pleasant vineyards,
      but you shall not drink their wine.
12 For I know how many are
      your transgressions
    and how great are your sins—
    you who afflict the righteous,
      who take a bribe,
    and turn aside the needy in the gate.
13 Therefore he who is prudent will
      keep silent in such a time,
    for it is an evil time.

14 Seek good, and not evil,
      that you may live;
    and so the Lord, the God of
      hosts, will be with you,
      as you have said.
15 Hate evil, and love good,
      and establish justice in the gate;
    it may be that the Lord,
      the God of hosts,
    will be gracious to the
      remnant of Joseph.

16 Therefore thus says the Lord, the God of hosts, the Lord:

    "In all the squares there
      shall be wailing,
    and in all the streets they
      shall say, 'Alas! Alas!'
    They shall call the farmers
      to mourning
    and to wailing those who are
      skilled in lamentation,
17 and in all vineyards there
      shall be wailing,
    for I will pass through your midst,"
                              says the Lord.

LET JUSTICE ROLL DOWN

18 Woe to you who desire the
      day of the Lord!
    Why would you have the
      day of the Lord?
    It is darkness, and not light,
19   as if a man fled from a lion,
      and a bear met him,
    or went into the house and leaned
      his hand against the wall,
      and a serpent bit him.
20 Is not the day of the Lord
      darkness, and not light,
    and gloom with no brightness in it?

21 "I hate, I despise your feasts,
    and I take no delight in your
      solemn assemblies.
22 Even though you offer me your burnt
      offerings and grain offerings,
      I will not accept them;
    and the peace offerings of your
      fattened animals,
      I will not look upon them.
23 Take away from me the noise
      of your songs;
    to the melody of your harps
      I will not listen.
24 But let justice roll down like waters,
    and righteousness like an
      ever-flowing stream.

25 "Did you bring to me sacrifices and offerings during the forty years in the wilderness, O house of Israel? 26 You shall take up Sikkuth your king, and Kiyyun your star-god—your images that you made for yourselves, 27 and I will send you into exile beyond Damascus," says the Lord, whose name is the God of hosts.

WOE TO THOSE AT EASE IN ZION

6 "Woe to those who are at ease in Zion,
    and to those who feel secure on the
      mountain of Samaria,
    the notable men of the first
      of the nations,
    to whom the house of Israel
      comes!
2   Pass over to Calneh, and see,
      and from there go to
      Hamath the great;
    then go down to Gath of
      the Philistines.
    Are you better than these kingdoms?
      Or is their territory greater
      than your territory,
3   O you who put far away the
      day of disaster
    and bring near the seat of violence?

---

[a] Or you tax

⁴ "Woe to those who lie on beds of ivory
  and stretch themselves out
    on their couches,
  and eat lambs from the flock
    and calves from the midst of the stall,
⁵ who sing idle songs to the
    sound of the harp
  and like David invent for themselves
    instruments of music,
⁶ who drink wine in bowls
  and anoint themselves with
    the finest oils,
  but are not grieved over
    the ruin of Joseph!
⁷ Therefore they shall now be the first
    of those who go into exile,
  and the revelry of those who stretch
    themselves out shall pass away."

⁸The Lord GOD has sworn by himself, declares the LORD, the God of hosts:

  "I abhor the pride of Jacob
    and hate his strongholds,
  and I will deliver up the city
    and all that is in it."

⁹And if ten men remain in one house, they shall die. ¹⁰And when one's relative, the one who anoints him for burial, shall take him up to bring the bones out of the house, and shall say to him who is in the innermost parts of the house, "Is there still anyone with you?" he shall say, "No"; and he shall say, "Silence! We must not mention the name of the LORD."

¹¹ For behold, the LORD commands,
    and the great house shall be struck
      down into fragments,
    and the little house into bits.
¹² Do horses run on rocks?
    Does one plough there*ᵃ* with oxen?
  But you have turned justice into poison
    and the fruit of righteousness
      into wormwood*ᵇ*—
¹³ you who rejoice in Lo-debar,*ᶜ*
    who say, "Have we not by
      our own strength
    captured Karnaim*ᵈ* for ourselves?"
¹⁴ "For behold, I will raise up
    against you a nation,
  O house of Israel," declares the
    LORD, the God of hosts;
  "and they shall oppress you
    from Lebo-hamath
  to the Brook of the Arabah."

WARNING VISIONS

7 This is what the Lord GOD showed me: behold, he was forming locusts when the latter growth was just beginning to sprout, and behold, it was the latter growth after the king's mowings. ²When they had finished eating the grass of the land, I said,

  "O Lord GOD, please forgive!
    How can Jacob stand?
    He is so small!"
³ The LORD relented concerning this:
    "It shall not be," said the LORD.

⁴This is what the Lord GOD showed me: behold, the Lord GOD was calling for a judgement by fire, and it devoured the great deep and was eating up the land. ⁵Then I said,

  "O Lord GOD, please cease!
    How can Jacob stand?
    He is so small!"
⁶ The LORD relented concerning this:
    "This also shall not be," said
      the Lord GOD.

⁷This is what he showed me: behold, the Lord was standing beside a wall built with a plumb line, with a plumb line in his hand. ⁸And the LORD said to me, "Amos, what do you see?" And I said, "A plumb line." Then the Lord said,

  "Behold, I am setting a plumb line
    in the midst of my people Israel;
    I will never again pass by them;
⁹ the high places of Isaac shall
      be made desolate,
    and the sanctuaries of Israel
      shall be laid waste,
    and I will rise against the house of
      Jeroboam with the sword."

AMOS ACCUSED

¹⁰Then Amaziah the priest of Bethel sent to Jeroboam king of Israel, saying, "Amos has conspired against you in the midst of the house of Israel. The land is not able to bear all his words. ¹¹For thus Amos has said,

  "'Jeroboam shall die by the sword,
    and Israel must go into exile
      away from his land.'"

---
*ᵃ*Or *the sea*   *ᵇ*Or *into bitter fruit*   *ᶜ*Lo-debar means *nothing*
*ᵈ*Karnaim means *horns* (a symbol of strength)

¹²And Amaziah said to Amos, "O seer, go, flee away to the land of Judah, and eat bread there, and prophesy there, ¹³but never again prophesy at Bethel, for it is the king's sanctuary, and it is a temple of the kingdom." ¹⁴Then Amos answered and said to Amaziah, "I was[a] no prophet, nor a prophet's son, but I was a herdsman and a dresser of sycamore figs. ¹⁵But the LORD took me from following the flock, and the LORD said to me, 'Go, prophesy to my people Israel.' ¹⁶Now therefore hear the word of the LORD.

> "You say, 'Do not prophesy against Israel,
>   and do not preach against the
>   house of Isaac.'

¹⁷Therefore thus says the LORD:

> "'Your wife shall be a prostitute
>   in the city,
> and your sons and your daughters
>   shall fall by the sword,
> and your land shall be divided
>   up with a measuring line;
> you yourself shall die in
>   an unclean land,
> and Israel shall surely go into
>   exile away from its land.'"

THE COMING DAY OF BITTER MOURNING

8 This is what the Lord GOD showed me: behold, a basket of summer fruit. ²And he said, "Amos, what do you see?" And I said, "A basket of summer fruit." Then the LORD said to me,

> "The end[b] has come upon
>   my people Israel;
>   I will never again pass by them.
> ³ The songs of the temple[c] shall
>   become wailings[d] in that day,"
>   declares the Lord GOD.
> "So many dead bodies!"
> "They are thrown everywhere!"
> "Silence!"

> ⁴ Hear this, you who trample
>   on the needy
>   and bring the poor of the
>   land to an end,
> ⁵ saying, "When will the new
>   moon be over,
>   that we may sell grain?
> And the Sabbath,
>   that we may offer wheat for sale,
> that we may make the ephah
>   small and the shekel[e] great
>   and deal deceitfully with
>   false balances,
> ⁶ that we may buy the poor for silver
>   and the needy for a pair of sandals
>   and sell the chaff of the wheat?"

> ⁷ The LORD has sworn by the
>   pride of Jacob:
> "Surely I will never forget
>   any of their deeds.
> ⁸ Shall not the land tremble
>   on this account,
>   and everyone mourn who
>   dwells in it,
> and all of it rise like the Nile,
>   and be tossed about and sink
>   again, like the Nile of Egypt?"

> ⁹ "And on that day," declares
>   the Lord GOD,
>   "I will make the sun go down at noon
>   and darken the earth in
>   broad daylight.
> ¹⁰ I will turn your feasts into mourning
>   and all your songs into lamentation;
> I will bring sackcloth on every waist
>   and baldness on every head;
> I will make it like the mourning
>   for an only son
>   and the end of it like a bitter day.

> ¹¹ "Behold, the days are coming,"
>   declares the Lord GOD,
>   "when I will send a famine
>   on the land—
> not a famine of bread, nor
>   a thirst for water,
>   but of hearing the words of the LORD.
> ¹² They shall wander from sea to sea,
>   and from north to east;
> they shall run to and fro, to seek
>   the word of the LORD,
>   but they shall not find it.

> ¹³ "In that day the lovely virgins
>   and the young men
>   shall faint for thirst.
> ¹⁴ Those who swear by the
>   Guilt of Samaria,
>   and say, 'As your god lives, O Dan',

---

[a] Or *am*; twice in this verse   [b] The Hebrew words for *end* and *summer fruit* sound alike   [c] Or *palace*   [d] Or *The singing women of the palace shall wail*   [e] An *ephah* was about 3/5 of a bushel or 22 litres; a *shekel* was about 2/5 of an ounce or 11 grams

and, 'As the Way of Beersheba lives',
    they shall fall, and never rise again."

THE DESTRUCTION OF ISRAEL

9 I saw the Lord standing beside[a] the altar, and he said:

"Strike the capitals until the
    thresholds shake,
    and shatter them on the heads
        of all the people;[b]
and those who are left of them I
    will kill with the sword;
not one of them shall flee away;
not one of them shall escape.

² "If they dig into Sheol,
    from there shall my hand take them;
if they climb up to heaven,
    from there I will bring them down.
³ If they hide themselves on
        the top of Carmel,
    from there I will search them
        out and take them;
and if they hide from my sight
        at the bottom of the sea,
    there I will command the serpent,
        and it shall bite them.
⁴ And if they go into captivity
        before their enemies,
    there I will command the sword,
        and it shall kill them;
and I will fix my eyes upon them
    for evil and not for good."

⁵ The Lord GOD of hosts,
he who touches the earth and it melts,
    and all who dwell in it mourn,
and all of it rises like the Nile,
    and sinks again, like the
        Nile of Egypt;
⁶ who builds his upper chambers
        in the heavens
    and founds his vault upon the earth;
who calls for the waters of the sea
    and pours them out upon the
        surface of the earth—
the LORD is his name.

⁷ "Are you not like the Cushites to me,
    O people of Israel?" declares
        the LORD.
"Did I not bring up Israel from
        the land of Egypt,
    and the Philistines from Caphtor
        and the Syrians from Kir?

⁸ Behold, the eyes of the Lord GOD
    are upon the sinful kingdom,
    and I will destroy it from the
        surface of the ground,
    except that I will not utterly
        destroy the house of Jacob,"
            declares the LORD.

⁹ "For behold, I will command,
    and shake the house of Israel
        among all the nations
as one shakes with a sieve,
    but no pebble shall fall to the earth.
¹⁰ All the sinners of my people
        shall die by the sword,
    who say, 'Disaster shall not
        overtake or meet us.'

THE RESTORATION OF ISRAEL

¹¹ "In that day I will raise up
        the booth of David that is fallen
    and repair its breaches,
        and raise up its ruins
    and rebuild it as in the days of old,
¹² that they may possess the
        remnant of Edom
    and all the nations who are
        called by my name,"[c]
            declares the LORD who does this.

¹³ "Behold, the days are coming,"
        declares the LORD,
    "when the ploughman shall
        overtake the reaper
    and the treader of grapes him
        who sows the seed;
the mountains shall drip sweet wine,
    and all the hills shall flow with it.
¹⁴ I will restore the fortunes of
        my people Israel,
    and they shall rebuild the ruined
        cities and inhabit them;
they shall plant vineyards
    and drink their wine,
    and they shall make gardens
        and eat their fruit.
¹⁵ I will plant them on their land,
    and they shall never again
        be uprooted
    out of the land that I have
        given them,"
            says the LORD your God.

---

[a]Or on [b]Hebrew *all of them* [c]Hebrew; Septuagint (compare Acts 15:17) *that the remnant of mankind and all the nations who are called by my name may seek the Lord*

OBADIAH

¹The vision of Obadiah.

EDOM WILL BE HUMBLED

Thus says the Lord GOD
  concerning Edom:
We have heard a report from the LORD,
  and a messenger has been sent
    among the nations:
"Rise up! Let us rise against
  her for battle!"
² Behold, I will make you small
    among the nations;
  you shall be utterly despised.ᵃ
³ The pride of your heart has
    deceived you,
  you who live in the clefts
    of the rock,ᵇ
  in your lofty dwelling,
  who say in your heart,
    "Who will bring me down
      to the ground?"
⁴ Though you soar aloft like the eagle,
    though your nest is set
      among the stars,
  from there I will bring you down,
      declares the LORD.

⁵ If thieves came to you,
    if plunderers came by night—
    how you have been destroyed!—
  would they not steal only
    enough for themselves?
  If grape gatherers came to you,
    would they not leave gleanings?
⁶ How Esau has been pillaged,
    his treasures sought out!
⁷ All your allies have driven
    you to your border;
  those at peace with you
    have deceived you;
  they have prevailed against you;
    those who eat your breadᶜ have
      set a trap beneath you—
  you haveᵈ no understanding.

⁸ Will I not on that day,
    declares the LORD,
  destroy the wise men out of Edom,
    and understanding out
      of Mount Esau?
⁹ And your mighty men shall be
    dismayed, O Teman,
  so that every man from Mount Esau
    will be cut off by slaughter.

EDOM'S VIOLENCE AGAINST JACOB

¹⁰ Because of the violence done
    to your brother Jacob,
  shame shall cover you,
    and you shall be cut off for ever.
¹¹ On the day that you stood aloof,
    on the day that strangers
      carried off his wealth
  and foreigners entered his gates
    and cast lots for Jerusalem,
  you were like one of them.
¹² But do not gloat over the day
    of your brother
    in the day of his misfortune;
  do not rejoice over the people
      of Judah
    in the day of their ruin;
  do not boastᵉ
    in the day of distress.
¹³ Do not enter the gate of my people
    in the day of their calamity;
  do not gloat over his disaster
    in the day of his calamity;
  do not loot his wealth
    in the day of his calamity.
¹⁴ Do not stand at the crossroads
    to cut off his fugitives;
  do not hand over his survivors
    in the day of distress.

THE DAY OF THE LORD IS NEAR

¹⁵ For the day of the LORD is near
    upon all the nations.
  As you have done, it shall
    be done to you;
  your deeds shall return on
    your own head.

ᵃOr *Behold, I have made you small among the nations; you are utterly despised* ᵇOr *of Sela* ᶜHebrew lacks *those who eat* ᵈHebrew *he has* ᵉHebrew *do not enlarge your mouth*

OBADIAH

16 For as you have drunk on my
  holy mountain,
   so all the nations shall
    drink continually;
  they shall drink and swallow,
   and shall be as though they
    had never been.
17 But in Mount Zion there shall
   be those who escape,
   and it shall be holy,
  and the house of Jacob shall possess
   their own possessions.
18 The house of Jacob shall be a fire,
   and the house of Joseph a flame,
   and the house of Esau stubble;
  they shall burn them and
   consume them,
   and there shall be no survivor
    for the house of Esau,
     for the LORD has spoken.

THE KINGDOM OF THE LORD

19 Those of the Negeb shall
   possess Mount Esau,
   and those of the Shephelah
    shall possess the land
    of the Philistines;
  they shall possess the land of Ephraim
   and the land of Samaria,
   and Benjamin shall possess Gilead.
20 The exiles of this host of the
   people of Israel
   shall possess the land of the
    Canaanites as far as Zarephath,
  and the exiles of Jerusalem
   who are in Sepharad
   shall possess the cities of the Negeb.
21 Saviours shall go up to Mount Zion
   to rule Mount Esau,
   and the kingdom shall be
    the LORD's.

JONAH

JONAH FLEES THE PRESENCE OF THE LORD

1 Now the word of the LORD came to Jonah the son of Amittai, saying, ²"Arise, go to Nineveh, that great city, and call out against it, for their evil[a] has come up before me." ³But Jonah rose to flee to Tarshish from the presence of the LORD. He went down to Joppa and found a ship going to Tarshish. So he paid the fare and went down into it, to go with them to Tarshish, away from the presence of the LORD.

⁴But the LORD hurled a great wind upon the sea, and there was a mighty tempest on the sea, so that the ship threatened to break up. ⁵Then the mariners were afraid, and each cried out to his god. And they hurled the cargo that was in the ship into the sea to lighten it for them. But Jonah had gone down into the inner part of the ship and had lain down and was fast asleep. ⁶So the captain came and said to him, "What do you mean, you sleeper? Arise, call out to your god! Perhaps the god will give a thought to us, that we may not perish."

JONAH IS THROWN INTO THE SEA

⁷And they said to one another, "Come, let us cast lots, that we may know on whose account this evil has come upon us." So they cast lots, and the lot fell on Jonah. ⁸Then they said to him, "Tell us on whose account this evil has come upon us. What is your occupation? And where do you come from? What is your country? And of what people are you?" ⁹And he said to them, "I am a Hebrew, and I fear the LORD, the God of heaven, who made the sea and the dry land." ¹⁰Then the men were exceedingly afraid and said to him, "What is this that you have done!" For the men knew that he was fleeing from the presence of the LORD, because he had told them.

¹¹Then they said to him, "What shall we do to you, that the sea may quiet down for us?" For the sea grew more and more tempestuous. ¹²He said to them, "Pick me up and hurl me into the sea; then the sea will quiet down for you, for I know it is because of me that this great tempest has come upon you."

¹³Nevertheless, the men rowed hard[b] to get back to dry land, but they could not, for the sea grew more and more tempestuous against them. ¹⁴Therefore they called out to the LORD, "O LORD, let us not perish for this man's life, and lay not on us innocent blood, for you, O LORD, have done as it pleased you." ¹⁵So they picked up Jonah and hurled him into the sea, and the sea ceased from its raging. ¹⁶Then the men feared the LORD exceedingly, and they offered a sacrifice to the LORD and made vows.

A GREAT FISH SWALLOWS JONAH

¹⁷[c] And the LORD appointed[d] a great fish to swallow up Jonah. And Jonah was in the belly of the fish three days and three nights.

JONAH'S PRAYER

2 Then Jonah prayed to the LORD his God from the belly of the fish, ²saying,

"I called out to the LORD, out
　of my distress,
and he answered me;
out of the belly of Sheol I cried,
　and you heard my voice.
³　For you cast me into the deep,
　into the heart of the seas,
　and the flood surrounded me;
all your waves and your billows
　passed over me.
⁴　Then I said, 'I am driven away
　from your sight;
yet I shall again look
　upon your holy temple.'
⁵　The waters closed in over
　me to take my life;
the deep surrounded me;
weeds were wrapped about my head
⁶　at the roots of the mountains.
I went down to the land
　whose bars closed upon me for ever;
yet you brought up my life from the pit,
　O LORD my God.

---

[a]The same Hebrew word can mean *evil* or *disaster*, depending on the context; so throughout Jonah [b]Hebrew *the men dug in* [their oars] [c]Ch 2:1 in Hebrew [d]Or *had appointed*

⁷ When my life was fainting away,
    I remembered the LORD,
  and my prayer came to you,
    into your holy temple.
⁸ Those who pay regard to vain idols
    forsake their hope of steadfast love.
⁹ But I with the voice of thanksgiving
    will sacrifice to you;
  what I have vowed I will pay.
    Salvation belongs to the LORD!"

¹⁰And the LORD spoke to the fish, and it vomited Jonah out upon the dry land.

JONAH GOES TO NINEVEH

3 Then the word of the LORD came to Jonah the second time, saying, ²"Arise, go to Nineveh, that great city, and call out against it the message that I tell you." ³So Jonah arose and went to Nineveh, according to the word of the LORD. Now Nineveh was an exceedingly great city,ᵃ three days' journey in breadth.ᵇ ⁴Jonah began to go into the city, going a day's journey. And he called out, "Yet forty days, and Nineveh shall be overthrown!" ⁵And the people of Nineveh believed God. They called for a fast and put on sackcloth, from the greatest of them to the least of them.

THE PEOPLE OF NINEVEH REPENT

⁶The word reachedᶜ the king of Nineveh, and he arose from his throne, removed his robe, covered himself with sackcloth, and sat in ashes. ⁷And he issued a proclamation and published through Nineveh, "By the decree of the king and his nobles: Let neither man nor beast, herd nor flock, taste anything. Let them not feed or drink water, ⁸but let man and beast be covered with sackcloth, and let them call out mightily to God. Let everyone turn from his evil way and from the violence that is in his hands. ⁹Who knows? God may turn and relent and turn from his fierce anger, so that we may not perish."

¹⁰When God saw what they did, how they turned from their evil way, God relented of the disaster that he had said he would do to them, and he did not do it.

JONAH'S ANGER AND THE LORD'S COMPASSION

4 But it displeased Jonah exceedingly,ᵈ and he was angry. ²And he prayed to the LORD and said, "O LORD, is not this what I said when I was yet in my country? That is why I made haste to flee to Tarshish; for I knew that you are a gracious God and merciful, slow to anger and abounding in steadfast love, and relenting from disaster. ³Therefore now, O LORD, please take my life from me, for it is better for me to die than to live." ⁴And the LORD said, "Do you do well to be angry?"

⁵Jonah went out of the city and sat to the east of the city and made a booth for himself there. He sat under it in the shade, till he should see what would become of the city. ⁶Now the LORD God appointed a plantᵉ and made it come up over Jonah, that it might be a shade over his head, to save him from his discomfort.ᶠ So Jonah was exceedingly glad because of the plant. ⁷But when dawn came up the next day, God appointed a worm that attacked the plant, so that it withered. ⁸When the sun rose, God appointed a scorching east wind, and the sun beat down on the head of Jonah so that he was faint. And he asked that he might die and said, "It is better for me to die than to live." ⁹But God said to Jonah, "Do you do well to be angry for the plant?" And he said, "Yes, I do well to be angry, angry enough to die." ¹⁰And the LORD said, "You pity the plant, for which you did not labour, nor did you make it grow, which came into being in a night and perished in a night. ¹¹And should not I pity Nineveh, that great city, in which there are more than 120,000 persons who do not know their right hand from their left, and also much cattle?"

ᵃHebrew *a great city to God* ᵇOr *a visit was a three days' journey*
ᶜOr *had reached* ᵈHebrew *it was exceedingly evil to Jonah* ᵉHebrew *qiqayon*, probably the castor oil plant; also verses 7, 9, 10 ᶠOr *his evil*

MICAH

1 The word of the Lord that came to Micah of Moresheth in the days of Jotham, Ahaz, and Hezekiah, kings of Judah, which he saw concerning Samaria and Jerusalem.

THE COMING DESTRUCTION

2 Hear, you peoples, all of you;[a]
  pay attention, O earth, and
    all that is in it,
  and let the Lord God be a
    witness against you,
  the Lord from his holy temple.
3 For behold, the Lord is coming
    out of his place,
  and will come down and tread upon
    the high places of the earth.
4 And the mountains will
    melt under him,
  and the valleys will split open,
  like wax before the fire,
    like waters poured down
      a steep place.
5 All this is for the transgression of Jacob
  and for the sins of the
    house of Israel.
  What is the transgression of Jacob?
  Is it not Samaria?
  And what is the high place of Judah?
  Is it not Jerusalem?
6 Therefore I will make Samaria a
    heap in the open country,
  a place for planting vineyards,
  and I will pour down her
    stones into the valley
  and uncover her foundations.
7 All her carved images shall
    be beaten to pieces,
  all her wages shall be
    burned with fire,
  and all her idols I will lay waste,
  for from the fee of a prostitute
    she gathered them,
  and to the fee of a prostitute
    they shall return.

8 For this I will lament and wail;
  I will go stripped and naked;
  I will make lamentation
    like the jackals,
  and mourning like the ostriches.
9 For her wound is incurable,
  and it has come to Judah;
  it has reached to the gate of my people,
    to Jerusalem.

10 Tell it not in Gath;
    weep not at all;
  in Beth-le-aphrah
    roll yourselves in the dust.
11 Pass on your way,
    inhabitants of Shaphir,
    in nakedness and shame;
  the inhabitants of Zaanan
    do not come out;
  the lamentation of Beth-ezel
    shall take away from you
      its standing place.
12 For the inhabitants of Maroth
    wait anxiously for good,
  because disaster has come
    down from the Lord
  to the gate of Jerusalem.
13 Harness the steeds to the chariots,
    inhabitants of Lachish;
  it was the beginning of sin
    to the daughter of Zion,
  for in you were found
    the transgressions of Israel.
14 Therefore you shall give parting gifts[b]
    to Moresheth-gath;
  the houses of Achzib shall
    be a deceitful thing
  to the kings of Israel.
15 I will again bring a conqueror to you,
    inhabitants of Mareshah;
  the glory of Israel
    shall come to Adullam.
16 Make yourselves bald and
    cut off your hair,
  for the children of your delight;
  make yourselves as bald as the eagle,
    for they shall go from you into
      exile.

---

[a]Hebrew *all of them* [b]Or *give dowry*

WOE TO THE OPPRESSORS

2 Woe to those who devise wickedness
   and work evil on their beds!
When the morning dawns,
      they perform it,
   because it is in the power
      of their hand.
² They covet fields and seize them,
      and houses, and take them away;
   they oppress a man and his house,
      a man and his inheritance.
³ Therefore thus says the LORD:
   behold, against this family I
      am devising disaster,[a]
   from which you cannot
      remove your necks,
   and you shall not walk haughtily,
      for it will be a time of disaster.
⁴ In that day they shall take up a
      taunt song against you
   and moan bitterly,
   and say, "We are utterly ruined;
   he changes the portion
      of my people;
   how he removes it from me!
   To an apostate he allots our fields."
⁵ Therefore you will have none
      to cast the line by lot
   in the assembly of the LORD.

⁶ "Do not preach"—thus they preach—
   "one should not preach
      of such things;
   disgrace will not overtake us."
⁷ Should this be said, O house of Jacob?
   Has the LORD grown impatient?[b]
   Are these his deeds?
   Do not my words do good
      to him who walks uprightly?
⁸ But lately my people have
      risen up as an enemy;
   you strip the rich robe from those
      who pass by trustingly
   with no thought of war.[c]
⁹ The women of my people you
      drive out
   from their delightful houses;
   from their young children
      you take away
   my splendour for ever.
¹⁰ Arise and go,
      for this is no place to rest,
   because of uncleanness that destroys
      with a grievous destruction.
¹¹ If a man should go about and
      utter wind and lies,
   saying, "I will preach to you of
      wine and strong drink",
   he would be the preacher
      for this people!
¹² I will surely assemble all
      of you, O Jacob;
   I will gather the remnant of Israel;
   I will set them together
      like sheep in a fold,
   like a flock in its pasture,
      a noisy multitude of men.
¹³ He who opens the breach
      goes up before them;
   they break through and
      pass the gate,
   going out by it.
   Their king passes on before them,
      the LORD at their head.

RULERS AND PROPHETS DENOUNCED

3 And I said:
   Hear, you heads of Jacob
   and rulers of the house of Israel!
Is it not for you to know justice?—
²   you who hate the good
         and love the evil,
   who tear the skin from off my people[d]
      and their flesh from off their bones,
³ who eat the flesh of my people,
   and flay their skin from off them,
   and break their bones in pieces
   and chop them up like meat in a pot,
      like flesh in a cauldron.

⁴ Then they will cry to the LORD,
      but he will not answer them;
   he will hide his face from
      them at that time,
   because they have made
      their deeds evil.

⁵ Thus says the LORD concerning
      the prophets
   who lead my people astray,
   who cry "Peace"
      when they have something to eat,
   but declare war against him
      who puts nothing into their mouths.
⁶ Therefore it shall be night to
      you, without vision,
   and darkness to you,
      without divination.

---

[a] The same Hebrew word can mean *evil* or *disaster*, depending on the context [b] Hebrew *Has the spirit of the LORD grown short?* [c] Or *returning from war* [d] Hebrew *from off them*

The sun shall go down on
      the prophets,
   and the day shall be black over them;
⁷ the seers shall be disgraced,
      and the diviners put to shame;
   they shall all cover their lips,
      for there is no answer from God.
⁸ But as for me, I am filled with power,
      with the Spirit of the LORD,
   and with justice and might,
   to declare to Jacob his transgression
      and to Israel his sin.

⁹ Hear this, you heads of the
      house of Jacob
   and rulers of the house of Israel,
   who detest justice
      and make crooked all that is straight,
¹⁰ who build Zion with blood
      and Jerusalem with iniquity.
¹¹ Its heads give judgement for a bribe;
   its priests teach for a price;
   its prophets practise
      divination for money;
   yet they lean on the LORD and say,
   "Is not the LORD in the midst of us?
      No disaster shall come upon us."
¹² Therefore because of you
      Zion shall be ploughed as a field;
   Jerusalem shall become
      a heap of ruins,
   and the mountain of the house
      a wooded height.

THE MOUNTAIN OF THE LORD

4 It shall come to pass in the latter days
   that the mountain of the
      house of the LORD
   shall be established as the
      highest of the mountains,
   and it shall be lifted up
      above the hills;
   and peoples shall flow to it,
² and many nations shall
      come, and say:
   "Come, let us go up to the
      mountain of the LORD,
   to the house of the God of Jacob,
   that he may teach us his ways
      and that we may walk in his paths."
   For out of Zion shall go forth the law,ᵃ
      and the word of the LORD
      from Jerusalem.
³ He shall judge between many peoples,
      and shall decide disputes for
         strong nations far away;
   and they shall beat their swords
      into ploughshares,
   and their spears into
      pruning-hooks;
   nation shall not lift up sword
      against nation,
   neither shall they learn
      war any more;
⁴ but they shall sit every man under
      his vine and under his fig tree,
   and no one shall make them afraid,
   for the mouth of the LORD of
      hosts has spoken.
⁵ For all the peoples walk
      each in the name of its god,
   but we will walk in the name
      of the LORD our God
      for ever and ever.

THE LORD SHALL RESCUE ZION

⁶ In that day, declares the LORD,
      I will assemble the lame
   and gather those who have
      been driven away
   and those whom I have afflicted;
⁷ and the lame I will make the remnant,
      and those who were cast
         off, a strong nation;
   and the LORD will reign over
      them in Mount Zion
   from this time forth and
      for evermore.

⁸ And you, O tower of the flock,
      hill of the daughter of Zion,
   to you shall it come,
      the former dominion shall come,
      kingship for the daughter
         of Jerusalem.

⁹ Now why do you cry aloud?
      Is there no king in you?
   Has your counsellor perished,
      that pain seized you like a
         woman in labour?
¹⁰ Writhe and groan,ᵇ O daughter
      of Zion,
   like a woman in labour,
   for now you shall go out from the city
      and dwell in the open country;
      you shall go to Babylon.
   There you shall be rescued;
      there the LORD will redeem you
      from the hand of your enemies.

ᵃOr teaching   ᵇOr push

MICAH 4–5

¹¹ Now many nations
   are assembled against you,
saying, "Let her be defiled,
   and let our eyes gaze upon Zion."
¹² But they do not know
   the thoughts of the LORD;
they do not understand his plan,
   that he has gathered them as
      sheaves to the threshing floor.
¹³ Arise and thresh,
   O daughter of Zion,
for I will make your horn iron,
   and I will make your hoofs bronze;
you shall beat in pieces many
      peoples;
   and shall devote^a their
      gain to the LORD,
   their wealth to the Lord of
      the whole earth.

THE RULER TO BE BORN IN BETHLEHEM

5 ^b Now muster your troops,
   O daughter^c of troops;
siege is laid against us;
with a rod they strike the
      judge of Israel
   on the cheek.
^{2d} But you, O Bethlehem Ephrathah,
   who are too little to be among
      the clans of Judah,
from you shall come forth for me
   one who is to be ruler in Israel,
whose coming forth is from of old,
   from ancient days.
³ Therefore he shall give them
      up until the time
   when she who is in labour
      has given birth;
then the rest of his brothers
      shall return
   to the people of Israel.
⁴ And he shall stand and shepherd his
      flock in the strength of the LORD,
   in the majesty of the name
      of the LORD his God.
And they shall dwell secure, for
      now he shall be great
   to the ends of the earth.
⁵ And he shall be their peace.

When the Assyrian comes
      into our land
   and treads in our palaces,
then we will raise against him
      seven shepherds
   and eight princes of men;
⁶ they shall shepherd the land of
      Assyria with the sword,
   and the land of Nimrod
      at its entrances;
and he shall deliver us
   from the Assyrian
when he comes into our land
   and treads within our border.

A REMNANT SHALL BE DELIVERED

⁷ Then the remnant of Jacob shall be
      in the midst of many peoples
   like dew from the LORD,
      like showers on the grass,
   which delay not for a man
      nor wait for the children of man.
⁸ And the remnant of Jacob shall
      be among the nations,
   in the midst of many peoples,
like a lion among the beasts
      of the forest,
   like a young lion among the
      flocks of sheep,
which, when it goes through,
      treads down
   and tears in pieces, and there
      is none to deliver.
⁹ Your hand shall be lifted up
      over your adversaries,
   and all your enemies shall be
      cut off.
¹⁰ And in that day, declares the LORD,
   I will cut off your horses
      from among you
   and will destroy your chariots;
¹¹ and I will cut off the cities of your land
   and throw down all your
      strongholds;
¹² and I will cut off sorceries
      from your hand,
   and you shall have no more
      tellers of fortunes;
¹³ and I will cut off your carved images
      and your pillars from among you,
   and you shall bow down no more
      to the work of your hands;
¹⁴ and I will root out your Asherah
      images from among you
   and destroy your cities.
¹⁵ And in anger and wrath I will
      execute vengeance
   on the nations that did not obey.

---

^aHebrew *devote to destruction*   ^bCh 4:14 in Hebrew   ^cThat is, city
^dCh 5:1 in Hebrew

THE INDICTMENT OF THE LORD

6 Hear what the LORD says:
   Arise, plead your case before the mountains,
      and let the hills hear your voice.
2 Hear, you mountains, the indictment of the LORD,
      and you enduring foundations of the earth,
   for the LORD has an indictment against his people,
      and he will contend with Israel.

3 "O my people, what have I done to you?
      How have I wearied you?
         Answer me!
4 For I brought you up from the land of Egypt
      and redeemed you from the house of slavery,
   and I sent before you Moses,
      Aaron, and Miriam.
5 O my people, remember what Balak king of Moab devised,
      and what Balaam the son of Beor answered him,
   and what happened from Shittim to Gilgal,
      that you may know the righteous acts of the LORD."

WHAT DOES THE LORD REQUIRE?

6 "With what shall I come before the LORD,
      and bow myself before God on high?
   Shall I come before him with burnt offerings,
      with calves a year old?
7 Will the LORD be pleased with[a] thousands of rams,
      with ten thousands of rivers of oil?
   Shall I give my firstborn for my transgression,
      the fruit of my body for the sin of my soul?"
8 He has told you, O man, what is good;
      and what does the LORD require of you
   but to do justice, and to love kindness,[b]
      and to walk humbly with your God?

DESTRUCTION OF THE WICKED

9 The voice of the LORD cries to the city—
      and it is sound wisdom to fear your name:
   "Hear of the rod and of him who appointed it![c]
10 Can I forget any longer the treasures[d] of wickedness in the house of the wicked,
      and the scant measure that is accursed?
11 Shall I acquit the man with wicked scales
      and with a bag of deceitful weights?
12 Your[e] rich men are full of violence;
      your inhabitants speak lies,
      and their tongue is deceitful in their mouth.
13 Therefore I strike you with a grievous blow,
      making you desolate because of your sins.
14 You shall eat, but not be satisfied,
      and there shall be hunger within you;
   you shall put away, but not preserve,
      and what you preserve I will give to the sword.
15 You shall sow, but not reap;
      you shall tread olives, but not anoint yourselves with oil;
      you shall tread grapes, but not drink wine.
16 For you have kept the statutes of Omri,[f]
      and all the works of the house of Ahab;
      and you have walked in their counsels,
   that I may make you a desolation,
      and your[g] inhabitants a hissing;
   so you shall bear the scorn of my people."

WAIT FOR THE GOD OF SALVATION

7 Woe is me! For I have become as when the summer fruit has been gathered,
      as when the grapes have been gleaned:
   there is no cluster to eat,
      no first-ripe fig that my soul desires.
2 The godly has perished from the earth,
      and there is no one upright among mankind;
   they all lie in wait for blood,
      and each hunts the other with a net.

---

[a]Or *Will the LORD accept* [b]Or *steadfast love* [c]The meaning of the Hebrew is uncertain [d]Or *Are there still treasures* [e]Hebrew *whose* [f]Hebrew *For the statutes of Omri are kept* [g]Hebrew *its*

3 Their hands are on what is
      evil, to do it well;
   the prince and the judge
      ask for a bribe,
   and the great man utters the
      evil desire of his soul;
   thus they weave it together.
4 The best of them is like a brier,
   the most upright of them
      a thorn hedge.
   The day of your watchmen, of your
      punishment, has come;
   now their confusion is at hand.
5 Put no trust in a neighbour;
   have no confidence in a friend;
   guard the doors of your mouth
      from her who lies in your arms;[a]
6 for the son treats the father
      with contempt,
   the daughter rises up
      against her mother,
   the daughter-in-law against
      her mother-in-law;
   a man's enemies are the men
      of his own house.
7 But as for me, I will look to the LORD;
   I will wait for the God of
      my salvation;
   my God will hear me.

8 Rejoice not over me, O my enemy;
      when I fall, I shall rise;
   when I sit in darkness,
      the LORD will be a light to me.
9 I will bear the indignation of the LORD
      because I have sinned against him,
   until he pleads my cause
      and executes judgement for me.
   He will bring me out to the light;
      I shall look upon his vindication.
10 Then my enemy will see,
      and shame will cover her
   who said to me,
      "Where is the LORD your God?"
   My eyes will look upon her;
      now she will be trampled down
      like the mire of the streets.
11 A day for the building of your walls!
   In that day the boundary
      shall be far extended.
12 In that day they[b] will come to you,
      from Assyria and the cities of Egypt,
   and from Egypt to the River,[c]
      from sea to sea and from
      mountain to mountain.
13 But the earth will be desolate
      because of its inhabitants,
   for the fruit of their deeds.

14 Shepherd your people with your staff,
      the flock of your inheritance,
   who dwell alone in a forest
      in the midst of a garden land;[d]
   let them graze in Bashan and Gilead
      as in the days of old.
15 As in the days when you came
      out of the land of Egypt,
   I will show them[e] marvellous things.
16 The nations shall see and be
      ashamed of all their might;
   they shall lay their hands
      on their mouths;
   their ears shall be deaf;
17 they shall lick the dust like a serpent,
      like the crawling things of the earth;
   they shall come trembling out
      of their strongholds;
   they shall turn in dread to
      the LORD our God,
   and they shall be in fear of you.

GOD'S STEADFAST LOVE AND COMPASSION
18 Who is a God like you,
      pardoning iniquity
   and passing over transgression
      for the remnant of his inheritance?
   He does not retain his anger for ever,
      because he delights in
      steadfast love.
19 He will again have compassion on us;
      he will tread our iniquities
      underfoot.
   You will cast all our[f] sins
      into the depths of the sea.
20 You will show faithfulness to Jacob
      and steadfast love to Abraham,
   as you have sworn to our fathers
      from the days of old.

---
[a]Hebrew *bosom* [b]Hebrew *he* [c]That is, the Euphrates
[d]Hebrew *of Carmel* [e]Hebrew *him* [f]Hebrew *their*

NAHUM

1

An oracle concerning Nineveh. The book of the vision of Nahum of Elkosh.

GOD'S WRATH AGAINST NINEVEH

2 The LORD is a jealous and
 avenging God;
 the LORD is avenging and wrathful;
the LORD takes vengeance
 on his adversaries
 and keeps wrath for his enemies.
3 The LORD is slow to anger
 and great in power,
 and the LORD will by no means
 clear the guilty.
His way is in whirlwind and storm,
 and the clouds are the
 dust of his feet.
4 He rebukes the sea and makes it dry;
 he dries up all the rivers;
Bashan and Carmel wither;
 the bloom of Lebanon withers.
5 The mountains quake before him;
 the hills melt;
the earth heaves before him,
 the world and all who dwell in it.

6 Who can stand before his
 indignation?
Who can endure the heat
 of his anger?
His wrath is poured out like fire,
 and the rocks are broken
 into pieces by him.
7 The LORD is good,
 a stronghold in the day of trouble;
he knows those who take
 refuge in him.
8 But with an overflowing flood
 he will make a complete end
 of the adversaries,[a]
 and will pursue his enemies
 into darkness.
9 What do you plot against the LORD?
 He will make a complete end;
 trouble will not rise up
 a second time.
10 For they are like entangled thorns,
 like drunkards as they drink;
they are consumed like
 stubble fully dried.
11 From you came one
 who plotted evil against the LORD,
 a worthless counsellor.

12 Thus says the LORD,
"Though they are at full
 strength and many,
 they will be cut down and pass away.
Though I have afflicted you,
 I will afflict you no more.
13 And now I will break his
 yoke from off you
 and will burst your bonds apart."

14 The LORD has given
 commandment about you:
"No more shall your name
 be perpetuated;
from the house of your
 gods I will cut off
 the carved image and the
 metal image.
I will make your grave, for you are vile."

15[b] Behold, upon the mountains,
 the feet of him
 who brings good news,
 who publishes peace!
Keep your feasts, O Judah;
 fulfil your vows,
for never again shall the worthless
 pass through you;
 he is utterly cut off.

THE DESTRUCTION OF NINEVEH

2

The scatterer has come up against you.
Man the ramparts;
watch the road;
dress for battle;[c]
 collect all your strength.

2 For the LORD is restoring the
 majesty of Jacob
 as the majesty of Israel,

---

[a]Hebrew *of her place* [b]Ch 2:1 in Hebrew [c]Hebrew *gird your loins*

for plunderers have plundered them
 and ruined their branches.

³ The shield of his mighty men is red;
 his soldiers are clothed in scarlet.
The chariots come with flashing metal
 on the day he musters them;
 the cypress spears are brandished.
⁴ The chariots race madly
 through the streets;
they rush to and fro through
 the squares;
they gleam like torches;
 they dart like lightning.
⁵ He remembers his officers;
 they stumble as they go,
they hasten to the wall;
 the siege tower[a] is set up.
⁶ The river gates are opened;
 the palace melts away;
⁷ its mistress[b] is stripped;[c]
 she is carried off,
her slave girls lamenting,
moaning like doves
 and beating their breasts.
⁸ Nineveh is like a pool
 whose waters run away.[d]
"Halt! Halt!" they cry,
 but none turns back.
⁹ Plunder the silver,
 plunder the gold!
There is no end of the treasure
 or of the wealth of all
 precious things.

¹⁰ Desolate! Desolation and ruin!
 Hearts melt and knees tremble;
anguish is in all loins;
 all faces grow pale!
¹¹ Where is the lions' den,
 the feeding place of the young lions,
where the lion and lioness went,
 where his cubs were, with
 none to disturb?
¹² The lion tore enough for his cubs
 and strangled prey for his
 lionesses;
he filled his caves with prey
 and his dens with torn flesh.

¹³Behold, I am against you, declares the Lord of hosts, and I will burn your[e] chariots in smoke, and the sword shall devour your young lions. I will cut off your prey from the earth, and the voice of your messengers shall no longer be heard.

WOE TO NINEVEH

3 Woe to the bloody city,
 all full of lies and plunder—
 no end to the prey!
² The crack of the whip, and
 rumble of the wheel,
galloping horse and
 bounding chariot!
³ Horsemen charging,
 flashing sword and glittering spear,
hosts of slain,
 heaps of corpses,
dead bodies without end—
 they stumble over the bodies!
⁴ And all for the countless whorings
 of the prostitute,
graceful and of deadly charms,
who betrays nations with
 her whorings,
 and peoples with her charms.

⁵ Behold, I am against you,
 declares the Lord of hosts,
and will lift up your skirts
 over your face;
and I will make nations look
 at your nakedness
and kingdoms at your shame.
⁶ I will throw filth at you
 and treat you with contempt
 and make you a spectacle.
⁷ And all who look at you will
 shrink from you and say,
"Wasted is Nineveh; who will
 grieve for her?"
Where shall I seek
 comforters for you?

⁸ Are you better than Thebes[f]
 that sat by the Nile,
with water round her,
 her rampart a sea,
 and water her wall?
⁹ Cush was her strength;
 Egypt too, and that without limit;
Put and the Libyans were
 her[g] helpers.

¹⁰ Yet she became an exile;
 she went into captivity;
her infants were dashed in pieces
 at the head of every street;

---

[a]Or *the mantelet* [b]The meaning of the Hebrew word rendered *its mistress* is uncertain [c]Or *exiled* [d]Compare Septuagint; the meaning of the Hebrew is uncertain [e]Hebrew *her* [f]Hebrew *No-amon* [g]Hebrew *your*

for her honoured men lots were cast,
   and all her great men were
      bound in chains.
11 You also will be drunken;
   you will go into hiding;
you will seek a refuge from the enemy.
12 All your fortresses are like fig trees
   with first-ripe figs —
if shaken they fall
   into the mouth of the eater.
13 Behold, your troops
   are women in your midst.
The gates of your land
   are wide open to your enemies;
   fire has devoured your bars.

14 Draw water for the siege;
   strengthen your forts;
go into the clay;
   tread the mortar;
   take hold of the brick mould!
15 There will the fire devour you;
   the sword will cut you off.
It will devour you like the locust.
Multiply yourselves like the locust;
   multiply like the grasshopper!

16 You increased your merchants
   more than the stars of the heavens.
   The locust spreads its wings
      and flies away.

17 Your princes are like grasshoppers,
   your scribes[a] like clouds of locusts
settling on the fences
   in a day of cold —
when the sun rises, they fly away;
   no one knows where they are.

18 Your shepherds are asleep,
   O king of Assyria;
   your nobles slumber.
Your people are scattered
   on the mountains
   with none to gather them.
19 There is no easing your hurt;
   your wound is grievous.
All who hear the news about you
   clap their hands over you.
For upon whom has not come
   your unceasing evil?

---

[a] Or *marshals*

HABAKKUK

1

The oracle that Habakkuk the prophet saw.

HABAKKUK'S COMPLAINT

2 O Lord, how long shall I cry for help,
  and you will not hear?
Or cry to you "Violence!"
  and you will not save?
3 Why do you make me see iniquity,
  and why do you idly look at wrong?
Destruction and violence
    are before me;
  strife and contention arise.
4 So the law is paralysed,
  and justice never goes forth.
For the wicked surround the righteous;
  so justice goes forth perverted.

THE LORD'S ANSWER

5 "Look among the nations, and see;
    wonder and be astounded.
For I am doing a work in your days
    that you would not believe if told.
6 For behold, I am raising up
    the Chaldeans,
  that bitter and hasty nation,
who march through the
    breadth of the earth,
  to seize dwellings not their own.
7 They are dreaded and fearsome;
  their justice and dignity go
    forth from themselves.
8 Their horses are swifter than leopards,
  more fierce than the evening wolves;
    their horsemen press proudly on.
Their horsemen come from afar;
  they fly like an eagle swift to devour.
9 They all come for violence,
  all their faces forward.
They gather captives like sand.
10 At kings they scoff,
    and at rulers they laugh.
They laugh at every fortress,
    for they pile up earth and take it.
11 Then they sweep by like the
    wind and go on,
  guilty men, whose own
    might is their god!"

HABAKKUK'S SECOND COMPLAINT

12 Are you not from everlasting,
    O Lord my God, my Holy One?
  We shall not die.
O Lord, you have ordained
    them as a judgement,
  and you, O Rock, have established
    them for reproof.
13 You who are of purer eyes
    than to see evil
  and cannot look at wrong,
why do you idly look at traitors
  and remain silent when the
    wicked swallows up
  the man more righteous than he?
14 You make mankind like the
    fish of the sea,
  like crawling things that have no ruler.
15 He[a] brings all of them up with a hook;
  he drags them out with his net;
  he gathers them in his dragnet;
    so he rejoices and is glad.
16 Therefore he sacrifices to his net
    and makes offerings to his dragnet;
  for by them he lives in luxury,[b]
    and his food is rich.
17 Is he then to keep on emptying his net
  and mercilessly killing
    nations for ever?

2

I will take my stand at my watchpost
and station myself on the tower,
and look out to see what he will
    say to me,
  and what I will answer
    concerning my complaint.

THE RIGHTEOUS SHALL LIVE BY HIS FAITH

2 And the Lord answered me:

"Write the vision;
  make it plain on tablets,
  so he may run who reads it.
3 For still the vision awaits its
    appointed time;
  it hastens to the end—it will not lie.

---

[a] That is, the wicked foe [b] Hebrew *his portion is fat*

If it seems slow, wait for it;
   it will surely come; it will not delay.

4 "Behold, his soul is puffed up; it is
      not upright within him,
   but the righteous shall live by
      his faith.[a]

5 "Moreover, wine[b] is a traitor,
      an arrogant man who is
         never at rest.[c]
   His greed is as wide as Sheol;
      like death he has never enough.
   He gathers for himself all nations
      and collects as his own all peoples."

WOE TO THE CHALDEANS

6 Shall not all these take up their taunt against him, with scoffing and riddles for him, and say,

   "Woe to him who heaps up
      what is not his own—
         for how long?—
      and loads himself with pledges!"
7 Will not your debtors suddenly arise,
      and those awake who will
         make you tremble?
   Then you will be spoil for them.
8 Because you have plundered
      many nations,
   all the remnant of the peoples
      shall plunder you,
   for the blood of man and
      violence to the earth,
   to cities and all who dwell in them.

9 "Woe to him who gets evil
      gain for his house,
   to set his nest on high,
   to be safe from the reach of harm!
10 You have devised shame
      for your house
   by cutting off many peoples;
      you have forfeited your life.
11 For the stone will cry out from the wall,
      and the beam from the
         woodwork respond.

12 "Woe to him who builds a
      town with blood
   and founds a city on iniquity!
13 Behold, is it not from the LORD of hosts
   that peoples labour merely for fire,
      and nations weary themselves
         for nothing?
14 For the earth will be filled
      with the knowledge of the
         glory of the LORD
   as the waters cover the sea.

15 "Woe to him who makes his
      neighbours drink—
   you pour out your wrath and
      make them drunk,
   in order to gaze at their nakedness!
16 You will have your fill of shame
      instead of glory.
   Drink, yourself, and show
      your uncircumcision!
   The cup in the LORD's right hand
      will come round to you,
   and utter shame will come
      upon your glory!
17 The violence done to Lebanon
      will overwhelm you,
   as will the destruction of the
      beasts that terrified them,
   for the blood of man and
      violence to the earth,
   to cities and all who dwell in them.

18 "What profit is an idol
      when its maker has shaped it,
   a metal image, a teacher of lies?
   For its maker trusts in his
      own creation
   when he makes speechless idols!
19 Woe to him who says to a
      wooden thing, Awake;
   to a silent stone, Arise!
   Can this teach?
   Behold, it is overlaid with
      gold and silver,
   and there is no breath at all in it.
20 But the LORD is in his holy temple;
   let all the earth keep silence
      before him."

HABAKKUK'S PRAYER

3 A prayer of Habakkuk the prophet, according to Shigionoth.

2 O LORD, I have heard the report of you,
      and your work, O LORD, do I fear.
   In the midst of the years revive it;
      in the midst of the years
         make it known;
      in wrath remember mercy.

---

[a] Or *faithfulness* [b] Masoretic Text; Dead Sea Scroll *wealth*
[c] The meaning of the Hebrew of these two lines is uncertain

³ God came from Teman,
  and the Holy One from
    Mount Paran.   *Selah*
  His splendour covered the heavens,
    and the earth was full of his praise.
⁴ His brightness was like the light;
    rays flashed from his hand;
    and there he veiled his power.
⁵ Before him went pestilence,
    and plague followed at his heels.ᵃ
⁶ He stood and measured the earth;
    he looked and shook the nations;
  then the eternal mountains
      were scattered;
    the everlasting hills sank low.
    His were the everlasting ways.
⁷ I saw the tents of Cushan in affliction;
    the curtains of the land of
      Midian did tremble.
⁸ Was your wrath against the
      rivers, O Lord?
  Was your anger against the rivers,
    or your indignation against the sea,
  when you rode on your horses,
    on your chariot of salvation?
⁹ You stripped the sheath
      from your bow,
    calling for many arrows.ᵇ   *Selah*
  You split the earth with rivers.
¹⁰ The mountains saw you and writhed;
    the raging waters swept on;
  the deep gave forth its voice;
    it lifted its hands on high.
¹¹ The sun and moon stood
      still in their place
    at the light of your arrows
      as they sped,
    at the flash of your glittering spear.
¹² You marched through the earth in fury;
    you threshed the nations in anger.
¹³ You went out for the salvation
      of your people,
    for the salvation of your anointed.
  You crushed the head of the
      house of the wicked,
    laying him bare from thigh
      to neck.ᶜ   *Selah*
¹⁴ You pierced with his own arrows
      the heads of his warriors,
    who came like a whirlwind
      to scatter me,
    rejoicing as if to devour
      the poor in secret.
¹⁵ You trampled the sea with your horses,
    the surging of mighty waters.
¹⁶ I hear, and my body trembles;
    my lips quiver at the sound;
  rottenness enters into my bones;
    my legs tremble beneath me.
  Yet I will quietly wait for
      the day of trouble
    to come upon people who
      invade us.

HABAKKUK REJOICES IN THE LORD

¹⁷ Though the fig tree should
      not blossom,
    nor fruit be on the vines,
  the produce of the olive fail
    and the fields yield no food,
  the flock be cut off from the fold
    and there be no herd in the stalls,
¹⁸ yet I will rejoice in the Lord;
    I will take joy in the God
      of my salvation.
¹⁹ God, the Lord, is my strength;
    he makes my feet like the deer's;
    he makes me tread on
      my high places.

To the choirmaster: with
    stringedᵈ instruments.

ᵃHebrew *feet*   ᵇThe meaning of the Hebrew line is uncertain
ᶜThe meaning of the Hebrew line is uncertain   ᵈHebrew *my stringed*

ZEPHANIAH

1 The word of the Lord that came to Zephaniah the son of Cushi, son of Gedaliah, son of Amariah, son of Hezekiah, in the days of Josiah the son of Amon, king of Judah.

THE COMING JUDGEMENT ON JUDAH

2 "I will utterly sweep away everything
    from the face of the earth,"
        declares the Lord.
3 "I will sweep away man and beast;
    I will sweep away the birds
        of the heavens
    and the fish of the sea,
    and the rubble[a] with the wicked.
    I will cut off mankind
        from the face of the earth,"
            declares the Lord.
4 "I will stretch out my hand
        against Judah
    and against all the inhabitants
        of Jerusalem;
    and I will cut off from this place
        the remnant of Baal
    and the name of the idolatrous
        priests along with the priests,
5 those who bow down on the roofs
        to the host of the heavens,
    those who bow down and
        swear to the Lord
    and yet swear by Milcom,[b]
6 those who have turned back
        from following the Lord,
    who do not seek the Lord
        or enquire of him."

THE DAY OF THE LORD IS NEAR

7 Be silent before the Lord God!
    For the day of the Lord is near;
    the Lord has prepared a sacrifice
        and consecrated his guests.
8 And on the day of the Lord's sacrifice—
    "I will punish the officials
        and the king's sons
    and all who array themselves
        in foreign attire.
9 On that day I will punish
    everyone who leaps over
        the threshold,
    and those who fill their master's[c] house
        with violence and fraud.
10 "On that day," declares the Lord,
    "a cry will be heard from
        the Fish Gate,
    a wail from the Second Quarter,
        a loud crash from the hills.
11 Wail, O inhabitants of the Mortar!
    For all the traders[d] are no more;
    all who weigh out silver are cut off.
12 At that time I will search
        Jerusalem with lamps,
    and I will punish the men
        who are complacent,[e]
    those who say in their hearts,
    'The Lord will not do good,
        nor will he do ill.'
13 Their goods shall be plundered,
        and their houses laid waste.
    Though they build houses,
        they shall not inhabit them;
    though they plant vineyards,
        they shall not drink wine
            from them."

14 The great day of the Lord is near,
        near and hastening fast;
    the sound of the day of the
        Lord is bitter;
    the mighty man cries aloud there.
15 A day of wrath is that day,
    a day of distress and anguish,
    a day of ruin and devastation,
    a day of darkness and gloom,
    a day of clouds and thick darkness,
16 a day of trumpet blast and battle cry
    against the fortified cities
    and against the lofty battlements.

17 I will bring distress on mankind,
    so that they shall walk like the blind,
    because they have sinned
        against the Lord;

---

[a] Or *stumbling blocks* (that is, idols) [b] Or *their king* [c] Or *their Lord's* [d] Or *all the people of Canaan* [e] Hebrew *are thickening on the dregs* [of their wine]

their blood shall be poured
  out like dust,
and their flesh like dung.
¹⁸ Neither their silver nor their gold
  shall be able to deliver them
  on the day of the wrath of the Lord.
In the fire of his jealousy,
  all the earth shall be consumed;
for a full and sudden end
  he will make of all the
    inhabitants of the earth.

JUDGEMENT ON JUDAH'S ENEMIES

2 Gather together, yes, gather,
    O shameless nation,
  ²before the decree takes effect*ᵃ*
    —before the day passes
      away like chaff—
  before there comes upon you
    the burning anger of the Lord,
  before there comes upon you
    the day of the anger of the Lord.
³ Seek the Lord, all you
    humble of the land,
  who do his just commands;*ᵇ*
  seek righteousness; seek humility;
    perhaps you may be hidden
    on the day of the anger of the Lord.
⁴ For Gaza shall be deserted,
    and Ashkelon shall become
      a desolation;
  Ashdod's people shall be
    driven out at noon,
    and Ekron shall be uprooted.

⁵ Woe to you inhabitants
    of the sea coast,
    you nation of the Cherethites!
  The word of the Lord is against you,
    O Canaan, land of the Philistines;
    and I will destroy you until
      no inhabitant is left.
⁶ And you, O sea coast, shall be
    pastures,
    with meadows*ᶜ* for shepherds
    and folds for flocks.
⁷ The sea coast shall become
    the possession
    of the remnant of the
      house of Judah,
    on which they shall graze,
    and in the houses of Ashkelon
    they shall lie down at evening.
  For the Lord their God will
    be mindful of them
    and restore their fortunes.

⁸ "I have heard the taunts of Moab
    and the revilings of the Ammonites,
  how they have taunted my people
    and made boasts against
      their territory.
⁹ Therefore, as I live," declares
    the Lord of hosts,
    the God of Israel,
  "Moab shall become like Sodom,
    and the Ammonites like Gomorrah,
  a land possessed by nettles
    and salt pits,
    and a waste for ever.
  The remnant of my people
    shall plunder them,
    and the survivors of my nation
    shall possess them."
¹⁰ This shall be their lot in
    return for their pride,
  because they taunted and boasted
    against the people of the
      Lord of hosts.
¹¹ The Lord will be awesome
    against them;
  for he will famish all the
    gods of the earth,
  and to him shall bow down,
    each in its place,
    all the lands of the nations.

¹² You also, O Cushites,
    shall be slain by my sword.

¹³ And he will stretch out his
    hand against the north
    and destroy Assyria,
  and he will make Nineveh
    a desolation,
    a dry waste like the desert.
¹⁴ Herds shall lie down in her midst,
    all kinds of beasts;*ᵈ*
  even the owl and the hedgehog*ᵉ*
    shall lodge in her capitals;
  a voice shall hoot in the window;
    devastation will be on the threshold;
    for her cedar work will be laid bare.
¹⁵ This is the exultant city
    that lived securely,
  that said in her heart,
    "I am, and there is no one else."
  What a desolation she has become,
    a lair for wild beasts!

---

*ᵃ*Hebrew *gives birth*   *ᵇ*Or *who carry out his judgement*   *ᶜ*Or *caves*
*ᵈ*Hebrew *beasts of every nation*   *ᵉ*The identity of the animals rendered *owl* and *hedgehog* is uncertain

Everyone who passes by her
   hisses and shakes his fist.

JUDGEMENT ON JERUSALEM AND THE NATIONS

3 Woe to her who is rebellious and defiled,
   the oppressing city!
2 She listens to no voice;
   she accepts no correction.
She does not trust in the Lord;
   she does not draw near to
     her God.

3 Her officials within her
   are roaring lions;
her judges are evening wolves
   that leave nothing till the morning.
4 Her prophets are fickle,
   treacherous men;
her priests profane what is holy;
   they do violence to the law.
5 The Lord within her is righteous;
   he does no injustice;
every morning he shows
   forth his justice;
     each dawn he does not fail;
but the unjust knows no shame.

6 "I have cut off nations;
   their battlements are in ruins;
I have laid waste their streets
   so that no one walks in them;
their cities have been made desolate,
   without a man, without
     an inhabitant.
7 I said, 'Surely you will fear me;
   you will accept correction.
Then your*a* dwelling would
   not be cut off
according to all that I have
   appointed against you.'*b*
But all the more they were eager
   to make all their deeds corrupt.

8 "Therefore wait for me,"
   declares the Lord,
"for the day when I rise up
   to seize the prey.
For my decision is to gather nations,
   to assemble kingdoms,
to pour out upon them my
   indignation,
   all my burning anger;
for in the fire of my jealousy
   all the earth shall be consumed.

THE CONVERSION OF THE NATIONS

9 "For at that time I will change the
   speech of the peoples
   to a pure speech,
that all of them may call upon
   the name of the Lord
and serve him with one accord.
10 From beyond the rivers of Cush
   my worshippers, the daughter
     of my dispersed ones,
   shall bring my offering.

11 "On that day you shall not
   be put to shame
because of the deeds by which you
   have rebelled against me;
for then I will remove from your midst
   your proudly exultant ones,
and you shall no longer be haughty
   in my holy mountain.
12 But I will leave in your midst
   a people humble and lowly.
They shall seek refuge in the
   name of the Lord,
13 those who are left in Israel;
they shall do no injustice
   and speak no lies,
nor shall there be found in
   their mouth
   a deceitful tongue.
For they shall graze and lie down,
   and none shall make them afraid."

ISRAEL'S JOY AND RESTORATION

14 Sing aloud, O daughter of Zion;
   shout, O Israel!
Rejoice and exult with all your heart,
   O daughter of Jerusalem!
15 The Lord has taken away the
   judgements against you;
he has cleared away your enemies.
The King of Israel, the Lord,
   is in your midst;
you shall never again fear evil.
16 On that day it shall be said
   to Jerusalem:
"Fear not, O Zion;
   let not your hands grow weak.
17 The Lord your God is in your midst,
   a mighty one who will save;
he will rejoice over you with gladness;
   he will quiet you by his love;
he will exult over you with
   loud singing.

---

a Hebrew *her* *b* Hebrew *her*

18 I will gather those of you who
        mourn for the festival,
    so that you will no longer
        suffer reproach.ᵃ
19 Behold, at that time I will deal
        with all your oppressors.
    And I will save the lame
        and gather the outcast,
    and I will change their shame into praise
        and renown in all the earth.

20 At that time I will bring you in,
        at the time when I gather
            you together;
    for I will make you renowned
            and praised
        among all the peoples of the earth,
    when I restore your fortunes
        before your eyes," says the LORD.

ᵃThe meaning of the Hebrew is uncertain

HAGGAI

THE COMMAND TO REBUILD THE TEMPLE

1 In the second year of Darius the king, in the sixth month, on the first day of the month, the word of the Lord came by the hand of Haggai the prophet to Zerubbabel the son of Shealtiel, governor of Judah, and to Joshua the son of Jehozadak, the high priest: ²"Thus says the Lord of hosts: These people say the time has not yet come to rebuild the house of the Lord." ³Then the word of the Lord came by the hand of Haggai the prophet, ⁴"Is it a time for you yourselves to dwell in your panelled houses, while this house lies in ruins? ⁵Now, therefore, thus says the Lord of hosts: Consider your ways. ⁶You have sown much, and harvested little. You eat, but you never have enough; you drink, but you never have your fill. You clothe yourselves, but no one is warm. And he who earns wages does so to put them into a bag with holes.

⁷"Thus says the Lord of hosts: Consider your ways. ⁸Go up to the hills and bring wood and build the house, that I may take pleasure in it and that I may be glorified, says the Lord. ⁹You looked for much, and behold, it came to little. And when you brought it home, I blew it away. Why? declares the Lord of hosts. Because of my house that lies in ruins, while each of you busies himself with his own house. ¹⁰Therefore the heavens above you have withheld the dew, and the earth has withheld its produce. ¹¹And I have called for a drought on the land and the hills, on the grain, the new wine, the oil, on what the ground brings forth, on man and beast, and on all their labours."

THE PEOPLE OBEY THE LORD

¹²Then Zerubbabel the son of Shealtiel, and Joshua the son of Jehozadak, the high priest, with all the remnant of the people, obeyed the voice of the Lord their God, and the words of Haggai the prophet, as the Lord their God had sent him. And the people feared the Lord. ¹³Then Haggai, the messenger of the Lord, spoke to the people with the Lord's message, "I am with you, declares the Lord." ¹⁴And the Lord stirred up the spirit of Zerubbabel the son of Shealtiel, governor of Judah, and the spirit of Joshua the son of Jehozadak, the high priest, and the spirit of all the remnant of the people. And they came and worked on the house of the Lord of hosts, their God, ¹⁵on the twenty-fourth day of the month, in the sixth month, in the second year of Darius the king.

THE COMING GLORY OF THE TEMPLE

2 In the seventh month, on the twenty-first day of the month, the word of the Lord came by the hand of Haggai the prophet: ²"Speak now to Zerubbabel the son of Shealtiel, governor of Judah, and to Joshua the son of Jehozadak, the high priest, and to all the remnant of the people, and say, ³'Who is left among you who saw this house in its former glory? How do you see it now? Is it not as nothing in your eyes? ⁴Yet now be strong, O Zerubbabel, declares the Lord. Be strong, O Joshua, son of Jehozadak, the high priest. Be strong, all you people of the land, declares the Lord. Work, for I am with you, declares the Lord of hosts, ⁵according to the covenant that I made with you when you came out of Egypt. My Spirit remains in your midst. Fear not. ⁶For thus says the Lord of hosts: Yet once more, in a little while, I will shake the heavens and the earth and the sea and the dry land. ⁷And I will shake all nations, so that the treasures of all nations shall come in, and I will fill this house with glory, says the Lord of hosts. ⁸The silver is mine, and the gold is mine, declares the Lord of hosts. ⁹The latter glory of this house shall be greater than the former, says the Lord of hosts. And in this place I will give peace, declares the Lord of hosts.'"

BLESSINGS FOR A DEFILED PEOPLE

¹⁰On the twenty-fourth day of the ninth month, in the second year of Darius, the word of the Lord came by Haggai the prophet, ¹¹"Thus says the Lord of hosts: Ask the priests about the law: ¹²'If someone carries holy meat in the fold of his garment and touches

with his fold bread or stew or wine or oil or any kind of food, does it become holy?'" The priests answered and said, "No." ¹³Then Haggai said, "If someone who is unclean by contact with a dead body touches any of these, does it become unclean?" The priests answered and said, "It does become unclean." ¹⁴Then Haggai answered and said, "So is it with this people, and with this nation before me, declares the LORD, and so with every work of their hands. And what they offer there is unclean. ¹⁵Now then, consider from this day onward.ᵃ Before stone was placed upon stone in the temple of the LORD, ¹⁶how did you fare? Whenᵇ one came to a heap of twenty measures, there were but ten. When one came to the wine vat to draw fifty measures, there were but twenty. ¹⁷I struck you and all the products of your toil with blight and with mildew and with hail, yet you did not turn to me, declares the LORD. ¹⁸Consider from this day onward, from the twenty-fourth day of the ninth month. Since the day that the foundation of the LORD's temple was laid, consider: ¹⁹Is the seed yet in the barn? Indeed, the vine, the fig tree, the pomegranate, and the olive tree have yielded nothing. But from this day on I will bless you."

ZERUBBABEL CHOSEN AS A SIGNET

²⁰The word of the LORD came a second time to Haggai on the twenty-fourth day of the month, ²¹"Speak to Zerubbabel, governor of Judah, saying, I am about to shake the heavens and the earth, ²²and to overthrow the throne of kingdoms. I am about to destroy the strength of the kingdoms of the nations, and overthrow the chariots and their riders. And the horses and their riders shall go down, every one by the sword of his brother. ²³On that day, declares the LORD of hosts, I will take you, O Zerubbabel my servant, the son of Shealtiel, declares the LORD, and make you like aᶜ signet ring, for I have chosen you, declares the LORD of hosts."

ᵃOr *backward*; also verse 18 ᵇProbable reading (compare Septuagint); Hebrew *LORD, since they were. When* ᶜHebrew *the*

ZECHARIAH

A CALL TO RETURN TO THE LORD

1 In the eighth month, in the second year of Darius, the word of the LORD came to the prophet Zechariah, the son of Berechiah, son of Iddo, saying, ²"The LORD was very angry with your fathers. ³Therefore say to them, Thus declares the LORD of hosts: Return to me, says the LORD of hosts, and I will return to you, says the LORD of hosts. ⁴Do not be like your fathers, to whom the former prophets cried out, 'Thus says the LORD of hosts, Return from your evil ways and from your evil deeds.' But they did not hear or pay attention to me, declares the LORD. ⁵Your fathers, where are they? And the prophets, do they live for ever? ⁶But my words and my statutes, which I commanded my servants the prophets, did they not overtake your fathers? So they repented and said, 'As the LORD of hosts purposed to deal with us for our ways and deeds, so has he dealt with us.'"

A VISION OF A HORSEMAN

⁷On the twenty-fourth day of the eleventh month, which is the month of Shebat, in the second year of Darius, the word of the LORD came to the prophet Zechariah, the son of Berechiah, son of Iddo, saying, ⁸"I saw in the night, and behold, a man riding on a red horse! He was standing among the myrtle trees in the glen, and behind him were red, sorrel, and white horses. ⁹Then I said, 'What are these, my lord?' The angel who talked with me said to me, 'I will show you what they are.' ¹⁰So the man who was standing among the myrtle trees answered, 'These are they whom the LORD has sent to patrol the earth.' ¹¹And they answered the angel of the LORD who was standing among the myrtle trees, and said, 'We have patrolled the earth, and behold, all the earth remains at rest.' ¹²Then the angel of the LORD said, 'O LORD of hosts, how long will you have no mercy on Jerusalem and the cities of Judah, against which you have been angry these seventy years?' ¹³And the LORD answered gracious and comforting words to the angel who talked with me. ¹⁴So the angel who talked with me said to me, 'Cry out, Thus says the LORD of hosts: I am exceedingly jealous for Jerusalem and for Zion. ¹⁵And I am exceedingly angry with the nations that are at ease; for while I was angry but a little, they furthered the disaster. ¹⁶Therefore, thus says the LORD, I have returned to Jerusalem with mercy; my house shall be built in it, declares the LORD of hosts, and the measuring line shall be stretched out over Jerusalem. ¹⁷Cry out again, Thus says the LORD of hosts: My cities shall again overflow with prosperity, and the LORD will again comfort Zion and again choose Jerusalem.'"

A VISION OF HORNS AND CRAFTSMEN

¹⁸ᵃ And I lifted my eyes and saw, and behold, four horns! ¹⁹And I said to the angel who talked with me, "What are these?" And he said to me, "These are the horns that have scattered Judah, Israel, and Jerusalem." ²⁰Then the LORD showed me four craftsmen. ²¹And I said, "What are these coming to do?" He said, "These are the horns that scattered Judah, so that no one raised his head. And these have come to terrify them, to cast down the horns of the nations who lifted up their horns against the land of Judah to scatter it."

A VISION OF A MAN WITH A MEASURING LINE

2ᵇ And I lifted my eyes and saw, and behold, a man with a measuring line in his hand! ²Then I said, "Where are you going?" And he said to me, "To measure Jerusalem, to see what is its width and what is its length." ³And behold, the angel who talked with me came forward, and another angel came forward to meet him ⁴and said to him, "Run, say to that young man, 'Jerusalem shall be inhabited as villages without walls, because of the multitude of people and livestock in it. ⁵And I will be to her a wall of fire all round, declares the LORD, and I will be the glory in her midst.'"

⁶Up! Up! Flee from the land of the north, declares the LORD. For I have spread you

---

ᵃCh 2:1 in Hebrew ᵇCh 2:5 in Hebrew

abroad as the four winds of the heavens, declares the LORD. ⁷Up! Escape to Zion, you who dwell with the daughter of Babylon. ⁸For thus said the LORD of hosts, after his glory sent me[a] to the nations who plundered you, for he who touches you touches the apple of his eye: ⁹"Behold, I will shake my hand over them, and they shall become plunder for those who served them. Then you will know that the LORD of hosts has sent me. ¹⁰Sing and rejoice, O daughter of Zion, for behold, I come and I will dwell in your midst, declares the LORD. ¹¹And many nations shall join themselves to the LORD in that day, and shall be my people. And I will dwell in your midst, and you shall know that the LORD of hosts has sent me to you. ¹²And the LORD will inherit Judah as his portion in the holy land, and will again choose Jerusalem."

¹³Be silent, all flesh, before the LORD, for he has roused himself from his holy dwelling.

A VISION OF JOSHUA THE HIGH PRIEST

3 Then he showed me Joshua the high priest standing before the angel of the LORD, and Satan[b] standing at his right hand to accuse him. ²And the LORD said to Satan, "The LORD rebuke you, O Satan! The LORD who has chosen Jerusalem rebuke you! Is not this a brand[c] plucked from the fire?" ³Now Joshua was standing before the angel, clothed with filthy garments. ⁴And the angel said to those who were standing before him, "Remove the filthy garments from him." And to him he said, "Behold, I have taken your iniquity away from you, and I will clothe you with pure vestments." ⁵And I said, "Let them put a clean turban on his head." So they put a clean turban on his head and clothed him with garments. And the angel of the LORD was standing by.

⁶And the angel of the LORD solemnly assured Joshua, ⁷"Thus says the LORD of hosts: If you will walk in my ways and keep my charge, then you shall rule my house and have charge of my courts, and I will give you the right of access among those who are standing here. ⁸Hear now, O Joshua the high priest, you and your friends who sit before you, for they are men who are a sign: behold, I will bring my servant the Branch. ⁹For behold, on the stone that I have set before Joshua, on a single stone with seven eyes,[d] I will engrave its inscription, declares the LORD of hosts, and I will remove the iniquity of this land in a single day. ¹⁰In that day, declares the LORD of hosts, every one of you will invite his neighbour to come under his vine and under his fig tree."

A VISION OF A GOLDEN LAMPSTAND

4 And the angel who talked with me came again and woke me, like a man who is awakened out of his sleep. ²And he said to me, "What do you see?" I said, "I see, and behold, a lampstand all of gold, with a bowl on the top of it, and seven lamps on it, with seven lips on each of the lamps that are on the top of it. ³And there are two olive trees by it, one on the right of the bowl and the other on its left." ⁴And I said to the angel who talked with me, "What are these, my lord?" ⁵Then the angel who talked with me answered and said to me, "Do you not know what these are?" I said, "No, my lord." ⁶Then he said to me, "This is the word of the LORD to Zerubbabel: Not by might, nor by power, but by my Spirit, says the LORD of hosts. ⁷Who are you, O great mountain? Before Zerubbabel you shall become a plain. And he shall bring forward the top stone amid shouts of 'Grace, grace to it!'"

⁸Then the word of the LORD came to me, saying, ⁹"The hands of Zerubbabel have laid the foundation of this house; his hands shall also complete it. Then you will know that the LORD of hosts has sent me to you. ¹⁰For whoever has despised the day of small things shall rejoice, and shall see the plumb line in the hand of Zerubbabel.

"These seven are the eyes of the LORD, which range through the whole earth." ¹¹Then I said to him, "What are these two olive trees on the right and the left of the lampstand?" ¹²And a second time I answered and said to him, "What are these two branches of the olive trees, which are beside the two golden pipes from which the golden oil[e] is poured out?" ¹³He said to me, "Do you not know what these are?" I said, "No, my lord." ¹⁴Then he said, "These are the two anointed ones[f] who stand by the Lord of the whole earth."

A VISION OF A FLYING SCROLL

5 Again I lifted my eyes and saw, and behold, a flying scroll! ²And he said to me, "What do you see?" I answered, "I see a flying scroll. Its length is twenty cubits,

---

[a] Or *he sent me after glory* [b] Hebrew *the Accuser* or *the Adversary* [c] That is, a burning stick [d] Or *facets* [e] Hebrew lacks *oil* [f] Hebrew *two sons of new oil*

and its width ten cubits."[a] ³Then he said to me, "This is the curse that goes out over the face of the whole land. For everyone who steals shall be cleaned out according to what is on one side, and everyone who swears falsely[b] shall be cleaned out according to what is on the other side. ⁴I will send it out, declares the LORD of hosts, and it shall enter the house of the thief, and the house of him who swears falsely by my name. And it shall remain in his house and consume it, both timber and stones."

A VISION OF A WOMAN IN A BASKET

⁵Then the angel who talked with me came forward and said to me, "Lift your eyes and see what this is that is going out." ⁶And I said, "What is it?" He said, "This is the basket[c] that is going out." And he said, "This is their iniquity[d] in all the land." ⁷And behold, the leaden cover was lifted, and there was a woman sitting in the basket! ⁸And he said, "This is Wickedness." And he thrust her back into the basket, and thrust down the leaden weight on its opening.

⁹Then I lifted my eyes and saw, and behold, two women coming forward! The wind was in their wings. They had wings like the wings of a stork, and they lifted up the basket between earth and heaven. ¹⁰Then I said to the angel who talked with me, "Where are they taking the basket?" ¹¹He said to me, "To the land of Shinar, to build a house for it. And when this is prepared, they will set the basket down there on its base."

A VISION OF FOUR CHARIOTS

6 Again I lifted my eyes and saw, and behold, four chariots came out from between two mountains. And the mountains were mountains of bronze. ²The first chariot had red horses, the second black horses, ³the third white horses, and the fourth chariot dappled horses—all of them strong.[e] ⁴Then I answered and said to the angel who talked with me, "What are these, my lord?" ⁵And the angel answered and said to me, "These are going out to the four winds of heaven, after presenting themselves before the Lord of all the earth. ⁶The chariot with the black horses goes towards the north country, the white ones go after them, and the dappled ones go towards the south country." ⁷When the strong horses came out, they were impatient to go and patrol the earth. And he said, "Go, patrol the earth." So they patrolled the earth. ⁸Then he cried to me, "Behold, those who go towards the north country have set my Spirit at rest in the north country."

THE CROWN AND THE TEMPLE

⁹And the word of the LORD came to me: ¹⁰"Take from the exiles Heldai, Tobijah, and Jedaiah, who have arrived from Babylon, and go the same day to the house of Josiah, the son of Zephaniah. ¹¹Take from them silver and gold, and make a crown, and set it on the head of Joshua, the son of Jehozadak, the high priest. ¹²And say to him, 'Thus says the LORD of hosts, 'Behold, the man whose name is the Branch: for he shall branch out from his place, and he shall build the temple of the LORD. ¹³It is he who shall build the temple of the LORD and shall bear royal honour, and shall sit and rule on his throne. And there[f] shall be a priest on his throne, and the counsel of peace shall be between them both.'' ¹⁴And the crown shall be in the temple of the LORD as a reminder to Helem,[g] Tobijah, Jedaiah, and Hen the son of Zephaniah.

¹⁵"And those who are far off shall come and help to build the temple of the LORD. And you shall know that the LORD of hosts has sent me to you. And this shall come to pass, if you will diligently obey the voice of the LORD your God."

A CALL FOR JUSTICE AND MERCY

7 In the fourth year of King Darius, the word of the LORD came to Zechariah on the fourth day of the ninth month, which is Chislev. ²Now the people of Bethel had sent Sharezer and Regem-melech and their men to entreat the favour of the LORD, ³saying to the priests of the house of the LORD of hosts and the prophets, "Should I weep and abstain in the fifth month, as I have done for so many years?"

⁴Then the word of the LORD of hosts came to me: ⁵"Say to all the people of the land and the priests, 'When you fasted and mourned in the fifth month and in the seventh, for these seventy years, was it for me that you fasted? ⁶And when you eat and when you drink, do you not eat for yourselves and drink for

---

[a] A *cubit* was about 18 inches or 45 centimetres [b] Hebrew lacks *falsely* (supplied from verse 4) [c] Hebrew *ephah*; also verses 7–11. An *ephah* was about 3/5 of a bushel or 22 litres [d] One Hebrew manuscript, Septuagint, Syriac; most Hebrew manuscripts *eye* [e] Or *and the fourth chariot strong dappled horses* [f] Or *he* [g] An alternate spelling of *Heldai* (verse 10)

yourselves? ⁷Were not these the words that the Lord proclaimed by the former prophets, when Jerusalem was inhabited and prosperous, with her cities round her, and the South and the lowland were inhabited?'"

⁸And the word of the Lord came to Zechariah, saying, ⁹"Thus says the Lord of hosts, Render true judgements, show kindness and mercy to one another, ¹⁰do not oppress the widow, the fatherless, the sojourner, or the poor, and let none of you devise evil against another in your heart." ¹¹But they refused to pay attention and turned a stubborn shoulder and stopped their ears that they might not hear.ᵃ ¹²They made their hearts diamond-hard lest they should hear the law and the words that the Lord of hosts had sent by his Spirit through the former prophets. Therefore great anger came from the Lord of hosts. ¹³"As Iᵇ called, and they would not hear, so they called, and I would not hear," says the Lord of hosts, ¹⁴"and I scattered them with a whirlwind among all the nations that they had not known. Thus the land they left was desolate, so that no one went to and fro, and the pleasant land was made desolate."

THE COMING PEACE AND PROSPERITY OF ZION

8 And the word of the Lord of hosts came, saying, ²"Thus says the Lord of hosts: I am jealous for Zion with great jealousy, and I am jealous for her with great wrath. ³Thus says the Lord: I have returned to Zion and will dwell in the midst of Jerusalem, and Jerusalem shall be called the faithful city, and the mountain of the Lord of hosts, the holy mountain. ⁴Thus says the Lord of hosts: Old men and old women shall again sit in the streets of Jerusalem, each with staff in hand because of great age. ⁵And the streets of the city shall be full of boys and girls playing in its streets. ⁶Thus says the Lord of hosts: If it is marvellous in the sight of the remnant of this people in those days, should it also be marvellous in my sight, declares the Lord of hosts? ⁷Thus says the Lord of hosts: Behold, I will save my people from the east country and from the west country, ⁸and I will bring them to dwell in the midst of Jerusalem. And they shall be my people, and I will be their God, in faithfulness and in righteousness."

⁹Thus says the Lord of hosts: "Let your hands be strong, you who in these days have been hearing these words from the mouth of the prophets who were present on the day that the foundation of the house of the Lord of hosts was laid, that the temple might be built. ¹⁰For before those days there was no wage for man or any wage for beast, neither was there any safety from the foe for him who went out or came in, for I set every man against his neighbour. ¹¹But now I will not deal with the remnant of this people as in the former days, declares the Lord of hosts. ¹²For there shall be a sowing of peace. The vine shall give its fruit, and the ground shall give its produce, and the heavens shall give their dew. And I will cause the remnant of this people to possess all these things. ¹³And as you have been a byword of cursing among the nations, O house of Judah and house of Israel, so will I save you, and you shall be a blessing. Fear not, but let your hands be strong."

¹⁴For thus says the Lord of hosts: "As I purposed to bring disaster to you when your fathers provoked me to wrath, and I did not relent, says the Lord of hosts, ¹⁵so again have I purposed in these days to bring good to Jerusalem and to the house of Judah; fear not. ¹⁶These are the things that you shall do: Speak the truth to one another; render in your gates judgements that are true and make for peace; ¹⁷do not devise evil in your hearts against one another, and love no false oath, for all these things I hate, declares the Lord."

¹⁸And the word of the Lord of hosts came to me, saying, ¹⁹"Thus says the Lord of hosts: The fast of the fourth month and the fast of the fifth and the fast of the seventh and the fast of the tenth shall be to the house of Judah seasons of joy and gladness and cheerful feasts. Therefore love truth and peace.

²⁰"Thus says the Lord of hosts: Peoples shall yet come, even the inhabitants of many cities. ²¹The inhabitants of one city shall go to another, saying, 'Let us go at once to entreat the favour of the Lord and to seek the Lord of hosts; I myself am going.' ²²Many peoples and strong nations shall come to seek the Lord of hosts in Jerusalem and to entreat the favour of the Lord. ²³Thus says the Lord of hosts: In those days ten men from the nations of every tongue shall take hold of the robe of a Jew, saying, 'Let us go with you, for we have heard that God is with you.'"

ᵃ Hebrew *and made their ears too heavy to hear*   ᵇ Hebrew *he*

JUDGEMENT ON ISRAEL'S ENEMIES

9 The oracle of the word of the Lord is
against the land of Hadrach
and Damascus is its resting-place.
For the Lord has an eye on mankind
and on all the tribes of Israel,[a]
2 and on Hamath also, which
borders on it,
Tyre and Sidon, though
they are very wise.
3 Tyre has built herself a rampart
and heaped up silver like dust,
and fine gold like the mud
of the streets.
4 But behold, the Lord will strip
her of her possessions
and strike down her power
on the sea,
and she shall be devoured by fire.

5 Ashkelon shall see it, and be afraid;
Gaza too, and shall writhe
in anguish;
Ekron also, because its hopes
are confounded.
The king shall perish from Gaza;
Ashkelon shall be uninhabited;
6 a mixed people[b] shall dwell in Ashdod,
and I will cut off the pride of Philistia.
7 I will take away its blood
from its mouth,
and its abominations from
between its teeth;
it too shall be a remnant for our God;
it shall be like a clan in Judah,
and Ekron shall be like the Jebusites.
8 Then I will encamp at my
house as a guard,
so that none shall march to and fro;
no oppressor shall again
march over them,
for now I see with my own eyes.

THE COMING KING OF ZION

9 Rejoice greatly, O daughter of Zion!
Shout aloud, O daughter
of Jerusalem!
Behold, your king is coming to you;
righteous and having salvation is he,
humble and mounted on a donkey,
on a colt, the foal of a donkey.
10 I will cut off the chariot from Ephraim
and the war horse from Jerusalem;
and the battle bow shall be cut off,
and he shall speak peace
to the nations;
his rule shall be from sea to sea,
and from the River[c] to the
ends of the earth.
11 As for you also, because of the blood
of my covenant with you,
I will set your prisoners free
from the waterless pit.
12 Return to your stronghold, O
prisoners of hope;
today I declare that I will
restore to you double.
13 For I have bent Judah as my bow;
I have made Ephraim its arrow.
I will stir up your sons, O Zion,
against your sons, O Greece,
and wield you like a warrior's sword.

THE LORD WILL SAVE HIS PEOPLE

14 Then the Lord will appear over them,
and his arrow will go forth
like lightning;
the Lord God will sound the trumpet
and will march forth in the
whirlwinds of the south.
15 The Lord of hosts will protect them,
and they shall devour, and tread
down the sling stones,
and they shall drink and roar
as if drunk with wine,
and be full like a bowl,
drenched like the corners of the altar.

16 On that day the Lord their
God will save them,
as the flock of his people;
for like the jewels of a crown
they shall shine on his land.
17 For how great is his goodness,
and how great his beauty!
Grain shall make the young
men flourish,
and new wine the young women.

THE RESTORATION FOR JUDAH AND ISRAEL

10 Ask rain from the Lord
in the season of the spring rain,
from the Lord who makes the
storm clouds,
and he will give them
showers of rain,
to everyone the vegetation
in the field.

---

[a] Or *For the eye of mankind, especially of all the tribes of Israel, is toward the Lord* [b] Or *a foreign people*; Hebrew *a bastard* [c] That is, the Euphrates

2 For the household gods
    utter nonsense,
  and the diviners see lies;
  they tell false dreams
    and give empty consolation.
  Therefore the people
    wander like sheep;
  they are afflicted for lack
    of a shepherd.

3 "My anger is hot against the shepherds,
    and I will punish the leaders;[a]
  for the LORD of hosts cares for his
    flock, the house of Judah,
  and will make them like his
    majestic steed in battle.
4 From him shall come the cornerstone,
    from him the tent peg,
  from him the battle bow,
    from him every ruler—all
    of them together.
5 They shall be like mighty
    men in battle,
  trampling the foe in the
    mud of the streets;
  they shall fight because the
    LORD is with them,
  and they shall put to shame
    the riders on horses.

6 "I will strengthen the house of Judah,
    and I will save the house of Joseph.
  I will bring them back because I
    have compassion on them,
  and they shall be as though I
    had not rejected them,
  for I am the LORD their God
    and I will answer them.
7 Then Ephraim shall become
    like a mighty warrior,
  and their hearts shall be
    glad as with wine.
  Their children shall see it and be glad;
    their hearts shall rejoice in the LORD.

8 "I will whistle for them and
    gather them in,
  for I have redeemed them,
    and they shall be as many
    as they were before.
9 Though I scattered them
    among the nations,
  yet in far countries they
    shall remember me,
  and with their children they
    shall live and return.

10 I will bring them home from
    the land of Egypt,
  and gather them from Assyria,
  and I will bring them to the land
    of Gilead and to Lebanon,
    till there is no room for them.
11 He shall pass through the
    sea of troubles
  and strike down the waves of the sea,
  and all the depths of the Nile
    shall be dried up.
  The pride of Assyria shall be laid low,
    and the sceptre of Egypt shall depart.
12 I will make them strong in the LORD,
    and they shall walk in his name,"
      declares the LORD.

THE FLOCK DOOMED TO SLAUGHTER

11 Open your doors, O Lebanon,
    that the fire may devour
    your cedars!
2 Wail, O cypress, for the
    cedar has fallen,
  for the glorious trees are ruined!
  Wail, oaks of Bashan,
    for the thick forest has been felled!
3 The sound of the wail of
    the shepherds,
  for their glory is ruined!
  The sound of the roar of the lions,
    for the thicket of the
    Jordan is ruined!

⁴Thus said the LORD my God: "Become shepherd of the flock doomed to slaughter. ⁵Those who buy them slaughter them and go unpunished, and those who sell them say, 'Blessed be the LORD, I have become rich', and their own shepherds have no pity on them. ⁶For I will no longer have pity on the inhabitants of this land, declares the LORD. Behold, I will cause each of them to fall into the hand of his neighbour, and each into the hand of his king, and they shall crush the land, and I will deliver none from their hand."

⁷So I became the shepherd of the flock doomed to be slaughtered by the sheep traders. And I took two staffs, one I named Favour, the other I named Union. And I tended the sheep. ⁸In one month I destroyed the three shepherds. But I became impatient with them, and they also detested me. ⁹So I said, "I will not be your shepherd. What is to die, let it die. What is to be destroyed, let

---
[a]Hebrew *the male goats*

it be destroyed. And let those who are left devour the flesh of one another." ¹⁰And I took my staff Favour, and I broke it, annulling the covenant that I had made with all the peoples. ¹¹So it was annulled on that day, and the sheep traders, who were watching me, knew that it was the word of the LORD. ¹²Then I said to them, "If it seems good to you, give me my wages; but if not, keep them." And they weighed out as my wages thirty pieces of silver. ¹³Then the LORD said to me, "Throw it to the potter"—the lordly price at which I was priced by them. So I took the thirty pieces of silver and threw them into the house of the LORD, to the potter. ¹⁴Then I broke my second staff Union, annulling the brotherhood between Judah and Israel.

¹⁵Then the LORD said to me, "Take once more the equipment of a foolish shepherd. ¹⁶For behold, I am raising up in the land a shepherd who does not care for those being destroyed, or seek the young or heal the maimed or nourish the healthy, but devours the flesh of the fat ones, tearing off even their hoofs.

¹⁷ "Woe to my worthless shepherd,
who deserts the flock!
May the sword strike his arm
and his right eye!
Let his arm be wholly withered,
his right eye utterly blinded!"

THE LORD WILL GIVE SALVATION

12 The oracle of the word of the LORD concerning Israel: Thus declares the LORD, who stretched out the heavens and founded the earth and formed the spirit of man within him: ²"Behold, I am about to make Jerusalem a cup of staggering to all the surrounding peoples. The siege of Jerusalem will also be against Judah. ³On that day I will make Jerusalem a heavy stone for all the peoples. All who lift it will surely hurt themselves. And all the nations of the earth will gather against it. ⁴On that day, declares the LORD, I will strike every horse with panic, and its rider with madness. But for the sake of the house of Judah I will keep my eyes open, when I strike every horse of the peoples with blindness. ⁵Then the clans of Judah shall say to themselves, 'The inhabitants of Jerusalem have strength through the LORD of hosts, their God.'

⁶"On that day I will make the clans of Judah like a blazing pot in the midst of wood, like a flaming torch among sheaves. And they shall devour to the right and to the left all the surrounding peoples, while Jerusalem shall again be inhabited in its place, in Jerusalem.

⁷"And the LORD will give salvation to the tents of Judah first, that the glory of the house of David and the glory of the inhabitants of Jerusalem may not surpass that of Judah. ⁸On that day the LORD will protect the inhabitants of Jerusalem, so that the feeblest among them on that day shall be like David, and the house of David shall be like God, like the angel of the LORD, going before them. ⁹And on that day I will seek to destroy all the nations that come against Jerusalem.

HIM WHOM THEY HAVE PIERCED

¹⁰"And I will pour out on the house of David and the inhabitants of Jerusalem a spirit of grace and pleas for mercy, so that, when they look on me, on him whom they have pierced, they shall mourn for him, as one mourns for an only child, and weep bitterly over him, as one weeps over a firstborn. ¹¹On that day the mourning in Jerusalem will be as great as the mourning for Hadad-rimmon in the plain of Megiddo. ¹²The land shall mourn, each family*ᵃ* by itself: the family of the house of David by itself, and their wives by themselves; the family of the house of Nathan by itself, and their wives by themselves; ¹³the family of the house of Levi by itself, and their wives by themselves; the family of the Shimeites by itself, and their wives by themselves; ¹⁴and all the families that are left, each by itself, and their wives by themselves.

13 "On that day there shall be a fountain opened for the house of David and the inhabitants of Jerusalem, to cleanse them from sin and uncleanness.

IDOLATRY CUT OFF

²"And on that day, declares the LORD of hosts, I will cut off the names of the idols from the land, so that they shall be remembered no more. And also I will remove from the land the prophets and the spirit of uncleanness. ³And if anyone again prophesies, his father and mother who bore him will say to him, 'You shall not live, for you speak lies in the name of the LORD.' And his father and mother who bore him shall pierce him through when he prophesies.

ᵃOr clan; throughout verses 12–14

⁴"On that day every prophet will be ashamed of his vision when he prophesies. He will not put on a hairy cloak in order to deceive, ⁵but he will say, 'I am no prophet, I am a worker of the soil, for a man sold me in my youth.'ᵃ ⁶And if one asks him, 'What are these wounds on your back?'ᵇ he will say, 'The wounds I received in the house of my friends.'

THE SHEPHERD STRUCK

⁷ "Awake, O sword, against my shepherd,
against the man who stands
next to me,"
declares the LORD of hosts.

"Strike the shepherd, and the
sheep will be scattered;
I will turn my hand against
the little ones.
⁸ In the whole land, declares the LORD,
two thirds shall be cut
off and perish,
and one third shall be left alive.
⁹ And I will put this third into the fire,
and refine them as one refines silver,
and test them as gold is tested.
They will call upon my name,
and I will answer them.
I will say, 'They are my people';
and they will say, 'The LORD is
my God.'"

THE COMING DAY OF THE LORD

14 Behold, a day is coming for the LORD, when the spoil taken from you will be divided in your midst. ²For I will gather all the nations against Jerusalem to battle, and the city shall be taken and the houses plundered and the women raped. Half of the city shall go out into exile, but the rest of the people shall not be cut off from the city. ³Then the LORD will go out and fight against those nations as when he fights on a day of battle. ⁴On that day his feet shall stand on the Mount of Olives that lies before Jerusalem on the east, and the Mount of Olives shall be split in two from east to west by a very wide valley, so that one half of the Mount shall move northwards, and the other half southwards. ⁵And you shall flee to the valley of my mountains, for the valley of the mountains shall reach to Azal. And you shall flee as you fled from the earthquake in the days of Uzziah king of Judah. Then the LORD my God will come, and all the holy ones with him.ᶜ

⁶On that day there shall be no light, cold, or frost.ᵈ ⁷And there shall be a uniqueᵉ day, which is known to the LORD, neither day nor night, but at evening time there shall be light.
⁸On that day living waters shall flow out from Jerusalem, half of them to the eastern seaᶠ and half of them to the western sea.ᵍ It shall continue in summer as in winter.
⁹And the LORD will be king over all the earth. On that day the LORD will be one and his name one.
¹⁰The whole land shall be turned into a plain from Geba to Rimmon south of Jerusalem. But Jerusalem shall remain aloft on its site from the Gate of Benjamin to the place of the former gate, to the Corner Gate, and from the Tower of Hananel to the king's wine presses. ¹¹And it shall be inhabited, for there shall never again be a decree of utter destruction.ʰ Jerusalem shall dwell in security.
¹²And this shall be the plague with which the LORD will strike all the peoples that wage war against Jerusalem: their flesh will rot while they are still standing on their feet, their eyes will rot in their sockets, and their tongues will rot in their mouths.
¹³And on that day a great panic from the LORD shall fall on them, so that each will seize the hand of another, and the hand of the one will be raised against the hand of the other. ¹⁴Even Judah will fight at Jerusalem.ⁱ And the wealth of all the surrounding nations shall be collected, gold, silver, and garments in great abundance. ¹⁵And a plague like this plague shall fall on the horses, the mules, the camels, the donkeys, and whatever beasts may be in those camps.
¹⁶Then everyone who survives of all the nations that have come against Jerusalem shall go up year after year to worship the King, the LORD of hosts, and to keep the Feast of Booths. ¹⁷And if any of the families of the earth do not go up to Jerusalem to worship the King, the LORD of hosts, there will be no rain on them. ¹⁸And if the family of Egypt does not go up and present themselves, then on them there shall be no rain;ʲ there shall be the plague with which the LORD afflicts the nations that do not go up to

---

ᵃOr *for the land has been my possession since my youth* ᵇOr *on your chest*; Hebrew *wounds between your hands* ᶜOther Hebrew manuscripts *you* ᵈCompare Septuagint, Syriac, Vulgate, Targum; the meaning of the Hebrew is uncertain ᵉHebrew *one* ᶠThat is, the Dead Sea ᵍThat is, the Mediterranean Sea ʰThe Hebrew term rendered *decree of utter destruction* refers to things devoted (or set apart) to the Lord (or by the Lord) for destruction ⁱOr *against Jerusalem* ʲHebrew lacks *rain*

keep the Feast of Booths. ¹⁹This shall be the punishment to Egypt and the punishment to all the nations that do not go up to keep the Feast of Booths.

²⁰And on that day there shall be inscribed on the bells of the horses, "Holy to the Lord." And the pots in the house of the Lord shall be as the bowls before the altar. ²¹And every pot in Jerusalem and Judah shall be holy to the Lord of hosts, so that all who sacrifice may come and take of them and boil the meat of the sacrifice in them. And there shall no longer be a trader[c] in the house of the Lord of hosts on that day.

---

[c] Or *Canaanite*

MALACHI

1

The oracle of the word of the LORD to Israel by Malachi.ᵃ

THE LORD'S LOVE FOR ISRAEL

²"I have loved you," says the LORD. But you say, "How have you loved us?" "Is not Esau Jacob's brother?" declares the LORD. "Yet I have loved Jacob ³but Esau I have hated. I have laid waste his hill country and left his heritage to jackals of the desert." ⁴If Edom says, "We are shattered but we will rebuild the ruins," the LORD of hosts says, "They may build, but I will tear down, and they will be called 'the wicked country', and 'the people with whom the LORD is angry for ever.'" ⁵Your own eyes shall see this, and you shall say, "Great is the LORD beyond the border of Israel!"

THE PRIESTS' POLLUTED OFFERINGS

⁶"A son honours his father, and a servant his master. If then I am a father, where is my honour? And if I am a master, where is my fear? says the LORD of hosts to you, O priests, who despise my name. But you say, 'How have we despised your name?' ⁷By offering polluted food upon my altar. But you say, 'How have we polluted you?' By saying that the LORD's table may be despised. ⁸When you offer blind animals in sacrifice, is that not evil? And when you offer those that are lame or sick, is that not evil? Present that to your governor; will he accept you or show you favour? says the LORD of hosts. ⁹And now entreat the favour of God, that he may be gracious to us. With such a gift from your hand, will he show favour to any of you? says the LORD of hosts. ¹⁰Oh that there were one among you who would shut the doors, that you might not kindle fire on my altar in vain! I have no pleasure in you, says the LORD of hosts, and I will not accept an offering from your hand. ¹¹For from the rising of the sun to its setting my name will beᵇ great among the nations, and in every place incense will be offered to my name, and a pure offering. For my name will be great among the nations, says the LORD of hosts. ¹²But you profane it when you say that the Lord's table is polluted, and its fruit, that is, its food may be despised. ¹³But you say, 'What a weariness this is', and you snort at it, says the LORD of hosts. You bring what has been taken by violence or is lame or sick, and this you bring as your offering! Shall I accept that from your hand? says the LORD. ¹⁴Cursed be the cheat who has a male in his flock, and vows it, and yet sacrifices to the Lord what is blemished. For I am a great King, says the LORD of hosts, and my name will be feared among the nations.

THE LORD REBUKES THE PRIESTS

2

"And now, O priests, this command is for you. ²If you will not listen, if you will not take it to heart to give honour to my name, says the LORD of hosts, then I will send the curse upon you and I will curse your blessings. Indeed, I have already cursed them, because you do not lay it to heart. ³Behold, I will rebuke your offspring,ᶜ and spread dung on your faces, the dung of your offerings, and you shall be taken away with it.ᵈ ⁴So shall you know that I have sent this command to you, that my covenant with Levi may stand, says the LORD of hosts. ⁵My covenant with him was one of life and peace, and I gave them to him. It was a covenant of fear, and he feared me. He stood in awe of my name. ⁶True instructionᵉ was in his mouth, and no wrong was found on his lips. He walked with me in peace and uprightness, and he turned many from iniquity. ⁷For the lips of a priest should guard knowledge, and peopleᶠ should seek instruction from his mouth, for he is the messenger of the LORD of hosts. ⁸But you have turned aside from the way. You have caused many to stumble by your instruction. You have corrupted the covenant of Levi, says the LORD of hosts, ⁹and so I make you despised and abased before all the people, inasmuch as you do not keep my ways but show partiality in your instruction."

ᵃ*Malachi* means *my messenger* ᵇOr *is* (three times in verse 11; also verse 14) ᶜHebrew *seed* ᵈOr *to it* ᵉOr *law*; also verses 7, 8, 9 ᶠHebrew *they*

JUDAH PROFANED THE COVENANT

¹⁰Have we not all one Father? Has not one God created us? Why then are we faithless to one another, profaning the covenant of our fathers? ¹¹Judah has been faithless, and abomination has been committed in Israel and in Jerusalem. For Judah has profaned the sanctuary of the LORD, which he loves, and has married the daughter of a foreign god. ¹²May the LORD cut off from the tents of Jacob any descendant*ᵃ* of the man who does this, who brings an offering to the LORD of hosts!

¹³And this second thing you do. You cover the LORD's altar with tears, with weeping and groaning because he no longer regards the offering or accepts it with favour from your hand. ¹⁴But you say, "Why does he not?" Because the LORD was witness between you and the wife of your youth, to whom you have been faithless, though she is your companion and your wife by covenant. ¹⁵Did he not make them one, with a portion of the Spirit in their union?*ᵇ* And what was the one God*ᶜ* seeking?*ᵈ* Godly offspring. So guard yourselves*ᵉ* in your spirit, and let none of you be faithless to the wife of your youth. ¹⁶"For the man who does not love his wife but divorces her,*ᶠ* says the LORD, the God of Israel, covers*ᵍ* his garment with violence, says the LORD of hosts. So guard yourselves in your spirit, and do not be faithless."

THE MESSENGER OF THE LORD

¹⁷You have wearied the LORD with your words. But you say, "How have we wearied him?" By saying, "Everyone who does evil is good in the sight of the LORD, and he delights in them." Or by asking, "Where is the God of justice?"

3 "Behold, I send my messenger, and he will prepare the way before me. And the Lord whom you seek will suddenly come to his temple; and the messenger of the covenant in whom you delight, behold, he is coming, says the LORD of hosts. ²But who can endure the day of his coming, and who can stand when he appears? For he is like a refiner's fire and like fullers' soap. ³He will sit as a refiner and purifier of silver, and he will purify the sons of Levi and refine them like gold and silver, and they will bring offerings in righteousness to the LORD.*ʰ* ⁴Then the offering of Judah and Jerusalem will be pleasing to the LORD as in the days of old and as in former years.

⁵"Then I will draw near to you for judgement. I will be a swift witness against the sorcerers, against the adulterers, against those who swear falsely, against those who oppress the hired worker in his wages, the widow and the fatherless, against those who thrust aside the sojourner, and do not fear me, says the LORD of hosts.

ROBBING GOD

⁶"For I the LORD do not change; therefore you, O children of Jacob, are not consumed. ⁷From the days of your fathers you have turned aside from my statutes and have not kept them. Return to me, and I will return to you, says the LORD of hosts. But you say, 'How shall we return?' ⁸Will man rob God? Yet you are robbing me. But you say, 'How have we robbed you?' In your tithes and contributions. ⁹You are cursed with a curse, for you are robbing me, the whole nation of you. ¹⁰Bring the full tithe into the storehouse, that there may be food in my house. And thereby put me to the test, says the LORD of hosts, if I will not open the windows of heaven for you and pour down for you a blessing until there is no more need. ¹¹I will rebuke the devourer*ⁱ* for you, so that it will not destroy the fruits of your soil, and your vine in the field shall not fail to bear, says the LORD of hosts. ¹²Then all nations will call you blessed, for you will be a land of delight, says the LORD of hosts.

¹³"Your words have been hard against me, says the LORD. But you say, 'How have we spoken against you?' ¹⁴You have said, 'It is vain to serve God. What is the profit of our keeping his charge or of walking as in mourning before the LORD of hosts? ¹⁵And now we call the arrogant blessed. Evildoers not only prosper but they put God to the test and they escape.'"

THE BOOK OF REMEMBRANCE

¹⁶Then those who feared the LORD spoke with one another. The LORD paid attention and heard them, and a book of remembrance was written before him of those who feared the LORD and esteemed his name. ¹⁷"They

---

*ᵃ*Hebrew *any who wakes and answers* *ᵇ*Hebrew *in it* *ᶜ*Hebrew *the one* *ᵈ*Or *And not one has done this who has a portion of the Spirit. And what was that one seeking?* *ᵉ*Or *So take care;* also verse 16 *ᶠ*Hebrew *who hates and divorces* *ᵍ*Probable meaning (compare Septuagint and Deuteronomy 24:1–4); or *"The LORD, the God of Israel, says that he hates divorce, and him who covers* *ʰ*Or *and they will belong to the LORD, bringers of an offering in righteousness* *ⁱ*Probably a name for some crop-destroying pest or pests

shall be mine, says the LORD of hosts, in the day when I make up my treasured possession, and I will spare them as a man spares his son who serves him. ¹⁸Then once more you shall see the distinction between the righteous and the wicked, between one who serves God and one who does not serve him.

THE GREAT DAY OF THE LORD

4 ᵃ "For behold, the day is coming, burning like an oven, when all the arrogant and all evildoers will be stubble. The day that is coming shall set them ablaze, says the LORD of hosts, so that it will leave them neither root nor branch. ²But for you who fear my name, the sun of righteousness shall rise with healing in its wings. You shall go out leaping like calves from the stall. ³And you shall tread down the wicked, for they will be ashes under the soles of your feet, on the day when I act, says the LORD of hosts.

⁴"Remember the law of my servant Moses, the statutes and rulesᵇ that I commanded him at Horeb for all Israel.

⁵"Behold, I will send you Elijah the prophet before the great and awesome day of the LORD comes. ⁶And he will turn the hearts of fathers to their children and the hearts of children to their fathers, lest I come and strike the land with a decree of utter destruction."ᶜ

ᵃCh 4:1-6 is ch 3:19-24 in Hebrew ᵇOr *and just decrees*
ᶜThe Hebrew term rendered *decree of utter destruction* refers to things devoted (or set apart) to the Lord (or by the Lord) for destruction

APOCRYPHA

APOCRYPHA

TOBIT

1 [a] The book of the words of Tobit son of Tobiel, son of Ananiel, son of Aduel, son of Gabael, son of Raphael, son of Raguel, of the descendants of Asiel from the tribe of Naphtali, ²who in the days of Shalmaneser[b], the king of the Assyrians, was taken into captivity from Thisbe, which is to the south[c] of Kedesh of Naphtali in Upper Galilee above Asher to the west, north[d] of Phogor.

TOBIT'S YOUTH AND VIRTUOUS LIFE

³I, Tobit, walked in the ways of truth and in righteous deeds all the days of my life, and I performed many acts of mercy for my brothers and my compatriots who went with me into captivity in the land of the Assyrians, to Nineveh. ⁴Now when I was in my own country, in the land of Israel, when I was young, the whole tribe of Naphtali my ancestor[e] broke away from the house of my ancestor David and from the city of Jerusalem, the place chosen from among all the tribes of Israel, where all the tribes should sacrifice. In it the temple of God's dwelling was consecrated and established for all generations for ever.

⁵All my brothers and the house of Naphtali my ancestor—those people used to sacrifice on all the high places of Galilee to the calf that Jeroboam, king of Israel, made in Dan. ⁶But I alone went often to Jerusalem at the time for the feasts, just as it is written for all Israel by an everlasting decree. I would hurry off to Jerusalem, taking the first fruits—the first fruits of my fields and the tithes of my livestock and the first shearings of the sheep—and I would give these to the priests, the sons of Aaron, at the altar. ⁷I would give a tenth of the corn, wine, olive oil, pomegranates, figs, and the produce from the other fruit trees to the sons of Levi who ministered in Jerusalem. I tithed a second tenth in silver for the six years, and I would go and spend this in Jerusalem each year. ⁸I would give these things to the orphans and widows and sojourners who had attached themselves to the sons of Israel: I would carry and give it to them in the third year and we would eat them according to the stipulation that had been stipulated concerning them in the Law of Moses and according to the commands which Deborah, the mother of Ananiel our father, had commanded me (for my father had died and left me an orphan). ⁹When I became a man I took a wife from the descendants of our family, and I fathered a son by her, and I called his name Tobias.

TAKEN CAPTIVE TO NINEVEH

¹⁰After I was carried away captive to Assyria, and while I was in captivity, I went to Nineveh. And all my brothers and my relatives ate the food[f] of the Gentiles; ¹¹but I preserved my soul from eating the Gentiles' food. ¹²And because[g] I had been mindful of my God with my whole soul, ¹³the Most High gave me favour and good standing in the sight of Shalmaneser, and I used to purchase for him whatever he needed. ¹⁴I used to go into Media and buy for him there until he died. And I entrusted sacks of money to Gabael, the brother of Gabri, in the land of Media—ten talents of silver. ¹⁵And when Shalmaneser died and his son Sennacherib reigned in his place, the roads to Media were unfit and I could no longer travel into Media.

COURAGE IN BURYING THE DEAD

¹⁶In the days of Shalmaneser I performed many acts of mercy for my brothers, for those of my kindred. ¹⁷I would give my bread to the hungry and garments to the naked; and if ever I saw anyone from my people dead and thrown out behind the wall of Nineveh, I would bury him. ¹⁸And if King Sennacherib put anyone to death at the time he came fleeing from Judea (in the days of the judgement that the King of Heaven visited upon him for the blasphemies he uttered), I buried him. For in his anger he

---

[a]Tobit is one of the seven deuterocanonical books that do not exist in their entirety in Hebrew or Aramaic, but which were included in the Greek Septuagint, and were likewise included in the Latin Vulgate version of the Bible translated by Jerome in the late fourth century AD. See further, Introduction, pages xiii to xiv. [b]Latin Enemessar; also verses 13, 15, 16 [c]Greek right [d]Greek left [e]Greek father; twice, and also verse 5 [f]Greek bread; also verse 11 [g]Latin; Greek when

put to death many of the sons of Israel, and I stole away their bodies and buried them. Sennacherib sought them out, but did not find them. ¹⁹Then a certain one of the Ninevites went and informed the king about me, that I was burying them, so I hid myself. When I learned that the king knew about me and that I was being sought out to be put to death, I was terrified and ran away. ²⁰Then everything that belonged to me was confiscated and nothing was left to me, that had not been taken for the royal treasury, except my wife Anna and my son Tobias.

²¹But not forty[a] days passed before two of Sennacherib's[b] sons killed him. They fled into the mountains of Ararat, and Esar-haddon,[c] his son, reigned after him. He appointed Ahikar son of my brother Anael over all the accounts of his kingdom and he himself had authority over the entire administration. ²²Then Ahikar interceded for me, and I returned to Nineveh. Now Ahikar was cupbearer, keeper of the signet ring, administrator and accountant under Sennacherib king of the Assyrians, and Esar-haddon had appointed him second to himself.[d] He was my nephew and a member of my family.

2 And during the time of King Esar-haddon[e] I came back to my house, and my wife Anna and my son Tobias were restored to me. And at our Feast of Pentecost, which is a sacred festival of seven days, a good meal was prepared for me and I reclined to eat. ²A table was set before me, and an abundance of cooked food was set before me, and I said to my son Tobias, "Child, go about and, bring back any poor person whom you might find among our kindred,[f] from among the captives of Nineveh, who is mindful with all his heart, so that he might eat together with us. Behold, child, I will wait until you return." ³So Tobias went to seek out any poor person from among our kindred. When he returned he said, "Father!" And I said, "Here I am, child!" And he, replying, said, "Behold, father! One from our nation has been murdered and thrown into the market-place, and now he lies there strangled." ⁴So leaping up, I left my meal before I had tasted it and took the body[g] out of the street and set it in one of my rooms until the sun set and I could bury it.[h] ⁵And when I returned, I washed myself and began to eat my food in sorrow. ⁶And I remembered the word of the prophet, what things Amos spoke against Bethel, saying:

"Your feasts shall be turned
into mourning,
and all your songs into
lamentation."

And I wept.

TOBIT BECOMES BLIND

⁷When the sun had set I went out, dug a grave, and buried him. ⁸And my neighbours were mocking me, saying, "Is he no longer afraid? For he was already sought out to be put to death for doing this deed, and he ran away. Now behold! He is back to burying the dead!" ⁹On the same night I washed myself and I went out into my courtyard and fell asleep beside the courtyard wall, and my face was uncovered because of the heat. ¹⁰I did not know that there were sparrows on the wall above me, and their warm droppings fell into my eyes and brought on white films. I went to the physicians to be healed, but the more they anointed me with their potions, the more my eyes were blinded by the white films until I was completely blind. For four years I had no use of my eyes. All my relatives[i] grieved over me and Ahikar took care of me for two years, before he went to Elymais.

TOBIT'S WIFE EARNS THEIR LIVELIHOOD

¹¹At that time my wife Anna earned money at women's work. ¹²She used to send the products to their employers and they would pay her wages. On the seventh of Dystros, she cut off a woven piece and sent it to the employers and they paid her the whole price and gave her a kid from the herd to take home.[j] ¹³When she returned to me the kid began to bleat. So I called her and said, "Where did you get this goat? It is not stolen, is it? Return it to its owners, for we do not have the right to eat anything stolen." ¹⁴And she said to me, "It was given to me as a gift in addition to my wage." But I did not believe her and kept telling her to return it to the owners, and I became flushed over this on her account. Then she replied to me, "And where are your deeds of mercy? Where are your righteous deeds? Behold! these things are known about you!"

---

[a]Some manuscripts *forty-five* or *fifty* [b]Greek *his* [c]Greek *Sacherdonus*; also verse 22 [d]Or *him a second time* [e]Greek *Sacherdonus* [f]Greek *brothers*; also verse 3 [g]Greek *him* [h]Greek *him* [i]Greek *brothers* [j]Greek *for the hearth*

TOBIT'S PRAYER

3 Then I became greatly depressed in my soul. Groaning out loud, I wept and I began to pray as I groaned: ²"Righteous are you, O Lord; all your deeds are just and all your ways are merciful and true. You judge the world.*ᵃ* ³And now, Lord, remember me and look favourably upon me*ᵇ*; do not punish me for my sins and for my unwitting offences and those of my fathers. They sinned before you ⁴and they disobeyed your commandments, and you gave us over to plunder and captivity and death; you made us an example and a byword and a reproach among all the nations among which you scattered us. ⁵And now your many judgements are true, to deal with me for my sins, because we did not do what you commanded and we did not walk before you with sincerity. ⁶And now deal with me according to your pleasure; command my spirit to withdraw from me, that I may be set free from the face of the earth and become earth myself. For it is better for me to die than to live, because I have heard false reproaches, and great sorrow is upon me. Lord, command that I be set free from this distress. Set me free to go to the eternal place and do not turn your face, Lord, away from me. It is better for me to die and not to hear reproaches than to continue to see so much distress in my life."

SARAH FALSELY ACCUSED

⁷On that day, it befell Sarah, daughter of Raguel in Ecbatana of Media, that she heard reproaches from one of her father's maidservants, ⁸because she had been given to seven husbands, and the evil demon Asmodeus killed them before they had been with her as it is prescribed for wives. So the maidservant said to her, "You are the one who kills your husbands! Behold! You have already been married to seven husbands and have not borne the name of any one of them. ⁹Why do you beat us over your dead husbands? Go along with them, and may we never see a son or daughter of yours!"

SARAH'S PRAYER FOR DEATH

¹⁰On that day she was grieved in her soul and began to weep. Ascending to the upper room in her father's house, she wanted to hang herself. But she reconsidered and said: "Let it not happen that they reproach my father and say to him, 'You had one beloved daughter and she hanged herself to escape her troubles.' I would bring the old age of my father down to Hades in grief. It is better for me not to hang myself, but to beg the Lord that I might die and no longer hear reproaches during my life." ¹¹At that very time, spreading out her hands towards the window, she prayed and said: "Blessed are you, merciful God, and blessed is your name for ever. May all your works bless you for ever. ¹²And now, O Lord, my face looks to you and I lift my eyes. ¹³Speak, that I might be set free from the earth and that I might no longer hear reproaches. ¹⁴You know, Master, that I am clean from any uncleanness with a man ¹⁵and that I did not stain my name or the name of my father in the land of my captivity. I am my father's only child, and he has no other child to be his heir, no near kinsman*ᶜ* or relative for whom I should keep myself to be a wife. Already seven have been lost to me. Why should I yet live? And if it does not seem right to you to kill me, Lord, hear now how I am reproached!"

ANSWER TO PRAYER

¹⁶At that very moment, the prayer of both was heard in the presence of the glory of God. ¹⁷And Raphael was sent to heal the two of them: with regard to Tobit, to remove the white films from his eyes, in order that he might see the light of God with his eyes; with regard to Sarah, daughter of Raguel, to give her as wife to Tobias son of Tobit and to send Asmodeus the evil demon away from her, because Tobias was entitled to inherit her before all those wishing to have her. At that very moment, Tobit returned from the courtyard into his house and Sarah, the daughter of Raguel, came down from the upper room.

TOBIT GIVES INSTRUCTIONS TO HIS SON

4 On that day Tobit remembered the silver that he had left in trust with Gabael at Rages in Media, ²and he said in his heart: "Behold! I have asked for death. Why do I not call my son Tobias and tell him about this silver before I die?" ³So he called his son Tobias, and he came to him, and Tobit*ᵈ* said to him, "Bury me honourably and respect your mother and do not abandon her all the days of her life. Do what is pleasing to her and do not grieve her spirit in any matter. ⁴Remember her, child, because she faced many dangers for you while you were in her

---

*ᵃ*Or *age* *ᵇ*Or *look down upon me* *ᶜ*Greek *brother* *ᵈ*Greek *he*

womb. And when she dies, bury her beside me in one grave.[a]

5"Remember the Lord all your days, child, and refuse to sin or to transgress his commandments. Do righteous deeds all the days of your life and do not walk in the paths of wrongdoing. **6**For those who practise what is true will prosper in their deeds. **7**Do deeds of mercy from your possessions to all who practise righteousness and do not let your eye begrudge the gift when you make it. Do not turn your face away from any poor man, and the face of God will not be turned away from you. **8**If you have many possessions, make your gift from them in proportion; if few, do not be afraid to give according to the little you have. **9**So you will be laying up a good treasure for yourself against the day of necessity. **10**For practising mercy delivers from death and keeps you from entering the darkness; **11**for practising mercy is an excellent offering in the sight of the Most High for all who do it.

12"Beware, child, of all fornication. First of all take a wife from among the descendants of your fathers and do not marry a foreign woman, who is not of your father's tribe; for we are the sons of the prophets. Noah, Abraham, Isaac, and Jacob, our fathers of old — remember, child, that these all took wives from among their kinsmen. They were blessed in their children, and their offspring will inherit the land. **13**So now, child, love your kinsfolk and do not disdain in your heart to take for yourself a wife from among your kinsfolk and from the sons and daughters of your people. For in arrogant disdain there is ruin and great confusion; and in idleness there is loss and great want, because idleness is the mother of famine.

14"Do not hold over till the next day the wages of any man who works for you, but pay him at once; and if you serve God you will receive payment. Watch yourself, my son, in everything you do and be disciplined in all your conduct. **15**And what you hate, do not do to anyone. Do not drink wine to excess or let drunkenness go with you on your way. **16**Give some of your bread to the hungry and some of your clothing to the naked. Give all your surplus to charity and do not let your eye begrudge the gift while you are making it. **17**Place your loaves on the grave of the righteous, but give none to sinners. **18**Seek advice from every wise man and do not despise any useful counsel. **19**Bless the Lord God on every occasion; ask him that your ways may be made straight and that all your paths and plans may prosper. For none of the nations has understanding; but the Lord will give them good counsel, and whomever he wishes he brings down as far as the lowest parts of Hades.

"And now, child, remember these commands and let them not be blotted out of your mind.[b] **20**And now, child, I tell you that I entrusted ten talents of silver to Gabael, the brother[c] of Gabri, at Rages in Media. **21**Do not be afraid, child, that we have become poor: Many good things are yours if you fear God and flee from every sin and do what is good in the sight of the Lord your God."

THE ANGEL RAPHAEL

5 Then Tobias answered his father Tobit, saying, "Father, everything that you have commanded me I will do; **2**but how will I be able to obtain the silver[d] from him when he does not know me and I do not know him? What sign am I to give him so that he will recognize me and believe me and give me the silver? And I do not know the roads leading into Media, that I might travel there." **3**Then Tobit answered his son Tobias, saying, "He gave me his handwritten receipt, and I gave a receipt to him. I divided one in two pieces and we each took one piece, and I put one with the silver. And now, behold! It is twenty years since I entrusted this silver. And now, child, seek out a reliable man for yourself, who will travel with you, and we will pay him wages until you return. Now obtain this silver from him."

4So Tobias went to look for a man who might go with him into Media, who knew the road. He went out and found the angel Raphael standing before him, though Tobias[e] did not know that he was an angel of God. **5**Tobias[f] said to him, "Where are you from, young man?" And he said, "From the sons of Israel, your brothers, and I have come here to find employment." Tobias[g] said to him, "Do you know the road to go into Media?" **6**He said to him, "Yes, I was there often, and I

---

[a]Tobit 4:5–19 is supplied from Greek Vaticanus (see Introduction, page xiii to xiv); Greek Sinaiticus reads: **5**"Remember the Lord all your days, child, and refuse to sin or to transgress his commandments. Do righteous deeds all the days of your life and do not walk in the paths of wrongdoing. **6**For those who practice what is true will prosper in their deeds. **7**And to all who practice righteousness, **19**the Lord will give them good counsel, and whomever the Lord wishes he brings down as far as Hades below. [b]Greek heart [c]Greek lacks the brother, but see 1:14 [d]Greek it [e]Greek he [f]Greek he [g]Greek he

know and have experience with all the roads. I have travelled many times into Media and lodged with Gabael, our brother, who lives at Rages in Media. It is a two-day journey from Ecbatana to Rages, for Rages lies on a mountain, but Ecbatana in the midst of a plain." [7]Then Tobias[a] said to him, "Wait for me, young man, until I go and tell my father, for I need you to go with me, and I will pay you your wages." [8]And he said to him, "I will linger; only do not delay." [9]So Tobias went and informed his father Tobit and said to him, "Behold! I have found a man from among our brothers, the sons of Israel." He said, "Call the man for me, so that I may learn what his ancestry is, from which tribe he comes, and whether he is a reliable man, that he should go with you, child."

[10]So Tobias went out, called him, and said to him, "Young man, my father is calling for you." And he entered the house and Tobit greeted him first. And the angel[b] said, "May many things come to be that will give you joy." Replying, Tobit said to him, "What is left to give me joy? I am a person with no power in his eyes. I do not see the light of heaven, but I lie in darkness like the dead, who no longer see the light. I am living among the dead: I hear people's voices, but I do not see them." And he said to him, "Take heart! Your healing from God is near. Take heart!" Then Tobit said to him, "My son Tobias wishes to journey into Media. If you are able to accompany him and guide him, I will give you your wages, brother." He replied, "I am able to go with him, and I know all the roads. I have gone often into Media and crossed all its plains, and I know the mountains and all its paths." [11]Then Tobit[c] said to him, "Brother, what is your lineage, and from what tribe do you come? Tell me, brother." [12]But he answered, "What need do you have of a tribe?" And Tobit[d] said to him, "I would like to know the truth about whose you are, brother, and what your name is." [13]He said to him, "I am Azarias son of the great Ananias, from among your brothers." [14]Then Tobit[e] said to him, "May you go in good health and be kept safe, brother. Do not be angry with me, brother, because I wanted to learn the truth about your lineage. You do turn out to be a brother, of a good and noble stock. I used to know Ananias and Nathan, the two sons of the great Shemeliah: they used to travel with me to Jerusalem and worship with me there, and they were not led astray. Your relatives[f] are good people; you are from good stock, and may you go rejoicing." [15]And he said to him, "I am giving you a daily wage of a drachma and any necessary expenses for you and likewise for my son. [16]Now go with my son, and I will add a bonus to your wages." And he replied to him, "I will go with him. Do not be afraid: we will be safe as we go, and we will return to you in safety, because the way is secure." [17]And Tobit[g] said to him, "Blessing be upon you, brother."

Then he called his son and said to him, "Child, get your things ready for the journey and go with your brother, and may God in heaven bring you both safely there and bring you both back to me safe and sound, and may his angel travel with you both in safety, child." So he went out to make his journey, and he kissed his father and mother, and Tobit said to him, "Go safely!"

[18]His mother wept and said to Tobit, "Why have you sent my child away? Is he not the staff in our hand as he goes in and out before us? [19]Do not pile silver upon silver, but let it be a ransom for our child. [20]For the life that is given to us by the Lord is enough for us." [21]And he said to her, "Do not make an issue of this; our child will go safely and come back to us safe and sound. You will see with your own eyes on that day that he returns to you safely. So do not make an issue of this, and do not be afraid for them, sister, [22]for a good angel will go with him. His journey will be successful, and he will come back safe and sound."

6

So she stopped weeping.

JOURNEY TO RAGES

[2]So the child went out, and the angel with him, and the dog came out and went along with them. The two journeyed along, and the first night came upon them, and they camped beside the Tigris river. [3]Then the child went down to wash his feet in the Tigris river. A large fish, leaping up from the river, tried to swallow the child's foot, and he cried out. [4]The angel said to the boy, "Grab hold of the fish and master it!" So the young man took hold of the fish and dragged it up on the land. [5]Then the angel said to him, "Split the fish open and take out its gall and heart and liver and keep them with you, but throw away the

---
[a]Greek he [b]Greek he [c]Greek he [d]Greek he [e]Greek he [f]Greek brothers [g]Greek he

entrails, for its gall and heart and liver are useful for medicine." ⁶So the boy split open the fish and gathered the gall, heart, and liver. And they broiled the fish and ate it, and left some to be salted.

And the two journeyed on together until they came near to Media. ⁷Then the boy questioned the angel and said to him, "Brother Azarias, what kind of medicine is in the fish's heart and liver and in its gall?" ⁸He said to him, "As for the fish's heart and the liver, burn these in the presence of a man or woman who meets misfortune from a demon or evil spirit, and every such misfortune will flee from that person and not abide with him ever after. ⁹And as for the gall, anoint the eyes of a person, upon which white films have formed, and breathe upon them (upon the white films), and they will be cured."

RAPHAEL'S INSTRUCTIONS

¹⁰When he entered Media and was already drawing near to Ecbatana, ¹¹Raphael said to the youth, "Brother Tobias?" And he said to him, "Here I am." And he said to him, "We must lodge tonight with the family of Raguel. The man is a relative of yours, and he has a daughter named Sarah. ¹²He has no male child nor daughter, but only Sarah, and you are nearest kin to her, more entitled than all other men to inherit her, and it is right for you to inherit all that belongs to her father. The girl is sensible, courageous, and very beautiful, and her father is honourable." ¹³And he continued,ᵃ "It has been shown to be right for you to take her. So listen to me, brother, and I will speak to her father about the girl this very night, that you might take her as your bride, and when we return from Rages we will celebrate her wedding feast. And I know that Raguel will certainly not be able to keep her from you nor to give her to another. He would be liable to the death penalty according to the judgement of the book of Moses, because he knows that the inheritance is proper for you to have, to take his daughter before any man. So now listen to me, brother, and we will speak about the girl this very night and we will get her betrothed to you. And when we return from Rages, we will take her and conduct her along with us to your house."

¹⁴Then Tobias answered Raphael, saying, "Brother Azarias, I heard that she has already been given to seven husbands and they died in the bridal chamber on the wedding night: when they were approaching her, they died.

I also heard people saying that a demon kills them. ¹⁵So now I am afraid, because it does not harm her, but if anyone wants to get close to her, it kills him. I am my father's only son, and I am afraidᵇ lest I die and bring the lives of my father and mother down to their graves in sorrow on my account. And they have no other son to bury them."

¹⁶But the angelᶜ said to him, "Do you not remember your father's commands, that he commanded you to take a wife from your father's household? So listen to me now, brother, and do not make an issue of this demon, and take her, for I know indeed that a wife will be given to you this very night. ¹⁷Now, when you enter the bridal chamber, take some of the liver of the fish, and the heart, and place these upon the ashes of the incense burner, and the smell will go forth, ¹⁸and the demon will sense it, and he will flee and never appear round her again for all time. And when you are about to be with her, rise up first, both of you, and pray and implore the Lord of heaven, that mercy and deliverance might come upon you both. And do not be afraid, for she was made your portion from before eternity. You will deliver her, and she will go with you, and I assume that you will have children by her, and they will be like brothers to you. So do not make an issue of this." When Tobias heard Raphael's words, and that she was a sister to him from his father's household, he loved her greatly and his heart fixed itself on her.

ARRIVAL AT RAGUEL'S HOME

7 When they entered Ecbatana, he said to him, "Brother Azarias, lead me directly to Raguel our brother." And he led him to the house of Raguel, and they found him seated beside the door of the courtyard. They greeted him first, and he said to them, "Many greetings, brothers; welcome, and good health to you." And he led them into his house. ²Then he said to Edna his wife, "How much this young man resembles Tobit, my kinsman!"ᵈ ³And Edna enquired of them, saying to them, "Where are you from, brothers?" They answered her, "We are from the sons of Naphtali, from among those taken captive in Nineveh." ⁴So she said to them, "Do you know our brother Tobit?" And they said to her, "We indeed know him." And she

---

ᵃGreek *said* ᵇGreek lacks *and I am afraid* ᶜGreek *he* ᵈGreek *brother*; also verse 7

asked them, "Is he in good health?" ⁵They said to her, "He is alive and in good health." And Tobias said, "He is my father." ⁶Then Raguel sprang up and kissed him and wept, ⁷and he spoke and said to him, "Blessing be upon you, child, son of that good and noble father! O most wretched of evils, that a just man, one who practised deeds of mercy, was rendered blind." Then he fell upon the neck of his kinsman Tobias and wept. ⁸And his wife Edna wept over him, and their daughter Sarah likewise wept. ⁹Then he killed a ram from the flock and welcomed them earnestly.

MARRIAGE OF TOBIAS AND SARAH

When they had bathed and washed themselves and reclined at table to eat, Tobias said to Raphael, "Brother Azarias, speak to Raguel, that he might give Sarah my sister to me." ¹⁰Raguel heard this and said to the youth, "Eat, drink, and be merry this night, for there is no person for whom it is proper to take Sarah my daughter besides you, brother. Likewise I myself do not have authority to give her to another man besides you, for you are nearest kin[a] to me. But I will nevertheless explain the truth to you, child. ¹¹I gave her to seven husbands from among our brothers, and they all died the night on which they were going in to be with her. But now, child, eat and drink, and the Lord will act among you." And Tobias said, "I will surely eat nothing here nor will I drink until you settle the matters that concern me." So Raguel said to him, "I hereby do it, and she is given to you according to the judgement of the book of Moses. It has been decided from heaven that she be given to you. Receive your sister. From now on you are her brother and she your sister. She is given to you from today and for ever, and may the Lord of heaven lead you both on a good path this night, child, and may he bring mercy and peace upon you both." ¹²Then Raguel called his daughter Sarah, and she came to him, and taking her by the hand he gave her to Tobias[b] and said, "Receive your wife, given to you according to the law and according to the judgement written in the book of Moses. Take her and go to your father safe and sound. And may the God of heaven prosper your way in peace." ¹³And he called her mother, and he told her to bring a scroll and he wrote a marriage contract in the scroll, to the effect that he gave her to him as a wife according to the judgement of the law of Moses. ¹⁴With that, they began to eat and drink.

¹⁵And Raguel called Edna his wife and said to her, "Sister, prepare the other room and lead Sarah[c] there." ¹⁶So she proceeded to furnish the room as he said to her and led her there. Then she wept over her and wiped away her tears and said to her, ¹⁷"Take heart, daughter; may the Lord of heaven grant you joy in place of your grief. Take heart, daughter." And she went out.

TOBIAS ROUTS THE DEMON

8 When they had finished eating and drinking, they wanted to go to sleep, so they escorted the youth and led him to the other room. ²Tobias remembered Raphael's words, and he took the fish's liver and the heart out of the sack where he had been keeping them and put them upon the live ashes in the incense burner. ³And the odour of the fish exercised a restraining force and the demon fled upwards to the districts of Egypt, and Raphael went and ensnared him there and bound him at once.

⁴And they came and shut the door of the private room. Tobias arose from the bed and said to Sarah,[d] "Sister, get up. Let us pray and plead with our Lord that he might bring us mercy and deliverance." ⁵So she arose and they began to pray and plead that deliverance might come to them, and he began to say:

"Blessed are you, O God of our fathers,
  and blessed is your name through
    all the ages and generations.
  Let the heavens and every creature
    bless you through the ages.
⁶ You made Adam, and you made
    his wife Eve for him
  as a helper and support.
  From them both the offspring of
    mankind came into being.
  You said, 'It is not good for
    the man to be alone;
  let us make a helper for
    him like himself.'

⁷And now, it is not because of lust that I am taking this sister of mine, but with sincerity. Grant that she and I may find mercy and that we may grow old together." ⁸And they said together, "Amen, Amen." ⁹Then they both went to sleep for the night.

---

[a] Greek omits *kin* [b] Greek *him* [c] Greek *her* [d] Greek *her*

But Raguel arose, called his household servants to him, and went off and dug a grave, ¹⁰for he said, "Perhaps he will die and we will become a laughing-stock and reproach." ¹¹When he had finished digging the grave, Raguel went into the house and called his wife ¹²and said, "Send one of the maidservants to go and see whether he is alive or if he has died, that we might bury him so that no one might know." ¹³So they sent the maid. They lit a lamp and opened the door, and she went in and found them lying down and sleeping together. ¹⁴And the maidservant came out and told them that he was alive and that there was no harm. ¹⁵Then they blessed the God of heaven and said:

"Blessed are you, O God, with
    every pure blessing.
Let them bless you
    throughout the ages.
¹⁶ Blessed are you, because you
    have made me glad,
And because it has not turned
    out as I was expecting;
but you have treated us according
    to your great mercy.
¹⁷ Blessed are you, because you have
    had mercy on two only children.
Bring them mercy and
    deliverance, Master;
and bring their lives to fulfilment
    with gladness and mercy."

¹⁸Then he ordered his servants to fill in the grave before morning came.

WEDDING FEAST

¹⁹He told his wife to bake many loaves of bread and he went out to the herd and selected two cows and four rams and gave orders to make them ready, and they began to make preparations. ²⁰And he called Tobias and said to him, "For fourteen days you shall surely not depart hence, but you will stay here eating and drinking with me, and you will bring gladness to my daughter's afflicted soul. ²¹And of all that belongs to me, take half and depart hence to your father safe and sound. As for the other half, when my wife and I die, it is yours. Take heart, child: I am your father and Edna your mother, and we will be by your side and that of your sister from now on and for ever. Take heart, child!"

THE MONEY RECOVERED

9 Then Tobias called Raphael and said to him, ²"Brother Azarias, take four servants and two camels with you and go to Media. Present yourself to Gabael, give him the receipt, take possession of the silver, and bring him back with you to the wedding feast. ³For you know that my father is counting the days, and if I delay even one day I will cause him much grief. And you see what Raguel has sworn, and I cannot transgress his oath." ⁵So Raphael made the journey to Rages in Media along with the four servants and the two camels, and they stayed overnight with Gabael. He gave him his receipt, and told him about Tobit's son Tobias, that he had taken a wife and that he was inviting Gabael*ᵃ* to the wedding feast. Gabael*ᵇ* arose and counted out the money bags with their seals intact and they agreed that all was in order. ⁶They both rose early in the morning and went to the wedding feast. They entered Raguel's home and found Tobias reclining at table. He got up and greeted him, and Gabael*ᶜ* wept and blessed him and said to him, "Noble and good seed of a noble and good man, a just and mercy-working man! May the Lord give you and your wife and your father and your wife's mother blessing from heaven! Blessed is God, for I see in Tobias the very likeness of my cousin Tobit!"

ANXIETY OF TOBIAS' PARENTS

10 Now day by day, Tobit was counting out how many days Tobias*ᵈ* had been travelling and how many days he would need to return. And when the days had been completed and his son did not yet arrive, ²he said, "Perhaps he has been held up there, or perhaps Gabael died and no one is there to give him the silver?" ³And he began to grieve. ⁴And Anna his wife said, "My child has perished and is no longer among the living!" Then she began to mourn and to lament over her son and said, ⁵"Woe to me, child, that I allowed you, the light of my eyes, to leave!" ⁶Tobit began to say to her, "Be still and stop making an issue, sister; he is safe and sound. Something has probably distracted them there. The man travelling with him is reliable and one of our brothers. Do not grieve over him, sister; he is just about here."*ᵉ* ⁷And she said to him, "You be

---

*ᵃ*Greek *him* *ᵇ*Greek *he* *ᶜ*Greek *he* *ᵈ*Greek *he* *ᵉ*Greek *he is already here*

quiet and stop deceiving me; my child has perished." And she rushed out every day to look down the road by which her son had left and would not listen to anyone. And whenever the sun had set, she would go back in and wail and weep the whole night long and would take no sleep.

TOBIAS AND SARAH HEAD FOR HOME

Now when the fourteen days of the wedding feast that Raguel had sworn to make for his daughter were completed, Tobias went to him and said, "Send me back, for I know that my father and mother do not believe that they will ever see me again. So now I ask you, father, that you dismiss me, so I may go to my father. I have already told you in what condition I left him." ⁸And Raguel said to Tobias, "Stay, child; stay with me, and I will send messengers to your father Tobit, and they will inform him how things are with you." ⁹And he replied, "By no means! I ask you to send me back from here to my father." ¹⁰So Raguel arose and gave Tobias his wife Sarah and half of all his belongings — male and female servants, cattle and sheep, donkeys and camels, garments, silver, and vessels. ¹¹And he sent them off safe and sound, and bade him farewell and said to him, "Be well, child, and go your way safe and sound. May the Lord of heaven prosper you and your wife Sarah, and may I see your children before I die." ¹²He said also to his daughter Sarah, "Go to your father-in-law and your mother-in-law,ᵃ because from now on they are your parents, as are the ones who gave you birth. Go in peace, daughter, and may I hear a good report about you as long as I live." And saying farewell, he allowed them to go. And Edna said to Tobias, "Child and beloved brother, may the Lord bring you back and may I live to see your children, yours and Sarah's,ᵇ before I die. Before the Lord I am entrusting my daughter to you for safekeeping. Do nothing to grieve her all the days of your life. Go in peace, child. From now on I am your mother and Sarah is your sister. May we all prosper together all the days of our lives." And she kissed them both and sent them off safe and sound. ¹³So Tobias left Raguel safe and sound, rejoicing and blessing the Lord of heaven and earth, the King of all, because he had made his journey a success. And he said to him, "May it pleaseᶜ you to honour them all the days of their lives."

11 As they were approaching Kaserein, which is across from Nineveh, ²Raphael said, "You know in what condition we left your father. ³Let us run ahead of your wife and prepare the house while they are coming." ⁴So they both went together, and he said to him, "Take the gall in your hands." And the dog went along behind them.

⁵Now Anna sat looking intently down the road her son had taken.ᵈ ⁶And she caught sight of him coming and said to his father, "Behold! your son is coming, and so is the man who went with him!"

TOBIT'S SIGHT RESTORED

⁷And Raphael said to Tobias before he drew near to his father, "I know that his eyes will be opened. ⁸Smear the fish's gall into his eyes, and the medicine will cause the white films to contract and peel away from his eyes, and your father will look up and see the light."

⁹Then Anna ran up and fell upon her son's neck and said to him, "I have seen you, child; from now on I am ready to die."ᵉ And she wept. ¹⁰And Tobit got up, stumbling over his feet, and emerged from the door of the courtyard. And Tobias went up to him ¹¹with the fish's gall in his hand, and he blew into his eyes and took hold of him and said, "Take heart, father", and he put the medicine on him, and Tobit allowed him.ᶠ ¹²And he peeled away the white filmsᵍ from the corners of his eyes with his two hands. Then he fell on his neck ¹⁴and he wept and said to him, "I see you, child, the light of my eyes!" And he said, "Blessed is God, and blessed is his great name, and blessed are all his holy angels. May your great name be over us, and may all your angels be blessed through all the ages. ¹⁵For he chastised me, and behold! I see my son Tobias!" And Tobias went in rejoicing and blessing God with his full voice,ʰ and Tobias reported to his father that his journey had prospered, and that he recovered the silver, and how he took Sarah the daughter of Raguel as his wife; and he said, "Behold! She has arrived and is at the very gate of Nineveh!"

¹⁶Then Tobit went out to the gate of Nineveh to meet his daughter-in-law, rejoicing and blessing God. When the Ninevites saw him as he was making his way and crossing through in his full strength with no one

---
ᵃThe main Greek manuscript lacks *and your mother-in-law*
ᵇGreek *my daughter Sarah* ᶜGreek uncertain ᵈGreek *her son's road*
ᵉGreek *I will die* ᶠGreek *he yielded* ᵍGreek lacks *the white films*
ʰGreek *with his whole mouth*

guiding him by the hand, they were amazed. ¹⁷And Tobit acknowledged before them that God had shown him mercy and opened his eyes. And Tobit came near to Sarah the wife of his son Tobias and blessed her and said to her, "May you enter safe and sound, daughter! Blessed is your God who has led you to us, daughter, and blessed is your father and your mother,ᵃ and blessed is Tobias my son, and blessed are you, daughter. Come into your home safe and sound, with blessing and joy. Come in, daughter!" There was joy that day among all the Judeans who were in Nineveh. ¹⁸And his nephews Ahikar and Nadabᵇ came to Tobit, rejoicing. ¹⁹The wedding was celebrated with joy for seven days, and many gifts were bestowed on them.ᶜ

RAPHAEL'S WAGES

12 When the wedding feast was completed, Tobit called his son Tobias and said to him, "Child, see that you give his wages to the man who went with you, and that you add something over and above." ²He said to him, "Father, how much am I to give him as his wages? It would not hurt me to give him half of the goods that he carried back with me. ³For he has led me on my way safe and sound, and he cured my wife, and he fetched the silver with me, and he healed you. How much more shall I give him as wages?" ⁴Tobit said to him, "It is right, child, for him to take half of all that he has come back carrying." ⁵So he called him and said, "Take for your wages half of all that you came back carrying, and depart safe and sound."

RAPHAEL'S EXHORTATION

⁶Then the angelᵈ called the two of them privately and said to them: "Bless God and acknowledge him before all the living with respect to the good things he has done for you. Bless and sing hymns to his name. Report the words of God to all people honourably, and do not hesitate to acknowledge him. ⁷It is an honourable thing to keep a king's secret hidden and gloriously to reveal and acknowledge the works of God. Keep doing what is good, and evil will not come upon you. ⁸Prayer with sincerity, practising mercy, and righteousness is better than wealth with injustice. It is a more honourable thing to do a work of mercy than to store up gold. ⁹Practising mercy delivers from death, and it purges away every sin. Those who do deeds of mercy will have full satisfaction from life; ¹⁰but those who practise sin and injustice are enemies of their own souls.

RAPHAEL DISCLOSES HIS IDENTITY

¹¹"I will tell you the whole truth and not conceal anything from you. I informed you already and said, 'It is an honourable thing to keep a king's secret hidden and gloriously to reveal the works of God.' ¹²So now, when you prayed, and Sarah too, I brought the remembrance of your prayers before the glory of the Lord, and likewise when you buried the dead. ¹³When you did not hesitate to rise and leave your meal and go and care for the dead, ¹⁴then I was sent to you, to test you, and at the same time God sent me to heal you and your daughter-in-lawᵉ Sarah. ¹⁵I am Raphael, one of the seven angels who stand and enter before the glory of the Lord."

¹⁶The two of them were troubled; they fell on their faces and they were greatly alarmed. ¹⁷And he said to them, "Do not be afraid; peace to you both. Bless God through all the ages. ¹⁸When I was with you, it was not by my favour that I was with you, but by God's will. Bless him all your days; sing hymns to him. ¹⁹And you were looking at me, butᶠ I was not eating anything, but it appeared this way to you in a vision. ²⁰And now bless God and acknowledge him on earth. Behold! I am ascending to him who sent me. Write down all these things that have happened to you." And he ascended. ²¹Then they stood up, and they were no longer able to see him. ²²So they began to bless and to sing praise to God and to acknowledge him concerning these great works of his, how an angel of God appeared to them.

TOBIT'S THANKSGIVING TO GOD

13 Then Tobitᵍ said:

"Blessed is God who lives for ever,
    and blessed is his kingdom,
² because he chastises, and
    he shows mercy;
he leads down to Hades
    below the earth,
and he himself raises up again
    from great devastation,

ᵃThe main Greek manuscript lacks *and your mother* ᵇSome manuscripts *Nabad* ᶜSome manuscripts and versions omit parts of verse 19 beginning at *The wedding was celebrated* ᵈGreek *Then he* ᵉGreek *bride* ᶠGreek *that* ᵍGreek *he*

and there is nothing that can
    escape his hand.
³ Acknowledge him, O sons of
    Israel, before the nations;
    for he himself has scattered
    you among them,
⁴ and he has shown you his
    greatness even there.
So exalt him in the presence
    of every living thing,
    because he himself is our Lord;
he is our God, and he is our Father,
    and he is God through all the ages.
⁵ He will chastise you for your
    unrighteous deeds,
    and he will have mercy upon you all,
from all the nations wherever
    you have been scattered.
⁶ When you turn to him with all your
    heart and with all your soul,
    to do what is true before him,
    then he will turn to you
    and will surely not hide his face
        from you any longer.
And now see what he has done with you;
    acknowledge him with
        your full voice,ᵃ
and bless the Lord of righteousness
    and exalt the King of the ages.ᵇ
I acknowledge him in the
    land of my captivity,
    and I show his power and majesty
    to a nation of sinners.
Turn back, you sinners, and do
    what is right before him;
    who knows if he will accept you
        and have mercy on you?
⁷ I exalt my God
    and my soul exalts the King of heaven,
    and will rejoice in his majesty.
⁸ Let all people speak
    and acknowledge him in Jerusalem.
⁹ O Jerusalem, the holy city,
    he will chastise you for the
        deeds of your sons,
    and will again show mercy to
        the sons of the righteous.
¹⁰ Acknowledge the Lord in good times
    and bless the King of the ages.
Your tabernacle will once again
    be built for you with joy.
May he cheer all those within
    you who are captives
    and love all those within you
        who are distressed,
    to all generations for ever.

¹¹ A bright light will shine into all
    the ends of the earth:
many nations will come to
    you from far off,
    and sojourners from all the
        farthest places of the earth will
            comeᶜ to your holy name,
    bearing in their hands their gifts
        for the King of heaven.
Generations of generations will render
    joyful worship within you,
    and the name of the chosen one will
        last for generations for ever.
¹² Cursed are all who speak a
    harsh word against you;
    cursed will be all those who
        overthrow and pull
            down your walls,
    and all who topple your towers
        and burn your dwellings.
But blessed will be all who
    revere you for ever.
¹³ Go, then, and rejoice over the
    sons of the righteous,
    because they will all be
        gathered together
    and will bless the Lord of the age.
¹⁴ Happy are those who love you,
    and happy are those who will rejoice
        over the peace you enjoy.
Happy are all the people who will
    grieve over all your chastisements,
    because they will rejoice over you,
    and they will see all your joy for ever.
¹⁵ Bless the Lord, the great
    King, O my soul,
¹⁶ because Jerusalem will be
    built up for a city,
    God'sᵈ house unto all ages.
Happy would I be, if the remnant
    of my line might be present
    to see your glory and to acknowledge
        the King of heaven.
The gates of Jerusalem will be built
    with sapphire and emerald,
    and all her walls with precious stone;
the towers of Jerusalem will
    be built with gold
    and her outer fortifications
        with pure gold.
¹⁷ The streets of Jerusalem will be paved
    withᵉ garnet and stone of Ophir;

ᵃGreek *with your whole mouth* ᵇTobit 13:6b–10a is supplied from Greek Vaticanus; see Introduction, page xiii to xiv. ᶜGreek lacks second *will come* ᵈGreek *his* ᵉOr *be inlaid with*

¹⁸ and the gates of Jerusalem will
speak songs of joyful worship,
and all her houses will say
'Hallelujah! Blessed is
the God of Israel,'
and the blessed will bless the holy
name for ever and beyond."

TOBIT'S FINAL COUNSEL

14 And the words of Tobit's confession came to an end. And he died in peace at one hundred and twelve years of age and was buried honourably in Nineveh. ²He was sixty-two years old when he was injured in his eyes, and after he regained sight he lived in prosperity*ᵃ* and practised deeds of mercy, and he continued to bless God and to acknowledge God's majesty. ³When he was dying, he called his son Tobias and commanded him, saying, "Child, take your children ⁴and run away to Media, because I trust God's word concerning Nineveh, which Nahum spoke, that all these things will come to pass and befall Assyria*ᵇ* and Nineveh. All things whatsoever that were spoken by the prophets of Israel, whom God sent, will come about, and nothing shall be lacking from all their words, but all things will come to pass in their appointed times. In Media there will be deliverance,*ᶜ* more so than in Assyria and in Babylon. Therefore, I know and believe that all things that God said will be fulfilled and come to be, and not a single word of his speech will prove wrong. Our brothers living in the land of Israel will be scattered*ᵈ* and taken from the good land into captivity, and all the land of Israel will be desolate, and Samaria and Jerusalem will be desolate, and the house of God will be in grief and will be burned down for a time. ⁵But God will again have mercy on them, and God will bring them back into the land of Israel, and they will rebuild the house, though for a time not as the first one, until the span of the times is fulfilled. After this they will all return from their captivity and will rebuild Jerusalem gloriously, and the house of God will be built therein, just as the prophets of Israel spoke concerning it. ⁶And all the nations throughout the whole earth, all will turn and fear God sincerely, and they will all abandon their lying idols, which*ᵉ* led them astray. ⁷And they will bless the God of the ages in righteousness. All the sons of Israel who are delivered in those days, being mindful of God with sincerity, will be gathered and will come into Jerusalem and will dwell for ever in the land of Abraham with security, and it will be given to them. And those who love God sincerely will rejoice, and those practising sin and injustice will depart from all the land.

⁸"So now, children, I am commanding you: serve God in sincerity and do what is pleasing before him. Your children also are to be instructed to practise righteousness and mercy and to remain mindful of God and to bless his name in every time with sincerity and with all their strength. And now you, child: leave Nineveh and do not remain here. ¹⁰In the day that you bury your mother with me, that very day do not lodge overnight within its boundaries. For I see that much injustice is within it, and much guile is perpetrated within it, and they have no shame. See, child, what Nadab did to Ahikar who had reared him: was he not brought down alive into the earth? And God repaid him to his face with dishonour, and Ahikar came out into the light and Nadab went into everlasting darkness, because he sought to kill Ahikar. By practising mercy, he stepped out of the fatal trap that Nadab set for him, and Nadab fell into the fatal trap and it destroyed him. ¹¹So now, children, see what practising mercy brings about, and what injustice brings about—that it kills. And now my soul is departing."

DEATH OF TOBIT AND ANNA

And they set him upon his bed, and he died and was buried honourably. ¹²And when his mother died, Tobias buried her with his father. Then he and his wife departed for Media, and they dwelt in Ecbatana with Raguel his father-in-law. ¹³He looked after them honourably in their old age and he buried them in Ecbatana of Media and he inherited the property of Raguel and of Tobit his father. ¹⁴He died honourably at the age of one hundred and seventeen years. ¹⁵And before he died, he saw and heard about the destruction of Nineveh, and he saw her captives being led into Media, which Cyaxares*ᶠ* the king of Media had taken captive, and he blessed God for all the things that he brought upon the sons of Nineveh and Assyria.*ᵍ* He rejoiced over Nineveh before he died, and blessed the Lord God for ages of ages.

---

*ᵃ*Greek *good things* *ᵇ*Latin; Greek *Athour* *ᶜ*Or *safety*
*ᵈ*Latin; Greek *numbered* *ᵉ*Correction; Greek *who* *ᶠ*Greek *Achiachar*
*ᵍ*Latin; Greek *Athouria*

JUDITH

ARPHAXAD FORTIFIES ECBATANA

1 ^{a} In the twelfth year of the reign of Nebuchadnezzar, who ruled over the Assyrians in the great city of Nineveh, in the days of Arphaxad, who ruled over the Medes in Ecbatana— ²he is the king who built walls round Ecbatana with hewn stones three cubits thick and six cubits long; he made the walls seventy cubits high and fifty cubits wide; ³at the gates he built towers a hundred cubits high and sixty cubits wide at the foundations; ⁴and he made its gates, which were seventy cubits high and forty cubits wide, so that his armies could march out in force and his infantry form their ranks— ⁵it was in those days that King Nebuchadnezzar made war against King Arphaxad in the great plain that is on the borders of Ragae. ⁶He was joined by all the people of the hill country and all those who lived along the Euphrates and the Tigris and the Hydaspes and in the plain of King Arioch of the Elymeans. Many nations joined the forces of the Chaldeans.

NEBUCHADNEZZAR ISSUES AN ULTIMATUM

⁷Then King Nebuchadnezzar of the Assyrians sent to all who lived in Persia and to all who lived in the west, those who lived in Cilicia and Damascus and Lebanon and Antilebanon and all who lived along the sea coast ⁸and those among the nations of Carmel and Gilead and Upper Galilee and the great Plain of Esdraelon ⁹and all who were in Samaria and its surrounding towns and beyond the Jordan as far as Jerusalem and Bethany and Chelous and Kadesh and the river of Egypt and Tahpanhes and Raamses and the whole land of Goshen, ¹⁰even beyond Tanis and Memphis and all who lived in Egypt as far as the borders of Ethiopia. ¹¹But all who lived in the whole region disregarded the orders of King Nebuchadnezzar of the Assyrians and refused to join him in the war; for they were not afraid of him, but looked upon him as only one^b man, and they sent back his messengers empty-handed and shamefaced.

ARPHAXAD IS DEFEATED

¹²Then Nebuchadnezzar was very angry with this whole region and swore by his throne and kingdom that he would surely take revenge on the whole territory of Cilicia and Damascus and Syria, that he would kill them by the sword and also all the inhabitants of the land of Moab and the people of Ammon and all Judea and everyone in Egypt, as far as the coasts of the two seas. ¹³In the seventeenth year he led his forces against King Arphaxad and defeated him in battle and overthrew the whole army of Arphaxad and all his cavalry and all his chariots. ¹⁴Thus he took possession of his cities and came to Ecbatana, captured its towers, plundered its markets, and turned its beauty into shame. ¹⁵He captured Arphaxad in the mountains of Ragae and struck him down with his spears; and he utterly destroyed him, to this day. ¹⁶Then he returned with them to Nineveh, he and all his combined forces, a vast body of troops; and there he and his forces rested and feasted for 120 days.

EXPEDITION AGAINST THE WEST

2 In the eighteenth year, on the twenty-second day of the first month, there was talk in the palace of King Nebuchadnezzar of the Assyrians about carrying out his revenge on the whole region, just as he had said. ²He called together all his officers and all his nobles and set forth to them his secret plan and recounted fully, with his own lips, all the wickedness of the region;^{c} ³and it was decided that everyone who had not obeyed his command should be destroyed. ⁴When he had finished setting forth his plan, King Nebuchadnezzar of the Assyrians called Holofernes, the chief general of his army, second only to himself, and said to him:

---

^{a}Judith is one of the seven deuterocanonical books that do not exist in their entirety in Hebrew or Aramaic, but which were included in the Greek Septuagint, and were likewise included in the Latin Vulgate version of the Bible translated by Jerome in the late fourth century AD. See further, *Introduction*, pages xiii to xiv. ^{b}Or *a* ^{c}The meaning of the Greek is uncertain

⁵"Thus says the great king, the lord of the whole earth: When you leave my presence, take with you men confident in their strength, to the number of 120,000 foot soldiers and 12,000 cavalry. ⁶Go and attack the whole west country, because they disobeyed my orders. ⁷Tell them to prepare earth and water, for I am coming against them in my anger and will cover the whole face of the earth with the feet of my army and will hand them over to be plundered by my troops,[a] ⁸till their wounded shall fill their valleys, and every brook and river shall be filled with their dead and overflow; ⁹and I will lead them away captive to the ends of the whole earth. ¹⁰You shall go and seize all their territory for me in advance. They will yield themselves to you, and you shall hold them for me till the day of their punishment. ¹¹But if they refuse, your eye shall not spare, and you shall hand them over to slaughter and plunder throughout your whole region. ¹²For as I live and by the power of my kingdom, what I have spoken my hand will execute. ¹³And you—take care not to transgress any of your sovereign's commands, but be sure to carry them out just as I have ordered you; and do not delay about it."

CAMPAIGN OF HOLOFERNES

¹⁴So Holofernes left the presence of his master and called together all the commanders, generals, and officers of the Assyrian army ¹⁵and mustered the picked troops by divisions as his lord had ordered him to do, 120,000 of them, together with 12,000 archers on horseback, ¹⁶and he organized them as a great army is marshalled for a campaign. ¹⁷He collected a vast number of camels and donkeys and mules for transport and innumerable sheep and oxen and goats for provision; ¹⁸also plenty of food for every man and a huge amount of gold and silver from the royal palace. ¹⁹So he set out with his whole army, to go ahead of King Nebuchadnezzar and to cover the whole face of the earth to the west with their chariots and horsemen and picked troops of infantry. ²⁰Along with them went a mixed crowd like a swarm of locusts, like the dust of the earth—a multitude that could not be counted.

²¹They marched for three days from Nineveh to the plain of Bectileth and camped opposite Bectileth near the mountain that is to the north of Upper Cilicia. ²²From there Holofernes[b] took his whole army, his infantry, cavalry, and chariots and went up into the hill country ²³and ravaged Put and Lud and plundered all the people of Rassis and the Ishmaelites who lived along the desert, south of the country of the Chelleans. ²⁴Then he followed[c] the Euphrates and passed through Mesopotamia and destroyed all the hilltop cities along the brook Abron, as far as the sea. ²⁵He also seized the territory of Cilicia and killed everyone who resisted him and came to the southern borders of Japheth, fronting towards Arabia. ²⁶He surrounded all the Midianites and burned their tents and plundered their sheepfolds. ²⁷Then he went down into the plain of Damascus during the wheat harvest and burned all their fields and destroyed their flocks and herds and sacked their cities and ravaged their lands and put to death all their young men with the edge of the sword.

²⁸So fear and terror of him fell upon all the people who lived along the sea coast, at Sidon and Tyre, and those who lived in Sur and Ocina and all who lived in Jamnia. Those who lived in Azotus and Ascalon feared him exceedingly.

ENTREATIES FOR PEACE

3 So they sent messengers to sue for peace and said, ²"Behold, we the servants of Nebuchadnezzar, the great king, lie prostrate before you. Do with us whatever you will. ³Behold, our buildings and all our land and all our wheat fields and our flocks and herds and all our sheepfolds with their tents lie before you; do with them whatever you please. ⁴Our cities also and their inhabitants are your slaves; come and deal with them in any way that seems good to you."

⁵The men came to Holofernes and told him all this. ⁶Then he went down to the sea coast with his army and stationed garrisons in the hilltop cities and took picked men from them as his allies. ⁷And these people and all in the country round about welcomed him with garlands and dances and tambourines. ⁸And he demolished all their shrines[d] and cut down their sacred groves; for it had been given to him to destroy all the gods of the land, so that all nations should worship only Nebuchadnezzar, and all their tongues and tribes should call upon him as god.

⁹Then he came to the edge of Esdraelon, near Dothan, fronting the great ridge of Judea; ¹⁰here he camped between Geba and

---
[a] Greek by them [b] Greek he [c] Or crossed [d] Greek borders

JUDEA ON ALERT

4 By this time the people of Israel living in Judea heard of everything that Holofernes, the general of King Nebuchadnezzar of the Assyrians, had done to the nations and how he had plundered and destroyed all their temples; ²they were therefore very greatly terrified at his approach and were alarmed both for Jerusalem and for the temple of the Lord their God. ³For they had only recently returned from the captivity, and all the people of Judea were newly gathered together, and the sacred vessels and the altar and the temple had been consecrated after their profanation. ⁴So they sent to every district of Samaria and to Kona and Beth-horon and Belmain and Jericho and to Choba and Aesora and the valley of Salem ⁵and immediately seized all the high hilltops and fortified the villages on them and stored up food in preparation for war—since their fields had recently been harvested. ⁶And Joakim, the high priest, who was in Jerusalem at that time, wrote to the people of Bethulia and Betomesthaim, which faces Esdraelon opposite the plain near Dothan, ⁷ordering them to seize the passes up into the hills, since by them Judea could be invaded, and it was easy to stop any who tried to enter, for the approach was narrow, wide enough for only two men at the most.

PRAYER AND PENANCE

⁸So the Israelites did as Joakim the high priest and the senate of the whole people of Israel, in session at Jerusalem, had given order. ⁹And every man of Israel cried out to God with great fervour, and they humbled themselves with much fasting. ¹⁰They and their wives and their children and their cattle and every resident alien and hired labourer and purchased slave—they all girded themselves with sackcloth. ¹¹And all the men and women of Israel, and their children, living at Jerusalem, prostrated themselves before the temple and put ashes on their heads and spread out their sackcloth before the Lord. ¹²They even surrounded the altar with sackcloth and cried out in unison, praying earnestly to the God of Israel not to give up their infants as prey and their wives as booty and the cities they had inherited to be destroyed and the sanctuary to be profaned and desecrated to the malicious joy of the Gentiles. ¹³So the Lord heard their prayers and looked upon their affliction; for the people fasted many days throughout Judea and in Jerusalem before the sanctuary of the Lord Almighty. ¹⁴And Joakim the high priest and all the priests who stood before the Lord and ministered to the Lord, with their loins girded with sackcloth, offered the continual whole burnt offering and the vows and voluntary gifts of the people. ¹⁵With ashes upon their turbans, they cried out to the Lord with all their might to look with favour upon the whole house of Israel.

COUNCIL AGAINST THE ISRAELITES

5 It was reported to Holofernes, the general of the Assyrian army, that the people of Israel had prepared for war and had closed the passes in the hills and had fortified all the high hilltops and set up barricades in the plains. ²He was very angry, so he called together all the princes of Moab and the commanders of Ammon and all the governors of the coastland ³and said to them, "Tell me, you Canaanites, what people is this that lives in the hill country? What cities do they inhabit? How large is their army, and in what does their power or strength consist? Who rules over them as king, leading their army? ⁴And why have they alone, of all who live in the west, refused to come out and meet me?"

ACHIOR'S REPORT

⁵Then Achior, the leader of all the Ammonites, said to him, "Let my lord now hear a word from the mouth of your servant, and I will tell you the truth about this people that dwells in the nearby mountain district. No falsehood shall come from your servant's mouth. ⁶This people is descended from the Chaldeans. ⁷At one time they lived in Mesopotamia, because they would not follow the gods of their fathers who were in Chaldea. ⁸For they had left the ways of their ancestors, and they worshipped the God of heaven, the God they had come to know; hence they drove them out from the presence of their gods; and they fled to Mesopotamia and lived there for a long time. ⁹Then their God commanded them to leave the place where they were living and go to the land of Canaan. There they settled and prospered, with much gold and silver and

very many cattle. ¹⁰When a famine spread over Canaan they went down to Egypt and lived there as long as they had food; and there they became a great multitude—so great that they could not be counted. ¹¹So the king of Egypt became hostile to them; he took advantage of them and set them to making bricks and humbled them and made slaves of them. ¹²Then they cried out to their God, and he afflicted the whole land of Egypt with incurable plagues; and so the Egyptians drove them out of their sight. ¹³Then God dried up the Red Sea before them, ¹⁴and he led them by the way of Sinai and Kadesh-barnea and drove out all the people of the wilderness. ¹⁵So they lived in the land of the Amorites and by their might destroyed all the inhabitants of Heshbon; and crossing over the Jordan they took possession of all the hill country. ¹⁶And they drove out before them the Canaanites and the Perizzites and the Jebusites and the Shechemites and all the Gergesites and lived there for a long time. ¹⁷As long as they did not sin against their God they prospered, for the God who hates iniquity is with them. ¹⁸But when they departed from the way that he had appointed for them, they were utterly defeated in very many battles and were led away captive to a foreign country; the temple of their God was razed to the ground, and their cities were captured by their enemies. ¹⁹But now they have returned to their God and have come back from the places to which they were scattered and have occupied Jerusalem, where their sanctuary is, and have settled in the hill country, because it was uninhabited. ²⁰Now therefore, my master and lord, if there is any unwitting error in this people and they sin against their God and we find out their offence, then we will go up and defeat them. ²¹But if there is no transgression in their nation, then let my lord pass them by; for their Lord will defend them, and their God will protect them, and we shall be put to shame before all the earth."

²²When Achior had finished saying this, all the men standing round the tent began to complain; Holofernes' officers and all the men from the sea coast and from Moab insisted that he must be put to death. ²³"For," they said, "we will not be afraid of the Israelites; they are a people with no strength or power for making war. ²⁴Therefore let us go up, Lord Holofernes, and they will be devoured by your vast army."

ACHIOR HANDED OVER TO THE ISRAELITES

6 When the disturbance made by the men outside the council died down, Holofernes, the commander of the Assyrian army, said to Achior and all the Moabites in the presence of all the foreign contingents:

²"And who are you, Achior, and you hirelings of Ephraim, to prophesy among us as you have done today and tell us not to make war against the people of Israel because their God will defend them? Who is God except Nebuchadnezzar? He will send his forces and will destroy them from the face of the earth, and their God will not deliver them— ³we the king's servants*ᵃ* will destroy them as one man. They cannot resist the might of our cavalry. ⁴We will overwhelm them with them, and their mountains will be drunk with their blood, and their fields will be full of their dead. Their footprints cannot withstand our attack, but will utterly perish. So says King Nebuchadnezzar, the lord of the whole earth. For he has spoken; none of his words shall be in vain.

⁵"But you, Achior, you Ammonite hireling, who has said these words on the day of your iniquity, you shall not see my face again from this day until I take revenge on this race that came out of Egypt. ⁶Then the sword of my army and the spear*ᵇ* of my servants shall pierce your sides, and you shall fall among their wounded, when I return. ⁷Now my slaves are going to take you back into the hill country and put you in one of the cities beside the passes, ⁸and you will not die until you perish along with them. ⁹If you really hope in your heart that they will not be taken, do not look downcast! I have spoken and none of my words shall fail."

¹⁰Then Holofernes ordered his slaves, who waited on him in his tent, to seize Achior and take him to Bethulia and hand him over to the Israelites. ¹¹So his slaves took him and led him out of the camp into the plain, and from the plain they went up into the hill country and came to the springs below Bethulia. ¹²When the men of the city saw them on the top of the hill, they caught up their weapons and ran out of the city to the top of the hill, and all the slingers kept them from coming up by casting stones at them. ¹³However, they got under the shelter of the hill, and they bound Achior and left him

---
*ᵃ*Greek *we his servants*   *ᵇ*Latin, Syriac; Greek *people*

thrown at the foot of the hill and returned to their master.

¹⁴Then the Israelites came down from their city and found him; and they untied him and brought him into Bethulia and placed him before the magistrates of their city, ¹⁵who in those days were Uzziah son of Micah, of the tribe of Simeon, and Chabris son of Gothoniel and Charmis son of Melchiel. ¹⁶They called together all the elders of the city, and all their young men and their women ran to the assembly; and they set Achior in the midst of all their people, and Uzziah asked him what had happened. ¹⁷He answered and told them what had taken place at the council of Holofernes and all that he had said in the presence of the Assyrian leaders and all that Holofernes had said so boastfully against the house of Israel. ¹⁸Then the people fell down and worshipped God and cried out to him and said:

¹⁹"O Lord God of heaven, note their arrogance and have pity on the humiliation of our people and look this day upon the faces of those who are consecrated to you."

²⁰Then they consoled Achior and praised him greatly. ²¹And Uzziah took him from the assembly to his own house and gave a banquet for the elders; and all that night they called on the God of Israel for help.

CAMPAIGN AGAINST BETHULIA

7 The next day Holofernes ordered his whole army and all the allies who had joined him to break camp and move against Bethulia and to seize the passes up into the hill country and make war on the Israelites. ²So all their warriors moved their camp that day; their force of men of war was 170,000 infantry and 12,000 cavalry, together with the baggage and the foot soldiers handling it, a very great multitude. ³They encamped in the valley near Bethulia, beside the spring, and they spread out in breadth over Dothan as far as Balbaim and in length from Bethulia to Cyamon, which faces Esdraelon.

⁴When the Israelites saw their vast numbers they were greatly terrified, and everyone said to his neighbour, "These men will now lick up the face of the whole land; neither the high mountains nor the valleys nor the hills will bear their weight." ⁵Then each man took up his weapons, and when they had kindled fires on their towers they remained on guard all that night.

⁶On the second day Holofernes led out all his cavalry in full view of the Israelites in Bethulia ⁷and examined the approaches to their city and visited the springs that supplied their water and seized them and set guards of soldiers over them and then returned to his army.

⁸Then all the chieftains of the people of Esau and all the leaders of the Moabites and the commanders of the coastland came to him and said, ⁹"Let our lord hear a word, lest his army be defeated. ¹⁰For these people, the Israelites, do not rely on their spears but on the height of the mountains where they live, for it is not easy to reach the tops of their mountains. ¹¹Therefore, my lord, do not fight against them in battle array, and not a man of your army will fall. ¹²Remain in your camp and keep all the men in your forces with you; only, let your servants take possession of the spring of water that flows from the foot of the mountain— ¹³for this is where all the people of Bethulia get their water. So thirst will destroy them, and they will give up their city. We and our people will go up to the tops of the nearby mountains and camp there to keep watch that not a man gets out of the city. ¹⁴They and their wives and children will waste away with famine, and before the sword reaches them they will be strewn round in the streets where they live. ¹⁵So you will pay them back with evil, because they rebelled and did not receive you peaceably."

¹⁶These words pleased Holofernes and all his servants, and he gave orders to do as they had said. ¹⁷So the army of the Ammonites moved forwards together with 5,000 Assyrians, and they encamped in the valley and seized the water supply and the springs of the Israelites. ¹⁸And the sons of Esau and the sons of Ammon went up and encamped in the hill country opposite Dothan; and they sent some of their men towards the south and the east, towards Acraba, which is near Chusi beside the brook Mochmur. The rest of the Assyrian army encamped in the plain and covered the whole face of the land, and their tents and supply trains spread out in great number, and they formed a vast multitude.

DISTRESS OF THE ISRAELITES

¹⁹The people of Israel cried out to the Lord their God, for their courage failed, because all their enemies had surrounded them and there was no way of escape from them. ²⁰The

whole Assyrian army, their infantry, chariots, and cavalry, surrounded them for thirty-four days, until all the vessels of water belonging to every inhabitant of Bethulia were empty; ²¹their cisterns were going dry, and they did not have enough water to drink their fill for a single day, because it was measured out to them to drink. ²²Their children lost heart, and the women and young men fainted from thirst and fell down in the streets of the city and in the passages through the gates; there was no strength left in them any longer.

²³Then all the people, the young men, the women, and the children, gathered round Uzziah and the rulers of the city and cried out with a loud voice and said before all the elders, ²⁴"God be judge between you and us! For you have done us a great injury in not making peace with the Assyrians. ²⁵For now we have no one to help us; God has sold us into their hands, to strew us on the ground before them with thirst and utter destruction. ²⁶Now call them in and surrender the whole city to the army of Holofernes and to all his forces, to be plundered. ²⁷For it would be better for us to be captured by them; for we will be slaves, but our lives will be spared, and we shall not witness the death of our infants before our eyes or see our wives and children draw their last breath. ²⁸We call to witness against you heaven and earth and our God, the Lord of our fathers, who punishes us according to our sins and the sins of our fathers. Let him not do this day the things that we have described!"

²⁹Then great and general lamentation arose throughout the assembly, and they cried out to the Lord God with a loud voice. ³⁰And Uzziah said to them, "Have courage, my brothers! Let us hold out for five more days; by that time the Lord our God will restore to us his mercy, for he will not forsake us utterly. ³¹But if these days pass by and no help comes for us, I will do what you say."

³²Then he dismissed the people to their various posts, and they went up on the walls and towers of their city. The women and children he sent home. And they were greatly depressed in the city.

CHARACTER OF JUDITH

8 At that time Judith heard about these things: she was the daughter of Merari son of Ox, son of Joseph, son of Oziel, son of Elkiah, son of Ananias, son of Gideon, son of Raphaim, son of Ahitub, son of Elijah, son of Hilkiah, son of Eliab, son of Nathanael, son of Salamiel, son of Sarasadai, son of Israel. ²Her husband Manasseh, who belonged to her tribe and family, had died during the barley harvest. ³For as he stood overseeing the men who were binding sheaves in the field, he was overcome by the burning heat and took to his bed and died in Bethulia his city. So they buried him with his fathers in the field between Dothan and Balamon. ⁴Judith had lived at home as a widow for three years and four months. ⁵She set up a tent for herself on the roof of her house and girded sackcloth round her loins and wore the garments of her widowhood. ⁶She fasted all the days of her widowhood, except the day before the Sabbath and the Sabbath itself, the day before the new moon and the day of the new moon, and the feasts and days of rejoicing of the house of Israel. ⁷She was beautiful in appearance and had a very lovely face; and her husband Manasseh had left her gold and silver and men and women slaves and cattle and fields; and she maintained this estate. ⁸No one spoke ill of her, for she feared God with great devotion.

JUDITH AND THE ELDERS

⁹When Judith heard the wicked words spoken by the people against the ruler, because they were faint for lack of water, and when she heard all that Uzziah said to them and how he promised them under oath to surrender the city to the Assyrians after five days, ¹⁰she sent her maid, who was in charge of all she possessed, to summon Uzziah and Chabris and Charmis, the elders of her city. ¹¹They came to her, and she said to them:

"Listen to me, rulers of the people of Bethulia! What you have said to the people today is not right; you have even sworn and pronounced this oath between God and you, promising to surrender the city to our enemies unless the Lord turns and helps us within so many days. ¹²Who are you, who have put God to the test this day and are setting yourselves up in the place of[a] God among the sons of men? ¹³You are questioning the Lord Almighty—but you will never know anything! ¹⁴You cannot plumb the depths of the human heart or find out what a man is thinking; how do you expect to search out God, who made all these things, and find out his mind or comprehend his thought? No,

---
[a] Or *yourselves above*

³Now Judith had told her maid to stand outside the bedchamber and to wait for her to come out, as she did every day; for she said she would be going out for her prayers. And she had said the same thing to Bagoas. ⁴So everyone went out, and no one, either small or great, was left in the bedchamber. Then Judith, standing beside his bed, said in her heart, "O Lord God of all might, look in this hour upon the work of my hands for the exaltation of Jerusalem. ⁵For now is the time to help your inheritance and to carry out my undertaking for the destruction of the enemies who have risen up against us."

⁶She went up to the post at the end of the bed, above Holofernes' head and took down his sword from it. ⁷She came close to his bed and took hold of the hair of his head and said, "Give me strength this day, O Lord God of Israel!" ⁸And she struck his neck twice with all her might and severed his head from his body. ⁹Then she tumbled his body off the bed and pulled down the canopy from the posts; after a moment she went out and gave Holofernes' head to her maid, ¹⁰who placed it in her food bag.

JUDITH RETURNS TO BETHULIA

Then the two of them went out together, as they were accustomed to go for prayer; and they passed through the camp and circled round the valley and went up the mountain to Bethulia and came to its gates. ¹¹Judith called out from afar to the watchmen at the gates, "Open, open the gate! God, our God, is still with us, to show his power in Israel and his strength against our enemies, even as he has done this day!"

¹²When the men of her city heard her voice, they hurried down to the city gate and called together the elders of the city. ¹³They all ran together, both small and great, for it was unbelievable that she had returned; they opened the gate and admitted them, and they kindled a fire for light and gathered round them. ¹⁴Then she said to them with a loud voice, "Praise God, O praise him! Praise God, who has not withdrawn his mercy from the house of Israel, but has destroyed our enemies by my hand this very night!"

¹⁵Then she took the head out of the bag and showed it to them and said, "See, here is the head of Holofernes, the commander of the Assyrian army, and here is the canopy beneath which he lay in his drunken stupor. The Lord has struck him down by the hand of a woman. ¹⁶As the Lord lives, who has protected me in the way I went, it was my face that tricked him to his destruction, and yet he committed no act of sin with me, to defile and shame me."

¹⁷All the people were greatly astonished and bowed down and worshipped God and said with one accord, "Blessed are you, our God, who has brought into contempt this day the enemies of your people."

¹⁸And Uzziah said to her, "O daughter, you are blessed by the Most High God above all women on earth; and blessed be the Lord God, who created the heavens and the earth, who has guided you to strike the head of the leader of our enemies. ¹⁹Your hope will never depart from the hearts of men, as they remember the power of God. ²⁰May God grant this to be a perpetual honour to you and may he visit you with blessings, because you did not spare your own life when our nation was brought low, but have avenged our ruin, walking in the straight path before our God." And all the people said, "So be it, so be it!"

JUDITH'S COUNSEL

14 Then Judith said to them, "Listen to me, my brothers, and take this head and hang it upon the parapet of your wall. ²And as soon as morning comes and the sun rises, let every valiant man take his weapons and go out of the city and set a captain over them, as if you were going down to the plain against the Assyrian outpost; only do not go down. ³Then they will seize their arms and go into their camp and rouse the officers of the Assyrian army; and they will rush into the tent of Holofernes and will not find him. Then fear will come over them, and they will flee before you, ⁴and taking pursuit, you and all who live within the borders of Israel cut them down as they flee. ⁵But before you do all this, bring Achior the Ammonite to me, and let him see and recognize the man who despised the house of Israel and sent him to us as if to his death."

⁶So they summoned Achior from the house of Uzziah. And when he came and saw the head of Holofernes in the hand of one of the men at the gathering of the people, he fell down on his face and his spirit failed him. ⁷And when they raised him up he fell at Judith's feet and knelt before her and said, "Blessed are you in every tent of Judah! In every nation those who hear your name will

be alarmed. ⁸Now tell me what you have done during these days."

Then Judith described to him in the presence of the people all that she had done, from the day she left until the moment of her speaking to them. ⁹And when she had finished speaking, the people raised a great shout and made a joyful noise in their city. ¹⁰And when Achior saw all that the God of Israel had done, he believed firmly in God and was circumcised and joined the house of Israel, remaining so to this day.

HOLOFERNES' DEATH IS DISCOVERED

¹¹As soon as it was dawn they hung the head of Holofernes on the wall, and every man took his weapons, and they went out in companies to the passes in the mountains. ¹²And when the Assyrians saw them they sent word to their commanders, and they went to the generals and the captains and to all their officers. ¹³So they came to Holofernes' tent and said to the steward in charge of all his personal affairs, "Wake up our lord, for the slaves have been so bold as to come down against us to give battle, in order to be destroyed completely."

¹⁴So Bagoas went in and knocked at the curtain of the tent, for he supposed that he was sleeping with Judith. ¹⁵But when no one answered, he drew it aside and went into the bedchamber and found him thrown down on the footstool dead, with his head cut off. ¹⁶And he cried out with a loud voice and wept and groaned and shouted and rent his garments. ¹⁷Then he went to the tent where Judith had stayed, and when he did not find her he rushed out to the people and shouted, ¹⁸"The slaves have tricked us! One Hebrew woman has brought disgrace upon the house of King Nebuchadnezzar! For look, Holofernes is lying on the ground, and his head is not on him!"

¹⁹When the leaders of the Assyrian army heard this, they rent their tunics and were greatly dismayed, and their cries and shouts were very loud in the midst of the camp.

ASSYRIANS FLEE IN PANIC

15 When the men in the tents heard it, they were amazed at what had happened. ²Fear and trembling came over them, so that they did not wait for one another, but with one impulse all rushed out and fled by every path across the plain and through the hill country. ³Those who had camped in the hills round Bethulia also took to flight. Then the Israelites, everyone that was a soldier, rushed out upon them. ⁴And Uzziah sent men to Betomasthaim and Bebai and Chobai and Kola and to all the frontiers of Israel to tell what had taken place and to urge all to rush out upon their enemies to destroy them. ⁵And when the Israelites heard it, with one accord they fell upon the enemy*ᵃ* and cut them down as far as Choba. Likewise those in Jerusalem and all the hill country also came, for they were told what had happened in the camp of the enemy; and those in Gilead and in Galilee outflanked them with great slaughter, until they came to Damascus and its borders. ⁶The rest of the people of Bethulia fell upon the Assyrian camp and plundered it and were greatly enriched. ⁷And the Israelites, when they returned from the slaughter, took control of what remained, and the villages and towns in the hill country and in the plain took possession of a great amount of booty, for there was a vast quantity of it.

ISRAELITES CELEBRATE THEIR VICTORY

⁸Then Joakim the high priest and the senate of the people of Israel who lived at Jerusalem came to witness the good things that the Lord had done for Israel and to see Judith and to greet her. ⁹And when they met her they all blessed her with one accord and said to her, "You are the exaltation of Jerusalem, you are the great glory of Israel, you are the great pride of our nation! ¹⁰You have done all this single-handed; you have done great good to Israel, and God is well pleased with it. May the almighty Lord bless you for ever!" And all the people said, "So be it!"

¹¹So all the people plundered the camp for thirty days. They gave Judith the tent of Holofernes and all his silver dishes and his beds and his bowls and all his furniture; and she took them and loaded her mule and hitched up her carts and piled the things on them.

¹²Then all the women of Israel gathered to see her and blessed her, and some of them performed a dance for her; and she took branches in her hands and gave them to the women who were with her; ¹³and they crowned themselves with olive wreaths, she and those who were with her; and she went before all the people in the dance, leading

---

ᵃGreek upon them

all the women, while all the men of Israel followed, bearing their arms and wearing garlands and with songs on their lips.

JUDITH'S HYMN OF PRAISE

14 Then Judith began this thanksgiving before all Israel, and all the people loudly sang this song of praise.

16 And Judith said:

Begin a song to my God with
  tambourines,
sing to my Lord with cymbals.
Raise to him a new psalm;[a]
  exalt him and call upon his name.
2 For God is the Lord who crushes wars;
  for into his camp, in the
    midst of the people
  he delivered me out of the
    hands of my pursuers.

3 The Assyrian came down from the
    mountains of the north;
  he came with myriads of his army;
  their multitude blocked up the valleys,
    their cavalry covered the hills.
4 He said he would burn up my territory
    and kill my young men
      with the sword
  and put my infants on the ground
    and hand over my children as prey
    and take my virgins as booty.

5 But the Lord Almighty has foiled them
    by the hand of a woman.
6 For their mighty one did not fall by
    the hands of the young men,
  nor did the sons of the
      Titans strike him,
  nor did tall giants set upon him;
  but Judith daughter of
      Merari undid him
    with the beauty of her face.

7 For she took off her widow's mourning
    to exalt the oppressed in Israel.
  She anointed her face with ointment
8 and fastened her hair with a tiara
    and put on a linen gown
      to deceive him.
9 Her sandal ravished his eyes,
    her beauty captivated his mind,
    and the sword severed his neck.
10 The Persians trembled at her boldness,
    the Medes were daunted
      at her daring.

11 Then my oppressed people
    raised the war cry;
  my weak people shouted.[b]
  And they trembled,
    they raised their cry and
      turned to flight.
12 The sons of maidservants have
    pierced them through;
  they wounded them like the
      children of fugitives,
    they perished before the
      army of my Lord.

13 I will sing to my God a new song:
  O Lord, you are great and glorious,
    wonderful in strength, invincible.
14 Let all your creatures serve you,
    for you spoke, and they were made.
  You sent forth your Spirit,[c]
    and it formed them;
    there is none that can
      resist your voice.
15 For the mountains shall be shaken to
    their foundations with the waters;
  at your presence the rocks
    shall melt like wax,
  but to those who fear you
    you will continue to show mercy.
16 For every sacrifice as a fragrant
    offering is a small thing,
  and all fat for whole burnt offerings
    to you is a very little thing,
  but he who fears the Lord
    shall be great for ever.

17 Woe to the nations that rise
    up against my people!
  The Lord Almighty will take
    vengeance on them in
      the day of judgement;
  fire and worms he will give
    to their flesh;
  they shall weep in pain for ever.

18 When they arrived at Jerusalem they worshipped God. As soon as the people were purified, they offered their whole burnt offerings, their freewill offerings, and their gifts. **19** Judith also dedicated to God all the vessels of Holofernes, which the people had given her; and the canopy that she took for herself from his bedchamber she gave as a votive offering to the Lord. **20** So the people continued feasting

---
[a]Some manuscripts *him a psalm and praise* [b]Some manuscripts *feared* [c]Or *breath*

in Jerusalem before the sanctuary for three months, and Judith remained with them.

RENOWN AND DEATH OF JUDITH

²¹After this everyone returned home to his own inheritance, and Judith went to Bethulia and remained on her estate and was honoured in her time throughout the whole country. ²²Many desired to marry her, but she remained a widow all the days of her life after Manasseh her husband died and was gathered to his people. ²³She became more and more famous and grew old in her husband's house, until she was 105 years old. She set her maid free. She died in Bethulia, and they buried her in the cave of her husband Manasseh, ²⁴and the house of Israel mourned for her seven days. Before she died she distributed her property to all those who were next of kin to her husband Manasseh and to her own nearest kinsmen. ²⁵And no one ever again spread terror among the people of Israel in the days of Judith or for a long time after her death.

ESTHER

MORDECAI'S DREAM

1 ¹ᵃᵃ In the second year when Artaxerxes the Great was reigning, on the first day of Nisan, Mordecai son of Jair, son of Shimei, son of Kish, of the tribe of Benjamin, had a dream. ¹ᵇHe was a Jew, dwelling in the city of Susa, a great man, serving in the court of the king. ¹ᶜHe was one of the captives whom King Nebuchadnezzar of Babylon had brought from Jerusalem with King Jeconiah of Judea. And this was his dream:

¹ᵈBehold, noise and confusion, thunders and earthquake, tumult upon the earth! ¹ᵉAnd behold, two great dragons came forwards, both ready to fight, and they roared terribly. ¹ᶠAnd at their roaring every nation prepared for war, to fight against the nation of the righteous. ¹ᵍAnd behold, a day of darkness and gloom, tribulation and distress, affliction and great tumult upon the earth! ¹ʰAnd the whole righteous nation was troubled; they feared the evils that threatened themselves and were ready to perish. ¹ⁱThen they cried to God; and from their cry, as though from a tiny spring, there came a great river, with abundant water; ¹ᵏlight came, and the sun rose, and the lowly were exalted and consumed those held in honour.

¹ˡMordecai saw in this dream what God had determined to do, and after he awoke he had it on his mind and sought all day to understand it in every detail.

PLOT AGAINST THE KING

¹ᵐᵇ Now Mordecai took his rest in the courtyard with Gabatha and Tharra, the two eunuchs of the king who kept watch in the courtyard. ¹ⁿHe overheard their conversation and enquired into their purposes and learned that they were preparing to lay hands upon King Artaxerxes; and he informed the king concerning them. ¹⁰Then the king examined the two eunuchs, and when they confessed they were led to execution. ¹ᵖThe king made a permanent record of these things, and Mordecai wrote an account of them. ¹ᵠAnd the king ordered Mordecai to serve in the court and rewarded him for these things. ¹ʳBut Haman son of Hamadathos, a Bougean, was in great honour with the king, and he sought to injure Mordecai and his people because of the two eunuchs of the king.

THE KING'S BANQUETS

1 Now in the days of Ahasuerus, the Ahasuerus who reigned from India to Ethiopia over 127 provinces, ²in those days when King Ahasuerus sat on his royal throne in Susa, the citadel, ³in the third year of his reign he gave a feast for all his officials and servants. The army of Persia and Media and the nobles and governors of the provinces were before him, ⁴while he showed the riches of his royal glory and the splendour and pomp of his greatness for many days, 180 days. ⁵And when these days were completed, the king gave for all the people present in Susa the citadel, both great and small, a feast lasting for seven days in the court of the garden of the king's palace. ⁶There were white cotton curtains and violet hangings fastened with cords of fine linen and purple to silver rodsᶜ and marble pillars, and also couches of gold and silver on a mosaic pavement of porphyry, marble, mother-of-pearl, and precious stones. ⁷Drinks were served in golden vessels, vessels of different kinds, and the royal wine was lavished according to the bounty of the king. ⁸And drinking was according to this edict: "There is no compulsion." For the king had given orders to all the staff of his palace to do as each man desired. ⁹Queen Vashti also gave a feast for

---

ᵃThe following three paragraphs in italic type, under the heading *Mordecai's Dream*, do not appear in the Hebrew text of Esther. These three paragraphs, however, are included in the Greek Septuagint text of Esther and were likewise included in the Latin Vulgate version of the Bible translated by Jerome in the late fourth century AD. Jerome placed these paragraphs at the end of Esther, along with explanatory notes to make them accessible to the reader. For the text of Esther in this publication of the ESV Catholic Edition Bible, these paragraphs have been placed in the narrative sequence as they appear in the Septuagint. The paragraphs under this heading (*Mordecai's Dream*) correspond to the following chapter and verse numbers used in the Vulgate: Esther 11:2-12. See further, *Introduction*, pages xiii to xiv. ᵇThe following paragraph in italic type, under the heading *Plot against the King*, does not appear in the Hebrew text of Esther. This paragraph, however, is included in the Greek Septuagint and the Latin Vulgate, where it corresponds to the following chapter and verse numbers used in the Vulgate: Esther 12:1-6. See further the asterisk note above and *Introduction*, pages xiii to xiv. ᶜOr *rings*

QUEEN VASHTI'S REFUSAL

¹⁰On the seventh day, when the heart of the king was merry with wine, he commanded Mehuman, Biztha, Harbona, Bigtha and Abagtha, Zethar and Carkas, the seven eunuchs who served in the presence of King Ahasuerus, ¹¹to bring Queen Vashti before the king with her royal crown,ᵃ in order to show the peoples and the princes her beauty, for she was lovely to look at. ¹²But Queen Vashti refused to come at the king's command delivered by the eunuchs. At this the king became enraged, and his anger burned within him.

¹³Then the king said to the wise men who knew the times (for this was the king's procedure towards all who were versed in law and judgement, ¹⁴the men next to him being Carshena, Shethar, Admatha, Tarshish, Meres, Marsena, and Memucan, the seven princes of Persia and Media, who saw the king's face, and sat first in the kingdom): ¹⁵"According to the law, what is to be done to Queen Vashti, because she has not performed the command of King Ahasuerus delivered by the eunuchs?" ¹⁶Then Memucan said in the presence of the king and the officials, "Not only against the king has Queen Vashti done wrong, but also against all the officials and all the peoples who are in all the provinces of King Ahasuerus. ¹⁷For the queen's behaviour will be made known to all women, causing them to look at their husbands with contempt,ᵇ since they will say, 'King Ahasuerus commanded Queen Vashti to be brought before him, and she did not come.' ¹⁸This very day the noble women of Persia and Media who have heard of the queen's behaviour will say the same to all the king's officials, and there will be contempt and wrath in plenty. ¹⁹If it please the king, let a royal order go out from him, and let it be written among the laws of the Persians and the Medes so that it may not be repealed, that Vashti is never again to come before King Ahasuerus. And let the king give her royal position to another who is better than she. ²⁰So when the decree made by the king is proclaimed throughout all his kingdom, for it is vast, all women will give honour to their husbands, high and low alike." ²¹This advice pleased the king and the princes, and the king did as Memucan proposed. ²²He sent letters to all the royal provinces, to every province in its own script and to every people in its own language, that every man be master in his own household and speak according to the language of his people.

ESTHER CHOSEN QUEEN

2 After these things, when the anger of King Ahasuerus had abated, he remembered Vashti and what she had done and what had been decreed against her. ²Then the king's young men who attended him said, "Let beautiful young virgins be sought out for the king. ³And let the king appoint officers in all the provinces of his kingdom to gather all the beautiful young virgins to the harem in Susa the citadel, under custody of Hegai, the king's eunuch, who is in charge of the women. Let their cosmetics be given to them. ⁴And let the young woman who pleases the kingᶜ be queen instead of Vashti." This pleased the king, and he did so.

⁵Now there was a Jew in Susa the citadel whose name was Mordecai, the son of Jair, son of Shimei, son of Kish, a Benjaminite, ⁶who had been carried away from Jerusalem among the captives carried away with Jeconiah king of Judah, whom Nebuchadnezzar king of Babylon had carried away. ⁷He was bringing up Hadassah, that is Esther, the daughter of his uncle, for she had neither father nor mother. The young woman had a beautiful figure and was lovely to look at, and when her father and her mother died, Mordecai took her as his own daughter. ⁸So when the king's order and his edict were proclaimed, and when many young women were gathered in Susa the citadel in the custody of Hegai, Esther also was taken into the king's palace and put in the custody of Hegai, who had charge of the women. ⁹And the young woman pleased him and won his favour. And he quickly provided her with her cosmetics and her portion of food, and with seven chosen young women from the king's palace, and advanced her and her young women to the best place in the harem. ¹⁰Esther had not made known her people or kindred, for Mordecai had commanded her not to make it known. ¹¹And every day Mordecai walked in front of the court of the harem to learn how Esther was and what was happening to her.

ᵃOr *headdress* ᵇHebrew *to disdain their husbands in their eyes* ᶜHebrew *who is good in the eyes of the king*

Mordecai and say, ¹¹"All the king's servants and the people of the king's provinces know that if any man or woman goes to the king inside the inner court without being called, there is but one law—to be put to death, except the one to whom the king holds out the golden sceptre so that he may live. But as for me, I have not been called to come in to the king these thirty days."

¹²And they told Mordecai what Esther had said. ¹³Then Mordecai told them to reply to Esther, "Do not think to yourself that in the king's palace you will escape any more than all the other Jews. ¹⁴For if you keep silent at this time, relief and deliverance will rise for the Jews from another place, but you and your father's house will perish. And who knows whether you have not come to the kingdom for such a time as this?" ¹⁵Then Esther told them to reply to Mordecai, ¹⁶"Go, gather all the Jews to be found in Susa, and hold a fast on my behalf, and do not eat or drink for three days, night or day. I and my young women will also fast as you do. Then I will go to the king, though it is against the law, and if I perish, I perish."ᵃ ¹⁷Mordecai then went away and did everything as Esther had ordered him.

MORDECAI'S PRAYER

¹⁷ᵃᵇ *Then Mordecaiᶜ prayed to the Lord, calling to remembrance all the works of the Lord. He said:*

¹⁷ᵇ*"O Lord, Lord, King who rules over all things, for the universe is in your power and there is no one who can oppose you when it is your will to save Israel.* ¹⁷ᶜ*For you have made heaven and earth and every wonderful thing in it under heaven,* ¹⁷ᵈ*and you are Lord of all, and there is no one who can resist you, the Lord.* ¹⁷ᵉ*You know all things; you know, O Lord, that it was not in insolence or pride or for any love of glory that I did this and refused to bow down to this proud Haman.* ¹⁷ᶠ*For I would have been willing to kiss the soles of his feet, to save Israel!* ¹⁷ᵍ*But I did this that I might not set the glory of man above the glory of God, and I will not bow down to anyone but you, my Lord; and I will not do these things in pride.* ¹⁷ʰ*And now, O Lord God and King, God of Abraham, spare your people; for they are looking to annihilate us, and they desire to destroy the inheritance that has been yours from the beginning.* ¹⁷ⁱ*Do not neglect your portion, which you redeemed for yourself out of the land of Egypt.* ¹⁷ᵏ*Hear my prayer and have mercy upon your allotment and turn our mourning into feasting, that we may live and sing praise to your name, O Lord; do not destroy the mouth of those who praise you."*

¹⁷ˡ*And all Israel cried out mightily, for their death was before their eyes.*

ESTHER'S PRAYER

¹⁷ᵐᵈ *And Esther the queen, seized with deathly anxiety, fled to the Lord;* ¹⁷ⁿ *she took off her splendid apparel and put on the garments of distress and mourning, and instead of costly perfumes she covered her head with ashes and excrement, and she utterly humbled her body and every part that she loved to adorn she covered with her tangled hair.* ¹⁷ᵒ*And she prayed to the Lord God of Israel and said:*

"O my Lord, you only are our King; help me, who am alone and have no helper but you, ¹⁷ᵖ*for my danger is in my hand.* ¹⁷ᑫ*Ever since I was born I have heard in the tribe of my family that you, O Lord, took Israel out of all the nations and our fathers from among all their ancestors for an everlasting inheritance and that you did for them all that you promised.* ¹⁷ʳ*And now we have sinned before you, and you have given us into the hands of our enemies,* ¹⁷ˢ*because we glorified their gods. You are righteous, O Lord!* ¹⁷ᵗ*And now they were not satisfied that we are in bitter slavery, but they have covenanted with their idols* ¹⁷ᵘ*to abolish what your mouth has ordained and to destroy your inheritance, to stop the mouths of those who praise you and to quench your altar and the glory of your house,* ¹⁷ᵛ*to open the mouth of the nations for the praise of vain idols and to magnify for ever a mortal king.* ¹⁷ʷ*O Lord, do not surrender your sceptre to what has no being; and do not let them mock at our downfall; but turn their plan against them and make an example of the man who began this against us.* ¹⁷ˣ*Remember, O Lord; make yourself known in this time of our affliction and give me courage, O King of the gods and Master of all dominion!* ¹⁷ʸ*Put eloquent speech in my mouth before the lion and turn his heart to hate the man who is fighting against us, so that there may be an end of him and those who agree with him.* ¹⁷ᶻ*But save us by your hand and help me, who am alone and have no helper but you, O Lord.* ¹⁷ᵃᵃ*You have knowledge of all things; and you*

ᵃHebrew *if I am destroyed, then I will be destroyed* ᵇThe following three paragraphs in italic type, under the heading *Mordecai's Prayer*, do not appear in the Hebrew text of Esther. These three paragraphs, however, are included in the Greek Septuagint and the Latin Vulgate, where they correspond to the following chapter and verse numbers used in the Vulgate: Esther 13:8-18. See further the asterisk note at the beginning of Esther (page 435) and *Introduction*, pages xiii to xiv. ᶜGreek *he* ᵈThe following two paragraphs in italic type, under the heading *Esther's Prayer*, do not appear in the Hebrew text of Esther. These two paragraphs, however, are included in the Greek Septuagint and the Latin Vulgate, where they correspond to the following chapter and verse numbers used in the Vulgate: Esther 14:1-19. See further the asterisk note at the beginning of Esther (page 435) and *Introduction*, pages xiii to xiv.

know that I hate the splendour of the wicked and abhor the bed of the uncircumcised and of any alien. ¹⁷ᵇᵇYou know my necessity—that I abhor the sign of my proud position, which is upon my head on the days when I appear in public. I abhor it like a menstrual rag, and I do not wear it on the days when I am at leisure. ¹⁷ᶜᶜAnd your servant has not eaten at Haman's table, and I have not honoured the king's feast or drunk the wine of the libations. ¹⁷ᵈᵈYour servant has had no joy since the day that I was brought here until now, except in you, O Lord God of Abraham. ¹⁷ᵉᵉO God, whose might is over all, hear the voice of the despairing and save us from the hands of evildoers. And save me from my fear!"

ESTHER PREPARES A BANQUET

5 On the third day Esther put on her royal robes and stood in the inner court of the king's palace, in front of the king's quarters, while the king was sitting on his royal throne inside the throne room opposite the entrance to the palace. ²And when the king saw Queen Esther standing in the court, she won favour in his sight, and he held out to Esther the golden sceptre that was in his hand. Then Esther approached and touched the tip of the sceptre.

ESTHER RECEIVED BY THE KING

²ᵃᵃ *And it happened on the third day, when she finished praying, she took off the garments of service and put on her glory.* ²ᵇ*Then, majestically adorned, after invoking the aid of the all-seeing God and Saviour, she took her two maids with her,* ²ᶜ*leaning daintily on one,* ²ᵈ*while the other followed carrying her train.* ²ᵉ*She was radiant with perfect beauty, and she looked happy, as if beloved, but her heart was frozen with fear.* ²ᶠ*When she had gone through all the doors, she stood before the king. He was seated on his royal throne, clothed in the full array of his majesty, all covered with gold and precious stones. And he was most terrifying.*

²ᵍ*Lifting his face, flushed with splendour, he looked at her in fierce anger. And the queen faltered and turned pale and faint and collapsed upon the head of the maid who went before her.* ²ʰ*Then God changed the spirit of the king to gentleness, and in alarm he sprang from his throne and took her in his arms until she came to herself. And he comforted her with soothing words and said to her,* ²ⁱ*"What is it, Esther? I am your brother. Take courage;* ²ᵏ*you shall not die, for our law applies only to the common person. Come near."*

²¹*Then he raised the golden rod and touched it to her neck;* ²ᵐ*and he embraced her and said, "Speak to me."* ²ⁿ*And she said to him, "I saw you, my lord, like an angel of God, and my heart was shaken with fear at your glory.* ²⁰*For you are wonderful, my lord, and your countenance is full of grace."* ²ᵖ*But as she was speaking, she fell fainting.* ²ᵠ*And the king was agitated, and all his servants sought to comfort her.*

³And the king said to her, "What is it, Queen Esther? What is your request? It shall be given you, even to the half of my kingdom." ⁴And Esther said, "If it please the king,ᵇ let the king and Haman come today to a feast that I have prepared for the king." ⁵Then the king said, "Bring Haman quickly, so that we may do as Esther has asked." So the king and Haman came to the feast that Esther had prepared. ⁶And as they were drinking wine after the feast, the king said to Esther, "What is your wish? It shall be granted you. And what is your request? Even to the half of my kingdom, it shall be fulfilled."ᶜ ⁷Then Esther answered, "My wish and my request is: ⁸If I have found favour in the sight of the king, and if it please the kingᵈ to grant my wish and fulfil my request, let the king and Haman come to the feast that I will prepare for them, and tomorrow I will do as the king has said."

HAMAN PLANS TO HANG MORDECAI

⁹And Haman went out that day joyful and glad of heart. But when Haman saw Mordecai in the king's gate, that he neither rose nor trembled before him, he was filled with wrath against Mordecai. ¹⁰Nevertheless, Haman restrained himself and went home, and he sent and brought his friends and his wife Zeresh. ¹¹And Haman recounted to them the splendour of his riches, the number of his sons, all the promotions with which the king had honoured him, and how he had advanced him above the officials and the servants of the king. ¹²Then Haman said, "Even Queen Esther let no one but me come with the king to the feast she prepared. And tomorrow also I am invited by her together with the king. ¹³Yet all this is worth nothing to me,

---

ᵃThe following three paragraphs in italic type, under the heading *Esther Received by the King*, do not appear in the Hebrew text of Esther. These three paragraphs, however, are included in the Greek Septuagint and the Latin Vulgate, where they correspond to the following chapter and verse numbers used in the Vulgate: Esther 15:1-16. See further the asterisk note at the beginning of Esther (page 435) and *Introduction*, pages xiii to xiv. ᵇHebrew *If it is good to the king* ᶜOr *done* ᵈHebrew *if it is good to the king*

so long as I see Mordecai the Jew sitting at the king's gate." ¹⁴Then his wife Zeresh and all his friends said to him, "Let a gallows*ᵃ* fifty cubits*ᵇ* high be made, and in the morning tell the king to have Mordecai hanged upon it. Then go joyfully with the king to the feast." This idea pleased Haman, and he had the gallows made.

THE KING HONOURS MORDECAI

6 On that night the king could not sleep. And he gave orders to bring the book of memorable deeds, the chronicles, and they were read before the king. ²And it was found written how Mordecai had told about Bigthana*ᶜ* and Teresh, two of the king's eunuchs, who guarded the threshold, and who had sought to lay hands on King Ahasuerus. ³And the king said, "What honour or distinction has been bestowed on Mordecai for this?" The king's young men who attended him said, "Nothing has been done for him." ⁴And the king said, "Who is in the court?" Now Haman had just entered the outer court of the king's palace to speak to the king about having Mordecai hanged on the gallows*ᵈ* that he had prepared for him. ⁵And the king's young men told him, "Haman is there, standing in the court." And the king said, "Let him come in." ⁶So Haman came in, and the king said to him, "What should be done to the man whom the king delights to honour?" And Haman said to himself, "Whom would the king delight to honour more than me?" ⁷And Haman said to the king, "For the man whom the king delights to honour, ⁸let royal robes be brought, which the king has worn, and the horse that the king has ridden, and on whose head a royal crown*ᵉ* is set. ⁹And let the robes and the horse be handed over to one of the king's most noble officials. Let them dress the man whom the king delights to honour, and let them lead him on the horse through the square of the city, proclaiming before him: 'Thus shall it be done to the man whom the king delights to honour.'" ¹⁰Then the king said to Haman, "Hurry; take the robes and the horse, as you have said, and do so to Mordecai the Jew, who sits at the king's gate. Leave out nothing that you have mentioned." ¹¹So Haman took the robes and the horse, and he dressed Mordecai and led him through the square of the city, proclaiming before him, "Thus shall it be done to the man whom the king delights to honour."

¹²Then Mordecai returned to the king's gate. But Haman hurried to his house, mourning and with his head covered. ¹³And Haman told his wife Zeresh and all his friends everything that had happened to him. Then his wise men and his wife Zeresh said to him, "If Mordecai, before whom you have begun to fall, is of the Jewish people, you will not overcome him but will surely fall before him."

ESTHER REVEALS HAMAN'S PLOT

¹⁴While they were yet talking with him, the king's eunuchs arrived and hurried to bring Haman to the feast that Esther had prepared.

7 So the king and Haman went in to feast with Queen Esther. ²And on the second day, as they were drinking wine after the feast, the king again said to Esther, "What is your wish, Queen Esther? It shall be granted you. And what is your request? Even to the half of my kingdom, it shall be fulfilled." ³Then Queen Esther answered, "If I have found favour in your sight, O king, and if it please the king, let my life be granted me for my wish, and my people for my request. ⁴For we have been sold, I and my people, to be destroyed, to be killed, and to be annihilated. If we had been sold merely as slaves, men and women, I would have been silent, for our affliction is not to be compared with the loss to the king." ⁵Then King Ahasuerus said to Queen Esther, "Who is he, and where is he, who has dared*ᶠ* to do this?" ⁶And Esther said, "A foe and enemy! This wicked Haman!" Then Haman was terrified before the king and the queen.

HAMAN IS HANGED

⁷And the king arose in his wrath from the wine-drinking and went into the palace garden, but Haman stayed to beg for his life from Queen Esther, for he saw that harm was determined against him by the king. ⁸And the king returned from the palace garden to the place where they were drinking wine, as Haman was falling on the couch where Esther was. And the king said, "Will he even assault the queen in my presence, in my own house?" As the word left the mouth of the king, they covered Haman's face. ⁹Then Harbona, one of the eunuchs in attendance on the king,

---

*ᵃ*Or *wooden beam*; twice in this verse (see note on 2:23) *ᵇ*A *cubit* was about 18 inches or 45 centimetres *ᶜBigthana* is an alternate spelling of *Bigthan* (see 2:21) *ᵈ*Or *wooden beam* (see note on 2:23) *ᵉ*Or *headdress* *ᶠ*Hebrew *whose heart has filled him*

said, "Moreover, the gallows[a] that Haman has prepared for Mordecai, whose word saved the king, is standing at Haman's house, fifty cubits[b] high." And the king said, "Hang him on that." ¹⁰So they hanged Haman on the gallows that he had prepared for Mordecai. Then the wrath of the king abated.

ESTHER SAVES THE JEWS

8 On that day King Ahasuerus gave to Queen Esther the house of Haman, the enemy of the Jews. And Mordecai came before the king, for Esther had told what he was to her. ²And the king took off his signet ring, which he had taken from Haman, and gave it to Mordecai. And Esther set Mordecai over the house of Haman.

³Then Esther spoke again to the king. She fell at his feet and wept and pleaded with him to avert the evil plan of Haman the Agagite and the plot that he had devised against the Jews. ⁴When the king held out the golden sceptre to Esther, Esther rose and stood before the king. ⁵And she said, "If it please the king, and if I have found favour in his sight, and if the thing seems right before the king, and I am pleasing in his eyes, let an order be written to revoke the letters devised by Haman the Agagite, the son of Hammedatha, which he wrote to destroy the Jews who are in all the provinces of the king. ⁶For how can I bear to see the calamity that is coming to my people? Or how can I bear to see the destruction of my kindred?" ⁷Then King Ahasuerus said to Queen Esther and to Mordecai the Jew, "Behold, I have given Esther the house of Haman, and they have hanged him on the gallows,[c] because he intended to lay hands on the Jews. ⁸But you may write as you please with regard to the Jews, in the name of the king, and seal it with the king's ring, for an edict written in the name of the king and sealed with the king's ring cannot be revoked."

⁹The king's scribes were summoned at that time, in the third month, which is the month of Sivan, on the twenty-third day. And an edict was written, according to all that Mordecai commanded concerning the Jews, to the satraps and the governors and the officials of the provinces from India to Ethiopia, 127 provinces, to each province in its own script and to each people in its own language, and also to the Jews in their script and their language. ¹⁰And he wrote in the name of King Ahasuerus and sealed it with the king's signet ring. Then he sent the letters by mounted couriers riding on swift horses that were used in the king's service, bred from the royal stud, ¹¹saying that the king allowed the Jews who were in every city to gather and defend their lives, to destroy, to kill, and to annihilate any armed force of any people or province that might attack them, children and women included, and to plunder their goods, ¹²on one day throughout all the provinces of King Ahasuerus, on the thirteenth day of the twelfth month, which is the month of Adar.

DECREE OF ARTAXERXES

¹²ᵃᵈ *The following is a copy of this letter:*
"The great king, Artaxerxes, to the rulers of the provinces from India to Ethiopia, 127 satrapies, and to those who are loyal to our government, greeting.

¹²ᵇ*"The more often they are honoured by the too great kindness of their benefactors, the prouder do many become.* ¹²ᶜ*They not only seek to injure our subjects, but in their inability to stand prosperity they even undertake to scheme against their own benefactors.* ¹²ᵈ*They not only take away thankfulness from among people, but, carried away by the boasts of those who know nothing of goodness, they suppose that they will escape the evil-hating justice of God, who always sees everything.* ¹²ᵉ*And often many of those who are set in places of authority have been made in part responsible for the shedding of innocent blood and have been involved in irremediable calamities, by the persuasion of friends who have been entrusted with the administration of public affairs,* ¹²ᶠ*when these people by the false trickery of their evil natures beguile the sincere goodwill of their sovereigns.*

¹²ᵍ*"What has been wickedly accomplished through the pestilent behaviour of those who exercise authority unworthily can be seen not so much from the more ancient records that we hand on as from investigation of matters close at hand.* ¹²ʰ*For the future we will take care to render our kingdom quiet and peaceable for all people,* ¹²ⁱ*by changing our methods and always judging what comes before our eyes with more*

---

[a]Or *wooden beam;* also verse 10 (see note on 2:23) [b]A *cubit* was about 18 inches or 45 centimetres [c]Or *wooden beam* (see note on 2:23) [d]The following nine paragraphs in italic type, under the heading *Decree of Artaxerxes,* do not appear in the Hebrew text of Esther. These nine paragraphs, however, are included in the Greek Septuagint and the Latin Vulgate, where they correspond to the following chapter and verse numbers used in the Vulgate: Esther 16:1-24. See further the asterisk note at the beginning of Esther (page 435) and *Introduction,* pages xiii to xiv.

equitable consideration. ¹²ᵏFor Haman son of Hamadathos, a Macedonian (really an alien to the Persian blood and quite devoid of our kindliness), having become our guest, ¹²ˡso far enjoyed the goodwill that we have for every nation that he was publicly proclaimed our father and was continually bowed down to by all as the person second to the royal throne. ¹²ᵐBut, unable to restrain his arrogance, he undertook to deprive us of our kingdom and our life ¹²ⁿand with intricate craft and deceit asked for the destruction of Mordecai, our saviour and perpetual benefactor, and of Esther, the blameless partner of our kingdom, together with their whole nation. ¹²ᵒHe thought that in this way he would find us undefended and would transfer the kingdom of the Persians to the Macedonians.

¹²ᵖ"But we find that the Jews, who were consigned to annihilation by this thrice-accursed man, are not evildoers but are governed by most righteous laws ¹²ᑫand are sons of the Most High, the mightiest living God, who has directed the kingdom both for us and for our ancestors in the most excellent order.

¹²ʳ"You will therefore do well not to put into execution the letters sent by Haman son of Hamadathos, ¹²ˢbecause the man himself who did these things has been hanged at the gates of Susa, with all his household. For God, who rules over all things, has speedily inflicted on him the punishment he deserved.

¹²ᵗ"Therefore post a copy of this letter publicly in every place and permit the Jews to live under their own laws. ¹²ᵘAnd give them reinforcements, so that on the thirteenth day of the twelfth month, Adar, on that very day they may defend themselves against those who attack them at the time of their affliction. ¹²ᵛFor God, who rules over all things, has made this day to be a joy to his chosen people instead of a day of destruction for them.

¹²ʷ"Therefore you shall observe this with all good cheer as a notable day among your commemorative festivals, ¹²ˣso that both now and hereafter it may mean salvation for us and the loyal Persians, but that for those who plot against us it may be a reminder of destruction.

¹²ʸ"Every city and country, without exception, which does not act accordingly, shall be destroyed in wrath with spear and fire. It shall be made not only impassable for people, but also most hateful for all time to beasts and birds."

¹³A copy of what was written was to be issued as a decree in every province, being publicly displayed to all peoples, and the Jews were to be ready on that day to take vengeance on their enemies. ¹⁴So the couriers, mounted on their swift horses that were used in the king's service, rode out hurriedly, urged by the king's command. And the decree was issued in Susa the citadel.

¹⁵Then Mordecai went out from the presence of the king in royal robes of blue and white, with a great golden crownᵃ and a robe of fine linen and purple, and the city of Susa shouted and rejoiced. ¹⁶The Jews had light and gladness and joy and honour. ¹⁷And in every province and in every city, wherever the king's command and his edict reached, there was gladness and joy among the Jews, a feast and a holiday. And many from the peoples of the country declared themselves Jews, for fear of the Jews had fallen on them.

THE JEWS DESTROY THEIR ENEMIES

9 Now in the twelfth month, which is the month of Adar, on the thirteenth day of the same, when the king's command and edict were about to be carried out, on the very day when the enemies of the Jews hoped to gain the mastery over them, the reverse occurred: the Jews gained mastery over those who hated them. ²The Jews gathered in their cities throughout all the provinces of King Ahasuerus to lay hands on those who sought their harm. And no one could stand against them, for the fear of them had fallen on all peoples. ³All the officials of the provinces and the satraps and the governors and the royal agents also helped the Jews, for the fear of Mordecai had fallen on them. ⁴For Mordecai was great in the king's house, and his fame spread throughout all the provinces, for the man Mordecai grew more and more powerful. ⁵The Jews struck all their enemies with the sword, killing and destroying them, and did as they pleased to those who hated them. ⁶In Susa the citadel itself the Jews killed and destroyed 500 men, ⁷and also killed Parshandatha and Dalphon and Aspatha ⁸and Poratha and Adalia and Aridatha ⁹and Parmashta and Arisai and Aridai and Vaizatha, ¹⁰the ten sons of Haman the son of Hammedatha, the enemy of the Jews, but they laid no hand on the plunder.

¹¹That very day the number of those killed in Susa the citadel was reported to the king. ¹²And the king said to Queen Esther, "In Susa the citadel the Jews have killed and destroyed 500 men and also the ten sons of Haman.

ᵃOr headdress

What then have they done in the rest of the king's provinces! Now what is your wish? It shall be granted you. And what further is your request? It shall be fulfilled." ¹³And Esther said, "If it please the king, let the Jews who are in Susa be allowed tomorrow also to do according to this day's edict. And let the ten sons of Haman be hanged on the gallows."ᵈ ¹⁴So the king commanded this to be done. A decree was issued in Susa, and the ten sons of Haman were hanged. ¹⁵The Jews who were in Susa gathered also on the fourteenth day of the month of Adar and they killed 300 men in Susa, but they laid no hands on the plunder.

¹⁶Now the rest of the Jews who were in the king's provinces also gathered to defend their lives, and got relief from their enemies and killed 75,000 of those who hated them, but they laid no hands on the plunder. ¹⁷This was on the thirteenth day of the month of Adar, and on the fourteenth day they rested and made that a day of feasting and gladness. ¹⁸But the Jews who were in Susa gathered on the thirteenth day and on the fourteenth, and rested on the fifteenth day, making that a day of feasting and gladness. ¹⁹Therefore the Jews of the villages, who live in the rural towns, hold the fourteenth day of the month of Adar as a day for gladness and feasting, as a holiday, and as a day on which they send gifts of food to one another.

THE FEAST OF PURIM INAUGURATED

²⁰And Mordecai recorded these things and sent letters to all the Jews who were in all the provinces of King Ahasuerus, both near and far, ²¹obliging them to keep the fourteenth day of the month Adar and also the fifteenth day of the same, year by year, ²²as the days on which the Jews got relief from their enemies, and as the month that had been turned for them from sorrow into gladness and from mourning into a holiday; that they should make them days of feasting and gladness, days for sending gifts of food to one another and gifts to the poor.

²³So the Jews accepted what they had started to do, and what Mordecai had written to them. ²⁴For Haman the Agagite, the son of Hammedatha, the enemy of all the Jews, had plotted against the Jews to destroy them, and had cast Pur (that is, cast lots), to crush and to destroy them. ²⁵But when it came before the king, he gave orders in writing that his evil plan which he had devised against the Jews should return on his own head, and that he and his sons should be hanged on the gallows. ²⁶Therefore they called these days Purim, after the term Pur. Therefore, because of all that was written in this letter, and of what they had faced in this matter, and of what had happened to them, ²⁷the Jews firmly bound themselves and their offspring and all who joined them, that without fail they would keep these two days according to what was written and at the time appointed every year, ²⁸that these days should be remembered and kept throughout every generation, in every clan, province, and city, and that these days of Purim should never fall into disuse among the Jews, nor should the commemoration of these days cease among their descendants.

²⁹Then Queen Esther, the daughter of Abihail, and Mordecai the Jew gave full written authority, confirming this second letter about Purim. ³⁰Letters were sent to all the Jews, to the 127 provinces of the kingdom of Ahasuerus, in words of peace and truth, ³¹that these days of Purim should be observed at their appointed seasons, as Mordecai the Jew and Queen Esther bound them, and as they had bound themselves and their offspring, with regard to their fasts and their lamenting. ³²The command of Esther confirmed these practices of Purim, and it was recorded in writing.

THE GREATNESS OF MORDECAI

10 King Ahasuerus imposed tax on the land and on the coastlands of the sea. ²And all the acts of his power and might, and the full account of the high honour of Mordecai, to which the king advanced him, are they not written in the Book of the Chronicles of the kings of Media and Persia? ³For Mordecai the Jew was second in rank to King Ahasuerus, and he was great among the Jews and popular with the multitude of his brothers, for he sought the welfare of his people and spoke peace to all his people.

MORDECAI'S DREAM FULFILLED

³ᵃᵇ *And Mordecai said, "These things have come from God.* ³ᵇ*For I remember the dream*

ᵈOr *wooden beam*; also verse 25 (see note on 2:23) ᵇThe following two paragraphs in italic type, under the two headings *Mordecai's Dream Fulfilled* and *Postscript*, do not appear in the Hebrew text of Esther. These two paragraphs, however, are included in the Greek Septuagint and the Latin Vulgate, where they correspond to the following chapter and verse numbers used in the Vulgate: Esther 10:4–11:1. See further the asterisk note at the beginning of Esther (page 435) and *Introduction*, pages xiii to xiv.

that I saw concerning these matters; and none of them has failed to be fulfilled. ³ᶜThe tiny spring that became a river, and there was light and the sun and abundant water—the river is Esther, whom the king married and made queen. ³ᵈThe two dragons are Haman and myself. ³ᵉThe nations are those that gathered to destroy the name of the Jews. ³ᶠAnd my nation, this is Israel, who cried out to God and were saved. The Lord has saved his people; the Lord has delivered us from all these evils; God has done great signs and wonders, which have not occurred among the nations. ³ᵍFor this purpose he made two lots, one for the people of God and one for all the nations. ³ʰAnd these two lots came to the hour and moment and day of decision before God and among all the nations. ³ⁱAnd God remembered his people and vindicated his inheritance. ³ᵏSo they will observe these days in the month of Adar, on the fourteenth and fifteenth of that month, with an assembly and joy and gladness before God, from generation to generation for ever among his people Israel."

POSTSCRIPT

³ˡIn the fourth year of the reign of Ptolemy and Cleopatra, Dositheus, who said that he was a priest and a Levite,ᵃ and Ptolemy his son brought the preceding Letter of Phrourai, which they said was genuine and had been translated by Lysimachus son of Ptolemy, one of the residents of Jerusalem.

ᵃOr was a priest, and Levitas

THE WISDOM OF SOLOMON

EXHORTATION TO UPRIGHTNESS

1 [a] Love righteousness, you rulers of
        the earth,
    think of the Lord with uprightness
    and seek him with sincerity of heart;
2 because he is found by those who
        do not put him to the test
    and manifests himself to those
        who do not distrust him.
3 For perverse thoughts separate
        people from God,
    and when his power is tested,
        it convicts the foolish;
4 because wisdom will not
        enter a deceitful soul
    or dwell in a body enslaved to sin.
5 For a holy and disciplined spirit
        will flee from deceit
    and will rise and depart from
        foolish thoughts
    and will be ashamed at the approach
        of unrighteousness.

6 For wisdom is a kindly spirit and
    will not free a blasphemer from
        the guilt of his words,
    because God is witness of
        his inmost feelings
    and a true observer of his heart
        and a hearer of his tongue.
7 Because the Spirit of the Lord
        has filled the world,
    and that which holds all things
        together knows what is said;
8 therefore no one who utters
        unrighteous things
        will escape notice,
    and justice, when it punishes,
        will not pass him by.
9 For enquiry will be made into the
        counsels of an ungodly man,
    and a report of his words will
        come to the Lord
    to convict him of his lawless deeds;
10 because a jealous ear hears all things,
    and the sound of murmurings
        does not go unheard.
11 Beware then of useless murmuring
    and keep your tongue from slander;
    because no secret word is
        without result,[b]
    and a lying mouth destroys the soul.

12 Do not invite death by the
        error of your life
    or bring on destruction by the
        works of your hands;
13 because God did not make death,
    and he does not delight in the
        death of the living.
14 For he created all things that
        they might exist,
    and the origins[c] of the world
        are wholesome,
    and there is no destructive
        poison in them;
    and the dominion[d] of Hades
        is not on earth.
15 For righteousness is immortal.

LIFE AS THE UNGODLY SEE IT

16 But the ungodly by their deeds and
        words summoned death;[e]
    considering him a friend,
        they pined away,
    and they made a covenant with him,
    because they are fit to belong to his party.

2 For they reasoned unsoundly,
        saying to themselves,
    "Short and sorrowful is our life,
    and there is no remedy at the
        death of a human being,

---

[a]The Wisdom of Solomon is one of the seven deuterocanonical books that do not exist in their entirety in Hebrew or Aramaic, but which were included in the Greek Septuagint, and were likewise included in the Latin Vulgate version of the Bible translated by Jerome in the late fourth century AD. See further, *Introduction*, pages xiii to xiv.
[b]Or *word will go unpunished* [c]Or *creatures* [d]Or *palace* [e]Greek *him*

and no one has been known
to return from death.
2 Because we were born by mere chance,
and hereafter we shall be as
though we had never been;
because the breath in our
nostrils is smoke,
and reason is a spark kindled by
the beating of our hearts.
3 When it is extinguished, the
body will turn to ashes,
and the spirit will dissolve
like empty air.
4 Our name will be forgotten in time,
and no one will remember our works;
our life will pass away like
the traces of a cloud
and be scattered like mist
that is chased by the rays of the sun
and overcome by its heat.
5 For our allotted time is the
passing of a shadow,
and there is no return from our death,
because it is sealed up and
no one turns back.

6 "Come, therefore, let us enjoy the
good things that exist
and make use of the creation
to the full as in youth.
7 Let us take our fill of costly
wine and perfumes,
and let no flower of spring pass by us.
8 Let us crown ourselves with
rosebuds before they wither.
9 Let none of us fail to share
in our revelry,
everywhere let us leave signs
of enjoyment,
because this is our portion
and this our lot.
10 Let us oppress the righteous
poor man;
let us not spare the widow
or regard the grey hairs of the aged.
11 But let our might be our law of right,
for what is weak proves
itself to be useless.

12 "Let us lie in wait for the righteous man,
because he is inconvenient to us
and opposes our actions;
he reproaches us for sins
against the law
and accuses us of sins against
our training.
13 He professes to have knowledge of God
and calls himself a child[a] of the Lord.
14 He became to us a reproof
of our thoughts;
15 the very sight of him is a burden to us,
because his manner of life is
unlike that of others
and his ways are strange.
16 We are considered by him
as something base,
and he avoids our ways as unclean;
he calls the last end of the
righteous happy
and boasts that God is his father.
17 Let us see if his words are true,
and let us test what will happen
at the end of his life;
18 for if the righteous man is God's
son, he will help him
and will deliver him from the
hand of his adversaries.
19 Let us test him with insult and torture,
that we may find out how gentle he is
and make trial of his forbearance.
20 Let us condemn him to a
shameful death
for, according to what he says,
he will be protected."

ERROR OF THE WICKED

21 Thus they reasoned, but they
were led astray,
for their wickedness blinded them,
22 and they did not know the
secret purposes of God
or hope for the wages of holiness
or discern the prize for blameless souls;
23 for God created mankind
for incorruption
and made him in the image of
his own character,[b]
24 but through the devil's envy
death entered the world,
and those who belong to his
party experience it.

DESTINY OF THE RIGHTEOUS

3 But the souls of the righteous are
in the hand of God,
and no torment will ever touch them.
2 In the eyes of the foolish they
seemed to have died,
and their departure was thought
to be an evil thing,

---

[a] Or *servant* [b] Some manuscripts *eternity*

WISDOM OF SOLOMON 3–4

3 and their going from us to be
  their destruction;
but they are at peace.
4 For though in the sight of men
  they were punished,
their hope is full of immortality.
5 Having been disciplined a little,
  they will receive great good,
because God tested them and found
  them worthy of himself;
6 like gold in the furnace he tried them,
and like a sacrificial whole burnt
  offering he accepted them.
7 In the time of their visitation
  they will shine forth
and will run like sparks
  through the stubble.
8 They will govern nations and
  rule over peoples,
and the Lord will reign over
  them for ever.
9 Those who trust in him will
  understand truth,
and the faithful will abide
  with him in love,
because grace and mercy are
  upon his holy ones,
and he watches over his chosen.[a]

DESTINY OF THE UNGODLY

10 But the ungodly will be punished
  as their reasoning deserves,
who disregarded the righteous man[b]
  and rebelled against the Lord;
11 for whoever despises wisdom and
  instruction is miserable.
Their hope is vain, their labours
  are unprofitable,
and their works are useless.
12 Their wives are foolish, and
  their children evil;
13 their offspring are accursed.

CHILDLESSNESS

For blessed is the barren woman
  who is undefiled,
who has not entered into
  a sinful union;
she will have fruit when God
  examines souls.
14 Blessed also is the eunuch whose
  hands have done no lawless deed
and who has not devised wicked
  things against the Lord;
for special favour will be shown
  him for his faithfulness

and a place of great delight in
  the temple of the Lord.
15 For the fruit of good labours
  is renowned,
and the root of understanding
  does not fail.
16 But children of adulterers will
  not come to maturity,
and the offspring of an unlawful
  union will perish.
17 Even if they live long they will
  be held of no account,
and finally their old age will
  be without honour.
18 If they die young, they will
  have no hope
and no consolation in the
  day of decision.
19 For the end of an unrighteous
  generation is grievous.

4 Better than this is childlessness
  with virtue,
for in the memory of virtue[c] is
  immortality,
because it is known both by
  God and by man.
2 When it is present, people imitate[d] it,
and they long for it when it has gone;
and throughout all time it marches
  crowned in triumph,
victor in the contest for prizes
  that are undefiled.
3 But the prolific brood of the
  ungodly will be of no use,
and none of their illegitimate
  seedlings will strike a deep root
  or take a firm hold.
4 For even if they put forth
  boughs for a while,
standing insecurely they will
  be shaken by the wind,
and by the violence of the winds
  they will be uprooted.
5 The branches will be broken off
  before they come to maturity,
and their fruit will be useless,
not ripe enough to eat and
  good for nothing.
6 For children born of unlawful unions
are witnesses of evil against their
  parents when God examines them.[e]

---

[a]The meaning of the Greek is uncertain; this verse omitted by some manuscripts; compare 4:15 [b]Or *disregarded what is right* [c]Greek *it* [d]Some manuscripts *honour* [e]Greek *parents at their examination*

7 But the righteous man, though
   he die early, will be at rest.
8 For old age is not honoured
   for length of time
   or measured by number of years;
9 but understanding is grey hair
   for human beings,
   and a blameless life is ripe old age.

10 There was one who pleased God
   and was loved by him,
   and while living among sinners
   he was taken up.
11 He was caught up lest evil change
   his understanding
   or guile deceive his soul.
12 For the fascination of wickedness
   obscures what is good,
   and roving desire perverts
   the innocent mind.
13 Being perfected in a short time,
   he fulfilled long years;
14 for his soul was pleasing to the Lord,
   therefore he took him quickly from
   the midst of wickedness.
15 Yet the peoples saw and did
   not understand
   or take such a thing to heart,
   that God's grace and mercy
   are with his elect,
   and he watches over his holy ones.

TRIUMPH OF THE RIGHTEOUS

16 The righteous man who has
   died will condemn the
   ungodly who are living,
   and youth whose life is quickly over
   will condemn the prolonged old
   age of the unrighteous man.
17 For the unrighteous will see the
   end of the wise man
   and will not understand what the
   Lord purposed for him
   and for what he kept him safe.
18 They will see and will have
   contempt for him,
   but the Lord will laugh them to scorn.
   After this they will become
   dishonoured corpses
   and an outrage among the dead for ever;
19 because he will dash them
   speechless to the ground
   and shake them from the foundations;
   they will be left utterly dry and barren,
   and they will suffer anguish,
   and the memory of them will perish.

FINAL JUDGEMENT

20 They will come with dread when
   their sins are reckoned up,
   and their lawless deeds will
   convict them to their face.

5 Then the righteous man will stand
   with great confidence
   in the presence of those who have
   afflicted him
   and those who make light
   of his labours.
2 When they see him, they will be
   shaken with dreadful fear,
   and they will be amazed at his
   unexpected salvation.
3 They will speak to one another
   in repentance,
   and in anguish of spirit they
   will groan and say:
4 "This is the man whom we
   once held in derision
   and made a byword of
   reproach—we fools!
   We thought that his life was madness
   and that his end was without honour.
5 Why has he been numbered
   among the sons of God?
   And why is his lot among the saints?
6 So it was we who strayed from
   the way of truth,
   and the light of righteousness
   did not shine on us,
   and the sun did not rise upon us.
7 We took our fill of the paths of
   lawlessness and destruction,
   and we journeyed through
   trackless deserts,
   but the way of the Lord we
   have not known.
8 What has our arrogance profited us?
   And what good has our boasted
   wealth brought us?
9 All those things have vanished
   like a shadow
   and like a rumour that passes by;
10 like a ship that sails through
   the billowy water,
   and when it has passed no
   trace can be found,
   nor track of its keel in the waves;
11 or as, when a bird flies through the air,
   no evidence of its passage is found;
   the light air, lashed by the
   beat of its pinions
   and pierced by the force of
   its rushing flight,

is traversed by the movement
of its wings,
and afterwards no sign of its
coming is found there;
¹² or as, when an arrow is shot at a target,
the air, thus divided, comes
together at once,
so that no one knows its pathway.
¹³ So we also, as soon as we were
born, ceased to be,
and we had no sign of virtue to show,
but were consumed in our
wickedness."
¹⁴ Because the hope of the ungodly man
is like chaff*ᵃ* carried by the wind
and like a light frost*ᵇ* driven
away by a storm;
it is dispersed like smoke
before the wind,
and it passes like the remembrance
of a guest who stays but a day.

REWARD OF THE RIGHTEOUS

¹⁵ But the righteous live for ever,
and their reward is with the Lord;
the Most High takes care of them.
¹⁶ Therefore they will receive
a glorious crown
and a beautiful diadem from
the hand of the Lord,
because with his right hand
he will cover them,
and with his arm he will shield them.
¹⁷ The Lord*ᶜ* will take his zeal as
his whole armour
and will arm all creation to
repel*ᵈ* his enemies;
¹⁸ he will put on righteousness
as a breastplate
and wear impartial justice as
a helmet;
¹⁹ he will take holiness as an
invincible shield
²⁰ and sharpen stern wrath for a sword,
and creation will join with him to
fight against the madmen.
²¹ Shafts of lightning will fly
with true aim
and will leap to the target as from
a well-drawn bow of clouds,
²² and hailstones full of wrath will be
hurled as from a catapult;
the water of the sea will
rage against them,
and rivers will relentlessly
overwhelm them;
²³ a mighty wind will rise against them,
and like a tempest it will
winnow them away.
Lawlessness will lay waste
the whole earth,
and evildoing will overturn
the thrones of rulers.

KINGS SHOULD SEEK WISDOM

6 Listen therefore, O kings, and
understand;
learn, O judges of the ends of
the earth.
² Give ear, you that rule over
multitudes
and boast of many nations.
³ For your dominion was given
you from the Lord,
and your sovereignty from
the Most High,
who will search out your works
and enquire into your plans.
⁴ Because as servants of his kingdom
you did not rule rightly
or keep the law
or walk according to the
purpose of God,
⁵ he will come upon you
terribly and swiftly,
because severe judgement falls
on those in high places.
⁶ For the lowliest may be
pardoned in mercy,
but the mighty will be mightily tested.
⁷ For the Lord of all will not
stand in awe of anyone
or show deference to greatness;
because he himself made
both small and great,
and he takes thought for all alike.
⁸ But a strict enquiry is in store
for the mighty.
⁹ To you then, O monarchs, my
words are directed
that you may learn wisdom
and not transgress.
¹⁰ For they will be made holy who
observe holy things in holiness,
and those who have been taught
them will find a defence.
¹¹ Therefore set your desire on my words;
long for them, and you will
be instructed.

---

*ᵃOr dust   ᵇSome manuscripts like a spider's web   ᶜGreek He
ᵈOr punish*

DESCRIPTION OF WISDOM

12 Wisdom is radiant and unfading,
 and she is easily discerned by
   those who love her
 and is found by those who seek her.
13 She hastens to make herself known
   to those who desire her.
14 He who rises early to seek her
   will have no difficulty,
 for he will find her sitting at
   his gates.
15 To fix one's thought on her is
   perfect understanding,
 and he who is vigilant on her account
   will soon be free from care,
16 because she goes about seeking
   those worthy of her,
 and she graciously appears to
   them in their paths
 and meets them in every thought.

17 The beginning of wisdom[a] is the
   sincerest desire for instruction,
 and concern for instruction
   is love of her,
18 and love of her is the keeping
   of her laws,
 and giving heed to her laws is
   assurance of immortality,
19 and immortality brings
   one near to God;
20 so the desire for wisdom
   leads to a kingdom.

21 Therefore if you delight in thrones
   and sceptres, O monarchs
   over the peoples,
 honour wisdom, that you
   may reign for ever.
22 I will tell you what wisdom is
   and how she came to be,
 and I will hide no secrets from you,
 but I will trace her course from
   the beginning of creation
 and make knowledge of her clear,
 and I will not pass by the truth;
23 neither will I travel in the
   company of sickly envy,
 for envy[b] does not associate
   with wisdom.
24 A multitude of the wise is the
   salvation of the world,
 and a sensible king is the
   stability of a people.
25 Therefore be instructed by my
   words, and you will profit.

SOLOMON LIKE OTHER MORTALS

7 I also am mortal, like all men,
 a descendant of the first-formed
   child of earth;
 and in the womb of a mother I
   was moulded into flesh,
2 within the period of ten months,
   compacted with blood,
 from the seed of a man and the
   pleasure of marriage.
3 And when I was born, I began to
   breathe the common air
 and fell upon the kindred earth,
 and my first sound was a
   cry, like that of all.
4 I was nursed with care in
   swaddling cloths.
5 For no king has had a different
   beginning of existence;
6 there is for all mankind one entrance
   into life and a common departure.

SOLOMON'S RESPECT FOR WISDOM

7 Therefore I prayed, and
   understanding was given me;
 I called upon God, and the spirit
   of wisdom came to me.
8 I preferred her to sceptres and thrones,
 and I accounted wealth as nothing
   in comparison with her.
9 Neither did I liken to her
   any priceless gem,
 because all gold is but a little
   sand in her sight,
 and silver will be accounted
   as clay before her.
10 I loved her more than
   health and beauty,
 and I chose to have her rather than light,
 because her radiance never ceases.
11 All good things came to me
   along with her,
 and in her hands uncounted wealth.
12 I rejoiced in them all, because
   wisdom leads them;
 but I did not know that she
   was their mother.
13 I learned without guile and I
   impart without grudging;
 I do not hide her wealth,
14 for it is an unfailing treasure
   for mankind;
 those who get it obtain
   friendship with God,

---
[a]Greek *Her beginning*   [b]Greek *this*

commended for the gifts that
     come from instruction.

SOLOMON PRAYS FOR WISDOM

15 May God grant that I speak
       with judgement
   and have thoughts worthy of
       what I have received,
   for he is the guide even of wisdom
   and the corrector of the wise.
16 For both we and our words
       are in his hand,
   as are all understanding
       and skill in crafts.
17 For it is he who gave me unerring
       knowledge of what exists,
   to know the structure of the world
       and the activity of the elements;
18 the beginning and end and
       middle of times,
   the alternations of the solstices and
       the changes of the seasons,
19 the cycles of the year and the
       constellations of the stars,
20 the natures of animals and the
       tempers of wild beasts,
   the powers of spirits[a] and the
       reasonings of human beings,
   the varieties of plants and
       the virtues of roots;
21 I learned both what is secret
       and what is manifest,
22 for wisdom, the fashioner of
       all things, taught me.

NATURE OF WISDOM

   For in her there is a spirit that
       is intelligent, holy,
   unique, manifold, subtle,
   mobile, clear, unpolluted,
   distinct, invulnerable, loving
       the good, keen,
   irresistible, 23beneficent, humane,
   steadfast, sure, free from anxiety,
   all-powerful, overseeing all,
   and penetrating through all spirits
       that are intelligent and
       pure and subtlest.
24 For wisdom is more mobile
       than any motion;
   because of her pureness she pervades
       and penetrates all things.
25 For she is a breath of the power
       of God
   and a pure emanation of the
       glory of the Almighty;

therefore nothing defiled gains
    entrance into her.
26 For she is a reflection of eternal light,
   a spotless mirror of the
       working of God,
   and an image of his goodness.
27 Though she is but one, she
       can do all things,
   and while remaining in herself,
       she renews all things;
   in every generation she passes
       into holy souls
   and makes them friends of
       God and prophets;
28 for God loves nothing so much as the
       man who lives with wisdom.
29 For she is more beautiful than the sun
   and excels every constellation
       of the stars.
   Compared with the light, she
       is found to be superior,
30 for it is succeeded by the night,
   but against wisdom evil
       does not prevail.

8 She reaches mightily from one end
       of the earth to the other,
   and she orders all things well.

SOLOMON'S LOVE FOR WISDOM

2 I loved her and sought her
       from my youth,
   and I desired to take her for my bride,
   and I became enamoured
       of her beauty.
3 She glorifies her noble birth
       by living with God,
   and the Lord of all loves her.
4 For she is an initiate in the
       knowledge of God
   and an associate in his works.
5 If riches are a desirable
       possession in life,
   what is richer than wisdom
       who effects all things?
6 And if understanding is effective,
   who more than she is fashioner
       of what exists?
7 And if anyone loves righteousness,
       her labours are virtues;
   for she teaches self-control
       and prudence,
   justice and courage;
   nothing in life is more profitable
       for humans than these.

---

[a] Or winds

8 And if anyone longs for wide experience,
she knows the things of old and infers the things to come;
she understands turns of speech and the solutions of riddles;
she has foreknowledge of signs and wonders
and of the outcome of seasons and times.

WISDOM INDISPENSABLE TO RULERS

9 Therefore I determined to take her to live with me,
knowing that she would give me good counsel
and encouragement in cares and grief.
10 Because of her I shall have glory among the multitudes
and honour in the presence of the elders, though I am young.
11 I shall be found keen in judgement, and in the sight of rulers I shall be admired.
12 When I am silent they will wait for me, and when I speak they will give heed;
and when I speak at greater length they will put their hands on their mouths.
13 Because of her I shall have immortality
and leave an everlasting remembrance to those who come after me.
14 I shall govern peoples, and nations will be subject to me;
15 fearsome monarchs will be afraid of me when they hear of me;
among the people I shall show myself capable and courageous in war.
16 When I enter my house, I shall find rest with her,
for companionship with her has no bitterness,
and life with her has no pain, but gladness and joy.
17 When I considered these things inwardly
and thought upon them in my mind, that in kinship with wisdom there is immortality,
18 and in friendship with her, pure delight,
and in the labours of her hands, unfailing wealth,
and in the experience of her company, understanding,
and renown in sharing her words,
I went about seeking how to get her for myself.
19 As a child I was naturally gifted, and a good soul fell to my lot;
20 or rather, being good, I entered an undefiled body.
21 But I perceived that I would not possess wisdom unless God gave her to me—
and it was a mark of insight to know whose gift she was—
so I appealed to the Lord and implored him,
and with my whole heart I said:

SOLOMON'S PRAYER FOR WISDOM

9 "O God of my fathers and Lord of mercy,
who has made all things by your word
2 and by your wisdom has formed man to have dominion over the creatures you have made
3 and rule the world in holiness and righteousness
and pronounce judgement in uprightness of soul,
4 give me the wisdom that sits by your throne,
and do not reject me from among your servants.
5 For I am your slave and the son of your maidservant,
a man who is weak and short-lived, with little understanding of judgement and laws;
6 for even if one is perfect among the sons of men,
yet without the wisdom that comes from you he will be regarded as nothing.
7 You have chosen me to be king of your people
and to be judge over your sons and daughters.
8 You have given command to build a temple on your holy mountain
and an altar in the city of your habitation,
a copy of the holy tent that you prepared from the beginning.
9 With you is wisdom, who knows your works
and was present when you made the world
and who understands what is pleasing in your sight

and what is right according to
   your commandments.
10 Send her forth from the holy heavens
   and from the throne of your
      glory send her,
that she may be with me and toil
   and that I may learn what
      is pleasing to you.
11 For she knows and understands
      all things,
   and she will guide me wisely
      in my actions
   and guard me with her glory.
12 Then my works will be acceptable,
   and I shall judge your people justly
   and shall be worthy of the
      throne[a] of my father.
13 For what human being can learn
      the counsel of God?
   Or who can discern what
      the Lord wills?
14 For the reasoning of mortals
      is worthless,
   and our designs are likely to fail,
15 for a perishable body weighs
      down the soul,
   and this earthy tent burdens the
      mind full of thoughts.[b]
16 We can hardly guess at
      what is on earth,
   and what is at hand we
      find with labour;
   but who has traced out what
      is in the heavens?
17 Who has learned your counsel,
      unless you have given wisdom
   and sent your holy spirit from on high?
18 And thus the paths of those on
      earth were set right,
   and people were taught
      what pleases you
   and were saved by wisdom."

WISDOM FROM ADAM TO MOSES

10 Wisdom[c] protected the
      first-formed
      father of the world, when he
         alone had been created;
   she delivered him from his
      transgression
2 and gave him strength to
      rule all things.
3 But when an unrighteous man
      departed from her in his anger,
   he perished because in rage
      he killed his brother.

4 When the earth was flooded because
      of him, wisdom again saved it,
   steering the righteous man by
      a paltry piece of wood.
5 Wisdom also, when the nations
      in wicked agreement had
         been confounded,
   recognized the righteous
      man and preserved him
         blameless before God
   and kept him strong in the face of
      his compassion for his child.
6 Wisdom rescued a righteous man
      when the ungodly were
         perishing;
   he escaped the fire that descended
      on the Five Cities.[d]
7 Evidence of their wickedness
      still remains:
   a continually smoking wasteland,
   plants bearing fruit that
      does not ripen,
   and a pillar of salt standing
      as a monument to an
         unbelieving soul.
8 For because they passed wisdom by,
   they were not only hindered from
      recognising the good,
   but also left for mankind a
      reminder of their folly,
   so that their failures could
      never go unnoticed.
9 Wisdom rescued from troubles
      those who served her.
10 When a righteous man fled from
      his brother's wrath,
   she guided him on straight paths;
   she showed him the reign of God
   and gave him knowledge
      of holy things;[e]
   she prospered him in his labours
   and increased the fruit of his toil.
11 When his oppressors were covetous,
   she stood by him and made him rich.
12 She protected him from his enemies
   and kept him safe from those
      who lay in wait for him;
   in his arduous contest she
      gave him the victory,
   so that he might learn that godliness
      is more powerful than anything.

---

[a] Greek *thrones* [b] Or *burdens the anxious mind* [c] Greek *She*; also verses 5, 6, 13, 15 [d] Or *on Pentapolis* [e] Or *of holy ones*

13 When a righteous man was sold,
    wisdom did not desert him,
  but delivered him from sin.
  She descended with him
    into the dungeon,
14 and when he was in prison
    she did not leave him,
  until she brought him the
    sceptre of a kingdom
  and authority over his masters.
  Those who accused him she
    showed to be false,
  and she gave him everlasting honour.

WISDOM LED THE ISRAELITES OUT OF EGYPT

15 A holy people and blameless race
  wisdom delivered from a
    nation of oppressors.
16 She entered the soul of a
    servant of the Lord
  and withstood fearsome kings
    with wonders and signs.
17 She gave holy people the reward
    of their labours;
  she guided them along a
    marvellous way
  and became a shelter to them by day
  and a starry flame through the night.
18 She brought them over the Red Sea
  and led them through deep waters;
19 but she drowned their enemies
  and cast them up from the
    depth of the sea.
20 Therefore the righteous
    plundered the ungodly;
  they sang hymns, O Lord,
    to your holy name
  and praised with one accord
    your defending hand,
21 because wisdom opened the mouth
    of those who could not speak
  and made the tongues of
    infants speak clearly.

WISDOM LED THE ISRAELITES THROUGH THE DESERT

11 Wisdom^a prospered their works by
    the hand of a holy prophet.
  ^{2}They journeyed through an
    uninhabited wilderness
  and pitched their tents in
    untrodden places.
3 They withstood their enemies
    and fought off their foes.
4 When they thirsted they
    called upon you,
  and water was given them
    out of flinty rock,
  and slaking of thirst from hard stone.
5 For through the very things by which
    their enemies were punished,
  they themselves received
    benefit in their need.
6 Instead of the fountain of an
    ever-flowing river,
  stirred up and defiled with blood
7 in rebuke for the decree to
    kill the infants,
  you gave them abundant
    water unexpectedly,
8 showing by their thirst at that time
  how you punished their enemies.
9 For when they were tried, though they
    were being disciplined in mercy,
  they learned how the ungodly were
    tormented when judged in wrath.
10 For you tested them as a father
    does in warning,
  but the ungodly^b you examined as a
    stern king does in condemnation.
11 Whether absent or present, they
    were equally distressed,
12 for a twofold grief possessed them,
  and a groaning at the memory
    of what had occurred.
13 For when they heard that through
    their own punishments
  the righteous^c had received
    benefit, they perceived it
    was the Lord's doing.
14 For though they had mockingly
    rejected him who long before
    had been cast out and exposed,
  at the end of the events they
    marvelled at him,
  for their thirst was not like
    that of the righteous.

PUNISHMENT OF THE WICKED

15 In return for their foolish and
    wicked thoughts,
  which led them astray to worship
    irrational serpents and
    worthless animals,
  you sent upon them a multitude
    of irrational creatures
    to punish them,
16 that they might learn that one
    is punished by the very
    things by which he sins.

---
^{a}Greek *She* ^{b}Greek *but those* ^{c}Greek *they*

WISDOM OF SOLOMON 11–12

17 For your all-powerful hand,
   which created the world out
      of formless matter,
   did not lack the means to send
      upon them a multitude
         of bears or bold lions
18 or newly created unknown
      beasts full of rage
   or such as breathe out fiery breath
   or belch forth a thick pall of smoke
   or flash terrible sparks from their eyes;
19 not only could their damage
      exterminate men,[a]
   but the mere sight of them
      could kill by fright.
20 Even apart from these, men[b]
      could fall at a single breath
   when pursued by justice
   and scattered by the breath
      of your power.
   But you have arranged all things by
      measure and number and weight.

GOD IS POWERFUL AND MERCIFUL

21 For it is always in your power
      to show great strength,
   and who can withstand the
      might of your arm?
22 Because the whole world before you
      is like a speck that tips the scales
   and like a drop of morning dew
      that falls upon the ground.
23 But you are merciful to all, for
      you can do all things,
   and you overlook people's sins,
      that they may repent.
24 For you love all things that exist
   and loathe none of the things
      that you have made,
   for you would not have made
      anything if you had hated it.
25 How would anything have endured
      if you had not willed it?
   Or how would anything not called
      forth by you have been preserved?
26 You spare all things, for they are yours,
      O Lord who loves the living.

12

For your immortal spirit is in
      all things.
2 Therefore you correct little by
      little those who trespass
   and remind and warn them of the
      things by which they sin
   that they may be freed from
      wickedness and put their
         trust in you, O Lord.

SINS OF THE CANAANITES

3 Those who used to live in
      your Holy Land
4 you hated for their detestable
      practises,
   their works of sorcery and
      unholy rites,
5 their merciless slaughter[c]
      of children,
   and their sacrificial feasting on
      human flesh and blood.
   These initiates from the midst
      of a pagan cult,[d]
6 these parents who murder
      helpless lives,
   you purposed to destroy by the
      hands of our fathers,
7 that the land most precious
      of all to you
   might receive a worthy colony
      of the servants[e] of God.
8 But even these you spared, since
      they were but men,
   and you sent wasps[f] as
      forerunners of your army,
   to destroy them little by little,
9 though you were not unable to give
      the ungodly into the hands
         of the righteous in battle
   or to destroy them at one blow
      by fearsome wild beasts
         or your stern word.
10 But judging them little by little you
      gave them a chance to repent,
   though you were not unaware
      that their origin[g] was evil
   and their wickedness inborn
   and that their way of thinking
      would never change.
11 For they were an accursed race
      from the beginning,
   and it was not through fear of
      anyone that you left them
         unpunished for their sins.

GOD IS SOVEREIGN

12 For who will say, "What
      have you done?"
   Or will resist your judgement?
   Who will accuse you for the
      destruction of nations
         that you made?

---

[a]Greek them [b]Greek they [c]Greek slaughterers [d]The meaning of the Greek is uncertain [e]Or children; also verse 20 [f]Or hornets [g]Or nature

Or who will come before you
to plead as an advocate
for the unrighteous?
13 For neither is there any God besides
you, whose care is for all,^a
to whom you should prove that you
have not judged unjustly;
14 nor can any king or monarch
confront you about those
whom you have punished.
15 You are righteous and rule all
things righteously,
deeming it alien to your power
to condemn him who does not
deserve to be punished.
16 For your strength is the source
of righteousness,
and your sovereignty over all
causes you to spare all.
17 For you show your strength
when men doubt the
completeness of your power,
and you rebuke any insolence
among those who know it.^b
18 You are sovereign in strength but
you judge with mildness,
and with great forbearance
you govern us;
for you have power to act
whenever you choose.

GOD'S LESSONS FOR ISRAEL

19 Through such works you have
taught your people
that the one who is righteous
must be kind,
and you have filled your sons
with good hope,
because you give repentance for sins.
20 For if you punished with such
great care and indulgence^c
the enemies of your servants and
those deserving of death,
granting them time and opportunity
to give up their wickedness,
21 with what strictness you have
judged your sons,
to whose fathers you gave oaths and
covenants full of good promises!
22 So while chastening us you
scourge our enemies ten
thousand times more,
so that we may meditate upon your
goodness when we judge,
and when we are judged we
may expect mercy.

PUNISHMENT OF THE EGYPTIANS

23 Therefore those who in folly of
life lived unrighteously
you tormented through their
own abominations.
24 For they went far astray on
the paths of error,
accepting as gods those animals that
even their enemies^d despised;
they were deceived like
foolish infants.
25 Therefore, as to unreasoning children,
you sent your judgement
to mock them.
26 But those who have not heeded the
warning of gentle rebukes
will experience the deserved
judgement of God.
27 For when in their suffering
they became incensed
at those creatures that they had
thought to be gods, being
punished by means of them,
they saw and recognized as the
true God him whom they had
before refused to know.
Therefore the utmost condemnation
came upon them.

FOOLISHNESS OF NATURE WORSHIP

13 For all men who were ignorant of
God were foolish by nature;
and they were unable from the
good things that are seen
to know him who exists,
nor did they recognize the artisan
while paying heed to his works;
2 but they supposed that either
fire or wind or swift air
or the circle of the stars or
turbulent water
or the luminaries of heaven were
the gods that rule the world.
3 If through delight in the beauty
of these things people
assumed them to be gods,
let them know how much better
than these is their Lord,
for the author of beauty created them.
4 And if people were amazed at
their power and working,
let them perceive from them

---

^aOr *for all things* ^bThe meaning of the Greek is uncertain
^cSome manuscripts *entreaty*; some manuscripts omit *and indulgence*
^dGreek *even they*

how much more powerful is
   he who formed them.
5 For from the greatness and
      beauty of created things
   comes a corresponding perception
      of their Creator.
6 Yet these people are little to
      be blamed,
   for perhaps they go astray
      while seeking God and
      desiring to find him.
7 For as they live among his works
      they keep searching,
   and they trust in what they see,
      because the things that
      are seen are beautiful.
8 Yet again, not even they
      are to be excused;
9 for if they had the power
      to know so much
   that they could investigate the world,
   how did they fail to find sooner
      the Lord of these things?

FOOLISHNESS OF IDOLATRY

10 But miserable, with their hopes
      set on dead things,
   are those who give the name "gods"
      to the works of human hands,
   gold and silver fashioned with skill
      and likenesses of animals
   or a useless stone, the work
      of an ancient hand.
11 A skilled woodcutter may saw
      down a tree easy to handle
   and skilfully strip off all its bark
   and then with pleasing workmanship
   make a useful vessel that
      serves life's needs
12 and burn the cast-off pieces
      of his work
   to prepare his food and eat his fill.
13 But a cast-off piece from among
      them, useful for nothing,
   a stick crooked and full of knots,
   he takes and carves with
      care in his leisure
   and shapes it with skill
      gained in idleness;*a*
   he forms it like the image of a man
14 or makes it like some
      worthless animal,
   giving it a coat of red paint and
      colouring its surface red
   and covering every blemish
      in it with paint;

15 then he makes for it a
      niche that suits it
   and sets it in the wall and fastens
      it there with iron.
16 So he takes thought for it,
      that it may not fall,
   because he knows that it
      cannot help itself,
   for it is only an image and
      has need of help.
17 When he prays about possessions
      and his marriage and children,
   he is not ashamed to address
      a lifeless thing.
18 For health he appeals to a
      thing that is weak;
   for life he prays to a thing that is dead;
   for aid he entreats a thing that
      is utterly inexperienced;
   for a prosperous journey, a thing
      that cannot take a step;
19 for moneymaking and work and
      success with his hands
   he asks strength of a thing whose
      hands have no strength.

FOLLY OF A NAVIGATOR PRAYING TO AN IDOL

14 Again, one preparing to sail and
      about to voyage over raging
      waves
   calls upon a piece of wood more fragile
      than the ship that carries him.
2 For it was desire for gain that
      planned that vessel,
   and wisdom was the artisan
      who built it;
3 but it is your providence, O Father,
      that steers its course,
   because you have given it
      a path in the sea
   and a safe way through the waves,
4 showing that you can save
      from every danger,
   so that even if someone lacks
      skill, he may put to sea.
5 It is your will that works of
      your wisdom should not
      be without effect;
   therefore men trust their lives even
      to the smallest piece of wood,
   and passing through the billows on
      a raft they come safely to land.
6 For even in the beginning, when
      arrogant giants were perishing,

---
*a*Some manuscripts *with intelligent skill*

the hope of the world took
    refuge on a raft
and guided by your hand left
    to the world the seed of
    a new generation.
7 For blessed is the wood by which
    righteousness comes.

8 But the idol made with hands
    is accursed, and so is the
    one who made it;
he because he made it, and the
    perishable thing because
    it was named a god.
9 For equally hateful to God are the
    ungodly man and his ungodliness,
10 for what was done will be punished
    together with him who did it.
11 Therefore there will be a visitation
    also upon the idols of the nations,
because, though part of what
    God created, they became
    an abomination
and became traps for human souls
    and a snare to the feet of the foolish.

ORIGIN AND EVILS OF IDOLATRY

12 For the beginning of fornication
    was the conception of idols,
and the invention of them was
    the corruption of life,
13 for neither have they existed
    from the beginning
nor will they exist for ever.
14 For through human vanity they
    entered the world,
and therefore their speedy end
    has been planned.
15 For a father, consumed with grief
    at an untimely bereavement,
made an image of his child, who had
    been suddenly taken from him;
and he now honoured as a god what
    was once a dead human being
and handed on to his dependants
    secret rites and initiations.
16 Then the ungodly custom,
    grown strong with time,
    was kept as a law,
and at the command of monarchs
    carved images were worshipped.
17 When people could not honour
    monarchs[a] in their presence,
    since they lived at a distance,
they imagined their appearance
    from far away
and made a visible image of the
    king whom they honoured,
so that by their zeal they might flatter
    the absent one as though present.
18 Then the ambition of the
    artisan impelled
even those who did not know the
    king to intensify their worship.
19 For he, perhaps wishing to
    please his ruler,
skilfully forced the likeness to
    take more beautiful form,
20 and the multitude, attracted by
    the charm of his work,
now regarded as an object of worship
    the one whom shortly before they
    had honoured as a human being.
21 And this became a hidden
    trap for mankind,
because people, in bondage to
    misfortune or to royal authority,
bestowed on objects of stone
    or wood the name that
    ought not to be shared.

22 Then it was not enough for them to
    err about the knowledge of God,
but even though they live in great
    strife due to ignorance,
they call such great evils peace.
23 For whether they kill children
    in their initiations or
    celebrate secret mysteries
or hold frenzied revels with
    strange customs,
24 they no longer keep either their
    lives or their marriages pure,
but they either treacherously
    kill one another or grieve
    one another by adultery,
25 and all is a raging riot of blood
    and murder, theft and deceit,
    corruption, faithlessness,
    tumult, perjury,
26 confusion over what is good,
    forgetfulness of favour,
pollution of souls, sexual perversion,
    disorder in marriage, adultery,
    and debauchery.
27 For the worship of idols not to be named
    is the beginning and cause
    and end of every evil.
28 For their worshippers[b] either rave
    in exultation or prophesy lies

---
[a] Greek them [b] Greek For they

or live unrighteously or readily
    commit perjury;
29 for because they trust in lifeless idols
    they swear wicked oaths and
    expect to suffer no harm.
30 But just penalties will overtake
    them on two counts:
  because they thought wickedly of God
    in devoting themselves to idols
  and because in deceit they swore
    unrighteously through
    contempt for holiness.
31 For it is not the power of the things
    by which men swear,[a]
  but the just penalty for those who sin,
  that always pursues the transgression
    of the unrighteous.

BENEFITS OF WORSHIPPING THE TRUE GOD

15 But you, our God, are kind and true,
    patient and ruling all things[b]
    in mercy.
2 For even if we sin we are yours,
    knowing your power;
  but we will not sin, because we know
    that we are accounted yours.
3 For to know you is complete
    righteousness,
  and to know your power is the
    root of immortality.
4 For neither has the evil intent
    of human art misled us
  nor the fruitless toil of painters,
  a figure stained with varied colours,
5 whose appearance arouses
    yearning in fools,
  so that they desire[c] the lifeless
    form of a dead image.
6 Lovers of evil things and fit for
    such objects of hope[d]
  are those who either make or
    desire or worship them.

FOOLISHNESS OF WORSHIPPING CLAY IDOLS

7 For a potter kneads the soft earth
    and laboriously moulds each
    vessel for our service,
  but out of the same clay he fashions
  both the vessels that serve clean uses
  and those for contrary uses,
    making all in like manner;
  but which shall be the use
    of each of these
  the worker in clay decides.
8 With misspent toil, he forms a futile
    god from the same clay —
  this man who was made of earth
    a short time before
  and after a little while goes to that
    from which he was taken,
  when he is required to return the
    soul that was lent him.
9 But he is not concerned that
    he is destined to die
  or that his life is brief,
  but he competes with workers
    in gold and silver
  and imitates workers in copper;
  and he counts it his glory that he
    moulds counterfeit gods.
10 His heart is ashes, his hope
    is cheaper than dirt,
  and his life is of less worth than clay,
11 because he failed to know the
    one who formed him
  and inspired in him an active soul
  and breathed into him a living spirit.
12 But he[e] considered our
    existence an idle game,
  and life a festival held for profit,
  for he says one must get
    money however one can,
    even by base means.
13 For this man, more than all
    others, knows that he sins
  when he makes from earthy matter
    fragile vessels and carved images.
14 But most foolish and more miserable
    than the soul of an infant
  are all the enemies who
    oppressed your people.
15 For they thought that all their
    heathen idols were gods,
  though these have neither the use
    of their eyes to see with
  nor nostrils with which to draw
    breath
  nor ears with which to hear
  nor fingers to feel with,
  and their feet are of no use
    for walking.
16 For a human being made them,
  and one whose spirit is
    borrowed formed them;
  for no man can form a god
    that is like himself.
17 He is mortal, and what he makes
    with lawless hands is dead,

---

[a] Or *of the oaths men swear* [b] Or *ruling the universe* [c] Greek *and he desires* [d] Greek *such hopes* [e] Some manuscripts *they*

for he is better than the
objects he worships,
since[a] he has life, but they never do.

SERPENTS IN THE DESERT

18 The enemies of your people[b] worship
even the most hateful animals,
which are worse than all others,
when judged by their
lack of intelligence;
19 and even as animals they are not
so beautiful in appearance
that one would desire them,
but they have escaped both the
praise of God and his blessing.

16

Therefore those men were
deservedly punished
through such creatures
and were tormented by a
multitude of animals.
2 Instead of this punishment you
showed kindness to your people,
and you prepared quails to eat,
a delicacy to satisfy the
desire of appetite;
3 in order that those men, when
they desired food,
might lose the least remnant
of appetite[c]
because of the odious creatures
sent to them,
while your people,[d] after suffering
want a short time,
might partake of delicacies.
4 For it was necessary that upon
those oppressors inexorable
want should come,
while to these it was merely
shown how their enemies
were being tormented.

5 For when the terrible rage of wild
beasts came upon your people[e]
and they were being destroyed by
the bites of writhing serpents,
your wrath did not continue to the end;
6 they were troubled for a little
while as a warning
and received a symbol of
deliverance to remind them
of your law's command.
7 For he who turned towards it was
saved, not by what he saw,
but by you, the Saviour of all.
8 And by this also you convinced
our enemies
that it is you who delivers
from every evil.
9 For they were killed by the bites
of locusts and flies,
and no healing was found for them,
because they deserved to be
punished by such things;
10 but your sons were not conquered even
by the teeth of venomous serpents,
for your mercy came to their
help and healed them.
11 To remind them of your oracles
they were bitten
and then were quickly delivered,
lest they should fall into
deep forgetfulness
and become indifferent to
your kindness.
12 For neither herb nor poultice
cured them,
but it was your word, O
Lord, that heals all.
13 For you have power over life and death;
you lead people down to the gates
of Hades and back again.
14 A man in his wickedness kills,
but he cannot bring back
the departed spirit
or set free the imprisoned soul.

DISASTROUS STORMS STRIKE EGYPT

15 To escape from your hand is impossible;
16 for the ungodly, refusing to know you,
were scourged by the strength
of your arm,
pursued by unusual rains and
hail and relentless storms,
and utterly consumed by fire.
17 For—most incredible of all—in the
water, which quenches all things,
the fire had still greater effect,
for the universe defends the righteous.
18 At one time the flame was restrained,
so that it might not consume the
creatures sent against the ungodly,
but that seeing this they might know
that they were being pursued by
the judgement of God;
19 and at another time even in the
midst of water it burned
more intensely than fire,
to destroy the crops of the
unrighteous land.

---

[a]Some manuscripts *of which* [b]Greek *They* [c]Greek *might loathe the necessary appetite* [d]Greek *while they* [e]Greek *upon them*

THE ISRAELITES RECEIVE MANNA

20 Instead of these things you gave
    your people food of angels,
and without their toil you
    supplied them from heaven
    with bread ready to eat,
providing every pleasure and
    suited to every taste.
21 For your sustenance manifested your
    sweetness towards your children;
and the bread,[a] ministering to the
    desire of the one who took it,
was changed to suit everyone's liking.
22 Snow and ice withstood fire
    without melting,
so that they might know that the
    crops of their enemies
were being destroyed by the fire
    that blazed in the hail
and flashed in the showers of rain;
23 whereas the fire,[b] in order that the
    righteous might be fed,
even forgot its native power.
24 For creation, serving you who made it,
    exerts itself to punish the
    unrighteous
and in kindness relaxes on behalf
    of those who trust in you.
25 Therefore at that time also,
    changed into all forms,
it served your all-nourishing bounty,
    according to the desire of
    those who had need,[c]
26 so that your sons, whom you
    loved, O Lord, might learn
that it is not the production of
    crops that feeds mankind,
but that your word preserves
    those who trust in you.
27 For what was not destroyed by fire
was melted when simply warmed
    by a fleeting ray of the sun,
28 to make it known that one must rise
    before the sun to give you thanks
and must pray to you at the
    dawning of the light;
29 for the hope of an ungrateful person
    will melt like wintry frost
and flow away like waste water.

TERROR STRIKES THE EGYPTIANS AT NIGHT

17 Great are your judgements and
    hard to describe;
therefore uninstructed souls
    have gone astray.

2 For when the lawless supposed
    that they held the holy
    nation in their power,
they themselves lay as captives
    of darkness and prisoners
    of long night,
shut in under their roofs, exiles
    from eternal providence.
3 For thinking that in their secret
    sins they were unobserved
behind a dark curtain of forgetfulness,
they were scattered, terribly alarmed,[d]
    and appalled by spectres.
4 For not even the inner chamber
    that held them protected
    them from fear,
but terrifying sounds rang
    out around them,
and dismal phantoms with
    gloomy faces appeared.
5 And no power of fire was
    able to give light,
nor did the brilliant flames of the stars
avail to illumine that hateful night.
6 Nothing was shining through to them
except a dreadful, self-kindled fire,
and in terror they deemed the
    things that they saw
to be worse than that unseen
    appearance.
7 The delusions of their magic
    art lay humbled,
and their boasted wisdom was
    scornfully rebuked.
8 For those who promised to
    drive off the fears and
    disorders of a sick soul
were themselves sick with
    ridiculous fear.
9 For even if nothing disturbing
    frightened them,
yet, scared by the passing of beasts
    and the hissing of serpents,
10 they perished in trembling fear,
refusing to look even at the air, though
    it nowhere could be avoided.
11 For wickedness is a cowardly thing,
    condemned by its own testimony;[e]
distressed by conscience, it has always
    exaggerated[f] the difficulties.
12 For fear is nothing but surrender of
    the helps that come from reason;

---

[a]Greek and it [b]Greek whereas this [c]Or who made supplication [d]Some manuscripts they were unobserved, they were darkened behind a dark curtain of forgetfulness, terribly alarmed [e]The meaning of the Greek is uncertain [f]Some manuscripts anticipated

13 and inner expectation, being weak,
   prefers ignorance of what
      causes the torment.
14 But throughout the night, which
      was really powerless
   and which beset them from the
      recesses of powerless Hades,
   they all slept the same sleep
15 and now were driven by
      monstrous spectres
   and now were paralysed by
      their souls' surrender,
   for sudden and unexpected fear
      overwhelmed them.
16 And whoever was there fell down
   and thus was kept shut up in a
      prison not made of iron;
17 for whether he was a farmer
      or a shepherd
   or a worker who toiled in
      the wilderness,
   he was seized and endured
      the inescapable fate;
   for with one chain of darkness
      they all were bound.
18 Whether there came a whistling wind
   or a melodious sound of birds in
      wide-spreading branches
   or the rhythm of violently
      rushing water
19 or the harsh crash of rocks
      hurled down
   or the unseen running of
      leaping animals
   or the sound of the most
      savage roaring beasts
   or an echo thrown back from a
      hollow of the mountains,
   it paralysed them with terror.
20 For the whole world was illumined
      with brilliant light
   and was engaged in unhindered work,
21 while over those people alone
      heavy night was spread,
   an image of the darkness that was
      about to receive them;
   but still heavier than darkness
      were they to themselves.

LIGHT SHINES ON THE ISRAELITES

18 But for your holy ones there was
      very great light.
   Their enemies[a] heard their voices
      but did not see their forms
   and counted them happy for
      not having suffered
2 and were thankful that your holy ones,[b]
      though previously wronged,
      were doing them no injury;
   and they begged their pardon
      for having been at
         variance with them.[c]
3 Therefore you provided a
      flaming pillar of fire
   as a guide for your people's[d]
      unknown journey
   and a harmless sun for their
      glorious wandering.
4 For those men deserved to
      be deprived of light and
         imprisoned in darkness,
   who had kept your sons imprisoned,
   through whom the imperishable
      light of the law was to be
         given to the world.

DEATH OF THE EGYPTIAN FIRSTBORN

5 When they had resolved to kill the
      infants of your holy ones,
   and one child had been
      exposed and rescued,
   you in punishment took away a
      multitude of their children;
   and you destroyed them all
      together by a mighty flood.
6 That night was made known
      beforehand to our fathers,
   so that they might rejoice in
      sure knowledge of the oaths
         in which they trusted.
7 The deliverance of the righteous and
      the destruction of their enemies
   were expected by your people.
8 For by the same means by which
      you punished our enemies
   you called us to yourself
      and glorified us.
9 For in secret the holy children of
      good people offered sacrifices
   and with one accord agreed
      to the divine law,
   that the saints would share
      alike the same things,
   both blessings and dangers;
   and already they were singing
      the praises of the fathers.[e]
10 But the discordant cry of their
      enemies echoed back,

---

[a]Greek *They* [b]Greek *that they* [c]The meaning of the Greek is uncertain [d]Greek *for their* [e]Some manuscripts *dangers, the fathers already leading the songs of praise*

and their piteous lament for their
children was spread abroad.
11 The slave was punished with the
same penalty as the master,
and the common man suffered
the same loss as the king;
12 and they all together, by the
one form of death,
had corpses too many to count.
For the living were not sufficient
even to bury them,
since in one instant their most valued
children had been destroyed.
13 For though they had disbelieved
everything because of
their magic arts,
yet, when their firstborn were
destroyed, they acknowledged
your people to be God's son.
14 For while gentle silence
enveloped all things,
and night in its swift course
was now half gone,
15 your all-powerful word leaped from
heaven, from the royal throne,
into the midst of the land
that was doomed,
a stern warrior ¹⁶carrying
the sharp sword of your
authentic command,
and stood and filled all
things with death
and touched heaven while
standing on the earth.
17 Then at once apparitions in dreadful
dreams greatly troubled them,
and unexpected fears assailed them;
18 and one here and another there,
hurled down half dead,
made known why they were dying;
19 for the dreams that disturbed them
forewarned them of this,
so that they might not perish without
knowing why they suffered.

THREAT OF ANNIHILATION IN THE DESERT

20 The experience of death touched
also the righteous,
and a plague came upon the
multitude in the desert,
but the wrath did not long continue.
21 For a blameless man was quick
to act as their champion;
he brought forward the shield
of his ministry,
prayer and propitiation by incense;
he withstood the anger and put
an end to the disaster,
showing that he was your servant.
22 He conquered the wrath*ᵃ* not
by strength of body
and not by force of arms,
but by his word he subdued
the punisher,
appealing to the oaths and covenants
given to our fathers.
23 For when the dead had already fallen
on one another in heaps,
he intervened and held back
the wrath
and cut off its way to the living.
24 For upon his long robe the whole
world was depicted,
and the glories of the fathers
were engraved on the
four rows of stones,
and your majesty on the
diadem upon his head.
25 To these the destroyer yielded,
these he*ᵇ* feared;
for merely to test the wrath
was enough.

RED SEA

19

But the ungodly were assailed
to the end by pitiless anger,
for God*ᶜ* knew in advance even
their future actions,
2 that, though they themselves had
permitted*ᵈ* your people to depart
and hastily sent them forth,
they would change their minds
and pursue them.
3 For while they were still
busy at mourning
and were lamenting at the
graves of their dead,
they reached another foolish
decision
and pursued as fugitives those
whom they had begged and
compelled to depart.
4 For the fate they deserved drew
them on to this end
and made them forget what
had happened,
in order that they might fill up
the punishment that their
torments still lacked

---

*ᵃ*Greek *multitude* *ᵇ*Some manuscripts *they* *ᶜ*Greek *he* *ᵈ*Some manuscripts *had changed their minds to permit*

5 and that your people might
　　experience[a] an incredible journey,
　but they themselves might
　　meet a strange death.

GOD GUIDES AND PROTECTS HIS PEOPLE

6 For the whole creation in its nature
　　was fashioned anew,
　complying with your commands,
　　that your children[b] might
　　be kept unharmed.
7 The cloud was seen
　　overshadowing the camp,
　and dry land emerging where
　　water had stood before,
　an unhindered way out of the Red Sea,
　and a grassy plain out of
　　the raging waves,
8 where those protected by your hand
　　passed through as one nation,
　after gazing on marvellous wonders.
9 For they ranged like horses
　　and leaped like lambs,
　praising you, O Lord, who
　　delivered them.
10 For they still recalled the events
　　of their sojourn,
　how instead of producing animals
　　the earth brought forth gnats,
　and instead of fish the river spewed
　　out vast numbers of frogs.
11 Afterwards they saw also a
　　new kind[c] of birds,
　when desire led them to ask
　　for luxurious food;
12 for, to give them relief, quails
　　came up from the sea.

PUNISHMENT OF THE EGYPTIANS

13 The punishments did not come
　　upon the sinners
　without prior signs in the
　　violence of thunder,
　for they justly suffered because
　　of their wicked acts;
　for they practised a more bitter
　　hatred of strangers.
14 Others had refused to receive strangers
　　when they came to them,
　but these made slaves of guests
　　who were their benefactors.
15 And not only so, but punishment
　　of some sort will come
　　upon the former
　because they received the
　　foreigners with hostility;
16 but the latter, after receiving
　　with festal celebrations
　those who had already shared
　　the same rights,
　afflicted them with terrible sufferings.
17 They were stricken also with
　　loss of sight—
　just as were those at the door
　　of the righteous man—
　when, surrounded by
　　yawning darkness,
　each tried to find the way
　　through his own door.

NEW HARMONY IN NATURE

18 For the elements changed[d]
　　places with one another,
　as on a harp the notes differ
　　in respect to rhythm,
　even though the sound of each
　　note remains what it is.
　This may be clearly inferred from
　　the sight of what took place.
19 For land animals were transformed
　　into water creatures,
　and creatures that swim moved
　　over to the land.
20 Fire even in water retained
　　its normal power,
　and water forgot its fire-
　　quenching nature.
21 Flames, on the contrary,
　　failed to consume
　the flesh of perishable creatures
　　that walked among them,
　nor did they melt[e] the frostlike, easily
　　melted kind of heavenly food.

CONCLUSION

22 For in everything, O Lord, you have
　　exalted and glorified your people;
　and you have not neglected to help them
　　at every time and in every place.

---

[a] Some manuscripts *accomplish*　[b] Or *servants*　[c] Or *production*
[d] Greek *changing*　[e] Greek *nor could be melted*

SIRACH

^a**PROLOGUE**^b

Since many and great things have been given to us through the Law and the Prophets and the others that followed them, on account of which we must praise Israel for instruction and wisdom; and since it is necessary not only that the readers themselves should acquire understanding but also that those who love learning should be able to help the outsiders by both speaking and writing, my grandfather Jesus, after devoting himself especially to the reading of the Law and the Prophets and the other books of our fathers and after acquiring considerable proficiency in them, was himself also led to write something pertaining to instruction and wisdom, in order that, by becoming conversant with this also, those who love learning should make even greater progress in living according to the law.

You are urged therefore to read with good will and attention and to be indulgent in cases where, despite our diligent labour in translating, we may seem to have rendered some expressions ineffectively. For what was originally expressed in Hebrew does not have the same force when translated into another language. Not only this work, but even the law itself, the prophecies, and the rest of the books differ not a little as originally expressed.

When I came to Egypt in the thirty-eighth year of the reign of Euergetes and stayed for some time, having found a copy affording no little instruction,[c] it seemed highly necessary that I should myself devote some industry and diligence to the translation of the following book, offering both sleeplessness and skill in that period of time in order to complete and publish the book for those living abroad who wished to gain learning, being prepared in character to live according to the law.

IN PRAISE OF WISDOM

1 All wisdom comes from the Lord
  and is with him for ever.
² The sand of the sea, the drops of rain,
  and the days of eternity—
    who will count them?
³ The height of heaven, the
    breadth of the earth,
  the Abyss and wisdom—who
    will search them out?
⁴ Wisdom was created before
    all things,
  and prudent understanding
    from eternity.
⁵ The source of wisdom is God's
    word in the highest heaven,
  and her ways are eternal
    commandments.
⁶ The root of wisdom—to whom
    has it been revealed?
  Her great deeds—who knows
    them?
⁷ The knowledge of wisdom—to
    whom was it manifested?
  And her abundant experience—
    who has understood it?
⁸ There is one who is wise,
    greatly to be feared,
  sitting upon his throne.
⁹ The Lord himself created
    wisdom;[d]
  he saw her and apportioned her,
  he poured her out upon
    all his works,
¹⁰ with all flesh according to his gift,
  and he supplied her to
    those who persisted
    in loving him.[e]

FEAR OF THE LORD IS TRUE WISDOM

¹¹ The fear of the Lord is glory
    and exultation
  and gladness and a crown
    of rejoicing.
¹² The fear of the Lord delights
    the heart

---

[a]The Wisdom of Sirach is one of the seven deuterocanonical books that do not exist in their entirety in Hebrew or Aramaic, but which were included in the Greek Septuagint, and were likewise included in the Latin Vulgate version of the Bible translated by Jerome in the late fourth century AD. See further, *Introduction*, pages xiii to xiv. [b]This heading is in the Greek text [c]Some manuscripts *found opportunity for no little instruction* [d]Greek *her* [e]The longer edition adds *Love for the Lord is notable wisdom; to whomever he appears, he apportions her as the vision of himself.*

and gives gladness and
joy and long life.[a]
13 With him who fears the Lord it
will go well at the end;
on the day of his death he
will be blessed.

14 To fear the Lord is the
beginning of wisdom;
she is created with the
faithful in the womb.
15 She made her nest among human
beings as an eternal foundation,
and among their descendants
she will be trusted.
16 To fear the Lord is wisdom's
full measure;
she inebriates people
with her fruits;
17 she fills their whole house
with desirable goods
and their storehouses
with her produce.
18 The fear of the Lord is the
crown of wisdom,
making peace and perfect
health to flourish.[b]
19 He saw her and apportioned her;[c]
he rained down knowledge and
discerning comprehension,
and he exalted the glory of
those who held her fast.
20 To fear the Lord is the root
of wisdom,
and her branches are long life.
21 The fear of the Lord drives away sins;
and where it abides, it will
turn away all anger.

22 Unrighteous anger cannot be justified,
for the weight of a person's anger
tips the scale to his ruin.
23 A patient man will endure until
the right moment,
and then joy will burst forth for him.
24 He will hide his words until
the right moment,
and the lips of many will tell
of his good sense.
25 In the treasuries of wisdom
are wise sayings,[d]
but godliness is an abomination
to a sinner.
26 If you desire wisdom, keep
the commandments,
and the Lord will supply it for you.

27 For the fear of the Lord is
wisdom and instruction,
and fidelity and meekness
are his delight.
28 Do not disobey the fear of the Lord;
do not approach him with
a divided heart.
29 Be not a hypocrite in the
sight[e] of people
and pay attention in your speech.
30 Do not exalt yourself lest you fall
and thus bring dishonour
upon yourself.
The Lord will reveal your secrets
and cast you down in the midst
of the congregation,
because you did not come in
the fear of the Lord,
and your heart was full of deceit.

DUTIES TOWARDS GOD

2 My son, if you come forwards to
serve the Lord,
prepare yourself for testing.
2 Set your heart right and be steadfast
and do not be hasty in
time of calamity.
3 Hold to him and do not depart,
that you may reach full growth
by the end of your life.
4 Accept whatever is brought upon you
and in changes that humble
you be patient.
5 For gold is tested in the fire,
and acceptable people in the
furnace of humiliation.[f]
6 Trust in him, and he will help you;
make your ways straight
and hope in him.

7 You who fear the Lord, wait
for his mercy;
and turn not aside, lest you fall.
8 You who fear the Lord, trust in him,
and your reward will certainly not fail;
9 you who fear the Lord, hope
for good things,
for everlasting joy and mercy.[g]

---

[a]The longer edition adds *Fear of the Lord is a gift from the Lord, for indeed he makes paths firm on the basis of love.* [b]The longer edition adds *Both are gifts from God for peace, and cause for boasting broadens for those who persist in loving him.* [c]Some manuscripts omit this line as a doublet from 1:9b [d]Some manuscripts *wisdom is an illustration of knowledge* [e]Syriac; Greek *mouths* [f]The longer edition adds *Trust in him amid diseases and poverty.* [g]The longer edition adds *because his reward is an eternal gift with joy*

10 Consider the ancient
    generations and see:
  who trusted in the Lord and
    was put to shame?
  Or who persevered in the fear of
    the Lord[a] and was forsaken?
  Or who called upon him and
    was overlooked?
11 For the Lord is compassionate
    and merciful;
  he forgives sins and saves in
    time of affliction.
12 Woe to cowardly hearts and
    to slack hands
  and to the sinner who walks
    along two ways!
13 Woe to the faint heart, for
    it does not trust!
  Therefore it will not be sheltered.
14 Woe to you who have lost
    your endurance!
  What will you do when the
    Lord punishes you?
15 Those who fear the Lord will
    not disobey his words,
  and those who love him
    will keep his ways.
16 Those who fear the Lord will
    seek his approval,
  and those who love him will
    be filled with the law.
17 Those who fear the Lord will
    prepare their hearts
  and will humble their
    souls before him.
18 We will fall into the hands of the Lord
    and not into the hands of people;
  for as his majesty is,
    so also is his mercy.

DUTIES TOWARDS PARENTS

3 Listen to me your father, O children,
    and act accordingly, that you may
    be kept in safety.
2 For the Lord honoured the father
    above the children,
  and he confirmed the judgement
    of the mother over her sons.
3 Whoever honours his father
    atones for sins,
4 and whoever glorifies his mother is
    like one who lays up treasure.
5 Whoever honours his father will be
    gladdened by his own children,
  and when he prays he will be heard.

6 Whoever glorifies his father
    will have long life,
  and whoever obeys the Lord
    will refresh his mother;
7b he will serve his parents
    as his masters.
8 Honour your father by word and deed,
    that a blessing from him
    may come upon you.
9 For a father's blessing strengthens
    the houses of the children,
  but a mother's curse uproots
    foundations.
10 Do not glorify yourself in your
    father's dishonour,
  for your father's dishonour
    is no glory to you.
11 For a person's glory comes from
    his father's honour,
  and a mother in dishonour is a
    reproach to her children.
12 O son, help your father in his old age
    and do not grieve him as
    long as he lives;
13 even if he is lacking in understanding,
    show indulgence;
  in all your strength do not
    despise him.
14 For kindness to a father will
    not be forgotten,
  and against your sins it will
    be credited to you;
15 in the day of your affliction it will be
    remembered in your favour;
  as frost in fair weather, your
    sins will melt away.
16 Whoever forsakes his father
    is like a blasphemer,
  and whoever angers his mother
    is cursed by the Lord.

HUMILITY

17 My son, perform your tasks in meekness;
  then you will be loved by those
    whom God accepts.
18 The greater you are, the more you
    must humble yourself;
  so you will find favour in the
    sight of the Lord.[c]
20 For great is the might of the Lord;
  he is glorified by the humble.
21 Seek not what is too difficult for you

---

[a] Greek *of him* [b] The longer edition adds *whoever fears the Lord will honour his father*, [c] The longer edition adds verse 19: *Many are lofty and renowned, but to the meek he reveals his secrets.*

or investigate what is
  beyond your power.
22 Reflect upon what has been
    assigned to you,
  for you do not need what is hidden.
23 Do not meddle in what is
    beyond your tasks,
  for matters too great for
    human understanding
    have been shown you.
24 For their speculation has led many astray,
  and false conjecture has caused
    their thoughts to slip.[a]

26 A hard heart will be afflicted at the end,
    and whoever loves danger
    will perish by it.
27 A hard heart will be burdened
    by troubles,
  and the sinner will heap sin upon sin.
28 The affliction of the proud
    has no healing,
  for a plant of wickedness has
    taken root in him.
29 The mind of the intelligent man
    will ponder a parable,
  and an attentive ear is the
    wise man's desire.

ALMS FOR THE POOR

30 Water will extinguish a blazing fire:
  and almsgiving will atone for sin.
31 Whoever requites favours gives
    thought to the future;
  at the moment of his falling
    he will find support.

DUTIES TOWARDS THE POOR AND THE OPPRESSED

4 My son, deprive not the poor of
    his living
  and do not keep needy eyes waiting.
2 Do not grieve the one who is hungry
    or anger a man in distress.
3 Do not add to the troubles
    of an angry heart
  or delay your gift to a beggar.
4 Do not reject an afflicted suppliant
    or turn your face away from
    a poor person.
5 Do not avert your eye from
    someone who begs
  or give him occasion to curse you;
6 for if in bitterness of soul he calls
    down a curse upon you,
  his Maker will hear his prayer.

7 Make yourself beloved in
    the congregation;
  bow your head low to a great man.
8 Incline your ear to the poor
  and answer him peaceably
    and gently.
9 Deliver him who is wronged from
    the hand of the wrongdoer;
  and do not be faint-hearted
    in judging a case.
10 Be like a father to orphans,
    and in the place of a husband
    to their mother;
  you will then be like a son
    of the Most High,
  and he will love you more than
    does your mother.

REWARDS OF WISDOM

11 Wisdom exalts her sons
  and gives help to those who seek her.
12 Whoever loves her loves life,
  and those who seek her early
    will be filled with joy.
13 Whoever holds her fast
    will inherit glory,
  and the Lord will bless the
    place she[b] enters.
14 Those who serve her will minister
    to the Holy One;[c]
  the Lord loves those who love her.
15 He who obeys her will judge nations,
  and whoever gives heed to
    her will dwell secure.
16 If he has faith he will inherit her;
  and his descendants will remain
    in possession of her.
17 For at first she will walk with
    him on tortuous paths,
  she will bring fear and
    cowardice upon him
  and will torment him by her discipline
    until she trusts his soul,
  and she will test him with
    her ordinances.
18 And again she will come straight
    back to him and gladden him
  and will reveal her secrets to him.
19 If he goes astray she will forsake him
    and give him over into the
    hand of his downfall.

---

[a]The longer edition adds verse 25: *If you have no pupils you will be without light; when you lack knowledge do not profess to have it.*
[b]Or he   [c]Or *minister at the holy place* or *minister to a holy person*

20 Watch for the right opportunity
     and beware of evil;^a
  and do not bring shame on
     yourself.
21 For there is a shame that brings sin,
     and there is a shame that is
     glory and favour.
22 Do not show partiality, to
     your own harm,
  or deference, to your downfall.
23 Do not refrain from speaking
     at the crucial time.[b]
24 For wisdom is known through speech,
     and education through the
     words of the tongue.
25 Never speak against the truth,
     but be ashamed concerning
     your ignorance.
26 Do not be ashamed to
     confess your sins
  and do not try to force the
     flow of a river.
27 Do not subject yourself to
     a foolish fellow
  or show partiality to a ruler.
28 Fight even to death for the truth,
     and the Lord God will fight for you.
29 Do not be reckless in your speech
     or sluggish and remiss
     in your deeds.
30 Do not be like a lion in your home,
     acting out a role among
     your servants.
31 Let not your hand be
     extended to receive,
  but withdrawn when it is
     time to repay.

PRECEPTS FOR EVERYDAY LIVING

5 Do not be preoccupied with your
     wealth
  or say, "I am self-sufficient."
2 Do not follow your inclination
     and strength,
  walking according to the
     desires of your heart.
3 Do not say, "Who will have
     power over me?"
  for the Lord will surely punish you.
4 Do not say, "I sinned, and what
     happened to me?"
  for the Lord is slow to anger.
5 Do not be so confident of atonement[c]
     that you add sin to sin.
6 Do not say, "His compassion is great,
     he will atone for[d] the
     multitude of my sins,"
  for both mercy and wrath
     are with him,
  and his anger rests on sinners.
7 Do not delay to turn to the Lord
     or postpone it from day to day;
  for suddenly the wrath of the
     Lord will go forth,
  and at the time of punishment
     you will perish.

8 Do not occupy yourself with
     dishonest wealth,
  for it will not benefit you in
     the day of calamity.
9 Do not winnow with every wind
     or follow every path;
  the double-tongued
     sinner does that.
10 Be steadfast in your understanding,
     and let your speech be consistent.
11 Be quick in your listening
     and in patience make a reply.
12 If you have understanding,
     answer your neighbour;
  but if not, put your hand
     over your mouth.
13 Good repute and dishonour
     come from speaking,
  and a person's tongue is
     his downfall.
14 Do not be called a slanderer
     and do not lie in ambush
     with your tongue;
  for shame comes to the thief,
     and severe condemnation to
     the double-tongued.
15 In great and small matters
     do not be unaware

6 and do not become an enemy
     instead of a friend;
  for a bad name inherits shame
     and reproach:
  so fares the double-tongued sinner.
2 Do not exalt yourself through
     your soul's counsel,
  lest your strength be
     plundered like a bull.[e]

---
[a]Or *of an evil man*   [b]Greek *at a time of salvation*; the longer edition adds *And do not hide your wisdom in the face of excellence*.
[c]Hebrew *forgiveness*   [d]Or *it will atone for*; Hebrew *he will forgive*
[e]The meaning of the Greek is uncertain

3 You will devour your leaves
  and destroy your fruit
 and will leave yourself like
  a withered tree.
4 An evil soul will destroy
  the one who has it
 and make him a laughing-
  stock of his enemies.

FRIENDSHIP, FALSE AND TRUE

5 A pleasant voice will multiply
  its friends,
 and a gracious tongue will
  multiply courtesies.
6 Let those that are at peace
  with you be many,
 but let your advisers be one
  in a thousand.
7 When you gain a friend, gain
  him through testing
 and do not trust him hastily.
8 For there is a friend who is such
  at his own convenience
 and who will never stand by you
  in your day of trouble.
9 And there is a friend who
  changes into an enemy
 and will disclose a quarrel
  to your disgrace.
10 And there is a friend who is
  a table companion,
 but who will never stand by you
  in your day of trouble.
11 In your prosperity he will make
  himself your equal
 and be bold with your servants;
12 but if you are brought low he
  will be against you
 and will hide himself from
  your presence.
13 Keep yourself far from your enemies
 and be on guard towards
  your friends.
14 A faithful friend is a sturdy shelter:
 he that has found one has
  found a treasure.
15 There is nothing so precious
  as a faithful friend,
 and no scales can measure
  his excellence.
16 A faithful friend is an elixir of life;
 and those who fear the
  Lord will find him.
17 Whoever fears the Lord directs
  his friendship aright,
 for as he is, so is his neighbour also.

BLESSINGS OF WISDOM

18 My son, from your youth up
  choose instruction,
 and until you are old you will
  keep finding wisdom.
19 Come to her like one who
  ploughs and sows
 and wait for her good fruits.
 For in cultivating her you
  will toil a little,
 and quickly you will eat
  of her produce.
20 She seems very harsh to
  the uninstructed;
 a weakling will not remain with her.
21 She will weigh him down like
  a heavy testing stone,
 and he will not be slow to cast
  her off.
22 For wisdom is like her name
 and is not manifest to many.
23 Listen, child, and accept my
  judgement;
 and do not reject my counsel.
24 Put your feet into her fetters
 and your neck into her collar.
25 Put your shoulder under
  her and carry her
 and do not chafe under her bonds.
26 Come to her with all your soul
 and keep her ways with
  all your might.
27 Search out and seek, and she will
  become known to you;
 and when you get hold of
  her, do not let her go.
28 For at last you will find the
  rest she gives,
 and she will be changed
  into joy for you.
29 Then her fetters will become
  for you a strong shelter,
 and her collar a glorious robe.
30 Her yoke[a] is a golden ornament,
 and her bonds are a cord of blue.
31 You will wear her like a glorious robe
 and put her on like a crown
  of gladness.
32 If you are willing, child,
  you will be taught,
 and if you apply yourself you
  will become clever.

---

[a] Hebrew; Greek *Jpon her*

33 If you love to listen you will receive,
and if you incline your ear
you will become wise.
34 Stand in the assembly of the elders
and cling to their wisdom.ᵃ
35 Be ready to listen to everyᵇ narrative
and do not let wise proverbs
escape you.
36 If you see an intelligent man,
visit him early;
let your foot wear out his doorstep.
37 Reflect on the statutes of the Lord
and attend to his commandments
at all times.
He himself will strengthen your heart,ᶜ
and your desire for wisdom
will be granted.

MISCELLANEOUS ADVICE

7 Do no evil, and evil will never
befall you.
² Stay away from wrong, and it
will turn away from you.
³ My son, do not sow the
furrows of injustice,
and you will not reap a
sevenfold crop.
⁴ Do not seek from the Lord
the highest office
or the seat of honour from the king.
⁵ Do not assert your righteousness
before the Lord
or display your wisdom
before the king.
⁶ Do not seek to become a judge,
lest you lack the strength to
remove iniquity,
lest you be partial to a powerful man,
and thus put a blot on your integrity.
⁷ Do not offend against the public
and do not disgrace yourself
among the people.
⁸ Do not commit a sin twice;
even for one you will not
go unpunished.
⁹ Do not say, "He will consider the
multitude of my gifts,
and when I make an offering to the
Most High God he will accept it."
¹⁰ Do not be faint-hearted in your prayer
or neglect to give alms.
¹¹ Do not ridicule a man who
is bitter in soul,
for there is one who abases
and exalts.
¹² Do not deviseᵈ a lie against
your brother
or do the like to a friend.
¹³ Refuse to utter any lie,
for the habit of lying serves no good.
¹⁴ Do not prattle in the assembly
of the elders
or repeat yourself in your prayer.
¹⁵ Do not hate toilsome labour
and farm work, which were
created by the Most High.
¹⁶ Do not count yourself among
the crowd of sinners;
remember that wrath does not delay.
¹⁷ Humble your soul greatly,
for the punishment of the ungodly
is fire and the worm.ᵉ

RELATIONS WITH OTHERS

¹⁸ Do not exchange a friend for money
or a real brother for the
gold of Ophir.
¹⁹ Do not depart from a wise
and good wife,
for her charm is worth
more than gold.
²⁰ Do not abuse a servant who
performs his work faithfully
or a hired labourer who
devotes himself to you.
²¹ Let your soul loveᶠ an
intelligent servant;
do not withhold from him
his freedom.
²² Do you have cattle? Look after them;
if they are profitable to
you, keep them.
²³ Do you have children? Discipline them
and make them obedientᵍ
from their youth.
²⁴ Do you have daughters? Be
concerned for their chastityʰ
and do not show yourself too
indulgent with them.
²⁵ Give a daughter in marriage, and you
will have finished a great task,
and give her to a man of
understanding.

ᵃOr *elders. Who is wise? Cling to him.* ᵇHebrew; Greek adds *divine* ᶜGreek; Hebrew *He will give insight to your mind* ᵈHebrew; Greek *plough* ᵉHebrew *for the expectation of man is worms* ᶠHebrew *Love like yourself* ᵍGreek *and bend their necks* ʰGreek *body*

26 Do you have a wife like your
    soul?[a] Do not cast her out;
    and do not trust yourself to
    one whom you detest.
27 With all your heart honour your father
    and do not forget the birth
    pains of your mother.
28 Remember that through your
    parents[b] you were born;
    and what can you give back to them
    that equals their gift to you?

29 With all your soul fear the Lord
    and admire his priests.
30 With all your might love your Maker
    and do not forsake his ministers.
31 Fear the Lord and honour the priest
    and give him his portion, as
    is commanded you:
    the firstfruits, the guilt offering,
    the gift of the shoulders,
    the sacrifice of sanctification, and
    the firstfruits of the holy things.

32 Stretch forth your hand to
    the poor person,
    so that your blessing may
    be complete.
33 The kindness of a gift is
    before all the living,
    and do not hinder a kindness
    for the dead.
34 Do not fail those who weep
    and mourn with those who mourn.
35 Do not hesitate to visit a sick man,
    because for such deeds
    you will be loved.
36 In all your affairs, remember
    the end of your life,
    and then you will never sin.

PRUDENCE AND COMMON SENSE

8 Do not contend with a powerful man,
    lest you fall into his hands.
2 Do not quarrel with a rich man,
    lest his resources outweigh yours;
    for gold has ruined many
    and has perverted the
    hearts of kings.
3 Do not argue with a chatterer
    or heap wood on his fire.
4 Do not jest with an ill-bred person,
    lest your ancestors be disgraced.
5 Do not reproach a man who is
    turning away from sin;
    remember that we all deserve
    punishment.
6 Do not disdain a man when he is old,
    for indeed some of us are
    growing old.
7 Do not rejoice over anyone's death;
    remember that we all must die.

8 Do not slight the discourse of
    the sages,
    but busy yourself with their maxims;
    because from them you will
    gain instruction
    and learn how to serve great ones.
9 Do not disregard the discourse
    of the aged,
    for they themselves learned
    from their fathers;
    because from them you will
    gain understanding
    and learn how to give an
    answer in time of need.

10 Do not kindle the coals of a sinner;
    do not be set ablaze by his fire.
11 Do not get up and leave an
    insolent fellow,
    lest he lie in ambush against
    your words.
12 Do not lend to a man who is
    stronger than you;
    and if you do lend anything, be
    as one who has lost it.
13 Do not give surety beyond your means,
    and if you give surety, be concerned
    as one who must pay.
14 Do not go to law against a judge,
    for they will decide for him
    because of his standing.
15 Do not travel on the road with
    a foolhardy fellow,
    so that your troubles will
    not burden you;
    for he will act as he pleases,
    and through his folly you
    will perish with him.
16 Do not fight with a wrathful man
    and do not cross the
    desert with him;
    because blood is as nothing in
    his sight,
    and where no help is at hand,
    he will strike you down.

---

[a] Hebrew, Syriac omit *like your soul* [b] Greek *through them*

17 Do not consult with a fool,
for he will not be able to
keep a secret.
18 In the presence of a stranger do
nothing that is to be kept secret,
for you do not know what
he will divulge.[a]
19 Do not reveal your heart to everyone,
lest you drive away your good luck.[b]

WOMEN

9 Do not be jealous of the wife of
your bosom
and do not teach her an evil lesson
to your own hurt.
2 Do not give your soul to a woman
so that she gains mastery
over your strength.
3 Do not go to meet a loose woman,
lest you fall into her snares.
4 Do not associate with a woman singer,
lest you be caught in her intrigues.
5 Do not look intently at a virgin,
lest you stumble and incur
penalties for her.
6 Do not give yourself to prostitutes,
lest you lose your inheritance.
7 Do not look around in the
alleys of a city
or wander about in its
deserted sections.
8 Turn away your eyes from
a shapely woman
and do not look intently at beauty
belonging to another;
many have been misled by
a woman's beauty,
and by it passion is kindled like a fire.
9 Never sit down with another
man's wife
or share a meal with her over wine;
lest your soul turn aside to her,
and in your spirit[c] you will
slip into destruction.

CHOICE OF FRIENDS

10 Do not abandon an old friend,
for a new one does not
compare with him.
A new friend is like new wine;
if it ages, you will drink it
with pleasure.
11 Do not envy a sinner's reputation,
for you do not know what
his end will be.

12 Do not delight in what
pleases the ungodly;
remember that they will not be
justified as far as Hades.
13 Keep far from a man who has
the authority to kill,
and you will not be worried
by the fear of death.
But if you approach him,
make no misstep,
lest he rob you of your life.
Know that you are walking in
the midst of snares
and that you are going about
on the city battlements.
14 As much as you can, aim at
those who are near you[d]
and consult with the wise.
15 Let your conversation be with
men of understanding,
and let all your discussion be about
the law of the Most High.
16 Let righteous men be your
dinner companions,
and let your boast be in the
fear of the Lord.

RULERS

17 In the hand of artisans a work
will be praised,
and so a people's leader is
wise in his speech.
18 A babbler is feared in his city,
and the man who is reckless
in speech will be hated.

10 A wise magistrate will educate
his people,
and the rule of an understanding
man will be well ordered.
2 Like the magistrate of the people,
so are his officials;
and like the ruler of the city, so
are all its inhabitants.
3 An uneducated king will
ruin his people,
but a city will grow through the
understanding of its rulers.
4 Authority over the land is in
the hands of the Lord,

---

[a] Or *what it will bring forth* [b] Hebrew; Greek *everyone, let him not return a favour to you* [c] Hebrew and some Greek manuscripts *blood*
[d] The meaning of the Greek is uncertain

and over it he will raise up the
    right man for the time.
5 The success of a man is in the
    hands of the Lord,
and he confers his honour upon
    the face of the scribe.[a]

SIN OF PRIDE

6 Do not be angry with your
    neighbour for every injury
and do not attempt anything
    by acts of insolence.
7 Arrogance is hateful before the
    Lord and before people,
and injustice is out of tune to both.
8 Sovereignty passes from
    nation to nation
on account of injustice and
    insolence and wealth.[b]
9 Why would dust and ash
    act arrogantly?
For even in life his bowels decay.[c]
10 A long illness baffles the physician;[d]
    the king of today will die tomorrow.
11 For when a man is dead,
    he will inherit creeping things
    and wild beasts and worms.
12 The beginning of a person's pride
    is to depart from the Lord;
his heart has forsaken his Maker.
13 For the beginning of pride is sin,
    and the man who clings to it will
    pour out abominations.
Therefore the Lord brought upon
    them extraordinary afflictions
    and destroyed them utterly.
14 The Lord has cast down the
    thrones of rulers
and has seated the lowly
    in their place.
15 The Lord has plucked up the
    roots of the nations[e]
and has planted the humble
    in their place.
16 The Lord has overthrown the
    lands of the nations
and has destroyed them to the
    foundations of the earth.
17 He has removed some of them
    and destroyed them
and has extinguished the memory
    of them from the earth.
18 Pride was not created for
    human beings,
nor fierce anger for those
    born of women.

PERSONS DESERVING HONOUR

19 What race is worthy of honour?
    The human race.
What race is worthy of honour?
    Those who fear the Lord.
What race is unworthy of honour?
    The human race.
What race is unworthy of honour?
    Those who transgress the
    commandments.
20 Among brothers their leader
    is worthy of honour,
and those who fear the Lord are
    worthy of honour in his eyes.[f]
22 The rich and the eminent
    and the poor—[g]
their boast is the fear of the Lord.
23 It is not right to despise an
    intelligent poor man,
nor is it proper to honour
    a sinful man.
24 The nobleman and the judge and
    the ruler will be honoured,
but none of them is greater than
    the one who fears the Lord.
25 Free persons will be at the
    service of a wise servant,
and a man of understanding
    will not grumble.

HUMILITY

26 Do not make a display of your wisdom
    when you do your work
or glorify yourself at a time
    when you are in want.
27 Better is a man who works and has
    an abundance of everything
than one who goes about
    boasting, but lacks bread.
28 My son, glorify your soul
    with humility
and ascribe to yourself honour
    according to your worth.
29 Who will justify the person who
    sins against himself?
And who will honour the man who
    dishonours his own life?
30 A poor man is honoured for
    his knowledge,

---

[a] Or official [b] The longer edition adds *For there is nothing more lawless than a lover of money: for such a person makes his own soul a commodity.* [c] Hebrew; the meaning of the Greek is uncertain [d] Hebrew, Vulgate; the meaning of the Greek is uncertain [e] Some manuscripts *of the proud nations* [f] The longer edition adds verse 21: *The fear of the Lord is the beginning of acceptance; obduracy and pride are the beginning of rejection.* [g] Hebrew; Greek *The proselyte and foreigner and poor person*

while a rich man is honoured
for his wealth.
31 A man honoured in poverty, how
much more in wealth!
And a man dishonoured in wealth,
how much more in poverty!

DECEPTIVENESS OF APPEARANCES

11 The wisdom of a humble person
will lift up his head
and will seat him among the great.
2 Do not praise a man for his good looks
or loathe a person because
of his appearance.
3 The bee is small among
flying creatures,
and her product is the origin
of sweet things.
4 Do not boast about wearing
fine clothes
or exalt yourself in the day
that you are honoured;
for the works of the Lord
are wonderful,
and his works are concealed
among human beings.
5 Many kings have had to sit
on the ground,
but one who was not anticipated
has worn a crown.
6 Many rulers have been
greatly disgraced,
and illustrious men have been
handed over to others.

DELIBERATION AND CAUTION

7 Do not find fault before
you investigate;
first consider and then reprove.
8 Do not answer before you have heard
or interrupt a speaker in the
midst of his words.
9 Do not argue about a matter that
does not concern you
or sit with sinners when
they judge a case.*a*
10 My son, do not busy yourself
with many matters;
if you multiply activities you
will not go unpunished,
and if you pursue you will
not overtake,
and by fleeing you will not escape.
11 There is a man who works and
toils and presses on,
but falls behind so much the more.
12 There is another who is slow
and needs help,
who lacks strength and
abounds in poverty;
and the eyes of the Lord looked
upon him for his good
and lifted him out of his low estate
13 and raised up his head,
and many were amazed at him.
14 Good things and bad, life and death,
poverty and wealth, come
from the Lord.
15 Wisdom, understanding, and
knowledge of the law
come from the Lord;
affection and the ways of good
works come from him.
16 Error and darkness were
created with sinners;
evil will grow old with those
who take pride in malice.
17 The gift of the Lord endures for
those who are godly,
and his favour will bring
lasting success.
18 There is a man who is rich through
his diligence and self-denial,
and this is the reward allotted to him:
19 when he says, "I have found rest,
and now I shall enjoy*b* my goods!"
he does not know how much
time will pass
until he leaves them to others and dies.
20 Stand by your covenant*c* and attend to it
and grow old in your work.
21 Do not wonder at the works of a sinner,
but trust in the Lord and
keep at your toil;
for it is easy in the sight of the Lord
to enrich a poor man quickly
and suddenly.
22 The blessing of the Lord is in
the reward of the godly,
and quickly his favour flourishes.
23 Do not say, "What do I need,
and what prosperity will be
mine in the future?"
24 Do not say, "I have sufficiency,
and what harm will befall
me in the future?"

---

*a*Or *sit in council in the trial of sinners*   *b*Greek *shall eat of*   *c*Hebrew *task*

²⁵ In the day of prosperity,
adversity is forgotten,
and in the day of adversity,
prosperity is not remembered.
²⁶ For it is easy in the sight of the Lord
to reward a person on the day of
death according to his conduct.
²⁷ The misery of an hour makes
one forget luxury,
and at the close of a person's life
his deeds will be revealed.
²⁸ Call no one happy before his death;
a man will be known through
his children.^a

CARE IN CHOOSING FRIENDS

²⁹ Do not bring every person
into your home,
for many are the wiles of the crafty.
³⁰ Like a decoy partridge in a cage, so
is the heart of a proud person,
and like a spy he observes
your weakness;^b
³¹ for he lies in wait, distorting
good things into evil,
and to desirable things he
adds a blemish.
³² From a spark of fire come
many burning coals,
and a sinner lies in wait to shed blood.
³³ Beware of a scoundrel, for he
devises evil things,
lest he give you a lasting blemish.
³⁴ Receive a stranger into your home, and
he will upset you with commotion
and will estrange you from your own.

12 If you do a kindness, know to
whom you do it,
and there will be thanks for your
good deeds.
² Do good to a godly man, and
you will be repaid—
if not by him, certainly by the Most High.
³ No good will come to the person
who persists in evil
or to him who does not give alms.
⁴ Give to the godly person and
do not help the sinner.
⁵ Do good to the humble and do
not give to the ungodly;
hold back his bread and do
not give it to him,
lest by means of it he subdue you;
for you will receive twice as
many bad things
for all the good things that
you might do for him.
⁶ For the Most High also hates sinners
and will inflict punishment
on the ungodly.^c
⁷ Give to the good person and do
not help the sinner.

⁸ A friend will not be known^d
in prosperity,
nor will an enemy be hidden
in adversity.
⁹ A person's enemies are grieved
when he prospers,
and in his adversity even his friend
will separate from him.
¹⁰ Never trust your enemy,
for like the rusting of copper,
so is his wickedness.
¹¹ Even if he humbles himself and
goes about cringing,
watch yourself and be on your
guard against him;
and you will be to him like one
who has polished a mirror,
and you will know that it was
not hopelessly tarnished.
¹² Do not put him next to you,
lest he overthrow you and
take your place;
do not have him sit at your right,
lest he try to take your seat,
and at last you will realize the
truth of my words
and be stung by what I have said.

¹³ Who will pity a snake charmer
bitten by a serpent
or all those who go near wild beasts?
¹⁴ So no one will pity one who
associates with a sinner
and becomes involved in his sins.
¹⁵ He will stay with you for a time,
but if you falter, he will surely
not stand by you.

¹⁶ An enemy will speak sweetly
with his lips,
but in his heart he will plan to
throw you into a pit;
an enemy will weep with his eyes,
but if he finds an opportunity his
thirst for blood will be insatiable.

---

^aGreek; Hebrew *a person is known in his end* ^bHebrew; Greek *downfall* ^cThe longer edition adds *and he is keeping them for the day of their punishment* ^dSome manuscripts *punished*

17 If bad things befall you, you will
    find him there ahead of you;
   and while pretending to help you,
    he will trip you by the heel;
18 he will shake his head and
    clap his hands
   and whisper much and change
    his expression.

CAUTION REGARDING ASSOCIATES

13
Whoever touches pitch will
    get dirty,
and whoever associates with a
    proud man will become
    like him.
2 Do not lift a weight beyond
    your strength
   or associate with one mightier
    and richer than you.
   How can the clay pot associate
    with the iron kettle?
   The pot will strike against it
    and will itself be broken.
3 A rich person inflicted injury, and he
    is the one who was indignant;
   a poor man was injured, and he
    is the one who will plead.
4 A rich man[a] will exploit you if
    you can be of use to him,
   but if you are in need he
    will forsake you.
5 If you own something, he
    will live with you;
   he will drain your resources
    and he will not care.
6 When he needs you he will deceive you,
    he will smile at you and give you hope.
   He will speak to you kindly and
    say, "What do you need?"
7 He will shame you with his foods,
    until he has drained you
    two or three times;
   and finally he will deride you.
   After this, he will see you
    and forsake you
    and shake his head at you.
8 Take care not to be led astray
    and not to be humiliated
    in your feasting.[b]
9 When a powerful man invites
    you, be reserved;
   and he will invite you
    the more often.
10 Do not push forward, lest
    you be repulsed;
   and do not remain at a distance,
    lest you be forgotten.
11 Do not try to treat him as an equal
    or trust his abundance of words;
   for he will test you through much talk,
    and while he smiles he will
    be examining you.
12 Merciless is the one who does
    not guard words;[c]
   he will surely not hesitate to
    injure or to imprison.
13 Keep words to yourself and
    be very watchful,
   for you are walking about with
    your own downfall.[d]

15 Every creature loves its like,
    and every person his neighbour;
16 all living beings associate by species,
    and a man clings to one like himself.
17 What fellowship has a wolf with a lamb?
    No more has a sinner with a godly man.
18 What peace is there between
    a hyena and a dog?
   And what peace between a rich
    man and a poor man?
19 Wild donkeys in the wilderness
    are the prey of lions;
   likewise the poor are
    pastures for the rich.
20 Humility is an abomination
    to a proud man;
   likewise a poor person is an
    abomination to a rich one.
21 When a rich man totters, he is
    steadied by friends,
   but when a humble man falls, he is
    even pushed away by friends.
22 If a rich man slips, his
    helpers are many;
   he spoke unseemly words,
    and they justified him.
   A humble man slipped, and
    they reproach him;
   he uttered insight and
    receives no attention.
23 A rich person spoke and
    all stood silent,
   and they extol to the clouds
    what he says.

---

[a]Greek *He* [b]Hebrew and some Greek manuscripts; one Greek manuscript *folly* [c]Some manuscripts *Mercilessly he will store up your words* [d]The longer edition adds verses 13c–14: *When you hear these things in your sleep, wake up!* 14 *During all your life love the Lord and call on him for your salvation.*

A poor person spoke and they
say, "Who is this fellow?"
And should he stumble, they
will even push him down.

24 Riches are good if they are
free from sin,
and poverty is evil in the
opinion of the ungodly.
25 A person's heart changes his face,
either for good or for evil.^a
26 The mark of a happy heart
is a cheerful face,
but to devise proverbs requires
painful thinking.

14 Blessed is the man who does not
blunder with his lips
and need not suffer grief for sin.
2 Blessed is the one whose heart
does not condemn him
and who has not given up his hope.

RESPONSIBLE USE OF WEALTH

3 Riches are not seemly for a stingy man;
and of what use is property
to an envious person?
4 Whoever accumulates by depriving
himself, accumulates for others;
and others will live in luxury
on his goods.
5 The one who is mean to himself, to
whom will he be generous?
And he will certainly not
enjoy his own riches.
6 No one is meaner than the man
who is grudging to himself,
and this is the retribution
for his baseness;
7 even if he does good, he does
it unintentionally
and reveals his baseness in the end.
8 Evil is the one with a grudging eye;
he averts his face and overlooks lives.
9 A greedy man's eye is not
satisfied with a portion,
and mean injustice withers the soul.
10 An evil eye begrudges bread,
and it is lacking at his table.

11 Child, treat yourself well,
according to your means,
and present worthy offerings
to the Lord.
12 Remember that death will not delay,
and the decree^b of Hades has
not been shown to you.

13 Do good to a friend before you die
and reach out and give to him
as much as you can.
14 Do not deprive yourself of a
happy day;
let not your share of desired
good pass by you.
15 Will you not leave the fruit of
your labours to another
and what you acquired by toil
to be divided by lot?
16 Give and take and beguile yourself,
because in Hades one cannot
look for luxury.
17 All living beings become
old like a garment,
for the decree from of old is,
"You will surely die!"
18 Like flourishing leaves on
a spreading tree
that sheds some and puts
forth others,
so are the generations of
flesh and blood:
one generation dies and
another is born.
19 Every product decays and
ceases to exist,
and the one who made it will
pass away with it.

HAPPINESS OF SEEKING WISDOM

20 Blessed is the man who
meditates on^c wisdom
and who reasons intelligently.
21 The one who reflects on her
ways in his heart
will also ponder her secrets.
22 Pursue wisdom^d like a hunter
and lie in wait on her paths.
23 The one who peers through
her windows
will also listen at her doors;
24 the one who encamps near her house
will also fasten his tent
peg to her walls;
25 he will pitch his tent near her
and will lodge in an excellent
lodging place;
26 he will place his children
under her shelter
and will camp under her boughs;

---

^aThe longer edition adds *and a glad heart makes a cheerful countenance* ^bGreek *covenant*; also verse 17 ^cSome manuscripts *who dies in* ^dGreek *her*

SIRACH 14–16

27 he will be sheltered by her
    from the heat
  and will dwell in the midst
    of her glory.

15

1 The person who fears the Lord
    will do this,
  and the one who holds to the law
    will obtain wisdom.[a]
2 She will come to meet him
    like a mother,
  and like a young bride she
    will welcome him.
3 She will feed him with the
    bread of understanding
  and give him the water of
    wisdom to drink.
4 He will lean on her and will not fall,
  and he will attend to her and
    will not be put to shame.
5 She will exalt him above his neighbours
  and will open his mouth in the
    midst of the assembly.
6 He will find gladness and a
    crown of rejoicing
  and will acquire an
    everlasting name.
7 Foolish people will not obtain her,
  and sinful men will not see her.
8 She is far from arrogance,
  and liars will never remember her.

9 A hymn of praise is not fitting
    on the lips of a sinner,
  for it has not been sent
    from the Lord.
10 For a hymn of praise will be
    uttered in wisdom,
  and the Lord will make it prosper.

FREEDOM OF CHOICE

11 Do not say, "Because of the Lord
    I left the right way";
  for he[b] will not do what he hates.
12 Do not say, "It was he who
    led me astray";
  for he had no need of a sinful man.
13 The Lord hates every abomination,
  and they are not loved by
    those who fear him.
14 It was he who created mankind
    in the beginning,
  and he left him in the power
    of his own choice.
15 If you desire, you will keep
    the commandments,
  and to act faithfully is a
    matter of choice.
16 He has placed before you fire and water:
  stretch out your hand for
    whichever you wish.
17 Life and death are in front of people,
  and whichever one chooses
    will be given to him.
18 For great is the wisdom of the Lord;
  he is mighty in power and
    sees everything;
19 his eyes are on those who fear him,
  and he knows a person's every deed.
20 He has not commanded
    anyone to be ungodly,
  and he has not given anyone
    permission to sin.

GOD'S PUNISHMENT OF SINNERS

16

1 Do not desire a multitude of
    useless children
  or rejoice in ungodly sons.
2 If they multiply, do not rejoice in them
  unless the fear of the Lord
    is with them.
3 Do not trust in their life
  and do not rely on their multitude;[c]
  for one is better than a thousand,
  and to die childless is better than
    to have ungodly children.
4 For through one person of
    understanding a city will
    be filled with people,
  but through a tribe of lawless people
    it will be made desolate.
5 Many such things my eye has seen,
  and my ear has heard things
    more striking than these.

6 In an assembly of sinners a
    fire will be kindled,
  and in a disobedient nation
    wrath was kindled.
7 He was not propitiated for
    the ancient giants
  who revolted in their might.
8 He did not spare the neighbours of Lot,
  whom he loathed on account
    of their insolence.
9 He showed no pity for a nation
    devoted to destruction,
  for those driven out in their sins[d]

---

[a]Greek her [b]Hebrew; Greek you [c]The longer edition adds for you will groan with untimely mourning, and you will learn suddenly of their end [d]Some manuscripts add He did all these things to hard-hearted nations, and he was not consoled by the multitude of his holy ones.

10 or for the 600,000 men on foot
   who assembled in their
      hardness of heart.ᵃ
11 Even if there is only one stiff-necked
      person,
   it will be a wonder if he
      remains unpunished.
   For mercy and wrath are with the Lord;ᵇ
   he is mighty to forgive, and
      he pours out wrath.
12 As great as his mercy, so great
      is also his reproof;
   he will judge a man according
      to his deeds.
13 The sinner will not escape
      with his plunder,
   and the patience of the godly
      will never be frustrated.
14 He will make room for every
      act of mercy;
   everyone will receive in
      accordance with his deeds.ᶜ

17 Do not say, "I shall be hidden
      from the Lord,
   and who from on high will
      remember me?
   Among so many people I
      shall not be known,
   for what is my soul in the
      boundless creation?
18 Behold, heaven and the highest heaven,
   the Abyss and the earth, will
      tremble at his visitation.ᵈ
19 The mountains also and the
      foundations of the earth
   shake with trembling when
      he looks upon them,
20 and no mind will reflect on these things.
      Who will ponder his ways?
21 Like a blast of wind that no
      person will see,
   so most of his works are concealed.
22 Who will announce acts of justice?
      Or who will await them? For
      the covenant is far off."ᵉ
23 This is what one devoid of
      understanding thinks;
   and a senseless and misguided
      man thinks foolish things.

GOD'S WISDOM SEEN IN CREATION

24 Listen to me, child, and
      learn knowledge
   and pay close attention in your
      heart to my words.

25 I will impart instruction by weight
   and declare knowledge accurately.

26 The works of the Lord have existed from
      the beginning by his creation,ᶠ
   and when he made them, he
      determined their divisions.
27 He arranged their tasks in
      an eternal order
   and their dominion for
      allᵍ generations;
   they neither hunger nor grow weary,
      and they do not cease from
      their labours.
28 They do not crowd one another aside,
      and they will never
      disobey his word.
29 After this the Lord looked
      upon the earth
   and filled it with his good things;
30 with all kinds of living beings
      he covered its surface,
   and to it they return.

17 The Lord created mankind out
      of earth
   and turned him back to it again.
2 He gave to them numbered
      days, a limited time,
   but granted them authority over
      the things upon the earth.ʰ
3 He endowed them with
      strength like his ownⁱ
   and made them in his own image.
4 He placed the fear of themʲ
      in all living beings
   and granted them dominion
      over beasts and birds.ᵏ
6 He made for them deliberation,
      speech, and eyes;
   he gave them ears and a
      mind for thinking.
7 He filled them with knowledge
      and understanding

ᵃSome manuscripts of the longer edition add *Chastening, showing mercy, striking, healing, the Lord kept watch in compassion and discipline.* ᵇGreek *with him* ᶜSome manuscripts of the longer edition add verses 15–16: *The Lord hardened Pharaoh so that he did not know him; in order that his works might be known under heaven.* ¹⁶*His mercy is manifest to the whole of creation, and he apportioned his light and darkness to Adam.* ᵈSome manuscripts of the longer edition add *the whole cosmos that has come into being and continues to be by his will* ᵉSome manuscripts of the longer edition add *And an investigation of all things comes at the end.* ᶠHebrew; Greek *judgement* ᵍGreek *their* ʰGreek *upon it* ⁱGreek *strength proper to them* ʲSyriac; Greek *him* ᵏSome manuscripts of the longer edition add verse 5: *They obtained the use of the five faculties of the Lord; as sixth he distributed to them the gift of mind, and as seventh reason, the interpreter of his faculties.*

and showed them good
  things and bad.
8 He set his eye[a] upon their hearts
  to show them the majesty
    of his works.[b]
10 And they will praise his holy name
  to proclaim the grandeur of his works.
11 He bestowed knowledge upon them
  and allotted to them the law of life.[c]
12 He established with them an
    eternal covenant
  and showed them his judgements.
13 Their eyes saw his glorious majesty,
  and their ears heard the
    glory of his voice.
14 And he said to them, "Beware
    all unrighteousness."[d]
  And he gave commandment to
    each of them concerning
    his neighbour.

15 Their ways are always before him,
  they will not be hid from his eyes.[e]
17 He appointed a ruler for every nation,
  and Israel is the Lord's own portion.[f]
19 All their works are as the
    sun before him,
  and his eyes are continually
    upon their ways.
20 Their iniquities are not
    hidden from him,
  and all their sins are before the Lord.[g]
22 A man's almsgiving is like a
    signet with the Lord,[h]
  and he will keep a person's kindness
    like the apple of his eye.[i]
23 Afterwards he will arise
    and requite them,
  and he will bring their recompense
    on their heads.
24 Yet to those who repented
    he granted a return,
  and he encouraged those whose
    endurance was failing.

CALL TO REPENTANCE

25 Turn to the Lord and forsake your sins;
  pray in his presence and
    lessen your offence.
26 Return to the Most High and
    turn away from iniquity[j]
  and hate abominations intensely.
27 Who will sing praises to the
    Most High in Hades,
  as do those who are alive
    and give thanks?
28 From the dead, as from one who does
    not exist, thanksgiving has ceased;
  he who is alive and well sings
    the Lord's praises.
29 How great is the mercy of the Lord,
  and his forgiveness for those
    who turn to him!
30 For not everything is possible
    among people,
  since a son of man is not immortal.
31 What is brighter than the sun?
    Yet its light fails.[k]
  So flesh and blood devise evil.
32 He marshals the host of the
    height of heaven;
  but all people are dust and ashes.

MAJESTY OF GOD

18 He who lives for ever created the
    whole universe;
  ²the Lord alone will be declared
    righteous.[l]
4 To none has he given power to
    proclaim his works;
  and who can search out
    his mighty deeds?
5 Who will measure his majestic power?
  And who will fully recount
    his mercies?
6 It is not possible to diminish
    or increase them,
  nor is it possible to trace the
    wonders of the Lord.
7 When a person has finished,
    then he is just beginning,
  and when he stops, he
    will be at a loss.
8 What is a human being, and
    of what use is he?
  What is his good and
    what is his evil?

---

[a]Some manuscripts *fear* [b]Some manuscripts of the longer edition add verse 9: *And he gave them to boast of his marvels for ever.* [c]Some manuscripts of the longer edition add *in order that they might know that those who now exist are mortal* [d]Or *Beware every unrighteous man* [e]Some manuscripts of the longer edition add verses 16–17a: *Their ways from youth tend towards evil, and they are unable to make for themselves hearts of flesh in place of their stony hearts. ¹⁷For in the division of the nations of the whole earth* [f]Some manuscripts of the longer edition add verse 18: *whom, being his firstborn, he brings up with discipline, and allotting to him the light of his love, he does not neglect him.* [g]Some manuscripts add verse 21: *But the Lord, who is gracious and knows his creatures, has neither left nor abandoned them, sparing them.* [h]Greek *with him* [i]Some manuscripts of the longer edition add *apportioning repentance to his sons and daughters* [j]Some manuscripts of the longer edition add *for he will lead you out of darkness to the light of health* [k]Or *light suffers eclipse* [l]Some manuscripts of the longer edition add verses 2b–3: *and there is no other besides him. ³He steers the world with the span of his hand, and all things obey his will; for he himself is king of all things by his power, separating among them the holy things from the profane.*

9 The number of a person's days is
 great if he reaches 100 years.
10 Like a drop of water from the
 sea and a grain[a] of sand
 so are a few years in the
 day of eternity.
11 Therefore the Lord is
 patient with them
 and pours out his mercy upon them.
12 He sees and recognizes that
 their end will be evil;
 therefore he grants them
 forgiveness in abundance.
13 The compassion of a person
 is for his neighbour,
 but the compassion of the Lord
 is for all living beings.
 He rebukes and trains and
 teaches them
 and turns them back, as a
 shepherd his flock.
14 He has compassion on those
 who accept his discipline
 and who are eager for his
 judgements.

THE RIGHT SPIRIT IN GIVING ALMS

15 Child, do not mix reproach
 with your good deeds
 or cause grief by your words
 when you present a gift.
16 Does not the dew assuage
 the scorching heat?
 So a word is better than a gift.
17 Indeed, does not a word
 surpass a good gift?
 Both are to be found in a
 gracious man.
18 A fool is ungracious and abusive,
 and the gift of a grudging person
 makes the eyes waste away.

NEED OF REFLECTION AND SELF-CONTROL

19 Before you speak, learn,
 and before you fall ill, take
 care of your health.
20 Before judgement, examine yourself,
 and in the hour of visitation you
 will find forgiveness.
21 Before falling ill, humble yourself,
 and when you are on the point
 of sinning, turn back.
22 Let nothing hinder you from
 paying a vow promptly,
 and do not wait until death
 to be released from it.

23 Before making a vow,[b] prepare yourself;
 and do not be like a person
 who tests the Lord.
24 Think of his wrath on the day of death
 and of the moment of vengeance
 when he turns away his face.
25 In the time of plenty think of
 the time of hunger;
 in the days of wealth think
 of poverty and need.
26 From morning to evening
 conditions change,
 and all things move swiftly
 before the Lord.

27 A wise person will be cautious
 in everything,
 and in days of sin he will guard
 against wrongdoing.
28 Every intelligent person
 knows wisdom,
 and he[c] will acknowledge the
 one who finds her.
29 Those who understand sayings
 become skilled themselves
 and pour forth apt proverbs.[d]

CONCERNING SELF-CONTROL[e]

30 Do not follow your desires
 and restrain yourself from
 your appetites.
31 If you give your soul the
 satisfaction of desire,
 it will make you the laughing-
 stock of your enemies.
32 Do not revel in great luxury,
 lest you become impoverished
 by its expense.
33 Do not become a beggar by feasting
 with borrowed money,
 when you have nothing
 in your purse.[f]

19 A worker who is a drunkard will
 not become rich;
 he who despises small things will
 fail little by little.
2 Wine and women lead
 intelligent men astray,
 and the man who consorts with
 prostitutes is very reckless.

---

[c] Greek pebble [b] Or Before offering a prayer [c] Or she [d] Some manuscripts add Better is confidence in the only Lord than clinging with a dead heart to a corpse. [e] This heading is in the Greek text [f] Some manuscripts of the longer edition add for you will be plotting against your own life

3 Decay and worms will inherit him,
    and the reckless soul will
      be snatched away.

AGAINST LOOSE TALK

4 One who trusts others too
    quickly is light-minded,
  and one who sins does
    wrong to himself.
5 One who rejoices in wickedness[a]
    will be condemned,[b]
6 and one who hates gossip
    lessens wickedness.
7 Never repeat a conversation,
    and you will lose nothing at all.
8 With friend or foe do not report it,
    and unless it would be a sin for
      you, do not disclose it;
9 for someone has heard you
    and watched you,
  and when the time comes
    he will hate you.
10 Have you heard a word? Let
     it die with you.
   Be brave! It will not make you burst!
11 With such a word a fool
     will suffer pains
   like a woman in labour with a child.
12 Like an arrow stuck in the
     flesh of the thigh,
   so is a word inside a fool.
13 Question a friend, perhaps
     he did not do it;
   and if he did anything, so that
     he may do it no more.
14 Question a neighbour, perhaps
     he did not say it;
   and if he said it, so that he
     may not say it again.
15 Question a friend, for often it is slander;
   so do not believe everything
     you hear.
16 A person may make a slip
     without intending it.
   Who has never sinned
     with his tongue?
17 Question your neighbour before
     you threaten him;
   and let the law of the Most
     High take its course.[c]

TRUE AND FALSE WISDOM

20 All wisdom is the fear of the Lord,
    and in all wisdom there is
     the doing of the law.[d]

22 But the knowledge of wickedness
     is not wisdom,
   nor is there prudence where
     sinners take counsel.
23 There is a cleverness that
     is abominable,
   and there is a fool who lacks wisdom.
24 Better is the God-fearing person
     who lacks intelligence
   than the highly prudent man
     who transgresses the law.
25 There is a cleverness that is
     scrupulous but unjust,
   and there are people who distort
     kindness to gain a verdict.
26 There is a rascal bowed down
     in mourning,[e]
   but inwardly he is full of deceit.
27 He hides his face and
     pretends not to hear;
   but where no one notices,
     he will forestall you.
28 And if by lack of strength he is
     prevented from sinning,
   he will do evil when he finds
     an opportunity.
29 A man is known by his appearance,
   and a sensible man is known by
     his face, when you meet him.
30 A man's attire and open-
     mouthed laughter,
   and a person's manner of
     walking, show what he is.

SILENCE AND SPEECH

20 There is a reproof that is not
     timely;
   and there is a man who keeps
     silent but is wise.
2 How much better it is to reprove
    than to stay angry!
3 And the one who confesses his
    fault will be kept from loss.
4 Like a eunuch's desire to
    violate a maiden
  is a man who executes
    judgements by violence.

---

[a]Some manuscripts *heart*   [b]Some manuscripts add verses 5b–6a: *but he who withstands pleasures crowns his life.* ⁶*He who controls his tongue will live without strife,*   [c]Some manuscripts of the longer edition add verses 18–19: *The fear of the Lord is the beginning of acceptance, and wisdom obtains his love.* ¹⁹*The knowledge of the Lord's commandments is life-giving discipline; and those who do what is pleasing to him will enjoy the fruit of the tree of immortality.*   [d]Some manuscripts of the longer edition add verses 20b–21: *and the knowledge of his omnipotence.* ²¹*When a servant says to his master, "I will not act as pleases you," even if later he does it, he angers the one who supports him.*   [e]Greek *blackness*

5 There is one who by keeping
        silent is found wise,
    while another is detested for
        being too talkative.
6 There is one who keeps silent
        because he has no answer,
    while another keeps silent because
        he knows when to speak.
7 A wise person will be silent
        until the right moment,
    but a braggart and fool goes
        beyond the right moment.
8 Whoever uses too many words
        will be loathed,
    and whoever usurps the right
        to speak will be hated.[a]

PARADOXES

9 There is success for a man in adversity,
    and there is a windfall that
        results in a loss.
10 There is a gift that profits you nothing,
    and there is a gift that brings
        a double return.
11 There are losses because of glory,
    and there is a person who
        has raised his head from
        humble circumstances.
12 There is a person who buys
        much for a little,
    but pays for it seven times over.

13 The wise man makes himself
        beloved through his words,
    but the courtesies of fools
        are wasted.
14 A fool's gift will profit you nothing,[b]
    for he has many eyes instead of one.
15 He gives little and upbraids much,
    he opens his mouth like a herald;
    today he lends and tomorrow
        he asks for it back;
    such a one is a hateful person.
16 A fool will say, "I have no friend,
    and there is no gratitude for
        my good deeds."
    Those who eat his bread are
        wicked in their speech:
17 how many will ridicule him,
        and how often![c]

INAPPROPRIATE SPEECH

18 A slip on the pavement is better
        than a slip of the tongue;
    so the downfall of the wicked
        will occur speedily.

19 An ungracious man is like a story
        told at the wrong time,
    which is continually on the
        lips of the ignorant.
20 A proverb from a fool's lips
        will be rejected,
    for he does not tell it at
        its proper time.

21 There is a person who is prevented
        from sinning by his poverty,
    so when he rests he feels no remorse.
22 There is a person who destroys his
        life on account of shame
    and who will destroy it from
        his foolish look.
23 There is a person who for shame
        makes promises to a friend
    and needlessly made him an enemy.

LYING

24 A lie is an ugly blot on a person;
    it is continually on the lips
        of the ignorant.
25 A thief is preferable to a habitual liar,
    but both will inherit ruin.
26 The disposition of a liar brings disgrace,
    and his shame is ever with him.

PROVERBIAL SAYINGS[d]

27 One who is wise in speech
        will advance himself,
    and a sensible person will
        please great ones.
28 Whoever cultivates the soil will
        heap up his harvest,
    and whoever pleases the great
        will atone for injustice.
29 Presents and gifts blind the
        eyes of the wise;
    like a muzzle on the mouth
        they avert reproofs.
30 Hidden wisdom and unseen treasure,
    what advantage is there in
        either of them?
31 Better is the person who hides his folly
    than the person who hides
        his wisdom.[e]

---

[a]Some manuscripts of the longer edition add *How good it is, when reproved, to show repentance, for thus you will escape wilful transgression.* [b]Some manuscripts of the longer edition add *likewise the gift of the begrudging person on account of compulsion* [c]Some manuscripts of the longer edition add *For he did not take his having in the right sense, and his not having was similarly undifferentiated for him.* [d]This heading is in the Greek text [e]Some manuscripts add verse 32: *Unwearied patience in seeking the Lord is better than a masterless charioteer of one's own life.*

SIRACH 21

VARIOUS SINS

21 ¹ Child, have you sinned? Do not
add more,
but pray about your former sins.
² Flee from sin as from a snake;
for if you approach sin,
it will bite you.
Its teeth are lion's teeth,
destroying human souls.
³ All lawlessness is like a two-
edged sword;
there is no healing for its wound.
⁴ Panic and insolence will
lay waste riches;
thus the house of the proud
will be laid waste.
⁵ The prayer of a poor man goes from
his lips to the ears of God,*a*
and his judgement comes
speedily.
⁶ Whoever hates reproof walks in
the steps of the sinner,
but the one who fears the Lord
will repent in his heart.
⁷ He who is mighty in speech
is known from afar;
but the sensible person, when
he slips, is aware of it.
⁸ A person who builds his house
with other people's money
is like one who gathers stones
for his burial mound.*b*
⁹ An assembly of the wicked is like
tow gathered together,
and their end is a flame of fire.
¹⁰ The way of sinners is smoothly
paved with stones,
but at its end is the pit of Hades.

WISDOM AND FOOLISHNESS

¹¹ Whoever keeps the law
controls his thoughts,
and wisdom is the fulfilment
of the fear of the Lord.
¹² He who is not clever will not
be taught,
but there is a cleverness that
increases bitterness.
¹³ The knowledge of a wise man
will increase like a flood,
and his counsel like a
flowing spring.*c*
¹⁴ The mind of a fool is like a broken jar;
it will hold no knowledge.

¹⁵ When a man of understanding
hears a wise saying,
he will praise it and add to it;
the self-indulgent person
heard it and disliked it
and cast it behind his back.
¹⁶ A fool's narration is like a
burden on a journey,
but grace will be found in the
speech of the intelligent.
¹⁷ The utterance of a sensible man will
be sought in the assembly,
and they will ponder his
words in their hearts.
¹⁸ Like a house that has vanished,
so is wisdom to a fool;
and the knowledge of the ignorant
is unexamined talk.
¹⁹ Education is like fetters on the
feet of a senseless person
and like manacles on his right hand.
²⁰ A fool raises his voice when he laughs,
but a clever man will at
most smile quietly.
²¹ Education is like a golden ornament
to a sensible person
and like a bracelet on the right arm.
²² The foot of a fool rushes into a house,
but a man of experience stands
respectfully before it.
²³ A boor peers into the house
from the door,
but a cultivated man
remains outside.
²⁴ It is ill-mannered for a person
to listen at a door,
and a person of sense is
grieved by the disgrace.
²⁵ The lips of strangers will speak
of these things,*d*
but the words of the prudent will
be weighed in the balance.
²⁶ The heart of fools is in their mouth,
but the mouth of wise people
is in*e* their heart.
²⁷ When an ungodly man curses
his adversary,*f*
he curses his own soul.
²⁸ A whisperer defiles his own soul
and is hated in his neighbourhood.

---

a Greek *to his ears* *b* Some manuscripts *for the winter* *c* Or *like a spring of life* *d* The meaning of the Greek is uncertain *e* Some manuscripts omit *in* *f* Or *curses Satan*

THE IDLER

22 The indolent may be compared
to a filthy stone,
and everyone hisses at his
disgrace.
2 The indolent may be compared
to the filth of dunghills;
anyone that picks it up will
shake it off his hand.

DEGENERATE CHILDREN

3 A father's disgrace is in the birth
of an undisciplined son,
and the birth of a daughter is a loss.
4 A sensible daughter will
obtain her husband,
but one who is put to shame
brings grief to her father.
5 An impudent daughter disgraces
father and husband
and will be despised by both.
6 Like music in mourning is a tale
told at the wrong time,
but chastising and discipline
are wisdom at all times.[a]

WISDOM AND FOLLY

9 He who teaches a fool is like one
who glues potsherds together
or who rouses a sleeper
from deep slumber.
10 He who tells a story to a fool
tells it to a drowsy man;
and at the end he will say,
"What is it?"
11 Weep for the dead, for he
lacks the light;
and weep for the fool, for he
lacks intelligence;
weep less bitterly for the dead,
for he has attained rest;
but the wicked life of the fool
is worse than death.
12 Mourning for the dead
lasts seven days,
but for a fool or an ungodly
person it lasts all his life.

13 Do not talk much with a foolish man
and do not visit an
unintelligent man;[b]
guard yourself from him to
escape trouble,
and you will not be soiled when
he shakes himself off;
avoid him and you will find rest,
and you will never be wearied
by his madness.
14 What is heavier than lead?
And what is its name except "Fool"?
15 Sand, salt, and a piece of iron
are easier to bear than a
stupid person.

16 A wooden beam firmly bonded
into a building
will not be torn loose by
an earthquake;
so a heart firmly fixed on a
reasonable counsel
will not be afraid in a crisis.
17 A heart settled on an
intelligent thought
is like the stucco decoration on
the wall of a colonnade.[c]
18 Fences set on a high place
will not stand firm against the wind;
so a timid heart with a fool's purpose
will not stand firm against any fear.

PRESERVATION OF FRIENDSHIP

19 One who pricks an eye will
make tears fall,
and one who pricks the heart
bares its feelings.
20 One who throws a stone at
birds scares them away,
and one who reviles a friend will
break off the friendship.
21 Even if you have drawn your
sword against a friend,
do not despair, for a renewal of
friendship is possible.
22 If you have opened your mouth
against your friend,
do not worry, for reconciliation
is possible;
but as for reviling, arrogance,
disclosure of secrets, or
a treacherous blow—
in these cases any friend will flee.

23 Gain the trust of your neighbour
in his poverty,
that you may rejoice with
him in his prosperity;
stand by him in time of affliction,

---

[a] Some manuscripts add verses 7–8: *Children who are brought up in a good life conceal the lowly birth of their parents. 8Children who are disdainfully and boorishly haughty stain the nobility of their kindred.*
[b] Some manuscripts of the longer edition add *for a senseless person will bring to naught all that is yours* [c] Or *on a smooth wall*

that you may share with him
in his inheritance.[a]
24 The vapour and smoke of the
furnace precede the fire;
so insults precede bloodshed.
25 I will not be ashamed to
protect a friend,
and I will not hide from him;
26 but if some harm should happen
to me because of him,
whoever hears of it will
beware of him.

PRAYER FOR HELP AGAINST SINNING

27 Who will set a guard over my mouth
and a seal of prudence upon
my lips,
in order that I may not fall
on their account,
and my tongue may not destroy me?

23

O Lord, Father and Ruler of
my life,
do not abandon me to their
counsel,
and let me not fall because of them!
2 Who will set whips over my thoughts
and the discipline of wisdom
over my heart,
that they may not spare me in
my errors of ignorance
and that it may not pass
over my[b] sins;
3 in order that my ignorant deeds
may not be multiplied
and my sins may not abound,
so that I fall before my adversaries,
and my enemy rejoices over me?
4 O Lord, Father and God of my life,
do not give me haughty eyes
5 and remove from me all
covetousness.
6 Let neither gluttony nor
lust overcome me
and do not surrender me to
a shameless soul.

DISCIPLINE OF THE TONGUE[c]

7 Listen, my children, to instruction
concerning speech;
the one who observes it will
never be caught.
8 The sinner is overtaken
through his lips,
the reviler and the arrogant
are tripped by them.
9 Do not accustom your mouth to oaths
and do not habitually utter the
name of the Holy One;
10 for as a servant who is
continually interrogated
will not lack bruises,
so also the man who always
swears and utters the name
will not be cleansed from sin.
11 A man who swears many oaths
will be filled with iniquity,
and the scourge will not
leave his house;
if he offends, his sin remains on him,
and if he disregards it,
he sins doubly;
if he has sworn needlessly, he
will not be justified,
for his house will be filled
with calamities.

FOUL LANGUAGE

12 There is an utterance that is
comparable to death;[d]
may it never be found in the
inheritance of Jacob!
For all these errors will be
far from the godly,
and they will not wallow in sins.
13 Do not accustom your mouth
to lewd vulgarity,
for it involves sinful speech.
14 Remember your father and mother
when[e] you sit in council
among the great;
lest you be forgetful in their presence
and be deemed a fool on
account of your habits;
then you will wish that you
had never been born,
and you will curse the day
of your birth.
15 A man accustomed to use
insulting words
will never become disciplined
all his days.

SEXUAL SINS

16 Two sorts of people multiply sins,
and a third incurs wrath.
The soul heated like a burning fire
will surely never be quenched
until it is consumed;

---

[a] Some manuscripts of the longer edition add *For one should not always despise restricted circumstances or admire a rich man who is stupid.* [b] Greek *their* [c] This heading is in the Greek text [d] Some manuscripts *that is clothed about with death* [e] Greek *for*

a person who has sexual intercourse
      with his near of kin[a]
   will never cease until the
      fire burns him up.
17 To a sexually immoral person
      all bread tastes sweet;
   he will never cease until he dies.
18 A person who breaks his
      marriage vows
   says to himself, "Who sees me?
   Darkness surrounds me, and
      the walls hide me,
   and no one sees me. Why
      should I fear?
   The Most High will surely not
      remember my sins."
19 His fear is confined to the eyes
      of human beings,
   and he does not realize that
      the eyes of the Lord
   are ten thousand times
      brighter than the sun;
   they look upon all the ways of people
   and peer into the hidden places.
20 Before the universe was created,
      it was known to him;
   so it was also after it was finished.
21 This person will be punished
      in the streets of the city,
   and where he does not expect
      it, he will be seized.
22 So it is also with a woman who
      leaves her husband
   and provides an heir by a stranger.
23 For first of all, she has disobeyed
      the law of the Most High;
   second, she has committed an
      offence against her husband;
   and third, she has committed adultery
      through illicit sexual encounters
   and brought forth children
      by another man.
24 She herself will be brought
      before the assembly,
   and punishment will fall
      on her children.
25 Her children will not take root,
   and her branches will not bear fruit.
26 She will leave her memory for a curse,
   and her disgrace will not
      be blotted out.
27 Those who survive her will recognize
   that nothing is better than
      the fear of the Lord,
   and nothing sweeter than to heed the
      commandments of the Lord.[b]

PRAISE OF WISDOM[c]

24 Wisdom will praise herself
       and will boast in the midst of
          her people.
2 In the assembly of the Most High
      she will open her mouth,
   and in the presence of his
      forces she will boast:
3 "I came forth from the mouth
      of the Most High
   and covered the earth like a mist.
4 I dwelt in high places,
   and my throne was in a
      pillar of cloud.
5 Alone I have made the circuit
      of the vault of heaven
   and have walked in the
      depths of the Abyss.
6 In the waves of the sea, in
      the whole earth,
   and in every people and nation I
      have obtained a possession.[d]
7 Among all these I sought a resting place;
   I sought in whose territory
      I might lodge.
8 Then the Creator of all things
      commanded me,
   and the one who created me gave
      my tent a resting place.
   And he said, 'Make your
      dwelling in Jacob
   and in Israel receive your
      inheritance.'
9 From eternity, in the beginning,
      he created me,
   and for eternity I shall not
      cease to exist.
10 In the holy tabernacle I
      ministered before him,
   and so I was established in Zion.
11 In the beloved city likewise he
      gave me a resting place,
   and in Jerusalem was my dominion.
12 So I took root in an honoured people,
      in the portion of the Lord,
      his inheritance.
13 I grew tall like a cedar in Lebanon
   and like a cypress on the
      heights of Hermon.
14 I grew tall like a palm tree in Engedi[e]
   and like rose plants in Jericho;

---

[a] Greek *sexual intercourse in the body of his flesh* [b] Some manuscripts add verse 28: *It is a great honour to follow God, and for you to be received by him is long life.* [c] This heading is in the Greek text [d] Some manuscripts *I exercised rule* [e] Some manuscripts *palm tree on the beaches*

like a beautiful olive tree in the field
and like a plane tree I grew tall.
15 Like cassia and camel's thorn I gave
forth the aroma of spices,
and like choice myrrh I spread
a pleasant odour,
like galbanum, onycha, and stacte
and like the fragrance of
frankincense in a tent.
16 Like a terebinth I spread
out my branches,
and my branches are branches
of glory and favour.
17 Like a vine I caused favour to bud,
and my blossoms became fruits
of glory and of wealth.[b]
19 Come to me, you who desire me,
and eat your fill of my produce.
20 For the remembrance of me is
sweeter than honey,
and my inheritance sweeter
than the honeycomb.
21 Those who eat me will hunger for more,
and those who drink me
will thirst for more.
22 The one who obeys me will
not be put to shame,
and those who work with
me will not sin."

WISDOM AND LAW
23 All this is the book of the covenant
of the Most High God,
the law that Moses commanded us
as an inheritance for the
congregations of Jacob.[c]
25 It fills up wisdom like the Pishon
and like the Tigris at the time
of the firstfruits.
26 It supplies understanding
like the Euphrates
and like the Jordan at harvest time.
27 It makes instruction shine
forth like light,
like the Gihon at the time of vintage.
28 Just as the first man did not
know her perfectly,
the last one has not fathomed her;
29 for her thought was filled from the sea,
and her counsel from the great Abyss.

30 I went forth like a canal from a river
and like a water channel
into a garden.
31 I said, "I will water my orchard
and drench my garden plot";
and lo, my canal became a river,
and my river became a sea.
32 I will again make instruction
shine forth like the dawn,
and I will make it shine afar;
33 I will again pour out teaching
like prophecy
and leave it to all future generations.
34 Observe that I have not laboured
for myself alone,
but for all who seek wisdom.[d]

THOSE WHO ARE WORTHY OF PRAISE

25 My soul takes pleasure in
three things,
and they are beautiful in the
sight of the Lord and of
people:[e]
agreement between brothers,
friendship between neighbours,
and a wife and a husband who
accommodate one another.
2 My soul hates three kinds of people,
and I am greatly offended
at their life:
a beggar who is arrogant, a
rich man who is a liar,
and an adulterous old man
who lacks good sense.

3 You have gathered nothing
in your youth;
how then can you find anything
in your old age?
4 What an attractive thing is
judgement in grey-haired men
and for the aged to possess
good counsel!
5 How attractive is wisdom in the aged
and understanding and counsel
in honourable men!
6 Rich experience is the
crown of the aged,
and their boast is the fear of the Lord.
7 Nine things I have called
blessed in my heart,
and a tenth I shall tell
with my tongue:

---

[b]Some manuscripts of the longer edition add verse 18: *I am the mother of beautiful love, of fear, of knowledge, and of holy hope; being eternal, I give, along with all my children, to those who are named by him.* [c]Some manuscripts of the longer edition add verse 24: *"Do not cease to be strong in the Lord, cling to him so that he may strengthen you; the Lord Almighty alone is God, and besides him there is no saviour."* [d]Greek *her* [e]Syriac, Vulgate; Greek *In three things I was beautiful, and I stood in beauty before the Lord and people*

a person rejoicing over children;
a man who lives to see the
downfall of his foes;
8 happy is he who lives with
an intelligent wife,
and he who has not made a
slip with his tongue,
and he who has not served a
person unworthy of himself;
9 happy is he who has gained
good sense,
and he who speaks to
attentive listeners.
10 How great is he who has
gained wisdom!
But there is no one superior to
him who fears the Lord.
11 The fear of the Lord surpasses
everything;
to whom shall be likened the
one who holds it fast?[a]

EXTREME FORMS OF EVIL

13 Any wound, but not a wound
of the heart!
Any wickedness, but not the
wickedness of a wife!
14 Any attack, but not an attack
from those who hate!
And any vengeance, but not the
vengeance of enemies!
15 There is no venom[b] worse
than a snake's venom,
and no wrath worse than
an enemy's[c] wrath.

THE EVIL OF A WICKED WOMAN

16 I would rather dwell with a
lion and a dragon
than dwell with an evil wife.
17 The wickedness of a wife
changes her appearance
and darkens her face like
that of a bear.
18 Her husband will take his meals
among the neighbours,
and he cannot help sighing[d] bitterly.
19 Any iniquity is insignificant
compared to a wife's iniquity;
may a sinner's lot befall her!
20 A sandy ascent for the feet
of the aged —
such is a garrulous wife for
a quiet husband.
21 Do not be ensnared by a
woman's beauty
and do not desire a woman
for her possessions.[e]
22 There is wrath and impudence
and great disgrace
when a wife supports her husband.
23 An evil wife means a dejected heart,
a gloomy face, and a wounded heart.
A wife who does not call her
husband blessed
means drooping hands
and weak knees.
24 From a woman sin had its beginning,
and because of her we all die.
25 Allow no outlet to water
and no boldness of speech
in an evil wife.
26 If she does not go as you direct,
separate her from yourself.

THE JOY OF A GOOD WIFE

26 Happy is the husband of a
good wife;
the number of his days will
be doubled.
2 A courageous wife rejoices
her husband,
and he will complete his
years in peace.
3 A good wife is a great blessing;
she will be granted among
the blessings of the man
who fears the Lord.
4 Whether rich or poor, his heart
is glad,
and at all times his face is cheerful.

THE WORST EVIL: A WICKED WIFE

5 Of three things my heart is afraid,
and at the appearance of a
fourth I am frightened:
the slander of a city, the
gathering of a mob,
and false accusation — all these
are worse than death.
6 There is grief of heart and sorrow
when a wife is envious of a rival,
and a tongue lashing makes
it known to all.
7 An evil wife is an ox yoke that chafes;
taking hold of her is like
grasping a scorpion.

---

[a]Some manuscripts add verse 12: *The fear of the Lord is the beginning of love for him, and faith is the beginning of clinging to him.* [b]Greek *head*; twice in this verse [c]Some manuscripts *a woman's* [d]Some manuscripts *and listening he sighs* [e]Hebrew, Syriac; some Greek manuscripts *beauty*

8 There is great anger when
　　a wife is drunken;
　　she will not hide her shame.
9 A wife's sexual immorality
　　shows in her lustful eyes,
　　and she is known by her eyelids.
10 Keep strict watch over a
　　headstrong daughter,
　　lest, when she finds liberty,
　　she use it to her hurt.
11 Be on guard against her impudent eye
　　and do not wonder if she
　　sins against you.
12 As a thirsty wayfarer opens his mouth
　　and drinks from any water near him,
　　so will she sit in front of every peg
　　and open her quiver to the arrow.

THE BLESSING OF A GOOD WIFE

13 A wife's charm will delight her husband,
　　and her skill will put fat on his bones.
14 A silent wife is a gift of the Lord,
　　and there is nothing so precious
　　as a disciplined soul.
15 A modest wife adds charm to charm,
　　and there is no fitting scale to weigh
　　the value of a chaste soul.[a]
16 Like the sun rising in the
　　heights of the Lord,
　　so is the beauty of a good wife in
　　her well-ordered home.
17 Like the shining lamp on the
　　holy lampstand,
　　so is a beautiful face on
　　a stately figure.
18 Like pillars of gold on a base of silver,
　　so are beautiful feet with a
　　steadfast heart.[b]

THREE DEPRESSING THINGS

28 At two things my heart is grieved,
　　and because of a third anger
　　comes over me:
　　a warrior in want through poverty,
　　and intelligent men who are
　　treated contemptuously;
　　a man who turns back from
　　righteousness to sin—
　　the Lord will prepare him
　　for the sword!

TEMPTATIONS OF COMMERCE

29 A merchant can hardly keep
　　from wrongdoing,
　　and a tradesman will not be
　　declared innocent of sin.

27

Many have committed sin
　　for gain,[c]
　　and whoever seeks to get rich
　　will avert his eyes.
2 As a stake is driven firmly into a
　　fissure between stones,
　　so sin is wedged in between
　　selling and buying.
3 If a person is not steadfast and
　　zealous in the fear of the Lord,
　　his house will be quickly overthrown.

TESTS IN LIFE

4 When a sieve is shaken, the
　　refuse appears;
　　so a person's filth in his thoughts.
5 The kiln tests the potter's vessels;
　　likewise the test of a person
　　is in his reasoning.
6 The fruit discloses the
　　cultivation of a tree;
　　so the expression of a thought
　　discloses the cultivation
　　of a person's mind.
7 Do not praise a man before
　　you hear him reason,
　　for this is the test of people.

REWARD AND RETRIBUTION

8 If you pursue justice, you will attain it
　　and wear it as a glorious robe.
9 Birds roost with their kind;
　　so truth returns to those
　　who practise it.
10 A lion lies in wait for prey;
　　so does sin for the workers
　　of iniquity.

VARIETIES OF SPEECH

11 The talk of the godly person
　　is always wise,
　　but the fool changes like the moon.

---

[a]The meaning of the Greek is uncertain   [b]Some manuscripts of the longer edition add verses 19–27: *Child, keep sound the bloom of your youth and do not give your strength to strangers.* [20]*Seek a fertile field within the whole plain and sow it with your own seed, trusting in your fine stock.* [21]*So your offspring will arise around you and, having confidence in their good descent, will grow great.* [22]*A prostitute is regarded as spittle, and a married woman as a tower of death to her lovers.* [23]*A godless wife is given as a portion to a lawless man, but a pious wife is given to the man who fears the Lord.* [24]*A shameless woman constantly acts disgracefully, but a modest daughter will show modesty even before her husband.* [25]*A headstrong wife is regarded as a dog, but one who has a sense of shame will fear the Lord.* [26]*A wife honouring her own husband will seem wise to all, but if she dishonours him in her pride she will be known to all as ungodly. Happy is the husband of a good wife; for the number of his years will be doubled.* [27]*A loud-voiced and garrulous wife is regarded as a war trumpet for putting the enemy to flight, and the soul of every person of similar constitution will live in the anarchy of war.*   [c]Some manuscripts *for a trifle*

12 Among stupid people watch
for a chance to leave,
but among thoughtful
people stay on.
13 The talk of fools is offensive,
and their laughter is wantonly sinful.
14 The speech of those given to swearing
makes one's hair stand on end,
and their quarrels make
one stop his ears.
15 The strife of the proud leads
to bloodshed,
and their abuse is grievous to hear.

BETRAYING SECRETS

16 Whoever betrays secrets
destroys confidence
and will never find a
congenial friend.
17 Love your friend and keep
faith with him;
but if you betray his secrets,
do not run after him.
18 For as a person destroys his corpse,[a]
so you have destroyed the
friendship of your neighbour.
19 And as you allow a bird to
escape from your hand,
so you have let your neighbour go
and will not catch him again.
20 Do not go after him, for he is too far off
and has escaped like a
gazelle from a snare.
21 For a wound may be bandaged,
and there is reconciliation
after abuse,
but whoever has betrayed
secrets is without hope.

HYPOCRISY AND RETRIBUTION

22 Whoever winks his eye
plans evil deeds,
and the one who knows him
will stay far from him.
23 In your presence his mouth
is all sweetness,
and he admires your words;
but later he will twist his speech
and with your own words he will
set you a stumbling block.
24 I have hated many things, but none
to be compared to him;
even the Lord will hate him.
25 Whoever throws a stone straight up
throws it on his own head;
and a treacherous blow
opens up wounds.
26 The one who digs a pit will fall into it,
and the one who sets a snare
will be caught in it.
27 If someone does evil, it will
roll back upon him,
and he will not know where
it came from.
28 Mockery and abuse issue from
the one who is proud,[b]
but vengeance lies in wait
for him like a lion.
29 Those who rejoice in the fall of the
godly will be caught in a snare,
and pain will consume them
before their death.

ANGER AND VENGEANCE

30 Anger and wrath, these also
are abominations,
and the sinful man will
hold them fast.

28 The one who seeks vengeance
will be paid vengeance
from the Lord,
and he who keeps a record will
have his own sins recorded.
2 Forgive your neighbour the
wrong he has done,
and then your sins will be
pardoned when you pray.
3 Does one person harbour
anger against another
and yet seek for healing
from the Lord?
4 Does he have no mercy towards
someone like himself
and yet pray concerning
his own sins?
5 If he himself, being flesh,
maintains wrath,
who will make atonement
for his sins?
6 Remember the end of your life[c]
and cease from enmity,
remember destruction and
death and be true to the
commandments.
7 Remember the commandments and do
not be angry with your neighbour;
remember the covenant of the Most
High and overlook error.

---

[a] Some manuscripts *enemy* [b] Some manuscripts *from proud men* [c] Greek *Remember the last things*

8 Refrain from strife, and you
    will lessen sins;
  for a person given to anger
    will kindle strife,
9 and a sinful man will disturb friends
    and inject enmity among
      those who are at peace.
10 In proportion to the fuel for
    the fire, so will it burn,
  and in proportion to the obstinacy
    of strife, so will it increase;*a*
  in proportion to a person's
    strength will be his anger,
  and in proportion to his wealth
    he will heighten his wrath.
11 A hasty quarrel kindles fire,
    and hasty strife sheds blood.

THE EVIL TONGUE

12 If you blow on a spark, it will glow;
    if you spit on it, it will be put out;
    and both come out of your mouth.
13 Curse the whisperer and
    double-tongued,
  for he has destroyed many
    who were at peace.
14 Slander*b* has shaken many
    and scattered them from
      nation to nation
  and destroyed strong cities
    and overturned the houses
      of great men.
15 Slander has driven away
    courageous women
  and deprived them of the
    fruit of their toil.
16 Whoever pays heed to it
    will not find rest,
  nor will he settle down in peace.
17 The blow of a whip raises a welt,
    but a blow of the tongue
      crushes the bones.
18 Many have fallen by the
    edge of the sword,
  but not so many as have fallen
    because of the tongue.
19 Happy is the one who is
    protected from it,
  who has not been exposed
    to its anger,
  who has not borne its yoke
    and has not been bound
      with its fetters;
20 for its yoke is a yoke of iron,
    and its fetters are fetters of bronze;
21 its death is an evil death,
    and Hades is preferable to it.
22 It will not be master over the godly,
    and they will not be burned
      in its flame.
23 Those who forsake the Lord
    will fall into its power;
  it will burn among them and
    will not be put out.
  It will be sent out against
    them like a lion;
  like a leopard it will mangle them.
24a See, you fence in your
    property with thorns,
25b so make a door and a bolt
    for your mouth.
24b You lock up your silver and gold;
25a likewise make balances and
    scales for your words,
26 beware lest you err with your tongue,*c*
    lest you fall before the one
      who lies in wait.

LENDING AND BORROWING

29 The one who shows mercy will
    lend to his neighbour,
  and the one who girds him up
    with his hand keeps the
      commandments.
2 Lend to your neighbour in
    the time of his need;
  and in turn, repay your
    neighbour promptly.
3 Confirm your word and keep
    faith with him,
  and on every occasion you will
    find what you need.
4 Many regard a loan as a windfall
    and cause trouble to those
      who help them.
5 One will kiss another's hands
    until he gets a loan
  and will talk humbly when speaking
    of his neighbour's money;
  but at the time for repayment
    he will delay
  and will pay in words of unconcern
    and will find fault with the time.
6 If he is able to pay, the lender*d*
    will hardly get back half
  and will regard that as a windfall.
  If he cannot, he has robbed
    him of his money,

---

a Some manuscripts *burn* *b* Greek *A third tongue*; also verse 15 *c* Greek *with it* *d* Greek *pay, he*

and he has needlessly made
him his enemy;
he will repay him with curses
and reproaches
and instead of glory will repay
him with dishonour.
7 Many have refused to lend not
because of wickedness;
they have been afraid of being
defrauded needlessly.

8 Nevertheless, be patient with a man
in humble circumstances
and do not make him wait
for your alms.
9 Help a poor man for the
commandment's sake
and because of his need do not
send him away empty.
10 Lose your silver for the sake of
a brother or a friend
and do not let it rust under
a stone and be lost.
11 Lay up your treasure according to the
commandments of the Most High,
and it will profit you more than gold.
12 Store up almsgiving in your treasury,
and it will rescue you from
all affliction;
13 more than a mighty shield and
more than a heavy spear,
it will fight on your behalf
against an enemy.

GUARANTEEING DEBTS

14 A good man will be surety
for his neighbour,
but the one who has lost a sense
of shame will fail him.
15 Do not forget all the kindness
of your guarantor,
for he has given his life for you.
16 A sinner will overthrow the
prosperity of his guarantor,
17 and an ingrate will abandon
his rescuer.
18 Being surety has ruined many
who were prosperous
and has shaken them like
a wave of the sea;
it has driven men of power into exile,
and they have wandered
among foreign nations.
19 The sinner falls into suretyship
and in pursuing gain will
fall into lawsuits.

20 Assist your neighbour according
to your ability,
but take heed to yourself
lest you fall.

HOME AND HOSPITALITY

21 The essentials for life are
water and bread
and clothing and a house to
cover one's nakedness.
22 Better is the life of a poor man
under the shelter of his roof
than sumptuous food in the
house of others.
23 Be content with little or much,
and you will never hear reproach
for being a stranger.
24 It is a miserable life to go
from house to house,
and where you are a stranger you
may not open your mouth;
25 you will serve as host and pour
drink without being thanked,
and besides this you will
hear bitter words:
26 "Come here, stranger, prepare the table,
and if you have anything at hand,
let me have it to eat."
27 "Give place, stranger, to an
honoured person;
my brother has come to stay with
me, I need my house."
28 These things are hard to bear for
anyone who has feeling:
scolding for being a stranger and the
reproach of the moneylender.

CONCERNING CHILDREN[a]

30 He who loves his son will whip
him often,
in order that he may rejoice at
the way he turns out.
2 He who disciplines his son
will profit by him
and will boast of him among
acquaintances.
3 He who teaches his son will make
his enemies envious
and will glory in him in the
presence of friends.
4 The[b] father may die, and
yet he is not dead,
for he has left behind him
one like himself;

---

[a]This heading is in the Greek text [b]Greek *His*

5 while alive he saw and rejoiced,
　　and when he died he was not grieved;
6 he has left behind him an avenger
　　against his enemies
　　and one to repay the kindness
　　　of his friends.

7 He who spoils his son will
　　bind up his wounds,
　　and his feelings will be
　　　troubled at every cry.
8 A horse untamed turns out stubborn,
　　and a son unrestrained
　　　turns out wilful.
9 Pamper a child, and he will terrify you;
　　play with him, and he will
　　　give you grief.
10 Do not laugh with him, lest you
　　have sorrow with him,
　　and in the end you will
　　　gnash your teeth.
11 Give him no authority in his youth
　　and do not ignore his errors.
12 Bow down his neck in his youth[a]
　　and beat his sides while he is young,
　　lest he become stubborn
　　　and disobey you,
　　and you have sorrow of
　　　soul from him.[b]
13 Discipline your son and take
　　pains with him[c]
　　that you may not be offended
　　　by his shamelessness.

HEALTH

14 Better off is a poor man who is well
　　and strong in constitution
　　than a rich man who is severely
　　　afflicted in body.
15 Health and soundness are
　　better than all gold,
　　and a robust body than
　　　countless riches.
16 There is no wealth better
　　than health of body,
　　and there is no gladness
　　　above joy of heart.
17 Death is better than a miserable life,
　　and eternal rest[d] than
　　　chronic sickness.

CONCERNING FOODS[e]

18 Good things poured out upon
　　a mouth that is closed
　　are like offerings of food
　　　placed upon a grave.

19 Of what use to an idol is an
　　offering of fruit?
　　For it can neither eat nor smell.
　　So is he who is afflicted by the Lord;
20 he sees with his eyes and groans,
　　as also a eunuch groans when
　　　he embraces a maiden.[f]

21 Do not give yourself over to sorrow
　　and do not afflict yourself
　　　deliberately.
22 Gladness of heart is the life of a person,
　　and the rejoicing of a man is long life.
23 Delight your soul and
　　comfort your heart
　　and remove sorrow far from you,
　　for sorrow has destroyed many,
　　　and there is no profit in it.
24 Jealousy and anger shorten life,
　　and anxiety brings on old
　　　age too soon.
25 At meals a cheerful and good heart
　　will give heed to the food.

RIGHT ATTITUDE TOWARDS RICHES

31 Wakefulness over wealth wastes
　　away one's flesh,
　　and anxiety about it removes sleep.
2 Wakeful anxiety prevents slumber,
　　and a severe illness carries off sleep.[g]
3 The rich person toils in the
　　accumulation of wealth,
　　and when he rests he fills
　　　himself with his dainties.
4 The poor person toils as his
　　livelihood diminishes,
　　and when he rests he
　　　becomes needy.

5 He who loves gold will not be justified,
　　and he who pursues money
　　　will be led astray[h] by it.
6 Many have come to ruin
　　because of gold,
　　and their destruction has met
　　　them face to face.
7 It is a stumbling block to those
　　who are devoted to it,
　　and every fool will be taken
　　　captive by it.

---

[a]Some manuscripts omit this and the preceding line [b]Some manuscripts omit this line [c]Greek; Hebrew *and make his yoke heavy* [d]Some manuscripts omit *eternal rest* [e]This heading is in the Greek text [f]Some manuscripts add *so is he who gives judgements by compulsion* [g]Some manuscripts *and sleep carries off a severe illness* [h]Hebrew, Syriac; Greek *will be filled*

8 Blessed is the rich man who
  is found blameless
  and who does not go after gold.
9 Who is he, that we may
  call him blessed,
  for he has done wonderful
  things among his people.
10 Who has been tested by it and
  been found perfect?
  Let it be for him a ground
  for boasting.
  Who has had the power to transgress
  and did not transgress
  and to do evil and did not do it?
11 His prosperity will be established,
  and the assembly will recount
  his acts of charity.

TABLE ETIQUETTE

12 Are you seated at the table
  of a great man?[b]
  Do not be gluttonous[c] at it
  and do not say, "There is
  certainly much upon it!"
13 Remember that a greedy
  eye[d] is a bad thing.
  What has been created
  greedier[e] than the eye?
  Therefore it sheds tears
  from every face.
14 Do not reach out your hand
  for everything you see
  and do not crowd your
  neighbour[f] at the dish.
15 Judge your neighbour's
  feelings by your own
  and in every matter be thoughtful.
16 Eat like a human being[g] what
  is set before you
  and do not chew greedily,
  lest you be hated.
17 Be the first to stop eating, for the
  sake of good manners,
  and do not be insatiable, lest
  you give offence.
18 If you are seated among many persons,
  do not reach out your hand
  before they do.
19 How ample a little is for a well-
  disciplined person!
  He does not wheeze when
  he is in bed.
20 Healthy sleep depends on
  moderate eating;
  he rises early and feels fit.[h]
  The distress of sleeplessness
  and of nausea
  and colic are with the glutton.
21 If you are overstuffed with food,
  get up and vomit at a distance,[i]
  and you will have relief.
22 Listen to me, my son, and do
  not disregard me,
  and in the end you will
  appreciate my words.
  In all your deeds be moderate,[j]
  and no sickness will overtake you.
23 Lips will praise the one who
  is liberal with food,
  and their testimony to his
  excellence is trustworthy.
24 The city will complain of the one
  who is stingy with food,
  and their testimony to his
  stinginess is accurate.

TEMPERANCE IN DRINKING WINE

25 Do not prove your valour by wine,
  for wine has destroyed many.
26 The furnace tests the work
  of the smith,[k]
  so wine tests hearts in the
  strife of the proud.
27 Wine is like life to men,
  if you drink it in moderation.
  What is life to a man who
  is without wine?
  It is created from the beginning
  to make men glad.
28 A rejoicing of heart and gladness of soul
  is wine drunk in season
  with self-control.
29 A bitterness to the soul is
  wine drunk to excess,
  with provocation and stumbling.
30 Drunkenness increases the anger
  of a fool to his injury,
  reducing his strength and
  adding wounds.
31 Do not reprove your neighbour
  at a banquet of wine
  and do not despise him in
  his merrymaking;

---

[b]Hebrew, Syriac; Greek *seated at a great table* [c]Greek *Do not open your throat* [d]Greek *thct an evil eye* [e]Greek *eviler* [f]Greek *crowd him* [g]Greek; Hebrew *like a well-mannered person* [h]Greek *early, and his soul is with him* [i]Some manuscripts *vomit in the midst of the meal* [j]Hebrew; Greek *industrious* [k]Hebrew; Greek *Fire and water prove the temper of steel*

speak no word of reproach to him
and do not afflict him by making
demands of him.

BANQUET ETIQUETTE

32 If they make you master of the
feast, do not exalt yourself;
be among them as one of them;
take good care of them and
then be seated;
2 when you have fulfilled your
duties, take your place,
that you may be merry on their
account
and receive a wreath for your
excellent leadership.
3 Speak, you who are older, for it
is fitting that you should,
but with accurate understanding,
and do not interrupt the music.
4 Where there is entertainment,
do not pour out talk;
do not display your cleverness
out of season.
5 A ruby seal in a setting of gold
is a concert of music at a
banquet of wine.
6 A seal of emerald in a rich
setting of gold
is the melody of music
with good wine.
7 Speak, you who are young, if
there is need of you,
but no more than twice,
and only if asked.
8 Speak concisely, say much
in few words;
be as one who knows and yet
holds his tongue.
9 Among the great do not act
as their equal;
and when another is speaking,
do not babble.
10 Lightning speeds before the thunder,
and approval precedes a
modest man.
11 Leave in good time and do
not be the last;
go home quickly and do not linger.
12 Amuse yourself there and
do what you like,
but do not sin through proud
speech.
13 And for these things bless the
one who made you
and satisfies you with his good gifts.

PROVIDENCE OF GOD

14 He who fears the Lord*a* will
accept his discipline,
and those who rise early
will find favour.
15 The one who seeks the law
will be filled with it,
but the hypocrite will stumble at it.
16 Those who fear the Lord will find justice,
and like a light they will kindle
righteous deeds.
17 A sinful person will shun reproof
and will find a decision
according to his liking.
18 A man of judgement will not
overlook an idea,
and an insolent*b* and proud man
will not cower in fear.*c*
19 Do nothing without counsel;
and when you have acted,
do not regret it.
20 Do not go on a path full of hazards
and do not stumble over
stony ground.*d*
21 Do not be overconfident
on a smooth way*e*
22 and give good heed to your paths.*f*
23 Guard*g* yourself in every act,
for this is the keeping of the
commandments.
24 He who believes the law gives heed
to the commandments,
and the one who trusts the
Lord will not suffer loss.

33 No evil will befall the man who
fears the Lord,
but in trial he will deliver him
again and again.
2 A wise man will not hate the law,
but he who is hypocritical about
it is like a boat in a storm.
3 A man of understanding will
trust in the law;
for him the law is as dependable as
an enquiry by means of Urim.

---

*a*Hebrew *who seeks God* *b*Greek *stranger* *c*The meaning of the Greek is uncertain; some manuscripts add *and after acting, with him, without deliberation* *d*Or *stumble twice at an obstacle* *e*Or *on an unexplored way* *f*Syriac, Vulgate; Greek *and beware of your children* *g*Hebrew; Greek *Be true to*

4 Prepare what to say, and thus
you will be heard;
bind together your instruction
and make your answer.
5 The heart of a fool is like a cart wheel,
and his thoughts like a turning axle.
6 A stallion is like a mocking friend;
he neighs under everyone
who sits on him.

DIFFERENCES IN NATURE AND IN MANKIND

7 Why is any day better than another,
when all the daylight in the
year is from the sun?
8 By the Lord's decision they
were distinguished,
and he appointed the different
seasons and festivals;
9 some of them he exalted and hallowed,
and some of them he made
ordinary days.
10 All human beings are from
the ground,
and Adam was created of the dust.
11 In the fullness of his knowledge
the Lord distinguished them
and appointed their different ways;
12 some of them he blessed and exalted,
and some of them he made holy
and brought near to himself;
but some of them he cursed
and brought low,
and he turned them out
of their place.
13 Like clay in the hand of the potter—
for all his ways are as he pleases—
so are human beings in the hand
of him who made them,
to give to them as he decides.

14 Good is the opposite of evil,
and life the opposite of death;
so the sinner is the opposite
of the godly.
15 Look upon all the works of
the Most High;
two by two, one the opposite
of the other.
16 I was the last on watch;
I was like one who gleans after
the grape-gatherers;
17 by the blessing of the Lord I arrived,
and like a grape-gatherer I
filled my wine press.
18 Consider that I have not laboured
for myself alone,
but for all who seek instruction.
19 Hear me, you who are great
among the people,
and you leaders of the
congregation, take note.

ADVANTAGE OF INDEPENDENCE

20 To son or wife, to brother or friend,
do not give power over yourself,
as long as you live;
and do not give your property
to another,
in case you change your mind
and must ask for it.
21 While you are still alive and
have breath in you,
do not let anyone take
your place.
22 For it is better that your children
should ask from you
than that you should look to
the hand of your sons.
23 Excel in all that you do;
bring no stain upon your honour.
24 At the time when you end
the days of your life,
in the hour of death, distribute
your inheritance.

TREATMENT OF SLAVES

25 Fodder and a stick and
burdens for a donkey;
bread and discipline and
work for a servant.
26 Set your slave to work, and
you will find rest;
leave his hands idle, and he
will seek liberty.
27 Yoke and thong will bow the neck,
and for a wicked servant there
are racks and tortures.
28 Put him to work, that he may not be idle,
29 for idleness teaches much evil.
30 Set him to work, as is fitting for him,
and if he does not obey, make
his fetters heavy.
Do not act immoderately
toward anybody
and do nothing without discretion.

31 If you have a servant, let
him be as yourself,
because you have bought
him with blood.
If you have a servant, treat
him as a brother,

for as your own soul you
will need him.
32 If you ill-treat him, and he
leaves and runs away,
33 which way will you go to seek him?

DREAMS MEAN NOTHING

34 A man of no understanding has
vain and false hopes,
and dreams give wings to fools.
2 As one who catches at a shadow
and pursues the wind,
so is he who gives heed to dreams.
3 The vision of dreams is
this against that,
the likeness of a face
confronting a face.
4 From an unclean thing what
will be made clean?
And from something false
what will be true?
5 Divinations and omens and
dreams are folly,
and like a woman in labour
the mind has fantasies.
6 Unless they are sent from the
Most High as a visitation,
do not give your mind to them.
7 For dreams have deceived many,
and those who put their hope
in them have failed.
8 Without such deceptions the
law will be fulfilled,
and wisdom in a faithful
mouth is perfection.

EXPERIENCE AS A TEACHER

9 A travelled man knows many things,
and one with much experience will
speak with understanding.
10 The one who is untried
knows few things,
11 but he that has travelled acquires
much cleverness.
12 I have seen many things in my travels,
and I understand more
than I can express.
13 I have often been in danger of death,
but have escaped because of
these experiences.

FEAR THE LORD

14 The spirit of those who fear
the Lord will live,
15 for their hope is in him
who saves them.
16 He who fears the Lord will not be timid
or play the coward, for he is his hope.
17 Blessed is the soul of the man
who fears the Lord!
18 To whom does he look? And
who is his support?
19 The eyes of the Lord are upon
those who love him,
a mighty protection and
strong support,
a shelter from the hot wind and a
shade from noonday sun,
a guard against stumbling and
a defence against falling.
20 He lifts up the soul and gives
light to the eyes;
he grants healing, life, and blessing.

OFFERING SACRIFICES

21 If one sacrifices from what has
been wrongfully obtained,
the offering is blemished;[a]
22 the gifts[b] of the lawless are
not acceptable.
23 The Most High is not pleased with
the offerings of the ungodly;
and he is not propitiated for sins
by a multitude of sacrifices.
24 Like one who slaughters a son in
the presence of his father
is the man who offers a sacrifice
from the property of the poor.
25 The bread of the needy is
the life of the poor;
whoever deprives them of
it is a man of blood.
26 To take away a neighbour's
living is to murder him;
27 to deprive an employee of his
wages is to shed blood.
28 One builds and another tears down;
what do they gain but toil?
29 One prays and another curses;
to whose voice will the Lord listen?
30 If someone washes after touching a
dead body and touches it again,
what has he gained by his washing?
31 So if a man fasts for his sins
and goes again and does
the same things,
who will listen to his prayer?
And what has he gained by
humbling himself?

---

[a] Some manuscripts *is made in mockery*   [b] Some manuscripts *mockeries*

LAW AND SACRIFICES

35 He who keeps the law makes many offerings;
² he who heeds the commandments sacrifices a peace offering.
³ He who returns a kindness offers fine flour,
⁴ and he who gives alms sacrifices a thank-offering.
⁵ To keep from wickedness is pleasing to the Lord,
and to forsake unrighteousness is atonement.
⁶ Do not appear before the Lord empty-handed,
⁷ for all these things are to be done because of the commandment.
⁸ The offering of a righteous man anoints the altar,
and its pleasing odour rises before the Most High.
⁹ The sacrifice of a righteous man is acceptable,
and the memory of it will not be forgotten.
¹⁰ Glorify the Lord generously and do not stint the firstfruits of your hands.
¹¹ With every gift show a cheerful face and dedicate your tithe with gladness.
¹² Give to the Most High as he has given and as generously as you are able.
¹³ For the Lord is the one who repays, and he will repay you sevenfold.

DIVINE JUSTICE

¹⁴ Do not offer him a bribe, for he will not accept it;
¹⁵ and do not trust to an unrighteous sacrifice;
for the Lord is the judge, and with him is no partiality.
¹⁶ He will not show partiality in the case of a poor man;
and he will listen to the prayer of one who is wronged.
¹⁷ He will not ignore the supplication of the orphan
or the widow when she pours out her story.
¹⁸ Do not the tears of the widow run down her cheek
¹⁹ as she cries out against him who has caused them to fall?
²⁰ He whose service is pleasing to the Lord will be accepted,
and his prayer will reach to the clouds.
²¹ The prayer of the humble pierces the clouds,
and he will not be consoled until it reaches the Lord;[a]
he will not desist until the Most High visits him
²² and does justice for the righteous and executes judgement.
And the Lord will not delay, neither will he be patient with them,
till he crushes the loins of the unmerciful
²³ and repays vengeance on the nations;
till he takes away the multitude of the insolent
and breaks the sceptres of the unrighteous;
²⁴ till he repays a person according to his deeds
and the works of men according to their devices;
²⁵ till he judges the case of his people and makes them rejoice in his mercy.
²⁶ Mercy is as welcome in time of affliction
as clouds of rain in the time of drought.

PRAYER FOR GOD'S PEOPLE

36 Have mercy upon us, O Lord,[b] the God of all, and look upon us
² and cause the fear of you to fall upon all the nations.
³ Lift up your hand against foreign nations
and let them see your might.
⁴ As in us you have been sanctified before them,
so in them be you magnified before us;
⁵ and let them know you, as we have known
that there is no God but you, O Lord.
⁶ Show signs anew and work further wonders;
⁷ make your hand and your right arm glorious.

---

[a] Or *until the Lord draws near* [b] Hebrew omits *O Lord*

8 Rouse your anger and pour
    out your wrath;
9 destroy the adversary and
    wipe out the enemy.
10 Hasten the day and remember
    the appointed time[a]
    and let people recount your
    mighty deeds.
11 Let him who survives be consumed
    in the fiery wrath,
    and may those who harm your
    people meet destruction.
12 Crush the heads of the rulers
    of the enemy
    who say, "There is no one
    but ourselves."
13 Gather all the tribes of Jacob[b]
16 and give[c] them their inheritance,
    as at the beginning.
17 Have mercy, O Lord, upon the
    people called by your name,
    upon Israel, whom you have
    likened to a[d] firstborn son.
18 Have pity on the city of
    your sanctuary,[e]
    Jerusalem, the place of your rest.[f]
19 Fill Zion with the celebration of
    your wondrous deeds[g]
    and your temple[h] with your glory.
20 Bear witness to those whom you
    created in the beginning
    and fulfil the prophecies
    spoken in your name.
21 Reward those who wait for you
    and let your prophets be
    found trustworthy.
22 Hear, O Lord, the prayer of
    your servants,
    according to your good will[i]
    for your people,
    and all who are on the earth will know
    that you are the Lord, the
    God of the ages.

DISCRIMINATION

23 The stomach will take any food,
    yet one food is better than another.
24 As the palate tastes the kinds of game,
    so an intelligent mind
    detects false words.
25 A perverse mind will cause grief,
    but a person of experience
    will pay him back.
26 Every male is accepted by a woman,
    but one daughter is better
    than another.
27 A woman's beauty lights up the face
    and surpasses every man's desire.
28 If kindness and humility
    mark her speech,
    her husband is not like other men.
29 He who acquires a wife gets
    his best possession,[j]
    a helper fit for him and a
    pillar of support.[k]
30 Where there is no fence, the
    property will be plundered;
    and where there is no wife, a man
    will wander about and sigh.[l]
31 For who will trust a nimble robber
    that skips from city to city?
    So who will trust a man that has no nest
    and lodges wherever night
    finds him?

FALSE FRIENDS

37 Every friend will say, "I too am
    a friend";
    but some friends are friends
    only in name.
2 Is it not a grief to the death
    when a companion and friend
    turns to enmity?
3 O evil imagination, why
    were you formed
    to cover the land with deceit?
4 Some companions rejoice in the
    happiness of a friend,
    but in time of trouble are
    against him.
5 Some companions help a friend
    for their stomach's sake
    and in the face of battle
    take up the shield.
6 Do not forget a friend in your heart[m]
    and be not unmindful of
    him in your wealth.[n]

CAUTION IN TAKING ADVICE

7 Every counsellor praises counsel,
    but some give counsel in
    their own interest.
8 Be wary of a counsellor
    and learn first what is his interest—

---

[a]Some manuscripts *remember your oath* [b]Due to dislocations in Greek manuscripts, numbers 14–15 are not used but no verses are missing [c]Some manuscripts *and I gave* [d]Hebrew *Israel, when you have named* [e]Or *pity on your holy city* [f]Hebrew *dwelling* [g]Hebrew *with your majesty* [h]Greek *people* [i]Hebrew; some Greek manuscripts *according to the blessing of Aaron* [j]Hebrew; Greek *He who acquires a wife enters upon a possession* [k]Hebrew; Greek *rest* [l]Hebrew *will be a fugitive and a wanderer* [m]Hebrew *a friend during the battle* [n]Hebrew *of him when you divide the spoil*

for he will take thought
  for himself—
lest he cast the lot against you
9 and tell you, "Your way is good",
  and then stand aloof to see
    what will happen to you.
10 Do not consult the one who looks
    at you suspiciously;
  hide your counsel from those
    who are jealous of you.
11 Do not consult with a woman
    about her rival
  or with a coward about war,
  with a merchant about barter
  or with a buyer about selling,
  with a grudging man about gratitude[a]
  or with a merciless man
    about kindness,
  with an idler about any work
  or with a man hired for a year
    about completing his work,
  with a lazy servant about a big task—
  pay no attention to these in
    any matter of counsel.
12 But stay constantly with a godly man
    whom you know to be a keeper
      of the commandments,
  whose soul is in accord with your soul
  and who will grieve with
    you if you fail.
13 And establish[b] the counsel
    of your own heart,
  for no one is more faithful
    to you than it is.
14 For a man's soul sometimes keeps
    him better informed
  than seven watchmen sitting
    high on a watchtower.
15 And above all these things,
    pray to the Most High
  that he may direct your way in truth.

TRUE AND FALSE WISDOM

16 Reason is the beginning of every work,
  and counsel precedes every
    undertaking.
17 As a clue to changes of heart
18 four turns of fortune appear:[c]
  good and evil, life and death;
  and it is the tongue that
    continually rules them.
19 A man may be shrewd and
    the teacher of many
  and yet be unprofitable to himself.
20 A man skilled in words may be hated;
  he will be destitute of all food,
21 for grace was not given him by the Lord,
  since he is lacking in all wisdom.
22 A man may be wise to his
    own advantage,
  and the fruits of his understanding
    are evident.[d]
23 A wise man will instruct
    his own people,
  and the fruits of his understanding
    will be trustworthy.
24 A wise man will have praise
    heaped upon him,
  and all who see him will
    call him happy.
25 The life of a man is numbered by days,
  but the days of Israel are
    without number.
26 One who is wise among his people
    will inherit honour,[e]
  and his name will live for ever.

MODERATION

27 My son, test your soul while you live;
    see what is bad for it and
      do not give it that.
28 For not everything is good
    for everyone,
  and no one enjoys everything.
29 Do not be greedy for every luxury
  and do not give yourself up to food;
30 for overeating brings sickness,
  and gluttony leads to nausea.
31 Many have died of gluttony,
  but he who is careful to avoid
    it prolongs his life.

PHYSICIANS AND HEALTH

38 Honour the physician[f] according
    to your need of him,
    for the Lord created him;
2 for healing comes from the
    Most High,
  and he will receive a gift
    from the king.
3 The skill of the physician
    lifts up his head,
  and in the presence of the
    great he is admired.
4 The Lord created medicines
    from the earth,

---

[a]Hebrew *generosity*   [b]Hebrew *And give heed to*
[c]Hebrew *The mind is the root of conduct; it sprouts four branches*
[d]Some manuscripts *praiseworthy*; some manuscripts *and the fruits of his understanding on his lips are trustworthy*; compare 37:23
[e]Some manuscripts *confidence*   [f]Some manuscripts add *with the honour due him*

and a sensible man will
not despise them.
⁵ Was not water made sweet with a tree
in order that his*a* power
might be known?
⁶ And he gave skill to human beings
that he*b* might be glorified in
his marvellous works.
⁷ By them he heals and takes
away pain;
⁸ the pharmacist makes of
them a compound.
His works will never be finished;
and from him health*c* is upon
the face of the earth.

⁹ My child, when you are sick
do not be negligent,
but pray to the Lord, and
he will heal you.
¹⁰ Give up your faults and direct
your hands aright
and cleanse your heart from all sin.
¹¹ Offer a sweet-smelling sacrifice and
a memorial portion of fine flour
and pour oil on your offering, as
much as you can afford.*d*
¹² And give the physician his place,
for the Lord created him;
let him not leave you, for
there is need of him.
¹³ There is a time when success lies
in the hands of physicians,*e*
¹⁴ for they too will pray to the Lord
that he should grant them
success in diagnosis*f*
and in healing, for the sake
of preserving life.
¹⁵ He who sins before his Maker,
may he fall into the care*g*
of a physician.

MOURNING FOR THE DEAD

¹⁶ My child, let your tears
fall for the dead,
and as one who is suffering
grievously begin the lament.
Lay out his body with the
honour due him
and do not neglect his burial.
¹⁷ Let your weeping be bitter and
your wailing fervent;
observe the mourning
according to his worth,
for one day, or two, to avoid criticism;
then be comforted for your sorrow.

¹⁸ For sorrow results in death,
and sorrow of heart saps
one's strength.
¹⁹ In calamity sorrow continues,
and the life of a poor man
weighs down his heart.
²⁰ Do not give your heart to sorrow;
drive it away, remembering
the end of life.
²¹ Do not forget, there is no coming back;
you do the dead*h* no good, and
you injure yourself.
²² Remember his doom, for
yours is like it:
"Yesterday it was mine, and
today it is yours."
²³ When the dead is at rest, let his
remembrance cease
and be comforted for him when
his spirit has departed.

TRADES AND CRAFTS

²⁴ The wisdom of the scribe depends
on the opportunity of leisure;
and the one who has little
business may become wise.
²⁵ How can he become wise who
handles the plough
and who glories in the
shaft of a goad,
who drives oxen and is occupied
with their work
and whose talk is about*i* bulls?
²⁶ He sets his heart on
ploughing furrows,
and he is concerned about
fodder for the heifers.
²⁷ So too is every artisan and
master worker
who labours by night as
well as by day;
those who cut the signets of seals,
each is diligent in making
a great variety;
he sets his heart on painting
a lifelike image,
and he is careful to finish his work.
²⁸ So too is the smith sitting by the anvil,
intent upon his handiwork in iron;
the breath of the fire melts his flesh,
and he struggles in the heat
of the furnace;

---

a Or *its* *b* Or *they* *c* Or *peace* *d* Hebrew; Vulgate omits *as much as you can afford*; the meaning of the Greek is uncertain *e* Greek *in their hands* *f* Hebrew; Greek *rest* *g* Greek *hands* *h* Greek *do him* *i* Or *among*

the sound of the hammer makes
his hearing strange[a]
and his eyes are on the
pattern of the object.
He sets his heart on finishing
his handiwork,
and he is careful to complete
its decoration.
29 So too is the potter sitting at his work
and turning the wheel with his feet;
he is always deeply concerned
over his work,
and all his output is counted.
30 He moulds the clay with his arm
and makes it pliable with his feet;
he sets his heart to finish the glazing,
and he is careful to clean the furnace.

31 All these rely upon their hands,
and each is skilful in his own work.
32 Without them a city cannot
be established,
and men can neither sojourn
nor live there.
Yet they are not sought out for
the council of the people,
33 nor do they attain eminence
in the public assembly.
They do not sit in the judge's seat,
nor do they understand the
dispensing of justice;
they cannot expound discipline
or judgement,
and they are not found using proverbs.
34 But they keep stable the
fabric of the world,
and their prayer is in the
practise of their trade.

ACTIVITY OF THE SCRIBE

39 On the other hand he who devotes himself
to the study of the law of the
Most High
will seek out the wisdom
of all the ancients
and will be concerned with
prophecies;
2 he will preserve the discourse
of notable men
and penetrate the subtleties
of parables;
3 he will seek out the hidden
meanings of proverbs
and be at home with the
obscurities of parables.

4 He will serve among the great
and appear before rulers;
he will travel through the lands
of foreign nations,
for he tests the good and the
evil among mankind.
5 He will set his heart to rise early
to seek the Lord who made him
and will make supplication
before the Most High;
he will open his mouth in prayer
and make supplication for his sins.

6 If the great Lord is willing,
he will be filled with the spirit
of understanding;
he will pour forth his words
of wisdom
and give thanks to the Lord in prayer.
7 He will direct his counsel and
knowledge aright
and meditate on his secrets.
8 He will reveal instruction
in his teaching
and will glory in the law of
the Lord's covenant.
9 Many will praise his understanding,
and it will never be blotted out;
his memory will not disappear,
and his name will live through
all generations.
10 Nations will declare his wisdom,
and the congregation will
proclaim his praise;
11 if he lives long, he will leave a name
greater than a thousand,
and if he goes to rest, it is
enough[b] for him.

HYMN OF PRAISE TO GOD

12 I have yet more to say, which
I have thought upon,
and I am filled, like the
moon at the full.
13 Listen to me, O you holy sons,
and bud like a rose growing
by a stream of water;
14 send forth fragrance like frankincense
and put forth blossoms like a lily.
Scatter the fragrance and sing
a hymn of praise;
bless the Lord for all his works;
15 ascribe majesty to his name
and give thanks to him with praise,

---

[a] Greek *hammer renews the ear* [b] The meaning of the Greek is uncertain

with songs on your lips and with harps;
and this you shall say in
thanksgiving:
16 "All things are the works of the
Lord, for they are very good,
and whatever he commands
will be done in its time."
17 No one can say, "What is
this?" "Why is that?"
for at the proper time all things
will be searched out.
At his word the waters stood in a heap,
and the reservoirs of water at
the word of his mouth.
18 At his command whatever
pleases him is done,
and none can limit his saving power.
19 The works of all are before him,
and nothing can be hid
from his eyes.
20 From everlasting to everlasting
he sees them,
and nothing is marvellous to him.
21 No one can say, "What is
this?" "Why is that?"
for everything has been
created for its use.
22 His blessing covers the dry
land like a river
and drenches it like a flood.
23 The nations will incur his wrath,
just as he turns freshwater into salt.
24 To the holy his ways are straight,
just as they are obstacles
to the wicked.
25 From the beginning good things
were created for good people,
so also evil things for sinners.
26 Basic to all the needs of human life
are water and fire and iron
and salt
and wheat flour and milk and honey,
the blood of the grape and
oil and clothing.
27 All these are for good to the godly,
but they turn into evils for sinners.
28 There are winds that have been
created for vengeance,
and in their anger they
scourge heavily;[a]
in the time of consummation they
will pour out their strength
and calm the anger of their Maker.
29 Fire and hail and famine and pestilence,
all these have been created
for vengeance;
30 the teeth of wild beasts and
scorpions and vipers
and the sword that punishes the
ungodly with destruction;
31 they will rejoice in his commands
and be made ready on earth
for their service,
and when their times come they
will not transgress his word.
32 Therefore from the beginning
I have been convinced
and have thought this out
and left it in writing:
33 The works of the Lord are all good,
and he will supply every
need in its hour.
34 And no one can say, "This is
worse than that",
for all things will prove good
in their season.
35 So now sing praise with all
your heart and voice
and bless the name of the Lord.

HUMAN WRETCHEDNESS

40 Great labour was created for
every man,
and a heavy yoke is upon the
sons of Adam,
from the day they come forth
from their mother's womb
till the day they return to[b]
the mother of all.
2 Their perplexities and fear of heart—
their anxious thought is
the day of death,
3 from the man who sits on
a splendid throne
to the one who is humbled
in dust and ashes,
4 from the one who wears
purple and a crown
to the one who is clothed
in sackcloth;
5 there is anger and envy and
trouble and unrest
and fear of death and fury and strife.
And when one rests upon his bed,
his sleep at night confuses his mind.

---
[a]Hebrew; Syriac *they can dislodge mountains* [b]Some manuscripts *they are buried in*

6 He gets little or no rest,
and afterwards in his sleep,
he struggles as though
it were daytime;[a]
he is troubled by the visions
of his mind
like one who has escaped
from the battlefront;
7 at the moment of his rescue
he wakes up
and wonders that his fear
was for nothing.
8 With all flesh, both human and beast,
and upon sinners seven times
more,
9 are death and bloodshed and
strife and sword,
calamities, famine and
affliction and plague.
10 All these were created for the wicked,
and on their account the flood
came.
11 All things that are from the earth
turn back to the earth,
and what is from the waters
returns to the sea.

INJUSTICE WILL NOT PROSPER

12 All bribery and injustice
will be blotted out,
but good faith will stand for ever.
13 The wealth of the unjust will
dry up like a torrent
and crash like a loud clap of
thunder in a rain.
14 A generous man will be made glad;
likewise transgressors
will utterly fail.
15 The children of the ungodly will
not put forth many branches;
they are unhealthy roots
upon sheer rock.
16 The reeds by any water or river bank
will be plucked up before
any grass.
17 Kindness is like a garden
of blessings,
and almsgiving endures for ever.

JOYS OF LIFE

18 Life is sweet for the self-reliant
and the worker,[b]
but he who finds treasure is
better off than both.
19 Children and the building of a city
establish a man's name,
but a blameless wife is accounted
better than both.
20 Wine and music gladden the heart,
but the love of wisdom is
better than both.
21 The flute and the harp make
pleasant melody,
but a sweet speech is
better than both.
22 The eye desires grace and beauty,
but the green shoots of corn
more than both.
23 A friend or a companion never
meets one amiss,
but a wife with her husband[c]
is better than both.
24 Brothers and help are for a
time of trouble,
but deeds of mercy rescue
better than both.
25 Gold and silver make the
foot stand sure,
but good counsel is esteemed
more than both.
26 Riches and strength lift up the heart,
but the fear of the Lord is
better than both.
There is no loss in the fear of
the Lord,
and with it there is no need
to seek for help.
27 The fear of the Lord is like a
garden of blessing
and covers a person[d] better
than any glory.

THE DISGRACE OF BEGGING

28 My child, do not lead the
life of a beggar;
it is better to die than to beg.
29 When a man looks to the
table of another,
his existence cannot be
considered as life.
He pollutes[e] himself with
the food of others,
but a man who is intelligent
and well instructed
guards against that.
30 In the mouth of the shameless,
begging is sweet,
but in his stomach a fire
is kindled.

---

[a]The meaning of the Greek is uncertain [b]Greek *for the self-reliant worker* [c]Hebrew *but a sensible wife* [d]Greek *covers him* [e]Or *ruins*

SIRACH 41

DEATH

41 ¹ O death, how bitter is the
    reminder of you
    to one who lives at peace among
        his possessions,
to a man without distractions, who
    is prosperous in everything
    and who still has the vigour
        to enjoy his food!
² O death, how welcome is your sentence
    to one who is in need and is
        failing in strength,
very old and distracted
    over everything,
    to one who is contrary and
        has lost his patience!
³ Do not fear the sentence of death;
    remember your former days
        and the end of life;
this is the decree from the
    Lord for all flesh,
⁴ and how can you reject the good
    pleasure of the Most High?
Whether life is for 10 or 100
    or 1,000 years,
    there is no enquiry about it in Hades.

FATE OF THE WICKED

⁵ The children of sinners are
    abominable children,
    and they frequent the haunts
        of the ungodly.
⁶ The inheritance of the children
    of sinners will perish,
    and on their posterity will be
        a perpetual disgrace.
⁷ Children will blame an ungodly father,
    for they suffer disgrace
        because of him.
⁸ Woe to you, ungodly men,
    who have forsaken the law of
        the Most High God!
⁹ For if you multiply, it is
    unto destruction.ᵃ
When you are born, you are
    born to a curse;
    and when you die, a curse is your lot.
¹⁰ Whatever is from the dust
    returns to dust;
    so the ungodly go from curse
        to destruction.
¹¹ The mourning of humans is
    about their bodies,
    but the evil name of sinners
        will be blotted out.
¹² Have regard for your name, since
    it will endure after you
    longer than a thousand
        great stores of gold.
¹³ The days of a good life are numbered,
    but a good name endures for ever.
¹⁴ My children, observe instruction
    and be at peace;
hidden wisdom and unseen treasure,
    what advantage is there in
        either of them?

A SERIES OF CONTRASTS

¹⁵ Better is the person who hides his folly
    than the one who hides his wisdom.
¹⁶ Therefore show respect for
    my judgements:
for not every kind of shame
    is good to retain,
    and not everything is confidently
        esteemed by everyone.
¹⁷ Be ashamed of sexual immorality,
    before your father or mother;
    and of a lie, before a leader or a ruler;
¹⁸ of a transgression, before a
    judge or magistrate;
    and of iniquity, before a
        congregation or the people;
of unjust dealing, before your
    partner or friend;
¹⁹ and of theft, in the place
    where you live.
Be ashamed of breaking an
    oath or a covenant.ᵇ
Be ashamed of selfish
    behaviour at meals,ᶜ
of surliness in receiving and giving
²⁰ and of silence, before those
    who greet you;
of looking at a woman who
    is a prostitute
²¹ and of rejecting the appeal
    of a kinsman;
of taking away someone's
    portion or gift
    and of gazing at another man's wife;
²² of meddling with his servant girl—
    and do not approach her bed;
of abusive words, before friends—
    and do not revile after making a gift;

ᵃHebrew; some Greek manuscripts omit this line ᵇHebrew; Greek *Be ashamed before the truth of God and his covenant* ᶜGreek *Be ashamed of fixing the elbow on the bread*

42

of repeating and telling what
you hear
and of revealing secrets.
Then you will show proper shame
and will find favour with
every man.

Of the following things do
not be ashamed
and do not show partiality
so as to sin:
2 of the law of the Most High
and his covenant
and of rendering judgement
to acquit the ungodly;
3 of keeping accounts with a partner
or with travelling companions
and of dividing the inheritance
of friends;
4 of accuracy with scales and weights
and of acquiring much or little;
5 of profit from dealing with merchants
and of much discipline of children
and of whipping a wicked
servant severely.[a]
6 Where there is an evil wife, a
seal is a good thing;
and where there are many
hands, lock things up.
Whatever dealings you have, let it
be by number and weight,
and make a record of all that
you give out or take in.
8 Do not be ashamed to instruct
the stupid or foolish
or the aged man who is guilty
of sexual immorality.
Then you will be truly instructed
and will be approved before
all the living.

DAUGHTERS AND FATHERS

9 A daughter keeps her father
secretly wakeful,
and worry over her robs
him of sleep;
when she is young, lest
she do not marry,
or if married, lest she be hated;
10 while a virgin, lest she be defiled
or become pregnant in her
father's house;
or having a husband, lest she
prove unfaithful,
or, though married, lest
she be barren.
11 Keep strict watch over a
headstrong daughter,
lest she make you a laughing-
stock to your enemies,
a byword in the city and notorious[b]
among the people,
and put you to shame before
the great multitude.

12 Do not look upon anyone
for comeliness
and do not sit in the midst
of women;
13 for from garments comes the moth,
and from a woman comes
woman's wickedness.
14 Better is the wickedness of a man
than a woman who does good;
and a shameful woman
brings disgrace.

WORKS OF GOD IN NATURE

15 I will now call to mind the
works of the Lord
and will declare what I have seen.
By the words[c] of the Lord his
works are done.
And by his good pleasure
justice is done.[d]
16 The sun looks down on
everything with its light,
and the work of the Lord is
full of his glory.
17 The Lord has not enabled
even his holy ones
to recount all his marvellous
works,
which the Lord the Almighty
has established
so that the universe may stand
firm in his glory.
18 He searches out the Abyss
and the heart
and considers their wonders.[e]
For the Most High knows all
that may be known,
and he has seen the signs[f] of
the age.[g]
19 He declares what has been
and what is to be,
and he reveals the tracks
of hidden things.

---

[a]Greek *and of making the side of a wicked servant bleed* [b]Greek *and called out* [c]Hebrew *word* [d]Some manuscripts omit this line [e]Some manuscripts *trickery* [f]Greek *sign* [g]Hebrew *seen from of old things yet to come*

20 No thought escapes him,
and not one thing[a] is
hidden from him.
21 He has ordained the splendours
of his wisdom,
and he is from everlasting
and to everlasting.
Nothing can be added or taken away,
and he needs no one to be
his counsellor.
22 How greatly to be desired
are all his works,
and how sparkling they are to see![b]
23 All these things live and
remain for ever
for every need, and all are obedient.
24 All things are twofold, one
opposite the other,
and he has made nothing
incomplete.
25 One confirms the good
things of the other,
and who can have enough
of seeing his glory?

SPLENDOUR OF THE SUN

43 The pride of the heavenly heights is the clear firmament,
the appearance of heaven in
a spectacle of glory.
2 The sun, when it appears, making
proclamation as it goes forth,
is a marvellous instrument, the
work of the Most High.
3 At noon it parches the land;
and who can withstand
its burning heat?
4 A man tending[c] a furnace
works in burning heat,
but the sun burns the mountains
three times as much;
it breathes out fiery vapours,
and with bright beams it
blinds the eyes.
5 Great is the Lord who made it;
and at his command it
hastens on its course.

SPLENDOUR OF THE MOON

6 He made the moon also, to
mark its season,
to show the times, and to
be a sign of the age.
7 From the moon comes the
sign for feast days,
a light that wanes when it
has reached the full.
8 The month is named for the moon,[d]
increasing marvellously
in its phases,
an instrument of the hosts on high
shining forth in the
firmament of heaven.

GLORY OF STARS AND RAINBOW

9 The glory of the stars is the
beauty of heaven,
a gleaming adornment in the
heights of the Lord.
10 At the command of the Holy One
they stand as ordered,
they never relax in their watches.
11 Look upon the rainbow and
praise him who made it,
exceedingly beautiful in
its brightness.
12 It encircles the heaven with
its glorious arc;
the hands of the Most High
have stretched it out.

MARVELS OF NATURE

13 By his command he sends
the driving snow
and speeds the lightnings
of his judgement.
14 Therefore the storehouses are opened,
and the clouds fly forth like birds.
15 In his majesty he amasses the clouds,
and the hailstones are
broken in pieces.
17a The voice of his thunder
convulses the earth;
16 at his appearing the mountains
are shaken;
at his will the south wind blows.
17b So do the tempest from the
north and the whirlwind.
He scatters the snow like
birds flying down,
and its descent is like
locusts alighting.
18 The eye marvels at the beauty
of its whiteness,
and the mind is amazed at
its falling.
19 He pours the frost upon
the earth like salt,

---

[a]Greek *word* [b]The meaning of the Greek is uncertain [c]Some manuscripts *blowing* [d]Hebrew *The new moon is renewed*

and when it freezes, it becomes
pointed thorns.
20 The cold north wind blows,
and ice freezes over the water;
it rests upon every pool of water,
and the water puts it on
like a breastplate.
21 He consumes the mountains and
burns up the wilderness
and withers the tender
grass like fire.
22 A mist quickly heals all things;
when the dew appears, it
refreshes from the heat.

23 By his counsel he stilled the
great deep
and planted islands in it.
24 Those who sail the sea tell
of its dangers,
and we marvel at what we hear,
25 for in it are strange and
marvellous works,
all kinds of living things, and
huge creatures of the sea.
26 Because of him his messenger
finds the way,
and by his word all things
hold together.

27 Though we could say more, we
would never finish,
and the sum of our words
is: "He is the all."
28 Where shall we find strength
to praise him?
For he is greater than all his works.
29 Fearsome is the Lord and very great,
and marvellous is his power.
30 When you praise the Lord, exalt
him as much as you can;
for he will surpass even that.
When you exalt him, put forth
all your strength
and do not grow weary, for you
cannot praise him enough.
31 Who has seen him and can
describe him?
Or who can extol him as he is?
32 Many things greater than
these lie hidden,
for we have seen but few
of his works.
33 For the Lord has made all things,
and to the godly he has
granted wisdom.

HYMN IN HONOUR OF OUR ANCESTORS[a]

44 Let us now praise famous men
and our fathers in their
generations.
2 The Lord apportioned to
them[b] great glory,
his majesty from the beginning.
3 There were those who ruled
in their kingdoms
and were men renowned
for their power,
giving counsel by their understanding
and proclaiming prophecies;
4 leaders of the people in
their deliberations
and in understanding of the
people's learning,
wise in their words of instruction;
5 those who composed musical tunes
and set forth verses in writing;
6 rich men furnished with resources,
living peaceably in their
dwelling places—
7 all these were honoured in
their generations
and were the glory of their times.
8 There are some of them who
have left a name,
so that their praises are declared.
9 And there are some who
have no memorial,
who have perished as though
they had not lived;
they have become as though
they had not been born,
and so have their children
after them.
10 But these were, nevertheless,
men of mercy,
whose righteous deeds have
not been forgotten;
11 with their descendants it will remain,
a goodly inheritance to
their posterity.[c]
12 Their descendants stand
by the covenants;
their children also, for their sake.
13 Their posterity will continue for ever,
and their glory will not be blotted out.
14 Their bodies were buried in peace,
and their name lives to
all generations.

---

[a]This heading is in the Greek text [b]Hebrew; Greek *The Lord created*
[c]Hebrew; compare Vulgate, Syriac; the meaning of the Greek is
uncertain

15 Peoples will declare their wisdom,
and the congregation
proclaims their praise.

ENOCH
16 Enoch pleased the Lord
and was taken up;
he was an example of repentance
to all generations.

NOAH
17 Noah was found perfect and righteous;
in the time of wrath he was what
is taken in exchange;[a]
therefore a remnant was left to the earth
when the flood came.
18 Everlasting covenants were
made with him
that all flesh should not be
blotted out by a flood.

ABRAHAM
19 Abraham was the great father of
a multitude of nations,
and no one has been found
like him in glory;
20 he kept the law of the Most High
and was taken into covenant
with him;
he established the covenant in his flesh,
and when he was tested he
was found faithful.
21 Therefore the Lord[b] assured
him by an oath
that the nations would be blessed
through his posterity;
that he would multiply him like
the dust of the earth
and exalt his posterity like the stars
and cause them to inherit
from sea to sea
and from the River to the
ends of the earth.

ISAAC AND JACOB
22 To Isaac also he gave the
same assurance
for the sake of Abraham his father.
23 The blessing of all men
and the covenant
he made to rest upon the
head of Jacob;
he acknowledged him with
his blessings
and gave him his[c] inheritance;

he determined his portions
and distributed them among
twelve tribes.

MOSES
45 From his descendants the Lord[d]
brought forth a man
of mercy,
who found favour in the
sight of all flesh
and was beloved by God and man,
Moses, whose memory is blessed.
2 He made him equal in glory
to the holy ones
and made him great in the
fears of his enemies.
3 By his words he caused signs to cease;[e]
the Lord[f] glorified him in the
presence of kings.
He gave him commands for his people
and showed him part of his glory.
4 He sanctified him through
faithfulness and meekness;
he chose him out of all mankind.
5 He made him hear his voice
and led him into the thick darkness
and gave him the commandments
face to face,
the law of life and knowledge,
to teach Jacob the covenant
and Israel his judgements.

AARON
6 He exalted Aaron the brother of Moses,[g]
a holy man like him, of
the tribe of Levi.
7 He made an everlasting
covenant with him
and gave him the priesthood
of the people.
He blessed him with
splendid vestments
and put a glorious robe upon him.
8 He clothed him with
consummate glory
and crowned[h] him with the
symbols of authority,
the linen breeches, the long
robe, and the ephod.
9 And he encircled him with
pomegranates,

---
[a]Hebrew *wrath he kept the race alive*   [b]Greek *Therefore he*
[c]Hebrew; Greek *by*   [d]Greek *From his descendants he*
[e]Hebrew *he performed rapid miracles*   [f]Greek *he*   [g]Greek *him*
[h]Some manuscripts *strengthened*

with very many golden
   bells round about,
to send forth a sound as he walked,
   to make their ringing heard
      in the temple
   as a reminder to the sons
      of his people;
10 with a holy garment, of gold and blue
      and purple, the work of
         an embroiderer;
   with the oracle of judgement,
      Urim and Thummim;
11 with twisted scarlet, the
      work of an artisan;
   with precious stones engraved
      like signets,
   in a setting of gold, the
      work of a jeweller,
   for a reminder, in engraved letters,
      according to the number of
         the tribes of Israel;
12 with a gold crown upon his turban,
      inscribed like a signet
         with "Holiness",
   a distinction to be prized, the
      work of an expert,
      the delight of the eyes,
         richly adorned.
13 Before his time there never were
      such beautiful things.
   No outsider ever put them on,
   but only his sons
      and his descendants perpetually.
14 His sacrifices shall be wholly burned
      twice every day continually.
15 Moses ordained him
      and anointed him with holy oil;
   it was an everlasting covenant for him
      and for his descendants all
         the days of heaven,
   to minister to the Lord[a] and
      serve as priest
   and bless his people in his name.
16 He chose him out of all the living
      to offer sacrifice to the Lord,
   incense and a pleasing odour
      as a memorial portion,
   to make atonement for the[b] people.
17 In his commandments he gave him
      authority and statutes
         and[c] judgements
   to teach Jacob the testimonies
      and to enlighten Israel with
         his law.
18 Outsiders conspired against him
      and envied him in the wilderness:
   Dathan and Abiram and their men
      and the company of Korah,
         in wrath and anger.
19 The Lord saw it and was not pleased,
      and in the wrath of his anger
         they were destroyed;
   he wrought wonders against them
      to consume them in flaming fire.
20 He added glory to Aaron
      and gave him a heritage;
   he allotted to him the first
      of the firstfruits,
   he prepared bread of firstfruits
      in abundance;
21 for they eat the sacrifices to the Lord,
      which he gave to him and
         his descendants.
22 But in the land of the people
      he has no inheritance,
   and he has no portion
      among the people;
   for the Lord[d] himself is his[e]
      portion and inheritance.

PHINEHAS

23 Phinehas son of Eleazar is
      the third in glory,
   for he was zealous in the
      fear of the Lord
   and stood fast, when the
      people turned away,
   in the ready goodness of his soul
      and made atonement for Israel.
24 Therefore a covenant of peace
      was established with him,
   that he should be leader of the
      sanctuary and of his people,
   that he and his descendants
      should have
   the dignity of the priesthood for ever.
25 A covenant was also established
      with David
   son of Jesse, of the tribe of Judah:
   the heritage of the king is
      from son to son only;
   so the heritage of Aaron is
      for his descendants.
   Now bless the Lord who has
      crowned you with glory.[f]
26 May the Lord[g] grant you
      wisdom in your heart
   to judge his people in righteousness,

---
[a]Greek *to him* [b]Some manuscripts *your* [c]Hebrew; Greek *statutes in covenants of* [d]Greek *for he* [e]Some manuscripts *your* [f]Hebrew; Greek omits this line [g]Greek *May he*

so that their prosperity may not vanish
and that their glory may endure
throughout their generations.[a]

JOSHUA AND CALEB

46 Joshua son of Nun was mighty
in war
and was the successor of
Moses in prophesying.
He became, in accordance
with his name,
a great saviour of God's[b]
chosen ones,
to take vengeance on the enemies
that rose against them,
so that he might give Israel
its inheritance.
2 How glorious he was when
he lifted his hands
and stretched out his sword
against the cities!
3 Who before him ever stood so firm?
For he waged the wars of the Lord.
4 Was not the sun held back by his hand?
And did not one day become
as long as two?
5 He called upon the Most High,
the Mighty One,
when enemies pressed
him on every side,
and the great Lord answered him
with hailstones of mighty power.
6 He hurled down war upon that nation,
and in the descent[c] he destroyed
those who resisted,
so that the nations might
know his armament,
that he was fighting in the
sight of the Lord;
for he wholly followed
the Mighty One.
7 And in the days of Moses he
did a loyal deed,
he and Caleb son of Jephunneh:
they withstood the congregation,[d]
restrained the people from sin
and stilled their wicked murmuring.
8 And these two alone were preserved
out of 600,000 people on foot,
to bring them into their inheritance,
into a land flowing with
milk and honey.
9 And the Lord gave Caleb strength,
which remained with him to old age,
so that he went up to the hill
country,
and his children obtained it
for an inheritance;
10 so that all the sons of Israel might see
that it is good to follow the Lord.

THE JUDGES

11 The judges also, with their
respective names,
those whose hearts did not
fall into idolatry
and who did not turn away
from the Lord—
may their memory be blessed!
12 May their bones revive from
where they lie,
and may the name of those who
have been honoured
live again in their sons![e]

SAMUEL

13 Samuel, beloved by his Lord,
a prophet of the Lord,
established the kingdom
and anointed rulers over his people.
14 By the law of the Lord he judged
the congregation,
and the Lord watched over Jacob.
15 By his faithfulness he was
proved to be a prophet,
and by his words he became
known as a trustworthy seer.
16 He called upon the Lord,
the Mighty One,
when his enemies pressed
him on every side,
and he offered in sacrifice
a sucking lamb.
17 Then the Lord thundered from heaven
and made his voice heard
with a mighty sound;
18 and he wiped out the leaders
of the people of Tyre
and all the rulers of the Philistines.
19 Before the time of his eternal sleep,
Samuel[f] called men to testify before
the Lord and his anointed:
"I have not taken anyone's property,
not so much as a pair of shoes."
And no man accused him.
20 Even after he had fallen
asleep he prophesied
and revealed to the king his death

---

[a] The meaning of the Greek is uncertain [b] Greek *his* [c] Or *and when he went down* [d] Some manuscripts *enemy* [e] The meaning of the Greek is uncertain [f] Greek *he*

and lifted up his voice out of
 the earth in prophecy,
to blot out the wickedness
 of the people.

NATHAN

47 And after him Nathan rose up
to prophesy in the days
of David.

DAVID

2 As the fat is selected from
 the peace offering,
so David was selected from
 the sons of Israel.
3 He played with lions as
 with young goats
and with bears as with
 lambs of the flock.
4 In his youth did he not kill a giant
 and take away reproach
 from the people,
when he lifted his hand with
 a stone in the sling
and struck down the
 boasting of Goliath?
5 For he appealed to the Lord,
 the Most High,
and he gave him strength
 in his right hand
to slay a man mighty in war,
 to exalt the power[a] of his
 people.
6 So they glorified him for
 his ten thousands
and praised him for the
 blessings of the Lord,
when the glorious diadem
 was brought to him.
7 For he wiped out his enemies
 on every side
and annihilated his adversaries
 the Philistines;
he crushed their power
 even to this day.
8 In all that he did he gave thanks
 to the Holy One, the Most High,
 with ascriptions of glory;
he sang praise with all his heart,
 and he loved his Maker.
9 He placed singers before the altar
 to make sweet melody
 with their voices.
10 He gave beauty to the feasts
 and arranged their times
 throughout the year,[b]
while they praised God's[c] holy name,
 and the sanctuary resounded
 from early morning.
11 The Lord took away his sins
 and exalted his power for ever;
he gave him the covenant of kings
 and a throne of glory in Israel.

SOLOMON

12 After him rose up a wise son
 who on his account lived
 expansively;[d]
13 Solomon reigned in days of peace,
 and God gave him rest on every side,
that he might build a house
 for his name
and prepare a sanctuary
 to stand for ever.
14 How wise you became in your youth!
 You overflowed like a river
 with understanding.
15 Your influence covered the earth,
 and you filled it with parables
 and riddles.
16 Your name reached to far-off islands,
 and you were loved for your peace.
17 For your songs and proverbs
 and parables
and for your interpretations, the
 countries marvelled at you.
18 In the name of the Lord God,
 who is called the God of Israel,
you gathered gold like tin
 and amassed silver like lead.
19 But you lay with women,
 and through your body you were
 brought into subjection.
20 You put a stain upon your honour
 and defiled your posterity,
so that you brought wrath
 upon your children;
and they were[e] grieved at your folly,
21 so that the sovereignty was divided
 and a disobedient kingdom
 arose out of Ephraim.
22 But the Lord will never give up his mercy
 or cause any of his works to perish;
he will never blot out the
 descendants of his chosen one
or destroy the posterity of
 him who loved him;
so he gave a remnant to Jacob
 and to David a root of his stock.

---

[a] Greek *horn*; also verses 7, 11 [b] Greek *times to completion* [c] Greek *his*
[d] Hebrew *lived in safety* [e] Some manuscripts *and I was*

REHOBOAM AND JEROBOAM

23 Solomon rested with his fathers
   and left behind him one of
      his sons,
   ample in*a* folly and lacking
      in understanding,
   Rehoboam, whose policy caused
      the people to revolt.
   And Jeroboam son of Nebat,
      who caused Israel to sin
   and gave to Ephraim a sinful way.
24 Their sins became exceedingly many,
   so that they were removed
      from their land.
25 For they sought out every
      sort of wickedness,
   till vengeance came upon them.

ELIJAH

48 Then the prophet Elijah arose
      like a fire,
   and his word burned like
      a torch.
2 He brought a famine upon them,
   and by his zeal he made them
      few in number.
3 By the word of the Lord he
      shut up the heavens,
   and also three times
      brought down fire.
4 How glorious you were, O Elijah,
      in your wondrous deeds!
   And who has the right to boast
      that which you have?
5 You who raised a corpse from death
   and from Hades, by the word
      of the Most High;
6 who brought kings down
      to destruction
   and famous men from their beds;
7 who heard rebuke at Sinai
   and judgements of
      vengeance at Horeb;
8 who anointed kings to
      inflict retribution
   and prophets to succeed you.*b*
9 You who were taken up by a
      whirlwind of fire
   in a chariot with horses of fire;
10 you who are ready*c* at the appointed
      time, it is written,
   to calm the wrath of God before
      it breaks out in fury,
   to turn the heart of the
      father to the son,
   and to restore the tribes of Jacob.

11 Blessed are those who saw you
   and those who have been
      fallen asleep*d* in love;
   for we also shall surely live.*e*

ELISHA

12 It was Elijah who was covered
      by the whirlwind,
   and Elisha was filled with his spirit;
   he performed twice as many signs
   and marvels with every
      utterance of his mouth.*f*
   In all his days he did not tremble
      before any ruler,
   and no one brought him
      into subjection.
13 Nothing was too hard for him,
   and when he was dead his
      body prophesied.
14 As in his life he did wonders,
   so in death his deeds were
      marvellous.
15 For all this the people did not repent,
   and they did not forsake their sins,
   till they were carried away
      captive from their land
   and were scattered over all the earth;
   the people were left, very
      few in number,
   and a ruler in the house of David.
16 Some of them did what was
      pleasing to God,*g*
   but others multiplied sins.

HEZEKIAH AND ISAIAH

17 Hezekiah fortified his city
   and brought water into the midst of it;
   he tunnelled the sheer rock with iron
   and built pools for water.
18 In his days Sennacherib came up,
   and he sent Rabshakeh and
      then departed;
   he lifted up his hand against Zion
   and made great boasts in
      his arrogance.
19 Then their hearts were shaken
      and their hands trembled,
   and they were in anguish,
      like women in travail.
20 But they called upon the Lord
      who is merciful,

---

*a*Hebrew, Syriac; Greek *sons, the people's*   *b*Hebrew; Greek *him*   *c*Hebrew; Greek *you who are for reproofs*   *d*Some manuscripts *have been adorned*   *e*The meaning of the Greek is uncertain   *f*Greek omits this and the preceding line   *g*Greek omits *to God*

spreading forth their hands
  towards him;
and the Holy One quickly heard
  them from heaven
and delivered them by the
  hand of Isaiah.
21 The Lord[a] struck down the
  camp of the Assyrians,
and his angel wiped them out.
22 For Hezekiah did what was
  pleasing to the Lord,
and he held strongly to the
  ways of David his father,
as Isaiah the prophet commanded,
  who was great and faithful
  in his vision.
23 In his days the sun went backwards,
  and he lengthened the
  life of the king.
24 By the spirit of might he
  saw the last things
and comforted those who
  mourned in Zion.
25 He revealed what was to occur
  to the end of time
and the hidden things before
  they came to pass.

JOSIAH AND OTHER WORTHIES

49

The memory of Josiah is like
  a blending of incense
  prepared by the art of
  the perfumer;
it is sweet as honey to every mouth
  and like music at a banquet of wine.
2 He was led aright in turning the people
  and took away the abominations
  of iniquity.
3 He set his heart upon the Lord;
  in the days of the lawless he
  strengthened godliness.

4 Except David and Hezekiah and Josiah,
  they all sinned greatly,
for they forsook the law of
  the Most High;
  the kings of Judah came to an end;
5 for they gave their power to others
  and their glory to a foreign nation,
6 who set fire to the chosen
  city of the sanctuary
and made her streets desolate,
  according to the word[b] of Jeremiah.
7 For they had afflicted him;
  yet he had been consecrated in
  the womb as prophet,
to pluck up and afflict and destroy
  and likewise to build and to plant.
8 It was Ezekiel who saw the
  vision of glory
that God[c] showed him above the
  chariot of the cherubim.
9 For God remembered his
  enemies with storm
and did good to those who
  directed their ways aright.[d]

10 May the bones of the twelve prophets
  revive from where they lie,
for they comforted the people of Jacob
  and delivered them with
  confident hope.

11 How shall we magnify Zerubbabel?
  He was like a signet on
  the right hand,
12 and so was Jeshua son of Jozadak;
  in their days they built the house
  and raised a temple[e] holy
  to the Lord,
  prepared for everlasting glory.
13 The memory of Nehemiah
  also is lasting;
he raised for us the walls
  that had fallen
and set up the gates and bars
  and rebuilt our ruined houses.

RETROSPECT

14 No one like Enoch has been
  created on earth,
for he was taken up from the earth.
15 And neither has there been
  any man like Joseph,[f]
  even his bones were cared for.
16 Shem and Seth were honoured
  among men,
and Adam above every living
  being in the creation.

SIMON SON OF ONIAS

50

The leader of his brothers and
  the pride of his people[g]
  was Simon the high priest,
  son of Onias,
who in his life repaired the house
  and in his time fortified the temple.

---

[a]Greek He [b]Greek desoate, by the hand [c]Greek he; also verse 9 [d]The meaning of the Greek is uncertain [e]Some manuscripts people [f]Hebrew, Syriac; Greek adds the leader of his brothers, the support of the people [g]Hebrew, Syriac; Greek omits this line; compare 49:15

SIRACH 50

2 He laid the foundations for the
high double walls,^a
the high retaining walls for
the temple enclosure.
3 In his days a cistern for water
was quarried out,^b
a reservoir like the sea in
circumference.
4 He considered how to save
his people from ruin
and fortified the city to
withstand a siege.
5 How glorious he was when the
people gathered round him
as he came out of the
inner sanctuary!^c
6 Like the morning star
among the clouds,
like the full moon on feast days;
7 like the sun shining upon the
temple of the Most High
and like the rainbow gleaming
in glorious clouds;
8 like roses in the days of the firstfruits,
like lilies by a spring of water,
like a green shoot on Lebanon^d
on a summer day;
9 like fire and incense in the censer,
like a vessel of hammered gold
adorned with all kinds of
precious stones;
10 like an olive tree putting forth its fruit
and like a cypress towering
in the clouds.
11 When he put on his glorious robe
and clothed himself with
superb perfection
and went up to the holy altar,
he made the court of the
sanctuary glorious.
12 And when he received the portions
from the hands of the priests,
as he stood by the hearth of the altar
with a garland of brothers round him,
he was like a young cedar
on Lebanon;
and they surrounded him like
the trunks of palm trees,
13 all the sons of Aaron in
their splendour
with the Lord's offering in their hands,
before the whole congregation
of Israel.
14 Finishing the service at the altars
and arranging the offering to the
Most High, the Almighty,
15 he reached out his hand to the cup
and poured a drink offering of
the blood of the grape;
he poured it out at the foot of the altar,
a pleasing odour to the Most
High, the King of all.
16 Then the sons of Aaron shouted,
they sounded the trumpets
of hammered work,
they made a great noise to be heard
for remembrance before
the Most High.
17 Then all the people together made haste
and fell to the ground
upon their faces
to worship their Lord,
the Almighty, God Most High.
18 And the singers praised him
with their voices
in sweet and full-toned melody.^e
19 And the people earnestly prayed
to the Lord Most High
in supplication before him
who is merciful,
till the order of worship of
the Lord was ended;
so they completed his service.
20 Then Simon^f came down and
lifted up his hands
over the whole congregation
of the sons of Israel,
to pronounce the blessing of
the Lord with his lips
and to glory in his name;
21 and they bowed down in
worship a second time,
to receive the blessing from
the Most High.

BENEDICTION

22 And now bless the God of all,
who in every way does great things;
who exalts our days from birth
and deals with us according
to his mercy.
23 May he give us^g gladness of heart
and grant that peace may be
in our days in Israel,
as in the days of old.
24 May he entrust to us his mercy!
And let him deliver us in our^h days!

---

^aSome manuscripts *for the height of the court*   ^bCompare Hebrew; Greek *was diminished*   ^cGreek *out of the house of the veil*   ^dOr *green shoot of frankincense*   ^eSome manuscripts *in sweet melody throughout the house*   ^fGreek *he*   ^gSome manuscripts *you*   ^hSome manuscripts *his*

EPILOGUE

25 With two nations my soul is vexed,
and the third is no nation:
26 those who live on Mount Seir[c]
and the Philistines
and the foolish people that
dwell in Shechem.

27 Instruction in understanding
and knowledge
I have written in this book,
Jesus son of Sirach, son of
Eleazar,[d] of Jerusalem,
who out of his heart poured
forth wisdom.
28 Blessed is he who concerns
himself with these things,
and he who lays them to heart
will become wise.
29 For if he does them, he will be
strong for all things,
for the fear of the Lord is
his strength.[e]

PRAYER OF JESUS SON OF SIRACH[f]

51 I will give thanks to you, O Lord
and King,
and will praise you as God my
Saviour.
I give thanks to your name,
2 for you have been my
protector and helper
and have delivered my body
from destruction
and from the snare of a
slanderous tongue,
from lips that utter lies.
Before the adversaries
you were my helper ³and
delivered me,
in the greatness of your mercy
and of your name,
from the gnashings of teeth
about to devour me,[g]
from the hand of those who
sought my life,
from the many afflictions
that I endured,
4 from choking fire on every side,
and from the midst of fire
that I did not kindle,
5 from the depths of the belly of Hades,
from an unclean tongue
and lying words —
6 the slander of an unrighteous
tongue.[h]

My soul drew near to death,
and my life was very near
to Hades beneath.
7 They surrounded me on every side,
and there was no one to help me;
I looked for human help,
and there was none.
8 Then I remembered your mercy, O Lord,
and your kindness[i] from of old,
that you deliver those who wait for you
and save them from the hand
of their enemies.
9 And I sent up my supplication
from the earth
and prayed for deliverance
from death.
10 I appealed to the Lord, the
Father of my lord,
not to forsake me in the
days of affliction,
at the time when there is no
help against the proud.
11 I will praise your name continually
and will sing praise with
thanksgiving.
My prayer was heard,
12 for you saved me from destruction
and rescued me from an evil time.
Therefore I will give thanks to
you and praise you,
and I will bless the name of the Lord.

AUTOBIOGRAPHICAL POEM ON WISDOM

13 While I was still young, before
I went on my travels,
I sought wisdom openly
in my prayer.
14 Before the temple I asked for her,
and I will search for her to the last.
15 From blossom to[a] ripening grape
my heart delighted in her;
my foot entered upon the straight path;
from my youth I followed her steps.
16 I inclined my ear a little
and received her,
and I found for myself
much instruction.
17 I made progress therein;
to him who gives wisdom
I will give glory.

---

[c]Hebrew, Vulgate; Greek *on the mountain of Samaria*   [d]Hebrew *Jesus son of Eleazar, son of Sirach*   [e]Some manuscripts *the light of the Lord is his lamp*; some manuscripts add *And to the godly he has given wisdom. Blessed be the Lord for ever. Amen, amen.*   [f]This heading is in the Greek text   [g]Compare Vulgate; Greek *name, when I was about to be devoured*   [h]Some manuscripts add *to the king*   [i]Some manuscripts *work*
[a]Some manuscripts *As from*

SIRACH 51

18 For I resolved to live according
      to wisdom,[a]
   and I was zealous for the good;
   and I shall never be put to shame.
19 My soul grappled with wisdom,
      and in my conduct I was strict;[b]
   I spread out my hands to the heavens
   and lamented my ignorance of her.
20 I directed my soul to her,
      and through purification I found her.
   I gained understanding[c] with
      her from the first,
   therefore I will not be forsaken.
21 My heart was stirred to seek her,
      therefore I have gained a
      good possession.
22 The Lord gave me a tongue
      as my reward,
   and I will praise him with it.

23 Draw near to me, you who are untaught,
      and lodge in the house of instruction.
24 Why do you say you are lacking
      in these things,[d]
   and why are your souls very thirsty?
25 I opened my mouth and said:
      Get these things[e] for yourselves
      without money.
26 Put your neck under the yoke
      and let your souls receive
      instruction;
   it is to be found close by.
27 See with your eyes that I
      have laboured little
   and found for myself much rest.
28 Get instruction with a large
      sum of silver,
   and you will gain by it much
      gold.
29 May your soul rejoice in his mercy,
      and may you not be put to shame
      when you praise him.
30 Do your work before the
      appointed time,
   and in God's[f] time he will
      give you your reward.

---

[a]Greek *her*; also verse 19 [b]The meaning of the Greek is uncertain
[c]Greek *heart* [d]Compare Hebrew, Syriac; the meaning of the Greek is
uncertain [e]Greek omits *these things* [f]Greek *his*

BARUCH

BARUCH AND THE JEWS IN BABYLON

1 [a] These are the words of the book that Baruch son of Neraiah, son of Mahseiah, son of Zedekiah, son of Hasadiah, son of Hilkiah, wrote in Babylon, ²in the fifth year, on the seventh day of the month, at the time when the Chaldeans took Jerusalem and burned it with fire. ³And Baruch read the words of this book in the hearing of Jeconiah son of King Jehoiakim of Judah and in the hearing of all the people who came to hear the book ⁴and in the hearing of the mighty men and the princes and in the hearing of the elders and in the hearing of all the people, small and great, all who dwelt in Babylon by the river Sud.

⁵Then they wept and fasted and prayed before the Lord; ⁶and they collected money, each giving what he could; ⁷and they sent it to Jerusalem to Jehoiakim the high priest,[b] son of Hilkiah, son of Shallum, and to the priests and to all the people who were present with him in Jerusalem. ⁸At the same time, on the tenth day of Sivan, Baruch[c] took the vessels of the house of the Lord, which had been carried away from the temple, to return them to the land of Judah — the silver vessels that Zedekiah son of King Josiah of Judah had made, ⁹after King Nebuchadnezzar of Babylon had carried away from Jerusalem Jeconiah and the princes and the prisoners and the mighty men and the people of the land and brought them to Babylon.

LETTER TO JERUSALEM

¹⁰And they said: Look, we are sending you money; so buy with the money whole burnt offerings and sin offerings and incense and prepare a corn offering and offer them upon the altar of the Lord our God; ¹¹and pray for the life of King Nebuchadnezzar of Babylon and for the life of Belshazzar his son, that their days on earth may be like the days of heaven. ¹²And the Lord will give us strength, and he will give light to our eyes, and we shall live under the protection[d] of King Nebuchadnezzar of Babylon and under the protection[e] of Belshazzar his son, and we shall serve them many days and find favour in their sight. ¹³And pray for us to the Lord our God, for we have sinned against the Lord our God, and to this day the anger of the Lord and his wrath have not turned away from us. ¹⁴And you shall read this book that we are sending you, to make a public declaration in the house of the Lord on the days of the feasts and at appointed seasons.

CONFESSION OF SINS

¹⁵And you shall say: Righteousness belongs to the Lord our God, but shame, as at this day, to us, to the people of Judah, to the inhabitants of Jerusalem, ¹⁶and to our kings and our princes and our priests and our prophets and our fathers, ¹⁷because we have sinned before the Lord ¹⁸and have disobeyed him and have not heeded the voice of the Lord our God, to walk in the statutes of the Lord that he set before us. ¹⁹From the day when the Lord brought our fathers out of the land of Egypt until today, we have been disobedient to the Lord our God, and we have been negligent, in not heeding his voice. ²⁰So to this day there have clung to us the calamities and the curse that the Lord declared through Moses his servant at the time when he brought our fathers out of the land of Egypt to give to us a land flowing with milk and honey. ²¹We did not heed the voice of the Lord our God in all the words of the prophets whom he sent to us, ²²but we each followed the intent of his own wicked heart by serving other gods and doing what is evil in the sight of the Lord our God.

2 So the Lord confirmed his word, which he spoke against us and against our judges who judged Israel and against our kings and against our princes and against

---

[a]Baruch is one of the seven deuterocanonical books that do not exist in their entirety in Hebrew or Aramaic, but which were included in the Greek Septuagint, and were likewise included in the Latin Vulgate version of the Bible translated by Jerome in the late fourth century AD. See further, *Introduction*, pages xiii to xiv.
[b]Greek *Jehoiakim the priest* [c]Greek *he* [d]Greek *live in the shadow*
[e]Greek *and in the shadow*

the people of Israel and Judah. ²Under the whole heaven there has not been done the like of what he has done in Jerusalem, in accordance with what is written in the law of Moses, ³that we should eat, one the flesh of his son and another the flesh of his daughter. ⁴And he gave them into subjection to all the kingdoms round us, to be a reproach and a desolation among all the surrounding peoples, where the Lord has scattered them. ⁵They were brought low and not raised up, because we sinned against the Lord our God, in not heeding his voice.

⁶Righteousness belongs to the Lord our God, but shame to us and our fathers, as at this day. ⁷All those calamities with which the Lord threatened us have come upon us. ⁸Yet we have not entreated the favour of the Lord by turning away, each of us, from the thoughts of his wicked heart. ⁹And the Lord has kept watch over the calamities, and the Lord has brought them upon us, for the Lord is righteous in all his works that he has commanded us, ¹⁰yet we have not obeyed his voice, to walk in the statutes of the Lord that he set before us.

PRAYER FOR DELIVERANCE

¹¹And now, O Lord God of Israel, you who brought your people out of the land of Egypt with a mighty hand and with signs and wonders and with great power and outstretched arm and have made for yourself a name, as at this day, ¹²we have sinned, we have been ungodly, we have done wrong, O Lord our God, against all your ordinances. ¹³Let your anger turn away from us, for few of us are left, among the nations where you have scattered us. ¹⁴Hear, O Lord, our prayer and our supplication, and for your own sake deliver us and grant us favour in the sight of those who have carried us into exile; ¹⁵that all the earth may know that you are the Lord our God, for Israel and his descendants are called by your name. ¹⁶O Lord, look down from your holy habitation and consider us. Incline your ear, O Lord, and hear; ¹⁷open your eyes, O Lord, and see; for the dead who are in Hades, whose spirit has been taken from their bodies, will not ascribe glory or justice to the Lord, ¹⁸but the person that is greatly distressed,*ᵃ* that goes about bent over and feeble, and the eyes that are failing and the person that hungers will ascribe to you glory and righteousness, O Lord. ¹⁹For it is not because of any righteous deeds of our fathers or our kings that we bring before you our prayer for mercy, O Lord our God. ²⁰For you have sent your anger and your wrath upon us, just as you declared by the hand of your servants the prophets, saying: ²¹Thus says the Lord: Bend your shoulders and serve the king of Babylon, and you will remain in the land that I gave to your fathers. ²²But if you will not obey the voice of the Lord and will not serve the king of Babylon, ²³I will make to cease from the cities of Judah and from the region round Jerusalem the voice of mirth and the voice of gladness, the voice of the bridegroom and the voice of the bride, and the whole land will be a desolation without inhabitants.

²⁴But we did not obey your voice, to serve the king of Babylon; and you have confirmed your words, which you spoke by the hands of your servants the prophets, that the bones of our kings and the bones of our fathers would be taken out of their place; ²⁵and look, they have been cast out to the heat of day and the frost of night. They perished in great misery, by famine and sword and dispatch. ²⁶And the house that is called by your name you have made as it is today, because of the wickedness of the house of Israel and the house of Judah.

GOD'S PROMISE RECALLED

²⁷Yet you have dealt with us, O Lord our God, in all your kindness and in all your great compassion, ²⁸as you spoke by the hand of your servant Moses on the day when you commanded him to write your law in the presence of the people of Israel, saying, ²⁹"If you will not obey my voice, this very great multitude of voices will surely turn into a small one among the nations, where I will scatter them. ³⁰For I know that they will not obey me, for they are a stiff-necked people. But in the land of their exile they will come to themselves, ³¹and they will know that I am the Lord their God. I will give them a heart that obeys and ears that hear; ³²and they will praise me in the land of their exile and will remember my name ³³and will turn from their stubbornness and their wicked deeds; for they will remember the way of their fathers, who sinned before the Lord. ³⁴I will bring them again into the land that I swore to give to their fathers, to Abraham

---

ᵃThe meaning of the Greek is uncertain

and to Isaac and to Jacob, and they will rule over it; and I will increase them, and they will not be diminished. ³⁵I will make an everlasting covenant with them to be their God and they shall be my people; and I will never again remove my people Israel from the land that I have given them."

3 O Lord Almighty, God of Israel, the soul in anguish and the wearied spirit cry out to you. ²Hear, O Lord, and have mercy, for we have sinned before you. ³For you are enthroned for ever, and we are perishing for ever. ⁴O Lord Almighty, God of Israel, hear now the prayer of those of Israel who have died and of the sons of those who sinned before you, who did not heed the voice of the Lord their God, so that calamities have clung to us. ⁵Remember not the iniquities of our fathers, but in this time remember your power and your name. ⁶For you are the Lord our God, and you, O Lord, will we praise. ⁷For you have put the fear of you in our hearts in order that we should call upon your name; and we will praise you in our exile, for we have put away from our hearts all the iniquity of our fathers who sinned before you. ⁸Behold, we are today in our exile where you have scattered us, to be reproached and cursed and punished for all the iniquities of our fathers who forsook the Lord our God.

IN PRAISE OF WISDOM

⁹ Hear the commandments
　　of life, O Israel;
　give ear and learn wisdom!
¹⁰ Why is it, O Israel, why is it that you
　　are in the land of your enemies,
　that you are growing old in
　　a foreign country,
　that you are defiled with the dead,
¹¹ that you are counted among
　　those in Hades?
¹² You have forsaken the
　　fountain of wisdom.
¹³ If you had walked in the way of God,
　you would be dwelling in
　　peace for ever.
¹⁴ Learn where there is wisdom,
　where there is strength,
　where there is understanding,
　that you may at the same time discern
　where there is length of
　　days and life,
　where there is light for the
　　eyes and peace.

¹⁵ Who has found her place?
　And who has entered her
　　storehouses?
¹⁶ Where are the princes of the nations
　and those who rule over the
　　beasts on earth;
¹⁷ those who have sport with
　　the birds of the air
　and who hoard up silver and gold,
　in which men trust,
　　and there is no end to their getting;
¹⁸ those who scheme to get silver
　　and are anxious,
　whose labours are beyond measure?
¹⁹ They have vanished and gone
　　down to Hades,
　and others have arisen in
　　their place.

²⁰ Young men have seen the light of day
　and have dwelt upon the earth;
　but they have not learned the
　　way to knowledge
　or understood her paths
　or laid hold of her.
²¹ Their sons have strayed far
　　from their way.
²² She has not been heard of in Canaan
　or seen in Teman;
²³ the sons of Hagar, who seek for
　　understanding on the earth,
　　the merchants of Merran
　　　and Teman,
　　the storytellers and the seekers
　　　for understanding,
　have not learned the way to wisdom
　　or given thought to her paths.

²⁴ O Israel, how great is the house of God!
　And how vast its estate!ᵃ
²⁵ It is great and has no bounds;
　it is high and immeasurable.
²⁶ The giants were born there, who
　　were famous of old,
　great in stature, expert in war.
²⁷ God did not choose them
　or give them the way to knowledge;
²⁸ so they perished because
　　they had no wisdom,
　they perished through their folly.
²⁹ Who has gone up into heaven
　　and taken her
　and brought her down
　　from the clouds?

ᵃOr *And how vast the territory that he possesses*

BARUCH 3–4

30 Who has gone over the sea
    and found her
    and will buy her for pure gold?
31 No one knows the way to her
    or is concerned about the path to her.
32 But he who knows all things knows her,
    he found her by his understanding.
    He who prepared the earth for all time
    filled it with four-footed creatures;
33 he who sends forth the
        light, and it goes,
    called it, and it obeyed him in fear;
34 the stars shone in their watches
    and were glad;
    he called them, and they
        said, "Here we are!"
    They shone with gladness for
        him who made them.
35 This is our God;
    no other can be compared to him!
36 He found the whole way to knowledge
    and gave her to Jacob his servant
    and to Israel whom he loved.
37 Afterwards she appeared upon earth
    and lived among humans.

4 This is the book of the
        commandments of God
    and the law that endures for ever.
    All who hold her fast will live,
    and those who forsake her will die.
2 Turn, O Jacob, and take her;
    walk towards the shining of her light.
3 Do not give your glory to another
    or your advantages to an alien people.
4 Happy are we, O Israel,
    for we know what is pleasing to God.

ENCOURAGEMENT FOR ISRAEL

5 Take courage, my people,
    O memorial of Israel!
6 It was not for destruction
    that you were sold to the nations,
    but you were handed over
        to your enemies
    because you angered God.
7 For you provoked him who made you,
    by sacrificing to demons
    and not to God.
8 You forgot the everlasting God,
    who brought you up,
    and you grieved Jerusalem,
    who reared you.
9 For she saw the wrath that came
    upon you from God,
    and she said:

"Listen, you neighbours of Zion,
    God has brought great
        sorrow upon me;
10 for I have seen the captivity of
    my sons and daughters,
    which the Everlasting
        brought upon them.
11 With joy I nurtured them,
    but I sent them away with
        weeping and sorrow.
12 Let no one rejoice over me, a widow
    and bereaved of many;
    I was left desolate because of
        the sins of my children,
    because they turned away
        from the law of God.
13 They had no regard for his statutes;
    they did not walk in the ways of
        God's commandments
    or tread the paths of discipline
        in his righteousness.
14 Let the neighbours of Zion come;
    remember the captivity of my
        sons and daughters,
    which the Everlasting
        brought upon them.
15 For he brought against them
    a nation from afar,
    a shameless nation, of a
        strange language,
    who had no respect for an old man
    and had no pity for a child.
16 They led away the widow's beloved sons
    and bereaved the lonely woman
        of her daughters.

17 "But I, how can I help you?
18 For he who brought these
    calamities upon you
    will deliver you from the hand
        of your enemies.
19 Go, my children, go;
    for I have been left desolate.
20 I have taken off the robe of peace
    and put on the sackcloth of
        my supplication;
    I will cry to the Everlasting
        all my days.

21 "Take courage, my children, cry to God,
    and he will deliver you from the
        power and hand of the enemy.
22 For I have put my hope in the
        Everlasting to save you,
    and joy has come to me
        from the Holy One,

because of the mercy that
    soon will come to you
from your everlasting Saviour.*

23 For I sent you out with sorrow
    and weeping,
but God will give you back to me
    with joy and gladness for ever.

24 For as the neighbours of Zion have
    now seen your capture,
so they soon will see your
    salvation by God,
which will come to you with great glory
    and with the splendour of
    the Everlasting.

25 My children, endure with patience
    the wrath that has come
    upon you from God.
Your enemy has overtaken you,
    but you will soon see their destruction
    and will tread upon their necks.

26 My tender sons have travelled
    rough roads;
they were taken away like a flock
    carried off by the enemy.

27 "Take courage, my children,
    and cry to God,
for you will be remembered by him
    who brought this upon you.

28 For just as you purposed to
    go astray from God,
return with tenfold zeal to seek him.

29 For he who brought these
    calamities upon you
will bring you everlasting joy
    with your salvation."

JERUSALEM IS ASSURED OF HELP

30 Take courage, O Jerusalem,
for he who named you
    will comfort you.

31 Wretched will be those
    who afflicted you
and rejoiced at your fall.

32 Wretched will be the cities that your
    children served as slaves;
wretched will be the city that
    received your sons.

33 For just as she rejoiced at your fall
    and was glad for your ruin,
so she will be grieved at her
    own desolation.

34 And I will take away her pride
    in her great population,
and her insolence will be
    turned to grief.

35 For fire will come upon her from the
    Everlasting for many days,
and for a long time she will be
    inhabited by demons.

36 Look towards the east, O Jerusalem,
    and see the joy that is coming
    to you from God!

37 Behold, your sons are coming,
    whom you sent away;
they are coming, gathered
    from east and west,
at the word of the Holy One,
    rejoicing in the glory of God.

5 Take off the garment of your sorrow
    and affliction, O Jerusalem,
and put on for ever the beauty of
    the glory from God.

2 Put on the robe of the
    righteousness from God;
put on your head the crown of the
    glory of the Everlasting.

3 For God will show your splendour
    everywhere under heaven.

4 For your name will for ever
    be called by God:
"Peace of righteousness and
    glory of godliness."

5 Arise, O Jerusalem, stand
    upon the height
and look towards the east
and see your children gathered
    from west and east,
at the word of the Holy One,
    rejoicing that God has
    remembered them.

6 For they went forth from you on foot,
    led away by their enemies;
but God will bring them back to you,
    carried in glory, as on a royal throne.

7 For God has ordered that every
    high mountain and the
    everlasting hills be made low
and the valleys filled up to
    make level ground,
so that Israel may walk safely
    in the glory of God.

8 The woods and every fragrant tree
    have shaded Israel at God's command.

9 For God will lead Israel with joy,
    in the light of his glory,
with the mercy and righteousness
    that come from him.

---

*Or *from the Everlasting, your Saviour*

THE LETTER OF JEREMIAH

¹A copy of a letter that Jeremiah sent to those who were to be taken to Babylon as captives by the king of the Babylonians, to give them the message that God had commanded him.

THE PEOPLE FACE A LONG CAPTIVITY

²Because of the sins that you have committed before God, you will be taken to Babylon as captives by King Nebuchadnezzar of the Babylonians. ³Therefore when you have come to Babylon you will remain there for many years, for a long time, up to seven generations; after that I will bring you away from there in peace. ⁴Now in Babylon you will see gods made of silver and gold and wood, which are carried aloft on the shoulders and inspire awe among the nations. ⁵So take care not to become at all like the foreigners or to let awe of these gods^a possess you, when you see the multitude before and behind them worshipping them. ⁶But say to yourself, "It is you, O Lord, whom we must worship." ⁷For my angel is with you, demanding an account of your souls.

HELPLESSNESS OF IDOLS

⁸Their tongues are smoothed by the carpenter, and they themselves are overlaid with gold and silver; but they are false and cannot speak. ⁹People^b take gold and make crowns for the heads of their gods, as they would for a girl who loves ornaments; ¹⁰and sometimes the priests secretly take gold and silver from their gods and spend it upon themselves ¹¹and even give some of it to the prostitutes in the brothel. They adorn their gods^c out with garments like people—these gods of silver and gold and wood, ¹²which cannot save themselves from rust and corrosion. When they have been dressed in purple robes, ¹³their faces are wiped because of the dust from the temple, which is thick upon them. ¹⁴Like a local ruler the god^d holds a sceptre, though unable to destroy anyone who offends it. ¹⁵It has a dagger in its right hand and has an axe; but it cannot save itself from war and robbers. ¹⁶Therefore they evidently are not gods; so do not revere them.

¹⁷For just as one's dish is useless when it is broken, so are their gods,^{e} when they have been set up in the temples. Their eyes are full of the dust raised by the feet of those who enter. ¹⁸And just as the gates are shut on every side upon a man who has offended a king, as though he were sentenced to death, so the priests make their temples secure with doors and locks and bars, in order that they may not be plundered by robbers. ¹⁹They light lamps, even more than they light for themselves, though their gods^f can see none of them. ²⁰They are^g just like a beam of the temple, but people say they melt their hearts. When worms from the earth devour them and their robes, they do not notice, ²¹since their faces have been blackened by the smoke of the temple. ²²Bats, swallows, and birds light on their bodies and heads; and so do cats. ²³From this you will know that they are not gods; so do not revere them.

²⁴As for the gold that they wear for beauty—they will not shine unless someone wipes off the rust; for even when they were being cast, they had no feeling. ²⁵They are bought at any cost, but there is no breath in them. ²⁶Having no feet, they are carried on attendants' shoulders, revealing their worthlessness to all. ²⁷And those who serve them are ashamed because through them these gods^h are made to stand, lest they fall to the ground. If anyone sets one of them upright, it cannot move by itself; and if it is tipped over, it will never straighten itself; but gifts are placed before them just as before the dead. ²⁸The

---

^{a}Greek *awe for them* ^{b}Greek *They* ^{c}Greek *adorn them* ^{d}Greek *ruler he* ^{e}Greek *so are they* ^{f}Greek *though they* ^{g}Greek *It is* ^{h}Greek *through them they* ^{i}Greek *to them*

priests sell the sacrifices that are offered to these gods[j] and use the money; and likewise their wives preserve some with salt, but share none with the poor or helpless. ²⁹Women in menstruation or after childbirth take part in their sacrifices. Since you know by these things that they are not gods, do not revere them.

³⁰For why should they be called gods? Because women serve meals for gods of silver and gold and wood? ³¹Or because priests rush into their temples with their clothes rent, their heads and beards shaved, and their heads uncovered, ³²howling and shouting before their gods as some do at a funeral feast for a man who has died? ³³The priests take some of the clothing of their gods[a] to clothe their wives and children. ³⁴Whether one does evil to them or good, they will not be able to repay it. They cannot set up a king or depose one. ³⁵Likewise they are unable to give either wealth or money; if one makes a vow to them and does not keep it, they will never enforce it. ³⁶They will never save anyone from death or rescue the weak from the strong. ³⁷They will never restore sight to a blind person or rescue anyone who is in distress. ³⁸They will never take pity on a widow or do good to an orphan. ³⁹These things that are made of wood and overlaid with gold and silver are like stones from the mountain, and those who serve them will be put to shame. ⁴⁰Why then must anyone think that they are gods or call them gods?

FOOLISHNESS OF WORSHIPPING IDOLS

Besides, even the Chaldeans themselves dishonour them; ⁴¹for when they see a mute person who cannot speak, they bring him before Bel[b] and think it appropriate to call out to him, as though Bel[c] were able to understand. ⁴²Yet they themselves cannot perceive this and abandon their gods,[d] for they have no sense. ⁴³And the women, with cords round them, sit along the passageways, burning bran for incense; and when one of them is led off by one of the passers-by and is lain with, she derides the woman next to her, because she was not as attractive as herself and her cord was not broken. ⁴⁴Whatever is done for them is false. Why then must anyone think that they are gods or call them gods?

⁴⁵They are made by carpenters and goldsmiths; they can be nothing but what the artisans wish them to be. ⁴⁶Those who make them will certainly not live very long themselves; how then can the things that are made by them be gods? ⁴⁷They have left only lies and reproach for those who come after. ⁴⁸For when war or calamity comes upon them, the priests consult together as to where they can hide themselves and their gods.[e] ⁴⁹How then can one fail to see that these are not gods, for they cannot save themselves from war or calamity? ⁵⁰Since they are made of wood and overlaid with gold and silver, it will afterwards be known that they are false. ⁵¹It will be apparent to all the nations and kings that they are not gods but the work of men's hands and that there is no work of God in them. ⁵²Who then can fail to know that they are not gods?[f]

⁵³For they will never set up a king over a country or give rain to the people. ⁵⁴They will never judge their own cause or deliver one who is wronged, for they have no power; they are like crows between heaven and earth. ⁵⁵When fire breaks out in a temple of gods made of wood or overlaid with gold or silver, their priests will flee and escape, but the gods[g] will be burnt in two like beams. ⁵⁶Besides, they will surely offer no resistance to a king or any enemies. Why then must anyone admit or think that they are gods?

⁵⁷Gods made of wood and overlaid with silver and gold will never save themselves from thieves and robbers. ⁵⁸Strong men will strip them of their gold and silver and of the robes they wear and go off with this booty, and they will not be able to help themselves. ⁵⁹So it is better to be a king who shows his courage or a useful household utensil that serves its owner's need than to be these false gods; better even the door of a house that protects its contents than these false gods; better also a wooden pillar in a palace than these false gods.

⁶⁰For sun and moon and stars, shining and sent forth for service, are obedient. ⁶¹So also the lightning, when it flashes, is widely seen; and the wind likewise blows in every land. ⁶²When God commands the clouds to go over the whole world, they carry out his command. ⁶³And the fire sent from above to consume mountains and woods does what it is ordered. But these idols[h] are not to be

---

[a] Greek *of them* [b] Or *they bring Bel and pray* [c] Greek *he* [d] Greek *abandon them* [e] Greek *and them* [f] The meaning of the Greek is uncertain [g] Greek *but they* [h] Greek *things*

compared with them in appearance or power. ⁶⁴Therefore one must not think that they are gods or call them gods, for they are unable either to decide a case or to do good to people. ⁶⁵Since you know then that they are not gods, do not revere them.

⁶⁶For they will never curse or bless kings; ⁶⁷they will never show signs in the heavens and[a] among the nations or shine like the sun or give light like the moon. ⁶⁸The wild beasts are better than they are, for they can flee to cover and help themselves. ⁶⁹So we have no evidence whatever that they are gods; therefore do not revere them.

⁷⁰Like a scarecrow in a cucumber bed, that guards nothing, so are their gods of wood, overlaid with gold and silver. ⁷¹In the same way, their gods of wood, overlaid with gold and silver, are like a thorn bush in a garden, on which every bird sits; or like a dead body cast out in the darkness. ⁷²By the purple and linen[b] that rot upon them you will know that they are not gods; and they will finally themselves be consumed and be a reproach in the land. ⁷³Better therefore is a just man who has no idols, for he will be far from reproach.

---

[a] Some manuscripts omit and   [b] Greek marble; Syriac silk

THE PRAYER OF AZARIAH

AND THE SONG OF THE THREE YOUNG MEN

PRAYER OF AZARIAH IN THE FURNACE

¹And they walked about in the midst of the flames, singing hymns to God and blessing the Lord. ²Then Azariah stood and offered this prayer; in the midst of the fire he opened his mouth and said:

3 "Blessed are you, O Lord, God of our
    ancestors, and worthy of praise;
    and your name is glorified for ever.
4 For you are just in all that you have done,
    and all your works are true
    and your ways right,
    and all your judgements are truth.
5 You have executed true judgements in
    all that you have brought upon us
    and upon Jerusalem, the holy
    city of our ancestors,
    for in truth and justice you have
    brought all these upon us
    because of our sins.
6 For we have sinfully and lawlessly
    departed from you,
    and have sinned in all things
7 and have not obeyed your
    commandments;
we have not observed them
    or done them,
    as you have commanded us that
    it might go well with us.
8 So all that you have brought upon us
    and all that you have done to us,
    you have done in true judgement.
9 You have given us into the
    hands of lawless enemies,
    most hateful rebels,
    and to an unjust king, the most
    wicked in all the world.
10 And now we cannot open our mouths;
    shame and disgrace have befallen
    your servants and worshippers.
11 For your name's sake do not
    give us up utterly
    and do not break your covenant
12 and do not withdraw your
    mercy from us,
    for the sake of Abraham your beloved
    and for the sake of Isaac your servant
    and Israel your holy one,
13 to whom you promised
    to make their descendants as
    many as the stars of heaven
    and as the sand on the
    shore of the sea.
14 For we, O Lord, have become
    fewer than any nation
    and are brought low this day in all
    the world because of our sins.
15 And at this time there is no prince
    or prophet or leader,
    no whole burnt offering or sacrifice
    or oblation or incense,
    no place to make an offering
    before you or to find mercy.
16 Yet with a contrite heart and a humble
    spirit may we be accepted,
17 as though it were with whole burnt
    offerings of rams and bulls
    and with tens of thousands
    of fat lambs;
    such may our sacrifice be in
    your sight this day,
    and may it accomplish after you,
    for there will be no shame for
    those who trust in you.
18 And now with all our heart
    we follow you,
    we fear you and seek your
    countenance.
19 Do not put us to shame,
    but deal with us in your forbearance
    and in your abundant mercy.

PRAYER OF AZARIAH

20 Deliver us in accordance with
    your marvellous works
  and give glory to your name, O Lord!
21 Let all who do harm to your
    servants be put to shame;
  let them be disgraced and
    deprived of all dominion
  and let their strength be broken.
22 Let them know that you are the
    Lord, the only God,
  glorious over the whole world."

SONG OF THE THREE JEWS

²³Now the king's servants who threw them in did not cease feeding the furnace fires with naphtha, pitch, tow, and brush. ²⁴And the flame streamed out above the furnace forty-nine cubits, ²⁵and it broke through and burned those of the Chaldeans whom it caught round the furnace. ²⁶But the angel of the Lord came down into the furnace to be with Azariah and his companions and drove the fiery flame out of the furnace ²⁷and made the midst of the furnace like a moist whistling wind, so that the fire did not touch them at all or hurt or trouble them.

²⁸Then the three, as with one mouth, praised and glorified and blessed God in the furnace, saying:

29 "Blessed are you, O Lord, God
    of our ancestors,
  and to be praised and highly
    exalted for ever;
30 and blessed is your glorious,
    holy name
  and to be highly praised and
    highly exalted for ever;
31 blessed are you in the shrine
    of your holy glory
  and to be extolled and highly
    glorified for ever.
32 Blessed are you, who sits
    upon cherubim and looks
    upon the deeps,
  and to be praised and highly
    exalted for ever.
33 Blessed are you upon the throne
    of your kingdom
  and to be extolled and highly
    exalted for ever.
34 Blessed are you in the
    firmament of heaven
  and to be sung and glorified
    for ever.
35 Bless the Lord, all works of the Lord,
  sing praise to him and highly
    exalt him for ever.
36 Bless the Lord, you heavens,
  sing praise to him and highly
    exalt him for ever.
37 Bless the Lord, you angels of the Lord,
  sing praise to him and highly
    exalt him for ever.
38 Bless the Lord, all waters
    above the heaven,
  sing praise to him and highly
    exalt him for ever.
39 Bless the Lord, all powers,
  sing praise to him and highly
    exalt him for ever.
40 Bless the Lord, sun and moon,
  sing praise to him and highly
    exalt him for ever.
41 Bless the Lord, stars of heaven,
  sing praise to him and highly
    exalt him for ever.
42 Bless the Lord, all rain and dew,
  sing praise to him and highly
    exalt him for ever.
43 Bless the Lord, all winds,
  sing praise to him and highly
    exalt him for ever.
44 Bless the Lord, fire and heat,
  sing praise to him and highly
    exalt him for ever.
45 Bless the Lord, winter cold
    and summer heat,
  sing praise to him and highly
    exalt him for ever.
46 Bless the Lord, dews and snows,
  sing praise to him and highly
    exalt him for ever.
47 Bless the Lord, nights and days,
  sing praise to him and highly
    exalt him for ever.
48 Bless the Lord, light and darkness,
  sing praise to him and highly
    exalt him for ever.
49 Bless the Lord, ice and cold,
  sing praise to him and highly
    exalt him for ever.
50 Bless the Lord, frosts and snows,
  sing praise to him and highly
    exalt him for ever.
51 Bless the Lord, lightnings and clouds,
  sing praise to him and highly
    exalt him for ever.
52 Let the earth bless the Lord;
  let it sing praise to him and
    highly exalt him for ever.

53 Bless the Lord, mountains and hills,
     sing praise to him and highly exalt him for ever.
54 Bless the Lord, all things that grow on the earth,
     sing praise to him and highly exalt him for ever.
55 Bless the Lord, seas and rivers,
     sing praise to him and highly exalt him for ever.
56 Bless the Lord, you springs,
     sing praise to him and highly exalt him for ever.
57 Bless the Lord, you whales and all creatures that move in the waters,
     sing praise to him and highly exalt him for ever.
58 Bless the Lord, all birds of the air,
     sing praise to him and highly exalt him for ever.
59 Bless the Lord, all beasts and cattle,
     sing praise to him and highly exalt him for ever.
60 Bless the Lord, you sons of men,
     sing praise to him and highly exalt him for ever.
61 Bless the Lord, O Israel,
     sing praise to him and highly exalt him for ever.
62 Bless the Lord, you priests,
     sing praise to him and highly exalt him for ever.
63 Bless the Lord, you servants,
     sing praise to him and highly exalt him for ever.
64 Bless the Lord, spirits and souls of the righteous,
     sing praise to him and highly exalt him for ever.
65 Bless the Lord, you who are holy and humble in heart,
     sing praise to him and highly exalt him for ever.
66 Bless the Lord, Hananiah, Azariah, and Mishael,
     sing praise to him and highly exalt him for ever;
   for he has rescued us from Hades and saved us from the hand of death
     and delivered us from the midst of the burning fiery furnace;
   from the midst of the fire he has delivered us.
67 Give thanks to the Lord, for he is good, for his mercy is for ever.
68 Bless him, all who worship the Lord, the God of gods,
     sing praise to him and give thanks to him,
   for his mercy is for ever."

SUSANNA

SUSANNA'S BEAUTY ATTRACTS TWO ELDERS

¹There was a man living in Babylon whose name was Joakim. ²And he took a wife named Susanna daughter of Hilkiah, a very beautiful woman and one who feared the Lord. ³Her parents were righteous and had taught their daughter according to the law of Moses. ⁴Joakim was very rich and had a spacious garden adjoining his house; and the Jews used to come to him because he was the most honoured of them all.

⁵In that year two elders from the people were appointed as judges. Concerning them the Lord had said: "Iniquity came forth from Babylon, from elders who were judges, who were supposed to govern the people." ⁶These men were frequently at Joakim's house, and all who had lawsuits came to them.

⁷When the people departed at noon, Susanna would go into her husband's garden to walk. ⁸The two elders used to see her every day, going in and walking about, and they began to desire her. ⁹And they perverted their minds and turned away their eyes from looking to heaven or remembering righteous judgements. ¹⁰Both were overwhelmed with passion for her, but they did not tell each other of their distress, ¹¹for they were ashamed to disclose their lustful desire to possess her. ¹²And they watched eagerly, day after day, to see her.

¹³They said to each other, "Let us go home, for it is mealtime." And when they went out, they parted from each other. ¹⁴But turning back, they met again; and when each pressed the other for the reason, they confessed their lust. And then together they arranged for a time when they could find her alone.

THE ELDERS ATTEMPT TO SEDUCE SUSANNA

¹⁵Once, while they were watching for an opportune day, she went in as before with only two maids and wished to bathe in the garden, for it was very hot. ¹⁶And no one was there except the two elders, who had hid themselves and were watching her. ¹⁷She said to her maids, "Bring me oil and ointments and shut the garden doors so that I may bathe." ¹⁸They did as she said, shut the garden doors, and went out by the side doors to bring what they had been commanded; and they did not see the elders, because they were hidden.

¹⁹When the maids had gone out, the two elders rose and ran to her and said: ²⁰"Look, the garden doors are shut, no one sees us, and we lust for you; so give your consent and be with us. ²¹If you refuse, we will testify against you that a young man was with you, and this was why you sent your maids away from you."

²²Susanna sighed deeply and said, "I am hemmed in on every side. For if I do this thing, it is death for me; and if I do not, I shall not escape your hands. ²³I choose not to do it and to fall into your hands, rather than to sin in the sight of the Lord."

²⁴Then Susanna cried out with a loud voice, and the two elders shouted against her. ²⁵And one of them ran and opened the garden doors. ²⁶When the household servants heard the shouting in the garden, they rushed in at the side door to see what had happened to her. ²⁷And when the elders told their tale, the servants were greatly ashamed, for nothing like this had ever been said about Susanna.

THE ELDERS TESTIFY AGAINST SUSANNA

²⁸The next day, when the people gathered to her husband Joakim, the two elders came, full of their wicked plot to have Susanna put to death. They said before the people, ²⁹"Send for Susanna daughter of Hilkiah, who is the wife of Joakim." So they sent for her. ³⁰And she came, with her parents, her children, and all her kindred.

³¹Now Susanna was a woman of great refinement and beautiful in appearance. ³²As she was veiled, the wicked men ordered her to be unveiled, that they might feast upon her beauty. ³³But her family and friends and all who saw her wept.

³⁴Then the two elders stood up in the midst of the people and laid their hands upon her

head. ³⁵And she, weeping, looked up towards heaven, for her heart trusted in the Lord. ³⁶The elders said, "As we were walking in the garden alone, this woman came in with two maids, shut the garden doors, and dismissed the maids. ³⁷Then a young man, who had been hidden, came to her and lay with her. ³⁸We were in a corner of the garden, and when we saw this wickedness we ran to them. ³⁹We saw them embracing, but we could not hold the man, for he was too strong for us, and he opened the doors and dashed out. ⁴⁰So we seized this woman and asked her who the young man was, ⁴¹but she would not tell us. These things we testify."

The assembly believed them, because they were elders of the people and judges; and they condemned her to death.

⁴²Then Susanna cried out with a loud voice and said, "O eternal God, who does discern what is secret, who is aware of all things before they come to be, ⁴³you know that these men have borne false witness against me. And now I am to die! Yet I have done none of the things that they have wickedly invented against me!"

⁴⁴The Lord heard her cry. ⁴⁵And as she was being led away to be put to death, God aroused the holy spirit of a young lad named Daniel; ⁴⁶and he cried with a loud voice, "I am innocent of the blood of this woman."

DANIEL RESCUES SUSANNA

⁴⁷All the people turned to him and said, "What is this that you have said?" ⁴⁸Taking his stand in the midst of them, he said, "Are you such fools, you sons of Israel? Have you condemned a daughter of Israel without examination and without learning the facts? ⁴⁹Return to the place of judgement. For these men have borne false witness against her."

⁵⁰Then all the people returned in haste. And the elders said to him, "Come, sit among us and inform us, for God has given you that right." ⁵¹And Daniel said to them, "Separate them far from each other, and I will examine them."

⁵²When they were separated from each other, he summoned one of them and said to him, "You old relic of wicked days, your sins have now come home, which you have committed in the past, ⁵³pronouncing unjust judgements, condemning the innocent, and letting the guilty go free, though the Lord said, 'Do not put to death an innocent and righteous person.' ⁵⁴Now then, if you really saw her, tell me this: Under what tree did you see them being intimate with each other?" He answered, "Under a mastic tree." ⁵⁵And Daniel said, "Very well! You have lied against your own head, for the angel of God has received the sentence from God and will immediately cut^a you in two."

⁵⁶Then he put him aside and commanded them to bring the other. And he said to him, "You offspring of Canaan and not of Judah, beauty has deceived you and lust has perverted your heart. ⁵⁷This is how you both have been dealing with the daughters of Israel, and they were intimate with you through fear; but a daughter of Judah would not endure your wickedness. ⁵⁸Now then, tell me: Under what tree did you catch them being intimate with each other?" He answered, "Under an evergreen oak." ⁵⁹And Daniel said to him, "Very well! You also have lied against your own head, for the angel of God is waiting with his sword to saw^b you in two, that he may destroy you both."

⁶⁰Then all the assembly shouted loudly and blessed God, who saves those who hope in him. ⁶¹And they rose against the two elders, for out of their own mouths Daniel had convicted them of bearing false witness; and they did to them as they had wickedly planned to do to their neighbour; ⁶²acting in accordance with the law of Moses, they put them to death. Thus innocent blood was saved that day.

⁶³And Hilkiah and his wife praised God for their daughter Susanna, and so did Joakim her husband and all her kindred, because nothing shameful was found in her. ⁶⁴And from that day onward Daniel had a great reputation among the people.

---

^{a}The Greek words for *mastic tree* and *cut* sound alike ^{b}The Greek words for *evergreen oak* and *saw* sound alike

BEL AND THE DRAGON

DANIEL AND THE PRIESTS OF BEL

¹When King Astyages was laid with his ancestors, Cyrus the Persian received his kingdom. ²And Daniel was a companion of the king and was the most honoured of his friends.

³Now the Babylonians had an idol called Bel, and every day they spent on it twelve bushels of fine flour and forty sheep and fifty gallons of wine. ⁴The king revered it and went every day to worship it. But Daniel kept worshipping his own God.

And the king said to him, "Why do you not worship Bel?" ⁵He answered, "Because I do not revere man-made idols, but the living God, who created heaven and earth and has dominion over all flesh."

⁶The king said to him, "Do you not think that Bel is a living God? Do you not see how much he eats and drinks every day?" ⁷Then Daniel laughed and said, "Do not be deceived, O king, for this is but clay inside and brass outside, and it never ate or drank anything."

⁸Then the king was angry, and he called his priests and said to them, "If you do not tell me who is eating these provisions, you shall die. ⁹But if you prove that Bel is eating them, Daniel shall die, because he blasphemed against Bel." And Daniel said to the king, "Let it be done as you have said."

¹⁰Now there were seventy priests of Bel, besides their wives and children. And the king went with Daniel into the temple of Bel. ¹¹And the priests of Bel said, "Behold, we are going outside; you yourself, O king, shall set forth the food and mix and place the wine and shut the door and seal it with your signet. ¹²And when you return in the morning, if you do not find that Bel has eaten it all, we will die; or else Daniel will, who is telling lies about us." ¹³They were unconcerned, for beneath the table they had made a hidden entrance, through which they used to go in regularly and consume the provisions.ᵃ

¹⁴When they had gone out, the king set forth the food for Bel. Then Daniel ordered his servants to bring ashes, and they sifted them throughout the whole temple in the presence of the king alone. Then they went out, shut the door, and sealed it with the king's signet and departed. ¹⁵In the night the priests came with their wives and children, as they were accustomed to do, and ate and drank everything.

¹⁶Early in the morning the king rose and came, and Daniel with him. ¹⁷And the kingᵇ said, "Are the seals unbroken, Daniel?" He answered, "They are unbroken, O king."

¹⁸As soon as the doors were opened, the king looked at the table and shouted in a loud voice, "You are great, O Bel; and with you there is no deceit, none at all."

¹⁹Then Daniel laughed and restrained the king from going in and said, "Look at the floor and notice whose footsteps these are." ²⁰The king said, "I see the footsteps of men and women and children."

²¹Then the king was enraged, and he seized the priests and their wives and children; and they showed him the secret doors through which they were accustomed to enter and devour what was on the table. ²²Therefore the king put them to death and gave Bel over to Daniel, who destroyed it and its temple.

DANIEL KILLS THE DRAGON

²³There was also a great dragon, which the Babylonians revered. ²⁴And the king said to Daniel, "You cannot deny that this is a living god; so worship him." ²⁵Daniel said, "I will worship the Lord my God, for he is the living God. ²⁶But if you, O king, will give me permission, I will slay the dragon without sword or club." The king said, "I give you permission."

ᵃGreek consume them ᵇGreek And he

²⁷Then Daniel took pitch, fat, and hair and boiled them together and made cakes, which he fed to the dragon. The dragon ate them and burst open. And Daniel said, "See what you have been worshipping!"

²⁸When the Babylonians heard it, they were very indignant and conspired against the king, saying, "The king has become a Jew; he has destroyed Bel and slain the dragon and slaughtered the priests." ²⁹Going to the king, they said, "Hand Daniel over to us or else we will kill you and your household." ³⁰The king saw that they were pressing him hard, and under compulsion he handed Daniel over to them.

DANIEL IN THE LIONS' DEN

³¹They threw Daniel into the lions' den, and he was there for six days. ³²There were seven lions in the den, and every day they had been given two human bodies and two sheep; but these were not given to them now, so that they might devour Daniel.

³³Now the prophet Habakkuk was in Judea. He had boiled pottage and had broken bread into a bowl and was going into the field to take it to the reapers. ³⁴But the angel of the Lord said to Habakkuk, "Take the dinner that you have to Babylon, to Daniel, in the lions' den." ³⁵Habakkuk said, "Sir, I have never seen Babylon, and I know nothing about the den." ³⁶Then the angel of the Lord took him by the crown of his head and lifted him by his hair and set him down in Babylon, right over the den, with the rushing sound of the wind itself.

³⁷Then Habakkuk shouted, "Daniel, Daniel! Take the dinner that God has sent you." ³⁸And Daniel said, "You have remembered me, O God, and have not forsaken those who love you." ³⁹So Daniel arose and ate. And the angel of God immediately returned Habakkuk to his own place.

⁴⁰On the seventh day the king came to mourn for Daniel. When he came to the den he looked in, and there sat Daniel. ⁴¹And the king shouted with a loud voice, "You are great, O Lord God of Daniel, and there is no other besides you." ⁴²And he pulled Daniel[a] out and threw into the den those who had attempted his destruction, and they were devoured immediately before his eyes.

---

[a] Greek *him*

1 MACCABEES

ALEXANDER THE GREAT

1 [a] After Alexander son of Philip the Macedonian, who came from the land of Kittim, had defeated[b] King Darius of the Persians and the Medes, he succeeded him as king. (He had previously become king of Greece.) [2] He fought many battles, conquered strongholds, and put to death the kings of the earth. [3] He advanced to the ends of the earth and plundered many nations. When the earth became quiet before him, he was exalted, and his heart was lifted up. [4] He gathered a very strong army and ruled over countries, nations, and princes, and they became tributary to him.

[5] After this he fell sick and perceived that he was dying. [6] So he summoned his most honoured officers, who had been brought up with him from youth, and divided his kingdom among them while he was still alive. [7] And after Alexander had reigned for twelve years, he died.

[8] Then his officers seized control, each in his own place. [9] They all put on crowns after his death, and so did their sons after them for many years; and they caused many evils on the earth.

ANTIOCHUS EPIPHANES AND RENEGADE JEWS

[10] From them came forth a sinful root, Antiochus Epiphanes son of King Antiochus; he had been a hostage in Rome. He began to reign in the 137th year[c] of the kingdom of the Greeks.

[11] In those days lawless men came forth from Israel and misled many, saying, "Let us go and make a covenant with the Gentiles round about us, for since we separated from them many evils have come upon us." [12] This proposal pleased them, [13] and some of the people eagerly went to the king. He authorized them to observe the ordinances of the Gentiles. [14] So they built a gymnasium in Jerusalem, according to Gentile custom, [15] and removed the marks of circumcision and abandoned the holy covenant. They joined with the Gentiles and sold themselves to do evil.

ANTIOCHUS IN EGYPT

[16] When Antiochus saw that his kingdom was established, he determined to become king of the land of Egypt, that he might reign over both kingdoms. [17] So he invaded Egypt with a strong force, with chariots and elephants and with a large fleet. [18] He engaged King Ptolemy of Egypt in battle, and Ptolemy turned and fled before him, and many were wounded and fell. [19] And they captured the fortified cities in the land of Egypt, and he plundered the land of Egypt.

PERSECUTION OF THE JEWS

[20] After subduing Egypt, Antiochus returned in the 143rd year.[d] He went up against Israel and came to Jerusalem with a strong force. [21] He arrogantly entered the sanctuary and took the golden altar, the lampstand for the light, and all its utensils. [22] He took also the table for the bread of the Presence, the cups for drink offerings, the bowls, the golden censers, the curtain, the crowns, and the gold decoration on the front of the temple; he stripped it all off. [23] He took the silver and the gold and the costly vessels; he took also the hidden treasures that he found. [24] Taking them all, he departed to his own land.

He committed deeds of murder
    and spoke with great arrogance.
[25] Israel mourned deeply in
    every community,
[26] rulers and elders groaned,
maidens and young men
    became faint,
the beauty of the women faded.
[27] Every bridegroom took up the lament;
she who sat in the bridal
    chamber was mourning.

---

[a] 1 Maccabees is one of the seven deuterocanonical books that do not exist in their entirety in Hebrew or Aramaic, but which were included in the Greek Septuagint, and were likewise included in the Latin Vulgate version of the Bible translated by Jerome in the late fourth century AD. See further, *Introduction*, pages xiii to xiv.
[b] Greek *Kittim, and he defeated* [c] 175 BC [d] 169 BC

28 Even the land shook for its inhabitants,
and all the house of Jacob was
clothed with shame.

OCCUPATION OF JERUSALEM

²⁹Two years later the king sent to the cities of Judah a chief collector of tribute, and he came to Jerusalem with a large force. ³⁰Deceitfully he spoke peaceable words to them, and they believed him; but he suddenly fell upon the city, dealt it a severe blow, and destroyed many people of Israel. ³¹He plundered the city, burned it with fire, and tore down its houses and its surrounding walls. ³²And they took captive the women and children and took possession of the cattle. ³³Then they fortified the city of David with a great strong wall and strong towers, and it became their citadel. ³⁴And they stationed there a sinful people, lawless men. These strengthened their position; ³⁵they stored up arms and food, and collecting the spoils of Jerusalem they stored them there and became a great snare.

36 It became an ambush against
the sanctuary,
an evil adversary of Israel
continually.
37 On every side of the sanctuary
they shed innocent blood;
they even defiled the sanctuary.
38 Because of them the residents
of Jerusalem fled;
she became a dwelling of strangers;
she became strange to her offspring,
and her children forsook her.
39 Her sanctuary became
desolate as a desert;
her feasts were turned
into mourning,
her Sabbaths into a reproach,
her honour into contempt.
40 Her dishonour now grew as
great as her glory;
her exaltation was turned
into mourning.

INSTALLATION OF GENTILE CULTS

⁴¹Then the king wrote to his whole kingdom that all should be one people ⁴²and that each should give up his customs. ⁴³All the Gentiles accepted the command of the king. Many even from Israel gladly adopted his religion; they sacrificed to idols and profaned the Sabbath. ⁴⁴And the king sent letters by messengers to Jerusalem and the cities of Judah; he directed them to follow customs strange to the land, ⁴⁵to forbid whole burnt offerings and sacrifice and drink offering in the sanctuary, to profane Sabbaths and feasts, ⁴⁶to defile the sanctuary and the priests, ⁴⁷to build altars and sacred precincts and shrines for idols, to sacrifice swine and unclean animals, ⁴⁸and to leave their sons uncircumcised. They were to make themselves abominable by everything unclean and profane, ⁴⁹so that they should forget the law and change all the ordinances. ⁵⁰"And whoever does not obey the command of the king shall die."

⁵¹In such words he wrote to his whole kingdom. And he appointed inspectors over all the people and commanded the cities of Judah to offer sacrifice, city by city. ⁵²Many of the people, everyone who forsook the law, joined them, and they did evil in the land; ⁵³they drove Israel into hiding in every place of refuge they had.

⁵⁴Now on the fifteenth day of Chislev, in the 145th year,[a] they erected a desolating sacrilege upon the altar of whole burnt offering. They also built altars in the surrounding cities of Judah ⁵⁵and burned incense at the doors of the houses and in the streets. ⁵⁶The books of the law that they found they tore to pieces and burned with fire. ⁵⁷Where the book of the covenant was found in the possession of anyone or if anyone adhered to the law, the decree of the king condemned him to death. ⁵⁸They kept using violence against Israel, against those found month after month in the cities. ⁵⁹And on the twenty-fifth day of the month they offered sacrifice on the altar that was upon the altar of whole burnt offering. ⁶⁰According to the decree, they put to death the women who had their children circumcised ⁶¹and their families and those who circumcised them; and they hung the infants from their mothers' necks.

⁶²But many in Israel stood firm and were resolved in their hearts not to eat unclean food. ⁶³They chose to die rather than to be defiled by food or to profane the holy covenant; and they did die. ⁶⁴And very great wrath came upon Israel.

MATTATHIAS AND HIS SONS

2 In those days Mattathias son of John, son of Simeon, a priest of the sons of Joarib, moved from Jerusalem and settled in Modein. ²He had five sons, John

---
[a] 167 BC

1 MACCABEES 2

surnamed Gaddi, ³Simon called Thassi, ⁴Judas called Maccabeus, ⁵Eleazar called Avaran, and Jonathan called Apphus. ⁶He saw the blasphemies being committed in Judah and Jerusalem ⁷and said:

"Alas! Why was I born to see this,
   the ruin of my people, the
      ruin of the holy city,
   and they lived there when it was
      given over to the enemy,
   the sanctuary given over to aliens?
⁸   Her temple has become like a
      man without honour;[a]
⁹   her glorious vessels have been
      carried into captivity.
   Her infants have been killed
      in her streets,
   her youths by the sword of the foe.
¹⁰   What nation has not possessed
      her in its kingdom
   and has not seized her spoils?
¹¹   All her adornment has
      been taken away;
   no longer free, she has
      become a slave.
¹²   And behold, our holy place, our beauty,
      and our glory have been laid waste;
   the Gentiles have profaned them.
¹³   Why should we live any longer?"

¹⁴And Mattathias and his sons rent their clothes, put on sackcloth, and mourned greatly.

PAGAN WORSHIP REFUSED

¹⁵Then the king's officers who were enforcing the apostasy came to the city of Modein to make them offer sacrifice. ¹⁶Many from Israel came to them; and Mattathias and his sons were assembled. ¹⁷Then the king's officers spoke to Mattathias as follows: "You are a leader, honoured and great in this city, and supported by sons and brothers. ¹⁸Now be the first to come and do what the king commands, as all the Gentiles and the men of Judah and those who are left in Jerusalem have done. Then you and your sons will be numbered among the friends of the king, and you and your sons will be honoured with silver and gold and many gifts."

¹⁹But Mattathias answered and said in a loud voice: "Even if all the nations which live under the rule of the king obey him and have chosen to do his commandments, departing each one from the religion of his fathers, ²⁰yet I and my sons and my brothers will live by the covenant of our fathers. ²¹Far be it from us to desert the law and the ordinances. ²²We will not obey the king's words by turning aside from our religion to the right hand or to the left."

²³When he had finished speaking these words, a Jew came forward in the sight of all to offer sacrifice upon the altar in Modein, according to the king's command. ²⁴When Mattathias saw it, he burned with zeal and his heart was stirred. He gave vent to righteous anger; he ran and slaughtered him upon the altar. ²⁵At the same time he killed the king's officer who was forcing them to sacrifice, and he tore down the altar. ²⁶Thus he burned with zeal for the law, as Phinehas did against Zimri son of Salom.

²⁷Then Mattathias cried out in the city with a loud voice, saying: "Let everyone who is zealous for the law and supports the covenant come out with me!" ²⁸And he and his sons fled to the hills and left all that they had in the city.

²⁹Then many who were seeking righteousness and justice went down to the wilderness to dwell there, ³⁰they, their sons, their wives, and their cattle, because evils pressed heavily upon them. ³¹And it was reported to the king's officers and to the troops in Jerusalem the city of David that men who had rejected the king's command had gone down to the hiding places in the wilderness. ³²Many pursued them, and overtaking them, they encamped opposite them and prepared for battle against them on the Sabbath day. ³³And they said to them, "Enough of this! Come out and do what the king commands, and you will live." ³⁴But they said, "We will not come out, nor will we do what the king commands and so profane the Sabbath day." ³⁵Then the enemy[b] hastened to attack them. ³⁶But they did not answer them or hurl a stone at them or block up their hiding places, ³⁷for they said, "Let us all die in our innocence; heaven and earth testify for us that you are killing us unjustly." ³⁸So they attacked them on the Sabbath, and they died, with their wives and children and cattle, to the number of 1,000 persons.

³⁹When Mattathias and his friends learned of it, they mourned for them deeply. ⁴⁰And each said to his neighbour: "If we all do as our brothers have done and refuse to fight with the Gentiles for our lives and our ordinances,

---

[a]The meaning of the Greek is uncertain [b]Greek Then they

they will quickly destroy us from the earth." ⁴¹So they made this decision that day: "Let us fight against every man who comes to attack us on the Sabbath day; let us not all die as our brothers died in their hiding places."

COUNTERATTACK

⁴²Then there united with them a company of Hasideans, mighty warriors of Israel, everyone who offered himself willingly for the law. ⁴³And all who became fugitives to escape their troubles joined them and reinforced them. ⁴⁴They organized an army and struck down sinners in their anger and lawless men in their wrath; the survivors fled to the Gentiles for safety. ⁴⁵And Mattathias and his friends went about and tore down the altars; ⁴⁶they forcibly circumcised all the uncircumcised boys that they found within the borders of Israel. ⁴⁷They hunted down the arrogant men, and the work prospered in their hands. ⁴⁸They rescued the law out of the hands of the Gentiles and kings, and they never let the sinner gain the upper hand.

LAST WORDS OF MATTATHIAS

⁴⁹Now the days drew near for Mattathias to die, and he said to his sons: "Arrogance and reproach have now become strong; it is a time of ruin and furious anger. ⁵⁰Now, my children, show zeal for the law and give your lives for the covenant of our fathers. ⁵¹"Remember the deeds of the fathers, which they did in their generations; and receive great honour and an everlasting name. ⁵²Was not Abraham found faithful when tested, and it was reckoned to him as righteousness? ⁵³Joseph in the time of his distress kept the commandment and became lord of Egypt. ⁵⁴Phinehas our father, because he was deeply zealous, received the covenant of everlasting priesthood. ⁵⁵Joshua, because he fulfilled the command, became a judge in Israel. ⁵⁶Caleb, because he testified in the assembly, received an inheritance in the land. ⁵⁷David, because he was merciful, inherited the throne of the kingdom for ever. ⁵⁸Elijah, because of great zeal for the law, was taken up into heaven. ⁵⁹Hananiah, Azariah, and Mishael believed and were saved from the flame. ⁶⁰Daniel, because of his innocence, was delivered from the mouth of the lions.

⁶¹"And so observe, from generation to generation, that none who hope in him will lack strength. ⁶²Do not fear the words of a sinner, for his splendour will turn into dung and worms. ⁶³Today he will be exalted, but tomorrow he will not be found, because he has returned to the dust, and his plans will perish. ⁶⁴My children, be courageous and grow strong in the law, for by it you will gain honour.

⁶⁵"Now behold, I know that Simeon your brother is wise in counsel; always listen to him; he shall be your father. ⁶⁶Judas Maccabeus has been a mighty warrior from his youth; he shall command the army for you and fight the battle against^a the peoples. ⁶⁷You shall rally about you all who observe the law and avenge the wrong done to your people. ⁶⁸Pay back the Gentiles in full and heed what the law commands."

⁶⁹Then he blessed them and was gathered to his fathers. ⁷⁰He died in the 146th year^b and was buried in the tomb of his fathers at Modein. And all Israel mourned for him with great lamentation.

EARLY VICTORIES OF JUDAS

3 Then Judas his son, who was called Maccabeus, took command in his place. ²All his brothers and all who had joined his father helped him; they gladly fought for Israel.

3   He extended the glory of his people.
      Like a giant he put on his
         breastplate;
      he girded on his armour of war
         and waged battles,
      protecting the host by his sword.
4   He was like a lion in his deeds,
      like a lion's cub roaring for prey.
5   He searched out and pursued
         the lawless;
      he burned those who
         troubled his people.
6   Lawless men shrank back
         for fear of him;
      all the evildoers were confounded;
      and deliverance prospered
         by his hand.
7   He embittered many kings,
      but he made Jacob glad by his deeds,
      and his memory is blessed for ever.
8   He went through the cities of Judah;
      he destroyed the ungodly
         out of the land;^{c}
      thus he turned away wrath
         from Israel.

---
^{a}Or *of* ^{b}166 BC ^{c}Greek *out of it*

⁹ He was renowned to the ends of the earth;
he gathered in those who were perishing.

¹⁰But Apollonius gathered together Gentiles and a large force from Samaria to fight against Israel. ¹¹When Judas learned of it, he went out to meet him, and he defeated and killed him. Many were wounded and fell, and the rest fled. ¹²Then they seized their spoils; and Judas took the sword of Apollonius and used it in battle the rest of his life.

¹³Now when Seron, the commander of the Syrian army, heard that Judas had gathered a large company, including a body of faithful men who stayed with him and went out to battle, ¹⁴he said, "I will make a name for myself and win honour in the kingdom. I will make war on Judas and his companions, who scorn the king's command." ¹⁵And again a strong army of ungodly men went up with him to help him, to take vengeance on the sons of Israel.

¹⁶When he approached the ascent of Beth-horon, Judas went out to meet him with a small company. ¹⁷But when they saw the army coming to meet them, they said to Judas, "How can we, few as we are, fight against so great and strong a multitude? And we are faint, for we have eaten nothing today." ¹⁸Judas replied, "It is easy for many to be hemmed in by few, for in the sight of heaven there is no difference between saving by many or by few. ¹⁹It is not on the size of the army that victory in battle depends, but strength comes from heaven. ²⁰They come against us in great pride and lawlessness to destroy us and our wives and our children and to despoil us; ²¹but we fight for our lives and our laws. ²²He himself will crush them before us; as for you, do not be afraid of them."

²³When he finished speaking, he rushed suddenly against Seron and his army, and they were crushed before him. ²⁴They pursued him down the descent of Beth-horon to the plain; 800 of them fell, and the rest fled into the land of the Philistines. ²⁵Then Judas and his brothers began to be feared, and terror fell upon the Gentiles round about them. ²⁶His fame reached the king, and the Gentiles talked of the battles of Judas.

POLICY OF ANTIOCHUS

²⁷When King Antiochus heard these reports, he was greatly angered; and he sent and gathered all the forces of his kingdom, a very strong army. ²⁸And he opened his coffers and gave a year's pay to his forces and ordered them to be ready for any need. ²⁹Then he saw that the money in the treasury was exhausted and that the revenues from the country were small because of the dissension and disaster that he had caused in the land by abolishing the laws that had existed from the earliest days. ³⁰He feared that he might not have such funds as he had before for his expenses and for the gifts that he used to give more lavishly than preceding kings. ³¹He was greatly perplexed in mind and determined to go to Persia and collect the revenues from those regions and raise a large fund.

³²He left Lysias, a distinguished man of royal lineage, in charge of the king's affairs from the river Euphrates to the borders of Egypt. ³³Lysias was also to take care of Antiochus his son until he returned. ³⁴And he turned over to Lysias[a] half of his troops and the elephants and gave him orders about all that he wanted done. As for the residents of Judea and Jerusalem, ³⁵Lysias was to send a force against them to wipe out and destroy the strength of Israel and the remnant of Jerusalem; he was to banish the memory of them from the place, ³⁶settle aliens in all their territory, and distribute their land. ³⁷Then the king took the remaining half of his troops and departed from Antioch his capital in the 147th year.[b] He crossed the Euphrates river and went through the upper provinces.

PREPARATIONS FOR BATTLE

³⁸Lysias chose Ptolemy son of Dorymenes and Nicanor and Gorgias, mighty men among the friends of the king, ³⁹and sent with them 40,000 and 7,000 cavalry to go into the land of Judah and destroy it, as the king had commanded. ⁴⁰So they departed with their entire force, and when they arrived they encamped near Emmaus in the plain. ⁴¹When the traders of the region heard what was said of them, they took silver and gold in immense amounts and fetters[c] and went to the camp to get the sons of Israel for slaves. And forces from Syria and the land of the Philistines joined with them.

⁴²Now Judas and his brothers saw that misfortunes had increased and that the forces were encamped in their territory. They also

---

[a] Greek *him*   [b] 165 BC   [c] Syriac; Greek *slaves*

learned what the king had commanded to do to the people to cause their final destruction. ⁴³But they said to one another, "Let us repair the destruction of our people and fight for our people and the sanctuary." ⁴⁴And the congregation assembled to be ready for battle and to pray and ask for mercy and compassion.

⁴⁵ Jerusalem was uninhabited
like a wilderness;
not one of her children
went in or out.
The sanctuary was trampled down,
and the sons of aliens
held the citadel;
it was a lodging place for
the Gentiles.
Joy was taken from Jacob;
the flute and the harp ceased to play.

⁴⁶So they assembled and went to Mizpah, opposite Jerusalem, because Israel formerly had a place of prayer in Mizpah. ⁴⁷They fasted that day, put on sackcloth and sprinkled ashes on their heads, and rent their clothes. ⁴⁸And they opened the book of the law to enquire into those matters about which the Gentiles were consulting the images of their idols. ⁴⁹They also brought the garments of the priesthood and the firstfruits and the tithes, and they stirred up the Nazirites who had completed their days; ⁵⁰and they cried aloud to heaven, saying:

"What shall we do with these?
Where shall we take them?
⁵¹ Your sanctuary is trampled
down and profaned,
and your priests mourn
in humiliation.
⁵² And behold, the Gentiles
are assembled against
us to destroy us;
you know what they plot against us.
⁵³ How will we be able to
withstand them,
if you do not help us?"

⁵⁴Then they sounded the trumpets and gave a loud shout. ⁵⁵After this Judas appointed leaders of the people, in charge of thousands and hundreds and fifties and tens. ⁵⁶And he said to those who were building houses or were betrothed or were planting vineyards or were faint-hearted that each should return to his home, according to the law. ⁵⁷Then the army marched out and encamped to the south of Emmaus.

⁵⁸And Judas said, "Gird yourselves and be valiant. Be ready early in the morning to fight with these Gentiles who have assembled against us to destroy us and our sanctuary. ⁵⁹It is better for us to die in battle than to see the misfortunes of our nation and of the sanctuary. ⁶⁰But as his will in heaven may be, so he will do."

BATTLE AT EMMAUS

4 Now Gorgias took 5,000 infantry and 1,000 picked cavalry, and this division moved out by night ²to fall upon the camp of the Jews and attack them suddenly. Men from the citadel were his guides. ³But Judas heard of it, and he and his mighty men moved out to attack the king's force in Emmaus ⁴while the division was still absent from the camp. ⁵When Gorgias entered the camp of Judas by night, he found no one there, so he looked for them in the hills, because he said, "These men are fleeing from us."

⁶At daybreak Judas appeared in the plain with 3,000 men, but they did not have armour[a] and swords such as they desired. ⁷And they saw the camp of the Gentiles, strong and fortified, with cavalry round about it; and these men were trained in war. ⁸But Judas said to the men who were with him, "Do not fear their numbers or be afraid when they charge. ⁹Remember how our fathers were saved at the Red Sea, when Pharaoh with his forces pursued them. ¹⁰And now let us cry to heaven, to see whether he will favour us and remember his covenant with our fathers and crush this army before us today. ¹¹Then all the Gentiles will know that there is one who redeems and saves Israel."

¹²When the foreigners looked up and saw them coming against them, ¹³they went forth from their camp to battle. Then the men with Judas blew their trumpets ¹⁴and engaged in battle. The Gentiles were crushed and fled into the plain, ¹⁵and all those in the rear fell by the sword. They pursued them to Gazara and to the plains of Idumea and to Azotus and Jamnia; and 3,000 of them fell. ¹⁶Then Judas and his force turned back from pursuing them, ¹⁷and he said to the people,

---
[a] Greek *coverings*

1 MACCABEES 4

"Do not be greedy for plunder, for there is a battle before us; **18**Gorgias and his force are near us in the hills. But stand now against our enemies and fight them and afterwards seize the plunder boldly."

19Just as Judas was finishing this speech, a detachment was seen, peering out of the hills. **20**They saw that their army[a] had been put to flight and that the Jews[b] were burning the camp, for the smoke that was seen showed what had happened. **21**When they perceived this they were greatly frightened and when they also saw the army of Judas drawn up in the plain for battle, **22**they all fled into the land of the Philistines. **23**Then Judas returned to plunder the camp, and they seized much gold and silver and cloth dyed blue and sea purple and great riches. **24**On their return they sang hymns and praises to heaven, for he is good, for his mercy endures for ever. **25**Thus Israel had a great deliverance that day.

FIRST CAMPAIGN OF LYSIAS

26Those of the foreigners who escaped went and reported to Lysias all that had happened. **27**When he heard it, he was perplexed and discouraged, for things had not happened to Israel as he had intended, nor had they turned out as the king had commanded him. **28**But the next year he mustered 60,000 picked infantrymen and 5,000 cavalry to subdue them. **29**They came into Idumea and encamped at Beth-zur, and Judas met them with 10,000 men.

30When he saw that the army was strong, he prayed, saying, "Blessed are you, O Saviour of Israel, who crushed the attack of the mighty warrior by the hand of your servant David and gave the camp of the Philistines into the hands of Jonathan son of Saul and of the man who carried his armour. **31**So do you hem in this army by the hand of your people Israel, and let them be ashamed of their troops and their cavalry. **32**Fill them with cowardice; melt the boldness of their strength; let them tremble in their destruction. **33**Strike them down with the sword of those who love you, and let all who know your name praise you with hymns."

34Then both sides attacked, and there fell of the army of Lysias 5,000 men; they fell from before them. **35**And when Lysias saw the rout of his troops and observed the boldness that inspired those of Judas and how ready they were either to live or to die nobly, he departed to Antioch and enlisted mercenaries, to invade Judea when they were numerous again.

CLEANSING AND DEDICATION OF THE TEMPLE

36Then said Judas and his brothers, "Behold, our enemies are crushed; let us go up to cleanse the sanctuary and dedicate it." **37**So all the army assembled and they went up to Mount Zion. **38**And they saw the sanctuary desolate, the altar profaned, and the gates burned. In the courts they saw bushes sprung up as in a thicket or as on one of the mountains. They saw also the chambers of the priests in ruins. **39**Then they rent their clothes and mourned with great lamentation and sprinkled themselves with ashes. **40**They fell face down on the ground and sounded the signal on the trumpets and cried out to heaven. **41**Then Judas detailed men to fight against those in the citadel until he had cleansed the sanctuary.

42He chose blameless priests devoted to the law, **43**and they cleansed the sanctuary and removed the defiled stones to an unclean place. **44**They deliberated what to do about the altar of whole burnt offering, which had been profaned. **45**And they thought it best to tear it down, lest it bring reproach upon them, for the Gentiles had defiled it. So they tore down the altar **46**and stored the stones in a convenient place on the temple hill until there should come a prophet to tell what to do with them. **47**Then they took whole stones, as the law directs, and built a new altar like the former one. **48**They also rebuilt the sanctuary and the interior of the temple and consecrated the courts. **49**They made new holy vessels and brought the lampstand, the altar of incense, and the table into the temple. **50**Then they burned incense on the altar and lit the lamps on the lampstand, and these gave light in the temple. **51**They placed the bread on the table and hung up the curtains. Thus they finished all the work they had undertaken.

52Early in the morning on the twenty-fifth day of the ninth month, which is the month of Chislev, in the 148th year,[c] **53**they rose and offered sacrifice, as the law directs, on the new altar of whole burnt offering that they had built. **54**At the very season and on the very day that the Gentiles had profaned it, it was

---

[a]Greek *saw that they* [b]Greek *and that they* [c]164 BC

dedicated with songs and harps and lutes and cymbals. ⁵⁵All the people fell on their faces and worshipped and blessed heaven, who had prospered them. ⁵⁶So they celebrated the dedication of the altar for eight days and offered whole burnt offerings with gladness; they offered a sacrifice of deliverance and praise. ⁵⁷They decorated the front of the temple with golden crowns and small shields; they restored the gates and the chambers for the priests and furnished them with doors. ⁵⁸There was very great gladness among the people, and the reproach of the Gentiles was removed.

⁵⁹Then Judas and his brothers and all the assembly of Israel determined that every year at that season the days of the dedication of the altar should be observed with gladness and joy for eight days, beginning with the twenty-fifth day of the month of Chislev.

⁶⁰At that time they fortified Mount Zion with high walls and strong towers round about, to keep the Gentiles from coming and trampling them down as they had done before. ⁶¹And he stationed a garrison there to hold it, and he fortified it to hold Beth-zur, so that the people might have a stronghold that faced Idumea.

WARS WITH NEIGHBOURING PEOPLES

5 When the Gentiles round about heard that the altar had been built and the sanctuary dedicated as it was before, they became very angry, ²and they determined to destroy the descendants of Jacob who lived among them. So they began to kill and destroy among the people. ³But Judas made war on the sons of Esau in Idumea, at Akrabattene, because they kept lying in wait for Israel. He dealt them a heavy blow and humbled them and despoiled them. ⁴He also remembered the wickedness of the sons of Baean, who were a trap and a snare to the people and ambushed them on the highways. ⁵They were shut up by him in their towers; and he encamped against them, vowed their complete destruction, and burned with fire its towers and all who were inside. ⁶Then he crossed over to attack the Ammonites, where he found a strong band and many people with Timothy as their leader. ⁷He engaged in many battles with them, and they were crushed before him; he struck them down. ⁸He also overtook Jazer and its villages; then he returned to Judea.

LIBERATION OF GALILEAN JEWS

⁹Now the Gentiles in Gilead gathered together against the Israelites who lived in their territory and planned to destroy them. But they fled to the stronghold of Dathema ¹⁰and sent to Judas and his brothers a letter that said, "The Gentiles around us have gathered together against us to destroy us. ¹¹They are preparing to come and capture the stronghold to which we have fled, and Timothy is leading their forces. ¹²Now then come and rescue us from their hands, for many of us have fallen, ¹³and all our brothers who were in the land of Tob have been killed; the enemy[a] have captured their wives and children and goods and have destroyed about 1,000 men there."

¹⁴While the letter was still being read, behold, other messengers, with their garments rent, came from Galilee and made a similar report; ¹⁵they said that against them had gathered together men of Ptolemais and Tyre and Sidon and all Galilee of the Gentiles[b] "to annihilate us". ¹⁶When Judas and the people heard these messages, a great assembly was called to determine what they should do for their brothers who were in distress and were being attacked by enemies.[c] ¹⁷Then Judas said to Simon his brother, "Choose your men and go and rescue your brothers in Galilee; I and Jonathan my brother will go to Gilead." ¹⁸But he left Joseph son of Zechariah and Azariah, a leader of the people, with the rest of the forces, in Judea for defence; ¹⁹and he gave them this command, "Take charge of this people, but do not engage in battle with the Gentiles until we return." ²⁰Then 3,000 men were assigned to Simon to go to Galilee, and 8,000 to Judas for Gilead.

²¹So Simon went to Galilee and fought many battles against the Gentiles, and the Gentiles were crushed before him. ²²He pursued them to the gate of Ptolemais, and as many as 3,000 of the Gentiles fell, and he despoiled them. ²³Then he took the Jews[d] of Galilee and Arbatta, with their wives and children and all they possessed, and led them to Judea with great rejoicing.

JUDAS AND JONATHAN IN GILEAD

²⁴Judas Maccabeus and Jonathan his brother crossed the Jordan and went three days' journey into the wilderness. ²⁵They encountered the Nabateans, who met them

---

[a] Greek *killed; they* [b] Greek *aliens* [c] Greek *them* [d] Greek *took those*

peaceably and told them all that had happened to their brothers in Gilead: [26]"Many of them have been shut up in Bozrah and Bosor, in Alema and Chaspho, Maked and Carnaim"— all these cities were strong and large — [27]"and some have been shut up in the other cities of Gilead; the enemy is[a] getting ready to attack the strongholds tomorrow and take and destroy all these people in one day."

[28]Then Judas and his army quickly turned back by the wilderness road to Bozrah; and he took the city and killed every male by the edge of the sword; then he seized all its spoils and burned it with fire. [29]He departed from there at night, and they went all the way to the stronghold of Dathema.[b] [30]At dawn they looked up, and behold, a large company, that could not be counted, carrying ladders and engines of war to capture the stronghold, and they were attacking them. [31]So Judas saw that the battle had begun and that the cry of the city went up to heaven with trumpets and loud shouts, [32]and he said to the men of his forces, "Fight today for your brothers!" [33]Then he came up behind them in three companies, who sounded their trumpets and cried aloud in prayer. [34]And when the army of Timothy realized that it was Maccabeus, they fled before him, and he dealt them a heavy blow. As many as 8,000 of them fell that day.

[35]Next he turned aside to Maapha[c] and fought against it and took it; and he killed every male in it, plundered it, and burned it with fire. [36]From there he marched on and took Chaspho, Maked, and Bosor and the other cities of Gilead.

[37]After these things Timothy gathered another army and encamped opposite Raphon, on the other side of the stream. [38]Judas sent men to spy out the camp, and they reported to him, "All the Gentiles round us have gathered to him; it is a very large force. [39]They also have hired Arabs to help them, and they are encamped across the stream, ready to come and fight against you." And Judas went to meet them.

[40]Now as Judas and his army drew near to the stream of water, Timothy said to the officers of his forces, "If he crosses over to us first, we will not be able to resist him, for he will surely defeat us. [41]But if he shows fear and camps on the other side of the river, we will cross over to him and defeat him." [42]When Judas approached the stream of water, he stationed the scribes of the people at the stream and gave them this command, "Permit no man to encamp, but make them all enter the battle." [43]Then he crossed over against them first, and the whole army followed him. All the Gentiles were defeated before him, and they threw away their arms and fled into the sacred precincts at Carnaim. [44]But he took the city and burned the sacred precinct with fire, together with all who were in it. Thus Carnaim was conquered; they could stand before Judas no longer.

RETURN TO JERUSALEM

[45]Then Judas gathered together all the Israelites in Gilead, the small and the great, with their wives and children and goods, a very large company, to go to the land of Judah. [46]So they came to Ephron. This was a large and very strong city on the road, and they could not go round it to the right or to the left; they had to go through the middle of it. [47]But the men of the city shut them out and blocked up the gates with stones. [48]And Judas sent them this friendly message, "Let us pass through your land to get to our land. No one will do you harm; we will simply pass by on foot." But they refused to open to him. [49]Then Judas ordered proclamation to be made to the army that each should encamp where he was. [50]So the men of the forces encamped, and he fought against the city all that day and all the night, and the city was delivered into his hands. [51]He destroyed every male by the edge of the sword and razed and plundered the city. Then he passed through the city over the slain.

[52]And they crossed the Jordan into the large plain before Beth-shan. [53]And Judas kept rallying the stragglers and encouraging the people all the way till he came to the land of Judah. [54]So they went up to Mount Zion with gladness and joy and offered whole burnt offerings, because not one of them had fallen before they returned in safety.

JOSEPH AND AZARIAH DEFEATED

[55]Now while Judas and Jonathan were in Gilead and Simon his brother was in Galilee before Ptolemais, [56]Joseph son of Zechariah and Azariah, the commanders of the forces, heard of their brave deeds and of the heroic war they had fought. [57]So they said, "Let us also make a name for ourselves; let

---

[a]Greek Gilead; they are [b]Greek omits of Dathema; see 5:9
[c]The Greek name is uncertain

us go and make war on the Gentiles round us." ⁵⁸And they issued orders to the men of the forces that were with them, and they marched against Jamnia. ⁵⁹And Gorgias and his men came out of the city to meet them in battle. ⁶⁰Then Joseph and Azariah were routed and were pursued to the borders of Judea; as many as 2,000 of the people of Israel fell that day. ⁶¹Thus the people suffered a great rout because, thinking to do a brave deed, they did not listen to Judas and his brothers. ⁶²But they did not belong to the family of those men through whom deliverance was given to Israel.

⁶³The man Judas and his brothers were greatly honoured in all Israel and among all the Gentiles, wherever their name was heard. ⁶⁴Men gathered to them and praised them.

SUCCESS AT HEBRON AND PHILISTIA

⁶⁵Then Judas and his brothers went forth and fought the sons of Esau in the land to the south. He struck Hebron and its villages and tore down its strongholds and burned its towers round about. ⁶⁶Then he marched off to go into the land of the Philistines and passed through Marisa.ᵃ ⁶⁷On that day some priests, who wished to do a brave deed, fell in battle, for they went out to battle unwisely. ⁶⁸But Judas turned aside to Azotus in the land of the Philistines; he tore down their altars, and the carved images of their gods he burned with fire; he plundered the cities and returned to the land of Judah.

LAST DAYS OF ANTIOCHUS EPIPHANES

6 King Antiochus was going through the upper provinces when he heard that Elymais in Persia was a city famed for its wealth in silver and gold. ²Its temple was very rich, containing golden shields,ᵇ breastplates, and weapons left there by Alexander son of Philip, the Macedonian king who first reigned over the Greeks. ³So he came and tried to take the city and plunder it, but he could not, because his plan became known to the men of the city ⁴and they withstood him in battle. So he fled and in great grief departed from there to return to Babylon. ⁵Then someone came to him in Persia and reported that the armies that had gone into the land of Judah had been routed; ⁶that Lysias had gone first with a strong force, but was turned back before the Jews;ᶜ that the Jewsᵈ had grown strong from the arms, supplies, and abundant spoils that they had taken from the armies they had cut down; ⁷that they had torn down the abomination that he had erected upon the altar in Jerusalem; and that they had surrounded the sanctuary with high walls as before and also Beth-zur, his city.

⁸When the king heard this news, he was astounded and badly shaken. He took to his bed and became sick from grief, because things had not turned out for him as he had planned. ⁹He lay there for many days, because deep grief continually gripped him, and he concluded that he was dying. ¹⁰So he called all his friends and said to them, "Sleep departs from my eyes and I am downhearted with worry. ¹¹I said to myself, 'To what distress I have come! And into what a great flood I now am plunged! For I was kind and beloved in my power.' ¹²But now I remember the evils I did in Jerusalem. I seized all her vessels of silver and gold; and I sent to destroy the inhabitants of Judah without good reason. ¹³I know that it is because of this that these evils have come upon me; and behold, I am perishing of deep grief in a strange land."

¹⁴Then he called for Philip, one of his friends, and made him ruler over all his kingdom. ¹⁵He gave him the crown and his robe and the signet, that he might guide Antiochus his son and bring him up to be king. ¹⁶Thus King Antiochus died there in the 149th year.ᵉ ¹⁷And when Lysias learned that the king was dead, he set up Antiochus the king's sonᶠ to reign. Lysiasᵍ had brought him up as a boy, and he named him Eupator.

RENEWED ATTACKS FROM SYRIA

¹⁸Now the men in the citadel kept hemming Israel in around the sanctuary. They were trying in every way to harm them and strengthen the Gentiles. ¹⁹So Judas decided to destroy them and assembled all the people to besiege them. ²⁰They gathered together and besieged the citadelʰ in the 150th year;ⁱ and he built siege towers and other engines of war. ²¹But some of the garrison escaped from the siege and some of the ungodly Israelites joined them. ²²They went to the king and said, "How long will you fail to do justice and to avenge our brothers? ²³We were happy to serve your father, to live by what he said and to follow his commands. ²⁴For

---

ᵃSome manuscripts *Samaria* ᵇGreek *coverings* ᶜGreek *before them*
ᵈGreek *that they* ᵉ163 BC ᶠGreek *set up Antiochus his son*
ᵍGreek *He* ʰGreek *besieged it* ⁱ162 BC

this reason the sons of our people besieged the citadel[a] and became hostile to us; moreover, they have put to death as many of us as they have caught, and they have seized our inheritances. 25And not against us alone have they stretched out their hands, but also against all the lands on their borders. 26And behold, today they have encamped against the citadel in Jerusalem to take it; they have fortified both the sanctuary and Beth-zur; 27and unless you quickly prevent them, they will do still greater things, and you will not be able to stop them."

28The king was enraged when he heard this. He assembled all his friends, the commanders of his forces and those over the cavalry.[b] 29And mercenary forces came to him from other kingdoms and from islands of the seas. 30The number of his forces was 100,000 foot soldiers, 20,000 horsemen, and 32 elephants accustomed to war. 31They came through Idumea and encamped against Beth-zur, and for many days they fought and built engines of war; but the Jews[c] sallied out and burned these with fire and fought manfully.

BATTLE AT BETH-ZECHARIAH

32Then Judas marched away from the citadel and encamped at Beth-zechariah, opposite the camp of the king. 33Early in the morning the king rose and took his army by a forced march along the road to Beth-zechariah, and his troops made ready for battle and sounded their trumpets. 34They showed the elephants the juice of grapes and mulberries, to arouse them for battle. 35And they distributed the beasts among the phalanxes; with each elephant they stationed 1,000 men armed with coats of mail and with brass helmets on their heads; and 500 picked horsemen were assigned to each beast. 36These took their position beforehand wherever the beast was; wherever it went they went with it, and they never left it. 37And upon the elephants[d] were wooden towers, strong and covered; they were fastened upon each beast by special harness, and upon each were four[e] armed men who fought from there, and also its Indian driver. 38The rest of the horsemen were stationed on either side, on the two flanks of the army, to harass the enemy while being themselves protected by the phalanxes. 39When the sun shone upon the shields of gold and brass, the hills were ablaze with them and gleamed like flaming torches.

40Now a part of the king's army was spread out on the high hills, and some troops were on the plain, and they advanced steadily and in good order. 41All who heard the noise made by their multitude, by the marching of the multitude and the clanking of their arms, trembled, for the army was very large and strong. 42But Judas and his army advanced to the battle, and 600 men of the king's army fell. 43And Eleazar called Avaran saw that one of the beasts was equipped with royal armour. It was taller than all the others, and he supposed that the king was upon it. 44So he gave his life to save his people and to win for himself an everlasting name. 45He courageously ran into the midst of the phalanx to reach it; he killed men right and left, and they parted before him on both sides. 46He got under the elephant, stabbed it from beneath, and killed it; but it fell to the ground upon him and there he died. 47And when the Jews[f] saw the royal might and the fierce attack of the forces, they turned away in flight.

SIEGE OF THE TEMPLE

48The soldiers of the king's army went up to Jerusalem against them, and the king encamped in Judea and at Mount Zion. 49He made peace with the men of Beth-zur, and they evacuated the city, because they had no provisions there to withstand a siege, since it was a sabbatical year for the land. 50So the king took Beth-zur and stationed a guard there to hold it. 51Then he encamped before the sanctuary for many days. He set up siege towers, engines of war to throw fire and stones, machines to shoot arrows, and catapults. 52The Jews[g] also made engines of war to match theirs and fought for many days. 53But they had no food in storage,[h] because it was the seventh year; those who found safety in Judea from the Gentiles had consumed the last of the stores. 54Few men were left in the sanctuary, because famine had prevailed over the rest and they had been scattered, each to his own place.

SYRIA OFFERS TERMS

55Then Lysias heard that Philip, whom King Antiochus while still living had appointed to bring up Antiochus his son to be king, 56had returned from Persia and Media with the

---

[a]The meaning of the Greek is uncertain [b]Greek *reins*
[c]Greek *but they* [d]Greek *upon them* [e]Some manuscripts *thirty*; some manuscripts *thirty-two* [f]Greek *when they* [g]Greek *They*
[h]Some manuscripts *in the sanctuary*

forces that had gone with the king and that he was trying to seize control of the government. ⁵⁷So he quickly gave orders to depart and said to the king, to the commanders of the forces, and to the men, "We daily grow weaker, our food supply is scant, the place against which we are fighting is strong, and the affairs of the kingdom press urgently upon us. ⁵⁸Now then let us come to terms with these men and make peace with them and with all their nation ⁵⁹and agree to let them live by their laws as they did before; for it was on account of their laws that we abolished that they became angry and did all these things."

⁶⁰The speech pleased the king and the commanders, and he sent to the Jews[a] an offer of peace, and they accepted it. ⁶¹So the king and the commanders gave them their oath. On these conditions the Jews[b] evacuated the stronghold. ⁶²But when the king entered Mount Zion and saw what a strong fortress the place was, he broke the oath he had sworn and commanded and tore down the wall all round. ⁶³Then he departed with haste and returned to Antioch. He found Philip in control of the city, but he fought against him and took the city by force.

EXPEDITION OF BACCHIDES AND ALCIMUS

7 In the 151st year[c] Demetrius son of Seleucus set forth from Rome, sailed with a few men to a city by the sea and there began to reign. ²As he was entering the royal palace of his fathers, the army seized Antiochus and Lysias to bring them to him. ³But when this act became known to him, he said, "Do not let me see their faces!" ⁴So the army killed them, and Demetrius took his seat upon the throne of his kingdom.

⁵Then there came to him all the lawless and ungodly Israelites; they were led by Alcimus, who wanted to be high priest. ⁶And they brought to the king this accusation against the people: "Judas and his brothers have destroyed all your friends and have driven us out of our land. ⁷Now then send a man whom you trust; let him go and see all the ruin that Judas[d] has brought upon us and upon the land of the king, and let him punish them and all who help them."

⁸So the king chose Bacchides, one of the king's friends, governor of the province Beyond the River; he was a great man in the kingdom and was faithful to the king. ⁹And he sent him and with him the ungodly Alcimus, whom he made high priest; and he commanded him to take vengeance on the sons of Israel. ¹⁰So they marched away and came with a large force into the land of Judah; and he sent messengers to Judas and his brothers with peaceable but treacherous words. ¹¹But they paid no attention to their words, for they saw that they had come with a large force.

¹²Then a group of scribes appeared in a body before Alcimus and Bacchides to ask for just terms. ¹³The Hasideans were first among the sons of Israel to seek peace from them, ¹⁴for they said, "A priest of the line of Aaron has come with the army, and he will not harm us." ¹⁵And he spoke peaceable words to them and swore this oath to them, "We will not seek to injure you or your friends." ¹⁶So they trusted him; but he seized sixty of them and killed them in one day, in accordance with the word that was written:

¹⁷ "The flesh of your saints and their blood
  they poured out round
   about Jerusalem,
  and there was none to bury them."

¹⁸Then the fear and dread of them fell upon all the people, for they said, "There is no truth or justice in them, for they have violated the agreement and the oath that they swore."

¹⁹Then Bacchides departed from Jerusalem and encamped in Beth-zaith. And he sent and seized many of the men who had deserted to him,[e] and some of the people, and killed them and threw them into the great pit. ²⁰He placed Alcimus in charge of the country and left with him a force to help him; then Bacchides went back to the king.

²¹Alcimus fought for the high priesthood, ²²and all who were troubling their people joined him. They gained control of the land of Judah and did great damage in Israel. ²³And Judas saw all the evil that Alcimus and those with him had done among the sons of Israel; it was more than the Gentiles had done. ²⁴So Judas went out into all the surrounding parts of Judea and took vengeance on the men who had deserted, and they were prevented from going out into the country. ²⁵When Alcimus saw that Judas and those with him had grown strong and realized that he could not withstand them, he returned to the king and brought wicked charges against them.

---

[a]Greek *to them* [b]Greek *conditions they* [c]161 BC [d]Greek *he*; also verse 24 [e]Or *many of his men who had deserted*

NICANOR IN JUDEA

26Then the king sent Nicanor, one of his honoured princes, who hated and detested Israel, and he commanded him to destroy the people. 27So Nicanor came to Jerusalem with a large force and treacherously sent to Judas and his brothers this peaceable message, 28"Let there be no fighting between me and you; I shall come with a few men to see you face to face in peace." 29So he came to Judas, and they greeted one another peaceably. But the enemy were ready to seize Judas. 30It became known to Judas that Nicanor[a] had come to him with treacherous intent, and he was afraid of him and would not meet him again. 31When Nicanor learned that his plan had been disclosed, he went out to meet Judas in battle near Caphar-salama. 32About 500 men of the army of Nicanor fell, and the rest[b] fled into the city of David.

NICANOR THREATENS THE TEMPLE

33After these events Nicanor went up to Mount Zion. Some of the priests came out of the sanctuary, and some of the elders of the people, to greet him peaceably and to show him the whole burnt offering that was being offered for the king. 34But he mocked them and derided them and defiled them and spoke arrogantly, 35and in anger he swore this oath, "Unless Judas and his army are delivered into my hands this time, then if I return safely I will burn up this house." And he went out in great anger. 36Then the priests went in and stood before the altar and the temple, and they wept and said:

37 "You chose this house to be
   called by your name
   and to be for your people a house
   of prayer and supplication.
38 Take vengeance on this man
   and on his army
   and let them fall by the sword;
   remember their blasphemies
   and let them live no longer."

DEATH OF NICANOR

39Now Nicanor went out from Jerusalem and encamped in Beth-horon, and the Syrian army joined him. 40And Judas encamped in Adasa with 3,000 men. Then Judas prayed and said, 41"When the messengers from the king spoke blasphemy, your angel went forth and struck down 185,000 of the Assyrians.[c] 42So also crush this army before us today; let the rest learn that Nicanor has spoken wickedly against your sanctuary, and judge him according to this wickedness." 43So the armies met in battle on the thirteenth day of the month of Adar. The army of Nicanor was crushed, and he himself was the first to fall in the battle. 44When his army saw that Nicanor had fallen, they threw down their arms and fled. 45The Jews[d] pursued them a day's journey, from Adasa as far as Gazara, and as they followed kept sounding the battle call on the trumpets. 46And men came out of all the villages of Judea round about, and they outflanked the enemy[e] and drove them back to their pursuers,[f] so that they all fell by the sword; not even one of them was left. 47Then the Jews[g] seized the spoils and the plunder, and they cut off Nicanor's head and the right hand that he had so arrogantly stretched out and brought them and displayed them just outside Jerusalem. 48The people rejoiced greatly and celebrated that day as a day of great gladness. 49And they decreed that this day should be celebrated each year on the thirteenth day of Adar. 50So the land of Judah had rest for a few days.

EULOGY OF THE ROMANS

8 Now Judas heard of the fame of the Romans, that they were very strong and were well disposed towards all who made an alliance with them, that they pledged friendship to those who came to them, 2and that they were very strong. Men told him of their wars and of the brave deeds that they were doing among the Gauls, how they had defeated them and forced them to pay tribute, 3and what they had done in the land of Spain to get control of the silver and gold mines there, 4and how they had gained control of the whole region by their planning and patience, even though the place was far distant from them. They also subdued the kings who came against them from the ends of the earth, until they crushed them and inflicted great disaster upon them; the rest paid them tribute every year. 5Philip and King Perseus of the Macedonians[h] and the others who rose up against them, they crushed in battle and conquered. 6They also defeated King Antiochus the Great of Asia, who went to fight against them with 120 elephants and

---

[a]Greek *he*; also verse 42 [b]Greek *and they* [c]Greek *of them*
[d]Greek *They* [e]Greek *outflanked them* [f]Greek *to these*
[g]Greek *Then they* [h]Or *Kittim*

with cavalry and chariots and a very large army. He was crushed by them; ⁷they took him alive and decreed that he and those who should reign after him should pay a heavy tribute and give hostages and surrender some of their best provinces, ⁸the country of India and Media and Lydia. These they took from him and gave to King Eumenes. ⁹The Greeks planned to come and destroy them, ¹⁰but this became known to them, and they sent a general against the Greeks*a* and attacked them. Many of them were wounded and fell, and the Romans*b* took captive their wives and children; they plundered them, conquered the land, tore down their strongholds, and enslaved them to this day. ¹¹The remaining kingdoms and islands, as many as ever opposed them, they destroyed and enslaved; ¹²but with their friends and those who rely on them they have kept friendship. They have subdued kings far and near, and as many as have heard of their fame have feared them. ¹³Those whom they wish to help and to make kings, they make kings, and those whom they wish depose; and they have been greatly exalted. ¹⁴Yet for all this not one of them has put on a crown or worn purple as a mark of pride, ¹⁵but they have built for themselves a senate chamber, and every day 320 senators constantly deliberate concerning the people, to govern them well. ¹⁶They trust one man each year to rule over them and to control all their land; they all heed the one man, and there is no envy or jealousy among them.

ALLIANCE WITH ROME

¹⁷So Judas chose Eupolemus son of John, son of Accos, and Jason son of Eleazar and sent them to Rome to establish friendship and alliance ¹⁸and to free themselves from the yoke; for they saw that the kingdom of the Greeks was completely enslaving Israel. ¹⁹They went to Rome, a very long journey; and they entered the senate chamber and spoke as follows: ²⁰"Judas, who is also called Maccabeus, and his brothers and the people of the Jews have sent us to you to establish alliance and peace with you, that we may be enrolled as your allies and friends." ²¹The proposal pleased them, ²²and this is a copy of the letter that they wrote in reply, on bronze tablets, and sent to Jerusalem to remain with them there as a memorial of peace and alliance:

²³"May all go well with the Romans and with the nation of the Jews at sea and on land for ever, and may sword and enemy be far from them. ²⁴If war comes first to Rome or to any of their allies in all their dominion, ²⁵the nation of the Jews shall act as their allies wholeheartedly, as the occasion may indicate to them. ²⁶And to the enemy who makes war they shall not give or supply corn, arms, money, or ships, as Rome has decided; and they shall keep their obligations without receiving any return. ²⁷In the same way, if war comes first to the nation of the Jews, the Romans shall willingly act as their allies, as the occasion may indicate to them. ²⁸And to the enemy allies shall be given no corn, arms, money, or ships, as Rome has decided; and they shall keep these obligations and do so without deceit. ²⁹Thus on these terms the Romans make a treaty with the Jewish people. ³⁰If after these terms are in effect both parties shall determine to add or delete anything, they shall do so at their discretion, and any addition or deletion that they may make shall be valid.

³¹"And concerning the wrongs that King Demetrius is doing to them we have written to him as follows: 'Why have you made your yoke heavy upon our friends and allies the Jews? ³²If now they appeal again for help against you, we will defend their rights and fight you on sea and on land.'"

BACCHIDES RETURNS TO JUDEA

9 When Demetrius heard that Nicanor and his army had fallen in battle, he sent Bacchides and Alcimus into the land of Judah a second time, and with them the right wing of the army. ²They went by the road that leads to Gilgal and encamped against Mesaloth in Arbela, and they took it and killed many people. ³In the first month of the 152nd year*c* they encamped against Jerusalem; ⁴then they marched off and went to Berea with 20,000 foot soldiers and 2,000 cavalry.

⁵Now Judas was encamped in Elasa, and with him were 3,000 picked men. ⁶When they saw the huge number of the enemy forces, they were greatly frightened, and many slipped away from the camp, until no more than 800 of them were left.

⁷When Judas saw that his army had slipped away and the battle was imminent, he was crushed in spirit, for he had no time to assemble them. ⁸He became faint, but he said to those who were left, "Let us rise and

---

a Greek *against them* *b* Greek *and they* *c* 160 BC

go up against our enemies. We may be able to fight them." ⁹But they tried to dissuade him, saying, "We are unable. Let us rather save our own lives now, and let us come back with our brothers and fight them; we are too few." ¹⁰But Judas said, "Far be it from us to do such a thing as to flee from them. If our time has come, let us die bravely for our brothers and leave no cause to question our honour."

LAST BATTLE OF JUDAS

¹¹Then the army of Bacchides[a] marched out from the camp and took its stand for the encounter. The cavalry was divided into two companies, and the slingers and the archers went ahead of the army, as did all the chief warriors. ¹²Bacchides was on the right wing. Flanked by the two companies, the phalanx advanced to the sound of the trumpets; and the men with Judas also blew their trumpets. ¹³The earth was shaken by the noise of the armies, and the battle raged from morning till evening.

¹⁴Judas saw that Bacchides and the strength of his army were on the right; then all the stout-hearted men went with him, ¹⁵and they crushed the right wing, and he pursued them as far as Mount Azotus. ¹⁶When those on the left wing saw that the right wing was crushed, they turned and followed close behind Judas and his men. ¹⁷The battle became desperate, and many on both sides were wounded and fell. ¹⁸Judas also fell, and the rest fled.

¹⁹Then Jonathan and Simon took Judas their brother and buried him in the tomb of their fathers at Modein ²⁰and wept for him. And all Israel made great lamentation for him; they mourned many days and said:

²¹   "How is the mighty fallen,
     the saviour of Israel!"

²²Now the rest of the acts of Judas and his wars and the brave deeds that he did and his greatness have not been recorded, for they were very many.

JONATHAN SUCCEEDS JUDAS

²³After the death of Judas, the lawless emerged in all parts of Israel; all the doers of injustice appeared. ²⁴In those days a very great famine occurred, and the country deserted with them to the enemy. ²⁵And Bacchides chose the ungodly and put them in charge of the country. ²⁶They sought and searched for the friends of Judas and brought them to Bacchides, and he took vengeance on them and made sport of them. ²⁷Thus there was great distress in Israel, such as had not been since the time that prophets ceased to appear among them.

²⁸Then all the friends of Judas assembled and said to Jonathan, ²⁹"Since the death of your brother Judas there has been no one like him to go against our enemies and Bacchides and to deal with those of our nation who hate us. ³⁰So now we have chosen you today to take his place as our ruler and leader, to fight our battle." ³¹And Jonathan at that time accepted the leadership and took the place of Judas his brother.

CAMPAIGNS OF JONATHAN

³²When Bacchides learned of this, he tried to kill him. ³³But Jonathan and Simon his brother and all who were with him heard of it, and they fled into the wilderness of Tekoa and camped by the water of the pool of Asphar. ³⁴Bacchides found this out on the Sabbath day, and he with all his army crossed the Jordan.

³⁵And Jonathan[b] sent his brother as leader of the multitude and begged the Nabateans, who were his friends, for permission to store with them the great amount of baggage that they had. ³⁶But the sons of Jambri from Medeba came out and seized John and all that he had and departed with it.

³⁷After these things it was reported to Jonathan and Simon his brother, "The sons of Jambri are celebrating a great wedding and are conducting the bride, a daughter of one of the great nobles of Canaan, from Nadabath with a large escort." ³⁸And they remembered the blood of John their brother and went up and hid under cover of the mountain. ³⁹They raised their eyes and looked and saw a tumultuous procession with much baggage; and the bridegroom came out with his friends and his brothers to meet them with tambourines and musicians and many weapons. ⁴⁰Then they rushed upon them from the ambush and began killing them. Many were wounded and fell, and the rest fled to the mountain; and they took all their goods. ⁴¹Thus the wedding was turned into mourning and the voice of their musicians into a funeral dirge. ⁴²And when they had fully avenged the blood of their brother, they returned to the marshes of the Jordan.

---

[a]Greek *Then the army*   [b]Greek *he*

⁴³When Bacchides heard of this, he came with a large force on the Sabbath day to the banks of the Jordan. ⁴⁴And Jonathan said to those with him, "Let us rise up now and fight for our lives, for today things are not as they were before. ⁴⁵For look! the battle is in front of us and behind us; the water of the Jordan is on this side and on that, with marsh and thicket; there is no place to turn. ⁴⁶Cry out now to heaven that you may be delivered from the hands of our enemies." ⁴⁷So the battle began, and Jonathan stretched out his hand to strike Bacchides, but he eluded him and went to the rear. ⁴⁸Then Jonathan and the men with him leaped into the Jordan and swam across to the other side, and the enemy[a] did not cross the Jordan to attack them. ⁴⁹And about 1,000 of Bacchides' men fell that day.

BACCHIDES BUILDS FORTIFICATIONS

⁵⁰Bacchides[b] then returned to Jerusalem and built strong cities in Judea: the fortress in Jericho and Emmaus and Beth-horon and Bethel and Timnath and Pharathon and Tephon, with high walls and gates and bars. ⁵¹And he placed garrisons in them to harass Israel. ⁵²He also fortified the city of Beth-zur and Gazara and the citadel, and in them he put troops and stores of food. ⁵³And he took the sons of the leading men of the land as hostages and put them under guard in the citadel at Jerusalem.

⁵⁴In the 153rd year,[c] in the second month, Alcimus gave orders to tear down the wall of the inner court of the sanctuary. He tore down the work of the prophets! ⁵⁵But he only began to tear it down, for at that time Alcimus was stricken and his work was hindered; his mouth was stopped and he was paralysed, so that he could no longer say a word or give commands concerning his house. ⁵⁶And Alcimus died at that time in great agony. ⁵⁷When Bacchides saw that Alcimus was dead, he returned to the king, and the land of Judah had rest for two years.

END OF THE WAR

⁵⁸Then all the lawless plotted and said, "See! Jonathan and his men are living in quiet and confidence. So now let us bring Bacchides back, and he will capture them all in one night." ⁵⁹And they went and consulted with him. ⁶⁰He started to come with a large force and secretly sent letters to all his allies in Judea, telling them to seize Jonathan and his men; but they were unable to do it, because their plan became known. ⁶¹And Jonathan's men[d] seized about fifty of the men of the country who were leaders in this treachery and killed them.

⁶²Then Jonathan with his men and Simon withdrew to Beth-basi in the wilderness; he rebuilt the parts of it that had been demolished, and they fortified it. ⁶³When Bacchides learned of this, he assembled all his forces and sent orders to the men of Judea. ⁶⁴Then he came and encamped against Beth-basi; he fought against it for many days and made machines of war.

⁶⁵But Jonathan left Simon his brother in the city, while he went out into the country; and he went with only a few men. ⁶⁶He struck down Odomera and his brothers and the sons of Phasiron in their tents. ⁶⁷Then he[e] began to attack and went into battle with his forces; and Simon and his men sallied out from the city and set fire to the machines of war. ⁶⁸They fought with Bacchides, and he was crushed by them. They distressed him greatly, for his plan and his expedition had been in vain. ⁶⁹So he was greatly enraged at the lawless men who had counselled him to come into the country, and he killed many of them. Then he decided to depart to his own land.

⁷⁰When Jonathan learned of this, he sent ambassadors to him to make peace with him and obtain release of the captives. ⁷¹He agreed and did as he said; and he swore to Jonathan[f] that he would not try to harm him as long as he lived. ⁷²He restored to him the captives whom he had formerly taken from the land of Judah; then he turned and departed to his own land and came no more into their territory. ⁷³Thus the sword ceased from Israel. And Jonathan dwelt in Michmash. And Jonathan began to judge the people, and he destroyed the ungodly out of Israel.

REVOLT OF ALEXANDER EPIPHANES

10 In the 160th year[g] Alexander Epiphanes son of Antiochus landed and occupied Ptolemais. They welcomed him, and there he began to reign. ²When King Demetrius heard of it, he assembled a very large army and marched out to meet him in battle. ³And Demetrius sent Jonathan a letter in peaceable words to honour

---
[a]Greek *and they* [b]Greek *He* [c]159 BC [d]Greek *And they* [e]Some manuscripts *they* [f]Greek *him* [g]152 BC; also verse 21

him; ⁴for he said, "Let us act first to make peace with them before he makes peace with Alexander against us, ⁵for he will remember all the wrongs that we did to him and to his brothers and his nation." ⁶So Demetrius[a] gave him authority to recruit troops, to equip them with arms, and to become his ally; and he commanded that the hostages in the citadel should be released to him.

⁷Then Jonathan came to Jerusalem and read the letter in the hearing of all the people and of the men in the citadel. ⁸They were greatly alarmed when they heard that the king had given him authority to recruit troops. ⁹But the men in the citadel released the hostages to Jonathan, and he returned them to their parents.

¹⁰And Jonathan dwelt in Jerusalem and began to rebuild and restore the city. ¹¹He directed those who were doing the work to build the walls and encircle Mount Zion with squared stones, for better fortification; and they did so.

¹²Then the foreigners who were in the strongholds that Bacchides had built fled; ¹³each left his place and departed to his own land. ¹⁴Only in Beth-zur did some remain who had forsaken the law and the commandments, for it served as a place of refuge.

¹⁵Now King Alexander heard of all the promises that Demetrius had sent to Jonathan, and men told him of the battles that Jonathan[b] and his brothers had fought, of the brave deeds that they had done, and of the troubles that they had endured. ¹⁶So he said, "Shall we find another such man? Come now, we will make him our friend and ally." ¹⁷And he wrote a letter and sent it to him, in the following words:

JONATHAN BECOMES HIGH PRIEST

¹⁸"King Alexander to his brother Jonathan, greetings. ¹⁹We have heard about you, that you are a mighty warrior and worthy to be our friend. ²⁰And so we have appointed you today to be the high priest of your nation; you are to be called the king's friend" (and he sent him a purple robe and a golden crown) "and you are to take our side and keep friendship with us."

²¹So Jonathan put on the holy garments in the seventh month of the 160th year, at the Feast of Tabernacles, and he recruited troops and equipped them with arms in abundance. ²²When Demetrius heard of these things he was grieved and said, ²³"What is this that we have done? Alexander has gotten ahead of us in forming a friendship with the Jews to strengthen himself. ²⁴I also will write them words of encouragement and promise them honour and gifts, that I may have their help." ²⁵So he sent a message to them in the following words:

LETTER FROM DEMETRIUS TO JONATHAN

"King Demetrius to the nation of the Jews, greetings. ²⁶Since you have kept your agreement with us and have continued your friendship with us and have not sided with our enemies, we have heard of it and rejoiced. ²⁷And now continue still to keep faith with us, and we will repay you with good for what you do for us. ²⁸We will grant you many immunities and give you gifts.

²⁹"And now I free you and exempt all the Jews from payment of tribute and salt tax and crown levies, ³⁰and instead of collecting the third of the corn and the half of the fruit of the trees that I should receive, I release them from this day and henceforth. I will not collect them from the land of Judah or from the three districts added to it from Samaria and Galilee, from this day and for all time. ³¹And let Jerusalem and her environs, her tithes and her revenues, be holy and free from tax. ³²I release also my control of the citadel in Jerusalem and give it to the high priest, that he may station in it men of his own choice to guard it. ³³And every one of the Jews taken as a captive from the land of Judah into any part of my kingdom, I set free without payment; and let all officials cancel also the taxes on their cattle.

³⁴"And all the feasts and Sabbaths and new moons and appointed days and the three days before a feast and the three after a feast—let them all be days of immunity and release for all the Jews who are in my kingdom. ³⁵No one shall have authority to exact anything from them or annoy any of them about any matter.

³⁶"Let Jews be enrolled in the king's forces to the number of 30,000 men, and let the maintenance be given them that is due to all the forces of the king. ³⁷Let some of them be stationed in the great strongholds of the king, and let some of them be put in positions of trust in the kingdom. Let their officers and leaders be of their own number, and let them live by their own laws, just as the king has commanded in the land of Judah.

---

[a] Greek *he*; also verse 46 [b] Greek *he*; also verse 78

38"As for the three districts that have been added to Judea from the country of Samaria, let them be so annexed to Judea that they are considered to be under one ruler and obey no other authority but the high priest. 39Ptolemais and the land adjoining it I have given as a gift to the sanctuary in Jerusalem, to meet the necessary expenses of the sanctuary. 40I also grant 15,000 shekels of silver yearly out of the king's revenues from appropriate places. 41And all the additional funds that the government officials have not paid as they did among the first nations,[a] they shall give from now on for the service of the temple.[b] 42Moreover, the 5,000 shekels of silver that my officials[c] have received every year from the income of the services of the temple, this too is cancelled, because it belongs to the priests who minister there. 43And whoever takes refuge at the temple in Jerusalem or in any of its precincts, because he owes money to the king or has any debt, let him be released and receive back all his property in my kingdom.

44"Let the cost of rebuilding and restoring the structures of the sanctuary be paid from the revenues of the king. 45And let the cost of rebuilding the walls of Jerusalem and fortifying it round about and the cost of rebuilding the walls in Judea also be paid from the revenues of the king."

DEATH OF DEMETRIUS

46When Jonathan and the people heard these words, they did not believe or accept them, because they remembered the great wrongs that Demetrius had done in Israel and how he had greatly oppressed them. 47They favoured Alexander, because he had been the first to speak peaceable words to them, and they remained his allies all his days.

48Now King Alexander assembled large forces and encamped opposite Demetrius. 49The two kings met in battle, and the army of Demetrius fled, and Alexander[d] pursued him and defeated them. 50He pressed the battle strongly until the sun set, and Demetrius fell on that day.

TREATY OF PTOLEMY AND ALEXANDER

51Then Alexander sent ambassadors to King Ptolemy of Egypt with the following message: 52"Since I have returned to my kingdom and have taken my seat on the throne of my fathers and established my rule — for I crushed Demetrius and gained control of our country; 53I met him in battle, and he and his army were crushed by us, and we have taken our seat on the throne of his kingdom — 54now therefore let us establish friendship with one another; give me now your daughter as my wife, and I will become your son-in-law and will make gifts to you and to her in keeping with your position."

55King Ptolemy replied and said, "Happy was the day on which you returned to the land of your fathers and took your seat on the throne of their kingdom. 56And now I will do for you as you wrote, but meet me at Ptolemais, so that we may see one another, and I will become your father-in-law, as you have said."

57So Ptolemy set out from Egypt, he and Cleopatra his daughter, and came to Ptolemais in the 162nd year.[e] 58King Alexander met him, and Ptolemy[f] gave him Cleopatra his daughter in marriage and celebrated her wedding at Ptolemais with great pomp, as kings do.

59Then King Alexander wrote to Jonathan to come to meet him. 60So he went with pomp to Ptolemais and met the two kings; he gave them and their friends silver and gold and many gifts and found favour with them. 61A group of pestilent men from Israel, lawless men, gathered together against him to accuse him; but the king paid no attention to them. 62The king gave orders to take off Jonathan's garments and to clothe him in purple, and they did so. 63The king also seated him at his side; and he said to his officers, "Go forth with him into the middle of the city and proclaim that no one is to bring charges against him about any matter, and let no one annoy him for any reason." 64And when his accusers saw the honour that was paid him, in accordance with the proclamation, and saw him clothed in purple, they all fled. 65Thus the king honoured him and enrolled him among his chief friends and made him general and governor of the province. 66And Jonathan returned to Jerusalem in peace and gladness.

APOLLONIUS IS DEFEATED BY JONATHAN

67In the 165th year[g] Demetrius son of Demetrius came from Crete to the land of his fathers. 68When King Alexander heard of it, he was greatly grieved and returned to

---
[a]The meaning of the Greek is uncertain [b]Greek *house*
[c]Greek *that they* [d]Some manuscripts *Alexander fled, and Demetrius*
[e]150 BC [f]Greek *he* [g]147 BC

Antioch. ⁶⁹And Demetrius appointed Apollonius the governor of Coelesyria, and he assembled a large force and encamped against Jamnia. Then he sent the following message to Jonathan the high priest:

⁷⁰"You are the only one to rise up against us, and I have become a laughing-stock and reproach because of you. Why do you assume authority against us in the hill country? ⁷¹If you now have confidence in your forces, come down to the plain to meet us, and let us match strength with each other there, for I have with me the power of the cities. ⁷²Ask and learn who I am and who the others are that are helping us. They will tell you that you cannot stand before us, for your fathers were twice put to flight in their own land. ⁷³And now you will not be able to withstand my cavalry and such an army in the plain, where there is no stone or pebble or place to flee."

⁷⁴When Jonathan heard the words of Apollonius, his spirit was aroused. He chose 10,000 men and set out from Jerusalem, and Simon his brother met him to help him. ⁷⁵He encamped before Joppa, but the men of the city closed its gates, for Apollonius had a garrison in Joppa. ⁷⁶So they fought against it, and the men of the city became afraid and opened the gates, and Jonathan gained possession of Joppa.

⁷⁷When Apollonius heard of it, he mustered 3,000 cavalry and a large army and went to Azotus as though he were going farther. At the same time he advanced into the plain, for he had a large troop of cavalry and put confidence in it. ⁷⁸Jonathan pursued him to Azotus, and the armies engaged in battle. ⁷⁹Now Apollonius had secretly left 1,000 cavalry behind them. ⁸⁰Jonathan learned that there was an ambush behind him, for they surrounded his army and shot arrows at his men from early morning till late afternoon. ⁸¹But his men stood fast, as Jonathan commanded, and the enemy's*ᵃ* horses grew tired.

⁸²Then Simon brought forward his force and engaged the phalanx in battle (for the cavalry was exhausted); they were overwhelmed by him and fled, ⁸³and the cavalry was dispersed in the plain. They fled to Azotus and entered Beth-dagon, the temple of their idol, for safety. ⁸⁴But Jonathan burned Azotus and the surrounding towns and plundered them; and the temple of Dagon and those who had taken refuge in it, he burned with fire. ⁸⁵The number of those who fell by the sword, with those burned alive, came to 8,000 men.

⁸⁶Then Jonathan departed from there and encamped against Ascalon, and the men of the city came out to meet him with great pomp. ⁸⁷And Jonathan and those with him returned to Jerusalem with much booty. ⁸⁸When King Alexander heard of these things, he honoured Jonathan still more; ⁸⁹and he sent to him a golden buckle,*ᵇ* such as it is the custom to give to the kinsmen of kings. He also gave him Ekron and all its environs as his possession.

PTOLEMY INVADES SYRIA

11 Then the king of Egypt gathered great forces, like the sand by the seashore, and many ships; and he tried to get possession of Alexander's kingdom by trickery and add it to his own kingdom. ²He set out for Syria with peaceable words, and the people of the cities opened their gates to him and went to meet him, for King Alexander had commanded them to meet him, since he was Alexander's*ᶜ* father-in-law. ³But when Ptolemy entered the cities he stationed forces as a garrison in each city.

⁴When he*ᵈ* approached Azotus, they showed him the temple of Dagon burned down and Azotus and its suburbs destroyed and the corpses lying about and the charred bodies of those whom Jonathan*ᵉ* had burned in the war, for they had piled them in heaps along his route. ⁵They also told the king what Jonathan had done, to throw blame on him; but the king kept silent. ⁶Jonathan met the king at Joppa with pomp, and they greeted one another and spent the night there. ⁷And Jonathan went with the king as far as the river called Eleutherus; then he returned to Jerusalem.

⁸So King Ptolemy gained control of the coastal cities as far as Seleucia by the sea, and he kept devising evil designs against Alexander. ⁹He sent envoys to King Demetrius, saying, "Come, let us make a covenant with each other, and I will give you in marriage my daughter who was Alexander's wife, and you shall reign over your father's kingdom. ¹⁰For I now regret that I gave him my daughter, for he has tried to kill me." ¹¹He threw blame on Alexander*ᶠ* because he coveted his kingdom. ¹²So he took his daughter away from him and gave her to Demetrius. He was estranged from Alexander, and their enmity became manifest.

---
*ᵃ*Greek *and their* *ᵇ*Or *a brooch* *ᶜ*Greek *his* *ᵈ*Some manuscripts *they* *ᵉ*Greek *he*; also verse 53 *ᶠ*Greek *him*

¹³Then Ptolemy entered Antioch and put on the crown of Asia. Thus he put two crowns upon his head, the crown of Egypt and that of Asia. ¹⁴Now King Alexander was in Cilicia at that time, because the people of that region were in revolt. ¹⁵And Alexander heard of it and came against him in battle. Ptolemy marched out and met him with a strong force and put him to flight. ¹⁶So Alexander fled into Arabia to find protection there, and King Ptolemy was exalted. ¹⁷And Zabdiel the Arab cut off the head of Alexander and sent it to Ptolemy. ¹⁸But King Ptolemy died three days later, and his troops in the strongholds were killed by the inhabitants of the strongholds. ¹⁹So Demetrius became king in the 167th year.[a]

JONATHAN'S DIPLOMACY

²⁰In those days Jonathan assembled the men of Judea to attack the citadel in Jerusalem, and he built many engines of war to use against it. ²¹But certain lawless men who hated their nation went to the king and reported to him that Jonathan was besieging the citadel. ²²When he heard this he was angry, and as soon as he heard it he set out and came to Ptolemais; and he wrote Jonathan not to continue the siege, but to meet him for a conference at Ptolemais as quickly as possible.

²³When Jonathan heard this, he gave orders to continue the siege; and he chose some of the elders of Israel and some of the priests and put himself in danger, ²⁴for he went to the king at Ptolemais, taking silver and gold and clothing and numerous other gifts. And he won his favour. ²⁵Although certain lawless men of his nation kept making complaints against him, ²⁶the king treated him as his predecessors had treated him; he exalted him in the presence of all his friends. ²⁷He confirmed him in the high priesthood and in as many other honours as he had formerly had and made him to be regarded as one of his chief friends. ²⁸Then Jonathan asked the king to free Judea and the three districts of[b] Samaria from tribute and promised him 300 talents. ²⁹The king consented and wrote a letter to Jonathan about all these things; its contents were as follows:

³⁰"King Demetrius to Jonathan his brother and to the nation of the Jews, greetings. ³¹This copy of the letter that we wrote concerning you to Lasthenes our kinsman we have written to you also, so that you may know what it says. ³²'King Demetrius to Lasthenes his father, greetings. ³³To the nation of the Jews, who are our friends and fulfil their obligations to us, we have determined to do good, because of the good will they show toward us. ³⁴We have confirmed as their possession both the territory of Judea and the three districts of Aphairema and Lydda and Ramathaim; these were added to Judea from Samaria, with all the region bordering them, for all those who offer sacrifice in Jerusalem in exchange for the royal taxes that the king formerly received from them each year, from the crops of the land and the fruit of the trees. ³⁵And the other payments henceforth due to us of the tithes, and the taxes due to us, and the salt pits and the crown taxes due to us — from all these we shall grant them release. ³⁶And not one of these grants shall be cancelled from this time forth for ever. ³⁷Now therefore take care to make a copy of this, and let it be given to Jonathan and put up in a conspicuous place on the holy mountain.'"

INTRIGUE OF TRYPHO

³⁸Now when King Demetrius saw that the land was quiet before him and that there was no opposition to him, he dismissed all his troops, each man to his own place, except the foreign troops that he had recruited from the islands of the nations. So all the troops who had served his fathers hated him. ³⁹Now Trypho had formerly been one of Alexander's supporters. He saw that all the troops were murmuring against Demetrius. So he went to Imalkue the Arab, who was bringing up Antiochus, the young son of Alexander, ⁴⁰and insistently urged him to hand Antiochus[c] over to him, to become king in place of his father. He also reported to Imalkue[d] what Demetrius had done and told of the hatred that the troops of Demetrius[e] had for him; and he stayed there many days.

⁴¹Now Jonathan sent to King Demetrius the request that he remove the troops of the citadel from Jerusalem and the troops in the strongholds; for they kept fighting against Israel. ⁴²And Demetrius sent this message to Jonathan, "Not only will I do these things for you and your nation, but I will confer great honour on you and your nation, if I find an opportunity. ⁴³Now then you will do well to send me men who will help me, for all my troops have revolted." ⁴⁴So Jonathan sent

---

[a]145 BC [b]Greek and [c]Greek him [d]Greek him [e]Greek him; also verse 55

3,000 stalwart men to him at Antioch, and when they came to the king, the king rejoiced at their arrival. ⁴⁵Then the men of the city assembled within the city, to the number of 120,000, and they wanted to kill the king. ⁴⁶But the king fled into the palace. Then the men of the city seized the main streets of the city and began to fight. ⁴⁷So the king called the Jews to his aid, and they all rallied round him and then spread out through the city; and they killed on that day as many as 100,000 men. ⁴⁸They set fire to the city and seized much spoil on that day, and they saved the king. ⁴⁹When the men of the city saw that the Jews had gained control of the city as they pleased, their courage failed and they cried out to the king with this entreaty, ⁵⁰"Grant us peace and make the Jews stop fighting against us and our city." ⁵¹And they threw down their arms and made peace. So the Jews gained glory in the eyes of the king and of all the people in his kingdom. And they became renowned in his kingdom, and they returned to Jerusalem with much spoil.

⁵²So King Demetrius sat on the throne of his kingdom, and the land was quiet before him. ⁵³But he broke his word about all that he had promised; and he became estranged from Jonathan and did not repay the favours that Jonathan had done him, but oppressed him greatly.

TRYPHO SEIZES POWER

⁵⁴After this Trypho returned, and with him the young boy Antiochus, who began to reign and put on the crown. ⁵⁵All the troops that Demetrius had cast off gathered around him, and they fought against Demetrius, and he fled and was routed. ⁵⁶And Trypho captured the elephants[a] and gained control of Antioch. ⁵⁷Then the young Antiochus wrote to Jonathan, saying, "I confirm you in the high priesthood and set you over the four districts and make you one of the friends of the king." ⁵⁸And he sent him gold plates and a table service and granted him the right to drink from gold cups and dress in purple and wear a gold buckle.[b] ⁵⁹Simon his brother he made governor from the Ladder of Tyre to the borders of Egypt.

CAMPAIGNS OF JONATHAN AND SIMON

⁶⁰Then Jonathan set forth and travelled beyond the river and among the cities, and all the army of Syria gathered to him as allies. When he came to Ascalon, the people of the city met him and paid him honour. ⁶¹From there he departed to Gaza, but the men of Gaza shut him out. So he besieged it and burned its suburbs with fire and plundered them. ⁶²Then the people of Gaza pleaded with Jonathan, and he made peace with them and took the sons of their rulers as hostages and sent them to Jerusalem. And he passed through the country as far as Damascus.

⁶³Then Jonathan heard that the officers of Demetrius had come to Kadesh in Galilee with a large army, intending to remove him from office. ⁶⁴He went to meet them, but left his brother Simon in the country. ⁶⁵Simon encamped before Beth-zur and fought against it for many days and hemmed it in. ⁶⁶Then they asked him to grant them terms of peace, and he did so. He removed them from there, took possession of the city, and set a garrison over it.

⁶⁷Jonathan and his army encamped by the waters of Gennesaret. Early in the morning they marched to the plain of Hazor, ⁶⁸and behold, the army of the foreigners met him in the plain; they had set an ambush against him in the mountains, but they themselves met him face to face. ⁶⁹Then the men in ambush emerged from their places and joined battle. ⁷⁰All the men with Jonathan fled; not one of them was left except Mattathias son of Absalom and Judas son of Chalphi, commanders of the forces of the army. ⁷¹Jonathan rent his garments and put dust on his head and prayed. ⁷²Then he turned back to the battle against the enemy[c] and routed them, and they fled. ⁷³When his men who were fleeing saw this, they returned to him and joined him in the pursuit as far as Kadesh, to their camp, and there they encamped. ⁷⁴As many as 3,000 of the foreigners fell that day. And Jonathan returned to Jerusalem.

ALLIANCES WITH ROME AND SPARTA

12 Now when Jonathan saw that the time was favourable for him, he chose men and sent them to Rome to confirm and renew the friendship with them. ²He also sent letters to the same effect to the Spartans and to other places. ³So they went to Rome and entered the senate chamber and said, "Jonathan the high priest and the Jewish nation have sent us to renew the former friendship and alliance with them."

---

[a] Greek *beasts*   [b] Or *a brooch*   [c] Greek *against them*

⁴And the Romans[a] gave them letters to the people in every place, asking them to provide for the envoys[b] safe conduct to the land of Judah.

⁵This is a copy of the letter that Jonathan wrote to the Spartans: ⁶"Jonathan the high priest, the senate of the nation, the priests, and the rest of the Jewish people to their brothers the Spartans, greetings. ⁷Already in time past a letter was sent to Onias the high priest from Arius,[c] who was king among you, stating that you are our brothers, as the appended copy shows. ⁸Onias welcomed the envoy with honour and received the letter, which contained a clear declaration of alliance and friendship. ⁹Therefore, though we have no need of these things, since we have as encouragement the holy books that are in our hands, ¹⁰we have undertaken to send to renew our brotherhood and friendship with you, so that we may not become estranged from you, for considerable time has passed since you sent your letter to us. ¹¹We therefore remember you constantly on every occasion, both in our feasts and on other appropriate days, at the sacrifices that we offer and in our prayers, as it is right and proper to remember brothers. ¹²And we rejoice in your glory. ¹³But as for ourselves, many afflictions and many wars have encircled us; the kings round about us have waged war against us. ¹⁴We were unwilling to annoy you and our other allies and friends with these wars, ¹⁵for we have the help that comes from heaven for our aid; and we were delivered from our enemies and our enemies were humbled. ¹⁶We therefore have chosen Numenius son of Antiochus and Antipater son of Jason and have sent them to Rome to renew our former friendship and alliance with them. ¹⁷We have commanded them to go also to you and greet you and deliver to you this letter from us concerning the renewal of our brotherhood. ¹⁸And now please send us a reply to this."

¹⁹This is a copy of the letter that they sent to Onias: ²⁰"King Arius of the Spartans, to Onias the great priest, greetings. ²¹It has been found in writing concerning the Spartans and the Jews that they are brothers and are of the family of Abraham. ²²And now that we have learned this, please write us concerning your welfare; ²³we on our part write to you that your cattle and your property belong to us, and ours belong to you. We therefore command that our envoys[d] report to you accordingly."

FURTHER CAMPAIGNS OF JONATHAN AND SIMON

²⁴Now Jonathan heard that the commanders of Demetrius had returned, with a larger force than before, to wage war against him. ²⁵So he marched away from Jerusalem and met them in the region of Hamath, for he gave them no opportunity to invade his own country. ²⁶He sent spies to their camp, and they returned and reported to him that the enemy[e] were being drawn up in formation to fall upon the Jews[f] by night. ²⁷So when the sun set, Jonathan commanded his men to be alert and to keep their arms at hand so as to be ready all night for battle, and he stationed outposts around the camp. ²⁸When the enemy heard that Jonathan and his men were prepared for battle, they were afraid and were terrified at heart; so they kindled fires in their camp. ²⁹But Jonathan and his men did not know it until morning, for they saw the fires burning. ³⁰Then Jonathan pursued them, but he did not overtake them, for they had crossed the Eleutherus river. ³¹So Jonathan turned aside against the Arabs who are called Zabadeans, and he crushed them and plundered them. ³²Then he broke camp and went to Damascus and marched through all that region.

³³Simon also went forth and marched through the country as far as Ascalon and the neighbouring strongholds. He turned aside to Joppa and took it by surprise, ³⁴for he had heard that they were ready to hand over the stronghold to the men whom Demetrius had sent. And he stationed a garrison there to guard it.

³⁵When Jonathan returned he convened the elders of the people and planned with them to build strongholds in Judea, ³⁶to build the walls of Jerusalem still higher, and to erect a high barrier between the citadel and the city to separate it from the city, in order to isolate it so that its garrison[g] could neither buy nor sell. ³⁷So they gathered together to build up the city; part of the wall on the valley to the east had fallen, and he repaired the section called Chaphenatha. ³⁸And Simon built Adida in the Shephelah; he fortified it and installed gates with bolts.

TRYPHO CAPTURES JONATHAN

³⁹Then Trypho attempted to become king of Asia and put on the crown and to raise his

---
[a]Greek And they [b]Greek for them [c]Or Darius [d]Greek that they
[e]Greek that they [f]Greek upon them [g]Greek that they

hand against King Antiochus. ⁴⁰He feared that Jonathan might not permit him to do so, but might make war on him, so he kept seeking to seize and kill him, and he marched forth and came to Beth-shan. ⁴¹Jonathan went out to meet him with 40,000 picked fighting men, and he came to Beth-shan. ⁴²When Trypho saw that he had come with a large army, he was afraid to raise his hand against him. ⁴³So he received him with honour and commended him to all his friends, and he gave him gifts and commanded his friends and his troops to obey him as they would himself. ⁴⁴Then he said to Jonathan, "Why have you wearied all these people when we are not at war? ⁴⁵Dismiss them now to their homes and choose for yourself a few men to stay with you and come with me to Ptolemais. I will hand it over to you as well as the other strongholds and the remaining troops and all the officials and will turn round and go home. For that is why I am here."

⁴⁶Jonathan[a] trusted him and did as he said; he sent away the troops, and they returned to the land of Judah. ⁴⁷He kept with himself 3,000 men, 2,000 of whom he left in Galilee, while 1,000 accompanied him. ⁴⁸But when Jonathan entered Ptolemais, the men of Ptolemais closed the gates and seized him, and all who had entered with him they killed with the sword.

⁴⁹Then Trypho sent troops and cavalry into Galilee and the Great Plain to destroy all Jonathan's soldiers. ⁵⁰But they realized that Jonathan had been seized and had perished along with his men, and they encouraged one another and kept marching in close formation, ready for battle. ⁵¹When their pursuers saw that they would fight for their lives, they turned back. ⁵²So they all reached the land of Judah safely, and they mourned for Jonathan and his companions and were in great fear; and all Israel mourned deeply. ⁵³And all the nations round about them tried to destroy them, for they said, "They have no leader or helper. Now therefore let us make war on them and blot out the memory of them from among men."

SIMON TAKES COMMAND

13 Simon heard that Trypho had assembled a large army to invade the land of Judah and destroy it, ²and he saw that the people were trembling and fearful. So he went up to Jerusalem, and gathering the people together ³he encouraged them, saying to them, "You yourselves know all that I and my brothers and the house of my father have done for the laws and the sanctuary; you know also the wars and the difficulties that we have seen. ⁴By reason of this all my brothers have perished for the sake of Israel, and I alone am left. ⁵And now, far be it from me to spare my life in any time of distress, for I am not better than my brothers. ⁶But I will avenge my nation and the sanctuary and your wives and children, for all the nations have gathered together out of hatred to destroy us."

⁷The spirit of the people was rekindled when they heard these words, ⁸and they answered in a loud voice, "You are our leader in place of Judas and Jonathan your brother. ⁹Fight our battles, and all that you say to us we will do." ¹⁰So he assembled all the warriors and hastened to complete the walls of Jerusalem, and he fortified it on every side. ¹¹He sent Jonathan son of Absalom to Joppa, and with him a considerable army; he drove out its occupants and remained there.

DECEIT AND TREACHERY OF TRYPHO

¹²Then Trypho departed from Ptolemais with a large army to invade the land of Judah, and Jonathan was with him under guard. ¹³And Simon encamped in Adida, facing the plain. ¹⁴Trypho learned that Simon had risen up in place of Jonathan his brother and that he was about to join battle with him, so he sent envoys to him and said, ¹⁵"It is for the money that Jonathan your brother owed the royal treasury, in connection with the offices he held, that we are detaining him. ¹⁶Send now 100 talents of silver and two of his sons as hostages, so that when released he will not revolt against us, and we will release him."

¹⁷Simon knew that they were speaking deceitfully to him, but he sent to get the money and the sons, lest he arouse great hostility among the people, who might say, ¹⁸"Because Simon[b] did not send him the money and the sons, he perished." ¹⁹So he sent the sons and 100 talents, but Trypho[c] broke his word and did not release Jonathan.

²⁰After this Trypho came to invade the country and destroy it, and he circled round by the way to Adora. But Simon and his army kept marching along opposite him to every place he went. ²¹Now the men in the citadel kept sending envoys to Trypho urging him

---

[a]Greek He; also verse 50 [b]Greek I [c]Greek he

to come to them by way of the wilderness and to send them food. ²²So Trypho got all his cavalry ready to go, but that night a very heavy snow fell, and he did not go because of the snow. He marched off and went into the land of Gilead. ²³When he approached Baskama, he killed Jonathan, and he was buried there. ²⁴Then Trypho turned back and departed to his own land.

JONATHAN'S TOMB

²⁵And Simon sent and took the bones of Jonathan his brother and buried him in Modein, the city of his fathers. ²⁶All Israel bewailed him with great lamentation and mourned for him many days. ²⁷And Simon built upon the tomb of his father and his brothers; he made it high that it might be seen, with polished stone at the front and back. ²⁸He also erected seven pyramids, opposite one another, for his father and mother and four brothers. ²⁹And for the pyramids^a he devised mechanisms, erecting about them great columns, and upon the columns he put suits of armour for a permanent memorial, and beside the suits of armour carved ships, so that they could be seen by all who sail the sea. ³⁰This is the tomb that he built in Modein; it remains to this day.

JUDEA GAINS INDEPENDENCE

³¹Trypho dealt treacherously with the young King Antiochus; he killed him ³²and became king in his place, putting on the crown of Asia; and he brought great calamity upon the land. ³³But Simon built up the strongholds of Judea and walled them all around, with high towers and great walls and gates and bolts, and he stored food in the strongholds. ³⁴Simon also chose men and sent them to King Demetrius with a request to grant relief to the country, for all that Trypho did was to plunder. ³⁵King Demetrius sent him a favourable reply to this request and wrote him a letter as follows: ³⁶"King Demetrius to Simon, the high priest and friend of kings, and to the elders and nation of the Jews, greetings. ³⁷We have received the gold crown and the palm branch that you^b sent, and we are ready to make a general peace with you and to write to our officials to grant you release from tribute. ³⁸All the grants that we have made to you remain valid, and let the strongholds that you have built be your possession. ³⁹We pardon any errors and offences committed to this day and cancel the crown tax that you owe; and whatever other tax has been collected in Jerusalem shall be collected no longer. ⁴⁰And if any of you are qualified to be enrolled in our bodyguard,^{c} let them be enrolled, and let there be peace between us."

⁴¹In the 170th year^d the yoke of the Gentiles was removed from Israel, ⁴²and the people began to write in their documents and contracts, "In the first year of Simon the great high priest and commander and leader of the Jews."

CAPTURE OF GAZARA BY SIMON

⁴³In those days Simon^e encamped against Gazara^f and surrounded it with troops. He made a siege engine, brought it up to the city, and battered and captured one tower. ⁴⁴The men in the siege engine leaped out into the city, and a great tumult arose in the city. ⁴⁵The men in the city, with their wives and children, went up on the wall with their clothes rent, and they cried out with a loud voice, asking Simon to make peace with them; ⁴⁶they said, "Do not treat us according to our wicked acts but according to your mercy." ⁴⁷So Simon reached an agreement with them and stopped fighting against them. But he expelled them from the city and cleansed the houses in which the idols were, and then entered it with hymns and praise. ⁴⁸He cast out of it all uncleanness and settled in it men who observed the law. He also strengthened its fortifications and built in it a house for himself.

SIMON REGAINS THE JERUSALEM CITADEL

⁴⁹The men in the citadel at Jerusalem were prevented from going out to the country and back to buy and sell. So they were very hungry, and many of them perished from famine. ⁵⁰Then they cried to Simon to make peace with them, and he did so. But he expelled them from there and cleansed the citadel from its pollutions. ⁵¹On the twenty-third day of the second month, in the 171st year,^{g} the Jews^h entered it with praise and palm branches and with harps and cymbals and stringed instruments and with hymns and songs, because a great enemy had been crushed and removed from Israel. ⁵²And Simon decreed that every year they should celebrate this day with rejoicing. He

---

^{a}Greek *for these* ^{b}Greek *you* in 13:37-40 is plural ^{c}Or *court* ^{d}142 BC ^{e}Greek *he*; also verse 52 ^{f}Greek *Gaza* ^{g}141 BC ^{h}Greek *year, they*

strengthened the fortifications of the temple hill alongside the citadel, and he and his men dwelt there. ⁵³And Simon saw that John his son had reached manhood, so he made him commander of all the forces, and he dwelt in Gazara.

CAPTURE OF DEMETRIUS

14 In the 172nd year[a] King Demetrius assembled his forces and marched into Media to secure help, so that he could make war against Trypho. ²When King Arsaces of Persia and Media heard that Demetrius had invaded his territory, he sent one of his commanders to take him alive. ³And he went and defeated the army of Demetrius and seized him and took him to Arsaces, who put him under guard.

EULOGY OF SIMON

4 The land[b] had rest all the
   days of Simon.
   He sought the good of his nation;
   his rule was pleasing to them,
   as was the honour shown
   him, all his days.
5 To crown all his honours he
   took Joppa for a harbor
   and opened a way to the
   isles of the sea.
6 He extended the borders of his nation
   and gained full control
   of the country.
7 He gathered a host of captives;
   he ruled over Gazara and Bethzur and the citadel,
   and he removed its
   uncleanness from it;
   and there was none to oppose him.
8 They tilled their land in peace;
   the ground gave its increase,
   and the trees of the plains their fruit.
9 Old men sat in the streets;
   they all talked together
   of good things;
   and the youths donned the glories
   and garments of war.
10 He supplied the cities with food
   and furnished them with the
   means of defence,
   till his renown spread to the
   ends of the earth.
11 He established peace in the land,
   and Israel rejoiced with great joy.
12 Each man sat under his vine
   and his fig tree,
   and there was none to
   make them afraid.
13 No one was left in the land
   to fight them,
   and the kings were crushed
   in those days.
14 He strengthened all the
   humble of his people;
   he sought out the law
   and did away with every lawless
   and wicked man.
15 He made the sanctuary glorious
   and added to the vessels
   of the sanctuary.

DIPLOMACY WITH ROME AND SPARTA

¹⁶It was heard in Rome and as far away as Sparta that Jonathan had died, and they were deeply grieved. ¹⁷When they heard that Simon his brother had become high priest in his place and that he was ruling over the country and the cities in it, ¹⁸they wrote to him on bronze tablets to renew with him the friendship and alliance that they had established with Judas and Jonathan his brothers. ¹⁹And these were read before the assembly in Jerusalem.

²⁰This is a copy of the letter that the Spartans sent: "The rulers and the city of the Spartans to Simon the great priest and to the elders and the priests and the rest of the Jewish people, our brothers, greetings. ²¹The envoys who were sent to our people have told us about your glory and honour, and we rejoiced at their coming. ²²And what they said we have recorded in our public decrees, as follows: 'Numenius son of Antiochus and Antipater son of Jason, envoys of the Jews, have come to us to renew their friendship with us. ²³It has pleased our people to receive these men with honour and to put a copy of their words in the public archives, so that the people of the Spartans may have a record of them. And they have sent a copy of this to Simon the high priest.'"

²⁴After this Simon sent Numenius to Rome with a large gold shield weighing 1,000 minas, to confirm the alliance with the Romans.[c]

OFFICIAL HONOURS FOR SIMON

²⁵When the people heard these things they said, "How shall we thank Simon and

---
[a] 140 BC; also verse 27   [b] Some manuscripts add *of Judah*   [c] Greek *with them*

his sons? ²⁶For he and his brothers and the house of his father have stood firm; they have fought and repulsed Israel's enemies and established its freedom." ²⁷So they made a record on bronze tablets and put it upon pillars on Mount Zion.

This is a copy of what they wrote: "On the eighteenth day of Elul, in the 172nd year, which is the third year of Simon the great high priest, ²⁸in Asaramel,ᵃ in the great assembly of the priests and the people and the rulers of the nation and the elders of the country, it was proclaimed to us ²⁹that when many times wars occurred in the country, Simon son of Mattathias, son of the sons of Joarib, and his brothers exposed themselves to danger and resisted the enemies of their nation, in order that their sanctuary and the law might be preserved; and they brought great glory to their nation. ³⁰Jonathan rallied his nation and became their high priest and was gathered to his people. ³¹And when their enemies decided to invade their country to devastate their country and to lay hands on their sanctuary, ³²then Simon rose up and fought for his nation. He spent great sums of his own money; he armed the men of his nation's forces and paid them wages. ³³He fortified the cities of Judea and Beth-zur on the borders of Judea, where formerly the arms of the enemy had been stored, and he placed there a garrison of Jews. ³⁴He also fortified Joppa, which is by the sea, and Gazara, which is on the borders of Azotus, where the enemy formerly dwelt. He settled Jews there and provided in those citiesᵇ whatever was necessary for their restoration.

³⁵"The people saw Simon's faithfulnessᶜ and the glory that he had resolved to win for his nation, and they made him their leader and high priest, because he had done all these things and because of the justice and loyalty that he had maintained towards his nation. He sought in every way to exalt his people. ³⁶And in his days things prospered in his hands, so that the Gentiles were put out of theᵈ country, as were also the men in the city of David in Jerusalem, who had built themselves a citadel from which they used to sally forth and defile the environs of the sanctuary and do great damage to its purity. ³⁷He settled Jews in it and fortified it for the safety of the country and of the city and built the walls of Jerusalem higher.

³⁸"In view of these things King Demetrius confirmed him in the high priesthood, ³⁹and he made him one of the king'sᵉ friends and paid him high honours. ⁴⁰For he had heard that the Jews were addressed by the Romans as friends and allies and brothers and that the Romansᶠ had received the envoys of Simon with honour ⁴¹and that the Jews and the priests were pleased that Simon would be their leader and high priest for ever, until a trustworthy prophet should arise, ⁴²and that he should be governor over them and that he should take charge of the sanctuary and appoint men over its tasks and over the country and the weapons and the strongholds and that he should take charge of the sanctuary ⁴³and that he should be obeyed by all and that all contracts in the country should be written in his name and that he should be clothed in purple and wear gold.

⁴⁴"And none of the people or priests shall be permitted to nullify any of these decisions or to oppose what he says or to convene an assembly in the country without his permission or to be clothed in purple or put on a gold buckle.ᵍ ⁴⁵Whoever acts contrary to these decisions or nullifies any of them shall be liable to punishment."

⁴⁶And all the people agreed to grant Simon the right to act in accord with these decisions. ⁴⁷So Simon accepted and agreed to be high priest, to be commander and ethnarch of the Jews and priests, and to be protector ofʰ them all. ⁴⁸And they gave orders to inscribe this decree upon bronze tablets, to put them up in a conspicuous place in the precincts of the sanctuary, ⁴⁹and to deposit copies of them in the treasury, so that Simon and his sons might have them.

LETTER OF ANTIOCHUS VII

15 Antiochus son of King Demetrius sent a letter from the islands of the sea to Simon, the priest and ethnarch of the Jews, and to all the nation; ²its contents were as follows: "King Antiochus to Simon the great priest and ethnarch and to the nation of the Jews, greetings. ³Whereas certain pestilent men have gained control of the kingdom of our fathers, and I intend to lay claim to the kingdom so that I may restore it as it formerly was and have recruited a host of mercenary troops and have equipped warships ⁴and intend to make a landing in the

---

ᵃThis word resembles Hebrew *the court/prince of the people of God* ᵇGreek *in them* ᶜSome manuscripts *conduct* ᵈGreek *their* ᵉGreek *one of his* ᶠGreek *that they* ᵍOr *a brooch* ʰOr *to preside over*

1 MACCABEES 15

country so that I may proceed against those who have destroyed our country and those who have devastated many cities in my kingdom, [5]now therefore I confirm to you all the tax remissions that the kings before me have granted you and release from all the other payments from which they have released you. [6]I permit you to mint your own coinage as money for your country, [7]and I grant freedom to Jerusalem and the sanctuary. All the weapons that you have prepared and the strongholds that you have built and now hold shall remain yours. [8]Every debt you owe to the royal treasury and any such future debts shall be cancelled for you from henceforth and for all time. [9]When we gain control of our kingdom, we will bestow great honour upon you and your nation and the temple, so that your glory will become manifest in all the earth."

[10]In the 174th year[a] Antiochus set out and invaded the land of his fathers. All the troops rallied to him, so that there were few with Trypho. [11]Antiochus pursued him, and he came in his flight to Dor, which is by the sea; [12]for he knew that troubles had converged upon him, and his troops had deserted him. [13]So Antiochus encamped against Dor, and with him were 120,000 warriors and 8,000 cavalry. [14]He surrounded the city, and the ships joined battle from the sea; he pressed the city hard from land and sea and permitted no one to leave or enter it.

ROME SUPPORTS THE JEWS

[15]Then Numenius and his companions arrived from Rome, with letters to the kings and countries, in which the following was written: [16]"Lucius, consul of the Romans, to King Ptolemy, greetings. [17]The envoys of the Jews have come to us as our friends and allies to renew our ancient friendship and alliance. They had been sent by Simon the high priest and by the people of the Jews [18]and have brought a gold shield weighing 1,000 minas. [19]We therefore have decided to write to the kings and countries that they should not seek their harm or make war against them and their cities and their country or make alliance with those who war against them. [20]And it has seemed good to us to accept the shield from them. [21]Therefore if any pestilent men have fled to you from their country, hand them over to Simon the high priest, that he may punish them according to their law."

[22]The consul[b] wrote the same thing to King Demetrius and to Attalus and Ariarathes and Arsaces [23]and to all the countries and to Sampsakes[c] and to the Spartans and to Delos and to Myndos and to Sicyon and to Caria and to Samos and to Pamphylia and to Lycia and to Halicarnassus and to Rhodes and to Phaselis and to Cos and to Side and to Aradus and Gortyna and Cnidus and Cyprus and Cyrene. [24]They also sent a copy of these things to Simon the high priest.

ANTIOCHUS VII THREATENS SIMON

[25]King Antiochus besieged Dor anew,[d] continually throwing his forces against it and making engines of war; and he shut Trypho up and kept him from going out or in. [26]And Simon sent to Antiochus 2,000 picked men to fight for him and silver and gold and much military equipment. [27]But he refused to receive them, and he broke all the agreements he formerly had made with Simon[e] and became estranged from him. [28]He sent to him Athenobius, one of his friends, to confer with him, saying, "You hold control of Joppa and Gazara and the citadel in Jerusalem; they are cities of my kingdom. [29]You have devastated their territory, you have done great damage in the land, and you have taken possession of many places in my kingdom. [30]Now then, hand over the cities that you have seized and the tribute money of the places that you have conquered outside the borders of Judea; [31]or else give me for them 500 talents of silver and, for the destruction that you have caused and the tribute money of the cities, 500 talents more. Otherwise we will come and conquer you."

[32]So Athenobius the friend of the king came to Jerusalem, and when he saw the splendour of Simon and the sideboard with its gold and silver plate and his great magnificence, he was amazed. He reported to him the words of the king, [33]but Simon gave him this reply: "We have neither taken foreign land nor seized foreign property, but only the inheritance of our fathers, which at one time had been unjustly taken by our enemies. [34]Now that we have the opportunity, we are firmly holding the inheritance of our fathers. [35]As for Joppa and Gazara, which you demand, they were causing great damage among the people and to our land; for them we will give

---

[a]138 BC [b]Greek He [c]The Greek name is uncertain [d]Or Dor a second time [e]Greek him

100 talents." Athenobius[a] did not answer him a word, ³⁶but returned in wrath to the king and reported to him these words and the splendour of Simon and all that he had seen. And the king was greatly angered.

VICTORY OVER CENDEBEUS

³⁷Now Trypho embarked on a ship and escaped to Orthosia. ³⁸Then the king made Cendebeus commander-in-chief of the coastal country and gave him troops of infantry and cavalry. ³⁹He commanded him to encamp against Judea and commanded him to build up Kedron and fortify its gates and to make war on the people; but the king pursued Trypho. ⁴⁰So Cendebeus came to Jamnia and began to provoke the people and invade Judea and take the people captive and kill them. ⁴¹He built up Kedron and stationed there horsemen and troops, so that they might go out and make raids along the highways of Judea, as the king had ordered him.

16 John went up from Gazara and reported to Simon his father what Cendebeus had done. ²And Simon called in his two older sons Judas and John and said to them: "I and my brothers and the house of my father have fought the wars of Israel from our youth until this day, and things have prospered in our hands so that we have delivered Israel many times. ³But now I have grown old, and you by his mercy are mature in years. Take my place and my brother's, and go out and fight for our nation, and may the help that comes from heaven be with you."

⁴So John[b] chose out of the country 20,000 warriors and horsemen, and they marched against Cendebeus and camped for the night in Modein. ⁵Early in the morning they arose and marched into the plain, and behold, a large force of infantry and horsemen was coming to meet them; and a stream lay between them. ⁶Then he and his army lined up against them. And he saw that the soldiers were afraid to cross the stream, so he crossed over first; and when his men saw him, they crossed over after him. ⁷Then he divided the army and placed the horsemen in the midst of the infantry, for the cavalry of the enemy were very numerous. ⁸And they sounded the trumpets, and Cendebeus and his army were put to flight, and many of them were wounded and fell; the rest fled into the stronghold. ⁹At that time Judas the brother of John was wounded, but John pursued them until Cendebeus[c] reached Kedron, which he had built. ¹⁰They also fled into the towers that were in the fields of Azotus, and John[d] burned it with fire, and about 2,000 of them fell. And he returned to Judea safely.

MURDER OF SIMON AND HIS SONS

¹¹Now Ptolemy son of Abubus had been appointed governor over the plain of Jericho, and he had much silver and gold, ¹²for he was son-in-law of the high priest. ¹³His heart was lifted up; he determined to get control of the country and made treacherous plans against Simon and his sons, to do away with them. ¹⁴Now Simon was visiting the cities of the country and attending to their needs, and he went down to Jericho with Mattathias and Judas his sons, in the 177th year,[e] in the eleventh month, which is the month of Shebat. ¹⁵The son of Abubus received them treacherously in the little stronghold called Dok, which he had built; he gave them a great banquet and hid men there. ¹⁶When Simon and his sons were drunk, Ptolemy and his men rose up, took their weapons, and rushed in against Simon in the banquet hall, and they killed him and his two sons and some of his servants. ¹⁷So he committed an act of great treachery and returned evil for good.

JOHN SUCCEEDS SIMON

¹⁸Then Ptolemy wrote a report about these things and sent it to the king, asking him to send troops to aid him and to turn over to him the cities and the country. ¹⁹He sent other men to Gazara to do away with John; he sent letters to the captains asking them to come to him so that he might give them silver and gold and gifts; ²⁰and he sent other men to take possession of Jerusalem and the temple hill. ²¹But someone ran ahead and reported to John at Gazara that his father and brothers had perished and that "he has sent men to kill you also". ²²When he heard this, he was greatly shocked; and he seized the men who came to destroy him and killed them, for he had found out that they were seeking to destroy him.

²³The rest of the acts of John and his wars and the brave deeds that he did and the building of the walls that he built and his achievements, ²⁴behold, they are written in the chronicles of his high priesthood, from the time that he became high priest after his father.

---

[a] Greek He [b] Some manuscripts he [c] Greek he [d] Greek he [e] 134 BC

2 MACCABEES

LETTER TO THE JEWS IN EGYPT

1 [a] The Jewish brothers in Jerusalem and those in the land of Judea to their Jewish brothers in Egypt: Greetings and good peace.

²May God do good to you, and may he remember his covenant with Abraham and Isaac and Jacob, his faithful servants. ³May he give you all a heart to worship him and to do his will with a strong heart and a willing spirit. ⁴May he open your heart to his law and his commandments, and may he bring peace. ⁵May he hear your prayers and be reconciled to you, and may he not forsake you in time of evil. ⁶We are now praying for you here.

⁷In the reign of Demetrius, in the 169th year,[b] we Jews wrote to you, in the critical distress that came upon us in those years after Jason and his company revolted from the Holy Land and the kingdom ⁸and burned the gate and shed innocent blood. We prayed to the Lord, and we were heard, and we offered sacrifice and corn offering, and we lit the lamps and we set out the loaves. ⁹And now we see that you keep the Feast of Booths in the month of Chislev, in the 188th year.[c]

LETTER TO ARISTOBULUS

¹⁰Those in Jerusalem and those in Judea and the senate and Judas to Aristobulus, who is of the family of the anointed priests, teacher of King Ptolemy, and to the Jews in Egypt: Greetings and good health.

¹¹Having been saved by God out of grave dangers, we thank him greatly for taking our side against the king.[d] ¹²For he drove out those who fought against the holy city. ¹³For when the leader reached Persia with a force that seemed irresistible, they were cut to pieces in the temple of Nanea by a deception employed by the priests of Nanea. ¹⁴For under pretext of intending to marry her, Antiochus came to the place together with his friends, to secure most of its treasures as a dowry. ¹⁵When the priests of the temple of Nanea had set out the treasures and Antiochus had come with a few men inside the wall of the sacred precinct, they closed the temple as soon as he entered it. ¹⁶Opening the secret door in the ceiling, they threw stones and struck down the leader and his men and dismembered them and cut off their heads and threw them to the people outside. ¹⁷Blessed in every way be our God, who has brought judgement upon those who have behaved impiously.

FIRE CONSUMES NEHEMIAH'S SACRIFICE

¹⁸Since on the twenty-fifth day of Chislev we shall celebrate the purification of the temple, we thought it necessary to notify you, in order that you also may celebrate the Feast of Booths and the Feast of the Fire given when Nehemiah, who built the temple and the altar, offered sacrifices.

¹⁹For when our fathers were being led captive to Persia, the pious priests of that time took some of the fire of the altar and secretly hid it in the hollow of a dry cistern, where they took such precautions that the place was unknown to anyone. ²⁰But after many years had passed, when it pleased God, Nehemiah, having been commissioned by the king of Persia, sent the descendants of the priests who had hidden the fire to get it. And when they reported to us that they had not found fire but thick liquid, he ordered them to dip it out and bring it. ²¹And when the materials for the sacrifices were presented, Nehemiah ordered the priests to sprinkle the liquid on the wood and on what was laid upon it. ²²When this was done and some time had passed and the sun, which had been clouded over, shone out, a great fire blazed up, so that all marvelled. ²³And while the sacrifice was being consumed, the priests offered prayer—the priests and everyone. Jonathan led, and the rest responded, as did Nehemiah. ²⁴The prayer was to this effect:

---

[a] 2 Maccabees is one of the seven deuterocanonical books that do not exist in their entirety in Hebrew or Aramaic, but which were included in the Greek Septuagint, and were likewise included in the Latin Vulgate version of the Bible translated by Jerome in the late fourth century AD. See further, Introduction, pages xiii to xiv. [b] 143 BC [c] 124 BC
[d] Greek greatly as those who array themselves against a king

"O Lord, Lord God, Creator of all things, who is awe-inspiring and strong and just and merciful, who alone is King and is kind, **²⁵**who alone is bountiful, who alone is just and almighty and eternal, who rescues Israel from every evil, who chose the fathers and consecrated them, ²⁶accept this sacrifice on behalf of all your people Israel and preserve your portion and make it holy. ²⁷Gather together our scattered people, set free those who are slaves among the Gentiles, look upon those who are rejected and despised, and let the Gentiles know that you are our God. ²⁸Afflict those who oppress and are insolent with pride. ²⁹Plant your people in your holy place, as Moses said." ³⁰Then the priests sang the hymns. ³¹And when the materials of the sacrifice were consumed, Nehemiah ordered that the liquid that was left should be poured upon large stones. ³²When this was done, a flame blazed up; but when the light from the altar shone back, it went out. ³³When this matter became known, and it was reported to the king of the Persians that, in the place where the exiled priests had hidden the fire, the liquid had appeared with which Nehemiah and his associates had burned the materials of the sacrifice, ³⁴the king investigated the matter and enclosed the place and made it sacred. ³⁵And with those persons whom the king favoured he exchanged many excellent gifts. ³⁶Nehemiah and his associates called this "nephthar", which means purification, but by most people it is called naphtha.*ᵃ*

JEREMIAH HIDES THE TENT, ARK, AND ALTAR

2 One finds in the records that Jeremiah the prophet ordered those who were being deported to take some of the fire, as has been told, ²and that the prophet, after giving them the law, instructed those who were being deported not to forget the commandments of the Lord or to be led astray in their thoughts upon seeing the gold and silver statues and their adornment. ³And with other similar words he exhorted them that the law should not depart from their hearts.

⁴It was also in the writing that the prophet, having received an oracle, ordered that the tent and the ark should follow with him and that he went out to the mountain where Moses had gone up and had seen the inheritance of God. ⁵And Jeremiah came and found a cave, and he brought there the tent and the ark and the altar of incense, and he sealed up the entrance. ⁶Some of those who followed him came up to mark the way, but could not find it. ⁷When Jeremiah learned of it, he rebuked them and declared: "The place shall be unknown until God gathers his people together again and shows his mercy. ⁸And then the Lord will disclose these things, and the glory of the Lord and the cloud will appear, as they were shown in the case of Moses, and as Solomon asked that the place should be specially consecrated."

⁹It was also made clear that being possessed of wisdom Solomon*ᵇ* offered sacrifice for the dedication and completion of the temple. ¹⁰Just as Moses prayed to the Lord, and fire came down from heaven and devoured the sacrifices, so also Solomon prayed, and the fire came down and consumed the whole burnt offerings. ¹¹And Moses said, "They were consumed because the sin offering had not been eaten." ¹²Likewise Solomon also kept the eight days.

¹³The same things are reported in the records and in the memoirs of Nehemiah, and also that he founded a library and collected the books about the kings and prophets and the writings of David and letters of kings about votive offerings. ¹⁴In the same way Judas also collected all the books that had been lost on account of the war that had come upon us, and they are in our possession. ¹⁵So if you have need of them, send people to get them for you.

¹⁶Since, therefore, we are about to celebrate the purification, we write to you. Will you therefore please keep the days? ¹⁷It is God who has saved all his people and has returned the inheritance to all, and the kingship and priesthood and consecration, ¹⁸as he promised through the law. For we have hope in God that he will soon have mercy upon us and will gather us from everywhere under heaven into his holy place, for he has rescued us from great evils and has purified the place.

COMPILER'S PREFACE

¹⁹The story of Judas Maccabeus and his brothers and the purification of the great temple and the dedication of the altar ²⁰and further the wars against Antiochus Epiphanes and his son Eupator ²¹and the appearances that came from heaven to those who fought zealously on behalf of Judaism, so that though few in number they seized the whole

---

*ᵃ*Greek *nephthai* *ᵇ*Greek *he*

land and pursued the barbarian hordes ²²and recovered the temple famous throughout the world and freed the city and restored the laws that were about to be abolished, while the Lord with great kindness became gracious to them — ²³all this, which has been set forth by Jason of Cyrene in five volumes, we shall attempt to condense into a single book. ²⁴For considering the flood of numerical data and the difficulty there is for those who wish to enter upon the narratives of history because of the mass of material, ²⁵we have aimed to please those who wish to read, to make it easy for those who are inclined to memorize and to profit all readers. ²⁶For us who have undertaken the toil of abbreviating, it is no light matter but calls for sweat and loss of sleep, ²⁷just as it is not easy for one who prepares a banquet and seeks the benefit of others. However, to secure the gratitude of many we will gladly endure the uncomfortable toil, ²⁸leaving the responsibility for exact details to the compiler, while devoting our effort to arriving at the outlines of the condensation. ²⁹For as the master builder of a new house must be concerned with the whole construction, while the one who undertakes its painting and decoration has to consider only what is suitable for its adornment, such in my judgement is the case with us. ³⁰It is the duty of the original historian to occupy the ground and to discuss matters from every side and to take trouble with details, ³¹but the one who recasts the narrative should be allowed to fight for brevity of expression and to forego exhaustive treatment. ³²At this point therefore let us begin our narrative, without adding further to what has already been said; for it is foolish to lengthen the preface while cutting short the history itself.

ARRIVAL OF HELIODORUS IN JERUSALEM

3 While the holy city was inhabited in unbroken peace and the laws were very well observed because of the piety of the high priest Onias and his hatred of wickedness, ²it came about that the kings themselves honoured the place and glorified the temple with the finest presents, ³so that even King Seleucus of Asia defrayed from his own revenues all the expenses connected with the service of the sacrifices. ⁴But a man named Simon, of the tribe of Benjamin, who had been made captain of the temple, had a disagreement with the high priest about the administration of the city market; ⁵and when he could not prevail over Onias he went to Apollonius of Tarsus,ᵃ who at that time was governor of Coelesyria and Phoenicia. ⁶He reported to him that the treasury in Jerusalem was full of untold sums of money, so that the amount of the funds could not be reckoned and that they did not belong to the account of the sacrifices, but that it was possible for them to fall under the control of the king. ⁷When Apollonius met the king, he told him of the money about which he had been informed. The kingᵇ chose Heliodorus, who was in charge of his affairs, and sent him with commands to effect the removal of the aforesaid money. ⁸Heliodorus at once set out on his journey, ostensibly to make an inspection tour of the cities of Coelesyria and Phoenicia, but in fact to carry out the king's purpose.

⁹When he had arrived at Jerusalem and had been kindly welcomed by the high priest ofᶜ the city, he told about the disclosure that had been made and stated why he had come, and he enquired whether this really was the situation. ¹⁰The high priest explained that there were some deposits belonging to widows and orphans ¹¹and also some money of Hyrcanus son of Tobias, a man of very prominent position, and that it totaled in all 400 talents of silver and 200 of gold. To such an extent the impious Simon had misrepresented the facts. ¹²And he said that it was utterly impossible that wrong should be done to those people who had trusted in the holiness of the place and in the sanctity and inviolability of the temple that is honoured throughout the whole world. ¹³But Heliodorus, because of the king's commands that he had, said that this money must in any case be confiscated for the king's treasury. ¹⁴So he set a day and went in to direct the inspection of these funds.

There was no little distress throughout the whole city.¹⁵The priests prostrated themselves before the altar in their priestly garments and called towards heaven upon him who had given the law about deposits, that he should keep them safe for those who had deposited them. ¹⁶To see the appearance of the high priest was to be wounded at heart, for his face and the change in his colour disclosed the anguish of his soul. ¹⁷For terror and bodily trembling had come over the man,

---
ᵃGreek *Apollonius son of Tharseas* ᵇGreek *He*
ᶜSome manuscripts *and*

which plainly showed to those who looked at him the pain lodged in his heart. ¹⁸People also hurried out of their houses in crowds to make a general supplication because the Holy Place was about to be brought into contempt. ¹⁹Women, girded with sackcloth under their breasts, thronged the streets. Some of the maidens who were kept indoors ran together to the gates, and some to the walls, while others peered out of the windows. ²⁰And holding up their hands to heaven, they all made entreaty. ²¹There was something pitiable in the prostration of the whole populace and the anxiety of the high priest in his great anguish.

THE LORD PROTECTS HIS TEMPLE

²²While they were calling upon the almighty Lord that he would keep what had been entrusted safe and secure for those who had entrusted it, ²³Heliodorus went on with what had been decided. ²⁴But when he arrived at the treasury with his bodyguard, then and there the Sovereign of spirits and of all authority caused so great a manifestation that all who had been so bold as to accompany him were astounded by the power of God and became faint with terror. ²⁵For there appeared to them a magnificently caparisoned horse, with a rider of frightening appearance, and it rushed furiously at Heliodorus and struck at him with its front hoofs. Its rider was seen to have armour and weapons of gold. ²⁶Two young men also appeared to him, remarkably strong, gloriously beautiful and splendidly dressed, who stood on each side of him and scourged him continuously, inflicting many blows on him. ²⁷When he suddenly fell to the ground and deep darkness came over him, his men took him up and put him on a stretcher ²⁸and carried him away—this man who had just entered the aforesaid treasury with a great retinue and all his bodyguard but was now unable to help himself—and they recognized clearly the sovereign power of God. ²⁹While he lay prostrate, speechless because of the divine intervention and deprived of any hope of recovery, ³⁰they praised the Lord who had acted marvellously for his own place. And the temple, which a little while before was full of fear and disturbance, was filled with joy and gladness, now that the almighty Lord had appeared.

ONIAS PRAYS FOR HELIODORUS

³¹Quickly some of Heliodorus' friends asked Onias to call upon the Most High and to grant life to one who was lying quite at his last breath. ³²And the high priest, fearing that the king might get the notion that some foul play had been perpetrated by the Jews with regard to Heliodorus, offered sacrifice for the man's recovery. ³³While the high priest was making the offering of atonement, the same young men appeared again to Heliodorus, dressed in the same clothing, and they stood and said, "Be very grateful to Onias the high priest, since for his sake the Lord has granted you your life. ³⁴And see that you, who have been scourged by heaven, report to everyone the majestic power of God." Having said this they vanished.

CONVERSION OF HELIODORUS

³⁵Then Heliodorus offered sacrifice to the Lord and made very great vows to the Saviour of his life, and having bidden Onias farewell, he marched off with his forces to the king. ³⁶And he bore testimony to everyone concerning the deeds of the supreme God, which he had seen with his own eyes. ³⁷When the king asked Heliodorus what sort of person would be suitable to send on another mission to Jerusalem, he replied, ³⁸"If you have any enemy or plotter against your government, send him there, for you will get him back thoroughly scourged, if he escapes at all, for there certainly is about the place some power of God. ³⁹For he who has his dwelling in heaven watches over that place himself and brings it aid, and he strikes and destroys those who come to do it injury." ⁴⁰This was the outcome of the episode of Heliodorus and the protection of the treasury.

SIMON ACCUSES ONIAS

4 The previously mentioned Simon, who had informed about the money against[a] his own country, slandered Onias, saying that it was he who had incited Heliodorus and had been the real cause of the misfortune. ²He dared to designate as a plotter against the government the man who was the benefactor of the city, the protector of his compatriots, and a zealot for the laws. ³When his hatred progressed to such a degree that even murders were committed by one of Simon's approved agents, ⁴Onias recognized that the rivalry was serious and that Apollonius son of Menestheus[b] and governor of

---

[a]Greek and [b]Vulgate; compare 4:21; the meaning of the Greek is uncertain

Coelesyria and Phoenicia was intensifying the malice of Simon. ⁵So he conveyed himself to the king, not accusing his fellow citizens but having in view the welfare, both public and private, of all the people. ⁶For he saw that without the king's attention public affairs could not again reach a peaceful settlement and that Simon would not stop his folly.

JASON'S REFORMS

⁷When Seleucus died and Antiochus who was called Epiphanes succeeded to the kingdom, Jason the brother of Onias obtained the high priesthood by corruption, ⁸promising the king at an interview*ᵃ* 360 talents of silver and, from another source of revenue, 80 talents. ⁹In addition to this he promised to pay 150 more if permission were given to establish by his authority a gymnasium and a body of youth for it and to enroll the people of Jerusalem as citizens of Antioch. ¹⁰When the king assented and Jason*ᵇ* came to office, he at once shifted his compatriots over to the Greek way of life. ¹¹He set aside the existing royal concessions to the Jews, secured through John the father of Eupolemus, who went on the mission to establish friendship and alliance with the Romans; and he destroyed the lawful ways of living and introduced new customs contrary to the law. ¹²For with alacrity he founded a gymnasium right under the citadel, and he induced the noblest of the young men*ᶜ* to wear the athlete's cap. ¹³There was such an extreme of hellenization and increase in the adoption of foreign ways because of the surpassing wickedness of Jason, who was ungodly and no true high priest, ¹⁴that the priests were no longer intent upon their service at the altar. Despising the sanctuary and neglecting the sacrifices, they hastened to take part in the unlawful proceedings in the wrestling arena after the call to the discus, ¹⁵disdaining the honours prized by their fathers and putting the highest value upon Greek forms of prestige. ¹⁶For this reason heavy disaster overtook them, and those whose ways of living they admired and wished to imitate completely became their enemies and punished them. ¹⁷For it is no light thing to show irreverence to the divine laws — which later events will make clear.

JASON INTRODUCES GREEK CUSTOMS

¹⁸When the quadrennial games were being held at Tyre and the king was present, ¹⁹the vile Jason sent envoys, chosen as being Antiochian citizens from Jerusalem, to carry 300 silver drachmas for the sacrifice to Hercules. Those who carried the money, however, thought best not to use it for sacrifice, because that was inappropriate, but to expend it for another purpose. ²⁰So this money was intended by the sender for the sacrifice to Hercules, but by the decision of its carriers it was applied to the construction of triremes.

²¹When Apollonius son of Menestheus was sent to Egypt for the coronation*ᵈ* of Philometor as king, Antiochus learned that Philometor*ᵉ* had become hostile to his government, and he took measures for his own security. Therefore upon arriving at Joppa he proceeded to Jerusalem. ²²He was welcomed magnificently by Jason and the city and ushered in with a blaze of torches and with shouts. Then he marched into Phoenicia.

MENELAUS BECOMES HIGH PRIEST

²³After a period of three years Jason sent Menelaus, the brother of the previously mentioned Simon, to carry the money to the king and to complete the records of essential business. ²⁴But he, when presented to the king, extolled him with an air of authority and secured the high priesthood for himself, outbidding Jason by 300 talents of silver. ²⁵After receiving the king's orders he returned, possessing no qualification for the high priesthood, but having the hot temper of a cruel tyrant and the rage of a savage wild beast. ²⁶So Jason, who after supplanting his own brother was supplanted by another man, was driven as a fugitive into the land of Ammon. ²⁷And Menelaus held the office, but he did not pay regularly any of the money promised to the king. ²⁸When Sostratus the captain of the citadel kept requesting payment, for the collection of the revenue was his responsibility, the two of them were summoned by the king on account of this issue. ²⁹Menelaus left his own brother Lysimachus as deputy in the high priesthood, while Sostratus left Crates, the commander of the Cyprian troops.

MURDER OF ONIAS

³⁰While such was the state of affairs, it happened that the people of Tarsus and of Mallus revolted because their cities had been given

---

*ᵃ*Or *king by a petition* *ᵇ*Greek *he* *ᶜ*Some manuscripts add *subjecting them* *ᵈ*The meaning of the Greek is uncertain *ᵉ*Greek *he*

as a present to Antiochis, the king's concubine. ³¹So the king went hastily to settle the trouble, leaving Andronicus, a man of high rank, to act as his deputy. ³²But Menelaus, thinking he had obtained a suitable opportunity, stole some of the gold vessels of the temple and gave them to Andronicus; other vessels, as it happened, he had sold to Tyre and the neighbouring cities. ³³When Onias became fully aware of these acts he publicly exposed them, having first withdrawn to a place of sanctuary at Daphne near Antioch. ³⁴Therefore Menelaus, taking Andronicus aside, urged him to kill Onias. Andronicus[a] came to Onias and resorting to treachery offered him sworn pledges and gave him his right hand and in spite of Onias' suspicion persuaded him to come out from the place of sanctuary; then, with no regard for justice, he immediately got rid of him. ³⁵For this reason not only Jews, but many also of other nations, were grieved and displeased at the unjust murder of the man. ³⁶When the king returned from the region of Cilicia, the Jews in the[b] city appealed to him with regard to the unreasonable murder of Onias, and the Greeks shared their hatred of the crime. ³⁷Therefore Antiochus was grieved at heart and filled with pity and wept because of the moderation and good conduct of the deceased; ³⁸and inflamed with anger, he immediately stripped off the purple robe from Andronicus, tore off his garments, and led him round the whole city to that very place where he had committed the outrage against Onias, and there he dispatched the bloodthirsty fellow. The Lord thus repaid him with the punishment he deserved.

UNPOPULARITY OF LYSIMACHUS AND MENELAUS

³⁹When many acts of sacrilege had been committed in the city by Lysimachus with the connivance of Menelaus, and when report of them had spread abroad, the populace gathered against Lysimachus, because many of the gold vessels had already been stolen. ⁴⁰And since the crowds were becoming aroused and filled with anger, Lysimachus armed about 3,000 men and launched an unjust attack, under the leadership of a certain Auranus, a man advanced in years and no less advanced in folly. ⁴¹But when the Jews[c] became aware of Lysimachus' attack, some picked up stones, some blocks of wood, and others took handfuls of the ashes that were lying round and threw them in wild confusion at Lysimachus and his men. ⁴²As a result, they wounded many of them and killed some and put them all to flight; and the temple robber himself they killed close by the treasury.

⁴³Charges were brought against Menelaus about this incident. ⁴⁴When the king came to Tyre, three men sent by the senate presented the case before him. ⁴⁵But Menelaus, already as good as beaten, promised a substantial bribe to Ptolemy son of Dorymenes to win over the king. ⁴⁶Therefore Ptolemy, taking the king aside into a colonnade as if for refreshment, induced the king to change his mind. ⁴⁷Menelaus, the cause of all the evil, he acquitted of the charges against him, while he sentenced to death those unfortunate men, who would have been freed uncondemned if they had pleaded even before Scythians. ⁴⁸And so those who had spoken for the city and the people and the holy vessels quickly suffered the unjust penalty. ⁴⁹Therefore even the Tyrians, showing their hatred of the crime, provided magnificently for their funeral. ⁵⁰But Menelaus, because of the cupidity of those in power, remained in office, growing in wickedness, having become the chief plotter against his fellow citizens.

JASON TRIES TO REGAIN CONTROL

5 About this time Antiochus made his second invasion of Egypt. ²And it happened that over all the city, for almost forty days, there appeared golden-clad horsemen charging through the air, in companies fully armed with lances and drawn swords — ³troops of horsemen drawn up, attacks and counter-attacks made on this side and on that, brandishing of shields, massing of spears, hurling of missiles, the flash of golden trappings, and armour of all sorts. ⁴Therefore everyone prayed that the apparition might prove to have been a good omen.

⁵When a false rumor arose that Antiochus was dead, Jason took no less than 1,000 men and suddenly made an assault upon the city. When the troops upon the wall had been forced back and at last the city was being taken, Menelaus took refuge in the citadel. ⁶But Jason kept relentlessly slaughtering his fellow citizens, not realizing that success at

---

[a] Greek He [b] Or each [c] Greek when they

the cost of one's kindred is the greatest misfortune, but imagining that he was setting up trophies of victory over enemies and not over compatriots. ⁷He did not gain control of the government, however, and in the end got only disgrace from his conspiracy and fled again into the country of the Ammonites. ⁸Finally he met a miserable end. Sentenced by Aretas the ruler of the Arabs, fleeing from city to city, pursued by all men, hated as a rebel against the laws, and abhorred as the executioner of his country and his fellow citizens, he was cast ashore in Egypt; ⁹and he who had driven many from their own country into exile died in exile, having embarked to go to the Lacedaemonians in hope of finding protection because of their kinship. ¹⁰He who had cast out many to lie unburied had no one to mourn for him; he had no funeral of any sort and no place in the tomb of his fathers.

¹¹When news of what had happened reached the king, he took it to mean that Judea was in revolt. So, raging inwardly, he left Egypt and took the city by storm. ¹²And he commanded his soldiers to cut down relentlessly everyone they met and to slay those who went into the houses. ¹³Then there was killing of young and old, destruction of women and children, and slaughter of virgins and infants. ¹⁴Within the total of three days 80,000 were destroyed, 40,000 in hand-to-hand fighting; and as many were sold into slavery as were slain.

PILLAGE OF THE TEMPLE

¹⁵Not content with this, Antiochus[a] dared to enter the holiest temple in all the world, guided by Menelaus, who had become a traitor both to the laws and to his country. ¹⁶He took the holy vessels with his polluted hands and swept away with profane hands the votive offerings that other kings had made to enhance the glory and honour of the place. ¹⁷Antiochus was elated in spirit and did not perceive that the Lord was angered for a little while because of the sins of those who dwelt in the city and that therefore he was disregarding the Holy Place. ¹⁸But if it had not happened that they were involved in many sins, this man would have been scourged and turned back from his rash act as soon as he came forwards, just as Heliodorus had been, whom King Seleucus sent to inspect the treasury. ¹⁹But the Lord did not choose the nation for the sake of the Holy Place, but the place for the sake of the nation. ²⁰Therefore the place itself shared in the misfortunes that befell the nation and afterwards participated in its benefits; and what was forsaken in the wrath of the Almighty was restored again in all its glory when the great Lord was reconciled.

²¹So Antiochus carried off 1,800 from the temple and hurried away to Antioch, thinking in his arrogance that he could sail on the land and walk on the sea, because his mind was elated. ²²And he left governors to afflict the people: at Jerusalem, Philip, by birth a Phrygian and in character more barbarous than the man who appointed him; ²³and at Gerizim, Andronicus; and besides these Menelaus, who lorded it over his fellow citizens worse than the others did. In his malice towards the Jewish citizens,[b] ²⁴Antiochus sent Apollonius, the captain of the Mysians, with an army of 22,000 and commanded him to slay all the grown men and to sell the women and boys as slaves. ²⁵When this man arrived in Jerusalem, he pretended to be peaceably disposed and waited until the holy Sabbath day; then, finding the Jews not at work, he ordered his men to parade under arms. ²⁶He put to the sword all those who came out to see them, then rushed into the city with his armed men and killed great numbers of people.

²⁷But Judas Maccabeus, with about nine others, got away to the wilderness and kept himself and his companions alive in the mountains as wild animals do; they continued to live on what grew wild, so that they might not share in the defilement.

SUPPRESSION OF JUDAISM

6 Not long after this, the king sent an Athenian senator[c] to compel the Jews to forsake the laws of their fathers and cease to live by the laws of God ²and also to pollute the temple in Jerusalem and call it the temple of Olympian Zeus and to call the one in Gerizim the temple of Zeus the Friend of Strangers, as did the people who dwelt in that place.

³Harsh and utterly grievous was the onslaught of evil. ⁴For the temple was filled with debauchery and revelling by the Gentiles, who dallied with prostitutes and had intercourse with women within the sacred

---

[a] Greek he; also verse 24 [b] Or worse than the others did in his malice towards the Jewish citizens. [c] Or sent Geron an Athenian; some manuscripts sent an Antiochian senator

precincts and besides brought in things for sacrifice that were unfit. ⁵The altar was covered with abominable offerings that were forbidden by the laws. ⁶No one could either keep the Sabbath or observe the feasts of his fathers or so much as confess to being a Jew.

⁷On the monthly celebration of the king's birthday, the Jews[a] were taken, under bitter constraint, to partake of the sacrifices; and when the Feast of Dionysus came, they were compelled to walk in the procession in honour of Dionysus, wearing wreaths of ivy. ⁸At the suggestion of Ptolemy[b] a decree was issued to the neighbouring Greek cities, that they should adopt the same policy towards the Jews and make them partake of the sacrifices ⁹and should slay those who did not choose to change over to Greek customs. One could see, therefore, the misery that had come upon them. ¹⁰For example, two women were brought in for having circumcised their children. These women they publicly paraded round the city, with their babies hung at their breasts, and then hurled them down headlong from the wall. ¹¹Others, who had assembled in the caves nearby to observe the seventh day secretly, were betrayed to Philip and were all burned together, because their piety kept them from defending themselves, in view of their regard for that holiest day.

PROVIDENTIAL SIGNIFICANCE OF THE PERSECUTION

¹²Now I urge those who read this book not to be depressed by such calamities, but to recognize that these punishments were designed not to destroy but to discipline our people. ¹³In fact, to punish the ungodly quickly rather than leave them alone for very long is a sign of great kindness. ¹⁴For in the case of the other nations the Lord waits patiently to punish them until they have reached the full measure of their sins; but he does not deal in this way with us, ¹⁵in order that he may not take vengeance on us afterwards when our sins have reached their height. ¹⁶Therefore he never withdraws his mercy from us. Though he disciplines us with calamities, he does not forsake his own people. ¹⁷Let what we have said serve as a reminder; we must go on briefly with the story.

MARTYRDOM OF ELEAZAR

¹⁸Eleazar, one of the scribes in high position, a man now advanced in age and of noble presence, was being forced to open his mouth to eat swine's flesh. ¹⁹But he, welcoming death with honour rather than life with pollution, went up to the rack of his own accord, spitting out the flesh, ²⁰as men ought to go who have the courage to refuse things that it is not right to taste, even for the natural love of life.

²¹Those who were in charge of that unlawful sacrifice took the man aside, because of their long acquaintance with him, and privately urged him to bring meat of his own providing, proper for him to use, and pretend that he was eating the flesh of the sacrificial meal that had been commanded by the king, ²²so that by doing this he might be saved from death and be treated kindly on account of his old friendship with them. ²³But making a high resolve, worthy of his years and the dignity of his old age and the grey hairs that he had reached with distinction and his excellent life even from childhood, and moreover according to the holy God-given law, he declared himself quickly, telling them to send him to the grave.

²⁴"Such pretence is not worthy of our time of life", he said, "lest many of the young should suppose that Eleazar in his ninetieth year has gone over to an alien religion, ²⁵and through my pretence, for the sake of living a brief moment longer, they should be led astray because of me, while I defile and disgrace my old age. ²⁶For even if for the present I should avoid the punishment of men, yet whether I live or die I shall not escape the hands of the Almighty. ²⁷Therefore, by manfully giving up my life now, I will show myself worthy of my old age ²⁸and leave to the young a noble example of how to die a good death willingly and nobly for the revered and holy laws."

When he had said this, he went[c] at once to the rack. ²⁹And those who a little before had acted towards him with good will now changed to ill will, because the words he had uttered were in their opinion sheer madness. ³⁰When he was about to die under the blows, he groaned aloud and said: "It is clear to the Lord in his holy knowledge that, though I might have been saved from death, I am enduring terrible sufferings in my body under this beating, but in my soul I am glad to suffer these things because I fear him."

---

[a] Greek *birthday, they* [b] Or *of Ptolemy's family* [c] Some manuscripts *he was dragged*

³¹So in this way he died, leaving in his death an example of nobility and a memorial of courage, not only to the young but to the great body of his nation.

MARTYRDOM OF SEVEN BROTHERS

7 It happened also that seven brothers and their mother were arrested and were being compelled by the king, under torture with whips and cords, to partake of unlawful swine's flesh. ²One of them, acting as their spokesman, said, "What do you intend to ask and learn from us? For we are ready to die rather than transgress the laws of our fathers."

³The king fell into a rage and gave orders that pans and cauldrons be heated. ⁴These were heated immediately, and he commanded that the tongue of their spokesman be cut out and that they scalp him and cut off his hands and feet, while the rest of the brothers and the mother looked on. ⁵When he was utterly helpless, the king[a] ordered them to take him to the fire, still breathing, and to fry him in a pan. The smoke from the pan spread widely, but the brothers[b] and their mother encouraged one another to die nobly, saying, ⁶"The Lord God is watching over us and in truth has compassion on us, as Moses declared in his song that bore witness against the people to their faces, when he said, 'And he will have compassion on his servants.'"

⁷After the first brother had died in this way, they brought forwards the second for their sport. They tore off the skin of his head with the hair and asked him, "Will you eat rather than have your body punished limb by limb?" ⁸He replied in the language of his fathers and said to them, "No". Therefore he in turn underwent tortures as the first brother had done. ⁹And when he was at his last breath, he said, "You accursed wretch, you dismiss us from this present life, but the King of the universe will raise us up to an everlasting renewal of life, because we have died for his laws."

¹⁰After him, the third was the victim of their sport. When it was demanded, he quickly put out his tongue and courageously stretched forth his hands ¹¹and said nobly, "I got these from heaven, and because of his laws I disdain them, and from him I hope to get them back again." ¹²As a result the king himself and those with him were astonished at the young man's spirit, for he regarded his sufferings as nothing.

¹³When he too had died, they maltreated and tortured the fourth in the same way. ¹⁴And when he was near death, he said, "One cannot but choose to die at the hands of men and to cherish the hope that God gives of being raised again by him. But for you there will be no resurrection to life!"

¹⁵Next they brought forwards the fifth and maltreated him. ¹⁶But he looked at the king[c] and said, "Because you have authority among men, mortal though you are, you do what you please. But do not think that God has forsaken our people. ¹⁷Keep on, then, and see his mighty power, when you and your descendants are in torment!"

¹⁸After him they brought forwards the sixth. And when he was about to die, he said, "Do not deceive yourself in vain. For we are suffering these things on our own account, because of our sins against our own God. Therefore[d] astounding things have happened. ¹⁹But do not think that you will go unpunished for having tried to fight against God!"

²⁰The mother was especially admirable and worthy of honourable memory. Though she saw her seven sons perish within a single day, she bore it with good courage because of her hope in the Lord. ²¹She encouraged each of them in the language of their fathers. Filled with a noble spirit, she fired her woman's reasoning with a man's courage and said to them, ²²"I do not know how you came into being in my womb. It was not I who gave you life and breath, nor I who set in order the elements within each of you. ²³Therefore the Creator of the world, who shaped the beginning of mankind and devised the origin of all things, will in his mercy give life and breath back to you again, since you now forget yourselves for the sake of his laws."

²⁴Antiochus felt that he was being treated with contempt, and he was suspicious of her reproachful tone. The youngest brother being still alive, Antiochus[e] not only appealed to him in words, but promised with oaths that he would make him rich and enviable if he would turn from the ways of his fathers and that he would take him for his friend and entrust him with public affairs. ²⁵Since the young man would not listen to him at all, the king called the mother to him and urged her to advise the youth to save himself. ²⁶After much urging on his part, she undertook to persuade

---

[a] Greek *helpless, he*   [b] Greek *but they*   [c] Greek *at him*   [d] Latin; some manuscripts omit *Therefore*   [e] Greek *he*

her son. ²⁷But, leaning close to him, she spoke in their native tongue as follows, deriding the cruel tyrant: "My son, have pity on me. I carried you nine months in my womb and nursed you for three years and have reared you and brought you up to this point in your life and have taken care of you.ᵃ ²⁸I urge you, my child, to look at the heaven and the earth and see everything that is in them and recognize that not out of things that already existed did God make them, and so too the human race comes into being. ²⁹Do not fear this butcher, but prove worthy of your brothers. Accept death, so that in God's mercy I may get you back again along with your brothers."

³⁰Now as she was speaking, the young man said, "What are youᵇ waiting for? I will not obey the king's command, but I obey the command of the law that was given to our fathers through Moses. ³¹But you,ᶜ who have contrived all sorts of evil against the Hebrews, will certainly not escape the hands of God. ³²For we are suffering because of our own sins. ³³And if our living Lord is angry for a little while, to rebuke and discipline us, he will again be reconciled with his own servants. ³⁴But you, unholy wretch, you most defiled of all men, do not be elated in vain and puffed up by uncertain hopes, when you raise your hand against the children of heaven. ³⁵You have not yet escaped the judgement of the almighty, all-seeing God. ³⁶For now our brothers after enduring a brief suffering have fallen to an ever-flowing life under God's covenant; but you, by the judgement of God, will receive just punishment for your arrogance. ³⁷I, like my brothers, give up body and life for the laws of our fathers, appealing to God to show mercy soon to our nation and by afflictions and plagues to make you confess that he alone is God ³⁸and through me and my brothers to bring to an end the wrath of the Almighty that has justly fallen on our whole nation."

³⁹The king fell into a rage and handled him worse than the others, being exasperated at his scorn. ⁴⁰So he died in his integrity, putting his whole trust in the Lord.

⁴¹Last of all, the mother died, after her sons. ⁴²Let this be enough, then, about the eating of sacrifices and the extreme tortures.

REVOLT OF JUDAS MACCABEUS

8 Judas, however, who was also called Maccabeus, and his companions secretly entered the villages and summoned their kinsmen and enlisted those who had continued in the Jewish faith, and so they gathered about 6,000 men. ²They earnestly prayed to the Lord to look upon the people who were oppressed by all and to have pity on the temple that had been profaned by ungodly men ³and to have mercy on the city that was being destroyed and about to be levelled to the ground and to listen to the blood that cried out to him ⁴and to remember also the lawless destruction of the innocent babies and the blasphemies committed against his name and to show his hatred of evil.

⁵As soon as Maccabeus got his army organized, the Gentiles could not withstand him, for the wrath of the Lord had turned to mercy. ⁶Coming without warning, he would set fire to towns and villages. He captured strategic positions and put to flight not a few of the enemy. ⁷He found the nights most advantageous for such attacks. And talk of his valour spread everywhere.

⁸When Philip saw that the man was gaining ground little by little and that he was pushing ahead with more frequent successes, he wrote to Ptolemy, the governor of Coelesyria and Phoenicia, to come to the aid of the king's government. ⁹And Ptolemyᵈ promptly appointed Nicanor son of Patroclus, one of the king's chief friends, and sent him, in command of no fewer than 20,000 Gentiles of all nations, to wipe out the whole race of Judea. He associated with him Gorgias, a general and a man of experience in military service. ¹⁰Nicanor determined to make up for the king the tribute due to the Romans, 2,000 talents, by selling the captured Jews into slavery. ¹¹And he immediately sent to the cities on the sea coast, inviting them to buy Jewish slaves and promising to hand over ninety slaves for a talent, not expecting the judgement from the Almighty that was about to overtake him.

PREPARATION FOR BATTLE

¹²Word came to Judas concerning Nicanor's invasion; and when he told his companions of the arrival of the army, ¹³those who were cowardly and distrustful of God's justice ran off and got away. ¹⁴Others sold all their remaining property and at the same time asked the Lord to rescue those who had been sold by the ungodly Nicanor before he ever

---

ᵃ Or *and have borne the burden of your education* ᵇ Greek *you* is plural ᶜ Greek *you* is singular ᵈ Greek *he*

met them, ¹⁵if not for their own sake, yet for the sake of the covenants made with their fathers, and because he had called them by his holy and glorious name. ¹⁶But Maccabeus gathered his men together, to the number of 6,000, and exhorted them not to be frightened by the enemy and not to fear the great multitude of Gentiles who were wickedly coming against them, but to fight nobly, ¹⁷keeping before their eyes the lawless outrage that the Gentiles[a] had committed against the Holy Place and the torture of the derided city and, besides, the overthrow of their ancestral way of life. ¹⁸"For they trust to arms and acts of daring", he said, "but we trust in the almighty God, who is able with a single nod to strike down those who are coming against us and even the whole world."

¹⁹Moreover, he told them of the times when help came to their ancestors; both the time of Sennacherib, when 185,000 perished, ²⁰and the time of the battle with the Galatians that took place in Babylonia, when 8,000 in all went into the affair, with 4,000 Macedonians; and when the Macedonians were hard pressed, the 8,000, by the help that came to them from heaven, destroyed 120,000 and took much booty.

JUDAS DEFEATS NICANOR

²¹With these words he filled them with good courage and made them ready to die for their laws and their country; then he divided his army into four parts. ²²He appointed his brothers also, Simon and Joseph and Jonathan, each to command a division, putting 1,500 men under each. ²³He also read aloud from the holy book the words "El-ezer", thus giving the watchword, "God's help"; then, leading the first division himself, he joined battle with Nicanor.

²⁴With the Almighty as their ally, they killed more than 9,000 of the enemy and wounded and disabled most of Nicanor's army and forced them all to flee. ²⁵They captured the money of those who had come to buy them as slaves. After pursuing them for some distance, they were obliged to return because the hour was late. ²⁶For it was the day before the Sabbath, and for that reason they did not continue their pursuit. ²⁷And when they had collected the arms of the enemy and stripped them of their spoils, they kept the Sabbath, giving great praise and thanks to the Lord, who had preserved them for that day and allotted it to them as the beginning of mercy. ²⁸After the Sabbath they gave some of the spoils to those who had been tortured and to the widows and orphans and distributed the rest among themselves and their children. ²⁹When they had done this, they made common supplication and begged the merciful Lord to be wholly reconciled with his servants.

JUDAS DEFEATS TIMOTHY AND BACCHIDES

³⁰In encounters with the forces of Timothy and Bacchides they killed more than 20,000 of them and got possession of some exceedingly high strongholds, and they divided very much plunder, giving to those who had been tortured and to the orphans and widows and also to the aged shares equal to their own. ³¹Collecting the arms of the enemy,[b] they stored them all carefully in strategic places and carried the rest of the spoils to Jerusalem. ³²They killed the commander of Timothy's forces, a most unholy man and one who had greatly troubled the Jews. ³³While they were celebrating the victory in the city of their fathers, they burned those who had set fire to the sacred gates, and Callisthenes,[c] who had fled into one little house; so these received the proper recompense for their impiety.[d]

³⁴The thrice-accursed Nicanor, who had brought 1,000 merchants to buy the Jews, ³⁵having been humbled with the help of the Lord by opponents whom he regarded as of the least account, took off his splendid uniform and made his way alone like a runaway slave across the country till he reached Antioch, having succeeded chiefly in the destruction of his own army! ³⁶Thus he who had undertaken to secure tribute for the Romans by the capture of the people of Jerusalem proclaimed that the Jews had a Defender and that therefore the Jews were invulnerable, because they followed the laws ordained by him.

LAST CAMPAIGN OF ANTIOCHUS EPIPHANES

9 About that time, as it happened, Antiochus had retreated in disorder from the region of Persia. ²For he had entered the city called Persepolis and attempted to rob the temples and control the city. Therefore the people rushed to the rescue with arms, and Antiochus and his men[e] were

---

[a]Greek *that they* [b]Greek *Collecting their arms* [c]Some manuscripts and versions add *and some others* [d]The meaning of the Greek is uncertain [e]Greek *and they*

defeated, with the result that Antiochus was put to flight by the inhabitants and beat a shameful retreat. ³While he was in Ecbatana, news came to him of what had happened to Nicanor and the forces of Timothy. ⁴Transported with rage, he conceived the idea of turning upon the Jews the injury done by those who had put him to flight; so he ordered his charioteer to drive without stopping until he completed the journey. But the judgement of heaven rode with him! For in his arrogance he said, "When I get there I will make Jerusalem a cemetery of Jews."

⁵But the all-seeing Lord, the God of Israel, struck him an incurable and invisible blow. As soon as he ceased speaking he was seized with a pain in his bowels for which there was no relief and with sharp internal tortures— ⁶and that very justly, for he had tortured the bowels of others with many and strange inflictions. ⁷Yet he did not in any way stop his insolence, but was even more filled with arrogance, breathing fire in his rage against the Jews and giving orders to hasten the journey. And so it came about that he fell out of his chariot as it was rushing along, and the fall was so hard as to torture every limb of his body. ⁸Thus he who had just been thinking in his superhuman arrogance that he could command the waves of the sea and imagining that he could weigh the high mountains in a balance was brought down to earth and carried in a litter, making the power of God manifest to all. ⁹And so the ungodly man's body swarmed with worms, and while he was still living in anguish and pain, his flesh rotted away, and because of his stench the whole army felt revulsion at his decay. ¹⁰Because of his intolerable stench no one was able to carry the man who a little while before had thought that he could touch the stars of heaven. ¹¹Then it was that, broken in spirit, he began to lose much of his arrogance and to come to his senses under the scourge of God, for he was tortured with pain every moment. ¹²And when he could not endure his own stench, he uttered these words: "It is right to be subject to God, and no mortal should think that he is equal to God."ᵃ

ANTIOCHUS MAKES A PROMISE TO GOD

¹³Then the abominable fellow made a vow to the Lord, who would no longer have mercy on him, stating ¹⁴that the holy city, which he had been hastening to level to the ground and to make a cemetery, he was now declaring to be free; ¹⁵and the Jews, whom he had not considered worth burying but had planned to throw out with their children to the beasts, for the birds to pick, he would make, all of them, equal to citizens of Athens; ¹⁶and the holy sanctuary, which he had formerly plundered, he would adorn with the finest offerings; and the holy vessels he would give back, all of them, many times over; and the expenses incurred for the sacrifices he would provide from his own revenues; ¹⁷and in addition to all this he also would become a Jew and would visit every inhabited place to proclaim the power of God. ¹⁸But when his sufferings did not in any way abate, for the judgement of God had justly come upon him, he gave up all hope for himself and wrote to the Jews the following letter, in the form of a supplication. This was its content:

ANTIOCHUS' LETTER AND DEATH

¹⁹"To his worthy Jewish citizens, Antiochus their king and general sends hearty greetings and good wishes for their health and prosperity. ²⁰If you and your children are well and your affairs are as you wish, I am glad. As my hope is in heaven, ²¹I remember with affection your esteem and good will. On my way back from the region of Persia I suffered an annoying illness, and I have deemed it necessary to take thought for the general security of all. ²²I do not despair of my condition, for I have good hope of recovering from my illness, ²³but I observed that my father, on the occasions when he made expeditions into the upper country, appointed his successor, ²⁴so that, if anything unexpected happened or any unwelcome news came, the people throughout the realm would not be troubled, for they would know to whom the government was left. ²⁵Moreover, I understand how the princes along the borders and the neighbours to my kingdom keep watching for opportunities and waiting to see what will happen. So I have appointed my son Antiochus to be king, whom I have often entrusted and commended to most of you when I hastened off to the upper provinces; and I have written to him what is written here. ²⁶I therefore urge and entreat you to remember the public and private services rendered to you and to maintain your present good will, each of you, towards me and

---

ᵃOr think thoughts proper only to God

my son. ²⁷For I am sure that he will follow my policy and will treat you with moderation and kindness."

²⁸So the murderer and blasphemer, having endured the most intense suffering, such as he had inflicted on others, came to the end of his life by a most pitiable fate, among the mountains in a strange land. ²⁹And Philip, one of his courtiers, took his body home; then, fearing the son of Antiochus, he conveyed himself to Ptolemy Philometor in Egypt.

PURIFICATION OF THE TEMPLE

10 Now Maccabeus and his followers, the Lord leading them on, recovered the temple and the city; ²and they tore down the altars that had been built in the public square by the foreigners and also destroyed the sacred precincts. ³They purified the sanctuary and made another altar of sacrifice; then, striking fire out of flint, they offered sacrifices, after a lapse of two years, and they burned incense and lighted lamps and set out the bread of the Presence. ⁴And when they had done this, they fell prostrate and prayed earnestly to the Lord that they might never again fall into such misfortunes, but that, if they should ever sin, they might be disciplined by him with forbearance and not be handed over to blasphemous and barbarous nations. ⁵It happened that on the same day on which the sanctuary had been profaned by the foreigners, the purification of the sanctuary took place, that is, on the twenty-fifth day of the same month, which was Chislev. ⁶And they celebrated it for eight days with rejoicing, in the manner of the Feast of Booths, remembering how not long before, during the Feast of Booths, they had been wandering in the mountains and caves like wild animals. ⁷Therefore bearing ivy-wreathed wands and beautiful branches and also fronds of palm, they offered hymns of thanksgiving to him who had given success to the purifying of his own Holy Place. ⁸They decreed by public ordinance and referendum that the whole nation of the Jews should observe these days every year.

⁹Such then was the end of Antiochus, who was called Epiphanes.

ACCESSION OF ANTIOCHUS EUPATOR

¹⁰Now we will tell what took place under Antiochus Eupator, who was the son of that ungodly man, and will give a brief summary of the principal calamities of the wars. ¹¹This man, when he succeeded to the kingdom, appointed one Lysias to have charge of the government and to be chief governor of Coelesyria and Phoenicia. ¹²Ptolemy, who was called Macron, took the lead in showing justice to the Jews because of the wrong that had been done to them and attempted to maintain peaceful relations with them. ¹³As a result he was accused before Eupator by the king's friends. He heard himself called a traitor at every turn, because he had abandoned Cyprus, which Philometor had entrusted to him, and had gone over to Antiochus Epiphanes. Unable to command the respect due his office,ᵃ he took poison and ended his life.

CAMPAIGN IN IDUMEA

¹⁴When Gorgias became governor of the region, he maintained a force of mercenaries and at every turn kept on warring against the Jews. ¹⁵Besides this, the Idumeans, who had control of important strongholds, were harassing the Jews; they received those who were banished from Jerusalem and endeavoured to keep up the war. ¹⁶But Maccabeus and his men, after making solemn supplication and asking God to fight on their side, rushed to the strongholds of the Idumeans. ¹⁷Attacking them vigorously, they gained possession of the places and beat off all who fought upon the wall and killed those whom they encountered, killing no fewer than 20,000.

¹⁸When no less than 9,000 took refuge in two very strong towers well equipped to withstand a siege, ¹⁹Maccabeus left Simon and Joseph, and also Zacchaeus and his men, a force sufficient to besiege them; and he himself set off for places where he was more urgently needed. ²⁰But the men with Simon, being lovers of money, were bribed by some of those who were in the towers and on receiving 70,000 drachmas let some of them slip away. ²¹When word of what had happened came to Maccabeus, he gathered the leaders of the people and accused these men of having sold their brothers for money by setting their enemies free to fight against them. ²²Then he killed these men who had turned traitor and immediately captured the two towers. ²³Having success at arms in everything he undertook, he destroyed more than 20,000 in the two strongholds.

ᵃThe meaning of the Greek is uncertain

JUDAS DEFEATS TIMOTHY

²⁴Now Timothy, who had been defeated by the Jews before, gathered a tremendous force of mercenaries and collected the cavalry from Asia in no small number. He came on, intending to take Judea by storm. ²⁵As he drew near, Maccabeus and his men sprinkled dust upon their heads and girded their loins with sackcloth, in supplication to God. ²⁶Falling upon the steps before the altar, they implored him to be gracious to them and to be an enemy to their enemies and an adversary to their adversaries, as the law declares. ²⁷And rising from their prayer they took up their arms and advanced a considerable distance from the city; and when they came near to the enemy they halted. ²⁸Just as dawn was breaking, the two armies joined battle, the one having as pledge of success and victory not only their valour but also their reliance upon the Lord, while the other made rage their leader in the fight.

²⁹When the battle became fierce, there appeared to the enemy from heaven five resplendent men on horses with golden bridles, and they were leading the Jews. ³⁰Two of them took Maccabeus in their midst, and protecting him with their own armour and weapons, they kept him from being wounded. And they showered arrows and thunderbolts upon the enemy, so that, confused and blinded, they were thrown into disorder and cut to pieces. ³¹And they slaughtered 20,500 men, plus 600 horsemen.

³²Timothy himself fled to a stronghold called Gazara, especially well garrisoned, where Chaereas was commander. ³³Then Maccabeus and his men were glad, and they besieged the fort for four days. ³⁴The men within, relying on the strength of the place, blasphemed terribly and hurled out wicked words. ³⁵But at dawn of the fifth day, twenty young men in the army of Maccabeus, fired with anger because of the blasphemies, bravely stormed the wall and with savage fury cut down everyone they met. ³⁶Others who came up in the same way wheeled round against the defenders and set fire to the towers; they kindled fires and burned the blasphemers alive. Others broke open the gates and let in the rest of the force, and they occupied the city. ³⁷They killed Timothy, who was hidden in a cistern, and his brother Chaereas and Apollophanes. ³⁸When they had accomplished these things, with hymns and thanksgivings they blessed the Lord who shows great kindness to Israel and gives them the victory.

LYSIAS BESIEGES BETH-ZUR

11 Very soon after this, Lysias, the king's guardian and kinsman, who was in charge of the government, being vexed at what had happened, ²gathered about 80,000 men and all his cavalry and came against the Jews. He intended to make the city a home for Greeks ³and to levy tribute on the temple as he did on the sacred places of the other nations and to put up the high priesthood for sale every year. ⁴He took no account whatever of the power of God, but was elated with his ten thousands of infantry and his thousands of cavalry and his eighty elephants. ⁵Entering Judea, he approached Beth-zur, which was a fortified place about five leagues^a from Jerusalem, and pressed it hard.

⁶When Maccabeus and his men got word that Lysias^b was besieging the strongholds, they and all the people, with lamentations and tears, begged the Lord to send a good angel to save Israel. ⁷Maccabeus himself was the first to take up arms, and he urged the others to risk their lives with him to aid their brothers. Then they eagerly rushed off together. ⁸And there, while they were still near Jerusalem, a horseman appeared at their head, clothed in white and brandishing weapons of gold. ⁹And they all together praised the merciful God and were strengthened in heart, ready to assail not only men but the wildest beasts or walls of iron. ¹⁰They advanced in battle order, having their heavenly ally, for the Lord had mercy on them. ¹¹They hurled themselves like lions against the enemy and threw down 11,000 of them and 1,600 horsemen and forced all the rest to flee. ¹²Most of those who got away were stripped and wounded, and Lysias himself escaped by fleeing in disgrace.

LYSIAS MAKES PEACE WITH THE JEWS

¹³And as he was not without intelligence, he pondered over the defeat that had befallen him and realized that the Hebrews were invincible because the mighty God fought on their side. So he sent to them ¹⁴and persuaded them to settle everything on just terms, promising that he would persuade the king, constraining him to be their friend.

---

^{a}About 20 miles; the meaning of the Greek is uncertain ^{b}Greek *he*

¹⁵Maccabeus, having regard for the common good, agreed to all that Lysias urged. For the king granted every request in behalf of the Jews that Maccabeus delivered to Lysias in writing.

¹⁶The letter written to the Jews by Lysias was to this effect:

"Lysias to the people of the Jews, greeting. ¹⁷John and Absalom, who were sent by you, have delivered your signed communication and have asked about the matters indicated therein. ¹⁸I have informed the king of everything that needed to be brought before him, and he has agreed to what was possible. ¹⁹If you will maintain your good will towards the government, I will endeavour for the future to help promote your welfare. ²⁰And concerning these matters and their details, I have ordered these men and my representatives to confer with you. ²¹Farewell. The 148th year,[a] Dioscorinthius twenty-fourth."

²²The king's letter ran thus:

"King Antiochus to his brother Lysias, greetings. ²³Now that our father has gone on to the gods, we desire that the subjects of the kingdom be undisturbed in caring for their own affairs. ²⁴We have heard that the Jews do not consent to our father's change to Greek customs but prefer their own way of living and ask that their own customs be allowed them. ²⁵Accordingly, since we choose that this nation also be free from disturbance, our decision is that their temple be restored to them and that they live according to the customs of their ancestors. ²⁶You will do well, therefore, to send word to them and give them pledges of friendship, so that they may know our policy and be of good cheer and go on happily in the conduct of their own affairs."

²⁷To the nation the king's letter was as follows:

"King Antiochus to the senate of the Jews and to the other Jews, greetings. ²⁸If you are well, it is as we desire. We also are in good health. ²⁹Menelaus has informed us that you wish to return home and look after your own affairs. ³⁰Therefore those who go home by the thirtieth day of Xanthicus will have our pledge of friendship and full permission ³¹for the Jews to enjoy their own food and laws, just as formerly, and none of them shall be molested in any way for what he may have done in ignorance. ³²And I have also sent Menelaus to encourage you. ³³Farewell. The 148th year, Xanthicus fifteenth."

³⁴The Romans also sent them a letter, which read thus:

"Quintus Memmius and Titus Manius, envoys of the Romans, to the people of the Jews, greetings. ³⁵With regard to what Lysias the kinsman of the king has granted you, we also give consent. ³⁶But as to the matters that he decided are to be referred to the king, as soon as you have considered them, send someone promptly, so that we may make proposals appropriate for you. For we are on our way to Antioch. ³⁷Therefore make haste and send some men, so that we may know your disposition. ³⁸Farewell. The 148th year, Xanthicus fifteenth."

INCIDENTS AT JOPPA AND JAMNIA

12 When this agreement had been reached, Lysias returned to the king, and the Jews went about their farming.

²But some of the governors in various places, Timothy and Apollonius son of Gennaeus, as well as Hieronymus and Demophon and in addition to these Nicanor the governor of Cyprus, would not let them live quietly and in peace. ³And the people of Joppa did so ungodly a deed as this: they invited the Jews who lived among them to embark, with their wives and children, on boats that they had provided, as though there were no ill will to the Jews;[b] ⁴and this was done by public vote of the city. And when they accepted, because they wished to live peaceably and suspected nothing, the men of Joppa[c] took them out to sea and drowned them, not less than 200. ⁵When Judas heard of the cruelty visited on his compatriots, he gave orders to his men ⁶and, calling upon God the righteous Judge, attacked the murderers of his kindred. He set fire to the harbour by night and burned the boats and massacred those who had taken refuge there. ⁷Then, because the city's gates were closed, he withdrew, intending to come again and root out the whole community of Joppa. ⁸But learning that the people in Jamnia meant in the same way to wipe out the Jews who were living among them, ⁹he attacked the people of Jamnia by night and set fire to the harbour and the fleet, so that the glow of the light was seen in Jerusalem, thirty miles[d] distant.

---

[a] 164 BC; also verses 32, 38   [b] Greek *to them*   [c] Greek *nothing, they*
[d] Greek *240 stadia*

CAMPAIGN IN GILEAD

¹⁰When they had gone more than a mile[a] from there, on their march against Timothy, no fewer than 5,000 Arabs with 500 horsemen attacked them. ¹¹After a hard fight Judas and his men won the victory, by the help of God. The defeated nomads begged Judas to grant them pledges of friendship, promising to give him livestock and to help his people[b] in all other ways. ¹²Judas, thinking that they might really be useful in many ways, agreed to make peace with them; and after receiving his pledges they went to their tents.

¹³He also attacked a certain city that was strongly fortified with earthworks[c] and walls and inhabited by all sorts of Gentiles. Its name was Caspin. ¹⁴And those who were within, relying on the strength of the walls and on their supply of provisions, behaved most insolently towards Judas and his men, railing at them and even blaspheming and saying unholy things. ¹⁵But Judas and his men, calling upon the great Sovereign of the world, who without battering rams or engines of war overthrew Jericho in the days of Joshua, rushed furiously upon the walls. ¹⁶They took the city by the will of God and slaughtered untold numbers, so that the adjoining lake, a quarter of a mile[d] wide, appeared to be running over with blood.

JUDAS DEFEATS TIMOTHY'S ARMY

¹⁷When they had gone ninety-five miles[e] from there, they came to Charax, to the Jews who are called Toubiani. ¹⁸They did not find Timothy in that region, for he had by then departed from the region without accomplishing anything, though in one place he had left a very strong garrison. ¹⁹Dositheus and Sosipater, who were captains under Maccabeus, marched out and destroyed those whom Timothy had left in the stronghold, more than 10,000 men. ²⁰But Maccabeus arranged his army in divisions, set men[f] in command of the divisions, and hastened after Timothy, who had with him 120,000 infantry and 2,500 cavalry. ²¹When Timothy learned of the approach of Judas, he sent off the women and the children and also the baggage to a place called Carnaim; for that place was hard to besiege and difficult of access because of the narrowness of all the approaches. ²²But when Judas' first division appeared, terror and fear came over the enemy at the manifestation to them of him who sees all things; and they rushed off in flight and were swept on, this way and that, so that often they were injured by their own men and pierced by the points of their swords. ²³And Judas pressed the pursuit with the utmost vigour, putting the sinners to the sword, and destroyed as many as 30,000 men.

²⁴Timothy himself fell into the hands of Dositheus and Sosipater and their men. With great guile he entreated them to let him go in safety, because he held the parents of most of them and the brothers of some, to whom no consideration would be shown. ²⁵And when with many words he had confirmed his solemn promise to restore them unharmed, they let him go, for the sake of saving their brothers.

JUDAS WINS OTHER VICTORIES

²⁶Then Judas[g] marched against Carnaim and the temple of Atargatis and slaughtered 25,000 people. ²⁷After the rout and destruction of these, he marched also against Ephron, a fortified city where there were multitudes of people of all nationalities.[h] Stalwart young men took their stand before the walls and made a vigorous defence; and great stores of war engines and missiles were there. ²⁸But the Jews[i] called upon the Sovereign who with power shatters the might of his enemies, and they got the city into their hands and killed as many as 25,000 of those who were within it

²⁹Setting out from there, they hastened to Scythopolis, which is seventy-five miles[j] from Jerusalem. ³⁰But when the Jews who lived there bore witness to the good will that the people of Scythopolis had shown them and their kind treatment of them in times of misfortune, ³¹they thanked them and exhorted them to be well disposed to their race in the future also. Then they went up to Jerusalem, as the Feast of Weeks was close at hand.

JUDAS DEFEATS GORGIAS

³²After the feast called Pentecost, they hastened against Gorgias, the governor of Idumea. ³³And he came out with 3,000 infantry and 400 cavalry. ³⁴When they joined battle, it happened that a few of the Jews fell. ³⁵But a certain Dositheus, one of

---

[a]Greek *nine stadia* [b]Greek *help them* [c]The meaning of the Greek is uncertain [d]Greek *two stadia* [e]Greek *750 stadia* [f]Greek *them* [g]Greek *he* [h]The meaning of the Greek is uncertain [i]Greek *But they* [j]Greek *600 stadia*

Bacenor's men, who was on horseback and was a strong man, caught hold of Gorgias and, grasping his cloak, was dragging him off by main strength, wishing to take the accursed man alive, when one of the Thracian horsemen bore down upon him and cut off his arm; so Gorgias escaped and reached Marisa.

36 As Esdris and his men had been fighting for a long time and were weary, Judas called upon the Lord to show himself their ally and leader in the battle. 37 In the language of their fathers he raised the battle cry, with hymns; then he charged against Gorgias' men when they were not expecting it and put them to flight.

PRAYERS FOR THOSE KILLED IN BATTLE

38 Then Judas assembled his army and went to the city of Adullam. As the seventh day was coming on, they purified themselves according to the custom, and they kept the Sabbath there.

39 On the next day, as by that time it had become necessary, Judas and his men went to take up the bodies of the fallen and to bring them back to lie with their kinsmen in the sepulchres of their fathers. 40 Then under the tunic of every one of the dead they found sacred tokens of the idols of Jamnia, which the law forbids the Jews to wear. And it became clear to all that this was why these men had fallen. 41 So they all blessed the ways of the Lord, the righteous Judge, who reveals the things that are hidden; 42 and they turned to prayer, imploring that the sin that had been committed might be wholly blotted out. And the noble Judas exhorted the people to keep themselves free from sin, for they had seen with their own eyes what had happened because of the sin of those who had fallen. 43 He also took up a collection, man by man, to the amount of 2,000 drachmas of silver and sent it to Jerusalem to provide for a sin offering. In doing this he acted very well and honourably, taking account of the resurrection. 44 For if he were not expecting that those who had fallen would rise again, it would have been superfluous and foolish to pray for the dead. 45 But if he was looking to the splendid reward that is laid up for those who fall asleep in godliness, it was a holy and pious thought. Therefore he made atonement for the dead, that they might be delivered from their sin.

MENELAUS PUT TO DEATH

13 In the 149th year[a] word came to Judas and his men that Antiochus Eupator was coming with a great army against Judea 2 and with him Lysias, his guardian, who had charge of the government. Each of them had a Greek force of 110,000 infantry, 5,300 cavalry, 22 elephants, and 300 chariots armed with scythes.

3 Menelaus also joined them and with utter hypocrisy urged Antiochus on, not for the sake of his country's welfare, but because he thought that he would be established in office. 4 But the King of kings aroused the anger of Antiochus against the scoundrel; and when Lysias informed him that this man was to blame for all the trouble, he ordered them to take him to Beroea and to put him to death by the method that is the custom in that place. 5 For there is a tower in that place, fifty cubits high, full of ashes, and it has a rim running round it that on all sides inclines precipitously into the ashes. 6 There they all push to destruction any man guilty of sacrilege or notorious for other crimes. 7 By such a fate it came about that Menelaus the lawbreaker died, without even burial in the earth. 8 And this was eminently just; because he had committed many sins against the altar whose fire and ashes were holy, he met his death in ashes.

BATTLE NEAR THE CITY OF MODEIN

9 The king with barbarous arrogance was coming to show the Jews things far worse than those[b] that had been done in his father's time. 10 But when Judas heard of this, he ordered the people to call upon the Lord day and night, now if ever to help those who were on the point of being deprived of the law and their country and the holy temple 11 and not to let the people who had just begun to revive fall into the hands of the blasphemous Gentiles. 12 When they had all joined in the same petition and had fervently prayed to the merciful Lord with weeping and fasting and lying prostrate for three days without ceasing, Judas exhorted them and ordered them to stand ready.

13 After consulting privately with the elders, he determined to march out and decide the matter by the help of God before the king's army could enter Judea and get possession of the city. 14 So, committing the decision to

---

[a] 163 BC [b] Or show the Jews the worst of the things

the Creator of the world and exhorting his men to fight nobly to the death for the laws, temple, city, country, and commonwealth, he pitched his camp near Modein. ¹⁵He gave his men the watchword, "God's victory", and with a picked force of the bravest young men, he attacked the king's pavilion at night and killed as many as 2,000 men in the camp and stabbed[a] the leading elephant with its occupant. ¹⁶In the end they filled the camp with terror and confusion and withdrew in triumph. ¹⁷This happened, just as day was dawning, because the Lord's help protected him.

ANTIOCHUS MAKES A TREATY WITH THE JEWS

¹⁸The king, having had a taste of the daring of the Jews, tried strategy in attacking their positions. ¹⁹He advanced against Beth-zur, a strong fortress of the Jews, was turned back, attacked again,[b] and was defeated. ²⁰Judas sent in to the garrison whatever was necessary. ²¹But Rhodocus, a man from the ranks of the Jews, gave secret information to the enemy; he was sought for, caught, and put in prison. ²²The king negotiated a second time with the people in Beth-zur, gave pledges, received theirs, withdrew, attacked Judas and his men, was defeated. ²³He got word that Philip, who had been left in charge of the government, had revolted in Antioch; he was dismayed, called in the Jews, yielded and swore to observe all their rights, settled with them and offered sacrifice, honoured the sanctuary and showed generosity to the Holy Place. ²⁴He received Maccabeus, left Hegemonides as governor from Ptolemais to Gerar, ²⁵and went to Ptolemais. The people of Ptolemais were indignant over the treaty; in fact they were so angry that they wanted to annul its terms.[c] ²⁶Lysias took the public platform, made the best possible defence, convinced them, appeased them, gained their good will, and set out for Antioch. This is how the king's attack and withdrawal turned out.

ALCIMUS SPEAKS AGAINST JUDAS

14 Three years later, word came to Judas and his men that Demetrius son of Seleucus had sailed into the harbour of Tripolis with a strong army and a fleet ²and had taken possession of the country, having made away with Antiochus and his guardian Lysias.

³Now a certain Alcimus, who had formerly been high priest but had willfully defiled himself in the times of separation,[d] realized that there was no way for him to be safe or to have access again to the holy altar ⁴and went to King Demetrius in about the 151st year,[e] presenting to him a crown of gold and a palm and besides these some of the customary olive branches from the temple. During that day he kept quiet. ⁵But he found an opportunity that furthered his mad purpose when he was invited by Demetrius to a meeting of the council and was asked about the disposition and intentions of the Jews. He answered:

⁶"Those of the Jews who are called Hasideans, whose leader is Judas Maccabeus, are keeping up war and stirring up sedition and will not let the kingdom attain tranquillity. ⁷Therefore I have laid aside my ancestral glory—I mean the high priesthood—and have now come here, ⁸first because I am genuinely concerned for the interests of the king, and second because I have regard also for my fellow citizens. For through the folly of those whom I have mentioned our whole nation is now in no small misfortune. ⁹Since you are acquainted, O king, with the details of this matter, please take thought for our country and our hard-pressed nation with the gracious kindness that you show to all. ¹⁰For as long as Judas lives, it is impossible for the government to find peace."

¹¹When he had said this, the rest of the king's friends, who were hostile to Judas, quickly inflamed Demetrius still more. ¹²And he immediately chose Nicanor, who had been in command of the elephants, appointed him governor of Judea, and sent him off ¹³with orders to kill Judas and scatter those with him and to set up Alcimus as high priest of the great temple. ¹⁴And the Gentiles throughout Judea, who had fled before[f] Judas, flocked to join Nicanor, thinking that the misfortunes and calamities of the Jews would mean prosperity for themselves.

NICANOR MAKES FRIENDS WITH JUDAS

¹⁵When the Jews[g] heard of Nicanor's coming and the gathering of the Gentiles, they sprinkled dust upon their heads and prayed to him who established his own people for

---

[a] Greek *and put together* [b] Or *back, faltered* [c] The meaning of the Greek is uncertain [d] Some manuscripts *mingling* [e] 161 BC [f] The meaning of the Greek is uncertain [g] Greek *When they*

ever and always upholds his own heritage by manifesting himself. ¹⁶At the command of the leader, they[a] set out from there immediately and engaged them in battle at a village called Dessau.[b] ¹⁷Simon the brother of Judas had encountered Nicanor, but had been temporarily[c] checked because of the sudden consternation created by the enemy.

¹⁸Nevertheless Nicanor, hearing of the valour of Judas and his men and their courage in battle for their country, shrank from deciding the issue by bloodshed. ¹⁹Therefore he sent Posidonius and Theodotus and Mattathias to give and receive pledges of friendship. ²⁰When the terms had been fully considered and the leader had informed the people, and it appeared that they were of one mind, they agreed to the covenant. ²¹And the leaders[d] set a day on which to meet by themselves. A chariot came forwards from each army; seats of honour were set in place; ²²Judas posted armed men in readiness at key places to prevent sudden treachery on the part of the enemy; they held the proper conference.

²³Nicanor stayed on in Jerusalem and did nothing out of the way, but dismissed the flocks of people that had gathered. ²⁴And he kept Judas always in his presence; he was warmly attached to the man. ²⁵And he urged him to marry and have children; so he married, settled down, and shared the common life.

NICANOR TURNS AGAINST JUDAS

²⁶But when Alcimus noticed their good will for one another, he took the covenant that had been made and went to Demetrius. He told him that Nicanor was disloyal to the government, for he had appointed that conspirator against the kingdom, Judas, to be his successor. ²⁷The king became excited and, provoked by the false accusations of that depraved man, wrote to Nicanor, stating that he was displeased with the covenant and commanding him to send Maccabeus to Antioch as a prisoner without delay.

²⁸When this message came to Nicanor, he was troubled and grieved that he had to annul their agreement when the man had done no wrong. ²⁹Since it was not possible to oppose the king, he watched for an opportunity to accomplish this by a stratagem. ³⁰But Maccabeus, noticing that Nicanor was more austere in his dealings with him and was meeting him more rudely than had been his custom, concluded that this austerity did not spring from the best motives. So he gathered not a few of his men and went into hiding from Nicanor.

³¹When the latter became aware that he had been cleverly outwitted by the man, he went to the great[e] and holy temple while the priests were offering the customary sacrifices and commanded them to hand the man over. ³²And when they declared on oath that they did not know where the man was whom he sought, ³³he stretched out his right hand towards the sanctuary and swore this oath: "If you do not hand Judas over to me as a prisoner, I will level this precinct of God to the ground and tear down the altar, and I will build here a splendid temple to Dionysus."

³⁴Having said this, he went away. Then the priests stretched forth their hands towards heaven and called upon the constant Defender of our nation, in these words: ³⁵"O Lord of all, who has need of nothing, you were pleased that there be a temple for your habitation among us; ³⁶so now, O Holy One, Lord of all holiness, keep undefiled for ever this house that has been so recently purified."

RAZIS DIES FOR HIS COUNTRY

³⁷A certain Razis, one of the elders of Jerusalem, was denounced to Nicanor as a man who loved his fellow citizens and was very well thought of and for his good will was called father of the Jews. ³⁸For in former times, when there was no mingling with the Gentiles, he had been accused of Judaism, and for Judaism he had with all zeal risked body and life. ³⁹Nicanor, wishing to exhibit the enmity that he had for the Jews, sent more than 500 soldiers to arrest him; ⁴⁰for he thought that by arresting[f] him he would do them an injury. ⁴¹When the troops were about to capture the tower and were forcing the door of the courtyard, they ordered that fire be brought and the doors burned. Being surrounded, Razis[g] fell upon his own sword, ⁴²preferring to die nobly rather than to fall into the hands of sinners and suffer outrages unworthy of his noble birth. ⁴³But in the heat of the struggle he did not hit exactly, and the crowd was now rushing in through the doors. He bravely ran up on the wall and manfully threw himself down into the crowd. ⁴⁴But as they quickly drew back,

---

[a]Greek he [b]The Greek name is uncertain [c]Some manuscripts slowly [d]Greek And they [e]Greek greatest [f]The meaning of the Greek is uncertain [g]Greek he

a space opened, and he fell in the middle of the empty space. ⁴⁵Still alive and aflame with anger, he rose, and though his blood gushed forth and his wounds were severe he ran through the crowd; and standing upon a steep rock, ⁴⁶with his blood now completely drained from him, he tore out his entrails, took them with both hands and hurled them at the crowd, calling upon the Lord of life and spirit to give them back to him again. This was the manner of his death.

NICANOR'S ARROGANCE

15 When Nicanor heard that Judas and his men were in the region of Samaria, he made plans to attack them with complete safety on the day of rest. ²And when the Jews who were compelled to follow him said, "Do not destroy so savagely and barbarously, but show respect for the day that he who sees all things has honoured and hallowed above other days," ³the thrice-accursed wretch asked if there were a sovereign in heaven who had commanded the keeping of the Sabbath day. ⁴And when they declared, "It is the living Lord himself, the Sovereign in heaven, who ordered us to observe the seventh day", ⁵he replied, "And I am a sovereign also, on earth, and I command you to take up arms and finish the king's business." Nevertheless, he did not succeed in carrying out his abominable design.

JUDAS PREPARES THE JEWS FOR BATTLE

⁶This Nicanor in his utter boastfulness and arrogance had determined to erect a public monument of victory over Judas and his men. ⁷But Maccabeus did not cease to trust with all confidence that he would get help from the Lord. ⁸And he exhorted his men not to fear the attack of the Gentiles, but to keep in mind the former times when help had come to them from heaven and now to look for the victory that the Almighty would give them. ⁹Encouraging them from the Law and the Prophets and reminding them also of the struggles they had won, he made them the more eager. ¹⁰And when he had aroused their courage, he gave his orders, at the same time pointing out the perfidy of the Gentiles and their violation of oaths. ¹¹He armed each of them not so much with confidence in shields and spears as with the inspiration of brave words, and he cheered them all by relating a dream, a sort of vision,ᵃ that was worthy of belief.

¹²What he saw was this: Onias, who had been high priest, a noble and good man, of modest bearing and gentle manner, one who spoke fittingly and had been trained from childhood in all that belongs to excellence, was praying with outstretched hands for the whole body of the Jews. ¹³Then likewise a man appeared, distinguished by his grey hair and dignity and of marvellous majesty and authority. ¹⁴And Onias spoke, saying, "This is a man who loves the brothers and prays much for the people and the holy city—Jeremiah the prophet of God." ¹⁵Jeremiah stretched out his right hand and gave to Judas a golden sword, and as he gave it he addressed him thus: ¹⁶"Take this holy sword, a gift from God, with which you will strike down your adversaries."

¹⁷Encouraged by the words of Judas, so noble and so effective in arousing valour and awaking manliness in the souls of the young, they determined not to carry on a campaignᵇ but to attack bravely and to decide the matter by fighting hand to hand with all courage, because the city and the sanctuary and the temple were in danger. ¹⁸Their concern for wives and children and also for brothers and relatives lay upon them less heavily; their greatest and first fear was for the consecrated sanctuary. ¹⁹And those who had to remain in the city were in no little distress, being anxious over the encounter in the open country.

DEFEAT AND DEATH OF NICANOR

²⁰When all were now looking forwards to the coming decision, and the enemy was already close at hand with their army drawn up for battle, the elephantsᶜ strategically stationed and the cavalry deployed on the flanks, ²¹Maccabeus, perceiving the hosts that were before him and the varied supply of arms and the savagery of the elephants, stretched out his hands towards heaven and called upon the Lord who works wonders; for he knew that it is not by arms, but as the Lordᵈ decides, that he gains the victory for those who deserve it. ²²And he called upon him in these words: "O Lord, in the time of King Hezekiah of Judea you sent your angel, and he killed fully 185,000 in the camp of Sennacherib. ²³So now, O Sovereign of the heavens, send a good angel to carry terror

---

ᵃThe meaning of the Greek is uncertain ᵇSome manuscripts *to remain in the camp* ᶜGreek *beasts*; also verse 21 ᵈGreek *as he*

and trembling before us. ²⁴By the might of your arm may these blasphemers who come against your holy people be struck down." With these words he ended his prayer.

²⁵Nicanor and his men advanced with trumpets and battle songs; ²⁶and Judas and his men met the enemy in battle with invocation to God and prayers. ²⁷So, fighting with their hands and praying to God in their hearts, they laid low no less than 35,000 men and were greatly gladdened by God's manifestation.

²⁸When the action was over and they were returning with joy, they recognized Nicanor, lying dead, in full armour. ²⁹Then there was shouting and tumult, and they blessed the Sovereign Lord in the language of their fathers. ³⁰And the man who was ever in body and soul the defender of his fellow citizens, the man who maintained his youthful good will towards his compatriots, ordered them to cut off Nicanor's head and arm and carry them to Jerusalem. ³¹And when he arrived there and had called his compatriots together and stationed the priests before the altar, he sent for those who were in the citadel. ³²He showed them the vile Nicanor's head and that profane man's arm, which had been boastfully stretched out against the holy house of the Almighty; ³³and he cut out the tongue of the ungodly Nicanor and said that he would give it piecemeal to the birds and hang up these rewards of his folly opposite the sanctuary. ³⁴And they all, looking to heaven, blessed the Lord who had manifested himself, saying, "Blessed is he who has kept his own place undefiled." ³⁵And he hung Nicanor's head from the citadel, a clear and conspicuous sign to everyone of the help of the Lord. ³⁶And they all decreed by public vote never to let this day go unobserved, but to celebrate the thirteenth day of the twelfth month—which is called Adar in the Syrian language—the day before Mordecai's day.

COMPILER'S EPILOGUE

³⁷This, then, is how matters turned out with Nicanor. And from that time the city has been in the possession of the Hebrews. So I too will here end my story. ³⁸If it is well told and to the point, that is what I myself desired; if it is poorly done and mediocre, that was the best I could do. ³⁹For just as it is harmful to drink wine alone or, again, to drink water alone, while wine mixed with water is sweet and delicious and enhances one's enjoyment, so also the style of the story delights the ears of those who read the work. And here will be the end.

1 ESDRAS

JOSIAH CELEBRATES THE PASSOVER

1 Josiah kept the Passover to his Lord in Jerusalem; he killed the Passover lamb on the fourteenth day of the first month, ²having placed the priests according to their divisions, arrayed in their garments, in the temple of the Lord. ³And he told the Levites, the temple servants of Israel, that they should sanctify themselves to the Lord and put the holy ark of the Lord in the house that King Solomon son of David had built; ⁴and he said, "You need no longer carry it upon your shoulders. Now worship the Lord your God and serve his people Israel and prepare yourselves by your families and tribes, ⁵in accordance with the directions of King David of Israel and the magnificence of Solomon his son. Stand in order in the temple according to the groupings of the fathers' houses of you Levites, who minister before your brothers the people of Israel, ⁶and kill the Passover lamb and prepare the sacrifices for your brothers and keep the Passover according to the commandment of the Lord that was given to Moses."

⁷And Josiah gave to the people who were present 30,000 lambs and kids and 3,000 calves; these were given from the king's possessions, as he promised, to the people and the priests and Levites. ⁸And Hilkiah, Zechariah, and Jehiel, the chief officers of the temple, gave to the priests for the Passover 2,600 sheep and 300 calves. ⁹And Jeconiah and Shemaiah and Nethanel his brother and Hashabiah and Ochiel and Joram, captains over thousands, gave the Levites for the Passover 5,000 sheep and 700 calves.

¹⁰And this is what took place. The priests and the Levites, properly arrayed and having the unleavened bread, stood according to ¹¹their tribes and the grouping of the fathers' houses, before the people, to make the offering to the Lord as it is written in the book of Moses; this they did in the morning. ¹²They roasted the Passover lamb with fire, as required; and they boiled the sacrifices in bronze pots and cauldrons, with a pleasing odour, ¹³and carried them to all the people. Afterwards they prepared the Passover for themselves and for their brothers the priests, the sons of Aaron, ¹⁴because the priests were offering the fat until night; so the Levites prepared it for themselves and for their brothers the priests, the sons of Aaron. ¹⁵And the temple musicians, the sons of Asaph, were in their place according to the arrangement made by David, and also Asaph, Zechariah, and Eddinus, who represented the king. ¹⁶The gatekeepers were at each gate; no one needed to depart from his duties, for their brothers the Levites prepared the Passover for them.

¹⁷So the things that had to do with the sacrifices to the Lord were accomplished that day: the Passover was kept ¹⁸and the sacrifices were offered on the altar of the Lord, according to the command of King Josiah. ¹⁹And the sons of Israel who were present at that time kept the Passover and the Feast of Unleavened Bread seven days. ²⁰No Passover like it had been kept in Israel since the times of Samuel the prophet; ²¹none of the kings of Israel had kept such a Passover as was kept by Josiah and the priests and Levites and the people of Judah and all of Israel who were dwelling in Jerusalem. ²²In the eighteenth year of the reign of Josiah this Passover was kept. ²³And the deeds of Josiah were upright in the sight of the Lord, for his heart was full of godliness. ²⁴The events of his reign have been recorded in the past, concerning those who sinned and acted wickedly towards the Lord beyond any other people or kingdom and how they perceptibly grieved the Lord,ᵃ so that the words of the Lord rose up against Israel.

END OF JOSIAH'S REIGN

²⁵After all these acts of Josiah, it happened that Pharaoh, king of Egypt, went to make war at Carchemish on the Euphrates, and Josiah went out against him. ²⁶And the king of Egypt sent word to him saying, "What have we to do with each other, king of Judea? ²⁷I was not sent against you by the Lord God, for

---
ᵃGreek *grieved him*

my war is at the Euphrates. And now the Lord is with me! The Lord is with me, urging me on! Stand aside and do not oppose the Lord."

²⁸But Josiah did not turn back to his chariot, but tried to fight with him and did not heed the words of Jeremiah the prophet from the mouth of the Lord. ²⁹He joined battle with him in the plain of Megiddo, and the commanders came down against King Josiah. ³⁰And the king said to his servants, "Take me away from the battle, for I am very weak." And immediately his servants took him out of the line of battle. ³¹And he got into his second chariot; and after he was brought back to Jerusalem he died and was buried in the tomb of his fathers. ³²And in all Judea they mourned for Josiah. Jeremiah the prophet lamented for Josiah, and the principal men, with the women,ᵃ have made lamentation for him to this day; it was ordained that this should always be done throughout the whole nation of Israel. ³³These things are written in the book of the histories of the kings of Judea; and every one of the acts of Josiah and his splendour and his understanding of the law of the Lord and the things that he had done before and these that are now told are recorded in the book of the kings of Israel and Judah.

LAST KINGS OF JUDAH

³⁴And the men of the nation took Jeconiahᵇ son of Josiah, who was twenty-three years old, and made him king in succession to Josiah his father. ³⁵And he reigned for three months in Judah and Jerusalem. Then the king of Egypt deposed him from reigning in Jerusalem ³⁶and fined the nation 100 talents of silver and a talent of gold. ³⁷And the king of Egypt made Jehoiakim his brother king of Judea and Jerusalem. ³⁸Jehoiakim put the nobles in prison and seized his brother Zarius and brought him up out of Egypt.

³⁹Jehoiakim was twenty-five years old when he began to reign in Judea and Jerusalem, and he did what was evil in the sight of the Lord. ⁴⁰And King Nebuchadnezzar of Babylon came up against him and bound him with a chain of bronze and took him away to Babylon. ⁴¹Nebuchadnezzar also took some holy vessels of the Lord and carried them away and stored them in his temple in Babylon. ⁴²But the things that are reported about Jehoiakimᶜ and his uncleanness and impiety are written in the chronicles of the kings.

⁴³Jehoiachin his son became king in his stead; when he was made king he was eighteen years old, ⁴⁴and he reigned for three months and ten days in Jerusalem. He did what was evil in the sight of the Lord. ⁴⁵And after a year Nebuchadnezzar sent and removed him to Babylon, with the holy vessels of the Lord, ⁴⁶and made Zedekiah king of Judea and Jerusalem.

FALL OF JERUSALEM

Zedekiah was twenty-one years old, and he reigned for eleven years. ⁴⁷He also did what was evil in the sight of the Lord and did not listen to the words that were spoken by Jeremiah the prophet from the mouth of the Lord. ⁴⁸And though King Nebuchadnezzar had made him swear by the name of the Lord, he broke his oath and rebelled; and he stiffened his neck and hardened his heart and transgressed the laws of the Lord, the God of Israel. ⁴⁹Also the leaders of the people and of the priests committed many acts of sacrilege and lawlessness beyond all the unclean deeds of all the nations and polluted the temple of the Lord that had been sanctified in Jerusalem. ⁵⁰So the God of their fathers sent word by his messenger to call them back, because he would have spared them and his dwelling place. ⁵¹But they mocked his messengers, and whenever the Lord spoke, they scoffed at his prophets, ⁵²until in his anger against his people because of their ungodly acts he gave command to bring against them the kings of the Chaldeans. ⁵³These killed their young men with the sword round their holy temple and did not spare young man or maiden, old man or youngster, for he gave them all into their hands. ⁵⁴And all the holy vessels of the Lord, great and small, and the treasure chests of the Lord and the royal stores, they took and carried away to Babylon. ⁵⁵And they burned the house of the Lord and broke down the walls of Jerusalem and burned their towers with fire ⁵⁶and utterly destroyed all its glorious things. The survivors he led away to Babylon with the sword, ⁵⁷and they were servants to him and to his sons until the Persians began to reign, in fulfilment of the word of the Lord by the mouth of Jeremiah: ⁵⁸"Until the land has enjoyed its Sabbaths, it shall keep Sabbath all the time of its desolation until the completion of seventy years."

ᵃ*Or with their wives* ᵇSome manuscripts *Jehoahaz*; compare 2 Kings 23:30 and 2 Chronicles 36:1 ᶜGreek *him*

CYRUS PERMITS THE EXILES TO RETURN

2 In the first year of Cyrus as king of the Persians, so that the word of the Lord by the mouth of Jeremiah might be accomplished, ²the Lord stirred up the spirit of King Cyrus of the Persians, and he made a proclamation throughout all his kingdom and also put it in writing:

³"Thus says King Cyrus of the Persians: The Lord of Israel, the Lord Most High, has made me king of the world, ⁴and he has commanded me to build him a house at Jerusalem, which is in Judea. ⁵If any one of you, therefore, is of his people, may his Lord be with him and let him go up to Jerusalem, which is in Judea, and build the house of the Lord of Israel—he is the Lord who dwells in Jerusalem, ⁶and let all, wherever they may live, be helped by the men of his place with gold and silver—⁷with gifts and with horses and cattle, besides the other things added as votive offerings for the temple of the Lord that is in Jerusalem."

⁸Then arose the heads of families of the tribes of Judah and Benjamin and the priests and the Levites and all whose spirit the Lord had stirred to go up to build the house in Jerusalem for the Lord; ⁹and their neighbours helped them with everything, with silver and gold, with horses and cattle, and with a very great number of votive offerings from many whose hearts were stirred.

¹⁰King Cyrus also brought out the holy vessels of the Lord that Nebuchadnezzar had carried away from Jerusalem and stored in his temple of idols. ¹¹When King Cyrus of the Persians brought these out, he gave them to Mithridates his treasurer, ¹²and by him they were given to Sheshbazzar the governor of Judea. ¹³The number of these was 1,000 gold cups, 1,000 silver cups, 29 silver censers, 30 gold bowls, 2,410 silver bowls, and 1,000 other vessels. ¹⁴All the vessels were handed over, gold and silver, 5,469, ¹⁵and they were carried back by Sheshbazzar with the returning exiles from Babylon to Jerusalem.

OPPOSITION TO REBUILDING JERUSALEM

¹⁶But in the time of King Artaxerxes of the Persians, Bishlam, Mithridates, Tabeel, Rehum, Beltethmus, Shimshai the scribe, and the rest of their associates living in Samaria and other places wrote him the following letter, against those who were living in Judea and Jerusalem:

¹⁷"To King Artaxerxes our lord, your servants Rehum the recorder and Shimshai the scribe and the other judges of their council in Coelesyria and Phoenicia: ¹⁸Now be it known to our lord the king that the Jews who came up from you to us have gone to Jerusalem and are building that rebellious and wicked city, repairing its market-places and walls, and laying the foundations for a temple. ¹⁹Now if this city is built and the walls finished, they will not only refuse to pay tribute but will even resist kings. ²⁰And since the building of the temple is now going on, we think it best not to neglect such a matter, ²¹but to speak to our lord the king, in order that, if it seems good to you, search may be made in the records of your fathers. ²²You will find in the chronicles what has been written about them and will learn that this city was rebellious, troubling both kings and other cities, ²³and that the Jews were rebels and kept setting up blockades in it from of old. That is why this city was laid waste. ²⁴Therefore we now make known to you, O lord and king, that if this city is built and its walls finished, you will no longer have access to Coelesyria and Phoenicia."

²⁵Then the king, in reply to Rehum the recorder and Beltethmus and Shimshai the scribe and the others associated with them and living in Samaria and Syria and Phoenicia, wrote as follows:

²⁶"I have read the letter you sent me. So I ordered search to be made, and it has been found that this city from of old has fought against kings ²⁷and that the men in it were given to rebellion and war and that mighty and cruel kings ruled in Jerusalem and exacted tribute from Coelesyria and Phoenicia. ²⁸Therefore I have now issued orders to prevent these men from building the city and to take care that nothing more be done ²⁹and that such wicked proceedings go no further to the annoyance of kings."

³⁰Then, when the letter from King Artaxerxes was read, Rehum and Shimshai the scribe and their associates went in haste to Jerusalem, with horsemen and a multitude in battle array, and began to hinder the builders. And the building of the temple in Jerusalem ceased until the second year of the reign of King Darius of the Persians.

DEBATE OF THE THREE BODYGUARDS

3 Now King Darius gave a great banquet for all that were under him and all that were born in his house and all the nobles of Media and Persia ²and all the satraps and generals and governors that were

under him in the 127 satrapies from India to Ethiopia. ³They ate and drank, and when they were satisfied they departed; and King Darius went to his bedroom and went to sleep and then awoke.

⁴Then the three young men of the bodyguard, who kept guard over the person of the king, said to one another, ⁵"Let each of us state what one thing is strongest; and to him whose statement seems wisest, King Darius will give rich gifts and great honours of victory. ⁶He shall be clothed in purple and drink from gold cups and sleep on a gold bed and have a chariot with gold bridles and a turban of fine linen and a necklace round his neck; ⁷and because of his wisdom he shall sit next to Darius and shall be called kinsman of Darius."

⁸Then each wrote his own statement, and they sealed them and put them under the pillow of King Darius ⁹and said, "When the king wakes, they will give him the writing; and to the one whose statement the king and the three nobles of Persia judge to be wisest the victory shall be given according to what is written." ¹⁰The first wrote, "Wine is strongest." ¹¹The second wrote, "The king is strongest." ¹²The third wrote, "Women are strongest, but truth is victor over all things."

¹³When the king awoke, they took the writing and gave it to him, and he read it. ¹⁴Then he sent and summoned all the nobles of Persia and Media and the satraps and generals and governors and prefects, ¹⁵and he took his seat in the council chamber, and the writing was read in their presence. ¹⁶And he said, "Call the young men, and they shall explain their statements." So they were summoned and came in. ¹⁷And they said to them, "Explain to us what you have written."

SPEECH ABOUT WINE

Then the first, who had spoken of the strength of wine, began and said: ¹⁸"Gentlemen, how is wine the strongest? It leads astray the minds of all who drink it. ¹⁹It makes equal the mind of the king and the orphan, of the slave and the free, of the poor and the rich. ²⁰It turns every thought to feasting and mirth and forgets all sorrow and debt. ²¹It makes all hearts feel rich, forgets kings and satraps, and makes everyone talk in vast sums.ᵃ ²²When men drink they forget to be friendly with friends and brothers, and before long they draw their swords. ²³And when they recover from the wine, they do not remember what they have done. ²⁴Gentlemen, is not wine the strongest, since it forces men to do these things?" When he had said this, he stopped speaking.

SPEECH ABOUT THE KING

4 Then the second, who had spoken of the strength of the king, began to speak: ²"Gentlemen, are not men strongest, who rule over land and sea and all that is in them? ³But the king is stronger; he is their lord and master, and whatever he says to them they obey. ⁴If he tells them to make war on one another, they do it; and if he sends them out against the enemy, they go and conquer mountains, walls, and towers. ⁵They kill and are killed and do not disobey the king's command; if they win the victory, they bring everything to the king—whatever spoil they take and everything else. ⁶Likewise those who do not serve in the army or make war but till the soil, whenever they sow, reap the harvest and bring some to the king; and they compel one another to pay taxes to the king. ⁷And yet he is only one man! If he tells them to kill, they kill; if he tells them to release, they release; ⁸if he tells them to attack, they attack; if he tells them to lay waste, they lay waste; if he tells them to build, they build; ⁹if he tells them to cut down, they cut down; if he tells them to plant, they plant. ¹⁰All his people and his armies obey him. Moreover, he reclines, he eats and drinks and sleeps, ¹¹but they keep watch round him and no one may go away to attend to his own affairs, nor do they disobey him. ¹²Gentlemen, why is not the king the strongest, since he is to be obeyed in this fashion?" And he stopped speaking.

SPEECH ABOUT WOMEN

¹³Then the third, who had spoken of women and truth—this was Zerubbabel—began to speak: ¹⁴"Gentlemen, is not the king great, and are not men many, and is not wine strong? Who then is their master, or who is their lord? Is it not women? ¹⁵Women gave birth to the king and to every people that rules over sea and land. ¹⁶From women they came; and women brought up the very men who plant the vineyards from which comes wine. ¹⁷Women make men's clothes; they bring men glory; men cannot exist without women. ¹⁸If men gather gold and silver or any

---
ᵃGreek *in talents*

other beautiful thing and then see a woman lovely in appearance and beauty, ¹⁹they let all those things go and gape at her and with open mouths stare at her, and all prefer her to gold or silver or any other beautiful thing. ²⁰A man leaves his own father, who brought him up, and his own country and holds fast to his wife. ²¹With his wife he ends his days, with no thought of his father or his mother or his country. ²²Hence you must realise that women rule over you!

"Do you not labour and toil and bring everything and give it to women? ²³A man takes his sword and goes out to travel and rob and steal and to sail the sea and rivers; ²⁴he faces lions, and he walks in darkness, and when he steals and robs and plunders, he brings it back to the woman he loves. ²⁵A man loves his wife more than his father or his mother. ²⁶Many men have lost their minds because of women and have become slaves because of them. ²⁷Many have perished or stumbled or sinned, because of women. ²⁸And now do you not believe me?

"Is not the king great in his power? Do not all lands fear to touch him? ²⁹Yet I have seen him with Apame, the king's concubine, the daughter of the illustrious Bartacus; she would sit at the king's right hand ³⁰and take the crown from the king's head and put it on her own and slap the king with her left hand. ³¹At this the king would gaze at her with mouth agape. If she smiles at him, he laughs; if she loses her temper with him, he flatters her, that she may be reconciled to him. ³²Gentlemen, why are not women strong, since they do such things?"

SPEECH ABOUT TRUTH

³³Then the king and the nobles looked at one another; and he began to speak about truth: ³⁴"Gentlemen, are not women strong? The earth is vast, and heaven is high, and the sun is swift in its course, for it makes the circuit of the heavens and returns to its place in one day. ³⁵Is he not great who does these things? But truth is great and stronger than all things. ³⁶The whole earth calls upon truth, and heaven blesses her. All God's*ᵃ* works quake and tremble, and with him there is nothing unrighteous. ³⁷Wine is unrighteous, the king is unrighteous, women are unrighteous, all the sons of men are unrighteous, all their works are unrighteous, and all such things. There is no truth in them, and in their unrighteousness they will perish. ³⁸But truth endures and is strong forever and lives and prevails for ever and ever. ³⁹With it there is no partiality or preference, but it does what is righteous instead of anything that is unrighteous or wicked. All men approve its deeds, ⁴⁰and there is nothing unrighteous in its judgement. To it belongs the strength and the kingship and the power and the majesty of all the ages. Blessed be the God of truth!" ⁴¹He ceased speaking; then all the people shouted and said, "Great is truth and strongest of all!"

ZERUBBABEL'S REWARD

⁴²Then the king said to him, "Ask what you wish, even beyond what is written, and we will give it to you, for you have been found to be the wisest. And you shall sit next to me and be called my kinsman." ⁴³Then he said to the king, "Remember the vow that you made to build Jerusalem, in the day when you became king, ⁴⁴and to send back all the vessels that were taken from Jerusalem, which Cyrus set apart when he vowed to destroy Babylon and vowed to send them back there. ⁴⁵You also vowed to build the temple, which the Edomites burned when Judea was laid waste by the Chaldeans. ⁴⁶And now, O lord the king, this is what I ask and request of you, and this suits your greatness. I pray therefore that you fulfil the vow whose fulfilment you vowed to the King of heaven with your own lips."

⁴⁷Then King Darius rose and kissed him and wrote letters for him to all the treasurers and governors and generals and satraps, that they should give escort to him and all who were going up with him to build Jerusalem. ⁴⁸And he wrote letters to all the governors in Coelesyria and Phoenicia and to those in Lebanon, to bring cedar timber from Lebanon to Jerusalem and to help him build the city. ⁴⁹And he wrote for all the Jews who were going up from his kingdom to Judea, in the interest of their freedom, that no officer or satrap or governor or treasurer should forcibly enter their doors; ⁵⁰that all the country that they would occupy should be theirs without tribute; that the Idumeans should give up the villages of the Jews that they held; ⁵¹that twenty talents a year should be given for the building of the temple until it was completed ⁵²and an additional ten talents a year for whole burnt offerings to be offered

---

*ᵃ*Greek *the*

on the altar every day, in accordance with the commandment to make seventeen offerings; ⁵³and that all who came from Babylonia to build the city should have their freedom, they and their children and all the priests who came. ⁵⁴He wrote also concerning their support and the priests' garments in which[a] they were to minister. ⁵⁵He wrote that the support for the Levites should be provided until the day when the temple should be finished and Jerusalem built. ⁵⁶He wrote that land and wages should be provided for all who guarded the city. ⁵⁷And he sent back from Babylon all the vessels that Cyrus had set apart; everything that Cyrus had ordered to be done, he also commanded to be done and to be sent to Jerusalem.

ZERUBBABEL'S PRAYER

⁵⁸When the young man went out, he lifted up his face to heaven towards Jerusalem and praised the King of heaven, saying, ⁵⁹"From you is the victory; from you is wisdom, and yours is the glory. I am your servant. ⁶⁰Blessed are you, who has given me wisdom; I give you thanks, O Lord of our fathers."

⁶¹So he took the letters and went to Babylon and told this to all his kinsmen. ⁶²And they praised the God of their fathers, because he had given them release and permission ⁶³to go up and build Jerusalem and the temple that is called by his name; and they feasted, with music and rejoicing, for seven days.

LIST OF RETURNING EXILES

5 After this the heads of fathers' houses were chosen to go up, according to their tribes, with their wives and sons and daughters and their menservants and maidservants and their livestock. ²And Darius sent with them 1,000 horsemen to take them back to Jerusalem in safety, with the music of drums and flutes; ³and all their brothers were making merry. And he made them go up with them.

⁴These are the names of the men who went up, according to their fathers' houses in the tribes, over their groups: ⁵the priests, the sons of Phinehas son of Aaron; Jeshua son of Jozadak, son of Seraiah, and Joakim son of Zerubbabel, son of Shealtiel, of the house of David, of the lineage of Phares, of the tribe of Judah, ⁶who spoke wise words before King Darius of the Persians in the second year of his reign, in the month of Nisan, the first month.

⁷These are the Judeans who came up out of their sojourn in captivity, whom King Nebuchadnezzar of Babylon had carried away to Babylon ⁸and who returned to Jerusalem and the rest of Judea, each to his own town. They came with Zerubbabel and Jeshua, Nehemiah, Seraiah, Resaiah, Enenius, Mordecai, Beelsarus, Aspharasus, Reeliah, Rehum, and Baanah, their leaders.

⁹The number of those from the nation and their leaders: the sons of Parosh: 2,172. The sons of Shephatiah: 472. ¹⁰The sons of Arah: 756. ¹¹The sons of Pahathmoab, of the sons of Jeshua and Joab: 2,812. ¹²The sons of Elam: 1,254. The sons of Zattu: 945. The sons of Chorbe: 705. The sons of Bani: 648. ¹³The sons of Bebai: 623. The sons of Azgad: 1,322. ¹⁴The sons of Adonikam: 667. The sons of Bigvai: 2,066. The sons of Adin: 454. ¹⁵The sons of Ater, namely of Hezekiah: 92. The sons of Kilan and Azetas: 67. The sons of Azaru: 432. ¹⁶The sons of Annias: 101. The sons of Arom. The sons of Bezai: 323. The sons of Arsiphurith: 112. ¹⁷The sons of Baiterus: 3,005. The sons of Bethlomon: 123. ¹⁸The men of Netophah: 55. The men of Anathoth: 158. The men of Bethasmoth: 42. ¹⁹The men of Kiriatharim: 25. The men of Chephirah and Beeroth: 743. ²⁰The Chadiasans and Ammidians: 422. The men of Kirama and Geba: 621. ²¹The men of Macalon: 122. The men of Betolio: 52. The sons of Niphish: 156. ²²The sons of the other Calamolalus and Ono: 725. The sons of Jerechus: 345. ²³The sons of Senaah: 3,330.

²⁴The priests: the sons of Jedaiah son of Jeshua, of the sons of Anasib: 972. The sons of Immer: 1,052. ²⁵The sons of Pashhur: 1,247. The sons of Charme: 1,017.

²⁶The Levites: the sons of Jeshua and Kadmiel and Bannas and Sudias: 74. ²⁷The temple musicians: the sons of Asaph: 128. ²⁸The gatekeepers: the sons of Shallum, the sons of Ater, the sons of Talmon, the sons of Akkub, the sons of Hatita, the sons of Shobai, in all 139.

²⁹The temple servants: the sons of Esau, the sons of Hasupha, the sons of Tabbaoth, the sons of Keros, the sons of Sua, the sons of Padon, the sons of Lebanah, the sons of Hagabah, ³⁰the sons of Akkub, the sons of Uthai, the sons of Ketab, the sons of Hagab, the sons of Subai, the sons of Hana, the sons of Cathua, the sons of Geddur, ³¹the sons of Jairus, the sons of Daisan, the sons of Noeba, the sons of Chezib, the sons of Gazera, the sons

---
[a] Greek *and in what priestly garments*

of Uzza, the sons of Phinoe, the sons of Hasrah, the sons of Basthai, the sons of Asnah, the sons of the Maani, the sons of Nephisim, the sons of Acuph, the sons of Hakupha, the sons of Asur, the sons of Pharakim, the sons of Bazluth, ³²the sons of Mehida, the sons of Cutha, the sons of Charea, the sons of Barkos, the sons of Serar, the sons of Temah, the sons of Neziah, the sons of Hatipha.

³³The sons of Solomon's servants: the sons of Assaphioth, the sons of Peruda, the sons of Jaalah, the sons of Lozon, the sons of Isdael, the sons of Shephatiah, ³⁴the sons of Agia, the sons of Pochereth-hazzebaim, the sons of Sarothie, the sons of Masiah, the sons of Gas, the sons of Addus, the sons of Subas, the sons of Apherra, the sons of Barodis, the sons of Shaphat, the sons of Allon.

³⁵All the temple servants and the sons of Solomon's servants were 372.

³⁶The following are those who came up from Tel-melah and Tel-harsha, under the leadership of Cherub, Addan, and Immer, ³⁷though they could not prove by their fathers' houses or lineage that they belonged to Israel: the sons of Delaiah son of Tobiah, the sons of Nekoda: 652.

³⁸Of the priests the following had assumed the priesthood but were not found registered: the sons of Habaiah, the sons of Hakkoz, the sons of Jaddus who had married Agia, one of the daughters of Barzillai, and was called by his name. ³⁹And when the genealogy of these men was sought in the register and was not found, they were excluded from serving as priests. ⁴⁰And Nehemiah and Attharias*ᵃ* told them not to share in the holy things until a high priest should appear wearing Urim and Thummim.*ᵇ*

⁴¹All those of Israel, twelve or more years of age, besides menservants and maidservants, were 42,360; ⁴²their menservants and maidservants were 7,337; there were 245 musicians and singers. ⁴³There were 435 camels and 7,036 horses, 245 mules, and 5,525 donkeys.

⁴⁴Some of the heads of families, when they came to the temple of God that is in Jerusalem, vowed that they would erect the house on its site, to the best of their ability ⁴⁵and that they would give to the sacred treasury for the work 1,000 minas of gold, 5,000 minas of silver, and 100 priests' garments.

⁴⁶The priests, the Levites, and some others of God's people*ᶜ* settled in Jerusalem and its vicinity; and the temple musicians, the gatekeepers, and all Israel in their towns.

WORSHIP BEGINS AGAIN

⁴⁷When the seventh month came and the sons of Israel were each in his own home, they gathered as of one mind in the square before the first gate towards the east. ⁴⁸Then Jeshua son of Jozadak, with his fellow priests, and Zerubbabel son of Shealtiel, with his kinsmen, took their places and prepared the altar of the God of Israel, ⁴⁹to offer whole burnt offerings upon it, in accordance with the directions in the book of Moses the man of God. ⁵⁰And some joined them from the other peoples of the land. And they erected the altar in its place, for all the peoples of the land were hostile to them and were stronger than they; and they offered sacrifices at the proper times and whole burnt offerings to the Lord morning and evening. ⁵¹They kept the Feast of Booths, as it is commanded in the law, and offered the proper sacrifices every day ⁵²and thereafter the continual offerings and sacrifices on Sabbaths and at new moons and at all the consecrated feasts. ⁵³And all who had made any vow to God began to offer sacrifices to God, from the new moon of the seventh month, though the temple of God was not yet built. ⁵⁴And they gave money to the masons and the carpenters and food and drink ⁵⁵and carts*ᵈ* to the Sidonians and the Tyrians, to bring cedar logs from Lebanon and convey them in rafts to the harbour of Joppa, according to the decree that they had in writing from King Cyrus of the Persians.

FOUNDATIONS OF THE TEMPLE LAID

⁵⁶In the second year after their coming to the temple of God in Jerusalem, in the second month, Zerubbabel son of Shealtiel and Jeshua son of Jozadak made a beginning, together with their brothers and the Levitical priests and all who had come to Jerusalem from the captivity; ⁵⁷and they laid the foundation of the temple of God on the new moon of the second month in the second year after they came to Judea and Jerusalem. ⁵⁸And they appointed the Levites who were twenty or more years of age to have charge of the work of the Lord. And Jeshua arose, and his sons and brothers and Kadmiel his brother and the sons of Jeshua Emadabun and the sons of Joda son of Iliadun, with their sons and brothers, all the Levites, as one man pressing forwards the work on the house of God.

ᵃOr and the governor *ᵇGreek wearing Manifestation and Truth*
ᶜOr and those who were of the people *ᵈThe meaning of the Greek is uncertain*

So the builders built the temple of the Lord. [59]And the priests stood arrayed in their garments, with musical instruments and trumpets, and the Levites, the sons of Asaph, with cymbals, [60]praising the Lord and blessing him, according to the directions of King David of Israel; [61]and they sang hymns, giving thanks to the Lord, because his goodness and his glory are for ever upon all Israel. [62]And all the people sounded trumpets and shouted with a great shout, praising the Lord for the erection of the house of the Lord. [63]Some of the Levitical priests and heads of fathers' houses, old men who had seen the former house, came to the building of this one with outcries and loud weeping, [64]while many came with trumpets and a joyful noise, [65]so that the people could not hear the trumpets because of the weeping of the people.

For the multitude sounded the trumpets loudly, so that the sound was heard from a great distance; [66]and when the enemies of the tribe of Judah and Benjamin heard it, they came to find out what the sound of the trumpets meant. [67]And they learned that those who had returned from captivity were building the temple for the Lord God of Israel. [68]So they approached Zerubbabel and Jeshua and the heads of the fathers' houses and said to them, "We will build with you. [69]For we obey your Lord just as you do, and we have been sacrificing to him ever since the days of King Esarhaddon of the Assyrians, who brought us here." [70]But Zerubbabel and Jeshua and the heads of the fathers' houses in Israel said to them, "You have nothing to do with us in building the house for the Lord our God, [71]for we alone will build it for the Lord of Israel, as King Cyrus of the Persians has commanded us." [72]But the peoples of the land pressed hard[a] upon those in Judea, cut off their supplies, and hindered their building; [73]and by plots and demagoguery and uprisings they prevented the completion of the building as long as King Cyrus lived. And they were kept from building for two years, until the reign of Darius.

WORK ON THE TEMPLE BEGINS AGAIN

6 Now in the second year of the reign of Darius, the prophets Haggai and Zechariah son of Iddo prophesied to the Jews who were in Judea and Jerusalem; they prophesied to them in the name of the Lord God of Israel. [2]Then Zerubbabel son of Shealtiel and Jeshua son of Jozadak arose and began to build the house of the Lord that is in Jerusalem, with the help of the prophets of the Lord who were with them.

[3]At the same time Sisinnes the governor of Syria and Phoenicia and Sathrabuzanes and their associates came to them and said, [4]"By whose order are you building this house and this roof and finishing all the other things? And who are the builders that are finishing these things?" [5]Yet the elders of the Jews were dealt with kindly, for the providence of the Lord was over the captives; [6]and they were not prevented from building until word could be sent to Darius concerning them and a report made.

[7]A copy of the letter that Sisinnes the governor of Syria and Phoenicia, and Sathrabuzanes, and their associates the local rulers in Syria and Phoenicia wrote and sent to Darius:

[8]"To King Darius, greetings. Let it be fully known to our lord the king that, when we went to the country of Judea and entered the city of Jerusalem, we found the elders of the Jews, who had been in captivity, [9]building in the city of Jerusalem a great new house for the Lord, of hewn stone, with costly timber laid in the walls. [10]These operations are going on rapidly, and the work is prospering in their hands and being completed with all splendour and care. [11]Then we asked these elders, 'At whose command are you building this house and laying the foundations of this structure?' [12]And in order that we might inform you in writing who the leaders are, we questioned them and asked them for a list of the names of those who are at their head. [13]They answered us, 'We are the servants of the Lord who created the heaven and the earth. [14]And the house was built many years ago by a king of Israel who was great and strong, and it was finished. [15]But when our fathers sinned against the Lord of Israel who is in heaven and provoked him, he gave them over into the hands of King Nebuchadnezzar of Babylon and the Chaldeans; [16]and they pulled down the house and burned it and carried the people away captive to Babylon. [17]But in the first year that Cyrus reigned over the country of Babylonia, King Cyrus wrote that this house should be rebuilt. [18]And the holy vessels of gold and of silver, which Nebuchadnezzar had taken out of the house in Jerusalem and stored in his own temple, these King Cyrus took out again from the

---
[a]The meaning of the Greek is uncertain

temple in Babylon, and they were delivered to Zerubbabel and Sheshbazzar the governor ¹⁹with the command that he should take all these vessels back and put them in the temple at Jerusalem and that this temple of the Lord should be rebuilt on its site. ²⁰Then this Sheshbazzar, after coming here, laid the foundations of the house of the Lord that is in Jerusalem, and although it has been in process of construction from that time until now, it has not yet reached completion.' ²¹Now therefore, if it seems wise, O king, let search be made in the royal archives of our lord[a] the king that are in Babylon; ²²and if it is found that the building of the house of the Lord in Jerusalem was done with the consent of King Cyrus and if it is approved by our lord the king, let him send us directions concerning these things."

OFFICIAL PERMISSION GRANTED

²³Then Darius commanded that search be made in the royal archives that were deposited in Babylon. And in Ecbatana, the fortress that is in the country of Media, a scroll[b] was found in which this was recorded: ²⁴"In the first year of the reign of Cyrus, King Cyrus ordered the building of the house of the Lord in Jerusalem, where they sacrifice with perpetual fire; ²⁵its height to be sixty cubits and its width sixty cubits, with three courses of hewn stone and one course of new native timber; the cost to be paid from the treasury of King Cyrus; ²⁶and that the holy vessels of the house of the Lord, both of gold and of silver, which Nebuchadnezzar took out of the house in Jerusalem and carried away to Babylon, should be restored to the house in Jerusalem, to be placed where they had been."

²⁷So Darius[c] commanded Sisinnes the governor of Syria and Phoenicia and Sathrabuzanes and their associates and those who were appointed as local rulers in Syria and Phoenicia to keep away from the place and to permit Zerubbabel, the servant of the Lord and governor of Judea, and the elders of the Jews to build this house of the Lord on its site. ²⁸"And I command that it be built completely and that full effort be made to help those who have returned from the captivity of Judea, until the house of the Lord is finished; ²⁹and that out of the tribute of Coelesyria and Phoenicia a portion be scrupulously given to these men, that is, to Zerubbabel the governor, for sacrifices to the Lord, for bulls and rams and lambs, ³⁰and likewise wheat and salt and wine and oil, regularly every year, without quibbling, for daily use as the priests in Jerusalem may indicate, ³¹in order that libations may be made to the Most High God for the king and his children and that prayers be offered for their life."

³²And he commanded that if any should transgress or nullify any of the things stated and written above,[d] a beam should be taken out of his house and he should be hanged upon it, and his property should be forfeited to the king.

³³"Therefore may the Lord, whose name is there called upon, destroy every king and nation that shall stretch out their hands to hinder or damage that house of the Lord in Jerusalem.

³⁴"I, King Darius, have decreed that it be done with all diligence as here prescribed."

THE TEMPLE IS DEDICATED

7 Then Sisinnes the governor of Coelesyria and Phoenicia and Sathrabuzanes and their associates following the orders of King Darius, ²supervised the holy work with very great care, assisting the elders of the Jews and the chief officers of the temple. ³And the holy work prospered while the prophets Haggai and Zechariah prophesied; ⁴and they completed it by the command of the Lord God of Israel. So with the consent of Cyrus and Darius and Artaxerxes, kings of the Persians, ⁵the holy house was finished by the twenty-third day of the month of Adar, in the sixth year of King Darius. ⁶And the sons of Israel, the priests, the Levites, and the rest of those from the captivity who joined them did according to what was written in the book of Moses. ⁷They offered at the dedication of the temple of the Lord 100 bulls, 200 rams, 400 lambs, ⁸and 12 male goats for the sin of all Israel, according to the number of the twelve leaders of the tribes of Israel; ⁹and the priests and the Levites stood arrayed in their garments, according to kindred, for the services of the Lord God of Israel in accordance with the book of Moses; and the gatekeepers were at each gate.

PASSOVER

¹⁰The sons of Israel who came from the captivity kept the Passover on the fourteenth day of the first month, after the priests and

---
[a] Some manuscripts *of Cyrus* [b] Some manuscripts *passage* [c] Greek *he* [d] Some manuscripts *and herein written* or *and added in writing*

the Levites were purified together. ¹¹Not all of the returned captives were purified, but the Levites were all purified together,ᵃ ¹²and they sacrificed the Passover lamb for all the returned captives and for their brothers the priests and for themselves. ¹³And the sons of Israel who had come from the captivity ate it, all those who had separated themselves from the abominations of the peoples of the land and sought the Lord. ¹⁴And they kept the Feast of Unleavened Bread seven days, rejoicing before the Lord, ¹⁵Because he had changed the will of the king of the Assyrians concerning them, to strengthen their hands for the service of the Lord God of Israel.

EZRA ARRIVES IN JERUSALEM

8 After these things, when King Artaxerxes of the Persians was reigning, Ezra came, son of Seraiah, son of Azariah, son of Hilkiah, son of Shallum, ²son of Zadok, son of Ahitub, son of Amariah, son of Uzzi, son of Bukki, son of Abishua, son of Phineas, son of Eleazar, son of Aaron the chief priest. ³This Ezra came up from Babylon as a scribe skilled in the law of Moses, which was given by the God of Israel; ⁴and the king showed him honour, for he found favour before the kingᵇ in all his requests. ⁵There came up with him to Jerusalem some of the sons of Israel and some of the priests and Levites and temple musicians and gatekeepers and temple servants, ⁶in the seventh year of the reign of Artaxerxes, in the fifth month (this was the king's seventh year); for they left Babylon on the new moon of the first month and arrived in Jerusalem on the new moon of the fifth month, by the prosperous journey that the Lord gave them.ᶜ ⁷For Ezra possessed great knowledge, so that he omitted nothing from the law of the Lord or the commandments, but taught all Israel all the ordinances and judgements.

THE KING'S MANDATE

⁸The following is a copy of the written commission from King Artaxerxes that was delivered to Ezra the priest and reader of the law of the Lord:

⁹"King Artaxerxes to Ezra the priest and reader of the law of the Lord, greetings. ¹⁰In accordance with my gracious decision, I have given orders that those of the Jewish nation and of the priests and Levites and others in our realm, who freely choose to do so, may go with you to Jerusalem. ¹¹Let as many as are so disposed, therefore, depart with you as I and the seven friends who are my counsellors have decided, ¹²in order to look into matters in Judea and Jerusalem, in accordance with what is in the law of the Lord, ¹³and to carry to Jerusalem the gifts for the Lord of Israel that I and my friends have vowed and to collect for the Lord in Jerusalem all the gold and silver that may be found in the country of Babylonia, ¹⁴together with what is given by the nation for the temple of their Lord that is in Jerusalem, both gold and silver for bulls and rams and lambs and what goes with them, ¹⁵so as to offer sacrifices upon the altar of their Lord that is in Jerusalem. ¹⁶And whatever you and your brothers are minded to do with the gold and silver, perform it in accordance with the will of your God; ¹⁷and deliver the holy vessels of the Lord that are given you for the use of the temple of your God that is in Jerusalem. ¹⁸And whatever else occurs to you as necessary for the temple of your God, you may provide out of the royal treasury.

¹⁹"And I, King Artaxerxes, have commanded the treasurers of Syria and Phoenicia that whatever Ezra the priest and reader of the law of the Most High God sends for, they shall take care to give him, ²⁰up to 100 talents of silver and likewise up to 100 cors of wheat, 100 baths of wine, and salt in abundance. ²¹Let all things prescribed in the law of God be scrupulously fulfilled for the Most High God, so that wrath may not come upon the kingdom of the king and his sons. ²²You are also informed that no tribute or any other tax is to be laid on any of the priests or Levites or temple musicians or gatekeepers or temple servants or persons employed in this temple and that no one has authority to impose any tax upon them.

²³"And you, Ezra, according to the wisdom of God, appoint judges and justices to judge all those who know the law of your God, throughout all Syria and Phoenicia; and those who do not know it you shall teach. ²⁴And all who transgress the law of your God or the law of the kingdom shall be strictly punished, whether by death or some other punishment, either fine or imprisonment."

EZRA PRAISES GOD

²⁵Blessed be the Lord alone, who put this into the heart of the king, to glorify his house

---

ᵃThe meaning of the Greek is uncertain ᵇGreek *before him*
ᶜSome manuscripts add *for/upon him*

that is in Jerusalem, ²⁶and who honoured me in the sight of the king and his counsellors and all his friends and nobles. ²⁷I was encouraged by the help of the Lord my God, and I gathered men from Israel to go up with me.

LEADERS WHO RETURNED

²⁸These are the principal men, according to their fathers' houses and their groups, who went up with me from Babylon, in the reign of King Artaxerxes: ²⁹Of the sons of Phineas: Gershom. Of the sons of Ithamar: Gamael. Of the sons of David: Hattush son of Shecaniah. ³⁰Of the sons of Parosh: Zechariah, and with him 150 men enrolled. ³¹Of the sons of Pahathmoab: Eliehoenai son of Zerahiah, and with him 200 men. ³²Of the sons of Zattu: Shecaniah son of Jahaziel, and with him 300 men. Of the sons of Adin: Obed son of Jonathan, and with him 250 men. ³³Of the sons of Elam: Jeshaiah son of Gotholiah, and with him 70 men. ³⁴Of the sons of Shephatiah: Zeraiah son of Michael, and with him 70 men. ³⁵Of the sons of Joab: Obadiah son of Jehiel, and with him 212 men. ³⁶Of the sons of Bani: Shelomith son of Josiphiah, and with him 160 men. ³⁷Of the sons of Bebai: Zechariah son of Bebai, and with him 28 men. ³⁸Of the sons of Azgad: Johanan son of Hakkatan, and with him 110 men. ³⁹Of the sons of Adonikam: the last ones, their names being Eliphelet, Jeuel, and Shemaiah, and with them 70 men. ⁴⁰Of the sons of Bigvai: Uthai son of Istalcurus, and with him 70 men.

⁴¹I assembled them at the river called Theras, and we encamped there for three days, and I inspected them. ⁴²When I found there none of the sons of the priests or of the Levites, ⁴³I sent word to Eliezar, Iduel, Maasmas, ⁴⁴Elnathan, Shemaiah, Jarib, Nathan, Elnathan, Zechariah, and Meshullam, who were leaders and men of understanding; ⁴⁵and I told them to go to Iddo, who was the leading man at the place of the treasury, ⁴⁶and ordered them to tell Iddo and his brothers and the treasurers at that place to send us men to serve as priests in the house of our Lord. ⁴⁷And by the mighty hand of our Lord they brought us competent men of the sons of Mahli son of Levi, son of Israel, namely Sherebiah with his sons and kinsmen: 18; ⁴⁸also Hashabiah and Annunus and Jeshaiah his brother, of the sons of Hananiah, and their sons: 20 men; ⁴⁹and of the temple servants, whom David and the leaders had given for the service of the Levites: 220 temple servants; the list of all their names was reported.

EZRA PROCLAIMS A FAST

⁵⁰There I proclaimed a fast for the young men before our Lord, to seek from him a prosperous journey for ourselves and for our children and the livestock that were with us. ⁵¹For I was ashamed to ask the king for foot soldiers and horsemen and an escort to keep us safe from our adversaries; ⁵²for we had said to the king, "The power of our Lord will be with those who seek him and will support them in every way." ⁵³And again we prayed to our Lord about these things, and we found him very merciful.

GIFTS FOR THE TEMPLE

⁵⁴Then I set apart twelve of the leaders of the priests, Sherebiah and Hashabiah and ten of their kinsmen with them; ⁵⁵and I weighed out to them the silver and the gold and the holy vessels of the house of our Lord, which the king himself and his counsellors and the nobles and all Israel had given. ⁵⁶I weighed and gave to them 650 talents of silver and silver vessels worth 100 talents and 100 talents of gold ⁵⁷and 20 golden bowls and 12 bronze vessels of fine bronze that glittered like gold. ⁵⁸And I said to them, "You are holy to the Lord, and the vessels are holy, and the silver and the gold are vowed to the Lord, the Lord of our fathers. ⁵⁹Be watchful and on guard until you deliver them to the leaders of the priests and the Levites and to the heads of the fathers' houses of Israel, in Jerusalem, in the chambers of the house of our Lord." ⁶⁰So the priests and the Levites who took the silver and the gold and the vessels that had been in Jerusalem carried them to the temple of the Lord.

RETURN TO JERUSALEM

⁶¹We departed from the river Theras on the twelfth day of the first month; and we arrived in Jerusalem by the mighty hand of our Lord that was upon us; he delivered us from every enemy on the way, and so we came to Jerusalem. ⁶²When we had been there three days, the silver and the gold were weighed and delivered in the house of our Lord to Meremoth the priest, son of Uriah; ⁶³and with him was Eleazar son of Phinehas, and with them were Jozabad son of Jeshua and Moeth son of Binnui, the Levites. ⁶⁴The total was counted and weighed, and the weight of everything

was recorded at that very time. ⁶⁵And those who had come back from captivity offered sacrifices to the Lord, the God of Israel, 12 bulls for all Israel, 96 rams, ⁶⁶72 lambs, and as a thank-offering 12 male goats—all as a sacrifice to the Lord. ⁶⁷And they delivered the king's orders to the royal stewards and to the governors of Coelesyria and Phoenicia; and these officials[a] honoured the people and the temple of the Lord.

EZRA'S PRAYER

⁶⁸After these things had been done, the leaders came to me and said, ⁶⁹"The people of Israel and the leaders and the priests and the Levites have not put away from themselves the alien peoples of the land and their pollutions, the Canaanites, the Hittites, the Perizzites, the Jebusites, the Moabites, the Egyptians, and the Edomites. ⁷⁰For they and their sons have married the daughters of these people,[b] and the holy race has been mixed with the alien peoples of the land; and from the beginning of this matter the leaders and the nobles have been sharing in this iniquity."

⁷¹As soon as I heard these things I rent my garments and my holy mantle and pulled out hair from my head and beard and sat down in anxiety and grief. ⁷²And all who were ever moved at[c] the word of the Lord of Israel gathered round me, as I mourned over this iniquity, and I sat grief-stricken until the evening sacrifice. ⁷³Then I rose from my fast, with my garments and my holy mantle rent, and kneeling down and stretching forth my hands to the Lord ⁷⁴I said:

"O Lord, I am ashamed and confounded before your face. ⁷⁵For our sins have risen higher than our heads, and our mistakes have mounted up to heaven ⁷⁶from the times of our fathers, and we are in great sin to this day. ⁷⁷And because of our sins and the sins of our fathers, we with our brothers and our kings and our priests were given over to the kings of the earth, to the sword and captivity and plundering, in shame until this day. ⁷⁸And now in some measure mercy has come to us from you, O Lord, to leave to us a root and a name in your Holy Place ⁷⁹and to uncover a light for us in the house of the Lord our God and to give us food in the time of our servitude. ⁸⁰Even in our bondage we were not forsaken by our Lord, but he brought us into favour with the kings of the Persians, so that they have given us food ⁸¹and glorified the temple of our Lord and raised Zion from desolation, to give us a stronghold in Judea and Jerusalem.

⁸²"And now, O Lord, what shall we say, when we have these things? For we have transgressed your commandments, which you gave by your servants the prophets, saying, ⁸³'The land into which you are entering to take possession of it is a land polluted with the pollution of the aliens of the land, and they have filled it with their uncleanness. ⁸⁴Therefore do not take their daughters in marriage to your sons and do not give your daughters to their sons; ⁸⁵and do not seek ever to have peace with them, in order that you may be strong and eat the good things of the land and leave it for an inheritance to your children for ever.' ⁸⁶And all that has happened to us has come about because of our evil deeds and our great sins. For you, O Lord, lifted the burden of our sins ⁸⁷and gave us such a root as this; but we turned back again to transgress your law by mixing with the uncleanness of the peoples of the land. ⁸⁸Were you not angry enough with us to destroy us without leaving a root or seed or name? ⁸⁹O Lord of Israel, you are true; for we are left as a root to this day. ⁹⁰Behold, we are now before you in our iniquities; for we can no longer stand in your presence because of these things."

PLAN FOR ENDING MIXED MARRIAGES

⁹¹While Ezra was praying and making his confession, weeping and lying upon the ground before the temple, there gathered round him a very great crowd from Jerusalem, men and women and youths; for there was great weeping among the multitude. ⁹²Then Jeconiah[d] son of Jehiel, one of the Israelites, called out and said to Ezra, "We have sinned against the Lord and have married foreign women from the peoples of the land; but even now there is hope for Israel. ⁹³Let us take an oath to the Lord about this, that we will put away all our foreign wives, with their children, ⁹⁴as seems good to you and to all who obey the law of the Lord. ⁹⁵Arise[e] and take action, for it is your task, and we are with you to take strong measures." ⁹⁶Then Ezra arose and had the leaders of the priests and Levites of all Israel take oath that they would do this. And they took the oath.

---

[a]Greek and they [b]Greek married their daughters [c]Or ever zealous for [d]Or Shecaniah; compare Ezra 10:2 [e]Some manuscripts as seems good to you." And all who obeyed the law of the Lord rose and said to Ezra, "Arise

EXPULSION OF FOREIGN WIVES

9 Then Ezra rose and went from the court of the temple to the chamber of Jehohanan son of Eliashib ²and spent the night there; and he did not eat bread or drink water, for he was mourning over the great iniquities of the multitude. ³And a proclamation was made throughout Judea and Jerusalem to all who had returned from the captivity that they should assemble at Jerusalem, ⁴and that if any did not meet there within two or three days, in accordance with the decision of the ruling elders, their livestock should be seized for sacrifice and the men themselves[a] expelled from the multitude of those who had returned from the captivity.

⁵Then the men of the tribe of Judah and Benjamin assembled at Jerusalem within three days; this was the ninth month, on the twentieth day of the month. ⁶And all the multitude sat in the open square before the temple, shivering because of the bad weather that prevailed. ⁷Then Ezra rose and said to them, "You have broken the law and married foreign women and so have increased the sin of Israel. ⁸Now then make confession and give glory to the Lord the God of our fathers ⁹and do his will; separate yourselves from the peoples of the land and from your foreign wives." ¹⁰Then all the multitude shouted and said with a loud voice, "We will do as you have said. ¹¹But the multitude is great and it is winter, and we are unable to stand in the open air. This is not a work we can do in one day or two, for we have sinned too much in these things. ¹²So let the leaders of the multitude stay, and let all those in our settlements who have foreign wives come at the time appointed, ¹³with the elders and judges of each place, until we are freed from the wrath of the Lord over this matter." ¹⁴Jonathan son of Asahel and Jahzeiah son of Tikvah undertook the matter on these terms, and Meshullam and Levi and Shabbethai served with them as judges. ¹⁵And those who had returned from the captivity acted in accordance with all this.

¹⁶Ezra the priest chose for himself the leading men of their fathers' houses, all of them by name; and on the new moon of the tenth month they began their sessions to investigate the matter. ¹⁷And the cases of the men who had foreign wives were brought to an end by the new moon of the first month.

¹⁸Of the priests those who were brought in and found to have foreign wives were ¹⁹of the sons of Jeshua son of Jozadak and his brothers: Maaseiah, Eliezar, Jarib, and Jodan. ²⁰They pledged themselves to put away their wives and to give rams in propitiation of their error. ²¹Of the sons of Immer: Hanani and Zebadiah and Maaseiah and Shemaiah and Jehiel and Azariah ²²Of the sons of Pashhur: Elioenai, Maaseiah, Ishmael and Nathanael and Gedaliah and Salthas.[b]

²³And of the Levites: Jozabad and Shimei and Kelaiah, who was Kelita, and Pethahiah and Judah and Jonah. ²⁴Of the temple musicians: Eliashib and Bacchurus ²⁵Of the gatekeepers: Shallum and Tolbanus.[c]

²⁶Of Israel: of the sons of Parosh: Ramiah, Izziah, Malchijah, Mijamin and Eleazar and Asibias and Benaiah. ²⁷Of the sons of Elam: Mattaniah and Zechariah, Jezrielus and Abdi, and Jeremoth and Elijah. ²⁸Of the sons of Zamoth: Eliadas, Eliashib, Othoniah, Jeremoth, and Zabad and Zerdaiah. ²⁹Of the sons of Bebai: Jehohanan and Hananiah and Zabbai and Emathis. ³⁰Of the sons of Mani: Olamos, Malluch, Jedaiah, Jashub, and Sheal and Jeremoth. ³¹Of the sons of Addi: Naathus and Moossias, Laccunus and Naidus, and Matthanias and Sesthel, and Belnuus and Manasseas. ³²Of the sons of Annan: Elionas and Asaias and Melchias and Sabbaias and Simon Chosamaeus. ³³Of the sons of Hashum: Mattenai and Mattattah and Zabad and Eliphelet and Manasseh and Shimei. ³⁴Of the sons of Bani: Jeremai, Moadios, Maeros, Joel, Mamdai and Bedeiah and Anos, Carabasion and Eliashib and Mamnitanaimos, Eliasis, Binnui, Elialis, Shimei, Shelemiah, Nethaniah. Of the sons of Ezora: Shashai, Azarel, Azael, Samatos, Zambris, Joseph. ³⁵Of the sons of Nooma: Mazitiah, Zabad, Iddo, Joel, Benaiah. ³⁶All these had married foreign women, and they put them away with their children.

EZRA READS THE LAW TO THE PEOPLE

³⁷The priests and the Levites and the people of Israel settled in Jerusalem and in the country. On the new moon of the seventh month, when the sons of Israel were in their settlements, ³⁸the whole multitude gathered with one accord into the open square before the east gate of the temple; ³⁹and they told Ezra the chief priest and reader to bring the law of Moses that had been given by the Lord God of Israel. ⁴⁰So Ezra the chief priest brought the

---

[a] Greek *and he himself* [b] Or *Elasah*; compare Ezra 10:22 [c] Or *Telem*; compare Ezra 10:24

law, for all the multitude, men and women, and all the priests to hear the law, on the new moon of the seventh month. **⁴¹**And he read aloud in the open square before the gate of the temple from early morning until midday, in the presence of both men and women; and all the multitude gave attention to the law. **⁴²**Ezra the priest and reader of the law stood on the wooden platform that had been prepared; **⁴³**and beside him stood Mattathiah, Shema, Ananiah, Azariah, Uriah, Hezekiah, and Baalsamus on his right hand, **⁴⁴**and on his left Pedaiah, Mishael, Malchijah, Lothasubus, Nabariah, and Zechariah. **⁴⁵**Then Ezra took up the book of the law in the sight of the multitude, for he had the place of honour in the presence of all. **⁴⁶**And when he opened the law, they all stood erect. And Ezra blessed the Lord God Most High, the God of hosts, the Almighty; **⁴⁷**and all the multitude answered, "Amen." And they lifted up their hands and fell to the ground and worshipped the Lord. **⁴⁸**Jeshua and Anniuth and Sherebiah, Jadin, Jacob, Shabbethai, Hodiah, Maiannas and Kelita, Azariah and Jozabad, Hanan, Pelaiah, the Levites, taught the law of the Lord and read the law of the Lord to the multitude,[a] at the same time explaining what was read.

⁴⁹Then Attharates[b] said to Ezra the chief priest and reader and to the Levites who were teaching the multitude and to all, **⁵⁰**"This day is holy to the Lord"—now they were all weeping as they heard the law—**⁵¹**"so go your way, eat the fat and drink the sweet, and send portions to those who have none; **⁵²**for the day is holy to the Lord; and do not be sorrowful, for the Lord will exalt you." **⁵³**And the Levites commanded all the people, saying, "This day is holy; do not be sorrowful." **⁵⁴**Then they all went their way, to eat and drink and enjoy themselves and to give portions to those who had none and to make great rejoicing; **⁵⁵**because they were inspired by the words that they had been taught. And they came together.[c]

---

[a] Some manuscripts omit *and read the law of the Lord to the multitude*
[b] Or *Then the governor* [c] Greek ends abruptly; compare Nehemiah 8:13

THE PRAYER OF MANASSEH

ASCRIPTION OF PRAISE

1 O Lord Almighty,
    the God of our fathers,
    of Abraham and Isaac and Jacob,
    and of their righteous descendants;
2 you who made heaven and earth
    with all their order;
3 who shackled the sea by your
        word of command,
    who closed up the deep
    and sealed it with your terrible
        and glorious name;
4 at whom all things shudder
    and tremble before your power,
5 for your glorious splendour
        is unendurable,
    and the wrath of your threat to
        sinners is overpowering;
6 yet immeasurable and unsearchable
        is your promised mercy,
7 for you are the Lord Most High,
    of great compassion, patient,
        and very merciful,
    repenting over the evils of
        human beings.[a]
8 Therefore you, O Lord, God
        of the righteous,
    did not appoint repentance
        for the righteous,
    for Abraham and Isaac and Jacob,
        who did not sin against you,
    but you have appointed repentance
        for me, the sinner.

CONFESSION OF SINS

9 For the sins I committed are more in
        number than the sand of the sea;
    my transgressions are multiplied,
        O Lord, they are multiplied!
    I am unworthy to look up and
        see the height of heaven
    because of the multitude
        of my iniquities.
10 I am weighted down with
        many an iron fetter,
    so that I am rejected
        because of my sins,
    and I have no relief;
    for I provoked your wrath
        and did what is evil in your sight,
    setting up abominations and
        multiplying offences.

SUPPLICATION FOR PARDON

11 And now I bend the knee of my heart,
        imploring you for your kindness.
12 I have sinned, O Lord, I have sinned,
        and I know my transgressions.
13 I earnestly implore you,
        forgive me, O Lord, forgive me!
    Do not destroy me with my
        transgressions!
    Do not be angry with me for ever
        or lay up evil for me;
    do not condemn me to the
        depths of the earth.
    For you, O Lord, are the God
        of those who repent,
14 and in me you will show
        forth your goodness;
    for, unworthy as I am, you will
        save me in your great mercy,
15 and I will praise you continually
        all the days of my life.
    For all the might of heaven
        sings your praise,
    and yours is the glory for
        ever. Amen.

---

[a]Latin, Syriac, later Greek manuscripts add *You, O Lord, according to your great goodness have promised repentance and forgiveness to those who have sinned against you; and in the multitude of your mercies you have appointed repentance for sinners, that they may be saved.*

PSALM 151

This psalm is ascribed to David as his own composition (though it is outside the number[a]), after he had fought in single combat with Goliath.

1. I was small among my brothers
    and youngest in my father's house;
    I tended my father's sheep.
2. My hands made a harp,
    my fingers fashioned a lyre.
3. And who will declare it to my Lord?
    The Lord himself;
    he himself listens.[b]
4. It was he who sent his messenger[c]
    and took me from my father's sheep
    and anointed me with his anointing oil.
5. My brothers were handsome and tall,
    but the Lord was not satisfied with them.
6. I went out to meet the Philistine,[d]
    and he cursed me by his idols.
7. But I drew his own sword;
    I beheaded him and removed reproach from the children of Israel.

---

[a]Some manuscripts add *of the 150 [psalms]*   [b]Some manuscripts *he himself will hear me*; some manuscripts add *to everything* or *to me*   [c]Or *angel*   [d]Or *foreigner*

3 MACCABEES

BATTLE OF RAPHIA

1 When Philopator learned from those who returned that the regions that he had controlled had been seized by Antiochus, he gave orders to all his forces, both infantry and cavalry, took with him his sister Arsinoë, and marched out to the region near Raphia, where Antiochus' supporters were encamped. ²But a certain Theodotus, determined to carry out the plot he had devised, took with him the best of the Ptolemaic soldiers[a] that had been previously issued to him and crossed over by night to the tent of Ptolemy, intending single-handed to kill him and thereby end the war. ³But Dositheus, known as son of Drimylus, a Jew by birth who later changed his religion and apostatised from the ancestral traditions, had led the king away and arranged that a certain insignificant man should sleep in the tent; and so it turned out that this man incurred the vengeance meant for the king.[b] ⁴When a bitter fight resulted, and matters were turning out rather in favour of Antiochus, Arsinoë went to the troops with wailing and tears, her hair all dishevelled, and exhorted them to defend themselves and their children and wives bravely, promising to give them each two minas of gold if they won the battle. ⁵And so it came about that the enemy was routed in the action, and many captives also were taken. ⁶Now that he had foiled the plot, Ptolemy[c] decided to visit the neighbouring cities and encourage them. ⁷By doing this and by endowing their sacred enclosures with gifts, he strengthened the morale of his subjects.

PHILOPATOR ATTEMPTS TO ENTER THE TEMPLE

⁸Since the Jews had sent some of their council and elders to greet him, to bring him gifts of welcome, and to congratulate him on what had happened, he was all the more eager to visit them as soon as possible. ⁹After he had arrived in Jerusalem, he offered sacrifice to the supreme[d] God and made thank offerings and did what was fitting for the place. Then, upon entering the place and being impressed by its excellence and its beauty, ¹⁰he marvelled at the good order of the temple and conceived a desire to enter the Most Holy Place. ¹¹When they said that this was not permitted, because not even members of their own nation were allowed to enter, nor even all of the priests, but only the high priest who was pre-eminent over all, and he only once a year, the king was by no means persuaded. ¹²Even after the law had been read to him, he did not cease to maintain that he ought to enter, saying, "Even if those men are deprived of this honour, I ought not to be." ¹³And he enquired why, when he entered every other temple,[e] no one there had stopped him. ¹⁴And someone heedlessly said that it was wrong to take this as a sign in itself. ¹⁵"But since this has happened," the king[f] said, "why should not I at least enter, whether they wish it or not?"

JEWISH RESISTANCE TO PTOLEMY

¹⁶Then the priests in all their vestments prostrated themselves and entreated the supreme God to aid in the present situation and to avert the violence of this evil design, and they filled the temple with cries and tears; ¹⁷and those who remained behind in the city were agitated and hurried out, supposing that something mysterious was occurring. ¹⁸The virgins who had been enclosed in their chambers rushed out with their mothers, sprinkled their hair with dust,[g] and filled the streets with groans and lamentations. ¹⁹Those women who had recently been arrayed for marriage abandoned the bridal chambers prepared for wedded union and, neglecting proper modesty, in a disorderly rush flocked together in the city. ²⁰Mothers and nurses abandoned even newborn children here and there, some in houses and some in the streets, and without a backwards look they crowded together at the highest temple. ²¹Various were the supplications of those gathered there because

---

[a] Or arms [b] Greek for that one [c] Greek he [d] Greek greatest; also verse 16 [e] Or every other sacred enclosure [f] Greek happened," he [g] Some manuscripts add and ashes

of what the king was profanely plotting. ²²In addition, the bolder of the citizens would not tolerate the completion of his plans or the fulfilment of his intended purpose. ²³They shouted to their fellows to take arms and die courageously for the ancestral law and created a considerable disturbance in the place; and being barely restrained by the old men[a] and the elders, they resorted to the same posture of supplication as the others. ²⁴Meanwhile the crowd, as before, was engaged in prayer, ²⁵while the elders near the king tried in various ways to change his arrogant mind from the plan that he had conceived. ²⁶But he, in his arrogance, took heed of nothing and began now to approach, determined to bring the aforesaid plan to a conclusion. ²⁷When those who were round him observed this, they turned, together with our people, to call upon the one having all power to defend them in the present trouble and not to overlook this unlawful and haughty deed. ²⁸The continuous, vehement, and concerted cry of the crowds[b] resulted in an immense uproar; ²⁹for it seemed that not only the people but also the walls and the whole earth round echoed, because indeed all at that time[c] preferred death to the profanation of the place.

PRAYER OF THE HIGH PRIEST SIMON

2 Then the high priest Simon, facing the sanctuary, bending his knees and extending his hands with calm dignity, prayed as follows:[d] ²"Lord, Lord, king of the heavens and sovereign of all creation, holy among the holy ones, the only ruler, almighty, give attention to us who are suffering grievously from an impious and profane man, puffed up in his audacity and power. ³For you, the Creator of all things and the governor of all, are a just Ruler, and you judge those who have done anything in insolence and arrogance. ⁴You destroyed those who in the past committed injustice, among whom were even giants who trusted in their strength and boldness, whom you destroyed by bringing upon them a boundless flood. ⁵You consumed with fire and sulphur the people of Sodom who acted arrogantly, who were notorious for[e] their vices; and you made them an example to those who should come afterwards. ⁶You made known your mighty power by inflicting many and varied punishments on the audacious pharaoh who had enslaved your holy people Israel. ⁷And when he pursued them with chariots and a mass of troops, you overwhelmed him in the depths of the sea, but carried through safely those who had put their confidence in you, the Ruler over the whole creation. ⁸And when they had seen the works of your hands, they praised you, the Almighty. ⁹You, O King, when you had created the boundless and immeasurable earth, chose this city and sanctified this place for your name, though you have no need of anything; and when you had glorified it by your magnificent self-manifestation,[f] you made it a firm foundation for the glory of your great and honoured name. ¹⁰And because you love the house of Israel, you promised that if we should have reverses and tribulation should overtake us, you would listen to our petition when we come to this place and pray. ¹¹And indeed you are faithful and true. ¹²And because often when our fathers were oppressed you helped them in their humiliation and rescued them from great evils, ¹³see now, O holy King, that because of our many and great sins we are crushed with suffering, subjected to our enemies, and overtaken by helplessness. ¹⁴In our downfall this audacious and profane man undertakes to violate the Holy Place on earth dedicated to your glorious name. ¹⁵For your dwelling, the heaven of heavens, is unapproachable by man. ¹⁶But because you graciously bestowed your glory upon your people Israel, you sanctified this place. ¹⁷Do not punish us for the defilement committed by these men or call us to account for this profanation, lest the transgressors boast in their wrath or exult in the arrogance of their tongue, saying, ¹⁸'We have trampled down the house of the sanctuary as the houses of the idols[g] are trampled down.' ¹⁹Wipe away our sins and disperse our errors and reveal your mercy at this hour. ²⁰Speedily let your mercies overtake us and put praises in the mouth of those who are downcast and broken in spirit and give us peace."

GOD'S PUNISHMENT OF PTOLEMY

²¹Thereupon God, who oversees all things, the first Father of all, holy among the holy ones, having heard the lawful supplication, scourged him who had exalted himself in insolence and audacity. ²²He shook him this

---
[a] Some manuscripts *by the priests* [b] Some manuscripts *and vehement cry of the assembled crowds* [c] Some manuscripts omit *at that time*
[d] Some manuscripts omit 2:1 [e] Some manuscripts *were secret in*
[f] Or *magnificent epiphany* [g] Greek *abominations*

way and that as a reed is shaken by the wind, so that he lay helpless on the ground and, besides being paralysed in his limbs, was unable even to speak, since he was smitten[a] by a righteous judgement. ²³Then both friends and bodyguards, seeing the severe punishment that had overtaken him and fearing lest he should lose his life, quickly dragged him out, panic-stricken in their exceedingly great fear. ²⁴After a while he recovered, and though he had been punished, he by no means repented, but went away uttering bitter threats.

HOSTILE MEASURES AGAINST THE JEWS

²⁵When he arrived in Egypt, he increased in his deeds of malice, abetted by the previously mentioned drinking companions and comrades, who were strangers to everything just. ²⁶He was not content with his innumerable licentious deeds, but he also continued with such audacity that he framed evil reports in the various localities; and many of his friends, intently observing the king's purpose, themselves also followed his will. ²⁷He proposed to inflict public disgrace upon the Jewish people,[b] and he set up a stone[c] on the tower in the courtyard with this inscription: ²⁸"None of those who do not sacrifice shall enter their sanctuaries, and all Jews shall be subjected to a registration involving poll tax and to being sold off as slaves. Those who object to this are to be taken by force and put to death; ²⁹those who are registered are also to be branded on their bodies by fire with the ivy-leaf symbol of Dionysus, and they shall also be reduced to their former limited status." ³⁰In order that he might not appear to be an enemy to all, he inscribed below: "But if any of them prefer to join those who have been initiated into the mysteries, they shall have equal citizenship with the Alexandrians."

³¹Now some, while apparently abhorring the price to be exacted for maintaining the religion of the city,[d] readily gave themselves up, since they expected to enhance their reputation by their future association with the king. ³²But the majority acted firmly with a courageous spirit and did not depart from their religion; and by paying money in exchange for life they confidently attempted to save themselves from the registration. ³³They remained resolutely hopeful of obtaining help, and they abhorred those who separated themselves from them, considering them to be enemies of the Jewish[e] nation and depriving them of common fellowship and mutual help.

THE JEWS AND THEIR NEIGHBOURS

3 When the impious king comprehended this situation, he became so infuriated that not only was he enraged against those Jews who lived in Alexandria, but was still more bitterly hostile towards those in the countryside; and he ordered that all should promptly be gathered into one place and put to death by the cruelest means. ²While these matters were being arranged, a hostile rumour was circulated against the Jewish[f] nation by men who conspired to do them ill, a pretext being given by a report that they hindered others[g] from the observance of their lawful customs. ³The Jews, however, continued to maintain goodwill and unswerving loyalty towards the dynasty; ⁴but because they worshipped God and conducted themselves by his law, they kept their separateness with respect to foods. For this reason they appeared hostile to some; ⁵but since they adorned their style of life with the good deeds of upright people, they were established in good repute among all people. ⁶Nevertheless those of other races paid no heed to their good service to their nation, which was common talk among all; ⁷instead they gossiped about the differences in worship and foods, alleging that these people were loyal neither to the king nor to his authorities, but were hostile and greatly opposed to his government. So they attached no ordinary reproach to them.

⁸The Greeks in the city, though wronged in no way, when they saw an unexpected tumult round these people and the crowds that suddenly were forming, were not strong enough to help them, for they lived under tyranny. They tried to console them, being grieved at the situation, and expected that matters would change; ⁹for such a great community ought not to be left to its fate in this way when it had committed no offence. ¹⁰And already some of their neighbours and friends and business associates had taken some of them aside privately and were pledging to protect them and to exert more earnest efforts for their assistance.

---

[a]Some manuscripts *pierced* [b]Greek *upon the nation* [c]Greek *stele*
[d]The meaning of the Greek is uncertain [e]Greek omits *Jewish*
[f]Greek omits *Jewish* [g]Greek *them*

PTOLEMY'S DECREE TO ARREST ALL JEWS

11Then the king, boastful of his present good fortune and not considering the might of the supreme[a] God, but assuming that he would persevere constantly in his same purpose, wrote this letter against them: **12**"King Ptolemy Philopator to his generals and soldiers in Egypt and all its districts, greetings and good health. **13**I myself and our government are faring well. **14**When our expedition took place in Asia, as you yourselves know, it was brought to conclusion, according to plan, by the gods' deliberate alliance with us in battle, **15**and we considered that we should not rule the nations inhabiting Coelesyria and Phoenicia by the power of the spear but should cherish them with clemency and great benevolence, gladly treating them well. **16**And when we had granted very great revenues to the temples in the cities, we came on to Jerusalem also and went up to honour the temple of those wicked people, who never cease from their folly. **17**They accepted our presence by word, but insincerely by deed, because when we proposed to enter their inner temple and honour it with magnificent and most beautiful offerings, **18**they were carried away by their traditional conceit and prevented us from entering; but they were spared the exercise of our power because of the benevolence that we have towards all. **19**By maintaining their manifest ill will towards us, they become the only people among all nations who hold their heads high in defiance of kings and their own benefactors and are unwilling to regard any action as sincere.

20"But we accommodated ourselves to their folly and, crossing again into Egypt after victory, greeted all nationals there with benevolence. We did as was proper, **21**among these things declaring amnesty towards their compatriots here. And both because of their alliance with us and the myriad affairs liberally entrusted to them from the beginning, we ventured to make a change, by deciding both to deem them worthy of Alexandrian citizenship and to make them participants in our regular religious rites.[b] **22**But they took this in a contrary spirit and, in their innate malice, disdained what is good. Since they incline constantly to what is base, **23**they not only spurn the priceless citizenship, but also both by speech and by silence they abominate those few among them who are sincerely disposed towards us; in every situation, in accordance with their infamous way of life, they secretly suspect that we may soon alter our policy. **24**Therefore, fully convinced by these indications that they are ill-disposed towards us in every way, we have taken precautions lest, if a sudden disorder should later arise against us, we should have these impious people behind our backs as traitors and barbarous enemies. **25**Therefore we have given orders that, as soon as this letter shall arrive, you are to send to us those who live among you, together with their wives and children, with insulting and harsh treatment, and bound securely with iron fetters, to suffer the sure and shameful death that suits enemies. **26**For when these all have been punished, we are sure that for the remaining time the government will be established for ourselves in good order and in the best state. **27**But whoever shelters any of the Jews, old people or children or even infants, will be tortured to death with the most hateful torments, together with his household. **28**Anyone willing to give information will receive the property of the one who incurs the punishment and also 2,000 drachmas from the royal treasury and will be awarded the crown of freedom.[c] **29**Every place detected sheltering a Jew is to be made unapproachable and burned with fire and shall become useless for all time to any mortal creature." **30**The original of the letter was written in the above form.

JEWS DEPORTED TO ALEXANDRIA

4 In every place, then, where this decree arrived, a feast at public expense was arranged for the Gentiles with shouts and gladness, for the inveterate enmity that had been in their minds since long ago was now made evident and outspoken. **2**But among the Jews there was incessant mourning, lamentation, and tearful cries; everywhere their hearts were burning, and they groaned because of the unexpected destruction that had suddenly been decreed for them. **3**What district or city or what habitable place at all or what streets were not filled with mourning and wailing for them? **4**For with such a harsh and ruthless spirit were they being sent off, all together, by the generals in the several cities, that at the sight of their

---

[a] Greek *greatest* [b] Some manuscripts *make them partners of our regular priests* [c] Or *will be awarded his freedom*; Greek *will be crowned with freedom*

unusual punishments, even some of their enemies, perceiving the common object of pity before their eyes and reflecting upon the uncertain outcome of life, shed tears at the most miserable expulsion of these people. ⁵For a multitude of grey-headed old men, sluggish of foot and bent with age, was being led away, forced to march at a swift pace by the violence with which they were driven in such a shameful manner. ⁶And young women who had just entered the bridal chamber to share married life exchanged joy for wailing, their myrrh-perfumed hair sprinkled with ashes, and were carried away unveiled, all together raising a lament instead of a wedding song, as they were torn by the harsh treatment of the Gentiles.ᵃ ⁷In bonds and in public view they were violently dragged along as far as the place of embarkation. ⁸Their husbands, in the prime of youth, their necks encircled with ropes instead of garlands, spent the remaining days of their marriage festival in lamentations instead of good cheer and youthful revelry, seeing the grave already lying open before them.ᵇ ⁹They were brought on board like wild animals, driven under the constraint of iron bonds; some were fastened by the neck to the benches of the boats, others had their feet secured by unbreakable fetters, ¹⁰and in addition they were confined under a solid deck, so that with their eyes in total darkness, they should undergo treatment suiting traitors during the whole voyage.

JEWS IMPRISONED AT SCHEDIA

¹¹When these men had been brought to the place called Schedia, and the voyage was concluded as the king had decreed, he commanded that they should be enclosed in the hippodrome that had been built with an immense perimeter wall in front of the city and that was well-suited to make them an obvious spectacle to all coming back into the city and to those from the cityᶜ going out into the country, so that they could neither communicate with the king's forces nor in any way claim to be inside the circuit of the city.ᵈ ¹²And when this had happened, the king, hearing that the Jews' compatriots from the city frequently went out in secret to lament bitterly the ignoble misfortune of their brothers, ¹³ordered in his rage that these men be dealt with in precisely the same fashion as the others, not omitting any detail of their punishment. ¹⁴The entire race was to be registered individually, not for the hard labour that has been briefly mentioned before, but to be tortured with the outrages that he had ordered and at the end to be destroyed in the space of a single day. ¹⁵The registration of these people was therefore conducted with bitter haste and zealous diligence from the rising of the sun till its setting, and though uncompleted it stopped after forty days.

¹⁶The king was greatly and continually filled with joy, organising drinking parties in honour of all his idols, with a mind alienated from truth and with a profane mouth, praising deaf things that are unable even to communicate or to come to one's help and uttering improper words against the supremeᵉ God. ¹⁷But after the previously mentioned interval of time the scribes declared to the king that they were no longer able to take the census of the Jews because of their innumerable multitude, ¹⁸although most of them were still in the country, some still residing in their homes, and some at the place; the task was impossible for all the generals in Egypt. ¹⁹After he had threatened them severely, charging that they had been bribed to contrive a means of escape, he was clearly convinced about the matter ²⁰when they said and proved that both the paperᶠ and the pens they used for writing had already given out. ²¹But this was an act of the invincible providence of him who was aiding the Jews from heaven.

EXECUTION OF THE JEWS IS TWICE THWARTED

5 Then the king, completely inflexible and filled with overpowering anger and wrath, summoned Hermon, keeper of the elephants, ²and ordered him on the following day to drug all the elephants—500 in number—with large handfuls of frankincense and plenty of unmixed wine and to drive them in, maddened by the lavish abundance of liquor, so that the Jews might meet their doom. ³When he had given these orders he returned to his feasting, together with those of his friends and of the army who were especially hostile towards the Jews. ⁴And Hermon, keeper of the elephants, proceeded faithfully to carry out the orders. ⁵The

---
ᵃOne manuscript *as though torn by heathen whelps* ᵇGreek *seeing Hades already lying at their feet* ᶜGreek *to those of them* ᵈOr *claim protection of the walls*; the meaning of the Greek is uncertain ᵉGreek *greatest* ᶠOr *the paper factory*

servants in charge of the Jews[a] went out in the evening and set about binding the hands of the wretched people and making arrangements for their continued custody through the night, convinced that the whole nation would experience its final destruction. **6**For to the Gentiles it appeared that the Jews were left without any aid, **7**because in their bonds they were forcibly confined on every side. But with tears and an irrepressible voice they all called upon the almighty Lord and Ruler of all power, their merciful God and Father, praying **8**that he avert with vengeance the unholy plot against them and in a glorious manifestation rescue them from the fate now prepared for them. **9**So their entreaty continued to ascend fervently to heaven.

10Hermon, however, when he had drugged the pitiless elephants until they had been filled with a great abundance of wine and satiated with frankincense, presented himself at the courtyard early in the morning to report to the king about these preparations. **11**But the Lord[b] sent upon the king a portion of sleep, that beneficence that from the beginning, night and day, is bestowed by him who grants it to whomever he wishes. **12**And by the action of the Lord he was overcome by so pleasant and deep a sleep[c] that he quite failed in his lawless purpose and was completely frustrated in his inflexible plan. **13**Then the Jews, since they had escaped the appointed hour, began praising their holy God and again begged him who is easily reconciled to show the might of his all-powerful hand to the arrogant Gentiles.

14But now, since it was nearly the middle of the tenth hour, the person who was in charge of the invitations, seeing that the guests were assembled, approached the king and nudged him. **15**And when he had with difficulty roused him, he pointed out that the hour of the banquet was already slipping by, and he gave him an account of the situation. **16**The king, after considering this, returned to his drinking and ordered those present for the banquet to recline opposite him. **17**When this was done he began urging them to give themselves over to revelry and to make the present[d] portion of the banquet joyful by celebrating all the more. **18**After the party had been going on for some time, the king summoned Hermon and with sharp threats demanded to know why the Jews had been allowed to remain alive through the present day. **19**But when he, with the corroboration of his friends, pointed out that while it was still night he had carried out completely the order given him, **20**the king,[e] possessed by a savagery worse than that of Phalaris, said that the Jews[f] could be thankful for today's sleep, "but," he added, "tomorrow without delay prepare the elephants in the same way for the destruction of the lawless Jews!" **21**When the king had spoken, all those present readily and joyfully with one accord gave their approval, and each departed to his own home. **22**But they did not so much employ the duration of the night in sleep as in devising all sorts of insults for those they thought to be doomed.

23Then, as soon as the cock had crowed in the early morning, Hermon, having equipped[g] the beasts, began to move them along in the great colonnade. **24**The crowds of the city had been assembled for this most pitiful spectacle, and they were eagerly waiting for daybreak. **25**But the Jews, at their last gasp, since the time had run out, stretched their hands towards heaven and with most tearful supplication and mournful dirges implored the supreme[h] God to help them again at once. **26**The rays of the sun were not yet shed abroad, and the king was still receiving his friends, when Hermon arrived and invited him to come out, indicating that what the king desired was ready for action. **27**But he, upon receiving the report and being struck by the unusual invitation to come out—since he had been completely overcome by incomprehension—enquired what the matter was for which this had been so zealously completed for him. **28**This was the act of God who rules over all things, for he had implanted in the king's mind a forgetfulness of the things he had previously devised. **29**Then Hermon and all the king's friends pointed out that the beasts and the armed forces were ready, "O king, according to your eager purpose."[i] **30**But at these words he was filled with an overpowering wrath, because by the providence of God his whole mind had been deranged in regards to these matters; and with a threatening look he said, **31**"Were your parents or children present, I would have prepared them to be a rich feast for the savage beasts instead of the Jews,

---

[a]Greek *of them* [b]Greek *But he* [c]Some manuscripts add *from evening to the ninth hour* [d]Some manuscripts *delayed*; Greek *untimely* [e]Greek *he* [f]Greek *that they* [g]Or *armed* [h]Greek *greatest* [i]Some manuscripts *pointed to the beasts and the armed forces, saying, "They are ready, O king, according to your eager purpose."*

who give me no ground for complaint and have exhibited to an extraordinary degree a full and firm loyalty to my ancestors. ³²In fact you would have been deprived of life instead of these, were it not for an affection arising from our nurture in common and your usefulness." ³³So Hermon suffered an unexpected and dangerous threat, and his eyes and his face showed his dismay. ³⁴The king's friends one by one sullenly slipped away, and they[a] dismissed the assembled people, each to his own occupation. ³⁵Then the Jews, upon hearing what the king had said, started praising the manifest Lord God, King of kings, since this also was his aid that they had received.

³⁶The king, however, reconvened the party in the same manner and went about urging the guests to return to their celebrating. ³⁷After summoning Hermon he said in a threatening tone, "How many times, you poor wretch, must I give you orders about these same things? ³⁸Equip[b] the elephants now once more for the destruction of the Jews tomorrow!" ³⁹But the officials who were reclining at table with him, wondering at his instability of mind, began to object as follows: ⁴⁰"O king, how long will you continue to test us, as though we are idiots, ordering now for a third time that they be destroyed and again revoking your decree in the matter?[c] ⁴¹As a result the city is in a tumult because of its expectation; it is crowded with masses of people and also in constant danger of being plundered." ⁴²Upon this the king, a Phalaris in everything and filled with madness, took no account of the changes of mind that had come about within him for the protection of the Jews, and he firmly swore an irrevocable[d] oath that he would send these people to death[e] without delay, mangled by the knees and feet of the beasts, ⁴³and would also march against Judea and rapidly level it to the ground with fire and spear and by burning to the ground the temple "inaccessible to us" would quickly render it for ever empty of those who offered sacrifices there. ⁴⁴Then the friends and officers departed with great joy, and they confidently started posting the armed forces at the places in the city most favourable for keeping guard. ⁴⁵Now when the beasts had been brought virtually to a state of madness, so to speak, by the very fragrant draughts of wine mixed with frankincense and had been equipped with frightful devices, the elephant keeper ⁴⁶entered at about dawn into the courtyard—the city now being filled with countless masses of people crowding their way into the hippodrome—and began urging the king on to the matter at hand. ⁴⁷So he, when he had filled his impious mind with a deep rage, rushed out in full force along with the beasts, wishing to witness, with invulnerable heart and with his own eyes, the grievous and pitiful destruction of the aforementioned people. ⁴⁸And when the Jews saw the dust raised by the elephants going out at the gate and by the following armed forces, as well as by the trampling of the crowd, and heard the loud and tumultuous noise, ⁴⁹they thought that this was their last moment of life, the end of their most miserable suspense, and giving way to lamentation and groans they started kissing one another, embracing relatives and falling upon one another's shoulders—parents and children, mothers and daughters, and others with babies at their breasts who were drawing their last milk. ⁵⁰Not only this, but when they considered the help that they had received before from heaven they prostrated themselves with one accord on the ground, removing the babies from their breasts, ⁵¹and cried out in a very loud voice, imploring the Ruler over every power to manifest himself and be merciful to them, as they stood now at the gates of death.

PRAYER OF ELEAZAR

6 Then a certain Eleazar, famous among the priests of the country, who had attained a ripe old age and throughout his life had been adorned with every virtue, directed the elders round him to cease calling upon the holy God and prayed as follows: ²"King of great power, almighty God Most High, governing all creation with mercy, ³look upon the descendants of Abraham, O Father, upon the children of the consecrated Jacob, a people of your consecrated portion, foreigners in a foreign land who are perishing unjustly. ⁴Pharaoh with his abundance of chariots, the former ruler of this Egypt, exalted with lawless insolence and boastful tongue, you destroyed together with his arrogant army by drowning them in the sea, manifesting the light of your mercy upon the nation of Israel. ⁵Sennacherib exulting in his countless forces, oppressive king of

---

[a] Some manuscripts *he* [b] Or *Arm* [c] Some manuscripts *decree when the matter is in hand* [d] Or *unfulfillable* [e] Greek *Hades*; also verse 51

the Assyrians, who had already gained control of the whole world by the spear and was moving against your holy city, speaking grievous words with boasting and insolence, you, O Lord, broke in pieces, showing your power to many nations. ⁶The three companions in Babylon who had voluntarily surrendered their lives to the flames so as not to serve vain things, you rescued unharmed, even to a hair, moistening the fiery furnace with dew and turning the flame against all their enemies. ⁷Daniel, who through envious slanders was cast down into the ground to lions as food for wild beasts, you brought up to the light unharmed. ⁸And Jonah, wasting away in the belly of a huge, sea-born monster, you, Father, watched over and restored[a] unharmed to all his family. ⁹And now, you who hate insolence, all-merciful and protector of all, reveal yourself quickly to those of the nation of Israel[b]—who are being outrageously treated by the abominable and lawless Gentiles. ¹⁰Even if our lives have become entangled in impieties in our exile, rescue us from the hand of the enemy and destroy us, Lord, by whatever fate you choose. ¹¹Let not the empty-minded praise their empty idols[c] at the destruction of your beloved people, saying, 'Not even their god has rescued them.' ¹²But you, O Eternal One, who have all might and all power, look upon us now: have mercy upon us who by the senseless insolence of the lawless are being deprived of life in the manner of traitors. ¹³And let the Gentiles cower today in fear of your invincible might, O honoured one, who have power to save the nation of Jacob. ¹⁴The whole throng of infants and their parents are entreating you with tears. ¹⁵Let it be shown to all the Gentiles that you are with us, O Lord, and have not turned your face from us; but just as you have said, 'Not even when they were in the land of their enemies did I neglect them,' so accomplish it, O Lord."

TWO ANGELS RESCUE THE JEWS

¹⁶Just as Eleazar was ending his prayer, the king arrived at the hippodrome with the beasts and all the arrogance of his power. ¹⁷And when the Jews observed this they raised great cries to heaven so that even the nearby valleys resounded with them and brought an uncontrollable terror upon the army. ¹⁸Then the most glorious, almighty, and true God revealed his holy face and opened the heavenly gates, from which two glorious angels of fearful aspect descended, visible to all but the Jews. ¹⁹They opposed the power of the enemy and filled them with confusion and terror, binding them with immovable shackles. ²⁰Even the king began to shudder bodily, and he forgot his sullen insolence. ²¹The beasts turned back upon the armed forces following them and began trampling and destroying them. ²²Then the king's anger was turned to pity and tears because of the things that he had devised beforehand. ²³For when he heard the shouting and saw them all fallen headlong to destruction, he wept and angrily threatened his friends, saying, ²⁴"You are committing treason and surpassing tyrants in savagery; and even me, your benefactor, you are now attempting to deprive of dominion and life by secretly devising acts of no advantage to the kingdom. ²⁵Who is it that has taken each man from his home and senselessly gathered here those who faithfully have held the fortresses of our country? ²⁶Who is it that has so lawlessly encompassed with outrageous treatment those who from the beginning differed from[d] all nations in their goodwill toward us and often have accepted willingly the worst of human dangers? ²⁷Loose and untie their unjust bonds! Send them back to their homes in peace, begging pardon for your former actions![e] ²⁸Release the sons of the almighty and living God of heaven, who from the time of our ancestors until now has granted an unimpeded and notable stability to our government." ²⁹These then were the things he said; and the Jews, immediately released, began to bless their holy God and Saviour, since they now had escaped death.

THE JEWS CELEBRATE THEIR DELIVERANCE

³⁰Then the king, when he had returned to the city, summoned the official in charge of the revenues and ordered him to provide to the Jews both wines and everything else needed for a festival of seven days, deciding that they should celebrate their rescue with all joyfulness in that same place in which they had expected to meet their destruction. ³¹Accordingly those disgracefully treated and near to death[f] or, rather, who stood at its very gates arranged for a banquet of deliverance

---

[a] Some manuscripts *Father, rescued and restored*; some manuscripts *Father, recognised and restored*; some manuscripts *Father, mercifully restored* [b] Some manuscripts *to the saints of Israel* [c] Greek *their things* [d] Or *beginning excelled above* [e] Or *peace, revoking your former commands* [f] Greek *Hades*

instead of a bitter and lamentable death, and full of joy they apportioned to celebrants the place that had been prepared for their destruction and burial. ³²They ceased their chanting of dirges and took up the ancestral song, praising God, their Saviour and worker of wonders.ᵃ Putting an end to all mourning and wailing, they formed choruses*ᵇ* as a sign of peaceful joy. ³³Likewise also the king, after convening a great banquet to celebrate these events, gave thanks to heaven unceasingly and lavishly for the unexpected rescue that heᶜ had experienced. ³⁴And those who had previously believed that the Jews would be destroyed and become food for birds and had joyfully registered them groaned as they themselves were overcome by disgrace, and their fire-breathing boldness was ignominiouslyᵈ quenched. ³⁵But the Jews, when they had arranged the aforementioned choral group, as we have said before, passed the time in feasting to the accompaniment of joyous thanksgiving and psalms. ³⁶And when they had ordained a public rite for these things for the duration of their sojourning throughout their generations, they instituted the observance of the aforesaid days as a festival, not for drinking and gluttony, but because of the deliverance that had come to them through God. ³⁷Then they petitioned the king, asking for dismissal to their homes. ³⁸So their registration was carried out from the twenty-fifth of Pachon to the fourth of Epeiph,ᵉ for forty days; and their destruction was set for the fifth to the seventh of Epeiph,*ᶠ* the three days ³⁹in which the Lord of all most gloriously revealed his mercy and rescued them all together and unharmed. ⁴⁰Then they feasted, provided with everything by the king, until the fourteenth day,*ᵍ* on which also they made the petition for their dismissal. ⁴¹The king granted their request at once and wrote the following letter for them to the generals in the cities, magnanimously expressing his concern:

PTOLEMY'S LETTER ON BEHALF OF THE JEWS

7 "King Ptolemy Philopator to the generals in Egypt and all in authority in his government, greetings and good health. ²We ourselves and our children are faring well, the great God guiding our affairs according to our desire. ³Certain of our friends, frequently urging us with malicious intent, persuaded us to gather together the Jews of the kingdom in a body and to punish them with barbarous penalties as traitors; ⁴for they declared that our government would never be firmly established until this was accomplished, because of the ill will that these people had towards all nations. ⁵They also led them out with harsh treatment as slaves, or rather as traitors, and, girding themselves with a cruelty more savage than that of Scythian custom, they tried without any enquiry or examination to put them to death. ⁶But we very severely threatened them for these acts, and in accordance with the clemency that we have towards all people we barely spared their lives. Since we have come to realise that the God of heaven surely shields the Jews, always fighting for them as a father does for his children, ⁷and since we have taken into account the friendly and firm goodwill that they had towards us and our ancestors, we justly have acquitted them of every charge of whatever kind. ⁸We also have ordered each and every one to return to his own home, with no one in any wayʰ doing them harm at all or reproaching them for the irrational things that have happened. ⁹For you should know that if we devise any evil against them or cause them any grief at all, we always shall have not a mortal, but the Ruler over every power, the Most High God, as an antagonist to avenge such acts thoroughly and inescapably. Farewell."

THE JEWS RETURN HOME WITH JOY

¹⁰Upon receiving this letter the Jews did not immediately hurry to make their departure, but they requested of the king that at their own hands those of the Jewish nation who had wilfully transgressed against the holy God and the law of God should receive the punishment they deserved. ¹¹For they declared that those who for the belly's sake had transgressed the divine commandments would also never be favourably disposed towards the king's government. ¹²The kingⁱ then, admitting and approving the truth of what they said, granted them a general licence so that freely and without royal authority or supervision they might destroy those everywhere in his kingdom who had transgressed the law of God. ¹³When they had applauded him in fitting manner, their

---

ᵃSome manuscripts *praising Israel and the wonder-working God* or *praising Israel's Saviour, the wonder-working God*   ᵇOr *formed choral groups*   ᶜSome manuscripts *they*   ᵈSome manuscripts *completely*   ᵉMay 20–June 28   *ᶠ*June 29–July 1   *ᵍ*July 8   ʰSome manuscripts *place*   ⁱGreek *He*

priests and the whole multitude shouted the hallelujah and joyfully departed. [14]And so on their way they set about punishing and putting to death as public examples any whom they met of their compatriots who had become defiled. [15]In that day they put to death more than 300 men; and they kept the day as a joyful festival, since they had destroyed the profaners. [16]But those who had held fast to God even to death and had received the full enjoyment of deliverance began their departure from the city, crowned with all sorts of very fragrant flowers, joyfully and loudly giving thanks to the one God of their fathers, the eternal Saviour[a] of Israel, in words of praise and all kinds of melodious songs.

[17]When they had arrived at Ptolemais, called "rose-bearing" because of a characteristic of the place, the fleet waited for them, in accord with the common desire, for seven days. [18]There they celebrated their deliverance,[b] for the king had generously provided all things to them for their journey, to each as far as his own house. [19]And when they had landed in peace with appropriate thanksgiving, there too in like manner they decided to observe these days as a joyous festival during the time of their sojourning. [20]Then, after inscribing them as holy on a pillar and dedicating a place of prayer at the site of the festival, they departed unharmed, free, and overjoyed, since at the king's command they had been brought safely by land and sea and river each to his own place. [21]They also possessed greater authority among their enemies than before, being held in honour and awe; and they were not subject at all to confiscation of their belongings by anyone. [22]Besides they all recovered all of their property, in accordance with the registration, so that those who held any restored it to them with extreme fear.[c] So the supreme God perfectly performed great deeds for their deliverance. [23]Blessed be the Deliverer of Israel through all times! Amen.

---

[a] Some manuscripts *the holy Saviour* or *the Holy One* [b] Greek *they made a cup of deliverance* [c] Some manuscripts *with a very large supplement*

2 ESDRAS

GENEALOGY OF EZRA

1 The second book of the prophet Ezra son of Seraiah, son of Azariah, son of Hilkiah, son of Shallum, son of Zadok, son of Ahitub, ²son of Ahijah, son of Phinehas, son of Eli, son of Amariah, son of Azariah, son of Meraioth, son of Arna, son of Uzzi, son of Borith, son of Abishua, son of Phinehas, son of Eleazar, ³son of Aaron, of the tribe of Levi, who was a captive in the country of the Medes in the reign of King Artaxerxes of the Persians.

EZRA'S PROPHETIC CALL

⁴The word of the Lord came to me, saying, ⁵"Go, declare to my people their evil deeds and to their children the iniquities that they have committed against me, so that they may tell their children's children ⁶that the sins of their parents have increased in them, for they have forgotten me and have offered sacrifices to strange gods. ⁷Was it not I who brought them out of the land of Egypt, out of the house of bondage? But they have angered me and despised my counsels. ⁸Pull out the hair of your head and hurl all evils upon them, for they have not obeyed my law—they are a rebellious people. ⁹How long shall I endure them, on whom I have bestowed such great benefits? ¹⁰For their sake I have overthrown many kings: I struck down Pharaoh with his servants and all his army. ¹¹I have destroyed all nations before them and scattered in the east the people of two provinces, Tyre and Sidon; I have slain all their enemies.

GOD'S MERCIES TO ISRAEL

¹²"But speak to them and say, Thus says the Lord: ¹³Surely it was I who brought you through the sea and made safe highways for you where there was no road; I gave you Moses as leader and Aaron as priest; ¹⁴I provided light for you from a pillar of fire and did great wonders among you. Yet you have forgotten me, says the Lord.

¹⁵"Thus says the Lord Almighty: The quails were a sign to you; I gave you camps for your protection, and in them you complained. ¹⁶You have not rejoiced in my name at the destruction of your enemies, but to this day you still complain. ¹⁷Where are the benefits that I bestowed on you? When you were hungry and thirsty in the wilderness, did you not cry out to me, ¹⁸saying, 'Why have you led us into this wilderness to kill us? It would have been better for us to serve the Egyptians than to die in this wilderness.' ¹⁹I pitied your groanings and gave you manna for food; you ate the bread of angels. ²⁰When you were thirsty, did I not split open the rock so that waters flowed in abundance? Because of the heat I covered you with the leaves of trees. ²¹I divided fertile lands among you; I drove out the Canaanites, the Perizzites, and the Philistines before you. What more can I do for you? says the Lord. ²²Thus says the Lord Almighty: When you were in the wilderness, at the bitter stream, thirsty and blaspheming my name, ²³I did not send fire upon you for your blasphemies, but threw a tree into the water and made the stream sweet.

ISRAEL'S DISOBEDIENCE AND REJECTION

²⁴"What shall I do to you, O Jacob? You would not obey me, O Judah. I will turn to other nations and will give them my name, that they may keep my statutes. ²⁵Because you have forsaken me, I also will forsake you. When you beg mercy of me, I will show you no mercy. ²⁶When you call upon me, I will not listen to you; for you have defiled your hands with blood, and your feet are swift to commit murder. ²⁷It is not as though you had forsaken me; you have forsaken yourselves, says the Lord.

²⁸"Thus says the Lord Almighty: Have I not entreated you as a father entreats his sons or a mother her daughters or a nurse her children, ²⁹that you should be my people and I should be your God and that you should be my children and I should be your father? ³⁰I gathered you as a hen gathers her hatchlings under her wings. But now, what shall I do to you? I will cast you out from my presence. ³¹When you offer oblations to me, I will turn my face from you; for I have rejected your

holy days and new moons and circumcisions of the flesh. ³²I sent to you my servants the prophets, but you have taken and slain them and torn their bodies in pieces; their blood I will require of you, says the Lord.

³³"Thus says the Lord Almighty: Your house is desolate; I will drive you out as the wind drives straw; ³⁴and your sons will have no children, because with you they have neglected my commandment and have done what is evil in my sight. ³⁵I will give your houses to a people that will come, that without having heard me will believe. Those to whom I have shown no signs will do what I have commanded. ³⁶They have seen no prophets, yet will recall their former state.ᵃ ³⁷I call to witness the gratitude of the people that is to come, whose children rejoice with gladness; though they do not see me with bodily eyes, yet with the spirit they will believe the things I have said.

³⁸"And now, father, look with pride and see the people coming from the east; ³⁹to them I will give as leaders Abraham, Isaac, and Jacob and Hosea and Amos and Micah and Joel and Obadiah and Jonah ⁴⁰and Nahum and Habakkuk, Zephaniah, Haggai, Zechariah and Malachi, who is also called the messenger of the Lord.

GOD'S JUDGEMENT ON ISRAEL

2 "Thus says the Lord: I brought this people out of bondage, and I gave them commandments through my servants the prophets; but they would not listen to them and made my counsels void. ²The mother who bore them says to them, 'Go, my children, because I am a widow and forsaken. ³I brought you up with gladness; but with mourning and sorrow I have lost you, because you have sinned before the Lord God and have done what is evil in my sight. ⁴But now what can I do for you? For I am a widow and forsaken. Go, my children, and ask for mercy from the Lord.' ⁵I call upon you, father, as a witness in addition to the mother of the children, because they would not keep my covenant, ⁶that you may bring confusion upon them and bring their mother to ruin, so that they may have no offspring. ⁷Let them be scattered among the nations, let their names be blotted out from the earth, because they have despised my covenant.

⁸"Woe to you, Assyria, who conceal the unrighteous in your midst! O wicked nation, remember what I did to Sodom and Gomorrah, ⁹whose land lies in lumps of pitch and piles of ashes. Thus will I do to those who have not listened to me, says the Lord Almighty."

¹⁰Thus says the Lord to Ezra: "Tell my people that I will give them the kingdom of Jerusalem, which I was going to give to Israel. ¹¹Moreover, I will take back to myself their glory and will give to these others the everlasting habitations, which I had prepared for Israel.ᵇ ¹²The tree of life shall give them fragrant perfume, and they shall neither toil nor become weary. ¹³Askᶜ and you will receive; pray that your days may be few, that they may be shortened. The kingdom is already prepared for you; watch! ¹⁴Call, O call heaven and earth to witness, for I left out evil and created good, because I live, says the Lord.

EXHORTATION TO GOOD WORKS

¹⁵"Mother, embrace your sons; bring them up with gladness, as does the dove; make their footing firm, because I have chosen you, says the Lord. ¹⁶And I will raise up the dead from their places and will bring them out from their tombs, because I recognise my name in them. ¹⁷Do not fear, mother of children, for I have chosen you, says the Lord. ¹⁸I will send you help, my servants Isaiah and Jeremiah.ᵈ According to their counsel I have consecrated and prepared for you twelve trees loaded with various fruits ¹⁹and the same number of springs flowing with milk and honey and seven mighty mountains on which roses and lilies grow; by these I will fill your children with joy. ²⁰Guard the rights of the widow, secure justice for the fatherless, give to the needy, defend the orphan, clothe the naked, ²¹care for the injured and the weak, do not ridicule a lame person, protect the maimed, and let the blind one have a vision of my splendour. ²²Protect the old and the young within your walls. ²³When you find any who are dead, commit them to the grave and markᵉ it,ᶠ and I will give you the first place in my resurrection. ²⁴Pause and be quiet, my people, because your rest will come. ²⁵Good nurse, nourish your children and strengthen their feet. ²⁶Not one of the servants whom I have given you will perish, for I will require them from among your number. ²⁷Do not be anxious, for when the day of tribulation and anguish comes, others

---

ᵃSome manuscripts *their iniquities* ᵇLatin *those* ᶜSome manuscripts *Go* ᵈSome manuscripts add *and Daniel* ᵉOr *seal* ᶠOr *dead, mark them and commit them to the grave*

shall weep and be sorrowful, but you shall rejoice and have abundance. ²⁸The nations shall envy you, but they shall not be able to do anything against you, says the Lord. ²⁹My hands will cover you, that your children may not see Gehenna. ³⁰Rejoice, O mother, with your children, because I will deliver you, says the Lord. ³¹Remember your children that sleep, because I will bring them out of the hiding places of the earth and will show mercy to them; for I am merciful, says the Lord Almighty. ³²Embrace your offspring until I come and proclaim mercy to them; because my springs run over, and my grace will not fail."

EZRA ON MOUNT HOREB

³³I, Ezra, received a command from the Lord on Mount Horeb to go to Israel. When I came to them they rejected me and refused the Lord's commandment. ³⁴Therefore I say to you, O nations that hear and understand, "Await your shepherd; he will give you everlasting rest, because he who will come at the end of the age is close at hand. ³⁵Be ready for the rewards of the kingdom, because endless light will shine upon you for evermore. ³⁶Flee from the shadow of this age, receive the joy of your glory; I publicly call on my Saviour to witness.[a] ³⁷Receive what the Lord has entrusted to you and be joyful, giving thanks to him who has called you to heavenly kingdoms. ³⁸Arise, stand upright, and see at the feast of the Lord the number of those who have been sealed. ³⁹Those who have departed from the shadow of this age have received glorious garments from the Lord. ⁴⁰Take again your full number, O Zion, and enfold your people who are clothed in white, who have fulfilled the law of the Lord. ⁴¹The number of your children, whom you desired, is full; ask the Lord's power that your people, who have been called from the beginning, may be made holy."

EZRA SEES THE SON OF GOD

⁴²I, Ezra, saw on Mount Zion a great multitude, which I could not number, and they all were praising the Lord with songs. ⁴³In their midst was a young man of great stature, taller than any of the others, and on the head of each of them he placed a crown, but he was more exalted than they. And I was held spellbound. ⁴⁴Then I asked an angel, "Who are these, my lord?" ⁴⁵He answered and said to me, "These are they who have put off mortal clothing and have put on the immortal, and they have confessed the name of God; now they are being crowned and receive palms." ⁴⁶Then I said to the angel, "Who is that young man who places crowns on them and puts palms in their hands?" ⁴⁷He answered and said to me, "He is the Son of God, whom they confessed in the world." So I began to praise those who had stood valiantly for the name of the Lord.[b] ⁴⁸Then the angel said to me, "Go, tell my people how great and many are the wonders of the Lord God that you have seen."

FIRST VISION: EZRA'S PRAYER OF COMPLAINT

3 In the thirtieth year after the destruction of our city, I, Salathiel, who am also called Ezra, was in Babylon. I was troubled as I lay on my bed, and my thoughts welled up in my heart, ²because I saw the desolation of Zion and the wealth of those who lived in Babylon. ³My spirit was greatly agitated, and I began to speak anxious words to the Most High and said, ⁴"O sovereign Lord, did you not speak at the beginning when you formed the earth—and that without help—and commanded the dust[c] ⁵and it gave[d] you Adam, a lifeless body? Yet he was the workmanship of your hands, and you breathed into him the breath of life, and he was made alive in your presence. ⁶And you led him into the garden that your right hand had planted before the earth appeared. ⁷And you laid upon him one commandment of yours; but he transgressed it, and immediately you appointed death for him and for his descendants. From him there sprang nations and tribes, peoples and clans, without number. ⁸And every nation walked after its own will and did ungodly things before you and scorned you, and you did not hinder them. ⁹But again, in its time you brought the flood upon the inhabitants of the world and destroyed them. ¹⁰And the same fate befell them: as death came upon Adam, so the flood upon them. ¹¹But you left one of them, Noah with his household, and all the righteous who have descended from him.

¹²"When those who dwelt on earth began to multiply, they produced children and peoples and many nations, and again they began to be more ungodly than were their ancestors. ¹³And when they were committing

---

[a]Some manuscripts *I testify that my Saviour has been commissioned by the Lord* [b]Some manuscripts *So I began to praise and glorify the Lord.* [c]Syriac, Ethiopic; Latin *people* or *world* [d]Syriac

iniquity before you, you chose for yourself one of them, whose name was Abraham; ¹⁴and you loved him, and to him only you revealed the end of the times, secretly by night. ¹⁵You made with him an everlasting covenant and promised him that you would never forsake his descendants; and you gave to him Isaac, and to Isaac you gave Jacob and Esau. ¹⁶And you set apart Jacob for yourself, but Esau you rejected; and Jacob became a great multitude. ¹⁷And when you led his descendants out of Egypt, you brought them to Mount Sinai. ¹⁸You bent down the heavens and shook*ᵃ* the earth and moved the world and made the depths to tremble and troubled the times.*ᵇ* ¹⁹And your glory passed through the four gates of fire and earthquake and wind and ice, to give the law to the descendants of Jacob and your commandment to the posterity of Israel.

²⁰"Yet you did not take away from them their evil heart, so that your law might bring forth fruit in them. ²¹For the first Adam, burdened with an evil heart, transgressed and was overcome, as were also all who were descended from him. ²²Thus the disease became permanent; the law was in the people's heart along with the evil root, but what was good departed, and the evil remained. ²³So the times passed and the years were completed, and you raised up for yourself a servant, named David. ²⁴And you commanded him to build a city for your name and in it to offer you oblations from what is yours. ²⁵This was done for many years; but the inhabitants of the city transgressed, ²⁶in everything doing as Adam and all his descendants had done, for they also bore the evil heart. ²⁷So you delivered the city into the hands of your enemies.

BABYLON COMPARED WITH ZION

²⁸"Then I said in my heart, Are the deeds of those who inhabit Babylon any better? Is that why she has gained dominion over Zion? ²⁹For when I came here I saw ungodly deeds without number, and my soul has seen many sinners during these thirty years.*ᶜ* And my heart failed me, ³⁰for I have seen how you endure those who sin and have spared those who act wickedly and have destroyed your people and have preserved your enemies ³¹and have not shown to anyone how your way may be comprehended.*ᵈ* Are the deeds of Babylon better than those of Zion? ³²Or has another nation known you besides Israel? Or what tribes have so believed your covenants as these tribes of Jacob? ³³Yet their reward has not appeared, and their labour has borne no fruit. For I have travelled widely among the nations and have seen that they abound in wealth, though they are unmindful of your commandments. ³⁴Now therefore weigh in a balance our iniquities and those of the inhabitants of the world; and so it will be found which way the turn of the scale will incline. ³⁵When have the inhabitants of the earth not sinned in your sight? Or what nation has kept your commandments so well? ³⁶You may indeed find individual people who have kept your commandments, but nations you will not find."

LIMITATIONS OF THE HUMAN MIND

4 Then the angel that had been sent to me, whose name was Uriel, answered ²and said to me, "Your understanding has utterly failed regarding this world, and do you wish*ᵉ* to comprehend the way of the Most High?" ³Then I said, "Yes, my lord." And he replied to me, "I have been sent to show you three ways and to put before you three problems. ⁴If you can solve one of them for me, I also will show you the way you desire to see and will teach you why the heart is evil."

⁵I said, "Speak on, my lord."

And he said to me, "Go, weigh for me the weight of fire or measure for me a measure*ᶠ* of wind or call back for me the day that is past."

⁶I answered and said, "Who of those that have been born can do this, that you ask me concerning these things?"

⁷And he said to me, "If I had asked you, 'How many dwellings are in the heart of the sea, or how many springs are at the source of the deep, or how many ways*ᵍ* are above the firmament, or which are the exits of hell, or which are the entrances*ʰ* of paradise?' ⁸perhaps you would have said to me, 'I never went down into the deep, nor as yet did I descend*ⁱ* into hell, neither did I ever ascend into heaven.'*ʲ* ⁹But now I have asked you only about fire and wind and the day, things through which you have passed and without which you cannot exist,*ᵏ* and you

---

*ᵃ*Syriac, Ethiopic, Arabic 1, Georgian; Latin *and set fast*   *ᵇ*Or *universe*
*ᶜ*Ethiopic, Arabic 1, Armenian; Latin, Syriac *sinners in this thirtieth year*
*ᵈ*Syriac; Latin *how this way should be forsaken*   *ᵉ*Some versions; Latin *think*   *ᶠ*Syriac, Ethiopic, Arabic, Georgian; Latin *blast*
*ᵍ*Some versions; Latin *springs*   *ʰ*Syriac; compare Ethiopic, Arabic 2, Armenian; Latin omits *of hell, or which are the entrances*   *ⁱ*Latin omits *did I descend*   *ʲ*Some manuscripts add *nor did I enter paradise*
*ᵏ*Some Latin manuscripts *and from which you cannot be separated*

have given me no answer about them!" ¹⁰And he said to me, "You cannot understand the things with which you have grown up; ¹¹how then can your mind comprehend the way of the Most High? For the way of the Most High is without measure. And how can one who is already corrupt[a] by the corrupt world understand the way of the incorruptible?"[b] When I heard this, I fell on my face[c] ¹²and said to him, "It would be better for us not to be here than to come here and live in ungodliness and to suffer and not understand why."

PARABLE OF FOREST AND SEA

¹³He answered me and said, "It happened one day that the forests of the trees of the plain went out,[d] and they made a plan ¹⁴and said, 'Come, let us go and make war against the sea, that it may recede before us and that we may make for ourselves more forests.' ¹⁵And in like manner the waves of the sea also made a plan and said, 'Come, let us go up and make war on[e] the forest of the plain so that there also we may gain more territory for ourselves.' ¹⁶But the plan of the forest was in vain, for the fire came and consumed it; ¹⁷likewise also the plan of the waves of the sea, for the sand stood firm and stopped them. ¹⁸If now you were a judge between them, which would you undertake to justify and which to condemn?"

¹⁹I answered and said, "Each has made a foolish plan, for the land is assigned to the forest, and to the sea is assigned a place to carry its waves."

²⁰He answered me and said, "You have judged rightly, but why have you not judged so in your own case? ²¹For as the land is assigned to the forest and the sea to its waves, so also those who dwell upon earth can understand only what is on the earth, and he who is above the heavens can understand what is above the height of the heavens."

NEW AGE TO MAKE ALL THINGS CLEAR

²²Then I answered and said, "I beg you, my lord, why[f] have I been endowed with the power of understanding? ²³For I did not wish to enquire about the ways above, but about those things that we daily experience: why Israel has been given over to the Gentiles as a reproach; why the people whom you loved has been given over to godless tribes, and the law of our fathers has been made of no effect and the written covenants no longer exist; ²⁴and why we pass from the world like locusts, and our life is like a mist,[g] and we are not worthy to obtain mercy. ²⁵But what will he do for his name, by which we are called? It is about these things that I have asked."

²⁶He answered me and said, "If you are alive, you will see, and if you live long,[h] you will often marvel, because the age is hastening swiftly to its end. ²⁷For it will not be able to bring the things that have been promised to the righteous in their appointed times, because this age is full of sadness and infirmities. ²⁸For the evil about which[i] you ask me has been sown, but the harvest of it has not yet come. ²⁹If therefore that which has been sown is not reaped and if the place where the evil has been sown does not pass away, the field where the good has been sown will not come. ³⁰For a grain of evil seed was sown in Adam's heart from the beginning, and how much ungodliness it has produced until now and will produce until the time of threshing comes! ³¹Consider now for yourself how much fruit of ungodliness a grain of evil seed has produced. ³²When heads of corn without number are sown, how great a threshing floor they will fill!"

WHEN WILL THE NEW AGE COME?

³³Then I answered and said, "How long[j] and when will these things be? For our years are few and evil."[k] ³⁴He answered me and said, "You do not hasten faster than the Most High, for your haste is for yourself,[l] but the Highest hastens on behalf of many. ³⁵Did not the souls of the righteous in their storerooms ask about these matters, saying, 'How long are we to remain here?[m] And when will come the harvest of our reward?' ³⁶And Jeremiel the archangel answered them and said, 'When the number of those like yourselves is completed;[n] for he has weighed the age in the balance ³⁷and measured the times by measure and numbered the times by number; and he will not move or arouse them until that measure is fulfilled.'"

³⁸Then I answered and said, "O sovereign Lord, but all of us also are full of ungodliness.

---

[a]Some versions; the meaning of the Latin is uncertain
[b]Syriac, Ethiopic; Latin *incorruption*   [c]Syriac, Ethiopic, Arabic 1
[d]Some versions; Latin *that I went into a forest of trees of the plain*
[e]Latin *and subdue*   [f]Syriac, Ethiopic, Armenian   [g]Syriac, Ethiopic, Arabic, Georgian; Latin *trembling*   [h]Syriac; Latin *if you live*
[i]Syriac, Ethiopic; the meaning of the Latin is uncertain
[j]Syriac, Ethiopic; the meaning of the Latin is uncertain   [k]So all versions; Latin *Why are our years few and evil?*   [l]Syriac, Ethiopic, Arabic, Armenian   [m]Syriac, Ethiopic, Arabic 2, Georgian; Latin *How long do I hope thus?*   [n]Syriac, Ethiopic, Arabic 2; Latin *number of seeds is completed for you*

³⁹And it is perhaps on account of us that the time of threshing is delayed for the righteous—on account of the sins of those who dwell on earth."

⁴⁰He answered me and said, "Go and ask a woman who is with child if, when her nine months have been completed, her womb can keep the child within her any longer."

⁴¹And I said, "No, lord, it cannot."

And he said to me, "In Hades the storerooms of the souls are like the womb. ⁴²For just as a woman who is in travail makes haste to escape the pains of birth, so also do these places hasten to give back those things that were committed to them from the beginning. ⁴³Then the things that you desire to see will be disclosed to you."

HOW MUCH TIME REMAINS?

⁴⁴I answered and said, "If I have found favour in your sight and if it is possible and if I am worthy, ⁴⁵show me this also: whether more time is to come than has passed or whether for us the greater part has gone by. ⁴⁶For I know what has gone by, but I do not know what is to come."

⁴⁷And he said to me, "Stand at my right side, and I will show you the interpretation of a parable."

⁴⁸So I stood and looked, and behold, a flaming furnace passed by before me, and when the flame had gone by I looked, and behold, the smoke remained. ⁴⁹And after this a cloud full of water passed before me and poured down a heavy and violent rain, and when the rainstorm had passed, drops remained in the cloud.

⁵⁰And he said to me, "Consider it for yourself; for as the rain is more than the drops, and the fire is greater than the smoke, so the quantity that passed was far greater; but drops and smoke remained."

⁵¹Then I prayed and said, "Do you think that I shall live until those days? And what will take place*ᵃ* in those days?"

⁵²He answered me and said, "Concerning the signs about which you ask me, I can tell you in part; but I was not sent to tell you concerning your life, for I do not know."

SIGNS OF THE END

5 "Now concerning the signs: behold, the days are coming when those who dwell on earth shall be seized with great terror,*ᵇ* and the lot*ᶜ* of truth shall be hidden, and the land shall be barren of faith. ²And unrighteousness shall be increased beyond what you yourself see and beyond what you heard of formerly. ³And the land that you now see ruling shall be waste and untrodden,*ᵈ* and men shall see it desolate. ⁴But if the Most High grants that you live, you shall see it thrown into confusion after the third period;*ᵉ*

> and the sun shall suddenly
>   shine forth at night,
>   and the moon during the day.
> ⁵ Blood shall drip from wood,
>   and the stone shall utter its voice;
>   the peoples shall be troubled,
>   and the atmosphere shall
>   be changed.*ᶠ*

⁶And one shall reign whom those who dwell on earth do not expect, and the birds shall fly away;*ᵍ* ⁷and the sea of Sodom shall cast up fish; and one whom the many do not know shall make his voice heard by night, and all shall hear his voice.*ʰ* ⁸There shall be chasms also in many places, and fire shall often break out, and the wild beasts shall roam beyond their haunts, and menstrual women shall bring forth monsters. ⁹And salt waters shall be found in the sweet, and all friends shall fight against one another; then shall reason hide itself, and wisdom shall withdraw into its storeroom, ¹⁰and it shall be sought by many but shall not be found, and unrighteousness and unrestraint shall increase on earth. ¹¹And one country shall ask its neighbour, 'Has righteousness or anyone who does right passed through you?' And it will answer, 'No.' ¹²And at that time men shall hope but not obtain; they shall labour but their ways shall not prosper. ¹³These are the signs that I am permitted to tell you, and if you pray again and weep as you do now and fast for seven days, you shall hear yet greater things than these."

CONCLUSION OF THE FIRST VISION

¹⁴Then I awoke, and my body shuddered violently, and my soul was so troubled that it fainted. ¹⁵But the angel who had come and

---
*ᵈ*Ethiopic, Georgian, Arabic; Syriac, Latin *Or who will be alive*
*ᵇ*Syriac; Ethiopic *confusion*; the meaning of the Latin is uncertain
*ᶜ*Syriac, Ethiopic, Georgian; Latin *way*   *ᵈ*Syriac   *ᵉ*Latin *after the third*; Ethiopic *after three months*; Armenian *after the third vision*; Georgian *after the third day*   *ᶠ*Syriac, Georgian, Arabic, Armenian; Ethiopic *and the stars shall fall*; the meaning of the Latin is uncertain   *ᵍ*Latin adds *together*   *ʰ*Latin *fish; and it shall make its voice heard by night, which the many have not known, but all shall hear its voice*

talked with me held me and strengthened me and set me on my feet.

¹⁶Now on the second night Phaltiel, a chief of the people, came to me and said, "Where have you been? And why is your countenance sad? ¹⁷Or do you not know that Israel has been entrusted to you in the land of their exile? ¹⁸Rise therefore and eat some bread, so that you may not forsake us, like a shepherd who leaves his flock in the power of cruel wolves."

¹⁹Then I said to him, "Depart from me and do not come near me for seven days, and then you may come to me and I will tell you the matter."ᵃ

He heard what I said and left me. ²⁰So I fasted seven days, mourning and weeping, as Uriel the angel had commanded me.

SECOND VISION: EZRA'S SECOND PRAYER OF COMPLAINT

²¹And after seven days the thoughts of my heart were very grievous to me again. ²²Then my soul recovered the spirit of understanding, and I began once more to speak words in the presence of the Most High. ²³And I said, "O sovereign Lord, from every forest of the earth and from all its trees you have chosen for yourself one vine, ²⁴and from all the lands of the world you have chosen for yourself one region,ᵇ and from all the flowers of the world you have chosen for yourself one lily, ²⁵and from all the depths of the sea you have filled for yourself one river, and from all the cities that have been built you have consecrated Zion for yourself, ²⁶and from all the birds that have been created you have named for yourself one dove, and from all the flocks that have been made you have acceptedᶜ for yourself one sheep, ²⁷and from all the multitude of peoples you have obtained for yourself one people; and to this people, whom you have loved, you have given the law that is approved by all. ²⁸And now, O Lord, why have you given over the one to the many and dishonouredᵈ the one root beyond the others and scattered your only one among the many? ²⁹And those who opposed your lawᵉ have trodden down those who believed your covenant. ³⁰If you do really hate your people, they should be punished at your own hands."

RESPONSE TO EZRA'S COMPLAINTS

³¹When I had spoken these words, the angel who had come to me on a previous night was sent to me, ³²and he said to me, "Listen to me, and I will instruct you; pay attention to me, and I will tell you more."

³³And I said, "Speak, my lord." And he said to me, "Are you greatly disturbed over Israel?ᶠ Or do you love him more than his Maker does?"

³⁴And I said, "No, my lord, but because of my grief I have spoken; for every hour I suffer agonies of heart, while I struggle to understand the way of the Most High and to search out part of his judgement."

³⁵And he said to me, "You cannot." And I said, "Why not, my lord? Why then was I born? Or why did not my mother's womb become my grave, that I might not see the travail of Jacob and the exhaustion of the people of Israel?"

³⁶He said to me, 'Count up for me those who have not yet come and gather for me the scattered raindrops and make the withered flowers bloom again for me; ³⁷open for me the closed storerooms and bring forth for me the winds shut up in them or show me the appearance of one whom you have never seenᵍ or show me the picture of a voice; and then I will explain to you the travail that you ask to understand."

³⁸And I said, "O sovereign Lord, who is able to know these things except he whose dwelling is not with men? ³⁹As for me, I am without wisdom and miserable,ʰ and how can I speak concerning the things that you have asked me?"

⁴⁰He said to me, "Just as you cannot do one of the things that were mentioned, so you cannot discover my judgement or the goal of the love that I have promised my people."

WHY SUCCESSIVE GENERATIONS HAVE BEEN CREATED

⁴¹And I said, "Yet behold, O Lord, you make promises to those who are alive at the end, but what will those do who were before us, or we, or those who come after us?"

⁴²He said to me, "I shall liken my judgement to a circle;ⁱ just as for those who are last there is no slowness, so for those who are first there is no haste."

⁴³Then I answered and said, "Could you not have created at one time those who have

---

ᵃSome versions; Latin omits *and I will tell you the matter*
ᵇEthiopic; Latin *pit*   ᶜSyriac, Arabic 1, Georgian; Latin *provided*
ᵈSyriac, Ethiopic, Arabic; Latin *prepared*   ᵉEthiopic, Georgian; compare Syriac; Latin *promises*   ᶠOr *You are greatly distracted over Israel*; Latin adds *in mind*   ᵍLatin omits *or show me the appearance of one whom you have never seen*   ʰLatin omits *and miserable*   ⁱOr *crown*

been and those who are and those who will be, that you might show your judgement the sooner?"

⁴⁴He replied to me and said, "The creation cannot make more haste than the Creator, neither can the world hold at one time those who have been created in it."

⁴⁵And I said, "How have you said to your servant that you^a will certainly give life at one time to your creation? If therefore all creatures will live at one time^b and the creation will sustain them, it might even now be able to support all of them present at one time."

⁴⁶He said to me, "Ask a woman's womb and say to it, 'If you bear ten^c children, why one after another?' Request it therefore to produce ten at one time."

⁴⁷I said, "Of course it cannot, but only each in its own time."

⁴⁸He said to me, "Even so have I given the womb of the earth to those who from time to time are sown in it. ⁴⁹For as an infant does not bring forth and a woman who has become old does not bring forth any longer, so have I organised the world that I created."

WHEN AND HOW WILL THE END COME?

⁵⁰Then I enquired and said, "Since you have now given me the opportunity, let me speak before you. Is our mother, of whom you have told me, still young? Or is she now approaching old age?"

⁵¹He replied to me, "Ask a woman who bears children, and she will tell you. ⁵²Say to her, 'Why are those whom you have borne recently not like those whom you bore before, but smaller in stature?' ⁵³And she herself will answer you, 'Those born in the strength of youth are different from those born during the time of old age, when the womb is failing.' ⁵⁴Therefore you also should consider that you and your contemporaries are smaller in stature than those who were before you ⁵⁵and those who come after you will be smaller than you, as born of a creation that already is ageing and passing the strength of youth."

⁵⁶And I said, "O Lord, I beg you, if I have found favour in your sight, show your servant through whom you visit your creation."

6 And he said to me, "The beginning is by the hand of man,^d but the end by my own hands. For before the circuit of the world existed and before^e the portals of the world were in place and before the assembled winds blew ²and before the rumblings of thunder sounded and before the flashes of lightning shone and before the foundations of paradise were laid ³and before the beautiful flowers were seen and before the powers of movement^f were established and before the innumerable hosts of angels were gathered together ⁴and before the heights of the air were lifted up and before the measures of the firmaments were named and before the footstool of Zion was established ⁵and before the present years were reckoned and before the imaginations of those who now sin were estranged and before those who stored up treasures of faith were sealed—⁶then I planned these things, and they were made through me and not through another."^g

DIVIDING THE TIMES

⁷And I answered and said, "What will be the dividing of the times? Or when will be the end of the first age and the beginning of the age that follows?"

⁸He said to me, "From Abraham to Isaac,^h because from him were born Jacob and Esau, for Jacob's hand held Esau's heel from the beginning. ⁹For Esau is the end of this age, and Jacob is the beginning of the age that follows. ¹⁰For the beginning of a man is his hand, and the end of a man is his heel;^i between the heel and the hand seek for nothing else, Ezra!"

MORE SIGNS OF THE END

¹¹I answered and said, "O sovereign Lord, if I have found favour in your sight, ¹²show your servant the end of your signs that you showed me in part on a previous night."

¹³He answered and said to me, "Rise to your feet and you will hear a full, resounding voice. ¹⁴And if the place where you are standing is greatly shaken ¹⁵while the voice is speaking, do not be terrified; because the word concerns the end, and the foundations of the earth will understand ¹⁶that the speech concerns them. They will tremble and be shaken, for they know that their end must be changed."

---

^a Syriac, Ethiopic, Arabic 1; the meaning of the Latin is uncertain
^b Latin omits *If therefore all creatures will live at one time*
^c Syriac, Ethiopic, Arabic 2, Armenian   ^d Ethiopic *by the Son of Man*
^e Syriac; compare Georgian, Ethiopic, Arabic, Armenian; Latin omits first sentence of quotation and reads *At the beginning of the circle of the earth*   ^f Or *before the earthquakes*   ^g Latin adds *just as the end shall come through me and not through another*   ^h Some manuscripts *From Abraham to Abraham*   ^i Syriac

¹⁷When I heard this, I rose to my feet and listened, and behold, a voice was speaking, and its sound was like the sound of many waters. ¹⁸And it said, "Behold, the days are coming, and it shall be that when I draw near to visit the inhabitants of the earth, ¹⁹and when I require from the doers of iniquity the penalty of their iniquity, and when the humiliation of Zion is complete, ²⁰and when the seal is placed upon the age that is about to pass away, then I will show these signs: the books shall be opened before the firmament, and all shall see it together. ²¹Infants a year old shall speak with their voices, and women with child shall give birth to premature children at three or four months, and these shall live and dance. ²²Sown places shall suddenly appear unsown,ᵃ and full storehouses shall suddenly be found to be empty; ²³and the trumpet shall sound aloud, and when all hear it, they shall suddenly be terrified. ²⁴At that time friends shall make war on friends like enemies, and the earth and those who inhabit it shall be terrified, and the springs of the fountains shall stand still, so that for three hours they shall not flow.

²⁵"And it shall be that whoever remains after all that I have foretold to you shall himself be saved and shall see my salvation and the end of my world. ²⁶And they shall see the men who were taken up, who from their birth have not tasted death; and the heart of the earth'sᵇ inhabitants shall be changed and converted to a different spirit. ²⁷For evil shall be blotted out, and deceit shall be quenched; ²⁸faithfulness shall flourish, and corruption shall be overcome; and the truth, which has been so long without fruit, shall be revealed."

CONCLUSION OF THE SECOND VISION

²⁹While he spoke to me, behold, little by little the place where I was standing began to rock to and fro.ᶜ ³⁰And he said to me, "I have come to show you these things this night.ᵈ ³¹If therefore you will pray again and fast again for seven days, I will again declare to you greater things than these,ᵉ ³²because your voice has surely been heard before the Most High; for the Mighty One has seen your uprightness and has also observed the purity that you have maintained from your youth. ³³Therefore he sent me to show you all these things and to say to you:ᶠ 'Believe and do not be afraid! ³⁴Do not be quick to think vain thoughts concerning the former times, lest you be hasty concerning the last times.'"

THIRD VISION: CREATION OF THE WORLD

³⁵Now after this I wept again and fasted seven days as before, in order to complete the three weeks as I had been told. ³⁶And on the eighth night my heart was troubled within me again, and I began to speak in the presence of the Most High. ³⁷For my spirit was greatly aroused, and my soul was in distress.

GOD'S WORK IN CREATION

³⁸I said, "O Lord, you spoke at the beginning of creation and said on the first day, 'Let heaven and earth be made,' and your word accomplished the work. ³⁹And then the Spirit was hovering, and darkness and silence embraced everything; the sound of man's voice was not yet there.ᵍ ⁴⁰Then you commanded that a ray of light be brought forth from your treasuries, so that your works might then appear.

⁴¹"Again, on the second day, you created the spirit of the firmament and commanded him to divide and separate the waters, that one part might move upwards and the other part remain beneath.

⁴²"On the third day you commanded the waters to be gathered together in the seventh part of the earth; six parts you dried up and kept so that some of them might be planted and cultivated and be of service before you. ⁴³For your word went forth, and at once the work was done. ⁴⁴For immediately fruit came forth in endless abundance and of varied appeal to the taste and flowers of inimitable colour and innumerable beautiful treesʰ and odours of inexpressible fragrance. These were made on the third day.

⁴⁵"On the fourth day you commanded the brightness of the sun, the light of the moon, and the arrangement of the stars to come into being; ⁴⁶and you commanded them to serve man, who was about to be formed.

⁴⁷"On the fifth day you commanded the seventh part, where the water had been gathered together, to bring forth living creatures, birds, and fishes; and so it was done. ⁴⁸The mute and lifeless water produced living creatures, as it was commanded,ⁱ that therefore the nations might declare your wondrous works.

ᵃLatin ambiguous; Syriac, Ethiopic *Unsown places shall suddenly appear sown* ᵇSyriac; compare Ethiop c, Arabic 1, Armenian; Latin omits *earth's* ᶜSyriac, Ethiopic; compare Arabic, Armenian ᵈSyriac; compare Ethiopic ᵉSyriac, Ethiopic, Arabic 1, Armenian; Latin adds *by day* ᶠLatin; Syriac, Ethiopic, Georgian *these things." And he said to me* ᵍSyriac, Ethiopic; Latin *yet from you* ʰSyriac, Ethiopic, Georgian, Arabic 1; Latin omits this phrase ⁱThe text is uncertain

⁴⁹"Then you kept in existence two living creatures that you created;ᵃ the name of one you called Behemoth and the name of the other Leviathan. ⁵⁰And you separated one from the other, for the seventh part where the water had been gathered together could not hold them both. ⁵¹And you gave Behemoth one of the parts that had been dried up on the third day, to live in it, where there are 1,000 mountains; ⁵²but to Leviathan you gave the seventh part of the watery part;ᵇ and you have kept them to be eaten by whom you will and when you will.

⁵³"On the sixth day you commanded the earth to bring forth before you cattle, beasts, and creeping things; ⁵⁴and over these you placed Adam, as ruler over all the works that you had made; and from him we have all come, the people whom you have chosen.

WHY DO GOD'S PEOPLE SUFFER?

⁵⁵"All this I have spoken before you, O Lord, because you have said that it was for us that you created this world.ᶜ ⁵⁶As for the other nations that have descended from Adam, you have said that they are nothing and that they are like spittle, and you have compared their abundance to a drop from a bucket. ⁵⁷And now, O Lord, behold, these nations, which are reputed as nothing, domineer over us and trampleᵈ us. ⁵⁸But we your people, whom you have called your firstborn, only begotten, zealous for you,ᵉ and dearest, have been given into their hands. ⁵⁹If the world has indeed been created for us, why do we not possess our world as an inheritance? How long will this be so?"

RESPONSE TO EZRA'S QUESTIONS

7 When I had finished speaking these words, the angel who had been sent to me on the former nights was sent to me again, ²and he said to me, "Rise, Ezra, and listen to the words that I have come to speak to you."

³I said, "Speak, my lord." And he said to me, "There is a sea set in a wide expanse so that it is broadᶠ and vast, ⁴but it has an entrance set in a narrow place, so that it is like a river. ⁵If anyone, then, wishes to reach the sea, to look at it, or to navigate it,ᵍ how can he come to the broad part unless he passes through the narrow part? ⁶Another example: there is a city built and set on a plain, and it is full of all good things; ⁷but the entrance to it is narrow and set in a precipitous place, so that there is fire on the right hand and deep water on the left; ⁸and there is only one path lying between them, that is, between the fire and the water, so that only one man can walk upon that path. ⁹If now that city is given to a man for an inheritance, how will the heir receive his inheritance unless he passes through the danger set before him?"ʰ

¹⁰I said, "He cannot, lord." And he said to me, "So also is Israel's portion. ¹¹For I made the world for their sake, and when Adam transgressed my statutes, what had been made was judged. ¹²And so the entrances of this world were made narrow and sorrowful and toilsome; they are few and evil, full of dangers and involved in great hardships. ¹³But the entrances of the greaterⁱ world are broad and safe and really yield the fruit of immortality. ¹⁴Therefore unless the living pass through the difficult and vain experiences, they can never receive those things that have been reserved for them. ¹⁵But now why are you disturbed, seeing that you are to perish? And why are you moved, seeing that you are mortal? ¹⁶And why have you not considered in your mind what is to come, rather than what is now present?"

FATE OF THE UNGODLY

¹⁷Then I answered and said, "O sovereign Lord, behold, you have ordained in your law that the righteous shall inherit these things, but that the ungodly shall perish. ¹⁸The righteous therefore can endure difficult circumstances while hoping for easier ones; but those who have done wickedly have suffered the difficult circumstances and will not see the easier ones."

¹⁹And he said to me, "You are not a better judge than God or wiser than the Most High! ²⁰Let many perish who are now living, rather than that the law of God that is set before them be disregarded! ²¹For God strictly commanded those who came into the world, when they came, what they should do to live, and what they should observe to avoid punishment. ²²Nevertheless they were not obedient and spoke against him:

ᵃSyriac, Ethiopic; Latin *Then you kept in existence two souls*
ᵇSyriac, Ethiopic, Georgian; Latin *the seventh part, the watery part*
ᶜSyriac, Ethiopic, Arabic 2; Latin *created the firstborn world;* compare Arabic 1 *created the first world* ᵈLatin *devour* ᵉThe meaning of the Latin is uncertain; Syriac, Ethiopic *kin* ᶠSyriac; compare Ethiopic, Arabic 1; Latin *deep* ᵍLatin *to rule over it* ʰLatin, Syriac; Arabic, Armenian *through the narrow way;* compare Georgian Ethiopic
ⁱLatin; Syriac, Ethiopic *coming*

They devised for themselves
    vain thoughts
²³ and proposed to themselves
    wicked frauds;
they even declared that the Most
    High does not exist,
and they ignored his ways!
²⁴ They scorned his law
    and denied his covenants;
they have been unfaithful
    to his statutes
and have not performed his works.

TEMPORARY MESSIANIC KINGDOM

²⁵"Therefore, Ezra, empty things are for the empty, and full things are for the full. ²⁶For behold, the time will come, when the signs that I have foretold to you will come to pass, that the city that now is not seen shall appear,ᵃ and the land that now is hidden shall be disclosed. ²⁷And everyone who has been delivered from the evils that I have foretold shall see my wonders. ²⁸For my son the Messiahᵇ shall be revealed with those who are with him, and those who remain shall rejoice 400 years. ²⁹And after these years my son the Messiah shall die, and all who draw human breath. ³⁰And the world shall be turned back to primeval silence for seven days, as it was at the first beginnings; so that no one shall be left. ³¹And after seven days the world, which is not yet awake, shall be roused, and that which is corruptible shall perish. ³²And the earth shall give up those who are asleep in it, and the dust those who dwell silently in it; and the storerooms shall give up the souls that have been committed to them. ³³And the Most High shall be revealed upon the seat of judgement, and compassion shall pass away, mercy shall grow distant,ᶜ and patience shall be withdrawn;ᵈ ³⁴but only judgement shall remain, truth shall stand, and faithfulness shall grow strong. ³⁵And recompense shall follow, and the reward shall be manifested; righteous deeds shall awake, and unrighteous deeds shall not sleep.ᵉ ³⁶Then the pitᶠ of torment shall appear, and opposite it shall be the place of rest; and the furnace of hellᵍ shall be disclosed, and opposite it the paradise of delight. ³⁷Then the Most High will say to the nations that have been raised from the dead, 'Look now and understand whom you have denied, whom you have not served, whose commandments you have despised! ³⁸Look on this side and on that; here are delight and rest, and there are fire and torments!' Thus he willʰ speak to them on the day of judgement—³⁹a day that has no sun or moon or stars ⁴⁰or cloud or thunder or lightning or wind or water or air or darkness or evening or morning ⁴¹or summer or spring or harvest or heatⁱ or frost or cold or hail or rain or dew ⁴²or noon or night or dawn or shining or brightness or light, but only the splendour of the glory of the Most High, by which all shall see what has been determined for them. ⁴³For it will last for about a week of years. ⁴⁴This is my judgement and its prescribed order; and to you alone have I shown these things."

ONLY A FEW WILL BE SAVED

⁴⁵"I answered and said, "O Lord, I said then and I say now:ʲ Blessed are those who are alive and keep your commandments! ⁴⁶But what of those for whom I prayed?ᵏ For who among the living is there that has not sinned, or who among those who have been born has not transgressed your covenant? ⁴⁷And now I see that the world to come will bring delight to few, but torments to many. ⁴⁸For an evil heart has grown up in us, which has alienated us from Godˡ and has brought us into corruption and the ways of death and has shown us the paths of perdition and removed us far from life—and that not just a few of us but almost all who have been created!"

⁴⁹He answered me and said, "Listen to me, Ezra,ᵐ and I will instruct you and will admonish you yet again. ⁵⁰For this reason the Most High has made not one world but two. ⁵¹For whereas you have said that the righteous are not many but few, while the ungodly abound, hear the explanation for this.

⁵²"If you have just a few precious stones, will you add to them lead and clay?"ⁿ

⁵³I said, "Lord, how could that be?"

⁵⁴And he said to me, 'Not only that, but ask the earth and she will tell you; defer to her, and she will declare it to you. ⁵⁵Say to her, 'You produce gold and silver and brass and also iron and lead and clay; ⁵⁶but silver is more abundant than gold, and brass than silver, and iron than brass, and lead than iron, and

---

ᵃArmenian; Latin, Syriac *pass, that the bride shall appear, even the city appearing* ᵇSyriac, Arabic 1; Ethiopic *For my Messiah*; Arabic 2 *For the Messiah*; Armenian *For the Messiah of God*; Latin *For my son Jesus* ᶜLatin omits this phrase ᵈLatin *shall gather together* ᵉA passage formerly missing, 7:36–105, has been restored and is indicated by italic verse numbers ᶠSyriac Ethiopic; Latin *place* ᵍLatin *gehenna* ʰSyriac, Ethiopic, Arabic 1; Latin *Thus you shall* ⁱLatin omits *or harvest* and adds *or winter* ʲSyriac; Latin *And I answered, "I said then, O Lord, and I say now* ᵏOr *those concerning whom I asked* ˡLatin, Syriac, Ethiopic *these* ᵐSyriac, Arabic 1, Georgian; Latin, Ethiopic omit *Ezra* ⁿArabic 1

clay than lead.' ⁵⁷"Judge therefore which things are precious and desirable, those that are abundant or those that are rare?"

⁵⁸I said, "O sovereign Lord, what is plentiful is of less worth, for what is rarer is more precious."

⁵⁹He answered me and said, "Weigh within yourself[a] what you have thought, for he who has what is hard to get rejoices more than he who has what is plentiful. ⁶⁰So also will be the judgement[b] that I have promised; for I will rejoice over the few who shall be saved, because it is they who have made my glory to prevail now, and through them my name has now been honoured. ⁶¹And I will not grieve over the multitude of those who perish; for it is they who are now like a mist and are similar to a flame and smoke—they are set on fire and burn hotly and are extinguished."

LAMENTATION OF EZRA, WITH RESPONSE

⁶²I replied and said, "O earth, what have you brought forth, if the mind is made out of the dust like the other created things! ⁶³For it would have been better if the dust itself had not been born, so that the mind might not have been made from it. ⁶⁴But now the mind grows with us, and therefore we are tormented, because we perish and know it. ⁶⁵Let the human race lament, but let the beasts of the field be glad; let all who have been born lament, but let the four-footed beasts and the flocks rejoice! ⁶⁶For it is much better with them than with us; for they do not look for a judgement, nor do they know of any torment or life[c] promised to them after death. ⁶⁷For what does it profit us that we shall be preserved alive but cruelly tormented? ⁶⁸For all who have been born are involved in iniquities and are full of sins and burdened with transgressions. ⁶⁹And if we were not to come into judgement after death, perhaps it would have been better for us."

⁷⁰He answered me and said, "When the Most High made the world and Adam and all who have come from him, he first prepared the judgement and the things that pertain to the judgement. ⁷¹And now understand from your own words, for you have said that the mind grows with us. ⁷²For this reason, therefore, those who dwell on earth shall be tormented, because though they had understanding they committed iniquity, and though they received the commandments they did not keep them, and though they obtained the law they dealt unfaithfully with what they received. ⁷³What, then, will they have to say in the judgement, or how will they answer in the last times? ⁷⁴For how long the time is that the Most High has been patient with those who inhabit the world, and not for their sake, but because of the times that he has foreordained!"

STATE OF THE DEAD BEFORE JUDGEMENT

⁷⁵I answered and said, "If I have found favour in your sight, O Lord, show this also to your servant: whether after death, as soon as every one of us yields up his soul, we shall be kept in rest until those times come when you will renew the creation, or whether we shall be tormented at once?"

⁷⁶He answered me and said, "I will show you that also, but do not be associated with those who have shown scorn or number yourself among those who are tormented. ⁷⁷For you have a treasure of works laid up with the Most High; but it will not be shown to you until the last times. ⁷⁸Now, concerning death, the teaching is: When the decisive decree has gone forth from the Most High that a person shall die, as the spirit leaves the body to return again to him who gave it, first of all it adores the glory of the Most High. ⁷⁹And if it is one of those who have shown scorn and have not kept the ways of the Most High and who have despised his law and who have hated those who fear God—⁸⁰such spirits shall not enter into habitations, but shall immediately wander about in torments, ever grieving and sad, in seven ways. ⁸¹The first way: because they have scorned the law of the Most High. ⁸²The second way: because they cannot now repent and do good[d] that they may live. ⁸³The third way: they shall see the reward laid up for those who have trusted the covenants of the Most High. ⁸⁴The fourth way: they shall consider the torment laid up for themselves in the last days. ⁸⁵The fifth way: they shall see how the habitations of the other souls[e] are guarded by angels in profound quiet. ⁸⁶The sixth way: they shall see how some of them will pass over into torments. ⁸⁷The seventh way, which is worse[f] than all the ways that have been mentioned: because they shall utterly waste away in confusion and be consumed with shame[g] and shall wither with

---

[a] Syriac, Ethiopic, Arabic 1 [b] Syriac, Arabic 1; Latin *creation*
[c] Syriac, Ethiopic; Armenian, Arabic *resurrection*; Latin *salvation*
[d] Syriac, Georgian; compare Armenian; Latin *and make a good repentance* [e] Latin *of the others* [f] Latin *greater* [g] Syriac, Ethiopic

fear at seeing the glory of the Most High before whom they sinned while they were alive and before whom they are to be judged in the last times.

⁸⁸"Now this is the order of those who have kept the ways of the Most High, when they shall be separated from their mortal body.ᵃ ⁸⁹During the time that they lived in it,ᵇ they laboriously served the Most High and withstood danger every hour, that they might keep the law of the Lawgiver perfectly. ⁹⁰Therefore this is the teaching concerning them: ⁹¹First of all, they shall see with great joy the glory of him who receives them, for they shall have rest in seven orders. ⁹²The first order: because they have struggled with great effort to overcome the evil thought that was formed with them, that it might not lead them astray from life into death. ⁹³The second order: because they see the perplexity in which the souls of the ungodly wander and the punishment that awaits them. ⁹⁴The third order: they see the witness that he who formed them bears concerning them, that while they were alive they kept the law that was given them in trust. ⁹⁵The fourth order: they understand the rest that they now enjoy, being gathered into their chambers and guarded by angels in profound quiet and the glory that awaits them in the last days. ⁹⁶The fifth order: they rejoice that they have now escaped what is corruptible and shall inherit what is to come; and besides they see the straits and toilᶜ from which they have been delivered and the spacious liberty that they are to receive and enjoy in immortality. ⁹⁷The sixth order: when it is shown to them how their countenance is to shine like the sun and how they are to be made like the light of the stars, being incorruptible from then on. ⁹⁸The seventh order, which is greater than all that have been mentioned: because they shall rejoice with boldness and shall be confident without confusion and shall be glad without fear, for they hasten to see the face of him whom they served in life and from whom they are to receive their reward when glorified. ⁹⁹This is the order of the souls of the righteous, as henceforth is announced;ᵈ and the aforesaid are the ways of torment that those who would not give heed shall suffer hereafter."

¹⁰⁰I answered and said, "Will time therefore be given to the souls, after they have been separated from the bodies, to see what you have described to me?"

¹⁰¹He said to me, "They shall have freedom for seven days, so that during these seven days they may see the things that have been predicted, and afterwards they shall be gathered in their habitations."

NO INTERCESSION FOR THE UNGODLY

¹⁰²I answered and said, "If I have found favour in your sight, show further to me, your servant, whether on the day of judgement the righteous will be able to intercede for the ungodly or to entreat the Most High for them, ¹⁰³fathers for sons or sons for parents, brothers for brothers, relatives for their kinsmen, or friends for friends."ᵉ

¹⁰⁴He answered me and said, "Since you have found favour in my sight, I will show you this also. The day of judgement is decisiveᶠ and displays to all the seal of truth. Just as now a father does not send his son or a son his father or a master his servant or a friend his dearest friend to be illᵍ or sleep or eat or be healed in his stead, ¹⁰⁵so no one shall ever pray for another on that day, neither shall anyone lay a burden on another;ʰ for then everyone shall bear his own righteousness and unrighteousness."

³⁶ ¹⁰⁶I answered and said, "How then do we find that first Abraham prayed for the people of Sodom, and Moses for our fathers who sinned in the desert, ³⁷ ¹⁰⁷and Joshua after him for Israel in the days of Achan, ³⁸ ¹⁰⁸and Samuel in the days of Saul,ⁱ and David for the plague, and Solomon for those in the sanctuary, ³⁹ ¹⁰⁹and Elijah for those who received the rain and for the one who was dead, that he might live, ⁴⁰ ¹¹⁰and Hezekiah for the people in the days of Sennacherib, and many others prayed for many? ⁴¹ ¹¹¹If therefore the righteous have prayed for the ungodly now, when corruption has increased and unrighteousness has multiplied, why will it not be so then as well?"

⁴² ¹¹²He answered me and said, "This present world is not the end;ʲ the glory of God does not abide in it;ᵏ therefore those who were strong prayed for the weak. ⁴³ ¹¹³But the day of judgement will be the end of this age and the

---

ᵃLatin *from the corruptible vessel* ᵇSyriac, Ethiopic ᶜSyriac, Ethiopic; Latin *fullness* ᵈSyriac ᵉSyriac, Ethiopic, Arabic 1; Latin *brothers for brothers, kinsmen for their nearest, friends for their dearest* ᶠLatin *bold* ᵍSyriac, Ethiopic, Armenian; Latin *to understand* ʰSyriac; Latin omits *on that day, neither shall any or e lay a burden on another* ⁱSyriac, Ethiopic, Arabic 1; Latin omits *in the days of Saul* ʲEthiopic, Georgian, and one Latin manuscript *The end of this word has not yet come to pass* ᵏSome versions; or *the glory of God does not continuously abide in it*; Latin omits *of God and not*

beginning[a] of the immortal age to come, in which corruption has passed away, [44][114]sinful indulgence has come to an end, unbelief has been cut off, and righteousness has increased and truth has appeared. [45][115]Therefore no one will then be able to have mercy on him who has been condemned in the judgement or to harm[b] him who is victorious."

LAMENTATION OVER THE FATE OF MOST PEOPLE

[46][116]I answered and said, "This is my first and last word, that it would have been better if the earth had not produced Adam or else, when it had produced him, had restrained him from sinning.[c] [47][117]For what good is it to all that they live in sorrow now and expect punishment after death? [48][118]O Adam, what have you done? For though it was you who sinned, the fall was not yours alone, but ours also who are your descendants. [49][119]For what good is it to us, if an eternal age has been promised to us, but we have done deeds that bring death? [50][120]And what good is it that an everlasting hope has been promised us, but we have miserably failed? [51][121]Or that safe and healthful habitations have been reserved for us, but we have lived[d] wickedly? [52][122]Or that the glory of the Most High will defend those who have led a pure life, but we have walked in the most wicked ways? [53][123]Or that a paradise shall be revealed, whose fruit remains unspoiled and in which are abundance and healing, but we shall not enter it, [54][124]because we have lived in unseemly places? [55][125]Or that the countenances of those who practised self-control shall shine more than the stars, but our countenances shall be blacker than darkness? [56][126]For while we lived and committed iniquity we did not consider what we should suffer after death."

[57][127]He answered and said, "This is the meaning of the contest that the person who is born on earth shall wage, [58][128]that if he is defeated he shall suffer what you have said, but if he is victorious he shall receive what I have said.[e] [59][129]For this is the way of which Moses, while he was alive, spoke to the people, saying, 'Choose for yourself life, that you may live!' [60][130]But they did not believe him or the prophets after him or even myself who have spoken to them. [61][131]Therefore there shall not be[f] grief at their destruction, so much as joy over the life of those who believed."[g]

EZRA APPEALS TO GOD'S MERCY

[62][132]I answered and said, "I know, O Lord, that the Most High is now called merciful, because he has mercy on those who have not yet come into the world; [63][133]and gracious, because he is gracious to those who turn in repentance to his law; [64][134]and patient, because he shows patience towards those who have sinned, since they are his own works; [65][135]and bountiful, because he would rather give than take away;[h] [66][136]and abundant in compassion, because he makes his compassions abound more and more to those now living and to those who are gone and to those yet to come, [67][137]for if he did not make them abound, the world with those who inhabit it would not have life; [68][138]and he is called giver, because if he did not give out of his goodness so that those who have committed iniquities might be relieved of them, not one ten-thousandth of mankind could have life; [69][139]and judge, because if he did not pardon those who were created by his word and blot out the multitude of their sins,[i] [70][140]there would[j] be left only very few of the innumerable multitude.

8 He answered me and said, "The Most High made this world for the sake of many, but the world to come for the sake of few. ²But I tell you a parable, Ezra. Just as, when you ask the earth, it will tell you that it provides very much clay from which earthenware is made, but only a little dust from which gold comes; so is the course of the present world. ³Many have been created, but few shall be saved."

EZRA AGAIN APPEALS TO GOD'S MERCY

⁴I answered and said, "Then take delight in[k] of understanding, O my soul, and drink wisdom, O my heart![l] ⁵For not of your own will did you come into the world,[m] and against your will you depart, for you have been given only a short time to live. ⁶O Lord,[n] grant to your servant that we may pray before you and give us seed for our heart and cultivation of our understanding so that fruit may be produced, by which every mortal who bears the likeness[o] of a human being may be

---

[a]Latin omits *the beginning* [b]Syriac, Ethiopic; Latin *overwhelm* [c]Latin; Syriac, Ethiopic, Arabic 1 *had taught him not to sin* [d]Syriac, Armenian *erred* [e]Syriac, Ethiopic, Arabic 1; Latin *what I say* [f]Syriac; Latin *there was not* [g]Syriac, Ethiopic, Georgian; Latin *of those to whom salvation is assured* [h]Or *he is ready to give according to requests* [i]Latin *contempts* [j]Latin adds *probably* [k]Some versions; Latin *Then drink your fill* [l]Syriac; Latin *soul, and let it feed on what it understands* [m]Syriac [n]Latin adds *over us* [o]Syriac; Latin *place*

able to live. ⁷For you alone exist, and we are a work of your hands, as you have declared. ⁸And because you give life to the body that is now fashioned in the womb and furnish it with members, what you have created is preserved in fire and water, and for nine months the womb that you have formed[a] endures your creation that has been created in it. ⁹But that which keeps and that which is kept shall both be kept by your keeping.[b] And when the womb gives up again what has been created in it, ¹⁰you have commanded that from the members themselves[c] milk should be supplied that is the fruit of the breasts, ¹¹so that what has been fashioned may be nourished for a time; and afterwards you will guide him in your mercy. ¹²You have brought him up in your righteousness and instructed him in your law and taught[d] him in your wisdom. ¹³You will take away his life, for he is your creation; and you will make him live, for he is your work. ¹⁴If then you will suddenly and quickly[e] destroy him who with so great labour was fashioned by your command, to what purpose was he made? ¹⁵And now I will speak out: About all mankind you know best; but I will speak about your people, for whom I am grieved; ¹⁶and about your inheritance, for whom I lament; and about Israel, for whom I am sad; and about the seed of Jacob, for whom I am troubled. ¹⁷Therefore I will pray before you for myself and for them, for I see the failings of us who dwell in the land ¹⁸and I have heard of the judgement[f] that is to come. ¹⁹Therefore hear my voice and understand my words, and I will speak before you."

EZRA'S PRAYER

The beginning of the words of Ezra's prayer, before he was taken up. He said: ²⁰"O Lord who inhabits eternity,[g] whose eyes are exalted[h] and whose upper chambers are in the air, ²¹whose throne is beyond measure and whose glory is beyond comprehension, before whom the hosts of angels stand trembling ²²and at whose command they are changed to wind and fire,[i] whose word is sure and whose utterances are certain, whose ordinance is strong and whose command is terrible, ²³whose look dries up the depths and whose indignation makes the mountains melt away and whose truth is established for ever[j]—²⁴hear, O Lord, the voice[k] of your servant and give ear to the petition of your creature; attend to my words.

²⁵For as long as I live I will speak, and as long as I have understanding I will answer. ²⁶O look not upon the sins of your people, but at those who have served you in truth. ²⁷Regard not[l] those who act wickedly, but those who have kept your covenants amid afflictions. ²⁸Think not on those who have lived wickedly in your sight; but remember those who have willingly acknowledged that you are to be feared. ²⁹Let it not be your will to destroy those who have had the ways of cattle; but regards those who have gloriously taught[m] your law. ³⁰Be not angry with those who are deemed worse than beasts; but love those who have always put their trust in your glory. ³¹For we and our forebears have passed our lives in ways that bring death;[n] but you, because of us sinners, are called merciful. ³²For if you have desired to have pity on us, who have no works of righteousness,[o] then you will be called merciful. ³³For the righteous, who have many works laid up with you, shall receive their reward in consequence of their own deeds. ³⁴But what is man, that you are angry with him; or what is a corruptible race, that you are so bitter against it? ³⁵For in truth there is no one among those who have been born who has not acted wickedly, and among those who have existed[p] there is no one who has not transgressed. ³⁶For in this, O Lord, your goodness[q] will be declared, when you are merciful to those who have no store of good works."

RESPONSE TO EZRA'S PRAYER

³⁷He answered me and said, "Some things you have spoken rightly, and it will come to pass according to your words. ³⁸For indeed I will not concern myself about the fashioning of those who have sinned or about their death, their judgement, or their destruction; ³⁹but I will rejoice over the creation of the righteous, over their pilgrimage also and their life[r] and their receiving their reward. ⁴⁰As I have spoken, therefore, so it shall be.

⁴¹"For just as the farmer sows many seeds upon the ground and plants a multitude

---
[a] Latin for nine months what you have formed [b] Syriac [c] Latin adds that is, from the breasts [d] Latin reproved [e] Syriac; Latin you will with a light command [f] Latin land. But I have heard of the swiftness of the judgement [g] Or who abides for ever [h] One Latin manuscript whose are the highest heavens [i] Syriac; Latin they whose service takes the form of wind and fire [j] Arabic 2; some manuscripts truth bears witness [k] Some versions; Latin prayer [l] Latin adds the endeavours of [m] Syriac have received the brightness of [n] Syriac, Ethiopic; the meaning of the Latin is uncertain [o] Ethiopic, Armenian, Arabic have no good works [p] Syriac [q] Latin your righteousness and goodness [r] Syriac, Ethiopic; Latin salvation

of seedlings and yet not all that have been sown will come up[a] in due season and not all that were planted will take root, so also those who have been sown in the world will not all live."[b]

⁴²I answered and said, "If I have found favour before you, let me speak. ⁴³For if the farmer's seed does not come up, because it has not received your rain in due season or if it has been ruined by too much rain, it perishes.[c] ⁴⁴But man, who has been formed by your hands and is called your own image because he is made like you and for whose sake you have formed all things—have you also made him like the farmer's seed? ⁴⁵No, O Lord[d] who is over us! But spare your people and have mercy on your inheritance, for you have mercy on your own creation."

EZRA'S FINAL APPEAL FOR MERCY

⁴⁶He answered me and said, "Things that are present are for those who live now, and things that are future are for those who will live hereafter. ⁴⁷For you come far short of being able to love my creation more than I love it. But you have often compared yourself[e] to the unrighteous. Never do so! ⁴⁸But even in this respect you will be praiseworthy before the Most High, ⁴⁹because you have humbled yourself, as is becoming for you, and have not deemed yourself to be among the righteous in order to receive[f] the greatest glory. ⁵⁰For many miseries will affect those who inhabit the world in the last times, because they have walked in great pride. ⁵¹But think of your own case and enquire concerning the glory of those who are like yourself, ⁵²because it is for you that paradise is opened, the tree of life is planted, the age to come is prepared, delight[g] is provided, a city is built, rest is appointed,[h] goodness is established, and wisdom perfected beforehand. ⁵³The root of evil is sealed up from you, illness is banished from you, and death is hidden; hell has fled and corruption has been forgotten;[i] ⁵⁴sorrows have passed away, and in the end the treasure of immortality is made manifest. ⁵⁵Therefore do not ask any more questions about the multitude of those who perish. ⁵⁶For they also received freedom, but they despised the Most High and were contemptuous of his law and forsook his ways. ⁵⁷Moreover they have even trampled upon his righteous ones ⁵⁸and said in their hearts that there is no God—though knowing full well that they must die. ⁵⁹For just as the things that have been predicted await[j] you, so the thirst and torment that are prepared await them. For the Most High did not intend that human beings should be destroyed; ⁶⁰but they themselves who were created have defiled the name of him who made them and have been ungrateful to him who prepared life for them. ⁶¹Therefore my judgement is now drawing near; ⁶²I have not shown this to all, but only to you and a few like you."

Then I answered and said, ⁶³"Behold, O Lord, you have now shown me a multitude of the signs that you will do in the last times, but you have not shown me when you will do them."

MORE SIGNS OF THE END

9 He answered me and said, "Measure carefully in your mind, and when you see that a certain part of the predicted signs are past, ²then you will know that it is the very time when the Most High is about to visit the world that he has made. ³So when there shall appear in the world earthquakes, tumult of peoples, intrigues of nations, wavering of leaders, confusion of princes, ⁴then you will know that it was of these that the Most High spoke from the days that were of old.[k] ⁵For just as with everything that has occurred in the world, the beginning is evident[l] and the end manifest; ⁶so also are the times of the Most High: the beginnings are manifest in wonders and mighty works, and the end in deeds and in signs. ⁷And it shall be that everyone who will be saved and will be able to escape on account of his works or on account of the faith by which he has believed ⁸will survive the dangers that have been predicted and will see my salvation in my land and within my borders, which I have sanctified for myself from the beginning. ⁹Then those who have now abandoned[m] my ways shall be amazed, and those who have rejected them with contempt shall dwell in torments. ¹⁰For as many as did not acknowledge me in their lifetime, although they received my

---

[a] Syriac, Ethiopic *will live*; Latin *will be saved* [b] Some versions; Latin, Georgian *not all be saved* [c] Compare Syriac, Arabic 1, Armenian, Georgian [d] Ethiopic, Arabic; compare Syriac; Latin omits *O Lord* [e] Syriac, Ethiopic; Latin *have brought yourself near* [f] Or *righteous; so that you will receive*; some Latin manuscripts *righteous. You will receive the greater glory, for* [g] Syriac, Ethiopic, Armenian, Georgian; Latin *plenty* [h] Syriac; Latin *allowed* [i] Syriac; Latin *hidden. Hades and corruption have fled into oblivion* or *hidden; corruption has fled into Hades to be forgotten* [j] Syriac; Latin *predicted will receive* [k] Latin, Arabic 2 add *were from the beginning* [l] Syriac; Ethiopic *is in the word* [m] Latin *abused*

benefits, ¹¹and as many as scorned my law while they still had freedom and did not understand but despised it*ᵃ* while an opportunity of repentance was still open to them, ¹²these must in torment acknowledge it after death. ¹³Therefore, do not continue to be curious as to how the ungodly will be punished; but enquire how the righteous will live,*ᵇ* those to whom the age belongs and for whose sake the age was made."*ᶜ*

ARGUMENT RECAPITULATED

¹⁴I answered and said, ¹⁵"I said before and I say now and will say it again: there are more who perish than those who will live, ¹⁶as a wave is greater than a drop of water."

¹⁷He answered me and said, "As is the field, so is the seed; and as are the flowers, so are the colours; and as is the work, so is the judgement; and as is the farmer, so is the threshing floor. ¹⁸For there was a time in this age when I was preparing for those who now exist, before the world was made for them to dwell in, and no one opposed me then, for no one existed; ¹⁹but now those who have been created in this world that is supplied both with an unfailing table and an inexhaustible pasture*ᵈ* have become corrupt in their ways. ²⁰So I considered my world, and behold, it was lost, and my earth, and behold, it was in peril because of the devices of those who*ᵉ* had come into it. ²¹And I saw and spared some*ᶠ* with great difficulty and saved for myself one grape out of a cluster and one plant out of a great forest.*ᵍ* ²²So let the multitude perish that has been born in vain, but let my grape and my plant be saved, because with much labour I have perfected them. ²³But if you will let seven days more pass—do not fast during them, however; ²⁴but go into a field of flowers where no house has been built and eat only of the flowers of the field and taste no meat and drink no wine, but eat only flowers, ²⁵and pray to the Most High continually—then I will come and talk with you."

FOURTH VISION: ABIDING GLORY OF THE MOSAIC LAW

²⁶So I went, as he directed me, into the field that is called Ardat;*ʰ* and there I sat among the flowers and ate of the plants of the field, and the nourishment they afforded satisfied me. ²⁷And after seven days, as I lay on the grass, my heart was troubled again as it was before. ²⁸And my mouth was opened, and I began to speak before the Most High and said, ²⁹"O Lord, you showed yourself*ⁱ* to our fathers in the wilderness when they came out from Egypt and when they came into the untrodden and unfruitful wilderness; ³⁰and you said, 'Hear me, O Israel, and give heed to my words, O descendants of Jacob. ³¹For behold, I sow my law in you, and it shall bring forth fruit in you and you shall be glorified through it for ever.' ³²But though our fathers received the law, they did not keep it and did not observe the statutes; yet the fruit of the law did not perish—for it could not perish, because it was yours. ³³Yet those who received it perished, because they did not keep what had been sown in them. ³⁴And behold, it is the rule that, when the ground has received seed or the sea a ship or any dish food or drink, and when it happens that what was sown or what was launched or what was put in is destroyed, ³⁵they are destroyed, but the things that held them remain; yet with us it has not been so. ³⁶For we who have received the law and sinned will perish, as well as our heart that received it; ³⁷the law, however, does not perish but remains in its glory."

A WEEPING WOMAN

³⁸When I said these things in my heart, I lifted up*ʲ* my eyes and saw a woman on my right, and*ᵏ* she was mourning and weeping with a loud voice and was deeply grieved at heart, and her clothes were rent, and there were ashes on her head. ³⁹Then I dismissed the thoughts with which I had been engaged and turned to her ⁴⁰and said to her, "Why are you weeping, and why are you grieved at heart?"

⁴¹And she said to me, "Let me alone, my lord, that I may weep for myself and continue to mourn, for I am greatly embittered in spirit and deeply afflicted."

⁴²And I said to her, "What has happened to you? Tell me."

⁴³And she said to me, "Your servant was barren and had no child, though I lived with my husband thirty years. ⁴⁴And every hour and every day during those thirty years I implored the Most High, night and day. ⁴⁵And after thirty years God heard your handmaid and looked upon my affliction*ˡ* and considered my distress and gave me a son. And I

---

*ᵃ*Or *me*; also verse 12   *ᵇ*Latin, Arabic 1 *will be saved*; also verse 15   *ᶜ*Latin adds *and when*   *ᵈ*Latin *law*   *ᵉ*Latin *those devices that*   *ᶠ*Latin *them*   *ᵍ*Syriac, Ethiopic, Arabic 1; Latin *tribe*   *ʰ*Syriac, Ethiopic *Arpad*; Armenian *Ardab*   *ⁱ*Latin adds *among us*   *ʲ*Syriac, Arabic, Armenian; Latin *I looked about me with*   *ᵏ*Latin adds *behold*   *ˡ*Latin *my low estate*

rejoiced greatly over him, I and my husband and all my neighbours;[a] and we gave great glory to the Mighty One. **46**And I brought him up with much care. **47**So when he grew up and I came to take a wife for him, I set a day for the marriage feast.

10 "But it happened that when my son entered his wedding chamber, he fell down and died. **2**Then we[b] put out the lamps, and all my neighbours[c] attempted to console me; and I remained quiet until evening of the second day. **3**But when they all had stopped consoling me, that I might be quiet, I got up in the night and fled and came to this field, as you see. **4**And now I intend not to return to the city, but to stay here, and I will neither eat nor drink, but without ceasing mourn and fast until I die."

5Then I broke off the reflections with which I was still engaged and answered her in anger and said, **6**"You most foolish of women, do you not see our mourning, and what has happened to us? **7**For Zion, the mother of us all, is in deep grief and great affliction. **8**It is most appropriate to mourn now, because we are all mourning, and to be sorrowful, because we are all sorrowing; you, however, are sorrowing for one son.[d] **9**Now ask the earth, and she will tell you that it is she who ought to mourn over so many who have come into being upon her. **10**And from the beginning all have been born of her, and others will come; and behold, almost all go to perdition, and a multitude of them are destined for destruction. **11**Who then ought to mourn the more, she[e] who lost so great a multitude or you who are grieving for one? **12**But if you say to me, 'My lamentation is not like the earth's, for I have lost the fruit of my womb, which I brought forth in pain and bore in sorrow; **13**but it is with the earth according to the way of the earth—the multitude that is now in it goes as it came'; **14**then I say to you, 'As you brought forth in sorrow, so the earth also has from the beginning given her fruit, that is, man, to him who made her.' **15**Now, therefore, keep your sorrow to yourself and bear bravely the troubles that have come upon you. **16**For if you acknowledge the decree of God to be just, you will receive your son back in due time and will be praised among women. **17**Therefore go into the city to your husband."

18She said to me, "I will not do so; I will not go into the city, but I will die here."

19So I spoke again to her and said, **20**"Do not do that thing, but let yourself be persuaded because of the troubles of Zion and be consoled because of the sorrow of Jerusalem. **21**For you see that our sanctuary has been laid waste, our altar thrown down, our temple destroyed; **22**our harp has been laid low, our song has been silenced, and our rejoicing has been ended; the light of our lampstand has been put out, the ark of our covenant has been plundered, our holy things have been polluted, and the name by which we are called has been profaned; our free men[f] have suffered abuse, our priests have been burned to death, our Levites have gone into captivity, our virgins have been defiled, and our wives have been ravished; our righteous men have been carried off, our little ones have been cast out, our young men have been enslaved and our strong men made powerless. **23**And, what is more than all, the seal of Zion—for she has now lost the seal of her glory and has been given over into the hands of those that hate us. **24**Therefore shake off your great sadness and lay aside your many sorrows, so that the Mighty One may be merciful to you,[g] and the Most High may give you rest, a relief from your troubles."

25While I was talking to her, behold, her countenance suddenly shone exceedingly, and her countenance flashed like lightning, so that I was too frightened to approach her, and my heart was terrified. While[h] I was wondering what this meant, **26**behold, she suddenly uttered a loud and fearful cry, so that the earth shook at the sound. **27**And I looked, and behold, the woman was no longer visible to me, but there was an established city,[i] and a place of huge foundations showed itself. Then I was afraid and cried with a loud voice and said, **28**"Where is the angel Uriel, who came to me at first? For it was he who brought me into this overpowering bewilderment; my end has become corruption, and my prayer a reproach."

URIEL'S INTERPRETATION OF THE FOURTH VISION

29As I was speaking these words, behold, the angel who had come to me at first came to me, and he looked upon me; **30**and behold, I lay there like a corpse and I was deprived of my understanding. Then he grasped my

---

[a]Latin *my fellow citizens* [b]Latin adds *all* [c]Latin *my fellow citizens* [d]Syriac adds *but we, the whole world, for our mother* [e]Syriac [f]Or *our children* [g]Latin adds *again* [h]Syriac, Ethiopic, Arabic 1; Latin omits *I was too frightened to approach her, and my heart was terrified. While* [i]Syriac, Ethiopic, Arabic; Latin *but a city was being built*

right hand and strengthened me and set me on my feet and said to me, ³¹"What is the matter with you? And why are you troubled? And why are your understanding and the thoughts of your mind troubled?"

³²I said, "Because you have forsaken me! I did as you directed,ᵃ and behold, I saw and still see what I am unable to explain."

³³He said to me, "Stand up like a man, and I will instruct you."

³⁴I said, "Speak, my lord; only do not forsake me, lest I die before my time.ᵇ ³⁵For I have seen what I did not know, and I have heard what I do not understand. ³⁶Or is my mind deceived, and my soul dreaming? ³⁷Now therefore I entreat you to give your servant an explanation of this."ᶜ

³⁸He answered me and said, "Listen to me and I will inform you and tell you about the things that you fear, for the Most High has revealed many secrets to you. ³⁹For he has seen your righteous conduct, that you have sorrowed continually for your people and mourned greatly over Zion. ⁴⁰This therefore is the explanation. ⁴¹The woman who appeared to you a little while ago, whom you saw mourning and began to console—⁴²but you do not now see the form of a woman, but an established cityᵈ has appeared to you—⁴³and as for her telling you about the misfortune of her son, this is the interpretation: ⁴⁴This woman whom you saw, whom you now see as an established city, is Zion.ᵉ ⁴⁵And as for her telling you that she was barren for thirty years, it is because there were 3,000ᶠ years in the world before any offering was offered in it.ᵍ ⁴⁶And after 3,000ʰ years Solomon built the city and offered offerings; then it was that the barren woman bore a son. ⁴⁷And as for her telling you that she brought him up with much care, that was the period of residence in Jerusalem. ⁴⁸And as for her saying to you, 'When my son entered his wedding chamber he died,' and that misfortune had overtaken her,ⁱ that was the destruction that befell Jerusalem. ⁴⁹And behold, you saw her likeness, how she mourned for her son, and you began to console her for what had happened.ʲ ⁵⁰For now the Most High, seeing that you are sincerely grieved and profoundly distressed for her, has shown you the brilliance of her glory and the loveliness of her beauty. ⁵¹Therefore I told you to remain in the field where no house had been built, ⁵²for I knew that the Most High would reveal these things to you. ⁵³Therefore I told you to go into the field where there was no foundation of any building, ⁵⁴for no work of human construction could endure in a place where the city of the Most High was to be revealed.

⁵⁵"Therefore do not be afraid and do not let your heart be terrified; but go in and see the splendour and vastness of the building, as far as it is possible for your eyes to see it, ⁵⁶and afterwards you will hear as much as your ears can hear. ⁵⁷For you are more blessed than many, and you have been called before the Most High, as but few have been. ⁵⁸But tomorrow night you shall remain here, ⁵⁹and the Most High will show you in those dream visions what the Most High will do to those who dwell on earth in the last days."

So I slept that night and the following one, as he had commanded me.

FIFTH VISION: THE EAGLE

11 On the second night I had a dream, and behold there came up from the sea an eagle that had twelveᵏ wings and three heads. ²And I looked, and behold, he spread his wings over all the earth, and all the winds of heaven blew upon him, and the clouds were gathered about him.ˡ ³And I looked, and out of his wings there grew opposing wings; and they became little, puny wings. ⁴But his heads were at rest; the middle head was larger than the other heads, but it also was at rest with them. ⁵And I looked, and behold, the eagle flew with his wings, to reign over the earth and over those who dwell in it. ⁶And I saw how all things under heaven were subjected to him, and no one spoke against him, not even one of the creatures that was on the earth. ⁷And I looked, and behold, the eagle rose upon his talons and uttered a cry to his wings, saying, ⁸"Do not all watch at the same time; let each sleep in his own place and watch in his turn; ⁹but let the heads be reserved for the last."

¹⁰And I looked, and behold, the voice did not come from his heads, but from the midst of his body. ¹¹And I counted his opposing wings, and behold, there were eight of them. ¹²And I looked, and behold, on the right side

---

ᵃLatin adds *and went out into the field* ᵇSyriac, Ethiopic, Arabic; Latin *die to no purpose* ᶜEthiopic, Arabic 2; Armenian *of these wonders*; Syriac, Latin add *bewildering vision* ᵈSyriac, Ethiopic, Arabic; Latin *but a city to be built* ᵉSyriac, Ethiopic, Arabic, Armenian ᶠSyriac, Ethiopic, Arabic, Armenian ᵍLatin, Syriac, Arabic, Armenian *her* ʰSyriac, Ethiopic, Arabic, Armenian ⁱOr *him* ʲSome Latin manuscripts and Arabic 2 add *these were the things to be opened to you* ᵏLatin adds *feathered* ˡSyriac; compare Ethiopic, Arabic; Latin omits *the clouds* and *about him*

one wing arose, and it reigned over all the earth. ¹³And while it was reigning it came to its end and disappeared, so that its place was not seen. Then the next wing arose and reigned, and it continued to reign a long time. ¹⁴And while it was reigning its end came also, so that it disappeared like the first. ¹⁵And behold, a voice sounded, saying to it. ¹⁶"Hear me, you who have ruled the earth all this time; I announce this to you before you disappear. ¹⁷After you no one shall rule as long as you or even half as long."

¹⁸Then the third wing raised itself up and held the rule like the former ones, and it also disappeared. ¹⁹And so it went with all the wings; they wielded power one after another and then were never seen again. ²⁰And I looked, and behold, in due course the wings that followed*a* also rose up on the right*b* side, in order to rule. There were some of them that ruled, yet disappeared suddenly; ²¹and others of them rose up, but did not hold the rule.

²²And after this I looked, and behold, the twelve wings and the two little wings disappeared; ²³and nothing remained on the eagle's body except the three heads that were at rest and six little wings. ²⁴And I looked, and behold, two little wings separated from the six and remained under the head that was on the right side; but four remained in their place. ²⁵And I looked, and behold, these four little wings*c* planned to set themselves up and hold the rule. ²⁶And I looked, and behold, one was set up, but suddenly disappeared; ²⁷a second also, and this disappeared more quickly than the first. ²⁸And I looked, and behold, the two that remained were planning between themselves to reign;*d* ²⁹and while they were planning, behold, one of the heads that were at rest (the one that was in the middle) awoke; for it was greater than the other two heads. ³⁰And I saw how it allied the two heads with itself, ³¹and behold, the head turned with those that were with it, and it devoured the two little wings*e* that were planning to reign. ³²Moreover this head gained control of the whole earth and with much oppression dominated its inhabitants; and it had greater power over the world than all the wings that had gone before.

³³And after this I looked, and behold, the middle head also suddenly disappeared, just as the wings had done. ³⁴But the two heads remained, which also ruled over the earth and its inhabitants. ³⁵And I looked, and behold, the head on the right side devoured the one on the left.

A LION ROUSED FROM THE FOREST

³⁶Then I heard a voice saying to me, "Look before you and consider what you see." ³⁷And I looked, and behold, a creature like a lion was aroused out of the forest, roaring; and I heard how he uttered a man's voice to the eagle and spoke, saying, ³⁸"Listen and I will speak to you. The Most High says to you, ³⁹'Are you not the one that remains of the four beasts that I had made to reign in my world, so that the end of my times might come through them? ⁴⁰You, the quarter that has come, have conquered all the beasts that have gone before; and you have held sway over the world with much terror and over all the earth with grievous oppression; and for so long you have dwelt*f* on the earth with deceit. ⁴¹And you have judged the earth, but not with truth; ⁴²for you have afflicted the meek and injured the peaceable; you have hated those who tell the truth and have loved liars; you have destroyed the fortifications*g* of those who brought forth fruit and have laid low the walls of those who did you no harm. ⁴³And so your insolence has come up before the Most High, and your pride to the Mighty One. ⁴⁴And the Most High has looked upon his times, and behold, they are ended, and his ages are completed! ⁴⁵Therefore you will surely disappear, you eagle, and your terrifying wings and your evilest little wings and your malicious heads and your evilest talons and your whole worthless body, ⁴⁶so that the whole earth, freed from your violence, may be refreshed and relieved and may hope for the judgement and mercy of him who made it.'"

12 While the lion was saying these words to the eagle, I looked, ²and behold, the remaining head disappeared. And the two wings that had gone over to it arose*h* and set themselves up to reign, and their reign was brief and full of tumult. ³And I looked, and behold, they also disappeared, and the whole body of the eagle was burned, and the earth was exceedingly terrified.

---

*a*Syriac, Arabic 2 *in due course the little wings*   *b*Some Ethiopic manuscripts *left*   *c*Syriac, Ethiopic, Arabic 2; Latin *these four underwings*   *d*Latin adds *together*   *e*Syriac; Latin *the two underwings*   *f*Syriac, Arabic, Armenian; Latin, Ethiopic *The quarter came, however, and conquered all the beasts that have gone before and held sway over the world with much terror and over all the earth with grievous oppression and for so long dwelt*   *g*Syriac, Ethiopic, Armenian; Latin *dwellings*   *h*Ethiopic; Latin omits *arose*

Then I awoke in great perplexity of mind and great fear, and I said to my spirit, ⁴"Behold, you have brought this upon me, because you search out the ways of the Most High. ⁵Behold, I am still weary in mind and very weak in my spirit, and not even a little strength is left in me, because of the great fear with which I have been terrified this night. ⁶Therefore I will now plead with the Most High that he may strengthen me to the end."

INTERPRETATION OF THE FIFTH VISION

⁷And I said, "O sovereign Lord, if I have found favour in your sight and if I have been privileged[a] before you beyond many others and if my prayer has indeed come up before your face, ⁸strengthen me and show me, your servant, the interpretation and meaning of this terrifying vision, that you may fully comfort my soul. ⁹For you have judged me worthy to be shown the end of the times and the last events of the times."

¹⁰He said to me, "This is the interpretation of this vision that you have seen: ¹¹The eagle that you saw coming up from the sea is the fourth kingdom that appeared in a vision to your brother Daniel. ¹²But it was not explained to him as I now explain or have explained it to you. ¹³Behold, the days are coming when a kingdom shall arise on earth, and it shall be more terrifying than all the kingdoms that have been before it. ¹⁴And twelve kings shall reign in it, one after another. ¹⁵But the second that is to reign shall hold sway for a longer time than any other of the twelve.[b] ¹⁶This is the interpretation of the twelve wings that you saw. ¹⁷As for your seeing[c] a voice that spoke, coming not from the eagle's[d] heads but from the midst of his body, this is the interpretation: ¹⁸In the midst of[e] the time of that kingdom great struggles shall arise, and it shall be in danger of falling; nevertheless it shall not fall then, but shall regain its former power.[f] ¹⁹As for your seeing eight little wings arising from[g] his wings, this is the interpretation: ²⁰Eight kings shall arise in it, whose times shall be short and their years swift; ²¹and two of them shall perish when the middle of its time draws near; and four shall be kept for the time when its end approaches; but two shall be kept until the end. ²²As for your seeing three heads at rest, this is the interpretation: ²³In its last days the Most High will raise up three kings,[h] and they[i] shall renew many things in it and shall rule the earth ²⁴and its inhabitants more oppressively than all who were before them; therefore they are called the heads of the eagle. ²⁵For it is they who shall sum up his wickedness and perform his last actions. ²⁶As for your seeing that the large head disappeared, one of the kings[j] shall die in his bed, but in agonies. ²⁷But as for the two who remained, the sword shall devour them. ²⁸For the sword of one shall devour him who was with him; but he also shall fall by the sword in the last days. ²⁹As for your seeing two little wings[k] passing over to[l] the head that was on the right side, ³⁰this is the interpretation: It is these whom the Most High has kept for the eagle's[m] end; this was the reign that was brief and full of tumult, as you have seen.

³¹"And as for the lion whom you saw rousing up out of the forest and roaring and speaking to the eagle and reproving him for his unrighteousness and as for all his words that you have heard, ³²this is the Messiah[n] whom the Most High has kept until the end of days, who will arise from the posterity of David and will come and speak to them;[o] he will denounce them for their ungodliness and for their wickedness and will cast up before them their contemptuous dealings. ³³For first he will set them living in judgement, and when he has reproved them, then he will destroy them. ³⁴But he will deliver in mercy the remnant of my people, those who have been saved throughout my borders, and he will make them joyful until the end comes, the day of judgement, of which I spoke to you at the beginning. ³⁵This is the dream that you saw, and this is its interpretation. ³⁶And you alone were worthy to learn this secret of the Most High. ³⁷Therefore write all these things that you have seen in a book and put it in a hidden place; ³⁸and you shall teach them to the wise among your people, whose hearts you know are able to comprehend and keep these secrets. ³⁹But wait here seven days more, so that you may be shown whatever it pleases the Most High to show you." Then he left me.

---

[a]Some versions; Latin *have been accounted righteous* [b]Latin *than the twelve* [c]Latin, Armenian *hearing* [d]Latin *from his* [e]Syriac, Armenian; Latin *After* [f]Ethiopic, Arabic 1, Armenian; Latin, Syriac *its beginning* [g]Syriac, Ethiopic, Armenian; Latin *eight underwings clinging to* [h]Syriac, Ethiopic, Arabic, Armenian; Latin *kingdoms* [i]Syriac, Ethiopic, Armenian; Latin *he* [j]Latin *of them* [k]Arabic 1; Latin *two underwings* [l]Syriac, Ethiopic; Latin omits *to* [m]Latin *for his* [n]Latin *the anointed one* [o]Syriac; Latin omits *of days, who will arise from the posterity of David and will come and speak to them*

THE PEOPLE COME TO EZRA

40 When all the people heard that the seven days were past and I had not returned to the city, they all gathered together, from the least to the greatest, and came to me and spoke to me, saying, **41** "How have we offended you, and what harm have we done you, that you have forsaken us and sit in this place? **42** For of all the prophets you alone are left to us, like a cluster of grapes from the vintage and like a lamp in a dark place and like a haven for a ship saved from a storm. **43** Are not the evils that have befallen us sufficient?^{a} **44** Therefore if you forsake us, how much better it would have been for us if we also had been consumed in the burning of Zion! **45** For we are no better than those who died there." And they wept with a loud voice.

Then I answered them and said, **46** "Take courage, O Israel; and do not be sorrowful, O house of Jacob; **47** for the Most High has you in remembrance, and the Mighty One has not forgotten you for ever.^{b} **48** As for me, I have neither forsaken you nor withdrawn from you; but I have come to this place to pray on account of the desolation of Zion and to seek mercy on account of the humiliation of our^c sanctuary. **49** Now go, every one of you to his house, and after these days I will come to you." **50** So the people went into the city, as I told them to do. **51** But I sat in the field seven days, as the angel^d had commanded me; and I ate only of the flowers of the field, and my food was of plants during those days.

SIXTH VISION: THE MAN FROM THE SEA

13 After seven days I dreamed a dream in the night; **2** and behold, a great^e wind arose from the sea and stirred up all its waves. **3** And I looked, and behold, this wind made something like the figure of a man come up out of the heart of the sea. And I looked, and behold,^{f} that man flew^g with the clouds of heaven; and wherever he turned his face to look, everything under his gaze trembled, **4** and whenever his voice issued from his mouth, all who heard his voice melted as wax melts^h when it feels the fire.

5 After this I looked, and behold, an innumerable multitude of people were gathered together from the four winds of heaven to make war against the man who came up out of the sea. **6** And I looked, and behold, he carved out for himself a great mountain and flew up upon it. **7** And I tried to see the region or place from which the mountain was carved, but I could not.

8 After this I looked, and behold, all who had gathered together against him, to wage war with him, were much afraid, yet dared to fight. **9** And behold, when he saw the onrush of the approaching multitude, he neither lifted his hand nor held a spear or any weapon of war; **10** but I saw only how he sent forth from his mouth as it were a stream of fire and from his lips a flaming breath, and from his tongue he shot forth a storm of fiery coals.^{i} **11** All these were mingled together, the stream of fire and the flaming breath and the great storm and fell on the onrushing multitude that was prepared to fight and burned them all up, so that suddenly nothing was seen of the innumerable multitude but only the dust of ashes and the smell of smoke. When I saw it, I was amazed.

12 After this I saw the same man come down from the mountain and call to him another multitude that was peaceable. **13** Then many people^j came to him, some of whom were joyful and some sorrowful; some of them were bound, and some were bringing others as offerings.

INTERPRETATION OF THE SIXTH VISION

Then in great fear I awoke; and I implored the Most High and said, **14** "From the beginning you have shown your servant these wonders and have deemed me worthy to have my prayer heard by you; **15** now show me also the interpretation of this dream. **16** For as I consider it in my mind, alas for those who will be left in those days! And still more, alas for those who are not left! **17** For those who are not left will be sad, **18** because they understand what is reserved for the last days, but cannot attain it. **19** But alas for those also who are left and for that very reason! For they shall see great dangers and much distress, as these dreams show. **20** Yet it is better^k to come into these things,^{l} though incurring peril than to pass from the world like a cloud and not to see what shall happen in the last days."

---

^{a}Latin, Ethiopic, Armenian, Arabic 1; Syriac, Arabic 2 add *that you forsake us as well* ^{b}Syriac, Armenian; Latin *forgotten you in your contest* ^{c}Syriac, Ethiopic; Latin *your* ^{d}Latin *as he* ^{e}Latin omits *great* ^{f}Syriac and some manuscripts; Latin omits *this wind made something like the figure of a man come up out of the heart of the sea. And I looked, and behold* ^{g}Syriac, Ethiopic, Arabic, Armenian; Latin *that man grew strong* ^{h}Syriac; Latin *voice burned as the earth rests* ^{i}Syriac, Ethiopic; Latin *of sparks* ^{j}Latin, Syriac, Arabic 2; Latin *Then the faces of many people* ^{k}Ethiopic; compare Arabic 2; Latin *easier* ^{l}Syriac; Latin *into this*

He answered me and said, ²¹"I will tell you the interpretation of the vision, and I will also explain to you the things that you have mentioned. ²²As for what you said about those who are left, this is the interpretation: ²³He who brings the peril at that time will himself protect those who fall into peril, who have works and have faith in the Almighty. ²⁴Understand therefore that those who are left are more blessed than those who have died. ²⁵This is the interpretation of the vision: As for your seeing a man come up from the heart of the sea, ²⁶this is he whom the Most High has been keeping for many ages, through whom he will deliver[a] his creation; and he will direct those who are left. ²⁷And as for your seeing fiery breath[b] and a storm coming out of his mouth ²⁸and as for his not holding a spear or weapon of war, yet destroying the onrushing multitude that came to conquer him, this is the interpretation: ²⁹Behold, the days are coming when the Most High will deliver those who are on the earth. ³⁰And bewilderment of mind shall come over those who dwell on the earth. ³¹And they shall plan to make war against one another, city against city, place against place, people against people, and kingdom against kingdom. ³²And when these things come to pass and the signs occur that I showed you before, then my Son[c] will be revealed, whom you saw as a man coming up from the sea.[d] ³³And when all the nations hear his voice, every man shall leave his own land and the warfare that they have against one another; ³⁴and an innumerable multitude shall be gathered together, as you saw, desiring to come and conquer him. ³⁵But he will stand on the top of Mount Zion. ³⁶And Zion will come and be made manifest to all people, prepared and built, as you saw the mountain carved out without hands. ³⁷And he, my Son, will reprove the assembled nations for their ungodliness (this was symbolised by the storm) ³⁸and will reproach them to their face with their evil deeds[e] and the torments with which they are to be tortured (which were symbolised by the flames) and will destroy them without effort by[f] the law (which was symbolised by the fire). ³⁹And as for your seeing him gather to himself another multitude that was peaceable, ⁴⁰these are the ten[g] tribes that were led away from their own land into captivity in the days of King Hoshea, whom King Shalmaneser of the Assyrians led captive; he took them across the river, and they were taken into another land. ⁴¹But they formed this plan for themselves, that they would leave the multitude of the nations and go to a more distant region, where mankind had never lived, ⁴²that there at least they might keep their statutes that they had not kept in their own land. ⁴³And they went in by the narrow passages of the Euphrates river. ⁴⁴For at that time the Most High performed signs for them and stopped the channels of the river until they had passed over. ⁴⁵Through that region[h] there was a long way to go, a journey of a year and a half; and that country is called Arzareth.[i]

⁴⁶"Then they dwelt there until the last times; and now, when they are about to come again, ⁴⁷the Most High will stop[j] the channels of the river again, so that they may be able to pass over. Therefore you saw the multitude gathered together in peace. ⁴⁸But those who are left of your people, who are found within my holy borders, shall be saved.[k] ⁴⁹Therefore when he destroys the multitude of the nations that are gathered together, he will defend the people who remain. ⁵⁰And then he will show them very many wonders."

⁵¹I said, "O sovereign Lord, explain this to me: Why did I see the man coming up from the heart of the sea?"

⁵²He said to me, "Just as no one can explore or know what is in the depths of the sea, so no one on earth can see my Son or those who are with him, except in the time of his day.[l] ⁵³This is the interpretation of the dream that you saw. And you alone have been enlightened about this, ⁵⁴because you have forsaken your own ways and have applied yourself to mine and have searched out my law; ⁵⁵for you have devoted your life to wisdom and called understanding your mother. ⁵⁶Therefore I have shown you this, for there is a reward laid up with the Most High. And after three more days I will tell you other things and explain weighty and wondrous matters to you."

⁵⁷Then I arose and walked in the field, giving great glory and praise to the Most High because of his wonders, which he did from time to time, ⁵⁸and because he governs the

---

[a] Some versions; Latin *ages, who will himself deliver* [b] Syriac, Armenian, Arabic 1; Latin *seeing wind and fire* [c] Latin, Syriac; Ethiopic, Armenian *then that man* [d] Syriac and some Latin manuscripts omit *from the sea* [e] Syriac, Ethiopic, Armenian; Latin *their thoughts* [f] Syriac; Latin *and* [g] Some witnesses *nine* or *nine and a half* [h] Latin; Ethiopic, Armenian *To that region*; Syriac omits [i] *Arzareth means Another Land* [j] Syriac; Latin *the Most High stops* [k] Syriac; Latin omits *shall be saved* [l] Syriac; Ethiopic *except when his time and his day have come*; Latin omits *his*

times and whatever things come to pass in their seasons. And I stayed there three days.

SEVENTH VISION: THE LORD COMMISSIONS EZRA

14 On the third day, while I was sitting under an oak, behold, a voice came out of a bush opposite me and said, "Ezra, Ezra." ²And I said, "Here I am, Lord," and I rose to my feet. ³Then he said to me, "I revealed myself in a bush and spoke to Moses, when my people were in bondage in Egypt; ⁴and I sent him and led*ᵃ* my people out of Egypt; and I led him up on Mount Sinai, where I kept him with me many days; ⁵and I told him many wondrous things and showed him the secrets of the times and declared to him*ᵇ* the end of the times. Then I commanded him, saying, ⁶'These words you shall publish openly, and these you shall keep secret.' ⁷And now I say to you: ⁸Lay up in your heart the signs that I have shown you, the dreams that you have seen, and the interpretations that you have heard; ⁹for you shall be taken up from among human beings, and henceforth you shall live with my Son and with those who are like you, until the times are ended. ¹⁰For the age has lost its youth, and the times begin to grow old. ¹¹For the age is divided into twelve parts, and nine*ᶜ* of its parts have already passed, ¹²as well as half of the tenth part; so two of its parts remain, besides half of the tenth part.*ᵈ* ¹³Now therefore, set your house in order and reprove your people; comfort the lowly among them and instruct those that are wise.*ᵉ* And now renounce the life that is corruptible ¹⁴and put away from you mortal thoughts; cast away from you the burdens of man and divest yourself now of your weak nature ¹⁵and lay to one side the thoughts that are most grievous to you and hasten to escape from these times. ¹⁶For evils worse than those that you have now seen happen shall be done hereafter. ¹⁷For the weaker the world becomes through old age, the more shall evils be multiplied among*ᶠ* its inhabitants. ¹⁸For truth shall go farther away, and falsehood shall come near. For the eagle*ᵍ* that you saw in the vision is already hastening to come."

EZRA'S CONCERN TO RESTORE THE SCRIPTURES

¹⁹Then I answered and said, "Let me speak*ʰ* in your presence, Lord. ²⁰For behold, I will go, as you have commanded me, and I will reprove the people who are now living; but who will warn those who will be born hereafter? For the world lies in darkness, and its inhabitants are without light. ²¹For your law has been burned, and so no one knows the things that have been done or will be done by you. ²²If then I have found favour before you, send the Holy Spirit into me, and I will write everything that has happened in the world from the beginning, the things that were written in your law, that people may be able to find the path, and that those who wish to live in the last days may live."*ⁱ*

²³He answered me and said, "Go and gather the people and tell them not to seek you for forty days. ²⁴But prepare for yourself many writing tablets and take with you Sarea, Dabria, Selemia, Elkana,*ʲ* and Asiel—these five, because they are trained to write rapidly; ²⁵and you shall come here, and I will light in your heart the lamp of understanding, which shall not be put out until what you are about to write is finished. ²⁶And when you have finished, some things you shall make public, and some you shall deliver in secret to the wise; tomorrow at this hour you shall begin to write."

EZRA'S LAST WORDS TO THE PEOPLE

²⁷Then I went as he commanded me, and I gathered all the people together and said to them,*ᵏ* ²⁸"Hear these words, O Israel. ²⁹At first our fathers dwelt as aliens in Egypt, and they were delivered from there ³⁰and received the law of life, which they did not keep, which you also have transgressed after them. ³¹Then land was given to you for a possession in the land of Zion; but you and your fathers committed iniquity and did not keep the ways that the Most High commanded you. ³²And because he is a righteous judge, in due time he took from you what he had given. ³³And now you are here, and your kindred are farther in the interior.*ˡ* ³⁴If you, then, will rule over your minds and discipline your hearts, you shall be kept alive, and after death you shall obtain mercy. ³⁵For after death the judgement will come, when

---

*ᵃ*Syriac, Arabic *and he led* *ᵇ*Syriac, Ethiopic, Arabic, Armenian; Latin omits *declared to him* *ᶜ*Latin, Ethiopic *ten* *ᵈ*Syriac omits 14:11–12; Ethiopic *For the world is divided into ten parts and has come to the tenth, and half of the tenth remains.* *ᵉ*Latin omits *and instruct those that are wise* *ᶠ*Latin *upon* *ᵍ*Syriac, Ethiopic, Arabic, Armenian *ʰ*Some Latin manuscripts omit *Let me speak* *ⁱ*Latin; Syriac, Georgian *may know the way* *ʲ*Syriac, Ethiopic, Armenian; Latin *Ethanus* *ᵏ*Syriac, Ethiopic, Armenian; Latin, Georgian omit *to them* *ˡ*Syriac, Ethiopic, Armenian; Latin *are among you*

we shall live again; and then the names of the righteous will become manifest, and the deeds of the ungodly will be disclosed. ³⁶But let no one come to me now, and let no one seek me for forty days."

RESTORATION OF THE SCRIPTURES

³⁷So I took the five men, as he commanded me, and we proceeded to the field and remained there. ³⁸And on the next day, behold, a voice called me, saying, "Ezra, open your mouth and drink what I give you to drink." ³⁹Then I opened my mouth, and behold, a full cup was offered to me; it was full of something like water, but its colour was like fire. ⁴⁰And I took it and drank; and when I had drunk it, my heart poured forth understanding, and wisdom increased in my breast, and[a] my spirit retained its memory; ⁴¹and my mouth was opened and was no longer closed. ⁴²And the Most High gave understanding to the five men, and by turns they wrote what was dictated, in characters that they did not know.[b] They sat forty days and wrote during the daytime and ate their bread at night. ⁴³As for me, I spoke in the daytime and was not silent at night. ⁴⁴So during the forty days ninety-four[c] books were written. ⁴⁵And when the forty days were ended, the Most High spoke to me, saying, "Make public the twenty-four[d] books that you wrote first, and let the worthy and the unworthy read them; ⁴⁶but keep the seventy that were written last, in order to give them to the wise among your people. ⁴⁷For in them is the spring of understanding, the fountain of wisdom, and the river of knowledge." ⁴⁸And I did so.[e]

VENGEANCE ON THE WICKED

15[f] The Lord says, Behold, speak in the ears of my people the words of the prophecy that I will put in your mouth ²and cause them to be written on paper; for they are trustworthy and true. ³Do not fear the plots against you and do not be troubled by the unbelief of those who oppose you. ⁴For every unbeliever shall die in his unbelief.

⁵Behold, says the Lord, I bring evils upon the world, the sword and famine and death and destruction. ⁶For iniquity has spread throughout every land, and their harmful deeds have reached their limit. ⁷Therefore, says the Lord, ⁸I will be silent no longer concerning their ungodly deeds that they impiously commit, neither will I tolerate their wicked practises. Behold, innocent and righteous blood cries out to me, and the souls of the righteous cry out continually. ⁹I will surely avenge them, says the Lord, and will receive to myself all the innocent blood from among them. ¹⁰Behold, my people are led like a flock to the slaughter; I will not allow them to live any longer in the land of Egypt, ¹¹but I will bring them out with a mighty hand and with an uplifted arm and will strike Egypt with a plague, as before, and will destroy all its land.

¹²Let Egypt and its foundations mourn on account of the plague of chastisement and punishment that the Lord will bring upon it. ¹³Let the farmers that till the ground mourn, because their seed shall fail and their trees shall be ruined by blight and hail and by a terrible tempest. ¹⁴Alas for the world and for those who live in it! ¹⁵For the sword and misery draw near them, and nation shall rise up to fight against nation, with swords in their hands. ¹⁶For there shall be unrest among people; growing strong against one another, they shall in their might have no respect for their king or the chief of their leaders. ¹⁷For a man will desire to go into a city and shall not be able. ¹⁸For because of their pride the cities shall be in confusion, the houses shall be destroyed, and people shall be afraid. ¹⁹A man shall have no pity upon their neighbours, but shall make an assault upon their houses with the sword and plunder their goods, because of hunger for bread and because of great tribulation.

²⁰Behold, says God, I call together all the kings of the earth to fear me, from the rising sun and from the south, from the east and from Lebanon; to turn and repay what they have given them. ²¹Just as they have done to my elect until this day, so I will do and will repay into their bosom. Thus says the Lord God: ²²My right hand will not spare the sinners, and my sword will not cease from those who shed innocent blood on earth. ²³And a fire will go forth from his wrath and will consume the foundations of the earth

---

[a]Some versions; Latin for [b]Syriac; compare Ethiopic, Arabic 2, Armenian [c]Syriac, Ethiopic Arabic 1, Armenian [d]Syriac, Arabic 1; Latin, Ethiopic, Armenian omit *twenty-four* [e]Syriac adds *in the seventh year of the sixth week, 5,000 years and three months and twelve days after creation. At that time Ezra was caught up and taken to the place of those who are like him, after he had written all these things. And he was called the scribe of the knowledge of the Most High for ever and ever.* Ethiopic, Arabic 1, Armenian have a similar ending [f]Chapters 15–16 are extant only in Latin (except 15:57–59, which has been found in Greek)

and the sinners, like straw that is kindled. ²⁴Woe to those who sin and do not observe my commandments, says the Lord; ²⁵I will not spare them. Depart, you faithless children! Do not pollute my sanctuary. ²⁶For the Lord*ᵃ* knows all who transgress against him; therefore he will hand them over to death and slaughter. ²⁷For now calamities have come upon the whole earth, and you shall remain in them; for God will not deliver you, because you have sinned against him.

TERRIFYING VISION OF WARFARE

²⁸Behold, a terrifying sight, appearing from the east! ²⁹The nations of the dragons of Arabia shall come out with many chariots, and from the day that they set out, their hissing shall spread over the earth, so that all who hear them fear and tremble. ³⁰Also the Carmonians, raging in wrath, shall go forth like wild boars*ᵇ* of the forest, and with great power they shall come and engage them in battle and shall devastate a portion of the land of the Assyrians with their teeth. ³¹And then the dragons, remembering their origin, shall become still stronger; and if they combine in great power and turn to pursue them, ³²then these shall be disorganised and silenced by their power and shall turn and flee. ³³And from the land of the Assyrians an enemy in ambush shall beset them and destroy one of them, and fear and trembling shall come upon their army, and indecision upon their kings.

JUDGEMENT ON BABYLON

³⁴Behold, clouds from the east and from the north to the south; and their appearance is very threatening, full of wrath and storm. ³⁵They shall throw themselves against one another and shall pour out a heavy tempest upon the earth, and their own tempest; and there shall be blood from the sword as high as a horse's belly ³⁶and a man's thigh and a camel's hock. ³⁷And there shall be fear and great trembling upon the earth; and those who see that wrath shall be horror-stricken, and they shall be seized with trembling. ³⁸And, after that, heavy storm clouds shall be stirred up from the south and from the north, and another part from the west. ³⁹And the winds from the east shall prevail over the cloud that was*ᶜ* raised in wrath and shall dispel it; and the tempest that was to cause destruction by the east wind shall be driven violently towards the south and west. ⁴⁰And great and mighty clouds, full of wrath and tempest, shall rise, to destroy all the earth and its inhabitants, and shall pour out upon every high and lofty place*ᵈ* a terrible tempest, ⁴¹fire and hail and flying swords and floods of water, in order that all the fields and all the streams may be filled with the abundance of those waters. ⁴²And they shall destroy cities and walls, mountains and hills, trees of the forests, and grass of the meadows and their corn. ⁴³And they shall go on steadily to Babylon and shall destroy her. ⁴⁴They shall come to her and surround her; they shall pour out the tempest and all its wrath upon her; then the dust and smoke shall go up to heaven, and all who are about her shall wail over her. ⁴⁵And those who survive shall serve those who have destroyed her.

JUDGEMENT ON ASIA

⁴⁶And you, Asia, who share in the glamour of Babylon and the glory of her person—⁴⁷woe to you, miserable wretch! For you have made yourself like her; you have decked out your daughters for sexual immorality to please and take pride in your lovers, who have always lusted after you. ⁴⁸You have imitated that hateful prostitute*ᵉ* in all her deeds and devices; therefore God says, ⁴⁹I will send evils upon you, widowhood, poverty, famine, sword, and pestilence, to devastate your houses and bring you to destruction and death. ⁵⁰And the glory of your power shall wither like a flower, when the heat rises that is sent upon you. ⁵¹You shall be weakened like a wretched woman who is beaten and wounded, so that you cannot receive your mighty lovers. ⁵²Would I have dealt with you so violently, says the Lord, ⁵³If you had not killed my chosen people at every opportunity, exulting and clapping your hands and talking about their death when you were drunk? ⁵⁴Beautify the appearance of your face! ⁵⁵The reward of a prostitute is in your bosom, therefore you shall receive your recompense. ⁵⁶As you will do to my chosen people, says the Lord, so God will do to you and will hand you over to adversities. ⁵⁷Your children shall die of hunger, and you shall fall by the sword, and your cities shall be wiped out, and all your people who are in the open country shall fall by the sword. ⁵⁸And those who are in the mountains and

---

*ᵃ*Some manuscripts *For God* *ᵇ*Some manuscripts omit *like wild boars* *ᶜ*Latin *that he* *ᵈ*Or *every eminent person* *ᵉ*Latin omits *prostitute*

highlands[a] shall perish of hunger, and they shall eat their own flesh in hunger for bread and drink their own blood in thirst for water. ⁵⁹Unhappy above all others, you shall come and suffer fresh afflictions. ⁶⁰And as they pass they shall wreck the hateful[b] city and shall destroy a part of your land and abolish a portion of your glory, as they return from devastated Babylon. ⁶¹And you shall be broken down by them like stubble, and they shall be like fire to you. ⁶²And they shall devour you and your cities, your land and your mountains; they shall burn with fire all your forests and your fruitful trees. ⁶³They shall carry your children away captive and shall plunder your wealth and abolish the splendour of your face.

FURTHER DENUNCIATIONS

16 Woe to you, Babylon and Asia! Woe to you, Egypt and Syria! ²Tie sackcloth and haircloth[c] around your waist and wail for your children and lament for them; for your destruction is at hand. ³The sword has been sent upon you, and who is there to turn it back? ⁴A fire has been sent upon you, and who is there to quench it? ⁵Calamities have been sent upon you, and who is there to drive them away? ⁶Can one drive off a hungry lion in the forest or quench a fire in the stubble once it has begun to burn? ⁷Can one turn back an arrow shot by a strong archer? ⁸The Lord God sends calamities, and who will drive them away? ⁹Fire will go forth from his wrath, and who is there to quench it? ¹⁰He will flash lightning, and who will not be afraid? He will thunder, and who will not be terrified? ¹¹The Lord will threaten, and who will not be utterly shattered at his presence? ¹²The earth and its foundations quake, the sea is churned up from the depths, and its waves and the fish also shall be troubled at the presence of the Lord and before the glory of his power. ¹³For his right hand that bends the bow is strong, and his arrows that he shoots are sharp and will not miss when they begin to be shot to the ends of the world. ¹⁴Behold, calamities are sent forth and shall not return until they come over the earth. ¹⁵The fire is kindled and shall not be put out until it consumes the foundations of the earth. ¹⁶Just as an arrow shot by a mighty archer does not return, so the calamities that are sent upon the earth shall not return. ¹⁷Alas for me! Alas for me! Who will deliver me in those days?

HORROR OF THE LAST DAYS

¹⁸The beginning of sorrows, when there shall be much lamentation; the beginning of famine, when many shall perish; the beginning of wars, when the powers shall be terrified; the beginning of calamities, when all shall tremble. What shall they do in these circumstances, when the calamities come? ¹⁹Behold, famine and plague, tribulation and anguish are sent as scourges for the correction of humanity.[d] ²⁰Yet for all this they will not turn from their iniquities, nor will they ever be mindful of the scourges. ²¹Behold, provision will be so cheap upon earth that they will imagine that peace is assured for them, and then the calamities shall spring up on the earth—the sword, famine, and great confusion. ²²For many of those who live on the earth shall perish by famine; and those who survive the famine shall die by the sword. ²³And the dead shall be cast out like excrement, and there shall be no one to console them; for the earth shall be left desolate, and its cities shall be demolished. ²⁴No one shall be left to cultivate the earth or to sow it. ²⁵The trees shall bear fruit, and who will gather it? ²⁶The grapes shall ripen, and who will tread them? For in all places there shall be great solitude; ²⁷one person will long to see another or even to hear his voice. ²⁸For out of a city, ten shall be left; and out of the field, two who have hidden themselves in thick groves and clefts in the rocks. ²⁹As in an olive orchard three or four olives may be left on every tree ³⁰or as when a vineyard is gathered some clusters may be left by those who search carefully through the vineyard, ³¹so in those days three or four shall be left by those who search their houses with the sword. ³²And the earth shall be left desolate, and its fields shall be for thorn bushes,[e] and its roads and all its paths shall bring forth thorns, because no sheep will go along them. ³³Virgins shall mourn because they have no bridegrooms; women shall mourn because they have no husbands; their daughters shall mourn, because they have no helpers. ³⁴Their bridegrooms shall be killed in war, and their husbands shall perish of famine.

GOD'S PEOPLE MUST PREPARE FOR THE END

³⁵Listen now to these things and understand them, O servants of the Lord. ³⁶See the

---

[a]Greek; Latin omits *and highlands* [b]Some manuscripts *idle* or *unprofitable* [c]Some manuscripts omit *and haircloth* [d]Latin *for correction* [e]Some manuscripts *shall be ploughed up*

word of the Lord; receive it, do not disbelieve what the Lord says.*ᵃ* ³⁷Behold, the calamities draw near and are not delayed. ³⁸Just as a woman with child, in the ninth month, when the time of her delivery draws near, has great pains about her womb for two or three hours beforehand, and when the child comes forth from the womb, there will not be a moment's delay, ³⁹so the calamities will not delay in coming forth upon the earth, and the world will groan, and pains will seize it on every side.

⁴⁰Hear my words, O my people; prepare for battle, and in the midst of the calamities be like strangers on the earth. ⁴¹Let him that sells be like one who will flee; let him that buys be like one who will lose; ⁴²let him that does business be like one who will not make a profit; and let him that builds a house be like one who will not live in it; ⁴³let him that sows be like one who will not reap; so also him that prunes the vines, like one who will not gather the grapes; ⁴⁴them that marry, like those who will have no children; and them that do not marry, like those who are widowed. ⁴⁵Because those who labour, labour in vain; ⁴⁶for strangers shall gather their fruits and plunder their goods and overthrow their houses and take their children captive; for in captivity and famine they will beget their children.*ᵇ* ⁴⁷Those who conduct business, do it only to be plundered; the more they adorn their cities, their houses and possessions, and their persons, ⁴⁸the angrier I will be with them for their sins, says the Lord. ⁴⁹Just as a respectable and virtuous woman abhors a prostitute, ⁵⁰so righteousness shall abhor iniquity, when she decks herself out, and shall accuse her to her face, when he comes who will defend him who searches out every sin on earth.

POWER AND WISDOM OF GOD

⁵¹Therefore do not be like her or her works. ⁵²For behold, just a little while, and iniquity will be removed from the earth, and righteousness shall reign over us. ⁵³Let no sinner say that he has not sinned; for God*ᶜ* will burn coals of fire on the head of him who says, "I have not sinned before God and his glory."*ᵈ* ⁵⁴Behold, the Lord knows all the works of men, their imaginations and their thoughts and their hearts. ⁵⁵He said, "Let the earth be made," and it was made; "Let the heaven be made," and it was made. ⁵⁶At his word the stars were fixed, and he knows the number of the stars. ⁵⁷It is he who searches the deep and its treasures; who has measured the sea and its contents; ⁵⁸who has enclosed the sea in the midst of the waters and by his word has suspended the earth over the water; ⁵⁹who has spread out the heaven like an arch and founded it upon the waters; ⁶⁰who has put springs of water in the desert and pools on the tops of the mountains, to send rivers from the heights to water the earth; ⁶¹who formed man and put a heart in the midst of his body and gave him breath and life and understanding ⁶²and the spirit of almighty God; who made all things and searches out hidden things in hidden places. ⁶³Surely he knows your imaginations and what you think in your hearts! Woe to those who sin and want to hide their sins! ⁶⁴Because the Lord will strictly examine all their works and will make a public spectacle of all of you. ⁶⁵And when your sins come out before men, you shall be put to shame; and your own iniquities shall stand as your accusers in that day. ⁶⁶What will you do? Or how will you hide your sins before God and his angels? ⁶⁷Behold, God is the judge, fear him! Cease from your sins and forget your iniquities, never to commit them again; so God will lead you forth and deliver you from all tribulation.

IMPENDING PERSECUTION OF GOD'S PEOPLE

⁶⁸For behold, the burning wrath of a great multitude is kindled over you, and they shall carry off some of you and shall feed you what was sacrificed to idols. ⁶⁹And those who consent to eat shall be held in*ᵉ* derision and contempt and be trodden under foot. ⁷⁰For in many places*ᶠ* and in neighbouring cities there shall be a great insurrection against those who fear the Lord. ⁷¹They shall be like mad men, sparing no one, but plundering and destroying those who continue to fear the Lord. ⁷²For they shall destroy and plunder their goods and drive them out of their houses. ⁷³Then the tested quality of my elect shall be manifest, as gold that is tested by fire.

PROMISE OF DIVINE DELIVERANCE

⁷⁴Hear, my elect, says the Lord. Behold, the days of tribulation are at hand, and I will deliver you from them. ⁷⁵Do not fear or

---

*ᵃ*Latin *do not believe the gods of whom the Lord speaks* *ᵇ*Or *for they will beget their children for captivity and famine* *ᶜ*Latin *he* *ᵈ*Some manuscripts *angels* *ᵉ*Latin *consent to them shall be for these in* *ᶠ*The meaning of the Latin is uncertain

doubt, for God is your guide. ⁷⁶You who keep my commandments and precepts, says the Lord God, do not let your sins pull you down or your iniquities prevail over you. ⁷⁷Woe to those who are choked by their sins and overwhelmed by their iniquities, as a field is choked with undergrowth and its path^a overwhelmed with thorns, so that no one can pass through! ⁷⁸It is shut off and given up to be consumed by fire.

---

^aSome manuscripts *seed*

4 MACCABEES

AUTHOR'S TASK

1 The subject that I am about to discuss is most philosophical, that is, whether devout reason is sovereign over the emotions.[a] So it is right for me to advise you to pay earnest attention to this philosophical enquiry. [2] For the subject is essential to everyone who is seeking knowledge, and in addition it includes the praise of the highest virtue — I mean, of course, rational judgment. [3] If, then, it is evident that reason rules over those emotions that hinder self-control, namely, gluttony and lust, [4] it is also clear that it masters the emotions that hinder one from justice, such as malice, and those that stand in the way of courage, namely anger, fear, and pain. [5] Some might perhaps ask, "If reason rules the emotions, why is it not sovereign over forgetfulness and ignorance?" Their attempt at argument is ridiculous![b] [6] For reason does not rule its own emotions, but those that are opposed to justice, courage, and self-control;[c] and it is not for the purpose of destroying them, but so that one may not give way to them.

[7] I could prove to you from many and various examples that reason[d] is absolute master over the emotions, [8] but I can demonstrate it best from the noble bravery of those who died for the sake of virtue, Eleazar and the seven brothers and their mother. [9] All of these, by despising sufferings that bring death, demonstrated that reason controls the emotions. [10] On this anniversary[e] it is fitting for me to praise for their virtues those who, with their mother, died for the sake of nobility and goodness, and I would also call them blessed for the honour in which they are held. [11] For all people, even their torturers, marvelled at their courage and endurance, and they became the cause of the downfall of tyranny over their nation. By their endurance they conquered the tyrant, and thus their native land was purified through them. [12] I shall shortly have an opportunity to speak of this; but, as my custom is, I shall begin by stating my main principle, and then I shall turn to their story, giving glory to the all-wise God.

SUPREMACY OF REASON

[13] Our enquiry, accordingly, is whether reason is sovereign over the emotions. [14] We shall decide just what reason is and what emotion is, how many kinds of emotions there are, and whether reason rules over all these. [15] Now reason is the mind that with sound logic prefers the life of wisdom. [16] Wisdom, next, is the knowledge of divine and human matters and the causes of these. [17] This, in turn, is education in the law, by which we learn divine matters reverently and human affairs to our advantage. [18] Now the kinds of wisdom are rational judgement, justice, courage, and self-control. [19] Rational judgement is supreme over all of these, since by means of it reason rules over the emotions. [20] The two most comprehensive types of the emotions are pleasure and pain; and each of these is by nature concerned with both body and soul. [21] The emotions of both pleasure and pain have many attendants. [22] Thus desire precedes pleasure and delight follows it. [23] Fear precedes pain and sorrow comes after. [24] Anger, as anyone will see if he reflects on this experience, is an emotion embracing pleasure and pain. [25] In pleasure there exists even a malevolent tendency, which is the most complex of all the emotions. [26] In the soul it is boastfulness, love of money, thirst for honour, rivalry, and malice; [27] in the body, indiscriminate eating, gluttony, and solitary gormandising.

[28] Just as pleasure and pain are two plants growing from the body and the soul, so there are many offshoots of these plants,[f] [29] each of which the master cultivator — reason — weeds and prunes and ties up and waters and thoroughly irrigates and so tames the jungle of habits and emotions. [30] For reason is the guide of the virtues, but over the emotions it is sovereign.

Observe now first of all that rational judgement is sovereign over the emotions by virtue of the restraining power of self-control.

---

[a] Or *passions* or *sensations* [b] Or *They are attempting to make my argument ridiculous!* [c] Some manuscripts add *and rational judgement* [d] Some manuscripts *that devout reason* [e] Greek *At this time* [f] Some manuscripts *emotions*

³¹Self-control, then, is mastery of the desires. ³²Some desires are mental, others are physical, and reason evidently rules over both. ³³Otherwise how is it that when we are attracted to forbidden foods we abstain from the pleasure to be had from them? Is it not because reason is able to rule over appetites? I for one think so. ³⁴Therefore when we crave seafood and fowl and animals and all sorts of foods that are forbidden to us by the law, we abstain because of domination by reason. ³⁵For the emotions of the appetites are restrained, checked by the temperate mind, and all the impulses of the body are bridled by reason.

COMPATIBILITY OF THE LAW WITH REASON

2 And why is it amazing that the desires of the soul for the enjoyment of beauty are rendered powerless? ²It is for this reason, certainly, that the temperate Joseph is praised, because by mental effort[a] he overcame sexual desire. ³For when he was young and in his prime for intercourse, by reason he nullified the frenzy[b] of the passions. ⁴Not only is reason proved to rule over the frenzied urge of sexual desire, but also over every desire.[c] ⁵Thus the law says, "You shall not covet[d] your neighbour's wife or anything that is your neighbour's." ⁶In fact, since the law has told us not to covet, I could prove to you all the more that reason is able to control desires.

Just so it is with the emotions that hinder one from justice. ⁷Otherwise how could it be that someone who is habitually a solitary gormandiser, a glutton, or even a drunkard can learn a better way, unless reason is clearly lord of the emotions? ⁸Thus, as soon as a man adopts a way of life in accordance with the law, even though he is a lover of money, he is forced to act contrary to his natural ways and to lend without interest to those who ask and to cancel the debt when the seventh year arrives. ⁹If one is greedy, he is restrained by the law on account of reason so that he neither gleans his harvest nor gathers the last grapes from the vineyard.

In all other matters we can recognise that reason rules the emotions. ¹⁰For the law prevails even over affection for parents, so that virtue is not abandoned for their sakes. ¹¹It rules over love for one's wife, so that one rebukes her when she breaks the law. ¹²It exercises lordship over love for children, so that one punishes them for misdeeds. ¹³It is sovereign over the relationship of friends, so that one rebukes friends when they act wickedly. ¹⁴Do not consider it paradoxical when reason, through the law, can prevail even over enmity. The fruit trees of the enemy are not cut down, but one preserves the property of enemies from the destroyers and helps raise up what has fallen.[e]

¹⁵It is evident that reason rules even[f] the more violent emotions: lust for power, vainglory, boasting, arrogance, and malice. ¹⁶For the temperate mind repels all these malicious emotions, just as it repels anger — for it is sovereign over even this. ¹⁷When Moses was angry with Dathan and Abiram he did nothing against them in anger, but controlled his anger by reason. ¹⁸For, as I have said, the temperate mind is able to get the better of the emotions, to correct some, and to render others powerless. ¹⁹Why else did Jacob, our wisest father, censure the households of Simeon and Levi for their irrational slaughter of the entire tribe of the Shechemites, saying, "Cursed be their anger"? ²⁰For if reason could not control anger, he would not have spoken thus. ²¹Now when God fashioned man, he planted in him emotions and inclinations, ²²but at the same time he enthroned the mind among the senses as a sacred governor over them all. ²³To the mind he gave the law; and one who lives subject to this will rule a kingdom that is temperate, just, good, and courageous.

²⁴How is it then, one might say, that if reason is master of the emotions, it does not control forgetfulness and ignorance?

3 This notion is entirely ridiculous; for it is evident that reason rules not over its own emotions, but over those of the body. ²No one of us can eradicate that kind of desire, but reason can provide a way for us not to be enslaved by desire. ³No one of you can eradicate anger from the mind, but reason can help to deal with anger. ⁴No one of you can eradicate malice, but reason can fight at our side so that we are not overcome by malice. ⁵For reason does not uproot the emotions but is their antagonist.

KING DAVID'S THIRST

⁶Now this can be explained more clearly by the story of King David's thirst. ⁷David

---

[a] Some manuscripts add *in reasoning* [b] Or *gadfly* [c] Or *over all covetousness* [d] Or *desire*; also verse 6 [e] Or *raise up the beasts that have fallen*; compare Exodus 23:4–5 [f] Some manuscripts *through*

had been attacking the Philistines all day long and together with the soldiers of his nation had slain many of them. [8]Then when evening fell, he[a] came, sweating and quite exhausted, to the royal tent, round which the whole army of our ancestors had encamped. [9]Now all the rest were at supper, [10]but the king was extremely thirsty, and although springs were plentiful there, he could not satisfy his thirst from them. [11]But a certain irrational desire for the water in the enemy's territory tormented and inflamed him, undid and consumed him. [12]When his guards complained bitterly because of the king's craving, two staunch young soldiers, respecting[b] the king's desire, armed themselves fully, and taking a pitcher climbed over the enemy's ramparts. [13]Eluding the sentinels at the gates, they went searching throughout the enemy camp [14]and found the spring and from it boldly brought the king a drink. [15]But David,[c] although he was burning with thirst, considered it an altogether fearful danger to his soul to drink what was regarded as equivalent to blood. [16]Therefore, opposing reason to desire, he poured out the drink as an offering to God. [17]For the temperate mind can conquer the drives of the emotions and quench the flames of frenzied desires; [18]it can overthrow bodily agonies even when they are extreme and by nobility of reason spurn all domination by the emotions.

AN ATTEMPT ON THE TEMPLE TREASURY

[19]The present occasion now invites us to a narrative demonstration of temperate reason.

[20]At a time when our fathers were enjoying profound peace because of their observance of the law and were prospering, so that even King Seleucus Nicanor of Asia had both appropriated money to them for the temple service and recognised their commonwealth—[21]at just that time certain men attempted a revolution against the public harmony and caused many and various disasters.

4 Now there was a certain Simon, a political opponent of the noble and good man, Onias, who then held the high priesthood for life. When he was unable to injure Onias despite bringing all manner of charges against him in the name of the state, he fled the country with the purpose of betraying it. [2]So he came to Apollonius, governor of Syria, Phoenicia, and Cilicia, and said, [3]"I have come here because I am loyal to the king's government, to report that in the Jerusalem treasuries there are deposited tens of thousands in private funds, which are not the property of the temple but are suitable for King Seleucus." [4]When Apollonius learned the details of these things, he praised Simon for his service to the king and went up to Seleucus to inform him of the rich treasure. [5]On receiving authority to deal with this matter, he proceeded quickly to our country accompanied by the accursed Simon and a very strong military force. [6]He said that he had come with the king's authority to seize the private funds in the treasury. [7]The people indignantly protested his words, considering it outrageous that those who had committed deposits to the sacred treasury should be deprived of them, and did all that they could to prevent it. [8]But, uttering threats, Apollonius went on to the temple. [9]While the priests together with women and children were imploring God in the temple to shield the Holy Place that was being treated so contemptuously, [10]and while Apollonius was going up with his armed forces to seize the money, angels on horseback with lightning flashing from their weapons appeared from heaven, instilling in them great fear and trembling. [11]Then Apollonius fell down half dead in the temple court that was open to all peoples, stretched out his hands towards heaven, and with tears implored the Hebrews to pray for him and propitiate the wrath of the heavenly army. [12]For he said that he had committed a sin deserving of death and that if he were delivered he would praise the blessedness of the Holy Place before all people. [13]Moved by these words, Onias the high priest, though in another way taking care lest King Seleucus suppose that Apollonius had been overcome by human treachery and not by divine justice, prayed for him. [14]So Apollonius, having been preserved beyond all expectations, went away to report to the king what had happened to him.

ANTIOCHUS' PERSECUTION OF THE JEWS

[15]When King Seleucus died, his son Antiochus Epiphanes succeeded to the throne, an arrogant and terrible man [16]who removed Onias from the priesthood and appointed Onias'[d] brother Jason as high priest. [17]Jason[e]

---
[a]Some manuscripts add *hurried and* [b]Or *soldiers, embarrassed because of* [c]Greek *he* [d]Greek *his* [e]Greek *He*; also verse 19

agreed that if the office were conferred upon him he would pay the king 3,660 talents annually. ¹⁸So the king appointed him high priest and ruler of the nation. ¹⁹Jason changed the nation's way of life and altered its form of government in complete violation of the law, ²⁰so that not only was a gymnasium constructed at the very citadel[a] of our native land, but also abolished the provisions for the care of the temple. ²¹The divine justice was angered by these acts and caused Antiochus himself to make war on them. ²²For when he was warring against Ptolemy in Egypt, he heard that a rumor of his death had spread and that the people of Jerusalem had rejoiced greatly. He speedily marched against them, ²³and after he had ravaged them he issued a decree that if any of them should be found observing the ancestral law they should die. ²⁴When, by means of his decrees, he had not been able in any way to put an end to the people's observance of the law, but saw that all his threats and punishments were being disregarded, ²⁵even to the point that women, because they had circumcised their sons, were thrown headlong from heights along with their infants, though they had known beforehand that they would suffer this—²⁶when, then, his decrees were despised by the people, he himself, through torture, tried to compel everyone in the nation to renounce Judaism by eating defiling foods.

ANTIOCHUS' ENCOUNTER WITH ELEAZAR

5 The tyrant Antiochus, sitting in state with his counsellors on a certain high place and with his armed soldiers standing round him, ²ordered the guards to seize each and every Hebrew and to compel them to eat pork and food sacrificed to idols. ³If any were not willing to eat defiling food, they were to be broken on the wheel and killed. ⁴And when many persons had been rounded up, one man, Eleazar by name, leader of the flock, was brought[b] before the king. He was a man of priestly family, learned in the law, advanced in age, and known to many in the tyrant's court because of his advanced age.

⁵When Antiochus saw him he said, ⁶"Before I begin to torture you, old man, I would advise you to save yourself by eating pork, ⁷for I respect your age and your grey hairs. Although you have had them for so long a time, it does not seem to me that you are a philosopher when you observe the piety of the Jews. ⁸Why, when nature has granted it to us, should you abhor eating the very excellent meat of this animal? ⁹It is senseless not to enjoy delicious things that are not shameful, and wrong to spurn the gifts of nature. ¹⁰It seems to me that you will do something even more senseless if, by holding a vain opinion concerning the truth, you continue to despise me to your own hurt. ¹¹Will you not awaken from your foolish philosophy, dispel your futile reasonings, adopt a mind appropriate to your years, philosophise according to the truth of what is beneficial, ¹²and have compassion on your old age by honouring my humane advice? ¹³For consider this, that if there is some power watching over this religion of yours, it may excuse you from any transgression that arises out of compulsion."

¹⁴When the tyrant urged him in this fashion to eat meat unlawfully, Eleazar asked to have a word. ¹⁵When he had received permission to speak, he began to address the people as follows: ¹⁶"We, O Antiochus, who have been persuaded to govern our lives by the divine law, think that there is no compulsion more powerful than our obedience to the law. ¹⁷Therefore we consider that we should not transgress it in any respect. ¹⁸Even if, as you suppose, our law were not truly divine and we were wrongly considering it to be divine, not even so would it be right for us to invalidate our reputation for piety. ¹⁹Therefore do not suppose that it would be a petty sin if we were to eat defiling food; ²⁰to transgress the law in matters either small or great is of equal seriousness, ²¹for in either case the law is equally despised. ²²You scoff at our philosophy as though living by it were irrational, ²³but it teaches us self-control, so that we master all pleasures and desires, and it also trains us in courage, so that we endure any suffering willingly; ²⁴it instructs us in justice, so that in all our dealings we act impartially,[c] and it teaches us piety, so that with proper reverence we worship the only real God.

²⁵"Therefore we do not eat defiling food; for since we believe that the law was established by God, we know that the Creator of the cosmic order in giving us the law in accordance with nature has shown sympathy towards us. ²⁶He has permitted us to eat

---

[a] Or *at the high place* [b] Or *was the first of the flock to be brought*
[c] Or *so that we give what is due in all our interactions*

what will be most suitable for our lives,[a] but he has forbidden us to eat meats that would be contrary to this. ²⁷It would be tyrannical for you to compel us not only to transgress the law, but also to eat in such a way that you may deride us for eating defiling foods, which are most hateful to us. ²⁸But you shall have no such occasion to laugh at me, ²⁹nor will I transgress the sacred oaths of my ancestors concerning the keeping of the law, ³⁰not even if you gouge out my eyes and burn my entrails. ³¹I am not so old and cowardly as not to be young in reason on behalf of piety. ³²Therefore get your torture wheels ready and fan the fire more vehemently! ³³I do not so pity my old age as to destroy the ancestral law by my own act. ³⁴I will not play false to you, O law that trained me, nor will I renounce you, beloved self-control. ³⁵I will not put you to shame, philosophical reason, nor will I reject you, honoured priesthood and knowledge of the law. ³⁶You, O king,[b] shall not defile the honourable mouth of my old age or my long life lived lawfully. ³⁷The fathers will receive me as pure, as one who does not fear your violence even to death. ³⁸You will tyrannise the ungodly, but you shall not dominate my religious principles either by words or by deeds."

MARTYRDOM OF ELEAZAR

6 When Eleazar in this manner had made eloquent response to the exhortations of the tyrant, the guards who were standing by dragged him violently to the instruments of torture. ²First they stripped the old man, who remained adorned with the gracefulness of his piety. ³And after they had tied his arms behind him they began to scourge him on either side, ⁴while a herald opposite him cried out, "Obey the king's commands!" ⁵But the courageous and noble man, as a true Eleazar,[c] was unmoved, as though being tortured in a dream; ⁶yet while the old man's eyes were raised to heaven, his flesh was being torn by scourges, his blood flowing, and his sides were being cut to pieces. ⁷And though he fell to the ground because his body could not endure the agonies, he kept his reason upright and unswerving. ⁸One of the cruel guards rushed at him and began to kick him in the side to make him get up again after he fell. ⁹But he continued to bear the pains and scorn the punishment and endure the tortures. ¹⁰And like a noble athlete the old man, while being beaten, was victorious over his torturers; ¹¹in fact, with his face bathed in sweat and gasping heavily for breath, he amazed even his torturers by his courageous spirit.

¹²At that point, partly out of pity for his old age, ¹³partly out of sympathy from their acquaintance with him, partly out of admiration for his endurance, some of the king's retinue came to him and said, ¹⁴"Eleazar, why are you so irrationally destroying yourself through these evil things? ¹⁵We will set before you some cooked meat; save yourself by pretending to eat pork."

¹⁶But Eleazar, as though more bitterly tormented by this counsel, cried out: ¹⁷"May we, the children[d] of Abraham, never think so basely that out of cowardice we feign a role unbecoming to us! ¹⁸For it would be irrational if we, who have lived in accordance with truth to old age and have maintained in accordance with law the reputation of such a life, should now change our course ¹⁹and ourselves become a pattern of impiety to the young, so as to set an example of the eating of defiling food. ²⁰It would be shameful if we should survive for a little while and during that time be a laughing stock to all for our cowardice ²¹and if we should be despised by the tyrant as unmanly and not protect our divine law even to death. ²²Therefore, O children of Abraham, die nobly on behalf of piety! ²³And you, guards of the tyrant, why do you delay?"

²⁴When they saw that he was so courageous in the face of the afflictions and that he had not been changed by their compassion, the guards brought him to the fire. ²⁵There they burned him with maliciously contrived instruments, threw him down, and poured stinking liquids into his nostrils. ²⁶When he was now burned to his very bones and about to expire, he lifted up his eyes to God and said, ²⁷"You know, O God, that though I might have saved myself, I am dying in burning torments for the sake of the law. ²⁸Be merciful to your people, and let our punishment on their behalf suffice. ²⁹Make my blood their purification and take my life in exchange for theirs." ³⁰And after he said this, the holy man died nobly in his tortures, and by reason he resisted even to the very tortures of death for the sake of the law.

---

[a] Or *souls* [b] Greek omits *O King* [c] Eleazar means *God helps*
[d] Or *May we, O children*

³¹Admittedly, then, devout reason is sovereign over the emotions. ³²For if the emotions had prevailed over reason, we would have testified to their domination. ³³But now that reason has conquered the emotions, we properly attribute to it the power to govern. ³⁴And it is right for us to acknowledge the dominance of reason when it masters even external agonies. It would be ridiculous to deny it.[a] ³⁵And I have proved not only that reason has mastered agonies, but also that it masters pleasures and in no respect yields to them.

AN ENCOMIUM ON ELEAZAR

7 For like a most skilful pilot, the reason of our father Eleazar steered the ship of piety over the sea of the emotions, ²and though buffeted by the stormings of the tyrant and overwhelmed by the mighty waves of tortures, ³in no way did he turn the rudder of piety until he sailed into the haven of immortal victory. ⁴No city besieged with many ingenious war machines has ever held out as did that holiest man. Although his sacred life was consumed by tortures and racks, he conquered the besiegers by shielding piety with reason. ⁵For in setting his mind firm like a jutting cliff, our father Eleazar broke the maddening waves of the emotions. ⁶O priest, worthy of the priesthood, you neither defiled your sacred teeth nor profaned your stomach, which had room only for reverence and purity, by eating defiling foods. ⁷O man in harmony with the law and philosopher of divine life! ⁸Such should be those who are administrators of the law, shielding it with their own blood and noble sweat in sufferings even to death. ⁹You, father, strengthened our obedience to the law through your endurance unto glory, and you did not abandon the holiness that you praised, but by your deeds you made your words of divine[b] philosophy credible. ¹⁰O aged man, more powerful than tortures; O elder, fiercer than fire; O supreme king over the passions, Eleazar! ¹¹For just as our father Aaron, armed with the censer, ran through the multitude of the people and conquered the fiery[c] angel, ¹²so the descendant of Aaron, Eleazar, though being consumed by the fire, remained unmoved in his reason. ¹³Most amazing, indeed, though he was an old man, his body no longer tense and firm,[d] his muscles flabby, his sinews feeble, he became young again ¹⁴in spirit through reason; and by reason like that of Isaac he rendered the many-headed rack ineffective. ¹⁵O man of blessed age and of venerable grey hair and of law-abiding life, whom the faithful seal of death has perfected!

¹⁶If, therefore, because of piety an aged man despised tortures even to death, most certainly devout reason is governor of the emotions. ¹⁷Some perhaps might say, "Not everyone has full command of his emotions, because not everyone has prudent reason." ¹⁸But as many as attend to piety with a whole heart, these alone are able to control the passions of the flesh, ¹⁹since they believe that they, like our patriarchs Abraham and Isaac and Jacob, do not die to God, but live to God. ²⁰No contradiction therefore arises when some persons appear to be dominated by their emotions because of the weakness of their reason. ²¹What person who lives as a philosopher by the whole rule of philosophy and trusts in God ²²and knows that it is blessed to endure any suffering for the sake of virtue would not be able to overcome the emotions through godliness? ²³For only the wise and courageous man is lord of his emotions.

SEVEN BROTHERS DEFY THE TYRANT

8 For this is why even the very young, by following a philosophy in accordance with devout reason, have prevailed over the most painful instruments of torture. ²For when the tyrant was conspicuously defeated in his first attempt, being unable to compel an old man to eat defiling foods, then in violent rage he commanded that others of the Hebrew captives be brought and that any who ate defiling food should be freed after eating, but if any were to refuse, these should be tortured even more cruelly.

³When the tyrant had given these orders, seven brothers—handsome, modest, noble, and gifted in every way—were brought before him along with their aged mother. ⁴When the tyrant saw them, grouped round their mother as if in a chorus, he was pleased with them. And struck by their appearance and nobility, he smiled at them and summoned them nearer and said, ⁵"Young men, I admire each and every one of you in a kindly manner and greatly respect the beauty and the number

---

[a]Syriac; the meaning of the Greek is uncertain [b]Some manuscripts omit *divine* [c]Some manuscripts omit *fiery* [d]Greek *man, the tautness of the body already loosed*

of such brothers. Not only do I advise you not to display the same madness as that of the old man who has just been tortured, but I also exhort you to yield to me and so enjoy my friendship. ⁶Just as I am able to punish those who disobey my orders, so I can be a benefactor to those who are disposed to obey me. ⁷Trust me, then, and you will receive positions of authority in my government after renouncing the ancestral tradition of your national life. ⁸And enjoy your youth by adopting the Greek way of life and by changing your manner of living. ⁹But if by disobedience you rouse my anger, you will compel me to destroy each and every one of you with dreadful punishments through tortures. ¹⁰Therefore take pity on yourselves. Even I, your enemy, have compassion for your youth and handsome appearance. ¹¹Will you not consider this, that if you disobey, nothing remains for you but to die on the rack?"

¹²When he had said these things, he ordered the instruments of torture to be brought forwards so as to persuade them out of fear to eat the defiling food. ¹³And when the guards had placed before them wheels and joint-dislocators, rack and hooks[a] and catapults[b] and cauldrons, brasiers and thumbscrews and iron claws and wedges and bellows, the tyrant resumed speaking: ¹⁴"Be afraid, young fellows, and whatever justice you revere will be merciful to you when you transgress under compulsion."

¹⁵But when they had heard the inducements and saw the dreadful devices, not only were they not afraid, but they also opposed the tyrant with their own philosophy and by their right reasoning nullified his tyranny. ¹⁶Let us consider, on the other hand, what arguments might have been used if some of them had been cowardly and unmanly. Would they not have been these? ¹⁷"O wretches that we are and so senseless! Since the king has summoned and exhorted us to accept kind treatment if we obey him, ¹⁸why do we take pleasure in vain resolves and venture upon a disobedience that brings death? ¹⁹O men and brothers, should we not fear the instruments of torture and consider the threats of torments and give up this vain opinion and this arrogance that threatens to destroy us? ²⁰Let us take pity on our youth and have compassion on our mother's age; ²¹and let us seriously consider that if we disobey we are dead! ²²Also, divine justice will excuse us for fearing the king when we are under compulsion. ²³Why do we banish ourselves from this most pleasant life and deprive ourselves of this delightful world? ²⁴Let us not struggle against compulsion[c] or take hollow pride in being put to the rack. ²⁵Not even the law itself would be inclined to slay us for fearing the instruments of torture. ²⁶Why does such contentiousness excite us and such a fatal stubbornness please us, when we can live in peace if we obey the king?"

²⁷But the youths, though about to be tortured, neither said any of these things nor even seriously considered them. ²⁸For they were contemptuous of the emotions and sovereign over agonies, ²⁹so that as soon as the tyrant had ceased counselling them to eat defiling food, all with one voice together, as from one mind, said:

9 "Why do you delay, O tyrant? For we are ready to die rather than transgress our ancestral commandments; ²we are obviously putting our ancestors to shame unless we should practise ready obedience to the law and to Moses[d] our counsellor. ³Tyrant and counsellor of lawlessness, in your hatred for us do not pity us more than we pity ourselves.[e] ⁴For we consider this pity of yours that ensures our safety through transgression of the law to be more grievous than death itself. ⁵You are trying to terrify us by threatening us with death by torture, as though a short time ago you learned nothing from Eleazar. ⁶And if the aged men of the Hebrews for the sake of piety fulfilled their religious duty[f] while enduring torture, it would be even more fitting that we young men should die despising your coercive tortures, which our aged instructor also overcame. ⁷Therefore, tyrant, put us to the test; and if you take our lives because of our religion, do not suppose that you can injure us by torturing us. ⁸For we, through this severe suffering and endurance, shall have the prises of virtue and shall be with God, for whom we suffer; ⁹but you, because of your bloodthirstiness towards us, will deservedly undergo from the divine justice eternal torment by fire."

THE TORTURE OF THE FIRST BROTHER

¹⁰When they had said these things the tyrant not only was angry, as at those who

---

[a] Or *clubs*; the meaning of the Greek is uncertain [b] Here and elsewhere in 4 Maccabees an instrument of torture [c] Or *fate* [d] Some manuscripts *knowledge* [e] The meaning of the Greek is uncertain [f] One manuscript *piety died*

are disobedient, but also was enraged, as at those who are ungrateful. ¹¹Then at his command the guards brought forward the oldest, and having torn off his tunic, they bound his hands and arms with thongs on each side. ¹²When they had worn themselves out beating him with scourges, without accomplishing anything, they placed him upon the wheel. ¹³When the noble youth was stretched out round this, his limbs were dislocated, ¹⁴and though broken in every member he denounced the tyrant, saying, ¹⁵"Most abominable tyrant, enemy of heavenly justice, savage of mind, you are mangling me in this manner, not because I am a murderer or as one who acts impiously, but because I protect the divine law." ¹⁶And when the guards said, "Agree to eat so that you may be released from the tortures," ¹⁷he replied, "You abominable lackeys, your wheel is not so powerful as to strangle my reason. Cut my limbs, burn my flesh, and twist my joints. ¹⁸Through all these tortures I will convince you that sons of the Hebrews alone are invincible on behalf of virtue." ¹⁹While he was saying these things, they spread fire under him, and while fanning the flames*ᵃ* they tightened the wheel further. ²⁰The wheel was completely smeared with blood, and the pile of coals was being quenched by the drippings of gore, and pieces of flesh were falling off the axles of the machine. ²¹Although the ligaments joining his bones were already severed, the courageous youth, worthy*ᵇ* of Abraham, did not groan, ²²but as though transformed by fire into immortality he nobly endured the rackings. ²³"Imitate me, brothers," he said. "Do not leave your post in my struggle*ᶜ* or renounce our courageous brotherhood. ²⁴Fight the sacred and noble battle for piety. Thereby the just providence of our ancestors may become merciful to our nation and take vengeance on the accursed tyrant." ²⁵When he had said this, the saintly youth broke the thread of life.

THE TORTURE OF THE SECOND BROTHER

²⁶While all were marvelling at his courageous spirit, the guards brought the next oldest forward, and after fitting themselves with iron gauntlets having sharp hooks, they bound him to the torture machine and catapult. ²⁷Before torturing him, they enquired if he were willing to eat, and they heard this noble decision.*ᵈ* ²⁸These leopard-like beasts tore out his sinews with the iron hands, flayed all his flesh up to his chin, and tore away his scalp. But he steadfastly endured this agony and said, ²⁹"How sweet is any kind of death for the sake of our ancestral piety!" ³⁰To the tyrant he said, "Do you not think, you most savage tyrant, that you are being tortured more than I, as you see the arrogant design of your tyranny being defeated by our endurance for the sake of piety? ³¹I lighten my pain by the joys that come from virtue, ³²but you suffer torture by the threats that come from impiety. You will not escape, most abominable tyrant, the punishments of the divine wrath."

THE TORTURE OF THE THIRD BROTHER

10 When he too had endured a glorious death, the third was led forward, and many repeatedly urged him to save himself by tasting the meat. ²But he shouted, "Do you not know that the same father begot me and those who died and the same mother bore me and that I was brought up on the same teachings? ³I do not renounce the noble kinship that binds me to my brothers."*ᵉ* ⁵Enraged by the man's boldness, they disjointed his hands and feet with their instruments, dismembering him by prying his limbs from their sockets ⁶and breaking his fingers and arms and legs and elbows. ⁷Since they were unable in any way to break his spirit,*ᶠ* they abandoned the instruments*ᵍ* and scalped him with their fingernails in Scythian fashion. ⁸They immediately brought him to the wheel, and while his vertebrae were being dislocated upon it he saw his own flesh torn all round and drops of blood flowing from his entrails. ⁹When he was about to die, he said, ¹⁰"We, most abominable tyrant, are suffering because of our godly training and virtue, ¹¹but you, because of your impiety and bloodthirstiness, will undergo unceasing torments."

THE TORTURE OF THE FOURTH BROTHER

¹²When he also had died in a manner worthy of his brothers, they dragged the fourth forward, saying, ¹³"As for you, do not give way to the same insanity as your brothers, but obey the king and save yourself." ¹⁴But

---

*ᵃ*The meaning of the Greek is uncertain *ᵇ*Some manuscripts *youth, a son* *ᶜ*Some manuscripts *post for ever* *ᵈ*Some manuscripts *and having heard his noble decision they tore him to shreds* *ᵉ*Some manuscripts add verse 4: *So if you have any instrument of torture, apply it to my body; for you cannot touch my soul, even if you wish.* *ᶠ*Greek *to strangle him* *ᵍ*Some manuscripts *they tore off his skin*

he said to them, "You do not have a fire hot enough to make me play the coward. ¹⁵No, by the blessed death of my brothers, by the eternal destruction of the tyrant, and by the everlasting life of the pious, I will not renounce our noble brotherhood. ¹⁶Contrive tortures, tyrant, so that you may learn from them that I am a brother to those who have just been tortured." ¹⁷When he heard this, the bloodthirsty, murderous, and utterly abominable Antiochus gave orders to cut out his tongue. ¹⁸But he said, "Even if you remove my organ of speech, God hears even those who are mute. ¹⁹See, here is my tongue; cut it off, for in spite of this you will not make our reason speechless. ²⁰Gladly, for the sake of God, we let our bodily members be mutilated. ²¹God will visit you swiftly, for you are cutting out a tongue that has been melodious with divine hymns."

THE TORTURE OF THE FIFTH BROTHER

11 When this one died also, after being cruelly tortured, the fifth leaped up, saying, ²"I will not refuse, tyrant, to be tortured for the sake of virtue. ³I have come of my own accord, so that by murdering me you will incur punishment from the heavenly justice for even more crimes. ⁴Hater of virtue, hater of mankind, for what act of ours are you destroying us in this way? ⁵Is it because[a] we revere the Creator of all things and live according to his virtuous law? ⁶But these deeds deserve honours, not tortures."[b] ⁹While he was saying these things, the guards bound him and dragged him to the catapult; ¹⁰they tied him to it on his knees, and fitting iron clamps on them, they twisted his back[c] round a wedge worked by a wheel,[d] so that he was completely curled back like a scorpion, and all his members were disjointed. ¹¹In this condition, gasping for breath and in anguish of body, ¹²he said, "Tyrant, they are splendid favours that you grant us against your will, because through these noble sufferings you give us an opportunity to show our steadfastness towards the law."

THE TORTURE OF THE SIXTH BROTHER

¹³After he too had died, the sixth, a mere boy, was led forward. When the tyrant enquired whether he was willing to eat and be released, he said, ¹⁴"I am younger in age than my brothers, but I am their equal in mind. ¹⁵Since to this end we were born and bred, we ought likewise to die for the same principles. ¹⁶So if it seems right to you to torture me for not eating defiling foods, go on torturing!" ¹⁷When he had said this, they led him to the wheel. ¹⁸He was carefully stretched tight upon it, his back was broken, and he was roasted[e] from underneath. ¹⁹To his back they applied sharp spits that had been heated in the fire and pierced his ribs so that his entrails were burned through. ²⁰While being tortured he said, "O contest suiting holiness, in which so many of us brothers have been summoned to an arena of sufferings for the sake of piety and in which we have not been defeated! ²¹For devout knowledge, O tyrant, is invincible. ²²I also, equipped with nobility, will die with my brothers, ²³and I myself will bring a great avenger upon you, you inventor of tortures and enemy of those who are truly devout. ²⁴We six boys have put an end to your tyranny! ²⁵Since you have not been able to persuade us to change our mind or to force us to eat defiling foods, is not this your downfall? ²⁶Your fire is cold to us, and the catapults painless, and your violence powerless. ²⁷For it is not the guards of the tyrant but those of the divine law that are set over us; therefore we hold our reason unconquered."

THE TORTURE OF THE SEVENTH BROTHER

12 When he also, thrown into the cauldron, had died a blessed death, the seventh and youngest of all came forward. ²Even though the tyrant had been fearfully reproached by the brothers, he felt strong compassion for this child when he saw that he was already in fetters. He summoned him to come nearer and tried to counsel him, saying, ³"You see the result of your brothers' stupidity, for they died in torments because of their disobedience. ⁴You too, if you do not obey, will die a tortured wretch before your time, ⁵but if you yield to persuasion you will be my friend and a leader in the government of the kingdom." ⁶When he had so pleaded, he sent for the boy's mother to show compassion on her who had been bereaved of so many sons and to influence her to persuade[f] the surviving son to obey and save himself. ⁷But once his mother had exhorted him in the

---

[a] Some manuscripts *Or does it seem evil to you that* [b] Some manuscripts add verses 7–8: *If of course you had human feelings and had hope of salvation from God—*⁸ *but, as it is, you are a stranger to God and persecute those who serve him.* [c] Greek *loins* [d] The meaning of the Greek is uncertain [e] Some manuscripts add *by fire* [f] One manuscript *influence her, so that she, taking pity on herself after being bereaved of so many sons, would persuade*

Hebrew language, as we shall tell a little later, [8]he said, "Let me loose, let me speak to the king and to all his friends that are with him." [9]Extremely pleased by the boy's declaration, they freed him at once. [10]Running to the nearest of the brasiers, [11]he said, "You profane tyrant, most impious of all the wicked, since you have received good things and also your kingdom from God, were you not ashamed to murder his servants and torture the athletes of piety? [12]Because of this, justice has laid up for you a more intense and eternal fire and tortures, and these throughout all time[a] will never let you go. [13]As a man, were you not ashamed, you most savage beast, to cut out the tongues of those who have feelings like yours and are made of the same elements as you and to maltreat and torture them in this way? [14]Surely they by dying nobly fulfilled their pious duty to God, but you will wail bitterly for having slain without cause the contestants for virtue." [15]Then because he too was about to die, he said, [16]"I do not desert the excellent example[b] of my brothers, [17]and I call on the God of our fathers to be merciful to our nation;[c] [18]but on you he will take vengeance both in this present life and when you are dead." [19]After he had uttered these imprecations, he flung himself into the brasiers and so ended his life.[d]

REASON'S SOVEREIGNTY IN THE SEVEN

13 Since, then, the seven brothers despised sufferings even unto death, everyone must concede that devout reason is sovereign over the emotions. [2]For if they had been slaves to their emotions and had eaten defiling food, we would say that they had been conquered by these emotions. [3]But in fact it was not so. Instead, by reason, which is praised before God, they prevailed over their emotions. [4]The supremacy of the mind over these cannot be overlooked, for the brothers[e] mastered both emotions and pains. [5]How then can one fail to confess the sovereignty of right reason over emotion in those who were not turned back by fiery agonies? [6]For just as towers jutting out over harbours hold back the threatening waves and make it calm for those who sail into the inner basin, [7]so the seven-towered right reason of the youths, by fortifying the harbour of piety, conquered the tempest of the emotions. [8]For they constituted a holy chorus of piety and emboldened one another, saying, [9]"Brothers, let us die like brothers for the sake of the law; let us imitate the three youths in Assyria who despised the same ordeal of the furnace. [10]Let us not be cowardly in the demonstration of our piety." [11]While one said, "Courage, brother," another said, "Bear up nobly," [12]and another reminded them, "Remember whence you came and the father by whose hand Isaac submitted to being slain for the sake of religion." [13]Each of them and all of them together looking at one another, cheerful and undaunted, said, "Let us with all our hearts consecrate ourselves to God, who gave us our lives,[f] and let us use our bodies as a bulwark for the law. [14]Let us not fear him who thinks he is killing us, [15]for great is the contest of the soul and the danger of eternal torment lying before those who transgress the commandment of God. [16]Therefore let us put on the full armour of the restraint of the passions that comes through divine reason. [17]For if we so die,[g] Abraham and Isaac and Jacob will welcome us, and all the fathers will praise us." [18]Those who were left behind said to each of the brothers who were being dragged away, "Do not put us to shame, brother, or betray the brothers who have died before us."

[19]You are not ignorant of the affection of brotherhood, which the divine and all-wise Providence has bequeathed through the fathers to their descendants and which was implanted in the mother's womb. [20]There the brothers dwelt the same length of time and were shaped during the same period of time; and growing from the same blood and through the same life, they were brought to the light of day. [21]When they were born after an equal time of gestation, they drank milk from the same fountains. From such embraces brotherly loving souls are nourished; [22]and they grow stronger from this common nurture and daily companionship and from both general education and our discipline in the law of God.

[23]Therefore, when sympathy and brotherly affection had been so established, the seven brothers were the more sympathetic to one another. [24]Since they had been educated by the same law and trained in the same virtues and brought up together in right living, they loved one another all the more. [25]A common zeal for nobility expanded their goodwill and

---

[a]Greek throughout the whole age [b]Some manuscripts witness [c]Some manuscripts to my race [d]Greek and so gave up; some manuscripts and so gave up his spirit/soul [e]Greek for they [f]Or souls [g]Some manuscripts suffer

harmony towards one another, ²⁶because, with the aid of piety, they rendered their brotherly love more fervent. ²⁷But although nature and companionship and virtuous habits had augmented the affection of brotherhood, those who were left endured, for the sake of piety, watching their brothers being maltreated and tortured to death.

14 Furthermore, they encouraged them to face the torture, so that they not only despised their agonies, but also mastered the emotions of brotherly love.

²O reason,ᵃ more royal than kings and freer than the free! ³O sacred music of the seven brothers, well tuned in regard to piety! ⁴None of the seven youths proved coward or shrank from death, ⁵but all of them, as though running the course towards immortality, hastened to death by torture. ⁶Just as the hands and feet are moved in harmony with the guidance of the mind, so those holy youths, as though moved by an immortal spirit of piety, agreed to go to death for its sake. ⁷O holiest seven, brothers in harmony! For just as the seven days of creation move in choral dance round piety, ⁸so these youths, forming a chorus of seven, encircled the fear of tortures and dissolved it. ⁹Even now, we ourselves shudder as we hear of the tribulations of these young men; they not only saw what was happening, yes, not only heard the direct word of threat, but also bore up steadfastly under the sufferings and in agonies of fire at that. ¹⁰What could be more excruciatingly painful than this? For the power of fire is intense and swift, and it consumed their bodies quickly.

AN ENCOMIUM ON THE MOTHER OF THE SEVEN

¹¹Do not consider it amazing that reason had full command over these men in their tortures, since even the mind of a woman despised more diverse agonies, ¹²for the mother of the seven young men bore up under the rackings of each one of her children.

¹³Observe how complex is a mother's love for her children, which draws everything towards a sympathy felt in her inmost parts. ¹⁴Even unreasoning animals, like mankind, have a sympathy and parental love for their offspring. ¹⁵For example, among birds, the ones that are tame protect their young by building on the housetops, ¹⁶and the others, by building in mountain peaks and precipitous chasms and in the holes and tops of trees, hatch the nestlings and ward off the intruder. ¹⁷If they are unable to keep him away, they do what they can to help their young by flying in circles round them in the anguish of love and warning them with their own calls. ¹⁸And why is it necessary to demonstrate sympathy for children by the example of unreasoning animals, ¹⁹since even bees at the time for making honeycombs defend themselves against intruders and, as though with an iron dart, sting those who approach their hive and defend it even to the death? ²⁰But sympathy for her children did not sway the mother of the young men; she was of the same mind as Abraham.

15 O reason of the children, tyrant over the emotions! O piety, more desirable to the mother than her children! ²Two courses were open to this mother, that of piety and that of preserving her seven sons for a time, as the tyrant had promised. ³She loved piety more, the piety that preserves them for eternal life according to God's promise. ⁴In what manner might I express the emotions of parents who love their children? We impress upon the character of a small child a wondrous likeness both of mind and of form. Especially is this true of mothers, who because of their birth pains have a deeper sympathy towards their offspring than do the fathers. ⁵For to the degree that mothers are weaker and the more children they bear, the more they are devoted to their children. ⁶The mother of the seven boys, more than any other mother, loved her children. In seven pregnancies she had implanted in herself tender love towards them, ⁷and because of the many pains she suffered with each of them she had sympathy for them; ⁸yet because of the fear of God she disdained the temporary safety of her children. ⁹Not only so, but also because of the nobility of her sons and their ready obedience to the law she felt a greater tenderness towards them. ¹⁰For they were just and self-controlled and courageous and magnanimous and loved their brothers and their mother, so that they obeyed her even to death in keeping the ordinances. ¹¹Nevertheless, though so many factors influenced the mother to suffer with them out of love for her children, in the case of none of them were the

---
ᵃOr *minds*

various tortures strong enough to pervert her reason. ¹²Instead, the mother urged them on, each child singly and all together, to death for the sake of piety. ¹³O sacred nature and parental love, yearning of parents towards offspring, nurture, and indomitable maternal feelings! ¹⁴This mother, who saw them tortured and burned one by one, for the sake of piety did not change her attitude. ¹⁵She watched the flesh of her children consumed by fire, their toes and fingers scattered*a* on the ground, and the flesh of the head to the chin exposed like masks. ¹⁶O mother, tried now by more bitter pains than even the birth pains you suffered for them! ¹⁷O woman, who alone gave birth to such perfect piety! ¹⁸When the firstborn breathed his last it did not turn you aside, nor when the second in torments looked at you piteously, nor when the third expired; ¹⁹nor did you weep when you looked at the eyes of each one in his tortures gazing boldly at the same agonies and saw in their nostrils signs of the approach of death. ²⁰When you saw the flesh of children burned*b* upon the flesh of other children, severed hands upon hands, detached heads upon heads, and corpses fallen on other corpses, and when you saw the place filled with many spectators of the torturings of your children, you did not shed tears. ²¹Neither the melodies of sirens nor the songs of swans attract the attention of their hearers as did the voices of the children in torture calling to their mother. ²²How great and how many torments the mother then suffered as her sons were tortured on the wheel and with the hot irons! ²³But devout reason, giving her heart a man's courage in the very midst of her emotions, strengthened her to disregard her temporal love for her children.

²⁴Although she witnessed the destruction of seven children and the ingenious and various rackings, this noble mother disregarded all these*c* because of faith in God. ²⁵For as in the council chamber of her own soul she saw mighty advocates—nature, family, parental love, and the instruments awaiting her children—²⁶this mother held two ballots, one bearing death and the other deliverance for her children. ²⁷She did not approve the deliverance that would preserve the seven sons for a short time, ²⁸but as the daughter of God-fearing Abraham she remembered his fortitude.

²⁹O mother of the nation, vindicator of the law and defender of piety, who carried away the prize of the contest in your heart! ³⁰O more noble than males in steadfastness and more manly than men in endurance! ³¹Just as Noah's ark, carrying the world in the universal flood, stoutly endured the waves, ³²so you, O guardian of the law, overwhelmed from every side by the flood and violent winds of your emotions, surrounded by the torture of your sons, endured nobly and withstood the wintry storms that assail piety.

16 If, then, a woman, advanced in years and mother of seven sons, endured seeing her children tortured to death, it must be admitted that devout reason is sovereign over the emotions. ²Thus I have demonstrated not only that men have ruled over the emotions, but also that a woman has despised the fiercest tortures. ³The lions surrounding Daniel were not so savage, nor was the raging fiery furnace of Mishael so intensely hot, as was the innate parental love that inflamed her as she saw her seven sons tortured in such varied ways. ⁴But the mother quenched so many and such great emotions by devout reason.

⁵Consider this also. If this woman, though a mother, had been faint-hearted, she would have mourned over them and perhaps have spoken as follows: ⁶"O how wretched am I and thrice unhappy time after time! After bearing seven children, I am now the mother of none! ⁷O seven childbirths all in vain, seven profitless pregnancies, fruitless nurturings, and wretched nursings! ⁸In vain, my sons, I endured many birth pains for you and the more grievous anxieties of your upbringing. ⁹Alas for my children, some unmarried, others married and without offspring.*d* I shall not see your children or have the happiness of being called grandmother. ¹⁰Alas, I who had so many and beautiful children am a widow and alone, with many sorrows.*e* ¹¹Nor when I die, shall I have any of my sons to bury me."

¹²Yet the sacred and God-fearing mother did not wail with such a lament for any of them, nor did she dissuade any of them from dying, nor did she grieve as they were dying, ¹³but, as though having a mind like adamant and giving rebirth for immortality to the whole number of her sons, she implored them and urged them on to death

---

*a*Or *quivering* *b*Some manuscripts *saw the amputated flesh of children* *c*Some manuscripts *this noble mother having bidden them farewell surrendered them* *d*Greek *benefit* *e*Or *alone, much to be pitied*

for the sake of piety. ¹⁴O mother, soldier of God in the cause of piety, elder and woman!ᵃ By steadfastness you have conquered even a tyrant, and in word and deed you have proved more powerful than a man. ¹⁵For when you and your sons were arrested together, you stood and watched Eleazar being tortured and said to your sons in the Hebrew language, ¹⁶"My sons, noble is the contest to which you are called to bear witness for the nation. Fight zealously for our ancestral law. ¹⁷For it would be shameful if, while an aged man endures such agonies for the sake of piety, you young men were to be terrified by tortures. ¹⁸Remember that it is through God that you have had a share in the world and have enjoyed life, ¹⁹and therefore you ought to endure every suffering for the sake of God. ²⁰For his sake also our father Abraham was zealous to sacrifice his son Isaac, the ancestor of our nation; and when Isaac saw his father's hand wielding a sword and descending upon him, he did not cower. ²¹And Daniel the righteous was thrown to the lions, and Hananiah, Azariah, and Mishael were hurled into the fiery furnace and endured it for the sake of God. ²²You too must have the same faith towards God and not be grieved. ²³It is unreasonable for people who have knowledge of piety not to withstand pain."

²⁴By these words the mother of the seven encouraged and persuaded each of her sons to die rather than violate God's commandment. ²⁵They knew also that those who die for the sake of God live to God, as do Abraham and Isaac and Jacob and all the patriarchs.

17 Some of the guards said that when she also was about to be seized and put to death she threw herself into the flames so that no one might touch her body.

²O mother, who with your seven sons nullified the violence of the tyrant, frustrated his evil designs, and showed the nobility of your faith! ³Nobly set like a roof on the pillars of your sons, you held firm and unswerving against the earthquake of the tortures. ⁴Take courage, therefore, O holy-minded mother, maintaining firm an enduring hope in God. ⁵The moon in heaven, with the stars, does not stand so august as you, who, after lighting the way to piety for your starlike seven sons, stand in honour before God and are firmly set in heaven with them. ⁶For your children were true descendants of father Abraham.ᵇ

THE EFFECT OF THE MARTYRDOMS

⁷If it were permitted for us to paint the history of your piety as an artist might, would not the viewers have shuddered as they saw the mother of the seven children enduring their varied tortures to death for the sake of piety? ⁸Indeed it would be proper to inscribe upon their tomb these words as a reminder to the people of our nation:ᶜ

⁹"Here lie buried an aged priest and an aged woman and seven children, because of the violence of the tyrant who wished to destroy the polity of the Hebrews. ¹⁰They vindicated their nation, looking to God and enduring torture even to death."

¹¹Truly the contest in which they were engaged was divine, ¹²for on that day virtue gave the awards and tested them for their endurance. Victory brought immortality in endless life. ¹³Eleazar was the first contestant, the mother of the seven sons entered the competition, and the brothers contended. ¹⁴The tyrant was the antagonist, and the world and the human race were the spectators. ¹⁵Reverence for God was victor and gave the crown to its own athletes. ¹⁶Who did not admire the athletes of the divineᵈ legislation? Who were not amazed?

¹⁷The tyrant himself and all his council marvelled at theirᵉ endurance, ¹⁸because of which they now stand before the divine throne and live through blessed eternity. ¹⁹For Moses says, "All who are consecrated are under your hands." ²⁰These, then, who have been consecrated for the sake of God,ᶠ are honoured, not only with this honour, but also because of them our enemies did not rule over our nation, ²¹the tyrant was punished, and the homeland purified—they having become, as it were, a ransom for the sin of our nation. ²²And through the blood of those devout ones and their death as a propitiatory offering, divine providence preserved Israel that previously had been afflicted.

²³For the tyrant Antiochus, when he saw the courage of their virtue and their endurance under the tortures, proclaimed the endurance of these people to his soldiers as an example, ²⁴and this made them noble and

---

ᵃOne manuscript O Mother—for the sake of piety towards God indeed the mother of a pious army—soldier, elder, and woman! ᵇGreek For your childbearing was from Abraham the father; some manuscripts For your children were true descendants of Abraham the servant. ᶜOr as a memorial to the heroes of our people ᵈSome manuscripts true ᵉSome manuscripts add virtue and ᶠSome manuscripts omit for the sake of God

courageous for infantry battle and siege, and he ravaged and conquered all his enemies.

18 O Israelite children, offspring of the seed of Abraham, obey this law and exercise piety in every way, ²knowing that devout reason is master of the emotions, not only of sufferings from within, but also of those from without.

³Therefore those who gave over their bodies in suffering for the sake of piety were not only admired by human beings, but also were deemed worthy to share in a divine inheritance. ⁴Because of them the nation gained peace, and by reviving observance of the law in the homeland they ravaged the enemy. ⁵The tyrant Antiochus was both punished on earth and is being chastised after his death. Since in no way whatever was he able to compel the Israelites to adopt foreign customs and to abandon their ancestral customs, he left Jerusalem and marched against the Persians.

THE MOTHER'S ADDRESS TO HER CHILDREN

⁶The mother of the seven sons expressed also these principles to her children: ⁷"I was a pure virgin and did not go outside my father's house; but I guarded the rib from which woman was made.ᵃ ⁸No seducer corrupted me on a desert plain, nor did the destroyer, the deceitful serpent, defile the purity of my virginity. ⁹In the time of my maturity I remained with my husband, and when these sons had grown up their father died. He was blessed to have lived out his life with good children and not have the grief of bereavement. ¹⁰While he was still with you, he taught you the Law and the Prophets. ¹¹He read to you about Abel slain by Cain and about Isaac who was offered as a whole burnt offering and about Joseph in prison. ¹²He told you of the zeal of Phineas, and he taught you about Hananiah, Azariah, and Mishael in the fire. ¹³He praised Daniel in the den of the lions and blessed him. ¹⁴He reminded you of the Scripture of Isaiah, which says, 'Even though you go through the fire, the flame shall not consume you.' ¹⁵He sang to you songs of the psalmist David, who said, 'Many are the afflictions of the righteous.' ¹⁶He recounted to you Solomon's proverb, 'Thereᵇ is a tree of life for those who do his will.' ¹⁷He confirmed the saying of Ezekiel, 'Shall these dry bones live?' ¹⁸For he did not forget to teach you the song that Moses taught, which says, ¹⁹'I kill and I make alive: this is your life and the length of your days.'"

²⁰O bitter was that day—and yet not bitter—when that bitter tyrant of the Greeks quenched fire with fire in his cruel cauldrons and in his burning rage brought those seven sons of the daughter of Abraham to the catapult and back again to moreᶜ tortures, ²¹pierced the pupils of their eyes and cut out their tongues and put them to death with various tortures. ²²For these crimes divine justice pursued and will pursue the accursed tyrant. ²³But the sons of Abraham with their victorious mother are gathered together intoᵈ the chorus of the fathers and have received pure and immortalᵉ souls from God, ²⁴to whom be glory for ever and ever. Amen.

ᵃGreek *the rib that was built*; compare Genesis 2:22   ᵇOr *He*
ᶜSome manuscripts *to all his*   ᵈOne manuscript *are being nobly proclaimed to*   ᵉSome manuscripts *victorious*

THE NEW TESTAMENT

THE GOSPEL ACCORDING TO
MATTHEW

THE GENEALOGY OF JESUS CHRIST

1 The book of the genealogy of Jesus Christ, the son of David, the son of Abraham. ²Abraham was the father of Isaac, and Isaac the father of Jacob, and Jacob the father of Judah and his brothers, ³and Judah the father of Perez and Zerah by Tamar, and Perez the father of Hezron, and Hezron the father of Ram,[a] ⁴and Ram the father of Amminadab, and Amminadab the father of Nahshon, and Nahshon the father of Salmon, ⁵and Salmon the father of Boaz by Rahab, and Boaz the father of Obed by Ruth, and Obed the father of Jesse, ⁶and Jesse the father of David the king.

And David was the father of Solomon by the wife of Uriah, ⁷and Solomon the father of Rehoboam, and Rehoboam the father of Abijah, and Abijah the father of Asaph,[b] ⁸and Asaph the father of Jehoshaphat, and Jehoshaphat the father of Joram, and Joram the father of Uzziah, ⁹and Uzziah the father of Jotham, and Jotham the father of Ahaz, and Ahaz the father of Hezekiah, ¹⁰and Hezekiah the father of Manasseh, and Manasseh the father of Amos,[c] and Amos the father of Josiah, ¹¹and Josiah the father of Jechoniah and his brothers, at the time of the deportation to Babylon.

¹²And after the deportation to Babylon: Jechoniah was the father of Shealtiel,[d] and Shealtiel the father of Zerubbabel, ¹³and Zerubbabel the father of Abiud, and Abiud the father of Eliakim, and Eliakim the father of Azor, ¹⁴and Azor the father of Zadok, and Zadok the father of Achim, and Achim the father of Eliud, ¹⁵and Eliud the father of Eleazar, and Eleazar the father of Matthan, and Matthan the father of Jacob, ¹⁶and Jacob the father of Joseph the husband of Mary, of whom Jesus was born, who is called Christ.

¹⁷So all the generations from Abraham to David were fourteen generations, and from David to the deportation to Babylon fourteen generations, and from the deportation to Babylon to the Christ fourteen generations.

THE BIRTH OF JESUS CHRIST

¹⁸Now the birth of Jesus Christ[e] took place in this way. When his mother Mary had been betrothed[f] to Joseph, before they came together she was found to be with child from the Holy Spirit. ¹⁹And her husband Joseph, being a just man and unwilling to put her to shame, resolved to divorce her quietly. ²⁰But as he considered these things, behold, an angel of the Lord appeared to him in a dream, saying, "Joseph, son of David, do not fear to take Mary as your wife, for that which is conceived in her is from the Holy Spirit. ²¹She will bear a son, and you shall call his name Jesus, for he will save his people from their sins." ²²All this took place to fulfil what the Lord had spoken by the prophet:

²³ "Behold, the virgin shall conceive
       and bear a son,
   and they shall call his
       name Immanuel"

(which means, God with us). ²⁴When Joseph woke from sleep, he did as the angel of the Lord commanded him: he took his wife, ²⁵but knew her not until she had given birth to a son. And he called his name Jesus.

THE VISIT OF THE WISE MEN

2 Now after Jesus was born in Bethlehem of Judea in the days of Herod the king, behold, wise men[g] from the east came to Jerusalem, ²saying, "Where is he who has been born king of the Jews? For we saw his star when it rose[h] and have come to worship him." ³When Herod the king heard this, he was troubled, and all Jerusalem with him; ⁴and assembling all the chief priests and scribes of the people, he enquired of them where the Christ was to be born. ⁵They told

---

[a]Greek *Aram*; also verse 4 [b]*Asaph* is probably an alternate spelling of *Asa*; some manuscripts *Asa*; also verse 8 [c]*Amos* is probably an alternate spelling of *Amon*; some manuscripts *Amon*; twice in this verse [d]Greek *Salathiel*; twice in this verse [e]Some manuscripts *of the Christ* [f]That is, legally pledged to be married [g]Greek *magi*; also verses 7, 16 [h]Or *in the east*; also verse 9

him, "In Bethlehem of Judea, for so it is written by the prophet:

⁶ "'And you, O Bethlehem, in the land
of Judah,
are by no means least among
the rulers of Judah;
for from you shall come a ruler
who will shepherd my
people Israel.'"

⁷Then Herod summoned the wise men secretly and ascertained from them what time the star had appeared. ⁸And he sent them to Bethlehem, saying, "Go and search diligently for the child, and when you have found him, bring me word, that I too may come and worship him." ⁹After listening to the king, they went on their way. And behold, the star that they had seen when it rose went before them until it came to rest over the place where the child was. ¹⁰When they saw the star, they rejoiced exceedingly with great joy. ¹¹And going into the house, they saw the child with Mary his mother, and they fell down and worshipped him. Then, opening their treasures, they offered him gifts, gold and frankincense and myrrh. ¹²And being warned in a dream not to return to Herod, they departed to their own country by another way.

THE FLIGHT TO EGYPT

¹³Now when they had departed, behold, an angel of the Lord appeared to Joseph in a dream and said, "Rise, take the child and his mother, and flee to Egypt, and remain there until I tell you, for Herod is about to search for the child, to destroy him." ¹⁴And he rose and took the child and his mother by night and departed to Egypt ¹⁵and remained there until the death of Herod. This was to fulfil what the Lord had spoken by the prophet, "Out of Egypt I called my son."

HEROD KILLS THE CHILDREN

¹⁶Then Herod, when he saw that he had been tricked by the wise men, became furious, and he sent and killed all the male children in Bethlehem and in all that region who were two years old or under, according to the time that he had ascertained from the wise men. ¹⁷Then was fulfilled what was spoken by the prophet Jeremiah:

¹⁸ "A voice was heard in Ramah,
weeping and loud lamentation,
Rachel weeping for her children;
she refused to be comforted,
because they are no more."

THE RETURN TO NAZARETH

¹⁹But when Herod died, behold, an angel of the Lord appeared in a dream to Joseph in Egypt, ²⁰saying, "Rise, take the child and his mother and go to the land of Israel, for those who sought the child's life are dead." ²¹And he rose and took the child and his mother and went to the land of Israel. ²²But when he heard that Archelaus was reigning over Judea in place of his father Herod, he was afraid to go there, and being warned in a dream he withdrew to the district of Galilee. ²³And he went and lived in a city called Nazareth, so that what was spoken by the prophets might be fulfilled, that he would be called a Nazarene.

JOHN THE BAPTIST PREPARES THE WAY

3 In those days John the Baptist came preaching in the wilderness of Judea, ²"Repent, for the kingdom of heaven is at hand."ᵃ ³For this is he who was spoken of by the prophet Isaiah when he said,

"The voice of one crying in
the wilderness:
'Prepareᵇ the way of the Lord;
make his paths straight.'"

⁴Now John wore a garment of camel's hair and a leather belt round his waist, and his food was locusts and wild honey. ⁵Then Jerusalem and all Judea and all the region about the Jordan were going out to him, ⁶and they were baptized by him in the river Jordan, confessing their sins.

⁷But when he saw many of the Pharisees and Sadducees coming to his baptism, he said to them, "You brood of vipers! Who warned you to flee from the wrath to come? ⁸Bear fruit in keeping with repentance. ⁹And do not presume to say to yourselves, 'We have Abraham as our father', for I tell you, God is able from these stones to raise up children for Abraham. ¹⁰Even now the axe is laid to the root of the trees. Every tree therefore that does not bear good fruit is cut down and thrown into the fire.

¹¹"I baptize you with water for repentance, but he who is coming after me is mightier

---

ᵃOr the kingdom of heaven has come near   ᵇOr crying: Prepare in the wilderness

than I, whose sandals I am not worthy to carry. He will baptize you with the Holy Spirit and fire. ¹²His winnowing fork is in his hand, and he will clear his threshing floor and gather his wheat into the barn, but the chaff he will burn with unquenchable fire."

THE BAPTISM OF JESUS

¹³Then Jesus came from Galilee to the Jordan to John, to be baptized by him. ¹⁴John would have prevented him, saying, "I need to be baptized by you, and do you come to me?" ¹⁵But Jesus answered him, "Let it be so now, for thus it is fitting for us to fulfil all righteousness." Then he consented. ¹⁶And when Jesus was baptized, immediately he went up from the water, and behold, the heavens were opened to him,ᵃ and he saw the Spirit of God descending like a dove and coming to rest on him; ¹⁷and behold, a voice from heaven said, "This is my beloved Son,ᵇ with whom I am well pleased."

THE TEMPTATION OF JESUS

4 Then Jesus was led up by the Spirit into the wilderness to be tempted by the devil. ²And after fasting forty days and forty nights, he was hungry. ³And the tempter came and said to him, "If you are the Son of God, command these stones to become loaves of bread." ⁴But he answered, "It is written,

"'Man shall not live by bread alone,
    but by every word that comes
        from the mouth of God.'"

⁵Then the devil took him to the holy city and set him on the pinnacle of the temple ⁶and said to him, "If you are the Son of God, throw yourself down, for it is written,

"'He will command his angels
    concerning you',

and

"'On their hands they will bear you up,
    lest you strike your foot
        against a stone.'"

⁷Jesus said to him, "Again it is written, 'You shall not put the Lord your God to the test.'" ⁸Again, the devil took him to a very high mountain and showed him all the kingdoms of the world and their glory. ⁹And he said to him, "All these I will give you, if you will fall down and worship me." ¹⁰Then Jesus said to him, "Be gone, Satan! For it is written,

"'You shall worship the Lord your God
    and him only shall you serve.'"

¹¹Then the devil left him, and behold, angels came and were ministering to him.

JESUS BEGINS HIS MINISTRY

¹²Now when he heard that John had been arrested, he withdrew into Galilee. ¹³And leaving Nazareth he went and lived in Capernaum by the sea, in the territory of Zebulun and Naphtali, ¹⁴so that what was spoken by the prophet Isaiah might be fulfilled:

¹⁵   "The land of Zebulun and the
            land of Naphtali,
    the way of the sea, beyond the
        Jordan, Galilee of the Gentiles—
¹⁶   the people dwelling in darkness
        have seen a great light,
    and for those dwelling in the
        region and shadow of death,
    on them a light has dawned."

¹⁷From that time Jesus began to preach, saying, "Repent, for the kingdom of heaven is at hand."ᶜ

JESUS CALLS THE FIRST DISCIPLES

¹⁸While walking by the Sea of Galilee, he saw two brothers, Simon (who is called Peter) and Andrew his brother, casting a net into the sea, for they were fishermen. ¹⁹And he said to them, "Follow me, and I will make you fishers of men."ᵈ ²⁰Immediately they left their nets and followed him. ²¹And going on from there he saw two other brothers, James the son of Zebedee and John his brother, in the boat with Zebedee their father, mending their nets, and he called them. ²²Immediately they left the boat and their father and followed him.

JESUS MINISTERS TO GREAT CROWDS

²³And he went throughout all Galilee, teaching in their synagogues and proclaiming the gospel of the kingdom and healing every disease and every affliction among

---

ᵃSome manuscripts omit *to him* ᵇOr *my Son, my* (or *the*) *Beloved*
ᶜOr *the kingdom of heaven has come near* ᵈThe Greek word *anthropoi* refers here to both men and women

the people. ²⁴So his fame spread throughout all Syria, and they brought him all the sick, those afflicted with various diseases and pains, those oppressed by demons, those having seizures, and paralytics, and he healed them. ²⁵And great crowds followed him from Galilee and the Decapolis, and from Jerusalem and Judea, and from beyond the Jordan.

THE SERMON ON THE MOUNT

5 Seeing the crowds, he went up on the mountain, and when he sat down, his disciples came to him.

THE BEATITUDES

²And he opened his mouth and taught them, saying:

³"Blessed are the poor in spirit, for theirs is the kingdom of heaven.

⁴"Blessed are those who mourn, for they shall be comforted.

⁵"Blessed are the meek, for they shall inherit the earth.

⁶"Blessed are those who hunger and thirst for righteousness, for they shall be satisfied.

⁷"Blessed are the merciful, for they shall receive mercy.

⁸"Blessed are the pure in heart, for they shall see God.

⁹"Blessed are the peacemakers, for they shall be called sons[a] of God.

¹⁰"Blessed are those who are persecuted for righteousness' sake, for theirs is the kingdom of heaven.

¹¹"Blessed are you when others revile you and persecute you and utter all kinds of evil against you falsely on my account. ¹²Rejoice and be glad, for your reward is great in heaven, for so they persecuted the prophets who were before you.

SALT AND LIGHT

¹³"You are the salt of the earth, but if salt has lost its taste, how shall its saltiness be restored? It is no longer good for anything except to be thrown out and trampled under people's feet.

¹⁴"You are the light of the world. A city set on a hill cannot be hidden. ¹⁵Nor do people light a lamp and put it under a basket, but on a stand, and it gives light to all in the house. ¹⁶In the same way, let your light shine before others, so that[b] they may see your good works and give glory to your Father who is in heaven.

CHRIST CAME TO FULFIL THE LAW

¹⁷"Do not think that I have come to abolish the Law or the Prophets; I have not come to abolish them but to fulfil them. ¹⁸For truly, I say to you, until heaven and earth pass away, not an iota, not a dot, will pass from the Law until all is accomplished. ¹⁹Therefore whoever relaxes one of the least of these commandments and teaches others to do the same will be called least in the kingdom of heaven, but whoever does them and teaches them will be called great in the kingdom of heaven. ²⁰For I tell you, unless your righteousness exceeds that of the scribes and Pharisees, you will never enter the kingdom of heaven.

ANGER

²¹"You have heard that it was said to those of old, 'You shall not murder; and whoever murders will be liable to judgement.' ²²But I say to you that everyone who is angry with his brother[c] will be liable to judgement; whoever insults[d] his brother will be liable to the council; and whoever says, 'You fool!' will be liable to the hell[e] of fire. ²³So if you are offering your gift at the altar and there remember that your brother has something against you, ²⁴leave your gift there before the altar and go. First be reconciled to your brother, and then come and offer your gift. ²⁵Come to terms quickly with your accuser while you are going with him to court, lest your accuser hand you over to the judge, and the judge to the guard, and you be put in prison. ²⁶Truly, I say to you, you will never get out until you have paid the last penny.[f]

LUST

²⁷"You have heard that it was said, 'You shall not commit adultery.' ²⁸But I say to you that everyone who looks at a woman with lustful intent has already committed adultery with her in his heart. ²⁹If your right eye causes you to sin, tear it out and throw it away. For it is better that you lose one of your members than that your whole body be thrown into hell. ³⁰And if your right hand causes you to sin, cut it off and throw it away. For it is better that you lose one of your members than that your whole body go into hell.

---

[a] Greek *huioi*; see Preface [b] Or *house. ¹⁶Let your light so shine before others that* [c] Some manuscripts insert *without cause* [d] Greek says *Raca* to (a term of abuse) [e] Greek *Gehenna*; also verses 29, 30 [f] Greek *kodrantes*, Roman copper coin (Latin *quadrans*) worth about 1/64 of a *denarius* (which was a day's wage for a labourer)

DIVORCE

31"It was also said, 'Whoever divorces his wife, let him give her a certificate of divorce.' 32But I say to you that everyone who divorces his wife, except on the ground of sexual immorality, makes her commit adultery, and whoever marries a divorced woman commits adultery.

OATHS

33"Again you have heard that it was said to those of old, 'You shall not swear falsely, but shall perform to the Lord what you have sworn.' 34But I say to you, Do not take an oath at all, either by heaven, for it is the throne of God, 35or by the earth, for it is his footstool, or by Jerusalem, for it is the city of the great King. 36And do not take an oath by your head, for you cannot make one hair white or black. 37Let what you say be simply 'Yes' or 'No'; anything more than this comes from evil.[a]

RETALIATION

38"You have heard that it was said, 'An eye for an eye and a tooth for a tooth.' 39But I say to you, Do not resist the one who is evil. But if anyone slaps you on the right cheek, turn to him the other also. 40And if anyone would sue you and take your tunic,[b] let him have your cloak as well. 41And if anyone forces you to go one mile, go with him two miles. 42Give to the one who begs from you, and do not refuse the one who would borrow from you.

LOVE YOUR ENEMIES

43"You have heard that it was said, 'You shall love your neighbour and hate your enemy.' 44But I say to you, Love your enemies and pray for those who persecute you, 45so that you may be sons of your Father who is in heaven. For he makes his sun rise on the evil and on the good, and sends rain on the just and on the unjust. 46For if you love those who love you, what reward do you have? Do not even the tax collectors do the same? 47And if you greet only your brothers,[c] what more are you doing than others? Do not even the Gentiles do the same? 48You therefore must be perfect, as your heavenly Father is perfect.

GIVING TO THE NEEDY

6 "Beware of practising your righteousness before other people in order to be seen by them, for then you will have no reward from your Father who is in heaven.

2"Thus, when you give to the needy, sound no trumpet before you, as the hypocrites do in the synagogues and in the streets, that they may be praised by others. Truly, I say to you, they have received their reward. 3But when you give to the needy, do not let your left hand know what your right hand is doing, 4so that your giving may be in secret. And your Father who sees in secret will reward you.

THE LORD'S PRAYER

5"And when you pray, you must not be like the hypocrites. For they love to stand and pray in the synagogues and at the street corners, that they may be seen by others. Truly, I say to you, they have received their reward. 6But when you pray, go into your room and shut the door and pray to your Father who is in secret. And your Father who sees in secret will reward you.

7"And when you pray, do not heap up empty phrases as the Gentiles do, for they think that they will be heard for their many words. 8Do not be like them, for your Father knows what you need before you ask him. 9Pray then like this:

"Our Father in heaven,
    hallowed be your name.[d]
10 Your kingdom come,
    your will be done,[e]
    on earth as it is in heaven.
11 Give us this day our daily bread,[f]
12 and forgive us our debts,
    as we also have forgiven our debtors.
13 And lead us not into temptation,
    but deliver us from evil.[g]

14For if you forgive others their trespasses, your heavenly Father will also forgive you, 15but if you do not forgive others their trespasses, neither will your Father forgive your trespasses.

FASTING

16"And when you fast, do not look gloomy like the hypocrites, for they disfigure their faces that their fasting may be seen by others.

---

[a]Or *the evil one* [b]Greek *chiton*, a long garment worn under the cloak next to the skin [c]Or *brothers and sisters*. In New Testament usage, depending on the context, the plural Greek word *adelphoi* (translated "brothers") may refer either to *brothers* or to *brothers and sisters* [d]Or *Let your name be kept holy*, or *Let your name be treated with reverence* [e]Or *Let your kingdom come, let your will be done* [f]Or *our bread for tomorrow* [g]Or *the evil one*; some manuscripts add *For yours is the kingdom and the power and the glory, for ever. Amen*

MATTHEW 6-7

Truly, I say to you, they have received their reward. **17**But when you fast, anoint your head and wash your face, **18**that your fasting may not be seen by others but by your Father who is in secret. And your Father who sees in secret will reward you.

LAY UP TREASURES IN HEAVEN

19"Do not lay up for yourselves treasures on earth, where moth and rust^a destroy and where thieves break in and steal, **20**but lay up for yourselves treasures in heaven, where neither moth nor rust destroys and where thieves do not break in and steal. **21**For where your treasure is, there your heart will be also.

22"The eye is the lamp of the body. So, if your eye is healthy, your whole body will be full of light, **23**but if your eye is bad, your whole body will be full of darkness. If then the light in you is darkness, how great is the darkness!

24"No one can serve two masters, for either he will hate the one and love the other, or he will be devoted to the one and despise the other. You cannot serve God and money.^{b}

DO NOT BE ANXIOUS

25"Therefore I tell you, do not be anxious about your life, what you will eat or what you will drink, nor about your body, what you will put on. Is not life more than food, and the body more than clothing? **26**Look at the birds of the air: they neither sow nor reap nor gather into barns, and yet your heavenly Father feeds them. Are you not of more value than they? **27**And which of you by being anxious can add a single hour to his span of life?^{c} **28**And why are you anxious about clothing? Consider the lilies of the field, how they grow: they neither toil nor spin, **29**yet I tell you, even Solomon in all his glory was not arrayed like one of these. **30**But if God so clothes the grass of the field, which today is alive and tomorrow is thrown into the oven, will he not much more clothe you, O you of little faith? **31**Therefore do not be anxious, saying, 'What shall we eat?' or 'What shall we drink?' or 'What shall we wear?' **32**For the Gentiles seek after all these things, and your heavenly Father knows that you need them all. **33**But seek first the kingdom of God and his righteousness, and all these things will be added to you.

34"Therefore do not be anxious about tomorrow, for tomorrow will be anxious for itself. Sufficient for the day is its own trouble.

JUDGING OTHERS

7 "Judge not, that you be not judged. **2**For with the judgement you pronounce you will be judged, and with the measure you use it will be measured to you. **3**Why do you see the speck that is in your brother's eye, but do not notice the log that is in your own eye? **4**Or how can you say to your brother, 'Let me take the speck out of your eye', when there is the log in your own eye? **5**You hypocrite, first take the log out of your own eye, and then you will see clearly to take the speck out of your brother's eye.

6"Do not give dogs what is holy, and do not throw your pearls before pigs, lest they trample them underfoot and turn to attack you.

ASK, AND IT WILL BE GIVEN

7"Ask, and it will be given to you; seek, and you will find; knock, and it will be opened to you. **8**For everyone who asks receives, and the one who seeks finds, and to the one who knocks it will be opened. **9**Or which one of you, if his son asks him for bread, will give him a stone? **10**Or if he asks for a fish, will give him a serpent? **11**If you then, who are evil, know how to give good gifts to your children, how much more will your Father who is in heaven give good things to those who ask him!

THE GOLDEN RULE

12"So whatever you wish that others would do to you, do also to them, for this is the Law and the Prophets.

13"Enter by the narrow gate. For the gate is wide and the way is easy^d that leads to destruction, and those who enter by it are many. **14**For the gate is narrow and the way is hard that leads to life, and those who find it are few.

A TREE AND ITS FRUIT

15"Beware of false prophets, who come to you in sheep's clothing but inwardly are ravenous wolves. **16**You will recognize them by their fruits. Are grapes gathered from thorn bushes, or figs from thorn bushes? **17**So, every healthy tree bears good fruit, but the diseased tree bears bad fruit. **18**A healthy tree cannot bear bad fruit, nor can a diseased tree bear good fruit. **19**Every tree that does

---

^{a}Or *worm*; also verse 20 ^{b}Greek *mammon*, a Semitic word for money or possessions ^{c}Or *a single cubit to his stature*; a cubit was about 18 inches or 45 centimetres ^{d}Some manuscripts *For the way is wide and easy*

I NEVER KNEW YOU

²¹"Not everyone who says to me, 'Lord, Lord', will enter the kingdom of heaven, but the one who does the will of my Father who is in heaven. ²²On that day many will say to me, 'Lord, Lord, did we not prophesy in your name, and cast out demons in your name, and do many mighty works in your name?' ²³And then will I declare to them, 'I never knew you; depart from me, you workers of lawlessness.'

BUILD YOUR HOUSE ON THE ROCK

²⁴"Everyone then who hears these words of mine and does them will be like a wise man who built his house on the rock. ²⁵And the rain fell, and the floods came, and the winds blew and beat on that house, but it did not fall, because it had been founded on the rock. ²⁶And everyone who hears these words of mine and does not do them will be like a foolish man who built his house on the sand. ²⁷And the rain fell, and the floods came, and the winds blew and beat against that house, and it fell, and great was the fall of it."

THE AUTHORITY OF JESUS

²⁸And when Jesus finished these sayings, the crowds were astonished at his teaching, ²⁹for he was teaching them as one who had authority, and not as their scribes.

JESUS CLEANSES A LEPER

8 When he came down from the mountain, great crowds followed him. ²And behold, a leper[a] came to him and knelt before him, saying, "Lord, if you will, you can make me clean." ³And Jesus[b] stretched out his hand and touched him, saying, "I will; be clean." And immediately his leprosy was cleansed. ⁴And Jesus said to him, "See that you say nothing to anyone, but go, show yourself to the priest and offer the gift that Moses commanded, for a proof to them."

THE FAITH OF A CENTURION

⁵When he had entered Capernaum, a centurion came forward to him, appealing to him, ⁶"Lord, my servant is lying paralysed at home, suffering terribly." ⁷And he said to him, "I will come and heal him." ⁸But the centurion replied, "Lord, I am not worthy to have you come under my roof, but only say the word, and my servant will be healed. ⁹For I too am a man under authority, with soldiers under me. And I say to one, 'Go', and he goes, and to another, 'Come', and he comes, and to my servant,[c] 'Do this', and he does it." ¹⁰When Jesus heard this, he marvelled and said to those who followed him, "Truly, I tell you, with no one in Israel[d] have I found such faith. ¹¹I tell you, many will come from east and west and recline at table with Abraham, Isaac, and Jacob in the kingdom of heaven, ¹²while the sons of the kingdom will be thrown into the outer darkness. In that place there will be weeping and gnashing of teeth." ¹³And to the centurion Jesus said, "Go; let it be done for you as you have believed." And the servant was healed at that very moment.

JESUS HEALS MANY

¹⁴And when Jesus entered Peter's house, he saw his mother-in-law lying sick with a fever. ¹⁵He touched her hand, and the fever left her, and she rose and began to serve him. ¹⁶That evening they brought to him many who were oppressed by demons, and he cast out the spirits with a word and healed all who were sick. ¹⁷This was to fulfil what was spoken by the prophet Isaiah: "He took our illnesses and bore our diseases."

THE COST OF FOLLOWING JESUS

¹⁸Now when Jesus saw a crowd around him, he gave orders to go over to the other side. ¹⁹And a scribe came up and said to him, "Teacher, I will follow you wherever you go." ²⁰And Jesus said to him, "Foxes have holes, and birds of the air have nests, but the Son of Man has nowhere to lay his head." ²¹Another of the disciples said to him, "Lord, let me first go and bury my father." ²²And Jesus said to him, "Follow me, and leave the dead to bury their own dead."

JESUS CALMS A STORM

²³And when he got into the boat, his disciples followed him. ²⁴And behold, there arose a great storm on the sea, so that the boat was being swamped by the waves; but he was asleep. ²⁵And they went and woke him, saying, "Save us, Lord; we are perishing." ²⁶And he said to them, "Why are you

---

[a] Leprosy was a term for several skin diseases; see Leviticus 13
[b] Greek he [c] Or bondservant [d] Some manuscripts not even in Israel

afraid, O you of little faith?" Then he rose and rebuked the winds and the sea, and there was a great calm. ²⁷And the men marvelled, saying, "What sort of man is this, that even winds and sea obey him?"

JESUS HEALS TWO MEN WITH DEMONS

²⁸And when he came to the other side, to the country of the Gadarenes,ᵃ two demon-possessedᵇ men met him, coming out of the tombs, so fierce that no one could pass that way. ²⁹And behold, they cried out, "What have you to do with us, O Son of God? Have you come here to torment us before the time?" ³⁰Now a herd of many pigs was feeding at some distance from them. ³¹And the demons begged him, saying, "If you cast us out, send us away into the herd of pigs." ³²And he said to them, "Go." So they came out and went into the pigs, and behold, the whole herd rushed down the steep bank into the sea and drowned in the waters. ³³The herdsmen fled, and going into the city they told everything, especially what had happened to the demon-possessed men. ³⁴And behold, all the city came out to meet Jesus, and when they saw him, they begged him to leave their region.

JESUS HEALS A PARALYTIC

9 And getting into a boat he crossed over and came to his own city. ²And behold, some people brought to him a paralytic, lying on a bed. And when Jesus saw their faith, he said to the paralytic, "Take heart, my son; your sins are forgiven." ³And behold, some of the scribes said to themselves, "This man is blaspheming." ⁴But Jesus, knowingᶜ their thoughts, said, "Why do you think evil in your hearts? ⁵For which is easier, to say, 'Your sins are forgiven,' or to say, 'Rise and walk'? ⁶But that you may know that the Son of Man has authority on earth to forgive sins"— he then said to the paralytic—"Rise, pick up your bed and go home." ⁷And he rose and went home. ⁸When the crowds saw it, they were afraid, and they glorified God, who had given such authority to men.

JESUS CALLS MATTHEW

⁹As Jesus passed on from there, he saw a man called Matthew sitting at the tax booth, and he said to him, "Follow me." And he rose and followed him.

¹⁰And as Jesusᵈ reclined at table in the house, behold, many tax collectors and sinners came and were reclining with Jesus and his disciples. ¹¹And when the Pharisees saw this, they said to his disciples, "Why does your teacher eat with tax collectors and sinners?" ¹²But when he heard it, he said, "Those who are well have no need of a physician, but those who are sick. ¹³Go and learn what this means: 'I desire mercy, and not sacrifice.' For I came not to call the righteous, but sinners."

A QUESTION ABOUT FASTING

¹⁴Then the disciples of John came to him, saying, "Why do we and the Pharisees fast,ᵉ but your disciples do not fast?" ¹⁵And Jesus said to them, "Can the wedding guests mourn as long as the bridegroom is with them? The days will come when the bridegroom is taken away from them, and then they will fast. ¹⁶No one puts a piece of unshrunk cloth on an old garment, for the patch tears away from the garment, and a worse tear is made. ¹⁷Neither is new wine put into old wineskins. If it is, the skins burst and the wine is spilled and the skins are destroyed. But new wine is put into fresh wineskins, and so both are preserved."

A GIRL RESTORED TO LIFE AND A WOMAN HEALED

¹⁸While he was saying these things to them, behold, a ruler came in and knelt before him, saying, "My daughter has just died, but come and lay your hand on her, and she will live." ¹⁹And Jesus rose and followed him, with his disciples. ²⁰And behold, a woman who had suffered from a discharge of blood for twelve years came up behind him and touched the fringe of his garment, ²¹for she said to herself, "If I only touch his garment, I will be made well." ²²Jesus turned, and seeing her he said, "Take heart, daughter; your faith has made you well." And instantlyᶠ the woman was made well. ²³And when Jesus came to the ruler's house and saw the flute players and the crowd making a commotion, ²⁴he said, "Go away, for the girl is not dead but sleeping." And they laughed at him. ²⁵But when the crowd had been put outside, he went in and took her by the hand, and the girl arose. ²⁶And the report of this went through all that district.

ᵃSome manuscripts Gergesenes; some Gerasenes ᵇGreek daimonizomai (demonized); also verse 33; elsewhere rendered oppressed by demons ᶜSome manuscripts perceiving ᵈGreek he ᵉSome manuscripts add much, or often ᶠGreek from that hour

JESUS HEALS TWO BLIND MEN

²⁷And as Jesus passed on from there, two blind men followed him, crying aloud, "Have mercy on us, Son of David." ²⁸When he entered the house, the blind men came to him, and Jesus said to them, "Do you believe that I am able to do this?" They said to him, "Yes, Lord." ²⁹Then he touched their eyes, saying, "According to your faith be it done to you." ³⁰And their eyes were opened. And Jesus sternly warned them, "See that no one knows about it." ³¹But they went away and spread his fame through all that district.

JESUS HEALS A MAN UNABLE TO SPEAK

³²As they were going away, behold, a demon-oppressed man who was mute was brought to him. ³³And when the demon had been cast out, the mute man spoke. And the crowds marvelled, saying, "Never was anything like this seen in Israel." ³⁴But the Pharisees said, "He casts out demons by the prince of demons."

THE HARVEST IS PLENTIFUL, THE LABOURERS FEW

³⁵And Jesus went throughout all the cities and villages, teaching in their synagogues and proclaiming the gospel of the kingdom and healing every disease and every affliction. ³⁶When he saw the crowds, he had compassion for them, because they were harassed and helpless, like sheep without a shepherd. ³⁷Then he said to his disciples, "The harvest is plentiful, but the labourers are few; ³⁸therefore pray earnestly to the Lord of the harvest to send out labourers into his harvest."

THE TWELVE APOSTLES

10 And he called to him his twelve disciples and gave them authority over unclean spirits, to cast them out, and to heal every disease and every affliction. ²The names of the twelve apostles are these: first, Simon, who is called Peter, and Andrew his brother; James the son of Zebedee, and John his brother; ³Philip and Bartholomew; Thomas and Matthew the tax collector; James the son of Alphaeus, and Thaddaeus;ᵃ ⁴Simon the Zealot,ᵇ and Judas Iscariot, who betrayed him.

JESUS SENDS OUT THE TWELVE APOSTLES

⁵These twelve Jesus sent out, instructing them, "Go nowhere among the Gentiles and enter no town of the Samaritans, ⁶but go rather to the lost sheep of the house of Israel. ⁷And proclaim as you go, saying, 'The kingdom of heaven is at hand.'ᶜ ⁸Heal the sick, raise the dead, cleanse lepers,ᵈ cast out demons. You received without paying; give without pay. ⁹Acquire no gold or silver or copper for your belts, ¹⁰no bag for your journey, or two tunicsᵉ or sandals or a staff, for the labourer deserves his food. ¹¹And whatever town or village you enter, find out who is worthy in it and stay there until you depart. ¹²As you enter the house, greet it. ¹³And if the house is worthy, let your peace come upon it, but if it is not worthy, let your peace return to you. ¹⁴And if anyone will not receive you or listen to your words, shake off the dust from your feet when you leave that house or town. ¹⁵Truly, I say to you, it will be more bearable on the day of judgement for the land of Sodom and Gomorrah than for that town.

PERSECUTION WILL COME

¹⁶"Behold, I am sending you out as sheep in the midst of wolves, so be wise as serpents and innocent as doves. ¹⁷Beware of men, for they will deliver you over to courts and flog you in their synagogues, ¹⁸and you will be dragged before governors and kings for my sake, to bear witness before them and the Gentiles. ¹⁹When they deliver you over, do not be anxious how you are to speak or what you are to say, for what you are to say will be given to you in that hour. ²⁰For it is not you who speak, but the Spirit of your Father speaking through you. ²¹Brother will deliver brother over to death, and the father his child, and children will rise against parents and have them put to death, ²²and you will be hated by all for my name's sake. But the one who endures to the end will be saved. ²³When they persecute you in one town, flee to the next, for truly, I say to you, you will not have gone through all the towns of Israel before the Son of Man comes.

²⁴"A disciple is not above his teacher, nor a servantᶠ above his master. ²⁵It is enough for the disciple to be like his teacher, and the servant like his master. If they have called the master of the house Beelzebul, how much more will they malignᵍ those of his household.

ᵃSome manuscripts *Lebbaeus*, or *Lebbaeus called Thaddaeus* ᵇGreek *kananaios*, meaning *zealot* ᶜOr *The kingdom of heaven has come near* ᵈ*Leprosy* was a term for several skin diseases; see Leviticus 13 ᵉGreek *chiton*, a long garment worn under the cloak next to the skin ᶠOr *bondservant*; also verse 25 ᵍGreek lacks *will they malign*

HAVE NO FEAR

26 "So have no fear of them, for nothing is covered that will not be revealed, or hidden that will not be known. 27 What I tell you in the dark, say in the light, and what you hear whispered, proclaim on the housetops. 28 And do not fear those who kill the body but cannot kill the soul. Rather fear him who can destroy both soul and body in hell.*ᵃ* 29 Are not two sparrows sold for a penny?*ᵇ* And not one of them will fall to the ground apart from your Father. 30 But even the hairs of your head are all numbered. 31 Fear not, therefore; you are of more value than many sparrows. 32 So everyone who acknowledges me before men, I also will acknowledge before my Father who is in heaven, 33 but whoever denies me before men, I also will deny before my Father who is in heaven.

NOT PEACE, BUT A SWORD

34 "Do not think that I have come to bring peace to the earth. I have not come to bring peace, but a sword. 35 For I have come to set a man against his father, and a daughter against her mother, and a daughter-in-law against her mother-in-law. 36 And a person's enemies will be those of his own household. 37 Whoever loves father or mother more than me is not worthy of me, and whoever loves son or daughter more than me is not worthy of me. 38 And whoever does not take his cross and follow me is not worthy of me. 39 Whoever finds his life will lose it, and whoever loses his life for my sake will find it.

REWARDS

40 "Whoever receives you receives me, and whoever receives me receives him who sent me. 41 The one who receives a prophet because he is a prophet will receive a prophet's reward, and the one who receives a righteous person because he is a righteous person will receive a righteous person's reward. 42 And whoever gives one of these little ones even a cup of cold water because he is a disciple, truly, I say to you, he will by no means lose his reward."

MESSENGERS FROM JOHN THE BAPTIST

11 When Jesus had finished instructing his twelve disciples, he went on from there to teach and preach in their cities.

2 Now when John heard in prison about the deeds of the Christ, he sent word by his disciples 3 and said to him, "Are you the one who is to come, or shall we look for another?" 4 And Jesus answered them, "Go and tell John what you hear and see: 5 the blind receive their sight and the lame walk, lepers*ᶜ* are cleansed and the deaf hear, and the dead are raised up, and the poor have good news preached to them. 6 And blessed is the one who is not offended by me."

7 As they went away, Jesus began to speak to the crowds concerning John: "What did you go out into the wilderness to see? A reed shaken by the wind? 8 What then did you go out to see? A man*ᵈ* dressed in soft clothing? Behold, those who wear soft clothing are in kings' houses. 9 What then did you go out to see? A prophet?*ᵉ* Yes, I tell you, and more than a prophet. 10 This is he of whom it is written,

> "'Behold, I send my messenger
> before your face,
> who will prepare your
> way before you.'

11 Truly, I say to you, among those born of women there has arisen no one greater than John the Baptist. Yet the one who is least in the kingdom of heaven is greater than he. 12 From the days of John the Baptist until now the kingdom of heaven has suffered violence,*ᶠ* and the violent take it by force. 13 For all the Prophets and the Law prophesied until John, 14 and if you are willing to accept it, he is Elijah who is to come. 15 He who has ears to hear,*ᵍ* let him hear.

16 "But to what shall I compare this generation? It is like children sitting in the market-places and calling to their playmates,

17 "'We played the flute for you,
and you did not dance;
we sang a dirge, and you
did not mourn.'

18 For John came neither eating nor drinking, and they say, 'He has a demon.' 19 The Son of Man came eating and drinking, and they say, 'Look at him! A glutton and a drunkard, a friend of tax collectors and sinners!' Yet wisdom is justified by her deeds."*ʰ*

---

*ᵃ*Greek *Gehenna*   *ᵇ*Greek *assarion*, Roman copper coin (Latin *quadrans*) worth about 1/16 of a *denarius* (which was a day's wage for a labourer)   *ᶜ*Leprosy was a term for several skin diseases; see Leviticus 13   *ᵈ*Or *Why then did you go out? To see a man ...*
*ᵉ*Some manuscripts *Why then did you go out? To see a prophet?*
*ᶠ*Or *has been coming violently*   *ᵍ*Some manuscripts omit *to hear*
*ʰ*Some manuscripts *children* (compare Luke 7:35)

WOE TO UNREPENTANT CITIES

²⁰Then he began to denounce the cities where most of his mighty works had been done, because they did not repent. ²¹"Woe to you, Chorazin! Woe to you, Bethsaida! For if the mighty works done in you had been done in Tyre and Sidon, they would have repented long ago in sackcloth and ashes. ²²But I tell you, it will be more bearable on the day of judgement for Tyre and Sidon than for you. ²³And you, Capernaum, will you be exalted to heaven? You will be brought down to Hades. For if the mighty works done in you had been done in Sodom, it would have remained until this day. ²⁴But I tell you that it will be more tolerable on the day of judgement for the land of Sodom than for you."

COME TO ME, AND I WILL GIVE YOU REST

²⁵At that time Jesus declared, "I thank you, Father, Lord of heaven and earth, that you have hidden these things from the wise and understanding and revealed them to little children; ²⁶yes, Father, for such was your gracious will.ᵃ ²⁷All things have been handed over to me by my Father, and no one knows the Son except the Father, and no one knows the Father except the Son and anyone to whom the Son chooses to reveal him. ²⁸Come to me, all who labour and are heavy laden, and I will give you rest. ²⁹Take my yoke upon you, and learn from me, for I am gentle and lowly in heart, and you will find rest for your souls. ³⁰For my yoke is easy, and my burden is light."

JESUS IS LORD OF THE SABBATH

12 At that time Jesus went through the cornfields on the Sabbath. His disciples were hungry, and they began to pluck ears of corn and to eat. ²But when the Pharisees saw it, they said to him, "Look, your disciples are doing what is not lawful to do on the Sabbath." ³He said to them, "Have you not read what David did when he was hungry, and those who were with him: ⁴how he entered the house of God and ate the bread of the Presence, which it was not lawful for him to eat nor for those who were with him, but only for the priests? ⁵Or have you not read in the Law how on the Sabbath the priests in the temple profane the Sabbath and are guiltless? ⁶I tell you, something greater than the temple is here. ⁷And if you had known what this means, 'I desire mercy, and not sacrifice', you would not have condemned the guiltless. ⁸For the Son of Man is lord of the Sabbath."

A MAN WITH A WITHERED HAND

⁹He went on from there and entered their synagogue. ¹⁰And a man was there with a withered hand. And they asked him, "Is it lawful to heal on the Sabbath?"—so that they might accuse him. ¹¹He said to them, "Which one of you who has a sheep, if it falls into a pit on the Sabbath, will not take hold of it and lift it out? ¹²Of how much more value is a man than a sheep! So it is lawful to do good on the Sabbath." ¹³Then he said to the man, "Stretch out your hand." And the man stretched it out, and it was restored, healthy like the other. ¹⁴But the Pharisees went out and conspired against him, how to destroy him.

GOD'S CHOSEN SERVANT

¹⁵Jesus, aware of this, withdrew from there. And many followed him, and he healed them all ¹⁶and ordered them not to make him known. ¹⁷This was to fulfil what was spoken by the prophet Isaiah:

¹⁸ "Behold, my servant whom
  I have chosen,
 my beloved with whom my
  soul is well pleased.
 I will put my Spirit upon him,
  and he will proclaim justice
  to the Gentiles.
¹⁹ He will not quarrel or cry aloud,
  nor will anyone hear his
  voice in the streets;
²⁰ a bruised reed he will not break,
  and a smouldering wick he
  will not quench,
 until he brings justice to victory;
²¹ and in his name the Gentiles
  will hope."

BLASPHEMY AGAINST THE HOLY SPIRIT

²²Then a demon-oppressed man who was blind and mute was brought to him, and he healed him, so that the man spoke and saw. ²³And all the people were amazed, and said, "Can this be the Son of David?" ²⁴But when the Pharisees heard it, they said, "It is only by Beelzebul, the prince of demons, that this man casts out demons." ²⁵Knowing their thoughts, he said to them, "Every kingdom divided against itself is laid waste,

---

ᵃOr for so it pleased you well

and no city or house divided against itself will stand. ²⁶And if Satan casts out Satan, he is divided against himself. How then will his kingdom stand? ²⁷And if I cast out demons by Beelzebul, by whom do your sons cast them out? Therefore they will be your judges. ²⁸But if it is by the Spirit of God that I cast out demons, then the kingdom of God has come upon you. ²⁹Or how can someone enter a strong man's house and plunder his goods, unless he first binds the strong man? Then indeed he may plunder his house. ³⁰Whoever is not with me is against me, and whoever does not gather with me scatters. ³¹Therefore I tell you, every sin and blasphemy will be forgiven people, but the blasphemy against the Spirit will not be forgiven. ³²And whoever speaks a word against the Son of Man will be forgiven, but whoever speaks against the Holy Spirit will not be forgiven, either in this age or in the age to come.

A TREE IS KNOWN BY ITS FRUIT

³³"Either make the tree good and its fruit good, or make the tree bad and its fruit bad, for the tree is known by its fruit. ³⁴You brood of vipers! How can you speak good, when you are evil? For out of the abundance of the heart the mouth speaks. ³⁵The good person out of his good treasure brings forth good, and the evil person out of his evil treasure brings forth evil. ³⁶I tell you, on the day of judgement people will give account for every careless word they speak, ³⁷for by your words you will be justified, and by your words you will be condemned."

THE SIGN OF JONAH

³⁸Then some of the scribes and Pharisees answered him, saying, "Teacher, we wish to see a sign from you." ³⁹But he answered them, "An evil and adulterous generation seeks for a sign, but no sign will be given to it except the sign of the prophet Jonah. ⁴⁰For just as Jonah was three days and three nights in the belly of the great fish, so will the Son of Man be three days and three nights in the heart of the earth. ⁴¹The men of Nineveh will rise up at the judgement with this generation and condemn it, for they repented at the preaching of Jonah, and behold, something greater than Jonah is here. ⁴²The queen of the South will rise up at the judgement with this generation and condemn it, for she came from the ends of the earth to hear the wisdom of Solomon, and behold, something greater than Solomon is here.

RETURN OF AN UNCLEAN SPIRIT

⁴³"When the unclean spirit has gone out of a person, it passes through waterless places seeking rest, but finds none. ⁴⁴Then it says, 'I will return to my house from which I came.' And when it comes, it finds the house empty, swept, and put in order. ⁴⁵Then it goes and brings with it seven other spirits more evil than itself, and they enter and dwell there, and the last state of that person is worse than the first. So also will it be with this evil generation."

JESUS' MOTHER AND BROTHERS

⁴⁶While he was still speaking to the people, behold, his mother and his brothers[a] stood outside, asking to speak to him.[b] ⁴⁸But he replied to the man who told him, "Who is my mother, and who are my brothers?" ⁴⁹And stretching out his hand towards his disciples, he said, "Here are my mother and my brothers! ⁵⁰For whoever does the will of my Father in heaven is my brother and sister and mother."

THE PARABLE OF THE SOWER

13 That same day Jesus went out of the house and sat beside the lake. ²And great crowds gathered about him, so that he got into a boat and sat down. And the whole crowd stood on the beach. ³And he told them many things in parables, saying: "A sower went out to sow. ⁴And as he sowed, some seeds fell along the path, and the birds came and devoured them. ⁵Other seeds fell on rocky ground, where they did not have much soil, and immediately they sprang up, since they had no depth of soil, ⁶but when the sun rose they were scorched. And since they had no root, they withered away. ⁷Other seeds fell among thorns, and the thorns grew up and choked them. ⁸Other seeds fell on good soil and produced grain, some a hundredfold, some sixty, some thirty. ⁹He who has ears,[c] let him hear."

THE PURPOSE OF THE PARABLES

¹⁰Then the disciples came and said to him, "Why do you speak to them in parables?"

---

[a] Or *brothers and sisters*; also verses 48, 49 [b] Some manuscripts insert verse 47: *Someone told him, "Your mother and your brothers are standing outside, asking to speak to you"* [c] Some manuscripts add here and in verse 43 *to hear*

¹¹And he answered them, "To you it has been given to know the secrets of the kingdom of heaven, but to them it has not been given. ¹²For to the one who has, more will be given, and he will have an abundance, but from the one who has not, even what he has will be taken away. ¹³This is why I speak to them in parables, because seeing they do not see, and hearing they do not hear, nor do they understand. ¹⁴Indeed, in their case the prophecy of Isaiah is fulfilled that says:

> "'You will indeed hear but
>   never understand,
>   and you will indeed see but
>   never perceive."
> ¹⁵ For this people's heart has grown dull,
>   and with their ears they
>   can barely hear,
>   and their eyes they have closed,
>   lest they should see with their eyes
>   and hear with their ears
>   and understand with their heart
>   and turn, and I would heal them.'

¹⁶But blessed are your eyes, for they see, and your ears, for they hear. ¹⁷For truly, I say to you, many prophets and righteous people longed to see what you see, and did not see it, and to hear what you hear, and did not hear it.

THE PARABLE OF THE SOWER EXPLAINED

¹⁸"Hear then the parable of the sower: ¹⁹When anyone hears the word of the kingdom and does not understand it, the evil one comes and snatches away what has been sown in his heart. This is what was sown along the path. ²⁰As for what was sown on rocky ground, this is the one who hears the word and immediately receives it with joy, ²¹yet he has no root in himself, but endures for a while, and when tribulation or persecution arises on account of the word, immediately he falls away.ᵃ ²²As for what was sown among thorns, this is the one who hears the word, but the cares of the world and the deceitfulness of riches choke the word, and it proves unfruitful. ²³As for what was sown on good soil, this is the one who hears the word and understands it. He indeed bears fruit and yields, in one case a hundredfold, in another sixty, and in another thirty."

THE PARABLE OF THE WEEDS

²⁴He put another parable before them, saying, "The kingdom of heaven may be compared to a man who sowed good seed in his field, ²⁵but while his men were sleeping, his enemy came and sowed weedsᵇ among the wheat and went away. ²⁶So when the plants came up and bore grain, then the weeds appeared also. ²⁷And the servantsᶜ of the master of the house came and said to him, 'Master, did you not sow good seed in your field? How then does it have weeds?' ²⁸He said to them, 'An enemy has done this.' So the servants said to him, 'Then do you want us to go and gather them?' ²⁹But he said, 'No, lest in gathering the weeds you root up the wheat along with them. ³⁰Let both grow together until the harvest, and at harvest time I will tell the reapers, "Gather the weeds first and bind them in bundles to be burned, but gather the wheat into my barn."'"

THE MUSTARD SEED AND THE LEAVEN

³¹He put another parable before them, saying, "The kingdom of heaven is like a grain of mustard seed that a man took and sowed in his field. ³²It is the smallest of all seeds, but when it has grown it is larger than all the garden plants and becomes a tree, so that the birds of the air come and make nests in its branches."

³³He told them another parable. "The kingdom of heaven is like leaven that a woman took and hid in three measures of flour, till it was all leavened."

PROPHECY AND PARABLES

³⁴All these things Jesus said to the crowds in parables; indeed, he said nothing to them without a parable. ³⁵This was to fulfil what was spoken by the prophet:ᵈ

> "I will open my mouth in parables;
>   I will utter what has been hidden
>   since the foundation of
>   the world."

THE PARABLE OF THE WEEDS EXPLAINED

³⁶Then he left the crowds and went into the house. And his disciples came to him, saying, "Explain to us the parable of the weeds of the field." ³⁷He answered, "The one who sows the good seed is the Son of Man. ³⁸The field is the world, and the good seed is the sons of the kingdom. The weeds are the sons of the evil one, ³⁹and the enemy who sowed

---

ᵃOr *stumbles* ᵇProbably *darnel*, a wheat-like weed ᶜOr *bondservants*; also verse 28 ᵈSome manuscripts *Isaiah the prophet*

them is the devil. The harvest is the end of the age, and the reapers are angels. *⁴⁰*Just as the weeds are gathered and burned with fire, so will it be at the end of the age. *⁴¹*The Son of Man will send his angels, and they will gather out of his kingdom all causes of sin and all law-breakers, *⁴²*and throw them into the fiery furnace. In that place there will be weeping and gnashing of teeth. *⁴³*Then the righteous will shine like the sun in the kingdom of their Father. He who has ears, let him hear.

THE PARABLE OF THE HIDDEN TREASURE

⁴⁴"The kingdom of heaven is like treasure hidden in a field, which a man found and covered up. Then in his joy he goes and sells all that he has and buys that field.

THE PARABLE OF THE PEARL OF GREAT VALUE

⁴⁵"Again, the kingdom of heaven is like a merchant in search of fine pearls, *⁴⁶*who, on finding one pearl of great value, went and sold all that he had and bought it.

THE PARABLE OF THE NET

⁴⁷"Again, the kingdom of heaven is like a net that was thrown into the sea and gathered fish of every kind. *⁴⁸*When it was full, men drew it ashore and sat down and sorted the good into containers but threw away the bad. *⁴⁹*So it will be at the end of the age. The angels will come out and separate the evil from the righteous *⁵⁰*and throw them into the fiery furnace. In that place there will be weeping and gnashing of teeth.

NEW AND OLD TREASURES

⁵¹"Have you understood all these things?" They said to him, "Yes." *⁵²*And he said to them, "Therefore every scribe who has been trained for the kingdom of heaven is like a master of a house, who brings out of his treasure what is new and what is old."

JESUS REJECTED AT NAZARETH

*⁵³*And when Jesus had finished these parables, he went away from there, *⁵⁴*and coming to his home town he taught them in their synagogue, so that they were astonished, and said, "Where did this man get this wisdom and these mighty works? *⁵⁵*Is not this the carpenter's son? Is not his mother called Mary? And are not his brothers James and Joseph and Simon and Judas? *⁵⁶*And are not all his sisters with us? Where then did this man get all these things?" *⁵⁷*And they took offence at him. But Jesus said to them, "A prophet is not without honour except in his home town and in his own household." *⁵⁸*And he did not do many mighty works there, because of their unbelief.

THE DEATH OF JOHN THE BAPTIST

14 At that time Herod the tetrarch heard about the fame of Jesus, *²*and he said to his servants, "This is John the Baptist. He has been raised from the dead; that is why these miraculous powers are at work in him." *³*For Herod had seized John and bound him and put him in prison for the sake of Herodias, his brother Philip's wife,*ᵃ* *⁴*because John had been saying to him, "It is not lawful for you to have her." *⁵*And though he wanted to put him to death, he feared the people, because they held him to be a prophet. *⁶*But when Herod's birthday came, the daughter of Herodias danced before the company and pleased Herod, *⁷*so that he promised with an oath to give her whatever she might ask. *⁸*Prompted by her mother, she said, "Give me the head of John the Baptist here on a platter." *⁹*And the king was sorry, but because of his oaths and his guests he commanded it to be given. *¹⁰*He sent and had John beheaded in the prison, *¹¹*and his head was brought on a platter and given to the girl, and she brought it to her mother. *¹²*And his disciples came and took the body and buried it, and they went and told Jesus.

JESUS FEEDS THE FIVE THOUSAND

*¹³*Now when Jesus heard this, he withdrew from there in a boat to a desolate place by himself. But when the crowds heard it, they followed him on foot from the towns. *¹⁴*When he went ashore he saw a great crowd, and he had compassion on them and healed their sick. *¹⁵*Now when it was evening, the disciples came to him and said, "This is a desolate place, and the day is now over; send the crowds away to go into the villages and buy food for themselves." *¹⁶*But Jesus said, "They need not go away; you give them something to eat." *¹⁷*They said to him, "We have only five loaves here and two fish." *¹⁸*And he said, "Bring them here to me." *¹⁹*Then he ordered the crowds to sit down on the grass, and taking the five loaves and the two fish,

---

*ᵃ*Some manuscripts *his brother's wife*

he looked up to heaven and said a blessing. Then he broke the loaves and gave them to the disciples, and the disciples gave them to the crowds. ²⁰And they all ate and were satisfied. And they took up twelve baskets full of the broken pieces left over. ²¹And those who ate were about five thousand men, besides women and children.

JESUS WALKS ON THE WATER

²²Immediately he made the disciples get into the boat and go before him to the other side, while he dismissed the crowds. ²³And after he had dismissed the crowds, he went up on the mountain by himself to pray. When evening came, he was there alone, ²⁴but the boat by this time was a long way[a] from the land,[b] beaten by the waves, for the wind was against them. ²⁵And in the fourth watch of the night[c] he came to them, walking on the sea. ²⁶But when the disciples saw him walking on the sea, they were terrified, and said, "It is a ghost!" and they cried out in fear. ²⁷But immediately Jesus spoke to them, saying, "Take heart; it is I. Do not be afraid."

²⁸And Peter answered him, "Lord, if it is you, command me to come to you on the water." ²⁹He said, "Come." So Peter got out of the boat and walked on the water and came to Jesus. ³⁰But when he saw the wind,[d] he was afraid, and beginning to sink he cried out, "Lord, save me." ³¹Jesus immediately reached out his hand and took hold of him, saying to him, "O you of little faith, why did you doubt?" ³²And when they got into the boat, the wind ceased. ³³And those in the boat worshipped him, saying, "Truly you are the Son of God."

JESUS HEALS THE SICK IN GENNESARET

³⁴And when they had crossed over, they came to land at Gennesaret. ³⁵And when the men of that place recognized him, they sent word around to all that region and brought to him all who were sick ³⁶and implored him that they might only touch the fringe of his garment. And as many as touched it were made well.

TRADITIONS AND COMMANDMENTS

15 Then Pharisees and scribes came to Jesus from Jerusalem and said, ²"Why do your disciples break the tradition of the elders? For they do not wash their hands when they eat." ³He answered them, "And why do you break the commandment of God for the sake of your tradition? ⁴For God commanded, 'Honour your father and your mother,' and, 'Whoever reviles father or mother must surely die.' ⁵But you say, 'If anyone tells his father or his mother, "What you would have gained from me is given to God,'[e] ⁶he need not honour his father.' So for the sake of your tradition you have made void the word[f] of God. ⁷You hypocrites! Well did Isaiah prophesy of you, when he said:

⁸ "'This people honours me
    with their lips,
  but their heart is far from me;
⁹ in vain do they worship me,
    teaching as doctrines the
    commandments of men.'"

WHAT DEFILES A PERSON

¹⁰And he called the people to him and said to them, "Hear and understand: ¹¹it is not what goes into the mouth that defiles a person, but what comes out of the mouth; this defiles a person." ¹²Then the disciples came and said to him, "Do you know that the Pharisees were offended when they heard this saying?" ¹³He answered, "Every plant that my heavenly Father has not planted will be rooted up. ¹⁴Let them alone; they are blind guides.[g] And if the blind lead the blind, both will fall into a pit." ¹⁵But Peter said to him, "Explain the parable to us." ¹⁶And he said, "Are you also still without understanding? ¹⁷Do you not see that whatever goes into the mouth passes into the stomach and is expelled?[h] ¹⁸But what comes out of the mouth proceeds from the heart, and this defiles a person. ¹⁹For out of the heart come evil thoughts, murder, adultery, sexual immorality, theft, false witness, slander. ²⁰These are what defile a person. But to eat with unwashed hands does not defile anyone."

THE FAITH OF A CANAANITE WOMAN

²¹And Jesus went away from there and withdrew to the district of Tyre and Sidon. ²²And behold, a Canaanite woman from that region came out and was crying, "Have mercy on me, O Lord, Son of David; my daughter is severely oppressed by a demon." ²³But he did not answer her a word. And his disciples came

---

[a]Greek *many stadia*, a *stadion* was about 607 feet or 185 metres
[b]Some manuscripts *was out on the sea* [c]That is, between 3 A.M. and 6 A.M. [d]Some manuscripts *strong wind* [e]Or *is an offering*
[f]Some manuscripts *law* [g]Some manuscripts add *of the blind*
[h]Greek *is expelled into the latrine*

and begged him, saying, "Send her away, for she is crying out after us." ²⁴He answered, "I was sent only to the lost sheep of the house of Israel." ²⁵But she came and knelt before him, saying, "Lord, help me." ²⁶And he answered, "It is not right to take the children's bread and throw it to the dogs." ²⁷She said, "Yes, Lord, yet even the dogs eat the crumbs that fall from their masters' table." ²⁸Then Jesus answered her, "O woman, great is your faith! Be it done for you as you desire." And her daughter was healed instantly.ᵃ

JESUS HEALS MANY

²⁹Jesus went on from there and walked beside the Sea of Galilee. And he went up on the mountain and sat down there. ³⁰And great crowds came to him, bringing with them the lame, the blind, the crippled, the mute, and many others, and they put them at his feet, and he healed them, ³¹so that the crowd wondered, when they saw the mute speaking, the crippled healthy, the lame walking, and the blind seeing. And they glorified the God of Israel.

JESUS FEEDS THE FOUR THOUSAND

³²Then Jesus called his disciples to him and said, "I have compassion on the crowd because they have been with me now three days and have nothing to eat. And I am unwilling to send them away hungry, lest they faint on the way." ³³And the disciples said to him, "Where are we to get enough bread in such a desolate place to feed so great a crowd?" ³⁴And Jesus said to them, "How many loaves do you have?" They said, "Seven, and a few small fish." ³⁵And directing the crowd to sit down on the ground, ³⁶he took the seven loaves and the fish, and having given thanks he broke them and gave them to the disciples, and the disciples gave them to the crowds. ³⁷And they all ate and were satisfied. And they took up seven baskets full of the broken pieces left over. ³⁸Those who ate were four thousand men, besides women and children. ³⁹And after sending away the crowds, he got into the boat and went to the region of Magadan.

THE PHARISEES AND SADDUCEES DEMAND SIGNS

16 And the Pharisees and Sadducees came, and to test him they asked him to show them a sign from heaven. ²He answered them,ᵇ "When it is evening, you say, 'It will be fair weather, for the sky is red.' ³And in the morning, 'It will be stormy today, for the sky is red and threatening.' You know how to interpret the appearance of the sky, but you cannot interpret the signs of the times. ⁴An evil and adulterous generation seeks for a sign, but no sign will be given to it except the sign of Jonah." So he left them and departed.

THE LEAVEN OF THE PHARISEES AND SADDUCEES

⁵When the disciples reached the other side, they had forgotten to bring any bread. ⁶Jesus said to them, "Watch and beware of the leaven of the Pharisees and Sadducees." ⁷And they began discussing it among themselves, saying, "We brought no bread." ⁸But Jesus, aware of this, said, "O you of little faith, why are you discussing among yourselves the fact that you have no bread? ⁹Do you not yet perceive? Do you not remember the five loaves for the five thousand, and how many baskets you gathered? ¹⁰Or the seven loaves for the four thousand, and how many baskets you gathered? ¹¹How is it that you fail to understand that I did not speak about bread? Beware of the leaven of the Pharisees and Sadducees." ¹²Then they understood that he did not tell them to beware of the leaven of bread, but of the teaching of the Pharisees and Sadducees.

PETER CONFESSES JESUS AS THE CHRIST

¹³Now when Jesus came into the district of Caesarea Philippi, he asked his disciples, "Who do people say that the Son of Man is?" ¹⁴And they said, "Some say John the Baptist, others say Elijah, and others Jeremiah or one of the prophets." ¹⁵He said to them, "But who do you say that I am?" ¹⁶Simon Peter replied, "You are the Christ, the Son of the living God." ¹⁷And Jesus answered him, "Blessed are you, Simon Bar-Jonah! For flesh and blood has not revealed this to you, but my Father who is in heaven. ¹⁸And I tell you, you are Peter, and on this rockᶜ I will build my church, and the gates of hellᵈ shall not prevail against it. ¹⁹I will give you the keys of the kingdom of heaven, and whatever you bind on earth shall be bound in heaven, and whatever you loose on earth shall be loosedᵉ in heaven."

ᵃGreek *from that hour* ᵇSome manuscripts omit the following words to the end of verse 3 ᶜThe Greek words for *Peter* and *rock* sound similar ᵈGreek *the gates of Hades* ᵉOr *shall have been bound . . . shall have been loosed*

²⁰Then he strictly charged the disciples to tell no one that he was the Christ.

JESUS FORETELLS HIS DEATH AND RESURRECTION

²¹From that time Jesus began to show his disciples that he must go to Jerusalem and suffer many things from the elders and chief priests and scribes, and be killed, and on the third day be raised. ²²And Peter took him aside and began to rebuke him, saying, "Far be it from you, Lord!ᵃ This shall never happen to you." ²³But he turned and said to Peter, "Get behind me, Satan! You are a hindranceᵇ to me. For you are not setting your mind on the things of God, but on the things of man."

TAKE UP YOUR CROSS AND FOLLOW JESUS

²⁴Then Jesus told his disciples, "If anyone would come after me, let him deny himself and take up his cross and follow me. ²⁵For whoever would save his lifeᶜ will lose it, but whoever loses his life for my sake will find it. ²⁶For what will it profit a man if he gains the whole world and forfeits his soul? Or what shall a man give in return for his soul? ²⁷For the Son of Man is going to come with his angels in the glory of his Father, and then he will repay each person according to what he has done. ²⁸Truly, I say to you, there are some standing here who will not taste death until they see the Son of Man coming in his kingdom."

THE TRANSFIGURATION

17 And after six days Jesus took with him Peter and James, and John his brother, and led them up a high mountain by themselves. ²And he was transfigured before them, and his face shone like the sun, and his clothes became white as light. ³And behold, there appeared to them Moses and Elijah, talking with him. ⁴And Peter said to Jesus, "Lord, it is good that we are here. If you wish, I will make three tents here, one for you and one for Moses and one for Elijah." ⁵He was still speaking when, behold, a bright cloud overshadowed them, and a voice from the cloud said, "This is my beloved Son,ᵈ with whom I am well pleased; listen to him." ⁶When the disciples heard this, they fell on their faces and were terrified. ⁷But Jesus came and touched them, saying, "Rise, and have no fear." ⁸And when they lifted up their eyes, they saw no one but Jesus only.

⁹And as they were coming down the mountain, Jesus commanded them, "Tell no one the vision, until the Son of Man is raised from the dead.' ¹⁰And the disciples asked him, "Then why do the scribes say that first Elijah must come?" ¹¹He answered, "Elijah does come, and he will restore all things. ¹²But I tell you that Elijah has already come, and they did not recognize him, but did to him whatever they pleased. So also the Son of Man will certainly suffer at their hands." ¹³Then the disciples understood that he was speaking to them of John the Baptist.

JESUS HEALS A BOY WITH A DEMON

¹⁴And when they came to the crowd, a man came up to him and, kneeling before him, ¹⁵said, "Lord, have mercy on my son, for he has seizures and he suffers terribly. For often he falls into the fire, and often into the water. ¹⁶And I brought him to your disciples, and they could not heal him." ¹⁷And Jesus answered, "O faithless and twisted generation, how long am I to be with you? How long am I to bear with you? Bring him here to me." ¹⁸And Jesus rebuked the demon,ᵉ and itᶠ came out of him, and the boy was healed instantly.ᵍ ¹⁹Then the disciples came to Jesus privately and said, "Why could we not cast it out?" ²⁰He said to them, "Because of your little faith. For truly, I say to you, if you have faith like a grain of mustard seed, you will say to this mountain, 'Move from here to there', and it will move, and nothing will be impossible for you."ʰ

JESUS AGAIN FORETELLS DEATH, RESURRECTION

²²As they were gatheringⁱ in Galilee, Jesus said to them, "The Son of Man is about to be delivered into the hands of men, ²³and they will kill him, and he will be raised on the third day." And they were greatly distressed.

THE TEMPLE TAX

²⁴When they came to Capernaum, the collectors of the two-drachma tax went up to Peter and said, "Does your teacher not pay the tax?" ²⁵He said, "Yes." And when he came into the house, Jesus spoke to him first, saying,

---

ᵃOr "[May God be] merciful to you, Lord!" ᵇGreek stumbling block ᶜThe same Greek word can mean either soul or life, depending on the context; twice in this verse and twice in verse 26 ᵈOr my Son, my (or the) Beloved ᵉGreek it ᶠGreek the demon ᵍGreek from that hour ʰSome manuscripts insert verse 21: But this kind never comes out except by prayer and fasting ⁱSome manuscripts remained

"What do you think, Simon? From whom do kings of the earth take toll or tax? From their sons or from others?" ²⁶And when he said, "From others", Jesus said to him, "Then the sons are free. ²⁷However, not to give offence to them, go to the lake and cast a hook and take the first fish that comes up, and when you open its mouth you will find a shekel.ᵃ Take that and give it to them for me and for yourself."

WHO IS THE GREATEST?

18 At that time the disciples came to Jesus, saying, "Who is the greatest in the kingdom of heaven?" ²And calling to him a child, he put him in the midst of them ³and said, "Truly, I say to you, unless you turn and become like children, you will never enter the kingdom of heaven. ⁴Whoever humbles himself like this child is the greatest in the kingdom of heaven.

⁵"Whoever receives one such child in my name receives me, ⁶but whoever causes one of these little ones who believe in me to sin,ᵇ it would be better for him to have a great millstone fastened round his neck and to be drowned in the depth of the sea.

TEMPTATIONS TO SIN

⁷"Woe to the world for temptations to sin!ᶜ For it is necessary that temptations come, but woe to the one by whom the temptation comes! ⁸And if your hand or your foot causes you to sin, cut it off and throw it away. It is better for you to enter life crippled or lame than with two hands or two feet to be thrown into the eternal fire. ⁹And if your eye causes you to sin, tear it out and throw it away. It is better for you to enter life with one eye than with two eyes to be thrown into the hellᵈ of fire.

THE PARABLE OF THE LOST SHEEP

¹⁰"See that you do not despise one of these little ones. For I tell you that in heaven their angels always see the face of my Father who is in heaven.ᵉ ¹²What do you think? If a man has a hundred sheep, and one of them has gone astray, does he not leave the ninety-nine on the mountains and go in search of the one that went astray? ¹³And if he finds it, truly, I say to you, he rejoices over it more than over the ninety-nine that never went astray. ¹⁴So it is not the will of myᶠ Father who is in heaven that one of these little ones should perish.

IF YOUR BROTHER SINS AGAINST YOU

¹⁵"If your brother sins against you, go and tell him his fault, between you and him alone. If he listens to you, you have gained your brother. ¹⁶But if he does not listen, take one or two others along with you, that every charge may be established by the evidence of two or three witnesses. ¹⁷If he refuses to listen to them, tell it to the church. And if he refuses to listen even to the church, let him be to you as a Gentile and a tax collector. ¹⁸Truly, I say to you, whatever you bind on earth shall be bound in heaven, and whatever you loose on earth shall be loosedᵍ in heaven. ¹⁹Again I say to you, if two of you agree on earth about anything they ask, it will be done for them by my Father in heaven. ²⁰For where two or three are gathered in my name, there am I among them."

THE PARABLE OF THE UNFORGIVING SERVANT

²¹Then Peter came up and said to him, "Lord, how often will my brother sin against me, and I forgive him? As many as seven times?" ²²Jesus said to him, "I do not say to you seven times, but seventy-seven times.

²³"Therefore the kingdom of heaven may be compared to a king who wished to settle accounts with his servants.ʰ ²⁴When he began to settle, one was brought to him who owed him ten thousand talents.ⁱ ²⁵And since he could not pay, his master ordered him to be sold, with his wife and children and all that he had, and payment to be made. ²⁶So the servantʲ fell on his knees, imploring him, 'Have patience with me, and I will pay you everything.' ²⁷And out of pity for him, the master of that servant released him and forgave him the debt. ²⁸But when that same servant went out, he found one of his fellow servants who owed him a hundred denarii,ᵏ and seizing him, he began to choke him, saying, 'Pay what you owe.' ²⁹So his fellow servant fell down and pleaded with him, 'Have patience with me, and I will pay you.' ³⁰He refused and went and put him in prison until he should pay the debt. ³¹When his fellow

---

ᵃGreek *stater*, a silver coin worth four drachmas or approximately one shekel ᵇGreek *causes . . . to stumble*; also verses 8, 9 ᶜGreek *stumbling blocks* ᵈGreek *Gehenna* ᵉSome manuscripts add verse 11: *For the Son of Man came to save the lost* ᶠSome manuscripts *your* ᵍOr *shall have been bound . . . shall have been loosed* ʰOr *bondservants*; also verses 28, 31 ⁱA *talent* was a monetary unit worth about twenty years' wages for a labourer ʲOr *bondservant*; also verses 27, 28, 29, 32, 33 ᵏA *denarius* was a day's wage for a labourer

servants saw what had taken place, they were greatly distressed, and they went and reported to their master all that had taken place. ³²Then his master summoned him and said to him, 'You wicked servant! I forgave you all that debt because you pleaded with me. ³³And should not you have had mercy on your fellow servant, as I had mercy on you?' ³⁴And in anger his master delivered him to the jailers,*ᵃ* until he should pay all his debt. ³⁵So also my heavenly Father will do to every one of you, if you do not forgive your brother from your heart."

TEACHING ABOUT DIVORCE

19 Now when Jesus had finished these sayings, he went away from Galilee and entered the region of Judea beyond the Jordan. ²And large crowds followed him, and he healed them there.

³And Pharisees came up to him and tested him by asking, "Is it lawful to divorce one's wife for any cause?" ⁴He answered, "Have you not read that he who created them from the beginning made them male and female, ⁵and said, 'Therefore a man shall leave his father and his mother and hold fast to his wife, and the two shall become one flesh'? ⁶So they are no longer two but one flesh. What therefore God has joined together, let not man separate." ⁷They said to him, "Why then did Moses command one to give a certificate of divorce and to send her away?" ⁸He said to them, "Because of your hardness of heart Moses allowed you to divorce your wives, but from the beginning it was not so. ⁹And I say to you: whoever divorces his wife, except for sexual immorality, and marries another, commits adultery."*ᵇ*

¹⁰The disciples said to him, "If such is the case of a man with his wife, it is better not to marry." ¹¹But he said to them, "Not everyone can receive this saying, but only those to whom it is given. ¹²For there are eunuchs who have been so from birth, and there are eunuchs who have been made eunuchs by men, and there are eunuchs who have made themselves eunuchs for the sake of the kingdom of heaven. Let the one who is able to receive this receive it."

LET THE CHILDREN COME TO ME

¹³Then children were brought to him that he might lay his hands on them and pray. The disciples rebuked the people, ¹⁴but Jesus said, "Let the little children come to me and do not hinder them, for to such belongs the kingdom of heaven." ¹⁵And he laid his hands on them and went away.

THE RICH YOUNG MAN

¹⁶And behold, a man came up to him, saying, "Teacher, what good deed must I do to have eternal life?" ¹⁷And he said to him, "Why do you ask me about what is good? There is only one who is good. If you would enter life, keep the commandments." ¹⁸He said to him, "Which ones?" And Jesus said, "You shall not murder, You shall not commit adultery, You shall not steal, You shall not bear false witness, ¹⁹Honour your father and mother, and, You shall love your neighbour as yourself." ²⁰The young man said to him, "All these I have kept. What do I still lack?" ²¹Jesus said to him, "If you would be perfect, go, sell what you possess and give to the poor, and you will have treasure in heaven; and come, follow me." ²²When the young man heard this he went away sorrowful, for he had great possessions.

²³And Jesus said to his disciples, "Truly, I say to you, only with difficulty will a rich person enter the kingdom of heaven. ²⁴Again I tell you, it is easier for a camel to go through the eye of a needle than for a rich person to enter the kingdom of God." ²⁵When the disciples heard this, they were greatly astonished, saying, "Who then can be saved?" ²⁶But Jesus looked at them and said, "With man this is impossible, but with God all things are possible." ²⁷Then Peter said in reply, "See, we have left everything and followed you. What then will we have?" ²⁸Jesus said to them, "Truly, I say to you, in the new world,*ᶜ* when the Son of Man will sit on his glorious throne, you who have followed me will also sit on twelve thrones, judging the twelve tribes of Israel. ²⁹And everyone who has left houses or brothers or sisters or father or mother or children or lands, for my name's sake, will receive a hundredfold*ᵈ* and will inherit eternal life. ³⁰But many who are first will be last, and the last first.

LABOURERS IN THE VINEYARD

20 "For the kingdom of heaven is like a master of a house who went out early in the morning to hire labourers for his vineyard. ²After agreeing

---

*ᵃ*Greek torturers *ᵇ*Some manuscripts add *and whoever marries a divorced woman commits adultery*; other manuscripts *except for sexual immorality, makes her commit adultery, and whoever marries a divorced woman commits adultery* *ᶜ*Greek *in the regeneration* *ᵈ*Some manuscripts *manifold*

with the labourers for a denarius[a] a day, he sent them into his vineyard. ³And going out about the third hour he saw others standing idle in the market-place, ⁴and to them he said, 'You go into the vineyard too, and whatever is right I will give you.' ⁵So they went. Going out again about the sixth hour and the ninth hour, he did the same. ⁶And about the eleventh hour he went out and found others standing. And he said to them, 'Why do you stand here idle all day?' ⁷They said to him, 'Because no one has hired us.' He said to them, 'You go into the vineyard too.' ⁸And when evening came, the owner of the vineyard said to his foreman, 'Call the labourers and pay them their wages, beginning with the last, up to the first.' ⁹And when those hired about the eleventh hour came, each of them received a denarius. ¹⁰Now when those hired first came, they thought they would receive more, but each of them also received a denarius. ¹¹And on receiving it they grumbled at the master of the house, ¹²saying, 'These last worked only one hour, and you have made them equal to us who have borne the burden of the day and the scorching heat.' ¹³But he replied to one of them, 'Friend, I am doing you no wrong. Did you not agree with me for a denarius? ¹⁴Take what belongs to you and go. I choose to give to this last worker as I give to you. ¹⁵Am I not allowed to do what I choose with what belongs to me? Or do you begrudge my generosity?'[b] ¹⁶So the last will be first, and the first last."

JESUS FORETELLS HIS DEATH A THIRD TIME

¹⁷And as Jesus was going up to Jerusalem, he took the twelve disciples aside, and on the way he said to them, ¹⁸"See, we are going up to Jerusalem. And the Son of Man will be delivered over to the chief priests and scribes, and they will condemn him to death ¹⁹and deliver him over to the Gentiles to be mocked and flogged and crucified, and he will be raised on the third day."

A MOTHER'S REQUEST

²⁰Then the mother of the sons of Zebedee came up to him with her sons, and kneeling before him she asked him for something. ²¹And he said to her, "What do you want?" She said to him, "Say that these two sons of mine are to sit, one at your right hand and one at your left, in your kingdom." ²²Jesus answered, "You do not know what you are asking. Are you able to drink the cup that I am to drink?" They said to him, "We are able." ²³He said to them, "You will drink my cup, but to sit at my right hand and at my left is not mine to grant, but it is for those for whom it has been prepared by my Father." ²⁴And when the ten heard it, they were indignant at the two brothers. ²⁵But Jesus called them to him and said, "You know that the rulers of the Gentiles lord it over them, and their great ones exercise authority over them. ²⁶It shall not be so among you. But whoever would be great among you must be your servant,[c] ²⁷and whoever would be first among you must be your slave,[d] ²⁸even as the Son of Man came not to be served but to serve, and to give his life as a ransom for many."

JESUS HEALS TWO BLIND MEN

²⁹And as they went out of Jericho, a great crowd followed him. ³⁰And behold, there were two blind men sitting by the roadside, and when they heard that Jesus was passing by, they cried out, "Lord,[e] have mercy on us, Son of David!" ³¹The crowd rebuked them, telling them to be silent, but they cried out all the more, "Lord, have mercy on us, Son of David!" ³²And stopping, Jesus called them and said, "What do you want me to do for you?" ³³They said to him, "Lord, let our eyes be opened." ³⁴And Jesus in pity touched their eyes, and immediately they recovered their sight and followed him.

THE TRIUMPHAL ENTRY

21 Now when they drew near to Jerusalem and came to Bethphage, to the Mount of Olives, then Jesus sent two disciples, ²saying to them, "Go into the village in front of you, and immediately you will find a donkey tied, and a colt with her. Untie them and bring them to me. ³If anyone says anything to you, you shall say, 'The Lord needs them', and he will send them at once." ⁴This took place to fulfil what was spoken by the prophet, saying,

⁵ "Say to the daughter of Zion,
   'Behold, your king is coming to you,
      humble, and mounted on a donkey,
      on a colt,[f] the foal of a
         beast of burden.'"

---

[a] A *denarius* was a day's wage for a labourer   [b] Or *is your eye bad because I am good?*   [c] Greek *diakonos*   [d] Or *bondservant*, or *servant* (for the contextual rendering of the Greek word *doulos*, see Preface)   [e] Some manuscripts omit *Lord*   [f] Or *donkey, and on a colt*

⁶The disciples went and did as Jesus had directed them. ⁷They brought the donkey and the colt and put on them their cloaks, and he sat on them. ⁸Most of the crowd spread their cloaks on the road, and others cut branches from the trees and spread them on the road. ⁹And the crowds that went before him and that followed him were shouting, "Hosanna to the Son of David! Blessed is he who comes in the name of the Lord! Hosanna in the highest!" ¹⁰And when he entered Jerusalem, the whole city was stirred up, saying, "Who is this?" ¹¹And the crowds said, "This is the prophet Jesus, from Nazareth of Galilee."

JESUS CLEANSES THE TEMPLE

¹²And Jesus entered the temple[a] and drove out all who sold and bought in the temple, and he overturned the tables of the money-changers and the seats of those who sold pigeons. ¹³He said to them, "It is written, 'My house shall be called a house of prayer', but you make it a den of robbers."

¹⁴And the blind and the lame came to him in the temple, and he healed them. ¹⁵But when the chief priests and the scribes saw the wonderful things that he did, and the children crying out in the temple, "Hosanna to the Son of David!" they were indignant, ¹⁶and they said to him, "Do you hear what these are saying?" And Jesus said to them, "Yes; have you never read,

"'Out of the mouth of infants
    and nursing babies
you have prepared praise'?"

¹⁷And leaving them, he went out of the city to Bethany and lodged there.

JESUS CURSES THE FIG TREE

¹⁸In the morning, as he was returning to the city, he became hungry. ¹⁹And seeing a fig tree by the wayside, he went to it and found nothing on it but only leaves. And he said to it, "May no fruit ever come from you again!" And the fig tree withered at once.

²⁰When the disciples saw it, they marvelled, saying, "How did the fig tree wither at once?" ²¹And Jesus answered them, "Truly, I say to you, if you have faith and do not doubt, you will not only do what has been done to the fig tree, but even if you say to this mountain, 'Be taken up and thrown into the sea', it will happen. ²²And whatever you ask in prayer, you will receive, if you have faith."

THE AUTHORITY OF JESUS CHALLENGED

²³And when he entered the temple, the chief priests and the elders of the people came up to him as he was teaching, and said, "By what authority are you doing these things, and who gave you this authority?" ²⁴Jesus answered them, "I also will ask you one question, and if you tell me the answer, then I also will tell you by what authority I do these things. ²⁵The baptism of John, from where did it come? From heaven or from man?" And they discussed it among themselves, saying, "If we say, 'From heaven', he will say to us, 'Why then did you not believe him?' ²⁶But if we say, 'From man', we are afraid of the crowd, for they all hold that John was a prophet." ²⁷So they answered Jesus, "We do not know." And he said to them, "Neither will I tell you by what authority I do these things.

THE PARABLE OF THE TWO SONS

²⁸"What do you think? A man had two sons. And he went to the first and said, 'Son, go and work in the vineyard today.' ²⁹And he answered, 'I will not', but afterwards he changed his mind and went. ³⁰And he went to the other son and said the same. And he answered, 'I go, sir', but did not go. ³¹Which of the two did the will of his father?" They said, "The first." Jesus said to them, "Truly, I say to you, the tax collectors and the prostitutes go into the kingdom of God before you. ³²For John came to you in the way of righteousness, and you did not believe him, but the tax collectors and the prostitutes believed him. And even when you saw it, you did not afterwards change your minds and believe him.

THE PARABLE OF THE TENANTS

³³"Hear another parable. There was a master of a house who planted a vineyard and put a fence round it and dug a wine press in it and built a tower and leased it to tenants, and went into another country. ³⁴When the season for fruit drew near, he sent his servants[b] to the tenants to get his fruit. ³⁵And the tenants took his servants and beat one, killed another, and stoned another. ³⁶Again he sent other servants, more than at first. And they did the same to them. ³⁷Finally he sent his son to them, saying, 'They will respect my son.' ³⁸But when the tenants saw the son, they said to themselves, 'This is the

---

[a]Some manuscripts add *of God* [b]Or *bondservants*; also verses 35, 36

heir. Come, let us kill him and have his inheritance.' ³⁹And they took him and threw him out of the vineyard and killed him. ⁴⁰When therefore the owner of the vineyard comes, what will he do to those tenants?" ⁴¹They said to him, "He will put those wretches to a miserable death and let out the vineyard to other tenants who will give him the fruits in their seasons."

⁴²Jesus said to them, "Have you never read in the Scriptures:

> " 'The stone that the builders rejected
>   has become the cornerstone;ᵃ
> this was the Lord's doing,
>   and it is marvellous in our eyes'?

⁴³Therefore I tell you, the kingdom of God will be taken away from you and given to a people producing its fruits. ⁴⁴And the one who falls on this stone will be broken to pieces; and when it falls on anyone, it will crush him."ᵇ

⁴⁵When the chief priests and the Pharisees heard his parables, they perceived that he was speaking about them. ⁴⁶And although they were seeking to arrest him, they feared the crowds, because they held him to be a prophet.

THE PARABLE OF THE WEDDING FEAST

22 And again Jesus spoke to them in parables, saying, ²"The kingdom of heaven may be compared to a king who gave a wedding feast for his son, ³and sent his servantsᶜ to call those who were invited to the wedding feast, but they would not come. ⁴Again he sent other servants, saying, 'Tell those who are invited, "See, I have prepared my dinner, my oxen and my fat calves have been slaughtered, and everything is ready. Come to the wedding feast." ' ⁵But they paid no attention and went off, one to his farm, another to his business, ⁶while the rest seized his servants, treated them shamefully, and killed them. ⁷The king was angry, and he sent his troops and destroyed those murderers and burned their city. ⁸Then he said to his servants, 'The wedding feast is ready, but those invited were not worthy. ⁹Go therefore to the main roads and invite to the wedding feast as many as you find.' ¹⁰And those servants went out into the roads and gathered all whom they found, both bad and good. So the wedding hall was filled with guests.

¹¹"But when the king came in to look at the guests, he saw there a man who had no wedding garment. ¹²And he said to him, 'Friend, how did you get in here without a wedding garment?' And he was speechless. ¹³Then the king said to the attendants, 'Bind him hand and foot and cast him into the outer darkness. In that place there will be weeping and gnashing of teeth.' ¹⁴For many are called, but few are chosen."

PAYING TAXES TO CAESAR

¹⁵Then the Pharisees went and plotted how to entangle him in his words. ¹⁶And they sent their disciples to him, along with the Herodians, saying, "Teacher, we know that you are true and teach the way of God truthfully, and you do not care about anyone's opinion, for you are not swayed by appearances.ᵈ ¹⁷Tell us, then, what you think. Is it lawful to pay taxes to Caesar, or not?" ¹⁸But Jesus, aware of their malice, said, "Why put me to the test, you hypocrites? ¹⁹Show me the coin for the tax." And they brought him a denarius.ᵉ ²⁰And Jesus said to them, "Whose likeness and inscription is this?" ²¹They said, "Caesar's." Then he said to them, "Therefore render to Caesar the things that are Caesar's, and to God the things that are God's." ²²When they heard it, they marvelled. And they left him and went away.

SADDUCEES ASK ABOUT THE RESURRECTION

²³The same day Sadducees came to him, who say that there is no resurrection, and they asked him a question, ²⁴saying, "Teacher, Moses said, 'If a man dies having no children, his brother must marry the widow and raise up offspring for his brother.' ²⁵Now there were seven brothers among us. The first married and died, and having no offspring left his wife to his brother. ²⁶So too the second and third, down to the seventh. ²⁷After them all, the woman died. ²⁸In the resurrection, therefore, of the seven, whose wife will she be? For they all had her."

²⁹But Jesus answered them, "You are wrong, because you know neither the Scriptures nor the power of God. ³⁰For in the resurrection they neither marry nor are given in marriage, but are like angels in heaven. ³¹And as for the resurrection of the dead, have

---
ᵃGreek *the head of the corner* ᵇSome manuscripts omit verse 44
ᶜOr *bondservants*; also verses 4, 6, 8, 10 ᵈGreek *for you do not look at people's faces* ᵉA *denarius* was a day's wage for a labourer

you not read what was said to you by God: ³²'I am the God of Abraham, and the God of Isaac, and the God of Jacob'? He is not God of the dead, but of the living." ³³And when the crowd heard it, they were astonished at his teaching.

THE GREAT COMMANDMENT

³⁴But when the Pharisees heard that he had silenced the Sadducees, they gathered together. ³⁵And one of them, a lawyer, asked him a question to test him. ³⁶"Teacher, which is the great commandment in the Law?" ³⁷And he said to him, "You shall love the Lord your God with all your heart and with all your soul and with all your mind. ³⁸This is the great and first commandment. ³⁹And a second is like it: You shall love your neighbour as yourself. ⁴⁰On these two commandments depend all the Law and the Prophets."

WHOSE SON IS THE CHRIST?

⁴¹Now while the Pharisees were gathered together, Jesus asked them a question, ⁴²saying, "What do you think about the Christ? Whose son is he?" They said to him, "The son of David." ⁴³He said to them, "How is it then that David, in the Spirit, calls him Lord, saying,

⁴⁴ "'The Lord said to my Lord,
"Sit at my right hand,
until I put your enemies
under your feet"'?

⁴⁵If then David calls him Lord, how is he his son?" ⁴⁶And no one was able to answer him a word, nor from that day did anyone dare to ask him any more questions.

SEVEN WOES TO THE SCRIBES AND PHARISEES

23 Then Jesus said to the crowds and to his disciples, ²"The scribes and the Pharisees sit on Moses' seat, ³so do and observe whatever they tell you, but not the works they do. For they preach, but do not practise. ⁴They tie up heavy burdens, hard to bear,ᵃ and lay them on people's shoulders, but they themselves are not willing to move them with their finger. ⁵They do all their deeds to be seen by others. For they make their phylacteries broad and their fringes long, ⁶and they love the place of honour at feasts and the best seats in the synagogues ⁷and greetings in the market-places and being called rabbiᵇ by others. ⁸But you are not to be called rabbi, for you have one teacher, and you are all brothers.ᶜ ⁹And call no man your father on earth, for you have one Father, who is in heaven. ¹⁰Neither be called instructors, for you have one instructor, the Christ. ¹¹The greatest among you shall be your servant. ¹²Whoever exalts himself will be humbled, and whoever humbles himself will be exalted.

¹³"But woe to you, scribes and Pharisees, hypocrites! For you shut the kingdom of heaven in people's faces. For you neither enter yourselves nor allow those who would enter to go in.ᵈ ¹⁵Woe to you, scribes and Pharisees, hypocrites! For you travel across sea and land to make a single proselyte, and when he becomes a proselyte, you make him twice as much a child of hellᵉ as yourselves.

¹⁶"Woe to you, blind guides, who say, 'If anyone swears by the temple, it is nothing, but if anyone swears by the gold of the temple, he is bound by his oath.' ¹⁷You blind fools! For which is greater, the gold or the temple that has made the gold sacred? ¹⁸And you say, 'If anyone swears by the altar, it is nothing, but if anyone swears by the gift that is on the altar, he is bound by his oath.' ¹⁹You blind men! For which is greater, the gift or the altar that makes the gift sacred? ²⁰So whoever swears by the altar swears by it and by everything on it. ²¹And whoever swears by the temple swears by it and by him who dwells in it. ²²And whoever swears by heaven swears by the throne of God and by him who sits upon it.

²³"Woe to you, scribes and Pharisees, hypocrites! For you tithe mint and dill and cumin, and have neglected the weightier matters of the law: justice and mercy and faithfulness. These you ought to have done, without neglecting the others. ²⁴You blind guides, straining out a gnat and swallowing a camel!

²⁵"Woe to you, scribes and Pharisees, hypocrites! For you clean the outside of the cup and the plate, but inside they are full of greed and self-indulgence. ²⁶You blind Pharisee! First clean the inside of the cup and the plate, that the outside also may be clean.

ᵃSome manuscripts omit *hard to bear* ᵇ*Rabbi* means *my teacher*, or *my master*; also verse 8 ᶜOr *brothers and sisters* ᵈSome manuscripts add here (or after verse 12) verse 14: *Woe to you, scribes and Pharisees, hypocrites! For you devour widows' houses and for a pretence you make long prayers; therefore you will receive the greater condemnation* ᵉGreek *Gehenna*; also verse 33

²⁷"Woe to you, scribes and Pharisees, hypocrites! For you are like whitewashed tombs, which outwardly appear beautiful, but within are full of dead people's bones and all uncleanness. ²⁸So you also outwardly appear righteous to others, but within you are full of hypocrisy and lawlessness.

²⁹"Woe to you, scribes and Pharisees, hypocrites! For you build the tombs of the prophets and decorate the monuments of the righteous, ³⁰saying, 'If we had lived in the days of our fathers, we would not have taken part with them in shedding the blood of the prophets.' ³¹Thus you witness against yourselves that you are sons of those who murdered the prophets. ³²Fill up, then, the measure of your fathers. ³³You serpents, you brood of vipers, how are you to escape being sentenced to hell? ³⁴Therefore I send you prophets and wise men and scribes, some of whom you will kill and crucify, and some you will flog in your synagogues and persecute from town to town, ³⁵so that on you may come all the righteous blood shed on earth, from the blood of righteous Abel to the blood of Zechariah the son of Barachiah,ᵃ whom you murdered between the sanctuary and the altar. ³⁶Truly, I say to you, all these things will come upon this generation.

LAMENT OVER JERUSALEM

³⁷"O Jerusalem, Jerusalem, the city that kills the prophets and stones those who are sent to it! How often would I have gathered your children together as a hen gathers her brood under her wings, and you were not willing! ³⁸See, your house is left to you desolate. ³⁹For I tell you, you will not see me again, until you say, 'Blessed is he who comes in the name of the Lord.'"

JESUS FORETELLS DESTRUCTION OF THE TEMPLE

24 Jesus left the temple and was going away, when his disciples came to point out to him the buildings of the temple. ²But he answered them, "You see all these, do you not? Truly, I say to you, there will not be left here one stone upon another that will not be thrown down."

SIGNS OF THE END OF THE AGE

³As he sat on the Mount of Olives, the disciples came to him privately, saying, "Tell us, when will these things be, and what will be the sign of your coming and of the end of the age?" ⁴And Jesus answered them, "See that no one leads you astray. ⁵For many will come in my name, saying, 'I am the Christ', and they will lead many astray. ⁶And you will hear of wars and rumours of wars. See that you are not alarmed, for this must take place, but the end is not yet. ⁷For nation will rise against nation, and kingdom against kingdom, and there will be famines and earthquakes in various places. ⁸All these are but the beginning of the birth pains.

⁹"Then they will deliver you up to tribulation and put you to death, and you will be hated by all nations for my name's sake. ¹⁰And then many will fall awayᵇ and betray one another and hate one another. ¹¹And many false prophets will arise and lead many astray. ¹²And because lawlessness will be increased, the love of many will grow cold. ¹³But the one who endures to the end will be saved. ¹⁴And this gospel of the kingdom will be proclaimed throughout the whole world as a testimony to all nations, and then the end will come.

THE ABOMINATION OF DESOLATION

¹⁵"So when you see the abomination of desolation spoken of by the prophet Daniel, standing in the holy place (let the reader understand), ¹⁶then let those who are in Judea flee to the mountains. ¹⁷Let the one who is on the housetop not go down to take what is in his house, ¹⁸and let the one who is in the field not turn back to take his cloak. ¹⁹And alas for women who are pregnant and for those who are nursing infants in those days! ²⁰Pray that your flight may not be in winter or on a Sabbath. ²¹For then there will be great tribulation, such as has not been from the beginning of the world until now, no, and never will be. ²²And if those days had not been cut short, no human being would be saved. But for the sake of the elect those days will be cut short. ²³Then if anyone says to you, 'Look, here is the Christ!' or 'There he is!' do not believe it. ²⁴For false christs and false prophets will arise and perform great signs and wonders, so as to lead astray, if possible, even the elect. ²⁵See, I have told you beforehand. ²⁶So, if they say to you, 'Look, he is in the wilderness', do not go out. If they say, 'Look, he is in the inner rooms', do not believe it. ²⁷For as the lightning comes from the east and shines as far as the west, so will

---
ᵃSome manuscripts omit *the son of Barachiah* ᵇOr *stumble*

be the coming of the Son of Man. ²⁸Wherever the corpse is, there the vultures will gather.

THE COMING OF THE SON OF MAN

²⁹"Immediately after the tribulation of those days the sun will be darkened, and the moon will not give its light, and the stars will fall from heaven, and the powers of the heavens will be shaken. ³⁰Then will appear in heaven the sign of the Son of Man, and then all the tribes of the earth will mourn, and they will see the Son of Man coming on the clouds of heaven with power and great glory. ³¹And he will send out his angels with a loud trumpet call, and they will gather his elect from the four winds, from one end of heaven to the other.

THE LESSON OF THE FIG TREE

³²"From the fig tree learn its lesson: as soon as its branch becomes tender and puts out its leaves, you know that summer is near. ³³So also, when you see all these things, you know that he is near, at the very gates. ³⁴Truly, I say to you, this generation will not pass away until all these things take place. ³⁵Heaven and earth will pass away, but my words will not pass away.

NO ONE KNOWS THAT DAY AND HOUR

³⁶"But concerning that day and hour no one knows, not even the angels of heaven, nor the Son,ᵃ but the Father only. ³⁷For as were the days of Noah, so will be the coming of the Son of Man. ³⁸For as in those days before the flood they were eating and drinking, marrying and giving in marriage, until the day when Noah entered the ark, ³⁹and they were unaware until the flood came and swept them all away, so will be the coming of the Son of Man. ⁴⁰Then two men will be in the field; one will be taken and one left. ⁴¹Two women will be grinding at the mill; one will be taken and one left. ⁴²Therefore, stay awake, for you do not know on what day your Lord is coming. ⁴³But know this, that if the master of the house had known in what part of the night the thief was coming, he would have stayed awake and would not have let his house be broken into. ⁴⁴Therefore you also must be ready, for the Son of Man is coming at an hour you do not expect.

⁴⁵"Who then is the faithful and wise servant,ᵇ whom his master has set over his household, to give them their food at the proper time? ⁴⁶Blessed is that servant whom his master will find so doing when he comes. ⁴⁷Truly, I say to you, he will set him over all his possessions. ⁴⁸But if that wicked servant says to himself, 'My master is delayed', ⁴⁹and begins to beat his fellow servantsᶜ and eats and drinks with drunkards, ⁵⁰the master of that servant will come on a day when he does not expect him and at an hour he does not know ⁵¹and will cut him in pieces and put him with the hypocrites. In that place there will be weeping and gnashing of teeth.

THE PARABLE OF THE TEN VIRGINS

25 "Then the kingdom of heaven will be like ten virgins who took their lampsᵈ and went to meet the bridegroom.ᵉ ²Five of them were foolish, and five were wise. ³For when the foolish took their lamps, they took no oil with them, ⁴but the wise took flasks of oil with their lamps. ⁵As the bridegroom was delayed, they all became drowsy and slept. ⁶But at midnight there was a cry, 'Here is the bridegroom! Come out to meet him.' ⁷Then all those virgins rose and trimmed their lamps. ⁸And the foolish said to the wise, 'Give us some of your oil, for our lamps are going out.' ⁹But the wise answered, saying, 'Since there will not be enough for us and for you, go rather to the dealers and buy for yourselves.' ¹⁰And while they were going to buy, the bridegroom came, and those who were ready went in with him to the marriage feast, and the door was shut. ¹¹Afterwards the other virgins came also, saying, 'Lord, lord, open to us.' ¹²But he answered, 'Truly, I say to you, I do not know you.' ¹³Watch therefore, for you know neither the day nor the hour.

THE PARABLE OF THE TALENTS

¹⁴"For it will be like a man going on a journey, who called his servantsᶠ and entrusted to them his property. ¹⁵To one he gave five talents,ᵍ to another two, to another one, to each according to his ability. Then he went away. ¹⁶He who had received the five talents went at once and traded with them, and he made five talents more. ¹⁷So also he who had the two talents made two talents more. ¹⁸But he who had received the one talent went and dug in the ground and hid his master's money. ¹⁹Now after a long time the master

---

ᵃSome manuscripts omit: *nor the Son* ᵇOr *bondservant*; also verses 46, 48, 50 ᶜOr *bondservants* ᵈOr *torches* ᵉSome manuscripts add *and the bride* ᶠOr *bondservants*; also verse 19 ᵍA *talent* was a monetary unit worth about twenty years' wages for a labourer

of those servants came and settled accounts with them. ²⁰And he who had received the five talents came forward, bringing five talents more, saying, 'Master, you delivered to me five talents; here, I have made five talents more.' ²¹His master said to him, 'Well done, good and faithful servant.ᵃ You have been faithful over a little; I will set you over much. Enter into the joy of your master.' ²²And he also who had the two talents came forward, saying, 'Master, you delivered to me two talents; here, I have made two talents more.' ²³His master said to him, 'Well done, good and faithful servant. You have been faithful over a little; I will set you over much. Enter into the joy of your master.' ²⁴He also who had received the one talent came forward, saying, 'Master, I knew you to be a hard man, reaping where you did not sow, and gathering where you scattered no seed, ²⁵so I was afraid, and I went and hid your talent in the ground. Here, you have what is yours.' ²⁶But his master answered him, 'You wicked and slothful servant! You knew that I reap where I have not sown and gather where I scattered no seed? ²⁷Then you ought to have invested my money with the bankers, and at my coming I should have received what was my own with interest. ²⁸So take the talent from him and give it to him who has the ten talents. ²⁹For to everyone who has will more be given, and he will have an abundance. But from the one who has not, even what he has will be taken away. ³⁰And cast the worthless servant into the outer darkness. In that place there will be weeping and gnashing of teeth.'

THE FINAL JUDGEMENT

³¹"When the Son of Man comes in his glory, and all the angels with him, then he will sit on his glorious throne. ³²Before him will be gathered all the nations, and he will separate people one from another as a shepherd separates the sheep from the goats. ³³And he will place the sheep on his right, but the goats on the left. ³⁴Then the King will say to those on his right, 'Come, you who are blessed by my Father, inherit the kingdom prepared for you from the foundation of the world. ³⁵For I was hungry and you gave me food, I was thirsty and you gave me drink, I was a stranger and you welcomed me, ³⁶I was naked and you clothed me, I was sick and you visited me, I was in prison and you came to me.' ³⁷Then the righteous will answer him, saying, 'Lord, when did we see you hungry and feed you, or thirsty and give you drink? ³⁸And when did we see you a stranger and welcome you, or naked and clothe you? ³⁹And when did we see you sick or in prison and visit you?' ⁴⁰And the King will answer them, 'Truly, I say to you, as you did it to one of the least of these my brothers,ᵇ you did it to me.'

⁴¹"Then he will say to those on his left, 'Depart from me, you cursed, into the eternal fire prepared for the devil and his angels. ⁴²For I was hungry and you gave me no food, I was thirsty and you gave me no drink, ⁴³I was a stranger and you did not welcome me, naked and you did not clothe me, sick and in prison and you did not visit me.' ⁴⁴Then they also will answer, saying, 'Lord, when did we see you hungry or thirsty or a stranger or naked or sick or in prison, and did not minister to you?' ⁴⁵Then he will answer them, saying, 'Truly, I say to you, as you did not do it to one of the least of these, you did not do it to me.' ⁴⁶And these will go away into eternal punishment, but the righteous into eternal life."

THE PLOT TO KILL JESUS

26 When Jesus had finished all these sayings, he said to his disciples, ²"You know that after two days the Passover is coming, and the Son of Man will be delivered up to be crucified."

³Then the chief priests and the elders of the people gathered in the palace of the high priest, whose name was Caiaphas, ⁴and plotted together in order to arrest Jesus by stealth and kill him. ⁵But they said, "Not during the feast, lest there be an uproar among the people."

JESUS ANOINTED AT BETHANY

⁶Now when Jesus was at Bethany in the house of Simon the leper,ᶜ ⁷a woman came up to him with an alabaster flask of very expensive ointment, and she poured it on his head as he reclined at table. ⁸And when the disciples saw it, they were indignant, saying, "Why this waste? ⁹For this could have been sold for a large sum and given to the poor." ¹⁰But Jesus, aware of this, said to them, "Why do you trouble the woman? For she has done a beautiful thing to me. ¹¹For you always have the poor with you, but you will not always have me. ¹²In pouring this ointment on my

---

ᵃOr *bondservant*; also verses 23, 26, 30   ᵇOr *brothers and sisters*
ᶜ*Leprosy* was a term for several skin diseases; see Leviticus 13

body, she has done it to prepare me for burial. ¹³Truly, I say to you, wherever this gospel is proclaimed in the whole world, what she has done will also be told in memory of her."

JUDAS TO BETRAY JESUS

¹⁴Then one of the twelve, whose name was Judas Iscariot, went to the chief priests ¹⁵and said, "What will you give me if I deliver him over to you?" And they paid him thirty pieces of silver. ¹⁶And from that moment he sought an opportunity to betray him.

THE PASSOVER WITH THE DISCIPLES

¹⁷Now on the first day of Unleavened Bread the disciples came to Jesus, saying, "Where would you have us prepare for you to eat the Passover?" ¹⁸He said, "Go into the city to a certain man and say to him, 'The Teacher says, My time is at hand. I will keep the Passover at your house with my disciples.'" ¹⁹And the disciples did as Jesus had directed them, and they prepared the Passover.

²⁰When it was evening, he reclined at table with the twelve.^{a} ²¹And as they were eating, he said, "Truly, I say to you, one of you will betray me." ²²And they were very sorrowful and began to say to him one after another, "Is it I, Lord?" ²³He answered, "He who has dipped his hand in the dish with me will betray me. ²⁴The Son of Man goes as it is written of him, but woe to that man by whom the Son of Man is betrayed! It would have been better for that man if he had not been born." ²⁵Judas, who would betray him, answered, "Is it I, Rabbi?" He said to him, "You have said so."

INSTITUTION OF THE LORD'S SUPPER

²⁶Now as they were eating, Jesus took bread, and after blessing it broke it and gave it to the disciples, and said, "Take, eat; this is my body." ²⁷And he took a cup, and when he had given thanks he gave it to them, saying, "Drink of it, all of you, ²⁸for this is my blood of the^b covenant, which is poured out for many for the forgiveness of sins. ²⁹I tell you I will not drink again of this fruit of the vine until that day when I drink it new with you in my Father's kingdom."

JESUS FORETELLS PETER'S DENIAL

³⁰And when they had sung a hymn, they went out to the Mount of Olives. ³¹Then Jesus said to them, "You will all fall away because of me this night. For it is written, 'I will strike the shepherd, and the sheep of the flock will be scattered.' ³²But after I am raised up, I will go before you to Galilee." ³³Peter answered him, "Though they all fall away because of you, I will never fall away." ³⁴Jesus said to him, "Truly, I tell you, this very night, before the cock crows, you will deny me three times." ³⁵Peter said to him, "Even if I must die with you, I will not deny you!" And all the disciples said the same.

JESUS PRAYS IN GETHSEMANE

³⁶Then Jesus went with them to a place called Gethsemane, and he said to his disciples, "Sit here, while I go over there and pray." ³⁷And taking with him Peter and the two sons of Zebedee, he began to be sorrowful and troubled. ³⁸Then he said to them, "My soul is very sorrowful, even to death; remain here, and watch^c with me." ³⁹And going a little farther he fell on his face and prayed, saying, "My Father, if it be possible, let this cup pass from me; nevertheless, not as I will, but as you will." ⁴⁰And he came to the disciples and found them sleeping. And he said to Peter, "So, could you not watch with me one hour? ⁴¹Watch and pray that you may not enter into temptation. The spirit indeed is willing, but the flesh is weak." ⁴²Again, for the second time, he went away and prayed, "My Father, if this cannot pass unless I drink it, your will be done." ⁴³And again he came and found them sleeping, for their eyes were heavy. ⁴⁴So, leaving them again, he went away and prayed for the third time, saying the same words again. ⁴⁵Then he came to the disciples and said to them, "Sleep and take your rest later on.^{d} See, the hour is at hand, and the Son of Man is betrayed into the hands of sinners. ⁴⁶Rise, let us be going; see, my betrayer is at hand."

BETRAYAL AND ARREST OF JESUS

⁴⁷While he was still speaking, Judas came, one of the twelve, and with him a great crowd with swords and clubs, from the chief priests and the elders of the people. ⁴⁸Now the betrayer had given them a sign, saying, "The one I will kiss is the man; seize him." ⁴⁹And he came up to Jesus at once and said, "Greetings, Rabbi!" And he kissed him. ⁵⁰Jesus said to him, "Friend, do what you came to do."^{e} Then they came up and laid hands on Jesus

---

^{a}Some manuscripts add *disciples* ^{b}Some manuscripts insert *new* ^{c}Or *keep awake*; also verses 40, 41 ^{d}Or *Are you still sleeping and taking your rest?* ^{e}Or *Friend, why are you here?*

and seized him. ⁵¹And behold, one of those who were with Jesus stretched out his hand and drew his sword and struck the servantᵃ of the high priest and cut off his ear. ⁵²Then Jesus said to him, "Put your sword back into its place. For all who take the sword will perish by the sword. ⁵³Do you think that I cannot appeal to my Father, and he will at once send me more than twelve legions of angels? ⁵⁴But how then should the Scriptures be fulfilled, that it must be so?" ⁵⁵At that hour Jesus said to the crowds, "Have you come out as against a robber, with swords and clubs to capture me? Day after day I sat in the temple teaching, and you did not seize me. ⁵⁶But all this has taken place that the Scriptures of the prophets might be fulfilled." Then all the disciples left him and fled.

JESUS BEFORE CAIAPHAS AND THE COUNCIL

⁵⁷Then those who had seized Jesus led him to Caiaphas the high priest, where the scribes and the elders had gathered. ⁵⁸And Peter was following him at a distance, as far as the courtyard of the high priest, and going inside he sat with the guards to see the end. ⁵⁹Now the chief priests and the whole councilᵇ were seeking false testimony against Jesus that they might put him to death, ⁶⁰but they found none, though many false witnesses came forward. At last two came forward ⁶¹and said, "This man said, 'I am able to destroy the temple of God, and to rebuild it in three days.'" ⁶²And the high priest stood up and said, "Have you no answer to make? What is it that these men testify against you?"ᶜ ⁶³But Jesus remained silent. And the high priest said to him, "I adjure you by the living God, tell us if you are the Christ, the Son of God." ⁶⁴Jesus said to him, "You have said so. But I tell you, from now on you will see the Son of Man seated at the right hand of Power and coming on the clouds of heaven." ⁶⁵Then the high priest tore his robes and said, "He has uttered blasphemy. What further witnesses do we need? You have now heard his blasphemy. ⁶⁶What is your judgement?" They answered, "He deserves death." ⁶⁷Then they spat in his face and struck him. And some slapped him, ⁶⁸saying, "Prophesy to us, you Christ! Who is it that struck you?"

PETER DENIES JESUS

⁶⁹Now Peter was sitting outside in the courtyard. And a servant girl came up to him and said, "You also were with Jesus the Galilean." ⁷⁰But he denied it before them all, saying, "I do not know what you mean." ⁷¹And when he went out to the entrance, another servant girl saw him, and she said to the bystanders, "This man was with Jesus of Nazareth." ⁷²And again he denied it with an oath: "I do not know the man." ⁷³After a little while the bystanders came up and said to Peter, "Certainly you too are one of them, for your accent betrays you." ⁷⁴Then he began to invoke a curse on himself and to swear, "I do not know the man." And immediately the cock crowed. ⁷⁵And Peter remembered the saying of Jesus, "Before the cock crows, you will deny me three times." And he went out and wept bitterly.

JESUS DELIVERED TO PILATE

27 When morning came, all the chief priests and the elders of the people took counsel against Jesus to put him to death. ²And they bound him and led him away and delivered him over to Pilate the governor.

JUDAS HANGS HIMSELF

³Then when Judas, his betrayer, saw that Jesusᵈ was condemned, he changed his mind and brought back the thirty pieces of silver to the chief priests and the elders, ⁴saying, "I have sinned by betraying innocent blood." They said, "What is that to us? See to it yourself." ⁵And throwing down the pieces of silver into the temple, he departed, and he went and hanged himself. ⁶But the chief priests, taking the pieces of silver, said, "It is not lawful to put them into the treasury, since it is blood money." ⁷So they took counsel and bought with them the potter's field as a burial place for strangers. ⁸Therefore that field has been called the Field of Blood to this day. ⁹Then was fulfilled what had been spoken by the prophet Jeremiah, saying, "And they took the thirty pieces of silver, the price of him on whom a price had been set by some of the sons of Israel, ¹⁰and they gave them for the potter's field, as the Lord directed me."

JESUS BEFORE PILATE

¹¹Now Jesus stood before the governor, and the governor asked him, "Are you the King of the Jews?" Jesus said, "You have said so." ¹²But

---

ᵃOr bondservant ᵇGreek *Sanhedrin* ᶜOr *Have you no answer to what these men testify against you?* ᵈGreek *he* when he was accused by the chief priests and elders, he gave no answer. ¹³Then Pilate said to him, "Do you not hear how many things they testify against you?" ¹⁴But he gave him no answer, not even to a single charge, so that the governor was greatly amazed.

THE CROWD CHOOSES BARABBAS

¹⁵Now at the feast the governor was accustomed to release for the crowd any one prisoner whom they wanted. ¹⁶And they had then a notorious prisoner called Barabbas. ¹⁷So when they had gathered, Pilate said to them, "Whom do you want me to release for you: Barabbas, or Jesus who is called Christ?" ¹⁸For he knew that it was out of envy that they had delivered him up. ¹⁹Besides, while he was sitting on the judgement seat, his wife sent word to him, "Have nothing to do with that righteous man, for I have suffered much because of him today in a dream." ²⁰Now the chief priests and the elders persuaded the crowd to ask for Barabbas and destroy Jesus. ²¹The governor again said to them, "Which of the two do you want me to release for you?" And they said, "Barabbas." ²²Pilate said to them, "Then what shall I do with Jesus who is called Christ?" They all said, "Let him be crucified!" ²³And he said, "Why? What evil has he done?" But they shouted all the more, "Let him be crucified!"

PILATE DELIVERS JESUS TO BE CRUCIFIED

²⁴So when Pilate saw that he was gaining nothing, but rather that a riot was beginning, he took water and washed his hands before the crowd, saying, "I am innocent of this man's blood;^{a} see to it yourselves." ²⁵And all the people answered, "His blood be on us and on our children!" ²⁶Then he released for them Barabbas, and having scourged^b Jesus, delivered him to be crucified.

JESUS IS MOCKED

²⁷Then the soldiers of the governor took Jesus into the governor's headquarters,^{c} and they gathered the whole battalion^d before him. ²⁸And they stripped him and put a scarlet robe on him, ²⁹and twisting together a crown of thorns, they put it on his head and put a reed in his right hand. And kneeling before him, they mocked him, saying, "Hail, King of the Jews!" ³⁰And they spat on him and took the reed and struck him on the head. ³¹And when they had mocked him, they stripped him of the robe and put his own clothes on him and led him away to crucify him.

THE CRUCIFIXION

³²As they went out, they found a man of Cyrene, Simon by name. They compelled this man to carry his cross. ³³And when they came to a place called Golgotha (which means Place of a Skull), ³⁴they offered him wine to drink, mixed with gall, but when he tasted it, he would not drink it. ³⁵And when they had crucified him, they divided his garments among them by casting lots. ³⁶Then they sat down and kept watch over him there. ³⁷And over his head they put the charge against him, which read, "This is Jesus, the King of the Jews." ³⁸Then two robbers were crucified with him, one on the right and one on the left. ³⁹And those who passed by derided him, wagging their heads ⁴⁰and saying, "You who would destroy the temple and rebuild it in three days, save yourself! If you are the Son of God, come down from the cross." ⁴¹So also the chief priests, with the scribes and elders, mocked him, saying, ⁴²"He saved others; he cannot save himself. He is the King of Israel; let him come down now from the cross, and we will believe in him. ⁴³He trusts in God; let God deliver him now, if he desires him. For he said, 'I am the Son of God.'" ⁴⁴And the robbers who were crucified with him also reviled him in the same way.

THE DEATH OF JESUS

⁴⁵Now from the sixth hour^e there was darkness over all the land^f until the ninth hour.^{g} ⁴⁶And about the ninth hour Jesus cried out with a loud voice, saying, "Eli, Eli, lema sabachthani?" that is, "My God, my God, why have you forsaken me?" ⁴⁷And some of the bystanders, hearing it, said, "This man is calling Elijah." ⁴⁸And one of them at once ran and took a sponge, filled it with sour wine, and put it on a reed and gave it to him to drink. ⁴⁹But the others said, "Wait, let us see whether Elijah will come to save him." ⁵⁰And Jesus cried out again with a loud voice and yielded up his spirit.

⁵¹And behold, the curtain of the temple was torn in two, from top to bottom. And the earth shook, and the rocks were split.

---

^{a}Some manuscripts *this righteous blood*, or *this righteous man's blood*
^{b}A Roman judicial penalty, consisting of a severe beating with a multi-lashed whip containing embedded pieces of bone and metal
^{c}Greek *the praetorium* ^{d}Greek *cohort*; a tenth of a Roman legion, usually about 600 men ^{e}That is, noon ^{f}Or *earth* ^{g}That is, 3 P.M.

⁵²The tombs also were opened. And many bodies of the saints who had fallen asleep were raised, ⁵³and coming out of the tombs after his resurrection they went into the holy city and appeared to many. ⁵⁴When the centurion and those who were with him, keeping watch over Jesus, saw the earthquake and what took place, they were filled with awe and said, "Truly this was the Son[a] of God!"

⁵⁵There were also many women there, looking on from a distance, who had followed Jesus from Galilee, ministering to him, ⁵⁶among whom were Mary Magdalene and Mary the mother of James and Joseph and the mother of the sons of Zebedee.

JESUS IS BURIED

⁵⁷When it was evening, there came a rich man from Arimathea, named Joseph, who also was a disciple of Jesus. ⁵⁸He went to Pilate and asked for the body of Jesus. Then Pilate ordered it to be given to him. ⁵⁹And Joseph took the body and wrapped it in a clean linen shroud ⁶⁰and laid it in his own new tomb, which he had cut in the rock. And he rolled a great stone to the entrance of the tomb and went away. ⁶¹Mary Magdalene and the other Mary were there, sitting opposite the tomb.

THE GUARD AT THE TOMB

⁶²The next day, that is, after the day of Preparation, the chief priests and the Pharisees gathered before Pilate ⁶³and said, "Sir, we remember how that impostor said, while he was still alive, 'After three days I will rise.' ⁶⁴Therefore order the tomb to be made secure until the third day, lest his disciples go and steal him away and tell the people, 'He has risen from the dead', and the last fraud will be worse than the first." ⁶⁵Pilate said to them, "You have a guard[b] of soldiers. Go, make it as secure as you can." ⁶⁶So they went and made the tomb secure by sealing the stone and setting a guard.

THE RESURRECTION

28 Now after the Sabbath, towards the dawn of the first day of the week, Mary Magdalene and the other Mary went to see the tomb. ²And behold, there was a great earthquake, for an angel of the Lord descended from heaven and came and rolled back the stone and sat on it. ³His appearance was like lightning, and his clothing white as snow. ⁴And for fear of him the guards trembled and became like dead men. ⁵But the angel said to the women, "Do not be afraid, for I know that you seek Jesus who was crucified. ⁶He is not here, for he has risen, as he said. Come, see the place where he[c] lay. ⁷Then go quickly and tell his disciples that he has risen from the dead, and behold, he is going before you to Galilee; there you will see him. See, I have told you." ⁸So they departed quickly from the tomb with fear and great joy, and ran to tell his disciples. ⁹And behold, Jesus met them and said, "Greetings!" And they came up and took hold of his feet and worshiped him. ¹⁰Then Jesus said to them, "Do not be afraid; go and tell my brothers to go to Galilee, and there they will see me."

THE REPORT OF THE GUARD

¹¹While they were going, behold, some of the guard went into the city and told the chief priests all that had taken place. ¹²And when they had assembled with the elders and taken counsel, they gave a sufficient sum of money to the soldiers ¹³and said, "Tell people, 'His disciples came by night and stole him away while we were asleep.' ¹⁴And if this comes to the governor's ears, we will satisfy him and keep you out of trouble." ¹⁵So they took the money and did as they were directed. And this story has been spread among the Jews to this day.

THE GREAT COMMISSION

¹⁶Now the eleven disciples went to Galilee, to the mountain to which Jesus had directed them. ¹⁷And when they saw him they worshiped him, but some doubted. ¹⁸And Jesus came and said to them, "All authority in heaven and on earth has been given to me. ¹⁹Go therefore and make disciples of all nations, baptizing them in[d] the name of the Father and of the Son and of the Holy Spirit, ²⁰teaching them to observe all that I have commanded you. And behold, I am with you always, to the end of the age."

---

[a] Or a son [b] Or Take a guard [c] Some manuscripts the Lord [d] Or into

THE GOSPEL ACCORDING TO MARK

JOHN THE BAPTIST PREPARES THE WAY

1 The beginning of the gospel of Jesus Christ, the Son of God.[a] ²As it is written in Isaiah the prophet,[b]

"Behold, I send my messenger
 before your face,
who will prepare your way,
³ the voice of one crying in
 the wilderness:
 'Prepare[c] the way of the Lord,
 make his paths straight,'"

⁴John appeared, baptizing in the wilderness and proclaiming a baptism of repentance for the forgiveness of sins. ⁵And all the country of Judea and all Jerusalem were going out to him and were being baptized by him in the river Jordan, confessing their sins. ⁶Now John was clothed with camel's hair and wore a leather belt round his waist and ate locusts and wild honey. ⁷And he preached, saying, "After me comes he who is mightier than I, the strap of whose sandals I am not worthy to stoop down and untie. ⁸I have baptized you with water, but he will baptize you with the Holy Spirit."

THE BAPTISM OF JESUS

⁹In those days Jesus came from Nazareth of Galilee and was baptized by John in the Jordan. ¹⁰And when he came up out of the water, immediately he saw the heavens being torn open and the Spirit descending on him like a dove. ¹¹And a voice came from heaven, "You are my beloved Son;[d] with you I am well pleased."

THE TEMPTATION OF JESUS

¹²The Spirit immediately drove him out into the wilderness. ¹³And he was in the wilderness forty days, being tempted by Satan. And he was with the wild animals, and the angels were ministering to him.

JESUS BEGINS HIS MINISTRY

¹⁴Now after John was arrested, Jesus came into Galilee, proclaiming the gospel of God, ¹⁵and saying, "The time is fulfilled, and the kingdom of God is at hand;[e] repent and believe in the gospel."

JESUS CALLS THE FIRST DISCIPLES

¹⁶Passing alongside the Sea of Galilee, he saw Simon and Andrew the brother of Simon casting a net into the sea, for they were fishermen. ¹⁷And Jesus said to them, "Follow me, and I will make you become fishers of men."[f] ¹⁸And immediately they left their nets and followed him. ¹⁹And going on a little farther, he saw James the son of Zebedee and John his brother, who were in their boat mending the nets. ²⁰And immediately he called them, and they left their father Zebedee in the boat with the hired servants and followed him.

JESUS HEALS A MAN WITH AN UNCLEAN SPIRIT

²¹And they went into Capernaum, and immediately on the Sabbath he entered the synagogue and was teaching. ²²And they were astonished at his teaching, for he taught them as one who had authority, and not as the scribes. ²³And immediately there was in their synagogue a man with an unclean spirit. And he cried out, ²⁴"What have you to do with us, Jesus of Nazareth? Have you come to destroy us? I know who you are—the Holy One of God." ²⁵But Jesus rebuked him, saying, "Be silent, and come out of him!" ²⁶And the unclean spirit, convulsing him and crying out with a loud voice, came out of him. ²⁷And they were all amazed, so that they questioned among themselves, saying, "What is this? A new teaching with authority! He commands even the unclean spirits, and they obey him." ²⁸And at once his fame spread everywhere throughout all the surrounding region of Galilee.

---

[a]Some manuscripts omit *the Son of God* [b]Some manuscripts *in the prophets* [c]Or *crying: Prepare in the wilderness* [d]Or *my Son, my (or the) Beloved* [e]Or *the kingdom of God has come near* [f]The Greek word *anthropoi* refers here to both men and women

JESUS HEALS MANY

²⁹And immediately he^a left the synagogue and entered the house of Simon and Andrew, with James and John. ³⁰Now Simon's mother-in-law lay ill with a fever, and immediately they told him about her. ³¹And he came and took her by the hand and lifted her up, and the fever left her, and she began to serve them.

³²That evening at sunset they brought to him all who were sick or oppressed by demons. ³³And the whole city was gathered together at the door. ³⁴And he healed many who were sick with various diseases, and cast out many demons. And he would not permit the demons to speak, because they knew him.

JESUS PREACHES IN GALILEE

³⁵And rising very early in the morning, while it was still dark, he departed and went out to a desolate place, and there he prayed. ³⁶And Simon and those who were with him searched for him, ³⁷and they found him and said to him, "Everyone is looking for you." ³⁸And he said to them, "Let us go on to the next towns, that I may preach there also, for that is what I came for." ³⁹And he went throughout all Galilee, preaching in their synagogues and casting out demons.

JESUS CLEANSES A LEPER

⁴⁰And a leper^b came to him, imploring him, and kneeling said to him, "If you will, you can make me clean." ⁴¹Moved with pity, he stretched out his hand and touched him and said to him, "I will; be clean." ⁴²And immediately the leprosy left him, and he was made clean. ⁴³And Jesus^c sternly charged him and sent him away at once, ⁴⁴and said to him, "See that you say nothing to anyone, but go, show yourself to the priest and offer for your cleansing what Moses commanded, for a proof to them." ⁴⁵But he went out and began to talk freely about it, and to spread the news, so that Jesus could no longer openly enter a town, but was out in desolate places, and people were coming to him from every quarter.

JESUS HEALS A PARALYTIC

2 And when he returned to Capernaum after some days, it was reported that he was at home. ²And many were gathered together, so that there was no more room, not even at the door. And he was preaching the word to them. ³And they came, bringing to him a paralytic carried by four men. ⁴And when they could not get near him because of the crowd, they removed the roof above him, and when they had made an opening, they let down the bed on which the paralytic lay. ⁵And when Jesus saw their faith, he said to the paralytic, "Son, your sins are forgiven." ⁶Now some of the scribes were sitting there, questioning in their hearts, ⁷"Why does this man speak like that? He is blaspheming! Who can forgive sins but God alone?" ⁸And immediately Jesus, perceiving in his spirit that they thus questioned within themselves, said to them, "Why do you question these things in your hearts? ⁹Which is easier, to say to the paralytic, 'Your sins are forgiven', or to say, 'Rise, take up your bed and walk'? ¹⁰But that you may know that the Son of Man has authority on earth to forgive sins"— he said to the paralytic— ¹¹"I say to you, rise, pick up your bed, and go home." ¹²And he rose and immediately picked up his bed and went out before them all, so that they were all amazed and glorified God, saying, "We never saw anything like this!"

JESUS CALLS LEVI

¹³He went out again beside the lake, and all the crowd was coming to him, and he was teaching them. ¹⁴And as he passed by, he saw Levi the son of Alphaeus sitting at the tax booth, and he said to him, "Follow me." And he rose and followed him.

¹⁵And as he reclined at table in his house, many tax collectors and sinners were reclining with Jesus and his disciples, for there were many who followed him. ¹⁶And the scribes of^d the Pharisees, when they saw that he was eating with sinners and tax collectors, said to his disciples, "Why does he eat^e with tax collectors and sinners?" ¹⁷And when Jesus heard it, he said to them, "Those who are well have no need of a physician, but those who are sick. I came not to call the righteous, but sinners."

A QUESTION ABOUT FASTING

¹⁸Now John's disciples and the Pharisees were fasting. And people came and said to him, "Why do John's disciples and the disciples of the Pharisees fast, but your disciples

---

^aSome manuscripts *they* ^b*Leprosy* was a term for several skin diseases; see Leviticus 13 ^cGreek *he*; also verse 45
^dSome manuscripts *and* ^eSome manuscripts add *and drink*

do not fast?" ¹⁹And Jesus said to them, "Can the wedding guests fast while the bridegroom is with them? As long as they have the bridegroom with them, they cannot fast. ²⁰The days will come when the bridegroom is taken away from them, and then they will fast in that day. ²¹No one sews a piece of unshrunk cloth on an old garment. If he does, the patch tears away from it, the new from the old, and a worse tear is made. ²²And no one puts new wine into old wineskins. If he does, the wine will burst the skins — and the wine is destroyed, and so are the skins. But new wine is for fresh wineskins."[a]

JESUS IS LORD OF THE SABBATH

²³One Sabbath he was going through the cornfields, and as they made their way, his disciples began to pluck ears of corn. ²⁴And the Pharisees were saying to him, "Look, why are they doing what is not lawful on the Sabbath?" ²⁵And he said to them, "Have you never read what David did, when he was in need and was hungry, he and those who were with him: ²⁶how he entered the house of God, in the time of[b] Abiathar the high priest, and ate the bread of the Presence, which it is not lawful for any but the priests to eat, and also gave it to those who were with him?" ²⁷And he said to them, "The Sabbath was made for man, not man for the Sabbath. ²⁸So the Son of Man is lord even of the Sabbath."

A MAN WITH A WITHERED HAND

3 Again he entered the synagogue, and a man was there with a withered hand. ²And they watched Jesus,[c] to see whether he would heal him on the Sabbath, so that they might accuse him. ³And he said to the man with the withered hand, "Come here." ⁴And he said to them, "Is it lawful on the Sabbath to do good or to do harm, to save life or to kill?" But they were silent. ⁵And he looked round at them with anger, grieved at their hardness of heart, and said to the man, "Stretch out your hand." He stretched it out, and his hand was restored. ⁶The Pharisees went out and immediately held counsel with the Herodians against him, how to destroy him.

A GREAT CROWD FOLLOWS JESUS

⁷Jesus withdrew with his disciples to the sea, and a great crowd followed, from Galilee and Judea ⁸and Jerusalem and Idumea and from beyond the Jordan and from around Tyre and Sidon. When the great crowd heard all that he was doing, they came to him. ⁹And he told his disciples to have a boat ready for him because of the crowd, lest they crush him, ¹⁰for he had healed many, so that all who had diseases pressed around him to touch him. ¹¹And whenever the unclean spirits saw him, they fell down before him and cried out, "You are the Son of God." ¹²And he strictly ordered them not to make him known.

THE TWELVE APOSTLES

¹³And he went up on the mountain and called to him those whom he desired, and they came to him. ¹⁴And he appointed twelve (whom he also named apostles) so that they might be with him and he might send them out to preach ¹⁵and have authority to cast out demons. ¹⁶He appointed the twelve: Simon (to whom he gave the name Peter); ¹⁷James the son of Zebedee and John the brother of James (to whom he gave the name Boanerges, that is, Sons of Thunder); ¹⁸Andrew, and Philip, and Bartholomew, and Matthew, and Thomas, and James the son of Alphaeus, and Thaddaeus, and Simon the Zealot,[d] ¹⁹and Judas Iscariot, who betrayed him.

²⁰Then he went home, and the crowd gathered again, so that they could not even eat. ²¹And when his family heard it, they went out to seize him, for they were saying, "He is out of his mind."

BLASPHEMY AGAINST THE HOLY SPIRIT

²²And the scribes who came down from Jerusalem were saying, "He is possessed by Beelzebul," and "by the prince of demons he casts out the demons." ²³And he called them to him and said to them in parables, "How can Satan cast out Satan? ²⁴If a kingdom is divided against itself, that kingdom cannot stand. ²⁵And if a house is divided against itself, that house will not be able to stand. ²⁶And if Satan has risen up against himself and is divided, he cannot stand, but is coming to an end. ²⁷But no one can enter a strong man's house and plunder his goods, unless he first binds the strong man. Then indeed he may plunder his house.

²⁸"Truly, I say to you, all sins will be forgiven the children of man, and whatever blasphemies they utter, ²⁹but whoever blasphemes against the Holy Spirit never has

---

[a]Some manuscripts omit *But new wine is for fresh wineskins* [b]Or *in the passage about* [c]Greek *him* [d]Greek *kananaios*, meaning *zealot*

forgiveness, but is guilty of an eternal sin"— ³⁰for they were saying, "He has an unclean spirit."

JESUS' MOTHER AND BROTHERS

³¹And his mother and his brothers came, and standing outside they sent to him and called him. ³²And a crowd was sitting around him, and they said to him, "Your mother and your brothers[a] are outside, seeking you." ³³And he answered them, "Who are my mother and my brothers?" ³⁴And looking about at those who sat around him, he said, "Here are my mother and my brothers! ³⁵For whoever does the will of God, he is my brother and sister and mother."

THE PARABLE OF THE SOWER

4 Again he began to teach beside the sea. And a very large crowd gathered about him, so that he got into a boat and sat in it on the sea, and the whole crowd was beside the sea on the land. ²And he was teaching them many things in parables, and in his teaching he said to them: ³"Listen! Behold, a sower went out to sow. ⁴And as he sowed, some seed fell along the path, and the birds came and devoured it. ⁵Other seed fell on rocky ground, where it did not have much soil, and immediately it sprang up, since it had no depth of soil. ⁶And when the sun rose, it was scorched, and since it had no root, it withered away. ⁷Other seed fell among thorns, and the thorns grew up and choked it, and it yielded no grain. ⁸And other seeds fell into good soil and produced grain, growing up and increasing and yielding thirtyfold and sixtyfold and a hundredfold." ⁹And he said, "He who has ears to hear, let him hear."

THE PURPOSE OF THE PARABLES

¹⁰And when he was alone, those around him with the twelve asked him about the parables. ¹¹And he said to them, "To you has been given the secret of the kingdom of God, but for those outside everything is in parables, ¹²so that

"'they may indeed see but not perceive,
  and may indeed hear but not understand,
lest they should turn and be forgiven.'"

¹³And he said to them, "Do you not understand this parable? How then will you understand all the parables? ¹⁴The sower sows the word. ¹⁵And these are the ones along the path, where the word is sown: when they hear, Satan immediately comes and takes away the word that is sown in them. ¹⁶And these are the ones sown on rocky ground: the ones who, when they hear the word, immediately receive it with joy. ¹⁷And they have no root in themselves, but endure for a while; then, when tribulation or persecution arises on account of the word, immediately they fall away.[b] ¹⁸And others are the ones sown among thorns. They are those who hear the word, ¹⁹but the cares of the world and the deceitfulness of riches and the desires for other things enter in and choke the word, and it proves unfruitful. ²⁰But those that were sown on the good soil are the ones who hear the word and accept it and bear fruit, thirtyfold and sixtyfold and a hundredfold."

A LAMP UNDER A BASKET

²¹And he said to them, "Is a lamp brought in to be put under a basket, or under a bed, and not on a stand? ²²For nothing is hidden except to be made manifest; nor is anything secret except to come to light. ²³If anyone has ears to hear, let him hear." ²⁴And he said to them, "Pay attention to what you hear: with the measure you use, it will be measured to you, and still more will be added to you. ²⁵For to the one who has, more will be given, and from the one who has not, even what he has will be taken away."

THE PARABLE OF THE SEED GROWING

²⁶And he said, "The kingdom of God is as if a man should scatter seed on the ground. ²⁷He sleeps and rises night and day, and the seed sprouts and grows; he knows not how. ²⁸The earth produces by itself, first the blade, then the ear, then the full grain in the ear. ²⁹But when the grain is ripe, at once he puts in the sickle, because the harvest has come."

THE PARABLE OF THE MUSTARD SEED

³⁰And he said, "With what can we compare the kingdom of God, or what parable shall we use for it? ³¹It is like a grain of mustard seed, which, when sown on the ground, is the smallest of all the seeds on earth, ³²yet when it is sown it grows up and becomes larger than all the garden plants and puts out large branches, so that the birds of the air can make nests in its shade."

---

[a]Other manuscripts add *and your sisters* [b]Or *stumble*

³³With many such parables he spoke the word to them, as they were able to hear it. ³⁴He did not speak to them without a parable, but privately to his own disciples he explained everything.

JESUS CALMS A STORM

³⁵On that day, when evening had come, he said to them, "Let us go across to the other side." ³⁶And leaving the crowd, they took him with them in the boat, just as he was. And other boats were with him. ³⁷And a great windstorm arose, and the waves were breaking into the boat, so that the boat was already filling. ³⁸But he was in the stern, asleep on the cushion. And they woke him and said to him, "Teacher, do you not care that we are perishing?" ³⁹And he awoke and rebuked the wind and said to the sea, "Peace! Be still!" And the wind ceased, and there was a great calm. ⁴⁰He said to them, "Why are you so afraid? Have you still no faith?" ⁴¹And they were filled with great fear and said to one another, "Who then is this, that even the wind and the sea obey him?"

JESUS HEALS A MAN WITH A DEMON

5 They came to the other side of the lake, to the country of the Gerasenes.ᵃ ²And when Jesusᵇ had stepped out of the boat, immediately there met him out of the tombs a man with an unclean spirit. ³He lived among the tombs. And no one could bind him any more, not even with a chain, ⁴for he had often been bound with shackles and chains, but he wrenched the chains apart, and he broke the shackles in pieces. No one had the strength to subdue him. ⁵Night and day among the tombs and on the mountains he was always crying out and cutting himself with stones. ⁶And when he saw Jesus from afar, he ran and fell down before him. ⁷And crying out with a loud voice, he said, "What have you to do with me, Jesus, Son of the Most High God? I adjure you by God, do not torment me." ⁸For he was saying to him, "Come out of the man, you unclean spirit!" ⁹And Jesus asked him, "What is your name?" He replied, "My name is Legion, for we are many." ¹⁰And he begged him earnestly not to send them out of the country. ¹¹Now a great herd of pigs was feeding there on the hillside, ¹²and they begged him, saying, "Send us to the pigs; let us enter them." ¹³So he gave them permission. And the unclean spirits came out and entered the pigs; and the herd, numbering about two thousand, rushed down the steep bank into the sea and drowned in the sea.

¹⁴The herdsmen fled and told it in the city and in the country. And people came to see what it was that had happened. ¹⁵And they came to Jesus and saw the demon-possessedᶜ man, the one who had had the legion, sitting there, clothed and in his right mind, and they were afraid. ¹⁶And those who had seen it described to them what had happened to the demon-possessed man and to the pigs. ¹⁷And they began to beg Jesusᵈ to depart from their region. ¹⁸As he was getting into the boat, the man who had been possessed with demons begged him that he might be with him. ¹⁹And he did not permit him but said to him, "Go home to your friends and tell them how much the Lord has done for you, and how he has had mercy on you." ²⁰And he went away and began to proclaim in the Decapolis how much Jesus had done for him, and everyone marvelled.

JESUS HEALS A WOMAN AND JAIRUS'S DAUGHTER

²¹And when Jesus had crossed again in the boat to the other side, a great crowd gathered about him, and he was beside the sea. ²²Then came one of the rulers of the synagogue, Jairus by name, and seeing him, he fell at his feet ²³and implored him earnestly, saying, "My little daughter is at the point of death. Come and lay your hands on her, so that she may be made well and live." ²⁴And he went with him.

And a great crowd followed him and thronged about him. ²⁵And there was a woman who had had a discharge of blood for twelve years, ²⁶and who had suffered much under many physicians, and had spent all that she had, and was no better but rather grew worse. ²⁷She had heard the reports about Jesus and came up behind him in the crowd and touched his garment. ²⁸For she said, "If I touch even his garments, I will be made well." ²⁹And immediately the flow of blood dried up, and she felt in her body that she was healed of her disease. ³⁰And Jesus, perceiving in himself that power had gone out from him, immediately turned about in the crowd and said, "Who touched my garments?" ³¹And

---

ᵃSome manuscripts *Cergesenes*; some *Gadarenes* ᵇGreek *he*; also verse 9 ᶜGreek *daimonizomai* (demonized); also verses 16, 18; elsewhere rendered *oppressed by demons* ᵈGreek *him*

his disciples said to him, "You see the crowd pressing around you, and yet you say, 'Who touched me?'" ³²And he looked round to see who had done it. ³³But the woman, knowing what had happened to her, came in fear and trembling and fell down before him and told him the whole truth. ³⁴And he said to her, "Daughter, your faith has made you well; go in peace, and be healed of your disease."

³⁵While he was still speaking, there came from the ruler's house some who said, "Your daughter is dead. Why trouble the Teacher any further?" ³⁶But overhearing[a] what they said, Jesus said to the ruler of the synagogue, "Do not fear, only believe." ³⁷And he allowed no one to follow him except Peter and James and John the brother of James. ³⁸They came to the house of the ruler of the synagogue, and Jesus[b] saw a commotion, people weeping and wailing loudly. ³⁹And when he had entered, he said to them, "Why are you making a commotion and weeping? The child is not dead but sleeping." ⁴⁰And they laughed at him. But he put them all outside and took the child's father and mother and those who were with him and went in where the child was. ⁴¹Taking her by the hand he said to her, "Talitha cumi", which means, "Little girl, I say to you, arise." ⁴²And immediately the girl got up and began walking (for she was twelve years of age), and they were immediately overcome with amazement. ⁴³And he strictly charged them that no one should know this, and told them to give her something to eat.

JESUS REJECTED AT NAZARETH

6 He went away from there and came to his home town, and his disciples followed him. ²And on the Sabbath he began to teach in the synagogue, and many who heard him were astonished, saying, "Where did this man get these things? What is the wisdom given to him? How are such mighty works done by his hands? ³Is not this the carpenter, the son of Mary and brother of James and Joses and Judas and Simon? And are not his sisters here with us?" And they took offence at him. ⁴And Jesus said to them, "A prophet is not without honour, except in his home town and among his relatives and in his own household." ⁵And he could do no mighty work there, except that he laid his hands on a few sick people and healed them. ⁶And he marvelled because of their unbelief.

And he went about among the villages teaching.

JESUS SENDS OUT THE TWELVE APOSTLES

⁷And he called the twelve and began to send them out two by two, and gave them authority over the unclean spirits. ⁸He charged them to take nothing for their journey except a staff—no bread, no bag, no money in their belts— ⁹but to wear sandals and not put on two tunics.[c] ¹⁰And he said to them, "Whenever you enter a house, stay there until you depart from there. ¹¹And if any place will not receive you and they will not listen to you, when you leave, shake off the dust that is on your feet as a testimony against them." ¹²So they went out and proclaimed that people should repent. ¹³And they cast out many demons and anointed with oil many who were sick and healed them.

THE DEATH OF JOHN THE BAPTIST

¹⁴King Herod heard of it, for Jesus'[d] name had become known. Some[e] said, "John the Baptist[f] has been raised from the dead. That is why these miraculous powers are at work in him." ¹⁵But others said, "He is Elijah." And others said, "He is a prophet, like one of the prophets of old." ¹⁶But when Herod heard of it, he said, "John, whom I beheaded, has been raised." ¹⁷For it was Herod who had sent and seized John and bound him in prison for the sake of Herodias, his brother Philip's wife, because he had married her. ¹⁸For John had been saying to Herod, "It is not lawful for you to have your brother's wife." ¹⁹And Herodias had a grudge against him and wanted to put him to death. But she could not, ²⁰for Herod feared John, knowing that he was a righteous and holy man, and he kept him safe. When he heard him, he was greatly perplexed, and yet he heard him gladly.

²¹But an opportunity came when Herod on his birthday gave a banquet for his nobles and military commanders and the leading men of Galilee. ²²For when Herodias's daughter came in and danced, she pleased Herod and his guests. And the king said to the girl, "Ask me for whatever you wish, and I will give it to you." ²³And he vowed to her, "Whatever you ask me, I will give you, up to half of my kingdom." ²⁴And she went out

---

[a]Or *ignoring*; some manuscripts *hearing* [b]Greek *he* [c]Greek *chiton*, a long garment worn under the cloak next to the skin [d]Greek *his* [e]Some manuscripts *He* [f]Greek *baptizer*; also verse 24

and said to her mother, "For what should I ask?" And she said, "The head of John the Baptist." ²⁵And she came in immediately with haste to the king and asked, saying, "I want you to give me at once the head of John the Baptist on a platter." ²⁶And the king was exceedingly sorry, but because of his oaths and his guests he did not want to break his word to her. ²⁷And immediately the king sent an executioner with orders to bring John's[a] head. He went and beheaded him in the prison ²⁸and brought his head on a platter and gave it to the girl, and the girl gave it to her mother. ²⁹When his disciples heard of it, they came and took his body and laid it in a tomb.

JESUS FEEDS THE FIVE THOUSAND

³⁰The apostles returned to Jesus and told him all that they had done and taught. ³¹And he said to them, "Come away by yourselves to a desolate place and rest a while." For many were coming and going, and they had no leisure even to eat. ³²And they went away in the boat to a desolate place by themselves. ³³Now many saw them going and recognized them, and they ran there on foot from all the towns and got there ahead of them. ³⁴When he went ashore he saw a great crowd, and he had compassion on them, because they were like sheep without a shepherd. And he began to teach them many things. ³⁵And when it grew late, his disciples came to him and said, "This is a desolate place, and the hour is now late. ³⁶Send them away to go into the surrounding countryside and villages and buy themselves something to eat." ³⁷But he answered them, "You give them something to eat." And they said to him, "Shall we go and buy two hundred denarii[b] worth of bread and give it to them to eat?" ³⁸And he said to them, "How many loaves do you have? Go and see." And when they had found out, they said, "Five, and two fish." ³⁹Then he commanded them all to sit down in groups on the green grass. ⁴⁰So they sat down in groups, by hundreds and by fifties. ⁴¹And taking the five loaves and the two fish, he looked up to heaven and said a blessing and broke the loaves and gave them to the disciples to set before the people. And he divided the two fish among them all. ⁴²And they all ate and were satisfied. ⁴³And they took up twelve baskets full of broken pieces and of the fish. ⁴⁴And those who ate the loaves were five thousand men.

JESUS WALKS ON THE WATER

⁴⁵Immediately he made his disciples get into the boat and go before him to the other side, to Bethsaida, while he dismissed the crowd. ⁴⁶And after he had taken leave of them, he went up on the mountain to pray. ⁴⁷And when evening came, the boat was out on the sea, and he was alone on the land. ⁴⁸And he saw that they were making headway painfully, for the wind was against them. And about the fourth watch of the night[c] he came to them, walking on the sea. He meant to pass by them, ⁴⁹but when they saw him walking on the sea they thought it was a ghost, and cried out, ⁵⁰for they all saw him and were terrified. But immediately he spoke to them and said, "Take heart; it is I. Do not be afraid." ⁵¹And he got into the boat with them, and the wind ceased. And they were utterly astounded, ⁵²for they did not understand about the loaves, but their hearts were hardened.

JESUS HEALS THE SICK IN GENNESARET

⁵³When they had crossed over, they came to land at Gennesaret and moored to the shore. ⁵⁴And when they got out of the boat, the people immediately recognized him ⁵⁵and ran about the whole region and began to bring the sick people on their beds to wherever they heard he was. ⁵⁶And wherever he came, in villages, cities, or countryside, they laid the sick in the market-places and implored him that they might touch even the fringe of his garment. And as many as touched it were made well.

TRADITIONS AND COMMANDMENTS

7 Now when the Pharisees gathered to him, with some of the scribes who had come from Jerusalem, ²they saw that some of his disciples ate with hands that were defiled, that is, unwashed. ³(For the Pharisees and all the Jews do not eat unless they wash their hands properly,[d] holding to the tradition of the elders, ⁴and when they come from the market-place, they do not eat unless they wash.[e] And there are many other traditions that they observe, such as the washing of cups and pots and copper vessels and dining couches.[f]) ⁵And the Pharisees

---

[a]Greek *his* [b]A *denarius* was a day's wage for a labourer [c]That is, between 3 A.M. and 6 A.M. [d]Greek *unless they wash the hands with a fist*, probably indicating a kind of ceremonial washing [e]Greek *unless they baptize*; some manuscripts *unless they purify themselves* [f]Some manuscripts omit *and dining couches*

and the scribes asked him, "Why do your disciples not walk according to the tradition of the elders, but eat with defiled hands?" ⁶And he said to them, "Well did Isaiah prophesy of you hypocrites, as it is written,

> "'This people honours me
> with their lips,
> but their heart is far from me;
> ⁷ in vain do they worship me,
> teaching as doctrines the
> commandments of men.'

⁸You leave the commandment of God and hold to the tradition of men."

⁹And he said to them, "You have a fine way of rejecting the commandment of God in order to establish your tradition! ¹⁰For Moses said, 'Honour your father and your mother'; and, 'Whoever reviles father or mother must surely die.' ¹¹But you say, 'If a man tells his father or his mother, "Whatever you would have gained from me is Corban"' (that is, given to God)*ᵃ*— ¹²then you no longer permit him to do anything for his father or mother, ¹³thus making void the word of God by your tradition that you have handed down. And many such things you do."

WHAT DEFILES A PERSON

¹⁴And he called the people to him again and said to them, "Hear me, all of you, and understand: ¹⁵There is nothing outside a person that by going into him can defile him, but the things that come out of a person are what defile him."*ᵇ* ¹⁷And when he had entered the house and left the people, his disciples asked him about the parable. ¹⁸And he said to them, "Then are you also without understanding? Do you not see that whatever goes into a person from outside cannot defile him, ¹⁹since it enters not his heart but his stomach, and is expelled?"*ᶜ* (Thus he declared all foods clean.) ²⁰And he said, "What comes out of a person is what defiles him. ²¹For from within, out of the heart of man, come evil thoughts, sexual immorality, theft, murder, adultery, ²²coveting, wickedness, deceit, sensuality, envy, slander, pride, foolishness. ²³All these evil things come from within, and they defile a person."

THE SYROPHOENICIAN WOMAN'S FAITH

²⁴And from there he arose and went away to the region of Tyre and Sidon.*ᵈ* And he entered a house and did not want anyone to know, yet he could not be hidden. ²⁵But immediately a woman whose little daughter had an unclean spirit heard of him and came and fell down at his feet. ²⁶Now the woman was a Gentile, a Syrophoenician by birth. And she begged him to cast the demon out of her daughter. ²⁷And he said to her, "Let the children be fed first, for it is not right to take the children's bread and throw it to the dogs." ²⁸But she answered him, "Yes, Lord; yet even the dogs under the table eat the children's crumbs." ²⁹And he said to her, "For this statement you may go your way; the demon has left your daughter." ³⁰And she went home and found the child lying in bed and the demon gone.

JESUS HEALS A DEAF MAN

³¹Then he returned from the region of Tyre and went through Sidon to the Sea of Galilee, in the region of the Decapolis. ³²And they brought to him a man who was deaf and had a speech impediment, and they begged him to lay his hand on him. ³³And taking him aside from the crowd privately, he put his fingers into his ears, and after spitting touched his tongue. ³⁴And looking up to heaven, he sighed and said to him, "Ephphatha", that is, "Be opened." ³⁵And his ears were opened, his tongue was released, and he spoke plainly. ³⁶And Jesus*ᵉ* charged them to tell no one. But the more he charged them, the more zealously they proclaimed it. ³⁷And they were astonished beyond measure, saying, "He has done all things well. He even makes the deaf hear and the mute speak."

JESUS FEEDS THE FOUR THOUSAND

8 In those days, when again a great crowd had gathered, and they had nothing to eat, he called his disciples to him and said to them, ²"I have compassion on the crowd, because they have been with me now three days and have nothing to eat. ³And if I send them away hungry to their homes, they will faint on the way. And some of them have come from far away." ⁴And his disciples answered him, "How can one feed these people with bread here in this desolate place?" ⁵And he asked them, "How many loaves do you have?" They said, "Seven." ⁶And he directed the crowd to sit down on the ground. And he took the seven loaves,

---

ᵃOr an offering *ᵇSome manuscripts add verse 16: If anyone has ears to hear, let him hear* *ᶜGreek goes out into the latrine* *ᵈSome manuscripts omit and Sidon* *ᵉGreek he*

and having given thanks, he broke them and gave them to his disciples to set before the people; and they set them before the crowd. ⁷And they had a few small fish. And having blessed them, he said that these also should be set before them. ⁸And they ate and were satisfied. And they took up the broken pieces left over, seven baskets full. ⁹And there were about four thousand people. And he sent them away. ¹⁰And immediately he got into the boat with his disciples and went to the district of Dalmanutha.[a]

THE PHARISEES DEMAND A SIGN

¹¹The Pharisees came and began to argue with him, seeking from him a sign from heaven to test him. ¹²And he sighed deeply in his spirit and said, "Why does this generation seek a sign? Truly, I say to you, no sign will be given to this generation." ¹³And he left them, got into the boat again, and went to the other side.

THE LEAVEN OF THE PHARISEES AND HEROD

¹⁴Now they had forgotten to bring bread, and they had only one loaf with them in the boat. ¹⁵And he cautioned them, saying, "Watch out; beware of the leaven of the Pharisees and the leaven of Herod."[b] ¹⁶And they began discussing with one another the fact that they had no bread. ¹⁷And Jesus, aware of this, said to them, "Why are you discussing the fact that you have no bread? Do you not yet perceive or understand? Are your hearts hardened? ¹⁸Having eyes do you not see, and having ears do you not hear? And do you not remember? ¹⁹When I broke the five loaves for the five thousand, how many baskets full of broken pieces did you take up?" They said to him, "Twelve." ²⁰"And the seven for the four thousand, how many baskets full of broken pieces did you take up?" And they said to him, "Seven." ²¹And he said to them, "Do you not yet understand?"

JESUS HEALS A BLIND MAN AT BETHSAIDA

²²And they came to Bethsaida. And some people brought to him a blind man and begged him to touch him. ²³And he took the blind man by the hand and led him out of the village, and when he had spat on his eyes and laid his hands on him, he asked him, "Do you see anything?" ²⁴And he looked up and said, "I see people, but they look like trees, walking." ²⁵Then Jesus[c] laid his hands on his eyes again; and he opened his eyes, his sight was restored, and he saw everything clearly. ²⁶And he sent him to his home, saying, "Do not even enter the village."

PETER CONFESSES JESUS AS THE CHRIST

²⁷And Jesus went on with his disciples to the villages of Caesarea Philippi. And on the way he asked his disciples, "Who do people say that I am?" ²⁸And they told him, "John the Baptist; and others say, Elijah; and others, one of the prophets." ²⁹And he asked them, "But who do you say that I am?" Peter answered him, "You are the Christ." ³⁰And he strictly charged them to tell no one about him.

JESUS FORETELLS HIS DEATH AND RESURRECTION

³¹And he began to teach them that the Son of Man must suffer many things and be rejected by the elders and the chief priests and the scribes and be killed, and after three days rise again. ³²And he said this plainly. And Peter took him aside and began to rebuke him. ³³But turning and seeing his disciples, he rebuked Peter and said, "Get behind me, Satan! For you are not setting your mind on the things of God, but on the things of man."

³⁴And calling the crowd to him with his disciples, he said to them, "If anyone would come after me, let him deny himself and take up his cross and follow me. ³⁵For whoever would save his life[d] will lose it, but whoever loses his life for my sake and the gospel's will save it. ³⁶For what does it profit a man to gain the whole world and forfeit his soul? ³⁷For what can a man give in return for his soul? ³⁸For whoever is ashamed of me and of my words in this adulterous and sinful generation, of him will the Son of Man also be ashamed when he comes in the glory of his Father with the holy angels."

9 And he said to them, "Truly, I say to you, there are some standing here who will not taste death until they see the kingdom of God after it has come with power."

THE TRANSFIGURATION

²And after six days Jesus took with him Peter and James and John, and led them up a high mountain by themselves. And he

---

[a]Some manuscripts *Magadan*, or *Magdala* [b]Some manuscripts *the Herodians* [c]Greek *he* [d]The same Greek word can mean either *soul* or *life*, depending on the context; twice in this verse and once in verse 36 and once in verse 37

was transfigured before them, ³and his clothes became radiant, intensely white, as no one[a] on earth could bleach them. ⁴And there appeared to them Elijah with Moses, and they were talking with Jesus. ⁵And Peter said to Jesus, "Rabbi,[b] it is good that we are here. Let us make three tents, one for you and one for Moses and one for Elijah." ⁶For he did not know what to say, for they were terrified. ⁷And a cloud overshadowed them, and a voice came out of the cloud, "This is my beloved Son;[c] listen to him." ⁸And suddenly, looking around, they no longer saw anyone with them but Jesus only.

⁹And as they were coming down the mountain, he charged them to tell no one what they had seen, until the Son of Man had risen from the dead. ¹⁰So they kept the matter to themselves, questioning what this rising from the dead might mean. ¹¹And they asked him, "Why do the scribes say that first Elijah must come?" ¹²And he said to them, "Elijah does come first to restore all things. And how is it written of the Son of Man that he should suffer many things and be treated with contempt? ¹³But I tell you that Elijah has come, and they did to him whatever they pleased, as it is written of him."

JESUS HEALS A BOY WITH AN UNCLEAN SPIRIT

¹⁴And when they came to the disciples, they saw a great crowd around them, and scribes arguing with them. ¹⁵And immediately all the crowd, when they saw him, were greatly amazed and ran up to him and greeted him. ¹⁶And he asked them, "What are you arguing about with them?" ¹⁷And someone from the crowd answered him, "Teacher, I brought my son to you, for he has a spirit that makes him mute. ¹⁸And whenever it seizes him, it throws him down, and he foams and grinds his teeth and becomes rigid. So I asked your disciples to cast it out, and they were not able." ¹⁹And he answered them, "O faithless generation, how long am I to be with you? How long am I to bear with you? Bring him to me." ²⁰And they brought the boy to him. And when the spirit saw him, immediately it convulsed the boy, and he fell on the ground and rolled about, foaming at the mouth. ²¹And Jesus asked his father, "How long has this been happening to him?" And he said, "From childhood. ²²And it has often cast him into fire and into water, to destroy him. But if you can do anything, have compassion on us and help us." ²³And Jesus said to him, "'If you can'! All things are possible for one who believes." ²⁴Immediately the father of the child cried out[d] and said, "I believe; help my unbelief!" ²⁵And when Jesus saw that a crowd came running together, he rebuked the unclean spirit, saying to it, "You mute and deaf spirit, I command you, come out of him and never enter him again." ²⁶And after crying out and convulsing him terribly, it came out, and the boy was like a corpse, so that most of them said, "He is dead." ²⁷But Jesus took him by the hand and lifted him up, and he arose. ²⁸And when he had entered the house, his disciples asked him privately, "Why could we not cast it out?" ²⁹And he said to them, "This kind cannot be driven out by anything but prayer."[e]

JESUS AGAIN FORETELLS DEATH, RESURRECTION

³⁰They went on from there and passed through Galilee. And he did not want anyone to know, ³¹for he was teaching his disciples, saying to them, "The Son of Man is going to be delivered into the hands of men, and they will kill him. And when he is killed, after three days he will rise." ³²But they did not understand the saying, and were afraid to ask him.

WHO IS THE GREATEST?

³³And they came to Capernaum. And when he was in the house he asked them, "What were you discussing on the way?" ³⁴But they kept silent, for on the way they had argued with one another about who was the greatest. ³⁵And he sat down and called the twelve. And he said to them, "If anyone would be first, he must be last of all and servant of all." ³⁶And he took a child and put him in the midst of them, and taking him in his arms, he said to them, ³⁷"Whoever receives one such child in my name receives me, and whoever receives me, receives not me but him who sent me."

ANYONE NOT AGAINST US IS FOR US

³⁸John said to him, "Teacher, we saw someone casting out demons in your name,[f] and we tried to stop him, because he was not following us." ³⁹But Jesus said, "Do not stop him, for no one who does a mighty work in my

---

[a] Greek *launderer (gnapheus)* [b] *Rabbi* means *my teacher*, or *my master*
[c] Or *my Son, my* (or *the*) *Beloved* [d] Some manuscripts add *with tears*
[e] Some manuscripts add *and fasting* [f] Some manuscripts add *who does not follow us*

name will be able soon afterwards to speak evil of me. ⁴⁰For the one who is not against us is for us. ⁴¹For truly, I say to you, whoever gives you a cup of water to drink because you belong to Christ will by no means lose his reward.

TEMPTATIONS TO SIN

⁴²"Whoever causes one of these little ones who believe in me to sin,ᵃ it would be better for him if a great millstone were hung round his neck and he were thrown into the sea. ⁴³And if your hand causes you to sin, cut it off. It is better for you to enter life crippled than with two hands to go to hell,ᵇ to the unquenchable fire.ᶜ ⁴⁵And if your foot causes you to sin, cut it off. It is better for you to enter life lame than with two feet to be thrown into hell. ⁴⁷And if your eye causes you to sin, tear it out. It is better for you to enter the kingdom of God with one eye than with two eyes to be thrown into hell, ⁴⁸'where their worm does not die and the fire is not quenched.' ⁴⁹For everyone will be salted with fire.ᵈ ⁵⁰Salt is good, but if the salt has lost its saltiness, how will you make it salty again? Have salt in yourselves, and be at peace with one another."

TEACHING ABOUT DIVORCE

10 And he left there and went to the region of Judea and beyond the Jordan, and crowds gathered to him again. And again, as was his custom, he taught them.

²And Pharisees came up and in order to test him asked, "Is it lawful for a man to divorce his wife?" ³He answered them, "What did Moses command you?" ⁴They said, "Moses allowed a man to write a certificate of divorce and to send her away." ⁵And Jesus said to them, "Because of your hardness of heart he wrote you this commandment. ⁶But from the beginning of creation, 'God made them male and female.' ⁷Therefore a man shall leave his father and mother and hold fast to his wife,ᵉ ⁸and the two shall become one flesh.' So they are no longer two but one flesh. ⁹What therefore God has joined together, let not man separate."

¹⁰And in the house the disciples asked him again about this matter. ¹¹And he said to them, "Whoever divorces his wife and marries another commits adultery against her, ¹²and if she divorces her husband and marries another, she commits adultery."

LET THE CHILDREN COME TO ME

¹³And they were bringing children to him that he might touch them, and the disciples rebuked them. ¹⁴But when Jesus saw it, he was indignant and said to them, "Let the children come to me; do not hinder them, for to such belongs the kingdom of God. ¹⁵Truly, I say to you, whoever does not receive the kingdom of God like a child shall not enter it." ¹⁶And he took them in his arms and blessed them, laying his hands on them.

THE RICH YOUNG MAN

¹⁷And as he was setting out on his journey, a man ran up and knelt before him and asked him, "Good Teacher, what must I do to inherit eternal life?" ¹⁸And Jesus said to him, "Why do you call me good? No one is good except God alone. ¹⁹You know the commandments: 'Do not murder, Do not commit adultery, Do not steal, Do not bear false witness, Do not defraud, Honour your father and mother.'" ²⁰And he said to him, "Teacher, all these I have kept from my youth." ²¹And Jesus, looking at him, loved him, and said to him, "You lack one thing: go, sell all that you have and give to the poor, and you will have treasure in heaven; and come, follow me." ²²Disheartened by the saying, he went away sorrowful, for he had great possessions.

²³And Jesus looked around and said to his disciples, "How difficult it will be for those who have wealth to enter the kingdom of God!" ²⁴And the disciples were amazed at his words. But Jesus said to them again, "Children, how difficult it isᶠ to enter the kingdom of God! ²⁵It is easier for a camel to go through the eye of a needle than for a rich person to enter the kingdom of God." ²⁶And they were exceedingly astonished, and said to him,ᵍ "Then who can be saved?" ²⁷Jesus looked at them and said, "With man it is impossible, but not with God. For all things are possible with God." ²⁸Peter began to say to him, "See, we have left everything and followed you." ²⁹Jesus said, "Truly, I say to you, there is no one who has left house or brothers or sisters or mother or father or children or lands, for my sake and for the gospel, ³⁰who will not receive a hundredfold now in this time,

---

ᵃGreek *to stumble*; also verses 43, 45, 47 ᵇGreek *Gehenna*; also verse 47 ᶜSome manuscripts add verses 44 and 46 (which are identical with verse 48) ᵈSome manuscripts add *and every sacrifice will be salted with salt* ᵉSome manuscripts omit *and hold fast to his wife* ᶠSome manuscripts add *for those who trust in riches* ᵍSome manuscripts *to one another*

houses and brothers and sisters and mothers and children and lands, with persecutions, and in the age to come eternal life. ³¹But many who are first will be last, and the last first."

JESUS FORETELLS HIS DEATH A THIRD TIME

³²And they were on the road, going up to Jerusalem, and Jesus was walking ahead of them. And they were amazed, and those who followed were afraid. And taking the twelve again, he began to tell them what was to happen to him, ³³saying, "See, we are going up to Jerusalem, and the Son of Man will be delivered over to the chief priests and the scribes, and they will condemn him to death and deliver him over to the Gentiles. ³⁴And they will mock him and spit on him, and flog him and kill him. And after three days he will rise."

THE REQUEST OF JAMES AND JOHN

³⁵And James and John, the sons of Zebedee, came up to him and said to him, "Teacher, we want you to do for us whatever we ask of you." ³⁶And he said to them, "What do you want me to do for you?" ³⁷And they said to him, "Grant us to sit, one at your right hand and one at your left, in your glory." ³⁸Jesus said to them, "You do not know what you are asking. Are you able to drink the cup that I drink, or to be baptized with the baptism with which I am baptized?" ³⁹And they said to him, "We are able." And Jesus said to them, "The cup that I drink you will drink, and with the baptism with which I am baptized, you will be baptized, ⁴⁰but to sit at my right hand or at my left is not mine to grant, but it is for those for whom it has been prepared." ⁴¹And when the ten heard it, they began to be indignant at James and John. ⁴²And Jesus called them to him and said to them, "You know that those who are considered rulers of the Gentiles lord it over them, and their great ones exercise authority over them. ⁴³But it shall not be so among you. But whoever would be great among you must be your servant,ᵃ ⁴⁴and whoever would be first among you must be slaveᵇ of all. ⁴⁵For even the Son of Man came not to be served but to serve, and to give his life as a ransom for many."

JESUS HEALS BLIND BARTIMAEUS

⁴⁶And they came to Jericho. And as he was leaving Jericho with his disciples and a great crowd, Bartimaeus, a blind beggar, the son of Timaeus, was sitting by the roadside. ⁴⁷And when he heard that it was Jesus of Nazareth, he began to cry out and say, "Jesus, Son of David, have mercy on me!" ⁴⁸And many rebuked him, telling him to be silent. But he cried out all the more, "Son of David, have mercy on me!" ⁴⁹And Jesus stopped and said, "Call him." And they called the blind man, saying to him, "Take heart. Get up; he is calling you." ⁵⁰And throwing off his cloak, he sprang up and came to Jesus. ⁵¹And Jesus said to him, "What do you want me to do for you?" And the blind man said to him, "Rabbi, let me recover my sight." ⁵²And Jesus said to him, "Go your way; your faith has made you well." And immediately he recovered his sight and followed him on the way.

THE TRIUMPHAL ENTRY

11 Now when they drew near to Jerusalem, to Bethphage and Bethany, at the Mount of Olives, Jesusᶜ sent two of his disciples ²and said to them, "Go into the village in front of you, and immediately as you enter it you will find a colt tied, on which no one has ever sat. Untie it and bring it. ³If anyone says to you, 'Why are you doing this?' say, 'The Lord has need of it and will send it back here immediately.'" ⁴And they went away and found a colt tied at a door outside in the street, and they untied it. ⁵And some of those standing there said to them, "What are you doing, untying the colt?" ⁶And they told them what Jesus had said, and they let them go. ⁷And they brought the colt to Jesus and threw their cloaks on it, and he sat on it. ⁸And many spread their cloaks on the road, and others spread leafy branches that they had cut from the fields. ⁹And those who went before and those who followed were shouting, "Hosanna! Blessed is he who comes in the name of the Lord! ¹⁰Blessed is the coming kingdom of our father David! Hosanna in the highest!"

¹¹And he entered Jerusalem and went into the temple. And when he had looked around at everything, as it was already late, he went out to Bethany with the twelve.

JESUS CURSES THE FIG TREE

¹²On the following day, when they came from Bethany, he was hungry. ¹³And seeing in the distance a fig tree in leaf, he went to see if he could find anything on it. When he

---

ᵃGreek *diakonos* ᵇOr *bondservant*, or *servant* (for the contextual rendering of the Greek word *doulos*, see Preface) ᶜGreek *he*

came to it, he found nothing but leaves, for it was not the season for figs. ¹⁴And he said to it, "May no one ever eat fruit from you again." And his disciples heard it.

JESUS CLEANSES THE TEMPLE

¹⁵And they came to Jerusalem. And he entered the temple and began to drive out those who sold and those who bought in the temple, and he overturned the tables of the money-changers and the seats of those who sold pigeons. ¹⁶And he would not allow anyone to carry anything through the temple. ¹⁷And he was teaching them and saying to them, "Is it not written, 'My house shall be called a house of prayer for all the nations'? But you have made it a den of robbers." ¹⁸And the chief priests and the scribes heard it and were seeking a way to destroy him, for they feared him, because all the crowd was astonished at his teaching. ¹⁹And when evening came they*ᵃ* went out of the city.

THE LESSON FROM THE WITHERED FIG TREE

²⁰As they passed by in the morning, they saw the fig tree withered away to its roots. ²¹And Peter remembered and said to him, "Rabbi, look! The fig tree that you cursed has withered." ²²And Jesus answered them, "Have faith in God. ²³Truly, I say to you, whoever says to this mountain, 'Be taken up and thrown into the sea', and does not doubt in his heart, but believes that what he says will come to pass, it will be done for him. ²⁴Therefore I tell you, whatever you ask in prayer, believe that you have received*ᵇ* it, and it will be yours. ²⁵And whenever you stand praying, forgive, if you have anything against anyone, so that your Father also who is in heaven may forgive you your trespasses."*ᶜ*

THE AUTHORITY OF JESUS CHALLENGED

²⁷And they came again to Jerusalem. And as he was walking in the temple, the chief priests and the scribes and the elders came to him, ²⁸and they said to him, "By what authority are you doing these things, or who gave you this authority to do them?" ²⁹Jesus said to them, "I will ask you one question; answer me, and I will tell you by what authority I do these things. ³⁰Was the baptism of John from heaven or from man? Answer me." ³¹And they discussed it with one another, saying, "If we say, 'From heaven', he will say, 'Why then did you not believe him?' ³²But shall we say, 'From man'?"—they were afraid of the people, for they all held that John really was a prophet. ³³So they answered Jesus, "We do not know." And Jesus said to them, "Neither will I tell you by what authority I do these things."

THE PARABLE OF THE TENANTS

12 And he began to speak to them in parables. "A man planted a vineyard and put a fence around it and dug a pit for the wine press and built a tower, and leased it to tenants and went into another country. ²When the season came, he sent a servant*ᵈ* to the tenants to get from them some of the fruit of the vineyard. ³And they took him and beat him and sent him away empty-handed. ⁴Again he sent to them another servant, and they struck him on the head and treated him shamefully. ⁵And he sent another, and him they killed. And so with many others: some they beat, and some they killed. ⁶He had still one other, a beloved son. Finally he sent him to them, saying, 'They will respect my son.' ⁷But those tenants said to one another, 'This is the heir. Come, let us kill him, and the inheritance will be ours.' ⁸And they took him and killed him and threw him out of the vineyard. ⁹What will the owner of the vineyard do? He will come and destroy the tenants and give the vineyard to others. ¹⁰Have you not read this Scripture:

"'The stone that the builders rejected
 has become the cornerstone;*ᵉ*
¹¹ this was the Lord's doing,
 and it is marvellous in our eyes'?"

¹²And they were seeking to arrest him but feared the people, for they perceived that he had told the parable against them. So they left him and went away.

PAYING TAXES TO CAESAR

¹³And they sent to him some of the Pharisees and some of the Herodians, to trap him in his talk. ¹⁴And they came and said to him, "Teacher, we know that you are true and do not care about anyone's opinion. For you are not swayed by appearances,*ᶠ* but truly teach the way of God. Is it lawful to pay taxes to Caesar, or not? Should we pay them, or should we not?" ¹⁵But, knowing their hypocrisy, he said

---

*ᵃ*Some manuscripts *he* *ᵇ*Some manuscripts *are receiving*
*ᶜ*Some manuscripts add verse 26: *But if you do not forgive, neither will your Father who is in heaven forgive your trespasses* *ᵈ*Or *bondservant*; also verse 4 *ᵉ*Greek *the head of the corner* *ᶠ*Greek *you do not look at people's faces*

to them, "Why put me to the test? Bring me a denarius[a] and let me look at it." [16]And they brought one. And he said to them, "Whose likeness and inscription is this?" They said to him, "Caesar's." [17]Jesus said to them, "Render to Caesar the things that are Caesar's, and to God the things that are God's." And they marvelled at him.

THE SADDUCEES ASK ABOUT THE RESURRECTION

[18]And Sadducees came to him, who say that there is no resurrection. And they asked him a question, saying, [19]"Teacher, Moses wrote for us that if a man's brother dies and leaves a wife, but leaves no child, the man[b] must take the widow and raise up offspring for his brother. [20]There were seven brothers; the first took a wife, and when he died left no offspring. [21]And the second took her, and died, leaving no offspring. And the third likewise. [22]And the seven left no offspring. Last of all the woman also died. [23]In the resurrection, when they rise again, whose wife will she be? For the seven had her as wife."

[24]Jesus said to them, "Is this not the reason you are wrong, because you know neither the Scriptures nor the power of God? [25]For when they rise from the dead, they neither marry nor are given in marriage, but are like angels in heaven. [26]And as for the dead being raised, have you not read in the book of Moses, in the passage about the bush, how God spoke to him, saying, 'I am the God of Abraham, and the God of Isaac, and the God of Jacob'? [27]He is not God of the dead, but of the living. You are quite wrong."

THE GREAT COMMANDMENT

[28]And one of the scribes came up and heard them disputing with one another, and seeing that he answered them well, asked him, "Which commandment is the most important of all?" [29]Jesus answered, "The most important is, 'Hear, O Israel: The Lord our God, the Lord is one. [30]And you shall love the Lord your God with all your heart and with all your soul and with all your mind and with all your strength.' [31]The second is this: 'You shall love your neighbour as yourself.' There is no other commandment greater than these." [32]And the scribe said to him, "You are right, Teacher. You have truly said that he is one, and there is no other besides him. [33]And to love him with all the heart and with all the understanding and with all the strength, and to love one's neighbour as oneself, is much more than all whole burnt offerings and sacrifices." [34]And when Jesus saw that he answered wisely, he said to him, "You are not far from the kingdom of God." And after that no one dared to ask him any more questions.

WHOSE SON IS THE CHRIST?

[35]And as Jesus taught in the temple, he said, "How can the scribes say that the Christ is the son of David? [36]David himself, in the Holy Spirit, declared,

" 'The Lord said to my Lord,
"Sit at my right hand,
until I put your enemies
under your feet." '

[37]David himself calls him Lord. So how is he his son?" And the great throng heard him gladly.

BEWARE OF THE SCRIBES

[38]And in his teaching he said, "Beware of the scribes, who like to walk around in long robes and like greetings in the market-places [39]and have the best seats in the synagogues and the places of honour at feasts, [40]who devour widows' houses and for a pretence make long prayers. They will receive the greater condemnation."

THE WIDOW'S OFFERING

[41]And he sat down opposite the treasury and watched the people putting money into the offering box. Many rich people put in large sums. [42]And a poor widow came and put in two small copper coins, which make a penny.[c] [43]And he called his disciples to him and said to them, "Truly, I say to you, this poor widow has put in more than all those who are contributing to the offering box. [44]For they all contributed out of their abundance, but she out of her poverty has put in everything she had, all she had to live on."

JESUS FORETELLS DESTRUCTION OF THE TEMPLE

13 And as he came out of the temple, one of his disciples said to him, "Look, Teacher, what wonderful stones and what wonderful buildings!" [2]And

---

[a] *A denarius* was a day's wage for a labourer [b]Greek *his brother*
[c]Greek *two lepta*, which make a *kodrantes*; a *kodrantes* (Latin *quadrans*) was a Roman copper coin worth about 1/64 of a *denarius* (which was a day's wage for a labourer)

Jesus said to him, "Do you see these great buildings? There will not be left here one stone upon another that will not be thrown down."

SIGNS OF THE END OF THE AGE

³And as he sat on the Mount of Olives opposite the temple, Peter and James and John and Andrew asked him privately, ⁴"Tell us, when will these things be, and what will be the sign when all these things are about to be accomplished?" ⁵And Jesus began to say to them, "See that no one leads you astray. ⁶Many will come in my name, saying, 'I am he!' and they will lead many astray. ⁷And when you hear of wars and rumours of wars, do not be alarmed. This must take place, but the end is not yet. ⁸For nation will rise against nation, and kingdom against kingdom. There will be earthquakes in various places; there will be famines. These are but the beginning of the birth pains.

⁹"But be on your guard. For they will deliver you over to councils, and you will be beaten in synagogues, and you will stand before governors and kings for my sake, to bear witness before them. ¹⁰And the gospel must first be proclaimed to all nations. ¹¹And when they bring you to trial and deliver you over, do not be anxious beforehand what you are to say, but say whatever is given you in that hour, for it is not you who speak, but the Holy Spirit. ¹²And brother will deliver brother over to death, and the father his child, and children will rise against parents and have them put to death. ¹³And you will be hated by all for my name's sake. But the one who endures to the end will be saved.

THE ABOMINATION OF DESOLATION

¹⁴"But when you see the abomination of desolation standing where he ought not to be (let the reader understand), then let those who are in Judea flee to the mountains. ¹⁵Let the one who is on the housetop not go down, nor enter his house, to take anything out, ¹⁶and let the one who is in the field not turn back to take his cloak. ¹⁷And alas for women who are pregnant and for those who are nursing infants in those days! ¹⁸Pray that it may not happen in winter. ¹⁹For in those days there will be such tribulation as has not been from the beginning of the creation that God created until now, and never will be. ²⁰And if the Lord had not cut short the days, no human being would be saved. But for the sake of the elect, whom he chose, he shortened the days. ²¹And then if anyone says to you, 'Look, here is the Christ!' or 'Look, there he is!' do not believe it. ²²For false christs and false prophets will arise and perform signs and wonders, to lead astray, if possible, the elect. ²³But be on guard; I have told you all things beforehand.

THE COMING OF THE SON OF MAN

²⁴"But in those days, after that tribulation, the sun will be darkened, and the moon will not give its light, ²⁵and the stars will be falling from heaven, and the powers in the heavens will be shaken. ²⁶And then they will see the Son of Man coming in clouds with great power and glory. ²⁷And then he will send out the angels and gather his elect from the four winds, from the ends of the earth to the ends of heaven.

THE LESSON OF THE FIG TREE

²⁸"From the fig tree learn its lesson: as soon as its branch becomes tender and puts out its leaves, you know that summer is near. ²⁹So also, when you see these things taking place, you know that he is near, at the very gates. ³⁰Truly, I say to you, this generation will not pass away until all these things take place. ³¹Heaven and earth will pass away, but my words will not pass away.

NO ONE KNOWS THAT DAY OR HOUR

³²"But concerning that day or that hour, no one knows, not even the angels in heaven, nor the Son, but only the Father. ³³Be on guard, keep awake.ᵃ For you do not know when the time will come. ³⁴It is like a man going on a journey, when he leaves home and puts his servantsᵇ in charge, each with his work, and commands the doorkeeper to stay awake. ³⁵Therefore stay awake—for you do not know when the master of the house will come, in the evening, or at midnight, or when the cock crows,ᶜ or in the morning—³⁶lest he come suddenly and find you asleep. ³⁷And what I say to you I say to all: Stay awake."

THE PLOT TO KILL JESUS

14 It was now two days before the Passover and the Feast of Unleavened Bread. And the chief priests and the scribes were seeking how to arrest

---

ᵃSome manuscripts add *and pray* ᵇOr *bondservants* ᶜThat is, the third watch of the night, between midnight and 3 A.M.

him by stealth and kill him, ²for they said, "Not during the feast, lest there be an uproar from the people."

JESUS ANOINTED AT BETHANY

³And while he was at Bethany in the house of Simon the leper,[a] as he was reclining at table, a woman came with an alabaster flask of ointment of pure nard, very costly, and she broke the flask and poured it over his head. ⁴There were some who said to themselves indignantly, "Why was the ointment wasted like that? ⁵For this ointment could have been sold for more than three hundred denarii[b] and given to the poor." And they scolded her. ⁶But Jesus said, "Leave her alone. Why do you trouble her? She has done a beautiful thing to me. ⁷For you always have the poor with you, and whenever you want, you can do good for them. But you will not always have me. ⁸She has done what she could; she has anointed my body beforehand for burial. ⁹And truly, I say to you, wherever the gospel is proclaimed in the whole world, what she has done will be told in memory of her."

JUDAS TO BETRAY JESUS

¹⁰Then Judas Iscariot, who was one of the twelve, went to the chief priests in order to betray him to them. ¹¹And when they heard it, they were glad and promised to give him money. And he sought an opportunity to betray him.

THE PASSOVER WITH THE DISCIPLES

¹²And on the first day of Unleavened Bread, when they sacrificed the Passover lamb, his disciples said to him, "Where will you have us go and prepare for you to eat the Passover?" ¹³And he sent two of his disciples and said to them, "Go into the city, and a man carrying a jar of water will meet you. Follow him, ¹⁴and wherever he enters, say to the master of the house, 'The Teacher says, Where is my guest room, where I may eat the Passover with my disciples?' ¹⁵And he will show you a large upper room furnished and ready; there prepare for us." ¹⁶And the disciples set out and went to the city and found it just as he had told them, and they prepared the Passover.

¹⁷And when it was evening, he came with the twelve. ¹⁸And as they were reclining at table and eating, Jesus said, "Truly, I say to you, one of you will betray me, one who is eating with me." ¹⁹They began to be sorrowful and to say to him one after another, "Is it I?" ²⁰He said to them, "It is one of the twelve, one who is dipping bread into the dish with me. ²¹For the Son of Man goes as it is written of him, but woe to that man by whom the Son of Man is betrayed! It would have been better for that man if he had not been born."

INSTITUTION OF THE LORD'S SUPPER

²²And as they were eating, he took bread, and after blessing it broke it and gave it to them, and said, "Take; this is my body." ²³And he took a cup, and when he had given thanks he gave it to them, and they all drank of it. ²⁴And he said to them, "This is my blood of the[c] covenant, which is poured out for many. ²⁵Truly, I say to you, I will not drink again of the fruit of the vine until that day when I drink it new in the kingdom of God."

JESUS FORETELLS PETER'S DENIAL

²⁶And when they had sung a hymn, they went out to the Mount of Olives. ²⁷And Jesus said to them, "You will all fall away, for it is written, 'I will strike the shepherd, and the sheep will be scattered.' ²⁸But after I am raised up, I will go before you to Galilee." ²⁹Peter said to him, "Even though they all fall away, I will not." ³⁰And Jesus said to him, "Truly, I tell you, this very night, before the cock crows twice, you will deny me three times." ³¹But he said emphatically, "If I must die with you, I will not deny you." And they all said the same.

JESUS PRAYS IN GETHSEMANE

³²And they went to a place called Gethsemane. And he said to his disciples, "Sit here while I pray." ³³And he took with him Peter and James and John, and began to be greatly distressed and troubled. ³⁴And he said to them, "My soul is very sorrowful, even to death. Remain here and watch."[d] ³⁵And going a little farther, he fell on the ground and prayed that, if it were possible, the hour might pass from him. ³⁶And he said, "Abba, Father, all things are possible for you. Remove this cup from me. Yet not what I will, but what you will." ³⁷And he came and found them sleeping, and he said to Peter, "Simon, are you asleep? Could you not watch one hour? ³⁸Watch and pray that you may not enter into temptation. The spirit indeed is willing, but the flesh is weak." ³⁹And again

---

[a] *Leprosy* was a term for several skin diseases; see Leviticus 13
[b] A *denarius* was a day's wage for a labourer [c] Some manuscripts insert *new* [d] Or *keep awake*; also verses 37, 38

he went away and prayed, saying the same words. ⁴⁰And again he came and found them sleeping, for their eyes were very heavy, and they did not know what to answer him. ⁴¹And he came the third time and said to them, "Are you still sleeping and taking your rest? It is enough; the hour has come. The Son of Man is betrayed into the hands of sinners. ⁴²Rise, let us be going; see, my betrayer is at hand."

BETRAYAL AND ARREST OF JESUS

⁴³And immediately, while he was still speaking, Judas came, one of the twelve, and with him a crowd with swords and clubs, from the chief priests and the scribes and the elders. ⁴⁴Now the betrayer had given them a sign, saying, "The one I will kiss is the man. Seize him and lead him away under guard." ⁴⁵And when he came, he went up to him at once and said, "Rabbi!" And he kissed him. ⁴⁶And they laid hands on him and seized him. ⁴⁷But one of those who stood by drew his sword and struck the servant[a] of the high priest and cut off his ear. ⁴⁸And Jesus said to them, "Have you come out as against a robber, with swords and clubs to capture me? ⁴⁹Day after day I was with you in the temple teaching, and you did not seize me. But let the Scriptures be fulfilled." ⁵⁰And they all left him and fled.

A YOUNG MAN FLEES

⁵¹And a young man followed him, with nothing but a linen cloth about his body. And they seized him, ⁵²but he left the linen cloth and ran away naked.

JESUS BEFORE THE COUNCIL

⁵³And they led Jesus to the high priest. And all the chief priests and the elders and the scribes came together. ⁵⁴And Peter had followed him at a distance, right into the courtyard of the high priest. And he was sitting with the guards and warming himself at the fire. ⁵⁵Now the chief priests and the whole council[b] were seeking testimony against Jesus to put him to death, but they found none. ⁵⁶For many bore false witness against him, but their testimony did not agree. ⁵⁷And some stood up and bore false witness against him, saying, ⁵⁸"We heard him say, 'I will destroy this temple that is made with hands, and in three days I will build another, not made with hands.'" ⁵⁹Yet even about this their testimony did not agree. ⁶⁰And the high priest stood up in the midst and asked Jesus, "Have you no answer to make? What is it that these men testify against you?"[c] ⁶¹But he remained silent and made no answer. Again the high priest asked him, "Are you the Christ, the Son of the Blessed?" ⁶²And Jesus said, "I am, and you will see the Son of Man seated at the right hand of Power, and coming with the clouds of heaven." ⁶³And the high priest tore his garments and said, "What further witnesses do we need? ⁶⁴You have heard his blasphemy. What is your decision?" And they all condemned him as deserving death. ⁶⁵And some began to spit on him and to cover his face and to strike him, saying to him, "Prophesy!" And the guards received him with blows.

PETER DENIES JESUS

⁶⁶And as Peter was below in the courtyard, one of the servant girls of the high priest came, ⁶⁷and seeing Peter warming himself, she looked at him and said, "You also were with the Nazarene, Jesus." ⁶⁸But he denied it, saying, "I neither know nor understand what you mean." And he went out into the gateway[d] and the cock crowed.[e] ⁶⁹And the servant girl saw him and began again to say to the bystanders, "This man is one of them." ⁷⁰But again he denied it. And after a little while the bystanders again said to Peter, "Certainly you are one of them, for you are a Galilean." ⁷¹But he began to invoke a curse on himself and to swear, "I do not know this man of whom you speak." ⁷²And immediately the cock crowed a second time. And Peter remembered how Jesus had said to him, "Before the cock crows twice, you will deny me three times." And he broke down and wept.[f]

JESUS DELIVERED TO PILATE

15 And as soon as it was morning, the chief priests held a consultation with the elders and scribes and the whole council. And they bound Jesus and led him away and delivered him over to Pilate. ²And Pilate asked him, "Are you the King of the Jews?" And he answered him, "You have said so." ³And the chief priests accused him of many things. ⁴And Pilate again asked him, "Have you no answer to make? See how many charges they bring against you." ⁵But Jesus made no further answer, so that Pilate was amazed.

---

[a]Or bondservant [b]Greek Sanhedrin [c]Or Have you no answer to what these men testify against you? [d]Or forecourt [e]Some manuscripts omit and the cock crowed [f]Or And when he had thought about it, he wept

PILATE DELIVERS JESUS TO BE CRUCIFIED

⁶Now at the feast he used to release for them one prisoner for whom they asked. ⁷And among the rebels in prison, who had committed murder in the insurrection, there was a man called Barabbas. ⁸And the crowd came up and began to ask Pilate to do as he usually did for them. ⁹And he answered them, saying, "Do you want me to release for you the King of the Jews?" ¹⁰For he perceived that it was out of envy that the chief priests had delivered him up. ¹¹But the chief priests stirred up the crowd to have him release for them Barabbas instead. ¹²And Pilate again said to them, "Then what shall I do with the man you call the King of the Jews?" ¹³And they cried out again, "Crucify him." ¹⁴And Pilate said to them, "Why? What evil has he done?" But they shouted all the more, "Crucify him." ¹⁵So Pilate, wishing to satisfy the crowd, released for them Barabbas, and having scourged*ª* Jesus, he delivered him to be crucified.

JESUS IS MOCKED

¹⁶And the soldiers led him away inside the palace (that is, the governor's headquarters),*ᵇ* and they called together the whole battalion.*ᶜ* ¹⁷And they clothed him in a purple cloak, and twisting together a crown of thorns, they put it on him. ¹⁸And they began to salute him, "Hail, King of the Jews!" ¹⁹And they were striking his head with a reed and spitting on him and kneeling down in homage to him. ²⁰And when they had mocked him, they stripped him of the purple cloak and put his own clothes on him. And they led him out to crucify him.

THE CRUCIFIXION

²¹And they compelled a passer-by, Simon of Cyrene, who was coming in from the country, the father of Alexander and Rufus, to carry his cross. ²²And they brought him to the place called Golgotha (which means Place of a Skull). ²³And they offered him wine mixed with myrrh, but he did not take it. ²⁴And they crucified him and divided his garments among them, casting lots for them, to decide what each should take. ²⁵And it was the third hour*ᵈ* when they crucified him. ²⁶And the inscription of the charge against him read, "The King of the Jews." ²⁷And with him they crucified two robbers, one on his right and one on his left.*ᵉ* ²⁹And those who passed by derided him, wagging their heads and saying, "Aha! You who would destroy the temple and rebuild it in three days, ³⁰save yourself, and come down from the cross!" ³¹So also the chief priests with the scribes mocked him to one another, saying, "He saved others; he cannot save himself. ³²Let the Christ, the King of Israel, come down now from the cross that we may see and believe." Those who were crucified with him also reviled him.

THE DEATH OF JESUS

³³And when the sixth hour*ᶠ* had come, there was darkness over the whole land until the ninth hour.*ᵍ* ³⁴And at the ninth hour Jesus cried with a loud voice, "Eloi, Eloi, lema sabachthani?" which means, "My God, my God, why have you forsaken me?" ³⁵And some of the bystanders hearing it said, "Behold, he is calling Elijah." ³⁶And someone ran and filled a sponge with sour wine, put it on a reed and gave it to him to drink, saying, "Wait, let us see whether Elijah will come to take him down." ³⁷And Jesus uttered a loud cry and breathed his last. ³⁸And the curtain of the temple was torn in two, from top to bottom. ³⁹And when the centurion, who stood facing him, saw that in this way he*ʰ* breathed his last, he said, "Truly this man was the Son*ⁱ* of God!"

⁴⁰There were also women looking on from a distance, among whom were Mary Magdalene, and Mary the mother of James the younger and of Joses, and Salome. ⁴¹When he was in Galilee, they followed him and ministered to him, and there were also many other women who came up with him to Jerusalem.

JESUS IS BURIED

⁴²And when evening had come, since it was the day of Preparation, that is, the day before the Sabbath, ⁴³Joseph of Arimathea, a respected member of the council, who was also himself looking for the kingdom of God, took courage and went to Pilate and asked for the body of Jesus. ⁴⁴Pilate was surprised to hear that he should have already died.*ʲ* And summoning the centurion, he asked him whether he was already dead. ⁴⁵And when he learned from the centurion that he was

---

*ª*A Roman judicial penalty, consisting of a severe beating with a multi-lashed whip containing embedded pieces of bone and metal *ᵇ*Greek *the praetorium* *ᶜ*Greek *cohort*; a tenth of a Roman legion, usually about 600 men *ᵈ*That is, 9 A.M. *ᵉ*Some manuscripts insert verse 28: *And the Scripture was fulfilled that says, "He was numbered with the transgressors"* *ᶠ*That is, noon *ᵍ*That is, 3 P.M. *ʰ*Some manuscripts insert *cried out and* *ⁱ*Or *a son* *ʲ*Or *Pilate wondered whether he had already died*

dead, he granted the corpse to Joseph. ⁴⁶And Joseph⁽ᵃ⁾ bought a linen shroud, and taking him down, wrapped him in the linen shroud and laid him in a tomb that had been cut out of the rock. And he rolled a stone against the entrance of the tomb. ⁴⁷Mary Magdalene and Mary the mother of Joses saw where he was laid.

THE RESURRECTION

16 When the Sabbath was past, Mary Magdalene, Mary the mother of James, and Salome bought spices, so that they might go and anoint him. ²And very early on the first day of the week, when the sun had risen, they went to the tomb. ³And they were saying to one another, "Who will roll away the stone for us from the entrance of the tomb?" ⁴And looking up, they saw that the stone had been rolled back—it was very large. ⁵And entering the tomb, they saw a young man sitting on the right side, dressed in a white robe, and they were alarmed. ⁶And he said to them, "Do not be alarmed. You seek Jesus of Nazareth, who was crucified. He has risen; he is not here. See the place where they laid him. ⁷But go, tell his disciples and Peter that he is going before you to Galilee. There you will see him, just as he told you." ⁸And they went out and fled from the tomb, for trembling and astonishment had seized them, and they said nothing to anyone, for they were afraid.

[SOME OF THE EARLIEST MANUSCRIPTS DO NOT INCLUDE 16:9–20.]⁽ᵇ⁾

JESUS APPEARS TO MARY MAGDALENE

⁹[[Now when he rose early on the first day of the week, he appeared first to Mary Magdalene, from whom he had cast out seven demons. ¹⁰She went and told those who had been with him, as they mourned and wept. ¹¹But when they heard that he was alive and had been seen by her, they would not believe it.

JESUS APPEARS TO TWO DISCIPLES

¹²After these things he appeared in another form to two of them, as they were walking into the country. ¹³And they went back and told the rest, but they did not believe them.

THE GREAT COMMISSION

¹⁴Afterwards he appeared to the eleven themselves as they were reclining at table, and he rebuked them for their unbelief and hardness of heart, because they had not believed those who saw him after he had risen. ¹⁵And he said to them, "Go into all the world and proclaim the gospel to the whole creation. ¹⁶Whoever believes and is baptized will be saved, but whoever does not believe will be condemned. ¹⁷And these signs will accompany those who believe: in my name they will cast out demons; they will speak in new tongues; ¹⁸they will pick up serpents with their hands; and if they drink any deadly poison, it will not hurt them; they will lay their hands on the sick, and they will recover."

¹⁹So then the Lord Jesus, after he had spoken to them, was taken up into heaven and sat down at the right hand of God. ²⁰And they went out and preached everywhere, while the Lord worked with them and confirmed the message by accompanying signs.]]

⁽ᵃ⁾Greek *he* ⁽ᵇ⁾Some manuscripts end the book with 16:8; others include verses 9–20 immediately after verse 8. At least one manuscript inserts additional material after verse 14; some manuscripts include after verse 8 the following: But they reported briefly to Peter and those with him all that they had been told. And after this, Jesus himself sent out by means of them, from east to west, the sacred and imperishable proclamation of eternal salvation. These manuscripts then continue with verses 9–20

THE GOSPEL ACCORDING TO
LUKE

DEDICATION TO THEOPHILUS

1 Inasmuch as many have undertaken to compile a narrative of the things that have been accomplished among us, ²just as those who from the beginning were eyewitnesses and ministers of the word have delivered them to us, ³it seemed good to me also, having followed all things closely for some time past, to write an orderly account for you, most excellent Theophilus, ⁴that you may have certainty concerning the things you have been taught.

BIRTH OF JOHN THE BAPTIST FORETOLD

⁵In the days of Herod, king of Judea, there was a priest named Zechariah,ᵃ of the division of Abijah. And he had a wife from the daughters of Aaron, and her name was Elizabeth. ⁶And they were both righteous before God, walking blamelessly in all the commandments and statutes of the Lord. ⁷But they had no child, because Elizabeth was barren, and both were advanced in years.

⁸Now while he was serving as priest before God when his division was on duty, ⁹according to the custom of the priesthood, he was chosen by lot to enter the temple of the Lord and burn incense. ¹⁰And the whole multitude of the people were praying outside at the hour of incense. ¹¹And there appeared to him an angel of the Lord standing on the right side of the altar of incense. ¹²And Zechariah was troubled when he saw him, and fear fell upon him. ¹³But the angel said to him, "Do not be afraid, Zechariah, for your prayer has been heard, and your wife Elizabeth will bear you a son, and you shall call his name John. ¹⁴And you will have joy and gladness, and many will rejoice at his birth, ¹⁵for he will be great before the Lord. And he must not drink wine or strong drink, and he will be filled with the Holy Spirit, even from his mother's womb. ¹⁶And he will turn many of the children of Israel to the Lord their God, ¹⁷and he will go before him in the spirit and power of Elijah, to turn the hearts of the fathers to the children, and the disobedient to the wisdom of the just, to make ready for the Lord a people prepared."

¹⁸And Zechariah said to the angel, "How shall I know this? For I am an old man, and my wife is advanced in years." ¹⁹And the angel answered him, "I am Gabriel. I stand in the presence of God, and I was sent to speak to you and to bring you this good news. ²⁰And behold, you will be silent and unable to speak until the day that these things take place, because you did not believe my words, which will be fulfilled in their time." ²¹And the people were waiting for Zechariah, and they were wondering at his delay in the temple. ²²And when he came out, he was unable to speak to them, and they realized that he had seen a vision in the temple. And he kept making signs to them and remained mute. ²³And when his time of service was ended, he went to his home.

²⁴After these days his wife Elizabeth conceived, and for five months she kept herself hidden, saying, ²⁵"Thus the Lord has done for me in the days when he looked on me, to take away my reproach among people."

BIRTH OF JESUS FORETOLD

²⁶In the sixth month the angel Gabriel was sent from God to a city of Galilee named Nazareth, ²⁷to a virgin betrothedᵇ to a man whose name was Joseph, of the house of David. And the virgin's name was Mary. ²⁸And he came to her and said, "Greetings, O favoured one, the Lord is with you!"ᶜ ²⁹But she was greatly troubled at the saying, and tried to discern what sort of greeting this might be. ³⁰And the angel said to her, "Do not be afraid, Mary, for you have found favour with God. ³¹And behold, you will conceive in your womb and bear a son, and you shall call his name Jesus. ³²He will be great and will be called the Son of the Most High. And the Lord God will give to him the throne of his father David, ³³and

---
ᵃGreek *Zacharias* ᵇThat is, legally pledged to be married
ᶜSome manuscripts add *Blessed are you among women!*

he will reign over the house of Jacob for ever, and of his kingdom there will be no end." ³⁴And Mary said to the angel, "How will this be, since I am a virgin?"[a] ³⁵And the angel answered her, "The Holy Spirit will come upon you, and the power of the Most High will overshadow you; therefore the child to be born[b] will be called holy—the Son of God. ³⁶And behold, your relative Elizabeth in her old age has also conceived a son, and this is the sixth month with her who was called barren. ³⁷For nothing will be impossible with God." ³⁸And Mary said, "Behold, I am the servant[c] of the Lord; let it be to me according to your word." And the angel departed from her.

MARY VISITS ELIZABETH

³⁹In those days Mary arose and went with haste into the hill country, to a town in Judah, ⁴⁰and she entered the house of Zechariah and greeted Elizabeth. ⁴¹And when Elizabeth heard the greeting of Mary, the baby leaped in her womb. And Elizabeth was filled with the Holy Spirit, ⁴²and she exclaimed with a loud cry, "Blessed are you among women, and blessed is the fruit of your womb! ⁴³And why is this granted to me that the mother of my Lord should come to me? ⁴⁴For behold, when the sound of your greeting came to my ears, the baby in my womb leaped for joy. ⁴⁵And blessed is she who believed that there would be[d] a fulfilment of what was spoken to her from the Lord."

MARY'S SONG OF PRAISE: THE MAGNIFICAT

⁴⁶And Mary said,

> "My soul magnifies the Lord,
> ⁴⁷ and my spirit rejoices in
>   God my Saviour,
> ⁴⁸ for he has looked on the humble
>   estate of his servant.
>   For behold, from now on
>   all generations will
>   call me blessed;
> ⁴⁹ for he who is mighty has done
>   great things for me,
>   and holy is his name.
> ⁵⁰ And his mercy is for those
>   who fear him
>   from generation to generation.
> ⁵¹ He has shown strength with his arm;
>   he has scattered the proud in the
>   thoughts of their hearts;
> ⁵² he has brought down the mighty
>   from their thrones
>   and exalted those of humble estate;
> ⁵³ he has filled the hungry
>   with good things,
>   and the rich he has sent away empty.
> ⁵⁴ He has helped his servant Israel,
>   in remembrance of his mercy,
> ⁵⁵ as he spoke to our fathers,
>   to Abraham and to his
>   offspring for ever."

⁵⁶And Mary remained with her about three months and returned to her home.

THE BIRTH OF JOHN THE BAPTIST

⁵⁷Now the time came for Elizabeth to give birth, and she bore a son. ⁵⁸And her neighbours and relatives heard that the Lord had shown great mercy to her, and they rejoiced with her. ⁵⁹And on the eighth day they came to circumcise the child. And they would have called him Zechariah after his father, ⁶⁰but his mother answered, "No; he shall be called John." ⁶¹And they said to her, "None of your relatives is called by this name." ⁶²And they made signs to his father, enquiring what he wanted him to be called. ⁶³And he asked for a writing tablet and wrote, "His name is John." And they all wondered. ⁶⁴And immediately his mouth was opened and his tongue loosed, and he spoke, blessing God. ⁶⁵And fear came on all their neighbours. And all these things were talked about through all the hill country of Judea, ⁶⁶and all who heard them laid them up in their hearts, saying, "What then will this child be?" For the hand of the Lord was with him.

ZECHARIAH'S PROPHECY

⁶⁷And his father Zechariah was filled with the Holy Spirit and prophesied, saying,

> ⁶⁸ "Blessed be the Lord God of Israel,
>   for he has visited and
>   redeemed his people
> ⁶⁹ and has raised up a horn of
>   salvation for us
>   in the house of his servant David,
> ⁷⁰ as he spoke by the mouth of his
>   holy prophets from of old,
> ⁷¹ that we should be saved
>   from our enemies

---

[a] Greek *since I do not know a man*   [b] Some manuscripts add *of you*
[c] Greek *bondservant*; also verse 48   [d] Or *believed, for there will be*

and from the hand of all
    who hate us;
⁷² to show the mercy promised
    to our fathers
and to remember his holy covenant,
⁷³ the oath that he swore to our
    father Abraham, to grant us
⁷⁴ that we, being delivered from
    the hand of our enemies,
might serve him without fear,
⁷⁵ in holiness and righteousness
    before him all our days.
⁷⁶ And you, child, will be called the
    prophet of the Most High;
for you will go before the Lord
    to prepare his ways,
⁷⁷ to give knowledge of salvation
    to his people
in the forgiveness of their sins,
⁷⁸ because of the tender
    mercy of our God,
whereby the sunrise shall
    visit us^a from on high
⁷⁹ to give light to those who sit
    in darkness and in the
        shadow of death,
to guide our feet into the
    way of peace."

⁸⁰And the child grew and became strong in spirit, and he was in the wilderness until the day of his public appearance to Israel.

THE BIRTH OF JESUS CHRIST

2 In those days a decree went out from Caesar Augustus that all the world should be registered. ²This was the first registration when^b Quirinius was governor of Syria. ³And all went to be registered, each to his own town. ⁴And Joseph also went up from Galilee, from the town of Nazareth, to Judea, to the city of David, which is called Bethlehem, because he was of the house and lineage of David, ⁵to be registered with Mary, his betrothed,^{c} who was with child. ⁶And while they were there, the time came for her to give birth. ⁷And she gave birth to her firstborn son and wrapped him in swaddling cloths and laid him in a manger, because there was no place for them in the inn.^{d}

THE SHEPHERDS AND THE ANGELS

⁸And in the same region there were shepherds out in the field, keeping watch over their flock by night. ⁹And an angel of the Lord appeared to them, and the glory of the Lord shone around them, and they were filled with great fear. ¹⁰And the angel said to them, "Fear not, for behold, I bring you good news of great joy that will be for all the people. ¹¹For unto you is born this day in the city of David a Saviour, who is Christ the Lord. ¹²And this will be a sign for you: you will find a baby wrapped in swaddling cloths and lying in a manger." ¹³And suddenly there was with the angel a multitude of the heavenly host praising God and saying,

¹⁴ "Glory to God in the highest,
    and on earth peace among those
        with whom he is pleased!"^{e}

¹⁵When the angels went away from them into heaven, the shepherds said to one another, "Let us go over to Bethlehem and see this thing that has happened, which the Lord has made known to us." ¹⁶And they went with haste and found Mary and Joseph, and the baby lying in a manger. ¹⁷And when they saw it, they made known the saying that had been told them concerning this child. ¹⁸And all who heard it wondered at what the shepherds told them. ¹⁹But Mary treasured up all these things, pondering them in her heart. ²⁰And the shepherds returned, glorifying and praising God for all they had heard and seen, as it had been told them.

²¹And at the end of eight days, when he was circumcised, he was called Jesus, the name given by the angel before he was conceived in the womb.

JESUS PRESENTED AT THE TEMPLE

²²And when the time came for their purification according to the Law of Moses, they brought him up to Jerusalem to present him to the Lord ²³(as it is written in the Law of the Lord, "Every male who first opens the womb shall be called holy to the Lord") ²⁴and to offer a sacrifice according to what is said in the Law of the Lord, "a pair of turtle-doves, or two young pigeons". ²⁵Now there was a man in Jerusalem, whose name was Simeon, and this man was righteous and devout, waiting for the consolation of Israel, and the Holy Spirit was upon him. ²⁶And it had been revealed to him by the Holy Spirit that he would not see death before he had seen the Lord's Christ.

---

^{a}Or *when the sunrise shall dawn upon us;* some manuscripts *since the sunrise has visited us* ^{b}Or *This was the registration before* ^{c}That is, one legally pledged to be married ^{d}Or *guest room* ^{e}Some manuscripts *peace, good will among men*

²⁷And he came in the Spirit into the temple, and when the parents brought in the child Jesus, to do for him according to the custom of the Law, ²⁸he took him up in his arms and blessed God and said,

²⁹ "Lord, now you are letting your
  servant[a] depart in peace,
  according to your word;
³⁰ for my eyes have seen your salvation
³¹ that you have prepared in the
  presence of all peoples,
³² a light for revelation to the Gentiles,
  and for glory to your people Israel."

³³And his father and his mother marvelled at what was said about him. ³⁴And Simeon blessed them and said to Mary his mother, "Behold, this child is appointed for the fall and rising of many in Israel, and for a sign that is opposed ³⁵(and a sword will pierce through your own soul also), so that thoughts from many hearts may be revealed."

³⁶And there was a prophetess, Anna, the daughter of Phanuel, of the tribe of Asher. She was advanced in years, having lived with her husband seven years from when she was a virgin, ³⁷and then as a widow until she was eighty-four.[b] She did not depart from the temple, worshipping with fasting and prayer night and day. ³⁸And coming up at that very hour she began to give thanks to God and to speak of him to all who were waiting for the redemption of Jerusalem.

THE RETURN TO NAZARETH

³⁹And when they had performed everything according to the Law of the Lord, they returned into Galilee, to their own town of Nazareth. ⁴⁰And the child grew and became strong, filled with wisdom. And the favour of God was upon him.

THE BOY JESUS IN THE TEMPLE

⁴¹Now his parents went to Jerusalem every year at the Feast of the Passover. ⁴²And when he was twelve years old, they went up according to custom. ⁴³And when the feast was ended, as they were returning, the boy Jesus stayed behind in Jerusalem. His parents did not know it, ⁴⁴but supposing him to be in the group they went a day's journey, but then they began to search for him among their relatives and acquaintances, ⁴⁵and when they did not find him, they returned to Jerusalem, searching for him. ⁴⁶After three days they found him in the temple, sitting among the teachers, listening to them and asking them questions. ⁴⁷And all who heard him were amazed at his understanding and his answers. ⁴⁸And when his parents[c] saw him, they were astonished. And his mother said to him, "Son, why have you treated us so? Behold, your father and I have been searching for you in great distress." ⁴⁹And he said to them, "Why were you looking for me? Did you not know that I must be in my Father's house?"[d] ⁵⁰And they did not understand the saying that he spoke to them. ⁵¹And he went down with them and came to Nazareth and was submissive to them. And his mother treasured up all these things in her heart.

⁵²And Jesus increased in wisdom and in stature[e] and in favour with God and man.

JOHN THE BAPTIST PREPARES THE WAY

3 In the fifteenth year of the reign of Tiberius Caesar, Pontius Pilate being governor of Judea, and Herod being tetrarch of Galilee, and his brother Philip tetrarch of the region of Ituraea and Trachonitis, and Lysanias tetrarch of Abilene, ²during the high priesthood of Annas and Caiaphas, the word of God came to John the son of Zechariah in the wilderness. ³And he went into all the region around the Jordan, proclaiming a baptism of repentance for the forgiveness of sins. ⁴As it is written in the book of the words of Isaiah the prophet,

  "The voice of one crying in
    the wilderness:
  'Prepare the way of the Lord,[f]
    make his paths straight.
⁵ Every valley shall be filled,
    and every mountain and hill
      shall be made low,
  and the crooked shall become straight,
    and the rough places shall
      become level ways,
⁶ and all flesh shall see the
    salvation of God.'"

⁷He said therefore to the crowds that came out to be baptized by him, "You brood of vipers! Who warned you to flee from the wrath to come? ⁸Bear fruits in keeping with repentance. And do not begin to say to yourselves,

---

[a]Or bondservant [b]Or as a widow for eighty-four years [c]Greek they [d]Or about my Father's business [e]Or years [f]Or crying, Prepare in the wilderness the way of the Lord

'We have Abraham as our father.' For I tell you, God is able from these stones to raise up children for Abraham. ⁹Even now the axe is laid to the root of the trees. Every tree therefore that does not bear good fruit is cut down and thrown into the fire."

¹⁰And the crowds asked him, "What then shall we do?" ¹¹And he answered them, "Whoever has two tunics[a] is to share with him who has none, and whoever has food is to do likewise." ¹²Tax collectors also came to be baptized and said to him, "Teacher, what shall we do?" ¹³And he said to them, "Collect no more than you are authorized to do." ¹⁴Soldiers also asked him, "And we, what shall we do?" And he said to them, "Do not extort money from anyone by threats or by false accusation, and be content with your wages."

¹⁵As the people were filled with expectation, and all were questioning in their hearts concerning John, whether he might be the Christ, ¹⁶John answered them all, saying, "I baptize you with water, but he who is mightier than I is coming, the strap of whose sandals I am not worthy to untie. He will baptize you with the Holy Spirit and fire. ¹⁷His winnowing fork is in his hand, to clear his threshing floor and to gather the wheat into his barn, but the chaff he will burn with unquenchable fire."

¹⁸So with many other exhortations he preached good news to the people. ¹⁹But Herod the tetrarch, who had been reproved by him for Herodias, his brother's wife, and for all the evil things that Herod had done, ²⁰added this to them all, that he locked up John in prison.

²¹Now when all the people were baptized, and when Jesus also had been baptized and was praying, the heavens were opened, ²²and the Holy Spirit descended on him in bodily form, like a dove; and a voice came from heaven, "You are my beloved Son;[b] with you I am well pleased."[c]

THE GENEALOGY OF JESUS CHRIST

²³Jesus, when he began his ministry, was about thirty years of age, being the son (as was supposed) of Joseph, the son of Heli, ²⁴the son of Matthat, the son of Levi, the son of Melchi, the son of Jannai, the son of Joseph, ²⁵the son of Mattathias, the son of Amos, the son of Nahum, the son of Esli, the son of Naggai, ²⁶the son of Maath, the son of Mattathias, the son of Semein, the son of Josech, the son of Joda, ²⁷the son of Joanan, the son of Rhesa, the son of Zerubbabel, the son of Shealtiel,[d] the son of Neri, ²⁸the son of Melchi, the son of Addi, the son of Cosam, the son of Elmadam, the son of Er, ²⁹the son of Joshua, the son of Eliezer, the son of Jorim, the son of Matthat, the son of Levi, ³⁰the son of Simeon, the son of Judah, the son of Joseph, the son of Jonam, the son of Eliakim, ³¹the son of Melea, the son of Menna, the son of Mattatha, the son of Nathan, the son of David, ³²the son of Jesse, the son of Obed, the son of Boaz, the son of Sala, the son of Nahshon, ³³the son of Amminadab, the son of Admin, the son of Arni, the son of Hezron, the son of Perez, the son of Judah, ³⁴the son of Jacob, the son of Isaac, the son of Abraham, the son of Terah, the son of Nahor, ³⁵the son of Serug, the son of Reu, the son of Peleg, the son of Eber, the son of Shelah, ³⁶the son of Cainan, the son of Arphaxad, the son of Shem, the son of Noah, the son of Lamech, ³⁷the son of Methuselah, the son of Enoch, the son of Jared, the son of Mahalaleel, the son of Cainan, ³⁸the son of Enos, the son of Seth, the son of Adam, the son of God.

THE TEMPTATION OF JESUS

4 And Jesus, full of the Holy Spirit, returned from the Jordan and was led by the Spirit in the wilderness ²for forty days, being tempted by the devil. And he ate nothing during those days. And when they were over, he was hungry. ³The devil said to him, "If you are the Son of God, command this stone to become bread." ⁴And Jesus answered him, "It is written, 'Man shall not live by bread alone.'" ⁵And the devil took him up and showed him all the kingdoms of the world in a moment of time, ⁶and said to him, "To you I will give all this authority and their glory, for it has been delivered to me, and I give it to whom I will. ⁷If you, then, will worship me, it will all be yours." ⁸And Jesus answered him, "It is written,

"'You shall worship the Lord your God,
and him only shall you serve.'"

⁹And he took him to Jerusalem and set him on the pinnacle of the temple and said to him, "If you are the Son of God, throw yourself down from here, ¹⁰for it is written,

---

[a] Greek *chiton*, a long garment worn under the cloak next to the skin [b] Or *my Son, my* (or *the*) *Beloved* [c] Some manuscripts *beloved Son; today I have begotten you* [d] Greek *Salathiel*

> " 'He will command his angels
> concerning you,
> to guard you',

¹¹and

> " 'On their hands they will bear you up,
> lest you strike your foot
> against a stone.' "

¹²And Jesus answered him, "It is said, 'You shall not put the Lord your God to the test.' " ¹³And when the devil had ended every temptation, he departed from him until an opportune time.

JESUS BEGINS HIS MINISTRY

¹⁴And Jesus returned in the power of the Spirit to Galilee, and a report about him went out through all the surrounding country. ¹⁵And he taught in their synagogues, being glorified by all.

JESUS REJECTED AT NAZARETH

¹⁶And he came to Nazareth, where he had been brought up. And as was his custom, he went to the synagogue on the Sabbath day, and he stood up to read. ¹⁷And the scroll of the prophet Isaiah was given to him. He unrolled the scroll and found the place where it was written,

> ¹⁸ "The Spirit of the Lord is upon me,
> because he has anointed me
> to proclaim good news to the poor.
> He has sent me to proclaim
> liberty to the captives
> and recovering of sight to the blind,
> to set at liberty those who
> are oppressed,
> ¹⁹ to proclaim the year of the
> Lord's favour."

²⁰And he rolled up the scroll and gave it back to the attendant and sat down. And the eyes of all in the synagogue were fixed on him. ²¹And he began to say to them, "Today this Scripture has been fulfilled in your hearing." ²²And all spoke well of him and marvelled at the gracious words that were coming from his mouth. And they said, "Is not this Joseph's son?" ²³And he said to them, "Doubtless you will quote to me this proverb, ' "Physician, heal yourself." What we have heard you did at Capernaum, do here in your home town as well.' " ²⁴And he said to them, "Truly, I say to you, no prophet is acceptable in his home town. ²⁵But in truth, I tell you, there were many widows in Israel in the days of Elijah, when the heavens were shut up three years and six months, and a great famine came over all the land, ²⁶and Elijah was sent to none of them but only to Zarephath, in the land of Sidon, to a woman who was a widow. ²⁷And there were many lepers[a] in Israel in the time of the prophet Elisha, and none of them was cleansed, but only Naaman the Syrian." ²⁸When they heard these things, all in the synagogue were filled with wrath. ²⁹And they rose up and drove him out of the town and brought him to the brow of the hill on which their town was built, so that they could throw him down the cliff. ³⁰But passing through their midst, he went away.

JESUS HEALS A MAN WITH AN UNCLEAN DEMON

³¹And he went down to Capernaum, a city of Galilee. And he was teaching them on the Sabbath, ³²and they were astonished at his teaching, for his word possessed authority. ³³And in the synagogue there was a man who had the spirit of an unclean demon, and he cried out with a loud voice, ³⁴"Ha![b] What have you to do with us, Jesus of Nazareth? Have you come to destroy us? I know who you are—the Holy One of God." ³⁵But Jesus rebuked him, saying, "Be silent and come out of him!" And when the demon had thrown him down in their midst, he came out of him, having done him no harm. ³⁶And they were all amazed and said to one another, "What is this word? For with authority and power he commands the unclean spirits, and they come out!" ³⁷And reports about him went out into every place in the surrounding region.

JESUS HEALS MANY

³⁸And he arose and left the synagogue and entered Simon's house. Now Simon's mother-in-law was ill with a high fever, and they appealed to him on her behalf. ³⁹And he stood over her and rebuked the fever, and it left her, and immediately she rose and began to serve them.

⁴⁰Now when the sun was setting, all those who had any who were sick with various diseases brought them to him, and he laid his hands on every one of them and healed them.

---

[a] *Leprosy* was a term for several skin diseases; see Leviticus 13
[b] Or *Leave us alone*

⁴¹And demons also came out of many, crying, "You are the Son of God!" But he rebuked them and would not allow them to speak, because they knew that he was the Christ.

JESUS PREACHES IN SYNAGOGUES

⁴²And when it was day, he departed and went into a desolate place. And the people sought him and came to him, and would have kept him from leaving them, ⁴³but he said to them, "I must preach the good news of the kingdom of God to the other towns as well; for I was sent for this purpose." ⁴⁴And he was preaching in the synagogues of Judea.ᵃ

JESUS CALLS THE FIRST DISCIPLES

5 On one occasion, while the crowd was pressing in on him to hear the word of God, he was standing by the lake of Gennesaret, ²and he saw two boats by the lake, but the fishermen had gone out of them and were washing their nets. ³Getting into one of the boats, which was Simon's, he asked him to put out a little from the land. And he sat down and taught the people from the boat. ⁴And when he had finished speaking, he said to Simon, "Put out into the deep and let down your nets for a catch." ⁵And Simon answered, "Master, we toiled all night and took nothing! But at your word I will let down the nets." ⁶And when they had done this, they enclosed a large number of fish, and their nets were breaking. ⁷They signalled to their partners in the other boat to come and help them. And they came and filled both the boats, so that they began to sink. ⁸But when Simon Peter saw it, he fell down at Jesus' knees, saying, "Depart from me, for I am a sinful man, O Lord." ⁹For he and all who were with him were astonished at the catch of fish that they had taken, ¹⁰and so also were James and John, sons of Zebedee, who were partners with Simon. And Jesus said to Simon, "Do not be afraid; from now on you will be catching men."ᵇ ¹¹And when they had brought their boats to land, they left everything and followed him.

JESUS CLEANSES A LEPER

¹²While he was in one of the cities, there came a man full of leprosy.ᶜ And when he saw Jesus, he fell on his face and begged him, "Lord, if you will, you can make me clean." ¹³And Jesusᵈ stretched out his hand and touched him, saying, "I will; be clean." And immediately the leprosy left him. ¹⁴And he charged him to tell no one, but "go and show yourself to the priest, and make an offering for your cleansing, as Moses commanded, for a proof to them." ¹⁵But now even more the report about him went abroad, and great crowds gathered to hear him and to be healed of their infirmities. ¹⁶But he would withdraw to desolate places and pray.

JESUS HEALS A PARALYTIC

¹⁷On one of those days, as he was teaching, Pharisees and teachers of the law were sitting there, who had come from every village of Galilee and Judea and from Jerusalem. And the power of the Lord was with him to heal.ᵉ ¹⁸And behold, some men were bringing on a bed a man who was paralysed, and they were seeking to bring him in and lay him before Jesus, ¹⁹but finding no way to bring him in, because of the crowd, they went up on the roof and let him down with his bed through the tiles into the midst before Jesus. ²⁰And when he saw their faith, he said, "Man, your sins are forgiven you." ²¹And the scribes and the Pharisees began to question, saying, "Who is this who speaks blasphemies? Who can forgive sins but God alone?" ²²When Jesus perceived their thoughts, he answered them, "Why do you question in your hearts? ²³Which is easier, to say, 'Your sins are forgiven you', or to say, 'Rise and walk'? ²⁴But that you may know that the Son of Man has authority on earth to forgive sins"—he said to the man who was paralysed—"I say to you, rise, pick up your bed and go home." ²⁵And immediately he rose up before them and picked up what he had been lying on and went home, glorifying God. ²⁶And amazement seized them all, and they glorified God and were filled with awe, saying, "We have seen extraordinary things today."

JESUS CALLS LEVI

²⁷After this he went out and saw a tax collector named Levi, sitting at the tax booth. And he said to him, "Follow me." ²⁸And leaving everything, he rose and followed him.

²⁹And Levi made him a great feast in his house, and there was a large company of tax collectors and others reclining at table with them. ³⁰And the Pharisees and their scribes grumbled at his disciples, saying, "Why do

---

ᵃSome manuscripts *Galilee* ᵇThe Greek word *anthropoi* refers here to both men and women ᶜ*Leprosy* was a term for several skin diseases; see Leviticus 13 ᵈGreek *he* ᵉSome manuscripts *was present to heal them*

you eat and drink with tax collectors and sinners?" ³¹And Jesus answered them, "Those who are well have no need of a physician, but those who are sick. ³²I have not come to call the righteous but sinners to repentance."

A QUESTION ABOUT FASTING

³³And they said to him, "The disciples of John fast often and offer prayers, and so do the disciples of the Pharisees, but yours eat and drink." ³⁴And Jesus said to them, "Can you make wedding guests fast while the bridegroom is with them? ³⁵The days will come when the bridegroom is taken away from them, and then they will fast in those days." ³⁶He also told them a parable: "No one tears a piece from a new garment and puts it on an old garment. If he does, he will tear the new, and the piece from the new will not match the old. ³⁷And no one puts new wine into old wineskins. If he does, the new wine will burst the skins and it will be spilled, and the skins will be destroyed. ³⁸But new wine must be put into fresh wineskins. ³⁹And no one after drinking old wine desires new, for he says, 'The old is good.'"ᵃ

JESUS IS LORD OF THE SABBATH

6 On a Sabbath,ᵇ while he was going through the cornfields, his disciples plucked and ate some ears of corn, rubbing them in their hands. ²But some of the Pharisees said, "Why are you doing what is not lawful to do on the Sabbath?" ³And Jesus answered them, "Have you not read what David did when he was hungry, he and those who were with him: ⁴how he entered the house of God and took and ate the bread of the Presence, which is not lawful for any but the priests to eat, and also gave it to those with him?" ⁵And he said to them, "The Son of Man is lord of the Sabbath."

A MAN WITH A WITHERED HAND

⁶On another Sabbath, he entered the synagogue and was teaching, and a man was there whose right hand was withered. ⁷And the scribes and the Pharisees watched him, to see whether he would heal on the Sabbath, so that they might find a reason to accuse him. ⁸But he knew their thoughts, and he said to the man with the withered hand, "Come and stand here." And he rose and stood there. ⁹And Jesus said to them, "I ask you, is it lawful on the Sabbath to do good or to do harm, to save life or to destroy it?" ¹⁰And after looking around at them all he said to him, "Stretch out your hand." And he did so, and his hand was restored. ¹¹But they were filled with fury and discussed with one another what they might do to Jesus.

THE TWELVE APOSTLES

¹²In these days he went out to the mountain to pray, and all night he continued in prayer to God. ¹³And when day came, he called his disciples and chose from them twelve, whom he named apostles: ¹⁴Simon, whom he named Peter, and Andrew his brother, and James and John, and Philip, and Bartholomew, ¹⁵and Matthew, and Thomas, and James the son of Alphaeus, and Simon who was called the Zealot, ¹⁶and Judas the son of James, and Judas Iscariot, who became a traitor.

JESUS MINISTERS TO A GREAT MULTITUDE

¹⁷And he came down with them and stood on a level place, with a great crowd of his disciples and a great multitude of people from all Judea and Jerusalem and the sea coast of Tyre and Sidon, ¹⁸who came to hear him and to be healed of their diseases. And those who were troubled with unclean spirits were cured. ¹⁹And all the crowd sought to touch him, for power came out from him and healed them all.

THE BEATITUDES

²⁰And he lifted up his eyes on his disciples, and said:

"Blessed are you who are poor, for yours is the kingdom of God.

²¹"Blessed are you who are hungry now, for you shall be satisfied.

"Blessed are you who weep now, for you shall laugh.

²²"Blessed are you when people hate you and when they exclude you and revile you and spurn your name as evil, on account of the Son of Man! ²³Rejoice in that day, and leap for joy, for behold, your reward is great in heaven; for so their fathers did to the prophets.

JESUS PRONOUNCES WOES

²⁴"But woe to you who are rich, for you have received your consolation.

²⁵"Woe to you who are full now, for you shall be hungry.

ᵃSome manuscripts *better* ᵇSome manuscripts *On the second first Sabbath* (that is, on the second Sabbath after the first)

"Woe to you who laugh now, for you shall mourn and weep.

²⁶"Woe to you, when all people speak well of you, for so their fathers did to the false prophets.

LOVE YOUR ENEMIES

²⁷"But I say to you who hear, Love your enemies, do good to those who hate you, ²⁸bless those who curse you, pray for those who abuse you. ²⁹To one who strikes you on the cheek, offer the other also, and from one who takes away your cloak do not withhold your tunic*ᵃ* either. ³⁰Give to everyone who begs from you, and from one who takes away your goods do not demand them back. ³¹And as you wish that others would do to you, do so to them.

³²"If you love those who love you, what benefit is that to you? For even sinners love those who love them. ³³And if you do good to those who do good to you, what benefit is that to you? For even sinners do the same. ³⁴And if you lend to those from whom you expect to receive, what credit is that to you? Even sinners lend to sinners, to get back the same amount. ³⁵But love your enemies, and do good, and lend, expecting nothing in return, and your reward will be great, and you will be sons of the Most High, for he is kind to the ungrateful and the evil. ³⁶Be merciful, even as your Father is merciful.

JUDGING OTHERS

³⁷"Judge not, and you will not be judged; condemn not, and you will not be condemned; forgive, and you will be forgiven; ³⁸give, and it will be given to you. Good measure, pressed down, shaken together, running over, will be put into your lap. For with the measure you use it will be measured back to you."

³⁹He also told them a parable: "Can a blind man lead a blind man? Will they not both fall into a pit? ⁴⁰A disciple is not above his teacher, but everyone when he is fully trained will be like his teacher. ⁴¹Why do you see the speck that is in your brother's eye, but do not notice the log that is in your own eye? ⁴²How can you say to your brother, 'Brother, let me take out the speck that is in your eye', when you yourself do not see the log that is in your own eye? You hypocrite, first take the log out of your own eye, and then you will see clearly to take out the speck that is in your brother's eye.

A TREE AND ITS FRUIT

⁴³"For no good tree bears bad fruit, nor again does a bad tree bear good fruit, ⁴⁴for each tree is known by its own fruit. For figs are not gathered from thorn bushes, nor are grapes picked from a bramble bush. ⁴⁵The good person out of the good treasure of his heart produces good, and the evil person out of his evil treasure produces evil, for out of the abundance of the heart his mouth speaks.

BUILD YOUR HOUSE ON THE ROCK

⁴⁶"Why do you call me 'Lord, Lord', and not do what I tell you? ⁴⁷Everyone who comes to me and hears my words and does them, I will show you what he is like: ⁴⁸he is like a man building a house, who dug deep and laid the foundation on the rock. And when a flood arose, the stream broke against that house and could not shake it, because it had been well built.*ᵇ* ⁴⁹But the one who hears and does not do them is like a man who built a house on the ground without a foundation. When the stream broke against it, immediately it fell, and the ruin of that house was great."

JESUS HEALS A CENTURION'S SERVANT

7 After he had finished all his sayings in the hearing of the people, he entered Capernaum. ²Now a centurion had a servant*ᶜ* who was sick and at the point of death, who was highly valued by him. ³When the centurion*ᵈ* heard about Jesus, he sent to him elders of the Jews, asking him to come and heal his servant. ⁴And when they came to Jesus, they pleaded with him earnestly, saying, "He is worthy to have you do this for him, ⁵for he loves our nation, and he is the one who built us our synagogue." ⁶And Jesus went with them. When he was not far from the house, the centurion sent friends, saying to him, "Lord, do not trouble yourself, for I am not worthy to have you come under my roof. ⁷Therefore I did not presume to come to you. But say the word, and let my servant be healed. ⁸For I too am a man set under authority, with soldiers under me: and I say to one, 'Go', and he goes; and to another, 'Come', and he comes; and to my servant, 'Do this', and he does it." ⁹When Jesus heard these things, he marvelled at him, and turning to the crowd

---

*ᵃ*Greek *chiton*, a long garment worn under the cloak next to the skin
*ᵇ*Some manuscripts *founded upon the rock* *ᶜ*Or *bondservant*; also verses 3, 8, 10 *ᵈ*Greek *he*

that followed him, said, "I tell you, not even in Israel have I found such faith." ¹⁰And when those who had been sent returned to the house, they found the servant well.

JESUS RAISES A WIDOW'S SON

¹¹Soon afterwards[a] he went to a town called Nain, and his disciples and a great crowd went with him. ¹²As he drew near to the gate of the town, behold, a man who had died was being carried out, the only son of his mother, and she was a widow, and a considerable crowd from the town was with her. ¹³And when the Lord saw her, he had compassion on her and said to her, "Do not weep." ¹⁴Then he came up and touched the bier, and the bearers stood still. And he said, "Young man, I say to you, arise." ¹⁵And the dead man sat up and began to speak, and Jesus[b] gave him to his mother. ¹⁶Fear seized them all, and they glorified God, saying, "A great prophet has arisen among us!" and "God has visited his people!" ¹⁷And this report about him spread through the whole of Judea and all the surrounding country.

MESSENGERS FROM JOHN THE BAPTIST

¹⁸The disciples of John reported all these things to him. And John, ¹⁹calling two of his disciples to him, sent them to the Lord, saying, "Are you the one who is to come, or shall we look for another?" ²⁰And when the men had come to him, they said, "John the Baptist has sent us to you, saying, 'Are you the one who is to come, or shall we look for another?'" ²¹In that hour he healed many people of diseases and plagues and evil spirits, and on many who were blind he bestowed sight. ²²And he answered them, "Go and tell John what you have seen and heard: the blind receive their sight, the lame walk, lepers[c] are cleansed, and the deaf hear, the dead are raised up, the poor have good news preached to them. ²³And blessed is the one who is not offended by me."

²⁴When John's messengers had gone, Jesus[d] began to speak to the crowds concerning John: "What did you go out into the wilderness to see? A reed shaken by the wind? ²⁵What then did you go out to see? A man dressed in soft clothing? Behold, those who are dressed in splendid clothing and live in luxury are in kings' courts. ²⁶What then did you go out to see? A prophet? Yes, I tell you, and more than a prophet. ²⁷This is he of whom it is written,

"'Behold, I send my messenger
before your face,
who will prepare your
way before you.'

²⁸I tell you, among those born of women none is greater than John. Yet the one who is least in the kingdom of God is greater than he." ²⁹(When all the people heard this, and the tax collectors too, they declared God just,[e] having been baptized with the baptism of John, ³⁰but the Pharisees and the lawyers rejected the purpose of God for themselves, not having been baptized by him.)

³¹"To what then shall I compare the people of this generation, and what are they like? ³²They are like children sitting in the market-place and calling to one another,

"'We played the flute for you,
and you did not dance;
we sang a dirge, and you
did not weep.'

³³For John the Baptist has come eating no bread and drinking no wine, and you say, 'He has a demon.' ³⁴The Son of Man has come eating and drinking, and you say, 'Look at him! A glutton and a drunkard, a friend of tax collectors and sinners!' ³⁵Yet wisdom is justified by all her children."

A SINFUL WOMAN FORGIVEN

³⁶One of the Pharisees asked him to eat with him, and he went into the Pharisee's house and reclined at table. ³⁷And behold, a woman of the city, who was a sinner, when she learned that he was reclining at table in the Pharisee's house, brought an alabaster flask of ointment, ³⁸and standing behind him at his feet, weeping, she began to wet his feet with her tears and wiped them with the hair of her head and kissed his feet and anointed them with the ointment. ³⁹Now when the Pharisee who had invited him saw this, he said to himself, "If this man were a prophet, he would have known who and what sort of woman this is who is touching him, for she is a sinner." ⁴⁰And Jesus answering said to him, "Simon, I have something to say to you." And he answered, "Say it, Teacher."

---

[a] Some manuscripts *The next day* [b] Greek *he* [c] *Leprosy* was a term for several skin diseases; see Leviticus 13 [d] Greek *he* [e] Greek *they justified God*

⁴¹"A certain money-lender had two debtors. One owed five hundred denarii, and the other fifty. ⁴²When they could not pay, he cancelled the debt of both. Now which of them will love him more?" ⁴³Simon answered, "The one, I suppose, for whom he cancelled the larger debt." And he said to him, "You have judged rightly." ⁴⁴Then turning towards the woman he said to Simon, "Do you see this woman? I entered your house; you gave me no water for my feet, but she has wet my feet with her tears and wiped them with her hair. ⁴⁵You gave me no kiss, but from the time I came in she has not ceased to kiss my feet. ⁴⁶You did not anoint my head with oil, but she has anointed my feet with ointment. ⁴⁷Therefore I tell you, her sins, which are many, are forgiven—for she loved much. But he who is forgiven little, loves little." ⁴⁸And he said to her, "Your sins are forgiven." ⁴⁹Then those who were at table with him began to say among[a] themselves, "Who is this, who even forgives sins?" ⁵⁰And he said to the woman, "Your faith has saved you; go in peace."

WOMEN ACCOMPANYING JESUS

8 Soon afterwards he went on through cities and villages, proclaiming and bringing the good news of the kingdom of God. And the twelve were with him, ²and also some women who had been healed of evil spirits and infirmities: Mary, called Magdalene, from whom seven demons had gone out, ³and Joanna, the wife of Chuza, Herod's household manager, and Susanna, and many others, who provided for them[b] out of their means.

THE PARABLE OF THE SOWER

⁴And when a great crowd was gathering and people from town after town came to him, he said in a parable, ⁵"A sower went out to sow his seed. And as he sowed, some fell along the path and was trampled underfoot, and the birds of the air devoured it. ⁶And some fell on the rock, and as it grew up, it withered away, because it had no moisture. ⁷And some fell among thorns, and the thorns grew up with it and choked it. ⁸And some fell into good soil and grew and yielded a hundredfold." As he said these things, he called out, "He who has ears to hear, let him hear."

THE PURPOSE OF THE PARABLES

⁹And when his disciples asked him what this parable meant, ¹⁰he said, "To you it has been given to know the secrets of the kingdom of God, but for others they are in parables, so that 'seeing they may not see, and hearing they may not understand'. ¹¹Now the parable is this: The seed is the word of God. ¹²The ones along the path are those who have heard; then the devil comes and takes away the word from their hearts, so that they may not believe and be saved. ¹³And the ones on the rock are those who, when they hear the word, receive it with joy. But these have no root; they believe for a while, and in time of testing fall away. ¹⁴And as for what fell among the thorns, they are those who hear, but as they go on their way they are choked by the cares and riches and pleasures of life, and their fruit does not mature. ¹⁵As for that in the good soil, they are those who, hearing the word, hold it fast in an honest and good heart, and bear fruit with patience.

A LAMP UNDER A JAR

¹⁶"No one after lighting a lamp covers it with a jar or puts it under a bed, but puts it on a stand, so that those who enter may see the light. ¹⁷For nothing is hidden that will not be made manifest, nor is anything secret that will not be known and come to light. ¹⁸Take care then how you hear, for to the one who has, more will be given, and from the one who has not, even what he thinks that he has will be taken away."

JESUS' MOTHER AND BROTHERS

¹⁹Then his mother and his brothers[c] came to him, but they could not reach him because of the crowd. ²⁰And he was told, "Your mother and your brothers are standing outside, desiring to see you." ²¹But he answered them, "My mother and my brothers are those who hear the word of God and do it."

JESUS CALMS A STORM

²²One day he got into a boat with his disciples, and he said to them, "Let us go across to the other side of the lake." So they set out, ²³and as they sailed he fell asleep. And a windstorm came down on the lake, and they were filling with water and were in danger. ²⁴And they went and woke him, saying, "Master, Master, we are perishing!" And he awoke and rebuked the wind and the raging waves, and they ceased, and there was a calm. ²⁵He

---
[a]Or to [b]Some manuscripts him [c]Or brothers and sisters. In New Testament usage, depending on the context, the plural Greek word adelphoi (translated "brothers") may refer either to brothers or to brothers and sisters; also verses 20, 21

said to them, "Where is your faith?" And they were afraid, and they marvelled, saying to one another, "Who then is this, that he commands even winds and water, and they obey him?"

JESUS HEALS A MAN WITH A DEMON

²⁶Then they sailed to the country of the Gerasenes,*ᵃ* which is opposite Galilee. ²⁷When Jesus*ᵇ* had stepped out on land, there met him a man from the city who had demons. For a long time he had worn no clothes, and he had not lived in a house but among the tombs. ²⁸When he saw Jesus, he cried out and fell down before him and said with a loud voice, "What have you to do with me, Jesus, Son of the Most High God? I beg you, do not torment me." ²⁹For he had commanded the unclean spirit to come out of the man. (For many a time it had seized him. He was kept under guard and bound with chains and shackles, but he would break the bonds and be driven by the demon into the desert.) ³⁰Jesus then asked him, "What is your name?" And he said, "Legion", for many demons had entered him. ³¹And they begged him not to command them to depart into the abyss. ³²Now a large herd of pigs was feeding there on the hillside, and they begged him to let them enter these. So he gave them permission. ³³Then the demons came out of the man and entered the pigs, and the herd rushed down the steep bank into the lake and drowned.

³⁴When the herdsmen saw what had happened, they fled and told it in the city and in the country. ³⁵Then people went out to see what had happened, and they came to Jesus and found the man from whom the demons had gone, sitting at the feet of Jesus, clothed and in his right mind, and they were afraid. ³⁶And those who had seen it told them how the demon-possessed*ᶜ* man had been healed. ³⁷Then all the people of the surrounding country of the Gerasenes asked him to depart from them, for they were seized with great fear. So he got into the boat and returned. ³⁸The man from whom the demons had gone begged that he might be with him, but Jesus sent him away, saying, ³⁹"Return to your home, and declare how much God has done for you." And he went away, proclaiming throughout the whole city how much Jesus had done for him.

JESUS HEALS A WOMAN AND JAIRUS'S DAUGHTER

⁴⁰Now when Jesus returned, the crowd welcomed him, for they were all waiting for him. ⁴¹And there came a man named Jairus, who was a ruler of the synagogue. And falling at Jesus' feet, he implored him to come to his house, ⁴²for he had an only daughter, about twelve years of age, and she was dying.

As Jesus went, the people pressed around him. ⁴³And there was a woman who had had a discharge of blood for twelve years, and though she had spent all her living on physicians,*ᵈ* she could not be healed by anyone. ⁴⁴She came up behind him and touched the fringe of his garment, and immediately her discharge of blood ceased. ⁴⁵And Jesus said, "Who was it that touched me?" When all denied it, Peter*ᵉ* said, "Master, the crowds surround you and are pressing in on you!" ⁴⁶But Jesus said, "Someone touched me, for I perceive that power has gone out from me." ⁴⁷And when the woman saw that she was not hidden, she came trembling, and falling down before him declared in the presence of all the people why she had touched him, and how she had been immediately healed. ⁴⁸And he said to her, "Daughter, your faith has made you well; go in peace."

⁴⁹While he was still speaking, someone from the ruler's house came and said, "Your daughter is dead; do not trouble the Teacher any more." ⁵⁰But Jesus on hearing this answered him, "Do not fear; only believe, and she will be well." ⁵¹And when he came to the house, he allowed no one to enter with him, except Peter and John and James, and the father and mother of the child. ⁵²And all were weeping and mourning for her, but he said, "Do not weep, for she is not dead but sleeping." ⁵³And they laughed at him, knowing that she was dead. ⁵⁴But taking her by the hand he called, saying, "Child, arise." ⁵⁵And her spirit returned, and she got up at once. And he directed that something should be given to her to eat. ⁵⁶And her parents were amazed, but he charged them to tell no one what had happened.

JESUS SENDS OUT THE TWELVE APOSTLES

9 And he called the twelve together and gave them power and authority over all demons and to cure diseases, ²and he sent them out to proclaim the kingdom of God and to heal. ³And he said to them, "Take

---

*ᵃ*Some manuscripts *Gadarenes*; others *Gergesenes*; also verse 37
*ᵇ*Greek *he*; also verses 38, 42 *ᶜ*Greek *daimonizomai* (demonized); elsewhere rendered *oppressed by demons* *ᵈ*Some manuscripts omit *and though she had spent all her living on physicians*
*ᵉ*Some manuscripts add *and those who were with him*

nothing for your journey, no staff, nor bag, nor bread, nor money; and do not have two tunics.[a] ⁴And whatever house you enter, stay there, and from there depart. ⁵And wherever they do not receive you, when you leave that town shake off the dust from your feet as a testimony against them." ⁶And they departed and went through the villages, preaching the gospel and healing everywhere.

HEROD IS PERPLEXED BY JESUS

⁷Now Herod the tetrarch heard about all that was happening, and he was perplexed, because it was said by some that John had been raised from the dead, ⁸by some that Elijah had appeared, and by others that one of the prophets of old had risen. ⁹Herod said, "John I beheaded, but who is this about whom I hear such things?" And he sought to see him.

JESUS FEEDS THE FIVE THOUSAND

¹⁰On their return the apostles told him all that they had done. And he took them and withdrew apart to a town called Bethsaida. ¹¹When the crowds learned it, they followed him, and he welcomed them and spoke to them of the kingdom of God and cured those who needed healing. ¹²Now the day began to wear away, and the twelve came and said to him, "Send the crowd away to go into the surrounding villages and countryside to find lodging and get provisions, for we are here in a desolate place." ¹³But he said to them, "You give them something to eat." They said, "We have no more than five loaves and two fish—unless we are to go and buy food for all these people." ¹⁴For there were about five thousand men. And he said to his disciples, "Make them sit down in groups of about fifty each." ¹⁵And they did so, and made them all sit down. ¹⁶And taking the five loaves and the two fish, he looked up to heaven and said a blessing over them. Then he broke the loaves and gave them to the disciples to set before the crowd. ¹⁷And they all ate and were satisfied. And what was left over was picked up, twelve baskets of broken pieces.

PETER CONFESSES JESUS AS THE CHRIST

¹⁸Now it happened that as he was praying alone, the disciples were with him. And he asked them, "Who do the crowds say that I am?" ¹⁹And they answered, "John the Baptist. But others say, Elijah, and others, that one of the prophets of old has risen." ²⁰Then he said to them, "But who do you say that I am?" And Peter answered, "The Christ of God."

JESUS FORETELLS HIS DEATH

²¹And he strictly charged and commanded them to tell this to no one, ²²saying, "The Son of Man must suffer many things and be rejected by the elders and chief priests and scribes, and be killed, and on the third day be raised."

TAKE UP YOUR CROSS AND FOLLOW JESUS

²³And he said to all, "If anyone would come after me, let him deny himself and take up his cross daily and follow me. ²⁴For whoever would save his life will lose it, but whoever loses his life for my sake will save it. ²⁵For what does it profit a man if he gains the whole world and loses or forfeits himself? ²⁶For whoever is ashamed of me and of my words, of him will the Son of Man be ashamed when he comes in his glory and the glory of the Father and of the holy angels. ²⁷But I tell you truly, there are some standing here who will not taste death until they see the kingdom of God."

THE TRANSFIGURATION

²⁸Now about eight days after these sayings he took with him Peter and John and James and went up on the mountain to pray. ²⁹And as he was praying, the appearance of his face was altered, and his clothing became dazzling white. ³⁰And behold, two men were talking with him, Moses and Elijah, ³¹who appeared in glory and spoke of his departure,[b] which he was about to accomplish at Jerusalem. ³²Now Peter and those who were with him were heavy with sleep, but when they became fully awake they saw his glory and the two men who stood with him. ³³And as the men were parting from him, Peter said to Jesus, "Master, it is good that we are here. Let us make three tents, one for you and one for Moses and one for Elijah"—not knowing what he said. ³⁴As he was saying these things, a cloud came and overshadowed them, and they were afraid as they entered the cloud. ³⁵And a voice came out of the cloud, saying, "This is my Son, my Chosen One;[c] listen to him!" ³⁶And when the voice had spoken, Jesus was found alone. And they kept silent and told no one in those days anything of what they had seen.

---

[a] Greek *chiton*, a long garment worn under the cloak next to the skin
[b] Greek *exodus* [c] Some manuscripts *my Beloved*

JESUS HEALS A BOY WITH AN UNCLEAN SPIRIT

³⁷On the next day, when they had come down from the mountain, a great crowd met him. ³⁸And behold, a man from the crowd cried out, "Teacher, I beg you to look at my son, for he is my only child. ³⁹And behold, a spirit seizes him, and he suddenly cries out. It convulses him so that he foams at the mouth, and shatters him, and will hardly leave him. ⁴⁰And I begged your disciples to cast it out, but they could not." ⁴¹Jesus answered, "O faithless and twisted generation, how long am I to be with you and bear with you? Bring your son here." ⁴²While he was coming, the demon threw him to the ground and convulsed him. But Jesus rebuked the unclean spirit and healed the boy, and gave him back to his father. ⁴³And all were astonished at the majesty of God.

JESUS AGAIN FORETELLS HIS DEATH

But while they were all marvelling at everything he was doing, Jesus*ᵃ* said to his disciples, ⁴⁴"Let these words sink into your ears: The Son of Man is about to be delivered into the hands of men." ⁴⁵But they did not understand this saying, and it was concealed from them, so that they might not perceive it. And they were afraid to ask him about this saying.

WHO IS THE GREATEST?

⁴⁶An argument arose among them as to which of them was the greatest. ⁴⁷But Jesus, knowing the reasoning of their hearts, took a child and put him by his side ⁴⁸and said to them, "Whoever receives this child in my name receives me, and whoever receives me receives him who sent me. For he who is least among all of you is the one who is great."

ANYONE NOT AGAINST US IS FOR US

⁴⁹John answered, "Master, we saw someone casting out demons in your name, and we tried to stop him, because he does not follow with us." ⁵⁰But Jesus said to him, "Do not stop him, for the one who is not against you is for you."

A SAMARITAN VILLAGE REJECTS JESUS

⁵¹When the days drew near for him to be taken up, he set his face to go to Jerusalem. ⁵²And he sent messengers ahead of him, who went and entered a village of the Samaritans, to make preparations for him. ⁵³But the people did not receive him, because his face was set towards Jerusalem. ⁵⁴And when his disciples James and John saw it, they said, "Lord, do you want us to tell fire to come down from heaven and consume them?"*ᵇ* ⁵⁵But he turned and rebuked them.*ᶜ* ⁵⁶And they went on to another village.

THE COST OF FOLLOWING JESUS

⁵⁷As they were going along the road, someone said to him, "I will follow you wherever you go." ⁵⁸And Jesus said to him, "Foxes have holes, and birds of the air have nests, but the Son of Man has nowhere to lay his head." ⁵⁹To another he said, "Follow me." But he said, "Lord, let me first go and bury my father." ⁶⁰And Jesus*ᵈ* said to him, "Leave the dead to bury their own dead. But as for you, go and proclaim the kingdom of God." ⁶¹Yet another said, "I will follow you, Lord, but let me first say farewell to those at my home." ⁶²Jesus said to him, "No one who puts his hand to the plough and looks back is fit for the kingdom of God."

JESUS SENDS OUT THE SEVENTY-TWO

10 After this the Lord appointed seventy-two*ᵉ* others and sent them on ahead of him, two by two, into every town and place where he himself was about to go. ²And he said to them, "The harvest is plentiful, but the labourers are few. Therefore pray earnestly to the Lord of the harvest to send out labourers into his harvest. ³Go your way; behold, I am sending you out as lambs in the midst of wolves. ⁴Carry no money bag, no knapsack, no sandals, and greet no one on the road. ⁵Whatever house you enter, first say, 'Peace be to this house!' ⁶And if a son of peace is there, your peace will rest upon him. But if not, it will return to you. ⁷And remain in the same house, eating and drinking what they provide, for the labourer deserves his wages. Do not go from house to house. ⁸Whenever you enter a town and they receive you, eat what is set before you. ⁹Heal the sick in it and say to them, 'The kingdom of God has come near to you.' ¹⁰But whenever you enter a town and they do not receive you, go into its streets and say, ¹¹'Even the dust of your town that clings to our feet we wipe off against you. Nevertheless know

---

*ᵃ*Greek *he* *ᵇ*Some manuscripts add *as Elijah did* *ᶜ*Some manuscripts add *And he said, "You do not know what manner of spirit you are of;* ⁵⁶*for the Son of Man came not to destroy people's lives but to save them"* *ᵈ*Greek *he* *ᵉ*Some manuscripts *seventy;* also verse 17

this, that the kingdom of God has come near.' **12**I tell you, it will be more bearable on that day for Sodom than for that town.

WOE TO UNREPENTANT CITIES

13"Woe to you, Chorazin! Woe to you, Bethsaida! For if the mighty works done in you had been done in Tyre and Sidon, they would have repented long ago, sitting in sackcloth and ashes. **14**But it will be more bearable in the judgement for Tyre and Sidon than for you. **15**And you, Capernaum, will you be exalted to heaven? You shall be brought down to Hades.

16"The one who hears you hears me, and the one who rejects you rejects me, and the one who rejects me rejects him who sent me."

THE RETURN OF THE SEVENTY-TWO

17The seventy-two returned with joy, saying, "Lord, even the demons are subject to us in your name!" **18**And he said to them, "I saw Satan fall like lightning from heaven. **19**Behold, I have given you authority to tread on serpents and scorpions, and over all the power of the enemy, and nothing shall hurt you. **20**Nevertheless, do not rejoice in this, that the spirits are subject to you, but rejoice that your names are written in heaven."

JESUS REJOICES IN THE FATHER'S WILL

21In that same hour he rejoiced in the Holy Spirit and said, "I thank you, Father, Lord of heaven and earth, that you have hidden these things from the wise and understanding and revealed them to little children; yes, Father, for such was your gracious will.*a* **22**All things have been handed over to me by my Father, and no one knows who the Son is except the Father, or who the Father is except the Son and anyone to whom the Son chooses to reveal him."

23Then turning to the disciples he said privately, "Blessed are the eyes that see what you see! **24**For I tell you that many prophets and kings desired to see what you see, and did not see it, and to hear what you hear, and did not hear it."

THE PARABLE OF THE GOOD SAMARITAN

25And behold, a lawyer stood up to put him to the test, saying, "Teacher, what shall I do to inherit eternal life?" **26**He said to him, "What is written in the Law? How do you read it?" **27**And he answered, "You shall love the Lord your God with all your heart and with all your soul and with all your strength and with all your mind, and your neighbour as yourself." **28**And he said to him, "You have answered correctly; do this, and you will live."

29But he, desiring to justify himself, said to Jesus, "And who is my neighbour?" **30**Jesus replied, "A man was going down from Jerusalem to Jericho, and he fell among robbers, who stripped him and beat him and departed, leaving him half dead. **31**Now by chance a priest was going down that road, and when he saw him he passed by on the other side. **32**So likewise a Levite, when he came to the place and saw him, passed by on the other side. **33**But a Samaritan, as he journeyed, came to where he was, and when he saw him, he had compassion. **34**He went to him and bound up his wounds, pouring on oil and wine. Then he set him on his own animal and brought him to an inn and took care of him. **35**And the next day he took out two denarii*b* and gave them to the innkeeper, saying, 'Take care of him, and whatever more you spend, I will repay you when I come back.' **36**Which of these three, do you think, proved to be a neighbour to the man who fell among the robbers?" **37**He said, "The one who showed him mercy." And Jesus said to him, "You go, and do likewise."

MARTHA AND MARY

38Now as they went on their way, Jesus*c* entered a village. And a woman named Martha welcomed him into her house. **39**And she had a sister called Mary, who sat at the Lord's feet and listened to his teaching. **40**But Martha was distracted with much serving. And she went up to him and said, "Lord, do you not care that my sister has left me to serve alone? Tell her then to help me." **41**But the Lord answered her, "Martha, Martha, you are anxious and troubled about many things, **42**but one thing is necessary.*d* Mary has chosen the good portion, which will not be taken away from her."

THE LORD'S PRAYER

11 Now Jesus*e* was praying in a certain place, and when he finished, one of his disciples said to him, "Lord, teach us to pray, as John taught his disciples." **2**And he said to them, "When you pray, say:

---

*a*Or *for so it pleased you well* *b*A *denarius* was a day's wage for a labourer *c*Greek *he* *d*Some manuscripts *few things are necessary, or only one* *e*Greek *he*

"Father, hallowed be your name.
Your kingdom come.
3 Give us each day our daily bread,[a]
4 and forgive us our sins,
for we ourselves forgive everyone
who is indebted to us.
And lead us not into temptation."

⁵And he said to them, "Which of you who has a friend will go to him at midnight and say to him, 'Friend, lend me three loaves, ⁶for a friend of mine has arrived on a journey, and I have nothing to set before him'; ⁷and he will answer from within, 'Do not bother me; the door is now shut, and my children are with me in bed. I cannot get up and give you anything'? ⁸I tell you, though he will not get up and give him anything because he is his friend, yet because of his impudence[b] he will rise and give him whatever he needs. ⁹And I tell you, ask, and it will be given to you; seek, and you will find; knock, and it will be opened to you. ¹⁰For everyone who asks receives, and the one who seeks finds, and to the one who knocks it will be opened. ¹¹What father among you, if his son asks for[c] a fish, will instead of a fish give him a serpent; ¹²or if he asks for an egg, will give him a scorpion? ¹³If you then, who are evil, know how to give good gifts to your children, how much more will the heavenly Father give the Holy Spirit to those who ask him!"

JESUS AND BEELZEBUL

¹⁴Now he was casting out a demon that was mute. When the demon had gone out, the mute man spoke, and the people marvelled. ¹⁵But some of them said, "He casts out demons by Beelzebul, the prince of demons", ¹⁶while others, to test him, kept seeking from him a sign from heaven. ¹⁷But he, knowing their thoughts, said to them, "Every kingdom divided against itself is laid waste, and a divided household falls. ¹⁸And if Satan also is divided against himself, how will his kingdom stand? For you say that I cast out demons by Beelzebul. ¹⁹And if I cast out demons by Beelzebul, by whom do your sons cast them out? Therefore they will be your judges. ²⁰But if it is by the finger of God that I cast out demons, then the kingdom of God has come upon you. ²¹When a strong man, fully armed, guards his own palace, his goods are safe; ²²but when one stronger than he attacks him and overcomes him, he takes away his armour in which he trusted and divides his spoil. ²³Whoever is not with me is against me, and whoever does not gather with me scatters.

RETURN OF AN UNCLEAN SPIRIT

²⁴"When the unclean spirit has gone out of a person, it passes through waterless places seeking rest, and finding none it says, 'I will return to my house from which I came.' ²⁵And when it comes, it finds the house swept and put in order. ²⁶Then it goes and brings seven other spirits more evil than itself, and they enter and dwell there. And the last state of that person is worse than the first."

TRUE BLESSEDNESS

²⁷As he said these things, a woman in the crowd raised her voice and said to him, "Blessed is the womb that bore you, and the breasts at which you nursed!" ²⁸But he said, "Blessed rather are those who hear the word of God and keep it!"

THE SIGN OF JONAH

²⁹When the crowds were increasing, he began to say, "This generation is an evil generation. It seeks for a sign, but no sign will be given to it except the sign of Jonah. ³⁰For as Jonah became a sign to the people of Nineveh, so will the Son of Man be to this generation. ³¹The queen of the South will rise up at the judgement with the men of this generation and condemn them, for she came from the ends of the earth to hear the wisdom of Solomon, and behold, something greater than Solomon is here. ³²The men of Nineveh will rise up at the judgement with this generation and condemn it, for they repented at the preaching of Jonah, and behold, something greater than Jonah is here.

THE LIGHT IN YOU

³³"No one after lighting a lamp puts it in a cellar or under a basket, but on a stand, so that those who enter may see the light. ³⁴Your eye is the lamp of your body. When your eye is healthy, your whole body is full of light, but when it is bad, your body is full of darkness. ³⁵Therefore be careful lest the light in you be darkness. ³⁶If then your whole body is full of light, having no part dark, it will be wholly bright, as when a lamp with its rays gives you light."

---

[a]Or our bread for tomorrow [b]Or persistence [c]Some manuscripts insert bread, will give him a stone; or if he asks for

WOES TO THE PHARISEES AND LAWYERS

37While Jesus[a] was speaking, a Pharisee asked him to dine with him, so he went in and reclined at table. 38The Pharisee was astonished to see that he did not first wash before dinner. 39And the Lord said to him, "Now you Pharisees cleanse the outside of the cup and of the dish, but inside you are full of greed and wickedness. 40You fools! Did not he who made the outside make the inside also? 41But give as alms those things that are within, and behold, everything is clean for you.

42"But woe to you Pharisees! For you tithe mint and rue and every herb, and neglect justice and the love of God. These you ought to have done, without neglecting the others. 43Woe to you Pharisees! For you love the best seat in the synagogues and greetings in the market-places. 44Woe to you! For you are like unmarked graves, and people walk over them without knowing it."

45One of the lawyers answered him, "Teacher, in saying these things you insult us also." 46And he said, "Woe to you lawyers also! For you load people with burdens hard to bear, and you yourselves do not touch the burdens with one of your fingers. 47Woe to you! For you build the tombs of the prophets whom your fathers killed. 48So you are witnesses and you consent to the deeds of your fathers, for they killed them, and you build their tombs. 49Therefore also the Wisdom of God said, 'I will send them prophets and apostles, some of whom they will kill and persecute', 50so that the blood of all the prophets, shed from the foundation of the world, may be charged against this generation, 51from the blood of Abel to the blood of Zechariah, who perished between the altar and the sanctuary. Yes, I tell you, it will be required of this generation. 52Woe to you lawyers! For you have taken away the key of knowledge. You did not enter yourselves, and you hindered those who were entering."

53As he went away from there, the scribes and the Pharisees began to press him hard and to provoke him to speak about many things, 54lying in wait for him, to catch him in something he might say.

BEWARE OF THE LEAVEN OF THE PHARISEES

12 In the meantime, when so many thousands of the people had gathered together that they were trampling one another, he began to say to his disciples first, "Beware of the leaven of the Pharisees, which is hypocrisy. 2Nothing is covered up that will not be revealed, or hidden that will not be known. 3Therefore whatever you have said in the dark shall be heard in the light, and what you have whispered in private rooms shall be proclaimed on the housetops.

HAVE NO FEAR

4"I tell you, my friends, do not fear those who kill the body, and after that have nothing more that they can do. 5But I will warn you whom to fear: fear him who, after he has killed, has authority to cast into hell.[b] Yes, I tell you, fear him! 6Are not five sparrows sold for two pennies?[c] And not one of them is forgotten before God. 7Why, even the hairs of your head are all numbered. Fear not; you are of more value than many sparrows.

ACKNOWLEDGE CHRIST BEFORE MEN

8"And I tell you, everyone who acknowledges me before men, the Son of Man also will acknowledge before the angels of God, 9but the one who denies me before men will be denied before the angels of God. 10And everyone who speaks a word against the Son of Man will be forgiven, but the one who blasphemes against the Holy Spirit will not be forgiven. 11And when they bring you before the synagogues and the rulers and the authorities, do not be anxious about how you should defend yourself or what you should say, 12for the Holy Spirit will teach you in that very hour what you ought to say."

THE PARABLE OF THE RICH FOOL

13Someone in the crowd said to him, "Teacher, tell my brother to divide the inheritance with me." 14But he said to him, "Man, who made me a judge or arbitrator over you?" 15And he said to them, "Take care, and be on your guard against all covetousness, for one's life does not consist in the abundance of one's possessions." 16And he told them a parable, saying, "The land of a rich man produced plentifully, 17and he thought to himself, 'What shall I do, for I have nowhere to store my crops?' 18And he said, 'I will do this: I will tear down my barns and build larger ones, and there I will store all my grain and

---

[a]Greek he [b]Greek Gehenna [c]Greek two assaria; an assarion was a Roman copper coin worth about 1/16 of a denarius (which was a day's wage for a labourer)

my goods. ¹⁹And I will say to my soul, "Soul, you have ample goods laid up for many years; relax, eat, drink, be merry." ' ²⁰But God said to him, 'Fool! This night your soul is required of you, and the things you have prepared, whose will they be?' ²¹So is the one who lays up treasure for himself and is not rich towards God."

DO NOT BE ANXIOUS

²²And he said to his disciples, "Therefore I tell you, do not be anxious about your life, what you will eat, nor about your body, what you will put on. ²³For life is more than food, and the body more than clothing. ²⁴Consider the ravens: they neither sow nor reap, they have neither storehouse nor barn, and yet God feeds them. Of how much more value are you than the birds! ²⁵And which of you by being anxious can add a single hour to his span of life?ᵃ ²⁶If then you are not able to do as small a thing as that, why are you anxious about the rest? ²⁷Consider the lilies, how they grow: they neither toil nor spin,ᵇ yet I tell you, even Solomon in all his glory was not arrayed like one of these. ²⁸But if God so clothes the grass, which is alive in the field today, and tomorrow is thrown into the oven, how much more will he clothe you, O you of little faith! ²⁹And do not seek what you are to eat and what you are to drink, nor be worried. ³⁰For all the nations of the world seek after these things, and your Father knows that you need them. ³¹Instead, seek hisᶜ kingdom, and these things will be added to you.

³²"Fear not, little flock, for it is your Father's good pleasure to give you the kingdom. ³³Sell your possessions, and give to the needy. Provide yourselves with money bags that do not grow old, with a treasure in the heavens that does not fail, where no thief approaches and no moth destroys. ³⁴For where your treasure is, there will your heart be also.

YOU MUST BE READY

³⁵"Stay dressed for actionᵈ and keep your lamps burning, ³⁶and be like men who are waiting for their master to come home from the wedding feast, so that they may open the door to him at once when he comes and knocks. ³⁷Blessed are those servantsᵉ whom the master finds awake when he comes. Truly, I say to you, he will dress himself for service and have them recline at table, and he will come and serve them. ³⁸If he comes in the second watch, or in the third, and finds them awake, blessed are those servants! ³⁹But know this, that if the master of the house had known at what hour the thief was coming, heᶠ would not have left his house to be broken into. ⁴⁰You also must be ready, for the Son of Man is coming at an hour you do not expect."

⁴¹Peter said, "Lord, are you telling this parable for us or for all?" ⁴²And the Lord said, "Who then is the faithful and wise manager, whom his master will set over his household, to give them their portion of food at the proper time? ⁴³Blessed is that servantᵍ whom his master will find so doing when he comes. ⁴⁴Truly, I say to you, he will set him over all his possessions. ⁴⁵But if that servant says to himself, 'My master is delayed in coming', and begins to beat the male and female servants, and to eat and drink and get drunk, ⁴⁶the master of that servant will come on a day when he does not expect him and at an hour he does not know, and will cut him in pieces and put him with the unfaithful. ⁴⁷And that servant who knew his master's will but did not get ready or act according to his will, will receive a severe beating. ⁴⁸But the one who did not know, and did what deserved a beating, will receive a light beating. Everyone to whom much was given, of him much will be required, and from him to whom they entrusted much, they will demand the more.

NOT PEACE, BUT DIVISION

⁴⁹"I came to cast fire on the earth, and would that it were already kindled! ⁵⁰I have a baptism to be baptized with, and how great is my distress until it is accomplished! ⁵¹Do you think that I have come to give peace on earth? No, I tell you, but rather division. ⁵²For from now on in one house there will be five divided, three against two and two against three. ⁵³They will be divided, father against son and son against father, mother against daughter and daughter against mother, mother-in-law against her daughter-in-law and daughter-in-law against mother-in-law."

INTERPRETING THE TIME

⁵⁴He also said to the crowds, "When you see a cloud rising in the west, you say at once, 'A shower is coming.' And so it happens. ⁵⁵And

---

ᵃOr *a single cubit to his stature*; a *cubit* was about 18 inches or 45 centimetres ᵇSome manuscripts *Consider the lilies; they neither spin nor weave* ᶜSome manuscripts *God's* ᵈGreek *Let your loins stay girded*; compare Exodus 12:11 ᵉOr *bondservants* ᶠSome manuscripts add *would have stayed awake and* ᵍOr *bondservant*; also verses 45, 46, 47

when you see the south wind blowing, you say, 'There will be scorching heat', and it happens. [56]You hypocrites! You know how to interpret the appearance of earth and sky, but why do you not know how to interpret the present time?

SETTLE WITH YOUR ACCUSER

[57]"And why do you not judge for yourselves what is right? [58]As you go with your accuser before the magistrate, make an effort to settle with him on the way, lest he drag you to the judge, and the judge hand you over to the officer, and the officer put you in prison. [59]I tell you, you will never get out until you have paid the very last penny."[a]

REPENT OR PERISH

13 There were some present at that very time who told him about the Galileans whose blood Pilate had mingled with their sacrifices. [2]And he answered them, "Do you think that these Galileans were worse sinners than all the other Galileans, because they suffered in this way? [3]No, I tell you; but unless you repent, you will all likewise perish. [4]Or those eighteen on whom the tower in Siloam fell and killed them: do you think that they were worse offenders than all the others who lived in Jerusalem? [5]No, I tell you; but unless you repent, you will all likewise perish."

THE PARABLE OF THE BARREN FIG TREE

[6]And he told this parable: "A man had a fig tree planted in his vineyard, and he came seeking fruit on it and found none. [7]And he said to the vine dresser, 'Look, for three years now I have come seeking fruit on this fig tree, and I find none. Cut it down. Why should it use up the ground?' [8]And he answered him, 'Sir, let it alone this year also, until I dig round it and put on manure. [9]Then if it should bear fruit next year, well and good; but if not, you can cut it down.'"

A WOMAN WITH A DISABLING SPIRIT

[10]Now he was teaching in one of the synagogues on the Sabbath. [11]And behold, there was a woman who had had a disabling spirit for eighteen years. She was bent over and could not fully straighten herself. [12]When Jesus saw her, he called her over and said to her, "Woman, you are freed from your disability." [13]And he laid his hands on her, and immediately she was made straight, and she glorified God. [14]But the ruler of the synagogue, indignant because Jesus had healed on the Sabbath, said to the people, "There are six days in which work ought to be done. Come on those days and be healed, and not on the Sabbath day." [15]Then the Lord answered him, "You hypocrites! Does not each of you on the Sabbath untie his ox or his donkey from the manger and lead it away to water it? [16]And ought not this woman, a daughter of Abraham whom Satan bound for eighteen years, be loosed from this bond on the Sabbath day?" [17]As he said these things, all his adversaries were put to shame, and all the people rejoiced at all the glorious things that were done by him.

THE MUSTARD SEED AND THE LEAVEN

[18]He said therefore, "What is the kingdom of God like? And to what shall I compare it? [19]It is like a grain of mustard seed that a man took and sowed in his garden, and it grew and became a tree, and the birds of the air made nests in its branches."

[20]And again he said, "To what shall I compare the kingdom of God? [21]It is like leaven that a woman took and hid in three measures of flour, until it was all leavened."

THE NARROW DOOR

[22]He went on his way through towns and villages, teaching and journeying towards Jerusalem. [23]And someone said to him, "Lord, will those who are saved be few?" And he said to them, [24]"Strive to enter through the narrow door. For many, I tell you, will seek to enter and will not be able. [25]When once the master of the house has risen and shut the door, and you begin to stand outside and to knock at the door, saying, 'Lord, open to us', then he will answer you, 'I do not know where you come from.' [26]Then you will begin to say, 'We ate and drank in your presence, and you taught in our streets.' [27]But he will say, 'I tell you, I do not know where you come from. Depart from me, all you workers of evil!' [28]In that place there will be weeping and gnashing of teeth, when you see Abraham and Isaac and Jacob and all the prophets in the kingdom of God but you yourselves cast out. [29]And people will come from east and west, and from north and south, and recline at table in the kingdom of God. [30]And behold,

---

[a]Greek *lepton*, a Jewish bronze or copper coin worth about 1/128 of a *denarius* (which was a day's wage for a labourer)

some are last who will be first, and some are first who will be last."

LAMENT OVER JERUSALEM

³¹At that very hour some Pharisees came and said to him, "Get away from here, for Herod wants to kill you." ³²And he said to them, "Go and tell that fox, 'Behold, I cast out demons and perform cures today and tomorrow, and the third day I finish my course. ³³Nevertheless, I must go on my way today and tomorrow and the day following, for it cannot be that a prophet should perish away from Jerusalem.' ³⁴O Jerusalem, Jerusalem, the city that kills the prophets and stones those who are sent to it! How often would I have gathered your children together as a hen gathers her brood under her wings, and you were not willing! ³⁵Behold, your house is forsaken. And I tell you, you will not see me until you say, 'Blessed is he who comes in the name of the Lord!'"

HEALING OF A MAN ON THE SABBATH

14 One Sabbath, when he went to dine at the house of a ruler of the Pharisees, they were watching him carefully. ²And behold, there was a man before him who had dropsy. ³And Jesus responded to the lawyers and Pharisees, saying, "Is it lawful to heal on the Sabbath, or not?" ⁴But they remained silent. Then he took him and healed him and sent him away. ⁵And he said to them, "Which of you, having a son^a or an ox that has fallen into a well on a Sabbath day, will not immediately pull him out?" ⁶And they could not reply to these things.

THE PARABLE OF THE WEDDING FEAST

⁷Now he told a parable to those who were invited, when he noticed how they chose the places of honour, saying to them, ⁸"When you are invited by someone to a wedding feast, do not sit down in a place of honour, lest someone more distinguished than you be invited by him, ⁹and he who invited you both will come and say to you, 'Give your place to this person', and then you will begin with shame to take the lowest place. ¹⁰But when you are invited, go and sit in the lowest place, so that when your host comes he may say to you, 'Friend, move up higher.' Then you will be honoured in the presence of all who sit at table with you. ¹¹For everyone who exalts himself will be humbled, and he who humbles himself will be exalted."

THE PARABLE OF THE GREAT BANQUET

¹²He said also to the man who had invited him, "When you give a dinner or a banquet, do not invite your friends or your brothers^b or your relatives or rich neighbours, lest they also invite you in return and you be repaid. ¹³But when you give a feast, invite the poor, the crippled, the lame, the blind, ¹⁴and you will be blessed, because they cannot repay you. For you will be repaid at the resurrection of the just."

¹⁵When one of those who reclined at table with him heard these things, he said to him, "Blessed is everyone who will eat bread in the kingdom of God!" ¹⁶But he said to him, "A man once gave a great banquet and invited many. ¹⁷And at the time for the banquet he sent his servant^c to say to those who had been invited, 'Come, for everything is now ready.' ¹⁸But they all alike began to make excuses. The first said to him, 'I have bought a field, and I must go out and see it. Please excuse me.' ¹⁹And another said, 'I have bought five yoke of oxen, and I am going to examine them. Please excuse me.' ²⁰And another said, 'I have married a wife, and therefore I cannot come.' ²¹So the servant came and reported these things to his master. Then the master of the house became angry and said to his servant, 'Go out quickly to the streets and lanes of the city, and bring in the poor and crippled and blind and lame.' ²²And the servant said, 'Sir, what you commanded has been done, and still there is room.' ²³And the master said to the servant, 'Go out to the highways and hedges and compel people to come in, that my house may be filled. ²⁴For I tell you,^{d} none of those men who were invited shall taste my banquet.'"

THE COST OF DISCIPLESHIP

²⁵Now great crowds accompanied him, and he turned and said to them, ²⁶"If anyone comes to me and does not hate his own father and mother and wife and children and brothers and sisters, yes, and even his own life, he cannot be my disciple. ²⁷Whoever does not bear his own cross and come after me cannot be my disciple. ²⁸For which of you, desiring to build a tower, does not first sit down and count the cost, whether he has enough to complete it? ²⁹Otherwise,

---

^{a}Some manuscripts *a donkey* ^{b}Or *your brothers and sisters*
^{c}Or *bondservant*; also verses 21 (twice), 22, 23 ^{d}The Greek word for *you* here is plural

when he has laid a foundation and is not able to finish, all who see it begin to mock him, ³⁰saying, 'This man began to build and was not able to finish.' ³¹Or what king, going out to encounter another king in war, will not sit down first and deliberate whether he is able with ten thousand to meet him who comes against him with twenty thousand? ³²And if not, while the other is yet a great way off, he sends a delegation and asks for terms of peace. ³³So therefore, any one of you who does not renounce all that he has cannot be my disciple.

SALT WITHOUT TASTE IS WORTHLESS

³⁴"Salt is good, but if salt has lost its taste, how shall its saltiness be restored? ³⁵It is of no use either for the soil or for the manure pile. It is thrown away. He who has ears to hear, let him hear."

THE PARABLE OF THE LOST SHEEP

15 Now the tax collectors and sinners were all drawing near to hear him. ²And the Pharisees and the scribes grumbled, saying, "This man receives sinners and eats with them."

³So he told them this parable: ⁴"What man of you, having a hundred sheep, if he has lost one of them, does not leave the ninety-nine in the open country, and go after the one that is lost, until he finds it? ⁵And when he has found it, he lays it on his shoulders, rejoicing. ⁶And when he comes home, he calls together his friends and his neighbours, saying to them, 'Rejoice with me, for I have found my sheep that was lost.' ⁷Just so, I tell you, there will be more joy in heaven over one sinner who repents than over ninety-nine righteous persons who need no repentance.

THE PARABLE OF THE LOST COIN

⁸"Or what woman, having ten silver coins,ᵃ if she loses one coin, does not light a lamp and sweep the house and seek diligently until she finds it? ⁹And when she has found it, she calls together her friends and neighbours, saying, 'Rejoice with me, for I have found the coin that I had lost.' ¹⁰Just so, I tell you, there is joy before the angels of God over one sinner who repents."

THE PARABLE OF THE PRODIGAL SON

¹¹And he said, "There was a man who had two sons. ¹²And the younger of them said to his father, 'Father, give me the share of property that is coming to me.' And he divided his property between them. ¹³Not many days later, the younger son gathered all he had and took a journey into a far country, and there he squandered his property in reckless living. ¹⁴And when he had spent everything, a severe famine arose in that country, and he began to be in need. ¹⁵So he went and hired himself out toᵇ one of the citizens of that country, who sent him into his fields to feed pigs. ¹⁶And he was longing to be fed with the pods that the pigs ate, and no one gave him anything.

¹⁷"But when he came to himself, he said, 'How many of my father's hired servants have more than enough bread, but I perish here with hunger! ¹⁸I will arise and go to my father, and I will say to him, "Father, I have sinned against heaven and before you. ¹⁹I am no longer worthy to be called your son. Treat me as one of your hired servants."' ²⁰And he arose and came to his father. But while he was still a long way off, his father saw him and felt compassion, and ran and embraced him and kissed him. ²¹And the son said to him, 'Father, I have sinned against heaven and before you. I am no longer worthy to be called your son.'ᶜ ²²But the father said to his servants,ᵈ 'Bring quickly the best robe, and put it on him, and put a ring on his hand, and shoes on his feet. ²³And bring the fattened calf and kill it, and let us eat and celebrate. ²⁴For this my son was dead, and is alive again; he was lost, and is found.' And they began to celebrate.

²⁵"Now his older son was in the field, and as he came and drew near to the house, he heard music and dancing. ²⁶And he called one of the servants and asked what these things meant. ²⁷And he said to him, 'Your brother has come, and your father has killed the fattened calf, because he has received him back safe and sound.' ²⁸But he was angry and refused to go in. His father came out and entreated him, ²⁹but he answered his father, 'Look, these many years I have served you, and I never disobeyed your command, yet you never gave me a young goat, that I might celebrate with my friends. ³⁰But when this son of yours came, who has devoured your property with prostitutes, you killed the fattened calf for him!' ³¹And he said to him, 'Son,

---

ᵃGreek *ten drachmas*; a *drachma* was a Greek coin approximately equal in value to a Roman *denarius*, worth about a day's wage for a labourer   ᵇGreek *joined himself to*   ᶜSome manuscripts add *treat me as one of your hired servants*   ᵈOr *bondservants*

you are always with me, and all that is mine is yours. ³²It was fitting to celebrate and be glad, for this your brother was dead, and is alive; he was lost, and is found.'"

THE PARABLE OF THE DISHONEST MANAGER

16 He also said to the disciples, "There was a rich man who had a manager, and charges were brought to him that this man was wasting his possessions. ²And he called him and said to him, 'What is this that I hear about you? Turn in the account of your management, for you can no longer be manager.' ³And the manager said to himself, 'What shall I do, since my master is taking the management away from me? I am not strong enough to dig, and I am ashamed to beg. ⁴I have decided what to do, so that when I am removed from management, people may receive me into their houses.' ⁵So, summoning his master's debtors one by one, he said to the first, 'How much do you owe my master?' ⁶He said, 'A hundred measures*a* of oil.' He said to him, 'Take your bill, and sit down quickly and write fifty.' ⁷Then he said to another, 'And how much do you owe?' He said, 'A hundred measures*b* of wheat.' He said to him, 'Take your bill, and write eighty.' ⁸The master commended the dishonest manager for his shrewdness. For the sons of this world*c* are more shrewd in dealing with their own generation than the sons of light. ⁹And I tell you, make friends for yourselves by means of unrighteous wealth,*d* so that when it fails they may receive you into the eternal dwellings.

¹⁰"One who is faithful in a very little is also faithful in much, and one who is dishonest in a very little is also dishonest in much. ¹¹If then you have not been faithful with the unrighteous wealth, who will entrust to you the true riches? ¹²And if you have not been faithful with that which is another's, who will give you that which is your own? ¹³No servant can serve two masters, for either he will hate the one and love the other, or he will be devoted to the one and despise the other. You cannot serve God and money."

THE LAW AND THE KINGDOM OF GOD

¹⁴The Pharisees, who were lovers of money, heard all these things, and they ridiculed him. ¹⁵And he said to them, "You are those who justify yourselves before men, but God knows your hearts. For what is exalted among men is an abomination in the sight of God.

¹⁶"The Law and the Prophets were until John; since then the good news of the kingdom of God is preached, and everyone forces his way into it.*e* ¹⁷But it is easier for heaven and earth to pass away than for one dot of the Law to become void.

DIVORCE AND REMARRIAGE

¹⁸"Everyone who divorces his wife and marries another commits adultery, and he who marries a woman divorced from her husband commits adultery.

THE RICH MAN AND LAZARUS

¹⁹"There was a rich man who was clothed in purple and fine linen and who feasted sumptuously every day. ²⁰And at his gate was laid a poor man named Lazarus, covered with sores, ²¹who desired to be fed with what fell from the rich man's table. Moreover, even the dogs came and licked his sores. ²²The poor man died and was carried by the angels to Abraham's side.*f* The rich man also died and was buried ²³and in Hades, being in torment, he lifted up his eyes and saw Abraham far off and Lazarus at his side. ²⁴And he called out, 'Father Abraham, have mercy on me, and send Lazarus to dip the end of his finger in water and cool my tongue, for I am in anguish in this flame.' ²⁵But Abraham said, 'Child, remember that you in your lifetime received your good things, and Lazarus in like manner bad things; but now he is comforted here, and you are in anguish. ²⁶And besides all this, between us and you a great chasm has been fixed, in order that those who would pass from here to you may not do so, and none may cross from there to us.' ²⁷And he said, 'Then I beg you, father, to send him to my father's house— ²⁸for I have five brothers—so that he may warn them, lest they also come into this place of torment.' ²⁹But Abraham said, 'They have Moses and the Prophets; let them hear them.' ³⁰And he said, 'No, father Abraham, but if someone goes to them from the dead, they will repent.' ³¹He said to him, 'If they do not hear Moses and the Prophets, neither will

---

a About 875 gallons or 3,200 litres *b* Between 1,000 and 1,200 bushels or 37,000 to 45,000 litres *c* Greek *age* *d* Greek *mammon*, a Semitic word for money or possessions; also verse 11; rendered *money* in verse 13 *e* Or *everyone is forcefully urged into it* *f* Greek *bosom*; also verse 23

they be convinced if someone should rise from the dead.'"

TEMPTATIONS TO SIN

17 And he said to his disciples, "Temptations to sin[a] are sure to come, but woe to the one through whom they come! ²It would be better for him if a millstone were hung round his neck and he were cast into the sea than that he should cause one of these little ones to sin.[b] ³Pay attention to yourselves! If your brother sins, rebuke him, and if he repents, forgive him, ⁴and if he sins against you seven times in the day, and turns to you seven times, saying, 'I repent', you must forgive him."

INCREASE OUR FAITH

⁵The apostles said to the Lord, "Increase our faith!" ⁶And the Lord said, "If you had faith like a grain of mustard seed, you could say to this mulberry tree, 'Be uprooted and planted in the sea', and it would obey you.

UNWORTHY SERVANTS

⁷"Will any one of you who has a servant[c] ploughing or keeping sheep say to him when he has come in from the field, 'Come at once and recline at table'? ⁸Will he not rather say to him, 'Prepare supper for me, and dress properly,[d] and serve me while I eat and drink, and afterwards you will eat and drink'? ⁹Does he thank the servant because he did what was commanded? ¹⁰So you also, when you have done all that you were commanded, say, 'We are unworthy servants;[e] we have only done what was our duty.'"

JESUS CLEANSES TEN LEPERS

¹¹On the way to Jerusalem he was passing along between Samaria and Galilee. ¹²And as he entered a village, he was met by ten lepers,[f] who stood at a distance ¹³and lifted up their voices, saying, "Jesus, Master, have mercy on us." ¹⁴When he saw them he said to them, "Go and show yourselves to the priests." And as they went they were cleansed. ¹⁵Then one of them, when he saw that he was healed, turned back, praising God with a loud voice; ¹⁶and he fell on his face at Jesus' feet, giving him thanks. Now he was a Samaritan. ¹⁷Then Jesus answered, "Were not ten cleansed? Where are the nine? ¹⁸Was no one found to return and give praise to God except this foreigner?" ¹⁹And he said to him, "Rise and go your way; your faith has made you well."[g]

THE COMING OF THE KINGDOM

²⁰Being asked by the Pharisees when the kingdom of God would come, he answered them, "The kingdom of God is not coming in ways that can be observed, ²¹nor will they say, 'Look, here it is!' or 'There!' for behold, the kingdom of God is in the midst of you."[h]

²²And he said to the disciples, "The days are coming when you will desire to see one of the days of the Son of Man, and you will not see it. ²³And they will say to you, 'Look, there!' or 'Look, here!' Do not go out or follow them. ²⁴For as the lightning flashes and lights up the sky from one side to the other, so will the Son of Man be in his day.[i] ²⁵But first he must suffer many things and be rejected by this generation. ²⁶Just as it was in the days of Noah, so will it be in the days of the Son of Man. ²⁷They were eating and drinking and marrying and being given in marriage, until the day when Noah entered the ark, and the flood came and destroyed them all. ²⁸Likewise, just as it was in the days of Lot—they were eating and drinking, buying and selling, planting and building, ²⁹but on the day when Lot went out from Sodom, fire and sulphur rained from heaven and destroyed them all— ³⁰so will it be on the day when the Son of Man is revealed. ³¹On that day, let the one who is on the housetop, with his goods in the house, not come down to take them away, and likewise let the one who is in the field not turn back. ³²Remember Lot's wife. ³³Whoever seeks to preserve his life will lose it, but whoever loses his life will keep it. ³⁴I tell you, in that night there will be two in one bed. One will be taken and the other left. ³⁵There will be two women grinding together. One will be taken and the other left."[j] ³⁷And they said to him, "Where, Lord?" He said to them, "Where the corpse[k] is, there the vultures[l] will gather."

THE PARABLE OF THE PERSISTENT WIDOW

18 And he told them a parable to the effect that they ought always to pray and not lose heart. ²He said, "In a certain city there was a judge who neither feared God nor respected man. ³And there was a widow in that city who kept

---

[a]Greek Stumbling blocks [b]Greek stumble [c]Or bondservant; also verse 9 [d]Greek gird yourself [e]Or bondservants [f]Leprosy was a term for several skin diseases; see Leviticus 13 [g]Or has saved you [h]Or within you, or within your grasp [i]Some manuscripts omit in his day [j]Some manuscripts add verse 36: Two men will be in the field; one will be taken and the other left [k]Greek body [l]Or eagles

coming to him and saying, 'Give me justice against my adversary.' ⁴For a while he refused, but afterwards he said to himself, 'Though I neither fear God nor respect man, ⁵yet because this widow keeps bothering me, I will give her justice, so that she will not beat me down by her continual coming.'" ⁶And the Lord said, "Hear what the unrighteous judge says. ⁷And will not God give justice to his elect, who cry to him day and night? Will he delay long over them? ⁸I tell you, he will give justice to them speedily. Nevertheless, when the Son of Man comes, will he find faith on earth?"

THE PHARISEE AND THE TAX COLLECTOR

⁹He also told this parable to some who trusted in themselves that they were righteous, and treated others with contempt: ¹⁰"Two men went up into the temple to pray, one a Pharisee and the other a tax collector. ¹¹The Pharisee, standing by himself, prayed*ᵃ* thus: 'God, I thank you that I am not like other men, extortioners, unjust, adulterers, or even like this tax collector. ¹²I fast twice a week; I give tithes of all that I get.' ¹³But the tax collector, standing far off, would not even lift up his eyes to heaven, but beat his breast, saying, 'God, be merciful to me, a sinner!' ¹⁴I tell you, this man went down to his house justified, rather than the other. For everyone who exalts himself will be humbled, but the one who humbles himself will be exalted."

LET THE CHILDREN COME TO ME

¹⁵Now they were bringing even infants to him that he might touch them. And when the disciples saw it, they rebuked them. ¹⁶But Jesus called them to him, saying, "Let the children come to me, and do not hinder them, for to such belongs the kingdom of God. ¹⁷Truly, I say to you, whoever does not receive the kingdom of God like a child shall not enter it."

THE RICH RULER

¹⁸And a ruler asked him, "Good Teacher, what must I do to inherit eternal life?" ¹⁹And Jesus said to him, "Why do you call me good? No one is good except God alone. ²⁰You know the commandments: 'Do not commit adultery, Do not murder, Do not steal, Do not bear false witness, Honour your father and mother.'" ²¹And he said, "All these I have kept from my youth." ²²When Jesus heard this, he said to him, "One thing you still lack. Sell all that you have and distribute to the poor, and you will have treasure in heaven; and come, follow me." ²³But when he heard these things, he became very sad, for he was extremely rich. ²⁴Jesus, seeing that he had become sad, said, "How difficult it is for those who have wealth to enter the kingdom of God! ²⁵For it is easier for a camel to go through the eye of a needle than for a rich person to enter the kingdom of God." ²⁶Those who heard it said, "Then who can be saved?" ²⁷But he said, "What is impossible with man is possible with God." ²⁸And Peter said, "See, we have left our homes and followed you." ²⁹And he said to them, "Truly, I say to you, there is no one who has left house or wife or brothers*ᵇ* or parents or children, for the sake of the kingdom of God, ³⁰who will not receive many times more in this time, and in the age to come eternal life."

JESUS FORETELLS HIS DEATH A THIRD TIME

³¹And taking the twelve, he said to them, "See, we are going up to Jerusalem, and everything that is written about the Son of Man by the prophets will be accomplished. ³²For he will be delivered over to the Gentiles and will be mocked and shamefully treated and spat upon. ³³And after flogging him, they will kill him, and on the third day he will rise." ³⁴But they understood none of these things. This saying was hidden from them, and they did not grasp what was said.

JESUS HEALS A BLIND BEGGAR

³⁵As he drew near to Jericho, a blind man was sitting by the roadside begging. ³⁶And hearing a crowd going by, he enquired what this meant. ³⁷They told him, "Jesus of Nazareth is passing by." ³⁸And he cried out, "Jesus, Son of David, have mercy on me!" ³⁹And those who were in front rebuked him, telling him to be silent. But he cried out all the more, "Son of David, have mercy on me!" ⁴⁰And Jesus stopped and commanded him to be brought to him. And when he came near, he asked him, ⁴¹"What do you want me to do for you?" He said, "Lord, let me recover my sight." ⁴²And Jesus said to him, "Recover your sight; your faith has made you well." ⁴³And immediately he recovered his sight and followed him, glorifying God. And all the people, when they saw it, gave praise to God.

---

*ᵃ*Or standing, prayed to himself *ᵇ*Or wife or brothers and sisters

LUKE 19

JESUS AND ZACCHAEUS

19 He entered Jericho and was passing through. ²And behold, there was a man named Zacchaeus. He was a chief tax collector and was rich. ³And he was seeking to see who Jesus was, but on account of the crowd he could not, because he was small in stature. ⁴So he ran on ahead and climbed up into a sycamore tree to see him, for he was about to pass that way. ⁵And when Jesus came to the place, he looked up and said to him, "Zacchaeus, hurry and come down, for I must stay at your house today." ⁶So he hurried and came down and received him joyfully. ⁷And when they saw it, they all grumbled, "He has gone in to be the guest of a man who is a sinner." ⁸And Zacchaeus stood and said to the Lord, "Behold, Lord, half of my goods I give to the poor. And if I have defrauded anyone of anything, I restore it fourfold." ⁹And Jesus said to him, "Today salvation has come to this house, since he also is a son of Abraham. ¹⁰For the Son of Man came to seek and to save the lost."

THE PARABLE OF THE TEN MINAS

¹¹As they heard these things, he proceeded to tell a parable, because he was near to Jerusalem, and because they supposed that the kingdom of God was to appear immediately. ¹²He said therefore, "A nobleman went into a far country to receive for himself a kingdom and then return. ¹³Calling ten of his servants,ᵃ he gave them ten minas,ᵇ and said to them, 'Engage in business until I come.' ¹⁴But his citizens hated him and sent a delegation after him, saying, 'We do not want this man to reign over us.' ¹⁵When he returned, having received the kingdom, he ordered these servants to whom he had given the money to be called to him, that he might know what they had gained by doing business. ¹⁶The first came before him, saying, 'Lord, your mina has made ten minas more.' ¹⁷And he said to him, 'Well done, good servant!ᶜ Because you have been faithful in a very little, you shall have authority over ten cities.' ¹⁸And the second came, saying, 'Lord, your mina has made five minas.' ¹⁹And he said to him, 'And you are to be over five cities.' ²⁰Then another came, saying, 'Lord, here is your mina, which I kept laid away in a handkerchief; ²¹for I was afraid of you, because you are a severe man. You take what you did not deposit, and reap what you did not sow.' ²²He said to him, 'I will condemn you with your own words, you wicked servant! You knew that I was a severe man, taking what I did not deposit and reaping what I did not sow? ²³Why then did you not put my money in the bank, and at my coming I might have collected it with interest?' ²⁴And he said to those who stood by, 'Take the mina from him, and give it to the one who has the ten minas.' ²⁵And they said to him, 'Lord, he has ten minas!' ²⁶'I tell you that to everyone who has, more will be given, but from the one who has not, even what he has will be taken away. ²⁷But as for these enemies of mine, who did not want me to reign over them, bring them here and slaughter them before me.'"

THE TRIUMPHAL ENTRY

²⁸And when he had said these things, he went on ahead, going up to Jerusalem. ²⁹When he drew near to Bethphage and Bethany, at the mount that is called Olivet, he sent two of the disciples, ³⁰saying, "Go into the village in front of you, where on entering you will find a colt tied, on which no one has ever yet sat. Untie it and bring it here. ³¹If anyone asks you, 'Why are you untying it?' you shall say this: 'The Lord has need of it.'" ³²So those who were sent went away and found it just as he had told them. ³³And as they were untying the colt, its owners said to them, "Why are you untying the colt?" ³⁴And they said, "The Lord has need of it." ³⁵And they brought it to Jesus, and throwing their cloaks on the colt, they set Jesus on it. ³⁶And as he rode along, they spread their cloaks on the road. ³⁷As he was drawing near—already on the way down the Mount of Olives—the whole multitude of his disciples began to rejoice and praise God with a loud voice for all the mighty works that they had seen, ³⁸saying, "Blessed is the King who comes in the name of the Lord! Peace in heaven and glory in the highest!" ³⁹And some of the Pharisees in the crowd said to him, "Teacher, rebuke your disciples." ⁴⁰He answered, "I tell you, if these were silent, the very stones would cry out."

JESUS WEEPS OVER JERUSALEM

⁴¹And when he drew near and saw the city, he wept over it, ⁴²saying, "Would that you, even you, had known on this day the things that make for peace! But now they are hidden from your eyes. ⁴³For the days will come

---

ᵃOr *bondservants*; also verse 15 ᵇA *mina* was about three months' wages for a labourer ᶜOr *bondservant*; also verse 22

upon you, when your enemies will set up a barricade round you and surround you and hem you in on every side ⁴⁴and tear you down to the ground, you and your children within you. And they will not leave one stone upon another in you, because you did not know the time of your visitation."

JESUS CLEANSES THE TEMPLE

⁴⁵And he entered the temple and began to drive out those who sold, ⁴⁶saying to them, "It is written, 'My house shall be a house of prayer', but you have made it a den of robbers."

⁴⁷And he was teaching daily in the temple. The chief priests and the scribes and the principal men of the people were seeking to destroy him, ⁴⁸but they did not find anything they could do, for all the people were hanging on his words.

THE AUTHORITY OF JESUS CHALLENGED

20 One day, as Jesus[a] was teaching the people in the temple and preaching the gospel, the chief priests and the scribes with the elders came up ²and said to him, "Tell us by what authority you do these things, or who it is that gave you this authority." ³He answered them, "I also will ask you a question. Now tell me, ⁴was the baptism of John from heaven or from man?" ⁵And they discussed it with one another, saying, "If we say, 'From heaven', he will say, 'Why did you not believe him?' ⁶But if we say, 'From man', all the people will stone us to death, for they are convinced that John was a prophet." ⁷So they answered that they did not know where it came from. ⁸And Jesus said to them, "Neither will I tell you by what authority I do these things."

THE PARABLE OF THE WICKED TENANTS

⁹And he began to tell the people this parable: "A man planted a vineyard and let it out to tenants and went into another country for a long while. ¹⁰When the time came, he sent a servant[b] to the tenants, so that they would give him some of the fruit of the vineyard. But the tenants beat him and sent him away empty-handed. ¹¹And he sent another servant. But they also beat and treated him shamefully, and sent him away empty-handed. ¹²And he sent yet a third. This one also they wounded and cast out. ¹³Then the owner of the vineyard said, 'What shall I do? I will send my beloved son; perhaps they will respect him.' ¹⁴But when the tenants saw him, they said to themselves, 'This is the heir. Let us kill him, so that the inheritance may be ours.' ¹⁵And they threw him out of the vineyard and killed him. What then will the owner of the vineyard do to them? ¹⁶He will come and destroy those tenants and give the vineyard to others." When they heard this, they said, "Surely not!" ¹⁷But he looked directly at them and said, "What then is this that is written:

"'The stone that the builders rejected
has become the cornerstone'?[c]

¹⁸Everyone who falls on that stone will be broken to pieces, and when it falls on anyone, it will crush him."

PAYING TAXES TO CAESAR

¹⁹The scribes and the chief priests sought to lay hands on him at that very hour, for they perceived that he had told this parable against them, but they feared the people. ²⁰So they watched him and sent spies, who pretended to be sincere, that they might catch him in something he said, so as to deliver him up to the authority and jurisdiction of the governor. ²¹So they asked him, "Teacher, we know that you speak and teach rightly, and show no partiality,[d] but truly teach the way of God. ²²Is it lawful for us to give tribute to Caesar, or not?" ²³But he perceived their craftiness, and said to them, ²⁴"Show me a denarius.[e] Whose likeness and inscription does it have?" They said, "Caesar's." ²⁵He said to them, "Then render to Caesar the things that are Caesar's, and to God the things that are God's." ²⁶And they were not able in the presence of the people to catch him in what he said, but marvelling at his answer they became silent.

SADDUCEES ASK ABOUT THE RESURRECTION

²⁷There came to him some Sadducees, those who deny that there is a resurrection, ²⁸and they asked him a question, saying, "Teacher, Moses wrote for us that if a man's brother dies, having a wife but no children, the man[f] must take the widow and raise up offspring for his brother. ²⁹Now there were seven brothers. The first took a wife, and died without children. ³⁰And the second ³¹and the

---

[a] Greek he [b] Or bondservant; also verse 11 [c] Greek the head of the corner [d] Greek and do not receive a face [e] A denarius was a day's wage for a labourer [f] Greek his brother

third took her, and likewise all seven left no children and died. ³²Afterwards the woman also died. ³³In the resurrection, therefore, whose wife will the woman be? For the seven had her as wife."

³⁴And Jesus said to them, "The sons of this age marry and are given in marriage, ³⁵but those who are considered worthy to attain to that age and to the resurrection from the dead neither marry nor are given in marriage, ³⁶for they cannot die any more, because they are equal to angels and are sons of God, being sons[a] of the resurrection. ³⁷But that the dead are raised, even Moses showed, in the passage about the bush, where he calls the Lord the God of Abraham and the God of Isaac and the God of Jacob. ³⁸Now he is not God of the dead, but of the living, for all live to him." ³⁹Then some of the scribes answered, "Teacher, you have spoken well." ⁴⁰For they no longer dared to ask him any question.

WHOSE SON IS THE CHRIST?

⁴¹But he said to them, "How can they say that the Christ is David's son? ⁴²For David himself says in the Book of Psalms,

"'The Lord said to my Lord,
"Sit at my right hand,
⁴³   until I make your enemies
        your footstool."'

⁴⁴David thus calls him Lord, so how is he his son?"

BEWARE OF THE SCRIBES

⁴⁵And in the hearing of all the people he said to his disciples, ⁴⁶"Beware of the scribes, who like to walk around in long robes, and love greetings in the market-places and the best seats in the synagogues and the places of honour at feasts, ⁴⁷who devour widows' houses and for a pretence make long prayers. They will receive the greater condemnation."

THE WIDOW'S OFFERING

21 Jesus[b] looked up and saw the rich putting their gifts into the offering box, ²and he saw a poor widow put in two small copper coins.[c] ³And he said, "Truly, I tell you, this poor widow has put in more than all of them. ⁴For they all contributed out of their abundance, but she out of her poverty put in all she had to live on."

JESUS FORETELLS DESTRUCTION OF THE TEMPLE

⁵And while some were speaking of the temple, how it was adorned with noble stones and offerings, he said, ⁶"As for these things that you see, the days will come when there will not be left here one stone upon another that will not be thrown down." ⁷And they asked him, "Teacher, when will these things be, and what will be the sign when these things are about to take place?" ⁸And he said, "See that you are not led astray. For many will come in my name, saying, 'I am he!' and, 'The time is at hand!' Do not go after them. ⁹And when you hear of wars and tumults, do not be terrified, for these things must first take place, but the end will not be at once."

JESUS FORETELLS WARS AND PERSECUTION

¹⁰Then he said to them, "Nation will rise against nation, and kingdom against kingdom. ¹¹There will be great earthquakes, and in various places famines and pestilences. And there will be terrors and great signs from heaven. ¹²But before all this they will lay their hands on you and persecute you, delivering you up to the synagogues and prisons, and you will be brought before kings and governors for my name's sake. ¹³This will be your opportunity to bear witness. ¹⁴Settle it therefore in your minds not to meditate beforehand how to answer, ¹⁵for I will give you a mouth and wisdom, which none of your adversaries will be able to withstand or contradict. ¹⁶You will be delivered up even by parents and brothers[d] and relatives and friends, and some of you they will put to death. ¹⁷You will be hated by all for my name's sake. ¹⁸But not a hair of your head will perish. ¹⁹By your endurance you will gain your lives.

JESUS FORETELLS DESTRUCTION OF JERUSALEM

²⁰"But when you see Jerusalem surrounded by armies, then know that its desolation has come near. ²¹Then let those who are in Judea flee to the mountains, and let those who are inside the city depart, and let not those who are out in the country enter it, ²²for these are days of vengeance, to fulfil all that is written. ²³Alas for women who are pregnant and

---

[a]Greek *huioi*; see Preface   [b]Greek *He*   [c]Greek *two lepta*; a *lepton* was a Jewish bronze or copper coin worth about 1/128 of a *denarius* (which was a day's wage for a labourer)   [d]Or *parents and brothers and sisters*

for those who are nursing infants in those days! For there will be great distress upon the earth and wrath against this people. ²⁴They will fall by the edge of the sword and be led captive among all nations, and Jerusalem will be trampled underfoot by the Gentiles, until the times of the Gentiles are fulfilled.

THE COMING OF THE SON OF MAN

²⁵"And there will be signs in sun and moon and stars, and on the earth distress of nations in perplexity because of the roaring of the sea and the waves, ²⁶people fainting with fear and with foreboding of what is coming on the world. For the powers of the heavens will be shaken. ²⁷And then they will see the Son of Man coming in a cloud with power and great glory. ²⁸Now when these things begin to take place, straighten up and raise your heads, because your redemption is drawing near."

THE LESSON OF THE FIG TREE

²⁹And he told them a parable: "Look at the fig tree, and all the trees. ³⁰As soon as they come out in leaf, you see for yourselves and know that the summer is already near. ³¹So also, when you see these things taking place, you know that the kingdom of God is near. ³²Truly, I say to you, this generation will not pass away until all has taken place. ³³Heaven and earth will pass away, but my words will not pass away.

WATCH YOURSELVES

³⁴"But watch yourselves lest your hearts be weighed down with dissipation and drunkenness and cares of this life, and that day come upon you suddenly like a trap. ³⁵For it will come upon all who dwell on the face of the whole earth. ³⁶But stay awake at all times, praying that you may have strength to escape all these things that are going to take place, and to stand before the Son of Man."

³⁷And every day he was teaching in the temple, but at night he went out and lodged on the mount called Olivet. ³⁸And early in the morning all the people came to him in the temple to hear him.

THE PLOT TO KILL JESUS

22 Now the Feast of Unleavened Bread drew near, which is called the Passover. ²And the chief priests and the scribes were seeking how to put him to death, for they feared the people.

JUDAS TO BETRAY JESUS

³Then Satan entered into Judas called Iscariot, who was of the number of the twelve. ⁴He went away and conferred with the chief priests and officers how he might betray him to them. ⁵And they were glad, and agreed to give him money. ⁶So he consented and sought an opportunity to betray him to them in the absence of a crowd.

THE PASSOVER WITH THE DISCIPLES

⁷Then came the day of Unleavened Bread, on which the Passover lamb had to be sacrificed. ⁸So Jesus[a] sent Peter and John, saying, "Go and prepare the Passover for us, that we may eat it." ⁹They said to him, "Where would you have us prepare it?" ¹⁰He said to them, "Behold, when you have entered the city, a man carrying a jar of water will meet you. Follow him into the house that he enters ¹¹and tell the master of the house, 'The Teacher says to you, Where is the guest room, where I may eat the Passover with my disciples?' ¹²And he will show you a large upper room furnished; prepare it there." ¹³And they went and found it just as he had told them, and they prepared the Passover.

INSTITUTION OF THE LORD'S SUPPER

¹⁴And when the hour came, he reclined at table, and the apostles with him. ¹⁵And he said to them, "I have earnestly desired to eat this Passover with you before I suffer. ¹⁶For I tell you I will not eat it[b] until it is fulfilled in the kingdom of God." ¹⁷And he took a cup, and when he had given thanks he said, "Take this, and divide it among yourselves. ¹⁸For I tell you that from now on I will not drink of the fruit of the vine until the kingdom of God comes." ¹⁹And he took bread, and when he had given thanks, he broke it and gave it to them, saying, "This is my body, which is given for you. Do this in remembrance of me." ²⁰And likewise the cup after they had eaten, saying, "This cup that is poured out for you is the new covenant in my blood.[c] ²¹But behold, the hand of him who betrays me is with me on the table. ²²For the Son of Man goes as it has been determined, but woe to that man by whom he is betrayed!" ²³And they began to question one another, which of them it could be who was going to do this.

---

[a]Greek *he* [b]Some manuscripts *never eat it again* [c]Some manuscripts omit, in whole or in part, verses 19b-20 (*which is given . . . in my blood*)

WHO IS THE GREATEST?

24 A dispute also arose among them, as to which of them was to be regarded as the greatest. 25 And he said to them, "The kings of the Gentiles exercise lordship over them, and those in authority over them are called benefactors. 26 But not so with you. Rather, let the greatest among you become as the youngest, and the leader as one who serves. 27 For who is the greater, one who reclines at table or one who serves? Is it not the one who reclines at table? But I am among you as the one who serves.

28 "You are those who have stayed with me in my trials, 29 and I assign to you, as my Father assigned to me, a kingdom, 30 that you may eat and drink at my table in my kingdom and sit on thrones judging the twelve tribes of Israel.

JESUS FORETELLS PETER'S DENIAL

31 "Simon, Simon, behold, Satan demanded to have you,[a] that he might sift you like wheat, 32 but I have prayed for you that your faith may not fail. And when you have turned again, strengthen your brothers." 33 Peter[b] said to him, "Lord, I am ready to go with you both to prison and to death." 34 Jesus[c] said, "I tell you, Peter, the cock will not crow this day, until you deny three times that you know me."

SCRIPTURE MUST BE FULFILLED IN JESUS

35 And he said to them, "When I sent you out with no money bag or knapsack or sandals, did you lack anything?" They said, "Nothing." 36 He said to them, "But now let the one who has a money bag take it, and likewise a knapsack. And let the one who has no sword sell his cloak and buy one. 37 For I tell you that this Scripture must be fulfilled in me: 'And he was numbered with the transgressors.' For what is written about me has its fulfilment." 38 And they said, "Look, Lord, here are two swords." And he said to them, "It is enough."

JESUS PRAYS ON THE MOUNT OF OLIVES

39 And he came out and went, as was his custom, to the Mount of Olives, and the disciples followed him. 40 And when he came to the place, he said to them, "Pray that you may not enter into temptation." 41 And he withdrew from them about a stone's throw, and knelt down and prayed, 42 saying, "Father, if you are willing, remove this cup from me. Nevertheless, not my will, but yours, be done." 43 And there appeared to him an angel from heaven, strengthening him. 44 And being in agony he prayed more earnestly; and his sweat became like great drops of blood falling down to the ground.[d] 45 And when he rose from prayer, he came to the disciples and found them sleeping for sorrow, 46 and he said to them, "Why are you sleeping? Rise and pray that you may not enter into temptation."

BETRAYAL AND ARREST OF JESUS

47 While he was still speaking, there came a crowd, and the man called Judas, one of the twelve, was leading them. He drew near to Jesus to kiss him, 48 but Jesus said to him, "Judas, would you betray the Son of Man with a kiss?" 49 And when those who were around him saw what would follow, they said, "Lord, shall we strike with the sword?" 50 And one of them struck the servant[e] of the high priest and cut off his right ear. 51 But Jesus said, "No more of this!" And he touched his ear and healed him. 52 Then Jesus said to the chief priests and officers of the temple and elders, who had come out against him, "Have you come out as against a robber, with swords and clubs? 53 When I was with you day after day in the temple, you did not lay hands on me. But this is your hour, and the power of darkness."

PETER DENIES JESUS

54 Then they seized him and led him away, bringing him into the high priest's house, and Peter was following at a distance. 55 And when they had kindled a fire in the middle of the courtyard and sat down together, Peter sat down among them. 56 Then a servant girl, seeing him as he sat in the light and looking closely at him, said, "This man also was with him." 57 But he denied it, saying, "Woman, I do not know him." 58 And a little later someone else saw him and said, "You also are one of them." But Peter said, "Man, I am not." 59 And after an interval of about an hour still another insisted, saying, "Certainly this man also was with him, for he too is a Galilean." 60 But Peter said, "Man, I do not know what you are talking about." And immediately, while he was still speaking, the cock crowed. 61 And the Lord turned and looked at Peter. And Peter

---

[a] The Greek word for *you* (twice in this verse) is plural; in verse 32, all four instances are singular [b] Greek *He* [c] Greek *He* [d] Some manuscripts omit verses 43 and 44 [e] Or *bondservant*

remembered the saying of the Lord, how he had said to him, "Before the cock crows today, you will deny me three times." ⁶²And he went out and wept bitterly.

JESUS IS MOCKED

⁶³Now the men who were holding Jesus in custody were mocking him as they beat him. ⁶⁴They also blindfolded him and kept asking him, "Prophesy! Who is it that struck you?" ⁶⁵And they said many other things against him, blaspheming him.

JESUS BEFORE THE COUNCIL

⁶⁶When day came, the assembly of the elders of the people gathered together, both chief priests and scribes. And they led him away to their council, and they said, ⁶⁷"If you are the Christ, tell us." But he said to them, "If I tell you, you will not believe, ⁶⁸and if I ask you, you will not answer. ⁶⁹But from now on the Son of Man shall be seated at the right hand of the power of God." ⁷⁰So they all said, "Are you the Son of God, then?" And he said to them, "You say that I am." ⁷¹Then they said, "What further testimony do we need? We have heard it ourselves from his own lips."

JESUS BEFORE PILATE

23 Then the whole company of them arose and brought him before Pilate. ²And they began to accuse him, saying, "We found this man misleading our nation and forbidding us to give tribute to Caesar, and saying that he himself is Christ, a king." ³And Pilate asked him, "Are you the King of the Jews?" And he answered him, "You have said so." ⁴Then Pilate said to the chief priests and the crowds, "I find no guilt in this man." ⁵But they were urgent, saying, "He stirs up the people, teaching throughout all Judea, from Galilee even to this place."

JESUS BEFORE HEROD

⁶When Pilate heard this, he asked whether the man was a Galilean. ⁷And when he learned that he belonged to Herod's jurisdiction, he sent him over to Herod, who was himself in Jerusalem at that time. ⁸When Herod saw Jesus, he was very glad, for he had long desired to see him, because he had heard about him, and he was hoping to see some sign done by him. ⁹So he questioned him at some length, but he made no answer. ¹⁰The chief priests and the scribes stood by, vehemently accusing him. ¹¹And Herod with his soldiers treated him with contempt and mocked him. Then, arraying him in splendid clothing, he sent him back to Pilate. ¹²And Herod and Pilate became friends with each other that very day, for before this they had been at enmity with each other.

¹³Pilate then called together the chief priests and the rulers and the people, ¹⁴and said to them, "You brought me this man as one who was misleading the people. And after examining him before you, behold, I did not find this man guilty of any of your charges against him. ¹⁵Neither did Herod, for he sent him back to us. Look, nothing deserving death has been done by him. ¹⁶I will therefore punish and release him."[a]

PILATE DELIVERS JESUS TO BE CRUCIFIED

¹⁸But they all cried out together, "Away with this man, and release to us Barabbas"— ¹⁹a man who had been thrown into prison for an insurrection started in the city and for murder. ²⁰Pilate addressed them once more, desiring to release Jesus, ²¹but they kept shouting, "Crucify, crucify him!" ²²A third time he said to them, "Why? What evil has he done? I have found in him no guilt deserving death. I will therefore punish and release him." ²³But they were urgent, demanding with loud cries that he should be crucified. And their voices prevailed. ²⁴So Pilate decided that their demand should be granted. ²⁵He released the man who had been thrown into prison for insurrection and murder, for whom they asked, but he delivered Jesus over to their will.

THE CRUCIFIXION

²⁶And as they led him away, they seized one Simon of Cyrene, who was coming in from the country, and laid on him the cross, to carry it behind Jesus. ²⁷And there followed him a great multitude of the people and of women who were mourning and lamenting for him. ²⁸But turning to them Jesus said, "Daughters of Jerusalem, do not weep for me, but weep for yourselves and for your children. ²⁹For behold, the days are coming when they will say, 'Blessed are the barren and the wombs that never bore and the breasts that never nursed!' ³⁰Then they will begin to say to the mountains, 'Fall on us',

---

[a]Here, or after verse 19, some manuscripts add verse 17: *Now he was obliged to release one man to them at the festival*

and to the hills, 'Cover us.' ³¹For if they do these things when the wood is green, what will happen when it is dry?"

³²Two others, who were criminals, were led away to be put to death with him. ³³And when they came to the place that is called The Skull, there they crucified him, and the criminals, one on his right and one on his left. ³⁴And Jesus said, "Father, forgive them, for they know not what they do."*ᵃ* And they cast lots to divide his garments. ³⁵And the people stood by, watching, but the rulers scoffed at him, saying, "He saved others; let him save himself, if he is the Christ of God, his Chosen One!" ³⁶The soldiers also mocked him, coming up and offering him sour wine ³⁷and saying, "If you are the King of the Jews, save yourself!" ³⁸There was also an inscription over him,*ᵇ* "This is the King of the Jews."

³⁹One of the criminals who were hanged railed at him,*ᶜ* saying, "Are you not the Christ? Save yourself and us!" ⁴⁰But the other rebuked him, saying, "Do you not fear God, since you are under the same sentence of condemnation? ⁴¹And we indeed justly, for we are receiving the due reward of our deeds; but this man has done nothing wrong." ⁴²And he said, "Jesus, remember me when you come into your kingdom." ⁴³And he said to him, "Truly, I say to you, today you will be with me in paradise."

THE DEATH OF JESUS

⁴⁴It was now about the sixth hour,*ᵈ* and there was darkness over the whole land until the ninth hour,*ᵉ* ⁴⁵while the sun's light failed. And the curtain of the temple was torn in two. ⁴⁶Then Jesus, calling out with a loud voice, said, "Father, into your hands I commit my spirit!" And having said this he breathed his last. ⁴⁷Now when the centurion saw what had taken place, he praised God, saying, "Certainly this man was innocent!" ⁴⁸And all the crowds that had assembled for this spectacle, when they saw what had taken place, returned home beating their breasts. ⁴⁹And all his acquaintances and the women who had followed him from Galilee stood at a distance watching these things.

JESUS IS BURIED

⁵⁰Now there was a man named Joseph, from the Jewish town of Arimathea. He was a member of the council, a good and righteous man, ⁵¹who had not consented to their decision and action; and he was looking for the kingdom of God. ⁵²This man went to Pilate and asked for the body of Jesus. ⁵³Then he took it down and wrapped it in a linen shroud and laid him in a tomb cut in stone, where no one had ever yet been laid. ⁵⁴It was the day of Preparation, and the Sabbath was beginning.*ᶠ* ⁵⁵The women who had come with him from Galilee followed and saw the tomb and how his body was laid. ⁵⁶Then they returned and prepared spices and ointments.

On the Sabbath they rested according to the commandment.

THE RESURRECTION

24 But on the first day of the week, at early dawn, they went to the tomb, taking the spices they had prepared. ²And they found the stone rolled away from the tomb, ³but when they went in they did not find the body of the Lord Jesus. ⁴While they were perplexed about this, behold, two men stood by them in dazzling apparel. ⁵And as they were frightened and bowed their faces to the ground, the men said to them, "Why do you seek the living among the dead? ⁶He is not here, but has risen. Remember how he told you, while he was still in Galilee, ⁷that the Son of Man must be delivered into the hands of sinful men and be crucified and on the third day rise." ⁸And they remembered his words, ⁹and returning from the tomb they told all these things to the eleven and to all the rest. ¹⁰Now it was Mary Magdalene and Joanna and Mary the mother of James and the other women with them who told these things to the apostles, ¹¹but these words seemed to them an idle tale, and they did not believe them. ¹²But Peter rose and ran to the tomb; stooping and looking in, he saw the linen cloths by themselves; and he went home marvelling at what had happened.

ON THE ROAD TO EMMAUS

¹³That very day two of them were going to a village named Emmaus, about seven miles*ᵍ* from Jerusalem, ¹⁴and they were talking with each other about all these things that had happened. ¹⁵While they were talking and discussing together, Jesus himself drew near and went with them. ¹⁶But their eyes were

---

ᵃSome manuscripts omit the sentence And Jesus . . . what they do
ᵇSome manuscripts add in letters of Greek and Latin and Hebrew
ᶜOr blasphemed him   ᵈThat is, noon   ᵉThat is, 3 P.M.   ᶠGreek was dawning   ᵍGreek sixty stadia; a stadion was about 607 feet or 185 metres

kept from recognizing him. ⁱ⁷And he said to them, "What is this conversation that you are holding with each other as you walk?" And they stood still, looking sad. ¹⁸Then one of them, named Cleopas, answered him, "Are you the only visitor to Jerusalem who does not know the things that have happened there in these days?" ¹⁹And he said to them, "What things?" And they said to him, "Concerning Jesus of Nazareth, a man who was a prophet mighty in deed and word before God and all the people, ²⁰and how our chief priests and rulers delivered him up to be condemned to death, and crucified him. ²¹But we had hoped that he was the one to redeem Israel. Yes, and besides all this, it is now the third day since these things happened. ²²Moreover, some women of our company amazed us. They were at the tomb early in the morning, ²³and when they did not find his body, they came back saying that they had even seen a vision of angels, who said that he was alive. ²⁴Some of those who were with us went to the tomb and found it just as the women had said, but him they did not see." ²⁵And he said to them, "O foolish ones, and slow of heart to believe all that the prophets have spoken! ²⁶Was it not necessary that the Christ should suffer these things and enter into his glory?" ²⁷And beginning with Moses and all the Prophets, he interpreted to them in all the Scriptures the things concerning himself.

²⁸So they drew near to the village to which they were going. He acted as if he were going farther, ²⁹but they urged him strongly, saying, "Stay with us, for it is towards evening and the day is now far spent." So he went in to stay with them. ³⁰When he was at table with them, he took the bread and blessed and broke it and gave it to them. ³¹And their eyes were opened, and they recognized him. And he vanished from their sight. ³²They said to each other, "Did not our hearts burn within us while he talked to us on the road, while he opened to us the Scriptures?" ³³And they rose that same hour and returned to Jerusalem. And they found the eleven and those who were with them gathered together, ³⁴saying, "The Lord has risen indeed, and has appeared to Simon!" ³⁵Then they told what had happened on the road, and how he was known to them in the breaking of the bread.

JESUS APPEARS TO HIS DISCIPLES

³⁶As they were talking about these things, Jesus himself stood among them, and said to them, "Peace to you!" ³⁷But they were startled and frightened and thought they saw a spirit. ³⁸And he said to them, "Why are you troubled, and why do doubts arise in your hearts? ³⁹See my hands and my feet, that it is I myself. Touch me, and see. For a spirit does not have flesh and bones as you see that I have." ⁴⁰And when he had said this, he showed them his hands and his feet. ⁴¹And while they still disbelieved for joy and were marvelling, he said to them, "Have you anything here to eat?" ⁴²They gave him a piece of broiled fish,ᵃ ⁴³and he took it and ate before them.

⁴⁴Then he said to them, "These are my words that I spoke to you while I was still with you, that everything written about me in the Law of Moses and the Prophets and the Psalms must be fulfilled." ⁴⁵Then he opened their minds to understand the Scriptures, ⁴⁶and said to them, "Thus it is written, that the Christ should suffer and on the third day rise from the dead, ⁴⁷and that repentance forᵇ the forgiveness of sins should be proclaimed in his name to all nations, beginning from Jerusalem. ⁴⁸You are witnesses of these things. ⁴⁹And behold, I am sending the promise of my Father upon you. But stay in the city until you are clothed with power from on high."

THE ASCENSION

⁵⁰And he led them out as far as Bethany, and lifting up his hands he blessed them. ⁵¹While he blessed them, he parted from them and was carried up into heaven. ⁵²And they worshipped him and returned to Jerusalem with great joy, ⁵³and were continually in the temple blessing God.

ᵃSome manuscripts add *and some honeycomb* ᵇSome manuscripts *and*

THE GOSPEL ACCORDING TO
JOHN

THE WORD BECAME FLESH

1 In the beginning was the Word, and the Word was with God, and the Word was God. ²He was in the beginning with God. ³All things were made through him, and without him was not any thing made that was made. ⁴In him was life,ᵃ and the life was the light of men. ⁵The light shines in the darkness, and the darkness has not overcome it.

⁶There was a man sent from God, whose name was John. ⁷He came as a witness, to bear witness about the light, that all might believe through him. ⁸He was not the light, but came to bear witness about the light.

⁹The true light, which gives light to everyone, was coming into the world. ¹⁰He was in the world, and the world was made through him, yet the world did not know him. ¹¹He came to his own,ᵇ and his own peopleᶜ did not receive him. ¹²But to all who did receive him, who believed in his name, he gave the right to become children of God, ¹³who were born, not of blood nor of the will of the flesh nor of the will of man, but of God.

¹⁴And the Word became flesh and dwelt among us, and we have seen his glory, glory as of the only Sonᵈ from the Father, full of grace and truth. ¹⁵(John bore witness about him, and cried out, "This was he of whom I said, 'He who comes after me ranks before me, because he was before me.'") ¹⁶For from his fullness we have all received, grace upon grace.ᵉ ¹⁷For the law was given through Moses; grace and truth came through Jesus Christ. ¹⁸No one has ever seen God; the only God,ᶠ who is at the Father's side,ᵍ he has made him known.

THE TESTIMONY OF JOHN THE BAPTIST

¹⁹And this is the testimony of John, when the Jews sent priests and Levites from Jerusalem to ask him, "Who are you?" ²⁰He confessed, and did not deny, but confessed, "I am not the Christ." ²¹And they asked him, "What then? Are you Elijah?" He said, "I am not." "Are you the Prophet?" And he answered, "No." ²²So they said to him, "Who are you? We need to give an answer to those who sent us. What do you say about yourself?" ²³He said, "I am the voice of one crying out in the wilderness, 'Make straightʰ the way of the Lord', as the prophet Isaiah said."

²⁴(Now they had been sent from the Pharisees.) ²⁵They asked him, "Then why are you baptizing, if you are neither the Christ, nor Elijah, nor the Prophet?" ²⁶John answered them, "I baptize with water, but among you stands one you do not know, ²⁷even he who comes after me, the strap of whose sandal I am not worthy to untie." ²⁸These things took place in Bethany across the Jordan, where John was baptizing.

BEHOLD, THE LAMB OF GOD

²⁹The next day he saw Jesus coming towards him, and said, "Behold, the Lamb of God, who takes away the sin of the world! ³⁰This is he of whom I said, 'After me comes a man who ranks before me, because he was before me.' ³¹I myself did not know him, but for this purpose I came baptizing with water, that he might be revealed to Israel." ³²And John bore witness: "I saw the Spirit descend from heaven like a dove, and it remained on him. ³³I myself did not know him, but he who sent me to baptize with water said to me, 'He on whom you see the Spirit descend and remain, this is he who baptizes with the Holy Spirit.' ³⁴And I have seen and have borne witness that this is the Sonⁱ of God."

JESUS CALLS THE FIRST DISCIPLES

³⁵The next day again John was standing with two of his disciples, ³⁶and he looked at Jesus as he walked by and said, "Behold, the Lamb of God!" ³⁷The two disciples heard him say this, and they followed Jesus. ³⁸Jesus turned and saw them following and said to

---

ᵃ Or *was not any thing made. That which has been made was life in him* ᵇ Greek *to his own things*; that is, to his own domain, or to his own people ᶜ *People* is implied in Greek ᵈ Or *only One*, or *unique One* ᵉ Or *grace in place of grace* ᶠ Or *the only One, who is God*; some manuscripts *the only Son* ᵍ Greek *in the bosom of the Father* ʰ Or *crying out, 'In the wilderness make straight* ⁱ Some manuscripts *the Chosen One*

them, "What are you seeking?" And they said to him, "Rabbi" (which means Teacher), "where are you staying?" ³⁹He said to them, "Come and you will see." So they came and saw where he was staying, and they stayed with him that day, for it was about the tenth hour.ᵃ ⁴⁰One of the two who heard John speak and followed Jesusᵇ was Andrew, Simon Peter's brother. ⁴¹He first found his own brother Simon and said to him, "We have found the Messiah" (which means Christ). ⁴²He brought him to Jesus. Jesus looked at him and said, "You are Simon the son of John. You shall be called Cephas" (which means Peterᶜ).

JESUS CALLS PHILIP AND NATHANAEL

⁴³The next day Jesus decided to go to Galilee. He found Philip and said to him, "Follow me." ⁴⁴Now Philip was from Bethsaida, the city of Andrew and Peter. ⁴⁵Philip found Nathanael and said to him, "We have found him of whom Moses in the Law and also the prophets wrote, Jesus of Nazareth, the son of Joseph." ⁴⁶Nathanael said to him, "Can anything good come out of Nazareth?" Philip said to him, "Come and see." ⁴⁷Jesus saw Nathanael coming towards him and said of him, "Behold, an Israelite indeed, in whom there is no deceit!" ⁴⁸Nathanael said to him, "How do you know me?" Jesus answered him, "Before Philip called you, when you were under the fig tree, I saw you." ⁴⁹Nathanael answered him, "Rabbi, you are the Son of God! You are the King of Israel!" ⁵⁰Jesus answered him, "Because I said to you, 'I saw you under the fig tree', do you believe? You will see greater things than these." ⁵¹And he said to him, "Truly, truly, I say to you,ᵈ you will see heaven opened, and the angels of God ascending and descending on the Son of Man."

THE WEDDING AT CANA

2 On the third day there was a wedding at Cana in Galilee, and the mother of Jesus was there. ²Jesus also was invited to the wedding with his disciples. ³When the wine ran out, the mother of Jesus said to him, "They have no wine." ⁴And Jesus said to her, "Woman, what does this have to do with me? My hour has not yet come." ⁵His mother said to the servants, "Do whatever he tells you."

⁶Now there were six stone water jars there for the Jewish rites of purification, each holding twenty or thirty gallons.ᵉ ⁷Jesus said to the servants, "Fill the jars with water." And they filled them up to the brim. ⁸And he said to them, "Now draw some out and take it to the master of the feast." So they took it. ⁹When the master of the feast tasted the water now become wine, and did not know where it came from (though the servants who had drawn the water knew), the master of the feast called the bridegroom ¹⁰and said to him, "Everyone serves the good wine first, and when people have drunk freely, then the poor wine. But you have kept the good wine until now." ¹¹This, the first of his signs, Jesus did at Cana in Galilee, and manifested his glory. And his disciples believed in him.

¹²After this he went down to Capernaum, with his mother and his brothersᶠ and his disciples, and they stayed there for a few days.

JESUS CLEANSES THE TEMPLE

¹³The Passover of the Jews was at hand, and Jesus went up to Jerusalem. ¹⁴In the temple he found those who were selling oxen and sheep and pigeons, and the money-changers sitting there. ¹⁵And making a whip of cords, he drove them all out of the temple, with the sheep and oxen. And he poured out the coins of the money-changers and overturned their tables. ¹⁶And he told those who sold the pigeons, "Take these things away; do not make my Father's house a house of trade." ¹⁷His disciples remembered that it was written, "Zeal for your house will consume me."

¹⁸So the Jews said to him, "What sign do you show us for doing these things?" ¹⁹Jesus answered them, "Destroy this temple, and in three days I will raise it up." ²⁰The Jews then said, "It has taken forty-six years to build this temple,ᵍ and will you raise it up in three days?" ²¹But he was speaking about the temple of his body. ²²When therefore he was raised from the dead, his disciples remembered that he had said this, and they believed the Scripture and the word that Jesus had spoken.

JESUS KNOWS WHAT IS IN MAN

²³Now when he was in Jerusalem at the Passover Feast, many believed in his name

---

ᵃThat is, about 4 P.M. ᵇGreek him ᶜCephas and Peter are from the word for rock in Aramaic and Greek, respectively ᵈThe Greek for you is plural; twice in this verse ᵉGreek two or three measures (metrētas); a metrētēs was about 10 gallons or 35 litres ᶠOr brothers and sisters. In New Testament usage, depending on the context, the plural Greek word adelphoi (translated "brothers") may refer either to brothers or to brothers and sisters. ᵍOr This temple was built forty-six years ago

when they saw the signs that he was doing. ²⁴But Jesus on his part did not entrust himself to them, because he knew all people ²⁵and needed no one to bear witness about man, for he himself knew what was in man.

YOU MUST BE BORN AGAIN

3 Now there was a man of the Pharisees named Nicodemus, a ruler of the Jews. ²This man came to Jesus^a by night and said to him, "Rabbi, we know that you are a teacher come from God, for no one can do these signs that you do unless God is with him." ³Jesus answered him, "Truly, truly, I say to you, unless one is born again^b he cannot see the kingdom of God." ⁴Nicodemus said to him, "How can a man be born when he is old? Can he enter a second time into his mother's womb and be born?" ⁵Jesus answered, "Truly, truly, I say to you, unless one is born of water and the Spirit, he cannot enter the kingdom of God. ⁶That which is born of the flesh is flesh, and that which is born of the Spirit is spirit.^{c} ⁷Do not marvel that I said to you, 'You^d must be born again.' ⁸The wind^e blows where it wishes, and you hear its sound, but you do not know where it comes from or where it goes. So it is with everyone who is born of the Spirit."

⁹Nicodemus said to him, "How can these things be?" ¹⁰Jesus answered him, "Are you the teacher of Israel and yet you do not understand these things? ¹¹Truly, truly, I say to you, we speak of what we know, and bear witness to what we have seen, but you^f do not receive our testimony. ¹²If I have told you earthly things and you do not believe, how can you believe if I tell you heavenly things? ¹³No one has ascended into heaven except he who descended from heaven, the Son of Man.^{g} ¹⁴And as Moses lifted up the serpent in the wilderness, so must the Son of Man be lifted up, ¹⁵that whoever believes in him may have eternal life.^{h}

FOR GOD SO LOVED THE WORLD

¹⁶"For God so loved the world,^{i} that he gave his only Son, that whoever believes in him should not perish but have eternal life. ¹⁷For God did not send his Son into the world to condemn the world, but in order that the world might be saved through him. ¹⁸Whoever believes in him is not condemned, but whoever does not believe is condemned already, because he has not believed in the name of the only Son of God. ¹⁹And this is the judgement: the light has come into the world, and people loved the darkness rather than the light because their works were evil. ²⁰For everyone who does wicked things hates the light and does not come to the light, lest his works should be exposed. ²¹But whoever does what is true comes to the light, so that it may be clearly seen that his works have been carried out in God."

JOHN THE BAPTIST EXALTS CHRIST

²²After this Jesus and his disciples went into the Judean countryside, and he remained there with them and was baptizing. ²³John also was baptizing at Aenon near Salim, because water was plentiful there, and people were coming and being baptized ²⁴(for John had not yet been put in prison). ²⁵Now a discussion arose between some of John's disciples and a Jew over purification. ²⁶And they came to John and said to him, "Rabbi, he who was with you across the Jordan, to whom you bore witness—look, he is baptizing, and all are going to him." ²⁷John answered, "A person cannot receive even one thing unless it is given him from heaven. ²⁸You yourselves bear me witness, that I said, 'I am not the Christ, but I have been sent before him.' ²⁹The one who has the bride is the bridegroom. The friend of the bridegroom, who stands and hears him, rejoices greatly at the bridegroom's voice. Therefore this joy of mine is now complete. ³⁰He must increase, but I must decrease."^{j}

³¹He who comes from above is above all. He who is of the earth belongs to the earth and speaks in an earthly way. He who comes from heaven is above all. ³²He bears witness to what he has seen and heard, yet no one receives his testimony. ³³Whoever receives his testimony sets his seal to this, that God is true. ³⁴For he whom God has sent utters the words of God, for he gives the Spirit without measure. ³⁵The Father loves the Son and has given all things into his hand. ³⁶Whoever believes in the Son has eternal life; whoever does not obey the Son shall not see life, but the wrath of God remains on him.

---

^{a}Greek him ^{b}Or from above; the Greek is purposely ambiguous and can mean both again and from above; also verse 7 ^{c}The same Greek word means both wind and spirit ^{d}The Greek for you is plural here ^{e}The same Greek word means both wind and spirit ^{f}The Greek for you is plural here; also four times in verse 12 ^{g}Some manuscripts add who is in heaven ^{h}Some interpreters hold that the quotation ends after verse 15 ^{i}Or For this is how God loved the world ^{j}Some interpreters hold that the quotation continues to the end of verse 36

JESUS AND THE WOMAN OF SAMARIA

4 Now when Jesus learned that the Pharisees had heard that Jesus was making and baptizing more disciples than John ²(although Jesus himself did not baptize, but only his disciples), ³he left Judea and departed again for Galilee. ⁴And he had to pass through Samaria. ⁵So he came to a town of Samaria called Sychar, near the field that Jacob had given to his son Joseph. ⁶Jacob's well was there; so Jesus, wearied as he was from his journey, was sitting beside the well. It was about the sixth hour.ᵃ

⁷A woman from Samaria came to draw water. Jesus said to her, "Give me a drink." ⁸(For his disciples had gone away into the city to buy food.) ⁹The Samaritan woman said to him, "How is it that you, a Jew, ask for a drink from me, a woman of Samaria?" (For Jews have no dealings with Samaritans.) ¹⁰Jesus answered her, "If you knew the gift of God, and who it is that is saying to you, 'Give me a drink', you would have asked him, and he would have given you living water." ¹¹The woman said to him, "Sir, you have nothing to draw water with, and the well is deep. Where do you get that living water? ¹²Are you greater than our father Jacob? He gave us the well and drank from it himself, as did his sons and his livestock." ¹³Jesus said to her, "Everyone who drinks of this water will be thirsty again, ¹⁴but whoever drinks of the water that I will give him will never be thirsty again.ᵇ The water that I will give him will become in him a spring of water welling up to eternal life." ¹⁵The woman said to him, "Sir, give me this water, so that I will not be thirsty or have to come here to draw water."

¹⁶Jesus said to her, "Go, call your husband, and come here." ¹⁷The woman answered him, "I have no husband." Jesus said to her, "You are right in saying, 'I have no husband'; ¹⁸for you have had five husbands, and the one you now have is not your husband. What you have said is true." ¹⁹The woman said to him, "Sir, I perceive that you are a prophet. ²⁰Our fathers worshipped on this mountain, but you say that in Jerusalem is the place where people ought to worship." ²¹Jesus said to her, "Woman, believe me, the hour is coming when neither on this mountain nor in Jerusalem will you worship the Father. ²²You worship what you do not know; we worship what we know, for salvation is from the Jews. ²³But the hour is coming, and is now here, when the true worshippers will worship the Father in spirit and truth, for the Father is seeking such people to worship him. ²⁴God is spirit, and those who worship him must worship in spirit and truth." ²⁵The woman said to him, "I know that Messiah is coming (he who is called Christ). When he comes, he will tell us all things." ²⁶Jesus said to her, "I who speak to you am he."

²⁷Just then his disciples came back. They marvelled that he was talking with a woman, but no one said, "What do you seek?" or, "Why are you talking with her?" ²⁸So the woman left her water jar and went away into town and said to the people, ²⁹"Come, see a man who told me all that I ever did. Can this be the Christ?" ³⁰They went out of the town and were coming to him.

³¹Meanwhile the disciples were urging him, saying, "Rabbi, eat." ³²But he said to them, "I have food to eat that you do not know about." ³³So the disciples said to one another, "Has anyone brought him something to eat?" ³⁴Jesus said to them, "My food is to do the will of him who sent me and to accomplish his work. ³⁵Do you not say, 'There are yet four months, then comes the harvest'? Look, I tell you, lift up your eyes, and see that the fields are white for harvest. ³⁶Already the one who reaps is receiving wages and gathering fruit for eternal life, so that sower and reaper may rejoice together. ³⁷For here the saying holds true, 'One sows and another reaps.' ³⁸I sent you to reap that for which you did not labour. Others have laboured, and you have entered into their labour."

³⁹Many Samaritans from that town believed in him because of the woman's testimony, "He told me all that I ever did." ⁴⁰So when the Samaritans came to him, they asked him to stay with them, and he stayed there two days. ⁴¹And many more believed because of his word. ⁴²They said to the woman, "It is no longer because of what you said that we believe, for we have heard for ourselves, and we know that this is indeed the Saviour of the world."

⁴³After the two days he departed for Galilee. ⁴⁴(For Jesus himself had testified that a prophet has no honour in his own home town.) ⁴⁵So when he came to Galilee, the Galileans welcomed him, having seen all that he had done in Jerusalem at the feast. For they too had gone to the feast.

ᵃThat is, about noon   ᵇGreek *for ever*

JESUS HEALS AN OFFICIAL'S SON

46So he came again to Cana in Galilee, where he had made the water wine. And at Capernaum there was an official whose son was ill. **47**When this man heard that Jesus had come from Judea to Galilee, he went to him and asked him to come down and heal his son, for he was at the point of death. **48**So Jesus said to him, "Unless you[a] see signs and wonders you will not believe." **49**The official said to him, "Sir, come down before my child dies." **50**Jesus said to him, "Go; your son will live." The man believed the word that Jesus spoke to him and went on his way. **51**As he was going down, his servants[b] met him and told him that his son was recovering. **52**So he asked them the hour when he began to get better, and they said to him, "Yesterday at the seventh hour[c] the fever left him." **53**The father knew that was the hour when Jesus had said to him, "Your son will live." And he himself believed, and all his household. **54**This was now the second sign that Jesus did when he had come from Judea to Galilee.

THE HEALING AT THE POOL ON THE SABBATH

5 After this there was a feast of the Jews, and Jesus went up to Jerusalem. **2**Now there is in Jerusalem by the Sheep Gate a pool, in Aramaic[d] called Bethesda,[e] which has five roofed colonnades. **3**In these lay a multitude of invalids—blind, lame, and paralysed.[f] **5**One man was there who had been an invalid for thirty-eight years. **6**When Jesus saw him lying there and knew that he had already been there a long time, he said to him, "Do you want to be healed?" **7**The sick man answered him, "Sir, I have no one to put me into the pool when the water is stirred up, and while I am going another steps down before me." **8**Jesus said to him, "Get up, take up your bed, and walk." **9**And at once the man was healed, and he took up his bed and walked.

Now that day was the Sabbath. **10**So the Jews[g] said to the man who had been healed, "It is the Sabbath, and it is not lawful for you to take up your bed." **11**But he answered them, "The man who healed me, that man said to me, 'Take up your bed, and walk.'" **12**They asked him, "Who is the man who said to you, 'Take up your bed and walk'?" **13**Now the man who had been healed did not know who it was, for Jesus had withdrawn, as there was a crowd in the place. **14**Afterwards Jesus found him in the temple and said to him, "See, you are well! Sin no more, that nothing worse may happen to you." **15**The man went away and told the Jews that it was Jesus who had healed him. **16**And this was why the Jews were persecuting Jesus, because he was doing these things on the Sabbath. **17**But Jesus answered them, "My Father is working until now, and I am working."

JESUS IS EQUAL WITH GOD

18This was why the Jews were seeking all the more to kill him, because not only was he breaking the Sabbath, but he was even calling God his own Father, making himself equal with God.

THE AUTHORITY OF THE SON

19So Jesus said to them, "Truly, truly, I say to you, the Son can do nothing of his own accord, but only what he sees the Father doing. For whatever the Father[h] does, that the Son does likewise. **20**For the Father loves the Son and shows him all that he himself is doing. And greater works than these will he show him, so that you may marvel. **21**For as the Father raises the dead and gives them life, so also the Son gives life to whom he will. **22**For the Father judges no one, but has given all judgement to the Son, **23**that all may honour the Son, just as they honour the Father. Whoever does not honour the Son does not honour the Father who sent him. **24**Truly, truly, I say to you, whoever hears my word and believes him who sent me has eternal life. He does not come into judgement, but has passed from death to life.

25"Truly, truly, I say to you, an hour is coming, and is now here, when the dead will hear the voice of the Son of God, and those who hear will live. **26**For as the Father has life in himself, so he has granted the Son also to have life in himself. **27**And he has given him authority to execute judgement, because he is the Son of Man. **28**Do not marvel at this, for an hour is coming when all who are in the tombs will hear his voice **29**and come out, those who have done good to the resurrection of life, and those who have done evil to the resurrection of judgement.

---

[a]The Greek for *you* is plural; twice in this verse [b]Or *bondservants* [c]That is, at 1 P.M. [d]Or *Hebrew* [e]Some manuscripts *Bethsaida* [f]Some manuscripts insert, wholly or in part, *waiting for the moving of the water;* [4]*for an angel of the Lord went down at certain seasons into the pool, and stirred the water: whoever stepped in first after the stirring of the water was healed of whatever disease he had* [g]The Greek word *Ioudaioi* refers specifically here to Jewish religious leaders, and others under their influence, who opposed Jesus in that time; also verses 15, 16, 18 [h]Greek *he*

WITNESSES TO JESUS

³⁰"I can do nothing on my own. As I hear, I judge, and my judgement is just, because I seek not my own will but the will of him who sent me. ³¹If I alone bear witness about myself, my testimony is not true. ³²There is another who bears witness about me, and I know that the testimony that he bears about me is true. ³³You sent to John, and he has borne witness to the truth. ³⁴Not that the testimony that I receive is from man, but I say these things so that you may be saved. ³⁵He was a burning and shining lamp, and you were willing to rejoice for a while in his light. ³⁶But the testimony that I have is greater than that of John. For the works that the Father has given me to accomplish, the very works that I am doing, bear witness about me that the Father has sent me. ³⁷And the Father who sent me has himself borne witness about me. His voice you have never heard, his form you have never seen, ³⁸and you do not have his word abiding in you, for you do not believe the one whom he has sent. ³⁹You search the Scriptures because you think that in them you have eternal life; and it is they that bear witness about me, ⁴⁰yet you refuse to come to me that you may have life. ⁴¹I do not receive glory from people. ⁴²But I know that you do not have the love of God within you. ⁴³I have come in my Father's name, and you do not receive me. If another comes in his own name, you will receive him. ⁴⁴How can you believe, when you receive glory from one another and do not seek the glory that comes from the only God? ⁴⁵Do not think that I will accuse you to the Father. There is one who accuses you: Moses, on whom you have set your hope. ⁴⁶For if you believed Moses, you would believe me; for he wrote of me. ⁴⁷But if you do not believe his writings, how will you believe my words?"

JESUS FEEDS THE FIVE THOUSAND

6 After this Jesus went away to the other side of the Sea of Galilee, which is the Sea of Tiberias. ²And a large crowd was following him, because they saw the signs that he was doing on the sick. ³Jesus went up on the mountain, and there he sat down with his disciples. ⁴Now the Passover, the feast of the Jews, was at hand. ⁵Lifting up his eyes, then, and seeing that a large crowd was coming towards him, Jesus said to Philip, "Where are we to buy bread, so that these people may eat?" ⁶He said this to test him, for he himself knew what he would do. ⁷Philip answered him, "Two hundred denarii*ᵃ* worth of bread would not be enough for each of them to get a little." ⁸One of his disciples, Andrew, Simon Peter's brother, said to him, ⁹"There is a boy here who has five barley loaves and two fish, but what are they for so many?" ¹⁰Jesus said, "Make the people sit down." Now there was much grass in the place. So the men sat down, about five thousand in number. ¹¹Jesus then took the loaves, and when he had given thanks, he distributed them to those who were seated. So also the fish, as much as they wanted. ¹²And when they had eaten their fill, he told his disciples, "Gather up the leftover fragments, that nothing may be lost." ¹³So they gathered them up and filled twelve baskets with fragments from the five barley loaves left by those who had eaten. ¹⁴When the people saw the sign that he had done, they said, "This is indeed the Prophet who is to come into the world!"

¹⁵Perceiving then that they were about to come and take him by force to make him king, Jesus withdrew again to the mountain by himself.

JESUS WALKS ON WATER

¹⁶When evening came, his disciples went down to the lake, ¹⁷got into a boat, and started across the lake to Capernaum. It was now dark, and Jesus had not yet come to them. ¹⁸The lake became rough because a strong wind was blowing. ¹⁹When they had rowed about three or four miles,*ᵇ* they saw Jesus walking on the lake and coming near the boat, and they were frightened. ²⁰But he said to them, "It is I; do not be afraid." ²¹Then they were glad to take him into the boat, and immediately the boat was at the land to which they were going.

I AM THE BREAD OF LIFE

²²On the next day the crowd that remained on the other side of the lake saw that there had been only one boat there, and that Jesus had not entered the boat with his disciples, but that his disciples had gone away alone. ²³Other boats from Tiberias came near the place where they had eaten the bread after the Lord had given thanks. ²⁴So when the crowd saw that Jesus was not there, nor his disciples, they themselves got into the boats and went to Capernaum, seeking Jesus.

ᵃA denarius was a day's wage for a labourer *ᵇGreek twenty-five or thirty stadia; a stadion was about 607 feet or 185 metres*

²⁵When they found him on the other side of the lake, they said to him, "Rabbi, when did you come here?" ²⁶Jesus answered them, "Truly, truly, I say to you, you are seeking me, not because you saw signs, but because you ate your fill of the loaves. ²⁷Do not work for the food that perishes, but for the food that endures to eternal life, which the Son of Man will give to you. For on him God the Father has set his seal." ²⁸Then they said to him, "What must we do, to be doing the works of God?" ²⁹Jesus answered them, "This is the work of God, that you believe in him whom he has sent." ³⁰So they said to him, "Then what sign do you do, that we may see and believe you? What work do you perform? ³¹Our fathers ate the manna in the wilderness; as it is written, 'He gave them bread from heaven to eat.'" ³²Jesus then said to them, "Truly, truly, I say to you, it was not Moses who gave you the bread from heaven, but my Father gives you the true bread from heaven. ³³For the bread of God is he who comes down from heaven and gives life to the world." ³⁴They said to him, "Sir, give us this bread always."

³⁵Jesus said to them, "I am the bread of life; whoever comes to me shall not hunger, and whoever believes in me shall never thirst. ³⁶But I said to you that you have seen me and yet do not believe. ³⁷All that the Father gives me will come to me, and whoever comes to me I will never cast out. ³⁸For I have come down from heaven, not to do my own will but the will of him who sent me. ³⁹And this is the will of him who sent me, that I should lose nothing of all that he has given me, but raise it up on the last day. ⁴⁰For this is the will of my Father, that everyone who looks on the Son and believes in him should have eternal life, and I will raise him up on the last day."

⁴¹So the Jews grumbled about him, because he said, "I am the bread that came down from heaven." ⁴²They said, "Is not this Jesus, the son of Joseph, whose father and mother we know? How does he now say, 'I have come down from heaven'?" ⁴³Jesus answered them, "Do not grumble among yourselves. ⁴⁴No one can come to me unless the Father who sent me draws him. And I will raise him up on the last day. ⁴⁵It is written in the Prophets, 'And they will all be taught by God.' Everyone who has heard and learned from the Father comes to me— ⁴⁶not that anyone has seen the Father except he who is from God; he has seen the Father. ⁴⁷Truly, truly, I say to you, whoever believes has eternal life. ⁴⁸I am the bread of life. ⁴⁹Your fathers ate the manna in the wilderness, and they died. ⁵⁰This is the bread that comes down from heaven, so that one may eat of it and not die. ⁵¹I am the living bread that came down from heaven. If anyone eats of this bread, he will live for ever. And the bread that I will give for the life of the world is my flesh."

⁵²The Jews then disputed among themselves, saying, "How can this man give us his flesh to eat?" ⁵³So Jesus said to them, "Truly, truly, I say to you, unless you eat the flesh of the Son of Man and drink his blood, you have no life in you. ⁵⁴Whoever feeds on my flesh and drinks my blood has eternal life, and I will raise him up on the last day. ⁵⁵For my flesh is true food, and my blood is true drink. ⁵⁶Whoever feeds on my flesh and drinks my blood abides in me, and I in him. ⁵⁷As the living Father sent me, and I live because of the Father, so whoever feeds on me, he also will live because of me. ⁵⁸This is the bread that came down from heaven, not like the bread*ᵃ* the fathers ate, and died. Whoever feeds on this bread will live for ever." ⁵⁹Jesus*ᵇ* said these things in the synagogue, as he taught at Capernaum.

THE WORDS OF ETERNAL LIFE

⁶⁰When many of his disciples heard it, they said, "This is a hard saying; who can listen to it?" ⁶¹But Jesus, knowing in himself that his disciples were grumbling about this, said to them, "Do you take offence at this? ⁶²Then what if you were to see the Son of Man ascending to where he was before? ⁶³It is the Spirit who gives life; the flesh is no help at all. The words that I have spoken to you are spirit and life. ⁶⁴But there are some of you who do not believe." (For Jesus knew from the beginning who those were who did not believe, and who it was who would betray him.) ⁶⁵And he said, "This is why I told you that no one can come to me unless it is granted him by the Father."

⁶⁶After this many of his disciples turned back and no longer walked with him. ⁶⁷So Jesus said to the twelve, "Do you want to go away as well?" ⁶⁸Simon Peter answered him, "Lord, to whom shall we go? You have the words of eternal life, ⁶⁹and we have believed, and have come to know, that you are the Holy One of God." ⁷⁰Jesus answered them, "Did I

---

*ᵃ*Greek lacks *the bread*   *ᵇ*Greek *He*

not choose you, the twelve? And yet one of you is a devil." ⁷¹He spoke of Judas the son of Simon Iscariot, for he, one of the twelve, was going to betray him.

JESUS AT THE FEAST OF BOOTHS

7 After this Jesus went about in Galilee. He would not go about in Judea, because the Jews[a] were seeking to kill him. ²Now the Jews' Feast of Booths was at hand. ³So his brothers[b] said to him, "Leave here and go to Judea, that your disciples also may see the works you are doing. ⁴For no one works in secret if he seeks to be known openly. If you do these things, show yourself to the world." ⁵For not even his brothers believed in him. ⁶Jesus said to them, "My time has not yet come, but your time is always here. ⁷The world cannot hate you, but it hates me because I testify about it that its works are evil. ⁸You go up to the feast. I am not[c] going up to this feast, for my time has not yet fully come." ⁹After saying this, he remained in Galilee.

¹⁰But after his brothers had gone up to the feast, then he also went up, not publicly but in private. ¹¹The Jews were looking for him at the feast, and saying, "Where is he?" ¹²And there was much muttering about him among the people. While some said, "He is a good man", others said, "No, he is leading the people astray." ¹³Yet for fear of the Jews no one spoke openly of him.

¹⁴About the middle of the feast Jesus went up into the temple and began teaching. ¹⁵The Jews therefore marvelled, saying, "How is it that this man has learning,[d] when he has never studied?" ¹⁶So Jesus answered them, "My teaching is not mine, but his who sent me. ¹⁷If anyone's will is to do God's[e] will, he will know whether the teaching is from God or whether I am speaking on my own authority. ¹⁸The one who speaks on his own authority seeks his own glory; but the one who seeks the glory of him who sent him is true, and in him there is no falsehood. ¹⁹Has not Moses given you the law? Yet none of you keeps the law. Why do you seek to kill me?" ²⁰The crowd answered, "You have a demon! Who is seeking to kill you?" ²¹Jesus answered them, "I did one work, and you all marvel at it. ²²Moses gave you circumcision (not that it is from Moses, but from the fathers), and you circumcise a man on the Sabbath. ²³If on the Sabbath a man receives circumcision, so that the law of Moses may not be broken, are you angry with me because on the Sabbath I made a man's whole body well? ²⁴Do not judge by appearances, but judge with right judgement."

CAN THIS BE THE CHRIST?

²⁵Some of the people of Jerusalem therefore said, "Is not this the man whom they seek to kill? ²⁶And here he is, speaking openly, and they say nothing to him! Can it be that the authorities really know that this is the Christ? ²⁷But we know where this man comes from, and when the Christ appears, no one will know where he comes from." ²⁸So Jesus proclaimed, as he taught in the temple, "You know me, and you know where I come from. But I have not come of my own accord. He who sent me is true, and him you do not know. ²⁹I know him, for I come from him, and he sent me." ³⁰So they were seeking to arrest him, but no one laid a hand on him, because his hour had not yet come. ³¹Yet many of the people believed in him. They said, "When the Christ appears, will he do more signs than this man has done?"

OFFICERS SENT TO ARREST JESUS

³²The Pharisees heard the crowd muttering these things about him, and the chief priests and Pharisees sent officers to arrest him. ³³Jesus then said, "I will be with you a little longer, and then I am going to him who sent me. ³⁴You will seek me and you will not find me. Where I am you cannot come." ³⁵The Jews said to one another, "Where does this man intend to go that we will not find him? Does he intend to go to the Dispersion among the Greeks and teach the Greeks? ³⁶What does he mean by saying, 'You will seek me and you will not find me', and, 'Where I am you cannot come'?"

RIVERS OF LIVING WATER

³⁷On the last day of the feast, the great day, Jesus stood up and cried out, "If anyone thirsts, let him come to me and drink. ³⁸Whoever believes in me, as[f] the Scripture has said, 'Out of his heart will flow rivers of living water.' " ³⁹Now this he said about the Spirit, whom those who believed in him were to receive, for as yet the Spirit had not been given, because Jesus was not yet glorified.

---

[a]Or *Judeans*; Greek *Ioudaioi* probably refers here to Jewish religious leaders, and others under their influence, in that time [b]Or *brothers and sisters*; also verses 5, 10 [c]Some manuscripts add *yet* [d]Or *this man knows his letters* [e]Greek *his* [f]Or *let him come to me, and let him who believes in me drink. As*

DIVISION AMONG THE PEOPLE

40When they heard these words, some of the people said, "This really is the Prophet." **41**Others said, "This is the Christ." But some said, "Is the Christ to come from Galilee? **42**Has not the Scripture said that the Christ comes from the offspring of David, and comes from Bethlehem, the village where David was?" **43**So there was a division among the people over him. **44**Some of them wanted to arrest him, but no one laid hands on him.

45The officers then came to the chief priests and Pharisees, who said to them, "Why did you not bring him?" **46**The officers answered, "No one ever spoke like this man!" **47**The Pharisees answered them, "Have you also been deceived? **48**Have any of the authorities or the Pharisees believed in him? **49**But this crowd that does not know the law is accursed." **50**Nicodemus, who had gone to him before, and who was one of them, said to them, **51**"Does our law judge a man without first giving him a hearing and learning what he does?" **52**They replied, "Are you from Galilee too? Search and see that no prophet arises from Galilee."

[THE EARLIEST MANUSCRIPTS DO NOT INCLUDE 7:53–8:11.][a]

THE WOMAN CAUGHT IN ADULTERY

8 **53**[[They went each to his own house, **1**but Jesus went to the Mount of Olives. **2**Early in the morning he came again to the temple. All the people came to him, and he sat down and taught them. **3**The scribes and the Pharisees brought a woman who had been caught in adultery, and placing her in the midst **4**they said to him, "Teacher, this woman has been caught in the act of adultery. **5**Now in the Law, Moses commanded us to stone such women. So what do you say?" **6**This they said to test him, that they might have some charge to bring against him. Jesus bent down and wrote with his finger on the ground. **7**And as they continued to ask him, he stood up and said to them, "Let him who is without sin among you be the first to throw a stone at her." **8**And once more he bent down and wrote on the ground. **9**But when they heard it, they went away one by one, beginning with the older ones, and Jesus was left alone with the woman standing before him. **10**Jesus stood up and said to her, "Woman, where are they? Has no one condemned you?" **11**She said, "No one, Lord." And Jesus said, "Neither do I condemn you; go, and from now on sin no more."]]

I AM THE LIGHT OF THE WORLD

12Again Jesus spoke to them, saying, "I am the light of the world. Whoever follows me will not walk in darkness, but will have the light of life." **13**So the Pharisees said to him, "You are bearing witness about yourself; your testimony is not true." **14**Jesus answered, "Even if I do bear witness about myself, my testimony is true, for I know where I came from and where I am going, but you do not know where I come from or where I am going. **15**You judge according to the flesh; I judge no one. **16**Yet even if I do judge, my judgement is true, for it is not I alone who judge, but I and the Father[b] who sent me. **17**In your Law it is written that the testimony of two people is true. **18**I am the one who bears witness about myself, and the Father who sent me bears witness about me." **19**They said to him therefore, "Where is your Father?" Jesus answered, "You know neither me nor my Father. If you knew me, you would know my Father also." **20**These words he spoke in the treasury, as he taught in the temple; but no one arrested him, because his hour had not yet come.

21So he said to them again, "I am going away, and you will seek me, and you will die in your sin. Where I am going, you cannot come." **22**So the Jews said, "Will he kill himself, since he says, 'Where I am going, you cannot come'?" **23**He said to them, "You are from below; I am from above. You are of this world; I am not of this world. **24**I told you that you would die in your sins, for unless you believe that I am he you will die in your sins." **25**So they said to him, "Who are you?" Jesus said to them, "Just what I have been telling you from the beginning. **26**I have much to say about you and much to judge, but he who sent me is true, and I declare to the world what I have heard from him." **27**They did not understand that he had been speaking to them about the Father. **28**So Jesus said to them, "When you have lifted up the Son of Man, then you will know that I am he, and that I do nothing on my own authority, but speak just as the Father taught me. **29**And he who sent me is with me. He has not left me alone, for I always do the things that are

---

[a]Some manuscripts do not include 7:53–8:11; others add the passage here or after 7:36 or after 21:25 or after Luke 21:38, with variations in the text [b]Some manuscripts *he*

pleasing to him." ³⁰As he was saying these things, many believed in him.

THE TRUTH WILL SET YOU FREE

³¹So Jesus said to the Jews who had believed him, "If you abide in my word, you are truly my disciples, ³²and you will know the truth, and the truth will set you free." ³³They answered him, "We are offspring of Abraham and have never been enslaved to anyone. How is it that you say, 'You will become free'?"

³⁴Jesus answered them, "Truly, truly, I say to you, everyone who practises sin is a slave^a to sin. ³⁵The slave does not remain in the house for ever; the son remains for ever. ³⁶So if the Son sets you free, you will be free indeed. ³⁷I know that you are offspring of Abraham; yet you seek to kill me because my word finds no place in you. ³⁸I speak of what I have seen with my Father, and you do what you have heard from your father."

YOU ARE OF YOUR FATHER THE DEVIL

³⁹They answered him, "Abraham is our father." Jesus said to them, "If you were Abraham's children, you would be doing the works Abraham did, ⁴⁰but now you seek to kill me, a man who has told you the truth that I heard from God. This is not what Abraham did. ⁴¹You are doing the works your father did." They said to him, "We were not born of sexual immorality. We have one Father—even God." ⁴²Jesus said to them, "If God were your Father, you would love me, for I came from God and I am here. I came not of my own accord, but he sent me. ⁴³Why do you not understand what I say? It is because you cannot bear to hear my word. ⁴⁴You are of your father the devil, and your will is to do your father's desires. He was a murderer from the beginning, and does not stand in the truth, because there is no truth in him. When he lies, he speaks out of his own character, for he is a liar and the father of lies. ⁴⁵But because I tell the truth, you do not believe me. ⁴⁶Which one of you convicts me of sin? If I tell the truth, why do you not believe me? ⁴⁷Whoever is of God hears the words of God. The reason why you do not hear them is that you are not of God."

BEFORE ABRAHAM WAS, I AM

⁴⁸The Jews answered him, "Are we not right in saying that you are a Samaritan and have a demon?" ⁴⁹Jesus answered, "I do not have a demon, but I honour my Father, and you dishonour me. ⁵⁰Yet I do not seek my own glory; there is One who seeks it, and he is the judge. ⁵¹Truly, truly, I say to you, if anyone keeps my word, he will never see death." ⁵²The Jews said to him, "Now we know that you have a demon! Abraham died, as did the prophets, yet you say, 'If anyone keeps my word, he will never taste death.' ⁵³Are you greater than our father Abraham, who died? And the prophets died! Who do you make yourself out to be?" ⁵⁴Jesus answered, "If I glorify myself, my glory is nothing. It is my Father who glorifies me, of whom you say, 'He is our God.'^{b} ⁵⁵But you have not known him. I know him. If I were to say that I do not know him, I would be a liar like you, but I do know him and I keep his word. ⁵⁶Your father Abraham rejoiced that he would see my day. He saw it and was glad." ⁵⁷So the Jews said to him, "You are not yet fifty years old, and have you seen Abraham?"^{c} ⁵⁸Jesus said to them, "Truly, truly, I say to you, before Abraham was, I am." ⁵⁹So they picked up stones to throw at him, but Jesus hid himself and went out of the temple.

JESUS HEALS A MAN BORN BLIND

9 As he passed by, he saw a man blind from birth. ²And his disciples asked him, "Rabbi, who sinned, this man or his parents, that he was born blind?" ³Jesus answered, "It was not that this man sinned, or his parents, but that the works of God might be displayed in him. ⁴We must work the works of him who sent me while it is day; night is coming, when no one can work. ⁵As long as I am in the world, I am the light of the world." ⁶Having said these things, he spat on the ground and made mud with the saliva. Then he anointed the man's eyes with the mud ⁷and said to him, "Go, wash in the pool of Siloam" (which means Sent). So he went and washed and came back seeing.

⁸The neighbours and those who had seen him before as a beggar were saying, "Is this not the man who used to sit and beg?" ⁹Some said, "It is he." Others said, "No, but he is like him." He kept saying, "I am the man." ¹⁰So they said to him, "Then how were your eyes opened?" ¹¹He answered, "The man called Jesus made mud and anointed my eyes and said to me, 'Go to Siloam and wash.' So I went and washed and received my sight." ¹²They said to him, "Where is he?" He said, "I do not know."

---

^{a}For the contextual rendering of the Greek word *doulos*, see Preface; also verse 35 ^{b}Some manuscripts *your God* ^{c}Some manuscripts *has Abraham seen you?*

¹³They brought to the Pharisees the man who had formerly been blind. ¹⁴Now it was a Sabbath day when Jesus made the mud and opened his eyes. ¹⁵So the Pharisees again asked him how he had received his sight. And he said to them, "He put mud on my eyes, and I washed, and I see." ¹⁶Some of the Pharisees said, "This man is not from God, for he does not keep the Sabbath." But others said, "How can a man who is a sinner do such signs?" And there was a division among them. ¹⁷So they said again to the blind man, "What do you say about him, since he has opened your eyes?" He said, "He is a prophet."

¹⁸The Jews[a] did not believe that he had been blind and had received his sight, until they called the parents of the man who had received his sight ¹⁹and asked them, "Is this your son, who you say was born blind? How then does he now see?" ²⁰His parents answered, "We know that this is our son and that he was born blind. ²¹But how he now sees we do not know, nor do we know who opened his eyes. Ask him; he is of age. He will speak for himself." ²²(His parents said these things because they feared the Jews, for the Jews had already agreed that if anyone should confess Jesus[b] to be Christ, he was to be put out of the synagogue.) ²³Therefore his parents said, "He is of age; ask him."

²⁴So for the second time they called the man who had been blind and said to him, "Give glory to God. We know that this man is a sinner." ²⁵He answered, "Whether he is a sinner I do not know. One thing I do know, that though I was blind, now I see." ²⁶They said to him, "What did he do to you? How did he open your eyes?" ²⁷He answered them, "I have told you already, and you would not listen. Why do you want to hear it again? Do you also want to become his disciples?" ²⁸And they reviled him, saying, "You are his disciple, but we are disciples of Moses. ²⁹We know that God has spoken to Moses, but as for this man, we do not know where he comes from." ³⁰The man answered, "Why, this is an amazing thing! You do not know where he comes from, and yet he opened my eyes. ³¹We know that God does not listen to sinners, but if anyone is a worshipper of God and does his will, God listens to him. ³²Never since the world began has it been heard that anyone opened the eyes of a man born blind. ³³If this man were not from God, he could do nothing." ³⁴They answered him, "You were born in utter sin, and would you teach us?" And they cast him out.

³⁵Jesus heard that they had cast him out, and having found him he said, "Do you believe in the Son of Man?"[c] ³⁶He answered, "And who is he, sir, that I may believe in him?" ³⁷Jesus said to him, "You have seen him, and it is he who is speaking to you." ³⁸He said, "Lord, I believe", and he worshipped him. ³⁹Jesus said, "For judgement I came into this world, that those who do not see may see, and those who see may become blind." ⁴⁰Some of the Pharisees near him heard these things, and said to him, "Are we also blind?" ⁴¹Jesus said to them, "If you were blind, you would have no guilt;[d] but now that you say, 'We see', your guilt remains.

I AM THE GOOD SHEPHERD

10 "Truly, truly, I say to you, he who does not enter the sheepfold by the door but climbs in by another way, that man is a thief and a robber. ²But he who enters by the door is the shepherd of the sheep. ³To him the gatekeeper opens. The sheep hear his voice, and he calls his own sheep by name and leads them out. ⁴When he has brought out all his own, he goes before them, and the sheep follow him, for they know his voice. ⁵A stranger they will not follow, but they will flee from him, for they do not know the voice of strangers." ⁶This figure of speech Jesus used with them, but they did not understand what he was saying to them.

⁷So Jesus again said to them, "Truly, truly, I say to you, I am the door of the sheep. ⁸All who came before me are thieves and robbers, but the sheep did not listen to them. ⁹I am the door. If anyone enters by me, he will be saved and will go in and out and find pasture. ¹⁰The thief comes only to steal and kill and destroy. I came that they may have life and have it abundantly. ¹¹I am the good shepherd. The good shepherd lays down his life for the sheep. ¹²He who is a hired hand and not a shepherd, who does not own the sheep, sees the wolf coming and leaves the sheep and flees, and the wolf snatches them and scatters them. ¹³He flees because he is a hired hand and cares nothing for the sheep. ¹⁴I am the good shepherd. I know my own and my own know me, ¹⁵just as the Father knows me and I know the Father; and I lay down my life for the sheep. ¹⁶And I have other

---

[a]Greek *Ioudaioi* probably refers here to Jewish religious leaders, and others under their influence, in that time; also verse 22 [b]Greek *him*
[c]Some manuscripts *the Son of God* [d]Greek *you would not have sin*

sheep that are not of this fold. I must bring them also, and they will listen to my voice. So there will be one flock, one shepherd. [17]For this reason the Father loves me, because I lay down my life that I may take it up again. [18]No one takes it from me, but I lay it down of my own accord. I have authority to lay it down, and I have authority to take it up again. This charge I have received from my Father."

[19]There was again a division among the Jews because of these words. [20]Many of them said, "He has a demon, and is insane; why listen to him?" [21]Others said, "These are not the words of one who is oppressed by a demon. Can a demon open the eyes of the blind?"

I AND THE FATHER ARE ONE

[22]At that time the Feast of Dedication took place at Jerusalem. It was winter, [23]and Jesus was walking in the temple, in the colonnade of Solomon. [24]So the Jews gathered around him and said to him, "How long will you keep us in suspense? If you are the Christ, tell us plainly." [25]Jesus answered them, "I told you, and you do not believe. The works that I do in my Father's name bear witness about me, [26]but you do not believe because you are not among my sheep. [27]My sheep hear my voice, and I know them, and they follow me. [28]I give them eternal life, and they will never perish, and no one will snatch them out of my hand. [29]My Father, who has given them to me,[a] is greater than all, and no one is able to snatch them out of the Father's hand. [30]I and the Father are one."

[31]The Jews picked up stones again to stone him. [32]Jesus answered them, "I have shown you many good works from the Father; for which of them are you going to stone me?" [33]The Jews answered him, "It is not for a good work that we are going to stone you but for blasphemy, because you, being a man, make yourself God." [34]Jesus answered them, "Is it not written in your Law, 'I said, you are gods'? [35]If he called them gods to whom the word of God came — and Scripture cannot be broken — [36]do you say of him whom the Father consecrated and sent into the world, 'You are blaspheming', because I said, 'I am the Son of God'? [37]If I am not doing the works of my Father, then do not believe me; [38]but if I do them, even though you do not believe me, believe the works, that you may know and understand that the Father is in me and I am in the Father." [39]Again they sought to arrest him, but he escaped from their hands.

[40]He went away again across the Jordan to the place where John had been baptizing at first, and there he remained. [41]And many came to him. And they said, "John did no sign, but everything that John said about this man was true." [42]And many believed in him there.

THE DEATH OF LAZARUS

11 Now a certain man was ill, Lazarus of Bethany, the village of Mary and her sister Martha. [2]It was Mary who anointed the Lord with ointment and wiped his feet with her hair, whose brother Lazarus was ill. [3]So the sisters sent to him, saying, "Lord, he whom you love is ill." [4]But when Jesus heard it he said, "This illness does not lead to death. It is for the glory of God, so that the Son of God may be glorified through it."

[5]Now Jesus loved Martha and her sister and Lazarus. [6]So, when he heard that Lazarus[b] was ill, he stayed two days longer in the place where he was. [7]Then after this he said to the disciples, "Let us go to Judea again." [8]The disciples said to him "Rabbi, the Jews were just now seeking to stone you, and are you going there again?" [9]Jesus answered, "Are there not twelve hours in the day? If anyone walks in the day, he does not stumble, because he sees the light of this world. [10]But if anyone walks in the night, he stumbles, because the light is not in him." [11]After saying these things, he said to them, "Our friend Lazarus has fallen asleep, but I go to awaken him." [12]The disciples said to him, "Lord, if he has fallen asleep, he will recover." [13]Now Jesus had spoken of his death, but they thought that he meant taking rest in sleep. [14]Then Jesus told them plainly, "Lazarus has died, [15]and for your sake I am glad that I was not there, so that you may believe. But let us go to him." [16]So Thomas, called the Twin,[c] said to his fellow disciples, "Let us also go, that we may die with him."

I AM THE RESURRECTION AND THE LIFE

[17]Now when Jesus came, he found that Lazarus had already been in the tomb four days. [18]Bethany was near Jerusalem, about two miles[d] off, [19]and many of the Jews had come to Martha and Mary to console them concerning their brother. [20]So when Martha

---

[a]Some manuscripts *What my Father has given to me* [b]Greek *he*; also verse 17 [c]Greek *Didymus* [d]Greek *fifteen stadia*; a *stadion* was about 607 feet or 185 metres

heard that Jesus was coming, she went and met him, but Mary remained seated in the house. ²¹Martha said to Jesus, "Lord, if you had been here, my brother would not have died. ²²But even now I know that whatever you ask from God, God will give you." ²³Jesus said to her, "Your brother will rise again." ²⁴Martha said to him, "I know that he will rise again in the resurrection on the last day." ²⁵Jesus said to her, "I am the resurrection and the life.ᵃ Whoever believes in me, though he die, yet shall he live, ²⁶and everyone who lives and believes in me shall never die. Do you believe this?" ²⁷She said to him, "Yes, Lord; I believe that you are the Christ, the Son of God, who is coming into the world."

JESUS WEEPS

²⁸When she had said this, she went and called her sister Mary, saying in private, "The Teacher is here and is calling for you." ²⁹And when she heard it, she rose quickly and went to him. ³⁰Now Jesus had not yet come into the village, but was still in the place where Martha had met him. ³¹When the Jews who were with her in the house, consoling her, saw Mary rise quickly and go out, they followed her, supposing that she was going to the tomb to weep there. ³²Now when Mary came to where Jesus was and saw him, she fell at his feet, saying to him, "Lord, if you had been here, my brother would not have died." ³³When Jesus saw her weeping, and the Jews who had come with her also weeping, he was deeply movedᵇ in his spirit and greatly troubled. ³⁴And he said, "Where have you laid him?" They said to him, "Lord, come and see." ³⁵Jesus wept. ³⁶So the Jews said, "See how he loved him!" ³⁷But some of them said, "Could not he who opened the eyes of the blind man also have kept this man from dying?"

JESUS RAISES LAZARUS

³⁸Then Jesus, deeply moved again, came to the tomb. It was a cave, and a stone lay against it. ³⁹Jesus said, "Take away the stone." Martha, the sister of the dead man, said to him, "Lord, by this time there will be an odour, for he has been dead four days." ⁴⁰Jesus said to her, "Did I not tell you that if you believed you would see the glory of God?" ⁴¹So they took away the stone. And Jesus lifted up his eyes and said, "Father, I thank you that you have heard me. ⁴²I knew that you always hear me, but I said this on account of the people standing around, that they may believe that you sent me." ⁴³When he had said these things, he cried out with a loud voice, "Lazarus, come out." ⁴⁴The man who had died came out, his hands and feet bound with linen strips, and his face wrapped with a cloth. Jesus said to them, "Unbind him, and let him go."

THE PLOT TO KILL JESUS

⁴⁵Many of the Jews therefore, who had come with Mary and had seen what he did, believed in him, ⁴⁶but some of them went to the Pharisees and told them what Jesus had done. ⁴⁷So the chief priests and the Pharisees gathered the council and said, "What are we to do? For this man performs many signs. ⁴⁸If we let him go on like this, everyone will believe in him, and the Romans will come and take away both our place and our nation." ⁴⁹But one of them, Caiaphas, who was high priest that year, said to them, "You know nothing at all. ⁵⁰Nor do you understand that it is better for you that one man should die for the people, not that the whole nation should perish." ⁵¹He did not say this of his own accord, but being high priest that year he prophesied that Jesus would die for the nation, ⁵²and not for the nation only, but also to gather into one the children of God who are scattered abroad. ⁵³So from that day on they made plans to put him to death.

⁵⁴Jesus therefore no longer walked openly among the Jews, but went from there to the region near the wilderness, to a town called Ephraim, and there he stayed with the disciples.

⁵⁵Now the Passover of the Jews was at hand, and many went up from the country to Jerusalem before the Passover to purify themselves. ⁵⁶They were looking forᶜ Jesus and saying to one another as they stood in the temple, "What do you think? That he will not come to the feast at all?" ⁵⁷Now the chief priests and the Pharisees had given orders that if anyone knew where he was, he should let them know, so that they might arrest him.

MARY ANOINTS JESUS AT BETHANY

12 Six days before the Passover, Jesus therefore came to Bethany, where Lazarus was, whom Jesus had raised from the dead. ²So they gave a dinner for him there. Martha served, and Lazarus was one of those reclining with him at table.

ᵃSome manuscripts omit *and the life* ᵇOr *was indignant*; also verse 38 ᶜGreek *were seeking for*

³Mary therefore took a pound[a] of expensive ointment made from pure nard, and anointed the feet of Jesus and wiped his feet with her hair. The house was filled with the fragrance of the perfume. ⁴But Judas Iscariot, one of his disciples (he who was about to betray him), said, ⁵"Why was this ointment not sold for three hundred denarii[b] and given to the poor?" ⁶He said this, not because he cared about the poor, but because he was a thief, and having charge of the money bag he used to help himself to what was put into it. ⁷Jesus said, "Leave her alone, so that she may keep it[c] for the day of my burial. ⁸For the poor you always have with you, but you do not always have me."

THE PLOT TO KILL LAZARUS

⁹When the large crowd of the Jews learned that Jesus[d] was there, they came, not only on account of him but also to see Lazarus, whom he had raised from the dead. ¹⁰So the chief priests made plans to put Lazarus to death as well, ¹¹because on account of him many of the Jews were going away and believing in Jesus.

THE TRIUMPHAL ENTRY

¹²The next day the large crowd that had come to the feast heard that Jesus was coming to Jerusalem. ¹³So they took branches of palm trees and went out to meet him, crying out, "Hosanna! Blessed is he who comes in the name of the Lord, even the King of Israel!" ¹⁴And Jesus found a young donkey and sat on it, just as it is written,

15   "Fear not, daughter of Zion;
    behold, your king is coming,
      sitting on a donkey's colt!"

¹⁶His disciples did not understand these things at first, but when Jesus was glorified, then they remembered that these things had been written about him and had been done to him. ¹⁷The crowd that had been with him when he called Lazarus out of the tomb and raised him from the dead continued to bear witness. ¹⁸The reason why the crowd went to meet him was that they heard he had done this sign. ¹⁹So the Pharisees said to one another, "You see that you are gaining nothing. Look, the world has gone after him."

SOME GREEKS SEEK JESUS

²⁰Now among those who went up to worship at the feast were some Greeks. ²¹So these came to Philip, who was from Bethsaida in Galilee, and asked him, "Sir, we wish to see Jesus." ²²Philip went and told Andrew; Andrew and Philip went and told Jesus. ²³And Jesus answered them, "The hour has come for the Son of Man to be glorified. ²⁴Truly, truly, I say to you, unless a grain of wheat falls into the earth and dies, it remains alone; but if it dies, it bears much fruit. ²⁵Whoever loves his life loses it, and whoever hates his life in this world will keep it for eternal life. ²⁶If anyone serves me, he must follow me; and where I am, there will my servant be also. If anyone serves me, the Father will honour him.

THE SON OF MAN MUST BE LIFTED UP

²⁷"Now is my soul troubled. And what shall I say? 'Father, save me from this hour'? But for this purpose I have come to this hour. ²⁸Father, glorify your name." Then a voice came from heaven: "I have glorified it, and I will glorify it again." ²⁹The crowd that stood there and heard it said that it had thundered. Others said, "An angel has spoken to him." ³⁰Jesus answered, "This voice has come for your sake, not mine. ³¹Now is the judgement of this world; now will the ruler of this world be cast out. ³²And I, when I am lifted up from the earth, will draw all people to myself." ³³He said this to show by what kind of death he was going to die. ³⁴So the crowd answered him, "We have heard from the Law that the Christ remains for ever. How can you say that the Son of Man must be lifted up? Who is this Son of Man?" ³⁵So Jesus said to them, "The light is among you for a little while longer. Walk while you have the light, lest darkness overtake you. The one who walks in the darkness does not know where he is going. ³⁶While you have the light, believe in the light, that you may become sons of light."

THE UNBELIEF OF THE PEOPLE

When Jesus had said these things, he departed and hid himself from them. ³⁷Though he had done so many signs before them, they still did not believe in him, ³⁸so that the word spoken by the prophet Isaiah might be fulfilled:

  "Lord, who has believed what
    he heard from us,

---

[a] Greek *litra*; a *litra* (or Roman pound) was equal to about 11 1/2 ounces or 327 grams   [b] A *denarius* was a day's wage for a labourer   [c] Or *Leave her alone; she intended to keep it*   [d] Greek *he*

and to whom has the arm of the
  Lord been revealed?"

[39]Therefore they could not believe. For again Isaiah said,

[40] "He has blinded their eyes
  and hardened their heart,
lest they see with their eyes,
  and understand with their
    heart, and turn,
  and I would heal them."

[41]Isaiah said these things because he saw his glory and spoke of him. [42]Nevertheless, many even of the authorities believed in him, but for fear of the Pharisees they did not confess it, so that they would not be put out of the synagogue; [43]for they loved the glory that comes from man more than the glory that comes from God.

JESUS CAME TO SAVE THE WORLD

[44]And Jesus cried out and said, "Whoever believes in me, believes not in me but in him who sent me. [45]And whoever sees me sees him who sent me. [46]I have come into the world as light, so that whoever believes in me may not remain in darkness. [47]If anyone hears my words and does not keep them, I do not judge him; for I did not come to judge the world but to save the world. [48]The one who rejects me and does not receive my words has a judge; the word that I have spoken will judge him on the last day. [49]For I have not spoken on my own authority, but the Father who sent me has himself given me a commandment—what to say and what to speak. [50]And I know that his commandment is eternal life. What I say, therefore, I say as the Father has told me."

JESUS WASHES THE DISCIPLES' FEET

13 Now before the Feast of the Passover, when Jesus knew that his hour had come to depart out of this world to the Father, having loved his own who were in the world, he loved them to the end. [2]During supper, when the devil had already put it into the heart of Judas Iscariot, Simon's son, to betray him, [3]Jesus, knowing that the Father had given all things into his hands, and that he had come from God and was going back to God, [4]rose from supper. He laid aside his outer garments, and taking a towel, tied it round his waist. [5]Then he poured water into a basin and began to wash the disciples' feet and to wipe them with the towel that was wrapped round him. [6]He came to Simon Peter, who said to him, "Lord, do you wash my feet?" [7]Jesus answered him, "What I am doing you do not understand now, but afterwards you will understand." [8]Peter said to him, "You shall never wash my feet." Jesus answered him, "If I do not wash you, you have no share with me." [9]Simon Peter said to him, "Lord, not my feet only but also my hands and my head!" [10]Jesus said to him, "The one who has bathed does not need to wash, except for his feet,[a] but is completely clean. And you[b] are clean, but not every one of you." [11]For he knew who was to betray him; that was why he said, "Not all of you are clean."

[12]When he had washed their feet and put on his outer garments and resumed his place, he said to them, "Do you understand what I have done to you? [13]You call me Teacher and Lord, and you are right, for so I am. [14]If I then, your Lord and Teacher, have washed your feet, you also ought to wash one another's feet. [15]For I have given you an example, that you also should do just as I have done to you. [16]Truly, truly, I say to you, a servant[c] is not greater than his master, nor is a messenger greater than the one who sent him. [17]If you know these things, blessed are you if you do them. [18]I am not speaking of all of you; I know whom I have chosen. But the Scripture will be fulfilled,[d] 'He who ate my bread has lifted his heel against me.' [19]I am telling you this now, before it takes place, that when it does take place you may believe that I am he. [20]Truly, truly, I say to you, whoever receives the one I send receives me, and whoever receives me receives the one who sent me."

ONE OF YOU WILL BETRAY ME

[21]After saying these things, Jesus was troubled in his spirit, and testified, "Truly, truly, I say to you, one of you will betray me." [22]The disciples looked at one another, uncertain of whom he spoke. [23]One of his disciples, whom Jesus loved, was reclining at table at Jesus' side,[e] [24]so Simon Peter motioned to him to ask Jesus[f] of whom he was speaking. [25]So that disciple, leaning back against Jesus, said to him, "Lord, who is it?" [26]Jesus

---

[a]Some manuscripts omit *except for his feet* [b]The Greek words for *you* in this verse are plural [c]Or *bondservant*, or *slave* (for the contextual rendering of the Greek word *doulos*, see Preface) [d]Greek *But in order that the Scripture may be fulfilled* [e]Greek *in the bosom of Jesus* [f]Greek lacks *Jesus*

answered, "It is he to whom I will give this morsel of bread when I have dipped it." So when he had dipped the morsel, he gave it to Judas, the son of Simon Iscariot. ²⁷Then after he had taken the morsel, Satan entered into him. Jesus said to him, "What you are going to do, do quickly." ²⁸Now no one at the table knew why he said this to him. ²⁹Some thought that, because Judas had the money bag, Jesus was telling him, "Buy what we need for the feast", or that he should give something to the poor. ³⁰So, after receiving the morsel of bread, he immediately went out. And it was night.

A NEW COMMANDMENT

³¹When he had gone out, Jesus said, "Now is the Son of Man glorified, and God is glorified in him. ³²If God is glorified in him, God will also glorify him in himself, and glorify him at once. ³³Little children, yet a little while I am with you. You will seek me, and just as I said to the Jews, so now I also say to you, 'Where I am going you cannot come.' ³⁴A new commandment I give to you, that you love one another: just as I have loved you, you also are to love one another. ³⁵By this all people will know that you are my disciples, if you have love for one another."

JESUS FORETELLS PETER'S DENIAL

³⁶Simon Peter said to him, "Lord, where are you going?" Jesus answered him, "Where I am going you cannot follow me now, but you will follow afterwards." ³⁷Peter said to him, "Lord, why can I not follow you now? I will lay down my life for you." ³⁸Jesus answered, "Will you lay down your life for me? Truly, truly, I say to you, the cock will not crow till you have denied me three times.

I AM THE WAY, AND THE TRUTH, AND THE LIFE

14 "Let not your hearts be troubled. Believe in God;ᵃ believe also in me. ²In my Father's house are many rooms. If it were not so, would I have told you that I go to prepare a place for you?ᵇ ³And if I go and prepare a place for you, I will come again and will take you to myself, that where I am you may be also. ⁴And you know the way to where I am going."ᶜ ⁵Thomas said to him, "Lord, we do not know where you are going. How can we know the way?" ⁶Jesus said to him, "I am the way, and the truth, and the life. No one comes to the Father except through me. ⁷If you had known me, you would have known my Father also.ᵈ From now on you do know him and have seen him."

⁸Philip said to him, "Lord, show us the Father, and it is enough for us." ⁹Jesus said to him, "Have I been with you so long, and you still do not know me, Philip? Whoever has seen me has seen the Father. How can you say, 'Show us the Father'? ¹⁰Do you not believe that I am in the Father and the Father is in me? The words that I say to you I do not speak on my own authority, but the Father who dwells in me does his works. ¹¹Believe me that I am in the Father and the Father is in me, or else believe on account of the works themselves.

¹²"Truly, truly, I say to you, whoever believes in me will also do the works that I do; and greater works than these will he do, because I am going to the Father. ¹³Whatever you ask in my name, this I will do, that the Father may be glorified in the Son. ¹⁴If you ask meᵉ for anything in my name, I will do it.

JESUS PROMISES THE HOLY SPIRIT

¹⁵"If you love me, you will keep my commandments. ¹⁶And I will ask the Father, and he will give you another Helper,ᶠ to be with you for ever, ¹⁷even the Spirit of truth, whom the world cannot receive, because it neither sees him nor knows him. You know him, for he dwells with you and will beᵍ in you.

¹⁸"I will not leave you as orphans; I will come to you. ¹⁹Yet a little while and the world will see me no more, but you will see me. Because I live, you also will live. ²⁰In that day you will know that I am in my Father, and you in me, and I in you. ²¹Whoever has my commandments and keeps them, he it is who loves me. And he who loves me will be loved by my Father, and I will love him and manifest myself to him." ²²Judas (not Iscariot) said to him, "Lord, how is it that you will manifest yourself to us, and not to the world?" ²³Jesus answered him, "If anyone loves me, he will keep my word, and my Father will love him, and we will come to him and make our home with him. ²⁴Whoever does not love me does not keep my words. And the word that you hear is not mine but the Father's who sent me.

ᵃOr *You believe in God* ᵇOr *In my Father's house are many rooms; if it were not so, I would have told you; for I go to prepare a place for you* ᶜSome manuscripts *Where I am going you know, and the way you know* ᵈOr *If you know me, you will know my Father also*, or *If you have known me, you will know my Father also* ᵉSome manuscripts omit *me* ᶠOr *Advocate*, or *Counsellor*; also 14:26; 15:26; 16:7 ᵍSome manuscripts *and is*

25"These things I have spoken to you while I am still with you. 26But the Helper, the Holy Spirit, whom the Father will send in my name, he will teach you all things and bring to your remembrance all that I have said to you. 27Peace I leave with you; my peace I give to you. Not as the world gives do I give to you. Let not your hearts be troubled, neither let them be afraid. 28You heard me say to you, 'I am going away, and I will come to you.' If you loved me, you would have rejoiced, because I am going to the Father, for the Father is greater than I. 29And now I have told you before it takes place, so that when it does take place you may believe. 30I will no longer talk much with you, for the ruler of this world is coming. He has no claim on me, 31but I do as the Father has commanded me, so that the world may know that I love the Father. Rise, let us go from here.

I AM THE TRUE VINE

15 "I am the true vine, and my Father is the vine dresser. 2Every branch in me that does not bear fruit he takes away, and every branch that does bear fruit he prunes, that it may bear more fruit. 3Already you are clean because of the word that I have spoken to you. 4Abide in me, and I in you. As the branch cannot bear fruit by itself, unless it abides in the vine, neither can you, unless you abide in me. 5I am the vine; you are the branches. Whoever abides in me and I in him, he it is that bears much fruit, for apart from me you can do nothing. 6If anyone does not abide in me he is thrown away like a branch and withers; and the branches are gathered, thrown into the fire, and burned. 7If you abide in me, and my words abide in you, ask whatever you wish, and it will be done for you. 8By this my Father is glorified, that you bear much fruit and so prove to be my disciples. 9As the Father has loved me, so have I loved you. Abide in my love. 10If you keep my commandments, you will abide in my love, just as I have kept my Father's commandments and abide in his love. 11These things I have spoken to you, that my joy may be in you, and that your joy may be full.

12"This is my commandment, that you love one another as I have loved you. 13Greater love has no one than this, that someone lay down his life for his friends. 14You are my friends if you do what I command you. 15No longer do I call you servants,*a* for the servant does not know what his master is doing; but I have called you friends, for all that I have heard from my Father I have made known to you. 16You did not choose me, but I chose you and appointed you that you should go and bear fruit and that your fruit should abide, so that whatever you ask the Father in my name, he may give it to you. 17These things I command you, so that you will love one another.

THE HATRED OF THE WORLD

18"If the world hates you, know that it has hated me before it hated you. 19If you were of the world, the world would love you as its own; but because you are not of the world, but I chose you out of the world, therefore the world hates you. 20Remember the word that I said to you: 'A servant is not greater than his master.' If they persecuted me, they will also persecute you. If they kept my word, they will also keep yours. 21But all these things they will do to you on account of my name, because they do not know him who sent me. 22If I had not come and spoken to them, they would not have been guilty of sin,*b* but now they have no excuse for their sin. 23Whoever hates me hates my Father also. 24If I had not done among them the works that no one else did, they would not be guilty of sin, but now they have seen and hated both me and my Father. 25But the word that is written in their Law must be fulfilled: 'They hated me without a cause.'

26"But when the Helper comes, whom I will send to you from the Father, the Spirit of truth, who proceeds from the Father, he will bear witness about me. 27And you also will bear witness, because you have been with me from the beginning.

16 "I have said all these things to you to keep you from falling away. 2They will put you out of the synagogues. Indeed, the hour is coming when whoever kills you will think he is offering service to God. 3And they will do these things because they have not known the Father, nor me. 4But I have said these things to you, that when their hour comes you may remember that I told them to you.

THE WORK OF THE HOLY SPIRIT

"I did not say these things to you from the beginning, because I was with you. 5But now

---

*a*Or *bondservants*, or *slaves* (for the contextual rendering of the Greek word *doulos*, see Preface); likewise for *servant* later in this verse and in verse 20   *b*Greek *they would not have sin*; also verse 24

I am going to him who sent me, and none of you asks me, 'Where are you going?' ⁶But because I have said these things to you, sorrow has filled your heart. ⁷Nevertheless, I tell you the truth: it is to your advantage that I go away, for if I do not go away, the Helper will not come to you. But if I go, I will send him to you. ⁸And when he comes, he will convict the world concerning sin and righteousness and judgement: ⁹concerning sin, because they do not believe in me; ¹⁰concerning righteousness, because I go to the Father, and you will see me no longer; ¹¹concerning judgement, because the ruler of this world is judged.

¹²"I still have many things to say to you, but you cannot bear them now. ¹³When the Spirit of truth comes, he will guide you into all the truth, for he will not speak on his own authority, but whatever he hears he will speak, and he will declare to you the things that are to come. ¹⁴He will glorify me, for he will take what is mine and declare it to you. ¹⁵All that the Father has is mine; therefore I said that he will take what is mine and declare it to you.

YOUR SORROW WILL TURN INTO JOY

¹⁶"A little while, and you will see me no longer; and again a little while, and you will see me." ¹⁷So some of his disciples said to one another, "What is this that he says to us, 'A little while, and you will not see me, and again a little while, and you will see me'; and, 'because I am going to the Father'?" ¹⁸So they were saying, "What does he mean by 'a little while'? We do not know what he is talking about." ¹⁹Jesus knew that they wanted to ask him, so he said to them, "Is this what you are asking yourselves, what I meant by saying, 'A little while and you will not see me, and again a little while and you will see me'? ²⁰Truly, truly, I say to you, you will weep and lament, but the world will rejoice. You will be sorrowful, but your sorrow will turn into joy. ²¹When a woman is giving birth, she has sorrow because her hour has come, but when she has delivered the baby, she no longer remembers the anguish, for joy that a human being has been born into the world. ²²So also you have sorrow now, but I will see you again, and your hearts will rejoice, and no one will take your joy from you. ²³In that day you will ask nothing of me. Truly, truly, I say to you, whatever you ask of the Father in my name, he will give it to you. ²⁴Until now you have asked nothing in my name. Ask, and you will receive, that your joy may be full.

I HAVE OVERCOME THE WORLD

²⁵"I have said these things to you in figures of speech. The hour is coming when I will no longer speak to you in figures of speech but will tell you plainly about the Father. ²⁶In that day you will ask in my name, and I do not say to you that I will ask the Father on your behalf; ²⁷for the Father himself loves you, because you have loved me and have believed that I came from God.ᵃ ²⁸I came from the Father and have come into the world, and now I am leaving the world and going to the Father."

²⁹His disciples said, "Ah, now you are speaking plainly and not using figurative speech! ³⁰Now we know that you know all things and do not need anyone to question you; this is why we believe that you came from God." ³¹Jesus answered them, "Do you now believe? ³²Behold, the hour is coming, indeed it has come, when you will be scattered, each to his own home, and will leave me alone. Yet I am not alone, for the Father is with me. ³³I have said these things to you, that in me you may have peace. In the world you will have tribulation. But take heart; I have overcome the world."

THE HIGH PRIESTLY PRAYER

17 When Jesus had spoken these words, he lifted up his eyes to heaven, and said, "Father, the hour has come; glorify your Son that the Son may glorify you, ²since you have given him authority over all flesh, to give eternal life to all whom you have given him. ³And this is eternal life, that they know you, the only true God, and Jesus Christ whom you have sent. ⁴I glorified you on earth, having accomplished the work that you gave me to do. ⁵And now, Father, glorify me in your own presence with the glory that I had with you before the world existed.

⁶"I have manifested your name to the people whom you gave me out of the world. Yours they were, and you gave them to me, and they have kept your word. ⁷Now they know that everything that you have given me is from you. ⁸For I have given them the words that you gave me, and they have received them and have come to know in truth that I came from you; and they have believed that you sent me. ⁹I am praying for them. I am not praying for the world but for those whom you have given me, for they are yours. ¹⁰All

---

ᵃSome manuscripts *from the Father*

mine are yours, and yours are mine, and I am glorified in them. **11**And I am no longer in the world, but they are in the world, and I am coming to you. Holy Father, keep them in your name, which you have given me, that they may be one, even as we are one. **12**While I was with them, I kept them in your name, which you have given me. I have guarded them, and not one of them has been lost except the son of destruction, that the Scripture might be fulfilled. **13**But now I am coming to you, and these things I speak in the world, that they may have my joy fulfilled in themselves. **14**I have given them your word, and the world has hated them because they are not of the world, just as I am not of the world. **15**I do not ask that you take them out of the world, but that you keep them from the evil one.*a* **16**They are not of the world, just as I am not of the world. **17**Sanctify them*b* in the truth; your word is truth. **18**As you sent me into the world, so I have sent them into the world. **19**And for their sake I consecrate myself,*c* that they also may be sanctified*d* in truth.

20"I do not ask for these only, but also for those who will believe in me through their word, **21**that they may all be one, just as you, Father, are in me, and I in you, that they also may be in us, so that the world may believe that you have sent me. **22**The glory that you have given me I have given to them, that they may be one even as we are one, **23**I in them and you in me, that they may become perfectly one, so that the world may know that you sent me and loved them even as you loved me. **24**Father, I desire that they also, whom you have given me, may be with me where I am, to see my glory that you have given me because you loved me before the foundation of the world. **25**O righteous Father, even though the world does not know you, I know you, and these know that you have sent me. **26**I made known to them your name, and I will continue to make it known, that the love with which you have loved me may be in them, and I in them."

BETRAYAL AND ARREST OF JESUS

18 When Jesus had spoken these words, he went out with his disciples across the brook Kidron, where there was a garden, which he and his disciples entered. **2**Now Judas, who betrayed him, also knew the place, for Jesus often met there with his disciples. **3**So Judas, having procured a band of soldiers and some officers from the chief priests and the Pharisees, went there with lanterns and torches and weapons. **4**Then Jesus, knowing all that would happen to him, came forward and said to them, "Whom do you seek?" **5**They answered him, "Jesus of Nazareth." Jesus said to them, "I am he."*e* Judas, who betrayed him, was standing with them. **6**When Jesus*f* said to them, "I am he", they drew back and fell to the ground. **7**So he asked them again, "Whom do you seek?" And they said, "Jesus of Nazareth." **8**Jesus answered, "I told you that I am he. So, if you seek me, let these men go." **9**This was to fulfil the word that he had spoken: "Of those whom you gave me I have lost not one." **10**Then Simon Peter, having a sword, drew it and struck the high priest's servant*g* and cut off his right ear. (The servant's name was Malchus.) **11**So Jesus said to Peter, "Put your sword into its sheath; shall I not drink the cup that the Father has given me?"

JESUS FACES ANNAS AND CAIAPHAS

12So the band of soldiers and their captain and the officers of the Jews*h* arrested Jesus and bound him. **13**First they led him to Annas, for he was the father-in-law of Caiaphas, who was high priest that year. **14**It was Caiaphas who had advised the Jews that it would be expedient that one man should die for the people.

PETER DENIES JESUS

15Simon Peter followed Jesus, and so did another disciple. Since that disciple was known to the high priest, he entered with Jesus into the courtyard of the high priest, **16**but Peter stood outside at the door. So the other disciple, who was known to the high priest, went out and spoke to the servant girl who kept watch at the door, and brought Peter in. **17**The servant girl at the door said to Peter, "You also are not one of this man's disciples, are you?" He said, "I am not." **18**Now the servants*i* and officers had made a charcoal fire, because it was cold, and they were standing and warming themselves. Peter also was with them, standing and warming himself.

*a*Or *from evil* *b*Greek *Set them apart* (for holy service to God)
*c*Or *I sanctify myself*; or *I set myself apart* (for holy service to God)
*d*Greek *may be set apart* (for holy service to God) *e*Greek *I am*;
also verses 6, 8 *f*Greek *he* *g*Or *bondservant*; twice in this verse
*h*Greek *Ioudaioi* probably refers here to Jewish religious leaders, and others under their influence, in that time; also verses 14, 31, 36, 38
*i*Or *bondservants*; also verse 26

THE HIGH PRIEST QUESTIONS JESUS

¹⁹The high priest then questioned Jesus about his disciples and his teaching. ²⁰Jesus answered him, "I have spoken openly to the world. I have always taught in synagogues and in the temple, where all Jews come together. I have said nothing in secret. ²¹Why do you ask me? Ask those who have heard me what I said to them; they know what I said." ²²When he had said these things, one of the officers standing by struck Jesus with his hand, saying, "Is that how you answer the high priest?" ²³Jesus answered him, "If what I said is wrong, bear witness about the wrong; but if what I said is right, why do you strike me?" ²⁴Annas then sent him bound to Caiaphas the high priest.

PETER DENIES JESUS AGAIN

²⁵Now Simon Peter was standing and warming himself. So they said to him, "You also are not one of his disciples, are you?" He denied it and said, "I am not." ²⁶One of the servants of the high priest, a relative of the man whose ear Peter had cut off, asked, "Did I not see you in the garden with him?" ²⁷Peter again denied it, and at once a cock crowed.

JESUS BEFORE PILATE

²⁸Then they led Jesus from the house of Caiaphas to the governor's headquarters.ᵃ It was early morning. They themselves did not enter the governor's headquarters, so that they would not be defiled, but could eat the Passover. ²⁹So Pilate went outside to them and said, "What accusation do you bring against this man?" ³⁰They answered him, "If this man were not doing evil, we would not have delivered him over to you." ³¹Pilate said to them, "Take him yourselves and judge him by your own law." The Jews said to him, "It is not lawful for us to put anyone to death." ³²This was to fulfil the word that Jesus had spoken to show by what kind of death he was going to die.

MY KINGDOM IS NOT OF THIS WORLD

³³So Pilate entered his headquarters again and called Jesus and said to him, "Are you the King of the Jews?" ³⁴Jesus answered, "Do you say this of your own accord, or did others say it to you about me?" ³⁵Pilate answered, "Am I a Jew? Your own nation and the chief priests have delivered you over to me. What have you done?" ³⁶Jesus answered, "My kingdom is not of this world. If my kingdom were of this world, my servants would have been fighting, that I might not be delivered over to the Jews. But my kingdom is not from the world." ³⁷Then Pilate said to him, "So you are a king?" Jesus answered, "You say that I am a king. For this purpose I was born and for this purpose I have come into the world—to bear witness to the truth. Everyone who is of the truth listens to my voice." ³⁸Pilate said to him, "What is truth?"

After he had said this, he went back outside to the Jews and told them, "I find no guilt in him. ³⁹But you have a custom that I should release one man for you at the Passover. So do you want me to release to you the King of the Jews?" ⁴⁰They cried out again, "Not this man, but Barabbas!" Now Barabbas was a robber.ᵇ

JESUS DELIVERED TO BE CRUCIFIED

19 Then Pilate took Jesus and flogged him. ²And the soldiers twisted together a crown of thorns and put it on his head and arrayed him in a purple robe. ³They came up to him, saying, "Hail, King of the Jews!" and struck him with their hands. ⁴Pilate went out again and said to them, "See, I am bringing him out to you that you may know that I find no guilt in him." ⁵So Jesus came out, wearing the crown of thorns and the purple robe. Pilate said to them, "Behold the man!" ⁶When the chief priests and the officers saw him, they cried out, "Crucify him, crucify him!" Pilate said to them, "Take him yourselves and crucify him, for I find no guilt in him." ⁷The Jewsᶜ answered him, "We have a law, and according to that law he ought to die because he has made himself the Son of God." ⁸When Pilate heard this statement, he was even more afraid. ⁹He entered his headquarters again and said to Jesus, "Where are you from?" But Jesus gave him no answer. ¹⁰So Pilate said to him, "You will not speak to me? Do you not know that I have authority to release you and authority to crucify you?" ¹¹Jesus answered him, "You would have no authority over me at all unless it had been given you from above. Therefore he who delivered me over to you has the greater sin."

¹²From then on Pilate sought to release him, but the Jews cried out, "If you release this man, you are not Caesar's friend. Everyone who makes himself a king opposes Caesar." ¹³So when Pilate heard these words,

---

ᵃGreek *the praetorium* ᵇOr *an insurrectionist* ᶜGreek *Ioudaioi* probably refers here to Jewish religious leaders, and others under their influence, in that time; also verses 12, 14, 31, 38

he brought Jesus out and sat down on the judgement seat at a place called The Stone Pavement, and in Aramaic[a] Gabbatha. [14]Now it was the day of Preparation of the Passover. It was about the sixth hour.[b] He said to the Jews, "Behold your King!" [15]They cried out, "Away with him, away with him, crucify him!" Pilate said to them, "Shall I crucify your King?" The chief priests answered, "We have no king but Caesar." [16]So he delivered him over to them to be crucified.

THE CRUCIFIXION

So they took Jesus, [17]and he went out, bearing his own cross, to the place called The Place of a Skull, which in Aramaic is called Golgotha. [18]There they crucified him, and with him two others, one on either side, and Jesus between them. [19]Pilate also wrote an inscription and put it on the cross. It read, "Jesus of Nazareth, the King of the Jews." [20]Many of the Jews read this inscription, for the place where Jesus was crucified was near the city, and it was written in Aramaic, in Latin, and in Greek. [21]So the chief priests of the Jews said to Pilate, "Do not write, 'The King of the Jews', but rather, 'This man said, I am King of the Jews.'" [22]Pilate answered, "What I have written I have written."

[23]When the soldiers had crucified Jesus, they took his garments and divided them into four parts, one part for each soldier; also his tunic.[c] But the tunic was seamless, woven in one piece from top to bottom, [24]so they said to one another, "Let us not tear it, but cast lots for it to see whose it shall be." This was to fulfil the Scripture which says,

> "They divided my garments
>   among them,
>   and for my clothing they cast lots."

So the soldiers did these things, [25]but standing by the cross of Jesus were his mother and his mother's sister, Mary the wife of Clopas, and Mary Magdalene. [26]When Jesus saw his mother and the disciple whom he loved standing nearby, he said to his mother, "Woman, behold, your son!" [27]Then he said to the disciple, "Behold, your mother!" And from that hour the disciple took her to his own home.

THE DEATH OF JESUS

[28]After this, Jesus, knowing that all was now finished, said (to fulfil the Scripture), "I thirst." [29]A jar full of sour wine stood there, so they put a sponge full of the sour wine on a hyssop branch and held it to his mouth. [30]When Jesus had received the sour wine, he said, "It is finished", and he bowed his head and gave up his spirit.

JESUS' SIDE IS PIERCED

[31]Since it was the day of Preparation, and so that the bodies would not remain on the cross on the Sabbath (for that Sabbath was a high day), the Jews asked Pilate that their legs might be broken and that they might be taken away. [32]So the soldiers came and broke the legs of the first, and of the other who had been crucified with him. [33]But when they came to Jesus and saw that he was already dead, they did not break his legs. [34]But one of the soldiers pierced his side with a spear, and at once there came out blood and water. [35]He who saw it has borne witness—his testimony is true, and he knows that he is telling the truth—that you also may believe. [36]For these things took place that the Scripture might be fulfilled: "Not one of his bones will be broken." [37]And again another Scripture says, "They will look on him whom they have pierced."

JESUS IS BURIED

[38]After these things Joseph of Arimathea, who was a disciple of Jesus, but secretly for fear of the Jews, asked Pilate that he might take away the body of Jesus, and Pilate gave him permission. So he came and took away his body. [39]Nicodemus also, who earlier had come to Jesus[d] by night, came bringing a mixture of myrrh and aloes, about seventy-five pounds[e] in weight. [40]So they took the body of Jesus and bound it in linen cloths with the spices, as is the burial custom of the Jews. [41]Now in the place where he was crucified there was a garden, and in the garden a new tomb in which no one had yet been laid. [42]So because of the Jewish day of Preparation, since the tomb was close at hand, they laid Jesus there.

THE RESURRECTION

20 Now on the first day of the week Mary Magdalene came to the tomb early, while it was still dark, and saw that the stone had been taken away from the tomb. [2]So she ran and went to Simon

---

[a] Or *Hebrew*; also verses 17, 20   [b] That is, about noon   [c] Greek *chiton*, a long garment worn under the cloak next to the skin   [d] Greek *him*   [e] Greek *one hundred litras*; a *litra* (or Roman pound) was equal to about 11 1/2 ounces or 327 grams

Peter and the other disciple, the one whom Jesus loved, and said to them, "They have taken the Lord out of the tomb, and we do not know where they have laid him." ³So Peter went out with the other disciple, and they were going towards the tomb. ⁴Both of them were running together, but the other disciple outran Peter and reached the tomb first. ⁵And stooping to look in, he saw the linen cloths lying there, but he did not go in. ⁶Then Simon Peter came, following him, and went into the tomb. He saw the linen cloths lying there, ⁷and the face cloth, which had been on Jesus'ᵃ head, not lying with the linen cloths but folded up in a place by itself. ⁸Then the other disciple, who had reached the tomb first, also went in, and he saw and believed; ⁹for as yet they did not understand the Scripture, that he must rise from the dead. ¹⁰Then the disciples went back to their homes.

JESUS APPEARS TO MARY MAGDALENE

¹¹But Mary stood weeping outside the tomb, and as she wept she stooped to look into the tomb. ¹²And she saw two angels in white, sitting where the body of Jesus had lain, one at the head and one at the feet. ¹³They said to her, "Woman, why are you weeping?" She said to them, "They have taken away my Lord, and I do not know where they have laid him." ¹⁴Having said this, she turned round and saw Jesus standing, but she did not know that it was Jesus. ¹⁵Jesus said to her, "Woman, why are you weeping? Whom are you seeking?" Supposing him to be the gardener, she said to him, "Sir, if you have carried him away, tell me where you have laid him, and I will take him away." ¹⁶Jesus said to her, "Mary." She turned and said to him in Aramaic,ᵇ "Rabboni!" (which means Teacher). ¹⁷Jesus said to her, "Do not cling to me, for I have not yet ascended to the Father; but go to my brothers and say to them, 'I am ascending to my Father and your Father, to my God and your God.'" ¹⁸Mary Magdalene went and announced to the disciples, "I have seen the Lord"—and that he had said these things to her.

JESUS APPEARS TO THE DISCIPLES

¹⁹On the evening of that day, the first day of the week, the doors being locked where the disciples were for fear of the Jews,ᶜ Jesus came and stood among them and said to them, "Peace be with you." ²⁰When he had said this, he showed them his hands and his side. Then the disciples were glad when they saw the Lord. ²¹Jesus said to them again, "Peace be with you. As the Father has sent me, even so I am sending you." ²²And when he had said this, he breathed on them and said to them, "Receive the Holy Spirit. ²³If you forgive the sins of any, they are forgiven them; if you withhold forgiveness from any, it is withheld."

JESUS AND THOMAS

²⁴Now Thomas, one of the twelve, called the Twin,ᵈ was not with them when Jesus came. ²⁵So the other disciples told him, "We have seen the Lord." But he said to them, "Unless I see in his hands the mark of the nails, and place my finger into the mark of the nails, and place my hand into his side, I will never believe."

²⁶Eight days later, his disciples were inside again, and Thomas was with them. Although the doors were locked, Jesus came and stood among them and said, "Peace be with you." ²⁷Then he said to Thomas, "Put your finger here, and see my hands; and put out your hand, and place it in my side. Do not disbelieve, but believe." ²⁸Thomas answered him, "My Lord and my God!" ²⁹Jesus said to him, "Have you believed because you have seen me? Blessed are those who have not seen and yet have believed."

THE PURPOSE OF THIS BOOK

³⁰Now Jesus did many other signs in the presence of the disciples, which are not written in this book; ³¹but these are written so that you may believe that Jesus is the Christ, the Son of God, and that by believing you may have life in his name.

JESUS APPEARS TO SEVEN DISCIPLES

21 After this Jesus revealed himself again to the disciples by the Sea of Tiberias, and he revealed himself in this way. ²Simon Peter, Thomas (called the Twin), Nathanael of Cana in Galilee, the sons of Zebedee, and two others of his disciples were together. ³Simon Peter said to them, "I am going fishing." They said to him, "We will go with you." They went out and got into the boat, but that night they caught nothing.

⁴Just as day was breaking, Jesus stood on the shore; yet the disciples did not know that

---

ᵃGreek *his* ᵇOr *Hebrew* ᶜGreek *Ioudaioi* probably refers here to Jewish religious leaders, and others under their influence, in that time ᵈGreek *Didymus* it was Jesus. ⁵Jesus said to them, "Children, do you have any fish?" They answered him, "No." ⁶He said to them, "Cast the net on the right side of the boat, and you will find some." So they cast it, and now they were not able to haul it in, because of the quantity of fish. ⁷That disciple whom Jesus loved therefore said to Peter, "It is the Lord!" When Simon Peter heard that it was the Lord, he put on his outer garment, for he was stripped for work, and threw himself into the sea. ⁸The other disciples came in the boat, dragging the net full of fish, for they were not far from the land, but about a hundred yards[a] off.

⁹When they got out on land, they saw a charcoal fire in place, with fish laid out on it, and bread. ¹⁰Jesus said to them, "Bring some of the fish that you have just caught." ¹¹So Simon Peter went aboard and hauled the net ashore, full of large fish, 153 of them. And although there were so many, the net was not torn. ¹²Jesus said to them, "Come and have breakfast." Now none of the disciples dared ask him, "Who are you?" They knew it was the Lord. ¹³Jesus came and took the bread and gave it to them, and so with the fish. ¹⁴This was now the third time that Jesus was revealed to the disciples after he was raised from the dead.

JESUS AND PETER

¹⁵When they had finished breakfast, Jesus said to Simon Peter, "Simon, son of John, do you love me more than these?" He said to him, "Yes, Lord; you know that I love you." He said to him, "Feed my lambs." ¹⁶He said to him a second time, "Simon, son of John, do you love me?" He said to him, "Yes, Lord; you know that I love you." He said to him, "Tend my sheep." ¹⁷He said to him the third time, "Simon, son of John, do you love me?" Peter was grieved because he said to him the third time, "Do you love me?" and he said to him, "Lord, you know everything; you know that I love you." Jesus said to him, "Feed my sheep. ¹⁸Truly, truly, I say to you, when you were young, you used to dress yourself and walk wherever you wanted, but when you are old, you will stretch out your hands, and another will dress you and carry you where you do not want to go." ¹⁹(This he said to show by what kind of death he was to glorify God.) And after saying this he said to him, "Follow me."

JESUS AND THE BELOVED APOSTLE

²⁰Peter turned and saw the disciple whom Jesus loved following them, the one who also had leaned back against him during the supper and had said, "Lord, who is it that is going to betray you?" ²¹When Peter saw him, he said to Jesus, "Lord, what about this man?" ²²Jesus said to him, "If it is my will that he remain until I come, what is that to you? You follow me!" ²³So the saying spread abroad among the brothers[b] that this disciple was not to die; yet Jesus did not say to him that he was not to die, but, "If it is my will that he remain until I come, what is that to you?"

²⁴This is the disciple who is bearing witness about these things, and who has written these things, and we know that his testimony is true.

²⁵Now there are also many other things that Jesus did. Were every one of them to be written, I suppose that the world itself could not contain the books that would be written.

---

[a] Greek *two hundred cubits*; a *cubit* was about 18 inches or 45 centimetres [b] Or *brothers and sisters*

THE
ACTS
OF THE APOSTLES

THE PROMISE OF THE HOLY SPIRIT

1 In the first book, O Theophilus, I have dealt with all that Jesus began to do and teach, ²until the day when he was taken up, after he had given commands through the Holy Spirit to the apostles whom he had chosen. ³He presented himself alive to them after his suffering by many proofs, appearing to them during forty days and speaking about the kingdom of God.

⁴And while staying[a] with them he ordered them not to depart from Jerusalem, but to wait for the promise of the Father, which, he said, "you heard from me; ⁵for John baptized with water, but you will be baptized with[b] the Holy Spirit not many days from now."

THE ASCENSION

⁶So when they had come together, they asked him, "Lord, will you at this time restore the kingdom to Israel?" ⁷He said to them, "It is not for you to know times or seasons that the Father has fixed by his own authority. ⁸But you will receive power when the Holy Spirit has come upon you, and you will be my witnesses in Jerusalem and in all Judea and Samaria, and to the end of the earth." ⁹And when he had said these things, as they were looking on, he was lifted up, and a cloud took him out of their sight. ¹⁰And while they were gazing into heaven as he went, behold, two men stood by them in white robes, ¹¹and said, "Men of Galilee, why do you stand looking into heaven? This Jesus, who was taken up from you into heaven, will come in the same way as you saw him go into heaven."

MATTHIAS CHOSEN TO REPLACE JUDAS

¹²Then they returned to Jerusalem from the mount called Olivet, which is near Jerusalem, a Sabbath day's journey away. ¹³And when they had entered, they went up to the upper room, where they were staying, Peter and John and James and Andrew, Philip and Thomas, Bartholomew and Matthew, James the son of Alphaeus and Simon the Zealot and Judas the son of James. ¹⁴All these with one accord were devoting themselves to prayer, together with the women and Mary the mother of Jesus, and his brothers.[c]

¹⁵In those days Peter stood up among the brothers (the company of persons was in all about 120) and said, ¹⁶"Brothers, the Scripture had to be fulfilled, which the Holy Spirit spoke beforehand by the mouth of David concerning Judas, who became a guide to those who arrested Jesus. ¹⁷For he was numbered among us and was allotted his share in this ministry." ¹⁸(Now this man acquired a field with the reward of his wickedness, and falling headlong[d] he burst open in the middle and all his bowels gushed out. ¹⁹And it became known to all the inhabitants of Jerusalem, so that the field was called in their own language Akeldama, that is, Field of Blood.) ²⁰"For it is written in the Book of Psalms,

"'May his camp become desolate,
 and let there be no one to dwell in it';

and

"'Let another take his office.'

²¹So one of the men who have accompanied us during all the time that the Lord Jesus went in and out among us, ²²beginning from the baptism of John until the day when he was taken up from us—one of these men must become with us a witness to his resurrection." ²³And they put forward two, Joseph called Barsabbas, who was also called Justus, and Matthias. ²⁴And they prayed and said, "You, Lord, who know the hearts of all, show which one of these two you have chosen ²⁵to take the place in this ministry and

---

[a]Or *eating* [b]Or *in* [c]Or *brothers and sisters*. In New Testament usage, depending on the context, the plural Greek word *adelphoi* (translated "brothers") may refer either to *brothers* or to *brothers and sisters*; also verse 15 [d]Or *swelling up*

apostleship from which Judas turned aside to go to his own place." ²⁶And they cast lots for them, and the lot fell on Matthias, and he was numbered with the eleven apostles.

THE COMING OF THE HOLY SPIRIT

2 When the day of Pentecost arrived, they were all together in one place. ²And suddenly there came from heaven a sound like a mighty rushing wind, and it filled the entire house where they were sitting. ³And divided tongues as of fire appeared to them and rested[a] on each one of them. ⁴And they were all filled with the Holy Spirit and began to speak in other tongues as the Spirit gave them utterance.

⁵Now there were dwelling in Jerusalem Jews, devout men from every nation under heaven. ⁶And at this sound the multitude came together, and they were bewildered, because each one was hearing them speak in his own language. ⁷And they were amazed and astonished, saying, "Are not all these who are speaking Galileans? ⁸And how is it that we hear, each of us in his own native language? ⁹Parthians and Medes and Elamites and residents of Mesopotamia, Judea and Cappadocia, Pontus and Asia, ¹⁰Phrygia and Pamphylia, Egypt and the parts of Libya belonging to Cyrene, and visitors from Rome, ¹¹both Jews and proselytes, Cretans and Arabians—we hear them telling in our own tongues the mighty works of God." ¹²And all were amazed and perplexed, saying to one another, "What does this mean?" ¹³But others mocking said, "They are filled with new wine."

PETER'S SERMON AT PENTECOST

¹⁴But Peter, standing with the eleven, lifted up his voice and addressed them: "Men of Judea and all who dwell in Jerusalem, let this be known to you, and give ear to my words. ¹⁵For these people are not drunk, as you suppose, since it is only the third hour of the day.[b] ¹⁶But this is what was uttered through the prophet Joel:

¹⁷ "'And in the last days it shall
be, God declares,
that I will pour out my
Spirit on all flesh,
and your sons and your daughters
shall prophesy,
and your young men shall see visions,
and your old men shall
dream dreams;
¹⁸ even on my male servants
and female servants
in those days I will pour out my
Spirit, and they shall prophesy.
¹⁹ And I will show wonders in
the heavens above
and signs on the earth below,
blood, and fire, and vapour
of smoke;
²⁰ the sun shall be turned to darkness
and the moon to blood,
before the day of the Lord comes,
the great and magnificent day.
²¹ And it shall come to pass that
everyone who calls upon the
name of the Lord shall be saved.'

²²"Men of Israel, hear these words: Jesus of Nazareth, a man attested to you by God with mighty works and wonders and signs that God did through him in your midst, as you yourselves know— ²³this Jesus,[c] delivered up according to the definite plan and foreknowledge of God, you crucified and killed by the hands of lawless men. ²⁴God raised him up, loosing the pangs of death, because it was not possible for him to be held by it. ²⁵For David says concerning him,

"'I saw the Lord always before me,
for he is at my right hand that
I may not be shaken;
²⁶ therefore my heart was glad,
and my tongue rejoiced;
my flesh also will dwell in hope.
²⁷ For you will not abandon
my soul to Hades,
or let your Holy One see corruption.
²⁸ You have made known to me
the paths of life;
you will make me full of gladness
with your presence.'

²⁹"Brothers, I may say to you with confidence about the patriarch David that he both died and was buried, and his tomb is with us to this day. ³⁰Being therefore a prophet, and knowing that God had sworn with an oath to him that he would set one of his descendants on his throne, ³¹he foresaw and spoke about the resurrection of the Christ, that he was not abandoned to Hades, nor did his flesh see corruption. ³²This Jesus God raised

---

[a] Or *And tongues as of fire appeared to them, distributed among them, and rested* [b] That is, 9 A.M. [c] Greek *this one*

up, and of that we all are witnesses. ³³Being therefore exalted at the right hand of God, and having received from the Father the promise of the Holy Spirit, he has poured out this that you yourselves are seeing and hearing. ³⁴For David did not ascend into the heavens, but he himself says,

> "'The Lord said to my Lord,
> "Sit at my right hand,
> ³⁵ until I make your enemies
> your footstool."'

³⁶Let all the house of Israel therefore know for certain that God has made him both Lord and Christ, this Jesus whom you crucified."

³⁷Now when they heard this they were cut to the heart, and said to Peter and the rest of the apostles, "Brothers, what shall we do?" ³⁸And Peter said to them, "Repent and be baptized every one of you in the name of Jesus Christ for the forgiveness of your sins, and you will receive the gift of the Holy Spirit. ³⁹For the promise is for you and for your children and for all who are far off, everyone whom the Lord our God calls to himself." ⁴⁰And with many other words he bore witness and continued to exhort them, saying, "Save yourselves from this crooked generation." ⁴¹So those who received his word were baptized, and there were added that day about three thousand souls.

THE FELLOWSHIP OF THE BELIEVERS

⁴²And they devoted themselves to the apostles' teaching and the fellowship, to the breaking of bread and the prayers. ⁴³And awe*ᵃ* came upon every soul, and many wonders and signs were being done through the apostles. ⁴⁴And all who believed were together and had all things in common. ⁴⁵And they were selling their possessions and belongings and distributing the proceeds to all, as any had need. ⁴⁶And day by day, attending the temple together and breaking bread in their homes, they received their food with glad and generous hearts, ⁴⁷praising God and having favour with all the people. And the Lord added to their number day by day those who were being saved.

THE LAME BEGGAR HEALED

3 Now Peter and John were going up to the temple at the hour of prayer, the ninth hour.*ᵇ* ²And a man lame from birth was being carried, whom they laid daily at the gate of the temple that is called the Beautiful Gate to ask alms of those entering the temple. ³Seeing Peter and John about to go into the temple, he asked to receive alms. ⁴And Peter directed his gaze at him, as did John, and said, "Look at us." ⁵And he fixed his attention on them, expecting to receive something from them. ⁶But Peter said, "I have no silver and gold, but what I do have I give to you. In the name of Jesus Christ of Nazareth, rise up and walk!" ⁷And he took him by the right hand and raised him up, and immediately his feet and ankles were made strong. ⁸And leaping up, he stood and began to walk, and entered the temple with them, walking and leaping and praising God. ⁹And all the people saw him walking and praising God, ¹⁰and recognized him as the one who sat at the Beautiful Gate of the temple, asking for alms. And they were filled with wonder and amazement at what had happened to him.

PETER SPEAKS IN SOLOMON'S PORTICO

¹¹While he clung to Peter and John, all the people, utterly astounded, ran together to them in the portico called Solomon's. ¹²And when Peter saw it he addressed the people: "Men of Israel, why do you wonder at this, or why do you stare at us, as though by our own power or piety we have made him walk? ¹³The God of Abraham, the God of Isaac, and the God of Jacob, the God of our fathers, glorified his servant*ᶜ* Jesus, whom you delivered over and denied in the presence of Pilate, when he had decided to release him. ¹⁴But you denied the Holy and Righteous One, and asked for a murderer to be granted to you, ¹⁵and you killed the Author of life, whom God raised from the dead. To this we are witnesses. ¹⁶And his name—by faith in his name—has made this man strong whom you see and know, and the faith that is through Jesus*ᵈ* has given the man this perfect health in the presence of you all.

¹⁷"And now, brothers, I know that you acted in ignorance, as did also your rulers. ¹⁸But what God foretold by the mouth of all the prophets, that his Christ would suffer, he thus fulfilled. ¹⁹Repent therefore, and turn back, that your sins may be blotted out, ²⁰that times of refreshing may come from the presence of the Lord, and that he may send the Christ appointed for you, Jesus, ²¹whom heaven must receive until the time

---

*ᵃ*Or *fear* *ᵇ*That is, 3 P.M. *ᶜ*Or *child*; also verse 26 *ᵈ*Greek *him*

for restoring all the things about which God spoke by the mouth of his holy prophets long ago. [22]Moses said, 'The Lord God will raise up for you a prophet like me from your brothers. You shall listen to him in whatever he tells you. [23]And it shall be that every soul who does not listen to that prophet shall be destroyed from the people.' [24]And all the prophets who have spoken, from Samuel and those who came after him, also proclaimed these days. [25]You are the sons of the prophets and of the covenant that God made with your fathers, saying to Abraham, 'And in your offspring shall all the families of the earth be blessed.' [26]God, having raised up his servant, sent him to you first, to bless you by turning every one of you from your wickedness."

PETER AND JOHN BEFORE THE COUNCIL

4 And as they were speaking to the people, the priests and the captain of the temple and the Sadducees came upon them, [2]greatly annoyed because they were teaching the people and proclaiming in Jesus the resurrection from the dead. [3]And they arrested them and put them in custody until the next day, for it was already evening. [4]But many of those who had heard the word believed, and the number of the men came to about five thousand.

[5]On the next day their rulers and elders and scribes gathered together in Jerusalem, [6]with Annas the high priest and Caiaphas and John and Alexander, and all who were of the high-priestly family. [7]And when they had set them in the midst, they enquired, "By what power or by what name did you do this?" [8]Then Peter, filled with the Holy Spirit, said to them, "Rulers of the people and elders, [9]if we are being examined today concerning a good deed done to a crippled man, by what means this man has been healed, [10]let it be known to all of you and to all the people of Israel that by the name of Jesus Christ of Nazareth, whom you crucified, whom God raised from the dead—by him this man is standing before you well. [11]This Jesus[a] is the stone that was rejected by you, the builders, which has become the cornerstone.[b] [12]And there is salvation in no one else, for there is no other name under heaven given among men[c] by which we must be saved."

[13]Now when they saw the boldness of Peter and John, and perceived that they were uneducated, common men, they were astonished. And they recognized that they had been with Jesus. [14]But seeing the man who was healed standing beside them, they had nothing to say in opposition. [15]But when they had commanded them to leave the council, they conferred with one another, [16]saying, "What shall we do with these men? For that a notable sign has been performed through them is evident to all the inhabitants of Jerusalem, and we cannot deny it. [17]But in order that it may spread no further among the people, let us warn them to speak no more to anyone in this name." [18]So they called them and charged them not to speak or teach at all in the name of Jesus. [19]But Peter and John answered them, "Whether it is right in the sight of God to listen to you rather than to God, you must judge, [20]for we cannot but speak of what we have seen and heard." [21]And when they had further threatened them, they let them go, finding no way to punish them, because of the people, for all were praising God for what had happened. [22]For the man on whom this sign of healing was performed was more than forty years old.

THE BELIEVERS PRAY FOR BOLDNESS

[23]When they were released, they went to their friends and reported what the chief priests and the elders had said to them. [24]And when they heard it, they lifted their voices together to God and said, "Sovereign Lord, who made the heaven and the earth and the sea and everything in them, [25]who through the mouth of our father David, your servant,[d] said by the Holy Spirit,

"'Why did the Gentiles rage,
 and the peoples plot in vain?
[26] The kings of the earth set themselves,
 and the rulers were
  gathered together,
 against the Lord and against
  his Anointed'[e]—

[27]for truly in this city there were gathered together against your holy servant Jesus, whom you anointed, both Herod and Pontius Pilate, along with the Gentiles and the peoples of Israel, [28]to do whatever your hand and your plan had predestined to take place. [29]And now, Lord, look upon their threats and grant to your servants to continue to speak

---
[a]Greek *This one* [b]Greek *the head of the corner* [c]The Greek word *anthropoi* refers here to both men and women [d]Or *child*; also verses 27, 30 [e]Or *Christ*

go into the land that I will show you.' ⁴Then he went out from the land of the Chaldeans and lived in Haran. And after his father died, God removed him from there into this land in which you are now living. ⁵Yet he gave him no inheritance in it, not even a foot's length, but promised to give it to him as a possession and to his offspring after him, though he had no child. ⁶And God spoke to this effect—that his offspring would be sojourners in a land belonging to others, who would enslave them and afflict them for four hundred years. ⁷'But I will judge the nation that they serve,' said God, 'and after that they shall come out and worship me in this place.' ⁸And he gave him the covenant of circumcision. And so Abraham became the father of Isaac, and circumcised him on the eighth day, and Isaac became the father of Jacob, and Jacob of the twelve patriarchs.

⁹"And the patriarchs, jealous of Joseph, sold him into Egypt; but God was with him ¹⁰and rescued him out of all his afflictions and gave him favour and wisdom before Pharaoh, king of Egypt, who made him ruler over Egypt and over all his household. ¹¹Now there came a famine throughout all Egypt and Canaan, and great affliction, and our fathers could find no food. ¹²But when Jacob heard that there was grain in Egypt, he sent out our fathers on their first visit. ¹³And on the second visit Joseph made himself known to his brothers, and Joseph's family became known to Pharaoh. ¹⁴And Joseph sent and summoned Jacob his father and all his kindred, seventy-five persons in all. ¹⁵And Jacob went down into Egypt, and he died, he and our fathers, ¹⁶and they were carried back to Shechem and laid in the tomb that Abraham had bought for a sum of silver from the sons of Hamor in Shechem.

¹⁷"But as the time of the promise drew near, which God had granted to Abraham, the people increased and multiplied in Egypt ¹⁸until there arose over Egypt another king who did not know Joseph. ¹⁹He dealt shrewdly with our race and forced our fathers to expose their infants, so that they would not be kept alive. ²⁰At this time Moses was born; and he was beautiful in God's sight. And he was brought up for three months in his father's house, ²¹and when he was exposed, Pharaoh's daughter adopted him and brought him up as her own son. ²²And Moses was instructed in all the wisdom of the Egyptians, and he was mighty in his words and deeds.

²³"When he was forty years old, it came into his heart to visit his brothers, the children of Israel. ²⁴And seeing one of them being wronged, he defended the oppressed man and avenged him by striking down the Egyptian. ²⁵He supposed that his brothers would understand that God was giving them salvation by his hand, but they did not understand. ²⁶And on the following day he appeared to them as they were quarrelling and tried to reconcile them, saying, 'Men, you are brothers. Why do you wrong each other?' ²⁷But the man who was wronging his neighbour thrust him aside, saying, 'Who made you a ruler and a judge over us? ²⁸Do you want to kill me as you killed the Egyptian yesterday?' ²⁹At this retort Moses fled and became an exile in the land of Midian, where he became the father of two sons.

³⁰"Now when forty years had passed, an angel appeared to him in the wilderness of Mount Sinai, in a flame of fire in a bush. ³¹When Moses saw it, he was amazed at the sight, and as he drew near to look, there came the voice of the Lord: ³²'I am the God of your fathers, the God of Abraham and of Isaac and of Jacob.' And Moses trembled and did not dare to look. ³³Then the Lord said to him, 'Take off the sandals from your feet, for the place where you are standing is holy ground. ³⁴I have surely seen the affliction of my people who are in Egypt, and have heard their groaning, and I have come down to deliver them. And now come, I will send you to Egypt.'

³⁵"This Moses, whom they rejected, saying, 'Who made you a ruler and a judge?'—this man God sent as both ruler and redeemer by the hand of the angel who appeared to him in the bush. ³⁶This man led them out, performing wonders and signs in Egypt and at the Red Sea and in the wilderness for forty years. ³⁷This is the Moses who said to the Israelites, 'God will raise up for you a prophet like me from your brothers.' ³⁸This is the one who was in the congregation in the wilderness with the angel who spoke to him at Mount Sinai, and with our fathers. He received living oracles to give to us. ³⁹Our fathers refused to obey him, but thrust him aside, and in their hearts they turned to Egypt, ⁴⁰saying to Aaron, 'Make for us gods who will go before us. As for this Moses who led us out from the land of Egypt, we do not know what has become of him.' ⁴¹And they made a calf in those days, and offered a sacrifice to the

idol and were rejoicing in the works of their hands. ⁴²But God turned away and gave them over to worship the host of heaven, as it is written in the book of the prophets:

> "'Did you bring to me slain
> beasts and sacrifices,
> during the forty years in the
> wilderness, O house of Israel?
> ⁴³ You took up the tent of Moloch
> and the star of your god Rephan,
> the images that you made
> to worship;
> and I will send you into exile
> beyond Babylon.'

⁴⁴"Our fathers had the tent of witness in the wilderness, just as he who spoke to Moses directed him to make it, according to the pattern that he had seen. ⁴⁵Our fathers in turn brought it in with Joshua when they dispossessed the nations that God drove out before our fathers. So it was until the days of David, ⁴⁶who found favour in the sight of God and asked to find a dwelling place for the God of Jacob.[a] ⁴⁷But it was Solomon who built a house for him. ⁴⁸Yet the Most High does not dwell in houses made by hands, as the prophet says,

> ⁴⁹ "'Heaven is my throne,
> and the earth is my footstool.
> What kind of house will you build
> for me, says the Lord,
> or what is the place of my rest?
> ⁵⁰ Did not my hand make all
> these things?'

⁵¹"You stiff-necked people, uncircumcised in heart and ears, you always resist the Holy Spirit. As your fathers did, so do you. ⁵²Which of the prophets did your fathers not persecute? And they killed those who announced beforehand the coming of the Righteous One, whom you have now betrayed and murdered, ⁵³you who received the law as delivered by angels and did not keep it."

THE STONING OF STEPHEN

⁵⁴Now when they heard these things they were enraged, and they ground their teeth at him. ⁵⁵But he, full of the Holy Spirit, gazed into heaven and saw the glory of God, and Jesus standing at the right hand of God. ⁵⁶And he said, "Behold, I see the heavens opened, and the Son of Man standing at the right hand of God." ⁵⁷But they cried out with a loud voice and stopped their ears and rushed together[b] at him. ⁵⁸Then they cast him out of the city and stoned him. And the witnesses laid down their garments at the feet of a young man named Saul. ⁵⁹And as they were stoning Stephen, he called out, "Lord Jesus, receive my spirit." ⁶⁰And falling to his knees he cried out with a loud voice, "Lord, do not hold this sin against them." And when he had said this, he fell asleep.

SAUL RAVAGES THE CHURCH

8 And Saul approved of his execution.
And there arose on that day a great persecution against the church in Jerusalem, and they were all scattered throughout the regions of Judea and Samaria, except the apostles. ²Devout men buried Stephen and made great lamentation over him. ³But Saul was ravaging the church, and entering house after house, he dragged off men and women and committed them to prison.

PHILIP PROCLAIMS CHRIST IN SAMARIA

⁴Now those who were scattered went about preaching the word. ⁵Philip went down to the city[c] of Samaria and proclaimed to them the Christ. ⁶And the crowds with one accord paid attention to what was being said by Philip, when they heard him and saw the signs that he did. ⁷For unclean spirits, crying out with a loud voice, came out of many who had them, and many who were paralysed or lame were healed. ⁸So there was much joy in that city.

SIMON THE MAGICIAN BELIEVES

⁹But there was a man named Simon, who had previously practised magic in the city and amazed the people of Samaria, saying that he himself was somebody great. ¹⁰They all paid attention to him, from the least to the greatest, saying, "This man is the power of God that is called Great." ¹¹And they paid attention to him because for a long time he had amazed them with his magic. ¹²But when they believed Philip as he preached good news about the kingdom of God and the name of Jesus Christ, they were baptized, both men and women. ¹³Even Simon himself believed, and after being baptized he continued with Philip. And seeing signs and great miracles[d] performed, he was amazed.

---

[a] Some manuscripts *for the house of Jacob* [b] Or *rushed with one mind*
[c] Some manuscripts *a city* [d] Greek *works of power*

¹⁴Now when the apostles at Jerusalem heard that Samaria had received the word of God, they sent to them Peter and John, ¹⁵who came down and prayed for them that they might receive the Holy Spirit, ¹⁶for he had not yet fallen on any of them, but they had only been baptized in the name of the Lord Jesus. ¹⁷Then they laid their hands on them and they received the Holy Spirit. ¹⁸Now when Simon saw that the Spirit was given through the laying on of the apostles' hands, he offered them money, ¹⁹saying, "Give me this power also, so that anyone on whom I lay my hands may receive the Holy Spirit." ²⁰But Peter said to him, "May your silver perish with you, because you thought you could obtain the gift of God with money! ²¹You have neither part nor lot in this matter, for your heart is not right before God. ²²Repent, therefore, of this wickedness of yours, and pray to the Lord that, if possible, the intent of your heart may be forgiven you. ²³For I see that you are in the gall[a] of bitterness and in the bond of iniquity." ²⁴And Simon answered, "Pray for me to the Lord, that nothing of what you have said may come upon me."

²⁵Now when they had testified and spoken the word of the Lord, they returned to Jerusalem, preaching the gospel to many villages of the Samaritans.

PHILIP AND THE ETHIOPIAN EUNUCH

²⁶Now an angel of the Lord said to Philip, "Rise and go towards the south[b] to the road that goes down from Jerusalem to Gaza." This is a desert place. ²⁷And he rose and went. And there was an Ethiopian, a eunuch, a court official of Candace, queen of the Ethiopians, who was in charge of all her treasure. He had come to Jerusalem to worship ²⁸and was returning, seated in his chariot, and he was reading the prophet Isaiah. ²⁹And the Spirit said to Philip, "Go over and join this chariot." ³⁰So Philip ran to him and heard him reading Isaiah the prophet and asked, "Do you understand what you are reading?" ³¹And he said, "How can I, unless someone guides me?" And he invited Philip to come up and sit with him. ³²Now the passage of the Scripture that he was reading was this:

"Like a sheep he was led to the slaughter
　and like a lamb before its
　　shearer is silent,
so he opens not his mouth.

³³ In his humiliation justice
　　was denied him.
　Who can describe his generation?
　For his life is taken away
　　from the earth."

³⁴And the eunuch said to Philip, "About whom, I ask you, does the prophet say this, about himself or about someone else?" ³⁵Then Philip opened his mouth, and beginning with this Scripture he told him the good news about Jesus. ³⁶And as they were going along the road they came to some water, and the eunuch said, "See, here is water! What prevents me from being baptized?"[c] ³⁸And he commanded the chariot to stop, and they both went down into the water, Philip and the eunuch, and he baptized him. ³⁹And when they came up out of the water, the Spirit of the Lord carried Philip away, and the eunuch saw him no more, and went on his way rejoicing. ⁴⁰But Philip found himself at Azotus, and as he passed through he preached the gospel to all the towns until he came to Caesarea.

THE CONVERSION OF SAUL

9 But Saul, still breathing threats and murder against the disciples of the Lord, went to the high priest ²and asked him for letters to the synagogues at Damascus, so that if he found any belonging to the Way, men or women, he might bring them bound to Jerusalem. ³Now as he went on his way, he approached Damascus, and suddenly a light from heaven shone around him. ⁴And falling to the ground, he heard a voice saying to him, "Saul, Saul, why are you persecuting me?" ⁵And he said, "Who are you, Lord?" And he said, "I am Jesus, whom you are persecuting. ⁶But rise and enter the city, and you will be told what you are to do." ⁷The men who were travelling with him stood speechless, hearing the voice but seeing no one. ⁸Saul rose from the ground, and although his eyes were opened, he saw nothing. So they led him by the hand and brought him into Damascus. ⁹And for three days he was without sight, and neither ate nor drank.

¹⁰Now there was a disciple at Damascus named Ananias. The Lord said to him in a vision, "Ananias." And he said, "Here I am,

---

[a] That is, a bitter fluid secreted by the liver; bile [b] Or *go at about noon* [c] Some manuscripts add all or most of verse 37: *And Philip said, "If you believe with all your heart, you may." And he replied, "I believe that Jesus Christ is the Son of God."*

Lord." ¹¹And the Lord said to him, "Rise and go to the street called Straight, and at the house of Judas look for a man of Tarsus named Saul, for behold, he is praying, ¹²and he has seen in a vision a man named Ananias come in and lay his hands on him so that he might regain his sight." ¹³But Ananias answered, "Lord, I have heard from many about this man, how much evil he has done to your saints at Jerusalem. ¹⁴And here he has authority from the chief priests to bind all who call on your name." ¹⁵But the Lord said to him, "Go, for he is a chosen instrument of mine to carry my name before the Gentiles and kings and the children of Israel. ¹⁶For I will show him how much he must suffer for the sake of my name." ¹⁷So Ananias departed and entered the house. And laying his hands on him he said, "Brother Saul, the Lord Jesus who appeared to you on the road by which you came has sent me so that you may regain your sight and be filled with the Holy Spirit." ¹⁸And immediately something like scales fell from his eyes, and he regained his sight. Then he rose and was baptized; ¹⁹and taking food, he was strengthened.

SAUL PROCLAIMS JESUS IN SYNAGOGUES

For some days he was with the disciples at Damascus. ²⁰And immediately he proclaimed Jesus in the synagogues, saying, "He is the Son of God." ²¹And all who heard him were amazed and said, "Is not this the man who made havoc in Jerusalem of those who called upon this name? And has he not come here for this purpose, to bring them bound before the chief priests?" ²²But Saul increased all the more in strength, and confounded the Jews who lived in Damascus by proving that Jesus was the Christ.

SAUL ESCAPES FROM DAMASCUS

²³When many days had passed, the Jews[a] plotted to kill him, ²⁴but their plot became known to Saul. They were watching the gates day and night in order to kill him, ²⁵but his disciples took him by night and let him down through an opening in the wall,[b] lowering him in a basket.

SAUL IN JERUSALEM

²⁶And when he had come to Jerusalem, he attempted to join the disciples. And they were all afraid of him, for they did not believe that he was a disciple. ²⁷But Barnabas took him and brought him to the apostles and declared to them how on the road he had seen the Lord, who spoke to him, and how at Damascus he had preached boldly in the name of Jesus. ²⁸So he went in and out among them at Jerusalem, preaching boldly in the name of the Lord. ²⁹And he spoke and disputed against the Hellenists.[c] But they were seeking to kill him. ³⁰And when the brothers learned this, they brought him down to Caesarea and sent him off to Tarsus.

³¹So the church throughout all Judea and Galilee and Samaria had peace and was being built up. And walking in the fear of the Lord and in the comfort of the Holy Spirit, it multiplied.

THE HEALING OF AENEAS

³²Now as Peter went here and there among them all, he came down also to the saints who lived at Lydda. ³³There he found a man named Aeneas, bedridden for eight years, who was paralyzed. ³⁴And Peter said to him, "Aeneas, Jesus Christ heals you; rise and make your bed." And immediately he rose. ³⁵And all the residents of Lydda and Sharon saw him, and they turned to the Lord.

DORCAS RESTORED TO LIFE

³⁶Now there was in Joppa a disciple named Tabitha, which, translated, means Dorcas.[d] She was full of good works and acts of charity. ³⁷In those days she became ill and died, and when they had washed her, they laid her in an upper room. ³⁸Since Lydda was near Joppa, the disciples, hearing that Peter was there, sent two men to him, urging him, "Please come to us without delay." ³⁹So Peter rose and went with them. And when he arrived, they took him to the upper room. All the widows stood beside him weeping and showing tunics[e] and other garments that Dorcas made while she was with them. ⁴⁰But Peter put them all outside, and knelt down and prayed; and turning to the body he said, "Tabitha, arise." And she opened her eyes, and when she saw Peter she sat up. ⁴¹And he gave her his hand and raised her up. Then, calling the saints and widows, he presented her alive. ⁴²And it became known throughout all Joppa, and many believed in the Lord. ⁴³And he stayed in Joppa for many days with one Simon, a tanner.

---

[a]The Greek word *Ioudaioi* refers specifically here to Jewish religious leaders, and others under their influence, who opposed the Christian faith in that time [b]Greek *through the wall* [c]That is, Greek-speaking Jews [d]The Aramaic name *Tabitha* and the Greek name *Dorcas* both mean *gazelle* [e]Greek *chiton*, a long garment worn under the cloak next to the skin

PETER AND CORNELIUS

10 At Caesarea there was a man named Cornelius, a centurion of what was known as the Italian Cohort, ²a devout man who feared God with all his household, gave alms generously to the people, and prayed continually to God. ³About the ninth hour of the day[a] he saw clearly in a vision an angel of God come in and say to him, "Cornelius." ⁴And he stared at him in terror and said, "What is it, Lord?" And he said to him, "Your prayers and your alms have ascended as a memorial before God. ⁵And now send men to Joppa and bring one Simon who is called Peter. ⁶He is lodging with one Simon, a tanner, whose house is by the sea." ⁷When the angel who spoke to him had departed, he called two of his servants and a devout soldier from among those who attended him, ⁸and having related everything to them, he sent them to Joppa.

PETER'S VISION

⁹The next day, as they were on their journey and approaching the city, Peter went up on the housetop about the sixth hour[b] to pray. ¹⁰And he became hungry and wanted something to eat, but while they were preparing it, he fell into a trance ¹¹and saw the heavens opened and something like a great sheet descending, being let down by its four corners upon the earth. ¹²In it were all kinds of animals and reptiles and birds of the air. ¹³And there came a voice to him: "Rise, Peter; kill and eat." ¹⁴But Peter said, "By no means, Lord; for I have never eaten anything that is common or unclean." ¹⁵And the voice came to him again a second time, "What God has made clean, do not call common." ¹⁶This happened three times, and the thing was taken up at once to heaven.

¹⁷Now while Peter was inwardly perplexed as to what the vision that he had seen might mean, behold, the men who were sent by Cornelius, having made enquiry for Simon's house, stood at the gate ¹⁸and called out to ask whether Simon who was called Peter was lodging there. ¹⁹And while Peter was pondering the vision, the Spirit said to him, "Behold, three men are looking for you. ²⁰Rise and go down and accompany them without hesitation,[c] for I have sent them." ²¹And Peter went down to the men and said, "I am the one you are looking for. What is the reason for your coming?" ²²And they said, "Cornelius, a centurion, an upright and God-fearing man, who is well spoken of by the whole Jewish nation, was directed by a holy angel to send for you to come to his house and to hear what you have to say." ²³So he invited them in to be his guests.

The next day he rose and went away with them, and some of the brothers from Joppa accompanied him. ²⁴And on the following day they entered Caesarea. Cornelius was expecting them and had called together his relatives and close friends. ²⁵When Peter entered, Cornelius met him and fell down at his feet and worshipped him. ²⁶But Peter lifted him up, saying, "Stand up; I too am a man." ²⁷And as he talked with him, he went in and found many persons gathered. ²⁸And he said to them, "You yourselves know how unlawful it is for a Jew to associate with or to visit anyone of another nation, but God has shown me that I should not call any person common or unclean. ²⁹So when I was sent for, I came without objection. I ask then why you sent for me."

³⁰And Cornelius said, "Four days ago, about this hour, I was praying in my house at the ninth hour,[d] and behold, a man stood before me in bright clothing ³¹and said, 'Cornelius, your prayer has been heard and your alms have been remembered before God. ³²Send therefore to Joppa and ask for Simon who is called Peter. He is lodging in the house of Simon, a tanner, by the sea.' ³³So I sent for you at once, and you have been kind enough to come. Now therefore we are all here in the presence of God to hear all that you have been commanded by the Lord."

GENTILES HEAR THE GOOD NEWS

³⁴So Peter opened his mouth and said: "Truly I understand that God shows no partiality, ³⁵but in every nation anyone who fears him and does what is right is acceptable to him. ³⁶As for the word that he sent to Israel, preaching good news of peace through Jesus Christ (he is Lord of all), ³⁷you yourselves know what happened throughout all Judea, beginning from Galilee after the baptism that John proclaimed: ³⁸how God anointed Jesus of Nazareth with the Holy Spirit and with power. He went about doing good and healing all who were oppressed by the devil, for God was with him. ³⁹And we are witnesses of all that he did both in the country

---

[a] That is, 3 P.M. [b] That is, noon [c] O- *accompany them, making no distinction* [d] That is, 3 P.M.

of the Jews and in Jerusalem. They put him to death by hanging him on a tree, **40**but God raised him on the third day and caused him to appear, **41**not to all the people but to us who had been chosen by God as witnesses, who ate and drank with him after he rose from the dead. **42**And he commanded us to preach to the people and to testify that he is the one appointed by God to be judge of the living and the dead. **43**To him all the prophets bear witness that everyone who believes in him receives forgiveness of sins through his name."

THE HOLY SPIRIT FALLS ON THE GENTILES

44While Peter was still saying these things, the Holy Spirit fell on all who heard the word. **45**And the believers from among the circumcised who had come with Peter were amazed, because the gift of the Holy Spirit was poured out even on the Gentiles. **46**For they were hearing them speaking in tongues and extolling God. Then Peter declared, **47**"Can anyone withhold water for baptizing these people, who have received the Holy Spirit just as we have?" **48**And he commanded them to be baptized in the name of Jesus Christ. Then they asked him to remain for some days.

PETER REPORTS TO THE CHURCH

11 Now the apostles and the brothers[a] who were throughout Judea heard that the Gentiles also had received the word of God. **2**So when Peter went up to Jerusalem, the circumcision party[b] criticized him, saying, **3**"You went to uncircumcised men and ate with them." **4**But Peter began and explained it to them in order: **5**"I was in the city of Joppa praying, and in a trance I saw a vision, something like a great sheet descending, being let down from heaven by its four corners, and it came down to me. **6**Looking at it closely, I observed animals and beasts of prey and reptiles and birds of the air. **7**And I heard a voice saying to me, 'Rise, Peter; kill and eat.' **8**But I said, 'By no means, Lord; for nothing common or unclean has ever entered my mouth.' **9**But the voice answered a second time from heaven, 'What God has made clean, do not call common.' **10**This happened three times, and all was drawn up again into heaven. **11**And behold, at that very moment three men arrived at the house in which we were, sent to me from Caesarea. **12**And the Spirit told me to go with them, making no distinction. These six brothers also accompanied me, and we entered the man's house. **13**And he told us how he had seen the angel stand in his house and say, 'Send to Joppa and bring Simon who is called Peter; **14**he will declare to you a message by which you will be saved, you and all your household.' **15**As I began to speak, the Holy Spirit fell on them just as on us at the beginning. **16**And I remembered the word of the Lord, how he said, 'John baptized with water, but you will be baptized with the Holy Spirit.' **17**If then God gave the same gift to them as he gave to us when we believed in the Lord Jesus Christ, who was I that I could stand in God's way?" **18**When they heard these things they fell silent. And they glorified God, saying, "Then to the Gentiles also God has granted repentance that leads to life."

THE CHURCH IN ANTIOCH

19Now those who were scattered because of the persecution that arose over Stephen travelled as far as Phoenicia and Cyprus and Antioch, speaking the word to no one except Jews. **20**But there were some of them, men of Cyprus and Cyrene, who on coming to Antioch spoke to the Hellenists[c] also, preaching the Lord Jesus. **21**And the hand of the Lord was with them, and a great number who believed turned to the Lord. **22**The report of this came to the ears of the church in Jerusalem, and they sent Barnabas to Antioch. **23**When he came and saw the grace of God, he was glad, and he exhorted them all to remain faithful to the Lord with steadfast purpose, **24**for he was a good man, full of the Holy Spirit and of faith. And a great many people were added to the Lord. **25**So Barnabas went to Tarsus to look for Saul, **26**and when he had found him, he brought him to Antioch. For a whole year they met with the church and taught a great many people. And in Antioch the disciples were first called Christians.

27Now in these days prophets came down from Jerusalem to Antioch. **28**And one of them named Agabus stood up and foretold by the Spirit that there would be a great famine over all the world (this took place in the days of Claudius). **29**So the disciples determined, every one according to his ability, to send relief to the brothers[d] living in Judea. **30**And they did so, sending it to the elders by the hand of Barnabas and Saul.

---

[a] Or *brothers and sisters* [b] Or *Jerusalem, those of the circumcision*
[c] Or *Greeks (that is, Greek-speaking non-Jews)* [d] Or *brothers and sisters*

JAMES KILLED AND PETER IMPRISONED

12 About that time Herod the king laid violent hands on some who belonged to the church. ²He killed James the brother of John with the sword, ³and when he saw that it pleased the Jews, he proceeded to arrest Peter also. This was during the days of Unleavened Bread. ⁴And when he had seized him, he put him in prison, delivering him over to four squads of soldiers to guard him, intending after the Passover to bring him out to the people. ⁵So Peter was kept in prison, but earnest prayer for him was made to God by the church.

PETER IS RESCUED

⁶Now when Herod was about to bring him out, on that very night, Peter was sleeping between two soldiers, bound with two chains, and sentries before the door were guarding the prison. ⁷And behold, an angel of the Lord stood next to him, and a light shone in the cell. He struck Peter on the side and woke him, saying, "Get up quickly." And the chains fell off his hands. ⁸And the angel said to him, "Dress yourself and put on your sandals." And he did so. And he said to him, "Wrap your cloak round you and follow me." ⁹And he went out and followed him. He did not know that what was being done by the angel was real, but thought he was seeing a vision. ¹⁰When they had passed the first and the second guard, they came to the iron gate leading into the city. It opened for them of its own accord, and they went out and went along one street, and immediately the angel left him. ¹¹When Peter came to himself, he said, "Now I am sure that the Lord has sent his angel and rescued me from the hand of Herod and from all that the Jewish people were expecting."

¹²When he realized this, he went to the house of Mary, the mother of John whose other name was Mark, where many were gathered together and were praying. ¹³And when he knocked at the door of the gateway, a servant girl named Rhoda came to answer. ¹⁴Recognizing Peter's voice, in her joy she did not open the gate but ran in and reported that Peter was standing at the gate. ¹⁵They said to her, "You are out of your mind." But she kept insisting that it was so, and they kept saying, "It is his angel!" ¹⁶But Peter continued knocking, and when they opened, they saw him and were amazed. ¹⁷But motioning to them with his hand to be silent, he described to them how the Lord had brought him out of the prison. And he said, "Tell these things to James and to the brothers."[a] Then he departed and went to another place.

¹⁸Now when day came, there was no little disturbance among the soldiers over what had become of Peter. ¹⁹And after Herod searched for him and did not find him, he examined the sentries and ordered that they should be put to death. Then he went down from Judea to Caesarea and spent time there.

THE DEATH OF HEROD

²⁰Now Herod was angry with the people of Tyre and Sidon, and they came to him with one accord, and having persuaded Blastus, the king's chamberlain,[b] they asked for peace, because their country depended on the king's country for food. ²¹On an appointed day Herod put on his royal robes, took his seat upon the throne, and delivered an oration to them. ²²And the people were shouting, "The voice of a god, and not of a man!" ²³Immediately an angel of the Lord struck him down, because he did not give God the glory, and he was eaten by worms and breathed his last. ²⁴But the word of God increased and multiplied.

²⁵And Barnabas and Saul returned from[c] Jerusalem when they had completed their service, bringing with them John, whose other name was Mark.

BARNABAS AND SAUL SENT OFF

13 Now there were in the church at Antioch prophets and teachers, Barnabas, Simeon who was called Niger,[d] Lucius of Cyrene, Manaen a lifelong friend of Herod the tetrarch, and Saul. ²While they were worshipping the Lord and fasting, the Holy Spirit said, "Set apart for me Barnabas and Saul for the work to which I have called them." ³Then after fasting and praying they laid their hands on them and sent them off.

BARNABAS AND SAUL ON CYPRUS

⁴So, being sent out by the Holy Spirit, they went down to Seleucia, and from there they sailed to Cyprus. ⁵When they arrived at Salamis, they proclaimed the word of God in the synagogues of the Jews. And they had John to assist them. ⁶When they had gone

---

[a] Or *brothers and sisters* [b] That is, trusted personal attendant [c] Some manuscripts *to* [d] *Niger* is a Latin word meaning *black*, or *dark*

through the whole island as far as Paphos, they came upon a certain magician, a Jewish false prophet named Bar-Jesus. ⁷He was with the proconsul, Sergius Paulus, a man of intelligence, who summoned Barnabas and Saul and sought to hear the word of God. ⁸But Elymas the magician (for that is the meaning of his name) opposed them, seeking to turn the proconsul away from the faith. ⁹But Saul, who was also called Paul, filled with the Holy Spirit, looked intently at him ¹⁰and said, "You son of the devil, you enemy of all righteousness, full of all deceit and villainy, will you not stop making crooked the straight paths of the Lord? ¹¹And now, behold, the hand of the Lord is upon you, and you will be blind and unable to see the sun for a time." Immediately mist and darkness fell upon him, and he went about seeking people to lead him by the hand. ¹²Then the proconsul believed, when he saw what had occurred, for he was astonished at the teaching of the Lord.

PAUL AND BARNABAS AT ANTIOCH IN PISIDIA

¹³Now Paul and his companions set sail from Paphos and came to Perga in Pamphylia. And John left them and returned to Jerusalem, ¹⁴but they went on from Perga and came to Antioch in Pisidia. And on the Sabbath day they went into the synagogue and sat down. ¹⁵After the reading from the Law and the Prophets, the rulers of the synagogue sent a message to them, saying, "Brothers, if you have any word of encouragement for the people, say it." ¹⁶So Paul stood up, and motioning with his hand said:

"Men of Israel and you who fear God, listen. ¹⁷The God of this people Israel chose our fathers and made the people great during their stay in the land of Egypt, and with uplifted arm he led them out of it. ¹⁸And for about forty years he put up with*ᵃ* them in the wilderness. ¹⁹And after destroying seven nations in the land of Canaan, he gave them their land as an inheritance. ²⁰All this took about 450 years. And after that he gave them judges until Samuel the prophet. ²¹Then they asked for a king, and God gave them Saul the son of Kish, a man of the tribe of Benjamin, for forty years. ²²And when he had removed him, he raised up David to be their king, of whom he testified and said, 'I have found in David the son of Jesse a man after my heart, who will do all my will.' ²³Of this man's offspring God has brought to Israel a Saviour, Jesus, as he promised. ²⁴Before his coming, John had proclaimed a baptism of repentance to all the people of Israel. ²⁵And as John was finishing his course, he said, 'What do you suppose that I am? I am not he. No, but behold, after me one is coming, the sandals of whose feet I am not worthy to untie.'

²⁶"Brothers, sons of the family of Abraham, and those among you who fear God, to us has been sent the message of this salvation. ²⁷For those who live in Jerusalem and their rulers, because they did not recognize him nor understand the utterances of the prophets, which are read every Sabbath, fulfilled them by condemning him. ²⁸And though they found in him no guilt worthy of death, they asked Pilate to have him executed. ²⁹And when they had carried out all that was written of him, they took him down from the tree and laid him in a tomb. ³⁰But God raised him from the dead, ³¹and for many days he appeared to those who had come up with him from Galilee to Jerusalem, who are now his witnesses to the people. ³²And we bring you the good news that what God promised to the fathers, ³³this he has fulfilled to us their children by raising Jesus, as also it is written in the second Psalm,

" 'You are my Son,
    today I have begotten you.'

³⁴And as for the fact that he raised him from the dead, no more to return to corruption, he has spoken in this way,

" 'I will give you the holy and sure
    blessings of David.'

³⁵Therefore he says also in another psalm,

" 'You will not let your Holy
    One see corruption.'

³⁶For David, after he had served the purpose of God in his own generation, fell asleep and was laid with his fathers and saw corruption, ³⁷but he whom God raised up did not see corruption. ³⁸Let it be known to you therefore, brothers, that through this man forgiveness of sins is proclaimed to you, ³⁹and by him everyone who believes is freed*ᵇ* from everything from which you could not

---

*ᵃ*Some manuscripts *he carried* (compare Deuteronomy 1:31)
*ᵇ*Greek *justified*; twice in this verse

be freed by the law of Moses. ⁴⁰Beware, therefore, lest what is said in the Prophets should come about:

⁴¹ "'Look, you scoffers,
be astounded and perish;
for I am doing a work in your days,
a work that you will not believe,
even if one tells it to you.'"

⁴²As they went out, the people begged that these things might be told them the next Sabbath. ⁴³And after the meeting of the synagogue broke up, many Jews and devout converts to Judaism followed Paul and Barnabas, who, as they spoke with them, urged them to continue in the grace of God.

⁴⁴The next Sabbath almost the whole city gathered to hear the word of the Lord. ⁴⁵But when the Jews[a] saw the crowds, they were filled with jealousy and began to contradict what was spoken by Paul, reviling him. ⁴⁶And Paul and Barnabas spoke out boldly, saying, "It was necessary that the word of God be spoken first to you. Since you thrust it aside and judge yourselves unworthy of eternal life, behold, we are turning to the Gentiles. ⁴⁷For so the Lord has commanded us, saying,

"'I have made you a light
for the Gentiles,
that you may bring salvation to
the ends of the earth.'"

⁴⁸And when the Gentiles heard this, they began rejoicing and glorifying the word of the Lord, and as many as were appointed to eternal life believed. ⁴⁹And the word of the Lord was spreading throughout the whole region. ⁵⁰But the Jews incited the devout women of high standing and the leading men of the city, stirred up persecution against Paul and Barnabas, and drove them out of their district. ⁵¹But they shook off the dust from their feet against them and went to Iconium. ⁵²And the disciples were filled with joy and with the Holy Spirit.

PAUL AND BARNABAS AT ICONIUM

14 Now at Iconium they entered together into the Jewish synagogue and spoke in such a way that a great number of both Jews and Greeks believed. ²But the unbelieving Jews stirred up the Gentiles and poisoned their minds against the brothers.[b] ³So they remained for a long time, speaking boldly for the Lord, who bore witness to the word of his grace, granting signs and wonders to be done by their hands. ⁴But the people of the city were divided; some sided with the Jews and some with the apostles. ⁵When an attempt was made by both Gentiles and Jews, with their rulers, to mistreat them and to stone them, ⁶they learned of it and fled to Lystra and Derbe, cities of Lycaonia, and to the surrounding country, ⁷and there they continued to preach the gospel.

PAUL AND BARNABAS AT LYSTRA

⁸Now at Lystra there was a man sitting who could not use his feet. He was crippled from birth and had never walked. ⁹He listened to Paul speaking. And Paul, looking intently at him and seeing that he had faith to be made well,[c] ¹⁰said in a loud voice, "Stand upright on your feet." And he sprang up and began walking. ¹¹And when the crowds saw what Paul had done, they lifted up their voices, saying in Lycaonian, "The gods have come down to us in the likeness of men!" ¹²Barnabas they called Zeus, and Paul, Hermes, because he was the chief speaker. ¹³And the priest of Zeus, whose temple was at the entrance to the city, brought oxen and garlands to the gates and wanted to offer sacrifice with the crowds. ¹⁴But when the apostles Barnabas and Paul heard of it, they tore their garments and rushed out into the crowd, crying out, ¹⁵"Men, why are you doing these things? We also are men, of like nature with you, and we bring you good news, that you should turn from these vain things to a living God, who made the heaven and the earth and the sea and all that is in them. ¹⁶In past generations he allowed all the nations to walk in their own ways. ¹⁷Yet he did not leave himself without witness, for he did good by giving you rains from heaven and fruitful seasons, satisfying your hearts with food and gladness." ¹⁸Even with these words they scarcely restrained the people from offering sacrifice to them.

PAUL STONED AT LYSTRA

¹⁹But Jews came from Antioch and Iconium, and having persuaded the crowds, they stoned Paul and dragged him out of the city, supposing that he was dead. ²⁰But when the disciples gathered about him, he rose up and

---

[a]Greek *Ioudaioi* probably refers here to Jewish religious leaders, and others under their influence, in that time; also verse 50 [b]Or *brothers and sisters* [c]Or *be saved*

entered the city, and on the next day he went on with Barnabas to Derbe. ²¹When they had preached the gospel to that city and had made many disciples, they returned to Lystra and to Iconium and to Antioch, ²²strengthening the souls of the disciples, encouraging them to continue in the faith, and saying that through many tribulations we must enter the kingdom of God. ²³And when they had appointed elders for them in every church, with prayer and fasting they committed them to the Lord in whom they had believed.

PAUL AND BARNABAS RETURN TO ANTIOCH IN SYRIA

²⁴Then they passed through Pisidia and came to Pamphylia. ²⁵And when they had spoken the word in Perga, they went down to Attalia, ²⁶and from there they sailed to Antioch, where they had been commended to the grace of God for the work that they had fulfilled. ²⁷And when they arrived and gathered the church together, they declared all that God had done with them, and how he had opened a door of faith to the Gentiles. ²⁸And they remained no little time with the disciples.

THE JERUSALEM COUNCIL

15 But some men came down from Judea and were teaching the brothers, "Unless you are circumcised according to the custom of Moses, you cannot be saved." ²And after Paul and Barnabas had no small dissension and debate with them, Paul and Barnabas and some of the others were appointed to go up to Jerusalem to the apostles and the elders about this question. ³So, being sent on their way by the church, they passed through both Phoenicia and Samaria, describing in detail the conversion of the Gentiles, and brought great joy to all the brothers.ᵃ ⁴When they came to Jerusalem, they were welcomed by the church and the apostles and the elders, and they declared all that God had done with them. ⁵But some believers who belonged to the party of the Pharisees rose up and said, "It is necessary to circumcise them and to order them to keep the law of Moses."

⁶The apostles and the elders were gathered together to consider this matter. ⁷And after there had been much debate, Peter stood up and said to them, "Brothers, you know that in the early days God made a choice among you, that by my mouth the Gentiles should hear the word of the gospel and believe. ⁸And God, who knows the heart, bore witness to them, by giving them the Holy Spirit just as he did to us, ⁹and he made no distinction between us and them, having cleansed their hearts by faith. ¹⁰Now, therefore, why are you putting God to the test by placing a yoke on the neck of the disciples that neither our fathers nor we have been able to bear? ¹¹But we believe that we will be saved through the grace of the Lord Jesus, just as they will."

¹²And all the assembly fell silent, and they listened to Barnabas and Paul as they related what signs and wonders God had done through them among the Gentiles. ¹³After they finished speaking, James replied, "Brothers, listen to me. ¹⁴Simeon has related how God first visited the Gentiles, to take from them a people for his name. ¹⁵And with this the words of the prophets agree, just as it is written,

¹⁶ "'After this I will return,
  and I will rebuild the tent of
    David that has fallen;
  I will rebuild its ruins,
    and I will restore it,
¹⁷ that the remnantᵇ of mankind
    may seek the Lord,
  and all the Gentiles who are
    called by my name,
  says the Lord, who makes these
    things ¹⁸known from of old.'

¹⁹Therefore my judgement is that we should not trouble those of the Gentiles who turn to God, ²⁰but should write to them to abstain from the things polluted by idols, and from sexual immorality, and from what has been strangled, and from blood. ²¹For from ancient generations Moses has had in every city those who proclaim him, for he is read every Sabbath in the synagogues."

THE COUNCIL'S LETTER TO GENTILE BELIEVERS

²²Then it seemed good to the apostles and the elders, with the whole church, to choose men from among them and send them to Antioch with Paul and Barnabas. They sent Judas called Barsabbas, and Silas, leading men among the brothers, ²³with the following letter: "The brothers, both the apostles and the elders, to the brothersᶜ who are of

---

ᵃOr *brothers and sisters*; also verse 22   ᵇOr *rest*   ᶜOr *brothers and sisters*; also verses 32, 33, 36

the Gentiles in Antioch and Syria and Cilicia, greetings. ²⁴Since we have heard that some persons have gone out from us and troubled you[a] with words, unsettling your minds, although we gave them no instructions, ²⁵it has seemed good to us, having come to one accord, to choose men and send them to you with our beloved Barnabas and Paul, ²⁶men who have risked their lives for the name of our Lord Jesus Christ. ²⁷We have therefore sent Judas and Silas, who themselves will tell you the same things by word of mouth. ²⁸For it has seemed good to the Holy Spirit and to us to lay on you no greater burden than these requirements: ²⁹that you abstain from what has been sacrificed to idols, and from blood, and from what has been strangled, and from sexual immorality. If you keep yourselves from these, you will do well. Farewell."

³⁰So when they were sent off, they went down to Antioch, and having gathered the congregation together, they delivered the letter. ³¹And when they had read it, they rejoiced because of its encouragement. ³²And Judas and Silas, who were themselves prophets, encouraged and strengthened the brothers with many words. ³³And after they had spent some time, they were sent off in peace by the brothers to those who had sent them.[b] ³⁵But Paul and Barnabas remained in Antioch, teaching and preaching the word of the Lord, with many others also.

PAUL AND BARNABAS SEPARATE

³⁶And after some days Paul said to Barnabas, "Let us return and visit the brothers in every city where we proclaimed the word of the Lord, and see how they are." ³⁷Now Barnabas wanted to take with them John called Mark. ³⁸But Paul thought best not to take with them one who had withdrawn from them in Pamphylia and had not gone with them to the work. ³⁹And there arose a sharp disagreement, so that they separated from each other. Barnabas took Mark with him and sailed away to Cyprus, ⁴⁰but Paul chose Silas and departed, having been commended by the brothers to the grace of the Lord. ⁴¹And he went through Syria and Cilicia, strengthening the churches.

TIMOTHY JOINS PAUL AND SILAS

16 Paul[c] came also to Derbe and to Lystra. A disciple was there, named Timothy, the son of a Jewish woman who was a believer, but his father was a Greek. ²He was well spoken of by the brothers[d] at Lystra and Iconium. ³Paul wanted Timothy to accompany him, and he took him and circumcised him because of the Jews who were in those places, for they all knew that his father was a Greek. ⁴As they went on their way through the cities, they delivered to them for observance the decisions that had been reached by the apostles and elders who were in Jerusalem. ⁵So the churches were strengthened in the faith, and they increased in numbers daily.

THE MACEDONIAN CALL

⁶And they went through the region of Phrygia and Galatia, having been forbidden by the Holy Spirit to speak the word in Asia. ⁷And when they had come up to Mysia, they attempted to go into Bithynia, but the Spirit of Jesus did not allow them. ⁸So, passing by Mysia, they went down to Troas. ⁹And a vision appeared to Paul in the night: a man of Macedonia was standing there, urging him and saying, "Come over to Macedonia and help us." ¹⁰And when Paul[e] had seen the vision, immediately we sought to go on into Macedonia, concluding that God had called us to preach the gospel to them.

THE CONVERSION OF LYDIA

¹¹So, setting sail from Troas, we made a direct voyage to Samothrace, and the following day to Neapolis, ¹²and from there to Philippi, which is a leading city of the[f] district of Macedonia and a Roman colony. We remained in this city some days. ¹³And on the Sabbath day we went outside the gate to the riverside, where we supposed there was a place of prayer, and we sat down and spoke to the women who had come together. ¹⁴One who heard us was a woman named Lydia, from the city of Thyatira, a seller of purple goods, who was a worshipper of God. The Lord opened her heart to pay attention to what was said by Paul. ¹⁵And after she was baptized, and her household as well, she urged us, saying, "If you have judged me to be faithful to the Lord, come to my house and stay." And she prevailed upon us.

PAUL AND SILAS IN PRISON

¹⁶As we were going to the place of prayer, we were met by a slave girl who had a spirit

---

[a]Some manuscripts *some persons from us have troubled you* [b]Some manuscripts insert verse 34: *But it seemed good to Silas to remain there* [c]Greek *He* [d]Or *brothers and sisters*; also verse 40 [e]Greek *he* [f]Or *that*

of divination and brought her owners much gain by fortune-telling. ¹⁷She followed Paul and us, crying out, "These men are servants of the Most High God, who proclaim to you the way of salvation." ¹⁸And this she kept doing for many days. Paul, having become greatly annoyed, turned and said to the spirit, "I command you in the name of Jesus Christ to come out of her." And it came out that very hour.

¹⁹But when her owners saw that their hope of gain was gone, they seized Paul and Silas and dragged them into the market-place before the rulers. ²⁰And when they had brought them to the magistrates, they said, "These men are Jews, and they are disturbing our city. ²¹They advocate customs that are not lawful for us as Romans to accept or practise." ²²The crowd joined in attacking them, and the magistrates tore the garments off them and gave orders to beat them with rods. ²³And when they had inflicted many blows upon them, they threw them into prison, ordering the jailer to keep them safely. ²⁴Having received this order, he put them into the inner prison and fastened their feet in the stocks.

THE PHILIPPIAN JAILER CONVERTED

²⁵About midnight Paul and Silas were praying and singing hymns to God, and the prisoners were listening to them, ²⁶and suddenly there was a great earthquake, so that the foundations of the prison were shaken. And immediately all the doors were opened, and everyone's bonds were unfastened. ²⁷When the jailer woke and saw that the prison doors were open, he drew his sword and was about to kill himself, supposing that the prisoners had escaped. ²⁸But Paul cried with a loud voice, "Do not harm yourself, for we are all here." ²⁹And the jailer[a] called for lights and rushed in, and trembling with fear he fell down before Paul and Silas. ³⁰Then he brought them out and said, "Sirs, what must I do to be saved?" ³¹And they said, "Believe in the Lord Jesus, and you will be saved, you and your household." ³²And they spoke the word of the Lord to him and to all who were in his house. ³³And he took them the same hour of the night and washed their wounds; and he was baptized at once, he and all his family. ³⁴Then he brought them up into his house and set food before them. And he rejoiced along with his entire household that he had believed in God.

³⁵But when it was day, the magistrates sent the police, saying, "Let those men go." ³⁶And the jailer reported these words to Paul, saying, "The magistrates have sent to let you go. Therefore come out now and go in peace." ³⁷But Paul said to them, "They have beaten us publicly, uncondemned, men who are Roman citizens, and have thrown us into prison; and do they now throw us out secretly? No! Let them come themselves and take us out." ³⁸The police reported these words to the magistrates, and they were afraid when they heard that they were Roman citizens. ³⁹So they came and apologized to them. And they took them out and asked them to leave the city. ⁴⁰So they went out of the prison and visited Lydia. And when they had seen the brothers, they encouraged them and departed.

PAUL AND SILAS IN THESSALONICA

17 Now when they had passed through Amphipolis and Apollonia, they came to Thessalonica, where there was a synagogue of the Jews. ²And Paul went in, as was his custom, and on three Sabbath days he reasoned with them from the Scriptures, ³explaining and proving that it was necessary for the Christ to suffer and to rise from the dead, and saying, "This Jesus, whom I proclaim to you, is the Christ." ⁴And some of them were persuaded and joined Paul and Silas, as did a great many of the devout Greeks and not a few of the leading women. ⁵But the Jews[b] were jealous, and taking some wicked men of the rabble, they formed a mob, set the city in an uproar, and attacked the house of Jason, seeking to bring them out to the crowd. ⁶And when they could not find them, they dragged Jason and some of the brothers before the city authorities, shouting, "These men who have turned the world upside down have come here also, ⁷and Jason has received them, and they are all acting against the decrees of Caesar, saying that there is another king, Jesus." ⁸And the people and the city authorities were disturbed when they heard these things. ⁹And when they had taken money as security from Jason and the rest, they let them go.

PAUL AND SILAS IN BEREA

¹⁰The brothers[c] immediately sent Paul and Silas away by night to Berea, and when they

---

[a]Greek *he* [b]Greek *Ioudaioi* probably refers here to Jewish religious leaders, and others under their influence, in that time; also verse 13
[c]Or *brothers and sisters*; also verse 14

arrived they went into the Jewish synagogue. ¹¹Now these Jews were more noble than those in Thessalonica; they received the word with all eagerness, examining the Scriptures daily to see if these things were so. ¹²Many of them therefore believed, with not a few Greek women of high standing as well as men. ¹³But when the Jews from Thessalonica learned that the word of God was proclaimed by Paul at Berea also, they came there too, agitating and stirring up the crowds. ¹⁴Then the brothers immediately sent Paul off on his way to the sea, but Silas and Timothy remained there. ¹⁵Those who conducted Paul brought him as far as Athens, and after receiving a command for Silas and Timothy to come to him as soon as possible, they departed.

PAUL IN ATHENS

¹⁶Now while Paul was waiting for them at Athens, his spirit was provoked within him as he saw that the city was full of idols. ¹⁷So he reasoned in the synagogue with the Jews and the devout persons, and in the market-place every day with those who happened to be there. ¹⁸Some of the Epicurean and Stoic philosophers also conversed with him. And some said, "What does this babbler wish to say?" Others said, "He seems to be a preacher of foreign divinities"—because he was preaching Jesus and the resurrection. ¹⁹And they took him and brought him to the Areopagus, saying, "May we know what this new teaching is that you are presenting? ²⁰For you bring some strange things to our ears. We wish to know therefore what these things mean." ²¹Now all the Athenians and the foreigners who lived there would spend their time in nothing except telling or hearing something new.

PAUL ADDRESSES THE AREOPAGUS

²²So Paul, standing in the midst of the Areopagus, said: "Men of Athens, I perceive that in every way you are very religious. ²³For as I passed along and observed the objects of your worship, I found also an altar with this inscription: 'To the unknown god.' What therefore you worship as unknown, this I proclaim to you. ²⁴The God who made the world and everything in it, being Lord of heaven and earth, does not live in temples made by man,ᵃ ²⁵nor is he served by human hands, as though he needed anything, since he himself gives to all mankind life and breath and everything. ²⁶And he made from one man every nation of mankind to live on all the face of the earth, having determined allotted periods and the boundaries of their dwelling place, ²⁷that they should seek God, and perhaps feel their way towards him and find him. Yet he is actually not far from each one of us, ²⁸for

"'In him we live and move and
   have our being';ᵇ

as even some of your own poets have said,

"'For we are indeed his offspring.'ᶜ

²⁹Being then God's offspring, we ought not to think that the divine being is like gold or silver or stone, an image formed by the art and imagination of man. ³⁰The times of ignorance God overlooked, but now he commands all people everywhere to repent, ³¹because he has fixed a day on which he will judge the world in righteousness by a man whom he has appointed; and of this he has given assurance to all by raising him from the dead."

³²Now when they heard of the resurrection of the dead, some mocked. But others said, "We will hear you again about this." ³³So Paul went out from their midst. ³⁴But some men joined him and believed, among whom also were Dionysius the Areopagite and a woman named Damaris and others with them.

PAUL IN CORINTH

18 After this Paulᵈ left Athens and went to Corinth. ²And he found a Jew named Aquila, a native of Pontus, recently come from Italy with his wife Priscilla, because Claudius had commanded all the Jews to leave Rome. And he went to see them, ³and because he was of the same trade he stayed with them and worked, for they were tentmakers by trade. ⁴And he reasoned in the synagogue every Sabbath, and tried to persuade Jews and Greeks.

⁵When Silas and Timothy arrived from Macedonia, Paul was occupied with the word, testifying to the Jews that the Christ was Jesus. ⁶And when they opposed and reviled him, he shook out his garments and said to them, "Your blood be on your own heads!

ᵃGreek *made by hands* ᵇProbably from Epimenides of Crete ᶜFrom Aratus's poem "Phainomena" ᵈGreek *he*

I am innocent. From now on I will go to the Gentiles." ⁷And he left there and went to the house of a man named Titius Justus, a worshipper of God. His house was next door to the synagogue. ⁸Crispus, the ruler of the synagogue, believed in the Lord, together with his entire household. And many of the Corinthians hearing Paul believed and were baptized. ⁹And the Lord said to Paul one night in a vision, "Do not be afraid, but go on speaking and do not be silent, ¹⁰for I am with you, and no one will attack you to harm you, for I have many in this city who are my people." ¹¹And he stayed a year and six months, teaching the word of God among them.

¹²But when Gallio was proconsul of Achaia, the Jews[a] made a united attack on Paul and brought him before the tribunal, ¹³saying, "This man is persuading people to worship God contrary to the law." ¹⁴But when Paul was about to open his mouth, Gallio said to the Jews, "If it were a matter of wrongdoing or vicious crime, O Jews, I would have reason to accept your complaint. ¹⁵But since it is a matter of questions about words and names and your own law, see to it yourselves. I refuse to be a judge of these things." ¹⁶And he drove them from the tribunal. ¹⁷And they all seized Sosthenes, the ruler of the synagogue, and beat him in front of the tribunal. But Gallio paid no attention to any of this.

PAUL RETURNS TO ANTIOCH

¹⁸After this, Paul stayed many days longer and then took leave of the brothers[b] and set sail for Syria, and with him Priscilla and Aquila. At Cenchreae he had cut his hair, for he was under a vow. ¹⁹And they came to Ephesus, and he left them there, but he himself went into the synagogue and reasoned with the Jews. ²⁰When they asked him to stay for a longer period, he declined. ²¹But on taking leave of them he said, "I will return to you if God wills", and he set sail from Ephesus. ²²When he had landed at Caesarea, he went up and greeted the church, and then went down to Antioch. ²³After spending some time there, he departed and went from one place to the next through the region of Galatia and Phrygia, strengthening all the disciples.

APOLLOS SPEAKS BOLDLY IN EPHESUS

²⁴Now a Jew named Apollos, a native of Alexandria, came to Ephesus. He was an eloquent man, competent in the Scriptures. ²⁵He had been instructed in the way of the Lord. And being fervent in spirit,[c] he spoke and taught accurately the things concerning Jesus, though he knew only the baptism of John. ²⁶He began to speak boldly in the synagogue, but when Priscilla and Aquila heard him, they took him aside and explained to him the way of God more accurately. ²⁷And when he wished to cross to Achaia, the brothers encouraged him and wrote to the disciples to welcome him. When he arrived, he greatly helped those who through grace had believed, ²⁸for he powerfully refuted the Jews in public, showing by the Scriptures that the Christ was Jesus.

PAUL IN EPHESUS

19 And it happened that while Apollos was at Corinth, Paul passed through the inland[d] country and came to Ephesus. There he found some disciples. ²And he said to them, "Did you receive the Holy Spirit when you believed?" And they said, "No, we have not even heard that there is a Holy Spirit." ³And he said, "Into what then were you baptized?" They said, "Into John's baptism." ⁴And Paul said, "John baptized with the baptism of repentance, telling the people to believe in the one who was to come after him, that is, Jesus." ⁵On hearing this, they were baptized in[e] the name of the Lord Jesus. ⁶And when Paul had laid his hands on them, the Holy Spirit came on them, and they began speaking in tongues and prophesying. ⁷There were about twelve men in all.

⁸And he entered the synagogue and for three months spoke boldly, reasoning and persuading them about the kingdom of God. ⁹But when some became stubborn and continued in unbelief, speaking evil of the Way before the congregation, he withdrew from them and took the disciples with him, reasoning daily in the hall of Tyrannus.[f] ¹⁰This continued for two years, so that all the residents of Asia heard the word of the Lord, both Jews and Greeks.

THE SONS OF SCEVA

¹¹And God was doing extraordinary miracles by the hands of Paul, ¹²so that even handkerchiefs or aprons that had touched his skin were carried away to the sick, and

---

[a]Greek *Ioudaioi* probably refers here to Jewish religious leaders, and others under their influence, in that time; also verses 14 (twice), 28
[b]Or *brothers and sisters*; also verse 27   [c]Or *in the Spirit*   [d]Greek *upper* (that is, highland)   [e]Or *into*   [f]Some manuscripts add *from the fifth hour to the tenth* (that is, from 11 A.M. to 4 P.M.)

their diseases left them and the evil spirits came out of them. ¹³Then some of the itinerant Jewish exorcists undertook to invoke the name of the Lord Jesus over those who had evil spirits, saying, "I adjure you by the Jesus whom Paul proclaims." ¹⁴Seven sons of a Jewish high priest named Sceva were doing this. ¹⁵But the evil spirit answered them, "Jesus I know, and Paul I recognize, but who are you?" ¹⁶And the man in whom was the evil spirit leaped on them, mastered all*a* of them and overpowered them, so that they fled out of that house naked and wounded. ¹⁷And this became known to all the residents of Ephesus, both Jews and Greeks. And fear fell upon them all, and the name of the Lord Jesus was extolled. ¹⁸Also many of those who were now believers came, confessing and divulging their practices. ¹⁹And a number of those who had practised magic arts brought their books together and burned them in the sight of all. And they counted the value of them and found it came to fifty thousand pieces of silver. ²⁰So the word of the Lord continued to increase and prevail mightily.

A RIOT AT EPHESUS

²¹Now after these events Paul resolved in the Spirit to pass through Macedonia and Achaia and go to Jerusalem, saying, "After I have been there, I must also see Rome." ²²And having sent into Macedonia two of his helpers, Timothy and Erastus, he himself stayed in Asia for a while.

²³About that time there arose no little disturbance concerning the Way. ²⁴For a man named Demetrius, a silversmith, who made silver shrines of Artemis, brought no little business to the craftsmen. ²⁵These he gathered together, with the workmen in similar trades, and said, "Men, you know that from this business we have our wealth. ²⁶And you see and hear that not only in Ephesus but in almost all of Asia this Paul has persuaded and turned away a great many people, saying that gods made with hands are not gods. ²⁷And there is danger not only that this trade of ours may come into disrepute but also that the temple of the great goddess Artemis may be counted as nothing, and that she may even be deposed from her magnificence, she whom all Asia and the world worship."

²⁸When they heard this they were enraged and were crying out, "Great is Artemis of the Ephesians!" ²⁹So the city was filled with the confusion, and they rushed together into the theatre, dragging with them Gaius and Aristarchus, Macedonians who were Paul's companions in travel. ³⁰But when Paul wished to go in among the crowd, the disciples would not let him. ³¹And even some of the Asiarchs,*b* who were friends of his, sent to him and were urging him not to venture into the theatre. ³²Now some cried out one thing, some another, for the assembly was in confusion, and most of them did not know why they had come together. ³³Some of the crowd prompted Alexander, whom the Jews had put forward. And Alexander, motioning with his hand, wanted to make a defence to the crowd. ³⁴But when they recognized that he was a Jew, for about two hours they all cried out with one voice, "Great is Artemis of the Ephesians!"

³⁵And when the town clerk had quietened the crowd, he said, "Men of Ephesus, who is there who does not know that the city of the Ephesians is temple keeper of the great Artemis, and of the sacred stone that fell from the sky?*c* ³⁶Seeing then that these things cannot be denied, you ought to be quiet and do nothing rash. ³⁷For you have brought these men here who are neither sacrilegious nor blasphemers of our goddess. ³⁸If therefore Demetrius and the craftsmen with him have a complaint against anyone, the courts are open, and there are proconsuls. Let them bring charges against one another. ³⁹But if you seek anything further,*d* it shall be settled in the regular assembly. ⁴⁰For we really are in danger of being charged with rioting today, since there is no cause that we can give to justify this commotion." ⁴¹And when he had said these things, he dismissed the assembly.

PAUL IN MACEDONIA AND GREECE

20 After the uproar ceased, Paul sent for the disciples, and after encouraging them, he said farewell and departed for Macedonia. ²When he had gone through those regions and had given them much encouragement, he came to Greece. ³There he spent three months, and when a plot was made against him by the Jews*e* as he was about to set sail for Syria, he decided to return through Macedonia. ⁴Sopater the Berean, son of Pyrrhus, accompanied

---

a Or *both* *b* That is, high-ranking officers of the province of Asia *c* The meaning of the Greek is uncertain *d* Some manuscripts *seek about other matters* *e* Greek *Ioudaioi* probably refers here to Jewish religious leaders, and others under their influence, in that time; also verse 19

him; and of the Thessalonians, Aristarchus and Secundus; and Gaius of Derbe, and Timothy; and the Asians, Tychicus and Trophimus. ⁵These went on ahead and were waiting for us at Troas, ⁶but we sailed away from Philippi after the days of Unleavened Bread, and in five days we came to them at Troas, where we stayed for seven days.

EUTYCHUS RAISED FROM THE DEAD

⁷On the first day of the week, when we were gathered together to break bread, Paul talked with them, intending to depart on the next day, and he prolonged his speech until midnight. ⁸There were many lamps in the upper room where we were gathered. ⁹And a young man named Eutychus, sitting at the window, sank into a deep sleep as Paul talked still longer. And being overcome by sleep, he fell down from the third storey and was taken up dead. ¹⁰But Paul went down and bent over him, and taking him in his arms, said, "Do not be alarmed, for his life is in him." ¹¹And when Paul had gone up and had broken bread and eaten, he conversed with them a long while, until daybreak, and so departed. ¹²And they took the youth away alive, and were not a little comforted.

¹³But going ahead to the ship, we set sail for Assos, intending to take Paul aboard there, for so he had arranged, intending himself to go by land. ¹⁴And when he met us at Assos, we took him on board and went to Mitylene. ¹⁵And sailing from there we came the following day opposite Chios; the next day we touched at Samos; and*ᵃ* the day after that we went to Miletus. ¹⁶For Paul had decided to sail past Ephesus, so that he might not have to spend time in Asia, for he was hastening to be at Jerusalem, if possible, on the day of Pentecost.

PAUL SPEAKS TO THE EPHESIAN ELDERS

¹⁷Now from Miletus he sent to Ephesus and called the elders of the church to come to him. ¹⁸And when they came to him, he said to them:

"You yourselves know how I lived among you the whole time from the first day that I set foot in Asia, ¹⁹serving the Lord with all humility and with tears and with trials that happened to me through the plots of the Jews; ²⁰how I did not shrink from declaring to you anything that was profitable, and teaching you in public and from house to house, ²¹testifying both to Jews and to Greeks of repentance towards God and of faith in our Lord Jesus Christ.*ᵇ* ²²And now, behold, I am going to Jerusalem, constrained by*ᶜ* the Spirit, not knowing what will happen to me there, ²³except that the Holy Spirit testifies to me in every city that imprisonment and afflictions await me. ²⁴But I do not account my life of any value nor as precious to myself, if only I may finish my course and the ministry that I received from the Lord Jesus, to testify to the gospel of the grace of God. ²⁵And now, behold, I know that none of you among whom I have gone about proclaiming the kingdom will see my face again. ²⁶Therefore I testify to you this day that I am innocent of the blood of all, ²⁷for I did not shrink from declaring to you the whole counsel of God. ²⁸Pay careful attention to yourselves and to all the flock, of which the Holy Spirit has made you overseers, to care for the church of God,*ᵈ* which he obtained with his own blood.*ᵉ* ²⁹I know that after my departure fierce wolves will come in among you, not sparing the flock; ³⁰and from among your own selves will arise men speaking twisted things, to draw away the disciples after them. ³¹Therefore be alert, remembering that for three years I did not cease night or day to admonish every one with tears. ³²And now I commend you to God and to the word of his grace, which is able to build you up and to give you the inheritance among all those who are sanctified. ³³I coveted no one's silver or gold or apparel. ³⁴You yourselves know that these hands ministered to my necessities and to those who were with me. ³⁵In all things I have shown you that by working hard in this way we must help the weak and remember the words of the Lord Jesus, how he himself said, 'It is more blessed to give than to receive.'"

³⁶And when he had said these things, he knelt down and prayed with them all. ³⁷And there was much weeping on the part of all; they embraced Paul and kissed him, ³⁸being sorrowful most of all because of the word he had spoken, that they would not see his face again. And they accompanied him to the ship.

PAUL GOES TO JERUSALEM

21 And when we had parted from them and set sail, we came by a straight course to Cos, and the next day to Rhodes, and from there to Patara.*ᶠ* ²And having found a ship crossing to Phoenicia, we

---

*ᵃ*Some manuscripts add *after remaining at Trogyllium* *ᵇ*Some manuscripts omit *Christ* *ᶜ*Or *bound in* *ᵈ*Some manuscripts *of the Lord* *ᵉ*Or *with the blood of his Own* *ᶠ*Some manuscripts add *and Myra*

went aboard and set sail. ³When we had come in sight of Cyprus, leaving it on the left we sailed to Syria and landed at Tyre, for there the ship was to unload its cargo. ⁴And having sought out the disciples, we stayed there for seven days. And through the Spirit they were telling Paul not to go on to Jerusalem. ⁵When our days there were ended, we departed and went on our journey, and they all, with wives and children, accompanied us until we were outside the city. And kneeling down on the beach, we prayed ⁶and said farewell to one another. Then we went on board the ship, and they returned home.

⁷When we had finished the voyage from Tyre, we arrived at Ptolemais, and we greeted the brothers[a] and stayed with them for one day. ⁸On the next day we departed and came to Caesarea, and we entered the house of Philip the evangelist, who was one of the seven, and stayed with him. ⁹He had four unmarried daughters, who prophesied. ¹⁰While we were staying for many days, a prophet named Agabus came down from Judea. ¹¹And coming to us, he took Paul's belt and bound his own feet and hands and said, "Thus says the Holy Spirit, 'This is how the Jews[b] at Jerusalem will bind the man who owns this belt and deliver him into the hands of the Gentiles.'" ¹²When we heard this, we and the people there urged him not to go up to Jerusalem. ¹³Then Paul answered, "What are you doing, weeping and breaking my heart? For I am ready not only to be imprisoned but even to die in Jerusalem for the name of the Lord Jesus." ¹⁴And since he would not be persuaded, we ceased and said, "Let the will of the Lord be done."

¹⁵After these days we got ready and went up to Jerusalem. ¹⁶And some of the disciples from Caesarea went with us, bringing us to the house of Mnason of Cyprus, an early disciple, with whom we should lodge.

PAUL VISITS JAMES

¹⁷When we had come to Jerusalem, the brothers received us gladly. ¹⁸On the following day Paul went in with us to James, and all the elders were present. ¹⁹After greeting them, he related one by one the things that God had done among the Gentiles through his ministry. ²⁰And when they heard it, they glorified God. And they said to him, "You see, brother, how many thousands there are among the Jews of those who have believed. They are all zealous for the law, ²¹and they have been told about you that you teach all the Jews who are among the Gentiles to forsake Moses, telling them not to circumcise their children or walk according to our customs. ²²What then is to be done? They will certainly hear that you have come. ²³Do therefore what we tell you. We have four men who are under a vow; ²⁴take these men and purify yourself along with them and pay their expenses, so that they may shave their heads. Thus all will know that there is nothing in what they have been told about you, but that you yourself also live in observance of the law. ²⁵But as for the Gentiles who have believed, we have sent a letter with our judgement that they should abstain from what has been sacrificed to idols, and from blood, and from what has been strangled,[c] and from sexual immorality." ²⁶Then Paul took the men, and the next day he purified himself along with them and went into the temple, giving notice when the days of purification would be fulfilled and the offering presented for each one of them.

PAUL ARRESTED IN THE TEMPLE

²⁷When the seven days were almost completed, the Jews from Asia, seeing him in the temple, stirred up the whole crowd and laid hands on him, ²⁸crying out, "Men of Israel, help! This is the man who is teaching everyone everywhere against the people and the law and this place. Moreover, he even brought Greeks into the temple and has defiled this holy place." ²⁹For they had previously seen Trophimus the Ephesian with him in the city, and they supposed that Paul had brought him into the temple. ³⁰Then all the city was stirred up, and the people ran together. They seized Paul and dragged him out of the temple, and at once the gates were shut. ³¹And as they were seeking to kill him, word came to the tribune of the cohort that all Jerusalem was in confusion. ³²He at once took soldiers and centurions and ran down to them. And when they saw the tribune and the soldiers, they stopped beating Paul. ³³Then the tribune came up and arrested him and ordered him to be bound with two chains. He enquired who he was and what he had done. ³⁴Some in the crowd were shouting one thing, some another. And as he could not learn the facts

---

[a] Or *brothers and sisters*; also verse 17 [b] Greek *Ioudaioi* probably refers here to Jewish religious leaders, and others under their influence, in that time [c] Some manuscripts omit *and from what has been strangled*

because of the uproar, he ordered him to be brought into the barracks. ³⁵And when he came to the steps, he was actually carried by the soldiers because of the violence of the crowd, ³⁶for the mob of the people followed, crying out, "Away with him!"

PAUL SPEAKS TO THE PEOPLE

³⁷As Paul was about to be brought into the barracks, he said to the tribune, "May I say something to you?" And he said, "Do you know Greek? ³⁸Are you not the Egyptian, then, who recently stirred up a revolt and led the four thousand men of the Assassins out into the wilderness?" ³⁹Paul replied, "I am a Jew, from Tarsus in Cilicia, a citizen of no obscure city. I beg you, permit me to speak to the people." ⁴⁰And when he had given him permission, Paul, standing on the steps, motioned with his hand to the people. And when there was a great hush, he addressed them in the Hebrew language,ᵃ saying:

22 "Brothers and fathers, hear the defence that I now make before you."

²And when they heard that he was addressing them in the Hebrew language,ᵇ they became even more quiet. And he said:

³"I am a Jew, born in Tarsus in Cilicia, but brought up in this city, educated at the feet of Gamalielᶜ according to the strict manner of the law of our fathers, being zealous for God as all of you are this day. ⁴I persecuted this Way to the death, binding and delivering to prison both men and women, ⁵as the high priest and the whole council of elders can bear me witness. From them I received letters to the brothers, and I journeyed towards Damascus to take those also who were there and bring them in bonds to Jerusalem to be punished.

⁶"As I was on my way and drew near to Damascus, about noon a great light from heaven suddenly shone around me. ⁷And I fell to the ground and heard a voice saying to me, 'Saul, Saul, why are you persecuting me?' ⁸And I answered, 'Who are you, Lord?' And he said to me, 'I am Jesus of Nazareth, whom you are persecuting.' ⁹Now those who were with me saw the light but did not understandᵈ the voice of the one who was speaking to me. ¹⁰And I said, 'What shall I do, Lord?' And the Lord said to me, 'Rise, and go into Damascus, and there you will be told all that is appointed for you to do.' ¹¹And since I could not see because of the brightness of that light, I was led by the hand by those who were with me, and came into Damascus.

¹²"And one Ananias, a devout man according to the law, well spoken of by all the Jews who lived there, ¹³came to me, and standing by me said to me, 'Brother Saul, receive your sight.' And at that very hour I received my sight and saw him. ¹⁴And he said, 'The God of our fathers appointed you to know his will, to see the Righteous One and to hear a voice from his mouth; ¹⁵for you will be a witness for him to everyone of what you have seen and heard. ¹⁶And now why do you wait? Rise and be baptized and wash away your sins, calling on his name.'

¹⁷"When I had returned to Jerusalem and was praying in the temple, I fell into a trance ¹⁸and saw him saying to me, 'Make haste and get out of Jerusalem quickly, because they will not accept your testimony about me.' ¹⁹And I said, 'Lord, they themselves know that in one synagogue after another I imprisoned and beat those who believed in you. ²⁰And when the blood of Stephen your witness was being shed, I myself was standing by and approving and watching over the garments of those who killed him.' ²¹And he said to me, 'Go, for I will send you far away to the Gentiles.'"

PAUL AND THE ROMAN TRIBUNE

²²Up to this word they listened to him. Then they raised their voices and said, "Away with such a fellow from the earth! For he should not be allowed to live." ²³And as they were shouting and throwing off their cloaks and flinging dust into the air, ²⁴the tribune ordered him to be brought into the barracks, saying that he should be examined by flogging, to find out why they were shouting against him like this. ²⁵But when they had stretched him out for the whips,ᵉ Paul said to the centurion who was standing by, "Is it lawful for you to flog a man who is a Roman citizen and uncondemned?" ²⁶When the centurion heard this, he went to the tribune and said to him, "What are you about to do? For this man is a Roman citizen." ²⁷So the tribune came and said to him, "Tell me, are you a Roman citizen?" And he said, "Yes." ²⁸The tribune answered, "I bought this citizenship for a large sum." Paul said, "But I am a citizen by birth." ²⁹So those who were about to

---

ᵃ Or *the Hebrew dialect* (probably Aramaic) ᵇ Or *the Hebrew dialect* (probably Aramaic) ᶜ Or *city at the feet of Gamaliel, educated* ᵈ Or *hear with understanding* ᵉ Or *when they had tied him up with leather strips*

examine him withdrew from him immediately, and the tribune also was afraid, for he realized that Paul was a Roman citizen and that he had bound him.

PAUL BEFORE THE COUNCIL

³⁰But on the next day, desiring to know the real reason why he was being accused by the Jews, he unbound him and commanded the chief priests and all the council to meet, and he brought Paul down and set him before them.

23 And looking intently at the council, Paul said, "Brothers, I have lived my life before God in all good conscience up to this day." ²And the high priest Ananias commanded those who stood by him to strike him on the mouth. ³Then Paul said to him, "God is going to strike you, you whitewashed wall! Are you sitting to judge me according to the law, and yet contrary to the law you order me to be struck?" ⁴Those who stood by said, "Would you revile God's high priest?" ⁵And Paul said, "I did not know, brothers, that he was the high priest, for it is written, 'You shall not speak evil of a ruler of your people.'"

⁶Now when Paul perceived that one part were Sadducees and the other Pharisees, he cried out in the council, "Brothers, I am a Pharisee, a son of Pharisees. It is with respect to the hope of the resurrection of the dead that I am on trial." ⁷And when he had said this, a dissension arose between the Pharisees and the Sadducees, and the assembly was divided. ⁸For the Sadducees say that there is no resurrection, nor angel, nor spirit, but the Pharisees acknowledge them all. ⁹Then a great clamour arose, and some of the scribes of the Pharisees' party stood up and contended sharply, "We find nothing wrong in this man. What if a spirit or an angel spoke to him?" ¹⁰And when the dissension became violent, the tribune, afraid that Paul would be torn to pieces by them, commanded the soldiers to go down and take him away from among them by force and bring him into the barracks.

¹¹The following night the Lord stood by him and said, "Take courage, for as you have testified to the facts about me in Jerusalem, so you must testify also in Rome."

A PLOT TO KILL PAUL

¹²When it was day, the Jews made a plot and bound themselves by an oath neither to eat nor drink till they had killed Paul. ¹³There were more than forty who made this conspiracy. ¹⁴They went to the chief priests and elders and said, "We have strictly bound ourselves by an oath to taste no food till we have killed Paul. ¹⁵Now therefore you, along with the council, give notice to the tribune to bring him down to you, as though you were going to determine his case more exactly. And we are ready to kill him before he comes near."

¹⁶Now the son of Paul's sister heard of their ambush, so he went and entered the barracks and told Paul. ¹⁷Paul called one of the centurions and said, "Take this young man to the tribune, for he has something to tell him." ¹⁸So he took him and brought him to the tribune and said, "Paul the prisoner called me and asked me to bring this young man to you, as he has something to say to you." ¹⁹The tribune took him by the hand, and going aside asked him privately, "What is it that you have to tell me?" ²⁰And he said, "The Jews have agreed to ask you to bring Paul down to the council tomorrow, as though they were going to enquire somewhat more closely about him. ²¹But do not be persuaded by them, for more than forty of their men are lying in ambush for him, who have bound themselves by an oath neither to eat nor drink till they have killed him. And now they are ready, waiting for your consent." ²²So the tribune dismissed the young man, charging him, "Tell no one that you have informed me of these things."

PAUL SENT TO FELIX THE GOVERNOR

²³Then he called two of the centurions and said, "Get ready two hundred soldiers, with seventy horsemen and two hundred spearmen to go as far as Caesarea at the third hour of the night.*ᵃ* ²⁴Also provide mounts for Paul to ride and bring him safely to Felix the governor." ²⁵And he wrote a letter to this effect:

²⁶"Claudius Lysias, to his Excellency the governor Felix, greetings. ²⁷This man was seized by the Jews and was about to be killed by them when I came upon them with the soldiers and rescued him, having learned that he was a Roman citizen. ²⁸And desiring to know the charge for which they were accusing him, I brought him down to their council. ²⁹I found that he was being accused about questions of their law, but charged with nothing deserving death or imprisonment. ³⁰And when it was disclosed to me

---
ᵃThat is, 9 P.M.

that there would be a plot against the man, I sent him to you at once, ordering his accusers also to state before you what they have against him."

³¹So the soldiers, according to their instructions, took Paul and brought him by night to Antipatris. ³²And on the next day they returned to the barracks, letting the horsemen go on with him. ³³When they had come to Caesarea and delivered the letter to the governor, they presented Paul also before him. ³⁴On reading the letter, he asked what province he was from. And when he learned that he was from Cilicia, ³⁵he said, "I will give you a hearing when your accusers arrive." And he commanded him to be guarded in Herod's praetorium.

PAUL BEFORE FELIX AT CAESAREA

24 And after five days the high priest Ananias came down with some elders and a spokesman, one Tertullus. They laid before the governor their case against Paul. ²And when he had been summoned, Tertullus began to accuse him, saying:

"Since through you we enjoy much peace, and since by your foresight, most excellent Felix, reforms are being made for this nation, ³in every way and everywhere we accept this with all gratitude. ⁴But, to detain*ᵃ* you no further, I beg you in your kindness to hear us briefly. ⁵For we have found this man a plague, one who stirs up riots among all the Jews throughout the world and is a ringleader of the sect of the Nazarenes. ⁶He even tried to profane the temple, but we seized him.*ᵇ* ⁸By examining him yourself you will be able to find out from him about everything of which we accuse him."

⁹The Jews also joined in the charge, affirming that all these things were so.

¹⁰And when the governor had nodded to him to speak, Paul replied:

"Knowing that for many years you have been a judge over this nation, I cheerfully make my defence. ¹¹You can verify that it is not more than twelve days since I went up to worship in Jerusalem, ¹²and they did not find me disputing with anyone or stirring up a crowd, either in the temple or in the synagogues or in the city. ¹³Neither can they prove to you what they now bring up against me. ¹⁴But this I confess to you, that according to the Way, which they call a sect, I worship the God of our fathers, believing everything laid down by the Law and written in the Prophets, ¹⁵having a hope in God, which these men themselves accept, that there will be a resurrection of both the just and the unjust. ¹⁶So I always take pains to have a clear conscience towards both God and man. ¹⁷Now after several years I came to bring alms to my nation and to present offerings. ¹⁸While I was doing this, they found me purified in the temple, without any crowd or tumult. But some Jews from Asia— ¹⁹they ought to be here before you and to make an accusation, should they have anything against me. ²⁰Or else let these men themselves say what wrongdoing they found when I stood before the council, ²¹other than this one thing that I cried out while standing among them: 'It is with respect to the resurrection of the dead that I am on trial before you this day.'"

PAUL KEPT IN CUSTODY

²²But Felix, having a rather accurate knowledge of the Way, put them off, saying, "When Lysias the tribune comes down, I will decide your case." ²³Then he gave orders to the centurion that he should be kept in custody but have some liberty, and that none of his friends should be prevented from attending to his needs.

²⁴After some days Felix came with his wife Drusilla, who was Jewish, and he sent for Paul and heard him speak about faith in Christ Jesus. ²⁵And as he reasoned about righteousness and self-control and the coming judgement, Felix was alarmed and said, "Go away for the present. When I get an opportunity I will summon you." ²⁶At the same time he hoped that money would be given him by Paul. So he sent for him often and conversed with him. ²⁷When two years had elapsed, Felix was succeeded by Porcius Festus. And desiring to do the Jews a favour, Felix left Paul in prison.

PAUL APPEALS TO CAESAR

25 Now three days after Festus had arrived in the province, he went up to Jerusalem from Caesarea. ²And the chief priests and the principal men of the Jews laid out their case against Paul, and they urged him, ³asking as a favour against Paul*ᶜ* that he summon him to Jerusalem — because

---

ᵃOr weary ᵇSome manuscripts add and we would have judged him according to our law. ⁷But the chief captain Lysias came and with great violence took him out of our hands, ⁸commanding his accusers to come before you. ᶜGreek him

they were planning an ambush to kill him on the way. ⁴Festus replied that Paul was being kept at Caesarea and that he himself intended to go there shortly. ⁵"So," said he, "let the men of authority among you go down with me, and if there is anything wrong about the man, let them bring charges against him."

⁶After he stayed among them not more than eight or ten days, he went down to Caesarea. And the next day he took his seat on the tribunal and ordered Paul to be brought. ⁷When he had arrived, the Jews who had come down from Jerusalem stood around him, bringing many and serious charges against him that they could not prove. ⁸Paul argued in his defence, "Neither against the law of the Jews, nor against the temple, nor against Caesar have I committed any offence." ⁹But Festus, wishing to do the Jews a favour, said to Paul, "Do you wish to go up to Jerusalem and there be tried on these charges before me?" ¹⁰But Paul said, "I am standing before Caesar's tribunal, where I ought to be tried. To the Jews I have done no wrong, as you yourself know very well. ¹¹If then I am a wrongdoer and have committed anything for which I deserve to die, I do not seek to escape death. But if there is nothing to their charges against me, no one can give me up to them. I appeal to Caesar." ¹²Then Festus, when he had conferred with his council, answered, "To Caesar you have appealed; to Caesar you shall go."

PAUL BEFORE AGRIPPA AND BERNICE

¹³Now when some days had passed, Agrippa the king and Bernice arrived at Caesarea and greeted Festus. ¹⁴And as they stayed there many days, Festus laid Paul's case before the king, saying, "There is a man left prisoner by Felix, ¹⁵and when I was at Jerusalem, the chief priests and the elders of the Jews laid out their case against him, asking for a sentence of condemnation against him. ¹⁶I answered them that it was not the custom of the Romans to give up anyone before the accused met the accusers face to face and had opportunity to make his defence concerning the charge laid against him. ¹⁷So when they came together here, I made no delay, but on the next day took my seat on the tribunal and ordered the man to be brought. ¹⁸When the accusers stood up, they brought no charge in his case of such evils as I supposed. ¹⁹Rather they had certain points of dispute with him about their own religion and about a certain Jesus, who was dead, but whom Paul asserted to be alive. ²⁰Being at a loss how to investigate these questions, I asked whether he wanted to go to Jerusalem and be tried there regarding them. ²¹But when Paul had appealed to be kept in custody for the decision of the emperor, I ordered him to be held until I could send him to Caesar." ²²Then Agrippa said to Festus, "I would like to hear the man myself." "Tomorrow", said he, "you will hear him."

²³So on the next day Agrippa and Bernice came with great pomp, and they entered the audience hall with the military tribunes and the prominent men of the city. Then, at the command of Festus, Paul was brought in. ²⁴And Festus said, "King Agrippa and all who are present with us, you see this man about whom the whole Jewish people petitioned me, both in Jerusalem and here, shouting that he ought not to live any longer. ²⁵But I found that he had done nothing deserving death. And as he himself appealed to the emperor, I decided to go ahead and send him. ²⁶But I have nothing definite to write to my lord about him. Therefore I have brought him before you all, and especially before you, King Agrippa, so that, after we have examined him, I may have something to write. ²⁷For it seems to me unreasonable, in sending a prisoner, not to indicate the charges against him."

PAUL'S DEFENCE BEFORE AGRIPPA

26 So Agrippa said to Paul, "You have permission to speak for yourself." Then Paul stretched out his hand and made his defence:

²"I consider myself fortunate that it is before you, King Agrippa, I am going to make my defence today against all the accusations of the Jews, ³especially because you are familiar with all the customs and controversies of the Jews. Therefore I beg you to listen to me patiently.

⁴"My manner of life from my youth, spent from the beginning among my own nation and in Jerusalem, is known by all the Jews. ⁵They have known for a long time, if they are willing to testify, that according to the strictest party of our religion I have lived as a Pharisee. ⁶And now I stand here on trial because of my hope in the promise made by God to our fathers, ⁷to which our twelve tribes hope to attain, as they earnestly worship night and day. And for this hope I am accused by Jews, O king! ⁸Why is it thought incredible by any of you that God raises the dead?

⁹"I myself was convinced that I ought to do many things in opposing the name of Jesus of Nazareth. ¹⁰And I did so in Jerusalem. I not only locked up many of the saints in prison after receiving authority from the chief priests, but when they were put to death I cast my vote against them. ¹¹And I punished them often in all the synagogues and tried to make them blaspheme, and in raging fury against them I persecuted them even to foreign cities.

PAUL TELLS OF HIS CONVERSION

¹²"In this connection I journeyed to Damascus with the authority and commission of the chief priests. ¹³At midday, O king, I saw on the way a light from heaven, brighter than the sun, that shone around me and those who journeyed with me. ¹⁴And when we had all fallen to the ground, I heard a voice saying to me in the Hebrew language,ᵃ 'Saul, Saul, why are you persecuting me? It is hard for you to kick against the goads.' ¹⁵And I said, 'Who are you, Lord?' And the Lord said, 'I am Jesus whom you are persecuting. ¹⁶But rise and stand upon your feet, for I have appeared to you for this purpose, to appoint you as a servant and witness to the things in which you have seen me and to those in which I will appear to you, ¹⁷delivering you from your people and from the Gentiles—to whom I am sending you ¹⁸to open their eyes, so that they may turn from darkness to light and from the power of Satan to God, that they may receive forgiveness of sins and a place among those who are sanctified by faith in me.'

¹⁹"Therefore, O King Agrippa, I was not disobedient to the heavenly vision, ²⁰but declared first to those in Damascus, then in Jerusalem and throughout all the region of Judea, and also to the Gentiles, that they should repent and turn to God, performing deeds in keeping with their repentance. ²¹For this reason the Jews seized me in the temple and tried to kill me. ²²To this day I have had the help that comes from God, and so I stand here testifying both to small and great, saying nothing but what the prophets and Moses said would come to pass: ²³that the Christ must suffer and that, by being the first to rise from the dead, he would proclaim light both to our people and to the Gentiles."

²⁴And as he was saying these things in his defence, Festus said with a loud voice, "Paul, you are out of your mind; your great learning is driving you out of your mind." ²⁵But Paul said, "I am not out of my mind, most excellent Festus, but I am speaking true and rational words. ²⁶For the king knows about these things, and to him I speak boldly. For I am persuaded that none of these things has escaped his notice, for this has not been done in a corner. ²⁷King Agrippa, do you believe the prophets? I know that you believe." ²⁸And Agrippa said to Paul, "In a short time would you persuade me to be a Christian?"ᵇ ²⁹And Paul said, "Whether short or long, I would to God that not only you but also all who hear me this day might become such as I am—except for these chains."

³⁰Then the king rose, and the governor and Bernice and those who were sitting with them. ³¹And when they had withdrawn, they said to one another, "This man is doing nothing to deserve death or imprisonment." ³²And Agrippa said to Festus, "This man could have been set free if he had not appealed to Caesar."

PAUL SAILS FOR ROME

27 And when it was decided that we should sail for Italy, they delivered Paul and some other prisoners to a centurion of the Augustan Cohort named Julius. ²And embarking in a ship of Adramyttium, which was about to sail to the ports along the coast of Asia, we put to sea, accompanied by Aristarchus, a Macedonian from Thessalonica. ³The next day we put in at Sidon. And Julius treated Paul kindly and gave him leave to go to his friends and be cared for. ⁴And putting out to sea from there we sailed under the lee of Cyprus, because the winds were against us. ⁵And when we had sailed across the open sea along the coast of Cilicia and Pamphylia, we came to Myra in Lycia. ⁶There the centurion found a ship of Alexandria sailing for Italy and put us on board. ⁷We sailed slowly for a number of days and arrived with difficulty off Cnidus, and as the wind did not allow us to go farther, we sailed under the lee of Crete off Salmone. ⁸Coasting along it with difficulty, we came to a place called Fair Havens, near which was the city of Lasea.

⁹Since much time had passed, and the voyage was now dangerous because even the Fastᶜ was already over, Paul advised them, ¹⁰saying, "Sirs, I perceive that the voyage will be with injury and much loss, not only of the cargo and the ship, but also of our lives." ¹¹But

---

ᵃOr *the Hebrew dialect* (probably Aramaic) ᵇOr *In a short time you would persuade me to act like a Christian!* ᶜThat is, the Day of Atonement

the centurion paid more attention to the pilot and to the owner of the ship than to what Paul said. ¹²And because the harbour was not suitable to spend the winter in, the majority decided to put out to sea from there, on the chance that somehow they could reach Phoenix, a harbour of Crete, facing both southwest and northwest, and spend the winter there.

THE STORM AT SEA

¹³Now when the south wind blew gently, supposing that they had obtained their purpose, they weighed anchor and sailed along Crete, close to the shore. ¹⁴But soon a tempestuous wind, called the northeaster, struck down from the land. ¹⁵And when the ship was caught and could not face the wind, we gave way to it and were driven along. ¹⁶Running under the lee of a small island called Cauda,[a] we managed with difficulty to secure the ship's boat. ¹⁷After hoisting it up, they used supports to undergird the ship. Then, fearing that they would run aground on the Syrtis, they lowered the gear,[b] and thus they were driven along. ¹⁸Since we were violently storm-tossed, they began the next day to jettison the cargo. ¹⁹And on the third day they threw the ship's tackle overboard with their own hands. ²⁰When neither sun nor stars appeared for many days, and no small tempest lay on us, all hope of our being saved was at last abandoned.

²¹Since they had been without food for a long time, Paul stood up among them and said, "Men, you should have listened to me and not have set sail from Crete and incurred this injury and loss. ²²Yet now I urge you to take heart, for there will be no loss of life among you, but only of the ship. ²³For this very night there stood before me an angel of the God to whom I belong and whom I worship, ²⁴and he said, 'Do not be afraid, Paul; you must stand before Caesar. And behold, God has granted you all those who sail with you.' ²⁵So take heart, men, for I have faith in God that it will be exactly as I have been told. ²⁶But we must run aground on some island."

²⁷When the fourteenth night had come, as we were being driven across the Adriatic Sea, about midnight the sailors suspected that they were nearing land. ²⁸So they took a sounding and found twenty fathoms.[c] A little farther on they took a sounding again and found fifteen fathoms.[d] ²⁹And fearing that we might run on the rocks, they let down four anchors from the stern and prayed for day to come. ³⁰And as the sailors were seeking to escape from the ship, and had lowered the ship's boat into the sea under pretence of laying out anchors from the bow, ³¹Paul said to the centurion and the soldiers, "Unless these men stay in the ship, you cannot be saved." ³²Then the soldiers cut away the ropes of the ship's boat and let it go.

³³As day was about to dawn, Paul urged them all to take some food, saying, "Today is the fourteenth day that you have continued in suspense and without food, having taken nothing. ³⁴Therefore I urge you to take some food. For it will give you strength,[e] for not a hair is to perish from the head of any of you." ³⁵And when he had said these things, he took bread, and giving thanks to God in the presence of all he broke it and began to eat. ³⁶Then they all were encouraged and ate some food themselves. ³⁷(We were in all 276[f] persons in the ship.) ³⁸And when they had eaten enough, they lightened the ship, throwing out the wheat into the sea.

THE SHIPWRECK

³⁹Now when it was day, they did not recognize the land, but they noticed a bay with a beach, on which they planned if possible to run the ship ashore. ⁴⁰So they cast off the anchors and left them in the sea, at the same time loosening the ropes that tied the rudders. Then hoisting the foresail to the wind they made for the beach. ⁴¹But striking a reef,[g] they ran the vessel aground. The bow stuck and remained immovable, and the stern was being broken up by the surf. ⁴²The soldiers' plan was to kill the prisoners, lest any should swim away and escape. ⁴³But the centurion, wishing to save Paul, kept them from carrying out their plan. He ordered those who could swim to jump overboard first and make for the land, ⁴⁴and the rest on planks or on pieces of the ship. And so it was that all were brought safely to land.

PAUL ON MALTA

28 After we were brought safely through, we then learned that the island was called Malta. ²The native people[h] showed us unusual kindness,

---

[a]Some manuscripts *Clauda*   [b]That is, the sea-anchor (or possibly the mainsail)   [c]About 120 feet; a fathom (Greek *orguia*) was about 6 feet or 2 metres   [d]About 90 feet (see previous note)   [e]Or *For it is for your deliverance*   [f]Some manuscripts *seventy-six*, or *about seventy-six*   [g]Or *sandbank*, or *crosscurrent*; Greek *place between two seas*   [h]Greek *barbaroi* (that is, non-Greek speakers); also verse 4

for they kindled a fire and welcomed us all, because it had begun to rain and was cold. ³When Paul had gathered a bundle of sticks and put them on the fire, a viper came out because of the heat and fastened on his hand. ⁴When the native people saw the creature hanging from his hand, they said to one another, "No doubt this man is a murderer. Though he has escaped from the sea, Justice[a] has not allowed him to live." ⁵He, however, shook off the creature into the fire and suffered no harm. ⁶They were waiting for him to swell up or suddenly fall down dead. But when they had waited a long time and saw no misfortune come to him, they changed their minds and said that he was a god.

⁷Now in the neighbourhood of that place were lands belonging to the chief man of the island, named Publius, who received us and entertained us hospitably for three days. ⁸It happened that the father of Publius lay sick with fever and dysentery. And Paul visited him and prayed, and putting his hands on him, healed him. ⁹And when this had taken place, the rest of the people on the island who had diseases also came and were cured. ¹⁰They also honoured us greatly,[b] and when we were about to sail, they put on board whatever we needed.

PAUL ARRIVES AT ROME

¹¹After three months we set sail in a ship that had wintered in the island, a ship of Alexandria, with the twin gods[c] as a figurehead. ¹²Putting in at Syracuse, we stayed there for three days. ¹³And from there we made a circuit and arrived at Rhegium. And after one day a south wind sprang up, and on the second day we came to Puteoli. ¹⁴There we found brothers[d] and were invited to stay with them for seven days. And so we came to Rome. ¹⁵And the brothers there, when they heard about us, came as far as the Forum of Appius and Three Taverns to meet us. On seeing them, Paul thanked God and took courage. ¹⁶And when we came into Rome, Paul was allowed to stay by himself, with the soldier who guarded him.

PAUL IN ROME

¹⁷After three days he called together the local leaders of the Jews, and when they had gathered, he said to them, "Brothers, though I had done nothing against our people or the customs of our fathers, yet I was delivered as a prisoner from Jerusalem into the hands of the Romans. ¹⁸When they had examined me, they wished to set me at liberty, because there was no reason for the death penalty in my case. ¹⁹But because the Jews objected, I was compelled to appeal to Caesar—though I had no charge to bring against my nation. ²⁰For this reason, therefore, I have asked to see you and speak with you, since it is because of the hope of Israel that I am wearing this chain." ²¹And they said to him, "We have received no letters from Judea about you, and none of the brothers coming here has reported or spoken any evil about you. ²²But we desire to hear from you what your views are, for with regard to this sect we know that everywhere it is spoken against."

²³When they had appointed a day for him, they came to him at his lodging in greater numbers. From morning till evening he expounded to them, testifying to the kingdom of God and trying to convince them about Jesus both from the Law of Moses and from the Prophets. ²⁴And some were convinced by what he said, but others disbelieved. ²⁵And disagreeing among themselves, they departed after Paul had made one statement: "The Holy Spirit was right in saying to your fathers through Isaiah the prophet:

²⁶ "'Go to this people, and say,
"You will indeed hear but
never understand,
and you will indeed see but
never perceive."
²⁷ For this people's heart has grown dull,
and with their ears they
can barely hear,
and their eyes they have closed;
lest they should see with their eyes
and hear with their ears
and understand with their heart
and turn, and I would heal them.'

²⁸Therefore let it be known to you that this salvation of God has been sent to the Gentiles; they will listen."[e]

³⁰He lived there two whole years at his own expense,[f] and welcomed all who came to him, ³¹proclaiming the kingdom of God and teaching about the Lord Jesus Christ with all boldness and without hindrance.

---

[a]Or *justice* [b]Greek *honoured us with many honours* [c]That is, the Greek gods Castor and Pollux [d]Or *brothers and sisters*; also verses 15, 21 [e]Some manuscripts add verse 29: *And when he had said these words, the Jews departed, having much dispute among themselves* [f]Or *in his own hired dwelling*

THE LETTER OF PAUL TO THE
ROMANS

GREETING

1 Paul, a servant[a] of Christ Jesus, called to be an apostle, set apart for the gospel of God, ²which he promised beforehand through his prophets in the holy Scriptures, ³concerning his Son, who was descended from David[b] according to the flesh ⁴and was declared to be the Son of God in power according to the Spirit of holiness by his resurrection from the dead, Jesus Christ our Lord, ⁵through whom we have received grace and apostleship to bring about the obedience of faith for the sake of his name among all the nations, ⁶including you who are called to belong to Jesus Christ,

⁷To all those in Rome who are loved by God and called to be saints:

Grace to you and peace from God our Father and the Lord Jesus Christ.

LONGING TO GO TO ROME

⁸First, I thank my God through Jesus Christ for all of you, because your faith is proclaimed in all the world. ⁹For God is my witness, whom I serve with my spirit in the gospel of his Son, that without ceasing I mention you ¹⁰always in my prayers, asking that somehow by God's will I may now at last succeed in coming to you. ¹¹For I long to see you, that I may impart to you some spiritual gift to strengthen you — ¹²that is, that we may be mutually encouraged by each other's faith, both yours and mine. ¹³I do not want you to be unaware, brothers,[c] that I have often intended to come to you (but thus far have been prevented), in order that I may reap some harvest among you as well as among the rest of the Gentiles. ¹⁴I am under obligation both to Greeks and to barbarians,[d] both to the wise and to the foolish. ¹⁵So I am eager to preach the gospel to you also who are in Rome.

THE RIGHTEOUS SHALL LIVE BY FAITH

¹⁶For I am not ashamed of the gospel, for it is the power of God for salvation to everyone who believes, to the Jew first and also to the Greek. ¹⁷For in it the righteousness of God is revealed from faith for faith,[e] as it is written, "The righteous shall live by faith."[f]

GOD'S WRATH ON UNRIGHTEOUSNESS

¹⁸For the wrath of God is revealed from heaven against all ungodliness and unrighteousness of men, who by their unrighteousness suppress the truth. ¹⁹For what can be known about God is plain to them, because God has shown it to them. ²⁰For his invisible attributes, namely, his eternal power and divine nature, have been clearly perceived, ever since the creation of the world,[g] in the things that have been made. So they are without excuse. ²¹For although they knew God, they did not honour him as God or give thanks to him, but they became futile in their thinking, and their foolish hearts were darkened. ²²Claiming to be wise, they became fools, ²³and exchanged the glory of the immortal God for images resembling mortal man and birds and animals and creeping things.

²⁴Therefore God gave them up in the lusts of their hearts to impurity, to the dishonouring of their bodies among themselves, ²⁵because they exchanged the truth about God for a lie and worshipped and served the creature rather than the Creator, who is blessed for ever! Amen.

²⁶For this reason God gave them up to dishonourable passions. For their women exchanged natural relations for those that are contrary to nature; ²⁷and the men likewise gave up natural relations with women and were consumed with passion for one another, men committing shameless acts with men and receiving in themselves the due penalty for their error.

²⁸And since they did not see fit to acknowledge God, God gave them up to a debased

---

[a] For the contextual rendering of the Greek word *doulos*, see Preface [b] Or *who came from the offspring of David* [c] Or *brothers and sisters*. In New Testament usage, depending on the context, the plural Greek word *adelphoi* (translated "brothers") may refer either to *brothers* or to *brothers and sisters* [d] That is, non-Greeks [e] Or *beginning and ending in faith* [f] Or *The one who by faith is righteous shall live* [g] Or *clearly perceived from the creation of the world*

mind to do what ought not to be done. ²⁹They were filled with all manner of unrighteousness, evil, covetousness, malice. They are full of envy, murder, strife, deceit, maliciousness. They are gossips, ³⁰slanderers, haters of God, insolent, haughty, boastful, inventors of evil, disobedient to parents, ³¹foolish, faithless, heartless, ruthless. ³²Though they know God's righteous decree that those who practise such things deserve to die, they not only do them but give approval to those who practise them.

GOD'S RIGHTEOUS JUDGEMENT

2 Therefore you have no excuse, O man, every one of you who judges. For in passing judgement on another you condemn yourself, because you, the judge, practise the very same things. ²We know that the judgement of God rightly falls on those who practise such things. ³Do you suppose, O man—you who judge those who practise such things and yet do them yourself—that you will escape the judgement of God? ⁴Or do you presume on the riches of his kindness and forbearance and patience, not knowing that God's kindness is meant to lead you to repentance? ⁵But because of your hard and impenitent heart you are storing up wrath for yourself on the day of wrath when God's righteous judgement will be revealed.

⁶He will render to each one according to his works: ⁷to those who by patience in well-doing seek for glory and honour and immortality, he will give eternal life; ⁸but for those who are self-seeking*ᵃ* and do not obey the truth, but obey unrighteousness, there will be wrath and fury. ⁹There will be tribulation and distress for every human being who does evil, the Jew first and also the Greek, ¹⁰but glory and honour and peace for everyone who does good, the Jew first and also the Greek. ¹¹For God shows no partiality.

GOD'S JUDGEMENT AND THE LAW

¹²For all who have sinned without the law will also perish without the law, and all who have sinned under the law will be judged by the law. ¹³For it is not the hearers of the law who are righteous before God, but the doers of the law who will be justified. ¹⁴For when Gentiles, who do not have the law, by nature do what the law requires, they are a law to themselves, even though they do not have the law. ¹⁵They show that the work of the law is written on their hearts, while their conscience also bears witness, and their conflicting thoughts accuse or even excuse them ¹⁶on that day when, according to my gospel, God judges the secrets of men by Christ Jesus.

¹⁷But if you call yourself a Jew and rely on the law and boast in God ¹⁸and know his will and approve what is excellent, because you are instructed from the law; ¹⁹and if you are sure that you yourself are a guide to the blind, a light to those who are in darkness, ²⁰an instructor of the foolish, a teacher of children, having in the law the embodiment of knowledge and truth— ²¹you then who teach others, do you not teach yourself? While you preach against stealing, do you steal? ²²You who say that one must not commit adultery, do you commit adultery? You who abhor idols, do you rob temples? ²³You who boast in the law dishonour God by breaking the law. ²⁴For, as it is written, "The name of God is blasphemed among the Gentiles because of you."

²⁵For circumcision indeed is of value if you obey the law, but if you break the law, your circumcision becomes uncircumcision. ²⁶So, if a man who is uncircumcised keeps the precepts of the law, will not his uncircumcision be regarded*ᵇ* as circumcision? ²⁷Then he who is physically*ᶜ* uncircumcised but keeps the law will condemn you who have the written code*ᵈ* and circumcision but break the law. ²⁸For no one is a Jew who is merely one outwardly, nor is circumcision outward and physical. ²⁹But a Jew is one inwardly, and circumcision is a matter of the heart, by the Spirit, not by the letter. His praise is not from man but from God.

GOD'S RIGHTEOUSNESS UPHELD

3 Then what advantage has the Jew? Or what is the value of circumcision? ²Much in every way. To begin with, the Jews were entrusted with the oracles of God. ³What if some were unfaithful? Does their faithlessness nullify the faithfulness of God? ⁴By no means! Let God be true though every one were a liar, as it is written,

> "That you may be justified
>   in your words,
> and prevail when you are judged."

⁵But if our unrighteousness serves to show the righteousness of God, what shall we say?

ᵃOr contentious *ᵇOr counted* *ᶜOr is by nature* *ᵈOr the letter*

That God is unrighteous to inflict wrath on us? (I speak in a human way.) ⁶By no means! For then how could God judge the world? ⁷But if through my lie God's truth abounds to his glory, why am I still being condemned as a sinner? ⁸And why not do evil that good may come?—as some people slanderously charge us with saying. Their condemnation is just.

NO ONE IS RIGHTEOUS

⁹What then? Are we Jews[a] any better off?[b] No, not at all. For we have already charged that all, both Jews and Greeks, are under sin, ¹⁰as it is written:

"None is righteous, no, not one;
¹¹   no one understands;
      no one seeks for God.
¹²   All have turned aside; together they
         have become worthless;
      no one does good,
         not even one."
¹³   "Their throat is an open grave;
      they use their tongues to deceive."
   "The venom of asps is under their lips."
¹⁴   "Their mouth is full of curses
         and bitterness."
¹⁵   "Their feet are swift to shed blood;
¹⁶   in their paths are ruin and misery,
¹⁷   and the way of peace they
         have not known."
¹⁸   "There is no fear of God
         before their eyes."

¹⁹Now we know that whatever the law says it speaks to those who are under the law, so that every mouth may be stopped, and the whole world may be held accountable to God. ²⁰For by works of the law no human being[c] will be justified in his sight, since through the law comes knowledge of sin.

THE RIGHTEOUSNESS OF GOD THROUGH FAITH

²¹But now the righteousness of God has been manifested apart from the law, although the Law and the Prophets bear witness to it— ²²the righteousness of God through faith in Jesus Christ for all who believe. For there is no distinction: ²³for all have sinned and fall short of the glory of God, ²⁴and are justified by his grace as a gift, through the redemption that is in Christ Jesus, ²⁵whom God put forward as a propitiation by his blood, to be received by faith. This was to show God's righteousness, because in his divine forbearance he had passed over former sins. ²⁶It was to show his righteousness at the present time, so that he might be just and the justifier of the one who has faith in Jesus.

²⁷Then what becomes of our boasting? It is excluded. By what kind of law? By a law of works? No, but by the law of faith. ²⁸For we hold that one is justified by faith apart from works of the law. ²⁹Or is God the God of Jews only? Is he not the God of Gentiles also? Yes, of Gentiles also, ³⁰since God is one—who will justify the circumcised by faith and the uncircumcised through faith. ³¹Do we then overthrow the law by this faith? By no means! On the contrary, we uphold the law.

ABRAHAM JUSTIFIED BY FAITH

4 What then shall we say was gained by Abraham, our forefather according to the flesh? ²For if Abraham was justified by works, he has something to boast about, but not before God. ³For what does the Scripture say? "Abraham believed God, and it was counted to him as righteousness." ⁴Now to the one who works, his wages are not counted as a gift but as his due. ⁵And to the one who does not work but believes in[d] him who justifies the ungodly, his faith is counted as righteousness, ⁶just as David also speaks of the blessing of the one to whom God counts righteousness apart from works:

⁷   "Blessed are those whose lawless
         deeds are forgiven,
      and whose sins are covered;
⁸   blessed is the man against whom the
         Lord will not count his sin."

⁹Is this blessing then only for the circumcised, or also for the uncircumcised? For we say that faith was counted to Abraham as righteousness. ¹⁰How then was it counted to him? Was it before or after he had been circumcised? It was not after, but before he was circumcised. ¹¹He received the sign of circumcision as a seal of the righteousness that he had by faith while he was still uncircumcised. The purpose was to make him the father of all who believe without being circumcised, so that righteousness would be counted to them as well, ¹²and to make him the father of the circumcised who are not merely circumcised but who also walk

---

[a]Greek *Are we* [b]Or *at any disadvantage?* [c]Greek *flesh* [d]Or *but trusts*; compare verse 24

in the footsteps of the faith that our father Abraham had before he was circumcised.

THE PROMISE REALIZED THROUGH FAITH

13 For the promise to Abraham and his offspring that he would be heir of the world did not come through the law but through the righteousness of faith. **14** For if it is the adherents of the law who are to be the heirs, faith is null and the promise is void. **15** For the law brings wrath, but where there is no law there is no transgression.

16 That is why it depends on faith, in order that the promise may rest on grace and be guaranteed to all his offspring—not only to the adherent of the law but also to the one who shares the faith of Abraham, who is the father of us all, **17** as it is written, "I have made you the father of many nations"—in the presence of the God in whom he believed, who gives life to the dead and calls into existence the things that do not exist. **18** In hope he believed against hope, that he should become the father of many nations, as he had been told, "So shall your offspring be." **19** He did not weaken in faith when he considered his own body, which was as good as dead (since he was about a hundred years old), or when he considered the barrenness[a] of Sarah's womb. **20** No unbelief made him waver concerning the promise of God, but he grew strong in his faith as he gave glory to God, **21** fully convinced that God was able to do what he had promised. **22** That is why his faith was "counted to him as righteousness". **23** But the words "it was counted to him" were not written for his sake alone, **24** but for ours also. It will be counted to us who believe in him who raised from the dead Jesus our Lord, **25** who was delivered up for our trespasses and raised for our justification.

PEACE WITH GOD THROUGH FAITH

5 Therefore, since we have been justified by faith, we[b] have peace with God through our Lord Jesus Christ. **2** Through him we have also obtained access by faith[c] into this grace in which we stand, and we[d] rejoice[e] in hope of the glory of God. **3** Not only that, but we rejoice in our sufferings, knowing that suffering produces endurance, **4** and endurance produces character, and character produces hope, **5** and hope does not put us to shame, because God's love has been poured into our hearts through the Holy Spirit who has been given to us.

6 For while we were still weak, at the right time Christ died for the ungodly. **7** For one will scarcely die for a righteous person—though perhaps for a good person one would dare even to die—**8** but God shows his love for us in that while we were still sinners, Christ died for us. **9** Since, therefore, we have now been justified by his blood, much more shall we be saved by him from the wrath of God. **10** For if while we were enemies we were reconciled to God by the death of his Son, much more, now that we are reconciled, shall we be saved by his life. **11** More than that, we also rejoice in God through our Lord Jesus Christ, through whom we have now received reconciliation.

DEATH IN ADAM, LIFE IN CHRIST

12 Therefore, just as sin came into the world through one man, and death through sin, and so death spread to all men[f] because all sinned—**13** for sin indeed was in the world before the law was given, but sin is not counted where there is no law. **14** Yet death reigned from Adam to Moses, even over those whose sinning was not like the transgression of Adam, who was a type of the one who was to come.

15 But the free gift is not like the trespass. For if many died through one man's trespass, much more have the grace of God and the free gift by the grace of that one man Jesus Christ abounded for many. **16** And the free gift is not like the result of that one man's sin. For the judgement following one trespass brought condemnation, but the free gift following many trespasses brought justification. **17** For if, because of one man's trespass, death reigned through that one man, much more will those who receive the abundance of grace and the free gift of righteousness reign in life through the one man Jesus Christ.

18 Therefore, as one trespass[g] led to condemnation for all men, so one act of righteousness[h] leads to justification and life for all men. **19** For as by the one man's disobedience the many were made sinners, so by the one man's obedience the many will be made righteous. **20** Now the law came in to increase the trespass, but where sin

---

[a] Greek *deadness* [b] Some manuscripts *let us* [c] Some manuscripts omit *by faith* [d] Or *let us*; also verse 3 [e] Or *boast*; also verses 3, 11 [f] The Greek word *anthropoi* refers here to both men and women; also twice in verse 18 [g] Or *the trespass of one* [h] Or *the act of righteousness of one*

increased, grace abounded all the more, ²¹so that, as sin reigned in death, grace also might reign through righteousness leading to eternal life through Jesus Christ our Lord.

DEAD TO SIN, ALIVE TO GOD

6 What shall we say then? Are we to continue in sin that grace may abound? ²By no means! How can we who died to sin still live in it? ³Do you not know that all of us who have been baptized into Christ Jesus were baptized into his death? ⁴We were buried therefore with him by baptism into death, in order that, just as Christ was raised from the dead by the glory of the Father, we too might walk in newness of life.

⁵For if we have been united with him in a death like his, we shall certainly be united with him in a resurrection like his. ⁶We know that our old self[a] was crucified with him in order that the body of sin might be brought to nothing, so that we would no longer be enslaved to sin. ⁷For one who has died has been set free[b] from sin. ⁸Now if we have died with Christ, we believe that we will also live with him. ⁹We know that Christ, being raised from the dead, will never die again; death no longer has dominion over him. ¹⁰For the death he died he died to sin, once for all, but the life he lives he lives to God. ¹¹So you also must consider yourselves dead to sin and alive to God in Christ Jesus.

¹²Let not sin therefore reign in your mortal body, to make you obey its passions. ¹³Do not present your members to sin as instruments for unrighteousness, but present yourselves to God as those who have been brought from death to life, and your members to God as instruments for righteousness. ¹⁴For sin will have no dominion over you, since you are not under law but under grace.

SLAVES TO RIGHTEOUSNESS

¹⁵What then? Are we to sin because we are not under law but under grace? By no means! ¹⁶Do you not know that if you present yourselves to anyone as obedient slaves,[c] you are slaves of the one whom you obey, either of sin, which leads to death, or of obedience, which leads to righteousness? ¹⁷But thanks be to God, that you who were once slaves of sin have become obedient from the heart to the standard of teaching to which you were committed, ¹⁸and, having been set free from sin, have become slaves of righteousness. ¹⁹I am speaking in human terms, because of your natural limitations. For just as you once presented your members as slaves to impurity and to lawlessness leading to more lawlessness, so now present your members as slaves to righteousness leading to sanctification.

²⁰For when you were slaves of sin, you were free in regard to righteousness. ²¹But what fruit were you getting at that time from the things of which you are now ashamed? For the end of those things is death. ²²But now that you have been set free from sin and have become slaves of God, the fruit you get leads to sanctification and its end, eternal life. ²³For the wages of sin is death, but the free gift of God is eternal life in Christ Jesus our Lord.

RELEASED FROM THE LAW

7 Or do you not know, brothers[d]—for I am speaking to those who know the law—that the law is binding on a person only as long as he lives? ²For a married woman is bound by law to her husband while he lives, but if her husband dies she is released from the law of marriage.[e] ³Accordingly, she will be called an adulteress if she lives with another man while her husband is alive. But if her husband dies, she is free from that law, and if she marries another man she is not an adulteress.

⁴Likewise, my brothers, you also have died to the law through the body of Christ, so that you may belong to another, to him who has been raised from the dead, in order that we may bear fruit for God. ⁵For while we were living in the flesh, our sinful passions, aroused by the law, were at work in our members to bear fruit for death. ⁶But now we are released from the law, having died to that which held us captive, so that we serve in the new way of the Spirit and not in the old way of the written code.[f]

THE LAW AND SIN

⁷What then shall we say? That the law is sin? By no means! Yet if it had not been for the law, I would not have known sin. For I would not have known what it is to covet if the law had not said, "You shall not covet." ⁸But sin, seizing an opportunity through the commandment, produced in me all kinds

---

[a] Greek man [b] Greek has been justified [c] For the contextual rendering of the Greek word doulos, see Preface; twice in this verse; also verses 17, 19 (twice), 20 [d] Or brothers and sisters; also verse 4 [e] Greek law concerning the husband [f] Greek of the letter

of covetousness. For apart from the law, sin lies dead. ⁹I was once alive apart from the law, but when the commandment came, sin came alive and I died. ¹⁰The very commandment that promised life proved to be death to me. ¹¹For sin, seizing an opportunity through the commandment, deceived me and through it killed me. ¹²So the law is holy, and the commandment is holy and righteous and good.

¹³Did that which is good, then, bring death to me? By no means! It was sin, producing death in me through what is good, in order that sin might be shown to be sin, and through the commandment might become sinful beyond measure. ¹⁴For we know that the law is spiritual, but I am of the flesh, sold under sin. ¹⁵For I do not understand my own actions. For I do not do what I want, but I do the very thing I hate. ¹⁶Now if I do what I do not want, I agree with the law, that it is good. ¹⁷So now it is no longer I who do it, but sin that dwells within me. ¹⁸For I know that nothing good dwells in me, that is, in my flesh. For I have the desire to do what is right, but not the ability to carry it out. ¹⁹For I do not do the good I want, but the evil I do not want is what I keep on doing. ²⁰Now if I do what I do not want, it is no longer I who do it, but sin that dwells within me.

²¹So I find it to be a law that when I want to do right, evil lies close at hand. ²²For I delight in the law of God, in my inner being, ²³but I see in my members another law waging war against the law of my mind and making me captive to the law of sin that dwells in my members. ²⁴Wretched man that I am! Who will deliver me from this body of death? ²⁵Thanks be to God through Jesus Christ our Lord! So then, I myself serve the law of God with my mind, but with my flesh I serve the law of sin.

LIFE IN THE SPIRIT

8 There is therefore now no condemnation for those who are in Christ Jesus.ᵃ ²For the law of the Spirit of life has set youᵇ free in Christ Jesus from the law of sin and death. ³For God has done what the law, weakened by the flesh, could not do. By sending his own Son in the likeness of sinful flesh and for sin,ᶜ he condemned sin in the flesh, ⁴in order that the righteous requirement of the law might be fulfilled in us, who walk not according to the flesh but according to the Spirit. ⁵For those who live according to the flesh set their minds on the things of the flesh, but those who live according to the Spirit set their minds on the things of the Spirit. ⁶For to set the mind on the flesh is death, but to set the mind on the Spirit is life and peace. ⁷For the mind that is set on the flesh is hostile to God, for it does not submit to God's law; indeed, it cannot. ⁸Those who are in the flesh cannot please God.

⁹You, however, are not in the flesh but in the Spirit, if in fact the Spirit of God dwells in you. Anyone who does not have the Spirit of Christ does not belong to him. ¹⁰But if Christ is in you, although the body is dead because of sin, the Spirit is life because of righteousness. ¹¹If the Spirit of him who raised Jesus from the dead dwells in you, he who raised Christ Jesusᵈ from the dead will also give life to your mortal bodies through his Spirit who dwells in you.

HEIRS WITH CHRIST

¹²So then, brothers,ᵉ we are debtors, not to the flesh, to live according to the flesh. ¹³For if you live according to the flesh you will die, but if by the Spirit you put to death the deeds of the body, you will live. ¹⁴For all who are led by the Spirit of God are sonsᶠ of God. ¹⁵For you did not receive the spirit of slavery to fall back into fear, but you have received the Spirit of adoption as sons, by whom we cry, "Abba! Father!" ¹⁶The Spirit himself bears witness with our spirit that we are children of God, ¹⁷and if children, then heirs—heirs of God and fellow heirs with Christ, provided we suffer with him in order that we may also be glorified with him.

FUTURE GLORY

¹⁸For I consider that the sufferings of this present time are not worth comparing with the glory that is to be revealed to us. ¹⁹For the creation waits with eager longing for the revealing of the sons of God. ²⁰For the creation was subjected to futility, not willingly, but because of him who subjected it, in hope ²¹that the creation itself will be set free from its bondage to corruption and obtain the freedom of the glory of the children of God. ²²For we know that the whole creation has been groaning together in the pains of childbirth until now. ²³And not only

---

ᵃSome manuscripts add *who walk not according to the flesh (but according to the Spirit)* ᵇSome manuscripts *me* ᶜOr *and as a sin offering* ᵈSome manuscripts lack *Jesus* ᵉOr *brothers and sisters*; also verse 29 ᶠSee discussion on "sons" in the Preface

the creation, but we ourselves, who have the firstfruits of the Spirit, groan inwardly as we wait eagerly for adoption as sons, the redemption of our bodies. ²⁴For in this hope we were saved. Now hope that is seen is not hope. For who hopes for what he sees? ²⁵But if we hope for what we do not see, we wait for it with patience.

²⁶Likewise the Spirit helps us in our weakness. For we do not know what to pray for as we ought, but the Spirit himself intercedes for us with groanings too deep for words. ²⁷And he who searches hearts knows what is the mind of the Spirit, because[a] the Spirit intercedes for the saints according to the will of God. ²⁸And we know that for those who love God all things work together for good,[b] for those who are called according to his purpose. ²⁹For those whom he foreknew he also predestined to be conformed to the image of his Son, in order that he might be the firstborn among many brothers. ³⁰And those whom he predestined he also called, and those whom he called he also justified, and those whom he justified he also glorified.

GOD'S EVERLASTING LOVE

³¹What then shall we say to these things? If God is for us, who can be[c] against us? ³²He who did not spare his own Son but gave him up for us all, how will he not also with him graciously give us all things? ³³Who shall bring any charge against God's elect? It is God who justifies. ³⁴Who is to condemn? Christ Jesus is the one who died—more than that, who was raised—who is at the right hand of God, who indeed is interceding for us.[d] ³⁵Who shall separate us from the love of Christ? Shall tribulation, or distress, or persecution, or famine, or nakedness, or danger, or sword? ³⁶As it is written,

> "For your sake we are being
> killed all the day long;
> we are regarded as sheep to
> be slaughtered."

³⁷No, in all these things we are more than conquerors through him who loved us. ³⁸For I am sure that neither death nor life, nor angels nor rulers, nor things present nor things to come, nor powers, ³⁹nor height nor depth, nor anything else in all creation, will be able to separate us from the love of God in Christ Jesus our Lord.

GOD'S SOVEREIGN CHOICE

9 I am speaking the truth in Christ—I am not lying; my conscience bears me witness in the Holy Spirit— ²that I have great sorrow and unceasing anguish in my heart. ³For I could wish that I myself were accursed and cut off from Christ for the sake of my brothers,[e] my kinsmen according to the flesh. ⁴They are Israelites, and to them belong the adoption, the glory, the covenants, the giving of the law, the worship, and the promises. ⁵To them belong the patriarchs, and from their race, according to the flesh, is the Christ, who is God over all, blessed for ever. Amen.

⁶But it is not as though the word of God has failed. For not all who are descended from Israel belong to Israel, ⁷and not all are children of Abraham because they are his offspring, but "Through Isaac shall your offspring be named." ⁸This means that it is not the children of the flesh who are the children of God, but the children of the promise are counted as offspring. ⁹For this is what the promise said: "About this time next year I will return, and Sarah shall have a son." ¹⁰And not only so, but also when Rebekah had conceived children by one man, our forefather Isaac, ¹¹though they were not yet born and had done nothing either good or bad—in order that God's purpose of election might continue, not because of works but because of him who calls— ¹²she was told, "The older will serve the younger." ¹³As it is written, "Jacob I loved, but Esau I hated."

¹⁴What shall we say then? Is there injustice on God's part? By no means! ¹⁵For he says to Moses, "I will have mercy on whom I have mercy, and I will have compassion on whom I have compassion." ¹⁶So then it depends not on human will or exertion,[f] but on God, who has mercy. ¹⁷For the Scripture says to Pharaoh, "For this very purpose I have raised you up, that I might show my power in you, and that my name might be proclaimed in all the earth." ¹⁸So then he has mercy on whomever he wills, and he hardens whomever he wills.

¹⁹You will say to me then, "Why does he still find fault? For who can resist his will?" ²⁰But who are you, O man, to answer back to God? Will what is moulded say to

---

[a]Or that [b]Some manuscripts God works all things together for good, or God works in all things for the good [c]Or who is [d]Or Is it Christ Jesus who died . . . for us? [e]Or brothers and sisters [f]Greek not of him who wills or runs

its moulder, "Why have you made me like this?" ²¹Has the potter no right over the clay, to make out of the same lump one vessel for honourable use and another for dishonourable use? ²²What if God, desiring to show his wrath and to make known his power, has endured with much patience vessels of wrath prepared for destruction, ²³in order to make known the riches of his glory for vessels of mercy, which he has prepared beforehand for glory— ²⁴even us whom he has called, not from the Jews only but also from the Gentiles? ²⁵As indeed he says in Hosea,

> "Those who were not my people
>   I will call 'my people',
> and her who was not beloved
>   I will call 'beloved'."
> ²⁶ "And in the very place where it was said to them, 'You are not my people',
>   there they will be called 'sons
>   of the living God'."

²⁷And Isaiah cries out concerning Israel: "Though the number of the sons of Israel[a] be as the sand of the sea, only a remnant of them will be saved, ²⁸for the Lord will carry out his sentence upon the earth fully and without delay." ²⁹And as Isaiah predicted,

> "If the Lord of hosts had not
>   left us offspring,
> we would have been like Sodom
>   and become like Gomorrah."

ISRAEL'S UNBELIEF

³⁰What shall we say, then? That Gentiles who did not pursue righteousness have attained it, that is, a righteousness that is by faith; ³¹but that Israel who pursued a law that would lead to righteousness[b] did not succeed in reaching that law. ³²Why? Because they did not pursue it by faith, but as if it were based on works. They have stumbled over the stumbling stone, ³³as it is written,

> "Behold, I am laying in Zion a stone of
>   stumbling, and a rock of offence;
> and whoever believes in him
>   will not be put to shame."

10 Brothers,[c] my heart's desire and prayer to God for them is that they may be saved. ²For I bear them witness that they have a zeal for God, but not according to knowledge. ³For, being ignorant of the righteousness of God, and seeking to establish their own, they did not submit to God's righteousness. ⁴For Christ is the end of the law for righteousness to everyone who believes.[d]

THE MESSAGE OF SALVATION TO ALL

⁵For Moses writes about the righteousness that is based on the law, that the person who does the commandments shall live by them. ⁶But the righteousness based on faith says, "Do not say in your heart, 'Who will ascend into heaven?'" (that is, to bring Christ down) ⁷"or 'Who will descend into the abyss?'" (that is, to bring Christ up from the dead). ⁸But what does it say? "The word is near you, in your mouth and in your heart" (that is, the word of faith that we proclaim); ⁹because, if you confess with your mouth that Jesus is Lord and believe in your heart that God raised him from the dead, you will be saved. ¹⁰For with the heart one believes and is justified, and with the mouth one confesses and is saved. ¹¹For the Scripture says, "Everyone who believes in him will not be put to shame." ¹²For there is no distinction between Jew and Greek; for the same Lord is Lord of all, bestowing his riches on all who call on him. ¹³For "everyone who calls on the name of the Lord will be saved."

¹⁴How then will they call on him in whom they have not believed? And how are they to believe in him of whom they have never heard?[e] And how are they to hear without someone preaching? ¹⁵And how are they to preach unless they are sent? As it is written, "How beautiful are the feet of those who preach the good news!" ¹⁶But they have not all obeyed the gospel. For Isaiah says, "Lord, who has believed what he has heard from us?" ¹⁷So faith comes from hearing, and hearing through the word of Christ.

¹⁸But I ask, have they not heard? Indeed they have, for

> "Their voice has gone out
>   to all the earth,
> and their words to the ends
>   of the world."

¹⁹But I ask, did Israel not understand? First Moses says,

---

[a] Or children of Israel [b] Greek a law of righteousness [c] Or Brothers and sisters [d] Or end of the law, that everyone who believes may be justified [e] Or him whom they have never heard

"I will make you jealous of those
who are not a nation;
with a foolish nation I will
make you angry."

²⁰Then Isaiah is so bold as to say,

"I have been found by those
who did not seek me;
I have shown myself to those
who did not ask for me."

²¹But of Israel he says, "All day long I have held out my hands to a disobedient and contrary people."

THE REMNANT OF ISRAEL

11 I ask, then, has God rejected his people? By no means! For I myself am an Israelite, a descendant of Abraham,[a] a member of the tribe of Benjamin. ²God has not rejected his people whom he foreknew. Do you not know what the Scripture says of Elijah, how he appeals to God against Israel? ³"Lord, they have killed your prophets, they have demolished your altars, and I alone am left, and they seek my life." ⁴But what is God's reply to him? "I have kept for myself seven thousand men who have not bowed the knee to Baal." ⁵So too at the present time there is a remnant, chosen by grace. ⁶But if it is by grace, it is no longer on the basis of works; otherwise grace would no longer be grace.

⁷What then? Israel failed to obtain what it was seeking. The elect obtained it, but the rest were hardened, ⁸as it is written,

"God gave them a spirit of stupor,
eyes that would not see
and ears that would not hear,
down to this very day."

⁹And David says,

"Let their table become a
snare and a trap,
a stumbling block and a
retribution for them;
¹⁰ let their eyes be darkened so
that they cannot see,
and bend their backs for ever."

GENTILES GRAFTED IN

¹¹So I ask, did they stumble in order that they might fall? By no means! Rather, through their trespass salvation has come to the Gentiles, so as to make Israel jealous. ¹²Now if their trespass means riches for the world, and if their failure means riches for the Gentiles, how much more will their full inclusion[b] mean!

¹³Now I am speaking to you Gentiles. Inasmuch then as I am an apostle to the Gentiles, I magnify my ministry ¹⁴in order somehow to make my fellow Jews jealous, and thus save some of them. ¹⁵For if their rejection means the reconciliation of the world, what will their acceptance mean but life from the dead? ¹⁶If the dough offered as firstfruits is holy, so is the whole lump, and if the root is holy, so are the branches.

¹⁷But if some of the branches were broken off, and you, although a wild olive shoot, were grafted in among the others and now share in the nourishing root[c] of the olive tree, ¹⁸do not be arrogant towards the branches. If you are, remember it is not you who support the root, but the root that supports you. ¹⁹Then you will say, "Branches were broken off so that I might be grafted in." ²⁰That is true. They were broken off because of their unbelief, but you stand fast through faith. So do not become proud, but fear. ²¹For if God did not spare the natural branches, neither will he spare you. ²²Note then the kindness and the severity of God: severity towards those who have fallen, but God's kindness to you, provided you continue in his kindness. Otherwise you too will be cut off. ²³And even they, if they do not continue in their unbelief, will be grafted in, for God has the power to graft them in again. ²⁴For if you were cut from what is by nature a wild olive tree, and grafted, contrary to nature, into a cultivated olive tree, how much more will these, the natural branches, be grafted back into their own olive tree.

THE MYSTERY OF ISRAEL'S SALVATION

²⁵Lest you be wise in your own sight, I do not want you to be unaware of this mystery, brothers:[d] a partial hardening has come upon Israel, until the fullness of the Gentiles has come in. ²⁶And in this way all Israel will be saved, as it is written,

"The Deliverer will come from Zion,
he will banish ungodliness
from Jacob";

---

[a]Or one of the offspring of Abraham [b]Greek their fullness [c]Greek root of richness; some manuscripts richness [d]Or brothers and sisters

²⁷ "and this will be my covenant
with them
when I take away their sins."

²⁸As regards the gospel, they are enemies for your sake. But as regards election, they are beloved for the sake of their forefathers. ²⁹For the gifts and the calling of God are irrevocable. ³⁰For just as you were at one time disobedient to God but now have received mercy because of their disobedience, ³¹so they too have now been disobedient in order that by the mercy shown to you they also may now[a] receive mercy. ³²For God has consigned all to disobedience, that he may have mercy on all.

³³Oh, the depth of the riches and wisdom and knowledge of God! How unsearchable are his judgements and how inscrutable his ways!

³⁴ "For who has known the
mind of the Lord,
or who has been his counsellor?"
³⁵ "Or who has given a gift to him
that he might be repaid?"

³⁶For from him and through him and to him are all things. To him be glory for ever. Amen.

A LIVING SACRIFICE

12 I appeal to you therefore, brothers,[b] by the mercies of God, to present your bodies as a living sacrifice, holy and acceptable to God, which is your spiritual worship.[c] ²Do not be conformed to this world,[d] but be transformed by the renewal of your mind, that by testing you may discern what is the will of God, what is good and acceptable and perfect.[e]

GIFTS OF GRACE

³For by the grace given to me I say to every one among you not to think of himself more highly than he ought to think, but to think with sober judgement, each according to the measure of faith that God has assigned. ⁴For as in one body we have many members,[f] and the members do not all have the same function, ⁵so we, though many, are one body in Christ, and individually members one of another. ⁶Having gifts that differ according to the grace given to us, let us use them: if prophecy, in proportion to our faith; ⁷if service, in our serving; the one who teaches, in his teaching; ⁸the one who exhorts, in his exhortation; the one who contributes, in generosity; the one who leads,[g] with zeal; the one who does acts of mercy, with cheerfulness.

MARKS OF THE TRUE CHRISTIAN

⁹Let love be genuine. Abhor what is evil; hold fast to what is good. ¹⁰Love one another with brotherly affection. Outdo one another in showing honour. ¹¹Do not be slothful in zeal, be fervent in spirit,[h] serve the Lord. ¹²Rejoice in hope, be patient in tribulation, be constant in prayer. ¹³Contribute to the needs of the saints and seek to show hospitality.

¹⁴Bless those who persecute you; bless and do not curse them. ¹⁵Rejoice with those who rejoice, weep with those who weep. ¹⁶Live in harmony with one another. Do not be haughty, but associate with the lowly.[i] Never be wise in your own sight. ¹⁷Repay no one evil for evil, but give thought to do what is honourable in the sight of all. ¹⁸If possible, so far as it depends on you, live peaceably with all. ¹⁹Beloved, never avenge yourselves, but leave it[j] to the wrath of God, for it is written, "Vengeance is mine, I will repay, says the Lord." ²⁰To the contrary, "if your enemy is hungry, feed him; if he is thirsty, give him something to drink; for by so doing you will heap burning coals on his head." ²¹Do not be overcome by evil, but overcome evil with good.

SUBMISSION TO THE AUTHORITIES

13 Let every person be subject to the governing authorities. For there is no authority except from God, and those that exist have been instituted by God. ²Therefore whoever resists the authorities resists what God has appointed, and those who resist will incur judgement. ³For rulers are not a terror to good conduct, but to bad. Would you have no fear of the one who is in authority? Then do what is good, and you will receive his approval, ⁴for he is God's servant for your good. But if you do wrong, be afraid, for he does not bear the sword in vain. For he is the servant of God, an avenger who carries out God's wrath on the wrongdoer. ⁵Therefore one must be in

---

[a] Some manuscripts omit *now* [b] Or *brothers and sisters* [c] Or *your rational service* [d] Greek *age* [e] Or *what is the good and acceptable and perfect will of God* [f] Greek *parts*; also verse 5 [g] Or *gives aid* [h] Or *fervent in the Spirit* [i] Or *give yourselves to humble tasks* [j] Greek *give place*

subjection, not only to avoid God's wrath but also for the sake of conscience. ⁶For because of this you also pay taxes, for the authorities are ministers of God, attending to this very thing. ⁷Pay to all what is owed to them: taxes to whom taxes are owed, revenue to whom revenue is owed, respect to whom respect is owed, honour to whom honour is owed.

FULFILLING THE LAW THROUGH LOVE

⁸Owe no one anything, except to love each other, for the one who loves another has fulfilled the law. ⁹For the commandments, "You shall not commit adultery, You shall not murder, You shall not steal, You shall not covet", and any other commandment, are summed up in this word: "You shall love your neighbour as yourself." ¹⁰Love does no wrong to a neighbour; therefore love is the fulfilling of the law.

¹¹Besides this you know the time, that the hour has come for you to wake from sleep. For salvation is nearer to us now than when we first believed. ¹²The night is far gone; the day is at hand. So then let us cast off the works of darkness and put on the armour of light. ¹³Let us walk properly as in the daytime, not in orgies and drunkenness, not in sexual immorality and sensuality, not in quarrelling and jealousy. ¹⁴But put on the Lord Jesus Christ, and make no provision for the flesh, to gratify its desires.

DO NOT PASS JUDGEMENT ON ONE ANOTHER

14 As for the one who is weak in faith, welcome him, but not to quarrel over opinions. ²One person believes he may eat anything, while the weak person eats only vegetables. ³Let not the one who eats despise the one who abstains, and let not the one who abstains pass judgement on the one who eats, for God has welcomed him. ⁴Who are you to pass judgement on the servant of another? It is before his own master*ᵃ* that he stands or falls. And he will be upheld, for the Lord is able to make him stand.

⁵One person esteems one day as better than another, while another esteems all days alike. Each one should be fully convinced in his own mind. ⁶The one who observes the day, observes it in honour of the Lord. The one who eats, eats in honour of the Lord, since he gives thanks to God, while the one who abstains, abstains in honour of the Lord and gives thanks to God. ⁷For none of us lives to himself, and none of us dies to himself. ⁸For if we live, we live to the Lord, and if we die, we die to the Lord. So then, whether we live or whether we die, we are the Lord's. ⁹For to this end Christ died and lived again, that he might be Lord both of the dead and of the living.

¹⁰Why do you pass judgement on your brother? Or you, why do you despise your brother? For we will all stand before the judgement seat of God; ¹¹for it is written,

> "As I live, says the Lord, every
>   knee shall bow to me,
> and every tongue shall
>   confess*ᵇ* to God."

¹²So then each of us will give an account of himself to God.

DO NOT CAUSE ANOTHER TO STUMBLE

¹³Therefore let us not pass judgement on one another any longer, but rather decide never to put a stumbling block or hindrance in the way of a brother. ¹⁴I know and am persuaded in the Lord Jesus that nothing is unclean in itself, but it is unclean for anyone who thinks it unclean. ¹⁵For if your brother is grieved by what you eat, you are no longer walking in love. By what you eat, do not destroy the one for whom Christ died. ¹⁶So do not let what you regard as good be spoken of as evil. ¹⁷For the kingdom of God is not a matter of eating and drinking but of righteousness and peace and joy in the Holy Spirit. ¹⁸Whoever thus serves Christ is acceptable to God and approved by men. ¹⁹So then let us pursue what makes for peace and for mutual upbuilding.

²⁰Do not, for the sake of food, destroy the work of God. Everything is indeed clean, but it is wrong for anyone to make another stumble by what he eats. ²¹It is good not to eat meat or drink wine or do anything that causes your brother to stumble.*ᶜ* ²²The faith that you have, keep between yourself and God. Blessed is the one who has no reason to pass judgement on himself for what he approves. ²³But whoever has doubts is condemned if he eats, because the eating is not from faith. For whatever does not proceed from faith is sin.*ᵈ*

ᵃOr lord ᵇOr shall give praise ᶜSome manuscripts add or be hindered or be weakened ᵈSome manuscripts insert here 16:25–27

THE EXAMPLE OF CHRIST

15 We who are strong have an obligation to bear with the failings of the weak, and not to please ourselves. ²Let each of us please his neighbour for his good, to build him up. ³For Christ did not please himself, but as it is written, "The reproaches of those who reproached you fell on me." ⁴For whatever was written in former days was written for our instruction, that through endurance and through the encouragement of the Scriptures we might have hope. ⁵May the God of endurance and encouragement grant you to live in such harmony with one another, in accord with Christ Jesus, ⁶that together you may with one voice glorify the God and Father of our Lord Jesus Christ. ⁷Therefore welcome one another as Christ has welcomed you, for the glory of God.

CHRIST THE HOPE OF JEWS AND GENTILES

⁸For I tell you that Christ became a servant to the circumcised to show God's truthfulness, in order to confirm the promises given to the patriarchs, ⁹and in order that the Gentiles might glorify God for his mercy. As it is written,

> "Therefore I will praise you
>   among the Gentiles,
>   and sing to your name."

¹⁰And again it is said,

> "Rejoice, O Gentiles, with his people."

¹¹And again,

> "Praise the Lord, all you Gentiles,
>   and let all the peoples extol him."

¹²And again Isaiah says,

> "The root of Jesse will come,
>   even he who arises to rule
>   the Gentiles;
> in him will the Gentiles hope."

¹³May the God of hope fill you with all joy and peace in believing, so that by the power of the Holy Spirit you may abound in hope.

PAUL THE MINISTER TO THE GENTILES

¹⁴I myself am satisfied about you, my brothers,ᵃ that you yourselves are full of goodness, filled with all knowledge and able to instruct one another. ¹⁵But on some points I have written to you very boldly by way of reminder, because of the grace given me by God ¹⁶to be a minister of Christ Jesus to the Gentiles in the priestly service of the gospel of God, so that the offering of the Gentiles may be acceptable, sanctified by the Holy Spirit. ¹⁷In Christ Jesus, then, I have reason to be proud of my work for God. ¹⁸For I will not venture to speak of anything except what Christ has accomplished through me to bring the Gentiles to obedience—by word and deed, ¹⁹by the power of signs and wonders, by the power of the Spirit of God—so that from Jerusalem and all the way around to Illyricum I have fulfilled the ministry of the gospel of Christ; ²⁰and thus I make it my ambition to preach the gospel, not where Christ has already been named, lest I build on someone else's foundation, ²¹but as it is written,

> "Those who have never been
>   told of him will see,
> and those who have never
>   heard will understand."

PAUL'S PLAN TO VISIT ROME

²²This is the reason why I have so often been hindered from coming to you. ²³But now, since I no longer have any room for work in these regions, and since I have longed for many years to come to you, ²⁴I hope to see you in passing as I go to Spain, and to be helped on my journey there by you, once I have enjoyed your company for a while. ²⁵At present, however, I am going to Jerusalem bringing aid to the saints. ²⁶For Macedonia and Achaia have been pleased to make some contribution for the poor among the saints at Jerusalem. ²⁷For they were pleased to do it, and indeed they owe it to them. For if the Gentiles have come to share in their spiritual blessings, they ought also to be of service to them in material blessings. ²⁸When therefore I have completed this and have delivered to them what has been collected,ᵇ I will leave for Spain by way of you. ²⁹I know that when I come to you I will come in the fullness of the blessingᶜ of Christ.

³⁰I appeal to you, brothers, by our Lord Jesus Christ and by the love of the Spirit, to strive together with me in your prayers to

---

ᵃOr *brothers and sisters*; also verse 30   ᵇGreek *sealed to them this fruit*
ᶜSome manuscripts insert *of the gospel*

God on my behalf, ³¹that I may be delivered from the unbelievers in Judea, and that my service for Jerusalem may be acceptable to the saints, ³²so that by God's will I may come to you with joy and be refreshed in your company. ³³May the God of peace be with you all. Amen.

PERSONAL GREETINGS

16 I commend to you our sister Phoebe, a servant[a] of the church at Cenchreae, ²that you may welcome her in the Lord in a way worthy of the saints, and help her in whatever she may need from you, for she has been a patron of many and of myself as well.

³Greet Prisca and Aquila, my fellow workers in Christ Jesus, ⁴who risked their necks for my life, to whom not only I give thanks but all the churches of the Gentiles give thanks as well. ⁵Greet also the church in their house. Greet my beloved Epaenetus, who was the first convert[b] to Christ in Asia. ⁶Greet Mary, who has worked hard for you. ⁷Greet Andronicus and Junia,[c] my kinsmen and my fellow prisoners. They are well known to the apostles,[d] and they were in Christ before me. ⁸Greet Ampliatus, my beloved in the Lord. ⁹Greet Urbanus, our fellow worker in Christ, and my beloved Stachys. ¹⁰Greet Apelles, who is approved in Christ. Greet those who belong to the family of Aristobulus. ¹¹Greet my kinsman Herodion. Greet those in the Lord who belong to the family of Narcissus. ¹²Greet those workers in the Lord, Tryphaena and Tryphosa. Greet the beloved Persis, who has worked hard in the Lord. ¹³Greet Rufus, chosen in the Lord; also his mother, who has been a mother to me as well. ¹⁴Greet Asyncritus, Phlegon, Hermes, Patrobas, Hermas, and the brothers[e] who are with them. ¹⁵Greet Philologus, Julia, Nereus and his sister, and Olympas, and all the saints who are with them. ¹⁶Greet one another with a holy kiss. All the churches of Christ greet you.

FINAL INSTRUCTIONS AND GREETINGS

¹⁷I appeal to you, brothers, to watch out for those who cause divisions and create obstacles contrary to the doctrine that you have been taught; avoid them. ¹⁸For such persons do not serve our Lord Christ, but their own appetites,[f] and by smooth talk and flattery they deceive the hearts of the naive. ¹⁹For your obedience is known to all, so that I rejoice over you, but I want you to be wise as to what is good and innocent as to what is evil. ²⁰The God of peace will soon crush Satan under your feet. The grace of our Lord Jesus Christ be with you.

²¹Timothy, my fellow worker, greets you; so do Lucius and Jason and Sosipater, my kinsmen.

²²I Tertius, who wrote this letter, greet you in the Lord.

²³Gaius, who is host to me and to the whole church, greets you. Erastus, the city treasurer, and our brother Quartus, greet you.[g]

DOXOLOGY

²⁵Now to him who is able to strengthen you according to my gospel and the preaching of Jesus Christ, according to the revelation of the mystery that was kept secret for long ages ²⁶but has now been disclosed and through the prophetic writings has been made known to all nations, according to the command of the eternal God, to bring about the obedience of faith — ²⁷to the only wise God be glory for evermore through Jesus Christ! Amen.

---

[a] Or deaconess [b] Greek firstfruit [c] Or Junias [d] Or messengers
[e] Or brothers and sisters; also verse 17 [f] Greek their own belly [g] Some manuscripts insert verse 24: The grace of our Lord Jesus Christ be with you all. Amen

THE FIRST LETTER OF PAUL TO THE CORINTHIANS

1 CORINTHIANS

GREETING

1 Paul, called by the will of God to be an apostle of Christ Jesus, and our brother Sosthenes,

² To the church of God that is in Corinth, to those sanctified in Christ Jesus, called to be saints together with all those who in every place call upon the name of our Lord Jesus Christ, both their Lord and ours:

³ Grace to you and peace from God our Father and the Lord Jesus Christ.

THANKSGIVING

⁴ I give thanks to my God always for you because of the grace of God that was given you in Christ Jesus, ⁵ that in every way you were enriched in him in all speech and all knowledge— ⁶ even as the testimony about Christ was confirmed among you— ⁷ so that you are not lacking in any gift, as you wait for the revealing of our Lord Jesus Christ, ⁸ who will sustain you to the end, guiltless in the day of our Lord Jesus Christ. ⁹ God is faithful, by whom you were called into the fellowship of his Son, Jesus Christ our Lord.

DIVISIONS IN THE CHURCH

¹⁰ I appeal to you, brothers,[a] by the name of our Lord Jesus Christ, that all of you agree, and that there be no divisions among you, but that you be united in the same mind and the same judgement. ¹¹ For it has been reported to me by Chloe's people that there is quarrelling among you, my brothers. ¹² What I mean is that each one of you says, "I follow Paul", or "I follow Apollos", or "I follow Cephas", or "I follow Christ." ¹³ Is Christ divided? Was Paul crucified for you? Or were you baptized in the name of Paul? ¹⁴ I thank God that I baptized none of you except Crispus and Gaius, ¹⁵ so that no one may say that you were baptized in my name. ¹⁶ (I did baptize also the household of Stephanas. Beyond that, I do not know whether I baptized anyone else.) ¹⁷ For Christ did not send me to baptize but to preach the gospel, and not with words of eloquent wisdom, lest the cross of Christ be emptied of its power.

CHRIST THE WISDOM AND POWER OF GOD

¹⁸ For the word of the cross is folly to those who are perishing, but to us who are being saved it is the power of God. ¹⁹ For it is written,

"I will destroy the wisdom of the wise,
 and the discernment of the
  discerning I will thwart."

²⁰ Where is the one who is wise? Where is the scribe? Where is the debater of this age? Has not God made foolish the wisdom of the world? ²¹ For since, in the wisdom of God, the world did not know God through wisdom, it pleased God through the folly of what we preach[b] to save those who believe. ²² For Jews demand signs and Greeks seek wisdom, ²³ but we preach Christ crucified, a stumbling block to Jews and folly to Gentiles, ²⁴ but to those who are called, both Jews and Greeks, Christ the power of God and the wisdom of God. ²⁵ For the foolishness of God is wiser than men, and the weakness of God is stronger than men.

²⁶ For consider your calling, brothers: not many of you were wise according to worldly standards,[c] not many were powerful, not many were of noble birth. ²⁷ But God chose what is foolish in the world to shame the wise; God chose what is weak in the world to shame the strong; ²⁸ God chose what is low and despised in the world, even things that are not, to bring to nothing things that are, ²⁹ so that no human being[d] might boast in the presence of God. ³⁰ And because of

---

[a] Or *brothers and sisters*. In New Testament usage, depending on the context, the plural Greek word *adelphoi* (translated "brothers") may refer either to *brothers* or to *brothers and sisters*; also verses 11, 26
[b] Or *the folly of preaching* [c] Greek *according to the flesh* [d] Greek *no flesh*

him[a] you are in Christ Jesus, who became to us wisdom from God, righteousness and sanctification and redemption, ³¹so that, as it is written, "Let the one who boasts, boast in the Lord."

PROCLAIMING CHRIST CRUCIFIED

2 And I, when I came to you, brothers,[b] did not come proclaiming to you the testimony[c] of God with lofty speech or wisdom. ²For I decided to know nothing among you except Jesus Christ and him crucified. ³And I was with you in weakness and in fear and much trembling, ⁴and my speech and my message were not in plausible words of wisdom, but in demonstration of the Spirit and of power, ⁵so that your faith might not rest in the wisdom of men[d] but in the power of God.

WISDOM FROM THE SPIRIT

⁶Yet among the mature we do impart wisdom, although it is not a wisdom of this age or of the rulers of this age, who are doomed to pass away. ⁷But we impart a secret and hidden wisdom of God, which God decreed before the ages for our glory. ⁸None of the rulers of this age understood this, for if they had, they would not have crucified the Lord of glory. ⁹But, as it is written,

"What no eye has seen, nor ear heard,
nor the heart of man imagined,
what God has prepared for
those who love him"—

¹⁰these things God has revealed to us through the Spirit. For the Spirit searches everything, even the depths of God. ¹¹For who knows a person's thoughts except the spirit of that person, which is in him? So also no one comprehends the thoughts of God except the Spirit of God. ¹²Now we have received not the spirit of the world, but the Spirit who is from God, that we might understand the things freely given us by God. ¹³And we impart this in words not taught by human wisdom but taught by the Spirit, interpreting spiritual truths to those who are spiritual.[e]

¹⁴The natural person does not accept the things of the Spirit of God, for they are folly to him, and he is not able to understand them because they are spiritually discerned. ¹⁵The spiritual person judges all things, but is himself to be judged by no one. ¹⁶"For who has understood the mind of the Lord so as to instruct him?" But we have the mind of Christ.

DIVISIONS IN THE CHURCH

3 But I, brothers,[f] could not address you as spiritual people, but as people of the flesh, as infants in Christ. ²I fed you with milk, not solid food, for you were not ready for it. And even now you are not yet ready, ³for you are still of the flesh. For while there is jealousy and strife among you, are you not of the flesh and behaving only in a human way? ⁴For when one says, "I follow Paul", and another, "I follow Apollos", are you not being merely human?

⁵What then is Apollos? What is Paul? Servants through whom you believed, as the Lord assigned to each. ⁶I planted, Apollos watered, but God gave the growth. ⁷So neither he who plants nor he who waters is anything, but only God who gives the growth. ⁸He who plants and he who waters are one, and each will receive his wages according to his labour. ⁹For we are God's fellow workers. You are God's field, God's building.

¹⁰According to the grace of God given to me, like a skilled[g] master builder I laid a foundation, and someone else is building upon it. Let each one take care how he builds upon it. ¹¹For no one can lay a foundation other than that which is laid, which is Jesus Christ. ¹²Now if anyone builds on the foundation with gold, silver, precious stones, wood, hay, straw— ¹³each one's work will become manifest, for the Day will disclose it, because it will be revealed by fire, and the fire will test what sort of work each one has done. ¹⁴If the work that anyone has built on the foundation survives, he will receive a reward. ¹⁵If anyone's work is burned up, he will suffer loss, though he himself will be saved, but only as through fire.

¹⁶Do you not know that you[h] are God's temple and that God's Spirit dwells in you? ¹⁷If anyone destroys God's temple, God will destroy him. For God's temple is holy, and you are that temple.

¹⁸Let no one deceive himself. If anyone among you thinks that he is wise in this age, let him become a fool that he may become wise. ¹⁹For the wisdom of this world is folly

---

[a] Greek *And from him* [b] Or *brothers and sisters* [c] Some manuscripts *mystery* (or *secret*) [d] The Greek word *anthropoi* can refer to both men and women [e] Or *interpreting spiritual truths in spiritual language*, or *comparing spiritual things with spiritual* [f] Or *brothers and sisters* [g] Or *wise* [h] The Greek for *you* is plural in verses 16 and 17

with God. For it is written, "He catches the wise in their craftiness", ²⁰and again, "The Lord knows the thoughts of the wise, that they are futile." ²¹So let no one boast in men. For all things are yours, ²²whether Paul or Apollos or Cephas or the world or life or death or the present or the future—all are yours, ²³and you are Christ's, and Christ is God's.

THE MINISTRY OF APOSTLES

4 This is how one should regard us, as servants of Christ and stewards of the mysteries of God. ²Moreover, it is required of stewards that they be found faithful. ³But with me it is a very small thing that I should be judged by you or by any human court. In fact, I do not even judge myself. ⁴For I am not aware of anything against myself, but I am not thereby acquitted. It is the Lord who judges me. ⁵Therefore do not pronounce judgement before the time, before the Lord comes, who will bring to light the things now hidden in darkness and will disclose the purposes of the heart. Then each one will receive his commendation from God.

⁶I have applied all these things to myself and Apollos for your benefit, brothers,[a] that you may learn by us not to go beyond what is written, that none of you may be puffed up in favour of one against another. ⁷For who sees anything different in you? What do you have that you did not receive? If then you received it, why do you boast as if you did not receive it?

⁸Already you have all you want! Already you have become rich! Without us you have become kings! And would that you did reign, so that we might share the rule with you! ⁹For I think that God has exhibited us apostles as last of all, like men sentenced to death, because we have become a spectacle to the world, to angels, and to men. ¹⁰We are fools for Christ's sake, but you are wise in Christ. We are weak, but you are strong. You are held in honour, but we in disrepute. ¹¹To the present hour we hunger and thirst, we are poorly dressed and buffeted and homeless, ¹²and we labour, working with our own hands. When reviled, we bless; when persecuted, we endure; ¹³when slandered, we entreat. We have become, and are still, like the scum of the world, the refuse of all things.

¹⁴I do not write these things to make you ashamed, but to admonish you as my beloved children. ¹⁵For though you have countless[b] guides in Christ, you do not have many fathers. For I became your father in Christ Jesus through the gospel. ¹⁶I urge you, then, be imitators of me. ¹⁷That is why I sent[c] you Timothy, my beloved and faithful child in the Lord, to remind you of my ways in Christ,[d] as I teach them everywhere in every church. ¹⁸Some are arrogant, as though I were not coming to you. ¹⁹But I will come to you soon, if the Lord wills, and I will find out not the talk of these arrogant people but their power. ²⁰For the kingdom of God does not consist in talk but in power. ²¹What do you wish? Shall I come to you with a rod, or with love in a spirit of gentleness?

SEXUAL IMMORALITY DEFILES THE CHURCH

5 It is actually reported that there is sexual immorality among you, and of a kind that is not tolerated even among pagans, for a man has his father's wife. ²And you are arrogant! Ought you not rather to mourn? Let him who has done this be removed from among you.

³For though absent in body, I am present in spirit; and as if present, I have already pronounced judgement on the one who did such a thing. ⁴When you are assembled in the name of the Lord Jesus and my spirit is present, with the power of our Lord Jesus, ⁵you are to deliver this man to Satan for the destruction of the flesh, so that his spirit may be saved in the day of the Lord.[e]

⁶Your boasting is not good. Do you not know that a little leaven leavens the whole lump? ⁷Cleanse out the old leaven that you may be a new lump, as you really are unleavened. For Christ, our Passover lamb, has been sacrificed. ⁸Let us therefore celebrate the festival, not with the old leaven, the leaven of malice and evil, but with the unleavened bread of sincerity and truth.

⁹I wrote to you in my letter not to associate with sexually immoral people— ¹⁰not at all meaning the sexually immoral of this world, or the greedy and swindlers, or idolaters, since then you would need to go out of the world. ¹¹But now I am writing to you not to associate with anyone who bears the name of brother if he is guilty of sexual immorality or greed, or is an idolater, reviler, drunkard, or swindler— not even to eat with such a one. ¹²For what have I to do with judging

---

[a]Or brothers and sisters [b]Greek you have ten thousand [c]Or am sending [d]Some manuscripts add Jesus [e]Some manuscripts add Jesus

outsiders? Is it not those inside the church[a] whom you are to judge? [13]God judges[b] those outside. "Purge the evil person from among you."

LAWSUITS AGAINST BELIEVERS

6 When one of you has a grievance against another, does he dare go to law before the unrighteous instead of the saints? [2]Or do you not know that the saints will judge the world? And if the world is to be judged by you, are you incompetent to try trivial cases? [3]Do you not know that we are to judge angels? How much more, then, matters pertaining to this life! [4]So if you have such cases, why do you lay them before those who have no standing in the church? [5]I say this to your shame. Can it be that there is no one among you wise enough to settle a dispute between the brothers, [6]but brother goes to law against brother, and that before unbelievers? [7]To have lawsuits at all with one another is already a defeat for you. Why not rather suffer wrong? Why not rather be defrauded? [8]But you yourselves wrong and defraud—even your own brothers![c]

[9]Or do you not know that the unrighteous[d] will not inherit the kingdom of God? Do not be deceived: neither the sexually immoral, nor idolaters, nor adulterers, nor men who practise homosexuality,[e] [10]nor thieves, nor the greedy, nor drunkards, nor revilers, nor swindlers will inherit the kingdom of God. [11]And such were some of you. But you were washed, you were sanctified, you were justified in the name of the Lord Jesus Christ and by the Spirit of our God.

FLEE SEXUAL IMMORALITY

[12]"All things are lawful for me", but not all things are helpful. "All things are lawful for me", but I will not be dominated by anything. [13]"Food is meant for the stomach and the stomach for food"—and God will destroy both one and the other. The body is not meant for sexual immorality, but for the Lord, and the Lord for the body. [14]And God raised the Lord and will also raise us up by his power. [15]Do you not know that your bodies are members of Christ? Shall I then take the members of Christ and make them members of a prostitute? Never! [16]Or do you not know that he who is joined[f] to a prostitute becomes one body with her? For, as it is written, "The two will become one flesh." [17]But he who is joined to the Lord becomes one spirit with him. [18]Flee from sexual immorality. Every other sin[g] a person commits is outside the body, but the sexually immoral person sins against his own body. [19]Or do you not know that your body is a temple of the Holy Spirit within you, whom you have from God? You are not your own, [20]for you were bought with a price. So glorify God in your body.

PRINCIPLES FOR MARRIAGE

7 Now concerning the matters about which you wrote: "It is good for a man not to have sexual relations with a woman." [2]But because of the temptation to sexual immorality, each man should have his own wife and each woman her own husband. [3]The husband should give to his wife her conjugal rights, and likewise the wife to her husband. [4]For the wife does not have authority over her own body, but the husband does. Likewise the husband does not have authority over his own body, but the wife does. [5]Do not deprive one another, except perhaps by agreement for a limited time, that you may devote yourselves to prayer; but then come together again, so that Satan may not tempt you because of your lack of self-control.

[6]Now as a concession, not a command, I say this.[h] [7]I wish that all were as I myself am. But each has his own gift from God, one of one kind and one of another.

[8]To the unmarried and the widows I say that it is good for them to remain single, as I am. [9]But if they cannot exercise self-control, they should marry. For it is better to marry than to burn with passion.

[10]To the married I give this charge (not I, but the Lord): the wife should not separate from her husband [11](but if she does, she should remain unmarried or else be reconciled to her husband), and the husband should not divorce his wife.

[12]To the rest I say (I, not the Lord) that if any brother has a wife who is an unbeliever, and she consents to live with him, he should not divorce her. [13]If any woman has a husband who is an unbeliever, and he consents to live with her, she should not divorce him. [14]For the unbelieving husband is made holy because of his wife, and the unbelieving wife is made holy because of her husband.

---

[a]Greek *those inside* [b]Or *will judge* [c]Or *brothers and sisters* [d]Or *wrongdoers* [e]The two Greek terms translated by this phrase refer to the passive and active partners in consensual homosexual acts [f]Or *who holds fast* (compare Genesis 2:24 and Deuteronomy 10:20); also verse 17 [g]Or *Every sin* [h]Or *I say this:*

Otherwise your children would be unclean, but as it is, they are holy. ⁱ⁵But if the unbelieving partner separates, let it be so. In such cases the brother or sister is not enslaved. God has called you*ᵃ* to peace. ¹⁶For how do you know, wife, whether you will save your husband? Or how do you know, husband, whether you will save your wife?

LIVE AS YOU ARE CALLED

¹⁷Only let each person lead the life*ᵇ* that the Lord has assigned to him, and to which God has called him. This is my rule in all the churches. ¹⁸Was anyone at the time of his call already circumcised? Let him not seek to remove the marks of circumcision. Was anyone at the time of his call uncircumcised? Let him not seek circumcision. ¹⁹For neither circumcision counts for anything nor uncircumcision, but keeping the commandments of God. ²⁰Each one should remain in the condition in which he was called. ²¹Were you a bondservant*ᶜ* when called? Do not be concerned about it. (But if you can gain your freedom, avail yourself of the opportunity.) ²²For he who was called in the Lord as a bondservant is a freedman of the Lord. Likewise he who was free when called is a bondservant of Christ. ²³You were bought with a price; do not become bondservants of men. ²⁴So, brothers,*ᵈ* in whatever condition each was called, there let him remain with God.

THE UNMARRIED AND THE WIDOWED

²⁵Now concerning*ᵉ* the betrothed,*ᶠ* I have no command from the Lord, but I give my judgement as one who by the Lord's mercy is trustworthy. ²⁶I think that in view of the present*ᵍ* distress it is good for a person to remain as he is. ²⁷Are you bound to a wife? Do not seek to be free. Are you free from a wife? Do not seek a wife. ²⁸But if you do marry, you have not sinned, and if a betrothed woman*ʰ* marries, she has not sinned. Yet those who marry will have worldly troubles, and I would spare you that. ²⁹This is what I mean, brothers: the appointed time has grown very short. From now on, let those who have wives live as though they had none, ³⁰and those who mourn as though they were not mourning, and those who rejoice as though they were not rejoicing, and those who buy as though they had no goods, ³¹and those who deal with the world as though they had no dealings with it. For the present form of this world is passing away.

³²I want you to be free from anxieties. The unmarried man is anxious about the things of the Lord, how to please the Lord. ³³But the married man is anxious about worldly things, how to please his wife, ³⁴and his interests are divided. And the unmarried or betrothed woman is anxious about the things of the Lord, how to be holy in body and spirit. But the married woman is anxious about worldly things, how to please her husband. ³⁵I say this for your own benefit, not to lay any restraint upon you, but to promote good order and to secure your undivided devotion to the Lord.

³⁶If anyone thinks that he is not behaving properly towards his betrothed,*ⁱ* if his*ʲ* passions are strong, and it has to be, let him do as he wishes: let them marry—it is no sin. ³⁷But whoever is firmly established in his heart, being under no necessity but having his desire under control, and has determined this in his heart, to keep her as his betrothed, he will do well. ³⁸So then he who marries his betrothed does well, and he who refrains from marriage will do even better.

³⁹A wife is bound to her husband as long as he lives. But if her husband dies, she is free to be married to whom she wishes, only in the Lord. ⁴⁰Yet in my judgement she is happier if she remains as she is. And I think that I too have the Spirit of God.

FOOD OFFERED TO IDOLS

8 Now concerning*ᵏ* food offered to idols: we know that "all of us possess knowledge". This "knowledge" puffs up, but love builds up. ²If anyone imagines that he knows something, he does not yet know as he ought to know. ³But if anyone loves God, he is known by God.*ˡ*

⁴Therefore, as to the eating of food offered to idols, we know that "an idol has no real existence", and that "there is no God but one". ⁵For although there may be so-called gods in heaven or on earth—as indeed there are many "gods" and many "lords"— ⁶yet for us there is one God, the Father, from whom are all things and for whom we exist, and one Lord, Jesus Christ, through whom are all things and through whom we exist.

---

*ᵃ*Some manuscripts *us* *ᵇ*Or *each person walk in the way* *ᶜ*For the contextual rendering of the Greek word *doulos*, see Preface; also verses 22 (twice), 23 *ᵈ*Or *brothers and sisters*; also verse 29 *ᵉ*The expression *Now concerning* introduces a reply to a question in the Corinthians' letter; see 7:1 *ᶠ*Greek *virgins* *ᵍ*Or *impending* *ʰ*Greek *virgin*, also verse 34 *ⁱ*Greek *virgin*; also verses 37, 38 *ʲ*Or *her* *ᵏ*The expression *Now concerning* introduces a reply to a question in the Corinthians' letter; see 7:1 *ˡ*Greek *him*

⁷However, not all possess this knowledge. But some, through former association with idols, eat food as really offered to an idol, and their conscience, being weak, is defiled. ⁸Food will not commend us to God. We are no worse off if we do not eat, and no better off if we do. ⁹But take care that this right of yours does not somehow become a stumbling block to the weak. ¹⁰For if anyone sees you who have knowledge eating*a* in an idol's temple, will he not be encouraged,*b* if his conscience is weak, to eat food offered to idols? ¹¹And so by your knowledge this weak person is destroyed, the brother for whom Christ died. ¹²Thus, sinning against your brothers*c* and wounding their conscience when it is weak, you sin against Christ. ¹³Therefore, if food makes my brother stumble, I will never eat meat, lest I make my brother stumble.

PAUL SURRENDERS HIS RIGHTS

9 Am I not free? Am I not an apostle? Have I not seen Jesus our Lord? Are not you my workmanship in the Lord? ²If to others I am not an apostle, at least I am to you, for you are the seal of my apostleship in the Lord.

³This is my defence to those who would examine me. ⁴Do we not have the right to eat and drink? ⁵Do we not have the right to take along a believing wife,*d* as do the other apostles and the brothers of the Lord and Cephas? ⁶Or is it only Barnabas and I who have no right to refrain from working for a living? ⁷Who serves as a soldier at his own expense? Who plants a vineyard without eating any of its fruit? Or who tends a flock without getting some of the milk?

⁸Do I say these things on human authority? Does not the Law say the same? ⁹For it is written in the Law of Moses, "You shall not muzzle an ox when it treads out the grain." Is it for oxen that God is concerned? ¹⁰Does he not certainly speak for our sake? It was written for our sake, because the ploughman should plough in hope and the thresher thresh in hope of sharing in the crop. ¹¹If we have sown spiritual things among you, is it too much if we reap material things from you? ¹²If others share this rightful claim on you, do not we even more?

Nevertheless, we have not made use of this right, but we endure anything rather than put an obstacle in the way of the gospel of Christ. ¹³Do you not know that those who are employed in the temple service get their food from the temple, and those who serve at the altar share in the sacrificial offerings? ¹⁴In the same way, the Lord commanded that those who proclaim the gospel should get their living by the gospel.

¹⁵But I have made no use of any of these rights, nor am I writing these things to secure any such provision. For I would rather die than have anyone deprive me of my ground for boasting. ¹⁶For if I preach the gospel, that gives me no ground for boasting. For necessity is laid upon me. Woe to me if I do not preach the gospel! ¹⁷For if I do this of my own will, I have a reward, but if not of my own will, I am still entrusted with a stewardship. ¹⁸What then is my reward? That in my preaching I may present the gospel free of charge, so as not to make full use of my right in the gospel.

¹⁹For though I am free from all, I have made myself a servant to all, that I might win more of them. ²⁰To the Jews I became as a Jew, in order to win Jews. To those under the law I became as one under the law (though not being myself under the law) that I might win those under the law. ²¹To those outside the law I became as one outside the law (not being outside the law of God but under the law of Christ) that I might win those outside the law. ²²To the weak I became weak, that I might win the weak. I have become all things to all people, that by all means I might save some. ²³I do it all for the sake of the gospel, that I may share with them in its blessings.

²⁴Do you not know that in a race all the runners run, but only one receives the prize? So run that you may obtain it. ²⁵Every athlete exercises self-control in all things. They do it to receive a perishable wreath, but we an imperishable. ²⁶So I do not run aimlessly; I do not box as one beating the air. ²⁷But I discipline my body and keep it under control,*e* lest after preaching to others I myself should be disqualified.

WARNING AGAINST IDOLATRY

10 For I do not want you to be unaware, brothers,*f* that our fathers were all under the cloud, and all passed through the sea, ²and all were baptized into Moses in the cloud and in the sea, ³and all ate the same spiritual food, ⁴and all drank the

---

*a*Greek *reclining at table* *b*Or *fortified*; Greek *built up* *c*Or *brothers and sisters* *d*Greek *a sister as wife* *e*Greek *I pummel my body and make it a slave* *f*Or *brothers and sisters*

same spiritual drink. For they drank from the spiritual Rock that followed them, and the Rock was Christ. ⁵Nevertheless, with most of them God was not pleased, for they were overthrown*a* in the wilderness.

⁶Now these things took place as examples for us, that we might not desire evil as they did. ⁷Do not be idolaters as some of them were; as it is written, "The people sat down to eat and drink and rose up to play." ⁸We must not indulge in sexual immorality as some of them did, and twenty-three thousand fell in a single day. ⁹We must not put Christ*b* to the test, as some of them did and were destroyed by serpents, ¹⁰nor grumble, as some of them did and were destroyed by the Destroyer. ¹¹Now these things happened to them as an example, but they were written down for our instruction, on whom the end of the ages has come. ¹²Therefore let anyone who thinks that he stands take heed lest he fall. ¹³No temptation has overtaken you that is not common to man. God is faithful, and he will not let you be tempted beyond your ability, but with the temptation he will also provide the way of escape, that you may be able to endure it.

¹⁴Therefore, my beloved, flee from idolatry. ¹⁵I speak as to sensible people; judge for yourselves what I say. ¹⁶The cup of blessing that we bless, is it not a participation in the blood of Christ? The bread that we break, is it not a participation in the body of Christ? ¹⁷Because there is one bread, we who are many are one body, for we all partake of the one bread. ¹⁸Consider the people of Israel:*c* are not those who eat the sacrifices participants in the altar? ¹⁹What do I imply then? That food offered to idols is anything, or that an idol is anything? ²⁰No, I imply that what pagans sacrifice they offer to demons and not to God. I do not want you to be participants with demons. ²¹You cannot drink the cup of the Lord and the cup of demons. You cannot partake of the table of the Lord and the table of demons. ²²Shall we provoke the Lord to jealousy? Are we stronger than he?

DO ALL TO THE GLORY OF GOD

²³"All things are lawful", but not all things are helpful. "All things are lawful", but not all things build up. ²⁴Let no one seek his own good, but the good of his neighbour. ²⁵Eat whatever is sold in the meat market without raising any question on the ground of conscience. ²⁶For "the earth is the Lord's, and the fullness thereof." ²⁷If one of the unbelievers invites you to dinner and you are disposed to go, eat whatever is set before you without raising any question on the ground of conscience. ²⁸But if someone says to you, "This has been offered in sacrifice", then do not eat it, for the sake of the one who informed you, and for the sake of conscience — ²⁹I do not mean your conscience, but his. For why should my liberty be determined by someone else's conscience? ³⁰If I partake with thankfulness, why am I denounced because of that for which I give thanks?

³¹So, whether you eat or drink, or whatever you do, do all to the glory of God. ³²Give no offence to Jews or to Greeks or to the church of God, ³³just as I try to please everyone in everything I do, not seeking my own advantage, but that of many, that they may be saved.

11

Be imitators of me, as I am of Christ.

HEAD COVERINGS

²Now I commend you because you remember me in everything and maintain the traditions even as I delivered them to you. ³But I want you to understand that the head of every man is Christ, the head of a wife*d* is her husband,*e* and the head of Christ is God. ⁴Every man who prays or prophesies with his head covered dishonours his head, ⁵but every wife*f* who prays or prophesies with her head uncovered dishonours her head, since it is the same as if her head were shaven. ⁶For if a wife will not cover her head, then she should cut her hair short. But since it is disgraceful for a wife to cut off her hair or shave her head, let her cover her head. ⁷For a man ought not to cover his head, since he is the image and glory of God, but woman is the glory of man. ⁸For man was not made from woman, but woman from man. ⁹Neither was man created for woman, but woman for man. ¹⁰That is why a wife ought to have a symbol of authority on her head, because of the angels.*g* ¹¹Nevertheless, in the Lord woman is not independent of man nor man of woman; ¹²for as woman was made from man, so man is now born of woman. And all things are from God. ¹³Judge for yourselves:

---

a Or *were laid low* *b* Some manuscripts *the Lord* *c* Greek *Consider Israel according to the flesh* *d* Greek *gunē*. This term may refer to a *woman* or a *wife*, depending on the context *e* Greek *anēr*. This term may refer to a *man* or a *husband*, depending on the context *f* In verses 5–13, the Greek word *gunē* is translated *wife* in verses that deal with wearing a veil, a sign of being married in first-century culture *g* Or *messengers*, that is, people sent to observe and report

is it proper for a wife to pray to God with her head uncovered? ¹⁴Does not nature itself teach you that if a man wears long hair it is a disgrace for him, ¹⁵but if a woman has long hair, it is her glory? For her hair is given to her for a covering. ¹⁶If anyone is inclined to be contentious, we have no such practice, nor do the churches of God.

THE LORD'S SUPPER

¹⁷But in the following instructions I do not commend you, because when you come together it is not for the better but for the worse. ¹⁸For, in the first place, when you come together as a church, I hear that there are divisions among you. And I believe it in part,ᵃ ¹⁹for there must be factions among you in order that those who are genuine among you may be recognized. ²⁰When you come together, it is not the Lord's supper that you eat. ²¹For in eating, each one goes ahead with his own meal. One goes hungry, another gets drunk. ²²What! Do you not have houses to eat and drink in? Or do you despise the church of God and humiliate those who have nothing? What shall I say to you? Shall I commend you in this? No, I will not.

²³For I received from the Lord what I also delivered to you, that the Lord Jesus on the night when he was betrayed took bread, ²⁴and when he had given thanks, he broke it, and said, "This is my body, which is forᵇ you. Do this in remembrance of me."ᶜ ²⁵In the same way also he took the cup, after supper, saying, "This cup is the new covenant in my blood. Do this, as often as you drink it, in remembrance of me." ²⁶For as often as you eat this bread and drink the cup, you proclaim the Lord's death until he comes.

²⁷Whoever, therefore, eats the bread or drinks the cup of the Lord in an unworthy manner will be guilty concerning the body and blood of the Lord. ²⁸Let a person examine himself, then, and so eat of the bread and drink of the cup. ²⁹For anyone who eats and drinks without discerning the body eats and drinks judgement on himself. ³⁰That is why many of you are weak and ill, and some have died.ᵈ ³¹But if we judgedᵉ ourselves truly, we would not be judged. ³²But when we are judged by the Lord, we are disciplinedᶠ so that we may not be condemned along with the world.

³³So then, my brothers,ᵍ when you come together to eat, wait forʰ one another— ³⁴if anyone is hungry, let him eat at home—so that when you come together it will not be for judgement. About the other things I will give directions when I come.

SPIRITUAL GIFTS

12 Now concerningⁱ spiritual gifts,ʲ brothers,ᵏ I do not want you to be uninformed. ²You know that when you were pagans you were led astray to mute idols, however you were led. ³Therefore I want you to understand that no one speaking in the Spirit of God ever says "Jesus is accursed!" and no one can say "Jesus is Lord" except in the Holy Spirit.

⁴Now there are varieties of gifts, but the same Spirit; ⁵and there are varieties of service, but the same Lord; ⁶and there are varieties of activities, but it is the same God who empowers them all in everyone. ⁷To each is given the manifestation of the Spirit for the common good. ⁸For to one is given through the Spirit the utterance of wisdom, and to another the utterance of knowledge according to the same Spirit, ⁹to another faith by the same Spirit, to another gifts of healing by the one Spirit, ¹⁰to another the working of miracles, to another prophecy, to another the ability to distinguish between spirits, to another various kinds of tongues, to another the interpretation of tongues. ¹¹All these are empowered by one and the same Spirit, who apportions to each one individually as he wills.

ONE BODY WITH MANY MEMBERS

¹²For just as the body is one and has many members, and all the members of the body, though many, are one body, so it is with Christ. ¹³For in one Spirit we were all baptized into one body—Jews or Greeks, slavesˡ or free—and all were made to drink of one Spirit.

¹⁴For the body does not consist of one member but of many. ¹⁵If the foot should say, "Because I am not a hand, I do not belong to the body", that would not make it any less a part of the body. ¹⁶And if the ear should say, "Because I am not an eye, I do not belong to the body", that would not make it any less a part of the body. ¹⁷If the whole body were an

---

ᵃOr I believe a certain report ᵇSome manuscripts broken for ᶜOr as my memorial; also verse 25 ᵈGreek have fallen asleep (as in 15:6, 20) ᵉOr discerned ᶠOr when we are judged we are being disciplined by the Lord ᵍOr brothers and sisters ʰOr share with ⁱThe expression Now concerning introduces a reply to a question in the Corinthians' letter; see 7:1 ʲOr spiritual persons ᵏOr brothers and sisters ˡFor the contextual rendering of the Greek word doulos, see Preface

eye, where would be the sense of hearing? If the whole body were an ear, where would be the sense of smell? ¹⁸But as it is, God arranged the members in the body, each one of them, as he chose. ¹⁹If all were a single member, where would the body be? ²⁰As it is, there are many parts,ᵃ yet one body.

²¹The eye cannot say to the hand, "I have no need of you", nor again the head to the feet, "I have no need of you." ²²On the contrary, the parts of the body that seem to be weaker are indispensable, ²³and on those parts of the body that we think less honourable we bestow the greater honour, and our unpresentable parts are treated with greater modesty, ²⁴which our more presentable parts do not require. But God has so composed the body, giving greater honour to the part that lacked it, ²⁵that there may be no division in the body, but that the members may have the same care for one another. ²⁶If one member suffers, all suffer together; if one member is honoured, all rejoice together.

²⁷Now you are the body of Christ and individually members of it. ²⁸And God has appointed in the church first apostles, second prophets, third teachers, then miracles, then gifts of healing, helping, administrating, and various kinds of tongues. ²⁹Are all apostles? Are all prophets? Are all teachers? Do all work miracles? ³⁰Do all possess gifts of healing? Do all speak with tongues? Do all interpret? ³¹But earnestly desire the higher gifts.

And I will show you a still more excellent way.

THE WAY OF LOVE

13 If I speak in the tongues of men and of angels, but have not love, I am a noisy gong or a clanging cymbal. ²And if I have prophetic powers, and understand all mysteries and all knowledge, and if I have all faith, so as to remove mountains, but have not love, I am nothing. ³If I give away all I have, and if I deliver up my body to be burned,ᵇ but have not love, I gain nothing.

⁴Love is patient and kind; love does not envy or boast; it is not arrogant ⁵or rude. It does not insist on its own way; it is not irritable or resentful;ᶜ ⁶it does not rejoice at wrongdoing, but rejoices with the truth. ⁷Love bears all things, believes all things, hopes all things, endures all things.

⁸Love never ends. As for prophecies, they will pass away; as for tongues, they will cease; as for knowledge, it will pass away. ⁹For we know in part and we prophesy in part, ¹⁰but when the perfect comes, the partial will pass away. ¹¹When I was a child, I spoke like a child, I thought like a child, I reasoned like a child. When I became a man, I gave up childish ways. ¹²For now we see in a mirror dimly, but then face to face. Now I know in part; then I shall know fully, even as I have been fully known.

¹³So now faith, hope, and love abide, these three; but the greatest of these is love.

PROPHECY AND TONGUES

14 Pursue love, and earnestly desire the spiritual gifts, especially that you may prophesy. ²For one who speaks in a tongue speaks not to men but to God; for no one understands him, but he utters mysteries in the Spirit. ³On the other hand, the one who prophesies speaks to people for their upbuilding and encouragement and consolation. ⁴The one who speaks in a tongue builds up himself, but the one who prophesies builds up the church. ⁵Now I want you all to speak in tongues, but even more to prophesy. The one who prophesies is greater than the one who speaks in tongues, unless someone interprets, so that the church may be built up.

⁶Now, brothers,ᵈ if I come to you speaking in tongues, how will I benefit you unless I bring you some revelation or knowledge or prophecy or teaching? ⁷If even lifeless instruments, such as the flute or the harp, do not give distinct notes, how will anyone know what is played? ⁸And if the bugle gives an indistinct sound, who will get ready for battle? ⁹So with yourselves, if with your tongue you utter speech that is not intelligible, how will anyone know what is said? For you will be speaking into the air. ¹⁰There are doubtless many different languages in the world, and none is without meaning, ¹¹but if I do not know the meaning of the language, I will be a foreigner to the speaker and the speaker a foreigner to me. ¹²So with yourselves, since you are eager for manifestations of the Spirit, strive to excel in building up the church.

¹³Therefore, one who speaks in a tongue should pray that he may interpret. ¹⁴For if I pray in a tongue, my spirit prays but my mind

---

ᵃOr *members*; also verse 22   ᵇSome manuscripts *deliver up my body [to death] that I may boast*   ᶜGreek *irritable and does not count up wrongdoing*   ᵈOr *brothers and sisters*; also verses 20, 26, 39

is unfruitful. ¹⁵What am I to do? I will pray with my spirit, but I will pray with my mind also; I will sing praise with my spirit, but I will sing with my mind also. ¹⁶Otherwise, if you give thanks with your spirit, how can anyone in the position of an outsider[a] say "Amen" to your thanksgiving when he does not know what you are saying? ¹⁷For you may be giving thanks well enough, but the other person is not being built up. ¹⁸I thank God that I speak in tongues more than all of you. ¹⁹Nevertheless, in church I would rather speak five words with my mind in order to instruct others, than ten thousand words in a tongue.

²⁰Brothers, do not be children in your thinking. Be infants in evil, but in your thinking be mature. ²¹In the Law it is written, "By people of strange tongues and by the lips of foreigners will I speak to this people, and even then they will not listen to me, says the Lord." ²²Thus tongues are a sign not for believers but for unbelievers, while prophecy is a sign[b] not for unbelievers but for believers. ²³If, therefore, the whole church comes together and all speak in tongues, and outsiders or unbelievers enter, will they not say that you are out of your minds? ²⁴But if all prophesy, and an unbeliever or outsider enters, he is convicted by all, he is called to account by all, ²⁵the secrets of his heart are disclosed, and so, falling on his face, he will worship God and declare that God is really among you.

ORDERLY WORSHIP

²⁶What then, brothers? When you come together, each one has a hymn, a lesson, a revelation, a tongue, or an interpretation. Let all things be done for building up. ²⁷If any speak in a tongue, let there be only two or at most three, and each in turn, and let someone interpret. ²⁸But if there is no one to interpret, let each of them keep silent in church and speak to himself and to God. ²⁹Let two or three prophets speak, and let the others weigh what is said. ³⁰If a revelation is made to another sitting there, let the first be silent. ³¹For you can all prophesy one by one, so that all may learn and all be encouraged, ³²and the spirits of prophets are subject to prophets. ³³For God is not a God of confusion but of peace.

As in all the churches of the saints, ³⁴the women should keep silent in the churches. For they are not permitted to speak, but should be in submission, as the Law also says. ³⁵If there is anything they desire to learn, let them ask their husbands at home. For it is shameful for a woman to speak in church.

³⁶Or was it from you that the word of God came? Or are you the only ones it has reached? ³⁷If anyone thinks that he is a prophet, or spiritual, he should acknowledge that the things I am writing to you are a command of the Lord. ³⁸If anyone does not recognize this, he is not recognized. ³⁹So, my brothers, earnestly desire to prophesy, and do not forbid speaking in tongues. ⁴⁰But all things should be done decently and in order.

THE RESURRECTION OF CHRIST

15 Now I would remind you, brothers,[c] of the gospel I preached to you, which you received, in which you stand, ²and by which you are being saved, if you hold fast to the word I preached to you—unless you believed in vain.

³For I delivered to you as of first importance what I also received: that Christ died for our sins in accordance with the Scriptures, ⁴that he was buried, that he was raised on the third day in accordance with the Scriptures, ⁵and that he appeared to Cephas, then to the twelve. ⁶Then he appeared to more than five hundred brothers at one time, most of whom are still alive, though some have fallen asleep. ⁷Then he appeared to James, then to all the apostles. ⁸Last of all, as to one untimely born, he appeared also to me. ⁹For I am the least of the apostles, unworthy to be called an apostle, because I persecuted the church of God. ¹⁰But by the grace of God I am what I am, and his grace towards me was not in vain. On the contrary, I worked harder than any of them, though it was not I, but the grace of God that is with me. ¹¹Whether then it was I or they, so we preach and so you believed.

THE RESURRECTION OF THE DEAD

¹²Now if Christ is proclaimed as raised from the dead, how can some of you say that there is no resurrection of the dead? ¹³But if there is no resurrection of the dead, then not even Christ has been raised. ¹⁴And if Christ has not been raised, then our preaching is in vain and your faith is in vain. ¹⁵We are even found to be misrepresenting God, because

---

[a] Or *of him that is without gifts* [b] Greek lacks *a sign* [c] Or *brothers and sisters* also verses 6, 31, 50, 58

we testified about God that he raised Christ, whom he did not raise if it is true that the dead are not raised. ¹⁶For if the dead are not raised, not even Christ has been raised. ¹⁷And if Christ has not been raised, your faith is futile and you are still in your sins. ¹⁸Then those also who have fallen asleep in Christ have perished. ¹⁹If in Christ we have hope[a] in this life only, we are of all people most to be pitied.

²⁰But in fact Christ has been raised from the dead, the firstfruits of those who have fallen asleep. ²¹For as by a man came death, by a man has come also the resurrection of the dead. ²²For as in Adam all die, so also in Christ shall all be made alive. ²³But each in his own order: Christ the firstfruits, then at his coming those who belong to Christ. ²⁴Then comes the end, when he delivers the kingdom to God the Father after destroying every rule and every authority and power. ²⁵For he must reign until he has put all his enemies under his feet. ²⁶The last enemy to be destroyed is death. ²⁷For "God[b] has put all things in subjection under his feet." But when it says, "all things are put in subjection", it is plain that he is excepted who put all things in subjection under him. ²⁸When all things are subjected to him, then the Son himself will also be subjected to him who put all things in subjection under him, that God may be all in all.

²⁹Otherwise, what do people mean by being baptized on behalf of the dead? If the dead are not raised at all, why are people baptized on their behalf? ³⁰Why are we in danger every hour? ³¹I protest, brothers, by my pride in you, which I have in Christ Jesus our Lord, I die every day! ³²What do I gain if, humanly speaking, I fought with beasts at Ephesus? If the dead are not raised, "Let us eat and drink, for tomorrow we die." ³³Do not be deceived: "Bad company ruins good morals."[c] ³⁴Wake up from your drunken stupor, as is right, and do not go on sinning. For some have no knowledge of God. I say this to your shame.

THE RESURRECTION BODY

³⁵But someone will ask, "How are the dead raised? With what kind of body do they come?" ³⁶You foolish person! What you sow does not come to life unless it dies. ³⁷And what you sow is not the body that is to be, but a bare seed, perhaps of wheat or of some other grain. ³⁸But God gives it a body as he has chosen, and to each kind of seed its own body. ³⁹For not all flesh is the same, but there is one kind for humans, another for animals, another for birds, and another for fish. ⁴⁰There are heavenly bodies and earthly bodies, but the glory of the heavenly is of one kind, and the glory of the earthly is of another. ⁴¹There is one glory of the sun, and another glory of the moon, and another glory of the stars; for star differs from star in glory.

⁴²So is it with the resurrection of the dead. What is sown is perishable; what is raised is imperishable. ⁴³It is sown in dishonour; it is raised in glory. It is sown in weakness; it is raised in power. ⁴⁴It is sown a natural body; it is raised a spiritual body. If there is a natural body, there is also a spiritual body. ⁴⁵Thus it is written, "The first man Adam became a living being";[d] the last Adam became a life-giving spirit. ⁴⁶But it is not the spiritual that is first but the natural, and then the spiritual. ⁴⁷The first man was from the earth, a man of dust; the second man is from heaven. ⁴⁸As was the man of dust, so also are those who are of the dust, and as is the man of heaven, so also are those who are of heaven. ⁴⁹Just as we have borne the image of the man of dust, we shall[e] also bear the image of the man of heaven.

MYSTERY AND VICTORY

⁵⁰I tell you this, brothers: flesh and blood cannot inherit the kingdom of God, nor does the perishable inherit the imperishable. ⁵¹Behold! I tell you a mystery. We shall not all sleep, but we shall all be changed, ⁵²in a moment, in the twinkling of an eye, at the last trumpet. For the trumpet will sound, and the dead will be raised imperishable, and we shall be changed. ⁵³For this perishable body must put on the imperishable, and this mortal body must put on immortality. ⁵⁴When the perishable puts on the imperishable, and the mortal puts on immortality, then shall come to pass the saying that is written:

"Death is swallowed up in victory."
⁵⁵ "O death, where is your victory?
O death, where is your sting?"

⁵⁶The sting of death is sin, and the power of sin is the law. ⁵⁷But thanks be to God, who gives us the victory through our Lord Jesus Christ.

---

[a]Or *we have hoped* [b]Greek *he* [c]Probably from Menander's comedy *Thais* [d]Greek *a living soul* [e]Some manuscripts *let us*

⁵⁸Therefore, my beloved brothers, be steadfast, immovable, always abounding in the work of the Lord, knowing that in the Lord your labour is not in vain.

THE COLLECTION FOR THE SAINTS

16 Now concerning[a] the collection for the saints: as I directed the churches of Galatia, so you also are to do. ²On the first day of every week, each of you is to put something aside and store it up, as he may prosper, so that there will be no collecting when I come. ³And when I arrive, I will send those whom you accredit by letter to carry your gift to Jerusalem. ⁴If it seems advisable that I should go also, they will accompany me.

PLANS FOR TRAVEL

⁵I will visit you after passing through Macedonia, for I intend to pass through Macedonia, ⁶and perhaps I will stay with you or even spend the winter, so that you may help me on my journey, wherever I go. ⁷For I do not want to see you now just in passing. I hope to spend some time with you, if the Lord permits. ⁸But I will stay in Ephesus until Pentecost, ⁹for a wide door for effective work has opened to me, and there are many adversaries.

¹⁰When Timothy comes, see that you put him at ease among you, for he is doing the work of the Lord, as I am. ¹¹So let no one despise him. Help him on his way in peace, that he may return to me, for I am expecting him with the brothers.

FINAL INSTRUCTIONS

¹²Now concerning our brother Apollos, I strongly urged him to visit you with the other brothers, but it was not at all his will[b] to come now. He will come when he has opportunity.

¹³Be watchful, stand firm in the faith, act like men, be strong. ¹⁴Let all that you do be done in love.

¹⁵Now I urge you, brothers[c]—you know that the household[d] of Stephanas were the first converts in Achaia, and that they have devoted themselves to the service of the saints—¹⁶be subject to such as these, and to every fellow worker and labourer. ¹⁷I rejoice at the coming of Stephanas and Fortunatus and Achaicus, because they have made up for your absence, ¹⁸for they refreshed my spirit as well as yours. Give recognition to such people.

GREETINGS

¹⁹The churches of Asia send you greetings. Aquila and Prisca, together with the church in their house, send you hearty greetings in the Lord. ²⁰All the brothers send you greetings. Greet one another with a holy kiss.

²¹I, Paul, write this greeting with my own hand. ²²If anyone has no love for the Lord, let him be accursed. Our Lord, come![e] ²³The grace of the Lord Jesus be with you. ²⁴My love be with you all in Christ Jesus. Amen.

---

[a] The expression *Now concerning* introduces a reply to a question in the Corinthians' letter; see 7:1; also verse 12   [b] Or *God's will for him*   [c] Or *brothers and sisters*; also verse 20   [d] Greek *house*   [e] Greek *Maranatha* (a transliteration of Aramaic)

THE SECOND LETTER OF PAUL TO THE CORINTHIANS

2 CORINTHIANS

GREETING

1 Paul, an apostle of Christ Jesus by the will of God, and Timothy our brother,

To the church of God that is at Corinth, with all the saints who are in the whole of Achaia:

²Grace to you and peace from God our Father and the Lord Jesus Christ.

GOD OF ALL COMFORT

³Blessed be the God and Father of our Lord Jesus Christ, the Father of mercies and God of all comfort, ⁴who comforts us in all our affliction, so that we may be able to comfort those who are in any affliction, with the comfort with which we ourselves are comforted by God. ⁵For as we share abundantly in Christ's sufferings, so through Christ we share abundantly in comfort too.ᵃ ⁶If we are afflicted, it is for your comfort and salvation; and if we are comforted, it is for your comfort, which you experience when you patiently endure the same sufferings that we suffer. ⁷Our hope for you is unshaken, for we know that as you share in our sufferings, you will also share in our comfort.

⁸For we do not want you to be unaware, brothers,ᵇ of the affliction we experienced in Asia. For we were so utterly burdened beyond our strength that we despaired of life itself. ⁹Indeed, we felt that we had received the sentence of death. But that was to make us rely not on ourselves but on God who raises the dead. ¹⁰He delivered us from such a deadly peril, and he will deliver us. On him we have set our hope that he will deliver us again. ¹¹You also must help us by prayer, so that many will give thanks on our behalf for the blessing granted us through the prayers of many.

PAUL'S CHANGE OF PLANS

¹²For our boast is this, the testimony of our conscience, that we behaved in the world with simplicityᶜ and godly sincerity, not by earthly wisdom but by the grace of God, and supremely so towards you. ¹³For we are not writing to you anything other than what you read and understand and I hope you will fully understand — ¹⁴just as you did partially understand us — that on the day of our Lord Jesus you will boast of us as we will boast of you.

¹⁵Because I was sure of this, I wanted to come to you first, so that you might have a second experience of grace. ¹⁶I wanted to visit you on my way to Macedonia, and to come back to you from Macedonia and have you send me on my way to Judea. ¹⁷Was I vacillating when I wanted to do this? Do I make my plans according to the flesh, ready to say "Yes, yes" and "No, no" at the same time? ¹⁸As surely as God is faithful, our word to you has not been Yes and No. ¹⁹For the Son of God, Jesus Christ, whom we proclaimed among you, Silvanus and Timothy and I, was not Yes and No, but in him it is always Yes. ²⁰For all the promises of God find their Yes in him. That is why it is through him that we utter our Amen to God for his glory. ²¹And it is God who establishes us with you in Christ, and has anointed us, ²²and who has also put his seal on us and given us his Spirit in our hearts as a guarantee.ᵈ

²³But I call God to witness against me — it was to spare you that I refrained from coming again to Corinth. ²⁴Not that we lord it over your faith, but we work with you for your joy, for you stand firm in your faith.

2 For I made up my mind not to make another painful visit to you. ²For if I cause you pain, who is there to make me glad but the one whom I have pained?

ᵃOr *For as the sufferings of Christ abound for us, so also our comfort abounds through Christ* ᵇOr *brothers and sisters*. In New Testament usage, depending on the context, the plural Greek word *adelphoi* (translated "brothers") may refer either to *brothers* or to *brothers and sisters* ᶜSome manuscripts *holiness* ᵈOr *down payment*

³And I wrote as I did, so that when I came I might not suffer pain from those who should have made me rejoice, for I felt sure of all of you, that my joy would be the joy of you all. ⁴For I wrote to you out of much affliction and anguish of heart and with many tears, not to cause you pain but to let you know the abundant love that I have for you.

FORGIVE THE SINNER

⁵Now if anyone has caused pain, he has caused it not to me, but in some measure — not to put it too severely — to all of you. ⁶For such a one, this punishment by the majority is enough, ⁷so you should rather turn to forgive and comfort him, or he may be overwhelmed by excessive sorrow. ⁸So I beg you to reaffirm your love for him. ⁹For this is why I wrote, that I might test you and know whether you are obedient in everything. ¹⁰Anyone whom you forgive, I also forgive. Indeed, what I have forgiven, if I have forgiven anything, has been for your sake in the presence of Christ, ¹¹so that we would not be outwitted by Satan; for we are not ignorant of his designs.

TRIUMPH IN CHRIST

¹²When I came to Troas to preach the gospel of Christ, even though a door was opened for me in the Lord, ¹³my spirit was not at rest because I did not find my brother Titus there. So I took leave of them and went on to Macedonia.

¹⁴But thanks be to God, who in Christ always leads us in triumphal procession, and through us spreads the fragrance of the knowledge of him everywhere. ¹⁵For we are the aroma of Christ to God among those who are being saved and among those who are perishing, ¹⁶to one a fragrance from death to death, to the other a fragrance from life to life. Who is sufficient for these things? ¹⁷For we are not, like so many, peddlers of God's word, but as men of sincerity, as commissioned by God, in the sight of God we speak in Christ.

MINISTERS OF THE NEW COVENANT

3 Are we beginning to commend ourselves again? Or do we need, as some do, letters of recommendation to you, or from you? ²You yourselves are our letter of recommendation, written on our^a hearts, to be known and read by all. ³And you show that you are a letter from Christ delivered by us, written not with ink but with the Spirit of the living God, not on tablets of stone but on tablets of human hearts.^{b}

⁴Such is the confidence that we have through Christ towards God. ⁵Not that we are sufficient in ourselves to claim anything as coming from us, but our sufficiency is from God, ⁶who has made us sufficient to be ministers of a new covenant, not of the letter but of the Spirit. For the letter kills, but the Spirit gives life.

⁷Now if the ministry of death, carved in letters on stone, came with such glory that the Israelites could not gaze at Moses' face because of its glory, which was being brought to an end, ⁸will not the ministry of the Spirit have even more glory? ⁹For if there was glory in the ministry of condemnation, the ministry of righteousness must far exceed it in glory. ¹⁰Indeed, in this case, what once had glory has come to have no glory at all, because of the glory that surpasses it. ¹¹For if what was being brought to an end came with glory, much more will what is permanent have glory.

¹²Since we have such a hope, we are very bold, ¹³not like Moses, who would put a veil over his face so that the Israelites might not gaze at the outcome of what was being brought to an end. ¹⁴But their minds were hardened. For to this day, when they read the old covenant, that same veil remains unlifted, because only through Christ is it taken away. ¹⁵Yes, to this day whenever Moses is read a veil lies over their hearts. ¹⁶But when one^c turns to the Lord, the veil is removed. ¹⁷Now the Lord^d is the Spirit, and where the Spirit of the Lord is, there is freedom. ¹⁸And we all, with unveiled face, beholding the glory of the Lord,^{e} are being transformed into the same image from one degree of glory to another.^{f} For this comes from the Lord who is the Spirit.

THE LIGHT OF THE GOSPEL

4 Therefore, having this ministry by the mercy of God,^{g} we do not lose heart. ²But we have renounced disgraceful, underhanded ways. We refuse to practise^h cunning or to tamper with God's word, but by the open statement of the truth we would commend ourselves to everyone's conscience

---

^{a}Some manuscripts *your* ^{b}Greek *fleshly hearts* ^{c}Greek *he* ^{d}Or *this Lord* ^{e}Or *reflecting the glory of the Lord* ^{f}Greek *from glory to glory* ^{g}Greek *having this ministry as we have received mercy* ^{h}Greek *to walk in*

in the sight of God. ³And even if our gospel is veiled, it is veiled to those who are perishing. ⁴In their case the god of this world has blinded the minds of the unbelievers, to keep them from seeing the light of the gospel of the glory of Christ, who is the image of God. ⁵For what we proclaim is not ourselves, but Jesus Christ as Lord, with ourselves as your servants*ᵃ* for Jesus' sake. ⁶For God, who said, "Let light shine out of darkness", has shone in our hearts to give the light of the knowledge of the glory of God in the face of Jesus Christ.

TREASURE IN JARS OF CLAY

⁷But we have this treasure in jars of clay, to show that the surpassing power belongs to God and not to us. ⁸We are afflicted in every way, but not crushed; perplexed, but not driven to despair; ⁹persecuted, but not forsaken; struck down, but not destroyed; ¹⁰always carrying in the body the death of Jesus, so that the life of Jesus may also be manifested in our bodies. ¹¹For we who live are always being given over to death for Jesus' sake, so that the life of Jesus also may be manifested in our mortal flesh. ¹²So death is at work in us, but life in you.

¹³Since we have the same spirit of faith according to what has been written, "I believed, and so I spoke", we also believe, and so we also speak, ¹⁴knowing that he who raised the Lord Jesus will raise us also with Jesus and bring us with you into his presence. ¹⁵For it is all for your sake, so that as grace extends to more and more people it may increase thanksgiving, to the glory of God.

¹⁶So we do not lose heart. Though our outer self*ᵇ* is wasting away, our inner self is being renewed day by day. ¹⁷For this light momentary affliction is preparing for us an eternal weight of glory beyond all comparison, ¹⁸as we look not to the things that are seen but to the things that are unseen. For the things that are seen are transient, but the things that are unseen are eternal.

OUR HEAVENLY DWELLING

5 For we know that if the tent that is our earthly home is destroyed, we have a building from God, a house not made with hands, eternal in the heavens. ²For in this tent we groan, longing to put on our heavenly dwelling, ³if indeed by putting it on*ᶜ* we may not be found naked. ⁴For while we are still in this tent, we groan, being burdened — not that we would be unclothed, but that we would be further clothed, so that what is mortal may be swallowed up by life. ⁵He who has prepared us for this very thing is God, who has given us the Spirit as a guarantee.

⁶So we are always of good courage. We know that while we are at home in the body we are away from the Lord, ⁷for we walk by faith, not by sight. ⁸Yes, we are of good courage, and we would rather be away from the body and at home with the Lord. ⁹So whether we are at home or away, we make it our aim to please him. ¹⁰For we must all appear before the judgement seat of Christ, so that each one may receive what is due for what he has done in the body, whether good or evil.

THE MINISTRY OF RECONCILIATION

¹¹Therefore, knowing the fear of the Lord, we persuade others. But what we are is known to God, and I hope it is known also to your conscience. ¹²We are not commending ourselves to you again but giving you cause to boast about us, so that you may be able to answer those who boast about outward appearance and not about what is in the heart. ¹³For if we are beside ourselves, it is for God; if we are in our right mind, it is for you. ¹⁴For the love of Christ controls us, because we have concluded this: that one has died for all, therefore all have died; ¹⁵and he died for all, that those who live might no longer live for themselves but for him who for their sake died and was raised.

¹⁶From now on, therefore, we regard no one according to the flesh. Even though we once regarded Christ according to the flesh, we regard him thus no longer. ¹⁷Therefore, if anyone is in Christ, he is a new creation.*ᵈ* The old has passed away; behold, the new has come. ¹⁸All this is from God, who through Christ reconciled us to himself and gave us the ministry of reconciliation; ¹⁹that is, in Christ God was reconciling*ᵉ* the world to himself, not counting their trespasses against them, and entrusting to us the message of reconciliation. ²⁰Therefore, we are ambassadors for Christ, God making his appeal through us. We implore you on behalf of Christ, be reconciled to God. ²¹For our sake he made him to be sin who knew no sin, so that in him we might become the righteousness of God.

---

*ᵃ*Or *slaves* (for the contextual rendering of the Greek word *doulos*, see Preface) *ᵇ*Greek *man* *ᶜ*Some manuscripts *putting it off* *ᵈ*Or *creature* *ᵉ*Or *God was in Christ, reconciling*

6 Working together with him, then, we appeal to you not to receive the grace of God in vain. ²For he says,

"In a favourable time I listened to you,
and in a day of salvation I
have helped you."

Behold, now is the favourable time; behold, now is the day of salvation. ³We put no obstacle in anyone's way, so that no fault may be found with our ministry, ⁴but as servants of God we commend ourselves in every way: by great endurance, in afflictions, hardships, calamities, ⁵beatings, imprisonments, riots, labours, sleepless nights, hunger; ⁶by purity, knowledge, patience, kindness, the Holy Spirit, genuine love; ⁷by truthful speech, and the power of God; with the weapons of righteousness for the right hand and for the left; ⁸through honour and dishonour, through slander and praise. We are treated as impostors, and yet are true; ⁹as unknown, and yet well known; as dying, and behold, we live; as punished, and yet not killed; ¹⁰as sorrowful, yet always rejoicing; as poor, yet making many rich; as having nothing, yet possessing everything.

¹¹We have spoken freely to you,ᵃ Corinthians; our heart is wide open. ¹²You are not restricted by us, but you are restricted in your own affections. ¹³In return (I speak as to children) widen your hearts also.

THE TEMPLE OF THE LIVING GOD

¹⁴Do not be unequally yoked with unbelievers. For what partnership has righteousness with lawlessness? Or what fellowship has light with darkness? ¹⁵What accord has Christ with Belial?ᵇ Or what portion does a believer share with an unbeliever? ¹⁶What agreement has the temple of God with idols? For we are the temple of the living God; as God said,

"I will make my dwelling among
them and walk among them,
and I will be their God,
and they shall be my people.
¹⁷ Therefore go out from their midst,
and be separate from them,
says the Lord,
and touch no unclean thing;
then I will welcome you,
¹⁸ and I will be a father to you,
and you shall be sons and
daughters to me,
says the Lord Almighty."

7 Since we have these promises, beloved, let us cleanse ourselves from every defilement of bodyᶜ and spirit, bringing holiness to completion in the fear of God.

PAUL'S JOY

²Make room in your heartsᵈ for us. We have wronged no one, we have corrupted no one, we have taken advantage of no one. ³I do not say this to condemn you, for I said before that you are in our hearts, to die together and to live together. ⁴I am acting with great boldness towards you; I have great pride in you; I am filled with comfort. In all our affliction, I am overflowing with joy.

⁵For even when we came into Macedonia, our bodies had no rest, but we were afflicted at every turn—fighting without and fear within. ⁶But God, who comforts the downcast, comforted us by the coming of Titus, ⁷and not only by his coming but also by the comfort with which he was comforted by you, as he told us of your longing, your mourning, your zeal for me, so that I rejoiced still more. ⁸For even if I made you grieve with my letter, I do not regret it—though I did regret it, for I see that that letter grieved you, though only for a while. ⁹As it is, I rejoice, not because you were grieved, but because you were grieved into repenting. For you felt a godly grief, so that you suffered no loss through us.

¹⁰For godly grief produces a repentance that leads to salvation without regret, whereas worldly grief produces death. ¹¹For see what earnestness this godly grief has produced in you, but also what eagerness to clear yourselves, what indignation, what fear, what longing, what zeal, what punishment! At every point you have proved yourselves innocent in the matter. ¹²So although I wrote to you, it was not for the sake of the one who did the wrong, nor for the sake of the one who suffered the wrong, but in order that your earnestness for us might be revealed to you in the sight of God. ¹³Therefore we are comforted.

And besides our own comfort, we rejoiced still more at the joy of Titus, because his spirit has been refreshed by you all. ¹⁴For whatever boasts I made to him about you, I was not put to shame. But just as everything we said to you was true, so also our boasting

---

ᵃGreek *Our mouth is open to you*   ᵇGreek *Beliar*   ᶜGreek *flesh*
ᵈGreek *lacks in your hearts*

before Titus has proved true. ¹⁵And his affection for you is even greater, as he remembers the obedience of you all, how you received him with fear and trembling. ¹⁶I rejoice, because I have complete confidence in you.

ENCOURAGEMENT TO GIVE GENEROUSLY

8 We want you to know, brothers,[a] about the grace of God that has been given among the churches of Macedonia, ²for in a severe test of affliction, their abundance of joy and their extreme poverty have overflowed in a wealth of generosity on their part. ³For they gave according to their means, as I can testify, and beyond their means, of their own accord, ⁴begging us earnestly for the favour[b] of taking part in the relief of the saints— ⁵and this, not as we expected, but they gave themselves first to the Lord and then by the will of God to us. ⁶Accordingly, we urged Titus that as he had started, so he should complete among you this act of grace. ⁷But as you excel in everything—in faith, in speech, in knowledge, in all earnestness, and in our love for you[c]—see that you excel in this act of grace also.

⁸I say this not as a command, but to prove by the earnestness of others that your love also is genuine. ⁹For you know the grace of our Lord Jesus Christ, that though he was rich, yet for your sake he became poor, so that you by his poverty might become rich. ¹⁰And in this matter I give my judgement: this benefits you, who a year ago started not only to do this work but also to desire to do it. ¹¹So now finish doing it as well, so that your readiness in desiring it may be matched by your completing it out of what you have. ¹²For if the readiness is there, it is acceptable according to what a person has, not according to what he does not have. ¹³For I do not mean that others should be eased and you burdened, but that as a matter of fairness ¹⁴your abundance at the present time should supply their need, so that their abundance may supply your need, that there may be fairness. ¹⁵As it is written, "Whoever gathered much had nothing left over, and whoever gathered little had no lack."

COMMENDATION OF TITUS

¹⁶But thanks be to God, who put into the heart of Titus the same earnest care I have for you. ¹⁷For he not only accepted our appeal, but being himself very earnest he is going[d] to you of his own accord. ¹⁸With him we are sending[e] the brother who is famous among all the churches for his preaching of the gospel. ¹⁹And not only that, but he has been appointed by the churches to travel with us as we carry out this act of grace that is being ministered by us, for the glory of the Lord himself and to show our good will. ²⁰We take this course so that no one should blame us about this generous gift that is being administered by us, ²¹for we aim at what is honourable not only in the Lord's sight but also in the sight of man. ²²And with them we are sending our brother whom we have often tested and found earnest in many matters, but who is now more earnest than ever because of his great confidence in you. ²³As for Titus, he is my partner and fellow worker for your benefit. And as for our brothers, they are messengers[f] of the churches, the glory of Christ. ²⁴So give proof before the churches of your love and of our boasting about you to these men.

THE COLLECTION FOR CHRISTIANS IN JERUSALEM

9 Now it is superfluous for me to write to you about the ministry for the saints, ²for I know your readiness, of which I boast about you to the people of Macedonia, saying that Achaia has been ready since last year. And your zeal has stirred up most of them. ³But I am sending[g] the brothers so that our boasting about you may not prove empty in this matter, so that you may be ready, as I said you would be. ⁴Otherwise, if some Macedonians come with me and find that you are not ready, we would be humiliated—to say nothing of you—for being so confident. ⁵So I thought it necessary to urge the brothers to go on ahead to you and arrange in advance for the gift[h] you have promised, so that it may be ready as a willing gift, not as an exaction.[i]

THE CHEERFUL GIVER

⁶The point is this: whoever sows sparingly will also reap sparingly, and whoever sows bountifully[j] will also reap bountifully. ⁷Each one must give as he has decided in his heart, not reluctantly or under compulsion, for God loves a cheerful giver. ⁸And God is able

---

[a] Or brothers and sisters [b] The Greek word charis can mean favour or grace or thanks, depending on the context [c] Some manuscripts in your love for us [d] Or he went [e] Or we sent; also verse 22 [f] Greek apostles [g] Or I have sent [h] Greek blessing; twice in this verse [i] Or a gift expecting something in return; Greek greed [j] Greek with blessings; twice in this verse

to make all grace abound to you, so that having all sufficiency^a in all things at all times, you may abound in every good work. ⁹As it is written,

> "He has distributed freely, he has given to the poor;
> his righteousness endures for ever."

¹⁰He who supplies seed to the sower and bread for food will supply and multiply your seed for sowing and increase the harvest of your righteousness. ¹¹You will be enriched in every way to be generous in every way, which through us will produce thanksgiving to God. ¹²For the ministry of this service is not only supplying the needs of the saints but is also overflowing in many thanksgivings to God. ¹³By their approval of this service, they^b will glorify God because of your submission that comes from your confession of the gospel of Christ, and the generosity of your contribution for them and for all others, ¹⁴while they long for you and pray for you, because of the surpassing grace of God upon you. ¹⁵Thanks be to God for his inexpressible gift!

PAUL DEFENDS HIS MINISTRY

10 I, Paul, myself entreat you, by the meekness and gentleness of Christ—I who am humble when face to face with you, but bold towards you when I am away!—²I beg of you that when I am present I may not have to show boldness with such confidence as I count on showing against some who suspect us of walking according to the flesh. ³For though we walk in the flesh, we are not waging war according to the flesh. ⁴For the weapons of our warfare are not of the flesh but have divine power to destroy strongholds. ⁵We destroy arguments and every lofty opinion raised against the knowledge of God, and take every thought captive to obey Christ, ⁶being ready to punish every disobedience, when your obedience is complete.

⁷Look at what is before your eyes. If anyone is confident that he is Christ's, let him remind himself that just as he is Christ's, so also are we. ⁸For even if I boast a little too much of our authority, which the Lord gave for building you up and not for destroying you, I will not be ashamed. ⁹I do not want to appear to be frightening you with my letters. ¹⁰For they say, "His letters are weighty and strong, but his bodily presence is weak, and his speech of no account." ¹¹Let such a person understand that what we say by letter when absent, we do when present. ¹²Not that we dare to classify or compare ourselves with some of those who are commending themselves. But when they measure themselves by one another and compare themselves with one another, they are without understanding.

¹³But we will not boast beyond limits, but will boast only with regard to the area of influence God assigned to us, to reach even to you. ¹⁴For we are not overextending ourselves, as though we did not reach you. For we were the first to come all the way to you with the gospel of Christ. ¹⁵We do not boast beyond limit in the labours of others. But our hope is that as your faith increases, our area of influence among you may be greatly enlarged, ¹⁶so that we may preach the gospel in lands beyond you, without boasting of work already done in another's area of influence. ¹⁷"Let the one who boasts, boast in the Lord." ¹⁸For it is not the one who commends himself who is approved, but the one whom the Lord commends.

PAUL AND THE FALSE APOSTLES

11 I wish you would bear with me in a little foolishness. Do bear with me! ²For I feel a divine jealousy for you, since I betrothed you to one husband, to present you as a pure virgin to Christ. ³But I am afraid that as the serpent deceived Eve by his cunning, your thoughts will be led astray from a sincere and pure devotion to Christ. ⁴For if someone comes and proclaims another Jesus than the one we proclaimed, or if you receive a different spirit from the one you received, or if you accept a different gospel from the one you accepted, you put up with it readily enough. ⁵Indeed, I consider that I am not in the least inferior to these super-apostles. ⁶Even if I am unskilled in speaking, I am not so in knowledge; indeed, in every way we have made this plain to you in all things.

⁷Or did I commit a sin in humbling myself so that you might be exalted, because I preached God's gospel to you free of charge? ⁸I robbed other churches by accepting support from them in order to serve you. ⁹And when I was with you and was in need, I did not burden anyone, for the brothers who

---

^{a}Or *all contentment* ^{b}Or *you*

came from Macedonia supplied my need. So I refrained and will refrain from burdening you in any way. ¹⁰As the truth of Christ is in me, this boasting of mine will not be silenced in the regions of Achaia. ¹¹And why? Because I do not love you? God knows I do!

¹²And what I am doing I will continue to do, in order to undermine the claim of those who would like to claim that in their boasted mission they work on the same terms as we do. ¹³For such men are false apostles, deceitful workmen, disguising themselves as apostles of Christ. ¹⁴And no wonder, for even Satan disguises himself as an angel of light. ¹⁵So it is no surprise if his servants, also, disguise themselves as servants of righteousness. Their end will correspond to their deeds.

PAUL'S SUFFERINGS AS AN APOSTLE

¹⁶I repeat, let no one think me foolish. But even if you do, accept me as a fool, so that I too may boast a little. ¹⁷What I am saying with this boastful confidence, I say not as the Lord would^a but as a fool. ¹⁸Since many boast according to the flesh, I too will boast. ¹⁹For you gladly bear with fools, being wise yourselves! ²⁰For you bear it if someone makes slaves of you, or devours you, or takes advantage of you, or puts on airs, or strikes you in the face. ²¹To my shame, I must say, we were too weak for that!

But whatever anyone else dares to boast of—I am speaking as a fool—I also dare to boast of that. ²²Are they Hebrews? So am I. Are they Israelites? So am I. Are they offspring of Abraham? So am I. ²³Are they servants of Christ? I am a better one—I am talking like a madman—with far greater labours, far more imprisonments, with countless beatings, and often near death. ²⁴Five times I received at the hands of the Jews the forty lashes less one. ²⁵Three times I was beaten with rods. Once I was stoned. Three times I was shipwrecked; for a night and a day I was adrift at sea; ²⁶on frequent journeys, in danger from rivers, danger from robbers, danger from my own people, danger from Gentiles, danger in the city, danger in the wilderness, danger at sea, danger from false brothers; ²⁷in toil and hardship, through many a sleepless night, in hunger and thirst, often without food,^b in cold and exposure. ²⁸And, apart from other things, there is the daily pressure on me of my anxiety for all the churches. ²⁹Who is weak, and I am not weak? Who is made to fall, and I am not indignant?

³⁰If I must boast, I will boast of the things that show my weakness. ³¹The God and Father of the Lord Jesus, he who is blessed for ever, knows that I am not lying. ³²At Damascus, the governor under King Aretas was guarding the city of Damascus in order to seize me, ³³but I was let down in a basket through a window in the wall and escaped his hands.

PAUL'S VISIONS AND HIS THORN

12 I must go on boasting. Though there is nothing to be gained by it, I will go on to visions and revelations of the Lord. ²I know a man in Christ who fourteen years ago was caught up to the third heaven—whether in the body or out of the body I do not know, God knows. ³And I know that this man was caught up into paradise—whether in the body or out of the body I do not know, God knows— ⁴and he heard things that cannot be told, which man may not utter. ⁵On behalf of this man I will boast, but on my own behalf I will not boast, except of my weaknesses— ⁶though if I should wish to boast, I would not be a fool, for I would be speaking the truth; but I refrain from it, so that no one may think more of me than he sees in me or hears from me. ⁷So to keep me from becoming conceited because of the surpassing greatness of the revelations,^c a thorn was given me in the flesh, a messenger of Satan to harass me, to keep me from becoming conceited. ⁸Three times I pleaded with the Lord about this, that it should leave me. ⁹But he said to me, "My grace is sufficient for you, for my power is made perfect in weakness." Therefore I will boast all the more gladly of my weaknesses, so that the power of Christ may rest upon me. ¹⁰For the sake of Christ, then, I am content with weaknesses, insults, hardships, persecutions, and calamities. For when I am weak, then I am strong.

CONCERN FOR THE CORINTHIAN CHURCH

¹¹I have been a fool! You forced me to it, for I ought to have been commended by you. For I was not at all inferior to these super-apostles, even though I am nothing. ¹²The signs of a true apostle were performed among you with utmost patience, with signs and wonders and mighty works. ¹³For in what were you less favoured than the rest of the

---

^a Greek *not according to the Lord* ^b Or *often in fasting* ^c Or *hears from me, even because of the surpassing greatness of the revelations. So to keep me from becoming conceited*

churches, except that I myself did not burden you? Forgive me this wrong!

¹⁴Here for the third time I am ready to come to you. And I will not be a burden, for I seek not what is yours but you. For children are not bound to save up for their parents, but parents for their children. ¹⁵I will most gladly spend and be spent for your souls. If I love you more, am I to be loved less? ¹⁶But granting that I myself did not burden you, I was crafty, you say, and got the better of you by deceit. ¹⁷Did I take advantage of you through any of those whom I sent to you? ¹⁸I urged Titus to go, and sent the brother with him. Did Titus take advantage of you? Did we not act in the same spirit? Did we not take the same steps?

¹⁹Have you been thinking all along that we have been defending ourselves to you? It is in the sight of God that we have been speaking in Christ, and all for your upbuilding, beloved. ²⁰For I fear that perhaps when I come I may find you not as I wish, and that you may find me not as you wish—that perhaps there may be quarrelling, jealousy, anger, hostility, slander, gossip, conceit, and disorder. ²¹I fear that when I come again my God may humble me before you, and I may have to mourn over many of those who sinned earlier and have not repented of the impurity, sexual immorality, and sensuality that they have practised.

FINAL WARNINGS

13 This is the third time I am coming to you. Every charge must be established by the evidence of two or three witnesses. ²I warned those who sinned before and all the others, and I warn them now while absent, as I did when present on my second visit, that if I come again I will not spare them—³since you seek proof that Christ is speaking in me. He is not weak in dealing with you, but is powerful among you. ⁴For he was crucified in weakness, but lives by the power of God. For we also are weak in him, but in dealing with you we will live with him by the power of God.

⁵Examine yourselves, to see whether you are in the faith. Test yourselves. Or do you not realize this about yourselves, that Jesus Christ is in you?—unless indeed you fail to meet the test! ⁶I hope you will find out that we have not failed the test. ⁷But we pray to God that you may not do wrong—not that we may appear to have met the test, but that you may do what is right, though we may seem to have failed. ⁸For we cannot do anything against the truth, but only for the truth. ⁹For we are glad when we are weak and you are strong. Your restoration is what we pray for. ¹⁰For this reason I write these things while I am away from you, that when I come I may not have to be severe in my use of the authority that the Lord has given me for building up and not for tearing down.

FINAL GREETINGS

¹¹Finally, brothers,[a] rejoice. Aim for restoration, comfort one another,[b] agree with one another, live in peace; and the God of love and peace will be with you. ¹²Greet one another with a holy kiss. ¹³All the saints greet you.

¹⁴The grace of the Lord Jesus Christ and the love of God and the fellowship of the Holy Spirit be with you all.

---

[a] Or *brothers and sisters* [b] Or *listen to my appeal*

THE LETTER OF PAUL TO THE
GALATIANS

GREETING

1 Paul, an apostle—not from men nor through man, but through Jesus Christ and God the Father, who raised him from the dead— ²and all the brothers[a] who are with me,

To the churches of Galatia:

³Grace to you and peace from God our Father and the Lord Jesus Christ, ⁴who gave himself for our sins to deliver us from the present evil age, according to the will of our God and Father, ⁵to whom be the glory for ever and ever. Amen.

NO OTHER GOSPEL

⁶I am astonished that you are so quickly deserting him who called you in the grace of Christ and are turning to a different gospel— ⁷not that there is another one, but there are some who trouble you and want to distort the gospel of Christ. ⁸But even if we or an angel from heaven should preach to you a gospel contrary to the one we preached to you, let him be accursed. ⁹As we have said before, so now I say again: If anyone is preaching to you a gospel contrary to the one you received, let him be accursed.

¹⁰For am I now seeking the approval of man, or of God? Or am I trying to please man? If I were still trying to please man, I would not be a servant[b] of Christ.

PAUL CALLED BY GOD

¹¹For I would have you know, brothers, that the gospel that was preached by me is not man's gospel.[c] ¹²For I did not receive it from any man, nor was I taught it, but I received it through a revelation of Jesus Christ. ¹³For you have heard of my former life in Judaism, how I persecuted the church of God violently and tried to destroy it. ¹⁴And I was advancing in Judaism beyond many of my own age among my people, so extremely zealous was I for the traditions of my fathers. ¹⁵But when he who had set me apart before I was born,[d] and who called me by his grace, ¹⁶was pleased to reveal his Son to[e] me, in order that I might preach him among the Gentiles, I did not immediately consult with anyone;[f] ¹⁷nor did I go up to Jerusalem to those who were apostles before me, but I went away into Arabia, and returned again to Damascus.

¹⁸Then after three years I went up to Jerusalem to visit Cephas and remained with him for fifteen days. ¹⁹But I saw none of the other apostles except James the Lord's brother. ²⁰(In what I am writing to you, before God, I do not lie!) ²¹Then I went into the regions of Syria and Cilicia. ²²And I was still unknown in person to the churches of Judea that are in Christ. ²³They only were hearing it said, "He who used to persecute us is now preaching the faith he once tried to destroy." ²⁴And they glorified God because of me.

PAUL ACCEPTED BY THE APOSTLES

2 Then after fourteen years I went up again to Jerusalem with Barnabas, taking Titus along with me. ²I went up because of a revelation and set before them (though privately before those who seemed influential) the gospel that I proclaim among the Gentiles, in order to make sure I was not running or had not run in vain. ³But even Titus, who was with me, was not forced to be circumcised, though he was a Greek. ⁴Yet because of false brothers secretly brought in—who slipped in to spy out our freedom that we have in Christ Jesus, so that they might bring us into slavery— ⁵to them we did not yield in submission even for a moment, so that the truth of the gospel might be preserved for you. ⁶And from those who seemed to be influential (what they were makes no difference to me; God shows no partiality)— those, I say, who seemed influential added

---

[a] Or *brothers and sisters*. In New Testament usage, depending on the context, the plural Greek word *adelphoi* (translated "brothers") may refer either to *brothers* or to *brothers and sisters*; also verse 11
[b] For the contextual rendering of the Greek word *doulos*, see Preface
[c] Greek *not according to man* [d] Greek *set me apart from my mother's womb* [e] Greek *in* [f] Greek *with flesh and blood*

nothing to me. ⁷On the contrary, when they saw that I had been entrusted with the gospel to the uncircumcised, just as Peter had been entrusted with the gospel to the circumcised ⁸(for he who worked through Peter for his apostolic ministry to the circumcised worked also through me for mine to the Gentiles), ⁹and when James and Cephas and John, who seemed to be pillars, perceived the grace that was given to me, they gave the right hand of fellowship to Barnabas and me, that we should go to the Gentiles and they to the circumcised. ¹⁰Only, they asked us to remember the poor, the very thing I was eager to do.

PAUL OPPOSES PETER

¹¹But when Cephas came to Antioch, I opposed him to his face, because he stood condemned. ¹²For before certain men came from James, he was eating with the Gentiles; but when they came he drew back and separated himself, fearing the circumcision party.ᵃ ¹³And the rest of the Jews acted hypocritically along with him, so that even Barnabas was led astray by their hypocrisy. ¹⁴But when I saw that their conduct was not in step with the truth of the gospel, I said to Cephas before them all, "If you, though a Jew, live like a Gentile and not like a Jew, how can you force the Gentiles to live like Jews?"

JUSTIFIED BY FAITH

¹⁵We ourselves are Jews by birth and not Gentile sinners; ¹⁶yet we know that a person is not justifiedᵇ by works of the law but through faith in Jesus Christ, so we also have believed in Christ Jesus, in order to be justified by faith in Christ and not by works of the law, because by works of the law no one will be justified.

¹⁷But if, in our endeavour to be justified in Christ, we too were found to be sinners, is Christ then a servant of sin? Certainly not! ¹⁸For if I rebuild what I tore down, I prove myself to be a transgressor. ¹⁹For through the law I died to the law, so that I might live to God. ²⁰I have been crucified with Christ. It is no longer I who live, but Christ who lives in me. And the life I now live in the flesh I live by faith in the Son of God, who loved me and gave himself for me. ²¹I do not nullify the grace of God, for if righteousnessᶜ were through the law, then Christ died for no purpose.

BY FAITH, OR BY WORKS OF THE LAW?

3 O foolish Galatians! Who has bewitched you? It was before your eyes that Jesus Christ was publicly portrayed as crucified. ²Let me ask you only this: Did you receive the Spirit by works of the law or by hearing with faith? ³Are you so foolish? Having begun by the Spirit, are you now being perfected byᵈ the flesh? ⁴Did you sufferᵉ so many things in vain—if indeed it was in vain? ⁵Does he who supplies the Spirit to you and works miracles among you do so by works of the law, or by hearing with faith— ⁶just as Abraham "believed God, and it was counted to him as righteousness"?

⁷Know then that it is those of faith who are the sons of Abraham. ⁸And the Scripture, foreseeing that God would justifyᶠ the Gentiles by faith, preached the gospel beforehand to Abraham, saying, "In you shall all the nations be blessed." ⁹So then, those who are of faith are blessed along with Abraham, the man of faith.

THE RIGHTEOUS SHALL LIVE BY FAITH

¹⁰For all who rely on works of the law are under a curse; for it is written, "Cursed be everyone who does not abide by all things written in the Book of the Law, and do them." ¹¹Now it is evident that no one is justified before God by the law, for "The righteous shall live by faith."ᵍ ¹²But the law is not of faith, rather "The one who does them shall live by them." ¹³Christ redeemed us from the curse of the law by becoming a curse for us— for it is written, "Cursed is everyone who is hanged on a tree"— ¹⁴so that in Christ Jesus the blessing of Abraham might come to the Gentiles, so that we might receive the promised Spiritʰ through faith.

THE LAW AND THE PROMISE

¹⁵To give a human example, brothers:ⁱ even with a man-made covenant, no one annuls it or adds to it once it has been ratified. ¹⁶Now the promises were made to Abraham and to his offspring. It does not say, "And to offsprings", referring to many, but referring to one, "And to your offspring", who is Christ. ¹⁷This is what I mean: the law, which came 430 years afterwards, does not annul

---

ᵃOr *fearing those of the circumcision* ᵇOr *counted righteous* (three times in verse 16); also verse 17 ᶜOr *justification* ᵈOr *now ending with* ᵉOr *experience* ᶠOr *count righteous*; also verses 11, 24 ᵍOr *The one who by faith is righteous will live* ʰGreek *receive the promise of the Spirit* ⁱOr *brothers and sisters*

a covenant previously ratified by God, so as to make the promise void. ⁱ⁸For if the inheritance comes by the law, it no longer comes by promise; but God gave it to Abraham by a promise.

¹⁹Why then the law? It was added because of transgressions, until the offspring should come to whom the promise had been made, and it was put in place through angels by an intermediary. ²⁰Now an intermediary implies more than one, but God is one.

²¹Is the law then contrary to the promises of God? Certainly not! For if a law had been given that could give life, then righteousness would indeed be by the law. ²²But the Scripture imprisoned everything under sin, so that the promise by faith in Jesus Christ might be given to those who believe.

²³Now before faith came, we were held captive under the law, imprisoned until the coming faith would be revealed. ²⁴So then, the law was our guardian until Christ came, in order that we might be justified by faith. ²⁵But now that faith has come, we are no longer under a guardian, ²⁶for in Christ Jesus you are all sons of God, through faith. ²⁷For as many of you as were baptized into Christ have put on Christ. ²⁸There is neither Jew nor Greek, there is neither slave[a] nor free, there is no male and female, for you are all one in Christ Jesus. ²⁹And if you are Christ's, then you are Abraham's offspring, heirs according to promise.

SONS AND HEIRS

4 I mean that the heir, as long as he is a child, is no different from a slave,[b] though he is the owner of everything, ²but he is under guardians and managers until the date set by his father. ³In the same way we also, when we were children, were enslaved to the elementary principles[c] of the world. ⁴But when the fullness of time had come, God sent forth his Son, born of woman, born under the law, ⁵to redeem those who were under the law, so that we might receive adoption as sons. ⁶And because you are sons, God has sent the Spirit of his Son into our hearts, crying, "Abba! Father!" ⁷So you are no longer a slave, but a son, and if a son, then an heir through God.

PAUL'S CONCERN FOR THE GALATIANS

⁸Formerly, when you did not know God, you were enslaved to those that by nature are not gods. ⁹But now that you have come to know God, or rather to be known by God, how can you turn back again to the weak and worthless elementary principles of the world, whose slaves you want to be once more? ¹⁰You observe days and months and seasons and years! ¹¹I am afraid I may have laboured over you in vain.

¹²Brothers,[d] I entreat you, become as I am, for I also have become as you are. You did me no wrong. ¹³You know it was because of a bodily ailment that I preached the gospel to you at first, ¹⁴and though my condition was a trial to you, you did not scorn or despise me, but received me as an angel of God, as Christ Jesus. ¹⁵What then has become of your blessedness? For I testify to you that, if possible, you would have gouged out your eyes and given them to me. ¹⁶Have I then become your enemy by telling you the truth?[e] ¹⁷They make much of you, but for no good purpose. They want to shut you out, that you may make much of them. ¹⁸It is always good to be made much of for a good purpose, and not only when I am present with you, ¹⁹my little children, for whom I am again in the anguish of childbirth until Christ is formed in you! ²⁰I wish I could be present with you now and change my tone, for I am perplexed about you.

EXAMPLE OF HAGAR AND SARAH

²¹Tell me, you who desire to be under the law, do you not listen to the law? ²²For it is written that Abraham had two sons, one by a slave woman and one by a free woman. ²³But the son of the slave was born according to the flesh, while the son of the free woman was born through promise. ²⁴Now this may be interpreted allegorically: these women are two covenants. One is from Mount Sinai, bearing children for slavery; she is Hagar. ²⁵Now Hagar is Mount Sinai in Arabia;[f] she corresponds to the present Jerusalem, for she is in slavery with her children. ²⁶But the Jerusalem above is free, and she is our mother. ²⁷For it is written,

> "Rejoice, O barren one who
> does not bear;
> break forth and cry aloud, you
> who are not in labour!

[a] For the contextual rendering of the Greek word *doulos*, see Preface
[b] For the contextual rendering of the Greek word *doulos*, see Preface; also verse 7 [c] Or *elemental spirits*; also verse 9 [d] Or *Brothers and sisters*; also verses 28, 31 [e] Or *by dealing truthfully with you*
[f] Some manuscripts *For Sinai is a mountain in Arabia*

> For the children of the desolate
> one will be more
> than those of the one who
> has a husband."

²⁸Now you,ᵃ brothers, like Isaac, are children of promise. ²⁹But just as at that time he who was born according to the flesh persecuted him who was born according to the Spirit, so also it is now. ³⁰But what does the Scripture say? "Cast out the slave woman and her son, for the son of the slave woman shall not inherit with the son of the free woman." ³¹So, brothers, we are not children of the slave but of the free woman.

CHRIST HAS SET US FREE

5 For freedom Christ has set us free; stand firm therefore, and do not submit again to a yoke of slavery.

²Look: I, Paul, say to you that if you accept circumcision, Christ will be of no advantage to you. ³I testify again to every man who accepts circumcision that he is obligated to keep the whole law. ⁴You are severed from Christ, you who would be justifiedᵇ by the law; you have fallen away from grace. ⁵For through the Spirit, by faith, we ourselves eagerly wait for the hope of righteousness. ⁶For in Christ Jesus neither circumcision nor uncircumcision counts for anything, but only faith working through love.

⁷You were running well. Who hindered you from obeying the truth? ⁸This persuasion is not from him who calls you. ⁹A little leaven leavens the whole lump. ¹⁰I have confidence in the Lord that you will take no other view, and the one who is troubling you will bear the penalty, whoever he is. ¹¹But if I, brothers,ᶜ still preachᵈ circumcision, why am I still being persecuted? In that case the offence of the cross has been removed. ¹²I wish those who unsettle you would emasculate themselves!

¹³For you were called to freedom, brothers. Only do not use your freedom as an opportunity for the flesh, but through love serve one another. ¹⁴For the whole law is fulfilled in one word: "You shall love your neighbour as yourself." ¹⁵But if you bite and devour one another, watch out that you are not consumed by one another.

KEEP IN STEP WITH THE SPIRIT

¹⁶But I say, walk by the Spirit, and you will not gratify the desires of the flesh. ¹⁷For the desires of the flesh are against the Spirit, and the desires of the Spirit are against the flesh, for these are opposed to each other, to keep you from doing the things you want to do. ¹⁸But if you are led by the Spirit, you are not under the law. ¹⁹Now the works of the flesh are evident: sexual immorality, impurity, sensuality, ²⁰idolatry, sorcery, enmity, strife, jealousy, fits of anger, rivalries, dissensions, divisions, ²¹envy,ᵉ drunkenness, orgies, and things like these. I warn you, as I warned you before, that those who doᶠ such things will not inherit the kingdom of God. ²²But the fruit of the Spirit is love, joy, peace, patience, kindness, goodness, faithfulness, ²³gentleness, self-control; against such things there is no law. ²⁴And those who belong to Christ Jesus have crucified the flesh with its passions and desires.

²⁵If we live by the Spirit, let us also keep in step with the Spirit. ²⁶Let us not become conceited, provoking one another, envying one another.

BEAR ONE ANOTHER'S BURDENS

6 Brothers,ᵍ if anyone is caught in any transgression, you who are spiritual should restore him in a spirit of gentleness. Keep watch on yourself, lest you too be tempted. ²Bear one another's burdens, and so fulfil the law of Christ. ³For if anyone thinks he is something, when he is nothing, he deceives himself. ⁴But let each one test his own work, and then his reason to boast will be in himself alone and not in his neighbour. ⁵For each will have to bear his own load.

⁶Let the one who is taught the word share all good things with the one who teaches. ⁷Do not be deceived: God is not mocked, for whatever one sows, that will he also reap. ⁸For the one who sows to his own flesh will from the flesh reap corruption, but the one who sows to the Spirit will from the Spirit reap eternal life. ⁹And let us not grow weary of doing good, for in due season we will reap, if we do not give up. ¹⁰So then, as we have opportunity, let us do good to everyone, and especially to those who are of the household of faith.

FINAL WARNING AND BENEDICTION

¹¹See with what large letters I am writing to you with my own hand. ¹²It is those who want to make a good showing in the flesh

---

ᵃSome manuscripts *we* ᵇOr *counted righteous* ᶜOr *brothers and sisters*; also verse 13 ᵈGreek *proclaim* ᵉSome manuscripts add *murder* ᶠOr *make a practice of doing* ᵍOr *Brothers and sisters*; also verse 18

who would force you to be circumcised, and only in order that they may not be persecuted for the cross of Christ. ¹³For even those who are circumcised do not themselves keep the law, but they desire to have you circumcised that they may boast in your flesh. ¹⁴But far be it from me to boast except in the cross of our Lord Jesus Christ, by which*a* the world has been crucified to me, and I to the world. ¹⁵For neither circumcision counts for anything, nor uncircumcision, but a new creation. ¹⁶And as for all who walk by this rule, peace and mercy be upon them, and upon the Israel of God.

¹⁷From now on let no one cause me trouble, for I bear on my body the marks of Jesus.

¹⁸The grace of our Lord Jesus Christ be with your spirit, brothers. Amen.

---

a Or through whom

THE LETTER OF PAUL TO THE
EPHESIANS

GREETING

1 Paul, an apostle of Christ Jesus by the will of God,

To the saints who are in Ephesus, and are faithful[a] in Christ Jesus:

²Grace to you and peace from God our Father and the Lord Jesus Christ.

SPIRITUAL BLESSINGS IN CHRIST

³Blessed be the God and Father of our Lord Jesus Christ, who has blessed us in Christ with every spiritual blessing in the heavenly places, ⁴even as he chose us in him before the foundation of the world, that we should be holy and blameless before him. In love ⁵he predestined us[b] for adoption to himself as sons through Jesus Christ, according to the purpose of his will, ⁶to the praise of his glorious grace, with which he has blessed us in the Beloved. ⁷In him we have redemption through his blood, the forgiveness of our trespasses, according to the riches of his grace, ⁸which he lavished upon us, in all wisdom and insight ⁹making known[c] to us the mystery of his will, according to his purpose, which he set forth in Christ ¹⁰as a plan for the fullness of time, to unite all things in him, things in heaven and things on earth.

¹¹In him we have obtained an inheritance, having been predestined according to the purpose of him who works all things according to the counsel of his will, ¹²so that we who were the first to hope in Christ might be to the praise of his glory. ¹³In him you also, when you heard the word of truth, the gospel of your salvation, and believed in him, were sealed with the promised Holy Spirit, ¹⁴who is the guarantee[d] of our inheritance until we acquire possession of it,[e] to the praise of his glory.

THANKSGIVING AND PRAYER

¹⁵For this reason, because I have heard of your faith in the Lord Jesus and your love[f] towards all the saints, ¹⁶I do not cease to give thanks for you, remembering you in my prayers, ¹⁷that the God of our Lord Jesus Christ, the Father of glory, may give you the Spirit of wisdom and of revelation in the knowledge of him, ¹⁸having the eyes of your hearts enlightened, that you may know what is the hope to which he has called you, what are the riches of his glorious inheritance in the saints, ¹⁹and what is the immeasurable greatness of his power towards us who believe, according to the working of his great might ²⁰that he worked in Christ when he raised him from the dead and seated him at his right hand in the heavenly places, ²¹far above all rule and authority and power and dominion, and above every name that is named, not only in this age but also in the one to come. ²²And he put all things under his feet and gave him as head over all things to the church, ²³which is his body, the fullness of him who fills all in all.

BY GRACE THROUGH FAITH

2 And you were dead in the trespasses and sins ²in which you once walked, following the course of this world, following the prince of the power of the air, the spirit that is now at work in the sons of disobedience—³among whom we all once lived in the passions of our flesh, carrying out the desires of the body[g] and the mind, and were by nature children of wrath, like the rest of mankind.[h] ⁴But[i] God, being rich in mercy, because of the great love with which he loved us, ⁵even when we were dead in our trespasses, made us alive together with Christ—by grace you have been saved— ⁶and raised us up with him and seated us with him in the heavenly places in Christ Jesus, ⁷so that in the coming ages he might show the immeasurable riches of his grace in kindness towards us in Christ Jesus. ⁸For by grace you have been saved through faith. And this is not your own doing; it is the gift of God, ⁹not a result

---

[a] Some manuscripts *saints who are also faithful* (omitting *in Ephesus*)
[b] Or *before him in love,* ⁵*having predestined us*   [c] Or *he lavished upon us in all wisdom and insight, making known . . .*   [d] Or *down payment*
[e] Or *until God redeems his possession*   [f] Some manuscripts omit *your love*
[g] Greek *flesh*   [h] Greek *like the rest*   [i] Or *And*

of works, so that no one may boast. ¹⁰For we are his workmanship, created in Christ Jesus for good works, which God prepared beforehand, that we should walk in them.

ONE IN CHRIST

¹¹Therefore remember that at one time you Gentiles in the flesh, called "the uncircumcision" by what is called the circumcision, which is made in the flesh by hands— ¹²remember that you were at that time separated from Christ, alienated from the commonwealth of Israel and strangers to the covenants of promise, having no hope and without God in the world. ¹³But now in Christ Jesus you who once were far off have been brought near by the blood of Christ. ¹⁴For he himself is our peace, who has made us both one and has broken down in his flesh the dividing wall of hostility ¹⁵by abolishing the law of commandments expressed in ordinances, that he might create in himself one new man in place of the two, so making peace, ¹⁶and might reconcile us both to God in one body through the cross, thereby killing the hostility. ¹⁷And he came and preached peace to you who were far off and peace to those who were near. ¹⁸For through him we both have access in one Spirit to the Father. ¹⁹So then you are no longer strangers and aliens,ᵃ but you are fellow citizens with the saints and members of the household of God, ²⁰built on the foundation of the apostles and prophets, Christ Jesus himself being the cornerstone, ²¹in whom the whole structure, being joined together, grows into a holy temple in the Lord. ²²In him you also are being built together into a dwelling place for God byᵇ the Spirit.

THE MYSTERY OF THE GOSPEL REVEALED

3 For this reason I, Paul, a prisoner of Christ Jesus on behalf of you Gentiles— ²assuming that you have heard of the stewardship of God's grace that was given to me for you, ³how the mystery was made known to me by revelation, as I have written briefly. ⁴When you read this, you can perceive my insight into the mystery of Christ, ⁵which was not made known to the sons of men in other generations as it has now been revealed to his holy apostles and prophets by the Spirit. ⁶This mystery isᶜ that the Gentiles are fellow heirs, members of the same body, and partakers of the promise in Christ Jesus through the gospel.

⁷Of this gospel I was made a minister according to the gift of God's grace, which was given me by the working of his power. ⁸To me, though I am the very least of all the saints, this grace was given, to preach to the Gentiles the unsearchable riches of Christ, ⁹and to bring to light for everyone what is the plan of the mystery hidden for ages inᵈ God, who created all things, ¹⁰so that through the church the manifold wisdom of God might now be made known to the rulers and authorities in the heavenly places. ¹¹This was according to the eternal purpose that he has realized in Christ Jesus our Lord, ¹²in whom we have boldness and access with confidence through our faith in him. ¹³So I ask you not to lose heart over what I am suffering for you, which is your glory.

PRAYER FOR SPIRITUAL STRENGTH

¹⁴For this reason I bow my knees before the Father, ¹⁵from whom every familyᵉ in heaven and on earth is named, ¹⁶that according to the riches of his glory he may grant you to be strengthened with power through his Spirit in your inner being, ¹⁷so that Christ may dwell in your hearts through faith—that you, being rooted and grounded in love, ¹⁸may have strength to comprehend with all the saints what is the breadth and length and height and depth, ¹⁹and to know the love of Christ that surpasses knowledge, that you may be filled with all the fullness of God.

²⁰Now to him who is able to do far more abundantly than all that we ask or think, according to the power at work within us, ²¹to him be glory in the church and in Christ Jesus throughout all generations, for ever and ever. Amen.

UNITY IN THE BODY OF CHRIST

4 I therefore, a prisoner for the Lord, urge you to walk in a manner worthy of the calling to which you have been called, ²with all humility and gentleness, with patience, bearing with one another in love, ³eager to maintain the unity of the Spirit in the bond of peace. ⁴There is one body and one Spirit—just as you were called to the one hope that belongs to your call— ⁵one Lord, one faith, one baptism, ⁶one God and Father of all, who is over all and through all

---

ᵃOr *sojourners* ᵇOr *in* ᶜThe words *This mystery is* are inferred from verse 4 ᵈOr *by* ᵉOr *from whom all fatherhood*; the Greek word *patria* in verse 15 is closely related to the word for *Father* in verse 14

and in all. ⁷But grace was given to each one of us according to the measure of Christ's gift. ⁸Therefore it says,

> "When he ascended on high he
> led a host of captives,
> and he gave gifts to men."[a]

⁹(In saying, "He ascended", what does it mean but that he had also descended into the lower regions, the earth?[b] ¹⁰He who descended is the one who also ascended far above all the heavens, that he might fill all things.) ¹¹And he gave the apostles, the prophets, the evangelists, the shepherds[c] and teachers,[d] ¹²to equip the saints for the work of ministry, for building up the body of Christ, ¹³until we all attain to the unity of the faith and of the knowledge of the Son of God, to mature manhood,[e] to the measure of the stature of the fullness of Christ, ¹⁴so that we may no longer be children, tossed to and fro by the waves and carried about by every wind of doctrine, by human cunning, by craftiness in deceitful schemes. ¹⁵Rather, speaking the truth in love, we are to grow up in every way into him who is the head, into Christ, ¹⁶from whom the whole body, joined and held together by every joint with which it is equipped, when each part is working properly, makes the body grow so that it builds itself up in love.

THE NEW LIFE

¹⁷Now this I say and testify in the Lord, that you must no longer walk as the Gentiles do, in the futility of their minds. ¹⁸They are darkened in their understanding, alienated from the life of God because of the ignorance that is in them, due to their hardness of heart. ¹⁹They have become callous and have given themselves up to sensuality, greedy to practise every kind of impurity. ²⁰But that is not the way you learned Christ! — ²¹assuming that you have heard about him and were taught in him, as the truth is in Jesus, ²²to put off your old self,[f] which belongs to your former manner of life and is corrupt through deceitful desires, ²³and to be renewed in the spirit of your minds, ²⁴and to put on the new self, created after the likeness of God in true righteousness and holiness.

²⁵Therefore, having put away falsehood, let each one of you speak the truth with his neighbour, for we are members one of another. ²⁶Be angry and do not sin; do not let the sun go down on your anger, ²⁷and give no opportunity to the devil. ²⁸Let the thief no longer steal, but rather let him labour, doing honest work with his own hands, so that he may have something to share with anyone in need. ²⁹Let no corrupting talk come out of your mouths, but only such as is good for building up, as fits the occasion, that it may give grace to those who hear. ³⁰And do not grieve the Holy Spirit of God, by whom you were sealed for the day of redemption. ³¹Let all bitterness and wrath and anger and clamour and slander be put away from you, along with all malice. ³²Be kind to one another, tender-hearted, forgiving one another, as God in Christ forgave you.

WALK IN LOVE

5 Therefore be imitators of God, as beloved children. ²And walk in love, as Christ loved us and gave himself up for us, a fragrant offering and sacrifice to God.

³But sexual immorality and all impurity or covetousness must not even be named among you, as is proper among saints. ⁴Let there be no filthiness nor foolish talk nor crude joking, which are out of place, but instead let there be thanksgiving. ⁵For you may be sure of this, that everyone who is sexually immoral or impure, or who is covetous (that is, an idolater), has no inheritance in the kingdom of Christ and God. ⁶Let no one deceive you with empty words, for because of these things the wrath of God comes upon the sons of disobedience. ⁷Therefore do not become partners with them; ⁸for at one time you were darkness, but now you are light in the Lord. Walk as children of light ⁹(for the fruit of light is found in all that is good and right and true), ¹⁰and try to discern what is pleasing to the Lord. ¹¹Take no part in the unfruitful works of darkness, but instead expose them. ¹²For it is shameful even to speak of the things that they do in secret. ¹³But when anything is exposed by the light, it becomes visible, ¹⁴for anything that becomes visible is light. Therefore it says,

> "Awake, O sleeper,
> and arise from the dead,
> and Christ will shine on you."

¹⁵Look carefully then how you walk, not as unwise but as wise, ¹⁶making the best use of the time, because the days are evil.

---

[a] The Greek word *anthropoi* can refer to both men and women
[b] Or *the lower parts of the earth*? [c] Or *pastors* [d] Or *the shepherd-teachers* [e] Greek *to a full-grown man* [k] Greek *man*; also verse 24

¹⁷Therefore do not be foolish, but understand what the will of the Lord is. ¹⁸And do not get drunk with wine, for that is debauchery, but be filled with the Spirit, ¹⁹addressing one another in psalms and hymns and spiritual songs, singing and making melody to the Lord with your heart, ²⁰giving thanks always and for everything to God the Father in the name of our Lord Jesus Christ, ²¹submitting to one another out of reverence for Christ.

WIVES AND HUSBANDS

²²Wives, submit to your own husbands, as to the Lord. ²³For the husband is the head of the wife even as Christ is the head of the church, his body, and is himself its Saviour. ²⁴Now as the church submits to Christ, so also wives should submit in everything to their husbands.

²⁵Husbands, love your wives, as Christ loved the church and gave himself up for her, ²⁶that he might sanctify her, having cleansed her by the washing of water with the word, ²⁷so that he might present the church to himself in splendour, without spot or wrinkle or any such thing, that she might be holy and without blemish.ᵃ ²⁸In the same way husbands should love their wives as their own bodies. He who loves his wife loves himself. ²⁹For no one ever hated his own flesh, but nourishes and cherishes it, just as Christ does the church, ³⁰because we are members of his body. ³¹"Therefore a man shall leave his father and mother and hold fast to his wife, and the two shall become one flesh." ³²This mystery is profound, and I am saying that it refers to Christ and the church. ³³However, let each one of you love his wife as himself, and let the wife see that she respects her husband.

CHILDREN AND PARENTS

6 Children, obey your parents in the Lord, for this is right. ²"Honour your father and mother" (this is the first commandment with a promise), ³"that it may go well with you and that you may live long in the land." ⁴Fathers, do not provoke your children to anger, but bring them up in the discipline and instruction of the Lord.

BONDSERVANTS AND MASTERS

⁵Bondservants,ᵇ obey your earthly mastersᶜ with fear and trembling, with a sincere heart, as you would Christ, ⁶not by the way of eye-service, as people-pleasers, but as bondservants of Christ, doing the will of God from the heart, ⁷rendering service with a good will as to the Lord and not to man, ⁸knowing that whatever good anyone does, this he will receive back from the Lord, whether he is a bondservant or is free. ⁹Masters, do the same to them, and stop your threatening, knowing that he who is both their Masterᵈ and yours is in heaven, and that there is no partiality with him.

THE WHOLE ARMOUR OF GOD

¹⁰Finally, be strong in the Lord and in the strength of his might. ¹¹Put on the whole armour of God, that you may be able to stand against the schemes of the devil. ¹²For we do not wrestle against flesh and blood, but against the rulers, against the authorities, against the cosmic powers over this present darkness, against the spiritual forces of evil in the heavenly places. ¹³Therefore take up the whole armour of God, that you may be able to withstand in the evil day, and having done all, to stand firm. ¹⁴Stand therefore, having fastened on the belt of truth, and having put on the breastplate of righteousness, ¹⁵and, as shoes for your feet, having put on the readiness given by the gospel of peace. ¹⁶In all circumstances take up the shield of faith, with which you can extinguish all the flaming darts of the evil one; ¹⁷and take the helmet of salvation, and the sword of the Spirit, which is the word of God, ¹⁸praying at all times in the Spirit, with all prayer and supplication. To that end, keep alert with all perseverance, making supplication for all the saints, ¹⁹and also for me, that words may be given to me in opening my mouth boldly to proclaim the mystery of the gospel, ²⁰for which I am an ambassador in chains, that I may declare it boldly, as I ought to speak.

FINAL GREETINGS

²¹So that you also may know how I am and what I am doing, Tychicus the beloved brother and faithful minister in the Lord will tell you everything. ²²I have sent him to you for this very purpose, that you may know how we are, and that he may encourage your hearts.

²³Peace be to the brothers,ᵉ and love with faith, from God the Father and the Lord Jesus Christ. ²⁴Grace be with all who love our Lord Jesus Christ with love incorruptible.

ᵃOr holy and blameless ᵇFor the contextual rendering of the Greek word *doulos*, see Preface; also verse 6; likewise for *bondservant* in verse 8 ᶜOr *your masters according to the flesh* ᵈGreek *Lord* ᵉOr *brothers and sisters*

THE LETTER OF PAUL TO THE
PHILIPPIANS

GREETING

1 Paul and Timothy, servants[a] of Christ Jesus,

To all the saints in Christ Jesus who are at Philippi, with the overseers[b] and deacons:[c]

²Grace to you and peace from God our Father and the Lord Jesus Christ.

THANKSGIVING AND PRAYER

³I thank my God in all my remembrance of you, ⁴always in every prayer of mine for you all making my prayer with joy, ⁵because of your partnership in the gospel from the first day until now. ⁶And I am sure of this, that he who began a good work in you will bring it to completion at the day of Jesus Christ. ⁷It is right for me to feel this way about you all, because I hold you in my heart, for you are all partakers with me of grace,[d] both in my imprisonment and in the defence and confirmation of the gospel. ⁸For God is my witness, how I yearn for you all with the affection of Christ Jesus. ⁹And it is my prayer that your love may abound more and more, with knowledge and all discernment, ¹⁰so that you may approve what is excellent, and so be pure and blameless for the day of Christ, ¹¹filled with the fruit of righteousness that comes through Jesus Christ, to the glory and praise of God.

THE ADVANCE OF THE GOSPEL

¹²I want you to know, brothers,[e] that what has happened to me has really served to advance the gospel, ¹³so that it has become known throughout the whole imperial guard[f] and to all the rest that my imprisonment is for Christ. ¹⁴And most of the brothers, having become confident in the Lord by my imprisonment, are much more bold to speak the word[g] without fear.

¹⁵Some indeed preach Christ from envy and rivalry, but others from good will. ¹⁶The latter do it out of love, knowing that I am put here for the defence of the gospel. ¹⁷The former proclaim Christ out of selfish ambition, not sincerely but thinking to afflict me in my imprisonment. ¹⁸What then? Only that in every way, whether in pretence or in truth, Christ is proclaimed, and in that I rejoice.

TO LIVE IS CHRIST

Yes, and I will rejoice, ¹⁹for I know that through your prayers and the help of the Spirit of Jesus Christ this will turn out for my deliverance, ²⁰as it is my eager expectation and hope that I will not be at all ashamed, but that with full courage now as always Christ will be honoured in my body, whether by life or by death. ²¹For to me to live is Christ, and to die is gain. ²²If I am to live in the flesh, that means fruitful labour for me. Yet which I shall choose I cannot tell. ²³I am hard pressed between the two. My desire is to depart and be with Christ, for that is far better. ²⁴But to remain in the flesh is more necessary on your account. ²⁵Convinced of this, I know that I will remain and continue with you all, for your progress and joy in the faith, ²⁶so that in me you may have ample cause to glory in Christ Jesus, because of my coming to you again.

²⁷Only let your manner of life be worthy[h] of the gospel of Christ, so that whether I come and see you or am absent, I may hear of you that you are standing firm in one spirit, with one mind striving side by side for the faith of the gospel, ²⁸and not frightened in anything by your opponents. This is a clear sign to them of their destruction, but of your salvation, and that from God. ²⁹For it has been granted to you that for the sake of Christ you should not only believe in him but also suffer for his sake, ³⁰engaged in the same conflict that you saw I had and now hear that I still have.

---

[a] For the contextual rendering of the Greek word *doulos*, see Preface [b] Or *bishops*; Greek *episkopoi* [c] Or *servants*, or *ministers*; Greek *diakonoi* [d] Or *you all have fellowship with me in grace* [e] Or *brothers and sisters*. In New Testament usage, depending on the context, the plural Greek word *adelphoi* (translated "brothers") may refer either to *brothers* or to *brothers and sisters*; also verse 14 [f] Greek *in the whole praetorium* [g] Some manuscripts add *of God* [h] Greek *Only behave as citizens worthy*

CHRIST'S EXAMPLE OF HUMILITY

2 So if there is any encouragement in Christ, any comfort from love, any participation in the Spirit, any affection and sympathy, ²complete my joy by being of the same mind, having the same love, being in full accord and of one mind. ³Do nothing from selfish ambition or conceit, but in humility count others more significant than yourselves. ⁴Let each of you look not only to his own interests, but also to the interests of others. ⁵Have this mind among yourselves, which is yours in Christ Jesus,ᵃ ⁶who, though he was in the form of God, did not count equality with God a thing to be grasped,ᵇ ⁷but emptied himself, by taking the form of a servant,ᶜ being born in the likeness of men. ⁸And being found in human form, he humbled himself by becoming obedient to the point of death, even death on a cross. ⁹Therefore God has highly exalted him and bestowed on him the name that is above every name, ¹⁰so that at the name of Jesus every knee should bow, in heaven and on earth and under the earth, ¹¹and every tongue confess that Jesus Christ is Lord, to the glory of God the Father.

LIGHTS IN THE WORLD

¹²Therefore, my beloved, as you have always obeyed, so now, not only as in my presence but much more in my absence, work out your own salvation with fear and trembling, ¹³for it is God who works in you, both to will and to work for his good pleasure.

¹⁴Do all things without grumbling or disputing, ¹⁵that you may be blameless and innocent, children of God without blemish in the midst of a crooked and twisted generation, among whom you shine as lights in the world, ¹⁶holding fast to the word of life, so that in the day of Christ I may be proud that I did not run in vain or labour in vain. ¹⁷Even if I am to be poured out as a drink offering upon the sacrificial offering of your faith, I am glad and rejoice with you all. ¹⁸Likewise you also should be glad and rejoice with me.

TIMOTHY AND EPAPHRODITUS

¹⁹I hope in the Lord Jesus to send Timothy to you soon, so that I too may be cheered by news of you. ²⁰For I have no one like him, who will be genuinely concerned for your welfare. ²¹For they all seek their own interests, not those of Jesus Christ. ²²But you know Timothy'sᵈ proven worth, how as a sonᵉ with a father he has served with me in the gospel. ²³I hope therefore to send him just as soon as I see how it will go with me, ²⁴and I trust in the Lord that shortly I myself will come also.

²⁵I have thought it necessary to send to you Epaphroditus my brother and fellow worker and fellow soldier, and your messenger and minister to my need, ²⁶for he has been longing for you all and has been distressed because you heard that he was ill. ²⁷Indeed he was ill, near to death. But God had mercy on him, and not only on him but on me also, lest I should have sorrow upon sorrow. ²⁸I am the more eager to send him, therefore, that you may rejoice at seeing him again, and that I may be less anxious. ²⁹So receive him in the Lord with all joy, and honour such men, ³⁰for he nearly diedᶠ for the work of Christ, risking his life to complete what was lacking in your service to me.

RIGHTEOUSNESS THROUGH FAITH IN CHRIST

3 Finally, my brothers,ᵍ rejoice in the Lord. To write the same things to you is no trouble to me and is safe for you.

²Look out for the dogs, look out for the evildoers, look out for those who mutilate the flesh. ³For we are the circumcision, who worship by the Spirit of Godʰ and glory in Christ Jesus and put no confidence in the flesh— ⁴though I myself have reason for confidence in the flesh also. If anyone else thinks he has reason for confidence in the flesh, I have more: ⁵circumcised on the eighth day, of the people of Israel, of the tribe of Benjamin, a Hebrew of Hebrews; as to the law, a Pharisee; ⁶as to zeal, a persecutor of the church; as to righteousness under the law,ⁱ blameless. ⁷But whatever gain I had, I counted as loss for the sake of Christ. ⁸Indeed, I count everything as loss because of the surpassing worth of knowing Christ Jesus my Lord. For his sake I have suffered the loss of all things and count them as rubbish, in order that I may gain Christ ⁹and be found in him, not having a righteousness of my own that comes from the law, but that which comes through faith in Christ, the righteousness from God that depends on faith— ¹⁰that I may know him and the power of his resurrection, and may share his sufferings, becoming like him

---

ᵃOr *which was also in Christ Jesus* ᵇOr *a thing to be held on to for advantage* ᶜOr *slave* (for the contextual rendering of the Greek word *doulos*, see Preface) ᵈGreek *his* ᵉGreek *child* ᶠOr *he drew near to the point of death*; compare verse 8 ᵍOr *brothers and sisters*; also verses 13, 17 ʰSome manuscripts *God in spirit* ⁱGreek *in the law*

in his death, ¹¹that by any means possible I may attain the resurrection from the dead.

STRAINING TOWARDS THE GOAL

¹²Not that I have already obtained this or am already perfect, but I press on to make it my own, because Christ Jesus has made me his own. ¹³Brothers, I do not consider that I have made it my own. But one thing I do: forgetting what lies behind and straining forward to what lies ahead, ¹⁴I press on towards the goal for the prize of the upward call of God in Christ Jesus. ¹⁵Let those of us who are mature think this way, and if in anything you think otherwise, God will reveal that also to you. ¹⁶Only let us hold true to what we have attained.

¹⁷Brothers, join in imitating me, and keep your eyes on those who walk according to the example you have in us. ¹⁸For many, of whom I have often told you and now tell you even with tears, walk as enemies of the cross of Christ. ¹⁹Their end is destruction, their god is their belly, and they glory in their shame, with minds set on earthly things. ²⁰But our citizenship is in heaven, and from it we await a Saviour, the Lord Jesus Christ, ²¹who will transform our lowly body to be like his glorious body, by the power that enables him even to subject all things to himself.

4 Therefore, my brothers,ᵃ whom I love and long for, my joy and crown, stand firm thus in the Lord, my beloved.

EXHORTATION, ENCOURAGEMENT, AND PRAYER

²I entreat Euodia and I entreat Syntyche to agree in the Lord. ³Yes, I ask you also, true companion,ᵇ help these women, who have labouredᶜ side by side with me in the gospel together with Clement and the rest of my fellow workers, whose names are in the book of life.

⁴Rejoice in the Lord always; again I will say, rejoice. ⁵Let your reasonablenessᵈ be known to everyone. The Lord is at hand; ⁶do not be anxious about anything, but in everything by prayer and supplication with thanksgiving let your requests be made known to God. ⁷And the peace of God, which surpasses all understanding, will guard your hearts and your minds in Christ Jesus.

⁸Finally, brothers, whatever is true, whatever is honourable, whatever is just, whatever is pure, whatever is lovely, whatever is commendable, if there is any excellence, if there is anything worthy of praise, think about these things. ⁹What you have learnedᵉ and received and heard and seen in me—practise these things, and the God of peace will be with you.

GOD'S PROVISION

¹⁰I rejoiced in the Lord greatly that now at length you have revived your concern for me. You were indeed concerned for me, but you had no opportunity. ¹¹Not that I am speaking of being in need, for I have learned in whatever situation I am to be content. ¹²I know how to be brought low, and I know how to abound. In any and every circumstance, I have learned the secret of facing plenty and hunger, abundance and need. ¹³I can do all things through him who strengthens me.

¹⁴Yet it was kind of you to shareᶠ my trouble. ¹⁵And you Philippians yourselves know that in the beginning of the gospel, when I left Macedonia, no church entered into partnership with me in giving and receiving, except you only. ¹⁶Even in Thessalonica you sent me help for my needs once and again. ¹⁷Not that I seek the gift, but I seek the fruit that increases to your credit.ᵍ ¹⁸I have received full payment, and more. I am well supplied, having received from Epaphroditus the gifts you sent, a fragrant offering, a sacrifice acceptable and pleasing to God. ¹⁹And my God will supply every need of yours according to his riches in glory in Christ Jesus. ²⁰To our God and Father be glory for ever and ever. Amen.

FINAL GREETINGS

²¹Greet every saint in Christ Jesus. The brothers who are with me greet you. ²²All the saints greet you, especially those of Caesar's household.

²³The grace of the Lord Jesus Christ be with your spirit.

ᵃOr brothers and sisters; also verses 8, 21 ᵇOr loyal Syzygus; Greek true yoke-fellow ᶜOr strived (see 1:27) ᵈOr gentleness ᵉOr these things—⁹which things you have also learned ᶠOr have fellowship in ᵍOr I seek the profit that accrues to your account

THE LETTER OF PAUL TO THE
COLOSSIANS

GREETING

1 Paul, an apostle of Christ Jesus by the will of God, and Timothy our brother, ²To the saints and faithful brothers¹ in Christ at Colossae:

Grace to you and peace from God our Father.

THANKSGIVING AND PRAYER

³We always thank God, the Father of our Lord Jesus Christ, when we pray for you, ⁴since we heard of your faith in Christ Jesus and of the love that you have for all the saints, ⁵because of the hope laid up for you in heaven. Of this you have heard before in the word of the truth, the gospel, ⁶which has come to you, as indeed in the whole world it is bearing fruit and increasing—as it also does among you, since the day you heard it and understood the grace of God in truth, ⁷just as you learned it from Epaphras our beloved fellow servant.¹ He is a faithful minister of Christ on your¹ behalf ⁸and has made known to us your love in the Spirit.

⁹And so, from the day we heard, we have not ceased to pray for you, asking that you may be filled with the knowledge of his will in all spiritual wisdom and understanding, ¹⁰so as to walk in a manner worthy of the Lord, fully pleasing to him: bearing fruit in every good work and increasing in the knowledge of God; ¹¹being strengthened with all power, according to his glorious might, for all endurance and patience with joy; ¹²giving thanks¹ to the Father, who has qualified you¹ to share in the inheritance of the saints in light. ¹³He has delivered us from the domain of darkness and transferred us to the kingdom of his beloved Son, ¹⁴in whom we have redemption, the forgiveness of sins.

THE PRE-EMINENCE OF CHRIST

¹⁵He is the image of the invisible God, the firstborn of all creation. ¹⁶For by¹ him all things were created, in heaven and on earth, visible and invisible, whether thrones or dominions or rulers or authorities—all things were created through him and for him. ¹⁷And he is before all things, and in him all things hold together. ¹⁸And he is the head of the body, the church. He is the beginning, the firstborn from the dead, that in everything he might be pre-eminent. ¹⁹For in him all the fullness of God was pleased to dwell, ²⁰and through him to reconcile to himself all things, whether on earth or in heaven, making peace by the blood of his cross.

²¹And you, who once were alienated and hostile in mind, doing evil deeds, ²²he has now reconciled in his body of flesh by his death, in order to present you holy and blameless and above reproach before him, ²³if indeed you continue in the faith, stable and steadfast, not shifting from the hope of the gospel that you heard, which has been proclaimed in all creation¹ under heaven, and of which I, Paul, became a minister.

PAUL'S MINISTRY TO THE CHURCH

²⁴Now I rejoice in my sufferings for your sake, and in my flesh I am filling up what is lacking in Christ's afflictions for the sake of his body, that is, the church, ²⁵of which I became a minister according to the stewardship from God that was given to me for you, to make the word of God fully known, ²⁶the mystery hidden for ages and generations but now revealed to his saints. ²⁷To them God chose to make known how great among the Gentiles are the riches of the glory of this mystery, which is Christ in you, the hope of glory. ²⁸Him we proclaim, warning everyone and teaching everyone with all wisdom, that we may present everyone mature in Christ. ²⁹For this I toil, struggling with all his energy that he powerfully works within me.

---

¹Or *brothers and sisters*. In New Testament usage, depending on the context, the plural Greek word *adelphoi* (translated "brothers") may refer either to *brothers* or to *brothers and sisters* ¹For the contextual rendering of the Greek word *sundoulos*, see Preface ¹Some manuscripts *our* ¹Or *patience, with joy giving thanks* ¹Some manuscripts *us* ¹That is, by means of; or *in* ¹Or *to every creature*

2 For I want you to know how great a struggle I have for you and for those at Laodicea and for all who have not seen me face to face, ²that their hearts may be encouraged, being knit together in love, to reach all the riches of full assurance of understanding and the knowledge of God's mystery, which is Christ, ³in whom are hidden all the treasures of wisdom and knowledge. ⁴I say this in order that no one may delude you with plausible arguments. ⁵For though I am absent in body, yet I am with you in spirit, rejoicing to see your good order and the firmness of your faith in Christ.

ALIVE IN CHRIST

⁶Therefore, as you received Christ Jesus the Lord, so walk in him, ⁷rooted and built up in him and established in the faith, just as you were taught, abounding in thanksgiving. ⁸See to it that no one takes you captive by philosophy and empty deceit, according to human tradition, according to the elemental spirits[a] of the world, and not according to Christ. ⁹For in him the whole fullness of deity dwells bodily, ¹⁰and you have been filled in him, who is the head of all rule and authority. ¹¹In him also you were circumcised with a circumcision made without hands, by putting off the body of the flesh, by the circumcision of Christ, ¹²having been buried with him in baptism, in which you were also raised with him through faith in the powerful working of God, who raised him from the dead. ¹³And you, who were dead in your trespasses and the uncircumcision of your flesh, God made alive together with him, having forgiven us all our trespasses, ¹⁴by cancelling the record of debt that stood against us with its legal demands. This he set aside, nailing it to the cross. ¹⁵He disarmed the rulers and authorities[b] and put them to open shame, by triumphing over them in him.[c]

LET NO ONE DISQUALIFY YOU

¹⁶Therefore let no one pass judgement on you in questions of food and drink, or with regard to a festival or a new moon or a Sabbath. ¹⁷These are a shadow of the things to come, but the substance belongs to Christ. ¹⁸Let no one disqualify you, insisting on asceticism and worship of angels, going on in detail about visions,[d] puffed up without reason by his sensuous mind, ¹⁹and not holding fast to the Head, from whom the whole body, nourished and knit together through its joints and ligaments, grows with a growth that is from God.

²⁰If with Christ you died to the elemental spirits of the world, why, as if you were still alive in the world, do you submit to regulations— ²¹"Do not handle, Do not taste, Do not touch" ²²(referring to things that all perish as they are used) — according to human precepts and teachings? ²³These have indeed an appearance of wisdom in promoting self-made religion and asceticism and severity to the body, but they are of no value in stopping the indulgence of the flesh.

PUT ON THE NEW SELF

3 If then you have been raised with Christ, seek the things that are above, where Christ is, seated at the right hand of God. ²Set your minds on things that are above, not on things that are on earth. ³For you have died, and your life is hidden with Christ in God. ⁴When Christ who is your[e] life appears, then you also will appear with him in glory.

⁵Put to death therefore what is earthly in you:[f] sexual immorality, impurity, passion, evil desire, and covetousness, which is idolatry. ⁶On account of these the wrath of God is coming.[g] ⁷In these you too once walked, when you were living in them. ⁸But now you must put them all away: anger, wrath, malice, slander, and obscene talk from your mouth. ⁹Do not lie to one another, seeing that you have put off the old self[h] with its practices ¹⁰and have put on the new self, which is being renewed in knowledge after the image of its creator. ¹¹Here there is not Greek and Jew, circumcised and uncircumcised, barbarian, Scythian, slave,[i] free; but Christ is all, and in all.

¹²Put on then, as God's chosen ones, holy and beloved, compassionate hearts, kindness, humility, meekness, and patience, ¹³bearing with one another and, if one has a complaint against another, forgiving each other; as the Lord has forgiven you, so you also must forgive. ¹⁴And above all these put on love, which binds everything together

---

[a] Or *elementary principles*; also verse 20 [b] Probably demonic rulers and authorities [c] Or *in it* (that is, the cross) [d] Or *about the things he has seen* [e] Some manuscripts *our* [f] Greek *therefore your members that are on the earth* [g] Some manuscripts add *upon the sons of disobedience* [h] Greek *man*; also as supplied in verse 10 [i] For the contextual rendering of the Greek word *doulos*, see Preface; likewise for *Bondservants* in verse 22

in perfect harmony. ¹⁵And let the peace of Christ rule in your hearts, to which indeed you were called in one body. And be thankful. ¹⁶Let the word of Christ dwell in you richly, teaching and admonishing one another in all wisdom, singing psalms and hymns and spiritual songs, with thankfulness in your hearts to God. ¹⁷And whatever you do, in word or deed, do everything in the name of the Lord Jesus, giving thanks to God the Father through him.

RULES FOR CHRISTIAN HOUSEHOLDS

¹⁸Wives, submit to your husbands, as is fitting in the Lord. ¹⁹Husbands, love your wives, and do not be harsh with them. ²⁰Children, obey your parents in everything, for this pleases the Lord. ²¹Fathers, do not provoke your children, lest they become discouraged. ²²Bondservants, obey in everything those who are your earthly masters,[a] not by way of eye-service, as people-pleasers, but with sincerity of heart, fearing the Lord. ²³Whatever you do, work heartily, as for the Lord and not for men, ²⁴knowing that from the Lord you will receive the inheritance as your reward. You are serving the Lord Christ. ²⁵For the wrongdoer will be paid back for the wrong he has done, and there is no partiality.

4 Masters, treat your bondservants[b] justly and fairly, knowing that you also have a Master in heaven.

FURTHER INSTRUCTIONS

²Continue steadfastly in prayer, being watchful in it with thanksgiving. ³At the same time, pray also for us, that God may open to us a door for the word, to declare the mystery of Christ, on account of which I am in prison—⁴that I may make it clear, which is how I ought to speak.

⁵Walk in wisdom towards outsiders, making the best use of the time. ⁶Let your speech always be gracious, seasoned with salt, so that you may know how you ought to answer each person.

FINAL GREETINGS

⁷Tychicus will tell you all about my activities. He is a beloved brother and faithful minister and fellow servant[c] in the Lord. ⁸I have sent him to you for this very purpose, that you may know how we are and that he may encourage your hearts, ⁹and with him Onesimus, our faithful and beloved brother, who is one of you. They will tell you of everything that has taken place here.

¹⁰Aristarchus my fellow prisoner greets you, and Mark the cousin of Barnabas (concerning whom you have received instructions—if he comes to you, welcome him), ¹¹and Jesus who is called Justus. These are the only men of the circumcision among my fellow workers for the kingdom of God, and they have been a comfort to me. ¹²Epaphras, who is one of you, a servant of Christ Jesus, greets you, always struggling on your behalf in his prayers, that you may stand mature and fully assured in all the will of God. ¹³For I bear him witness that he has worked hard for you and for those in Laodicea and in Hierapolis. ¹⁴Luke the beloved physician greets you, as does Demas. ¹⁵Give my greetings to the brothers[d] at Laodicea, and to Nympha and the church in her house. ¹⁶And when this letter has been read among you, have it also read in the church of the Laodiceans; and see that you also read the letter from Laodicea. ¹⁷And say to Archippus, "See that you fulfil the ministry that you have received in the Lord."

¹⁸I, Paul, write this greeting with my own hand. Remember my chains. Grace be with you.

---

[a] Or your masters according to the flesh [b] For the contextual rendering of the Greek word *doulos*, see Preface; likewise for *servant* in verse 12
[c] For the contextual rendering of the Greek word *sundoulos*, see Preface
[d] Or brothers and sisters

THE FIRST LETTER OF PAUL TO THE THESSALONIANS

1 THESSALONIANS

GREETING

1 Paul, Silvanus, and Timothy,

To the church of the Thessalonians in God the Father and the Lord Jesus Christ:

Grace to you and peace.

THE THESSALONIANS' FAITH AND EXAMPLE

²We give thanks to God always for all of you, constantly[a] mentioning you in our prayers, ³remembering before our God and Father your work of faith and labour of love and steadfastness of hope in our Lord Jesus Christ. ⁴For we know, brothers[b] loved by God, that he has chosen you, ⁵because our gospel came to you not only in word, but also in power and in the Holy Spirit and with full conviction. You know what kind of men we proved to be among you for your sake. ⁶And you became imitators of us and of the Lord, for you received the word in much affliction, with the joy of the Holy Spirit, ⁷so that you became an example to all the believers in Macedonia and in Achaia. ⁸For not only has the word of the Lord sounded forth from you in Macedonia and Achaia, but your faith in God has gone forth everywhere, so that we need not say anything. ⁹For they themselves report concerning us the kind of reception we had among you, and how you turned to God from idols to serve the living and true God, ¹⁰and to wait for his Son from heaven, whom he raised from the dead, Jesus who delivers us from the wrath to come.

PAUL'S MINISTRY TO THE THESSALONIANS

2 For you yourselves know, brothers,[c] that our coming to you was not in vain. ²But though we had already suffered and been shamefully treated at Philippi, as you know, we had boldness in our God to declare to you the gospel of God in the midst of much conflict. ³For our appeal does not spring from error or impurity or any attempt to deceive, ⁴but just as we have been approved by God to be entrusted with the gospel, so we speak, not to please man, but to please God who tests our hearts. ⁵For we never came with words of flattery,[d] as you know, nor with a pretext for greed—God is witness. ⁶Nor did we seek glory from people, whether from you or from others, though we could have made demands as apostles of Christ. ⁷But we were gentle[e] among you, like a nursing mother taking care of her own children. ⁸So, being affectionately desirous of you, we were ready to share with you not only the gospel of God but also our own selves, because you had become very dear to us.

⁹For you remember, brothers, our labour and toil: we worked night and day, that we might not be a burden to any of you, while we proclaimed to you the gospel of God. ¹⁰You are witnesses, and God also, how holy and righteous and blameless was our conduct towards you believers. ¹¹For you know how, like a father with his children, ¹²we exhorted each one of you and encouraged you and charged you to walk in a manner worthy of God, who calls you into his own kingdom and glory.

¹³And we also thank God constantly[f] for this, that when you received the word of God, which you heard from us, you accepted it not as the word of men[g] but as what it really is, the word of God, which is at work in you believers. ¹⁴For you, brothers, became imitators of the churches of God in Christ Jesus that are in Judea. For you suffered the same things from your own countrymen as they did from the Jews,[h] ¹⁵who killed both the Lord Jesus and the prophets, and drove us out, and

---

[a] Or *without ceasing* [b] Or *brothers and sisters*. In New Testament usage, depending on the context, the plural Greek word *adelphoi* (translated "brothers") may refer either to *brothers* or to *brothers and sisters* [c] Or *brothers and sisters*; also verses 9, 14, 17 [d] Or *with a flattering speech* [e] Some manuscripts *infants* [f] Or *without ceasing* [g] The Greek word *anthropoi* can refer to both men and women [h] The Greek word *Ioudaioi* can refer to Jewish religious leaders, and others under their influence, who opposed the Christian faith in that time

1 THESSALONIANS 2–4

displease God and oppose all mankind ¹⁶by hindering us from speaking to the Gentiles that they might be saved—so as always to fill up the measure of their sins. But wrath has come upon them at last![1]

PAUL'S LONGING TO SEE THEM AGAIN

¹⁷But since we were torn away from you, brothers, for a short time, in person not in heart, we endeavoured the more eagerly and with great desire to see you face to face, ¹⁸because we wanted to come to you—I, Paul, again and again—but Satan hindered us. ¹⁹For what is our hope or joy or crown of boasting before our Lord Jesus at his coming? Is it not you? ²⁰For you are our glory and joy.

3 Therefore when we could bear it no longer, we were willing to be left behind at Athens alone, ²and we sent Timothy, our brother and God's co-worker[1] in the gospel of Christ, to establish and exhort you in your faith, ³that no one be moved by these afflictions. For you yourselves know that we are destined for this. ⁴For when we were with you, we kept telling you beforehand that we were to suffer affliction, just as it has come to pass, and just as you know. ⁵For this reason, when I could bear it no longer, I sent to learn about your faith, for fear that somehow the tempter had tempted you and our labour would be in vain.

TIMOTHY'S ENCOURAGING REPORT

⁶But now that Timothy has come to us from you, and has brought us the good news of your faith and love and reported that you always remember us kindly and long to see us, as we long to see you—⁷for this reason, brothers,[1] in all our distress and affliction we have been comforted about you through your faith. ⁸For now we live, if you are standing fast in the Lord. ⁹For what thanksgiving can we return to God for you, for all the joy that we feel for your sake before our God, ¹⁰as we pray most earnestly night and day that we may see you face to face and supply what is lacking in your faith?

¹¹Now may our God and Father himself, and our Lord Jesus, direct our way to you, ¹²and may the Lord make you increase and abound in love for one another and for all, as we do for you, ¹³so that he may establish your hearts blameless in holiness before our God and Father, at the coming of our Lord Jesus with all his saints.

A LIFE PLEASING TO GOD

4 Finally, then, brothers,[1] we ask and urge you in the Lord Jesus, that as you received from us how you ought to walk and to please God, just as you are doing, that you do so more and more. ²For you know what instructions we gave you through the Lord Jesus. ³For this is the will of God, your sanctification:[1] that you abstain from sexual immorality; ⁴that each one of you know how to control his own body[1] in holiness and honour, ⁵not in the passion of lust like the Gentiles who do not know God; ⁶that no one transgress and wrong his brother in this matter, because the Lord is an avenger in all these things, as we told you beforehand and solemnly warned you. ⁷For God has not called us for impurity, but in holiness. ⁸Therefore whoever disregards this, disregards not man but God, who gives his Holy Spirit to you.

⁹Now concerning brotherly love you have no need for anyone to write to you, for you yourselves have been taught by God to love one another, ¹⁰for that indeed is what you are doing to all the brothers throughout Macedonia. But we urge you, brothers, to do this more and more, ¹¹and to aspire to live quietly, and to mind your own affairs, and to work with your hands, as we instructed you, ¹²so that you may walk properly before outsiders and be dependent on no one.

THE COMING OF THE LORD

¹³But we do not want you to be uninformed, brothers, about those who are asleep, that you may not grieve as others do who have no hope. ¹⁴For since we believe that Jesus died and rose again, even so, through Jesus, God will bring with him those who have fallen asleep. ¹⁵For this we declare to you by a word from the Lord,[1] that we who are alive, who are left until the coming of the Lord, will not precede those who have fallen asleep. ¹⁶For the Lord himself will descend from heaven with a cry of command, with the voice of an archangel, and with the sound of the trumpet of God. And the dead in Christ will rise first. ¹⁷Then we who are alive, who are left, will be caught up together with them in the clouds to meet the Lord in the air, and so we will always be

---

[1] Or *completely*, or *for ever* [1] Some manuscripts *servant* [1] Or *brothers and sisters* [1] Or *brothers and sisters*; also verses 10, 13 [1] Or *your holiness* [1] Or *how to take a wife for himself*; Greek *how to possess his own vessel* [1] Or *by the word of the Lord*

with the Lord. ⁱ⁸Therefore encourage one another with these words.

THE DAY OF THE LORD

5 Now concerning the times and the seasons, brothers,ᵃ you have no need to have anything written to you. ²For you yourselves are fully aware that the day of the Lord will come like a thief in the night. ³While people are saying, "There is peace and security", then sudden destruction will come upon them as labour pains come upon a pregnant woman, and they will not escape. ⁴But you are not in darkness, brothers, for that day to surprise you like a thief. ⁵For you are all childrenᵇ of light, children of the day. We are not of the night or of the darkness. ⁶So then let us not sleep, as others do, but let us keep awake and be sober. ⁷For those who sleep, sleep at night, and those who get drunk, are drunk at night. ⁸But since we belong to the day, let us be sober, having put on the breastplate of faith and love, and for a helmet the hope of salvation. ⁹For God has not destined us for wrath, but to obtain salvation through our Lord Jesus Christ, ¹⁰who died for us so that whether we are awake or asleep we might live with him. ¹¹Therefore encourage one another and build one another up, just as you are doing.

FINAL INSTRUCTIONS AND BENEDICTION

¹²We ask you, brothers, to respect those who labour among you and are over you in the Lord and admonish you, ¹³and to esteem them very highly in love because of their work. Be at peace among yourselves. ¹⁴And we urge you, brothers, admonish the idle,ᶜ encourage the faint-hearted, help the weak, be patient with them all. ¹⁵See that no one repays anyone evil for evil, but always seek to do good to one another and to everyone. ¹⁶Rejoice always, ¹⁷pray without ceasing, ¹⁸give thanks in all circumstances; for this is the will of God in Christ Jesus for you. ¹⁹Do not quench the Spirit. ²⁰Do not despise prophecies, ²¹but test everything; hold fast what is good. ²²Abstain from every form of evil.

²³Now may the God of peace himself sanctify you completely, and may your whole spirit and soul and body be kept blameless at the coming of our Lord Jesus Christ. ²⁴He who calls you is faithful; he will surely do it.

²⁵Brothers, pray for us.

²⁶Greet all the brothers with a holy kiss.

²⁷I put you under oath before the Lord to have this letter read to all the brothers.

²⁸The grace of our Lord Jesus Christ be with you.

ᵃOr *brothers and sisters*; also verses 4, 12, 14, 25, 26, 27   ᵇOr *sons*; twice in this verse   ᶜOr *disorderly*, or *undisciplined*

THE SECOND LETTER OF PAUL TO THE THESSALONIANS
2 THESSALONIANS

GREETING

1 Paul, Silvanus, and Timothy,
To the church of the Thessalonians in God our Father and the Lord Jesus Christ: ²Grace to you and peace from God our Father and the Lord Jesus Christ.

THANKSGIVING

³We ought always to give thanks to God for you, brothers,ᵃ as is right, because your faith is growing abundantly, and the love of every one of you for one another is increasing. ⁴Therefore we ourselves boast about you in the churches of God for your steadfastness and faith in all your persecutions and in the afflictions that you are enduring.

THE JUDGEMENT AT CHRIST'S COMING

⁵This is evidence of the righteous judgement of God, that you may be considered worthy of the kingdom of God, for which you are also suffering— ⁶since indeed God considers it just to repay with affliction those who afflict you, ⁷and to grant relief to you who are afflicted as well as to us, when the Lord Jesus is revealed from heaven with his mighty angels ⁸in flaming fire, inflicting vengeance on those who do not know God and on those who do not obey the gospel of our Lord Jesus. ⁹They will suffer the punishment of eternal destruction, away fromᵇ the presence of the Lord and from the glory of his might, ¹⁰when he comes on that day to be glorified in his saints, and to be marvelled at among all who have believed, because our testimony to you was believed. ¹¹To this end we always pray for you, that our God may make you worthy of his calling and may fulfil every resolve for good and every work of faith by his power, ¹²so that the name of our Lord Jesus may be glorified in you, and you in him, according to the grace of our God and the Lord Jesus Christ.

THE MAN OF LAWLESSNESS

2 Now concerning the coming of our Lord Jesus Christ and our being gathered together to him, we ask you, brothers,ᶜ ²not to be quickly shaken in mind or alarmed, either by a spirit or a spoken word, or a letter seeming to be from us, to the effect that the day of the Lord has come. ³Let no one deceive you in any way. For that day will not come, unless the rebellion comes first, and the man of lawlessnessᵈ is revealed, the son of destruction,ᵉ ⁴who opposes and exalts himself against every so-called god or object of worship, so that he takes his seat in the temple of God, proclaiming himself to be God. ⁵Do you not remember that when I was still with you I told you these things? ⁶And you know what is restraining him now so that he may be revealed in his time. ⁷For the mystery of lawlessness is already at work. Only he who now restrains it will do so until he is out of the way. ⁸And then the lawless one will be revealed, whom the Lord Jesus will kill with the breath of his mouth and bring to nothing by the appearance of his coming. ⁹The coming of the lawless one is by the activity of Satan with all power and false signs and wonders, ¹⁰and with all wicked deception for those who are perishing, because they refused to love the truth and so be saved. ¹¹Therefore God sends them a strong delusion, so that they may believe what is false, ¹²in order that all may be condemned who did not believe the truth but had pleasure in unrighteousness.

STAND FIRM

¹³But we ought always to give thanks to God for you, brothers beloved by the Lord,

---

ᵃOr *brothers and sisters*. In New Testament usage, depending on the context, the plural Greek word *adelphoi* (translated "brothers") may refer either to *brothers* or to *brothers and sisters*   ᵇOr *destruction that comes from*   ᶜOr *brothers and sisters*; also verses 13, 15   ᵈSome manuscripts *sin*   ᵉGreek *the son of perdition* (a Hebrew idiom)

because God chose you as the firstfruits[a] to be saved, through sanctification by the Spirit and belief in the truth. ¹⁴To this he called you through our gospel, so that you may obtain the glory of our Lord Jesus Christ. ¹⁵So then, brothers, stand firm and hold to the traditions that you were taught by us, either by our spoken word or by our letter.

¹⁶Now may our Lord Jesus Christ himself, and God our Father, who loved us and gave us eternal comfort and good hope through grace, ¹⁷comfort your hearts and establish them in every good work and word.

PRAY FOR US

3 Finally, brothers,[b] pray for us, that the word of the Lord may speed ahead and be honoured,[c] as happened among you, ²and that we may be delivered from wicked and evil men. For not all have faith. ³But the Lord is faithful. He will establish you and guard you against the evil one.[d] ⁴And we have confidence in the Lord about you, that you are doing and will do the things that we command. ⁵May the Lord direct your hearts to the love of God and to the steadfastness of Christ.

WARNING AGAINST IDLENESS

⁶Now we command you, brothers, in the name of our Lord Jesus Christ, that you keep away from any brother who is walking in idleness and not in accord with the tradition that you received from us. ⁷For you yourselves know how you ought to imitate us, because we were not idle when we were with you, ⁸nor did we eat anyone's bread without paying for it, but with toil and labour we worked night and day, that we might not be a burden to any of you. ⁹It was not because we do not have that right, but to give you in ourselves an example to imitate. ¹⁰For even when we were with you, we would give you this command: If anyone is not willing to work, let him not eat. ¹¹For we hear that some among you walk in idleness, not busy at work, but busybodies. ¹²Now such persons we command and encourage in the Lord Jesus Christ to do their work quietly and to earn their own living.[e]

¹³As for you, brothers, do not grow weary in doing good. ¹⁴If anyone does not obey what we say in this letter, take note of that person, and have nothing to do with him, that he may be ashamed. ¹⁵Do not regard him as an enemy, but warn him as a brother.

BENEDICTION

¹⁶Now may the Lord of peace himself give you peace at all times in every way. The Lord be with you all.

¹⁷I, Paul, write this greeting with my own hand. This is the sign of genuineness in every letter of mine; it is the way I write. ¹⁸The grace of our Lord Jesus Christ be with you all.

---

[a]Some manuscripts *chose you from the beginning* [b]Or *brothers and sisters*; also verses 6, 13 [c]Or *glorified* [d]Or *evil* [e]Greek *to eat their own bread*

THE FIRST LETTER OF PAUL TO TIMOTHY

1 TIMOTHY

GREETING

1 Paul, an apostle of Christ Jesus by command of God our Saviour and of Christ Jesus our hope, ²To Timothy, my true child in the faith: Grace, mercy, and peace from God the Father and Christ Jesus our Lord.

WARNING AGAINST FALSE TEACHERS

³As I urged you when I was going to Macedonia, remain at Ephesus so that you may charge certain persons not to teach any different doctrine, ⁴nor to devote themselves to myths and endless genealogies, which promote speculations rather than the stewardship*ᵃ* from God that is by faith. ⁵The aim of our charge is love that issues from a pure heart and a good conscience and a sincere faith. ⁶Certain persons, by swerving from these, have wandered away into vain discussion, ⁷desiring to be teachers of the law, without understanding either what they are saying or the things about which they make confident assertions.

⁸Now we know that the law is good, if one uses it lawfully, ⁹understanding this, that the law is not laid down for the just but for the lawless and disobedient, for the ungodly and sinners, for the unholy and profane, for those who strike their fathers and mothers, for murderers, ¹⁰the sexually immoral, men who practise homosexuality, enslavers,*ᵇ* liars, perjurers, and whatever else is contrary to sound*ᶜ* doctrine, ¹¹in accordance with the gospel of the glory of the blessed God with which I have been entrusted.

CHRIST JESUS CAME TO SAVE SINNERS

¹²I thank him who has given me strength, Christ Jesus our Lord, because he judged me faithful, appointing me to his service, ¹³though formerly I was a blasphemer, persecutor, and insolent opponent. But I received mercy because I had acted ignorantly in unbelief, ¹⁴and the grace of our Lord overflowed for me with the faith and love that are in Christ Jesus. ¹⁵The saying is trustworthy and deserving of full acceptance, that Christ Jesus came into the world to save sinners, of whom I am the foremost. ¹⁶But I received mercy for this reason, that in me, as the foremost, Jesus Christ might display his perfect patience as an example to those who were to believe in him for eternal life. ¹⁷To the King of the ages, immortal, invisible, the only God, be honour and glory for ever and ever.*ᵈ* Amen.

¹⁸This charge I entrust to you, Timothy, my child, in accordance with the prophecies previously made about you, that by them you may wage the good warfare, ¹⁹holding faith and a good conscience. By rejecting this, some have made shipwreck of their faith, ²⁰among whom are Hymenaeus and Alexander, whom I have handed over to Satan that they may learn not to blaspheme.

PRAY FOR ALL PEOPLE

2 First of all, then, I urge that supplications, prayers, intercessions, and thanksgivings be made for all people, ²for kings and all who are in high positions, that we may lead a peaceful and quiet life, godly and dignified in every way. ³This is good, and it is pleasing in the sight of God our Saviour, ⁴who desires all people to be saved and to come to the knowledge of the truth. ⁵For there is one God, and there is one mediator between God and men, the man*ᵉ* Christ Jesus, ⁶who gave himself as a ransom for all, which is the testimony given at the proper time. ⁷For this I was appointed a preacher and an apostle (I am telling the truth, I am not lying), a teacher of the Gentiles in faith and truth.

ᵃOr good order ᵇThat is, those who take someone captive in order to sell him into slavery ᶜOr healthy ᵈGreek to the ages of ages ᵉmen and man render the same Greek word that is translated people in verses 1 and 4

⁸I desire then that in every place the men should pray, lifting holy hands without anger or quarrelling; ⁹likewise also that women should adorn themselves in respectable apparel, with modesty and self-control, not with braided hair and gold or pearls or costly attire, ¹⁰but with what is proper for women who profess godliness—with good works. ¹¹Let a woman learn quietly with all submissiveness. ¹²I do not permit a woman to teach or to exercise authority over a man; rather, she is to remain quiet. ¹³For Adam was formed first, then Eve; ¹⁴and Adam was not deceived, but the woman was deceived and became a transgressor. ¹⁵Yet she will be saved through childbearing—if they continue in faith and love and holiness, with self-control.

QUALIFICATIONS FOR OVERSEERS

3 The saying is trustworthy: If anyone aspires to the office of overseer, he desires a noble task. ²Therefore an overseer[a] must be above reproach, the husband of one wife,[b] sober-minded, self-controlled, respectable, hospitable, able to teach, ³not a drunkard, not violent but gentle, not quarrelsome, not a lover of money. ⁴He must manage his own household well, with all dignity keeping his children submissive, ⁵for if someone does not know how to manage his own household, how will he care for God's church? ⁶He must not be a recent convert, or he may become puffed up with conceit and fall into the condemnation of the devil. ⁷Moreover, he must be well thought of by outsiders, so that he may not fall into disgrace, into a snare of the devil.

QUALIFICATIONS FOR DEACONS

⁸Deacons likewise must be dignified, not double-tongued,[c] not addicted to much wine, not greedy for dishonest gain. ⁹They must hold the mystery of the faith with a clear conscience. ¹⁰And let them also be tested first; then let them serve as deacons if they prove themselves blameless. ¹¹Their wives likewise[d] must be dignified, not slanderers, but sober-minded, faithful in all things. ¹²Let deacons each be the husband of one wife, managing their children and their own households well. ¹³For those who serve well as deacons gain a good standing for themselves and also great confidence in the faith that is in Christ Jesus.

THE MYSTERY OF GODLINESS

¹⁴I hope to come to you soon, but I am writing these things to you so that, ¹⁵if I delay, you may know how one ought to behave in the household of God, which is the church of the living God, a pillar and buttress of the truth. ¹⁶Great indeed, we confess, is the mystery of godliness:

> He[e] was manifested in the flesh,
> vindicated[f] by the Spirit,[g]
> seen by angels,
> proclaimed among the nations,
> believed on in the world,
> taken up in glory.

SOME WILL DEPART FROM THE FAITH

4 Now the Spirit expressly says that in later times some will depart from the faith by devoting themselves to deceitful spirits and teachings of demons, ²through the insincerity of liars whose consciences are seared, ³who forbid marriage and require abstinence from foods that God created to be received with thanksgiving by those who believe and know the truth. ⁴For everything created by God is good, and nothing is to be rejected if it is received with thanksgiving, ⁵for it is made holy by the word of God and prayer.

A GOOD SERVANT OF CHRIST JESUS

⁶If you put these things before the brothers,[h] you will be a good servant of Christ Jesus, being trained in the words of the faith and of the good doctrine that you have followed. ⁷Have nothing to do with irreverent, silly myths. Rather train yourself for godliness; ⁸for while bodily training is of some value, godliness is of value in every way, as it holds promise for the present life and also for the life to come. ⁹The saying is trustworthy and deserving of full acceptance. ¹⁰For to this end we toil and strive,[i] because we have our hope set on the living God, who is the Saviour of all people, especially of those who believe.

¹¹Command and teach these things. ¹²Let no one despise you for your youth, but set the believers an example in speech, in conduct,

---

[a] Or bishop; Greek episkopos; a similar term occurs in verse 1 [b] Or a man of one woman; also verse 12 [c] Or devious in speech [d] Or Wives likewise, or Women likewise [e] Greek Who; some manuscripts God; others Which [f] Or justified [g] Or vindicated in spirit [h] Or brothers and sisters. In New Testament usage, depending on the context, the plural Greek word adelphoi (translated "brothers") may refer either to brothers or to brothers and sisters [i] Some manuscripts and suffer reproach

in love, in faith, in purity. ¹³Until I come, devote yourself to the public reading of Scripture, to exhortation, to teaching. ¹⁴Do not neglect the gift you have, which was given you by prophecy when the council of elders laid their hands on you. ¹⁵Practise these things, immerse yourself in them,ᵃ so that all may see your progress. ¹⁶Keep a close watch on yourself and on the teaching. Persist in this, for by so doing you will save both yourself and your hearers.

INSTRUCTIONS FOR THE CHURCH

5 Do not rebuke an older man but encourage him as you would a father, younger men as brothers, ²older women as mothers, younger women as sisters, in all purity.

³Honour widows who are truly widows. ⁴But if a widow has children or grandchildren, let them first learn to show godliness to their own household and to make some return to their parents, for this is pleasing in the sight of God. ⁵She who is truly a widow, left all alone, has set her hope on God and continues in supplications and prayers night and day, ⁶but she who is self-indulgent is dead even while she lives. ⁷Command these things as well, so that they may be without reproach. ⁸But if anyone does not provide for his relatives, and especially for members of his household, he has denied the faith and is worse than an unbeliever.

⁹Let a widow be enrolled if she is not less than sixty years of age, having been the wife of one husband,ᵇ ¹⁰and having a reputation for good works: if she has brought up children, has shown hospitality, has washed the feet of the saints, has cared for the afflicted, and has devoted herself to every good work. ¹¹But refuse to enrol younger widows, for when their passions draw them away from Christ, they desire to marry ¹²and so incur condemnation for having abandoned their former faith. ¹³Besides that, they learn to be idlers, going about from house to house, and not only idlers, but also gossips and busybodies, saying what they should not. ¹⁴So I would have younger widows marry, bear children, manage their households, and give the adversary no occasion for slander. ¹⁵For some have already strayed after Satan. ¹⁶If any believing woman has relatives who are widows, let her care for them. Let the church not be burdened, so that it may care for those who are truly widows.

¹⁷Let the elders who rule well be considered worthy of double honour, especially those who labour in preaching and teaching. ¹⁸For the Scripture says, "You shall not muzzle an ox when it treads out the grain", and, "The labourer deserves his wages." ¹⁹Do not admit a charge against an elder except on the evidence of two or three witnesses. ²⁰As for those who persist in sin, rebuke them in the presence of all, so that the rest may stand in fear. ²¹In the presence of God and of Christ Jesus and of the elect angels I charge you to keep these rules without prejudging, doing nothing from partiality. ²²Do not be hasty in the laying on of hands, nor take part in the sins of others; keep yourself pure. ²³(No longer drink only water, but use a little wine for the sake of your stomach and your frequent ailments.) ²⁴The sins of some people are conspicuous, going before them to judgement, but the sins of others appear later. ²⁵So also good works are conspicuous, and even those that are not cannot remain hidden.

6 Let all who are under a yoke as bondservantsᶜ regard their own masters as worthy of all honour, so that the name of God and the teaching may not be reviled. ²Those who have believing masters must not be disrespectful on the ground that they are brothers; rather they must serve all the better since those who benefit by their good service are believers and beloved.

FALSE TEACHERS AND TRUE CONTENTMENT

Teach and urge these things. ³If anyone teaches a different doctrine and does not agree with the soundᵈ words of our Lord Jesus Christ and the teaching that accords with godliness, ⁴he is puffed up with conceit and understands nothing. He has an unhealthy craving for controversy and for quarrels about words, which produce envy, dissension, slander, evil suspicions, ⁵and constant friction among people who are depraved in mind and deprived of the truth, imagining that godliness is a means of gain. ⁶But godliness with contentment is great gain, ⁷for we brought nothing into the world, andᵉ we cannot take anything out of the world. ⁸But if we have food and clothing, with these we will be content. ⁹But those

---

ᵃGreek *be in them*   ᵇOr *a woman of one man*   ᶜFor the contextual rendering of the Greek word *doulos*, see Preface   ᵈOr *healthy*
ᵉGreek *for*; some manuscripts insert [it is] *certain* [that]

who desire to be rich fall into temptation, into a snare, into many senseless and harmful desires that plunge people into ruin and destruction. ¹⁰For the love of money is a root of all kinds of evils. It is through this craving that some have wandered away from the faith and pierced themselves with many pangs.

FIGHT THE GOOD FIGHT OF FAITH

¹¹But as for you, O man of God, flee these things. Pursue righteousness, godliness, faith, love, steadfastness, gentleness. ¹²Fight the good fight of the faith. Take hold of the eternal life to which you were called and about which you made the good confession in the presence of many witnesses. ¹³I charge you in the presence of God, who gives life to all things, and of Christ Jesus, who in his testimony before*ᵃ* Pontius Pilate made the good confession, ¹⁴to keep the commandment unstained and free from reproach until the appearing of our Lord Jesus Christ, ¹⁵which he will display at the proper time — he who is the blessed and only Sovereign, the King of kings and Lord of lords, ¹⁶who alone has immortality, who dwells in unapproachable light, whom no one has ever seen or can see. To him be honour and eternal dominion. Amen.

¹⁷As for the rich in this present age, charge them not to be haughty, nor to set their hopes on the uncertainty of riches, but on God, who richly provides us with everything to enjoy. ¹⁸They are to do good, to be rich in good works, to be generous and ready to share, ¹⁹thus storing up treasure for themselves as a good foundation for the future, so that they may take hold of that which is truly life.

²⁰O Timothy, guard the deposit entrusted to you. Avoid the irreverent babble and contradictions of what is falsely called "knowledge", ²¹for by professing it some have swerved from the faith.

Grace be with you.*ᵇ*

---

*ᵃ*Or *in the time of*   *ᵇ*The Greek for *you* is plural

THE SECOND LETTER OF PAUL TO TIMOTHY

2 TIMOTHY

GREETING

1 Paul, an apostle of Christ Jesus by the will of God according to the promise of the life that is in Christ Jesus, ²To Timothy, my beloved child:

Grace, mercy, and peace from God the Father and Christ Jesus our Lord.

GUARD THE DEPOSIT ENTRUSTED TO YOU

³I thank God whom I serve, as did my ancestors, with a clear conscience, as I remember you constantly in my prayers night and day. ⁴As I remember your tears, I long to see you, that I may be filled with joy. ⁵I am reminded of your sincere faith, a faith that dwelt first in your grandmother Lois and your mother Eunice and now, I am sure, dwells in you as well. ⁶For this reason I remind you to fan into flame the gift of God, which is in you through the laying on of my hands, ⁷for God gave us a spirit not of fear but of power and love and self-control.

⁸Therefore do not be ashamed of the testimony about our Lord, nor of me his prisoner, but share in suffering for the gospel by the power of God, ⁹who saved us and called us to*ᵃ* a holy calling, not because of our works but because of his own purpose and grace, which he gave us in Christ Jesus before the ages began,*ᵇ* ¹⁰and which now has been manifested through the appearing of our Saviour Christ Jesus, who abolished death and brought life and immortality to light through the gospel, ¹¹for which I was appointed a preacher and apostle and teacher, ¹²which is why I suffer as I do. But I am not ashamed, for I know whom I have believed, and I am convinced that he is able to guard until that day what has been entrusted to me.*ᶜ* ¹³Follow the pattern of the sound*ᵈ* words that you have heard from me, in the faith and love that are in Christ Jesus. ¹⁴By the Holy Spirit who dwells within us, guard the good deposit entrusted to you.

¹⁵You are aware that all who are in Asia turned away from me, among whom are Phygelus and Hermogenes. ¹⁶May the Lord grant mercy to the household of Onesiphorus, for he often refreshed me and was not ashamed of my chains, ¹⁷but when he arrived in Rome he searched for me earnestly and found me— ¹⁸may the Lord grant him to find mercy from the Lord on that day!—and you well know all the service he rendered at Ephesus.

A GOOD SOLDIER OF CHRIST JESUS

2 You then, my child, be strengthened by the grace that is in Christ Jesus, ²and what you have heard from me in the presence of many witnesses entrust to faithful men,*ᵉ* who will be able to teach others also. ³Share in suffering as a good soldier of Christ Jesus. ⁴No soldier gets entangled in civilian pursuits, since his aim is to please the one who enlisted him. ⁵An athlete is not crowned unless he competes according to the rules. ⁶It is the hard-working farmer who ought to have the first share of the crops. ⁷Think over what I say, for the Lord will give you understanding in everything.

⁸Remember Jesus Christ, risen from the dead, the offspring of David, as preached in my gospel, ⁹for which I am suffering, bound with chains as a criminal. But the word of God is not bound! ¹⁰Therefore I endure everything for the sake of the elect, that they also may obtain the salvation that is in Christ Jesus with eternal glory. ¹¹The saying is trustworthy, for:

If we have died with him, we
  will also live with him;
¹² if we endure, we will also
  reign with him;
if we deny him, he also will deny us;

ᵃOr with ᵇGreek before times eternal ᶜOr what I have entrusted to him; Greek my deposit ᵈOr healthy ᵉThe Greek word anthropoi can refer to both men and women, depending on the context

¹³ if we are faithless, he
  remains faithful—

for he cannot deny himself.

A WORKER APPROVED BY GOD

¹⁴Remind them of these things, and charge them before God[a] not to quarrel about words, which does no good, but only ruins the hearers. ¹⁵Do your best to present yourself to God as one approved,[b] a worker who has no need to be ashamed, rightly handling the word of truth. ¹⁶But avoid irreverent babble, for it will lead people into more and more ungodliness, ¹⁷and their talk will spread like gangrene. Among them are Hymenaeus and Philetus, ¹⁸who have swerved from the truth, saying that the resurrection has already happened. They are upsetting the faith of some. ¹⁹But God's firm foundation stands, bearing this seal: "The Lord knows those who are his", and, "Let everyone who names the name of the Lord depart from iniquity."

²⁰Now in a great house there are not only vessels of gold and silver but also of wood and clay, some for honourable use, some for dishonourable. ²¹Therefore, if anyone cleanses himself from what is dishonourable,[c] he will be a vessel for honourable use, set apart as holy, useful to the master of the house, ready for every good work.

²²So flee youthful passions and pursue righteousness, faith, love, and peace, along with those who call on the Lord from a pure heart. ²³Have nothing to do with foolish, ignorant controversies; you know that they breed quarrels. ²⁴And the Lord's servant[d] must not be quarrelsome but kind to everyone, able to teach, patiently enduring evil, ²⁵correcting his opponents with gentleness. God may perhaps grant them repentance leading to a knowledge of the truth, ²⁶and they may come to their senses and escape from the snare of the devil, after being captured by him to do his will.

GODLESSNESS IN THE LAST DAYS

3 But understand this, that in the last days there will come times of difficulty. ²For people will be lovers of self, lovers of money, proud, arrogant, abusive, disobedient to their parents, ungrateful, unholy, ³heartless, unappeasable, slanderous, without self-control, brutal, not loving good, ⁴treacherous, reckless, swollen with conceit, lovers of pleasure rather than lovers of God, ⁵having the appearance of godliness, but denying its power. Avoid such people. ⁶For among them are those who creep into households and capture weak women, burdened with sins and led astray by various passions, ⁷always learning and never able to arrive at a knowledge of the truth. ⁸Just as Jannes and Jambres opposed Moses, so these men also oppose the truth, men corrupted in mind and disqualified regarding the faith. ⁹But they will not get very far, for their folly will be plain to all, as was that of those two men.

ALL SCRIPTURE IS BREATHED OUT BY GOD

¹⁰You, however, have followed my teaching, my conduct, my aim in life, my faith, my patience, my love, my steadfastness, ¹¹my persecutions and sufferings that happened to me at Antioch, at Iconium, and at Lystra—which persecutions I endured; yet from them all the Lord rescued me. ¹²Indeed, all who desire to live a godly life in Christ Jesus will be persecuted, ¹³while evil people and impostors will go on from bad to worse, deceiving and being deceived. ¹⁴But as for you, continue in what you have learned and have firmly believed, knowing from whom[e] you learned it ¹⁵and how from childhood you have been acquainted with the sacred writings, which are able to make you wise for salvation through faith in Christ Jesus. ¹⁶All Scripture is breathed out by God and profitable for teaching, for reproof, for correction, and for training in righteousness, ¹⁷that the man of God[f] may be complete, equipped for every good work.

PREACH THE WORD

4 I charge you in the presence of God and of Christ Jesus, who is to judge the living and the dead, and by his appearing and his kingdom: ²preach the word; be ready in season and out of season; reprove, rebuke, and exhort, with complete patience and teaching. ³For the time is coming when people will not endure sound[g] teaching, but having itching ears they will accumulate for themselves teachers to suit their own passions, ⁴and will turn away from listening to the truth and wander off into myths. ⁵As for

---

[a]Some manuscripts *the Lord* [b]That is, one approved after being tested [c]Greek *from these things* [d]For the contextual rendering of the Greek word *doulos*, see Preface [e]The Greek for *whom* is plural [f]That is, a messenger of God (the phrase echoes a common Old Testament expression) [g]Or *healthy*

you, always be sober-minded, endure suffering, do the work of an evangelist, fulfil your ministry.

⁶For I am already being poured out as a drink offering, and the time of my departure has come. ⁷I have fought the good fight, I have finished the race, I have kept the faith. ⁸Henceforth there is laid up for me the crown of righteousness, which the Lord, the righteous judge, will award to me on that day, and not only to me but also to all who have loved his appearing.

PERSONAL INSTRUCTIONS

⁹Do your best to come to me soon. ¹⁰For Demas, in love with this present world, has deserted me and gone to Thessalonica. Crescens has gone to Galatia,ᵃ Titus to Dalmatia. ¹¹Luke alone is with me. Get Mark and bring him with you, for he is very useful to me for ministry. ¹²Tychicus I have sent to Ephesus. ¹³When you come, bring the cloak that I left with Carpus at Troas, also the books, and above all the parchments. ¹⁴Alexander the coppersmith did me great harm; the Lord will repay him according to his deeds. ¹⁵Beware of him yourself, for he strongly opposed our message. ¹⁶At my first defence no one came to stand by me, but all deserted me. May it not be charged against them! ¹⁷But the Lord stood by me and strengthened me, so that through me the message might be fully proclaimed and all the Gentiles might hear it. So I was rescued from the lion's mouth. ¹⁸The Lord will rescue me from every evil deed and bring me safely into his heavenly kingdom. To him be the glory for ever and ever. Amen.

FINAL GREETINGS

¹⁹Greet Prisca and Aquila, and the household of Onesiphorus. ²⁰Erastus remained at Corinth, and I left Trophimus, who was ill, at Miletus. ²¹Do your best to come before winter. Eubulus sends greetings to you, as do Pudens and Linus and Claudia and all the brothers.ᵇ

²²The Lord be with your spirit. Grace be with you.ᶜ

ᵃSome manuscripts *Gaul* ᵇOr *brothers and sisters*. In New Testament usage, depending on the context, the plural Greek word *adelphoi* (translated "brothers") may refer either to *brothers* or to *brothers and sisters* ᶜThe Greek for *you* is plural

THE LETTER OF PAUL TO
TITUS

GREETING

1 Paul, a servant[a] of God and an apostle of Jesus Christ, for the sake of the faith of God's elect and their knowledge of the truth, which accords with godliness, ²in hope of eternal life, which God, who never lies, promised before the ages began[b] ³and at the proper time manifested in his word[c] through the preaching with which I have been entrusted by the command of God our Saviour;

⁴To Titus, my true child in a common faith: Grace and peace from God the Father and Christ Jesus our Saviour.

QUALIFICATIONS FOR ELDERS

⁵This is why I left you in Crete, so that you might put what remained into order, and appoint elders in every town as I directed you — ⁶if anyone is above reproach, the husband of one wife,[d] and his children are believers[e] and not open to the charge of debauchery or insubordination. ⁷For an overseer,[f] as God's steward, must be above reproach. He must not be arrogant or quick-tempered or a drunkard or violent or greedy for gain, ⁸but hospitable, a lover of good, self-controlled, upright, holy, and disciplined. ⁹He must hold firm to the trustworthy word as taught, so that he may be able to give instruction in sound[g] doctrine and also to rebuke those who contradict it.

¹⁰For there are many who are insubordinate, empty talkers and deceivers, especially those of the circumcision party.[h] ¹¹They must be silenced, since they are upsetting whole families by teaching for shameful gain what they ought not to teach. ¹²One of the Cretans,[i] a prophet of their own, said, "Cretans are always liars, evil beasts, lazy gluttons."[j] ¹³This testimony is true. Therefore rebuke them sharply, that they may be sound in the faith, ¹⁴not devoting themselves to Jewish myths and the commands of people who turn away from the truth. ¹⁵To the pure, all things are pure, but to the defiled and unbelieving, nothing is pure; but both their minds and their consciences are defiled. ¹⁶They profess to know God, but they deny him by their works. They are detestable, disobedient, unfit for any good work.

TEACH SOUND DOCTRINE

2 But as for you, teach what accords with sound[k] doctrine. ²Older men are to be sober-minded, dignified, self-controlled, sound in faith, in love, and in steadfastness. ³Older women likewise are to be reverent in behaviour, not slanderers or slaves to much wine. They are to teach what is good, ⁴and so train the young women to love their husbands and children, ⁵to be self-controlled, pure, working at home, kind, and submissive to their own husbands, that the word of God may not be reviled. ⁶Likewise, urge the younger men to be self-controlled. ⁷Show yourself in all respects to be a model of good works, and in your teaching show integrity, dignity, ⁸and sound speech that cannot be condemned, so that an opponent may be put to shame, having nothing evil to say about us. ⁹Bondservants[l] are to be submissive to their own masters in everything; they are to be well-pleasing, not argumentative, ¹⁰not pilfering, but showing all good faith, so that in everything they may adorn the doctrine of God our Saviour.

¹¹For the grace of God has appeared, bringing salvation for all people. ¹²training us to renounce ungodliness and worldly passions, and to live self-controlled, upright, and godly lives in the present age, ¹³waiting for our blessed hope, the appearing of the glory of our great God and Saviour Jesus Christ, ¹⁴who gave himself for us to redeem us from all lawlessness and to purify for himself a people for his own possession who are zealous for good works.

---

[a] For the contextual rendering of the Greek word *doulos*, see Preface [b] Greek *before times eternal* [c] Or *manifested his word* [d] Or *a man of one woman* [e] Or *are faithful* [f] Or *bishop*; Greek *episkopos* [g] Or *healthy*; also verse 13 [h] Or *especially those of the circumcision* [i] Greek *One of them* [j] Probably from Epimenides of Crete [k] Or *healthy*; also verses 2, 8 [l] For the contextual rendering of the Greek word *doulos*, see Preface

¹⁵Declare these things; exhort and rebuke with all authority. Let no one disregard you.

BE READY FOR EVERY GOOD WORK

3 Remind them to be submissive to rulers and authorities, to be obedient, to be ready for every good work, ²to speak evil of no one, to avoid quarrelling, to be gentle, and to show perfect courtesy towards all people. ³For we ourselves were once foolish, disobedient, led astray, slaves to various passions and pleasures, passing our days in malice and envy, hated by others and hating one another. ⁴But when the goodness and loving kindness of God our Saviour appeared, ⁵he saved us, not because of works done by us in righteousness, but according to his own mercy, by the washing of regeneration and renewal of the Holy Spirit, ⁶whom he poured out on us richly through Jesus Christ our Saviour, ⁷so that being justified by his grace we might become heirs according to the hope of eternal life. ⁸The saying is trustworthy, and I want you to insist on these things, so that those who have believed in God may be careful to devote themselves to good works. These things are excellent and profitable for people. ⁹But avoid foolish controversies, genealogies, dissensions, and quarrels about the law, for they are unprofitable and worthless. ¹⁰As for a person who stirs up division, after warning him once and then twice, have nothing more to do with him, ¹¹knowing that such a person is warped and sinful; he is self-condemned.

FINAL INSTRUCTIONS AND GREETINGS

¹²When I send Artemas or Tychicus to you, do your best to come to me at Nicopolis, for I have decided to spend the winter there. ¹³Do your best to speed Zenas the lawyer and Apollos on their way; see that they lack nothing. ¹⁴And let our people learn to devote themselves to good works, so as to help cases of urgent need, and not be unfruitful.

¹⁵All who are with me send greetings to you. Greet those who love us in the faith.

Grace be with you all.

THE LETTER OF PAUL TO PHILEMON

GREETING

¹Paul, a prisoner for Christ Jesus, and Timothy our brother,

To Philemon our beloved fellow worker ²and Apphia our sister and Archippus our fellow soldier, and the church in your house:

³Grace to you and peace from God our Father and the Lord Jesus Christ.

PHILEMON'S LOVE AND FAITH

⁴I thank my God always when I remember you in my prayers, ⁵because I hear of your love and of the faith that you have towards the Lord Jesus and for all the saints, ⁶and I pray that the sharing of your faith may become effective for the full knowledge of every good thing that is in us for the sake of Christ.[a] ⁷For I have derived much joy and comfort from your love, my brother, because the hearts of the saints have been refreshed through you.

PAUL'S PLEA FOR ONESIMUS

⁸Accordingly, though I am bold enough in Christ to command you to do what is required, ⁹yet for love's sake I prefer to appeal to you—I, Paul, an old man and now a prisoner also for Christ Jesus— ¹⁰I appeal to you for my child, Onesimus,[b] whose father I became in my imprisonment. ¹¹(Formerly he was useless to you, but now he is indeed useful to you and to me.) ¹²I am sending him back to you, sending my very heart. ¹³I would have been glad to keep him with me, in order that he might serve me on your behalf during my imprisonment for the gospel, ¹⁴but I preferred to do nothing without your consent in order that your goodness might not be by compulsion but of your own accord. ¹⁵For this perhaps is why he was parted from you for a while, that you might have him back for ever, ¹⁶no longer as a bondservant[c] but more than a bondservant, as a beloved brother—especially to me, but how much more to you, both in the flesh and in the Lord.

¹⁷So if you consider me your partner, receive him as you would receive me. ¹⁸If he has wronged you at all, or owes you anything, charge that to my account. ¹⁹I, Paul, write this with my own hand: I will repay it—to say nothing of your owing me even your own self. ²⁰Yes, brother, I want some benefit from you in the Lord. Refresh my heart in Christ.

²¹Confident of your obedience, I write to you, knowing that you will do even more than I say. ²²At the same time, prepare a guest room for me, for I am hoping that through your prayers I will be graciously given to you.

FINAL GREETINGS

²³Epaphras, my fellow prisoner in Christ Jesus, sends greetings to you, ²⁴and so do Mark, Aristarchus, Demas, and Luke, my fellow workers.

²⁵The grace of the Lord Jesus Christ be with your spirit.

---

[a] Or *for Christ's service*   [b] *Onesimus* means *useful* (see verse 11) or *beneficial* (see verse 20)   [c] For the contextual rendering of the Greek word *doulos*, see Preface; twice in this verse

THE LETTER TO THE HEBREWS

THE SUPREMACY OF GOD'S SON

1 Long ago, at many times and in many ways, God spoke to our fathers by the prophets, ²but in these last days he has spoken to us by his Son, whom he appointed the heir of all things, through whom also he created the world. ³He is the radiance of the glory of God and the exact imprint of his nature, and he upholds the universe by the word of his power. After making purification for sins, he sat down at the right hand of the Majesty on high, ⁴having become as much superior to angels as the name he has inherited is more excellent than theirs.

⁵For to which of the angels did God ever say,

"You are my Son,
    today I have begotten you"?

Or again,

"I will be to him a father,
    and he shall be to me a son"?

⁶And again, when he brings the firstborn into the world, he says,

"Let all God's angels worship him."

⁷Of the angels he says,

"He makes his angels winds,
    and his ministers a flame of fire."

⁸But of the Son he says,

"Your throne, O God, is for
        ever and ever,
    the sceptre of uprightness is the
        sceptre of your kingdom.
⁹ You have loved righteousness
        and hated wickedness;
    therefore God, your God,
        has anointed you
    with the oil of gladness beyond
        your companions."

¹⁰And,

"You, Lord, laid the foundation of
        the earth in the beginning,
    and the heavens are the
        work of your hands;
¹¹ they will perish, but you remain;
        they will all wear out like a garment,
¹² like a robe you will roll them up,
        like a garment they will be changed.ᵃ
    But you are the same,
        and your years will have no end."

¹³And to which of the angels has he ever said,

"Sit at my right hand
    until I make your enemies a
        footstool for your feet"?

¹⁴Are they not all ministering spirits sent out to serve for the sake of those who are to inherit salvation?

WARNING AGAINST NEGLECTING SALVATION

2 Therefore we must pay much closer attention to what we have heard, lest we drift away from it. ²For since the message declared by angels proved to be reliable, and every transgression or disobedience received a just retribution, ³how shall we escape if we neglect such a great salvation? It was declared at first by the Lord, and it was attested to us by those who heard, ⁴while God also bore witness by signs and wonders and various miracles and by gifts of the Holy Spirit distributed according to his will.

THE FOUNDER OF SALVATION

⁵For it was not to angels that God subjected the world to come, of which we are speaking. ⁶It has been testified somewhere,

"What is man, that you are
    mindful of him,

ᵃSome manuscripts omit *like a garment*

or the son of man, that
you care for him?
⁷ You made him for a little while
lower than the angels;
you have crowned him with
glory and honour,ᵃ
⁸ putting everything in subjection
under his feet."

Now in putting everything in subjection to him, he left nothing outside his control. At present, we do not yet see everything in subjection to him. ⁹But we see him who for a little while was made lower than the angels, namely Jesus, crowned with glory and honour because of the suffering of death, so that by the grace of God he might taste death for everyone.

¹⁰For it was fitting that he, for whom and by whom all things exist, in bringing many sons to glory, should make the founder of their salvation perfect through suffering. ¹¹For he who sanctifies and those who are sanctified all have one source.ᵇ That is why he is not ashamed to call them brothers,ᶜ ¹²saying,

"I will tell of your name to my brothers;
in the midst of the congregation
I will sing your praise."

¹³And again,

"I will put my trust in him."

And again,

"Behold, I and the children
God has given me."

¹⁴Since therefore the children share in flesh and blood, he himself likewise partook of the same things, that through death he might destroy the one who has the power of death, that is, the devil, ¹⁵and deliver all those who through fear of death were subject to lifelong slavery. ¹⁶For surely it is not angels that he helps, but he helps the offspring of Abraham. ¹⁷Therefore he had to be made like his brothers in every respect, so that he might become a merciful and faithful high priest in the service of God, to make propitiation for the sins of the people. ¹⁸For because he himself has suffered when tempted, he is able to help those who are being tempted.

JESUS GREATER THAN MOSES

3 Therefore, holy brothers,ᵈ you who share in a heavenly calling, consider Jesus, the apostle and high priest of our confession, ²who was faithful to him who appointed him, just as Moses also was faithful in all God'sᵉ house. ³For Jesus has been counted worthy of more glory than Moses — as much more glory as the builder of a house has more honour than the house itself. ⁴(For every house is built by someone, but the builder of all things is God.) ⁵Now Moses was faithful in all God's house as a servant, to testify to the things that were to be spoken later, ⁶but Christ is faithful over God's house as a son. And we are his house, if indeed we hold fast our confidence and our boasting in our hope.ᶠ

A REST FOR THE PEOPLE OF GOD

⁷Therefore, as the Holy Spirit says,

"Today, if you hear his voice,
⁸ do not harden your hearts
as in the rebellion
on the day of testing in
the wilderness,
⁹ where your fathers put me to the test
and saw my works for forty years.
¹⁰ Therefore I was provoked
with that generation,
and said, 'They always go
astray in their heart;
they have not known my ways.'
¹¹ As I swore in my wrath,
'They shall not enter my rest.'"

¹²Take care, brothers, lest there be in any of you an evil, unbelieving heart, leading you to fall away from the living God. ¹³But exhort one another every day, as long as it is called "today", that none of you may be hardened by the deceitfulness of sin. ¹⁴For we have come to share in Christ, if indeed we hold our original confidence firm to the end. ¹⁵As it is said,

"Today, if you hear his voice,
do not harden your hearts
as in the rebellion."

ᵃSome manuscripts insert *and set him over the works of your hands* ᵇGreek *all are of one* ᶜOr *brothers and sisters*. In New Testament usage, depending on the context, the plural Greek word *adelphoi* (translated "brothers") may refer either to *brothers* or to *brothers and sisters*; also verse 12 ᵈOr *brothers and sisters*; also verse 12 ᵉGreek *his*; also verses 5, 6 ᶠSome manuscripts insert *firm to the end*

¹⁶For who were those who heard and yet rebelled? Was it not all those who left Egypt led by Moses? ¹⁷And with whom was he provoked for forty years? Was it not with those who sinned, whose bodies fell in the wilderness? ¹⁸And to whom did he swear that they would not enter his rest, but to those who were disobedient? ¹⁹So we see that they were unable to enter because of unbelief.

4 Therefore, while the promise of entering his rest still stands, let us fear lest any of you should seem to have failed to reach it. ²For good news came to us just as to them, but the message they heard did not benefit them, because they were not united by faith with those who listened.ᵃ ³For we who have believed enter that rest, as he has said,

"As I swore in my wrath,
'They shall not enter my rest'",

although his works were finished from the foundation of the world. ⁴For he has somewhere spoken of the seventh day in this way: "And God rested on the seventh day from all his works." ⁵And again in this passage he said,

"They shall not enter my rest."

⁶Since therefore it remains for some to enter it, and those who formerly received the good news failed to enter because of disobedience, ⁷again he appoints a certain day, "Today," saying through David so long afterwards, in the words already quoted,

"Today, if you hear his voice,
do not harden your hearts."

⁸For if Joshua had given them rest, Godᵇ would not have spoken of another day later on. ⁹So then, there remains a Sabbath rest for the people of God, ¹⁰for whoever has entered God's rest has also rested from his works as God did from his.

¹¹Let us therefore strive to enter that rest, so that no one may fall by the same sort of disobedience. ¹²For the word of God is living and active, sharper than any two-edged sword, piercing to the division of soul and of spirit, of joints and of marrow, and discerning the thoughts and intentions of the heart. ¹³And no creature is hidden from his sight, but all are naked and exposed to the eyes of him to whom we must give account.

JESUS THE GREAT HIGH PRIEST

¹⁴Since then we have a great high priest who has passed through the heavens, Jesus, the Son of God, let us hold fast our confession. ¹⁵For we do not have a high priest who is unable to sympathize with our weaknesses, but one who in every respect has been tempted as we are, yet without sin. ¹⁶Let us then with confidence draw near to the throne of grace, that we may receive mercy and find grace to help in time of need.

5 For every high priest chosen from among men is appointed to act on behalf of men in relation to God, to offer gifts and sacrifices for sins. ²He can deal gently with the ignorant and wayward, since he himself is beset with weakness. ³Because of this he is bound to offer sacrifice for his own sins just as he does for those of the people. ⁴And no one takes this honour for himself, but only when called by God, just as Aaron was.

⁵So also Christ did not exalt himself to be made a high priest, but was appointed by him who said to him,

"You are my Son,
today I have begotten you";

⁶as he says also in another place,

"You are a priest for ever,
after the order of Melchizedek."

⁷In the days of his flesh, Jesusᶜ offered up prayers and supplications, with loud cries and tears, to him who was able to save him from death, and he was heard because of his reverence. ⁸Although he was a son, he learned obedience through what he suffered. ⁹And being made perfect, he became the source of eternal salvation to all who obey him, ¹⁰being designated by God a high priest after the order of Melchizedek.

WARNING AGAINST APOSTASY

¹¹About this we have much to say, and it is hard to explain, since you have become dull of hearing. ¹²For though by this time you ought to be teachers, you need someone to teach you again the basic principles of the oracles of God. You need milk, not solid food, ¹³for everyone who lives on milk is unskilled

---

ᵃSome manuscripts *it did not meet with faith in the hearers*   ᵇGreek *he*   ᶜGreek *he*

in the word of righteousness, since he is a child. ¹⁴But solid food is for the mature, for those who have their powers of discernment trained by constant practice to distinguish good from evil.

6 Therefore let us leave the elementary doctrine of Christ and go on to maturity, not laying again a foundation of repentance from dead works and of faith towards God, ²and of instruction about washings,ᵃ the laying on of hands, the resurrection of the dead, and eternal judgement. ³And this we will do if God permits. ⁴For it is impossible, in the case of those who have once been enlightened, who have tasted the heavenly gift, and have shared in the Holy Spirit, ⁵and have tasted the goodness of the word of God and the powers of the age to come, ⁶and then have fallen away, to restore them again to repentance, since they are crucifying once again the Son of God to their own harm and holding him up to contempt. ⁷For land that has drunk the rain that often falls on it, and produces a crop useful to those for whose sake it is cultivated, receives a blessing from God. ⁸But if it bears thorns and thistles, it is worthless and near to being cursed, and its end is to be burned.

⁹Though we speak in this way, yet in your case, beloved, we feel sure of better things—things that belong to salvation. ¹⁰For God is not unjust so as to overlook your work and the love that you have shown for his name in serving the saints, as you still do. ¹¹And we desire each one of you to show the same earnestness to have the full assurance of hope until the end, ¹²so that you may not be sluggish, but imitators of those who through faith and patience inherit the promises.

THE CERTAINTY OF GOD'S PROMISE

¹³For when God made a promise to Abraham, since he had no one greater by whom to swear, he swore by himself, ¹⁴saying, "Surely I will bless you and multiply you." ¹⁵And thus Abraham,ᵇ having patiently waited, obtained the promise. ¹⁶For people swear by something greater than themselves, and in all their disputes an oath is final for confirmation. ¹⁷So when God desired to show more convincingly to the heirs of the promise the unchangeable character of his purpose, he guaranteed it with an oath, ¹⁸so that by two unchangeable things, in which it is impossible for God to lie, we who have fled for refuge might have strong encouragement to hold fast to the hope set before us. ¹⁹We have this as a sure and steadfast anchor of the soul, a hope that enters into the inner place behind the curtain, ²⁰where Jesus has gone as a forerunner on our behalf, having become a high priest for ever after the order of Melchizedek.

THE PRIESTLY ORDER OF MELCHIZEDEK

7 For this Melchizedek, king of Salem, priest of the Most High God, met Abraham returning from the slaughter of the kings and blessed him, ²and to him Abraham apportioned a tenth part of everything. He is first, by translation of his name, king of righteousness, and then he is also king of Salem, that is, king of peace. ³He is without father or mother or genealogy, having neither beginning of days nor end of life, but resembling the Son of God he continues a priest for ever.

⁴See how great this man was to whom Abraham the patriarch gave a tenth of the spoils! ⁵And those descendants of Levi who receive the priestly office have a commandment in the law to take tithes from the people, that is, from their brothers,ᶜ though these also are descended from Abraham. ⁶But this man who does not have his descent from them received tithes from Abraham and blessed him who had the promises. ⁷It is beyond dispute that the inferior is blessed by the superior. ⁸In the one case tithes are received by mortal men, but in the other case, by one of whom it is testified that he lives. ⁹One might even say that Levi himself, who receives tithes, paid tithes through Abraham, ¹⁰for he was still in the loins of his ancestor when Melchizedek met him.

JESUS COMPARED TO MELCHIZEDEK

¹¹Now if perfection had been attainable through the Levitical priesthood (for under it the people received the law), what further need would there have been for another priest to arise after the order of Melchizedek, rather than one named after the order of Aaron? ¹²For when there is a change in the priesthood, there is necessarily a change in the law as well. ¹³For the one of whom these things are spoken belonged to another tribe, from which no one has ever served at the altar. ¹⁴For it is evident that our Lord was descended from Judah, and in connection with that tribe Moses said nothing about priests.

ᵃOr *baptisms* (that is, cleansing rites) ᵇGreek *he* ᶜOr *brothers and sisters*

¹⁵This becomes even more evident when another priest arises in the likeness of Melchizedek, ¹⁶who has become a priest, not on the basis of a legal requirement concerning bodily descent, but by the power of an indestructible life. ¹⁷For it is witnessed of him,

"You are a priest for ever,
    after the order of Melchizedek."

¹⁸For on the one hand, a former commandment is set aside because of its weakness and uselessness ¹⁹(for the law made nothing perfect); but on the other hand, a better hope is introduced, through which we draw near to God.

²⁰And it was not without an oath. For those who formerly became priests were made such without an oath, ²¹but this one was made a priest with an oath by the one who said to him:

"The Lord has sworn
    and will not change his mind,
'You are a priest for ever.'"

²²This makes Jesus the guarantor of a better covenant.

²³The former priests were many in number, because they were prevented by death from continuing in office, ²⁴but he holds his priesthood permanently, because he continues for ever. ²⁵Consequently, he is able to save to the uttermost[a] those who draw near to God through him, since he always lives to make intercession for them.

²⁶For it was indeed fitting that we should have such a high priest, holy, innocent, unstained, separated from sinners, and exalted above the heavens. ²⁷He has no need, like those high priests, to offer sacrifices daily, first for his own sins and then for those of the people, since he did this once for all when he offered up himself. ²⁸For the law appoints men in their weakness as high priests, but the word of the oath, which came later than the law, appoints a Son who has been made perfect for ever.

JESUS, HIGH PRIEST OF A BETTER COVENANT

8 Now the point in what we are saying is this: we have such a high priest, one who is seated at the right hand of the throne of the Majesty in heaven, ²a minister in the holy places, in the true tent[b] that the Lord set up, not man. ³For every high priest is appointed to offer gifts and sacrifices; thus it is necessary for this priest also to have something to offer. ⁴Now if he were on earth, he would not be a priest at all, since there are priests who offer gifts according to the law. ⁵They serve a copy and shadow of the heavenly things. For when Moses was about to erect the tent, he was instructed by God, saying, "See that you make everything according to the pattern that was shown you on the mountain." ⁶But as it is, Christ[c] has obtained a ministry that is as much more excellent than the old as the covenant he mediates is better, since it is enacted on better promises. ⁷For if that first covenant had been faultless, there would have been no occasion to look for a second.

⁸For he finds fault with them when he says:[d]

"Behold, the days are coming,
    declares the Lord,
when I will establish a new covenant
    with the house of Israel
    and with the house of Judah,
⁹ not like the covenant that I
    made with their fathers
on the day when I took them
    by the hand to bring them
    out of the land of Egypt.
For they did not continue
    in my covenant,
    and so I showed no concern for
    them, declares the Lord.
¹⁰ For this is the covenant that I will
    make with the house of Israel
after those days, declares the Lord:
I will put my laws into their minds,
    and write them on their hearts,
and I will be their God,
    and they shall be my people.
¹¹ And they shall not teach, each
    one his neighbour
    and each one his brother,
    saying, 'Know the Lord',
for they shall all know me,
    from the least of them
    to the greatest.
¹² For I will be merciful towards
    their iniquities,
    and I will remember their
    sins no more."

---

[a]That is, completely; or at all times [b]Or tabernacle; also verse 5 [c]Greek he [d]Some manuscripts For finding fault with it he says to them

¹³In speaking of a new covenant, he makes the first one obsolete. And what is becoming obsolete and growing old is ready to vanish away.

THE EARTHLY HOLY PLACE

9 Now even the first covenant had regulations for worship and an earthly place of holiness. ²For a tent[a] was prepared, the first section, in which were the lampstand and the table and the bread of the Presence.[b] It is called the Holy Place. ³Behind the second curtain was a second section[c] called the Most Holy Place, ⁴having the golden altar of incense and the ark of the covenant covered on all sides with gold, in which was a golden urn holding the manna, and Aaron's staff that budded, and the tablets of the covenant. ⁵Above it were the cherubim of glory overshadowing the mercy seat. Of these things we cannot now speak in detail.

⁶These preparations having thus been made, the priests go regularly into the first section, performing their ritual duties, ⁷but into the second only the high priest goes, and he but once a year, and not without taking blood, which he offers for himself and for the unintentional sins of the people. ⁸By this the Holy Spirit indicates that the way into the holy places is not yet opened as long as the first section is still standing ⁹(which is symbolic for the present age).[d] According to this arrangement, gifts and sacrifices are offered that cannot perfect the conscience of the worshipper, ¹⁰but deal only with food and drink and various washings, regulations for the body imposed until the time of reformation.

REDEMPTION THROUGH THE BLOOD OF CHRIST

¹¹But when Christ appeared as a high priest of the good things that have come,[e] then through the greater and more perfect tent (not made with hands, that is, not of this creation) ¹²he entered once for all into the holy places, not by means of the blood of goats and calves but by means of his own blood, thus securing an eternal redemption. ¹³For if the blood of goats and bulls, and the sprinkling of defiled persons with the ashes of a heifer, sanctify[f] for the purification of the flesh, ¹⁴how much more will the blood of Christ, who through the eternal Spirit offered himself without blemish to God, purify our[g] conscience from dead works to serve the living God.

¹⁵Therefore he is the mediator of a new covenant, so that those who are called may receive the promised eternal inheritance, since a death has occurred that redeems them from the transgressions committed under the first covenant.[h] ¹⁶For where a will is involved, the death of the one who made it must be established. ¹⁷For a will takes effect only at death, since it is not in force as long as the one who made it is alive. ¹⁸Therefore not even the first covenant was inaugurated without blood. ¹⁹For when every commandment of the law had been declared by Moses to all the people, he took the blood of calves and goats, with water and scarlet wool and hyssop, and sprinkled both the book itself and all the people, ²⁰saying, "This is the blood of the covenant that God commanded for you." ²¹And in the same way he sprinkled with the blood both the tent and all the vessels used in worship. ²²Indeed, under the law almost everything is purified with blood, and without the shedding of blood there is no forgiveness of sins.

²³Thus it was necessary for the copies of the heavenly things to be purified with these rites, but the heavenly things themselves with better sacrifices than these. ²⁴For Christ has entered, not into holy places made with hands, which are copies of the true things, but into heaven itself, now to appear in the presence of God on our behalf. ²⁵Nor was it to offer himself repeatedly, as the high priest enters the holy places every year with blood not his own, ²⁶for then he would have had to suffer repeatedly since the foundation of the world. But as it is, he has appeared once for all at the end of the ages to put away sin by the sacrifice of himself. ²⁷And just as it is appointed for man to die once, and after that comes judgement, ²⁸so Christ, having been offered once to bear the sins of many, will appear a second time, not to deal with sin but to save those who are eagerly waiting for him.

CHRIST'S SACRIFICE ONCE FOR ALL

10 For since the law has but a shadow of the good things to come instead of the true form of these realities, it can never, by the same sacrifices that are

---

[a]Or *tabernacle*; also verses 11, 21 [b]Greek *the presentation of the loaves* [c]Greek *tent*; also verses 6, 8 [d]Or *which is symbolic for the age then present* [e]Some manuscripts *good things to come* [f]Or *For if the sprinkling of defiled persons with the blood of goats and bulls and with the ashes of a heifer sanctifies* [g]Some manuscripts *your* [h]The Greek word means both *covenant* and *will*; also verses 16, 17

continually offered every year, make perfect those who draw near. ²Otherwise, would they not have ceased to be offered, since the worshippers, having once been cleansed, would no longer have any consciousness of sins? ³But in these sacrifices there is a reminder of sins every year. ⁴For it is impossible for the blood of bulls and goats to take away sins.

⁵Consequently, when Christ[a] came into the world, he said,

> "Sacrifices and offerings you
>   have not desired,
>   but a body have you prepared for me;
> ⁶ in burnt offerings and sin offerings
>   you have taken no pleasure.
> ⁷ Then I said, 'Behold, I have come
>   to do your will, O God,
>   as it is written of me in the
>   scroll of the book.'"

⁸When he said above, "You have neither desired nor taken pleasure in sacrifices and offerings and burnt offerings and sin offerings" (these are offered according to the law), ⁹then he added, "Behold, I have come to do your will." He does away with the first in order to establish the second. ¹⁰And by that will we have been sanctified through the offering of the body of Jesus Christ once for all.

¹¹And every priest stands daily at his service, offering repeatedly the same sacrifices, which can never take away sins. ¹²But when Christ[b] had offered for all time a single sacrifice for sins, he sat down at the right hand of God, ¹³waiting from that time until his enemies should be made a footstool for his feet. ¹⁴For by a single offering he has perfected for all time those who are being sanctified.

¹⁵And the Holy Spirit also bears witness to us; for after saying,

> ¹⁶ "This is the covenant that I
>   will make with them
>   after those days, declares the Lord:
>   I will put my laws on their hearts,
>   and write them on their minds",

¹⁷then he adds,

> "I will remember their sins and their
>   lawless deeds no more."

¹⁸Where there is forgiveness of these, there is no longer any offering for sin.

THE FULL ASSURANCE OF FAITH

¹⁹Therefore, brothers,[c] since we have confidence to enter the holy places by the blood of Jesus, ²⁰by the new and living way that he opened for us through the curtain, that is, through his flesh, ²¹and since we have a great priest over the house of God, ²²let us draw near with a true heart in full assurance of faith, with our hearts sprinkled clean from an evil conscience and our bodies washed with pure water. ²³Let us hold fast the confession of our hope without wavering, for he who promised is faithful. ²⁴And let us consider how to stir up one another to love and good works, ²⁵not neglecting to meet together, as is the habit of some, but encouraging one another, and all the more as you see the Day drawing near.

²⁶For if we go on sinning deliberately after receiving the knowledge of the truth, there no longer remains a sacrifice for sins, ²⁷but a fearful expectation of judgement, and a fury of fire that will consume the adversaries. ²⁸Anyone who has set aside the law of Moses dies without mercy on the evidence of two or three witnesses. ²⁹How much worse punishment, do you think, will be deserved by the one who has trampled underfoot the Son of God, and has profaned the blood of the covenant by which he was sanctified, and has outraged the Spirit of grace? ³⁰For we know him who said, "Vengeance is mine; I will repay." And again, "The Lord will judge his people." ³¹It is a fearful thing to fall into the hands of the living God.

³²But recall the former days when, after you were enlightened, you endured a hard struggle with sufferings, ³³sometimes being publicly exposed to reproach and affliction, and sometimes being partners with those so treated. ³⁴For you had compassion on those in prison, and you joyfully accepted the plundering of your property, since you knew that you yourselves had a better possession and an abiding one. ³⁵Therefore do not throw away your confidence, which has a great reward. ³⁶For you have need of endurance, so that when you have done the will of God you may receive what is promised. ³⁷For,

> "Yet a little while,
>   and the coming one will come
>   and will not delay;

---

[a]Greek he [b]Greek this one [c]Or brothers and sisters

38 but my righteous one shall
live by faith,
and if he shrinks back,
my soul has no pleasure in him."

³⁹But we are not of those who shrink back and are destroyed, but of those who have faith and preserve their souls.

BY FAITH

11 Now faith is the assurance of things hoped for, the conviction of things not seen. ²For by it the people of old received their commendation. ³By faith we understand that the universe was created by the word of God, so that what is seen was not made out of things that are visible.

⁴By faith Abel offered to God a more acceptable sacrifice than Cain, through which he was commended as righteous, God commending him by accepting his gifts. And through his faith, though he died, he still speaks. ⁵By faith Enoch was taken up so that he should not see death, and he was not found, because God had taken him. Now before he was taken he was commended as having pleased God. ⁶And without faith it is impossible to please him, for whoever would draw near to God must believe that he exists and that he rewards those who seek him. ⁷By faith Noah, being warned by God concerning events as yet unseen, in reverent fear constructed an ark for the saving of his household. By this he condemned the world and became an heir of the righteousness that comes by faith.

⁸By faith Abraham obeyed when he was called to go out to a place that he was to receive as an inheritance. And he went out, not knowing where he was going. ⁹By faith he went to live in the land of promise, as in a foreign land, living in tents with Isaac and Jacob, heirs with him of the same promise. ¹⁰For he was looking forward to the city that has foundations, whose designer and builder is God. ¹¹By faith Sarah herself received power to conceive, even when she was past the age, since she considered him faithful who had promised. ¹²Therefore from one man, and him as good as dead, were born descendants as many as the stars of heaven and as many as the innumerable grains of sand by the seashore.

¹³These all died in faith, not having received the things promised, but having seen them and greeted them from afar, and having acknowledged that they were strangers and exiles on the earth. ¹⁴For people who speak thus make it clear that they are seeking a homeland. ¹⁵If they had been thinking of that land from which they had gone out, they would have had opportunity to return. ¹⁶But as it is, they desire a better country, that is, a heavenly one. Therefore God is not ashamed to be called their God, for he has prepared for them a city.

¹⁷By faith Abraham, when he was tested, offered up Isaac, and he who had received the promises was in the act of offering up his only son, ¹⁸of whom it was said, "Through Isaac shall your offspring be named." ¹⁹He considered that God was able even to raise him from the dead, from which, figuratively speaking, he did receive him back. ²⁰By faith Isaac invoked future blessings on Jacob and Esau. ²¹By faith Jacob, when dying, blessed each of the sons of Joseph, bowing in worship over the head of his staff. ²²By faith Joseph, at the end of his life, made mention of the exodus of the Israelites and gave directions concerning his bones.

²³By faith Moses, when he was born, was hidden for three months by his parents, because they saw that the child was beautiful, and they were not afraid of the king's edict. ²⁴By faith Moses, when he was grown up, refused to be called the son of Pharaoh's daughter, ²⁵choosing rather to be mistreated with the people of God than to enjoy the fleeting pleasures of sin. ²⁶He considered the reproach of Christ greater wealth than the treasures of Egypt, for he was looking to the reward. ²⁷By faith he left Egypt, not being afraid of the anger of the king, for he endured as seeing him who is invisible. ²⁸By faith he kept the Passover and sprinkled the blood, so that the Destroyer of the firstborn might not touch them.

²⁹By faith the people crossed the Red Sea as on dry land, but the Egyptians, when they attempted to do the same, were drowned. ³⁰By faith the walls of Jericho fell down after they had been encircled for seven days. ³¹By faith Rahab the prostitute did not perish with those who were disobedient, because she had given a friendly welcome to the spies.

³²And what more shall I say? For time would fail me to tell of Gideon, Barak, Samson, Jephthah, of David and Samuel and the prophets— ³³who through faith conquered kingdoms, enforced justice, obtained promises, stopped the mouths of lions, ³⁴quenched

the power of fire, escaped the edge of the sword, were made strong out of weakness, became mighty in war, put foreign armies to flight. ³⁵Women received back their dead by resurrection. Some were tortured, refusing to accept release, so that they might rise again to a better life. ³⁶Others suffered mocking and flogging, and even chains and imprisonment. ³⁷They were stoned, they were sawn in two,ᵃ they were killed with the sword. They went about in skins of sheep and goats, destitute, afflicted, mistreated—³⁸of whom the world was not worthy—wandering about in deserts and mountains, and in dens and caves of the earth.

³⁹And all these, though commended through their faith, did not receive what was promised, ⁴⁰since God had provided something better for us, that apart from us they should not be made perfect.

JESUS, FOUNDER AND PERFECTER OF OUR FAITH

12 Therefore, since we are surrounded by so great a cloud of witnesses, let us also lay aside every weight, and sin which clings so closely, and let us run with endurance the race that is set before us, ²looking to Jesus, the founder and perfecter of our faith, who for the joy that was set before him endured the cross, despising the shame, and is seated at the right hand of the throne of God.

DO NOT GROW WEARY

³Consider him who endured from sinners such hostility against himself, so that you may not grow weary or faint-hearted. ⁴In your struggle against sin you have not yet resisted to the point of shedding your blood. ⁵And have you forgotten the exhortation that addresses you as sons?

> "My son, do not regard lightly the
>   discipline of the Lord,
>   nor be weary when reproved by him.
> ⁶ For the Lord disciplines
>   the one he loves,
>   and chastises every son
>   whom he receives."

⁷It is for discipline that you have to endure. God is treating you as sons. For what son is there whom his father does not discipline? ⁸If you are left without discipline, in which all have participated, then you are illegitimate children and not sons. ⁹Besides this, we have had earthly fathers who disciplined us and we respected them. Shall we not much more be subject to the Father of spirits and live? ¹⁰For they disciplined us for a short time as it seemed best to them, but he disciplines us for our good, that we may share his holiness. ¹¹For the moment all discipline seems painful rather than pleasant, but later it yields the peaceful fruit of righteousness to those who have been trained by it.

¹²Therefore lift your drooping hands and strengthen your weak knees, ¹³and make straight paths for your feet, so that what is lame may not be put out of joint but rather be healed. ¹⁴Strive for peace with everyone, and for the holiness without which no one will see the Lord. ¹⁵See to it that no one fails to obtain the grace of God; that no "root of bitterness" springs up and causes trouble, and by it many become defiled; ¹⁶that no one is sexually immoral or unholy like Esau, who sold his birthright for a single meal. ¹⁷For you know that afterwards, when he desired to inherit the blessing, he was rejected, for he found no chance to repent, though he sought it with tears.

A KINGDOM THAT CANNOT BE SHAKEN

¹⁸For you have not come to what may be touched, a blazing fire and darkness and gloom and a tempest ¹⁹and the sound of a trumpet and a voice whose words made the hearers beg that no further messages be spoken to them. ²⁰For they could not endure the order that was given, "If even a beast touches the mountain, it shall be stoned." ²¹Indeed, so terrifying was the sight that Moses said, "I tremble with fear." ²²But you have come to Mount Zion and to the city of the living God, the heavenly Jerusalem, and to innumerable angels in festal gathering, ²³and to the assemblyᵇ of the firstborn who are enrolled in heaven, and to God, the judge of all, and to the spirits of the righteous made perfect, ²⁴and to Jesus, the mediator of a new covenant, and to the sprinkled blood that speaks a better word than the blood of Abel. ²⁵See that you do not refuse him who is speaking. For if they did not escape when they refused him who warned them on earth, much less will we escape if we reject him who warns from heaven. ²⁶At that time his voice shook the earth, but now he has promised,

---

ᵃSome manuscripts add *they were tempted*   ᵇOr *church*

"Yet once more I will shake not only the earth but also the heavens." ²⁷This phrase, "Yet once more", indicates the removal of things that are shaken—that is, things that have been made—in order that the things that cannot be shaken may remain. ²⁸Therefore let us be grateful for receiving a kingdom that cannot be shaken, and thus let us offer to God acceptable worship, with reverence and awe, ²⁹for our God is a consuming fire.

SACRIFICES PLEASING TO GOD

13 Let brotherly love continue. ²Do not neglect to show hospitality to strangers, for thereby some have entertained angels unawares. ³Remember those who are in prison, as though in prison with them, and those who are mistreated, since you also are in the body. ⁴Let marriage be held in honour among all, and let the marriage bed be undefiled, for God will judge the sexually immoral and adulterous. ⁵Keep your life free from love of money, and be content with what you have, for he has said, "I will never leave you nor forsake you." ⁶So we can confidently say,

"The Lord is my helper;
 I will not fear;
 what can man do to me?"

⁷Remember your leaders, those who spoke to you the word of God. Consider the outcome of their way of life, and imitate their faith. ⁸Jesus Christ is the same yesterday and today and for ever. ⁹Do not be led away by diverse and strange teachings, for it is good for the heart to be strengthened by grace, not by foods, which have not benefited those devoted to them. ¹⁰We have an altar from which those who serve the tent^a have no right to eat. ¹¹For the bodies of those animals whose blood is brought into the holy places by the high priest as a sacrifice for sin are burned outside the camp. ¹²So Jesus also suffered outside the gate in order to sanctify the people through his own blood. ¹³Therefore let us go to him outside the camp and bear the reproach he endured. ¹⁴For here we have no lasting city, but we seek the city that is to come. ¹⁵Through him then let us continually offer up a sacrifice of praise to God, that is, the fruit of lips that acknowledge his name. ¹⁶Do not neglect to do good and to share what you have, for such sacrifices are pleasing to God.

¹⁷Obey your leaders and submit to them, for they are keeping watch over your souls, as those who will have to give an account. Let them do this with joy and not with groaning, for that would be of no advantage to you.

¹⁸Pray for us, for we are sure that we have a clear conscience, desiring to act honourably in all things. ¹⁹I urge you the more earnestly to do this in order that I may be restored to you the sooner.

BENEDICTION

²⁰Now may the God of peace who brought again from the dead our Lord Jesus, the great shepherd of the sheep, by the blood of the eternal covenant, ²¹equip you with everything good that you may do his will, working in us^b that which is pleasing in his sight, through Jesus Christ, to whom be glory for ever and ever. Amen.

FINAL GREETINGS

²²I appeal to you, brothers,^{c} bear with my word of exhortation, for I have written to you briefly. ²³You should know that our brother Timothy has been released, with whom I shall see you if he comes soon. ²⁴Greet all your leaders and all the saints. Those who come from Italy send you greetings. ²⁵Grace be with all of you.

---

^{a}Or *tabernacle* ^{b}Some manuscripts *you* ^{c}Or *brothers and sisters*

THE LETTER OF JAMES

GREETING

1 James, a servant[a] of God and of the Lord Jesus Christ,
   To the twelve tribes in the Dispersion: Greetings.

TESTING OF YOUR FAITH

²Count it all joy, my brothers,[b] when you meet trials of various kinds, ³for you know that the testing of your faith produces steadfastness. ⁴And let steadfastness have its full effect, that you may be perfect and complete, lacking in nothing.
⁵If any of you lacks wisdom, let him ask God, who gives generously to all without reproach, and it will be given him. ⁶But let him ask in faith, with no doubting, for the one who doubts is like a wave of the sea that is driven and tossed by the wind. ⁷For that person must not suppose that he will receive anything from the Lord; ⁸he is a double-minded man, unstable in all his ways.
⁹Let the lowly brother boast in his exaltation, ¹⁰and the rich in his humiliation, because like a flower of the grass[c] he will pass away. ¹¹For the sun rises with its scorching heat and withers the grass; its flower falls, and its beauty perishes. So also will the rich man fade away in the midst of his pursuits.
¹²Blessed is the man who remains steadfast under trial, for when he has stood the test he will receive the crown of life, which God has promised to those who love him. ¹³Let no one say when he is tempted, "I am being tempted by God", for God cannot be tempted with evil, and he himself tempts no one. ¹⁴But each person is tempted when he is lured and enticed by his own desire. ¹⁵Then desire when it has conceived gives birth to sin, and sin when it is fully grown brings forth death.
¹⁶Do not be deceived, my beloved brothers. ¹⁷Every good gift and every perfect gift is from above, coming down from the Father of lights, with whom there is no variation or shadow due to change.[d] ¹⁸Of his own will he brought us forth by the word of truth, that we should be a kind of firstfruits of his creatures.

HEARING AND DOING THE WORD

¹⁹Know this, my beloved brothers: let every person be quick to hear, slow to speak, slow to anger; ²⁰for the anger of man does not produce the righteousness of God. ²¹Therefore put away all filthiness and rampant wickedness and receive with meekness the implanted word, which is able to save your souls.
²²But be doers of the word, and not hearers only, deceiving yourselves. ²³For if anyone is a hearer of the word and not a doer, he is like a man who looks intently at his natural face in a mirror. ²⁴For he looks at himself and goes away and at once forgets what he was like. ²⁵But the one who looks into the perfect law, the law of liberty, and perseveres, being no hearer who forgets but a doer who acts, he will be blessed in his doing.
²⁶If anyone thinks he is religious and does not bridle his tongue but deceives his heart, this person's religion is worthless. ²⁷Religion that is pure and undefiled before God the Father is this: to visit orphans and widows in their affliction, and to keep oneself unstained from the world.

THE SIN OF PARTIALITY

2 My brothers,[e] show no partiality as you hold the faith in our Lord Jesus Christ, the Lord of glory. ²For if a man wearing a gold ring and fine clothing comes into your assembly, and a poor man in shabby clothing also comes in, ³and if you pay attention to the one who wears the fine clothing and say, "You sit here in a good place", while you say to the poor man, "You stand over there",

---

[a] For the contextual rendering of the Greek word *doulos*, see Preface
[b] Or *brothers and sisters*. In New Testament usage, depending on the context, the plural Greek word *adelphoi* (translated "brothers") may refer either to *brothers* or to *brothers and sisters*; also verses 16, 19
[c] Or *a wild flower*   [d] Some manuscripts *variation due to a shadow of turning*   [e] Or *brothers and sisters*; also verses 5, 14

or, "Sit down at my feet", ⁴have you not then made distinctions among yourselves and become judges with evil thoughts? ⁵Listen, my beloved brothers, has not God chosen those who are poor in the world to be rich in faith and heirs of the kingdom, which he has promised to those who love him? ⁶But you have dishonoured the poor man. Are not the rich the ones who oppress you, and the ones who drag you into court? ⁷Are they not the ones who blaspheme the honourable name by which you were called?

⁸If you really fulfil the royal law according to the Scripture, "You shall love your neighbour as yourself", you are doing well. ⁹But if you show partiality, you are committing sin and are convicted by the law as transgressors. ¹⁰For whoever keeps the whole law but fails in one point has become guilty of all of it. ¹¹For he who said, "Do not commit adultery", also said, "Do not murder." If you do not commit adultery but do murder, you have become a transgressor of the law. ¹²So speak and so act as those who are to be judged under the law of liberty. ¹³For judgement is without mercy to one who has shown no mercy. Mercy triumphs over judgement.

FAITH WITHOUT WORKS IS DEAD

¹⁴What good is it, my brothers, if someone says he has faith but does not have works? Can that faith save him? ¹⁵If a brother or sister is poorly clothed and lacking in daily food, ¹⁶and one of you says to them, "Go in peace, be warmed and filled", without giving them the things needed for the body, what good[a] is that? ¹⁷So also faith by itself, if it does not have works, is dead.

¹⁸But someone will say, "You have faith and I have works." Show me your faith apart from your works, and I will show you my faith by my works. ¹⁹You believe that God is one; you do well. Even the demons believe — and shudder! ²⁰Do you want to be shown, you foolish person, that faith apart from works is useless? ²¹Was not Abraham our father justified by works when he offered up his son Isaac on the altar? ²²You see that faith was active along with his works, and faith was completed by his works; ²³and the Scripture was fulfilled that says, "Abraham believed God, and it was counted to him as righteousness" — and he was called a friend of God. ²⁴You see that a person is justified by works and not by faith alone. ²⁵And in the same way was not also Rahab the prostitute justified by works when she received the messengers and sent them out by another way? ²⁶For as the body apart from the spirit is dead, so also faith apart from works is dead.

TAMING THE TONGUE

3 Not many of you should become teachers, my brothers, for you know that we who teach will be judged with greater strictness. ²For we all stumble in many ways. And if anyone does not stumble in what he says, he is a perfect man, able also to bridle his whole body. ³If we put bits into the mouths of horses so that they obey us, we guide their whole bodies as well. ⁴Look at the ships also: though they are so large and are driven by strong winds, they are guided by a very small rudder wherever the will of the pilot directs. ⁵So also the tongue is a small member, yet it boasts of great things.

How great a forest is set ablaze by such a small fire! ⁶And the tongue is a fire, a world of unrighteousness. The tongue is set among our members, staining the whole body, setting on fire the entire course of life,[b] and set on fire by hell.[c] ⁷For every kind of beast and bird, of reptile and sea creature, can be tamed and has been tamed by mankind, ⁸but no human being can tame the tongue. It is a restless evil, full of deadly poison. ⁹With it we bless our Lord and Father, and with it we curse people who are made in the likeness of God. ¹⁰From the same mouth come blessing and cursing. My brothers,[d] these things ought not to be so. ¹¹Does a spring pour forth from the same opening both fresh and salt water? ¹²Can a fig tree, my brothers, bear olives, or a grapevine produce figs? Neither can a salt pond yield fresh water.

WISDOM FROM ABOVE

¹³Who is wise and understanding among you? By his good conduct let him show his works in the meekness of wisdom. ¹⁴But if you have bitter jealousy and selfish ambition in your hearts, do not boast and be false to the truth. ¹⁵This is not the wisdom that comes down from above, but is earthly, unspiritual, demonic. ¹⁶For where jealousy and selfish ambition exist, there will be disorder and every vile practice. ¹⁷But the wisdom from

---

[a] Or benefit [b] Or wheel of birth [c] Greek Gehenna [d] Or brothers and sisters; also verse 12

above is first pure, then peaceable, gentle, open to reason, full of mercy and good fruits, impartial and sincere. ⁱ⁸And a harvest of righteousness is sown in peace by those who make peace.

WARNING AGAINST WORLDLINESS

4 What causes quarrels and what causes fights among you? Is it not this, that your passions*ᵃ* are at war within you?*ᵇ* ²You desire and do not have, so you murder. You covet and cannot obtain, so you fight and quarrel. You do not have, because you do not ask. ³You ask and do not receive, because you ask wrongly, to spend it on your passions. ⁴You adulterous people!*ᶜ* Do you not know that friendship with the world is enmity with God? Therefore whoever wishes to be a friend of the world makes himself an enemy of God. ⁵Or do you suppose it is to no purpose that the Scripture says, "He yearns jealously over the spirit that he has made to dwell in us"? ⁶But he gives more grace. Therefore it says, "God opposes the proud but gives grace to the humble." ⁷Submit yourselves therefore to God. Resist the devil, and he will flee from you. ⁸Draw near to God, and he will draw near to you. Cleanse your hands, you sinners, and purify your hearts, you double-minded. ⁹Be wretched and mourn and weep. Let your laughter be turned to mourning and your joy to gloom. ¹⁰Humble yourselves before the Lord, and he will exalt you.

¹¹Do not speak evil against one another, brothers.*ᵈ* The one who speaks against a brother or judges his brother, speaks evil against the law and judges the law. But if you judge the law, you are not a doer of the law but a judge. ¹²There is only one lawgiver and judge, he who is able to save and to destroy. But who are you to judge your neighbour?

BOASTING ABOUT TOMORROW

¹³Come now, you who say, "Today or tomorrow we will go into such and such a town and spend a year there and trade and make a profit"— ¹⁴yet you do not know what tomorrow will bring. What is your life? For you are a mist that appears for a little time and then vanishes. ¹⁵Instead you ought to say, "If the Lord wills, we will live and do this or that." ¹⁶As it is, you boast in your arrogance. All such boasting is evil. ¹⁷So whoever knows the right thing to do and fails to do it, for him it is sin.

WARNING TO THE RICH

5 Come now, you rich, weep and howl for the miseries that are coming upon you. ²Your riches have rotted and your garments are moth-eaten. ³Your gold and silver have corroded, and their corrosion will be evidence against you and will eat your flesh like fire. You have laid up treasure in the last days. ⁴Behold, the wages of the labourers who mowed your fields, which you kept back by fraud, are crying out against you, and the cries of the harvesters have reached the ears of the Lord of hosts. ⁵You have lived on the earth in luxury and in self-indulgence. You have fattened your hearts in a day of slaughter. ⁶You have condemned and murdered the righteous person. He does not resist you.

PATIENCE IN SUFFERING

⁷Be patient, therefore, brothers,*ᵉ* until the coming of the Lord. See how the farmer waits for the precious fruit of the earth, being patient about it, until it receives the early and the late rains. ⁸You also, be patient. Establish your hearts, for the coming of the Lord is at hand. ⁹Do not grumble against one another, brothers, so that you may not be judged; behold, the Judge is standing at the door. ¹⁰As an example of suffering and patience, brothers, take the prophets who spoke in the name of the Lord. ¹¹Behold, we consider those blessed who remained steadfast. You have heard of the steadfastness of Job, and you have seen the purpose of the Lord, how the Lord is compassionate and merciful.

¹²But above all, my brothers, do not swear, either by heaven or by earth or by any other oath, but let your "yes" be yes and your "no" be no, so that you may not fall under condemnation.

THE PRAYER OF FAITH

¹³Is anyone among you suffering? Let him pray. Is anyone cheerful? Let him sing praise. ¹⁴Is anyone among you sick? Let him call for the elders of the church, and let them pray over him, anointing him with oil in the name of the Lord. ¹⁵And the prayer of faith will save the one who is sick, and the Lord will raise him up. And if he has committed sins, he will be forgiven. ¹⁶Therefore, confess your sins to one another and pray for

---

*ᵃ*Greek *pleasures*; also verse 3   *ᵇ*Greek *in your members*   *ᶜ*Or *You adulteresses!*   *ᵈ*Or *brothers and sisters*   *ᵉ*Or *brothers and sisters*; also verses 9, 10, 12, 19

one another, that you may be healed. The prayer of a righteous person has great power as it is working.[a] ¹⁷Elijah was a man with a nature like ours, and he prayed fervently that it might not rain, and for three years and six months it did not rain on the earth. ¹⁸Then he prayed again, and heaven gave rain, and the earth bore its fruit.

¹⁹My brothers, if anyone among you wanders from the truth and someone brings him back, ²⁰let him know that whoever brings back a sinner from his wandering will save his soul from death and will cover a multitude of sins.

---

[a] Or *The effective prayer of a righteous person has great power*

THE FIRST LETTER OF PETER
1 PETER

GREETING

1 Peter, an apostle of Jesus Christ,
To those who are elect exiles of the Dispersion in Pontus, Galatia, Cappadocia, Asia, and Bithynia, ²according to the foreknowledge of God the Father, in the sanctification of the Spirit, for obedience to Jesus Christ and for sprinkling with his blood:

May grace and peace be multiplied to you.

BORN AGAIN TO A LIVING HOPE

³Blessed be the God and Father of our Lord Jesus Christ! According to his great mercy, he has caused us to be born again to a living hope through the resurrection of Jesus Christ from the dead, ⁴to an inheritance that is imperishable, undefiled, and unfading, kept in heaven for you, ⁵who by God's power are being guarded through faith for a salvation ready to be revealed in the last time. ⁶In this you rejoice, though now for a little while, if necessary, you have been grieved by various trials, ⁷so that the tested genuineness of your faith—more precious than gold that perishes though it is tested by fire—may be found to result in praise and glory and honour at the revelation of Jesus Christ. ⁸Though you have not seen him, you love him. Though you do not now see him, you believe in him and rejoice with joy that is inexpressible and filled with glory, ⁹obtaining the outcome of your faith, the salvation of your souls.

¹⁰Concerning this salvation, the prophets who prophesied about the grace that was to be yours searched and enquired carefully, ¹¹enquiring what person or time*ᵃ* the Spirit of Christ in them was indicating when he predicted the sufferings of Christ and the subsequent glories. ¹²It was revealed to them that they were serving not themselves but you, in the things that have now been announced to you through those who preached the good news to you by the Holy Spirit sent from heaven, things into which angels long to look.

CALLED TO BE HOLY

¹³Therefore, preparing your minds for action,*ᵇ* and being sober-minded, set your hope fully on the grace that will be brought to you at the revelation of Jesus Christ. ¹⁴As obedient children, do not be conformed to the passions of your former ignorance, ¹⁵but as he who called you is holy, you also be holy in all your conduct, ¹⁶since it is written, "You shall be holy, for I am holy." ¹⁷And if you call on him as Father who judges impartially according to each one's deeds, conduct yourselves with fear throughout the time of your exile, ¹⁸knowing that you were ransomed from the futile ways inherited from your forefathers, not with perishable things such as silver or gold, ¹⁹but with the precious blood of Christ, like that of a lamb without blemish or spot. ²⁰He was foreknown before the foundation of the world but was made manifest in the last times for the sake of you ²¹who through him are believers in God, who raised him from the dead and gave him glory, so that your faith and hope are in God.

²²Having purified your souls by your obedience to the truth for a sincere brotherly love, love one another earnestly from a pure heart, ²³since you have been born again, not of perishable seed but of imperishable, through the living and abiding word of God; ²⁴for

> "All flesh is like grass
> and all its glory like the flower of grass.
> The grass withers,
> and the flower falls,
> ²⁵ but the word of the Lord
> remains for ever."

And this word is the good news that was preached to you.

A LIVING STONE AND A HOLY PEOPLE

2 So put away all malice and all deceit and hypocrisy and envy and all slander. ²Like newborn infants, long for

---

ᵃOr what time or circumstances *ᵇGreek girding up the loins of your mind*

the pure spiritual milk, that by it you may grow up into salvation — ³if indeed you have tasted that the Lord is good.

⁴As you come to him, a living stone rejected by men but in the sight of God chosen and precious, ⁵you yourselves like living stones are being built up as a spiritual house, to be a holy priesthood, to offer spiritual sacrifices acceptable to God through Jesus Christ. ⁶For it stands in Scripture:

> "Behold, I am laying in Zion a stone,
>   a cornerstone chosen and precious,
> and whoever believes in him
>   will not be put to shame."

⁷So the honour is for you who believe, but for those who do not believe,

> "The stone that the builders rejected
>   has become the cornerstone",ᵃ

⁸and

> "A stone of stumbling,
>   and a rock of offence."

They stumble because they disobey the word, as they were destined to do.

⁹But you are a chosen race, a royal priesthood, a holy nation, a people for his own possession, that you may proclaim the excellencies of him who called you out of darkness into his marvellous light. ¹⁰Once you were not a people, but now you are God's people; once you had not received mercy, but now you have received mercy.

¹¹Beloved, I urge you as sojourners and exiles to abstain from the passions of the flesh, which wage war against your soul. ¹²Keep your conduct among the Gentiles honourable, so that when they speak against you as evildoers, they may see your good deeds and glorify God on the day of visitation.

SUBMISSION TO AUTHORITY

¹³Be subject for the Lord's sake to every human institution,ᵇ whether it be to the emperorᶜ as supreme, ¹⁴or to governors as sent by him to punish those who do evil and to praise those who do good. ¹⁵For this is the will of God, that by doing good you should put to silence the ignorance of foolish people. ¹⁶Live as people who are free, not using your freedom as a cover-up for evil, but living as servantsᵈ of God. ¹⁷Honour everyone. Love the brotherhood. Fear God. Honour the emperor.

¹⁸Servants, be subject to your masters with all respect, not only to the good and gentle but also to the unjust. ¹⁹For this is a gracious thing, when, mindful of God, one endures sorrows while suffering unjustly. ²⁰For what credit is it if, when you sin and are beaten for it, you endure? But if when you do good and suffer for it you endure, this is a gracious thing in the sight of God. ²¹For to this you have been called, because Christ also suffered for you, leaving you an example, so that you might follow in his steps. ²²He committed no sin, neither was deceit found in his mouth. ²³When he was reviled, he did not revile in return; when he suffered, he did not threaten, but continued entrusting himself to him who judges justly. ²⁴He himself bore our sins in his body on the tree, that we might die to sin and live to righteousness. By his wounds you have been healed. ²⁵For you were straying like sheep, but have now returned to the Shepherd and Overseer of your souls.

WIVES AND HUSBANDS

3 Likewise, wives, be subject to your own husbands, so that even if some do not obey the word, they may be won without a word by the conduct of their wives, ²when they see your respectful and pure conduct. ³Do not let your adorning be external — the braiding of hair and the putting on of gold jewellery, or the clothing you wear — ⁴but let your adorning be the hidden person of the heart with the imperishable beauty of a gentle and quiet spirit, which in God's sight is very precious. ⁵For this is how the holy women who hoped in God used to adorn themselves, by submitting to their own husbands, ⁶as Sarah obeyed Abraham, calling him lord. And you are her children, if you do good and do not fear anything that is frightening.

⁷Likewise, husbands, live with your wives in an understanding way, showing honour to the woman as the weaker vessel, since they are heirs with youᵉ of the grace of life, so that your prayers may not be hindered.

SUFFERING FOR RIGHTEOUSNESS' SAKE

⁸Finally, all of you, have unity of mind, sympathy, brotherly love, a tender heart, and

---
ᵃGreek *the head of the corner* ᵇOr *every institution ordained for people* ᶜOr *king*; also verse 17 ᵈFor the contextual rendering of the Greek word *doulos*, see Preface ᵉSome manuscripts *since you are joint heirs*

a humble mind. ⁹Do not repay evil for evil or reviling for reviling, but on the contrary, bless, for to this you were called, that you may obtain a blessing. ¹⁰For

> "Whoever desires to love life
>   and see good days,
> let him keep his tongue from evil
>   and his lips from speaking deceit;
> ¹¹   let him turn away from
>   evil and do good;
>   let him seek peace and pursue it.
> ¹² For the eyes of the Lord are
>   on the righteous,
>   and his ears are open to their prayer.
> But the face of the Lord is against
>   those who do evil."

¹³Now who is there to harm you if you are zealous for what is good? ¹⁴But even if you should suffer for righteousness' sake, you will be blessed. Have no fear of them, nor be troubled, ¹⁵but in your hearts honour Christ the Lord as holy, always being prepared to make a defence to anyone who asks you for a reason for the hope that is in you; yet do it with gentleness and respect, ¹⁶having a good conscience, so that, when you are slandered, those who revile your good behaviour in Christ may be put to shame. ¹⁷For it is better to suffer for doing good, if that should be God's will, than for doing evil.

¹⁸For Christ also suffered[a] once for sins, the righteous for the unrighteous, that he might bring us to God, being put to death in the flesh but made alive in the spirit, ¹⁹in which[b] he went and proclaimed[c] to the spirits in prison, ²⁰because[d] they formerly did not obey, when God's patience waited in the days of Noah, while the ark was being prepared, in which a few, that is, eight persons, were brought safely through water. ²¹Baptism, which corresponds to this, now saves you, not as a removal of dirt from the body but as an appeal to God for a good conscience, through the resurrection of Jesus Christ, ²²who has gone into heaven and is at the right hand of God, with angels, authorities, and powers having been subjected to him.

STEWARDS OF GOD'S GRACE

4 Since therefore Christ suffered in the flesh,[e] arm yourselves with the same way of thinking, for whoever has suffered in the flesh has ceased from sin, ²so as to live for the rest of the time in the flesh no longer for human passions but for the will of God. ³For the time that is past suffices for doing what the Gentiles want to do, living in sensuality, passions, drunkenness, orgies, drinking parties, and lawless idolatry. ⁴With respect to this they are surprised when you do not join them in the same flood of debauchery, and they malign you; ⁵but they will give account to him who is ready to judge the living and the dead. ⁶For this is why the gospel was preached even to those who are dead, that though judged in the flesh the way people are, they might live in the spirit the way God does.

⁷The end of all things is at hand; therefore be self-controlled and sober-minded for the sake of your prayers. ⁸Above all, keep loving one another earnestly, since love covers a multitude of sins. ⁹Show hospitality to one another without grumbling. ¹⁰As each has received a gift, use it to serve one another, as good stewards of God's varied grace: ¹¹whoever speaks, as one who speaks oracles of God; whoever serves, as one who serves by the strength that God supplies—in order that in everything God may be glorified through Jesus Christ. To him belong glory and dominion for ever and ever. Amen.

SUFFERING AS A CHRISTIAN

¹²Beloved, do not be surprised at the fiery trial when it comes upon you to test you, as though something strange were happening to you. ¹³But rejoice insofar as you share Christ's sufferings, that you may also rejoice and be glad when his glory is revealed. ¹⁴If you are insulted for the name of Christ, you are blessed, because the Spirit of glory[f] and of God rests upon you. ¹⁵But let none of you suffer as a murderer or a thief or an evildoer or as a meddler. ¹⁶Yet if anyone suffers as a Christian, let him not be ashamed, but let him glorify God in that name. ¹⁷For it is time for judgement to begin at the household of God; and if it begins with us, what will be the outcome for those who do not obey the gospel of God? ¹⁸And

> "If the righteous is scarcely saved,
>   what will become of the ungodly
>   and the sinner?"[g]

---

[a] Some manuscripts *died* [b] Or *the Spirit, in whom* [c] Or *preached*
[d] Or *when* [e] Some manuscripts add *for us; some for you*
[f] Some manuscripts insert *and of power* [g] Greek *where will the ungodly and sinner appear?*

¹⁹Therefore let those who suffer according to God's will entrust their souls to a faithful Creator while doing good.

SHEPHERD THE FLOCK OF GOD

5 So I exhort the elders among you, as a fellow elder and a witness of the sufferings of Christ, as well as a partaker in the glory that is going to be revealed: ²shepherd the flock of God that is among you, exercising oversight,[a] not under compulsion, but willingly, as God would have you;[b] not for shameful gain, but eagerly; ³not domineering over those in your charge, but being examples to the flock. ⁴And when the chief Shepherd appears, you will receive the unfading crown of glory. ⁵Likewise, you who are younger, be subject to the elders. Clothe yourselves, all of you, with humility towards one another, for "God opposes the proud but gives grace to the humble."

⁶Humble yourselves, therefore, under the mighty hand of God so that at the proper time he may exalt you, ⁷casting all your anxieties on him, because he cares for you. ⁸Be sober-minded; be watchful. Your adversary the devil prowls around like a roaring lion, seeking someone to devour. ⁹Resist him, firm in your faith, knowing that the same kinds of suffering are being experienced by your brotherhood throughout the world. ¹⁰And after you have suffered for a little while, the God of all grace, who has called you to his eternal glory in Christ, will himself restore, confirm, strengthen, and establish you. ¹¹To him be the dominion for ever and ever. Amen.

FINAL GREETINGS

¹²By Silvanus, a faithful brother as I regard him, I have written briefly to you, exhorting and declaring that this is the true grace of God. Stand firm in it. ¹³She who is at Babylon, who is likewise chosen, sends you greetings, and so does Mark, my son. ¹⁴Greet one another with the kiss of love.

Peace to all of you who are in Christ.

---

[a]Some manuscripts omit *exercising oversight* [b]Some manuscripts omit *as God would have you*

THE SECOND LETTER OF PETER
2 PETER

GREETING

1 Simeon[a] Peter, a servant[b] and apostle of Jesus Christ,

To those who have obtained a faith of equal standing with ours by the righteousness of our God and Saviour Jesus Christ: ²May grace and peace be multiplied to you in the knowledge of God and of Jesus our Lord.

CONFIRM YOUR CALLING AND ELECTION

³His divine power has granted to us all things that pertain to life and godliness, through the knowledge of him who called us to[c] his own glory and excellence,[d] ⁴by which he has granted to us his precious and very great promises, so that through them you may become partakers of the divine nature, having escaped from the corruption that is in the world because of sinful desire. ⁵For this very reason, make every effort to supplement your faith with virtue,[e] and virtue with knowledge, ⁶and knowledge with self-control, and self-control with steadfastness, and steadfastness with godliness, ⁷and godliness with brotherly affection, and brotherly affection with love. ⁸For if these qualities[f] are yours and are increasing, they keep you from being ineffective or unfruitful in the knowledge of our Lord Jesus Christ. ⁹For whoever lacks these qualities is so short-sighted that he is blind, having forgotten that he was cleansed from his former sins. ¹⁰Therefore, brothers,[g] be all the more diligent to confirm your calling and election, for if you practise these qualities you will never fall. ¹¹For in this way there will be richly provided for you an entrance into the eternal kingdom of our Lord and Saviour Jesus Christ.

¹²Therefore I intend always to remind you of these qualities, though you know them and are established in the truth that you have. ¹³I think it right, as long as I am in this body,[h] to stir you up by way of reminder, ¹⁴since I know that the putting off of my body will be soon, as our Lord Jesus Christ made clear to me. ¹⁵And I will make every effort so that after my departure you may be able at any time to recall these things.

CHRIST'S GLORY AND THE PROPHETIC WORD

¹⁶For we did not follow cleverly devised myths when we made known to you the power and coming of our Lord Jesus Christ, but we were eyewitnesses of his majesty. ¹⁷For when he received honour and glory from God the Father, and the voice was borne to him by the Majestic Glory, "This is my beloved Son,[i] with whom I am well pleased", ¹⁸we ourselves heard this very voice borne from heaven, for we were with him on the holy mountain. ¹⁹And we have the prophetic word more fully confirmed, to which you will do well to pay attention as to a lamp shining in a dark place, until the day dawns and the morning star rises in your hearts, ²⁰knowing this first of all, that no prophecy of Scripture comes from someone's own interpretation. ²¹For no prophecy was ever produced by the will of man, but men spoke from God as they were carried along by the Holy Spirit.

FALSE PROPHETS AND TEACHERS

2 But false prophets also arose among the people, just as there will be false teachers among you, who will secretly bring in destructive heresies, even denying the Master who bought them, bringing upon themselves swift destruction. ²And many will follow their sensuality, and because of them the way of truth will be blasphemed. ³And in their greed they will exploit you with false words. Their condemnation from long ago is not idle, and their destruction is not asleep.

⁴For if God did not spare angels when they sinned, but cast them into hell[j] and committed them to chains[k] of gloomy darkness

---

[a] Some manuscripts *Simon* [b] For the contextual rendering of the Greek word *doulos*, see Preface [c] Or *by* [d] Or *virtue* [e] Or *excellence*; twice in this verse [f] Greek *these things*; also verses 9, 10, 12
[g] Or *brothers and sisters*. In New Testament usage, depending on the context, the plural Greek word *adelphoi* (translated "brothers") may refer either to *brothers* or to *brothers and sisters* [h] Greek *tent*; also verse 14 [i] Or *my Son, my* (or *the*) *Beloved* [j] Greek *Tartarus*
[k] Some manuscripts *pits*

to be kept until the judgement; ⁵if he did not spare the ancient world, but preserved Noah, a herald of righteousness, with seven others, when he brought a flood upon the world of the ungodly; ⁶if by turning the cities of Sodom and Gomorrah to ashes he condemned them to extinction, making them an example of what is going to happen to the ungodly;*ᵃ* ⁷and if he rescued righteous Lot, greatly distressed by the sensual conduct of the wicked ⁸(for as that righteous man lived among them day after day, he was tormenting his righteous soul over their lawless deeds that he saw and heard); ⁹then the Lord knows how to rescue the godly from trials,*ᵇ* and to keep the unrighteous under punishment until the day of judgement, ¹⁰and especially those who indulge*ᶜ* in the lust of defiling passion and despise authority.

Bold and wilful, they do not tremble as they blaspheme the glorious ones, ¹¹whereas angels, though greater in might and power, do not pronounce a blasphemous judgement against them before the Lord. ¹²But these, like irrational animals, creatures of instinct, born to be caught and destroyed, blaspheming about matters of which they are ignorant, will also be destroyed in their destruction, ¹³suffering wrong as the wage for their wrongdoing. They count it pleasure to revel in the daytime. They are blots and blemishes, revelling in their deceptions,*ᵈ* while they feast with you. ¹⁴They have eyes full of adultery,*ᵉ* insatiable for sin. They entice unsteady souls. They have hearts trained in greed. Accursed children! ¹⁵Forsaking the right way, they have gone astray. They have followed the way of Balaam, the son of Beor, who loved gain from wrongdoing, ¹⁶but was rebuked for his own transgression; a speechless donkey spoke with human voice and restrained the prophet's madness.

¹⁷These are waterless springs and mists driven by a storm. For them the gloom of utter darkness has been reserved. ¹⁸For, speaking loud boasts of folly, they entice by sensual passions of the flesh those who are barely escaping from those who live in error. ¹⁹They promise them freedom, but they themselves are slaves*ᶠ* of corruption. For whatever overcomes a person, to that he is enslaved. ²⁰For if, after they have escaped the defilements of the world through the knowledge of our Lord and Saviour Jesus Christ, they are again entangled in them and overcome, the last state has become worse for them than the first. ²¹For it would have been better for them never to have known the way of righteousness than after knowing it to turn back from the holy commandment delivered to them. ²²What the true proverb says has happened to them: "The dog returns to its own vomit, and the sow, after washing herself, returns to wallow in the mire."

THE DAY OF THE LORD WILL COME

3 This is now the second letter that I am writing to you, beloved. In both of them I am stirring up your sincere mind by way of reminder, ²that you should remember the predictions of the holy prophets and the commandment of the Lord and Saviour through your apostles, ³knowing this first of all, that scoffers will come in the last days with scoffing, following their own sinful desires. ⁴They will say, "Where is the promise of his coming? For ever since the fathers fell asleep, all things are continuing as they were from the beginning of creation." ⁵For they deliberately overlook this fact, that the heavens existed long ago, and the earth was formed out of water and through water by the word of God, ⁶and that by means of these the world that then existed was deluged with water and perished. ⁷But by the same word the heavens and earth that now exist are stored up for fire, being kept until the day of judgement and destruction of the ungodly.

⁸But do not overlook this one fact, beloved, that with the Lord one day is as a thousand years, and a thousand years as one day. ⁹The Lord is not slow to fulfil his promise as some count slowness, but is patient towards you,*ᵍ* not wishing that any should perish, but that all should reach repentance. ¹⁰But the day of the Lord will come like a thief, and then the heavens will pass away with a roar, and the heavenly bodies*ʰ* will be burned up and dissolved, and the earth and the works that are done on it will be exposed.*ⁱ*

¹¹Since all these things are thus to be dissolved, what sort of people ought you to be in lives of holiness and godliness, ¹²waiting for and hastening the coming of the day of God, because of which the heavens will be set on

---

*ᵃ*Some manuscripts *an example to those who were to be ungodly* *ᵇ*Or *temptations* *ᶜ*Greek *who go after the flesh* *ᵈ*Some manuscripts *love feasts* *ᵉ*Or *eyes full of an adulteress* *ᶠ*For the contextual rendering of the Greek word *doulos*, see Preface *ᵍ*Some manuscripts *on your account* *ʰ*Or *elements*; also verse 12 *ⁱ*Greek *found*; some manuscripts *will be burned up*

fire and dissolved, and the heavenly bodies will melt as they burn! ¹³But according to his promise we are waiting for new heavens and a new earth in which righteousness dwells.

FINAL WORDS

¹⁴Therefore, beloved, since you are waiting for these, be diligent to be found by him without spot or blemish, and at peace. ¹⁵And count the patience of our Lord as salvation, just as our beloved brother Paul also wrote to you according to the wisdom given him, ¹⁶as he does in all his letters when he speaks in them of these matters. There are some things in them that are hard to understand, which the ignorant and unstable twist to their own destruction, as they do the other Scriptures. ¹⁷You therefore, beloved, knowing this beforehand, take care that you are not carried away with the error of lawless people and lose your own stability. ¹⁸But grow in the grace and knowledge of our Lord and Saviour Jesus Christ. To him be the glory both now and to the day of eternity. Amen.

THE FIRST LETTER OF JOHN
1 JOHN

THE WORD OF LIFE

1 That which was from the beginning, which we have heard, which we have seen with our eyes, which we looked upon and have touched with our hands, concerning the word of life — ²the life was made manifest, and we have seen it, and testify to it and proclaim to you the eternal life, which was with the Father and was made manifest to us — ³that which we have seen and heard we proclaim also to you, so that you too may have fellowship with us; and indeed our fellowship is with the Father and with his Son Jesus Christ. ⁴And we are writing these things so that our[a] joy may be complete.

WALKING IN THE LIGHT

⁵This is the message we have heard from him and proclaim to you, that God is light, and in him is no darkness at all. ⁶If we say we have fellowship with him while we walk in darkness, we lie and do not practise the truth. ⁷But if we walk in the light, as he is in the light, we have fellowship with one another, and the blood of Jesus his Son cleanses us from all sin. ⁸If we say we have no sin, we deceive ourselves, and the truth is not in us. ⁹If we confess our sins, he is faithful and just to forgive us our sins and to cleanse us from all unrighteousness. ¹⁰If we say we have not sinned, we make him a liar, and his word is not in us.

CHRIST OUR ADVOCATE

2 My little children, I am writing these things to you so that you may not sin. But if anyone does sin, we have an advocate with the Father, Jesus Christ the righteous. ²He is the propitiation for our sins, and not for ours only but also for the sins of the whole world. ³And by this we know that we have come to know him, if we keep his commandments. ⁴Whoever says "I know him" but does not keep his commandments is a liar, and the truth is not in him, ⁵but whoever keeps his word, in him truly the love of God is perfected. By this we may know that we are in him: ⁶whoever says he abides in him ought to walk in the same way in which he walked.

THE NEW COMMANDMENT

⁷Beloved, I am writing you no new commandment, but an old commandment that you had from the beginning. The old commandment is the word that you have heard. ⁸At the same time, it is a new commandment that I am writing to you, which is true in him and in you, because[b] the darkness is passing away and the true light is already shining. ⁹Whoever says he is in the light and hates his brother is still in darkness. ¹⁰Whoever loves his brother abides in the light, and in him[c] there is no cause for stumbling. ¹¹But whoever hates his brother is in the darkness and walks in the darkness, and does not know where he is going, because the darkness has blinded his eyes.

¹² I am writing to you, little children,
   because your sins are forgiven
      for his name's sake.
¹³ I am writing to you, fathers,
   because you know him who
      is from the beginning.
   I am writing to you, young men,
   because you have overcome
      the evil one.
   I write to you, children,
   because you know the Father.
¹⁴ I write to you, fathers,
   because you know him who
      is from the beginning.
   I write to you, young men,
   because you are strong,
   and the word of God abides in you,
   and you have overcome the evil one.

DO NOT LOVE THE WORLD

¹⁵Do not love the world or the things in the world. If anyone loves the world, the love of the Father is not in him. ¹⁶For all that is

---

[a] Some manuscripts *your* [b] Or *that* [c] Or *it*

in the world—the desires of the flesh and the desires of the eyes and pride of life[a]—is not from the Father but is from the world. ¹⁷And the world is passing away along with its desires, but whoever does the will of God abides for ever.

WARNING CONCERNING ANTICHRISTS

¹⁸Children, it is the last hour, and as you have heard that antichrist is coming, so now many antichrists have come. Therefore we know that it is the last hour. ¹⁹They went out from us, but they were not of us; for if they had been of us, they would have continued with us. But they went out, that it might become plain that they all are not of us. ²⁰But you have been anointed by the Holy One, and you all have knowledge.[b] ²¹I write to you, not because you do not know the truth, but because you know it, and because no lie is of the truth. ²²Who is the liar but he who denies that Jesus is the Christ? This is the antichrist, he who denies the Father and the Son. ²³No one who denies the Son has the Father. Whoever confesses the Son has the Father also. ²⁴Let what you heard from the beginning abide in you. If what you heard from the beginning abides in you, then you too will abide in the Son and in the Father. ²⁵And this is the promise that he made to us[c]—eternal life.

²⁶I write these things to you about those who are trying to deceive you. ²⁷But the anointing that you received from him abides in you, and you have no need that anyone should teach you. But as his anointing teaches you about everything, and is true, and is no lie—just as it has taught you, abide in him.

CHILDREN OF GOD

²⁸And now, little children, abide in him, so that when he appears we may have confidence and not shrink from him in shame at his coming. ²⁹If you know that he is righteous, you may be sure that everyone who practises righteousness has been born of him.

3 See what kind of love the Father has given to us, that we should be called children of God; and so we are. The reason why the world does not know us is that it did not know him. ²Beloved, we are God's children now, and what we will be has not yet appeared; but we know that when he appears[d] we shall be like him, because we shall see him as he is. ³And everyone who thus hopes in him purifies himself as he is pure.

⁴Everyone who makes a practice of sinning also practises lawlessness; sin is lawlessness. ⁵You know that he appeared in order to take away sins, and in him there is no sin. ⁶No one who abides in him keeps on sinning; no one who keeps on sinning has either seen him or known him. ⁷Little children, let no one deceive you. Whoever practises righteousness is righteous, as he is righteous. ⁸Whoever makes a practice of sinning is of the devil, for the devil has been sinning from the beginning. The reason the Son of God appeared was to destroy the works of the devil. ⁹No one born of God makes a practice of sinning, for God's[e] seed abides in him; and he cannot keep on sinning, because he has been born of God. ¹⁰By this it is evident who are the children of God, and who are the children of the devil: whoever does not practise righteousness is not of God, nor is the one who does not love his brother.

LOVE ONE ANOTHER

¹¹For this is the message that you have heard from the beginning, that we should love one another. ¹²We should not be like Cain, who was of the evil one and murdered his brother. And why did he murder him? Because his own deeds were evil and his brother's righteous. ¹³Do not be surprised, brothers,[f] that the world hates you. ¹⁴We know that we have passed out of death into life, because we love the brothers. Whoever does not love abides in death. ¹⁵Everyone who hates his brother is a murderer, and you know that no murderer has eternal life abiding in him.

¹⁶By this we know love, that he laid down his life for us, and we ought to lay down our lives for the brothers. ¹⁷But if anyone has the world's goods and sees his brother in need, yet closes his heart against him, how does God's love abide in him? ¹⁸Little children, let us not love in word or talk but in deed and in truth.

¹⁹By this we shall know that we are of the truth and reassure our heart before him; ²⁰for whenever our heart condemns us,

---

[a] Or *pride in possessions* [b] Some manuscripts *you know everything*
[c] Some manuscripts *you* [d] Or *when it appears* [e] Greek *his*
[f] Or *brothers and sisters*. In New Testament usage, depending on the context, the plural Greek word *adelphoi* (translated "brothers") may refer either to *brothers* or to *brothers and sisters*; also verses 14, 16

God is greater than our heart, and he knows everything. ²¹Beloved, if our heart does not condemn us, we have confidence before God; ²²and whatever we ask we receive from him, because we keep his commandments and do what pleases him. ²³And this is his commandment, that we believe in the name of his Son Jesus Christ and love one another, just as he has commanded us. ²⁴Whoever keeps his commandments abides in God,[a] and God[b] in him. And by this we know that he abides in us, by the Spirit whom he has given us.

TEST THE SPIRITS

4 Beloved, do not believe every spirit, but test the spirits to see whether they are from God, for many false prophets have gone out into the world. ²By this you know the Spirit of God: every spirit that confesses that Jesus Christ has come in the flesh is from God, ³and every spirit that does not confess Jesus is not from God. This is the spirit of the antichrist, which you heard was coming and now is in the world already. ⁴Little children, you are from God and have overcome them, for he who is in you is greater than he who is in the world. ⁵They are from the world; therefore they speak from the world, and the world listens to them. ⁶We are from God. Whoever knows God listens to us; whoever is not from God does not listen to us. By this we know the Spirit of truth and the spirit of error.

GOD IS LOVE

⁷Beloved, let us love one another, for love is from God, and whoever loves has been born of God and knows God. ⁸Anyone who does not love does not know God, because God is love. ⁹In this the love of God was made manifest among us, that God sent his only Son into the world, so that we might live through him. ¹⁰In this is love, not that we have loved God but that he loved us and sent his Son to be the propitiation for our sins. ¹¹Beloved, if God so loved us, we also ought to love one another. ¹²No one has ever seen God; if we love one another, God abides in us and his love is perfected in us.

¹³By this we know that we abide in him and he in us, because he has given us of his Spirit. ¹⁴And we have seen and testify that the Father has sent his Son to be the Saviour of the world. ¹⁵Whoever confesses that Jesus is the Son of God, God abides in him, and he in God. ¹⁶So we have come to know and to believe the love that God has for us. God is love, and whoever abides in love abides in God, and God abides in him. ¹⁷By this is love perfected with us, so that we may have confidence for the day of judgement, because as he is so also are we in this world. ¹⁸There is no fear in love, but perfect love casts out fear. For fear has to do with punishment, and whoever fears has not been perfected in love. ¹⁹We love because he first loved us. ²⁰If anyone says, "I love God", and hates his brother, he is a liar; for he who does not love his brother whom he has seen cannot[c] love God whom he has not seen. ²¹And this commandment we have from him: whoever loves God must also love his brother.

OVERCOMING THE WORLD

5 Everyone who believes that Jesus is the Christ has been born of God, and everyone who loves the Father loves whoever has been born of him. ²By this we know that we love the children of God, when we love God and obey his commandments. ³For this is the love of God, that we keep his commandments. And his commandments are not burdensome. ⁴For everyone who has been born of God overcomes the world. And this is the victory that has overcome the world — our faith. ⁵Who is it that overcomes the world except the one who believes that Jesus is the Son of God?

TESTIMONY CONCERNING THE SON OF GOD

⁶This is he who came by water and blood — Jesus Christ; not by the water only but by the water and the blood. And the Spirit is the one who testifies, because the Spirit is the truth. ⁷For there are three that testify: ⁸the Spirit and the water and the blood; and these three agree. ⁹If we receive the testimony of men, the testimony of God is greater, for this is the testimony of God that he has borne concerning his Son. ¹⁰Whoever believes in the Son of God has the testimony in himself. Whoever does not believe God has made him a liar, because he has not believed in the testimony that God has borne concerning his Son. ¹¹And this is the testimony, that God gave us eternal life, and this life is in his Son. ¹²Whoever has the Son has life; whoever does not have the Son of God does not have life.

---

[a]Greek *him* [b]Greek *he* [c]Some manuscripts *how can he*

THAT YOU MAY KNOW

[13] I write these things to you who believe in the name of the Son of God, that you may know that you have eternal life. [14] And this is the confidence that we have towards him, that if we ask anything according to his will he hears us. [15] And if we know that he hears us in whatever we ask, we know that we have the requests that we have asked of him.

[16] If anyone sees his brother committing a sin not leading to death, he shall ask, and God[a] will give him life—to those who commit sins that do not lead to death. There is sin that leads to death; I do not say that one should pray for that. [17] All wrongdoing is sin, but there is sin that does not lead to death.

[18] We know that everyone who has been born of God does not keep on sinning, but he who was born of God protects him, and the evil one does not touch him.

[19] We know that we are from God, and the whole world lies in the power of the evil one.

[20] And we know that the Son of God has come and has given us understanding, so that we may know him who is true; and we are in him who is true, in his Son Jesus Christ. He is the true God and eternal life. [21] Little children, keep yourselves from idols.

---

[a] Greek *he*

THE SECOND LETTER OF JOHN
2 JOHN

GREETING

¹The elder to the elect lady and her children, whom I love in truth, and not only I, but also all who know the truth, ²because of the truth that abides in us and will be with us for ever:

³Grace, mercy, and peace will be with us, from God the Father and from Jesus Christ the Father's Son, in truth and love.

WALKING IN TRUTH AND LOVE

⁴I rejoiced greatly to find some of your children walking in the truth, just as we were commanded by the Father. ⁵And now I ask you, dear lady—not as though I were writing you a new commandment, but the one we have had from the beginning—that we love one another. ⁶And this is love, that we walk according to his commandments; this is the commandment, just as you have heard from the beginning, so that you should walk in it. ⁷For many deceivers have gone out into the world, those who do not confess the coming of Jesus Christ in the flesh. Such a one is the deceiver and the antichrist. ⁸Watch yourselves, so that you may not lose what we[a] have worked for, but may win a full reward. ⁹Everyone who goes on ahead and does not abide in the teaching of Christ, does not have God. Whoever abides in the teaching has both the Father and the Son. ¹⁰If anyone comes to you and does not bring this teaching, do not receive him into your house or give him any greeting, ¹¹for whoever greets him takes part in his wicked works.

FINAL GREETINGS

¹²Though I have much to write to you, I would rather not use paper and ink. Instead I hope to come to you and talk face to face, so that our joy may be complete.

¹³The children of your elect sister greet you.

---

[a] Some manuscripts *you*

THE THIRD LETTER OF JOHN
3 JOHN

GREETING

¹The elder to the beloved Gaius, whom I love in truth.

²Beloved, I pray that all may go well with you and that you may be in good health, as it goes well with your soul. ³For I rejoiced greatly when the brothers[a] came and testified to your truth, as indeed you are walking in the truth. ⁴I have no greater joy than to hear that my children are walking in the truth.

SUPPORT AND OPPOSITION

⁵Beloved, it is a faithful thing you do in all your efforts for these brothers, strangers as they are, ⁶who testified to your love before the church. You will do well to send them on their journey in a manner worthy of God. ⁷For they have gone out for the sake of the name, accepting nothing from the Gentiles. ⁸Therefore we ought to support people like these, that we may be fellow workers for the truth.

⁹I have written something to the church, but Diotrephes, who likes to put himself first, does not acknowledge our authority. ¹⁰So if I come, I will bring up what he is doing, talking wicked nonsense against us. And not content with that, he refuses to welcome the brothers, and also stops those who want to and puts them out of the church.

¹¹Beloved, do not imitate evil but imitate good. Whoever does good is from God; whoever does evil has not seen God. ¹²Demetrius has received a good testimony from everyone, and from the truth itself. We also add our testimony, and you know that our testimony is true.

FINAL GREETINGS

¹³I had much to write to you, but I would rather not write with pen and ink. ¹⁴I hope to see you soon, and we will talk face to face.

¹⁵Peace be to you. The friends greet you. Greet the friends, each by name.

---

[a] Or *brothers and sisters*. In New Testament usage, depending on the context, the plural Greek word *adelphoi* (translated "brothers") may refer either to *brothers* or to *brothers and sisters*; also verses 5, 10

THE LETTER OF JUDE

GREETING

¹Jude, a servant[a] of Jesus Christ and brother of James,

To those who are called, beloved in God the Father and kept for[b] Jesus Christ:

²May mercy, peace, and love be multiplied to you.

JUDGEMENT ON FALSE TEACHERS

³Beloved, although I was very eager to write to you about our common salvation, I found it necessary to write appealing to you to contend for the faith that was once for all delivered to the saints. ⁴For certain people have crept in unnoticed who long ago were designated for this condemnation, ungodly people, who pervert the grace of our God into sensuality and deny our only Master and Lord, Jesus Christ.

⁵Now I want to remind you, although you once fully knew it, that Jesus, who saved[c] a people out of the land of Egypt, afterwards destroyed those who did not believe. ⁶And the angels who did not stay within their own position of authority, but left their proper dwelling, he has kept in eternal chains under gloomy darkness until the judgement of the great day— ⁷just as Sodom and Gomorrah and the surrounding cities, which likewise indulged in sexual immorality and pursued unnatural desire,[d] serve as an example by undergoing a punishment of eternal fire.

⁸Yet in like manner these people also, relying on their dreams, defile the flesh, reject authority, and blaspheme the glorious ones. ⁹But when the archangel Michael, contending with the devil, was disputing about the body of Moses, he did not presume to pronounce a blasphemous judgement, but said, "The Lord rebuke you." ¹⁰But these people blaspheme all that they do not understand, and they are destroyed by all that they, like unreasoning animals, understand instinctively. ¹¹Woe to them! For they walked in the way of Cain and abandoned themselves for the sake of gain to Balaam's error and perished in Korah's rebellion. ¹²These are hidden reefs[e] at your love feasts, as they feast with you without fear, shepherds feeding themselves; waterless clouds, swept along by winds; fruitless trees in late autumn, twice dead, uprooted; ¹³wild waves of the sea, casting up the foam of their own shame; wandering stars, for whom the gloom of utter darkness has been reserved for ever.

¹⁴It was also about these that Enoch, the seventh from Adam, prophesied, saying, "Behold, the Lord comes with ten thousands of his holy ones, ¹⁵to execute judgement on all and to convict all the ungodly of all their deeds of ungodliness that they have committed in such an ungodly way, and of all the harsh things that ungodly sinners have spoken against him." ¹⁶These are grumblers, malcontents, following their own sinful desires; they are loud-mouthed boasters, showing favouritism to gain advantage.

A CALL TO PERSEVERE

¹⁷But you must remember, beloved, the predictions of the apostles of our Lord Jesus Christ. ¹⁸They[f] said to you, "In the last time there will be scoffers, following their own ungodly passions." ¹⁹It is these who cause divisions, worldly people, devoid of the Spirit. ²⁰But you, beloved, building yourselves up in your most holy faith and praying in the Holy Spirit, ²¹keep yourselves in the love of God, waiting for the mercy of our Lord Jesus Christ that leads to eternal life. ²²And have mercy on those who doubt; ²³save others by snatching them out of the fire; to others show mercy with fear, hating even the garment[g] stained by the flesh.

---

[a] For the contextual rendering of the Greek word *doulos*, see Preface [b] Or *by* [c] Some manuscripts *although you fully knew it, that the Lord who once saved* [d] Greek *different flesh* [e] Or *are blemishes* [f] Or *Christ, because they* [g] Greek *chiton*, a long garment worn under the cloak next to the skin

JUDE

DOXOLOGY

²⁴Now to him who is able to keep you from stumbling and to present you blameless before the presence of his glory with great joy, ²⁵to the only God, our Saviour, through Jesus Christ our Lord, be glory, majesty, dominion, and authority, before all time¹ and now and for ever. Amen.

---

¹Or *before any age*

THE REVELATION
TO JOHN

PROLOGUE

1 The revelation of Jesus Christ, which God gave him to show to his servants[a] the things that must soon take place. He made it known by sending his angel to his servant John, ²who bore witness to the word of God and to the testimony of Jesus Christ, even to all that he saw. ³Blessed is the one who reads aloud the words of this prophecy, and blessed are those who hear, and who keep what is written in it, for the time is near.

GREETING TO THE SEVEN CHURCHES

⁴John to the seven churches that are in Asia:

Grace to you and peace from him who is and who was and who is to come, and from the seven spirits who are before his throne, ⁵and from Jesus Christ the faithful witness, the firstborn of the dead, and the ruler of kings on earth.

To him who loves us and has freed us from our sins by his blood ⁶and made us a kingdom, priests to his God and Father, to him be glory and dominion for ever and ever. Amen. ⁷Behold, he is coming with the clouds, and every eye will see him, even those who pierced him, and all tribes of the earth will wail[b] on account of him. Even so. Amen.

⁸"I am the Alpha and the Omega," says the Lord God, "who is and who was and who is to come, the Almighty."

VISION OF THE SON OF MAN

⁹I, John, your brother and partner in the tribulation and the kingdom and the patient endurance that are in Jesus, was on the island called Patmos on account of the word of God and the testimony of Jesus. ¹⁰I was in the Spirit on the Lord's day, and I heard behind me a loud voice like a trumpet ¹¹saying, "Write what you see in a book and send it to the seven churches, to Ephesus and to Smyrna and to Pergamum and to Thyatira and to Sardis and to Philadelphia and to Laodicea."

¹²Then I turned to see the voice that was speaking to me, and on turning I saw seven golden lampstands, ¹³and in the midst of the lampstands one like a son of man, clothed with a long robe and with a golden sash round his chest. ¹⁴The hairs of his head were white, like white wool, like snow. His eyes were like a flame of fire, ¹⁵his feet were like burnished bronze, refined in a furnace, and his voice was like the roar of many waters. ¹⁶In his right hand he held seven stars, from his mouth came a sharp two-edged sword, and his face was like the sun shining in full strength.

¹⁷When I saw him, I fell at his feet as though dead. But he laid his right hand on me, saying, "Fear not, I am the first and the last, ¹⁸and the living one. I died, and behold I am alive for evermore, and I have the keys of Death and Hades. ¹⁹Write therefore the things that you have seen, those that are and those that are to take place after this. ²⁰As for the mystery of the seven stars that you saw in my right hand, and the seven golden lampstands, the seven stars are the angels of the seven churches, and the seven lampstands are the seven churches.

TO THE CHURCH IN EPHESUS

2 "To the angel of the church in Ephesus write: 'The words of him who holds the seven stars in his right hand, who walks among the seven golden lampstands.

²"'I know your works, your toil and your patient endurance, and how you cannot bear with those who are evil, but have tested those who call themselves apostles and are not, and found them to be false. ³I know you are enduring patiently and bearing up for my

---

[a]For the contextual rendering of the Greek word *doulos*, see Preface; likewise for *servant* later in this verse [b]Or *mourn*

name's sake, and you have not grown weary. ⁴But I have this against you, that you have abandoned the love you had at first. ⁵Remember therefore from where you have fallen; repent, and do the works you did at first. If not, I will come to you and remove your lampstand from its place, unless you repent. ⁶Yet this you have: you hate the works of the Nicolaitans, which I also hate. ⁷He who has an ear, let him hear what the Spirit says to the churches. To the one who conquers I will grant to eat of the tree of life, which is in the paradise of God.'

TO THE CHURCH IN SMYRNA

⁸"And to the angel of the church in Smyrna write: 'The words of the first and the last, who died and came to life.

⁹"'I know your tribulation and your poverty (but you are rich) and the slander[a] of those who say that they are Jews and are not, but are a synagogue of Satan. ¹⁰Do not fear what you are about to suffer. Behold, the devil is about to throw some of you into prison, that you may be tested, and for ten days you will have tribulation. Be faithful unto death, and I will give you the crown of life. ¹¹He who has an ear, let him hear what the Spirit says to the churches. The one who conquers will not be hurt by the second death.'

TO THE CHURCH IN PERGAMUM

¹²"And to the angel of the church in Pergamum write: 'The words of him who has the sharp two-edged sword.

¹³"'I know where you dwell, where Satan's throne is. Yet you hold fast my name, and you did not deny my faith[b] even in the days of Antipas my faithful witness, who was killed among you, where Satan dwells. ¹⁴But I have a few things against you: you have some there who hold the teaching of Balaam, who taught Balak to put a stumbling block before the sons of Israel, so that they might eat food sacrificed to idols and practise sexual immorality. ¹⁵So also you have some who hold the teaching of the Nicolaitans. ¹⁶Therefore repent. If not, I will come to you soon and war against them with the sword of my mouth. ¹⁷He who has an ear, let him hear what the Spirit says to the churches. To the one who conquers I will give some of the hidden manna, and I will give him a white stone, with a new name written on the stone that no one knows except the one who receives it.'

TO THE CHURCH IN THYATIRA

¹⁸"And to the angel of the church in Thyatira write: 'The words of the Son of God, who has eyes like a flame of fire, and whose feet are like burnished bronze.

¹⁹"'I know your works, your love and faith and service and patient endurance, and that your latter works exceed the first. ²⁰But I have this against you, that you tolerate that woman Jezebel, who calls herself a prophetess and is teaching and seducing my servants to practise sexual immorality and to eat food sacrificed to idols. ²¹I gave her time to repent, but she refuses to repent of her sexual immorality. ²²Behold, I will throw her onto a sickbed, and those who commit adultery with her I will throw into great tribulation, unless they repent of her works, ²³and I will strike her children dead. And all the churches will know that I am he who searches mind and heart, and I will give to each of you according to your works. ²⁴But to the rest of you in Thyatira, who do not hold this teaching, who have not learned what some call the deep things of Satan, to you I say, I do not lay on you any other burden. ²⁵Only hold fast what you have until I come. ²⁶The one who conquers and who keeps my works until the end, to him I will give authority over the nations, ²⁷and he will rule[c] them with a rod of iron, as when earthen pots are broken in pieces, even as I myself have received authority from my Father. ²⁸And I will give him the morning star. ²⁹He who has an ear, let him hear what the Spirit says to the churches.'

TO THE CHURCH IN SARDIS

3 "And to the angel of the church in Sardis write: 'The words of him who has the seven spirits of God and the seven stars.

"'I know your works. You have the reputation of being alive, but you are dead. ²Wake up, and strengthen what remains and is about to die, for I have not found your works complete in the sight of my God. ³Remember, then, what you received and heard. Keep it, and repent. If you will not wake up, I will come like a thief, and you will not know at what hour I will come against you. ⁴Yet you have still a few names in Sardis, people who have not soiled their garments, and they will walk with me in white, for they are worthy. ⁵The one who conquers will be clothed thus

---

[a] Greek *blasphemy* [b] Or *your faith in me* [c] Greek *shepherd*

in white garments, and I will never blot his name out of the book of life. I will confess his name before my Father and before his angels. ⁶He who has an ear, let him hear what the Spirit says to the churches.'

TO THE CHURCH IN PHILADELPHIA

⁷"And to the angel of the church in Philadelphia write: 'The words of the holy one, the true one, who has the key of David, who opens and no one will shut, who shuts and no one opens.

⁸"'I know your works. Behold, I have set before you an open door, which no one is able to shut. I know that you have but little power, and yet you have kept my word and have not denied my name. ⁹Behold, I will make those of the synagogue of Satan who say that they are Jews and are not, but lie—behold, I will make them come and bow down before your feet, and they will learn that I have loved you. ¹⁰Because you have kept my word about patient endurance, I will keep you from the hour of trial that is coming on the whole world, to try those who dwell on the earth. ¹¹I am coming soon. Hold fast what you have, so that no one may seize your crown. ¹²The one who conquers, I will make him a pillar in the temple of my God. Never shall he go out of it, and I will write on him the name of my God, and the name of the city of my God, the new Jerusalem, which comes down from my God out of heaven, and my own new name. ¹³He who has an ear, let him hear what the Spirit says to the churches.'

TO THE CHURCH IN LAODICEA

¹⁴"And to the angel of the church in Laodicea write: 'The words of the Amen, the faithful and true witness, the beginning of God's creation.

¹⁵"'I know your works: you are neither cold nor hot. Would that you were either cold or hot! ¹⁶So, because you are lukewarm, and neither hot nor cold, I will spit you out of my mouth. ¹⁷For you say, I am rich, I have prospered, and I need nothing, not realizing that you are wretched, pitiable, poor, blind, and naked. ¹⁸I counsel you to buy from me gold refined by fire, so that you may be rich, and white garments so that you may clothe yourself and the shame of your nakedness may not be seen, and salve to anoint your eyes, so that you may see. ¹⁹Those whom I love, I reprove and discipline, so be zealous and repent. ²⁰Behold, I stand at the door and knock. If anyone hears my voice and opens the door, I will come in to him and eat with him, and he with me. ²¹The one who conquers, I will grant him to sit with me on my throne, as I also conquered and sat down with my Father on his throne. ²²He who has an ear, let him hear what the Spirit says to the churches.'"

THE THRONE IN HEAVEN

4 After this I looked, and behold, a door standing open in heaven! And the first voice, which I had heard speaking to me like a trumpet, said, "Come up here, and I will show you what must take place after this." ²At once I was in the Spirit, and behold, a throne stood in heaven, with one seated on the throne. ³And he who sat there had the appearance of jasper and carnelian, and round the throne was a rainbow that had the appearance of an emerald. ⁴Round the throne were twenty-four thrones, and seated on the thrones were twenty-four elders, clothed in white garments, with golden crowns on their heads. ⁵From the throne came flashes of lightning, and rumblings[a] and peals of thunder, and before the throne were burning seven torches of fire, which are the seven spirits of God, ⁶and before the throne there was as it were a sea of glass, like crystal.

And round the throne, on each side of the throne, are four living creatures, full of eyes in front and behind: ⁷the first living creature like a lion, the second living creature like an ox, the third living creature with the face of a man, and the fourth living creature like an eagle in flight. ⁸And the four living creatures, each of them with six wings, are full of eyes all round and within, and day and night they never cease to say,

"Holy, holy, holy, is the Lord God Almighty,
 who was and is and is to come!"

⁹And whenever the living creatures give glory and honour and thanks to him who is seated on the throne, who lives for ever and ever, ¹⁰the twenty-four elders fall down before him who is seated on the throne and worship him who lives for ever and ever. They cast their crowns before the throne, saying,

---

[a] Or *voices*, or *sounds*

¹¹ "Worthy are you, our Lord and God,
 to receive glory and honour
  and power,
for you created all things,
 and by your will they existed
  and were created."

THE SCROLL AND THE LAMB

5 Then I saw in the right hand of him who was seated on the throne a scroll written within and on the back, sealed with seven seals. ²And I saw a mighty angel proclaiming with a loud voice, "Who is worthy to open the scroll and break its seals?" ³And no one in heaven or on earth or under the earth was able to open the scroll or to look into it, ⁴and I began to weep loudly because no one was found worthy to open the scroll or to look into it. ⁵And one of the elders said to me, "Weep no more; behold, the Lion of the tribe of Judah, the Root of David, has conquered, so that he can open the scroll and its seven seals."

⁶And between the throne and the four living creatures and among the elders I saw a Lamb standing, as though it had been slain, with seven horns and with seven eyes, which are the seven spirits of God sent out into all the earth. ⁷And he went and took the scroll from the right hand of him who was seated on the throne. ⁸And when he had taken the scroll, the four living creatures and the twenty-four elders fell down before the Lamb, each holding a harp, and golden bowls full of incense, which are the prayers of the saints. ⁹And they sang a new song, saying,

"Worthy are you to take the scroll
 and to open its seals,
for you were slain, and by your blood
 you ransomed people for God
from every tribe and language
 and people and nation,
¹⁰ and you have made them a kingdom
 and priests to our God,
and they shall reign on the earth."

¹¹Then I looked, and I heard around the throne and the living creatures and the elders the voice of many angels, numbering myriads of myriads and thousands of thousands, ¹²saying with a loud voice,

"Worthy is the Lamb who was slain,
to receive power and wealth
 and wisdom and might
and honour and glory and blessing!"

¹³And I heard every creature in heaven and on earth and under the earth and in the sea, and all that is in them, saying,

"To him who sits on the throne
 and to the Lamb
be blessing and honour and glory
 and might for ever and ever!"

¹⁴And the four living creatures said, "Amen!" and the elders fell down and worshipped.

THE SEVEN SEALS

6 Now I watched when the Lamb opened one of the seven seals, and I heard one of the four living creatures say with a voice like thunder, "Come!" ²And I looked, and behold, a white horse! And its rider had a bow, and a crown was given to him, and he came out conquering, and to conquer.

³When he opened the second seal, I heard the second living creature say, "Come!" ⁴And out came another horse, bright red. Its rider was permitted to take peace from the earth, so that people should slay one another, and he was given a great sword.

⁵When he opened the third seal, I heard the third living creature say, "Come!" And I looked, and behold, a black horse! And its rider had a pair of scales in his hand. ⁶And I heard what seemed to be a voice in the midst of the four living creatures, saying, "A quart[a] of wheat for a denarius,[b] and three quarts of barley for a denarius, and do not harm the oil and wine!"

⁷When he opened the fourth seal, I heard the voice of the fourth living creature say, "Come!" ⁸And I looked, and behold, a pale horse! And its rider's name was Death, and Hades followed him. And they were given authority over a quarter of the earth, to kill with sword and with famine and with pestilence and by wild beasts of the earth.

⁹When he opened the fifth seal, I saw under the altar the souls of those who had been slain for the word of God and for the witness they had borne. ¹⁰They cried out with a loud voice, "O Sovereign Lord, holy and true, how long before you will judge and avenge our blood on those who dwell on the earth?" ¹¹Then they were each given a white robe and told to rest a little longer, until the number of their fellow servants and their

---

[a] Greek *choinix*, a dry measure equal to about a quart   [b] A *denarius* was a day's wage for a labourer

brothers[a] should be complete, who were to be killed as they themselves had been.

¹²When he opened the sixth seal, I looked, and behold, there was a great earthquake, and the sun became black as sackcloth, the full moon became like blood, ¹³and the stars of the sky fell to the earth as the fig tree sheds its winter fruit when shaken by a gale. ¹⁴The sky vanished like a scroll that is being rolled up, and every mountain and island was removed from its place. ¹⁵Then the kings of the earth and the great ones and the generals and the rich and the powerful, and everyone, slave[b] and free, hid themselves in the caves and among the rocks of the mountains, ¹⁶calling to the mountains and rocks, "Fall on us and hide us from the face of him who is seated on the throne, and from the wrath of the Lamb, ¹⁷for the great day of their wrath has come, and who can stand?"

THE 144,000 OF ISRAEL SEALED

7 After this I saw four angels standing at the four corners of the earth, holding back the four winds of the earth, that no wind might blow on earth or sea or against any tree. ²Then I saw another angel ascending from the rising of the sun, with the seal of the living God, and he called with a loud voice to the four angels who had been given power to harm earth and sea, ³saying, "Do not harm the earth or the sea or the trees, until we have sealed the servants of our God on their foreheads." ⁴And I heard the number of the sealed, 144,000, sealed from every tribe of the sons of Israel:

⁵ 12,000 from the tribe of Judah
were sealed,
12,000 from the tribe of Reuben,
12,000 from the tribe of Gad,
⁶ 12,000 from the tribe of Asher,
12,000 from the tribe of Naphtali,
12,000 from the tribe of Manasseh,
⁷ 12,000 from the tribe of Simeon,
12,000 from the tribe of Levi,
12,000 from the tribe of Issachar,
⁸ 12,000 from the tribe of Zebulun,
12,000 from the tribe of Joseph,
12,000 from the tribe of Benjamin
were sealed.

A GREAT MULTITUDE FROM EVERY NATION

⁹After this I looked, and behold, a great multitude that no one could number, from every nation, from all tribes and peoples and languages, standing before the throne and before the Lamb, clothed in white robes, with palm branches in their hands, ¹⁰and crying out with a loud voice, "Salvation belongs to our God who sits on the throne, and to the Lamb!" ¹¹And all the angels were standing round the throne and round the elders and the four living creatures, and they fell on their faces before the throne and worshipped God, ¹²saying, "Amen! Blessing and glory and wisdom and thanksgiving and honour and power and might be to our God for ever and ever! Amen."

¹³Then one of the elders addressed me, saying, "Who are these, clothed in white robes, and from where have they come?" ¹⁴I said to him, "Sir, you know." And he said to me, "These are the ones coming out of the great tribulation. They have washed their robes and made them white in the blood of the Lamb.

¹⁵ "Therefore they are before
the throne of God,
and serve him day and night
in his temple;
and he who sits on the throne will
shelter them with his presence.
¹⁶ They shall hunger no more,
neither thirst any more;
the sun shall not strike them,
nor any scorching heat.
¹⁷ For the Lamb in the midst of the
throne will be their shepherd,
and he will guide them to
springs of living water,
and God will wipe away every
tear from their eyes."

THE SEVENTH SEAL AND THE GOLDEN CENSER

8 When the Lamb opened the seventh seal, there was silence in heaven for about half an hour. ²Then I saw the seven angels who stand before God, and seven trumpets were given to them. ³And another angel came and stood at the altar with a golden censer, and he was given much incense to offer with the prayers of all the saints on the golden altar before the throne, ⁴and the smoke of the incense, with the prayers of the saints, rose before God

---

[a] Or *brothers and sisters*. In New Testament usage, depending on the context, the plural Greek word *adelphoi* (translated "brothers") may refer either to *brothers* or to *brothers and sisters* [b] For the contextual rendering of the Greek word *doulos*, see Preface

from the hand of the angel. [5]Then the angel took the censer and filled it with fire from the altar and threw it on the earth, and there were peals of thunder, rumblings,[a] flashes of lightning, and an earthquake.

THE SEVEN TRUMPETS

[6]Now the seven angels who had the seven trumpets prepared to blow them.

[7]The first angel blew his trumpet, and there followed hail and fire, mixed with blood, and these were thrown upon the earth. And a third of the earth was burned up, and a third of the trees were burned up, and all green grass was burned up.

[8]The second angel blew his trumpet, and something like a great mountain, burning with fire, was thrown into the sea, and a third of the sea became blood. [9]A third of the living creatures in the sea died, and a third of the ships were destroyed.

[10]The third angel blew his trumpet, and a great star fell from heaven, blazing like a torch, and it fell on a third of the rivers and on the springs of water. [11]The name of the star is Wormwood.[b] A third of the waters became wormwood, and many people died from the water, because it had been made bitter.

[12]The fourth angel blew his trumpet, and a third of the sun was struck, and a third of the moon, and a third of the stars, so that a third of their light might be darkened, and a third of the day might be kept from shining, and likewise a third of the night.

[13]Then I looked, and I heard an eagle crying with a loud voice as it flew directly overhead, "Woe, woe, woe to those who dwell on the earth, at the blasts of the other trumpets that the three angels are about to blow!"

9 And the fifth angel blew his trumpet, and I saw a star fallen from heaven to earth, and he was given the key to the shaft of the bottomless pit.[c] [2]He opened the shaft of the bottomless pit, and from the shaft rose smoke like the smoke of a great furnace, and the sun and the air were darkened with the smoke from the shaft. [3]Then from the smoke came locusts on the earth, and they were given power like the power of scorpions of the earth. [4]They were told not to harm the grass of the earth or any green plant or any tree, but only those people who do not have the seal of God on their foreheads. [5]They were allowed to torment them for five months, but not to kill them, and their torment was like the torment of a scorpion when it stings someone. [6]And in those days people will seek death and will not find it. They will long to die, but death will flee from them.

[7]In appearance the locusts were like horses prepared for battle: on their heads were what looked like crowns of gold; their faces were like human faces, [8]their hair like women's hair, and their teeth like lions' teeth; [9]they had breastplates like breastplates of iron, and the noise of their wings was like the noise of many chariots with horses rushing into battle. [10]They have tails and stings like scorpions, and their power to hurt people for five months is in their tails. [11]They have as king over them the angel of the bottomless pit. His name in Hebrew is Abaddon, and in Greek he is called Apollyon.[d]

[12]The first woe has passed; behold, two woes are still to come.

[13]Then the sixth angel blew his trumpet, and I heard a voice from the four horns of the golden altar before God, [14]saying to the sixth angel who had the trumpet, "Release the four angels who are bound at the great river Euphrates." [15]So the four angels, who had been prepared for the hour, the day, the month, and the year, were released to kill a third of mankind. [16]The number of mounted troops was twice ten thousand times ten thousand; I heard their number. [17]And this is how I saw the horses in my vision and those who rode them: they wore breastplates the colour of fire and of sapphire[e] and of sulphur, and the heads of the horses were like lions' heads, and fire and smoke and sulphur came out of their mouths. [18]By these three plagues a third of mankind was killed, by the fire and smoke and sulphur coming out of their mouths. [19]For the power of the horses is in their mouths and in their tails, for their tails are like serpents with heads, and by means of them they wound.

[20]The rest of mankind, who were not killed by these plagues, did not repent of the works of their hands nor give up worshipping demons and idols of gold and silver and bronze and stone and wood, which cannot see or hear or walk, [21]nor did they repent of their murders or their sorceries or their sexual immorality or their thefts.

---

[a]Or *voices*, or *sounds* [b]*Wormwood* is the name of a plant and of the bitter-tasting extract derived from it [c]Greek *the abyss*; also verses 2, 11 [d]*Abaddon* means *destruction*; *Apollyon* means *destroyer* [e]Greek *hyacinth*

THE ANGEL AND THE LITTLE SCROLL

10 Then I saw another mighty angel coming down from heaven, wrapped in a cloud, with a rainbow over his head, and his face was like the sun, and his legs like pillars of fire. ²He had a little scroll open in his hand. And he set his right foot on the sea, and his left foot on the land, ³and called out with a loud voice, like a lion roaring. When he called out, the seven thunders sounded. ⁴And when the seven thunders had sounded, I was about to write, but I heard a voice from heaven saying, "Seal up what the seven thunders have said, and do not write it down." ⁵And the angel whom I saw standing on the sea and on the land raised his right hand to heaven ⁶and swore by him who lives for ever and ever, who created heaven and what is in it, the earth and what is in it, and the sea and what is in it, that there would be no more delay, ⁷but that in the days of the trumpet call to be sounded by the seventh angel, the mystery of God would be fulfilled, just as he announced to his servants the prophets.

⁸Then the voice that I had heard from heaven spoke to me again, saying, "Go, take the scroll that is open in the hand of the angel who is standing on the sea and on the land." ⁹So I went to the angel and told him to give me the little scroll. And he said to me, "Take and eat it; it will make your stomach bitter, but in your mouth it will be sweet as honey." ¹⁰And I took the little scroll from the hand of the angel and ate it. It was sweet as honey in my mouth, but when I had eaten it my stomach was made bitter. ¹¹And I was told, "You must again prophesy about many peoples and nations and languages and kings."

THE TWO WITNESSES

11 Then I was given a measuring rod like a staff, and I was told, "Rise and measure the temple of God and the altar and those who worship there, ²but do not measure the court outside the temple; leave that out, for it is given over to the nations, and they will trample the holy city for forty-two months. ³And I will grant authority to my two witnesses, and they will prophesy for 1,260 days, clothed in sackcloth."

⁴These are the two olive trees and the two lampstands that stand before the Lord of the earth. ⁵And if anyone would harm them, fire pours from their mouth and consumes their foes. If anyone would harm them, this is how he is doomed to be killed. ⁶They have the power to shut the sky, that no rain may fall during the days of their prophesying, and they have power over the waters to turn them into blood and to strike the earth with every kind of plague, as often as they desire. ⁷And when they have finished their testimony, the beast that rises from the bottomless pit*ᵃ* will make war on them and conquer them and kill them, ⁸and their dead bodies will lie in the street of the great city that symbolically*ᵇ* is called Sodom and Egypt, where their Lord was crucified. ⁹For three and a half days some from the peoples and tribes and languages and nations will gaze at their dead bodies and refuse to let them be placed in a tomb, ¹⁰and those who dwell on the earth will rejoice over them and make merry and exchange presents, because these two prophets had been a torment to those who dwell on the earth. ¹¹But after the three and a half days a breath of life from God entered them, and they stood up on their feet, and great fear fell on those who saw them. ¹²Then they heard a loud voice from heaven saying to them, "Come up here!" And they went up to heaven in a cloud, and their enemies watched them. ¹³And at that hour there was a great earthquake, and a tenth of the city fell. Seven thousand people were killed in the earthquake, and the rest were terrified and gave glory to the God of heaven.

¹⁴The second woe has passed; behold, the third woe is soon to come.

THE SEVENTH TRUMPET

¹⁵Then the seventh angel blew his trumpet, and there were loud voices in heaven, saying, "The kingdom of the world has become the kingdom of our Lord and of his Christ, and he shall reign for ever and ever." ¹⁶And the twenty-four elders who sit on their thrones before God fell on their faces and worshipped God, ¹⁷saying,

"We give thanks to you, Lord God Almighty,
  who is and who was,
for you have taken your great power
  and begun to reign.
¹⁸ The nations raged,
  but your wrath came,
  and the time for the dead
    to be judged,

---

*ᵃ*Or the abyss *ᵇ*Greek spiritually

and for rewarding your servants,
　　the prophets and saints,
　　and those who fear your name,
　　　both small and great,
　　and for destroying the
　　　destroyers of the earth."

¹⁹Then God's temple in heaven was opened, and the ark of his covenant was seen within his temple. There were flashes of lightning, rumblings,ᵃ peals of thunder, an earthquake, and heavy hail.

THE WOMAN AND THE DRAGON

12 And a great sign appeared in heaven: a woman clothed with the sun, with the moon under her feet, and on her head a crown of twelve stars. ²She was pregnant and was crying out in birth pains and the agony of giving birth. ³And another sign appeared in heaven: behold, a great red dragon, with seven heads and ten horns, and on his heads seven diadems. ⁴His tail swept down a third of the stars of heaven and cast them to the earth. And the dragon stood before the woman who was about to give birth, so that when she bore her child he might devour it. ⁵She gave birth to a male child, one who is to ruleᵇ all the nations with a rod of iron, but her child was caught up to God and to his throne, ⁶and the woman fled into the wilderness, where she has a place prepared by God, in which she is to be nourished for 1,260 days.

SATAN THROWN DOWN TO EARTH

⁷Now war arose in heaven, Michael and his angels fighting against the dragon. And the dragon and his angels fought back, ⁸but he was defeated, and there was no longer any place for them in heaven. ⁹And the great dragon was thrown down, that ancient serpent, who is called the devil and Satan, the deceiver of the whole world—he was thrown down to the earth, and his angels were thrown down with him. ¹⁰And I heard a loud voice in heaven, saying, "Now the salvation and the power and the kingdom of our God and the authority of his Christ have come, for the accuser of our brothersᶜ has been thrown down, who accuses them day and night before our God. ¹¹And they have conquered him by the blood of the Lamb and by the word of their testimony, for they loved not their lives even unto death. ¹²Therefore, rejoice, O heavens and you who dwell in them! But woe to you, O earth and sea, for the devil has come down to you in great wrath, because he knows that his time is short!"

¹³And when the dragon saw that he had been thrown down to the earth, he pursued the woman who had given birth to the male child. ¹⁴But the woman was given the two wings of the great eagle so that she might fly from the serpent into the wilderness, to the place where she is to be nourished for a time, and times, and half a time. ¹⁵The serpent poured water like a river out of his mouth after the woman, to sweep her away with a flood. ¹⁶But the earth came to the help of the woman, and the earth opened its mouth and swallowed the river that the dragon had poured from his mouth. ¹⁷Then the dragon became furious with the woman and went off to make war on the rest of her offspring, on those who keep the commandments of God and hold to the testimony of Jesus. And he stoodᵈ on the sand of the sea.

THE FIRST BEAST

13 And I saw a beast rising out of the sea, with ten horns and seven heads, with ten diadems on its horns and blasphemous names on its heads. ²And the beast that I saw was like a leopard; its feet were like a bear's, and its mouth was like a lion's mouth. And to it the dragon gave his power and his throne and great authority. ³One of its heads seemed to have a mortal wound, but its mortal wound was healed, and the whole earth marvelled as they followed the beast. ⁴And they worshipped the dragon, for he had given his authority to the beast, and they worshipped the beast, saying, "Who is like the beast, and who can fight against it?"

⁵And the beast was given a mouth uttering haughty and blasphemous words, and it was allowed to exercise authority for forty-two months. ⁶It opened its mouth to utter blasphemies against God, blaspheming his name and his dwelling,ᵉ that is, those who dwell in heaven. ⁷Also it was allowed to make war on the saints and to conquer them.ᶠ And authority was given it over every tribe and people and language and nation, ⁸and all who dwell on earth will worship it, everyone whose name has not been written before the

---

ᵃOr *voices, or sounds*　ᵇGreek *shepherd*　ᶜOr *brothers and sisters*
ᵈSome manuscripts *And I stood*, connecting the sentence with 13:1
ᵉOr *tabernacle*　ᶠSome manuscripts omit this sentence

foundation of the world in the book of life of the Lamb who was slain. ⁹If anyone has an ear, let him hear:

¹⁰ If anyone is to be taken captive,
  to captivity he goes;
 if anyone is to be slain with the sword,
  with the sword must he be slain.

Here is a call for the endurance and faith of the saints.

THE SECOND BEAST

¹¹Then I saw another beast rising out of the earth. It had two horns like a lamb and it spoke like a dragon. ¹²It exercises all the authority of the first beast in its presence,ᵃ and makes the earth and its inhabitants worship the first beast, whose mortal wound was healed. ¹³It performs great signs, even making fire come down from heaven to earth in front of people, ¹⁴and by the signs that it is allowed to work in the presence ofᵇ the beast it deceives those who dwell on earth, telling them to make an image for the beast that was wounded by the sword and yet lived. ¹⁵And it was allowed to give breath to the image of the beast, so that the image of the beast might even speak and might cause those who would not worship the image of the beast to be slain. ¹⁶Also it causes all, both small and great, both rich and poor, both free and slave,ᶜ to be marked on the right hand or the forehead, ¹⁷so that no one can buy or sell unless he has the mark, that is, the name of the beast or the number of its name. ¹⁸This calls for wisdom: let the one who has understanding calculate the number of the beast, for it is the number of a man, and his number is 666.ᵈ

THE LAMB AND THE 144,000

14 Then I looked, and behold, on Mount Zion stood the Lamb, and with him 144,000 who had his name and his Father's name written on their foreheads. ²And I heard a voice from heaven like the roar of many waters and like the sound of loud thunder. The voice I heard was like the sound of harpists playing on their harps, ³and they were singing a new song before the throne and before the four living creatures and before the elders. No one could learn that song except the 144,000 who had been redeemed from the earth. ⁴It is these who have not defiled themselves with women, for they are virgins. It is these who follow the Lamb wherever he goes. These have been redeemed from mankind as firstfruits for God and the Lamb, ⁵and in their mouth no lie was found, for they are blameless.

THE MESSAGES OF THE THREE ANGELS

⁶Then I saw another angel flying directly overhead, with an eternal gospel to proclaim to those who dwell on earth, to every nation and tribe and language and people. ⁷And he said with a loud voice, "Fear God and give him glory, because the hour of his judgement has come, and worship him who made heaven and earth, the sea and the springs of water."

⁸Another angel, a second, followed, saying, "Fallen, fallen is Babylon the great, she who made all nations drink the wine of the passionᵉ of her sexual immorality."

⁹And another angel, a third, followed them, saying with a loud voice, "If anyone worships the beast and its image and receives a mark on his forehead or on his hand, ¹⁰he also will drink the wine of God's wrath, poured full strength into the cup of his anger, and he will be tormented with fire and sulphur in the presence of the holy angels and in the presence of the Lamb. ¹¹And the smoke of their torment goes up for ever and ever, and they have no rest, day or night, these worshippers of the beast and its image, and whoever receives the mark of its name."

¹²Here is a call for the endurance of the saints, those who keep the commandments of God and their faith in Jesus.ᶠ

¹³And I heard a voice from heaven saying, "Write this: Blessed are the dead who die in the Lord from now on." "Blessed indeed," says the Spirit, "that they may rest from their labours, for their deeds follow them!"

THE HARVEST OF THE EARTH

¹⁴Then I looked, and behold, a white cloud, and seated on the cloud one like a son of man, with a golden crown on his head, and a sharp sickle in his hand. ¹⁵And another angel came out of the temple, calling with a loud voice to him who sat on the cloud, "Put in your sickle, and reap, for the hour to reap has come, for the harvest of the earth is fully ripe." ¹⁶So he who sat on the cloud

---

ᵃOr *on its behalf* ᵇOr *on behalf of* ᶜFor the contextual rendering of the Greek word *doulos*, see Preface ᵈSome manuscripts *616* ᵉOr *wrath* ᶠGreek *and the faith of Jesus*

swung his sickle across the earth, and the earth was reaped.

¹⁷Then another angel came out of the temple in heaven, and he too had a sharp sickle. ¹⁸And another angel came out from the altar, the angel who has authority over the fire, and he called with a loud voice to the one who had the sharp sickle, "Put in your sickle and gather the clusters from the vine of the earth, for its grapes are ripe." ¹⁹So the angel swung his sickle across the earth and gathered the grape harvest of the earth and threw it into the great wine press of the wrath of God. ²⁰And the wine press was trodden outside the city, and blood flowed from the wine press, as high as a horse's bridle, for 1,600 stadia.*ᵃ*

THE SEVEN ANGELS WITH SEVEN PLAGUES

15 Then I saw another sign in heaven, great and amazing, seven angels with seven plagues, which are the last, for with them the wrath of God is finished.

²And I saw what appeared to be a sea of glass mingled with fire—and also those who had conquered the beast and its image and the number of its name, standing beside the sea of glass with harps of God in their hands. ³And they sing the song of Moses, the servant of God, and the song of the Lamb, saying,

"Great and amazing are your deeds,
   O Lord God the Almighty!
Just and true are your ways,
   O King of the nations!*ᵇ*
⁴ Who will not fear, O Lord,
   and glorify your name?
For you alone are holy.
All nations will come
   and worship you,
for your righteous acts have
   been revealed."

⁵After this I looked, and the sanctuary of the tent*ᶜ* of witness in heaven was opened, ⁶and out of the sanctuary came the seven angels with the seven plagues, clothed in pure, bright linen, with golden sashes round their chests. ⁷And one of the four living creatures gave to the seven angels seven golden bowls full of the wrath of God who lives for ever and ever, ⁸and the sanctuary was filled with smoke from the glory of God and from his power, and no one could enter the sanctuary until the seven plagues of the seven angels were finished.

THE SEVEN BOWLS OF GOD'S WRATH

16 Then I heard a loud voice from the temple telling the seven angels, "Go and pour out on the earth the seven bowls of the wrath of God."

²So the first angel went and poured out his bowl on the earth, and harmful and painful sores came upon the people who bore the mark of the beast and worshipped its image.

³The second angel poured out his bowl into the sea, and it became like the blood of a corpse, and every living thing died that was in the sea.

⁴The third angel poured out his bowl into the rivers and the springs of water, and they became blood. ⁵And I heard the angel in charge of the waters*ᵈ* say,

"Just are you, O Holy One, who
   is and who was,
for you brought these judgements.
⁶ For they have shed the blood of
   saints and prophets,
   and you have given them
      blood to drink.
   It is what they deserve!"

⁷And I heard the altar saying,

"Yes, Lord God the Almighty,
   true and just are your judgements!"

⁸The fourth angel poured out his bowl on the sun, and it was allowed to scorch people with fire. ⁹They were scorched by the fierce heat, and they cursed*ᵉ* the name of God who had power over these plagues. They did not repent and give him glory.

¹⁰The fifth angel poured out his bowl on the throne of the beast, and its kingdom was plunged into darkness. People gnawed their tongues in anguish ¹¹and cursed the God of heaven for their pain and sores. They did not repent of their deeds.

¹²The sixth angel poured out his bowl on the great river Euphrates, and its water was dried up, to prepare the way for the kings from the east. ¹³And I saw, coming out of the mouth of the dragon and out of the mouth of the beast and out of the mouth of the false prophet, three unclean spirits like frogs. ¹⁴For they are demonic spirits, performing signs,

---
*ᵃ*About 184 miles; a *stadion* was about 607 feet or 185 metres *ᵇ*Some manuscripts *the ages* *ᶜ*Or *tabernacle* *ᵈ*Greek *angel of the waters* *ᵉ*Greek *blasphemed*; also verses 11, 21

who go abroad to the kings of the whole world, to assemble them for battle on the great day of God the Almighty. ¹⁵("Behold, I am coming like a thief! Blessed is the one who stays awake, keeping his garments on, that he may not go about naked and be seen exposed!") ¹⁶And they assembled them at the place that in Hebrew is called Armageddon.

THE SEVENTH BOWL

¹⁷The seventh angel poured out his bowl into the air, and a loud voice came out of the temple, from the throne, saying, "It is done!" ¹⁸And there were flashes of lightning, rumblings,^{a} peals of thunder, and a great earthquake such as there had never been since man was on the earth, so great was that earthquake. ¹⁹The great city was split into three parts, and the cities of the nations fell, and God remembered Babylon the great, to make her drain the cup of the wine of the fury of his wrath. ²⁰And every island fled away, and no mountains were to be found. ²¹And great hailstones, about one hundred pounds^b each, fell from heaven on people; and they cursed God for the plague of the hail, because the plague was so severe.

THE GREAT PROSTITUTE AND THE BEAST

17 Then one of the seven angels who had the seven bowls came and said to me, "Come, I will show you the judgement of the great prostitute who is seated on many waters, ²with whom the kings of the earth have committed sexual immorality, and with the wine of whose sexual immorality the dwellers on earth have become drunk." ³And he carried me away in the Spirit into a wilderness, and I saw a woman sitting on a scarlet beast that was full of blasphemous names, and it had seven heads and ten horns. ⁴The woman was arrayed in purple and scarlet, and adorned with gold and jewels and pearls, holding in her hand a golden cup full of abominations and the impurities of her sexual immorality. ⁵And on her forehead was written a name of mystery: "Babylon the great, mother of prostitutes and of earth's abominations." ⁶And I saw the woman, drunk with the blood of the saints, the blood of the martyrs of Jesus.^{c}

When I saw her, I marvelled greatly. ⁷But the angel said to me, "Why do you marvel? I will tell you the mystery of the woman, and of the beast with seven heads and ten horns that carries her. ⁸The beast that you saw was, and is not, and is about to rise from the bottomless pit^d and go to destruction. And the dwellers on earth whose names have not been written in the book of life from the foundation of the world will marvel to see the beast, because it was and is not and is to come. ⁹This calls for a mind with wisdom: the seven heads are seven mountains on which the woman is seated; ¹⁰they are also seven kings, five of whom have fallen, one is, the other has not yet come, and when he does come he must remain only a little while. ¹¹As for the beast that was and is not, it is an eighth but it belongs to the seven, and it goes to destruction. ¹²And the ten horns that you saw are ten kings who have not yet received royal power, but they are to receive authority as kings for one hour, together with the beast. ¹³These are of one mind, and they hand over their power and authority to the beast. ¹⁴They will make war on the Lamb, and the Lamb will conquer them, for he is Lord of lords and King of kings, and those with him are called and chosen and faithful."

¹⁵And the angel^e said to me, "The waters that you saw, where the prostitute is seated, are peoples and multitudes and nations and languages. ¹⁶And the ten horns that you saw, they and the beast will hate the prostitute. They will make her desolate and naked, and devour her flesh and burn her up with fire, ¹⁷for God has put it into their hearts to carry out his purpose by being of one mind and handing over their royal power to the beast, until the words of God are fulfilled. ¹⁸And the woman that you saw is the great city that has dominion over the kings of the earth."

THE FALL OF BABYLON

18 After this I saw another angel coming down from heaven, having great authority, and the earth was made bright with his glory. ²And he called out with a mighty voice,

"Fallen, fallen is Babylon the great!
She has become a dwelling
place for demons,
a haunt for every unclean spirit,
a haunt for every unclean bird,
a haunt for every unclean
and detestable beast.

---

^{a}Or *voices, or sounds* ^{b}Greek *a talent in weight* ^{c}Greek *the witnesses to Jesus* ^{d}Greek *the abyss* ^{e}Greek *he*

3 For all nations have drunk[a]
    the wine of the passion of her
        sexual immorality,
    and the kings of the earth have
        committed immorality with her,
    and the merchants of the earth have
        grown rich from the power
        of her luxurious living."

4 Then I heard another voice from heaven saying,

  "Come out of her, my people,
      lest you take part in her sins,
      lest you share in her plagues;
5   for her sins are heaped high
          as heaven,
      and God has remembered
          her iniquities.
6   Pay her back as she herself
          has paid back others,
      and repay her double for her deeds;
      mix a double portion for her
          in the cup she mixed.
7   As she glorified herself and
          lived in luxury,
      so give her a like measure of
          torment and mourning,
      since in her heart she says,
      'I sit as a queen,
      I am no widow,
      and mourning I shall never see.'
8   For this reason her plagues will
          come in a single day,
      death and mourning and famine,
      and she will be burned up with fire;
      for mighty is the Lord God
          who has judged her."

9 And the kings of the earth, who committed sexual immorality and lived in luxury with her, will weep and wail over her when they see the smoke of her burning. 10 They will stand far off, in fear of her torment, and say,

  "Alas! Alas! You great city,
      you mighty city, Babylon!
   For in a single hour your
      judgement has come."

11 And the merchants of the earth weep and mourn for her, since no one buys their cargo any more, 12 cargo of gold, silver, jewels, pearls, fine linen, purple cloth, silk, scarlet cloth, all kinds of scented wood, all kinds of articles of ivory, all kinds of articles of costly wood, bronze, iron and marble, 13 cinnamon, spice, incense, myrrh, frankincense, wine, oil, fine flour, wheat, cattle and sheep, horses and chariots, and slaves, that is, human souls.[b]

14 "The fruit for which your soul longed
        has gone from you,
    and all your delicacies and
        your splendours
    are lost to you,
        never to be found again!"

15 The merchants of these wares, who gained wealth from her, will stand far off, in fear of her torment, weeping and mourning aloud,

16 "Alas, alas, for the great city
        that was clothed in fine linen,
        in purple and scarlet,
        adorned with gold,
        with jewels, and with pearls!
17 For in a single hour all this wealth
        has been laid waste."

And all shipmasters and seafaring men, sailors and all whose trade is on the sea, stood far off 18 and cried out as they saw the smoke of her burning,

  "What city was like the great city?"

19 And they threw dust on their heads as they wept and mourned, crying out,

  "Alas, alas, for the great city
      where all who had ships at sea
      grew rich by her wealth!
   For in a single hour she has
      been laid waste.
20 Rejoice over her, O heaven,
      and you saints and apostles
          and prophets,
      for God has given judgement
          for you against her!"

21 Then a mighty angel took up a stone like a great millstone and threw it into the sea, saying,

  "So will Babylon the great city be
      thrown down with violence,
      and will be found no more;

[a] Some manuscripts *fallen by* [b] Or *and slaves, and human lives*

²² and the sound of harpists and
musicians, of flute players
and trumpeters,
will be heard in you no more,
and a craftsman of any craft
will be found in you no more,
and the sound of the mill
will be heard in you no more,
²³ and the light of a lamp
will shine in you no more,
and the voice of bridegroom and bride
will be heard in you no more,
for your merchants were the
great ones of the earth,
and all nations were deceived
by your sorcery.
²⁴ And in her was found the blood
of prophets and of saints,
and of all who have been
slain on earth."

REJOICING IN HEAVEN

19 After this I heard what seemed to be the loud voice of a great multitude in heaven, crying out,

"Hallelujah!
Salvation and glory and power
belong to our God,
² for his judgements are true and just;
for he has judged the great prostitute
who corrupted the earth
with her immorality,
and has avenged on her the
blood of his servants."

³Once more they cried out,

"Hallelujah!
The smoke from her goes up
for ever and ever."

⁴And the twenty-four elders and the four living creatures fell down and worshipped God who was seated on the throne, saying, "Amen. Hallelujah!" ⁵And from the throne came a voice saying,

"Praise our God,
all you his servants,
you who fear him,
small and great."

THE MARRIAGE SUPPER OF THE LAMB

⁶Then I heard what seemed to be the voice of a great multitude, like the roar of many waters and like the sound of mighty peals of thunder, crying out,

"Hallelujah!
For the Lord our God
the Almighty reigns.
⁷ Let us rejoice and exult
and give him the glory,
for the marriage of the Lamb
has come,
and his Bride has made
herself ready;
⁸ it was granted her to clothe herself
with fine linen, bright and pure"—

for the fine linen is the righteous deeds of the saints.

⁹And the angel said*ᵃ* to me, "Write this: Blessed are those who are invited to the marriage supper of the Lamb." And he said to me, "These are the true words of God." ¹⁰Then I fell down at his feet to worship him, but he said to me, "You must not do that! I am a fellow servant with you and your brothers who hold to the testimony of Jesus. Worship God." For the testimony of Jesus is the spirit of prophecy.

THE RIDER ON A WHITE HORSE

¹¹Then I saw heaven opened, and behold, a white horse! The one sitting on it is called Faithful and True, and in righteousness he judges and makes war. ¹²His eyes are like a flame of fire, and on his head are many diadems, and he has a name written that no one knows but himself. ¹³He is clothed in a robe dipped in*ᵇ* blood, and the name by which he is called is The Word of God. ¹⁴And the armies of heaven, arrayed in fine linen, white and pure, were following him on white horses. ¹⁵From his mouth comes a sharp sword with which to strike down the nations, and he will rule*ᶜ* them with a rod of iron. He will tread the wine press of the fury of the wrath of God the Almighty. ¹⁶On his robe and on his thigh he has a name written, King of kings and Lord of lords.

¹⁷Then I saw an angel standing in the sun, and with a loud voice he called to all the birds that fly directly overhead, "Come, gather for the great supper of God, ¹⁸to eat the flesh of kings, the flesh of captains, the flesh of mighty men, the flesh of horses and their riders, and the flesh of all men, both free and

---

*ᵃ*Greek *he said* *ᵇ*Some manuscripts *sprinkled with* *ᶜ*Greek *shepherd*

slave,[a] both small and great." [19]And I saw the beast and the kings of the earth with their armies gathered to make war against him who was sitting on the horse and against his army. [20]And the beast was captured, and with it the false prophet who in its presence[b] had done the signs by which he deceived those who had received the mark of the beast and those who worshipped its image. These two were thrown alive into the lake of fire that burns with sulphur. [21]And the rest were slain by the sword that came from the mouth of him who was sitting on the horse, and all the birds were gorged with their flesh.

THE THOUSAND YEARS

20 Then I saw an angel coming down from heaven, holding in his hand the key to the bottomless pit[c] and a great chain. [2]And he seized the dragon, that ancient serpent, who is the devil and Satan, and bound him for a thousand years, [3]and threw him into the pit, and shut it and sealed it over him, so that he might not deceive the nations any longer, until the thousand years were ended. After that he must be released for a little while.

[4]Then I saw thrones, and seated on them were those to whom the authority to judge was committed. Also I saw the souls of those who had been beheaded for the testimony of Jesus and for the word of God, and those who had not worshipped the beast or its image and had not received its mark on their foreheads or their hands. They came to life and reigned with Christ for a thousand years. [5]The rest of the dead did not come to life until the thousand years were ended. This is the first resurrection. [6]Blessed and holy is the one who shares in the first resurrection! Over such the second death has no power, but they will be priests of God and of Christ, and they will reign with him for a thousand years.

THE DEFEAT OF SATAN

[7]And when the thousand years are ended, Satan will be released from his prison [8]and will come out to deceive the nations that are at the four corners of the earth, Gog and Magog, to gather them for battle; their number is like the sand of the sea. [9]And they marched up over the broad plain of the earth and surrounded the camp of the saints and the beloved city, but fire came down from heaven[d] and consumed them, [10]and the devil who had deceived them was thrown into the lake of fire and sulphur where the beast and the false prophet were, and they will be tormented day and night for ever and ever.

JUDGEMENT BEFORE THE GREAT WHITE THRONE

[11]Then I saw a great white throne and him who was seated on it. From his presence earth and sky fled away, and no place was found for them. [12]And I saw the dead, great and small, standing before the throne, and books were opened. Then another book was opened, which is the book of life. And the dead were judged by what was written in the books, according to what they had done. [13]And the sea gave up the dead who were in it, Death and Hades gave up the dead who were in them, and they were judged, each one of them, according to what they had done. [14]Then Death and Hades were thrown into the lake of fire. This is the second death, the lake of fire. [15]And if anyone's name was not found written in the book of life, he was thrown into the lake of fire.

THE NEW HEAVEN AND THE NEW EARTH

21 Then I saw a new heaven and a new earth, for the first heaven and the first earth had passed away, and the sea was no more. [2]And I saw the holy city, new Jerusalem, coming down out of heaven from God, prepared as a bride adorned for her husband. [3]And I heard a loud voice from the throne saying, "Behold, the dwelling place[e] of God is with man. He will dwell with them, and they will be his people,[f] and God himself will be with them as their God.[g] [4]He will wipe away every tear from their eyes, and death shall be no more, neither shall there be mourning, nor crying, nor pain any more, for the former things have passed away."

[5]And he who was seated on the throne said, "Behold, I am making all things new." Also he said, "Write this down, for these words are trustworthy and true." [6]And he said to me, "It is done! I am the Alpha and the Omega, the beginning and the end. To the thirsty I will give from the spring of the water of life without payment. [7]The one who conquers will have this heritage, and I will be his God

---

[a]For the contextual rendering of the Greek word *doulos*, see Preface [b]Or *on its behalf* [c]Greek *the abyss*; also verse 3 [d]Some manuscripts *from God, out of heaven*, or *out of heaven from God* [e]Or *tabernacle* [f]Some manuscripts *peoples* [g]Some manuscripts omit *as their God*

and he will be my son. ⁸But as for the cowardly, the faithless, the detestable, as for murderers, the sexually immoral, sorcerers, idolaters, and all liars, their portion will be in the lake that burns with fire and sulphur, which is the second death."

THE NEW JERUSALEM

⁹Then came one of the seven angels who had the seven bowls full of the seven last plagues and spoke to me, saying, "Come, I will show you the Bride, the wife of the Lamb." ¹⁰And he carried me away in the Spirit to a great, high mountain, and showed me the holy city Jerusalem coming down out of heaven from God, ¹¹having the glory of God, its radiance like a most rare jewel, like a jasper, clear as crystal. ¹²It had a great, high wall, with twelve gates, and at the gates twelve angels, and on the gates the names of the twelve tribes of the sons of Israel were inscribed — ¹³on the east three gates, on the north three gates, on the south three gates, and on the west three gates. ¹⁴And the wall of the city had twelve foundations, and on them were the twelve names of the twelve apostles of the Lamb.

¹⁵And the one who spoke with me had a measuring rod of gold to measure the city and its gates and walls. ¹⁶The city lies foursquare, its length the same as its width. And he measured the city with his rod, 12,000 stadia.[a] Its length and width and height are equal. ¹⁷He also measured its wall, 144 cubits[b] by human measurement, which is also an angel's measurement. ¹⁸The wall was built of jasper, while the city was pure gold, like clear glass. ¹⁹The foundations of the wall of the city were adorned with every kind of jewel. The first was jasper, the second sapphire, the third agate, the fourth emerald, ²⁰the fifth onyx, the sixth carnelian, the seventh chrysolite, the eighth beryl, the ninth topaz, the tenth chrysoprase, the eleventh jacinth, the twelfth amethyst. ²¹And the twelve gates were twelve pearls, each of the gates made of a single pearl, and the street of the city was pure gold, like transparent glass.

²²And I saw no temple in the city, for its temple is the Lord God the Almighty and the Lamb. ²³And the city has no need of sun or moon to shine on it, for the glory of God gives it light, and its lamp is the Lamb. ²⁴By its light will the nations walk, and the kings of the earth will bring their glory into it, ²⁵and its gates will never be shut by day — and there will be no night there. ²⁶They will bring into it the glory and the honour of the nations. ²⁷But nothing unclean will ever enter it, nor anyone who does what is detestable or false, but only those who are written in the Lamb's book of life.

THE RIVER OF LIFE

22 Then the angel[c] showed me the river of the water of life, bright as crystal, flowing from the throne of God and of the Lamb ²through the middle of the street of the city; also, on either side of the river, the tree of life[d] with its twelve kinds of fruit, yielding its fruit each month. The leaves of the tree were for the healing of the nations. ³No longer will there be anything accursed, but the throne of God and of the Lamb will be in it, and his servants will worship him. ⁴They will see his face, and his name will be on their foreheads. ⁵And night will be no more. They will need no light of lamp or sun, for the Lord God will be their light, and they will reign for ever and ever.

JESUS IS COMING

⁶And he said to me, "These words are trustworthy and true. And the Lord, the God of the spirits of the prophets, has sent his angel to show his servants what must soon take place."

⁷"And behold, I am coming soon. Blessed is the one who keeps the words of the prophecy of this book."

⁸I, John, am the one who heard and saw these things. And when I heard and saw them, I fell down to worship at the feet of the angel who showed them to me, ⁹but he said to me, "You must not do that! I am a fellow servant with you and your brothers the prophets, and with those who keep the words of this book. Worship God."

¹⁰And he said to me, "Do not seal up the words of the prophecy of this book, for the time is near. ¹¹Let the evildoer still do evil, and the filthy still be filthy, and the righteous still do right, and the holy still be holy."

¹²"Behold, I am coming soon, bringing my recompense with me, to repay each one for what he has done. ¹³I am the Alpha and the Omega, the first and the last, the beginning and the end."

---

[a]About 1,380 miles; a *stadion* was about 607 feet or 185 metres
[b]A *cubit* was about 18 inches or 45 centimetres [c]Greek *he* [d]Or *the Lamb. In the midst of the street of the city, and or either side of the river, was the tree of life*

REVELATION 22

¹⁴Blessed are those who wash their robes,ᵃ so that they may have the right to the tree of life and that they may enter the city by the gates. ¹⁵Outside are the dogs and sorcerers and the sexually immoral and murderers and idolaters, and everyone who loves and practises falsehood.

¹⁶"I, Jesus, have sent my angel to testify to you about these things for the churches. I am the root and the descendant of David, the bright morning star."

¹⁷The Spirit and the Bride say, "Come." And let the one who hears say, "Come." And let the one who is thirsty come; let the one who desires take the water of life without price.

¹⁸I warn everyone who hears the words of the prophecy of this book: if anyone adds to them, God will add to him the plagues described in this book, ¹⁹and if anyone takes away from the words of the book of this prophecy, God will take away his share in the tree of life and in the holy city, which are described in this book.

²⁰He who testifies to these things says, "Surely I am coming soon." Amen. Come, Lord Jesus!

²¹The grace of the Lord Jesus be with all.ᵇ Amen.

ᵃSome manuscripts *do his commandments* ᵇSome manuscripts *all the saints*

TABLE OF
WEIGHTS AND MEASURES
AND MONETARY UNITS

The following table is based on the best generally accepted information available for biblical weights, measures, and monetary units. All equivalents are approximate. Weights and measures also varied somewhat in different times and places in the ancient world. Most weights, measures, and monetary units are also explained in footnotes on the pages where they occur in the ESV text.

BIBLICAL UNIT	APPROXIMATE AMERICAN AND METRIC EQUIVALENTS	BIBLICAL EQUIVALENT
bath	A *bath* was about 6 gallons or 22 liters	1 ephah
beka	A *beka* was about 1/5 ounce or 5.5 grams	10 gerahs
cor	A *cor* was about 6 bushels or 220 liters	10 ephahs
cubit	A *cubit* was about 18 inches or 45 centimeters	6 handbreadths
daric	A *daric* was a coin of about 1/4 ounce or 8.5 grams	
denarius	A *denarius* was a day's wage for a laborer	
ephah	An *ephah* was about 3/5 bushel or 22 liters	10 omers
gerah	A *gerah* was about 1/50 ounce or 0.6 gram	1/10 beka
handbreadth	A *handbreadth* was about 3 inches or 7.5 centimeters	1/6 cubit
hin	A *hin* was about 4 quarts or 3.5 liters	1/6 bath
homer	A *homer* was about 6 bushels or 220 liters	10 ephahs
kab	A *kab* was about 1 quart or 1 liter	1/22 ephah
lethech	A *lethech* was about 3 bushels or 110 liters	5 ephahs
log	A *log* was about 1/3 quart or 0.3 liter	1/72 bath
mina	A *mina* was about 1 1/4 pounds or 0.6 kilogram	50 shekels
omer	An *omer* was about 2 quarts or 2 liters	1/10 ephah
pim	A *pim* was about 1/3 ounce or 7.5 grams	2/3 shekel
seah	A *seah* was about 7 quarts or 7.3 liters	1/3 ephah
shekel	A *shekel* was about 2/5 ounce or 11 grams	2 bekas
span	A *span* was about 9 inches or 22 centimeters	3 handbreadths
stadion	A *stadion* was about 607 feet or 185 meters	
talent	A *talent* was about 75 pounds or 34 kilograms	60 minas

TABLE OF
WEIGHTS AND MEASURES
AND MONETARY UNITS

The following table is based on the best generally accepted information available in biblical weights, measures, and monetary units. All equivalents are approximate. Weights and measures also varied somewhat in different times and places in the ancient world. Most weight, measures, and monetary units are also explained in footnotes on the pages where they occur in the RSV text.

BIBLICAL UNIT	APPROXIMATE AMERICAN AND METRIC EQUIVALENTS	BIBLICAL EQUIVALENT
bath	A bath was about 6 gallons or 22 liters	1 ephah
beka	A beka was about 1/5 ounce or 5.5 grams	10 gerahs
cor	A cor was about 6 bushels or 220 liters	10 ephahs
cubit	A cubit was about 18 inches or 45 centimeters	6 handbreadths
daric	A daric was a coin of about 1/4 ounce or 8.5 grams	
denarius	A denarius was a day's wage for a laborer	
ephah	An ephah was about 3/5 bushel or 22 liters	10 omers
gerah	A gerah was about 1/50 ounce or 0.6 gram	1/10 beka
handbreadth	A handbreadth was about 3 inches or 7.5 centimeters	1/6 cubit
hin	A hin was about 4 quarts or 3.5 liters	1/6 bath
homer	A homer was about 6 bushels or 220 liters	10 ephahs
kab	A kab was about 1 quart or 1 liter	1/12 ephah
lethech	A lethech was about 3 bushels or 110 liters	5 ephahs
log	A log was about 1/3 quart or 0.3 liter	1/72 hin
mina	A mina was about 1 1/4 pounds or 0.6 kilogram	50 shekels
omer	An omer was about 2 quarts or 2 liters	1/10 ephah
pim	A pim was about 1/3 ounce or 7.5 grams	2/3 shekel
seah	A seah was about 7 quarts or 7.3 liters	1/3 ephah
shekel	A shekel was about 2/5 ounce or 11 grams	2 bekas
span	A span was about 9 inches or 22 centimeters	3 handbreadths
stadion	A stadion was about 607 feet or 185 meters	
talent	A talent was about 75 pounds or 34 kilograms	60 minas

MAPS

The world of Genesis

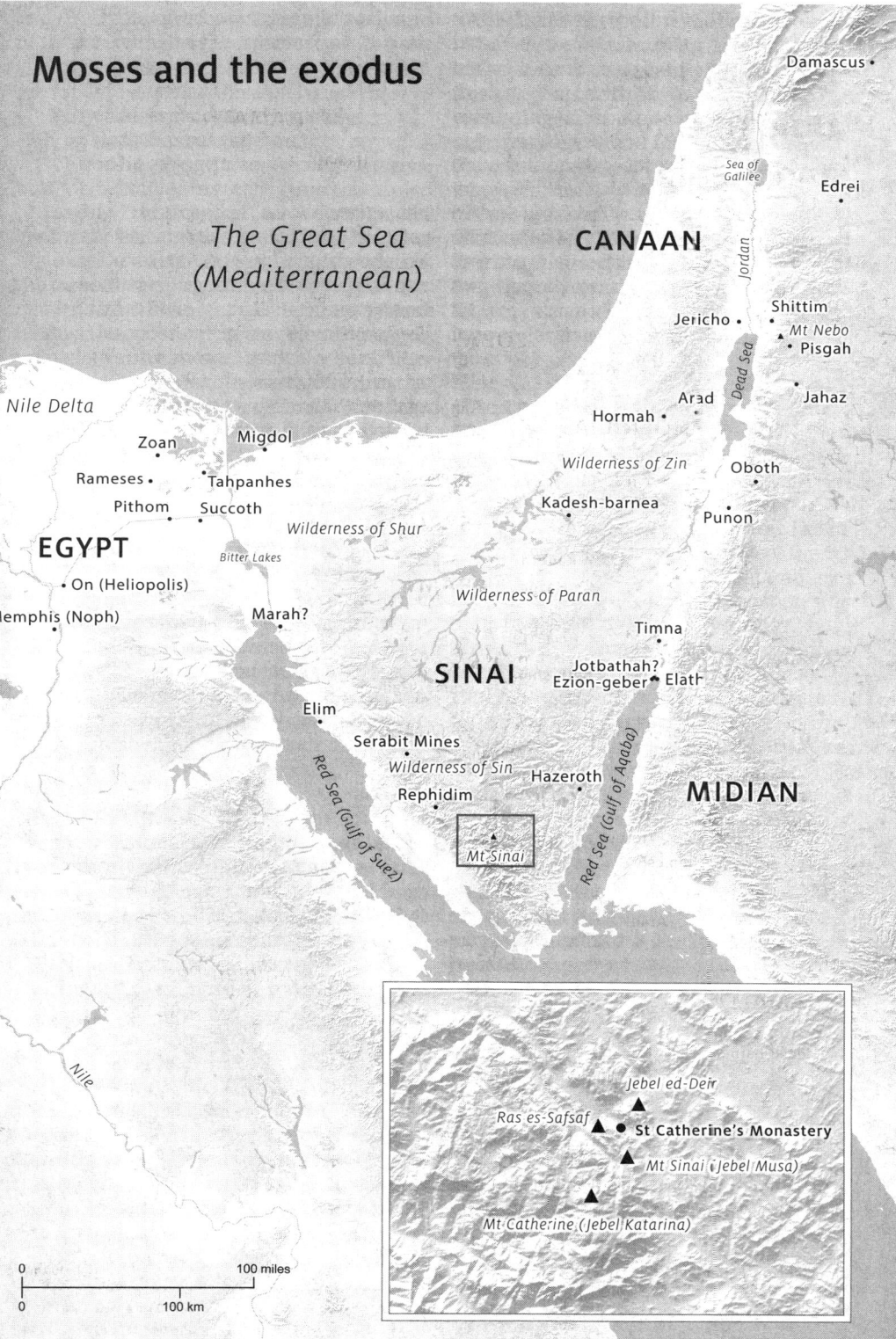

Israel at the time of David and Solomon

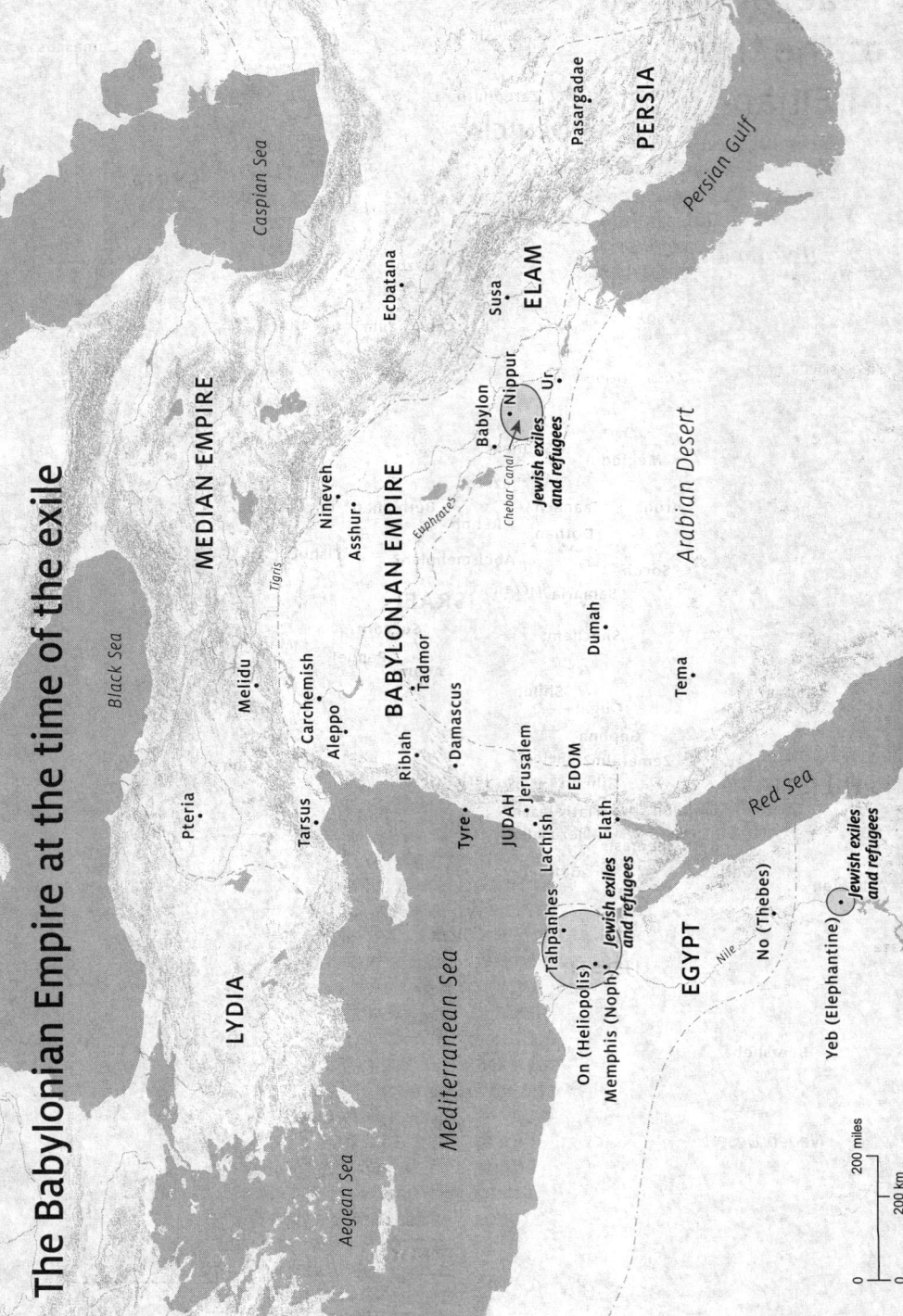

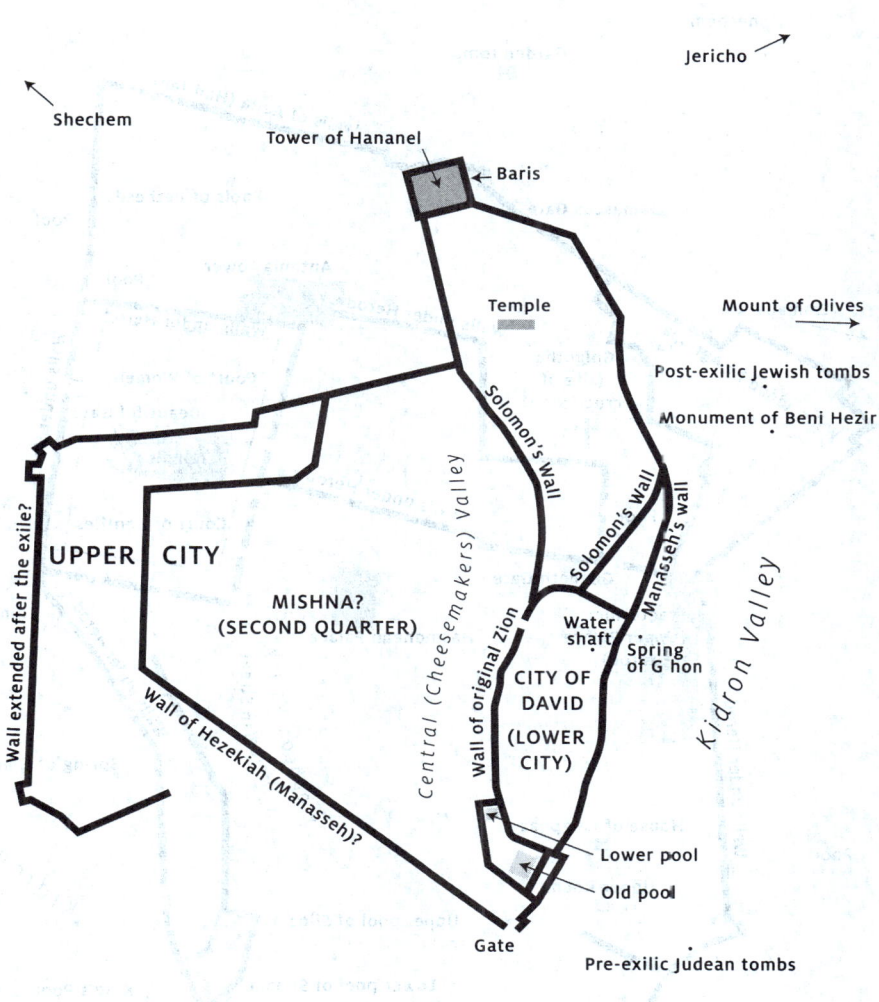

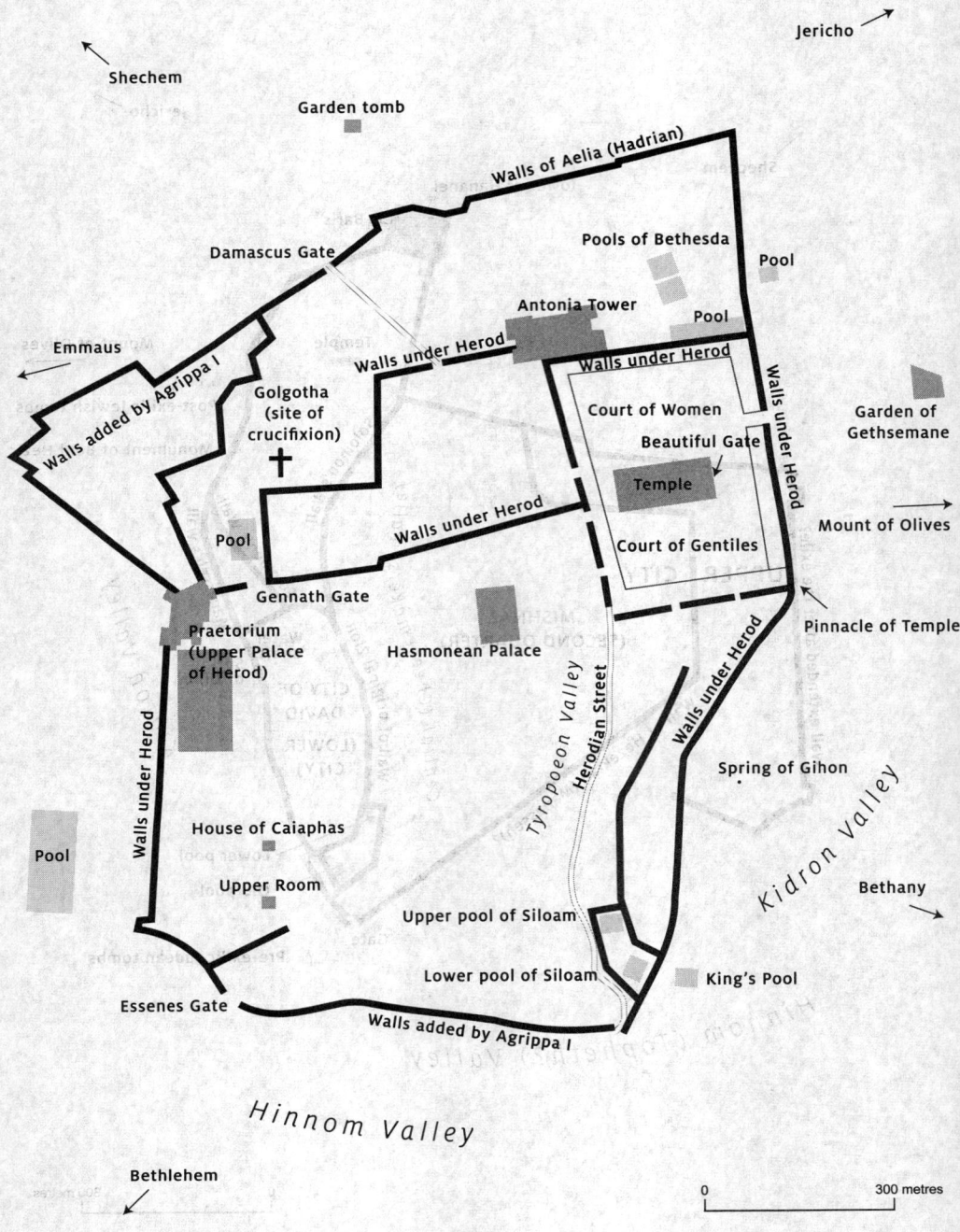

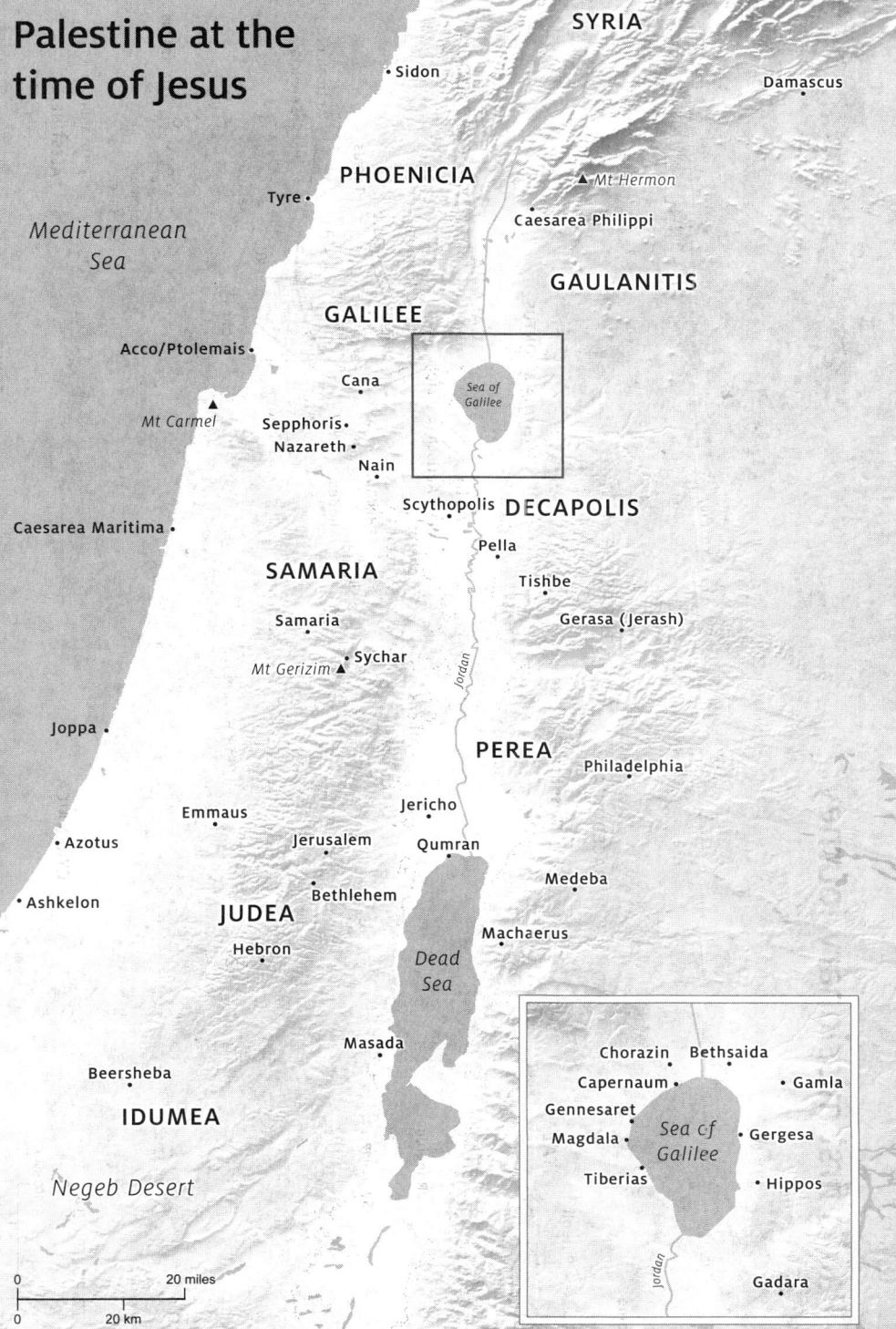

Paul's first missionary journey

Paul's second missionary journey

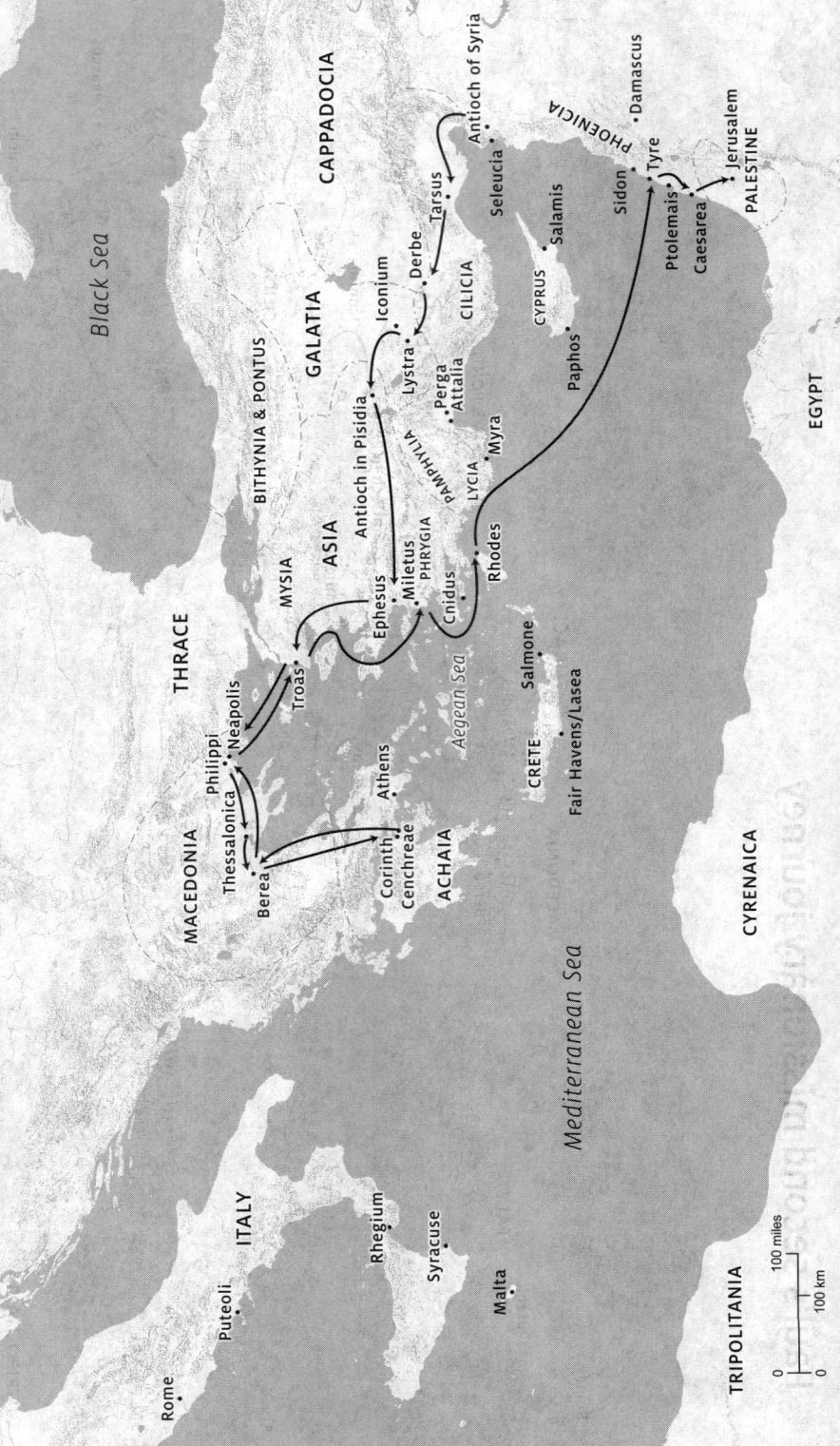

Paul's fourth missionary journey